LITTLE, BROWN AND COMPANY

Law School Casebook Series

The Employment Relation and the Law. Edited by BENJAMIN AARON, Professor of Law and Director, Institute of Industrial Relations, University of California at Los Angeles

Federal Income Taxation: Cases, Problems, Notes. WILLIAM D. ANDREWS, Professor of law, Harvard University

Antitrust Analysis: Problems, Text, Cases. PHILLIP AREEDA, Professor of Law, Harvard University

Land Transfer and Finance. ALLAN AXELROD, Professor of Law, Rutgers University, CURTIS J. BERGER, Professor of Law, Columbia University, and QUINTIN JOHNSTONE, Justus S. Hotchkiss Professor of Law, Yale University

Land Ownership and Use: Cases, Statutes, and Other Materials. CURTIS J. BERGER, Professor of Law, Columbia University

International Law: Cases and Materials. Third Edition. WILLIAM W. BISHOP, JR., Edwin M. Dickinson Professor of Law, University of Michigan

Federal Income, Estate and Gift Taxation. Fourth Edition. BORIS I. BITTKER, Southmayd Professor of Law, Yale University, and LAWRENCE M. STONE, Professor of Law, University of California at Berkeley

Materials on Reorganization, Recapitalization and Insolvency. WALTER J. BLUM, Professor of Law, University of Chicago, and STANLEY A. KAPLAN, Professor of Law, University of Chicago

Civil Procedure: Cases and Comments on the Process of Adjudication. PAUL D. CARRINGTON, Professor of Law, University of Michigan

Estate Planning. Third Edition. A. JAMES CASNER, Weld Professor of Law, Harvard University

Cases and Text on Property. Second Edition. A. JAMES CASNER, Weld Professor of Law, Harvard University, and W. BARTON LEACH, Story Professor of Law, Emeritus, Harvard University

International Legal Process. ABRAM CHAYES, Professor of Law, Harvard University, THOMAS EHRLICH, Professor of Law, Stanford University, and ANDREAS F. LOWENFELD, Professor of Law, New York University

Cases and Materials on Debtor and Creditor. VERN COUNTRYMAN, Professor of Law, Harvard University

The Lawyer in Modern Society. VERN COUNTRYMAN, Professor of Law, Harvard University, and TED FINMAN, Professor of Law, University of Wisconsin

Commercial Law: Cases and Materials. VERN COUNTRYMAN, Professor of Law, Harvard University, and ANDREW L. KAUFMAN, Professor of Law, Harvard University

Law, Medicine and Forensic Science. WILLIAM J. CURRAN, Frances Glessner Lee Professor of Legal Medicine, Harvard Medical School, Harvard School of Public Health, and E. DONALD SHAPIRO, Adjunct Professor of Law, New York University

Family Wealth Transactions. JESSE DUKEMINIER, Professor of Law, University of California at Los Angeles, and STANLEY M. JOHANSON, Professor of Law, University of Texas

Political and Civil Rights in the United States. Third Edition. THOMAS I. EMERSON, Lines Professor of Law, Yale University, DAVID HABER, Professor of Law, Rutgers University, and NORMAN DORSEN, Professor of Law and Director, Arthur Garfield Hays Civil Liberties Program, New York University

Cases and Materials on Family Law. CALEB FOOTE, Professor of Law and Criminology, University of California at Berkeley, ROBERT J. LEVY, Professor of Law, University of Minnesota, and FRANK E. A. SANDER, Professor of Law, Harvard University

Constitutional Law: Cases and Other Problems. Third Edition. PAUL A. FREUND, Carl M. Loeb University Professor, Harvard University, ARTHUR E. SUTHERLAND, Bussey Professor of Law, Emeritus, Harvard University, MARK DE WOLFE HOWE, late Charles Warren Professor of American Legal History, Harvard University, and ERNEST J. BROWN, Langdell Professor of Law, Harvard University

Cases and Materials on Corporations. ALEXANDER H. FREY, Algernon Sidney Biddle Professor of Law, Emeritus, University of Pennsylvania, C. ROBERT MORRIS, JR., Professor of Law, University of Minnesota, and JESSE CHOPER, Professor of Law, University of California at Berkeley

Cases and Materials on Torts. Second Edition. CHARLES O. GREGORY, John B. Minor Professor of Law, Emeritus, University of Virginia, and HARRY KALVEN, JR., Professor of Law, University of Chicago

Land-Use Planning: A Casebook on the Use, Misuse, and Re-use of Urban Land. Second Edition. CHARLES M. HAAR, Professor of Law, Harvard University

Administrative Law: Cases and Materials. Third Edition. LOUIS L. JAFFE, Byrne Professor of Administrative Law, Harvard University, and NATHANIEL L. NATHANSON, Frederic P. Vose Professor of Law, Northwestern University

Criminal Law and Its Processes: Cases and Materials. Second Edition. SANFORD H. KADISH, Professor of Law, University of California at Berkeley, and MONRAD G. PAULSEN, Dean and John B. Minor Professor of Law, University of Virginia

Constitutional Law: Cases and Materials. Fourth Edition. PAUL G. KAUPER, Henry M. Butzel Professor of Law, University of Michigan

Contracts: Cases and Materials. Second Edition. FRIEDRICH KESSLER, Professor of Law, University of California at Berkeley, and GRANT GILMORE, Harry A. Bigelow Professor of Law, University of Chicago

Basic Business Associations: Cases, Text and Problems. ELVIN R. LATTY, Dean Emeritus and William R. Perkins Professor of Law, Duke University, and GEORGE T. FRAMPTON, Professor of Law and Vice-Chancellor for Campus Affairs, University of Illinois

Cases and Text on the Law of Wills. Second Edition, 1960 Revision. W. BARTON LEACH, Story Professor of Law, Emeritus, Harvard University

Labor Law: Cases, Materials, and Problems. BERNARD D. MELTZER, Professor of Law, University of Chicago

Commercial Transactions: Cases and Materials. SOIA MENTSCHIKOFF, Professor of Law, University of Chicago

Legislation: Cases and Materials. FRANK C. NEWMAN, Professor of Law, University of California at Berkeley, and STANLEY S. SURREY, Jeremiah Smith, Jr., Professor of Law, Harvard University

Family Law: Cases and Materials. Second Edition. MORRIS PLOSCOWE, Adjunct Professor of Law, New York University, and HENRY H. FOSTER, JR., Professor of Law, New York University and DORIS JONAS FREED, of the New York and Maryland Bars

State and Local Government Law. SHO SATO, Professor of Law, University of California at Berkeley, and ARVO VAN ALSTYNE, Professor of Law, University of Utah

Problems and Materials on Decedents' Estates and Trusts. EUGENE F. SCOLES, Dean and Professor of Law, University of Oregon, and EDWARD C. HALBACH, JR., Dean and Professor of Law, University of California at Berkeley

Cases and Other Materials on Civil Procedure. AUSTIN WAKEMAN SCOTT, Dane Professor of Law, Emeritus, Harvard University, and ROBERT B. KENT, Professor of Law, Boston University

Select Cases and Other Authorities on the Law of Trusts. AUSTIN WAKEMAN SCOTT, Dane Professor of Law, Emeritus, Harvard University, and AUSTIN WAKEMAN SCOTT, JR., late Professor of Law, University of Colorado

The Civil Law System: Cases and Materials for the Comparative Study of Law. ARTHUR TAYLOR VON MEHREN, Professor of Law, Harvard University

The Law of Multistate Problems: Cases and Materials on Conflict of Laws. ARTHUR TAYLOR VON MEHREN, Professor of Law, Harvard University, and DONALD THEODORE TRAUTMAN, Professor of Law, Harvard University

Labor Relations and the Law. Third Edition. THE LABOR LAW GROUP TRUST Under the Editorship of JERRE WILLIAMS, Rex G. and Edna Heflin Baker Professor of Constitutional Law, University of Texas, and Others

Federal Income Taxation of Business Enterprise. BERNARD WOLFMAN, Dean and Professor of Law, University of Pennsylvania

Law School Textbook Series

Public Law Perspectives on a Private Law Problem: Auto Compensation Plans. WALTER J. BLUM, Professor of Law, University of Chicago, and HARRY KALVEN, JR., Professor of Law, University of Chicago

American Civil Procedure. WILLIAM WIRT BLUME, Professor of Law, University of California, Hastings College of Law

Readings in Jurisprudence and Legal Philosophy. MORRIS R. COHEN, late Professor of Law, City College of New York, and FELIX S. COHEN, late Visiting Professor of Law, City College of New York, and Visiting Lecturer, Yale University

Handbook of Modern Equity. Second Edition. WILLIAM Q. DE FUNIAK, Visiting Professor of Law, McGeorge School of Law, University of the Pacific

The Fundamentals of Legal Drafting. F. REED DICKERSON, Professor of Law, University of Indiana (Bloomington)

The Growth of American Law: The Law Makers. JAMES WILLARD HURST, Vilas Professor of Law, University of Wisconsin

Judicial Control of Administrative Action. Abridged Student Edition. LOUIS L. JAFFE, Byrne Professor of Administrative Law, Harvard University

Civil Procedure. FLEMING JAMES, JR., Sterling Professor of Law, Yale University

Trial Tactics and Methods. ROBERT E. KEETON, Professor of Law, Harvard University

Securities Regulation. Student Edition. LOUIS LOSS, William Nelson Cromwell Professor of Law, Harvard University

A Concise History of the Common Law. Fifth Edition. THEODORE F. T. PLUCKNETT, Late Professor of Legal History in the University of London

Effective Legal Research. Third Edition. MILES O. PRICE, late Professor of Law and Law Librarian, Columbia University, and HARRY BITNER, Professor of Law and Law Librarian, Cornell University

Scott's Abridgment of The Law of Trusts. AUSTIN WAKEMAN SCOTT, Dane Professor of Law, Emeritus, Harvard University

Handbook of Law Study. FERDINAND FAIRFAX STONE, W. R. Irby Professor of Law and Director of Institute of Comparative Law, Tulane University

Estate Planning

A. JAMES CASNER

ASSOCIATE DEAN AND WELD PROFESSOR OF LAW
HARVARD LAW SCHOOL

THIRD EDITION

LITTLE, BROWN AND COMPANY

Boston • Toronto

1961

Published simultaneously in Canada
by Little, Brown & Company (Canada) Limited

PRINTED IN THE UNITED STATES OF AMERICA

Preface to the Third Edition

The first edition of this work was published in 1953 under the title Estate Planning: Cases, Statutes, Text and Other Materials. The second carried the same title and became available in 1956. For convenience of reference, the name of the book has been shortened to Estate Planning for the third edition.

The organization of the material in this edition follows the pattern set by the two which preceded it. Developments in the five years since the publication of the second edition, however, have been so extensive that a substantial portion of the text has been completely rewritten. A chapter dealing with the income taxation of estates has been added. The quoted statutory material and regulations, which previously were carried in footnotes throughout the book, have been collected in appendices and cross references are made to the page on which such material is quoted whenever it is relevant to the matter under consideration. The result is that material which occupied 1092 pages in the second edition now covers 1572 pages.

The sample estate plans have been thoroughly revised to reflect ideas and suggestions that have come to light during the last five years.

The following paragraphs quoted from the Preface of the first edition are still relevant:

"Estate planning has been a function of lawyers for centuries. Even under the feudal system in England, there were distinct advantages to be gained by careful advance planning for the devolution of a person's estate on his death. The nature and scope of these advantages have changed from time to time through the years, but it can surely be said that proper estate planning has always made a contribution to the financial welfare of a person's family and to the preservation of the family wealth.

"Estate planning is an inherently complex task because of the technicalities of the applicable law, the foresight required to provide for appropriate disposition of property under varying circumstances, and the extreme difficulty of drafting property arrangements so that the language employed carries the same connotations for all persons. The successful completion of this task in any given situation requires a background of study which enables the lawyer to visualize all the considerations which may be relevant. This book is designed to present for critical examination all these considerations and thereby to develop the framework within which the lawyer's process of thinking must operate in carrying out his estate planning responsibility.

"An examination of the Table of Contents will reveal that this volume is designed to present for consecutive study and consideration the various types of arrangements with respect to the disposition of wealth which may be employed in an estate plan. The material included for discussion in each chapter has been selected because of its relevance in determining the circumstances under which the particular property arrangement should be used. Tax materials predominate when the choice is influenced largely by tax consequences, but this is by no means a book concerned solely with tax planning.

"Some of the material in the book is relevant only when substantial estates are involved. Most of it, however, deals with problems which may and do arise with respect to small estates as well as large ones. In my opinion, estate planning should not be sharply divided into planning for small estates and planning for large estates. I believe, rather, that one who has a thorough comprehension of the problems involved in handling a very complicated estate will be best qualified to deal with the less complicated ones, for he will be in a position to select from his background of knowledge what is most suitable for the particular situation he faces.

"Though essential, a study of the various types of arrangements for the disposition of wealth which may be employed in an estate plan is not of itself sufficient to give a full appreciation of the estate planning task. In addition, it is necessary to consider carefully the work of a person faced with a particular factual situation and to observe how the various types of arrangements available may be woven together to produce an over-all estate plan. Such an opportunity is presented in the estate plans in the Appendices."

Estate planning arrangements may significantly influence the lives of the beneficiaries. This human factor in estate planning is too frequently overlooked or given a subordinate position. The development of a plan that produces maximum tax avoidance is justified only if it also is a plan that is appropriate for the human beings who will be affected by it.

SUPPLEMENTS

Estate planning is a dynamic and changing field, and no book in such a field would be reliable for very long unless kept up to date. It is planned to keep this book abreast of new developments by annual supplementation.

ACKNOWLEDGMENTS

I am especially indebted to the following persons in the preparation of this third edition: Andrew H. Cox of the Boston Bar, who read Chapter IX and made many valuable suggestions; my wife, Margaret S. Casner, who assisted in many ways; and my secretary, Margret S. Candee, who spent countless hours assembling the manuscript and checking various details. I also express my appreciation to the many others who in one way or another contributed to the final product.

Various portions of the text are based on published law review articles of mine and permission to use these articles in whole or in part has been given by the law reviews concerned. The Old Colony Trust Company, of Boston, consented to the printing of its Estate Administration Guide in Chapter II. Little, Brown and Company authorized the use of parts of *American Law of Property*. The sample business purchase agreements in Chapter XV have been reproduced with the permission of the New York Life Insurance Company. For these courtesies I am deeply grateful.

A. JAMES CASNER

Harvard Law School
April, 1961

Summary of Contents

Table of Contents

CHAPTER VII

NON-TRUST GIFTS

CHAPTER XII

POWERS OF APPOINTMENT INCLUDING DISCRETIONARY TRUSTS

CHAPTER XIII

THE MARITAL DEDUCTION

CHAPTER XIV

CHARITABLE DISPOSITIONS

CHAPTER XV

DISPOSAL OF A BUSINESS INTEREST OR A FARM

CHAPTER XVI

MULTIPLE STATE DEATH TAXATION

CHAPTER XVII

MULTIPLE STATE INCOME TAXATION

CHAPTER XVIII

ESTATE PLANS WHICH CROSS STATE OR NATIONAL BORDERS

APPENDIX II

APPENDIX III

APPENDIX IV

APPENDIX V

APPENDIX V

APPENDIX VI

ESTATE PLANNING

CHAPTER I

Introduction

Even in these days of high taxes and high living costs, wealth or the control over wealth is acquired by many people. Careful consideration should be given to the disposition of this wealth if the maximum amount is to be preserved for the intended bene- *Estate plan* ficiaries and if the benefits which flow from this wealth are to do *arrangement* the maximum good for the beneficiaries. An arrangement for the *for devol* devolution of one's wealth is an estate plan. Estate planning is *of (1)'s* the process by which the arrangement is brought into existence. *wealth*

The statutes on descent and distribution of property in force in each state determine to whom the benefits of a person's owned *Intestacy* property pass on his death intestate. Thus the question each per- *Indiv* son faces is not whether he will have an estate plan, but whether *estate pla* he will have an estate plan of his own selection rather than one created by operation of law.

An estate plan of one's own selection is frequently worked out in a will. It must be kept in mind, however, that a will is not the only medium of expressing a person's desires as to the devolution of his estate. Under some circumstances, it may be appropriate to make inter vivos arrangements for the disposition of some of the wealth. These inter vivos arrangements may vary considerably as to the degree of control which is given up by a person during his lifetime. The more control he retains while he lives, the more the inter vivos arrangement operates like a will, which, of course, has no legal operation during the testator's lifetime. The following are typical inter vivos arrangements for the devolution of a portion of a person's wealth:

1. The outright gift
2. The joint ownership (tenancy by the entirety, joint tenancy, joint bank account, jointly owned government bonds) *Inter*
3. The irrevocable inter vivos trust *vivos*
4. The revocable inter vivos trust *arranger*
5. The legal present and future interest created inter vivos
6. The Settlement of the Proceeds of Life Insurance (pay-

able in a lump sum to a beneficiary or a trustee, or payable under the interest option or the installment option)

The importance of the will in the estate plan varies depending on the extent to which inter vivos arrangements have taken care of the devolution of the estate involved. However, it is very difficult to bring completely within the orbit of inter vivos arrangements all the wealth one may accumulate in his lifetime. For example, suppose that a husband purchases a family residence and takes title in the name of his wife and himself as tenants by the entirety. The husband needs no will to dispose of the family residence on his death if his wife survives him, because the complete title to the residence passes to his wife automatically under the right of survivorship which is an incident of the tenancy by the entirety. If, however, the wife predeceases the husband, the inter vivos arrangement of a tenancy by the entirety makes no disposition of the residence on the husband's death and he may need a will to cover that situation. The husband should make his will now to cover this eventuality and not wait to see whether his wife survives him, because he may not have time to make his will after his wife dies and before he dies.

From what has been said above, it should be obvious that a comprehensive estate plan not only deals with the property owned outright by the person whose estate is involved but also takes into consideration many other items of property. The following classification of property items may be useful to keep in mind:

1. Tangible personal property owned outright
2. Tangible personal property owned jointly
3. Real estate owned outright
4. Real estate owned jointly
5. Securities owned outright
6. Securities owned jointly
7. Cash in an individual account
8. Cash in a joint account
9. Business interest owned individually
10. Business interest in a partnership
11. Business which is incorporated where the stock is closely held
12. Property over which there is a power of appointment
13. Life insurance proceeds
14. Life insurance policy owned by someone other than the insured
15. Social security benefits
16. Retirement benefits other than from social security

17. Benefits under trusts established by other people[1]
18. Benefits which may come in the future as a result of the death of a relative (by inheritance or by will) [2]

A great many factors may be relevant in determining what is the most intelligent arrangement of a particular estate. An estate plan should not necessarily take the form which saves the most in taxes, but it is certainly the responsibility of the lawyer, in carrying out the objectives of the person whose estate is involved, to avoid unnecessary tax impacts on the estate and to show how additional tax savings may result, if that is the case, by some alterations in the objectives. Some typical considerations, other than taxes, which may influence the arrangement of a particular estate are as follows:

[handwritten margin note: Consider when making an estate plan]

1. The wife and her business ability
2. Whether minor children are involved
3. Whether some of the children are daughters
4. Whether some of the intended beneficiaries are legally incapacitated
5. Amount of wealth now benefiting wife and children
6. Nature of the property that is subject to the estate plan
7. Location of the property that is subject to the estate plan
8. Importance of flexibility in the estate plan to meet changing conditions
9. Significance of probate costs and delay
10. Costs of operating a trust

Estate planning is not something that concerns only the wealthy. In fact it may be more important for a person with a small estate to have a carefully worked out plan, because the effect on the beneficiaries will be far more serious if dollars are wasted.

[handwritten margin note: Estate plan = needed for both rich & poor]

Estate planning as it relates to small and large estates is not basically different. In both instances the objectives of the estate owner should be accomplished in the most sensible manner, with the least diminution in the value of the estate. It is true that a large estate usually presents a multitude of problems, whereas the average small estate presents only a few. But almost any problem which may arise in a large estate may be involved in a

---

[1] A person's estate plan should be prepared in the light of benefits which may accrue to him and his family under presently operative trusts established by other people. If one's children may receive benefits under a trust established by the will of their grandfather, it may be appropriate for the father of the children to take this fact into account in the disposition of his wealth.

[2] Whenever possible, a son's estate plan should be prepared with the background of what benefits will accrue to him and his family on the death of his father. It may be somewhat embarrassing for a son to ask his father about the terms of his father's will but an estate plan of the son which is prepared without such information may be a very unwise one.

small one. Thus, if a lawyer can work effectively with large es
tates, he should be able to adjust his sights so as to deal with
situations presented in small estates.

No dollar dividing line has been established between small
and large estates so far as estate planning is concerned. A particular dollar amount may be too small to justify the employment
of certain arrangements, and the same estate may be classified as a
large one in relation to others.

The dollar worth of an estate is a significant factor in determining the desirability of employing irrevocable inter vivos gifts
as a part of an estate plan. Such gifts are not sensible estate
planning arrangements unless the donor, after the gift, will have
adequate funds for his own needs. Thus, typically, inter vivos
gifts do not come into the picture when a small estate is involved. However, such gifts to the donor's spouse may be appropriate because of the practical assurance that the property so
given will continue to be available, if necessary, to meet the
donor's needs, and because, by splitting his estate with his spouse,
when his estate is between $60,000 and $120,000 in value, all
federal estate taxes may be eliminated, no matter in which order
the donor and his spouse die. The exact dollar line between a
small estate and a large one for the purpose of determining when
inter vivos gifts should be made cannot be fixed. It depends on
the age of the donor, his foreseeable needs, the nature of his
wealth, etc.

It may be appropriate, nevertheless, for a person whose estate
is too small to make inter vivos gifts, to place his property in a
revocable inter vivos trust. Such an arrangement may be just as
advantageous to a small estate as to a large one in the avoidance
of probate delays and expenses. Of course, if a professional
trustee's fees are to be paid for operating the trust, it may be too
costly to create such a trust unless the amount going into it is
sufficient to obtain the full benefit of the minimum charges of
the professional trustee. But trustees may be available for family
revocable trusts who will charge no fees or who will charge at a
lesser rate than the professional.

The dollar worth of the property subject to disposition will be
significant in determining the types of interests to create in the
intended beneficiaries. It must be kept in mind, however, that
the age of the beneficiary, his own dollar worth, his experience
in managing income-producing property, etc., may justify placing very small dollar amounts in trust, even in a discretionary
trust. Normally, long-range trusts will not be employed for small
dollar amounts, but for a short period of time almost any type of

trust may be employed when a small dollar amount is involved. If the dollar amount placed in trust is small, it may not be financially feasible to employ a professional trustee, but again a family or nonfamily individual trustee may be available at little or no cost.

In the case of a small estate, life insurance is quite frequently the principal asset involved. Here the major estate planning decision is the intelligent choice between leaving the proceeds with the insurance company under one of the options in the policy and having the proceeds paid outright either to a beneficiary or to an insurance trust. Obviously many factors bear on this choice. Whether the insured should continue to own the policies on his life becomes increasingly important as his estate expands in size.

Life ins often found in small estates.

It is not uncommon today for a person who has practically no owned property to have a power to appoint a substantial amount (witness the wife who has a general power of appointment under a marital deduction trust). In determining whether to exercise the power and what types of interests to create in the appointees, the same problems may be involved as when a large amount of owned assets is to be disposed of by the estate plan.

POA =

The lawyer who engages in estate planning must have a thorough knowledge of many fields of the law. He may be confronted with problems which can be solved intelligently only on the basis of a knowledge of the law relating to trusts, corporations, income taxes, gift taxes, estate taxes, state inheritance taxes, conflict of laws, future interests, class gifts, powers of appointment, rule against perpetuities, rule against accumulations, joint ownership, gifts of personal property, formalities of a will, incorporation by reference, insurance, divorce, intestate succession, contracts and almost any other topic that can be named. Some of these fields of the law, of course, predominate in estate planning so far as the frequency with which they are involved is concerned.

The lawyer's ability as a draftsman comes into play in the preparation of the instrument or instruments which go to make up the estate plan. A lawyer may give his client the best possible advice as to what the client should do in disposing of his accumulated wealth, but such advice will go for naught if the lawyer fails to carry out the desires of his client in the way he drafts the necessary documents. In order to be a good draftsman, one must be able to recognize inadequate draftsmanship. The ability of a person to discern that someone else has done a poor job of drafting an instrument, however, does not in and of itself mean that such a

Lawyers m/b good draftsmen

person is capable of doing a proper job of drafting himself. In the final analysis, one becomes a good draftsman only by doing a great deal of drafting.

The drafting phase of estate planning, broadly speaking, involves the drafting of both dispositive provisions and administrative provisions in wills and inter vivos trusts. The draftsman must provide in clear and unambiguous language who are to be benefited and under what circumstances they are to be benefited; and if, as is usually the case, the property is to be managed for any period of time by a fiduciary, the draftsman must give the fiduciary clear and unambiguous directions as to the powers and discretions he is to have in the administration of the property involved.

CHAPTER II

Estate Plan Created by Operation of Law — *i.e. intestacy*

If a decedent has not taken advantage of the methods available
to direct the disposition of his accumulated wealth on his death,
in other words if he dies intestate, the law has established an *Intestacy*
orderly process for the distribution of his estate among the living. *statutes*
The plan thus established by law is the estate plan created by *apply only*
operation of law. Keep in mind that even though a decedent has *to gross estate*
not left a will, the estate plan created by operation of law may
operate only with respect to a part of the assets that are includible *def.*
in his <u>gross estate</u>, that is, the estate which is subject to the federal *Gross*
estate tax.[1] In other words, the <u>probate estate</u> and the <u>gross estate</u> *estate*
are usually not the same.

The laws now in force in the various states with respect to the *Intestacy*
descent and distribution of the property of an intestate decedent *statutes*
are based largely on English law.[2] Because of this common origin, *based on*
the statutory scheme of distribution of intestate estates follows a *Eng. law*
similar pattern in the various states; but since there are local peculiarities, it is essential that one be familiar with the law of intestacy of the governing state in order to answer specific questions
as to the estate plan created by operation of law in regard to any
particular person.

It should be obvious that any statutory scheme for the distribution of a decedent's estate must follow a rather fixed and rigid
pattern. It would be impossible to draft a statute which would
give appropriate effect to the infinite variety of factors which may
be presented in connection with the family situation of different
decedents. In other words, when a person elects to have his own
estate plan, he can adjust it to meet the peculiarities of his own
family situation; but when he allows the estate plan created by *dispose*
operation of law to control the devolution of his estate, he is *of intestacy*

[1] Sections 2031-2044 of the 1954 Code describe a decedent's gross estate for
federal estate tax purposes. These sections are quoted infra page 1395.
[2] For a summary of the English law, see Leach, Cases and Text on the Law
of Wills 1-5 (2d ed. 1960 rev.).

accepting an assembly line product that pours everyone into the same mold.

The intestate mold of today is not in many respects in harmony with the realities of a modern society. The laws of intestacy could conceivably be improved and modernized, but legislative action in this area is slow and cumbersome, and in view of the fact that each individual, generally speaking, has the opportunity to avoid the operation of the intestacy laws, it is difficult to build up public demand for legislative change. Some of the undesirable features of the intestacy laws are as follows:

Disadv. of intestacy laws:

1. Beneficiaries usually take outright interests without regard to their individual competency to manage the property involved.
2. The wife's share is frequently inadequate.
3. The estate is unnecessarily diminished by taxes and other expenses as a result of a succession of intestate distributions.
4. The marital deduction allowable by the federal estate tax is normally not fully available when the wife survives.
5. When the beneficiaries are minors, complications are presented as a result of minors receiving property outright.
6. Certain people who frequently should receive benefits from the estate of a decedent are entirely omitted as takers — a daughter-in-law, a stepchild, a particularly needy relative, a faithful and loyal employee.

When should a person be advised to die intestate

The principal question which should be answered at this point is: Under what circumstances, if any, should a person be advised to die intestate? If a person fully understands who will receive his property on his death intestate, under the various combinations of circumstances which may exist at that time, and knows what share each one will receive, and if he then says that such disposition of his property is in accordance with his wishes, the estate plan created by operation of law meets his situation so far as the selection of beneficiaries is concerned. In addition to the selection of beneficiaries, however, he should be familiar with the administration of a decedent's estate under the estate plan created by operation of law, before finally concluding that death intestate is satisfactory in all respects.

Homestead R+ = personal right to beneficial, peaceful & uninterrupted use of home property free from claims of creditors!

[*Ch. II*   ESTATE PLAN CREATED BY OPERATION OF LAW   11

1.   INTESTATE TAKERS AND THEIR RESPECTIVE SHARES

a. *Homestead Rights*[3]

In determining how a person's property will pass on his death intestate, the picture would not be complete without some reference to homestead rights. It should be noted, however, that homestead rights may also be significant when a person dies testate and when there are inter vivos transfers.

The statutory provisions relating to homestead rights in Massachusetts[4] are fairly typical. In the light of the governing statute on homestead rights, three estate planning questions are considered here:

1. Under what circumstances would you advise a person to acquire an estate of homestead?
2. If a husband acquires an estate of homestead, will the value of his widow's interest be available for the federal estate tax marital deduction?
3. If a husband acquires an estate of homestead, will he thereby make a gift to anyone for federal gift tax purposes?

These questions can only be answered against the background of a particular statute and thus the discussion which follows in relation to them is based on the assumption that Massachusetts is the controlling jurisdiction. Such a localized consideration has broad significance, however, as it highlights the factors which should be kept in mind in attempting to answer the questions when other statutory language is controlling.

It would in general seem unwise for a husband in Massachusetts to curtail the alienability of residential property to the extent provided in the homestead laws, unless the exemption of homestead property from attachment, levy on execution and sale for the payment of debts is of particular importance to him. The estate of homestead in the widow is subject to Massachusetts inheritance taxes.[5] Very little use of the estate has been made.[6]

The estate of homestead in Massachusetts continues on the death of the husband for the benefit of the widow and minor children until the youngest child is twenty-one and until the marriage or death of the widow. If there are minor children,

---

[3] Homestead rights are discussed in detail in 1 American Law of Property §§5.75-5.120 (Casner ed. 1952).

[4] See Mass. Ann. Laws, c. 188, §§1-10, quoted infra page 1446.

[5] CCH State Tax Rep. (Mass.), vol. 1, p. 182.

[6] See Newhall, Settlement of Estates and Fiduciary Law in Massachusetts §§217, 218 (4th ed. 1958).

Probate homestead = a homestead set apart by ct for use of a surviving H or W & minor children out of common property or out of real estate belonging to the deceased

If kids, a terminable unt c/f qualify for estate tax marital deduction. If no kids, it can

12   ESTATE PLANNING   [Ch. II

then they may succeed to any interest in the estate of homestead which passes to the widow. Such a terminable interest cannot qualify for the estate tax marital deduction.[7] If, however, there are no minor children, so that the estate of homestead continues only for the benefit of the widow until her death or remarriage, the terminable interest she receives may qualify for the estate tax marital deduction. This will be true if, on its termination, the possession of the property in which the estate of homestead existed will pass to the widow or her estate.[8]

In Massachusetts, property in which an estate of homestead exists cannot be conveyed by the owner so as to defeat the right of the wife and the minor children to a homestead therein unless the wife joins in the deed for the purpose of releasing such right. Even so, it is submitted that, at the time the estate of homestead is created, there is not a transfer from the husband to the wife, which will constitute a gift for federal gift tax purposes. During the lifetime of the husband, the wife's right with respect to the estate of homestead is similar to inchoate dower, and it is recognized that a husband has made no gift to his wife by simply acquiring real property in which his wife will have inchoate dower.[9] If there is a transfer for federal gift tax purposes from the husband to the wife at the time the estate of homestead is created, the wife's interest would clearly seem to be a future interest and the annual gift tax exclusion would not be available with respect to the gift.[10]

b. Allowances to Widows and Children

The controlling local law may give to the decedent's widow and his children allowances which are designed to take care of

[7] Detailed examination of terminable interests in relation to the estate tax marital deduction is made infra page 832.

[8] See 1954 I.R.C. §2056(b)(1)(A), quoted infra page 1407.

Estate of Irvin C. Nelson v. Commissioner, 232 F.2d 720 (5th Cir. 1956), refers to homestead property under Florida law as property in which the wife acquires a terminable interest excluded from the marital deduction.

[9] Revenue Ruling 58-13, 1958-1 C.B. 342, holds that where a husband gives real property to his children, and his wife refuses to release her inchoate dower in the transferred land, the value of the property given to the children is not affected by the fact that it passes to them subject to the wife's dower right. This result seems to justify the conclusion that no previous transfer had been made by the husband to the wife for federal gift tax purposes at the time her inchoate dower right was born. See also D. L. Hopkins v. Magruder, 122 F.2d 693 (4th Cir. 1941); C. J. Carlton v. Commissioner, 190 F.2d 183 (5th Cir. 1951); C. M. Thompson, 37 B.T.A. 793 (1938); Estate of K. Bartman, 10 T.C. 1073 (1948).

[10] The annual gift tax exclusion is described in 1954 I.R.C. §2503(b), quoted infra page 1418.

them during a reasonable period for adjustment and which may be available whether the decedent dies intestate or testate.[11] The availability of these allowances makes it possible, within fairly narrow limits, to recast the decedent's plan of disposition after his death.

From an estate planning standpoint, probably the most important question is whether the amounts allowed and paid pursuant to state law for the support of the surviving spouse during the period of the settlement of the estate of the deceased spouse qualify for the estate tax marital deduction. The answer to this question has turned largely on whether the widow's allowance under the controlling local law is a terminable interest.[12]

The following is quoted from Revenue Ruling 83,[13] which is concerned with the widow's allowance and the estate tax marital deduction:

Under the general rule of subparagraph (A) of Section 812(e)(1) of the Code [1954 I.R.C. §2056(a)] the marital deduction will be allowed with respect to any interest in property included in the gross estate which passes from a decedent to his surviving spouse as absolute owner. In order to qualify under this subparagraph, any right of a widow to an allowance in her husband's estate must be a vested right of property which is not terminated by her death or other contingency. Therefore, if a widow's allowance for the full period of settlement of the estate is such that the allowance, or any unpaid balance thereof, will survive as an asset of her estate in case she dies at any time following the decedent's death, the interest thus taken by the widow would clearly constitute a deductible interest under Section 812(e)(1)(A) of the Code. Whether any interest thus taken by a widow satisfies the statutory requirement in this respect is to be determined in the light of the applicable provisions of the State statutes, as interpreted by the local courts.

There are cases, however, where it appears that the provisions of State statutes providing for allowances for support during the period of settlement of an estate do not confer upon the surviving spouse of a decedent any vested indefeasible right of property which would constitute a deductible interest under Section 812(e) of the Code. In many States

[11] See, for example, Mass. Ann. Laws, c. 196, §§1 and 2, quoted infra page 460.

[12] Detailed examination of terminable interests in relation to the estate tax marital deduction is made infra page 832.

[13] 1953-1 C.B. 395.

local courts have held that such allowances, or any rights
thereto, terminate ipso facto upon remarriage and that death
also terminates any rights to subsequent allowances. Under
such circumstances, the interests passing to the surviving
spouses of decedents in the forms of allowances made for
their support, pursuant to local law, amount to no more than
annuities payable out of the assets of the estates during the
periods of settlement or until prior death or remarriage of
the surviving spouses and, as such, constitute terminable
interests within the meaning of Section 812(e)(1)(B) [1954
I.R.C. §2056(b)], no portion of the values of which qualify
for the marital deduction.

In view of the foregoing, it is held that the interest in an
estate which passes to a surviving spouse pursuant to State
law in the form of an allowance for support during the period
of settlement of the deceased spouse's estate must constitute
a vested right of property such as will, in the event of her
death as of any moment or time following the decedent's
death, survive as an asset of her estate, in order to qualify
under Section 812(e)(1)(A) of the Internal Revenue Code for
the estate tax marital deduction.

The Internal Revenue Code of 1954, as passed by the House of
Representatives, contained a specific provision relating to widows'
allowances and the estate tax marital deduction, which stated in
substance that support allowances paid to the surviving spouse
within one year of the deceased spouse's death would qualify for
the deduction. This provision was deleted by the Senate, and the
Conference Committee report in commenting on the deletion said
in effect that the complications of the proposed section were largely
unnecessary because many of the widows' allowances should qualify
for the marital deduction under present law without regard to the
time of payment. The confusion which has developed over this
matter indicates that it might have been desirable to cover it specifically in the 1954 Code.

In order for any benefit received by a surviving spouse to qualify
for the estate tax marital deduction, it must be deemed to pass or
to have passed from the deceased spouse to the surviving spouse.[14]
Does the widow's allowance meet this test? The Treasury Regulations answer this question in the affirmative.[15] The Tax Court,
however, has taken a contrary position.[16]

[14] Detailed consideration of the passing test is given infra page 827.
[15] See Reg. §20.2056(e)-2(a), quoted infra page 1540.
[16] See Estate of Proctor D. Rensenhouse, 27 T.C. 107 (1956). This case was
remanded by the Sixth Circuit, 252 F.2d 566 (1958), when the issue as to the

The most troublesome question in regard to widows' allowances and the marital deduction has been whether the allowance is a terminable interest. In this regard it must be kept in mind that though the allowance is terminable, it may still qualify for the marital deduction if, on its termination, nothing passes to any person other than the surviving spouse or her estate. Thus, if the surviving spouse is the sole beneficiary of the decedent spouse's estate, a widow's allowance, though terminable, may qualify for the marital deduction because on its termination nothing passes to anyone but the surviving spouse or her estate.[17] Several courts have taken the position that the widow's allowance consists of only what is paid to her and that no part of her allowance can possibly pass to anyone else when the widow's right to future payments comes to an end, and thus the terminable interest in her is not a disqualified one.[18] This view should save all widows' allowances for the marital deduction to the extent amounts are in fact paid.

In several instances determinations have been made that the widow's allowance is not a terminable interest under the controlling local law.[19] The view that it is a terminable interest that does

---

passing requirement was dropped and the issue as to whether the allowance was a terminable interest was raised. For further litigation of this case see note 19 infra.

In Estate of John H. Denman, 33 T.C. 361 (1959), an Ohio law was involved under which a widow is entitled to $2500 as personal property exempt from administration and to an allowance sufficient to support her for twelve months. The decedent's estate had only tangible personalty, which was used for the payment of debts, and real property in which the widow was given a life interest. The widow advanced money from her own funds to the estate and then as executrix satisfied her own claims for $2500 and the widow's allowance ($3000). The court held that the amounts paid to the widow did not qualify for the marital deduction because they did not pass from the decedent to her. The court commented that "had the widow here compelled the estate to sell sufficient assets [real estate] to pay her allowances the amounts thereof might have qualified for the marital deduction."

. [17] See Reg. §20.2056(b)-1(g), Ex. (8), quoted infra page 1531.

[18] Quivey v. United States, 176 F. Supp. 433 (D. Neb. 1959); Shafer v. United States, 60-1 U.S.T.C. ¶11949 (S.D. Iowa, 1960).

. [19] In Estate of Proctor D. Rensenhouse, 31 T.C. 818 (1959), the court determined that under Michigan law the widow's allowance was not a terminable interest because, though it was payable in monthly installments over a year, the widow's death or remarriage would not terminate the payments. The court pointed out that the fact that the award had to be applied for and granted by a court was not a contingency that made the interest terminable. Molner v. United States, 175 F. Supp. 271 (N.D. Ill. 1959), held that an award to a surviving spouse under Illinois law for her proper support for the period of nine months after the decedent's death qualified for the marital deduction because an award does not terminate or abate upon the death or remarriage of the surviving spouse. In Estate of Margaret R. Gale, 35 T.C. —, No. 27 (1960), the law of Maine was involved and a single lump-sum award of $3000 to the decedent's widower was deemed to qualify for the marital deduction.

See also King v. Wiseman, 147 F. Supp. 156 (W.D. Okla. 1956), which held

not qualify for the marital deduction, however, has some support.[20]

Various distributions out of an estate of a decedent will carry to the distributee estate income for the year of distribution, so that the distributee will have to include such distributions in his gross income.[21] Will the payments which go to make up a widow's allowance carry estate income to the widow to any extent? If they do, the net worth of the widow's allowance may be significantly reduced. The Regulations exclude from such payments estate income except to the extent they are payable out of, and charge-able to, income under an order or a decree or local law.[22]

If the surviving spouse should die within ten years of the death of the deceased spouse, it will be necessary to ascertain the amount of the credit available to the estate of the surviving spouse with respect to the tax paid by the deceased spouse's estate on the transfers made to the surviving spouse.[23] Is the widow's allowance transferred to her by the deceased spouse for the purpose of the credit for tax paid on prior transfers? Revenue Ruling 58-167[24] points out that in most jurisdictions the widow's allowance is treated as a charge against the estate in the same manner as an expense of administration, but nevertheless it does pass to the surviving spouse by operation of law and, to the extent actually paid, is a transfer from the deceased spouse for the purpose of the credit for tax paid on prior transfers. The payment of the widow's

that the full amount of the widow's allowance qualified for the marital deduction under Oklahoma law.

[20] See Estate of Edward Cunha v. Commissioner, 279 F.2d 292 (9th Cir. 1960), which held that under California law an allowance to the decedent's widow did not qualify for the marital deduction because the right to the allowance was subject to termination in the event of the widow's death or remarriage. In United States National Bank of Portland v. United States, 188 F. Supp. 332 (D. Ore. 1960), a widow's allowance in the amount of $12,000 was granted under Oregon law, to be paid from corpus. The court construed the Oregon statute relating to a widow's allowance and determined that it gave no vested property right to the widow in estate assets but only a personal privilege which would terminate on her death or remarriage and which was subject to specified conditions precedent. On the basis of the Cunha case, the court concluded that the widow's allowance did not qualify for the marital deduction. The court regarded Shafer v. United States, supra note 18, as in conflict with the Cunha case.

[21] Income taxation of estates and estate beneficiaries is examined infra page 77.

[22] See Reg. §1.661(a)-2 (e), quoted infra page 1492.

H.R. 9662, which failed of passage in the Eighty-sixth Congress, contained a specific provision that would exclude from the gross income of the distributee any amount properly paid or credited from the corpus of a decedent's estate during the period beginning with the day following the death of the decedent and ending thirty-six months thereafter, in full or partial satisfaction of an award or allowance under applicable local law for the support of a surviving spouse or dependents for a limited period during the administration of the estate.

[23] See 1954 I.R.C. §2013, quoted infra page 1391.

[24] 1958-1 C.B. 340.

[handwritten top margin: In order for WA to count as a tax credit, it m/ come out of prine, + ~~income~~]

allowance, however, must be made out of principal, not income, in order for it to count in determining the credit.

The widow's allowance normally is a claim against the estate which takes precedence over debts, legacies and charges of administration. Even though the controlling local law so provides, the surviving spouse who receives a widow's allowance is a transferee of estate assets who may be required to pay income taxes of the deceased spouse which are assessed against his estate after his death.[25] *[handwritten: SS who receives WA m/h to pay income]*

[right margin handwritten: widow's allowance prevails over other debts — taxes levied against estate of deed]

If the widow's allowance escapes state inheritance taxes, its net worth to her may be increased. The controlling local law must be examined to determine whether it passes free of this tax burden.[26] *[handwritten: Ck to see if state inherit taxes m/b pd on WA]*

PROBLEMS

2.1. Under what circumstances would you advise a widow to claim her widow's allowance?

2.2. It is provided by 48 Stat. 760 (1934), 31 U.S.C., c. 6, §192 (1958):

[right margin handwritten: See p 78 + p 123]

> Every executor, administrator or assignee, or other person, who pays, in whole or in part, any debt due by the person or estate for whom or for which he acts before he satisfies and pays the debts due the United States from such person or estate, shall become answerable in his own person and estate to the extent of such payments for the debts so due to the United States, or for so much thereof as may remain due and unpaid.

Section 20.2002-1 of the Regulations states that the word "debt" as used in the above-quoted statute includes a beneficiary's distributive share of an estate.

If the executor pays a widow's allowance pursuant to a decree of a court, has he paid a "debt due by the . . . estate . . . for which he acts," so that he may be personally liable for debts due the United States to the extent of such payment if the remaining estate assets are not sufficient to discharge such debts?

2.3. If the widow dies before the expiration of the period of

---

[25] See 1954 I.R.C. §6901, quoted infra page 1434. The statement in the text in regard to the operation of §6901 is supported by Davis v. Birdsong, 275 F.2d 113 (5th Cir. 1960).

[26] For example, see the wording of the Massachusetts inheritance tax law (Mass. Ann. Laws, c. 65, §1), quoted infra page 1441. A widow's allowance in Massachusetts is treated as a deduction for inheritance tax purposes, like an administration expense, and is not subject to an inheritance tax. Newhall, Settlement of Estates and Fiduciary Law in Massachusetts §140 (4th ed. 1958).

time during which a widow's allowance can be claimed, without having claimed such an allowance, will there be includible in her gross estate the amount she might have claimed, on the ground that she died possessed of a general power of appointment with respect to such amount? [27] If the widow is alive at the expiration of the period of time during which a widow's allowance can be claimed and she has not claimed it, will she be deemed to have released a general power of appointment and thus have made a gift for federal gift tax purposes to the persons who benefit from her failure to claim her allowance? [28]

c. *Advancements*

A father may make payments to or for the benefit of his children during his lifetime, with various intentions. If his desire is that the expenditures for each child are to be totaled and the total treated as an advance payment on each child's share as an heir, will his desire be effectuated if he does not leave a will in which this intent is manifested? The statute on advancements which is operative in the controlling jurisdiction must be consulted in connection with answering this question.

An examination of the Massachusetts statutory provisions on advancements[29] reveals the following:

1. Advancements may be made only to a child or other lineal descendant.
2. Either real or personal property may be the subject matter of an advancement.
3. If the advancement exceeds the intestate share of the recipient, he does not have to return the excess.
4. The intention of the intestate that the transfer to the child or other lineal descendant is to be treated as an advancement must be expressed in the gift, or charged in writing as such by the intestate, or acknowledged in writing as such by the recipient.[30]

[27] The inclusion in a decedent's gross estate of the value of property over which he has a general power of appointment is explained infra page 689. Section 2041 of the 1954 Code, which deals with powers of appointment, is quoted infra page 1409.

[28] The release of a general power of appointment is deemed a transfer of property by the individual possessing the power. See 1954 I.R.C. §2514(b), quoted infra page 1426.

[29] See Mass. Ann. Laws, c. 196, §§3-8, quoted infra page 1460.

[30] In Bigelow v. Poole, 10 Gray 104, 105 (Mass. 1857), the following statement appears: "It is the settled law of this commonwealth, that an advancement, whether of real or personal property, made by an intestate to his child or other descendant, must be proved by the evidence prescribed by our statutes, and by no other."

5. The value of the property on the date it is given will control in determining the amount of the advancement unless some other value is stated in the instrument which is the basis of proving that an advancement has been made.
6. If the recipient of an advancement dies before the intestate, leaving issue, the advancement will be attributed to his issue in determining their distributive shares of the intestate's estate.

The consequences which payments made by a decedent in his lifetime should have when a final distribution of his estate is made can be controlled by him through a will.[31]   If the will is silent, advancements prior to the date of the will are eliminated from consideration on the theory that the testator took them into consideration in his determination of the distributive shares under the will.[32]   Transfers to a legatee which postdate the will may be deemed in partial or total satisfaction of the legacy.[33]

If the intestate share of a surviving spouse is based on the deceased spouse's estate as augmented by advancements made to lineal descendants, the portion of his estate which she will receive may be significantly increased and the available estate tax marital

[31] In In re Baum's Estate, 4 Utah 2d 375, 294 P.2d 711 (1956), the testator stated in his will that he desired to treat all of his children alike and that he had made advancements to two of his named sons, which were equivalent to their full share in his estate. The sons who were thus excluded undertook to establish that their father was mistaken in his belief that he had made advancements to them, but the court held that such evidence was inadmissible.

If payments are made during the testator's lifetime to one who can claim a certain share of the testator's estate on his death regardless of the terms of the will, such as a surviving spouse in some jurisdictions, the testator may not by the terms of his will force such a person to regard payments made to her to be treated as part of the share she is entitled to on death, except to the extent the controlling law on advancements would permit the payment to be regarded as an advancement.

[32] In Gilmore v. Jenkins, 129 Iowa 686, 106 N.W. 193 (1906), the court considered whether an advancement should be taken into consideration in the disposition of the decedent's property where he left a will but the will did not dispose of all his property, so that there was a partial intestacy. At page 689 the court uses this language: "We are of opinion that under our statute, which provides for bringing advancements into hotchpot when given by an 'intestate' to his heir, no property so given can be taken into account in the distribution of an estate, where the ancestor leaves a will, although he may not have disposed of all of his property thereby. The general rule, both in England and in this country, is that the law of advancements, in the absence of statute, does not apply unless the ancestor dies wholly intestate. [Citations omitted.] The reason for this rule is obvious. If it were otherwise, it would be impossible for one to make a will which, in cases of partial intestacy, would give to one heir more than to another. The testator is conclusively presumed to have considered the advancements and the bequests made in the will collectively, and to have made distribution as he intended to make it."

[33] See discussion at page 272 infra.

deduction may be enlarged with a significant resultant tax advantage. This was dramatically illustrated in a case controlled by Kansas law.[34]

PROBLEM

2.4. H dies intestate, a resident of Massachusetts, and survived by his wife, W, his son, S, and his daughter, D. Assume that H's net distributable estate (exclusive of the sums hereinafter mentioned) is $30,000. During his lifetime H delivered $9000 to his son. If this sum was an advancement, what dollar amount will W, S and D each receive on distribution of H's net distributable estate? If this sum was a loan to S and has not been repaid, what dollar amount will W, S and D each receive on distribution of H's net distributable estate? If the $9000 was an advancement, did H make a gift to his son for federal gift tax purposes? Suppose that the amount delivered by H to S during his lifetime was $20,000 and that this sum was an advancement. What dollar amount will W, S and D each receive on distribution of H's net distributable estate of $30,000? To answer the questions presented in this problem, it will be necessary to examine Massachusetts Annotated Laws, c. 190, §§1-3, quoted infra page 1451.

[34] In Brodrick v. Moore, 226 F.2d 105 (10th Cir. 1955), a husband acquired $89,500 worth of United States government bonds with his own funds and named his daughter as co-owner. He died testate and in his will gave all of his estate, except one item, to his daughter. His widow renounced his will and elected to take her statutory share. In Kansas, the governing state, the wife's statutory share on renunciation of her husband's will is one half. The Probate Court in Kansas determined that the $89,500 worth of bonds constituted an advancement. Under Kansas law (Kan. Gen. Stat. Ann. §59-510 (1949)), it is provided that property which has been given by an intestate decedent by way of an advancement to one to whom the decedent's property would pass by intestate succession shall be counted as a part of the distributive share of such property to such person and to that extent shall be taken into account in determining the estate to be distributed among those to whom it passes by intestate succession. When a widow renounces a will and elects to take under the Kansas statute, the estate is distributed as though there were no will. Thus, in determining the widow's distributive share, the Probate Court took into account the $89,500 advancement to the daughter. Consequently, the amount passing to the widow was substantially increased and the marital deduction available was likewise increased. The Court of Appeals held that the determination of the Kansas Probate Court that the $89,500 in bonds constituted an advancement to the daughter was controlling. The court said: . . . "the fact that the action of the widow may have had the effect of reducing taxes makes no difference. Taxes may be decreased, or avoided altogether, by means which the law permits." It appeared that the widow in this case had renounced her husband's will and claimed her statutory share solely to avoid taxes on his estate as evidenced by the fact that she later gave the property outright to her daughter. Note that the problem presented in this case could not arise in Massachusetts, because advancements are not taken into account in determining a widow's share.

d. *Spouse's Share*

(1) Dower and Curtesy [35]

In some states dower and curtesy have been abolished, so that the surviving spouse's share is dependent on the terms of the governing statutes on descent and distribution.[36] In many states, however, dower and curtesy continue to exist and the surviving spouse is forced to elect between dower or curtesy and the share in the real property given to the spouse under the statute of descent.[37]

Dower at common law was a life estate in one third of the real property of which the husband was seised of an estate of inheritance during the marriage, which estate the issue of the marriage might possibly inherit.[38] Prior to the death of the husband, the wife had inchoate dower, which became consummate on his death.[39]

Generally an absolute divorce puts an end to inchoate dower.[40] The statutes in the controlling jurisdiciton, however, must be examined because in some states the dower rights of the wife in land owned by the husband prior to the divorce will outlive the termination of the marriage if the husband's misconduct caused the divorce.[41] Even though divorce does not affect the wife's right

[35] For a detailed consideration of dower and curtesy, see 1 American Law of Property §§5.1-5.74 (Casner ed. 1952).

[36] The New York statute provides that when the parties intermarried prior to September 1, 1930, a widow shall be entitled to dower in all lands of which her husband was, prior to September 1, 1930, seized of an estate of inheritance at any time during the marriage. Except as thus provided, after August 31, 1930, no inchoate right of dower shall be possessed by a wife during coverture and no widow shall be endowed in any lands whereof her husband became seized of an estate of inheritance. N.Y. Real Property Law §190.

[37] Provisions operative in Massachusetts with respect to dower and curtesy are Chapter 189, §§1 et seq., quoted infra page 1448.

In Meyer v. Roberts, 19 Ill. 2d 141, 166 N.E.2d 27 (1960), a first wife claimed dower some five years after her husband died, stating that she had just learned of his death. The court held that her failure to make her election in the time stated in the statute was fatal to her claim.

[38] In Seaman v. Harmon, 192 Mass. 5, 7, 78 N.E. 301 (1906), the court states: "There is no statute in this Commonwealth which gives a wife dower in the estate of which her husband has only an equitable title. At common law the wife has no dower in the estate of which the husband did not have a legal seisin at some time during the coverture."

[39] The significance of the wife's inchoate dower in connection with federal gift tax matters is mentioned supra page 12, note 9.

[40] The result stated in the text is codified in Mass. Ann. Laws, c. 208, §27.

[41] See 1 American Law of Property §5.36 (Casner ed. 1952).

to dower in certain land, she will lose her right to waive dower and take a statutory share as an heir.[42]

The trend in the recent legislation relating to dower is to curtail it, if not to abolish it.[43]   If this new legislation is to be immediately significant on a wide front, it must be made applicable to existing inchoate dower rights.   To make it so effective may raise a serious constitutional question.[44]   During the husband's lifetime, he cannot dispose of his lands free of the wife's inchoate dower unless she acquiesces, and on his death her dower claim takes precedence over the husband's creditors.   If the husband becomes indebted to the federal government because of unpaid income taxes, will the federal government be in a position subordinate to the inchoate dower of the wife where it undertakes to collect for such unpaid income taxes out of the husband's realty?   If the husband dies leaving unpaid federal income taxes, will the wife take precedence over the federal government to the extent of her dower claim?[45]

[42] If a decree nisi is entered in a divorce case and the husband dies before the decree becomes absolute, the wife's marital rights in the husband's property are unaffected. See Diggs v. Diggs, 291 Mass. 399, 196 N.E. 858 (1935).

[43] See Mass. Ann. Laws, c. 189, §16, quoted infra page 1451.

[44] In Opinion of the Justices, 337 Mass. 786, 151 N.E.2d 475 (1958), a proposed statute which would limit dower and curtesy to the property owned by the deceased spouse at his or her death was deemed constitutional, even though it would destroy inchoate rights of dower and curtesy as they existed prior to the effective date of the proposed statute.

[45] In First National Bank of Elkhorn v. White, 58-2 U.S.T.C. ¶9568 (Walworth County Ct., Wis. 1958), the government enforced its claim for unpaid taxes during the lifetime of the husband and the court held that the inchoate right of dower could not be given priority over the government's claim. Compare, however, United States v. Ettelson, 67 F. Supp. 257 (E.D. Wis. 1946), where the court held that the lien for income taxes alleged to exist in favor of the United States did not affect or supersede the widow's dower interest in the Wisconsin realty. In Chandler v. Pilley, 60-1 U.S.T.C. ¶9238 (Shelby County Prob. Ct., Tenn. 1959), the court recognized that where the government had perfected its lien for unpaid income taxes against land of the taxpayer before his death, the lien took priority over the wife's claim of dower, but was not superior to her homestead right which was guaranteed her by the Tennessee Constitution.

United States v. Hicks, 212 F.2d 356 (5th Cir. 1954), held that where a widow was being sued by the government for the payment of unpaid federal income taxes of her husband, the District Court erred in granting her motion for a summary judgment without trying the case on the merits, when in her answer she simply alleged that she had received from the estate only her dower interest and sums for which she gave consideration.

In United States v. American National Bank of Jacksonville, 255 F.2d 504 (5th Cir. 1958), cert. denied sub nom. American National Bank of Jacksonville v. United States, 358 U.S. 835 (1958), rehearing denied, 359 U.S. 1006 (1959), a tenancy by the entirety governed by Florida law was involved, and the court held that the husband, during his wife's lifetime, would not have any interest in the property to which a lien for federal taxes owed by him, but not by her, could attach. Upon the wife's death, the tax lien attached to the

If the wife elects to take dower rather than her statutory share as an heir in the real property, the value of her one-third interest for life will not qualify for the estate tax marital deduction because it is a disqualified terminable interest.[46] The dower interest is deemed to pass from the husband to the wife,[47] so that, if the terminable character of it could be eliminated, it could qualify for the deduction. If the controlling local law provides that the wife may take a lump sum payment equal in value to a life interest in one third of the realty in lieu of one third for life in the realty, and the wife takes the lump sum payment, will this payment to her qualify for the estate tax marital deduction?[48]

property as of the time of her death. Thus a mortgage executed by the husband and wife had priority over the tax lien of the government.

[46] Terminable interests and the estate tax marital deduction are considered infra page 832.

[47] See Reg. §20.2056(e)-1(a), quoted infra page 1539.

[48] Revenue Ruling 279, 1953-2 C.B. 275, discusses the situation where, under state law, a surviving wife is entitled to dower in the real property of her husband of a life interest in one third of his lands. Under the state law, if the land in which the wife is entitled to dower is not capable of equitable division, the executor or administrator may sell the land with the consent of the surviving spouse and give her outright a sum of money equivalent to the value of her life interest, the amount in no event exceeding one third of the sale price. In such a state, if the land is sold and the wife receives outright a sum of money in payment of her dower interest, this sum does not qualify for the marital deduction because it stems from the life interest received under the statute, which is a terminable interest. The ruling provides that the sum of money received by the wife is not "a statutory interest in lieu of dower" and therefore it cannot be regarded as separate and distinct from the basic dower interest to which the wife is entitled. The state law under consideration in Rev. Rul. 279 was that of Alabama. Evidently the ruling did not please the persons representing the wife, because the case of Crosby v. United States, 148 F. Supp. 810 (N.D. Fla. 1956, Supplemental opinion, 1957), is concerned with the question whether the amount received by a wife in satisfaction of her dower interest in Alabama land is available for the marital deduction. The court held that under Alabama law the wife has an election to take the life interest in land or to receive outright a sum of money equal to the value of such life interest, and thus what she elects to receive outright does not stem from the life interest and is not a terminable interest for the purposes of the marital deduction. Additional proceedings in the Crosby case are reported in Crosby v. United States, 151 F. Supp. 497 (N.D. Fla. 1957), aff'd sub nom. United States v. Crosby, 257 F.2d 515 (5th Cir. 1958). In accord with the Crosby case is Traders National Bank of Kansas City v. United States, 148 F. Supp. 278 (W.D. Mo. 1956) (Missouri law), aff'd sub nom. United States v. Traders National Bank of Kansas City, 248 F.2d 667 (8th Cir. 1957). Dougherty v. United States, 175 F. Supp. 339 (E.D. Ky. 1959), held that the lump sum paid to a wife in satisfaction of her dower claim was not a "statutory interest in lieu of dower" because the Kentucky statute which authorized a money payment was not complied with. The amount paid to the wife was determined by agreement of the parties. If the statute had been complied with, the inference is that it would have been a "statutory interest in lieu of dower," and the amount paid her would have qualified for the marital deduction.

PROBLEMS

2.5. A conveys Blackacre, which is located in Massachusetts, to B for life, remainder to C and his heirs. C dies survived by his wife, W. Is W entitled to dower in Blackacre?

2.6. Under what circumstances will you advise a widow in Massachusetts to elect to take her dower and thereby give up her statutory right as an heir to a share of her husband's real property?

(2) Statutory Share as an Heir

When the deceased spouse dies intestate, the share in the estate which the surviving spouse is entitled to take as an heir depends, of course, on the terms of the controlling local law. Typically, the statutes on descent and distribution give the surviving spouse an outright interest and its size depends on the nearness to the decedent of other surviving relatives.[49] Although at one time the statutes on the descent of real property differed from those on the distribution of personal property, generally the two categories of property now pass to the same persons in the same proportions, but the title to the real property may pass directly to the described taker, whereas the title to the personal property may pass through the personal representative of the decedent on its way to the described taker.

Suppose that the deceased spouse dies intestate and leaves surviving him his wife and one child, and that the controlling local law under these conditions gives the surviving wife outright a one-third share of her deceased husband's estate. This one-third share, though given to the surviving wife by operation of law, is deemed to pass to her from her husband for purposes of the estate tax marital deduction,[50] and thus it qualifies for the marital deduction because it is not a terminable interest. Whether the maximum allowable marital deduction will be exceeded,[51] so that the gross estate of the surviving spouse will be augmented without the benefit of any compensating reduction in the deceased spouse's estate as to such excess,[52] will depend on the amount of the non-probate

---

[49] For an example of statutory provisions which describe a surviving spouse's share in the estate of a deceased spouse when the latter dies intestate, see Mass. Ann. Laws, c. 190, §1 (Supp. 1959), quoted infra page 1451.

[50] See Reg. §20.2056(e)-1(a)(5), quoted infra page 1539.

[51] The maximum allowable marital deduction is 50 percent of the deceased spouse's adjusted gross estate. See discussion at page 785 infra.

[52] The undesirability of making gifts to the surviving spouse which exceed the maximum allowable marital deduction is considered infra page 791.

items in the deceased spouse's gross estate which pass, or have passed, to the surviving spouse in a form which qualifies for the marital deduction.[53]

The amount of the available marital deduction as a result of the surviving spouse being entitled outright to a one-third share as an intestate taker will depend on whether her one-third share is carved out before or after the payment of various estate obligations. In other words, the available deduction is limited to the net worth of what passes to the surviving spouse.[54]

The estate obligations will consist of funeral expenses, debts, expenses of administration, and death taxes (federal and state). Assume for a moment that the one third passing outright to the surviving spouse is one third of what is left after all these estate obligations have been paid. A circle has been created because the value of the one third which qualifies for the marital deduction cannot be determined until the amount of the federal estate taxes is known, and that amount cannot be determined until the value of the one third is determined.[55] The circle is not avoided where the one third is carved out before federal estate taxes are paid, if it must contribute proportionately to the federal estate tax bill.

The statutes on descent and distribution were not drafted with the estate tax marital deduction in mind. Hence some difficulty may be encountered in attempting to reach what may be the ideal solution from the standpoint of preserving the worth of the estate, which is to carve out the surviving spouse's one third before the payment of federal estate taxes and then to free it from contributing to the payment of the federal estate tax bill. Even this solution will not make available for the marital deduction the full value of the one third if the surviving spouse must pay a state inheritance tax on its value.

The statutory share of the surviving spouse on the death of the deceased spouse intestate in Massachusetts, and the law of that Commonwealth is typical in this regard, is determined "after payment of the debts of the deceased and charges of his last sickness and funeral and of the settlement of his estate . . ." [56] Does the word "debts" or the words "charges . . . of the settlement of his

---

[53] An example of a non-probate item in the deceased spouse's gross estate which would pass to the surviving spouse in a form which qualifies for the marital deduction is the proceeds of life insurance on the life of the deceased spouse where the insured retained the incidents of ownership with respect to the insurance until his death and the proceeds are payable outright to the surviving spouse.

[54] See Reg. §20.2056(b)-4, quoted infra page 1534.

[55] See supplemental instructions for Form 706 for computation of interrelated death taxes and marital or charitable deduction.

[56] Mass. Ann. Laws, c. 190, §1 (Supp. 1959), quoted infra page 1451.

estate" include federal estate taxes? If so, then the circle is created
and the available marital deduction so far as the surviving spouse's
one third is concerned will be reduced. If not, then the circle is
avoided and the available marital deduction is increased if the one
third does not have to contribute to the federal estate tax bill.
Whether or to what extent it must so contribute depends on the
interpretation of the so-called Apportionment Act in Massachusetts.[57]

It is not possible to generalize about whether the surviving
spouse's one third will be determined before or after the payment
of federal estate taxes or whether the one third, if determined before the payment of federal estate taxes, will be free of any obligation to contribute to such taxes. The wording of the controlling
local law and the presence or absence of an apportionment act
may produce different results in different jurisdictions.[58]

PROBLEM

2.7. If it should be determined in Massachusetts that the surviving spouse's statutory share as an intestate taker is carved out
of the deceased spouse's estate after it has been reduced by the
payment of debts, funeral expenses, and expenses of administration
but before the payment of any death taxes, would the statutory
share so determined have to be reduced to any extent in determining the available marital deduction with respect to it because
of the amount of the death taxes?

e. *Shares of Persons Other than the Spouse*

After the decedent's estate is diminished by the payment of the
various estate obligations and the allocation to the surviving spouse
of whatever she is entitled to receive, the intestate shares of persons other than the surviving spouse will be carved out of what
is left, taking into account, as may be required, any advancements.

[57] Mass. Ann. Laws, c. 65A, §5 (Supp. 1959), quoted infra page 1444.
[58] In Pitts v. Hamrick, 228 F.2d 486 (4th Cir. 1955), the decedent died intestate, and under the controlling South Carolina law (S.C. Code §19-52
(1952)) his widow was entitled to one third of his estate. Furthermore, under
South Carolina law, the widow's share is not reduced by the federal estate
taxes chargeable against estate assets. Consequently, the court held that the
marital deduction otherwise allowable on account of the one-third interest
passing to the decedent's wife was not reduced by the taxes payable with
respect to the other two thirds.
A problem similar to the one considered in the text is presented when the
deceased spouse leaves a will and the surviving spouse renounces the will and
claims her statutory share. This problem is examined infra page 58.

The statute of descent and distribution in the controlling state will determine such intestate shares.[59]

The typical pattern of intestate distribution to others than a surviving spouse is to prefer the relatives of the decedent in the following order:

1. Lineal descendants
2. Parents
3. Brothers and sisters and their descendants
4. Other collateral kindred

If the decedent leaves no relatives and no surviving spouse, then his property escheats to the state.[60]

The governing local law must be examined to determine the manner of distribution among lineal descendants. Suppose, for example, that the decedent is survived by two children and six grandchildren, that three of the grandchildren are children of a deceased child of his, and the other three are children of his two living children. In such a case, the statute of descent and distribution will most likely call for a division among the lineal descendants on a per stirpes basis, that is, each living child will take one third and the one third that would have gone to the deceased child, had he lived, will go to the deceased child's three children.

When the intestate takers are brothers and sisters and their descendants, usually the per stirpes plan of distribution is followed. But intestate distributees who are collaterals other than brothers and sisters and their descendants are normally limited to those in the nearest degree of relationship to the decedent.[61]

---

[59] See, for example, Mass. Ann. Laws, c. 190, §§2-8, quoted infra page 1452.

[60] See Reg. §20.0-2(a), quoted infra page 1501, which points out that the escheat of a decedent's property to the state for lack of heirs is a transfer which causes the property to be included in the decedent's gross estate. Will the value of such a transfer be deductible in determining the taxable estate of the decedent? See 1954 I.R.C. §2055(a), quoted infra page 1405. Notice that though §2055(a) makes provision, in determining a decedent's taxable estate, for a deduction of the value of transfers to a state, Reg. §20.2055-1(a), quoted infra page 1529, refers to the deduction as being available with respect to property transferred by the decedent to any state "during his lifetime or by will."

[61] Under the civil law method of computing degrees of relationship, the relationship of the decedent and the claimant is ascertained by counting upwards from the decedent to the common ancestor and downwards from the common ancestor to the claimant, the total of the steps up and down being the degree of relationship between the claimant and the decedent. For example, if the claimant is a cousin of the decedent, their common ancestors will be a grandfather and grandmother of the decedent. The grandfather and grandmother will be two steps up from the decedent, and the cousin will be two steps down, so that the cousin will be in the fourth degree of relationship to the decedent. The civil law method of computing degrees of relationship is to be contrasted with the common law (or canon law) method. Under the latter method the degree of relationship is established by taking the num-

See local law re: adopted kids

The extent to which adopted children occupy the same position on an intestacy as other children is not the same in all states.[62] Inheritance from an adopted child may also have its peculiarities.[63]

PROBLEMS

2.8. A dies on September 1, 1960, domiciled in Belmont, Massachusetts. He is survived by a wife and three minor children. The following property is in his estate:

	Value
a. Tangible personal property (an automobile, house furnishings, some jewelry, etc.)	$ 3,000
b. Real estate (the family residence in Belmont, Massachusetts, the title to which was in the name of A at the time of his death)	25,000
c. Securities (in A's name at the time of his death)	40,000
d. Life insurance (payable to A's executors or administrators)	50,000
e. Cash (in a checking account in A's name)	1,000
f. Cash (in a savings account in A's name)	5,000
Total	$124,000

Describe the disposition of A's net estate.

2.9. Same as Problem 2.8 except that A had two children, but both of them predeceased him; one of A's children had three children, all of whom survive A, and his other child left one child, who survives A. Describe the disposition of A's net estate.

2.10. Same as Problem 2.8 except that A had no descendants; his parents predeceased him; he is survived by a brother and by two children of a deceased sister. Describe the disposition of A's net estate.

2.11. Same as Problem 2.8 except that A had no descendants; his parents predeceased him; he is not survived by any brother or sister or descendants of a brother or sister; he is survived by a cousin of his father and a child of his father's nephew. Describe the disposition of A's net estate.

---

ber of steps up or the number of steps down, whichever is greater. See Woerner, American Law of Administration §72 (3d ed. 1923).

[62] For an example of a statute describing the rights of adopted children on intestacy, see Mass. Ann. Laws, c. 210, §§7, 9 and 10, quoted infra page 1464.

[63] See the references in note 62 supra.

f. *Disclaimer by Intestate Taker of His Share*

If an intestate taker refuses to take his intestate share and the controlling local law makes no provision for such a situation, what happens to his share? The following are possible results:

1. The disclaimer or refusal is fully effective to prevent the passing of any title to him under the statutes of descent and distribution, and the intestate takers and their respective shares will be determined as though he were dead.

2. The title conferred on an intestate taker by the statutes of descent and distribution cannot be rejected and thus the title passes to him in spite of his disclaimer or refusal and will be deemed to pass from him to the person or persons who take as a consequence of the disclaimer or refusal.

Whether or not the disclaiming intestate taker has made a gift for federal gift tax purposes may turn on which result is reached, as the Hardenburgh case which follows illustrates.

[handwritten margin notes: States = divided on whether intestate heir c/ reject his intestate share. This = imp in deciding if intestate taker h/ made a gift for fed gift tax purpose]

HARDENBERGH v. COMMISSIONER OF INTERNAL REVENUE
198 F.2d 63 (8th Cir. 1952), cert. denied,
344 U.S. 836 (1952)

RIDDICK, Circuit Judge.

On April 2, 1944, George S. Hardenbergh, a resident of St. Paul, Minnesota, died intestate survived by his widow Ianthe and daughter Gabrielle and a son of a former marriage, Geoge Hardenbergh, as his sole heirs at law. Decedent left an estate consisting of real property of the value of $29,378.08 and personalty of the value of $291,281.33. All of the real estate was sold under order of the State Probate Court for the payment of debts and expenses of the administration, leaving $252,317.63 for distribution to the surviving heirs, of which each of the heirs was entitled to one-third by virtue of the Minnesota law of Intestate Succession, M.S.A. §525.13 et seq.

Some time prior to his death decedent had proposed leaving practically his entire estate to his son George in order to equalize to some extent the financial worth of his survivors. At this time his wife, Ianthe, was worth $2,000,000 and the daughter, Gabrielle, was worth a large sum in her own right. All of decedent's family agreed to this proposal, and decedent arranged with his attorney for the preparation of his will to carry it into effect. On Saturday, April 1, 1944, the attorney brought the will to decedent for execution, but because the decedent was then seriously ill, it was decided to delay the execution until Monday, April 3. Decedent died April 2 before the will could be executed.

In April 1944 the proceedings for the administration of decedent's estate began in a Minnesota Probate Court, and on September 20, 1944, Ianthe and Gabrielle filed in the administration proceedings a relinquishment of their respective interests in the estate as follows:

"We, Ianthe B. Hardenbergh and Gabrielle Hardenbergh, widow and daughter respectively of the above named George S. Hardenbergh, deceased, do hereby, coincidentally and jointly, definitely and finally renounce and reject, as of April 2, 1944, the date of death of said George S. Hardenbergh, any and all interest which we may then have had or may now have in and to the estate of said George S. Hardenbergh. We do hereby release and forever discharge the said estate and every part thereof from any claim or interest which may heretofore have accrued or might at any time hereafter accrue to us or either of us by reason of the laws of succession of the State of Minnesota; and we further agree that we will not at any time hereafter assert any claim or interest of any kind, nature or description in or to said estate or any portion thereof.

"We further respectfully state to the above named Court and to anyone interested in said estate that our purpose in renouncing any and all interest we may have in said estate is as follows: just prior to the death of George S. Hardenbergh, he, knowing that I, Ianthe B. Hardenbergh, had a large independent estate, and that I, Gabrielle Hardenbergh, had been amply provided for by trusts created by my grandfather, R. H. Bronson, and by my mother, Ianthe B. Hardenbergh, with our full knowledge and consent, had prepared a Last Will and Testament in which he devised and bequeathed substantially all of his estate to certain named trustees in trust for the sole benefit of his son, George Adams Hardenbergh. The provisions of said Last Will and Testament were agreeable to us. However, George S. Hardenbergh died before execution of said Last Will and Testament could be completed. We renounce all of interest in said estate so that the intention of the said George S. Hardenbergh may be carried out without delay or the intervention of other interests."

Thereafter, the Probate Court made its final decree of distribution reading in part:

". . . that . . . Ianthe B. Hardenbergh and Gabrielle Hardenbergh have filed with this court a renunciation of their interest in the above named estate, and that George Adams Hardenbergh is the person entitled to the residue of said estate of said decedent.

"Now, Therefore, on motion of Matt W. Miller, representative of said estate, and by virtue of the power and authority vested in this court by law, It Is Hereby Ordered, Adjudged and Decreed and the said court does hereby Order, Adjudge and Decree, that all and singular the above described property and all other estate of said decedent in the State of Minnesota, subject to any lawful disposition heretofore made, be and the same is hereby assigned to and vested in George Adams Hardenbergh."

Pursuant to the above decree the net estate was delivered to George Hardenbergh. The Commissioner determined that Ianthe and Gabrielle had each made a gift to George of one-third of the net estate, and the Tax Court sustained his action, 17 T.C. 166. These petitions for review challenge the Tax Court's decision on the ground that the Minnesota Probate Court by its order of final distribution of decedent's estate made the only effective transfer thereof to George Hardenbergh. The taxpayers (Ianthe and Gabrielle) contend that the State Probate Court, as an incident to its jurisdiction of decedent's estate, was invested with jurisdiction to determine decedent's heirs and to adjudicate the taxpayers' right to renounce any claim or interest in the estate; that the Tax Court had erroneously determined a question of State law contrary to the determination thereof by the State Probate Court; and that the decree of the Probate Court, and not the act of the taxpayers in relinquishing their claims to decedent's estate, is the source of the right and title in the property of the estate acquired by George Hardenbergh.

Section 1000 of the Internal Revenue Code, 26 U.S.C.A. §1000 imposes a tax upon the transfer of property by gift whether the property is real or personal, tangible or intangible, and whether the gift is direct or indirect.[64] Section 86.2 of Treasury Regulations 108 provides that all transactions whereby property or rights or interests in property "are gratuitously passed or conferred upon another, regardless of the means or device employed, constitute gifts subject to tax."[65] The words "property," "transfer," "gift," and "indirect," as used in the section of the Revenue Code, are to be read in the broadest and most comprehensive sense. Smith v. Shaughnessy, 318 U.S. 176. The question here is whether under the facts stated the taxpayers each made a gift to

---

[64] The corresponding section in the 1954 Code is §2511(a), quoted infra page 1419. — Ed.

[65] The corresponding section of the Regulations under the 1954 Code is §25.2511-1(c), quoted infra page 1544. — Ed.

George Hardenbergh of their respective interests in decedent's estate. If the gifts were made, there is no dispute as to the value of the gifts or as to the amount of tax for which each donor is liable.

We think the decision of the Tax Court is right. The general rule as to intestate succession is that the title to the property of an intestate passes by force of the rule of law, in this case the Minnesota Statute of Intestate Succession, and that those so entitled by law have no power to prevent the vesting of title in themselves. Bostian v. Milens, 239 Mo. App. 555, 193 S.W.2d 797; Coomes v. Finegan, 233 Iowa 448, 7 N.W.2d 729; and Annotation on Renunciation of benefit under statute of descent and distribution, 170 A.L.R. 435. The rule is otherwise as to legatees or devisees under a will. Brown v. Routzahn, 6 Cir., 63 F.2d 914, since the beneficiary under a will may accept or reject a testamentary gift.[66] The controlling fact here is that title to an interest in decedent's estate vested in the taxpayers by operation of law which neither had the power to prevent.

[66] Consider Rodgers v. United States, 218 F.2d 760 (5th Cir. 1955), *rehearing denied* 220 F.2d 170 (5th Cir. 1955), where a husband, shortly after his wife's death, executed deeds in which he granted to his children and grandchildren land that was community property owned by his wife and himself. His wife had devised to him her entire interest in the community property. Some years after the deeds were executed, the husband filed a renunciation of the devise to him under his wife's will. The court pointed out that under the Texas law which was applicable, the title to devised real estate vests immediately in the devisee, even though the will devising the land is not probated. In this case the husband had not probated his wife's will. Thus the court held that the husband had made a gift to his children and grandchildren not only of his one-half undivided interest in the community property but also of the wife's share of the community property, which was devised to him by her will. It is not clear that the same result would have been reached if the husband had renounced the gift to him under his wife's will, and his children and grandchildren had become entitled to it as a result of his renunciation.

In William L. Maxwell, 17 T.C. 1589 (1952), a husband was the sole beneficiary under his wife's will. The husband and wife were residents of California. The wife had no separate property of her own, and consequently, the property disposed of by her will was only her share of the community property. The husband undertook to renounce and disclaim the property given to him by her will and also any property to which he might be entitled under the laws of succession in California. Under California law the husband was the sole heir of his wife as to the community property. As a result of his renunciation and disclaimer, the California court directed distribution of the wife's share of the community property to her children. The Tax Court held that the husband made a gift of the wife's share of the community property to the children. The gift did not result from the husband's renunciation and disclaimer of the gift to him under his wife's will, because the court recognized that a legatee or devisee under a will is not bound to accept the gift made to him. Rather, the result was based on the husband's renunciation of his wife's property which passed to him on intestacy because of his refusal to accept the gift under his wife's will, for under California law an heir may not prevent intestate property from passing to himself. — Ed.

It is true, as taxpayers contend, that the Minnesota Probate Court acquired jurisdiction of decedent's estate; that the administration of the estate was a proceeding in rem; that during the administration the Probate Court held possession and control of all the estate property and had jurisdiction to determine "who is entitled to share therein, the proportions in which they take, and to assign to each his share"; and that the final decree of distribution is for the distributees the conclusive evidence of their rights. Bengtson v. Setterberg, 227 Minn. 337, 35 N.W.2d 623; Murray v. Calkins, 191 Minn. 460, 252 N.W. 605. It may also be conceded that a Minnesota Probate Court, as such, had no jurisdiction to enforce contracts made by or between heirs relative to the distribution of an estate, which does not mean, however, that such agreements are not binding and enforceable in a proper action in a court having jurisdiction. Barnes v. Verry, 174 Minn. 173, 218 N.W. 551; In re Butler's Estate, 205 Minn. 60, 284 N.W. 889, 890-891.

But it is also true, as shown by the Bengtson and Murray cases relied on by taxpayers, that the exercise of a probate court's jurisdiction is circumscribed by the Minnesota Statute of Intestate Succession. All that these cases hold of importance on the question here is that the probate court having jurisdiction of the property of the estate in administration to determine the identity of the parties entitled to take the estate has jurisdiction to make a wrong decision. Its decision, erroneous in law or fact, is final and binding upon the world, except upon direct attack by appellate review. That is to say, that if in the present case the Probate Court, without the intervention of the taxpayers, had vested the decedent's estate in George, its decree, though contrary to the Minnesota Statute, would be binding on taxpayers until vacated on appeal. The probate decree acquired the effect claimed for it as a transfer of decedent's property to George Hardenbergh because and only because of the consent or acquiescence of the taxpayers. It could not have survived a direct attack.

That the probate decree derived its vitality from the consent of the taxpayers clearly appears from the language of the taxpayers' renunciation and the final decree of distribution. The source of the rights acquired by George Hardenbergh was not the decree of the Probate Court, but the affirmative acts of taxpayers in relinquishing the shares of the estate which Minnesota law vested in them. And in this lies the distinction between the present case and cases like Harris v. Commissioner, 340 U.S. 106, where the reverse of this proposition was true. The Harris case involved the transfer of property rights between husband and wife in preparation for a divorce. The divorce court had jurisdiction to settle the property rights of the parties in any manner justified by the evidence as just and equitable and, as an incident of its jurisdiction, the power to accept or reject the property disposition made by the parties and submitted to the court. The Supreme Court, four justices dissenting, held that the decree of the divorce court and not the agreement between husband and wife disposing of their property interests was the source of the respective rights acquired by them in the property transferred, emphasizing the jurisdiction of the divorce court to approve or reject the agreement. The Court said, 340 U.S. at page 111:

"We, however, think that the gift tax statute is concerned with the source of rights, not with the manner in which rights at some distant time may be enforced. . . . It is 'the transfer' of the property with which the gift tax statute is concerned, not the sanctions which the law supplies to enforce transfer."

The taxpayers agree that upon the death of decedent intestate his sole surviving heirs were George Hardenbergh and the taxpayers, each by Minnesota law entitled, subject to the administration proceedings, to receive equal shares in the estate remaining for distribution. Under Minnesota law title to the real estate of an intestate decedent vests immediately upon his death in the heirs, Bengtson v. Setterberg, subject only to the jurisdiction of the probate court to divest title when necessary in administration proceedings. Where there are no debts, personal property of decedent vests in the heirs without administration. Holtan v. Fischer, 218 Minn. 81, 15 N.W.2d 206. While in cases of administration the administrator takes legal title to the personal property of an estate, the title so vested in him is a qualified one and is limited to the purposes of the administration. His possession and title are that of a custodian or trustee during administration. Subject to this right of possession and qualified title, the property descends to the heirs. The law of Minnesota on intestate succession rather than the decree of distribution in administration proceedings is the heirs' source of title. In re Butler's Estate, supra.

And so, here, the taxpayers realized that some affirmative action on their part was necessary to carry out decedent's wishes in reference to the distribution of his property. To this end they renounced their interests in decedent's estate which vested in them upon his death. Their interests in the estate were assignable, Cooper v. Hayward, 71 Minn. 374, 74 N.W. 152, and subject to the liens of judgment creditors, Kolars v. Brown, 108 Minn. 60, 124 N.W. 229. What the court did was to deliver to George at taxpayers' request what the taxpayers had given him.

The decision of the Tax Court is affirmed.[67]

PROBLEM

2.12. If the intestate estate includes income-producing realty and the right to possess it vests immediately in the intestate takers, the income from such realty will be taxable to the intestate takers from the date of the decedent's death.[68] If one of the intestate takers disclaims his intestate share in the decedent's realty, to whom will the income from such realty for the period between the decedent's death and the date of the disclaimer be taxable? See Frances Marcus, 22 T.C. 824 (1954). Would the result be the same in a state which has a statute like the ones referred to in note 67, supra? Would the result be the same if a devisee of realty disclaimed the devise in his favor? If an heir disclaims in a state which has a statute like the ones referred to in note 67, supra, or if a beneficiary under a will disclaims, on what basis will the state inheritance tax be assessed?

2.   ADMINISTRATION OF DECEDENT'S ESTATE[69]

The administration of a decedent's estate is in charge of an administrator (person originally appointed when the decedent

---

[67] The Hardenbergh case is discussed in 31 Texas L. Rev. 599 (1953) and 5 Vand. L. Rev. 852 (1952).

In Louisiana it has been held that an individual may renounce property transferred by will or by operation of law. Aurienne v. Mt. Olivet, Inc., 153 La. 451, 96 So. 29 (1923). The Model Probate Code (1946), prepared by a committee of the American Bar Association, provides in §58 that an heir as well as a devisee may renounce, and in the comment recognizes that it is changing the common law rule as to heirs. See the following state statutes which undertake to permit an heir to disclaim his inheritance: Ind. Ann. Stat. §6-604 (Burns, 1953), quoted infra page 1440; N.C. Gen. Stat. §28-149, 13(b) (1950, Supp. 1959), quoted infra page 1470; R.I. Gen. Laws Ann. §§34-5-1 to 34-5-12 (1956), quoted in part infra page 1473; W. Va. Code §4095a (1955, Supp. 1960), quoted infra page 1476; and Wis. Stat. Ann. §237.01(8) (1957, Supp. 1960), quoted infra page 1477.

Section 25.2511-1(c) of the Regulations, quoted infra page 1544, deals with the problem presented in the Hardenbergh case.

See also Roehner and Roehner, Renunciation as Taxable Gift — An Unconstitutional Federal Tax Decision, 8 Tax L. Rev. 289 (1953); 9 id. 100-101; Note, Disclaimers in Federal Taxation, 63 Harv. L. Rev. 1047 (1950). — Ed.

[68] The income taxation of estates is examined infra page 77.

[69] For an excellent summary of the administration of decedent estates, see Leach, Cases and Text on the Law of Wills 176-202 (2d ed. 1960 rev.).

Massachusetts Ann. Laws, c. 195, §16 (Supp. 1959), quoted infra page 1458, describes certain circumstances under which a formal administration of an estate of a decedent is unnecessary.

*Know terms

dies intestate);[70] or of an executor (person named in the decedent's will); or of an administrator with the will annexed (person originally appointed when the will does not name an executor or the one named fails to qualify), who is also known as an administrator cum testamento annexo or administrator c.t.a.;[71] or of an administrator of goods not administered (person appointed to complete the administration when the administrator originally appointed has not done so), who is also known as an administrator de bonis non or administrator d.b.n. The person who succeeds an executor or administrator c.t.a. is called an administrator c.t.a.d.b.n.[72] If no other suitable person is available to administer the decedent's estate, a permanent official known as the public administrator takes charge.[73]

The procedure which must be followed in securing the appointment of the decedent's personal representative normally results in a gap of significant proportions between the date of death and the date of appointment. If a will contest is involved, the gap is widened. It may be important that someone be authorized to act for the estate during this interim. In this case a special administrator may be appointed.[74]

If the assets of the decedent are not all located in the domiciliary state, it is usually necessary for a personal representative of the decedent to be appointed in each state where there are assets. Such a personal representative is called the ancillary administrator.[75] In so far as the personal representative of the decedent is acting in a representative capacity, he exists only in the state where the court that appointed him is located. Thus, if a person indebted to the decedent resides in a state other than the state of the decedent's domicile, the domiciliary personal representative cannot go to the other state and sue the debtor. The cause of action is derived from the decedent and a personal representative cannot maintain a derivative suit outside the jurisdiction of his appointment. However, causes of action which arise

---

[70] See Mass. Ann. Laws, c. 193, §§1, 2, quoted infra page 1456.

[71] See Mass. Ann. Laws, c. 193, §§7, 8, quoted infra page 1457.

[72] See Mass. Ann. Laws, c. 193, §9, quoted infra page 1457.

[73] See Mass. Ann. Laws, c. 194.

[74] See Mass. Ann. Laws, c. 193, §10, quoted infra page 1458.

[75] In Matter of the Estate of Katherine S. De Lano, 181 Kan. 729, 315 P.2d 611 (1957), a Kansas statute (Kan. Gen. Stat. Ann. §59-303 (1949, Supp. 1957)), which purports to confer on the courts of Kansas exclusive jurisdiction to determine the devolution, by will or by descent, of real property located in Kansas and tangible or intangible personal property wherever located, of all persons who are residents of Kansas at the time of their death, was held unconstitutional in so far as it attempted to confer such exclusive jurisdiction with respect to tangible and intangible personal property having a situs in another state.

in favor of the personal representative, such as the cause of action against one who wrongfully takes property from the possession of the representative, can be maintained wherever service on the defendant can be obtained.

Normally, it is highly desirable that the manager of a decedent's estate be a person who has been selected in advance by the decedent. He is in the best position to know what kind of personal representative should be selected in view of the nature of his assets and the peculiarities, if any, of his intended beneficiaries. Part of estate planning is the intelligent choice of the executor.[76] When the decedent names his executor in his will he can also excuse him from giving any sureties on his bond and thereby save for the estate the money which otherwise might be spent in the payment of charges for a professional surety.[77]

If the body of the alleged decedent has not been found, there is always the possibility that he may not be dead. It is widely recognized that if a person has not been seen or heard from for seven years he is presumed to be dead. If such a person's estate is administered by someone who is appointed by a court, the jurisdiction of which depends on the alleged decedent being dead, the acts of the administrator will be entirely void if the alleged decedent later puts in an appearance. To remedy this situation many states have enacted so-called absentee statutes in which the jurisdiction of the court to appoint a person to administer an estate is based on the fact of absence and not on the fact of death.[78]

If an administrator is appointed in the belief that the decedent died intestate and later a will is found, the result is not nearly so devastating as when the alleged decedent returns.[79] It is now

---

[76] See Chapter XX, which is entitled Selection of the Fiduciary.

[77] See Mass. Ann. Laws, c. 205, §4, quoted infra page 1462.

[78] See Mass. Ann. Laws, c. 200, §§1-14, for statutory provisions dealing with the settlement of estates of absentees. The Massachusetts provisions call for the appointment of a receiver to take over and manage the property of the absentee, and permit distribution of his estate upon the expiration of fourteen years after the date of his disappearance.

In Rev. Rul. 55-387, 1955-1 C.B. 131, it is held that a legally appointed guardian of a taxpayer who has disappeared must file the required federal income tax returns for the missing person for the taxable year in which he disappeared and for any subsequent taxable year prior to the time he is found or is declared dead by the appropriate court. The fact that the taxpayer's spouse is appointed guardian does not preclude the filing of a joint return by her.

See Rev. Rul. 56-682, 1956-2 C.B. 935, in regard to the requirements for filing a federal estate tax return for the estate of a missing person.

[79] In Walkden v. United States, 57-2 U.S.T.C. ¶11732 (N.D. Ohio, 1957), an executor had paid an estate tax on the basis of a will, and then a later document was found which was the last will of the decedent. Since the last will

generally recognized that persons who have dealt with the administrator prior to the discovery of the will are protected.[80] The personal representative of the decedent has many functions to perform during the period of administration. He collects and preserves the assets; pays claims against the estate which are presented by the various creditors, whose claims must be presented in the time allowed by the governing local law;[81] prepares and files the last personal income tax return of the decedent, the income tax return of the estate, federal estate tax Form 704 (preliminary notice due sixty days from the date personal representative qualifies) and Form 706 (tax return due fifteen months after the decedent's death), and the state tax return, and pays the amount due under these returns;[82] collects all relevant data about the decedent and his beneficiaries; distributes the assets in accordance with the will or, if the decedent died intestate, in accordance with the laws of descent and distribution; and files his final account. The Estate Administration Guide beginning on page 41 infra provides a check list of the various things which must be done by the personal representative from death to distribution.

The fee payable to the administrator or executor as compensation for administering the decedent's estate is normally based

contained a charitable bequest, the estate tax payable under it was less than the estate tax originally paid. Because of the length of time that the litigation took to establish the later document as the decedent's final will, the executor was unable to file a refund claim until more than three years after the payment of the tax under the earlier will. The court held that under these circumstances the statute of limitations for filing a refund claim ran from the date the later will was established as the valid one, and not from the date of the payment of the tax under the earlier will. In Walkden v. United States, 58-2 U.S.T.C. ¶11802 (N.D. Ohio, 1957), aff'd, 255 F.2d 681 (6th Cir. 1958), cert. denied, 358 U.S. 825 (1958), the District Court pointed out that, at the time of the original decision, it did not have before it the fact that the second will was admitted to probate some years prior to the completion of the litigation regarding it, and thus the court determined that the claim for refund was barred because it was made more than three years after the date the second will was admitted to probate.

[80] See Mass. Ann. Laws, c. 193, §6, quoted infra page 1457, and c. 195, §12, quoted infra page 1458.

[81] If the personal representative rejects a claim made against the decedent's estate, in many states there are statutes which require that an action must be brought against the estate within a stipulated short time after such a rejection or be permanently barred. In these states it becomes important to determine what amounts to a rejection of a claim which will invoke the short statute of limitations. In this connection, see In re Douglass Estate, 144 N.E.2d 924 (Preble County Prob. Ct., Ohio, 1957).

[82] Section 20.2002-1 of the Regulations, quoted infra page 1501, points out that the executor or administrator of a decedent's estate is responsible for the payment of the federal estate tax and that this responsibility applies to the entire tax, even though the gross estate consists in part of property which does not come within the possession of the executor or administrator.

on the value of the probate estate. In view of the fact, however, that the personal representative must interest himself in more than the probate assets in order to prepare the federal estate tax return, he should be permitted to make a reasonable charge with respect to non-probate assets as to which he performs tax and other services. In some states the fees for executors and administrators are set by statute.[83] In others the fees are subject to approval by the probate court and the only standard is one of reasonableness.[84] If an executor does not want any compensation for his services, he should make known this fact before the ser-

---

[83] See N.Y. Surrogate's Court Act §285.

[84] The reasonable compensation allowable to an executor or administrator appointed by a Massachusetts probate court is subject to court approval. Printed below is the Standard Charge Schedule of the Old Colony Trust Company, of Boston, Massachusetts, published in September, 1955, with respect to estates, and these charges conform to the general practice of probate courts in Massachusetts.

1. *With reference to personal property* — The sum of:
    (a) A charge based on probate inventory value at the following rates:
        —3% on the first $200,000
        —2½% on the next $800,000
        —2% on the second million
        —1½% on the third million
        —1% on the remainder.
        [*Minimum charge:* $350, plus $22 for each $1,000 of probate inventory value in excess of $5,000 and not in excess of $30,000.]
    (b) A charge of 6% of gross income collected. (With respect to interest on mortgages not disposed of within eighteen months of the date of appointment: A charge with respect to any period after such eighteen months, determined in accordance with Table A (page 13 of Standard Charge Schedules).)
    (c) A reasonable charge with respect to personal property not included in the probate estate as to which the Trust Company performs tax or other services.
2. *With reference to real property* —
    (a) included in the estate subject to administration: A reasonable principal charge dependent on services performed plus a charge as provided in Table B (pages 13-14 of Standard Charge Schedules).
    (b) not included in the estate subject to administration, but owned by the decedent and as to which the Trust Company performs services: A charge by appraisal, based on the services performed.

NOTES: (1) The Trust Company as executor or administrator performs all the normal services of settling the estate.
    (2) In the case of one or more co-executors or co-administrators, the Trust Company receives 100% of the charge in respect to an estate affected by the minimum rate, or 75% of the charge (but not less than $900) in respect to an estate not affected by the minimum rate. If giving effect to this provision does not afford reasonable compensation for a co-executor or co-administrator, such co-executor or co-administrator may be compensated through an additional charge.
    (3) To the extent that the residue of an estate not affected by the minimum rate is payable for charitable, educational, or religious purposes, the charge in 1(a) referable to the portion so payable may be reduced up to 10%.
    (4) For extraordinary services or responsibilities of the Trust Company, or

vices are rendered.[85] The fee paid to an executor or administrator is deductible for federal estate tax purposes.[86] If a bequest or devise is made to an executor in lieu of commissions, the amount of the bequest or devise is not deductible but presumably the amount of the bequest or devise would not be taxable income to the executor.[87] If the will fixes the compensation payable to the executor, a deduction for federal estate tax purposes may be taken to the extent that the amount so fixed does not exceed the compensation allowable by the local law or practice.[88]

A properly drafted estate plan will give the executor various powers and discretions to assist him in the administration of the estate. The administrative provisions in the plan will specify where various tax burdens are to fall; give the executor liberal powers of sale and reinvestment; and if one of the estate assets is a business, grant the executor ample authority to carry on the business or liquidate it, as may be the more desirable, etc.[89] The various legal and tax pitfalls which must be avoided in the drafting of administrative provisions are considered later.[90]

---

for Special Administration, an additional charge will be made.

(5) For performing the above services as agent for the executor(s) or administrator(s) of an estate, the Trust Company's compensation is computed in accordance with the above schedule as for a sole fiduciary.

[85] Revenue Ruling 56-472, 1956-2 C.B. 21, deals with a situation where an executor is entitled under state law to a fixed compensation and waives his right to receive such compensation and enters into an agreement to receive a stipulated amount which is less than the amount allowed by law. It is held that the executor does not realize taxable income by waiving his right to such commissions when the waiver is made before he renders any services or otherwise becomes entitled to them, and furthermore, no gift for federal gift tax purposes is made by virtue of such a waiver. See also Commissioner v. Mott, 85 F.2d 315 (6th Cir. 1936), which is concerned with a case where a trustee refused to accept compensation for his services. In Rosemary Kenny, 32 T.C. 748 (1959), a person named as one of the executors declined to serve, on the understanding that she would receive the same amount she would receive if she were to serve as executor, and it was held that the amount paid to her was income and not a gift.

[86] See Reg. §20.2053-3(b)(1), quoted infra page 1526. See the discussion at page 122, infra, as to whether certain estate tax deductions should be taken as income tax deductions.

[87] See Reg. §20.2053-3(b)(2), quoted infra page 1526.

[88] See note 87 supra.

[89] See the charter of administration given the executor under the wills in Appendix I, pages 1283 and 1298.

[90] See Chapter XIX.

3. ESTATE ADMINISTRATION GUIDE[91]

Estate of .... Trust Officer .... No. ....

Legal residence .... Adm. Assoc. ....

.... Inv. Officer ....

When established? .... Citizenship (nationality) ....

Capacity: Executor(s) u/will ....

      Administrator(s) (c.t.a.) (c.t.a.d.b.n.) (d.b.n.) (Special)

Co-exec. or Co-adm. .... Address ....

Date of death .... Cause ....

Place of death .... Length of last illness ....

If in hospital within three years before death, state its name and address ....

Physician .... Address ....

Undertaker .... Address ....

Place of burial .... Cemetery duties ....

Birth: Date of .... Place of ....

Business .... Address ....

If retired, state former business ....

Date of will .... Return day on probate ....

Date of appointment) .... 20-day certificate received ....

   Approval of bond) ....

State .... County .... Court No. ....

Counsel .... Fee .... Paid ....

.... Expenses ....

Appraisers ....

      (1)   (2)   (3)

   Addresses ....

   Amount paid and date ....

Consent to distribute tangible personal property received

   Federal [92] .... Mass. ....

Federal Form 704 (Preliminary Notice — 60-day) Filed ....

   Obtain ruling of counsel re method of allocating taxes.

Federal Form 706 (Estate Tax Return) Obtain factors, if necessary, for charity remainder.

   Due[93] .... Filed .... Amount paid [94] ....

[91] This guide was prepared by Old Colony Trust Company, of Boston, Massachusetts, for the guidance of its officers in administering estates.

[92] The procedure which should be followed in obtaining the consent of the federal taxing authorities to a distribution of tangible personal property is described in Reg. §20.2031-6(c), quoted infra page 1507. — ED.

[93] Fifteen months after death. — ED.

[94] Section 6511 of the 1954 Code, as amended by §82 of the Technical Amendments Act of 1958, allows a claim for refund to be brought within two

[handwritten margin note: Estate tax return m b filed w in 15 mos after death]

Deficiency .... Overassessment .... Audit ....
Discharge requested .... Filed in Probate Court ....
State tax on jointly held property and transfers
    Due[95] .... Date and amount paid ....
State inheritance tax (Mass. or state of domicile)
    Due[96] .... Date and amount paid ....
    Tax receipt filed in Probate Court ....
Additional estate tax payable to Mass.[97] .... Other states ....
Personal property tax return (if necessary) ....
    Diary card filed ....
    Return filed ....
On estates with bequests to public charities, copies of papers to be filed
    with Department of Attorney General, State House, Boston 33.
        Petition for Probate and copy of will
        Inventory
        Accountings
        Petitions of all kinds, with citations

	Name	Address	Date of Birth
Widow or husband			
Date of marriage to surviving spouse			
Domicile at date of marriage			
Name and date of death of deceased spouse			
Representative of spouse's estate			
Heirs-at-law			
A. Children			
and issue of			
deceased children			

years from the time the tax was paid or three years from the date the return
was filed, whichever is later. Hill v. United States, 167 F. Supp. 96 (D.N.J.
1958), aff'd, 263 F.2d 885 (3d Cir. 1959), considered what constitutes payment
of the estate tax by the executor for the purpose of starting the limitation
period for a refund. In Bowcut v. United States, 175 F. Supp. 218 (D. Mont.
1959), the executrix paid income taxes assessed against the decedent for past
years, after having paid the decedent's estate taxes, and did not file a claim for
a refund of estate taxes in time. The court allowed a claim of a refund of
income taxes, however, on the theory of equitable recoupment of estate tax
overpayment. The case was affirmed in 61-1 U.S.T.C. ¶11992 (9th Cir. 1961).
    First National Bank of Montgomery v. United States, 60-2 U.S.T.C. ¶11959
(Ct. Cl. 1960), illustrates the difference between a refund claim which has
been timely filed but fails to state the grounds for demanding the refund,
which can be amended at any time before the claim has been rejected, and a
refund claim which has been timely filed and does state the grounds, which
cannot be amended after the period of limitations, even though the claim has
not been rejected. — Ed.
    [95] In Massachusetts, fifteen months after death. — Ed.
    [96] In Massachusetts, fifteen months after death. — Ed.
    [97] Due eighteen months after death. — Ed.

Or

B. If NO children
   or issue of
   deceased children
   (1) Father ....
       and
       Mother ....

       or survivor..

       Or

   (2) Brothers,
       Sisters ....
       and/or issue
       of deceased
       Brothers ....
       and
       Sisters ....

       Other relationships
       if necessary ....

Analysis of Will

Are inheritance taxes payable from residue?..

	Distributed	*Insurance terminated*
Disposition of household furniture and personal effects	....	....

	Distributed	*Insurance terminated*
Bequests of specific property other than household furniture and personal effects (and income adjusted if securities)	....	....

	Distributed	*Insurance terminated*
Specific devises	....	....

Trusts other than residue: $................No. ....
Residue: Trusts $................No. ....
$................No. ....
Total cash legacies $................No. ....
Other provisions: ....

Parties Interested	Names	Addresses and Legal Domicile if Different	Relation- ship	Date of Birth and Living at Date of Death	Amount of Legacy and Date Paid

Have decedent's relations with other departments been investigated? ....

Have decedent's records and income tax returns been examined? ....

Has Postmaster been advised of death and requested to send all mail to us? ....

Has Trust Index been furnished with names and addresses of legatees? ....

Have makers of notes been notified to remit to us? ....

Did decedent own property in any other state or country? ....

State place of ancillary administration ....

Name and address of ancillary administrator ....

Assignments ....

Have debts and funeral expenses been paid? ....

Inventory due .... Inventory filed in Probate Court ....

Real Estate .... Personal .... Total ....

Has Investment Officer been given copy of "Estimate of Cash Requirements"? ....

Has estimate been prepared of residue of estate? ....

Have Instrument Control and Estate Tax Units been given estimate of residue in order to obtain appointment as trustee of residue? ....

Have securities been made free for sale or transfer? ....

Are vouchers required for filing with accounting? ....

Real estate   Note if mortgage outstanding

....

....

Vested owners to sign letter appointing Bank Agent or assuming liabilities

....

Papers delivered to Real Estate Department

....

Safe deposit boxes located ....   Name and address
        Contents removed ....   of joint depositor
        Box given up ....   and relationship ....
Brokerage Accounts   Closed?

....

Bank Accounts	Balances as of Date of Death	Collected?

Cash ....

Mortgages ....

Contract by decedent to sell land....................

Loans and Promissory Notes	Maker	Amount	Due Date	Rate of Interest	Paid	Collateral Delivered

Life Insurance	Amount	Policy No.	Beneficiary	Form 712 Required [98]

Accident and Health Insurance		Collected?

Jointly held property. Obtain name and address of surviving joint owners (real and personal). Ascertain full value and amount, if any, which originally belonged to survivor.

Business interests

Interests of decedent as beneficiary or fiduciary

Due from fiduciaries	Amount	Collected?

Goods in storage	Appraised?	Insured?	Disposed of?

Household furniture and personal effects	Appraised?	Insured?	Disposed of?

[98] This form, which consists of a statement by an insurance company as to the insurance on the decedent's life, must be filed with the federal estate tax return. — ED.

Location of jewelry   Appraised?   Insured?   Disposed of?

....

Automobiles   Appraised?   Insured?   Disposed of?

....

Did decedent own any insurance on life of another?

....

Was decedent war veteran?..............Benefits collected by whom..............
Social Security No...........................Benefits collected by whom..............
Other property

....

....

Has decedent's estate, spouse or any other person received or will any of them receive any bonus or awards as result of decedent's employment or death? If "yes," obtain full details.

....

Did decedent make any transfer described in the first paragraph (including the six subparagraphs) of the instructions for Schedule G of Federal Estate Tax Return? Obtain details.

....

Any transfer of $5000 or more at any time? Obtain name of transferor, date, amount, character of transfer and motive.[99]

....

Any transfer outright or in trust within 3 years preceding death?...........
     If $1000 or more, obtain name of transferor, date, amount, character of transfer and motive.[100]

....

Were there in existence any trusts created by decedent? Obtain full details and copies of trust instrument.[101]

....

....

[99] This information is required in order to complete Form 706. Outright transfers not in trust which were made more than three years preceding death do not have to be reported. See Special Ruling, dated September 22, 1960, CCH Fed. Est. & Gift Tax Rep. ¶ 8086. — Ed.
[100] This information is required in order to complete Form 706. — Ed.
[101] This information is required in order to complete Form 706. — Ed.

Powers of Appointment

Did decedent, at the time of death, possess a general power of appointment created after October 21, 1942?..

On or before such date?..

Did decedent, at any time by will or otherwise, exercise or release (to any extent) a general power of appointment created after October 21, 1942?..

On or before such date?..

Were there in existence at decedent's death any trusts not created by him under which he possessed any power, beneficial interest, or trusteeship?..

Annuities   *Joint and Survivor*   *Value for Mass.*   *Value for Federal*
(Including Employee Retirement Fund benefits)

In describing an annuity, the name and address of the grantor of the annuity should be given, or if payable out of a trust or other fund, such a description as will fully identify it. If payable for a term of years, the duration of the term and the date on which it began should be given, and if payable for the life of a person other than the decedent, the date of birth of such other person should be stated.

Liabilities — endorsements — leases — guarantees

Credit for Tax on Prior Transfers

List property received from a transferor who died within 10 years before or 2 years after the decedent.[102] There is no requirement that

[102] Section 2013 of the 1954 Code, quoted infra page 1391, sets up a credit for the federal estate tax paid with respect to prior transfers by a transferor who died within ten years before or two years after the transferee-decedent. It is possible for transferred property to be subject to double taxation in rapid succession without the benefit of any credit, in spite of §2013. Consider the following case: A transfers property to B and shortly thereafter B dies. More than two years after B dies, but within three years of the date of the transfer to B, A dies. The transfer by A is deemed a gift in contemplation of death and thus the value of the transferred property is includible in A's gross estate for federal estate tax purposes; the property is also includible in B's gross estate for federal estate tax purposes and no credit will be available with respect to the tax imposed on B's estate under §2013, because A did not die within two years after B. This possibility of double taxation in rapid succession is present every time an outright gift is made by one person to another.

See Rev. Rul. 58-167, 1958-1 C.B. 340, considered supra page 16, note 24, with regard to whether the widow's allowance is a transfer of property from the decedent within the meaning of §2013.

The computation of the credit is described in 1954 I.R.C. §2013(b), quoted infra page 1392, and Rev. Rul. 59-73, 1959-1 C.B. 234, sets forth the method

~~the property must be identified in the estate of the decedent or that it will be in existence on the date of his death.~~ Obtain copy of the transferor's Federal Estate Tax Return as well as audit letter, if there was one. Ascertain amounts of death taxes paid to state of domicile, other states, or foreign governments.

Closing of Administration

Have addresses been checked?..

Necessary votes and acceptances procured?........................

Legacies assigned noted?..

Has Income Tax Division cleared all prior to death and estate returns?

Has Income Tax Division been advised of changes in valuations? Federal and Massachusetts..

Any outstanding petty charges?.....................................

Have worthless securities been disposed of?.......................

Have decedent's personal papers been disposed of?................

Transfers completed?..

Income distributed to trusts?..

Has Chief of Public Relations been advised of pending termination? ....

Have papers in estate been transferred to trust file?..............

	Principal	*Income*
Has compensation been taken?......		
Report from Probate Court on any claims filed?......		
Closing notice sent to Instrument Control Unit?......		

	Accounts			*Appeal Period*	*Guardian ad*
No.	*Period Covered*	*Filed*	*Allowed*	*Expires*	*Litem Required*

Has surety been discharged?..

of computation where the decedent's estate includes property previously taxed in estates of prior decedents.

Section 2013(c)(1), quoted infra page 1392, places a limit on the amount of the credit, in that it may not exceed the amount by which the estate tax, computed before the credit, exceeds the tax computed by excluding from the gross estate the value of the transferred property. Revenue Ruling 60-161, I.R.B. 1960-17, 10, points out that in determining the estate tax computed by excluding from the gross estate the value of the transferred property, §2013(c)(1) expressly provides only for an adjustment in cases involving charitable gifts. Thus no proportionate adjustment to deductions otherwise allowable (expenses, losses or marital deductions) is to be made, but in cases where a marital deduction is allowable, the maximum deduction applicable is 50 percent of the reduced adjusted gross estate. — ED.

CHAPTER III

The Will as an Instrument in the Estate Plan

A will may be the only instrument in a person's estate plan or it may be one of a number of instruments. For example, if a person retains the complete ownership of his wealth — that is, makes no inter vivos arrangements which will control the devolution of his property in the event of his death — his will is his estate plan. On the other hand, if he sets up various inter vivos arrangements with respect to his property (such as joint ownerships where the survivor becomes the complete owner, inter vivos trusts, insurance settlements which keep the proceeds of the insurance out of his estate, etc.), there may be very little property left at the time of his death to pass under his will. In the latter situation his will may not be a very significant document in his estate plan but, even so, it is a necessary document if the estate plan is to be complete, because it is practically impossible to make inter vivos arrangements with respect to one's property which are certain to include all the property he may ever own. A person can have a complete estate plan represented solely by a will but he cannot have a complete estate plan of his own selection without a will.

Practically every problem that one may face in connection with estate planning may be presented in the consideration of the will as an instrument in an estate plan. Most of the problems of estate planning dealt with in later chapters in this book may and usually do arise when a will is involved, but it is not the function of this chapter to anticipate the consideration of material developed later.[1] Rather, it is the function of this chapter to present

[1] Thus questions of the following types will come up later for consideration in regard to wills:
  a. What are the significant factors in choosing between a will and a revocable inter vivos trust as the medium of disposing of a substantial portion of one's wealth? See Chapter V.
  b. What types of dispositions under a will have the effect of minimizing the impacts of taxation on one's estate and on one's beneficiaries? See Chapters XII and XIII.

two things a lawyer who is working on an estate plan should constantly bear in mind in regard to wills. They are

1. The standard which should be applied in the execution of a will; and
2. The extent to which a surviving spouse (or anyone else) may claim a share in the estate contrary to the terms of the will.

1.   STANDARD WHICH SHOULD BE APPLIED IN THE EXECUTION OF A WILL

A will should obviously be executed with the formalities required in the state in which the testator is domiciled.[2] But is that a sufficient standard to adopt? The testator may be domiciled in one state when his will is executed, and in another when he dies. At the time he executes the will or at the time of his death, he may own real property which is located in a state other than the one in which he is domiciled. In the light of these possibilities, a standard should be applied to the execution of a will, which will increase to the maximum the acceptability of the will in the various states.[3]

---

c. What are the considerations which should be influential in determining whether to make outright gifts in a will or gifts in trust in a will? See Chapter VII.

d. What are the pitfalls to avoid in drafting dispositive provisions in wills so that the intention of the testator will be carried out? See Chapter XI.

e. Who should be selected as executor and trustee under a will? See Chapter XX.

f. What administrative powers and discretions should be given in the will to the executor and trustee? See Chapter XIX.

g. What directions should be given in the will in regard to the payment of taxes? See Chapter XIX.

[2] See Mass. Ann. Laws, c. 191, §§1, 4, quoted infra page 1454, for an example of the statutory formalities which must be met in the execution of a will. Massachusetts and other jurisdictions relax the rigid formal requirements in a few restricted situations (soldiers and sailors) and allow oral wills to be effective. These oral wills are commonly referred to as nuncupative wills. See Mass. Ann. Laws, c. 191, §6, quoted infra page 1454.

In some states, a holographic will (a will written entirely in the testator's handwriting and signed by him but not witnessed) is permitted. See Cal. Prob. Code §53 (Deering, 1959), quoted infra page 1436.

[3] The standard suggested in the text should be adopted even though now many states by statute recognize as valid a will executed in the mode prescribed by law, either of the place where the will is executed or of the testator's domicile. For an example of such a statute, see Mass. Ann. Laws, c. 191, §5, quoted infra page 1454. Although Massachusetts has no statute recognizing the validity of a holographic will, such a will would be valid to control the devolution of the property of a Massachusetts domiciliary if he executed it in California where such wills are permitted. Until all states

The following is recommended as minimum standard operating procedure with respect to the execution of wills, no matter in which state the testator is domiciled or where the will is executed.

1. The testator should read the will in its entirety and the lawyer should make certain that the testator understands the terms of the will.

2. The testator and three persons who have no interest vested or contingent in the property disposed of by the testator's will or in the testator's estate in the event of an intestacy,[4] along with the lawyer supervising the execution of the will, should be in a room from which everyone else is excluded. No one should enter or leave this room until the execution of the will is completed.

3. The lawyer supervising the execution of the will should ask the testator the following question: "Do you declare in the presence of Mr. ...., Mr. .... and Mr. ....[5] that the document before you is your will, that you have read the document, that you understand the document and that the document expresses your desires as to the disposition of the property referred to therein on your death?" The testator should answer "yes" and his answer should be audible to the three mentioned witnesses.

4. The lawyer supervising the execution of the will should then ask the testator the following question: "Do you re-

---

have such a statute, a will may be valid under the law of the place where it is executed and yet be ineffective to control the devolution of the testator's property on his death.

[4] A will may be totally invalid because there are not the required number of witnesses who are *competent*. In order for a witness to be competent he must be able to understand what is transpiring. At one time, a witness was disqualified if he had any beneficial interest at stake, but now statutes generally recognize the competency of a witness, though he is beneficially interested, but void the devise or legacy in his favor. The statute may even void a devise or legacy to the spouse of a witness. If the witness was competent at the time the will was executed, his subsequent incompetency will not prevent the allowance of the will. See Mass. Ann. Laws, c. 191, §§2, 3, quoted infra page 1454.

In Haines v. George, 11 Ill. App. 2d 359, 137 N.E.2d 555 (1956), it was held that where a will designated that a person should be the attorney for the executor, and the attorney was a witness to the will, he was precluded from receiving compensation for services rendered to the executor, because the local law did not permit a witness to a will to receive any financial remuneration by reason of the will.

[5] The names of the three disinterested witnesses should be inserted in these blank spaces.

quest Mr. ...., Mr. .... and Mr. .... to witness your signing of your will?" Again the testator should answer "yes" and his answer should be audible to the three mentioned witnesses.

5. The three mentioned witnesses should then be so placed that each can see the testator sign his name and then the testator should sign his name in the place provided for his signature at the end of the will.[6]

6. One of the witnesses should then read aloud the attestation clause, which should provide in substance that the foregoing instrument was signed on such and such a date by the testator (giving his name); that the instrument was declared by the testator to be his will in the presence of the three witnesses; that the testator requested each of the witnesses to witness his signing of the document; that each of the witnesses did witness his signing of the document; that each witness in the presence of the testator and in the presence of the other witnesses does hereunto subscribe his name as witness, and that each witness does declare that he believes the testator to be of sound mind and memory.[7]

7. Each witness should declare that the attestation clause is a correct statement.

8. Each witness should then sign his name in the place provided for the signatures of the witnesses, following the attestation clause. As each witness signs, the testator and the other two witnesses should be so placed that each one

---

[6] In some states the statute relating to the execution of wills specifically provides that the will shall be subscribed by the testator at the end of the will. See, for example, N.Y. Decedent Estate Law §21, quoted infra page 1467. It may be desirable to have the testator initial or sign each page of the will when it is a multiple page document, so that there can be no substitution of pages. A clause at the end of the will may provide as follows: "For identification I have signed each of the foregoing seven pages of this will, which consists of eight pages." When such a clause is in the will, the testator should sign the preceding pages of the will before placing his signature at the end of the will. It may also be desirable to have the witnesses place their initials on each page of the will opposite the place where the testator has signed his name.

[7] An attestation clause makes out a prima facie case of the due execution of a will. Consequently, if witnesses are dead, unavailable, unable to testify or recollect, or even if they testify that certain requirements were not met, the presumption of due execution from a complete attestation clause may entitle the will to probate. Thus such a clause is very important.

For a case illustrating the significance of an attestation clause, see McIntyre v. Saltysiak, 205 Md. 415, 109 A.2d 70 (1954). In this case the will was executed seventeen years before probate, and it was held that the attestation was prima facie evidence of due execution. The person attacking a will must overcome such prima facie evidence by clear and convincing proof.

can see the witness sign his name.[8]   The witness should place his full address opposite his signature.[9]

There may be circumstances which require some variation in the procedure outlined above, as when the testator is unable to sign his own name or is blind, etc.   Whenever such special circumstances are presented, a careful check of applicable local laws should be made to determine what course of action should be followed.[10]

The procedure outlined above may require some supplementation when the circumstances indicate the possibility of a contest of the will on the ground of mental capacity or undue influence.[11] Of course, no lawyer should prepare a will for a client who is not mentally competent or who is not acting free of undue influence. Even though the lawyer is satisfied as to the mental competency of the testator and is satisfied that the testator is not unduly influenced, the circumstances may indicate the possibility of a contest on either of these grounds, and it may be desirable to discuss with the testator in the presence of witnesses the details of his will to establish to the satisfaction of the witnesses that the testator has the mental capacity to understand what he is doing and

[8] Notice that the Massachusetts statute (Mass. Ann. Laws, c. 191, §1, quoted infra page 1454) does not require that the witnesses sign in the presence of each other. Most states are like Massachusetts in this respect. A few, however, require the witnesses to sign in the presence of each other.   See, for example, Wis. Stat. Ann. §238.06 (1957), quoted infra page 1478.

[9] New York requires a witness to a will to write opposite his name his place of residence, and failure to do so subjects the witness to a fifty-dollar penalty. The omission of the place of residence of the witness does not affect the validity of the will in New York. See N.Y. Decedent Estate Law §22, quoted infra page 1467.

[10] If the testator is unable to write because of his physical condition, his hand should be taken and guided in making a mark. The witnesses should be able to testify that the mark so made was intended by the testator to serve as his signature. If the testator is unable to see, he should be informed, in a voice that the witnesses can hear, of each step in the execution of the will. See Pa. Stat. Ann., tit. 20, §192 (Purdon), quoted infra page 1471.

[11] For a discussion of the contest of wills on grounds of mental capacity, undue influence, and fraud, see Leach, Cases and Text on the Law of Wills 115-122 (2d ed. 1960 rev.).

When should you insert in the will a provision forfeiting a beneficiary's legacy in the event that the beneficiary contests the will? If the local jurisdiction construes such a forfeiture provision as not being violated if an action is brought in good faith for probable cause, the provision is of little significance. See Ryan v. Wachovia Bank and Trust Co., 235 N.C. 585, 70 S.E.2d 853 (1952), for a case which took the position that the forfeiture clause is not violated by an action brought in good faith for probable cause. It has also been held that a suit to construe the will will not result in the forfeiture clause being violated. See Dravo v. Liberty National Bank & Trust Co., 267 S.W.2d 95 (Ky. 1954). It is usually held that the forfeiture clause is entirely void if there is not a gift over in case of its breach. See In re Arrowsmith, 162 App. Div. 623, 147 N.Y. Supp. 1016 (1914), aff'd, 213 N.Y. 704, 108 N.E. 1089 (1915).

that, of his own free choice, he is disposing of his property in the manner provided in his will. The witnesses to such a discussion should promptly record in a written document their version of the discussion and the views formulated by them at the time as to the mental competency of the testator and as to his freedom from undue influence.[12]

It is possible that the situation may be such that the lawyer should advise a medical examination before the will is executed. Only in extraordinary circumstances would such a course of action seem to be necessary or desirable.[13]

The testator should be advised of the importance of keeping the executed original of his will in a safe place.[14] A conformed copy of the will should be given to the testator, which he can keep readily available for reference.

The will executed by the testator normally should have a clause revoking all prior wills and codicils, although, even if such a clause is not in the will, the new will revokes all prior wills and codicils to the extent that it is inconsistent with them. The problem should be faced, however, as to whether a prior will should be physically destroyed. A determination to destroy a prior will should be made only after it is concluded that there are no foreseeable circumstances under which its existence may be of any value.

If a prior will is destroyed as a result of the making a subsequent will and the subsequent will is for some reason ineffective, the prior will may still be effective on the ground that it was destroyed with the intention of revoking it on condition that the subsequent will was valid and effective. This is sometimes referred to as the doctrine of dependent relative revocation.[15] If an effective subse-

---

[12] Genovese v. Genovese, 338 Mass. 50, 153 N.E.2d 662 (1958), held that the proper execution of a will does not require that each attesting witness form an opinion as to whether the testator was of sound mind. The court also recognizes that the witnesses need not know that the paper is a will.

[13] See Note, Psychiatric Assistance in the Determination of Testamentary Capacity, 66 Harv. L. Rev. 1116 (1953). See also Sharpe, Medication as a Threat to Testamentary Capacity, 35 N.C.L. Rev. 380 (1957).

[14] The safe-deposit box of the testator is an appropriate place in which to deposit his will. Access to such a box is normally obtainable immediately after the testator's death in order to locate a will. Even though state law requires that the contents of a safe-deposit box be inventoried in the presence of some representative of the state before the removal of items from the box, access to the box should be permitted for the sole purpose of examining any will located there. The will may be left for safekeeping with the lawyer who drew it or with the executor named in the will. In some states statutory provisions exist which provide for the deposit of a will with the register of probate. See Mass. Ann. Laws, c. 191, §§10-12, quoted infra page 1455.

[15] See Warren, Dependent Relative Revocation, 33 Harv. L. Rev. 337 (1920). In re Field's Estate, 194 Misc. 47, 84 N.Y.S.2d 886 (1948), approved the

quent will revokes a prior will, will the prior will be revived by
a revocation of the subsequent one? Not all jurisdictions answer
this question in the same way and hence it may be desirable to destroy the prior will with the intention of permanently revoking
it to eliminate any danger of its revival.[16]

Burning, tearing, canceling, obliterating, and similar physical
acts with respect to a will, done with the intention of revoking
the same, will effectively revoke the will.[17] If the testator marries
after executing his will, the marriage may revoke the will under
the controlling law, unless possibly the will was executed in contemplation of a particular marriage.[18] A divorce may also revoke
a will.[19]

PROBLEMS

3.1. In a jurisdiction having a statute relating to witnesses to a
will like the one in Massachusetts referred to supra note 4, in
which of the following cases would the described legacy be void if
it is assumed that the described legatee was one of three witnesses
to a will in a jurisdiction requiring three witnesses to a will?

    a. A will witnessed by a Harvard Law School professor con-
       tains a pecuniary gift to the President and Fellows of
       Harvard College for the use of the Harvard Law School.

---

following quotation from another opinion of the Surrogate's Court: "The
history of our statutes, the decisions and our public policy exclude the existence of the doctrine of dependent relative revocation as a rule of law in this
State."

[16] In Estate of Adelene Moffat, 5 Misc. 2d 991, 158 N.Y.S.2d 975 (1956), a
codicil of the testatrix revoked her will in part, but after her death the
executed original of the codicil could not be found. The court presumed
that the codicil had been destroyed by the testatrix with the intent to revoke
it. The court held, however, that the subsequent revocation of the codicil
did not cause a revival of the revoked provisions of the will.

The court in Agricultural National Bank of Pittsfield v. Bernard, 338 Mass.
54, 153 N.E.2d 761 (1958), recognized that a subsequent will which contains
a clause revoking prior wills has the effect of revoking the prior wills, though
it cannot be found and its terms, other than the provision revoking prior
wills, cannot be established.

See page 56, note 22 infra, which illustrates why it may be desirable not
to destroy a prior will when a subsequent will provides for charitable gifts
similar to the ones in the prior will.

[17] See Mass. Ann. Laws, c. 191, §8, quoted infra page 1454.

In Payne v. Payne, 213 Ga. 613, 100 S.E.2d 450 (1957), the testator threw
his will into the fireplace with the intention of destroying and revoking
it, but his wife withdrew it before it had burned. The court held that the
will had not been revoked. Under the controlling statute, an intent to revoke
must be accompanied by actual destruction of the will.

[18] See Mass. Ann. Laws, c. 191, §9, quoted infra page 1455.

[19] See Wash. Rev. Code, §11.12.050 (1959), quoted infra page 1476.

b. A will witnessed by a stockholder in X Corporation contains a pecuniary legacy in favor of X Corporation.

3.2. Check the items listed below which, if they occur, may under some circumstances render the will inoperative in whole or in part in some states. Assume that the only possible argument against the will is the one mentioned in the item under consideration.

a. The will is written entirely in the handwriting of the deceased.

b. The will is written entirely in the handwriting of the deceased's wife.[20]

c. One of the witnesses to the will is the attorney who drew the will.[21]

d. One of the witnesses to the will is 19 years of age.

e. The will is not signed at the end.

f. There are only two witnesses to the will.

g. The will contains no attestation clause.

h. The will was executed in a state other than the state in which the decedent was domiciled.

i. The will consists of six pages and the decedent's signature does not appear on the first five pages.

j. One of the witnesses died before the other witnesses had placed their signatures on the will.

k. The decedent was a married woman.

l. The will names no one to serve as executor.

m. The will gives all the decedent's property to a charity.[22]

---

[20] In Tarricone v. Cummings, — Mass. — , 166 N.E.2d 737 (1960), the fact that the will was entirely in the handwriting of the principal beneficiary, who was also named as executrix, was stressed by the court in determining that the evidence was sufficient to present a jury issue as to fraud and undue influence.

[21] See Haines v. George, 11 Ill. App. 2d 359, 137 N.E.2d 555 (1956), referred to supra note 4.

 Canon 19 of the Canons of Professional Ethics of the American Bar Association provides as follows: "When a lawyer is a witness for his client, except as to merely formal matters, such as the attestation or custody of an instrument and the like, he should leave the trial of the case to other counsel. Except when essential to the ends of justice, a lawyer should avoid testifying in court in behalf of his client."

[22] See N.Y. Decedent Estate Law §17, quoted infra page 1467; Ohio Rev. Code Ann. §2107.06 (Page, 1954), quoted infra page 1470.

In Pennsylvania, in 1946, a bequest for religious or charitable uses made by a will executed less than thirty days prior to the testator's death was void under Pa. Stat. Ann., tit. 20, §195 (Purdon). A woman domiciled in Pennsylvania executed a 1945 will in which she gave the residue of her estate to a charity. In December, 1946, she executed a new will in which she specifically revoked the 1945 will. The 1946 will also gave the residue of her estate to the same charity as that described in the 1945 will. Two days after executing the 1946 will, she executed a codicil in which she provided that, should she die within thirty days after the execution of her 1946 will, it was her intention

—n. The decedent never read the will.

o. The decedent was under 21 years of age.

p. The will is typewritten but contains various interlineations in the handwriting of the deceased.

—q. The decedent married subsequent to the execution of the will. *yes, unless will = made in contemplat of (M)*

—r. The decedent was divorced subsequent to the execution of the will.

s. Subsequent to the execution of the will a child was born to the testator.[23]

t. One of the witnesses is the person named as executor in the will.[24]

2. THE EXTENT TO WHICH A SURVIVING SPOUSE (OR ANYONE ELSE) MAY CLAIM A SHARE IN THE ESTATE CONTRARY TO THE TERMS OF THE WILL

a. *The Spouse*

It is not uncommon for a surviving spouse to have the right to renounce the deceased spouse's will and claim a statutory share in

SS m/ renounce will & claim her statutory share.

---

that the 1946 will should be null and void and that her 1945 will should be and remain her last will and testament. She died within thirty days after executing her 1946 will. Did she make a valid charitable bequest under Pennsylvania law so as to entitle her estate to a deduction for a charitable gift? In Estate of Riddle, 21 T.C. 1109 (1954), the court held that the charitable gift was void and hence no deduction was allowed. It is interesting to note that in 1947 the Pennsylvania statute was amended to include the following: "Unless the testator directs otherwise, if such a will or codicil shall revoke or supersede a prior will or codicil executed at least thirty days before the testator's death, and not theretofore revoked or superseded and the original of which can be produced in legible condition, and if each instrument shall contain an identical gift for substantially the same religious or charitable purpose, the gift in the later will or codicil shall be valid; or if each instrument shall give for substantially the same religious or charitable purpose a cash legacy or a share of the residuary estate or a share of the same asset, payable immediately or subject to identical prior estates and conditions, the later gift shall be valid to the extent to which it shall not exceed the prior gift." Pa. Stat. Ann., tit. 20, §180.7(I) (Purdon). In McGuigen Estate, 388 Pa. 475, 131 A.2d 124 (1957), the 1947 amendment was considered, and the court held that a gift to charity in each of two wills was substantially the same, even though the gift in the earlier will was the income from the residue, whereas in the later will the gift was to the charity outright. Section 731.19 of Fla. Stat. (1959) is similar to the 1947 amendment in Pennsylvania.

[23] See Mass. Ann. Laws, c. 191, §20, quoted infra page 1456; N.J. Rev. Stat. §3A:3-10 (1951), quoted infra page 1466.

[24] It may be contended that the executor will lose his right to compensation when he is a witness under a statute like Mass. Ann. Laws, c. 191, §2, quoted infra page 1454. This contention was rejected in Blankner v. Lathrop, 169 Ohio St. 229, 159 N.E.2d 229 (1959).

his estate.[25]   In states where the surviving spouse has such a right,
the plan of disposition provided in a deceased spouse's will may be
seriously upset by the renunciation, because it will have to operate
as best it can on what is left after the withdrawal of the property
required to make up the share to which the surviving spouse is entitled as a result of the renunciation of the will.[26]

The statutory share which the surviving spouse takes when she
renounces the will is deemed to pass to her from the deceased
spouse,[27] so that it may qualify for the estate tax marital deduction
if it is not a disqualified terminable interest.[28]   The amount of the
available marital deduction, however, will turn on whether the
statutory share is carved out of what is left after all death costs, including taxes, are paid, or is carved out of the decedent's estate before death taxes are paid and is freed of any obligation to contribute to the payment of such taxes.   This is the same problem as was
previously considered in connection with the determination of a
surviving spouse's share when the deceased spouse dies intestate.[29]

[25] See, for example, Mass. Ann. Laws, c. 191, §§15-17, quoted infra page
1455.

[26] In various foreign countries there exists legislation designed to assure a
decedent's surviving family adequate maintenance out of the testator's property, in the court's discretion, whenever his will does not provide for it.   The
temporary allowances which a court in the United States may give to a widow
and children for support during administration of a decedent's estate are a
step in the same direction but one that is quite short of the power given the
courts in foreign countries to provide for permanent maintenance for the
family contrary to the terms of a will.   The extent to which a court may go in
modifying a decedent's will is illustrated by a report which appears in a
Christchurch, New Zealand, newspaper in March, 1959, where, on application
to the Supreme Court of Greymouth, the will of Bridget O'Leary, which
divided the decedent's estate between J. C. O'Leary and Mrs. Harley, two of
the six children of the decedent, was modified so as to divide the decedent's
estate between Arthur J. O'Leary and J. C. O'Leary except that provision was
made for the payment of £200 to Mrs. Harley, to be drawn equally from the
two shares, in lieu of the half share bequeathed to her.   A detailed discussion
of the system of flexible restraints on testamentary freedom in various foreign
countries is presented in Laufer, Flexible Restraints on Testamentary Freedom — A Report on Decedents' Family Maintenance Legislation, 69 Harv. L.
Rev. 277 (1955).

The nearest approach in this country to "post-death judicial estate planning" is in Maine, where it is provided in Me. Rev. Stat. Ann., c. 156, §14
(1954) that in the settlement of any testate estate where no provision is made
for the widow in her husband's will or where she duly waives the provisions
made, the judge may allow her so much of the personal estate as he deems
necessary according to the estate of her husband and the state of the family
under her care.   Under this statute permanent allowances for the widow and
not just temporary allowances may be made.

[27] Reg. §20.2056(e)-2(c), quoted infra page 1541.

[28] Terminable interests with respect to the estate tax marital deduction are
examined infra page 832.

[29] See discussion at page 25 supra.

The case reported in full immediately below deals with this problem.

In re WILLIAM G. BARNHART'S ESTATE
— *N.H.* —, *162 A.2d 168 (1960)*

Certification, of questions of law to the Supreme Court by the Probate Court of Grafton County pursuant to R.S.A. 547:30.

William G. Barnhart died testate September 14, 1956 leaving a widow, Elizabeth J. Barnhart and no children. The estate consists entirely of personal property having an approximate valuation of $2,000,000. The will contained a specific bequest to the widow of $200,000, and after numerous substantial bequests, the residue was bequeathed to trustees of the estate to pay the income to the widow, with the right to make payments out of the principal "for her care, support, maintenance and comfort," and upon her death and after payment of certain specific bequests the residue was bequeathed to William S. Crapser with the "hope and wish that he use it for such public purpose as to him may seem best." William S. Crapser is not related to the testator and both he and the widow were named as co-executors and co-trustees.

The twenty-third paragraph of the will provided as follows: "Twenty-third. I direct that all transfer, inheritance, legacy and succession and estate taxes that may be imposed in any jurisdiction upon any part of my estate or upon any of the gifts, legacies, bequests or devises herein, or in any codicil hereto, unless such codicil explicitly provides to the contrary, shall be paid by my residuary estate, and I direct that such taxes and charges be not charged against respective legatees, devisees or beneficiaries, nor deducted from the amount of any such gift, legacy, bequest or devise."

The widow seasonably filed a waiver of the provisions of the will in her favor in order that she might take her statutory share of the personal property, there being no real property in the estate.

In computing the widow's statutory share, the executors did not deduct from her share any portion of the federal estate taxes but took the maximum marital deduction on the federal estate tax return of one-half of the gross estate before computation of federal estate taxes. The Internal Revenue Service then claimed that the widow's statutory share under state law was to be computed by deducting federal estate taxes as well as debts and expenses of administration. This would, in effect, reduce the widow's statutory share, increase the federal estate tax, increase the state inheritance tax and also the state estate tax (R.S.A. ch. 87) and would result in an increase in the amount of the residuary estate bequeathed to William S. Crapser.

Thereupon the executors filed a petition for instructions in the Grafton County Probate Court to determine the question as to the proper method of computing the widow's statutory share. The Probate Court (Jones, J.) certified and transferred to this court the following questions of law:

"1. Is Elizabeth J. Barnhart, widow, entitled as her statutory share to receive Seven Thousand Five Hundred Dollars ($7,500) and one-half of the balance of the personal estate remaining after the payment of debts and expenses of administration, without the inclusion of Federal Estate Taxes in expenses of administration, or Seven Thousand Five Hundred Dollars ($7,500) plus one-half of the balance of the personal estate remaining after payment of debts and expenses of administration, including federal estate taxes as expenses of administration?

"2. Is any portion of the federal estate taxes to be apportioned to or charged to the share of Elizabeth J. Barnhart, widow?"

Additional facts appear in the opinion.

KENISON, C.J. The major issue in this case is concisely stated in Casner, Estate Planning (2d ed. 1956 and 1959 supp.) p. 55, note 25 in the following language: "Will the surviving spouse's share be based on what is left after payment of debts, funeral and administration expenses, and the estate tax, or on what is left after the payment of debts, funeral and administration expenses but before the payment of the estate tax." The cases are conflicting as appears from the citations in Casner pp. 22, 55 and annotation, 37 A.L.R.2d 7, 56. See Sutter, How to Plan for Apportionment of Estate Taxes (1955 and 1959 supp.) in 2 Lasser, Estate Tax Techniques 2137 (1959). This conflict is due in part to differences in testamentary clauses and variations in state statutes controlling the apportionment of estate taxes and rights of a surviving spouse to elect to take against the provisions of a will.

When the widow waived the provisions of her husband's will she was entitled by statute to $7,500 and one-half the remainder above that sum from his personal estate "remaining after the payment of debts and expenses of administration." R.S.A. 560:10, subd. II. The meaning of this statute is a matter of state law and not federal tax law. Riggs v. Del Drago, 317 U.S. 95; note, The Role of State Law in Federal Tax Determinations, 72 Harv. L. Rev. 1350 (1959); 2 Rabkin and Johnson, Federal Income, Gift and Estate Taxation §53.04(5) (1958).

The binding effect of state court decisions for federal tax purposes in the construction of wills and the interpretation of state statutes regulating the devolution of property is well established. Babcock's Estate v. Commissioner, 3 Cir., 1956, 234 F.2d 837; Oliver, The Nature of the Compulsive Effect of State Law in Federal Tax Proceedings, 41 Calif. L. Rev. 638 (1953). See Gallagher v. Smith, 3d Cir., 1953, 223 F.2d 218. There is some authority for an exception to this general rule if the probate proceedings are nonadversary. Merchants Nat. Bank & Trust v. United States, 7 Cir., 1957, 246 F.2d 410. Whatever the effect of this exception may be, it has no application to the present case since the proceedings in it are devoid of any semblance of collusion and are truly adversary in character. See Northrup, The Marital Deduction: The Street Case and the Need for Indiana Legislation, 34 Notre Dame Lawy. 195 (1959).

In this state the widow's statutory share in personal property "remaining after the payment of debts and expenses of administration" is $7,500 and one-half the remainder. R.S.A. 560:10, subd. II. The state taxing authorities contend that the federal estate tax is either a debt or an expense of administration within the meaning of R.S.A. 560:10, subd. II and in any event should be treated as one or the other in computing the marital deduction. Int. Rev. Code of 1954 §2056, 26 U.S.C.A. §2056. Cf. Amoskeag Trust Co. v. Trustees of Dartmouth College, 89 N.H. 471, 473, 200 A.2d 786, 117 A.L.R. 1186. While the federal estate tax constitutes a lien on the gross estate which in all events must be paid, it is not a debt within the meaning of R.S.A. 560:10, subd. II. The payment of debts under this section refers to debts of the testator such as real estate taxes, income taxes and other obligations incurred by the deceased before his death. See In re Grondin's Estate, 98 N.H. 313, 316, 100 A.2d 160. This meaning is indicated by R.S.A. 554:19, subd. IV which gives priority over legacies to the "just debts owed by the deceased." Nor are federal estate taxes considered to be "expenses of administration" in this state. The frequent practice of attorneys in providing in wills that federal and state taxes shall be paid *"as* an expense of administration" is an indication that the federal estate tax is not in the same category as the executor's and his attorney's fees, commissions and probate expenses generally in this state. We conclude that the payment of the federal estate tax is not a debt or an expense of administration in computing the widow's share under R.S.A. 560:10, subd. II. *} Held*

By the twenty-third paragraph of the will the testator provided that "transfer, inheritance, succession and estate taxes that may be imposed in any jurisdiction" should be paid out of the residuary estate and this was not limited to bequests in the will but also included taxes "upon any part of my estate." This was a testamentary declaration of a purpose to charge the residue with the payment of estate taxes upon any part of his estate whether transferred by probate or inter vivos, and whether passing as testate or intestate. This he had a right to do under state law. Although New Hampshire is one of the few states that have enacted the Uniform Estate Tax Apportionment Act (R.S.A. ch. 88-A (supp.), Laws 1959, c. 158), this act applies only to decedents dying after October 1, 1959 and has no application to this case. See Scholes and Stephens, The Proposed Uniform Estate Tax Apportionment Act, 43 Minn. L. Rev. 907 (1959). The limited equitable apportionment of estate taxes in certain cases required by R.S.A. ch. 88 does not apply here because of the exception contained in R.S.A. 88:2 that it is not effective "in any case in which a testator otherwise directs or provides in his will," 95 Trusts and Estates 898 (1956).

The further contention is made that the widow by waiving the will and taking her statutory share cannot receive any benefit or rights under the will direct or indirect, state or federal, taxwise or otherwise. This sweeps with too broad a brush. The fact that the testator designated his wife as co-executor and co-trustee is not changed because she took her statutory rights rather than her testamentary bequests. Annotation, 71 A.L.R. 665. If a provision of the will in the widow's favor is ineffective because of a widow's renunciation of such provision, it does not follow that other provisions of the will lose their efficacy. Jacobs v. Bean, 99 N.H. 239, 108 A.2d 559. If it may be to the widow's financial advantage to take her statutory share, she is not to be penalized by taxation or otherwise for taking a course of action which the state law expressly allows. In the post-mortem quietude of the testator's easy chair it is always facile to do some Sunday morning quarterbacking by saying what the testator could have provided in his will for the specific contingency of a widow's waiver of the will. A better formula could have been used but we think that the twenty-third clause of the will in its administrative provisions for the payment of taxes was adequate to take care of the payment of all death taxes, state and federal, upon all transfers, including that portion of the estate that passed to the widow by operation of state law. See Casner, How to Use Fractional Share Marital Deduction Gifts, 99 Trusts and Estates 190 (1960); Westfall, Estate Planning and the Widow's Election, 71 Harv. L. Rev. 1269 (1958).

While, as already indicated, the decisions of other jurisdictions are conflicting we conclude that the construction of this will and the applicable state law (R.S.A. 560:10, subd. II) require the answer to the first transferred question to be that the widow takes her statutory share after the payment of debts and expenses of administration without the inclusion of federal estate taxes in expenses of administration. Kramer, Federal Estate and Gift Taxation in 1957 Annual Survey of American Law 161, 175-176; Pitts v. Hamrick, 4 Cir., 1955, 228 F.2d 486; Casner, Estate Planning (2d ed. 1956 & 1959 supp.) p. 55, note 25; 2 Beveridge, Law of Federal Estate Taxation, §14.10 (1959 supp.); 33 Conn. Bar J. 397 (1959); 1 Lasser, Estate Tax Techniques, pp. 101, 113-116 (1959 supp.).

The second transferred question is whether any portion of the federal estate taxes is to be apportioned to or charged to the share of the widow. Both parties agree that the answer to this question is "no" and we see no occasion to consider it further.

Remanded.

All concurred.[30]

[30] In Merchants National Bank and Trust Co. of Indianapolis v. United States, 57-1 U.S.T.C. ¶11657 (S.D. Ind. 1956), a widow renounced her husband's will and elected to take the share given to her under state law. The will contained a provision that all federal and state death taxes should be paid out of his residuary estate. The Probate Court determined that in view of this provision no part of such taxes should be paid out of the share the widow received on renunciation. The District Court held that the decision of the Probate Court was controlling and, consequently, that the property passing to the widow which qualified for the marital deduction should not be reduced by the amount of the federal estate tax and state inheritance tax which could be said to be attributable to such property. The case was reversed in 246 F.2d 410 (7th Cir. 1957), cert. denied, 355 U.S. 881 (1957), rehearing denied, 355 U.S. 920 (1958).

Traders National Bank of Kansas City v. United States, 148 F. Supp. 278 (W.D. Mo. 1956), involved a marital deduction gift resulting from a wife's renunciation of her husband's will, which equaled 37.13 percent of the decedent's entire estate, and the court held that under Missouri law the marital deduction should be reduced by an amount equal to 37.13 percent of the federal estate tax paid by the estate. The Court of Appeals affirmed the District Court in United States v. Traders National Bank of Kansas City, 248 F.2d 667 (8th Cir. 1957). Although the Commissioner contended that, since the taxes were payable out of personal property, there should be attributed to the widow 50 percent of the estate tax because she was entitled to one half of the decedent's personal property, the court held that there would be attributed to her only the percentage of the estate tax which corresponded to the percentage of the over-all estate which the widow received. In re Laws Estate, 318 P.2d 767 (Cal. Dist. Ct. App. 1957), aff'd, 50 Cal. 2d 345, 325 P.2d 449 (1958), considers the problem in California with respect to both the marital deduction under federal estate tax law and the marital deduction given by the state inheritance tax law.

See also Estate of Rose Gerber Jaeger v. Commissioner, 252 F.2d 790 (6th Cir. 1958) (court followed Ohio law as announced in Campbell case infra); Provident Trust Company of Philadelphia v. United States, 58-2 U.S.T.C. ¶11815 (E.D. Pa. 1958), aff'd, 268 F.2d 779 (3d Cir. 1959) (point under consideration not involved on appeal; District Court opinion should therefore be examined); Old Colony Trust Co. v. McGowan, — Me. —, 163 A.2d 538 (1960) (spouse's share subject to federal estate taxes); Wachovia Bank and Trust Co. v. Green, 236 N.C. 654, 73 S.E.2d 879 (1953) (spouse's share subject to federal estate taxes); Campbell v. Lloyd, 162 Ohio St. 203, 122 N.E.2d 695 (1954) (spouse's share subject to federal estate taxes but result is contra to

NY law

In New York the surviving spouse is not entitled to elect against the will where the will gives her outright the sum of $2500 and the income for life from a trust, the principal of which equals or exceeds the difference between $2500 and her intestate share.[31] If the deceased spouse establishes a trust in his will for the benefit of the surviving spouse for life and the trust principal equals or exceeds the surviving spouse's intestate share but no outright gift of $2500 is made, the surviving spouse is entitled to elect to take the sum of $2500, which will be deducted from the principal of the trust. Where the aggregate of the provisions under the will for the surviving spouse, including the principal of a trust, is less than her intestate share, her right of election is limited to the difference between such aggregate and her intestate share. In no event can the surviving spouse by electing against a will obtain more than one half of the decedent's net estate. The intestate share of the surviving spouse is determind without regard to estate taxes, and whether the surviving spouse is relieved of contributing to such taxes is determined by the New York Apportionment Act.[32]

The trust for the surviving spouse in New York must give her the income for life in order for it to count in determining the aggregate of the provisions under the will for her. Thus, if the trust

---

earlier case of Miller v. Hammond, 156 Ohio St. 475, 104 N.E.2d 9 (1952)); In re Uihlein's Will, 264 Wis. 362, 59 N.W.2d 641 (1953) (spouse's share subject to federal estate taxes but compare the Uihlein case with Weyenberg v. United States, 135 F. Supp. 299 (E.D. Wis. 1955)). — Ed.

[31] See N.Y. Decedent Estate Law §18 in regard to a surviving spouse's right of election. By Laws 1959, c. 689, New York amended its intestate laws to give the surviving spouse one half of the property where not more than one child survives and there is no issue of a deceased child, or where no child survives and issue of not more than one deceased child survive. The new rule applies only to persons who die after July 1, 1959, and it *does not apply to right of election cases* (see N.Y. Decedent Estate Law §83).

In Matter of Ruppert, 3 N.Y.2d 731, 143 N.E.2d 517, 163 N.Y.S.2d 970 (1957), a widow claimed the right to elect to take against her husband's will on the grounds that the trust for her benefit under his will did not qualify for the marital deduction, and that thus the amount in her trust was less than her intestate share after the taxes assessed against it had been deducted, but the court held that she had no right of election.

[32] See N.Y. Decedent Estate Law §18-1(a) (Supp. 1959) and §124; the latter section is the N.Y. Apportionment Act.

Prezzano v. United States, 58-1 U.S.T.C. ¶11741 (S.D.N.Y. 1957), holds that, in New York, where the will provides for the payment of all estate taxes from the residuary estate and where only part of the residuary estate is bequeathed to the decedent's spouse, the marital deduction is computed on the wife's share without reduction for the estate tax allocable thereto, and that under §124 of the Decedent Estate Law, the share of the tax charged to her shall be in the proportion that the value of the property of the estate passing to her, less so much of such property with respect to which a marital deduction is allowed in computing the federal estate tax on the estate, bears to the total value of the net taxable estate.

under the will gives the income to the decedent's widow until her death or remarriage, the principal of such a trust would not count in determining what she could obtain by electing to take against the will.[33]

Where a surviving spouse is given a right to elect against the deceased spouse's will, can this right be asserted by her guardian if she is incompetent? Or by her personal representative if she dies before any definitive action is taken by her and she was competent? Or by her guardian after her death if she was incompetent? The statutory provisions giving the surviving spouse the right of election would have to be examined in order to supply answers.[34]

[33] In In re Shupack's Will, 1 A.D.2d 841, 149 N.Y.S.2d 20 (1956), a husband in his will established for his wife a trust of one third of his estate, which equaled her intestate share. The other two thirds went outright to his two children on their attainment of designated ages. The husband's estate consisted principally of stock in closely held corporations. The court held that the wife could elect against the will because the two children, when they attained the designated ages, would have effective control of the corporations, the stock of which made up the trust property of the wife's trust, by virtue of the children owning two thirds of the stock. Thus the children could control to a considerable extent the declaration of dividends and thereby control the flow of income to the wife under her trust. Consequently, the trust established for the wife's benefit might not be of substantial benefit to her. In such a situation, though the wife's trust comes within the literal wording of §18 of the New York Decedent Estate Law, she may elect to take against the will. By a divided court, the decision of the Appellate Division regarding the wife's election to take against the will was reversed in In re Shupack's Will, 1 N.Y.2d 482, 136 N.E.2d 513 (1956), further appeal denied, 3 A.D.2d 933, 163 N.Y.S.2d 1019 (1957).
In re Allan's Will, 5 A.D.2d 453, 172 N.Y.S.2d 447 (1958), considered the question whether in New York a widow who had filed notice of election to take against her husband's will could revoke her election, and the court held that she could revoke in the absence of any limitation in the statute and in the further absence of prejudice or objection by anyone interested in her husband's estate.
[34] See Mass. Ann. Laws, c. 201, §45 (Supp. 1959), quoted infra page 1461, which recognizes that a waiver may be filed by the guardian of an incompetent spouse. In Miller v. Miller, 339 Mass. 262, 158 N.E.2d 674 (1959), the court held that, although the waiver must be filed by the guardian in the time specified in the statute (within six months after probate of the will), it does not have to be approved by the Probate Court within that time. Furthermore, the court held that the acceptance by the surviving spouse of benefits which are not mentioned or incorporated in the will and which accrue to her on the death of her husband (e.g., life insurance proceeds) will not prevent the waiver of the will. See also First National Bank of Danville v. McMillan, 12 Ill. 2d 61, 145 N.E.2d 60 (1957); In re Callan's Estate, 101 Ohio App. 114, 135 N.E.2d 464 (1956).
The Pennsylvania statute provides that the right of election in the surviving spouse is personal to her and may not be exercised after her death. Pa. Stat. Ann., tit. 20, §180.12 (Purdon). Under this statute, the Pennsylvania court has held that where the surviving spouse was incompetent, her administrator could not make the election after her death. See Strecher Estate, 20 D. & C. 2d 652 (O.C. Phila. 1960). Illinois on the other hand has held that the right of election does not die with an incompetent spouse. See Aagesen v. Munson, 25 Ill. App. 2d 336, 166 N.E.2d 637 (1960).

Under the terms of an antenuptial agreement, the marital rights of a spouse may be relinquished. The relinquishment may be in return for a promise by the other spouse to leave her certain property by will at his death. The relinquishment of marital rights is not deemed a consideration in money or money's worth that will entitle the deceased spouse's estate to a debt deduction for federal estate tax purposes when the promised gift is made to the surviving spouse in his will.[35] The transfer by will to the surviving spouse in such a case, though in fulfillment of the antenuptial agreement, is considered as passing from the decedent to his surviving spouse and thus can qualify for the estate tax marital deduction.[36]

PROBLEMS

3.3. In a jurisdiction which permits the surviving spouse to elect against the deceased spouse's will and take outright a fractional share of his estate, how much estate income will be taxable to the surviving spouse in the year distribution is made to her? See Chapter IV, which deals with the income taxation of estates. See also Eugene C. Delmar, 25 T.C. 1015 (1956).

3.4. A is domiciled in a jurisdiction where there are statutes in regard to the marital rights of a surviving spouse, which are similar to those in force in Massachusetts. A desires to buy a tract of land located in the jurisdiction of his domicile and he does not want his freedom to convey the land inter vivos or by his will to be curtailed by the marital rights of his wife. Advise A as to the courses of action open to him to accomplish his objective.

3.5. A is domiciled in a jurisdiction where there are statutes in regard to the marital rights of a surviving spouse, which are similar to those in force in Massachusetts. A furnishes the following information in regard to his personal and financial affairs:

    a. He married W in 1920.

    b. He has three children, all over 21 years of age.

    c. He inherited Blackacre, located in the jurisdiction of his domicile, from his father in 1932. Blackacre is now worth $60,000.

    d. The title to the family residence is in A's name. The family residence is now worth $30,000.

    e. He owns $90,000 worth of securities and the title to these securities is in his own name.

A's present will gives the family residence outright to W; gives

[35] See 1954 I.R.C. §2053(e), quoted infra page 1404, and §2043(b), quoted infra page 1402.

[36] Rev. Rul. 54-446, 1954-2 C.B. 303.

Blackacre outright to his three children as tenants in common; and establishes a trust of the residue of his estate. During W's lifetime, the trustee has discretion to pay the income to any one or more of the group consisting of W and A's issue, and any income not paid to any one or more of the group is to be added to the principal. On W's death the principal and undistributed income are to be divided among his children then living, with the issue of any deceased child taking the share such deceased child would have taken if he had lived. Explain to A what the result will be if W survives him and elects to renounce his will.

3.6. H dies a resident of Massachusetts. W, his wife, renounces his will and claims her statutory share. Will the property interest which passes to her as a result of her renunciation qualify for the estate tax marital deduction?

3.7. H dies a resident of Massachusetts. He gives his wife, W, only a nominal amount under the terms of his will. W does not renounce his will and elect to take her statutory share. Has W made a gift for federal gift tax purposes to the other beneficiaries under the will because her failure to renounce the will prevented their shares under the will from being decreased? Consider in connection with this problem Hardenbergh v. Commissioner, supra page 29.

3.8. H dies a resident of Massachusetts. He gives his wife, W, a substantial amount under the terms of his will. W renounces the will and elects to take her statutory share. As a result of her renunciation, W's share in H's estate is less than the share given her under his will. Has W made a gift for federal gift tax purposes to the other beneficiaries designated in H's will, because her renunciation of the will has increased their respective shares? Consider in connection with this problem Hardenbergh v. Commissioner, supra page 29.

b. *A Child*

A child and other descendants of a decedent may be disinherited in most states.[37] To accomplish such a result, however, it may be necessary for the decedent's will to indicate that the omission of

---

[37] In Louisiana the doctrine of forced heirship exists and only a designated share of a person's property can be disposed of by his will to others when he has descendants.

To the extent the controlling local law permits the judicial award of allowances for a decedent's family, a child cannot be disinherited. See the discussion at page 12 supra.

In some states, if the decedent undertakes to give his property by will to charities, his children may defeat his desires. See page 56 supra, note 22.

beneficial provisions for the descendant was intentional and not occasioned by accident or mistake.[38]   Such manifestation would be present if the primary beneficiary was the decedent's wife, with his issue being designated as alternative or contingent beneficiaries.

The omission of any reference in a will to the children of the testator living on the date the will is executed is not nearly so likely as the omission of any reference to after-born and after-adopted children.[39]   The language employed in the will should be broad enough to show that the testator gave due consideration to the claims on his estate of all of his descendants, including adopted ones.

If the decedent has a power to appoint by will certain property, and the objects of the power include his descendants, will the appointive assets be treated the same as owned assets if he exercises the power by appointing to others than his descendants without indicating whether the omission of any appointment to his descendants was intentional?   It has been held that the omitted descendants have no basis for claiming any share of the appointive assets because such assets were not part of the estate of the decedent (the donee of the power).[40]

Re: rts of child omitted in will

The controlling local law will have to be examined to ascertain whether the right in the omitted child to take part of the decedent's estate is like an intestate share which cannot be refused without possible gift tax consequences,[41] or is like a devise or legacy that can be disclaimed without such consequences.   A will which gives all the decedent's property to his wife, with no reference to his children, combined with a will of the wife which gives all of her property to their children, may present an estate tax problem.   If the omitted children in such a case take some of their father's property from him, rather than through their mother, the mother's gross estate for federal estate tax purposes will be less than it otherwise would be.   If the amount the children take from their father reduces their mother's interest in their father's estate to less than 50 percent of his adjusted gross estate, the full marital deduction may not be available in determining his taxable estate.[42]

[38] See Mass. Ann. Laws, c. 191, §§20, 25, quoted infra page 1456.

[39] In regard to children adopted by the testator after the will is executed, see Ala. Code, tit. 61, §10 (1958), quoted infra page 1436.

[40] Fiske v. Warner, 99 N.H. 236, 109 A.2d 37 (1954).

[41] See Hardenbergh v. Commissioner, supra page 29.

[42] In First National Bank of Montgomery v. United States, 176 F. Supp. 768 (N.D. Ala. 1959), the court held that, in a nonadversary proceeding, a state court decree that the child took from the father was not binding, and then determined that on the facts under Alabama law the property all passed

c. *Particular Property*[43]

The testator may have no power of disposition by will over certain interests in particular property and, if that is the case, obviously a person who has such an interest is not bound by the testator's will if it undertakes to deprive him of the interest.[44]   Such a person may be required to allow his property interest to pass in accordance with the terms of the testator's will, however, if the testator in effect gives him something under the will on condition that he will abide by all the terms of the will and he accepts the disposition in his favor under the will.   The beneficiary under a will is put to this election whenever the will undertakes to give a property interest of his to someone else, unless a contrary intention on the part of the testator is appropriately manifested.[45]

The election by a beneficiary to abide by the terms of a will, even though the consequence will be that property owned by him will pass to another as provided in the will, should not cause the beneficiary's property to be included in the testator's gross estate for estate tax purposes.   The beneficiary, however, should be

---

to the wife and then from her to the child, so that it was all includible in the wife's gross estate.   The case was affirmed in 61-1 U.S.T.C. ¶11996 (5th Cir. 1961).

If the child can disclaim his share when he is omitted, and the effect of such a disclaimer is to leave the wife's gift under the will undiminished, whereas, if he had claimed his share, her gift under the will would have been diminished, will the entire amount of the wife's gift be available for the estate tax marital deduction?   See 1954 I.R.C. §2056(d)(2), quoted infra page 1410, and the discussion in regard thereto at page 828 infra.

[43] Various parts of a decedent's body may be of value to the living.   To be of value, however, the decedent's body must be made available shortly after death.   Can this availability be accomplished by provisions in a will?   A recent Illinois statute (Ill. Rev. Stat., c. 3, §193a-1 (1959)) provides as follows: "Every person of testamentary capacity may give by will or other written instrument executed during that person's lifetime, the whole or any part of his body to a charitable, educational or research institution, university, college, State Director of Public Health, State Director of Public Welfare, legally licensed hospital or any other organization intended and equipped to distribute human bodies or parts thereof, either for use as such institution, organization, university, college, Director or hospital may see fit, or for use as expressly designated in the will or other instrument, and the gift shall become effective immediately upon death."   Additional Illinois statutory provisions exonerate any person who acts under the will in good faith without knowledge of its revocation and allows the executor to carry out the gift before issuance of letters.

[44] For example, a testator by his will cannot deprive his wife of her rights in homestead property.   See page 11 supra.

[45] For a note on the election required of a devisee or legatee whose property is devised or bequeathed by a testator to another, see Leach, Cases and Text on Law of Wills 168 (2d ed. 1960 rev.).   See also Westfall, Estate Planning and the Widow's Election, 71 Harv. L. Rev. 1269 (1958).

deemed to have made a gift of his property to the recipient, if the value of what he receives under the will is less than the value of what he gives up.[46]

In a community property state,[47] the husband's power of disposition by will relates only to his share of the community property.[48] Consequently, if the husband undertakes to give his wife a life interest in all the community property, not in just his share, and to dispose of all the community property from and after her death, she may be put to an election. If she accepts the life interest given to her in his share of the community property, she may have to allow his will to control the devolution of her share of the community property from and after her death.[49]

---

[46] See Reg. §25.2511-1(h)(2) and (3), quoted infra page 1544.

[47] Special consideration is given to estate planning in community property states at page 426 infra.

[48] Under Nevada law the wife's interest in community property cannot be disposed of by her will when she is survived by her husband, unless the husband has abandoned his wife and is living separate and apart from her without such cause as would entitle him to a divorce. In In re Williams Estate, 40 Nev. 241, 161 Pac. 741 (1916), it was held that the wife's one-half community interest was always vested in her and therefore was not subject to inheritance tax when her husband predeceased her. On the basis of this case, Rev. Rul. 55-605, 1955-2 C.B. 382, holds that, on the death of the wife before her husband, her one-half interest in the community property, as well as one half of the jointly held property acquired with community funds, is includible in her gross estate for federal estate tax purposes. See Nev. Rev. Stat. §123.225 (1959), which is designed to make it clear that husband and wife have a present and equal right to community property subject to the right of the husband to exercise control.

[49] Coffman-Dobson Bank & Trust Co. v. Commissioner, 20 B.T.A. 890 (1930), held that a widow's interest in community property was not included in her husband's gross estate when he purported to dispose of her interest in the community property in his will and she elected to take under his will.

In Commissioner v. Chase Manhattan Bank, 259 F.2d 231 (5th Cir. 1958), *cert. denied,* 359 U.S. 913 (1959), the court considered three trusts established by a husband domiciled in Texas. One was a residuary trust under his will, which gave the income to his wife for life with remainder over to others. As to this trust the court held that the husband's will did not purport to dispose of the wife's share of the community property and thus the wife was not put to any election which might result in a gift on her part as to the amount by which the value of her share of the community property exceeded her life interest in the whole of the community property. The fact that she allowed her share of the community to go to the trustee would mean only that she had created a revocable trust of her share, because under Texas law all inter vivos trusts are revocable unless otherwise specified. Another trust was an insurance trust and the insurance made payable to it was purchased with community funds. The court recognized that under Texas law the husband as manager of the community could make a definitive selection of the beneficiaries of the policies. Thus, on the husband's death, the wife had no election, but was bound by the selected destination of the insurance proceeds. Nevertheless, at the husband's death a gift was made by her of her community share of the insurance proceeds minus her retained life interest in her share. See, in accord, Reg. §25.2511-1(h)(9), quoted infra page 1546. The final trust was a revocable inter vivos trust and community property was placed therein.

PROBLEMS

3.9. H in his will devises Blackacre, which he owns, to his wife, W, and purports to devise Whiteacre, owned by W, to his son, S. If W elects to take Blackacre, will the gift to her of Blackacre qualify for the estate tax marital deduction? See Section 20.2056(b)-4(b) of the Regulations, quoted infra page 1534.

3.10. H dies a resident of a community property state. Under the governing law, H can by will dispose of only one half of the community property, and his wife, W, is entitled to the other half. In his will H purports to dispose of all the community property, giving W a right to the income therefrom for her life, with remainder on her death to other designated beneficiaries. W, of course, is not required to accept the terms of the will so far as it purports to dispose of her share of the community property, but nevertheless she elects to abide by its terms. On W's death, will the value of her share of the community property be includible in her gross estate? In answering this problem, consider Section 2036 of the 1954 Code, quoted infra page 1396, and the discussion in regard thereto at page 193 infra.

———

A person's freedom of disposition with respect to owned assets may be curtailed by a contract to devise or bequeath his property in a certain manner.[50] This result may obtain where a joint and mutual will (a single document designed to serve as the wills of two people, under which the survivor takes the property of the first to die and their combined assets pass in a designated manner

———

The Court held that this was not invalid as a testamentary disposition and that the husband as manager of the community could make donations which would become irrevocable on his death, so that on the husband's death the wife made a gift of her share of the community minus the value of her retained life interest therein. In Estate of Lela Barry Vardell, 35 T.C. —, No. 8 (1960), the decedent's husband in his will purported to dispose of all the community property (Texas law was involved) and gave his wife the election to take a life interest in all the community, with a power to "handle, manage, sell, and in any manner dispose of said properties or any part thereof" as long as she remained a widow, or to take her share of the community property. The decedent elected to take under her husband's will and the court held that the value of her interest in the community was includible in her gross estate as a transfer with a retained life interest.

See also Giannini v. Commissioner, 148 F.2d 285 (9th Cir. 1945), *cert. denied,* 326 U.S. 730 (1945); Commissioner v. Siegel, 250 F.2d 339 (9th Cir. 1957); Westfall, Estate Planning and the Widow's Election, 71 Harv. L. Rev. 1269 (1958); Surrey, Federal Taxation of the Family — The Revenue Act of 1948, 61 Harv. L. Rev. 1097, 1150 n.189 (1948).

[50] See Sparks, Contract to Devise or Bequeath as an Estate Planning Device, 20 Mo. L. Rev. 1 (1955).

on the death of the survivor) is involved because the conclusion may be justified that the document was executed pursuant to an underlying contract that the survivor will not revoke the will.[51] If the survivor revokes the will and executes a new one, the beneficiaries under the revoked will may not be able to require the probate of the revoked will but may have to sue at law or in equity on the contract.[52]

Tax prob → The tax problems which may be presented as a result of the execution of joint and mutual wills are quite varied.[53] Particularly

[51] The same conclusion may be justified where the wills are mutual but not joint.

The following cases consider what evidence is sufficient to justify a finding that a joint and mutual will (or mutual wills) was executed pursuant to an underlying contract that the survivor will not revoke his will: Hoff v. Armbruster, 125 Colo. 198, 242 P.2d 604 (1952); In re Johnson's Estate, 233 Iowa 782, 10 N.W.2d 664 (1943); Gromek v. Gidzela, 36 N.J. Super. 212, 115 A.2d 144 (1955); Nye v. Bradford, 144 Tex. 618, 193 S.W.2d 165 (1946).

In Levis v. Hammond, — Iowa — , 100 N.W.2d 638 (1960), the court refused to enforce an agreement to name a wife's nephew as beneficiary subject to a life estate in the survivor of the wife and husband — an arrangement which was spelled out in mutual wills — when the wife died first and the husband then changed his will because the wife owned no property and thus the agreement was not sufficiently fair and reasonable to be enforced.

[52] See Isaacson's Estate, 77 Idaho 12, 285 P.2d 1061 (1955); Oursler v. Armstrong, 170 N.Y.S.2d 458 (1958), *aff'd,* 8 A.D.2d 194, 186 N.Y.S.2d 829 (1959), *appeal dismissed,* 6 N.Y.2d 998, 161 N.E.2d 754 (1959).

[53] Newman v. United States, 176 F. Supp. 364 (S.D. Ill. 1959), considered a case where a husband and wife made mutual wills in which the property of each was given to the other if the other survived, and otherwise went to the same alternate takers. Each will contained a recital that the wills were reciprocal and irrevocable. The wife died first, and the court held that the interest which passed to the husband qualified for the marital deduction. It was emphasized that the husband was free to dispose of the property received during his lifetime and that the persons who would take the property under his will would take from him and through him, so that he did not have a terminable interest.

In Estate of Charles Elson, 28 T.C. 442 (1957), the decedent and his wife executed a joint and mutual will, under the terms of which the survivor was to receive a life estate in all the property left by the first to die, and upon the death of the survivor, the entire estate was to pass to their son. Under Iowa law, such a will cannot be defeated by the surviving spouse. Nevertheless, the surviving spouse, by agreement with her son, elected to take her statutory interest, and this election was approved by the Iowa court. The Tax Court held that such action cannot operate to convert the interest of the surviving spouse from a terminable interest to one which will qualify for the marital deduction. It was pointed out that the Iowa court's decree was not made pursuant to any hearing on the merits in an adversary proceeding.

In McFarland v. Campbell, Jr., 213 F.2d 855 (5th Cir. 1954), a husband and wife made an irrevocable joint will in which they provided for a life estate in the survivor in the one-half interest in the community property owned by the first to die, and further provided that, on the death of the survivor of the two, all the community property would pass to a charity. The husband died first, and the question was whether the allowable charitable deduction should be limited to the remainder interest in the husband's one-half of the community property or whether it should extend to a remainder interest in all of

is this true when the agreement of the parties is to apply to the interest of the survivor with respect to property owned by them jointly with the right of survivorship.[54]

the community property, in view of the irrevocable nature of the joint will. The court held that, in spite of the irrevocable nature of the joint will, nothing had passed to the charity from the widow's estate and, consequently, the deduction was limited to the value of the interest passing to the charity from the husband's estate.

[54] In Estate of Awtry, 22 T.C. 91 (1954), a decedent and his wife, residents of Iowa, owned property jointly with the right of survivorship, and all of the consideration for the acquisition of the property was furnished by the decedent. They executed a joint and mutual will, agreeing that the survivor should have the use, income and control of the jointly owned property so long as the survivor should live. Under Iowa law the surviving wife could not change the terms of this joint and mutual will. Thus the court held that the interest passing to the surviving wife in the jointly owned property was a terminable interest and that no marital deduction therefor was allowable. Under the terms of the joint and mutual will, the property passed to named relatives on the death of the surviving spouse. The decision of the Tax Court was reversed on the ground that property owned in joint tenancy becomes the absolute property of the survivor and the survivor's rights therein cannot be cut down under Iowa law to any terminable interest by any joint and mutual will executed by husband and wife. 221 F.2d 749 (8th Cir. 1955). For a comment on Awtry v. Commissioner, see 69 Harv. L. Rev. 1140 (1956). Schildmeier v. United States, 171 F. Supp. 328 (S.D. Ind. 1959), was a case where husband and wife had a joint and mutual will, and the court regarded the Awtry case as controlling in deciding that the surviving spouse did not have a terminable interest in property vesting in her under a right of survivorship.

Olson v. Reisimer, 170 F. Supp. 541 (E.D. Wis. 1959), involved a husband and wife who owned realty in joint tenancy and executed a joint and mutual will whereby the survivor was to have a life estate in the realty, with a power to invade for comfort and maintenance, and the remainder was to go to their son in trust. The wife died in 1933, and in 1948 a state court determined that the husband had only a life estate in the realty as a result of the wife's will and the agreement between them as to the disposition on the husband's death. When the husband died, the Commissioner included the entire value of the realty in his gross estate, but the District Court held that the state court's determination as to what the husband had was conclusive and that under that determination no tax was due even on his share in which he retained a life interest, because he had in effect transferred a remainder interest in his half worth $8306.24 for a life interest in the wife's one half, which was worth $9193.76, and thus he had not given away any property in which he retained a life interest. The case was reversed and remanded in 271 F.2d 623 (7th Cir. 1959), on the ground that the transfer by the husband of the remainder interest in his share was without any consideration in money or money's worth and thus was includible in his gross estate as a transfer with life income retained.

In Lindsey v. United States, 167 F. Supp. 136 (D. Md. 1958), a decedent executed a will in which he gave the residue of his estate in trust for his wife for life with remainders over. The wife agreed to accept his will, to waive any legal rights in his estate, and to assign to the trust real estate which was owned by them as tenants by the entirety and which would pass to her as the survivor. The decedent agreed in return to make her the beneficiary under his life insurance policies. The court held that the effect of the agreement was to disqualify for the marital deduction the interest in the real estate which passed to the wife as the survivor, and that no deduction was available to the estate of the husband for the value of the real estate under 1954 I.R.C. §2053.

PROBLEM

3.11. H and W, husband and wife, execute a joint and mutual will (or mutual wills) whereby each gives his or her estate to the survivor, and on the survivor's death their combined assets are to pass to designated beneficiaries. The will is executed pursuant to an agreement as to the disposition of their property, so that under the governing law the agreement will be enforceable against the estate of the survivor if the survivor revokes the will and executes a different will (see Smith v. Thompson, 250 Mich. 302, 230 N.W. 156 (1930)). Has either H or W made a gift for federal gift tax purposes to the other or to the ultimate beneficiaries? On the death of the first to die, will the property passing under his will be included in his gross estate? On the death of the survivor, will their combined assets be included in the survivor's gross estate?

d. *A Compromise*

The plan of the testator for the disposition of his property may be significantly upset by a controversy arising in regard to his will which is settled by a compromise.[55] The following is a list of tax questions which may be presented as a result of a compromise agreement with respect to dispositions under a will:

1. Will the amount received under the compromise by the one contesting the will be income to him for federal income tax purposes?[56]

2. Will the expenses incurred in effecting a compromise agreement be deductible for federal income tax purposes under Section 212 of the 1954 Code, quoted infra page 1336.[57]

3. When distribution in settlement of a compromise is made by an estate to one who was not designated as a beneficiary under the will, will any part of the distributable net income for the year of payment be carried out of the estate and become taxable to the distributee? [58]

4. In view of the fact that the compromise agreement will re-

[55] See Mass. Ann. Laws, c. 204, §§15-17, quoted infra page 1462.
Are there any limits placed on the rewriting of a will by a compromise agreement? See Adams v. Link, 145 Conn. 634, 145 A.2d 753 (1958), where the court refused to approve a compromise which had the effect of abolishing a testamentary trust, because such a trust cannot be terminated, even though all interested parties agree, when a material purpose of the testator in creating the trust would thereby be defeated.
[56] See Lyeth v. Hoey, 305 U.S. 188, 59 Sup. Ct. 155, 83 L. Ed. 119 (1938).
[57] See Helen A. P. Merriman, 21 B.T.A. 67 (1930).
[58] See Chapter IV, which deals with the income taxation of estates.

sult in each claimant giving up to some extent what he would have been entitled to if he had refused to compromise and his contention had prevailed, has each claimant made a gift for federal gift tax purposes? [59] *ct below said no*

5. If the compromise agreement results in the establishment of a trust, who will be deemed the settlor thereof when federal tax consequences turn on who is the settlor? [60] *Decedent*

6. Will the entire amount which the decedent's wife receives under the compromise agreement be deemed to pass to her from her husband so that it may qualify for the estate tax marital deduction? [61]

7. If the will gives property to a charity and the compromise agreement results in the charity receiving a lesser amount than that stated in the will, what will be the charitable deduction available for federal estate tax purposes? [62] *lesser amt actually → charity.*

8. Will state inheritance taxes be assessed on the basis of the takers under the compromise agreement? [63] *cts divided*

[59] In Irma Lampert, 15 CCH T.C. Mem. 1184 (1956), a mother made a transfer of stock to her children in settlement of their lawsuits and claims against her for breach of her fiduciary obligations in the management of a trust. The court held that such transfers were not gifts but were made without donative intent and for full and adequate consideration in money or money's worth.

[60] In Bailey v. Ratterre, 144 F. Supp. 449 (N.D.N.Y. 1956), aff'd, 243 F.2d 454 (2d Cir. 1957), it was necessary to determine whether the decedent was the settlor of a trust that was created for the benefit of the decedent's son as a result of the son's dissatisfaction with his father's will, which gave all of the father's property to his wife, the decedent. Under the trust which was established, the decedent had the power of alteration and amendment and thus, if she was the settlor, the value of the trust property would be includible in her gross estate. On the basis of all the facts, the court concluded that the decedent was the settlor of the trust. The court recognized that under some circumstances a compromise of a will contest, which results in the establishment of a trust would not cause the beneficiary under the will who gives up some part of the property received by her under the will to be the settlor of the trust. In affirming, the Second Circuit pointed out that the trust was created after the son's rights to contest his father's will had expired.

[61] See Reg. §20.2056(e)-2(d), quoted infra page 1541.

[62] See Reg. §20.2055-2(d), quoted infra page 1530.

In Irving Trust Co. v. United States, 221 F.2d 303 (2d Cir. 1955), a will was involved which gave the property to charities. An amount was paid to various heirs in return for the withdrawal of their objections to the probate of the will. The court held that the charitable deduction was limited to the value of the property actually passing to the charities. Furthermore, the payments in accordance with the compromise were not deductible as claims against the estate.

Wilcox v. United States, 185 F. Supp. 385 (N.D. Ohio, 1960), held that where a will contest was compromised and the charitable beneficiary paid the will contestant the sum of $59,000 out of other property of the charity, for which the charity was reimbursed by gifts, the charitable deduction under the will was reduced by the amount of the payment.

[63] Pulliam v. Thrash, 245 N.C. 636, 97 S.E.2d 253 (1957), held that the

e. *Libelous Wills*

Sometimes a testator uses his will as a vehicle to comment on the character of certain persons for whom he has an intense dislike. Such a memorial to one not in his favor may result in part of the testator's estate going to the one he desires to exclude. In one case,[64] a wife in her will made no provision for her husband and as a parting gesture stated: "I do so intentionally because of the fact that during my lifetime he abandoned me, made no provision for my support, treated me with complete indifference and did not display any affection or regard for me." The husband brought suit against the executor of the will for damages because of an alleged testamentary libel. His recovery in the lower court was affirmed on appeal.[65]

inheritance tax was properly assessed against the three devisees named in the will, even though the property was divided into four parts as a result of a compromise and one part given to a person not named in the will. The three named devisees were attempting to make the fourth person contribute part of the state inheritance tax so assessed, but the court held that he had made no agreement, expressed or implied, to pay any part of the inheritance tax and thus was not liable for any part.

In Hart v. Mercantile Trust Company of Baltimore, 180 Md. 218, 23 A.2d 682 (1941), the state inheritance tax was applied as though the will had given the property initially to those who took under the compromise agreement.

See Emanuelson, Jr. v. United States and Emanuelson, Jr. v. Sullivan, cited and discussed infra page 882.

[64] Brown v. Du Frey, 1 N.Y.2d 190, 134 N.E.2d 469 (1956).

[65] See also Kleinschmidt v. Matthieu, 201 Ore. 406, 266 P.2d 686 (1954). Compare Citizens & Southern National Bank v. Hendricks, 176 Ga. 692, 168 S.E. 313 (1933); Carver v. Morrow, 213 S.C. 199, 48 S.E.2d 814 (1948).

In Schell Estate, 20 D. & C. 2d 628 (Montgomery County Orphan's Ct., Pa. 1960), the executors of the decedent requested the probate of a will, with libelous matter contained therein deleted. It was held that this request should be complied with where the libelous matter had no bearing on the dispositive provisions. It was recognized that the estate could be liable for testamentary libel.

CHAPTER IV

Income Taxation of Estates

A decedent's estate is recognized as a separate tax entity and, with some modifications, the federal income tax imposed on such an entity in regard to estate income is computed in the same manner as in the case of an individual.[1] This chapter is primarily concerned with the circumstances under which estate income will be deemed to have been distributed to an estate beneficiary and to be taxable to such a beneficiary and not to the estate.[2]

The situation where the executor is entitled to estate income, so that it will be taxed to the estate if it is not deemed to have been distributed, should be distinguished from the situation where the title to and the right to possession of property passes on the decedent's death directly to the beneficiary. In the latter case the beneficiary is entitled to collect and retain any income from the property and the income is taxable to him directly, not as a distributee of estate income.[3]

[1] See 1954 I.R.C. §641, quoted infra page 1361.

In Horace Greeley Hill, Jr., 24 T.C. 1133 (1955), it was held that where the executors of an estate were authorized by the decedent's will to waive or require refunding bonds as a condition for distribution of current income, the beneficiaries were not taxable for their share of the undistributed income of the estate because they did not have an enforceable and vested right to such income.

[2] To the extent that the executor has a choice as to whether estate income will be taxed to the estate or to a beneficiary, he should make that choice only after a thorough consideration of all the relevant facts.

In regard to the federal income tax consequences when the executor distributes estate property pursuant to a court order as an allowance or an award under local law for the support of the decedent's widow or other dependent, see discussion at page 16 supra.

[3] The decedent's real property usually passes directly to the beneficiary. In Revenue Ruling 57-133, 1957-1 C.B. 200, it is held that where, under applicable state law, real property is subject to administration, the income derived therefrom is includible in the gross income of the estate for the period that the estate is under administration; and that if, under the terms of the decedent's will, the net income from such property is to be used exclusively for a charitable purpose, it is deductible by the estate under the provisions of 1954 I.R.C. §642(c), quoted infra page 1362.

Revenue Ruling 59-375, 1959-2 C.B. 161, considers a situation where real

The extent to which an executor or other personal representative may with reasonable safety make distributions from time to time during administration must be determined in the light of the possible personal liability that may be imposed on him if he does not retain estate assets to meet estate liabilities. In this regard the following federal statute is relevant: "Every executor, administrator, or assignee, or other person who pays, in whole or in part, any debt due by the person or estate for whom or for which he acts before he satisfies and pays the debts due to the United States from such person or estate, shall become answerable in his own person and estate to the extent of such payments for the debts so due the United States, or for so much thereof as may remain due and unpaid." [4]

In the comment in the Regulations on this statutory provision, it is pointed out that the words "debt due by the person or estate," as used in the quoted federal statute, include a beneficiary's distributive share.[5] In most cases the executor can determine whether the property which will remain in his control after a partial distribution is adequate to cover the debts due to the United States. If there is any real doubt in a particular case, he can protect himself by requiring the distributee to give him a bond with surety that the distributed property or its equivalent will be forthcoming, if needed, to prevent him from being subjected to any personal liability.

The controlling state law may also place a personal liability on the executor who does not retain sufficient estate assets to meet various death costs. The extent to which this is a significant im-

---

property which passed directly to the decedent's heirs was needed in part to pay estate obligations. Partition in kind of the real property among the heirs was impracticable. The heirs and the administrator joined together in a petition for a sale to raise the necessary funds and to effect a partition of the property among the several heirs, and a gain was realized on the sale. Only that part of the gain was taxable to the estate which was proportionate to the portion of the proceeds payable to the administrator for discharge of estate obligations.

If the controlling local law vests the title to, and control of, real property directly in the devisee or heir, subject only to the power in the executor to make such devisee or heir account to the executor for income received, and if the income is required to meet estate obligations, what is the position of the devisee or heir who has received the income, paid a tax on it and then is required to turn over to the executor an amount equal to it? See 1954 I.R.C. §1341.

[4] 48 Stat. 760 (1934), 31 U.S.C., c. 6, §192 (1958). This statutory provision is also quoted in Problem 2.2, supra page 17, and is referred to infra page 123 in connection with the discussion of the federal income tax consequences with respect to the property in a revocable inter vivos trust on the death of the settlor of the trust.

[5] See Reg. §20.2002-1, quoted infra page 1501.

pediment to distributions by an executor from time to time during administration will depend on the same factors as are relevant in determining this issue with respect to his possible personal liability for debts due to the United States.

There may be other deterrents under controlling state law to partial distributions by an executor, including distributions in one year to one estate beneficiary and in a later year to another beneficiary.[6] In the discussion which follows, it will be assumed that such deterrents to partial distributions as may exist do not rule them out so that he in fact has discretion whether to make such distributions.

Three typical situations will be considered. They are as follows:

1. A partial distribution of the residue
2. A distribution in satisfaction, in whole or in part, of a pecuniary legacy
3. A distribution, in whole or in part, of property specifically bequeathed

In each case there will be discussion of the federal income tax consequences of the distribution under present law and then under H.R. 9662, a bill which failed of passage in the Eighty-sixth Congress.[7]

---

[6] If a pecuniary legacy is involved and the controlling state law requires that the interest on such a legacy at the legal rate will commence one year from the date of the testator's death, and the executor pays the legacy before the first year is up, can the residuary legatee hold the executor personally liable for the amount of the income which would have fallen into the residue if the legacy had not been paid until the expiration of the year? If the residuary estate is to be divided equally between A and B and the executor distributes to A his share and the value of B's share decreases between the time A's share is paid to him and the time B's share is paid to him, can B hold the executor personally liable for the decrease in value? If there is any possibility that an affirmative answer would be given to either question, the executor should make the distribution only with the consent of the person who might undertake to impose such a personal liability on him. Consideration should be given to the appropriateness of a provision in the will which gives the executor discretion in regard to distributions during administration.

Kinney-Lindstrom Foundation, Inc. v. United States, 60-2 U.S.T.C. ¶9662 (N.D. Iowa, 1960), held that where a claim against the United States (such as a tax refund) was an asset in a decedent's estate, the right to collect on it remained with the executor as long as the estate was open, even though it had been transferred to the estate beneficiary. This result was required by the anti-assignment statute (31 U.S.C., c. 6, §203) which prohibits the assignment of claims against the United States. When the estate is closed, then estate assets pass to the beneficiaries by operation of law, and thereafter the beneficiaries can sue on the claim. Any transfer prior to that time is voluntary and not by operation of law, even though approved by a court.

[7] It is relevant to examine the changes proposed in H.R. 9662 because it is likely that this bill will be revived in the Eighty-seventh Congress.

1.   THE RESIDUARY GIFT

Under present law, whenever the executor makes a distribution of a portion of a residuary gift, a deduction is allowed in computing the taxable income of the estate, and the gross income of the distributee is increased, but such a deduction and such an increase cannot exceed the distributable net income of the estate for the year of distribution.[8]   There is no throwback rule applicable to estates.[9]   If there are multiple distributees, then an allocation of the distributable net income is made among them, so that the gross income of each distributee will be increased by an amount which bears the same ratio to the distributable net income as the amount given to the distributee bears to the total distributed to all distributees.[10]   The character rule applies, which means that the amount paid to a beneficiary will have the same character in the hands of the beneficiary as in the hands of the estate.[11]

If the executor is not extremely careful in planning residuary distributions, he may place on a residuary distributee a larger portion of the income tax burden with respect to estate income than is placed on other residuary takers.   Suppose, for example, that the testator gives one half of his residuary estate to A and the other half to B; that the distributable net income of the estate in the second year of administration is $10,000; and that in that year the executor distributes to A stock in the residue worth $15,000 and to B stock in the residue worth $5000.   A is required to include in his gross income $7500 (he received three fourths of the total distribution for the year) and B is required to include in his gross income only $2500 (he received one fourth of the total distribution

---

[8] Section 643(a) of the 1954 Code quoted infra page 1363, defines distributable net income. The distribution deduction allowed the estate is described in §661, quoted infra page 1365.   The amount of the distribution includible in the beneficiary-recipient's gross income is governed by §662, quoted infra page 1366.

If the distributee is a charity or if the income of the estate is permanently set aside for a charity, the estate does not take a distribution deduction, but is allowed a deduction under §642(c), quoted infra page 1362, in computing the estate's taxable income.

[9] The throwback rule applicable to trusts is discussed infra page 742.

[10] See 1954 I.R.C. §662(a), quoted infra page 1366.

[11] See 1954 I.R.C. §662(b), quoted infra page 1366.

In Rev. Rul. 55-728, 1955-2 C.B. 36, it is pointed out that the taxpayer who receives dividends from stock owned individually by him and also from stock held by an estate is limited to a dividend exclusion of $50, but in computing his credit allowance he may include the dividends received from both sources, because §662(b) makes it clear that the dividend income received from an estate retains the same character in the hands of a beneficiary as in the hands of an estate.

for the year). ~~Thus, though in a final accounting A and B are to share equally in the estate income that falls into the residue, more of the income will have been included in A's gross income than in B's.~~[12]

The present law normally makes it undesirable, from the standpoint of federal income taxes, for an executor to make unequal distributions of residuary shares during administration.[13] Thus, if the residue includes stock in a closely held corporation, and a distribution to one residuary taker of his portion of the stock would give him control of the business — a desirable result from a business standpoint — such a distribution to him, without distributions to the other residuary takers of their portions, might place a heavy income tax burden on him.[14]

Even if all the residuary takers are given their respective portions of the closely held stock so that each will be deemed to receive a portion of the current year's distributable net income, the distributees will receive what is basically a nonliquid asset, and if their respective gross incomes will be augmented substantially by such distributions, they may be in a difficult position so far as the availability of liquid funds to meet the income tax load placed on them is concerned.[15]

Three significant changes in the present law would be made by

[12] In the textual illustration, if it is assumed that B is a charity, then the distributable net income would be only $5000, instead of $10,000, because a deduction would be allowed in the amount of the one half of the estate income which is permanently set aside for charity in determining the estate's taxable income. Consequently, $5000 would be includible in A's gross income. In applying the character rule, the charitable contributions deduction is (in the absence of specific allocation under the terms of the governing instrument or the requirement under local law of a different allocation) allocated among the classes of income entering into the computation of estate income in a designated manner. See Reg. §1.662(b)-2.

[13] The income tax bracket of a distributee or the deductions available to him may, ~~however, prevent the unequal distributions from producing~~ an unfavorable income tax result.

Section 2 of the 1954 Code provides that under certain circumstances a return of a surviving spouse shall be treated as a joint return of a husband and wife. When the circumstances described in §2 are present, it may be desirable to distribute part of the estate income to the surviving spouse, so that in effect the estate income will be divided into three parts for income tax purposes.

[14] If one share of the residue is to go outright and another share is to go in trust, a distribution of the outright share could be made without destroying an election by a small business corporation to be taxed like a "partnership" under 1954 I.R.C. §§1371-1377 (as added by the Technical Amendments Act of 1958, §64), but as soon as the distribution is made in trust, the election is destroyed.

[15] The difficult position of the distributees is created as a result of a distribution by the executor of nonliquid assets, but it may not be feasible for him to include with such a distribution liquid assets sufficient in amount to cover the income tax imposed on the distributees by the distribution. Thus, in the final analysis the present income tax laws make it difficult for the executor to make distribution of nonliquid assets during ~~administration.~~

H.R. 9662. One proposal is to extend the separate share rule[16] to estates. If this proposal is adopted, the beneficiary of each portion of the residue will be treated as though his portion was a separate estate and a distribution to him will never carry more of the current year's distributable net income than would be properly allocated to it as a separate estate.[17]

Another proposal has several parts and is designed to permit certain distributions from the residuary estate which will not carry out to the distributee estate income. Any real property, tangible personal property (other than money) or closely held stock owned by the decedent at the time of his death, which is properly distributed before the close of the thirty-sixth calendar month which begins after the date of the death of the decedent, in full or partial satisfaction of a share of the corpus of the residue, would not carry out to the distributee any estate income.[18] Furthermore, in the case of an estate in which the value (determined as of the date of

[16] See 1954 Code §663(c), quoted infra page 1367.

[17] H.R. 9662 also proposes that §642(h) of the 1954 Code, quoted infra page 1363, be amended so that on the termination of a separate share, unused loss carryovers and excess deductions allocable to the separate share may be available to the beneficiary.

Revenue Ruling 57-31, 1957-1 C.B. 201, holds that where a residuary testamentary trust is a beneficiary succeeding to the property of an estate and has deductions in excess of its gross income after the allowance of the excess deductions from the estate as authorized by §642(h)(2), the amount in excess of the gross income of the trust is not deductible by the income beneficiaries of the trust; but, if the trust terminates in the same year, then such excess deductions will be available to the remaindermen under the trust. Revenue Ruling 60-134, I.R.B. 1960-15, 16, considers the allocation of the deduction allowed by §642(h) among the intestate takers of Louisiana property. Under Louisiana law the property passes to the descendants subject to the usufruct of the widow. Perfect usufruct is where the property is used by the wife until her death or remarriage and is then turned over to the children. Imperfect usufruct is where the property is such that it cannot be used and later turned over, but its use involves its disappearance and the widow must turn over on death or remarriage the same quantity, quality and value as she received. The ruling recognizes that the phrase "beneficiaries succeeding to the estate or trust" in §642(h) has reference only to those persons who have a right to receive property as distinguished from a mere right to income from such property. The widow in effect gets only income from perfect usufruct but receives the property subject to imperfect usufruct, and §642(h) operates accordingly.

Section 642(h) does not deal with net operating loss carrybacks (see §172). Mellott v. United States, 257 F.2d 798 (3d Cir. 1958), cert. denied, 358 U.S. 864 (1959), brings out that the heirs of an estate to whom estate income was currently distributable could not assert the benefits of a carryback of a net operating loss available to the estate under the 1939 Code.

[18] Closely held stock would be limited to stock in a corporation of ten or less stockholders, where 20 percent or more in value of the voting stock of the corporation is included in the decedent's gross estate and the value of such stock in the decedent's gross estate exceeds either 35 percent of the value of his gross estate or 50 percent of the value of his taxable estate. This test is taken from 1954 I.R.C. §6166, discussed infra page 1429.

the decedent's death) of the gross estate is $100,000 or less,[19] any amount which is properly distributed before the close of the thirty-sixth month from the corpus of the estate — whether it is from corpus will depend on what the executor properly designates it — will not carry out to the distributee estate income. The effect of this proposal is to give the executor considerable discretion during the 36-month period to determine whether a partial distribution of the residue will cause any shift from the estate to the distributee of the income tax load with respect to the current year's estate income. The discretion exists because residuary takers will typically be entitled to income and corpus and if the executor designates the distribution as income, he will cause the shift, and if he designates it as corpus, there will be no shift.

If this proposal is adopted, the partial distribution of closely held stock can be designated as a distribution of corpus and the distributable net income attributable to the separate share of the residue will still be taxable to the estate so that the distributee will not be faced with an increased income tax load when he receives the nonliquid asset.

The proposal's operation, however, is not limited in cases where the gross estate is $100,000 or less to the situation where nonliquid assets are being distributed. If a liquid asset is involved, its liquidation by the distributee to raise funds needed to pay an increased income tax bill may force the distributee to sell the property at an undesirable time, and if it has increased in value since the date it was valued for estate purposes, the liquidation will subject the distributee to a tax on the gain.[20]

Under present law, the executor determines income tax consequences by his decision whether or not to distribute part of the residue. Under H.R. 9662 he would determine such consequences in the described cases by the designation he gives the distribution, that is, whether he designates it as a distribution of income or corpus. After the 36-month period has expired, the present law would be re-established, as modified by the extension of the separate share rule to estates.[21]

An executor who is not fully aware of the present rules which govern the income taxation of estates can produce some unfortu-

[19] For this purpose the decedent's gross estate would not contain items included therein only by reason of 1954 I.R.C. §§2035-2041 or of §2042(2).

[20] When a distribution in kind of a share of the residue is made, the basis of the distributee is the same as the basis of the estate.

[21] If administration is prolonged unduly, then the period of administration may be deemed to have ended, and the gross income, deductions and credits of the estate may thereafter be considered the gross income, deductions and credits of the person or persons succeeding to the property of the estate. See Reg. §1.641(b)-3.

nate income tax consequences, so far as estate beneficiaries are concerned, as a result of distributions of the residue during administration, even though, taxes to one side, he is doing a normal and natural thing. Under H.R. 9662 the normal action by the executor uninformed as to taxes will not produce such unfortunate results in most cases. In the hands of the tax-conscious executor, the H.R. 9662 proposals narrow to some extent the area of manipulation for tax avoidance purposes by the extension of the separate share rule to estates,[22] but within each separate share, the area of such manipulation is broadened during the 36-month period. The broadening may be justified if thereby simplicity in the income taxation of estates is obtained for a period that is long enough to conclude the administration of most estates.

A third proposal in H.R. 9662 would result in treating estate distributions to a charity like distributions to other estate beneficiaries, that is, as entitling the estate to a distribution deduction. The tier system would be modified, however, so that amounts paid to a charity would fall in the third tier along with amounts required to be paid from corpus in determining when some of the estate's income would be deemed to reach the distributee. The consequence of this would not be important if the estate income payable to a charity, or permanently set aside for it, constituted a separate share. In such a case the estate income would not be taxed. But if under a separate share the executor had discretion to pay the income or corpus either to an individual or a charity and in any year he paid amounts to each which equaled or exceeded the distributable net income of the estate attributable to such a separate share, the distribution to the individual would carry to him all the income and be taxed to him. Thus if H.R. 9662 is adopted, an executor will have to exercise more care in certain cases than now is required where estate income will pass to a charity.

2.   THE PECUNIARY LEGACY

Section 663(a)(1) of the 1954 Code[23] provides in substance that an amount distributed in satisfaction of a bequest of a specific sum of money will not be deductible in computing the taxable income of the estate for the year of distribution and will not increase the

[22] Under present law the executor can divide the income tax load among the residuary beneficiaries by controlling the amount of the distribution to each, but under the separate share rule he cannot place on any distributee more than the income tax load with respect to the portion of the estate income attributable to his share, no matter how he varies the distributions to each.

[23] Quoted, infra page 1367.

gross income of the distributee for such year, if the distribution is made all at once or in not more than three installments. The Regulations recognize that the distribution will not be in more than three installments, even though the executor in fact pays the legacy in more than three installments, if the terms of the will do not provide for such payments.[24] In other words, a bequest for which no time of payment is specified and which is to be paid in the ordinary course of administration is considered as required to be paid in a single installment.

If the bequest of a specific sum of money is by the terms of the will required to be paid in more than three installments, then each distribution will be deductible by the estate in computing its taxable income and each distribution will be added to the gross income of the legatee, but such a deduction and such an addition cannot exceed the distributable net income of the estate for the year of distribution.[25] If there are multiple distributees, then an allocation of the distributable net income is made among them.[26] The character rule also applies.[27]

If some limitation on installment payments is not placed on bequests of specific sums of money, a tax-free annuity could be established. The income tax avoidance feature of installment payments, however, is not in the number of installments but in the number of taxable years in which payments may be made. H.R. 9662 would modify the three-installment rule by protecting a bequest of a specific sum of money from the consequence of carrying out estate income to the distributee when distribution is made, if distribution is made all at once or in one taxable year of the estate and the will does not require the bequest to be paid in more than one taxable year of the estate, or if distribution is made before the close of the thirty-sixth calendar month which begins after the date of the death of the testator and the will does not require any part of the bequest to be paid after the close of that month.

The discussion so far indicates that the executor cannot affect the federal income tax consequences by the timing of distributions made in whole or partial satisfaction of a bequest of a specific sum of money as long as the will does not require payment to be made in more than three installments. The executor, however, will usually have discretion to satisfy the bequest of a specific sum of money by a distribution in kind of estate property. If he so elects, the federal income tax consequences are the same as if he sold the

---

24 See Reg. §§1.663(a)-1(a), 1.663(a)-1(c).
25 See page 80 supra, note 8.
26 See page 80 supra, note 10.
27 See page 80 supra, note 11.

property distributed in kind to the legatee for the amount of money given to the legatee by the will. Thus the estate may realize a gain or loss depending on whether the distributed property has gone up or down in value since the date it was valued for estate tax purposes. However, if the distribution in kind is made during the first year after the testator's death, the value on the date it is distributed will control for federal estate tax purposes, provided the alternate valuation date is selected under Section 2032 of the 1954 Code.[28] Thus no gain or loss on a distribution in kind during the first year would be possible if the alternate valuation date is selected. H.R. 9662 would make no change in the tax consequences of a distribution in kind.

The controlling state law may require, in the absence of a contrary manifestation of intent in the will, that the legatee receive some payment in addition to the specified sum, to compensate him for any delay in receiving his legacy. Thus, in many states an *outright* legatee is entitled to interest, at the legal rate, to commence a year from the date of the testator's death.[29] This payment must be made even though the estate in fact has no income. If, however, the legacy is payable to a *trustee*, the executor may have to pay the trustee, in addition to the specified sum of money, a share of the income in fact earned by the estate, or possibly an amount equal to the usual rate of return from such a sum held in trust, with the additional payment to be calculated from the date of the testator's death.[30]

The additional payment which the executor may be required to make is not itself a bequest of a specific sum of money protected by Section 663(a)(1), if the test given in the Regulations is applied, because that test requires that the amount of money be ascertainable under the terms of the testator's will as of the date of his death.[31] The amount of any such additional payment will always depend on when the executor exercises his discretion to make payment of the specified sum of money. When that payment is made, the total additional payment that is required can be calculated and not before.

The operation of the test set forth in the Regulations as to what is a bequest of a specific sum of money protected by Section

[28] Quoted infra page 1395.

[29] See 3 Scott, Trusts §234.2 (2d ed. 1956). In New York a legacy is by statute payable seven months after the granting of letters testamentary, and interest begins to run on legacies unpaid at that time. See P-H Wills, Est. & Trusts Serv. §443.10.

[30] See 3 Scott, Trusts, §234.2 (2d ed. 1956).

[31] See Reg. §1.663(a)-1(b). If the additional payment can be made only from the income of the estate, then §663(a)(1) provides that it "shall not be considered as a gift or bequest of a specific sum of money."

663(a)(1) is illustrated by a formula pecuniary legacy which may be used to describe the amount of a marital deduction gift.[32] Such a pecuniary legacy is not deemed a gift of a specific sum of money protected under Section 663(a)(1), because its amount is dependent on the amount in the adjusted gross estate of the deceased spouse, which is, in turn, dependent on the ascertainment of his funeral expenses, debts and the expenses of administration of his estate, and on the exercise of discretions given by the Code to the executor to select the valuation date and to determine whether to take certain deductions as income or estate tax deductions. Thus the amount of the pecuniary legacy is not ascertainable on the date of the testator's death.[33]

The entire formula pecuniary marital deduction gift, including any additional payment which may have to be made to compensate the legatee-spouse for delay in paying it to her, is outside the protection of Section 663(a)(1). If, however, a bequest of what is clearly a specific sum of money is made, it is not removed from the protection of Section 663(a)(1) by virtue of the fact that under controlling local law an additional payment may have to be made to compensate the legatee for delay in paying the legacy. Only the additional payment is outside such protection.

When a dollar amount is payable but it is not a bequest of a specific sum of money within the meaning of those words in Section 663(a)(1) because the dollar amount is not ascertainable on the testator's death, nevertheless, when the dollar amount is later ascertained, if it is then satisfied by the executor electing to distribute property in kind and the distributed property has increased in value since the date it was valued for estate tax purposes, the gain will be taxable to the estate.[34] In addition to this tax consequence, however, the distribution in satisfaction of the dollar amount, whether in kind or in cash, may give the estate a deduction for federal income tax purposes and increase the gross income

---

[32] Formula pecuniary marital deduction gifts are discussed infra page 793.

[33] The Regulations do recognize as a bequest of a specific sum of money one that is subject to the performance of a condition precedent to be performed after the testator's death, so that the bequest may never become payable. Section 1.663(a)-1(b)(4) of the Regulations provides as follows: "A gift or bequest of a specific sum of money or of specific property is not disqualified under this paragraph solely because its payment is subject to a condition. For example, provision for a payment by a trust to beneficiary A of $10,000 when he reaches age 25, and $10,000 when he reaches age 30, with payment over to B of any amount not paid to A because of his death, is a gift to A of a specific sum of money payable in two instalments, within the meaning of this paragraph, even though the exact amount payable to A cannot be ascertained with certainty under the terms of the trust instrument."

[34] See Rev. Rul. 56-270, 1956-1 C.B. 325; Reg. §1.1014-4(a)(3), quoted infra page 1499.

Is so-called "interest" payable on a legacy true interest for tax purps?

of the distributee. Thus the timing by the executor of such a distribution may have far-reaching federal income tax consequences.

What if interest = pd?

If the dollar amount that is to be satisfied by the distribution is the so-called interest that is payable on a pecuniary legacy from a date one year after the testator's death, is such a payment to be regarded the same as the payment by the executor of interest on a debt? If so, then the estate will be entitled to an interest deduction in the year of payment and the entire amount of the interest payment will be income to the distributee in the year of payment. If that result prevails, then the executor does affect significantly the federal income tax result, depending on whether he pays the interest as it accrues from year to year or lets it build up in amount and discharges it all in one year.[35]

If it = regarded as true int →

If it + regarded as true int

If the dollar payment is not to be regarded as true interest, then a distribution in satisfaction of it is like any other distribution to an estate beneficiary that is not protected by the exclusionary rule of Section 663(a)(1).

Suppose, for example, that a testator bequeaths $100,000 to T in trust for A; that under controlling local law the executor is required to distribute to T, in addition to $100,000, the portion of the income earned by the estate that is attributable to $100,000; that the estate earns income at the rate of 4 percent, so that when the executor makes the distribution to T at the end of the second year he must pay him $8000 as income for the two years; and that the distributable net income of the estate for the second year exceeds $8000. If the only distribution made by the executor in the second year is the distribution to T of $108,000, the gross income of the trust will be $8000 and the estate will have a deduction in the amount of $8000. Thus, though the throwback rule does not apply to distributions by an estate, the distributee here is required to include in his gross income more than his share of the current year's income.

A more dramatic illustration can be presented. Suppose that a will contains a marital deduction formula pecuniary gift in favor of the testator's wife and gives the residue of his estate to his son; that the formula produces a gift of $50,000; and that in the second year of administration, when the distributable net income of the

[35] In Davidson v. United States, 149 F. Supp. 208 (Ct. Cl. 1957), the total amount of so-called interest that was paid exceeded the amount of the current year's income of the estate, so that the excess was of no help as a deduction to the estate and if the entire amount of the so-called interest was taxable to the legatee in the year of payment, the income tax cost to him would reduce the worth of the payment substantially. The court held that the so-called interest payment was not true interest and should be regarded as a distribution taxable to the recipient only to the extent it did not exceed the current year's income. See also Wolf v. Commissioner, 84 F.2d 390 (3d Cir. 1936).

This ct held it + true interest

estate is $25,000, the executor elects to distribute to the wife
$25,000 (one half of her legacy).   No other distribution is made.
The entire $25,000 will be includible in the gross income of the
wife, a very costly result so far as she is concerned, and a windfall
to the residuary beneficiary due to the fact that the estate will pay
no income tax in that year on the $25,000 of taxable income.

H.R. 9662 would not change the present law in regard to what
constitutes a bequest of a specific sum of money.   Furthermore, it
would not determine whether so-called interest payable on a legacy
is true interest for tax purposes.   If, however, a payment of a dollar amount that is not a bequest of a specific sum of money is not
true interest, then H.R. 9662 might change the present situation
significantly.

The word "might" in the preceding sentence is used designedly
because it is not clear whether a pecuniary legacy can be a separate
share for purposes of the separate share rule if that rule is extended
to estates.   A somewhat similar problem is raised in connection
with the marital deduction where a power of appointment arrangement is permitted to qualify for such a deduction if the
power relates to a "specific portion" of an interest in property.[36]
In this situation, the Regulations take the position that a specific
sum of money cannot be a "specific portion" of an interest in property.[37]   If a pecuniary legacy cannot be a separate share, then the
only change in present law that would be made by H.R. 9662, so
far as pecuniary legacies are concerned, is in the discretion given
to the executor during the 36-month period to determine whether
he is distributing income or corpus.[38]

It is submitted that a proper analysis of the proposal in H.R.
9662 to extend the separate share rule to estates should lead to the
conclusion that within certain limits a pecuniary legacy should be
recognized as a separate share.   The discussion that follows assumes this result.   Consequently, if a bequest of $20,000 is made to
a person, any additional amount which has to be paid, and which
is not true interest, would pick up only a proportionate amount of
the distributable net income of the year of distribution and hence
would be income to the distributee only to that extent.

Suppose for example, that the distributable net income for the
third year of administration is $6000; that a legacy in trust in
the amount of $20,000 is paid at the end of the third year; that the
controlling local law requires the executor to pay the legatee, in

[36] So-called portion marital deduction gifts are examined infra page 861.
[37] See Reg. §20.2056(b)-5(c), quoted infra page 1536.
[38] This change alone would enable the executor to keep the taxation of
estate income almost in balance during the 36-month period.   After the 36-
month period, the present situation would fully apply if the specific sum of
money cannot be a separate share.

addition to the $20,000, his share of the income earned by the estate and that this share is $1800; and that $20,000, the amount of the legacy, is 10 percent of the total estate. If the $20,000 is a separate estate, then only 10 percent of the distributable net income of the entire estate for the year of distribution should be allocated to it.[39] Consequently, the legatee's gross income would be augmented by only $600 as a result of the payment to him of the $20,000 legacy and the additional amount of $1800 for the delay. It is possible that the extension of the separate share rule to estates would result in a requirement, imposed by local law, that the executor allocate to the separate share the income tax cost to the estate of the separate share's income for the first two years, when no distribution was made, so that the legatee would not be entitled to the full $1800. If this is not the case, the residuary takers will in effect be paying the income tax on the first two years' income of the separate share.[40]

The significance of the extension of the separate share rule to estates with respect to formula pecuniary marital deduction bequests would again be more dramatic. Such a bequest is like the additional payment that may be required in connection with a bequest of a specific sum of money in that it is not protected under Section 663(a)(1) of the present law. It is like the bequest of a specific sum of money, however, in that it is a gift of estate corpus, whereas the additional payment in connection with the bequest of a specific sum of money is a gift of estate income, at least if there is any. If an additional payment is required in connection with a formula pecuniary marital deduction gift to compensate the distributee spouse for delay in the payment of the legacy, such an additional payment will be chargeable to estate income. If the separate share rule should be extended to estates, the formula pecuniary marital

---

[39] The percentage of the total estate that is represented by the pecuniary legacy would have to be determined annually. Probably this percentage should be determined at the beginning of the taxable year on the basis of the amount then owing to the pecuniary legatee. If this is done, then probably the income for the preceding years already allocable to the specific sum should be added to the specific sum in determining the percentage of the total estate payable to the legatee. For a somewhat analogous problem where the value of the trust property at the beginning of the taxable year was selected, see Reg. §1.671-3(a)(3).

[40] See the following cases which consider what adjustments may have to be made by the executor when he elects to take certain administration expenses as income tax deductions rather than estate tax deductions, and, as a result of such election, certain beneficiaries receive more and others less than would have been the case if these expenses had been taken as estate tax deductions: Estate of Fred H. Bixby, 140 Cal. App. 2d 326, 295 P.2d 68 (1956); Estate of Edwin H. Warms, 140 N.Y.S.2d 169 (1955); In re Samuel Levy's Estate, 9 Misc. 2d 561, 167 N.Y.S.2d 16 (1957).

deduction gift should be regarded as a separate estate, and only if the total payment which has to be made exceeds the sum produced by the formula should any of the distributable net income of the estate for the year of distribution be attributable to the marital gift. In other words, the portion of the distributable net income of the year of distribution attributable to the separate marital gift share would be determined on the same basis as though the formula pecuniary marital deduction gift were a gift of a specific sum of money.

Once the portion of the current year's distributable net income allocable to a separate share is determined, what would be the result if a distribution is made only in partial satisfaction of the amount due? Under H.R. 9662 the executor would be allowed to determine during the 36-month period following the testator's death, within the limits prescribed, whether the payment to the distributee is corpus or income, and only to the extent that it is determined to be income would the payment carry distributable net income of the current year which has been allocated to the separate share.[41]

The separate share rule should not be applied in such a manner as to undermine the exclusion from Section 663(a)(1) of certain installment gifts. Thus, if the testator bequeaths to A the sum of $50,000, to be paid in five annual installments of $10,000 each, the separate share rule should either be deemed completely inapplicable, or, if applied, the separate share of the legatee should be regarded as $50,000, decreasing annually as each $10,000 payment is made, and the distributable net income apportioned to such a share annually should be determined accordingly.

3. THE SPECIFIC BEQUEST

When a specific bequest is made in a will, the executor normally must account to the legatee for the income from the specifically bequeathed property from the date of the testator's death.[42] Though

[41] If the extension of the separate share rule to estates is made but no other change in present law is operative (for example, if the 36-month period has ended), the result ought to be the same, provided the separate share is a bequest of a specific sum of money, because in such a case the executor under present law should be able to designate whether his partial payment is directed at the bequest of the specific sum of money or at the additional payment that is required to be made on account of the delay in paying the legacy. However, the result should be different if a pecuniary formula marital deduction gift is involved, because no part of such a payment is protected by §663(a)(1) and thus the current year's distributable net income properly allocable to the separate marital gift share would be deemed to go out first in any distribution.

[42] See 3 Scott, Trusts §234.2 (2d ed. 1956).

Tax w/h to be pd on income

the distribution of the specifically bequeathed property is protected under Section 663(a)(1) to the same extent as a bequest of a specific sum of money, the additional payment of the income from such property is not so protected. It is like the additional payment which may be required in connection with a bequest of a specific sum of money. Consequently, the previous discussion relating to such additional payment is relevant here and is incorporated by reference. H.R. 9662 would affect specific bequests in the same manner as it would affect bequests of a specific sum of money.

PROBLEMS

4.1. Why should the executor plan to make a distribution in satisfaction of a formula pecuniary marital deduction gift in a short taxable year of the estate?

4.2. Under what circumstances will the distributee of the family automobile be required to include the value of the car in his gross income for the year of distribution?

4.3. It is suggested that the following provision be included in a will:

> I authorize my executor to make distributions of estate property to the beneficiaries of my estate from time to time during administration. A distribution may be made to one estate beneficiary in any year without any requirement that a similar distribution be made to any other estate beneficiary. A distribution may be made of the entire interest of a beneficiary in my estate or of a part of his interest. A distribution to a beneficiary who is entitled to both corpus and income from my estate may be charged against the beneficiary's interest in corpus or his interest in income as my executor in his uncontrolled discretion may determine. Nothing contained herein shall be construed as authorizing my executor to distribute to any estate beneficiary more than his proper share in my estate.

Would you approve the inclusion of this provision?

4. STATE INCOME TAXATION

In jurisdictions which impose a state income tax, the executor must familiarize himself with the scope of the tax so far as the estate is concerned. Normally he will not be confronted here with the complexity that is involved in the federal income tax field.

CHAPTER V

The Revocable Inter Vivos Trust as an Instrument in the Estate Plan

1. REVOCABLE TRUSTS DEFINED

What is meant by a revocable inter vivos trust? Before answering this question, consider the following illustrations:

1. A transfers property to T in trust. T is to pay the income to B for life and, on B's death, he is to pay the corpus to C and his heirs. A, however, is given the power by the trust instrument to revoke the trust. If the trust is revoked, the corpus is to be paid to A.

    Note: In this illustration, A *alone* may revoke the trust.

2. A transfers property to T in trust. T is to pay the income to B for life and, on B's death, he is to pay the corpus to C and his heirs. A and T, however, are given the power by the trust instrument to revoke the trust. If the trust is revoked, the corpus is to be paid to A.

    Note: In this illustration, A in conjunction with another (T), who does not have a substantial adverse interest, may revoke the trust.[1]

3. A transfers property to T in trust. T is to pay the income to B for life and, on B's death, he is to pay the corpus to C and his heirs. A and B, however, are given the power by the trust instrument to revoke the trust. If the trust is revoked, the corpus is to be paid to A.

    Note: In this illustration, A in conjunction with another (B), who does have a substantial adverse interest, may revoke the trust.[2]

4. A transfers property to T in trust. T is to pay the income to B for life and, on B's death, he is to pay the corpus to

---

[1] The income, estate and gift tax consequences with respect to a trust which is revocable by the settlor in conjunction with someone who does not have a substantial adverse interest are considered in Chapter VI.

[2] The income, estate and gift tax consequences with respect to a trust which is revocable by the settlor in conjunction with someone who does have a substantial adverse interest are considered in Chapter VI.

Talone c/revoke

C and his heirs. T, however, is given the power by the trust instrument to revoke the trust. If the trust is revoked, the corpus is to be paid to A.

Note: In this illustration, T *alone* may revoke the trust.[3]

In all four of the above illustrations, a revocation of the trust results in the return of the corpus to the settlor of the trust. The illustrations differ with respect to the person or persons in whom the power of revocation rests. *In this chapter a revocable inter vivos trust means one in which the settlor alone has the power to revoke and in which the effect of his revocation is to force the return of the corpus to himself or to force the payment of the corpus as he may direct.[4]*

Def. of revocable trust

Before considering the usefulness of a revocable inter vivos trust as an instrument in an estate plan, the following questions should be answered:

1. Is a revocable inter vivos trust a testamentary disposition? The first Massachusetts case printed below deals with this question.

2. Can a wife, on the death of her husband, assert her marital rights against the property placed by her husband in a revocable inter vivos trust? The second Massachusetts case printed below considers this question.

3. Can the settlor direct by his will that property subject to disposition by his will is to be added to the revocable inter vivos trust? The third Massachusetts case printed below considers this question.

---

[3] The income, estate and gift tax consequences with respect to a trust which is revocable by someone other than the settlor, whether the person does or does not have a substantial adverse interest, are considered in Chapter VI.

[4] This type of revocable inter vivos trust has been selected for separate study here because it most nearly resembles the will. Other types of inter vivos trusts are treated in Chapter VI.

A California statute provides that unless a trust is expressly made irrevocable, it shall be revocable by the settlor, and on revocation the trustee shall transfer to the settlor the trust estate. Cal. Civ. Code §2280 (Deering, 1960). See Newman v. Commissioner, 222 F.2d 131 (9th Cir. 1955), in which the court held that because of the California statute, no completed gift was made for gift tax purposes as the result of the establishment of a trust which did not expressly state that the trust was irrevocable. Statutes similar to the California statute exist in Oklahoma (Okla. Stat., tit. 60, §175.41 (1951)) and Texas (Tex. Rev. Civ. Stat., art. 7425b-41 (1960)). In Frensley v. Phinney, 59-1 U.S.T.C. ¶11876 (W.D. Tex. 1959), the court found that the settlor had manifested an intent that the trust was not to be revocable.

When a parent establishes a bank account for a minor child and places the account in his own name as trustee for the minor, is the trust a revocable one so that the parent can withdraw the funds and use them for his own benefit? The answer to the question is one of intention, but what intention will be inferred if none is manifested? Estate of Michael A. Doyle, 32 T.C. 1209 (1959), regarded such an account as one revocable by the parent.

2. REVOCABLE TRUSTS AS NONTESTAMENTARY DISPOSITIONS

NATIONAL SHAWMUT BANK OF BOSTON v. JOY
315 Mass. 457, 53 N.E.2d 113 (1944)

LUMMUS, J.

This petition, filed October 31, 1942, is brought by The National Shawmut Bank of Boston and Haven Parker as trustees under an indenture of trust under seal entered into by them as trustees with William W. Nicholls of Boston as settlor, dated March 12, 1936, for instructions as to the distribution of the trust property at the termination of the trust.

The evidence is reported, but the material facts are not in dispute. William W. Nicholls, who was born in England on October 24, 1860, migrated to Massachusetts with his mother and sister in 1872. He grew up in Boston, where he became a naturalized citizen on May 12, 1886. He never married. Apparently before 1890 he went to the Azores to live, and there became agent for a steamship line and for a time was American consul. He lived there at Brown's Hotel, kept by Miss Sophia Brown, at Ponta Delgada on the island of São Miguel. But he retained his domicil in Boston and always described himself as of Boston. [Citations omitted.]

After he went to the Azores, his mother and sister continued to live in Boston in a house maintained by him until they died about thirty years ago. Even after their deaths he continued to visit Boston every year or two, although he no longer maintained a house there.

He had friends of long standing in New England, some of whom he made legatees in his will. At some time he told one of them that his friends meant much more to him than his relatives in England. One of his friends was Louis G. Neville, a dealer and broker in securities in Boston, who from about 1920 was given a free hand in buying and selling securities for Nicholls.

On October 21, 1926, while on a visit to Boston, Nicholls made his will, which was under seal. He named the petitioning bank as executor, and devised and bequeathed to it as trustee all his property. The income was made payable to Sophia Brown during her life, and after her death to another person (who in fact died before Sophia Brown) for his life. At the death of the survivor of them, pecuniary legacies were made payable to the respondent Minnie B. Joy and several other persons, and the residue was given to the

respondents Bettencourt and DeCosta. The will when executed
was put into the custody of the petitioning bank, and remained in
its custody until after Nicholls died on October 7, 1937. The will
was proved and allowed, and the bank was appointed executor, by
the Probate Court in and for the county of Suffolk at Boston on
June 5, 1939.

In 1936, while Nicholls was in the Azores, Neville, his son-in-law
Haven Parker, an attorney at law, and the bank decided that it
would be advisable for Nicholls to establish a voluntary trust. It
does not appear that Nicholls had been consulted. An instrument
of trust was drawn and sent to Nicholls, and he executed it in the
Azores on March 12, 1936. It was in form an indenture, and when
executed bore the signatures and seals of Nicholls as settlor and the
bank and Mr. Parker as trustees. It was amended, under a power
reserved by Nicholls, by another instrument similarly executed,
dated May 29, 1936. The combined instruments will be described
as though one. The property thereby conveyed by Nicholls to the
trustees consisted entirely of corporate stocks and bonds. It was
provided that the trust was established under the laws of Massachusetts, and was to be governed by those laws. Codman v. Krell, 152
Mass. 214, 218. Proctor v. Clark, 154 Mass. 45, 48. Harvey
v. Fiduciary Trust Co., 299 Mass. 457, 464. Loring, Trustee's
Handbook (5th ed. 1940) secs. 118-120. Commonwealth v. Stewart, 338 Penn. St. 9, affirmed Stewart v. Commonwealth, 312 U.S.
649. There is nothing to show that Nicholls did not understand
the effect of the trust instrument upon his property and upon his
earlier will. But whether he did or not, the terms of the trust instrument, as far as they are valid, bound him and bind all who
claim under him.

By those terms, Nicholls was to be paid $230 a month out of the
income or, if necessary, out of the principal.[5] It was provided
that "the trustees may make other payments from the principal of
the trust fund as they in their absolute discretion may deem necessary for the benefit of William W. Nicholls." After his death, the
income, and so much of the principal as the trustees in their absolute discretion might deem necessary, were to be paid to Sophia
Brown during her life. After the deaths of both Nicholls and

---

[5] (*Court footnote.* Court footnotes in this book have been renumbered so
as to give all footnotes in each chapter numerical sequence.) This provision
was substituted by the amendment of May 29, 1936, for one which made payable to Nicholls during his life only the income and so much of the principal
as the trustees in their absolute discretion might deem necessary. The only
other change made by that amendment was the insertion of the words "or sale"
after the word "purchase" in a provision, hereinafter quoted, giving certain
powers to Neville.

Sophia Brown, the principal and any accumulated income were to be paid over free from trust "to such person, persons or corporation as the donor (Nicholls) may appoint by an instrument duly acknowledged by him and under his seal and deposited with the trustees," and in default of such appointment "to such person or persons as are entitled to take from the donor (Nicholls) under the laws of intestacy of the Commonwealth of Massachusetts." It does not appear that Sophia Brown knew during the life of Nicholls of the existence of the trust, but such knowledge was not necessary to its validity. Aronian v. Asadoorian [315 Mass.], 274.

After Nicholls died on October 7, 1937, the trustees made payments under the trust instrument to Sophia Brown until her death on July 24, 1942. They now hold personalty, comprising the principal of the trust property, amounting to more than $29,000, besides nearly $1,000 of income remaining unpaid at the death of Sophia Brown. The Probate Court instructed the trustees to pay over the accumulated income as though it were principal, and the administrator of the estate of Sophia Brown did not appeal.[6] The

---

[6] On the death of a life beneficiary of a trust, the trustee may have in hand some income that he has not distributed to the life income beneficiary, and there may be some income that is due but has not been received by the trustee, and there may be some income that has accrued but is not yet payable to the trustee. The estate of the life income beneficiary is entitled to income received and due, and the income accrued but payable later is apportioned unless the trust instrument manifests a different intent. Ordinary dividends on shares of stock received by a trustee are not apportionable. See 3 Scott, Trusts §235A (2d ed. 1956). The trust instrument in National Shawmut Bank v. Joy provided that the principal and any accumulated income were to be paid over on the death of the life income beneficiaries. Does such language eliminate the estate of the life income beneficiary from sharing in the accumulated income? Evidently the administrator of the estate of Sophia Brown did not think it was worth raising the question on appeal. In Loring v. Cotter, 339 Mass. 689, 162 N.E.2d 294 (1959), the executor of the life income beneficiary did raise the question where the trust provided that the trustee was to "pay over the principal fund with any accumulations of income and additions thereto" to the remainderman. The court held that the remainderman was entitled to accumulated net income, to interest accrued on bonds to the date of the life beneficiary's death, and to dividends declared on stock of record prior to the life beneficiary's death. In the absence of the provision regarding accumulated income, these items would have gone to the executor of the life beneficiary. See Mass. Ann. Laws, c. 197, §27. Thorndike v. Dexter, 340 Mass. 387, 164 N.E.2d 338 (1960), was a case where the will called for the payment of income quarterly, or oftener if convenient, to the designated beneficiaries *living* at the time of such payment. On the termination of the trust, the capital, together with any income which had accrued since the last payment of income, was to be distributed to the designated takers. The court determined that the quarterly payments of income should be measured in quarters beginning with the testator's death. The direction to pay the income to beneficiaries *living* on the payment date overcame the apportionment provisions of Mass. Ann. Laws, c. 197, §27. However, the payment of income was delayed because of a tort claim against the estate, so that the quarterly payments could not begin, and during this delay a beneficiary died. The court

Probate Court instructed the trustees to distribute the principal and accumulated income equally among the three first cousins of Nicholls in England (including the administrator of the estate of one of them who died on April 11, 1939) living at the death of Nicholls on October 7, 1937. They were his statutory next of kin under the Massachusetts statute of distributions, G.L. (Ter. Ed.) c. 190, secs. 2, 3 (6). Am. Law Inst. Restatement: Property, secs. 310, 311.[7] Some of the legatees named in his will appealed. Apart from the trust property, Nicholls left less than $1,000, and what he left has been consumed in paying debts and expenses of his estate.[8] . . . .

3. The remaining contention of the legatees presents another important question. They contend that Nicholls reserved full do-

---

gave to the deceased beneficiary's estate the amount of income which the beneficiary would have received if the quarterly payments had been made. Cash received after the last quarterly payment date prior to the beneficiary's death on items then accrued and payable, which were the equivalent of cash on hand, such as overdue coupons on bearer bonds, was to be accounted for as though on hand on the last quarterly payment date and thus was payable to the beneficiary's estate. — ED.

[7] Restatement of Property §314(1) reads as follows: "When a person makes an otherwise effective inter vivos conveyance of an interest in land to his heirs, or of an interest in things other than land, to his next of kin, then, unless a contrary intent is found from additional language or circumstances, such conveyance to his heirs or next of kin is a nullity in the sense that it designates neither a conveyee nor the type of interest of a conveyee." In another part of the opinion, the court referred to the above-quoted section of the Restatement of Property and approved it, but decided that the next of kin of Nicholls nevertheless would take as purchasers under the trust. The court recognized that the so-called doctrine of worthier title as applied to inter vivos transfers was a rule of construction only and that the terms of the trust instrument justified the conclusion that the settlor intended the next of kin to take as purchasers. In reaching this result the court stressed the presence of the power of appointment in the settlor as supporting such a conclusion. Notice also that the next of kin were ascertained as of the death of the settlor and not as of the death of the life beneficiaries. — ED.

[8] The next of kin of the settlor would not have been entitled to take if the settlor had exercised his power of appointment by appointing the trust property to others. It was contended that his 1926 will, though it antedated the trust, exercised the power of appointment he had under the trust. The requirements for the exercise of the power were that the instrument exercising the power be one that was duly acknowledged, under seal, and deposited with the trustees. The 1926 will was in fact under seal and one of the attesting witnesses was in fact a notary qualified to take acknowledgments and the will was in fact deposited with the bank which was one of the trustees under the trust. Nevertheless, the court determined that the requirements for the execution of the power had not been met because the notary did not act as such in attesting the will and the will was not deposited with the bank in its capacity as trustee. A power may be exercised by an instrument which antedates the creation of the power, unless the instrument creating the power specifies otherwise, and a power may be exercised by a general residuary clause in a will though no specific mention of the power is made. See discussion of powers of appointment at page 690 infra. — ED.

minion over the trust property; that the provisions for persons other than Nicholls himself were testamentary in nature, intended to take effect only at or after his death, and were invalid because the trust instrument was not attested and subscribed by three witnesses as required for a will by G.L. (Ter. Ed.) c. 191, sec. 1; and that the trust instrument created merely an agency for Nicholls and not a genuine trust for other persons as cestuis after his death.

If that contention should prevail, the trust property would be deemed either the unqualified property of Nicholls, or property held for him under a resulting trust, and would pass under his will, either at his death or at the latest at the death of Sophia Brown, to the executor of his will for the benefit of the legatees named therein.

From the statute allowing the testamentary disposition of property by a will signed and witnessed as required by law (G.L. (Ter. Ed.) c. 191, sec. 1) and duly proved and allowed after death (sec. 7; Loring v. Massachusetts Horticultural Society, 171 Mass. 401, 402-403) the inference is plain that a testamentary disposition of property in any other manner is void.[9] [Citations omitted.] The statutes formerly contained an express provision to this effect (Gen. Sts. (1860) c. 92, sec. 6), and when it was omitted from Pub. Sts. (1882) c. 127, sec. 1, there was no intent to change the law. [Citation omitted.]

The distinguishing feature of a testamentary disposition is that it remains ambulatory until the death of the one who makes it. Until he dies, his title remains unimpaired and unaffected. A testamentary disposition becomes operative only upon and by reason of the death of the owner who makes it. It operates only upon what he leaves at his death. If the interest in question passes from the owner presently, while he remains alive, the transfer is inter vivos and not testamentary.[10] [Citations omitted.]

---

[9] (*Court footnote*) A gift causa mortis is no exception, for it must be perfected and title must pass inter vivos. It differs from an absolute gift mainly in being defeasible upon an express or implied condition subsequent. Duryea v. Harvey, 183 Mass. 429. Peck v. Scofield, 186 Mass. 108. Day v. Richards, 197 Mass. 86. Cronin v. Chelsea Savings Bank, 201 Mass. 146. Nelson v. Peterson, 202 Mass. 369. Stratton v. Athol Savings Bank, 213 Mass. 46. Stevens v. Provident Institution for Savings, 226 Mass. 138. Simpkins v. Old Colony Trust Co., 254 Mass. 576. Greeley v. O'Connor, 294 Mass. 527, 533. Rock v. Rock, 309 Mass. 44.

[10] (*Court footnote*) The validity of a conveyance delivered presently in escrow, beyond the control of the grantor, but not to be delivered to the grantee until the death of the grantor, is established. Tewksbury v. Tewksbury, 222 Mass. 595, 598. Wilson v. Jones, 280 Mass. 488. Scott, Trusts (1939) sec. 56.1. Bogert, Trusts (1935) sec. 103, page 334. 16 Am. Bar Asso. Journal, 779. Compare Stratton v. Athol Savings Bank, 213 Mass. 46; Russell v. Webster, 213 Mass. 491.

In some cases in this court it has apparently been thought of consequence that the settlor sought to avoid making a will, or to "evade" or "circumvent" the statutory requirements for a will, or to make a disposition of his property that would make a will unnecessary and in a popular sense would be a substitute for a will. We deem such considerations immaterial. The law prohibits only an unattested disposition that takes effect in a testamentary manner. If an owner of property can find a means of disposing of it inter vivos that will render a will unnecessary for the accomplishment of his practical purposes, he has a right to employ it. The fact that the motive of a transfer is to obtain the practical advantages of a will without making one is immaterial. [Citations omitted.]

We take up in order the provisions relied on by the legatees.

(a) Nicholls reserved to himself not only a life interest but also a power of appointment, subject to the life interests of himself and Sophia Brown, in favor of "such person, persons or corporation" as he might select, and the trustees were to pay over all the trust property accordingly upon the deaths of both Nicholls and Sophia Brown.

No one contends that the reservation by a settlor of an interest for his life, taken by itself, impairs the validity of a trust. [Citations omitted.]

As to the added power of appointment, it is true that the actual exercise of a power of appointment may sometimes have the result, even the unintended result, of making the property appointed the property of the donee of the power, especially for the benefit of his creditors. [Citations omitted.] But the power itself, however general, is not property, even though the donee of the power is also the settlor and the life beneficiary.[11] [Citations omitted.] And

---

[11] (*Court footnote*) But for the purpose of taxation the exercise or non-exercise of a general power of appointment may be treated as property, or the property may be treated as owned by the person having such a power. Chase National Bank v. United States, 278 U.S. 327. Curry v. McCanless, 307 U.S. 357, 371. Graves v. Elliott, 307 U.S. 383, 386. Pearce v. Commissioner of Internal Revenue, 315 U.S. 543, 544. Graves v. Schmidlapp, 315 U.S. 657, 141 Am. L.R. 948. Chickering v. Commissioner of Internal Revenue, 118 Fed. (2d) 254, 139 Am. L.R. 508. See also Boston Safe Deposit & Trust Co. v. Commissioner of Corporations & Taxation, 294 Mass. 551, 556, relating to a power to revoke or alter a trust. Compare Welch v. Commissioner of Corporations and Taxation, 309 Mass. 293, 297, et seq. (power to change life insurance beneficiary and to revoke or alter trust).

So, too, in bankruptcy the trustee in bankruptcy is vested with all "powers which he (the bankrupt) might have exercised for his own benefit, but not those which he might have exercised solely for some other person." Bankruptcy Act, sec. 70a(3) (U.S.C. Title 11, sec. 110(a)(3), as amended June 22, 1938, c. 575, sec. 1 (52 U.S. Sts. at Large, 879, 880)). This seems not to apply to powers exercisable by will. Montague v. Silsbee, 218 Mass. 107, 111.

but of remaindermen ≠ affected until POf = exercised

"where an estate is given over in default of appointment, the nature of the estate of the remaindermen is not affected by the power of disposition until that power is exercised." [Citations omitted.]

Accordingly, where a settlor reserves to himself not only a life interest but also a general power of appointment, the exercise of which would defeat provisions for the distribution of the trust property in default of appointment, the existence of that power does not make the trust property the property of the settlor nor make testamentary the provisions made in default of appointment.[12] [Citations omitted.]

HELD

(b) Nicholls reserved to himself also power to "alter, amend or revoke" the trust. The power to revoke, if not a kind of power of appointment [citations omitted], is akin to such a power. It is not property, and apart from the bankruptcy act cannot be reached by creditors. [Citations omitted.] Until a power to revoke is exercised, the interests created by the trust instrument remain unaffected. [Citations omitted.]

Power to revoke ≠ prop.

The reservation by the settlor, in addition to an interest for life, of a power to revoke the trust, did not make incomplete or testamentary the gift over to the statutory next of kin. [Citations omitted.]

Power to revoke ≠ make it testamentary

The same is true, a fortiori, of a reservation of the lesser powers to alter or amend the trust, or to withdraw principal from it, either with or without the consent of the trustee. Obviously an exercise of the power to revoke would enable the settlor to establish a new trust changed as he might desire. There is no reason why he may not reserve the right to take a short cut by altering or amending the original trust instrument. [Citations omitted.] The reservation of such powers does not make testamentary a gift over to the statutory next of kin. [Citations omitted.]

(c) The trust instrument contained this provision: "During the

---

Forbes v. Snow, 245 Mass. 85, 93. But it seems to apply to a general power, exercisable by an instrument inter vivos, to appoint, or to revoke a trust. 4 Collier, Bankruptcy (14th ed. 1942) 992. Board of Trade of Chicago v. Johnson, 264 U.S. 1. Cohen v. Samuels, 245 U.S. 50. Cohn v. Malone, 248 U.S. 450. Am. Law Inst. Restatement: Property, sec. 331. Griswold, 52 Harv. Law Rev. 929. Leach, 52 Harv. Law Rev. 961. Alexander, 56 Harv. Law Rev. 742.

These are exceptions to the general rule that a power of appointment, or a power of revocation of a trust (Scott, Trusts (1939) secs. 330, 330.12), is not property, and cannot be reached by creditors. Am. Law Inst. Restatement: Property, secs. 327-331.

[12] (*Court footnote*) As to the power to change the beneficiary in a life insurance policy, see Tyler v. Treasurer & Receiver General, 226 Mass. 306, 309; Goldman v. Moses, 287 Mass. 393, 396; Tolman v. Crowell, 288 Mass. 397, 400; Kruger v. John Hancock Mutual Life Ins. Co., 298 Mass. 124, 126. Ponlain v. Sullivan, 308 Mass. 58; Welch v. Commissioner of Corporations & Taxation, 309 Mass. 293, 297, et seq.; Scott, Trusts (1939) sec. 57.3.

life of Louis Gregg Neville of Wellesley, Massachusetts, the trustees are specifically directed without liability for any loss or depreciation which may result therefrom, to hold, retain, invest and reinvest the trust property solely in accordance with the written instructions of said Louis Gregg Neville, it being the intention and desire of the donor to vest in said Louis Gregg Neville the absolute control over the investment of the trust property held hereunder at any time during the life of said Louis Gregg Neville or until he shall notify the trustees in writing that he no longer wishes to instruct, direct and control the investment of the trust property. The said Louis Gregg Neville may charge any commissions due him on account of any investment of trust property made through him, and may take any profit accruing to him as a result of the purchase or sale by the trustees of investments directed by him, and the trustees are directed to pay such commission and profit."

Neville was not, as contended by the legatees, thereby given a right to all capital gains, so that the trust could never keep any. He was a dealer and broker in securities. As such he doubtless profited by commissions on purchases and sales made by him as broker. Where he bought or sold as principal, doubtless he made a profit. The trust instrument provided merely that he might receive such commissions and profits though in full control of the investments.

The powers given to Neville had little or no tendency to show that the trust instrument was to take effect in a testamentary manner. They did not make the trust a merely passive one. Important duties were left for the trustees. We think that the powers given to Neville did not impair the validity of the gift over to the statutory next of kin of Nicholls. Am. Law Inst. Restatement: Trusts, sec. 37. Scott, Trusts (1939) sec. 185.

But the legatees contend that by reserving power to alter, amend or revoke the trust the settlor made it possible for him as a practical matter to dominate Neville, and that the power to control the investments was in effect reserved to Nicholls himself. We assume without deciding that this contention is true. It does not follow that the gift over to the statutory next of kin is therefore testamentary and void. We need not decide whether the trust would have been invalid had the trustees been reduced to passive impotence, or something near it. A reservation by a settlor of the power to control investments does not impair the validity of a trust. [Citations omitted.] In Greeley v. Flynn, 310 Mass. 23, the settlor was herself the trustee and had every power of control, including the right to withdraw principal for her own use. Yet the gift over at her death was held valid and not testamentary.

It remains to speak of one Massachusetts case which has been thought inconsistent with the result here reached. In McEvoy v. Boston Five Cents Savings Bank, 201 Mass. 50, a wife conveyed under seal to a trustee a savings bank deposit, in trust to pay her whatever she might demand during her life, and at her death, if enough should remain, to pay to her husband a small sum weekly, and at his death to divide any remaining amount among certain cousins. She expressly reserved a power of revocation. The husband survived the wife. After his death the trustee sued the savings bank for the deposit. The administrator of the wife's estate appeared as adverse claimant, and a decision of the trial judge in his favor was affirmed by this court. The trustee admitted in his testimony that the wife told him that she intended by the trust instrument "to dispose of the property after she was dead as well as while she was living," and that "she intended this instrument in place of any will she might leave." This testimony was taken by this court as true, since the trial judge had found for the claimant. The opinion holds first that as a matter of law the provisions of the trust instrument for the disposition of the property after the death of the settlor were testamentary, and then adds that if that be thought too favorable to the claimant the decision of the trial judge for the claimant should be supported on the ground that "the evidence justified a finding by the trial judge that the paper was intended as a mere testamentary disposition of property, and not as a creation of a trust for any other purpose." In Jones v. Old Colony Trust Co., 251 Mass. 309, the McEvoy case is distinguished and supported on the ground that there "the nominal trustee had none of the ordinary powers of a trustee and was in substance and effect only an agent of the donor." See Scott, Trusts (1939) sec. 57.2.

In the McEvoy case the terms of the trust were fully stated in a formal document. Nothing was left to oral testimony or to inference from circumstances. The question whether the trust instrument was testamentary was to be determined solely by its terms. That the power of revocation did not make it testamentary, had been decided in Stone v. Hackett, 12 Gray, 227, 232. That the power to withdraw principal did not make it testamentary, had been decided in Davis v. Ney, 125 Mass. 590. Those cases were not cited. The trust instrument in the McEvoy case does not appear testamentary to us. The alternative or additional ground of decision implies that a purpose on the part of a settlor to employ a trust deed in order to avoid making a will makes testamentary and void what otherwise would be a valid settlement inter vivos. We think that that proposition is not law. We do not agree with the characterization of the McEvoy case, contained in the opinion in the Jones case, whereby the McEvoy case was distinguished and supported. The case of McEvoy v. Boston Five Cents Savings Bank, 201 Mass. 50, is overruled.

It may be added, that the principles of this opinion are not necessarily controlling in cases which concern the effectiveness of a voluntary trust in subjecting a settlor to a gift tax, or in freeing him from income taxes or his estate or the beneficiaries from estate or succession taxes, with respect to the trust property. Helvering v. F. & R. Lazarus & Co., 308 U.S. 252. Griffiths v. Commissioner of Internal Revenue, 308 U.S. 355. Helvering v. Clifford, 309 U.S. 331. Harrison v. Schaffner, 312 U.S. 579, 581, 582. Helvering v. Stuart, 317 U.S. 154, 168. Welch v. Commissioner of Corporations & Taxation, 309 Mass. 293, 298, 299.

Decree affirmed.[13]

---

[13] See comments on the Joy case in 24 B.U.L. Rev. 193 (1944) and 43 Mich. L. Rev. 976 (1945).

For cases involving revocable inter vivos trusts in which it is held that the terms of the trust which are designed to control the devolution of the trust property from and after the death of the settlor are effecive against the attack that the trust is a testamentary disposition, see President of Bowdoin College v. Merritt, 75 Fed. 480 (C.C.N.D. Cal. 1896); Commissioner v. Chase Manhattan Bank, 259 F.2d 231 (5th Cir. 1958), cert. denied, 359 U.S. 913 (1959) (for discussion of this case, see page 70 supra, note 49); United Building & Loan Assn. v. Garrett, 64 F. Supp. 460 (W.D. Ark. 1946) (construing Arkansas law); Hall v. Burkham, 59 Ala. 349 (1877); Cribbs v. Walker, 74 Ark. 104, 85 S.W. 244 (1905); Nichols v. Emory, 109 Cal. 323, 41 Pac. 1089 (1895); Denver National Bank v. Von Brecht, 137 Colo. 88, 322 P.2d 667 (1958); Cramer v. Hartford-Conn. Trust Co., 110 Conn. 22, 147 Atl. 139 (1929); Wilson v. Fulton National Bank of Atlanta, 188 Ga. 691, 4 S.E.2d 660 (1939); Bear v. Millikin Trust Co., 336 Ill. 366, 168 N.E. 349 (1929); Merchants National Bank of Aurora v. Weinold, 12 Ill. App. 2d 209, 138 N.E.2d 840 (1956); Keck v. McKinstry, 206 Iowa 1121, 221 N.W. 851 (1928); DeLeuil's Executors v. DeLeuil, 255 Ky. 406, 74 S.W.2d 474 (1934); Brown v. Fidelity Trust Co., 126 Md. 175, 94 Atl. 523 (1915); Rose v. Union Guardian Trust Co., 300 Mich. 73, 1 N.W.2d 458 (1942); Hiserodt v. Hamlett, 74 Miss. 37, 20 So. 143 (1896); Savings Investment & Trust Co. v. Little, 135 N.J. Eq. 546, 39 A.2d 392 (1944); Van Cott v. Prentice, 104 N.Y. 45, 10 N.E. 257 (1887); Witherington v. Herring, 140 N.C. 495, 53 S.E. 303 (1906); Ridge v. Bright, 244 N.C. 345, 93 S.E.2d 607 (1956); Bolles v. Toledo Trust Co., 144 Ohio St. 195, 58 N.E.2d 381 (1944); Shapley's Deed of Trust, 353 Pa. 499, 46 A.2d 227 (1946); Talbot v. Talbot, 32 R.I. 72, 78 Atl. 535 (1911); Leggroan v. Zion's Savings Bank, 120 Utah 93, 232 P.2d 746 (1952). See also Barlow v. Loomis, 19 Fed. 677 (C.C.D. Vt. 1884); Adams v. Haggerott, 34 F.2d 899 (8th Cir. 1929); Board of National Missions v. Smith, 182 F.2d 362 (7th Cir. 1950) (construing Illinois law); Sims v. Brown, 252 Mo. 58, 158 S.W. 624 (1913); Whalen v. Swircin, 141 Neb. 650, 4 N.W.2d 737 (1942); Beverly Hills National Bank v. Martin, 185 Okla. 254, 91 P.2d 94 (1939); Allen v. Hendrick, 104 Ore. 202, 206 Pac. 733 (1922); Koppelkam v. First Wisconsin Trust Co., 240 Wis. 254, 3 N.W.2d 350 (1942).

See, however, the following cases in which what purported to be an inter vivos trust was held to be a testamentary document: Betker v. Nalley, 140 F.2d 171 (D.C. Cir. 1944); Smith v. Simmons, 99 Colo. 227, 61 P.2d 589

PROBLEMS

5.1. In a jurisdiction which follows National Shawmut Bank of Boston v. Joy, will it make any difference in the result if the settlor himself is the sole trustee of the revocable inter vivos trust? See Farkas v. Williams, 5 Ill. 2d 417, 125 N.E.2d 600 (1955).

5.2. Under what circumstances, if any, should the revocable inter vivos trust be executed with the formalities required for a will?

3. SURVIVING SPOUSE'S ATTACKS ON A REVOCABLE TRUST

KERWIN v. DONAGHY
317 *Mass. 559, 59 N.E.2d 299 (1945)*

LUMMUS, J.

The widow of William J. Kerwin, late of New Bedford, brought this petition in equity in the Probate Court under G.L. (Ter. Ed.) c. 230, sec. 5, as amended (Walsh v. Mullen, 314 Mass. 241), against his daughter Gladys M. Donaghy and the executors of his will (the executors having refused to bring suit) to recover for the estate a large number of stocks, bonds and deposits in banks, standing in the name of or held by the respondent Gladys M. Donaghy, but

---

(1936); Johns v. Bowden, 68 Fla. 32, 66 So. 155 (1914); Coon v. Stanley, 230 Mo. App. 524, 94 S.W.2d 96 (1936); McGillivray v. First National Bank of Dickenson, 56 N.D. 152, 217 N.W. 150 (1927); Tunnell's Estate, 325 Pa. 554, 190 Atl. 906 (1937); Warsco v. Oshkosh Savings and Trust Co., 183 Wis. 156, 196 N.W. 829 (1924). See also Demartini v. Allegretti, 146 Cal. 214, 79 Pac. 871 (1905); Ferry v. Bryant, 19 Tenn. App. 612, 93 S.W.2d 344 (1936); Alexander v. Zion's Savings Bank & Trust Co., 2 Utah 2d 317, 273 P.2d 173 (1954), aff'd, 4 Utah 2d 90, 287 P.2d 665 (1955); Smith v. Deshaw, 116 Vt. 441, 78 A.2d 479 (1951).

In Magoon v. Cleveland Trust Co., 101 Ohio App. 194, 134 N.E.2d 879 (1956), it was held that where a settlor had retained the power to alter, amend or revoke an inter vivos trust by written notice to the trustee, he could not revoke the trust by his last will and testament. *Accord:* Merchants National Bank of Aurora v. Weinold, 22 Ill. App. 2d 219, 160 N.E.2d 174 (1959). In New York the so-called Totten trusts are revocable by will. See In re Hattan's Will, 19 Misc. 2d 500, 191 N.Y.S.2d 980 (1959); In re Poma's Will, 20 Misc. 2d 671, 192 N.Y.S.2d 156 (1959). In re Berry's Trust, 194 N.Y.S.2d 23 (1959), refused to allow a revocable trust to be revoked by will where the trust instrument stated that it was revocable by a written instrument executed and acknowledged in a manner required for the recording of realty deeds.

In re Lundgren's Estate, 250 Iowa 1233, 98 N.W.2d 839 (1959), upheld, as against an attack that it was a testamentary disposition, a contract for the sale of real estate entered into between a mother and her daughter, under which the title was to be conveyed on the mother's death and the daughter agreed to pay at that time $20,000. The mother was to receive all the income from the property during her lifetime. — ED.

owned, it was alleged, by the estate of William J. Kerwin. One of his two sons, Ernest W. Kerwin, intervened, and joined with the widow in seeking relief against Gladys M. Donaghy. The Probate Court, on May 28, 1943, entered a decree ordering the respondent Gladys M. Donaghy to transfer and deliver the stocks, bonds and bank deposits in question to the executors of the will of William J. Kerwin. She appealed. The case comes here upon a report of the evidence, with a finding of material facts.

William J. Kerwin died on April 20, 1941, leaving as his widow his second wife, Lillian A. Kerwin, whom he had married on February 15, 1926, when he was fifty-seven years old and she was thirty-nine. They had no children. She was a widow with a young son when they married. William J. Kerwin left three adult children by his first marriage, Harold E. Kerwin, Gladys M. Donaghy, and Ernest W. Kerwin. The eldest son, William J. Kerwin, Junior, had died about a year before his father, leaving a widow, Estelle C. Kerwin, but no issue. Gladys was unmarried when her father married the second time, and lived with her father and his second wife until she herself married one Paul A. Donaghy in July, 1926.

At that time William J. Kerwin was worth, according to his own judgment, half a million dollars. He had been superintendent of the Beacon Manufacturing Company for twenty-five years, and his annual income from that company alone amounted to $25,000. He retired from business in June, 1927, and thereafter had no regular occupation. Although his property evidently diminished in value afterwards, he always seemed to have plenty of money for his needs and those of his family, until his last illness.

On December 12, 1928, William J. Kerwin executed his will,[14] which after his death was duly proved and allowed. On November 12, 1941, his widow filed a waiver of the will, and claimed the interest in the estate that she would have taken had he died intestate.

The judge found in substance that from a time as early as 1923 William J. Kerwin was addicted to the folly of carrying most of his property in the names of some of his children, with the under-

[14] (*Court footnote*) In the will he used the adjective "beloved" in speaking of his wife and his children as well. He appointed his children Gladys and Harold, and Thomas M. Quinn, Esquire, as executors. He divided the household effects among his wife and children. He gave pecuniary legacies to grandchildren, but those were revoked by a codicil executed on November 28, 1936, which also was proved and allowed. He spoke of gifts made to residuary legatees, and declared that "all of said gifts were complete and outright and not advancements." He provided that any gifts to any legatee made after the execution of the will should be on account of the legacy. The seventeenth paragraph of the will divided the residue into five equal parts, and gave one part to each of the following: his widow, his daughter Gladys, and his sons William, Harold and Ernest. The codicil ratified and confirmed the will except as changed by the codicil.

standing that it should remain his and should be turned back to him at his request. His purpose was to defraud the Federal government by pretending to divide his income so as to avoid large surtaxes. The parts of his property held by his children other than Gladys were conveyed either to Gladys or back to him. In 1929 and thereafter the bulk of his property was held by and in the name of Gladys, and was kept in a safe deposit box of which she was the proprietor, although he had access to the box and kept the key to it in his desk. Many of the stock certificates, standing in her name, bore and still bear her indorsement in blank. In 1934, apparently with his consent, she cancelled his right of access, but that, the judge found, "was entirely consistent with a desire on Mr. Kerwin's part to make it appear, in case it should be questioned, that Gladys and not he was the owner of the contents of the box. He would have no difficulty in having Gladys go to the box with him and he kept the key to the box in his desk. It was customary when Mr. Kerwin wanted money to telephone Gladys to put it in his bank account which she promptly did whenever he called, excepting towards the last" of his life, during his last illness. During 1940 she paid him at his request about $15,000. It is hard to see how the surtaxes could be lessened by holding the bulk of his property in the name of Gladys after he ceased in 1927 to earn money, unless upon the tax returns the income was divided between him and Gladys. Whether it was or not does not appear.

Nothing in the relations of William J. Kerwin with his children made it likely that he would wish at any time to give all his property to Gladys and cut the others off. The judge found that "Mr. Kerwin and his wife got along well excepting for occasional times when there were some disagreements, but not very serious, and towards the last of his life they were very close to each other and he was solicitous for her welfare." Nevertheless the judge found that "he told Harold that he had put stock in Gladys' name because Mrs. Kerwin made so many demands for money he was going to see when he passed on that his children were going to have the money." It was, the judge found, "as a result of a temporary disagreement between William J. Kerwin and his wife" that he executed two trust agreements in August, 1936.

At that time William J. Kerwin consulted John D. Kenney, Esquire, a lawyer in New Bedford. Kerwin came alone at the first visit to the lawyer, but on later occasions Gladys accompanied him. He told the lawyer that he wished to make sure that at his death Gladys would own the property that she was holding for him. The lawyer advised him that a will would be ineffective, for his wife could waive the will. The lawyer advised a trust, and two formal trust agreements were drawn, and were executed by William J. Kerwin and by Gladys. One agreement dealt with the stocks and bonds, the other with the bank deposits. The agreements were substantially identical in their terms.

In these agreements Gladys declared herself trustee of a large number of specified stocks, bonds and bank deposits[15] "to pay the net income therefrom to said William J. Kerwin for and during the term of his natural life . . . and upon the decease of said William J. Kerwin to hold said fund, together with any undistributed income therefrom, to her own use and behoof absolutely forever." He reserved the right during his life "to alter, amend or revoke this agreement in whole or in part, by giving written notice thereof to said Gladys M. Donaghy." He covenanted, agreed and declared that he had no interest in the trust property except that set forth in the agreements. It was provided that "this trust agreement shall be binding upon the heirs, executors and administrators of the parties hereto." It was provided that the trustee "shall not be obligated to disclose the existence of this trust to any person, nor shall she be required to have said securities registered or recorded in her name as trustee, nor shall she be forbidden to mingle said securities or the income therefrom with her own funds . . ."

The stocks, bonds and bank deposits to which the trust agreements related were in the main the same as those which the decree ordered Gladys M. Donaghy to transfer to the executors.[16]

---

[15] (*Court footnote*) The trust agreements, which were under seal, included the following provisions: "That whereas, said William J. Kerwin has heretofore transferred and delivered to said Gladys M. Donaghy certain . . . (property) a schedule of which is annexed hereto . . . and whereas the parties hereto are desirous of definitely setting forth their respective rights and duties relative thereto . . . said Gladys M. Donaghy hereby covenants and agrees with said William J. Kerwin that she will hold said . . . (property) and the proceeds thereof, together with any additions and accumulations thereto (all of which property shall hereinafter be called 'the fund') upon the following uses and trusts . . ." — REPORTER.

[16] (*Court footnote*) But in addition to the stocks specified in the trust agreements, Gladys M. Donaghy held certificates for three hundred fifty shares of the stock of Beacon Manufacturing Company, one hundred fifty of them in her name, one hundred fifty of them in the name of Harold E. Kerwin, indorsed by him in blank, and fifty of them in the name of Ernest W. Kerwin, indorsed by him in blank. She held also a certificate for eighty-seven shares of the probably worthless stock of Dexdale Hosiery Mills in the name of Harold E. Kerwin but indorsed by him in blank. She testified that she held the Beacon stock on the terms stated in the trust agreements, but that she intended to turn over to Harold and Ernest the shares standing in their names. The judge found that there was no understanding that these stocks should belong to Gladys, subject to a life interest in her father, to the exclusion of the widow and the other children. Accordingly the final decree included these stocks in the property which Gladys was ordered to transfer to the executors.

The property covered by the two trust agreements comprised substantially all the property that William J. Kerwin had, except a comparatively small amount that he transferred to Lillian A. Kerwin in 1940 and 1941, and that forms the subject matter of the companion case which is hereinafter dealt with.   Late in 1940 he was disturbed about the condition of his affairs, and was trying to reach Gladys for the purpose of arranging his affairs so that what he considered his property would form part of his estate if he should die, to the end that his wife and all his children would be protected.   Gladys apparently avoided any considerable talk with him.   He was in bad health, and entirely dependent on Gladys for money.   On October 9, 1940, he got Gladys and Harold together, and asked them whether they would do the "right thing" by his wife.   When they said they would, he fell on his knees and said "Thank God for that."   He apparently rested content with that vague assurance, and did not then remember or appreciate the fact that under the trust agreements he had reserved a power of revocation of the trusts.   Not unlikely he was then too ill to take decisive action, and still trusted Gladys, although he was beginning to doubt her.   When he died there was little if anything remaining in his hands.

The judge had the task of discovering the truth in the tangled web of deceit that had been woven about the ownership of the property.   As to the basic facts dependent upon the credibility of the witnesses, his findings are entitled to great weight, and we see no reason to disagree with them.   But his inferences of fact from those basic facts, and his conclusions of law, are fully open to review by this court.   [Citations omitted.]

Those inferences and conclusions are as follows: "Said securities and bank accounts were at no time given to Gladys by her father to have as her own property.   Said pretended trust instruments were made as a result of a temporary disagreement between William J. Kerwin and his wife . . . they never intended to be carried out according to their terms but constituted an illusive device to deprive the wife of any substantial interest in her husband's estate as his widow.   It was not intended thereby to give the property all to Gladys upon her father's death, or to deprive his sons of any share therein as heirs or legatees of William J. Kerwin.   Said trusts are collusive and invalid and the securities and bank accounts . . . are the property of the estate of William J. Kerwin."   The main question before us is whether these inferences of fact and conclusions of law are correct.

Up to the time of the execution of the trust agreements, it could have been shown by oral evidence that there had been no beneficial gift of the property to Gladys because of the absence of a deed, or of proof of donative intent coupled with delivery (Rock v. Rock, 309 Mass. 44, 47; Reardon v. Whalen, 306 Mass. 579; Murphy v. Smith, 291 Mass. 93; Bedirian v. Zorian, 287 Mass. 191, 195), or because of proof that she took title to the property upon an oral trust in favor of her father and his estate. Rock v. Rock, 309 Mass. 44, 47. Russell v. Meyers, 316 Mass. 669, 672. And even after the trust agreements were executed, a third person not a party to them nor claiming under them, whose rights might be affected by them — for example, the Federal taxing authorities — could show by extrinsic evidence that they were false and illusory and did not express the real transaction between Gladys and her father. [Citations omitted.]

But in this case Lillian A. Kerwin and Ernest W. Kerwin claim under William J. Kerwin. They stand in his shoes. If title passed to Gladys as against William J. Kerwin, it passed to her as against his legatees. When the trust agreements were executed, the property to which they related was already in the possession of Gladys, and most if not all of it stood in her name. Those agreements contemplated the holding by her of the legal title. Under those circumstances no formal delivery of the property itself was necessary to vest the legal title in her. [Citations omitted.]

The trust agreements furnish incontrovertible internal evidence that they were intended to express the whole transaction between Gladys and her father. He covenanted, agreed and declared under seal that he had no right, power or interest in the trust property except such as was set forth in the trust agreements. The beneficial interest was completely disposed of by giving him an equitable life estate and Gladys the remainder "to her own use and behoof absolutely forever." His apparent purpose to render a will practically unnecessary, and his reserved power to alter, amend or revoke the trust, did not make the trust testamentary in its nature. National Shawmut Bank v. Joy, 315 Mass. 457, 469-475, 477-478. The reserved power could be exercised only according to its terms, and since there was never even an attempt to exercise it there was no impairment of the rights in remainder given to Gladys. [Citations omitted.] There was no mistake in drafting the trust agreements. Plainly they conformed to the purpose of William J. Kerwin at the time, that of disinheriting his wife. He could hardly have been so obtuse as to fail to see that they disinherited his sons also in plain words.

As matter of law the trust instruments must be taken as intended to accomplish the very purpose of the so-called "parol evidence rule," that of fixing beyond all question the rights of the parties to those agreements in accordance with their terms, and to preclude resort to extrinsic evidence apart from exceptional and strictly limited instances of need that are not applicable to this case. [Footnote omitted.] As to trusts, a learned author has said, "Under the parol evidence rule, if the manifestation of intention of the settlor is integrated in a writing, that is, if a written instrument is adopted by him as the complete expression of his intention, extrinsic evidence, in the absence of fraud, duress, mistake or other ground for reformation or rescission, is not admissible to contradict or vary it." Scott, Trusts (1939) secs. 38, 164.1. That statement finds support in our decisions. [Citations omitted.] Though often stated in terms of the admissibility of evidence, the so-called "parol evidence rule" is really a rule of substantive law. Extrinsic evidence, even though admitted, cannot control the words of a document that purports to express the whole transaction. [Footnote omitted.] [Citations omitted.]

It is true that a written contract or other instrument may be invalidated by extrinsic proof that it was executed as a joke or even in some instances as a pretense, with no intention on the part of either party that it should create any legal right or obligation. [Footnote omitted.] [Citations omitted.] [Footnote omitted.] We need not decide whether that rule can be extended to sealed instruments, in view of the common law theory that the obligor in such an instrument is conclusively bound by its terms. [Citations omitted.] "Where a seal (is) not required for the validity of a contract (it) has been treated as surplusage in order to carry out the expressed intention of the parties through resort to the rules applicable to simple contracts." Johnson-Foster Co. v. D'Amore Construction Co., 314 Mass. 416, 421. The reason why we need not decide that question is that in our opinion an inference of fact could not properly be drawn that the trust agreements were intended merely as shams. The evident purpose at the time was to disinherit the wife. The husband was careful to reserve the right to revoke the trusts, and revest the trust property in himself. The correct conclusion, we think, is that the trust agreements express the actual intention of the parties at the time.

Even if, notwithstanding the terms of the trust agreements, the remainder passing to Gladys under those agreements might be subjected to a trust in favor of her brothers and Lillian A. Kerwin by proof of an oral promise by Gladys to share the remainder with them (Ham v. Twombly, 181 Mass. 170, 172, 173; Beals v. Villard, 268 Mass. 129, 132, 133; compare Scott, Trusts (1939) sec. 38), the difficulty in this case would be that there is little evidence of such an oral promise. The trust agreements themselves, and all that was said when they were drawn and executed, negative any promise that would benefit Lillian A. Kerwin, for the plain purpose was to disinherit her. Neither was there anything said or done at that time to show a promise to hold for the other children. If there had been such a promise, it would not support the present petition which is brought for the benefit of the estate generally. The only conduct of Gladys that might be thought to recognize the claim of Lillian A. Kerwin was her promise, jointly with Harold who had no property in his hands, made on October 9, 1940, when their father was in his last illness and mentally disturbed, to "do the right thing" by Lillian. Such a promise by Harold could hardly have reference to a money settlement out of property of his father in his hands, for there was no such property. The promise by Gladys was in identical words. We cannot find that such a vague promise amounted to an understanding to hold for the distributees of the father's estate the remainder given to Gladys by the trust agreements.

At various times after the trust agreements were executed William J. Kerwin made statements indicating that he considered that all the stocks, bonds and bank deposits held by Gladys were really his and would form part of his estate. For example, in 1934 and again in 1938 Ernest told his father that he thought it was unfair to put only fifty shares of the Beacon stock into his name while Gladys and Harold held one hundred fifty shares each. His father denied any unfairness, saying that the stock was all his, and "if anything happened to him we were all to be treated alike." He said that the way the stock was held "didn't mean a thing." In 1940, when William J. Kerwin and his wife opened his safe deposit box and found in it only twenty-five shares of Beacon stock, he told his wife that everything else he owned was in the safe deposit box which was in the name of Gladys, and about the same time he gave his wife a memorandum of securities of the value of about $64,000 that he said he owned. Those securities must have been among those held by Gladys, for he himself held no such amount. Besides, there is his act of November 28, 1936, of ratifying and confirming his will after the bulk of his property had been covered by the trust agreements. A simple explanation of most of this testimony is that Kerwin knew that he had reserved the power to alter, amend or revoke the trust agreements, and concluded that that reserved power left him substantially the master of the trust property. Very likely he intended sooner or later to make an equitable division of it among his wife and children. But we cannot infer from this testimony any promise on the part of Gladys.

The judge found that the trust agreements "constituted an

illusive device to deprive the wife of any substantial interest in her husband's estate as his widow." It has been shown already that that "device" was not "illusory," but was one that fixed the rights of the parties to those agreements. The judge found further that William J. Kerwin, if the trust agreements were intended to be effective, "intended to cheat his wife." He could not "cheat" her in any legal sense by means of those agreements unless she had rights that were paramount to his right to do what he pleased in his lifetime with his own personal property.

The right of a wife to waive her husband's will, and take, with certain limitations, "the same portion of the property of the deceased, real and personal, that . . . she would have taken if the deceased had died intestate" (G.L. (Ter. Ed.) c. 191, sec. 15), does not extend to personal property that has been conveyed by the husband in his lifetime and does not form part of his estate at his death. Fiske v. Fiske, 173 Mass. 413, 419. Shelton v. Sears, 187 Mass. 455. In this Commonwealth a husband has an absolute right to dispose of any or all of his personal property in his lifetime, without the knowledge or consent of his wife, with the result that it will not form part of his estate for her to share under the statute of distributions (G.L. (Ter. Ed.) c. 190, secs. 1, 2), under his will, or by virtue of a waiver of his will. That is true even though his sole purpose was to disinherit her. [Citations omitted.] So far as it may conflict with the foregoing decisions, the case of Brownell v. Briggs, 173 Mass. 529, is no longer controlling. The right of a wife as distributee stands no higher than the similar right of a child. [Citations omitted.]

The limitation found in some of our cases upon the right of a husband to disinherit his wife by a conveyance or gift of personal property inter vivos, that the conveyance or gift must not be "colorable" (Kelley v. Snow, 185 Mass. 288, 299; Roche v. Brickley, 254 Mass. 584, 588), means merely that the conveyance or gift must be one legally binding on the settlor or donor, accomplished in his lifetime, and not testamentary in its effect. In other words, it must be an actual conveyance or gift. Potter Title & Trust Co. v. Braum, 294 Penn. St. 482, 64 Am. L.R. 463. In Newman v. Dore, 275 N.Y. 371, 112 Am. L.R. 643, complete control of the trustee, reserved to the settlor, was held to make testamentary and invalid a settlement designed to disinherit his wife. See also Krause v. Krause, 285 N.Y. 27; Brown v. Crafts, 98 Maine, 40, 45. The soundness of that ground was recently left open by us in National Shawmut Bank v. Joy, 315 Mass. 457, 476. In the present case no such control was reserved.[17]

[17] What was left open in National Shawmut Bank of Boston v. Joy? — ED.

Cases are not in point that hold invalid a conveyance by a husband to defeat a possible decree for the support of his wife. Shepherd v. Shepherd, 196 Mass. 179. Doane v. Doane, 238 Mass. 106, 112. Caines v. Sawyer, 248 Mass. 368, 374. 26 Am. Jur., Husband & Wife, sec. 197. Neither are cases holding invalid a gift made by a husband for the purpose of reducing the share of his estate to which his wife is entitled under an antenuptial contract. Eaton v. Eaton, 233 Mass. 351, 369, et seq. Nor are cases in which a woman married a man of supposed means in ignorance of the fact that on the eve of marriage he had conveyed away all his property for the purpose of defeating her expectations. Gedart v. Ejdrygiewicz, 305 Mass. 224. LeStrange v. LeStrange, 242 App. Div. (N.Y.) 74. Collins v. Collins, 98 Md. 473. Kirk v. Kirk, 340 Penn. St. 203. Hanson v. McCarthy, 152 Wis. 131. 26 Am. Jur., Husband & Wife, secs. 185-195.

The judge was right in ordering, upon the petition brought by Lillian A. Kerwin, a conveyance to the executors of the Beacon and Dexdale stocks. Even if the actually innocent wife could be affected by the fraudulent purpose of her late husband in holding those stocks in the name of his daughter Gladys, the wife has made out her case without reliance upon any fraud. [Citations omitted.]

But the other findings and orders contained in the final decree upon that petition are to be struck out. As so modified that decree is affirmed. There was no error in the final decree dismissing the petition brought by Gladys M. Donaghy and others, executors. Discussion of that petition is unnecessary The final decree dismissing it is affirmed.

So ordered.[18]

---

[18] For cases involving revocable inter vivos trusts in which it is held that the surviving spouse cannot reach or take into account the trust property for purposes of satisfying marital rights, see DeLeuil's Executors v. DeLeuil, 255 Ky. 406, 74 S.W.2d 474 (1934); Brown v. Fidelity Trust Co., 126 Md. 175, 94 Atl. 523 (1915); Ascher v. Cohen, 333 Mass. 397, 131 N.E.2d 198 (1956) (settlor was co-trustee); Rose v. Union Guardian Trust Co., 300 Mich. 73, 1 N.W.2d 458 (1942); Beirne v. Continental-Equitable Title & Trust Co., 307 Pa. 570, 161 Atl. 721 (1932); Dunnett v. Shields, 97 Vt. 419, 123 Atl. 626 (1926).

For cases involving revocable inter vivos trusts in which it is held that the surviving spouse of the settlor can reach or take into account the trust property for purposes of satisfying marital rights, see Smith v. Northern Trust Co., 322 Ill. App. 168, 54 N.E.2d 75 (1944); Wanstrath v. Kappel, 356 Mo. 210, 201 S.W.2d 327 (1947); Newman v. Dore, 275 N.Y. 371, 9 N.E.2d 966 (1937); MacGregor v. Fox, 280 App. Div. 435, 114 N.Y.S.2d 286 (1952), aff'd, 305 N.Y. 576, 111 N.E.2d 445 (1953); Harris v. Harris, 147 Ohio St. 437, 72 N.E.2d 378 (1947); Pengelly's Estate, 374 Pa. 358, 97 A.2d 844 (1953). See Note, 58 Dick. L. Rev. 70 (1953). See also Padfield v. Padfield, 78 Ill. 16 (1875); Cameron v. Cameron, 10 Smedes & M. 394 (Miss. 1848); Walker v. Walker, 66 N.H. 390, 31 Atl. 14 (1891) (semble); Norris v. Barbour. 188 Va.

PROBLEM

5.3. H establishes a revocable inter vivos trust. He dies leaving his wife, W.

    a. If the governing jurisdiction determines that the revocable inter vivos trust is a testamentary disposition, what will be the effect of the establishment of the revocable inter vivos trust so far as W's marital rights are concerned?

    b. If the governing jurisdiction determines that the revocable inter vivos trust is valid but that it is to be treated as a testamentary disposition at W's election so far as W is concerned, what will be the effect of the establishment of the revocable inter vivos trust on W's marital rights?

4. POUR-OVER FROM WILL TO REVOCABLE TRUST

OLD COLONY TRUST CO. v. CLEVELAND

291 Mass. 380, 196 N.E. 920 (1935)

LUMMUS, J.

On March 22, 1926, Willis H. Chandler conveyed what apparently was the bulk of his property to Old Colony Trust Company,

---

723, 51 S.E.2d 334 (1949); Burnet v. First National Bank of Chicago, 12 Ill. App. 2d 514, 140 N.E.2d 362 (1957), should be compared with the Smith v. Northern Trust Co., supra. The Ohio view was restated in Smyth v. Cleveland Trust Co., 81 Ohio Abs. 581 (Cuyahoga County C.P. 1959), but the court said that the revocable trust was a valid and subsisting one save and except for the portion which the widow was entitled to as her distributive share.

In some jurisdictions any inter vivos transfer made with intent to deprive the surviving spouse of marital rights is ineffective to so deprive the spouse. Payne v. Tatem, 236 Ky. 306, 33 S.W.2d 2 (1930); Wanstrath v. Kappel, 356 Mo. 210, 201 S.W.2d 327 (1947); Walker v. Walker, 66 N.H. 390, 31 Atl. 14 (1891). In Potter v. Winter, 280 S.W.2d 27 (Mo. 1955), no intent to deprive the surviving spouse of her marital rights was found to exist when the revocable trust gave her the income for life on one half of the property, with the power to appoint this half, and the trustee had discretion to invade the income of the other half and all of the corpus for her benefit. Compare Dunnett v. Shields, 97 Vt. 419, 123 Atl. 626 (1926) (fraud necessary to upset the trust was not found), and Williams v. Collier, 120 Fla. 248, 158 So. 815, reargument denied, 120 Fla. 258, 162 So. 868 (1935) (in upholding the trust the court stressed the settlor's good faith in providing for grandchildren, and the fact that ample provision had been made for the widow).

In some states statutory provisions undertake to protect the surviving spouse. See, for example, Mo. Ann. Stat. §474.150-1 (1952, Supp. 1959), quoted infra page 1466; Pa. Stat. Ann., tit. 20, §301.11 (Purdon, Supp. 1959), quoted infra page 1471.

Behan's Estate. — Pa. —, 160 A.2d 209 (1960), holds that the Pennsylvania statute applies even though the settlor spouse reserved only a restricted power of appointment. — ED.

in trust to pay the income to himself for life, and afterwards to his wife Susie E. Chandler for life. The second paragraph of the trust deed provided: "Upon my decease or upon the decease of my wife, provided she survives me, the Trustee shall pay from the principal of the trust estate" various sums ranging from $250 to $5,000 to thirty-seven persons named. The third paragraph of the trust deed provided that the income of the residue of the trust property shall then be paid in equal shares to Ella C. Cleveland, Josephine S. Haven, Luella A. Corbett and Sara K. Corbett, for their lives, with cross remainders for life between Ella C. Cleveland and Josephine S. Haven and between Luella A. Corbett and Sara K. Corbett. The fourth paragraph of the trust deed provided for ultimate remainders in fee to certain charities, after the life estates.

On June 21, 1926, Willis H. Chandler executed his will, by which he gave his household belongings to his wife Susie E. Chandler and the residue of his estate to Old Colony Trust Company to be held by it upon the trusts set forth in the trust deed just described.

The fifth paragraph of the trust deed reserved to the settlor the right to change the provisions and limitations of the trust deed. Acting under that authority, the settlor, on February 28, 1928, struck out the second paragraph of the original trust deed, and substituted a somewhat similar provision by which upon the death of the survivor of himself and his wife he directed the trustee to pay various sums ranging from $100 to $8,000 to fifty-two persons named, including all the persons named in the second paragraph of the original trust deed. None of such persons was reduced in amount. Luella A. Corbett having died, he substituted Emma F. Frye in her place as remainderman for life.

Willis H. Chandler died on December 13, 1932. Susie E. Chandler died on September 22, 1933. The trustee has paid out of the original trust estate all the amounts specified in the second paragraph of the trust deed as changed on February 28, 1928. It now seeks instructions as to the disposition of the residue which came to it by the will of Willis H. Chandler, consisting of personal property of the value of $16,320.51. The Probate Court entered a decree that such residue be held by the trustee "in trust upon the terms of Articles (Paragraphs) Third and Fourth of said deed of trust unamended for the benefit of the surviving life tenants and the residuary legatees named therein." Various persons included in the list of thirty-seven persons to whom various sums were given by the second paragraph of the original trust deed of March 22, 1926, appealed to this court.

Obviously the will did not, and could not, give the residue in

Here — deed-TR t/feder. power to modify:
HELD → Testam gift s/b upheld, but construed as a gift on terms of Trust as it = in existence when will = erle — i.e amendm s/b disregard

trust for purposes which had not then been defined, but remained to be defined by a later amendment of the trust deed.[19]   A document not in existence cannot be covered by the attestation of a will.   The will gave the residue to the trustee upon the trusts originally defined, and did not purport to do otherwise.   Thayer v. Wellington, 9 Allen, 283.   Olliffe v. Wells, 130 Mass. 221.   Bushby v. Newhall, 212 Mass. 432.   Compare Bemis v. Fletcher, 251 Mass. 178, 186.   Even though the testator so expected, the residue passing by the will cannot simply be added to the trust fund established during the life of Willis H. Chandler, and be made to follow the course of that fund to its ultimate destination under the amended trust deed.

It does not follow, however, that the fund passing under the will is to be treated as a completely independent fund as to which all the provisions of the original trust deed are to be duplicated as far as the amount passing under the will permits.   The testator did not intend that the thirty-seven persons named in the second paragraph of the original trust deed should be paid twice, once out of the original trust fund under the amendment of February 28, 1928, and again out of the fund passing under the will.   All the beneficiaries under the second paragraph of the original trust deed have already received as much as was therein given them, or more.   Since these beneficiaries have been paid, the Probate Court was right in its decree that the fund passing under the will be held for the purposes of the third and fourth paragraphs of the original deed of trust, which remain unchanged.[20]   The case is not governed by Bemis v. Fletcher, 251 Mass. 178.

The decree is affirmed.   The matter of additional costs and expenses is to be in the discretion of the Probate Court.   It is to be noticed that the right of the estate of Susie E. Chandler to the income of the fund during her life is not involved in the petition for instructions nor adjudicated by the decree.[21]

Ordered accordingly.[22]

---

[19] Why isn't any later amendment a fact of independent significance that can control a disposition under a will?

See Loring v. Clapp, 337 Mass. 53, 147 N.E.2d 836 (1958), where, in footnote 9, the court refers to the Old Colony case as follows: "Its result was influenced by a legal principle there expressed (but not here involved) with respect to testamentary gifts to revocable, amendable trusts, later amended, which may be inconsistent with present legal thought."   The statement to which this note is appended was repudiated in Second Bank-State Street Trust Co. v. Pinion, — Mass. —, 170 N.E.2d 350 (1960). — ED.

[20] The third paragraph was amended in 1928 to insert the name of Emma F. Frye in place of Luella A. Corbett, who had died.   Is the court holding that Emma is entitled to a share in the income received from the property added to the trust by the terms of Mr. Chandler's will? — ED.

[21] Susie E. Chandler survived her husband by about nine months.   The

STATUTORY NOTE

In recent years, many states have enacted statutes which under-take to deal with a pour-over from a will to a revocable inter vivos trust. Most of these enactments adopt a liberal approach to the

---

normal period of time for the administration of her husband's estate had not expired and no part of her husband's residuary estate had been turned over to the trustee of the inter vivos trust before she died. When does the right of a life beneficiary to income begin in a situation like this? When the trust is established, the life beneficiary of a residuary trust should be entitled to income from the date of the testator's death, in the absence of a contrary manifestation of intent. See 3 Scott, Trusts §234.3 (2d ed. 1956). See also Me. Rev. Stat. Ann., c. 160, §34 (1954, Supp. 1959), quoted infra page 1440; N.Y. Personal Property Law §17b, quoted infra page 1469. — ED.

[22] In Koeninger v. Toledo Trust Co., 49 Ohio App. 490, 197 N.E. 419 (1934), the same result was reached. A pour-over into a revocable or amend-able trust has been uniformly upheld where (1) *the trust was never amended or revoked:* Montgomery v. Blankenship, 217 Ark. 357, 230 S.W.2d 51 (1950); Willey's Estate, 128 Cal. 1, 60 Pac. 471 (1900); (2) *the trust was amended prior to the execution of the will:* Matter of Bremer, 156 Misc. 160, 281 N.Y. Supp. 264 (1935), *aff'd on reargument,* 157 Misc. 221, 283 N.Y. Supp. 159 (1936); Shawan v. City Bank Farmers Trust Co., 6 Ohio Ops. 309, 21 Ohio L. Abs. 432, 10 Ohio Supp. 297 (Lucas County Prob. Ct. 1936); In re Glatfelter's Estate, 60 York Leg. Rec. 77 (Pa. 1946); (3) *the trust was amended prior to the execution of a later codicil to the will:* First-Central Trust Co. v. Claflin, 49 Ohio L. Abs. 29, 73 N.E.2d 388 (Summit County C.P. 1947).

But where the trust was amended subsequent to the execution of the will, several courts have refused to incorporate the trust as it existed at the date of the execution of the will. Atwood v. Rhode Island Hospital Trust Co., 275 Fed. 513 (1st Cir. 1921); President & Directors of Manhattan Co. v. Janowitz, 172 Misc. 290, 14 N.Y.S.2d 375 (1939), *modified,* 260 App. Div. 174, 21 N.Y.S.2d 232 (1940).

Generally the courts have not upheld a pour-over into a trust as amended subsequent to the execution of the will, but where the trust amendment has been approved as a fact of independent significance, it would seem that amend-ing the trust subsequent to the execution of the will should not interfere with the validity of the pour-over. In re York's Estate, 95 N.H. 435, 65 A.2d 282 (1946); Swetland v. Swetland, 102 N.J. Eq. 294, 140 Atl. 279 (1928); Matter of Tiffany, 157 Misc. 873, 285 N.Y. Supp. 971 (1935); Matter of Tower, N.Y.L.J., May 13, 1946, p. 1889, col. 7 (N.Y. County Surr.). In Matter of Ivie, 155 N.Y.S.2d 544 (1956), *aff'd,* 3 A.D.2d 914, 163 N.Y.S.2d 380 (1957), *aff'd,* 4 N.Y.2d 178, 149 N.E.2d 725 (1958), the court upheld a pour-over to an inter vivos trust which had been amended, where the changes made subsequent to the execution of the will consisted of revoking an amendment that had named certain successor trustees and extended to them certain investment powers, and of adding an amendment in which all power to make further amendments was surrendered. This development in New York is significant in view of the Janowitz case, cited supra, a case which the court undertook to distinguish.

Restatement of Trusts Second §54, Comment *i*, takes the position that there can be a pour-over from a will to a trust amended subsequent to the date the will is executed. Such a pour-over cannot be supported on the ground of in-corporation by reference, but it can be upheld on the ground of resorting to a fact of independent significance. The Restatement position is adopted in Second Bank-State Street Trust Co. v. Pinion, — Mass. —, 170 N.E.2d 350 (1960). — ED.

matter and permit the pour-over to the trust even though it is amended after the execution of the will. See, for example, Ill. Rev. Stat., c. 3, §194a (1959), quoted infra page 1438; R.I. Gen. Laws Ann. §33-6-33 (1956, Supp. 1959), quoted infra page 1473. See also Colo. Laws 1959, c. 286; Del. Code Ann., tit. 12, §111 (1953, Supp. 1958); Fla. Stat. §736.17 (1959); Ind. Stat. Ann. §6-601(j) (Burns, 1953); Md. Code Ann., art. 93, §§350A, 350B (1957, Supp. 1960) (includes pour-over from will to trust under another will); Miss. Code Ann. §661.5 (1956, Supp. 1958); Neb. Rev. Stat. §30-1806 (1943, Supp. 1957); N.C. Gen. Stat. §31-47 (1950, Supp. 1959); Pa. Stat. Ann., tit. 20, §180.14a (Purdon, Supp. 1959); Va. Code Ann. §64-71.1 (1950, Supp. 1960); Wis. Stat. Ann. §231.205 (1957, Supp. 1960); Wyo. Comp. Stat. Ann. §6-310 (1945, Supp. 1957).

Several states have taken a different statutory road and have codified the view that a pour-over from a will fails if the trust is amended subsequent to the execution of the will and if the testator intended the terms of the trust as amended to govern the property coming to it from the will. See Conn. Gen. Stat. Rev. §45-173 (1958, Supp. 1959), quoted infra page 1437; Ore. Rev. Stat. §114.-070 (1957), quoted infra page 1471. Wisconsin originally adopted the narrow position (Wis. Stat. §231.205, as amended by Laws 1955, c. 85) but the broader view was taken in 1957 by the statute referred to in the preceding paragraph. The narrow position is still controlling in Wisconsin, however, where the testator died prior to July 26, 1957.[23]

PROBLEMS

5.4. H, who resides in Illinois, establishes a revocable inter vivos trust and places therein the sum of one dollar. Thereafter he makes his will and in it he pours over the residue of his estate to the trust. From time to time after the will is executed, H amends the revocable inter vivos trust. He dies. Will the property poured over to the trust from the will be governed by the terms of the trust as amended, or by the terms of the trust as originally executed?

5.5. In a jurisdiction which follows Old Colony Trust Company v. Cleveland, what is the result if there is a pour-over from a will to a so-called revocable inter vivos trust and the latter is executed with all of the formalities of a will and each amendment thereto is executed in the same manner? See Atwood v. Rhode

---

[23] For a discussion of the statutes which allow a testator to pour over property by will into an inter vivos trust as amended subsequent to the execution of his will, see 69 Harv. L. Rev. 1147 (1956).

Island Hospital Trust Co., 275 Fed. 513 (1st Cir. 1921); Merrill v.
Boal, 47 R.I. 274, 132 Atl. 721 (1926). See also 3 Restatement of
Property §348, Comments *e* and *f;* Stouse v. First National Bank
of Chicago, 245 S.W.2d 914, 32 A.L.R.2d 1261 (Ky. 1951).

5.6. In a jurisdiction which follows Old Colony Trust Company
v. Cleveland, what should be done to assure, as far as possible, that
the property poured over by the will will be governed by the terms
of the trust as amended?

5.7. In a jurisdiction which follows Old Colony Trust Company
v. Cleveland, what is the result if the pour-over is to a revocable
inter vivos trust that is established by one other than the testator
and (1) the trust is amended by the settlor thereof after the testator's will is executed but before the testator dies, and (2) the trust
is amended by the settlor after the death of the testator?

5.8. A establishes a revocable inter vivos trust with B as trustee.
The trust provides that the income is to be paid to A for his lifetime, and on his death, the trust corpus is to be paid to the trustee
under A's will if A should leave a will under which a trust is established, and otherwise the corpus is to be paid to A's executors and
administrators. A dies. A's will establishes a trust of the residue
of his estate with the X Trust Company as trustee. The executor
under A's will is his wife, W. Should B transfer the trust corpus
to W or to the X Trust Company? If W renounces A's will, is the
trust corpus deemed a part of A's estate for the purpose of determining her marital rights?

5. PROS AND CONS IN REGARD TO THE USE OF THE
REVOCABLE TRUST AS A KEY DOCUMENT [24]

a. *Federal Tax Considerations*

(1) Income Taxes

In considering the federal income tax consequencs which flow
from the establishment of a revocable inter vivos trust, the period
prior to the death of the settlor should be examined separately
from the period following his death. Generally speaking, for the
period which precedes his death (assuming he retains the power
to revoke until he dies) the income from the trust property is taxed
to the settlor just as it would have been if the trust had not been
set up, whether the income is paid to him, retained in the trust, or
turned over to someone else.[25] This means that the taxable year

[24] See generally Casner, Estate Planning — Avoidance of Probate, 60 Colum.
L. Rev. 108 (1960).
[25] See 1954 I.R.C. §§676, 677, quoted infra page 1374.

of, and the method of accounting used by, the revocable trust should be disregarded and the gross income from the trust properties should be determined by the settlor as though the trust had not been created.[26] The trustee's fees which may be charged for the operation of the revocable inter vivos trust will be borne in part by the federal government because such fees are incurred for the management, conservation or maintenance of property held for the production of income and are deductible for federal income tax purposes to a considerable extent.[27] The principal restriction on the deductibility of such fees relates to the portion allocable to the management, conservation or maintenance of property held for the production of income which is not included in gross income.[28]

Legal fees which the settlor must pay to bring the revocable inter vivos trust into existence should be deductible on the same basis as that on which trustee's fees are deductible. While it is true that a considerable portion of the instrument which is drafted by the lawyer will relate to the operation of the trust subsequent to the death of the settlor, there is no certainty that that portion will ever be used, because of the reserved power of revocation. Consequently, it does not seem unreasonable to regard the entire charge made by the lawyer as allocable to the establishment of an arrangement for the management, conservation or maintenance of property held for the production of income.[29]

If the trustee sells property in the revocable inter vivos trust during the lifetime of the settlor, what will be the basis of the trust property sold? It will be the same as it would be in the hands of the settlor.[30]

For the period following the death of the settlor during which the settlor's estate is in administration, the federal income tax con-

---

[26] Rev. Rul. 57-390, 1957-2 C.B. 326.

[27] See 1954 I.R.C. §212, quoted infra page 1336.
As to the amount of the trustee's fees, see page 139 infra, note 83.

[28] See Reg. §1.212-1(e), quoted infra page 1486.

[29] See Nancy R. Bagley, 8 T.C. 130 (1947); McDonald, Deduction of Attorney's Fees for Federal Income Tax Purposes, 103 U. of Pa. L. Rev. 168 (1954); Tax Note, When Are Lawyers' Fees and Legal Expenses Deductible? 40 A.B.A.J. 1095 (1954). See also the proposal of the American Bar Association to make all estate planning fees deductible, in 1955 Program and Committee Reports, Section of Taxation 69-75.
In Joseph Lewis, 27 T.C. 158 (1956), *aff'd,* 253 F.2d 821 (2d Cir. 1958), the settlor of a revocable inter vivos trust incurred legal fees in connection with the revocation of the trust because his wife had questioned his mental capacity to revoke it. The court held that these expenses were not deductible by him, since they were concerned with securing title to property rather than with the management, conservation or maintenance of property held for the production of income.

[30] See 1954 I.R.C. §1015(b), quoted infra page 1383.

sequences with regard to the trust property are not the same in all respects as they would be if the trust had not been established and the trust property had passed through probate administration. The differences result from the fact that the law governing trust items includible in the decedent's gross estate but not includible in his probate estate is not in all respects the same as the law governing probate items during the period of administration.[31]

During the period of administration of a decedent's estate, his estate is a separate tax entity for federal income tax purposes. The over-all economic benefit to the decedent's family that will be produced by estate income being taxed to this entity rather than to the beneficiaries will, of course, depend on various factors. The availability of the entity, however, makes it possible to take advantage of it if the circumstances warrant such a course of action. If a significant portion of what would otherwise be probate assets is eliminated by arrangements that keep gross estate items out of the probate estate, the significance of the estate as a separate tax entity is diminished.

Certain amounts that are allowable as deductions for estate tax purposes may be taken as deductions against estate income rather than as estate tax deductions.[32] Some of the benefits of the availability of this choice may be lost if the estate income is diminished by a reduction in the amount of probate assets.[33]

The revocable inter vivos trust which continues after the settlor's death is, like the estate, a separate tax entity, but the federal income tax consequences may differ depending on which entity is involved. For example, the so-called throwback rule, which may apply to distributions by a trust, does not apply to distributions by an estate.[34]

Because the executor is initially responsible for seeing that all death costs are paid, he may withhold estate distributions until he is discharged from personal liability for such payments. Thus the executor may accumulate estate income during administration.

[31] Income taxation of estates is developed supra page 77.

[32] See 1954 I.R.C. §642(g), quoted infra page 1363.

[33] Section 642(g) of the 1954 Code, by its terms, prevents a double deduction for expenses of administration that are deductible for both estate income tax purposes and estate tax purposes only when these expenses are incurred by the estate. If expenses are incurred by the trustee of a revocable inter vivos trust subsequent to the death of the settlor, which are deductible both for trust income tax purposes and estate tax purposes, will the trustee be required to elect whether to take such expenses as an income tax deduction or will the double deduction be allowed? If §642(g) is necessary to prevent the double deduction so far as the estate is concerned, it may be contended that the double deduction is allowable when the trust route is followed, because of the absence of any provision prohibiting the double deduction.

[34] The throwback rule is discussed infra page 742.

The accumulated income is taxed to the estate, and when it is finally distributed on the termination of administration, it is not taxed to the distributee under the throwback doctrine.

Suppose that a revocable trust continues after the settlor's death, and that under its terms the trustee has discretion to pay out or accumulate the income. If the trustee accumulates the income and then pays it out at the end of the period of administration of the settlor's estate, the same thing the executor may do, the throwback rule will apply. The fact that the throwback rule will apply does not necessarily mean that the over-all tax result will be significantly worse than the result that would be produced if the assets were in the estate of the settlor and were paid out by his executor.

The executor is privileged to withhold distributions until he is discharged of any personal liability to pay taxes, because his potential personal liability is the amount of payments he may make before the debts due the United States have been paid.[35] The trustee's potential personal liability, however, is limited to the value of the trust property at the time of the settlor's death.[36] Thus, if the terms of the trust as it continues after the settlor's death require the income to be paid out, it would seem that the trustee has no right to withhold income payments on the ground that he needs to do so to protect himself from possible personal liability. Consequently, a difference in income tax consequences during administration may be produced where the belief is that the beneficiary is entitled to all income from the date of the decedent's death.

One of the requirements of a power of appointment marital deduction trust is that the income of the trust be "payable annually or at more frequent intervals." [37] If the marital deduction trust is provided for under a will, it is possible, no matter what form of language is used to describe the amount that is to go into such trust, that the trust may not be established within a year after the decedent's death, and thus at least the initial payment of income under the trust will not be made annually. When the trust is finally established, there will be an accounting of income back to the date of the decedent's death and all such income will be paid to the decedent's wife by the trustee. The marital trust does not fail to qualify for the deduction because of this situation. In fact, the

[35] 48 Stat. 760 (1934), 31 U.S.C., c. 6, §192 (1958), quoted supra page 17, and supra page 78.

Section 20.2002-1 of the Regulations, quoted infra page 1501, points out that the possible personal liability of the executor under the above-mentioned statute is present if he makes distributions to beneficiaries of the estate.

[36] See 1954 I.R.C. §6324(a)(2), quoted infra page 1432.

[37] See discussion of power of appointment marital deduction trusts at page 839 infra.

Regulations recognize that the requirement that the income be "payable annually or at more frequent intervals" is met even though "the spouse is not entitled to the income from estate assets for the period before the distribution of those assets by the executor." [38]

If the revocable inter vivos trust is the principal instrument in the estate plan and the marital deduction trust is provided therein, the trust may be established immediately after the settlor's death and the income payments may begin immediately, unless the amount going into the marital trust is described by a formula designed to produce a marital trust that will provide the maximum allowable marital deduction. When such a formula is used, certain factors that must be known before the amount called for by the formula can be ascertained will not be known until some period of time has elapsed after the settlor's death.[39] Under these circumstances, the trustee will not be in a position to establish the marital trust definitively until later, and until it is so established he will not be able to make income payments with the certainty that he is paying the surviving spouse exactly what she is entitled to receive. When the marital trust is finally set up, the trustee will have to account to the spouse for all the income she was entitled to receive from the date of the death of the settlor.[40] Under these circumstances, it is clear that the income is "payable annually or more frequently," particularly in view of what is regarded as meeting this requirement in connection with testamentary trusts. Of course, the same reasons for delay in setting up the marital trust are present when it is created by will and described as to amount by a formula.

If the revocable inter vivos trust is employed as the medium for

[38] See Reg. §20.2056(b)-5(f)(9), quoted infra page 845.

[39] The formula will be based on the decedent's adjusted gross estate, which is the gross estate minus the deductions allowed by 1954 I.R.C. §§2053 and 2054, quoted infra page 1403. The ascertainment of the amount of the gross estate may be delayed because of uncertainty as to whether certain items are included in the gross estate, uncertainty as to the value of included items, or uncertainty as to whether certain deductions will be taken as income tax deductions or estate tax deductions. The precise amount of the §2053 and §2054 deductions may not be known until more than a year after the death of the decedent spouse. Formula gifts are examined infra page 793.

[40] When the trustee pays to the surviving spouse the income from the date of the death of the settlor, if some of it relates to a preceding taxable year, will the spouse be taxed under the throwback rule or will she be required to file an amended return for the preceding year? Since she was entitled to the income withheld from her and did not receive it only because of certain unresolved questions, it is submitted that when the questions are resolved, the situation should be treated in the same way as it would have been treated if the question had been resolved in the year of entitlement. For an analogous problem, see United States v. Higginson, 238 F.2d 439 (1st Cir. 1956).

disposing of a portion of the settlor's estate after his death and a portion is also allowed to pass through probate, then during the period of administration the trust may be available as a separate entity for part of the gross estate items and the estate may also be available as a separate entity for another part. If the trust permits (but does not require) the trustee to pay various death costs, the income-producing assets in the estate can be preserved during administration, if it is more desirable in the over-all picture to tax income to the estate than to the trust, by using trust assets rather than estate assets to meet such death obligations. In any event, consideration should be given to the inclusion in the revocable inter vivos trust of a provision that gives the trustee, after the settlor's death, discretion to pay the costs that arise as a result of his death.

Gross estate items that are subject to probate acquire a new basis on the death of the owner, the new basis being the value at which such items are included in the decedent's gross estate.[41] Non-probate gross estate items also acquire a new basis on the settlor's death if the property transferred has not been sold, exchanged or otherwise disposed of before his death by the person to whom the property was transferred before his death.[42] If the trustee of a re-

[41] See 1954 I.R.C. §1014(a), quoted infra page 1381.

Commissioner v. Estate of Fred T. Murphy, 229 F.2d 569 (6th Cir. 1956), recognizes that there may be an adjustment of basis for determining gain or loss as a result of events occurring after the death of a person and before the distribution of the property by the executors.

Mary Duerr, 30 T.C. 944 (1958), holds that in the absence of a federal estate tax return, the state inheritance tax valuation may control in determining the basis of stock owned by the decedent.

When a new basis is acquired from a decedent under §1014, will the value at which the property is included in the decedent's gross estate be controlling in determining the new basis? See Reg. §1.1014-3(a), quoted infra page 1497. The language of this regulation appeared in the 1939 Code Regulations and has been interpreted to mean that the figure arrived at by such an evaluation is only prima facie correct and may be shown to be erroneous. See McEwan v. Commissioner, 241 F.2d 887 (2d Cir. 1957). For a case in which the Commissioner attempted to reduce the estate tax valuation for the purpose of determining the income tax liability, see Estate of A. G. Johnson v. Commissioner, 270 F.2d 134 (4th Cir. 1959). See also Ford v. United States, 276 F.2d 17 (Ct. Cl. 1960), where the taxpayers, who were minors at the time they acquired stock by inheritance, were not estopped by the estate tax valuation made by their father's executors from establishing a correct market value basis for the purpose of reporting capital gains.

Under §1014 a new basis is acquired when property passes from the decedent by devise, even though the value of the property so passing is not included in the testator's gross estate. Thus foreign real estate passing by will acquires a new basis.

[42] See 1954 I.R.C. §1014(b)(2), (3) and (9), quoted infra page 1381. The language of §1014(b)(9) is not so clear as it might be. It refers to "property acquired from the decedent by reason of death, form of ownership, or other conditions (including property acquired through the exercise or nonexercise

vocable inter vivos trust sells the trust property before the settlor's death and reinvests the proceeds of the sale, will a new basis for the trust property be acquired on the death of the settlor? The Regulations take the position that the basis of any property acquired by the trustee of a revocable inter vivos trust in exchange for the original trust property, or of any property acquired by the trustee through reinvesting the proceeds of the sale of the original trust property, is the fair market value of the property thus acquired at the date of the settlor's death (or the applicable alternate valuation date) if the property thus acquired is properly included in his gross estate for federal estate tax purposes.[43] Since it is the property in the revocable inter vivos trust as of the date of the settlor's death which is properly included in his gross estate, a new basis is acquired on his death.

The holding period for capital gains purposes so far as an executor is concerned begins as of the date of the decedent's death.[44] The trustee of a revocable inter vivos trust will have been holding the trust property prior to the settlor's death, and though he acquires a new basis for the trust property on the settlor's death, the fact that the trustee's holding period antedated the settlor's death may put the trustee in a better position than the executor's to make sales shortly after the settlor's death.[45]

---

of a power of appointment), if by reason thereof the property is required to be included in determining the value of the decedent's gross estate . . ." If a revocable inter vivos trust is established and the income thereof is payable to a person other than the settlor, and the settlor dies, it should be concluded that property is acquired from the decedent by "other conditions," because if the failure to exercise a power of appointment is one of the "other conditions," the nonexercise of a power to revoke should be similarly treated. Section 1014(b)(9) applies only in the case of decedents dying after December 31, 1953.

Section 113(a)(5) of the 1939 Code was much narrower and included only what is §1014(b)(2) of the 1954 Code, though an amendment applicable to persons dying after December 31, 1951, extended it to include what is now §1014(b)(3).

[43] See Reg. §1.1014-3(d), quoted infra page 1498.

[44] See Brewster v. Gage, 280 U.S. 327 50 Sup. Ct. 115, 74 L. Ed. 457 (1930).

[45] If a person makes a gift that is deemed one in contemplation of death, so that a new basis is picked up by the donee under 1954 I.R.C. §1014, quoted infra page 1381, when does the holding period for capital gains purposes begin for the donee — on the date of the gift or on the date he acquires the new basis? Revenue Ruling 59-86, 1959-1 C.B. 209, holds that the period begins on the date of the gift if none of the provisions of 1954 I.R.C. §1223 apply.

The holding period problem is presented when community property is involved, and the surviving spouse obtains a new basis for her share of the community even though it is not included in her deceased husband's gross estate (see §1014(b)(6)). Revenue Ruling 59-220, 1959-1 C.B. 210, states that the holding period with respect to the wife's share of the community dates from the date the community property is acquired and that the holding period with respect to the husband's share, which passes to her on his death, dates from his death.

On the death of the settlor of a revocable trust, the trust becomes a separate entity for federal income tax purposes for the first time, and consequently, the trustee may elect to file the return of the trust either on the basis of a calendar year or a fiscal year, without the consent of the Commissioner.[46]

(2) Estate Taxes

The value of the trust property in a revocable inter vivos trust is includible in the settlor's gross estate for federal estate tax purposes.[47] The trust property that is valued is property that is subject to the power of revocation at the time of the settlor's death.[48]

Prior to the enactment of the Internal Revenue Code of 1954, consideration had to be given to the effect of the elimination of gross estate items from the probate estate on the estate tax deduction for debts, expenses of administration, and the like. Under the 1939 Code, the total allowance for such deductions was restricted to the value of the property in the decedent's gross estate subject to the payment of claims.[49] Thus, if the gross estate items not subject to probate were also not subject to claims against the decedent's estate under local law, and if most of the gross estate consisted of such non-probate items, part of the estate tax deduction might be lost even though the claims against the estate were paid in full. The 1954 Code remedies this situation by allowing a deduction in excess of the value of the property subject to claims, if the excess is paid before the date prescribed for the filing of the estate tax return.[50] Consequently, it is now possible to place practically all of a person's property in an arrangement that avoids probate and to preserve the benefit of the estate tax deduction for debts, expenses of administration, and the like, even though the amount of the deduction exceeds the property subject to claims.

The 1939 Code contained no provision permitting an estate tax deduction for the expenses of administering property not subject to claims. The 1954 Code, however, makes these expenses deductible if paid before the expiration of the period for the assessment of the tax, that is, within three years from the date the return is filed.[51]

[46] Rev. Rul. 57-51, 1957-1 C.B. 171.
[47] See 1954 I.R.C. §2038, quoted infra page 1397.
[48] See Howard v. United States, 125 F.2d 986 (5th Cir. 1942).
[49] See 1939 I.R.C. §812(b).
[50] See 1954 I.R.C. §2053, quoted infra page 1403.
[51] See 1954 I.R.C. §2053(b), quoted infra page 1403.

In Emma Peabody Abbett, 17 T.C. 1293 (1952), the decedent had established an inter vivos trust and the value of the trust property was included in his gross estate. As a result of the decedent's death there was an accounting

There are some items that may be subject to disposition by a person and that will be includible in his gross estate for federal estate tax purposes only if he sends them through his probate estate. If they are included in the assets of a revocable inter vivos trust, will their exemption from his gross estate be endangered? The following discussion relates to this problem.

---

proceeding as to the trust, and attorney's fees and guardian's fees were incurred. The Tax Court held that such portion of the fees as was properly allocable to the usual issues involved in a trust accounting was deductible from the decedent's gross estate under 1939 I.R.C. §812(b). As a result of this decision, Rev. Rul. 293, 1953-2 C.B. 257, was issued, in which it is stated: "It is usually not material whether attorney's fees or expenses paid in connection with an accounting of an inter vivos trust which is included in the grantor's gross estate are treated as a reduction in the value of the trust property or as an administration expense under Section 812(b) of the Code. It is material, however, in some cases. For example, if the revocable trust qualifies for the marital deduction, the surviving spouse will receive the net amount after payment of the expenses chargeable against the trust and the deduction should be limited to what passes to the surviving spouse. However, if the expenses chargeable to the inter vivos trust are held deductible as ordinary administration expenses, a marital deduction will be allowed in some cases for an amount in excess of that passing to the surviving spouse. In such cases treatment of the expenses incurred in connection with the inter vivos trust as deductible administration expenses would result in a double deduction to the extent of the trust expenses." Thus Rev. Rul. 293 states that the trust expenses should be deducted from the net value of the trust property rather than be deducted as an administration expense under §812(b).

In Rev. Rul. 55-601, 1955-2 C.B. 606, the question is raised as to whether the value of the assets of a revocable inter vivos trust includible in the decedent's gross estate for federal estate tax purposes should be reduced by any of the income taxes incurred by the trust before and after the decedent's death. By analogy to Rev. Rul. 293 it is held that the value of the trust property as of the applicable valuation date should be reduced by the amount of the income tax liability incurred by the trust prior to the date of the decedent's death. This value should not be reduced, however, by any income tax liability incurred by the trust subsequent to the decedent's death, and that means not even for the income tax liability incurred by the trust in the year following the decedent's death, even though the optional valuation date is selected for valuing the property in the trust.

In Fidelity-Philadelphia Trust Co. v. Smith, 142 F. Supp. 561 (E.D. Pa. 1956), the trustee of a revocable inter vivos trust which continued after the death of the settlor filed its account as trustee on the settlor's death. In the estate tax return of the settlor, a deduction was claimed for attorney's fees and expenses of filing the account and also for an interim trustee's commission taken out of principal. It was held that as to the legal fees and expenses, the situation was controlled by Haggart's Estate v. Commissioner, 182 F.2d 514 (3d Cir. 1950), where a deduction was allowed for the expenses of an accounting when there was a change in the trustees on the death of the settlor. Even though there is no change of trustees, where proper and orderly trust administration makes an accounting necessary, expenses of that accounting are deductible with respect to the trust assets included in the gross estate of the settlor. However, as to the interim commissions based upon principal at the time of the decedent's death, Pennsylvania law did not permit such commissions and the fact that the Probate Court in Pennsylvania allowed them, no one objecting, does not make them deductible. The District Court recognizes that commissions paid upon income of a trust are proper credits to the trustees

If O is an employee and his employer has established a noncontributory qualified pension, profit-sharing or stock bonus plan, the death benefits payable under such a plan will be includible in O's gross estate for federal estate tax purposes if, and only if, they are payable to his executor.[52]

When all of the incidents of ownership are in someone other than O, the insurance on O's life will not be includible in O's gross estate for federal estate tax purposes unless the proceeds of the insurance are receivable by his executor.[53]

Employee death benefits and life insurance proceeds are payable in cash and thus constitute a liquid asset that it may be desirable to have directed into a channel that will enable the funds to be utilized in some appropriate manner to meet the various death costs arising as a result of O's death. If O has established a revocable inter vivos trust containing provisions authorizing the trustee to pay such obligations, to loan money to O's executors or administrators, and to buy assets out of O's estate and retain them as a part of the trust property, can the employee death benefits and the life insurance proceeds safely be channeled into this trust?[54]

The answer to the question, so far as employee death benefits are concerned, will turn on whether the payment of such benefits to the trust will be deemed a payment to O's executor. If the payment is so regarded, then the employee death benefit will be brought into O's gross estate and be subjected to federal estate taxes. It is submitted that the payment to the trustee is not a payment to O's executor even though the trustee has the powers in regard to the use of the money paid to him which are described above. The trustee and the executor are two different personalities and the trustee must take into account, in determining whether

---

and will not be includible in the taxable estate. The case points out that Pennsylvania law has been changed, so that now interim commissions out of principal are permitted.

Does §2053(b) of the 1954 Code require that all of the expenses referred to above in this note be taken as a deduction for expenses of administering property not subject to claims, so that in no case will it now be proper to reduce the value of the trust property includible in the gross estate by the amount of such expenses? See Reg. §20.2053-8, quoted infra page 1527.

[52] See 1954 I.R.C. §2039, quoted infra page 1398.

[53] See 1954 I.R.C. §2042, quoted infra page 1402.

[54] Where employee death benefits are concerned, it should be kept in mind that a lump sum payment of such benefits to the trust will cause the entire amount of the payment (since the plan under consideration is a noncontributory one), less $5000, to be taxed for income tax purposes as a capital gain in the year of payment. See 1954 I.R.C. §101(b), quoted infra page 1329, and §402(a), quoted infra page 1342. If the payment of the employee death benefit is spread over a period of years, then each payment will be ordinary income to the recipient in the year of receipt, provided that the qualified plan is a noncontributory one.

to exercise his power, whether the exercise will be in the over-all interest of the beneficiaries of the trust. If the trust instrument requires the trustee to use the employee death benefits to pay estate obligations, then it may very well be that the payment to the trustee will be deemed the equivalent of a payment to O's executor. In some states, on O's death his creditors may be able to reach assets in a revocable inter vivos trust that he has established.[55] Even in these states, the payment of employee death benefits to a revocable inter vivos trust established by O should not be deemed the equivalent of a payment to his executor, because such additions to the revocable inter vivos trust on O's death should not be reachable by O's creditors if the property so added would not otherwise be reachable by his creditors. In other words, where the assets in a revocable inter vivos trust are deemed subject to the claims of O's creditors on his death, the law has developed on the theory that such property was under O's control until he died and was generally available to his creditors, and the fact of O's death should not place it beyond creditors' claims. This reasoning is not applicable, however, when the property added to the trust on O's death is property that was not reachable by O's creditors during his lifetime.

The proceeds of insurance on the life of O which are added to the trust on O's death are not payable to O's executor, and therefore there is no danger of having the proceeds so paid when the only reason that might be advanced is that they would be subject to a death tax otherwise not payable. If the insurance on the life of O is owned by someone other than O and the proceeds are made payable to the revocable inter vivos trust established by O, O may be deemed to have a reversionary interest in the insurance because he may affect the ultimate devolution of the proceeds by the way in which he exercises his powers of control over the revocable inter vivos trust. If he is deemed to have a reversionary interest in the insurance, then he has an incident of ownership, and its value will be includible in his gross estate on that ground, unless the reversionary interest does not meet the 5 percent value test.[56]

[55] See 5 American Law of Property §23.18 (Casner ed. 1952); 3 Scott, Trusts §330.12 (2d ed. 1956).

[56] Section 2042 of the 1954 Code, quoted infra page 1402, provides that the term "incident of ownership" includes a reversionary interest in the insured if the value of such reversionary interest exceeds 5 percent of the value of the policy immediately before the death of the insured, and also provides that the term "reversionary interest" includes a possibility that the policy, or the proceeds of the policy, may be subject to a power of disposition by the insured. In the case under consideration, even though the insured may be said to have a reversionary interest, it may be that it would never meet the 5 percent test because the owner of the policy could at any time before the insured dies change the beneficiary of the policy from the trust to someone else.

An executor may obtain a discharge from personal liability for estate taxes by following certain procedures prescribed in the 1954 Code.[57]   Where the assets of an inter vivos trust created by a decedent are included in his gross estate, the trustees of the trust are not entitled to a discharge from personal liability, as is an executor, because the statutory provision that protects executors does not apply to trustees.[58]

(3) Gift Taxes

No gift is made by the settlor of a revocable inter vivos trust so far as the federal gift tax is concerned, except to the extent that the income or the corpus of the trust is in fact paid to one other than the settlor.[59]

PROBLEM

5.9. A establishes a revocable inter vivos trust under which the income is payable to him for his lifetime, and on his death the trust continues for the benefit of his wife and issue. A becomes hopelessly insane, so that he no longer has the legal capacity to act to revoke the trust. Has A made a completed gift for federal gift tax purposes of the remainder interest under the trust as of the date of his insanity?   Consider in connection with this problem Revenue Ruling 55-518, 1955-2 C.B. 384.   See also 1 Scott, Trusts §58.4 n.9 (2d ed. 1956).

(4) Transfer Taxes

It should be kept in mind that the transfer of securities from the settlor to a revocable inter vivos trust is subject to a tax.[60]   Quite frequently the revocable trust will call for the division of the trust property into several separate trusts on the death of the settlor. Another transfer tax will be payable when such a division is made.[61]   Thus two transfer taxes may be payable before the prop-

---

[57] See §2204, quoted infra page 1415.

[58] Rev. Rul. 57-424, 1957-2 C.B. 623.

[59] See discussion at page 218 infra.

[60] See 1954 I.R.C. §4321, quoted infra page 1427.   If the tax is not paid on the date prescribed for payment, interest at the rate of 6 percent is charged. See 1954 I.R.C. §6601(a).

[61] Rev. Rul. 56-688, 1956-2 C.B. 889.   Though a division of trust property into shares is a transfer for purposes of the transfer tax, it is not a distribution of property within the meaning of 1954 I.R.C. §2032, quoted infra page 1395, so that the trust property is not valued as of the date of division when that occurs during the first year following the settlor's death and the executor selects the alternate valuation date.   See Rev. Rul. 57-495, 1957-2 C.B. 616.

erty comes to rest in the post-death arrangement, whereas only one such tax would be payable on the property if the several trusts were set up under a will rather than under a revocable inter vivos trust, because the transfer from the testator to his executor is by operation of law and hence exempt from any transfer tax.[62] Transfers from one revocable trust to another are exempt from the tax on transfers of stock and certificates of indebtedness if both trusts have the same settlor and the settlor is taxable on the income of both trusts.[63] Transfer taxes are so small in amount, however, that the fact that they may or may not be payable should not be a significant factor in reaching a decision.

[62] See 1954 I.R.C. §4343(a)(1), quoted infra page 1427.

Revenue Ruling 56-55, 1956-1 C.B. 682, points out that in a community property state a transfer tax is imposed when the deceased husband's share in the securities held as community property passes from him to his heirs (his heirs thus becoming tenants in common with his wife), and a further tax is imposed when the tenants in common divide the shares among themselves. Revenue Ruling 58-228, 1958-1 C.B. 460, deals with a situation where a testator, a resident of California, bequeathed the residue of his estate, which consisted of shares of stock, to named legatees, with a provision that, should any of the named persons die before becoming entitled to distribution of his or her share, then that share should be distributed to the survivors. California law provides that title to real and personal property of a California decedent vests immediately in the heirs or beneficiaries named in the will. Accordingly, a transfer tax is due upon the transfer of title to the beneficiaries as a class and again when their undivided interests in the stock are partitioned at the time of distribution.

Revenue Ruling 57-532, 1957-2 C.B. 774, holds that the transfer of securities issued in the name of an individual, without showing his capacity as trustee, to a surviving trustee is exempt from the documentary stamp tax under §4343(a)(8), where it is established by court order that such securities are, in fact, trust assets, and the individual in whose name the securities were issued was a trustee of the trust estate. Revenue Ruling 59-183, 1959-1 C.B. 440, discusses the applicability of the documentary stamp tax to the transfer of stock which is community property, when the decedent in his will bequeaths and devises all his property to his wife for life with remainder to his children.

Transfers of worthless certificates of indebtedness and worthless stock (where the value of the item transferred is not greater than the amount of the tax which would otherwise be imposed upon its delivery or transfer) by an executor to a legatee, heir or distributee are exempt from the transfer tax. See §4344(b) as amended by §141(a) of the Act to Make Technical Changes in the Federal Excise Tax Laws, and for Other Purposes, which was passed in 1958.

If a donee of a power of appointment can, by an exercise of the power, either cause a transfer of the trust property to new trustees to be held on such terms as the donee may designate, or provide for the retention by the present trustees of the trust property on such terms as the donee may designate, will one course of action be better than the other from a tax standpoint? Revenue Ruling 58-573, 1958-2 C.B. 843, holds that a transfer tax is due when the donee appoints the property to a new trustee.

For additional transfer tax matters, see Rev. Rul. 54-346, 1954-2 C.B. 386; Rev. Rul. 54-347, 1954-2 C.B. 386; Rev. Rul. 55-685, 1955-2 C.B. 643; Rev. Rul. 55-686, 1955-2 C.B. 644; Rev. Rul. 55-687, 1955-2 C.B. 645; Rev. Rul. 57-519, 1957-2 C.B. 772.

[63] See 1954 I.R.C. §4344(c), quoted infra page 1427.

(5) Closely Held Stock

If stock in a closely held corporation is transferred to a revocable inter vivos trust, the corporation will no longer be able to be taxed in accordance with Subchapter S.[64] Such a transfer, however, does not rule out the availability of Section 303 of the 1954 Code[65] but may cut down on the amount of stock redeemable under that section if expenses of administration are diminished as a result of reducing the probate estate.

If a corporation redeems all of its stock owned by a shareholder, the redemption will not be deemed a dividend.[66] In determining whether all of the shareholder's stock is redeemed, the shareholder under some circumstances is treated as the constructive owner of stock in the corporation that is in fact owned by someone else.[67] If O owns stock in a closely held corporation and his stock is to be redeemed by the corporation on his death, it will be redeemed from O's estate. In such a case the estate will be treated as owning any stock in the corporation which is owned by a beneficiary of the estate for purposes of determining whether all of the stock owned by a shareholder is redeemed.[68] Thus, if a contemplated beneficiary of O owns stock in the corporation, it may be advisable for O to establish a revocable inter vivos trust under which the beneficiary will be given benefits on the death of O, so that he will not be a beneficiary of O's estate. In this way, the stock in the corporation owned by the beneficiary will not be attributed to O's estate.[69]

[64] See 1954 I.R.C. §§1371-1377 and Reg. §1.1371-1(e); the latter is quoted infra page 1501.

[65] Quoted infra page 1338.

[66] See 1954 I.R.C. §302(b)(3).

[67] See 1954 I.R.C. §318.

[68] See 1954 I.R.C. §318(a)(2)(A).

[69] Section 1.318-3(a) of the Regulations points out that the beneficiary's stock will not be attributed to the estate after he ceases to be a beneficiary, and he ceases to be a beneficiary when all the property to which he is entitled has been received by him and there is only a remote possibility that it will be necessary for the estate to seek the return of the property or to seek payment from him to satisfy claims against the estate or expenses of administration. Thus it is within the power of the executor to avoid the attribution rules by making the distribution to the beneficiary before the redemption by the corporation. Revenue Ruling 60-18, I.R.B. 1960-3, 14, however, states that a residuary beneficiary does not cease to have an interest as a beneficiary of an estate in the process of administration until the estate is closed, even though the estate has known assets only sufficient to pay its existing liabilities; consequently, Reg. §1.318-3(a) is relevant only with respect to a specific legatee. Revenue Ruling 58-111, 1958-1 C.B. 173, considers the possible effect of partial distributions to a beneficiary of an estate and holds that in all cases (partial distributions as well as complete distributions) the date of redemption is the

(6) Installment Obligations

Under certain defined circumstances, income from the sale of property may be reported on the installment method.[70] If an installment obligation is disposed of, the general rule is that, when the disposition is otherwise than by sale or exchange, gain or loss results to the extent of the difference between the basis of the obligation and the fair market value of the obligation at the time it is disposed of.[71] A special rule is set up, however, to govern the transmission of an installment obligation by death.[72] If an installment obligation is transferred to a revocable inter vivos trust, is this a disposition that will invoke the general rule or will the disposition be regarded as taking place on the death of the settlor, so that the special rule governs? Until a definitive answer can be given to this question, installment obligations should not be transferred to a revocable inter vivos trust.

(7) United States Treasury Bonds

Treasury bonds of certain issues are redeemable at par and accrued interest upon the death of the owner for the purpose of having the proceeds applied in the payment of the estate taxes on the decedent's estate. Such bonds held by a trust created by the decedent, however, are so redeemable for such a purpose only in an amount not to exceed the amount of the federal tax which the trustee of the trust is required to pay under the terms of the trust instrument. Thus it may be desirable to keep the ownership of such bonds in the name of the decedent himself.

b. *State Tax Considerations*

State income, gift and death tax consequences should be explored before going forward with a revocable inter vivos trust. Usually this exploration will not make it undesirable to proceed

---

date to be used in determining the beneficiaries' proportionate interest in an estate when §318(a) is applied to determine the ownership of stock for the purpose of §302(b)(2).

Example (1) under Reg. §1.318-3(a) brings out that one having only a future interest in the assets of an estate is not a beneficiary of the estate under §318(a).

[70] See 1954 I.R.C. §453, quoted infra page 1353.

[71] See 1954 I.R.C. §453(d), quoted infra page 1454; Rev. Rul. 60-362, I.R.B. 1960-46, 10.

[72] See 1954 I.R.C. §453(d)(3), quoted infra page 1355.

with the trust if other considerations recommend it.[73]   In many states, life insurance proceeds are subject to state inheritance taxes only if they are payable to the insured's estate.   For the reasons indicated previously,[74] an arrangement which calls for the payment of such proceeds to a revocable inter vivos trust should not in and of itself be deemed the equivalent of having them paid to the insured's executor.

PROBLEM

5.10.   T owns insurance on his life in the amount of $50,000. The proceeds of the insurance are payable to the trustee of an insurance trust which T has executed.   A provision in the trust instrument requires the trustee to pay all federal and state death taxes arising as a result of T's death, regardless of the property subject to such taxes.   T in his will bequeaths $10,000 to A, $10,000 to B, and the residue of his estate to C.   Point out how this ar-

[73] State law should be examined to determine whether the property in a revocable inter vivos trust acquires a new basis for state income tax purposes on the death of the settlor.   In Massachusetts, for example (Mass. Ann. Laws, c. 62, §7 (Supp. 1959), as clarified in 1958), the basis of property acquired by gift after June 30, 1954, and prior to taxable years commencing after December 31, 1958, was the basis to the settlor or the last preceding owner by whom it was not acquired by gift, or the fair market value at the date of the gift, whichever was lower, and the date of the gift when a revocable trust was involved was the date on which the settlor died (or such earlier date as he gave up his power of revocation).   In Massachusetts, however, the basis of property acquired by bequest, devise or inheritance is the fair market value of the property on the date acquired.   Thus, from the basis standpoint, a testamentary trust might have produced a more favorable result than a revocable inter vivos trust in Massachusetts.   In Second Bank-State Street Trust Co. v. State Tax Commission, 337 Mass. 203, 148 N.E.2d 647 (1958), the court considered various situations in applying the rule of §7 of Chapter 62, that the extent of a taxable gain or loss must be measured with reference to the value of the securities at the date when the beneficiary's interest was acquired.   In 1958 the Massachusetts situation was changed with respect to taxable years commencing after December 31, 1958, so that "the basis of property acquired by gift shall, from and after the death of the donor, be the fair market value of the property at the date of such death if such property was subject to the inheritance tax imposed by section one of chapter sixty-five, or would have been subject to such tax if it had been real estate or tangible personal property within the Commonwealth of a value exceeding the exemptions provided in said section."   Mass. Ann. Laws, c. 62, §7 (Supp. 1959).

In Massachusetts the revocable inter vivos trust is a taxpayer and thus any excess losses sustained by the trust, though they are available to the settlor for federal income tax purposes, are not available to the settlor for Massachusetts income tax purposes.   The excess losses in the trust, however, may be applied to reduce the net capital gains of the trust in each of the three succeeding taxable years.   See Mass. Ann. Laws, c. 62, §5(c).   If a sale of trust property is to be made at a loss and it is important to have the loss available to the settlor, the trust property should be distributed to him and sold by him.   A transfer tax would of course be payable on such a distribution to the settlor.

[74] See discussion at page 129 supra.

rangement for the payment of death taxes may cause the state inheritance taxes to be greater than if some other arrangement had been adopted.

c. *Availability of Beneficial Rights on the Death of O, the Settlor*

Probate assets on O's death are in a suspended state until an executor or administrator has been appointed to take them over and manage them. When the personal representative is appointed, he must bear in mind that until the claims of creditors have been satisfied and death tax obligations met, he may be subjected to personal liability if he does not retain sufficient assets to meet such claims and obligations.[75] This potential personal liability naturally deters an executor or administrator from making estate assets available to the intended beneficiaries until such liability is eliminated.[76]

If gross estate items are placed by O in a revocable inter vivos trust that provides for the devolution of the trust property from and after the death of O, a managerial arrangement is established for these items that is uninterrupted by O's death. Before the trustee moves to make the trust assets available to the post-death beneficiaries, however, he should examine the extent of his possible personal liability if the claims of creditors of O are not satisfied or if tax obligations arising as a result of O's death are not met.

The extent to which the assets of a revocable inter vivos trust can be reached by the creditors of the settlor on the settlor's death is not the same in the various states.[77] But even where such assets

---

[75] See page 123 supra, note 35.

[76] In many estates, of course, the executor can, within a reasonable time, prepare a fairly reliable estimate of the death obligations and make partial distributions to estate beneficiaries without running a material risk. Partial distributions of estate assets, however, may create undesirable income tax results. See discussion of income taxation of estates at page 77 supra.

Section 2204 of the 1954 Code provides a method whereby the executor can obtain a discharge from personal liability, but this discharge is not obtainable until after the passage of an appreciable period of time.

[77] See 5 American Law of Property §23.18 (Casner ed. 1952); 3 Scott, Trusts §330.12 (2d ed. 1956).

United States v. Peelle, 159 F. Supp. 45 (E.D.N.Y. 1958), held that the settlor of a revocable inter vivos trust established under New York law is deemed to be the owner of securities in the trust for the purpose of the attachment of income tax liens of the United States against the settlor, and that the court can exercise the power of revocation to collect federal income taxes on the securities when the settlor has become incompetent. Furthermore, the life beneficiary of a trust who has an unlimited power to invade corpus will be deemed to be the owner of the corpus in regard to income tax liens against the life beneficiary.

are reachable by a creditor, the trustee does not apparently incur any personal liability when, after the death of the settlor and in accordance with the terms of the trust, he makes distributions before the creditor has taken appropriate steps to reach the trust assets. Thus, in this respect, gross estate items placed in a revocable inter vivos trust may be more readily available to post-death beneficiaries than probate assets.

The trustee of the revocable inter vivos trust may be subject to personal liability for death taxes that come into the picture as a result of O's death.[78]   A comparison of the possible personal liability for federal estate taxes of an executor with that of the trustee of a revocable inter vivos trust reveals that the executor's possible liability is greater because it may equal the sum of any payments the executor makes before the debts due the United States are paid, whereas the trustee's possible liability cannot exceed the value, at the time of O's death, of the property in the trust. Thus the trustee, because of his freedom from possible liability for debts if he makes distributions and because of his lesser potential liability for estate taxes, should feel freer to make the trust property available to the beneficiaries during the period of administration than the executor may feel so far as probate property is concerned.[79]

d. Cost of Establishing the Post-death Plan of O, the Settlor

Probate expenses include the executor's fee and the attorney's fee. These charges are usually a percentage of the probate estate.[80] Thus they should be reduced in amount when gross estate items come to rest in the post-death arrangement by a non-probate route. In view of the fact that the executor will have to take into account non-probate assets in fulfilling certain duties (such as the preparation of the federal estate tax return), a special charge over and above the charge based on a percentage of the probate estate ought to be allowed;[81] but even so, the probate costs should be less than when all gross estate items are sent through probate.

The net saving produced by a reduction in the executor's fee and the attorney's fee when probate is avoided depends on various factors. Such charges are deductible for federal estate tax pur-

[78] See 1954 I.R.C. §6325(a)(2), quoted infra page 1432.
The controlling state law will determine the extent to which a trustee of a revocable inter vivos trust may be personally liable for state death taxes.
[79] See page 131 supra note 58.
[80] See discussion of executors' fees at page 38 supra.
[81] See discussion of executors' fees at page 39 supra.

Factors to consider

poses.[82] Consequently, the amount saved by reducing these charges is offset to the extent the estate tax becomes larger. Furthermore, if gross estate items are kept from the probate estate by the use of

[82] See 1954 I.R.C. §2053, quoted infra page 1403.

For cases allowing the deduction of the executor's fee for estate tax purposes, see Estate of Elizabeth L. Audenried, 26 T.C. 120 (1956); Estate of Debe W. Hubbard, 26 T.C. 183 (1956) (deduction allowed even though part of fee was based on income of estate earned after decedent's death), *rev'd on another ground sub nom.* Estate of Debe W. Hubbard v. Commissioner, 250 F.2d 492 (5th Cir. 1957).

In Bohnen v. Harrison, 232 F.2d 406 (7th Cir. 1956), it was held that the attorney's fee incurred in prosecuting a claim for refund was deductible for estate tax purposes, as long as the claim was made in the executor's original complaint, even though the claim was not filed with the Commissioner. Goyette v. United States, 57-2 U.S.T.C. ¶11710 (S.D. Cal. 1957), held that additional attorney's and executor's fees for services rendered in connection with a refund claim of an assessed tax deficiency were deductible in computing the estate tax. The same result was reached in Greene v. United States, 57-2 U.S.T.C. ¶11713 (N.D. Ill. 1957). Also in accord is Commerce Trust Co. v. United States, 167 F. Supp. 643 (W.D. Mo. 1958). See Reg. §20.2053-3(c)(2).

In Fidelity-Philadelphia Trust Co. v. United States, 122 F. Supp. 551 (E.D. Pa. 1954), the question was presented as to whether the fees actually paid to an executor are deductible for estate tax purposes if the state court recognizes only part of such fees as the proper amount deductible with respect to state inheritance taxes. This question had been previously decided in favor of allowing as a deduction the full amount paid in Estate of Cardeza, 5 T.C. 202 (1946), *aff'd without this point being at issue,* 173 F.2d 19 (3d Cir. 1949). The Fidelity case held that there can be deducted only so much of the amount actually paid as is determined to be proper under the law of the jurisdiction involved. The decision was affirmed by the Third Circuit. 222 F.2d 379 (3d Cir. 1955).

Gordon v. United States, 163 F. Supp. 542 (W.D. Mo. 1958), considered a case where, after the decedent's property had been distributed pursuant to the decree of the Probate Court, expenses were incurred by the distributees in a controversy with the Internal Revenue Service, which would have been deductible as expenses of administration if incurred by the executor. The court held that these expenses were deductible even though there was no formal allowance of them by the Probate Court. See Reg. §20.2053-1(b)(2), which provides that a deduction for the amount of a bona fide indebtedness of the decedent, or of a reasonable expense of administration, will not be denied because no court decree has been entered, if the amount would be allowable under local law.

Section 20.2053-3(b)(2) of the Regulations, quoted infra page 1526, points out that a bequest or devise to the executor in lieu of commissions is not deductible. If, however, the decedent fixed by his will the compensation payable to the executor for services to be rendered in the administration of the estate, deduction may be taken to the extent that the amount so fixed does not exceed the compensation allowable by the local law or practice.

Some expenses of administration may be claimed as an income tax deduction in determining the net taxable income of the estate rather than as an estate tax deduction. See 1954 I.R.C. §642(g), quoted infra page 1363.

Section 1.642(g)-1 of the Regulations, quoted infra page 1491, recognizes that the allowance of a deduction in computing estate's taxable income is not precluded by claiming a deduction in the estate tax return, so long as the estate tax deduction is not finally allowed and the statement is filed. Revenue Ruling 58-484, 1958-2 C.B. 363, holds that the phrase "finally allowed" as used in the Regulations means an estate tax return in which the deduction in quesa revocable inter vivos trust, there may be trustees' fees during O's lifetime, which would not have been incurred if the assets had been allowed to pass through probate.[83]   Since such charges, how-

---

tion has been allowed and with respect to which the statute of limitations on assessment has expired, or in which, for any other reason, an assessment of a deficiency resulting from disallowance of the deduction is prohibited (such as a closing agreement).

Revenue Ruling 59-32, 1959-1 C.B. 245, recognizes that the portion of any administration expenses which is attributable under 1954 I.R.C. §265(1) to the earning of tax-exempt income, and hence not deductible for income tax purposes, may nevertheless be taken as a deduction for estate tax purposes under §2053(a), quoted infra page 1403, and the filing of the required statement under §642(g) will not prevent this result.

Expenses incurred in the sale of property, other than those of a dealer, go to reduce the sale price and are not deductible as an ordinary and necessary business expense.   Revenue Ruling 56-43, 1956-1 C.B. 210, points out that if such selling expenses are taken as a deduction in computing the taxable estate for estate tax purposes, §642(g) prevents them from also being used to reduce the sales price for income tax purposes.

[83] The Standard Charge Schedule of the Old Colony Trust Company, of Boston, Massachusetts, published in September, 1955, with respect to personal trusts is as follows:

A. *Annual Charge:*
    1. *Personal property collectively invested in Common Trust Fund A —*
        (a) 4% of gross income; and
        (b) $2 per $1,000 of principal
        [*Minimum charge:* $65 plus $2 per $1,000 of principal]
    2. *Personal property individually invested* (except mortgages) —
        The sum of:
        (a) 5% of gross income; and
        (b) $3 per $1,000 of principal up to $200,000;
            $2 per $1,000 of the next $300,000 of principal;
            $1 per $1,000 of the next $500,000 of principal;
            90¢ per $1,000 of the next $2,500,000 of principal; and
            Progressively diminishing rates on the remainder.
        [*Minimum charge:* $250; plus $5 per $1,000 of principal from $15,001 to $20,000; plus $3 per $1,000 of principal from $20,001 to $30,000; plus $1 per $1,000 of principal from $30,001 to $75,000.]
    3. *Mortgages* — A charge as provided in Table A (page 13 of Standard Charge Schedules).
    4. *Real Property* — A charge as provided in Table B (pages 13-14 of Standard Charge Schedules).
B. *Distribution Charge:*
    1. *Personal property* — 1½% of the market value on the distribution date of property distributed.   In cases of distribution within five years of the initial receipt of property, a smaller charge may be made.
    2. *Real property* — 1½% of the appraised value of the property on the distribution date.

NOTES: (1) As trustee, the Trust Company performs all the normal services of Trusteeship.
    (2) A co-trustee may be compensated out of the above charges, provided: (1) that the presence of an inactive or family trustee shall not diminish the Trust Company's compensation, (2) that the Trust Company receives 100% of the above minimum charges, and (3) that the Trust Company in no event

ever, may be fully deductible for income tax purposes, the full amount of the charges is not the net cost to O.[84] If the post-death arrangement under the revocable inter vivos trust provides for a

---

receives less than 75% of the above charges. If application of these provisos results in inadequate compensation of a co-trustee, he may be compensated through an additional charge.

(3) No charge is made against an account for entry in or withdrawal from Common Trust Fund A.

(4) If all the income of a trust is payable for charitable, educational, or religious purposes, the Annual Charge may be reduced up to 10%. If over half of the principal of a trust is payable upon termination for charitable, educational, or religious purposes, the Distribution Charge referable to the portion so payable may be reduced up to 10%.

(5) In the absence of other agreement, the Annual Charge is made in semi-annual instalments.

(6) The Annual Charge computed on principal is based on the average of market values at the beginning and the end of the charge period.

(7) For extraordinary services or responsibilities of the Trust Company, such as administration of close corporation holdings, appropriate departure from the Standard Charge will be made, by appraisal.

(8) For performing the above services as agent for the trustee(s) of a trust, the Trust Company's compensation is computed in accordance with the above schedule as if it were co-trustee of an individually invested account.

The reasonable compensation allowable to the Executor, Administrator, Trustee, Conservator, or Guardian, appointed by the Probate Court, is subject to Court approval. The charges shown . . . conform to the general practice of Probate Courts in Massachusetts, as evidenced from time to time.

In some states statutory fees for trustees have been established, e.g., N.Y. Surrogate's Court Act §§285a, 285b and 285c, and N.Y. Civil Practice Act §§1548, 1548a and 1548b.

The standard charge schedule set out above provides for a distribution charge. Suppose the settlor of a revocable inter vivos trust is dissatisfied with the trustee and removes him and appoints someone else in his place. Will the trustee who is removed and who must distribute the trust property to the successor trustee be entitled to a distribution charge? It is believed that some corporate trustees would claim a distribution charge under these circumstances, particularly if the corporate trustee which is removed believes it has rendered satisfactory service as trustee. It should be kept in mind that a distribution charge may also be collected if a revocable inter vivos trust is revoked and the trust property returned to the settlor.

[84] See discussion at page 121 supra.

If the trustee during O's lifetime is O or some member of his family, trustees' fees may be declined. If it is necessary to employ a professional trustee, then it is also very likely that O has been employing investment counsel, and the change to the trustee as investment manager will not significantly change the existing cost picture.

Revenue Ruling 58-53, 1958-1 C.B. 152, deals with a situation where the settlor of a revocable inter vivos trust paid, in the first year of the trust, trustee's commissions for subsequent years as well as for the first year. The settlor filed his income tax returns on a cash basis, and claimed in the year the trust was created a deduction for the entire amount of the commissions paid in the first year of the trust. The ruling holds that he was entitled to deduct only the portion of the commissions paid which was attributable to the services performed by the trustee in the first year of the trust. In succeeding years he may deduct the portion attributable to each such year. In no year, however, may he deduct the portion of the commissions which is allocable to the production or collection of income which is tax-exempt.

continuance of the property in trust, <u>trustees' fees may begin immediately on O's death,</u> whereas under a <u>testamentary trust they</u> would <u>not begin until the executor made distributions to the trustees under the will.</u> If the post-death arrangement under the revocable inter vivos trust calls for outright dispositions that cause a total or partial termination of the trust, it should be kept in mind that the trustee may be entitled to a distribution fee and, if so, the savings produced by avoiding expenses of probate may be significantly reduced.

e. Preservation of Secrecy as to Post-death Plan of O, the Settlor, and Amount of Property Subject to It

The destination of probate assets as revealed in a decedent's will and the amount and nature of them are a matter of public record, open to examination by anyone who desires to go to the place the public records are kept. O may wish to keep his lifetime financial record and his method of caring for his family from the prying eyes of the curious, and to a considerable extent he can do this if he makes arrangements that avoid probate.

Gross estate items that are not subject to probate will be disclosed in the final federal estate tax return, and a document such as the instrument creating a revocable inter vivos trust will be filed with the return;[85] but the return and its accompanying papers are not open to general public scrutiny as are the probate records. State death tax reports may also include information about nonprobate property, and the availability to the public of these records will affect the over-all secrecy that is maintainable.

If a revocable inter vivos trust is used and it provides for the continuance of the property in trust subsequent to O's death, it may be desirable to provide in O's will that the probate assets are to be added to the non-probate property in the trust, thereby subjecting both types of assets to the same governing plan for post-death operation. If we assume that the pour-over arrangement is effective,[86] will the desired secrecy as to the post-death plan and the amount of property subject to it be disturbed? The answer to this question is no, unless the local law requires the trust instrument to be probated with the will.[87] Even if the trust instrument is re-

[85] The instructions applicable to Schedule G (transfers during decedent's life) of the federal estate tax return (Form 706) provide that in case a transfer, by trust or otherwise, is made by a written instrument, a copy must be filed with the return.

[86] See page 118 supra, note 22.

[87] For a case that holds that a revocable inter vivos trust must be probated with the will when the will makes a pour-over to the trust, see Estate of Florence Harzfeld, 27 Kansas City B.J. No. 2, p. 19 (Jackson County Prob. Ct., Mo. 1952), with supplemental opinion at page 24.

quired to be probated, secrecy will be maintained as to the amount of the non-probate assets in the trust.

f. Freedom of Decision as to Nature of Post-death Plan of O, the Settlor

Various restrictions may be imposed by state law on O's freedom to decide who will be the beneficiaries of his bounty when he dies and in what manner the benefits will be conferred on them. To the extent that these restrictions are applicable only to probate assets, they can be avoided by avoiding probate. To the extent that they are not limited to probate assets, they may be avoided by placing the property under the more favorable law of another state.

In many states, as has been pointed out, a surviving spouse may renounce her husband's will and claim her statutory share of his estate.[88] Such renunciation on her part may upset O's over-all plans for his family. If gross estate items not subject to probate cannot be reached on the renunciation, then the significance of a renunciation is nullified to the extent of the elimination of probate assets.[89] The law of the most favorable state is available to a citizen of any other state if he establishes the revocable inter vivos trust there with the intention that its law control the trust, and if the trustee and the trust property are located there.[90]

If O desires to pass property by his will to charities, he may find himself restricted as to the amount he can dispose of in such a manner,[91] or he may be confronted with the difficulty that the charitable gifts will fail if he dies within a stated period of time after he executes his will.[92] The statutes imposing these restrictions on charitable gifts have been strictly construed as being applicable only to dispositions by will, and hence they are not applicable to

[88] See discussion at page 57 supra.

[89] See page 114 supra, note 18.

[90] See National Shawmut Bank v. Cumming, 325 Mass. 457, 91 N.E.2d 337 (1950) (widow of Vermont settlor had no greater right than widow of Massachusetts settlor when trustee and trust property were located in Massachusetts and trust instrument provided that Massachusetts law was to control). See also Hanson v. Denckla, 357 U.S. 235, 78 Sup. Ct. 1228, 2 L. Ed. 2d 235 (1958), printed infra page 1088, where it is recognized that if neither the trustee nor the trust property is located in a state, a decision by the state court that the trust is a testamentary disposition is not entitled to full faith and credit in the state where the trustee and the trust property are located. It may be, however, that a state, other than the one in which the trustee and the trust are located, in which a beneficiary of the trust resides could exercise jurisdiction over the resident beneficiary, after the trust has made a distribution to the beneficiary, and require him to turn over the property received to someone else.

[91] See N.Y. Decedent Estate Law §17, quoted infra page 1467.

[92] See Ohio Rev. Code Ann. §2107.06 (Page, 1954), quoted infra page 1470.

post-death charitable gifts under a revocable inter vivos trust.[93] Even if the local statute were by construction or by amendment made applicable to charitable gifts under a revocable inter vivos trust, its effect could easily be avoided by placing the trust under the governing law of a jurisdiction that imposes no restriction on such charitable dispositions.

The rule against perpetuities and the rule against accumulations both play a very important part in modern estate planning. If the estate plan that O adopts is one that properly restricts the beneficial rights of the beneficiaries, the benefits can pass from one beneficiary to another on the occurrence of stated contingencies or after the passage of stated periods of time without the imposition of death taxes on the distribution of such benefits.[94] The length of time this succession to benefits can go on without the imposition of such taxes is the period of the governing rule against perpetuities.

The statutory provisions that govern the federal income taxation of trusts make it possible to establish a trust under which income not distributed but accumulated by the trustee will be taxed to the trust as a separate tax entity.[95] The extent to which an accumulation trust may be employed will depend on the governing rule against accumulations.

In a revocable inter vivos trust, the governing law, so far as the rule against perpetuities and the rule against accumulations are concerned, can be selected by placing the trustee and the trust property in the jurisdiction of choice and by manifesting in the trust instrument an intention that the laws of that jurisdiction shall control.[96] Thus the most favorable of available rules as to perpetuities and accumulations may be available to O with respect to non-probate assets.[97] If O manifests an intention in his will that a trust under his will is to be governed by the laws of a jurisdiction other than his domicile, his desires may also be given effect if significant elements of the trust (the trustee and the trust prop-

---

[93] City Bank Farmers Trust Co. v. Charity Organization Soc., 238 App. Div. 720, 265 N.Y. Supp. 267, *aff'd,* 264 N.Y. 441, 191 N.E. 504 (1934); Cleveland Trust Co. v. White, 134 Ohio St. 1, 15 N.E.2d 627 (1938).

[94] No beneficiary should be given a descendable interest in the property involved nor should he be given what amounts to a general power of appointment under 1954 I.R.C. §2041, quoted infra page 1400, if he is not to have an interest includible in his gross estate for federal estate tax purposes on his death.

[95] See discussion at page 734 infra.

[96] See discussion at page 1073 infra.

[97] The rules as to perpetuities and accumulations in the several states are discussed in Parts 24 and 25 of 6 American Law of Property 1-405 (Casner ed. 1952).

erty) are located in the jurisdiction of his choice.[98] The conservative way to attain this objective, however, is the non-probate route.

Some of the advantages O gains by the use of the revocable inter vivos trust, under which he is able to select the governing rules against perpetuities and accumulations, will be lost if the periods of these respective rules begin to run from the date the trust is established. If the trust is set up under his will, of course, the periods will begin to run at O's death. When the trust is revocable by O alone, the interests under the trust do not restrict the disposability of the trust property in any significant manner as long as O retains his power. Thus the periods of the rules under consideration should and do run from the date O's power terminates, which will usually be on his death.[99] Consequently, the beginning of the measuring period for the validity of arrangements under a revocable inter vivos trust and under a will are usually the same.

O may be unable to designate as the manager of his probate assets the person of his choice. In some states, a nonresident individual is not qualified to serve as executor,[100] and in at least one state the statutory provision is broad enough to exclude a nonresident individual from serving as testamentary trustee.[101] In another state, a resident executor and testamentary trustee must be appointed to serve with a nonresident executor and testamentary trustee.[102] There may be restrictions as to the appointment of a foreign corporation as executor or testamentary trustee.[103] All of these restrictions on O can be avoided by the use of a revocable inter vivos trust. Where there is any danger that the restric-

---

[98] See Amerige v. Attorney General, 324 Mass. 648, 88 N.E.2d 126 (1949), printed infra page 771. It should be noted that in the Amerige case the question arose in a court in the jurisdiction the testator had selected. The result might not be the same if the question arose initially in a court in the state of the testator's domicile.

[99] See discussion at page 656 infra.

[100] See Ill. Rev. Stat., c. 3, §229 (1959), quoted infra page 1438.

[101] See Mich. Stat. Ann. §27.3178(278) (1943), quoted infra page 1465.

In Roby v. Smith, 131 Ind. 342, 30 N.E. 1093 (1891), it was held that an Indiana statute that prohibited the appointment of a nonresident trustee who was a citizen of the United States violated Article IV, §2 and the Fourteenth Amendment of the Constitution of the United States.

[102] See Va. Code Ann. §26-59 (1950, Supp. 1960), quoted infra page 1475. See also Pa. Stat. Ann., tit. 20, §320.903 (Purdon), quoted infra page 1473.

[103] New Hampshire is an example of a state that does not permit a foreign corporation to be appointed as trustee. See Bank of New York & Trust Co. v. Tilton, 82 N.H. 81, 129 Atl. 492 (1925). See also La. Rev. Stat. Ann. §9:1871 (1950). Massachusetts is an example of a state that does allow such an appointment. See Mass. Ann. Laws, c. 167, §45A; c. 172, §52. But in Massachusetts, as well as in many other states that allow a foreign corporation to be appointed a fiduciary, the appointment can be made only if the jurisdiction in which the foreign corporation is located permits a Massachusetts corporation to serve as a fiduciary in that jurisdiction.

tions will apply to the revocable inter vivos trust if the trust is to be governed by the law of O's domicile, then he will have to move the trust out from under such jurisdiction.

It is difficult to justify a law, regardless of the soundness of the reasons that motivated its enactment, when it restricts freedom of decision only as to probate assets. Such a law applies only to those who choose to have it apply to them. To a considerable extent, the same thing can be said of a state law that restricts O's freedom of decision more than it would be restricted if he resided in another state. If the more favorable law of another state is available to O if he chooses to move his dispositive arrangement in under it, then the restrictive effect of the law of his domicile is largely eliminated.

g. *Miscellaneous Considerations for O, the Settlor*

It may be desirable for O to place most of his income-producing property in a revocable inter vivos trust to accomplish during his lifetime certain objectives that cannot be fully accomplished in other ways. Under such a trust, O may select the person (the trustee) who is to provide for O's economic welfare in the event he should become incapacitated. If O were to become incapacitated without such provision being made for his care, then his economic welfare would be in the hands of a person appointed by the court. In at least one state,[104] a nonresident cannot be appointed conservator of the estate of an incompetent person. In that state, however, a nonresident could be the trustee of a revocable inter vivos trust and he could thus be in the position to manage O's estate were O to become incompetent.

If O decides to withdraw from the active management of his financial affairs, the revocable inter vivos trust offers a vehicle to carry on the management. It is true that the managerial responsibility could be transferred from O to an agent rather than to a trustee, but the agency arrangement will not survive the incompetency of O, whereas the trust arrangement will.

The management of O's financial affairs may require some special training, or O may desire to satisfy himself as to the competency of the person who is to succeed him in the role of manager. In either case, the successor to O can be given a trial run while O is still available to assist and advise if the successor is put in as the trustee of a revocable inter vivos trust. Again, this could be done under an agency arrangement, but if the successor is to

---

[104] See Ill. Rev. Stat., c. 3, §272 (1959), quoted infra page 1439.

carry on under a trust after O's death, the trial run will be more realistic if the trust format is used during O's lifetime.

The management of property that is placed in a revocable inter vivos trust during O's lifetime is uninterrupted as a result of O's death. The management of the probate assets inevitably shifts on O's death from the person who was managing them during O's lifetime to O's executor or administrator. When the period of administration of O's estate comes to an end, the management again shifts to the estate distributee. The shifts in management of probate assets may in fact be accomplished without any change in the identity of the manager by naming the same person as the inter vivos manager under an agency arrangement, the executor under the will, and the trustee who will succeed to the management of the property on the termination of estate administration. Nevertheless, the frequent changing of the managerial hat involves expenses and delays that may be avoided by using a revocable inter vivos trust under which there will be only one managerial arrangement for the duration of the trust. This factor of continuity of management uninterrupted by death may be particularly important when the property to be managed is a business.

If O owns assets physically located in several states and it is not possible or feasible to move them to the state of his domicile, ancillary administration may be necessary on O's death. The costs of ancillary administration when combined with the costs of domiciliary administration may justify using a revocable inter vivos trust to eliminate at least the necessity of ancillary administration.

When O's plans call for a trust as the medium for conferring benefits on persons who are to enjoy holdings on his death, it may be significant whether the trust is a so-called court trust or a so-called non-court trust. If O establishes a revocable inter vivos trust and under it a trust continues after O dies, such a trust comes into being without the intervention of any court and in most states will not become subject to any court orders unless it is brought into court by the trustee or the beneficiary for the settlement of some trust matter. This is a non-court trust. A testamentary trust is brought into being by a court and is, from the beginning, under court supervision in most states. It is a court trust.

One of the differences between a court trust and a non-court trust may be in the effectiveness of a provision that enables certain beneficiaries to approve the trustee's accounts. Such a provision may avoid both the necessity of going to court to obtain such approval and the expense of a guardian ad litem to represent unborn and unascertained persons who may have interests under the trust. The provision with respect to the approval of accounts is fairly common in non-court trusts. Its absence in court trusts is probably due to the belief that if the court brings the trust into being, the court cannot be deprived of its authority to direct how the trustee's work shall be approved.

When a will pours over to a trust that the testator established in his lifetime, it may be contended that the combined assets form one trust and that it is a non-court trust; or that they form one trust and that it is a court trust; or that the assets in the inter vivos trust at the testator's death form a non-court trust and the assets added by his will form a court trust. Recent state statutes in this area adopt the view that one trust is formed and that it is a non-court trust.[105] The view adopted by these statutes should be adopted judicially without the aid of a statute.[106]

The objective of having the post-death benefits administered under a non-court trust may be accomplished without any serious diversion of probate assets. The revocable inter vivos trust may be only a shell with a nominal amount placed therein in O's lifetime. If the governing local law is to the effect that the assets poured from the will take on the character of the assets already in the receptacle that receives the pour-over assets, there is not likely to be any different result based on the quantum poured over as compared with the quantum previously in the receptacle. In fact, one kind of inter vivos trust, namely, an insurance trust, frequently has nothing of significance in it during O's lifetime, but on his death it becomes the collector of assets not only from life insurance but also from his will.

---

[105] See Colo. Laws 1959, c. 286; Conn. Gen. Stat. Rev. §45-173 (1958, Supp. 1959); Del. Code Ann., tit. 12, §3521 (1953); Fla. Stat. §737.19 (1959); Neb. Rev. Stat. §30-1806 (1943, Supp. 1957); N.C. Gen. Stat. §31-47 (1950, Supp. 1959); Pa. Stat. Ann., tit. 20, §180.14a (Purdon, Supp. 1959).

[106] See 1 Scott, Trusts §54.3 (2d ed. 1956). See also Wells-Fargo Bank & Union Trust Co. v. Superior Court, 32 Cal. 2d 1, 193 P.2d 721 (1948); State ex rel. Citizens National Bank v. Superior Court, 236 Ind. 135, 138 N.E.2d 900 (1956); In re York's Estate, 95 N.H. 435, 65 A.2d 282 (1949).

CHAPTER VI
Other Types of Inter Vivos Trusts and Family Annuities

The types of inter vivos trusts considered at this point range from the inter vivos trust which is subject to revocation by the settlor in conjunction with someone who will probably acquiesce in his wishes, so that for all practical purposes it is the same as the revocable inter vivos trust, to the inter vivos trust that completely and unequivocally removes the trust property from any semblance of control by the settlor. Usually, when the settlor decides to create an inter vivos trust other than a revocable one, he desires to accomplish two tax results: (1) that the income from the trust property not be attributable to him and (2) that the value of the trust property be eliminated from his gross estate. The cost of achieving these results is frequently the payment of a federal gift tax.

If the inter vivos trust employed in the estate plan does not eliminate the value of the trust property from the settlor's gross estate for federal estate tax purposes, will the trust property included in the settlor's gross estate pick up a new basis for federal income tax purposes on the death of the settlor? If the trust is one under which the income is payable to or on the order or direction of the settlor for life and is subject to a power to revoke or a power to alter, amend or terminate which rests in the settlor alone or in conjunction with one who does not have an adverse interest, the trust property included in the settlor's gross estate will acquire a new basis on his death.[1] If trust property of any other type of trust is

---

[1] See 1954 I.R.C. §1014(b)(2) and (3), quoted infra page 1381.

Revenue Ruling 58-395, 1958-2 C.B. 398, holds that where the power to revoke is in the settlor and others who do not have an adverse interest, the provisions of §1014(b)(2) and (3) apply to give a new basis to the trust property.

Section 113(a)(5) of the 1939 Code, as amended by the Technical Changes Act of 1953, 67 Stat. 615, covered the same situations as are described in §1014(b)(2) and (3).

In Rev. Rul. 55-502, 1955-2 C.B. 560, an inter vivos trust was involved. The trust provided that it could be modified, altered or revoked by the settlor and

included in the settlor's gross estate, it will also acquire a new basis on his death but by a different route and with slightly different consequences.[2]

In situations like those described in the preceding paragraph, what will be the basis of the trust property during the lifetime of the settlor? The answer to this question depends on whether the transfer in trust is or is not a gift. If it is a gift, then the basis to the trust of the property placed therein by the settlor will be the same as it would be in the hands of the settlor, except that if the basis (adjusted for the period before the date of the gift) is greater than the fair market value of the property at the time of the gift, then for the purpose of determining a loss, the basis will be the fair market value.[3] This basis, however, will be increased if a federal gift tax is paid with respect to the transfer, but such an increase cannot bring the basis up above the fair market value of the property at the time of the gift.[4] If the transfer in trust is not a gift or sale, then during the lifetime of the settlor the trust prop-

---

her husband during their joint lives and, if the settlor survived her husband, then by the settlor alone. The question to be resolved was whether, on the death of the settlor before her husband, the trust property obtained a new basis under 1939 I.R.C. §113(a)(5), as amended by the Technical Changes Act of 1953. The ruling holds that a new basis was not obtained because the power to revoke or change the trust was not completely in the settlor but was held by the settlor in conjunction with her husband. As a result of the decision in Hazel B. Beckman Trust, 26 T.C. 1172 (1956), Rev. Rul. 55-502 has been modified by Rev. Rul. 57-287, 1957-1 C.B. 517, in so far as the earlier ruling holds that §113(a)(5) of the 1939 Code is applicable only if the right to revoke or change the trust is completely and unqualifiedly in the settlor. Bankers Trust Co. v. United States, 156 F. Supp. 931 (Ct. Cl. 1957), is in accord.

[2] Section 1014(b)(9) of the 1954 Code, quoted infra page 1382, governs when the situation is not one covered by §1014(b)(2) and (3). When a trust comes under §1014(b)(9) and is also one where the income is not attributable to the settlor (as when the income is payable to another and the power to revoke is in the settlor in conjunction with a person who has a substantial adverse interest), §1014(b)(9) requires that the value at the date of the settlor's death (or one year after his death) be "reduced by the amount allowed to the taxpayer as deductions in computing taxable income . . . for exhaustion, wear and tear, obsolescence, amortization, and depletion on such property before the death of the decedent" in arriving at the new basis. The coverage given by §1014(b)(9) was not available under the 1939 Code.

[3] See 1954 I.R.C. §1015(a), quoted infra page 1383. In regard to adjustments in basis, see §1016. See also page 234 infra, note 152.

Revenue Ruling 57-543, 1957-2 C.B. 518, deals with a situation where the settlor of a trust died before January 1, 1954, so that §1014(b)(9) did not apply, and points out that, even though the trust property was includible in the gross estate of the settlor because of the power he retained to determine who would get the income, no new basis was obtained for the trust property as of the time of the settlor's death, but rather the basis provisions of §1015(a) applied.

[4] See 1954 I.R.C. §1015(d), quoted infra page 1384.

erty transferred will have the same basis it would have in the hands of the settlor.[5]

If the settlor successfully eliminates the value of the trust property from his gross estate by the transfer in trust, no change in the basis picture will be produced by his death.[6]

Even though the inter vivos trust does not eliminate the value of the trust property from the settlor's gross estate for federal estate tax purposes, the trust property may not be subject to claims on his death, and the significance of this fact in relation to the allowance of an estate tax deduction for various expenses of administration is the same as when a revocable trust is involved.[7]

1.   NON-TAX REASONS FOR CREATING TRUSTS OTHER THAN REVOCABLE INTER VIVOS TRUSTS

There are some instances where the settlor of an inter vivos trust that is not revocable is motivated by considerations which do not involve taxes or, at least, tax considerations are secondary.

a. *Desire of Settlor to Protect Himself Against His Own Indiscretions*

A revocable inter vivos trust is no protection against the settlor's own indiscretions because he can reach the property for any reason. A trust under which the settlor retains the right to the income for

---

[5] See 1954 I.R.C. §1015(b), quoted infra page 1383.

If under §1014(b)(9) a new basis is acquired on the death of the settlor because the value of the trust property is includible in the settlor's gross estate, will that basis take precedence over the basis that would otherwise be applicable under §1015? In Rosalie W. Post, 26 T.C. 1055 (1956), the settlor of a trust had retained the right to alter the terms of the trust, including the power to change the beneficiaries, as long as he did not revoke the trust or revest himself with any of the principal of the trust. The Commissioner contended that the gift was not completed until the settlor's death, so that the basis of the trust property was the value at the date of the settlor's death. However, the court held that, because of the irrevocability of the trust, the settlor's basis when the trust was established (the basis was lower than the market value at that time) controlled in determining the loss sustained by a beneficiary of the trust to whom the property had been distributed after the settlor's death. In this case the settlor died in 1945, and §113(a)(5) of the 1939 Code did not give a new basis to the property of the trust, even though its value was included in the settlor's gross estate for federal estate tax purposes.

[6] See notes 3 and 4 supra.

In Trust of Harold B. Spero, 30 T.C. 845 (1958), the court held that the basis of stock sold by a trustee under a trust which gave the trustee the right to invade corpus for the benefit of the settlor was the cost of the stock and not its fair market value at the date of the settlor's death. The settlor had the power to name anyone as trustee in the event of the death, resignation, or removal of the original trustee but had no power to remove the trustee.

[7] See discussion at page 127 supra.

his life but which cannot be revoked by him alone, or cannot be revoked at all, does prevent him from dissipating the principal on indiscreet adventures. The settlor, of course, is taxable on the income from such a trust because he has the right to receive it,[8] and the value of the principal of such a trust is includible in his gross estate for federal estate tax purposes.[9] The establishment of a trust under which the settlor reserves the right to the income for his life with remainder in someone else and with no power in himself, alone or in conjunction with another, to revoke, alter or amend the trust means that he has made a gift, for federal gift tax purposes, of the value of the remainder interest, even though the value of the principal of the trust is includible in his gross estate for federal estate tax purposes.[10]

b. *Importance of Making a Dependent Financially Independent*

There are circumstances which arise from time to time in a family where it may be desirable to make a dependent financially independent. No feeling of financial independence on the part of a beneficiary is engendered by a revocable inter vivos trust because the financial benefits to him may be cut off by the settlor at any time. The desired financial security may come, however, from an inter vivos trust that is not revocable by the settlor. Nevertheless, the settlor will normally desire that the trust be set up in such a manner that the income will not be attributed to him for federal income tax purposes and that the value of the principal will not be included in his gross estate for federal estate tax purposes.[11]

[8] See 1954 I.R.C. §677, quoted infra page 1374.

[9] See 1954 I.R.C. §2036, quoted infra page 1396.

[10] If the settlor in conjunction with one who has a substantial adverse interest may revoke the trust, he will have made a gift of the remainder interest to the same extent as when there is no power to revoke. See discussion of gifts at page 218 infra.

In Alice S. Paolozzi, 23 T.C. 182 (1954), a trust was involved under which the trustees were to pay the settlor so much of the net income as they in their absolute discretion deemed best for her interest. A gift over of the remainder was to take effect on the death of the settlor. Under the applicable state law (Massachusetts), the settlor's creditors had recourse to the full amount of the trust income for the settlement of their claims, even though the income was payable to her only in the discretion of the trustees. Consequently, it was held that the only gift for gift tax purposes made by the settlor was the value of the remainder interest. See also page 222 infra, note 146.

The federal gift tax that is paid may be taken as a credit against the estate tax to the extent allowed under 1954 I.R.C. §2012, quoted infra page 1390.

The advantageous tax result which may be produced if the remainder is given to charity is considered infra page 893.

[11] Where the settlor is legally obligated to support or maintain the beneficiary, §677(b) of the 1954 Code, quoted infra page 1375, must be kept in mind

c. *Protection of Family of Settlor Against His Financially Hazardous Business Ventures*

The settlor may be about to undertake a business venture that is financially hazardous. He may wish to make provision for his dependents so that they will not suffer financially if the business venture does not turn out as he hopes. A revocable inter vivos trust does not accomplish his objective because under some circumstances the power of the settlor to revoke the trust may be exercised for the benefit of his creditors.[12] If the trust is not revocable by him, however, creditors of the business venture may not be able to reach the property placed in trust. The transfer of the property in trust, of course, must be such that it cannot be set aside as a transfer in fraud of creditors, or the objective the settlor has in mind will not be accomplished.[13] Even though such a trust is motivated primarily by considerations other than those involving taxes, the settlor will normally desire that it be set up in such a manner that the income from the trust will not be attributed to him for federal income tax purposes and that the value of the principal will not be included in his gross estate for federal estate tax purposes.[14]

---

if anyone is given discretion to apply or distribute the income for such support. Likewise §677(a), quoted infra page 1374, may cause the income to be taxable to the settlor if the terms of the trust require that the income be applied for the beneficiary's support and maintenance. If the settlor has the power alone or in conjunction with another to apply the income for the support and maintenance of the beneficiary, or if the income must be applied for his support and maintenance, undesirable estate tax consequences may also result. See discussion at page 208 infra.

If the beneficiary is a dependent of someone other than the settlor, the points covered in the discussion at pages 713 and 730 infra must be kept in mind.

[12] See page 100 supra, note 11.

[13] The Uniform Fraudulent Conveyances Act provides as follows in §5: "Every conveyance made without fair consideration when the person making it is engaged or is about to engage in a business or transaction for which the property remaining in his hands after the conveyance is unreasonably small capital is fraudulent . . . without regard to his actual intent." And it is provided in §6: "Every conveyance made and every obligation incurred without fair consideration when the person making the conveyance . . . intends or believes that he will incur debts beyond his ability to pay as they mature, is fraudulent as to present and future creditors."

[14] See page 151 supra, note 11.

2. WHEN SETTLOR IS NOT TAXABLE ON TRUST INCOME

a. *Warning*

The federal laws which now govern in determining whether the income of an inter vivos trust will be taxable to the settlor are extremely complicated. It is easy to stumble in undertaking to eliminate from the settlor's gross income the income of the property transferred in trust. Although the goal may be attained under the law of today, the achievement may be nullified under the law of tomorrow. While tomorrow's law will not apply to previous years, it may apply to future years with respect to the income of trusts created today.

Natural human instincts cause most people to desire to retain control over their accumulated wealth as long as they live. The retention of such control is very costly from a federal income tax standpoint if the income from the accumulated wealth will be taxed in the higher brackets. Thus it is a phase of estate planning to explore with the client the over-all income tax advantage to his family if the income from his accumulated wealth is taxed to some other member of the family or to a trust as a separate tax entity rather than to himself. The client's enthusiasm for the results of the exploration will normally decrease as his control over family wealth must be decreased to accomplish the goal.

Experience shows that it is not sound long-range planning to place reliance on arrangements which, though presently effective, do not rest on a stable foundation, when the objective is to eliminate the income of the trust property from the settlor's gross income. The laws operating in this area are under constant examination and study and it is reasonable to prophesy that the results of this process will make it more and more difficult to shift the taxability of income from the head of the family to others in the family or to a trust by a transfer in trust for the benefit of the family.

One's background in this field would be incomplete without having a familiarity with the Clifford case, on the basis of which the so-called Clifford regulations were promulgated in the 1940's. The judicial reception of these regulations in at least one instance should be noted. Consequently, the case of Helvering v. Clifford is printed in full below and the case of Commissioner of Internal Revenue v. Clark, famous for its attack on the Clifford regulations, is also reported in full. The present-day detailed statutory provisions which are subsequently examined in detail stem from this background.

HELVERING v. CLIFFORD
309 U.S. 331, 60 Sup. Ct. 554, 84 L. Ed. 788 (1940)

MR. JUSTICE DOUGLAS delivered the opinion of the Court.

In 1934 respondent declared himself trustee of certain securities which he owned. All net income from the trust was to be held for the "exclusive benefit" of respondent's wife. The trust was for a term of five years, except that it would terminate earlier on the death of either respondent or his wife. On termination of the trust the entire corpus was to go to respondent, while all "accrued or undistributed net income" and "any proceeds from the investment of such net income" was to be treated as property owned absolutely by the wife. During the continuance of the trust respondent was to pay over to his wife the whole or such part of the net income as he in his "absolute discretion" might determine. And during that period he had full power (a) to exercise all voting powers incident to the trusteed shares of stock; (b) to "sell, exchange, mortgage, or pledge" any of the securities under the declaration of trust "whether as part of the corpus or principal thereof or as investments or proceeds and any income therefrom, upon such terms and for such consideration" as respondent in his "absolute discretion may deem fitting"; (c) to invest "any cash or money in the trust estate or any income therefrom" by loans, secured or unsecured, by deposits in banks, or by purchase of securities or other personal property "without restriction" because of their "speculative character" or "rate of return" or any "laws pertaining to the investment of trust funds"; (d) to collect all income; (e) to compromise, etc., any claims held by him as trustee; (f) to hold any property in the trust estate in the names of "other persons or in my own name as an individual" except as otherwise provided. Extraordinary cash dividends, stock dividends, proceeds from the sale of unexercised subscription rights, or any enhancement, realized or not, in the value of the securities were to be treated as principal, not income. An exculpatory clause purported to protect him from all losses except those occasioned by his "own wilful and deliberate" breach of duties as trustee. And finally it was provided that neither the principal nor any future or accrued income should be liable for the debts of the wife; and that the wife could not transfer, encumber, or anticipate any interest in the trust or any income therefrom prior to actual payment thereof to her.

It was stipulated that while the "tax effects" of this trust were considered by respondent they were not the "sole consideration" involved in his decision to set it up, as by this and other gifts he intended to give "security and economic independence" to his wife and children. It was also stipulated that respondent's wife had substantial income of her own from other sources; that there was no restriction on her use of the trust income, all of which income was placed in her personal checking account, intermingled with her other funds, and expended by her on herself, her children and relatives; that the trust was not designed to relieve respondent from liability for family or household expenses and that after execution of the trust he paid large sums from his personal funds for such purposes.

Respondent paid a federal gift tax on this transfer. During the year 1934 all income from the trust was distributed to the wife who included it in her individual return for that year. The Commissioner, however, determined a deficiency in respondent's return for that year on the theory that income from the trust was taxable to him. The Board of Tax Appeals sustained that redetermination. 38 B.T.A. 1532. The Circuit Court of Appeals reversed. 105 F.2d 586. We granted certiorari because of the importance to the revenue of the use of such short term trusts in the reduction of surtaxes.

Sec. 22(a) of the Revenue Act of 1934, 48 Stat. 680, includes among "gross income" all "gains, profits, and income derived . . . from professions, vocations, trades, businesses, commerce, or sales, or dealings in property, whether real or personal, growing out of the ownership or use of or interest in such property; also from interest, rent, dividends, securities, or the transaction of any business carried on for gain or profit, or gains or profits and income derived from any source whatever." The broad sweep of this language indicates the purpose of Congress to use the full measure of its taxing power within those definable categories. Cf. Helvering v. Midland Mutual Life Insurance Co., 300 U.S. 216. Hence our construction of the statute should be consonant with that purpose. Technical considerations, niceties of the law of trusts or conveyances, or the legal paraphernalia which inventive genius may construct as a refuge from surtaxes should not obscure the basic issue. That issue is whether the grantor after the trust has been established may still be treated, under this statutory scheme, as the owner of the corpus. See Blair v. Commissioner, 300 U.S. 5, 12. In absence of more precise standards or guides supplied by statute or appropriate regulations, [footnote omitted] the answer to that question must depend on an analysis of the terms of the trust and all the circumstances attendant on its creation and operation. And where the grantor is the trustee and the beneficiaries are members of his family group, special scrutiny of the arrangement is necessary lest what is in reality but one economic unit be multiplied into two or more [footnote omitted] by devices which, though valid under state law, are not conclusive so far as sec. 22(a) is concerned.

In this case we cannot conclude as a matter of law that respondent ceased to be the owner of the corpus after the trust was created. Rather, the short duration of the trust, the fact that the wife was the beneficiary, and the retention of control over the corpus by respondent all lead irresistibly to the conclusion that respondent continued to be the owner for purposes of sec. 22(a).

So far as his dominion and control were concerned it seems clear that the trust did not effect any substantial change. In substance his control over the corpus was in all essential respects the same after the trust was created, as before. The wide powers which he retained included for all practical purposes most of the control which he as an individual would have. There were, we may assume, exceptions, such as his disability to make a gift of the corpus to others during the term of the trust and to make loans to himself. But this dilution in his control would seem to be insignificant and immaterial, since control over investment remained. If it be said that such control is the type of dominion exercised by any trustee, the answer is simple. We have at best a temporary reallocation of income within an intimate family group. Since the income remains in the family and since the husband retains control over the investment, he has rather complete assurance that the trust will not effect any substantial change in his economic position. It is hard to imagine that respondent felt himself the poorer after this trust had been executed or, if he did, that it had any rational foundation in fact. For as a result of the terms of the trust and the intimacy of the familial relationship respondent retained the substance of full enjoyment of all the rights which previously he had in the property. That might not be true if only strictly legal rights were considered. But when the benefits flowing to him indirectly through the wife are added to the legal rights he retained, the aggregate may be said to be a fair equivalent of what he previously had. To exclude from the aggregate those indirect benefits would be to deprive sec. 22(a) of considerable vitality and to treat as immaterial what may be highly relevant considerations in the creation of such family trusts. For where the head of the household has income in excess of normal needs, it may well make but little difference to him (except income-tax-wise) where portions of that income are routed — so long as it stays in the family group. In those circumstances the all-important factor might be retention by him of control over the principal. With that control in his hands he would keep direct command over all that he needed to remain in substantially the same financial situation as before.   Our point here is that no one fact is normally decisive but that all considerations and circumstances of the kind we have mentioned are relevant to the question of ownership and are appropriate foundations for findings on that issue.   Thus, where, as in this case, the benefits directly or indirectly retained blend so imperceptibly with the normal concepts of full ownership, we cannot say that the triers of fact committed reversible error when they found that the husband was the owner of the corpus for the purposes of sec. 22(a).   To hold otherwise would be to treat the wife as a complete stranger; to let mere formalism obscure the normal consequences of family solidarity; and to force concepts of ownership to be fashioned out of legal niceties which may have little or no significance in such household arrangements.

The bundle of rights which he retained was so substantial that respondent cannot be heard to complain that he is the "victim of despotic power when for the purpose of taxation he is treated as owner altogether."   See DuPont v. Commissioner, 289 U.S. 685, 689.

We should add that liability under sec. 22(a) is not foreclosed by reason of the fact that Congress made specific provision in sec. 166 for revocable trusts, but failed to adopt the Treasury recommendation in 1934, Helvering v. Wood [309 U.S.], p. 344, that similar specific treatment should be accorded income from short term trusts.   Such choice, while relevant to the scope of sec. 166, Helvering v. Wood, supra, cannot be said to have subtracted from sec. 22(a) what was already there.   Rather, on this evidence it must be assumed that the choice was between a generalized treatment under sec. 22(a) or specific treatment under a separate provision [footnote omitted] (such as was accorded revocable trusts under sec. 166); not between taxing or not taxing grantors of short term trusts.   In view of the broad and sweeping language of sec. 22(a), a specific provision covering short term trusts might well do no more than to carve out of sec. 22(a) a defined group of cases to which a rule of thumb would be applied.   The failure of Congress to adopt any such rule of thumb for that type of trust must be taken to do no more than to leave to the triers of fact the initial determination of whether or not on the facts of each case the grantor remains the owner for purposes of sec. 22(a).

In view of this result we need not examine the contention that the trust device falls within the rule of Lucas v. Earl, 281 U.S. 111 and Burnet v. Leininger, 285 U.S. 136, relating to the assignment of future income; or that respondent is liable under sec. 166, taxing grantors on the income of revocable trusts.

The judgment of the Circuit Court of Appeals is reversed and that of the Board of Tax Appeals is affirmed.

Reversed.

[Mr. Justice Roberts wrote a dissenting opinion and Mr. Justice McReynolds joined in the dissenting opinion.]

PROBLEM

6.1. Today there is in general no federal income tax advantage as a result of an inter vivos arrangement which causes the income from property to be attributed to a wife rather than to her husband. Why? See Section 2 of the 1954 Code.

COMMISSIONER OF INTERNAL REVENUE
v. CLARK
202 F.2d 94 (7th Cir. 1953)

Major, Chief Judge.

These are petitions to review a decision of the Tax Court holding that the income of certain charitable trusts for the year 1946 was not properly taxable to the respondents, as asserted by the Commissioner. The two cases were considered together by the Tax Court inasmuch as each presented identical questions for decision. They are similarly presented to this court and will be treated accordingly.

There is no dispute concerning the facts as found by the Tax Court, which follow a stipulation entered into by the parties. However, even though only a question of law is involved, we think a statement of the facts is material.

Respondents (sometimes referred to as petitioners) are sisters. Forest Park Home Foundation (called the Foundation) was organized as an Illinois not-for-profit corporation in 1939. It is a donee, contributions to which are deductible under Section 23(o)(2) of the Internal Revenue Code. The purpose of the Foundation was to meet the need in the Peoria, Illinois, community for the care, maintenance and establishment of a home for the aged. Under its charter and by-laws, gifts could not revert to the donors and, in the event of the dissolution of the Foundation, its assets were distributable to other charities. The Foundation was organized by three Peoria citizens, of whom one, W. H. Sommer, was the father of the petitioners. Petitioners being interested in the Foundation's program, each, on December 1, 1941, executed separate and identical deeds of trust.   Such trusts contained the following provisions (in the language of the Tax Court):

"Each petitioner transferred 15,000 shares of the common stock of the Keystone Steel and Wire Company of Peoria, Illinois, to the Foundation which was trustee and beneficiary.   Each trust was to be irrevocable for five years, though it could be extended.   At the expiration of the term, the corpus of each trust, but no accumulation of income, would be returned to the settlor.   The trust agreements expressly provided that all income from the trust estate was to be applied to the general charitable purposes of the Foundation and was not in any way to be retained as part of the trust corpus. During the period of the trusts, the trustee was to have 'full and complete control of the trust assets, and all the powers and rights in and in connection with said trust assets, to the same extent as though the stock had been transferred to the name of Forest Park Home Foundation on the books of the Corporation.'   In the event of dissolution of the Foundation, the trusts' assets were to go to other charities, expressly prohibiting return to the grantors.   The trust agreements provided that the trusts could be extended, but forbade any shortening.   The trusts further provided that only a currently equivalent number of shares of Keystone stock were to be returned to the settlors at the end of the trust term without accruals or additions because of income or profits."

Six days after the creation of the trusts came the attack upon Pearl Harbor.   It shortly became apparent that the original schedule of five years for establishing the home was inadequate.   The rising costs of construction and the war economy made it evident that more funds, as well as more time, would be necessary.   Accordingly, on December 1, 1942, petitioners extended the irrevocable period of the trusts for at least five additional years to December 1, 1951, all other provisions remaining unchanged.   In the taxable year 1946, the Foundation was directed by a board of directors of nine members representing a cross-section of the Peoria community.   Neither of the petitioners was a director, but three of their relatives were.

Also (in the language of the Tax Court):

"Under the terms of the trusts petitioners had no power with respect to the administration of the trusts or the distribution of the income therefrom.   Moreover, the petitioners did not and have not attempted, either directly or indirectly, to influence or control the decisions of the board of directors of the Foundation as trustee or beneficiary under the trusts.

"The program contemplated by the Foundation has been carried out during the 10-year period in that a 125-bed home has been built and is occupied by inmates and the charity is functioning as intended by its founders.

"During the taxable year 1946, the Foundation received dividends of $42,750 on the 15,000 shares of stock transferred originally by each petitioner to the trusts dated December 1, 1941."

Further (in the language of the Tax Court):

"Petitioners received no benefits directly or indirectly from the trusts. Under the terms of the trusts petitioners retained no powers of disposition of income or corpus by revocation, alteration, or otherwise."

For the year 1946, petitioner Clark returned a net taxable income of $13,585.83, and petitioner Rutherford returned a net taxable income of $14,903.92. The Commissioner assessed a deficiency on the basis of $42,750.00 additional income to each petitioner, which represented the income received by the Foundation from dividends on the shares of stock transferred by the trust indentures to the Foundation. A deficiency was assessed against petitioner Clark for $27,946.62, and against petitioner Rutherford for $28,801.93. In view of the discussion to follow, it is interesting and perhaps of some pertinency to note that the Commissioner determined deficiencies against each of the petitioners for the years 1944 and 1945, upon the same basis that deficiencies were determined for the year 1946. However, as pointed out by the Tax Court, it was stipulated that there were no deficiencies for those years. Also, each of the petitioners created a trust indenture dated June 29, 1943, which was irrevocable until June 29, 1953, or for a period of ten years. These indentures contained the same provisions and were for the same purpose as the trusts created December 1, 1941 and now in dispute. The Commissioner determined deficiencies on the income from these 1943 trusts but, as the Tax Court stated:

"The respondent (Commissioner) now concedes that the dividends . . . are not taxable to petitioners because each trust had a duration of 10 years."

The Tax Court stated the question of law before it as:

". . . whether the settlor-petitioners should be taxed on the charitable trust income solely because the duration of the trust is nine instead of 10 years, since the settlors have given up all other economic and legal aspects of ownership. Respondent (Commissioner) concedes in his brief that if the trusts in question were for a period of 10 years, the income therefrom is not taxable to petitioners."

The Tax Court stated:

"Respondent contends that under the Clifford regulations, Regulations 111, section 29.22(a)-21, these trusts are nine year trusts and taxable."

The Tax Court, after pointing out that the trusts were irrevocable, were to run for a period of at least nine years as extended on December 1, 1942, and that petitioners during such time retained no power or control over either the corpus or the income, none of which was to be applied for the benefit of any member of petitioners' family group, concluded:

"We hold that the income of the trusts for the taxable year in question was not taxable to petitioners under section 22(a) of the Internal Revenue Code or Helvering v. Clifford . . . 309 U.S. 331 or Treasury Regulations 111, section 29.22(a)-21. We do not think Helvering v. Clifford, supra, or section 29.22(a)-21 of Regulations 111 were intended to or do apply to the income of a trust such as we have here."

It is not clear on what basis the Tax Court refused to give effect to the regulation relied upon by the Commissioner. It could have been because the court treated the duration of the trusts as of ten years, in which case the regulation was inapplicable; it could have been because the court thought the regulation should not be given effect retroactively, and it is possible that the court regarded the regulation as unreasonable and, therefore, void as beyond the power of the Treasury to promulgate.

Obviously, the question for decision here is whether the Tax Court erred in rejecting the Commissioner's determination of a deficiency in the income tax returns of the petitioners for the year 1946 and in holding that the income of the trusts for said year was not taxable to petitioners.

Section 22(a) of the Internal Revenue Code (26 U.S.C.A. 1946 ed., section 22) generally defines "gross income" as follows:

" 'Gross income' includes gains, profits, and income derived from . . . interest, rent, dividends, securities, or the transaction of any business carried on for gain or profit, or gains or profits and income derived from any source whatever. . . ."

The full sweep of this provision has been often explored by courts and others and we supect the process will continue indefinitely. Particularly is this so when the income in question is derived from property held in trust, as in the instant situation. Whether such income is that of the settlor, the trustee, or the beneficiary is oftentimes difficult to ascertain. The many cases furnish numerous guides to be employed in making such determination but the adjudicated law can hardly be said to be settled. In Helvering v. Stuart, 317 U.S. 154, 168, the court stated:

"Economic gain realized or realizable by the taxpayer is necessary to produce a taxable income under our statutory scheme. That gain need not be collected by the taxpayer. He may give away the right to receive it, as was done in Helvering v. Horst, 311 U.S. 112, Helvering v. Eubank, 311 U.S. 122, 125, and Harrison v. Schaffner, 312 U.S. 579. But the donor nevertheless had the 'use (realization) of his economic gain.' 311 U.S. at 117. In none of the cases had the taxpayer really disposed of the res which produced the income."

The cases disclose that many factors have been utilized by courts in ascertaining whether a trust-settlor has from the trust income realized an economic gain. The most important case perhaps and certainly the most controversial is that of Helvering v. Clifford, 309 U.S. 331. There, the court sustained the decision of the Tax Court which had held that the settlor was the owner of the corpus after the trust was created and was, therefore, chargeable with its income. The court mentions numerous factors which led to this conclusion, such as the short duration of the trust, the fact that the wife was the beneficiary, and the control which the settlor retained over the corpus. The court pointed out (page 335):

"In substance his control over the corpus was in all essential respects the same after the trust was created, as before. . . . We have at best a temporary reallocation of income within an intimate family group. Since the income remains in the family and since the husband retains control over the investment, he has rather complete assurance that the trust will not effect any substantial change in his economic position. It is hard to imagine that respondent felt himself the poorer after this trust had been executed or, if he did, that it had any rational foundation in fact."

The Court further stated (page 336):

"Thus, where, as in this case, the benefits directly or indirectly retained blend so imperceptibly with the normal concepts of full ownership, we cannot say that the triers of fact committed reversible error when they found that the husband was the owner of the corpus for the purposes of Section 22(a)."

It was the "bundle of rights" retained by the settlor from which the court concluded that the husband remained the owner of the trust property and, therefore, chargeable with its income.

Many cases have been decided since Clifford. A reading of these cases reveals that the doctrine there announced has led to some confusion and that its application has been found difficult in particular cases. We shall not attempt to discuss these many cases but we think it can be rather firmly asserted that they all in the main employ the factors enumerated in Clifford. The Commissioner appears to so recognize because he concedes that his determination of deficiencies in petitioners' tax returns for 1944 and 1945 was erroneous.

The Commissioner, in support of his determination of deficiencies for 1946, relies solely upon Treasury Regulation 111, promulgated under the Internal Revenue Code on December 29, 1945, and applicable to taxable years commencing January 1, 1946. The pertinent portion of this regulation is Section 29.22(c)-21, which provides:

"Income of a trust is taxable to the grantor where the grantor has a reversionary interest in the corpus or the income therefrom which will or may reasonably be expected to take effect in possession or enjoyment—

(1) within ten years commencing with the date of the transfer . . ."

Petitioners attack the regulation upon three grounds: (1) its application to the instant situation would give it a retroactive effect and, in any event, the trusts are not merely for nine years, as asserted by the Commissioner, but are ten-year trusts; (2) the regulation is unreasonable and arbitrary and, therefore, void, and (3) it is unconstitutional inasmuch as it deprives petitioners of their property without due process, that is, without a hearing on the issues existing between the taxpayer and the Commissioner and whch arise because of the deficiencies asserted by the Commissioner.

We agree with the petitioners in all three contentions. Assuming that the regulation is valid, it is not discernible on what basis it should be applied to the income of trusts which had been in existence for some four or five years prior to its promulgation. By such application, income from the trust property which the Commissioner concedes was not that of petitioners prior to 1946 becomes that of the petitioners in 1946 and thereafter. Moreover, we think the trusts were for the duration of not less than ten years, and certainly this was so on January 1, 1946, when the regulation became effective, and for that reason the regulation cannot be properly applied.

More important, the regulation is void because it is unreasonable and arbitrary. Our conclusion in this respect is closely intertwined with our view that it is also unconstitutional, and the two issues can be treated together. We recognize that courts have indulged in considerable liberality in sustaining regulations adopted by administrative agencies. But, as was stated in Manhattan General Equipment Co. v. Commissioner, 297 U.S. 129, 134:

"The power of an administrative officer or board to administer a federal statute and to prescribe rules and regulations to that end is not the power to make law — for no such power can be delegated by Congress — but the power to adopt regulations to carry into effect the will of Congress as expressed by the statute. A regulation which does not do this, but operates to create a rule out of harmony with the statute, is a mere nullity."

Under the relevant section of the Revenue Act, the question as to whether the income from the trusts was that of petitioners was one of fact. It has been so treated and regarded from time immemorial. It was a factual issue upon which the Tax Court was charged with hearing all relevant testimony and making its findings. As was stated in Hormel v. Helvering, 312 U.S. 552, 556:

"And the basic reasons which support this general principle applicable to trial courts make it equally desirable that parties should have an opportunity to offer evidence on the general issues involved in the less formal proceedings before administrative agencies entrusted with the responsibility of fact finding."

And again, on page 560, the court stated:

"Congress has entrusted the Board with exclusive authority to determine disputed facts. Under these circumstances we do not feel that petitioner should be foreclosed from all opportunity to offer evidence before the Board on this issue, however remote may be his chance to take his case out of the Clifford rule."

In the Clifford case (309 U.S. 331) the court stated (page 336):

"Our point here is that no one fact is normally decisive but that all considerations and circumstances of the kind we have mentioned are relevant to the question of ownership and are appropriate foundations for findings on that issue."

It must be kept in mind that the regulation does not merely create a rebuttable presumption; it is conclusive. When it appears that the trust is for a period of less than ten years, that ipso facto determines that the income is that of the settlor. If this regulation is to stand, it means that in reality there is no issue for the Tax Court to determine. There could be no purpose in the taxpayer offering or in the Tax Court hearing evidence as to the factors involved in the situation. In the instant case, if the Tax Court had given effect to this regulation, as the Commissioner urged, there would have been no occasion and no reason for it to consider the facts and make findings. They would have been immaterial.

Petitioners, after the creation of these trusts, rested secure in the belief that they were not the owners of the income derived therefrom and that it was of no economic benefit or gain to them. Every adjudicated case of which we are aware would have sustained that belief and we doubt if a competent lawyer could have been found who would have disagreed. The Commissioner tacitly concedes as much because he admits that the income was not that of petitioners for the years 1944 and 1945. Without any alteration in the trust indentures and without any change in the relation of any of the parties thereto, that which was not income of petitioners in 1944 and 1945 became such in 1946. This remarkable transformation results, according to the Commissioner, from the regulation under discussion. It is a result based upon fiction rather than the actualities of the situation. The result is so unreasonable and unfair as to be shocking. The regulation is in conflict with Section 22(a) and with all adjudicated cases. We think it is void.

As noted, the regulation which decrees that the income from a trust is that of the settlor for the sole reason that its duration is for a period of less than ten years creates a conclusive or irrebuttable presumption. Such a presumption states a rule of substantive law. This is in contrast to a rebuttable presumption which only states a rule of evidence and which the opposing party is entitled to overcome by proof. United States v. Jones, 176 Fed. (2d) 278, 288. And the Supreme Court has held that a statute which creates a conclusive presumption under circumstances closely akin to those of the instant case contravenes the Fourteenth Amendment if enacted by state legislature and the Fifth Amendment if enacted by Congress.

In Schlesinger et al. v. Wisconsin et al., 270 U.S. 230, the Supreme Court struck down as violative of the Fourteenth Amendment a statute of the State of Wisconsin which provided in effect that gifts of a decedent's estate made within six years of his death were made in contemplation thereof. The court (page 239) stated:

"The challenged enactment plainly undertakes to raise a conclusive presumption that all material gifts within six years of death were made in anticipation of it and to lay a graduated inheritance tax upon them without regard to the actual intent. The presumption is declared to be conclusive and cannot be overcome by evidence. It is no mere prima facie presumption of fact."

In Heiner v. Donnan et al., 285 U.S. 312, the court likewise struck down a congressional enactment which created a conclusive presumption that gifts made within two years prior to the death of the donor were made in contemplation of death, on the ground that the provision violated the Fifth Amendment of the Constitution. The court pointed out (page 324) that Congress had the power to create a rebuttable presumption, and stated:

"But the presumption here created is not of that kind. It is made definitely conclusive — incapable of being overcome by proof of the most positive character."

The court discussed the Schlesinger case (270 U.S. 230) and pointed out (page 325) that the only difference between the two cases was that the former considered an enactment of the Wisconsin legislature which violated the Fourteenth Amendment, while the case under consideration involved a congressional enactment which violated the Fifth Amendment. The court (page 327) stated:

"The presumption here excludes consideration of every fact and circumstance tending to show the real motive of the donor. The young man in abounding health, bereft of life by a stroke of lightning within two years after making a gift, is conclusively presumed to have acted under the inducement of the thought of death, equally with the old and ailing who already stands in the shadow of the inevitable end."

And further the court stated (page 329):

"This court has held more than once that a statute creating a presumption which operates to deny a fair opportunity to rebut it violates the due process clause of the Fourteenth Amendment."

In Hoeper v. Tax Commissioner of Wisconsin et al., 284 U.S. 206, a statute of the State of Wisconsin which authorized an assessment of tax against a husband computed on the combined total of his and his wife's income was held unconstitutional, in violation of the Fourteenth Amendment. The court reaffirmed its holding in the Schlesinger case (270 U.S. 230). The court stated (page 215):

"That which is not in fact the taxpayer's income cannot be made such by calling it income."

It thus appears that even Congress would be without power to create the conclusive presumption which the Treasury has done in the regulation under attack. It is even more certain that an administrative agency is without authority to promulgate such a regulation. We conclude it is void because it violates the Constitution and, in any event, is in conflict with the congressional enactment on the subject and is arbitrary and unreasonable.

The decision of the Tax Court is affirmed.[15]

---

[15] In Rev. Rul. 54-48, 1954-1 C.B. 24, it is stated that "the Internal Revenue Service will follow that Decision [Clark] in the disposition of other cases only if the issue and the facts in such cases are identical to those in the Clark case."

In Rev. Rul. 54-9, 1954-1 C.B. 20, it is concluded that "the transfer of real property to a trust for a 10-year period, for the benefit of grantor's children, with his wife as one of two trustees, with the corpus to go to the grantor's wife in the event of his death prior to the expiration of a 10-year period, and with a privilege of leasing back such property from the trustees constitutes a

b. *Factors Which Are Relevant in Determining Whether Settlor Has Eliminated the Trust Income from His Gross Income.*

The Internal Revenue Code of 1954 undertook to spell out in detail the circumstances under which the settlor would be taxable on trust income on the ground of dominion and control.[16]   If the sole basis of taxing the settlor on trust income is dominion and control, the justification must be found in these sections of the Code.[17]

An examination of the Code provisions discloses that the following factors are relevant in determining whether the settlor has eliminated the trust income from his gross income:

1. Can the income or principal of the trust return to the settlor?
2. Can the income or principal of the trust be used to discharge the settlor's legal obligations, including his obligation to support or maintain some person?
3. Can the income or principal of the trust be used to pay insurance premiums on policies of insurance on the life of the settlor?
4. If there is a power to control beneficial enjoyment, though no benefit may be conferred on the settlor, is the power in the settlor, in the settlor's wife, in a subordinate party, in an independent party or in an adverse party?
5. If there is a power to control beneficial enjoyment, though

---

transfer in form rather than substance.   Rental payments made to the trust by the grantor will not constitute deductible business expenses.   The grantor will remain the owner of the property during the term of the trust for purposes of federal income and gift taxes, and the rental payments when made will constitute gifts."   Revenue Ruling 54-9 is modified by Rev. Rul. 57-315, 1957-2 C.B. 624, in so far as the earlier ruling provides that the rental payments constitute gifts when made.   The later ruling holds that the rental payments constitute a completed gift for federal gift tax purposes, the value of which is measured by the present worth of the right to receive the net rentals from the property during the term of the trust, provided that the right to receive such rentals is, under the terms of the transfer and applicable state law, fixed or vested.

In Holdeen v. Ratteree, 270 F.2d 701 (2d Cir. 1959), the court held that the settlor of a trust was not taxable on the income where the only basis for claiming that he was taxable was that he exercised influence over the trustee's investment policies.   Additional litigation in this case is reported in Holdeen v. Ratterree, 60-2 U.S.T.C. ¶9671 (N.D.N.Y. 1960), and 61-1 U.S.T.C. ¶9184 (N.D.N.Y. 1960).

The following is a valuable article on the Clifford regulations: Alexandre, A Case Method Restatement of the New Clifford Regulations, 3 Tax L. Rev. 189 (1947). — Ed.

16 See 1954 I.R.C. §§671-677, quoted beginning infra page 1370.
17 See 1954 I.R.C. §671, quoted infra page 1370.

no benefit may be conferred on the settlor, does the power relate to income only, or to principal only, or to both income and principal?

6. If there is a power to control beneficial enjoyment, though no benefit may be conferred on the settlor, is the power extensive or limited as to the variations in beneficial enjoyment which may be made?

7. Do certain administrative powers exist?

The discussion which follows will reveal additional factors which may be significant in determining the taxibility of the settlor on trust income, but the ones listed are the most prominent.

c. Short-Term Trusts

While a person in a high income tax bracket may not be in a position to divorce himself permanently from any portion of his accumulated wealth, he may be able to part with it for some limited period of time. This would be true if his present high income tax bracket is largely attributable to earned income, which will substantially decrease on retirement, at which time he will need to depend more on his accumulated wealth and the income therefrom. If he can transfer the taxability of the income from his accumulated wealth to someone in a lower income tax bracket for the limited time he can get along without that income, its net worth will be increased. The Internal Revenue Code of 1954 permits such a tax result through the creation of so-called short-term trusts to last for ten years or more.[18]

The settlor of a short-term trust will be deemed to have made a gift of the short-term interest for federal gift tax purposes. The gift tax regulations provide tables for determining the value of gifts of various types of limited interests.[19] For example, a gift of an income interest to last for ten years certain is worth a little less than 30 percent of the value of the property from which the income is to come. If, however, the trustee is given discretion to pay the income beneficiary some of the principal, so that it becomes uncertain how much of the principal will return to the settlor at the end of the short-term period, the valuation of the gift becomes complicated.[20] The short-term interest is a present inter-

[18] See 1954 I.R.C. §673, quoted infra page 1371. It must be kept in mind that, though the requirements of §673 are met, the trust income may still be taxed to the settlor under §674, 675, 676 or 677, and thus a short-term trust must always be tested against these sections also.

[19] See Reg. §25.2512-5(f).

[20] In McHugh v. United States, 142 F. Supp. 927 (Ct. Cl. 1956), a trust was involved which was to endure for ten years or until the death of the income beneficiary, whichever event should first occur. The trust instrument gave the

est, so that the annual exclusion for federal gift tax purposes will be available, if the income is required to be paid periodically to the beneficiary.[21]

The value of the reversionary interest which the settlor has when he establishes a short-term trust is in his gross estate for federal estate tax purposes if he dies prior to the expiration of the short-term trust. The possible undesirability of carrying in the settlor's gross estate such an item must be weighted in determining whether to go forward with a short-term trust.[22]

[handwritten marginalia: "my qualify for gift tax exclu"]

[handwritten marginalia: "Revers int = in his GE"]

---

trustee discretion to invade corpus for the benefit of the income beneficiary when the trustee considered the income payable under the trust and the funds available to the beneficiary from other sources "insufficient to provide properly for the essential needs — such as food, clothing, shelter and illness expenses." The question presented was whether, because of the power in the trustee to pay out corpus to the income beneficiary, the entire value of the trust property should be included in determining the value of the gift. The court applied by analogy the charitable remainder cases where the trustee has the power to pay out corpus for the life income beneficiary of the trust, and concluded that there was a sufficient standard here to entitle the settlor of the trust to attempt to establish that payments of principal would not be made under this trust, and if he was able to establish that such payments would not be made, the value of the gift would be restricted to the value of the ten-year interest in the income from the trust property. Thus the court dismissed a request for a summary judgment in favor of the United States. For a collection of charitable remainder cases, see page 918 infra, note 53.

The court in Karl T. Wiedemann, 26 T.C. 565 (1956), was faced with the problem of determining the value of the gift of a remainder interest when a trust was established pursuant to the provisions of a decree of divorce. Under the terms of the trust the net income was payable to the divorced wife for life, with a provision authorizing the trustee to invade the principal for her support. The remainder interest was given to the settlor's daughter, and the court held that the value of the remainder interest was not to be reduced by the remote possibility that the trust principal might be invaded for the benefit of the divorced wife.

In Mildred Irene Siegel, 26 T.C. 743 (1956), a wife in a community property state accepted the terms of her husband's will, in which he purported to dispose of all the community property, giving her a life interest therein. In determining whether what the wife gave up exceeded in value what she received (if it did, the excess value would be a gift), the court held that the discretionary power in the trustees to invade corpus to insure the maintenance of the wife's standard of living did not increase the value of what she received to a point which exceeded the value of what she gave. The case was affirmed sub nom. Commissioner v. Siegel, 250 F.2d 339 (9th Cir. 1957).

[21] See Rev. Rul. 58-242, 1958-1 C.B. 251. The annual exclusion for federal gift tax purposes, which is restricted to gifts of present interests, is described in 1954 I.R.C. §2503(b), quoted infra page 1418.

If the short-term trust is one which gives the trustee discretion to pay out or accumulate income during the short-term period, the gift will not be a present interest and the annual exclusion will not be available with respect to it.

[22] If, after the death of the settlor, the trustee sells securities held in trust, what will be their basis? Suppose that the trustee does not sell the securities but delivers them, on the termination of the trust, to the person then entitled to receive them and this person sells them. What will be the basis of the securities thus sold? See Comment, Basis Problems Under Section 1014(b)(9)

When a short-term trust is established, it will normally be desirable to prevent the estate of an income beneficiary from becoming entitled to the income if his death occurs before the trust ends. A provision which terminates the trust in the event the income beneficiary dies before the designated term has expired will prevent such a result.[23] Another way of accomplishing the same purpose is to provide for a shift of the right to income to another designated person in the event the original income beneficiary dies.[24] Furthermore, it should be kept in mind that the death of the settlor before the expiration of the designated term might make it undesirable from the family standpoint to continue the original plan of distribution of the income. For example, it might be advantageous to make the income from the short-term trust available to the settlor's wife. A provision which shifts the income on the death of the settlor from the original income beneficiary to the wife will accomplish this result.[25] A provision which termi-

---

Resulting from Death of the Settlor-Reversioner of an Inter Vivos Trust, 23 U. of Chi. L. Rev. 672 (1956).

In Miriam Coward Pierson, 27 T.C. 330 (1956), the taxpayer's grandfather established trusts in which the taxpayer's father had a remainder interest. The taxpayer received part of this remainder interest by devise from her father on his death in 1925, and the balance from her mother on her death in 1940. The trust terminated in 1941, on the death of the life beneficiary, and the trust property was distributed to the taxpayer. The court held that, even though the trustee's basis with respect to the distributed property was greater than the value of the property distributed, no loss was allowable. The court then determined that the taxpayer's basis of the distributed property was the same as the trustee's basis so far as the portion of the remainder interest which came to her from her father was concerned, because the trustee had sold and reinvested the trust property after her father's death, and consequently, it could no longer be said that the taxpayer received the property by bequest, devise or inheritance from her father within the meaning of §113(a)(5) of the 1939 Code. As to the portion of the remainder interest which came to her from her mother, however, the taxpayer's basis was the fair market value at the time of her mother's death, because no sale and reinvestment by the trustee had occurred since that time. The case was affirmed in 253 F.2d 928 (3d Cir. 1958). See also Brandeis v. United States, 251 F.2d 719 (8th Cir. 1958), where the court held that a contingent beneficiary under a trust established by a will acquired the stock distributed to him on the death of the life beneficiary, as of the time of the testator's death, for the purpose of determining the basis of such stock. In Bauer v. United States, 168 F. Supp. 539 (Ct. Cl. 1958), the taxpayer acquired by inheritance a remainder interest in stock, and her basis following the death of the life tenant was the value of the stock at the date of the death of the decedent-remainderman from whom she acquired the remainder interest.

23 See Reg. §1.673(a)-1(b), quoted infra page 1493.

24 If a secondary beneficiary is given a contingent interest in the short-term income interest, such a beneficiary's interest is a future interest and the annual gift tax exclusion will not be available with respect to it.

25 If the settlor's wife is given a contingent interest in the short-term income interest, §2513 of the 1954 Code, quoted infra page 1419, will not be available to the extent of the value of the contingent interest in her.

nates the short-term trust in the event of the death of the settlor cannot be used without adverse income tax consequences unless the life expectancy of the settlor is more than ten years at the time the trust is established,[26] and even then such a provision will cause the entire value of the trust property to be included in his gross estate on his death; whereas, if the trust continues, some part of the value may be excluded.

When the settlor sets up a trust under which the income is to be paid to another for ten years and the principal is to revert to him at the end of that period, the income of the trust which under the controlling local law is allocated to principal — capital gains for example — will be taxed to the settlor each year.[27] Such income is held for future distribution to the settlor and is specifically made taxable to him by the Internal Revenue Code.[28]

Gains (as well as other income allocated to principal) can be prevented from being attributable to the settlor of a short-term trust by inserting in the trust instrument a direction to the trustee that gains be currently distributed to someone else, or a direction that they be accumulated until the trust terminates, at which time they are to be distributed to a person other than the settlor. In the latter case, the gains will be attributable to the trust in each year except the final year of the trust, and in that year they will be attributable to the distributee. It should be noted, however, that provisions which prevent the capital gains from being taxed to the settlor may increase the amount of the gift made by the settlor for federal gift tax purposes and that it may be difficult, if not impossible, to determine the extent of such an increase. If, however, the settlor is the trustee or one of the trustees, no gift of the capital gains should be deemed to have been made until the gains are realized.

The short-term trust may be one which gives the trustee discretion to pay the income to a designated beneficiary or to accumulate it.[29] The accumulated income, however, must not pass to the settlor on the termination of the trust.[30] Furthermore, if the trustee is the settlor or a related or subordinate person and has the power to pay out or accumulate income, the income will be

---

[26] See Rev. Rul. 56-601, 1956-2 C.B. 458; Rev. Rul. 58-567, 1958-2 C.B. 365.

[27] See Rev. Rul. 58-242, 1958-1 C.B. 251; Reg. §1.673(a)-1(a), quoted infra page 1493.

[28] See 1954 I.R.C. §677(a)(2), quoted infra page 1374.

[29] As to gift tax consequences if the trustee may accumulate income, see page 169 supra, note 21.

[30] See 1954 I.R.C. §677(a)(2), quoted infra page 1374.

When the short-term period ends, the principal could be returned to the settlor and the trust could continue on with respect to the accumulated income.

taxable to the settlor unless proper safeguards are provided.[31] Compliance with these safeguards, however, permits a husband to establish a trust to last for ten years, with himself as trustee, with power in himself to pay out the income to his wife or to accumulate it, with the requirement that all accumulated income go to his wife or her estate on the termination of the trust, and with a proviso that the trust will terminate on the death of his wife if she dies before the expiration of the ten-year period.[32] This trust will be a separate tax entity for the family income to the extent that it is not paid out to the wife.

If an accumulation trust is established and accumulated income of a previous year is paid out, the accumulation distribution may be subject to the throwback rule.[33] A distribution on the termination of the trust, however, even though it will include accumulated income, will fall within one of the exceptions to the throwback rule if the trust must last at least ten years.[34]

The short-term trust arrangement is available only to a person who has accumulated income-producing wealth which can be transferred to a trust. Thus the high-salaried executive who has not been able to accumulate income-producing wealth cannot avail himself of such a trust. Is there any way in which the high-salaried executive can make use of a short-term trust by borrowing money and placing the borrowed funds in the trust? In answering this question, keep in mind that in certain cases interest is not deductible where the interest paid for a loan exceeds the return from the borrowed funds.[35]

If a person desires to start a life insurance program for his son while the premiums on the insurance on the son's life are low because of his age, but he realizes that he will have to carry the premiums for a considerable period of time until his son is financially able to take them over, a short-term trust may be the answer. The policies on the son's life, once acquired, could be transferred to the short-term trust along with enough income-producing property to provide sufficient income to pay the premiums. The trustee would be required to use the income to pay the premiums. If the son died before the end of the short-term period, on the termination of the trust the trustee would be required to turn over the collected proceeds and undistributed income in a manner which would exclude the settlor as a possible

---

[31] The safeguards which must be provided are described in 1954 I.R.C. §674, quoted infra page 1371.

[32] See 1954 I.R.C. §674(b)(6), quoted infra page 1372.

[33] This rule is discussed at page 742 infra.

[34] See 1954 I.R.C. §665(b)(4), quoted infra page 1368.

[35] See Rev. Rul. 54-94, 1954-1 C.B. 53.

recipient.   The proceeds would not be in the son's gross estate for federal estate tax purposes as long as he had no incidents of ownership in the policy at his death and they were not payable to his executors or administrators.[36]   If the son survived the short-term period, the trustee would deliver the policy to him or to such other person as might be designated in the trust to receive it.

Once a short-term trust is established, care must be taken not to add any property to it unless the trust has at least ten years to run at the time of the addition.   Also, any postponement of the date specified for its termination should be such that the postponed date will be at least ten years from the date on which the postponement is made.[37]

It should be noted that a trust which is to last for the lifetime of the designated income beneficiary is protected by the short-term trust rules without regard to the life expectancy of the beneficiary.[38]

If the income of the short-term trust is irrevocably payable to a certain type of charity, then the short-term period can be reduced from ten years to two years.[39]   Where a person desires to make gifts to a charity of the type which qualifies for the two-year rule, and the gifts in any one year will exceed the maximum amount he can deduct for federal income tax purposes,[40] he would be better off to provide at least such excess from the income of a short-term trust so that it will not be taxable to him on its way to the charity.[41]

---

[36] See 1954 I.R.C. §2042, quoted infra page 1402.

[37] See 1954 I.R.C. §673(d), quoted infra page 1371.

[38] See 1954 I.R.C. §673(c), quoted infra page 1371.

[39] See 1954 I.R.C. §673(b), quoted infra page 1371.   The type of charity to which the income must be payable is described in §170(b)(1)(A)(i), (ii) and (iii), quoted infra page 1334.

The two-year rule will not apply if the income is not payable throughout the two-year period to one specific charity (although specified portions of income can be made payable to different charities) or if the trustee is given discretion to pay the income to any one or more of several designated charities. See Reg. §1.673(b)-1(b), quoted infra page 1494.

[40] See 1954 I.R.C. §170(b), quoted infra page 1334.

[41] It should be noted that the value of the two-year interest in the trust property is not deductible for income tax purposes.   Section 170(b)(1)(D) of the 1954 Code provides in substance that no charitable income tax deduction is allowable with respect to the value of any interest in property transferred in trust after March 9, 1954, if the settlor has a reversionary interest and at the time of transfer his reversionary interest exceeds 5 percent of the value of the property.   A reversionary interest is defined to include "a power exercisable by the grantor or a nonadverse party (within the meaning of section 672(b)), or both, to revest in the grantor property or income therefrom."   A power to control beneficial enjoyment without thereby revesting in the grantor the property or income therefrom (a power under §674) is evidently not a reversionary interest for the purpose of applying §170(b)(1)(D).   Thus a two-year

The Code provisions under examination apply only to trusts. If a legal short-term interest is transferred, will the transferor be taxed on the income of the legal short-term interest if the short-term period is less than ten years? The answer to this question will depend (1) on whether the transfer of the legal interest is deemed an anticipatory assignment of income, and (2) if it is not so regarded, on the extent to which the courts evolve a Clifford doctrine in connection with legal interests.[42]

---

trust for a proper charity, with a power in the grantor to commence at the end of the two-year period (which, even though it causes the income to be taxable to the grantor, under §674, after the two-year period has elapsed, does not permit the property or income to be revested in the grantor), would seem to be outside §170(b)(1)(D), so that the value of the two-year interest in the charity would be deductible by the grantor in the year in which the trust was established. Section 170(b)(1)(D) does not apply if the grantor retains a reversionary interest in property in which a short-term *legal* interest is given to a charity, and the value of the short-term interest should be deductible in the year of the gift. See Priscilla M. Sullivan, 16 T.C. 228 (1951).

If a trust for a term of years for the benefit of a charity is established and the remainder is given to a member of the settlor's family, the value of the interest given to the charity will be deductible for income tax purposes in the year the trust is established, up to the limit permitted by §170. A gift for gift tax purposes will have been made of the remainder interest. Section 25.2512-5(f), Table II, of the Regulations is used to determine the present worth of the right to income from property for a term certain for gift tax purposes, and presumably the table would be applicable for determining the value of a term certain in a charity for income tax purposes. The table is based on a $3\frac{1}{2}$ percent return. Thus, suppose a trust is established to pay to charity for ten years the entire income annually or an amount equal to a return of $3\frac{1}{2}$ percent per year based on the value of the trust property on the date the trust is established, whichever is smaller, with a provision that any income not payable to the charity in any year shall be accumulated, and with a direction that the principal and accumulated income shall be paid to a member of the settlor's family at the end of the ten-year period. Would a charitable deduction for the full value of the right to the income for the designated term be available if the amount did not exceed the limit set by §170? The points discussed above also have some relevance in connection with testamentary gifts of income considered infra page 893. For a case where the income was given to charities for a limited time with remainder to the family of the transferor, and the court recognized that a charitable deduction was available in the year the transfer was made, see Winthrop v. Meisels, 281 F.2d 694 (2d Cir. 1960), discussed infra page 896, note 38.

[42] Revenue Ruling 56-221, 1956-1 C.B. 58, holds that the income derived from property after the transfer of a legal life interest therein is includible in the gross income of the life beneficiary.

In Winters v. Dallman, 56-1 U.S.T.C. ¶9204 (S.D. Ill. 1956), a husband who had farms out on lease made what was in effect a lease of his interest in the farms, subject to the outstanding leases, for a period of five years in favor of his wife. The court held that the income during the five-year period was taxable to the husband and not to the wife. The case was affirmed in 238 F.2d 912 (7th Cir. 1956). It should be noted that the basis of the Court of Appeals decision was that the taxpayer had made an anticipatory assignment of income. Suppose that a person owning a farm transfers a five-year interest in the farm to his son, and his son then leases the farm to a tenant for the

PROBLEMS

6.2. A transfers property to T in trust. The trust is to last for eight years, after which the corpus is to revert to A or to his estate. The trustee is to pay the net income to the X charity. Will the income from the trust be includible in A's gross income? If so, how much of the trust income will be deductible in computing A's net income?

6.3. A transfers property to T in trust. The trust is to last for ten years unless A's son, S, dies sooner, in which event the trust is to terminate on S's death. On the termination of the trust, the corpus is to revert to A or to his estate. The trustee is to pay the net income to S. Will the income from the trust be includible in A's gross income? What is the basis of the securities placed in the trust by A? If the trustee sells securities placed in the trust by A, at a loss, to whom is the loss attributable? If the trustee sells securities placed in the trust by A, at a gain, to whom is the gain taxable? See Graff v. Commissioner, 117 F.2d 247 (7th Cir. 1941); Commissioner v. Wilson, 125 F.2d 307 (7th Cir. 1942). If A adds property to the trust one year after the date of its creation, will the

---

five-year period and collects the rents under the lease. Will the income during the five-year period be taxable to the transferor or to the son?

The taxpayer in Napoleon Palmieri, Jr., 27 T.C. 720 (1957), owned a house and permitted his parents to occupy it. The parents rented one room and collected the rent for it. The court held that the rental income received by the parents was taxable to the taxpayer on the ground that the arrangement involved an anticipatory assignment of rental income.

See, however, Shafto v. United States, 57-1 U.S.T.C. ¶9334 (E.D.S.C. 1957), in which the taxpayer assigned leases for five- and ten-year terms to his wife in writing. The court held that he had assigned a valuable property interest in the written leases to his wife and that the rents were the product of that interest and were taxable to the wife. The case was reversed in 246 F.2d 338 (4th Cir. 1957). In reversing the District Court, the Court of Appeals characterized the transactions involved as of the same general character as those in the Clifford case.

Revenue Ruling 58-337, 1958-2 C.B. 13, considered a case where a husband and wife executed a lease that was to continue for a period of ten years, with an option in the lessee to make two successive renewals for a period of five years each, and with a further provision that, in the event of the sale of the property, the lessee was to be given a thirty-day option to purchase. The lessors established a ten-year trust and assigned to the trust the right to receive all rentals payable under the lease. The trustee, however, had no authority to assign or in any way encumber the lease. At the end of the ten-year period, the trustee was required to turn the lease over to the lessors, including any extension or renewal thereof. The ruling held that where a fee-owner-lessor assigns a lease without assigning the reversion, only the right to the rents passes to the assignee and thus there is only an assignment of income. Furthermore, the ruling stressed the fact that the trustee was prohibited from transferring the lease and thus did not have full power and control over the assigned property. The ruling held that the income was taxable to the lessors.

income from the property so added be includible in A's gross income?

6.4. A transfers property to T in trust. The trust is to last for ten years unless A's son, S, dies sooner, in which event the trust is to terminate on S's death. The value of the property placed in the trust is $10,000. Under the terms of the trust, when it terminates, the trustee is to pay A $10,000 or the value of the property then in the trust, whichever is lower in amount. While the trust lasts, the trustee is to pay the net income to S, and on the termination of the trust he is to pay S (or his estate if he is not living) the corpus to the extent that it exceeds $10,000. If the trustee sells securities placed in the trust by A, to whom is any gain attributable?

6.5. A transfers property to T in trust. The trust is to last for ten years unless A's son, S, graduates from college before the end of that time, in which event the trust is to terminate when S graduates. On the termination of the trust, the corpus is to revert to A or to his estate. At the time the trust is established, A is in his first year in high school. The trustee is to pay the net income to S. Will the income from the trust be includible in A's gross income?

6.6. A transfers property to T in trust. The trust is to last for five years, after which the corpus is to revert to A or to his estate. The trustee is to pay the net income to A's son, S. Two years after the execution of the trust, A executes an instrument in which he postpones the date specified for the termination of the trust to a date five years beyond the original date. For what years will the trust income be includible in A's gross income?

6.7. A's will establishes a trust under which the income is to be paid to B for life. B directs the trustee to pay the income from the trust to C for the next ten years. Is the income during this ten-year period includible in the gross income of B if we assume that B has a life expectancy in excess of ten years? See Revenue Ruling 55-38, 1955-1 C.B. 389. Will the answer be any different if the life expectancy of B is less than ten years? See Revenue Ruling 55-34, 1955-1 C.B. 226.

d. *Power to Control Beneficial Enjoyment* [43]

Although the settlor has parted, either temporarily or permanently, with the right to the beneficial enjoyment of the income

---

[43] See generally 1954 I.R.C. §674, quoted infra page 1371; Westfall, Trust Grantors and Section 674: Adventures in Income Tax Avoidance, 60 Colum. L. Rev. 326 (1960).

and principal of a trust, he may be taxable on the income of the trust if the beneficial rights under the trust depend on the manner in which an outstanding power is exercised. Whether an outstanding power to affect beneficial enjoyment has such a consequence depends in some instances on the nature of the power,[44] in others on who are the possible beneficiaries of the trust,[45] and in still others on who possesses the power.[46]

A power to control beneficial enjoyment is one which enables the power holder to determine who will enjoy the income or principal of a trust. The power may relate only to income, only to principal, or to both. The tests which must be applied to determine whether the existence of the power will cause the income to be taxable to the settlor are not always the same when the power relates to income as when it relates to principal.[47]

From an estate planning standpoint, the important question is whether sensible trusts can be established which take advantage of the exceptions to the general rule that a power to control beneficial enjoyment will cause the settlor to be taxed on the trust income. Consider the feasibility of the following types of trusts; each one takes advantage of a particular exception to the general rule:

1. A transfers property to T (A's brother) in trust. The trustee is given discretion whether to pay income to B or to accumulate it. On the death of B, the trust property, including all the accumulated income, is to be distributed, free of the trust, to T, the trustee, if he is living, and otherwise to his issue then living, such issue to take per stirpes. Further provisions eliminate the possibility of any reversionary interest in the settlor. T has a substantial beneficial interest in the trust, which would be adversely affected by the exercise of the power and thus the exception

---

[44] For example, if the power relates to the principal and is limited by a reasonably definite standard which is set forth in the trust instrument, the power can be possessed by anyone, including the settlor, and the settlor will not be taxable on the income because of the existence of the power. See 1954 I.R.C. §674(b)(5), quoted infra page 1372.

[45] For example, if the only posible beneficiaries of the trust are charities, the power can be possessed by anyone, including the settlor, and the settlor will not be taxable on the income because of the existence of the power. See 1954 I.R.C. §674(b)(4), quoted infra page 1372. See also Winthrop v. Meisels, 180 F. Supp. 29 (S.D.N.Y. 1959), aff'd, 281 F.2d 694 (2d Cir. 1960).

[46] Section 674(c) of the 1954 Code, quoted infra page 1373, describes the situations in which an independent trustee must be in the picture and the power must not be in the settlor if the income is not to be taxed to the settlor.

[47] Compare the test which must be met under 1954 I.R.C. §674(b)(5), quoted infra page 1372, which relates only to principal, with the test which must be met under §674(d), quoted infra page 1373, which relates only to income.

to the general rule based on the power to affect beneficial enjoyment resting in an adverse party is applicable.[48]

2. A transfers property to T (A's brother) in trust. The trustee is required to pay the income to B and, in addition, the trustee is given discretion to pay the principal to B. On the death of B, the then remaining principal is to be disposed of for the benefit of persons other than T and in such a manner as to eliminate any possibility of a reversionary interest in the settlor. Although T, A's brother, is within the group presumed to be subservient to the settlor, a so-called subordinate party,[49] any distribution of principal pursuant to the exercise of the discretionary power given to T must be charged against the principal held in trust for the payment of income to B. A special exception covers this situation no matter who possesses the power.[50] A, the settlor, could possess the power in this case without adverse federal income tax results, but if he did, the value of the trust property would be includible in his gross estate for federal estate tax purposes.[51]

3. A transfers property to T (A's brother) in trust. The trustee is given discretion to pay the income to B or to accumulate it. On the death of B, the trust property, including all the accumulated income, is to be distributed, free of the trust, to B's estate. No matter who possesses the power to accumulate the income of this trust, the settlor is insulated from taxation on the income because the arrangement comes within the exception made to the general rule where the power is only one to withhold the income temporarily from the income beneficiary.[52] It is this exception that makes possible the establishment of an additional tax entity for husband and wife through the use of a short-term

[48] Section 674(a) of the 1954 Code, quoted infra page 1371, makes it clear that the general rule is inapplicable if the power is in an adverse party. See §672(a), quoted infra page 1370, for the definition of an adverse party. Section 1.672(a)-1(a) of the Regulations points out that a person has a substantial beneficial interest if its value in relation to the total value of the property subject to his power is not insignificant. See page 184 infra, note 66. The adverse party may be in some tax difficulty himself if he exercises the power. See Westfall, Trust Grantors and Section 674: Adventures in Income Tax Avoidance, 60 Colum. L. Rev. 326, 333, n.21 (1960).

[49] The definition of a "related or subordinate party" is set forth in 1954 I.R.C. §672(c), quoted infra page 1370. The terms "brother" and "sister" as used in §672(c) include a brother and sister of either the whole or half blood. See Rev. Rul. 58-19, 1958-1 C.B. 251.

[50] See 1954 I.R.C. §674(b)(5)(B), quoted infra page 1372.

[51] See 1954 I.R.C. §2038, quoted infra page 1397, and Lober v. United States, printed in full infra page 210.

[52] See 1954 I.R.C. §674(b)(6), quoted infra page 1372.

trust, without any significant change in their financial situation.[53]

4. A transfers property to T (A's brother) in trust. The trustee is given discretion to pay the income to B (a minor) or to accumulate it, and is also given discretion to pay the principal to B. If B lives to attain twenty-one, the trustee is required to pay him the then remaining principal and accumulated income. If B dies before that date, the trustee is required to pay the then remaining principal and accumulated income as B may appoint under a general power to appoint by will, and in default of appointment, the trustee is required to dispose of the principal and income for the benefit of persons other than T and in such a manner as to eliminate any possibility of a reversionary interest in the settlor. Two exceptions, the power to appoint by will exception[54] and the minority exception,[55] operate to protect the settlor from being taxed on the income of the trust no matter who is serving as trustee.[56]

5. A transfers property to T (an independent trustee) in trust. The trustee is given discretion to pay, in such amount or amounts as he may determine, the income to any one or more of the group including B, B's spouse, and B's issue who are living from time to time, or to accumulate it, and is given the same discretion with respect to the principal. On the death of B, the then remaining principal and accumulated income are to be disposed of for the benefit of persons other than T and in such a manner as to eliminate any possibility of a reversionary interest in the settlor. The independent trustee exception protects the settlor from the operation of the general rule in this case.[57] It should be noted that the independent trustee exception is not available if the settlor is a co-holder of the powers.

Most of the exceptions to the general rule are themselves subject to an exception which will cause the reinstatement of the general rule. This is sometimes referred to as the exception to the exception.[58]

[53] See discussion at page 172 supra.
[54] See 1954 I.R.C. §674(b)(3), quoted infra page 1372.
[55] See 1954 I.R.C. §674(b)(7), quoted infra page 1373.
[56] The utility of this type of trust will become apparent when §2503(c) trusts are examined. See page 243 infra.
[57] See 1954 I.R.C. §674(c), quoted infra page 1373.
[58] Section 674, subsection (b), paragraphs (5), (6) and (7), and subsections (c) and (d) of the 1954 Code, quoted infra page 1372, all except from the protection of the exception to the general rule certain powers to affect the beneficiary or beneficiaries or the class of beneficiaries designated to receive income

The income of a trust will not be considered taxable to the settlor under the general rule merely because, it may be applied or distributed, in the discretion of another person, the trustee, or the settlor acting as trustee or co-trustee, for the support or maintenance of a beneficiary whom the settlor is legally obligated to support or maintain, except to the extent that it is so applied or distributed.[59]

If the power to control beneficial enjoyment is not within one of the exceptions to the general rule, but relates only to a portion of the income or to a portion of the corpus, then the settlor is subject to the general rule only with respect to such portion.

---

or corpus. A power of the type referred to above which makes an exception to the exception otherwise available is not necessarily a power to determine who receives income or corpus. It need only be a power to add to the originally described beneficiary or beneficiaries or class of beneficiaries with respect to whom there is another power in someone to determine whether distributions of income or corpus are to be made.

If the power to add to the beneficiary or beneficiaries or class of beneficiaries is in a person who has a substantial beneficial interest in the trust, which would be adversely affected by the exercise of the power, will the exception to the exception operate? Section 1.674(d)-2(b) of the Regulations contains this sentence: "This limitation [the exception to the exception] does not apply to a power held by a beneficiary to substitute other beneficiaries to succeed to his interest in the trust (so that he would be an adverse party as to the exercise or nonexercise of that power)."

If the power to add to the beneficiary or beneficiaries or class of beneficiaries is one exercisable only by will, will the exception to the exception operate? In this connection §674(b)(3), quoted infra page 1372, must be examined. Section 1.674(d)-2(b) of the Regulations contains the following sentence: "Nor does the limitation [the exception to the exception] apply to a power held by any person which would qualify as an exception under section 674(b)(3) (relating to testamentary powers)."

Suppose that A establishes a trust with the X Corporation, an independent trustee, as trustee and gives the trustee discretion to spray income among his son S and S's issue or to accumulate it. If the trust instrument should provide that at the end of five years, the group among whom the income may be sprayed shall be enlarged to include A's daughter and her issue, the exception to the exception does not apply because the class of beneficiaries among whom the income can be distributed is defined by the settlor, A, and no power exists in anyone to enlarge the class. The outer limits of the class of beneficiaries is set by A, and the fact that within these outer limits the class changes from time to time in accordance with a formula set by A does not give any person a power to add to the beneficiaries designated by A to receive income or corpus. Suppose, however, the trust instrument provides that the trustee shall have discretion to spray income among such one or more of A's issue as A's wife may designate annually, or to accumulate it. A's wife does not have the power to direct the payment of income to anyone, but may merely determine annually the members of the group among whom the income may be distributed in the trustee's discretion, for A has designated the outer limits of the group. Is the exception to the exception applicable to such a case?

[59] See 1954 I.R.C. §674(b)(1), quoted infra page 1371.

PROBLEMS

6.8. A transfers property to the X Trust Company in trust. The trust is to last until the death of A's son, S, and on his death the trustee is to distribute the corpus to the Y charity. The trustee has the power at any time to alter or amend the trust, but no alterations or amendment may result in the payment of income or corpus to A or to his estate. The trustee is to pay the net income to S. Will the income from the trust be includible in A's gross income?

6.9. A transfers property to himself and S, his son, in trust. The trust is to last until the death of S, and on his death the trustees are to distribute the corpus to the Y charity. The trustees have the power at any time to alter or amend the trust, but no alteration or amendment may result in the payment of income or corpus to A or to his estate. The trustees are to pay the net income to S. Will the income from the trust be includible in A's gross income?

6.10. A establishes an irrevocable inter vivos trust. He is the sole trustee. The trust property consists only of shares of stock in a corporation, and A in his individual capacity owns a controlling interest in the corporation. A, as trustee, is required to pay the net income in equal shares to his children living on each income payment date. Is he taxable on the income from the trust on the ground that he can control the flow of income to the beneficiaries by virtue of his control over the corporation? See D. D. Query, 13 CCH T.C. Mem. 891 (1954). See also Babson v. Delaney, 56-2 U.S.T.C. ¶9828 (D. Mass. 1956).[60]

[60] Section 20.2055-2(b) of the Regulations provides in part as follows. in regard to the allowance of a charitable deduction in determining the taxable estate of a decedent: "The deduction is not allowed in the case of a transfer in trust conveying to charity a present interest in income if by reason of all the conditions and circumstances surrounding the transfer it appears that the charity may not receive the beneficial enjoyment of the interest. For example, assume that assets placed in trust by the decedent consist of stock in a corporation the fiscal policies of which are controlled by the decedent and his family, that the trustees and remaindermen are likewise members of the decedent's family, and that the governing instrument contains no adequate guarantee of the requisite income to the charitable organization. Under such circumstances, no deduction will be allowed. Similarly, if the trustees are not members of the decedent's family but have no power to sell or otherwise dispose of the closely held stock, or otherwise insure the requisite enjoyment of income to the charitable organization, no deduction will be allowed."

Consideration should also be given, in connection with Problem 6.10, to the possibility that the settlor may be deemed to have a power to designate the persons who shall enjoy the income from the trust property, a power which may cause the value of the trust property to be includible in his gross estate under 1954 I.R.C. §2036, quoted infra page 1396.

6.11. A transfers property to B, his brother, and the X Trust Company in trust. The trust is to last until all of A's children living on the date of the execution of the trust are dead, at which time the trustees are to distribute the corpus to A's issue then living, such issue to take per stirpes, and if no issue of A is then living, the trustees are to distribute the corpus to the Y charity. The trustees may pay the income to, or apply it for the benefit of, such one or more of A's children who are living from time to time, and in such amount or amounts as the trustees in their uncontrolled discretion may determine; and in addition, the trustees may pay the principal to, or apply it for the benefit of, such one or more of A's issue who are living from time to time, and in such amount or amounts as the trustees in their uncontrolled discretion may determine. Will the income from the trust be includible in A's gross income? If A retains the power to remove the X Trust Company as trustee and appoint someone other than himself in its place, will the answer be the same? See Harvey v. Commissioner 227 F.2d 526 (6th Cir. 1955); Warren H. Corning, 24 T.C. 907 (1955), aff'd sub nom. Corning v. Commissioner, 239 F.2d 646 (6th Cir. 1956). Compare Murray, Short-Term Trusts, 93 Trusts & Estates 1078, 1128 (1954).[61]

6.12. A is a surgeon, and his principal source of income is from his professional practice. He establishes an irrevocable inter vivos trust for a minor child of his, with the X Corporation as trustee. The trust agreement provides that the income from the trust property shall be accumulated until the beneficiary reaches the age of twenty-one years, and that when he reaches that age the principal and income are to be paid to him in regular installments. In the event of the death of the beneficiary prior to the exhaustion of the

[61] Section 1.674(d)-2(a) of the Regulations provides as follows: "A power in the grantor to remove, substitute, or add trustees (other than a power exercisable only upon limited conditions which do not exist during the taxable year, such as the death or resignation of, or breach of fiduciary duty by, an existing trustee) may prevent a trust from qualifying under section 674(c) or (d). For example, if a grantor has an unrestricted power to remove an independent trustee and substitute any person including himself as trustee, the trust will not qualify under section 674(c) or (d). On the other hand if the grantor's power to remove, substitute, or add trustees is limited so that its exercise could not alter the trust in a manner that would disqualify it under section 674(c) or (d), as the case may be, the power itself does not disqualify the trust. Thus, for example, a power in the grantor to remove or discharge an independent trustee on the condition that he substitute another independent trustee will not prevent a trust from qualifying under section 674(c)."

Suppose that the trustees designated in Problem 6.11 exercised their discretion to pay out principal by creating a new trust for the benefit of A's issue. Will A be regarded as the settlor of the new trust for the purpose of determining whether under 1954 I.R.C. §674, quoted infra page 1371, the income of the new trust is taxable to him?

trust funds, the balance then in the trust is to be paid to the beneficiary's estate. A assigns annually to the trust selected accounts receivable. In the year in which the assigned accounts receivable are collected, will the amount collected be includible in A's gross income for income tax purposes? See Revenue Ruling 55-2, 1955-1 C.B. 211.[62]

e. *Administrative Powers*

Although the settlor has parted, either temporarily or permanently, with the right to the beneficial enjoyment of the income and principal of a trust, and although no power to control beneficial enjoyment exists which would cause the income of the trust to be taxable to the settlor, he may be taxable on the income of the trust if certain administrative powers exist.[63] Thus a power to deal with the trust property for less than an adequate and full consideration, or a power which enables the settlor to borrow from the trust without paying an adequate interest and without giving adequate security, or the fact that the settlor has borrowed from the trust and has not repaid the loan before the beginning of the taxable year,[64] or the fact that a power of administration is exercisable

[62] Suppose that the author of a book assigns all his rights in the book, including the copyright and right to future royalties, to a short-term trust for the benefit of his child. If there is no basis on which the income of the trust is taxable to the settlor so far as §673 and §674, quoted infra page 1371, are concerned, will the income of the trust nevertheless be taxable to him? See Rev. Rul. 54-599, 1954-2 C.B. 52, which provides in part as follows: "Where a taxpayer by deed of gift transfers and divests himself of all rights, title and interest in the dramatization rights to his novel necessary for its production in a specific medium, such as radio, television, motion pictures or on stage, he is not liable for Federal income tax with respect to any income deriving from his former interest in these rights." See also Dwan, Splitting of Ordinary Income from Patents and Copyrights, 45 A.B.A.J. 513 (1959), in which are considered Commissioner v. Reece, 233 F.2d 30 (1st Cir. 1956), and Heim v Fitzpatrick, 262 F.2d 887 (2d Cir. 1959), two recent cases which held that an inventor was not taxable on income from a patent after the assignment of the patent.

[63] See 1954 I.R.C. §675, quoted infra page 1373.

[64] See D. D. Query, 13 CCH T.C. Mem. 891 (1954), where the court refused to include the trust income in the gross income of the settlor-trustee when the settlor had borrowed trust funds for his own use. The court said: ". . . the fact that the taxpayer borrowed the trust funds for his own use, repaying the amount in full with interest, is not sufficient cause when all other facts are considered, to hold that the income of the trust was taxable to him." It does not appear whether the loan had been repaid before the beginning of the taxable year in question. The Query case was decided under the 1939 Code, which did not contain any section like §675 of the 1954 Code.

Will the settlor of a trust be entitled to an interest deduction for interest he pays on a loan — first, where the income of the trust is taxable to him because of the existence of the loan and, second, where the existence of the loan to him does not cause the income of the trust to be taxable to him?

in a nonfiduciary capacity, is a danger signal but not necessarily fatal.

Is it desirable to include in the trust instrument a provision which describes the administrative powers referred to in Section 675 and which specifically negates their existence to the extent that their existence would cause the income from the trust property to be includible in the settlor's gross income? Such a provision is essential in any jurisdiction where local trust law recognizes that such administrative powers do exist in the absence of specific negation. Otherwise it is necessary only to make certain that the trust instrument does not affirmatively grant such administrative powers.

f. *Power to Pay Income or Principal to Settlor*

Although all the hurdles previously considered with respect to the elimination of trust income from the gross income of the settlor have been successfully negotiated, all may be for naught if there exists a power to pay income or principal to the settlor himself.[65] The existence of such a power will not cause the settlor to be taxable on the trust income, however, if the power rests in an adverse party.[66] The correlation of the provisions of the Code relating to a power to pay income or principal to the settlor with the short-term trust provisions eliminates the significance of a power that can affect only beneficial enjoyment for a period commencing after the expiration of the short-term period.[67]

[65] See 1954 I.R.C. §§676, 677, quoted infra page 1374.

[66] The words "adverse party" are defined in 1954 I.R.C. §672(a), quoted infra page 1370. In Peter B. Barker, 25 T.C. 1230 (1956), it was held that a person having a remote contingent interest under a trust was not an adverse party. To the effect that a family member may be deemed to have a substantial adverse interest, see Lillian M. Newman, 1 T.C. 921 (1943). If, however, the so-called adverse party is merely a sham, he will be disregarded. See L. B. Foster, 8 T.C. 197 (1947). See also page 178 supra, note 48.

In Inez De Amodio, 34 T.C. —, No. 92 (1960), the taxpayers were grantors and equal beneficiaries of a trust which was revocable by their joint action, and the court held that the net long-term capital gains were taxable to the grantors as though the trust did not exist. In so holding, the court rejected the contention that the interests of the taxpayers were adverse to one another.

Laganas v. Commissioner, 281 F.2d 731 (1st Cir. 1960), involved a trust and the settlor and his wife were trustees. The wife was entitled to 10 percent of the income and, on the termination of the trust, to 10 percent of the corpus. The trustees had a power to amend the trust. Under these circumstances the court held that all but 10 percent of the income was taxable to the settlor. Ten percent was excluded because as to that the wife, the co-holder of the power to amend, had an adverse interest.

[67] See 1954 I.R.C. §676(b), quoted infra page 1374, and §677(a), quoted infra page 1374.

Section 1.677(a)-1(f) of the Regulations, quoted infra page 1496, provides that

If the power to benefit the settlor relates only to a portion of the income or principal, the settlor will be taxable on the trust income on the ground of dominion and control only with respect to such portion.[68]   If the settlor is deemed to have dominion and control over only the income, he will not be taxable on the income allocated to principal, such as capital gains.[69]

The settlor may be taxable on trust income on the ground of dominion and control if the income is or may be applied to the payment of premiums on policies of insurance on the life of the settlor.[70]   Consideration should be given to the desirability of

---

the short-term exception does not apply merely because the grantor must await the expiration of a period of time before he can receive or exercise discretion over previously accumulated income of the trust.   Thus, if the income of a trust is to be accumulated for ten years and then will be, or at the discretion of the grantor may be, distributed to the grantor, the grantor is treated as the owner of the trust from its inception.

Revenue Ruling 57-363, 1957-2 C.B. 326, considers an irrevocable twelve-year trust under which income not distributed to the beneficiary is to be accumulated, and, on the termination of the trust, such accumulated income may be paid by the trustee to either the beneficiary or the settlor.   The ruling holds that the settlor will be treated as the owner of the trust property under the provisions of §677(a)(2), quoted infra page 1374, and the income therefrom will be taxable to him.

If at the end of the short-term period the accumulated income is to be added to corpus, and the settlor is to receive only current income produced thereafter by the augmented corpus, will the income accumulated during the ten-year period be taxable to the trust or to the settlor?

[68] In Barber v. United States, 57-1 U.S.T.C. ¶9377 (N.D. Ala. 1956), aff'd, 251 F.2d 436 (5th Cir. 1958), the settlor transferred $180,000 to a trust and reserved the right to retake $150,000.   It was held that 83 percent ($150,000 divided by $180,000) of the net income of the trust was taxable to the settlor.

[69] See Reg. §1.677(a)-1(g), Ex. (1), quoted infra page 1496.   See also Estate of Hiram Solomon, 27 T.C. 426 (1956).

See Rev. Rul. 57-8, 1957-1 C.B. 204, where it was held that the settlor of a trust was taxable on the capital gains as well as the ordinary income where the net income or principal of the trust was distributable to him in the discretion of the trustee, even though the trust could not be revoked without the consent of the settlor's wife, who had an adverse interest.

In Estate of Edward H. Wadewitz, 32 T.C. 538 (1959), the settlor of a trust was deemed taxable on accumulated income, even though she could not become entitled to any of the accumulated income unless she survived her husband.   Such income was considered accumulated for future distribution to her.

If it is determined that the income of a trust is taxable to the settlor on the ground of dominion and control, and as a consequence, the trust becomes entitled to a refund with interest, to whom is the interest on the refund taxable?   See Easley v. Commissioner, 228 F.2d 810 (9th Cir. 1955), cert. denied, 351 U.S. 923 (1956).

[70] See 1954 I.R.C. §677(a)(3), quoted infra page 1375.

H.R. 9662, which failed of passage in the Eighty-sixth Congress, contained a proposal to add a new subsection (c) to §677, under which discretion would be deemed to exist to distribute income to the settlor, or to apply income in the payment of premiums on policies of insurance on his life, or to apply or distribute income for the support and maintenance of a beneficiary whom the

specifically negating the existence of any power to so use the income where the objective is to eliminate the trust income from the gross income of the settlor.[71]

Income of a trust is not taxable to the settlor merely because it may be applied or distributed for the support or maintenance of a beneficiary whom the settlor is legally obligated to support or maintain, if the power to so use the income rests in the settlor acting as trustee or co-trustee or in any other person whether acting as trustee or not.[72] If the power is exercised, then the settlor will be taxed on the income to the extent that it is so applied or distributed.[73] There is no relaxation in the rules applicable to the taxability of trust income to the settlor where the income may be used to satisfy obligations of the settlor other than his legal obligation to support or maintain a person.[74]

---

settlor is legally obligated to support or maintain, even though the terms of the trust specify that the discretion relates only to corpus, to the extent the income is not required to be distributed currently.

[71] It has been suggested that if, under the applicable local law, a proper trust investment for a trustee is the purchase of life insurance on the life of the settlor of the trust, a literal reading of 1954 I.R.C. §677(a)(3), quoted infra page 1375, would cause the income of the trust to be taxable to the settlor, whether the trustee purchased such an investment or not. Section 1.677(a)-1 of the Regulations, quoted infra page 1495, does not deal with this matter. If such an interpretation should be given to §677(a)(3), it would be necessary to insert in a trust a provision prohibiting the trustee from so investing the trust property in order to avoid that section. It is believed that a proper interpretation of §677(a)(3) limits its operation to situations where the income of a trust is in fact used to pay premiums on insurance on the life of the settlor or where there is some guide in the trust instrument as to the amount of income that may be so used, as, for example, when there is a specific provision in regard to the use of income to pay insurance premiums or when there is in fact life insurance of the settlor owned by the trustee. See Corning v. Commissioner, 104 F.2d 329 (6th Cir. 1939).

[72] See 1954 I.R.C. §677(b), quoted infra page 1375. See also the reference to H.R. 9662 in note 70 supra.

[73] Section 1.677(b)-1(e) of the Regulations, quoted infra page 1497, provides that the general rule of 1954 I.R.C. §677(a), quoted infra page 1374, is applicable if discretion to apply or to distribute the income of a trust rests solely in the grantor, or in the grantor in conjunction with other persons, unless in either case the grantor has such discretion as trustee or co-trustee.
Revenue Ruling 59-110, 1959-1 C.B. 45, recognizes that a father may establish an employer-employee relationship between himself and a minor child so that the payments made to the minor will be deductible under 1954 I.R.C. §162, even though the minor uses the wages for his own support. If, however, the father *requires* the child to purchase things which the father is obligated to furnish, the deduction is disallowed.

[74] See Reg. §1.677(b)-1(d), quoted infra page 1497.
The role played by state law in determining the existence of a legal obligation of support is examined in Note, The Role of State Law in Federal Tax Determinations, 72 Harv. L. Rev. 1350, 1359 (1959). See also Reg. §1.662(a)-4, quoted infra page 1493.
Raymond M. McKay, 34 T.C. —, No. 110 (1960), brings out that in determining whether a person has contributed more than half of a child's support,

The rules applicable to the taxability of a settlor of a trust on the ground of dominion and control can be applied only if the settlor can be identified. Where a trust has several settlors, then the portion of the trust of which each is settlor must be determined.[75]

PROBLEMS

6.13. When will the settlor of an inter vivos trust be taxable on the income under Section 676 and not under any other section of the 1954 Code?

6.14. When will the settlor of an inter vivos trust be taxable on the income under Section 677 and not under any other section of the 1954 Code?

6.15. A transfers income-producing real property to T in trust. The property is subject to a mortgage on which A is personally liable. The trust is irrevocable. Under its terms the trustee is to use the income to pay off the interest and principal on the mortgage indebtedness, and the balance of the income, if any, is to be paid to designated beneficiaries. Will the income used to pay the interest and principal on the mortgage indebtedness be taxable to A? See Hays' Estate v. Commissioner, 181 F.2d 169 (5th Cir. 1950). Compare with the Hays case Revenue Ruling 54-516, 1954-2 C.B. 54. See also Edwards v. Greenwald, 217 F.2d 632 (5th Cir. 1954). Consider also Herff v. Rountree, 140 F. Supp. 201 (M.D. Tenn. 1956), *appeal dismissed without prejudice sub nom.* Rountree v. Herff, 234 F.2d 658 (6th Cir. 1956).[76]

6.16. A establishes a trust and assigns to the trustee policies of insurance on his life. A's wife transfers to the trust securities owned by her, and the income from these securities is to be used to pay the premiums on A's life insurance. What are the income tax consequences of this type of arrangement as compared with one

---

so that the contributor may claim the child as a dependent and take a $600 exemption for him under 1954 I.R.C. §151(e), payments made for singing and dancing lessons could be included. The court recognizes that expenditures for a college education would also count. What is relevant in determining contributions for support for the purpose of §151(e), however, should not be controlling in determining whether payments made out of a trust discharge the settlor's, or someone else's, legal obligation to support another.

[75] A similar problem is presented in connection with the federal estate tax provisions. See discussion at page 197 infra.

[76] Section 25.2503-3(c), Ex. (5) of the Regulations provides as follows: "The corpus of a trust created by J consists of certain real property, subject to a mortgage. The terms of the trust provide that the net income from the property is to be used to pay the mortgage. After the mortgage is paid in full the net income is to be paid to K during his lifetime. Since K's right to receive the income payments will not begin until after the mortgage is paid in full the transfer in trust represents a gift of a future interest in property against which no exclusion is allowable."

where the husband transfers securities owned by himself to the trust, to provide funds to pay the premiums? Will the income tax consequences be the same if the husband gives securities to his wife so that she will have property to place in the trust? See Goldsmith v. Sturr, 241 F.2d 797 (2d Cir. 1957). What will be the effect if the wife is the beneficiary of the trust or of the insurance?

6.17. A transfers property to the X Trust Company in trust. The trust is irrevocable. It is to last until the death of A's surviving child and then the corpus is to be distributed to designated beneficiaries.

  a. *First assumption:* Assume that the trustee is directed to apply all the income for the support and maintenance of A's children. To whom will the income that is applied for the support and maintenance of a minor child of A be taxable? See Estate of D. E. Hamiel v. Commissioner, 253 F.2d 787 (6th Cir. 1958).

  b. *Second assumption:* Assume that the trustee in his discretion may apply the income for the support and maintenance of A's children. To whom will the income that is applied for the support and maintenance of a minor child of A be taxable?

  c. *Third assumption:* Assume that the trustee is directed to pay all the income to A's children. To whom will the income that is paid to a minor child of A be taxable?

  d. *Fourth assumption:* Assume that the settlor, who is not a trustee, may direct the trustee to apply the income to discharge a legal obligation of the settlor. Will the income be taxable to the settlor if not so applied? See Hopkins v. Commissioner, 144 F.2d 683 (6th Cir. 1944).

g. *State Income Tax Considerations*

The preceding discussion is concerned only with the federal income tax rules which must be kept in mind when the objective is the elimination of trust income from the gross income of the settlor. The full story as to the taxation of the trust income will not be known until the state income tax laws of the governing jurisdiction are also examined.

3. WHEN THE VALUE OF TRUST PROPERTY IS NOT INCLUDIBLE IN THE SETTLOR'S GROSS ESTATE

An inter vivos trust which is effective to cause the income from the trust property to be attributed to someone other than the settlor for federal income tax purposes is *not* necessarily also effective to eliminate the value of the trust property from the settlor's gross estate for federal estate tax purposes. Likewise, an inter vivos trust which is effective to eliminate the value of the trust property from the settlor's gross estate for federal estate tax purposes is *not* necessarily also effective to cause the income from the trust property to be attributed to someone other than the settlor for federal income tax purposes. Thus one must make certain that the inter vivos trust meets the tests of both the federal income and estate tax laws, if the objective is to remove the trust property from the settlor's estate for both federal income and estate tax purposes.

a. *Valuation of Gross Estate Items*

Before examining the various federal estate tax tests, a brief consideration will be given to the valuation of items includible in a decedent's gross estate for federal estate tax purposes. The executor may determine the value of all gross estate items as of the decedent's death or as of the alternate valuation date (for most purposes, though not all, this is one year after the decedent's death) as provided in Section 2032 of the 1954 Code.[77] The intelligent exercise by the executor of his power of choice is a very important factor in the post-death handling of an estate.

The nature of gross estate items may present some special and difficult problems of valuation.[78] The asset which typically causes the most trouble is stock in a closely held corporation which has not been traded on the open market.[79] Another item which presents difficulty is a contingent interest.[80]

---

[77] Quoted infra page 1395.

[78] Certain United States Treasury bonds are acceptable at par in payment of estate taxes. Revenue Ruling 156, 1953-2 C.B. 253, holds that they must be included in the decedent's gross estate at par when used for such a purpose, though their value in the open market is less. If such bonds are not in fact so used, but could be, they nevertheless will be includible in the gross estate at par value, according to Revenue Ruling 156. But Bankers Trust Co. v. United States, 178 F. Supp. 267 (S.D.N.Y. 1959), disagrees and holds that the bonds are includible in the decedent's gross estate at their fair market value on the date of death (when alternate valuation date is not selected), whether used to pay estate taxes or not. The case was reversed in 284 F.2d 537 (2d Cir. 1960). See CCH Fed. Est. & Gift Tax Rep. ¶4220.45 for a list of United States bonds which may be redeemed to pay estate taxes.

[79] See discussion of closely held stock at page 976 infra.

[80] On the problem of the valuation of a contingent interest included in the decedent's gross estate, see Duffield v. United States, 136 F. Supp. 944 (E.D. Pa. 1955). In this case the court held that where the decedent had at his death a contract for contingent fees in the event of a recovery in a lawsuit, and these fees became collectible four years after his death as a result of the decision in the lawsuit, there was includible in the decedent's gross estate the value of the contract at the time of his death. The court distinguished be-

If the value of trust property in an inter vivos trust is includible in the gross estate of the settlor, the property in the trust on the selected valuation date which stems from the transfer by the settlor must be valued.[81] In Commissioner v. McDermott,[82] the settlor

---

tween including the value of such a fee contract and including the amount of the fees themselves. The latter is not permissible under the decision of Bull v. United States, 295 U.S. 247, 55 Sup. Ct. 695, 79 L. Ed. 1421 (1935).

In Estate of Joseph Nemerov, 15 CCH T.C. Mem. 855 (1956), the decedent was an attorney who had performed services on a contingent fee basis, and at the time of his death, the issues involved had not been determined. More than a year after his death, the issues were settled favorably to his claim and the contingent fees were collected. The court held that at the time of the decedent's death, the value of his services could not have been determined, and the subsequently recovered fees are not includible in his gross estate.

Estate of Isaac W. Baldwin, 18 CCH T.C. Mem. 902 (1959), held that a claim based on another's fraud and breach of fiduciary duty must be valued as of the decedent's death, and the amount so determined is includible in the gross estate, though it turns out that subsequent events substantially reduce the value of the claim.

In Estate of Samuel Want, 29 T.C. 1223 (1958), the settlor of an inter vivos trust retained a power during his life to change the beneficiaries who were given contingent interests under the trust, and the court held that the value, if any, of such contingent interests was includible in his gross estate. The case was modified, reversed and remanded on other points sub nom. Want v. Commissioner, 280 F.2d 777 (2d Cir. 1960).

[81] See Igleheart v. Commissioner, 77 F.2d 704 (5th Cir. 1935), in which the court apparently adopted the view that if the property placed in an irrevocable inter vivos trust is a gift in contemplation of death, the property in the trust at the date of the settlor's death is the property that will be valued for purposes of determining the amount includible in his gross estate. See also, in accord with the Igleheart case, Kroger v. Commissioner, 145 F.2d 901 (6th Cir. 1944).

Commissioner v. Gidwitz' Estate, 196 F.2d 813 (7th Cir. 1952), and Burns v. Commissioner, 177 F.2d 739 (5th Cir. 1949), both recognize that in determining the value of property in a trust when the value of such property is includible in the settlor's gross estate as a gift in contemplation of death, the income between the date of transfer and the donor's death from the property placed in the trust and property purchased with such income will not be included in determining the value of the trust property. See also Reg. §20.2035-1(e), quoted infra page 1509.

In Estate of Delia Crawford McGehee, 28 T.C. 412 (1957), the court considered the valuation of stock given in contemplation of death, when stock dividends were paid after the gift was made and before the death of the donor. The court held that the value of the stock dividends was includible in the donor's gross estate as part of the value of the transfers in contemplation of death. The case was reversed sub nom. McGehee v. Commissioner, 260 F.2d 818 (5th Cir. 1958), on the point of what is includible in a gift in contemplation of death. In reversing, the court held that stock dividends distributed as a capitalization of income of the corporation earned subsequent to the gift were not part of the gift. In regard to the consequences if the stock dividend had represented a capitalization of profits earned prior to the transfer, see Tuck v. United States, 172 F. Supp. 890 (N.D. Cal. 1959), aff'd, 282 F.2d 405 (9th Cir. 1960).

In Seaboard Citizens National Bank of Norfolk v. United States, 58-1 U.S.T.C. ¶11738 (E.D. Va. 1957), the court instructed the jury to determine the fair market value, on the date of the decedent's death, of certain real

established a trust with himself as trustee, and under the terms of the trust the trustee could pay out income or accumulate it and add it to corpus. When the settlor died, the question raised was whether the portion of the value of the corpus attributable to the income accumulations was includible in the settlor's gross estate. The court held that the accumulations were not transferred to the trust by the settlor, but instead represented a benefit derived from a prior transfer, and consequently that portion of the value of the corpus attributable to such accumulations was not includible in the settlor's gross estate.[83]

b. *Transfers in Contemplation of Death*

If the settlor of an inter vivos trust survives the creation of the trust by three years or more, the transfer in trust cannot be attacked as one in contemplation of death. If the settlor dies within three years after the creation of the trust, however, the transfer in trust will, unless there is proof to the contrary, be deemed to have been made in contemplation of death,[84] and the value of the trust property will be included in the gross estate of the settlor, regardless of the terms of the trust.[85]

PROBLEMS

6.18. The lawyer preparing an inter vivos trust designed to eliminate the value of the trust property from the gross estate of the settlor for federal estate tax purposes should anticipate the possibility of an attack on the transfer in trust on the ground that it is in contemplation of death. What can he do, prior to and at

---

property allegedly transferred in contemplation of death, and outlined for the jury the factors which are relevant in determining such value.

[82] 222 F.2d 665 (7th Cir. 1955).

[83] Compare Michigan Trust Co. v. Kavanagh, 171 F. Supp. 227 (W.D. Mich. 1959), where the court included in the settlor's gross estate accumulated income when the settlor had a §2038 power. The court referred to the McDermott case with respect but said, "We are satisfied that it should be limited to the particular facts, and that the reasoning of the court cannot be applied to the trust instruments involved in this case." The case was reversed and remanded in 284 F.2d 502 (6th Cir. 1960).

[84] See 1954 I.R.C. §2035, quoted infra page 1396.

[85] Suppose that a gift in contemplation of death is made by a husband to a third person, and his wife consents to have one half of the gift charged to her for gift tax purposes under 1954 I.R.C. §2513, quoted infra page 1419. Section 20.2012-1(e) of the Regulations, in discussing the credit for gift taxes paid under 1954 I.R.C. §2012, quoted infra page 1390, provides in part as follows: "If a decedent made a gift of property which is thereafter included in his gross estate, and, under the provisions of section 2513 of the Internal Revenue Code of 1954 or section 1000(f) of the Internal Revenue Code of 1939, the gift was considered as made one-half by the decedent and one-half by his spouse, credit against the estate tax is allowed for the gift tax paid with respect to both halves of the gift."

the time of the transfer, to defeat such an attack if it is made as a result of the settlor's death within three years? [86]

6.19. If the guardian of an incurably insane person makes a transfer of the person's property under court sanction, can the transfer be one in contemplation of death if the insane person dies within three years? See City Bank Farmers Trust Co. v. McGowan, 323 U.S. 594, 65 Sup. Ct. 496, 89 L. Ed. 483 (1944).

6.20. A transfers property to B. A dies within three years and the transfer from A to B is deemed one in contemplation of death. B is required to pay the proportionate amount of the federal estate tax that is attributable to the inclusion of the transferred property

[86] See Estate of M. Selnes v. United States, 58-1 U.S.T.C. ¶11749 (D. Minn. 1957); Gordon v. United States, 163 F. Supp. 542 (W.D. Mo. 1958); Des Portes v. United States, 171 F. Supp. 598 (E.D.S.C. 1959) (gift of insurance policies involved; court suggested that fact that transaction was carried through without legal advice indicated insured was not concerned with disposing of his property in contemplation of death); American Trust Co. v. United States, 175 F. Supp. 185 (N.D. Cal. 1959) (fact that gift was made by wife to her husband to enable him to retire completely and still be in position to afford travel was cited by court in holding that gift was not in contemplation of death); Butterworth v. Usry, 177 F. Supp. 197 (E.D. La. 1959); Smith v. United States, 59-2 U.S.T.C. ¶11900 (D. Utah 1959); Lockwood v. United States, 181 F. Supp. 748 (S.D.N.Y. 1959) (in holding that gift was one not in contemplation of death, court stressed fact that donor was unalterably opposed to theory of income tax and that avoidance of income taxes was dominant motive of gift); Siebrecht v. United States, 60-1 U.S.T.C. ¶11917 (D.S.D. 1959); Metzger v. United States, 181 F. Supp. 830 (N.D. Ohio, 1960) (gifts to son and daughter made within 18 months of death were claimed by Commissioner to have been made in contemplation of death, and to support his position, Commissioner referred to will of donor in which he said he was giving his entire estate to his wife because he had made provision for his son and daughter; court held gifts were not made in contemplation of death, relying on donor's lifetime desire to provide a home for his son and income for his daughter, to maintain good family relations); Hoover v. United States, 180 F. Supp. 601 (Ct. Cl. 1960) (evidence showed 86-year-old mother made substantial gifts to children to make up for failure of her husband to give children money while the husband was alive and in control of the funds; court found the gifts by the mother were not made in contemplation of death); Estate of May Hicks Sheldon, 27 T.C. 194 (1956); Estate of Salim Ackel, 17 CCH T.C. Mem. 110 (1958); Estate of Maggie M. Holding, 30 T.C. 988 (1958); Florence M. Harrison, 17 CCH T.C. Mem. 776 (1958); Estate of Louise A. Schneller, 18 CCH T.C. Mem. 654 (1959) (fact that decedent was contemplating marriage did not conclusively rebut presumption that gifts were made in contemplation of death); Estate of Hilda M. Lenna, CCH T.C. Mem. 1960-153 (transfers were made to keep control of family corporation in family and were deemed prompted by lifetime motives); Estate of Helen Brown Goodman, 19 CCH T.C. Mem. 1960-173 (fact that at time inter vivos gift was made to one child, decedent's will was drawn and equalizing gifts were made in will to other children was deemed basis of holding that inter vivos gift was made in contemplation of death as one step in an integrated plan for the disposition of the decedent's estate); Estate of William Block, 19 CCH T.C. Mem. 1960-220 (gift was deemed in contemplation of death, though there was evidence that decedent's attorney had advised him to make gifts to his children because there was some doubt that an out-of-state divorce obtained by his second wife was valid and, if it was not valid, she might claim a share of property owned by him at his death); Estate of Carl C. Lynch, 35 T.C. —, No. 18 (1960).

in A's gross estate.   Under Section 1014(b)(9) of the 1954 Code, quoted infra page 1382, B may acquire a new basis as a result of the inclusion of the transferred property in A's gross estate.   Can B increase the new basis by the amount of the estate tax paid by him? See Jules S. Bache Trust, 24 T.C. 960 (1955), *aff'd sub nom.* Michel v. Commissioner, 239 F.2d 385 (2d Cir. 1956).   See also Trust of Harold B. Spero, 30 T.C. 845 (1958).

6.21.   A transfers property to B and pays the federal gift tax due on the transfer.   Shortly after B receives the property he dies. More than two years after B dies but less than three years from the date of the transfer from A to B, A dies.   The transfer from A to B is deemed one in contemplation of death and the value of the transferred property is included in A's gross estate.   Will the gift tax paid by A be available to any extent as a credit against the estate tax imposed on A's taxable estate?   See Section 2012 of the 1954 Code, quoted infra page 1390.   Will the gift tax paid by A be available to any extent as a credit against the estate tax imposed on B's taxable estate?   See Section 2013(a), quoted infra page 1391. Will the estate tax paid on A's taxable estate be available to any extent as a credit against the estate tax imposed on B's taxable estate?   See Section 2013(a).[87]

c. *Transfers Subject to Sections 2036 and 2038 of the 1954 Code*[88]

Sections 2036 and 2038 overlap one another to a considerable extent and that is why they are considered together, but there are situations with which each deals exclusively.   If the income of a trust is required to be paid to the settlor, the value of the trust property is includible in his gross estate solely because of the provisions of Section 2036.[89]   Furthermore, only Section 2036 can apply if the power to designate who shall possess or enjoy the trust

[87] When a credit is available in the amount of the estate tax paid on a prior transfer, §2013(b), quoted infra page 1392, provides that the federal estate tax paid on the prior transfer is increased by any credit allowed against such a tax under §2012, quoted infra page 1390.

[88] Section 2036 is quoted infra page 1396, and §2038 infra page 1397.

[89] Suppose that the settlor releases his retained life interest and that the release is deemed made in contemplation of death.   Will the entire value of the trust property be includible in his gross estate as would have been the case if his life interest had not been released?   See Rev. Rul. 56-324, 1956-2 C.B. 999, which holds that under such circumstances the entire value of the property is includible in the decedent's gross estate.

In Allen v. United States, 60-2 U.S.T.C. ¶ 11965 (D. Colo. 1960), the settlor of a trust who was also the life income beneficiary sold her life interest shortly before her death.   The price was established by using actuarial tables.   Although the transfer of the life interest was made in contemplation of death, no part of the value of the trust property was includible in the settlor's gross estate because it was a sale and not a gift of the life interest.

property or the income therefrom is subject to a contingency beyond the settlor's control at the time of his death, such as the death of another person during the settlor's lifetime.[90] On the other hand, Section 2036 can apply only to retained powers of the settlor, whereas Section 2038 applies to acquired powers as well.[91] Section 2038 alone is applicable when the power involved enables the settlor to terminate a trust and thereby accelerate enjoyment by a beneficiary whose rights under the trust are already indefeasibly vested.[92]

Transfers which may come under Sections 2036 and 2038 are not limited to transfers in trust.[93] A trust is usually involved, however, when these sections are applicable.

Neither of the sections under consideration applies to a transfer by the settlor for an adequate and full consideration in money or money's worth.[94] While it is not usual for a transfer in trust to be made for a consideration, a transfer of this type now and then occurs.[95]

[90] See Reg. §20.2038-1(b), quoted infra page 1513. But note 1954 I.R.C. §2038(b), quoted infra page 1398.

[91] As to transfers made before June 23, 1936, §2038 also applies only to retained powers. See Reg. §20.2038-1(c), quoted infra page 1513.

In Fabian v. United States, 127 F. Supp. 726 (D. Conn. 1954), it was held that 1939 I.R.C. §811(c)(1)(B), which is substantially the same as §2036, did not apply to acquired powers. In this case the powers were vested in the trustee, and the settlor became a trustee subsequent to the date the trust was established.

Section 20.2036-1(a) of the Regulations, quoted infra page 1510, provides in substance that the settlor will be deemed to have retained a power under §2036 if at the time of the transfer there was an understanding, express or implied, that it would later be conferred on him.

[92] See Lober v. United States, printed in full infra page 210.

[93] In Estate of Oei Tjong Swan, 24 T.C. §29 (1955), a transfer was made to a family foundation not technically a trust, and the transferor had the power to amend and revoke the foundation. It was held that the value of the transferred property was includible in the transferor's gross estate under 1939 I.R.C. §811(d) (1954 I.R.C. §2038). The case was reversed and remanded on another point in Swan v. Commissioner, 247 F.2d 144 (2d Cir. 1957).

[94] See 1954 I.R.C. §2043, quoted infra page 1402.

[95] In Rev. Rul. 55-378, 1955-1 C.B. 447, there was considered the situation where property was transferred in trust for the benefit of the children of the transferor but the latter reserved the right to withdraw up to $2500 a year or all his living expenses. The children paid all the transferor's living expenses, which exceeded the net income, and thus the transferor never made any withdrawals. It was held that these facts did not establish a sale of the trust property.

In Chase National Bank v. Commissioner, 225 F.2d 621 (8th Cir. 1955), the court recognized that when the consideration for the transfer in trust is the discharge of the transferor's legal obligation of support for his children, such a transfer is supported by full and adequate consideration. The court in Estate of Robert Manning McKeon, 25 T.C. 697 (1956), held that the transfer of property for the support of the decedent's minor children, when the transferred property was to be used to discharge the decedent's legal obliga-

The powers referred to in Sections 2036 and 2038 are significant so far as the settlor's estate tax situation is concerned only if they are in the settlor alone or in him in conjunction with another. What appears to be a power covered by these sections may in fact be no power at all because it is controlled by a standard. If this is true, the sections may be inapplicable.[96] Also, if the power set

---

tion to support them, was a transfer for an adequate and full consideration in money's worth, so that only the excess of the value of the trust corpus at the time of his death over the cost of the children's support was includible in his gross estate. The relinquishment by the decedent's wife of her marital rights and right to support were not deemed a transfer for an adequate consideration in money's worth. In National Bank of Commerce in Memphis v. Henslee, 179 F. Supp. 346 (M.D. Tenn. 1959), the decedent was given custody of his daughter and he set up a trust under which he retained the right to use income to support her; the court held that he had not made a transfer for a consideration, distinguishing the McKeon case on the ground that there the custody of the child went to another and the trust set up to support the child was executed to release the father of any further obligation of support.

In Nourse v. Riddell, 143 F. Supp. 759 (S.D. Cal. 1956), the decedent and her two children transferred property owned by each to a trust under which all the income was payable to the decedent for her life, and on her death all of the principal passed to her two children. In the light of the decedent's life expectancy at the time the trust was established, the decedent gave away more than she received in return, and a gift tax return was filed on that basis. At the time of the decedent's death, however, it was established that, because of the length of time she had actually lived, she had received more than she had given away. The court held that the facts as they actually developed could be taken into account and that thus no part of the value of the trust property was includible in the decedent's gross estate because she did not give away any property in which she retained the right to the income for life. The filing of the gift tax return did not constitute an estoppel in this case because, almost immediately after it was filed, a contest was initiated on the ground that no gift had been made, and this contest was settled by a compromise agreement.

In Estate of Thomas W. Tebb, 27 T.C. 671 (1957), the decedent, in order to prevent any dispute with his widow over stock in a closely held corporation after his death, executed what was called an agreement with his sons, wherein he requested them to continue the business after his death and deposited the shares of stock in the corporation in escrow, with instructions that they be delivered to his sons on his death. The stock was delivered to the sons when the decedent died, and the value of the stock was included in his gross estate. The Commissioner contended that the sons should report the value of the stock in their income in the year of its receipt because it was paid to them as compensation for agreeing to continue the business. The court held that the stock was properly includible in the decedent's gross estate for estate tax purposes, and that the Commissioner erred in determining that the transfer was a bona fide sale for an adequate and full consideration in money or money's worth.

The decedent in Klein v. Halpin, 57-1 U.S.T.C. ¶11679 (S.D. Iowa, 1957), had transferred two farms to his wife in return for the right to receive the income for life from the two farms transferred and from two other farms owned by his wife. At the time of the transfer the decedent was seventy-two years of age. A jury found that the transfer of the two farms by the decedent was a transfer for an adequate consideration, and that consequently, the value of the two farms was not includible in his gross estate.

[96] In Jennings v. Smith, 161 F.2d 74 (2d Cir. 1947), it was held that the settlor of a trust did not have a power to alter, amend or revoke the trust

forth in the trust instrument does nothing more than spell out the rights the parties would have anyway, it is not a Section 2036 or a Section 2038 power.[97]

---

when the trustees, one of whom was the settlor, had a power to invade principal for the settlor's son or his issue if any one or more of them "should suffer prolonged illness or be overtaken by financial misfortune which the trustees deem extraordinary . . ." In Michigan Trust Co. v. Kavanagh, 137 F. Supp. 52 (E.D. Mich. 1955), the settlor as a trustee had the power to distribute corpus "in any manner or amount, should what the trustee deems a special emergency arise." The court agreed with the principle of the Jennings case, namely, that where a power of invasion is measurable by a definite external standard, there is no power to alter, amend or revoke the trust. However, the court held that the language did not constitute a definite external standard and it reached this result, even though a state court decision had held that the settlor's power was limited. The question as to whether there is a sufficient standard to prevent the power from being one to alter, amend or revoke is a federal question which a state court has no power to answer. Subsequent to the entry of the partial summary judgment, the case was transferred to the District Court for the Western District of Michigan, and in Michigan Trust Co. v. Kavanagh, 171 F. Supp. 227 (W.D. Mich. 1959), the court concluded that the principal and accumulated income were subject to such a power and hence were includible in the settlor's gross estate. The Court of Appeals affirmed the District Court for the Eastern District, but reversed and remanded the case in the Western District. 284 F.2d 502 (6th Cir. 1960). Biscoe v. United States, 148 F. Supp. 224 (D. Mass. 1957), also agreed with the Jennings case but determined that the standard must be set forth wholly in the trust instrument and cannot be supplied in part by external factors. Goyette v. United States, 57-2 U.S.T.C. ¶11710 (S.D. Cal. 1957), held that there was no power to alter, amend, revoke or terminate the trust involved, when the provisions for invasion of corpus were subject to a fixed external standard limiting the discretion of the trustee to invade corpus only if the beneficiaries were in need of funds for their proper maintenance and support. Also, it was held that the power in the trustee to determine what was principal and what was income did not invest the trustee with power to arbitrarily determine income to be principal or vice versa, and was not a power to change the beneficial enjoyment of the trust income or corpus. State Street Trust Co. v. United States, 160 F. Supp. 877 (D. Mass. 1958), follows the Jennings case in holding that where the settlor of a trust who is also a trustee has the power to invade corpus for the "comfortable maintenance and/or support" of the beneficiary, the settlor's power will not cause the value of the trust property to be included in his gross estate because the standard set forth creates enforceable rights in the beneficiary, and this result was reached even though the payments of corpus were to be made by the trustees "in their sole and uncontrolled discretion." The court held, however, that the value of the trust property was includible in the settlor's gross estate because the trustees had the power "to exchange property for other property" and because the terms of the trust did not require that the exchange be for assets of equal value, and thus the power existed to affect the interests of the life beneficiaries and remaindermen. The case was affirmed in 263 F.2d 635 (1st Cir. 1959).

In Estate of Pierre Jay Wurts, 19 CCH T.C. Mem. 544 (1960), the settlor retained the power to remove the trustee and substitute himself, and the court considered the case as one where the settlor retained the powers given to the trustee. The income of the trust was payable to the settlor's wife for life and thereafter to his daughter for life. The trustee was authorized to pay to the wife any part of the principal which the trustee deemed advisable "by reason of any emergency or by reason of any change in circumstances." Up to $30,000 of the principal could be withdrawn by the daughter during the wife's

Powers that are within Sections 2036 and 2038 are not always obvious. They may be concealed in the form of administrative powers given to the trustee.[98]

(1) Who Is the Settlor?

In order to apply Sections 2036 and 2038 where several different persons have contributed to the trust over the years, the identity of each settlor and the property contributed by each must be known.[99] In connection with the preceding discussion relating to federal income taxes, it was observed that the income tax rules could not be applied without knowing the identity of the settlor and the portion of which he was settlor,[100] although there a finding that the settlor did not have a power would not necessarily prevent the income from being taxable to him, whereas here the power must be in the settlor, alone or in conjunction with another, for a Section 2036 or Section 2038 power to be involved. It should also be noted in passing, by way of comparison of the income and estate tax rules, that the fact that a power is held by the settlor in conjunction with one who has an adverse interest will not take it out of Section 2036 or Section 2038 but will eliminate its significance for income tax purposes.

lifetime and additional amounts could be withdrawn by her with the wife's consent. The trustee had broad administrative powers including the power to borrow from anyone, the power to charge expenses against principal or income, the power to determine whether certain dividends constituted income or principal, and the power to do all acts that an owner might do. The settlor had no reversionary interest. Under the circumstances, the Commissioner determined that the value of the trust property was includible in the settlor's gross estate either on the basis that he had retained the power to designate who would enjoy income or principal or that he had retained the power to alter, amend, or revoke the trust. The court held otherwise on the ground that the powers of the trustee were not so broad as to permit the trustee to materially vary the enjoyment of the interests between the beneficiaries.

[97] See Reg. §20.2038-1(a)(2), quoted infra page 1512.

[98] See State Street Trust Co. v. United States, referred to supra note 96, and compare with it the case of Estate of Pierre Jay Wurts discussed in the same note. The following quotation from the Court of Appeals in the former case mentions various administrative powers: "Perhaps no single power conferred by the decedent on the trustees would be enough to warrant the inclusion of the corpora of the trusts in his estate. But we believe that the powers conferred on the trustees, considered as a whole, are so broad and all inclusive that within any limits a Massachusetts court of equity could impose, the trustees, within the scope of their discretionary powers, could very substantially shift the economic benefits of the trusts between the life tenants and the remainderman."

[99] In Rev. Rul. 55-683, 1955-2 C.B. 603, it is held that where the decedent contributed to a trust established by his wife, the value of the property contributed to the trust by the decedent is includible in his gross estate because his wife retained the right to revoke or modify the trust with his approval.

[100] See discussion at page 187 infra. For an income tax case concerned with the identity of the settlor, see Nicholas A. Stavroudis, 27 T.C. 583 (1956).

The transfer in trust by the settlor may be a completed gift, in whole or in part, for federal gift tax purposes, even though the value of the trust property is includible in the settlor's gross estate under Section 2036 or Section 2038. Where a completed gift is involved and the settlor's wife consents to have one half of the value of the gift attributed to her for gift tax purposes,[101] will she be deemed the settlor of one half of the transferred property? If so, the powers in the husband as to her half might not cause its value to be included in his gross estate.[102] If neither of the sections would apply to the husband as settlor, but one of them might apply to the wife as settlor, then it would be important to know whether the wife is regarded as the settlor of the one half she consents to have attributed to her for federal gift tax purposes. Revenue Ruling 54-246 [103] takes the position that the wife is not the settlor of any portion of the trust when she gives such consent for gift tax purposes.

The rearrangement of property disposed of by will, either pursuant to a compromise or an agreement, when as a result of the rearrangement property is put in trust, may create some difficulty in determining who is the settlor of the trust.[104]

---

[101] See 1954 I.R.C. §2513, quoted infra page 1419 and discussed infra page 236.

[102] If the husband is not the settlor, the powers in him would be controlled by 1954 I.R.C. §2041, quoted infra page 1409, for estate tax purposes.

[103] 1954-1 C.B. 179.

[104] See Bailey v. Ratterre discussed supra page 75, note 60.

In Estate of Nettie M. Adams, 16 CCH T.C. Mem. 1130 (1957), a will disposing of Iowa land was involved. The will provided that the distribution of the land was to be subject to the dower rights of the testator's widow. The widow entered into an agreement with the recipient of the Iowa land, under which she would receive one third of the proceeds from the operation of the land. On the death of the widow, the Commissioner included in her gross estate one third of the value of the Iowa farm, contending that her dower interest preserved by the will meant one third in fee, and that thus she had made a transfer with a life interest retained. The court held that the testator's intention was to give his widow only a life interest, and that therefore she had made no transfer with a life interest reserved.

Peoples First National Bank and Trust Co. v. United States, 137 F. Supp. 482 (W.D. Pa. 1956), involved a beneficiary under a will who waived her rights in return for a conveyance to her, by other beneficiaries under the will, of a life interest in land, with a general power to dispose of the land by deed. Under these circumstances, the court held that she created the life interest in the land and created the power of appointment she had over it. If she had not been deemed the creator of the life interest and of the power, she would have had a pre-1942 general power of appointment which would not have caused the value of the land to be included in her gross estate, because the power had not been exercised. The case was reversed in 241 F.2d 420 (3d Cir. 1957). In reversing the District Court's decision the Court of Appeals advanced two grounds: (1) that there was no transfer by the decedent; and (2) that even if there had been a transfer, the waiver by the decedent of her rights

The nominal settlor of a trust may not be the one that counts for tax purposes. Such is the case when a person receives property from another with the understanding that he will place it in trust.[105]

In Lehman v. Commissioner[106] reciprocal trusts were set up by two brothers. Each brother, in the trust that he established, made the other brother the life income beneficiary, with remainder to the life income beneficiary's issue. The court held that each brother set up the trust established by him in consideration of the other brother doing likewise and, consequently, each brother would be deemed the settlor, not of the trust which he in fact established, but of the trust of which he was the income beneficiary.[107]

---

amounted to a compromise and a bona fide sale for an adequate consideration in money's worth.

In Estate of Bernard E. Denzer, 29 T.C. 237 (1957), the decedent was a beneficiary under a trust established by his father, and under its terms the decedent could alter and amend the trust with the consent of the trustee and could designate by his will who would take the property on his death. Litigation developed between the trustee and the beneficiaries under the trust and was settled by giving the decedent one half of the corpus and the income from the other half, but the decedent had to relinquish all power over the other half, including his power to dispose of it by will. It was held that the decedent did not create the trust as to the half of the corpus from which he was entitled to receive only income, and that therefore the trust property was not includible in his gross estate.

[105] In Bartron v. United States, 59-2 U.S.T.C. ¶11879 (D.S.D. 1959), the decedent was not deemed the settlor of a trust where she signed the trust agreement as settlor because she was acting pursuant to the demand which had been made by her husband, who furnished the property that went into the trust. The decedent had a life interest, and hence it was essential to determine whether she was the creator of the trust.

In Mary Lois K. McIntosh, 25 T.C. 794 (1956), *aff'd, sub nom.* Estate of Mary Lois K. McIntosh v. Commissioner, 248 F.2d 181 (2d Cir. 1957), *cert. denied,* 355 U.S. 923 (1958), a trust was established through a nominee, and it was held that though the decedent was not the nominal settlor of the trust, she was the real settlor.

An interesting variant on the problem of who is the settlor is presented by Marva Trotter Barrow Spaulding, 27 T.C. 479 (1956), which relates to transfers made by Joe Louis, the former heavyweight champion of the world. He entered into an agreement with his wife, pending divorce, under which he was to pay her a certain portion of his earnings from professional boxing and other activities, and she was obligated to apply 50 percent of the amounts received by her for the purpose of creating trusts for their children. He made transfers to her in years in which he was insolvent, and she used 50 percent of the funds received to establish the trusts. The court held that Joe Louis was the settlor of these trusts, and, consequently, the trustee of the funds could be held to a transferee liability with respect to the income taxes owed by Joe Louis in the years in which he made the transfers to his wife. The case was affirmed sub nom. First National Bank of Chicago v. Commissioner, 255 F.2d 759 (7th Cir. 1958).

[106] 109 F.2d 99 (2d Cir. 1940), *cert. denied,* 310 U.S. 637 (1940).

[107] See Kanter v. United States, 262 F.2d 761 (9th Cir. 1959), where a mother

PROBLEMS

6.22. H creates an irrevocable trust for the benefit of his children and names himself and his wife as trustees. Only his wife has the power to shift the interests of the children in the event they should make marriages not deemed suitable. W, H's wife, creates an identical irrevocable trust, but in her trust only H has the power to shift the interests of children in the event they make undesirable marriages. W dies. Should the value of the property in

---

created three trusts for her children and made each child a trustee of another child's trust, and it was held that the beneficiary had control of his trust for income tax purposes.

For a case in which the taxpayer, rather than the government, sought to invoke the reciprocal trust doctrine, see Hill v. Commissioner, 229 F.2d 237 (2d Cir. 1956).

In Estate of Carl J. Guenzel, 28 T.C. 59 (1957), a husband and wife each established irrevocable trusts wherein each named the other as the initial income beneficiary, but each reserved a secondary life income in the trust actually established by him or her. The wife died first and the value of the property in the trust created by the husband was included in the wife's gross estate on the ground that she was the creator of the trust under the reciprocal trust doctrine. Thereafter the husband gave up his life interest in the trust which was in fact created by his wife, but retained the life interest that came to him on the death of his wife in the trust which he had actually established. Later, when the husband died, the Commissioner claimed that the value of the trust actually created by the husband should be included in his gross estate. The court held that the Commissioner was correct and it was no defense that the value of the property in this same trust had been included in the wife's gross estate on the theory that she would be deemed the creator of it under the reciprocal trust doctrine. Also, the husband's estate was not entitled to any relief under the property previously taxed doctrine because he succeeded to the enjoyment of this property by a trust instrument which he himself had executed and not by gift or inheritance from another. The case was affirmed sub nom. Estate of Carl J. Guenzel v. Commissioner, 258 F.2d 248 (8th Cir. 1958).

The court in Estate of Florence B. Moreno, 28 T.C. 889 (1957), *aff'd, sub nom.* Estate of Florence B. Moreno v. Commissioner, 260 F.2d 389 (8th Cir. 1958), followed the Lehman case and applied the reciprocal trust doctrine where the subject matter of each trust was paid-up life insurance.

Revenue Ruling 57-422, 1957-2 C.B. 617, follows the Lehman case in a situation where a husband transferred 1000 shares of stock in trust to pay the income to his wife for her life, with the remainder over to their children, and at the same time his wife transferred 750 shares of the same stock in trust to pay the income to him for life, with remainder over to their children. To the extent of 750 shares of stock, each transferror is treated as the settlor of the trust in which he or she is the life beneficiary.

In Estates of Laura Carter and Ernest Trow Carter, 31 T.C. 1148 (1959), husband and wife established trusts on successive days. Under the husband's trust, the income was to go to the wife, with remainder to children and grandchildren. Under the wife's trust, the income was to go to the husband, with remainder in slightly different terms to children and grandchildren. The court included the value of the husband's trust in the wife's gross estate and the value of the wife's trust in the husband's gross estate.

H's trust, the one in which W has a power to alter or amend, be included in the wife's gross estate for federal estate tax purposes? See Newberry's Estate v. Commissioner, 201 F.2d 874 (3d Cir. 1953); McLain v. Jarecki, 232 F.2d 211 (7th Cir. 1956). See also Hepler and Bebeneck, The Taxation of Reciprocal Trusts, 30 Notre Dame Law. 149 (1954).

6.23. Suppose that H in his will establishes a trust under which his wife, W, is entitled to the income for her life, and on her death the principal is to be paid to her children. Under the applicable local law the wife is entitled to renounce her husband's will and take outright one third of his property. In order to prevent the wife from exercising her power to renounce, all interested parties agree that the testamentary trust shall be terminated and the trust property placed in a new trust under which the wife will be entitled to all the income and, in the discretion of the trustees, to certain benefits from the principal. Is the wife the settlor of the new trust to any extent? See National Bank of Commerce of Portland v. Clauson, 127 F. Supp. 386 (D. Me. 1955), *aff'd*, 226 F.2d 446 (1st Cir. 1955).

6.24. S establishes a trust under which all the income is to be paid to his mother for life. On his mother's death one half of the income is to be paid to S if he is then living, or if he is not then living, to his wife and children; the other half of the income is to be paid to F, his father. On the death of the survivor of S's mother and father, the trust is to terminate and the principal is to be paid to S if then living, otherwise to his wife and children. F gives to his son certain funds on the understanding that the son will place in the trust, property equivalent in value. The property given to S by F does not go into the trust. Is F the settlor of the trust to any extent? On F's death before his wife, to what extent, if any, will the value of the trust property be includible in his gross estate? See Farmers & Merchants Bank of Los Angeles v. United States, 125 F. Supp. 587 (S.D. Cal. 1954).

6.25. A bequeaths and devises the residue of his estate outright to his son S. Following this outright gift the will contains the following provisions:

> If my said son disclaims in whole or in part the outright gift to him of my residuary estate, I give to my trustees hereinafter named my residuary estate, or the portion thereof so disclaimed, to hold in trust as follows:
> (1) The disinterested trustee may pay the net income to my said son in such amount or amounts as the disinterested trustee in his uncontrolled discretion may

determine. Any net income in any year not paid to my said son shall be added to the principal.

(2) On the death of my said son, the trustees shall pay the principal and undistributed income as my said son may appoint by his will among his issue.

(3) On the death of my said son, to whatever extent he does not exercise his power to appoint by will, the trustees shall pay the principal and undistributed income to my said son's issue then living, such issue to take *per stirpes*, and if no issue of my said son is then living, the trustees shall pay the same to the X charity.

Shortly after A's death S disclaims his outright gift. Will income from the trust which comes into being as a consequence of the disclaimer be taxable to S if the disinterested trustee elects to accumulate it? On S's death, will the value of the trust property be includible in his gross estate for federal estate tax purposes? See Hardenbergh v. Commissioner, printed in full supra page 29.

(2)   Does the Settlor Have the Power?

The power to designate the persons who shall possess or enjoy the property or the income therefrom (Section 2036), or the power to alter, amend, revoke or terminate the trust (Section 2038), may have been relinquished by the settlor. If such a relinquishment is within three years of the settlor's death, however, it is subject to attack as having been made in contemplation of death. The terms of the instrument relinquishing the power must be carefully prepared or it may be found that some residue of the power still remains in the settlor.[108]

---

[108] In Estate of Thomas E. Steere, 22 T.C. 79 (1954), the decedent executed an inter vivos trust in which he reserved the power to revoke the trust and also, in a separate clause, reserved the power to "annul, change or modify in any respect whatsoever any of the trusts or powers hereby created . . ." Subsequently the decedent executed a document in which he expressly declared the deed of trust "to be irrevocable." The court held that in view of the separation in the original trust instrument of his powers to "revoke" and to "change or modify," the later instrument in which he declared the trust to be "irrevocable" did not release his power to alter or amend the trust, and hence he retained until his death the power to alter or amend and the value of the trust property was includible in his gross estate under 1939 I.R.C. §811(d) (1954 I.R.C. §2038).

In Rhode Island Hospital Trust Co. v. Commissioner, 219 F.2d 923 (1st Cir. 1955), the value of the trust property was included in the gross estate of the settlor of a trust that was originally revocable by the settlor and subject to alteration and amendment by him, even though the settlor had executed an instrument modifying the trust and had stated in this instrument that the trust as modified was to be irrevocable. Also, the settlor paid a gift tax on the

If the trustee of an inter vivos trust has a power which, if held by the settlor, would be a Section 2036 power or a Section 2038 power, and the settlor has the power to remove the trustee and appoint himself the trustee, the settlor will be deemed to possess the powers of the trustee.[109]   Where the settlor cannot remove the trus-

---

inter vivos trust after executing the modifying agreement.   The court held that the declaration that the trust was to be irrevocable only eliminated the power of revocation and left the trust subject to a power in the settlor to alter or amend.

[109] See Reg. §20.2036-1(b)(3), quoted infra page 1510, and Reg. §20.2038-1(a)(3), quoted infra page 1513.

See Loughridge's Estate v. Commissioner, 183 F.2d 294 (10th Cir. 1950), *cert. denied*, 340 U.S. 830 (1950), and, in accord with Loughridge's Estate, Jennings v. Smith, 161 F.2d 74 (2d Cir. 1947); Clark v. United States, 167 F. Supp. 54 (D. Me. 1958); Estate of Pierre Jay Wurts, 19 CCH T.C. Mem. 544 (1960), discussed supra page 196, note 96.   The case of Clark v. United States, supra, was remanded to the District Court for consideration, in the first instance, of a new argument in Clark v. United States, 267 F.2d 501 (1st Cir. 1959), to the effect that even though the settlor could substitute herself for the person given the power to terminate the trust, she would be forbidden by local law to exercise the power of termination under the controlling New York law, Real Property Law §141, quoted infra page 1470.   On remand, the District Court held that if the settlor had substituted herself for the person who had the power to terminate the trust, she would not have been precluded from exercising the power to terminate.   This conclusion was based on the fact that the power to terminate was not in the trustee but in others, and thus the settlor did not have the power to substitute herself as *trustee*. Section 141 of the Real Property Law in terms applies only when the power to distribute principal to himself is vested in a person "as trustee of an express trust."   The court admitted that §141 would apply by analogy to a power in trust, but this power in the hands of the settlor would not be such a power. The court heard Professor Richard R. Powell of Columbia University Law School, who testified as an expert on New York law, but the court did not agree with his conclusion that the settlor, if she had appointed herself in place of the power holder, would not have been able to exercise the power to terminate the trust.   See Clark v. United States, 180 F. Supp. 696 (D. Me. 1960).

In Van Beuren v. McLoughlin, 161 F. Supp. 944 (D.R.I. 1958), the settlor in 1932 established a trust which was to continue until the death of the survivor of herself and her husband.   The trust agreement provided that the trust was amendable "with the consent of the Trustee and adult Beneficiaries or adult Beneficiary then receiving the income by an instrument in writing duly executed by the Trustee and such Beneficiary or Beneficiaries."   No amendment, however, could alter the provision for distribution upon the termination of the trust.   The settlor was neither a trustee nor a beneficiary. In 1946, the trust was amended by an instrument in writing, not signed by the settlor, to provide for an additional trustee and to permit the settlor to remove and appoint trustees.   The court construed the language quoted above to mean that the settlor could amend the trust with the consent of the described persons and thus the value of the trust property was includible in her gross estate for estate tax under 1939 I.R.C. §811(d)(2).   The court did not pass on the effect of the power in the settlor to remove and appoint trustees. The case was affirmed in 262 F.2d 315 (1st Cir. 1958), *cert. denied*, 359 U.S. 991 (1959).   In affirming, the Court of Appeals did not adopt the District Court's reasoning but based the decision on the ground that the settlor could remove a trustee at any time and appoint a new one, including herself, and thus she was deemed to have the same powers as the trustees.   The court

tee, but has the power to appoint a successor trustee when the present trustee resigns or dies, and he may name himself as trustee, he will not be deemed to have a Section 2038 power until such time as a vacancy in the office of trustee in fact exists, because until that time the power to appoint himself will be subject to a contingency which has not yet occurred.[110] In the situation just described, however, if a Section 2036 power is involved, the result may well be different because, under that section, when the settlor has the right to designate the person or persons who are to possess or enjoy the transferred property or the income therefrom, it is immaterial whether the exercise of the power is subject to a contingency beyond his control which has not occurred before his death.[111]

In a trust where the settlor is not the trustee and cannot remove the trustee and cannot be appointed a trustee to fill any vacancy in the office of trustee, it should be safe to allow the settlor to desig-

---

pointed out that a power to remove a trustee and replace him is "an extremely potent power, even if she could not substitute herself."

In Walter v. United States, 60-2 U.S.T.C. ¶11952 (N.D. Ohio, 1960), the decedent established a trust under which the trustee had the power to pay the designated beneficiary at any time all or any part of the corpus as he deemed advisable. The decedent retained the power to remove the trustee and appoint a successor. The court held that the decedent could have appointed herself the successor trustee and therefore she possessed a power to terminate the trust and the value of the trust property was includible in her gross estate.

[110] See Reg. §20.2038-1(b), quoted infra page 1513.

In Rev. Rul. 55-393, 1955-1 C.B. 448, it is held that where an inter vivos trust is subject to change or amendment by the trustee with the consent of the income beneficiaries, and the settlor reserves the right to remove the trustee and appoint another trustee (including himself), the settlor has a power to alter, amend or revoke the trust in conjunction with the income beneficiaries. If, however, the settlor reserves the right to appoint a new trustee (including himself) only in the event of a vacancy in the office of trustee, he does not have any power to alter, amend or revoke at the time of his death if no vacancy then exists.

Winchell v. United States, 180 F. Supp. 710 (S.D. Cal. 1960), recognized that the settlor is not treated as holding trustee's powers merely because the settlor can fill a vacancy in the office of trustee when no vacancy exists at the time of the settlor's death.

Estate of Frederick M. Kasch, 30 T.C. 102 (1958), held that the value of trust property involved was not includible in the decedent's gross estate when he created the trust, and his written consent was required for an invasion of the trust corpus and such an invasion could be made only in the event his wife or child or grandchild suffered a period of illness or other incapacity for which other funds were insufficient, because his power was contingent and the event on which it was contingent did not occur during his lifetime.

In Bank of New York v. United States, 174 F. Supp. 911 (S.D.N.Y. 1957), it was held that the corpus of a trust was not includible in the settlor's gross estate where she had retained a power to appoint among her children and the power was subject to a contingency which did not occur.

[111] See Reg. §20.2036-1(b)(3), quoted infra page 1510.

nate who is to fill a vacancy in the office of trustee, no matter what powers are given to the trustee by the trust instrument.[112]

The federal estate tax law contains no provisions which attribute to the settlor powers possessed by parties who are classified for income tax purposes as related or subordinate parties.[113] Thus a power is not possessed by the settlor for the purposes of Section 2036 or Section 2038 merely because it is possessed by someone who might be, but is not legally required to be, subordinate to the settlor's wishes. The development of such an attribution rule in the estate tax field is always a possibility, however, and should be kept in mind in selecting the person to hold a power which, if held by the settlor, would be a Section 2036 or Section 2038 power.

If the power in the settlor is to amend only the administrative provisions and not to change the beneficial enjoyment, the settlor does not have a power that will cause the value of the trust property to be includible in his gross estate.[114] In Winchell v. United States[115] the court recognized the soundness of the statement in the preceding sentence and construed language in an inter vivos trust as giving the settlor only the power to amend administrative provisions, with the result that the value of the trust property was not includible in his gross estate.[116]

If the settlor has a power to revoke the trust but he has entered

---

[112] Winchell v. United States, 180 F. Supp. 710 (S.D. Cal. 1960), pointed out that if the settlor can give the trustee additional powers and cannot appoint himself as trustee, the settlor has no power alone or in conjunction with another to alter or amend the trust. In other words, if one has the power to give another the power to do things it is not the equivalent of having the power to do them oneself.

In Fidelity Union Trust Co. v. United States, 126 F. Supp. 527 (Ct. Cl. 1954), the settlor of an inter vivos trust was deemed to have a 1939 I.R.C. §811(d) (1954 I.R.C. §2038) power under the following circumstances: The trust instrument listed various powers in the trustee which were administrative in nature, and then it provided: "The trustee shall have such additional powers as the grantor . . . may grant to it. . . ." It was contended that the settlor could grant only additional administrative powers, but the court construed the power reserved to the settlor as extending to dispositive as well as administrative provisions.

Estate of Newcomb Carlton, 34 T.C. —, No. 104 (1960), stated that a decedent-settlor's retained power to appoint a successor trustee is not a power to alter, amend or revoke the trust.

[113] See 1954 I.R.C. §672(c), quoted infra page 1370.

[114] If the administrative powers are in fact powers to affect beneficial enjoyment, the result may be different. See State Street Trust Co. v. United States, referred to supra page 196, note 96, and supra page 197, note 98.

[115] 180 F. Supp. 710 (S.D. Cal. 1960).

[116] See Fidelity Union Trust Co. v. United States, discussed supra note 112.

In Holdeen v. Ratterree, 60-2 U.S.T.C. ¶9671 (S.D.N.Y. 1960), the court held that the power to modify the terms of a trust was broad enough to permit the power holder to merge the trust with another trust.

into a contract not to revoke, will he still be deemed to have a power to revoke for estate tax purposes? Such a contract may be the equivalent of a release of the power.[117]

If the settlor cannot initiate action under the power but must consent to any action that is taken, it may be contended that he has the power in conjunction with the person who can initiate the action. In Estate of Marion B. Gebbie[118] the court so held.

Suppose that the power reserved to the settlor is one exercisable only by his will. In such a case, if the settlor cannot benefit himself, his creditors, his estate or creditors of his estate by any exercise of the power, he will not have a general power of appointment.[119] Thus, if the value of the trust property is to be included in his gross estate because of the power to change the trust by his will, it will have to be on the ground that Sections 2036 and 2038 include powers exercisable only by the will of the settlor.[120]

PROBLEM

6.26. A transfers property to T in trust. A reserves to himself the power to alter or amend the trust, but no benefit may be conferred on him by any alteration or amendment. A becomes incurably insane and then dies. Will the value of the trust property be included in A's gross estate? See Hurd v. Commissioner, 160 F.2d 610 (1st Cir. 1947).

---

[117] In Kurz v. United States, 156 F. Supp. 99 (S.D.N.Y. 1957), a trust was created pursuant to a marital separation agreement, and the trust instrument provided that it could be revoked by the settlor with the consent of his wife and of other designated persons. The value of the trust property was held to be includible in the settlor's gross estate because of the reserved power to revoke or modify the trust instrument. It was contended that where the trust was made pursuant to the marital separation agreement, the reserved power was invalid because it violated the contract which called for its creation. The court, however, found nothing in the contract to prevent the reservation in the trust instrument of the power to revoke or modify it, and in addition, concluded that even if the contract was violated by the reservation, the tax consequences would not be altered thereby. The case was affirmed in 254 F.2d 811 (2d Cir. 1958).

[118] 13 CCH T.C. Mem. 136 (1954).

[119] See 1954 I.R.C. §2041(a)(2), quoted infra page 1400.

[120] In Antonina T. Halberstam, 13 CCH T.C. Mem. 1081 (1954), it was held that a power to change the trust by the will of the settlor made the value of the trust property includible in the settlor's gross estate under 1939 I.R.C. §811(d) (1954 I.R.C. §2038).

(3) Is the Possession or Enjoyment of, or the Right to the Income from, the Property Retained by the Settlor?

Section 2036 may apply if the settlor has retained the possession or enjoyment of, or the right to the income from, the transferred property.[121] If his right to the income is postponed until after a life interest given to someone else, the value of the trust property minus the value of such a life interest will be includible in his gross estate if he dies while the life interest is outstanding.[122]

If the settlor has retained the right to only part of the income, then only the portion of the trust property that is needed to produce such part of the income will be includible in his gross estate under Section 2036.[123]

[121] In National Bank of Commerce in Memphis v. Henslee, 179 F. Supp. 346 (M.D. Tenn. 1959), the decedent transferred to a trust the family home, retaining the right to reside in the home, and the court held that he had retained a life interest therein, so that its value would be includible in his gross estate.

The value of stock was includible in the settlor's gross estate in Estate of Ambrose Fry, 9 T.C. 503 (1947), where he gave it to his daughter subject to her giving him the dividends up to $15,000, and he died before he had received the full $15,000.

The decedent in Estate of Daniel McNichol, 29 T.C. 1179 (1958), executed a deed conveying certain income-producing real property to his children. Although the deed was unqualified on its face, the decedent, until his death, continued to receive and claim as his own all rents from the transferred real property. He included the rental income in his income for tax purposes. The court held that the decedent had retained for his life the possession or enjoyment of the income from the transferred property, so that its value was includible in his gross estate. The case was *affirmed sub nom.* Estate of Daniel McNichol v. Commissioner, 265 F.2d 667 (3d Cir. 1959), *cert. denied,* 361 U.S. 829 (1959).

[122] In Commissioner v. Nathan, 159 F.2d 546 (7th Cir. 1947), *cert. denied,* 334 U.S. 843 (1948), where the settlor reserved the right to the income for life, after the death of the first life beneficiary, the court held that the value of the trust property minus the first life interest was includible in the settlor's gross estate. See also Estate of Herman Hohensee, 25 T.C. 1258 (1956); Rev. Rul. 57-448, 1957-2 C.B. 618.

The settlor in Estate of Theodore Geddings Tarver, 26 T.C. 490 (1956), *aff'd,* 255 F.2d 913 (4th Cir. 1958), *sub nom.* Estate of Theodore Geddings Tarvar v. Commissioner, was deemed to retain the income for life in the trust property when the income was first to be used to pay an annuity to his wife, then to pay expenses on the trust property, and then was to be paid to the settlor. The value of the trust property less the value of the life interest in the wife was included in the settlor's gross estate.

[123] In Uhl v. Commissioner, 241 F.2d 867 (7th Cir. 1957), the settlor was entitled to receive $100 a month from trust income, and that part of the trust property which was necessary to produce a monthly income of $100 was includible in his gross estate.

In United States National Bank of Portland v. United States, 188 F. Supp. 332 (D. Ore. 1960), the decedent established an irrevocable inter vivos

The fact that the trust income from the transferred property is actually paid to the settlor does not establish conclusively that he retained the right to income. There may be some other explanation for such result.[124]

If the terms of the trust require that the income, or part thereof, be used for the support and maintenance of persons whom the settlor is legally obligated to support, he should be regarded as having retained the right to the income within the meaning of Section 2036.[125] If, however, the terms of the trust do not require that the

---

trust under which the income was to be accumulated and added to principal for a period of six years. Thereafter the decedent was to receive $100 a month from the net income, or principal if necessary, for his life, and his wife was to receive a like payment. In addition, the trustee had discretion to make additional payments of income to the decedent and his wife in the event of illness or other emergency, but the additional payments were not to exceed the sum of $5000 during the entire period of the trust. On the death of the survivor of the decedent and his wife, the trust was to terminate and the principal was to be paid to designated beneficiaries. The decedent died before the monthly income payments began. The court held that the amount includible in the decedent's gross estate with respect to the trust property would be the amount required to yield $100 a month to commence on the date such payments were to begin. In addition, there would also be includible, because of the discretion in the trustee to pay out $5000 of income, that percentage of such sum as would equal the percentage of the nontaxable portion of the corpus of the trust.

[124] In Goethe v. United States, 56-1 U.S.T.C. ¶11609 (S.D. Fla. 1956), the jury found that the decedent had not retained possession or enjoyment for his life when he made transfers to his sons of certain real property and, after the transfers, continued to collect and retain the income from the property. The beneficiaries had contended that the income received by the decedent, after the transfer, was in discharge of or payment for services rendered in connection with their business.

[125] See Reg. §20.2036-1(b)(2), quoted infra page 1510.

In Commissioner v. Estate of Dwight, 205 F.2d 298 (2d Cir. 1953), cert. denied, 346 U.S. 871 (1953), the value of the trust property was included in the settlor's gross estate under 1939 I.R.C. §811(c)(1)(B) (1954 I.R.C. §2036), where he had established a trust, the income of which was to be used for the support and maintenance of his wife, on the ground that the income was to be used to discharge the settlor's legal obligations.

In Estate of Robert Manning McKeon, 25 T.C. 697 (1956), the court recognized that the settlor of a trust retains the income of the trust if the income is to be used to discharge his legal obligation to support his wife or his minor children.

In Colonial-American National Bank of Roanoke v. United States, 243 F.2d 312 (4th Cir. 1957), the settlor transferred securities to a trust for the benefit of his insane wife, with gifts over to others upon her death. The terms of the trust required the trustees to pay the net income to the wife; if she did not use all of the income, any excess was to be added to corpus, and if the income was not sufficient to pay for her support, the trustees were to invade corpus. During his lifetime, the settlor in fact continued to pay for her support out of his own funds, and the trust income was never used for her support except for one hospital bill. The court held that the decedent's purpose was to provide for his wife after his death and, therefore, the trust was not one in

income be so used but only give the trustee discretion to so use it, then the settlor has not retained the right to the income and he does not have the right, either alone or in conjunction with another, to determine who will enjoy it,[126] unless, of course, the settlor is the trustee.

The terms of the transferring instrument may not specify that the transferor has reserved any life interest but he may be allowed to continue to use the transferred property in a manner similar to the use he was making of it prior to the transfer. Suppose, for example, a husband transfers the family residence to his wife but thereafter he continues to live in the house with his wife just as before the transfer. In such a situation has the transferor retained the possession of the property for his lifetime? Section 2036 does not specify that the retained life interest must be provided for in the instrument of transfer, but if it is not provided for there, it would seem that the facts must establish that the transferor has an enforceable right to it.[127]

---

which he had reserved to himself any right to have the income applied to his wife's support. The value of the trust property was not includible in his gross estate.

National Bank of Commerce in Memphis v. Henslee, 179 F. Supp. 346 (M.D. Tenn. 1959), was a case where the decedent had executed a trust under which he reserved the right to receive the income for use in the support of his dependent daughter during her minority. The court held that he had reserved the income for a period that did not end before his death, and therefore the value of the trust property was includible in his gross estate.

In Estate of William H. Lee, 33 T.C. —, No. 120 (1960), an irrevocable inter vivos trust was involved under which the trust income was to be paid to the settlor's wife for life for her maintenance and support. The entire value of the trust property was includible in the settlor's gross estate because the income was restricted to use in satisfaction of the settlor's obligation to support his wife, and in view of the settlor's over-all wealth, the amount of the income did not exceed the support the law would have required of him. The Dwight case, supra, was followed.

If, as a matter of right, the settlor's creditors can reach the trust income, since the settlor has it within his power to run up bills of sufficient amount to exhaust the trust income, he should be regarded as having retained the right to the income for the purposes of §2036. See Uhl v. Commissioner, supra note 123.

[126] Commissioner v. Douglass' Estate, 143 F.2d 961 (3d Cir. 1944); McCullough v. Granger, 128 F. Supp. 611 (W.D. Pa. 1955); Estate of Paul F. Donnelly, 38 B.T.A. 1234 (1938); Estate of Berman Barad, 13 CCH T.C. Mem. 223 (1954).

[127] Harter v. United States, 55-1 U.S.T.C. ¶11503 (N.D. Okla. 1954). The tax consequences when the transferor retains incidental benefits is discussed in 1 CCH 1955 Fed. Est. & Gift Tax Rep. ¶1460.387, and the conclusion there stated is: "No cases seem to hold or give a basis for holding that a transfer of a home to one's wife or children can be taxed merely because the transferor continues to live in the home." See also Estate of Louis Richards, 20 T.C. 904 (1953), aff'd, 221 F.2d 808 (9th Cir. 1955).

In Estate of George H. Burr, 4 CCH T.C. Mem. 1054 (1945), property was

PROBLEM

6.27. A transfers property to T in trust. Under the terms of the trust T is required to pay the income to A for his lifetime. On A's death, the trust property is to be distributed to A's issue then living, such issue to take per stirpes, and if no issue of A is then living, the trust property is to be distributed to the X charity. A desires to eliminate the value of the trust property from his gross estate for federal estate tax purposes. Which of the following steps, if taken by A, will accomplish his objective?

    a. A transfers his life interest under the trust to his wife, W. Thereafter, until A's death, A and W file joint income tax returns. See page 193 supra, note 89.

    b. A transfers his life interest under the trust to his son S for a lump sum which equals the present worth of his life interest. See Estate of Robert J. Cuddihy, 32 T.C. 1171 (1959), discussed infra page 439, note 11.

    c. A transfers his life interest under the trust to his son S in return for the son's promise to pay to A, as long as A lives, an amount equal to the income of the trust that is paid out each year.

(4) Lober v. United States

This case was decided under the 1939 Code but the decision is fully applicable to Section 2038. It should be noted that the trust involved in the Lober case has characteristics identical with the so-called present interest trust for a minor later developed.[128] Thus the estate tax consequences, if the settlor is a trustee of such a trust, are a major factor in determining whether he should be a trustee.

LOBER v. UNITED STATES
346 U.S. 335, 74 Sup. Ct. 98, 98 L. Ed. 15 (1953)

Mr. Justice Black delivered the opinion of the Court.

This is an action for an estate tax refund brought by the execu-

---

not included in the husband's gross estate when he gave a country home to his wife and continued to use it after the gift.

In Estate of Ethel M. Bullock, 19 CCH T.C. Mem. 1960-204, where the decedent had transferred property by deeds unrecorded until after her death and had continued to use the property described in the deeds and to collect the income therefrom until she died, the entire value of the transferred property was included in her gross estate on the ground that she had retained the income for life.

[128] See discussion at page 243 infra.

tors of the estate of Morris Lober. In 1924 he signed an instrument conveying to himself as trustee money and stocks for the benefit of his young son. In 1929 he executed two other instruments, one for the benefit of a daughter, the other for a second son. The terms of these three instruments were the same. Lober was to handle the funds, invest and reinvest them as he deemed proper. He could accumulate and reinvest the income with the same freedom until his children reached twenty-one years of age. When twenty-one they were to be paid the accumulated income. Lober could hold the principal of each trust until the beneficiary reached twenty-five. In case he died his wife was to be trustee with the same broad powers Lober had conveyed to himself. The trusts were declared to be irrevocable, and as the case reaches us we may assume that the trust instruments gave Lober's children a "vested interest" under state law, so that if they had died after creation of the trusts their interest would have passed to their estates. A crucial term of the trust instruments was that Lober could at any time he saw fit turn all or any part of the principal of the trusts over to his children. Thus, he could at will reduce the principal or pay it all to the beneficiaries, thereby terminating any trusteeship over it.

Lober died in 1942. By that time the trust property was valued at more than $125,000. The Internal Revenue Commissioner treated this as Lober's property and included it in his gross estate. That inclusion brought this lawsuit. The Commissioner relied on Section 811(d)(2) of the Internal Revenue Code, 26 U.S.C. Section 811 (1946 ed.). That section, so far as material here, required inclusion in a decedent's gross estate of the value of all property that the decedent had previously transferred by trust "where the enjoyment thereof was subject at the date of his death to any change through the exercise of a power . . . to alter, amend, or revoke . . . ." In Commissioner of Internal Revenue v. Holmes' Estate, 326 U.S. 480, we held that power to terminate was the equivalent of power to "alter, amend, or revoke" it, and we approved taxation of the Holmes estate on that basis. Relying on the Holmes case, the Court of Claims upheld inclusion of these trust properties in Lober's estate. 108 F. Supp. 731, 124 Ct. Cl. 44. This was done despite the assumption that the trust conveyances gave the Lober children an indefeasible "vested interest" in the properties conveyed. The Fifth Circuit Court of Appeals had reached a contrary result where the circumstances were substantially the same, in Hays' Estate v. Commissioner of Internal Revenue, 5 Cir., 181 F.2d 169, 172-174. Because of this conflict, we granted certiorari. 345 U.S. 969.

Petitioners stress a factual difference between this and the Holmes case. The Holmes trust instrument provided that if a beneficiary died before expiration of the trust his children succeeded to his interest, but if he died without children, his interest would pass to his brothers or their children. Thus the trustee had power to eliminate a contingency that might have prevented passage of a beneficiary's interest to his heirs. Here we assume that upon a death of the Lober beneficiaries their part in the trust estate would, under New York law, pass to their heirs. But we cannot agree that this difference should change the Holmes result.

We pointed out in the Holmes case that Section 811(d)(2) was more concerned with "present economic benefit" than with "technical vesting of title or estates." And the Lober beneficiaries, like the Holmes beneficiaries, were granted no "present right to immediate enjoyment of either income or principal." The trust instrument here gave none of Lober's children full "enjoyment" of the trust property, whether it "vested" in them or not. To get this full enjoyment they had to wait until they reached the age of twenty-five unless their father sooner gave them the money and stocks by terminating the trust under the power of change he kept to the very date of his death. This father could have given property to his children without reserving in himself any power to change the terms as to the date his gift would be wholly effective, but he did not. What we said in the Holmes case fits this situation too: "A donor who keeps so strong a hold over the actual and immediate enjoyment of what he puts beyond his own power to retake has not divested himself of that degree of control which Section 811(d)(2) requires in order to avoid the tax." Commissioner of Internal Revenue v. Holmes, supra, 326 U.S. at page 487.

Affirmed.

MR. JUSTICE DOUGLAS and MR. JUSTICE JACKSON dissent.[129]

---

[129] See Reg. §20.2038-1(a), quoted infra page 1512. For comments on the Lober case see 4 Duke B.J. 28 (1954); 37 Minn. L. Rev. 405 (1953); 28 St. John's L. Rev. 303 (1954); 1 U.C.L.A.L. Rev. 625 (1954).

In Struthers v. Kelm, 218 F.2d 810 (8th Cir. 1955), the court held that the Lober case was controlling and that the value of the trust property was includible in the settlor's gross estate when the trustees, one of whom was the settlor, had the power to pay the net income to the beneficiary or accumulate it or invest it for the beneficiary, and also had the power to use so much of the principal for the care, support and maintenance of the beneficiary as they in their discretion might determine. It should be noted that in this case the decedent expressly gave up the right, either alone or in conjunction with any other person, to revoke, change, amend or terminate the trust.

In Estate of Carrie Grossman, 27 T.C. 707 (1957), the settlor-trustee reserved the power to apply to the use of the income beneficiaries so much of the corpus as she in her discretion might deem advisable, and the trust could be terminated if the settlor-trustee consented thereto and any two of her children requested its termination. Both of these powers were deemed powers to terminate the trust reserved by the settlor, and consequently, the value of the trust property was includible in the settlor's gross estate. — ED.

d. *Transfers Taking Effect at Death*[130]

As to transfers made after October 7, 1949, it was not possible under the 1939 Code to make any beneficiary's possession or enjoyment turn on his surviving the settlor, without causing the value of at least some of the trust property to be included in the settlor's gross estate.[131] This result followed even though the settlor retained no beneficial interest of any kind under the trust. Thus, if A established an inter vivos trust and directed the trustee to accumulate the income until his, A's, death and then to distribute the corpus and accumulated income to A's issue then living, such issue to take per stirpes, and, if no issue of A were then living, to distribute the corpus and accumulated income to the X charity, the value of the entire trust property would be includible in A's gross estate.

Section 2037 of the 1954 Code re-enacts in substance Section 811(c)(2) of the 1939 Code, which was applicable to transfers prior to October 8, 1949. Thus no transfer in trust will be deemed one to take effect in possession or enjoyment at or after the death of the settlor if the settlor has no reversionary interest in the trust property, though some beneficiaries under the trust may not possess or enjoy their interests without surviving the settlor. Even if the settlor has a reversionary interest, unless immediately prior to his death it exceeds 5 percent of the value of the trust property,[132] the

---

[130] See 1954 I.R.C. §2037, quoted infra page 1397.

[131] See 1939 I.R.C. §811(c)(3)(A).

[132] See Reg. §20.2037-1(c)(3) and (4), quoted infra page 1511, for a discussion of the method of computing the value of a reversionary interest for purposes of the 5 percent test.

In Costin v. Cripe, 55-2 U.S.T.C. ¶11556 (S.D. Ind. 1955), aff'd, 235 F.2d 162 (7th Cir. 1956), it was held that the retention by a settlor of an irrevocable inter vivos trust of the power to designate other beneficiaries of the trust, exclusive of himself or his creditors, in the event of the prior death of his wife (aged 82) and of his son (aged 48), constituted the retention of an express reversionary interest, the value of which was 8.5 percent of the total value of the trust corpus when the settlor at the time of his death was seventy-three years of age. Thus the value of the trust corpus was included in his gross estate.

Estate of Theodore Geddings Tarver, 26 T.C. 490 (1956) aff'd, sub nom. Theodore Geddings Tarver v. Commissioner, 255 F.2d 913 (4th Cir. 1958), involved a contingent power of testamentary disposition in the settlor which was deemed sufficient to cause the transfer to take effect at death, where there was no showing that the reversionary interest did not exceed 5 percent of the value of the trust corpus. The Court of Appeals also held that the value of the corpus of the trust should be reduced by the value of a life estate created for the settlor's daughter, even though the life estate in the daughter would not continue after the settlor's death unless the daughter's mother survived the settlor. The Tax Court had not deducted the value of the life estate.

In Cardeza v. United States, 57-1 U.S.T.C. ¶11681 (E.D. Pa. 1957), the

transfer cannot be one to take effect in possession or enjoyment at or after his death. As to transfers prior to October 8, 1949, the reversionary interest must be created by the express terms of the trust instrument, but as to all other transfers it makes no difference whether the reversionary interest is created expressly or by operation of law.[133]

The 1954 Code gives a wider range of choice to the settlor of an inter vivos trust as to the type of trust to establish when one of his objectives is to eliminate the value of the trust property from his gross estate. It is possible now to give effect to the natural desire of the settlor of an inter vivos trust to have significant consequences

---

decedent, who was eighty-five years of age at the time of her death, had a reversionary interest which would come into possession if she survived her children and their issue. She had one son then living, who was sixty-four. He had no issue. The court held that the reversionary interest did not have any ascertainable value under applicable valuation principles and, therefore, it must be considered to have a value of zero. The case was affirmed sub nom. Estate of Charlotte D. M. Cardeza v. United States, 261 F.2d 423 (3d Cir. 1958).

The decedent in Smith v. United States, 158 F. Supp. 344 (D. Colo. 1957), made an inter vivos transfer of income-producing property to his wife for life, with the power in her to withdraw the principal at any time, and on her death the property was to revert to him. Since the wife could enjoy the benefit of the principal without surviving her husband, no gift to take effect from and after his death was made. The court held that nothing was includible in the gross estate of the husband when he predeceased his wife.

Dunk v. United States, 58-1 U.S.T.C. ¶11748 (S.D. Fla. 1958), involved a trust under which the corpus was to return to the decedent if the beneficiary, who was the decedent's grandson, died before the decedent and before attaining his thirtieth birthday, when the corpus was to be paid to him. The court held that the value of the decedent's reversionary interest was less than 5 percent of the trust fund.

Estate of Arthur Klauber, 34 T.C. —, No. 102 (1960), considered when a power of disposition in the settlor constitutes a reversionary interest that may cause the transfer by him to be one taking effect at his death. The court pointed out that in order for a power of disposition to be a reversionary interest it must be exercisable by the settlor alone, but that where the settlor can remove the trustees he has such a power to dominate them that he alone will be deemed to possess the powers of disposition given the trustees. In this case the power of disposition in the trustees related to $4000 each year, which represented 8.8 percent of the value of the corpus on the basis of the settlor's life expectancy just prior to his death. The Commissioner sought to include in the settlor's gross estate the entire value of the trust property but the court included only 8.8 percent because that was the settlor's entire reversionary interest based on the power of disposition. He also had a contingent reversionary right in all the trust corpus but that had to be considered separately and could not be aggregated with the power of disposition.

[133] See Reg. §20.2037-1(f)(2), quoted infra page 1512, which points out that if a gift to the settlor's heirs is a nullity under the doctrine of worthier title as applied to inter vivos transfers to the heirs of the transferor (see discussion of the doctrine at page 447 infra), so that as a consequence the settlor has a reversionary interest, this reversionary interest is regarded as arising by the express terms of the instrument of transfer and not by operation of law.

under the trust turn on the event of his death.[134]   If such an inter vivos trust is established, however, care must be taken to eliminate any possibility that the trust property may revert to the settlor or his estate.[135]

PROBLEM

6.28. A transfers property to T in trust. The trust instrument requires T to pay the net income to B for life.   On B's death, if A is then living, the principal is to revert to him, but if A is not then living, the principal is to be paid to C if he is then living.   A dies before B.

   a. In determining whether the value of A's reversionary interest exceeds 5 percent of the value of the trust property, is the value of B's life interest included or excluded from the value of the trust property?   See Section 20.2037-1(c)(4) of the Regulations, quoted infra page 1512.
   b. If the value of A's reversionary interest exceeds 5 percent of the value of the trust property, what is included in A's gross estate for federal estate tax purposes?
   c. If the value of A's reversionary interest is less than 5 per-

---

[134] Suppose that A desires to establish an irrevocable inter vivos trust for the benefit of his issue and that he believes that during his own lifetime he can meet the financial needs of his issue out of his funds not put in the trust. In such a case A may now provide in the trust, without adverse estate tax consequences, that during his lifetime the trustee will have discretion to pay out income or accumulate it but that on his death, the trustee will be required to pay out the income each year.

[135] See Reg. §20.2037-1(c)(2), quoted infra page 1511, which recognizes that the possibility that the settlor may receive back an interest in transferred property by inheritance is not a reversionary interest.

   A reversionary interest is a dangerous thing to have in the picture so far as taxes are concerned.   In addition to the difficulty it may create under §2037, consider the following sections of the 1954 Code:
   1. Section 673, quoted infra page 1371 (short-term trusts which are discussed supra page 168)
   2. Section 677(a)(2), quoted infra page 1374 (if a grantor has a reversionary interest, capital gains which represent income allocated to corpus may be taxable to him; this result may follow even though certain contingencies must occur before the reversionary interest can come into possession; see Kent v. Rothensies, 120 F.2d 476 (3d Cir. 1941), cert. denied, 314 U.S. 659 (1941))
   3. Section 170(b)(1)(D), quoted infra page 1334 (a charitable deduction for income tax purposes may be lost when the donor has a reversionary interest)
   4. Section 2042, quoted infra page 1402 (a reversionary interest may be an "incident of ownership" of a life insurance policy)
   5. Section 2031, quoted infra page 1395 (a reversionary interest, if descendable, is owned property)
   6. Section 2512, quoted infra page 1419 (in the valuation of a gift for gift tax purposes, a reversionary interest, if its value is not determinable, will not reduce the value of the gift)

cent of the value of the trust property, should the trust property be ignored so far as A's gross estate is concerned?

e. *State Death Taxes*

Most of the states impose death taxes of one type or another. When the objective of the settlor is to eliminate the imposition of death taxes by a transfer to an inter vivos trust, the controlling local law as to such taxes must be considered as well as the federal estate tax law.

4. GIFT TAX CONSIDERATIONS

The federal gift tax cost which may be incurred by the settlor of an inter vivos trust depends on a number of factors such as, for example:[136] the date on which the gift was completed; the aggregate value of taxable gifts for preceding years; the availability of some or all of the specific gift tax exemption; whether the gift is of a present interest so that the annual exclusion is available; whether the settlor's wife consents to have part of the gift charged to her for gift tax purposes; and the deductibility of some or all of the

---

[136] Section 2502(d) of the 1954 Code, quoted infra page 1418, provides that the gift tax imposed on the transfer of property shall be paid by the donor. Revenue Ruling 57-564, 1957-2 C.B. 328, holds that where the donor makes a gift to a trust and the gift is made upon the express condition that the trustees assume and agree to pay any federal gift tax imposed, the income of the trust property which is used to pay off sums borrowed to pay the gift tax is taxable to the donor under 1954 I.R.C. §677, quoted infra page 1374.

If the gift tax payable by the donor is not paid, the donee is liable for it under 1954 I.R.C. §§6324(b) and 6901(c)(1) to the extent of the value of his gift. Fred J. LaFortune, 29 T.C. 479 (1957), aff'd, sub nom. LaFortune v. Commissioner, 263 F.2d 186 (10th Cir. 1958), pointed out that the donee is responsible to the extent of the value of his gift for the gift tax due on all of the gifts made by the donor during the taxable year.

Bonnyman v. United States, 156 F. Supp. 625 (E.D. Tenn. 1957), aff'd, sub nom. United States v. Bonnyman, 261 F.2d 835 (6th Cir. 1958), recognized that a donee has standing to contest the government's valuation of the subject matter of a gift on which a deficiency assessment is based, since he may be held liable for the gift tax due on a gift.

In Love v. Fulton National Bank of Atlanta, 213 Ga. 887, 102 S.E.2d 488 (1958), a trust was involved which provided that the trustees could not use the income or corpus of the trust for the purpose of discharging any legal obligations or debts of the settlor. The court held that such a provision did not prevent the collection from the trustee, under §6324(b), of the gift tax due on the gifts to the trust, without regard to whether any attempt had been made to collect such a tax from the settlor.

Want v. Commissioner, 280 F.2d 777 (2d Cir. 1960), held that a trustee's liability as fiduciary of a transferee's estate was satisfiable to the extent of the value of the property transferred to the trust during the year in question, but only out of any assets in the trust at the time the notice of deficiency was served.

gift under the marital deduction or charitable deduction provisions.

The federal gift tax cost cannot, of course, be computed without taking some stand as to the value of the gift. This may or may not be easy depending on the nature of the gift.[137] The value of the property on the date the gift is made is controlling.[138] This value, however, must be reduced by the value of any consideration in money or money's worth which the settlor receives for the transfer.[139]

It is important to know to whom the transfer by gift is made. The form of the gift may appear to transfer the property to one person, when in fact the intent of the transferor is to confer the benefit on another.[140]

[137] The valuation of closely held stock is considered at page 942 infra.

See R. D. Mills, 17 CCH T.C. Mem. 108 (1958), where the valuation for gift tax purposes of an undivided interest in gas, oil and mineral rights is considered; and Estate of Julien W. Vose, 18 CCH T.C. Mem. 765 (1959), which deals with the valuation of so-called "certificates of indebtedness" that were subject to restrictions as to transfer and collectibility. The case was reversed and remanded on another point sub nom. Vose v. Commissioner, 284 F.2d 65 (1st Cir. 1960).

Section 25.2511-1(e) of the Regulations, quoted infra page 1544, points out that if the settlor has retained a reversionary interest but the value of it cannot be ascertained, no deduction for it is allowed in determining the value of his gift.

Farha Schayek, 33 T.C. 629, 71 (1960), held that where money was transferred to a trust and the trust instrument provided that at the inception of the trust the corporate trustee was entitled to a fee as its initial commission, the value of the gift was the amount which passed from the donor undiminished by the trustee's initial commission.

Suppose that the subject matter of the gift is something that will be worth either a great deal or nothing, such as a sweepstakes ticket. What is the value of such an item for gift tax purposes? If the ticket is a winning one, what amount is includible in the gross income of the donee? In Rev. Rul. 55-638, 1955-2 C.B. 35, it is held that the proceeds of a sweepstakes ticket acquired by gift before it became a winning ticket are includible in the gross income of the donee to the extent that the proceeds exceed the value of the gift, which is the price paid for the ticket by the donor.

[138] See 1954 I.R.C. §2512(a), quoted infra page 1419.

[139] See 1954 I.R.C. §2512(b), quoted infra page 1419. See also Irma Lampert, discussed supra page 75, note 59.

Shelton v. Lockhart, 154 F. Supp. 244 (W.D. Mo. 1957), held that where the Bureau of Indian Affairs required an Indian princess, as a condition of issuing to her a certificate of competency, which would grant her citizenship, to execute an instrument placing some of her property in trust for the benefit of her children, no gift tax was payable because the establishment of the trust represented a business venture by her and the Bureau, was negotiated at arm's length and was free from donative intent.

[140] In Weber v. United States, 60-1 U.S.T.C. ¶11925 (N.D. Okla. 1960), the decedent devised property to the plaintiff. On the face of the will the devise was outright. The plaintiff, however, agreed to hold the devised property in trust for the benefit of the decedent's children. The secret trust device was used to prevent the possibility of creditors of the decedent's children seizing the property. Under these circumstances, a constructive trust was created and distributions by the plaintiff to the decedent's children were not gifts.

a. When a Gift Is Complete

If an inter vivos trust is effective to cause the income from the trust property to be attributed to someone other than the settlor for federal income tax purposes, and if it is also effective to eliminate the value of the trust property from the settlor's gross estate for federal estate tax purposes, a gift of the trust property has been made for federal gift tax purposes. Is it equally certain as to whether a gift of the trust property has been made for federal gift tax purposes in the following situations?

1. *The inter vivos trust is effective to cause the income from the trust property to be attributed to someone other than the settlor for federal income tax purposes but it is not effective to eliminate the value of the trust property from the settlor's gross estate for federal estate tax purposes.* The inter vivos trust may be ineffective to eliminate the value of the trust property from the settlor's gross estate for federal estate tax purposes for any one of the following reasons, none of which will cause the income from the trust property to be attributed to the settlor:

   a. The transfer in trust is made in contemplation of death (§2035).
   b. Interests under the trust cannot be enjoyed by certain persons unless they survive the settlor, and the settlor has a reversionary interest which exceeds in value the 5 percent test (§2037).
   c. The settlor in conjunction with a person who has a substantial adverse interest may alter, amend or revoke the trust (§2038), or may designate who is to receive income or corpus (§2036).

It is believed that in all the above-described situations a gift has been made for federal gift tax purposes, though the value of the trust property is not eliminated from the settlor's gross estate for federal estate tax purposes.[141] Any gift tax paid may, of course, be

---

[141] In Publicker v. Miles, 55-1 U.S.T.C. ¶11531 (E.D. Pa. 1955), the settlor of a trust reserved the right to alter or amend the trust only with the consent of her husband, and under the terms of the trust her husband as trustee was authorized to pay income to the settlor, to himself or to the settlor's children, and was also authorized to invade corpus. The court held that because of the adverse interest of the husband, the settlor would have made a completed gift if the terms of the trust instrument alone were considered. There was, however, ample evidence that the settlor and her husband had an understanding that she could alter or revoke the trust at any time and this understanding caused the court to hold that the gift was incomplete. The result is clearly correct if the so-called understanding is one that would be enforceable by the settlor in the event the husband declined to acquiesce in the settlor's desires.

taken as a credit against the estate tax to the extent allowed by Section 2012 of the 1954 Code.

2. *The inter vivos trust is effective to eliminate the value of the trust property from the settlor's gross estate for federal estate tax purposes but it is not effective to cause the income from the trust property to be attributed to someone other than the settlor for federal income tax purposes.* The inter vivos trust may be ineffective to cause the income from the trust to be attributed to someone other than the settlor for federal income tax purposes for any one of the following reasons, none of which will cause the value of the trust property to be included in the gross estate of the settlor for federal estate tax purposes:

   a. A power to revest in the settlor title to the trust property is vested solely in a person who does not have a substantial adverse interest (§676).

   b. Discretion to distribute income to the settlor is given solely to a person who does not have a substantial adverse interest (§677).

   c. A power to alter or amend the trust (no alteration or amendment to benefit the settlor) is vested solely in a person who does not have a substantial adverse interest (§674).

It is believed that in all the above-described situations a gift has been made for federal gift tax purposes, though the income from the trust is attributed to the settlor for federal income tax purposes.[142]

3. *The inter vivos trust is not effective to cause the income from the trust property to be attributed to someone other than the settlor for federal income tax purposes and is not effective to eliminate the value of the trust property from the settlor's gross estate for federal estate tax purposes.* If an inter vivos trust, other than a revocable inter vivos trust, is created, the settlor may give up control, at least legally, and yet not remove the trust property from his

[142] In Galt v. Commissioner, 216 F.2d 41 (7th Cir. 1954), *cert. denied*, 348 U.S. 951 (1955), a father made a lease of certain land for twenty years. Under the terms of the lease, he was to receive (1) a fixed annual rental and (2) a percentage of the total annual amount wagered at the race track on the leased property. On the date the lease was executed the father irrevocably gave to each of his three sons a portion of the amount realized from the second of the funds payable by the lessee. The court held that the entire amount payable under the lease was income to the father, and that for gift tax purposes, the entire gift was made on the date the lease was signed, and thus no annual gift of the income was attributable to the father.

In Camiel Thorrez, 31 T.C. 655 (1958), a transfer of a partnership interest was not effective for income tax purposes but was regarded as a completed gift for gift tax purposes. The case was affirmed sub nom. Thorrez v. Commissioner, 272 F.2d 945 (6th Cir. 1959), but this point was not involved on appeal.

estate for either federal income or estate tax purposes. The following are examples of such inter vivos trusts:

    a. The trust provides that the settlor in conjunction with a person who does not have a substantial adverse interest may revest in the settlor the title to the trust property (§§676, 2038).

    b. The trust provides that the settlor in conjunction with a person who does not have a substantial adverse interest may alter or amend the trust but no alteration or amendment is to benefit the settlor (§§674, 2038).

It is believed that in neither of the above-described situations has the settlor made a gift for federal gift tax purposes, though legally he has given up control.[143]

---

[143] See Reg. §25.2511-2, quoted infra page 1546, for illustrations of powers retained by the settlor which will cause the transfer to be an incomplete gift.

For holdings that a gift has not been made by the settlor on the establishment of a trust in which the settlor, in conjunction with the trustee, has a power to affect the beneficial interests under the trust, see Camp v. Commissioner, 195 F.2d 999 (1st Cir. 1952); Latta v. Commissioner, 212 F.2d 164 (3d Cir. 1954), *cert. denied,* 348 U.S. 825 (1954).

In Rev. Rul. 54-537, 1954-2 C.B. 316, it is recognized that a gift is incomplete when the settlor of the trust possesses the power to revest in himself the beneficial title in the property.

Revenue Ruling 58-395, 1958-2 C.B. 398, recognizes that no completed gift is made when a trust is established which is revocable by the settlor in conjunction with others who have no adverse interest.

State Tax Commission v. Fitts, — Mass. —, 165 N.E.2d 586 (1960), involved a case where the settlor of a trust could amend or revoke it with the consent of his brother, who was one of the trustees. The issue before the court was whether the settlor could be deemed to have "received" trust property which was reachable only with the consent of his brother, when he had not in fact received it in hand. If he could be said to have "received" the property, then he would be subject to a state income tax and otherwise not. The court concluded he had "received" the property, saying: "The taxpayers [settlors] could have received the liquidating dividends and, indeed, the entire trust corpus whenever they desired, by merely exercising any of the powers they had reserved to amend, alter or revoke the trusts. The only limitation upon the exercise of these powers was the consent of Mr. Osmer C. Fitts who, it is agreed, had no substantial adverse interest in either trust. The exercise of this power of consent was subject to no standards, express or implied, and Mr. Fitts, as the taxpayers concede, could properly 'give or withhold his consent as he wishes as long as he does not act dishonestly.' In these circumstances Mr. Fitts was not a trustee of this power and owed no duty to the beneficiaries to resist alteration or revocation of the trusts."

In Jeannette B. Causey, CCH T.C. Mem. 1960-108, a settlor was attempting to establish that he had made no gift for gift tax purposes in 1953, so that he had a greater specific exemption available to him in 1955 than would otherwise be the case. In 1953, he executed a trust covering certain property described in a Schedule A but no schedule was ever prepared or attached. He filed a gift tax return listing 121 shares of stock as a gift to the trust. The securities referred to were at all times in a custodian account with a broker, in his name, and he received the income, spent it for family purposes and included it in his income tax return. On these facts it was held that he had not established by the preponderance of the evidence that he had not made

An inter vivos trust may be ineffective to remove the trust property from the settlor's estate for either federal income or estate tax purposes, but the settlor nevertheless will be deemed to have made a gift for federal tax purposes. Such a result follows when the trust creates a life interest in the settlor and an irrevocable remainder in another. The value of the gift, of course, is the value of the remainder interest.[144]

If the life interest retained by the settlor is in the form of discretion given to the trustee (who is not the settlor) to pay the income to the settlor or someone else, such a life interest should not detract from the completeness of the gift for federal gift tax purposes.[145] The power given the trustee to pay the income to the set-

---

a completed gift in 1953. The court referred to the validity of a parol declaration of trust.

Eleanor A. Bradford, 34 T.C. —, No. 107 (1960), is illustrative of the unusual ways in which one may become involved in a dispute over whether a completed gift has been made for gift tax purposes. Here a wife substituted her note in the amount of $205,000 for notes of her husband but the bank which held the note retained the husband's security as collateral. The Commissioner claimed that the wife had made a gift to the husband in the amount of $205,000, but the court held that a taxable transfer would not take place until the bank took judgment against the wife and levied on her property. The court mentioned that donative intent is material and that the wife had none when she signed the note. The reason why the wife substituted her note for her husband's was to enable him to satisfy certain New York Stock Exchange requirements.

[144] In Pamela M. W. Lingo, 13 CCH T.C. Mem. 436 (1954), an irrevocable inter vivos trust was involved under which the income was payable to the settlor until her death or remarriage. The trust instrument also provided that the trustee should pay any gift tax finally determined to be due from the settlor. It was held that in valuing the remainder interest, no deduction in value should be allowed for the value of the settlor's right to income, because the right was incapable of valuation due to the fact that it would end on her remarriage. The gift tax which the trustee was required to pay, however, was deductible. See Rev. Rul. 57-564, 1957-2 C.B. 328, discussed supra page 216, note 136.

In Estate of Franklin Lewis Hazelton, 29 T.C. 637 (1957), the decedent was the primary beneficiary of both principal and income of two separate trusts. Prior to his death, and at his request, a portion of the property of one trust — a portion he had placed in that trust — was transferred to the other trust. This transfer was made only after obtaining the consent of all contingent beneficiaries. The receiving trust differed from the transferring trust in that the decedent's wife was entitled to one half of the income and principal of the receiving trust, for her life, whereas she received only one third of the income from the transferring trust. The court held that the decedent made no taxable gift as a result of the transfer from one trust to the other, because he had exactly the same interest in the property before and after the transfer and he had no dominion or control over the property which was the subject of the transfer.

See also James Richard Bowden, 14 CCH T.C. Mem. 1102 (1955) *aff'd*, 234 F.2d 937 (5th Cir. 1956), *cert. denied*, 352 U.S. 916 (1957), *rehearing denied*, 352 U.S. 976 (1957), discussed infra page 265, note 215.

[145] Section 25.2511-2(b) of the Regulations, quoted infra page 1546, is in accord with the textual statement.

tlor may be found to give fixed rights to the settlor because of the existence of a standard which controls the trustee's action or because of some other reason, and if so, the gift is not complete as to such rights in the settlor if their value is ascertainable.[146]

All the circumstances surrounding what purports to be a transfer by way of gift must be closely scrutinized so that the real substance of the transaction will be revealed. Substance rather than form should control in determining if and when a gift for gift tax purposes has been made.[147]

[146] Revenue Ruling 54-538, 1954-2 C.B. 316, provides that where a trustee is authorized to use income and corpus, if necessary, for the settlor's support, the gift in trust is not rendered wholly incomplete. The amount required annually for the settlor's support according to his accustomed mode of living may be ascertained and valued as an annuity. The value of the gift is the value of the transferred property less the value of the settlor's retained support rights. This is to be distinguished from Estate of Christianna K. Gramm, 17 T.C. 1063 (1952), where the entire gift was deemed incomplete because of the fact that the amount of property placed in trust was so small that complete invasion of the corpus for the benefit of settlor was very probable. In Sarah Gilkey Vander Weele, 27 T.C. 340 (1956), the trustees of a trust were to pay the settlor such amounts of income as they in their discretion deemed desirable and ample for the settlor's comfortable well-being and enjoyment. If the income was insufficient, they were authorized to invade the trust principal. The court held that the settlor retained sufficient dominion and control over the income and corpus of the trust so that the transfer in trust did not constitute a completed gift. It was pointed out that under Michigan law, which governed the trust, a trust created for the benefit of the settlor does not protect his interest from the claims of his creditors. The case was affirmed sub nom. Commissioner v. Vander Weele, 254 F.2d 895 (6th Cir. 1958).

See Alice S. Paolozzi, discussed supra page 151, note 10.

Minnie E. Deal, 29 T.C. 730 (1958), considered a case where non-income-producing property was placed in trust, and the trustee was given discretion to pay the settlor as much of the income as she required during her life. On her death, the corpus was to go to her daughters, and the trustees had broad discretionary powers as to invasion of the corpus and the termination of the trust. The court held that in the absence of income from the property, a reservation of a discretionary right to income was without value, so that the value of the remainder interest transferred to the daughters was the total market value of the land, and the gift of the remainder interest to them was of a future interest.

[147] In William Herbert Brown, 25 T.C. 920 (1956), the taxpayer, in 1947, redeemed notes for $32,500 which were secured by a deed of trust on real estate that he and his wife owned. The notes were not then canceled nor was the deed of trust released of record. The taxpayer held the uncanceled notes as the property of his two minor children and, in 1947, reported that he had made cash gifts of $16,250 to each of them. When, in 1949, he had to raise money on the real estate, he canceled the notes and secured a record release of the deed of trust. He then gave each child his personal note for $16,250. In 1951 and 1952, he made interest payments to the children on these notes and deducted the interest on his income tax return. The court held that the interest deduction was properly disallowed. No valid debt existed and no bona fide gift resulted until the notes were paid in 1954. The case was affirmed sub nom. Brown v. Commissioner, 241 F.2d 827 (8th Cir. 1957).

When the subject matter of a gift is stock in a corporation, some time will elapse between the delivery of the stock to the settlor's broker for transfer to the name of the trustee and the actual transfer to the name of the trustee on the books of the corporation. As long as the stock is in the hands of the settlor's broker, the settlor can recall it and revoke his instructions, so the gift will not be completed while this situation continues.[148] The gift is completed on the date of the delivery of the stock, however, if delivery is made directly to the donee or his agent.[149]

In Clement v. Smith, 167 F. Supp. 369 (E.D. Pa. 1958), the settlor of a trust was held to have made no gift when he established a trust under which the trustees could pay any accumulated income to the settlor's father if they deemed it advisable or necessary, and the father was one of the trustees. Although this arrangement was irrevocable, no gift was deemed to have been made, because the father had substantial funds of his own and it was therefore unlikely that it would ever be proper for the trustees to pay him anything. If the trustees made a proper determination that the father needed money, a gift would be made at that time.

[148] See Rev. Rul. 54-135, 1954-1 C.B. 205. In Special Ruling dated December, 1958, CCH Fed. Est. & Gift Tax Rep. ¶8026, it is held that Rev. Rul. 54-135 governs when the donor instructs his broker (who is also the donee's broker) to transfer stock to the donee and at the same time informs the donee of the gift. Hence the gift is made on the date the stock is transferred on the books of the corporation, the broker being regarded as the donor's agent for the transaction.

The date of the completion of the gift in this situation also has importance for income tax purposes. For example, the amount of a deductible charitable contribution is the fair market value of the donated property at the time of the gift; and the amount of the deductible loss on the subsequent sale by the donee of the property is computed on either the donor's basis or the fair market value of the property at the time of the gift, whichever is lower.

The date of the completion of a gift is also significant in determining the actual value of stock for purposes of the documentary stamp tax. Special Ruling, dated December 23, 1958, CCH Fed. Excise Tax Rep. ¶6388, holds that in the case of a gift or bequest, the mean between the high and low selling prices on the day of the gift or bequest shall be considered to be the "actual value." Special Ruling dated July 30, 1959, CCH Fed. Excise Tax Rep. ¶6389, points out that the day of a gift for this purpose is the day the donor sends the stock to the transfer agent.

Mark G. Anton, 34 T.C. —, No. 86 (1960), considered a case where stock was the subject matter of a gift and prior to the date of the gift it had been announced that a dividend would be paid to holders of record on a designated date which was subsequent to the date of the gift. In such circumstances would the dividend be taxable to the donor or to the donee who was entitled to receive it? The Court held that the dividend was taxable to the donor, treating the situation as an assignment by the donor of the right to income.

[149] See Reg. §25.2511-2(h), quoted infra page 1547, and Reg. §1.170-1(b), quoted infra page 1485.

Revenue Ruling 54-554, 1954-2 C.B. 317, specifically provides that where a donor endorses a stock certificate and physically delivers it to the donee, the gift is complete for federal gift tax purposes on the date of delivery.

In Estate of Eli B. Witt v. Fahs, 160 F. Supp. 521 (S.D. Fla. 1956), it was held that a charitable contribution of an individual mailed to an agent of a charity on December 31, 1946, was a proper deduction in 1946, although the

Estate of Sanford v. Commissioner is printed in full below because it is a landmark decision as to when a gift has been made for federal gift tax purposes.

ESTATE OF SANFORD v. COMMISSIONER OF INTERNAL REVENUE
308 U.S. 39, 60 Sup. Ct. 51, 84 L. Ed. 20 (1939)

MR. JUSTICE STONE delivered the opinion of the Court.

This and its companion case, Rasquin v. Humphreys [308 U.S. 54] present the single question of statutory construction whether in the case of an inter vivos transfer of property in trust, by a donor reserving to himself the power to designate new beneficiaries other than himself, the gift becomes complete and subject to the gift tax imposed by the federal revenue laws at the time of the relinquishment of the power. Corelative questions, important only if a negative answer is given to the first one, are whether the gift becomes complete and taxable when the trust is created or, in the case where the donor has reserved a power of revocation for his own benefit and has relinquished it before relinquishing the power to change beneficiaries, whether the gift first becomes complete and taxable at the time of relinquishing the power of revocation.

In 1913, before the enactment of the first gift tax statute of 1924, decedent created a trust of personal property for the benefit of named beneficiaries, reserving to himself the power to terminate the trust in whole or in part, or to modify it. In 1919 he surrendered the power to revoke the trust by an appropriate writing in which he reserved "the right to modify any or all of the trusts" but provided that this right "shall in no way be deemed or construed to include any right or privilege" in the donor "to withdraw principal or income from any trust." In August, 1924, after the effective date of the gift tax statute, decedent renounced his remaining power to modify the trust. After his death in 1928, the Commissioner following the decision in Hesslein v. Hoey, 91 F.2d 954, in 1937, ruled that the gift became complete and taxable only upon decedent's final renunciation of his power to modify the trusts and gave notice of a tax deficiency accordingly.

The order of the Board of Tax Appeals sustaining the tax was affirmed by the Court of Appeals for the Third Circuit, 103 F.2d 81, which followed the decision of the Court of Appeals for the

check was not cashed until January 4, 1947. The United States mail was deemed an agent of the contributor and of the recipient, and the date of mailing was the date of payment.

Second Circuit in Hesslein v. Hoey, supra, in which we had denied certiorari, 302 U.S. 756. In the Hesslein case, as in the Humphreys case now before us, a gift in trust with the reservation of a power in the donor to alter the disposition of the property in any way not beneficial to himself, was held to be incomplete and not subject to the gift tax under the 1932 Act so long as the donor retained that power.

We granted certiorari in this case, 307 U.S. 618, and in the Humphreys case, id. 619, upon the representation of the Government that it has taken inconsistent positions with respect to the question involved in the two cases and that because of this fact and of the doubt of the correctness of the decision in the Hesslein case decision of the question by this Court is desirable in order to remove the resultant confusion in the administration of the revenue laws.

It has continued to take these inconsistent positions here, stating that it is unable to determine which construction of the statute will be most advantageous to the Government in point of revenue collected. It argues in this case that the gift did not become complete and taxable until surrender by the donor of his reserved power to designate new beneficiaries of the trusts. In the Humphreys case it argues that the gift upon trust with power reserved to the donor, not afterward relinquished, to change the beneficiaries was complete and taxable when the trust was created. It concedes by its brief that "a decision favorable to the government in either case will necessarily preclude a favorable decision in the other."

In ascertaining the correct construction of the statutes taxing gifts, it is necessary to read them in the light of the closely related provisions of the revenue laws taxing transfers at death, as they have been interpreted by our decisions. Section 319 et seq. of the Revenue Act of 1924, 43 Stat. 253, reenacted as Sec. 501 et seq. of the 1932 Act, 47 Stat. 169, imposed a graduated tax upon gifts. It supplemented that laid on transfers at death, which had long been a feature of the revenue laws. When the gift tax was enacted Congress was aware that the essence of a transfer is the passage of control over the economic benefits of property rather than any technical changes in its title. See Burnet v. Guggenheim, 288 U.S. 280, 287. Following the enactment of the gift tax statute this Court in Reinecke v. Northern Trust Co., 278 U.S. 339 (1929), held that the relinquishment at death of a power of revocation of a trust for the benefit of its donor was a taxable transfer, cf. Saltonstall v. Saltonstall, 276 U.S. 260; Chase National Bank v. United States, 278 U.S. 327; and similarly in Porter v. Commissioner, 288

U.S. 436 (1933), that the relinquishment by a donor at death of a reserved power to modify the trust except in his own favor is likewise a transfer of the property which could constitutionally be taxed under the provisions of Section 302(d) of the 1926 Revenue Act (reenacting in substance 302(d) of the 1924 Act) although enacted after the creation of the trust. Cf. Bullen v. Wisconsin, 240 U.S. 625; Curry v. McCanless, 307 U.S. 357; Graves v. Elliott, 307 U.S. 383. Since it was the relinquishment of the power which was taxed as a transfer and not the transfer in trust, the statute was not retroactively applied. Cf. Nichols v. Coolidge, 274 U.S. 531; Helvering v. Helmholz, 296 U.S. 93, 98.

The rationale of decision in both cases is that "taxation is not so much concerned with the refinements of title as it is with the actual command over the property taxed" (see Corliss v. Bowers, 281 U.S. 376, 378; Saltonstall v. Saltonstall, supra, 261; Burnet v. Guggenheim, supra, 287) and that a retention of control over the disposition of the trust property, whether for the benefit of the donor or others, renders the gift incomplete until the power is relinquished whether in life or at death. The rule was thus established, and has ever since been consistently followed by the Court, that a transfer of property upon trust, with power reserved to the donor either to revoke it and recapture the trust property or to modify its terms so as to designate new beneficiaries other than himself is incomplete, and becomes complete so as to subject the transfer to death taxes only on relinquishment of the power at death.

There is nothing in the language of the statute, and our attention has not been directed to anything in its legislative history to suggest that Congress had any purpose to tax gifts before the donor had fully parted with his interest in the property given, or that the test of the completeness of the taxed gift was to be any different from that to be applied in determining whether the donor has retained an interest such that it becomes subject to the estate tax upon its extinguishment at death. The gift tax was supplementary to the estate tax. The two are in pari materia and must be construed together. Burnet v. Guggenheim, supra, 286. An important, if not the main, purpose of the gift tax was to prevent or compensate for avoidance of death taxes by taxing the gifts of property inter vivos which, but for the gifts, would be subject in its original or converted form to the tax laid upon transfers at death. [Footnote omitted.]

Section 322 of the 1924 Act provides that when a tax has been imposed by Section 319 upon a gift, the value of which is required by any provision of the statute taxing the estate to be included in the gross estate, the gift tax is to be credited on the estate tax. The two taxes are thus not always mutually exclusive as in the case of gifts made in contemplation of death which are complete and taxable when made, and are also required to be included in the gross estate for purposes of the death tax. But Section 322 is without application unless there is a gift inter vivos which is taxable independently of any requirement that it shall be included in the gross estate. Property transferred in trust subject to a power of control over its disposition reserved to the donor is likewise required by Sec. 302(d) to be included in the gross estate. But it does not follow that the transfer in trust is also taxable as a gift. The point was decided in the Guggenheim case where it was held that a gift upon trust, with power in the donor to revoke it is not taxable as a gift because the transfer is incomplete, and that the transfer whether inter vivos or at death becomes complete and taxable only when the power of control is relinquished. We think, as was pointed out in the Guggenheim case, supra, 285, that the gift tax statute does not contemplate two taxes upon gifts not made in contemplation of death, one upon the gift when a trust is created or when the power of revocation, if any, is relinquished, and another on the transfer of the same property at death because the gift previously made was incomplete.

It is plain that the contention of the taxpayer in this case that the gift becomes complete and taxable upon the relinquishment of the donor's power to revoke the trust cannot be sustained unless we are to hold, contrary to the policy of the statute and the reasoning in the Guggenheim case, that a second tax will be incurred upon the donor's relinquishment at death of his power to select new beneficiaries, or unless as an alternative we are to abandon our ruling in the Porter case. The Government does not suggest, even in its argument in the Humphreys case, that we should depart from our earlier rulings, and we think it clear that we should not do so both because we are satisfied with the reasoning upon which they rest and because departure from either would produce inconsistencies in the law as serious and confusing as the inconsistencies in administrative practice from which the Government now seeks relief.

There are other persuasive reasons why the taxpayer's contention cannot be sustained. By Sections 315(b), 324, and more specifically by Section 510 of the 1932 Act, the donee of any gift is made personally liable for the tax to the extent of the value of the gift if the tax is not paid by the donor. It can hardly be supposed that Congress intended to impose personal liability upon the donee of a gift of property, so incomplete that he might be deprived of it by the donor the day after he had paid the tax. Further, Sec. 321(b)(1) exempts from the tax, gifts to religious, charitable, and educational corporations and the like. A gift would seem not to be complete, for purposes of the tax, where the donor has reserved the power to determine whether the donees ultimately entitled to receive and enjoy the property are of such a class as to exempt the gift from taxation. Apart from other considerations we should hesitate to accept as correct a construction under which it could plausibly be maintained that a gift in trust for the benefit of charitable corporations is then complete so that the taxing statute becomes operative and the gift escapes the tax even though the donor should later change the beneficiaries to the non-exempt class through exercise of a power to modify the trust in any way not beneficial to himself.

The argument of petitioner that the construction which the Government supports here, but assails in the Humphreys case, affords a ready means of evasion of the gift tax is not impressive. It is true, of course, that under it gift taxes will not be imposed on transactions which fall short of being completed gifts. But if for that reason they are not taxed as gifts they remain subject to death taxes assessed at higher rates, and the Government gets its due, which was precisely the end sought by the enactment of the gift tax.

Nor do we think that the provisions of Section 219(g) of the 1924 Act have any persuasive influence on the construction of the gift tax provisions with which we are now concerned. One purpose of the gift tax was to prevent or compensate for the loss of surtax upon income where large estates are split up by gifts to numerous donees. [Footnote omitted.] Congress was aware that donors in trust might distribute income among several beneficiaries, although the gift remains so incomplete as not to be subject to the tax. It dealt with that contingency in Section 219(g) which taxes to the settlor the income of a trust paid to beneficiaries where he reserved to himself an unexercised power to "revest in himself title" to the trust property producing the income. Whether this section is to be read as relieving the donor of the income tax where the power reserved is to modify the trust, except for his own benefit, we do not now decide. If Congress, in enacting it, undertook to define the extent to which a reserved power of control over the disposition of the income is equivalent to ownership of it so as to mark the line between those cases on the one hand where the income is to be taxed to the donor and those on the other where, by related sections, the income is to be taxed to the trust or its beneficiaries, we do not perceive that the section presents any question so comparable to that now before us as to affect our decision. We are concerned here with a question to which Congress has given no answer in the words of the statute, and it must be decided in conformity to the course of judicial decision applicable to a unified scheme of taxation of gifts whether made inter vivos or at death. If Congress, for the purpose of taxing income, has defined precisely the amount of control over the income which it deems equivalent to ownership of it, that definition is controlling on the courts even though without it they might reach a different conclusion, and even though retention of a lesser degree of control be deemed to render a transfer incomplete for the purpose of laying gift and death taxes.

The question remains whether the construction of the statute which we conclude is to be derived from its language and history, should be modified because of the force of treasury regulations or administrative practice. Article I of Regulations 67, under the 1924 Act (adopted without any change of present significance in Article III, Regulations 79, under the 1932 Act) provides that the creation of a trust where the grantor retains the power to revest in himself title to the corpus of the trust does not constitute a gift subject to the tax and declares that "where the power retained by the grantor to revest in himself title to the corpus is not exercised, a taxable transfer will be treated as taking place in the year in which such power is terminated." Petitioner urges that the regulation is in terms applicable to the trust presently involved because it was subject to a power of revocation in favor of the donor before the enactment of the gift tax which was later relinquished. But we think, as the court below thought, that the regulation was not directed to the case of the relinquishment of a reserved power to select new beneficiaries other than the donor and did not purport to lay down any rule for cases where there was a reserved power different from or in addition to the power to revest the title in the donor. At most the regulation is ambiguous and without persuasive force in determining the true construction of the statute. Burnet v. Chicago Portrait Co., 285 U.S. 1, 16, 20. The amended regulation of 1936 under the 1932 Act, Art. III, Reg. 79, removed the ambiguity by declaring that the gift is complete and subject to the tax when "the donor has so parted with dominion and control as to leave in him no power to cause the beneficial title to be revested in himself." But this regulation is by its terms applicable only to gifts made after June 6, 1932, and is of significance here only so far as it is declaratory of the correct construction of the 1924 Act.

Petitioner also insists that the construction of the statute for which he contends is sustained by the administrative practice. That practice is not disclosed by any published Treasury rulings or decisions and our only source of information on the subject is a stipulation appearing in the record. It states that in the administration of the gift tax under the 1924 and 1932 Acts and until the decision in the Hesslein case it was "the uniform practice of the Commissioner of Internal Revenue in adjusting cases of the character of that here involved to treat the taxable transfer subject to gift tax as occurring when the transferor relinquished all power to revest in himself title to the property constituting the subject of the transfer"; and that three hundred cases "of such character" have been closed or adjusted in conformity to this practice.

This definition of the practice appears as a part of a stipulation of facts setting forth in some 126 printed pages the original trust deed of December 24, 1913, and thirteen modifications of it between that date and the final relinquishment of the power of modification on August 20, 1924. They reveal a varied and extensive power of control by the donor over the disposition of the trust property which survived the relinquishment, in 1919, of the power of revocation for his own benefit, and with which he finally parted after enactment of the gift tax. The description of the practice as that resorted to in adjusting "cases of the character of that here involved," presupposes some knowledge on our part of what the signers of the stipulation regarded as the salient features of the present case which, although not specified by the stipulation, were necessarily embraced in the practice. Administrative practice, to be accepted as guiding or controlling judicial decision, must at least be defined with sufficient certainty to define the scope of the decision. If relinquishment of the power of revocation mentioned by the stipulation was of controlling significance in defining the practice, that circumstance was not present in the Hesslein case or in the Humphreys case. Whether in any of the three hundred cases mentioned in the stipulation the relinquishment of the power of revocation was followed by the relinquishment inter vivos of a power of changing the beneficiaries like that in this case, does not appear.

Such a stipulated definition of the practice is too vague and indefinite to afford a proper basis for a judicial decision which undertakes to state the construction of the statute in terms of the practice. Moreover, if we regard the stipulation as agreeing merely that the legal questions involved in the present case have uniformly been settled administratively in favor of the contention now made by the petitioner, it involves conclusions of law of the stipulators, both with respect to the legal issues in the present case and those resolved by the practice. We are not bound to accept, as controlling, stipulations as to questions of law.   Swift & Co. v. Hocking Valley Ry. Co., 243 U.S. 281, 289.

Without attempting to say what the administrative practice has actually been we may, for present purposes, make the assumption most favorable to the taxpayer in this case that the practice was as stated by the Government in its brief in the Humphreys case, viz., that until the decision in the Hesslein case "the Bureau consistently took the position that the gift tax applied to a transfer in trust where the grantor reserved the right to modify the trust but no right to revest title in himself."

But the record here shows that no such practice was recognized as controlling in 1935 when the present case first received the attention of the Bureau.   On February 21, 1935, the Assistant General Counsel gave an opinion reviewing at length the facts of the present case and the applicable principles of law, and concluded on the reasoning and authority of the Guggenheim and Porter cases that the gift was not complete and taxable until the relinquishment in August, 1924 of the power to modify the trust by the selection of new beneficiaries.   In April, 1935, the matter was reconsidered and a new opinion was given which was finally adopted by the Assistant Secretary who had intervened in the case.   This opinion reversed the earlier one on the authority of the Guggenheim case.   It was at pains to point out that in that case the Court had held that the relinquishment of the power of revocation was a taxable gift but it made no mention of the fact that there, unlike the present case, there was no power of modification which survived the relinquishment of the power of revocation, which was crucial in the Porter case.   Neither opinion rested upon or made any mention of any practice affecting cases where such a power of modification is reserved.   After the decision in the Hesslein case the ruling of the Bureau in this case was again reversed and notice of deficiency sent to the taxpayer.

From this record it is apparent that there was no established administrative practice before the opinion of April, 1935, [footnote omitted] and if the practice was adopted then it was because of a mistaken departmental ruling of law based on an obvious misinterpretation of the decisions in the Porter and Guggenheim cases.

Administrative practice may be of persuasive weight in determining the construction of a statute of doubtful meaning where the practice does not conflict with other provisions of the statute and is not so inconsistent with applicable decisions of the courts as to produce inconsistency and confusion in the administration of the law.   Such a choice, in practice, of one of two possible constructions of a statute by those who are experts in the field and specially informed as to administrative needs and convenience, tends to the wise interpretation and just administration of the laws. This is the more so when reliance has been placed on the practice by those affected by it.

But courts are not bound to accept the administrative construction of a statute regardless of consequences, even when disclosed in the form of rulings. See Helvering v. New York Trust Co., 292 U.S. 455, 468. Here the practice has not been revealed by any published rulings or action of the Department on which taxpayers could have relied. The taxpayers in the present cases are contending for different rulings. In Harriet Rosenau, 37 B.T.A. 468 (1938), as in the Humphreys case, the taxpayer contended that the date when the power to change the beneficiary is renounced is controlling. The petitioner here, who contends that the date of relinquishment of the power of revocation is controlling, rather than the date of surrender of power of modification, set up his trust and relinquished the power of revocation before the gift tax was enacted. The reenactment of the gift tax statute by the 1932 Act cannot be said to be a legislative approval of the practice which had not been disclosed by Treasury regulation, ruling or decision, and which does not appear to have been established before the adoption of the 1932 Act. Cf. McCaughn v. Hershey Chocolate Co., 283 U.S. 488, 492; Massachusetts Mutual Life Ins. Co. v. United States, 288 U.S. 269, 273; Helvering v. New York Trust Co., 292 U.S. 455, 468.

The very purpose sought to be accomplished by judicial acceptance of an administrative practice would be defeated if we were to regard the present practice as controlling. If a practice is to be accepted because of the superior knowledge of administrative officers of the administrative needs and convenience, see Brewster v. Gage, 280 U.S. 327, 336, there is no such reason for its acceptance here. The Government by taking no position confesses that it is unable to say how administrative need and convenience will best be served. If, as we have held, we may reject an established administrative practice when it conflicts with an earlier one and is not supported by valid reasons, see Burnet v. Chicago Portrait Co., 285 U.S. 1, 16, we should be equally free to reject the practice when it conflicts with our own decisions. A change of practice to conform to judicial decision, such as has occurred since the decision in the Hesslein case, or to meet administrative exigencies, will be accepted as controlling when consistent with our decisions. Morrissey v. Commissioner, 296 U.S. 344, 354. Here we have an added, and we think conclusive reason for rejecting the earlier practice and accepting the later. The earlier, because in sharp conflict with our own decisions. as we have already indicated, cannot be continued without the perpetuation of inconsistency and confusion comparable to that of which the Government asks to be relieved by our decision.

Affirmed.[150]

MR. JUSTICE BUTLER took no part in the consideration or decision of this case.

PROBLEMS

6.29. The terms of an irrevocable inter vivos trust provide that the net income is to be paid to the settlor for her life, and upon her death the principal of the trust is to be paid to or applied for any one or more of her issue and religious, charitable, scientific, literary, or educational corporations in such amounts as the settlor may in her last will appoint. Furthermore, during the lifetime of the settlor the trustees are authorized to pay her so much of the principal as they in their absolute discretion determine. Has the settlor made a completed gift for federal gift tax purposes with respect to any interest under the trust? See Revenue Ruling 54-342, 1954-2 C.B. 315.

6.30. A transfers property to T in trust. Under the terms of the trust instrument, until the death of A, T may pay the net income to A's son S or accumulate it. On the death of A, the trust property is to be paid to A's issue as A may appoint by his will, and in

---

[150] In Smith v. Shaughnessy, 318 U.S. 176, 178, 63 Sup. Ct. 545, 546, 87 L. Ed. 690, 692 (1943), the Court said:

"The taxpayer's principal argument here is that under our decision in the Hallock case, the value of the remainder will be included in the grantor's gross estate for estate tax purposes; and that in the Sanford case we intimated a general policy against allowing the same property to be taxed both as an estate and as a gift.

"This view, we think, misunderstands our position in the Sanford case. As we said there, the gift and estate tax laws are closely related and the gift tax serves to supplement the estate tax. [At this point there is the following footnote: "The gift tax was passed not only to prevent estate tax avoidance, but also to prevent income tax avoidance through reducing yearly income and thereby escaping the effect of progressive surtax rates." Citations are omitted.] We said that the taxes are not 'always mutually exclusive,' and called attention to Section 322 of the 1924 Act there involved (reenacted with amendments in Section 801 of the 1932 Act) which charts the course for granting credits on estate taxes by reason of previous payment of gift taxes on the same property. The scope of that provision we need not now determine. It is sufficient to note here that Congress plainly pointed out that 'some' of the 'total gifts subject to gift taxes . . . may be included for estate tax purposes and some not.' House Report No. 708, 72nd Cong., 1st Sess., p. 45. Under the statute the gift tax amounts in some instances to a security, a form of down-payment on the estate tax which secures the eventual payment of the latter; it is in no sense double taxation as the taxpayers suggest." — ED.

default of appointment by A, the trust property is to be paid to A's issue then living, such issue to take per stirpes, and if no issue of A is then living, the trust property is to be paid to the X charity.

    a. To what extent, if any, has A made a completed gift for federal gift tax purposes?

    b. If the income of the trust is paid to S, will it be includible in S's gross income for federal income tax purposes?

    c. On A's death, what will be includible in his gross estate for federal estate tax purposes so far as the trust property is concerned?

6.31. A transfers shares of stock to B, but possession of the certificates is given to X. It is agreed between A and B that B is to turn over to A all dividends from the stock during A's lifetime and that, if B complies, then on A's death, X is to deliver the certificates to B.

    a. Has A made a completed gift to B for gift tax purposes, and if so, what method should be employed to value the gift?

    b. Assume that prior to A's death, A and B have a difference of opinion regarding their rights in connection with the stock, and that the difference is voluntarily settled by an agreement between them whereby a portion of the stock in question is transferred back to A. If the answer to Part (a) above is that A made a completed gift to B when the stock was transferred to the name of B, will this subsequent development entitle A to a refund on the gift tax paid? See Short v. United States, 120 F. Supp. 755 (S.D.W. Va. 1954).

b. *Basis in the Hands of the Trustee of Trust Property Transferred by Gift*

At the beginning of this chapter, consideration was given generally to the basis for federal income tax purposes of trust property in the hands of the trustee.[151] The selection of the property to be placed in an irrevocable inter vivos trust must be made with these basis rules in mind. The federal gift tax payable will always be based on the value of the subject matter of the gift on the date the gift is made. Thus, if property having a low basis to the settlor is placed in trust, the gift tax due will be determined on the basis of the present high value of the property, whereas the net worth of the property to the trust after a sale has been made and the tax has been paid on the capital gain will be substantially less than the value on which the gift tax is calculated.[152]

----

[151] See discussion at page 148 supra.

[152] The discussion at page 125, supra, reveals that the trust property will

PROBLEM

6.32. A desires to place $100,000 worth of securities in an inter vivos trust. Assume that the trust instrument will be so drafted that he will be deemed to have made a gift of the trust property for federal gift tax purposes. A has 1000 shares of the X Corporation which have a present worth of $100 a share and which he acquired at $10 a share; 1000 shares of the Y Corporation which have a present worth of $100 a share and which he acquired at $80 a share; and 1000 shares of the Z Corporation which have a present worth of $100 a share and which he acquired at $120 a share. Advise A as to which securities should be placed in the trust.[153]

---

pick up a new basis if it is includible in the settlor's gross estate for federal estate tax purposes.

Under some circumstances, the basis of the property can be ascertained only after it has been determined whether the inter vivos arrangement was a completed gift. In Hahn v. United States, 123 F. Supp. 767 (S.D. Ohio, 1954), the taxpayer's mother desired to leave the taxpayer certain real estate on her death, and to accomplish this she executed deeds to the real estate but did not deliver them to the taxpayer. Ten years later she recorded the deeds. She continued to collect the rents and pay the taxes on the real estate. In the year in which the deeds were recorded the taxpayer wrote a letter to her mother stating that she held the property described in the deeds in trust for her mother. The mother's will gave the property outright to the taxpayer. The court held that the taxpayer acquired the property by gift and that her basis was that of her mother and not the fair market value at her mother's death.

In Caldwell & Co. v. Commissioner, 234 F.2d 660 (6th Cir. 1956), the court held that the Commissioner's determination that the basis of stock which was the subject matter of a gift was zero because there was no proof of the basis of the stock in the hands of the last preceding owner who had not acquired it by gift was arbitrary. There was nothing in the record to indicate the impossibility of finding the fair market value of the stock when it was acquired by the last preceding owner who had not acquired it by gift, and the court said, ". . . in the event insufficient probative evidence upon this issue is adduced, then neither gain nor loss can be allowed . . ."

If a gift of a going business is made, and on the date of the gift the business has some items available for sale, what is the basis of these items in the hands of the donee? See Wren Bowyer, 33 T.C. 660 (1960).

[153] If the settlor of a trust transfers to the trust money received from the sale of securities, and the trustee uses the money to buy securities of the same type as the ones sold by the settlor, what will be the tax consequences if the settlor sells the securities at a loss? If he sells them at a gain? In connection with these questions examine 1954 I.R.C. §267, quoted infra page 1337, and the wash-sales provisions of 1954 I.R.C. §1091. United States v. Norton, 250 F.2D 902 (5th Cir. 1958), held that a taxpayer could not deduct losses on the sale of stock by his broker when his broker at the same time bought a similar amount of the same stock for the taxpayers's mother, for whom the broker also acted as investment counsel; the taxpayer could, however, deduct the loss sustained on the sale of stock by the broker, even though the broker purchased an equal number of shares of the same stock for the taxpayer's mother twenty-eight days later. In Boehm v. Commissioner, 255 F.2d 684

c. *Exclusion, Specific Exemption, Gifts by Married Person to Person Other than Spouse and to Spouse*

Even though the transfer in trust by the settlor of an inter vivos trust constitutes a gift for federal gift tax purposes, it does not necessarily follow that a gift tax will be payable. So far as the trust creates present interests, the $3000 annual exclusion is applicable.[154] The $3000 annual exclusion, of course, does not apply to gifts of future interests and it is very likely that the inter vivos trust will have created some future interests.[155]

(2d Cir. 1958), the taxpayer sold shares in her wholly owned corporation to her father-in-law, and at the same time the corporation purchased the same amount at the same price. The court held that this was an indirect sale from her to her corporation, so that the deduction of the taxpayer for a loss was denied under 1939 I.R.C. §24(b)(1)(B) (1954 I.R.C. §267). For the application of the wash-sale rules where Treasury bonds are sold and repurchased, see Rev. Rul. 58-210, 1958-1 C.B. 523; Rev. Rul. 58-211, 1958-1 C.B. 529.

[154] See 1954 I.R.C. §2503(b), quoted infra page 1418.

For a special type of gift to minors which will be deemed a gift of only a present interest, so that the annual exclusion will be available with respect to it, see page 243 infra.

Suppose that A establishes an irrevocable inter vivos trust containing only future interests and then gives property outright to his son, and his son, after receiving the property, transfers it to the trust. Will A be deemed to have made a gift of a present interest to his son, and his son be deemed to have made a gift of a future interest? Or will the son be disregarded and A be deemed to have made a gift of a future interest? In Emil Klempner, 14 CCH T.C. Mem. 1185 (1955), the court held that absent any direct evidence of any agreement by the son to retransfer the property, plus the uncontradicted testimony that the transfer to the son was absolute, A will be deemed to have made a gift of a present interest to his son.

Harbeck Halsted, 28 T.C. 1069 (1957), held that where a designated beneficiary was given the right to call for the corpus of the trust at any time, gifts to the trust were gifts of a present interest, even though the terms of the trust created present and future interests.

In Estate of G. A. Buder, 25 T.C. 1012 (1956), the donor made separate gifts to his son and his son's wife, and then made a third gift to his son and his son's wife as "joint tenants" and not as tenants in common. He claimed that the third gift was to an entity separate from the other two and that he was entitled to an additional annual exclusion with respect to it. The court did not agree.

[155] In Estate of Louise Jardell, 24 T.C. 652 (1955), the court considered a case where certain gifts were made in October, 1949, of shares in royalty interests owned by and to be paid or delivered to the donor from the production of minerals, but the gift was to become effective only on production commencing January 1, 1950. The court held that the gift was of future interests because the eventual donees and the extent of their respective interests could not be definitely determined, since by January, 1950, one or more of them might have died.

It was held in Shefner and Gainsley v. Knox, 131 F. Supp. 936 (D. Minn. 1955), that the interests of beneficiaries under a trust which was set up to

If an inter vivos trust is established under which the income is to be paid to a designated person for his life, or for some other specified period of time, the income beneficiary's interest under the trust is a present interest and the $3000 annual gift tax exclusion is available with respect to it.[156] The gift is a present interest even

---

provide for the repurchase by a corporation of its own stock were future interests.

In Wyss v. United States, 55-1 U.S.T.C. ¶11543 (S.D. Ill. 1955), a trust was involved which provided that the trustees were authorized in their sole discretion to apply so much of the income and principal as they deemed expedient for the "support, maintenance, medical care, and education" of the beneficiary, and to pay accumulated income to the beneficiary at twenty-five and corpus at thirty. It was held that only future interests were involved and that hence there was no annual exclusion.

If the income beneficiaries of a trust are described by a class designation, such as "children" or "grandchildren," and during the period that income is to be paid, the class may increase in size by the birth of additional members or may decrease in size by the death of a member, will the gift to any one of such income beneficiaries be deemed a gift of a present interest, so that the $3000 annual exclusion will be available? The answer to this question can be found in Rev. Rul. 55-678, 1955-2 C.B. 389, and Rev. Rul. 55-679, 1955-2 C.B. 390.

In Celia Goldstein, 26 T.C. 506 (1956), stock in a family corporation was transferred to trustees, with the provision that the corporation could purchase each year so much of the stock as it should determine, paying the proceeds of the sale over to the beneficiaries of the trust. The court held that the gift to the beneficiaries under the trust was a gift of a future interest because the enjoyment of the gift was entirely contingent upon the discretion of the corporation in deciding whether it would or would not purchase the stock from the trustees.

Heringer v. Commissioner, 235 F.2d 149 (9th Cir. 1956), cert. denied, 352 U.S. 927 (1956), involved the owner of 40 percent of the stock in a closely held corporation who transferred property to the corporation. Without deciding whether the gift should be deemed a gift to the corporation or a gift to the stockholders thereof, the court determined that if the gift were deemed one to the stockholders it would be a gift of a future interest, and the $3000 annual exclusion would not be available because any benefit to the stockholders would be dependent upon the corporation declaring dividends. The court, however, pointed out that only 60 percent of the value of the property transferred should be deemed a gift because the donor owned 40 percent of the stock.

In George M. Street, 29 T.C. 428 (1957), the petitioner created six irrevocable trusts for the primary benefit of six minor grandchildren, and each trust provided that the income or principal could be used at any time it was needed for the support, comfort and education of the beneficiary. The court held that all interests under each trust were future interests. The case was affirmed sub nom. Street v. Commissioner, 261 F.2d 666 (5th Cir. 1958).

156 See Reg. §25.2503-3(b), quoted infra page 1542.

Hugh McK. Jones, 29 T.C. 200 (1957), involved two types of trusts. The first gave the entire trust income to a child of the settlor for life, with power in the corporate trustee to pay the child principal when proper to do so. The court held that the right of the child to receive income was a present interest which qualified for the annual $3000 exclusion; the power to encroach on the principal was deemed limited by a standard, and the chance of encroachment under the standard was deemed so remote as to be negligible, so that the flow of the income would not be affected. The other trust gave the trustee power

though the trust instrument contains a clause prohibiting a beneficiary from alienating, assigning, or otherwise anticipating the income.[157]   Furthermore, if the trustee is given the power to pay

---

to apply income and principal for the benefit of a grandchild of the settlor in such amounts as the trustee might deem necessary for the education, maintenance and support of the grandchild until the grandchild reached age twenty-one, with additional provisions disposing of the income and principal at that time.   The court held that all interests under the trust were future interests, so that no annual exclusion was available.

In George Fischer, 19 CCH T.C. Mem. 327 (1960), the court held that although the gifts of rights to receive trust income were present interests, the contingencies which might reduce or defeat the gifts were such (trust property was mortgaged rental realty and net income was defined as excess of rents and other income over disbursements and operating expenses and cost of amortization of mortgages) that the record did not justify finding that the present gifts had any value.   Thus all value was deemed attributable to the future interests.

The court in Munger v. United States, 154 F. Supp. 417 (M.D. Ala. 1957), found that the income beneficiaries under a trust were entitled to receive the income, and that the trustee's discretion was limited to the manner and means of paying the income to the beneficiaries.   Consequently, the interest of each income beneficiary under the trust was a present interest.   See also Fred J. LaFortune, 29 T.C. 479 (1957).   The case was affirmed sub nom. LaFortune v. Commissioner, 263 F.2d 186 (10th Cir. 1958).

In Frances Carroll Brown, 30 T.C. 831 (1958), the Commissioner disallowed the annual exclusion with respect to the income beneficiaries' interests under a trust because the trustees were given the power to allocate receipts of, and accretions to, the trust estate to principal.   The court, however, held that the annual exclusion was available because the trustees could not properly exercise their powers in such a manner as to diminish the value of the interests of the income beneficiaries.   Furthermore, the court held that the powers of the trustees did not render the interests of the income beneficiaries incapable of valuation.

[157] See Rev. Rul. 54-344, 1954-2 C.B. 319.

Estate of Julien W. Vose, 18 CCH T.C. Mem. 765 (1959), dealt with a case where the settlor of a trust under which he retained the income for life, with a general power of appointment, annually bestowed on members of his family "certificates of indebtedness" purporting to be obligations of the trust which he had created.   The obligations bore 6 percent interest, but the principal was not payable until the termination of the trust.   The certificates could not be transferred without the consent of the trustees.   The issue before the court was whether these gifts by the settlor were gifts of present or future interests.   The court held that the certificates were not "definitely enforceable legal obligations payable on a day certain and immediately disposable by the obligee" and hence were not "contractual rights such as exist in a bond or note," which were specifically excluded from the definition of a future interest by the Regulations (see Reg. 108, §86.11, relating to the 1939 Code; the corresponding regulation under the 1954 Code is §25.2503-3(a), quoted infra page 1542).   Thus the annual exclusion was not available.   (The Commissioner conceded that the gifts of 6 percent interest were gifts of present interests.)   The court also held that the face amount of the certificates would be their value for gift tax purposes, though they were not transferable and the principal was not collectible until the trust terminated.   The court was influenced by the fact that the face value of the certificates of indebtedness had been excluded from the settlor's gross estate for estate tax purposes.   The case was reversed and remanded sub nom. Vose v. Commissioner, 284 F.2d 65 (1st Cir. 1960), on

principal to such an income beneficiary, Section 2503(b) makes it clear that the income beneficiary's present interest is capable of being evaluated.[158]

The federal gift tax specific exemption is $30,000.[159] This is a lifetime exemption and not a per donee exemption as is the annual exclusion. What otherwise would be taxable gifts, whether of present or future interests, can be charged off against it until it is gone. It is not available to a nonresident who is not a citizen, unless an applicable tax convention provides differently.[160]

If the settlor of an irrevocable inter vivos trust (or any other donor) is married, the value of the beneficial rights conferred on persons other than his spouse may be divided equally between the settlor and his spouse if each is a citizen or resident of the United States, and each will be treated as having made a gift of one half for federal gift tax purposes.[161] The non-donor spouse must con-

---

the ground that the gifts of the certificates were outright gifts, not in trust, and qualified for the annual exclusion.

[158] In Rev. Rul. 54-92, 1954-1 C.B. 207, it is stated that the gift tax annual exclusion does not apply to a gift in trust under an instrument which provides for the distribution of income to a designated beneficiary but gives the trustee uncontrolled discretion to determine whether or not to distribute the principal to the income beneficiary. In such a case the beneficiary's present interest in the income is incapable of determination. See also Evans v. Commissioner, 198 F.2d 435 (3d Cir. 1952); Herrmann v. Commissioner, 235 F.2d 440 (5th Cir. 1956); Saul Reinfeld, 14 CCH T.C. Mem. 1326 (1955); Estate of Brigid Angela Casey, 25 T.C. 707 (1956); Fred J. LaFortune, 29 T.C. 479 (1957), *aff'd sub nom.* LaFortune v. Commissioner, 263 F.2d 186 (10th Cir. 1958); Farha Schayek, 33 T.C. 629 (1960). But compare J. J. Newlin, 31 T.C. 451 (1958). Section 2503(b) of the 1954 Code, quoted infra page 1418, which is not applicable to gifts made prior to January 1, 1955, is contra.

If a trust is established under which the trustee is required to pay the income to A for life and the trustee has discretion to pay the principal to A or his issue, the $3000 gift tax annual exclusion is not available with respect to the interest given to A under the trust. Raymond J. Funkhouser, 17 CCH T.C. Mem. 1094 (1958), *aff'd, sub nom.* Funkhouser's Trusts v. Commissioner, 275 F.2d 245 (4th Cir. 1960), *cert. denied,* 363 U.S. 804 (1960), holds that the annual exclusion is not available when the trustee has a power to pay corpus to one other than the income beneficiary, because the gift of the present interest cannot be valued. In Lorch v. Campbell, 59-2 U.S.T.C. ¶11901 (N.D. Tex. 1959), however, the court held that the life interest under the trust could be valued and the annual exclusion claimed where the trustee, who was the life income beneficiary, could terminate the trust and distribute the property to the remainderman.

[159] See 1954 I.R.C. §2521, quoted infra page 1423.

[160] See Reg. §25.2521-1 (a), quoted infra page 1554.

[161] See 1954 I.R.C. §2513, quoted infra page 1419.

If the wife consents to have one half of a gift charged to her for gift tax purposes and then the gift made by her husband is deemed one in contemplation of death, can the wife reclaim any of her specific exemption that was used up in consenting to the gift? A negative answer is given to this question in a discussion of it in CCH Fed. Est. & Gift Tax Rep. ¶8081, though no direct authority is cited.

sent to have the gift so regarded and this consent must be evidenced in a certain manner.[162] When a spouse dies, the executor may be faced with a decision as to whether to allow one half of the gifts made by the surviving spouse to be attributed to the deceased spouse and as to whether to seek the consent of the surviving spouse to allow one half of the gifts made by the deceased spouse to be attributed to the surviving spouse.[163]

Gift-splitting between husband and wife with respect to gifts to persons other than the spouse of the donor is not available if the gift is in part to the non-donor spouse and the value of the interest in the non-donor spouse is not ascertainable.[164] If the settlor establishes an irrevocable inter vivos trust which provides that a disinterested trustee may pay income and principal to any one or more of a group consisting of the settlor's spouse and his issue living from time to time, no part of such a gift can be attributed to the spouse because it cannot be separated from the other interests given and valued.[165]

[162] Revenue Ruling 54-252, 1954-2 C.B. 322, points out that where a husband has made gifts not exceeding a total of $6000 during the calendar year to a third party donee, and his wife has made no gifts during the calendar year, the wife is not required to file a gift tax return. She signifies her consent, on her husband's return, that one half of the gifts are chargeable to her. If the gifts made by the husband are of future interests, however, and one half of the value thereof is to be charged to the wife, she must file a return regardless of the value of the gifts.

Alex Frieder, 28 T.C. 1156 (1957), held that the consent of a wife signified on her husband's gift tax return was made in time, even though she had filed a gift tax return covering gifts for the same year, made by her prior to her marriage. In Camiel Thorrez, 31 T.C. 655 (1958), a husband filed a 1951 gift tax return and his wife did not execute the required consent; in 1954 he filed an amended return for 1951, prior to issuance of deficiency notice, and the wife did execute the consent on the amended return. The court held that the consent of the wife could not be signified after the 1951 return had been filed. The case was affirmed sub nom. Thorrez v. Commissioner, 272 F.2d 945 (6th Cir. 1959), but this point was not involved on appeal.

Revenue Ruling 59-39, 1959-1 C.B. 639, holds that where a gift is made by a husband to a third party, and one half the value of the gift is included in his gift tax return and the other half in the wife's return, an overassessment of the tax on the wife's return may be applied against a deficiency assessed against the husband.

In Rev. Rul. 55-241, 1955-1 C.B. 470, it is determined that a prenuptial agreement under which each spouse waived all marital rights in the property of the other does not prevent a husband and wife from taking advantage of the gift-splitting provision of the gift tax law in making gifts to third persons.

[163] In making his decision the executor should take into account the fact that the liability with respect to the entire tax of each spouse will be joint and several if the non-donor spouse consents. See also Reg. §25.2513-2(c), quoted infra page 1549.

[164] See Reg. §25.2513-1(b)(4), quoted infra page 1549.

[165] The spouse in the situation referred to in the text is an object of the power of appointment given to the disinterested trustee. Restatement of Property, §338, Comment b provides: "The interest of an object of a power,

Section 2513 of the 1954 Code specifically provides that gift-splitting is not available if the non-donor spouse has a general power of appointment over the subject matter of the gift. Presumably, the mere fact that the non-donor spouse has a power of

---

as such is essentially similar to the interest of an expectant distributee (see §315) . . ." Section 315 of the Restatement defines an expectant distributee as a person who may be an heir or devisee of a living person. If the settlor should make a gift to his spouse's mother, no one would contend that the availability of §2513 is eliminated on the ground that the settlor's spouse has an expectancy in the subject matter of the gift as an heir of her mother, which is incapable of valuation. If all the settlor's spouse has is an expectancy as an object of the power of appointment given the disinterested trustee, should it not also be disregarded in determining the availability of §2513? The material which follows in this footnote answers this question in the negative.

See Matthew P. Whittall, 24 T.C. 808 (1955), where the wife of the settlor of a trust was to receive "so much of the net income in quarter-annual installments in each calendar year as she shall request and said trustee shall deem wise for her comfort, maintenance and support." The court held that it was not possible on the record to ascertain the value of the interest transferred to the wife and thus the gift-splitting privilege was not available. Petition for review was dismissed for want of diligent prosecution. 230 F.2d 948 (1st Cir. 1956). In William H. Robertson, 26 T.C. 246 (1956), a husband created a trust giving his wife the income for life, with power in the corporate trustee to pay her so much of the principal as it deemed necessary for her maintenance and support, having due regard for her other assets, and with remainders over to others. The annual exclusion was allowed for the life interest given to the wife and gift-splitting was allowed with respect to the remainder, the court holding that the wife's interest in the principal by virtue of the power in the trustee to pay her principal could be valued under the same tests that permit valuation of charitable remainders when subject to a power to invade for the benefit of a life beneficiary. Revenue Ruling 56-439, 1956-2 C.B. 605, holds that where a gift is made in trust and the trustee has discretion to pay the income or principal to or among the spouse of the donor and others, the value of the income or principal to be distributed to the wife is not susceptible of determination and is not severable from the gifts to others, and hence the gift may not to any extent be considered as made one half by the donor and one half by his spouse under §2513. This Revenue Ruling is amplified in a Special Ruling dated November 16, 1956, CCH Fed. Est. & Gift Tax Rep. ¶8099. Compare with Rev. Rul. 56-439 the case of O'Connor v. O'Malley, 57-1 USTC ¶11690 (D. Neb. 1957), where the trustee was given discretion to pay principal to the settlor's husband in such amounts as the trustee might "from time to time deem advisable." The trust was created primarily for the benefit of the settlor's children, and the court found that in the light of the circumstances the settlor did not intend to make any gift to the husband by virtue of the power given the trustee, and the court therefore concluded that §1000(f) of the 1939 Code (1954 I.R.C. §2513) was available. In Max Kass, 16 CCH T.C. Mem. 1035 (1957), the settlor's spouse was the life beneficiary under the trust, and the trustees were given discretion to invade the corpus for her general welfare. The court determined that the value of the interests of other beneficiaries under the trust was not ascertainable and, therefore, the gift-splitting provisions of the Code did not apply.

If the wife consents to have one half of the gift charged to her and thereby uses up her $30,000 specific exemption, and it is later determined that such consent is ineffective because she is deemed to have an interest

appointment that is not a general one will not rule out the section.

The gift tax marital deduction is available with respect to certain gifts from one spouse to another.[166] The discussion of this deduction is postponed so that it may be considered with the estate tax marital deduction, which in many respects is similar.[167]

Gift tax rates are somewhat lower than estate tax rates, so that it may be advantageous from a tax standpoint for the settlor to place property in an inter vivos trust, even though a federal gift tax will have to be paid. The property placed in the inter vivos trust (assuming it is effective to remove the value of the trust property from the settlor's gross estate) is eliminated from the top bracket for estate tax purposes and taxed for gift tax purposes at the bottom rates if the settlor has not previously made taxable gifts.[168]

PROBLEMS

6.33. Shortly before his death A makes a gift to his son, S. The value of this gift is included in A's gross estate as a gift in contemplation of death. A's executor files a gift tax return and pays the gift tax that is due. The amount of the tax is deductible under Section 2053 of the 1954 Code, quoted infra page 1403. Suppose that A's surviving spouse agrees to have half of the gift charged to her for gift tax purposes under Section 2513 and that A's executor pays the entire gift tax liability. Will the entire amount paid by the executor be deductible under Section 2053? See Revenue Ruling 55-334, 1955-1 C.B. 449. Compare Revenue Ruling 55-506, 1955-2 C.B. 609. See also Section 20.2053-6(d) of the Regulations, quoted infra page 1526.

6.34. A transfers property to T in trust. Under the terms of the

---

in the appointive assets, and the existence of such an interest makes it impossible to evaluate the interests in other persons, will she have available as to gifts in future years her $30,000 specific exemption? In Rev. Rul. 55-709, 1955-2 C.B. 609, it was held that a husband who used his specific exemption when an equal division of community property was made did not eliminate its availability with respect to gifts made in subsequent years when later it was held by the courts that a division of community property into equal shares did not result in a gift by the husband to his wife.

[166] See 1954 I.R.C. §2523, quoted infra page 1425.

[167] For a treatment of marital deduction gifts, see page 783 infra.

[168] If the $30,000 specific exemption has not been used up, it cannot be carried over and added to the $60,000 federal estate tax exemption.

In calculating the tax saving that may be produced by making an inter vivos gift, one should take into consideration the fact that the subject matter of the gift will not get a stepped-up basis for federal income tax purposes (except to a limited extent if gift taxes are payable), whereas a stepped-up basis will be acquired if such property is retained in the donor's gross estate. See the discussion in regard to basis at page 234 supra.

trust, T is required to pay out all the income to three named beneficiaries for their joint lives but he is given discretion as to the
amount each beneficiary is to receive. On the death of one of
the named beneficiaries, the trust corpus is to be distributed to the
other named beneficiaries. Is the annual gift tax exclusion available with respect to any of the interests under the trust? See
Revenue Ruling 55-303, 1955-1 C.B. 471. See also Section 25.2503-
3(c), Ex. (3) of the Regulations, quoted infra page 1543.

d. *Present Interest Gifts to Minors*

Annual gifts to minors, designed to take advantage of the $3000
annual gift tax exclusion, may well be a significant part of any
comprehensive estate plan. The subject matter of a gift may be
transferred directly to the minor and such a transfer will qualify
for the annual exclusion, even though the minor does not have
the legal capacity to act for himself with respect to the transferred
property, and no legal guardian has been appointed for him.[169]
The inherent disadvantages of placing the ownership of property
in a minor make this route an undesirable one to use to take
advantage of the annual exclusion.

Section 2503(c) of the 1954 Code[170] recognizes that a transfer

[169] In Rev. Rul. 54-400, 1954-2 C.B. 319, it is held that where a gift of
shares of stock is made to a minor and the shares are issued in the name
of the minor, it is a gift of a present interest, even though no legal guardian
exists for the minor, unless the use or enjoyment of the property is in some
manner limited or restricted by the terms of the donor's conveyance. The
disability placed upon minors by state statutes is indecisive in determining
whether a minor has the immediate enjoyment of the property or the income
therefrom within the purport of the federal gift tax law.

In Rev. Rul. 55-469, 1955-2 C.B. 519, a case was considered which involved
a grandparent making an outright gift to his grandchildren. The controlling
state law prohibited stocks from being registered in the names of minors, and
consequently, the stocks were registered in the names of the parents of the
grandchildren. Dividends on the stocks were placed in separate bank accounts and proceeds from the sale of stocks were also deposited in separate
bank accounts. Under these circumstances it was determined that no taxable
trust existed and the income from the stocks was taxable to the minor grandchildren. The ruling referred to Prudence Miller Trust, 7 T.C. 1245 (1946).

Revenue Ruling 58-65, 1958-1 C.B. 13, holds that dividends received from
a savings and loan account which legally belongs to a minor are taxable
to the minor even though the account is in the name of the parents as
trustees.

In Snyder v. United States, 134 F. Supp. 319 (W.D.N.C. 1955), stock was
given to a minor's guardian. The court held that the gift was a gift of a
present interest and the annual exclusion was available because, under state
law concerning guardians, no delay in the enjoyment of the stock was involved. The title vested in the minor absolutely and the guardian was no
barrier to present enjoyment.

[170] Quoted infra page 1418. This provision of the 1954 Code is applicable
only with respect to gifts made after January 1, 1955.

will be deemed to create only a present interest in the minor beneficiary if the following tests are met:

1. The principal and income of the subject matter of the gift may be expended by the beneficiary or for his benefit before he attains twenty-one; and

2. The unexpended principal and income will pass to the beneficiary when he attains twenty-one, or to his estate or as he may appoint under a general power of appointment, if he dies under twenty-one.[171]

Each state has now enacted a so-called custodianship statute in one form or another.[172] The custodianship arrangement is designed to take advantage of Section 2503(c) and permits the ownership of the gift property to be placed in the name of a selected custodian, to be expended for the benefit of the minor or retained until he is twenty-one or dies, at which time the property is to be turned over to him or to his estate. These custodianship statutes have passed the tests laid down by Section 2503(c), so that only a present interest is created by a transfer in accordance with them.[173] Where the donor makes himself the custodian, however, he will have a Section 2038 power and the value of the property held by him as custodian will be includible in his gross estate for federal estate tax purposes if he dies possessed of the power.[174]   The in-

[171] Section 2503(c) as originally passed by the House of Representatives required that the income "will" be expended by or for the benefit of the minor prior to his attaining twenty-one. The Senate amended §2503(c) by inserting the word "may" for the word "will." The Senate Finance Committee report states: "Your Committee has amended the provisions of the House bill to provide that it is not necessary that the property or income therefrom be actually expended by or for the benefit of a minor during minority so long as all such amounts not so expended will pass to the donee upon attaining majority and, in the event of his prior death, will be payable to his estate or as he may appoint under a general power of appointment." S. Rep. No. 1622, 83d Cong., 2d Sess. 479 (1954).

[172] See Note, Recent Legislation to Facilitate Gifts of Securities to Minors, 69 Harv. L. Rev. 1476 (1956).

[173] Revenue Ruling 56-86, 1956-1 C.B. 449, deals with the Colorado statute and concludes that compliance with it results in a gift of a present interest in property within the meaning of §2503(c).

Revenue Ruling 59-357, 1959-2 C.B. 212, compares the Uniform Gifts to Minors Act and the Model Gifts of Securities to Minors Act and concludes that their differences do not justify any differences in tax consequences. The ruling reaffirms previous rulings applicable to these custodianship arrangements and states: "No taxable gift occurs for Federal gift tax purposes by reason of a subsequent resignation of the custodian or termination of the custodianship." After pointing out that the transferred property may be includible in the donor's gross estate if the transfer is in contemplation of death or if the donor is the custodian and dies while serving in that capacity, the ruling states: "In all other circumstances custodial property is includible only in the gross estate of the donee."

[174] Revenue Ruling 57-366, 1957-2 C.B. 618, holds that where the donor is custodian for a minor under a model custodianship act, the value of the

come of the gift property under the custodial arrangement is taxable to the minor, except to the extent that it is used to discharge someone's legal obligation to support the minor.[175]

Is it better to make present interest gifts to a minor by taking advantage of Section 2503(c) through the medium of a custodianship arrangement or through the medium of a trust drafted to comply with Section 2503(c)? There is no one answer to this question. The pros and cons of the custodianship arrangement must be weighed [176] against the pros and cons of the trust arrangement.

---

property given to the minor is includible in the donor's gross estate for federal estate tax purposes where he dies before the donee attains the age of twenty-one. The ruling is based on Lober v. United States, the opinion of which is printed supra page 210.

[175] Revenue Ruling 56-484, 1956-2 C.B. 23, deals with the taxation of income from stock that is transferred under the Model Custodianship Act adopted by Colorado. It is pointed out that under Colorado law a father must support and maintain his minor children without resort to their separate estates. Revenue Ruling 55-469, referred to supra note 169, is explained on the ground that under the facts dealt with, the income was not available for the support of the minors to whom the stock was given and thus would not be taxable to the parent under any circumstances. Where, however, a gift expressly provides that the property may be used for the support of the minor, the subject matter of the gift may be so applied without reference to the ability of the parent to furnish such support. The Colorado Custodian Act provides that the custodian may use the income for the support of the minor without regard to any other funds which may be available for the purpose. Under these circumstances, the Revenue Ruling concludes that the income will be taxable to the person who is obligated to support the minor, regardless of the relationship of the donor or of the custodian to the donee, to the extent that it is used in discharge of the legal obligation of support. The tax is imposed under 1954 I.R.C. §61, quoted infra page 1325. To the extent that the income is not used to discharge the legal obligation of support, it is taxable to the minor. It should be noted that Rev. Rul. 56-484 makes no mention of 1954 I.R.C. §102, which provides that gross income does not include the value of property acquired by gift unless one of the exceptions set forth in §102(b) applies. Section 102(b) clearly covers the situation of trust income, but is it clear that non-trust income, such as is involved when a custodianship arrangement for a minor is established, is excepted by §102(b)?

[176] Two Surrogate's Court cases in New York have considered the problem of the appointment of a successor custodian under the New York Gifts of Securities to Minors Act. In one case the custodian had died, and it was held that an application to a court had to be made to appoint a successor custodian and that the court should make a sufficient inquiry to insure that the appointee would serve the best interests of the minor. The court outlined the facts which should appear in the application. See Matter of Susan A. Bushing, 8 Misc. 2d 755, 167 N.Y.S.2d 132 (1957). In the other case the donor had originally designated himself as custodian for his minor children, and in order to avoid the inclusion in his gross estate for estate tax purposes of the value of the securities if he died before the children became of age, he resigned as custodian and sought to have his wife appointed as his successor. The court directed that there be submitted in an accounting proceeding an order to show cause, which provided for the representation of the children. See Mat-

Before examining the Section 2503(c) trust arrangement, consideration is given to the creation of present interest trust arrangements for the benefit of a minor, unaided by Section 2503(c), by the inclusion of the opinions in the Kieckhefer and Stifel cases.

KIECKHEFER v. COMMISSIONER OF INTERNAL REVENUE
189 F.2d 118 (7th Cir. 1951)

MAJOR, Chief Judge.

This appeal involves a deficiency in petitioner's gift tax for the taxable year 1945, during which he made a gift in trust to a minor grandson. The question for decision is whether the Tax Court correctly sustained the Commissioner's determination that such gift was of a future interest so as to preclude the statutory exclusion of $3,000, as provided for in sec. 1003(b)(3) of the Internal Revenue Code, Title 26 U.S.C.A. sec. 1003(b)(3).

The taxpayer, a resident of Prescott, Arizona, but for many years engaged in business in Milwaukee, Wisconsin, in the year 1944 consulted his attorney, Malcolm K. Whyte, also of Milwaukee, and advised him of the birth of a grandchild and that he would like to make a gift in trust to such child of $3,000. Counsel advised him that if the gift was one of a future interest the statutory exclusion would not be allowable but that he thought he could draw a trust instrument which would evidence a gift of a present and not a future interest. As a result of this conference, counsel prepared a trust instrument which was executed by the taxpayer on August 23, 1944. The grandson and beneficiary, John Irving Kieckhefer, was born on July 30, 1944. Robert H. Kieckhefer, son of the taxpayer and father of the grandson, was named as trustee. The trustee was also a resident of the State of Arizona, and admittedly during the

---

ter of Strauss, 8 Misc. 2d 277, 176 N.Y.S.2d 1014 (1957). Revenue Ruling 58-73, 1958-1 C.B. 458, holds that a transfer from a donor to a custodian under the New York act is a transfer of legal title and is subject to the documentary stamp tax imposed by 1954 I.R.C. §§4321 and 4331; however, under §4343(a), the later transfer of the securities from the custodian to the minor upon the latter's attaining his majority is tax-exempt. Revenue Ruling 60-12, I.R.B. 1960-2, 40, holds that no transfer tax is due when securities are transferred from the custodian to the name of the minor (the ruling is specifically made with respect to the New York statute), since the transfer does not involve the transfer of the legal title to such securities. To the extent that Rev. Rul. 58-73 held that §4343(a)(2) was the basis of holding that no transfer tax is due, it is modified. The effect of the change is to eliminate the necessity of filing an exemption certificate to make the transfer not taxable. A transfer from a guardian to a minor comes under §4343(a)(2), and the exemption certificate must accompany the transfer to make it not taxable.

taxable year was amply able financially to support and educate his son.

Only paragraphs 5 and 13 of the trust instrument need be considered. In fact, the controversy in the main revolves around the latter paragraph.

Paragraph 5, so far as here material, provides: "The trustee shall pay to the beneficiary or apply on his behalf such income from the trust and so much of the principal thereof as may be necessary for the education, comfort and support of the beneficiary and shall accumulate for such beneficiary all income not so needed. . . . The trust estate shall be deemed vested absolutely in said beneficiary and shall be his property, but the trustee is authorized and directed to hold said estate, *unless the trust be prior terminated as hereinafter provided,* until such beneficiary arrives at the age of twenty-one (21) years, at which time the trustee shall pay over to him the said trust estate including all accumulations. In the event that the said beneficiary shall die prior to his becoming twenty-one (21) years of age, the said trust estate and any accumulations shall belong to his estate and shall be paid over to his administrator." (Italics ours.)

In the absence of the italicized phrase, we agree with the Tax Court that the provisions of this paragraph would require a holding adverse to the taxpayer as they come squarely within both the reasoning and the decisions in Fondren v. Commissioner, 324 U.S. 18, and Commissioner v. Disston, 325 U.S. 442. In fact, that such is the case appears to be conceded on all sides.

Paragraph 13 provides: "This trust has been created by the donor after full consideration and advice. Upon such consideration and advice the donor has determined that this said trust shall not contain any right in the donor to alter, amend, revoke or terminate it. *The beneficiary shall be entitled to all or any part of the trust estate or to terminate the trust estate in whole or in part at any time whenever said John Irving Kieckhefer or the legally appointed guardian for his estate shall make due demand therefor by instrument in writing filed with the then trustee* and upon such demand being received by the trustee the trustee shall pay said trust estate and its accumulations, or the part thereof for which demand is made, over to said John Irving Kieckhefer or to the legally appointed guardian for his estate who made such demand on his behalf." (Italics ours.)

The italicized language of this paragraph forms the basis for the controversy as to whether the taxpayer's gift to his grandson was of a present or future interest. Again the Commissioner, as well as the Tax Court, relies upon the Fondren and Disston cases in support of the conclusion that it falls within the latter category. Other cases cited and relied upon both by the Commissioner and the taxpayer are of little, if any, aid because they each deal with a different factual situation. In fact, there is no case, so far as we are aware, where a court has decided the issue before us upon the same or even a similar state of facts.

The Commissioner's argument rests upon two premises, (1) that the infant beneficiary, being of tender years, could not make an effective demand, and (2) that the minor beneficiary had no legally appointed guardian at the time of the execution of the trust or since its establishment. In connection with this latter premise, it is urged that under the law of Arizona (the residence and domicile of the beneficiary as well as his father), it is doubtful if the court would appoint a guardian for the purpose of making a demand and, even so, that his actions would be subject to court review.

Section 86.11 of Treasury Regulation 108, promulgated under the Internal Revenue Code, so far as here pertinent, provides: "No part of the value of a gift of a future interest may be excluded in determining the total amount of gifts made during the calendar year. 'Future interests' is a legal term, and includes reversions, remainders, and other interests or estates, whether vested or contingent, and whether or not supported by a particular interest or estate, which are limited to commence in use, possession, or enjoyment at some future date or time."

We think the Fondren and Disston cases on the facts are readily distinguishable. In each of those cases, the court was dealing with trust agreements which by their terms contained the restrictions and conditions which led the court to decide that the gifts were of a future interest. As was pointed out in the Fondren case, 324 U.S. at page 24 (the Disston case is to the same effect), "That contingency by the explicit terms of the trust, was the existence of need which was then nonexistent and, in the stated contemplation of the donors, was not likely to occur in the future, at any rate during the child's minority." In contrast, the trustee in the instant situation is required "at any time" to pay the trust estate to the minor beneficiary upon demand made as provided. Thus, the conditions and restrictions upon which the Commissioner relies to convert this gift into one of a future interest are not imposed by the trust instrument but, if they exist, are the result solely of the disability of the beneficiary due to the fact that he is a minor.

The taxpayer in the Fondren case argued (the same argument is made here) that the position of the Commissioner means that every gift to a minor is of a future interest. The court, in response to this argument, stated 324 U.S. at page 29, "The argument is appealing, in so far as it seeks to avoid imputing to Congress the intention to 'penalize gifts to minors merely because the legal disability of their years precludes them for a time from receiving their income in hand currently.' " Following this, the court made a statement which again emphasizes the factual distinction between that case and this. The court stated, "But we think it is not applicable in the facts of this case, since by the terms of the trusts and the facts recited in the instruments none of the fund, whether income or corpus, could be applied immediately for the child's use or enjoyment." And the court further on the same page stated, "Whenever provision is made for immediate application of the fund for such a purpose, whether of income or of corpus, the exemption applies." The court in the same case also noted 324 U.S. at page 28, "The statute in this respect purports to make no distinction between gifts to minors and gifts to adults." The Commissioner in his brief states, "Gifts to minor beneficiaries are placed on an equality with gifts to adults by applying to both the principle that a right to enjoy the gift only upon the exercise of a trustee's or guardian's discretion, or conditioned upon some other factor, is a gift of a future interest."

Without expressly so stating, the Commissioner's position appears to be that the words in the Treasury Regulation, "use, possession, or enjoyment," mean that the beneficiary must have the actual, physical use, possession or enjoyment of the property, in other words, that the beneficiary occupies the same position relative to the gift that a boy sustains to his top or a girl to her doll. At any rate, the Commissioner's contention irresistibly leads to such a result. It is not, however, the use, possession or enjoyment by the beneficiary which marks the dividing line between a present and a future interest, but it is the right conferred upon the beneficiary to such use, possession or enjoyment. As was said in the Fondren case 324 U.S. at page 20, ". . . it is not enough to bring the exclusion into force that the donee has vested rights. In addition he must have the right presently to use, possess or enjoy the property."

The Commissioner emphasizes and relies upon a statement in the Disston case 325 U.S. at page 449: "In the absence of some indication from the face of the trust or surrounding circumstances that a steady flow of some ascertainable portion of income to the minor would be required, there is no basis for a conclusion that there is a gift of anything other than for the future." That statement, however, as already noted, was made in connection with a trust which lodged in the trustee a discretion as to when and how much would be paid to the beneficiary. Obviously, the statement has no relevancy to the instant case.

The Commissioner's reasoning reduces to a myth his concession that "gifts to minor beneficiaries are placed on an equality with gifts to adults." At any rate, no illustration is given as to how a gift of a present interest could be made to a minor of tender years. In fact, in oral argument, counsel for Commissioner, when pressed to give an illustration, was unable to do so other than to suggest that it might be made to an existing guardian. But even so, the use, possession or enjoyment of such gift would not immediately fall to the minor. It could only be used for his benefit and under the law of guardianship in such amounts and at such times as the guardian might deem proper. And it would seem, under the argument here advanced, that its use, possession and enjoyment would be restricted and subject to contingencies which would make it a gift of future interest.

Suppose in the instant situation that the beneficiary had been an adult rather than a minor. Such adult, of course, could immediately have made a demand upon the trustee and have received the trust property. We suppose that such a gift unquestionably would be one of a present interest. But because the beneficiary is a minor, with the disabilities incident thereto, it is reasoned that the gift is of a future interest because the disabled beneficiary is not capable of making demand.

Further hypothetical cases immediately come to mind illustrative of the Commissioner's untenable position. Suppose the instant taxpayer instead of creating a trust had deposited in a bank $3,000 in a savings account (or even in a checking account) in the name of his grandson or had purchased government bonds in his name. Obviously, the grandson could not have made demand upon the bank in the one instance for a withdrawal of the money, or on the government in the other instance for the bonds or the proceeds thereof, and he could not have obtained the use, possession or enjoyment of either. What he would have acquired would have been the right to the use, possession or enjoyment of the money or of the bonds through the means provided in all jurisdictions, so far as we are aware, that is, through a legally appointed guardian. However, we think under either supposition that the minor would have been the beneficiary of a gift of present rather than future interest. Certainly that would have been true if the beneficiary of the gift in either case had been an adult, and applying the Commissioner's concession that the same principle is to be applied in each case, it would seem to follow that it would be equally so where the beneficiary was a minor. At any rate, no court, so far as we are aware, has held to the contrary and we are not disposed to be the first. Further suppose that the taxpayer had conveyed by proper deed two farms, one to an adult and the other to a minor grandson. Again, the former no doubt would have been a gift of a present interest and we see no reason why the latter should not be accorded the same status, and this notwithstanding that the adult would have had the immediate use, possession and enjoyment of the farm to do with as he pleased, while the latter would only have had the right to such use, possession and enjoyment, acting through a legally appointed guardian and subject to such restrictions as the law of the jurisdiction might impose.

In all these suppositious instances, however, the reasoning of the Commissioner would inevitably lead to the result that the minor beneficiary acquired only a future interest because his right to the use, possession and enjoyment would be subject to the appointment of a guardian, with such restrictions as required by law. Thus, this reasoning, contrary to the Commissioner's assertion, would call for the application of not the same but a different principle, depending upon whether the beneficiary was an adult or a minor.

As heretofore shown, the fallaciousness of the Commissioner's contention is the failure to distinguish between restrictions and contingencies imposed by the donor (in this case the trust instrument), and such restrictions and contingencies as are due to disabilities always incident to and associated with minors and other incompetents. As to the former, it is authoritatively settled that a gift upon which the donor imposes such conditions or restrictions is of a future interest. In the latter, such restrictions as exist are imposed by law due to the fact that the beneficiary is incapable of acting on his own. It is our view, and we so hold, that such restrictions do not transform what otherwise would be a gift of present interest to one of future interest.

The decision of the Tax Court is reversed and the cause remanded, with directions to redetermine petitioner's deficiency, if any, in accordance with this decision.

KERNER, Circuit Judge (dissenting).

I believe the decision of the Tax Court, reported in 15 T.C. 111, is based on substantial evidence and is consistent with the law, hence I would affirm for the reasons stated in the opinion of the Tax Court.

STIFEL v. COMMISSIONER OF
INTERNAL REVENUE
197 F.2d 107 (2d Cir. 1952)

Taxpayer, a New York resident, set up in 1948 three separate irrevocable trusts for his children, aged eleven, seven and four years. The trustee in each trust was directed to apply the income from the trust to the use of the children during their lifetime and upon their death to pay it over to their executors. Articles Second, Third and Eleventh, the only ones pertinent here, provided:

"Article Second: The Trustee may at any time apply to the use of the Settlor's said daughter so much of the principal of the trust, and at such time or times, as the Trustee, in its discretion may deem necessary or advisable to provide for her proper education, medical care, living expenses and financial obligations, after giving full consideration to her age, health, abilities or limitations, other financial resources, and economic and social station in life.

"Article Third: The Trustee, during the minority of Settlor's said daughter, may make payment of income or principal applicable to the use of the Settlor's said daughter by paying the same to her mother, guardian or other person having the care and control of such daughter (but not in any event to the Settlor) or by payment directly to said daughter, or by expending it in such other manner as the Trustee, in its discretion, believes will benefit such daughter, as if the interest of said daughter in the trust property was held by the Trustee as guardian for said daughter and as if the Trustee were making payments and distributions in that capacity for the benefit of said daughter. Any payment herein authorized shall be a full discharge to the Trustee with respect thereto. Any payment or distribution by the Trustee to any duly appointed guardian for said daughter may be made directly to such guardian, whether qualified or appointed under the laws of the State of the domicile of the Trustee or not, without resort to any court for an order authorizing or directing such payment or distribution. Said daughter shall have the right at any time to demand payment to her or for her account of any unexpended income, but subject thereto the Trustee may accumulate for the benefit of such daughter so much of the income applicable to her use as the Trustee, in its discretion, may deem advisable, and any income so accumulated shall be paid to her upon her attaining the age of twenty-one (21) years or to her estate in the event of her death before attaining such age.

"Article Eleventh: The Settlor's daughter, Karen Stifel, shall

have the right (which may be exercised during her minority by her
general guardian, if any, or by any special guardian appointed for
such purpose by a court of competent jurisdiction, but in no event
by the Settlor) at any time to terminate this trust either in whole
or in part, and during minority to demand payment of all or any
part of any unexpended income, in which event such part or all of
the principal of the trust, or any accumulated income of the trust,
as to which the trust is so terminated, or such part or all of the income so demanded, as the case may be, shall be paid over to the
Settlor's said daughter, or, if she be a minor, to her general guardian or to such special guardian, but in no event to the Settlor."

Taxpayer deposited $3,500 in each trust, and treated $9,000 as
tax-free under Section 1003(b)(3), excluding from tax the first
$3,000 of gifts made annually by the donor to any one person, ex-
cept gifts of future interests in property.[177] The Commissioner
ruled that the gifts were not tax-free because they were gifts of

[177] (*Court footnote*)
Internal Revenue Code:
"Sec. 1003.   Net gifts
"(a) General definition.   The term 'net gifts' means the total amount of
gifts made during the calendar year, less the deductions provided in section
1004.
"(b) Exclusion from gifts . . .
"(3) (As added by Sec. 454 of the Revenue Act of 1942, c. 619, 56 Stat. 798)
Gifts after 1942.   In the case of gifts (other than gifts of future interests in
property) made to any person by the donor during the calendar year 1943
and subsequent calendar years, the first $3,000 of such gifts to such person
shall not, for the purposes of subsection (a), be included in the total amount
of gifts made during such year."   26 U.S.C. 1946 ed. sec. 1003.
"Treasury Regulations 108, promulgated under the Internal Revenue Code:
"Sec. 86.10.   Total Amount of Gifts.   Except with respect to any gift of
a future interest in property, the first $3,000 of gifts made to any one donee
during the calendar year 1943 or during any calendar year thereafter shall
be excluded in determining the total amount of gifts for such calendar year.
In the case of a gift in trust, the beneficiary of the trust is the donee of the
gift. . . .   The entire value of any gift of a future interest in property, and
the entire value of any gift made by a transfer in trust during the calendar
years 1939 to 1942, inclusive, must be included in the total amount of gifts
for the calendar year in which such a gift is made.
"Sec. 86.11.   Future Interests in Property.   No part of the value of a gift
of a future interest may be excluded in determining the total amount of gifts
made during the calendar year.   'Future interests' is a legal term, and includes
reversions, remainders, and other interests or estates, whether vested or contingent, and whether or not supported by a particular interest or estate, which
are limited to commence in use, possession or enjoyment at some future date
or time.   The term has no reference to such contractual rights as exist in a
bond, note (though bearing no interest until maturity), or in a policy of life
insurance, the obligations of which are to be discharged by payment in the
future.   But a future interest or interests in such contractual obligations may
be created by the limitations contained in a trust or other instrument of transfer employed in effecting a gift.   For the valuation of future interests see
section 86.19(g)."

future interests, and the Tax Court upheld him. 17 T.C. 647. The taxpayer has appealed.

Before SWAN, Chief Judge, and AUGUSTUS N. HAND and FRANK, Circuit Judges.

FRANK, Circuit Judge.

If an adult had been the beneficiary of each of these trusts, of course the gifts would not have been of future interests, since then (under Article Third) each such adult at any time could have demanded payment of income and (under Article Eleventh) of the corpus.[178] But here we have the following differentiating facts: (1) None of the children could himself make such a demand; he could do so only through a guardian. (2) The donor testified as follows: He had set up the trusts for the express purpose of teaching the three children how to invest their own money; his attorney had suggested naming a guardian in the instrument, but the donor had objected, because a guardian would be limited by law in what use he could make of the income on the children's behalf, and would be unable to allow them free play in the pecuniary education the donor wanted them to have. (3) No guardian was appointed during the period of three years from the creation of the trusts to the date of the trial here, although in New York, consent of the donor, the father, would not apparently have been necessary to the appointment of a guardian.[179] On these facts the Tax Court concluded, and we agree, that only future interests were conveyed at the time the trusts were set up.

It is urged that neither the Tax Court nor we may properly consider these items, since they involve restrictions not contained in the trust instrument. Cf. Kieckhefer v. Commissioner, 7 Cir., 189 F.2d 118, 122. But in Fondren v. Commissioner, 324 U.S. 18, 24, and Commissioner v. Disston, 325 U.S. 442, 449, the Supreme

---

[178] (*Court footnote*) The trust instrument itself seems to confer the rights — to demand income (Article Third) and to terminate the trust (Article Eleventh) — on the beneficiary directly, without making the intervention of a guardian necessary even during minority. The Commissioner, however, has argued that the instrument itself, in Article Eleventh, requires that the election to terminate be made by a guardian. The Tax Court was not entirely clear in its opinion whether the necessity of a guardian stemmed from the instrument or from legal disqualifications. In any event, whether the need for a guardian was intrinsic or extrinsic here is immaterial to the outcome; taking the view more favorable to the taxpayer, we are here considering the need as extrinsic. Cf. Kieckhefer v. Commissioner, 7 Cir., 189 F.2d 118.

[179] (*Court footnote*) Surrogate's Court Act, secs. 173, 175; see Matter of Stuart, 280 N.Y. 245, 249, 20 N.E.2d 741; Matter of Gustow, 220 N.Y. 373, 115 N.E. 995. No one of the children here was over 14, however, and therefore none could himself petition for a guardian's appointment. See Spyrous Skouras, 14 T.C. 523. Surrogate's Court Act, sec. 175.

Court, in determining the nature of the rights conferred by the trust instruments, took account of "surrounding circumstances"; the Court, in reaching its determinations, did not irrevocably lock itself inside the "four corners" of the writings but held that the key might lie outside. Were this not the rule, a donor could make gifts which on paper were 100% present but in practice were 100% future.

The Court of Appeals, in the Kieckhefer case, expressed the fear that no gift to a minor would be tax-free if the child's right at once to enjoy the fruits of the gift constituted the sole test of a present interest, since (it was said) the child's guardian or parent will always exercise control of some sort over the disposition of the child's property, so that only if the child's rights were those of "a boy to his top" or a "girl to her doll" would the gift be tax-free.[180] We believe this view under-estimates the traditional judicial knack of line-drawing. If here, for instance, the donor had, in the instrument, appointed a guardian to exercise the children's election rights, or indeed even if a next best friend of the children had successfully petitioned for one at the time the trust first was set up, the result might very well be different.[181] Then there would have been someone who, on the children's behalf, could have made an effective demand for income or corpus on the trustees under Articles Third and Eleventh. Here, there was no one who could exercise their election rights for them; consequently they acquired only "future interests," not subject to immediate capture.

Affirmed.[182]

---

[180] (*Court footnote*) See Note, 37 A.B.A.J. 78; cf. Fleming, Gifts for the Benefit of Minors, 49 Mich. L. Rev. 529; Note, 100 Un. of Pa. L. Rev. 905.

[181] (*Court footnote*) It would then seem to be proper to consider the actual facts as to the father's influence on the guardian appointed.

[182] For a comment on the Stifel case, see 22 Ford. L. Rev. 105 (1953).

See the following authorities which stressed the necessity of a legal guardian in order for a gift in trust for the benefit of the minor to be a gift of only a present interest: Rev. Rul. 54-91, 1954-1 C.B. 207 (if the trustee has discretion whether to expend or withhold the funds); Robert C. Ross, 14 CCH T.C. Mem. 1075 (1955). See, however, the following authorities which found that only a present interest was involved, though no guardian had been appointed: Rev. Rul. 59-78, 1959-1 C.B. 690 (if trustee is required to use property for benefit of minor as if it were held by trustee as guardian for minor); Gilmore v. Commissioner, 213 F.2d 520 (6th Cir. 1954); United States v. Baker, 236 F.2d 317 (4th Cir. 1956); Cannon v. Robertson, 98 F. Supp. 331 (W.D.N.C. 1951); Welles v. Sauber, 142 F. Supp. 449 (N.D. Ill. 1956); George W. Perkins, 27 T.C. 601 (1956). See also Glenn v. Pitts, 145 F. Supp. 779 (W.D.S.C. 1956); Freed v. Fox, 58-1 U.S.T.C. ¶11754 (D. Utah 1958); Josephine B. Crane, 16 CCH T.C. Mem. 12 (1957); Abraham M. Katz, 27 T.C. 783 (1957); William Goehner, 28 T.C. 542 (1957); Camiel Thorrez, 31 T.C. 655 (1958), aff'd sub nom. Thorrez v. Commissioner, 272 F.2d 945 (6th Cir. 1959); Farha Schayek, 33 T.C. 629 (1960). — ED.

Suppose that A transfers property to T to hold in trust, and under the terms of the trust T may pay the income and principal to S, A's minor son, from time to time, in such amount or amounts as T in his uncontrolled discretion may determine. If S lives to attain twenty-one, the then remaining principal and undistributed income are to be paid to him; if he dies under twenty-one, the then remaining principal and undistributed income are to be paid to his estate. Does such a trust qualify under Section 2503(c)? The principal and income may be expended by T for the benefit of the minor prior to his attaining twenty-one, and on his attaining twenty-one the unexpended principal and income pass to him or, if he dies before he attains twenty-one, to his estate. The trust qualifies under Section 2503(c) and no part of any gift to the trust is considered a gift of a future interest.[183]

The safest way to set up a trust for a minor that is intended to create only a present interest is by following closely the rules of Section 2503(c). It should be noted, however, that there are other types of trusts that establish only a present interest in the minor.[184]

Frequently the settlor of an inter vivos trust for a minor is the

---

[183] See Reg. §25.2503-4(b)(1), quoted infra page 1544, which points out that the trustee may be given discretion as to what amount of trust property, if any, is to be expended for the benefit of the minor and the purpose for which an expenditure is to be made, provided there are no substantial restrictions under the terms of the trust instrument on the exercise of such discretion.

De Concini v. Wood, 60-1 U.S.T.C. ¶11938 (D. Ariz. 1960), recognizes that the requirements of §2503(c) are met in that case, even though it might be necessary to resort to a court of equity to obtain the results which are required by that section.

If the property placed in the trust is non-income-producing property (as, for example, an insurance policy on the life of the settlor), will the trust qualify as a present interest trust under §2503(c)? In De Concini v. Wood, supra, the court upheld as a §2503(c) trust one to which an interest in unimproved vacant land was transferred.

If life insurance on the life of the settlor of a §2503(c) trust is placed in the trust and thereafter the settlor pays the annual premiums on the insurance, will such a cash gift qualify as a gift of a present interest in its entirety? Will the answer to the question be the same if the insurance given to the trust is on the life of a minor and the settlor pays the annual premiums? In considering these questions, it should be noted that part of the premium payment is not reflected in the augmentation of the cash surrender value but goes to cover the cost of pure insurance. Can such a part be deemed to have been expended for the "benefit of the minor"?

[184] See Reg. §25.2503-4(c), quoted infra page 1544.

Duffey v. United States, 182 F. Supp. 765 (D. Minn. 1960), considered a case where a trust was established for the benefit of a minor on December 30, 1954, two days before the effective date of §2503(c), and the trust complied with all the requirements of that section. The interest under the trust was deemed a future interest because of the power in the trustee to accumulate the income, and the annual exclusion was not available for the 1954 gift.

minor's father. If the trust property is payable to the minor's estate on his death under twenty-one and if the minor dies under twenty-one, the settlor will normally be the heir, or one of the heirs, of the minor and will get back by inheritance some or all of the property that he was seeking to remove from his estate. Since the minor cannot make a will in most states, this possibility is not avoidable so long as the trust provides for payments to the minor's estate on his death under twenty-one.

Suppose that, instead of providing for the property to go to the minor's estate if the minor dies under twenty-one, the trust provides that in the event of the death of the minor before twenty-one, the property shall go as he may appoint by will to anyone and, in default of appointment, to other designated beneficiaries. Will such a trust qualify under Section 2503(c)? That section requires that if the minor dies under twenty-one, the trust property "be payable to the estate of the donee or as he may appoint under a general power of appointment as defined in Section 2514(c)."

In most states the minor will not be able to exercise his general power of appointment,[185] and thus, if a gift over to others on his death under twenty-one in the event he does not exercise effectively his power of appointment will not disqualify the trust for Section 2503(c) treatment, an effective means is available to prevent the trust property from being inherited by the minor's parents on his death under twenty-one. The Regulations have taken the position that the trust for the minor is not disqualified for Section 2503(c) treatment by virtue of the fact that it contains a gift over in default of appointment by the minor.[186]

The general power of appointment referred to in Section 2503(c)

---

[185] See 5 American Law of Property §23.42 (Casner ed. 1952).

If the donor of a power stipulates that the power may be exercised by the donee-minor, will the stipulation be effective? See 3 Restatement of Property §345.

If the trust instrument provides that the minor may appoint "by a last will and testament or instrument in the nature of a will," will the words "instrument in the nature of a will" permit a minor to exercise the power by an instrument that would be his will if he had attained his majority? See In re Pulitzer's Estate, 152 Misc. 554, 274 N.Y. Supp. 907 (1934), aff'd, 245 App. Div. 720, 281 N.Y. Supp. 1012 (1935), aff'd, 270 N.Y. 524, 200 N.E. 300 (1936).

[186] See Reg. §25.2503-4(b), quoted infra page 1543.

Bonnie M. Heath, 34 T.C. —, No. 59 (1960), considered a trust for the benefit of a minor until he was twenty-one, with a requirement that the trust property be distributed to the minor at twenty-one, but with alternative provisions in favor of others if he should die under twenty-one. The annual gift tax exclusion was disallowed with respect to contributions to the trust because, in the event the minor died before twenty-one, the trust property would not pass "to the estate of the donee or as he may appoint under a general power of appointment."

may be a general power to appoint by deed only, or by will only, or by both deed and will.[187] Though the trust property of a Section 2503(c) trust must be payable to the minor beneficiary when he attains twenty-one, provision may be made for the extension of the trust by the minor-beneficiary.[188]

Rather than use a Section 2503(c) trust, it may be desirable under some circumstances to establish a trust which requires the trustee to pay the income to the minor for his lifetime, gives the trustee the discretion to pay the principal to the minor, and provides that on the minor's death the then remaining principal will pass to other designated beneficiaries. The life interest given the minor under such a trust is a present interest and the annual exclusion may be used with respect to gifts to the trust to the extent of the value of the minor's life interest. The value of the future interest in each annual gift can be charged against the $30,000 specific exemption. Many years will elapse before the value of the future interest in each annual gift will use up the specific exemption, so that a substantial amount may be placed in the trust over the years without the payment of any gift tax.[189]

Suppose that a person desires to establish a Section 2503(c) trust for each of his seven grandchildren. If the seven separate trusts are set up in one instrument and the trustee is authorized to mingle the trust property of each separate trust, alloting to each an undivided interest in the mingled funds, will such authorization prevent the trusts from meeting the requirements of Section 2503(c)? That section contains no prohibition against the mingling of trust funds. The mingling of funds of such trusts may be highly de-

---

[187] See Reg. §25.2503-4(b), quoted infra page 1543.

[188] Section 25.2503-4(b)(2) of the Regulations, quoted infra page 1544, points out that a trust which otherwise qualifies under §2503(c) is not disqualified merely because the minor, "upon reaching 21, has the right to extend the term of the trust." Revenue Ruling 59-144, 1959-1 C.B. 249, holds, however, that if at twenty-one the minor can demand the trust property or elect to extend the term and receive distribution according to terms set forth in the trust instrument, the trust will not qualify under §2503(c). Revenue Ruling 59-144 is superseded by Rev. Rul. 60-218, I.R.B. 1960-23, 12, which revises and restates the earlier ruling in order to clarify it. The new ruling points out that the minor must be given the unequivocal and unconditional right to receive the property at twenty-one, without any necessity of affirmative action on his part. Accordingly, the gift does not qualify under §2503(c) if the minor, on reaching twenty-one, may compel immediate distribution of the trust or may elect to extend the term of the trust and receive distribution of the corpus according to provisions set forth in the trust instrument.

[189] The possible undesirability of forcing the trust property into the hands of the beneficiary at what may be an immature age, which is a requisite of the §2503(c) trust, is not presented in the type of trust described in the text to which this footnote is appended.

sirable, in that a better diversification of investments may be obtained.

The language of Section 2503(c) states that the property and the income therefrom may be expended by, or for the benefit of, the minor-beneficiary. If the trust instrument prohibits the use of the trust property under circumstances which would result in the discharge of someone's legal obligation to support and maintain the minor, will such a restriction disqualify the trust for Section 2503(c) treatment? Before answering this question, it should be noted that the custodianship statutes previously considered [190] allow the expenditure of the custodial property for the benefit of the minor, even though the result may be the discharge of someone's legal obligation to support the minor, and that this fact does not prevent the custodianship arrangement from meeting the tests of Section 2503(c).[191] Thus a trust should not fail to meet the requirements of Section 2503(c) if it is equally broad as to the use of trust property. But the question asked is whether the trust can be more restrictive in this regard. The Regulations recognize that the test in regard to the discretion which may be given the trustee as to the expenditure of income and principal is met if there are no substantial restrictions under the terms of the trust instrument on the exercise of such discretion. A restriction which prohibits the expenditure of the trust property in the discharge of someone's legal obligation to support the minor should not be regarded as a substantial restriction on the trustee's discretion to expend the income and principal for the benefit of the minor.[192]

If the income of a Section 2503(c) trust can be and is used to discharge someone's legal obligation to support the minor, the income, to the extent it is so used, will be taxable to the one having

---

[190] See discussion at page 244 supra.

[191] See page 245 supra, note 175.

[192] See Reg. §25.2503-4(b)(1), quoted infra page 1544.

Beatrice B. Briggs, 34 T.C. —, No. 117 (1960), considered a case under the 1939 Code where gifts were made to the legally appointed guardians of minor beneficiaries, the guardians being the parents of the minors, and authorization was given to the guardians to use the property for the support and education of the minors. The controlling state law prohibited the parents from using a minor's property for the support and education of the minor unless the parents' estates were insufficient for this purpose. The Commissioner claimed the gifts were gifts of future interests because the parents were willing and able to support and educate their children, but the court held the authorization to the guardians overcame the prohibition as to use of the state law and thus the gifts were present interests. The implication of this case may be that a gift to a minor would not be a present interest if the prohibition of state law as to use were not removed. Section 2503(c), however, should be construed differently.

such legal obligation.[193] Otherwise the income will be taxable to the trust to the extent that it is not distributed to or for the benefit of the minor-beneficiary. To the extent that it is so distributed, it will be taxable to the minor-beneficiary. Thus, whereas the custodianship arrangement provides for only one income tax entity, the minor, the Section 2503(c) trust may make available two such entities, the trust and the minor.

The income tax consequences will not change no matter who is trustee of the Section 2503(c) trust. If the settlor is trustee he is insulated from taxation on the income, except to the extent that it is used to discharge his legal obligation to support the minor-beneficiary, by Section 674(b)(5)[194] and Section 674(b)(7)(B)[195] of the 1954 Code.

The settlor of a Section 2503(c) trust will not eliminate the trust property from his gross estate for federal estate tax purposes if he is the trustee. As trustee he will have a power to terminate the trust, which is a Section 2038 power.[196]

The Regulations state, in substance, that one who has a power to use trust property to discharge his own legal obligations has a general power of appointment for federal gift and estate tax purposes.[197] If the trustee of a Section 2503(c) trust is the person legally obligated to support the minor, is there any danger that the gift may be deemed to be to him if he can use the trust property to discharge his legal obligation to support the minor, so that when the power lapses, there will be a gift from him to the minor and so that the value of the trust property may be includible in his gross estate for federal estate tax purposes if he dies possessing the power? Revenue Ruling 59-357[198] seems to justify a negative answer to this question.

e. Prior Gift Tax Valuations

In the past, the amount of gifts made in a prior year was subject to adjustment for the purpose of computing the tax for a current year, even though the statutory period within which an additional tax might be assessed for the prior year had expired.[199] Thus, if the subject matter of gifts made in prior years was property which might on re-examination be valued at a greater amount than re-

---

[193] See page 245 supra, note 175.
[194] Quoted infra page 1372.
[195] Quoted infra page 1373.
[196] See Lober v. United States, printed in full supra page 210.
[197] See Reg. §20.2041-1(c)(1), quoted infra page 1517; Reg. §25.2514-1(c)(1), quoted infra page 1550.
[198] Discussed supra page 244, note 173.
[199] See S. Rep. No. 1622, 82d Cong., 2d Sess. 479 (1954).

ported in the prior gift tax return, it was impossible to know for certain what gift tax would be payable on gifts in the current year. This uncertainty in some cases made it unwise to proceed with what otherwise would have been desirable inter vivos transfers.

Section 2504(c) of the 1954 Code[200] eliminates in certain cases the significance of a possible change in the valuations placed on past gifts in calculating the tax on current gifts in 1955 and thereafter. The value of a gift made in a prior year is not subject to adjustment in cases where a tax was paid for such prior year and the time has expired within which a gift tax may be assessed on the transfer. Section 2504(c), however, will not prevent an adjustment if no tax was paid for the prior year or if issues other than the valuation of property are involved.[201]

PROBLEM

6.35. A desires to know the federal gift tax cost of making certain gifts in the current year. What information will be relevant in answering A's inquiry?

f. *State Gift Tax Considerations*

Some states have enacted a gift tax. The full story of the gift tax costs of making particular transfers of property cannot be determined without examining the controlling local law to ascertain whether there must be added to the federal gift tax costs any state gift tax costs. In this connection, it should be noted that Section 164(b)(4) of the 1954 Code prevents any federal income tax deduction for state gift taxes which are paid.

5. FAMILY ANNUITIES

The family trust considered in previous parts of this chapter may be used effectively in situations where the property owner of the family is willing to divorce himself from any personal economic benefit with respect to the property transferred in trust. He can afford to take such action, however, only if he retains control over assets not transferred to the trust which are adequate in amount to assure his own future financial security.

If the property owner of the family desires to have his own future financial security assured out of the transferred property, the trust device produces expensive income, estate, and gift tax results. On the other hand, if he purchases an annuity with the

[200] Quoted infra page 1419.
[201] See Reg. §25.2504-1(d), quoted infra page 1544.

transferred property, the tax results may be more favorable. He may choose a commercial annuity with the financial backing of the company selling the annuity, but this means that the property transferred in payment of the annuity will be permanently removed from the family. His other choice of annuity is to transfer the property to a member of his family, thereby keeping the property in the family, in return for the promise of the family member to pay him an annuity — a promise giving him financial security only as long as the promisor remains solvent.[202]

a. *Income Tax Considerations*

If the transferor sells his property in return for the unsecured promise of the family member who is the transferee, is any gain or loss realized on the sale? In Commissioner v. Kann's Estate,[203] the court said, ". . . an agreement by an individual to pay a life annuity to another has no 'fair market value' for purpose of computing capital gain."[204] If no gain is realized at the time of the

[202] If the transferor requires the promisor to give security for the performance of the promise, then it may be contended that he has retained the right to the income from the transferred property, and if the contention prevails, the income, estate and gift tax consequences will not be those applicable to annuities. See Estate of Cornelia B. Schwartz, 9 T.C. 229 (1947). Compare, however, Greene v. United States, 55-2 U.S.T.C. ¶11570 (N.D. Ill. 1955), where the decedent transferred various stocks, bonds and cash worth about $50,000 to her daughters. They agreed to manage the property and pay all the income to the decedent for her life. The daughters also promised that if the income did not amount to $1500 in any year, they would make up the difference, so that the decedent would be certain to receive $1500 annually. At the time of the transfer, the income from the transferred property was barely sufficient to cover the $1500 annual amount. After the transfer, however, the property increased in value and the income exceeded $1500 in each year. The court held that the transfer was a bona fide sale for an adequate consideration in money or money's worth and that the value of the transferred property was not includible in the decedent's gross estate. The Greene case was reversed in 237 F.2d 848 (7th Cir. 1956). It came before the District Court again in Greene v. United States, 57-2 U.S.T.C. ¶11713 (N.D. Ill. 1957), because the Court of Appeals had remanded for a determination of the excess of the fair market value of the transferred property, at the time of the decedent's death, over the value of the money or money's worth, if any, of the contingent annuity agreements of the daughters. In view of the fact that the District Court was not provided with any basis for determining whether the promises of the daughters had a monetary value or, if they had such a value, what the value was, there was a failure to sustain the burden of proving overpayment of the estate tax. In Frank v. Granger, 139 F. Supp. 497 (W.D. Pa. 1956), the court decided that a trust which called for the payment of $75,000 annually to a designated beneficiary did not mean that the amount was to be made up out of principal to the extent that the income was insufficient.

[203] 174 F.2d 357, 359 (3d Cir. 1949).

[204] Section 1241 of H.R. 8300, 83d Cong., 2d Sess. (1954), purported to deal with the exchange of property for an annuity contract. The Senate deleted

transfer, will any part of the annual payments be reportable as a gain? Section 72 of the 1954 Code[205] is applied to determine what portion of each annual payment is ordinary income. To ascertain this portion, it is necessary to determine the "investment in the contract." [206] It may be contended that some part of the portion of each annual payment that is excluded from ordinary income as a return of the investment is reportable as a gain.[207]

If the transferor purchases a joint and survivor annuity, it should be noted that the survivor no longer picks up a new basis with respect to the annuity, even though the value of the survivor's annuity is included in the deceased annuitant's gross estate.[208] However, the survivor is entitled to a deduction for the portion of the estate tax attributable to the inclusion of the value of the survivor's annuity in the deceased annuitant's gross estate.[209]

The income tax situation of the transferee of the family prop-

---

the House provisions as to annuity contracts and thus the 1954 Code does not deal expressly with the matter.

[205] Quoted infra page 1325.

[206] Section 72(c) of the 1954 Code, quoted infra page 1326, deals with the investment in the contract.

When family annuities are involved, the investment in the contract within the meaning of §72(c) should not mean the value of the transferred property when that value exceeds the value of the annuity. The excess should not be regarded as part of the consideration for the contract. Otherwise no part of the annual payment would be included in ordinary income in many cases. It is possible to imagine a case where the transferor and the transferee would bargain at arm's length, so that no donative intent of any kind could be inferred to the transferor. In such a case, the investment in the contract might very well be the value of what is transferred, though such value exceeds the value of the annuity according to the usual method of valuing an annuity. In family situations, however, it would be very rare that such arm's-length bargaining would take place.

In Jane J. de Canizares, 32 T.C. 345 (1959), a promise by a corporation to make yearly payments to the taxpayer in return for a transfer of its own stock to it was considered to be an annuity, the basis of which was the fair market value of the stock on the date it was transferred to the corporation and not what the taxpayer would have had to pay for a similar commercial annuity.

[207] Consider the following situation which, though it relates to the 3 percent annuity rule under the 1939 Code, is relevant in determining the probable attitude of the Internal Revenue Service in regard to the gain. A transferred to his son property having a basis of $10,000 and a market value of $20,000 in exchange for a promise of $1500 annual payments for life. In Rev. Rul. 239, 1953-2 C.B. 53, it is stated that of the $1500 annual payment, 600 (3 percent of the $20,000) is ordinary income under the 3 percent annuity rule, and $900 is excludable until the $10,000 basis is recovered. Thereafter, $600 is ordinary income and $900 is capital gain until the $10,000 gain ($20,000 minus the $10,000 basis) has been so reported. Then the full $1500 annual payment is ordinary income.

[208] See 1954 I.R.C. 1014(b)(9)(A), quoted infra page 1383. Section 1014(b)(8), quoted infra page 1382, adopts the 1939 Code rule as to annuitants dying after December 31, 1950, and before January 1, 1954.

[209] See 1954 I.R.C. §691(c) and (d), quoted infra page 1377.

erty is also relevant. What is his basis for computing depreciation and for determining gain or loss on a subsequent sale of the property? These matters are considered in Revenue Ruling 55-119, 1955-1 C.B. 352.[210]

b. *Estate Tax Consequences*

If the value of the transferred property is not greater than the value of the annuity received therefor, the value of the transferred property is not includible in the gross estate of the transferor.[211] When the value of the transferred property is greater, however, a gift probably has been made of the excess, and such a gift may be one in contemplation of death if the transferor dies within three years of the date of transfer.

When a joint and survivor annuity is involved, that part of the

[210] See also Kaufman's Inc., 28 T.C. 1179 (1957). An example of a private annuity transaction appears in 58 CCH Fed. Tax Rep. ¶8981.

In Dana S. Beane, 15 CCH T.C. Mem. 38 (1956), the taxpayer purchased a funeral business from his former employer, and the purchase price was $100 per week for ten years, or a total of $52,000, unless the vendor should die during that period. If his death occurred, the contract would be terminated and the purchaser would not be required to make payments beyond the year of the vendor's death. The vendor died after payments totaling $20,800 had been made, and the court held that the $20,800 rather than the $52,000 which the purchaser might have paid if the vendor had lived ten years constituted the cost.

Section 267 of the 1954 Code, quoted infra page 1337, should be kept in mind if the transferee sustains a loss on a subsequent sale of the transferred property, because such loss is disallowed as a deduction if the sale is to his brothers, sisters, spouse, ancestors or lineal descendants.

[211] In United States National Bank of Portland v. Earle, 54-1 U.S.T.C. ¶10937 (D. Ore. 1953), the court decided that property which had been transferred by the decedent to her daughter in 1937, in return for a promise by the daughter to pay the decedent an annuity of $5000 for life, was not includible in the gross estate of the decedent upon her death in 1949. The court held that the 1937 transfer constituted a bona fide sale for an adequate consideration in money or money's worth. The transfer was not deemed to be one whereby the decedent retained the right to income for life, or to have been made in contemplation of death, or to have been intended to take effect at or after the decedent's death. The court also determined that there was no reversionary interest retained by the decedent.

In Estate of Maria Becklenberg, 31 T.C. 402 (1958), the decedent and other members of her family contributed to a trust, the decedent's contributions amounting to 26.78 percent of the whole. The decedent was entitled to $10,000 per year out of trust income. The 26.78 percent of the trust property clearly earned more than $10,000. The court held that the value of the portion of the trust property needed to produce $10,000 in income was includible in the decedent's gross estate. The case was reversed sub nom. Estate of Maria Becklenberg v. Commissioner, 273 F.2d 297 (7th Cir. 1959), on the ground that the $10,000 a year which the decedent was entitled to receive was payable whether there was income to pay it or not, and since the decedent received the payments, "there was nothing left to be included in her gross estate."

value of the survivor's annuity which corresponds to the proportionate part of the purchase price of the annuity contributed by the deceased annuitant is included in the latter's gross estate.[212] If the surviving annuitant is the spouse of the deceased annuitant, the value of the survivor's annuity, to the extent that it is included in the deceased annuitant's gross estate, is available for the estate tax marital deduction. Even though the surviving annuitant's interest is terminable, nothing passes to any other person on its termination. Such a terminable interest is not a disqualified one.[213]

c. *Gift Tax Considerations*

If the value of the transferred property exceeds the value of the annuity, there is a gift for gift tax purposes with respect to the excess unless it is determined that no donative intent was present. If the annuity was purchased pursuant to a bona fide sale at which the purchase price was arrived at by arm's-length bargaining, no donative intent would be present. It is unlikely, however, that such will be the case where family annuities are involved.

When a joint and survivor annuity is purchased, the transferor of the family property will have made a gift to the other annuitant. If the other annuitant is the spouse of the transferor, no gift tax marital deduction is available with respect to the gift because the donee-spouse's interest is a terminable one and on its termination, the donor-spouse may enjoy the interest transferred. Such a terminable interest is disqualified so far as the gift tax marital deduction is concerned.[214]

PROBLEMS

6.36. The value of an annuity must be ascertained for income tax purposes to determine the investment in the contract under Section 72 of the 1954 Code. It must also be known because, if it is less than the value of the property transferred, the gift tax must be considered.[215] The value of a survivor's annuity must be cal-

---

[212] See 1954 I.R.C. §2039, quoted infra page 1398.

[213] Terminable interests and the marital deduction are examined infra page 832.

[214] See 1954 I.R.C. §2523(b), quoted infra page 1425, Reg. §25.2523(b)-1(c)(2), quoted infra page 1554.

[215] In James Richard Bowden, 14 CCH T.C. Mem. 1102 (1955), the petitioner transferred funds aggregating about $100,000 to a trust fund. Under the terms of the trust agreement he was to receive $400 a month for his life, and on his death, the remainder was to go to designated beneficiaries. The petitioner contended that the value of the gift of the remainder should be the difference between the value of the transferred property and the cost to him

culated, if the deceased annuitant contributed to the purchase price of a joint and survivor annuity, to ascertain the total value of the deceased annuitant's gross estate. How is the value of the annuity determined? See Gillespie v. Commissioner, 128 F.2d 140 (9th Cir. 1942); McMurtry v. Commissioner, 203 F.2d 659 (1st Cir. 1953); Grant v. Smyth, 226 F.2d 407 (9th Cir. 1955).

6.37. A transfers property to his son, S, in return for S's promise to pay him a stated sum monthly as long as he lives. The value of the annuity exceeds the value of the transferred property. What will be the tax consequences?

6.38. A transfers property to his son, S, in return for S's promise to pay him a stated sum monthly as long as he lives. S dies. What would you advise A to do?

6.39. Under what circumstances would you advise the purchase of an annuity by one member of a family from another member?[216]

---

of a commercial annuity that would pay him $400 a month for his lifetime. Such an annuity would cost him about $93,000. The court held, however, that the actuarial tables in Reg. 108, §86.19(f) (now Reg. §25.2512-5(f)) should be used to determine the value, and under these tables the value of the remainder interest came to about $42,000, which was deemed the value of the gift for gift tax purposes. The case was affirmed sub nom. Bowden v. Commissioner, 234 F.2d 937 (5th Cir. 1956), *cert. denied,* 352 U.S. 916 (1957), *rehearing denied,* 352 U.S. 976 (1957).

[216] A valuable article on family annuities, though written with respect to the 1939 Code, is Galvin, Income Tax Consequences of Agreements Involving Noncommercial Annuities, 29 Texas L. Rev. 469 (1951).

CHAPTER VII

Non-trust Gifts

1. CHOOSING BETWEEN TRUST GIFTS AND NON-TRUST GIFTS

In disposing of property by way of a gift, whether the gift is inter vivos or in a will, an intelligent choice should be made between a trust gift and a non-trust gift. There is no reason to place the subject matter of the gift in a trust unless desired objectives can thereby be accomplished which cannot be accomplished as effectively, or at all, by a non-trust gift.

The following variations in the types of non-trust gifts should be kept in mind:

1. A gift during the lifetime of the donor and a gift by his will
2. A gift of personal property inter vivos as distinguished from a gift causa mortis
3. A gift of a present interest
4. A gift of concurrent interest[1]
5. A gift of a future interest[2]

If a non-trust gift of land is to be made by a will or inter vivos, or if a non-trust gift of personal property is to be made by a will, the need for compliance with proper formalities to accomplish the gift is readily apparent from the very nature of the contemplated transfer and a lawyer is consulted.[3] When it comes to an

---

[1] The various types of concurrent interests and their use in an estate plan are examined infra page 400.

[2] Future interests, whether created under a trust or outside a trust, are considered in detail infra page 435. Almost every comprehensive estate plan will create some future interests.

[3] If the donor of an intended inter vivos trust fails to accomplish his goal, the value of the subject matter of the intended gift will not be removed from the donor's gross estate for federal estate tax purposes. In Kirkpatrick v. Sanders, 261 F.2d 480 (4th Cir. 1958), *cert. denied,* 359 U.S. 1000 (1959), a deed of gift of real property was not recorded within two years and hence was deemed void under the controlling law. Consequently, the value of the real property was includible in the gross estate of the one who attempted to make the gift. In Estate of Isaac W. Baldwin, 18 CCH T.C. Mem. 902 (1959), a recorded deed to real property named one of decedent's sons as grantee, but neither the deed itself nor possession and control of the property was actually delivered to the named grantee. The court held that the value of the realty

inter vivos gift of personal property, however, the order of the day seems to be complete casualness in regard to the steps taken to effectuate the gift. This casualness is probably due to the belief of the average layman that he can give away personal property just by making up his mind that the property is to belong to someone else and that there is no need to consult a lawyer about such matters.

The law requires that an inter vivos gift of personal property be effectuated by a delivery of the subject matter of the gift with the intention to make a gift, or by the delivery of a deed of gift in which the subject matter is adequately described. A lawyer should always insist on the delivery of a deed of gift as the method of making an inter vivos gift of personal property, because a written manifestation of the intention of the donor is then available. A delivery of the subject matter of the gift itself as the method of accomplishing a gift of personal property always leaves open to attack the question of the intention of the person who made the delivery — that is, did he intend to make a gift?[4]

---

was includible in the decedent's gross estate. If the donor is not mentally competent on the date a gift is allegedly made, the value of the property allegedly given away will be in the gross estate of the donor. See, for example, Estate of Barbara F. Thompson, 18 CCH T.C. Mem. 801 (1959).

On the death of a person, the beneficiaries of his estate may find it advantageous to contend that an inter vivos arrangement for their benefit made by the decedent was not a completed gift, so that the property passed to them under the decedent's will. Such would be the case if there were unpaid gift taxes with respect to the inter vivos arrangement which would exceed in amount any estate taxes that would be imposed by including the property in question in the decedent's gross estate. The new basis which would be acquired if the property in question were included in the decedent's gross estate might be more advantageous than the basis which would be applicable to property received by an inter vivos gift. In Estate of Daniel W. Kelly, 31 T.C. 493 (1958), the alleged donees attempted to establish that the decedent had not made valid gifts to them during his lifetime, so that no gift tax was due, but they failed. In Klee v. United States, 59-1 U.S.T.C. ¶9375 (D. Kan. 1959), the decedent transferred real property by a quitclaim deed which was unqualified on its face. The grantees, the heirs of the decedent, who died intestate, conveyed the land, and the question presented was whether the property conveyed had acquired a new basis on the death of the decedent. The grantees in the deed claimed they held the title to the land under an oral trust which ended on the grantor's death, so that the property passed on intestacy to them as the grantor's heirs. The court found that under Kansas law an oral trust of land was voidable, not void, and was unassailable by a third party, and thus the heirs acquired the land by descent and acquired a new basis. In Taylor v. United States, 59-2 U.S.T.C. ¶9521 (D. Kan. 1959), it became important to determine whether a deed of land became effective during the decedent's lifetime or was ineffective, so that the property passed by inheritance because a new basis would be acquired in the latter case and not in the former. It was held that the deed had not become effective.

4 For a collection of cases involving gifts of personal property, see Casner and Leach, Cases and Text on Property 105-178 (1950, with 1959 Supplement). In Graham v. United States, 60-2 U.S.T.C. ¶11961 (W.D. Wash. 1960), a

PROBLEMS

7.1. A person desires to adopt a program of making inter vivos gifts each year to each of his children, which will take full advantage of the $3000 annual exclusion under the federal gift tax. Can this program be carried out better by making trust gifts or non-trust gifts?[5]

7.2. A person desires to make an inter vivos arrangement with respect to part of his property, which will result in his having control over the property until his death, but on his death the property will pass in accordance with the terms of the inter vivos arrangement. Can this objective be carried out better by a trust arrangement or by a non-trust arrangement?[6]

---

claim for refund was made for estate taxes paid, because of the improper inclusion in the decedent's gross estate of some government bonds and jewelry. The bonds, which were payable to the decedent or his daughter, and the jewelry were located in a safe-deposit box to which the daughter did not have access. It was contended that the decedent had given this property to his daughter in his lifetime. She had even included the interest on the bonds in her gross income. The property had been purchased by the decedent with community funds but the decedent's wife had consented to the gift to the daughter. The court concluded that the decedent had made no gift because there had been no delivery.

In Woolsey v. United States, 138 F. Supp. 952 (N.D.N.Y. 1955), aff'd, 230 F.2d 948 (2d Cir. 1956), cert. denied, 352 U.S. 832 (1956), a father in each of the years 1942 through 1949 recorded in his permanent and daily ledger accounts gifts of stock to each of his daughters. None of the recorded gifts exceeded the $3000 annual exclusion. He did not make delivery of any of the stock until 1950. It was held that the failure to make a delivery prevented the gifts from being completed. All the stock was given in 1950, and in that year the aggregate value of the stock given to each daughter constituted the gift to each. This aggregate value exceeded the annual $3000 exclusion for the year 1950, and the donor was subject to the 25 percent penalty for failure to file a gift tax return within the time prescribed by law.

In Estate of Albert Rand, 28 T.C. 1002 (1957), a wife was the principal support of her husband and her family, and in order to avoid a feeling of inadequacy and lack of security on the part of her husband, she allowed him to handle part of her finances. He deposited money in bank accounts and safe-deposit boxes under his own or assumed names and he took title to two parcels of real estate in his own name. On the husband's death, the Commissioner included the value of these assets in the husband's gross estate, but the court held that the assets in his possession were proceeds of a business owned by his wife, were therefore her property and thus were not includible in the husband's estate.

[5] If stock in a closely held corporation is the subject matter of the transfer, one must keep in mind that a transfer of such stock in trust will eliminate the availability of any election under 1954 I.R.C. §1372 to have the corporate income taxed directly to the shareholders. Reg. §1.1371-1(e), quoted infra page 1501. The custodianship arrangement applicable to gifts to minors, which is discussed supra page 244, does not create a trust in so far as the operation of §1372 is concerned. (T.I.R. 113, Nov. 26, 1958, 58 CCH Fed. Tax Rep. ¶6816).

[6] The material relating to revocable inter vivos trusts at page 93 supra,

7.3. In choosing between a trust gift and a non-trust gift, of what significance is it that the subject matter of the gift is tangible personal property? Is income-producing personal property? Is land?[7]

7.4. In choosing between a trust gift and a non-trust gift, of what significance is it that the beneficiary is a wife? Is a daughter? Is a son? Is a minor?

7.5. If a person desires to make an inter vivos arrangement with respect to part of his property, which will result in eliminating the income from such property from his gross income and also in eliminating the value of such property from his gross estate, can his objective be accomplished better by a trust gift or a non-trust gift?[8]

7.6. Will the federal gift taxes payable on an inter vivos gift always be the same whether the particular gift is made in trust or not in trust?[9]

7.7. If a person's objective is to make an arrangement of his property for the benefit of his family, which is highly flexible so that financial benefits may be apportioned among the family from time to time in equal or unequal shares as someone may determine to be in the best financial interest of all concerned, is a trust arrangement or a non-trust arrangement better suited to the accomplishment of such an objective?[10]

---

and to the development of concurrent interests at page 400 supra are pertinent to this problem.

[7] In Rev. Rul. 54-583, 1954-2 C.B. 158, it is pointed out that where a trustee purchases a home for a beneficiary out of trust corpus and later sells the residence and, with the proceeds of the sale, acquires a new home for the beneficiary, the benefit of 1939 I.R.C. §112(n) (1954 I.R.C. §1034) is not available. This section provides that if property used by the taxpayer as his principal residence is sold by him and within a period beginning one year prior to the sale and ending one year after the sale a new residence is purchased, a gain is recognized only to the extent that the sale price exceeds what is paid for the new residence. The reason is that the taxpayer is the trustee and is not a person who uses the property as a residence. This ruling is of significance in determining whether to transfer a family residence by means of a trust gift or a non-trust gift.

[8] In so far as the elimination of income of the transferred property from the gross income of the settlor is concerned, if the elimination is to be made only for a short period of time, detailed statutory rules exist as to short-term trusts (see the discussion at page 168 supra) but there is no such detailed guidance available with respect to short-term legal interests.

[9] The federal gift tax law is examined supra page 216.

[10] The income, estate, and gift tax consequences with regard to the transferor in an arrangement which is like the one here described and which is established by inter vivos transfer are developed supra page 153. The income, estate, and gift tax consequences with regard to the beneficiaries in such a flexible arrangement are developed infra page 689.

2. PECUNIARY LEGACIES

A testator may desire to make some non-trust gifts in his will in the form of pecuniary legacies of specified amounts to designated persons. For example, he may desire to give $5000 to a brother, $5000 to a sister, $1000 to an employee, $10,000 to a charity, and to place his residuary estate in trust for the benefit of his wife and children. If the total amount of the pecuniary legacies is not in some way restricted to a percentage of the testator's total estate, they may bulk so large in relation to the testator's total estate that there will be very little left for his primary beneficiaries under the residuary trust.[11]

It must also be kept in mind that if the testator desires to give the designated persons the stipulated amounts free of taxes, so that the net amount each one receives will be the stipulated amount, the will should contain provisions which free such legacies from any tax burdens imposed by reason of the testator's death.[12]

If a pecuniary legacy is payable to a minor, the will should contain a provision permitting the executor to make the payment to the minor personally or to some other person for the minor, even though the other person is not a legal guardian. Otherwise a legal guardian may have to be appointed to receive payment for the minor, or the funds may be kept under the supervision of the court in some way until the minor attains his majority.

The will should state the intention of the testator as to whether a pecuniary legatee is to receive the amount of his legacy with interest or without interest, and if the former, the will should state the date from which interest should be calculated and at what rate. In the absence of any provisions in the will in regard to interest, the general rule is that legacies bear interest from one year after the testator's death.[13]

Whenever a pecuniary legacy is involved, a gift by the testator to the legatee made subsequent to the date of the execution of the will may raise the question whether such a gift is intended to be in satisfaction — in whole or in part — of the legacy. There is a presumption that the gift is in satisfaction of the legacy if the testator

[11] Careful thought should be given to whether the total amount of the pecuniary legacies should be restricted to a percentage of the testator's probate estate or gross estate or taxable estate.

[12] Provisions in a will relating to the payment of taxes imposed as a result of the testator's death are considered infra page 1132.

[13] See Atkinson, Wills 751-753 (2d ed. 1953).

stands in loco parentis to the legatee and the subject matter of the gift is the same as the subject matter of the legacy. There is no presumption that the legacy is satisfied if the testator does not stand in loco parentis to the legatee or if the subject matter of the gift differs from the subject matter of the legacy. When a pecuniary legacy is inserted in a will, the testator should be warned that if future inter vivos gifts are made to the legatee, he should manifest in writing whether he intends such gifts to be in satisfaction of the legacy.[14]

The net worth of the pecuniary legacy to the beneficiary will depend on whether the amount he receives will be includible in his gross income to any extent, and if the legacy is satisfied by distributions in kind of estate property, on what will be the basis for income tax purposes of such distributed property in his hands. The discussion of income taxation of estates deals with these matters.[15] A point not previously stressed is whether testamentary provisions which appear to be pecuniary legacies in fact constitute payment to the recipient for services rendered and, on this ground, are income to him.[16]

The pecuniary legatee may be indebted to the testator. If this

[14] On the satisfaction of legacies see Leach, Cases and Text on the Law of Wills 168 (2d ed. 1960 rev.). Compare with the doctrine of satisfaction of legacies, the doctrine of advancements, considered supra page 18.

[15] See page 77 supra.

[16] Revenue Ruling 57-398, 1957-2 C.B. 93, considers a case where a testator bequeathed a specific sum to an employee in appreciation of her work for him and, in the same clause of the will, stipulated that this fixed amount was to include all compensation for her services as executrix. It was held that the entire amount of the legacy was excludable from the beneficiary's gross income under 1954 I.R.C. §102(a), quoted infra page 1331, because the right to the legacy was not contingent upon her acting as executrix. See also Reg. §20.2053-3(b)(2), quoted infra page 1526.

In Ethel West Cotnam, 28 T.C. 947 (1957), the taxpayer, at the request of the decedent, performed various services for him in consideration of his promise to bequeath her one fifth of his estate. The taxpayer performed the services but the decedent died intestate. The taxpayer obtained a judgment for $120,000 and claimed that the amount thus paid to her was in the nature of a bequest and thus was not taxable to her. The court, however, held that the amount she received was income. The case was affirmed in part and reversed in part sub nom. Cotnam v. Commissioner, 263 F.2d 119 (5th Cir. 1959) (reversal related to treatment of $50,000 in attorney's fees, which reduced amount of judgment payable to taxpayer to $70,000, and so only that amount was income to her).

In Wilbur D. Jones, 17 CCH T.C. Mem. 952 (1958), the taxpayer did various things for a husband and wife, and it was indicated that she would be taken care of on the death of the wife. The husband died without leaving a will and then the wife died without a will. The taxpayer made a claim for services rendered after attempting to obtain probate of an unsigned paper as the will of the wife. The taxpayer was paid by representatives of the estate, and the court held that the amount received was income and not property acquired by bequest, devise or inheritance.

is the case, it should be made clear in the will whether the debt owed to the testator by the pecuniary legatee is to be deducted from the amount of the legacy. If, on the other hand, the testator is indebted to the pecuniary legatee, the will should specify whether the legacy is to be deemed to satisfy this indebtedness in whole or in part.[17]

The result desired if the pecuniary legatee dies before the testator should not be left to conjecture.[18] In this regard, it must be kept in mind that it is not unusual for several people to be killed in a common disaster and for it be be impossible to determine the order of their deaths.[19]

PROBLEM

7.8. H provides in his will that if W, his wife, survives him, all of his property is to go to her, and if she does not survive him, $5000 is to go to A, $5000 to B, and the residue of his estate to C. W provides in her will that if H survives her, all of her property is to go to him, and if he does not survive her, $5000 is to go to A, $5000 to B, and the residue of her estate to C.   H and W are killed simultaneously in an automobile accident.   The executor of H and the executor of W ask you whether each executor should pay A $5000 and B $5000.   What is your conclusion?   In reaching your conclusion, apply the Uniform Simultaneous Death Law referred to supra note 19.

3.   SPECIFIC BEQUESTS AND DEVISES; DEMONSTRATIVE LEGACIES; AND ADEMPTIONS

Whenever a specific bequest or devise of property is a phase of an estate plan, careful consideration should be given to several matters which may arise with respect to such bequests and devises. It should be kept in mind that many things may happen to the specified property between the date the will is executed and the date the testator dies. If, for example, the property is sold by the testator before he dies, the legatee takes nothing.   In other

---

[17] See Lopez v. Lopez, 96 So.2d 463 (Fla. 1957).   In Maney v. Maney, — Mass. —, 164 N.E.2d 146 (1960), the court held that where the will did not provide that assertion of claims against the estate by creditors who were also legatees was to result in forfeiture of legacies to such creditors, the testator would not be deemed to have intended that the creditors' acceptance of their legacies was to be treated as an election to forego their claims.

[18] See discussion regarding lapsed bequests or devises at page 278 infra.

[19] See the Uniform Simultaneous Death Law as adopted in Massachusetts (Mass. Ann. Laws, c. 190A, §§1-8), quoted infra page 1453.

words, the specific bequest and devise are subject to ademption.[26] Under such circumstances, the plan of the testator to divide his property fairly among the members of his family may be seriously upset.

If the property specifically devised is tangible personal property and the beneficiary is located at a considerable distance from the testator, the cost of delivering the item to the beneficiary my be substantial. In such a case the will should show that the testator contemplated that the executor would incur necessary expenses in making delivery.

[20] In Walsh v. Gillespie, 338 Mass. 278, 154 N.E.2d 906 (1959), a specific bequest of shares of stock was involved. The testator became incompetent and part of the stock specifically bequeathed was sold by her conservator to provide funds for her support. The court held that though the general rule is that an ademption takes place if the subject matter of the bequest is not in existence, a different rule applies when a sale is made for an incompetent. In the latter case, the funds realized from the sale, to the extent they are traceable on the death of the testator, will pass to the specific legatee.

In Bool v. Bool, 165 Ohio St. 262, 135 N.E.2d 372 (1956), there was a specific bequest of stock. Prior to the death of the testator, the corporation whose stock was involved notified the shareholders of its intention to redeem the stock in accordance with its terms, and funds for the stock redemption were deposited in a bank. Shareholders were directed to surrender the stock certificates before a designated date, and after that date, they had no rights other than the right to receive the redemption price. The testator died after the date designated for the surrender of the stock certificates. The court held that the specific bequest of the stock had not been adeemed.

Suppose that a specific bequest of a designated number of shares of stock is made and, prior to the death of the testator, a stock dividend is declared. Will the legatee receive only the stated number of shares or will he also be entitled to the stock dividend paid on those shares? In Harlan National Bank v. Brown, 317 S.W.2d 903 (Ky. 1958), the court held that the legatee was not entitled to any portion of the stock dividend. In accord is Central National Bank of Cleveland v. Cottier. 163 N.E.2d 709 (Cuyahoga County Prob. Ct., Ohio, 1958). But compare Allen v. National Bank of Austin, 19 Ill. App. 2d 149, 153 N.E.2d 260 (1958), where a specific bequest of a designated number of shares of stock was involved, and the court held that the legatee was entitled to additional shares issued as a result of a stock split occurring after the execution of the will. See also the following cases in accord with the Illinois case: In re Parker's Estate, 110 S.2d 498 (Dist. Ct. App. Fla. 1959); Clegg v. Lippold, 123 N.E.2d 549 (Montgomery County Prob. Ct., Ohio, 1951); In re McFerren's Estate, 365 Pa. 490, 76 A.2d 759 (1950).

An ademption may result from the destruction of the subject matter of the bequest. If the subject matter is insured, it may be desirable to provide that, in the event it is destroyed, an amount equal to the insurance proceeds will pass to the designated beneficiary. In Matter of Wright, 8 A.D.2d 158, 187 N.Y.S.2d 306 (1959), aff'd, 7 N.Y.2d 365, 165 N.E.2d 561 (1960), a bequest of a diamond ring was considered adeemed when it could not be found, even though the executor collected the value of the ring under an insurance policy.

If a decedent's partnership interest is purchased by the surviving partners, pursuant to a buy-and-sell agreement, will a specific bequest of the partnership interest be adeemed? See Partridge v. Pidgeon, 166 Ohio St. 496, 143 N.E.2d 840 (1957).

If land is specifically devised, it may be subject to a mortgage at the time the will is executed, or may become subject to a mortgage after the will is executed and before the testator dies. Does the testator intend that the mortgage indebtedness is to be discharged out of his other assets on his death so that the devisee will receive the land free and clear of the mortgage?[21] The intent of the testator in this regard should be clearly expressed in the will.[22]

A problem somewhat related to the one referred to in the preceding paragraph is presented when the testator gives a designated person an option to buy real property at a stipulated price and this property is subject to an encumbrance at the time of the testator's death. Is the person entitled to buy only the encumbered property at the stipulated price, or is he entitled to receive the described

[21] See Mass. Ann. Laws, c. 191, §23, quoted infra page 1456. It should be noted that the Massachusetts statute applies only if the mortgage is "given by the testator." In this situation, in the absence of any applicable statute, the prevailing view is that the testator intends the beneficiary to receive the devised real estate unencumbered, so that the executor is required to pay off the indebtedness. If the will contains a general clause that all debts are to be paid out of the residue, will such a clause overcome the operation of a statute like the one in Massachusetts which applies "unless the contrary shall plainly appear"? If the devised land was acquired by the testator subject to a mortgage, whether he assumes the indebtedness or not, a statute like the one in Massachusetts does not apply. In such cases the prevailing view is that the devisee takes the land without any right to have the encumbrance removed. See P-H Wills, Est. & Trust Serv. ¶436.

See the discussion at page 821 infra, note 76, in regard to whether the beneficiary named in an insurance policy is entitled to reimbursement from the insured's estate for the amount of the loan made to the insured when the insurance policy is the security for the loan.

Suppose a husband and wife acquire property as tenants by the entirety, execute a joint note for the purchase price and execute a mortgage to secure the note. If the husband dies, and the wife, who succeeds to the property as the survivor, pays the indebtedness, can she obtain a contribution from the estate of her husband? Compare Lopez v. Lopez, 90 So.2d 456 (Fla. 1956), with Cunningham v. Cunningham, 158 Md. 372, 148 Atl. 444 (1930). Whether the surviving tenant by the entirety is entitled to a contribution from the deceased tenant's estate when the tenancy is subject to a mortgage indebtedness on which both tenants are liable was considered in Florio v. Greenspan, — Mass. —, 165 N.E.2d 753 (1960), and the court held that despite the fact that both spouses originally were equally liable for the mortgage debt, it is inequitable to require the estate of the deceased spouse to contribute to the discharge of an encumbrance on property, the entire ownership of which is in the surviving spouses. The court refers to a contrary body of authority. It leaves undecided its position if the value of the property is less than the indebtedness. For another view, see In re Dowler's Estate, 368 Pa. 519, 84 A.2d 209 (1951).

[22] If the devisee of mortgaged land is entitled to have the underlying debt discharged out of other assets, and if the only assets available are specifically devised parcels of land, will all the devisees have to contribute to the payment of the debt? Eaton v. MacDonald, 154 Me. 227 145 A.2d 369 (1958), says yes.

property at the stipulated price free and clear of any encumbrance?[23] The testator's intention in this regard should be clearly expressed in the will.

A specific legacy should be contrasted with a demonstrative legacy. The latter is a legacy of a dollar amount, providing that the proceeds of the sale of specifically described property are to be applied to the payment of the dollar amount. Thus, if the testator gives A $10,000 and directs that his 100 shares of General Motors stock be sold and the proceeds be applied to the payment of this legacy, A has a demonstrative legacy. Unlike a specific bequest, a demonstrative legacy is not defeated if the property which is designated to be sold is not owned by the testator at his death; in other words, a demonstrative legacy is not subject to ademption. However, in determining the order in which property will be used to pay the debts of the testator, the demonstrative legacy is classified with the specific bequest to the extent of the value of the property that is to be sold to provide funds to pay the stated dollar amount.[24]

The will should specify the order in which the assets of the estate are to be used to pay the various death obligations of the testator. In the absence of an appropriate provision in the will, specific bequests and devises and the property which is to be sold

[23] See Hirlinger v. Hirlinger, 267 S.W.2d 46 (Kansas City, Mo., Ct. App. 1954). For cases determining whether the option can be exercised after the death of the person to whom it is given, see Stern v. Stern, 410 Ill. 377, 102 N.E.2d 104 (1951); In re Ludwick's Estate, 269 Pa. 365, 112 Atl. 543 (1921).

For a consideration of the cost basis for the purpose of determining gain or loss when the beneficiary of an option created by a will sells the option, see page 999 infra, note 74. Compare, however, the establishment of basis for the purpose of determining a gain or loss if the option is exercised by the beneficiary and then the property acquired by the option is sold. See Mack v. Commissioner, 148 F.2d 62 (3d Cir. 1945), *cert. denied,* 326 U.S. 719 (1945); Valleskey v. Nelson, 168 F. Supp. 636 (E.D. Wis. 1958), *aff'd,* 271 F.2d 6 (7th Cir. 1959), *cert. denied,* 361 U.S. 960 (1960) (where testamentary provision authorized sale of property to X at bargain price, and X purchased property pursuant to provision, it was held that X acquired property by purchase and not by bequest, and his basis was cost to him plus certain selling expenses). See also Death and Options, 42 A.B.A.J. 466 (1956). If the decedent owned an option which is exercisable, after his death, by the beneficiary under his will, there would seem to be no logical difference, so far as cost basis is concerned, from the situation where the option is created by the decedent. In connection with options, see the text concerning employee stock options at page 374 infra.

[24] On demonstrative legacies, see Leach, Cases and Text on the Law of Wills 150 (2d ed. 1960 rev.).

For a decision which held that a gift of a specified number of shares of stock, with an alternative gift of a dollar amount equal to the value of specified stock in case the stock has been sold, was a general legacy and not a specific bequest or a demonstrative legacy, see Park Lake Presbyterian Church v. Henry's Estate, 106 So.2d 215 (Dist. Ct. App. Fla., 1959)

to pay a demonstrative legacy will be used last to meet such death obligations.[25]

If the property specifically bequeathed or devised is to pass free of death tax burdens imposed as a result of the testator's death, the will may have to contain appropriate provisions in this regard.[26]

The extent to which a distribution to the beneficiary by the executor of property specifically bequeathed or devised will be deemed a distribution of estate income has been considered.[27] In this connection it should be kept in mind that if the title to the decedent's realty passes directly to the devisee (or heir) and the devisee (or heir) is entitled to immediate possession and to the income from the realty, the income is taxable to the devisee (or heir) and not to the estate.[28] Income from specifically bequeathed or devised property that comes under the control of the executor must eventually be accounted for to the beneficiary, though the executor is entitled to receive it initially.[29]

The comments previously made in regard to the failure of a pecuniary legatee to survive the testator are equally applicable to a beneficiary of specifically bequeathed or devised property.[30]

[25] For a discussion of the order in which the assets of the estate are used to meet various death obligations in the absence of appropriate provisions in the will, see Atkinson, Wills 754-763 (2d ed. 1953). For a case where the provisions in a will as to the order in which property was to be used to pay various legacies required interpretation by the court, see Sibley v. Livermore, 332 Mass. 730, 128 N.E.2d 329 (1955).

If the will contains a formula pecuniary marital deduction gift and various specific bequests, will the specific bequests abate in favor of the pecuniary marital deduction gift if there are not sufficient other assets to make up the amount called for by the formula? In Osborn v. Osborn, 334 S.W.2d 48 (Mo. 1960), the court concluded that the testator intended that the widow should receive the full amount of her bequest and that the estate should have the benefit of the maximum allowable marital deduction. Consequently, specific devises and bequests had to abate to provide the funds necessary to make up the full amount of the bequest to the widow.

[26] See page 271 supra, note 12.

[27] See discussion of income taxation of estates at page 77 supra.

[28] See page 77 supra, note 3.

[29] In Estate of Amelia Kern MacCulloch, N.Y.L.J., Oct. 30, 1957, p. 12, the Surrogate's Court was confronted with a bequest of the proceeds of specified shares of stock, and it became necessary to determine whether the bequest was a specific one or a general pecuniary legacy, because after the death of the testator and before the sale of the securities a cash dividend was paid. The court held that the cash dividend went to the legatee of the proceeds of the sale of the stock, just as it would have done if the stock itself had been given to the legatee.

[30] See page 273 supra, notes 18 and 19.

PROBLEMS

7.9. T in his will gives his interest in a partnership to his son S. After the execution of the will, the partnership is converted into a corporation and T receives a certain number of shares of the corporation. T dies. Is S entitled to the shares of stock in the corporation which succeeded the partnership? See Baldwin v. Davidson, 37 Tenn. App. 606, 267 S.W.2d 756 (1954).

7.10. A owns 100 shares of stock in the Canadian Pacific Railway Co. He makes a will, which contains the following provision: "I give 100 shares of stock in the Canadian Pacific Railway Co. to my son S." A sells his 100 shares of stock. He dies. Is A's executor required to buy 100 shares of stock in the Canadian Pacific Railway Co. and transfer them to S? See In re Harris' Estate, 143 N.Y.S.2d 157 (1955).

4.   LAPSED AND VOID LEGACIES

At common law, a bequest or devise to a person deceased on the date the will is executed (a void legacy), or to a person who dies after the will is executed but before the testator (a lapsed legacy), fails. You cannot make a gift to a dead man and the gift in terms to the dead man is not regarded as a gift to him or to his estate. What happens to the property which would have passed to the deceased beneficiary had he lived? If the bequest or devise is to a class, the members of the class who survive the testator take the gift.[31] If the bequest or devise is a nonresiduary one to an individual, the subject matter of the bequest or devise falls into the residue; if it is a residuary one, the subject matter falls through the residue into intestacy in most states. Such are the consequences if the testator does not manifest a different intent and if there is no applicable statute changing the result.

The various states have enacted what are called lapse statutes, which make substantial changes in the common law result unless the testator manifests an intent that rules out the applicability of the lapse statute.[32] These statutes do not apply to all bequests and devises, and the ones not covered by the statute continue to be

---

[31] This result is based on the presumed intention of the testator when he makes a gift to a defined group rather than to a separate individual. See the discussion as to class gifts at page 521 infra.

[32] An illustrative lapse statute is Mass. Ann. Laws, c. 191, §22, quoted infra page 1456.

governed by common law rules. A substantial controversy has developed as to whether they apply to class gifts.[33] At least one statute prevents a lapsed legacy of a part of the residue from falling through the residue into intestacy, by giving the lapsed residuary share to the other residuary takers.[34]

An estate planning job is not well done if the destination of a disposition under a will has to be worked out under either common law rules or a lapse statute in the event a beneficiary dies before the testator. The will itself should spell out the consequences of a beneficiary predeceasing the testator, because such manifested intent will overcome the otherwise governing effect of a common law or statutory rule.[35]

PROBLEM

7.11. A's will provides as follows: "I give the sum of $10,000 to my wife W and I give Blackacre to my son S and I give the residue of my estate to my daughter D." W dies. S dies leaving a minor child. D dies leaving a minor child. A dies a resident of Massachusetts. Who is entitled to the $10,000 legacy in favor of W? Who is entitled to Blackacre? Who is entitled to the residue of the estate? See State Street Trust Co. v. White, 305 Mass. 547, 26 N.E.2d 356 (1940).

---

[33] See page 522 infra.

[34] See Ill. Rev. Stat., c. 3, §200 (1959), quoted infra page 1438.

Several other states have statutory provisions like those in Illinois, where the share of a deceased residuary beneficiary passes to the surviving residuary beneficiaries if the lapse statute is not applicable. For an example see N.J. Rev. Stat. §3A:3-10 (1951), quoted infra page 1466. This result as to residuary beneficiaries has also been reached judicially (see Corbett v. Skaggs, 111 Kan. 380, 207 Pac. 819 (1922)), but the rule generally followed in the absence of statute is that the deceased residuary beneficiary's share becomes intestate property.

[35] If a beneficiary who is named in a revocable inter vivos trust to take the trust property outright after the settlor's death dies before the settlor, will the gift to the beneficiary lapse? See First National Bank of Cincinnati v. Tenney, 165 Ohio St. 513, 138 N.E.2d 15 (1956), in which it was held that the interest in the designated beneficiary was vested and, consequently, was not defeated by her death before the settlor's. If a person deposits money in a bank account in his own name as trustee for another, such a deposit may be deemed to create only a revocable trust and, if so, is called a "Totten trust" because of its similarity to the trust in Matter of Totten, 179 N.Y. 112, 71 N.E. 748 (1904). In United States v. Williams, 160 F. Supp. 761 (D.N.J. 1958), the beneficiary of a Totten trust predeceased the depositor, and it was held that the government was not entitled to the bank account where its claim arose through a levy and distraint for income tax deficiencies assessed against the beneficiary. When the beneficiary of a Totten trust predeceases the depositor, the trust is terminated.

CHAPTER VIII

Life Insurance

Life insurance may be owned by the insured or by someone other than the insured. If the insurance is owned by the insured, in the formulation of his estate plan consideration should be given to the desirability of his retaining the ownership until his death; if the insurance is owned by someone other than the insured, particular attention must be paid to the devolution of this asset in the event the owner dies before the insured.

If the ownership of life insurance is retained by the insured until his death, the settlement arrangement with respect to the proceeds becomes a significant part of his estate plan. It must be kept in mind, however, that the settlement should be worked out in conjunction with the development of the plan of disposition of other assets so that an integrated plan covering all assets will result. Life insurance proceeds may be disposed of on the death of the insured in any one of the following ways:

1. The proceeds may be made payable outright in a lump sum to a designated beneficiary (a non-trust gift).[1]
2. The proceeds may be made payable to the executors or administrators of the insured, in which case the proceeds will be added to the other probate assets of the insured.[2]

[1] The terms of the insurance policy usually give the lump sum payee the right to elect to leave the proceeds with the company, to be paid out under one of the options in the policy. See page 285 infra, note 14. The insurance policy normally provides the method of designating the beneficiary of the proceeds and of changing a beneficiary designation. In Austin v. Sears, 180 F. Supp. 485 (N.D. Cal. 1960), the designation of the beneficiary was initially made in the insured's will, a method not specified in the policy. Nevertheless, the court upheld the designation. It pointed out that the provisions in the policy with respect to designation and change of beneficiary were for the benefit of the insurer, not the insured, and that the required formalities would be relaxed when the controversy was between conflicting claimants (with the insurer not involved) in order to effectuate the insured's intent.

[2] If the insurance proceeds are added to the other probate assets of the insured, they become subject to the claims of his creditors, to the marital rights of his wife, and to state inheritance tax laws to the same extent as other probate assets.

In Beall Estate, 384 Pa. 14, 119 A.2d 216 (1956), it was held that National Service Life Insurance passes free of the claims of the insured's creditors, even though the proceeds are payable to the insured's estate.

Consider the effect of Florida Stat. §222.13 (1959) on the rules normally

3. The proceeds may be made payable to a testamentary trustee.[3] Such a method of settlement might provide in substance that in the event the insured leaves a will which is admitted to probate within one year after the insured's death, and that if a trust is established under the will and the named trustee qualifies as such within one year after the death of the insured, the proceeds will be paid to the named trustee and otherwise to the executors or administrators of the insured. The question raised by this method of settlement, if it is effective, though not attested in the manner required for testamentary disposition, is whether it means anything different from when the beneficiary designation is the executors or administrators of the insured.[4]

4. The proceeds may be made payable to a designated trustee to be held in trust pursuant to the terms of a trust instrument executed by the insured and the designated trustee (an insurance trust).[5] It seems safe to conclude that such

---

applicable where life insurance proceeds are made payable to the estate of the insured or to his executors or administrators. The case of Equitable Life Assurance Society of the United States v. McRee, 75 Fla. 257, 78 So. 22 (1918), should be read in conjunction with an examination of the Florida statute.

[3] In Frost v. Frost, 202 Mass. 100, 88 N.E. 446 (1909), the insured purported to assign a policy on his life to "the trustees to be named in my will." The court held that the purported assignment was testamentary and ineffective because it was not attested as a will. The following is a quotation from the opinion: "Upon the facts in the case these assignments never took effect within the lifetime of the assignor, for want of assignees, and never took effect after his death for want of proper attestation. There was therefore nothing upon which to base the contemplated trust, and it never was perfected."

[4] For excellent analyses of the problems presented by the designation of a testamentary trustee as the beneficiary of life insurance proceeds, see Lawthers, Testamentary Trusts as Beneficiaries Under Life Insurance Policies, 9 J. Am. Soc. C.L.U. 307 (1955); Schipper, Jr., Designating Trustee Under Will as Beneficiary of Insurance Policy, A.B.A. Proceedings of Probate and Trust Law Divisions 57 (1955).

Several states have passed statutes which specifically permit a trustee under the will of the insured to be named as the beneficiary of life insurance proceeds. These statutes are designed to assure that insurance proceeds under such a beneficiary designation will be treated in the same way as proceeds made payable to a trustee of an inter vivos trust. See Colo. Laws 1959, c. 293; N.Y. Decedent Estate Law §47-f, added by N.Y. Laws 1960, c. 1066, quoted infra page 1468; Pa. Stat. Ann., tit. 20, §301.7A (Purdon, Supp. 1959), as amended by Pa. Laws 1957, Act 377; Wis. Stat. Ann. §206.52(2) (1957), quoted infra page 1477.

[5] When insurance proceeds are payable to a minor, the Fidelity Mutual Life Insurance Company, Philadelphia, Pennsylvania, offers the following beneficiary designation:

"Any sum payable as herein provided to any of said beneficiaries designated in Class B of Article 1 during such beneficiary's minority shall be paid to JOHN DOE, brother of the insured, as trustee for such beneficiary. In the event said brother shall fail to serve or shall cease to serve as trustee for such beneficiary, because of death or otherwise, any sum payable as herein pro-an insurance trust will now be upheld against an attack on the ground that it is a testamentary disposition.[6] The question may well be asked, though, when does the trust in fact come into existence — when the instrument is executed or when a policy is made payable to the designated trustee or when the proceeds of a policy are received by the trustee? It is believed that the trust comes into existence when a policy is made payable to the designated trustee.[7] Nor-

---

vided to such beneficiary during such beneficiary's minority shall be paid to RICHARD DOE, nephew of the insured, as successor trustee. Any permissible right of withdrawal or election of options by such beneficiary during his minority shall be exercisable by said trustee. Such sums shall be held and expended for the maintenance, support and education of such minor beneficiary in the discretion of the trustee, except as may be otherwise provided in a separate trust instrument, and when such beneficiary shall attain the age of 21, the trustee shall pay over any unexpended funds. As respects any payment made to said trustee, the Company shall be under no liability to see to or be responsible for the proper discharge of the trust or any part thereof, and any such payment to said trustee shall fully discharge the Company for the amount so paid. The Company shall not be charged with notice of a separate trust instrument, a change of trustee, the death of such beneficiary, the termination of the trust, or of rights under the trust, until written evidence thereof is received at the Home Office."

[6] In Gordon v. Portland Trust Bank, 201 Ore. 648, 271 P.2d 653 (1954), the court considered, for the first time in Oregon, whether a life insurance trust was a testamentary disposition, and concluded that it was not. Compare Bickers v. Shenandoah Valley National Bank, 197 Va. 145, 88 S.E.2d 889 (1955), *rehearing denied*, 197 Va. 732, 90 S.E.2d 865 (1956). See N.Y. Personal Property Law §24-a, which expressly validates the designation of a beneficiary to receive payments from life insurance and payments due on the death of an employee under pension, retirement, death benefit, stock bonus and profit-sharing plans.

[7] See 1 Scott, Trusts §57.3 (2d ed. 1956); State v. Superior Court of Madison County, 236 Ind. 135, 138 N.E.2d 900 (1956). Statutes in several states specifically provide that it is not necessary to the validity of a trust agreement that it have a trust corpus other than the right of the trustee to receive insurance proceeds as beneficiary. See Colo. Laws 1959, c. 293; N.Y. Decedent Estate Law §47-f, added by N.Y. Laws 1960, c. 1066, quoted infra page 1468; Wis. Stat. Ann. §206.52(1), (3) (1957), quoted infra page 1477.

When the insured has reserved the right to change the beneficiary designated to receive the proceeds of a policy, what are the rights of the beneficiary prior to the maturity of the policy? See The Life Insurance Policy Contract 86 et seq. (Krueger and Waggoner eds. 1953), where it is brought out that the majority of the states hold that the beneficiary does not obtain any vested rights in the policy prior to the insured's death and that the insured may therefore assign the policy, obtain loans from the company, obtain the cash surrender value, etc., without the consent of the beneficiary. See, however, Estate of James Belden Bourland, 17 CCH T.C. Mem. 449 (1958), where the proceeds of an insurance policy which named the children of the decedent as beneficiaries were used by the decedent as part of the purchase price of a partnership interest, and the court held that a trust was thereby imposed, for the benefit of the children, on that portion of the partnership interest represented by the insurance proceeds so invested and the subsequent accumulation thereto. Consequently, the trust property held by the decedent on his death was not properly includible in his gross estate. The court applied Texas law.

mally, no policy is made payable to the designated trustee until after the instrument is executed, so there is a period of time after the execution of the instrument and before a trust comes into existence. If the settlor's will contains a provision directing that some part of his estate which is subject to disposition by his will shall be added to the insurance trust, the will is usually executed immediately after the execution of the insurance trust instrument. Is there any danger in executing a will which contains a pour-over provision to an insurance trust before the trust in fact comes into existence? In any jurisdiction recognizing the doctrine of incorporation by reference there is no difficulty in upholding the validity of the pour-over because the trust instrument is in existence prior to the execution of the will. If for any reason it is also desired to have the trust itself in existence when the will is executed, a nominal sum such as five dollars can be placed in the trust at the time it is executed, to be withdrawn later when a policy is made payable to the designated trustee.

If the proceeds of life insurance are made payable to an insurance trust, as long as the trust remains otherwise unfunded the trustee's fees will not begin until the proceeds are collected, even though a professional trustee is named in the trust agreement.[8] The insurance trust is also widely used as the means of carrying out a buy-and-sell agreement with respect to the interest of a deceased person in a business. Its use in this connection involves the collection, by the trustee, of the insurance proceeds on the insured's death and their application, as directed in the trust instrument, to finance the purchase of the decedent's interest in a business for the

---

[8] The Standard Charge Schedule of the Old Colony Trust Co., of Boston, Massachusetts, published in September, 1955, with respect to unfunded insurance trusts is as follows:

UNFUNDED INSURANCE TRUSTS

Standard Charge Schedule

A. *Individual Unfunded Insurance Trust:*
    Charge for Collecting and Dealing with Insurance Proceeds:
        $1\frac{1}{2}\%$ of the insurance proceeds collected; except that, as to any such proceeds which remain with the Trust Company after settlement of the estate, the charge will be reduced: to $\frac{1}{4}$ of 1% in case of trusteeship or an investment management account; to $\frac{3}{4}$ of 1% in case of custodianship.
    Charge for Acting as Trustee:
        The Trust Company makes no charge prior to collecting the insurance proceeds. Its charges for acting as trustee after collection of the insurance proceeds are the same as for a Personal Trust, page 12 of Standard Charge Schedules. [See page 139 supra, note 83.]

benefit of those interested in the business who survive.[9] The professional trustee makes no charge for acting as trustee under such a trust agreement prior to collecting the insurance proceeds.[10]

In addition to the methods described above for settling the proceeds of life insurance, the proceeds may be left with the company, to be paid out under one of the options in the policy or under some combination of these options.[11] A thorough understanding of the options set forth in the policy is essential if an intelligent choice is to be made with respect to the settlement of life insurance proceeds.

1.   THE OPTIONS UNDER THE POLICY[12]

PAYMENT AT MATURITY

Policy Proceeds

Payments under this Policy shall be made by the Company at the Home Office. The Company has the right to require sur-

---

[9] In regard to buy-and-sell agreements, see the discussion at page 942 infra.

[10] The Old Colony Trust Co., of Boston, Massachusetts, quotes the following charges with respect to an insurance trust designed to be the vehicle for carrying out a buy-and-sell agreement with respect to a decedent's interest:

B. *Close Corporation Insurance Trust; Partnership Insurance Trust:*
    Charge for Collecting and Dealing with Insurance Proceeds and Paying Purchase Price:
        Based on the amount of insurance proceeds collected and paid over or the amount of the purchase price paid for the decedent's interest, whichever amount is greater, for each settlement: $1\frac{1}{2}\%$ of the first $100,000; 1% of the next $100,000; and $\frac{1}{2}$ of 1% of the remainder.
    Minimum Charge: $250.00 for each settlement.
    Charge for Acting as Trustee:
        The Trust Company makes no charge prior to collecting the insurance proceeds.

[11] When the insured selects the option which is to control the payment of the insurance proceeds, it seems safe to conclude that such an arrangement is now safe from attack on the ground that it is a testamentary disposition, even though he reserves the right to change the beneficiary designation and the method of settlement at any time prior to his death.

In Toulouse v. New York Life Insurance Co., 40 Wash. 2d 538, 245 P.2d 205 (1952), the insured exercised an option in an endowment policy, and under the option which was selected the proceeds were left with the insurance company, to be paid to named beneficiaries of the insured on his death. The insured could not substitute other beneficiaries in place of those named but he could terminate their rights by withdrawing the cash surrender value. The court held that the exercise of the option in this manner was not a testamentary disposition.

For a comment on whether the arrangement is testamentary when the beneficiary elects the option after the death of the insured, see page 285 infra, note 14.

[12] The provisions of an insurance policy printed at this point are taken from a sample policy of the New England Mutual Life Insurance Company, of Boston, Massachusetts. The footnotes appended to the provisions of the policy are not footnotes prepared by the insurance company.

render of the Policy at the time of claim. The proceeds payable at maturity by death or as an endowment shall be the face amount, increased by any additions, accumulated dividends[13] and unpaid dividends, and reduced by any indebtedness to the Company on the Policy, and shall be paid in accordance with the beneficiary provisions. When death occurs within the grace period, any premium which is due but unpaid shall be deducted from the proceeds. Any amount of premium paid but not due when the Insured dies, shall be remitted in one sum to the person entitled to receive the policy proceeds upon the death of the Insured, or for whose immediate benefit such proceeds are then being applied.

Interest at the rate of two per cent per annum on the proceeds shall be paid from the date of maturity to the date of payment if the proceeds are to be paid in one sum, or to the date when the Option becomes operative if the proceeds are to be applied by the Company under an Option of Payment.

Options of Payment

The whole or part of the proceeds payable at maturity of this Policy by death or as an endowment, or of the net cash value payable on surrender, may be made payable under one of the first five Options, subject to the conditions hereinafter provided, or in any manner agreed upon with the Company. The provisions governing change of beneficiary shall apply to any election or change of election of an Option prior to maturity. After an Option becomes operative it may not be changed unless otherwise agreed upon with the Company at the time of election. If no election is in effect at maturity, the Payee entitled to the proceeds may then make the election for his or her own benefit.[14]

[13] When dividends are left with the insurance company, the interest on them is income for federal income tax purposes. Revenue Ruling 57-441, 1957-2 C.B. 45, brings out that such interest is not exempt from taxation when it is interest credited to the account of a veteran on dividends accrued by the Veterans' Administration on a converted United States government policy or on a National Service Life Insurance policy.

[14] In Hall v. Mutual Life Ins. Co. of New York, 201 Misc. 203, 109 N.Y.S.2d 646 (1952), the court held that the arrangement made by the payee of the life insurance policy involved, which provided for the disposition of the balance of the proceeds on the payee's death, was a testamentary disposition by the payee and that as such it was ineffective to control the disposition of the balance of the proceeds on the payee's death because the arrangement did not comply with the Statute of Wills. See N.Y. Personal Property Law §24-a (a 1952 amendment designed to overcome the result of the Hall case). The Hall case was reversed on appeal, 282 App. Div. 203, 122 N.Y.S.2d 239 (1953), and the Appellate Division was affirmed by the Court of Appeals without opinion, 306 N.Y. 909, 119 N.E.2d 598 (1954). See also Mutual Benefit Life Insurance Co. v. Ellis, 125 F.2d 127 (2d Cir. 1942).

In Wilhoit v. Peoples Life Insurance Co., 218 F.2d 887 (7th Cir. 1955), the beneficiary of an insurance policy received payment in a lump sum on the death of the insured, and twenty-three days later she and the insurance com-

First Option. Monthly instalments certain for a definite number of years, not exceeding thirty.

Second Option. Monthly payments (a) during the life of the Payee; or (b) for ten or twenty years certain, as may be elected, and thereafter during the life of the Payee.[15]

Third Option. Monthly payments during the life of the Payee. Upon receipt of due proof of death of the Payee before the sum of the instalments paid equals the amount applied to this Option, a sum equal to the difference shall be paid.

Fourth Option. Monthly interest payments at the rate of $1.65 for each One Thousand Dollars of the amount applied to this Option, commencing one month after this Option becomes operative and continuing during the life of the payee, or such other period as may be agreed upon with the Company. This interest is the equivalent of two per cent at the end of the year.[16] At the death of the Payee or at the end of the period agreed upon, the amount then retained, with any accrued interest, shall be paid in one sum, unless otherwise agreed upon with the Company.

Fifth Option. Instalments payable in such amounts and at such times as may be agreed upon with the Company, and continuing until the amount applied to this Option, with interest at two per cent per annum[17] and dividends as hereinafter provided, is exhausted. The final instalment shall be for the balance only.

Sixth Option. If this Policy is surrendered at the end of a policy year when the insurance age is between 55 and 70, the net cash value may be made payable in monthly instalments during the joint lifetime of the Insured and one other Payee then between 50 and 75 years of age, two-thirds of such monthly income to be

---

pany entered into an agreement whereby the proceeds were returned to the company, and the company agreed to pay her interest and return the principal to her on demand. In the event of the death of the beneficiary, the amount on deposit with the company was to be paid to a designated person. The court held that under Indiana law this arrangement was ineffectual to dispose of the money on deposit with the company after the death of the beneficiary, because of a failure to comply with the Statute of Wills.

[15] If it is important that some funds be available in the event of the early death of the primary beneficiary, the use of the second option with the ten- or twenty-year certain provision may be very costly. Such an arrangement involves dividing the proceeds into two portions, namely, an amount which will provide the payments for the fixed period and an amount which is sufficient to provide the deferred life annuity. In the event of the death of the beneficiary during the fixed period, there is no refund on the latter amount.

[16] The guaranteed rate of interest in the policy is an important factor in determining whether to leave the insurance proceeds with the company, to be paid out under one of the options. In older policies the guaranteed rate of interest is usually higher than in more recent policies.

[17] See note 16 supra.

continued during the balance of the lifetime of the survivor of such Payees.

Dividends. An Option elected before maturity shall become operative at maturity. An Option elected after maturity shall become operative upon receipt at the Home Office of the executed request. The first payment under the First, Second, Third or Sixth Option shall be payable when the Option becomes operative, and each payment shall be in accordance with the table for that Option.

Payments under the Second, Third and Sixth Options shall be based upon the sex of the Payee and the age of the Payee when the Option becomes operative, and shall be subject to satisfactory proof of the age of the Payee. If either the sex or age is misstated, the amount payable by the Company hereunder shall be that which the proceeds would have purchased on the correct basis. The Company may at any time require proof that a Payee is living, when payment is contingent upon survival of such Payee.

If the Second or Third Option is elected prior to maturity and becomes operative immediately at the death of the Insured, and if the original Payee dies on or before the thirtieth day after the date of the death of the Insured, notwithstanding and in lieu of any other provision, the amount then payable under such Option shall be the proceeds applied under the Option less any payment made thereunder, and such amount shall be paid in the same manner as the proceeds applied to said Option would have been payable if the original Payee had died before the Insured.[18]

The Options shall be available only with the consent of the Company, (a) if the amount applicable thereto is less than One Thousand Dollars, or (b) if an Option is elected by, or if payments under an Option are to be made to, a corporation, a partnership, association or fiduciary,[19] or (c) if the Policy is assigned other than to the Company.[20] If necessary to bring the amount of each guaranteed periodic payment to at least Ten Dollars, the Company may change the period of payment to quarterly, semiannual or annual.

Dividends. The First, Fourth and Fifth Options, the Second Option during any certain period, and the Third Option until an

[18] The desirability of this common disaster clause should be carefully considered whenever the insurance proceeds are settled in such a manner as to qualify for the estate tax marital deduction. See the discussion relating to a common disaster clause and the marital deduction at page 836 infra.

[19] Why should the insurance company be concerned about whether an option is elected by a fiduciary?

[20] A factor in determining whether the insured should assign the ownership of the policy to someone else is the availability of the options under the policy to the assignee.

amount equal to the proceeds has been paid, shall be credited with any dividends apportioned thereto by the Company. Any dividend under the First, Second, Third or Fourth Option shall be paid with the periodic instalments. Any dividend under the Fifth Option shall be added each year to the unpaid balance.

Final Payment. At the death of any Payee after the Option elected becomes operative, the then present value of any unpaid instalments certain under the First or Second Option, or any amount due under the provisions of the Third Option, or any principal amount and accrued interest then remaining unpaid under the Fourth or Fifth Option, shall be paid in one sum to the executors or administrators of such Payee, unless otherwise agreed upon with the Company; and such payment shall terminate the liability of the Company. Any unpaid instalments certain under the First Option shall be commuted at two per cent per annum, compounded annually, and under the Second Option at two and one-half per cent per annum, compounded annually. The liability of the Company shall terminate with the last payment due prior to the death (a) of the Payee under the Second or Third Option when payment is contingent upon survival of such Payee, or (b) of the surviving Payee under the Sixth Option.

Anticipation or Alienation. Unless otherwise agreed upon with the Company at the time of the election of the Option, no Payee shall have any right to assign, alienate, anticipate or commute any instalments or payments, to make withdrawals of proceeds, or to make any change in the provisions elected; and, except as otherwise prescribed by law, no payment of interest or of principal shall be subject to the debts, contracts or engagements of any Payee, nor to any judicial process to levy upon or attach the same for the payment thereof.[21]

---

[21] The validity of spendthrift provisions in insurance policies is considered in The Life Insurance Policy Contract 118 et seq. (Krueger and Waggoner eds. 1953). This book presents a thorough analysis of all phases of the life insurance contract. If the beneficiary selects the option under the policy which is to control the payment of the proceeds, the situation is somewhat comparable to the case where the settlor of a trust undertakes to spendthrift his interest under the trust. See Wilmington Trust Co. v. Carpenter, printed in full infra page 556. If the insured selects the option but gives the beneficiary an unlimited right of withdrawal as to the proceeds left with the company, what effect will the unlimited right of withdrawal have on the spendthrift provision? See Genesee Valley Trust Co. v. Glazer, 295 N.Y. 219, 66 N.E.2d 169 (1946). But compare Griswold, Spendthrift Trusts 72 (2d ed. 1947).

In New York, when proceeds of a life insurance policy which become a claim at the death of the insured are left with the insurance company under a trust or other agreement, the benefits accruing thereunder after the death of the insured are not transferable, or subject to commutation or encumbrance or to legal process except in an action to recover for necessaries, if the parties to the trust or other agreement so agree. See N.Y. Personal Property Law §15, quoted infra page 1468.

FIRST OPTION

Monthly Instalments for Each $1,000 Applied to Provide Income

Years	Instalment	Years	Instalment
1	$84.09	16	$6.07
2	42.46	17	5.77
3	28.59	18	5.50
4	21.65	19	5.26
5	17.49	20	5.04
6	14.72	21	4.85
7	12.74	22	4.67
8	11.25	23	4.51
9	10.10	24	4.36
10	9.18	25	4.22
11	8.42	26	4.10
12	7.80	27	3.98
13	7.26	28	3.87
14	6.81	29	3.77
15	6.42	30	3.68

SECOND AND THIRD OPTIONS

Monthly Instalments for Each $1,000 Applied to Provide Income

Guaranteed as long as Payee lives

		SECOND OPTION			THIRD OPTION
Age of Payee Nearest Birthday		Life	Instalments	Certain	Refund
Male	Female	Annuity	10 years	20 years	Annuity
under 6	under 12	$2.64	$2.63	$2.61	$2.59
6	12	2.65	2.64	2.63	2.60
7	13	2.67	2.66	2.65	2.62
8	14	2.68	2.67	2.66	2.63
9	15	2.70	2.69	2.68	2.65
10	16	2.72	2.71	2.70	2.67
11	17	2.73	2.72	2.71	2.68
12	18	2.75	2.74	2.73	2.70
13	19	2.77	2.76	2.75	2.72
14	20	2.79	2.78	2.77	2.74
15	21	2.81	2.80	2.79	2.76
16	22	2.83	2.82	2.81	2.78
17	23	2.86	2.85	2.84	2.80
18	24	2.88	2.87	2.86	2.82
19	25	2.91	2.90	2.88	2.84
20	26	2.93	2.92	2.91	2.87
21	27	2.96	2.95	2.93	2.89
22	28	2.99	2.98	2.96	2.92

		SECOND OPTION			THIRD OPTION
Age of Payee Nearest Birthday		Life Annuity	Instalments 10 years	Certain 20 years	Refund Annuity
Male	Female				
23	29	3.02	3.01	2.99	2.94
24	30	3.05	3.04	3.02	2.97
25	31	3.08	3.07	3.05	3.00
26	32	3.12	3.11	3.08	3.02
27	33	3.15	3.14	3.11	3.05
28	34	3.19	3.18	3.15	3.08
29	35	3.23	3.22	3.18	3.11
30	36	3.27	3.26	3.22	3.15
31	37	3.31	3.30	3.25	3.18
32	38	3.36	3.34	3.29	3.22
33	39	3.41	3.39	3.33	3.25
34	40	3.45	3.43	3.37	3.29
35	41	3.50	3.48	3.41	3.33
36	42	3.56	3.53	3.45	3.37
37	43	3.61	3.59	3.50	3.41
38	44	3.67	3.64	3.54	3.45
39	45	3.73	3.70	3.59	3.50
40	46	3.79	3.76	3.64	3.54
41	47	3.86	3.82	3.69	3.59
42	48	3.93	3.88	3.74	3.64
43	49	4.00	3.95	3.79	3.69
44	50	4.08	4.02	3.84	3.74
45	51	4.15	4.09	3.90	3.80
46	52	4.24	4.17	3.95	3.86
47	53	4.33	4.25	4.01	3.92
48	54	4.42	4.33	4.07	3.98
49	55	4.51	4.42	4.12	4.04
50	56	4.61	4.50	4.18	4.11
51	57	4.72	4.60	4.24	4.18
52	58	4.83	4.69	4.30	4.25
53	59	4.95	4.79	4.36	4.33
54	60	5.07	4.90	4.41	4.40
55	61	5.20	5.01	4.47	4.49
56	62	5.34	5.12	4.53	4.57
57	63	5.48	5.23	4.59	4.66
58	64	5.64	5.35	4.64	4.75
59	65	5.80	5.48	4.70	4.85
60	66	5.97	5.61	4.75	4.95
61	67	6.15	5.74	4.80	5.05

		SECOND OPTION			THIRD OPTION
Age of Payee Nearest Birthday		Life Annuity	Instalments 10 years	Certain 20 years	Refund Annuity
Male	Female				
62	68	6.34	5.87	4.85	5.16
63	69	6.54	6.01	4.90	5.27
64	70	6.75	6.16	4.94	5.39
65	71	6.97	6.30	4.98*	5.52
66	72	7.21	6.45	....	5.65
67	73	7.46	6.60	....	5.78
68	74	7.73	6.76	....	5.92
69	75	8.02	6.91	....	6.07
70	76	8.32	7.07	....	6.23
71	77	8.64	7.23	....	6.39
72	78	8.98	7.38	....	6.56
73	79	9.34	7.54	....	6.74
74	80	9.72	7.69	....	6.92
75	81	10.13	7.84	....	7.12
76	82	10.57	7.98	....	7.33
77	83	11.03	8.13	....	7.55
78	84	11.53	8.26	....	7.78
79	85	12.06*	8.39*	....	8.02*

* This amount payable for all older ages.

SIXTH OPTION

Monthly Instalments for Each $1,000 Applied to Provide Income

Guaranteed while both Payees live and two-thirds of amount
continued as long as Survivor lives

[*Note:* Only part of the table is set out below]

Age of Beneficiary Nearest Birthday		Age of Insured Nearest Birthday — Male							
		55	56	57	58	59	60	61	62
		Age of Insured Nearest Birthday — Female							
Male	Female	61	62	63	64	65	66	67	68
	50	$4.25	$4.29	$4.33	$4.37	$4.41	$4.45	$4.49	$4.53
	51	4.30	4.34	4.38	4.42	4.46	4.50	4.54	4.58
	52	4.34	4.39	4.43	4.47	4.51	4.56	4.60	4.64
	53	4.39	4.44	4.48	4.53	4.57	4.61	4.66	4.70
	54	4.44	4.49	4.54	4.58	4.63	4.67	4.72	4.77
	55	4.50	4.54	4.59	4.64	4.69	4.73	4.78	4.83
50	56	4.55	4.60	4.65	4.70	4.75	4.80	4.85	4.90
51	57	4.60	4.65	4.70	4.76	4.81	4.86	4.91	4.97
52	58	4.66	4.71	4.76	4.82	4.87	4.93	4.98	5.03

Age of Beneficiary Nearest Birthday		Age of Insured Nearest Birthday — Male							
Male	Female	55	56	57	58	59	60	61	62
		Age of Insured Nearest Birthday — Female							
		61	62	63	64	65	66	67	68
53	59	4.71	4.77	4.82	4.88	4.94	4.99	5.05	5.11
54	60	4.77	4.83	4.88	4.94	5.00	5.06	5.12	5.18
55	61	4.83	4.89	4.95	5.01	5.07	5.13	5.19	5.25
56	62	4.89	4.95	5.01	5.07	5.14	5.20	5.26	5.33
57	63	4.95	5.01	5.07	5.14	5.20	5.27	5.34	5.41
58	64	5.01	5.07	5.14	5.21	5.27	5.34	5.41	5.49
59	65	5.07	5.14	5.20	5.27	5.35	5.42	5.49	5.57
60	66	5.13	5.20	5.27	5.34	5.42	5.49	5.57	5.65
61	67	5.19	5.26	5.34	5.41	5.49	5.57	5.65	5.73
62	68	5.25	5.33	5.41	5.49	5.57	5.65	5.73	5.81
63	69	5.32	5.39	5.47	5.56	5.64	5.72	5.81	5.90
64	70	5.38	5.46	5.54	5.63	5.72	5.80	5.89	5.98
65	71	5.44	5.53	5.61	5.70	5.79	5.88	5.98	6.07
66	72	5.51	5.59	5.68	5.77	5.87	5.96	6.06	6.16
67	73	5.57	5.66	5.75	5.85	5.95	6.04	6.15	6.25
68	74	5.63	5.73	5.82	5.92	6.02	6.12	6.23	6.34
69	75	5.70	5.79	5.89	6.00	6.10	6.21	6.32	6.43
70		5.76	5.86	5.96	6.07	6.18	6.29	6.40	6.52
71		5.83	5.93	6.03	6.14	6.25	6.37	6.49	6.61
72		5.89	6.00	6.10	6.22	6.33	6.45	6.57	6.70
73		5.95	6.06	6.17	6.29	6.41	6.53	6.66	6.79
74		6.02	6.13	6.24	6.36	6.49	6.61	6.74	6.88
75		6.08	6.19	6.31	6.43	6.56	6.69	6.83	6.97

2. EXAMPLES OF SETTLEMENT ARRANGEMENTS WITH AN INSURANCE COMPANY

In working out with the insurance company the settlement of the proceeds of a policy under the available optional methods of settlement, various combinations of options and special provisions may result. Set forth below are two illustrations of special settlements worked out with an insurance company. These settlements are on forms especially prepared for the purpose by the New England Mutual Life Insurance Company of Boston. The portions of the form which are printed in italics were drafted to meet the particular situation.

Illustration 1

[Marital deduction arrangement with trustee of
insurance trust as secondary beneficiary] [22]

SPECIAL SETTLEMENT REQUEST
AND
REVOCATION OF PREVIOUS BENEFICIARIES

Request is hereby made that the amount due under Policy No.
0,000,000 be applied upon the death of the Insured for the benefit
of the following beneficiaries in accordance with the following provisions.   Any and all previous provisions for beneficiaries or for
policy control are hereby revoked.

Primary Beneficiary: .... *PRISCILLA ALDEN, wife of the*
Insured.

Secondary Beneficiary: .... *None.*

Option under which proceeds are
to be applied for each Primary
Beneficiary: .... *Fourth Option for life.*

Rights to withdraw or change reserved to each Primary Benefici-
ary: .... *While the Fourth Option is oper-*
ative, right: (a), to make with-
drawals up to $1,200. each con-
tract year, non-cumulative; (b),
on or after age 65, to elect settle-
ment for her sole benefit under
the Second Option, 10 or 20 years
certain and thereafter for life.

Option under which the value of
any guaranteed amounts unpaid
will be applied for each Secondary Beneficiary if at any time no
Primary Beneficiary is living: ...... *Not applicable.*

Rights to withdraw or change reserved to each Secondary Beneficiary (if at any time no Primary
Beneficiary is living): .... *Not applicable.*

[22] Marital deduction arrangements with respect to life insurance are discussed generally infra page 866.

Frequency of payments to Primary and Secondary Beneficiary: ....   *Fourth Option: Monthly, commencing after one month.*

Final Beneficiary to receive in one sum: ....   *See "Special Provisions."*

Owner of the Policy: ....   *The Insured.*

Order of Payment to Classes of Beneficiaries

Any payments due will be made exclusively to the Primary Beneficiary, if living. If at any time there be no Primary Beneficiary living, any payments due will be made to the Secondary Beneficiary, if living. If at any time there be no living Primary or Secondary Beneficiary, the then present value of any guaranteed amounts unpaid will be paid in one sum to the Final Beneficiary, if any be living, otherwise to the executors or administrators of the last survivor of the Insured and all beneficiaries, except as may be otherwise provided in this Request.

Settlements if More Than One Primary or Secondary Beneficiary

If at the death of the Insured there be more than one Primary Beneficiary living, or if at the death of the last survivor of the Insured and all Primary Beneficiaries there be more than one Secondary Beneficiary living, the then present value of any guaranteed amounts unpaid will be first divided into equal shares among the Primary Beneficiaries then living or among the Secondary Beneficiaries then living, as the case may be, and each person's share will be separately applied to the designated Option for his or her benefit. If any such beneficiary shall die after such division is made, the then present value of any guaranteed amounts unpaid on such beneficiary's share will be redivided into such number of equal shares as there shall be other beneficiaries of the same class then living. Each such share shall be added to and become a part of any amount then being retained under the Fourth or Fifth Option of the share or shares previously apportioned to the surviving beneficiary, but without increasing the amount of any Fifth Option instalment, except as may be otherwise provided in this Request. If, however, no amount is being retained under a Fourth or Fifth Option for such surviving beneficiary when an additional share is apportioned to such beneficiary, the additional share will be paid to such beneficiary in one sum.

SPECIAL PROVISIONS

Any provision included in this section shall supersede any conflicting provision on the first page, or above on this second page.

1. *Subject to the provisions of paragraph "4" below, upon the death of the survivor of the Insured and the Primary Beneficiary, the then present value of any guaranteed amounts unpaid will be paid in one sum to ABC TRUST COMPANY, of Boston, Massachusetts, Trustee, and its successors, hereinafter referred to as Trustee, to be held and disposed of according to the terms of the Trust created in the Trust Agreement dated March 20, 1961, between the Insured (JOHN A. ALDEN) and said Trustee. HOWEVER, if said Trust Agreement shall have been revoked during the life of the Insured, or the trust created thereby shall have terminated, or if the Trustee disclaims all right to receive payment, then, in any of such events, such amount will be paid in one sum to the executors or administrators of the survivor of the Insured and the Primary Beneficiary.*

2. *The Interest of the aforesaid Trustee, and its successors, in the policy and this Request shall be limited to receiving such amount as may, by the terms of this Request, be payable to the Trustee, and its successors, upon the death of the survivor of the Insured and the Primary Beneficiary if the Trustee shall then be named as beneficiary to receive any amount then due.*

3. *Unless notified of the revocation or termination of said Trust Agreement dated March 20, 1961, the Insurance Company shall be fully protected in making payment at the death of the survivor of the Insured and the Primary Beneficiary to said Trustee, or to any successor of whose appointment it has due notice, the receipt or release of either to be a full discharge to said Insurance Company of all liability in connection with any such payment, without any responsibility on the part of the Insurance Company to see to the distribution or application, in accordance with the terms of said Trust Agreement, of any amount paid to said Trustee, or any such successor.*

4. *All other provisions of this Request and the policy to the contrary notwithstanding, the interests of all beneficiaries other than the Primary Beneficiary are subject to the right hereby reserved to the Primary Beneficiary, while living, at all times after the death of the Insured, to revoke any and all provisions for payees to receive in any manner at*

or after the Primary Beneficiary's death, and in place thereof to designate that the value of any guaranteed amounts unpaid at the Primary Beneficiary's death be paid: (a), in one sum to the executors or administrators of the Primary Beneficiary; or (b), in such manner and for the benefit of such payee or payees as may be mutually agreed upon with the Insurance Company. Any such request must be in writing in a form meeting reasonable requirements of the Insurance Company, and shall take effect as of the date of such request but only when endorsed by the Insurance Company on the policy or any Certificate issued in lieu thereof, whether or not the said Primary Beneficiary be living at the time of endorsement; provided that any right so created shall be subject to any action taken or payment made by the Insurance Company prior to such endorsement.

Illustration 2

[Marital deduction arrangement with provision for
education of secondary beneficiary]

SPECIAL SETTLEMENT REQUEST
AND
REVOCATION OF PREVIOUS BENEFICIARIES

Request is hereby made that the amount due under Policy No. *0,000,000* be applied upon the death of the Insured for the benefit of the following beneficiaries in accordance with the following provisions. Any and all previous provisions for beneficiaries or for policy control are hereby revoked.

Primary Beneficiary: ....   *PRISCILLA ALDEN, wife of the Insured.*
   JOHN A. ALDEN, JR., son of
Secondary Beneficiary: ....   *the Insured.*

Option under which proceeds are
to be applied for each Primary
Beneficiary: ....   *Fourth Option for life.*

Rights to withdraw or change
reserved to each Primary Beneficiary: ....
   While the Fourth Option is operative, right: (a), to make withdrawals in whole or in part; (b),

to elect settlement for her sole benefit under any other Option, with such further withdrawal or commutation privilege as may then be agreed upon with the Insurance Company.

Option under which the value of any guaranteed amounts unpaid will be applied for each Secondary Beneficiary if at any time no Primary Beneficiary is living: ....

Fourth Option for life.

Rights to withdraw or change reserved to each Secondary Beneficiary (if at any time no Primary Beneficiary is living): ....

While the Fourth Option is operative or the Fifth Option provided in "Special Provisions" is operative, right, on and after age 25, or prior thereto upon submitting evidence satisfactory to the Insurance Company of graduation from an institution of higher learning: (a), to make withdrawals in whole or in part; (b), to elect settlement for his sole benefit under any other Option, with such further withdrawal or commutation privilege as may then be agreed upon with the Insurance Company. For other right see "Special Provisions."

Frequency of payments to Primary and Secondary Beneficiary:

Fourth Option: Monthly, commencing after one month.

Final Beneficiary to receive in one sum: ....

In equal shares, per stirpes, the living issue of the Secondary Beneficiary, if any, otherwise in equal shares such of the children of the Insured as may be living, and, per stirpes, the living issue of any or all of said children who may be dead.

Owner of the Policy: .... *The Insured.*

Order of Payment to Classes of Beneficiaries

Any payments due will be made exclusively to the Primary Beneficiary, if living. If at any time there be no Primary Beneficiary living, any payments due will be made to the Secondary Beneficiary, if living. If at any time there be no living Primary or Secondary Beneficiary, the then present value of any guaranteed amounts unpaid will be paid in one sum to the Final Beneficiary, if any be living, otherwise to the executors or administrators of the last survivor of the Insured and all beneficiaries, except as may be otherwise provided in this Request.

Settlement if More Than One Primary or Secondary Beneficiary

If at the death of the Insured there be more than one Primary Beneficiary living, or if at the death of the last survivor of the Insured and all Primary Beneficiaries there be more than one Secondary Beneficiary living, the then present value of any guaranteed amounts unpaid will be first divided into equal shares among the Primary Beneficiaries then living or among the Secondary Beneficiaries then living, as the case may be, and each person's share will be separately applied to the designated Option for his or her benefit. If any such beneficiary shall die after such division is made, the then present value of any guaranteed amounts unpaid on such beneficiary's share will be redivided into such number of equal shares as there shall be other beneficiaries of the same class then living. Each such share shall be added to and become a part of any amount then being retained under the Fourth or Fifth Option of the share or shares previously apportioned to the surviving beneficiary, but without increasing the amount of any Fifth Option instalment, except as may be otherwise provided in this Request. If, however, no amount is being retained under a Fourth or Fifth Option for such surviving beneficiary when an additional share is apportioned to such beneficiary, the additional share will be paid to such beneficiary in one sum.

SPECIAL PROVISIONS

Any provision included in this section shall supersede any conflicting provision on the first page, or above on this second page.

1. *Other Right reserved to the Secondary Beneficiary (if at any time no Primary Beneficiary is living):*
    a. *While the Fourth Option is operative, right, prior to age 25, upon submitting evidence satisfactory to the Insurance Company of attendance at an institution of higher learning, to elect settlement under the Fifth*

Option with payments of such amounts and payable at such times as may be agreed upon with the Insurance Company, except that the aggregate of specified payments is not to exceed $1,500. during each 12 months period. Unless before October 1st of the succeeding year the Insurance Company is furnished with a new election of the Fifth Option upon further proof of attendance at an institution of higher learning, the Fourth Option will be operative as of October 1st for any balance remaining, subject to further election, prior to age 25, upon proof again being furnished that the Secondary Beneficiary is in attendance at an institution of higher learning. If, however, such election is not made by October 1st of any year and the balance remaining is less than One Thousand Dollars ($1,000.), such balance will be paid in one sum on October 1st.

2. *An institution of higher learning is hereby defined as any college or university, any institution for professional or specialized training, or any school offering an educational course of a generally higher grade than high school. The decision of the New England Mutual Life Insurance Company shall be final as to whether or not the Secondary Beneficiary is in attendance at, or has graduated from, an institution of higher learning, within the meaning of this Request. Fifth Option payments conditional upon attendance at an institution of higher learning once in effect for any academic year shall not terminate prior to the following October 1st, except as otherwise provided, even though the Secondary Beneficiary shall, during such academic year, cease attendance at an institution of higher learning.*

3. *All other provisions of this Request and the policy to the contrary notwithstanding, the interests of all beneficiaries other than the Primary Beneficiary are subject to the right hereby reserved to the Primary Beneficiary, while living, at all times after the death of the Insured, to revoke any and all provisions for payees to receive in any manner at or after the Primary Beneficiary's death, and in place thereof to designate that the value of any guaranteed amounts unpaid at the Primary Beneficiary's death be paid: (a), in one sum to the executors or administrators of the Primary Beneficiary; or (b), in such manner and for the benefit of such payee or payees as may be mutually agreed upon with the Insurance Company. Any such request must be in writing in a form meeting reasonable require-*

*ments of the Insurance Company, and shall take effect as
of the date of such request but only when endorsed by the
Insurance Company on the policy or any Certificate issued
in lieu thereof, whether or not the said Primary Beneficiary be living at the time of endorsement; provided that
any right so created shall be subject to any action taken
or payment made by the Insurance Company prior to such
endorsement.*

PROBLEMS

8.1. If the insured does not want the insurance proceeds to be
paid in a lump sum to the intended beneficiaries at the time of
his death, but does want to introduce a high degree of flexibility
into the method of settling the proceeds, point out the flexibility
that may be attained in an insurance trust which it is not possible
to attain if the proceeds are left with the company to be paid out
under one of the options.

8.2. Each of the following factors is relevant in the selection of
the method of settling the proceeds of life insurance. Point out
which method of settlement is suggested by the stated factor.

a. The intended primary beneficiary is the insured's wife.
b. The intended primary beneficiary is a minor child of the
   insured.
c. The other assets of the insured are substantial.
d. The other assets of the insured are nominal.
e. Financial security for the intended beneficiary is of paramount importance.

3.   TAX CONSIDERATIONS

Life insurance proceeds are usually paid on the death of the
insured but they may be paid before that time. If they are to be
paid on the death of the insured, a relevant factor in determining
whether to adopt one method of settlement or another is the income tax consequences to the beneficiary. If the proceeds are to
be drawn down before the death of the insured, the income tax
consequences of one method of receiving the proceeds as compared
with another must be examined if an intelligent decision as to the
method of payment is to be adopted.[23]

When life insurance policies are involved in any estate, consid-

[23] If the insured receives back less than he has paid in in premiums, does he
have a deductible loss for income tax purposes? See Arnold v. United States,
180 F. Supp. 746 (N.D. Tex. 1960), where the court held that there was no
ascertainable loss under the circumstances before the court.

eration must be given to the estate tax consequences for the insured's estate and for the estate of the owner of the policies, should he be someone other than the insured. In some cases it may be possible and appropriate to eliminate from the insured's gross estate the proceeds of insurance on his life; if this is accomplished by someone else taking over the ownership of the policies, it must be kept in mind that such an owner may die before the insured and that, if so, the value of the policies will be includible in his gross estate.

If the insured arranges for the proceeds of a policy to be paid to himself and his wife under a joint and survivor annuity and he dies first, is anything includible in his gross estate for estate tax purposes with respect to the annuity? What are the income tax consequences of selecting such an annuity?

The gift tax consequences of inter vivos dealings with a life insurance policy must not be overlooked in determining whether such dealings are desirable.

a. *Income Tax Consequences*

(1) Proceeds Paid by Reason of the Death of the Insured [24]

An examination of Section 101 of the 1954 Code reveals that if the proceeds of a life insurance policy are paid in a lump sum by reason of the death of the insured, they are not includible in the gross income of the beneficiary-recipient for federal income tax purposes.[25] Any interest payable on them because of delay in

[24] See 1954 I.R.C. §101, quoted infra page 1329.

In order for the provisions of the 1954 Code relating to life insurance to govern, the proceeds payable must be life insurance. Sometimes there may be doubt as to whether life insurance is involved. In Estate of Clarence L. Moyer, 32 T.C. 515 (1959), amounts received from the so-called Gratuity Fund of the Philadelphia-Baltimore Stock Exchange by reason of the death of members of the exchange were held to be benefits received under life insurance contracts.

[25] In Francis H. W. Ducros, 30 T.C. 1337 (1958), a corporation took out a policy of insurance on the life of its president, paid the premiums thereon and reserved the right to designate the beneficiary. The plan was to bestow the proceeds of the policy upon the stockholders in proportion to their interests in the corporation. A stockholder was named a beneficiary in the policy and collected the proceeds on the death of the insured. The court held that what she received was income and not excludable as life insurance proceeds under 1939 I.R.C. §22(b)(1)(A) (1954 I.R.C. §101(a)(1)) because the policy was a wager policy and not a life insurance contract. The case was reversed sub nom. Ducros v. Commissioner, 272 F.2d 49 (6th Cir. 1959), and in reversing the court held that the policy was not a wagering contract and the insurance proceeds were not a dividend, since they were paid directly to the shareholder by the insurance company and not by the corporation.

payment will of course be includible in gross income. If the transferee for value rule is applicable, then, as we shall see, the result changes.

The adoption of the so-called interest option under the policy[26] means that for federal income tax purposes the interest payments will be includible in the beneficiary-recipient's gross income, but the proceeds retained by the company when finally paid will not be included in the recipient's gross income.

(a) *Installment Payments*

Prior to the 1954 Code, a powerful inducement existed to adopt an installment option for the payment of the proceeds of life insurance on the death of the insured because the guaranteed interest element in such payments was not subject to income tax. Interest payments in excess of the guaranteed interest rate, called "excess interest," were, however, reportable as income.[27]

Section 101 of the 1954 Code in effect eliminates the income tax advantage of the selection of the installment option except where the surviving spouse of the insured is the beneficiary. Section 101(d)(1)(B) allows the surviving spouse to exclude from her gross income annually for federal income tax purposes the first $1000 of the interest element in the payment.[28] She may even exclude "excess interest" included in the payment to her to the extent that such "excess interest" comes within the annual $1000 exclusion.

[26] The fourth option printed supra page 286 is the so-called interest option.
In Handelman v. United States, 144 F. Supp. 153 (S.D.N.Y. 1956), the court was required to determine whether a settlement arrangement under an insurance policy, which called for the payment by the insurance company to the primary beneficiary of an annuity of 5 percent of the $35,000 face amount of the policy during her life and, on her death, required the payment of the face amount of the policy to a secondary beneficiary, was an installment payment arrangement. If installment payments were involved, then, under 1939 I.R.C. §22(b)(1), no part of each installment payment would be income. The court held that in view of the fact that the entire amount of the policy was to be paid to the secondary beneficiary on the death of the primary beneficiary, the insured had adopted the interest option.

[27] See 1939 I.R.C. §22(b)(1); Law v. Rothensies, 155 F.2d 13 (3d Cir. 1946). These provisions continue to apply to settlement arrangements if the insured died before the date of the enactment of 1954 I.R.C. §101. See §101(f), quoted infra page 1331. Note, however, that "excess interest" under the fifth option (see page 286 supra) is not paid out when declared but is added to the unpaid balance. Under the 1939 Code this excess interest apparently escaped taxation when the fifth option was adopted.

[28] It is not strictly accurate to refer to the exclusion of the first $1000 of the *interest element* in the payment because the exclusion is available as to the first $1000 over the amount that is deemed the annual return of the amount held by the insurer whether it is really interest or not. For convenience of expression, however, it is referred to herein as the *interest element*.

Thus the 1954 Code makes it even more desirable than before to adopt the installment option if the spouse of the insured is the beneficiary and if the amount of life insurance so settled is such that the interest element in the payments is not likely to exceed the $1000 annual interest exclusion.

An example of the way Section 101 operates may be helpful. Suppose that A has $296,000 of insurance on his own life. He adopts a policy option for paying the proceeds of the life insurance to his wife, which provides for monthly payments during her life. At A's death his wife is fifty years of age and, for purposes of this illustration, it is assumed that under the applicable mortality table her life expectancy is 29.6 years.[29] The guaranteed monthly payment to her under the selected option is $1207.68.[30] The first step in determining the income tax consequences is to determine what portion of the $296,000 the wife will receive each year on the basis of her life expectancy. The amount proves to be $10,000. It is completely excluded from the wife's gross income because it is not deemed to be income at all, and would be equally excluded if the recipient were someone other than the wife of the insured. The annual amount received by the wife under the selected option is $14,492.16. Thus the interest element is $4492.16 and, since this exceeds by $3492.16 the allowable $1000 annual interest exclusion given to a recipient who is the wife of the insured, $3492.16 is included annually in her gross income. If the wife lives beyond her 29.6 years, the first $10,000 of the annual payment to her will still not be regarded as income and she will still be entitled to the $1000 annual interest exclusion as to the amount of each annual payment in excess of $10,000.[31] If the recipient of the payments in the above illustration is a person having a 29.6-year life expectancy, but is not A's wife, such a person will include in his gross income the entire amount in excess of the first $10,000 of each annual payment.[32]

[29] The applicable mortality table is the one used by the insurer in determining the benefits to be paid. See Reg. §1.101-4(c), quoted infra page 1482.

[30] The guaranteed monthly payment for each $1000 of insurance under the selected option is obtained by reference to the table at page 289 supra. This table provides that a female aged fifty is entitled to $4.08 a month for each $1000 of insurance when the straight life annuity option is selected, and 296 times $4.08 equals $1207.68.

[31] See Reg. §1.104-4(c), quoted infra page 1482.

[32] What are the state income tax consequences when the installment option is adopted? See Allen v. State Tax Commission, 337 Mass. 502, 150 N.E.2d 14 (1958), where the court considered this problem in the light of Mass. Ann. Laws, c. 62, §1(a) (Supp. 1959). It ruled that the language of the statute, which imposes an income tax on interest from bonds, notes, money at interest and all debts due the person to be taxed, did not justify the imposition of an income tax on the interest element in the installments paid to the beneficiary

If it is desired to adopt an installment payment arrangement that will have an interest element of about $1000, so that no part of the payment, or not more than a small part thereof, will be includible in the gross income of the wife-beneficiary, what amount of life insurance should be so settled? To answer this question, the age of the wife at the time the payments are to begin would have to be estimated if a straight life annuity or any other installment payment arrangement based on her life expectancy is involved.[33] For example, where the wife is fifty years of age on the husband's death and her life expectancy is 29.6 years, $88,800 of life insurance would produce a little over $300 in excess of the $1000 interest element in each annual installment if the life annuity option is adopted. In such a case $3000 of each annual payment will be deemed a return of the face amount of the policy. The annual payment under the life annuity option would amount to $4347.60,[34] so that the interest element in each annual payment would be $1347.60.[35]

If the selected beneficiary is the wife of the insured and the insured does not elect one of the optional methods of settlement under the policy and the wife elects to have the proceeds paid to her in installments rather than in a lump sum, are the income tax consequences with respect to the installment payments to the wife

of life insurance under an option which provided for equal payments for a stipulated number of years. On the basis of this case the Commissioner of Corporations and Taxation in Massachusetts issued Income Tax Ruling No. 21, July 11, 1958, CCH Mass. State Tax Rep. ¶15-204A, 10, which provides in substance that where, on the death of the insured, life insurance proceeds are payable to a beneficiary in a stated number of periodic installments or in an amount certain, no part of such payment or payments will be taxable as interest under Chapter 62, §1(a) "unless a segregation has been made by the insurer as between principal and interest." On the other hand, if the payment is based on the life expectancy of the payee, such payments are taxable in their entirety as an annuity under Chapter 62, §5(a) (Supp. 1959).

[33] Of course, the age of the wife at the start of the payments under the policy on her husband's life will not be known until his death, so this variable will make somewhat inaccurate any calculation of the amount of life insurance that can be left her under an installment option completely free of income tax.

[34] This figure is obtained in the same manner as is outlined supra page 303, note 30.

[35] If the mode of settlement contains refund features — for example, further payments are to be made after the death of the primary beneficiary if the primary beneficiary dies before receiving a specified number of payments or a specified total amount — the value of the refund feature must be ascertained and deducted from the face amount of the policy in order to obtain the amount to be prorated over the life expectancy of the beneficiary. The value of the refund feature is determined by the use of the interest rate and mortality tables used by the insurer in determining the benefits to be paid. See Reg. §1.101-4(e), quoted infra page 1484, and Reg. §1.101-4(g), Ex. (7), quoted infra page 1484.

determined by Section 101 or Section 72 (applicable if the wife with her own funds purchased an annuity)? [36] If Section 101 controls, the $1000 annual interest exclusion is available; if Section 72 applies, the exclusion is not available. The following case, though decided under the 1939 Code, is relevant in formulating an answer to the question asked above.

COMMISSIONER OF INTERNAL REVENUE
v. PIERCE
146 F.2d 388 (2d Cir. 1944)

L. HAND, Circuit Judge.

Both the Commissioner and the taxpayer appeal from an order of the Tax Court, which expunged in part, and affirmed in part, a deficiency assessment for income taxes against the taxpayer for the year 1940. (The taxpayer has not pressed her appeal before us, and we understand it to be abandoned.) The taxpayer's husband died on March 18, 1940, leaving a life insurance policy in the sum of $100,000, in which he had named her as the beneficiary. The policy first contained an unconditional promise to pay to the taxpayer on the death of her husband, "the sum of $100,000," and later provided as follows: "The Insured shall have the right with the privilege of revocation and change, to elect in lieu of payment in one sum either Option 'A,' 'B' or 'C,' or that the amount payable be distributed under two or more of said Options. The Beneficiary . . . when this Policy becomes payable, shall have the same right and privilege if no such election effected by the insured shall then be in force." The taxpayer's husband did not during his life elect any of the opitions, but after his death, in accordance with the language just quoted, the taxpayer elected to take under "Option 'C'," which gave her the right to have the net proceeds of the policy paid "in either 10, 15, 20 or 25 stipulated installments of an amount corresponding in the Table below to the age of the Beneficiary at the death of the Insured, provided that if the Beneficiary shall survive to receive the number of installments selected, similar installments shall be continued during the lifetime of the Beneficiary." She chose to be paid in ten installments: i.e., 120 monthly installments spread over 10 years. At her age each payment came to $597, and they were to continue as long as she lived. To these installments the insurer added such monthly dividends as were declared upon the policy — these being the subject of the taxpayer's appeal. For the year 1940 she received ten installments, aggregating $6,294, together with nine monthly dividends for $36

[36] Section 72 of the 1954 Code is quoted infra page 1325.

each. She did not return any of these as income, relying upon Section 22(b)(1) of the Internal Revenue Code, 26 U.S.C.A. Int. Rev. Code, Section 22(b)(1), which excludes from gross income and exempts from taxes the following: "Life insurance. Amounts received under a life insurance contract paid by reason of the death of the insured, whether in a single sum or otherwise (but if such amounts are held by the insurer under an agreement to pay interest thereon, the interest payments shall be included in gross income)." The Commisisoner assessed a deficiency against her of $2,009.51, which he computed as follows. He divided the principal of the policy — $100,000 — by the figure 19.45 — that being the taxpayer's expectancy in 1940 — this gave a quotient of $5,141.39, of which he took five-sixths — there being only ten monthly payments in the year 1940. The result was $4,284.49, and this he treated as the proper amortization payment of the capital sum of $100,000; the difference — $6,294 minus $4,284.49 — he treated as income and taxed accordingly. Upon review by all the judges of the Tax Court, it was held, two judges dissenting, that the taxpayer was right; the deficiency was expunged, except as to the nine dividends already mentioned; and from this order the Commissioner appealed.

Four Circuit Courts of Appeals have held that Section 22(b)(1) does not mean to separate such installments as are here in question into principal and interest and to include the interest in gross income; but that it exempts the whole installment. Commissioner v. Winslow, 1 Cir., 113 F.2d 418, 133 A.L.R. 405; Commissioner v. Bartlett, 2 Cir., 113 F.2d 766; Commissioner v. Buck, 2 Cir., 120 F.2d 775; Allis v. La Budde, 7 Cir., 128 F.2d 838; Kaufman v. United States, 4 Cir., 131 F.2d 854. The parenthesis applies to cases where the capital sum is retained for a season undiminished, and only the interest is paid to the beneficiary (United States v. Heilbroner, 2 Cir., 100 F.2d 379); and in economic theory there is no difference between such interest, and the interest concealed in an installment; for, when an insurer pays the beneficiary in a series of installments, it always does add something as interest upon those installments which for the time being it retains. Nevertheless, although for this reason the distinction is to some extent formal, the courts have thought that they saw adequate ground for it in the language used; and the Commissioner, after many unsuccessful efforts, has finally yielded and amended his regulations accordingly (Regulations 103, Section 19.22(b)(1)-1). We are, therefore, to take it as datum that, if the insured had during his life elected to take under "Option 'C'," the Tax Court would have been right. The Commissioner insists, however, that his earlier position is still valid when, as here, it was the beneficiary, not the insured, who made the choice. The argument is that, since she had the option of choosing between the principal and one of the options, it is as though she had actually received the principal and had reinvested it with the insurer, instead of upon some other security. Were that done, the resulting payments would have to be broken down into earnings and amortization installments, and, qua earnings, would be taxable.

It cannot be seriously argued that, literally at any rate, the installments are not "paid by reason of the death of the insured"; they are all conditional upon that event, and they begin to be payable at once thereafter. Pro tanto, they are precisely like any other life insurance, all of which is payable "by reason of the death of the insured." We recognize, however, that that is not a final answer; for, granting that the insured's death is a condition precedent, it is not the only condition precedent to the payments in question, as it is when the insured himself makes the choice. If the words should be read: "only by reason of the death of the insured," the meaning would be as the Commissioner maintains; and our decision turns upon whether that is their right interpretation.

The policy offered the beneficiary a choice between rights already in existence, with whose creations she had had nothing whatever to do; they came to her ready made by the insured. To say that her position was the same as though, having the principal in hand, she had exchanged it with the insurer for the option, is untrue in fact and unwarranted in law. Perhaps, if the policy had not contained the options, the beneficiary might still have been able to buy "Option 'C'" from the insurer by a direct bargain; but nothing in the record supports that assumption, and we have no right to make it. Life insurance is a technical subject, and it would be hazardous to say that it made no difference in the beneficiary's powers in dealing with the insurer that the policy contained the options. But even if it did make no difference, it is a fiction to treat the situation as though she had made such a bargain; it is as untrue as it would be to say that if the policy permitted her to be paid in dollars or pounds, and she took pounds, she had bought the pounds from the insurer with the dollars. It is as untrue as it would be to say that, if a testator gives a legatee the choice of money or a chattel and he takes the chattel, he has bought it of the executor. In such situations the beneficiary makes no bargain whatever with the decedent's representative; all that happens is that, not having the power to take both benefits, and being therefore put to a choice, he takes one of those already provided. Nothing will justify the violence to the language necessary to the Commissioner's interpretation, unless it is necessary to effectuate the underlying purpose of the statute. In this instance it would defeat that purpose.

We are to assume that Congress wished to favor the class of dependents in whose behalf life insurance is ordinarily secured — the wife and children of the insured. Although that involves an exemption from taxation and exemptions are viewed with jealousy, when the purpose is evident enough, we should not defeat or multilate its realization. The proposed distinction does not rest upon any difference in the class who will profit by the exemption; it does not rest upon any difference in the kind of property exempted; it does not rest upon any language in the statute — on the contrary it demands that we import a word which is not there: "only." Moreover, it would make a difference which in practice would impair the underlying purpose. If the Commissioner is right, an insured who has taken out such a policy, and who wishes to give the beneficiary — ordinarily his wife — the power to decide how she will use the proceeds, must consult her in advance, and act while he lives, unless he is willing to forego the exemption. As he cannot tell when he will die, he must make sure that he keeps abreast of all changes in their financial position, and provides for them; he will be unable to give her the power after his death to adapt her means to her needs. True, that extension will be short; she cannot wait long before electing; but at least she has some time within which to act, and this may be extremely important in those cases — which are apt to be frequent — in which through inattention, or through the assumption, common to us all, that death is not at hand, the insured has failed to do what the new situation demanded. For these reasons, as we have said, to import the necessary word would positively defeat the purpose of Congress.

In conclusion, we think that there are one or two analogies, which, while by no means on all fours, nevertheless look in the same direction. When a widow accepts her husband's testamentary provision in lieu of dower, she is held to take under the will, though it is only by performing the condition — releasing the dower — that she can take. Helvering v. Butterworth, 290 U.S. 365. Again, when an heir who contests a will, the contest remaining undecided, settles with the executor, he takes by inheritance, though it is again only by conforming to a condition that he gets his share. Lyeth v. Hoey, 305 U.S. 188. These decisions do not of course declare that the widow, or the heir, takes "only" from the husband or the ancestor; yet they are instances in which we do think of the property as passing only "by reason of" death, although some concurring act of the transferee is necessary. And indeed it is always true of any devise, and of any legacy, that the devisee or the legatee must accept it in order to pass the property. Acceptance is a condition not always fulfilled — as for example, when the testator has attached obligations to it — ; yet we should suppose that nobody would hesitate to say of such a devise or legacy that it passed "by reason of the death" of the testator.

Order affirmed.

FRANK, Circuit Judge (dissenting). [Dissenting opinion omitted.]

PROBLEMS

8.3. Re-examine the first five options in the sample life insurance policy printed supra page 286, and determine the federal income tax consequences under each of these options so far as the designated beneficiary is concerned.

8.4. Re-examine Illustration 1, page 293 supra, and determine the federal income tax consequences under this illustration so far as the designated beneficiary is concerned.

8.5. Re-examine Illustration 2, page 296 supra, and determine the federal income tax consequences under this illustration so far as the designated beneficiary is concerned.

8.6. A conveys Blackacre to B for life with remainder to "C and his heirs if C survives B." C sells his contingent remainder in Blackacre to D. D takes out insurance on the life of C so that he will be protected in the event that C predeceases B, thereby wiping out the interest which D purchased from C. Can D deduct the annual premiums paid by him for such a policy on the ground that it is an expense incurred for the conservation of property held for the production of income (1954 I.R.C., §212, quoted infra page 1336). See Donald B. Jones, 25 T.C. 4 (1955), *aff'd sub nom.* Jones v. Commissioner, 231 F.2d 655 (3d Cir. 1956).

8.7. A purchases a single premium deferred annuity contract which provides that on the death of the annuitant prior to the due date of the first annuity payment, the insurance company will pay to the designated beneficiary, if the policy is then in force, an amount equal to the consideration paid for the contract or the cash surrender value of the contract on the date of the death of the annuitant, whichever is greater. A dies before the due date of the first annuity payment, and the cash surrender value is greater than the amount paid for the contract. Thus the cash surrender value is paid to the designated beneficiary. Is any part of the amount paid to the designated beneficiary includible in his gross income? See Revenue Ruling 55-313, 1955-1 C.B. 219.

8.8. A takes out insurance on his life. He designates his wife, W, as beneficiary and elects to have the proceeds payable to her in 180 monthly installments. A dies. W induces the insurance company to agree to reduce the monthly payments from $106.80 to $44.98, such reduced payments to continue for ten years certain and thereafter for her life. Are the payments made to W under the new arangement paid to her by reason of the death of the insured? See Jones v. Commissioner, 222 F.2d 891 (7th Cir. 1955).

8.9. A takes out insurance on his life and designates his wife, W, as the primary beneficiary. He adopts the fifth option in the policy (see the fifth option in the sample life insurance policy printed supra page 286). The amount agreed upon between A and the company as the amount of each installment payment is $1 more than the amount W would receive if the straight interest option had been adopted. If the installments do not exhaust the amount retained by the company during W's lifetime, it is agreed that the balance will be paid in a lump sum to designated beneficiaries. Will W be entitled to the $1000 annual interest exclusion with respect to the installment payments made to her? See Section 1.101-3 of the Regulations, quoted infra page 1482. See also page 302 supra, note 26.

(b) *Transferee for Value Rule*

Under the 1939 Code, a transferee for value of a life insurance contract was required to include in his gross income, and pay a tax thereon as ordinary income, the difference between the proceeds received by reason of the death of the insured and the total consideration paid for the contract plus the premiums and other sums subsequently paid by the transferee.[37] Section 101(a)(2)(B) of the 1954 Code[38] eliminates the transferee for value rule "if such trans-

---

[37] See 1939 I.R.C. §22(b)(2)(A). The transferee for value rule did not apply "if such contract or interest therein has a basis for determining gain or loss in the hands of a transferee determined in whole or in part by reference to such basis of such contract or interest therein in the hands of the transferor." Ibid. This language is also found in 1954 I.R.C. §101(a)(2)(A), quoted infra page 1329.

Regulations 118, §39.22(b)(2)-3 uses the following language with reference to the above quotation: "Thus, where a corporation acquires a life insurance policy from a predecessor corporation in a tax-free reorganization, if the proceeds received under the policy by reason of the death of the insured would be exempt from taxation in the hands of the transferor, such proceeds received by reason of the death of the insured will be exempt from taxation in the hands of the transferee, because the basis is determined with reference to the basis in the hands of the transferor."

[38] Quoted infra page 1329.

fer is to the insured; to a partner of the insured, to a partnership in which the insured is a partner, or to a corporation in which the insured is a shareholder or officer." [39] This elimination is particularly significant in business purchase agreements.

Suppose that a business purchase agreement is executed by three partners and each partner takes out insurance on the life of the other two in an amount sufficient to give him the funds to finance the purchase of a deceased partner's interest. When one partner dies, his estate has a policy on the life of each of the surviving partners. If the surviving partners desire to execute a business purchase agreement between themselves, it would be desirable, in carrying out this new agreement, for each surviving partner to buy from the deceased partner's estate the policy on the life of the other surviving partner. Under Section 22(b)(2)(A) of the 1939 Code such purchases by each surviving partner made each a transferee for value, with the resultant income tax consequences when the proceeds were collected by reason of the death of the insured. Under the 1954 Code the transferee for value rule is eliminated in such cases. Notice, however, that if three shareholders in a corporation execute a business purchase agreement under which the stock of the first to die is to be bought by the survivors and the agreement is funded by each buying insurance on the life of the other two, and one shareholder dies, a purchase by each survivor of the insurance on the life of the other survivor from the estate of the decedent is not protected from the transferee for value rule under the 1954 Code.

To the extent that the 1954 Code has not eliminated the transferee for value rule, the transferee will include the same amount in his gross income as heretofore. Thus, if the transferee is paid the proceeds in installments, the amount prorated over the period of the payments to determine the annual amount that is not income will be the total of the consideration paid for the policy plus the premiums and other sums subsequently paid for the policy by the transferee, rather than the total proceeds of the policy.[40]

[39] Regulations 118, §39.22(b)(2)-3 indicates that the transferee for value rule does not apply under the pre-1954 law when the transferee is the insured. If a partner transfers life insurance on his own life to the partnership as part of the capital contribution, the transferee for value rule does not apply under the pre-1954 law because §113(a)(13) of the 1939 Code makes it clear that the basis for determining gain or loss in the hands of the transferee is determined by reference to the basis of such contracts in the hands of the transferor.

[40] See Reg. §1.101-4(b)(3), quoted infra page 1482.

If an employer purchases insurance on the life of an employee and pays the premiums thereon and then sells the policy to the employee at a time when further premiums are to be paid, the employee may receive taxable compensation to the extent of the difference between the value of the policy and what he pays for it. Revenue Ruling 59-195, 1959-1 C.B. 18, takes the position that in such a case the taxable gain to the employee is computed by determining

PROBLEMS

8.10. A pays premiums totaling $500 for an insurance policy in the face amount of $1000 on his life and subsequently transfers the policy to his wife, W, for $600. W later transfers the policy without consideration to S, who is the son of A and W. S receives the proceeds of $1000 upon the death of A. After the transfer from A to W, W paid premiums totaling $100, and after the transfer from W to S, S paid premiums totaling $100. What amount, if any, will be includible in S's gross income with respect to the $1000 paid him on the death of A? See Section 1.101-1(b)(5), Ex. (6) of the Regulations, quoted infra page 1481.

8.11. A takes out a policy of insurance on his life in the face amount of $10,000. A number of years later when the policy has a cash surrender value of $3000, A assigns the policy to B as collateral for a loan of $3000 from B. Under the terms of the assignment any amount collected by B in excess of the amount of the indebtedness is to be turned over to A or his estate. Premium payments made by B are to be added to the amount of the indebtedness. After the assignment, B makes two premium payments of $200 each. A dies. What amount, if any, will be includible in the gross income of B with respect to the $10,000 of insurance on the life of A which is collected by B? See Section 1.101-1(b)(4) of the Regulations, quoted infra page 1480.

8.12. A pays premiums totaling $5000 for an insurance policy in the face amount of $10,000 on his life. He then transfers the policy to his son, S, for $6000, and after the transfer S pays premiums totaling $1000. S then transfers the policy without consideration to A. A designates S as the beneficiary of the policy. A dies. S collects the face amount of the insurance. How much, if anything, will be includible in S's gross income with respect to the $10,000 of insurance on the life of A which is collected by S? See Section 1.101-1(b)(5), Ex. (7) of the Regulations, quoted infra page 1481.

8.13. A pays premiums of $5000 for an insurance policy in the face amount of $10,000 on his life. He then transfers the policy without consideration to his son, S. After the transfer, S pays premiums totaling $1000. S then transfers the policy to B for $6500, and after this transfer B pays premiums totaling $1000. A dies. What amount will be includible in the gross income of B with respect to the $10,000 of insurance on the life of A which

---

the value of the policy in the same way as its value would be determined for gift tax purposes. See page 326 infra, note 78.

is collected by B? See Section 1.101-1(b)(3) of the Regulations, quoted infra page 1480.

(2) Proceeds Paid for a Reason Other than the Death of the Insured

(a) *Proceeds Collected in a Lump Sum*

Before enactment of the 1954 Code, if an endowment policy matured and no election had been made prior to maturity to take payment over a period of time under one of the options in the contract rather than in a lump sum, the owner of the contract was required to include in his gross income in the year in which the policy matured the difference between the lump sum collectible and the aggregate premiums or other consideration paid.[41] An election after maturity to take payment over a period of time was treated as though the insured had received a lump sum payment and purchased an annuity therewith.[42]

The 1954 Code makes two important changes in relation to the endowment contract which is allowed to mature without any election to receive payment in installments. First, Section 72(h) of the 1954 Code[43] gives the owner of the contract sixty days after the date on which the contract matures and the lump sum becomes payable, to avoid the tax consequences of a lump sum payment by electing an annuity in lieu of the lump sum, thus becoming subject to the tax consequences of annuity payments.[44] Second, if such an election is not made, so that the tax consequences of a lump sum payment are applicable, Section 72(e)(3)[45] lightens the tax burden to some extent by providing that the tax attributable to the portion of the lump sum payment that is includible in gross income (the portion is the same as under the 1939 Code) "shall not be greater

---

[41] See Blum v. Higgins, 150 F.2d 471 (2d Cir. 1945). Cf. Lucas v. Alexander, 279 U.S. 573, 49 Sup. Ct. 426, 73 L. Ed. 851 (1929).

[42] See Estate of Harry Snider, 31 T.C. 1064 (1959), where, three years before the maturity of an annuity policy, the taxpayer elected to receive payment in installments, with the right to withdraw any amount. The company, however, could defer for six months compliance with a request for withdrawal. The policy matured in September, and the court held there was no constructive receipt of the difference between the cost and the cash surrender value because of the power in the company to delay compliance with the withdrawal request for six months. The court said that since the six months would expire in the next year, "it may be . . . that [taxpayer] can be charged with this income in that year."

[43] Quoted infra page 1328.

[44] The federal income tax consequences of annuity payments are set forth in 1954 I.R.C. §72, quoted infra page 1325.

[45] Quoted infra page 1327.

than the aggregate of the taxes attributable to such part had it been included in the gross income of the taxpayer ratably over the taxable year in which received and the preceding 2 taxable years."

(b) *Installment Payments Not Related in Duration to Anyone's Life*

If a decision was made in the pre-1954 Code era to have the proceeds of a life insurance contract or endowment contract paid out in installments before the death of the insured under an option which did not relate the duration of the installment payments to anyone's life, the installments were not includible in the recipient's gross income under Section 22(b)(2)(A) of the 1939 Code until the total amount paid out equaled the aggregate premiums and other consideration paid. Thereafter the entire amount of the installment payments was includible.

Section 72 of the 1954 Code[46] makes no differentiation in the treatment of installment payments between those for a certain period and those measured by one or more lives. The following comments on the new treatment of installment payments related in duration to someone's life are applicable to both. This treatment differs from the pre-1954 treatment and is applicable to installment payments (whether for a certain period or measured by one or more lives) received after January 1, 1954, even though the election to receive the installment payments antedates 1954 and installment payments have been received in prior years. The prior payments are taken into account in determining the income element in the post-1954 payments.[47]

(c) *Installment Payments Related in Duration to One or More Lives*

The so-called 3 percent annuity rule which applied prior to 1954 to installment payments related in duration to one or more lives[48] has been abolished. Section 72(b) of the 1954 Code[49] substitutes a new rule designed to exclude from the gross income of the recipient that part of each amount received as an annuity which is considered to represent a return of capital. When the amount to be excluded from each payment is once determined, it is ex-

[46] Quoted infra page 1325.
[47] See 1954 I.R.C. §72(c)(1)(B), quoted infra page 1326.
[48] See 1939 I.R.C. §22(b)(2)(A).
[49] Quoted infra page 1325.

cluded throughout the course of the installment payments.[50] There is no $1000 annual interest exclusion for payments to a spouse with respect to installment payments governed by Section 72.

(d) *Joint and Survivor Annuities*

The 3 percent annuity rule applied to joint and survivor annuities prior to the 1954 Code, with a stepped-up basis for the survivor based on the value at which the annuity interest was required to be included in the gross estate of the decedent annuitant.[51] Under Section 72 of the 1954 Code, the annual exclusion which is to be deemed a return of capital is fixed at the beginning of the annuity starting date on the basis of the ages of the two annuitants and this exclusion carries through to the end of the installment payments. However, if the value of the annuity on the death of one of the annuitants is includible in the decedent's gross estate,[52] an income tax deduction is allowable under Section 691(d)[53] (the section dealing with income in respect of a decedent) to compensate for the estate tax imposed on the income element in the annuity.[54]

[50] The Senate Finance Committee report gives this illustration: Where A, sixty-five years of age on the annuity starting date, has purchased an annuity for payments to him for life of $1000 per annum, his expected return will be $1000 times the multiple he finds in the actuarial tables. Assuming this multiple to be 15.5, A would have an expected return of $15,500. Assuming that A had paid $12,000 for the contract, his exclusion ratio would be 12,000/15,500, or 24/31, and A would exclude from his gross income $774.19 of each $1000 payment received in his taxable year. If instead A had purchased a contract calling for monthly payments of $100 each, his expected return would be $100 × 12 × 15.5, or $18,600; assuming he had paid $15,000 for such a contract his exclusion ratio would then be 15,000/18,600, or 25/31, and A would exclude from his gross income $80.65 of each $100 payment received in his taxable year. S. Rep. No. 1622, 83d Cong., 2d Sess. 174-175 (1954).

In Table I of Reg. §1.72-9, the multiple for a male aged sixty-five is 15, not 15.5 as used above.

If a refund annuity is involved, an adjustment must be made by employing Table III of Reg. §1.72-9 to obtain the percentage which must be set aside to cover the refund feature. Ruling 60-325, I.R.B. 1960-42, 9, outlines what is called the "approximate method of computing the adjusted investment in an annuity contract" to be used in connection with Reg. §1.72-9 in determining adjustments for a refund feature.

[51] See 1939 I.R.C. §§22(b)(2)(C), 113(a)(5). See also 1954 I.R.C. §72(i), which correlates pre-1954 joint and survivor annuities with the 1954 Code.

[52] See 1954 I.R.C. §2039, quoted infra page 1398.

[53] Quoted infra page 1377.

[54] Section 1.72-9 of the Regulations gives the basis of determining the part of each payment under a joint and survivor annuity that is excluded as a return of cost.

If the joint and survivor annuity provides for uniform payments to be made to the designated annuitants, Table II is used to obtain the combined life ex-

PROBLEMS

8.14. A owns an endowment policy which will mature in thirty days and pay $10,000. The aggregate premiums and other consideration paid by A with respect to the policy over the years are $7000. A wants a lump sum payment made to him on maturity. B is willing to pay A $9800 for the policy. Under what circumstances would it be advisable for A to accept B's offer? See Commissioner v. Phillips, 275 F.2d 33 (4th Cir. 1960); Arnfeld v. United States, 163 F. Supp. 865 (Ct. Cl. 1958), *cert. denied*, 359 U.S. 943 (1959).

8.15. In determining the aggregate amount of premiums and other consideration paid for the contract when such a determination is relevant, will the portion of the premiums paid which is attributable to some other benefit such as a disability benefit be includible? See Revenue Ruling 55-349, 1955-1 C.B. 232.

8.16. In determining the aggregate amount of premiums and other consideration paid for the contract when such a determination is relevant, will the premiums which have been paid by someone other than the recipient of the insurance proceeds be included? See Card and Adams v. Commissioner, 216 F.2d 93 (8th Cir. 1954).

---

pectancy of the annuitants, and the annual payments to be made are multiplied by the combined life expectancy to obtain the expected return. A fraction is then formed of which the numerator is the cost of the joint and survivor annuity and the denominator is the expected return; the annual payment is multiplied by that fraction; the result is the amount of each annual payment that is excluded as a return of cost, and the balance is the interest element in each annual payment to be included in the gross income of the payee annuitant.

If the joint and survivor annuity provides for a different amount for the second annuitant, the calculation of the exclusion ratio as to each payment is slightly more complicated. Table I in Reg. §1.72-9 must be used first to obtain the life expectancy of the first annuitant, and then Table II must be used to obtain the combined life expectancy of the two annuitants. The life expectancy of the first annuitant is subtracted from the combined life expectancy figure to produce the period for which payments are expected to continue for the second annuitant. The annual payment to the first annuitant is multiplied by his life expectancy and the annual payment to the second annuitant is multiplied by the difference between the life expectancy of the first annuitant and the combined life expectancy of both; the total of these two multiplications equals the expected return under the joint and survivor annuity. A fraction is then formed of which the numerator is the cost of the joint and survivor annuity and the denominator is the expected return. That fraction represents the percentage of each payment that is deemed a return of cost, and the balance of each payment is the interest element. If the annuity is one for a stated amount during the joint lives of the annuitants and then one for a lesser amount during the life of the surviving annuitant, Table II must be used in conjunction with Table II A in order to ascertain the interest element in each payment.

(3) Exchange of Policies

In the course of advising a person in regard to his life insurance, consideration should be given to the wisdom of exchanging one of his policies for another policy. An important factor in this regard is whether any taxable income may result merely from such an exchange. Revenue Ruling 54-264,[55] which was issued shortly before the enactment of the 1954 Code, holds that under the 1939 Code taxable income was realized when a single premium endowment policy was surrendered, pursuant to an election made at or prior to the maturity of the policy, in exchange for cash and a paid-up life insurance policy. The amount of this taxable income was the excess of the cash plus the value of the policy received over the premiums paid, reduced by any dividends paid or credited to the policyholder. The 1954 Code contains a new section, Section 1035,[56] which deals specifically with the exchange of life insurance policies. This new section, however, leaves a number of questions unanswered.[57]

PROBLEM

8.17. Shortly before the maturity date of a ten-year endowment policy owned by A, the insurance company agrees to defer payment of the maturity value for ten years. During the postponed period, interest on the sum retained by the company is to be added to the principal each year. Is the agreement postponing the maturity date an exchange of policies which results in any taxable income to A? See Section 1035, quoted infra page 1387, and Revenue Ruling 54-264, 1954-2 C.B. 57. Will the interest declared annually and added to principal be taxable to A each year? See William Fleming, 24 T.C. 818 (1955), *rev'd sub nom.* Fleming v. Commissioner, 241 F.2d 78 (5th Cir. 1957), *Tax Court decision reinstated,* 356 U.S. 260 (1958); Special Ruling dated March 19, 1958, 58 CCH Fed. Tax Rep. ¶6443. See also Phil Zimmermann, 25 T.C. 233 (1955), *aff'd sub nom.* Zimmermann v. Commissioner, 241 F.2d 338 (8th Cir. 1957). Additional litigation in the Zimmermann case is found in Zimmermann v. United States, 160 F. Supp. 1 (E.D. Mo. 1958).

[55] 1954-2 C.B. 57.
[56] Quoted infra page 1386.
[57] For an excellent analysis of §1035 and its effect on Rev. Rul. 54-264, see Freyburger, Tax Problems Relating to Life Insurance and Annuity Contracts, Ins. L.J. No. 389, pp. 375-384 (1955); Lawthers and Snyder, Taxation of Policy Changes, 9 J. Am. Soc. C.L.U. 213, 220 (1955).

(4) Deduction of Interest on Sums Borrowed to Pay Insurance Premiums

Section 163 of the 1954 Code enunciates as the general rule that all interest paid or accrued within a taxable year on an indebtedness is deductible in computing taxable income.[58] One of the exceptions to the general rule is in regard to certain amounts paid in connection with insurance contracts.[59]

[58] Revenue Ruling 58-239, 1958-1 C.B. 94, discusses the amount of the interest deduction which can be taken where a partial payment of the tax, penalty and interest, assessed for one or more years, is made by a taxpayer regularly employing the cash receipts and disbursement method of accounting. This ruling points out that where a lump sum is accepted in compromise of the tax, penalty and interest, and the sum is less than the tax and penalty claimed by the government, no part of the amount of the compromise is deductible as interest.

Revenue Ruling 54-94, 1954-1 C.B. 53, disapproved the interest deduction on obligations incurred in order to purchase taxable securities where a transaction was said to lack commercial substance. Under the plan dealt with in the ruling, a taxpayer borrowed the money required to buy Treasury notes. The notes were held by the lender as collateral. They were purchased at a discount and sold at or near par, so that a capital gain was realized on their sale. The capital gain and interest income taken together did not equal the interest cost of the borrowing. The profit came from the tax-saving through the deduction of interest cost.

In John Fox, 17 CCH T.C. Mem. 1006 (1958), no deduction was allowed for interest on a loan (to the extent that the interest exceeded the return on the purchased securities) where the lender took the securities purchased as security for the loan and agreed to look only to the securities for payment of the debt. See also Haggard v. United States, 59-1 U.S.T.C. ¶9299 (D. Ariz. 1959); Broome v. United States, 170 F. Supp. 613 (Ct. Cl. 1959); Eli D. Goodstein, 30 T.C. 1178 (1958), *aff'd sub nom.* Goodstein v. Commissioner, 267 F.2d 127 (1st Cir. 1959); Matthew M. Becker, 18 CCH T.C. Mem. 95 (1959), *aff'd on denial of interest deduction but remanded sub nom.* Becker v. Commissioner, 277 F.2d 146 (2d Cir. 1960); George G. Lynch, 31 T.C. 990 (1959), *aff'd sub nom.* Lynch v. Commissioner, 273 F.2d 867 (2d Cir. 1959); Leslie Julian, 31 T.C. 998 (1959), *aff'd sub nom.* Julian v. Commissioner, 273 F.2d 867 (2d Cir. 1959); Egbert J. Miles, 31 T.C. 1001 (1959); Oliver L. Williams, 18 CCH T.C. Mem. 205 (1959); Gordon MacRae, 34 T.C. —, No. 2 (1960). The Goodstein case is followed in Sonnabend v. Commissioner, 267 F.2d 319 (1st Cir. 1959); Morris R. De Woskin, 35 T.C. —, No. 44 (1960). Compare L. Lee Stanton, 34 T.C. —, No. 1 (1960).

The material in this note is reviewed in 60 CCH Fed. Tax Rep. ¶8709, where it is stated that the conclusion to be drawn from the decisions is that although a taxpayer has the right to conduct his affairs in a manner that will minimize and even to avoid taxes, he cannot create a tax deduction by engaging in transactions that are lacking in economic reality.

[59] See 1954 I.R.C. §264, quoted infra page 1337.

Section 264(a)(1) is examined and applied in Special Rulings, April 2 and May 15, 1956, 1956 CCH Fed. Tax Rep. ¶6624. For cases denying the interest deduction with respect to interest on sums borrowed to purchase an annuity contract under the 1939 Code, see Knetsch v. United States, 58-2 U.S.T.C. ¶9935 (S.D. Cal. 1958), *aff'd,* 272 F.2d 200 (9th Cir. 1959), *aff'd,* 81 Sup. Ct. 132 (1960); W. Stuart Emmons, 31 T.C. 26 (1958), *aff'd sub nom.* Emmons

PROBLEM

8.18. Do you see how a person in a high income tax bracket can make a profit by purchasing an annual premium retirement income annuity with borrowed money? See United States v. Bond, 258 F.2d 577 (5th Cir. 1958); Roderick v. United States, 59-2 U.S.T.C. ¶9650 (W.D. Tex. 1959).

(5) Liability of a Beneficiary of a Life Insurance Policy for Unpaid Income Taxes of the Insured[60]

The net worth to the designated beneficiary of the life insurance proceeds will depend, of course, on whether the proceeds can be reached to pay obligations of the insured. The fact that the state law may provide that life insurance proceeds cannot be reached by the creditors of the insured does not necessarily mean that the beneficiary will take the proceeds free of any liability in regard to the unpaid income taxes of the insured. Commissioner v. Stern[61] recognizes that where no lien for the unpaid income taxes of the insured attached prior to his death, the proceeds of the insurance passed to the beneficiary free of any liability in regard to such taxes.[62] United States v. Bess[63] establishes that when a lien for the

---

v. Commissioner, 270 F.2d 294 (3d Cir. 1959); Carl E. Weller, 31 T.C. 33 (1958), *aff'd sub nom.* Weller v. Commissioner, 270 F.2d 294 (3d Cir. 1959); Robert M. Diggs, 18 CCH T.C. Mem. 443 (1959), *aff'd sub nom.* Diggs v. Commissioner, 281 F.2d 326 (2d Cir. 1960); John Loughran, CCH T.C. Mem. 1960-214; Estate of M. H. Bennett, CCH T.C. Mem. 1960-253. See, however, the cases cited in Problem 8.18.

In Chapin v. McGowan, 58-1 U.S.T.C. ¶9469 (W.D.N.Y. 1958), *aff'd,* 271 F.2d 856 (2d Cir. 1959), where a taxpayer borrowed money to purchase single-premium endowment policies, the court, in applying the 1939 Code, held that in the computation of the gain realized on their maturity the interest paid to the lender did not constitute part of the cost or consideration paid for the policies.

[60] Section 6901 of the 1954 Code deals with the liability of the transferee of property for the unpaid income taxes of the transferor. Whether the beneficiary of an insurance policy is a transferee within the meaning of this section is not specifically stated. The section is quoted infra page 1433.

[61] 357 U.S. 39, 78 Sup. Ct. 1047, 2 L. Ed. 2d 1126 (1958).

[62] In United States v. Ott, 166 F. Supp. 13 (E.D. Mich. 1958), the court followed Commissioner v. Stern in holding that the widow-beneficiary prevailed over creditors under Michigan law and hence prevailed over the government when no tax lien existed on her husband's death. In Vernon M. Bingham, 30 T.C. 900 (1958), the court followed Commissioner v. Stern, pointing out that under the law of North Carolina, which controlled, life insurance proceeds are protected from the claims of the creditors of the insured unless there is a payment of premiums with intent to defraud. Estate of Harry Schneider, 30 T.C. 929 (1958), where New York Law was involved, also follows

insured's unpaid income taxes attaches during the insured's life-time, the beneficiary-recipient of the life insurance proceeds is sub-ject to transferee liability up to the cash surrender value of the policy immediately prior to the insured's death.[64] The cash sur-render value of a life insurance policy can be reached to pay the insured's income taxes in his lifetime as well as on his death.[65]

Commissioner v. Stern, holding that under New York law, creditors cannot reach life insurance proceeds when paid to an original beneficiary and can reach them when paid to a substitute beneficiary only if the change in bene-ficiaries was made with intent to delay, hinder, or defraud creditors, as long as the insured was not insolvent at the time of the payment of the initial pre-mium. For a consideration of the desirability of looking to state law in a situation like the one dealt with in Commissioner v. Stern, see Note, The Role of State Law in Federal Tax Determinations, 72 Harv. L. Rev. 1350, 1357 (1959).

[63] 357 U.S. 51, 78 Sup. Ct. 1054, 2 L. Ed. 2d 1135 (1958).

[64] In Flax v. United States, 179 F. Supp. 408 (D.N.J. 1959), the insured had taken a series of policy loans on his policies before the government lien attached, and the court held the beneficiary was liable as transferee only to the extent of the cash surrender value just prior to the insured's death minus the amount of the outstanding loans. In accord is United States v. Pilley, 60-2 U.S.T.C. ¶9794 (W. D. Tenn. 1960).

The Supreme Court decision in the Bess case was followed in United States v. Bridgeforth, 59-1 U.S.T.C. ¶9447 (M.D. Tenn. 1959). In McMahon v. United States, 172 F. Supp. 490 (D.R.I. 1959), the court applied United States v. Bess and allowed the widow-beneficiary to recover the amount in excess of the cash surrender value that was used to discharge the tax lien, even though she had consented to the use of the excess before the Supreme Court decided the Bess case. Pollard v. United States, 60-2 U.S.T.C. ¶9569 (E.D. Va. 1960), where the beneficiary had possession of the policy and paid most of the pre-miums, but the ownership of the policy was vested in the insured, follows United States v. Bess.

[65] United States v. Bosk, 180 F. Supp. 869 (S.D. Fla. 1960), considered the question whether the government can enforce its lien against the cash sur-render value of a policy while the insured is still alive, and held that it can. It contended that this result was foreshadowed by the dictum in United States v. Bess. United States v. Hancock, 60-2 U.S.T.C. ¶9724 (N.D. Ill. 1960), also recognizes the validity of the lien on the cash surrender value of a policy on the life of the taxpayer.

In United States v. Lucido, 59-2 U.S.T.C. ¶9700 (E.D. Mich. 1959), where a policy was owned by the insured, and his wife was named as beneficiary of the policy, the government was allowed to satisfy a tax lien for back income taxes of the insured out of the cash surrender and dividend values.

The court in United States v. Metropolitan Life Insurance Co., 256 F.2d 17 (4th Cir. 1958), held that the insured's interest in life insurance policies could be subjected to a lien for taxes; that the government could demand the cash surrender value of the policy to the extent necessary to satisfy the lien, even though the insured was not subject to the jurisdiction of the court; and, further, that a decree directing the insurance company to pay the cash sur-render value of the policy to the government would protect the company from further liability under the policy.

United States v. Fried, 183 F. Supp. 371 (E.D.N.Y. 1960), held, however, that the life insurance policy beneficiary is an indispensable party to a suit by the government to subject the cash surrender value of a policy to payment of the income taxes of the insured.

In United States v. Roark, 57-2 U.S.T.C. ¶9883 (W.D. Mo. 1957), *dismissed*

The availability of the cash surrender value of life insurance proceeds for the payment of the insured's income taxes is not the only point to keep in mind with respect to transferee liability but it is the one which most frequently presents itself.[66]

---

without prejudice, 257 F.2d 810 (8th Cir. 1958), the taxpayer was directed to execute applications for the cash value of his life insurance policies to be paid to the court to be applied in satisfaction of the government's lien for taxes. The court pointed out that the amount to be so paid should be reduced by any indebtedness due the insurance companies before they received notice of the tax lien. United States v. Grobe, 60-1 U.S.T.C. ¶9463 (D. Colo. 1960), held that the Government could enforce the lien arising as a result of assessments against the taxpayer for income taxes on the cash surrender value of a life insurance policy owned by the taxpayer. The court ordered the taxpayer to make such application to the insurance company as would cause the cash surrender value of the policy to be paid into court.

United States v. Bess was applied in United States v. Budak, 185 F. Supp. 697 (N.D. Ohio, 1960), where the lien was enforced during the lifetime of the insured. It was recognized that the insurer cannot deduct from the amount collectible by an enforcement of the lien any amount loaned to the insured after notice of the lien. The fact that on the death of the insured the rights of the beneficiaries to the amount of the policy in excess of the cash surrender value will be destroyed does not prevent enforcement of the lien in the insured's lifetime. See United States v. Reisor, 60-2 U.S.T.C. ¶9684 (E.D. Okla. 1960), where the court enforced a lien of the United States on property of a tax delinquent against the cash surrender value of his life insurance.

Revenue Ruling 56-48, 1956-1 C.B. 561, protects the insurance company from liability when the proceeds are paid to the insured or a beneficiary and there is outstanding against the insured or the beneficiary a federal tax lien, if the insurance company is not negligent or fraudulent and does not have actual notice of the lien.

[66] The court in Fried v. New York Life Insurance Co., 241 F.2d 504 (2d Cir. 1957), *cert. denied,* 354 U.S. 922 (1957), held that monthly disability benefit payments made to a delinquent taxpayer under a contract of insurance which provided payments for permanent disability were subject to a federal tax lien. A state law exempting such payments from execution for "any debt or liability of the insured" is ineffective against a federal lien for taxes.

The transferee liability of a beneficiary of life insurance for estate and gift taxes is different from transferee liability for income taxes. This difference is explained in Commissioner v. Chase Manhattan Bank, 259 F.2d 231, 256 (5th Cir. 1958), *cert. denied,* 359 U.S. 913 (1959).

A problem somewhat similar to the liability of a beneficiary of a life insurance policy for unpaid income taxes of the insured was presented in United States v. Helfenbein, 58-1 U.S.T.C. ¶11752 (N.D. Ill. 1958), where a decedent, shortly before his death, made a transfer in trust which left him insolvent at the time of his death. A deficiency assessment for unpaid income taxes was made against his estate, but his administratrix was not allowed a deduction in the amount of the assessment in determining the estate taxes due. In a suit to recover the income tax deficiency from the trust property, the court held that in determining the amount of income tax which could be recovered from the trustees, the trustees were allowed a credit for the estate tax paid as a result of the disallowance of a deduction for the amount of the income tax now being recovered. In Estate of Harry Schneider, 30 T.C. 929 (1958), the court held that the decedent's wife, who as survivor acquired the ownership of United States savings bonds, was not subject to transferee liability for the unpaid taxes of her husband, since he was not insolvent at the time the bonds were placed in co-ownership. However, the court held that the beneficiary of a

b. *Estate and Gift Tax Consequences*

Prior to the 1954 Code, the estate tax provision specially applicable to life insurance[67] provided for the inclusion of life insurance proceeds in the gross estate of the insured if:

1. The proceeds were payable to the insured's personal representative; or

2. The insured possessed at his death any of the incidents of ownership, exercisable either alone or in conjunction with any other person;[68] or

3. The insured paid the premiums directly or indirectly.[69]

---

revocable inter vivos trust was subject to transferee liability because the transfer to the trust was made when the decedent was indebted to the government and the transfer rendered him insolvent. On this later point, see also Estate of Harry Schneider, 29 T.C. 940 (1958).

See also United States v. Peelle, 159 F. Supp. 45 (E.D.N.Y. 1958), where the taxpayer was the beneficiary of an insurance trust with unlimited power to withdraw the principal in trust, and the court held that the insurance trust was subject to invasion for the payment of a tax lien against the beneficiary.

In United States v. Gilmore, 222 F.2d 167 (S.D. Fla. 1955), *cert. denied,* 350 U.S. 843 (1955), the taxpayer was administratrix of her deceased husband's estate and also the beneficiary of his life insurance. She used the assets of the estate other than his life insurance proceeds to pay his federal estate taxes, thereby exhausting these assets. The court pointed out that the taxpayer, as beneficiary of her husband's insurance, was personally liable for such portion of the total estate tax as the proceeds of the policies bore to the sum of the net estate and the amount of the exemption allowed in computing the net estate. In her capacity as administratrix she had a duty to collect from herself the portion of the estate tax payable out of the life insurance proceeds. Consequently, to that extent she was personally liable to pay deficiency assessments against her husband's estate for his unpaid income tax. See 69 Harv. L. Rev. 766 (1956). Citing with approval the Gilmore case, Steinbaugh v. Barday, — Colo. —, 352 P.2d 276 (1960), held that where assets were distributed to the decedent's daughter in compromise of her claim, and thereafter the sole testamentary heir, who was the executor, distributed estate assets to himself before discharging the tax debts of the estate, he could not obtain any contribution to the tax debts of the estate from the daughter.

The impact of the Stern and Bess cases on some of the questions involving transferees other than beneficiaries of life insurance is examined in Tax Note, Federal Tax Transferee Liability, 46 A.B.A.J. 207 (1960).

[67] See 1939 I.R.C. §811(g).

[68] Section 811(g) of the 1939 Code specifically provided that a reversionary interest in the insured did not constitute an incident of ownership.

[69] If the sole basis of the inclusion of the life insurance proceeds in the insured's gross estate was the payment of premiums and he had not paid all the premiums, then only that portion of the proceeds was includible that corresponded to the portion of the premiums he had paid. In determining this portion, §404(c) of the Revenue Act of 1942, 56 Stat. 945, as amended by §503(a) of the Revenue Act of 1950, 64 Stat. 962, provided that the amount paid by the insured on or before January 10, 1941, would be excluded if the insured at no time after that date possessed an incident of ownership in the policy. For this limited purpose a reversionary interest arising by express terms of the policy or other instrument was an incident of ownership if at

Section 2042 of the 1954 Code,[70] the estate tax provision now specially applicable to life insurance,[71] eliminates the premium

---

some time after January 10, 1941, its value exceeded 5 percent of the value of the policy. Section 404(c) applies only to estates of decedents dying after October 21, 1942. Section 209 of the Technical Changes Act of 1953 extends the operation of Section 404(c) to estates of decedents dying after January 10, 1941, and before October 22, 1942. In Bennett v. United States, 60-2 U.S.T.C. ¶11958 (N.D. Ill. 1960), the insured transferred securities to an irrevocable trust, and the principal of the trust was to be used to pay premiums on policies which the insured had assigned prior to January 10, 1941. The court held that the portion of the life insurance proceeds attributable to the premiums paid after January 10, 1941, was includible in the insured's gross estate because these premiums had been paid indirectly by the insured.

Kohl v. United States, 226 F.2d 381 (7th Cir. 1955), held that §404 of Revenue Act of 1942 is unconstitutional in so far as it undertakes to impose an estate tax on gifts made on or before January 10, 1941. In Rev. Rul. 56-250, 1956-1 C.B. 659, it was held that the decision in the Kohl case will not be considered by the Internal Revenue Service as a precedent in the disposition of other cases involving a similar factual situation. The Kohl case is rejected in Estate of Ellis Baker, 30 T.C. 776 (1958). In Schwarz v. United States, 170 F. Supp. 2 (E.D. La. 1959), the court upheld as constitutional the provisions of the 1939 Code which require the inclusion in the insured's gross estate of the portion of the proceeds that is proportional to the amount of premiums paid by him prior to the assignment of the policies. To the same effect is Shults v. United States, 60-2 U.S.T.C. ¶11977 (N.D.N.Y. 1960). The Kohl case was followed in Manufacturers National Bank of Detroit v. United States, 175 F. Supp. 291 (E.D. Mich. 1959), where the court said that no transfer of the proceeds of the policies of insurance on the decedent's life occurred on his death, because he had transferred all incidents of ownership prior to January 10, 1940, and consequently §811(g)(2) of the 1939 Code, as sought to be applied in the case to the insurance proceeds involved, is unconstitutional. The Manufacturers National Bank case was reversed sub nom. United States v. Manufacturers National Bank of Detroit, 363 U.S. 194, 80 Sup. Ct. 1103, 4 L. Ed. 2d 1158 (1960). Estate of Newcomb Carlton, 34 T.C. — , No. 104 (1960), states that §811(g)(2)(A) of the 1939 Code is not unconstitutional in requiring the inclusion in the insured's gross estate of some portion of the proceeds on the basis of the premium payment test, even though the insured retained no incidents of ownership in the policy.

For a recent case which, in applying the premium payment test of the 1939 Code, held that the premiums were paid indirectly by the insured, see Loeb v. Commissioner, 261 F.2d 232 (2d Cir. 1958).

[70] Quoted infra page 1402.

[71] It is important to know whether a particular arrangement involves the acquisition of insurance, so that §2042 will be applicable, or whether it involves the acquisition of an annuity, which will be governed by §2039, quoted infra page 1398. See, for example, Reg. §20.2039-1(d), quoted infra page 1514. In Stewart v. United States, 158 F. Supp. 25 (N.D. Cal. 1957), the decedent, who lived in a community property state, owned some annuity policies. She elected to take a specified number of equal payments, with the balance of the payments remaining at her death to go to her daughter and her daughter's children. Her husband joined with her in these arrangements for the payment of the annuity policies and, as to some of the policies, he also released his community interest. The court held that the annuity policies were not insurance and were therefore includible in her gross estate only to the extent of her interest therein. This meant that the policies in which her husband had relinquished his community rights were includible in full, but the policies in which he had retained his community

payment test as a ground for inclusion[72] and brings into the category of incidents of ownership of the policy a reversionary interest in the insured, whether arising by the express terms of the policy or other instrument, or by operation of law, if the value of the reversionary interest exceeds 5 percent of the value of the policy immediately before the insured's death. Even if all the hurdles of Section 2042 are cleared, the life insurance proceeds may still be includible in the insured's gross estate under some other section of the 1954 Code. For example, the transfer of the incidents of ownership of the policy may be deemed a transfer in contemplation of death.[73]

Under the 1939 Code, once the insured had started to pay the premiums on a policy of insurance on his life it was not possible for him, by giving away the policy, to remove all proceeds from his gross estate. The premium payment test was a permanent block to such a result.[74] Under Section 2042, it is now just as easy

---

interest were includible only to the extent of one half the value. The case was affirmed on this point (though reversed on another) sub nom. United States v. Stewart, 270 F.2d 894 (9th Cir. 1959), *cert. denied,* 361 U.S. 960 (1960).

In ascertaining income tax consequences, it may be essential to determine whether life insurance proceeds or something else is being paid to a designated beneficiary. See 1954 I.R.C. §101, quoted supra page 1339, and §72, quoted infra page 1325.

[72] If the premium payment test is restored by any future Act of Congress, will such legislation apply where the insured never possesses any of the incidents of ownership of the policy after the restoration of the test but does pay premiums after such restoration? See page 322 supra, note 69.

[73] See 1954 I.R.C. §2035, quoted infra page 1396. In Estate of Isaac W. Baldwin, 18 CCH T.C. Mem. 902 (1959), the court held that insurance policies transferred to a trust were transferred in contemplation of death and were therefore includible in the insured's gross estate.

Suppose that a person purchases a single premium life insurance policy in combination with a life annuity contract and immediately assigns the insurance policy to the beneficiaries thereof. Revenue Ruling 54-552, 1954-2 C.B. 284, states that the Internal Revenue Service will regard such a transaction as one in which the insured has retained during his lifetime the possession and enjoyment of the policy within the meaning of 1939 I.R.C. §811(c)(1)(B). In this announcement the Service is not following Harrison v. Bohnen, 345 U.S. 946, 73 Sup. Ct. 863, 97 L. Ed. 1371 (1953), *rehearing denied,* 345 U.S. 978 (1953), on the theory that because the Court's affirmance of the lower court's decision was by an equally divided Court, it is not authority for the determination of other cases. The Service's view is supported by Burr v. Commissioner, 156 F.2d 871 (2d Cir. 1946), and Conway v. Glenn, 193 F.2d 965 (6th Cir. 1952). In Fidelity-Philadelphia Trust Co. v. Smith, 142 F. Supp. 561 (E.D. Pa. 1956), *rev'd,* 241 F.2d 690 (3d Cir. 1957), the District Court reviewed various cases, including Burr v. Commissioner, Conway v. Glenn, and Harrison v. Bohnen, and decided to follow Harrison v. Bohnen. In reversing the District Court, the Court of Appeals followed the Burr and Conway cases. The Court of Appeals decision was reversed by the Supreme Court in 356 U.S. 274, 78 Sup. Ct. 730, 2 L. Ed. 2d 765 (1958), *rehearing denied,* 358 U.S. 802 (1958).

[74] Under the 1939 Code, the insured could surrender the policy and receive its cash surrender value and then give away the cash, but this caused a sacrifice

to eliminate from the insured's gross estate the proceeds of insurance on his life as it is to eliminate the value of other property. As long as the insurance proceeds are not made payable to the personal representative of the insured,[75] the insured need only deprive himself of, or never acquire, the incidents of ownership of the insurance, and the insurance proceeds are excluded from his gross estate so far as Section 2042 is concerned.[76]

---

of the benefits which would flow from keeping the policy alive. The insured could sell the policy and, if the purchaser paid him its full value, no part of the proceeds of the policy would be included in the gross estate of the insured, assuming he paid no premiums after the transfer (1939 I.R.C. §811(g)(2)), but such an arrangement produced undersirable income tax results because the transferee for value rule was applicable. See discussion of this rule at page 310 supra.

[75] Section 20.2042-1(b)(1) of the Regulations, quoted infra page 1525, comments on the arrangements as to the disposition of insurance proceeds which will be deemed the equivalent of having them payable to the insured's personal representative.

Revenue Ruling 57-54, 1957-1 C.B. 298, considers whether the amount paid to the personal representative of a decedent is includible in the decedent's gross estate under §2042 when the amount is paid pursuant to a contract between an insurance company and the owner of an airplane in which the decedent died as a result of an accident while a passenger on the plane.

Consider the estate tax consequences when an insurance policy is payable to the estate of the insured and the disposition of the proceeds is covered by a statute similar to Fla. Stat. §222.13 (1959). The case of Equitable Life Assurrance Society of the United States v. McRee, 75 Fla. 257, 78 So. 22 (1918), should be read in conjunction with an examination of the Florida statute.

[76] In Estate of Michael Collino, 25 T.C. 1026 (1956), proceeds of life insurance were included in the insured's gross estate, although the policies were taken out by the insured's mother and she paid all the premiums and retained possession of the policies, because it was conceded that the insured had the right to change the beneficiary of the policies. Such a right gave the insured an incident of ownership with respect to each policy.

Estate of Edmund W. Mudge, 27 T.C. 188 (1956), involved an irrevocable life insurance trust established by the insured, and under the terms of the trust agreement, it was provided that the trustee should follow the insured's instructions in the management of the trust property. It was held that the decedent had not retained any incidents of ownership in the policies transferred to the trust.

In Altschuler v. United States, 169 F. Supp. 456 (W.D. Mo. 1958), the death benefit under a retirement income policy, acquired pursuant to a pension trust agreement executed by an employer, was included in the employee's gross estate because he was deemed to have an incident of ownership when he, in conjunction with the pension committee and the trustee, could change the beneficiary.

Farwell v. United States, 243 F.2d 373 (7th Cir. 1957), pointed out that where the insured makes the proceeds of insurance on his life payable to an irrevocable inter vivos trust but retains the right to change the designated beneficiary of the policy, he has retained an incident of the ownership of the policy, so that the proceeds will be includible in his gross estate. In Hall v. Wheeler, 174 F. Supp. 418 (D. Me. 1959), the insured named as beneficiary the corporation of which he was president and gave the corporation possession of the policy; the corporation carried the policy on its books as an asset and paid the premiums. Nevertheless, the proceeds were includible in the insured's

If a person now owns insurance on his life, what are the factors to consider in determining whether to transfer the incidents of ownership of the insurance?

In the first place, the entire property situation of the insured must be carefully examined to determine whether, in the light of his own probable personal need for liquid funds and the possible need for such funds in the settlement of the obligations which will arise on his death, his life insurance asset should be permanently placed beyond his control. The savings in estate taxes made by the elimination of the life insurance proceeds from his gross estate may be lost many times over if other assets will have to be liquidated at a sacrifice to meet obligations on his death.

In the second place, the gift tax cost of transferring the life insurance asset must be taken into account.[77] A transfer of the incidents of ownership of the life insurance will result in a gift for federal gift tax purposes of the present value of the insurance. The method of determining this value in different situations is described in the Regulations.[78]

It will be important to know whether the gift of the life insurance is a gift of a present interest or of a future interest, because the $3000 annual gift tax exclusion will be available only with respect to the value of a present interest. If the incidents of ownership are transferred outright to an adult, it is submitted that only a present interest is created in the transferee.[79] This result should

---

gross estate, because he retained the right to change the beneficiary, either alone or in conjunction with the corporation, which constitutes an incident of ownership.

[77] Where a gift of life insurance is made, Form 938 must be filed by the donor with the federal gift tax return.

[78] See Reg. §25.2512-6, quoted infra page 1548. See also Guggenheim v. Rasquin, which is printed in full infra page 333.

If it is necessary to value a life insurance policy for the purpose of determining the extent of the gain a person may have realized in a transaction where the policy was taken in payment of some transferred item, the fair market value of a single-premium insurance policy is the same price a person of the same age, sex and condition of health as the insured would have to pay for a life insurance policy with the same insurance company on the significant date. The same principle applies in determining the value of a policy that is fully paid up. Gravois Planing Mill Co., CCH T.C. Mem. 1960-122.

[79] See Reg. §25.2503-3, quoted infra page 1542. See also Chittenden v. Hassett, 43-1 U.S.T.C. ¶10047 (D. Mass. 1943); Sidney R. Baer, 2 CCH T.C. Mem. 285 (1943), aff'd, 149 F.2d 637, 638, 639 (8th Cir. 1945). In the following cases the assignment of the insurance policy was deemed to create a future interest because of the nature of the assignment: Spyros P. Skouras, 14 T.C. 523 (1950), aff'd sub nom. Skouras v. Commissioner, 188 F.2d 831 (2d Cir. 1951) (assignment to the five children of insured, with right of survivorship; unanimous consent of transferees necessary to destroy right of survivorship); John M. Smyth, 2 CCH T.C. Mem. 4 (1943) (incidents of ownership exercisable only by joint action of primary and secondary beneficiaries named in policy); Nash-

follow no matter how the proceeds of the policy are payable at the time of the assignment, because the transferee acquires complete power to change the beneficiary arrangement on acquiring the incidents of ownership. If it is desired to make a present interest gift of the life insurance to or for the benefit of a minor, the previous discussion on gifts to minors is relevant.[80] On the basis of what is said there, it is apparent that a present interest gift of life insurance can be made outright to a minor or in trust for the minor provided the trust meets all the requirements of Section 2503(c) of the 1954 Code.[81] If the gift is in trust, and the minor-beneficiary has a general power of appointment, provision can be made for the disposition of the trust property in default of any exercise of the power by the minor, so that in the event of his death before he attains twenty-one, the beneficial interest under the trust will not pass to his estate.[82] Whether a transfer of a life insurance policy to a trust, other than a Section 2503(c) trust, for the benefit of either a minor or an adult will create only a present interest will depend on the terms of the trust.

The fact that on the date of transfer the beneficiary designated in the life insurance policy is a person other than the transferee is of no concern if the controlling local law is that the assignee of the policy takes precedence over the beneficiary designated therein at the time of the assignment.[83] If local law is otherwise, will the gift then be a gift of a future interest? As is mentioned above, the answer is no if the transferee is an adult who acquires complete power to change the beneficiary designation. If the transferee is a minor or is a trustee, the result should be the same but it would seem desirable to eliminate any doubt by changing the beneficiary designation before the transfer is made.

---

ville Trust Co., 2 CCH T.C. Mem. 992 (1943) (multiple transferees who had to join in exercising incidents of ownership); Joe J. Perkins, 1 T.C. 982 (1943) (assignment denied transferee right to take cash surrender value and to borrow on policy). Cf. Roberts v. Commissioner, 143 F.2d 657 (5th Cir. 1944), *cert. denied*, 324 U.S. 841 (1945) (annuity policies).

Revenue Ruling 55-408, 1955-1 C.B. 113, holds that where a policy of life insurance is transferred or assigned to a donee as absolute owner, and the donee or his guardian is not restricted in any manner from exercising all legal incidents of ownership in the policy, a gift of the policy and subsequent payment of premiums thereon by the donor will constitute gifts of present interest whether or not the policy has any cash value at the date of the transfer.

[80] See discussion at page 243 supra.

[81] Quoted infra page 1418. But compare with the statement in the text J. S. Phillips, 12 T.C. 216 (1949).

[82] See Reg. §25.2503-4(b)(3), quoted infra page 1544.

[83] See The Life Insurance Policy Contract 171 (Krueger and Waggoner eds. 1953), where it is pointed out that the majority view is that the assignee or his estate takes ahead of the beneficiary designated in the policy at the time of the assignment.

If the insured continues to pay the premiums on the insurance he has transferred, a gift for federal gift tax purposes is made at the time each premium payment is made. Is the amount of the gift the amount of the premium or the amount of increase in the value of the insurance brought about by the payment of the premium? For the answer to this question, see Guggenheim v. Rasquin, which is printed in full infra page 333. If the transfer of the policy creates no future interests, then the premium payment gift creates none.[84]

Since the reason for the transfer of the incidents of ownership of the life insurance is to remove the proceeds of the insurance from the insured's gross estate, contingencies which may prevent the accomplishment of that objective must be kept in mind, and as far as possible avoided in the making of the transfer.

If the gift is deemed one in contemplation of death, what amount will be included in the insured's gross estate? Will it be the face amount of the policy, which becomes collectible on his death, the value of the policy on the date of the gift, or the value of the policy just before he died? In Liebmann v. Hassett[85] it was held that the face amount of the policy less the proportionate amount of the insurance purchased with the premiums paid by the transferee was to be included in the insured's gross estate. Thus it may be highly desirable during the first three years after the transfer, when the gift is vulnerable to attack as a gift in contemplation of death, to make certain that the transferor does not pay the premiums directly or indirectly.

If the insured continues to pay the premiums after the transfer of the insurance, the payments made in the last three years before his death will be open to attack as gifts in contemplation of death. If such an attack is made and is successful, will the amount includible in the insured's gross estate be the premiums so paid, or the proportionate amount of the total insurance collected on death which these premium payments purchased? The Liebmann case may be the basis of a contention that it is the latter. Accordingly it may be advantageous, wherever possible, to avoid the payment of premiums directly or indirectly by the insured at any time after the date of the transfer.

Finally it must be kept in mind that if the insured has a reversionary interest which exceeds 5 percent of the value of the policy immediately prior to his death, he has an incident of ownership of the policy and the proceeds will be includible in his gross estate under the incidents of ownership test. If an outright transfer of

---

[84] See Reg. §25.2503-3(c), Ex. (6), quoted infra page 1543.
[85] 148 F.2d 247 (1st Cir. 1945).

the incidents of ownership of insurance is made, the beneficiary provisions of the policy should eliminate the estate of the insured as a possible beneficiary.[86]

Suppose that the insured is the presumptive heir of the transferee and thus may inherit all or a portion of the incidents of ownership of the policy or policies transferred. Will this possibility alone be enough to establish a reversionary interest in the insured, so that if he dies before the transferee, the proceeds of the insurance may be included in his gross estate if the 5 percent value test is met? The expectancy of an heir should not be deemed a reversionary interest within the meaning of Section 2042. The term "reversionary interest" is a property law term and in that field it has never been used to include the expectancy of an heir. In Estate of Ellen P. C. Goodyear,[87] the contention that the expectancy of an heir was a reversionary right that might make the gift one to take effect in possession or enjoyment at or after death was rejected. The Regulations recognize that the possibility that the insured may receive a policy or its proceeds by inheritance through the estate of another person, or as a surviving spouse under a statutory right of election or similar right, is not a reversionary interest.[88] The question may be largely academic because it is unlikely that the 5 percent test will ever be satisfied, even if the insured's expectancy as an heir is deemed a reversionary interest.

Even though the possibility that the insured may inherit the incidents of ownership of the transferred policies is not a reversionary interest, the transferee should immediately make certain that the incidents of ownership will not pass to the insured by inheritance if the transferee predeceases the insured, because if the incidents of ownership do in fact pass to the insured by inheritance, he will have to start all over again to remove them from his ownership and he may die before he has transferred them. If the transfer is outright to an adult, the transferee can make a will at the time of the transfer which will control the devolution of the ownership of the policy in the event of the death of the insured before the transferee and thereby keep the policy from passing back to the insured. If the transfer is for the benefit of a minor under a Section 2503(c) trust, the use of a gift in default of appointment by the minor can keep the insured out of the picture if the minor dies before the insured.[89]

If a policy of insurance is transferred to a trust, the terms of

---

[86] See page 327 supra, note 83.
[87] 2 T.C. 885 (1943).
[88] See Reg. §20.2042-1(c)(3), quoted infra page 1525.
[89] See page 327 supra, note 82.

the trust must provide for a disposition of the trust property in all possible contingencies or the insured may have a reversionary interest under the trust. The language of Section 2042 expressly recognizes that the reversionary interest may arise as a result of an instrument other than the policy of insurance itself.

At the time of the transfer of the life insurance, it must be decided whether to make the transfer in a form that will cause the value of the policy to be included in some person's estate for federal estate tax purposes if he or she dies before the insured.[90] If the transfer is only of a present interest, obviously the value of the policy will be so included because control over the policy must be given to the transferee in order for only a present interest to be transferred.[91] Even if it is decided that the value of the policy is to be includible in the gross estate of someone, it may be desirable to make the transfer in a form that will keep the policy out of the transferee's probate estate if he dies before the insured. This can be accomplished by making the initial transfer of the policy to a trust or in other ways.[92]

[90] If the transfer of the life insurance is to a trustee, the terms of the trust can be such that the death of a beneficiary under the trust, whether before or after the insured, will not cause the value of the policy or of its proceeds to be included in the deceased beneficiary's gross estate for federal estate tax purposes.

[91] On the question of the valuation of a life insurance policy when it is includible in the gross estate of someone other than the insured, see Reg. §20.2031-8(c), Ex. (3), quoted infra page 1508.

For a case which considers the method of determining the value for estate tax purposes of insurance held by the decedent on the life of another, see Estate of R. C. du Pont v. Commissioner, 233 F.2d 210 (3d Cir. 1956), *cert. denied,* 352 U.S. 878 (1956).

If a husband in a community property state takes out insurance on his life and pays the premiums with community funds, and his wife predeceases him, will any portion of the cash surrender value of the policy be includible in her gross estate? See Stewart v. United States, 158 F. Supp. 25 (N.D. Cal. 1957), *reversed on this point sub nom.* United States v. Stewart, 270 F.2d 894 (9th Cir. 1959), *cert. denied,* 361 U.S. 960 (1960); Quigley v. United States, 59-2 U.S.T.C. ¶11887 (W.D. Wash. 1959).

Revenue Ruling 55-379, 1955-1 C.B. 449, holds that when the decedent's executor elects the optional valuation date (1954 I.R.C. §2032) for valuing the assets in the gross estate of the decedent and among such assets is a policy on the life of another, the increase in the value of the insurance attributable to the payment of premiums or accrual of interest during the year after the decedent's death is excluded.

[92] In Estate of Ethel M. Donaldson, 31 T.C. 729 (1959), the insured named the decedent as primary beneficiary in policies on his life, and others as contingent beneficiaries. He waived his right to change the beneficiaries and assigned the policies to the beneficiaries. The decedent took out other policies on the insured and in these policies the decedent was designated as primary beneficiary and others as contingent beneficiaries, and no right existed in the decedent to change the beneficiary designations. Under these circumstances, though the policies did not pass to the estate of the decedent when she died before the insured, their value was includible in her gross estate because as

At this point it is appropriate to mention several other consequences which relate to the assignee of a life insurance policy. Although the value of the policy may not be reachable by the creditors of the insured when he retains the ownership of the policy, the creditors of the assignee may not be so barred.[93] The as-

---

primary beneficiary she could exercise rights under the policies to take the cash surrender value, borrow on the policies, etc.

The New York Life Insurance Company policy contains in its general provisions the following:

"At any time while the Insured is living the Owner can arrange for a transfer of his entire ownership to take effect either (a) immediately or (b) upon receipt by the Company of due proof of the Owner's death, as follows:

(a) Such ownership can be transferred immediately to a new Owner by written request satisfactory to the Company accompanied by the policy for appropriate indorsement.

(b) If the Owner is a natural person other than the Insured, he can, in the same manner, designate an Owner's Designee who, if living when the Company receives due proof of the death of the Owner who designated him and if such Owner's rights of ownership have not terminated, will then become the new Owner of this policy. Any such designation of Owner's Designee can be terminated or changed by the Owner from time to time in a similar manner."

The New York Life Insurance Company form titled Designation of Owner's Designee provides:

"With respect to Policy Number *000000* on the life of JOHN DOE, the Insured, RICHARD ROE is hereby designated Owner's Designee, subject to the terms and conditions of said policy, and the interest of any existing Owner's Designee is hereby terminated.

Dated *June 12, 1960*

/s/ *Robert Moe*   /s/ *Harry Loe*

---------------------------------------   ---
WITNESS   OWNER"

Is this designation on the part of the owner of the policy a testamentary disposition?

The New York Life Insurance Company will arrange for a succession of owners. The following is an example of such an arrangement:

"A, father of the Insured, is the Owner of this policy. Upon Receipt by the Company of due proof of the death of said A, B, mother of the Insured, if living, shall be the new Owner of the policy. If said B is not living when the Company receives due proof of the death of said A, or if after said B has succeeded to ownership, the Company receives due proof of her death, C, grandmother of the Insured, if living, shall be the new Owner of the policy. If said C is not living when the Company receives due proof of the death of said B, or if after said C has succeeded to ownership, the Company receives due proof of her death, the Insured shall be the new Owner of this policy.

"When ownership passes to a new Owner in accordance with this designation of Owner, the new Owner will succeed to the benefits, rights and privileges of the previous Owner, subject to the terms and conditions of this policy and subject to the interest of any existing collateral assignee.

"Notwithstanding anything in this policy to the contrary, the Owner may not exercise the Arrangements for Transfer of Ownership provisions of the policy without the consent of the Company, and the interest of persons designated to succeed to ownership shall be subordinate to the interest of any assignee and may be assigned by the Owner while living."

[93] See Redeker and Reid, Life Insurance Settlement Options 135 (1957).

signee of the policy may not be free to select a settlement under one of the options in the policy.[94]

If the insured needs additional insurance, it should be determined whether this should be taken out in such a way that incidents of ownership will never originate in the insured. Almost everything that is said above in regard to the transfer by the insured of the incidents of ownership of insurance he now holds is relevant in determining who should take out new insurance.

If the proceeds of the policy become payable before the death of the insured, or, even though they do not become payable before his death, if he decides to draw down the cash surrender value of the policy, and if in either case he elects to take payment in the form of a joint and survivor annuity, the value of the survivor annuity may be includible in his gross estate under Section 2039 of the 1954 Code.[95] Section 2039 will also be applicable when the original contract is the purchase of a joint and survivor annuity with no life insurance feature. Prior to the 1954 Code, other sections caused the inclusion of the value of the survivor annuity in the decedent's gross estate.[96]

---

[94] Some policies of insurance provide in substance that the options under the policy shall be available only with the consent of the company if the policy is assigned (see page 287 supra). If the options under a particular policy are very valuable and the policy contains such a clause, this factor should be taken into account in determining whether to remove the proceeds from the insured's gross estate by an assignment of the policy.

[95] Quoted infra page 1398.

[96] Revenue Ruling 55-302, 1955-1 C.B. 446, holds that where the decedent purchased a single premium joint life and survivorship annuity policy from an insurance company subsequent to March 3, 1931, the value of the survivor's annuity or the present worth of refund payments due under the contract if the survivor annuitant predeceased the decedent, is includible in the decedent's gross estate under 1939 I.R.C. §811(c) (§2036 of the 1954 Code is similar). See also Rev. Rul. 55-682, 1955-2 C.B. 601; Special Ruling dated March 16, 1956, CCH Fed. Est. & Gift Tax Rep. ¶8105 (this ruling relates to a retired serviceman who elects a joint and survivor annuity); Grant v. Smyth, 226 F.2d 407 (9th Cir. 1955); Forster v. Sauber, 57-1 U.S.T.C. ¶11695 (N.D. Ill. 1957), aff'd, 249 F.2d 379 (7th Cir. 1957), cert. denied, 356 U.S. 913 (1958).

Christiernin v. Manning, 138 F. Supp. 923 (D.N.J. 1956), held that the value of the survivor's contract is determined by a comparison with the cost of single-life annuities with guaranteed returns like the annuity of the survivor. In Dalton, Jr. v. Campbell, 56-2 U.S.T.C. ¶11621 (S.D. Ind. 1956), the court was confronted with the problem of determining the value of the survivor annuity of the decedent's wife for estate tax purposes. It concluded that the actual life expectancy of the widow, based on her physical condition at the time of the decedent's death, should control rather than her normal life expectancy as given in the mortality tables.

Revenue Ruling 54-144, 1954-1 C.B. 15, points out that annuities paid to beneficiaries under the Uniformed Services Contingency Option Act are made in consideration of annuity premiums paid by retired members rather than by the employer in consideration of past services. Revenue Ruling 59-254, 1959-2 C.B. 33, holds that since the retired member of the uniformed services bears

In selecting the method of settlement of life insurance proceeds, consideration should be given to the estate and gift tax consequences, with respect to both the estate of the insured and the beneficiaries, of one method of settlement as compared with another. From the standpoint of the estate of the insured, it may be desirable to adopt a method of settlement that qualifies for the estate tax marital deduction.[97] Furthermore, it may be important to know whether a transfer of the ownership of a life insurance policy to the insured's wife will qualify for the gift tax marital deduction.[98] From the standpoint of the beneficiaries, it must be kept in mind that the method of settlement may be such that the life insurance proceeds will be added to the gross estate of the beneficiary for estate tax purposes and will cause the beneficiary to be subject to a gift tax if any transfer of the proceeds is made by the beneficiary in his lifetime, whereas some other method of settlement may give the beneficiary all of the desired benefits without such estate and gift tax consequences.[99]

The case of Guggenheim v. Rasquin printed below is concerned with the valuation of an insurance policy for gift tax purposes.

GUGGENHEIM v. RASQUIN
312 U.S. 254, 61 Sup. Ct. 507, 85 L. Ed. 813 (1941)

MR. JUSTICE DOUGLAS delivered the opinion of the Court.

It is provided in the Revenue Act of 1932 (47 Stat. 169, 248) that for gift-tax purposes the amount of a gift of property shall be "the value thereof at the date of the gift." Sec. 506. This controversy involves the question of whether such "value" in case of single-premium life insurance policies, which are irrevocably assigned simultaneously with issuance, is cost to the donor or cash-surrender value of the policies. The case is here on a petition for certiorari which we granted because of a conflict among the Circuit Courts of Appeals [footnote omitted] as respects the proper method for valuation of such gifts made prior to 1936. [Footnote omitted.]

---

the entire cost of the annuity, and the circumstances under which the annuities are paid does not meet the requirements of 1954 I.R.C. §401(a), the entire value of the annuity payable on the death of the retired member is includible in his gross estate under §2039.

[97] See the discussion of settlement of life insurance proceeds so as to qualify them for the estate tax marital deduction at page 866 infra.

[98] See page 866 infra.

[99] The material in Chapters XI and XII is relevant in determining the settlement arrangements with respect to life insurance that will produce the most favorable estate and gift tax consequences so far as the beneficiary is concerned.

In December, 1934, petitioner purchased, at a cost of $852,438.50, single-premium life insurance policies on her own life in the aggregate face amount of $1,000,000. At substantially the same time she assigned them irrevocably to three of her children. Her gift-tax return listed the policies at their asserted cash-surrender value [footnote omitted] of $717,344.81. The Commissioner determined that the "value" of the policies was their cost and assessed a deficiency which petitioner paid. This is a suit for a refund. Judgment for petitioner in the District Court was reversed by the Circuit Court of Appeals. 110 F.2d 371.

We agree with the Circuit Court of Appeals that cost rather than cash-surrender value is the proper criterion for valuation of such gifts under Section 506 of the Act.

Cash-surrender value is the reserve less a surrender charge. And in case of a single-premium policy the reserve is the face amount of the contract discounted at a specified rate of interest on the basis of the insured's expected life. If the policy is surrendered, the company will pay the cash-surrender value. It is asserted that the market for insurance contracts is usually the issuing companies or the banks who will lend money on them; that banks will not loan more than the cash-surrender value; and that if policies had an actual realizable value in excess of their cash-surrender value, there would arise a business of purchasing such policies from those who otherwise would surrender them. From these facts it is urged that cash-surrender value represents the amount which would be actually obtained for the policies in a willing buyer-willing seller market — the test suggested by Treasury Regulations 79, Art. 19(1), promulgated October 30, 1933. [Footnote omitted.]

That analysis, however, overlooks the nature of the property interest which is being valued. Surrender of a policy represents only one of the rights of the insured or beneficiary. Plainly that right is one of the substantial legal incidents of ownership. See Chase National Bank v. United States, 278 U.S. 327, 335; Vance on Insurance (2d ed.) pp. 54-56. But the owner of a fully paid life insurance policy has more than the mere right to surrender it; he has the right to retain it for its investment virtues and to receive the face amount of the policy upon the insured's death. That these latter rights are deemed by purchasers of insurance to have substantial value is clear from the difference between the cost of a single-premium policy and its immediate or early cash-surrender value — in the instant case over $135,000. All of the economic benefits of a policy must be taken into consideration in determining its value for gift-tax purposes. To single out one and to disregard the others is in effect to substitute a different property interest for the one which was the subject of the gift. In this situation as in others (Susquehanna Power Co. v. State Tax Comm'n, 283 U.S. 291, 296) an important element in the value of the property is the use to which it may be put. Certainly the petitioner here did not expend $852, 438.50 to make an immediate gift limited to $717,344.81. Presumptively the value of these policies at the date of the gift was the amount which the insured had expended to acquire them. Cost is cogent evidence of value. And here it is the only sugested criterion which reflects the value to the owner of the entire bundle of rights in a single-premium policy — the right to retain it as well as the right to surrender it. Cost in this situation is not market price in the normal sense of the term. But the absence of market price is no barrier to valuation. [Footnote omitted.] Lucas v. Alexander, 279 U.S. 573, 579.

Petitioner, however, argues that cash-surrender value was made the measure of value by Art. 2(5), Treasury Regulations 79, promulgated October 30, 1933, which provided that the "irrevocable assignment of a life insurance policy . . . constitutes a gift in the amount of the net cash surrender value, if any, plus the prepaid insurance adjusted to the date of the gift." The argument is that under this regulation the reserve in case of a single-premium policy covers the prepaid insurance and represents the entire value of the policy. The regulation is somewhat ambiguous. But in our view it applied only to policies upon which current premiums were still being paid at the date of the gift, not to single-premium policies. Accordingly, the problem here involves an interpretation of the meaning of "value" in Section 506 unaided by an interpretative regulation.

Affirmed.[100]

PROBLEMS

8.19. A acquires a $10,000 policy of insurance on his life on July 1, 1935. The annual premium is $200. A pays the annual premiums for ten years and then transfers by gift all his rights under the policy to B, and thereafter B pays the annual premiums. The

---

[100] See comments on the Guggenheim v. Rasquin case in 54 Harv. L. Rev. 894 (1941), 25 Minn. L. Rev. 653 (1941), 14 So. Calif. L. Rev. 485 (1941).

In Rev. Rul. 58-372, 1958-2 C.B. 99, it was held that a corporation which acquired policies of insurance on the lives of certain of its officers and assigned the policies irrevocably to a charity on the date of payment of the initial premium could deduct an amount equal to the initial premium within the limitations of 1954 I.R.C. §170. — Ed.

proceeds of the policy are payable to B. A dies on June 30, 1953. With respect to the life insurance, what amount is includible in A's gross estate for federal estate tax purposes? [101] What is the answer if A dies on June 30, 1955?

8.20. H acquires a $10,000 policy of insurance on his life on July 1, 1950. H designates W, his wife, as the beneficiary but does not direct that payment of the proceeds be made under any particular option in the policy. H dies and W, in accordance with the provisions of the policy which allow a beneficiary to elect to receive payment under one of the options in the policy if the insured has not selected an option, elects to take only interest during her lifetime and directs that on her death the face amount be paid to S, son of H and W. W dies shortly after making this election. Will the value of the face amount of the insurance be includible in W's gross estate for federal estate tax purposes? [102] See Rundle v. Welch, 184 F. Supp. 777 (S.D. Ohio, 1960); Estate of Mabel E. Morton, 12 T.C. 380 (1949); Estate of John J. Tuohy, Jr., 14 T.C. 245 (1950).

8.21. In Problem 8.20, will the amount of the insurance qualify for the estate tax marital deduction in determining the taxable estate of H? See Section 20.2056(d)-1 of the Regulations, quoted infra page 1538.

8.22. A transfers property valued at $100,000 to the X Trust Company in trust. The trustee is directed to take out insurance on the life of A in the amount of $100,000 and to pay the premiums on such life insurance out of the income (and to the extent necessary, out of the principal) of the trust fund. The proceeds of the life insurance, when collected, are to be added to the principal of the trust. The trust is irrevocable. The trustee may pay the net income to, or apply it for the benefit of, such one or more of A's children who are living from time to time, and in such amount or amounts, as the trustee in its uncontrolled discretion may determine; and on the death of the survivor of A's children living on the date the trust was executed, the trustee is to pay the then remaining principal and undistributed income to A's issue then living, such issue to take per stirpes, and if no issue of A is then living,

---

[101] Section 811(g)(2) of the 1939 Code required that there be included in the gross estate of the insured the value of the proceeds of life insurance "to the extent of the amount receivable by all other beneficiaries as insurance under policies upon the life of the decedent (A) purchased with premiums, or other consideration, paid directly or indirectly by the decedent, in proportion that the amount so paid by the decedent bears to the total premiums paid for the insurance . . ."

[102] Re-examine the Pierce case at page 305 supra.

the trustee is to pay the then remaining principal and undistributed income to the Y charity.

During A's lifetime, to what extent will the income from the trust be includible in his gross income? See Section 677(a)(3) of the 1954 Code, quoted infra page 1374.

On A's death, will the proceeds of the insurance on his life be includible in his gross estate for federal estate tax purposes? See Section 2042 of the 1954 Code, quoted infra page 1402.

Will the value of the property in the trust, other than the proceeds of the insurance on A's life, be includible in A's gross estate for federal estate tax purposes? See First National Bank of Birmingham, 36 B.T.A. 651 (1937). See also Commissioner v. Beck's Estate, 129 F.2d 243 (2d Cir. 1942).[103]

8.23. The insured's wife applied for and received an insurance policy on his life. She transferred the policy to a trust. The insured and his estate had no interest, vested or contingent, under the terms of the trust, but the trust provided that the insured's wife retained the right to alter, amend or revoke the trust with the consent of the insured. The insured's wife transferred property of her own to the trust, and from time to time the insured himself transferred property to the trust. The income of the trust property is to be used, first, to pay premiums on the insurance, and any excess income is to be paid to the insured's wife for her life. The insured dies. Will the value of the proceeds of the insurance paid to the trust be includible in the insured's gross estate for federal estate tax purposes? During the insured's lifetime, should any portion of the income of the trust be includible in his gross income

---

[103] In Estate of Resch, 20 T.C. 171 (1953), a husband gave his wife property outright, and she then placed it in a trust. The trust income was to be used to pay insurance premiums on the life of the husband, with the balance of the net income going to the wife. It was held that the insurance premiums were paid indirectly by the husband and thus the proceeds of the insurance were includible in his gross estate under the premium payment test. But the property placed in the trust created by the wife was held not includible in the husband's gross estate because the wife was the settlor of the trust, even though she received from the husband the property that went into the trust, and thus it was not a trust created by the husband in which he reserved the income for his life.

In Bennett v. United States, 185 F. Supp. 577 (N.D. Ill. 1960), the court held that the value of securities transferred to an irrevocable trust were not includible in the settlor's gross estate on the ground of retention by him of income for life where the principal of the trust property was to be used to pay premiums on insurance on his life which was also transferred to the trust. Although the court stressed the fact that the premiums were to be paid out of principal, and the income was to be paid to designated beneficiaries, the implication is that the result would have been the same, even though the income of the trust was used to pay the premiums.

for federal income tax purposes? See Karagheusian v. Commissioner, 233 F.2d 197 (2d Cir. 1956). See also Farwell v. United States, 243 F.2d 373 (7th Cir. 1957).

8.24. Will the insured be deemed to possess any of the incidents of ownership of a policy of insurance on his life in either of the following situations?

a. The insured has transferred the ownership of the policy to his wife, W, but his consent must be obtained in connection with the exercise by her of any of the rights under the policy. See Estate of Louis Goldstein v. United States, 122 F. Supp. 677 (Ct. Cl. 1954), cert. denied, 348 U.S. 942 (1955).

b. The insured has transferred the ownership of the policy to his wife, W, but he has retained the right to receive any dividends declared after the transfer. See Estate of Chester H. Bowers, 23 T.C. 911 (1955).

c. The power to change the beneficiary is in a corporation of which the insured is the sole stockholder. See Section 20.2042-1(c)(2) of the Regulations, quoted infra page 1525.

8.25. The life insurance policies issued under the World War Veterans' Act of 1924, the National Service Life Insurance Act of 1940, and the Servicemen's Indemnity Act of 1951 are all issued subject to a statutory exemption from taxation. Does this statutory exemption from taxation operate to exclude from the gross estate of the insured the proceeds of such policies? See Revenue Ruling 55-622, 1955-2 C.B. 385. See also Section 20.2033-1(a) of the Regulations, quoted infra page 1509.[104]

8.26. A owns a policy of insurance on his life. The present value of this policy is $5000, but its face amount is $10,000. A transfers the ownership of the policy to his son, S, in return for the payment to him of $5000. A dies shortly after making the transfer. Will there be includible in A's gross estate for estate tax purposes any portion of the $10,000 collected by S? See Bourne Bean, 14 CCH T.C. Mem. 786 (1955).

8.27. Under what circumstances, if any, should the insured be advised to surrender his present insurance for its present cash value and to have the insurance replaced by his wife taking out new insurance on his life rather than to transfer the ownership of his present insurance to his wife?

8.28. A transfers the ownership of a policy of insurance on his

---

[104] In Greene v. United States, 171 F. Supp. 459 (Ct. Cl. 1959), cert. denied, 360 U.S. 933 (1959), Panama Canal loan bonds were involved which were issued under a statute providing that they were "exempt from all taxes," but it was held that this phrase did not exempt them from estate taxes.

life to his wife, W. W dies. W's will directs that the residue of her estate be held in trust for the benefit of her issue. The will names A as executor and trustee. A has no beneficial rights under the will. A dies. Will the value of the insurance on A's life be includible in A's gross estate for estate tax purposes? See Section 20.2042-1(c)(4) of the Regulations, quoted infra page 1526.

8.29. A transfers the ownership of a policy of insurance on his life to his wife, W. W establishes an irrevocable inter vivos trust and designates as the beneficiary of the policy the trustee of this irrevocable inter vivos trust. A dies. Will W be deemed to have made a gift for gift tax purposes of the proceeds of the insurance which passed to the trustee of the irrevocable inter vivos trust on the death of A? See Goodman v. Commissioner, 156 F.2d 218 (2d Cir. 1946).

c. *State Taxes*

In many states, life insurance proceeds are subject to state inheritance taxes only if the proceeds are payable to the insured's executors or administrators, whether or not the insured retains the incidents of ownership until his death.[105] In view of the fact that it is frequently desirable for the liquid life insurance proceeds to be available to meet the death costs of the insured, how can they be made available without at the same time being subject to state inheritance taxes? This can be done by having the proceeds paid to an insurance trust under which the trustee is authorized (not required) to pay various death costs of the insured.[106] The trustee should also be permitted to buy estate assets and to make loans to the insured's executors.

The state income tax picture with respect to insurance proceeds may differ from the federal one.[107]

---

[105] If the owner of a policy is a person other than the insured and he dies before the insured, the value of the policy will be an asset in his estate and will be subject to state inheritance taxes.

[106] State inheritance taxes on the residue should not be greater if the trustee relieves the residue of the payment of various death costs, because the net residue on which such taxes are assessed should be deemed to be what would have passed had the trustee decided not to give the relief. If this is not the case, the insurance proceeds used to give the relief to the residue are in effect being subjected to state inheritance taxes.

[107] See page 303 supra, note 32.

CHAPTER IX

Employee Benefits, Income in Respect of Decedents, and Social Security

1. INTRODUCTION

This chapter is restricted to a consideration of the estate planning aspects of employee benefits, income in respect of a decedent, and social security benefits. Whenever the client's financial picture includes any of these items, particular attention should be paid to them because they may have characteristics requiring that special treatment should be given to them or to other items so that the estate plan may achieve maximum benefits for the family.

2. EMPLOYEE BENEFITS

a. *In General*

Employee benefits may take various forms. There are so-called "qualified" pension, profit-sharing or stock bonus plans; non-qualified deferred compensation plans; restricted stock options; group insurance plans; and accident and health plans. Whatever the employee benefit arrangement may be, its net worth will depend on the tax benefits which attach to it. In some instances, these tax benefits are quite substantial.

b. *Qualified Pension, Profit-sharing or Stock Bonus Plans*[1]

A typical pension plan is one established and maintained by an employer primarily to provide systematically for the payment of

[1] The requirements which must be met in order for a plan to be a qualified one are set forth in 1954 I.R.C. §401, quoted infra page 1340.

A compilation of guides applicable to the qualification of stock bonus, pension, profit-sharing and annuity plans under §401(a) is found in Rev. Rul. 57-163, 1957-1 C.B. 128, as modified by Rev. Rul. 58-151, 1958-1 C.B. 192. Revenue Ruling 58-604, 1958-2 C.B. 147, answers various questions raised by

definitely determinable benefits to his employees over a period of years, usually for life, after retirement. Retirement benefits generally are measured by, and based on, such factors as years of service

---

Rev. Rul. 57-163 as modified by Rev. Rul. 58-151. Revenue Ruling 59-185, 1959-1 C.B. 86, amplifies Part 4(g) of Rev. Rul. 57-163. Revenue Ruling 60-2, I.R.B. 1960-1, 16, discusses the factors which are relevant in determining whether a suspension of employer contributions to an employee's profit-sharing plan constitutes a discontinuance within the meaning of Part 5(b)(4) of Rev. Rul. 57-163.

Revenue Ruling 57-213, 1957-1 C.B. 157, amplifies Rev. Rul. 54-51, 1954-1, C.B. 147, in regard to the purchase of ordinary life insurance with funds of a profit-sharing trust. Qualification under §401(a) is not prevented if such a purchase is properly restricted. Revenue Ruling 54-51 (as well as Rev. Rul. 57-163 referred to above) is further amplified in Rev. Rul. 60-84, I.R.B. 1960-10, 11, which holds that where a paid-up life insurance policy is distributed to a participant of an exempt trust forming part of a profit-sharing plan, a failure to convert the contract so that no portion is used to continue life insurance protection beyond retirement will not cause the trust and plan to fail of qualification if they otherwise meet the requirements of §401(a). Furthermore, the employee may treat the entire cash value of the policy as a gain from the sale or exchange of a capital asset held for more than six months, to the extent that it exceeds the net amount contributed by the employee, if he does not convert the contract into an annuity contract within sixty days after distribution to him. Revenue Ruling 60-83, I.R.B. 1960-10, 9, holds that the investment of current contributions under a profit-sharing plan in insurance protection by the purchase of paid-up units of endowment insurance, where, upon retirement, the total value of all units of such insurance purchased will be used to pay to the participant retirement income in the form of monthly annuities, will be allowed under a qualified plan. The life insurance element is incidental to the primary purpose to provide for deferred benefits.

Revenue Ruling 56-693, 1956-2 C.B. 282, brings out that a pension plan cannot qualify under §401(a) if the participants are permitted, prior to any severance of their employment or the termination of the plan, to withdraw, in times of financial need or otherwise, all or part of the funds accumulated on their behalf. A similar provision, however, will not necessarily prevent qualification of a profit-sharing plan. Revenue Ruling 57-587, 1957-2 C.B. 260, points out that although the participants' undistributed interests in an employees' trust may not be available to them by reason of a restricted right of withdrawal, the plan itself may eventually be disqualified in the event that, as a result of withdrawals by employees of their interests, the plan becomes one which is operated primarily for the benefit of employees who are officers, shareholders, persons whose principal duty consists in supervising the work of other employees or persons who are highly compensated employees. Revenue Ruling 60-323, I.R.B. 1960-41, 9, modifies both Rev. Rul. 56-693 and Rev. Rul. 57-163, referred to above, in holding that a pension plan will not be denied qualification because it contains provisions permitting a participant to withdraw his voluntary contributions which are made in addition to his compulsory contributions, where such withdrawals do not affect the member's participation in the plan, the employer's past or future contributions on his behalf, the basic benefits provided by both the participant's and the employer's compulsory contributions, and where, under the provisions of the plan, no interest is allowable with respect to the contributions withdrawn either at the time of the withdrawal or in computing benefits on retirement.

Section 401(a)(2) sets up as one of the requirements for a qualified plan that it be impossible to divert anything from the employees or their beneficiaries.

and compensation received by the employees. The determination of the amount of retirement benefits and the contributions to provide such benefits are not dependent upon profits. A qualified pension plan may include a trust (which may be called a "pension trust") or it may be established without a trust by the purchase of an annuity contract, in which case the plan may be called an "annuity plan." [2]

A profit-sharing plan is one established and maintained by an employer and is designed to provide for the participation in his profits by his employees or their beneficiaries. In order for the plan to be qualified, it must provide a predetermined formula for allocating the contributions made to the plan among the participants and for distributing the funds accumulated under the plan after a fixed number of years, on the attainment of a stated age, or on the prior occurrence of some event such as illness, disability, retirement or death, or severance of employment for some other reason. A plan is not a qualified one if the contributions to the plan are made at such time or in such amounts that the plan in operation discriminates in favor of officers, shareholders, persons whose

---

Revenue Ruling 59-309, 1959-2 C.B. 117, holds that a provision in a newly established plan that provides for the return of the employer's contributions if the plan does not initially qualify does not prevent qualification because no diversion is possible by reason of the provision if the plan is otherwise qualified. The view of the ruling is adopted in Branham Co., CCH T.C. Mem. 1960-31. Revenue Ruling 59-309 is superseded by Rev. Rul. 60-276, I.R.B. 1960-34, 12, which reaches the same result.

Revenue Ruling 60-73, I.R.B. 1960-9, 20, considers the requirement for qualified pension plans under §401(a) — that the plan provide for the payment of definitely determinable benefits to the employees — in a plan which provided that a forfeiture arising from termination of employment was to be reallocated to the accounts of the remaining participants. Such a plan fails to meet the requirement and the ruling describes three ways of amending the plan so as to meet the requirement.

Revenue Ruling 60-281, I.R.B. 1960-37, 20, recognizes that prior to termination of employment a participant in an employee pension plan may be given the right to withdraw his own contributions, including any increment actually earned by him, without disqualifying the plan, but any right of withdrawal that goes beyond this and constitutes a right to withdraw some of the employer's contributions will disqualify the plan.

Revenue Ruling 60-337, I.R.B. 1960-44, 7, considers the integration with social security benefits of a trusteed pension plan as provided for in §401(a)(5). This provision permits the plan to be restricted to employees earning in excess of $4800 a year.

Revenue Ruling 60-338, I.R.B. 1960-44, 6, deals with a profit-sharing plan for employees established by a cooperative and holds that the plan can be a qualified one, though the payments to the plan come from funds which otherwise would be distributed to the members of the cooperative.

[2] See Reg. §1.401-1(b)(1)(i), quoted infra page 1487.

Some insurance companies now sell what are called "variable annuities" designed to cushion the effects of inflation. These contracts pay the retired person, for life, an income varying with the earnings of the company's investments in common stocks.

principal duties consist in supervising the work of other employees, or highly compensated employees.[3]

A stock bonus plan is one established and maintained by an employer to provide benefits similar to those of a profit-sharing plan, except that the contributions by the employer are not necessarily dependent upon profits, and the benefits are distributed in the stock of the employer company. In order for the plan to be a qualified one, the provisions regarding the allocation and distribution of the stock of the employer which is to be shared among his employees or their beneficiaries are subject to the same requirements as a profit-sharing plan.[4]

A pension plan may be contributory in that the employee as well as the employer contributes to it, or it may be wholly noncontributory in that only the employer contributes to it. Whether the plan is contributory or noncontributory will be significant in connection with certain tax matters.

The contributions made by the employer to a qualified plan are deductible in the year made (subject to some limitations) for income tax purposes.[5] The build-up of the contributions to a qualified plan through accumulations of income and growth in value also escape income taxation during the build-up period. Even though the employee has a nonforfeitable right in the contribution by his employer to a qualified plan made on his behalf, he is not taxed on the contribution until the pay-out period arrives.[6]

---

[3] See Reg. §1.401-1(b)(1)(ii), quoted infra page 1487.

[4] See Reg. §1.401-1(b)(1)(iii), quoted infra page 1488.

[5] See 1954 I.R.C. §404, quoted infra page 1346, which describes the extent to which an employer's contributions to a qualified plan are deductible for income tax purposes. Revenue Ruling 60-379, I.R.B. 1960-51, 25, holds that in computing the limit on deductible contributions under §404(a)(3)(A) which may be made by an employer to a qualified profit-sharing plan, the employer may take into account its distributive share of compensation paid by a joint venture, in which it is participating, to employees covered by the employer's profit-sharing plan.

The extent to which the employer's contributions may be deductible for state income tax purposes will depend on the law of the controlling state. See, for example, Mass. Ann. Laws, c. 63, §30(5), which allows the employer a deduction if it is allowed one for federal income tax purposes.

[6] See 1954 I.R.C. §501(a), quoted infra page 1355. The income tax exemption during the build-up period may be lost under §503, which deals with certain prohibited transactions, or under §511, which is concerned with unrelated business income. In Rev. Rul. 58-526, 1958-2 C.B. 269, an exempt trust of a subsidiary corporation which purchased debentures of the parent corporation was considered, and it was held that the purchase was not a prohibited transaction under §503. Revenue Ruling 59-29, 1959-1 C.B. 123, held that the deposit of funds of an exempt employee's trust in a checking account with the employer-grantor bank is not a prohibited transaction under §503(c)(1) or §503(c)(6). Revenue Ruling 60-206, I.R.B. 1960-21, 10, determined that an exempt trust had unrelated business income on which it was taxable when it received rent under a lease of personal property.

Pension trusts may continue indefinitely, and accumulations under them

The federal income, gift and estate tax consequences in regard to the pay-out of employee benefits under a qualified plan will have considerable influence on the selection of the pay-out arrangement. Certainly any selection that is made without adequate consideration of the tax consequences may cause a substantial diminution in the worth of the employee benefit. Furthermore, the selection should be made in the light of the disposition of the employee's other assets so that a completely integrated plan of all his assets will be adopted.[7]

(1) Income Taxes

The benefits under a qualified plan may be paid to the distributee in a lump sum or in installments. The distributee may be the employee or, if he is not living, his designated beneficiary.

A lump sum payment to the distributee, whoever he is, may place in his hands a significant amount of liquid funds. The desirability, in the over-all picture, of having liquid funds available will be a factor in determining whether a lump sum payment is particularly appropriate.[8]

It might be prohibitively costly to have the employee benefit paid in a lump sum if the distributee will be required to include all or most of the payment in his gross income for the year in which distribution is made. The general rule is that the distributee will

---

may last for a long period of time. Specific statutory provisions now exist quite widely which exempt these arrangements from the rule against perpetuities and the rule against accumulations. See, for example, Mass. Ann. Laws, c. 203, §3A, quoted infra page 1461. Notice that this statute is not limited in its application to trusts under qualified pension plans.

The controlling state law will determine the extent to which the accumulated income is exempt from state income taxation during the build-up period. See, for example, Mass. Ann. Laws, c. 62, §8(j), which exempts the accumulated income from state income taxation. Massachusetts Ann. Laws, c. 62, §8(i) makes it clear that the employee is not subjected to state income taxation on the employer's contribution at the time it is made. See also Mass. Ann. Laws, c. 32, §41, which exempts, under limited circumstances, from state income taxation even the employee's contribution to a pension arrangement.

[7] The availability to an employee of substantial retirement benefits may justify the making of inter vivos gifts to other members of the family so that the employee's gross estate for federal estate tax purposes will be diminished in value.

[8] The most urgent need for liquid funds may be on the death of the employee so as to avoid a sale of nonliquid estate assets, at a sacrifice, to meet death costs. As is pointed out later in connection with the discussion of estate taxes (see page 355 infra), it will be undesirable from an estate tax standpoint to have the employee benefits under a qualified plan paid to the employee's executor, but as has already been indicated (see page 129 supra), the benefits may be made payable in a lump sum to an inter vivos trust, where they can be effectively used, without an adverse tax result, to prevent a sale of estate assets at a sacrifice.

be required to include in his gross income the amounts received under a qualified plan for the year in which they are received, as provided in Section 72 of the 1954 Code,[9] except that Section 72(e)(3)[10] will not apply.[11] In the case of a lump sum payment this means that if the plan is a noncontributory one, the entire payment will be taxable in one year as ordinary income under the general rule. If the plan is a contributory one, then only the excess over the amount contributed by the employee will be so taxable.[12]

---

[9] Quoted infra page 1325.

[10] Quoted infra page 1327. The effect of §72(e)(3) not being available is to deny in the case of a lump sum payment the right to spread the payment ratably over a three-year period for purposes of determining the income tax payable.

[11] The general rule as applied to qualified trusts is set forth in 1954 I.R.C. §402(a)(1), quoted infra page 1342, and as to qualified annuity plans in §403 (a)(1), quoted infra page 1344.

In Ned R. Harman, CCH T.C. Mem. 1960-159, a retired state employee contended that §72 could not constitutionally be applied to his annuity because (1) a new method for taxing annuities was established under which his unrecovered cost was apportioned on the basis of his life expectancy as of the effective date of the new Code, thus reducing his actuarial life expectancy as of his retirement date, and (2) part of his retirement pay represented "inheritances" received from deceased members of the retirement group and could not be taxed as income, and (3) at the time of his retirement he had a vested property right to continued employment and that he exchanged this right for an annuity for life and a tax on this would represent a capital levy. The court rejected these contentions.

[12] Section 72(f), quoted infra page 1327, sets forth the special rules for computing an employee's contribution. In this regard it should be noted that if an amount contributed by an employer was includible in the gross income of the employee, or if it would not have been includible in his gross income if it had been given to him by the employer at the time the employer made the contribution, then such amount will be deemed contributed by the employee.

It should be noted that where a qualified trust is involved, there is not included in the amount made available to a distributee the net unrealized appreciation in securities of the employer corporation attributable to the amount contributed by the employee. See §402(a)(1). See also Rev. Rul. 55-354, 1955-1 C.B. 396, for a discussion of the method of determining net unrealized appreciation. Revenue Ruling 57-514, 1957-2 C.B. 261, considers the method of determining the basis of the employer's stock received as a distribution from an employees' trust.

An example of a payment which would not have been includible in the employee's gross income if it had been given to him at the time the employer made the contribution is a payment to a foreign service employee under 1954 I.R.C. §911. See Rev. Rul. 55-294, 1955-1 C.B. 368, which considers the income tax consequences with respect to the pension of a foreign service employee. See also Rev. Rul. 56-123, 1956-1 C.B. 60, and Rev. Rul. 56-125, 1956-1 C.B. 627, dealing with foreign service employees. Consider Rev. Rul. 56-524, 1956-2 C.B. 504, and Rev. Rul. 56-571, 1956-2 C.B. 982, in relation to what constitutes exempt income within the purview of §911. Revenue Ruling 59-278, 1959-2 C.B. 174, supersedes Rev. Rul. 56-571 in regard to what may be excluded from gross income as consideration paid for an annuity because it is attributable to services rendered outside the United States. Revenue Ruling 60-36, I.R.B. 1960-5, 28, holds that an employee of the American Red Cross does not

An important exception to the general rule is operative in the case of a pay-out under a qualified plan if the total payments with respect to an employee are made within one taxable year of the distributee and certain tests are met.[13] The exception permits the amount which would otherwise be taxable as ordinary income under the general rule to be taxed as a gain from the sale or exchange of a capital asset held for more than six months.[14] The most important test which must be met in order for capital gains treatment

---

include in his gross income, to the extent allowed by §911(a)(2), amounts received for his services performed outside the United States which are attributable to any 18-consecutive-month period during which he was physically present within a foreign country or countries for at least 510 days, because the Red Cross is not an agency of the United States within the meaning of §911(a)(2).

Revenue Ruling 56-82, 1956-1 C.B. 59, holds that under §72(f), payments withheld from a state employee at a time when such payments would not have been taxable as income to him if they had been paid to him, may be included in figuring the cost of the annuity to the employee. See also Rev. Rul. 57-75, 1957-1 C.B. 28, which deals with some special situations regarding the consideration paid for annuities by employees of states and their political subdivisions, where their salaries were not subject to federal income taxes prior to 1939.

Revenue Ruling 58-236, 1958-1 C.B. 37, holds that an alien residing in the United States may include as his investment in the contract for an annuity, under an employees' trust established in a foreign country by a foreign corporation, the amount contributed on his behalf by his employer for services rendered in the foreign country. It also points out that if the foreign country is a community property country, the resident wife of the employee must include in her gross income her community property share in the annuity payments.

[13] The tests which must be met for qualified trusts are indicated in §402(a)(2), quoted infra page 1342, and those for qualified annuity plans in §403(a)(2), quoted infra page 1344.

Section 402(a)(3)(C) defines total distributions payable under a qualified trust as "the balance to the credit of an employee which becomes payable to a distributee on account of the employee's death or other separation from the service, or on account of his death after separation from the service." Section 403(a)(2)(B) similarly defines total amounts payable under a qualified annuity plan. Thus, the fact that partial distributions have been made prior to the specified event will not defeat the application of capital gains treatment.

[14] In determining the gain that is taxable, if a contributory plan is involved, the amount contributed by the employee (see note 12, supra, in regard to the determination of the employee's contribution) must be reduced by any amounts previously distributed to the employee which were not includible in gross income. See §§402(a)(2) and 403(a)(2).

Furthermore, if a qualified trust is involved and the total distributions include securities of the employer corporation, there must be excluded from the gain the net unrealized appreciation attributable to that part of the total distributions which consists of securities of the employer corporation so distributed. See §402(a)(2). See also Rev. Rul. 55-354, 1955-1 C.B. 396, for a discussion of the method of determining the net unrealized appreciation. Revenue Ruling 57-514, 1957-2 C.B. 261, considers the method of determining the basis of the employer's stock received as a distribution from an employees' trust.

to be available is that the total payments made within the taxable year are "on account of the employee's death or other separation from the service, or on account of the death of the employee after his separation from the service." [15] An employee who wants to

---

[15] The quoted language is found in §402(a)(2) as to qualified trusts, and there is similar language in §403(a)(2)(A)(iii) as to qualified annuity plans. Section 403(a)(2)(A)(ii) imposes the additional requirement that qualified annuity plans provide "that refunds of contributions with respect to annuity contracts purchased under such plan be used to reduce subsequent premiums on the contracts under the plan."

It was held in Harry K. Oliphint, 24 T.C. 744 (1955), *aff'd sub nom.* Oliphint v. Commissioner, 234 F.2d 699 (5th Cir. 1956), that there was not a distribution on account of the taxpayer's "separation from service" of his employer when the taxpayer was re-elected an officer of the corporation on the same day that distribution was made to him.

In Commissioner v. Miller, 226 F.2d 618 (6th Cir. 1955), one corporation sold out to another and at the time of the sale voted to discontinue a qualified trust and to distribute the trust assets. The employees of the selling corporation continued to work for the buying corporation in the same capacities. The court held that the payment of the trust fund to the employees was "on account of the employee's separation from service" within the meaning of the language of 1939 I.R.C. §165(b), so that capital gains treatment was accorded the distributees.

In Lester B. Martin, 26 T.C. 100 (1956), a corporation having a pension plan was dissolved, and the employee in question went to work immediately for the transferee corporation. It was held that the payment of a lump sum to the employee by the transferor corporation's pension trust was on account of the employee's separation from service within the meaning of 1939 I.R.C. §165(b). In Clarence F. Buckley, 29 T.C. 455 (1957), the taxpayer became an employee of the corporation which acquired all the assets of the corporation where he had been previously employed. The selling corporation had had a qualified pension plan which the buying corporation continued for five years, after which time the plan was terminated and the taxpayer received a lump sum payment. The court held that the payment to the taxpayer was not on account of his separation from service and that, therefore, the entire payment was ordinary income.

In Rev. Rul. 56-214, 1956-1 C.B. 196, it was held that an employee who, for any reason, terminates his participation in a qualified plan but who continues his employment with his employer is not deemed to have been separated from service and thus is not entitled to long-term capital gains treatment in connection with a lump sum distribution.

Revenue Ruling 57-115, 1957-1 C.B. 160, dealt with a lump sum distribution from an employees' qualified profit-sharing plan and held that the distribution was taxable at ordinary tax rates when the corporate officer, although uncompensated, continued to act in the capacity of an officer and director for limited service. In other words, the payment was not on account of his separation from service.

Revenue Ruling 58-94, 1958-1 C.B. 194, Rev. Rul. 58-95, 1958-1 C.B. 197, Rev. Rul. 58-96, 1958-1 C.B. 200, Rev. Rul. 58-97, 1958-1 C.B. 201, Rev. Rul. 58-98, 1958-1 C.B. 202, and Rev. Rul. 58-99, 1958-1 C.B. 202, consider the tax consequences of lump sum distributions by employee trusts where the employer has been reorganized, merged, liquidated, etc., and the employees work for the succeeding corporation. In the first five rulings referred to, the lump sum payments were held to be the result of a separation from service, resulting in capital gain benefits, but in the last ruling it was held that, under the circumstances involved, the payments were not made on account of the employees' separation from service and the payments were therefore taxable

draw down his pension benefits in a lump sum but to continue to serve his employer in some kind of consultative capacity may find it very costly taxwise.[16]   He may, however, select an installment payment plan with a lump sum payment of the commuted value of the unpaid installments to be made on his death to a designated beneficiary so that the lump sum payment will be made on account of his death.[17]

---

under the provisions of §72.   Revenue Ruling 58-383, 1958-2 C.B. 149, followed Rev. Rul. 58-94 on substantially similar facts.

Thomas E. Judkins, 31 T.C. 1022 (1959), held that a lump sum distribution under a qualified plan which was being terminated by new owners of the business was paid to an employee because of his separation from the employer's service two months before, although the lump sum payment (rather than an annuity) was made because the plan itself was being terminated.

In McGowan v. United States, 175 F. Supp. 364 (E.D. Wis. 1959), a corporation transferred some of its stock in a subsidiary to employees of the subsidiary, and as a result the subsidiary employees ceased to participate in the parent's pension fund.   The court held that the amount owing to and withdrawn by a continuing employee of the subsidiary from the parent's pension fund was ordinary income since there was no "separation from service."   The case was affirmed in 277 F.2d 613 (7th Cir. 1960).

In Estate of Edward I. Rieben, 32 T.C. 1205 (1959), a corporate employer discontinued a phase of its business and at the same time terminated its pension plan.   The taxpayer stayed on as an employee but received an annuity policy on the termination of the pension trust, which he surrendered to the issuing company for cash.   Since he did not receive the distributions from the pension trust because of his separation from service, the amount distributed to him was ordinary income, not capital gain.

[16] Revenue Ruling 57-260, 1957-1 C.B. 164, holds that when an employee continues to work beyond the specified retirement age and, prior to such age, makes an irrevocable election to receive upon the termination of his service with his employer, and only then, the total amount credited to his account, such amount will not be deemed to have been made available to him until he terminates his employment.

Revenue Ruling 60-292, I.R.B. 1960-37, 22, points out that where an employee is paid within one taxable year of the employee everything he is entitled to receive, capital gains treatment is available, though this payment is made some years after his separation from service (it was not made "available" to him prior to payment).   Any increment credited to the employee's account subsequent to his separation from service, however, is taxable to him as ordinary income in the year of distribution, since it is not part of the balance of his account which becomes payable on account of his separation from service, unless the increment is attributable to delay in distribution occasioned by administrative problems of the plan, in which case all will be subject to capital gains treatment.

[17] Section 165(b) of the 1939 Code, which dealt with total distributions under qualified trusts, provided for capital gains treatment but did not include total distributions "on account of the death of the employee after his separation from the service."   See Janet H. Gordon, 26 T.C. 763 (1956).   Furthermore, there was no provision under the 1939 Code giving capital gains treatment to lump sum payments under qualified annuity plans.

Revenue Ruling 55-298, 1955-1 C.B. 394, recognizes that where an employee receives from the trustee of a qualified profit-sharing plan an annuity contract on the termination of his service, he is entitled to capital gains treatment if he

Several different distributees may be designated to receive total payments with respect to an employee, and if the total distributions payable are paid or includible in the gross income of the several distributees within one taxable year on account of the employee's death or other separation from the service or on account of his death after separation from the service, capital gains treatment is applicable. However, if the share of any distributee is not paid or includible in his gross income within the same taxable year in which the shares of other distributees are paid or includible in

surrenders the annuity contract for its cash value in the year in which the distribution is made to him. Capital gains treatment will not be accorded him, however, if he defers the surrender of the contract to a later year, because then payment will not be on account of his separation from service. In this connection, see Reg. §1.402(a)-1(a)(2), quoted infra page 1488.

Revenue Ruling 56-446, 1956-2 C.B. 1065, deals with the United States-Canada tax convention and points out that under this convention, where the total distributions payable under a qualified plan with respect to an employee for services rendered outside the United States are paid in one lump sum to a nonresident alien residing in Canada on account of the employee's separation from service, the distribution is exempt from federal income taxation. Revenue Ruling 56-446, was modified in Rev. Rul. 58-247, 1958-1 C.B. 623, to make clear that the exemption from taxation is under Article VIII of the United States-Canada tax convention. Revenue Ruling 58-248, 1958-1 C.B. 621, points out that the tax convention between the United States and Australia does not apply to an amount constituting, with respect to any employee, the "total distributions payable" on account of the employee's death or other separation from service as defined in §402(a)(3)(C), when paid in one taxable year to an alien residing in Australia. Such a distribution, to the extent that it exceeds the employees' contributions, reduced by any amounts previously distributed which were not includible in gross income, is subject in the United States to a tax of not less than the 30 percent imposed by §871 and to the 30 percent withholding thereon required by §1441(a).

Revenue Ruling 56-558, 1956-2 C.B. 290, deals with the situation where, on account of his retirement, an employee receives the total distribution payable to him under an employees' trust in the year of his separation from service and then, in the following year, receives an additional distribution representing his pro rata portion of the current year's profits contributed by the employer to the plan. The ruling holds that capital gains treatment is available in regard to the distributions made in the year of retirement, but the additional distribution made in the following year is not treated as a capital gain but is taxable under §402(a)(1).

Revenue Ruling 58-423, 1958-2 C.B. 151, recognizes that long-term capital gains treatment is available when the distributee is a trust.

Revenue Ruling 59-94, 1959-1 C.B. 25, holds that where a qualified employees' profit-sharing trust gives the employee the unrestricted right to a lump sum payment on the termination of his services unless within sixty days after payment becomes due he elects to take an annuity, and the employee within such period so elects, §72(h) is applicable and no part of the lump sum will be considered as includible in gross income at the time the lump sum first became payable.

Revenue Ruling 59-401, 1959-2 C.B. 121, holds that the fact that benefits under an exempt employees' trust are paid directly by the insurer issuing the group annuity contract under which the benefits are funded, rather than by the trustee of the trust, does not affect the applicability of §402(a).

their gross income, none of the distributees is entitled to capital gains treatment.[18]

If the pay-out arrangement under a qualified plan does not qualify for capital gains treatment, then it may be desirable to spread the payments over a number of taxable years so that the amount annually subjected to income taxation as ordinary income under the general rule will be lessened. In this connection, notice that the amount taxable in any one year under the general rule is the amount actually distributed "or made available" to the distributee.[19] Also, the distributee is taxable on the distribution to him without regard to whether it stems from interest on tax-exempt securities in the qualified plan.[20]

A slight difference in the wording of the general rule as applied to annuity plans is worth noting. Whereas the general rule with respect to pay-outs under a qualified trust applies no matter who is the distributee,[21] if the pay-out is under an annuity plan the general rule as stated applies only when the payee is the employee.[22] What is the tax consequence if a lump sum payment is made to a distributee other than an employee under an annuity plan, under circumstances which eliminate the availability of capital gains treatment? [23] It might be contended that Section 72 would then be applicable, including the benefit of Section 72(e)(3), which is

---

[18] See Reg. §1.402(a)-(1)(a)(6)(iv), quoted infra page 1489.

[19] The following rulings consider whether an amount has been made available to an employee under a qualified plan: Rev. Rul. 54-265, 1954-2 C.B. 239; Rev. Rul. 55-368, 1955-1 C.B. 40; Rev. Rul. 55-423, 1955-1 C.B. 41; Rev. Rul. 55-424, 1955-1 C.B. 42; Rev. Rul. 55-425, 1955-1 C.B. 43; Rev. Rul. 55-427, 1955-2 C.B. 27. See also note 16 supra.

Revenue Ruling 58-230, 1958-1 C.B. 204, considered an employees' profit-sharing plan which allowed an employee to make withdrawals at certain periods, but a withdrawal would cause a suspension of participation in the plan by the employee for a specified period during which no contributions would be made to the plan for the employee by the employer. It was held that such a suspension represented a substantial restriction, so that the amounts which the employee could withdraw were not "made available" to him until a withdrawal was actually made. A partial withdrawal by him, however, was held to "make available" to him the difference between the amount actually withdrawn and the maximum he could have withdrawn, even though the difference could be withdrawn later only by incurring another similar suspension of participation.

Revenue Ruling 60-292, I.R.B. 1960-37, 22, holds that an employee's interest under an exempt trust is not made available to him on his separation from service where the plan provides that on withdrawal of his interest the employee will lose all prior service credits to which he was entitled. This is a substantial restriction on his right of withdrawal.

[20] See Rev. Rul. 55-61, 1955-1 C.B. 40.

[21] See 1954 I.R.C. §402(a)(1), quoted infra page 1342.

[22] See 1954 I.R.C. §403(a)(1), quoted infra page 1344.

[23] Where capital gains treatment is available, it is available no matter who is the distributee, even under an annuity plan. See 1954 I.R.C. §403(a)(2), quoted infra page 1344.

not available under the general rule normally applicable to pay-outs under qualified plans.

If the pay-out under a qualified plan is on account of the death of the employee, whether the pay-out is controlled by the general rule for income tax purposes or by the exception to the general rule which permits capital gains treatment, an additional income tax benefit may be available. Section 101(b) of the 1954 Code[24] lays down as a general rule that gross income does not include amounts received (whether in a single sum or otherwise) by beneficiaries or the estate of an employee if such amounts are paid by or on behalf of an employer[25] and are paid by reason of the death of the employee. The aggregate amount excludable from gross income on this ground, however, cannot exceed $5000,[26] and even this amount is not excludable where the employee possessed, immediately before his death, a nonforfeitable right to receive the amounts while living,[27] unless the nonforfeitable right falls within

[24] Quoted infra page 1329.

[25] It may be necessary under some arrangements to determine whether a payment as a result of an employee's death is one by or on behalf of the employer, so that §101(b) applies, or whether it represents an amount received under a life insurance contract, so that §101(a), quoted infra page 1329, applies. In Rhodes v. Gray, 59-2 U.S.T.C. ¶9646 (W.D. Ky. 1959), the arrangement involved a policy of insurance on the life of an employee, with premiums paid by the employer. The policy was owned by the employer, and the employer was named as beneficiary. Under the employee contract, however, the proceeds of the policy inured to the benefit of the person designated by the employee. The court held that the beneficiary designated by the employee received the proceeds of life insurance on the death of the employee for the purposes of 1939 I.R.C. §22(b)(1)(B), which is similar to §101.

[26] See §101(b)(2)(A), quoted infra page 1329.

Section 22(b)(1)(B) of the 1939 Code gave the $5000 exclusion only when the payment was pursuant to a contract. The 1954 Code has eliminated this requirement. It is more strict, however, in that it limits the exclusion to $5000 no matter how many employers make payments by reason of the employee's death, whereas the old law allowed a $5000 exclusion as to payments by each employer. See also Rev. Rul. 54-531, 1954-2 C.B. 56.

In determining whether the $5000 exclusion referred to in §101(b)(2)(A) is available, an employer-employee relationship must be found to exist. Revenue Ruling 54-547, 1954-2 C.B. 57, provides that where it is determined that a common law employer-employee relationship exists for federal employment tax purposes under §§1426(d) and 1607(i) of the 1939 Code, this relationship will be considered to exist for purposes of §22(b)(1)(B) of the 1939 Code.

Revenue Ruling 59-401, 1959-2 C.B. 121, holds that the fact that benefits under an exempt employees' trust are paid directly by the insurer issuing the group annuity contract under which the benefits are funded, rather than by the trustee of the trust, does not affect the applicability of §101(b).

[27] The amount payable by reason of the death of the employee may be made up of two segments: one may be the amount which would have been available to the employee if he had resigned on the day he died, and which, consequently, would not have been forfeitable; the other may consist of the amount which would be forfeited if he had resigned on the day he died, but which is payable as a result of his death. In such a case the exclusion should

the exception to the general rule, which accords capital gains treatment to total distributions within one taxable year.[28] Thus, if a beneficiary of a deceased employee receives a lump sum payment of $10,000 from a qualified trust under circumstances that make capital gains treatment available, and the employee had contributed $1000, the beneficiary can exclude $5000 of the $9000 gain.[29]

If the pay-out under the qualified plan is in installments over a period of years, and the $5000 exclusion is available, it is given effect by treatment as additional consideration paid by the employee in determining the amount of each installment payment that is taxable under Section 72.[30]

A further qualification on the normal operation of Section 72 should be kept in mind when the pay-out is in installments. If the employee's contributions under the installment pay-out plan are recoverable in three years, then all amounts received as an annuity are excluded from gross income until there has been excluded an amount equal to the employee's contributions, and thereafter the full amount of each installment payment is includible in gross income.[31] The operation of this rule must be correlated with the operation of the rule as to the $5000 exclusion when it is available in connection with installment payments taxable under Section 72.[32]

---

apply only to the segment of the payment made by reason of death, which was forfeitable at the time of the death of the employee. See Rev. Rul. 55-64, 1955-1 C.B. 228. The same principle may be applicable when death benefits are paid under a group annuity contract and payment is made upon death from the reserve which could have been applied to the purchase of an immediate or deferred annuity for the employee if had he separated from the employer's service prior to death. In this case the exclusion applies only to that part of the payment which is specifically designated as made only by reason of the employee's death. See Rev. Rul. 55-74, 1955-1 C.B. 230.

Revenue Ruling 59-255, 1959-2 C.B. 36, considers whether the $5000 excludable from gross income under §101(b) is available when the employee's right to a benefit is lost if he withdraws his own contributions to the plan, and holds that in such a case the employee's rights are forfeitable, and hence the $5000 exclusion is available.

In H. Lloyd Hess, 31 T.C. 165 (1958), a divided court allowed the $5000 exclusion under 1939 I.R.C. §22(b)(1)(B) with respect to a qualified plan, though the employee did possess a nonforfeitable right to receive, while living, the amounts of the death benefits in question. The case was reversed on the point sub nom. Hess v. Commissioner, 271 F.2d 104 (3d Cir. 1959), on the strength of regulations under the 1939 Code.

28 See 1954 I.R.C. §101(b)(2)(B), quoted infra page 1329.

29 See Reg. §1.101-2(d)(3)(ii), Ex. (2), quoted infra page 1481.

30 See 1954 I.R.C. §101(b)(2)(D), quoted infra page 1330.

31 See 1954 I.R.C. §72(d), quoted infra page 1326.

32 Section 101(b)(2)(D) may in some cases even operate to take an annuity out of §72(d) by increasing the consideration contributed by the employee, so that it exceeds the amounts to be received by the distributee during the first three years of the annuity.

The qualified plan may be funded with retirement income policies having a life insurance feature. If the life insurance is payable to a beneficiary of the employee, then the portion of the premiums paid for the life insurance protection from either contributions of the employer or earnings of the trust fund will constitute income to the employee for the year in which the contributions or earnings are applied toward the purchase of the life insurance.[33] When the proceeds of such a policy are paid on the

---

Revenue Ruling 57-483, 1957-2 C.B. 92, deals with a survivor benefit plan under which the employee's interest was forfeitable and the survivor benefit was payable in equal installments over a period of sixty months. It holds that the $5000 exclusion cannot be prorated over the period of payment but must be excluded from gross income until there has been received and excluded an amount not in excess of $5000. Revenue Ruling 58-153, 1958-1 C.B. 43, revokes Rev. Rul. 57-483 and holds that where, on account of the death of an employee, survivor benefit payments are received in installments over a period of years pursuant to a noncontributory plan of an employer, the amount not in excess of $5000 excludable from gross income under §101(b) shall be treated as consideration paid by the employee for purposes of §72; also, if the amount receivable in three years is equal to or greater than the amount excludable, the entire amount of each installment shall be excluded from gross income until the beneficiary has received the total amount so excludable, not in excess of $5000, after which all amounts received shall be included in gross income.

Revenue Ruling 58-497, 1958-2 C.B. 34, holds that "for purposes of determining whether section 72(d) of the Code is applicable to a contract where the date on which an amount is first received under the contract as an annuity is prior to January 1, 1954, the consideration for the contract contributed by the employee within the meaning of section 72(d)(1)(B) of the Code includes, in addition to amounts actually contributed by the employee, amounts which would have been treated as contributed by the employee as of that date under sections 72(f) and 101(b) of the Code and section 1.72-8 of the regulations as if these provisions were then in effect."

[33] See Reg. §1.402(a)-1(a)(3)(i), quoted infra page 1488.

See Rev. Rul. 55-747, 1955-2 C.B. 228, for the bases upon which one-year term premiums may be computed in determining the amount required to be included in the income of an employee on account of current life insurance protection provided for him under a life or endowment insurance contract held by an employees' trust qualified under 1954 I.R.C. §401(a).

Compare Rev. Rul. 55-193, 1955-1 C.B. 266, which states that where an employer establishes a nontrusteed pension and insurance plan for the benefit of his employee, funded by means of a contract which is the equivalent of a combination group term life insurance and group annuity contract, the premiums paid by the employer which are attributable to the insurance protection are not taxable to the employees. Revenue Ruling 56-633, 1956-2 C.B. 279, deals with the same type of insurance contract as the one referred to in Rev. Rul. 55-193, with the added feature of accident and health insurance. Separate premiums are specified for each type of benefit, and separate reserves are maintained. It is held that the annuity portion of the contract may qualify the arrangement under §401(a). Only the premiums paid by the employer for the annuity benefits, however, are deductible under §404. The other premiums paid are deductible under §162. Also, for the purpose of applying the provisions of §72, only the contributions for the annuity benefits may be included as consideration paid. The extent to which premiums paid by an individual for disability insurance are deductible under §162 is considered in Rev. Rul. 55-264, 1955-1 C.B. 11, Rev. Rul. 55-331, 1955-1 C.B. 271, and Rev.

death of the employee, the portion of the payment which exceeds the cash value of the policy immediately before the death of the insured employee is life insurance and is excludable from the recipient's gross income.[34] So much of the pay-out as equals the cash value is governed as to income tax consequences in the same manner as any other similar pay-out under a qualified plan.[35]

When a contributory qualified plan is involved, the income accumulations which will be tax-free until the pay-out period arrives will include not only income attributable to the employer's contributions but also income attributable to the employee's contributions. The income accumulations attributable to the employee's contributions will be income in respect of a decedent.[36] As is pointed out later,[37] the income accumulations attributable to the employer's contributions are not includible in the employee's gross estate for estate tax purposes, and thus they must be distinguished from the income accumulations attributable to the employee's contributions which are includible in the employee's gross estate.

Rul. 58-480, 1958-2 C.B. 62. In general, no such deduction is available unless the payments are to reimburse the taxpayer, to the extent specified in the policy, for certain business overhead expenses incurred by him during prolonged periods of disability due to injury or sickness.

In Rev. Rul. 55-748, 1955-2 C.B. 234, there is considered a case where an employees' pension trust purchases for the employees retirement income contracts which provide that on the death of an employee the life insurance benefits under the contracts shall be paid to the trustee. Under the terms of the pension plan the trustee is required to apply the proceeds to the payment of subsequent premiums on behalf of the other employees. The contributions of the employer attributable to such insurance are not costs of the pension plan for the purpose of determining the limitations on contributions under §404(a)(1) and may not be currently deducted, but they may be deducted as contributions to the trust in later years in accordance with the provisions of §404(a)(1)(D).

[34] See 1954 I.R.C. §101(a), quoted infra page 1329, and Reg. §1.402(a)-1(a)(4)(ii)(b), quoted infra page 1489.

[35] See Reg. §1.402(a)-1(a)(4)(ii)(c), quoted infra page 1489. In this connection it should be noted that the amounts the employee had to include in his gross income as payments for the life insurance feature are considered as premiums or other consideration paid or contributed by the employee only with respect to any benefits attributable to the contract providing the life insurance protection. See Reg. §1.402(a)-1(a)(3)(i), quoted infra page 1488.

See also Rev. Rul. 57-191, 1957-1 C.B. 162, for an analysis of the income tax consequences of retirement income policies having a life insurance feature.

[36] In H. Lloyd Hess, 31 T.C. 165 (1958), a divided court, in applying the 1939 Code provisions, held that the death benefits under a qualified plan were not income in respect of a decedent. The case was reversed on this point sub nom. Hess. v. Commissioner, 271 F.2d 104 (3d Cir. 1959).

The significance, from an estate planning standpoint, of the presence of income in respect of a decedent in the assets subject to disposition is considered infra page 389.

[37] See discussion relating to employee benefits and estate taxes at page 355 infra.

PROBLEMS

9.1. Under what circumstances should you advise an employee under a qualified pension plan to take payment thereunder in one taxable year?

9.2. A is an employee in the X Company, which has established a qualified pension plan set up under a trust and funded with individual retirement income policies having a life insurance feature. The pension plan is a noncontributory one. Assume that A dies before retirement and that on the date of his death the cash surrender value of his policies is $40,000, but the death benefit payable under the policies is $50,000. The death benefit is payable to W, his wife, in a lump sum. What will be the amount of the gain includible in W's gross income? Assume that A leaves the employment of the X Company prior to the date scheduled for his retirement and that the trustee of the pension trust delivers to him the individual retirement income policies applicable to him. Is the value of such a contract at the time of the distribution made available to A, so that it will be includible in his gross income under Section 402? See Revenue Ruling 55-639, 1955-2 C.B. 230, and Section 1.402(a)-1(a)(2) of the Regulations.

9.3. Under the terms of a qualified noncontributory pension trust, a lump sum is paid to S, the employee's son, on his father's death. S immediately gives the amount paid to him to W, the employee's widow. What tax consequences are produced by these events? See Revenue Ruling 55-460, 1955-2 C.B. 591.

(2) Estate Taxes[38]

Section 2039 (c) of the 1954 Code[39] excludes from the employee's gross estate for federal estate tax purposes the value of an annuity or other payment receivable by any beneficiary, other than the employee's executor, under an employees' trust (or under a contract purchased by an employees' trust) forming part of a pension, stock bonus, or profit-sharing plan which, at the time of the decedent's separation from employment (whether by death or otherwise), or at the time of the termination of the plan if earlier, met the requirements of a qualified plan under Section 401(a) of the 1954 Code.[40] Also, the value of an annuity or other payment under a

---

[38] See generally Comment, Estate Taxation of Employee Death Benefits, 66 Yale L.J. 1217 (1957).

[39] Quoted infra page 1399.

[40] See 1954 I.R.C. §2039(c)(1), quoted infra page 1399.

Revenue Ruling 59-401, 1959-2 C.B. 121. holds that the fact that benefits

retirement annuity contract purchased by an employer (and not by an employees' trust) pursuant to a plan which, at the time of the decedent's separation from employment (by death or otherwise), or at the time of the termination of the plan if earlier, met the requirements of Section 401(a)(3), (4), (5) and (6) is excluded from the employee's gross estate.[41] In both instances, however, the exclusion of the value from the employee's gross estate is restricted to the portion of the value that is not attributable to payments or contributions made by the deceased employee.[42]

If an employee is domiciled in a community property state and his wife dies first, will the value of any portion of the benefits under a qualified plan be includible in her gross estate? If the employee dies first, to what extent can he control the devolution of the death benefits under the plan? If the death benefits are paid to the employee's wife and she then dies, will any part of the payment to her be kept out of her gross estate by Section 2039(c)? It may not be possible at this time to give definitive answers to all the questions which may arise in connection with qualified plans in community property states.[43]

It should be kept in mind that property not includible in the decedent's gross estate is not available for the estate tax marital de-

---

under an exempt employees' trust are paid directly by the insurer issuing the group annuity contract under which the benefits are funded, rather than by the trustee of the trust, does not affect the applicability of §2039(c)(1).

In the instances where a distributee will be entitled to capital gains treatment as provided in §402(a)(2), quoted infra page 1342, the value of the lump sum payment will not be includible in the employee's gross estate when the distribution is made on account of his death, because §2039(c) will exclude the value of the payment from his gross estate.

See Reg. §20.2039-1(b), which points out that the words "annuity or other payment" in §2039(c) includes a lump sum payment.

[41] See 1954 I.R.C. §2039(c)(2), quoted infra page 1399.

[42] If the qualified plan is a noncontributory one, the total payments made on the employee's death will be excluded from his gross estate under §2039(c). See Reg. §20.2040-1(c), quoted infra page 1516, in connection with determining the portion of the total payment made on the employee's death that is excludable from his gross estate when the plan is a contributory one. It should be noted that the portion excludable is not the total payments made minus the amount of the employee's contributions.

[43] In connection with the problems raised in the text, see Kemp v. Metropolitan Life Insurance Co., 205 F.2d 857 (5th Cir. 1953); Boyd v. Curran, 166 F. Supp. 193 (S.D.N.Y. 1958).

For a discussion of the application of §2039 in determining the amount includible in the gross estate of a deceased civil service employee as a result of the annuity payable to his surviving spouse under the United States Civil Service Retirement System, see Rev. Rul. 56-1, 1956-1 C.B. 444. Revenue Ruling 57-446, 1957-2 C.B. 619, holds that state community property laws do not apply to annuities, death benefits, or refunds payable under the Civil Service Retirement Act, as amended, and thus, in applying Rev. Rul. 56-1, there will be no situation where only one half of the value will be includible in the decedent's gross estate.

duction.[44]   Thus, if the employee's wife is to be a beneficiary of employee death benefits that will not be includible in the employee's gross estate, it may be desirable to restrict her beneficial interest in such a manner that her own gross estate will not be augmented by the employee death benefits.[45]

The employee death benefits may be subject to state death taxes, even though they are not subject to any federal estate taxes.[46]

In determining what is includible in the deceased employee's gross estate if a qualified plan is funded with retirement income policies which have a life insurance feature, will Section 2039(c) or Section 2042 [47] (relating to life insurance) apply? Or will one section apply to part and the other section to part? The Regulations take the position that Section 2039(c) applies.[48] The estate tax result where a qualified plan is funded with retirement income policies with a life insurance feature should be compared with the income tax result in such a situation.[49]

PROBLEMS

9.4. Point out the undesirable tax consequences which may result when employee death benefits under a qualified noncontributory plan are paid outright to the employee's widow.

[44] See page 824 infra.

[45] The employee death benefits can be made payable in a lump sum to a trust under which the wife is given beneficial interests that are so restricted that the value of the trust property will not be includible in her gross estate.

[46] For a case which holds that death benefits payable under an employees' retirement plan are subject to state death taxes, see Dolak v. Sullivan, 145 Conn. 497, 144 A.2d 312 (1958). See also Morphet v. Morphet, 19 Ill. App. 304, 152 N.E.2d 492 (1958), as to rights of creditors against an employees' benefit plan.

If the employees' benefit plan provides that the interests of the beneficiaries are not subject to voluntary or involuntary alienation (a spendthrift provision), will such a provision be valid in view of the general policy to the effect that a restraint on involuntary alienation in a trust created by a person for his own benefit will not be given effect? Hines v. Sands, 312 S.W.2d 275 (Tex. Civ. App. 1958), upholds the provision in a profit-sharing trust. See comment on the case in 72 Harv. L. Rev. 1185 (1959).

State income tax consequences are also relevant. A letter from the Chairman of the State Tax Commission of Massachusetts, to Commerce Clearing House, Inc., dated December 22, 1959, CCH Mass. Tax Rep., p. 1593, states that payments from a pension plan after the death of a retired worker to a widow or other surviving relative do not constitute business income and it is not material whether or not the deceased employee contributed to the plan. The result may be different if the payments are made to the deceased employee's estate. See Mass. Ann. Laws C. 62, §9.

[47] Quoted infra page 1402.

[48] See Reg. §20.2039-1(d), quoted infra page 1514, and Reg. §20.2039-2(b), Ex. (3), quoted infra page 1515.

[49] See discussion at page 353 supra.

9.5. If the employee's owned assets are such that a public sale of them on his death will result in their being sold below their real value (for example, stock in a closely held corporation), how can the employee death benefits under a qualified noncontributory plan be made available to the employee's executors to meet death obligations of the employee, without causing the benefits to be includible in his gross estate?

9.6. An employee elects to leave with the trustee of a pension trust the benefits payable to him on retirement. Under the arrangement, the income from the amount left with the trustee is to accumulate and on the employee's death the amount plus accumulated income is to be paid to a designated beneficiary in a lump sum. Consequently, the payment will be made within one taxable year "on account of the death of the employee after his separation from service." Will the distributee be entitled to capital gains treatment under Section 402(a)(2)? Such a payment will be made under a plan which was qualified "at the time of the decedent's separation from employment." Will the payment be excluded from the gross estate of the employee under Section 2039(c)? If the arrangement made by the employee on retirement is irrevocable, will any income tax be payable on the accumulated income and, if so, by whom? See Revenue Ruling 56-656, 1956-2 C.B. 280; Revenue Ruling 60-59, I.R.B. 1960-7, 26.

9.7. Pursuant to a profit-sharing plan, the employer made contributions to a trust which were allocated to the employee's individual account. Under the plan, the employee would, upon his retirement at age sixty, be given the option to have the amount credited to his account (a) paid to him in a lump sum, (b) used to purchase a joint and survivor annuity for him and his designated beneficiary, or (c) left with the trustee under an arrangement whereby interest would be paid to him for his lifetime, with the principal to be paid, at his death, to his designated beneficiary. The plan further provided that if the third method of settlement were selected, the employee would retain the right to have the principal paid to himself in a lump sum up to the time of his death. At the time of the employee's retirement, the profit-sharing plan met the requirements of Section 401(a). Assume that the employee, upon reaching his retirement age, elected to have the amount credited to his account left with the trustee under the interest arrangement; assume, further, that the employee did not exercise his right to have the amount paid to him before his death. Describe the tax consequences. See Section 20.2039-2(b), Ex. (4) of the Regulations.

(3) Gift Taxes

The gift tax provisions have been correlated with the estate tax provisions so that in any case where the value of an annuity or other payment would not be includible in the employee's gross estate under Section 2039(c) of the 1954 Code, no transfer for gift tax purposes will be produced by the exercise or nonexercise by an employee of an election or option whereby an annuity or other payment will become payable to any beneficiary at or after the employee's death.[50]

(4) Self-employed Individuals

Self-employed individuals are placed in a distinctly disadvantageous position economically as compared with individuals employed by others, where the employer has arranged for a qualified retirement plan with all its tax benefits. Self-employed individuals have sought, with some success, to obtain the tax advantages available to those employed by others under qualified plans, by forming associations which are treated as corporations for all purposes under the Internal Revenue Code.[51]

---

[50] See 1954 I.R.C. §2517, quoted infra page 1423. Section 2517 was added by §§23(f) and 68 of the Technical Amendments Act of 1958. Section 68(c) of that act describes the effective date of §2517 as follows: "The amendments made by this section shall apply with respect to the calendar year 1955 and all calendar years thereafter. For calendar years before 1955, the determination as to whether the exercise or nonexercise by an employee of an election or option described in section 2517 of the Internal Revenue Code of 1954 (as added by subsection (a)) is a transfer for purposes of chapter 4 of the Internal Revenue Code of 1939 shall be made as if this section had not been enacted and without inferences drawn from the fact that this section is not made applicable with respect to calendar years before 1955."

[51] Section 7701(a)(3) of the 1954 Code provides that the term "corporation" includes associations, joint stock companies and insurance companies.

In United States v. Kintner, 216 F.2d 418 (9th Cir. 1954), the court held that a group of doctors who had formed an association in which they would be employees could set up an exempt employees' pension trust in which they were the beneficiaries and their income would be limited to their salaries and other sums allowed by agreement rather than consist of a proportionate share of the profits. The Treasury Department originally ruled that it would not follow the Kintner case so far as the pension trust part of the opinion is concerned. Rev. Rul. 56-23, 1956-1 C.B. 598. Such an association of doctors is basically a partnership, the members of which may not be treated as employees. Technical Information Release 61, dated October 10, 1957 (printed in Rev. Rul. 57-546, 1957-2 C.B. 886), modifies the position of the Internal Revenue Service under Rev. Rul. 56-23, by holding that the fact that an association establishes a pension plan is not determinative of whether such organization will be classified as a partnership or an association taxable as a corporation. In Galt v. United States, 175 F. Supp. 360 (N.D. Tex. 1959), corporate status for tax pur-

Set out immediately below are two examples, taken from the Regulations,[52] which illustrate arrangements made by self-employed individuals.

(1) A group of seven doctors forms a clinic for the purpose of furnishing, for profit, medical and surgical services to the public. They each transfer assets to the clinic, and their agreement provides that except upon complete liquidation of the organization on the vote of three-fourths of its members, no member has any individual interest in its assets. Their agreement also provides that neither the death, insanity, bankruptcy, retirement, resignation, nor expulsion of a member shall cause the dissolution of the organization. Under the applicable local law, on the occurrence of such an event, no member has the power to dissolve the organization. The management of the clinic is vested exclusively in an executive committee of four members elected by all the members, and under the applicable local law, no one acting without the authority of this committee has the power to bind the organization by his acts. Members of the clinic are personally liable for all debts of, or claims against, the clinic. Every member has the right to transfer his interest to a doctor who is not a member of the organization, but he must first advise the organization of the proposed transfer and give it the opportunity on a vote of the majority to purchase the interest at its fair market value. The organization has associates and an objective to carry on business and divide the gains therefrom. While it does not have the corporate characteristic of limited liability, it does have the characteristics of centralized management, continuity of life, and a modified form of free transferability of interests. The organization will be classified as an association for all the purposes of the Internal Revenue Code.

(2) A group of seven doctors forms a clinic for the purpose of furnishing, for profit, medical and surgical services to the public. They each transfer assets to the clinic, and their

---

poses was attributed to an association of doctors organized to operate a clinic and practice medicine. The fact that under local law a corporation could not be formed to do these things did not prevent such a tax result.

[52] §301.7701-2(g), Examples (1) and (2). In general, these regulations are applicable only to taxable years beginning after December 31, 1960.

In T.I.R. 262, dated October 28, 1960, 60 CCH Fed. Tax Rep. ¶6670, the Service announced that no determination letters would be issued under §401(a) with respect to the qualification of pension, annuity, profit-sharing or stock bonus plans established by organized professional groups, until the regulations under §7701 had been promulgated. These regulations were filed with the Federal Register on November 15, 1960.

agreement provides that except upon complete liquidation of the organization on the vote of three-fourths of its members, no member has any individual interest in its assets. Their agreement also provides that neither the death, insanity, bankruptcy, retirement, resignation, nor expulsion of a member shall cause the dissolution of the organization. However, under the applicable local law, a member who withdraws does have the power to dissolve the organization. While the agreement provides that the management of the clinic is to be vested exclusively in an executive committee of four members elected by all the members, this provision is ineffective as against outsiders who had no notice of it; and, therefore, the act of any member within the scope of the organization's business binds the organization insofar as such outsiders are concerned. While the agreement declares that each individual doctor alone is liable for acts of malpractice, members of the clinic are, nevertheless, personally liable for all debts of the clinic including claims based on malpractice. No member has the right, without the consent of all the other members, to transfer his interest to a doctor who is not a member of the clinic. The organization has associates and an objective to carry on business and divide the gains therefrom. However, it does not have the corporate characteristics of continuity of life, centralized management, limited liablity, and free transferability of interests. The organization will be classified as a partnership for all purposes of the Internal Revenue Code.

Strenuous efforts have been made and are being made by various groups representing self-employed individuals to obtain legislation that will make available qualified retirement plans to self-employed individuals. The latest version of this legislation is H.R. 10, which was reported to the Senate by the Senate Finance Committee on June 17, 1960, but failed of passage in the Eighty-sixth Congress. The tax benefits under this bill were not as advantageous as the ones available under qualified plans set up by an employer for its employees.[53]

(5) Employees of Charities

Special statutory provisions deal with an annuity contract purchased for an employee of a charity as described in Section 501(c)(3)

---

[53] For example, H.R. 10 did not permit capital gains treatment for lump sum distributions, and there was no exclusion from the gross estate of the self-employed of the value of any annuity or other payment receivable by a beneficiary.

of the 1954 Code.[54]   If the requisite conditions are met, the employee of the charity need not include in his income the annual payments made by the employer for the purchase of the annuity contract; death benefits under the annuity contract are excluded from the employee's gross estate; and the $5000 exclusion from gross income may be available.   The employee of the charity is not as well off from a tax standpoint, however, as he would be if his employer adopted a fully qualified plan, because no capital gains treatment is available for lump sum distributions.

Some charitable organizations enter into contracts with their employees under which certain financial benefits are promised to the employee on retirement, but no funds are segregated to back up the promise of the employer.   The employee is dependent solely on the financial ability of the employer to fulfill the promise when the time comes.   Such an arrangement does not result in current income to the employee because the promise has no present ascertainable dollar worth.   Will such arrangements be deemed the equivalent of an annuity contract purchased by an employer for the employee so that the special statutory provisions referred to in the preceding paragraph will be fully applicable?   This question has not been definitively answered.

c.   Nonqualified Plans[55]

Obviously, nonqualified plans which provide retirement security for an employee are not given the tax benefits available to qualified plans.   Nevertheless, the tax benefits that do exist may justify the use of nonqualified plans in many situations.

An employer may make contributions to a nonqualified plan under which the employee is given nonforfeitable rights.   In such a situation, the employer's contributions are deductible in the year

[54] Section 501(c)(3) is quoted infra page 1356.   The special statutory provisions are §403(b) and (d), quoted infra page 1344, §2039(c)(3), quoted infra page 1399, and §101(b)(2)(B)(iii), quoted infra page 1330.

In Morris Zeltzerman, 34 T.C. —, No. 8 (1960), the court took cognizance of the present form of §403(b), which was brought into being by §23a of the Technical Amendments Act of 1958, and held that nothing in it affected the court's conclusion that compensation which a doctor-taxpayer was to receive from an exempt organization and which at his request was used to buy annuities for him was constructively received by him and currently reportable. The case was affirmed sub nom. Zeltzerman v. Commissioner, 60-2 U.S.T.C. ¶9807 (1st Cir. 1960).   See also Maxwell B. Llewellyn, 19 CCH T.C. Mem 1023 (1960).

See generally Piga, Special Retirement Income Exclusion for Employees of Charitable Organizations, 46 A.B.A.J. 319 (1960).

[55] For a consideration of certain types of nonqualified plans when the employer who adopts the plan is a charitable organization, see discussion at page 361 supra.

made,[56] and are includible in the employee's gross income in that same year.[57]   During the pay-out period, the amount actually dis-

[56] See 1954 I.R.C. §404(a)(5), quoted infra page 1348.

In Rev. Rul. 55-525, 1955-2 C.B. 543, there was considered the situation where a corporation transferred to a revocable inter vivos trust certain shares of its stock. Eventually the shares in the trust were to be transferred to key employees as deferred compensation bonus payments. The ruling held that in view of the fact that the trust was revocable, the income from the trust funds was taxable under 1939 I.R.C. §166 and a deduction was allowed to the corporation for the deferred bonus payments in the year in which distributions were made to the employees and then only to the extent that they were deemed reasonable compensation for services rendered under 1939 I.R.C. §23(p).

In Russell Manufacturing Co. v. United States, 175 F. Supp. 159 (Ct. Cl. 1959), the employer was not allowed to deduct contributions to a nonexempt trust when they were made, even though the rights of the employers as a group were nonforfeitable, when the rights of any one of them could be forfeited. As amounts were paid by the trust, the employer could then deduct them. Technical Information Release 182, dated October 23, 1959, announced that the Internal Revenue Service will not follow the decision in the Russell case, as it is contrary to a long-standing interpretation of the Service. The Release is printed in Rev. Rul. 59-383, 1959-2 C.B. 456.

Mississippi River Fuel Corp. v. Koehler, 164 Supp. 844 (E.D. Mo. 1958), held that contributions by a taxpayer to a trust implementing a deferred compensation plan were not deductible under §23(p)(1)(C) of the 1939 Code (1954 I.R.C. §404(a)(3)), where the plan did not limit the taxpayer's contributions to the profits but, instead, determined its contributions on the basis of the amounts the employees contributed to the plan. The contributions were not deductible under §23(p)(1)(D) (1954 I.R.C. §404(a)(5)), as the employees' rights were forfeitable in the event of discharge for cause, voluntary withdrawal from the plan or termination of employment. The case was affirmed in 266 F.2d 190 (8th Cir. 1959), cert. denied, 361 U.S. 827 (1959). See also Mississippi River Fuel Corp., 29 T.C. 1248 (1958), aff'd sub nom. Mississippi River Fuel Corp. v. Commissioner, 266 F.2d 190 (8th Cir. 1959), cert. denied, 361 U.S. 827 (1959); Wesley Heat Treating Co., 30 T.C. 10 (1958), aff'd sub nom. Wesley Heat Treating Co. v. Commissioner, 267 F.2d 853 (7th Cir. 1959).

[57] See 1954 I.R.C. §402(b), quoted infra page 1343, and §403(c), quoted infra page 1345.

See Rev. Rul. 56-673, 1956-2 C.B. 281, in which it was held that employees were not entitled to deferred tax treatment in regard to employer's contributions to the purchase of individual retirement income endowment contracts where the employees were the owners of the contracts and the plan could not be considered a qualified one. See also Rev. Rul. 57-37, 1957-1 C.B. 18, where it was held that contributions made by an employer to separate and independently controlled trusts for each employee were taxable to the employees in the year they were made, when the employee's rights under the trust were fully vested and nonforfeitable. Revenue Ruling 57-37 held that the employee was taxable under §61 of the 1954 Code, quoted infra page 1325; Rev. Rul. 57-528, 1957-2 C.B. 263, modifies Rev. Rul. 57-37 by holding that the employee is taxable under the provisions of §402(b). Revenue Rulings 57-37 and 57-528 are distinguished in Rev. Rul. 60-31, I.R.B. 1960-5, 17, which is quoted at length infra page 372. George W. Drysdale, 32 T.C. 378 (1959), held that the employee was taxable on payments made by an employer to a trust in consideration of services rendered, as the payments were made to the trust when the employee's rights under the trust were nonforfeitable. The case was reversed and remanded sub nom. Drysdale v. Commissioner, 277 F.2d 413 (6th Cir. 1960), on the ground that the payments were not constructively received where, under the terms of the employment contract, the taxpayer did not have

tributed or made available to any distributee[58] will be taxable to him in the year it is distributed or made available under Section 72 of the 1954 Code,[59] except that Section 72(e)(3) does not apply.[60] In view of the fact that the contributions of the employer will have been included in the employee's gross income for the year in which the employer made them, the taxable income during the pay-out period is likely to be small.[61] The value of the annuity or other payment receivable by any beneficiary by reason of surviving the employee is includible in the employee's gross estate for federal estate tax purposes[62] and to the extent that the value is represented

---

any right to immediate possession of the payments; also the economic benefit theory was not applicable, since the taxpayer was restricted from exercising any dominion over the funds in the possession of the trustees. Revenue Ruling 58-307, 1958-1 C.B. 206, considered a nonexempt plan under which an employee's interest did not become vested until he reached age sixty and then was made available to him only in the discretion of the trustee until he retired. The employee, after he reached sixty, relinquished to the trustee all his rights under the plan, and it was held that such a relinquishment did not result in federal income tax liability to the employee or to the trust, but his interest was sufficiently vested so that the relinquishment was a transfer for gift tax purposes. Furthermore, since the benefits to the other employees from the relinquishment depended so much on the discretion in the trustee, no gift of a present interest was involved and no annual exclusion was available.

Revenue Ruling 55-691, 1955-2 C.B. 21, held that where an employee's salary is guaranteed by two individuals who propose to eliminate their liability as guarantors by placing a stated sum in trust or by buying an annuity with it, either arrangement to be used to make up the present deficiency in salary but to continue to be paid to the employee whether he continues in employment or not, the employer will receive income in the year the arrangment is set up in the amount placed in the trust or the annuity.

[58] Sections 402(b) and 403(c), which govern the taxability of a beneficiary under a nonqualified plan where the employee has a nonforfeitable right, differ in that the former applies no matter who is the distributee but the latter applies only when the distributee is the employee. For a similar difference in connection with pay-outs under a qualified plan, see the discussion at page 350 supra, which is equally applicable here.

[59] Quoted infra page 1325.

[60] Quoted infra page 1327.

[61] See 1954 I.R.C. §72(f), quoted infra page 1327. Section 72(d), quoted infra page 1326, which changes the normal operation of §72 when the employee's contributions are recoverable in three years, is not applicable unless part of the consideration for the employee annuity has been contributed by the employer.

[62] See 1954 I.R.C. §2039(a) and (b), quoted infra page 1398.

In Libbey v. United States, 147 F. Supp. 383 (N.D. Cal. 1956), an employer purchased a ten-year annuity for an employee and the annuity contract provided that if the employee should die after the commencement of the monthly payments and before their completion, the payments should be continued to his widow. Under the annuity contract the employee had an option to convert the ten-year annuity to a life annuity prior to the commencement of the annuity payments. It was held that no part of the value of the annuity was includible in the employee's gross estate because no transfer of property to anyone was made by him. His failure to exercise the option did not have the effect of a transfer.

by property which will be taxable income when paid out, income in respect of a decedent is involved.[63]   If the employee makes an irrevocable election as to the pay-out of the fund in which he has nonforfeitable rights, and persons other than the employee receive beneficial rights in the pay-out arrangement, he will have made a gift for federal gift tax purposes.[64]   The $5000 income tax exclusion available under some circumstances in connection with employee death benefits is not available where, as here, the employee's rights in a nonqualified plan are nonforfeitable.[65]   Capital gains treatment, of course, is not accorded a lump sum distribution under any nonqualified plan.

If the employee's rights under the nonqualified plan are forfeitable, then the employer's contributions to the plan are not deductible in the year made[66] and are not includible in the employee's gross income in that year.[67]   If the employee's forfeitable rights later become nonforfeitable, from that time on, the tax consequences are those attaching to a nonqualified plan where the employee has nonforfeitable rights.[68]   During the pay-out period under a nonqualified plan which, prior to the pay-out period, gave the employee only forfeitable rights, the amount of each payment should be taxable income to the distributee.[69]   The value of the

---

The court held in Glenn v. Hanner, 212 F.2d 483 (6th Cir. 1954), that benefits paid to a widow of a deceased employee (who died at age forty-six) were not includible in the estate of the deceased employee for estate tax purposes where they were paid under a limited power of appointment exercised by the employee under a profit-sharing trust, to which only his employer made contributions, and the amount of the contributions was in the sole discretion of the employer.   The trust provided that benefits were not payable to the employee until he reached age sixty-one or ceased to be an employee, and that on the death of the employee all his rights should cease and determine, and the principal and interest should be paid over to the employee's widow or descendants in such shares as he might appoint by his will.

[63] The significance from an estate planning standpoint of income being income in respect of a decedent is discussed infra page 389.

[64] See Reg. §25.2511-1(h)(10), quoted infra page 1546.

[65] See 1954 I.R.C. §101(b), quoted infra page 1329.

[66] See discussion in note 56 supra.   In Samuel J. Coppola, 36 T.C. —, No. 48 (1960), the court determined that the employee's rights under a nonqualified plan were forfeitable.

[67] See 1954 I.R.C. §402(b), quoted infra page 1343, and §403(c), quoted infra page 1345.

[68] See Reg. §1.402(b)-1(a)(1), quoted infra page 1489, Reg. §1.403(b)-1(a), quoted infra page 1491.

[69] If the payment is made in a lump sum and §72 is deemed to apply, §72(e)(3) should be available because there is no section of the 1954 Code that specifically excludes the availability of §72(e)(3) in regard to pay-outs under nonqualified plans under which the employee's rights are forfeitable.

If the pay-out is by reason of the death of the employee, the $5000 income tax exclusion is available under §101(b), quoted infra page 1329.

annuity or payment receivable by a beneficiary by reason of surviving the employee will be includible in his gross estate[70] and to the extent that this value is represented by property which will be taxable income when paid out, income in respect of a decedent is involved.[71]

The employer may elect to make payments of some kind to the employee on his retirement or to some member of the employee's family on his death. In either case, the employee does not have forfeitable rights in a nonqualified plan. He has no rights in any plan. If payments are made to the employee on retirement where no obligation existed to make the payments, will the payments be deemed gifts by the employer to the employee or will they be considered compensation for services rendered and be includible in the employee's gross income? The answer to this question is "it depends." [72] If the payments are made to a member of the em-

[70] See 1954 I.R.C. §2039(a) and (b), quoted infra page 1398.

[71] The significance of the presence of income in respect of a decedent in estate planning is discussed infra page 389.

[72] For holdings that the employee has received a gift from the employer, see the following: Peters v. Smith, 221 F.2d 721 (3d Cir. 1955); Neville v. Brodrick, 235 F.2d 263 (10th Cir. 1956); Adams v. Riordan, 57-2 U.S.T.C. ¶9770 (D. Vt. 1957). For opposite holdings, see Deasy v. Smith, 56-1 U.S.T.C. ¶9120 (E.D. Pa. 1955); Goethals v. United States, 147 F. Supp. 757 (Ct. Cl. 1957); Joseph Martin Umstead, 14 CCH T.C. Mem. 591 (1955); Hampton Leedom, 15 CCH T.C. Mem. 1180 (1956); Stuart L. Baltimore, 17 CCH T.C. Mem. 388 (1958); Fannie Brittelle, 32 T.C. 1332 (1959).

In Richard L. Harrington, 17 CCH T.C. Mem. 960 (1958), an employee of a partnership desired to build an addition to his house, which would cost $10,-000, and his employers supplied him with the money. The partners did not take a deduction for the payment, and no gift tax returns were filed by them. The court concluded that although no single factor was sufficient to establish a donative intent, when all factors were considered together they were conclusive evidence that the partners intended a gift.

In Stanton v. United States, 268 F.2d 727 (2d Cir. 1959), a payment was made by the Corporation of Trinity Church to its resigning president and was described as a "gratuity," but the resolution authorizing payment also said it was in "appreciation of services rendered," and the corporation was released from all rights and claims to pension and retirement benefits. The payment was deemed additional compensation. The case was vacated and remanded in 363 U.S. 278, 80 Sup. Ct. 1190, 4 L. Ed. 2d 1218 (1960). On remand, in Stanton v. United States, 186 F. Supp. 393 (E.D.N.Y. 1960), the payment was deemed a gift rather than severance pay, on the basis of findings of fact concerning the basic reasons for the payment of $20,000 to the retiring officer.

Duberstein v. Commissioner, 265 F.2d 28 (6th Cir. 1959), involved a Cadillac automobile received by the taxpayer for furnishing the names of potential customers to a business friend. The court reversed the Tax Court decision holding that the car was intended as remuneration for services rendered, because the taxpayer's evidence that the car was in fact a gift was not challenged by contrary or destructive analysis. The Court of Appeals, however, was reversed in 363 U.S. 278, 80 Sup. Ct. 1190, 4 L. Ed. 2d 1218 (1960). Its decision is vacated in Duberstein v. Commissioner, 60-2 U.S.T.C. ¶9788 (6th C.r. 1960). In Kaiser v. United States, 262 F.2d 367 (7th Cir. 1958), aff'd, 363 U.S. 299, 80 Sup. Ct. 1204, 4 L. Ed. 2d 1233 (1960), the value of foods and

ployee's family on his death, they may or may not be income in the hands of the recipient, depending on the facts.[73]   If they are income, the $5000 exclusion under Section 101(b) of the 1954 Code[74]

other items received from a union by an employee on strike was held to be a nontaxable gift.

The Supreme Court decisions in Duberstein, Kaiser and Stanton are considered in Beatty, Supreme Court Gift-Income Cases, 46 A.B.A.J. 1242 (1960). In applying the test of the Duberstein case, that whether a transfer is a gift is essentially one of fact, the lower court determination that a gift was made was not clearly erroneous and thus was affirmed in United States v. Kasynsky, 284 F.2d 143 (10th Cir. 1960).   Under the Duberstein test, the transfer was not deemed a gift in Abe A. Danish, CCH T.C. Mem. 1960-240.

In Willi v. United States, 60-1 U.S.T.C. ¶9164 (S.D.N.Y. 1959), it was held that stock transferred to an employee by stockholders of the employer was a gift and not compensation.

Revenue Ruling 60-14, I.R.B. 1960-3, 7, holds that the taxpayer received income and not a gift when the money he received came from a committee composed of officials in the organization in which he was an official, and the money was raised by the committee to pay his legal expenses in connection with litigation of a personal nature because the litigation would focus national attention on the organization.

Alvin T. Perkins, 34 T.C. —, No. 13 (1960), was a case concerned with payments to a retired minister.   The payments were deemed income to him because they were made in accordance with an established plan and past practice, because there was no close relationship between the recipient and the bulk of the contributing congregations, and because the amounts paid were not determined in the light of the needs of the individual recipients.   In view of these facts, Rev. Rul. 55-422, 1955-1 C.B. 14, which held that payments to a retired minister were not income to him but a gift, where they were not made in accordance with past practice and where there was a close relationship, etc., was not controlling.

In Stephen S. Jackson, 25 T.C. 1106 (1956), the taxpayer left a law practice in New York and took a position in California with a corporation.   After a year the corporation terminated his employment and paid him a sum in excess of his salary.   The payment was conditional upon the taxpayer agreeing to keep confidential certain information he had acquired and upon discharging the corporation of all claims.   The additional payment was taken as a salary deduction for past service on the books of the corporation.   The court held that the additional payment was not a gift but was income to the taxpayer, though there was no legal obligation to make the payment.

L. Gordon Walker, 25 T.C. 832 (1956), held that the employer's gift of six months' salary to a retiring corporate officer was income to the officer where the stockholders had not been asked to approve the gift and the employer treated it as an operating expense.

[73] For recent cases holding that the recipient does not receive taxable income, see Bounds v. United States, 262 F.2d 876 (4th Cir. 1958); United States v. Allinger, 275 F.2d 421 (6th Cir. 1960); Estate of Frank J. Foote, 28 T.C. 547 (1957); Estate of John A. Maycann, Sr., 29 T.C. 81 (1957).   For opposite holdings, see Beggy v. Commissioner, 226 F.2d 584 (3d Cir. 1955); Lengsfield v. Commissioner, 241 F.2d 508 (5th Cir. 1957); Fisher v. United States, 129 F. Supp. 759 (D. Mass. 1955); Ivan Y. Nickerson, CCH T.C. Mem. 1960-270.

[74] Quoted infra page 1329.

Revenue Ruling 59-64, 1959-1 C.B. 31, points out that where an employee dies in the middle of the month and the whole month's salary is paid to his beneficiary, the portion paid for the period subsequent to his death is not an amount to which the employee possessed a nonforfeitable right while living and hence qualifies under §101(b) for the exclusion up to $5000.

will be available.[75] Nothing should be added to the employee's gross estate for federal estate tax purposes as a consequence of a

[75] Does §101(b), have the effect of causing the inclusion in the gross income of the employee's spouse of so much of the voluntary payments as exceeds $5000? In Rodner v. United States, 149 F. Supp. 233 (S.D.N.Y. 1957), the court used the following language on this point: "Section 101(b) . . . eliminates the provisions limiting to contractual death benefits the application of the $5,000 exemption. To me the effect of this would seem to be to withdraw the complete exemption that gratuitous death benefits had enjoyed and to substitute an exemption up to $5,000. In the complete revision effected by the 1954 Code the general language exempting gifts is controlled by the particular language of section 101(b) limiting the exemption of death benefits to $5,000. Gifts in general are exempt but gifts in the form of death benefits are taxable insofar as they exceed $5,000." Reed v. United States, 177 F. Supp. 205 (W.D. Ky. 1959), *aff'd sub nom.* United States v. Reed, 277 F.2d 456 (6th Cir. 1960), however, held that a gift to an employee's widow was not subject to the $5000 limitation of §101(b). The Reed case is followed in Cowan v. United States, 60-2 U.S.T.C. ¶9674 (N.D. Ga. 1960). In Rev. Rul. 60-326, 60 CCH Fed. Tax Rep. ¶6615, the Internal Revenue Service announced that it will not follow the Reed case. The Service's position is that these payments are employee death benefits controlled by §101(b) and that the gift exclusion provisions of §102 are inapplicable. In Estate of Melvin Pierpont, 35 T.C. —, No. 10 (1960), the court, relying on the Duberstein case, concluded, that the payments to the taxpayer in excess of the $5000 death benefit provided for by §101(b) were taxable to her when they were made pursuant to a resolution of the corporation, of which the taxpayer's deceased husband was president, and the resolution stated that the payments were a continuation of the salary of the deceased president. The court declined to examine the Reed case. The Pierpont case is followed in Estate of Martin Kuntz, Sr., CCH T.C. Mem. 1960-247.

In Friedlander v. United States, 58-1 U.S.T.C. ¶9182 (E.D. Wis. 1958), a corporation paid the widow of a deceased employee an amount equal to one year's salary for the employee, and paid a state gift tax on the amount. The widow owned shares of stock in the corporation and the Commissioner contended that any payment to her out of corporate earnings must be taxed to her as a dividend regardless of the corporation's intent in making the payment. The court held that the payment was a gift and not taxable income. George M. Ryder v. Commissioner, 60-1 U.S.T.C. ¶9370 (8th Cir. 1960), held that payments to the widow of an officer of a corporation made pursuant to an agreement to deter her from selling her stock represented a distribution to her of company profits.

Florence S. Luntz, 29 T.C. 647 (1958), held that the payments to the widow of a deceased employee equaling two years' salary were gifts, even though the payments were made by a family corporation and were made pursuant to a resolution which, in addition to authorizing the payments to the widow in question, also authorized payments to the wives of two other living officers in the event of the death of those officers.

In Estate of Charles J. Ginsberg, 17 CCH T.C. Mem. 472 (1958), the corporation paid $25,000 to the widow of a deceased officer, and even though the corporate resolution represented the payments as a gratuity, the court held that the amount paid was taxable as the officer's salary where it appeared that he had received a considerably smaller salary than that of a comparable officer for preceding years. The case was affirmed sub nom. Estate of Charles J. Ginsberg v. Commissioner, 271 F.2d 511 (5th Cir. 1959).

Technical Information Release 87, dated August 25, 1958, 58 CCH Fed. Tax Rep. ¶6662, announces that the Internal Revenue Service will no longer litigate, under the 1939 Code, cases involving the taxability of payments to a

voluntary payment by the employer to a member of the employee's family on his death.[76]

deceased employee's widow unless there is clear evidence that they were intended as compensation for services or the payments may be considered as dividends. Revenue Ruling 58-613, 1958-2 C.B. 914, incorporates T.I.R. 87.

Packard v. United States, 179 F. Supp. 508 (S.D.N.Y. 1959), upheld the denial of motions for a summary judgment by the government and by the taxpayer where the taxpayer had received $40,000 from her deceased husband's employer "in recognition of your husband's long and valued relationship to our office and in line with an office custom," and the government was claiming that the sum was income to the widow. The court said that there was no convincing evidence that the payments were compensation for past services or that the employer intended the payments to be a gift.

The related problem is the right of the corporation to take a deduction for the payment to the widow. The deduction is allowed in Fort Orange Paper Co., CCH T.C. Mem. 1960-170. Fifth Avenue Coach Lines, Inc., 31 T.C. 1080 (1959), holds that tax treatment of payments made to an employee's widow is not conclusive as to whether the payments are ordinary and necessary business expenses. The case was affirmed in part and reversed in part on other issues sub nom. Commissioner v. Fifth Avenue Coach Lines, Inc., 281 F.2d 556 (2d Cir. 196).

[76] See Estate of Albert L. Salt, 17 T.C. 92 (1951). See also Rev. Rul. 55-581, 1955-2 C.B. 381 (the value of gratuitous payments to the widow, children or other dependent relatives of a member of the armed forces who dies while on active duty are not includible in his gross estate); Rev. Rul. 55-609, 1955-2 C.B. 34 (the value of a gratuity paid to a widow of a deceased congressman is a gift and is not includible in his gross estate).

In Molter v. United States, 146 F. Supp. 497 (E.D.N.Y. 1956), an employer provided for a death benefit on termination of service prior to normal retirement of an employee, in an amount equal to two years' pay. The employer reserved the right to terminate, withdraw, or modify the plan at its discretion, but such modification or withdrawal was to have no effect on any survivorship benefit which had accrued prior thereto as the result of the death of the employee. Under these circumstances the court held that at the time of his death, the employee possessed no property interest which he could have transferred to the survivor-beneficiary, and consequently the amount credited to the survivor beneficiary was not includible in the employee's gross estate.

The court in Graybar Electric Co., 29 T.C. 818 (1958), found that so-called "special death benefits" were actually payments made to supplement the low price at which stock was required to be offered to the corporation after the death of the stockholder. Under these circumstances the payments were not deductible by the corporation, and presumably, the value of the stock in the stockholder's estate for estate tax purposes would include the additional payments under the "special death benefits." The case was affirmed sub nom. Graybar Electric Co. v. Commissioner, 267 F.2d 403 (2d Cir. 1959), *cert. denied*, 361 U.S. 822 (1959).

In Estate of Eli L. Garber, 17 CCH T.C. Mem. 646 (1958), the decedent's employer paid to his estate the entire salary for the salary period in which the decedent died, and it was held that even though the amount was paid "as salary," it nevertheless was a gratuity, except as to the amount due for the portion of the salary period which preceded the decedent's death. Consequently, only the latter amount was includible in the decedent's gross estate. The estate had paid an income tax on the entire salary and the court refused to permit the estate to credit any excess income tax payment against any deficiency found in the estate tax, because the court determined that it was without jurisdiction to grant the application sought by the estate as long as no deficiency had been determined for the income tax of the estate for the period

Finally, the employer may contract to make payments to the employee on his retirement or to a member of his family on his death[77] where the employee and his family must rely solely on the continued solvency of the employer for the fulfillment of the promise. In such a situation the employee will be required to include the deferred compensation in his gross income only in the taxable years in which he receives the payments, because the promise made to him by the employer is unsecured. The payments made to a member of the employee's family on his death are likewise includible in the recipient's gross income in the year of payment.[78] The value of the rights under the contract are includible in his gross estate for federal estate tax purposes[79] and to the extent

---

in question. Further, the case considered whether the decedent's interest in a pension trust created by his employer constituted property includible in his gross estate. Various provisions in the pension trust placed considerable control in the pension boards, but the court held that the decedent's interest was includible in his gross estate because the pension boards did not have absolute power and authority over the rights of the employees to benefits under the plan but had to make payments to the beneficiaries designated by the employee. An appeal was taken only on the portion of the Tax Court's decision which is considered in the preceding sentence, and the case was affirmed sub nom. Estate of Eli L. Garber v. Commissioner, 271 F.2d 97 (3d Cir. 1959).

In Estate of John C. Morrow, 19 T.C. 1068 (1954), an employer paid all of the premiums on, and held all of the incidents of ownership of, a $10,000 policy of insurance on the life of a key employee, and the insurance was payable to the employer as sole beneficiary. The employer notified the employee that its purpose was to pay $5000 from the proceeds to a member of the immediate family of the employee designated by him. It was held that no part of the proceeds of the policy was includible in the gross estate of the employee under 1939 I.R.C. §811(g)(2). The agreement between the employer and the employee was not a contract of insurance, and the sum paid to the employee's daughter thereunder was not a payment of insurance. It was held that the employee did not pay the premiums on the policy indirectly, even though the Commissioner contended that he did, because the premiums paid by the employer were really extra compensation to the employee. The payment of the premiums by the employer did not represent income taxable to the employee.

[77] The contract to make payments to a member of the employee's family on his death may be to make the deferred payments which would have been made to the employee had he lived, or to make payments to the employee's family on his death which have no relationship to deferred payments promised the employee.

[78] Whether the $5000 exclusion under 1954 I.R.C. §101(b), quoted infra page 1329, will be available will depend on whether the employee possessed, immediately before his death, a nonforfeitable right to receive the amounts while living. If he had such a nonforfeitable right, the $5000 exclusion is not available to the recipient.

[79] See 1954 I.R.C. §2039(a) and (b) quoted infra page 1398.

In Estate of Albert B. King, 20 T.C. 930 (1953), the employee's rights to bonus payments existed pursuant to a contract, but they were subject to forfeiture so far as undelivered portions of any bonus payments were concerned

that the value is represented by what will be income when paid to the recipient, income in respect of a decedent is involved.[80] If the employee, during his lifetime, makes an irrevocable arrangement

---

if he left the employ of the company. If the employee died, his bonus rights were payable to his estate. The court held that the employee had property in the bonus rights under 1939 I.R.C. §811(a), and consequently the value of the bonus rights was includible in his gross estate.

In Goodman v. Granger, 56-1 U.S.T.C. ¶11595 (W.D. Pa. 1956), the decedent employee entered into a contract with his employer calling for contingent payments to him, or in event of his death, to his nominee, in the amount of $6000 a year for fifteen years. These payments were forfeitable on the occurrence of events within the personal control of the employee, such as failing to devote his best efforts to his job or engaging in a competing business, etc. The court held that the value of these contract rights immediately before the decedent employee's death was zero because no one would pay anything for rights forfeitable by conduct within the control of the employee. Thus no estate tax could be assessed with respect to these rights. The case was reversed in 243 F.2d 264 (3d Cir. 1957), where the court held that the contracts should be valued immediately after the decedent's death rather than at the moment before, so that such contracts did have a value. Certiorari was denied in 355 U.S. 835 (1957).

Revenue Ruling 60-70, I.R.B. 1960-8, 21, is concerned with annuities, lump sum distributions and residual death benefits paid to any person specified in subsection (a), (b), (c), (d) or (f)(1) of §5 of the Railroad Retirement Act of 1937, as amended, and holds that they are not includible in the gross estate of a deceased railroad employee under 1954 I.R.C. §2039, or under any other section of the Code. Section 2039 is not applicable because such payments are made pursuant to a law enacted by Congress rather than as a result of any contract or agreement entered into by the decedent or arising by reason of his employment. No other section is applicable because the decedent has no control over the designation of the beneficiary or the amount of the payment, since these are fixed by statute and since the decedent has no interest in the fund from which the payment is made. It is held, however, that payments under §5(f)(2) of the Railroad Retirement Act which pass to persons designated by the decedent are includible in his gross estate under 1954 I.R.C. §2033, quoted infra page 1396.

In Provident Trust Co. v. United States, 170 F. Supp. 74 (E.D. Pa. 1959), an employee's retirement plan was involved under which an annuity contract was acquired for the decedent, and he paid part of the premiums and the company paid part. The court held that the portion of the death payment to the employee's beneficiary which was attributable to the employer's contribution was not includible in the employee's gross estate because the company did not make such payments as a part of the terms of the employment but did it voluntarily. This case was decided under the 1939 Code. It would seem that the employer's contribution was made by reason of the employee's employment and thus would be under §2039(b) unless the arrangement was exempt under §2039(c).

In Beaver Trust Co. v. United States, 184 F. Supp. 553 (W.D. Pa. 1960), a corporation acquired an annuity for its president on his life and the corporation was named the beneficiary of the proceeds on his death. The corporation, after the death of the president, assigned the policy to his estate. The court found that the decedent possessed a contractual right to the policy and included it in his gross estate under the 1939 Code.

[80] The significance of the presence of income in respect of a decedent in estate planning is discussed page 389 infra.

for the disposition of the deferred compensation under which a person other than himself is benefited, he may have made a gift for federal gift tax purposes.[81]

Printed below are two illustrations of deferred compensation contracts which appear in Revenue Ruling 60-31, I.R.B. 1960-5, 17. As to both of these illustrations, the ruling recognizes that the additional compensation to be received by the taxpayer will be includible in his gross income only in the taxable years in which he actually receives installment payments. The ruling also points out that under these unfunded plans the employer is not entitled to any deduction except in a year of payment.[82]

(1) On January 1, 1958, the taxpayer and corporation X executed an employment contract under which the taxpayer is to be employed by the corporation in an executive capacity for a period of five years. Under the contract, the taxpayer is entitled to a stated annual salary and to additional compensation of $10x$ dollars for each year. The additional compensation will be credited to a bookkeeping reserve account and will be deferred, accumulated, and paid in annual installments equal to one-fifth of the amount in the reserve as of the close of the year immediately preceding the year of first payment. The payments are to begin only upon (a) termination of the taxpayer's employment by the corporation; (b) the taxpayer's becoming a part-time employee of the corporation; or (c) the taxpayer's becoming partially or totally incapacitated. Under the terms of the agreement, corporation X is under a merely contractual obligation to make the payments when due, and the parties did not intend that the amounts in the reserve be held by the corporation in trust for the taxpayer.

The contract further provides that if the taxpayer should fail or refuse to perform his duties, the corporation will be relieved of any obligation to make further credits to the reserve (but not of the obligation to distribute amounts previously contributed); but, if the taxpayer should become incapacitated from performing his duties, then credits to the reserve will continue for one year from the date of the incapacity, but not beyond the expiration of the five-year term of the contract. There is no specific provision in the contract for forfeiture by the taxpayer of his right to distribution from the reserve; and, in the event he should die prior to his receipt

[81] See Reg. §25.2511-1(h)(10), quoted infra page 1546.
[82] Even in a year of payment, the employer is entitled to a deduction only to the extent allowable under 1954 I.R.C. §404(a), quoted infra page 1346.

in full of the balance in the account, the remaining balance is distributable to his personal representative at the rate of one-fifth per year for five years, beginning three months after his death.

(2) The taxpayer is an officer and director of corporation *A*, which has a plan for making future payments of additional compensation for current services to certain officers and key employees designated by its board of directors. This plan provides that a percentage of the annual net earnings (before Federal income taxes) in excess of 4,000x dollars is to be designated for division among the participants in proportion to their respective salaries. This amount is not currently paid to the participants; but, the corporation has set up on its books a separate account for each participant and each year it credits thereto the dollar amount of his participation for the year, reduced by a proportionate part of the corporation's income taxes attributable to the additional compensation. Each account is also credited with the net amount, if any, realized from investing any portion of the amount in the account.

Distributions are to be made from these accounts annually beginning when the employee (1) reaches age 60, (2) is no longer employed by the company, including cessation of employment due to death, or (3) becomes totally disabled to perform his duties, whichever occurs first. The annual distribution will equal a stated percentage of the balance in the employee's account at the close of the year immediately preceding the year of first payment, and distributions will continue until the account is exhausted. However, the corporation's liability to make these distributions is contingent upon the employee's (1) refraining from engaging in any business competitive to that of the corporation, (2) making himself available to the corporation for consultation and advice after retirement or termination of his services, unless disabled, and (3) retaining unencumbered any interest or benefit under the plan. In the event of his death, either before or after the beginning of payments, amounts in an employee's account are distributable in installments computed in the same way to his designated beneficiaries or heirs-at-law. Under the terms of the compensation plan, corporation *A* is under a merely contractual obligation to make the payments when due, and the parties did not intend that the amounts in each account be held by the corporation in trust for the participants.

d. Stock Options

If an employee has an option to purchase stock of his corporate employer at a specified price, the employee owns an asset of value as soon as the market price of the employer's stock exceeds the employee's option price. The estate plan for the owner of such an asset must take into account the special problem the asset presents. These problems may be particularly complicated when the option is what is called a "restricted stock option." The discussion which follows relates first to restricted stock options and concludes with some observations relating to other stock options.

(1) Restricted Stock Options[83]

Substantial tax benefits attach to an option that qualifies as a restricted stock option. In order to qualify, the option must meet the tests laid down in the 1954 Code.[84] At the time the option is granted,[85] the optionee must be an employee of the optionor.[86]

[83] See generally Schlesinger, Selected Problems in the Use of Restricted Stock Options, 36 Taxes 709 (1958).

Where the employee owns stock in the employer corporation at the time a restricted stock option is granted, he must keep in mind 1954 I.R.C. §1091 if he plans to make any sale of the stock which he already owns and the stock will be sold at a loss. Section 1091 prevents any loss deduction in the event that, within a period beginning thirty days before the date of the sale and ending thirty days after such date, the taxpayer has acquired by purchase, or has entered into a contract or option so to acquire, substantially identical stock. Revenue Ruling 56-452, 1956-2 C.B. 525, holds that for the purpose of §1091, an employee who is granted a restricted stock option will be held to have entered into the option to acquire the stock on the date on which the option is granted to him and will also be deemed to have acquired the shares of stock pursuant to the option on the date on which the certificate for such shares of stock is issued. Thus he should not sell the stock he already owns within the period specified in §1091 with respect to the time the option is acquired, and likewise he should not make a sale within such period with respect to the date on which the option is exercised and the certificates are issued to him.

Revenue Ruling 59-297, 1959-2 C.B. 124, holds that an option to purchase stock of an employer corporation in combination with some other property interest is not a restricted stock option within the meaning of §421(d)(1).

[84] See 1954 I.R.C. §421(d), quoted infra page 1350. The original statutory treatment of restricted stock options was brought into the picture by §218 of the Revenue Act of 1950, 64 Stat. 942, which became 1939 I.R.C. §130A.

[85] The ascertainment of the time and date of granting an option may present problems. See Reg. §1.421-1(b).

[86] See Reg. §1.421-2(a)(3) as to what is essential to establish the relationship of employer and employee. Section 1.421-1(b)(2) brings out that if an option is granted to an individual upon condition that he will become an employee of the corporation, the option is not deemed granted until the date he becomes an employee.

Revenue Ruling 59-140, 1959-1 C.B. 92, discusses the effect on restricted

The option must not be transferable by the employee otherwise than by will or by the laws of descent and distribution and must be exercisable, during the employee's life, only by him.[87]   The option must not be exercisable after the expiration of ten years from the date it is granted.   The employee at the time the option is granted must not own stock possessing more than 10 percent of the total combined voting power of all classes of stock of the employer corporation.[88]   Finally, the option price must be at least 85 percent of the fair market value of the stock subject to the option at the time it is granted, but for the purpose of applying this test, where the option price is determined by a formula,[89] the price is computed as if the option were exercised on the day it was granted.[90]

---

stock options of leaves of absence due to military service or other bona fide leaves.   If the option is granted while the optionee is on leave, it will not qualify as a restricted stock option.   If, however, it was granted before the leave, it can be exercised while on leave, or by his estate if he dies on leave, and may qualify.   Also, if it was granted before the leave and exercised after the return from the leave, it may qualify.

[87] See Reg. §1.421-2(a)(4).

[88] The 10 percent rule is not applicable if, at the time the option is granted, the option price is at least 110 percent of the fair market value of the stock subject to the option and the option by its terms is not exercisable after the expiration of five years from the date it is granted.   See 1954 I.R.C. §421(d)(1)(C), quoted infra page 1350.   See also Reg. §1.421-2(a)(2).

In determining whether the 10 percent test is met, stock owned by certain relatives of the employee will be attributed to him as well as stock in an estate or trust of which he is a beneficiary.   See Reg. §1.421-2(b).   Revenue Ruling 58-325, 1958-1 C.B. 212, holds that the individual is considered to own proportionately the present interests of qualifying relatives in a trust but not remainder interests, whether vested or contingent.   No opinion is advanced as to whether an interest is a present interest, for this purpose, when the income of a trust is to be accumulated and later paid to a definitely designated beneficiary.

[89] The formula method of determining the option price is described in Reg. §1.421-1(d)(2).   In a declining market, the option loses its value when the option price is a fixed amount.   The formula method of determining the option price is designed to preserve some value for the option in a declining market.   See Webster, Restricted Stock Options in a Declining Market, 44 A.B.A.J. 68 (1958).

[90] Section 1.421-2(a)(5) of the Regulations points out that any reasonable valuation methods may be used for the purpose of determining whether, at the time the option is granted, the option price is at least 85 percent of the fair market value of the stock subject to the option.

Revenue Ruling 59-243, 1959-2 C.B. 123, holds that an employee stock option issued under a plan which imposes on the Treasury Department the function of making determinations of fair market value for the purpose of fixing the option price does not qualify as a restricted stock option under §421, as it does not provide a price determinable at the date of the option as required in §421(d)(1)(A).   Revenue Ruling 60-242, I.R.B. 1960-29, 10, holds that because the provision referred to in Rev. Rul. 59-243 as preventing an option from qualifying as a restricted one has been widely included in good faith, Rev. Rul. 59-243 will not apply retroactively.   This means that if an

In order for stock options to qualify as restricted stock options it is not necessary that they be offered to various employees on a nondiscriminatory basis. Each option granted can be entirely separate and distinct in its terms from other options granted to other employees of the corporation.[91]

The modification, extension or renewal of a restricted stock option may be deemed the equivalent of the granting of a new option, so that all the tests which must be met if the option is to be a restricted one will have to be met at the time of the modification, extension or renewal.[92] The effect of corporate reorganizations, liquidations, etc., on restricted stock options depends on various factors.[93]

The tax benefits available on the exercise of a stock option are lost if the option is exercised by the optionee three months or more after the date he ceases to be an employee of the corporation.[94] This requirement as to employment in connection with the exercise of the option is not applicable when the option is exercised by the estate of a deceased employee or by a person who acquired the right to exercise the option by bequest or inheritance or by reason of the death of the employee.[95]

---

option was granted prior to Rev. Rul. 59-243 and otherwise qualifies, the inclusion of the provision condemned in the ruling will not prevent the option from qualifying as a restricted one.

[91] See Rev. Rul. 59-198, 1959-1 C.B. 91.

[92] See 1954 I.R.C. §421(e) and Reg. §1.421-4.

Revenue Ruling 59-55, 1959-1 C.B. 94, holds that where an optionee of a restricted stock option does not accept an invitation to surrender his option in the hope of receiving a new option at a more favorable price, there is no modification of his option for the purposes of §421(e). Revenue Ruling 59-68, 1959-1 C.B. 95, holds the action of the stock option plan committee in construing that an employee's employment had not terminated when he was directed to serve as an officer of an affiliated company did not constitute a modification of the stock option within the meaning of §421(e).

[93] See 1954 I.R.C. §421(g) and Reg. §1.421-4(d).

A substitution of a new stock option for an old one, or an assumption of an old one, within the meaning of §421(g) is considered in Rev. Rul. 58-499, 1958-2 C.B. 157, and Rev. Rul. 60-168, I.R.B. 1960-18, 13.

[94] See 1954 I.R.C. §421(a), quoted infra page 1349, and Reg. §1.421.3.

Revenue Ruling 58-324, 1958-1 C.B. 214, recognizes that an optionee under a restricted stock option plan who exercised his option while employed by a corporation that became a subsidiary of the corporation which had previously granted him the option qualifies for the income tax treatment provided by §421.

[95] See 1954 I.R.C. §421(d)(6), quoted infra page 1351, and Reg. §1.421-5(d), which brings out that the option does not have to be exercised within three months after the death of the employee but, of course, it must be exercised pursuant to its terms. The optionee, however, must have been an employee at his death or within three months before his death.

In McTighe v. United States, 187 F. Supp. 606 (W.D. Pa. 1960), an executor exercised a stock option which had been given to the decedent and claimed the "no income" benefit provided in 1954 I.R.C. §421(a)(1). The op-

The tax benefit that is available on the exercise of a restricted stock option is that no income results to the employee at the time he exercises the option,[96] or to the person who has acquired the right to exercise the option by reason of the employee's death, at the time that person exercises the option.[97] This tax benefit is lost, however, if the employee exercises the option and then disposes of the stock thus acquired within two years from the date of the granting of the option or within six months after the transfer of the stock to him.[98] If the option is exercised by a person who acquired the right to exercise it by reason of the employee's death, then the holding period requirement is not applicable[99] and the tax benefit is not lost no matter how rapidly the stock is disposed of after its acquisition.[100] The effect, if an employee

---

tion granted to the decedent qualified as a restricted stock option but the decedent retired two years before his death, so that if he had exercised the option just before he died, he would not have met the requirement that the option be exercised within three month after he ceased to be an employee in order to have the "no income" benefit. The executor contended that the elimination in §421(d)(6)(A)(i) of the employee requirement when a restricted stock option is exercised by an estate permitted the estate to exercise this option and get the "no income" benefit. The court held that the estate could be in no better position in regard to the option than the decedent was when he died. Thus the difference between the option price and the value when the option was exercised was taxable as ordinary income.

[96] See 1954 I.R.C. §421(a), quoted infra page 1349. The employer does not get a deduction at the time the option is exercised and only the price paid under the option is considered received by the corporation for the stock transferred.

[97] See 1954 I.R.C. §421(d)(6)(A), quoted infra page 1351.

[98] See 1954 I.R.C. §421(a), quoted infra page 1349; Reg. §1.421-5(a)(2).

Section 1222(3) of the 1954 Code defines a long-term capital gain as one realized from the sale or exchange of a capital asset held for more than six months. Thus an employee could comply with the holding period necessary to avoid making a disqualifying disposition and yet not comply with the holding period essential if he is to realize a long-term capital gain on a sale of the stock acquired by the exercise of the option. This would be true if he acquired the stock under the option more than two years after the date the option is granted and sold the stock exactly six months after he acquired it. In such a case, he would not have disposed of it within six months after he acquired it but he would not have held it for more than six months as required by §1222(3).

[99] See 1954 I.R.C. §421(d)(6)(A)(i), quoted infra page 1352.

[100] Although the holding period requirement is not applicable, it should be kept in mind that the person who acquires the option by reason of the employee's death and exercises it must hold the stock for more than six months after its acquisition, to be entitled to treat any gain on the sale of the stock as a long-term gain. Where the deceased employee's executor exercises the option and distributes the stock shortly thereafter as part of the residue to the residuary taker, the latter can tack the period the stock is held by the estate to the period he holds it, to determine whether he has held it for more than six months if he sells it. See 1954 I.R.C. §1222(3). Where, however, the executor uses the stock acquired by an exercise of the option to satisfy a pecuniary legacy, and he does not hold the stock for more than six months,

makes a disqualifying disposition, is to cause the income attributable to the transfer to be treated as income received in the taxable year in which the disposition occurs.[101]

The estate plan of the employee should avoid any disposition of stock acquired by him as a result of exercising a restricted stock option, which is a disqualifying disposition.[102] Thus, until the holding period has expired the stock should not be used in any inter vivos program of gifts.[103] The title to the stock acquired by the exercise of the restricted stock option can be taken initially in the name of the employee and another jointly with the right of survivorship, or can be subsequently transferred into a joint ownership, without any disposition being deemed made by the employee.[104] But such a course of action during the holding period is dangerous because if the employee should die prior to the end of the holding period, thereby terminating the joint ownership, a disqualifying disposition would take place on his death when the full title passed to the survivor.[105] This danger is removed as soon as the employee outlives the expiration of the holding period.

If the option price is at least 95 percent of the fair market value

---

any gain realized by the estate as a result of such a distribution will not be a long-term capital gain.

In order to eliminate profits resulting from the use of "inside" information, §16(b) of the Securities Exchange Act of 1934 (15 U.S.C.A. §78p(b)) provides for the recovery by a listed corporation of all the profits realized by its directors, officers, or principal stockholders from the purchase and sale, or sale and purchase, within less than six months, of securities in that corporation. In September, 1952, the Securities and Exchange Commission amended its own rules so as to exempt from the application of §16(b) stock acquired pursuant to certain types of stock bonus and similar plans. In regard to this action of the Commission, see Greene v. Dietz, 247 F.2d 689 (2d Cir. 1957). See also Gruber v. Chesapeake & Ohio Railway, 158 F. Supp. 593 (N.D. Ohio, 1957).

[101] See 1954 I.R.C. §421(f), quoted infra page 1353; and Reg. §1.421-5(e).

[102] Section 421(d)(4) of the 1954 Code, quoted infra page 1351, describes dispositions which will be disqualifying dispositions, if made by the employee during the holding period.

What constitutes a disposition of stock within the meaning of §421(d)(4) is considered in Rev. Rul. 57-451, 1957-2 C.B. 295. Revenue Ruling 59-242, 1959-2 C.B. 125, holds that the purchase of an option ("put") to sell stock acquired upon the exercise of a restricted stock option does not, in and of itself, constitute a "disposition" as defined in §421(d)(4). The disposition occurs on the date the "put" is exercised.

[103] Such stock should not be transferred by the employee during the holding period even to a revocable inter vivos trust.

See Reg. §1.421-5(a)(3). A mere pledge or hypothecation of the stock cannot be a disqualifying disposition, but a disposition of the stock pursuant to the pledge or hypothecation can be.

[104] See 1954 I.R.C. §421(d)(4)(B), quoted infra page 1351.

[105] This result seems to be required by the language of 1954 I.R.C. §421(d)(4), quoted infra page 1351. See note 102 supra.

of the stock subject to the option at the time the option is granted, then, assuming that no disqualifying disposition is made, the tax consequences of any inter vivos disposition by the employee of the stock acquired by the exercise of the option are the same as the transfer by him of any owned stock, the basis of which is the option price. The tax story is different, however, if the option price is between 85 and 95 percent, assuming again that no disqualifying disposition is made, when the employee makes an inter vivos disposition of the stock he acquires by the exercise of the option. On such a disposition by him, there will be includible in his gross income as compensation (and not as a gain upon the sale or exchange of a capital asset), for the taxable year in which the disposition falls, an amount equal to the amount (if any) by which the option price is exceeded by the lesser of the fair market value of the stock at the time of the disposition, or the fair market value of the stock at the time the option was granted.[106] The basis of the stock in the hands of the employee is increased over the option price by an amount equal to the amount includible in his gross income, and the further tax consequences resulting from the inter vivos transfer are judged accordingly.[107]

The discussion in the preceding paragraph should make it clear that for estate planning purposes stock acquired under 95 percent options is like any other stock, after the holding period has expired, so far as inter vivos transfers are concerned. Stock acquired under 85-95 percent options, however, should not be used in inter vivos transfers, even after the holding period has expired, unless it is wise in the over-all picture for the employee to incur the augmentation in gross income that will thereby be produced.[108]

The importance of distinguishing between stock acquired under a 95 percent option and under an 85-95 percent option continues when the disposition of the acquired stock occurs on the death of the employee while owning the stock. On the death of the owner the tax consequences so far as the former stock is concerned are no

---

[106] See 1954 I.R.C. §421(b), quoted infra page 1349. If the option price is determined by a formula, the amount included in gross income is determined in a slightly different manner.

[107] See 1954 I.R.C. §421(b). If the employee dies after the disposition and the stock is includible in his gross estate for federal estate tax purposes, a new basis for it will be acquired under 1954 I.R.C. §1014, quoted infra page 1381.

[108] Such stock should not be placed even in a revocable inter vivos trust. The ownership of such stock can be placed in the name of the employee and another as joint owners with the right of survivorship, without the employee being deemed to have made a disposition but a disposition will be deemed to have been made by the employee on the termination of the joint ownership except to the extent the employee acquires the ownership of the stock on such termination. See 1954 I.R.C. §421(d)(4)(B), quoted infra page 1351. Also a mere pledge or hypothecation of the stock is not a disposition.

different from those with respect to any other stock he may own.[109] As regards the stock the employee acquired under the 85-95 percent option, there will be includible, as compensation, in his gross income for the taxable year closing with his death an amount equal to an amount (if any) by which the option price is exceeded by the lesser of the fair market value of the stock at the time of his death or the fair market value of the stock at the time the option was granted.[110]

Finally, it is important to distinguish between 95 percent options and 85-95 percent options when the option is exercised by a person who acquired the right to the option by reason of the death of the employee, that is, by his executor or by one to whom the option is bequeathed or by one who inherits it, and a disposition is made by the one who acquires the stock pursuant to such exercise. A disposition of the stock acquired under a 95 percent option presents no special tax problems.[111] A disposition of stock acquired under an 85-95 percent option, however, will result in the one making the disposition[112] having ordinary income to the same limited extent as the employee would have had ordinary income if he had exercised the option and made a disposition after the expiration of the holding period.[113] The ordinary income which the one making the disposition will be deemed to have received is treated as income in respect of a decedent.[114]

The estate plan of an employee who now owns or may own at his death some unexercised restricted stock options should ease the

[109] The basis of the stock will be determined in accordance with 1954 I.R.C. §1014, quoted infra page 1381.

[110] See 1954 I.R.C. §421(b), quoted infra page 1349. If the option price is determined by a formula, the amount included in gross income as compensation is determined in a slightly different manner. The basis of the stock will be determined as provided by 1954 I.R.C. §1014, quoted infra page 1381.

[111] Prior to 1958, when §421(d)(6)(C), quoted infra page 1352, was added to the 1954 Code, the Code contained a §1014 (d), which prevented any new basis for a restricted stock option which the employee had not exercised at his death. In this situation, it was highly desirable for the employee to exercise the option before he died, so that the stock acquired would have a new basis on his death. If he let the option fall into his estate, though its value was includible in his gross estate, the stock acquired by the exercise of the option by his executor had as its basis only the option price. In 1958, §1014(d) was repealed, so that now the option gets a new basis, and §421(b)(6)(C) describes how that basis is reflected in the basis of the stock acquired by the exercise of the option.

[112] Any transfer of stock acquired by an employee's estate as a result of exercising an option is considered a disposition.

[113] See 1954 I.R.C. §421(b), quoted infra page 1349.

[114] See 1954 I.R.C. §421(d)(6)(B), quoted infra page 1352, and Reg. §1.421-5(d)(3)(ii).

The significance for estate planning purposes of the presence of income in respect of a decedent is discussed infra page 389.

way, so far as that is possible, for the exercise of the options after the employee's death.[115]

The illustrations set out below may be helpful in understanding the preceding textual discussion.

1. On June 1, 1959, the X Corporation grants to E, an employee, a restricted stock option to purchase 100 shares of its stock at $95 per share. On that date the fair market value of the X Corporation stock is $100 per share. On June 1, 1960, while employed by the X Corporation, E exercises the option in full and pays the X Corporation $9500, and on the same day the X Corporation transfers to E 100 shares of its stock having a fair market value of $12,000. E retains the shares until after June 1, 1961 (this retention is necessary to comply with the holding period requirement). E realizes no income on June 1, 1960, and his basis for the 100 shares is $9500. If he sells the stock after June 1, 1961, for $15,000, he will have a long-term capital gain (having held the stock for more than six months) of $5500.

2. On June 1, 1959, the X Corporation grants to E, an employee, a restricted stock option to purchase a share of its stock for $85. The fair market value of the stock on that date is $100 per share. On June 1, 1960, E exercises the restricted stock option, and on that date the X Corporation transfers the share of stock to him. On June 2, 1961, after expiration of the required holding period, E sells the share for $150, its fair market value on that date. He makes his income tax return on the basis of the calendar year. Compensation in the amount of $15 is includible in his gross income for 1961, the year of the disposition of the share. The $15 represents the difference between the option price of $85 and the fair market value of the share on the date the option was granted ($100), since this value is less than the fair market value of the share on the date of disposition ($150). For purposes of computing a gain or loss on the share, E's cost basis of $85 is increased by $15, the amount includible in his gross income as compensation. Thus E's basis is 100, and since he sold the share for $150 after holding it for more than six months, he realized a long-term capital gain of $50.

[115] The need for a provision in a will which authorizes the executor to use estate assets to raise money to exercise an option may be extremely important because of margin requirements limiting what can be borrowed against the stock subject to the option.

3. On June 1, 1959, E was granted a restricted stock option to purchase for $85 one share of the stock of his employer. On that day, the fair market value of the stock was $100 per share. E died on February 1, 1960, without having exercised the option. It was, however, exercisable by his estate, and for purposes of the estate tax was valued at $30. On March 1, 1960, the estate exercised the option and on March 15, 1960, sold for $150 the share of stock so acquired. For its taxable year including March 15, 1960, the estate is required to include in its gross income $15 as compensation. During the taxable year no distributions were made to estate beneficiaries. The estate is entitled to an income tax deduction of the estate tax attributable to the $15 includible in the estate's gross income, because of the income in respect of a decedent, assuming there are no other items of income in respect of a decedent and no deductions in respect of a decedent. If the value of the option in the gross estate was $30 and the estate tax attributable to the $30 is $10, the estate tax attributable to the $15 will be $5, which is the amount of the income tax deduction allowed to the estate because of the income in respect of a decedent. The basis of the stock acquired by the estate will be the price paid under the option ($85) plus the value of the option in E's gross estate ($30) less the excess of what would have been includible in the gross income of the employee, had he exercised the option and held the share until his death, over the amount which is includible in the estate's gross income as compensation (here that would be 0) and plus an amount equal to the excess of the amount includible in the estate income as compensation over the basis of the option (here that would be 0). Thus the basis of the stock in the estate is $115 and the estate realized a capital gain of $35 but it is not a long-term capital gain because the stock was not held by the estate for a period in excess of six months after it was acquired.

(2) Other Stock Options

The main issue to be resolved when an employee has a stock option which does not qualify as a restricted stock option is when will the employee be deemed to have realized compensation for income tax purposes. This issue will have to be dealt with not only when the employee is given initially an unqualified option but also when a restricted stock option is so modified that it no longer qualifies or when a disqualifying disposition is made of the stock acquired by the exercise of a restricted stock option.

The Supreme Court of the United States, in Commissioner v. LoBue,[116] held that where the option was nontransferable, the employee received compensation in the amount of the difference between the option price and the market value of the stock at the time the option was exercised.[117] The Regulations[118] set forth the following rules with respect to the options without a readily ascertainable fair market value (as to options with a readily ascertainable fair market value, compensation is realized when the option is granted in an amount equal to the excess, if any, of such fair market value over any amount paid for the option):

1. Except as provided in 2 below, if the option is exercised by the person to whom it was granted, the employee realizes compensation at the time an unconditional right to receive the property subject to the option is acquired by such person.[119]

---

[116] 351 U.S. 243, 76 Sup. Ct. 800, 100 L. Ed. 1142 (1956).

[117] In Philip J. LoBue, 28 T.C. 1317 (1957), the Tax Court considered when an option was exercised (the issue which was remanded to it by the Supreme Court), and concluded that the taxpayer exercised the option on the date when he gave his unconditional promissory note in the amount of the purchase price rather than on the date when the note was paid. The case was affirmed sub nom. Commissioner v. LoBue, 256 F.2d 735 (3d Cir. 1958).

[118] See Reg. §1.421-6. The rules in the Regulations are applicable only to options granted on or after February 26, 1945, and even then they are not applicable to property transferred pursuant to an option exercised before September 25, 1959, if the property is transferred subject to a restriction which has a significant effect on its value, or to property transferred pursuant to an option granted before September 25, 1959, and exercised on or after that date, if under the terms of the option the property to be transferred is to be subject to a restriction which has a significant effect on its value and if the property is actually transferred subject to the restriction. However, if an option granted before September 25, 1959, and on or after February 26, 1954, is sold or otherwise disposed of before exercise, the rules set out in the Regulations fully apply. See Reg. §1.421-6(a)(2).

[119] See Reg. §1.421-6(d)(1), which also describes the amount includible in the employee's gross income under the described conditions.

Joseph Kane, 25 T.C. 1112 (1956), *aff'd sub nom.* Kane v. Commissioner, 238 F.2d 624 (2d Cir. 1956), *cert. denied,* 353 U.S. 931 (1957), held that an option granted to the wife of an employee to buy stock in the employer corporation was compensation to the employee in the year in which the option was exercised (compensation was the difference between price paid and real value), even though the option was not granted by the corporation but by the president of the corporation, and the wife paid for the stock out of her own funds.

In Estate of James S. Ogsbury, 28 T.C. 93 (1957), the taxpayer received an unassignable option to purchase stock of his employer corporation at a bargain price. The option permitted the taxpayer to delay payment and passage of title to the stock after its exercise for the period he was still employed or for six months after his death if he died while in the employ of the corporation. An exercise of the option, however, bound the employee unconditionally to

2. If the option is exercised by the person to whom it was granted but, at the time an unconditional right to receive the property subject to the option is acquired by such person, the property is subject to a restriction which has a significant effect on its value, the employee realizes compensation at the time the restriction lapses or at the time the property is sold or exchanged in an arm's-length transaction, whichever occurs earlier.[120]

3. If the option is not exercised by the person to whom it was granted, but is transferred in an arm's-length transaction,

---

pay for the stock. The court held that the taxpayer received income when he exercised the option in 1945, and not when he paid for the stock in 1948. The case was affirmed sub nom. Commissioner v. Estate of James S. Ogsbury, 258 F.2d 294 (2d Cir. 1958).

In Frank Champion, CCH T.C. Mem. 1960-51, the court held that an employee received taxable compensation in the difference between the fair market value and the option price at the time he exercised the option, and the fair market value as determined by the Commissioner was upheld even though its intrinsic value may have been less.

In Joy Manufacturing Co. v. Commissioner, 230 F.2d 740 (3d Cir. 1956), the taxpayer's wholly owned subsidiary owed it a sum for engineering services rendered to it. The taxpayer agreed to invest the fees in shares of the subsidiary's increased capital stock. It was held that no income accrued to the stockholder when it rendered the services, but that in substance the services rendered were a capital contribution. Thus, should the stock later be sold by the taxpayer, the latter would have a capital gain, not ordinary income.

[120] See Reg. §1.421-6(d)(2), which also describes the amount includible in the employee's gross income under the described conditions. In Robert Lehman, 17 T.C. 652 (1951), the court held that income was not realized when restrictions relating to options terminated, and in T.I.R. 248, dated August 29, 1960, 60 CCH Fed. Tax Rep. ¶6601, acquiescence in this case is withdrawn, as it is contrary to the position taken in Reg. §1.421-6(d)(2).

In MacDonald v. Commissioner, 230 F.2d 534 (7th Cir. 1956), a taxpayer was given an option to buy stock at a price much below market to induce him to take an executive position in the corporation. He agreed not to sell the stock during the time he was in the employ of the corporation. It was held that the Tax Court was in error in holding that in the year the option was exercised, he realized income in the amount of the difference between the option price and the market price. In holding that the Tax Court erred in the method of determining the gain when the stock was acquired, the Court of Appeals relied on the agreement not to sell and also the provision in the Securities Exchange Act of 1934, §16(b), which would subject him to a suit by the corporation or stockholders if he sold the stock within six months. If a person cannot sell (or if he sells and will have to account to others for his profit), he has not realized the difference between the option price and the market price. The Tax Court in Harold E. MacDonald, 16 CCH T.C. Mem. 208 (1956), denied the Commissioner's motion for an additional hearing, on the ground that there was no other proper or meritorious method for computing the gain realized on the exercise of the stock option. The case was reversed sub nom. Commissioner v. MacDonald, 248 F.2d 552 (7th Cir. 1957), with instructions that the Tax Court should hear additional evidence and render its decision.

the employee realizes compensation only at the time of the transfer of the option.[121]

4. If the option is not exercised by the person to whom it was granted, but is transferred in a transaction which is not at arm's length, the employee realizes compensation at the time of the transfer of the option and additional compensation later when the option is exercised or further transferred in accordance with rules 1, 2 and 3.[122]

The basis of the property acquired by an exercise of the option by the person to whom it was granted is increased by any amount that is includible in the employee's gross income.[123]

PROBLEMS

9.8. E has been granted certain restricted stock options by his corporate employer. He has established an insurance trust to receive the proceeds of insurance on his life when he dies. The restricted stock options are exercisable by E's estate if he does not exercise them in his lifetime. Consider the appropriateness of inserting the following provisions in the insurance trust and in E's will:

---

[121] See Reg. §1.421-6(d)(3), which also describes the amount includible in the employee's gross income under the described conditions.

[122] See Reg. §1.421-6(d)(4), which also describes the amount includible initially in the employee's gross income and includible subsequently as additional compensation.

Robert C. Enos, 31 T.C. 100 (1958), held that where an option to buy 25,000 shares of unissued stock at a stated price was given to an employee and he transferred the option to his wife and daughters for $300 and they later surrendered the option for $2 a share, the gain realized on the surrender was taxable as compensation to the employee. At all times the price stated in the option was higher than the market price.

Section 1.421-6(d)(5) of the Regulations describes the consequences if the employee dies before realizing compensation. In this situation it should be noted that income in respect of a decedent may be involved.

Section 1.421-6(d)(7) of the Regulations points out that if the rules as to unqualified options are applicable because a disqualifying disposition is made of stock acquired by the exercise of a restricted stock option, the taxable year of the employee for which he is required to include in his gross income the compensation resulting from such an option is determined under 1954 I.R.C. §421(f), quoted infra page 1353.

[123] See Reg. §1.421-6(e).

If an employee fails to exercise an option to buy stock given to him by the employer, how is his loss treated? In Royal Little, 31 T.C. 607 (1958), *aff'd sub nom.* Little v. Commissioner, 273 F.2d 746 (1st Cir. 1960), the Tax Court applied §117(g) of the 1939 Code and held that the employee had a short-term capital loss. Section 1234 of the 1954 Code, which corresponds to §117(g), should be examined to determine what changes have been made in §117(g).

1. *Insurance Trust Provision*

The trustee is authorized to make loans or advances to the settlor's executors or administrators on such terms as the trustee deems advisable. The settlor may own stock options at the time of his death which are exercisable, under their terms, by his executors after his death, and the trustee is authorized to make loans or advances to the settlor's executors for the purpose of enabling them to exercise such stock options.

2. *Provision in Will*

My executor is authorized to exercise any stock options which are exercisable, under their terms, by my executor after my death if, in the opinion of my executor, the exercise of such stock options, will be beneficial to my estate; and to borrow money on such terms as my executor may determine in order to raise the funds necessary to exercise such stock options and to give as security for such loan or loans any part of my residuary estate. The attention of my executor is directed to [describe provision in insurance trust] which authorizes the trustee under said insurance trust to loan money to my executor to enable my executor to exercise stock options.

9.9. Under what circumstances, if any, should you advise that a restricted stock option be made the subject matter of a specific bequest rather than be allowed to pass as a part of the employee's residuary estate?

9.10. What type of life insurance should be obtained and by whom should it be owned if the sole purpose of the acquisition of the insurance is to assure the availability of the funds which will be necessary to take full advantage of restricted stock options?

e. *Insurance on the Employee's Life*

Generally, life insurance premiums paid by an employer with respect to insurance on the life of his employee, where the proceeds of the policy are payable to beneficiaries of the employee, are includible in the employee's gross income.[124] The premiums paid by an employer on policies of group term life insurance covering the lives of his employees, however, are not gross income to the employees, even though they designate the beneficiaries to receive the proceeds.[125] If an effective transfer of the incidents of

124 See Reg. §1.61-2(d)(2), quoted infra page 1479.
125 See Reg. §1.61-2(d)(2), quoted infra page 1479.
See Rev. Rul. 55-357, 1955-1 C.B. 13 (government employee not required to

ownership of the group insurance can be made by the employee, the proceeds collectible on his death may be removed from his gross estate for federal estate tax purposes.[126]

An employee can increase the protection that life insurance gives to his family, without any increase in his financial burden if he can get his employer to loan him money, free of interest, to pay premiums, the employer to be paid back when the insurance proceeds are collected. If the money loaned by the employer never exceeds the cash surrender value of the policy, the employer's loan is fairly well secured. This arrangement can be worked out under a contract whereby the employer agrees to pay the annual premiums to the extent of the annual increases in the cash surrender value of the policy, the employee paying the balance of the premiums, with the employer being entitled to be reimbursed, out of the proceeds, by an amount equal to the cash surrender value. The mere furnishing of money in this situation does not result in realized income to the employee or in a deduction to the employer.[127]

f. *Accident and Health Plans*

The existence of an accident and health plan for the benefit of an employee may provide security for the employee that will make it easier for him, in appropriate cases, to make inter vivos gifts. The tax benefits which attach to employee accident and health plans encourage their establishment.[128] The gross income of an

---

include in his gross income the portion of premium paid by government on his federal employees group life insurance).

Revenue Ruling 56-400, 1956-2 C.B. 116, provides that insurance premiums paid by an employer on behalf of his employees for group hospitalization and group term life insurance are not includible in the gross income of the employees, but this exclusion does not apply to premiums paid for group permanent life insurance.

Funds used by the trustee of a qualified employees' trust to pay premiums on a group life insurance contract, however, are currently included in the gross income of the employee-participant in the trust. Revenue Ruling 54-52, 1954-1 C.B. 150. Revenue Ruling 54-52 is amplified in Rev. Rul. 56-634, 1956-2 C.B. 291, where it is brought out that the expiration of the period during which the life insurance protection has been provided does not result in a loss deductible by the employee.

[126] See the discussion relating to life insurance and federal estate taxes at page 322 supra.

[127] Revenue Ruling 55-713, 1955-2 C.B. 23, considers the so-called "split-dollar" life insurance premium arrangement.

Insurance companies promote a policy in connection with what is called "minimum deposit plans," under which the insured borrows against the annual increase in the cash surrender value, to pay a substantial portion of the annual premiums. The New York restriction on the use of this device is discussed in CCH Fed. Est. & Gift Tax Rep. ¶8054.

[128] Sections 104, 105 and 106 of the 1954 Code, quoted infra page 1331, are the ones applicable particularly to accident and health plans.

employee does not include the employer's contributions to an accident and health plan which provides compensation to the employee for personal injuries or sickness incurred by him, his spouse or his dependents.[129] The pay-out to the employee may also be excludable from the employee's gross income.[130]

g. *Miscellaneous Matters*

Although they will have little, if any, effect on estate planning decisions, mention should be made of the retirement income tax

---

[129] See Reg. §1.106-1.

[130] See 1954 I.R.C. §§104, 105, quoted infra page 1331.

In Haynes v. United States, 353 U.S. 81, 77 Sup. Ct. 649, 1 L. Ed. 2d 671 (1957), the Supreme Court considered the extent to which an employee may exclude from his gross income sickness disability benefits received under an employees' plan. The following cases applied the rules established by the Haynes case: Branham v. United States, 245 F.2d 235 (6th Cir. 1957); United States v. Herbkersman, 245 F.2d 244 (6th Cir. 1957); Hanna v. United States, 57-2 U.S.T.C. ¶9716 (5th Cir. 1957); United States v. Pfleiderer, 58-1 U.S.T.C. ¶9225 (7th Cir. 1957); Charles J. Jackson, 28 T.C. 36 (1957); J. Wesley Sibole, 28 T.C. 40 (1957); Adam S. H. Trappey, 34 T.C. —, No. 40 (1960); Estate of Harold C. Wright, CCH T.C. Mem. 1960-156. In connection with disallowed claims for refund of taxes paid on benefits conferred under an uninsured employees' plan similar to the one in the Haynes case, see the Technical Amendments Act of 1958, §98, which extended to September 2, 1959, the period within which suits may be filed upon such a claim. Revenue Ruling 60-184, I.R.B. 1960-19, 37, brings various previously published rulings into line with the Haynes case.

Revenue Ruling 57-76, 1957-1 C.B. 66, points out that if an employee is absent from work because he has reached retirement age, payments that may be made to him cannot be excluded from gross income under §105(d), which gives an exclusion from gross income up to a weekly rate of $100 on account of payments for personal injuries or sickness. Thus, if an employee is receiving disability payments, they are excludable to the extent allowed in Section 105(d); they are not excludable to the extent allowed in Section 105(d) after he reaches retirement age. The ruling defines "retirement age" in this connection. See also Rev. Rul. 58-544, 1958-2 C.B. 43, which allows only payments received prior to the time the employee reaches normal retirement age to be excluded from his gross income to the extent provided in §105(d). Revenue Ruling 57-178, 1957-1 C.B. 71, points out that if a disability pension constitutes an amount which is excludable under §105(d), the fact that the employee engages in a gainful occupation does not require different treatment in regard to the disability pension.

Revenue Ruling 59-64, 1959-1 C.B. 31, recognizes that if an employee dies and his beneficiary receives something that would not have been income to the employee under §105(d) if he had received it, it will not be income to the beneficiary.

Revenue Ruling 59-159, 1959-1 C.B. 26, examines the operation of §105(d) with respect to earnings of a husband in a community property state and holds that, though such earnings are owned one half by the husband and one half by the wife, if the husband is sick, the exclusion from gross income under §105(d) is taken as though the earnings were owned entirely by the husband. If the wife is sick, no exclusion from gross income is available under §105(d) as to her share of the husband's earnings.

credit[131] and the special benefits that may be payable to a veteran under veterans' legislation.[132]

3. INCOME IN RESPECT OF DECEDENTS[133]

Income in respect of a decedent, broadly speaking, refers to those amounts to which a decedent was entitled as gross income but which were not properly includible in computing his taxable income for the taxable year ending with the date of his death or for a previous taxable year under the method of accounting employed by the decedent.[134]   The following are examples of income in respect of a decedent:

1. Renewal commissions on life insurance sold by an agent, which, if not paid to the agent in his lifetime, will be paid to his designated beneficiary after his death[135]

[131] See 1954 I.R.C. §37.

[132] See 1954 I.R.C. §692.

Section 104(a)(4) excludes from gross income amounts received as a pension, annuity or similar allowance for personal injuries or sickness resulting from active service in the armed forces.   McNair v. Commissioner, 250 F.2d 147 (4th Cir. 1957), held that amounts received by a naval officer who was retired from active duty because he had become permanently disabled were excluded from gross income, even though he was entitled to the same amount as a retired naval officer, irrespective of disability.   In accord is Freeman v. United States, 265 F.2d 66 (9th Cir. 1959).   Compare, however, Riley v. United States, 156 F. Supp. 751 (Ct. Cl. 1957).   Revenue Ruling 58-43, 1958-1 C.B. 45, holds that a member of the armed forces retired for reasons other than physical disability is not absent from work on account of personal injuries or sickness within the meaning of §105(d) and no part of his retirement pay may be excluded from gross income under §105(d), even though he is sick or injured and hospitalized as a result thereof.   The ruling points out that the provisions of §402 of the Career Compensation Act of 1949, 63 Stat. 802, and Title 10, c. 61, of the United States Code concern wage continuation plans, and therefore disability retirement pay received pursuant to those provisions, which is in excess of the amount excluded under §104(a)(4), may be excluded from gross income under §105(d) if received before the member reaches retirement age but not after he reaches such age.   Revenue Ruling 58-599, 1958-2 C.B. 45, clarifies Rev. Rul. 58-43 by pointing out that a member of the armed forces on the retired list because of a physical disability is no longer "absent from work" for purposes of the exclusion under §105(d) when he performs services as an employee of the United States.   Retirement ages for various members of the armed forces are set forth in Rev. Rul. 59-26, 1959-1 C.B. 29.

[133] See 1954 I.R.C. §691, quoted infra page 1375.

[134] See Reg. §1.691(a)-1(b).

[135] See Estate of Thomas F. Remington, 9 T.C. 99 (1947).   See also Latendresse v. Commissioner, 243 F.2d 577 (7th Cir. 1957), *cert. denied,* 355 U.S. 830 (1957); Estate of Abraham Goldstein, 33 T.C. —, No. 116 (1960). Revenue Ruling 59-162, 1959-1 C.B. 224, recognizes that renewal commissions are income in respect of a decedent.

In Commissioner v. Oates, 207 F.2d 711 (7th Cir. 1953), a general insurance agent entered into a new agreement with the insurance company under which he was to be paid his terminal commissions on insurance sales at the rate of $1000 a month for a period of not more than 180 months rather than as the

2. Accounts receivable of a cash-basis taxpayer[136]
3. Amount includible in the gross income of a successor in interest of a deceased partner[137]

---

commissions accrued. Payments were made in accordance with the new agreement. Although the commissions as they accrued were credited to the agent on the books of the company, the excess over the stipulated payments was held not to be income to the agent on the theory of constructive receipt. The agent was taxable only on the amounts actually received. Query: Would such an agreement be equally effective as to renewal commissions to be paid after the agent's death? The nonacquiescence in Commissioner v. Oates is withdrawn and acquiescence substituted by Rev. Rul. 60-31, I.R.B. 1960-5, 17. The Oates case is followed in Olmsted Incorporated Life Agency, 35 T.C. —, No. 51 (1960).

The court in Hall v. United States, 242 F.2d 412 (7th Cir. 1957), cert. denied, 355 U.S. 821 (1957), held that an insurance agent continued to be taxable on the renewal commissions when he made a purported gift assignment of the employment contract, because he made a transfer of income derived from an obligation to pay compensation and not a transfer of income-producing property.

In Florence E. Carr, 28 T.C. 779 (1957), the taxpayer's husband was president and majority stockholder of a corporation engaged in an insurance brokerage business. In 1927 the corporation owed the husband in excess of $100,000 for unpaid commissions, and in that year an agreement was entered into under which the corporation agreed to pay, after the husband's death, $100,000 at the rate of $10,000 a year for ten years to the taxpayer. The husband died in 1951, and the court held that the payments made to the taxpayer pursuant to the agreement were not taxable income to her. The court stated that cases relating to income in respect of a decedent were not in point because the Commissioner did not rely on the section dealing with such income, and cases involving payments to a widow after the death of her employee-husband were not in point because the payments were made pursuant to a contract.

[136] Accounts receivable are frequently a significant asset in the estate of a doctor or a lawyer.

[137] See 1954 I.R.C. §753, quoted infra page 1381.

United States v. Ellis, 154 F. Supp. 32 (S.D.N.Y. 1957), applies the 1939 Code to a partnership agreement under which the taxpayer, the widow of a former partner, was to receive certain shares of the insurance brokerage partnership income for ten years after her husband's death. The court held that the value of this right was includible in the deceased partner's gross estate and that the taxpayer's share of the partner's profits was income in respect of a decedent. The case was affirmed in 264 F.2d 325 (2d Cir. 1959).

In Mandel v. Sturr, 57-1 U.S.T.C. ¶9668 (S.D.N.Y. 1957), the executor of a deceased partner entered into an agreement with the surviving partner whereby the deceased partner's beneficiaries would receive a stated sum in lieu of any share of profits or other accruals of the business for the period after his death, and a stated sum as interest on the capital account of the deceased partner. The stated amounts were includible in the gross estate of the deceased partner and were taxable to the designated beneficiaries, when received, as income in respect of a decedent under the 1939 Code. The case was reversed in part and remanded in 266 F.2d 321 (2d Cir. 1959) (amount paid as interest on capital account of deceased partner was not in gross estate and was ordinary income to recipients; stated sum paid in lieu of any share in profits for period after death was deemed payment in settlement of possible claim due to delay in paying deceased partner's estate what it was entitled to, and hence this payment was not in gross estate and was ordinary income to recipients).

4. Certain portions of payments under installment obligations received by the decedent[138]
5. Certain payments under employee benefit plans[139]
6. Amount received by the estate of a decedent from a claim which was in the process of litigation at the time of the decedent's death, when the claim involved was for infringement of patent rights, because such an amount if collected by the decedent would have been income to him[140]
7. Lump sum payment made to the estate of a federal government employee for accumulated or accrued annual leave which is in effect compensation for services rendered[141]
8. Interest on a Series E United States savings bond not includible in income by the decedent[142]

Compare Estate of Charles A. Riegelman, 27 T.C. 833 (1957), *aff'd sub nom.* Estate of Charles A. Riegelman v. Commissioner, 253 F.2d 315 (2d Cir. 1958).

[138] See 1954 I.R.C. §691(a)(4), quoted infra page 1376.
[139] See discussion at page 354 supra.
[140] See Rev. Rul. 55-463, 1955-2 C.B. 277.
[141] See Rev. Rul. 55-229, 1955-1 C.B. 75.
[142] See Reg. §1.691(a)-2(b), Ex. (3).

Revenue Ruling 58-435, 1958-2 C.B. 370, considers a situation involving Series E United States savings bonds. Some of the bonds were purchased by the decedent and registered in her name alone, some were purchased by the decedent and registered in the names of the decedent and her husband, and some were purchased by the husband and registered in the names of the husband and the decedent. The husband died first. On the decedent's death, her executor elected to include in the income of the estate the interest on the Series E bonds (no income tax had previously been paid on the interest). The ruling recognizes that the interest on the bonds purchased by the decedent was income in respect of a decedent and the interest on the bonds purchased by the husband was income in respect of a prior decedent to the extent that it was attributable to interest earned prior to the husband's death and was income in respect of decedent as to the balance. Furthermore, when the bonds were distributed by the estate to the trustee under the will, the trustee could elect to postpone payment of the tax on interest which subsequently accrued. A Federal Savings & Loan Association encourages savings by paying 4 percent interest plus a bonus interest if the savings are not withdrawn until after the lapse of designated periods, and the Internal Revenue Service has ruled that the penalty of losing the bonus prevents both the 4 percent interest and the bonus from being taxed to the depositor before final maturity or earlier withdrawal (see Special Ruling, dated April 21, 1959, 59 CCH Fed. Tax Rep. ¶6514). Thus such arrangements should in all respects operate like the interest element in Series E bonds.

Estate of William P. Cooper, CCH T.C. Mem. 1960-98, decided that where the decedent acquired for $2300 prepaid installment share accounts of the Perpetual Building and Loan Association and over the years Perpetual credited so-called stock dividends from its earnings, which could not be withdrawn until the account matured or was surrendered in its entirety, the accumulation that was collected by the decedent's executor (amounting to some $115,000) was income in respect of a decedent.

9. Royalty payments in connection with a book of which the decedent was author[143]

10. Interest owed to a decedent and received after his death[144]

The illustrations given above are not exhaustive but they illustrate the wide variety of situations where income in respect of a decedent may be involved.[145]

The Senate Finance Committee report notes that Section 126 of the 1939 Code (which corresponds with Section 691 of the 1954

---

[143] See Rev. Rul. 57-544, 1957-2 C.B. 361, where the contract entered into by and between the author and the publisher constituted a sale of the manuscript by the former to the latter. Thus all royalties were items to which the author had a right, as having been earned in his lifetime, and the royalties which accrued after his death were income in respect of a decedent. This clarification is made in Rev. Rul. 60-227, I.R.B. 1960-25, 13, in distinguishing a contract entered into between an inventor and a manufacturer which gave the latter a license to use the inventor's patent in return for the payment of royalties. Revenue Ruling 60-227 holds that such arrangement is not a sale but merely a license, and that in such a case royalty payments which accrue after the date of the death of the inventor are ordinary income, not income in respect of a decedent, includible in the gross income of the recipient under 1954 I.R.C. §61, quoted infra page 1325.

[144] Richardson v. United States, 177 F. Supp. 394 (E.D. Mich. 1959).

[145] See generally on this topic, Drye, The Taxation of a Decedent's Income, 8 Tax L. Rev. 201-209 (1953); Louthan, Income in Respect of Decedents, 36 Trust Bull. No. 7, p. 44 (1957); Note, Income in Respect of Decedents: The Scope of Section 126 [of the 1939 Code (1954 I.R.C. §691)], 65 Harv. L. Rev. 1024 (1952); Commissioner v. Linde, 213 F.2d 1 (9th Cir. 1954), cert. denied, 348 U.S. 871 (1955).

Revenue Ruling 58-436, 1958-2 C.B. 366, holds that livestock and farm crops (harvested or unharvested, raised by a decedent prior to his death or received from tenants as rent for farm lands held for sale or feeding purposes) owned by a cash-basis decedent are items of property and not income in respect of a decedent.

Revenue Ruling 59-64, 1959-1 C.B. 31, recognizes that where an employee dies and his beneficiary receives something that would not have been income to the employee, had he received it, because of §105(d), the payment to the beneficiary is not income in respect of a decedent to such an extent. To the extent it would not have been excluded from the gross income of the employee under §105(d), it is income in respect of a decedent.

In Lacomble v. United States, 177 F. Supp. 373 (N.D. Cal. 1959), the court held that reduced pension payments received by a widow of a deceased employee did not qualify as income in respect of a decedent because under no circumstances would the decedent ever have received the payments, for they were payable only to his widow. The widow claimed that the payments should be regarded as income in respect of a decedent so that they would have the same character in her hands as in her husband's hands and she could then exclude a portion as deferred compensation for services rendered abroad by her husband while a nonresident of the United States. The court said that the fact that under §691(d) a special deduction is given to the surviving annuitant does not make amounts received by the surviving annuitant income in respect of a decedent.

Edna S. Ullman, 34 T.C. — , No. 114 (1960), held that payments to a widow under an award from the Mixed Claims Commission, United States and Germany, were income in respect of a decedent.

Code) was enacted "to overcome the pre-existing requirement that there be included in the income of a decedent for the taxable period in which his death occurred all the income accrued up to the date of his death, if not otherwise includible in respect of such period or a prior period."[146]   Section 126 prevented this bunching of income in the decedent's final return, by making the income which accrued solely by reason of his death taxable to the person who received it and at the time he received it.   While this change in the law took care of the situation on the death of the initial decedent, if the beneficiary of the initial decedent also died before payment to him, Section 126 as worded did not prevent the pyramiding of income in the subsequent decedent's final return.[147] But, under Sections 691(a)(1), (2), and (3), an item of gross income in respect of a subsequent decedent includes an item of gross income in respect of a *prior* decedent, provided the right to receive such amount was acquired by the subsequent decedent by reason of the death of the prior decedent or by bequest, devise, or inheritance from him.   This change made by the 1954 Code should be kept in mind whenever the item of income in respect of a decedent may continue on through successive decedents.

Property which constitutes a right to receive an item of income in respect of a decedent under Section 691 does not receive a new basis on the decedent's death, though it is includible in his gross estate for federal estate tax purposes.[148]   The harshness of the result that subjects such a right to income to the federal estate tax, and also subjects the income when collected to a federal income tax, without the benefit of any improvement in basis, is somewhat alleviated by the fact that the one who has to pay the income tax is allowed a deduction from his gross income in the amount of the estate tax attributable to the income in respect of a decedent on which he has to pay an income tax.[149]   This deduction is available

---

[146] S. Rep. No. 1622, 83d Cong., 2d Sess. 373 (1954).

[147] The Senate Finance Committee report gives the following example of successive decedents: "[I]f a widow of a life insurance agent acquires by reason of the death of her husband the right to receive renewal commissions on life insurance sold by him in his lifetime and payable over a period of years, but the widow dies prior to the receipt of such commissions, leaving the right to receive the commissions to her son, no income in respect of the commissions is required to be included in the final return of the husband.   However, upon the subsequent death of his widow, the fair market value of the right to receive such commissions must, under existing law, be included in her final return."   S. Rep. No. 1622, 83d Cong., 2d Sess. 373 (1954).

[148] See 1954 I.R.C. §1014(c), quoted infra page 1383.

[149] See 1954 I.R.C. §691(c), quoted infra page 1377.

In Rev. Rul. 55-481, 1955-2 C.B. 279, it is held that since 100 percent of a long-term capital gain is included in the gross estate of a decedent for fed-in the case of successive decedents, so that if an item of income in respect of a prior decedent is subjected to the federal estate tax, the deduction is available. This complements the revision referred to above which permits the inclusion in income in respect of a subsequent decedent of items of income in respect of a prior decedent.

Whenever rights to income in respect of a decedent are or may be in the portfolio of assets of the person whose estate plan is being prepared, careful thought must be given to the destination of such rights so that the impact of income taxation in regard to them will be lessened as much as is appropriate under the circumstances, and the deduction for the estate tax attributable to them will be fully available. The impact of income taxation may be lessened by spreading the rights to income in respect of a decedent over several tax entities.

The rights to income in respect of a decedent should be distinguished from the amounts received as a result of the enforcement of the rights. If the rights are distributed by the decedent's estate to the estate beneficiaries entitled to them, and the latter enforce them, the amount collected is includible in the gross income of the beneficiaries and they are entitled to the deduction for the estate tax attributable to the rights. Suppose, however, that the decedent's estate enforces the rights, or they are distributed to the trustee of a trust who is entitled to receive them and the trustee enforces them, can the income in respect of a decedent which is now possessed by the estate or the trust be passed on through to estate or trust beneficiaries so that they, and not the estate or trust, will be taxable on the income and be entitled to the deduction for the estate tax attributable to it?

The Senate Finance Committee report notes that under the 1939 Code "items of income in respect of a decedent distributed by an estate or trust are ordinarily not includible in the gross income of the beneficiary, because such items represent 'corpus' as distinguished from 'income' in the hands of the estate or trust.[150]

---

eral estate tax purposes, and 100 percent of a long-term capital gain is taken into account in computing gross income for federal income tax purposes, the same percentage is taken into consideration in computing the deduction authorized to recipients of income in respect of decedents under §691(c).

[150] S. Rep. No. 1622, 83d Cong., 2d Sess. 375 (1954). See also Estate of Robert L. Clymer, 13 CCH T.C. Mem. 715 (1954), in which it was held that an estate was not entitled to a charitable deduction for the amount of 1939 I.R.C. §126 income it received and paid over to a charity, because §126 income is not income after collection by the estate, but is then corpus. The case was reversed sub nom. Clymer v. Commissioner, 221 F.2d 680 (3d Cir. 1955). In Estate of Ostella Carruth, 27 T.C. 871 (1957), a case covered by the 1939 Code, rents which accrued prior to the lessor's death were collected after his death and

However, the revised income tax provisions relating to estates, trusts and beneficiaries generally do not preserve this distinction for income tax purposes of a beneficiary." [151]   If the income in respect of a decedent that is paid, credited, or required to be distributed to a beneficiary of an estate or trust is now taxable to the beneficiary, there should be available to the beneficiary a deduction for the estate taxes paid on such income.   Section 691(c)(1)(B) provides for this by excluding any such income actually paid, credited, or distributed to the beneficiary from the gross income of the estate or trust for the purpose of determining the deduction allowable under Section 691(c).   Such income is taxable to the beneficiary under Section 662(a)(2), and is considered under Section 662(b) to "have the same character in the hands of the beneficiary as in the hands of the estate or trust."   Thus it is now possible to give discretion to the fiduciary as to the distribution of income in respect of a decedent, and by the exercise of that discretion the fiduciary can determine to which tax entity the income will be attributed.[152]

It must be kept in mind that certain transfers of the right to receive income in respect of a decedent will cause the amount of the consideration, if any, received for the right or the fair market value of the right at the time of the transfer, whichever is greater, to be

---

placed in a trust pursuant to the terms of his will.   The amount of the accrued rents was deemed corpus of the trust.   In Midland National Bank of Billings v. United States, 168 F. Supp. 736 (D. Mont. 1959), it was held that income in respect of a decedent when distributed by an estate to a beneficiary was deductible by the estate in determining the estate's taxable income under §162(c) of the 1939 Code (the court referred to the quotation from the Senate Finance Committee Report which appears in the text and pointed out that it is not controlling as to law under the 1939 Code). — ED.

[151] See 1954 I.R.C. §§641-663, quoted infra page 1361. — ED.

[152] The state law may require that income in respect of a decedent be added to the trust corpus, and thus the discretion given to the trustee should be broad enough to permit him to pay out corpus as well as income.   If income in respect of a decedent is added to corpus, is such an addition an accumulation for purposes of applying the controlling statute in regard to accumulations? Matter of Pennock, 285 N.Y. 475, 35 N.E.2d 177 (1941), answers this question in the negative.

See Reg. §1.691(c)-2(a), which describes how the amount of the deduction which passes through to the beneficiary of an estate or trust is determined. H.R. 9662, which failed of enactment in the Eighty-sixth Congress, proposed an amendment (§102(f) of the bill) of §642 of the 1954 Code under which subsection (i) would be redesignated subsection (j) and a new subsection (i) would be inserted as follows: "An estate or trust shall be allowed the deduction provided by section 691(c) (relating to the deduction allowed for estate tax on income in respect of a decedent) only in respect of so much of the income in respect of a decedent as is not properly allocable to a beneficiary under section 652 or section 662."   This proposed insertion is said by the Senate Finance Committee Report to be declaratory of existing law.

Discretionary trusts are examined infra page 733.

included in the gross income of the transferor for the taxable period in which the transfer occurs. A transfer of the right by the decedent's estate to one to whom it is specifically bequeathed or to a residuary beneficiary when the right is a part of the residue will not cause such a result. A transfer of the right by the trustee of a trust, to which the right is bequeathed, to a beneficiary of the trust is like the transfer by the estate to a specific or residuary beneficiary. If, however, the executor of the decedent's estate distributes the right to a pecuniary legatee in satisfaction of his legacy, the gross income of the estate will be augmented in the manner described in the first sentence of this paragraph. Likewise, an estate beneficiary to whom the right had been distributed as part of his share of the residue will suddenly increase his gross income if he makes a gift of such a right to his son or anyone else.[153]

The deduction for income tax purposes of the estate tax attributable to income in respect of a decedent will cause this income in the hands of a particular beneficiary to be taxed less than the same amount of other income.[154] If income is to be given to a charity, it would be unwise to make up the gift of income in any part by using income in respect of a decedent, because the portion of the deduction allocable to income which passes to the charity would be lost. The inclusion of income in respect of a decedent in a marital deduction gift [155] may not decrease the amount of the deduction,[156]

---

[153] See Reg. §1.691(a)-4.

It must be kept in mind that if the executor distributes to an estate beneficiary a right to income in respect of a decedent, the distribution of such an item of estate property will carry out to the distributee estate income for the year of distribution to the same extent as the distribution of other estate property to the distributee would carry out estate income. See Chapter IV on income taxation of estates.

[154] The deduction is fully explained in Reg. §1.691(c)-1.

[155] Marital deduction gifts are discussed infra page 783.

[156] See Thomas A. Desmond, 13 CCH T.C. Mem. 889 (1954). In this case a deduction was allowed for the estate tax paid on income with respect to a decedent, even though the income was included in calculating the marital deduction. The Commissioner argued that since the income in respect of the decedent was an item included in computing the marital deduction, no estate tax was attributable thereto, and hence the estate was entitled to no deduction. But the Tax Court did not agree.

In the Final Report of the Advisory Group on Subchapter J, to the Committee on Ways and Means of the House of Representatives, dated February 4, 1959, a recommendation was made to amend §691 of the 1954 Code so that no part of the deduction for the estate tax paid on income in respect of a decedent would be allowed to the widow who received such income under a marital deduction gift which did not bear any estate tax. The full deduction was given to the recipients of such income whose share of the estate in fact bore the burden of the only estate tax imposed on the income in respect of a decedent. This recommendation was not included in H.R. 9662, the bill which was based on the Advisory Group's recommendations. That bill failed of passage in the Eighty-sixth Congress.

but it will mean that the wife will get the benefit of income to which a deduction attaches when in the over-all family picture it might be better to place such income elsewhere.[157] One of the requirements of a power of appointment marital deduction trust is that the wife be entitled to all the income from the entire interest, or all the income from a specific portion thereof.[158] If the controlling local law requires the addition to corpus of income in respect of a decedent in the absence of a contrary manifestation of intent, and the income is in the marital trust, will this income requirement as to power of appointment trusts be satisfied? The answer to this question should be in the affirmative.[159] If the controlling local law, however, requires such income to be paid out to the income beneficiary in the absence of a contrary manifestation of intent, a direction that the income be added to corpus might disqualify the trust for marital deduction purposes. Thus considerable thought should be given to the most desirable course of action to recommend in regard to income in respect of a decedent when a marital deduction gift is involved.[160]

The amount of any income tax deduction for expenses, interest, taxes, and depletion, or of the foreign tax credit, in respect of a decedent, which is not properly allowable to the decedent with regard to the taxable period on which falls the date of his death, or a prior period, is not lost. The 1954 Code specifies when such an amount is allowed to the decedent's estate, and when to others.[161] These deductions and the credit are relevant in deter-

---

[157] If a nonmarital trust is established under which the trustee is given discretion to spray the income and corpus among a group, including the wife, the trustee may be able to produce a better income tax result by the intelligent exercise of his power to spray, so far as the income in respect of a decedent is concerned, than will be produced if such income is given outright to the wife.

[158] See the discussion at page 839 supra.

[159] The Regulations refer to the principles of the law of trusts as controlling in determining whether the wife is given the requisite right to income. See Reg. §20.2056(b)-5(f), quoted infra page 842.

[160] See Drye, The Taxation of a Decedent's Income, 8 Tax L. Rev. 201, 214 (1953).

If a widow is the life income beneficiary under a trust, and if a particular item in the husband's estate is deemed income in respect of a decedent and all of the item passes to the widow as income beneficiary pursuant to the decree of a state court, will the value of the item qualify for the marital deduction? Beaver Trust Co. v. United States, 184 F. Supp. 553 (W.D. Pa. 1960), refused to regard as binding the state court decree and held that the income in respect of a decedent (the court did not so designate the income) was an item in which the widow received only a life interest (a terminable interest) and therefore the gift to her did not qualify for the marital deduction.

[161] See 1954 I.R.C. §691(b), quoted infra page 1376.

Revenue Ruling 58-69, 1958-1 C.B. 254, holds that in those jurisdictions which require the executor or administrator of the estate of a decedent to pay real estate taxes which, prior to the death of the decedent, have become a charge against the real estate of the decedent, the taxes so paid by the executor

mining the estate tax attributable to income in respect of a decedent.[162]

It should not be assumed that the state income tax consequences
and the state death tax costs in regard to income in respect of a
decedent follow the federal tax pattern. The controlling local
law must be examined.

4. SOCIAL SECURITY

The social security benefits available on the attainment of certain ages, as well as the benefits which will be available to family
members when someone dies, should be taken into account in making decisions in regard to other assets governed by the estate plan.
The periodic social security payments made to the insured worker,
or to his wife or children after his death, are not includible in
gross income for federal income tax purposes[163] and may not be
subject to state income taxes.[164] Social security benefits must be
taken into account, however, when received by a child and used
for his support as the child's contribution toward his support, in
determining whether the child qualifies as a dependent.[165]

---

or administrator are allowable under the provisions of §691(b)(1)(A) as a deduction on the fiduciary income tax return of the estate for the taxable year
in which paid. On the other hand, if the executor or administrator is not
required to pay the taxes, but does so, and if the payment was in behalf of
a beneficiary entitled to the income from the estate and was made in lieu of
a direct payment to the beneficiary, a deduction would be allowable under
§661.

It should be noted that §642(g), which disallows income tax deductions for
certain items allowed as deductions under the estate tax, is by its terms made
inapplicable to income in respect of a decedent.

[162] See 1954 I.R.C. §691(c)(2)(B), quoted infra page 1377.

[163] See Reg. §1.61-11(b).

See Stark v. Flemming, 181 F. Supp. 539 (N.D. Cal. 1959), in which a woman
organized a corporation, remained connected with the corporation for the
precise period required to give her an insured status under the social security
law, and had her salary fixed at precisely the amount which during the period
would entitle her to maximum social security benefits, and it was held that
this was not a bona fide employment that would render her eligible for social
security benefits.

[164] Social security payments are not subject to state income taxes in Massachusetts, as they do not constitute income from professions, employments,
trade or business and are not retirement allowances subject to taxation under
Mass. Ann. Laws, c. 62, §5(b). See Gray v. State Tax Commission, CCH Mass.
Tax Rep. ¶200-092 (App. Tax Bd. 1959), aff'd sub nom. State Tax Commission
v. Gray, 340 Mass. 535, 165 N.E.2d 404 (1960).

[165] Revenue Ruling 57-344, 1957-2 C.B. 112, brings out that social security
benefits received by a child and used for the support of the child must be
considered as the child's contribution toward his support in determining, for
purposes of 1954 I.R.C. §151(e), who furnished more than half of the child's
support.

Revenue Ruling 58-419, 1958-2 C.B. 57, recognizes that social security bene-

On the death of an insured worker his unclaimed social security benefits are not recoverable by his executor.[166]   The value of the payments that may be due someone on and after the death of the insured worker is not includible in his gross estate for federal estate tax purposes.[167]   The controlling local law must be consulted as to whether any state death taxes may be payable.

---

fits must be taken into consideration in determining the amount of support furnished a recipient for purposes of ascertaining whether the recipient qualifies as a dependent under §152 and in computing retirement income credit under §37.

[166] Coy v. Folsom, 228 F.2d 276 (3d Cir. 1955), so held, even though the reason the decedent had not claimed his social security benefits was that he was not mentally competent to handle his affairs.

[167] In Rev. Rul. 55-87, 1955-1 C.B. 112, consideration was given to the estate tax consequences of the lump sum payment provided by §202(i) of the Social Security Act, as amended.   This section provides, in substance, that upon the death of a person who died after August, 1950, fully or currently insured, an amount equal to three times the individual's primary insurance amount shall be paid in a lump sum to his widow or, if there is no widow, to any person or persons equitably entitled thereto to the extent and in the proportion that such person or persons have paid the expenses of burial of the insured individual.   The ruling stated that the decedent had no control over the designation of the beneficiary of the payment and had no property interest in the federal old age and survivor's insurance trust fund.   Consequently the payment did not constitute property of the decedent at the time of his death, within the meaning of 1954 I.R.C. §2033 (1939 I.R.C. §811(a)). Accordingly, the lump sum death payment was not includible in the decedent's gross estate for federal estate tax purposes.

Revenue Ruling 56-637, 1956-2 C.B. 600, brings out that compensation benefits awarded to a widow of an employee under a workmen's compensation act of a state are not includible in the employee's gross estate where the employee dies as a result of an occupational disease contracted in the course of his employment.   Revenue Ruling 54-19, 1954-1, C.B. 179, holds that amounts receivable in the settlement of claims under the New Jersey Death by Wrongful Act statute are not includible in the decedent's gross estate for federal estate tax purposes.

CHAPTER X

Concurrent Interests Including Community Property

Concurrent interests are widely used in estate planning. Not always, however, is the decision to use them wisely made. They have a place in estate planning, but it is a fairly restricted one. In order to determine their proper function in estate planning, it is essential to know the basic characteristics of each type of concurrent interest and the tax consequences produced by each.

1. THE TENANCY BY THE ENTIRETY

The tenancy by the entirety can exist only where a husband and wife are the co-owners, and it has the characteristic that on the death of one, the survivor becomes the owner in severalty of the property formerly jointly held. This right of survivorship is not destructible except with the consent of both the husband and the wife.

This form of tenancy can exist in both real and personal property in some states; in others only in real property. In some states it has been completely abolished.

At common law, the husband had full control of the property held by the entirety during the joint lives of his wife and himself and consequently was entitled to all the income therefrom.[1] The wife had only an indestructible right to the whole if she survived her husband. The controlling local law must be examined to ascertain the extent to which the rigors of the common law have been modified.[2]

---

[1] In Massachusetts, the tenancy by the entirety is recognized in all its common law vigor. Licker v. Gluskin, 265 Mass. 403, 164 N.E. 613 (1929), holds that the husband is entitled to all the income. In Ronan v. Ronan, 339 Mass. 460, 159 N.E.2d 653 (1959), the court held that the proceeds received on the condemnation of a tenancy by the entirety should be deposited in a savings institution in the names of the husband and wife as tenants by the entirety, the interest during their joint lives to be payable to the husband, and the survivor to be entitled to the deposited sum.

[2] A comprehensive review of the tenancy by the entirety is found in King v. Greene, 30 N.J. 395, 153 A.2d 49 (1959). The court concluded that at common law the husband had full control of the property during the joint lives of him-

2. THE JOINT TENANCY

The joint tenancy, like the tenancy by the entirety, has the right of survivorship. One of the joint tenants acting alone, however, can destroy this right as to his undivided interest in the jointly held property. This can be done by a conveyance of his interest to another, but such a conveyance must be made in his lifetime. In other words, he cannot dispose of his interest in the joint tenancy by his will.

The control of property held by joint tenancy is not exclusively vested in any one of the joint tenants. If the jointly held property is income-producing, each joint tenant is entitled to an equal share of the income.

3. THE TENANCY IN COMMON

The right of survivorship does not attach to a tenancy in common. When one tenant in common dies, his undivided interest in the common property passes as would an asset owned by the decedent in severalty. Whereas joint tenants always have the same undivided interest in the jointly held property, the undivided interests of tenants in common may or may not be equal.

At common law, a conveyance to husband and wife was presumed to create a tenancy by the entirety, and a conveyance to two or more other persons was presumed to create a joint tenancy. Statutes now exist which set up a presumption in favor of a tenancy in common. Thus, if it is desired to create another form of tenancy, this desire must be clearly and unequivocally manifested.

---

self and his wife and that he could convey the fee simple title to the property subject only to the right of his wife to the property if she in fact survived. The New Jersey Married Women's Act, N.J. Rev. Stat. §§37:2-16 et seq. (1954), did not abolish the tenancy, as such an act has been held to do in some states, but had the effect of making husband and wife each entitled to the control of an undivided one half during their joint lives, with the right to full control in the survivor, this survivorship right not being destructible by either alone. Either, however, could convey his or her control over an undivided one half during their joint lives and either could convey his or her right to full control under the survivorship rights. What a person can convey can be taken by creditors of that person.

Pilip v. United States, 186 F. Supp. 397 (D. Alaska 1960), is concerned with the tenancy by the entirety in Alaska and holds that the government was entitled to only one half of the income from the tenancy in enforcing a lien against the property for the unpaid income taxes of the husband. Moore v. Glotzbach, 188 F. Supp. 267 (E.D. Va. 1960), held that under Virginia law, which was controlling, the income from property owned by a husband and wife as tenants by the entirety was not subject to levy for internal revenue taxes due by the husband only.

4. THE JOINT BANK ACCOUNT

Money can be deposited in a joint checking account or joint savings account which provides that withdrawals may be made by either one of the designated persons, and that on the death of one the survivor will be the sole owner of the account.[3] The joint bank account is not a true joint tenancy because the true joint tenant can withdraw only his undivided interest.

5. JOINTLY OWNED GOVERNMENT BONDS

Government bonds may be held in the name of "A or B," which means that either can cash the bond and on the death of one the survivor becomes the sole owner.[4] Such bonds may be held in the

[3] In Rev. Rul. 55-187, 1955-1 C.B. 197, it is pointed out that a joint checking account is subject to levy to satisfy an outstanding tax liability of one of the designated joint owners only to the extent of the taxpayer's interest therein. Factors bearing on the question of the extent of a taxpayer's interest in such an account include the nature of the tenancy created under state law; the source of the funds deposited; the intent of the person opening the joint account; and whether in actual practice the account was under the control of one party, even though the other had authority to withdraw funds from the account.

[4] It should be noted, however, that bonds payable "to A or B" can be re-registered only by both A and B joining to have the bonds reregistered. Silverman v. McGinnes, 57-2 U.S.T.C. ¶11719 (E.D. Pa. 1957), held that although the decedent during his lifetime made a gift of Series E bonds which he purchased and registered in the joint names of himself and various other persons, the registration of the bonds created a conclusive presumption as to their ownership for tax purposes, and therefore the evidence as to a gift was inadmissible and the entire value of the bonds was included in the decedent's gross estate. The case was reversed and remanded in 259 F.2d 731 (3d Cir. 1958), on the ground that no part of the value of the bonds was includible in the decedent's gross estate, since he had effectively parted with his economic interest in the bonds prior to his death. In Silverman v. McGinnes, 170 F. Supp. 813 (E.D. Pa. 1959), the court held that the executors could amend their complaint to claim a deduction for attorneys' fees because, as a result of the remand, the case was still being prosecuted, no final judgment having been rendered. For a recent state court case which went behind the form of the registration of government bonds to determine ownership, see Estate of Joseph DeNat, N.Y.L.J., Oct. 10, 1958, p. 13 (N.Y. City Surr.). In Tanner v. Ervin, 250 N.C. 602, 109 S.E.2d 460 (1959), a husband and wife owned Series E bonds payable to either or the survivor and under a separation agreement the husband was given the title to the bonds; he died before changing the registration and under applicable Treasury Regulations the wife was the only one entitled to collect the proceeds, but the court held that she was required to turn the proceeds over to the husband's estate. In accord with the Tanner case is Alexander v. Mermel, — Ill. App. —, 169 N.E.2d 569 (1960). See also Graham v. United States, 60-2 U.S.T.C. ¶11961 (W.D. Wash. 1960), discussed supra page 268, note 4.

In Byer v. Byer, 180 Kan. 258, 303 P.2d 137 (1956), the court held that the Treasury Regulations which permit payment to be made to either of the co-owners of a United States savings bond are only for administrative convenience

name of "A payable on his death to B." [5]   In such a case the bonds can be cashed only by A during his lifetime, and B will succeed to their ownership on A's death if A has not cashed them.

There are dollar limits placed on purchases of Series E and H savings bonds, and the Treasury Department has issued an informational bulletin as to how these limits operate where bonds are jointly owned.[6]

---

and do not determine the rights of the parties to the proceeds when one cashes the bond.

If United States Series E bonds are acquired by A and registered in the name of A or B and kept throughout A's life in A's safe-deposit box, will the attempted gift to B as the survivor fail because of lack of delivery of the subject matter? Horstman Estate, 398 Pa. 506, 159 A.2d 514 (1960), held that the federal regulations which allow such registration of a Series E bond control the purchase of the bond, and registration of it constitutes a contract between the purchaser and the United States government, with the surviving co-owner standing in the position of a third party beneficiary. See generally on the requirement of delivery to perfect a gift page 268 supra.

[5] Where government bonds are in the name of "A payable on his death to B" and A becomes incompetent, what is the legal effect if a guardian appointed for A cashes the bonds? In Cornelison v. Walters, 178 Kan. 607, 290 P.2d 1016 (1955), it was held that the person in the position of B could obtain from A's estate, on A's death, the amount B would have received had the bonds not been cashed. A similar problem may arise where bonds are payable "to A or B," and A's guardian cashes the bonds. As to this situation, see In re Barletta's Estate, 2 Misc. 2d 135, 150 N.Y.S.2d 479 (1956); Morris v. Morris, 195 Tenn. 133, 258 S.W.2d 732 (1953). In these cases B as the survivor was allowed to obtain the proceeds from A's estate.

[6] The ownership of the government bonds is not a true joint tenancy for the reasons stated supra page 402, in connection with joint bank accounts.

The Treasury Department has issued the following informational bulletin (mailed to attorneys as an enclosure in its letter dated November 23, 1955) regarding Series E and H United States savings bonds:

"Purchases by one individual in any one calendar year of Series E Savings Bonds are limited to $20,000 maturity value ($15,000 purchase price), and of Series H Savings Bonds to $20,000 (purchase at par).

"*However, additional holdings* by individuals are permitted in cases where either Series E or H Bonds are registered in *co-ownership* form. Bonds issued to co-owners may, for the purpose of computing the amount held, be applied to the holdings of either or apportioned between them.

"This is how the co-ownership feature allows for additional holdings by individuals in the case, *for example,* of a family of four, none of whom are registered owners or co-owners of Series E Bonds purchased in this calendar year: the husband can purchase $20,000 (maturity value) in Series E Bonds in his own name, and if he wishes, he can also purchase an additional $60,000 (maturity value) in Series E Bonds registered as follows: $20,000 in his name with his wife as co-owner; $20,000 in his name with one child as co-owner, and $20,000 in his name with the other child as co-owner. The family unit is cited merely as an example, but any person may be named as co-owner. In the case illustrated, the husband as the sole owner of $20,000 (maturity value) and as a co-owner of $60,000 (maturity value) in Series E Bonds, would be entitled under the regulations to redeem all or part of the Bonds without obtaining the signature of any of the other co-owners.

"The same co-ownership provisions apply to Series H Bonds inasmuch as purchase limits of E and H Bonds are applied separately. In the example

6. NON-TAX CONSIDERATIONS

The main non-tax reason for the creation of concurrent interests which have the characteristic of the right of survivorship is the avoidance of probate. The advantages of avoiding probate are considered in another connection.[7] These advantages, however, must be recognized as only part of the total picture and not be given more weight than they deserve.

Whenever property is jointly owned with the right of survivorship, the will of the survivor will dispose of the property. The will of each joint owner should therefore be prepared with this in mind because there may not be time to draw an appropriate will when the survivor is determined. In fact, in the preparation of the will of each joint owner, consideration should be given to the disposition of the jointly owned property in the event that the joint owners die under circumstances which make it impossible to establish the order of their death.[8]

---

above, the husband not only can purchase $80,000 in Series E Bonds, but can also buy $80,000 in Series H Bonds as well. Semi-annual interest checks on the full $80,000 in H Bonds would be mailed to the owner and he would be entitled to redeem all or part of the Bonds without obtaining the signature of any of the other co-owners."

[7] See discussion of the pros and cons of revocable inter vivos trusts at page 120 supra.

[8] See the Uniform Simultaneous Death Act as adopted in Massachusetts, Mass. Ann. Laws, c. 190A, §3, quoted infra page 1453, which deals specifically with the disposition of jointly owned property with the right of survivorship, when the survivor cannot be determined.

In CCH 1955 Fed. Est. & Gift Tax Rep. ¶2070.035, there is a discussion of the availability of the marital deduction with respect to property owned by a husband and wife in joint tenancy or in tenancy by the entirety, if the husband and wife die simultaneously and the governing jurisdiction has adopted the Uniform Simultaneous Death Act. The discussion includes the following: "Since, in the case of simultaneous deaths, one-half of the property does pass to the decedent's spouse, and since it is includible in her estate, it should qualify for the marital deduction to the extent that it is included in decedent's gross estate. For all practical purposes, however, it usually does not matter whether the entire value of the joint property is first included in decedent's estate (assuming he paid for all of it) and then the marital deduction taken as to the one-half which passes to his spouse, or whether one-half is included in his gross estate and the other half included in the spouse's estate without considering any of it for the marital deduction. The result, taxwise, will be the same whichever method is used for determining decedent's estate tax."

7. TAX CONSIDERATIONS[9]

a. *Income Taxes*

If the jointly owned property is income-producing, each joint owner will normally include in his gross income the portion of the income which he is entitled to receive.[10] Where, however, the donor-joint-owner is entitled to withdraw all of the donation, as in the case of a joint bank account, or to cash a jointly owned government bond, then he will be taxable on the income in proportion to the amount of his donation to the joint arrangement.[11] The income tax on Series E savings bonds, of course, can be deferred.[12]

[9] See generally Young, Tax Incidents of Joint Ownership, 1959 U. Ill. L.F. 972-1021.

[10] In Lipsitz v. Commissioner, 220 F.2d 871 (4th Cir. 1955), a tenancy by the entirety was involved that was controlled by Maryland law, under which the husband and wife are each entitled to one half of the income from property owned by them as tenants by the entirety. Nevertheless, the court ruled that if the spouses had agreed that all of the income was to go to one of them, such an agreement modified the ordinary consequences of the tenancy by the entirety, and for income tax purposes the income was all attributable to the spouse who was entitled to receive it under the agreement. Certiorari was denied in 350 U.S. 845 (1955).

In Lannan v. Kelm, 221 F.2d 725 (8th Cir. 1955), business property was put in the name of husband and wife as joint tenants and used in the husband's business. When the property was sold, the question arose as to whether the gain on the sale was attributable one half to each of the two joint tenants or all to the husband, in whose business the property was used. The court reversed the lower court's determination that the gain was taxable one half to each, and said: "We have not been referred to any cases . . . that hold that capital gain and income resulting from jointly owned realty is taxable according to the ownership thereof under state law regardless of any other consideration. The trial court held that the motive and intent of the husband are immaterial. It is with this we disagree." In other words, the court was saying that though a joint tenancy exists in form, if the control of the husband remains unchanged in regard to the income, for income tax purposes he may continue to be regarded as the owner.

[11] Revenue Ruling 54-143, 1954-1 C.B. 12, provides that where a Series E bond is issued to two persons as co-owners, the interest increment on the bond is taxable to them in proportion to the amount of the purchase price contributed by each.

In United States v. Stock Yards Bank, 55-1 USTC ¶9113 (W.D. Ky. 1954) *aff'd,* 231 F.2d 628 (6th Cir. 1956), United States Series E bonds, payable to a husband and/or his wife, which were held by a bank as collateral for the husband's note were not subject to levy by the United States for unpaid income taxes of the husband. The court stated that the wife's right in the bonds could not be taken from her "by a levy or distraint based upon an assessment against her husband."

[12] In Rev. Rul. 55-278, 1955-1 C.B. 471, it is determined that when government bonds are acquired with the money of A and put in the name of A or B and then are reissued in the name of B alone, a gift from A to B is made at the time the bonds are issued in B's name alone, and the value of the gift is the redemption value of the bonds at the time they are reissued. Furthermore, the interest on the bonds that accrued before the reissue is includible in A's

Deductions for taxes and interest paid in relation to the jointly held property should turn on the extent to which the joint owner who makes the payment is entitled to reimbursement from the other joint owner.[13]   The same should be true as to any deduction for repairs to and maintenance of the jointly owned property.[14] Losses sustained in the operation of the jointly held property should be divided on the same basis as the joint owners are entitled to income.[15]

Section 116 of the 1954 Code[16] permits a dividends-received exclusion in the amount of $50. This dividends-received exclusion as applied to married couples permits the exclusion of dividends only on stock owned by each spouse. Thus a husband who receives $100 in dividends cannot attribute $50 of this to his wife, so that

income for the year in which the gift is made. Revenue Ruling 58-2, 1958-1 C.B. 236, deals with a case where the owner of Series E United States savings bonds transferred them to a revocable inter vivos trust. He had not reported the interest on the bonds in his individual income tax returns for the past years. The ruling holds that under 1954 I.R.C. §676 the settlor of the trust is considered as the owner of the bonds, and since he did not realize the benefit of the interest at the time of the transfer, he is not required to include in his income tax return the amount of the interest that had accumulated to the date of the transfer.

Non-interest-bearing Growth Savings Certificates issued by banks at a discount, which increase in value by a specified progressively higher amount at stated intervals, and the increment in the value of which is payable only upon surrender of the certificate, are to be treated the same as Series E savings bonds for income tax purposes, according to Revenue Ruling 57-452, 1957-2 C.B. 302. Revenue Ruling 60-145, I.R.B. 1960-16, 18, holds that interest on nonnegotiable savings certificates issued by a bank, which is credited periodically to a certificate holder but paid only upon redemption of the certificate and at a different date prior to maturity, is includible in the holder's gross income for the taxable year in which the interest was received prior to the first maturity date or credited thereafter.

[13] In Theodore Milgroom, 31 T.C. 1256 (1959), it is pointed out that in Massachusetts the husband is obligated to pay all taxes and interest on property held by the entireties and is entitled to the possession of the proceeds of the sale of such property.   Hence he is entitled to deduct on his separate return the total amount of taxes and mortgage interest paid as a part of the sale transaction with respect to such property.

[14] In Estate of Elmer B. Boyd, 28 T.C. 564 (1957), a tenant in common who owned an undivided one-half interest in rental property paid for the repairs to and the maintenance of the property and claimed a deduction for the total of such payments.   The court held that he was entitled to deduct only one half of the total because he was entitled to reimbursement from the other co-owner for any payments for repairs and maintenance in excess of one half. On the right of one co-tenant to contribution, however, compare 2 American Law of Property §6.18 (Casner ed. 1952).

[15] In George E. Reynolds, 26 T.C. 1225 (1956), the court held that where a husband and wife owned land in Florida as tenants by the entirety, the income from the operation of the property was equally the property of the husband and wife, even though the purchase money was provided by the husband. Thus the loss suffered in the operation of the land was attributable to them jointly and was not the individual loss of the husband.

[16] Quoted infra page 1333.

the couple can exclude the entire $100. If, however, the stock is held by husband and wife in joint tenancy or in tenancy by the entirety, and under applicable local law each spouse is entitled to half of the dividends, then if the total dividends received amount to $100, $50 will be attributable to each spouse and the entire amount will be excluded under the dividends-received exclusion.[17]

If property is concurrently owned with a right of survivorship, then, on the death of one of the concurrent owners, there will be included in the decedent's gross estate for federal estate tax purposes the entire value of such concurrently owned property if the decedent furnished all the consideration for its acquisition, or that portion of its value that corresponds to the portion of the consideration furnished by the decedent if he did not supply all the consideration, or its value divided by the number of concurrent owners if the concurrent interest was acquired by gift, devise, or inheritance.[18] Under the 1939 Code, no matter how much was included in the gross estate of the decedent concurrent owner, the survivor retained the old basis of the property when he succeeded to the ownership under the right of survivorship.[19]

Section 1014(b)(9) of the 1954 Code[20] provides that property acquired from the decedent by "form of ownership," if by reason thereof "the property is required to be included in determining the value of the decedent's gross estate," takes on a new basis which is the value of the property at the date of the decedent's death (or at the controlling date after death if the optional valuation date is selected). It is believed that the ownership in severalty which vests in the survivor of two concurrent owners by the right of survivor-

[17] See Rev. Rul. 55-476, 1955-2 C.B. 35.

[18] See 1954 I.R.C. §2040, quoted infra page 1399.

[19] Section 113(a)(5) described all the circumstances where a new basis was acquired for property transmitted at death; concurrent interests with the right of survivorship were not mentioned.

Under the 1939 Code, an estate tax might be payable on the full value of the concurrently owned property, as when the first to die furnished all the consideration, but the value of the property to the survivor might be much less because the property carried a low basis, making a substantial capital gains tax payable on a sale by the survivor. In Gits v. United States, 58-2 U.S.T.C. ¶9759 (N.D. Ill. 1958), the 1939 Code was applied in determining the basis of the surviving joint tenant for depreciation purposes. In G. Loutrell Timanus, 32 T.C. 631 (1959), aff'd, 278 F.2d 297 (4th Cir. 1960), where the testator devised land to his wife and son as joint tenants, the son's basis as the survivor, under 1939 I.R.C. §113(a)(5), was the value of the land at the death of his father. In Marie D. Bouchard, 34 T.C. —, No. 68 (1960), the 1939 Code was applicable and the surviving joint tenant of stock did not obtain a new basis therefor, even though the value of the stock was includible in the deceased joint owner's gross estate. The case was reversed and remanded, 285 F.2d 556 (1st Cir. 1961), on the ground that no joint tenancy had been created and hence the survivor took under the decedent's will.

[20] Quoted infra page 1382.

ship is property acquired from the decedent by "form of ownership" and thus comes under Section 1014(b)(9). It must be kept in mind that this section applies only in the case of decedents dying after December 31, 1953.[21]

Where only a portion of the value of the concurrently owned property is included in the gross estate of the first of the concurrent owners to die (where, for example, the decedent furnished only a portion of the consideration), there will be included in the decedent's gross estate the value of an undivided interest in the concurrently owned property that corresponds to the fractional share of the consideration furnished by the decedent for the acquisition of the property. Thus, under Section 1014(b)(9) a new basis will be acquired by the survivor as to such undivided interest, but the old basis will continue as to the other undivided interest. Notice that Section 1014(b)(9) applies only when the "property" is included in determining the value of the decedent's gross estate. It is submitted that the "property" is so included when only the value of part of the joint interest is included in the gross estate.[22]

The basis of the jointly held property during the joint lives of the owners, as well as its basis after one dies, to the extent a new basis is not picked up on his death, will depend on various factors. The following are illustrative:

1. If X devises Blackacre to A and B as joint tenants, the basis

----

[21] Section 1014(b)(9) contains the limitation that "if the property is acquired before the death of the decedent, the basis shall be the amount determined under subsection (a) reduced by the amount allowed to the taxpayer as deductions in computing taxable income under this subtitle or prior income tax laws for exhaustion, wear and tear, obsolescence, amortization, and depletion on such property before the death of the decedent." It would seem that the interest of the survivor in the property is "acquired before the death of the decedent," where, on the transfer, a right is acquired, of which the transferee cannot be deprived, so that the new basis should be reduced by the amount allowed to the survivor as deductions for depreciation in computing the survivor's taxable income during the lifetime of the decedent. Section 1.1014-6(a)(3), Ex. (2) of the Regulations, quoted infra page 1500, is in accord with these observations. If, however, a tenancy by the entirety in real property (or a joint tenancy between husband and wife in real property) is involved and the donor spouse is the decedent and did not elect to treat the creation of the tenancy as a transfer under 1954 I.R.C. §2515, quoted infra page 1422, is the interest of the survivor "acquired before the death of the decedent"? Yes, it is, because §2515 only defines a transfer in such a situation for gift tax purposes, and nothing therein should be determinative for income tax purposes.

[22] Revenue Ruling 56-215, 1956-1 C.B. 324, holds that a new basis is obtained under §1014(b)(9) as to the portion of the jointly held property includible in the decedent's gross estate under 1954 I.R.C. §2040. The fact that no estate tax may be due or that no estate tax return is required does not preclude obtaining a new basis. However, no alternate valuation may be elected for property where the valuation of the estate does not exceed $60,000 at the time of the decedent's death.

of the jointly owned property in the hands of A and B will be governed by Section 1014 of the 1954 Code.[23]

2. If A purchases Blackacre and takes title in the name of A and B as joint tenants, the basis in the hands of A and B will be governed by Section 1012 of the 1954 Code,[24] with such adjustment as may be required so far as B's basis for his interest is concerned by virtue of the fact that he acquired his interest by gift.[25]

Those sections of the 1954 Code providing for the nonrecognition of gain or loss in certain situations are equally applicable if jointly held property is involved. Thus, if property jointly held is compulsorily or involuntarily converted, no gain will be recognized to the extent provided by Section 1033 of the 1954 Code.[26] Accordingly, there is no reason to avoid creating concurrent interests just because these possibilities exist.

A problem similar to the transferee liability of one who takes life insurance proceeds for the unpaid income taxes of the insured[27] is the transferee liability of a surviving joint tenant for the unpaid income taxes of the deceased joint tenant. The applicable rules should be similar.[28]

b. *Estate Taxes*

Prior to the 1954 Code, a factor which had to be taken into account in determining whether to create a concurrent interest with a right of survivorship was the effect that the resultant diminution in the value of property subject to claims would have on the estate tax deductions. The 1939 Code[29] did not allow an estate tax deduction for debts, expenses of administration, and the like, to the extent that such items exceeded the value, at the time of the de-

---

[23] Quoted infra page 1381.

[24] Quoted infra page 1381.

[25] See 1954 I.R.C. §1015, quoted infra page 1383.

[26] Quoted infra page 1384.
Revenue Ruling 57-408, 1957-2 C.B. 525, illustrates the operation of §1033 where proceeds of insurance resulting from the involuntary conversion of property held by tenants in common are used to purchase for them as tenants in common 85 percent of the stock of a corporation owning property similar to or related in service or use to the property involuntarily converted.

[27] See discussion at page 319 supra.

[28] Payne v. United States, 247 F.2d 481 (8th Cir. 1957), *cert. denied,* 355 U.S. 923 (1958), held that where a taxpayer-husband transferred real property to his wife and himself as tenants by the entirety, and the transfer made the taxpayer insolvent, the husband and wife as tenants by the entirety were liable as transferees of the real property under 1939 I.R.C. §311 (1959 I.R.C. §6901) for the husband's unpaid income taxes.

[29] See 1939 I.R.C. §812(b).

cedent's death, of property subject to claims.[30] Section 2053(c)(2) of the 1954 Code[31] continues the disallowance of the estate tax deduction for such excess "except to the extent that such deductions represent amounts paid before the date prescribed for the filing of the estate tax return." [32] Thus this factor can now be disregarded in determining whether to create concurrent interests provided that the survivor keeps in mind the requirement that the expenses be paid before the filing of the estate tax return.

Section 2053(b) of the 1954 Code,[33] which has no counterpart in the 1939 Code, allows a deduction for "amounts representing expenses incurred in administering property not subject to claims which is included in the gross estate to the same extent such amounts would be allowable as a deduction under subsection (a) if such property were subject to claims, and such amounts are paid before the expiration of the period of limitation for assessment provided in section 6501." [34] Various expenses incurred in connection with administering concurrent interests, such as determining the value of the property and ascertaining the proportionate contribution of each concurrent owner to the purchase price, should thus be deductible.

The most objectionable tax feature of the 1939 Code in regard to concurrent interests with a right of survivorship was the possibility of double estate taxation in rapid succession when husband and wife were the concurrent owners.[35] The deduction for prop-

[30] Section 812(b) of the 1939 Code defines property subject to claims as "property includible in the gross estate of the decedent which, or the avails of which, would under the applicable law, bear the burden of the payment of such deductions in the final adjustment and settlement of the estate."

[31] Quoted infra page 1403.

[32] In describing this change, the Senate Finance Committee report gives an illustration: "For example, if the decedent's estate includes only property held by the decedent and his surviving spouse as tenants by the entirety, such items as funeral expenses, debts and other valid claims if allowable under local law and paid by the spouse prior to the time for filing the estate tax return, will be allowed by this section." S. Rep. No. 1622, 83d Cong., 2d Sess. 474 (1954).

[33] Quoted infra page 1403.

[34] Section 6501 of the 1954 Code imposes a three-year limitation on the assessment of taxes commencing with the date the return was filed.

[35] Suppose, for example, that a husband purchased with his own funds securities worth $250,000 and took the ownership of the securities in the name of himself and his wife as joint tenants with a right of survivorship. Assume that the husband and the wife then died in a common accident, the wife surviving the husband for a short period of time, and that the jointly owned securities constituted their entire estates. The full value of the securities would be included in the husband's gross estate, since he furnished all the consideration for their acquisition. Likewise the full value of the securities would be included in the wife's gross estate, since she became the complete owner of the securities by surviving her husband. In determining the net estate of the husband, a marital deduction was available, but that deduction was limited to

erty previously taxed within five years under the 1939 Code[36] did not apply to transfers from one spouse to another.

Section 2013 of the 1954 Code[37] eliminates entirely the deduction for property previously taxed and substitutes a credit against the decedent's estate tax equal to all or part of the estate tax paid on a transfer of the property to the decedent from a person who died within ten years prior to the decedent's death. The credit diminishes in amount as the time between the deaths of the transferor and the decedent increases. For the first two years following the death of the transferor 100 percent of the credit is available, during the third and fourth years 80 percent, and so on, down to 20 percent in the ninth and tenth years. Significantly, the credit is available with respect to transfers from one spouse to another and thus the possibility, outlined above, of double taxation in rapid succession where spouses own a concurrent interest with a right of survivorship is eliminated. Of course, if the surviving spouse survives for more than two years, the double taxation feature will begin to reappear, but the surviving spouse may be able to nullify this by a program of inter vivos gifts.

It should be noted, however, that the total amount of the taxes payable may be greater than the total amount which would be payable if the surviving spouse had received only one half of the husband's estate in a form which would be includible in her gross estate on her death. For example, if the husband's gross estate is $200,000 and his wife has little or no property, the federal estate tax on his estate will be approximately $4800, and on her death shortly after his, assuming she retains until her death all of the property given outright to her on his death, the federal estate tax on her estate will be approximately $30,000 and, though the credit of $4800 is available in determining the tax payable on her death, a tax of approximately $25,000 will be payable on her death, making an over-all total of some $30,000 payable in taxes. On the other hand, if the husband had given his wife only approximately half of his estate, the tax on his death would have been $4800 and the tax on her later death would have been $4800, making a total of $9600 in taxes. In other words, an additional $20,000 in taxes

---

50 percent of the husband's adjusted gross estate. Thus the deductions would not eliminate any net estate. The excess of the gross estate over the deductions, the husband's net estate, would be taxable, and no deduction would be available, in determining the wife's net estate, for the property which was previously taxed in her husband's estate and which is includible in her gross estate.

[36] See 1939 I.R.C. §812(c).

[37] Quoted infra page 1391.

has to be paid as a result of the husband giving all of his property to his wife in a form that causes its value to be includible in her gross estate on her death.

As has been mentioned, the factors that are relevant in determining the extent to which the value of concurrently owned property with the right of survivorship will be included in the gross estate of the first of the joint owners to die are set out in Section 2040 of the 1954 Code.[38] When the consideration test is applicable, that is, when the jointly held property was not acquired by gift, bequest, devise or inheritance, so that it is essential to determine what proportion of the purchase price was furnished by the first of the joint owners to die, very careful records should be maintained.[39] If a joint bank account is established, only the money of one of the joint owners should be placed in this account because a mixture of the funds of the two joint owners will make it almost impossible to determine, on the death of one, the proportionate contributions of each where, over the years, there have been many withdrawals and deposits.[40]

[38] Quoted infra page 1399. It should be noted that §2040 affirmatively excepts from inclusion in the gross estate of a decedent the value of such part of the jointly held property as may be shown to have belonged originally to the surviving joint owner and not acquired by him from the decedent joint owner for less than an adequate consideration. Thus, if the first to die of the joint owners made no contribution, directly or indirectly, to the joint property, but the entire contribution was made by the survivor, nothing is includible in the decedent's gross estate under §2040 or any other section of the Code.

[39] Section 20.2040-1(a) of the Regulations, quoted infra page 1515, brings out that the entire value of the jointly held property is includible in the gross estate of the first of the joint owners to die, unless his executor submits facts sufficient to show that the property was not acquired entirely with consideration furnished by the decedent. See the following cases where the contribution of the surviving joint owner was not proved and hence the entire value of the jointly owned property was includible in the gross estate of the first to die: English v. United States, 270 F.2d 876 (7th Cir. 1959); Tuck v. United States, 172 F. Supp. 890 (N.D. Cal. 1959), aff'd, 282 F.2d 405 (9th Cir. 1960); Estate of Paul S. Brown, 19 CCH T.C. Mem. 1960-265.

[40] In Murphy v. Shaughnessy, 54-2 U.S.T.C. ¶10970 (N.D.N.Y. 1953), the decedent and his son opened a joint bank account. The initial deposit was $2500, made up of $1700 supplied by the decedent and $800 by his son. On the death of the decedent, the balance in the account was $1265.36. It was established that no withdrawals were made by the decedent and no additional deposits were made either by the decedent or by his son. How much is includible in the decedent's gross estate for estate tax purposes so far as the joint bank account is concerned? The court held that the full amount was includible in his gross estate.

In Estate of Joseph J. Mulconroy, 15 CCH T.C. Mem. 887 (1956) the court included in the decedent's gross estate the entire value of United States Treasury bonds issued in the name of himself or his sister, because there was not sufficient evidence to justify a finding that the sister had paid for the bonds.

Is it possible for that one of the joint owners of a bank account who furnished the money in the account, or that one of the joint owners of a govern-

In applying the consideration test, it must be kept in mind that money or property given by one concurrent owner to the other which is applied to the purchase price of the jointly held property will be deemed to have been furnished by the donor-concurrent-owner. Even though the donated property has increased in value after the gift and before it is applied to the purchase price, its entire value will be deemed to be the contribution of the donor.[41] To the extent, however, that the donee uses income only from the donated property in paying the purchase price, he is deemed to make the contribution and not the donor.[42]

Suppose that H purchases land with his own funds and takes title thereto in the name of himself and his wife as tenants by the entirety; that the original purchase price is $10,000; that five years later, when the value of the property is $15,000, the $5000 increase being due to economic conditions, H's wife, W, with funds of her own makes a $5000 addition to the land; and that two years later H dies and the value of the land at the time of his death, and one year after his death, is $25,000. What portion of the value of the land will be includible in H's gross estate? At the time W made

---

ment bond who paid for it, to give the other all rights in the account or the bond without the form of ownership being changed, so that if the donor dies, no part of the value of the account or the bond will be includible in his gross estate? See Silverman v. McGinnes, 259 F.2d 731 (3d Cir. 1958), discussed supra page 402, note 4. See also Estate of Michael A. Doyle, 32 T.C. 1209 (1959), where the court concluded, on the evidence presented, that the account was still a joint one with right of survivorship when the decedent died, although there was some evidence that the decedent intended to give the other the entire account.

[41] See Reg. §20.2040-1(c)(4), quoted infra page 1516.

Swartz v. United States, 182 F. Supp. 540 (D. Mass. 1960), refuses to apply Reg. §20.2040-1(c)(4) in a case where the property given by the decedent to the survivor was sold by the survivor and the gain realized and the money then used to buy the property jointly held by the decedent and the survivor. Thus the survivor was deemed the contributor of the portion of the purchase price that corresponded to the gain realized on the sale of the property given to her by the decedent. The implication of the opinion is that the Regulations would not be followed even if the gain is not realized, as when the property given to the survivor by decedent is itself transferred into joint ownership after it has appreciated in value.

[42] See Reg. §20.2040-1(c)(5), quoted infra page 1516. In accord with the Regulations is Harvey v. United States, 185 F.2d 463 (7th Cir. 1950).

In Tuck v. United States, 172 F. Supp. 890 (N.D. Cal. 1959), a husband gave stock to his wife, and on the date of the gift the corporation declared a stock dividend. The dividend was later given by the wife to the husband and placed by him in joint tenancy with her. Is the contribution of the stock dividend attributable to the wife or the husband? The court held that it was traceable to the original gift by the husband to the wife, since it represented a capitalization of profits earned prior to the original gift. The case was affirmed in 282 F.2d 405 (9th Cir. 1960). McGehee v. Commissioner, discussed supra page 190, note 81, is distinguished on the ground that in that case the stock dividend represented a capitalization of current earnings.

her $5000 contribution, the land was worth $15,000, and the entire $15,000 was attributable to the original $10,000 contribution made by H. Thus, immediately after the $5000 addition, when the land was presumably worth $20,000, three fourths of this value was attributable to H and one fourth to W. The subsequent increase in value of $5000 does not change the fractional contributions of H and W, so that three fourths of the value of the land arguably might be includible in H's gross estate.[43]

A concurrent owner who takes as survivor by right of survivorship may have to contribute to the deceased joint owner's death taxes. Thus, if it is desired to free the survivor of this burden, the will of the deceased joint owner should relieve the jointly held property of it.[44]

On the death of a tenant in common, only the value of his undivided interest in the common property is includible in his gross estate no matter who furnished the consideration for the acquisition of the property, unless some basis for including more than the value of his undivided interest exists under some section of the 1954 Code other than Section 2040. Thus the deceased tenant in common may have made a gift in contemplation of death of some other undivided interest in the common property and, on this ground, more than the value of the undivided interest in the common property owned by him may be includible in his gross estate.[45]

An undivided interest in property, such as is held by a tenant in common, may be difficult to sell. Should this fact depress its

[43] The result suggested in the text is supported by analogy in Reg. §25.2515-1(c)(2), Ex. (2), quoted infra page 1551. On the basis of the literal wording of 1954 I.R.C. §2040, quoted infra page 1399, one could strongly contend that the result in the problem posed in the text should be that two thirds of the value of the land is included in H's gross estate.

[44] Revenue Ruling 56-144, 1956-1 C.B. 563, holds that though the surviving joint tenant is personally liable for the estate tax of a decedent to the extent of the value of the joint property at the time of the decedent's death if tax is not paid when due, where the property is transferred to a bona fide purchaser, the tax lien is divested. "Bona fide purchaser" means one who acquires property by arm's-length dealings and pays full consideration. The fact that the purchaser is presumed to know of the lien by reason of the recital of the death of the joint tenant in the chain of title does not prevent him from being a bona fide purchaser.

[45] Each tenant in common is entitled to the possession of the entire property with the other. To the extent that a transfer has been made by one of the tenants in common to the other, has the transferor retained for his lifetime "the possession or enjoyment of" the transferred property within the meaning of those words under 1954 I.R.C. §2036, quoted infra page 1396, so that the value of the transferred interest will be includible in his gross estate? I think not, for such a right to enjoy the possession of the whole is entirely subject to the transferee's desires because of the right of partition available to the transferee.

value in determining its value for federal estate tax purposes? Probably not, because of the right in a tenant in common to partition.[46]

c. *Gift Taxes*

In many jurisdictions it is quite common for husband and wife to own real property as tenants by the entirety or as joint tenants with a right of survivorship. A phase of estate planning is advising husband and wife whether to take the ownership of real property in one of these forms or, if either form of ownership now exists, whether to continue it, in the light of the gift tax consequences of one course of action as compared with another. Section 2515 of the 1954 Code,[47] which has no counterpart in the 1939 Code, is significant in determining these consequences. In order to evaluate this new section, however, the gift tax situation as it has existed in this area in the past and as it will continue in the future where Section 2515 does not apply, or is ruled out because of an election not to have it apply, must be explored.

Section 2515 aside, the gift tax situation on the creation of a tenancy by the entirety or a joint tenancy with a right of survivorship in real property depends on the characteristics of such a joint interest under the governing local law.[48] The following characteristics are significant:

1. Under the applicable local law, who is entitled to the income from the jointly held property?
2. Under the applicable local law, can either spouse acting alone destroy the right of survivorship?

[46] In Tishman v. United States, 59-1 U.S.T.C. ¶11875 (E.D. Va. 1959), it was determined that an undivided one-half interest in real estate is not to be valued at one half of the total value of the property but rather is to be discounted by 15 percent for federal estate tax purposes. If this approach is sound for federal estate tax purposes, it should also be used for gift tax purposes. But compare Estate of Isaac W. Baldwin, 18 CCH T.C. Mem. 902 (1959), where the court held a one-half undivided interest was worth one half of the full interest. In Blackburn v. United States, 60-2 U.S.T.C. ¶11964 (S.D. Ind. 1960), even though an expert witness testified that it was reasonable and customary to discount property which had multiple owners of undivided interests from 15 to 20 percent, the court allowed no discount in valuing an undivided one-fourth interest, because the several interests in the property were in unity for disposal purposes.

Stewart F. Hancock, CCH T.C. Mem. 1960-230, deals with the valuation for gift tax purposes of a one-thirtieth interest in commercial real estate owned totally by members of a real estate syndicate and occupied by tenants with long-term leases.

[47] Quoted infra page 1422.

[48] For a discussion of the characteristics of such tenancies, see 2 American Law of Property §§6.2, 6.3, 6.6 (Casner ed. 1952).

The donee-spouse, in case either spouse acting alone can sever the joint ownership, clearly receives a present interest, so that the annual exclusion is available in ascertaining the net taxable gift.[49] If neither spouse acting alone can sever the joint ownership but the donee-spouse is entitled to receive a portion of the income and to share in the possession of the land, a present interest clearly exists to that extent.   In such a case, however, the indestructible right to take all, if the donee-spouse survives the donor-spouse, may be a future interest.[50]   If neither spouse acting alone can sever the joint ownership and the donee-spouse is not entitled to income or possession, but receives only an indestructible right to the whole on surviving, the entire interest given might well be thought to be a future interest.[51]   The valuation of the gift to the donee-spouse where neither spouse acting alone can sever the joint ownership will depend on the age of the donee-spouse as compared with the age of the donor-spouse.[52]

The 1939 Code made it clear,[53] as does the 1954 Code likewise,[54] that the value of the gift to the donee-spouse qualifies for the gift tax marital deduction.   Thus only half the value of the gift is deemed a gift from the donor-spouse to the donee-spouse.[55]   To the extent that the donor-spouse has not used up his $30,000 specific gift tax exemption,[56] of course a further deduction is available in computing the taxable gift for the year.[57]

---

[49] See Reg. §25.2511-1(h)(5), quoted infra page 1544.

[50] See Reg. §25.2512-2, quoted infra page 1553.

[51] In Massachusetts the husband is entitled to all the income from, and the exclusive possession of, a tenancy by the entirety.   The wife has an indestructible right to the whole if she survives.   See page 400 supra, note 1.   The practice in Massachusetts, however, evidently concurred in by the Internal Revenue Service, is to regard the wife's interest in a tenancy by the entirety as a present interest.

[52] See Reg. §25.2515-2(b), (c), quoted infra page 1553.

[53] See 1939 I.R.C. §1004(a)(3)(D).

[54] See 1954 I.R.C. §2523(d), quoted infra page 1425.

[55] For example, suppose that a husband buys Blackacre out of his own funds, paying $24,000, and takes title thereto in the name of himself and his wife as joint tenants with a right of survivorship.   Blackacre is located in a jurisdiction where either spouse, acting alone, may sever his or her interest. One half the value of the gift is deductible under the gift tax marital deduction, leaving $6000.   The annual exclusion of $3000 is available because the gift to the wife is of a present interest.   Thus the net taxable gift is $3000. See Reg. §25.2523(d)-1, quoted infra page 1555.

[56] See 1954 I.R.C. §2521, quoted infra page 1423.

[57] If a person decides to give certain property which he owns to his children, the gift tax cost can be kept to a minimum by giving each child annually an undivided interest in the subject matter of the gift, but this undivided interest should not exceed in value the annual gift tax exclusion.   If the donor lives long enough, the property involved can be passed to his children without any gift tax cost by a series of such annual gifts.   In Howells v. Fox, 251 F.2d 94 (10th Cir. 1957), cert. denied, 356 U.S. 974 (1958), the owner of a promissory

To complete the background necessary to a proper evaluation of Section 2515, one other point needs to be examined. Suppose that real property is owned by husband and wife as joint tenants with a right of survivorship in a jurisdiction which allows either spouse, acting alone, to sever the tenancy. If the right of survivorship is destroyed by dividing the property in kind or by selling it and dividing the proceeds of the sale, has either spouse made any gift to the other? The answer to this question should be no, because the right of survivorship was always destructible at the will of either party and so no gift is made from the younger, who had the better chance of surviving, to the elder.[58] If, however, a tenancy by the entirety is involved and the controlling jurisdiction does not allow either spouse acting alone to destroy the right of survivorship, a different situation is presented on such a division. In this case the younger has conceivably enriched the elder by making it certain that the elder will have an interest, not defeasible on the elder's prior death, in some of the property.[59]

Section 2515(a) provides that the creation of a tenancy by the entirety or joint tenancy with a right of survivorship between a husband and wife in real property is not to be treated as a transfer for gift tax purposes unless the donor-spouse elects to have it so

---

note made partial assignments thereof to her children in stated dollar amounts, along with the interest attributable to such amounts. When the assignor died, the face value of the note was less than its face value at the time of the partial assignments. The court was presented with the question whether the partial assignments were of the specified dollar amounts or of an undivided interest in the whole of the note in the proportion that the stated sum bore to the face amount of the note. The amount includible in the assignor's estate for estate tax purposes depended on what had been assigned. The court held that an undivided interest in the whole of the note had been assigned to each child rather than a guaranteed sum of money, which would be a lien on the face value of the note.

[58] Under what circumstances, if any, will the elimination of the right of survivorship as to Blackacre produce a gain which will be subject to a tax as a capital gain?

Revenue Ruling 56-437, 1956-2 C.B. 507, holds that for the purposes of eliminating a survivorship feature, the conversion of a joint tenancy in capital stock of a corporation into a tenancy in common, whether done voluntarily or pursuant to a partition proceeding, is a nontaxable transaction for federal income tax purposes and neither concurrent owner realizes a taxable gain or sustains a deductible loss.

Revenue Ruling 57-209, 1957-1 C.B. 413, holds that the transfer of stock from the husband and wife as joint tenants to their names as tenants in common is subject to the documentary stamp tax imposed under 1954 I.R.C. §§4321 and 4333.

[59] In a Special Ruling dated October 1, 1948, CCH 1954 Fed. Est. & Gift Tax Rep. ¶5470.15, the Treasury Department held that the conversion of a tenancy by the entirety into a tenancy in common is not a taxable gift if the spouses are the same age. If their ages differ, the transfer is taxable as a gift from the younger to the elder to the extent that the value of the rights of the younger under the tenancy exceeds one half the value of the property.

treated. To exercise the election, he must file a gift tax return reporting the gift for the calendar year in which the gift was made "within the time prescribed by law, irrespective of whether or not the gift exceeds the exclusion provided by section 2503(b)," [60] that is, irrespective of whether the value of the gift exceeds the annual $3000 exclusion for gifts of present interests. Since the gift tax sections of the 1954 Code "shall apply with respect to the calendar year 1955 and all calendar years thereafter," [61] the gift tax consequences of the creation of a tenancy by the entirety or a joint tenancy with right of survivorship in real property in 1954 or a prior year will not be affected by the failure to make the election.[62] However, if an addition is made to the tenancy after January 1, 1955, it will be governed by Section 2515.

In the area where Section 2515 operates, what is the significance of a failure to make the election provided for? Section 2515(b) provides: "In the case of the termination of a tenancy by the entirety [or joint tenancy with right of survivorship between husband and wife], other than by reason of the death of a spouse, the creation of which, or additions to which, were not deemed to be transfers by reason of subsection (a), a spouse shall be deemed to have made a gift to the extent that the proportion of the total consideration furnished by such spouse multiplied by the proceeds of such termination (whether in form of cash, property, or interest in property) exceeds the value of such proceeds of termination received by such spouse." [63]

The question now is when the donor-spouse should elect, after January 1, 1955, to treat the creation of a tenancy by the entirety or joint tenancy with a right of survivorship in real property or an addition to the value thereof in the form of an improvement,

[60] The quotation in the text is from 1954 I.R.C. §2515(c), quoted in full infra page 1422.

[61] See 1954 I.R.C. §7851(a)(2)(B).

[62] Where real property is not involved or where the joint owners of real property are not husband and wife, §2515 does not apply at all.

[63] The Senate Finance Committee report (S. Rep. No. 1622, 83d Cong., 2d Sess. 480 (1954)) gives the following illustration of the quoted language: "Under the rule in this section, if the husband furnished $30,000 and the wife $10,000 as consideration for the purchase of real property held as tenants by the entirety and, when the property was sold for $60,000, the husband received $35,000 and the wife $25,000, the gift at the time of sale would be computed as follows:

Value of husband's interest equals $60,000 × 30,000/40,000 = $45,000.

Value of gift equals value of interest minus value of proceeds received.

Gift equals $45,000 minus $35,000 equals $10,000."

The consideration furnished by each spouse is not always easy to calculate. See, for example, Reg. §25.2515-1(c)(2), Ex. (2), quoted infra page 1551. For a discussion of the difficulties in determining the contribution by each joint owner for estate tax purposes, see page 412 supra.

reduction in indebtedness, or otherwise, as a transfer for gift tax purposes. The answer would be easy if it could be said with certainty that the tenancy would not terminate until the death of one of the spouses, because then there could be no possible advantage in electing to treat any of the described events as a transfer for gift tax purposes.[64] No one, however, can foretell with certainty how the tenancy will end, or what division of the proceeds of the sale of the joint property may be appropriate at some future date when a sale may be made.[65]

In some cases, as, for example, where the value of the property increases sharply after the creation of the concurrent interest, it may be highly advantageous to elect to treat the creation of the interest as a transfer.[66] A sharp increase in value is unusual, but the

[64] If it could be known that on the termination of the tenancy for a reason other than the death of a spouse, the share each spouse would take would correspond exactly to the share of the total consideration furnished by that spouse, in which case no gift would be made under §2515(b) at the time of division, there could again be no possible advantage in electing to treat any of the described events as a transfer for gift tax purposes.

[65] Suppose that H buys a house, contributing all the money, and takes title as joint tenant with W. H does not make an election. Several years later the house is sold and another one is bought immediately. Will the proceeds from the sale of the first be deemed a distribution, with one half taxed as a gift to W? The presumption ought to be that the proceeds are a return of consideration to H. In any event, it might be advisable for the parties to preserve evidence showing that the proceeds were not distributed. Section 25.2515-1(d)(2)(ii) of the Regulations, quoted infra page 1552, recognizes that no gift is made to W in this situation.

[66] Suppose that after January 1, 1955, a husband buys a farm, paying $60,000 out of his own funds and taking the title in the name of himself and his wife as joint tenants with a right of survivorship. The farm is located in a jurisdiction in which either spouse, acting alone, can sever the joint tenancy. Five years later, after the discovery of oil in the area, the farm is worth $1,000,000. The farm is then sold and the situation of the husband at that time makes it desirable to divide the $1,000,000 equally between the husband and the wife. What are the gift tax consequences (1) if the husband elected to treat the creation of the joint tenancy as a transfer to the wife for gift tax purposes, and (2) if he did not make such an election?

If the creation of the joint tenancy was treated as a transfer for gift tax purposes, the value of the gift to the wife was one half the total purchase price, or $30,000. One half the value of the gift was deductible as the gift tax marital deduction, leaving $15,000. The annual exclusion of $3000 reduces the amount to $12,000. On the assumption that the residue of the husband's $30,000 cumulative exemption exceeded $12,000, no net taxable gift was involved. When the property is later sold and each joint tenant takes one half, no new gift is made by either one.

If the husband did not elect to treat the creation of the joint tenancy as a transfer for gift tax purposes, then, when the property is sold and the proceeds are divided equally, he will be deemed to have made a gift to his wife at that time. The value of the gift is determined as follows:

Value of husband's interest equals $1,000,000 × 60,000/60,000 = $1,000,000.
Value of gift equals value of interest minus value of proceeds received.
Gift equals $1,000,000 minus $500,000 equals $500,000. One half of the

possibility of some increase in value is almost always present. An analysis of the particular case must be made to determine the possible disadvantages that may result if no election is made to treat the creation of the concurrent interest as a transfer for gift tax purposes, of which the possibility of increase in value of the property is one important factor. Other factors are:

1. If the election is made to treat the creation of the joint tenancy as a transfer for gift purposes, and then on the sale of the land it is found desirable to turn over all the proceeds of the sale to the husband, who furnished all of the consideration, a gift will be made at that time by the wife to the husband. Whereas, if no election is made, no gift will be made at any time.

2. If a joint tenancy or tenancy by the entirety is created in a jurisdiction in which neither spouse, acting alone, can destroy the right of survivorship, an election to treat the creation of the tenancy as a transfer will result in a gift from the younger spouse to the elder spouse on an equal division of the proceeds obtained from the sale of the property. If no election is made, however, and the spouses contributed equal portions of the consideration, no gift will result under Section 2515(b) on an equal division of the proceeds obtained from the sale of the property.[67]

---

value of the gift is deductible as the gift tax marital deduction, leaving $250,-000. The annual exclusion of $3000 reduces the amount to $247,000. On the assumption that the husband's $30,000 cumulative exemption is fully available, the net taxable gift will be $217,000 and a gift tax will be payable on this amount.

Notice that the income tax law will exact a sizable tax on the gain in connection with such a sale, but, evidently, in applying §2515(b) to determine the amount of the gift from one spouse to another on the termination of the joint tenancy the amount of the capital gain is of no significance.

Suppose that H owns an oil well having an expected producing life of ten years and that he places this property in tenancy by the entirety with W, his wife. Under the governing local law, half of the income from the tenancy by the entirety is payable to W. As oil is extracted from the well, half of the income from its sale is paid to W. Do these payments constitute any termination of the tenancy so as to impose a gift tax on the husband in regard to them if he has not elected to treat the creation of the tenancy as a transfer for gift tax purposes? If the answer to the question is no, and the well runs dry in ten years, half the value of the oil property will have been transferred to W without the payment of a gift tax.

[67] If local law permits, it may be desirable to make the right of survivorship destructible by either spouse, acting alone, so that no gift can possibly be involved on an equal division of the proceeds of the sale of the jointly owned property when an election is made to treat the creation as a transfer.

A tenancy by the entirety is converted into a tenancy in common by the divorce of the owners. See 2 American Law of Property §6.6 (Casner ed. 1952). A joint tenancy between husband and wife, however, may not be destroyed under local law if the owners are divorced. If the joint tenancy is not de-

PROBLEMS

10.1. H and W, husband and wife, own concurrently the following assets:

a. Blackacre as tenants by the entirety; title to Blackacre was taken in this form in 1940; H paid the entire purchase price of $30,000; Blackacre is now worth $50,000.

b. Whiteacre as joint tenants; title to Whiteacre was taken in this form in 1946; the purchase price was $60,000; H paid two thirds of the purchase price and W paid one third out of funds raised by the sale of securities given to her outright by her husband in 1944; Whiteacre is now worth $48,000.

c. United States Series E bonds payable "to H or W"; H furnished one half of the money for the purchase of these bonds and W furnished the other half out of her share of the net income from Whiteacre; the bonds were purchased in July, 1950, at a price of $15,000; the present value of the bonds is between $16,000 and $17,000.

d. A savings account payable to either or the survivor; this account was opened in 1940; the present balance is $6000; H has made deposits from his funds; W has deposited income from the securities given her by her husband and income from Whiteacre; withdrawals have been made from time to time by H and from time to time by W; the total interest on the account over the years amounts to $1200.

Determine the answers to the following questions:

(1) H dies and W survives him. What amounts will be includible in H's gross estate for federal estate tax purposes with respect to Blackacre, Whiteacre, the government bonds and the savings account?

(2) W dies and H survives her. What amounts will be includible in W's gross estate for federal estate tax purposes with respect to Blackacre, Whiteacre, the government bonds and the savings account?

(3) H dies and W survives him. What amounts will be available for the estate tax marital deduction with respect to Blackacre, Whiteacre, the government bonds and the savings account? [68]

---

stroyed by divorce, will the tenancy be deemed terminated by a divorce for the purpose of applying §2515(b)? If not, then §2515 can be significant in cases of property owned in joint tenancy by persons who are no longer husband and wife.

[68] Kingery v. Granquist, 56-1 U.S.T.C. ¶11587 (D. Ore. 1956), recognized

(4) W dies and H survives her. What amounts will be available for the estate tax marital deduction with respect to Blackacre, Whiteacre, the government bonds and the savings account?

(5) H dies and W survives him. W sells Blackacre for $45,000. What is the basis of Blackacre for the purpose of determining whether W has a gain or loss on such a sale for federal income tax purposes? See Revenue Ruling 56-519, 1956-2 C.B. 123. See also Antoinette M. Faraco, 29 T.C. 674 (1958), *aff'd sub nom.* Faraco v. Commissioner, 261 F.2d 387 (4th Cir. 1958), *cert. denied,* 359 U.S. 925 (1959), dealing with Section 113(a)(5) of the 1939 Code as it applies to this question.

(6) H dies and W survives him. W sells Whiteacre for $50,000. What is the basis of Whiteacre for the purpose of determining whether W has a gain or loss on such a sale for federal income tax purposes?

(7) Assume that W dies and H survives her and H makes the sales referred to in (5) and (6) above. What is the basis for the purpose of determining whether H has a gain or loss on such sales for federal income tax purposes?

(8) During the joint lifetime of H and W, what part of the income from Blackacre, Whiteacre, the government bonds and the savings account is attributable to H for federal income tax purposes and what part of the income is attributable to W?

(9) In what years did H make a gift to W for federal gift tax purposes with respect to Blackacre, Whiteacre, the government bonds and the savings account? Will such gifts qualify for the federal gift tax marital deduction?

(10) H dies and W survives him. Will Blackacre, Whiteacre, the government bonds and the savings account be includible in the probate estate of H?

10.2. Under what circumstances may it be advisable from an estate planning standpoint to eliminate the right of suvivorship with respect to some or all concurrent interests of the person whose estate plan is being prepared?

10.3. In Problem 10.1, if H and W eliminate the right of survivorship as to Blackacre, will such an elimination constitute a gift by H to W or by W to H for federal gift tax purposes?

10.4. In Problem 10.1, if H and W eliminate the right of survi-

that demand notes made payable to a husband and wife jointly, with right of survivorship, qualify for the marital deduction when the wife survives the husband.

vorship as to Whiteacre, will such an elimination constitute a gift by H to W or by W to H for federal gift tax purposes?

10.5. In Problem 10.1, if H sells an undivided one-fourth interest in Whiteacre to X for $20,000, will H have realized any gain?[69]

10.6. H and W own Blackacre as joint tenants, and the purchase price for Blackacre was contributed by H. Shortly before H's death, H and W join in making a transfer of Blackacre to their son, S. H is deemed to have made a gift in contemplation of death. Will the entire value of Blackacre be includible in H's gross estate, or will only one half of its value be so includible? See Estate of D. M. Brockway, 18 T.C. 488 (1954), *aff'd sub nom.* Brockway v. Commissioner, 219 F.2d 400 (9th Cir. 1954); Baltimore National Bank v. United States, 136 F. Supp. 642 (D. Md. 1955); Estate of A. Carl Borner, 25 T.C. 584 (1955); Estate of Edward Carnall, 25 T.C. 654 (1955).[70]

10.7. A purchases a United States savings bond entirely with his own funds. He has the bond registered in co-ownership form in the names of himself and B. He delivers the bond to B. The pertinent savings bond regulation permits either co-owner to redeem the bond upon his separate request, without requiring the signature of the other, and in the event of a redemption by one of the co-owners, the other "shall cease to have any interest in the Bond." The regulation also points out that on the death of one co-owner the surviving co-owner will become the sole owner.

    a. Has A made a gift to B for federal gift tax purposes of all or any part of the value of the bond?

    b. If B survives A, will all or any part of the bond be included in A's gross estate for federal estate tax purposes? See Estate of John H. Boogher, 22 T.C. 1167 (1954). See also page 402 supra, note 4.

---

[69] In Rev. Rul. 59-121, 1959-1 C.B. 212, it was held that the consideration received by an owner of land for the granting of an easement therein should be applied as a reduction of the basis of the land subject to the easement; any excess over the basis constitutes recognized gain.

[70] See Note, Joint Tenancy and Estate Tax Avoidance: A Widening Loophole for Transfers in Contemplation of Death, 66 Yale L.J. 142 (1956).

Revenue Ruling 57-448, 1957-2 C.B. 618, deals with a situation where a husband purchased property with his own funds and took title thereto in the name of himself and his wife as tenants by the entirety, and later they transferred the property to a trust. Under the terms of the trust, the income was to be paid to them in equal shares for their joint lives, and on the death of one, the income was to go to the survivor. The husband died. The ruling holds that the entire value of the trust property, less the life interest in the wife's one half thereof, is includible in the husband's gross estate under 1954 I.R.C. §2036(a), quoted infra page 1396. It does not state whether the trust was revocable or irrevocable, so that it may be inferred that the result would be the same in either case.

10.8. Effective January 1, 1955, the Treasury Department changed the regulations governing United States savings bonds to permit the purchase of Series E and H bonds by trustees of personal trust estates. The annual purchase limit of $20,000 (maturity value) of each series, which applies to individual owners, will also apply to a single trust estate, regardless of the number of beneficiaries. If a bond is of a series which may be originally issued in the name of a trustee, it may be reissued in the name of a trustee of an inter vivos trust. A owns Series E bonds in the amount of $20,000 (maturity value). He establishes an irrevocable inter vivos trust with T as trustee. Under the terms of the trust T is to pay the net income to A's son, S, and on the termination of the trust, the principal is to be paid to designated beneficiaries. A has his Series E bonds reissued in the name of T as trustee under the trust. T collects the $20,000 on the bonds on their maturity date. A never included any portion of the interest in his income during the period he held the bonds. To whom is the interest taxable when collected by T?

10.9. A and B own Blackacre as tenants in common. Blackacre was purchased in 1950 by A and B for $30,000. A paid two thirds of the purchase price and B one third. The deed to A and B reads as follows: "to A and B as tenants in common and not as joint tenants." A dies and B survives him. What amount is includible in A's gross estate for federal estate tax purposes with respect to Blackacre? See Estate of Charles A. Trafton, 27 T.C. 610 (1956).

10.10. If an arrangement by two persons provides for the survivor to become the outright owner of the property involved, such an arrangement, if inexpertly drawn, may leave doubt as to what was intended: a joint tenancy, life interests in undivided portions with a remainder in the survivor, or a fee interest in undivided portions with an executory interest in favor of the survivor. In determining the value of what is includible in the gross estate of the first to die, what difference does it make whether the arrangement is construed in one or another of the suggested ways? See Brockway v. Commissioner, 219 F.2d 400 (9th Cir. 1954).

10.11. In a state which does not recognize a tenancy by the entirety, H has real estate conveyed to himself and his wife as tenants by the entirety. H furnishes all of the consideration. H dies. How much of the value of the real estate is includible in II's gross estate for estate tax purposes? See Dane v. Delaney, 125 F. Supp. 594 (D. Mass. 1954).

10.12. H plans to purchase a house as a family residence. He seeks your advice as to the best way to take title to it. Under what circumstances will you advise him to take title in the name of himself and his wife with the right of survivorship?

10.13. H owns the family residence. He desires to place the title to it in the name of himself and his wife as tenants by the entirety. What steps should be taken to accomplish this result? See Mass. Ann. Laws, c. 184, §8, as amended by Acts of 1954, c. 395, and approved on May 4, 1954. (The 1954 amendment provides: ". . . a conveyance of real estate by a person to himself and his spouse as tenants by the entirety shall, when recorded in accordance with the provisions of section three of chapter two hundred and nine, create a tenancy by the entirety.")

10.14. H desires to give his farm to his two sons in such a way that they will enjoy the benefits of the farm concurrently as long as both of them live, and that the survivor will become the owner in severalty of the farm. Describe the disposition you would advise him to make to accomplish his objective.

10.15. H purchases a family residence and the title thereto is taken in the names of his wife, W, and of his son, S, as joint tenants with the right of survivorship. Will the gift to the wife qualify for the federal gift tax marital deduction? See Section 25.2523(e)-1(g)(2) of the Regulations, quoted infra page 1555.

d. *State Taxes*

The extent to which the pattern of state death taxes as applied to concurrent interests follows the federal plan requires, of course, an examination of the statutory provisions of the controlling state.[71] Massachusetts is an example of a state which gives particularly favorable state inheritance tax treatment to a residence owned by husband and wife as tenants by the entirety.[72] State income

[71] In Bradley v. State, 100 N.H. 232, 123 A.2d 148 (1956), the decedent established a joint bank account with his sister-in-law. Apparently, at no time during the decedent's lifetime did the sister-in-law have access to the bank books. On the death of the decedent, the sister-in-law assigned the bank books to the decedent's executor, waiving her statutory right to claim the deposits as the surviving joint tenant. The question presented to the court was whether the state inheritance taxes should be assessed on the basis of the amount in the bank deposits less the expenses of administration of the decedent's estate, or whether they should be assessed on the basis of the full amount in the bank account. The court held that the surviving joint tenant could refuse to accept the interest passing to her as the survivor and that her refusal would cause the amount in the bank account to fall into the estate and be subject to the claims against the estate. The court noted that if the survivor had taken the bank account under her right of survivorship, the amount in the account would not have been subject to claims against the estate, and the state inheritance taxes would have been assessed on the full amount in the account.

[72] See Mass. Ann. Laws, c. 65, §1 (Supp. 1959), quoted infra page 1441,

taxes and state gift taxes must not be overlooked in completing the
tax picture of jointly owned property.

8.　COMMUNITY PROPERTY[73]

Estate planning in a community property state involves all the
considerations relevant in a noncommunity property state with
respect to the property of an unmarried person and the separate
property of a married person. Such considerations are also relevant in planning the disposition of the portion of the community
property which is subject to disposition by the person whose estate
plan is being formulated. The fact that a community property
state is in the picture does introduce additional estate planning
considerations, however, and the more significant ones are listed
below:[74]

---

which exempts entirely from state inheritance taxes single family residential
property occupied by the husband and wife as a domicile and owned by them
as tenants by the entirety, and exempts up to $25,000 in value multiple-family
residential property so occupied and so owned.

The Commissioner of Corporations and Taxation in Massachusetts has
ruled that the $25,000 exemption allowable in the case of multiple-family
residential property applies only to the portion of such property actually
occupied by the husband and wife as a residence at the time of the decedent's
death. The illustration given in the ruling is of an apartment building containing ten apartments, which was purchased with funds contributed solely by
the husband. The total fair market value of the building is $100,000, and the
fair market value of the apartment occupied by the husband and wife is
$10,000. The exemption allowable under the Massachusetts statute on the
death of the husband is only $10,000. See 42 Mass. L.Q. No. 1, p. 20 (1957).
Evans v. Commissioner of Corporations and Taxation, 339 Mass. 754, 162
N.E.2d 310 (1959), does not agree with the Commissioner. The case holds that
the full $25,000 exemption is available on multiple-residence property, even
though the husband and wife do not occupy the entire property.

[73] An analysis of community property is found in 2 American Law of
Property §§7.1-7.36 (Casner ed. 1952).

Community property exists in Arizona, California, Idaho, Louisiana,
Nevada, New Mexico, Texas and Washington. Prior to the Revenue Act
of 1948, the community property states had a distinct income tax advantage
and this fact induced the following other states to adopt the system: Hawaii
(1945), Michigan (1947), Nebraska (1947), Oklahoma (1945), Oregon (1947)
and Pennsylvania (1947). Michigan repealed its statute in 1948, and Hawaii,
Nebraska, Oklahoma and Oregon did likewise in 1949. The Pennsylvania
Supreme Court eliminated community property in that state by holding the
statute unconstitutional. Wilcox v. Penn Mutual Life Ins. Co., 357 Pa. 581,
55 A.2d 521 (1947). Revenue Ruling 60-102, I.R.B. 1960-21, 7, examines the
laws of the Panama Canal Zone, which are based on the California laws as
they existed prior to July 29, 1927 (on that date the California laws were
amended so as to give the wife an interest in community property that would
cause one half of the income to be attributed to her for federal income tax
purposes), and holds that the Panama Canal Zone is not a community
property jurisdiction for federal income tax purposes.

[74] The statutes in the various community property states are not uniform.

1. Probably the most significant difference in estate planning in a common law state and a community property state is the minor role normally played by the estate tax marital deduction in a community property state. This is because the computation of the adjusted gross estate in a community property state requires the subtraction from the gross estate of the value of the community property included therein,[75] so that the adjusted gross estate will be very small where, as is usually the case, the gross estate consists principally of community property. The maximum estate tax marital deduction is 50 percent of the adjusted gross estate, and thus, if the adjusted gross estate is small in amount, the available estate tax marital deduction will be of little significance. It should be kept in mind, however, that if a spouse owns substantial separate property, so that he will have a sizeable adjusted gross estate,[76] the community property which is subject to disposition by him can be used to make estate tax marital deduction gifts.

2. The gift tax marital deduction normally will play a minor role also in estate planning in a community property state. If a husband gives his wife outright his share of the community property, a gift tax will be payable thereon without the benefit of any gift tax marital deduction.[77] An equal division of the community property between husband and wife does not constitute a gift for federal gift tax purposes by either one to the other. If the separate property of one spouse is given to the other, then the gift tax marital deduction comes into the picture.[78]

3. The management of the community property during the joint lives of the husband and wife may be placed by

---

Thus, if any problem turns on the law as to community property in a particular state, care must be taken to examine the law. An analysis of the estate of a resident of Louisiana is set forth as an example at page 1304 infra.

[75] See 1954 I.R.C. §2056(c)(2)(B), quoted infra page 1409.

[76] It must be kept in mind that community property which is converted into the separate property of the deceased spouse may continue to be regarded as community property in determining the adjusted gross estate. See 1954 I.R.C. §2056(c)(2)(C), quoted infra page 1410.

[77] See 1954 I.R.C. §2523(f), quoted infra page 1426.

For a case in which it was important to determine whether a husband had made a gift to his wife of a portion of the community property, see *Jacques v. Jarecki*, 56-2 U.S.T.C. ¶11625 (N.D. Ill. 1956).

[78] Community property which is converted into the separate property of the donor-spouse may continue to be regarded as community property for purposes of determining the availability of the gift tax marital deduction. See 1954 I.R.C. §2523(f)(3), (4), quoted infra page 1426.

the controlling community property law in one spouse or the other. An important aspect of estate planning in a community property state is the extent to which the manager of the community can make inter vivos arrangements, such as revocable inter vivos trusts, insurance trusts, irrevocable inter vivos trusts, outright gifts, etc., that will be effective even as to the non-manager's share of the community property.[79]

4. Where the wife is allowed to elect whether to stand by property arrangements with respect to community property made by her husband, the tax consequences of an election by her to accept them become important.[80]

5. Life insurance purchased with community funds may present special problems, particularly if the spouse of the insured dies first.[81] The extent to which the surviving

---

[79] See Commissioner v. Chase Manhattan Bank, 259 F.2d 231 (5th Cir. 1958), *cert. denied,* 359 U.S. 913 (1959), where the court held that on the husband's death the wife could not withdraw her share of the community property which he had transferred to a revocable inter vivos trust, and that she had no election as to the destination of any portion of the proceeds of insurance on his life, even though the life insurance had been purchased with community funds. Furthermore, the wife was deemed to have made a gift, at the time of the husband's death, of her share of the community property placed in the trust and her share of the life insurance proceeds to the beneficiaries which had been selected by her deceased husband. Texas law was applied in this case.

Revenue Ruling 56-408, 1956-2 C.B. 600, points out that in a community property state, where the husband is the managing member of the community and may make valid gifts of the community property to third persons, such gifts made by him in contemplation of his wife's death are includible, under 1954 I.R.C. §2035, quoted infra page 1396, in her gross estate to the extent of her one-half interest in the property.

[80] See discussion at page 70 supra.

In Stapf v. United States, 189 F. Supp. 830 (N.D. Tex. 1960), the husband disposed of his wife's share of the community as well as his own, and she elected to abide by the will. The question was whether gifts in the will to the wife were on condition that she allow her property to go as provided in the will, so that the gifts to her could qualify for the marital deduction only to the extent to which the gifts to her exceeded the value of what she had to give up. The court held the gifts to her could qualify because, at the most, the will imposed on her an election or condition and not any pecuniary obligation.

[81] Stewart v. United States, 158 F. Supp. 25 (N.D. Cal. 1957), held that where the insured owned insurance policies on his life which had been purchased with community funds, and the insured's wife predeceased him, one half of the cash surrender value of the policies was not includible in her gross estate, even though she had a vested right in the policies and could have prevented their disposition to a third party by gift, because her interest was not one which her executor could in any way reduce to cash or possession in her estate. Thus no transfer of interest took place as a result of the wife's death. This case was reversed on this point sub nom. United States v. Stewart, 270 F.2d 894 (9th Cir. 1959). Quigley v. United States, 59-2 U.S.T.C. ¶11887 (W.D. Wash. 1959), held that one half of the cash surrender value of policies issued

spouse is bound by the selection made by the insured spouse as to the disposition of the insurance proceeds is particularly significant from an estate planning standpoint.[82] The fact that veterans' insurance has been held not to be subject to the community property laws is also important.[83]

6. Because of the fact that many tax consequences turn on whether particular property is separate property or community property, careful records should be kept by husband and wife in a community property state so that proper identification can easily be made.[84] Unfortunately, family

---

on the life of the husband was includible in the wife's gross estate when she died first and premiums had been paid from community funds.

California Trust Co. v. Riddell, 136 F. Supp. 7 (S.D. Cal. 1955), held that one half of the cash surrender value of policies of insurance on the life of the husband was includible in the wife's gross estate because, under California law, life insurance on the life of the husband purchased with his earnings is community property. This result was reached even though the husband had the power to change the beneficiaries, the court saying, "the fact that the policies in question were retained by the husband and that he had a right to change the beneficiaries at will does not mean he could deprive the wife of her community interest therein without her consent."

In Stapf v. United States, 60-2 U.S.T.C. ¶11967 (N.D. Tex. 1960), the decedent acquired insurance on his life and paid some of the premiums out of separate property prior to his marriage and some out of community property after his marriage. The court, applying the 1939 Code, included in the decedent's gross estate the portion of the insurance proceeds that corresponded to the portion of the premiums paid out of his separate property plus one half of the premiums paid out of community property.

[82] See page 428 supra, note 79.

[83] Revenue Ruling 56-603, 1956-2 C.B. 601, points out that the proceeds of life insurance policies issued by the Veterans' Administration are not subject to the community property laws of any state, and accordingly, the full value of the proceeds of such insurance is includible in the insured's gross estate. The ruling relies on Wissner v. Wissner, 338 U.S. 655, 70 Sup. Ct. 398, 94 L. Ed. 424 (1950).

In Estate of L. C. Hunt v. United States, 175 F. Supp. 665 (E.D. Tex. 1959), the decedent owned two United States Government War Risk Life Insurance policies on his own life, in the amount of $5000 each, and paid the premiums thereon out of community funds. The court held that the entire $10,000 worth of life insurance was includible in the decedent's gross estate under the 1939 Code.

[84] If a dispute arises as to whether certain property of a decedent is his separate property or his community property, and it is advantageous to a person to establish that the property is community property or separate property, will the attorney's fees paid by such a person in settling the dispute be deductible under 1954 I.R.C. §212, quoted infra page 1336? In the following cases the deduction was allowed: Day v. United States, 57-1 U.S.T.C. ¶9270 (D. Ariz. 1956); Lytton-Smith v. United States, 57-1 U.S.T.C. ¶9272 (D. Ariz. 1956).

In Estate of J. Leslie Vogel, 30 T.C. 125 (1958), the court determined that various assets standing in the name of the surviving spouse alone were community property, on the ground that the evidence failed to establish that what was community property had been transmuted to separate property by an

records are not usually complete and accurate in this regard. The intermixture of separate and community property, and the consequent elimination of the separate identity of each, are facilitated in those states which regard the income from separate property as community property because of the natural tendency to intermingle income and the property from which it is derived.[85]

7. Generally a new basis is obtained with respect to property on the death of a person, only if the value of the property is included in the gross estate of the decedent. The surviving spouse's share of community property, however, acquires a new basis, even though the value of the share is not included in the gross estate of the deceased spouse.[86]

8. The income and estate tax consequences in relation to property placed in an inter vivos trust may turn on a de-

---

alleged oral agreement or that such assets had been acquired with income from the surviving spouse's separate property. The case was affirmed sub nom. Estate of J. Leslie Vogel v. Commissioner, 278 F.2d 548 (9th Cir. 1960).

[85] In Idaho, Louisiana and Texas, with some exceptions, the income from separate property is regarded as community property. See 2 American Law of Property §7.12 (Casner ed. 1952).

[86] See 1954 I.R.C. §1014(b)(6), (7), quoted infra page 1382.

Under the 1939 Code, §113(a)(5) did not give the surviving joint tenant a new basis, even though the value of the property held in joint tenancy was included in the gross estate of the deceased joint tenant for federal estate tax purposes. The result is different under 1954 I.R.C. §1014, quoted infra page 1381. However, like the 1954 Code, the 1939 Code gave a new basis to community property. Thus, prior to the 1954 Code it was important to determine whether property held by husband and wife was community property or was held by them as joint tenants. For a case which determined that the husband and wife held the property as joint tenants under California law, see Bordenave v. United States, 150 F. Supp. 820 (N.D. Cal. 1957). In McCollum v. United States, 58-2 U.S.T.C. ¶9957 (N.D. Okla. 1958), the court held that the fact that property was conveyed to husband and wife as joint tenants did not prevent it from being community property under Oklahoma law, and thus, on the death of the husband a new basis was acquired under the 1939 Code.

The date on which the holding period begins for the purpose of determining the tax on a gain with respect to the wife's share of the community and with respect to the deceased husband's share which comes to her on his death is considered supra page 126, note 45.

If husband and wife in a community property state convert their community property into a tenancy in common, on the husband's death the wife does not get a new basis as to her share of the tenancy in common. Laura Massaglia, 33 T.C. 379 (1959), is a case where it was not until after the husband's death that the court in the controlling state recognized that a husband and wife could convert community property into a tenancy in common, but the effect of such a decision was to cause an agreement made by the husband and wife to be operative and thus deprive her of a new basis as to her share of the tenancy in common. (New Mexico law was involved.) The case was affirmed in 61-1 U.S.T.C. ¶9208 (10th Cir. 1961).

termination of who is the settlor.[87]   In a noncommunity
property state, if the husband transfers property to such a
trust and his wife consents to have one half of the gift
charged to her for gift tax purposes,[88] the wife is not regarded to any extent as the settlor of the trust by virtue of
her giving her consent.[89]   In a community property state,
on the other hand, if one spouse acquiesces in a transfer of
community property by the other spouse, it would seem
that the acquiescing spouse should be regarded as the transferor of his or her share of the community property.[90]

9. The community property laws may come into the picture
when the preparation of an estate plan for a domiciliary
of a common law state is involved. This may happen if
the client once resided in a community property state, because in such a situation the community property acquired
during that period of residence will retain it character
when moved to a noncommunity property state.[91] Also, a
resident of a noncommunity property state who acquires
real property in a community property state may find he
has some community property on his hands.[92]

10. If a husband and wife move from a common law state to a
community property state, will the property they bring
with them take on the mantle of community property if it
would have been community property had they acquired
it while residents of a community property state? The answer to this question is no, but such property may be sub-

[87] As to the importance of determining who is the settlor of an inter vivos
trust, see discussion at page 197 supra.
[88] See 1954 I.R.C. §2513, quoted infra page 1419.
[89] See Rev. Rul. 54-246, 1954-1 C.B. 179, which holds that the consenting
spouse is not the settlor for estate tax purposes. It would seem that the same
result should be reached in determining whether she is the settlor for income
tax purposes.
[90] If a spouse has no right to elect against a transfer in trust of community
property made by the other spouse, will she nevertheless be a settlor of the
trust? The answer is probably yes. See page 428 supra, note 79.
[91] The community property which a husband and wife bring into a noncommunity property state, and the income therefrom, should be segregated
from their other property so that they can at all times be identified.
[92] In Rev. Rul. 55-461, 1955-2 C.B. 608, reference is made to the case of
Noble v. Commissioner, 138 F.2d 444 (10th Cir. 1943), where it was held that
a resident of a noncommunity property state who acquires real property in a
community property state with his own separate funds holds the property as
his own separate property without expressly designating it as such in the deed.
The ruling states, however, that the Noble case is not applicable when land
is purchased in Louisiana, because in that state real property purchased by a
married man becomes community property when it is not stipulated that it is
purchased with separate property; and this rule applies to the purchase of real
property in Louisiana by a nonresident.

ject to special treatment that makes it quite similar to community property.[93]

11. If the husband is domiciled in a community property state, the wife will also be regarded as so domiciled for the purpose of determining whether certain property is community property.[94] Thus the determination of the domicile of the husband becomes an important factor.[95]

12. In a community property state, the entire community property of the two spouses must be administered on the

---

[93] See California Prob. Code Ann. §201.5 (Deering, 1959) as amended in 1957, quoted infra page 1436. Section 201.5 and related sections of the Code are examined in Parker, Surviving Spouses Elective Rights in Community and Foreign Marital Property, 39 Trust Bull. No. 6, p. 24 (1960).

Estate of Frank Sbicca, 35 T.C. —, No. 14 (1960), points out that §201.5 of the California Probate Code does not convert a husband's personal property into community property. The full value of such property is includible in the husband's gross estate, and the wife's interest therein is a mere expectancy, so that any relinquishment by her of such property would not be giving up anything so far as she is concerned.

[94] Revenue Ruling 56-269, 1956-1 C.B. 318, points out that the domicile of a husband in a community property state fixes the domicile of his wife in that state and that the community property is divisible for federal income taxes. Thus, where a husband, a United States citizen, received income for personal services for the United States government in a foreign country, one half of the income was attributable to his wife. She was a nonresident alien who did not reside in the United States during the year. Under these circumstances, though the husband's share of the income was taxable pursuant to the provisions of 1954 I.R.C. §911(a) because the income was received for services to the United States government, the wife's share of the income was not deemed taxable because, under §871 a nonresident alien may be taxed only on income derived from sources within the United States, and the source of her income was not deemed from within the United States, though it was derived from personal services performed by her husband for the United States government, since the services were performed in a foreign country. Revenue Ruling 60-57, I.R.B. 1960-6, 74, also considers the situation of the nonresident alien wife whose husband is a United States citizen and is domiciled in a community property state. It points out that if the husband's income is derived from a trade or business within the United States, the nonresident alien wife is taxed under §871(c) as a nonresident alien engaged in a trade or business within the United States, but she must file Form 1040B to get the benefits of §871(c). If no portion of the community income is derived from a trade or business within the United States, the nonresident alien wife is taxed under §871(a) or §871(b) as a nonresident alien not engaged in a trade or business within the United States. See also United States v. Rexach, 185 F. Supp. 465 (D. Puerto Rico, 1960), where the domicile of the taxpayer (a citizen) and his alien wife was the Dominican Republic and the wife's one half of the community property income was deemed not taxable.

[95] In Richard M. Gooding, 27 T.C. 627 (1956), the taxpayer, a resident of Virginia, married a resident of Texas. The taxpayer never established a permanent residence in Texas but visited his wife a total of forty-one days during their marriage, which lasted approximately seven months. The court held that the taxpayer had not established that he had changed his domicile to Texas and, therefore, he and his former wife were not entitled, pursuant to the community property law of Texas, to divide their incomes earned during the period of their marriage. The case was affirmed in 250 F.2d 765 (D.C. Cir. 1957).

death of the first to die. This fact raises a number of questions in regard to tax consequences during the period of
administration.[96]

[96] See the following cases which deal with the taxation of the income derived from the surviving spouse's share of the community property during the
period of administration: Bishop v. Commissioner, 152 F.2d 389 (9th Cir.
1946); Commissioner v. Estate of J. T. Sneed, Jr., 220 F.2d 313 (5th Cir. 1955);
Estate of Bessie A. Woodward, 24 T.C. 883 (1955) *aff'd,* 241 F.2d 496 (5th Cir.
1957); but cf. Wells-Fargo Bank and Union Trust Co. v. United States, 134 F.
Supp. 340 (N.D. Cal. 1955), *rev'd,* 245 F.2d 524 (9th Cir. 1957). In Rev. Rul.
55-726, 1955-2 C.B. 24, it was held that in Washington and California and
all community property states having similar community property laws,
the estate of a deceased spouse should not, for federal income tax purposes,
be regarded as embracing the whole of the community property; the surviving spouse is the proper taxable person with respect to one half of the
income therefrom.
  The allocation between the deceased spouse's share of the community property and the surviving spouse's share of various obligations which must be
met during administration is considered in the following: Commissioner v.
Estate of J. T. Sneed, Jr., supra; McCullough v. United States, 134 F. Supp.
957 673 (W.D. La. 1955); Estate of Thomas Gannett, 24 T.C. 654 (1955); Rev.
Rul. 55-524, 1955- 2 C.B. 535.
  In Estate of William G. Helis, 26 T.C. 143 (1956), it was held that full administration expenses were deductible in Louisiana because they had been incurred in solving the complex problems involved in the calculation of the
federal and state taxes and had not been incurred for the administration of
the community generally. The court in Duncan v. United States, 143 F. Supp.
356 (W.D. Tex. 1956), held that it was proper to disallow as an estate tax
deduction so much of the attorney's fees and the executor's commissions as
was attributable to the surviving spouse's interest in the community property.
The case was reversed and remanded on a different point in 247 F.2d 845
(5th Cir. 1957), *rehearing denied,* 57-2 U.S.T.C. ¶11724 (5th Cir. 1957). In
Bosworth v. United States, 57-1 U.S.T.C. ¶11662 (W.D. Wash. 1956), the Commissioner allowed as a deduction only part of the attorney's fees, administration expenses, and monthly payments for family allowances to the surviving
spouse, but the District Court held that these items were deductible in full.
In Estate of L. C. Hunt v. United States, 59-2 U.S.T.C. ¶11891 (E.D. Tex.
1959), the descedent's estate incurred attorney's fees and court costs in the sum
of $917.50 in the administration of the estate, and the Commissioner allowed
only one half of this sum as a deductible administration expense. The court
held that the full sum was deductible.
  Dickson v. Phinney, 57-2 U.S.T.C. ¶9696 (W.D. Tex. 1957), dealt with the
effect which the remarriage of a surviving spouse during administration of the
estate of the decedent spouse had on income taxation. In re Algee's Estate,
158 Cal. App. 2d 691, 323 P.2d 221 (1958), held that the personal representative of a husband is entitled to the possession of the entire community property and is charged with it upon his accounting, and the wife's share of the
community property is properly included in the base for determining statutory attorney's fees.
  In Stapf v. United States, 189 F. Supp. 830 (N.D. Tex. 1960), the husband's will disposed of the wife's share of the community property as well as
his own, and the wife elected to abide by the will. Sixty-five percent of the
estate being administered consisted of the decedent's separate estate and his
share of the community, and the other 35 percent consisted of the wife's share
of the community. Sixty-five percent of the expenses of administration were
held deductible. Also, only one half of the community debts were deductible,
even though the decedent directed in his will that all community debts be
paid from his share.

PROBLEM

10.16. H and his wife, W, are residents of a community property state. W dies intestate, and under the controlling local law, her share of the community property passes outright to their two children. H, after W's death, continues to manage all of the property which constituted community property during her lifetime. The two children take no action to recover the possession of their share of the community property from H during his lifetime. H dies intestate and the two children are his only heirs. Is the value of W's share of the community property includible in H's gross estate if it is assumed that the children could not have recovered the possession of W's share of the community property from H immediately prior to his death if H had elected to set up the statute of limitations as a defense? See Guitar v. United States, 135 F. Supp. 509 (N.D. Tex. 1955).

CHAPTER XI

Future Interests Including the Rule Against Perpetuities and Related Rules

A thorough knowledge of the law of future interests is essential in the field of estate planning because every estate plan either will create future interests or will reject them in circumstances where they could be created. Such creation or rejection can be made intelligently only by someone with a background of knowledge as to what can be accomplished by the employment of future interests. Furthermore, the person whose estate plan is being drawn up may already own a future interest, and the disposal of such an asset will have to be taken into consideration. An evaluation of what he has by virtue of the ownership of the future interest must be made in order to plan properly for its disposal, and this evaluation can be made only by someone who has an adequate knowledge of the law of future interests.

1. TAX CONSIDERATIONS

The tax advantage that results from the creation of future interests in an estate plan is that federal and state death taxes can be avoided as the beneficial enjoyment of the property passes successively to the designated beneficiaries. Thus, if T in his will establishes a trust under which the income is to be paid to his wife for life and then to his son for life, and finally the corpus is to be distributed to the son's issue then surviving, no federal or state death taxes will be imposed on the property in the trust as the beneficial enjoyment passes from the wife to the son and from the son to his issue.[1] Of course, the creation of such a trust in T's will does not diminish the federal and state death taxes imposed at the time of his death.[2]

[1] Federal and state death taxes are also avoided to the same extent if such a trust is created by an inter vivos transfer.

[2] The creation of such an inter vivos trust may eliminate the imposition of federal and state death taxes on the value of the trust property on the death of the settlor, but the settlor may have to pay a federal gift tax. See page 153 supra.

If a future interest is created in a person, and it is descendible — that is, the person is not required to survive to the period of beneficial enjoyment — it is an asset in his estate and is subject to federal and state death taxes just as is any other asset. *For this reason, it is normally undesirable in an estate plan to create a future interest that may pass through the estate of a deceased person while it is still a future interest.*[3]

If the death tax is an estate tax, as is the federal death tax, the creation of a future interest by the decedent does not present any complication in determining the amount of the tax because the tax is assessed on the estate as a whole and not on the beneficial interests created. If, however, the value of a future interest that is created is deductible as a charitable deduction or as a marital deduction, then its value must be determined in order to ascertain the decedent's taxable estate.

State death taxes are frequently inheritance taxes — a tax on the value of the interest given to a particular beneficiary — and the creation of a future interest, particularly one subject to various contingencies, can create some difficulties in determining the amount of the tax. The controlling inheritance tax statute will have to be examined to answer specific questions, but generally the statute will allow the payment of the tax to be postponed until the future interest becomes possessory, or will permit the amount of the tax to be settled by negotiation and paid immediately.[4]

Even though a state has an inheritance tax, it will usually also have a so-called "sponge tax," which is designed to make certain that the over-all death tax paid as the result of the decedent's death will at least equal the maximum credit which could be taken for state death taxes in determining the federal estate tax bill.[5]

If a decedent's estate includes a descendible future interest, then the determination of the amount of the death taxes, whether under an estate tax or an inheritance tax, is somewhat complicated. Here again the typical statutory provisions will allow the payment of the tax to be postponed.[6]

---

[3] In McElroy v. Hinds, 54-2 U.S.T.C. ¶10957 (W.D. Okla. 1954), the court held that a person who, just prior to her death, owned an interest in property contingent on her surviving certain life beneficiaries, owned nothing includible in her gross estate for estate tax purposes when she predeceased the designated life beneficiaries.

[4] For an example of state inheritance tax provisions applicable to future interests, see Mass. Ann. Laws, c. 65, §§13-15, quoted infra page 1443.

[5] See 1954 I.R.C. §2011, quoted infra page 1388.

[6] See the following sections of the 1954 Code: §6163, quoted infra page 1428; §6601(b), quoted infra page 1433; §6165, quoted infra page 1428; §7101, quoted infra page 1435; §2015, quoted infra page 1394.

The possible complications which may be introduced in determining death taxes by the use of future interests in an estate plan are not sufficiently significant to deter their use in situations where they are otherwise appropriate. It is desirable, of course, to anticipate these complications and give the fiduciary administering the estate adequate power to cope with them in the way that may be most advantageous for all concerned.[7]

When future interests are used in inter vivos transfers, it should be kept in mind that the $3000 annual federal gift tax exclusion is not available with respect to them.[8]

A future interest may qualify for either the estate tax marital deduction or the gift tax marital deduction. It will qualify if it is not a terminable interest. In some limited situations it may qualify even though it is a terminable interest.[9]

The federal income tax consequences of dispositions in trust where the trust contains present and future interests are considered elsewhere.[10] In this chapter additional federal income tax material will be introduced from time to time.

PROBLEMS

11.1. T dies and under the terms of his will the residue of his estate is given to a named trustee to hold in trust. The trustee is to pay the net income to T's wife for her life; on the death of T's wife, he is to pay the net income to T's son for his life; on the death of the survivor of T's wife and T's son, he is to pay the corpus to the issue of T's son then living, such issue to take per stirpes; if no issue of T's son is living on the death of the survivor of T's wife and T's son, the trustee is to pay the corpus to the X charity.

a. In determining the federal estate tax on T's estate, will

For a comment on §§6163 and 6601(b), see Rev. Rul. 56-622, 1956-2 C.B. 956, which makes it clear that the interest on any deficiency attributable to the inclusion of a reversionary or remainder interest in the decedent's gross estate is computed at a rate of 4 percent per annum from the due date of the tax.

[7] The fiduciary normally should be authorized to compromise and to pay as soon as practicable all death taxes assessed on future or contingent interests. The fiduciary holding such power ought not to be one who can benefit himself by the way in which he exercises the power, or he may have a general power of appointment. See page 1132 infra.

[8] See discussion of the $3000 annual gift tax exclusion at page 236 supra.

[9] See discussion relating to terminable interests at page 832 infra.

[10] The circumstances under which the settlor of a trust will be taxed on trust income on the ground of dominion and control are examined supra page 153. The income taxation of trusts when the settlor is out of the picture in whole or in part is explored infra page 729.

a separate valuation of the future interests under the residuary trust be necessary?

b. In determining the state inheritance taxes with respect to the gifts under T's will, will a separate valuation of the future interests under the residuary trust be necessary?

11.2. T dies and under the terms of his will the residue of his estate is given to a named trustee to hold in trust. The trustee is to pay the net income to T's wife for her life; on the death of T's wife, he is to pay the corpus to T's son, and the interest in T's son is indefeasibly vested.

a. T's son dies. In determining the federal estate tax on the estate of T's son, will a valuation of the future interest in T's son under the residuary trust established by T's will be necessary?

b. T's son dies. The son's will gives his interest under the residuary trust to his wife. (1) Will the gift to the son's wife qualify for the estate tax marital deduction? (2) In determining the state inheritance tax with respect to the gift to the son's wife, will a valuation of the future interest in T's son under the residuary trust be necessary?

c. T's son makes an inter vivos gift to his wife of his interest under the residuary trust. (1) Will the gift to the son's wife qualify for the federal gift tax marital deduction? See Revenue Ruling 54-470, 1954-2 C.B. 320. (2) Will the annual federal gift tax exclusion be available with respect to the gift to the son's wife? See Revenue Ruling 54-401, 1954-2 C.B. 320. (3) Will a valuation of the future interest in T's son under the residuary trust be necessary in determining the amount of the federal gift tax payable by T's son?

11.3. A transfers Blackacre to B for life with remainder to C and his heirs. C buys B's life estate in Blackacre. The Federal Government contends that the life estate purchased by C merges with his indefeasibly vested remainder in fee simple and is destroyed, and that C is therefore not entitled to recover his cost of B's life estate through amortization over the period of B's life expectancy. Should such a contention prevail? See Bell v. United States, 212 F.2d 253 (7th Cir. 1954); William N. Fry, Jr., 31 T.C. 522 (1958), *aff'd sub nom.* Commissioner v. Fry, 60-2 U.S.T.C. ¶9738 (6th Cir. 1960).[11]

---

[11] In Eisele v. Rountree, 59-2 U.S.T.C. ¶9687 (M.D. Tenn. 1959), the court found that under the facts a life interest was not purchased, and thus denied as a deduction a claim which was based on the purchase of a wasting asset. Revenue Ruling 60-180, I.R.B. 1960-19, 13, recognizes that a lessee who would

2.　CLASS GIFTS

Almost every estate plan which creates future interests will describe some beneficiaries by a group designation.　The reason is that a plan which provides for a succession to property at some

---

normally depreciate his unrecovered basis in depreciable improvements on the property over their estimated useful life or the remaining term of the lease, whichever is shorter, must depreciate his unrecovered basis in such improvements over their remaining estimated useful life, without regard to the remaining term of the lease, when he acquires the lessor's interest and thus becomes the fee simple owner.

Will the payment made to B by C in Problem 11.3 be ordinary income or taxed as the sale of a capital asset?　In Gladys Cheesman Evans, 30 T.C. 798, (1958), an irrevocable inter vivos trust created prior to 1930 was involved, under which the settlor retained the right to the income for life and a reversionary interest which would take effect if she should survive all the remaindermen.　On December 1, 1950, the settlor transferred all her interests under the trust to her husband in consideration of the payment to her by him of $50,000 in 1950, $40,000 in 1951, $30,000 in 1952, $20,000 in 1953, and $10,000 in 1954 and each succeeding year during her lifetime.　The settlor treated the payments as proceeds from the sale of her trust interests, no portion of which was taxable until she recovered her basis for such interests, and thereafter as capital gain.　The court sustained the settlor's position.　In Rosen v. United States, 59-2 U.S.T.C. ¶9587 (N.D. Ala. 1959), amounts which were received by a widow in exchange for her dower interest in lands of her deceased husband and which were fixed monthly payments for life were held to be an annuity rather than ordinary income.

The sale by a life beneficiary of his interest to the remainderman as a means of converting ordinary income into a tax-free recovery of capital is discussed in 59 CCH Fed. Tax Rep. ¶8738.　In this connection §1239 of the 1954 Code must be kept in mind.　This section says, in substance, that if there is a sale of depreciable property (the life interest is of this character) between a husband and wife, or between an individual and a corporation, more than 80 percent in value of the outstanding stock of which is owned by such an individual, any gain to the transferor from the sale will be considered as a gain from the sale of property which is neither a capital asset nor property described in §1231.

In Estate of Robert J. Cuddihy, 32 T.C. 1171 (1959), the court relied in part on several income tax cases holding that a transfer by a life beneficiary of his interest in trust property is a transfer of a capital asset, and that the lump sum consideration received is not regarded as an accelerated receipt of future income in reaching the conclusion that the value of such property would not be includible in the gross estate of one who reserved to himself the income of a trust for life and then released his right to receive the income for a lump sum consideration on the theory that he "retained for his life . . . the possession or enjoyment of, or the right to the income from, the property" within the meaning of 1939 I.R.C. §811(c)(1)(B) (1954 I.R.C. §2036).

If a sale of a property interest is made under a deferred payment arrangement, and the buyer's promise to pay cannot be valued, no taxable income is received by the seller until after his basis is recovered, and thereafter he is taxable only on the amount of the yearly payments.　It has been held that the mere contractual promise of the buyer has no fair market value.　See Ruprecht v. Commissioner, 39 F.2d 458 (5th Cir. 1930).　But compare Frank Cowden, Sr., 32 T.C. 853 (1959), discussed infra page 1002.　In cases of doubt as to whether the buyer's arrangement can be valued, the installment method of purchase

future date should involve beneficiaries who are unborn or unascertained, and such beneficiaries can only be described with reference to their membership in some group. The drafting of gifts to designated groups — that is, the drafting of class gifts — can be done competently only by someone with a background of knowledge that enables him to appreciate the inherent ambiguities present in class designations. The diminution in the assets of an estate which results from the costs of litigation to construe dispositive provisions in an estate plan is a waste that should be entirely eliminated by proper drafting. Furthermore, though the court in construing the language of a dispositive provision in an estate plan purports to ascertain the intention of the transferor, there can be no assurance that the court's decision will accomplish that objective. Thus an ambiguously drafted dispositive provision not only is costly to the estate involved but also makes it doubtful whether the real desires of the transferor will be effectuated.

The group designations typically employed in an estate plan to describe beneficiaries are "children," "issue" and "heirs." There may be other group designations occasionally employed such as "grandchildren," "brothers and sisters," and "nephews and nieces," but on the whole they do not present problems basically different from the group designations more commonly used. Therefore an awareness of the inherent ambiguities in gifts to "children," "issue" and "heirs" will make one appreciative of the inherent ambiguities in other class designations.

It is suggested that five points be kept constantly in mind in connection with the drafting of class gifts. These five points are considered immediately below.

---

under 1954 I.R.C. §453 can be used to avoid bunching all the income in one year. The points discussed above may be relevant in arranging for the sale of a life interest.

In Voloudakis v. Commissioner, 274 F.2d 209 (9th Cir. 1960), a lessee transferred his leasehold interest in return for a monthly payment and claimed that the monthly payments were not ordinary income but rather represented installment payments on a sale of the leasehold. The court held the payments were ordinary income and, in reaching this result, stressed the fact that the lessee had retained the right to repossess in case of a default in the payments and thus had made a sublease and not a sale. In Metropolitan Building Co. v. Commissioner, 282 F.2d 592 (9th Cir. 1960), the court held that a lessee who transferred his leasehold to the lessor on payment to him of a sum of money by his sublessee was taxable on the money received as a capital gain.

What is the basis of the life interest sold by B in Problem 11.3? See Reg. §1.1014-5.

a. *Words of Purchase*

Language in a disposition that purports to create an interest in a described group as purchasers may fail to do so because of certain historical property rules which continue in effect in the governing jurisdiction. The historical rules which are significant in this regard and which may be applicable when a disposition purports to create an interest in a described group are (1) the rule in Shelley's Case, (2) the rule of construction that a gift to the heirs of the grantor of an inter vivos conveyance is not intended to create any interest in such heirs as purchasers, (3) the rule that when a gift is made to the heirs of the testator, the heirs will take by descent and not by purchase, and (4) the rule in Wild's Case.

(1) The Rule in Shelley's Case

BISHOP v. WILLIAMS
221 Ark. 617, 255 S.W.2d 171 (1953)

George Rose Smith, J. This is an ejectment suit brought by the appellees to recover possession of a tract of land in Arkansas County. In our view the decisive issue is whether a deed executed by W. E. Meacham in 1916 vested the fee simple in the two grantees or merely gave them life estates with remainder to their heirs. The trial court, finding that life tenancies existed, entered judgment for the plaintiffs.

In 1916 Meacham conveyed ninety-five acres to two brothers, C. H. and C. F. Williams, the granting clause containing this language: "to have and to hold to them during their natural lives with remainder after their death to their heirs, the term heirs herein used is a term of purchase and not of limitations." In the following year the Williams brothers divided the land by an exchange of deeds, C. H. receiving the tract now in controversy. C. H. conveyed this tract to R. C. Wills in 1926, and by later conveyances that title has passed to the appellants. C. H. Williams died in 1950, and his heirs now seek to recover the land upon the theory that C. H. had a mere life estate which terminated upon his death.

It is at once apparent that, standing alone, the grant to the Williams brothers "during their natural lives with remainder after their death to their heirs" would undeniably convey the fee simple by operation of the Rule in Shelley's Case. This fact is readily admitted by the appellees, but they insist that since the Rule necessarily involves the construction of the term "heirs" as a word of limitation rather than as one of purchase, the principle is rendered inapplicable by Meacham's recital that he used the term in the latter sense. By this recital, the appellees say, "the grantor has clearly shown his intention . . . to convey a life estate in the lands."

This argument is fallacious in that it assumes that the Rule in Shelley's Case is a rule of construction, designed to assist the court in determining the grantor's intention. But the contrary is true; the Rule is one of law, to be applied without regard to the conveyor's intention. Indeed, it is safe to say that in almost every instance the Rule has the effect of creating a fee when the grantor or testator meant to bring into being some other estate. For example, in the leading case of Hardage v. Stroope, 58 Ark. 303, 24 S.W. 490, the deed was to Tennessee M. Carroll for life and then to her bodily heirs in fee, and if she left no bodily heirs then according to the law of descent and distribution. Of course, the grantors did not mean for Mrs. Carroll to take the fee title; but, following a rule that has been in force for some six centuries, we held that to be the effect of their conveyance. Our cases have announced the doctrine so frequently that it has become a rule of property which we are not free to disregard.

We know of no jurisdiction in which the grantor's intention is permitted to defeat the application of the Rule. As Powell writes in his admirable work on Real Property, Sec. 379, "the Rule in Shelley's Case is a rule of law which applies despite the conveyor's most explicit manifestation of his desire that it not apply." Illustrative cases included those in which the grantor, after having conveyed to A for life with remainder to his heirs, attempts to qualify his action by stating his intention to create a life estate only in the first taker. In such instances it is uniformly held that the grantee takes the fee simple. Fowler v. Black, 136 Ill. 363, 26 N.E. 596, 11 L.R.A. 670; Daniels v. Dingman, 140 Iowa 386, 118 N.W. 373; Edgerton v. Harrison, 230 N.C. 158, 52 S.E.2d 357; Bullock v. Waterman St. Baptist Soc., 5 R.I. 273. The testator could hardly have been more emphatic than he was in Lauer v. Hoffman, 241 Pa. 315, 88 A. 496, 47 L.R.A., N.S. 676, where, after using words that came within the Rule, he added that "in no event whatever shall the fee simple vest [in my daughter]." Nevertheless it did.

In the case at bar it is plain that Meacham, after having created a fee simple by reason of the Rule in Shelley's Case, could not have rendered that action ineffective by adding that he intended for the Williams brothers to be mere life tenants. Nor could he achieve that result in a more roundabout way by asserting that the term "heirs" was used as a word of purchase. It has been pointed out that the Rule applies "even though the conveyor specifically provides . . . that the heirs shall take as purchasers." Rest., Property, Sec. 312, Comment k. We adopted that view in the Hardage case, supra, when we approved this familiar language from the opinion in Doebler's Appeal, 64 Pa. St. 9: "It [the Rule] declares inexorably that where the ancestor takes a preceding freehold by the same instrument, a remainder shall not be limited to the heirs . . . as purchasers. If given as an immediate remainder after the freehold, it shall vest as an executed estate of inheritance in the ancestor; if immediately after some other interposed estate, then it shall vest in him as a remainder. Wherever this is so, it is not possible for the testator to prevent this legal consequence by any declaration, no matter how plain, of a contrary intention."

We conclude that the effect of Meacham's deed was to convey the fee title to C. F. and C. H. Williams as tenants in common. They were then free to divide the property between themselves. Title to the tract allotted to C. H. has now passed to these appellants, who are clearly entitled to retain possession.

Reversed and dismissed.

ED. F. McFADDIN, Justice (dissenting). The germane portions of the deed here involved read as follows:

"Know All Men By These Presents: That I, W. E. Meacham, a single man, for and in consideration of the sum of ($2,500) twenty-five hundred dollars, to me in hand paid by H. J. Williams, the receipt of which is hereby acknowledged, do hereby grant, bargain, sell and convey unto C. H. Williams and C. F. Williams, *to have and to hold to them during their natural lives with remainder after their death to their heirs, the term heirs herein used is a term of purchase and not of limitations,* the following lands lying in the county of Arkansas, State of Arkansas, to-wit: The Frl. N½ of NE¼, right bank of Bayou, and SW¼ NE¼ Section Seventeen (17), Township Four (4) South, Range Six (6) West, Northern District, Arkansas County, Arkansas.

"To have and to hold the same unto the said C. H. Williams and C. F. Williams *as above set forth* and unto their heirs and assigns forever, and all appurtenances thereunto belonging." (Italics my own.)

The majority opinion holds that the italicized words are without effect, because "the rule in Shelley's case applies"; and I cannot agree with that holding. For some time our Court has held that the intention of the parties, as ascertained from all the language of the deed, should govern in the construction of the instrument, rather than any hard and fast formulae anciently established. Luther v. Patman, 200 Ark. 853, 141 S.W.2d 42; Carter Oil Co.,

v. Weil, 209 Ark. 653, 192 S.W.2d 215; Coffelt v. Decatur School
District No. 17, 208 S.W.2d 1; McBride v. Conyers, 212 Ark. 1034,
208 S.W.2d 1006.   Here the grantor (in actuality the payor of the
consideration, H. J. Williams, father of the life tenants) used an
apt phrase to clearly and definitely express his intent to create a
life estate only in the two sons of H. J. Williams, namely, C. H. and
C. F. Williams.

In the italicized portion of the deed above, there are these
words: ". . . the term heirs herein used is a term of purchase and
not of limitations, . . ." Thus, the deed itself described what was
meant by the words "heirs"; and every time the word "heirs" appears in the deed, it means that the heirs of C. H. Williams and
C. F. Williams take by purchase and not by limitations.   The
grantor used legal words to have a legal meaning, and I think we
should give some effect to them: but the majority opinion is that
when the "Rule in Shelley's case" enters, then the intent of a party
goes out the window.   I still believe that we should give effect to
what was the clear intent of H. J. Williams in having this deed
made as it was in 1916. . . .

Therefore, I dissent from the holding of the majority on the
point at issue.[12]

SANDBERG v. HEIRS OF CHAMPLIN
152 Neb. 161, 40 N.W.2d 411 (1950)

CHAPPELL, J.

This action was brought to obtain a decree construing the will
of August Sandberg, deceased, and adjudicating that plaintiff Tom
Sandberg was the owner in fee simple of lands devised therein,
subject only to the life estate of plaintiff Albina Sandberg.   Tom
Sandberg and Marie Sandberg are husband and wife, and Albina
Sandberg, widow of August Sandberg, deceased, is the mother of
Tom Sandberg.   Defendant Arlyn Sandberg is a minor daughter
and only child of Tom Sandberg.   Her duly appointed guardian
ad litem filed answer denying that Tom Sandberg was the owner
in fee simple of the property, alleging that she was by virtue of the
will the owner of an interest therein, the right to possession and
enjoyment of which was contingent upon the life estates of Albina
Sandberg and Tom Sandberg.

Upon trial to the court, a decree was entered, awarding plaintiff
the relief sought, upon the premise that the decision was controlled

[12] For a comment on Bishop v. Williams, see 7 Ark. L. Rev. 411 (1953). —
ED.

by the rule in Shelley's case, which was effective as a rule of property at the time of the death of August Sandberg on February 22, 1941. It was also held that the purported general limitations upon encumbrance or alienation by Albina Sandberg and Tom Sandberg were respectively precatory only, or ineffective and void. From that decree, the guardian ad litem appealed, assigning that the decree was contrary to law. We conclude that the assignment should not be sustained.

Concededly, August Sandberg's death occurred before the Uniform Property Act, now Chapter 76, article 1, R.S. 1943, came into full force and effect in this state. Without dispute, also, at the time of his death, August Sandberg was the fee simple title owner of the property described in plaintiff's petition.

The will, insofar as important here, provided: "All of my real property of whatever nature and wherever located shall be placed in the custody of my wife, Albina Sandberg for her to enjoy the rents and profits therefrom so long as she shall live. It is my expressed wish however that no mortgage, lien, or other incumbrance be placed upon this land or that it be sold or disposed of in any manner. At her death possession shall pass to my son, Tom Sandberg, and he likewise shall enjoy the rents and profits therefrom but with the same restrictions as above outlined, namely, that he shall not place any mortgage, lien or other incumbrance upon this land or that it shall not be sold or disposed of in any manner. At his death it is my expressed wish that this real estate be distributed to his heirs."

That Albina Sandberg had a life estate there can be no doubt. It is obvious also that testator attempted by the foregoing provision to devise only a life estate to Tom Sandberg after the death of Albina Sandberg, with remainder to his heirs at law. Under the circumstances, however, such provision comes within the rule promulgated in Myers v. Myers, 109 Neb. 230, 190 N.W. 491, approved and followed in O'Shea v. Zessin, 138 Neb. 380, 293 N.W. 240, to the effect that where a testator by his will has devised a life estate in real property to a person, and at his death to his heirs at law, the word heirs is to be taken as a word of limitation as distinguished from purchase, and such person becomes vested with a fee simple title to the property devised. That rule was a rule of property at the time of August Sandberg's death, (Sutphen v. Joslyn, 111 Neb. 777, 198 N.W. 164), which rule does not yield to the expression of testator's intention and is controlling in the case at bar.

Viewed in that light, Tom Sandberg, upon the death of August

Sandberg, became vested under the will with an absolute remainder in fee simple, subject only to Albina Sandberg's life estate, in which event the provision in the will attempting without limitation to prevent any encumbrance or alienation by him, being repugnant to the estate devised, was ineffective and void. State Bank of Jensen v. Thiessen, 137 Neb. 426, 289 N.W. 791.

With regard to the purported restraint against encumbrance or alienation by Albina Sandberg, owner of the life estate, it will be observed that the language used was precatory, not mandatory. That is, the language was advisory only in character, and not a command as appeared in Drury v. Hickinbotham, 129 Neb. 499, 262 N.W. 37. The life estate was devised to her absolutely, without qualifying the interest so devised, without limitation over or provision for forfeiture or reversion for breach of any condition, and also without retaining any interest in the property, as appeared in Majerus v. Santo, 143 Neb. 774, 10 N.W.2d 608. Also, the relevant language used was directed to and concerned only the owner of the life estate, and did not relate to testator's ultimate intended disposition of the estate to another so as to indicate a trust intent, as appeared in Tucker v. Heirs of Myers, 151 Neb. 359, 37 N.W.2d 585.

The relevant language in the will must be construed in the light of testator's intention, and applicable rules of law. In that regard, the language of a will, addressed to and concerning only a beneficiary therein, expressing testator's wish, request, desire, or the like, as distinguished from a command, will not ordinarily be construed as mandatory but precatory only, unless from a construction of the entire will it appears that the language used was intended to be and was in fact lawfully testamentary and dispositive of the property to another. 69 C.J., Wills, Sec. 1132, p. 78, Sec. 1133, p. 79; 57 Am. Jur. Wills, Sec. 1180, p. 771. We therefore conclude that the attempt of the testator to prevent encumbrance or alienation by the owner of the life estate was not mandatory but precatory only.[13]

[13] In most states a disabling restraint upon a legal life estate is void. See 6 American Law of Property §26.49 (Casner ed. 1952). Nebraska is the principal state in which such a disabling restraint is upheld. Therefore, it is particularly important to note the extent to which the court avoids the Nebraska law in this case by regarding the words restraining alienation as being only precatory. The language in Sandberg v. Heirs of Champlin restraining alienation by the remainderman is evidently construed as mandatory rather than precatory, and the court holds that such a restraint on a fee is void. If the court had held it valid, it should be noted that the restraint would apply, for the life of the son, to a legal future interest in fee simple as a result of the operation of the rule in Shelley's Case. The validity of restraints on the alienation of legal future interests is considered in 6 American Law of Property §§26.52-26.54 (Casner ed. 1952). — ED.

For the reasons heretofore stated, we conclude that the judgment should be and hereby is affirmed.

Affirmed.[14]

PROBLEMS

11.4. A owns land in a jurisdiction in which the rule in Shelley's Case is in force. A desires to dispose of the land in such a manner that his son, S, will have the use of the land for his life and then, on his death, the land will be owned in fee simple by his heirs. Draft the terms of a disposition which will accomplish A's desires.

(2) Doctrine of Worthier Title as Applied to Inter Vivos Transfers and to Testamentary Dispositions

McKENNA v. SEATTLE–FIRST NATIONAL BANK
35 Wash. 2d 662, 214 P.2d 664 (1950)

ROBINSON, J. — This is an appeal from a decree entered after trial, in the Superior court of King county, of two actions which were consolidated for trial because they grew out of the same facts and presented essentially the same questions of law. One of the actions was instituted by the Seattle-First National Bank for the purpose of obtaining a declaration as to the person or persons to whom it should convey certain real property held by it in trust. The other action was brought by one John A. McKenna, and certain others, claiming title to the real property in question, plaintiffs praying that their title be quieted as against the bank and as against certain other persons claiming interests in the property as heirs of the settlor of the trust. The trial court entered a decree quieting title in favor of McKenna and the other parties plaintiff in the second action. This appeal has been taken by the heirs of the settlor. Although the trustee bank is named as one of the respondents, we shall, for convenience, use that term to designate only McKenna and those claiming under him.

The appeal presents no issues of fact, since the facts are stipu-

---

[14] The rule in Shelley's Case is developed in 1 American Law of Property §§4.40-4.52 (Casner ed. 1952) and 3 Restatement of Property §§312, 313. The rule has been abolished in many states by statute and was abolished as recently as 1953 in Illinois. It appears to be operative in Arkansas, Delaware, Indiana, North Carolina and Texas.

The significance of the rule in Shelley's Case for federal estate tax purposes is illustrated in Estate of Zachary Smith Reynolds, 42 B.T.A. 145 (1940), *rev'd on other grounds sub nom.* Helvering v. Safe Deposit & Trust Co., 316 U.S. 56, 62 Sup. Ct. 925, 86 L. Ed. 1266 (1942). — ED.

lated. The background of the consolidated cases may be epito-mized as follows:

On June 9, 1921, or thereabouts, a cause of action in tort for damages arose in favor of respondent John A. McKenna, and against Hugh L. Watson, now deceased. July 18, 1921, or there-abouts, Hugh L. Watson delivered the sum of six thousand three hundred dollars to the predecessor of respondent Seattle-First National Bank, with written instructions to the bank to purchase certain real property and to hold it in trust for the benefit of the settlor's grandmother, Helen Langston, and mother, Nellie C. Watson, for their respective lives, and for the life of the survivor of them. Pursuant to these instructions, the bank purchased the property in question and executed a declaration of trust, in terms substantially identical to those of the trust instructions. This document read, in part, as follows:

"2. The said Helen Langston and Nellie C. Watson during their lifetimes, and during the lifetime of the survivor of them, have the right to occupy and use said property as a home for the two of them jointly so long as they both live, and as a home for the sur-vivor of them until the death of such survivor, irrevocable by any act of said trustee or of the said Hugh L. Watson or by any act of them the said trustee and the said Hugh L. Watson.

"3. Upon the death of the survivor of the said Helen Langston and said Nellie C. Watson said property shall be by said trustee conveyed to the said Hugh L. Watson in case he shall then be alive; or in case he shall have died prior to the death of the survivor of them as aforesaid, then in such case said property shall be con-veyed by the trustee to the legal heirs of the said Hugh L. Watson."

This case turns entirely upon the interpretation to be given paragraph No. 3.

December 30, 1921, a default judgment was entered in favor of respondent McKenna and against Hugh Watson, the settlor, in connection with the tort cause of action. April 26, 1924, execution having been issued upon the judgment, the interest of Hugh Wat-son in the real property held in trust was sold at sheriff's sale and conveyed to respondent McKenna by sheriff's deed. Such interest as respondent McKenna acquired by the sheriff's deed was held by respondents McKenna, Gilbert, Tucker, Hyland, and Elvidge at the time of trial.

In 1935, the settlor, Hugh Watson, died; in 1937, Helen Lang-ston, one of the two life tenants, died; and in 1947, Nellie C. Watson, the second of the two life tenants, died. The sole heirs at law of the settlor, Hugh Watson, were appellants, Margaret Watson, his widow, and Nellie C. Watson, his mother. Appellant

Cecil Langston is the brother of Nellie C. Watson and her sole heir at law.

Appellants contend that this trust instrument created concurrent contingent remainders in Hugh Watson, as settlor, and in his "legal heirs." Their argument, as we understand it, is as follows: Hugh Watson's interest, being entirely contingent upon his surviving the life tenants, terminated with his death. Upon this event, the contingent remainder in the heirs became a vested remainder in Margaret Watson, his widow, and Nellie C. Watson, his mother, these being his heirs as determined at the date of his death. Nellie C. Watson, of course, was also life tenant of the property by virtue of the terms of the declaration of trust. Upon her death, her share of the remainder interest descended to Cecil Langston, her brother, and the remainder became possessory in him and in Margaret Watson, the surviving widow. Appellants argue that respondents, whose claim is based solely upon their status as successors in interest to Hugh Watson, can now make no claim to the property, the only contingency upon which it was limited to return to the settlor having failed to occur.

Putting aside, for the moment, the question of whether the heirs held a contingent remainder, we may note that in no event could Hugh Watson's interest be so described. The trustee bank took only such an interest as would enable it to carry out the objects and purposes of the trust. The trust itself was to expire with the death of the life tenants, Hobbie v. Ogden, 178 Ill. 357, 53 N.E. 104, and the provision directing the bank to convey the trust property upon that event was superfluous, Doctor v. Hughes, 225 N.Y. 305, 122 N.E. 221, since it would have been required to do so in any case. Livingston v. Ward, 247 N.Y. 97, 159 N.E. 875. The bank, therefore, took an interest which could endure for a term no greater than that embraced by the life estates. "The result is, therefore, the same as it would have been if the estate of the trustees had only been an estate pour autre vie, . . ." Ellis v. Page, 61 Mass. (7 Cush.) 161. See In re Kenyon, 17 R.I. 149, 158, 20 Atl. 294. Consequently, the settlor, Hugh Watson, retained a reversion (1 Simes, Law of Future Interests, p. 67, Sec. 46); for, when an owner in fee simple transfers a life estate, even if it is to be followed by a contingent remainder in fee, the transferor, having disposed of less than his entire interest, has a reversion by operation of law. Burby on Real Property, p. 459, Sec. 287; Clark v. Hillis, 134 Ind. 421, 34 N.E. 13. The nature of this estate cannot be changed by calling it a remainder. Robinson v. Blankenship, 116 Tenn. 394, 92 S.W. 854. As is said in the last cited case:

"So that if after the creation of this life estate . . . , he [the grantor] had simply reserved a remainder to himself without more, the law fixing the character of the estate which remained in him as a reversion, would have let him into the possession upon the determination of the estate granted as a reversion, rather than as remainderman."

It is true that the limitation to Hugh Watson was conditional in form, providing that the property "shall be by said trustee conveyed to the said Hugh L. Watson *in case* he shall then be alive; or in case he shall have died . . . to the legal heirs of the said Hugh L. Watson." But since Hugh Watson already possessed the estate in reversion, from which he had never been parted, and since it is axiomatic that all reversions are vested estates (Gray, The Rule Against Perpetuities (4th ed.), p. 102, Sec. 114), this limitation cannot be said to have imposed a condition precedent to the vesting of his interest. If it had any effect, it imposed a condition subsequent, which might operate to divest that interest. Thus, Gray states (p. 105, Sec. 113.2):

"When an estate is given on a condition, the condition is always both precedent and subsequent; it is precedent as to the estate which is given on the condition, it is subsequent as to the estate which now exists and will continue to exist if the condition is not fulfilled. The vesting of an estate is not affected by the fact that it may be divested by a condition subsequent."

Appellants' claim, therefore, must rest on the argument that, even though Hugh Watson's estate was vested, it was subject to be divested by his decease prior to the termination of the life estates; that, by this instrument, Hugh Watson intended to create life estates in his mother and grandmother, and to create a remainder in fee in his heirs, contingent on his predeceasing the life tenant; and that, as the contingency happened, the remainder vested. Wells v. Kuhn (Mo.), 221 S.W. 19. Had the ultimate remainder been to specifically named persons, rather than to heirs, this view would doubtless be correct (Limitation to the Heirs of a Settlor, 34 Ill. L. Rev. 835, 843), and the death of Hugh Watson, occurring during the period of the continuance of the life estates, would have operated to divest his reversion and vest a remainder in those persons. Appellants urge that, even if we consider that Hugh Watson retained a reversion, this is precisely what happened here.

Respondents do not appear to contend, on this appeal, that the transfer of the purchase money for the property from the settlor to the trustee bank amounted to a fraudulent conveyance, and they agree that the trust instruments created valid life interests in the real property in the two life tenants and the survivor of them. They contend, however, that the limitation to heirs was null and void, and that it had no other effect than to confirm the reversion in Hugh Watson. They argue that this reversion passed to respondent McKenna by virtue of the sheriff's deed, and, the life estates having terminated, that they, as McKenna's successors, are now entitled to the property.

Respondents base their contention upon a very old and well-established principle of property law, which is sometimes referred to as the doctrine of worthier title, and sometimes — perhaps more accurately — as the inter vivos branch of the doctrine of worthier title, but which is perhaps best designated as the rule against a remainder to the grantor's heirs. (A case drawing a distinction between the "doctrine of worthier title" in its technical or orthodox sense and the rule with which we are here concerned, is Mitchell v. Dauphin Deposit Trust Co., 283 Ky. 532, 142 S.W.(2d) 181. Compare Professors Harper and Heckel, The Doctrine of Worthier Title, 24 Ill. L. Rev., with Morris, The Inter Vivos Branch of the Doctrine of Worthier Title, 2 Okla. L. Rev. 133; and note Professor Warren's somewhat polemical article, A Remainder to the Grantor's Heirs, 22 Tex. L. Rev. 22.)

The rule has been defined in 125 A.L.R. 548, at p. 551, as

". . . the doctrine that an inter vivos conveyance for life, with attempted remainder to the heirs or next of kin of the conveyor, is ineffective to create a remainder, but leaves a reversion in the conveyor."

Like the rule in Shelley's case, to which it is related (National Shawmut Bank of Boston v. Joy, 315 Mass. 457, 53 N.E.(2d) 113; "Remainders" to Conveyors' Heirs or Next of Kin, 44 Dickinson L. Rev. 247) and with which it has often been confused (Doctor v. Hughes, 225 N.Y. 305, 122 N.E. 221), the rule against a remainder to the grantor's heirs had its origin in the feudal system, in the principle that "a man cannot raise a fee-simple to his own right heirs by the name of heirs, as a purchase, neither by conveyance of land, nor by use, nor by devise." Counden v. Clerke, 80 Eng. Reprint (Hob. 30) 180. Godolphin v. Abingdon, 2 Atkyns 57, 26 Eng. Reprint 432.

It is now generally conceded that whatever may have been the original reasons for its adoption, they have long since disappeared. In re Burchell's Estate, 299 N.Y. 351, 87 N.E.(2d) 293; 1 Simes, Law of Future Interests, p. 265, Sec. 147; "Limitations to Settlors' Heirs," 37 Cal. L. Rev. 283. Nevertheless, the rule has been adopted in nearly all of the American jurisdictions which have had occasion to consider it. See annotation at 125 A.L.R. 541, and, in addition to the cases there cited, Beach v. Busey, 156 F.(2d) 496 (1946); Wilson v. Pharris, 203 Ark. 614, 158 S.W.(2d) 274

(1941); Bixby v. California Trust Co., 33 Cal. (2d) 495, 202 P.(2d) 1018 (1949); May v. Marx, 300 Ill. App. 144, 20 N.E.(2d) 821 (leave to appeal denied, 300 Ill. App. xiii) (1939); Corwin v. Rheims, 390 Ill. 205, 61 N.E.(2d) 40 (1945); Pewitt v. Workman, 289 Ky. 459, 159 S.W.(2d) 21 (1942); National Shawmut Bank of Boston v. Joy, 315 Mass. 457, 53 N.E.(2d) 113 (1944); Davidson v. Davidson, 350 Mo. 639, 167 S.W.(2d) 641 (1943); Fidelity Union Trust Co. v. Parfner, 135 N.J. Eq. 133, 37 A.(2d) 675 (1944); Richardson v. Richardson, 298 N.Y. 135, 81 N.E.(2d) 54. The strictness with which it is applied varies greatly among the different jurisdictions, however, one extreme being represented by Pennsylvania, which holds the rule one of property, to be applied, presumably, regardless of intent (In re Brolasky's Estate, 302 Pa. 439, 153 Atl. 739);[15] the other being represented by New York, which holds:

"But this rule . . . is with us no more than a prima facie precept of construction which may serve to point the intent of the author, when the interpretation of a writing like this trust agreement is not otherwise plain. Inasmuch as for us that rule has now no other effect, it must give place to a sufficient expression by a grantor of his purpose to make a gift of a remainder to those who will be his distributees." Engel v. Guaranty Trust Co., 280 N.Y. 43, 19 N.E.(2d) 673.

See, also, In re Burchell's Estate, 299 N.Y. 351, 87 N.E.(2d) 293 (1949).

Probably, none of the courts applying the rule, however, would dissent from the proposition that it should be followed, at least in cases where

". . . there is nothing which shows an intent . . . to create remainder interests in his heirs at law or to justify a departure from the usual rule of construction." Bixby v. California Trust Co., 33 Cal. (2d) 495, 202 P.(2d) 1018.

The New York approach, as well as the general concept of the rule as one of construction, developed from the leading case of Doctor v. Hughes, 225 N.Y. 305, 122 N.E. 221. In that case, realty was conveyed to a trustee, who, upon the death of the grantor, was to convey to the heirs of the latter. While the grantor was still

---

[15] If the grantor's heirs are to be ascertained at some time other than the date of the grantor's death, the doctrine of worthier title as applied to inter vivos transfers is eliminated. In Pennsylvania, by Pa. Stat. Ann., tit. 20, §301.14 (Purdon), it has been established as a rule of interpretation that a conveyance of real or personal property to the conveyor's heirs means his heirs ascertained when the conveyance is to take effect in enjoyment. Statutes that created a presumption that a gift to the heirs of a designated person is also a gift to the person's children reduce the situations to which the doctrine of worthier title as applied to inter vivos transfers is applicable. See Ga. Code Ann. §85-504 (1955); N.C. Gen. Stat. §41-6 (1950). — Ed.

living, one of his daughters conveyed to her husband all her interest in the realty. The plaintiffs, judgment creditors of the husband, sought to subject his interest to their lien. It was held that the interest of the husband was a mere expectancy and not subject to execution, the grantor having reserved a reversion in the property rather than having created a remainder in his heirs. In the course of the opinion, however, Judge Cardozo, after observing that, at common law, the direction to transfer the estate to the heirs of the grantor would "indubitably have been equivalent to the reservaation of a reversion," stated:

"But in the absence of modifying statute, the rule persists to-day, at least as a rule of construction, if not as one of property. . . . We do not say that the ancient rule survives as an absolute prohibition limiting the power of a grantor. . . . There may be times . . . when a reference to the heirs of the grantor will be regarded as the gift of a remainder, and will vest title in the heirs presumptive as upon a gift to the heirs of others . . . Even at common law, a distinction was taken between grants to the heirs as such, and grants where the reference to heirs was a mere descriptio personarum . . . But at least the ancient rule survives to this extent, that to transform into a remainder what would ordinarily be a reversion, the intention to work the transformation must be clearly expressed. Here there is no clear expression of such a purpose."

In a later paragraph, the opinion suggests an explanation for the remarkable vitality of the rule:

"There is no adequate disclosure of a purpose in the mind of this grantor to vest his presumptive heirs with rights which it would be beyond his power to defeat. No one is heir to the living; and seldom do the living mean to forego the power of disposition during life by the direction that upon death there shall be a transfer to their heirs."

This assumption does not seem unwarranted. Vague end limitations to "heirs" or "heirs at law" or "next of kin" are frequent in inter vivos conveyances, as where a grantor conveys property in trust, either for his own benefit (the Doctor case) or for the benefit of another (the present case), for the life of the beneficiary, providing that, upon the death of the latter, the trust corpus should "revert" or "descend" or "be conveyed" to his heirs. If these interests in favor of the heirs (a class of persons which cannot be ascertained until the grantor's death) which may not be destroyed by the grantor. Even with the consent of the life beneficiary, he limitations are treated as remainders, the effect will be to create may not revoke the trust which, though it contain an express prevision that it should be irrevocable, he would otherwise (ordinarily) be able to do. Restatement, Trusts, p. 1033, Sec. 338 (1), comment (a). Should he obtain the consent of the heirs presumptive to the revocation, it has been held that even that might be insufficient (Engel v. Guaranty Trust Co., 280 N.Y. 43, 19 N.E.(2d) 673); and it would unquestionably be insufficient if the heirs presumptive were minors or for some other reason incapable of consent (Whittemore v. Equitable Trust Co., 250 N.Y. 298, 165 N.E. 454).

Furthermore, the grantor would be unable to convey or devise an interest in the property remaining after the life estate, for the very reason that he would have already granted the whole of such interest; and this would be so even though his conveyees, or devisees were friends of long standing, while his heirs at law presumptive, entitled to the property by virtue of the end limitation considered as a remainder, were distant relatives. See National Shawmut Bank of Boston v. Joy, 315 Mass. 457, 53 N.E. (2d) 113.

It seems more probable that the average grantor, in making a limitation to heirs in a conveyance of this kind, is merely providing for what should be done in the event that he is no longer living and capable of taking the property himself at the termination of the trust estate; and that he actually has no thought of creating an indestructible interest in his as yet undetermined heirs. This is the view of the Restatement of Property, which would accept the rule against a remainder to the grantor's heirs "unless a contrary intent is found from additional language or circumstances" (Restatement, Property, p. 1776, Sec. 314(1)), and, in explanation, states:

"The continuance of the rule stated in Subsection (1) as a rule of construction is justified on the basis that it represents the probable intention of the average conveyor. Where a person makes a gift in remainder to his own heirs (particularly where he also gives himself an estate for life) he seldom intends to create an indestructible interest in those persons who take his property by intestacy, but intends the same thing as if he had given the remainder 'to my estate.' " Restatement, Property, p. 1778, Sec. 314, comment (a).

See, also, Fidelity Union Trust Co. v. Parfner, 135 N.J. Eq. 133, 37 A.(2d) 675.

It is, of course, true that, if a grantor has his children in mind, when he creates an end limitation to "heirs," he may well intend to create an indestructible interest in them. But, as is suggested in the preceding quotation from Doctor v. Hughes, it was held, even at common law, that, where it could be gathered from the whole of the instrument that the grantor intended "heirs" to refer to children, or to any other specified group save his heirs at law, the rule would not apply. In such cases, courts have generally not hesitated to find a remainder in the children. Boone v. Baird, 91 Miss. 420, 44 So. 929; Shirey v. Clark, 72 Ark. 539, 81 S.W. 1057; Huss v. Stephens, 51 Pa. 282.[16]

Appellants argue that at least the rule should not be regarded as a rigid mandate of law, to be applied in every case without consideration of the probable intent of the grantor; and with this position we are inclined to agree. There may well be occasions when a grantor, by the use of an end limitation to heirs, intends to express his desire that indestructible interests should be created in those individuals who will turn out to be his heirs upon his death. If this is his purpose, there would seem to be no reason in modern times why it should not be effectuated. The fact that this purpose may exist in but a minority of cases presents a convincing argument against the desirability of wholly abandoning the rule; but, if its chief contemporary justification lies in the circumstance that it serves to implement probable intention, it would be anomalous to invoke it in cases where its effect would be to defeat the grantor's plain design.

That the rule should not be treated as one of law has been the view of almost all of the commentators on the subject, both of those who have favored its continuance as a rule of construction (Professor Edward H. Warren, A Remainder to the Grantor's Heirs, 22 Tex. L. Rev. 22; Limitations to Settlors' Heirs, 37 Cal. L. Rev. 283; J. Wesley Oler, "Remainders" to Conveyors' Heirs or Next of Kin, 44 Dickinson L. Rev. 247 (by the author of the extensive comment on the rule at 125 A.L.R. 548); Professor Russell R. Reno, The Doctrine of Worthier Title as Applied in Maryland, 4 Md. L. Rev. 50; Joseph W. Morris, The Inter Vivos Branch of the Worthier Title Doctrine, 2 Okla. L. Rev. 133; Joseph W. Morris, Bixby v. California Trust Co., An Answer, 25 Cal. State Bar Jour. 324; The Worthier Title Doctrine in California, 1 Stanford L. Rev. 774); and, needless to say, of those who have urged its complete abolition (Limitations to Heirs of the Grantor, 39 Col. L. Rev. 628, at p. 656; Inter Vivos Trusts and the Doctrine of Worthier Title, 48 Yale L. Jour. 874; Walter L. Nossaman, Gifts to Heirs, Remainder or Reversion, 24 Cal. State Bar Jour. 59 and 329; Limitation to the Heirs of a Settlor, 34 Ill. L. Rev. 835). Professor Simes, who does not favor the rule (Simes, Fifty Years of Future Interests, 50 Harv. L. Rev. 749, 756), nevertheless states that its invocation as a matter of construction "would

---

[16] See page 452 supra, note 15. — Ed.

seem to be the only reasonable basis for its application today."
1 Simes, Law of Future Interests, p. 265, Sec. 147.[17]

Even if regarded as a rule of construction, the rule against a remainder to the grantor's heirs is subject to the uncertainties of any rule based on intent, and its application may, in peculiar circumstances, bring about unfortunate or inequitable results. (See comment on City Bank Farmers Trust Co. v. Miller, 278 N.Y. 134, 15 N.E.(2d) 553, in 48 Yale L. Jour. 874.) But an examination of the case invoking the rule, as cited earlier in this opinion, does not indicate that this is the usual consequence. Rather, it shows that the rule has, on the whole, proved a useful device to aid courts in ascertaining the probable intent of the grantor where his actual intent is not clear.

We, therefore, have no hesitation in holding that, in an inter vivos conveyance, where nothing in the instrument discloses a contrary intent, a remainder limited to the grantor's heirs will be regarded as the equivalent of a reservation of a reversion in the grantor himself. . . .

Appellants place much reliance on Norman v. Horton, 344 Mo. 290, 126 S.W.(2d) 187, 125 A.L.R. 531. In that case, the court held that an ultimate limitation to the heirs at law of a grantor resulted in a remainder rather than a reversion, on the ground that this interpretation was in accord with the grantor's intention. In the course of reaching this result, the court seems to have abandoned entirely the rule against a remainder to the grantor's heirs, although this "ancient rule of feudal tenure," as it was termed, had apparently been previously applied in the Missouri cases of Wells v. Kuhn (Mo.), 221 S.W. 19, and Stephens v. Moore, 298 Mo. 215, 249 S.W. 601, neither of which the court mentioned. However, in the later case of Davidson v. Davidson, 350 Mo. 639, 167 S.W.(2d) 641, the author of the opinion in the Norman case specifically adopted the rule as set forth in the Restatement and quoted extensively therefrom. A reversion was found, and the Norman case distinguished, on the ground that the instrument being construed in the Davidson case lacked several features present in the instrument involved in the Norman case, which, the court felt, had been inescapably indicative of intent to create a remainder. Without discussing these features at length, we may note that they are lacking in the case at bar as well, and we cannot, for that reason, regard the Norman case as authoritative, except

[17] In Tennessee the rule still seems to be a rule of law. See Cochran v. Frierson, 195 Tenn. 174, 258 S.W.2d 748 (1953); Comment, Feudal Tenure in Tennessee: The Doctrine of the Worthier Title, 24 Tenn. L. Rev. 350 (1956). — ED.

in so far as it emphasizes the importance of attempting to carry out the grantor's intent in cases of this kind.

Appellants also rely on Whittemore v. Equitable Trust Co., 250 N.Y. 298, 165 N.E. 454, one of numerous New York cases which, though adhering to the rule against a remainder to the grantor's heirs as a rule of construction, have nevertheless held, in particular instances, that such remainders had been created; and they contend that the indicia of intent which influenced the court to reach this result in the Whittemore and similar cases, are present in the case at bar, and, providing we follow the rule as one of construction, require us to reach the same result here.

In the Whittemore case, three settlors placed property in trust for two named beneficiaries for life. Upon their death, the trust estate was to be returned to the settlors in equal shares, but, if any of them was then dead, his or her share was to be paid to his appointee by will. In default of appointment, it was to be paid to such persons as would take in the event the deceased settlor died intestate. Section 23 of the New York Personal Property Law permits the settlor to revoke a trust of personalty with the consent of all persons beneficially interested. All of the adult parties to this trust desired its revocation, but the trustee resisted their efforts to bring it about, on the ground that the children of the settlors, as heirs presumptive, had a beneficial interest in the trust, and, being minors, could not consent to revocation. The court agreed, holding that the intent of the settlors, as construed from the instrument, had been to create a remainder, and that the children were, therefore, beneficially interested parties whose consent would be required in order for the trust to be revoked.[18]

[18] In New York, Real Property Law §118 and Personal Property Law §23 provide that the settlor of a trust can revoke it with the consent of all the persons beneficially interested therein. These provisions have been construed as allowing a revocation if all *living* persons beneficially interested consent. In other words, the possibility that unborn persons may become beneficially interested does not prevent a revocation. In re Peabody, 5 N.Y.2d 541, 158 N.E.2d 841 (1959), held that a child en ventre sa mère is not one whose consent is required under the New York Personal Property Law §23. Prior to 1951, however, if the beneficiaries under a trust were described as the "heirs" of someone and these heirs were purchasers, then the consent of the living persons who fulfilled such a description evidently was necessary. In that year, New York amended §118 and §23 as follows: "For the purpose of this section, a gift or limitation, contained in a trust created on or after September first, nineteen hundred fifty-one, in favor of a class of persons described only as heirs or next of kin or distributees of the creator of the trust, or by other words of like import, does not create a beneficial interest in such persons." See also Md. Code Ann., art. 16, §108 (1957), which also permits the interest limited in favor of heirs to be disregarded in determining whether the settlor and persons having a beneficial interest have consented to the termination of a trust.

California Laws 1959, c. 270, added a new §771 to the Civil Code, which

The same court, in construing the decision in the later case of Engel v. Guaranty Trust Co., 280 N.Y. 43, 19 N.E.(2d) 673, said:
"The chief reason for that view was the circumstance that the only provision which the settlors made for control by them of the trust principal gave them no power save that of testamentary disposition thereof. (Id. [250 N.Y. 298] 301, 303.)"

In other words, the court was of the opinion that the reservation of the power of appointment indicated that the settlors believed that their ultimate limitation had created an interest in the heirs, and that they reserved the power in order to be able to defeat that interest. Under this theory, had they intended to retain a reversion, the power would have been superfluous, since, in that circumstance, the settlors could have transferred their interest, not only by will, but by inter vivos conveyance, without any provision in the trust instrument permitting them to do so. Richardson v. Richardson, 298 N.Y. 135, 81 N.E.(2d) 54, and 39 Col. L. Rev. 628, 665, cited therein; In re Burchell's Estate, 299 N.Y. 351, 87 N.E.(2d) 293. Or, as respondents have succinctly put the matter in their brief:
"The settlor was to have the right to dispose of the property only by will. The retention of the power of testamentary disposition was emphasized by the court as a factor in showing intention to create a remainder by purchase in the next of kin. If the settlor were to have a reversion of all remaining after the life estates, the express reservation of the power of disposition would be meaningless. The express provision for only one of the powers that would belong to the settlor if there were a reversion gives rise to the inference that the power reserved is the only right reserved, thus negativing the usual presumption in favor of a reversion in the settlor."

Other courts, even in New York, have not invariably taken this view of the effect of the reservation of a power of appointment,

---

provides that a clause in an inter vivos trust stating that the trust may not be terminated shall not prevent termination by the joint action of all the creators of the trust and all the beneficiaries thereunder if all concerned are competent and if the beneficiaries are all of the age of majority.

If the trust instrument provides a method of revocation, can this method be ignored if the settlor and all beneficiaries consent to a revocation? In Matter of Mordecai, N.Y.L.J., April 13, 1960, p. 8 (Sup. Ct., N.Y. County), the court answered the question in the negative where the settlor had the only interest under the trust, the trust instrument provided that the trust could be revoked with the approval of the trustees, and such consent was reasonably withheld. Also, where the settlor was the only beneficiary he could not revoke the trust alone when he had transferred stock to a trustee under an indenture which provided that the stock was to be voted by a voting committee, without whose consent the trust could not be revoked. See Mundet v. Mundet Cork Corp., 10 A.D.2d 795, 198 N.Y.S.2d 754 (1960). — ED.

and have found reversions even where such reservations were present. Fidelity & Columbia Trust Co. v. Williams, 268 Ky. 671, 105 S.W.(2d) 814; Sinnott v. City Bank Farmers Trust Co., 71 N.Y.S.(2d) 514; Davies v. City Bank Farmers Trust Co., 248 App. Div. 380, 288 N.Y.S. 398. See Fidelity Union Trust Co. v. Parfner, 135 N.J. Eq. 133, 37 A.(2d) 675, and cases there cited. Indeed it has specifically been held that such a reservation aids the presumption that a reversion was intended. Green v. City Bank Farmers Trust Co., 72 N.Y.S.(2d) 442. In Stephens v. Moore, 298 Mo. 215, 249 S.W. 601, the court said:

"The words, 'and the trust shall pass to and vest in my legal heirs, or as may be directed in my will,' is a mere statement, by way of further limitation of the trustee's estate, that the grantor reserves full authority to dispose of the reversion as he sees fit."

But, in any event, such a power was not involved in the case here under consideration, and we need not concern ourselves with this aspect of the problem more than to note that the circumstance of the reservation of the power of appointment by will, in an instrument which made full and formal disposition of the trust property, and yet contained no provision reserving a corresponding power to grant or assign an interest in the property during the life of the settlor, seems to have been the principal factor in causing the New York court to find an intention to create a remainder, not only in the Whittemore, Engel, and Richardson cases, supra, but in Hussey v. City Bank Farmers Trust Co., 236 App. Div. 117, 258 N.Y.S. 396, affirmed 261 N.Y. 533, 185 N.E. 726. It is quite plain, from the following language in the Whittemore case, that had the instrument there under consideration been of the type with which we are here concerned, the court would have found, not a remainder, but a reversion:

"If the trust deed had said that upon the death of the life beneficiary the net principal of the trust estate was to be paid over and delivered to the settlor or his next of kin in equal shares, the addition in this place of the words 'next of kin,' would not have been sufficient in all probability to create a remainder. Rather it would indicate that the settlor intended all above a life interest to remain with him as a reversion to be disposed of in any way he pleased. The words would indicate a limitation, not a gift, (Whittemore v. Equitable Trust Co., 162 App. Div. 607; Doctor v. Hughes, 225 N.Y. 305.) But that is not this case."

This language was quoted with approval in the Richardson case, which, except for In re Burchell's Estate, 299 N.Y. 351, 87 N.E.(2d) 293, is the latest decision of the New York Court of Appeals on this subject.

Close scrutiny of the instruments in the case at bar reveals nothing which would tend to indicate that it was the intention of this settlor to create remainder interests in favor of those who might, in the event of his decease before the expiration of the trust period, become entitled to benefits thereunder. The main purpose of the entire transaction appears to have been the acquisition of the property and the protection of the settlor's mother and grandmother in their occupancy thereof. That purpose being accomplished, it seems reasonable to suppose that the settlor intended that the property should return to him, and naturally, in the event he were no longer living, to any who might inherit from him. The fact that he specified that the property should pass to him, if he survived the life tenants, would seem, if anything, to strengthen the presumption that he reserved a reversion. The courts have generally taken this view when construing instruments containing similar provisions. Wells v. Kuhn (Mo.), 221 S.W. 19; Wilcoxen v. Owen, 237 Ala. 169, 185 So. 897, 125 A.L.R. 539; Due v. Woodward, 151 Ala. 136, 44 So. 44; Berlenbach v. Chemical Bank & Trust Co., 235 App. Div. 170, 256 N.Y.S. 563; Genesee Valley Trust Co. v. Newborn, 168 Misc. 703, 6 N.Y.S.(2d) 498.

In Green v. City Bank Farmers Trust Co., 72 N.Y.S.(2d) 442, four settlors had established a trust for their own benefit, scheduled to terminate at the end of a specified period when the property was to revert to the settlors. In the event of a settlor's death prior to the expiration of the trust, the principal was to pass to those whom he might appoint by will, and, in default of such appointment, to his intestate distributees. Particularly in view of the fact that the trust in the present case was set up for the benefit of the settlor's mother and grandmother, whom he might normally be expected to outlive, the following language from the Green case seems appropriate in this connection:

"In seeking to determine the settlor's intent herein, major significance must manifestly be given to the fact that the trust is not to run for the life of the settlor, but is to terminate upon the happening of an independent event, whereupon the principal of the trust is to revert to the settlor and the trust is to terminate. The provisions for payment of income and principal, in the event of testator's intestacy, from which respondent trustee would spell out an intention on the part of the settlor to create a remainder, is itself wholly contingent upon the settlor's decease before the expiration of the trust period. Such expiration during the life of the settlor, would completely cut off even the expectancy of those whom the trustee characterizes as remaindermen."

See dicta to similar effect in Engel v. Guaranty Trust Co., 280

N.Y. 43, 19 N.Y.(2d) 673, and Richardson v. Richardson, 298 N.Y. 135, 81 N.E.(2d) 54.

As we are unable to find anything in the circumstances of this case which would warrant us in disregarding the usual common-law rule, we hold that the settlor, in establishing the trust under consideration, created neither concurrent contingent remainders in himself and his heirs, nor a single contingent remainder in his heirs, which would vest in the event of his decease prior to the termination of the life estates; but that, on the contrary, he did nothing more than reserve to himself an indefeasible reversion, which was reached by execution and passed to respondent Mc-Kenna by virtue of the sheriff's deed. The life estates having terminated, respondents McKenna, Gilbert, Tucker, Hyland, and Elvidge, are now entitled to a fee simple estate in the property.

The decree is affirmed.

MALLERY, HILL, and HAMLEY, JJ., concur.

SIMPSON, C.J., concurs in the result.[19]

PROBLEMS

11.5. If an inter vivos gift is made to the heirs of the grantor and the heirs take as purchasers, in which of the following cases will the value of the transferred property be includible, in whole or in part, in the grantor's gross estate for federal estate tax purposes?

    a. A transfers property to T in trust to pay the net income to A for his life and then to transfer the trust property to A's heirs. See Section 2036 of the 1954 Code, quoted infra page 1396.

    b. A transfers property to T in trust to pay the net income to B for life and then to transfer the trust property to A's heirs. See Section 2037 of the 1954 Code, quoted infra page 1397.

    c. A transfers property to T in trust to pay the net income to B for the life of A and then to transfer the trust property to A's heirs.

11.6. In New York, A transfers property to T in trust to pay the

[19] For a comment on McKenna v. Seattle-First National Bank, see 26 Wash. L. Rev. 139 (1951).

When an inter vivos trust creates a life interest in a person other than the settlor and the reversion following the life interest is in the settlor, and the settlor dies before the life beneficiary, what is the basis, for income tax purposes, of the life interest under the trust, of the reversion which passes to the settlor's heirs or beneficiaries under his will, and of the trust corpus? See Comment, Basis Problems Under Section 1014(b)(9), Resulting from Death of the Settlor-Reversioner of an Inter Vivos Trust, 23 U. of Chi. L. Rev. 672 (1956). — ED.

income to B for the life of A and then to transfer the trust property to A's heirs. In view of the fact that A and B, acting together, can terminate the trust, even though the heirs of A are purchasers under the disposition (see page 457 supra, note 18), does A have a power, in conjunction with another, to terminate the trust that will cause the value of the trust property to be includible in his gross estate under Section 2038 of the 1954 Code, quoted infra page 1397, if A dies before B? See Section 20.2038-1(a) of the Regulations, quoted infra page 1512. See also Bartlett v. United States, 146 F. Supp. 719 (Ct. Cl. 1956).

ELLIS v. PAGE
7 Cush. 161 (Mass. 1851)

BIGELOW, J. This is a bill in equity in the nature of a bill of interpleader, brought by the executors of the last will and testament of Ephraim Marsh, against sundry persons, legatees and heirs at law of said Marsh.

The facts, as they appear by the bill, answers and documents in the case, are substantially as follows: Ephraim Marsh, the testator, died in the year 1837, leaving a will and codicil, which were duly proved and allowed, March 22, 1847. In and by said will, he devised a part of his real estate, in different proportions, to his children and other relations in fee, and a part to his executors, in trust for his children and other persons. Among that part of his real estate devised in trust, were four dwelling-houses in Fayette, and two lots of land in Knox Street, in Boston, which were given to said trustees "their heirs and assigns forever, in trust to pay over the net rents and income thereof to" his "son Charles Marsh during his life, and, on his decease, to convey in fee, and pay to his children said houses and lots, or the proceeds thereof, in case they have been sold; and in default of such children, to convey and pay the same to his [does "his" refer to the son or to the testator? Ed.] heirs at law." The trustees had full power, by the will, to sell at their discretion any of the real estate devised to them in trust for said Charles Marsh, but no sale had been made by them of any part of it at the time of death of Charles Marsh, the cestui que trust, which took place in August, 1849, he leaving no issue. The testator also gave to sundry persons pecuniary legacies, amounting in all to fifteen thousand four hundred dollars, none of which have been paid by the executors. The personal estate of the testator falls short of paying debts and legacies, in the sum of about twenty-two hundred dollars. The bill further states that, in order to settle the estate, it is requisite, either that said legacies should be proportionably abated, or that the real estate devised to said trustees, in trust for said Charles Marsh for life, and on his decease without children to be conveyed in fee to the heirs at law, should be sold, and the proceeds applied, so far as may be necessary, to the payment of said legacies in full.

The bill prays that said legatees and heirs at law may interplead and settle their rights to said estate, under the direction of the court, and that the executors may be advised how to proceed in the settlement thereof.

The question, whether the real estate devised to said trustees, by the clause of the will above cited, can be sold to make up the deficiency of personal estate and to pay the legacies in full, depends on the construction to be given to that part of the will.   If it is to be considered as a specific devise to the heirs at law, after the death of Charles Marsh, so that they take by the will, then it is very clear, that it cannot be sold to pay legacies, for the reason that lands, specifically devised, are not subject to be sold for the payment of specific legacies.   Scott v. Scott, 1 Eden, 458, 461; Hubbell v. Hubbell, 9 Pick. 561.   See also Hays v. Jackson, 6 Mass. 151.   But if the heirs at law do not take under the will by purchase, but take by descent as heirs, then so much of the real estate as is included in this devise would come within the provision of Rev. Sts. c. 71, Sec. 20, and may be sold as undevised real estate, for the payment of said legacies.

It is a well settled rule of real property, that a limitation to an heir in a devise is void, and that the heir cannot be a purchaser; Co. Lit. 22b; or, to state the rule more fully, if a man devises by his will his land to his heir at law and his heirs, in such case the devise, as such, is void, and the heir will take by descent and not by purchase, for the reason that the title by descent is the worthier and better title, by taking away the entry of those who might have a right to the land.   Powell on Devises, 427, 430; 6 Cruise, Greenl. ed. 151; 1 Jarman on Wills, 67.   And it makes no difference as to the operation of this rule, that the land comes to the heir charged with payment of annuities or legacies, nor that the testator devises the land to one for life, remainder to his heir at law in fee, in which latter case the heir is in, on the termination of the life estate, by descent and not by purchase.   So, too, it has been held, that the limitation to the heir, by devise in fee, after an estate tail, or the ingrafting of an executory devise, or the carving out of a contingent interest, or the limiting of the reversion in fee, or the alternate fee, to the heir at law, will not break the descent, and that when the estate devolves to the heir, he takes by descent and not by purchase.   Powell on Devises, 427, 430; 1 Jarman on

Wills, 67; Fearne's Post. Works, 128, 229; 1 Eden, 462 note; Doe v. Timins, 1 B. & Ald. 530; Manbridge v. Plummer, 2 Myl. & K. 93.

This rule of law, established in England by a long series of judicial decisions, was altered by statute of 3 & 4 William 4, c. 106. But it has been fully recognized as the common law of this state, and has not been changed by statute. Parsons v. Winslow, 6 Mass. 178; Whitney v. Whitney, 14 Mass. 90.

There would have been no difficulty in the application of this rule to the devise in question, if the estate had been given to the trustees for the life of Charles Marsh, and, on his decease without issue, then in fee to the heirs at law. It would then have come within the letter of the rule. But the devise in this case was to the trustees and their heirs, who, on the death of the cestui que trust without children, are to convey the estate in fee to the heirs at law. Does this so change the estate which the heirs take, or so break the descent, that the rule is inapplicable to this devise? In considering this question, it is to be remembered, that one of the great tests, by which to try the application of the rule, is to ascertain whether the tenure or quality of the estate which the heirs take is changed by the devise, i.e., whether they take an estate different in quantity or quality from that which they would have taken if the estate had not been devised, but had been left to descend to them. Fearne's Post. Works, 229. Apply this test to the estate which the heirs at law take in this case on the death of Charles Marsh without issue. They take a fee simple, precisely what they would have taken, if no will had been made. Perhaps a clearer test is given by Chancellor Kent, who says: "Strike out the particular devise to the heir, and if, without that, he would take by descent exactly the same estate which the devise purports to give him, he is in by descent and not by purchase." 4 Kent Com. (6th ed.) 507. Now it is very clear, that, on the conveyance by the trustees of the estate in question to the heirs at law in fee, as provided by the will, the heirs will take exactly what they would have taken if no will had been made.

On looking into the will, it is manifest that the testator intended, in case Charles Marsh died without issue, his heirs at law should at once take the estate in question equally in fee. But as it might become necessary, during the life of the cestui que trust, to sell some portion or all of the real estates devised in trust, the testator gave to the trustees a power to sell at their discretion, directing them, on the death of the cestui que trust, "if the estate shall have been sold," to pay the proceeds to the heirs at law, otherwise to convey to them in fee. The main purpose in devising the estates to the trustees and their heirs was, to enable them to execute this power of sale, if necessary, and convey a good title to the premises. As this power of sale was not exercised by the trustees during the life of Charles Marsh, as it was to have been, if exercised at all, it would not perhaps be a very forced construction to say that, after his death, the devise came within those cases where it has been held that a devise to trustees and their heirs may be construed so as to vest only a life estate in the trustees. Doe v. Hicks, 7 T.R. 433; Curtis v. Price, 12 Ves. 89.

But without deciding this point, and assuming that, on the death of Charles Marsh without issue, the legal estate was still in said trustees, yet they held it only to convey it in fee to the heirs at law. The main purpose of the devise in trust had been accomplished. The heirs have the entire absolute interest in the estate, and can compel the trustees to convey the legal estate to them. 1 Cruise, Greenl. ed. 418. The result is therefore, the same as it would have been if the estate of the trustees had only been an estate pour autre vie, remainder to the heirs at law in fee. The equitable estate being thus vested in the heirs at law with a right to an immediate conveyance of the legal estate in fee, we see no good reason why it should not be subject to all the legal incidents to which it would have been liable, if both the legal and equitable estates had been directly vested in the heirs at law by the terms of the devise. It has been often held to be of the utmost importance to preserve a strict analogy between legal and equitable estates, in all respects, for the reason that it would destroy the whole harmony of the laws of real property, if the legal estate was subject to one set of rules and the equitable estate to another. Wykham v. Wykham, 18 Ves. 423, note. A fortiori is this important and necessary, when the entire equitable estate is in the same persons who have also the immediate right to the legal estate.

On these principles, we think the real estates included in this devise cannot be considered as lands specifically devised by the will but that they fall within the provisions of the Rev. Sts. c. 71, Sec. 20, and are liable to be sold for the payment of legacies. This conclusion, we are satisfied, carries out the intent of the testator, while at the same time it conforms to the rules of law.

Decree accordingly.[20]

[20] The doctrine of worthier title as applied to inter vivos transfers is developed in 1 American Law of Property §§4.19-4.23 (Casner ed. 1952) and 3 Restatement of Property §314. The doctrine of worthier title as applied to testamentary dispositions is considered in 1 American Law of Property §4.19 (Casner ed. 1952) and 3 Restatement of Property §314.

In some states both the inter vivos aspect and the testamentary aspect of the doctrine of worthier title have been abolished, so that the presumption is that the heirs take as purchasers. See Ill. Rev. Stat., c. 30, §§188, 189 (1959), quoted

PROBLEMS

11.7. A, a resident of California, transfers property to T in trust. Under the terms of the trust T is to pay the income to A for life, and on A's death he is to distribute the corpus to A's heirs. Section 779 of the California Civil Code (Deering, 1960) provides as follows:

"When a remainder is limited to the heirs, or heirs of the body, of a person to whom a life estate in the same property is given, the persons who, on the termination of the life estate, are the successors or heirs of the body of the owner for life, are entitled to take by virtue of the remainder so limited to them, and not as mere successors of the owner for life."

A dies leaving a will in which he devises and bequeathes all of his property to his daughter, D. A's heirs at his death are D and his son, S. Is S entitled to any portion of the property held by T as trustee? See Bixby v. California Trust Co., 190 P.2d 321 (Cal. App. 1948), *rev'd*, 33 Cal. 2d 495, 202 P.2d 1018 (1949).

11.8. A is domiciled in a jurisdiction in which an inter vivos gift to the heirs of the grantor is presumed to create no interest in the heirs as purchasers. A desires to establish an irrevocable inter vivos trust under the terms of which he is to enjoy the income for his life, and on his death, the corpus is to be paid to his heirs as purchasers. Draft the terms of the gift to A's heirs which will accomplish his desires.

11.9. Michigan Statutes Annotated §27.3178(150) (1943) provides in part as follows: ". . . and if the intestate shall leave no issue, father or mother, his or her estate shall descend, subject to the provisions herein made for the widow or husband, if a widow or husband survive the deceased, to his or her brothers and sisters and the children of deceased brothers and sisters, and if such persons are in the same degree of kindred to the intestate, they shall take equally, otherwise they shall take by right of representation: Provided, however, that if such intestate shall die under the age of 21 years and not having been married, all the estate that came to such intestate by inheritance from a parent, which has not been

---

infra page 439; Neb. Rev. Stat. §§76-114, 76-115 (1943), quoted infra page 1446. See also Minn. Stat. §500.14, subd. 4 (1957). In Kansas the testamentary aspect of the rule has been abolished. See Kan. Gen. Stat. Ann. §58-506 (1949). California has abolished both aspects of the worthier title rule, and the effect of a gift to the heirs of the grantor or testator is to be determined on the basis of general rules of construction unaided by any presumption against the creation of an interest in the heirs as purchasers. Cal. Laws 1959, c. 122. — Ed.

lawfully disposed of, shall descend to the other children and the issue of the deceased children of the same parent, if there be such children or issue, and if such persons are in the same degree of kindred to said intestate they shall take equally, otherwise they shall take by right of representation. . . ." A devises and bequeaths the residue of his estate to his son and sole heir, S. Under what circumstances will it make any difference whether S takes by descent or by purchase if the above-quoted Michigan statute is applicable? See Morris, the Wills Branch of the Worthier Title Doctrine, 54 Mich. L. Rev. 451 (1956).

11.10. In a jurisdiction which recognizes the testamentary aspect of the doctrine of worthier title, suppose that T devises Blackacre to his son and sole heir, S; that he devises and bequeaths the residue of his estate to his mother; and that S declines to accept the devise in his favor. Who is the owner of Blackacre as a result of S's refusal to accept the devise in his favor? Has S made a gift for federal gift tax purposes? See Hardenbergh v. Commissioner, printed in full supra page 29.

11.11. Assume the same facts as in problem 11.10 except that S dies before A, leaving a child who survives A. Who is the owner of Blackacre? See Estate of Warren, 211 Iowa 940, 234 N.W. 835 (1931)

11.12. A owns land in a jurisdiction which holds that when a devise of land is made to the heirs of the testator, the heirs will take by descent and not by purchase. Under what circumstances, if any, will the operation of this rule affect the disposition of A's land under an estate plan?

(3) The Rule in Wild's Case

SILLIMAN v. WHITAKER
119 N.C. 89, 25 S.E. 742 (1896)

[An action of ejectment is brought to recover certain land which was owned by Richard Ward at the time of his death in 1849. The testator was survived by a daughter Sarah and he devised the land in question (which at the time of his death was represented by an undivided interest in a larger tract) to his sons in trust for Sarah "and all her children, if she should have any." In 1850, the land in question was set off as Sarah's share by the Court of Equity pursuant to a petition. Sarah attained her majority in 1859. She married in 1868 and her daughter, the plaintiff in this action, was born in 1869. The defendants established that a petition was filed in 1857 on behalf of the infant Sarah, for the sale of the land in question for reinvestment. The defendants also established they had been in open, notorious and exclusive possession under mesne conveyances, running back to the title conveyed in pursuance of that sale. The jury was charged that on this evidence the plaintiff was not entitled to recover. The plaintiff excepted and appealed from the judgment rendered.]

CLARK, J.: The devise was to trustees "in trust for Sarah Ward and all her children, if she shall have any." It was settled in Wild's case, 6 Rep., 17, (3 Coke's Rep., 288,) decided in the 41st year of Elizabeth, that a devise to B and his (or her) children, B having no children when the testator died, is an estate tail. If he have children at that time, the children take as joint tenants with the parent. This has been uniformly followed in England. In the late case in the House of Lords of Clifford v. Koe, 5 App., 447, Wild's case was reaffirmed, opinions being delivered seriatim by Lord Chancellor Selborn, Lord Hatherly, Lord Blackburn and Lord Watson, unanimously sustaining Wild's case, and stating that "for these three hundred years it has been the uniform ruling" in England. Theobald on Wills, 334; Hawkins on Wills, 198.

In this country, estates tail having been turned into fee-simple, while Wild's case has been as uniformly followed as in England, it has been with the necessary modification that where the devise is to B and his children, if he have no children at the testator's death, B takes a fee-simple instead of an estate tail, and further, (by virtue of our statutes), if there are children of B at the testator's death, the father and children take as tenants in common instead of joint tenants. Wheatland v. Dodge, 10 Metc., 502; Nightingale v. Burrell, 15 Pick., 104 (on p. 114); 3 Jarman on Wills, 174; Schouler on Wills, Secs. 555, 556. This has always been the ruling in North Carolina, as was held in Hunt v. Satterwaite, 85 N.C., 73, citing with approval Wild's case and precedents in our reports, and Smith, C.J., adds that the interposition of a trustee is obviously to secure the property for the use of the mother and her children, and cannot change the construction of the devise. This case in turn was approved by Merrimon, J., in Hampton v. Wheeler, 99 N.C., 222, in which he cites the additional cases of Moore v. Leach, 50 N.C., 88; Chestnut v. Meares, 56 N.C., 416; Gay v. Baker, 58 N.C., 344, and states that "the rule is clearly settled and we need not advert further to it."

It is true the words here are to "Sarah and her children, *if she shall have any.*" We do not see that these added words change the construction in any wise. At most, they merely indicate that at the time of writing the will the testator knew his daughter had no children, and doubtless the same was true in all the numerous cases

above cited in which the devise was to "B and his children," in
which uniformly when B had no children at the testator's death
he was held in England to take an estate tail, and in this country
a fee-simple. In the present case there is nothing on the face of
the will to show a contrary intent to take it out of the long-settled
rule. From the allegations of the complaint it appears that Sarah
was eleven or twelve years of age at the testator's death, but non
constat that he might not have expected that at his death she would
have been married and the mother of a child.

In a very similar case — Gillespie v. Shumann, 62 Ga., 252
(1879), where the devise was to a woman and "her children, if
any living," it was held to mean living at the death of the testator
— almost our very case — and as none were then living, the
woman took a fee-simple estate, and the birth of a child subsequently to the death of her testator could not divest the fee —
and parol testimony to show a contrary intent in the testator was
held inadmissible. The rulings above cited are not only uniform
in England and in this country, but they are consonant with our
public policy, which is adverse to tying up estates; and further, in
the present case the ruling is consonant with justice, which would
be outraged by turning out the parties who have held the realty
undisturbed for forty years under mesne conveyances from a purchaser who bought in reliance upon the decree of a court of equity,
which, after careful investigation, had adjudged that it had power
to order the sale, and by whom the purchase money in full (which
is doubtless more than the property would bring now) was paid
over to the trustee named in the will for the benefit of the mother,
whose only child is now seeking to recover the premises which have
passed from hand to hand in reliance upon the solemn adjudication of the Court of Equity.

It is proper to say that if the devise had been to A for life remainder to such children as may be living at her death, a very
different case would have been presented. Williams v. Hassell,
73 N.C., 174; 74 N.C., 434; Young v. Young, 97 N.C., 132; or even
if the devise had been to A for life, with remainder to her children.
But here the devise to "B and her children (if she shall have any)"
is in substance that which has been construed in Wild's case and
others above cited to confer upon B, when she has no children at
the death of the testator, not a life estate, but an estate tail in England and a fee-simple in this country. When words used in a will
have received a settled judicial construction the testator is taken
as using them in that sense, unless a different intent plainly appears. Applying that rule, the devise here was, in legal effect, to
"Sarah and her children, if she shall have any at the death of the

testator, and if not, then to Sarah in fee simple," and the law hath been so written "these three hundred years," say the authorities. No Error.

CHAMBERS v. UNION TRUST CO.
235 Pa. 610, 84 Atl. 512 (1912)

Opinion by MR. JUSTICE MOSCHZISKER, April 8, 1912:

The matter here for decision is the question of the proper interpretation of the following provision contained in the will of Joseph Barnsley: "Item. I give and devise my farm (devised by my father to me) to my nephew, Joseph Barnsley and to his children; but in case he should die without legal issue, then it is to go to the heirs of my father, as directed by the intestate laws of Pennsylvania; subject, nevertheless, to the yearly payment of one hundred dollars to my sister, Mary Ann Barnsley, during her life."

The testator died January 12, 1888. Mary Ann Barnsley, the annuitant, died January 16, 1889. Joseph Barnsley, the devisee, entered into possession of the farm in the year 1888 and retained the same until October 11, 1909, when he died unmarried and without children, no issue ever having been born to him. He left a will in which he devised all of his property. The plaintiffs claim as the heirs of William Barnsley who was the father of the testator, and the defendants under this will of the testator's nephew and devisee. In a well stated opinion, after reviewing various authorities, the learned Court below determined the case thus: "Invoking either the rule in Shelley's case, or the rule in Wild's Case, we are of the opinion that the word 'children' was a synonym for 'heirs of his body,' and that the devise being 'immediate' and there being no children to take, the farm was devised in tail and this is enlarged by the Act of April 27, 1855, P.L. 368, into an estate in fee. . . . In accordance with the foregoing reasons . . . judgment is entered for the defendant for the whole of the above described property." The plaintiffs have appealed.

In Graham v. Flower, 13 S. & R. 439, it is stated: "In Wild's Case, 6 Coke, 16b, this distinction is taken: (1) 'If A devises land to B and to his children or issues, and he hath not any issue at the time of the devise, the same is an estate-tail, for the intent is manifest and certain, that his children or issue should take, and as immediate devisees they cannot take, because they are not in rerum natura, and by way of remainder they cannot take, for that was not his intent, for the gift is immediate; therefore, then, such words shall be taken as words of limitation. (2) But if a man devises land to A and to his children or issue, and he then has issue, his express intent may take effect, according to the rule of the common law, and no manifest and certain intent appears to the contrary; and therefore, in such case, they shall have but a joint-estate for life.'" In the case just cited, and in Shirlock v. Shirlock, 5 Pa. 367, the second resolution of the rule was followed, and it was decided that living children take immediately with their parent. The resolutions are mentioned in Ellet v. Paxson, 2 W. & S., 418, 434; Cote v. Von Bonnhorst, 41 Pa. 243, 251; Myers's Appeal, 49 Pa. 111, 114; Taylor v. Taylor, 63 Pa. 481, 488; Seibert v. Wise, 70 Pa. 147, 150; Cressler's Estate, 161 Pa. 427, 434; Oyster v. Orris, 191 Pa. 606, 609; but in none of these cases does the decision rest upon the rule in question. In Coursey v. Davis, 46 Pa. 25, we decided that a grant to a woman and her children vested in her a life-estate with remainder in fee to the children as a class, so that those in being at the date of the deed, as well as those subsequently born, would be entitled to take in the distribution, on the termination of the life estate at the death of the mother. In Hague v. Hague, 161 Pa. 643, we determined a gift to "Sarah Jane Hague and her children" to be a life-estate in the mother with remainder in fee to the children as a class; thus in effect overruling the earlier cases which held the mother and children to be tenants in common, and expressly announcing that Shirlock v. Shirlock, supra, "cannot now be regarded as authority." In Crawford v. Forest Oil Co., 208 Pa. 5, a devise to a son "and to his children" was construed to vest a life estate in the former and an estate in remainder in the children living at the testator's death, subject to open and let in afterborn children. In Elliott v. Diamond Coal and Coke Co., 230 Pa. 423, a devise to a daughter "To have and to hold unto my said daughter and her children forever" was held to vest an estate for life in the daughter, remainder in fee to the children as a class. Finally, in Vaughan's Estate, 230 Pa. 554, a life-estate was given to a wife, at her death one-third of the property was given to a trustee to hold for a daughter, "for her and her children's sole use and benefit;" held, that the daughter took a life-estate with remainder to her children in fee.

In all of the cases just referred to children were living at the death of the testator, so we may take it as firmly established that the second resolution in Wild's case is not the law in Pennsylvania. But the question arises, does the first resolution apply when there are no children? Although several of the cases to which we have already referred apparently indicate that this court has recognized the first resolution, yet in none of them have we had occasion actually to apply it in order to rule on the matter before us for decision.

In fact, this appears to be the first instance where a case has been presented without children in being to take. After an exhaustive examination of the authorities and much thought, we are brought to the conclusion that the resolution does not control under such circumstances, for the reason upon which it rests fails because of the different interpretation which we place upon a devise to a parent and children. Under the second resolution in Wild's case, as applied in England and originally accepted in Pennsylvania, it was held that such a devise gave the parent and children a joint estate, the children taking immediately and not in remainder. The theory was that, if there were no children in existence at the time of the devise the provision in their favor would fail altogether, unless the parent were given a fee-tail; hence, and for that reason alone, the first resolution. But with us, where the children take in remainder, it is immaterial whether they are, or are not, in existence at the time of the devise or at the time of the death of the testator: Cote v. Von Bonnhorst, 41 Pa. 243, 251; Curtis v. Longstreth, 44 Pa. 297, 303; Taylor v. Taylor, 63 Pa. 481, 488; therefore it is not necessary to give an artificial meaning to the devise in order to care for the interests of the children, and there is no apparent reason for adhering to the first resolution in Wild's case. In Cote v. Von Bonnhorst, supra, where the devise was to a daughter "to have and to hold to her for and during the term of her natural life and at and immediately after her decease, . . . to her children in fee; but if she should die without having children," then over, we held that the daughter took but an estate for life, and after refusing to treat the word "children" as a word of limitation, and referring to the rule in Wild's case, Strong, J., said (p. 252): "Where a limitation is to a parent for life, and to his children by way of remainder, there seems to be no ground, whether there are children or not, for holding the parent to be a tenant in tail," and (p. 251), "the reason ceases entirely when the gift to the children instead of being immediate is by way of remainder."

We shall now consider the applicability of the rule in Shelley's case. In the present instance, as in all other cases, our first inquiry is, looking at the words of the will, what did the testator intend? We entertain no doubt that when Joseph Barnsley devised the farm to "my nephew and to his children," and provided if the nephew should die without legal issue it was to go to the heirs of his, the testator's father, he did not at all contemplate that, if the nephew should leave no descendants his heirs should take to the exclusion of the heirs of the testator's father. Yet, if the words used express an intention that the land shall go to the testator's nephew and then descend lineally through him to his issue, the rule in Shelley's case applies and the Court below must be affirmed on that theory. But on the other hand, if the words show that the testator intended the children of his nephew to take as purchaser's directly from him, the testator, then the rule in Shelley's case has no application: Kemp v. Reinhard, 228 Pa. 143.

Under the settled decisions of this Court, the language employed by the testator, "to my nephew and to his children" was tantamount to saying, "to my nephew for life with remainder to his children." The only question is, does the use of the phrase "in case he should die without legal issue," make it necessary to construe the prior use of the word "children" as though it were "issue," which would mean an indefinite failure of issue, thus creating an estate tail and bringing the devise within the rule in Shelley's case? We think not. "Children" is prima facie a word of purchase and not of limitation, and we are convinced that the present testator intended so to use it. Moreover there is no necessity for giving the word an enlarged meaning, for here, under the devise as framed, the estate would vest in the children of the nephew as a class immediately upon any of them coming into existence before his death and there could, therefore, be no possibility of an exclusion of descendants. As to the phrase "without issue," "there is less reluctance to narrow the prima facie meaning of the word 'issue' than of" other words; that word may be "applied only to children:" Taylor v. Taylor, 63 Pa. 481, 483. "It is an unbending rule that when a fee-simple . . . is given in remainder after an estate for life to the children of the first-taker, words following containing a limitation over on default of his issue are held not to raise an estate-tail by implication. In this class of cases 'issue' is construed to mean 'such issue;' that is, children:" Sheets' Estate, 52 Pa. 257, 268; Curtis v. Longstreth, 44 Pa. 297, 302-3. "It is well settled also that words importing a failure of issue without the word 'such,' following a devise to children in fee-simple or fee-tail, refer to the objects of that prior devise and not to the issue at large: "Dailey v. Koons, 90 Pa. 246, 249. The present case falls within these authorities and the words of the devise, "legal issue," should have been construed to mean, "such children," and to import a definite failure of issue.

Since the nephew was dead, without issue, the devise over to the heirs of William Barnsley, the father of the testator, would take effect as an alternative limitation. Sheets' Estate, 52 Pa. 257; Fetrow's Estate, 58 Pa. 424, and the Court below should have determined this case accordingly. The assignments of error are sustained, the judgment for the defendants is reversed and judgment is here entered for the plaintiffs.[21]

PROBLEM

11.13. A owns land in a jurisdiction which follows the rules of construction in Wild's Case. A desires to devise the land in such a manner that his son and his son's children as they are born will be tenants in common of the land, each having an equal undivided interest in fee simple. The son has no children now and may have none before the death of A. Draft the terms of the devise which will accomplish A's desires.

b. *Definitional Aspects*

When a gift is made to the "children" of a designated person as purchasers, are adopted children included? Are his illegitimate children included? (Bear in mind that children of parents who have gone through a marriage ceremony may be technically illegitimate if one of the parents has been divorced and the governing jurisdiction does not recognize the divorce.) Are his stepchildren included? Are his grandchildren included? Are his children by a former marriage included?

When a gift is made to the "issue" of a designated person as purchasers, are descendants of any degree within the group designation? Are adopted children included? Are illegitimate children included?

When a gift is made to the "heirs" of a designated person, is some statute on the descent and distribution of property to be employed to ascertain who are the heirs? If so, will the statute applicable to real property or the statute applicable to personal property be employed? Will the statute in force when the will is drafted, or the statute in force when the testator dies, or the statute in force when the designated ancestor dies be employed? Will any of the persons described as takers under the applicable statute be excluded? As of what time will the statute be applied to ascertain the heirs?

There may be rules of construction recognized in the governing

---

[21] In regard to the rule in Wild's Case, see 5 American Law of Property §§22.15-22.28 (Casner ed. 1952) and 3 Restatement of Property §283.

By Kansas law it is provided that the rule in Wild's Case does not apply in the case of an instrument disposing of property to "B and his children" but, instead, such an instrument will create a life interest in B and a remainder in his children. See Kan. Gen. Stat. Ann. §58-505 (1949), quoted infra page 1440. — Ed.

jurisdiction which are designed to answer the questions in the three preceding paragraphs in the absence of evidence that manifests some different intention on the part of the transferor. The answers to these questions, however, should not be left to the operation of a rule of construction. They should be found in the terms of the dispositive instrument.

(1) Gifts to "Children," "Issue," and the Like

In re PIERCE'S ESTATE
32 Cal. 2d 265, 196 P.2d 1 (1948)

TRAYNOR, J. — By a holographic will dated March 1, 1933, Edwin Pierce left his entire estate in trust. The will provided that a monthly annuity be paid to his widow, Edna Dyer Pierce and that the residue of the net income be divided in ten equal shares, two shares to each of the four children of a deceased brother and one share to each of the two children of a deceased niece. The provisions requiring construction are:

(1) "Should any of the *annuitants,* children or grandchildren of my late brother, W. A. Pierce, die before the final distribution of my estate, his or her annuity shall be distributed in equal shares to his or her children (*lawful* issue), until final distribution.

(2) "At the death of the last of the annuitants, Edna Dyer Pierce, William J. Pierce, Grace P. Holland, Chas. A. Pierce and Harry A. Pierce, it is my will that my estate be liquidated and distributed in equal shares, to and among the surviving grandchildren of my late brother, William A. Pierce, said grandchildren being the *lawful issue,* of the children of my late brother, William A. Pierce." (Underlining by the testator.)

At the date of the testator's death on April 14, 1935, Harry A. Pierce, one of the designated beneficiaries of the trust, had no children. In 1943, he and his wife, Marjorie A. Pierce, adopted Iola Ann Pierce, and in 1944, they adopted Dolores Amelia Pierce. Harry A. Pierce died in 1945 and Marjorie A. Pierce, acting as guardian *ad litem* for the two children, made a claim in their behalf for his annuity upon the trustee. The trustee then petitioned the trial court for instructions to determine whether the adopted children were enitled to receive the annuity. The trial court entered an order that they were. The trustee and beneficiaries appeal.

The question for determination on this appeal is whether the testator used the term "lawful issue" to exclude adopted children. Respondent contends that the statutes governing the status of the children and their rights to inherit control the construction of this term. Section 228 of the Civil Code establishes the relationship of parent and child between an adopted child and the adoptive parent, and section 257 of the Probate Code, incorporating the rule of In re Newman, 75 Cal. 213, 219, 16 P. 887, 7 Am. St. Rep. 146, provides that an adopted child succeeds to the estate of an adoptive parent in the same manner as a natural child. It was held in In re Newman, supra, that an adopted child is included within the meaning of the term "issue" as then used in the statute of succession. "If the adopted child is by virtue of its *status* to be 'regarded and treated in all respects as the child of the person adopting,' and is to 'have all the rights and be subject to all the duties of the legal relation of parent and child,' the right to succeed to the estate of the deceased parent must be included." (In re Newman, supra, 75 Cal. 213, 219.)

Even though an adopted child has a status with respect to its adoptive parent identical to that of a child born of such parent and succeeds to the estate of an adoptive parent in the same manner as a child born of such parent, it does not follow that such status is determinative in construing the terms of a will. It is fundamental in the interpretation of wills that the testator's intent be derived from the language of the will itself and, under Probate Code, section 105, when an uncertainty appears upon the face of the will, from the circumstances under which it was executed.

The procedure for adoption, unknown at common law, is entirely statutory. (Matter of Cozza, 163 Cal. 514, 522, 126 P. 161, Ann. Cas. 1914A, 214.) Adoption creates a status to which attach the legal incidents of the relation of parent and child. Section 228 of the Civil Code defines the rights and duties between an adoptive parent and the adopted child and requires adoptive parents to regard adopted children as children born of such parents. It does not, however, require persons other than adoptive parents to regard them as such in the drafting of private instruments such as wills, trusts, and deeds. "The adoption statutes of this state do not purport to affect the relationship of any person other than that of the parents by blood, the adopting parents, and the child. It is the person adopting the child who, by the express terms of the section, after adoption 'shall sustain towards each other the legal relation of parent and child and have all the rights and be subject to all the duties of that relation . . .'" (In re Darling, 173 Cal. 221, 225, 159 P. 606.) Even under the statute of succession, adopted children are not regarded as children born of the adoptive parents with respect to inheritance from relatives of the adoptive parents. (Estate of Pence, 117 Cal. App. 323, 333, 4 P.2d 202; Estate of

Jones, 3 Cal. App. 2d 395, 400, 39 P.2d 847.) "The adoption simply fixes the *status* of the child as to its former and adopted parents. To its grandparents by blood it continues to be a grandchild, and the child of its parents by blood. It does not acquire new grandparents in the persons of the father and mother of an adopting parent." (In re Darling, supra, 173 Cal. 221, 226.)

In the determination of the rights of an adopted child under a will, the controlling question is not whether the adopted child would inherit from its adoptive parent under the statute of succession, but whether the adopted child is included among the persons the testator intended to share in his estate. (Puterbaugh's Estate, 261 Pa. 235, 241, 104 A. 601, 5 A.L.R. 1277; Comer v. Comer, 195 Ga. 79, 23 S.E.2d 420, 424, 144 A.L.R. 664; see 1 Am. Jur. 665.)[22]

Section 108 of the Probate Court provides: "A testamentary disposition to 'heirs,' 'relations,' 'nearest relations,' 'representatives,' 'legal representatives,' 'personal representatives,' 'family,' 'nearest (or next) of kin' of any person, without other words of qualification, . . . vests the property of such person, according to the provisions of Division II of this Code. . . ." Before its amendment in 1931 this section also included the term "issue." This amendment clearly indicates that the statute of succession was not to control the interpretation of the term "issue" as used in a will. When statutes like section 108 are not applicable, the rules of intestate succession apply only if the testator expresses an intention in the will to adopt such rules. (See Estate of Watts, 179 Cal. 20, 22, 175 P. 415.)

Respondent also relies on Estate of Moore, 7 Cal. App. 2d 722, 724, 47 P.2d 533, 48 P.2d 28, Estate of Tibbetts, 48 Cal. App. 2d 177, 178, 119 P.2d 368, and Estate of Esposito, 57 Cal. App. 2d 859, 865, 135 P.2d 167, holding that adopted children are "lineal descendants" within the meaning of Section 92 of the Probate Code, which prevents the lapse of a testamentary devise or bequest to kindred, if the devisee or legatee predeceases the testator but leaves lineal descendants surviving the testator. Although a beneficiary takes directly under the will of the testator under such an

[22] In 1955, the California statute relating to inheritance by and from an adopted child was amended to read as follows: "An adopted child shall be deemed a descendant of one who has adopted him, the same as a natural child, for all purposes of succession by, from or through the adopting parent the same as a natural parent. An adopted child does not succeed to the estate of a natural parent when the relationship between them has been severed by adoption, nor does such natural parent succeed to the estate of such adopted child, nor does such adopted child succeed to the estate of a relative of the natural parent, nor does any relative of the natural parent succeed to the estate of an adopted child." Cal. Prob. Code §257 (Deering, 1959). — ED.

anti-lapse statute, he does so because the statute substitutes him for the predeceased devisee or legatee. He takes, not by virtue of the expressed intentions of the testator, but solely by virtue of the statute. Section 228 of the Civil Code compels the result in these cases as it does in the succession cases. As stated in Estate of Moore (supra, at 724): "The law applicable to the present controversy and creating the status is found in section 228 of the Civil Code providing that 'after adoption the two shall sustain towards each other the legal relation of parent and child, and have all the rights and be subject to all the duties of that relation.' . . . That such adopted child is to be considered as 'issue' and a lineal descendant of the adopting parent, has been on several occasions recognized by our courts. . . . To exclude adopted children from its scope would be to say that they are not entitled as to the adopting parent, to the full rights of natural children, which is contrary to the express provision of the statute."

In construing the statutes of succession and the anti-lapse statute, the courts were concerned primarily with carrying out the intention of the Legislature (Civ. Code, Sec. 228) that adopted children be given the same rights under the statutes of this state as those enjoyed by natural children. (See, also, Estate of Winchester, 140 Cal. 468, 469, 74 P. 10.) These statutes and the cases thereunder, however, unlike section 108 of the Probate Code, do not purport to prescribe a standard meaning for the terms "lineal descendant" or "lawful issue" as used in wills or other private instruments, and are therefore not controlling in the interpretation of wills or other private instruments.

The question whether an adopted child is included within the meaning of "lawful issue" as used in a will usually turns on the particular circumstance of each case. Thus the meaning of "lawful issue" has been determined from the general scheme or purpose of a will considered as a whole (Middletown Trust Co. v. Gaffey, 96 Conn. 61, 69, 112 A. 689; Mooney v. Tolles, 111 Conn. 1, 11, 149 A. 515, 70 A.L.R. 608; New York Life Ins. & Trust Co. v. Viele, 161 N.Y. 11, 20, 55 N.E. 311, 76 Am. St. Rep. 238; Comer v. Comer, supra, 195 Ga. 79, 23 S.E.2d 420, 424, 144 A.L.R. 664; Woods v. Crump, 283 Ky. 675, 681, 142 S.W.2d 680), or from the fact that the testator used different terms such as heirs, issue, and children interchangeably to identify the same persons (Hall v. Crandall, 25 Del. Ch. 339, 20 A.2d 545, 547; Smith v. Thomas, 317 Ill. 150, 158-159, 147 N.W. 788; Cook v. Underwood, 209 Iowa 641, 644, 228 N.W. 629; see Everitt v. La Speyre, 195 Ga. 377, 24 S.E.2d 381, 384). Moreover, the meaning of the term has frequently been determined by the circumstances surrounding the execution of the will, such as the testator's knowledge of the adoption and his approval or disapproval thereof (Ansonia Nat. Bank v. Kunkel, 105 Conn. 744, 748, 136 A. 588; Middletown Trust Co. v. Gaffey, supra, 96 Conn. 61, 71; Munie v. Gruenewald, 289 Ill. 468, 472, 124 N.E. 605; In re McEwan, 128 N.J. Eq. 140, 147, 15 A.2d 340; Trowbridge v. Trowbridge, 127 Conn. 469, 474-475, 17 A.2d 517; see notes, 70 A.L.A. 621, 144 A.L.R. 670), or the testator's knowledge of the inability of persons, whose "issue" are provided for in the will, to bear children. (Ansonia Nat. Bank v. Kunkel, supra, 753; Beck v. Dickinson, 99 Ind. App. 463, 466, 192 N.E. 899; see Bray v. Miles, 23 Ind. App. 432, 54 N.E. 446, 55 N.E. 510.) "Since the language of different wills is so varied and the circumstances surrounding the testators are so different, decisions in will construction cases are of less value as guides or authority than is the case in almost any other branch of the law. . . . each will must be construed in the light of its own particular phraseology and the facts and circumstances surrounding the testator at the time of its execution." (Thompson on Wills (3d ed.), pp. 324-325.)

The circumstances preceding the execution of the will in the present case indicate that the testator intended to use "lawful issue" in its ordinary meaning as offspring of parentage (3 Page on Wills 152; cases collected in 117 A.L.R. 691) to exclude adopted children. At the trial there was introduced into evidence the testimony of Edna Dyer Pierce, the widow of the testator, who testified to an oral conversation that took place in the presence of the testator and to other circumstances that occurred before the making of the will. The widow testified that at a time before the execution of the will she had a conversation with the testator in the presence of a nephew relating to the plans of Harry A. Pierce to adopt Iola Ann, who at that time was approximately 2 years of age; that during the conversation the nephew had informed the testator of the contemplated adoption and the testator then said: "If God spares my life until tomorrow, and I can get down to my bank, I am going to disinherit Harry"; that Harry, being informed of the testator's state of mind, promised him that he would not adopt Iola Ann or Dolores Amelia; that the testator destroyed a will that he had executed for the very purpose of disinheriting Harry. The disinheriting will, which was torn and thrown into a wastebasket, was retrieved by the widow and preserved; this document was introduced into evidence at the trial. Edna Dyer Pierce further testified that one of the reasons that the testator did not like these minor children was the fact that the husband of the mother of the children stated to the testator that he was not the father of the second child, since he was in jail at the time the child was conceived and could not have been the father. This was the only evidence received at the trial relating to the construction of the language of the will.

Section 105 of the Probate Code provides: "When there is an imperfect description, or no person or property exactly answers the description, mistakes and omissions must be corrected, if the error appears from the context of the will or from extrinsic evidence, excluding the oral declarations of the testator as to his intentions; and when an uncertainty arises upon the face of a will, as to the application of any of its provisions, the testator's intention is to be ascertained from the words of the will, taking into view the circumstances under which it was made, excluding such oral declarations."

If the terms of the will are unambiguous and are susceptible of only one meaning the intent of the testator must be gathered from the face of the instrument itself. (Estate of Watts, supra, 179 Cal. 20, 23; Estate of Soulie, 72 Cal. App. 2d 332, 335, 164 P.2d 565; Estate of Owens, 62 Cal. App. 2d 772, 774, 145 P.2d 376; Vincent v. Security-First Nat. Bank, 67 Cal. App. 2d 602, 610, 155 P.2d 63.) This will, however, is not clear on its face. The testator used "lawful issue" to qualify or restrict the meaning of children or grandchildren. As a layman using the words "lawful issue" in a holographic will he may have intended to distinguish legitimate from illegitimate children, adopted from natural children, legitimate children of the blood of the testator from adopted or illegitimate children, or he may have intended to include children of his legatees that they regard as their lawful issue. In view of the uncertainty appearing on the face of the will, it was proper for the trial court to admit evidence of the circumstances preceding the execution of the instrument to determine what the testator meant by "children (*lawful issue*)" in the first provision quoted above, and by "grandchildren being the *lawful issue*" in the second provision quoted above.

Respondent contends that the extrinsic evidence was inadmissible on the ground that it was too remote from the date of the execution of the will. That contention, however, relates to the probative value to be given such evidence, not to its admissibility. It cannot be seriously contended that such evidence was not sufficiently relevant to the testator's attitude toward the adopted children. (Trowbridge v. Trowbridge, supra, 127 Conn. 469, 471; Munie v. Gruenewald, supra, 298 Ill. 468, 472; see Beck v. Dickinson, supra 99 Ind. App. 463.) In any event, since the respondent interposed only a general objection to the admission of the testimony of the widow, the question of its admissibility on the specific ground of remoteness cannot now be considered on appeal. It is well settled that when a general objection to the admission of certain evidence is overruled by the trial court, the party against whom the ruling is made cannot raise for the first time on appeal a specific objection thereto, unless the evidence is not admissible for any purpose. Crocker v. Carpenter, 98 Cal. 418, 421, 33 P. 271; Christiansen v. Hollings, 44 Cal. App. 2d 332, 340, 112 P.2d 723; Gularte v. Martins, 65 Cal. App. 2d 817, 821, 151 P.2d 570.)

The circumstances under which the will was executed may relate to events occurring before its execution, if they have relevance concerning the intention of the testator at the time the will was executed. (See Thompson on Wills supra, at p. 488.) Accordingly, in several California cases circumstances existing years before the execution of a will have been considered in the interpretation of wills to determine the testator's intentions as they existed at the time of the execution of the will. (Estate of Dominici, 151 Cal. 181, 188, 90 P. 448; Estate of Mitchell, 160 Cal. 618, 623, 117 P. 774; Estate of Hotaling, 72 Cal. App. 2d 848, 165 P.2d 681; Estate of Johnson, 107 Cal. App. 236, 239, 290 P. 314; Estate of Wierzbicky, 69 Cal. App. 2d 690, 693, 159 P.2d 699.)

Although section 105 of the Probate Code clearly permits the introduction of evidence of circumstances surrounding the execution of a will, when there is an uncertainty on the face of the will as to the application of any of its provisions, it specifically provides that oral declarations of the testator cannot be considered to determine his intentions. This section has been construed, however, not to exclude oral declarations that consist of instructions to a scrivener. (Estate of Dominici, supra, 151 Cal. 181; Estate of Little, 170 Cal. 52, 148 P. 194; Estate of Donnellan, 164 Cal. 14, 127 P. 166; Estate of Hotaling, supra, 72 Cal. App. 2d 848, 856.) The testator's statements relating to the disinheritance of Harry A. Pierce were not instructions to a scrivener and therefore do not come within this exception. (See Estate of Johnson, supra, 107 Cal. App. 236, 240; Estate of Maloney, 27 Cal. App. 2d 332, 335, 80 P.2d 998.)

There is sufficient evidence of circumstances before the execution of the will, exclusive of the testator's declarations, however, to support the conclusion that the testator intended to exclude adopted children from taking under the will. The uncontradicted testimony shows that the testator was opposed to the adoption of these children and that his opposition was manifested by the execution of a will disinheriting the adoptive parent; that the testator destroyed the disinheriting will on the promise of Harry A. Pierce that he would not adopt these children. This appeal is upon an agreed statement of facts, and therefore rule 52 of the Rules on

Appeal is controlling: "If a record on appeal does not contain all of the papers, records and oral proceedings, but is certified by the judge or the clerk, or stipulated to by the parties, in accordance with these rules, it shall be presumed in the absence of proceedings or augmentation that it includes all matters material to a determination of the points on appeal." Thus, this court must determine from this record alone whether there was any evidence to support the judgment of the trial court. (See Alkus v. Johnson-Pacific Co., 80 Cal. App. 2d 1, 8, 181 P.2d 72, 76.) Since the only evidence in the agreed statement shows that the testator did not intend that the adopted children should take under the will, there is no evidence to support the order of the trial court.

The order is reversed.

GIBSON, C.J., SHENK, J., EDMONDS, J., and SPENCE, J., concurred.

CARTER, J. — I dissent. [Dissenting opinion omitted; Schauer, J., concurred in dissenting opinion.] [23]

MEEK v. AMES
177 Kan. 565, 280 P.2d 957 (1955)

THIELE, Justice.

This was an action in which plaintiffs sought to recover damages for the alleged wrongful detention of real estate and to have themselves declared the owners of the real estate under the will of Benjamin Reeder and entitled to possession thereof. In a former appeal the ruling of the trial court striking certain allegations of their petition was sustained and reference is made to the opinion in Meek v. Ames, 175 Kan. 564, 266 P.2d 270, for the statement of facts therein. After the above opinion was filed the plaintiffs filed a second amended petition, hereafter referred to as the petition.

For present purposes it may be said that the petition alleged the status of the plaintiffs and their relationship to Benjamin Reeder and Maude Reeder Ames; that Benjamin Reeder died June 12, 1914, leaving a last will which was duly admitted to probate; that under the terms of his will he devised to his daughter, Maude Reeder, a half section of land for her natural life only, subject to the life use of his wife Diana S. Reeder, and at the death of his daughter Maude Reeder, all the land devised should go to and be the absolute property of her children. Similar devises were made

---

[23] For a comment on In re Pierce's Estate, see 22 So. Calif. L. Rev. 89 (1948). In New England Trust Co. v. Sanger, 151 Me., 295, 118 A.2d 760 (1955), an adopted child was not regarded as included in a gift under a will to "lineal descendants" of the adopting parent, but as included in the alternative gift to the "heirs at law" of the adopting parent. — ED.

to other daughters. The testator further provided that if at the death of any of his daughters she should have no children living then the real estate devised to her should be divided equally between his other daughters; that Diana S. Reeder died October 10, 1928; that Maude Reeder Ames died May 10, 1951, leaving no children living entitled to inherit under the will of Benjamin F. Reeder, and as of the last date all of the title to the above half section of land vested in and became the property of the plaintiffs who had made demand upon the defendant for possession, which had been refused to plaintiffs' damage. They prayed for possession of the real estate and damages for its detention.

The record as abstracted does not disclose that any defendant other than Earl Ames filed any pleadings or participated in the trial.

The defendant Earl Ames filed an answer admitting that Benjamin Reeder died leaving a will, the relationship of the plaintiffs to him and that Maude Reeder Ames died May 10, 1951. He denied that Maude Reeder Ames left no children entitled to take under the will of Benjamin Reeder and alleged that she was survived by one child, Mary Jane Jeffress Ames, who was entitled to take under the will; that on or about September 7, 1937, defendant Ames and his wife Maude Reeder Ames adopted Mary Jane Jeffress as their own child and heir under proceedings had in the probate court of Johnson county, Kansas, a copy of the order and decree of adoption being attached to the petition, and that at the time of the death of Maude Reeder Ames the said Mary Jane Jeffress Ames was the child and heir of Maude Reeder Ames and the answering defendant and was entitled to and did inherit the described real estate; that on May 18, 1951, Mary Jane Jeffress Ames, then an adult, conveyed all her interest in the real estate to Earl Ames, the warranty deed of conveyance being duly recorded and a copy being attached to the petition; that by virtue of all of the aforesaid Earl Ames was now the owner and in possession of the real estate and was entitled to an order and judgment of the court to that effect and he so prayed and asked that his title be quieted as against the plaintiffs. We here note that the adoption proceedings show that Mary Jane Jeffress was 19 years of age at the time of her adoption, and that the deed above mentioned expressed a consideration of $1, settlement of property rights "and other valuable considerations."

The plaintiffs' demurrer to the above answer was overruled and they filed a reply that an adoption proceeding was had in which Earl Ames and Maude Reeder Ames purported to adopt Mary Jane Jeffress, but they alleged that such proceeding was instituted and prosecuted in bad faith and pursuant to a conspiracy between

Earl Ames, Mary Jane Jeffress and her natural mother Claribel Jeffress for the sole purpose of obtaining the above real property described in the will of Benjamin Reeder and for the purpose of defrauding plaintiffs of their rights of inheritance and ownership in said real estate and in disregard of the purposes and intents of Benjamin Reeder as expressed in his will in view of the circumstances and law in effect when the will was made; that the adoption proceedings were had with an oral understanding Ames and his wife would adopt Mary Jane Jeffress for the purpose of permitting her to inherit the property involved and that she was to receive it only for the purpose of conveying the fee to Earl Ames; that she was to continue to be known as Jeffress, to reside with her mother, to use the name Ames only on legal documents, and to continue as the child of her natural mother and the Ameses were to assume no obligation, financial or otherwise, have no parental control as to Mary Jane and that she would not live at their home, which agreement was carried out. Plaintiffs set forth the language in the statute providing for adoption proceedings in the probate court appearing as G.S. 1935, 38-105; that the adoption was had in 1937 and that at the date of Benjamin Reeder's death certain statutes were in effect, which provided that the period of minority of females extended only to 18 years and that adoption proceedings affected only minors. Other allegations enlarged upon those reviewed, contained an admission Mary Jane Jeffress Ames executed a warranty deed to Earl Ames on May 18, 1951, and a denial that, on account of the alleged fraud, it conveyed any title to Earl Ames. They alleged they were entitled to a judgment that Maude Reeder Ames died leaving no child or children entitled to take under the will of Benjamin Reeder.

We here note that plaintiffs filed a motion demanding a trial by jury and a motion for a change of venue on account of disqualification of the trial judge. These motions were denied and a trial was had, following which the trial court made findings of fact, and conclusions of law, which include the status of the parties; that Benjamin Reeder died June 12, 1914; that Maude Reeder married Earl Ames in 1913 and died Mary 10, 1951; that Maude Reeder Ames and her husband legally adopted Mary Jane Jeffress, a minor female child, as their own child and heir on September 7, 1937, in the probate court of Johnson county; that the decree of adoption had never been set aside, modified or appealed from; that the adoption proceedings were regular and valid on their face; that the probate court had jurisdiction to enter the decree of adoption; that the time for appeal had expired and the decree had become final and was not subject to collateral attack; that upon the death of Maude Reeder Ames she was survived by her husband and by Mary Jane Jeffress Ames, her adopted daughter, and that she left no other child or children, natural or adopted, and no descendants of any deceased child or deceased adopted child. The trial court further found that on September 6, 1939, Mary Jane Jeffress Ames made a warranty deed, now of record, conveying a part of the real estate to Earl Ames in fee and another part to him for life, all on conditions which need not be noticed, and that on May 18, 1951, she conveyed the fee simple title to all of the real estate to him, and that he was at the commencement of this action the owner of the fee simple title to the property and in possession; that none of the plaintiffs had any right, title or interest in the real estate; that Earl Ames was entitled to a judgment quieting his title and it entered judgment accordingly.

The plaintiffs' motion for a new trial was denied and they perfected an appeal to this court. . . .

We first take note of the following: Benjamin Reeder made his will on August 17, 1904, and by a codicil made June 28, 1911, he changed the executor. He died June 12, 1914. At all times just mentioned the statutes provided only for the adoption of a minor child, Laws 1903, Ch. 361; G.S. 1905, Sec. 4378, et seq., and G.S. 1915, Sec. 6361 et seq., and that the period of minority of the female extended to eighteen years, G.S. 1901, Sec. 4182 and G.S. 1915, Sec. 6357. By laws 1917, Ch. 184, the period was extended for females to the age of 21 years and although that section has been amended in other particulars, that period persists to this day, G.S. 1949, 38-101.

Among others, appellants make a contention the gist of which is that while a will speaks as of the date of the testator's death, his intention must be ascertained in the light of the circumstances when he made it; that at the time the will was made adoption could not be had of a female child over eighteen years of age; that it is apparent that in construing the word "children" as used in the will, the statutes above mentioned as to age and adoption are controlling insofar as the testator's intentions are concerned, and it is not to be presumed he intended that a female nineteen years of age could be adopted so as to take under the will; that under Smith v. Smith, 104 Kan. 629, 180 P. 231, it was held the above act of 1917 extending the period of minority of females to the age of twenty-one years did not change the status of a daughter who had already reached majority under the former law; that the proceedings attached to the answer showed that Mary Jane Jeffress was nineteen years of age when she was adopted, and in view of the law and the fact, appellants' demurrer to appellees' answer should have been sustained. Neither the petition nor the answer disclose the age of Maude Reeder. The will was made in 1904. She did not marry Earl Ames until 1913, and there is no evidence she was previously married. If we look to the date of the will as reflecting the testator's intention, we can only assume that he expected his daughter to marry and have a family for he made it clear from his will that at the end of her life estate in the real estate devised to her, all of the land "shall go to and be the absolute property of her children." He was aware of her marriage in 1913 and died in 1914 without making any change in his will. He did not limit the devise to the issue of Maude's body, but used the general term children. It must be assumed the testator knew that any child adopted by his daughter would have the same right of inheritance from and under him as a natural child, Riley v. Day, 88 Kan. 503, 129 P. 524, 44 L.R.A., N.S., 296 [decided in 1913]. It must also be assumed that even though he knew at the time he made his will that adoptions were of minors only and that the age of minority extended only to eighteen years for females, he also knew that both statutes were subject to change at any time by the legislature. Knowing these things he provided in his will that the remainder after the death of his daughter should go to her children living at the time of her death. Insofar as Mary Jane Jeffress is concerned she was not born until after the will had been made, the testator had died, and the statute of 1917 increasing the period of minority for females to the age of 21 years had been passed. The contention of appellants cannot be sustained. . . .

Even though we were to hold that at this late date the appellants could make a collateral attack on the judgment of adoption, an examination of the allegations of their reply and of their proffered evidence in support discloses that the gist thereof was that the adoption was a fraud on them. They seem to concede that had the child been of tender years there would have been no fraud, but because she was nineteen years of age, the obtaining of the adoption was fraudulent. It is not debatable but that Mr. and Mrs. Ames could have deliberately had a natural child for the very purpose of its receiving the remainder in the devised real estate if it survived its mother and that their act in so doing would not be a fraud on any one. It is also clear Mr. and Mrs. Ames had a legal right to adopt a minor child in 1937, and that adoption having been duly had, thereafter that adopted child had the same rights of person and property as a natural child. In our opinion it may not be said that because of the adoption and that the child survived its adoptive mother and therefore succeeded to the remainder, a fraud was perpetrated against those persons who would otherwise have received it. . . .

No error has been made to appear and the judgment of the trial court is affirmed.[24]

PROBLEMS

11.14. A has a son, S. S is adopted by B. A's father dies and in his will he devises Blackacre "to the children of A." Will S be entitled to share in the gift to A's children? See Stamford Trust Co. v. Lockwood, 98 Conn. 337, 119 Atl. 218 (1922). See also La Bove v. Metropolitan Life Insurance Co., 264 F.2d 233 (3d Cir. 1959).

11.15. A has a son, S. A marries W. S is adopted by W. A's father dies and in his will he devises Blackacre "to the children of A." Will S be entitled to share in the gift to A's children? See Ind. Stat. Ann. §6-601(d) (Burns, 1953), quoted infra page 1439.

11.16. A has a son, S. S is adopted by A's sister. A's father dies and in his will he devises Blackacre "to my issue who survive me, such issue to take per stirpes." Assume that A and his sister both predeceased their father and that A left two children, S and an-

[24] See the following references in 5 American Law of Property (Casner ed. 1952): §22.34 (inclusion of adopted children in a gift to children); §22.36 (inclusion of adopted children in a gift to issue); §22.33 (inclusion of illegitimate children in a gift to children); §22.36 (inclusion of illegitimate children in a gift to issue); §22.34 (inclusion of stepchildren in a gift to children); §§22.32, 22.33 (inclusion of grandchildren in a gift to children); §22.33 (inclusion of children of several marriages in gift to children), §22.36 (inclusion primarily of descendants of any degree in gifts to issue). See also 3 Restatement of Property §§285-293.

In Massachusetts a statutory presumption has been established in favor of the inclusion of an adopted child. See Mass. Ann. Laws, c. 210, §8 (Supp. 1959). As to instruments executed prior to August 26, 1958, however, the presumption in favor of adopted children is restricted to the case where the adopting parent is the transferor.

See also Ind. Stat. Ann. §6-601(d), (e) (Burns, 1953), quoted infra page 1439.

In Bedinger v. Graybill's Executor and Trustee, 302 S.W.2d 594 (Ky. 1957), the court considered a case where a man adopted his wife in order to make her his heir so that she could take under a remainder gift to his heirs at law in his mother's will. The court held that the adoption was valid and that as a result of the adoption the son's wife could take as a child of his under the remainder gift. If the wife could have taken only a wife's share, she would not have been entitled to all the property.

In re Cilley, 400 Pa. 567, 163 A.2d 302 (1960), applies the Pennsylvania statute to a disposition under a revocable life insurance trust and concludes that the statute which equates adopted and natural children when the adoption antedates the conveyance causes the inclusion of an adopted child, even though the gift under the trust was to "lawful issue" and even though the settlor excluded the adopted child from sharing in the property disposed of by his will. — ED.

other, who both survived A's father, and that his sister left one natural-born child and one adopted child, S, who both survived A's father. What will be S's undivided share in Blackacre?

11.17. A in his will makes gifts to the "children" of one designated person and to the "issue" of another designated person. Determine the adequacy of the following provision in A's will:

"References in this will to 'child' or 'children' mean lawful blood descendants in the first degree of the parent designated, and references to 'issue' mean lawful blood descendants in the first, second or any other degree of the ancestor designated, provided always, however, that

    a. an adopted child and such adopted child's lawful blood descendants shall be considered in this will as lawful blood descendants of the adopting parent or parents and of anyone who is by blood or adoption an ancestor of the adopting parents or of either of the adopting parents; and

    b. a child born to persons who are openly living together as husband and wife after the performance of a marriage ceremony between them and such child's lawful blood descendants shall be considered in this will as lawful blood descendants of such child's parents and of any ancestor of either of such parents, regardless of the fact that a purported divorce of one or both of such persons with reference to a prior marriage is invalid."

(2) Gifts to "Heirs" and the Like

NEW ENGLAND TRUST CO. v. WATSON
330 Mass. 265, 112 N.E.2d 799 (1953)

WILKINS, J. This is a petition for instructions by the trustee under the will of George S. Winslow, who died on October 9, 1880, leaving a widow and four unmarried children. The principal question is who are the distributees upon the termination of a residuary trust. The language for interpretation is: "Upon the death of the last survivor of my wife and children, I direct my trustees to pay over and distribute that portion of the principal of the trust fund, which shall then remain in their hands, among my heirs at law, the division to be made in all cases per stirpes and not per capita." In the Probate Court a decree was entered based upon the construction that "my heirs at law" means heirs at the testator's death, and directing distribution to the estates of the four children. Respondents who have appealed are grandchildren, who contend that issue is meant, or that the heirs are to be determined at the death of Charles G. Winslow, the last surviving child, on October 14, 1950.

When the will was executed on June 30, 1870, three of the four children, George, Junior, Eleanor, and Amabel, had been born, and Charles was born the following year. Eleanor and Charles died without issue. The appellants are the respondents Beatrice I. Nicolls and Enid A. Gore, children of Amabel; and the respondents Katherine W. Pollock, Anna W. Winslow, and Eleanora S. Watson, children of George, Junior.

Subject to annuities to the testator's mother-in-law, to two brothers, and to two sisters, the residuary trust income was to be paid one third to the widow and the balance to the children in equal shares. Of the principal each son was to receive a prescribed fraction at the age of twenty-five, or if he died before that age he could appoint it by will. A daughter could appoint the same prescribed fraction by will. In default of appointment by a child the unappointed principal was to go to the surviving issue of that child, and if no issue, was to be added to the principal of the other children, and if neither children nor issue, was to go to the widow and brothers and sisters of the testator. In fact, the sons received their prescribed fraction of principal at the age of twenty-five and the daughters exercised their powers of appointment. As matters eventuated, this prescribed fraction was one twelfth in the case of each of the four children. It is the balance of principal, amounting to eight twelfths, with which we are concerned.

As the testator left both realty and personalty, a remainder to his heirs is to those entitled to his real estate by descent. Such a gift determines both the persons who take and in what manner and proportions, the statute in substance being incorporated in the will. Tyler v. City Bank Farmers Trust Co., 314 Mass. 528, 529-530. In the case cited, the applicable rule was stated in these words: "In the accurate use of language, only those entitled to inherit at the death of another can be called his heirs. Accordingly, unless a contrary intention appears, a gift in a will to the heirs of a person, whether he be the testator or a life tenant or another, will be construed as a gift to such heirs determined as of the time of death of that person" (page 531). Old Colony Trust Co. v. Johnson, 314 Mass. 703, 711-712. Loring v. Sargent, 319 Mass. 127, 129-130. Bagley v. Kuhn, 322 Mass. 372, 373-374.

We now turn to the various arguments which have been addressed to us in an effort to show that the Probate Court judge erred in failing to discover in the will the expression of an intention to use "heirs at law" in other than its normal sense.

The words "per stirpes and not per capita" (Bradlee v. Converse, 318 Mass. 117, 119) following "my heirs at law" shed no light on the time as of which the heirs are to be determined. Old Colony Trust Co. v. Clarke, 291 Mass. 17, 23. In this connection it is convenient to consider the contention that "heirs at law" means "issue." The paragraph in which the sentence to be construed is found is the only one in the will where "heirs at law" are mentioned, whereas the word "issue" is carefully used elsewhere. Merchants National Bank v. Church, 285 Mass. 217, 221. It is argued that by the construction adopted in the court below the phrase "per stirpes and not per capita" becomes surplusage. It happens that in the event which occurred, where the children are the heirs, no additional effect is contributed by the phrase, but in another situation it might have had an effect. See Balch v. Stone, 149 Mass. 39, 42. While not decisive, let it be noted that if "heirs at law" means merely "issue," there would have been a partial intestacy had the children died without issue. It should also be noted that when the testator was dealing with issue, as he was with the prescribed fraction which each child might appoint and there was a gift in default of appointment to the issue of a deceased child or, if none, to other children, he was careful to make a gift over to his widow and brothers and sisters.

The normal interpretation that heirs are to be determined at the testator's death is not inapplicable because the heirs are life beneficiaries, or because the gift is in the form of a direction to pay over and distribute at a future time without any words of present gift. Tyler v. City Bank Farmers Trust Co., 314 Mass. 528, 531, 532. We see no indication in the will that the testator did not expect the life beneficiaries to have any future interest in principal. Compare Worcester County Trust Co. v. Marble, 316 Mass. 294. In Taylor v. Albree, 317 Mass. 57, the gift was "to my legal heirs and representatives whoever they may be" (page 61). No authority has been cited for the suggestion that the determination of heirs at the later time was intended because the gift to the heirs is an initial gift and not "a catch-all after the testator had exhausted his specific intentions." Examples to the contrary are Blume v. Kimball, 222 Mass. 412, Calder v. Bryant, 282 Mass. 231, and Old Colony Trust Co. v. Clarke, 291 Mass 17.

There is no inconsistency in this will between a vested remainder and the powers of appointment given to the children over four twelfths only of the trust property. The sons could appoint by will between the ages of twenty-one and twenty-five years; at twenty-five they would take outright. The daughters, on the other hand, might only appoint by will, a provision which was manifestly to equal what the sons might receive at twenty-five or earlier appoint by will. In these circumstances, such cases as Warren v. Sears, 303 Mass. 578, Commissioner of Corporations & Taxation v. Baker, 303 Mass. 606, and McKay v. Audubon Society, Inc., 318 Mass. 482, are not controlling.

Many points of argument serve to suggest the provision the testator might have made had the precise question occurred to him. It must be kept in mind that the will was drawn when the oldest child was but eight years of age. The testator must have realized that the residuary trust might last for many, even seventy, years, as it actually did. There was a paragraph showing that he anticipated that there might be further children, and a later child was in fact born. But it is apparent that he had not anticipated all questions. There was no express provision for the disposition of income should a child die after attaining the age of twenty-one. In the case of Amabel, who died leaving children, instructions of the Probate Court were sought and obtained in 1929. In the case of Eleanor, who died leaving no children, instructions are sought in the present case. It is not surprising that the testator was not closely concerned about his unmarried children's unborn children.

Viewing the will as a whole, we see no clear intention that the testator used "heirs at law" in other than the normal sense. We do not agree with some appellants that "the only reasonable purpose for delaying the possession of the remaindermen was to determine who the distributees would be." More reasonable, in our opinion, was a purpose to enlarge the respective payments of income to those who continued to live to receive it.

The widow was not an heir in 1880 when the testator died. St. 1876, c. 220. Brown v. Spring, 241 Mass. 565, 568. Seavey v. O'Brien, 307 Mass, 33, 35-36. Taylor v. Albree, 317 Mass. 57, 62. Compare R.L. c. 140, Sec. 3, Third. See now G.L. (Ter. Ed.) c. 190, Sec. 1, as amended by St. 1945, c. 238.

There is a minor question as to the disposition of income accruing between September 19, 1950, the date of the death of Eleanor, and October 14, 1950, the date of the death of Charles. This was not mentioned in the decree. We think that the income on that part of the principal not affected by the exercise of Eleanor's power of appointment and on which she had been receiving the income should go one third to the children of Amabel in equal shares, one third to the children of George in equal shares, and one third to the executors of the will of Charles.

The decree is to be modified by adding an instruction that the income which would have been payable to Eleanor Winslow if she had lived (other than on the part of the principal appointed by her) and which accrued between September 19, 1950, and October 14, 1950, shall be paid one sixth each to Beatrice I. Nicolls and Enid A. Gore; one ninth each to Katherine W. Pollock, Anna W. Winslow, and Eleanora S. Watson; and one third to the executors of the will of Charles G. Winslow. The decree is also to be modified by omitting the reference to income appearing in the record at page 51, lines 1 to 4, which was agreed at the arguments before us to have been inserted in error. As so modified, the decree is affirmed. Costs and expenses of appeal are to be in the discretion of the Probate Court.

So ordered.

COLONY v. COLONY
97 N.H. 386, 89 A.2d 909 (1952)

Probate Appeal, from a decree of distribution on a petition by John J. Colony, and Horatio Colony sole surviving trustees of the estate of John E. Colony, a resident of Keene, who died testate October 6, 1883. His will, dated December 28, 1877, was proved and allowed October 19, 1883.

The testator, a widower since 1870, had, at the time he made his will, one child, a daughter Julia, born November 5, 1870. He also had then living four brothers, viz: Timothy, George, Henry and Horatio and a half-brother Josiah Dean Colony. About a year before the will was made, another brother, Alfred, had died leaving a widow, two sons and a daughter. His brother Timothy predeceased the testator by some ten months leaving children and grandchildren.

John E. Colony's will bequeathed to his daughter Julia a policy of insurance on his life in the sum of $20,000 and a substitute gift up to that amount to make up part or all thereof which might not be paid by the insurance company. In addition he gave Julia $5,000. The remaining dispositive clauses of his will are as follows:

"Third. I further direct my executor to invest one hundred thousand dollars in good, safe dividend paying stocks, securities & property and hold the same & the income thereof for the use of my said daughter as herein after described & to other uses hereafter stated. It is my will that my executor shall pay for & give to my said daughter from time to time freely, for her education & support & for the education & support of her lineal descendants & for the proper maintenance of family position, if any such descendants & family she shall have, a sum not exceeding Five thousand dollars a year, and the balance of such income, if any, I direct my executor to invest in such stocks & estate as are herein before described.

"Fourth. I give & bequeath to each of my brothers, Henry Colony and George D. Colony the sum of ten thousand dollars.

"Fifth. All the rest residue & remainder of my property, I direct my executor to keep well invested in manner herein before stated, & also the income which shall be realized from the same, and upon the decease of my said daughter, I give bequeath & devise all my property & estate of every kind & description which shall be held in trust or otherwise, to the children or lineal descendants of my said daughter then living, if any there shall be, for their use & benefit forever. But if my said daughter shall die leaving no children or lineal descendants, then I give five thousand dollars to each of my brothers Henry Colony & George D. Colony in the first place — and the balance thereof I direct to be divided into five equal shares — and one share each to be given & paid over to my brothers Timothy Colony, Henry Colony, George D. Colony & Horatio Colony if living, otherwise to their heirs — and one share to the heirs of my late brother Alfred T. Colony, deceased."

Testator's daughter, Julia Colony Ames, died on January 5, 1950, without leaving issue or lineal descendants. Shortly thereafter the trustees filed their account praying that it be allowed and that the trust fund in their hands be distributed to the persons entitled thereto. Their account was allowed without objection but appeals to the Superior Court were taken from the decree of distribution made after hearing by the Judge of Probate.

The exceptions of the parties taken during the hearings in the Superior Court on said appeals and to the findings of fact, rulings of law and decree of the Court were reserved and transferred by Sullivan, J.

Other facts appear in the opinion.

James I. Hines, A. James Casner and Paul V. Rutledge of Massachusetts (Mr. Casner orally), for Paul V. Rutledge, adm'r d.b.n., w.w.a. of Kate Colony Frye.

Sulloway, Piper, Jones, Hollis & Godfrey (Mr. Godfrey orally), for John J. Colony, Jr. and Ernest W. Johnson, co-executors of will of George T. Colony.

Hamblett, Griffith, Moran & Hamblett (Mr. Charles K., Hamblett orally), for Ethel M. Aspin, Doris M. Hall, Marjorie R. McQuesten, Edna D. Winslow and Dorothy A. Plett.

Howard B. Lane, Joseph A. Locke and Roger P. Stokey of Massachusetts (Mr. Stokey and Mr. Lane orally), for Murray S. Colony, James Colony, Frank H. Colony and Eleanor W. Colony.

McLane, Davis, Carleton & Graf, Stanley M. Brown and Tyler & Reynolds of Massachusetts; Choate, Hall & Stewart of Massachusetts (Mr. Brown orally), for Karl Adams and Katherine Adams Heard.

Devine & Milliment (Mr. Milliment orally), for Louise Colony Johnson.

William H. Watson and William H. Watson, Jr. (Mr. Wm. H. Watson orally), for Wm. H. Watson as guardian ad litem and as attorney for Davis Ellsworth Clarkson.

Arwe & Arwe (Mr. Henry C. Arwe orally), for Laurence D. Colony, Jr.

Upton, Sanders & Upton (Mr. Richard F. Upton orally), for John J. Colony and Horatio Colony.

Howard W. Robbins, James D. Dow and Howard S. Whiteside all of Massachusetts (Mr. Dow orally), for John K. Colony and Donald G. Colony.

Philip H. Faulkner and N. Michael Plaut (Mr. Plaut orally), for Alfred T. Colony.

Homer S. Bradley, guardian ad litem for the allowance of trustee's account, pro se, furnished no brief.

Harlath Slattery, guardian ad litem against the allowance of trustees' account, pro se, furnished no brief.

Arthur Olson, for Ruth Cutter, Harriette M. Creedon, Ruby Bills Fuller and Elizabeth Kennedy, furnished no brief.

Edgar L. Ryerson of Massachusetts, for Stuart C. Hymes, adm'r of Mary L. Hymer's estate.

Roy M. Pickard, for trustees, furnished no brief.[25]

LAMPRON, J. The main issues before us for decision are the following, viz; (1) Julia, the testator's daughter, having died "leaving no children or lineal descendants" who is entitled to the five thousand dollar bequests made to testator's brothers Henry and George Colony; (2) Julia having so died and none of testator's brothers Timothy, Henry, George and Horatio being alive at her decease, as of what time are their heirs and those of Alfred (a brother already deceased at the making of the will) to whom the residue is given to be determined; (3) if their heirs are to be determined as of the date of death of Julia, there being then no children or lineal descendants of the brother Timothy, although there are of all the other brothers, (a) is the residue to be distributed per capita to the heirs of the five brothers as a class or

---

[25] The detailed listing of the attorneys has been retained as an illustration of the tremendous expense which is involved in ascertaining the intention of the testator when his will contains language which does not clearly and unequivocally express his desires. — ED.

(b) is to be divided into four equal shares and distributed equally among the lineal descendants of the four brothers having same or (c) is the residue to be nevertheless divided into five equal shares and Timothy's share distributed to his heirs according to R.L., c. 360, §1 III; (4) as to Henry's share where there are seven grand-children and two great grandchildren, the latter two issue of a deceased grandchild, all being the lineal descendants of four of Henry's children, is the share to be divided into eight or four equal parts.

All the parties are in agreement that, except for the last issue which involves for the most part the interpretation of R.L., c. 360, §1, these questions are to be resolved by a determination of the testator's intent relative thereto gathered from his will read in the light of the competent evidence bearing upon its interpretation. Osgood v. Vivada, 94 N.H. 222, 224; Amoskeag Trust Co. v. Has-kell, 96 N.H. 89. As to what the testator intended by his will there is, however, no such unanimity among them.

The task of determining his intent is not an easy one as plausible and able arguments have been presented for different views. No useful purpose would be served in a seriate consideration of the merits and fallacies of these arguments. It is sufficient to say that they will be duly considered in arriving at our decision and only those will be mentioned in the opinion as are needed to set forth our conclusions.

The gifts of $5,000 each to Henry and George Colony were not intended by the testator to be subject to the requirement that the legatees survive Julia. The will contained no words expressly evidencing such an intention. Cole v. Society, 64 N.H. 445, 457; Dana v. Sanborn, 70 N.H. 152; Stearns v. Matthews, 94 N.H. 435, 437. And the fact that their gifts were postponed as to enjoyment in possession to a date subsequent to the death of the testator did not in and of itself justify an inference that no gift was intended if they failed to survive to the end of the postponed period. Holmes v. Alexander, 82 N.H. 380, 386; Osgood v. Vivada, 94 N.H. 222, 225. Nor could such an inference be drawn from the express condition attached to their gift that Julia "shall die leaving no children or lineal descendants." Restatement, Property, §261.

On the other hand the fact that the bequest to the children or lineal descendants of Julia which immediately precedes their gift, and that of the residue to Timothy, Henry, George and Horatio which immediately follows it, are both expressly made subject to the condition that the beneficiaries be living at the time of distribution, which condition is absent in the gifts to Henry and George, is a strong indication that the testator did not intend to attach the condition of survival to their legacy. Their bequests should therefore be distributed to their respective legal representatives. Upton v. White, 92 N.H. 221, 226; Stearns v. Matthews, supra, 438.

The testator having died in 1883 and the life tenant, his daughter Julia, on January 5, 1950, without ever having had children, and testator's brothers all having predeceased her, we now consider that portion of article "Fifth" of the will of John E. Colony which reads: "But if my said daughter shall die leaving no children or lineal descendants . . . the balance thereof I direct to be divided into five equal shares — and one share each to be given & paid over to my brothers Timothy Colony, Henry Colony, George D. Colony & Horatio Colony if living, otherwise to their heirs. . . ."

What is the meaning of the word "heirs" as used by the testator in the above quoted portion of his will?

Argument is made that the word "heirs" has an ordinary well-accepted legal meaning, viz: those persons who succeed to a decedent's property at his death if he dies intestate (Simes v. Ward, 78 N.H. 533, 534), and that in the absence of appropriate evidence there is no reason to assume that a testator has used the word "heirs" in other than its ordinary meaning. It is further argued that there is no evidence in this case that the testator intended any other use; that consequently the word "heirs" in the above clause of the will "otherwise to their heirs" was intended by him to mean those persons who, at the time of the death of each brother or at the time of death of the testator, as to those brothers who predeceased him (53 Harv. L. Rev. 207, 235), were entitled to inherit the property of the designated brother under New Hampshire law in force at that time.

Those who oppose this view argue that there is sufficient evidence to show that the testator intended to designate by the word "heirs" those persons who would have suceeded to each brother's property if he had died intestate at the termination of the life estate, namely, at Julia's death.

Under our decisions there is no presumption either way on this question. It is determined in each case by ascertaining the testator's intent by such competent evidence as tends to place the court in his position. Burpee v. Pickard, 94 N.H. 307; Amoskeag Trust Co. v. Haskell, supra, 91. And cases differ so widely in their facts that little aid can be derived from them in attempting to apply their law to the facts of a particular case. Harris v. Ingalls, 74 N.H. 339, 342; Remick v. Merrill, 80 N.H. 225, 227; Rogers v. Scagliotti, 96 N.H. 134, 135.

After giving careful consideration to all the factors involved, we are of the opinion that, when the testator used the words "otherwise to their heirs" in the fifth clause of his will, he intended to have the heirs of his respective brothers determined at the time when his "said daughter [Julia] shall die leaving no children or lineal descendants," on January 5, 1950, as the events turned out.

It seems to us that the wording of the fifth clause has overtones of futurity, viz; "And upon the decease of my said daughter"; "to the children or lineal descendants . . . then living, if any there shall be"; "if living." This language indicates to us that the testator intended to postpone selection of the remaindermen till Julia's death. Cf. Romprey v. Brothers, 95 N.H. 258. We arrived at this conclusion not by applying rules of law (Amoskeag Trust Co. v. Haskell, supra) or canons of construction (Redman v. Ring, 94 N.H. 195, 197) to his words or because he used certain technical terms (Osgood v. Vivada, 94 N.H. 222, 224) but merely by trying under all the circumstances to place ourselves in the position of the testator.

We think that even though the words "living at the decease of my said daughter" are absent after the phrase "otherwise to their heirs" the situation existing at the time he drew his will indicates an intention on the part of John E. Colony to benefit persons living at the time of distribution. When he drew his will his daughter Julia was 7 years of age, his brother Timothy 59, George 56, Henry 54, and Horatio 42. His brother Alfred had died leaving a widow and three children, 18, 12, and 5 years old. He had eighteen nephews and nieces ranging in age from 5 to 37 years, only two being younger than Julia. All the nephews and nieces who survived him were living when he executed his will and no child was born to any of his brothers thereafter.

If he had intended to limit these remainders to the heirs of his brothers determined as of the date of his death, he could have so indicated by designating the then heirs of Alfred by name; he could also have made a codicil to his will after Timothy's death to designate his heirs by name as they were then known to him. As a matter of fact had he intended to grant remainders which were to vest early he could have named all of his nephews and nieces in his will. His failure so to do indicates to us a realization on his part that the final distribution might be in the distant future (Holmes v. Alexander, 82 N.H. 380, 383; Romprey v. Brothers, supra, 261) and he was content to have the heirs of his brothers determined as of the time for distribution at Julia's death.

No worthwhile purpose would be accomplished by expanding on the other arguments advanced for determining the heirs as of

Julia's death such as (1) by doing otherwise, seventeen of the eighteen children of the brothers having predeceased Julia, it would be necessary to trace the interest of seventeen of them through their estates and further through the estates of any deceased successors in title (Crockett v. Robinson, 46 N.H. 454, 458; Remick v. Merrill, 80 N.H. 225, 229; Cowan v. Cowan, 90 N.H. 198, 201); (2) if there was early vesting a substantial part of the estate would go to non-Colonys contrary to testator's intent to provide for "proper maintenance of family position." [26]

Having determined that the heirs of each of the five brothers who are to take the residue are to be determined as of January 5, 1950, the date of Julia's death, we now turn our attention to the method of distribution. Here again our problem is to determine by a balance of probabilities the intent of John E. Colony in that respect. Romprey v. Brothers, supra, 260.

And as stated at the beginning of this opinion different solutions have been proposed by the parties. One view is that the testator was more interested in the Colony family and its tradition than in particular individuals of that family. He therefore had no preference among his many nephews and nieces, and grandnephews and nieces, some born, some unborn. Such a man with equal feelings towards his relatives would want equal treatment of them. This result can only be accomplished by treating all of the heirs of his brothers as a class and distributing the residue per capita among them, regardless of their degree of relationship.

It has been argued by others that it is true that equality of treatment was intended by the testator as between the heirs of his brothers if all the brothers died before the life estate terminated, but he intended those heirs to be only the heirs of the body and descendants of each of his brothers. Timothy having no lineal

---

[26] See St. Aubin, Jr. v. Sheehan, 138 F. Supp. 154 (D.R.I. 1956), for a case where an estate tax would be imposed on the decedent if the described heirs were ascertained on the death of the designated ancestor, but would not be imposed on the decedent if the heirs were ascertained at the period of distribution.

It should be noted that in 1877, when John E. Colony executed his will, and in 1883, when he died, the tax consequences of descendable future interests were quite different from what they are today. Thus, if the court tries "under all the circumstances to place ourselves in the position of the testator," it should view any argument based on tax consequences in the way John E. Colony would have viewed such arguments in the period 1877-1883. In 1882, a year before John E. Colony died, the court in Curry v. Spencer, 61 N.H. 624, 632 (1882), had the following to say about a New Hampshire death tax imposed by 1878 legislation: "Under the reservations of the bill of rights and the limitations of the constitution, it is plainly founded upon pure inequality, and is simply extortion in the name of taxation; and it can therefore never be sustained in this jurisdiction so long as equality and justice continue to be the basis of constitutional taxation." — ED.

descendants the testator did not intend that his collateral heirs take but rather that the remainder be divided into as many equal shares as there were lineal descendants of full brothers, each such brother's descendants being considered as a class substituted for the brother.

The final view advanced is that the testator intended the residue to be divided into five equal shares, each share to be distributed to those persons who were the heirs of a particular brother on the date of the death of Julia, January 5, 1950, as determined by the statute of descent and distribution in force on that date, to be distributed to them in accordance with the provisions of that statute. We agree with that view.

The language of the will itself, in our judgment, is a strong indication in that direction, viz; "and the balance thereof I direct to be divided into five equal shares — and one share each to be given & paid over to my brothers Timothy Colony, Henry Colony, George D. Colony & Horatio Colony if living, otherwise to their heirs — and one share to the heirs of my late brother Alfred T. Colony, deceased." There would be no purpose in directing that his estate be divided into five equal shares unless he intended to provide separate shares for the five branches of his family. This clause, read as a whole, indicates the testator's desire to keep each brother's share intact for such brother or for such brother's heirs. The words "equal" and "one share each" clearly show this intention and the fact that he expressly left "one share to the heirs of my late brother, Alfred T. Colony, deceased" is further confirmation of his desire that in case any of the other brothers died before the date of distribution his one fifth share was to go to his heirs. McLane v. Crosby, 77 N.H. 596 (299 Briefs & Cases 393).

Also if the testator had intended to have only the lineal descendants of his brothers share the residue instead of those who would have succeeded to each brother's share if the brother had died intestate as to that part of his estate (Simes v. Ward, 78 N.H. 533, 534), he would not have used the word "heirs" but the words "children or lineal descendants" as he did twice in this same clause. Souhegan National Bank v. Kenison, 92 N.H. 117, 119; Bedell v. Colby, 94 N.H. 384, 386.

We now direct our attention to the problem, previously mentioned, involving the interpretation of our statute of descent and distribution (R.L., c. 360, §§1, 6) which interest particularly the Henry Colony line. To repeat it, at Julia's death the living lineal descendants of Henry consisted of seven grandchildren and two great grandchildren, the latter two issue of a deceased grandchild, all being the lineal descendants of four of Henry's children. It is contended by some that this share is to be divided into four parts each to be distributed equally among the living lineal descendants of each child of Henry because the inheritance should be *per stirpes* and the grandchildren and great grandchildren inherit as representatives of each *stirpes*. Others maintain that there being seven grandchildren and the representatives of an eighth grandchild, deceased, the grandchildren being all in an equal degree of kinship to the deceased ancestor Henry, the division should be *per capita* and each of the seven grandchildren should take an equal share and the eighth share should be divided equally between the two great grandchildren as representatives of their deceased parent.

An able and well documented argument has been made to the effect that the rule of taking *per capita* among relatives of the same degree applies only in situations involving next of kin and not where we are dealing with lineal descendants and the right of representation. In the latter event it is argued lineal descendants, however remote, never inherit as next of kin and always inherit *per stirpes*. 22 & 23 Charles II, c. 10; 118th Novel, Cooper's Justinian (3d ed.) 393. See Kelsey v. Hardy, 20 N.H. 479; Smith, N.H. Reports, 447.

The advocates of this view admit that there is language in Nichols v. Shepard, 63 N.H. 391, and in Preston v. Cole, 64 N.H. 459, to the effect that when all the claimants stand in equal degree to the testators such as "three grandchildren" they take *per capita*. They point out, however, and correctly, that each of these cases involved next of kin and not lineal descendants and they argue that although these decisions on their facts are sound the statements made in dictum are erroneous.

The parties could not find a previous decision in New Hampshire on the particular issue involved here and we know of none. Nichols v. Shepard, supra, was decided in June, 1885, and Preston v. Cole, supra, in 1887. Louis G. Hoyt in his work entitled "Practice in Proceedings in The Probate Courts of New Hampshire" which has been generally used by the members of our bar as a source of authority on probate matters since 1901, states on page 242, that if the only descendants are grandchildren, being of equal degree of kinship to the intestate, they take *per capita*. He cites in support of that proposition the above cases.

Although there are instances to the contrary (the decree of the probate court in this case being one) it is our understanding that the interpretation of our statute set forth in the above cases and in Hoyt's has been followed by our courts of probate and by the members of our bar in the distribution of estates. The reasons advanced for a contrary interpretation are not of such a compelling nature as to necessitate an overturning of this long standing interpretation of our statute with the disastrous consequences which would inevitably result in numerous cases. Green v. Bancroft, 75 N.H. 204, 207. We have not found it necessary however to place our decision on that basis as we are of the opinion that the statements in Nichols v. Shepard, supra, and in Preston v. Cole, supra, and in Hoyt's to the effect that when the claimants all stand related to the intestate in equal degree they take *per capita*, enunciate the proper construction of the statutory provisions in question.

Distribution is to be made in accordance with the decree of the Superior Court which is affirmed subject to the following modifications, viz; (1) the share of the heirs of George D. Colony is to be distributed in accordance with the terms of agreements entered into among the parties concerned, (2) the $5,000 bequests each to Henry and George are to be distributed to their respective legal representatives.

Case discharged.

All concurred.[27]

PROBLEM

11.18. A in his will makes gifts to the "heirs" of a designated person. Determine the adequacy of the following provision which is in A's will:

"References in this will to 'heirs' mean those persons other than creditors who would take the personal property of the person whose heirs are designated under the laws of the Commonwealth of Massachusetts in force at the time stipulated for distribution, whether or not such persons are related by blood to him (or her), if he (or she) had died intestate at such time and domiciled in such Commonwealth. In determining who such persons are, it shall be assumed that all decrees of divorce rendered by a court of record, wherever located, are valid. Distribution to such persons shall

[27] See the following references in 5 American Law of Property (Casner ed. 1952) dealing with gifts to heirs and the like: §22.57 (when statute dealing with intestate succession of property is to be employed); §22.58 (what statute is to be used); §22.59 (circumstances under which a person described by the applicable statute is to be excluded); §22.60 (the time as of which the statute is applied). See also 3 Restatement of Property §§305-311.

In some states a statutory presumption has been established in favor of ascertaining the heirs of a designated person on the date enjoyment in possession is to begin. See Ind. Stat. Ann. §6-601(c) (Burns, 1953), quoted infra page 1439; Pa. Stat. Ann., tit. 20, §301.14 (Purdon), quoted infra page 1472. — ED.

be made in the manner and in the proportion that personal property of the person whose heirs are designated would be distributed under the laws of the Commonwealth of Massachusetts in force at the time stipulated for distribution, if he (or she) had died intestate at such time, owning the property available for distribution and no other property and domiciled in such Commonwealth."

c.   *Time Within Which a Class Member Must Be Born*

When a gift is made by T in his will "to A for life, then to the children of B," within what period of time must a child of B be born in order to be included in the gift? The same question stated another way is: At what time will the class close, so that class members born thereafter will be excluded from the gift? In the example given, it may be contended that T intended only the children of B born when he executed his will to share in the gift; or that he intended to include those born before he died; or that he intended to include all born before A died; or that he intended to include all whenever born. There may be established rules of construction in the governing jurisdiction which determine when the class closes in the absence of evidence that manifests some different intention on the part of the transferor. Even if there are such rules of construction, the terms of the dispositive instrument should establish definitely when the class closes to after-born members.

EARLE ESTATE
369 Pa. 52, 85 A.2d 90 (1951)

Opinion by Mr. JUSTICE LADNER, December 27, 1951:

George H. Earle, Jr. died February 19, 1928, leaving a will dated January 24, 1928. In that will he provided by the third paragraph of the Fifth Item of his will as follows: "In the event that my estate, after the payment of taxes, shall at least amount to the net sum of Five Million ($5,000,000) Dollars or over, I give and bequeath to my Trustees in Trust for the benefit of each and every male child of my sons who shall by birth inherit and bear the name of Earle, the sum of One Hundred Thousand ($100,000) Dollars for each one of such male children. Said sum shall be held in Trust upon the same terms, conditions and uses as provided in ITEM THIRD in the trust for the benefit of my granddaughter LOUISE DILWORTH BEGGS, and in ITEM FOURTH in trust for the benefit of my granddaughter EDITH EARLE LEE."

The reference to the other items of the will makes clear that only the *income* not the principal is given to these grandsons.

The sole question before us on these appeals [footnote omitted] is whether Anthony Wayne Earle, who was born July 11, 1949, i.e., *after* the testator's death, is entitled to have a $100,000 trust set up for him in accordance with the paragraph quoted.

At the audit of the Trustees' Third Account such application was made on behalf of the minor by C. Brewster Rhoads, Esq., as guardian ad litem appointed by the Auditing Judge to protect the minor's interest. It was opposed by Frank Rodgers Donahue, Esq., appointed by the Auditing Judge to represent all minor and unascertained remainder interests of the trust estate which comprises the whole residuary estate.

The learned Auditing Judge refused the application, holding that the provision of the will in question must be so construed as to *exclude* grandsons born *after* testator's death, which ruling was confirmed on exceptions by the court en banc, Judge Bolger dissenting.

With all due deference to the learned judges of the court below, who are distinguished in their respective branch of the law, we must conclude they erred and the decree appealed from must be reversed.

It is well settled that the intention of a testator is the polar star in the construction of wills: [citations omitted]. Equally well settled is the corollary proposition that where the language used by the testator is plain and clearly discloses his intention, no rules of construction are necessary to arrive at an interpretation, a principle repeatedly emphasized by Mr. Justice (now Chief Justice) Drew in Boyer v. Campbell, 312 Pa. 460, 167 A. 284 (1933); Haydon's Estate, 334 Pa. 403, 6 A.2d 581 (1939); Brown Estate, 349 Pa. 23, 36 A.2d 335 (1944). And as held in the recent case of Clark Est., 359 Pa. 411, 59 A.2d 109 (1948), it is the actual intent, as ascertained from the language of the will that must prevail in the light of the circumstances surrounding testator at the date of the execution of the will. Hence it is our duty to examine the will and if possible ascertain its meaning without reference to canons of construction. [Citations omitted.]

When we peruse the provision in question we see that the testator establishes a class composed of such of his grandsons as are born to his sons and defines the qualifications of members of that class explicitly by the words, "I give and bequeath . . . for the benefit of *each* and *every male* child of my *sons*, who *shall* by birth inherit and bear the name of Earle," etc. Analyzing this language it becomes clear that the phrase "each and every" is an emphatic way of saying "all" and can indicate only an intent that no son of his sons be excluded.

Next we note the testator adds to the phrase "each and every male child" the words *"of my sons,"* which indicates *all* male progeny of both sons are intended to be included. The use of the plural becomes more important when we view the extraneous circumstances of the family situation from the testator's armchair. (This, as pointed out by Mr. Justice Allen M. Stearne in Schmick Estate, 349 Pa. 65, 70, 36 A.2d 305 (1940), we must do. See also Jackson's Estate, 337 Pa. 561, 12 A.2d 338 (1940); McGlathery's Estate, 311 Pa. 351, 166 A. 886 (1933)). The testator at the date of the will had two sons, George H. III, age 37 and married, who had three sons living at the date of the will and at the date of testator's death and one en ventre sa mere born thereafter on September 26, 1928, and Ralph Earle, 35 years of age, who though married had *no* children living at either the date of the will or of testator's death and none so far born since testator's death. Testator was on cordial terms with *both* of his sons for he designated both sons as co-trustees of the trust under his will. These circumstances confirm testator's intent to include any male offsprings of both of his sons whenever born. Certainly it is unthinkable that he intended to cut off sons of Ralph, his younger son, just because he had no sons *then*.

Significant also is the future tense indicated by the word "shall" in the phrase, "who *shall* by birth inherit and bear the name of Earle." To give effect to the future tense, it is reasonable to regard the testator's intent as including in the described class those born *after* his death as well as *before*.

It is equally clear that the motivating purpose that influenced these special bequests of income was pride in the family name and desire to have that name perpetuated by as many lineal male descendants of the *blood and name* as possible. To exclude grandsons that came within the described class merely because they happened to be born after the testator's death would do violence to the very purpose that actuated the gifts. To which may be added that normally if a testator has in mind individual members of a group he would describe them by name; therefore, when he uses a class designation he would seem to mean not only those known to him but all that may come into the class described unless there is some contrary intent manifested.

We have here then a clear case for the application of the principle referred to in Witman v. Webner, 351 Pa. 503, 41 A.2d 686 (1945), where Mr. Justice Horace Stern said, at page 507, "It is well settled that if a person qualifies within the exact meaning of

language describing a class he will be held to be a member of that
class unless other language in the instrument expressly or by clear
implication indicates a contrary intent: Robinson's Estate, 266
Pa. 251, 109 A. 924; Hogg's Estate, 329 Pa. 163, 196 A. 503;
Rosengarten Estate, 349 Pa. 32, 39, 36 A.2d 310, 313, 314.''

We have examined the whole will to ascertain if there be any
other language that impels such contrary intent and find nothing
that compels a narrower construction of the testator's explicit language.   In doing so we have been greatly assisted by the learned
opinions of the three eminent judges of the court below and the
excellent briefs of the able guardians ad litem.   Our respect for
the learned judges below requires us to examine the reasons advanced in the adjudication and the opinion of the court en banc
which led the court below to a different conclusion.

Judge Hunter in his adjudication begins by applying the general
rule of construction known as "the rule of convenience" which he
states as follows: "that in the case of an *immediate* gift to a class,
the class closes as of the death of the testator."   However, unless
the word "immediate" is understood to mean a gift of principal
distributable at the testator's death, the rule is too broadly stated
because the rule must be applied with due regard to its origin.
As the learned Auditing Judge points out, this rule had its origin
in the English case of Ringrose v. Bramham, 2 Cox 384, 30 Eng.
Reprint 177 (1794), where the testator provided, "I also give to
Joseph Ringrose's children £50 to every child he hath by his wife
Elizabeth . . . I also give to Christopher Rhodes's children, that
he hath by his wife Peggy, £50 to every child. . . ."   The court
there said: ". . . if I am to let in all the children of these two
persons born at any future time, I must *postpone* the *distribution*
of the testator's personal estate until the death of Joseph Ringrose
and Christopher Rhodes, or their wives . . . until I know how
many legacies of £50 are payable."   (Italics supplied.)   It must
be remembered this was an executor's account and the rule there
adopted solved the very practical difficulty of reserving a sufficient
sum to meet the contingency of an unknown number of future
births, or in the alternative withhold *all* distribution for an *indefinite* period from other distributees presently entitled.   It is to
be noted also that the words of this testator "children that he hath
by his wife" were of equivocal import so that the rule there
adopted was no doubt a proper solution.

However, the danger of such rules of construction is their tendency in the progress of time to become inflexible and in their application to circumstances where there is neither reason nor necessity
until finally they become controlling.   A familiar example of that

eventuality is the Rule in Shelley's Case, which became so fixed that it more often thwarted a grantor or testator's intent than observed it. [Footnote omitted.] The case of Storrs v. Benbow, 2 My. & K. 46, 39 Eng. Reprint 862 (1833), cited by the Auditing Judge also illustrates this tendency. In that case testator gave ". . . the sum of £500 apiece to each child that *may be born* to either of the children of either of my brothers, lawfully begotten, etc. . . ." (Italics supplied.) It was held the class closed as of the death of the testator thus extending the rule of convenience to a case where the testator's words clearly indicated futurity. The decision seeks to explain away the words "may be born" by asserting these words would be satisfied by the period of time between the date of the will and the date of the death, yet this is no explanation at all because even *without* such words of futurity, children born between the date of the will and testator's death were always regarded as being within the class: 3 Jarman on Wills, 7th Ed. 1930, page 1669.

Therefore, we must be constantly alert to see that artificial rules of construction should be resorted to only where the intent of a testator as gleaned from his language is obscure, or where there is compelling practical necessity for their application; and when the reasons on which they are founded do not exist they ought not be applied. In this case the basic reason, which gave rise to the "rule of convenience" is *not* present. There is here no gift of principal to any member of the class in question that vested at testator's death. Aside from a few minor legacies given outright to nonmembers of the family by Item Second only *income* is given. No distribution is made of the principal to any family beneficiary and the whole of it is withheld until the date of the termination of the trust as hereinafter noted. Indeed, the learned Auditing Judge admits the reason giving rise to the rule does not here exist and frankly says, "If this testator intended that the executors pay $100,-000 [income] legacies to grandsons living at his death, and that the trustees of residuary estate pay similar legacies to the afterborn, it must be admitted that there is no practical difficulty in so doing. The residuary trust will remain intact until 'the expiration of twenty-one (21) years after the death of my (the testator's) last surviving grandchild or greatgrandchild living at the time of my decease.' Distribution at the termination of the residuary trust will not be delayed, because it does not seem possible that the trust can terminate before the death of testator's two sons, when the class of grandsons will be complete." It therefore serves no purpose to restrict words of futurity of the gifts here made to the period between the date of the will and testator's death because when such restriction serves no purpose, words of futurity are not to be restricted to date of testator's *death* but are projected at least to the *date of distribution* and it was expressly so held in Heisse v. Markland, 2 Rawle 274 (1830), and Austin's Estate, 315 Pa. 449, 173 A. 278 (1934).

That the rule should not be applied when the reason therefor does not exist has been recognized by respectable authority as noted by text writers.[28] In Mogg v. Mogg, 1 Mer. 654, 35 Eng. Reprint 811 (1811), where a testator devised certain property in trust to pay rents toward the support and maintenance of "children begotten and to be begotten" of his daughter Sarah Mogg, it was held the class remained open so as to include five children born after the testator's death because the gift was an aggregate sum to the whole class and *did not delay distribution*. It should be noted that the restricted view of the words importing futurity, "children begotten and to be begotten" were not explained away by asserting they were satisfied by the period of time between the date of the will and the date of testator's death, thereby indicating that the real basis and perhaps the only justification for the application of the "rule of convenience" is where it delays indefinitely distribution to other distributees. So, too, as pointed out by Judge Bolger in his dissenting opinion, the Restatement of Property, Sec. 294, comment *q,* indicates that the rule need not be applied to close a class at testator's death when distribution is not actually delayed for the reasons therein set forth. This whether separate sums are given to each member of the class or an aggregate to the whole class: [citations omitted].

Judge Bolger in his dissenting opinion calls attention to another exception to the application of the "rule of convenience," which is that when there are no members of the class in existence at the date of the will or of testator's death the rule is inapplicable. He then demonstrates that this exception might well be applied to the instant case for the testator cannot be presumed to have intended that his gift to the sons of Ralph should be a nullity as he well knew Ralph then had no sons. All of which is analogous to the recognized principle that a devise to children of a living person who has no children is an executory devise to children when born: Hunter's Common Place Book, p. 388, citing Mitchell v. Long, 80 Pa. 516 (1876) and Leisenring's Estate, 237 Pa. 60 (1912).

In justice to the learned Auditing Judge we should say it is evident from his adjudication that he does not rely with too much

---

[28] (*Court footnote*) See, for example, those collected in the comprehensive article by Casner, entitled Class Gifts to Others Than to "Heirs" or "Next of Kin" Increase in Class Membership, 51 Harv. L.R. 254 (1937).

confidence on the rule of convenience for he concludes, "Aside from the question of the testator's intent, I agree with the claimant in his contention that there is no reason for applying the rule of convenience, and that the class could remain open until the final termination of the residuary trust, without inconvenience to the estate."

He then proceeds to search the will for other light on testator's provision which he regards as ambiguous. While we have come to the conclusion that the provision in question is *not* ambiguous, we will proceed nevertheless to answer the other reasons advanced in the adjudication. It is argued that the establishment of the trust for an afterborn grandson is not consistent with the general plan of the will because his life estate under Item Fifth of the will may continue beyond the termination date of the residuary trust under Item Eleventh, the minor appellant being 20 years and 10 months younger than his youngest half brother. This argument assumes too much.

The *terms* of the $100,000 trusts for the male offsprings of testator's sons are not set out in paragraph 3 of Item Fifth which creates them, but by reference the terms and conditions of the two named granddaughter trusts set up in Item Third and Fourth are incorporated. Item Fourth is identical with Item Third under which the trust set up for the granddaughter, Louise, is stated to be, ". . . for the term of her life." Upon her death the trustees are to pay the income from this trust to her issue ". . . until the time for the distribution of the principal of my estate arrives, as fixed in ITEM ELEVENTH hereof." When the time arrives for the distribution of the principal of testator's estate, the principal of this trust is to be paid to the issue of Louise per stirpes. In the event that she should die without issue "her surviving," the principal of the trust falls back into the residuary estate.

As we understand the argument made by learned counsel for the appellee and accepted by the Auditing Judge it is, that in case of a trust for a grandson born in testator's lifetime such grandson cannot be living at the date of the termination of the trust which must, under Item Eleventh, end 21 years after the life of the longest liver of testator's grandchildren or great grandchildren living at testator's death. But to give a grandson born *after* the *testator's* death a life estate would not only offend the rule against perpetuities but be inconsistent with the pattern of testator's will. However, as Judge Bolger correctly points out in his dissenting opinion, this argument assumes that the trust for the two granddaughters fit in with the pattern of the will, whereas, in fact, they do not. This because Item Eleventh which fixes the date of the termination of the trust expressly excludes these two granddaughters as measuring lives as well as from participation[29] in the corpus of the residue, and passes the corpus of their trusts on to their issue in default of which it falls into the residue.

From this it follows that these two granddaughters not being measuring lives may survive the termination of the trust. Hence, what happens in such event poses a problem equally inconsistent with the pattern of the will. It shows also that testator failed to provide for that contingency, but such failure is no reason to deny the trusts for the granddaughters in face of the express language creating them. Neither does the fact that the testator failed to provide for the contingency of the after born grandson surviving by more than 21 years the last surviving measuring life of the trust furnish any reason for refusing to give due effect to the express language which standing alone is applicable to after born grandsons as well as those born in his lifetime. In other words, as said by Judge Bolger, "The patterning of the gifts to grandsons . . . does not involve the question of whether an after born grandchild shall take, but only as to *how and to what extent* he shall take: Bowen's Estate, 139 Superior Ct. 523."

Nor is the possibility of the appellant minor living beyond the date of the trust termination a controlling factor, for if the estate, granted by reference, be treated as one per autre vie (measured by the granddaughters' lives) then there is no perpetuity. On the other hand, if treated as an estate for *his* life it would naturally be interpreted as an income for his life or *until the termination of the trust,* which interpretation easily avoids violation of the rule against perpetuities without denying him the benefit of his trust.

We need not speculate nor now pass on what may happen if the various contingencies occur that are mentioned as possibly affecting the ultimate disposition of the trusts to the two granddaughters or the trust to the appellant minor if any of them should survive the termination of the residuary trust. None of the contingencies may ever happen, but if any of them do, that situation can then be met in the light of circumstances then existing. For the present, it is sufficient to state none of these possibilities is any valid reason for refusing to give full effect to what we regard as unambiguous language of the provision which by description, clearly includes the after born grandson.

Turning now to the opinion of the court en banc, we observe the eminent jurist who wrote its opinion falls into the same error

---

[29] (*Court footnote*) Except as to granddaughter Edith whom the testator's son, Ralph, adopted, if he appoints her to share as he is given the right to do under par. 3, Item Ninth of the will.

that runs through the adjudication. Disavowing the need to apply the rule of convenience, the opinion nevertheless begins by applying it, calling it the general rule which is stated to be, that where there is "any immediate gift to a class, the class closes as of the date of the testator's death." But as we hereinbefore observed, this rule can only be applied where the estate is *distributable* at the death.[30] This is because, as Chief Justice Gibson says, "the *time of distribution* is, itself, a circumstance of paramount consideration"; (italics supplied). Heisse v. Markland, 2 Rawle 274, 276 (1830), and see Judge Gest's opinion, affirmed on appeal, in Austin's Estate, 315 Pa. 449, 453, 173 A. 278 (1934).

Of course the rationale of the opinion of the court en banc is that the time of distribution here was actually the date of the audit of the executor's account as evidenced by the award to the executors in their capacity of trustees. Technically such an award *is* a distribution but it is not the *kind* of distribution which warrants the application of the rule of convenience. What Judge Ashman stated in Bonaffon's Estate, 14 W.N.C. 501, 502 (1884), is peculiarly appropriate on this point. Said that learned jurist in dismissing exceptions to Judge Penrose's adjudication, "In a gift to children as a class, the law aims to postpone as far as possible the period of distribution, in order to bring within the scope of the testator's bounty the largest number of beneficiaries. But the rule has been broken, upon the ground of convenience, where a literal adherence to it would sacrifice the interests of living children to secure the possible rights of children who may yet be born."

In order to justify his taking the executor's audit as distribution date[31] for the application of the rule, the learned opinion writer for the court en banc felt it necessary to find some intent of the testator so indicating. Consequently he points out that the increase provisions for the named granddaughter trusts appearing in the first and second paragraphs of the same item (Fifth) each begin with the same condition as the paragraph 3 creating the grandson trusts, viz., "In the event my estate . . . shall at least amount to a net sum of 5 million." Since, proceeds the opinion, the time of the determination though not fixed must necessarily be at the audit

---

[30] (*Court footnote*) The controlling rule is more accurately stated as follows: "The general rule of construction adopted with respect to increase in the class membership is that the class will increase in size until the *period of distribution* but not after that time." (Italics supplied.) Casner, Increase in Class Membership, 51 Harv. L.R. 254, 260.

[31] (*Court footnote*) While the court en banc states the applicable rule as being the class closed at the date of the *death,* the opinion treats this date as though it was the date of the *audit* of the executors' account. To regard the actual *date of death* as the controlling time would make the reasoning of the opinion inconsistent.

of the executor's account, and not thereafter, so far as the first two paragraphs are concerned the testator must have so intended as to the third. Waiving aside the obvious answer that this does not necessarily follow because had the testator *not* repeated the same condition the gifts in the third paragraph would have been free of it, it is clear that if the testator in paragraph 3 had added (what we hold is clearly implied) the additional words, "whether born before my death or after," the fact that the increase of the granddaughter trusts was properly determinable at the time of the audit could not be held to overcome such words. Nor can that fact overcome the words which the testator actually used which we have demonstrated at the beginning of this opinion clearly imply the same thing.

In holding the real distribution date for the application of the rule to be the *distribution of principal* at the termination of the trust, we need not be concerned with the fancied disadvantages (recited in both the opinion and appellees' brief) that might arise if a later time than executors' audit were fixed for the fulfillment of the 5 million condition, e.g., such as the necessity of continuous reappraisement of the corpus, or the possibility of its future diminution below that figure and thereby exclude some after born child or reduce the income of the widow and children of the testator. All these speculations are unimportant in face of the facts that testator's net estate was approximately ten million at the time of the executors' audit and at the present time is still over eight million.

But assuming the proper time when the 5 million condition must be fulfilled was at the audit of the executors' account and not thereafter, we still find no difficulty because that situation was fully met by Judge Henderson who audited the executors' account and who *expressly reserved the rights* of afterborn children against the estate awarded to the trustees. Though he did not think it necessary to decide that question, he took care, in effect, to charge any future claims of afterborn children on the fund awarded by him to the executors-trustees, thereby properly leaving the question to be decided if and when it might arise. In passing we note that counsel for the accountant at that audit was Mr., later, Justice Barnes, who had been testator's personal counsel and witnessed his will. His acquiescence is somewhat indicative of the fact that afterborn children were intended to be included, otherwise he would no doubt have had a guardian or trustee ad litem appointed for that audit and the question *then* settled.

The opinion finally suggests that in the first paragraph of the Ninth Item of his will the testator used the phrase, *either before my death or thereafter* and thereby demonstrated he knew how to so specify when that was his intent. This is usually a persuasive argument but it loses its force when we observe testator did not use that phrase in the second paragraph nor in the fourth, fifth, or sixth paragraphs of the same Item where it would have been equally appropriate; instead he seems to have relied on the plain implication of such words. So, too, it might also be answered by pointing out that in Item Fifth the testator had already used the all inclusive words, ". . . each and every male child of my sons," which coupled with the words of futurity, "who *shall* by birth inherit and bear the name of Earle," made the additional words redundant. Judge Bolger sets forth in his dissenting opinion other equally cogent reasons why the argument based on the omission of those words cannot prevail but which we find unnecessary to repeat.

To sum up our position briefly, we say that since the minor claimant here qualifies within the exact meaning of the language used in describing the class, he cannot be excluded by the application of a rule of construction which can only be invoked when it delays distribution beyond the time fixed in a will.

We conclude by saying that we have carefully read the entire will in the light of the learned opinions of the three judges of the court below and of the able arguments and briefs of the learned counsel and find nothing to shake the plain implication of the explicit words which bring the minor claimant within the class described by the testator. To hold otherwise would do violence not only to testator's unambiguous language but also to the clearly apparent motive, the sole reason for the gifts, namely, family pride and a desire to perpetuate an honored name.

We hold until the time fixed by the testator for the distribution of the corpus of his estate arrives, any son's male child born before that time who qualifies as a member of the class described in par. 3, of Item Fifth, cannot be excluded.

Decree reversed, costs to be paid out of the estate.

Dissenting Opinion by MR. JUSTICE ALLEN M. STEARNE:

I am unable to join in this opinion. It is an ancient well established canon of will construction that where there is an immediate gift of *a separate sum to each member of a class,* the class closes as of the date of death of testator. This was precisely what happened here. By the will testator erected a $100,000 trust "for the benefit of each and every male child of my sons who shall by birth inherit and bear the name of Earle." This was followed by a gift of the residue, under which testator erected a trust, disposing of both income and principal which is to endure to the utmost limit of permissive remoteness — lives in being and twenty-one years thereafter: Warren's Estate, 320 Pa. 112, 113, 182 A. 396. The beneficiaries under the residuary trust were the widow (since deceased) and each of testator's five named children and their issue.

Now the crux of this case is this: if the $100,000 trust now claimed by the afterborn child of George H. Earle III is taken from the residuary trust, such payment diminishes the shares of income and principal not only of George H. Earle III and his four other sons, and their issue, but also of testator's other children and their issue. In other words, *the estate already given and bequeathed is necessarily cut down and diminished.* To accomplish this effectively requires clear and unequivocal language: Haydon's Estate, 334 Pa. 403, 6 A.2d 581; Harris Estate, 351 Pa. 368, 41 A.2d 715; Fink et al. v. Stein, 158 Pa. Superior Ct. 464, 45 A.2d 249. It must be conceded that testator used no *express language* directing that afterborn grandsons of the name of Earle should have their $100,000 trust funds paid out of the residuary trust. It is only by *necessary implication* that such an intent may be declared. The majority in their opinion seek to demonstrate such implied intent. To attempt to analyze and answer the many points submitted in substantiation of the claim of proof of implied intent, would result in entering a labyrinth of generalities and legal principles, most of which I freely concede, but which clearly have no application to this case. The inferences of testamentary intent which are so voluminously submitted become less convincing the more they are advanced. And strange as it may seem, apparently in an effort still further to strengthen their contentions, the majority not only conjecture what *testator* intended but venture to suggest what *counsel* regarded as testator's intent. In the opinion it is said: "In passing we note that counsel for the accountant at that audit was Mr., later, Justice Barnes, who had been testator's personal counsel and witnessed his will. His acquiescence is somewhat indicative of the fact that afterborn children were intended to be included, otherwise he would no doubt have had a guardian or trustee ad litem appointed for that audit and the question *then* settled."

In construing wills it is my opinion that there should be no straying from the solid and well defined highway of testamentary construction. We should refrain from entering the misty swamp of testamentary conjecture, following an illusory will-o'-the-wisp seeking to determine what we *surmise* was testator's true intent. It is axiomatic that in expounding a will it is not what the testator may have meant, but what is the meaning of his words. This principle is analogous to a provision of the Statutory Construction

Act: "The object of all interpretation and construction of laws is to ascertain and effectuate the intention of the Legislature; . . . the letter of [the statute] is not to be disregarded under the pretext of pursuing its spirit."

Judge Hunter's adjudication and Judge Klein's opinion in the court below comprehensively and accurately state the applicable authorities and reach the correct construction of this will. It would be unnecessarily repetitious for me to restate what they have so well said, and with which I thoroughly agree.

It is for these reasons I note my dissent.[32]

ROGERS v. MUTCH
10 Ch. D. 25 (1878)

Elizabeth Hill, Widow, by her will, dated the 3rd of June, 1873, bequeathed "the sum of £100 to each of the children of my niece Eliza Mutch, who shall live to attain the age of twenty-one years."

The testatrix died on the 31st of October, 1873.

Eliza Mutch was still living, and she and her husband were Defendants in this action, which was for the administration of the estate of the testatrix. Mrs. Mutch had not yet had any children. In distributing the estate the question arose whether any, and, if so, what amount should be set apart to answer the legacies to the "children" of Mrs. Mutch.

JESSEL, M.R.: —

As I understand the rule, its object is simply one of convenience.

In the old case of Ringrose v. Bramham, the gift was of £50 to every child of Joseph Ringrose and Christopher Rhodes by their present wives who came of age, and the Master of the Rolls says this: "Here there are distinct legacies of £50 to each of the children, and therefore if I am to let in all the children of these two persons born at any future time, I must postpone the distribution of the testator's personal estate until the death of Joseph Ringrose and Christopher Rhodes, or their wives, for I can never divide the

---

[32] For comments on Earle Estate, see 100 U. of Pa. L. Rev. 908 (1952); 38 Va. L. Rev. 525 (1952).

In Crockett v. Crockett, 332 Mass. 564, 126 N.E.2d 363 (1955), a bequest read "to all of my nieces and nephews, I wish that my estate would provide a four year college course to any wishing to accept such," and it was upheld as a present gift of an ascertainable sum. The court pointed out that delay in determining what amount should be paid under the bequest would prevent the computation of the shares of the residue. After-born nephews and nieces were excluded from the bequest, even though no niece had been born. The Probate Court was instructed to fix the time within which a guardian of a nephew should determine whether to accept the gift for his ward and to do whatever else was necessary to carry out the testator's intent. — ED.

residue until I know how many legacies of £50 are payable." And he distinguishes the case of Gilmore v. Severn, 1 Bro. C.C. 582, that in that case a gross sum of £350 was given to the children of Jane Gilmore, to be paid to them in equal shares at twenty-one, and that there was no inconvenience in postponing the vesting of those shares until some one of them attained that age, so as to let in the children born in the meantime, because there was nothing to do but to set apart the sum of £350, and the residue of the testator's personal estate might be immediately divided. So that the rule is a rule of convenience; unless you adopt it you cannot divide the estate.

In Ringrose v. Bramham, 2 Cox, 384, there were children living at the death of the testator, but the same rule applies, where, as in the present case, there are no children living at the testator's death. If, in such a case, you are to let in children born after the death, the estate is no more divisible in the one case than in the other; and so Lord Hatherley, when Vice-Chancellor, points out in Mann v. Thompson, Kay, 638. He says this [id. 642]: "The next case is not a bequest of a sum to be divided among a class, but a gift of a certain sum to each individual of the class, where no time is fixed by the will at which the class is to be ascertained. I do not find any decided case in which the point has arisen, which occurs here with regard to children, who were neither in esse at the date of the will, nor at the testator's death." He then refers to Ringrose v. Bramham, and says: "The reason which he (the Master of the rolls) gave for excluding them (the afterborn children), seems to be very sound, namely, the extreme inconvenience of postponing the distribution of the testator's personal estate until all the children who might be born should be ascertained, which would not happen until the death of their respective parents."

The actual point in this case did not arise in Ringrose v. Bramham, but still the *ratio decidendi* clearly applies.

[His Lordship then read several other passages from the Vice-Chancellor's judgment, Kay, 643, 644, and continued:] It appears, therefore, that the Vice-Chancellor approves of the decision in Ringrose v. Bramham, and also of the reason for that decision, and would have applied it to the case before him but that the language of the will was sufficient to shew the testator contemplated those children only who should be living at his death.

Then I find the rule is laid down in Mr. Hawkins' well-known and valuable book, where he says [Page 73]: "The rule which admits objects born after the testator's death and before the period of distribution, to share in the bequest, only applies where the total amount of the gift is independent of the number of objects among whom it is to be divided, and is therefore not increased by the construction adopted. But a gift of a certain sum to each of a class of objects at a future period is confined to those living at the testator's death." He then illustrates the rule by referring to the two authorities I have mentioned, and proceeds: "The reason given is, that in the latter case, if afterborn children were admitted, the distribution of the personal estate of the testator would have to be postponed till it could be ascertained how many legacies of the given amount would be payable." So he obviously takes the same view as has been taken by the authorities, namely, that no children born after the testator's death can be admitted unless the total amount of the gift is independent of the number of objects.

So I apply the rule in this case, and hold that no child Mrs. Mutch may have can take under this bequest.

SHERIDAN v. BLUME
290 Ill. 508, 125 N.E. 353 (1919)

Mr. Justice Carter delivered the opinion of the court:

Appellee, Jessie Sheridan, filed a bill in the circuit court of Cook county for the partition of certain real estate devised by the will of her mother. The decision required the construction of said will. After the pleadings were settled the circuit court construed the will and ordered partition of the real estate in a certain manner, whereupon the appellants appealed to this court.

The principal if not the sole question to be decided is the proper construction of the will of Mrs. Anna Pochmann. Mrs. Pochmann died testate April 7, 1916. Her will was duly probated, disposing of all her estate, including the real estate here sought to be partitioned. The third paragraph of the will is the only portion that requires construction. The will first provides for the payment of debts and a money legacy, which is not involved here, and for the appointment of an executrix and trustee. The clause in question reads:

"Third — Subject to the foregoing two paragraphs, I direct that all of the residue of my estate, real, personal and mixed, of which I may die seized, possessed or entitled, be divided into five equal parts, share and share alike; and I give, devise and bequeath one of such parts to my daughter Jessie Sheridan, one of such parts to my daughter Emily T. Blume, one of such parts to my daughter Laura Hedemark and one of such parts to my daughter Meta Pochmann, each to have and to hold the same to them and their respective heirs and assigns forever; and the remaining one of such parts I give, devise and bequeath in equal parts, share and share alike, unto the children of my daughter Annie Bell that are living, when the youngest living thereof shall have attained his or her majority, each to have and to hold the same to them and their respective heirs and assigns forever, — the part mentioned in this sentence to be held in trust by my hereinafter named executrix until the youngest living child of said Annie Bell shall have reached his or her majority, it being my intention that the part of my estate which would otherwise go to my daughter Annie Bell shall go to such of her children as attain their majority."

Mrs. Pochmann left her surviving her five daughters, Jessie Sheridan, Emily T. Blume, Laura Hedemark, Meta Pochmann and Annie Bell, and also Russell Davy, only child of a deceased daughter. Mrs. Pochmann at her death was sixty-nine years of age. Her will was executed November 9, 1913. At the date the will was executed and at the death of testatrix there were born and surviving the following children of her daughter Annie Bell: Roy S. Bell, twenty-five years old at the time of hearing in the trial court; Allen C. Bell, then twenty-three years of age; Grace M. Bell, thirteen years, and Frank P. Bell, eleven years. The cause was referred to a master in chancery, who construed the third paragraph with reference to the interests of Mrs. Bell's children that they were not vested with any interest until the youngest reached majority. On a hearing in the circuit court a decree was entered, which found, among other things, that it was the intention of the testatrix by said will "to devise a one-fifth interest of the residue of her estate in trust for such of the children of said defendant, Annie Bell, as were living when all the living children should have attained their majority; that therefore the interests of the children of Annie Bell in and to such one-fifth interest cannot be determined until such time after the death of said defendant, Annie Bell, as all her living children shall have attained legal age."

The portion of the will relating to the share going to the children of Mrs. Bell contains two statements that may not be considered in entire harmony as to the disposition of the property. In the first part of the third clause it is stated that the share in question shall go to the children of Annie Bell "that are living, when the youngest living thereof shall have attained his or her majority," and at the end of the third clause it is stated, "it being my intention that the part of my estate which would otherwise go to my daughter Annie Bell shall go to such of her children as attain their majority." It is argued that the last clause of the will, if there is any inconsistency, should have the greater weight in construing the will. The rule that where there are inconsistent clauses in a will the last prevails is only applicable when the real intention of the testator cannot be discovered and where the two provisions are so utterly inconsistent that it is impossible for both to coincide with the general intention of the testator. (Hunt v. Hawes, 181 Ill. 343.) The usual rule, however, is that the intention of the testator is to be gathered, not from one clause of the will alone but from a view of the whole will and all its parts, or that such construction shall be adopted, if it can be reasonably found, as to give force and effect to every word and clause in the will. (Morrison v. Schorr, 197 Ill. 554.) We think the intention of the testatrix, as shown by the entire will, clearly indicates that the one-fifth portion of the estate which, if the general scheme had been followed out, would have gone to the mother, Annie Bell, will, under the will as drawn, go to such of her children as reach their majority.

The law favors the vesting of estates, and in cases where the instrument is susceptible of two constructions the law is inclined to favor the construction most favorable to the devisee rather than the construction that would be against his interest. (Mettler v. Warner, 243 Ill. 600; see, also, Armstrong v. Barber, 239 Ill. 389.) Subject to certain other provisions which will be referred to later, each of the children of Annie Bell will take a vested interest in his or her share upon reaching the age of majority, — that is, eighteen years if a daughter and twenty-one years if a son. After reaching that age, as their share is then vested, it would pass upon the death of such devisee, the same as other property. Up to the time of reaching the age of majority the interest of each of Annie Bell's children is contingent upon their reaching that age, and if they die before reaching majority their share is to be divided among their surviving brothers and sisters, this added portion being subject to the same rules, as to vesting or contingency, as the original portion. There being a possibility of more children being born to Annie Bell, it cannot be told until her death who will be entitled, finally, to a possible share, hence the share of each of her children already born, so long as contingent, is subject to the further contingency of being decreased pro tanto to raise the portion for such after-born child, and the shares of those that have vested are thereafter subject to be opened up to that extent to contribute their part of such share for an after-born child.

The third clause of the will further provides that "the part mentioned in this sentence to be held in trust by my hereinafter named executrix until the youngest living child of said Annie Bell shall have reached his or her majority," hence the shares above mentioned, whether contingent or vested, are not to pass at once into the possession of the various devisees. Until after the death of the mother, Annie Bell, and until the youngest living child has reached majority, each devisee, on becoming of age, becomes vested only with an equitable interest. Until the time mentioned, such interests are to be held by the person named as executrix, as a trustee. Said trustee should keep the funds properly invested, and may pay over, from time to time, the proper part of the income to the beneficiaries who have become vested with their equitable interests on account of their reaching majority, and at the death of Annie Bell, and when the youngest living child has attained majority, the trustee should distribute the fund among those entitled to the various shares. This is a partition proceeding, and hence the fund in question to be held by the trustee will consist of the share in the proceeds of sale of the real estate paid over by the master in chancery. Under the doctrine of representation, the after-born children of Annie Bell, if any, will be bound by these proceedings, and their interest in the real estate sold by the master in chancery will cease and in its place will be substituted the right to participate in the fund held by said trustee. Dole v. Shaw, 282 Ill. 642; Gavin v. Curtin, 171 id. 640.

It is further suggested by counsel for appellants that if the will is construed to the effect that the property must be held by the trustee until the death of Annie Bell it will be contrary to section 155, chapter 30, of the statute concerning restraining accumulations in conveyances.[33] We are of the opinion that the trustee may properly divide and pay over the income, from time to time, of the shares belonging to those children of Annie Bell who have become of age. The only reason for withholding the portion of the income going to the children who are still minors is, that their interest may be defeated by their death before reaching majority. This distribution should take place along the lines commonly followed by trustees where there is no specified direction in the instrument creating the trust. As to the share of any after-born child who might reach majority more than twenty-one years after the death of the testatrix, we think this is fully covered by the portion of that statute already referred to which reads, "or for any longer than during the minority . . . of any person . . . who, under the uses or trusts of the . . . will, . . . would, for the time being, if of full age, be entitled unto the rents, issues and profits . . . so directed to be accumulated." As to any part of the income earned

[33] At the time this case was decided, Illinois law provided that accumulation could not be made to last longer than the term of twenty-one years from the death of the testator or longer than the minority of any person who would for the time being, if of full age, be entitled to the income. In 1953, Illinois adopted the common law rule against accumulations, but the change applies only to instruments which become operative after the effective date of the 1953 law. See Ill. Rev. Stat., c. 30, §153 (1959). — ED.

before the birth of an after-born child and paid out to the adult children, we deem it unnecessary to consider and decide at the present time just on what conditions or terms said part should be refunded, if at all, to such after-born child. That matter may be adjusted from the corpus of the trust fund at the proper time.

It is suggested that the wording of the will confines the distribution to the children of Annie Bell that are living at the death of the testatrix. We cannot so hold. The testatrix had in mind that the youngest child might die before reaching the age of majority, and then, if Annie Bell were dead, it would not be necessary to wait until such youngest child would have reached the age of majority had he or she survived, but the distribution would take place when all the children of Annie Bell that lived to reach the age of majority had reached that age, provided their mother had died so that it was possible to know that there would be no more children.

The decree of the circuit court should be so modified as to provide for the distribution of the share going to Annie Bell's children according to the rules above stated and entered with such modifications.

Reversed and remanded, with directions.[34]

PROBLEMS

11.19. A desires to make a gift of $1000 to each of his grandchildren, whenever born, on the grandchild's twenty-first birthday. A has five children now living, and no child of his is deceased. He has four grandchildren now living and the likelihood is that there will be many additional grandchildren born. Draft the provision you would insert in A's will to accomplish his objective.

11.20. A desires to make a gift of $100,000 to be equally divided among his grandchildren whenever born. A has five children now living, and no child of his is deceased. He has four grandchildren now living and the likelihood is that there will be many additional grandchildren born. Draft the provision you would insert in A's will to accomplish his objective.

11.21. In his will T gives the residue of his estate to a trustee and directs the trustee to pay the income to his wife for life; and "on the death of my said wife, the trustee is to accumulate the income until my youngest grandchild attains twenty-one, at which time the trustee shall distribute the corpus and accumulated income in equal shares to my grandchildren then living." Is it pos-

---

[34] A discussion of various situations which present a problem as to the time within which a class member must be born in order to share in a gift to the class is to be found in 5 American Law of Property §§22.39-22.46 (Casner ed. 1952). See also 3 Restatement of Property §§294, 295. — ED.

sible that a grandchild of the testator may be excluded from the gift to grandchildren on the ground that he is born too late?

d. *Requirement of Survival*

In connection with each class gift, consideration should be given to the effect of the death of a class member before the date set for beneficial enjoyment by the class. If the interest of a class member is not subject to a requirement of survival to the date set for beneficial enjoyment, his interest may be subject to death taxes as a future interest. Normally it is unwise to create in an estate plan an interest in a class member (or in an individual to whom a future interest is given) that is not subject to a requirement of survival to the date set for beneficial enjoyment.

If a gift is made to the "heirs" of a designated person and the statute which is to be employed to ascertain the designated heirs is not to be applied until the date set for beneficial enjoyment by the designated heirs, it is obvious that a person must survive to that date in order to be an heir. If, however, the statute which is to be employed to ascertain the designated heirs is to be applied at a date which precedes the date of beneficial enjoyment by the designated heirs, will the heirs so ascertained have interests subject to a requirement of survival to the date of beneficial enjoyment?

If the word "issue" is used to describe the class, is there any more of a basis for implying a requirement of survival to the date of beneficial enjoyment than if some other class designation is employed?

The language of the dispositive instrument should make it clear (1) whether there is a requirement of survival; (2) if there is such a requirement, to what date the class member must survive to satisfy the requirement; and (3) if there is such a requirement, what disposition is to be made of the interest of the class member when he fails to meet the requirement of survival. Rules of construction may exist in the governing jurisdiction which resolve the questions as to survival in the absence of a manifestation of intention in regard to the matter in the dispositive instrument, but a properly drafted estate plan will not require recourse to such rules of construction to obtain the answers.

(1) Death of a Class Member Before the Death of the Testator

DOWNING v. NICHOLSON
115 Iowa 493, 88 N.W. 1064 (1902)

DEEMER, J. — John Nicholson died testate June 2, 1898. His will was executed May 19th of the same year. This will made certain bequests to relatives and others, and contained the following residuary clause: "After paying all the foregoing amounts, I give and bequeath the balance of my property to be divided equally between all my nephews and nieces." John Downing, the applicant herein, is a son of Mary Fitzpatrick, nee Nicholson; and Mary Fitzpatrick was a daughter of Michael Nicholson, a brother of the deceased. Mrs. Fitzpatrick, applicant's mother, died June 15, 1883, which, as will be observed, was long prior to the time John Nicholson made his will. John Downing, who is a grandnephew of the deceased, claims that he is entitled to take, under the residuary clause of the will, the share his mother would have received, had she outlived the testator. This clause devises the remainder of his property to testator's nephews and nieces as a class, and applicant is not one of that class. His claim, however, is that he is a substituted legatee, and as such is entitled to the share his mother would have received had she outlived the testator. A devise to nephews will not include grandnephews unless there be something in the context which shows that testator intended to include them, or unless there be such an ambiguity as authorizes extrinsic evidence for the purpose of showing that grandnephews were intended to be included. The case was decided by the trial court on the pleadings, and the facts we have recited are the only ones admitted by the parties. True, something is said in the petition about the intention of the testator; but this is denied in the answer, and therefore cannot be treated as a fact in the disposition of the case. The proposition of law announced is too plain for controversy, and we need only cite in its support In re Woodward, 117 N.Y. 522 (23 N.E. Rep. 120, 7 L.R.A. 367), and cases therein cited. Applicant practically concedes this rule, but he relies on section 3281 of the Code, which reads as follows: "If a devisee die before a testator, his heirs shall inherit the property devised to him, unless from the terms of the will a contrary intent is manifest." The mischief this statute was enacted to cure was the common law rule to the effect that a devise to one who dies before the death of the testator lapses. McMenomy v. McMenomy, 22 Iowa, 148. Nearly every state in the Union has adopted statutes similar to this, although few are as comprehensive. Some of them apply only to cases where the original beneficiary was a child or other lineal descendant of the testator; some to cases where the beneficiary is a child or other relative, and dies leaving issue surviving the testator (and in some of the states of this group the statute applies only to certain classes of relatives, who are clearly pointed out by the statute); and some to all cases, no matter what relation the beneficiary is to the testator, or whether the beneficiary leaves descendants or not. See statutes and cases cited and referred to in 18 Am. & Eng. Enc. Law, pp. 755, 756, et seq. The remedy for this mischief of the common law was first adopted in this state with the Code of 1851, which was in the same language as the statute under consideration, save that in place of the word "property" the word "amount" is used. Section 2319 of the Revision is a copy of section 1287 of the Code of 1851, and this same language is carried into section 2337 of the Code of 1873. For more than 50 years it has been the policy of this state to prevent lapses where a devisee dies before the death of the testator, and this has been done by the use of the broadest and most comprehensive language. We are now, for the first time, called upon to determine whether or not this section applies to a devise to a class, and, if so, whether or not it applies to such devisees when one of that class is dead at the time testator made his will; and this without the aid of other extrinsic evidence, save such as identifies the persons belonging to the class, and identifies the claimant as a grandnephew of the testator. On entering this field, we, as usual, find quite a number of conflicting decisions, and are again reminded that it seems almost impossible to write a statute in language so clear that it may not be the subject of controversy.

Since a will speaks from the day of the testator's death, the members of the class, where the devise is to a class, are prima facie to be determined upon the death of the testator. Ruggles v. Randall, 70 Conn. 44 (38 Atl. Rep. 885); Richardson v. Willis, 163 Mass. 130 (39 N.E. Rep. 1015); Buzby v. Roberts, 53 N.J. Eq. 566 (32 Atl. Rep. 9). But this is not an unyielding rule, even at common law. The will itself may indicate a contrary intent, and if that be so this intent will be adopted and enforced. In re Swenson's Estate, 55 Minn. 300 (56 N.W. Rep. 1115); Bailey v. Brown, 19 R.I. 669 (36 Atl. Rep. 581). Under the common law rule, the members of the class to whom testator left his residue estate would be determined upon the day of his death; and, as applicant herein is neither a nephew nor a niece, he would be excluded. Applicant's counsel contend, however, that the statute which we have quoted modifies this rule to this extent: that, although the members of the class are to be determined as upon the day of the testator's death, yet, as the applicant is an heir of one of that class, who would have taken under the will, had his mother survived, he is entitled to her share, and that the decree of the trial court, so holding, is correct. Some of the cases hold that the general common law rule with reference to gifts to a class is not affected by these statutes, for the reason that they are only intended to apply where something is given by will to one who dies before the testator, and have no application to gifts to a class, where the gift is, in legal effect, only to the members of that class in existence at a designated time. See In re Harvey's Estate, [1893] 1 Ch. 567; Martin v. Trustees, 98 Ga. 320 (25 S.E. Rep. 522). This is also the rule in England. Olney v. Bates, 3 Drew, 319; Browne v. Hammond, Johns. Eng. Ch. 210. But in other states these statutes are held applicable to gifts to a class as well as to individuals. Howland v. Slade, 155 Mass. 415 (29 N.E. Rep. 631); Bray v. Pullen, 84 Me. 185 (24 Atl. Rep. 811); Strong v. Smith, 84 Mich. 567 (48 N.W. Rep. 183); Parker v. Leach, 66 N.H. 416 (31 Atl. Rep. 19); In re Bradley's Estate, 166 Pa. 300 (31 Atl. Rep. 96); Jones v. Hunt, 96 Tenn. 369 (34 S.W. Rep. 693); Wildberger v. Cheek's Ex'rs, 94 Va. 517 (27 S.E. Rep. 441). The numerical weight of authority seems to favor this rule, although it also will yield to the intent of the testator as found in the context of the will, or as shown by competent and legitimate evidence. White v. Institute, 171 Mass. 84 (50 N.E. Rep. 512); Bigelow v. Clap, 166 Mass. 88 (43 N.E. Rep. 1037); Almy v. Jones, 17 R.I. 265 (21 Atl. Rep. 616, 12 L.R.A. 414). The reason for this general rule appears to be that, as the statute is remedial in character, it should receive a liberal construction, so as to advance the remedy and suppress the mischief; that wills are presumed to be drawn with reference to existing laws and that in arriving at a testator's intent we must presume that he had knowledge of the law, and drafted his will accordingly; that in gifts of the class in question a testator is presumed to treat all members of the class as surviving, although some of them be dead, and that, in the absence of other evidence, this presumption will be conclusive; and that there is no substantial difference between a gift to all of a class and a gift to each member thereof, naming them. Where there is such conflict in authority, much may be said in support of either rule. Despite the temptation, we will not enter into a further discussion of the matter, but content ourselves with saying that we prefer the doctrine announced by the greater number of the cases as a rule of general application, but that, like all other rules on the subject, it must yield to the intent of the testator when that can be ascertained; for that is the polar star of all inquiry in such cases. Daboll v. Field, 9 R.I. 266.

With these rules settled, we are now brought down to the pivotal point in the case, to-wit, does the statute apply to a case where the devise is to a class, one of the members of which is dead at the time the will was executed, so that the heirs of the deceased member take by substitution or representation? Here, again, there is a decided and irreconcilable conflict in the cases. Holding to the affirmative of the proposition are Bray v. Pullen, 84 Me. 185 (24 Atl. Rep. 811); Wildberger v. Cheek's Ex'rs, 94 Va. 517 (27 S.E. Rep. 441); Winter v. Winter, 5 Hare, 306; Moses v. Allen, 81 Me. 268 (17 Atl. Rep. 66); Jamison v. Hay, 46 Mo. 546; Chenault's Guardian v. Chenault's Estate, 88 Ky. 83 (9 S.W. Rep. 775). On the other hand, statutes to prevent lapses are held not to apply where the supposed devisee is dead at the time the will is made. White v. Institute, supra; Billingsley v. Tongue, 9 Md. 575; Lindsay v. Pleasants, 39 N.C. 320; Almy v. Jones, 17 R.I. 265 (21 Atl. Rep. 216, 12 L.R.A. 414); Tolbert v. Burns, 82 Ga. 213 (8 S.E. Rep. 79). We cannot take the time or space necessary to review these authorities. Some of them were decided on facts indicating the testator's intent to be in accord with the statutory construction, and at least one on a statute which provided that the issue of a devisee who is dead at the time of the making of the will shall take the property given to him. We do not favor any arbitrary rule with reference to this matter, preferring to leave each case to be determined on its own peculiar facts. We may say, however, that at common law a legacy or devise to a person who was dead at the time of the making of the will was void, or, as some cases put it, lapsed. And it is only perforce of a somewhat strained construction of language that statutes similar to the one under construction are held to modify this rule. In Kentucky there is an express statute which does so. See cases heretofore cited. And we understand Tennessee has a like statute. See Dixon v. Cooper, 88 Tenn. 177 (12 S.W. Rep. 445). This general rule also obtained even where the testator knew that the donee was dead. Dildine v. Dildine, 32 N.J. Eq. 78. If a deceased beneficiary is specifically named in the will, this, perhaps, is a sufficient indication that the testator intended his heirs to take, under the statute before quoted, as substitutional or representative devisees. But where the gift is to a class, of which there are many members, it is reasonable to suppose that the testator had in mind only those of that class who were living at the time he made his will. To apply the rule to the instant case, when testator made his will he had several nephews and nieces living. He also had at least one grandnephew, whose mother had been dead for more than 10 years. In the residuary clause of his will he devised his remaining property to his "nephews and nieces," share and share alike. Did he intend by this description to give any part of it to this grandnephew? Surely not, for it would have been easy to include him if he had so desired. Taking the will by its "four corners," and reading it in the light of the admitted facts, we hardly think one unversed in the law would say that testator intended to include applicant in the class described as "nephews and nieces." If he had intended to include the grandnephew, we think it more likely that he would have named him. Nephews and nieces are here the primary devisees. Nothing whatever is given to their issue, except as they may be substituted under the statute. In order to claim under the will, this substituted legatee must point out the original legatee in whose place he would stand. At the date of the will none but living nephews and nieces of the testator could have taken. The issue of the one who was dead at that time can show no object of substitution, and to give him an original legacy would be, in effect, to make a new will for the testator. Of course, if the proposed legatee or devisee is living at the time the will is made, and subsequently dies before the death of the testator, a different intent is manifest, which will be given in effect in virtue of the statute under which applicant claims. But where, as in this case, the gift is to a class, it is perfectly clear that testator had in mind only those members of the class who were then in existence. This conclusion is not in harmony with some of the cases we have cited, which hold that it makes no difference whether the devise is to a class or to designated beneficiaries, but we think that in arriving at the testator's intent there is a manifest difference. In the one case there is a devise to a particular person, showing an intent that that person or his heirs are the objects of his bounty, while in the other there is a devise to all of a class, and not to one of a different class, who is in no manner referred to in the will. Mrs. Fitzpatrick was never a devisee under the will, for she was dead and incapable of taking when the will was executed. True, her son was living; but that the testator intended to exclude him is manifest from the fact that he makes no mention of him by name, nor is he included in the class which is to take the residuary estate. The primary rule in the construction of all wills is the intent of the testator. When this is ascertained, almost all arbitrary and judge made rules will yield, and the intent prevail. The statute in question is based on the assumption that the testator would prefer his estate to go to the legatee's descendants rather than to have it lapse. And it was not intended, we think, to apply to a case like this, where the persons whom he intended to take are clearly pointed out as a class. There was no devise in this case which would lapse, unless we arbitrarily say that he intended a part of his estate to go to one whom he knew to be dead when he made his last will and testament. Although it has been a difficult task to pioneer our way through the conflicting authorities which have been cited by counsel, and others which we have discovered on an independent investigation, we reach the quite satisfactory conclusion that the applicant is not entitled to take under the will, and that the court was in error in declaring him a beneficiary on the pleadings as they stood at the time the motion for decree was submitted.

It follows that the decree must be reversed.[35]

(2) Death of a Class Member After the Death of the Testator or After the Effective Date of an Inter Vivos Transfer, and Before the Period of Distribution

STRAWHACKER v. STRAWHACKER
132 Neb. 614, 272 N.W. 772 (1937)

CARTER, J.

Plaintiffs brought this suit to have a deed to 80 acres of Jefferson county land construed and for a decree that they are the owners of an undivided one-half interest therein. From an adverse decree, plaintiffs appeal.

The record discloses that on December 1, 1883, John Jury and

[35] For a recent case in accord with Downing v. Nicholson, see Drafts v. Drafts, 114 So.2d 473 (Fla. Dist. Ct. App. 1959).

For the effect of the death of a class member before the death of the testator, see 5 American Law of Property §§22.47-22.55 (Casner ed. 1952); 3 Restatement of Property §§296, 298.

The Massachusetts lapse statute, Mass. Ann. Laws, c. 191, §22, quoted infra page 1456, does not expressly apply to class gifts. This statute was applied to a gift to a class in Stockbridge, Petitioner, 145 Mass. 517, 14 N.E. 928 (1887), the court saying, "the circumstances that the gift to him [a class member who was last seen before the testator made his will, and more than seven years had elapsed by the time the testator died] was only as one of a class does not prevent the operation of this statute." The statute is applicable to a gift to a relative who is dead at the date the will is executed. Lewis v. Corbin, 195 Mass. 520, 81 N.E. 248 (1907) (deceased legatee referred to by his name). The word "issue" in the Massachusetts statute does not include an adopted child of a deceased legatee. Gammons v. Gammons, 212 Mass. 454, 99 N.E. 95 (1912).

Illinois Rev. Stat., c. 3, §200 (1959), quoted infra page 1438, and Maryland Code Ann., art. 93, §§354, 355 (1957), quoted infra page 1441, both expressly apply to class gifts. See also the lapse statutes in the following states which expressly apply to class gifts: Arkansas, Kentucky, Nebraska, Pennsylvania and Tennessee. — ED.

Mary E. Jury, his wife, conveyed the above-mentioned lands "to Andrew M. Strawhacker for and during his natural life and at his death, to his present wife Genevieve and her children. Now of the town of Minonk, county of Woodford and the state of Illinois." On the date of the execution and delivery of the deed, Genevieve Strawhacker had one child, Orville Strawhacker, then about one year of age. Subsequent to the execution and delivery of the deed, seven additional children were born to Andrew M. Strawhacker and his wife, Genevieve Strawhacker. Orville Strawhacker died December 28, 1918, leaving surviving his widow and one son, the plaintiffs in this action. Another child, Storis I. Strawhacker, died April 15, 1891, at the age of six years. Andrew M. Strawhacker, the grantee of the life estate, died on October 15, 1922. The question for determination is the rights of the parties in the land in question, as fixed by the provisions of the deed above quoted.

Plaintiffs contend that the language employed by the grantor of the deed indicates an intent that the remainder interest should vest only in those persons in being at the time the deed was executed and delivered. The evidence shows that Genevieve Strawhacker had only one child at that time. The use of the word "children" in the clause "to his present wife Genevieve and her children" seems to us to indicate an intent to include after-born children, otherwise the grantor would have named the then living child as a grantee of the remainder interest. Unless this be true, there would have been no reason for the use of the plural in designating the grantees of the estate in remainder. The contention is also advanced that the use of the words "now of the town of Minonk" indicates that the grantor of the lands in question indicated an intent that only those "now" in being should receive an interest in the realty. It will be observed that a period precedes the use of the word "now" and that the word "now" is capitalized, indicating the beginning of a new sentence. We conclude that the use of the words "now of the town of Minonk" refers solely to the then residence of Andrew M. Strawhacker, Genevieve Strawhacker and Orville Strawhacker and contains no inference whatever to the extent of the class intended as grantees in the deed by the use of the words, "to his present wife Genevieve and her children."

We are convinced that, at the time of the execution and delivery of the deed, Andrew M. Strawhacker became vested with a life estate and that the remainder interest vested in his wife, Genevieve, and her only son then in being, Orville Strawhacker, subject to the condition that the class will open up and let in other children born during the continuance of the life estate. The rule is aptly stated by a text-writer as follows: "A bequest or devise to a class of the remainder over after a life estate vests the title to the estate in remainder in those of the class in esse at the death of the testator; the right of enjoyment of possession, however, is deferred until the expiration of the preceding estate. The estate in remainder, when once vested as upon the death of the testator, does not lapse by reason of the death of a beneficiary prior to the expiration of the life estate unless the will so provides, as by a limitation over in the event of death of a remainderman before that of the life tenant. But the class will open up and let in those born during the continuance of the life estate, who belong to the class designated in the will. This general rule is held to apply particularly to gifts to children as a class, and in all such cases the estate in remainder vests in such of them as are living at the time of the death of the testator and in those born during the continuance of the life estate, from the moment of their birth." 2 Alexander, Commentaries on Wills, sec. 890.

The rule is also well stated in 2 Underhill, Law of Wills, sec. 558, as follows: "Where the distribution to or among children is to come after a prior life estate, a different rule is applicable than where it is immediate; for if the distribution or the possession of the property devised in remainder to children is not to be made or enjoyed until a period has elapsed subsequent to the death of the testator, a gift to children as a class will embrace not only all children who are living at the testator's death, and compose the class at that time, but also all who are born before the period of distribution arrives. The rule as thus stated is applicable to a remainder to the children of some person other than the testator himself. Thus, suppose the testator shall give property to A. for his life, and after his death to the children of A. in remainder; all the children of A. who are living at the death of the testator, and all of A.'s children who are born during his life, will constitute the class at the period of distribution. And the same rule would apply where the gift is of a remainder to the children of B. at the death of A., or the children of the testator after a prior life estate to be enjoyed by his widow. If the gift of the remainder is a present gift, that is to say, if it vests a present interest, the possession only being postponed, all the children take who are in esse at the death of the testator, and they will take vested interests, subject to open and let in after-born children who come into being during the existence of the prior life estate; and both classes will compose the class at the time appointed for distribution. And if any child in whom the remainder has become vested dies during the life tenancy, his or her issues, if any survive until the time of distribution, will take *per stirpes* the share of the parent."

In Restatement, Property, sec. 157, the following pertinent statements appear:

"A remainder can be (a) indefeasibly vested; or (b) vested subject to open; or (c) vested subject to complete defeasance; or (d) subject to a condition precedent. . . .

"Illustration to Clause (b): 2. A, owning Blackacre in fee simple absolute, transfers Blackacre 'to B for life, remainder to the children of B.' B has a child C. C has a remainder vested subject to open and let in other children born to B."

"When an otherwise effective conveyance of either land or a thing other than land creates one or more prior interests, the maximum duration of which is measured by lives, and then limits a remainder estate in fee simple absolute, or a corresponding remainder interest in a thing other than land, which is construed to be in favor of the 'children' of a designated living person who has one or more living children, these children have a 'remainder vested subject to open.' It is immaterial whether this designated person is the transferor, a transferee in favor of whom one of the prior life interests has been created or a person having no other relation to the affected thing." Restatement, Property, sec. 157, comment n.

We necessarily conclude that the life estate in the case at bar immediately vested in Andrew M. Strawhacker and that the remainder interest immediately vested in Genevieve Strawhacker and her then only son, Orville Strawhacker, at the time the deed was executed and delivered, and as each subsequent child was born to Genevieve Strawhacker during the continuance of the life estate he became a member of the class and his interests in the land immediately vested. Yates v. Yates, 104 Neb. 678, 178 N.W. 262; Wilkins v. Rowan, 107 Neb. 180, 185 N.W. 437; DeWitt v. Searles, 123 Neb. 129, 242 N.W. 370; Drury v. Hickinbotham, 129 Neb. 499, 262 N.W. 37.

It will be noted that the clause in the deed does not provide for a defeasance of the vested interest of any child, either by the death of the child or otherwise. In such case the vested interest of a child does not lapse at his death but descends to his heirs. In the instant case, each of the eight children and Genevieve Strawhacker became vested with an undivided interest in the land as they entered the class. At the termination of the life estate by the death of Andrew M. Strawhacker, the grantee of the life estate, the number within the class became fixed and the absolute interest of each at that time would necessarily be an undivided one-ninth interest in the premises.

The contention of plaintiffs that a one-half interest in the premises vested in Orville Strawhacker absolutely when the deed was executed and delivered and that, as his heirs, they are now entitled to a one-half interest therein is without merit. The vested interest of Orville Strawhacker was subject to being opened to let in children born during the continuance of the life estate, and as each subsequent child was born into the class, the interest of each was thereby proportionately decreased.

We therefore hold that each of the six surviving children is entitled to an undivided one-ninth interest in and to said lands by virtue of his being a member of the designated class. Genevieve Strawhacker is also entitled to an undivided one-ninth interest in her own right, as she was designated by name as a member of the class. Likewise, the estates of Orville Strawhacker and Storis I. Strawhacker are each entitled to an undivided one-ninth interest in and to said lands.

The trial court properly denied the claim of plaintiffs that they were entitled to one-half of the property involved in this action. The trial court erred, however, in not permitting the estates of Orville Strawhacker and Storis I. Strawhacker, deceased members of the class, to share in the estate.

The judgment of the trial court is reversed and the cause is remanded, with directions to enter a decree in accordance with this opinion.

Reversed.[36]

---

[36] For the effect of the death of a class member after the testator's death and before the period of distribution, see 5 American Law of Property §§21.11-21.13 (Casner ed. 1952); 3 Restatement of Property §296.

Tennessee has taken the view that there is a requirement of survival to the period of distribution when a class gift is involved and the entire subject matter of the gift passes to the class members who meet the requirement of survival (see Denison v. Jowers, 192 Tenn. 356, 241 S.W.2d 427 (1951)) unless Tennessee Code Annotated §32-306 (1955), quoted infra page 1475, is applicable. This Tennessee statute is in effect a lapse statute which operates where a class member dies after the testator and before the end of a required period of survival.

As to whether, if a gift is made to the heirs of a designated person and the heirs are ascertained prior to the period of distribution, the heirs so ascertained must survive to the period of distribution, see 5 American Law of Property §22.61 (Casner ed. 1952). As to whether, if a gift is made to the issue of a designated person, a requirement of survival to the period of distribution is implied from the fact that the beneficiaries are described by the word "issue," see id. §21.13. — ED.

PROBLEM

11.22. T in his will gives the residue of his estate to a trustee and directs the trustee "to pay the net income to my wife for her life; and on the death of my said wife, to pay the corpus to my children in equal shares." T has four children. One child dies before T. One of the three children who survive T dies before T's wife. On the death of T's wife, to whom should the corpus of the trust be distributed and in what shares?

In considering this problem, point out the variations in the answer:

    a. If the lapse statute in the governing state is not applicable to class gifts;

    b. If the lapse statute in the governing state is applicable to class gifts and the deceased child of T is survived by issue;

    c. If the lapse statute in the governing state is applicable to class gifts and the deceased child of T is not survived by issue.

(3) Meanings Attributable to the Word "Surviving"

In re PATTERSON'S ESTATE
227 Mich. 486, 198 N.W. 958 (1924)

SHARPE, J.   The last will and testament of Andrew J. Patterson, long a resident of Shiawassee county, executed on January 21, 1889, contained the following provision:

"I give, devise and bequeath to my beloved wife, Nancy A. Patterson, all of my estate, of which I may die possessed of whatever nature, real, personal and mixed, for her lifetime, and at her decease the remainder over unto the surviving children, the issue of myself and my said wife, Nancy A. Patterson, share and share alike. My said wife to have the use and profits of my said estate, and if the same are not sufficient for her proper maintenance and support then she is to use of the principal estate sufficient for her proper maintenance and support."

At the time the will was executed, the testator had four children living, Charles J. Patterson, Arthur D. Patterson, Carrie A. Patterson (Terbush), and Fred R. Patterson. Charles and Arthur died before the testator, leaving no issue. Carrie then had two children, Jay M. Terbush, Jr., and Rispah Terbush, while Fred had one child, Ivah Patterson. Before the death of the widow, which occurred on February 6, 1923, both Carrie and Fred had died. Carrie's two children were then living. Fred's first wife, the mother of Ivah, had died. He had remarried, and his widow, Carrie E., and a son, Frederick G., as well as Ivah, who had married a man named Wilson, survived him.

The question here presented is whether the remainder over after the termination of the life estate in the widow, Nancy, vested on the death of the testator, or on the death of Nancy. If it vested on the death of the testator, then the widow of Frederick is entitled to her distributive share of his estate; if not, she has no interest therein. The trial court, in a carefully prepared opinion, concluded that the remainder vested on the death of the testator. Ivah Patterson-Wilson here reviews by writ of error the order of distribution made pursuant to such conclusion. Carefully prepared and helpful briefs have been filed, and the case was ably presented on the hearing.

Counsel are not in dispute over the general rules by which we must be governed. We must ascertain the intent of the testator if possible (Kirsher v. Todd, 195 Mich. 297); so construe the will that every word "means something, if possible" (Rivenett v. Bourquin, 53 Mich. 10), and give "force and vitality to all parts and all expressions in the will" (In re Blodgett's Estate, 197 Mich. 455). Counsel for appellees also insist upon the application of the rule that "the law favors the vesting of estates at the earliest possible moment" (1 Schouler on Wills [6th ed.], Sec. 1258; In re Shumway's Estate, 194 Mich. 245, 254, L.R.A. 1918A, 578), and also strongly urge that the construction which this court has placed upon wills wherein similar language was used has become an established rule of property in this State and should not be disregarded.

Had not the words "at her decease" and "surviving" been inserted in the provision, it is clear that the remainder would have vested in Carrie and Fred at the death of the testator. We are of the opinion that the decisions of this court in Rood v. Hovey, 50 Mich. 395, and in Porter v. Porter, 50 Mich. 456, are conclusive as to the construction which we should place upon the provision in this will. In the Porter Case, after giving the widow an estate for life in all the property of the testator, the will provided:

"*On the decease* of my wife, Eliza G. Porter, I desire my property to be divided equally between my *surviving* children," etc.

Mr. Justice Campbell, speaking for the court, said:

"We think, on the rules of construction which have always prevailed in this State, that immediately on George F. Porter's death his children took vested estates subject only to the life estate and other burdens imposed by law or by the will."

He further said:

"We can discover nothing in the will indicating any different intent, and we do not think the purposes of justice or the policy of the laws would be subserved by attempting to change this rule. Wills have been made in this region from a period when the concurrent views of most of the authorities from which we derive our analogies agreed on this interpretation. The statutes have been during that interval so changed as to further and not to destroy that interpretation. It can hardly be expected that all minds will concur in the same view as an original matter. Neither is it always safe to infer that local laws and policy may not account for many of the conflicts among courts. But it is generally true that terms are used in wills as they are used in other documents, with the meaning which has become generally accepted. It would be dangerous to act on any other presumption; and it would be dangerous and unjust to have fluctuating rules. It is now and always has been proper and obligatory to give every will the meaning fairly to be deduced from its whole terms. The same words standing alone may have a different meaning than what should be given them when qualified or affected by other parts of the will. But there is nothing in this will to indicate any different meaning, and we do not think we are called on to change the law of the State. It is easy enough in drawing wills to fix the time of vesting beyond any peradventure. But local law and reason both, in our judgment, favor vested estates, and subserve justice. If the rule once established seems unreasonable to the legislature it is easily changed, and persons drawing wills are supposed to understand what they are doing, and those who act on their advice take no greater risks in these than in other cases."

In Re Shumway's Estate, supra, the will, after creating a life estate in the wife, provided that — "after her decease I give, devise and bequeath all of said real estate to my legal heirs to be divided between them according to the provisions of the statute."

It was urged that, under this and other provisions of the will from which an intent might be ascertained, the estate in remainder did not vest until the death of the widow. It was, however, held that it vested on the death of the testator. An exhaustive opinion, in which the text-book law and the decisions of this and other courts are reviewed and discussed, was written by Mr. Justice Brooke. We feel that we can add nothing to the reasoning employed by those Justices in reaching the conclusions stated.

We have not overlooked the claim of counsel for appellant that the use of the words "the surviving children" is expressive of the intent that the remainder should pass to the children surviving at the death of the widow. Similar language was used in Porter v. Porter, supra. We find no intent to apply any different rule of construction in the recent cases of In re Blodgett's Estate, supra; Hadley v. Henderson, 214 Mich. 157; and Rozell v. Rozell, 217 Mich. 324. The many cases cited by counsel from other jurisdictions have been considered. We think the rule has become one of property in this State, and that it should not be disturbed.

The judgment is affirmed, with costs against appellant.[37]

CLARK, C.J., and McDONALD, BIRD, MOORE, STEERE, FELLOWS, and WIEST, JJ., concurred.

(4) Language Deemed Sufficient to Eliminate the Applicability of a Lapse Statute

BURLET v. BURLET
246 Ill. 563, 92 N.E. 965 (1910)

MR. JUSTICE COOKE delivered the opinion of the court:

On September 14, 1895, Frank Burlet, Sr., being the owner of lots 4 and 5 in block 2 and lot 6 in block 11, in Berrian's addition to the city of Peoria, conveyed the same to Anna Burlet, his wife. Lot 6 was the homestead of Frank and Anna Burlet and the wife did not join in the conveyance. On June 3, 1900, Anna Burlet made a will. At that time she had living five children, viz., John, Mary, Anna, Peter and Frank, Jr. Frank, Jr., died December 1, 1908, leaving surviving him as his only child and only heir, his

---

[37] As to the meanings attributable to the word "surviving," see 5 American Law of Property §21.15 (Casner ed. 1952); 3 Restatement of Property §§249-251.

See Cal. Prob. Code §122 (Deering, 1959), quoted infra page 1436, which provides that words of survivorship will refer to the time of possession when possession is postponed to a date subsequent to the testator's death. But examine Ga. Code Ann. §85-708 (1955), quoted infra page 1437, which provides that words of survivorship shall refer to the testator's death so as to vest remainders.

It is not uncommon to give a remainder interest to a described group with a provision that if one of the described remaindermen dies before the life beneficiary, his share will pass to the "survivors." Do you see what construction problems this type of disposition raises? First, if one remainderman dies before the life beneficiary and his share passes over to the survivors, and then a second remainderman dies before the life beneficiary, will the share the second remainderman received on the death of the first remainderman go over to his survivors along with his initial share or will only his initial share go over? Leahy v. Murray, 16 Ill. 2d 453, 158 N.E.2d 30 (1959), held that only the initial share went over, and that if all members of the group died before the life beneficiary, the initial share of the last one to die was not divested because there were no "survivors" to take it — ED.

daughter, Elizabeth. Anna Burlet died testate on December 15, 1908, leaving as her last will and testament the instrument executed by her on June 3, 1900. Her husband, the four remaining children and the grandchild, Elizabeth, survived her. By the first clause of her will she directed that all her just debts and funeral expenses be paid, and the second and last clause is as follows: "After the payment of such funeral expenses and debts, I give, devise and bequeath unto my beloved husband, Frank Burlet, any and all real estate, personal estate and mixed property, of whatsoever kind or character, for and during his natural life, and all that remains at his death I give, devise and bequeath unto my beloved children, share and share, or the survivor or survivors of them, and their heirs." Frank Burlet, Sr., died intestate June 5, 1909, leaving the said four children and the grandchild Elizabeth, surviving him as his only heirs-at-law. Thereafter the daughter Anna conveyed her interest in said real estate to her sister Mary and her brother John. After the death of Frank Burlet, Sr., the children, John, Mary and Peter, and John as the administrator with the will annexed of the estate of Anna Burlet, filed their bill for partition in the circuit court of Peoria county, making the grandchild, Elizabeth Burlet, a party defendant. The bill set up the facts already stated and prayed for a division and partition of the premises according to the respective rights and interests of the parties. A guardian ad litem was appointed for the minor defendant, Elizabeth, and the cause was referred to the master in chancery to take the proof and report his conclusions of law and fact. The master found that there was no provision made in the will of Anna Burlet for the contingency of the death of Frank Burlet, Jr., prior to the death of the testatrix, and that therefore Elizabeth, as the only child of Frank Burlet, Jr., is entitled, under section 11 of the Statute of Descent, to take the same share in the premises which her father would have taken as one of the devisees had he survived the testatrix, and that the interests of the parties in the premises were as follows: John and Mary each the three-tenths part, and Peter and the grandchild, Elizabeth, each the one-fifth part. The complainants objected and excepted to the report of the master, but the chancellor overruled the exceptions and entered a decree of partition in accordance with the findings of the master, from which decree the complainants in the bill have appealed to this court.

The only question for consideration here is the proper construction to be given to the second clause of the will of Anna Burlet. If, as a proper construction of this clause, it be found that the testatrix made no provision for the contingency of the death of her son Frank before her death, then section 11 of "An act in regard to the descent of property," approved April 9, 1872, will govern. That section is as follows: "Whenever a devisee or legatee in any last will and testament, being a child or grandchild of the testator, shall die before such testator, and no provision shall be made for such contingency, the issue, if any there be, of such devisee or legatee, shall take the estate devised or bequeathed as the devisee or legatee would have done had he survived the testator, and if there be no such issue at the time of the death of such testator, the estate disposed of by such devise or legacy shall be considered and treated in all respects as intestate estate."

The point in dispute between the parties is narrowed down to the construction to be placed upon the words, "or the survivor or survivors of them, and their heirs," being the concluding words of the second clause of the will. It is contended on the part of appellants that the survivors at the death of the testatrix took the whole property. Appellee contends, on the other hand, that the gift, being preceded by a life estate, took effect in favor of those, only, who survived the period of distribution at the termination of the life interest. Should the contention of appellants be upheld then the grand-daughter, Elizabeth, took nothing whatever under the will of her grandmother, as it would be apparent that provision had been made for the contingency of the death of her father during the lifetime of the testatrix, whereas if the contention of appellee is sustained, under the rule laid down in Pirrung v. Pirrung, 228 Ill. 441, section 11 of the Statute of Descent would apply and the grand-daughter, Elizabeth, would take the interest her father would have taken had he survived the death of Frank Burlet, Sr.

The decisions in regard to determining when, in cases such as this, the survivorship is referred to the time of the death of the testator and when to the death of the person to whom has been given an intervening interest are not in entire harmony. The rule now prevailing, and which we follow, is, that where a gift to survivors is preceded by a life or other prior interest it takes effect in favor of those who survive the period of distribution, and those only, unless a special contrary intent is found in the will. This is the rule now generally accepted and which we have followed and approved in Ridgeway v. Underwood, 67 Ill. 419, Blatchford v. Newberry, 99 id. 11, and Schuknecht v. Schultz, 212 id. 43. Applying this rule of construction to the clause in question, it is apparent that the testatrix made no provision whatever for the contingency of the death of her son Frank before the time of her decease, and under the rule laid down in Rudolph v. Rudolph, 207 Ill. 266, Frail v. Carstairs, 187 id. 310, and Pirrung v. Pirrung, supra, the chancellor properly held that section 11 of the Statute of Descent applied, and the appellee took the interest which her father would have taken in the premises had he survived the decease of Frank Burlet, Sr.

Appellants rely upon the case of Hempstead v. Dickson, 20 Ill. 194, which announces a contrary doctrine. The rule there laid down designating the period to which survivorship is referred, so far as it applies to a case where a gift to survivors is preceded by a life or other prior interest, has not been followed by us in later cases and is not approved.

Appellants contend that the addition of the words "and their heirs" to this clause indicates that the testatrix meant this devise to apply only to such of her children as should survive the time of her decease, and rely, in support of this contention, upon the case of Grimmer v. Friederich, 164 Ill. 245. In that case the clause construed was as follows: "After the death of my said wife, Magdalena Grimmer, all the remainder of my estate, both personal and real, shall be equally divided among my surviving children and their heirs, share and share alike," and we there held that the words "and their heirs," contained in that clause, were important and significant, as showing an express intention on the part of the testator that the survivorship was not to be referred to the death of his widow but to the time of his own decease. The language in the clause under consideration here is quite different from the language employed in the Grimmer will. There the residue was to be divided equally *among* his surviving children *and their heirs,* while here the devise is *"unto* my beloved children, share and share, or the survivor or survivors of them, and their heirs." In the Grimmer case it is apparent that the testator, by the use of the word "among," meant that should the contingency arise his estate should be divided among his children living at the time of the widow's death and the heirs of such as should die between the time of his decease and the death of his widow, while in the clause here under consideration the devise is to the children of the testatrix or the survivor or survivors of them and their heirs, — i.e., the heirs of the survivors, — clearly indicating that the words "and their heirs" were used simply as words of limitation to characterize the estate devised. This clause has the same meaning precisely as though the testatrix had used, instead of the words "and their heirs," the expression "in fee simple."

A proper construction of the will of Anna Burlet was given by

the chancellor and a proper application of the statute made. The
decree of the circuit court is affirmed.

Decree affirmed.[38]

CARTWRIGHT and DUNN, JJ., dissenting.

PROBLEM

11.23. T in his will gives the residue of his estate to a trustee and
directs the trustee "to pay the net income to my wife for her life;
and on the death of my said wife, to pay the corpus to my surviving children in equal shares." T has four children. One child
dies before T. One of the three children who survive T dies before T's wife. On the death of T's wife, to whom should the
corpus be distributed and in what shares?

(5) Gifts "to Be Paid" When Beneficiary Attains a Specified Age

In re WILL OF MANSUR
98 Vt. 296, 127 Atl. 297 (1925)

SLACK, J. This is an appeal from a decree of the probate court
within and for the probate district of Orleans dismissing a petition
brought by appellant, as administrator of the estate of Sallie Storrs
Tate, for the purpose of affecting a final settlement, and distribution of the assets, of the estate of the late Zophar M. Mansur, on
the ground that appellant, as such administrator, has no interest
in the Mansur estate because the legacy bequeathed to the said
Sallie by the said Mansur did not vest in the legatee, but lapsed at
her death.

The agreed facts in the case, so far as material to the question
before us, are these: Zophar M. Mansur died March 28, 1914. He
was survived by one son, Arthur G., and two grandchildren, John

---

[38] In Hartwick v. Heberling, 364 Ill. 523, 4 N.E.2d 965 (1936), there was a
gift to A and the heirs of his body, and in case A should die leaving no heirs
of his body, to B and C and the survivor of them. A predeceased the testator
and the contention was made that the gift to B and C failed. The court said
at page 531: "Our decisions in . . . Burlet v. Burlet . . . are cited to support
the contention that the testator meant the death of [A] after the death of the
[testator]. In all those decisions [the lapse statute] was involved, and in all
but one of them there were children or grandchildren who would be disinherited, but for the operation of that section, if the death had been interpreted
as death at any time . . . Those decisions must be considered only in the
light of their facts . . ."

For a consideration of the language which is deemed sufficient to make a
lapse statute inapplicable, see 5 American Law of Property §§21.29, 22.51
(Casner ed. 1952). — ED.

D. Storrs and Sallie L. Storrs, children of a daughter who died December 1, 1911. Mr. Mansur left a will bearing date of January 15, 1914, which was allowed by the probate court in said district April 21, 1914, which contained the following provision: "I give to my granddaughter, Sallie L. Storrs, the sum of thirty thousand dollars, to be placed in the hands of a trustee, the income thereof to be paid to the said Sallie L. Storrs semi-annually, one half of the principle to be paid to the said Sallie L. Storrs when she shall become thirty years of age and the remaining one-half when she shall become thirty-five years of age." It contained a like provision for the grandson, John D. Storrs. The granddaughter, Sallie L., was born November 18, 1894, she married the appellant August 4, 1920, and died, intestate, November 23, 1921. She was survived by one daughter, the fruit of said marriage, born October 29, 1921, who is still living. The appellant is the duly appointed administrator of Sallie's estate. Mr. Mansur's son, Arthur G., is executor of the Mansur will and, as such, has in his hands a large amount of property that belongs to the Mansur estate. No part of the legacy bequeathed to the said Sallie has ever been paid.

Whether the court erred in dismissing the petition depends, entirely, upon whether the provision in the Mansur will, above quoted, created a vested or a contingent legacy, and this, in turn, depends upon whether the contingency, namely, the attainment of a certain age by the legatee, attached to the substance of the gift or to the time of payment thereof.

In construing wills, the first and chief object is to ascertain the intention of the testator, since, so far as it may be legally carried out, that governs. Harris et al. v. Harris' Estate, 82 Vt. 199, 72 Atl. 912. To aid in ascertaining this fact certain well-recognized rules have been established. One is that the law favors the vesting of estates on the death of the testator when the will becomes operative, and if the language used is consistent with an intention to postpone the enjoyment only, such will be presumed to have been the testator's intention. This presumption is so favorably regarded that no estate will be held contingent unless positive terms are employed in the will indicating that such is the intention. In re Robinson's Estate, 90 Vt. 328, 98 Atl. 826; Harris et al. v. Harris' Estate, supra; Burton v. Provost, 75 Vt. 199, 54 Atl. 189; Jones' Admr. v. Knappen, 63 Vt. 391, 22 Atl. 630, 14 L.R.A. 293; In re Tucker's Will, 63 Vt. 104, 21 Atl. 272, 25 A.S.R. 743; Weatherhead v. Stoddard, 58 Vt. 623, 5 Atl. 517, 56 A.R. 573. Another rule is that when futurity is annexed to the substance of the gift, the vesting is postponed; but if annexed to the time of payment only, the legacy vests immediately. Perhaps this rule is nowhere better stated than by Blackstone; he says: "And if a *contingent* legacy be left to anyone, as *when* he attains, or *if* he attains, the age of twenty-one, and he dies before that time, it is a lapsed legacy: But a legacy to one *to be paid* when he attains the age of twenty-one years, is a *vested* legacy; an interest which commences in *praesenti*, although it be *solvendum in futuro*, and if the legatee dies before that age, his representatives shall receive it out of the testator's personal estate, at the same time it would have become payable in case the legatee had lived." 2 Bl. Comm. 513. See also 2 Williams on Executors (11th ed.), 973. In the first instance, futurity being annexed to the substance of the gift, the vesting is postponed; in the latter instance, futurity being annexed to the time of enjoyment only, the legacy vests immediately. Regardless of its origin, or the reason for its adoption, this rule is now recognized by the great weight of authority both in this country and in England. Among the numerous cases where the language of the bequest is held to affect a postponement of payment or enjoyment only — the legacy vesting immediately upon the death of the testator — are, Staples v. D'Wolf, 8 R.I. 118; Dale v. White, 33 Conn. 294; Austin v. Bristol, 40 Conn. 420, 16 A.R. 23; Harrison v. Moore, 64 Conn. 344, 30 Atl. 55; Brown v. Brown, 44 N.H. 281; Sanborn v. Clough, 64 N.H. 315, 10 Atl. 678; Zartman v. Ditmars, 37 App. Div. 173, 55 N.Y.S. 908; Goebel v. Wolf, 113 N.Y. 405, 21 N.E. 388, 10 A.S.R. 464; Williams v. Boul, 101 App Div. 593, 92 N.Y.S. 177; Id., 184 N.Y. 605, 77 N.E. 1198; Kimble v. White, 50 N.J. Eq. 28, 24 Atl. 400; Furness v. Fox, 1 Cush. (Mass.) 134, 48 A.D. 593; Eldridge v. Eldridge, 9 Cush. (Mass.) 516; Wardwell v. Hale, 161 Mass. 396, 37 N.E. 196, 42 A.S.R. 413; Kerlin v. Bull, 1 Dall. (Pa.) 175, 1 L. ed. 88; Cropley v. Cooper, 19 Wall. 167, 22 L. ed. 109; McArthur v. Scott, 113 U.S. 340, 28 L. ed. 1015, 5 Sup. Ct. 642; Goodlittle v. Whitby, 1 Burr. 228; Lyman v. Vanderspiegel, 1 Aik. 275; Boraston's Case, 3 Coke 19. See also, Warren's Admr. v. Bronson, 81 Vt. 121, 133, 69 Atl. 655; In re Robinson's Estate, 90 Vt. 328, 98 Atl. 826; and note Goebel v. Wolf, supra.

In Staples v. D'Wolf it is said: "The question is always — is futurity annexed to the substance of the gift? If so, the vesting is postponed; or is it annexed to the time of payment only? If so, the legacy vests immediately. 1 Harman, 759, 760. And if the gift be expressly to A, and expressed to be payable or to be paid at a certain time, time is held to relate to the payment only, and not to the gift itself, and it confers a vested interest on the testator's death."

In Brown v. Brown, where the language of the bequest was, "I do give and bequeath to Hiram S. Brown . . . the sum of $1,200, to be paid to him by the executor of my said will, when he shall attain the age of 21 years," it was held, Hiram having survived the testator but died before reaching the age of 21 years, that the gift vested in him and was payable to his representative. The court said: "Where the gift is of a sum of money to the legatee 'payable,' or 'to be paid' at the age of twenty-one, the legacy vests immediately, and, upon the legatee's death before that age, goes to his representative; and this is upon the ground that the testator intended the gift to be absolute, but chose to postpone the payment to the period when the legatee might make better use of his bounty. This distinction is established by a weight of authority too great to be shaken, and it may well be supposed that wills are made with reference to it."

In Dale v. White, it is said: "It is a well settled rule of construction that a legacy given to a person or a class, to be paid or divided at a future time, takes effect in point of right on the death of the testator. In such case the contingency attaches, not to the substance of the gift, but to the time of payment." In the latter case we also find this rule of construction laid down: "Where words are equivocal, leaving it in doubt whether the words of contingency or condition apply to the gift itself or the time of payment, courts are inclined to construe them as applying to the time of payment, and to hold the gift as vested rather than contingent."

Applying the rules of construction already referred to, in the light of the application given them in the cases cited, to the case at bar it would seem that but one conclusion could be reached. Other provisions of the bequest aside, the language, "I give to my grand-daughter, Sallie L. Storrs, the sum of thirty thousand dollars, . . . one half of the principal to be paid to the said Sallie L. Storrs when she shall become thirty years of age and the remaining one-half when she shall become thirty-five years of age" would seem to leave no doubt of the testator's intention to create a vested legacy with postponed enjoyment.

But the provision that the legacy shall be placed in the hands of a trustee, and the income thereof paid to the legatee semi-annually, makes the intent of the testator doubly certain. Under this provision not only is the legacy to be segregated instanter from the rest of the testator's estate, but the legatee receives an immediate beneficial interest therein. Similar provisions have been before the courts in other jurisdictions. See Eldridge v. Eldridge, supra; Equitable Guarantee & Trust Co. v. Bowe, 9 Del. Ch. 336, 82 Atl. 693; Warner v. Durant, 76 N.Y. 133; Gifford v. Thorn,

9 N.J. Eq. 702; and Reed's Appeal, 118 Pa. 215; 11 Atl. 787, 4 A.S.R. 588.

In Eldridge v. Eldridge, Shaw, C.J., said: "But it is a decisive circumstance, in the present case, that the legacy is charged with the support of the legatee during her minority. In the first clause, he directs his son, James, the executor and residuary devisee, to pay to his grand-daughter, Sarah Malvina, $1,000, at twenty-one years of age, and proceeds to direct that she be supported out of it during her minority. If it stood upon this clause alone, it appears to us that the intent would be quite clear, because it creates an immediate beneficial interest in the legatee, and the payment only is postponed."

In Equitable Guarantee & Trust Co. v. Bowe, the testator gave to a trustee $10,000 for each of his grandchildren to hold as a trust fund, and "to pay over the net income for the maintenance and education of said grandchildren until they arrive at the age of thirty years, and as they respectively arrive at the age of thirty years, to pay over to them the share of the principal sum to which they are entitled, free and discharged from all trusts. One of the grandchildren died at the age of 14 years, and it was held that the gift vested and that the administrator of the deceased child was entitled to the legacy. Speaking to this point the court said: "The principles of law applicable to such a gift are clear and well settled. In bequests of personal estate, a gift of the whole interim interest to or for the benefit of the legatee, prima facie, vests the principal, though if such words had not been used the legacy would not have been treated as vested."

In Warner v. Durant, it is said: "Where the gift is to be severed instanter from the general estate, for the benefit of the legatee; and in the meantime, the interest thereof is to be paid to him; that is indicative of the intent of the testator that the legatee shall, at all events, have the principal, and is to wait, only for the payment, until the day fixed."

In Gifford v. Thorn, it is said: "Where the interest of the legacy is directed to be paid to the legatee until he receives the principal, or where the legacy is placed in the hands of trustees for the exclusive benefit of the legatee until it is directed to be paid over, the legacy will be deemed vested."

In Reed's Appeal, it is said: "And while it is true as a general rule, as before observed, that where the time or other condition is annexed to the substance of the gift, and not merely to the payment, the legacy is contingent; yet it is equally true that a well-recognized exception to the rule is, that where interest, whether by way of maintenance or otherwise, is given to the legatee in the meantime, the legacy shall, notwithstanding the gift appears to be postponed, vest immediately on the death of the testator."

Other circumstances are called to our attention by the appellant which it is claimed are indicative of the testator's intention to create a vested legacy, but it is needless to consider them, since, notwithstanding the ingenious argument of appellee, we are satisfied from what has already been said that no other conclusion is warranted.

We hold, therefore, that the legacy of $30,000 vested in Sallie Storrs Tate immediately upon the death of the testator and, consequently, that the appellant, as her legal representative, is entitled to receive the same out of the testator's estate.

The appellant insists that since the legatee had the entire beneficial interest in the legacy he is entitled to recover the full amount of the principal at once, and calls attention to numerous authorities that seem to support this view, but the disposition of the petition below was such that the court was not called upon to, nor did it, pass upon this question, hence, it is not before us.

Decree of the probate court reversed and cause remanded for further proceedings and decree not inconsistent with the views herein expressed. Let the appellant recover his costs in this Court. To be certified to the probate court.[39]

PROBLEM

11.24. T in his will provides, "I give the sum of $50,000 to A in trust for the benefit of the children of B, each child of B to be paid his share of the trust fund on attaining the age of twenty-one years, the income in the meantime to be divided equally among the children of B who are born prior to each income payment date." T dies. B has two children, C and D. C is fifteen and D is twelve. Three years after T's death another child, E, is born to B. D dies four years after T's death. Five years after T's death another child, F, is born to B. Seven years after T's death another child, G, is born to B. Is any child of B excluded from the gift on the ground that he is born too late?

---

[39] Whether there is a requirement of survival to the designated age is considered in connection with the following types of dispositions in 5 American Law of Property (Casner ed. 1952): "$1000 to A at twenty-one" (§21.18); "$1000 to be paid to A at twenty-one without interest thereon in the meantime" (§21.18); "$1000 to A at twenty-one, income on such amount to be paid to A prior to twenty-one," or "$1000 to be paid to A at twenty-one, income on such amount to be paid to A prior to twenty-one" (§21.20).

For a consideration of the so-called divide-and-pay-over rule as a basis of implying a requirement of survival to some date subsequent to the effective date of the dispositive instrument, see id. §21.21. — ED.

e. *Share of Each Class Member*

If the class members are all in the same degree of relationship to the person who gives the class an identity, as, for example, when the class is "the children of A," the share of each class member in the subject matter of the disposition will be the same in the absence of a manifestation of intention that the division is to be on some other basis. When the class is described as the "issue" of some person, however, the class members may be in different degrees of relationship to the designated person, and the dispositive instrument should make it clear whether the class members are to take on a per capita basis or on a per stirpes basis or on some other basis.

If the class is described as the "heirs" of some person, the heirs when ascertained by the applicable statute may be in different degrees of relationship to the person. The dispositive instrument should make it clear whether the statute which is applied to ascertain the heirs is also to be applied to determine the proportionate share each heir takes in the property that is to be distributed.

If a gift is made to several classes (a gift to the children of A and the children of B), is each class to take one half of the property for division among its members, or is the property to be divided among the several classes on a straight per capita basis? A similar question is presented if a gift is made to an individual and to a class (a gift to A and the children of B).

B. M. C. DURFEE TRUST CO. v. BORDEN
329 Mass. 461, 109 N.E.2d 129 (1952)

WILKINS, J. The will of Philip D. Borden in its residuary clause created a trust for the benefit of his wife and daughter, and directed that upon their deaths without issue the trust property "shall be paid over to the issue of my nephews, James Edgar Borden, Frank H. Borden, and Sydney F. Borden, living at the time of the death of the last survivor of my said wife and my said daughter or at the time of my death in case I shall survive both of them, share and share alike." The testator died in 1936. His wife died in 1937, and his daughter in 1951, both without issue. At the daughter's death, which became the time for distribution, all three nephews were dead, two having predeceased the testator. There were then living Hildreth Crapo, Marjorie Brown, and Donald D. Borden, children of Frank H. Borden; Philip P. Borden, child of James Edgar Borden; and Freeman S. Borden, child

of Sydney F. Borden.   In the next generation there were living
Donald B. Brown, child of Marjorie Brown; and Joanne Borden
and Bradford P. Borden, children of Philip P. Borden.

The question raised by this petition for instructions by the
trustee is whether the distribution should be in five parts, as was
decreed in the court below, to the five children of the nephews
per capita; or in three parts to the children of the three nephews
per stirpes; or, treating the children and grandchildren of the
nephews on an equal footing, in eight parts per capita to the five
children and the three grandchildren.

When the will was executed in 1922, the three nephews were
living, and so were the five children of the nephews to whom distribution has been decreed, as well as a daughter of J. Edgar
Borden, who predeceased the testator leaving no issue.   The three
grandchildren were born after the will was executed.

It seems clear that there should not be a division in three parts
among the issue of the nephews per stirpes.   There are no words
indicating such an intent.   Indeed, the testator's language shows
the contrary.   The nephews themselves were not made beneficiaries.   The bequest was to their issue "share and share alike."
The word "living" modifies "issue," not "nephews."   The issue
living at the daughter's death would not share equally should the
distribution be made one third to each set of children of the
nephews.   Language calling for a per stirpes division would not
have been difficult to find.   This case in this aspect is within the
authority of Cammann v. Abbe, 258 Mass. 427, 429, and Gleason
v. Hastings, 278 Mass. 409, 413.   See Hall v. Hall, 140 Mass. 267,
271.   The describing of the nephews by name does not lead to a
different result.   See Leslie v. Wilder, 228 Mass. 343, 345; Russell v. Welch, 237 Mass. 261, 263.   The language of Jackson v.
Jackson, 153 Mass. 374, 377-378, is not contrary to our holding.

It seems equally clear that the three grandchildren should not
take along with their parents and the other children of the
nephews.   "The word 'issue,' in the absence of any indication to
the contrary, . . . refers to lineal descendants of the ancestor who
would be entitled, at the death of such ancestor, to take his property under the law of intestate succession, and, in conformity to
this principle, grandchildren of the ancestor and their descendants 'will not be allowed to compete with their parents unless such
was the intention of the testator.'   Ernst v. Rivers, 233 Mass. 9,
14."   Boston Safe Deposit & Trust Co. v. Park, 307 Mass. 255, 264.
Manning v. Manning, 229 Mass. 527, 529.   Agricultural National
Bank v. Miller, 316 Mass. 288, 292.   No such intention here appears.   The decree appealed from was right.

Costs and expenses of appeal are to be in the discretion of the Probate Court.

Decree affirmed.[40]

PROBLEM

11.25. T in his will makes a gift "to the issue of A, such issue to take per stirpes." Determine the adequacy of the following provision which is in T's will:

"Whenever distribution is to be made to issue on a per stirpes basis, that means the property is to be distributed in the manner and in the proportions that personal property of the named ancestor would be distributed under the laws of the Commonwealth of Massachusetts in force at the time stipulated for distribution if he died intestate at such time, domiciled in such Commonwealth and having only issue as next of kin." See Mass. Ann. Laws. c. 190, §3, quoted infra page 1451.[41]

3.   VESTED AND CONTINGENT INTERESTS[42]

The term "vested" has not always been used in the property field with one precise meaning.[43] The term is used here with reference to an interest in property which is created by the trans-

---

[40] In Welch v. Phinney, 337 Mass. 594, 150 N.E.2d 723 (1958), the gift on the death of the income beneficiary was to the "issue then living of my said nephews . . . *per capita* and not *per stirpes.*" Issue of different generations were allowed to share in the gift without regard to whether the parents were living or deceased.

The share that each class member is to receive is considered in 5 American Law of Property (Casner ed. 1952): §21.13 (whether in a gift to "issue" distribution is per capita or per stirpes); §22.62 (division of the subject matter of the gift when the beneficiaries are described as "heirs" and the like); §§22.12-22.14 (gifts to an individual and a group, and gifts to several groups). See also 3 Restatement of Property §§300-304, 310, 311. — Ed.

[41] Re-examine the language of the testamentary provision in Problem 11.18, page 501 supra, to determine the adequacy of the language in that provision, which is designed to describe the shares each described heir is to receive.

[42] The textual material under this heading is based on 5 American Law of Property §§21.5-21.7 and 21.31 (Casner ed. 1952).

[43] The term "vested" has sometimes been associated with interests that are descendible. For example, A devises land "to B for life, then to C and his heirs if D marries E." C's interest is subject to an unperformed condition precedent but is descendible on C's death if the possibility that the condition may be performed is still outstanding. In Hills v. Barnard, 152 Mass. 67, 73, 25 N.E. 96, 97-98 (1890), the court said that C's interest is a vested interest in a contingent remainder.

Occasionally the term "vested" seems to be reserved for present interests as distinguished from future interests. A present interest may always be vested, but the term "vested" should not be confined exclusively to present interests.

feror and which is not subject to an unfulfilled condition precedent.

An interest created by the transferor which is subject to an unfulfilled condition precedent is either a remainder or an executory interest. Normally such interests are created by the express language of the disposition but they may be created by implication. Reversions, possibilities of reverter, and rights of entry are not regarded herein as interests created by the transferor, although, of course, they are vested interests in so far as the rule against perpetuities is concerned.[44] The exclusion of reversions, possibilities of reverter, and rights of entry in a discussion of vesting is justified because the situations which typically require construction to determine whether an interest is vested relate to interests created by the transferor in others.[45]

An interest in property may be incapable of becoming a present interest until some event occurs without being subject to any unfulfilled condition precedent. Thus, if A devises property "to B for life, then to C and his heirs," C's interest cannot become a present interest until B's life interest comes to an end, but C's interest is not subject to an unfulfilled condition precedent. Likewise, if A devises property "to B during widowhood, then to C and his heirs," C's interest is not subject to any unfulfilled condition precedent. In both of these illustrations, C has a remainder and no remainder is subject to an unfulfilled condition precedent if the remainder is ready, throughout its existence, to become a present interest whenever and however the precedent interest or interests come to an end.[46]

An executory interest, on the other hand, is always regarded as being subject to an unfulfilled condition precedent unless the event on which it is to become a present interest is the passage of a stipulated or computable period of time. Thus, if A devises property "to B and his heirs twenty-five years from the date of my

[44] Section 154 of the Restatement of Property defines a possibility of reverter as a reversionary interest subject to a condition precedent, and §155 defines a power of termination (a right of entry) as a future interest created in the transferor, or his successor in interest, subject to a condition precedent.

[45] Whether or not the transferor, or his successor in interest, has a reversion normally turns on whether an interest created by the transferor is subject to a condition precedent, so that this material is relevant to any consideration of reversions.

[46] The classic definition of a vested remainder is given in Gray, The Rule Against Perpetuities §9 (4th ed., Roland Gray, 1942): "A remainder is vested if, at every moment during its continuance, it becomes a present estate, whenever and however the preceding freehold estates determine. A remainder is contingent if, in order for it to become a present estate, the fulfillment of some condition precedent, other than the determination of the preceding freehold estates, is necessary."

death," B's executory interest is not subject to any unfulfilled condition precedent.[47]

Not every vested future interest is certain to become a present interest, because a vested future interest may expire by its own terms before the time arrives for it to become a present interest,[48] or a vested future interest may be subject to divestiture upon the happening of an event, and the divesting event may occur before the time arrives for it to become a present interest.[49] In other words, a future interest is certain to become a present interest only when it is not subject to any unfulfilled condition precedent and is not subject to complete defeasance on the happening of any event.[50]

In the light of what is stated in the preceding paragraph, it should be apparent that a vested future interest may be less likely to become a present interest than an interest subject to an unfulfilled condition precedent, or vice versa.[51] It all depends on the circumstances. Thus, a weighing of the probabilities that a future interest will become a present interest is of no significance in determining whether the interest is vested and hence free of any unfulfilled condition precedent.

Historically, many legal consequences turned on whether a legal interest in land was vested or was subject to an unfulfilled condition precedent.[52] Some of these anachronisms continue to be of significance even in modern times.[53]

[47] See 4 Restatement of Property §370, Comment *h*.

[48] A devises property "to B for life, then to C for life." C's interest is vested, but if C dies before B's life interest ends, C's vested interest expires by its own terms and will never become a present interest.

[49] A devises property "to B for life, then to C and his heirs, but if C marries D, then to E and his heirs." C's interest is vested, but if C marries D before B's life interest ends, C's vested interest is divested and will never become a present interest.

[50] A future interest that is certain to become a present interest is either indefeasibly vested (A devises property "to B for life, then to C and his heirs") or is vested subject only to partial divestiture (A devises property "to B for life, then to B's children," and B has a child now living whose interest is construed to be subject only to partial divestiture by the birth of more children to B).

[51] A devises property "to B for life, then to C for life," and A devises property "to D for life, then to E and his heirs if E survives D." Whether C's vested life interest is more likely to become a present interest than E's contingent remainder in fee depends, of course, on the age of C as compared with the age of B, and the age of E as compared with the age of D.

[52] A contingent remainder was destroyed if it did not vest at or before the termination of the prior supporting estate (see 1 American Law of Property §4.60 (Casner ed. 1952)); vested remainders were freely transferable but contingent remainders were not (id. §4.65); vested remainders were subject to the claims of creditors but contingent remainders were not (id. §4.78).

[53] The extent to which the doctrine of destructibility of contingent remainders is significant in modern times is discussed in 1 American Law of Property

Today, if a created interest in property is subject to an unfulfilled condition precedent, the two principal questions which must
be considered are:

1. Does the created interest violate the rule against perpetuities?
2. What disposition is to be made of the property pending
   the performance of the condition precedent?

Other questions may be presented, but they are not significant in
comparison with the two just mentioned.[54]

If the dispute in connection with a particular donative transaction is whether the language used imposes a requirement that
the designated beneficiary survive to some date, the solution of
such a dispute may be significant in relation to tax matters[55] and
in relation to the applicability of a lapse statute.[56] In these respects, however, the result is the same whether the requirement of
survival is a condition precedent or a divesting contingency.

The situation which forces a determination as to whether a
condition is a condition precedent or a divesting contingency is
one in which the legal problem presented is solved one way if
the created interest is vested and another way if it is contingent.

It is well established that a power to appoint or to dispose of
the subject matter of a gift is presumed to operate by way of
divestiture and does not render the interest in default of appointment contingent.[57] Thus, if the gift is "to B for life, then as B
shall appoint, and in default of appointment, to C and his heirs,"
C is presumed to have a vested remainder subject to divestment
by B's exercise of the power of appointment.

Suppose the gift is "to B for life, then to C and his heirs, but
if C dies without issue during the life of B, to D and his heirs."
C's interest is generally regarded as being vested subject to divestment on his death without issue during the life of B, rather than
as being contingent on his not dying without issue during that

---

§4.63 (Casner ed. 1952). The modern law as to the transferability of contingent interests and as to the rights of creditors to reach contingent interests
is developed in id. §§4.67 and 4.79.

[54] As to the right of the owner of a contingent interest in an undivided
share to demand partition, see 2 id. §6.23; as to the right of the owner of a
contingent interest to enjoin waste, see 5 id. §20.22.

[55] If a person owns an interest in property that is contingent on his survival
to some date and if he dies before the designated date, his gross estate for
federal estate tax purposes will not include such an interest.

[56] If a person is given by will an interest in property that is expressly contingent on his surviving the testator, the applicability of a lapse statute in the
event he predeceases the testator is overcome.

[57] The leading English case is Doe dem. Willis v. Martin, 4 Durn. & E. 39
(K.B. 1790). This position has been adopted in 3 Restatement of Property
§276.

period.[58] The same result is reached even though the supplanting limitation covers all possible failures of C to survive to a given date.[59] Such is the case where the gift is "to B for life, then to C and his heirs, but if C dies with issue during the life of B, to such issue, and if C dies without issue during the life of B, to D and his heirs." Of course, the property will not pass to C's estate if C dies before B, since whether he dies before B with or without issue, the property will go over to someone else. Nevertheless, C's interest is regarded as vested subject to divestment on his death before B, not contingent.

Suppose the gift is "to B for life, then to C or his heirs [or children or issue or representatives]." In this situation it may be determined that the alternative takers — C's heirs, etc. — are to be substituted for C only on his death before the death of the testator. In that case, C on surviving the testator takes an indefeasibly vested interest. If, however, the determination is that C's interest is subject to a condition of survival of B, the cases are divided as to whether C's interest is defeasibly vested or contingent.[60]

It is fundamental that no vested interest may be created in favor of an unascertained person. The problem will often prove to be one of determining whether the condition inheres in the description of the taker, so that the taker is unascertained, or whether the takers are ascertained independently of the condition which they are required to meet, so that the condition may operate as a divesting contingency.[61] Obviously, the distinction is a difficult one to make, and no uniform rule can be formulated.

Of course, a gift to an unborn person is subject to the condition precedent that he be born alive.[62] When the taker is described as the "husband," "wife," or "widow" of some designated person and at the effective date of the instrument it is impossible to state with certainty what person will meet that description, the gift is subject to a condition precedent.

---

[58] This view is embodied in 3 Restatement of Property §254.

[59] See id. §253.

[60] Section 252 of the Restatement of Property has taken the position that C's interest is subject to a condition precedent.

[61] Section 250 of the Restatement of Property has taken the position that a description of takers as persons "who survive" or are "living" at a future time tends to indicate that there is a requirement of survival to that time, as a condition precedent.

[62] See id. §273.

EDWARDS v. HAMMOND
3 Lev. 132 (C.P. 1683)

Ejectment upon not guilty, and special verdict, the case was. A copyholder of land, burrough English, surrendered to the use of himself for life, and after to the use of his eldest son and his heirs, if he live to the age of 21 years: provided, and upon condition, that if he die before 21, that then it shall remain to the surrenderer and his heirs. The surrenderer died, the youngest son entered; and the eldest son being 17 brought an ejectment; and the sole question was, whether the devise to the eldest son be upon condition precedent, or if the condition be subsequent? scil. that the estate in fee shall vest immediately upon the death of the father, to be divested if he die before 21. For the defendant it was argued, that the condition was precedent, and that the estate should descend to the youngest son in the mean time, or at least shall be in contingency and in abeyance 'til the first son shall attain to one and twenty; and so the eldest son has no title now, being no more than 17. On the other side it was argued, and so agreed by the Court; that though by the first words this may seem to be a condition precedent, yet, taking all the words together, this was not a condition precedent, but a present devise to the eldest son, subject to and defeasible by this condition subsequent, scil. his not attaining the age of 21; and they resembled this to the case of Spring and Caesar reported by Jones Justice and abridged by Roll. 1 Abr. 415, nu. 12. A fine to the use of B. and his heirs if C. pays him not 20s. upon Septemb. 10, and if C. does pay, to the use of B. for life, remainder to C. and his heirs, where the word si does not create a condition precedent, but the estate in fee vests presently in C. to be divested by payment afterwards; so here: accordingly this case was adjudged in Mich. term next following.

FESTING v. ALLEN
12 Mees. & Wels. 279 (Ex. 1843)

ROLFE, B. . . .

The question for our opinion arises on the will of Roger Belk, which, so far as it is material to state it, is as follows: — "I give and devise unto George Allen, Thomas Youle, and John Gillatt, all and every my messuages, lands, tenements, and hereditaments, both freehold and copyhold, and all my other messuages, lands, tenements, hereditaments, and real estate whatsoever and wheresoever, to have and to hold the same unto the said George Allen, Thomas Youl, and John Gillatt, their heirs and assigns, to the uses, upon and for the trusts, intents, and purposes, and with, under, and subject to the powers, provisions, and declarations hereinafter expressed and contained of and concerning the same; viz., to the use of my said dear wife and her assigns, for and during the term of her natural life, if she shall so long continue my widow and unmarried, without impeachment of waste; and from and after her decease, or second marriage, which shall first happen, to the use of my said granddaughter, Martha Hannah Johnson, and her assigns, for and during the term of her natural life, and from and after her decease to the use of all and every the child or children of her, the said Martha Hannah Johnson, who shall attain the age of twenty-one years, if more than one, equally to be divided amongst them, share and share alike, to hold as tenants in common, and not as joint tenants, and to their several and respective heirs and assigns for ever, and if but one such child, then to the use of such one child, his or her heirs and assigns for ever; and for want of any such issue, then it is my will and mind, and I do hereby direct, that my said trustees, and the survivor of them, and the heirs and assigns of such survivor, do and shall stand seised and possessed thereof in trust, as to one equal half part or share thereof, to permit and suffer Ann Johnson, the wife of my grandson Thomas Roger Belk Johnson, or any other wife, whom he may happen to marry, to receive and take the rents, issues, and profits, thereof, for and during the term of her natural life, for the maintenance and education of all and every the child or children of my said grandson Thomas Roger Belk Johnson; and from and after her decease, to the use of all and every the child and children of my said son [sic], Thomas Roger Belk Johnson, lawfully begotten, who shall attain the age of twenty-one years, if more than one, equally to be divided amongst them, share and share alike, to hold as tenants in common, and not as joint tenants, and to their several and respective heirs and assigns for ever; and if but one such child, then to the use of such one child, his or her heirs and assigns for ever.   And as to the other equal half part or share thereof, to stand seised and possessed thereof to the use of the said Sarah Rhodes, for and during the term of her natural life, and from and after her decease, to the use of all and every the child or children of the said Sarah Rhodes, lawfully begotten, who shall attain the age of twenty-one years, if more than one, to be equally divided amongst them, share and share alike, to hold as tenants in common and not as joint tenants, and to their several and respective heirs and assigns for ever."

Martha Hannah Johnson survived the testator's widow, and after his death, namely, in the year 1825, married Maurice Green Festing. She died in 1833, leaving three infant children; and the main question is, whether those children took on her death any interest in the devised estates.

We think that they did not. It was contended on their behalf that they took vested estates in fee immediately on the death of their mother, subject only to be devested in the event of their dying under twenty-one, and the case, it was said, must be treated as coming within the principle of the decision of the House of Lords in Phipps v. Ackers, and the cases there referred to. To this, however, we cannot accede. In all those cases there was an absolute gift to some ascertained person or persons, and the Courts held, that words accompanying the gift, though apparently importing a contingency or contingencies, did in reality only indicate certain circumstances on the happening or not happening of which the estate previously devised should be devested, and pass from the first devisee into some other channel. The clear distinction in the present case is, that here there is no gift to any one who does not answer the whole of the requisite description. The gift is not to the children of Mrs. Festing, but to the children who shall attain twenty-one, and no one who has not attained his age of twenty-one years is an object of the testator's bounty, any more than a person who is not a child of Mrs. Festing. Even if there were no authority establishing this to be a substantial and not an imaginary distinction, still we should not feel inclined to extend the doctrine of Doe v. Moore and Phipps v. Ackers to cases not precisely similar. But, in fact, the distinction to which we have adverted in a great measure forms the ground of the decision in the case of Duffield v. Duffield, in the House of Lords, and Russell v. Buchanan (2 C. & M. 561) in this Court, and on this short ground our opinion is founded. We think that Mrs. Festing was tenant for life, with contingent remainders in fee to such of her children as should attain twenty-one, and as no child had attained twenty-one when the particular estate determined by her death, the remainder was necessarily defeated. It is equally clear that all the other limitations were defeated by the same event, namely, the death of Mrs. Festing leaving several infant children, but no child who had then attained the age of twenty-one years. For the limitations to take effect at her decease were all of them contingent remainders in fee, one or other of which was to take effect according to the events pointed out. If Mrs. Festing had left at her decease a child who had then attained the age of twenty-one years, her child or children would have taken absolutely, to the exclusion of all the other contingent remaindermen. If, on the other hand, there had at her decease been a failure of her child or children who should attain twenty-one, then the alternative limitations would have taken effect; but this did not happen, for though she left no child of the age of twenty-one years, and therefore capable of taking under the devise in favour of her children, yet neither is it possible to say that there was at her decease a failure of her issue who should attain the age of twenty-one years, for she left three children, all or any of whom might and still may attain the prescribed age; so that the contingency on which alone the alternative limitations were to take effect had not happened when the particular estate determined, and those alternative limitations, all of which were clearly contingent remainders, were therefore defeated. On these short grounds, we think it clear, that neither the infant children of Mrs. Festing, nor the parties who were to take the estate in case of her leaving no child who should attain twenty-one, take any interest whatever, but that on her death the whole estate and interest vested in the heir-at-law.

We shall certify our opinion to Vice-Chancellor Wigram accordingly.[63]

4.   INCOMPLETE DISPOSITIONS

An incomplete disposition exists whenever the dispositive instrument does not make it clear what is to be done with the property under all conceivable circumstances. The danger of leaving gaps as to the disposition of the property is ever present when future interests are created.

In determining whether a gap in a disposition exists, it should be kept in mind that a beneficiary may disclaim or renounce the interest given to him. If a prior interest is disclaimed or renounced, is it clear under the terms of the dispositive instrument whether subsequent interests are to be accelerated as a result of such a disclaimer or renunciation? If a subsequent interest is for some reason ineffective, is it clear under the terms of the dispositive instrument what the consequences will be so far as a prior interest is concerned?

If a legal contingent remainder in land is created, there is necessarily present the possibility that the remainderman may not be ready to take over the possession of the property when the prior supporting estate ends. If the remainderman is not ready when the prior supporting estate ends, the contingent remainder is de-

---

[63] Edwards v. Hammond and Festing v. Allen are discussed in 5 American Law of Property §21.32 (Casner ed. 1952). — Ed.

stroyed if the doctrine of destructibility of contingent remainders is still in force in the governing state. If the doctrine is not in force, a determination will have to be made as to the disposition of the land during the gap.

An instrument in an estate plan is not properly drafted if it contains any gap as to the disposition of the property under reasonably foreseeable circumstances.

a. *Failure of Prior Interest*

WILMINGTON TRUST CO. v. CARPENTER
31 Del. Ch. 411, 75 A.2d 815 (1950)

HARRINGTON, Chancellor: The plaintiff trustee under an agreement executed by Margaretta duPont Carpenter, dated September 22, 1930, seeks instructions with respect to the persons entitled to the income therefrom during the remainder of Mrs. Carpenter's life. That instrument in part provides (1) that the trust so created

". . . shall continue until the death of the last survivor of the Settlor, Margaretta duPont Carpenter, Robert R. M. Carpenter, husband of the said Settlor, Pierre S. duPont, brother of the said Settlor, and Alice Belin duPont, wife of the said Pierre S. du-Pont;"

(2) That the trustees

". . . pay over and deliver unto the said Robert R. M. Carpenter the entire net income of the trust estate for and during the term of his life and, upon his death, to pay over and deliver such entire net income unto the said Settlor, if she be then living, for and during the term of her life;

(3) "Upon the death of the said Robert R. M. Carpenter and the said Settlor, if the trust hereby created shall still be in existence, it shall be the duty of the said Trustee, until the termination of the trust hereby created . . . to divide such net income into four equal parts and to pay over one of such equal parts unto each of the four children of the said Settlor, to wit, Louisa C. Jenney (now Louisa d'A. Carpenter), Irene duPont Carpenter (now Irene Carpenter Morgan), Robert R. M. Carpenter, Jr., and William K. duPont Carpenter, and unto the lawful issue of any of them that may be deceased leaving lawful issue her or him surviving, such lawful issue to take, equally among them if more than one, his, her or their parent's share of such net income; . . .

(4) "No part of the principal or income of the trust estate hereby created shall be subject to the control, debts, liabilities, and/or engagements of any of the beneficiaries thereof and no

part of such principal or income shall be subject to assignment or alienation by them or any of them, nor to execution or process for the enforcement of judgments or claims of any sort against such beneficiaries or any of them. All payments of income from said trust estate shall be made only as the same accrue and not by way of anticipation. It is hereby expressly understood and agreed that any attempt to so anticipate, alienate or assign shall not be binding upon the Trustee and shall be wholly disregarded by the Trustee."

The trust corpus is substantial, consisting of 45,000 shares of the common stock of Delaware Realty & Investment Corporation and of other securities and cash of the face amount of approximately $68,000.

On February 24, 1947, and April 16, of the same year, Margaretta duPont Carpenter executed and delivered to the plaintiff trustee certain documents which stated, in substance, that if at any time there should be no one entitled under the terms of the said trust agreement of September 22, 1930, to receive the principal or the income from the trust created thereby, it should be paid over absolutely to The Carpenter Foundation and should not revert to her, or to her heirs, executors or administrators. She further stated that these directions should not affect the life estate in the trust reserved to her.

Robert R. M. Carpenter died June 11, 1949, survived by his wife, Margaretta duPont Carpenter, the settlor of the trust, to whom the plaintiff trustee paid the income therefrom after his death until January 10, 1950. Pierre S. duPont, the brother of the settlor, is living. The four children of Mrs. Carpenter are also living, and of age. The living issue of such children are the defendants, Renee Carpenter Kitchell, Margaretta duPont Kitchell, Nancy Gardiner Kitchell, Carol Victoria Kitchell, Leslie Halsey Kitchell, Robert R. M. Carpenter, III, Mary Kaye Carpenter, II, Kemble duPont Carpenter, Keith Carpenter and Belle Morgan Carpenter, all of whom are minors.

On the same day that Margaretta duPont Carpenter created the trust in question by the said agreement dated September 22, 1930, Robert R. M. Carpenter, her husband, likewise created a similar, though smaller, trust from which Mrs. Carpenter was to receive the income during her lifetime, and on her death the income was to be paid to Robert R. M. Carpenter should he survive her.

It is unnecessary to state the tax status of such trusts created in 1930 and their subsequent history. It is sufficient to state that on October 24, 1949, and more than four months after the death of

Robert R. M. Carpenter, the Congress of the United States enacted what is known as the "Technical Changes Act of 1949," which was duly approved by the President. Section 8 of that Act, Public Law 378, 81st Congress, Act Oct. 25, 1949, Chapter 720, 26 U.S.C.A. Sec. 811 note, provides:

"In the case of a transfer of property made prior to June 7, 1932, under which the grantor retained (1) the possession or enjoyment of, or the right to the income from, the property, or (2) the right, either alone or in conjunction with any person, to designate the persons who shall possess or enjoy the property or the income therefrom, then an assignment by the grantor of such possession, enjoyment, or right to income, or a relinquishment by him of such right of designation, shall, if made in 1949 or 1950, not be deemed a transfer of property for the purposes of chapter 4 of the Internal Revenue Code, and shall, if made prior to 1951, not be deemed to have been made in contemplation of death within the meaning of chapter 3 of such code. The foregoing provisions shall not apply —

"(A) if the transfer was made after March 3, 1931, and prior to June 7, 1932, and if the property transferred would have been includible in the grantor's gross estate upon his death by reason of the amendatory language of the joint resolution of March 3, 1931 (45 Stat. 1516); or

"(B) if the property transferred would have been includible in the grantor's gross estate under section 811(d) of the Internal Revenue Code had he died on October 7, 1949."

Under certain circumstances, which do not exist here, the Internal Revenue Department of the United States, for the purpose of federal taxation, regards trusts such as were created by Margaretta duPont Carpenter and Robert R. M. Carpenter as reciprocal or cross trusts and holds that the wife is the settlor not of the trust which she actually creates but of the trust her husband creates and vice versa. Mrs. Carpenter was the actual settlor of the trust before the court, but counsel advised her that it could not be definitely stated which trust the Commissioner of Internal Revenue would rule was created by her though she should attempt to take the proper steps to relinquish her rights before 1951. On November 23, 1949, Mrs. Carpenter, therefore, applied to the Commissioner of Internal Revenue of the United States for a ruling and a closing agreement with respect to the tax status of the trust created by her in September of 1930. There was a favorable ruling by the Commissioner on January 9, 1950, and on the following day, January 10th, Mrs. Carpenter entered into a closing agreement with him which was approved by the Secretary of the Treasury February 23, 1950. Under this ruling and agreement, the Internal Revenue Department of the United States recognized Margaretta duPont Carpenter's right to relinquish her life interest in the income from the trust created by her, and by a renunciation or assignment prior to 1951, to cause such right to become vested in her children, or their issue, without any liability for the payment of gift taxes, provided that instrument was effective under the laws of Delaware to divest her right to such trust income. On January 10, 1950, Mrs. Carpenter executed and delivered to the Wilmington Trust Company, the plaintiff trustee, an instrument under seal which in part stated:

"I, the said Margaretta duPont Carpenter, for reasons satisfactory to myself and which are known to my children, do hereby forever renounce and disclaim all my life estate in the said trust estate and all right, title and interest of whatsoever nature therein given to me by the provisions of the said trust instrument. I do hereby solemnly declare and affirm that I will not hereafter accept, either at present or in the future, from the trustee of said trust, its successor or assigns, any portion of the income of said trust estate, or any interest therein which may be sought to be paid to me in accordance with any right, title or interest which I had at any time before the execution of this instrument, it being my intention in executing this instrument to terminate my life estate in the said trust estate as effectively as would my death. . . ."

In the same instrument, she further stated:

"I Margaretta duPont Carpenter, supplementing, but without in any manner limiting or conditioning the foregoing renunciation, do hereby give, grant, bargain, sell, release and convey my right hereafter to receive the entire net income from said trust estate during the term of my life, and all my right, title and interest of whatsoever nature, legal or equitable, absolute or contingent, vested or hereafter to accrue, in and to the said trust estate and any part thereof, unto my said four children, to wit, the said Louisa d'A. Carpenter, Irene Carpenter Morgan, Robert R. M. Carpenter, Jr., and William K. duPont Carpenter, and unto the lawful issue of any of them that may be deceased leaving lawful issue her or him surviving, such lawful issue to take, equally among them if more than one, his, her or their parent's share of such net income, and if any of said children should die without leaving lawful issue surviving, the share of such net income of any child so dying shall be equally distributed among the remaining children and the lawful issue of any of them that shall have died leaving such issue, as provided for in said . . . trust agreement."

The questions on which the plaintiff trustee seeks instructions are:

(1) Did the instrument executed by Margaretta duPont Carpenter on January 10, 1950 terminate her right to receive the income during her lifetime from the trust created by her on September 22, 1930?

(2) If so, is such life income payable during the continuance of the trust to her four children and to the issue of any of them, *per stirpes,* who may die during her lifetime leaving children?

(3) If Mrs. Carpenter's right to receive the income from the trust during her lifetime was terminated by the instrument of January 10, 1950, must it be accumulated until her death and then paid to her children and to their issue *per stirpes?*

(4) If Mrs. Carpenter's right to receive such income was so terminated by the instrument of January 10, 1950, is it payable to The Carpenter Foundation until her death?

In general, the right of a life beneficiary of a trust created by another person to refuse to accept its benefits has been recognized in this State. Scotton v. Moore, 5 Boyce (28 Del.) 545, 93 A. 373, Ann. Cas. 1918C, 409; Equitable Trust Co. v. Proctor, 27 Del. Ch. 151, 32 A.2d 422. The textbooks made the broad general statement, however, that a beneficiary cannot renounce the gift after having accepted it. Griswold, Spendthrift Trusts, Sec. 524; Scott on Trusts, Sec. 337.7; 1 Bogert, Trusts & Trustees, Sec. 173; but cf. Compton, et al., v. Rixey, 124 Va. 548, 98 S.E. 651, 5 A.L.R. 465. This would seem to depend upon the intent of the donor of the fund and is usually determined by the provisions of the instrument creating the trust. See Blackwell v. Virginia Trust Co., 177 Va. 299, 14 S.E.2d 301; Malatesta's Estate, 29 Pa. Dist. R. 113. Cf. Griswold, Spendthrift Trusts, Sec. 528. But this case is governed by somewhat different principles as Margaretta DuPont Carpenter was both the settlor of the trust and after her husband's death the sole life beneficiary of the income therefrom.

Without determining whether spendthrift trusts were valid in this State prior to the enactment of Chapter 186, Volume 38, Laws of Delaware, some Delaware cases have apparently assumed they were. See Wilmington Trust Co. v. Wilmington Trust Co., 21 Del. Ch. 188, 186 A. 903; Wilmington Trust Co. v. Wilmington Trust Co., 25 Del. Ch. 193, 15 A.2d 655. That question was not determined by Gray, Administrator v. Corbit, 4 Del. Ch. 135, and it is unnecessary to determine it here. In any event, it is a settled rule of policy in most states which recognize spendthrift trusts that if a person creates such a trust for his own benefit and is not under some incapacity, he can terminate it at will so far as his interest is concerned, and compel a reconveyance of that interest. Weymouth v. Delaware Trust Co., 29 Del. Ch. 1, 45 A.2d 427; Griswold, Spendthrift Trusts, Secs. 497, 498; 2 Restatement, Trusts, Sec. 339. That rule was applied in the Weymouth Case six years after the creation of the trust, though the agreement provided that it was irrevocable. Under its terms the income was payable to the settlor during his lifetime and at his death the principal was payable to his executors or administrators. The court in discussing the question said:

"A rule which seems more consistent with our law concerning revocability is that the mere existence of 'spendthrift trust provisions' in a trust created by the sole beneficiary should not prevent revocation." 29 Del. Ch. 1, 5, 45 A.2d 429.

Mrs. Carpenter could not terminate the trust as other persons had interests in the fund in remainder, and did not seek to compel a reconveyance of any interest. But in the formal renunciation of her rights in the instrument executed by her and delivered to the plaintiff trustee on January 10, 1950, she stated:

"It is my intention in executing this instrument to terminate my life interest in the trust as effectively as would my death."

Applying the above principles, that statement clearly and unequivocally indicated Mrs. Carpenter's intent and effectively terminated her life interest in the trust. Cf. Griswold on Spendthrift Trusts, Sec. 528; In re Bowers' Estate, 346 Pa. 85, 29 A.2d 519. Cases like Claflin v. Claflin, 149 Mass. 19, 20 N.E. 454, 3 L.R.A. 370, 14 Am. St. Rep. 393, are not in conflict with this conclusion. See Griswold, Spendthrift Trusts, supra, Sec. 498.

It is true that Chapter 186, Volume 38, Laws of Delaware, enacted in 1933, par. 4415, Revised Code, 1935, provides:

"Creditors and Assignees of a Beneficiary of a Trust: — The creditors of a beneficiary of a trust shall have only such rights against such beneficiary's interest in the trust property or the income therefrom as shall not be denied to them by the terms of the instrument creating or defining the trustor (trust or) by the laws of this State; provided, however, that if such beneficiary shall have transferred property to the trust in defraud of his creditors the foregoing shall in no way limit the rights of such creditors with respect to the property so transferred. Every interest in trust property or the income therefrom which shall not be subject to the rights of the creditors of the beneficiary, as aforesaid, shall be exempt from execution, attachment, distress for rent, and all other legal or equitable process instituted by or on behalf of such creditors. Every assignment by a beneficiary

of a trust of his interest in the trust property or the income therefrom which is, by the terms of the instrument creating or defining
the trust unassignable, shall be void."

Retroactive laws are not favored and statutes are not held to
have that effect unless it clearly appears to have been the legislative intent. Equitable Trust Co. v. Richards, (Del. Orph.) post
p. 564, 73 A.2d 437. But it is unnecessary to determine whether
Chapter 186, Volume 38, Laws of Delaware, was intended to be
retroactive or, if it was, whether it could affect the Carpenter
trust. See Equitable Trust Co. v. Richards, supra. In any event,
its provisions have been construed strictly. Weymouth v. Delaware Trust Co., supra; see also Tracey v. Curtis Franklin, post
p. . . . , 67 A.2d 56.

The trust in the Weymouth case was created in 1940 and
though the retroactive question was not before the court, the Vice
Chancellor, in discussing the Delaware statute of 1933, said:

"This section deals specifically with restrictions upon the rights
of creditors of a beneficiary with respect to trust property, and
restrictions upon assignments by a beneficiary. Assuming, without deciding, that a settlor-beneficiary may, as the respondent
argues, validly create such restrictions, this will not aid the
respondent. The statute prescribes express consequences of restrictions of the particular kinds dealt with, and makes no mention of revocability. It would seem to me unwarranted to construe the language of the act as requiring the alteration urged
by the respondent in the law otherwise applicable with respect
to revocability. . . ." 29 Del. Ch. 1, 6, 45 A.2d 429.

The same reasoning leads to the conclusion that if the statute
was applicable to this case, it did not prevent Margaretta duPont
Carpenter from effectively renouncing her life rights under the
trust created by her.[64]

---

[64] If a trust is established which contains a spendthrift provision, under what
circumstances should the terms of the trust authorize a beneficiary to disclaim
or release his interest under the trust? If such an authorization is given,
should the terms of the trust provide for the disposition of the trust property
in the event of a disclaimer or release? It is provided by Pa. Stat. Ann., tit.
20, §301.3 (Purdon, Supp. 1959) that an income beneficiary of a spendthrift
trust can release his right to income if thereby such income will pass to one or
more of his descendants. Prior to this relaxation, the Internal Revenue
Service had ruled that the income from a Pennsylvania spendthrift trust is
taxable to the income beneficiary, even though he assigns the income to another. I.T. 4035, 1950-2 C.B. 60.

The validity of a renunciation by a beneficiary under a testamentary trust
was questioned by the trustees in In re Suter's Estate, 207 Misc. 1002, 142
N.Y.S.2d 353 (1955). The beneficiary was a minor when the trust was established, and when he attained his majority, he renounced all claims to his
father's estate "for moral and political reasons." At the time of the litigation

The solicitors for the parties disagree, however, with respect to the proper disposition of the income from the trust fund during the remainder of Mrs. Carpenter's life. In the assignment part of the renunciation of January 10, 1950, she purported to grant and convey her life interest in the trust to her four named children, all of whom are living, and "to the lawful issue of any of them that may be deceased leaving lawful issue, her or her surviving . . . ," as provided in said trust agreement. That part of the instrument was preceded by the statement "supplementing but without in any manner limiting or conditioning the foregoing renunciation." It is likewise unnecessary to determine, however, whether this was an effective assignment of Margaretta duPont Carpenter's life rights in the trust. As to the general powers of a settlor-beneficiary of a spendthrift trust in that respect, see Griswold on Trusts, Secs. 493, 494; cf. cases cited in Weymouth v. Delaware Trust Co., supra. In any event, upon the premature termination of a prior life right to the income from a trust fund, the rights of the succeeding beneficiaries will be accelerated unless contrary to the intent of the settlor of the trust. Scotton v. Moore, 5 Boyce (28 Del.) 545, 93 A. 373, Ann. Cas. 1918C, 469; Equitable Trust Co. v. Proctor, 27 Del. Ch. 151, 32 A.2d 422; 2 Restatement, Trusts, Sec. 231. That rule usually applies if the possession and enjoyment of the fund by other beneficiaries is merely postponed for the benefit of a life taker of the income. Scotton v. Moore, supra; Equitable Trust Co. v. Proctor, supra. It also applies even if there is a substituted gift to others should a subsequent beneficiary die prior to the death of the life taker. Id.

As was pointed out in Scotton v. Moore, supra,

"If the principle is based upon the presumed intention of the testator, there need be no distinction made between vested and contingent remainders in its application." 5 Boyce (28 Del.) 545, 93 A. 375.

---

he was a senior at Yale University. The court agreed with the beneficiary's insistence that as a member of a free society, with freedom of choice, he could not be yoked to this inheritance against his will. This result, the court holds, does not violate the New York statute prohibiting the transfer of income of a trust (see N.Y. Personal Property Law §15, quoted infra page 1468). Under the trust, the son was to receive income until he was thirty, then part of the corpus, additional corpus at thirty-five, and the balance at forty. If he died before forty, the corpus was to go to the son's issue, with gifts over to others if he had no issue. The court directed that the trust continue at least until the son attained age thirty and that in the meantime the income should be paid to those presumptively entitled to the next estate. When the son attains thirty or dies, whichever first occurs, application may be made to the court to determine the distribution of part or all of the corpus. — ED.

The income rights of Margaretta duPont Carpenter's children and the issue of any child who might have died leaving children, were to take effect in possession "upon the death of the said Robert R. M. Carpenter and the said settlor"; but I am not satisfied that the quoted words were intended to be a condition precedent to the acquisition of any rights whatever under the agreement.

In Equitable Trust Company v. Proctor, supra, the court said:

"Expressions used in connection with a gift of succeeding interests, such as 'after the death of,' or 'then living,' though they refer unequivocally to the time of the death of the donee of a prior interest, do not necessarily evince an intent contrary to acceleration upon renunciation by the donee of the prior interest." 27 Del. Ch. 151, 32 A.2d 424.

See also 2 Restatement, Law of Property, Sec. 233, Comment (b).

From the language of the Carpenter agreement it seems reasonable to conclude that the possessory rights of the subsequent beneficiaries under the trust were merely postponed for the benefit of the prior life takers of the income and were acceleratd on the premature termination of that interest. See Equitable Trust Co. v. Proctor, supra. If any of Mrs. Carpenter's children should die during her lifetime their issue would take their shares of the income per stirpes. The settlor of the trust at least indicated her intent with respect to the rights of such beneficiaries when she executed the assignment of January 10, 1950. See Griswold, Spendthrift Trusts, Sec. 528.

In Blackwell v. Virginia Trust Company, supra, the court held that, under its provisions, the acceleration of the rights of subsequent beneficiaries, on the renunciation of the life interest of a prior beneficiary under a spendthrift trust agreement, executed by another person would clearly defeat the intent of the settlor of the trust. Furthermore, under the law of Virginia, acceleration does not apply to contingent interests. It follows that that case is not pertinent to the determination of this controversy.

On Margaretta duPont Carpenter's renunciation of her right to the income from the trust fund during her lifetime it was legally payable, in accordance with the provisions of the agreement, to her four named children, the next beneficiaries of the trust during their respective lives and cannot be held and accumulated by the trustee for them or their issue until her death. It follows that The Carpenter Foundation has no rights in the income from the trust accruing during Mrs. Carpenter's lifetime.

An appropriate order will be entered in accordance with this opinion.[65]

[65] Section 207(a) of the Technical Changes Act of 1953 eliminated the need for the settlor to relinquish her income rights as a prerequisite to escape from estate taxes, so that if Margaretta duPont Carpenter had done nothing, the value of the trust property would not have been includible in her gross estate and she would have had the benefit of the income for life. Section 2036(b) of the 1954 Code provides: "This section shall not apply to a transfer made before March 4, 1931; nor to transfers made after March 3, 1931, and before June 7, 1932 unless the property transferred would have been includible in the decedent's gross estate by reason of the amendatory language of the joint resolution of March 3, 1931 (46 Stat. 1516)." In Smith v. United States, 139 F. Supp. 305 (Ct. Cl. 1956), it was held that a trust established on October 1, 1923, in which the settlor reserved the income for life and which was revocable by the settlor and the trustee until the death of the trustee in 1933, did not result in a transfer before March 4, 1931, but rather resulted in a transfer in 1933 when the power to revoke came to an end. Thus, on the settlor's death in 1950, the value of the trust property was includible in his gross estate under 1939 I.R.C. §811 (c) (1)(B) (1954 I.R.C. §2036). Maclean v. United States, 59-1 U.S.T.C. ¶11864 (S.D. Cal. 1959), dealt with a situation where the settlor established a trust in 1923, reserving the income for life and the power to revoke the trust, and she revoked it on May 27, 1931, and immediately set up another trust in which she reserved the income for life. The court held the actions she took in 1931 resulted in a new trust, so that it could not be deemed one created before March 4, 1931, and hence the value of the trust property was includible in her gross estate on her death in 1954. The case was affirmed in 275 F.2d 936 (9th Cir. 1960). Did the transfer by Margaretta duPont Carpenter occur in 1947 when she gave up any reversionary interest rather than in 1930 when the trust was established? In Estate of Robert J. Cuddihy, 32 T.C. 1171 (1959), and Estate of Ellis Branson Ridgway, 33 T.C. 1000 (1960), the transfers in trust were deemed made before March 4, 1931, though the grantor retained powers with respect to the trust which were not released until after that date. In Estate of Newcomb Carlton, 34 T.C. —, No. 104 (1960), the decedent made a transfer in trust in 1930 under which he retained the right to some income for life and the power to change the age at which a beneficiary would receive the corpus. After 1932, he released his power in regard to the corpus. The court held that the transfer was made in 1930 and not when he released his power over the corpus, and thus the value of the trust property was not includible in his gross estate as the subject of a transfer with a retained right to income. To the same effect is Estate of Ellie G. Canfield, 34 T.C.—, No. 103 (1960), where the power that was released after 1932 was a general testamentary power.

In Estate of Debe W. Hubbard, 26 T.C. 183 (1956), a transfer in trust was made after March 3, 1931, and before June 7, 1932, and the court held that under the circumstances presented, the value of the property was includible in the decedent's gross estate by reason of the joint resolution of March 3, 1931, as the subject of a transfer with possession or enjoyment retained. The case was reversed, 250 F.2d 492 (5th Cir. 1957), on the ground that under the law in effect in 1932, a transfer was not taxable because of the existence of a contingent reversionary right to income; and the right of the decedent, at the time of the decedent's death, to any income in excess of the required payments to others did not cause the inclusion of any of the trust property in the decedent's gross estate, since no excess income was in fact available in any year. Estate of Lena R. Arents, 34 T.C. —, No. 29 (1960), held that where an inter vivos transfer in trust occurred during the interval between March 3, 1931,

PROBLEMS

11.26. In a jurisdiction in which the rule in Shelley's Case is in force, A devises land as follows: "To B for life, then to B's heirs." A dies. B disclaims all interest given to him under the terms of the devise. What is the state of the title to the land? See 3 Restatement of Property §312, Comment *c*, Illustration 5-II. Is the answer the same if B predeceases A? Compare Bellville Savings Bank v. Aneshaensel, 298 Ill. 292, 131 N.E. 682 (1921), with 2 Restatement of Property §230, Comment *e*.

11.27. In a jurisdiction in which the doctrine of destructibility of contingent remainders is in force, A devises land as follows: "To B for life, then to C and his heirs if C attains twenty-one." B dies, then A dies. Two years after A's death C attains twenty-one. Is C entitled to possession of the land? Suppose that B survives A and disclaims the life estate given to him, and two years after the disclaimer, C attains twenty-one. Will C be entitled to possession of the land? See 5 American Law of Property §21.39 (Casner ed. 1952).

11.28. A transfers property to T in trust to pay the income to B for life and then to distribute the corpus in specified ways. If B's life interest is subject to a spendthrift provision, he cannot sell it and obtain the possible tax advantage discussed supra page 438, note 11. The availability of this possible tax advantage may be

---

and June 7, 1932, under which the settlor-decedent reserved a life interest in the trust income, commencing after the death of another person who actually survived the decedent, the transferred property was not includible in the decedent's gross estate.

The acceleration of the succeeding interest as a result of the failure of a prior interest is examined in 5 American Law of Property §§21.43-21.45 (Casner ed. 1952).

In 1955, Illinois enacted a statute which provides that when a will is renounced by the testator's spouse, any future interest which is to take effect in possession or enjoyment at or after the termination of an estate or other interest given by the will to the surviving spouse shall take effect as though the surviving spouse had predeceased the testator, unless the will expressly provides that in case of renunciation such a future interest shall not be accelerated. The act by its express terms applies only to wills of decedents dying after it takes effect. Ill. Rev. Stat., c. 3, §168a (1959). Consideration should be given to the desirability of including in a dispositive instrument a provision which would require solution along the lines of the Illinois statute, in the event of a disclaimer or renunciation of a prior interest. Such a provision might be as follows: "In the event that a beneficiary hereunder disclaims or renounces the interest limited in his favor, succeeding interests shall take effect as though such beneficiary had died on the date of the disclaimer or renunciation." — ED.

less desirable than the protection given to B by the spendthrift clause. Is the effectiveness of the spendthrift clause undermined if B is given a general power to appoint the trust property by deed? Is the effectiveness of the spendthrift clause undermined if B is given a nongeneral power to appoint the trust property by deed? A general power of appointment for estate tax purposes is defined in Section 2041(b) of the 1954 Code, quoted infra page 1401. See Griswold, Spendthrift Trusts 72 (2d ed. 1947).

b. *Ineffective Subsequent Interest*

BROWN v. INDEPENDENT BAPTIST CHURCH OF WOBURN
325 Mass. 645, 91 N.E.2d 922 (1950)

QUA, C.J. The object of this suit in equity, originally brought in this court, is to determine the ownership of a parcel of land in Woburn and the persons entitled to share in the proceeds of its sale by a receiver.

Sarah Converse died seised of the land on July 19, 1849, leaving a will in which she specifically devised it "to the Independent Baptist Church of Woburn, to be holden and enjoyed by them so long as they shall maintain and promulgate their present religious belief and faith and shall continue a Church; and if the said Church shall be dissolved, or if its religious sentiments shall be changed or abandoned, then my will is that this real estate shall go to my legatees hereinafter named, to be divided in equal portions between them. And my will further is, that if my beloved husband, Jesse Converse, shall survive me, that then this devise to the aforesaid Independent Church of Woburn, shall not take effect till from and after his decease; and that so long as he shall live he may enjoy and use the said real estate, and take the rents and profits thereof to his own use." Then followed ten money legacies in varying amounts to different named persons, after which there was a residuary clause in these words, "The rest and residue of my estate I give and bequeath to my legatees above named, saving and except therefrom the Independent Baptist Church; this devise to take effect from and after the decease of my husband; I do hereby direct and will that he shall have the use and this rest and residue during his life."

The husband of the testatrix died in 1864. The church named by the textatrix ceased to "continue a church" on October 19, 1939.

The parties apparently are in agreement, and the single justice ruled, that the estate of the church in the land was a determinable fee. We concur. First Universalist Society of North Adams v. Boland, 155 Mass. 171, 174. Institution for Savings v. Roxbury Home for Aged Women, 244 Mass. 583, 585-586. Dyer v. Siano, 298 Mass. 537, 540. The estate was a fee, since it might last forever, but it was not an absolute fee, since it might (and did) "automatically expire upon the occurrence of a stated event." Restatement: Property, Sec. 44. It is also conceded, and was ruled, that the specific executory devise over to the persons "hereinafter named" as legatees was void for remoteness. This conclusion seems to be required by Proprietors of the Church in Brattle Square v. Grant, 3 Gray, 142, 155-156, First Universalist Society of North Adams v. Boland, 155 Mass. 171, 173, and Institution for Savings v. Roxbury Home for Aged Women, 244 Mass. 583, 587. See Restatement: Property, Sec. 44, illustration 20. The reason is stated to be that the determinable fee might not come to an end until long after any life or lives in being and twenty-one years, and in theory at least might never come to an end, and for an indefinite period no clear title to the entire estate could be given.

Since the limitation over failed, it next becomes our duty to consider what became of the possibility of reverter which under our decisions remained after the failure of the limitation. First Universalist Society of North Adams v. Boland, 155 Mass. 171, 175. Institution for Savings v. Roxbury Home for Aged Women, 244 Mass. 583, 587. Restatement: Property, Sec. 228, illustration 2, and Appendix to Volume II, at pages 35-36, including note 2. A possibility of reverter seems, by the better authority, to be assignable inter vivos (Restatement: Property, Sec. 159; Simes, Future Interests, Sec. 715; see Tiffany, Real Property [3d ed.] Sec. 314, note 31) and must be at least as readily devisable as the other similar reversionary interest known as a right of entry for condition broken, which is devisable, though not assignable. Dyer v. Siano, 298 Mass. 537, 539. Hayden v. Stoughton, 5 Pick. 528, 535-540. Brigham v. Shattuck, 10 Pick. 306. Austin v. Cambridgeport Parish, 21 Pick. 215, 223-224. Clapp v. Wilder, 176 Mass. 332, 337. Battistone v. Banulski, 110 Conn. 267. G.L. (Ter. Ed.) c. 191, Secs. 1, 24. Restatement: Property, Sec. 165 (see comment f). Simes, Future Interests, Sec. 732. See Tiffany, Real Property (3d ed.) Sec. 314, note 34; Steel v. Cook, 1 Met. 281. It follows that the possibility of reverter passed under the residuary clause of the will to the same persons designated in the invalid executory devise. It is of no consequence that the persons designated in the two provisions were the same. The same result must be reached as if they were different.

The single justice ruled that the residuary clause was void for remoteness, apparently for the same reason that rendered the executory devise void. With this we cannot agree, since we consider it settled that the rule against perpetuities does not apply to reversionary interests of this general type, including possibilities of reverter. Proprietors of the Church in Brattle Square v. Grant, 3 Gray, 142, 148. French v. Old South Society in Boston, 106 Mass. 479, 488-498. Tobey v. Moore, 130 Mass. 448, 450. First Universal Society of North Adams v. Boland, 155 Mass. 171, 175-176. Restatement: Property, Sec. 372. Tiffany, Real Property (3d ed.) Sec. 404. See Gray, Rule Against Perpetuities (4th ed.) Secs. 41, 312, 313. For a full understanding of the situation here presented it is necessary to keep in mind the fundamental difference in character between the attempted executory devise to the legatees later named in the will and the residuary gift to the same persons. The executory devise was in form and substance an attempt to limit or create a new future interest which might not arise or vest in anyone until long after the permissible period. It was obviously not intended to pass such a residuum of the testatrix's existing estate as a possibility of reverter, and indeed if the executory devise had been valid according to its terms the whole estate would have passed from the testatrix and no possibility of reverter could have been left to her or her devisees. The residuary devise, on the other hand, was in terms and purpose exactly adapted to carry any interest which might otherwise remain in the testatrix, whether or not she had it in mind or knew it would exist. Thayer v. Wellington, 9 Allen, 283, 295. Wellman v. Carter, 286 Mass. 237, 249-250.

We cannot accept the contention made in behalf of Mrs. Converse's heirs that the words of the residuary clause "saving and except therefrom the Independent Baptist Church" were meant to exclude from the operation of that clause any possible rights in the *land* previously given to the church. We construe these words as intended merely to render the will consistent by excluding the church which also had been "above named" from the list of "legatees" who were to take the residue.

The interlocutory decree entered December 16, 1947, is reversed, and a new decree is to be entered providing that the land in question or the proceeds of any sale thereof by the receiver shall go to the persons named as legatees in the will, other than the Independent Baptist Church of Woburn, or their successors in interest. Further proceedings are to be in accord with the new decree. Costs and expenses are to be at the discretion of the single justice.

So ordered.[66]

STATUTORY NOTE RELATING TO RIGHTS OF ENTRY AND POSSIBILITIES OF REVERTER

In recent years, statutes relating to rights of entry and possibilities of reverter have been enacted in several states. The statutes are of two types: (1) those that are designed to place some limit on the duration of these property interests; (2) those that seek to make these property interests with a somewhat ancient vintage more easily discoverable by one making a search of the title to land.

Statutes of the first type have been enacted because rights of entry and possibilities of reverter are not subject to the rule against perpetuities and it is thought, at least by some, that they should be subject to some rule to prevent the disturbance of the present

[66] For a comment on Brown v. Independent Baptist Church of Woburn, see 64 Harv. L. Rev. 864 (1951). The effect of the failure of a divesting interest on a prior interest is examined in 5 American Law of Property §§21.47, 21.48 (Casner ed. 1952).

In Edward John Noble Hospital v. Board of Foreign Missions, 176 N.Y.S.2d 157 (1958), the grantor conveyed property to a hospital, reserving to herself the possession of the property for her lifetime. The interest in the hospital was made subject to specified conditions, and on the violation of the conditions, the property "shall thereupon revert and become part of the residuary estate of the party of the first part [the grantor]." The court held the gift over violated the rule against perpetuities and the interest in the hospital was unqualified.

In Industrial National Bank v. Drysdale, 83 R.I. 172, 114 A.2d 191 (1955), a testamentary trust in the amount of $10,000 was established for the benefit of a designated charitable corporation. The transfer to the trustee was "in perpetual trust." Eighteen years after the testator's death the charitable beneficiary was discontinued and the question arose as to the disposition of the trust funds. The court determined there was no general charitable intent and thus no cy pres, so the trust property reverted to the next of kin by way of a resulting trust. Reargument was allowed on whether the trust property passed to the next of kin or residuary legatees in 83 R.I. 175, 119 A.2d 729 (1955). The court confirmed the original decision on this matter in 84 R.I. 385, 125 A.2d 87 (1956). Is this case distinguishable from the Brown case? See also Knowles v. South County Hospital, — R.I. — , 140 A.2d 499 (1958), where the testator devised land and provided that it was to remain part of his estate upon failure of the grantee to comply with stated conditions (the conditions might occur beyond the period of the rule against perpetuities) and to pass to a named beneficiary, and the court held that the gift of what remained in the estate to the named beneficiary did not violate the rule. — Ed.

In re Pruner's Estate, 400 Pa. 629, 162 A.2d 626 (1960), held that a gift over following a determinable fee to charity violated the rule against perpetuities and that the possibility of reverter passed as intestate property since the will contained no residuary clause.

situation by the enforcement of an out-of-date right. Massachusetts Annotated Laws, Chapter 184A, Section 3, which was enacted in 1954 and is quoted infra page 1445, places a thirty-year limit on the duration of rights of entry and possibilities of reverter unless the specified contingency must occur, if at all, within the period of the rule against perpetuities. The thirty-year period is allowed even though it will exceed the period of the rule against perpetuities. The Massachusetts statute, however, does not apply to a case where both the fee simple determinable and the possibility of reverter, or both the fee simple subject to a condition subsequent and the right of entry, are in charities, nor does it apply when the grantor is the Commonwealth of Massachusetts or any political subdivision thereof.

Illinois Revised Statutes, Chapter 30, Section 37e (1959), provides that neither possibilities of reverter nor rights of entry, whether created before or after the enactment of the statute, shall be valid for a period longer than fifty years from the date of their creation. This statute was upheld as constitutional, even though it applied to property rights in existence before its enactment, in Trustees of Schools of Township No. 1 v. Batdorf, 6 Ill. 2d 486, 130 N.E.2d 111 (1955).

In 1960, Kentucky enacted a statute abolishing determinable fees and possibilities of reverter. Words which would have created a determinable fee henceforth will create a fee simple subject to a right of entry, and the contingency must occur within thirty years or the fee will become absolute. The right of entry may be created in a person other than the creator of the interest and is valid for the thirty-year period regardless of the rule against perpetuities. Possibilities of reverter and rights of entry created before the new statute are subject to the thirty-year limitation unless recorded before 1965 as directed. Kentucky Laws 1960, S.B. 180. Nebraska Laws 1959, Chapter 350 adopts the thirty-year rule as to rights of entry and possibilities of reverter and provides that such interests owned by a corporation will be terminated if the corporation is dissolved.

An example of a statute of the second type is Massachusetts Annotated Laws, Chapter 260, Section 31A, which was enacted in 1956, and is quoted infra page 1465. If a possibility of reverter or a right of entry is one created prior to January 2, 1955, the statute takes away the remedy to enforce it from and after January 1, 1966, unless the owner of the interest makes a prescribed recording of it. See also Illinois Revised Statutes, Chapter 30, Section 37f (1959), which provides that if a possibility of reverter was created more than fifty years prior to the effective date of the act, and if the reverter has come into existence prior to the effective date, no person shall commence an action for the reverter of the land based upon such a possibility of reverter after one year from the effective date. This Illinois statute was held constitutional in Trustees of Schools of Township No. 1 v. Batdorf, 6 Ill. 2d 486, 130 N.E.2d 111 (1955).

c. *Incompleteness Avoided by Implied Gift*

KIESLING v. WHITE
411 Ill. 493, 104 N.E.2d 291 (1952)

MR. JUSTICE SCHAEFER delivered the opinion of the court:

This appeal is from a decree of the circuit court of Mason County construing the will of Martin Kiesling who died testate on April 8, 1948. He left no widow and no children, but he was survived by five sisters, one brother and seven nephews and nieces. The will created life estates in the testator's property for his brother and his sisters with remainders to his nephews and nieces. The principal issue is whether, upon the death of each of the life tenants, one sixth of the testator's property should be distributed to the nephews and nieces, or whether cross remainders among the life tenants in the income from the property are to be implied, and distribution to the remaindermen postponed until the life estates have terminated.

The case turns upon the construction of paragraphs 3 and 4 of the will. By paragraph 3 of his will, Kiesling bequeathed "unto my brothers and sisters equal shares of the income of my property that I may own at the time of my death, whether the same be real estate, mixed or personal property, meaning hereby to give each one of them, my said brothers and sisters 'share and share alike' their fractional part of the income from my said property . . . [and] meaning hereby to give to my said brothers and sisters a life estate only in my said property." Then follows paragraph 4, "It is my will, and I hereby give, devise and bequeath unto my nephews and nieces 'share and share alike,' the rest and residue of all of my property after the life estates hereinabove provided in Paragraph Three (3) of this my Last Will and Testament have come to an end."

The plaintiffs, Lawrence Kiesling, the testator's brother, and his three children, filed their complaint seeking a construction of Martin Kiesling's will, and incidentally involving also the will of George Kiesling, Sr., deceased, who was the father of Lawrence Kiesling and his brothers and sisters. When the complaint was filed on April 23, 1949, Lawrence Kiesling was seventy-three years old and the ages of his five sisters ranged from seventy to eighty-seven years. By their complaint, plaintiffs proposed alternative constructions of the third and fourth paragraphs of the will of Martin Kiesling, with relief depending upon the construction adopted. Their first interpretation, and the one which they actually espouse, is that each of the brothers and sisters is to take an undivided one-sixth interest for life in the testator's property, and that as each brother or sister dies, one sixth of the property is to be distributed among the nieces and nephews. Should the court adopt this construction, plaintiffs asked for partition of the testator's property and also of specified property devised to Lawrence Kiesling and certain of his brothers and sisters under the will of their father, George Kiesling, Sr. who died in 1908. Under the alternative construction advanced by plaintiffs, the brothers and sisters of Martin Kiesling have life estates in the income from his property, the entire estate to pass to the nephews and nieces, the ultimate remaindermen, upon the death of the last surviving brother or sister. Under this construction, cross remainders in the income are created by implication in the surviving brothers and sisters. Should the court adopt this interpretation, plaintiffs asked that a trustee be appointed to hold and manage the funds derived from the personal property of the testator, and to distribute the income therefrom to the brothers and sisters and the corpus to the remaindermen upon the death of the last surviving life tenant.

Four of the testator's sisters, (hereinafter defendant-appellees,) answered the complaint, denying the first alternative construction sought and asserting the validity of the interpretation favoring cross remainders among the life tenants. These defendant-appellees also filed a counter-claim in which they requested the appointment of a trustee to handle the entire estate of the testator and distribute the income and eventually the corpus in accordance with the second construction proposed by plaintiffs. The counter-claim also sought a construction of the will of George Kiesling, Sr., so that interests of the various parties thereunder might be determined, and prayed for the granting of such additional relief as was appropriate.

One of the testator's nieces, (also hereinafter a defendant-appellee,) answered the complaint, asking that a construction creating cross remainders be adopted but opposing the appointment of a trustee to hold and manage the property.

The remaining sister of the testator, and her three children (hereinafter defendant-appellants,) by their answer accepted the first alternative construction, denied the validity of a construction establishing cross remainders, and questioned the right to appoint a trustee to care for and manage the personal property.

Plaintiffs and defendant-appellants answered the counterclaim of defendant-appellees, and defendant-appellees replied to both of the answers to the counterclaim. The cause was referred to a master in chancery. The master's report recommended the entry of a decree adopting the first construction of Martin Kiesling's will proposed by plaintiffs. Objections to his report were ordered to stand as exceptions, the exceptions were sustained, and a decree entered finding the equities to be with the defendant-appellees and construing the will as establishing cross remainders in the income among the life tenants. In accordance with the prayer for relief in the counterclaim, the chancellor designated a trustee to care for and manage the real and personal property of Martin Kiesling, deceased, to distribute the net income to the life tenants or to the survivor or survivors of them, and to distribute the corpus of the personal property to the ultimate remaindermen, the nieces and nephews living at the time of the death of the testator, upon the death of the last surviving life tenant. The trustee was also to collect the rents and profits from specified portions of the real estate of George Kiesling, Sr., deceased. Plaintiffs prosecute this appeal, and defendant-appellants cross appeal. A freehold is necessarily involved.

Before analyzing the precise language of Martin Kiesling's will, it is appropriate to isolate the factors which have heretofore been held controlling in determining whether or not cross limitations will be implied. In Cheney v. Teese, 108 Ill. 473, (where cross limitations would have been implied had the question been raised, see Addicks v. Addicks, 266 Ill. 349, 357,) the testator, after giving life estates to his two surviving daughters, devised the remainder in fee to his grandchildren "share and share alike, to take possession only after the death of my said daughters." Stressing the word "only," this court held that under a proper interpretation of the will, the grandchildren could not be let into possession of the land until after the death of *both* daughters. The remainder to the grandchildren "share and share alike" obviously denoted *per capita* distribution.

In Addicks v. Addicks, 266 Ill. 349, the testator gave to his two sons "to share alike the rent and income" of certain property "during their natural lives" and "after the death of my said sons, [naming them]," directed that the property be sold and the proceeds "be equally divided between all of my grandchildren, share and share alike." Since the testator clearly must have contemplated one sale and one division of the proceeds among his grandchildren *per capita*, cross remainders for life were implied.

In Martin v. Casner, 383 Ill. 260, the will provided for the remainder of all the property to go to the surviving children of the life tenant, *per capita,* "at the death of all of" the life tenants. The court held that cross limitations were created.

It is clear from these authorities and others (Glaser v. Chicago Title and Trust Co., 393 Ill. 447; Whittaker v. Porter, 321 Ill. 368; Randolph v. Wilkinson, 294 Ill. 508; Kramer v. Sangamon Loan and Trust Co., 293 Ill. 553; Fussey v. White, 113 Ill. 637;) that the intention of the testator as to the time when the remaindermen are to come into use and possession has been the controlling element in determining whether cross limitations are to be implied. Unless from the language used it appears that the testator intended to postpone the enjoyment of the remainder until the death of all the life tenants, the terms "at their death" or "at their decease," referring to the death of the life tenants, will be construed to mean "as they respectively die." The question in each case is thus narrowed to ascertaining whether there is "language in this will which evidences an intent to postpone the enjoyment of the remainder." Martin v. Casner, 383 Ill. 260, 268.

The intention of a testator must of course be ascertained from a consideration of his entire will, and, to the extent possible, that construction must be adopted which will uphold and give effect to all the language employed. (Glaser v. Chicago Title and Trust Co. 393 Ill. 447, 456; Golstein v. Handley, 390 Ill. 118.) Here, the provisions of paragraph 3, establishing the life estates, aid but little in determining the principal issue. Plaintiffs and defendant-appellants argue that the phrases "equal shares," " 'share and share alike,' " and "their fractional part of the income, "support their view that each life tenant is to receive only the income from one sixth of the estate. But these expressions are also consistent with an intention that the testator's brothers and sisters, whatever the number living either at or after his death, should always divide the income equally. The argument that, under cross limitations, the longer-lived life tenants will receive more and thus violate this intention of equality is not persuasive; even under the alternative construction, those living the longest will enjoy greater benefits as life tenants than those less fortunate. The contention is also advanced that since eventually one brother or sister will receive all the income under cross limitations, such a construction is incompatible with the word "fractional." But a strict, technical approach to the issue is unwarranted, particularly where, as here, the testator's intention becomes apparent from other provisions of the will. Papa v. Papa, 377 Ill. 316, 320; Pollock v. Pollock, 328 Ill. 179, 192.

The fourth paragraph, since it deals with the actual division of the estate upon the death of the life tenants, is really the determinative portion of the will. This paragraph devises and bequeaths "unto my nephews and nieces 'share and share alike' the rest and residue of all my property after the life estates hereinabove provided in Paragraph Three (3) . . . have come to an end." It indicates an intention to postpone the remainder. But plaintiffs and defendant-appellants argue that just as the phrase "after or upon their death" means "upon their respective deaths," (Martin v. Casner, 383 Ill. 260; Whittaker v. Porter, 321 Ill. 368;) so here, "after the life estates . . . have come to an end," under the same authorities, means "after the respective life estates are ended." As for the phrase, "rest and residue of all my property," they point out that if the remaindermen receive one sixth as each life tenant dies, they will ultimately take all.

It is true that the will is susceptible of that interpretation; but the alternative construction is more reasonable and appears to adhere more closely to the intention of the testator. Giving proper emphasis to the phrases, "rest and residue of *all* my property" and "life estates" (Italics supplied,) the intention reflected is simply this: The testator desired that his aged brothers and sisters, whatever their number, receive the income as long as any of them lived, and that after the life estates had come to an end, all of his property should then go simultaneously to the other designated class, the nieces and nephews. Any other construction requires that the phrase "all my property" be ignored, or given a distorted and abnormal meaning. "All my property" states what is to be distributed to the nephews and nieces, and "after the life estates . . . have come to an end" states when the distribution is to be made. In our opinion the testator contemplated two classes: one, his surviving brothers and sisters who were to receive equal shares of the income so long as any lived, and, the other, his nieces and nephews who were to take the remainder. We are also of the opinion that the intention of the testator was to postpone the enjoyment of the remainder, and accordingly, cross limitations should be implied.

Another approach leads to the same result. Without question, the remainder here, being to the "nephews and nieces 'share and share alike,' " calls for a *per capita* division. (See: Beall v. Beall, 331 Ill. 28, 34; Cheney v. Teese, 108 Ill. 473, 482-483; Hardcastle v. Potter Matlock Trust Co., 215 Ky. 136, 284 S.W. 1032; Carey and Schuyler, Illinois Law of Future Interests, pp. 391-392.) The general rule is that where distribution is postponed, a class gift will comprehend all members of the class born up to the period of distribution. (Way v. Geiss, 280 Ill. 152; Dime Savings and

Trust Co. v. Watson, 254 Ill. 419; Schuknecht v. Schultz, 212 Ill. 43; Cheney v. Teese, 108 Ill. 473, 482.) Because of the possibility of the birth of new members of the class of nieces and nephews, an interpretation which would allow multiple distributions of the remainder in this case would disregard the testator's expressed intention that the remainder go to his nephews and nieces " 'share and share alike.' " The proposition has been stated generally in these terms: ". . . a determination in favor of a *per capita* division to a class in remainder requires the ambiguous words to be interpreted in favor of a single point of division upon the termination of the last of the preceding limited interests with the consequent implication of cross interests to the takers of preceding estates in the property. On the other hand, a determination that remaindermen take *per stirpes* impels no such result." (Carey and Schuyler, Illinois Law of Future Interests, p. 326.) Here, the parties agree that the interests of the remaindermen are vested, and the distribution is to be *per capita*.

Since the circuit court correctly found that distribution was to be postponed until the death of the last surviving life tenant, the latter event and not the testator's death is the critical point for determination of the class. This being so, the decree is erroneous to the extent that it found and adjudged that the remainder was to go to the nephews and nieces in existence at the time of the testator's death, *per capita*. The decree will be modified to provide that the remainder be distributed among the nephews and nieces born up to the time of the death of the last surviving life tenant, *per capita*.

The finding of cross limitations disposes of all issues concerning partition, inasmuch as the complaint requests partition only if the construction of the will denying cross limitations is adopted. Ashmore v. Hawkins, 145 Ill. 447.

The final issue is the propriety of the appointment of a trustee to invest the personal property and to manage the real estate of the testator, and to distribute the income of the life tenants and the corpus to the remaindermen upon the death of the last surviving life tenant. Defendant-appellees argue that the will itself calls for the establishment of such a trust, since it bestows the income and not the property on the life tenants and since the income is to be divided equally. A gift of income, however, is equivalent to a devise of the property and merely delineates the usual life estate. (Schmidt v. Schmidt, 292 Ill. 275, 281; Mather v. Mather, 103 Ill. 607, 613.) Equal division of the income could be accomplished by appointment of an agent to handle the real estate for the life tenants, whether such an agent be one of them or a stranger. But although the will does not create the trust, its creation is within the broad powers of a court of equity. In the trial court the two principal groups of contestants both requested the appointment of a trustee for the personal property, and, in addition, one of these factions asked for a trustee to handle the entire estate. We cannot say that the chancellor, faced with this situation, abused his judicial discretion in establishing a trust as a most effective means of administering the property until the death of the aged life tenants.

The property passing under the will of George Kiesling, Sr., to certain of his children was included in the trust. This was proper, since a construction of the will of George Kiesling, Sr., and an ascertainment of the respective interests of the parties in his estate was requested. These surviving beneficiaries under that will are also recipients as tenants in common of the income of the life estates established under Martin Kiesling's will. Partition of the land passing under the will of George Kiesling, Sr., was not sought in the event of a construction of cross limitations in the main will issue and may not therefore be properly considered here.

The decree of the circuit court of Mason County is modified by eliminating from paragraph three the phrase "in existence at the time of the testator's death," and substituting therefor the following: "born up to the time of the death of the last surviving brother or sister." The decree, as modified, is affirmed.

Decree modified and affirmed.[67]

PROBLEM

11.29. T in his will gives the residue of his estate to a trustee and directs him "to pay the net income in equal shares to A, B and C; and on the death of the survivor of A, B and C, to pay the corpus to the issue then living of A, such issue to take per stirpes." Point out the gaps in T's disposition of the residue of his estate.

5. GIFTS OVER ON DEATH WITHOUT ISSUE, GIFTS
OVER ON DEATH, AND IMPLIED GIFTS TO ISSUE

If a devise of land is made "to A and his heirs, but if A dies without issue, to B and his heirs," or "to A for life, then to B and his heirs, but if B dies without issue, to C and his heirs," the mean-

---

[67] Compare with Kiesling v. White the case of New England Trust Co. v. Watson printed in full supra page 488.

Gifts by implication are considered in 5 American Law of Property §§21.33-21.36 (Casner ed. 1952). — Ed.

ing of the words "dies without issue" becomes significant. If the governing state still recognizes the common law presumption that the words "dies without issue" connote an indefinite failure of issue, this presumption must be reckoned with in drafting a disposition that uses such words. A question is also presented, in connection with gifts over on death without issue, whether the gift over is substitutional or successive. For example, in the second illustration given above, will C take if B dies without issue at any time, or only if B dies without issue before the life tenant, or only if B dies without issue before the testator?

Other ambiguities are inherent in the words "dies without issue," such as, Is an adopted child an issue? Is an illegitimate child an issue? If the designated person has issue but dies without any issue surviving him, does he die without issue?

If a devise of land is made "to A for life, then to B and his heirs, but if B dies, to C and his heirs," is B's interest cut down to a life estate because he is certain to die? Or do the words "but if B dies" mean that his interest is to be defeated if, and only if, he dies before A?

ADAMS v. VIDAL
60 So.2d 545 (Fla. 1952)

HOBSON, Justice.

This case originated in the Circuit Court in and for Alachua County by the filing of a bill for a declaratory decree. Adolphe L. Vidal and Albert Vidal as Executors and Trustees under the will of John W. Vidal, deceased, and Milton Vidal Hodgson were plaintiffs below and Leonard Clinton Adams, Jr. and the appellants Leonard C. Adams, and Leonard C. Adams as Administrator of the Estate of Irma Vidal Adams, deceased, were defendants.

The bill sought a construction of the will of John W. Vidal, deceased, and to have determined the question whether the surviving minor nephews and niece of the testator, Milton Vidal Hodgson, Leonard Clinton Adams, Jr., and Irma Susan Adams took an absolute fee simple title to undivided interests in certain properties left to the above named Trustees to be held in trust until Leonard Clinton Adams, Jr., should arrive at the age of twenty-one years, he being the youngest of the three cestui que trustent, or whether the title of such devisees and legatees was subject to defeasance or divestment. The Trustees were directed to use the net income from the trust property for the maintenance, care and education of said nephews and nieces until the youngest of the beneficiaries and devisees arrived at twenty-one years of age when it is obvious it was the intention of the testator that the trust be terminated.

On May 21, 1945, when Leonard Clinton Adams, Jr., became twenty-one years of age, he, the other nephew and the niece were all living. Thereafter, in March, 1946, the niece, Irma Susan Adams, died intestate without spouse or issue her surviving. She was, however, survived by her mother, Irma Vidal Adams, who died intestate on or about June 27, 1950, and by her father, Leonard C. Adams, who were her sole surviving heirs at law, and her brother, Leonard Clinton Adams, Jr.

The provisions of the will which are pertinent to the determination of whether the two nephews and niece of the testator took an absolute fee simple title to the subject property on the date Leonard Clinton Adams, Jr., became twenty-one years of age, not subject to defeasance or divestment, are sub-paragraphs (e), (f), (g) and (h) of the Twelfth Article of the will. These sub-paragraphs follow:

"e. In the event Milton Vidal Hodgson, Irma Susan Adams and Leonard Clinton Adams, Jr., are each living at the time Leonard Clinton Adams, Jr. arrives at the age of twenty-one (21) years, and providing that they have each made their home and resided in Gainesville at the old home place as provided herein, then I do hereby give, devise, and bequeath all of said property under Paragraph 12 to Milton Vidal Hodgson, Irma Susan Adams and Leonard Clinton Adams, Jr. in fee simple absolute, share and share alike, or to the survivor of them, subject to conditions named in sub-paragraphs f, g, and h.

"f. In the event of the death of Milton Vidal Hodgson before marriage, or in the event of his marriage and his subsequent demise leaving no widow, children or descendants of children him surviving, then the entire interest held by Milton Vidal Hodgson shall vest in Irma Susan Adams and Leonard Clinton Adams, Jr. equally, or in the survivor of them, and if the said Irma Susan Adams and Leonard Clinton Adams, Jr. have predeceased Milton Vidal Hodgson, then the entire interest held by him shall vest in Adolphe L. Vidal and Albert Vidal, in fee simple absolute, share and share alike, if living, and if deceased, then to his or their heir or heirs.

"g. In the event of the death of Irma Susan Adams before marriage, or in the event of her marriage and her subsequent demise leaving no surviving spouse, children or descendants of children her surviving, then the entire interest held by Irma Susan Adams shall vest in Leonard Clinton Adams, Jr. and Milton Hodgson equally, or in the survivor of them, and if the said

Leonard Clinton Adams, Jr. and Milton Vidal Hodgson have pre-deceased Irma Susan Adams, then the entire interest held by her shall vest in Adolphe L. Vidal and Albert Vidal, in fee simple absolute, share and share alike, if living, and if deceased, then to his or their heir or heirs.

"h. In the event of the death of Leonard Clinton Adams, Jr. before marriage, or in the event of his marriage and his subse-quent demise leaving no widow, children or descendants of chil-dren him surviving, then the entire interest held by Leonard Clinton Adams, Jr. shall vest in Irma Susan Adams and Milton Vidal Hodgson equally or in the survivor of them, and if the said Irma Susan Adams and Milton Vidal Hodgson have pre-deceased Leonard Clinton Adams, Jr., then the entire interest held by him shall vest in Adolphe L. Vidal and Albert Vidal, in fee simple absolute, share and share alike, if living, and if deceased, then to his or their heir or heirs."

It is admitted that the two nephews and the niece of the testator made their home "at the old home place" as required by the terms of the will.

It was determined in and by the declaratory decree entered in the Circuit Court by the Judge thereof that the undivided in-terests of Milton Vidal Hodgson, Irma Susan Adams and Leonard Clinton Adams, Jr. were subject to being divested "on the death of either [sic] without spouse, children or descendants of children surviving"; that upon the death of Irma Susan Adams, it having been determined that she died "without spouse, children or de-scendants of children her surviving, the interest held by her in the trust properties inured in equal shares to Milton Vidal Hodg-son and Leonard Clinton Adams, Jr. in fee simple absolute and not subject to divestment"; and that the appellants were only entitled to an accounting for the period between the date Leonard Clinton Adams, Jr. arrived at the age of twenty-one years and the date of the death of Irma Susan Adams.

We need not, but as a convenience to the bench and bar will, cite authority for the well established principle that in construing a will the intention of the testator is the controlling factor and it should be gleaned from the four corners of the will unless the language employed by the testator is ambiguous, in which case the testimony of competent witnesses may be received and con-sidered as an aid to the court in its quest for the testator's intent. [Citations omitted.] The learned Chancellor declared in his de-cree, which was entered upon plaintiff's motion for final decree on bill and answer, that it was the testator's primary concern and intention to provide "that the several properties left in trust for his niece and nephews, Milton Vidal Hodgson, Irma Susan Adams and Leonard Clinton Adams, Jr., should pass to them or to their surviving spouses and lineal descendants, or if all three of these named beneficiaries should die without surviving spouses or lineal descendants, then to Adolphe L. Vidal and Albert Vidal or their heirs, but not to the heirs generally of Milton Vidal Hodgson, Irma Susan Adams and Leonard Clinton Adams, Jr."

We have no difficulty in agreeing that such was the testator's intent and dominant purpose.

Counsel for appellants contend the Chancellor was in error in holding that all three beneficiaries at the time Leonard Clinton Adams, Jr. became twenty-one years of age took a defeasible fee simple interest in the trust properties subject to being divested upon the death of any one of said beneficiaries without spouse, children or descendants of children him or her surviving.

It is further their view that the provisions of sub-paragraphs f, g and h of the Twelfth paragraph of the will if valid should be limited in their application to the period of time from testator's death to the date upon which Leonard Clinton Adams, Jr. became twenty-one years of age, to-wit: May 21, 1945. They also assert that the provisions of sub-paragraphs f, g, and h of Item Twelve of the will violate the rule against perpetuities and should for such reason be held to be invalid and inoperative.

Appellants' contentions are bottomed upon two conclusions with reference to the testator's intent one of which is, if indeed both are not, directly in conflict with the Chancellor's holding upon the subject of the testator's intent. The first of these erroneous conclusions is that it was the testator's primary intent and purpose to provide the "old home place" as a home for and to maintain, care for and educate his two minor nephews and his minor niece until each had attained his or her majority. The second of these conclusions which we deem to be fallacious is that the testator intended the dying without leaving spouse, children or descendants of children, the devisee surviving, was meant to be effective only if such devisee should die before Leonard Clinton Adams, Jr. became or would have become twenty-one years of age.

Although it was undoubtedly one of the testator's purposes to provide his nephews and niece with a home during the minority of each and to have them live together for such period in the milieu of the family circle, his primary concern and intent with reference to the vesting of title to the properties which he placed in trust was, as the Chancellor decreed, that such property should go to the nephews and niece or to a surviving spouse or spouses, child or children, descendant or descendants of child or children who might be living upon the death of, and survive, the beneficiaries or any one of them, or to the surviving devisee or devisees, otherwise to Adolphe L. Vidal and Albert Vidal and their heirs in fee simple absolute.

We cannot agree that the testator intended sub-paragraphs f, g and h of Item Twelve of the will to apply only in the case of the death of either nephew or the niece, or all three, before the twenty-first anniversary of the birth of Leonard Clinton Adams, Jr. The testator expressly stated that should either nephew or his niece die before marriage or without spouse, children or descendants of children him or her surviving, then the interest of the one dying would vest in the survivor or survivors. We apprehend that had he intended such provision to be effective only from the date of his death until the date upon which the youngest beneficiary or devisee became twenty-one years of age he would have said so. Moreover, his use of the words "descendants of children" is indicative of a contrary intent. John W. Vidal executed his will on September 9, 1936, and departed this life on or about November 19, 1936. Leonard Clinton Adams, Jr. became twenty-one years of age on May 21, 1945. If the testator had intended sub-paragraphs f, g and h, supra, to apply only in case of the death of either nephew or the niece before May 21, 1945, he would not have used the expression "descendants of children." Although it might have been possible, it is indeed far fetched, not to say preposterous, to assume he thought that his niece or either nephew would marry and have a child and such child, who upon May 21, 1945 could not have been more than seven and a fraction years of age, would have married and have become a parent.

Consequently, we hold the view that the testator intended sub-paragraphs f, g and h, supra, to apply both prior and subsequent to May 21, 1945 and that the property which was the subject of the trust should ultimately vest in fee simple absolute in a spouse or spouses, child or children or descendants of children who might survive one or all of the beneficiaries or devisees and if there be no surviving spouse or spouses and in the event of a definite failure of issue upon the death of all three first takers or devisees the entire trust property should finally so vest in Adolphe L. Vidal and Albert Vidal or his or their heirs.

We now give our attention to the remaining pertinent question, whether the provisions of sub-paragraphs f, g and h, supra, violate the rule against perpetuities or, more accurately speaking, the rule against remoteness or remote vesting of an estate or interest therein. This rule, as has ofttimes been stated, is a restraint on the right to create future interests, or in a broad sense a limitation upon the jus disponendi of property. We have defined the rule against perpetuities as being that an estate or interest in order to be good must vest within the period of life or lives in being at testator's death or within twenty-one years thereafter with the term of gestation added in case of posthumous birth. [Citations omitted.]

The old English, many of the early American and some modern decisions disclose a definite leaning toward the view that since the law favors early vesting of estates, an executory limitation must contain language which expressly declares the testator's intent that the failure of issue take place at the expiration of the life of the first taker, otherwise the expressions "die without issue," "die leaving no issue" or words of similar import should be construed as connoting an indefinite failure of issue. These cases track the common law which favors the presumption of an indefinite failure of issue construction in the absence of an expressed intent to the contrary. This rule of the common law has not been abrogated by statute in this jurisdiction, hence it is in full force and effect. So it is we must determine whether the language used by the testator in the will now before us when considered in the light of the testator's dominant purpose and plan of distribution of his estate, is sufficient to overcome the presumption raised by the common law. See Russ v. Russ, 9 Fla. 105, 106; In re Miller's Estate, 145 Pa. 561, 22 A. 1044; Armstrong v. Douglass, 89 Tenn. 219, 14 S.W. 604, 10 L.R.A. 85; A.L.I. Restatement, Property Sec. 266. If we give an indefinite failure of issue construction to sub-paragraphs f, g and h they must be stricken down and declared void as being violative of the rule against perpetuities or remoteness.[68]

A judicious contemplation of the entire will of John W. Vidal, deceased, of his dominant purpose and plan of distribution, convinces us that he intended the expression "descendants of children *him [or her]* surviving" to mean descendants of children in esse at the time of the death of each of the first takers or devisees. As we construe the will, the testator had in mind a definite rather than an indefinite failure of issue. The words "him [or her] surviving"

[68] In 1936, when John W. Vidal died, Florida Revised Statutes (1920) §3616 provided: ". . . no real estate shall be entailed in this State." The present corresponding section (Fla. Stat. §689.14 (1959)) reads as follows: "No property, real or personal, shall be entailed in this state. Any instrument purporting to create an estate tail, express or implied, shall be deemed to create an estate for life in the first taker with remainder per stirpes to the lineal descendants of the first taker in being at the time of his death. If the remainder fails for want of such remainderman, then it shall vest in any other remaindermen designated in such instrument, or, if there is no such designation, then it shall revert to the original donor or to his heirs." If the present wording of the Florida statute had applied to the will of John W. Vidal, would the statement in the opinion to which this note is appended be correct? — Ed.

when considered in the light of the testator's plan or scheme with reference to the disposition of his estate clearly signify a testamentary intent that the failure of issue must occur at a precise time, i.e. upon the death of each of the first takers or devisees. Indeed, these words alone would ordinarily be sufficient to justify such an interpretation unless a definite failure of issue construction should be clearly inconsistent with the testator's dominant purpose and plan of distribution.

Having determined that the testator intended a definite failure of issue, we are unable to envisage the possibility of a situation developing which could cause the vesting of the subject property in fee simple absolute at a time beyond lives in being and twenty-one years thereafter; nor has counsel for appellants demonstrated that such a situation might possibly arise. Should Milton Vidal Hodgson die without having married and without leaving a spouse, children or descendants of children him surviving and thereafter Leonard Clinton Adams, Jr. should also die without having married and without leaving a spouse, children or descendants of children him surviving, the subject property would vest in fee simple absolute in Adolphe L. Vidal and Albert Vidal or his or their heir or heirs. The fee simple title to the entire property will surely vest absolutely in some one within the period of lives in being and twenty-one years thereafter.

Counsel for both appellants and all of the appellees except Leonard Clinton Adams, Jr., are of the opinion the Chancellor erred in holding that upon the death of Irma the two nephews, Milton and Leonard, Jr., became vested share and share alike with her interest in the trust property in fee simple absolute and not subject to divestment. We are forced to agree that such holding is inconsistent with the testator's intent as declared by the Chancellor, to-wit: "that *the several properties left in trust* for his niece and nephews Milton Vidal Hodgson, Irma Susan Adams and Leonard Clinton Adams, Jr., should pass to them or to their surviving spouses and lineal descendants, or if all three of these named beneficiaries should die without surviving spouses or lineal descendants, *then to Adolphe L. Vidal and Albert Vidal or their heirs,* but not to the heirs generally of Milton Vidal Hodgson, Irma Susan Adams and Leonard Clinton Adams, Jr." (Italics supplied.)

To hold, as did the Chancellor, that Milton and Leonard, Jr. became vested share and share alike with Irma's interest in the trust property in fee simple absolute not subject to divestment would surely disrupt and defeat the primary intent and object of the testator. Such determination would lead inevitably to the conclusion as a matter of law that the share of Irma's interest which went to each of the nephews would, upon their deaths, descend under the law of descent and distribution to their heirs generally or pass to those devisees who might be named by them in their wills and "the *entire* interest held by" (Italics supplied) each would not vest in the survivor, or if none "in Adolphe L. Vidal and Albert Vidal in fee simple absolute, share and share alike, if living, and if deceased then to his or their heir or heirs," in the event neither nephew left a spouse, children or descendants of children him surviving. Assuredly, such was not the testator's intent. Moreover, we find nothing in the will to justify even an assumption that the testator had in mind a different plan or scheme of distribution with reference to any portion of the properties that might go to a surviving beneficiary or beneficiaries from that which he had with respect to the original one-third of the trust property which was devised to each cestui que trust.

We do not deem it necessary to discuss other contentions of appellants because we find them to be devoid of merit.

We conclude that the decree from which this appeal was prosecuted should be affirmed except insofar as it held that the interest of Irma, which upon divestment went to Milton and Leonard, Jr., share and share alike, vested in them in fee simple absolute not subject to divestment.

Affirmed in part and reversed in part.

SEBRING, C.J., and TERRELL, CHAPMAN, THOMAS, ROBERTS and MATHEWS, JJ., concur.[69]

PROBLEM

11.30. In a jurisdiction in which the rule in Shelley's Case is in force, A devises land as follows: "To B for life, then to B's issue,

[69] See the following references in 5 American Law of Property (Casner ed. 1952) which deal with the various aspects of gifts over on death without issue: §§21.49 and 21.50 (difference between indefinite failure of issue and definite failure of issue, and the modern status of the common law presumption in favor of indefinite failure of issue); §§21.51-21.54 (substitutional gift construction of contrasted with the successive gift construction); §21.55 (whether death without issue means without having had issue or without issue surviving). See also 3 Restatement of Property §§265-271.

Statutes which abolish the common law presumption in favor of indefinite failure of issue and thus set up a presumption in favor of definite failure of issue have been widely adopted. For example, see Mass. Ann. Laws, c. 184, §6, quoted infra page 1445. Hayes v. Hammond, 336 Mass. 233, 143 N.E.2d 693 (1957), illustrates the operation of the presumption in favor of indefinite failure of issue where the dispositive instrument is not governed by the Massachusetts statute because of the early date of the execution of the instrument.

Usually the statutes do not undertake to deal with the substitutional or successive gift problem. See, however, Neb. Rev. Stat. §76-111 (1943), quoted infra page 1466, which does deal with this problem.

but if B dies without issue, to C and his heirs." A dies. What estates in the land are created by A's will? See 5 American Law of Property §21.57 (Casner ed. 1952).

HARRIS TRUST AND SAVINGS BANK
v. JACKSON
412 Ill. 261, 106 N.E.2d 188 (1952)

Mr. Justice Schaefer delivered the opinion of the court:

The Harris Trust and Savings Bank, as trustee, under the will of Howard B. Jackson, brought an action in the circuit court of Cook County seeking a construction of the will and a determination of certain questions which had arisen upon the termination of the trust. Lou B. Jackson, widow of a nephew of the testator, and Suzanne and Audrey Jackson, granddaughters of the nephew and great grandnieces of the testator, prosecute this appeal from the ensuing decree. A freehold is necessarily involved.

Howard B. Jackson died testate on January 19, 1923. He was survived by his widow, Florence, his brother, Frank G. Jackson, and his nephew, Arthur S. Jackson. The questions presented concern the ultimate disposition of the trust assets. The will directed the trustee, upon the cessation of two prior life estates, to transfer and deliver the assets to the testator's nephew, Arthur S. Jackson, or if he be dead, as in fact he was, then to his lawful heirs. The issues are: (1) whether the gift over upon Arthur's death refers to his death before that of the last surviving life tenant rather than to his death before that of the testator, and, (2) if so, whether Arthur's "lawful heirs" include his widow.

The case turns upon the construction of paragraph 4 of the will, which provided: "If either my wife, Florence May Jackson, or my brother, Frank G. Jackson, shall survive me, then I give, devise and bequeath to Harris Trust and Savings Bank . . . as Trustee, all of the property, real, personal or mixed, which I may own at my death . . . to be held on the following trusts . . . : (a) All of the income from the trust estate shall be paid to my wife, Florence May Jackson, if she be alive, for and during the remainder of her lifetime, and from and after her death (or from and after my death if my said wife dies before I do) it shall be paid to my brother, Frank G. Jackson, for and during the remainder of his lifetime. . . . (b) On the death of my said wife, Florence May Jackson, if she survive my said brother, Frank G. Jackson, or upon the death of my said brother, if he survives my said wife, the trust shall cease and terminate and the principal thereof with any accumulated income shall be transferred and delivered by my Trustee to my nephew, Arthur S. Jackson, or if he be dead, then to his lawful heirs." By paragraph 5, the testator provided: "If neither my said wife, nor my said brother survive me, then I give, devise and bequeath all my property . . . to my said nephew, Arthur S. Jackson, and if he also be dead, then to the heirs at law of said Arthur S. Jackson."

The testator's wife, Florence, and his brother, Frank, both survived him so that the trust became effective and the trustee entered upon its duties and paid the income to Florence Jackson during her lifetime. Florence died on June 5, 1946, six years after the death of the brother, Frank Jackson. Her death thus became the event fixed by the testator for the termination of the trust and the distribution of its assets under paragraph 4(b). Arthur, however, was also dead, his death having occurred on September 28, 1933. He was survived by his widow, Lou B. Jackson, and a son, Arthur S. Jackson, Jr. The latter died intestate on June 3, 1942, leaving as his only heirs-at-law his two daughters, Suzanne and Audrey Jackson.

In the action brought by the trustee, Suzanne and Audrey Jackson, and Lou B. Jackson argued that Arthur S. Jackson, to receive the trust assets under paragraph 4(b), had to survive the last life tenant and therefore, under the substitutionary provision of the paragraph the trustee is required to deliver the principal and accumulated income to those persons who come within the classification "lawful heirs" of Arthur. Lou B. Jackson further urged that she falls within that classification under the amendment to the Illinois law of descent which became effective on June 30, 1923, even though the will was executed and the testator died prior to that date. On the other hand, the administrator of the estate of Florence Jackson contended that Arthur, having survived the testator, took an absolutely vested remainder, and hence the trust assets should be transferred to Arthur's estate and not to his lawful heirs.

Evidence was taken by a master in chancery and the cause then heard by the chancellor upon exceptions to his report. The chancellor entered a decree confirming the master's recommendation and holding that Arthur S. Jackson, "because he survived the testator, acquired an irrevocably vested interest in the corpus of the trust." The decree entered therefore directed the trustee to deliver the trust assets to Lou B. Jackson, as executrix of the will of Arthur S. Jackson. From that decree this appeal has been taken.

The chancellor also found that the remainder limited to Arthur was vested, subject to being divested. This finding was correct. (Storkan v. Ziska, 406 Ill. 259; Smith v. Shepard, 370 Ill. 491).

The critical consideration is the effect of the language of divestiture employed by the will. Does the reference to the death of Arthur contemplate only his death at a time prior to the testator's death or does it refer to his death prior to the death of the last life tenant? In a written opinion, the chancellor deemed the answer to be clear because of two recent decisions of this court, assertedly establishing the rule that where there are substitutionary gifts in remainder after limited intermediate gifts, the death of the primary remainderman is referable to a time prior to that of the testator, and, therefore, if the primary remainderman survives the testator, the property belongs to him absolutely. Three cases, Knight v. Pottgieser, 176 Ill. 368, Murphy v. Westhoff, 386 Ill. 136, and Peadro v. Peadro, 400 Ill. 482, are cited to support this proposition, but since the holding of the Knight case is subject to considerable doubt, (Warrington v. Chester, 294 Ill. 524, 528-529; Carey and Schuyler, Illinois Law of Future Interests, p. 259,) it was upon the latter two decisions that the trial court placed reliance, stating: ". . . Murphy v. Westhoff and Peadro v. Peadro, supra, left no doubt that the [above] rule was one of general application and freed it from all supposed restrictions. The reason for such a result cannot be predicated so much upon interpretation, as it can upon the policy of the law to make future interests irrevocably vested at the earliest possible moment."

The cardinal rule of testamentary construction to which all other rules must yield is to ascertain the intention of the testator from the will itself and to effectuate this intention, unless contrary to some established rule of law or public policy. (Vollmer v. McGowan, 409 Ill. 306, 311.) However difficult its application may be in particular fact situations, this statement is no empty platitude. Rules of construction, such as the one urged by appellee and adopted by the chancellor, govern only where the language of the will is so ambiguous as to place the testator's intention in doubt. Trabue v. Gillham, 408 Ill. 508; Storkan v. Ziska, 406 Ill. 259.

The case last cited is illuminating. A trust agreement after requiring the trustee to pay over the income to the settlor during his life and after his death in equal shares to his five named children, specified that the trust estate was to be divided among the children in the event the property held in trust was not sold within twenty-one years after the settlor's death. Then followed a provision that "And in case of the death of any of said children, then such shares [of the estate] coming to such deceased child or children shall descend to the heirs of such deceased child or children." After the death of the settlor but before the expiration of the twenty-one years, one of the settlor's children, Adela, died leaving all her property by will to certain beneficiaries. The trial court held that Adela, having survived the testator, had an indefeasibly vested interest which passed under her will, and the Appellate Court affirmed, relying upon the rule of construction supposedly laid down in Murphy v. Westhoff, 386 Ill. 136, and Peadro v. Peadro, 400 Ill. 482. Upon further appeal, this court reversed, observing: "The same rules of construction used in regard to wills are alike applicable to the construction of trust agreements. . . . The question then of paramount importance is the settlor's intention. This seems to be the general purpose, rather than to determine which technical rule of construction can be applied to the facts and adopted regardless of the stated and apparent intention and desire of the settlor. . . . If the intention may be gathered from its language without reference to rules of construction, there is no occasion to use the latter. Where the use of rules as a presumed intention so twist and warp the evident meaning of a will as to render it ambiguous or unreasonable, and when, on the other hand, the words used in their ordinary sense are plain and their meaning clear, construction demands the use of the plain intention over the presumed intention, which is fixed by rules used only where the actual intent cannot be ascertained." Since the court found that the language of the trust instrument clearly directed that in the event one of the named children should die before the termination of the trust, that child's share should go to his or her heirs, the decree of the trial court and the judgment of the Appellate Court were reversed.

While the language of the two instruments involved is, of course, different, the analogy between the Storkan case and the instant one is obvious. Here, also, the intent of the testator is so clearly expressed as to completely negate the application of any technical rules of construction. This is apparent from the scheme of the will. Paragraph 4(a) and paragraph 5 are concerned with events at the death of the testator; the provision at issue — paragraph 4(b) — covers the subsequent situation, — what is to occur on the death of the life tenants. In such a scheme, the phrase "or if he [Arthur] be dead," cannot logically be separated from the key words introducing the sentence, "On the death of [the life tenants]." These words fix the time for termination of the trust; they fix also the time for Arthur's interest to take effect in possession. The duty of the trustee is specified — to deliver the assets to Arthur, "or if he be dead, then to his lawful heirs." In this language there is no intimation that the trustee, having ascertained that Arthur is dead, must make further inquiry as to the date of his death, and must then correlate that date with the date of the testator's death. Any such suggestion must come from a source other than the words of the testator. This conclusion is fortified by the fact that the language of the will demonstrates that the testator knew how to correlate the death of a beneficiary with his own death. Thus, in paragraph 4(a) he employs the phrase, "If my said wife dies before I do." That the termination of the trust is the pivotal feature of paragraph 4(b) is of further significance upon examination of the court's opinion in Murphy v. Westhoff, 386, 136, relied upon so heavily by appellee. It was there noted, as a major basis for distinguishing Smith v. Shepard, 370 Ill. 491, "that the will in that case [Smith v. Shepard] provided for the disposition of that portion of the estate remaining at the death of his [the testator's] wife and that the time of the division was the death of the wife." In view of the foregoing factors, we are of the opinion that, as in the Storkan case, "it is unnecessary to resort to technical rules of construction to ascertain the intent" of the testator because the testator has plainly and clearly directed that in the event of Arthur's death before that of the last life tenant, the trust estate should go to Arthur's lawful heirs.

While it becomes unnecessary to consider the application of Murphy v. Westhoff, 386 Ill. 136, and Peadro v. Peadro, 400 Ill. 482, it is apparent from the history and development of this case and of the Storkan case that the law has become unsettled on the point here involved. (Carey and Schuyler, Illinois Law of Future Interests, Cumulative Pocket Part (1947), pp. 104-107, 80-81; 13 Ill. Law Review 859, 861; 1949 Ill. Law Forum 530; 37 Ill. Bar Journal, 266.). Since this is so, we deem it appropriate to state that the scope of Murphy v. Westhoff and Peadro v. Peadro is limited to their particular factual situations, and that the rule, as laid down in Burlet v. Burlet, 246 Ill. 563, and Smith v. Shepard, 370 Ill. 491, is still the law in this field, i.e., ". . . when a gift over is preceded by a particular estate the gift over will usually take effect if the contingency happens at any time during the period of the particular estate." (Smith v. Shepard, at p. 495.) Therefore, unless a contrary intent appears from the language of the will, in cases where the gifts are substitutionary, "death" is referable to that point of time when the first gift takes effect in possession, and the first taker must survive to that time. The argument that there is no contingency in the instant situation because the death of the primary remainderman is certain to occur ignores what is obviously the controlling consideration, — the sequence of deaths among the life tenants and the primary remainderman, which is not at all certain.

The remaining issue for consideration is whether Arthur Jackson's "lawful heirs" included his widow. The word "heirs" is a technical word with a fixed legal meaning when used in a will, and, unless controlled by or inconsistent with the context, must be interpreted according to its strict legal meaning. When thus construed it includes and designates all those persons, whether many or few, upon whom the law would cast the inheritance in case of intestacy. Dillman v. Dillman, 409 Ill. 494; Richards v. Miller, 62 Ill. 417.

At the time of the testator's death and for some years before, a surviving spouse could be a "lawful heir" with respect to personalty, even though there were also children surviving. (Walker v. Walker, 283 Ill. 11.) However, prior to 1923, the widow did not inherit any portion of the real estate where there were surviving children, but took an estate of dower. The Statute of Descent was amended in 1923 (Laws of 1923, p. 325,) to provide that where an intestate died leaving a widow and also a child or children, the widow was to receive as her absolute estate, in lieu of dower, one third of the personal property and one third of each parcel of real estate in which dower was waived. While the estate is not immediately vested by law, it may become vested if the widow so chooses and manifests her choice by failing to elect to take dower within the statutory period. She is to be considered as an heir, because her own act determines whether or not she has that status. Dillman v. Dillman, 409 Ill. 494; Bundy v. Solon, 384 Ill. 137.

We come thus to the question whether the scope of the phrase "lawful heirs" is to be determined at the death of the testator, six months before the 1923 amendment became effective, or at the time of Arthur Jackson's death in 1933. It seems clear that the testator, having employed the phrase in its technical sense, was saying, in effect, "Now let the law take its course." Had he desired a particular group as defined by the statute then in effect to be the recipients of the gift over, he could easily have so specified. The reasonable inference is that, absent a contrary intent of the testator as shown by additional language or circumstances, the law of intestacy in force at the death of the named ancestor, here Arthur Jackson, was intended. (Butterfield v. Sawyer, 187 Ill. 598; see, Casner, 53 Harv. Law Rev. 207, 214, 228, and cases there cited.) In this case, therefore, since Lou B. Jackson failed to elect to take dower within the statutory period she falls within the classification "lawful heirs."

The decree of the circuit court of Cook County is reversed and the cause remanded, with directions to enter a decree in accordance with the views expressed in this opinion.

Reversed and remanded, with directions.[70]

In re ROUSE'S ESTATE
369 Pa. 568, 87 A.2d 281 (1952)

ALLEN M. STEARNE, Justice.

This appeal relates to a will construction. The question is whether there is an implied gift of corpus to testator's two minor great-grandchildren or whether there is a partial *intestacy*. Appellant is the widow of testator's grandson (claiming as executrix under the will of her husband, the grandson, and in her individual right), and appellees are the testamentary guardians of her two minor children. The Orphans' Court of Philadelphia County decreed that the corpus amounting to $1,222,123.53 passed to the minor children. The appeal followed.

Josiah G. Rouse, testator, died February 21, 1926. His will, which was duly probated, is dated June 2, 1903. At his death his grandson, Josiah Rouse Burns, was his sole heir.

By the will testator placed the residue of his estate in trust. The dispositive provisions relating to his residuary estate are contained in the sixth item, which he divided into four numbered clauses. The first clause relates to the care of the cemetery lot, while the second has to do with the maintenance of the family home during the widow's life, neither of which affect the present appeal.

The objects of testator's bounty as specified in clauses three and four are: his wife, Sabra G. Rouse; his wife's sister, Julia Swanton; his grandson, Josiah Rouse Burns; his grandson's "child or children or issue of deceased child or children" (hereafter termed issue) and the Grand Lodge of Free and Accepted Masons of the Jurisdiction of Pennsylvania (hereafter termed Masonic Lodge).

The testamentary scheme, for the present purpose, may be summarized as follows: the trustees were directed to divide the net income into eight equal parts; his wife Sabra was given the income from six of the eight shares for life; the sister-in-law Julia was given the income from one of the eight shares for her life; and the remaining eighth share of income was given to the grandson, Josiah Rouse Burns, for his life. Testator contemplated and pro-

---

[70] For a comment on Harris Trust and Savings Bank v. Jackson, see 1952 U. of Ill. L.F. 456. Gifts over on death as distinguished from gifts over on death without issue are examined in 5 American Law of Property §§21.58-21.61 (Casner ed. 1952). See also 3 Restatement of Property §§263, 264. — ED.

vided against the deaths of his wife, his sister-in-law and grandson in their various lifetimes, as well as the death of the grandson with and without leaving issue. We need not recite in detail these elaborate testamentary provisions. Testator's wife and sister-in-law predeceased him. The grandson survived and received the entire net income until his decease on September 19, 1949. The grandson left issue, two minor children, the appellees. He died testate and, as above stated, his widow (appellant) claims seven-eighths share of the corpus, as executrix and in her individual right.

It is apparent what disposition testator intended concerning the corpus of the residuary trust estate following the decease of the grandson. The narrow question is whether the words which he employed accomplished such purpose.

As to one-eighth share there is no question. Upon the death of the grandson, the life tenant, the remainder is given to his "child or children and issue of deceased child or children then living."

As testator's sister-in-law Julia predeceased him, the income on the eighth share given to her was bequeathed and was paid to the grandson for life. It was only in case the grandson died in the lifetime of Julia that the grandson's issue were given the corpus of this share. As this event did not occur we need not consider other provisions respecting this share.

By the fourth clause testator provided for the disposition of the corpus of the remaining shares of the residuary trust estate in the event that the grandson survived testator's wife and sister-in-law. He employed the following language: "In the event of my said grandson, Josiah Rouse Burns, surviving my said wife and the said Julia Swanton [which he did] and then dying without leaving child or children or issue of deceased child or children him surviving . . . to the [Masonic Lodge]. . . ."

It is a well established canon of will construction that where there is a gift to A for life, and if A dies without issue then to B, this constitutes an implied gift to A's issue, should A leave any such issue; Estate of Noble, 182 Pa. 188, 37 A. 852; Beilstein v. Beilstein, 194 Pa. 152, 45 A. 73; In re Lippincott's Estate, 276 Pa. 283, 120 A. 136; In re List's Estate, 283 Pa. 255, 129 A. 64; In re Clayton's Estate, 302 Pa. 468, 153 A. 742; In re Murray's Estate, 313 Pa. 359, 169 A. 103; In re Cope's Estate, 353 Pa. 306, 45 A.2d 52; In re Africa's Estate, 359 Pa. 567, 59 A.2d 925. It is upon this principle that the guardians of the minor children claim the corpus, and upon which it was awarded to them by the court below. The executrix under the will of the grandson, who was testator's sole heir, contends, upon the contrary, that such gift being merely implied, constitutes but an inference or presumption, which may be rebutted as any other presumption. Regarding the will from its four corners, it is urged that such presumption is rebutted and that an intestacy results. To rebut such implied gift, appellant points to the fact that when testator devised and bequeathed a one-eighth share of the corpus to such children he did so by a specific grant to the children or their issue in plain and unequivocal language. Also he employed the same language in two other instances in case of the death of the grandson leaving issue (1) prior to the death of testator's wife and (2) prior to the death of the sister-in-law. It is therefore urged with great vigor that when testator devised and bequeathed the seven-eighths share of the corpus he gave it to the Masonic Lodge only in the event that the grandson left no issue; that he made no gift to issue in case the grandson left issue. Because of the absence of such express grant to the issue, it is urged that this constituted an omission, which was either intentional or accidental, which in either case resulted in an intestacy.

First considering whether there was an intentional omission, resulting in intestacy, there is a presumption testator intends to dispose of his whole estate. Such presumption, however, is met by an equally potent presumption that an heir is not to be disinherited except by plain words or necessary implication. The effect of the conflict of rules is well stated by Judge Hunter in his Pennsylvania Orphans' Court Commonplace Book, Vol. 2, Wills, sec. 4(b), p. 1436, in the following language: "These presumptions are of like force and effect, and in applying one we must not overlook the other. Neither presumption, however, can be permitted to defeat the intention of the testator which is expressed in apt words or appears by clear implication." See In re Grothe's Estate, 229 Pa. 186, 78 A. 88; In re French's Estate, 292 Pa. 37, 140 A. 549; In re Loving's Estate, 159 Pa. Super. 339, 48 A.2d 39. This language does not reveal an express intent by testator to die intestate as to this portion of the trust corpus.

We do not subscribe to the conjecture of the court in banc that "the absence of express language as to the event which occurred as an oversight of the scrivener." If there were an omission, such omission might not be remedied by judicial construction. In re Grothe's Estate, supra, Justice Mestrezat said, 229 Pa. at page 192, 78 A. at page 90 ". . . if it was an oversight, the courts have no authority to insert a provision . . . under the assumption that it was the intention of the testator. It is only when the language of the will expressly or by clear implication discloses the intention of the testator that the courts may carry it out. It will not do for the courts to undertake to guess at the intention of a testator and declare that to be his will. If he sees fit for any reason not to dispose of any part of his estate, or such is the result of ignorance or oversight, the courts cannot supply the gap or hiatus and reconstruct the will. To do so would be a perversion of the functions of the court and deprive a testator of the right to dispose of his property." See: In re Morrison's Will, 361 Pa. 419, 65 A.2d 384, and cases therein cited.

As we construe this will, there is no sound basis for the contention that there was an omission which was either intentional or accidental. A testator is not required to employ the same words or use the same phraseology in expressing the same testamentary design, even in the same document. In devising and bequeathing the one-eighth share the grandson and his children were the sole objects of testator's consideration. The same exclusive consideration is apparent when he contemplated the possibility of his grandson predeceasing testator's wife and sister-in-law. However, when testator was disposing of the seven-eighths share, he was not only considering the grandson and his issue but he was also providing for his wife and sister-in-law. It was only in this connection that testator contemplated the possibility of his grandson dying without issue. In that event, but in that event only, did he pass the corpus to the Masonic Lodge. It would, of course, have removed all possible doubt had testator said in unambiguous language that upon the death of the grandson, his children or their issue should take the remainder, but if the grandson left no such children, then the corpus should pass to the Masonic Lodge. We see no difference in the use of the language which testator did employ in so expressing his intent. Such testamentary provision discloses a clear and unequivocal implication, which is not substantially rebutted, that testator passed the entire residuary trust estate to the children and issue of his grandson — life tenant. There is no other language in the will which could be fairly held to demonstrate a contrary intent. We agree with the court below that In re Cope's Estate, 353 Pa. 306, 45 A.2d 52, rules the present will construction.

Decree affirmed. Costs to be paid from the estate.[71]

6. CHILD IN GESTATION

The terms of a dispositive instrument in an estate plan should specify the extent to which a child in gestation which is later

[71] Whether a remainder will be implied in favor of the life tenant's issue when the only gift following the life interest is a gift to others if the life tenant dies without issue is discussed in 5 American Law of Property §21.34 (Casner ed. 1952). See also 3 Restatement of Property §272. — ED.

born alive is to be regarded as a child in being during the period of gestation. For example, if T in his will gives the residue of his estate to a trustee and directs him "to pay the net income to A for life and on A's death to distribute the corpus to A's issue then living, such issue to take per stirpes, and if no issue of A is then living, to distribute the corpus to the X charity," and if A dies after T, leaving no issue born but leaving a child of his in gestation, does such a child when born alive take under the gift "to A's issue then living," or is no issue of A then living, so that the gift over to the X charity takes effect? [72]

PROBLEM

11.31. T in his will provides that "a child in gestation, which child is later born alive, shall be regarded in this will as a child in being during the period of gestation." Comment on the appropriateness and adequacy of such a provision.

7. LEGAL FUTURE INTERESTS

The property with which an estate plan will normally deal consists of tangible personal property, land, income-producing personal property such as stocks and bonds, and cash. If the income-producing personal property is not given outright to designated beneficiaries, it is usually placed in trust because the trust offers the best managerial arrangement for the property, and consequently future interests in the property are normally equitable.

Legal future interests in land, that is, the reversion, the right of entry, the possibility of reverter, the remainder (indefeasibly vested, vested subject only to partial divestiture, vested subject to complete divestiture, or contingent) and the executory interest (springing or shifting), have been a significant part of land law for centuries.[73] There are many situations presented in estate

---

[72] As to whether a child in gestation at the period of distribution is included in a class gift, see 5 American Law of Property §§22.42-22.46 (Casner ed. 1952); as to whether a child in gestation defeats a gift over on death without issue, see id. §21.56.

In some states statutes exist which deal specifically with the rights of a child in gestation under dispositive instruments. See, for example, N.Y. Real Property Law §56, quoted infra page 1469, which provides that where a future interest is limited to a group, a posthumous child shall be entitled to take in the same manner as if living on the death of his parent, and that a divesting contingency shall not be deemed to have occurred where it is dependent on the death of a person without issue if a posthumous child of such person comes into the picture.

[73] Familiarity with the historical background of the development of legal

planning where their use may be appropriate. Whenever a legal future interest is employed, however, it will usually be highly desirable to spell out a detailed list of powers which may be exercised by the owner of the present interest for the benefit of himself and the owners of the legal future interests. In this way, an administrative mechanism is provided during the period of divided ownership of the legal title.

The enjoyment of tangible personal property is in its physical use and consequently such property, except in unusual situations, should be given outright or in the form of successive legal interests.

UNDERWOOD v. UNDERWOOD

162 Ala. 553, 50 So. 305 (1909)

MAYFIELD, J. — This was a bill filed by a remainderman as to personal property, to require an account of the items and value of the property received by the life tenant under the will of the testator, which also vested a remainder in the complainant, and prayed that all of said property, or such of it as should be, be sold and converted into cash in order to secure to orator, as remainderman, his rights under the fifth clause of the will, and that the use of the property not sold, and the interest of the proceeds of that sold, be secured to the life tenant, and that the property not sold and the net proceeds of that sold be secured to orator as remainderman. The life tenant, who was the wife of the testator (the complainant, remainderman, being the son of the testator), interposed demurrers to the original bill, which were sustained upon a hearing, with leave to amend on the 9th day of August, 1907. On the 20th day of August, 1907, in response to a request, the court assigned definite grounds for sustaining the demurrers. The order states that each and every ground of the demurrer is well taken, except the one which recites that the allegations of the bill are merely a statement of the conclusions of the pleader. Complainant amended his bill on the 30th day of August, 1907, and to the amended bill the respondent again interposed her demurrers, upon the same grounds interposed to the original, and certain additional grounds. This demurrer was heard on the 7th day of September, 1907. The demurrer was sustained by the court, and the complainant was allowed until the first day of the next term in which to amend his bill. On the 24th day of Octo-

---

future interests in land is essential to a thorough understanding of the subject. In this regard, see Casner and Leach, Cases and Text on Property 247-270 (1950, with 1959 Supplement); 1 American Law of Property §§1.1-1.50 (Casner ed. 1952).

ber complainant applied for an appeal and gave security for the costs, and notice of the appeal was on the same day issued by the register and served upon the respondent. On the 13th day of November, 1907, the judge of the court set aside or annulled the order allowing an appeal from the decree on demurrer, on the ground that it was taken after the lapse of 30 days, and, the complainant standing by his bill and declining to amend, the judge dismissed the bill out of the court and taxed the complainant with the costs. From this decree of dismissal the appeal is taken, and complainant here asigns as error the sustaining of the demurrers to the original bill and to the amended bill and the dismissing of the bill without prejudice.

The appellee moves to dismiss the appeal for that it was not taken within the time required by law, in that the first appeal allowed by the register was more than 30 days after the sustaining of the demurrer, and for that, after this appeal was taken, the judge or chancellor had no power or authority to make any further orders or to set aside the appeal allowed by the register. It requires no argument or authority to show that, if the first appeal is the only one shown by the record, it should be dismissed, because it is upon a decree on demurrer and was taken more than 30 days from the rendition of the decree; but, of course, no appeal could be taken at the time the attempt was made by the complainant and the register to perfect the appeal. It was wholly void because not authorized. The trial court, or this court, could not give or accord it any validity, and there was nothing improper in the trial court's disregarding it. Consequently the appeal is taken from the decree of November 13, 1907.

It does not appear that any application was made by the complainant to be allowed to further amend; but it is affirmatively shown that he declined so to do. It likewise does not appear that he requested that the bill be dismissed without prejudice or upon the motion of the complainant; all that the record shows being that the complainant had failed to amend his bill from the 7th day of September, 1907, until the 13th day of November, 1907, and that he was allowed time within which to amend his bill, when the demurrer was sustained. There was no other course open to the trial court than to dismiss the bill; the demurrer having been sustained, and the complainant declining to amend. We find no error in any of the orders or decrees of the trial court in this matter. The bill, we think, is wholly insufficient as one upon which to grant the relief prayed, or any other relief, so far as its allegations show.

It is true, as stated by this court in the case of Bethea v. Bethea,

116 Ala. 271, 22 South. 563 (quoting from the language of Mr. Justice Story), that: "Where there is a future right of enjoyment of personal property, courts of equity will now interpose and grant relief upon a bill quia timet, where there is any danger of loss or deterioration, or injury to it in the hands of the party who is entitled to the present possession" — citing a number of Alabama cases. We cannot agree with counsel for the appellant that the case made by this bill is as strong as, or stronger than, any of the cases referred to. It appears from the bill that the testator was the husband of the life tenant and the father of the remainderman, and that, after disposing of his real estate by the fourth item of his will, he gave all his personal property to his wife, the respondent, during her life, and at her death, to complainant, her son. The language of the will is as follows: "Item 4. I further hereby will to my wife, Piety J. Underwood, for her use and benefit during her life, all of my personal property including horses, mules, cattle, hogs, wagons, buggy, etc., and all household and kitchen furniture, and at her death said personal property I will to my son, William H. Underwood."

The bill contains an inventory of the property, which is made an exhibit, which shows one mule, one horse, cow and calf, a wagon, a buggy, and harness, from $125 to $140 in cash, the proceeds of the sale of cotton raised upon the lands, cotton seed, plow tools, 50 bushels or more of corn, fodder, etc., a watch and chain, and household and kitchen furniture. It clearly appears that it was the intention of the testator that his wife should have the use of this property during her life, and that if anything remained at her death it would go to the complainant or remainderman. To sell this property and allow the wife the interest only would entirely defeat the purpose of the will; while to require her to give bond or security for the same, to the remainderman, to secure his rights under the will, might entirely deprive her of any benefit to be derived from the property, and might impose upon her a burden which she could not discharge. The use of by far the greater part of the property — that is, the most valuable portion of it — would of necessity consume the property. The life tenant may outlive the mule, the horse, or the cow; and the use of the wagon, buggy and harness, the cash, cotton seed, corn, and fodder, and farming utensils, for any great length of time, of course would consume them. It is this use, during her life, whether that period be long or short, to which she is entitled, and to take this property and sell it, or to sell the other property which might not be destroyed by its use, such as household and kitchen furniture, would be something clearly beyond the intention of the testator.

If any wrong or fraud, on the part of the life tenant, was shown, or if it appeared that the property was being claimed by some person not entitled to it, or that one was claiming the interest of the remainderman rather than that of the life tenant, there would be some ground for equity to interpose, to preserve the property; but interposition of a court of equity, so far as appears from this bill, would defeat the rights of the life tenant, rather than protect the rights of the remainderman.   It certainly cannot be a reason for depriving the life tenant of property, or of the use of property, to which she is legally and equitably entitled, that that is the only property she has, and that if she dies soon enough some other party will have a reversion or remainder in the same property. Nor is it any ground for such a deprivation that the life tenant has denied the remainderman the right to the possession of the property, or that she has converted a part of it.   Both in law and in equity she was entitled to the possession of all the property, and was entitled to convert a part of it, because, by its very nature and character, the use thereof by the life tenant would of necessity consume it — and this is especially true of all the most valuable — if the life tenant should live long enough.   In cases of bequests of specific things, such as the most valuable in this case — horses, mules, wagons, buggies, corn, cotton seed — for the use and benefit of a person for life, the use of such property of necessity consists in the consumption of it.   Consequently a gift of such property for life, in most cases, though not necessarily in all, amounts to an absolute gift, for the very apparent reason that the use of the property and the property itself cannot exist separately.   It is true that the bill contains a general averment that the life tenant would convert it all; but no facts are shown to justify this presumption or conclusion, and it is something that the trial court nor this court could not know.   It is a conclusion to be drawn from the facts, and there are certainly no facts set forth which would justify the conclusion.

The inventory shows one article to be cash arising from rent of land of deceased.   The bill does not show whether the respondent was given a life estate in these lands or not.   If she was, she was entitled to the rents; that is to say, if she had the same interest in the lands that she did in the personal property.   This was the very interest which she acquired.   Consequently it was her property, and as to it the complainant would have no interest.   On the other hand, if the lands belonged to the complainant after the death of the testator, then the item has no place in this bill.   Personal property is so transitory and destructible in its nature that the right to enjoy it during life necessarily carries with it privileges which do not belong to the grant of life estate in lands. A life estate in personal property undoubtedly gives the donee the right to consume such articles as cannot be enjoyed without consuming them, as well as the right to wear out, by use, such as cannot be used without wearing out. The extent of liability over, to a remainderman, is to be governed by the intention of the donor, as manifested in the instrument which evidences the gift; and, if the parties claim under a will, the intention of the testator is to be collected, not from the particular clause, but from the whole instrument. Personal property is either wholly consumed or at least impaired by use. The person entitled to the use has the right to enjoy and use all the property, according to its character and nature. Those to be consumed become his absolute property, while things not to be consumed may be put to the use for which they were designed, and at the termination of the life estate they go to the remainderman — Holman's Case, 24 Pa. 174; Stoner & Barr's Case, 2 Pa. 428, 45 Am. Dec. 608; Baskin's Case, 3 Pa. 304, 45 Am. Dec. 641; Arminger v. Reitz, 91 Md. 334, 46 Atl. 990; Sutphen v. Ellis, 35 Mich. 446.

We know of no reason why the intention of the testator should not control, in determining what rights, interest, etc., the respective legatees shall take, in cases like this — whether the property shall be sold for its preservation for the remainderman, whether the life tenant shall be required to give security for its preservation and its delivery to the remainderman at the termination of the life estate. While the entire will is not set out in this case — and consequently we cannot construe it as a whole — yet, from what does appear, it seems that a farmer left a will, by which he devised and bequeathed a part at least of his lands to his wife, for life, with a remainder to his son, and all of his personal property (some of which is specified by items, showing that they were necessary for farming and housekeeping) to his wife, during her life, with a remainder to his son. The conclusion is irresistible that it was not intended that this property should be sold, and the interest of the fund, only, be used by the wife, the principal and accumulation to go to the remainderman; but that the wife should use it, during her life, for the purposes for which it was suitable and intended to be used, and for her own benefit during her life, and that the remainder, if any, at her death, should go to his son. To sell this property for the purposes sought in this bill, or to require the life tenant to give security for its preservation and delivery, would clearly defeat the intention of the testator, rather than promote it.

The bill was unquestionably subject to demurrer interposed,

and, complainant declining to amend, no other course was open but to dismiss it; and, if any injury resulted from dismissing his bill, it was his own fault.

The decree of the lower court is affirmed.

DOWDELL, C.J., and SIMPSON and McCLELLAN, JJ., concur.[74]

PROBLEMS

11.32. T owns a portrait of his grandfather. He has a son who is thirty-five years of age and a daughter who is thirty. He wants his son to have the use of the portrait until the son dies, and then his daughter to have the use of the portrait until she dies. On the death of the survivor of his son and daughter, he wants the portrait to go to his son's eldest son. Is this situation one where it is advisable for T to provide in his will for legal present and future interests in the portrait? If so, what problems, if any, may arise over the years with respect to the portrait, which can and should be settled by the terms of T's will?

11.33. T in his will bequeathed certain tangible personal property to his wife to hold and to enjoy for her lifetime, and the terms of his will relieved her from any liability for waste with respect to the property and excused her from any liability for failure to insure it. Upon her death the property is to go to certain designated relatives of T. T's executor delivered to the wife the described tangible personal property, which was worth approximately $4000. After making other distributions called for under the will, the executor filed what was termed a first and final accounting, in which was shown the distribution to the wife of the

---

[74] Legal future interests in personal property are dealt with in 1 American Law of Property §§4.4, 4.108-4.112 (Casner ed. 1952).

Statutes which are concerned with legal future interests in personal property have taken various forms. In Alabama, the present interest owner cannot remove the property from the jurisdiction without the consent of the future interest owner. See Alabama Code, tit. 47, §64 (1958), quoted infra page 1436. In Ohio, personal property may be delivered to the person given the limited present interest, with or without bond, as the court may determine, or the property may be ordered held by a fiduciary, with or without bond, for the benefit of the person with the limited interest, that is, the arrangement may be converted from one involving legal interests to one involving the use of a trust. The bond may be increased or decreased, and if not required originally, may be required subsequently. See Ohio Rev. Code Ann. §2113.58 (Page, 1954), quoted infra page 1470.

In Pennsylvania, the owner of a present interest in personal property is deemed a trustee of such property except that he is not required to change the form of investment to one authorized for Pennsylvania fiduciaries, and he is not entitled to compensation as a trustee. The court may require such security to protect the remainderman as it determines is necessary. See Pa. Stat. Ann., tit. 20, §301.13 (Purdon), quoted infra page 1472. — ED.

$4000 worth of tangible personal property. Objection is made to the allowance of the executor's account as a final one on the ground that title to the tangible personal property remains in the executor until the wife's death. Should the executor's account be allowed as a final one? See Old Colony Trust Co. v. Swift, 331 Mass. 755, 122 N.E.2d 757 (1954). But compare Vaughn v. Vaughn, 118 So.2d 620 (Miss. 1960).

QUIGLEY v. QUIGLEY

370 Ill. 151, 18 N.E.2d 186 (1938)

MR. JUSTICE JONES delivered the opinion of the court:

Appellants, nephews of the testatrix, filed in the circuit court of Cook county, a bill to construe the will of Alice M. Quigley, deceased. The will, written in longhand by the testatrix, provides: "I hereby give, devise and bequeath to my brother, Charles L. Quigley, all my property, real estate, personal and of whatever form for his personal use during his lifetime." It then provides for the payment of all her debts and obligations and the expenses of her last sickness and death, and provides for the payment of $100 to the Catholic Extension Society for masses for the repose of her soul. The will further provides: "After the death of my brother, I wish that whatever is left of my estate be divided among my four nephews." The question presented is the extent of the interest given to Charles L. Quigley. The circuit court held he was given a life estate with full power to dispose of the corpus of the estate during his lifetime, by proper deed or deeds of conveyance, but not by his last will or testament. It is the contention of appellants that Charles was given only a life estate, with no power to dispose of the corpus.

The testatrix was a spinster sixty-nine years of age at the time of her death. She had been a teacher in the public schools of Chicago for about thirty years and had retired a few years before her death. She lived with her brother Charles, for the last seven or eight years of her life. Charles and her four nephews were her only heirs and next of kin. Her estate consisted of two vacant lots worth about $1000 each, and personal property valued at approximately $29,000. The personal property included capital stock in various corporations, of a market value of $27,000, and the rest consisted of bank deposits, checks and a promissory note.

In determining the interests created by the will, we must ascertain and give effect to the intention of the testatrix as expressed by all the provisions of the will, interpreted in view of the circumstances surrounding the testatrix. (Hollenbeck v. Smith, 231 Ill.

484.) Appellees argue that the expressions "for his personal use during his lifetime" and "whatever is left of my estate" show an intention to give the life tenant a power of disposal of the corpus and to give the nephews only so much as the life tenant should not dispose of in his lifetime. It is contended that "for his personal use during his lifetime" has a different and larger meaning than "for his lifetime," in that it means the life tenant may "use up" the estate. No authority is cited in support of this contention. In several analogous cases similar language has been employed, and in none of them has it been suggested that such language has a different meaning than the usual words creating a life estate. In Welsch v. Belleville Savings Bank, 94 Ill. 191, the language was "for her own free, independent and uncontrollable use and benefit for the term of her natural life." In Thompson v. Adams, 205 Ill. 552, the language was "for the sole use and benefit of my wife, Elizabeth Adams, so long as she shall live and remain my widow." In Strickland v. Strickland, 271 Ill. 614, the property was devised "for her use during the term of her natural life, she is to have absolute control of same during her lifetime." It is our opinion that a gift "for his personal use during his lifetime" has no different meaning than "for life." No significance is to be attached to the words employed here. It cannot be said that those words manifest an intention to add to the life estate a power to consume or dispose of the corpus of the estate.

It is next argued by appellees that the words "whatever is left" show an intention to create a power of disposal. Appellants agree the rule is that when a will creating a life estate contains a subsequent clause granting remainderman whatever is left of the estate, no power to dispose of the corpus of the estate is created unless the expression "whatever is left" can be given no other reasonable meaning than that of a grant of such power of disposal. (Vanatta v. Carr, 223 Ill. 160.) Here the expression "whatever is left" can, in our opinion, be given another reasonable meaning. After creating a life estate the will provides the life tenant, as executor, shall pay all the debts and obligations the testatrix may have incurred, including the expense of her last sickness and death. She also directs the payment of $100 to a certain society for the saying of masses. The amount of such payments was uncertain, and they would undoubtedly result in a diminution of the corpus of the estate. She then gave to her nephews "whatever is left." The reasonable meaning of this expression, as used here, is that she meant "whatever is left" after the specified payments had been made and after her brother had enjoyed the use of and returns from her property during his life. She might also have foreseen that some of the assets would be destroyed or diminished in value through insolvency of the corporations, banks or the maker of the note, or in some other manner. We cannot agree that the creation of a power of disposal of the corpus is the only reasonable meaning that can be given to this expression. There is, in the will before us, no provision, either preceding or following the words "whatever is left," which indicates any purpose of the testatrix to vest Charles L. Quigley with a power of sale or disposal. There is here no doubtful power of sale which can be made a certain one by a consideration of these words in the will. Thompson v. Adams, supra. . . .

It is argued by appellees that the character of the testatrix's property is such that unless the power of disposal is granted, the life tenant can receive but little benefit from the estate. In support of this contention the life tenant says that $500 was cash in bank, upon which no interest is being paid, and that it is absurd to think that the testatrix would want him to keep the money on deposit during his entire life just for the benefit of the remaindermen. One or two other items of property are also mentioned in this category. The contention of the life tenant is predicated upon an erroneous view of the law. It is well settled that a gift of the use of money to a life tenant is a gift of interest and not of the corpus. A life tenant has, under proper restrictions, the right to invest and reinvest money or its equivalent in order that his bequest may be made remunerative. It would be idle to say that he must leave such assets dormant. The executor or trustee, as the case may be, is bound to invest the money for the benefit of the usee. If the life tenant desires to have possession of the property he may do so under such reasonable restrictions as the courts may impose. The matter of requiring security is now, ordinarily, one of discretion with the court having jurisdiction over the property. 17 R.C.L. "Life Estates," sec. 17, p. 626, et seq.; 21 Corpus Juris "Estates," sec. 245, p. 1040; Scott v. Scott, 137 Iowa, 239, 23 L.R.A. (N.S.) 716, and annotations thereto; Welsch v. Belleville Savings Bank, supra.

After considering the entire will and all the competent evidence of the surrounding circumstances, we conclude the will created only a life estate in Charles L. Quigley, with a remainder to appellants.

The decree is reversed and the cause is remanded to the circuit court, with directions to enter a decree in conformity with the views herein expressed.

Reversed and remanded, with directions.

COLLINGS v. COLLINGS' EXECUTORS
260 S.W.2d 935 (Ky. 1953)

STEWART, Justice.

This action was brought below by the widow, Bess H. Collings, and the executors of the will of Ben H. Collings, deceased, as plaintiffs, against the decedent's cousin, Lowell Anderson Collings, the latter's infant daughter, and the other known heirs of the decedent, primarily to construe the above-mentioned will. The following clauses of the instrument, dated May 10, 1946, are the pertinent ones so far as this litigation is concerned.

"3. All the rest and residue of my estate, real, personal and mixed, of whatever kind and description and wherever situated, I will, devise and bequeath to my beloved wife, Bess H. Collings.

"4. Any part of my estate remaining undisposed of at the time of the death of my said wife, I will and bequeath to my cousin, Lowell Anderson Collings. Should he not survive her, then to his decedents[sic], if he leaves any, and if not, to my heirs at law."

The widow and the executors contend paragraphs three and four of the will when read together vest in the widow, Bess H. Collings, the fee simple title to the residuary estate, whereas Lowell Anderson Collings maintains the widow received only a life estate in the residue and at her death he will be entitled, if alive, to decedent's entire residuary estate, or, in the alternative, to so much thereof as the widow does not dispose of for her own use and benefit during her lifetime. The Chancellor filed a written opinion holding in effect that Item 3 of the will devised the residuary estate in fee simple to the widow and that Item 4 is "fatally vague and uncertain" and therefore void. Lowell Anderson Collings and the other defendants below have appealed.

It is often difficult to determine whether a particular will devises a fee or a life estate. But out of many decisions written by this Court on this issue there have emerged two controlling principles. The first of these is thus summarized in Sisson v. Sisson, 208 Ky. 843, 272 S.W. 15: "The pivotal question in every case is, Did the first devisee take a fee or life estate? and one of the tests is, Was he given the unlimited power of disposition?"

The second principle, followed in this jurisdiction for many years, is that the intention of the testator as gathered from the will as a whole and from the language employed by the testator in writing it is to control. To attempt to arrive at the intention of the testator by any other method would be to indulge in a piecemeal interpretation of his will rather than a construction of all the clauses contained in a single instrument as a unit. Points v. Points, 312 Ky. 348, 227 S.W.2d 913.

It should be pointed out that, in construing any will as a whole in order to ascertain the intent of the testator, we departed many years ago from the rigid and often harsh common law rule that where the instrument contains technical phrases appropriate to create an apparent fee, it is legally impossible by subsequent clauses to qualify or limit the effect of the language in the prior part of the will. This Court is now committed to the following doctrine set forth in Greenway v. White, 196 Ky. 745, 246 S.W. 137, 139, 32 A.L.R. 1385:

"It may be admitted that some of the earlier decisions, including, perhaps, some from this court, under the ancient common-law doctrine that there could be no limitation upon a fee, held that, where a will or other instrument of conveyance gave an estate absolutely to one with express or implied power of unrestricted disposition, the estate could not be reduced by any subsequent provision of the instrument, but the courts generally, including this one, have long since come to the conclusion that the rule requiring the intention of the maker, either of a will or deed, as gathered from the entire instrument, to prevail, overshadows and dispenses with the ancient technical, common-law rule, and that, where it appears from the entire language of the will or deed that it was the intention of the maker to limit the estate given or granted to less than an absolute one, that intention will prevail."

In Hanks v. McDanell, 307 Ky. 243, 210 S.W.2d 784, 17 A.L.R.2d 1, we declared that the gift over of a remanent of the estate is no longer conclusively presumed to be void. See Weakley v. Weakley, Ky., 237 S.W.2d 524. However, before the McDanell case was decided, the opinion of Berner v. Luckett, 299 Ky. 744, 186 S.W.2d 905, handed down in 1945, unquestionably recognized and gave support to the proposition that the gift over may serve to define the estate of the first taker as a life interest.

Whether the will in controversy devised to the widow a fee or a life estate is dependent upon the answer to this question: Did the testator invest his widow with power to deed and to devise in fee simple all the property embraced in his will? If the widow can only dispose of the devised estate while she is living, that is, by inter vivos conveyances, then, although she can pass a fee simple title by deed, all that she has is a life estate with power to encroach on the corpus. An absolute fee is bestowed when the testator endows his widow with an unlimited power of disposition as to the property devised not only during her lifetime but also on her death.[75] Wintuska v. Peart, 237 Ky. 666, 36 S.W.2d 50, Evans v. Leer, 232 Ky. 358, 23 S.W.2d 553, Spicer v. Spicer, 177 Ky. 400, 197 S.W. 959, and Angel v. Wood, 153 Ky. 195, 154 S.W. 1103.

With the foregoing principles to guide us, we now turn our attention to the language of the will, and we note that there is no express power of disposition vested in the widow in either of the foregoing items. Such power must be implied and we shall elaborate on this point hereinafter. In Item 4 the testator unqualifiedly devises and bequeaths, and we quote, "any part of my estate remaining undisposed of at the time of the death of my said wife" to "my cousin, Lowell Anderson Collings." This same paragraph definitely provides for the further disposition of his property if certain contingencies develop. When Items 3 and 4 are considered together they merely invest the widow with the authority to use and enjoy the estate for her needs and comfort as she may deem it necessary during her natural life. It is unmistakably clear under the fourth clause that the widow cannot dispose of the remainder of the estate by will because the testator not only reserved this right exclusively to himself but he has already fully exercised it. Therefore, to sum up, the will gives the widow full power to dispose of the property for her own use and benefit during her lifetime but it limits her disposition of it at her death, and we therefore conclude that the testator did not intend to give her the devised property in fee.

Appellees argue that KRS 381.060(1) compels us to declare the estate to be vested in fee simple in the widow. We do not agree with this contention. This subsection does nothing more than dispense with the necessity to use "words of inheritance" in a deed or will in order to create a fee. The provision did not change the rule that where there are words in a conveyance or a devise indicating the intent they will nevertheless govern. In Hall v. Wright, 121 Ky. 16, 87 S.W. 1129, 1130, in construing Section 2342 of the Kentucky Statutes of 1903, now KRS 381.060(1), we succinctly set forth the foregoing point in this language:

"Under the common law, when a grant was made to a person

---

[75] In Estate of Edward F. Pipe v. Commissioner, 241 F.2d 210 (2d Cir. 1957), *cert. denied,* 355 U.S. 814 (1957), the court considered N.Y. Real Property Law §149, which provides, in substance, that where an absolute power of disposition is given to a life beneficiary, the estate is changed into a fee simple with respect to the rights of creditors, purchasers and encumbrancers, but is subject to any future estates limited thereon in case the power of disposition is not exercised and in case the property is not sold for the satisfaction of debts. The court held that under this New York statute a life beneficiary with a power of disposition did not have a fee simple interest. — ED.

without words of inheritance, the estate would not pass to the heirs, and the grantee would not take the fee-simple title; hence the necessity for this statute to pass the fee-simple title to purchasers when no words of inheritance were contained in the conveyance. But this statute does not apply where there are any words in the conveyance indicating how the title is to pass."

Inherent in the will is the plain meaning that there was bestowed upon the widow an implied power to encroach upon the corpus of the estate during her lifetime. The testator undoubtedly intended that his widow should have a free hand in the use and management of his property and he meant, we believe, for her to have this use and management untrammelled by court proceedings or other interference. In short, we are of the opinion and we hold that it was the testator's intention that his widow should possess all right as to the use and enjoyment of the devised estate during her natural life; nevertheless, she may not willfully waste it, nor give it away, nor dispose of it by will.

Wherefore, the judgment is reversed with directions that it be set aside and that a judgment be entered in conformity with this opinion.

DUNCAN and MOREMEN, JJ., dissenting.[76]

ATTEBERY v. PRENTICE
158 Neb. 795, 65 N.W.2d 138 (1954)

WENKE, J.

This is an appeal from the district court for Sioux County. It primarily involves the construction of the last will and testament of O. T. Attebery, deceased.

[76] For a comment on Collings v. Collings' Executors, see 42 Ky. L.J. 717 (1954). Compare with Collings v. Collings' Executors the case of Ramsey v. Holder, 291 S.W.2d 556 (Ky. 1956).

In Brunton v. Easthampton Savings Bank, 336 Mass. 345, 145 N.E.2d 696 (1957), the testator gave his estate to his wife for life and then provided: "In case there shall be any part of my estate, given, devised, and bequeathed as aforesaid to my wife . . . not used by her for her comfort and support during her natural life, and shall be remaining upon her decease, such property [is to pass to other designated persons]." The court held that this language gave the testator's wife a life interest with a power to consume principal, but that the wife had no power to mortgage the property. Another Massachusetts case, Kent v. Morrison, 153 Mass. 137, 26 N.E. 427 (1891), where a life tenant with a power to sell was allowed to mortgage the property, was distinguished on the ground that the power given the life tenant in the Kent case was broader. Even though a life tenant is not given a power to sell or mortgage the property, the Massachusetts statute (Mass. Ann. Laws, c. 183, §49) establishes a procedure whereby land which is divided into present and future interests may be sold or mortgaged on the petition of anyone interested, if the sale or mortgage appears to the court to be desirable. The interests of the various persons in the land are transformed into interests in the proceeds of the sale or mortgage as provided in Chapter 183, §51. — ED.

O. T. Attebery died on August 24, 1942, a resident of Scotts Bluff County. He left a last will and testament which was duly allowed and admitted to probate by the county court of Scotts Bluff County on September 22, 1942. This will, insofar as here material, is as follows:

"Second: I give, devise, and bequeath unto my wife, Ellelia Attebery, all of my real estate wheresoever situated, to have and to hold during the period of her natural life, but with full power and authority to sell and convey the same or any part or portion thereof at any time when it may be advantageous or profitable to do so or when it becomes necessary for her support, said support to be such as is suitable for persons of her age and social position, and of a like character to which she was accustomed during the later years of our married life. The remainder of said real estate, if any, on the death of my wife, I give, devise, and bequeath to Henry B. Attebery, Richard L. Attebery, Fred M. Attebery, Charles W. Attebery, Harry E. Attebery, Lena Fuhrer Francil, Susie Wissenberg, and Sadie Strufing, share and share alike.

"Third: I give, devise, and bequeath unto my said wife, Ellelia Attebery, all my personal property of every description, with the request and direction that she shall execute a will leaving the remainder of such personal property as she shall be possessed of at her death to the beneficiaries named in the paragraph numbered second, of this my will, share and share alike.

"Fourth: In case of the death of myself and wife in a common disaster all of my said property of every description, real, personal, or mixed, shall immediately descend to and vest in the beneficiaries named in the paragraph numbered second of this my will, share and share alike."

Among the assets of the estate was a ranch consisting of 8,360 acres of deeded land and a lease on a section of state school land. On July 1, 1951, the widow conveyed this land and assigned the lease on the section of school land to O. D. Prentice.

The consideration for the deed was an annuity contract secured by a mortgage on the real estate conveyed. By the terms of this contract O. D. Prentice agreed to pay the widow, during each year of her natural life the sum of $6,000, the same to be paid on the first day of July of each year commencing with July 1, 1951; to pay to her executor or administrator, upon her death, that part of the annual payment which had accrued up to the time of her death; to satisfy any and all claims which he had against her for professional services already rendered as her doctor; to make no charge for any professional services he might render to her in the future; and to pay any and all doctor and hospital bills which she might incur.

The widow died on December 16, 1952. Shortly after her death some of the parties named as remaindermen in the will of O. T. Attebery learned they were such. Thereafter, on December 29, 1952, the living remaindermen named in the will, and the heirs or successors of those who had died, commenced this action against O. D. Prentice and his wife, Mary Lou. The purpose of the action is to have the deed and conveyance from Ellelia Attebery to O. D. Prentice vacated, canceled, and annulled; to have the mortgage, dated June 30, 1951, and recorded in book 28 of mortgages, pages 191-192, canceled and annulled, and the purported lien thereof removed; to have the title to the real estate above described quieted in the plaintiffs; to require O. D. Prentice and Mary Lou Prentice to make an assignment to plaintiffs of the lease from the State of Nebraska covering section 16, Township 25 North, Range 57 West of the Sixth P.M., Sioux County, Nebraska, upon the payment by plaintiffs to defendants of a sum equal to the amount of the bonus paid to the State of Nebraska for said lease; and to have O. D. Prentice account to plaintiffs for the rents and income from said property.

The trial court found generally for the plaintiffs and decreed, insofar as here material, that upon payment by the plaintiffs into court the sum of $3,694.64 for the benefit of O. D. Prentice that the purported deed from Ellelia Attebery to the defendant O. D. Prentice dated July 1, 1951, be vacated, canceled, and annulled; that the mortgage dated June 30, 1951, be vacated, canceled, and annulled, and the purported lien of said mortgage upon the real property described in said mortgage be removed; that title to the real property described in the above-described deed be quieted in plaintiffs; and that the defendants assign to plaintiffs the school land lease from the State of Nebraska.

Defendants filed a motion for a new trial and have perfected this appeal from the overruling thereof.

Under the will the widow became possessed of a life estate in the ranch with a power of sale. See, Perigo v. Perigo, ante p. 733, 64 N.W.2d 789; Annable v. Ricedorff, 140 Neb. 93, 299 N.W. 373; Abbott v. Wagner, 108 Neb. 359, 188 N.W. 113.

The character of the remainder as a vested estate is not affected by the conferring upon the life tenant the power to sell and convey the premises for certain purposes. Abbott v. Wagner, supra; Ashbaugh v. Wright, 152 Minn. 57, 188 N.W. 157. In other words, the widow did not become vested of the fee by reason of the authority vested in her by the will.

Based on the many cases and authorities cited it seems to be appellant's thought that the power of sale given the widow was sufficiently broad that thereunder she had an absolute and unlimited

power of disposition and could dispose of the real estate of which
her husband died seized, or any part thereof, whenever she
pleased as long as she felt it was in any way advantageous or profitable to her, provided she acted in good faith and did not waste
or squander the property for the purpose of preventing the remainder from going to the remaindermen.

Also, it appears to be appellants' thought that her decisions on
the question of what was necessary for her support required the
exercise of judgment and discretion on her part and, if fairly and
honestly made, would be conclusive.

In Perigo v. Perigo, supra, quoting from Kramer v. Larson, ante
p. 404, 63 N.W.2d 349, with approval, we held:

"In searching for the intention of the testator, the court must
examine the entire will, consider all its provisions, give words
their generally accepted literal and grammatical meaning, and indulge the presumption that the testator understood the meaning
of the words used.

"The intention of the testator as determined from the will must
be given effect if it is not inconsistent with any rule of law."

Therein we also held, by quoting from Hill v. Hill, 90 Neb. 43,
132 N.W. 738, 38 L.R.A.N.S. 198, that: " 'It is the duty of the
courts in construing a will to carry into effect the true intent of
the testator, so far as that intent can be collected from the whole
instrument, if not inconsistent with the rules of law; but the law
imputes to the testator a knowledge of those rules, and he will be
presumed to have executed his will with an understanding that
the objects of his bounty may demand their portions in accordance therewith.' "

Taking his will as a whole, O. T. Attebery gave to his wife,
Ellelia Attebery, the life use of all his real estate with the remainder to "Henry B. Attebery, Richard L. Attebery, Fred M.
Attebery, Charles W. Attebery, Harry E. Attebery, Lena Fuhrer
Francil, Susie Wissenberg, and Sadie Strufing, share and share
alike." In connection therewith he gave the owner of the life use
full power and authority to sell and convey the same, or any part
or portion thereof, at any time when it became advantageous or
profitable to do so, that is, advantageous or profitable to all parties
interested therein. In addition to the income therefrom, in order to be sure his widow would always have sufficient for her support in a manner suitable for a person of her age and social position and in keeping with the standard to which she had become
accustomed, he gave her full power and authority to sell and convey such real estate, or any part or portion thereof, when it became necessary for her to do so for that purpose.

The right here given the widow to dispose of the corpus of the property was a limited right and could only be exercised by her consistent with the objects and purposes for which the authority was given. Abbott v. Wagner, supra.

Ordinarily courts will not interfere with the discretion of the life tenant in the exercise of this authority but he is not necessarily the sole and ultimate judge thereof. A court of equity will review his judgment and, if the evidence adduced shows he has exceeded the authority given him, revise his judgment. Abbott v. Wagner, supra; Beliveau v. Beliveau, 217 Minn. 235, 14 N.W.2d 360; Morford v. Dieffenbacker, 54 Mich. 593, 20 N.W. 600.

We will consider first the widow's authority to sell and convey in case it became necessary for her support. Under the terms of the will we think the widow was entitled to support solely from the estate without regard to her own separate means of support. See, Annotation, 101 A.L.R. 1465; In re Worman's Estate, 231 Iowa 1351, 4 N.W.2d 373.

In considering the record we apply the following: "It is the duty of this court in an equity case to try the issues de novo and to reach an independent decision without being influenced by the findings of the trial court except if the evidence is in irreconcilable conflict this court may consider that the trial court saw the witnesses, observed their manner of testifying, and accepted one version of the facts rather than the opposite." Keim v. Downing, 157 Neb. 481, 59 N.W.2d 602.

The evidence shows that when the estate of her husband was settled the widow had a bank account of about $14,644; United States Government bonds, purchased in 1941 and 1942, with a value at maturity of $1,200; the life use of the home in which she lived; and the income from the ranch. That on July 1, 1951, when she conveyed the ranch, she had bank accounts totalling about $36,000; United States Government bonds with a value at maturity of $12,200, of which $11,000 had been purchased since the year of her husband's death; the life use of the home, and the life income from the ranch. On July 1, 1951, the ranch was leased until May 1, 1953, for a rental of $2,800 per year, and had an oil and gas lease thereon which was yielding delay rentals of $2,020 per year. The taxes on the ranch were between $900 and $1,000 per year.

It is self-evident, from the foregoing, that the income which the widow had been and was receiving from the ranch since her husband's death up to July 1, 1951, had been more than adequate for her support and had permitted her to substantially increase her own funds. In this regard the evidence establishes she was leasing the ranch for less than its fair rental value. There was absolutely no necessity or need for her selling the ranch for her support.

We come then to the question of whether or not she was authorized under the power and authority to sell and convey the same, or any part thereof, because it was advantageous or profitable to do so. We think this authority relates to all those interested therein, which would include remaindermen. It is apparent the widow,· whose duty it was to keep the improvements on the ranch in repair, had neglected this duty although the income was sufficient for that purpose.

The only advantage gained by the sale flowed to the widow. She was of the age of 68 years and 5 months at the time and it appears she did not like the responsibility of looking after the ranch, which included making necessary improvements and keeping the improvements thereon in repair; that the sale relieved her of this worry and gave her a feeling of security and peace of mind; and that it gave her some increase in her annual income, although not needed for her support. On the other hand it completely deprived the remaindermen of all rights therein as, under the contract, there would be nothing left for them whenever she died.

The relation of a life tenant to his remaindermen is that of a quasi trustee. The relation is the same if a power of disposal is annexed to the life estate. See, Beliveau v. Beliveau, supra; Mallett v. Hall, 129 Me. 148, 150 A. 531; Johnson v. Johnson, 51 Ohio St. 446, 38 N.E. 61.

As stated in Mallett v. Hall, supra: "The life tenant is a trustee for the benefit of the remainderman only in the sense that the duty rests upon him merely to have due regard for the rights of those in remainder."

And, as stated in Beliveau v. Beliveau, supra: ". . . a life tenant is a quasi trustee of the property in the sense that he cannot injure or dispose of it to the injury of the remainderman, even though a power of disposition and encroachment are annexed to the life estate."

Here a ranch, reasonably worth at the time not less than $133,000, was conveyed by the widow at a time when no need existed for doing so, as far as her support is concerned, and certainly the benefits she would gain would not overcome the large loss the remaindermen would suffer. To permit this conveyance to stand would not only be unfair to the remaindermen but would permit the life tenant to perpetrate a fraud on them.

We think the evidence requires that the deed be set aside, the mortgage canceled and the lien thereof removed from the records of Sioux County, and the title to the lands quieted in the appellees. The trial court having so decreed, we affirm its action in so doing. . . .[77]

PROBLEMS

11.34. To what extent, if any, will the value of the 8360-acre tract of land dealt with in Attebery v. Prentice be included in the gross estate of Ellelia Attebery? See Section 2041(a)(1) of the 1954 Code, quoted infra page 1400.

11.35. T in his will gives Blackacre "to my wife for life with power in my said wife to sell Blackacre in fee simple and use or dispose of the proceeds of such sale as she may desire; on the death of my said wife, if she has not sold Blackacre, the same shall pass to my children then living."

  a. T dies. His wife dies and she has not sold Blackacre. Will the value of Blackacre be included in the wife's gross estate for federal estate tax purposes? See Section 2041(a)(2) of the 1954 Code, quoted infra page 1400.

  b. On T's death, if his wife survives him, will the gift of Blackacre by T to his wife be available for the estate tax marital deduction? See Section 2056(b)(5) of the 1954 Code, quoted infra page 1408.

11.36. T owns a family residence. He wants his wife to have the use of the residence as long as she lives, and then he wants the residence to be added to the residue of his estate. He desires to create a trust of the residue of his estate for the benefit of his wife and his issue. Is this situation one where it is advisable for T to provide in his will for a legal life estate in the residence in his wife with a legal remainder in the residence in the trustee of the residuary trust? If so, what problems, if any, may arise over the years with respect to the residence property which can and should be settled by the terms of the will? See Revenue Ruling 54-583, 1954-2 C.B. 158, which is considered supra page 270, note 7.

[77] Virginia by statute has undertaken to make it clear that the fact that the life tenant is given a power to dispose absolutely of the property by deed or will does not cause the remainder to fail except to the extent that the power is exercised. See Va. Code Ann. §55-7 (1950), quoted infra page 1476.

If a person is given an estate in fee simple with a gift over, on his death, of so much of the property as is not disposed of by him in his lifetime, it may be contended that the purported gift over fails because to uphold it would result in a restraint on the alienation of a fee by will. New Jersey Revised Statutes §3A:3-16 (1951), quoted infra page 1467, specifically states that the gift over in such case in not void. Notice that if a person is given an estate in fee simple with a gift over to others if he dies intestate, it may be contended that the gift over is invalid because to uphold it would result in a restraint on the alienation of a fee by intestacy. The New Jersey statute does not cover this situation. — Ed.

INCOME TAX NOTE RELATING TO LEGAL
PRESENT AND FUTURE INTERESTS

If a legal life interest is created and the life tenant has a power to sell and reinvest the property in which his life interest exists, who is taxable on any gain realized on a sale? Who is entitled to take a loss realized on a sale? In Weil v. United States, 180 F. Supp. 407 (Ct. Cl. 1960), the court concluded that under Alabama law the legal life tenant has the same fiduciary obligation toward the remainderman as the trustee of a life interest, and therefore, just as in the case of the trustee, he must pay the tax on any gain realized by a sale of the property in which the life interest exists. In reaching this result, the court disagreed with United States v. Cooke, 228 F.2d 667 (9th Cir. 1955), which took the position that the gain was not taxable to anyone because the life tenant was not the equivalent of a fiduciary, and thus there was no provision in the Code on the basis of which the gain could be taxed. It could not be taxed to the life tenant because he was not entitled to it, and it could not be taxed to the remainderman because he would not be entitled to it until the life interest came to an end. In United States v. De Bonchamps, 278 F.2d 127 (9th Cir. 1960), *cert. denied*, 81 Sup. Ct. 58 (1960), the Court of Appeals for the Ninth Circuit reversed its own decision in United States v. Cooke and held that the life tenant was taxable on the gain as a trustee.[78]

---

[78] In Security-First National Bank v. United States, 181 F. Supp. 911 (S.D. Cal. 1960), a life tenant under a will had power to sell an indefeasible title and power to consume as she might from time to time find necessary for her support, comfort, health and service. The court concluded that the life tenant was a trustee for the remainderman, and thus gains were taxable to her as trustee. United States v. Cooke was distinguished on the ground that there the life tenant had unfettered dominion and therefore was not a trustee for the remainderman. For additional material on this matter see Case Comment, Who Pays a Capital Gains Tax on a Gift to a Life Tenant and Contingent Remainderman, 51 Nw. U.L. Rev. 487 (1956). See also the following cases: Brown v. United States, 58-2 U.S.T.C. ¶9861 (D. Hawaii, 1958); Matter of United States Trust Co. v. Lynch, 267 N.Y. 22, 195 N.E. 537 (1935).

Revenue Ruling 59-99, 1959-1 C.B. 158, considers a case where a life tenant in land petitioned the appropriate court in Michigan for authority to sell the land and requested the court to appoint a trustee to take charge of the proceeds received from the sale. The authority was granted, and the life tenant sold the land. The ruling holds that the gain from the sale must be reported by the court-appointed trustee and a tax paid thereon by the trustee. Section 641(a)(1) of the 1954 Code, quoted infra page 1361, applies, though the sale was in fact made by the legal life tenant. The case of United States v. National City Bank of New York, 21 F. Supp. 791 (S.D.N.Y. 1937), is referred to with approval as a case finding that a person holding income for future distribution under the terms of a will or trust must pay the tax regardless of whether the trust existed at the time of the sale from which the income was realized.

In Gaskill v. United States, 188 F. Supp. 507 (N.D. Tex. 1960), the life

Thus the use of this tax haven as a means of avoiding a tax on a gain seems to have been eliminated.

In Katherine B. Bliss, 27 T.C. 770 (1957), a severe windstorm damaged the property in which the taxpayer had a life interest. The difference in the value of the property before and after the storm was $30,000. The court apportioned the loss between the life tenant and the remainderman by the use of actuarial tables. The case was reversed sub nom. Bliss v. Commissioner, 256 F.2d 533 (2d Cir. 1958). In reversing, the Courts of Appeals held that all the loss was deductible by the life tenant, pointing out, however, that it should be understood "as not formulating any rule of general application but only as deciding this case on the basis of the unusual fact situation now before us." Since the Tax Court did not determine the basis of the life tenant in the property in question, the case was remanded to the Tax Court to make such a determination. In Lena L. Steinert, 33 T.C. 447 (1959), a casualty-loss deduction was allowed the life tenant of real property for clean-up expense actually paid by her after a hurricane and for that part of the loss in value of the property attributable to her life estate.

In United States v. Schofield, 179 F. Supp. 332 (E.D. Pa. 1959), a life tenant, while he was insolvent, made expenditures for the improvement of land. After his death, the government instituted suit to recover income taxes due from the life tenant, by impressing a lien, to the extent of the improvements, on the land held by the remainderman. The court held that the United States had no lien, since the assessment and demand were made after the life tenant's death at a time when he had no interest in the real estate. For subsequent litigation in this matter, see United States v. Schofield, 60-2 U.S.T.C. ¶9729 (E.D. Pa. 1960), where it was held that the life tenant's actions amounted to a fraudulent conveyance under the Uniform Fraudulent Conveyance Act and that the government was entitled to a lien for the taxes. On the basis of the cost of the improvements the lien was computed at $2000.

In E. Eugene King, 31 T.C. 108 (1958), the taxpayer and his wife entered into a property settlement that was later incorporated in a divorce decree, under which he gave her a life interest with

---

tenant procured a court order to sell the property in which her life interest existed, and the court order required the payment of the proceeds to a trust company to hold for the benefit of the life tenant and the remainderman. The court concluded that the trustee should pay the tax on the gain. In the course of its opinion the court said that it was inclined to agree with United States v. Cooke in a situation like the one in that case rather than with United States v. De Bonchamps.

remainder to their children. She received the life interest in full satisfaction of alimony. The court held that he had realized a taxable gain but only to the extent of the gain allocable to the life estate transferred to his wife, since the conveyance of the remainder to the children was found to be a gift. Under state law it could not be in discharge of any legal obligation to the children.

Hope existed for a while that a transferor would be entitled to capital gains treatment where he sold for some stated amount his oil rights, the interest in the transferee to last until the transferee had collected from the oil rights the stated amount plus interest. This hope has disappeared as a result of the decision in Commissioner v. P. G. Lake, Inc., 356 U.S. 260 (1958), in which such a transfer was treated as an anticipatory assignment of rights to future income.[79] This situation should be compared with the one considered supra page 438, note 11, where ordinary income was successfully converted into amounts taxable as a gain from the sale of a capital asset.

8.   ALIENABILITY

In connection with estate planning, the alienability of future interests is important from two standpoints. If a person owns a future interest, the alienability of that interest is significant in determining what dispositions of it are possible in his estate plan. If he is creating future interests in his estate plan, the extent to which he can control the alienability of such interests by the beneficiaries may be significant.

In the absence of any prohibition as to alienability in the instrument which creates a future interest, there is generally freedom of alienation as to all types of future interests that are likely to be involved in an estate plan, but the governing state law must be examined.[80] Attempts to control the alienability of future in-

---

[79] For cases in which the Supreme Court's decision in Commissioner v. P. G. Lake, Inc., is applied and followed, see Eugene T. Flewellan, 32 T.C. 317 (1959); Estate of O. W. Killam, 33 T.C. 345 (1959). See also Note, Distinguishing Ordinary Income from Capital Gains Where Rights to Future Income Are Sold, 69 Harv. L. Rev. 737 (1956).

[80] Reversions and vested remainders have always been alienable. It has been held that the right of entry not only is inalienable but an attempt to alienate it will destroy it. See Rice v. Boston and Worcester R.R., 12 Allen 141 (Mass. 1866). The alienability of possibilities of reverter is now generally recognized. In Trustees of Schools of Township No. 1 v. Batdorf, 6 Ill. 2d 486, 130 N.E.2d 111 (1955), the court pointed out that a possibility of reverter can pass by descent but it is incapable of alienation, devise or partition. In Nichols v. Haehn, 8 A.D.2d 405, 187 N.Y.S.2d 773 (1959), the court held that a possibility of reverter is alienable. Various views have been taken as to the alienability of contingent remainders and executory interests. For a thorough discussion

terests in an estate plan present problems in the field of restraints on alienation. These restraints may be of the forfeiture type (an attempted alienation either extinguishes the interest subject to the restraint or else makes the interest subject to destruction at the will of the creator or his heirs) or of the disabling type (an attempted transfer of the interest subject to the restraint is of no effect).

a. *Restraint on the Alienation of a Legal Interest*

ANDREWS v. HALL
156 Neb. 817, 58 N.W.2d 201 (1953)

CARTER, J.

This is a suit for the partition of real estate devised to the plaintiff by her father, N. J. Hall. The appellant, Hilda B. Robinson, is the widow of Frank B. Hall, a son of the testator, N. J. Hall. The only question for determination is whether or not Frank B. Hall, who was devised a one-ninth interest in the real estate here involved, forfeited such interest when he attempted to sell, mortgage, and dispose of his interest in such real estate contrary to the provisions of the will of his father, N. J. Hall. The trial court held that Frank B. Hall had forfeited the interest in the real estate devised to him under the will of his father, N. J. Hall, and consequently that the appellant, the former wife of Frank B. Hall, acquired no interest therein under a deed from her husband. From a decree so holding, Hilda B. Robinson appeals.

The record shows that N. J. Hall died testate on January 28, 1930. By his will the real estate here involved could not be sold during the life of his wife, Minta A. Hall, the owner of the life estate. The will then provided: "After the death of my wife Minta A. Hall I wish all of my property both personal and real estate devided (divided) share and share alike with my children, with the following understanding that should any of my children during the life of my wife Minta A. Hall attempt to break this will or change the terms stated therein or attempt to sell, mort-

---

of the alienability, devisability and descendibility of future interests, see 1 American Law of Property §§4.64-4.81 (Casner ed. 1952).

A future interest that is contingent on the beneficiary surviving to some specified time is not a readily marketable item. The beneficiary, however, can protect the purchaser of such an interest by taking out insurance on his life and making it payable to the purchaser in the event that the beneficiary dies before the specified time. Will the premiums paid by the insured be deductible under I.R.C. 1954 Code §212 quoted infra page 1336? Joseph J. O'Donohue, 33 T.C. 698 (1960), says no.

gage or dispose of their interest in my estate before the death of my wife Minta A. Hall, it is my will that such heir shall forfeit all of his or her share except ten dollars, and that the balance of their share shall be divided share and share alike with the other children."

The answer discloses that Frank B. Hall, during his lifetime and prior to the death of Minta A. Hall, widow of the testator, conveyed his interest in the real estate to his wife, Hilda B. Hall, now Hilda B. Robinson, the appellant. It is the contention of appellant that the provision of the will herein quoted devised an undivided one-ninth interest in and to the real estate involved, in fee simple absolute, which interest vested in said Frank B. Hall upon the death of his father, subject to the life estate of his mother. It is then urged that the restriction imposed by the will against selling, mortgaging, or disposing of such interest in the real estate before the death of testator's widow, Minta A. Hall, is invalid and ineffectual for that purpose, and null, void, and repugnant to the fee simple estate devised.

The widow of the testator had a life estate in the property here involved. The will contained a general provision to the effect that none of the real estate devised to testator's children could be sold during the lifetime of the owner of the life estate. In view of the specific restrictions against alienation directed to his children in the portion of the will hereinbefore quoted, we assume that testator intended this general provision to restrict the partition of the real estate subject to the life tenancy of testator's widow. If this assumption is not the correct one, the restraint against alienation therein imposed would be subject to the same rules of law as those set forth heretofore in the quoted provision of the will. We are not here concerned with provisions intended to preserve the life estate of the widow. The sole question is the validity of the restriction against selling, mortgaging, or disposing of the fee simple estate granted by the testator to his children.

The intent of the testator is clear in the present case. He gave a life estate to his widow and the remainder in fee simple to his children, share and share alike. It is clear, also, that testator intended to restrict the alienation of the vested remainders he had devised to his children. The question is whether or not his plainly expressed intent against alienation can properly be given effect under controlling rules of law.

The appellee contends that the intent of the testator must be ascertained from the four corners of the will and, when once ascertained, it must be given effect under the intent statute, section 76-205, R.R.S. 1943. As a general proposition the foregoing states the correct rule. We reiterate, however, that this intent statute does not have the effect of changing substantive law and is, in fact, declaratory of a rule of construction long adopted by the courts. We have held that it relates only to rules of construction and does not enlarge or limit, or in any way modify, any rule of substantive law that existed at the time of its passage or that thereafter has been created. Stuehm v. Mikulski, 139 Neb. 374, 297 N.W. 595, 137 A.L.R. 327; Majerus v. Santo, 143 Neb. 774, 10 N.W.2d 608. We adhere to these holdings.

The children of the testator were devised a fee simple title to the remainder. It was alienable and devisable by the remaindermen, unless the restriction in question prevents. The will of the testator was effective at the death of the testator and it devised the entire interest of the testator to his wife and children. It is the general rule that a grant or devise of real estate to a designated person in fee simple, with provisions therein that are inconsistent or repugnant thereto such as a restriction against the power to sell, mortgage, or otherwise encumber, conveys an absolute fee and such restrictions are void. Watson v. Dalton, on rehearing, 146 Neb. 86, 20 N.W.2d 610; State Bank of Jansen v. Thiessen, 137 Neb. 426, 289 N.W. 791. One of the primary incidents of ownership of property in fee simple is the right to convey or encumber it. It is the general rule that a testator may not create a fee simple estate to vest at his death and at the same time restrict alienation thereof. Restatement, Property, Sec. 406, subd. e, p. 2397.

Appellee cites the case of Peters v. Northwestern Mutual Life Ins. Co., 119 Neb. 161, 227 N.W. 917, 67 A.L.R. 1311. There can be no question that it supports the position taken by appellee. The rule therein cited does not conform to the general rule applicable to restrictions upon alienation of fee simple estates. We do not agree that there has been a judicial relaxation of rules governing the creation and vesting of fee simple estates. The validity or extent of one's title to real estate ought not to rest upon considerations of reasonableness in the imposing of restrictions. Such a relaxation by judicial interpretation can only bring confusion where certainty ought to exist. We think the case of Peters v. Northwestern Mutual Life Ins. Co. supra is unsound in its reasoning on this question and that it should be overruled. The general rule that restrictions against alienation of real estate vested in fee simple are against public policy and void is a rule of substantive law which remains unaffected by the intent statute. It is a rule to be applied in all cases falling within it.

We do not say that a testator may not create a vested fee simple estate subject to a condition subsequent, or a determinable or defeasible fee. What we do say is that a restriction against alienation of a vested fee simple estate is not any one of these, nor, since it is void, can it be used as the sole basis for the creation of any of these estates. A restraint on alienation in the form of a condition subsequent, forfeiting or terminating the fee simple estate, or providing for a limitation over upon breach of the condition, is void. 41 Am. Jur., Perpetuities and Restraints on Alienation, Sec. 70, p. 111; 31 C.J.S., Estates, Sec. 8, p. 20. The right of alienation is inherent in the vested fee simple estate and it arises by virtue of the fact that such an estate is created. The nature of estates in fee simple determinable, estates in fee simple subject to a condition subsequent, and estates in fee simple defeasible upon a condition subsequent, are fully discussed in Ohm v. Clear Creek Drainage Dist., 153 Neb. 428, 45 N.W.2d 117. A perusal of that case will demonstrate that a restriction against alienation of a vested estate in fee simple is no part of, nor incidental to, any one of these estates. Consequently, cases dealing with the creation of recognized common-law estates have no application to a restriction against alienation of a vested fee simple estate. The rules announced in Sandberg v. Heirs of Champlin, 152 Neb. 161, 40 N.W.2d 411, Watson v. Dalton, supra, State Bank of Jansen v. Thiessen, supra, and Myers v. Myers, 109 Neb. 230, 190 N.W. 491, control in the present case and require a holding that Frank B. Hall was the owner in fee simple of a one-ninth interest in the real estate in question and that the purported restriction against alienation contained in the will is against public policy and void. This being so, the conveyance made by him to Hilda B. Robinson was valid and operated to convey his interest in the real estate to her.

The judgment of the district court is reversed and the cause remanded with directions to enter a decree in conformity with the holdings of this opinion.

Reversed and remanded with directions.[81]

[81] For a comment on Andrews v. Hall, see 52 Mich. L. Rev. 616 (1954). The following references in 6 American Law of Property (Casner ed. 1952) relate to forfeiture restraints and disabling restraints on legal interests: §§26.13-26.47 (restraints on alienation of present legal fees simple or other absolute interests); §§26.48-26.51 (restraints on present legal life estates or terms of years); §§26.52-26.54 (restraints on legal future interests). See also Sandberg v. Heirs of Champlin, quoted supra page 444, and see page 446 supra, note 13, and page 616 supra, note 77. — ED.

b. *Restraint on the Alienation of an Equitable Interest*

RICHARDSON v. WARFIELD
252 Mass. 518, 148 N.E. 141 (1925)

SANDERSON, J. This is a petition by the trustees under the will of Clement Willis, who died June 20, 1889, for instructions as to the disposition of the principal of the trust fund held by them and of certain income which has accumulated in their hands. The clauses of the will providing for the payment of this income and the division of the principal are in the following language: "Tenth. I give to my Trustees hereinafter named all the rest and residue of my property both real, personal and mixed, of every kind and sort, and wherever situated, to have and hold the same and to pay over the income to my heirs as often as once in six months. Eleventh. The real and personal estate given to my Trustees the income of which is made payable to my children and their heirs at law, shall not be subject to any assignment, sale or draft, or order, voluntary or by process at law, and this extends to all my bequests to my children and their heirs at law, and after the decease of my children the property is to be divided among my grandchildren share and share alike."

The testator had four children. His son Edward H. Willis predeceased him leaving two children; Charles J. Willis died in 1895, leaving six children, two having been born after the testator's decease; Henry C. Willis died in 1898 leaving one child; and Mary E. Willis Sparhawk died July 19, 1924, leaving two children. At the time of the death of Mrs. Sparhawk two of the six children of Charles J. Willis had died: George A. Willis in December, 1922, leaving three children, and Rachel N. Willis, one of the children born after the death of the testator, in 1906. No one has appeared in these proceedings to represent the estate of Rachel N. Willis. After her death the fractional part of the income which she had been receiving was divided among her surviving brothers and sisters. At the time of the testator's death there were nine living grandchildren and when his last surviving child died there were nine surviving grandchildren. In the meantime two grandchildren had been born and two had died. The total number of grandchildren, living and dead, was eleven.

In 1912 George A. Willis assigned to George F. West and Son all his interest in the estate of Clement Willis upon the death of his last surviving child. George F. West and Son have been made parties to these proceedings and are contending that all interest which George A. Willis had in the estate belongs to them. One Kenneth S. Domett also has been made a party, contending that by reason of an agreement between him and George F. West and Son concerning this assignment, he has a claim against the administrator of the estate of George A. Willis which should be determined in this proceeding.

The clause in the will providing that the property given to the trustees should not be subject to any assignment, sale or order, made it impossible for George A. Willis to pass any title by the assignment which he undertook to make. Broadway National Bank v. Adams, 133 Mass. 170. Boston Safe Deposit & Trust Co. v. Collier, 222 Mass. 390. The trust was an active one which required for its accomplishment that the legal title should be in the trustees. The title of the beneficiaries was an equitable one and inalienable under the terms of the will. Such a restraint on alienation is valid as to both principal and income, and neither George F. West and Son nor the claimant under them is entitled to share in the estate. Haskell v. Haskell, 234 Mass. 442.[82]

The trustees have permitted the portion of income which was formerly payable to George A. Willis to accumulate since his death, and they now ask instructions as to its disposition and also as to the persons who are to take, and the proportions in which they are to take, the principal of the fund.

The provision that the property is to be divided after the decease of the testator's children means that the whole fund should be divided as of July 19, 1924, the date of death of the last surviving child. Dole v. Keyes, 143 Mass. 237. Estates are considered vested unless it plainly appears that the testator intended otherwise, and this is especially true where the limitation over is made to children of the testator or his relatives by blood or marriage. Bosworth v. Stockbridge, 189 Mass. 266. Minot v. Purrington, 190 Mass. 336. Porter v. Porter, 226 Mass. 204, 206. Boston Safe Deposit & Trust Co. v. Abbott, 242 Mass. 92. In the case under consideration the income is made payable to the testator's children and their heirs, while the property, in the end, is to be divided

---

[82] In Sproul-Bolton v. Sproul-Bolton, 383 Pa. 85, 117 A.2d 688 (1955), the court considered whether a spendthrift provision as to principal would continue after the beneficiary had a right to the principal but prior to the time the trustee in fact distributed it to him. The court conceded that the settlor can effectively provide against attachment or alienation until the actual payment of principal to the beneficiary by the trustee. It found, however, that in this case the settlor had not extended the spendthrift provision to cover this period. — ED.

among the testator's grandchildren share and share alike. It is apparent from a reading of the eleventh clause of the will that when the testator used the word "heirs" in the tenth, he meant children; and from reading the two together that he meant his children and their children when he used the words "my children and their heirs" in the eleventh clause. He did not attempt to control the disposition of his estate beyond his grandchildren, nor of the income of it beyond the death of his last surviving child. The record discloses that no great-grandchild was born until after his death. Clause three of the will, which provides for grandchildren at the testator's decease, was held in Richardson v. Willis, 163 Mass. 130, not to include grandchildren born after the testator's death. The omission in the provision for the final disposition of the property of the words "at my decease" indicates a purpose to include in this clause all grandchildren. The basic testamentary purpose to benefit children and grandchildren which appears in different parts of the will and codicil will be best accomplished by construing their interests as vested. The words "after the decease of my children" do not express a contingency but an inevitable future event. They do not fix the time when the remaindermen will be ascertained or when their titles spring into existence, but only when the possession and enjoyment of the shares begin. In cases where the testator intends to include in his benefactions all persons who come within the description of grandchildren, not only at the time of his death but up to the time when the property vests in possession, the estate vests in interest at the death of the testator, but the devise or bequest will open to let in after-born grandchildren up to the time fixed for distribution. Bosworth v. Stockbridge, supra. Weston v. Foster, 7 Met. 297. Blanchard v. Blanchard, 1 Allen, 223. Hatfield v. Sohier, 114 Mass. 48, 52. Dole v. Keyes, 143 Mass. 237. McArthur v. Scott, 113 U.S. 340. The estate vests in such after-born children at their birth. Weston v. Foster, supra. Hatfield v. Sohier, supra. A vested interest in an estate passes upon the death of his owner to his legal representative in so far as it is personal, and to his heirs in so far as it is real property. Winslow v. Goodwin, 7 Met. 363. Hatfield v. Sohier, supra. Goddard v. Whitney, 140 Mass. 92. Boston Safe Deposit & Trust Co. v. Nevin, 212 Mass. 232.

The income that accumulated up to July 19, 1924, which would have been paid to George A. Willis, if living, is to be paid to his legal representative. The principal of the trust fund is to be divided into eleven equal parts; one part to be paid to each of the nine living grandchildren, one part to the legal representative of George A. Willis, and one part to the legal representative of Rachel N. Willis. Costs out of the fund as between solicitor and client are to be in the discretion of the single justice.

Decree accordingly.[83]

9. RULE AGAINST PERPETUITIES

Whenever future interests are created in an estate plan, the rule against perpetuities must be kept in the forefront of one's thinking. It is obvious that by no stretch of the imagination can an estate plan which violates the rule against perpetuities be deemed properly drafted.[84]

The common-law rule against perpetuities is operative in most states. However, statutory rules which are substantially different from the common law rule exist in a number of states. It is essential to know what state law as to perpetuities will govern the estate plan in the absence of any attempt to select the governing

---

[83] Re-examine Wilmington Trust Co. v. Carpenter, printed in full supra page 556, which considers the effectiveness of a trust provision restraining alienation by the settlor of his interest under the trust. In regard to whether a spendthrift provision is undermined by giving to the one whose interest is subject to the spendthrift provision a general power to appoint the trust property by deed or a special power to appoint the trust property by deed, see Griswold, Spendthrift Trusts 72 (2d ed. 1947).

The following references in 6 American Law of Property (Casner ed. 1952) relate to forfeiture and disabling restraints on equitable interests: §§26.88-26.100 (validity of restraints on alienation of equitable interests apart from statutory provisions); §§26.101-26.107 (statutes creating, authorizing or forbidding restraints on equitable interests). See also a state-by-state analysis as to the validity of spendthrift trusts in 34 A.L.R.2d 1335 (1954). On the effect of inserting an invalid spendthrift provision, see 9 id. 1361 (1950).

In New York a statutory spendthrift provision as to income attaches to trusts. See N.Y. Personal Property Law §15 (N.Y. Real Property Law §103 is similar), quoted infra page 1468. This New York statute is particularly significant in applying the New York rule against perpetuities because every trust whereby the income is payable to a person suspends the power of alienation and the New York rule is aimed at property dispositions which suspend the power of alienation as well as at remoteness of vesting. — Ed.

[84] If an inter vivos trust is established which is designed to eliminate the value of the trust property from the settlor's gross estate, and some interests under the trust violate the rule against perpetuities, there will be a reversionary interest in the settlor, the value of which will be includible in his gross estate. In Old Colony Trust Co. v. United States, 165 F. Supp. 669 (D. Mass. 1958), the Commissioner claimed that an interest under an inter vivos trust violated the Massachusetts rule against perpetuities, so that the settlor had an interest under the trust that was includible in his gross estate. The settlor's executor filed a petition in the Probate Court seeking a declaration as to rights under the trust and making interested persons parties. The Commissioner was informed of the proceedings by registered mail but did not appear. After a vigorous contest by interested parties, the Probate Court determined that the rule against perpetuities was not violated, and no appeal was taken. The District Court decided that the state court's determination was controlling and, therefore, the settlor's gross estate did not include any interest under the trust.

state, and if the law as to perpetuities in the state is too restrictive
in the particular case, to know to what extent the law as to perpetuities in some other state may be made controlling.[85]

The date from which the period of the rule against perpetuities
commences to run in different situations must be kept in mind.
When does the period commence to run in the following situations?

1. An irrevocable inter vivos trust
2. A revocable inter vivos trust
3. Settlement of insurance proceeds by adoption of one of the
   options in the policy
4. A will [86]

JEE v. AUDLEY
1 Cox 324 (Ch. 1787)

Edward Audley, by his will, bequeathed as follows, "Also my
will is that £1000 shall be placed out at interest during the life
of my wife, which interest I give her during her life, and at her
death I give the said £1000 unto my niece Mary Hall and the issue of her body lawfully begotten, and to be begotten, and in default of such issue I give the said £1000 to be equally divided
between the daughters then living of my kinsman John Jee and his
wife Elizabeth Jee."

It appeared that John Jee and Elizabeth Jee were living at the
time of the death of the testator, had four daughters and no son,
and were of a very advanced age. Mary Hall was unmarried and
of the age of about 40; the wife was dead. The present bill was
filed by the four daughters of John and Elizabeth Jee to have the
£1000 secured for their benefit upon the event of the said Mary
Hall dying without leaving children. And the question was,

---

[85] The extent to which the law of a particular state as to the rule against
perpetuities may be selected to control the estate plan is examined in Amerige
v. Attorney General, printed in full infra page 771. The material at page
1068 infra, is also relevant.

[86] When the period commences to run in the following situations is considered in Chapter XII:
1. The exercise of a general power to appoint by deed alone or by deed
   or will (page 702 infra).
2. The exercise of a general power to appoint by will (page 702 infra).
3. The exercise of a special power to appoint by deed alone or by deed
   or will (page 702 infra).
4. The exercise of a special power to appoint by will (page 702 infra).
5. The gift in default of the exercise of a power of appointment (page 703
   infra).

The application of the rule against perpetuities to charitable gifts is dealt
with infra page 876. For a consideration of administrative provisions and
the rule against perpetuities, see page 1120 infra.

whether the limitation to the daughters of John and Elizabeth Jee was not void as being too remote; and to prove it so, it was said that this was to take effect on a general failure of issue of Mary Hall; and though it was to the daughters of John and Elizabeth Jee, yet it was not confined to the daughters living at the death of the testator, and consequently it might extend to after-born daughters, in which case it would not be within the limit of a life or lives in being and 21 years afterwards, beyond which time an executory devise is void.

On the other side it was said, that though the late cases had decided that on a gift to children generally, such children as should be living at the time of the distribution of the fund should be let in, yet it would be very hard to adhere to such a rule of construction so rigidly, as to defeat the evident intention of the testator in this case, especially as there was no real possibility of John and Elizabeth Jee having children after the testator's death, they being then 70 years old; that if there were two ways of construing words, that should be adopted which would give effect to the disposition made by the testator; that the cases, which had decided that after-born children should take, proceeded on the implied intention of the testator, and never meant to give an effect to words which would totally defeat such intention. . . .

MASTER OF THE ROLLS [Sir Lloyd Kenyon]. Several cases determined by Lord Northington, Lord Camden, and the present Chancellor, have settled that children born after the death of the testator shall take a share in these cases; the difference is, where there is an immediate devise, and where there is an interest in remainder; in the former case the children living at the testator's death only shall take; in the latter those who are living at the time the interest vests in possession; and this being now a settled principle, I shall not strain to serve an intention at the expense of removing the land marks of the law; it is of infinite importance to abide by decided cases, and perhaps more so on this subject than any other. The general principles which apply to this case are not disputed: the limitations of personal estate are void, unless they necessarily vest, if at all, within a life or lives in being and 21 years or 9 or 10 months afterwards. This has been sanctioned by the opinion of judges of all times, from the time of the Duke of Norfolk's case to the present: it is grown reverend by age, and is not now to be broken in upon; I am desired to do in this case something which I do not feel myself at liberty to do, namely to suppose it impossible for persons in so advanced an age as John and Elizabeth Jee to have children; but if this can be done in one case it may in another, and it is a very dangerous experiment, and introductive of the greatest inconvenience to give a latitude to such sort of conjecture. Another thing pressed upon me, is to decide on the events which have happened; but I cannot do this without overturning very many cases. The single question before me is, not whether the limitation is good in the events which have happened, but whether it was good in its creation; and if it were not, I cannot make it so. Then must this limitation, if at all, necessarily take place within the limits prescribed by law? The words are "in default of such issue I give the said £1000 to be equally divided between the daughters then living of John Jee and Elizabeth his wife." If it had been to "daughters now living," or "who should be living at the time of my death," it would have been very good; but as it stands, this limitation may take in after-born daughters; this point is clearly settled by Ellison v. Airey, and the effect of law on such limitation cannot make any difference in construing such intention. If then this will extended to after-born daughters, is it within the rules of law? Most certainly not, because John and Elizabeth Jee might have children born ten years after the testator's death, and then Mary Hall might die without issue 50 years afterwards; in which case it would evidently transgress the rules prescribed. I am of opinion therefore, though the testator might possibly mean to restrain the limitation to the children who should be living at the time of the death, I cannot, consistently with decided cases, construe it in such restrained sense, but must intend it to take in after-born children. This therefore not being within the rules of law, and as I cannot judge upon subsequent events, I think the limitation void. Therefore dismiss the bill, but without costs.[87]

Matter of WILCOX
194 N.Y. 288, 87 N.E. 497 (1909)

CULLEN, Ch. J. Bethuel McCoy died testate in 1874. He left him surviving three children, William McCoy, Charles McCoy and Frances D. Wilcox. A daughter, Maria E. Sanders, predeceased him, leaving a husband and two children. This controversy relates to the validity and effect of the seventh clause of his will, which is as follows: "I give, devise and bequeath all the rest, residue and remainder of my estate, both real and personal, as follows: . . . and the remaining third thereof to my said executors in trust for the purpose of paying the income thereof to my daughter,

[87] The common-law rule against perpetuities is considered in 6 American Law of Property §§24.1-24.64 (Casner ed. 1952) and 4 Restatement of Property §§370-403. — ED.

Frances D. Wilcox, for and during the term of her natural life, annually, and at her decease I give, devise and bequeath to her issue, share and share alike, such income, and as each of her said issue shall attain the age of 21 years, I give, devise and bequeath to it one equal undivided share of the principal of said remaining third, and in case my said daughter, Frances D. Wilcox, shall die, leaving no issue born to her, which shall attain the age of 21 years, then and in such case, said remaining third of my residuary estate, I give, devise and bequeath to my daughter, Maria E. Sanders, and my son Charles McCoy, share and share alike forever." By the will the testator's son Charles McCoy was appointed executor thereof.

By one of the codicils the provision of his will in favor of Maria E. Sanders was modified so as to give her the income of this share for life, and on her death the principal to her husband and children. Maria, as already said, died before the testator. The will was proved and the executor qualified. On the settlement of the executor's accounts in 1880 it was found that the fund for the benefit of Frances D. Wilcox under the seventh clause of the will amounted to $7,512. The executor was directed to invest said sum and apply the income to said Frances during her life, and upon her death to distribute it in accordance with the provisions of the will. The executor died in 1898, when the beneficiary Frances was appointed trustee of the fund. She received the income during her lifetime. On her death in January, 1906, the executor of her will instituted these proceedings for the settlement of her accounts as trustee.

Frances was married at the decease of her father, the testator. She left no issue her surviving, having had but one child, who was born March 6th, 1859, and died on the 3rd of June following. The contest is between Charles B. McCoy and Frank G. McCoy, the children of the testator's son William McCoy, who contend that the whole of the seventh clause of the will is invalid and that the fund passed, as in case of intestacy, and the legatees to whom by that clause the fund is bequeathed on the contingency that Frances should leave no issue who should reach majority. These legatees contend that the gift over is valid regardless of the invalidity of any provisions directing the prior disposition of the fund. The surrogate decided in favor of the legatees. That decision has been affirmed by the Appellate Division by a divided court, and the next of kin now appeal to this court.

It is conceded by both the learned courts below that the provision creating a trust in favor of the issue whom Frances might leave surviving until such issue respectively should reach their majority was illegal and invalid, in that it might suspend the absolute ownership of personal property during lives not in being at the death of the testator. This conclusion was undoubtedly correct (1 R.S. p. 723, Sec. 15), though it would have been valid in the case of real estate if it could be assumed that the trust was several as to the share of each issue. (Manice v. Manice, 43 N.Y. 303.) [88] The trust during the lifetime of Frances was plainly valid and is readily severable from the ulterior provisions and limitations. (Tiers v. Tiers, 98 N.Y. 568.) But it was also held that the invalidity of the provision for the issue of Frances did not affect the validity of the gift over. It was considered that such gift being made to named beneficiaries in being at the death of the testator, and the interests of such persons being at all times susceptible of alienation by them, did not suspend the absolute ownership of the property for any period. The learned judge who wrote for the Appellate Division said that the estates provided for by the will were alternative and that as the first and invalid one in favor of the issue of Frances had not taken effect, the second was in no way affected by such invalidity. In one sense the will provided for alternative dispositions of the property, but only in the sense that every gift over may be said to be alternative on the failure of the contingency on which the gift is dependent to occur. The dispositions were not, however, alternative in the ordinary use of that term. If the learned court intended to assert that the gift over by itself implied alternatives, to wit, a gift on the contingency that Frances died without issue her surviving — a gift that would have been unquestionably good — and a gift on the contingency that no issue that she might leave should reach majority, such a doctrine seems to be in direct opposition to the decided cases.

It is said by Professor Gray in his work on Perpetuities (Sec. 331): "Very often, indeed generally, a future contingency which is too remote may in fact happen within the limit prescribed by the rule against perpetuities, and a gift conditioned on such contingency may be put into one of two classes according as the contingency happens or does not happen within those limits; but unless this division into classes is made by the donor, the law will not make it for him, and the gift will be bad altogether. . . . (Sec. 331.) This is the law even when the division is of the most obvi-

---

[88] The New York minority provision was extended in 1929 to personal property. This minority provision as it applies to both real and personal property is explained in 6 American Law of Property §25.17 (Casner ed. 1952). It was eliminated as of April 12, 1960, by the 1960 New York legislation that added to the permissible period of the rule against perpetuities a twenty-one-year period for all cases. See Note on the New York Statutory Rule Against Perpetuities, infra page 639. — Ed.

ous character. Thus a gift to B, if no child of A reaches twenty-five is bad, although A dies without children; while if the gift over had been if A dies without children, or if his children all die under twenty-one,[89] then on A's death without children the gift over would have taken effect." It was said in In re Bence (L.R. 3 Ch. Div. 1891, 242, 251), alluding to another decision: "The case is, therefore, no authority for the proposition that every gift over may be analyzed into as many events as are included within its language, and be held good or bad as the events happen."

It is in this respect that the case before us differs essentially from that of Schettler v. Smith (41 N.Y. 328), relied upon by the Appellate Division. In that case the testator himself expressly made alternative gifts, the first upon the death of the widow of his son if the son should leave a widow, which was held bad, because such widow might be a person not in being at the death of the testator, and the other in the case of the death of the son without a widow, or of his death without issue, in either of which contingencies the gift over was good. So in that case the gift over upon the death of the son leaving a widow was held void in entirety, though it was entirely possible that the son's widow might be a person in being at the death of the testator. At this point we must recall two elementary principles in determining the validity of wills. First. Such validity must be determined not in the light of what has actually transpired, but from exactly the same point of view from which it would be regarded had a suit been brought to determine the validity of the will at the time of the death of the testator, instead of at a subsequent period. That is to say, the validity of a will depends not on what has happened since the death of the testator, but on what might have happened. Second. In determining the validity of limitations of estates, under the above statutes, (the provisions of the Revised Statutes in reference to absolute ownership and restraint of alienation) it is not sufficient that the estates attempted to be created may, by the happening of subsequent events, be terminated within the prescribed period, if such events might so happen that such estates might extend beyond such period. In other words, to render such future estates valid, they must be so limited that in every possible contingency, they will absolutely terminate at such period, or such estates will be held void." (Schettler v. Smith, p. 334, supra.)

The first question is, what is the effect of the invalidity of the trust which the testator attempted to create or continue during

---

[89] "Twenty-one" should be "twenty-five." The court has misquoted Professor Gray. See Gray, The Rule Against Perpetuities §332 (4th ed., Roland Gray, 1942). — ED.

the minority of the issue of his daughter Frances. The words of the will are "and as each of her said issue shall attain the age of 21 years, I give, devise and bequeath to it one equal undivided share," etc. The general rule is that such terms, although apparently making the gift depend on a contingency, should be construed as applying merely to the futurity of possession. So also the presence of a gift over in case of failure to attain the age of twenty-one years confirms the construction that the gift is vested. It was decided in Manice v. Manice (supra), where the trust during the minority of the issue of the daughter was held invalid as to personalty, that such personalty vested in the daughter's issue on the death of their mother. In this case, therefore, on the death of the testator's daughter Frances her issue would have been entitled to the principal of the trust fund subject only to the limitation in favor of the testator's two children Maria Sanders and Charles McCoy if that limitation is valid. It must be here remembered that the gift over is only in case of Frances leaving no issue who should attain the age of twenty-one years, and that there might have been issue some of whom might arrive at the age of twenty-one years and some of whom might fail to attain that age, in which case the gift over would not take effect.

The remaining question is as to the validity of the gift over. That this gift was contingent, not vested, was settled by the decision of this court in Hennessy v. Patterson (85 N.Y. 91). But though contingent, the legatees were certain and their interests at all times alienable. It must, therefore, be conceded that the gift did in no degree suspend the absolute power of alienation. But the question remains did it suspend the absolute ownership of personal property for more than two lives in being, which is the rule prescribed by the Revised Statutes. (1 R.S. 723, Sec. 15.)

At common law the suspension of the power of alienation was no factor of the rule against perpetuities either as to real estate or personalty. That rule was against remoteness in vesting and certain future estates were held bad for remoteness, though they did not affect the power of alienation. (Gray on Perpetuities, Secs. 1-4, 268, et seq.) That rule was that a future estate must vest, if at all, within lives in being and the term of twenty-one years. Under our Revised Statutes a new rule was substituted for that which had been evolved at common law by the courts and with us, of course, the only question is what does our statute forbid. In the first place it substituted two lives in being for any number of lives in being, and as to real estate a minority instead of a definite period of twenty-one years and for the prevention of perpetuities in real estate beyond the prescribed limit the first and chief enactment of the statute is found in sections 13, 14 and 15 of Chapter 1, part 2 of the Revised Statutes, the last of which provides that "the absolute power of alienation, shall not be suspended by any limitation or condition whatever, for a longer period than during the continuance of not more than two lives in being at the creation of the estate, except in the single case mentioned in the next section." That it is the application of this provision which has most frequently come before the courts in the determination of the legality of testamentary dispositions is unquestionable, and this fact has led at times to the assertion that since the enactment of the Revised Statutes there is only one rule against perpetuities in this state and that is that the absolute power of alienation shall not be suspended for more than two lives in being. There are, to me, two unanswerable objections to such contention. The revisers were men of great erudition and professional experience. They understood thoroughly the common-law rule under which they had been educated and had practiced and also the result of the alterations in that rule which they intended to effect. Section 17 prohibits the creation of successive life estates to more than two persons in being and renders all subsequent life estates limited thereon void.[90] It was common

---

[90] As the text to which this note is appended points out, legal life estates do not suspend the power of alienation. To make somewhat similar the results with respect to both legal and equitable interests, New York by statute provided a set of special rules applicable to legal interests which invalidated certain interests, though the power of alienation was not suspended and though the interests would vest within the required time. The most prominent of these rules was the one prohibiting the creation of successive legal life estates in more than two persons. Thus, if a conveyance was made "to A for life, then to B for life, then to C for life," C's life estate was void. As long as the two-lives rule controlled the creation of interests under a trust, a rough approximation existed as to permissible legal and equitable life interests. Notice, however, that more than two successive equitable life interests could validly be created as long as the maximum trust term was properly measured by two lives. In regard to the New York rule as to successive legal life estates, see 6 American Law of Property §§25.92-25.96 (Casner ed. 1952). When the New York rule against perpetuities was changed from a two-lives rule to a multiple-lives rule (see Note on the New York Statutory Rule Against Perpetuities at page 639 infra), a corresponding correlating change was made in the rule as to successive legal life estates so that, effective as to inter vivos instruments executed on and after September 1, 1959, and as to wills of persons dying after that date (including exercise, by such instruments or wills, of powers granted or reserved prior to that date), successive legal life estates may be created in more than two persons. The latest chapter in this drama is the repeal of the rule as to successive legal life estates as of April 12, 1960, when New York added to its multiple-lives rule a twenty-one-year period in gross, so that it no longer is necessary to have a set of separate rules applicable to legal interests.

Other special rules applicable to legal interests which followed the same path as the one outlined above with respect to successive legal life estates, even to their elimination as of April 12, 1960, were the following: successive

knowledge then, as now, that no number of legal life estates of persons in being could suspend the absolute power of alienation for a single instant of time. At least in this respect the revisers intended to enact some further limitation on the power to create future estates than the provision that they should not suspend the power of alienation.

Secondly, we have the provisions of sections 18 to 24 with reference to the creation of remainders. The last of these sections prescribes, "subject to the rules established in the preceding sections of this Article, a freehold estate as well as a chattel real, may be created, to commence at a future day; an estate for life may be created, in a term of years, and a remainder limited thereon; a remainder of a freehold or chattel real, either contingent or vested, may be created expectant on the determination of a term of years; *and a fee may be limited on a fee*, upon a contingency, which, if it should occur, must happen within the period prescribed in this Article." (Id. Sec. 24.) If the revisers intended, as is claimed, to establish the single rule that the power of alienation should not be suspended for more than two lives in being, it is impossible to understand why these elaborate and minute provisions for the creation of remainders were enacted. Sections 14 and 15 covered the whole subject. Their provisions were absolute and unqualified that the absolute power of alienation should not be suspended by any limitation or condition whatever for longer than the prescribed period. If suspension of the power of alienation was the only rule, what possible object was to be gained by the provisions of the later sections? They added nothing to the efficacy of the former inhibitions, and we can hardly credit the idea that the revisers were under delusion as to their necessity. It seems to me clear that the revisers did intend, so far as remainders were concerned, in addition to the provision against inalienability, to provide against remoteness of vesting which, as already said, was the test of validity under the common-law rule, with which they were familiar. It may be said that this view also accords with that entertained by Mr. Chaplin in his text book on Suspension of the Power of Alienation, where he says (p. 1): "The provisions of the Revised Statutes

---

legal life estates could be created only in persons in being; an estate for life after a term of years could be created only in a person in being; only a remainder in fee could be limited after a life estate pur auter vie, and if more than two lives measured the duration of a life estate pur auter vie, the remainder would take effect upon the death of the two persons first named as the measuring lives; a contingent remainder limited on a term of years had to be one which would vest within two lives. — ED.

furnish two rules concerning the alienability and the vesting of estates. These rules may be stated as follows:

"Rule I. Alienability. The power of conveying the absolute fee, in possession, shall not be suspended beyond the statutory period. . . .

"Rule II. Vesting. Estates in remainder shall be so limited that within the statutory period, if ever, they must vest in interest.

"This rule is thus seen to apply to only one class of future estates, namely, 'remainders;' but to insist not only on absolute alienability, but also on vesting, which is a broader term, and (except in certain cases of vesting in trust) includes alienability."

That section 17 imposes an additional restriction on the power to create future estates in land is settled by the decision of this court in Purdy v. Hayt (92 N.Y. 446, 451), where, in giving effect to it, Chief Judge Andrews said: "The prohibition against the creation of more than two successive life estates in the same property has no necessary connection with the law of perpetuities. There is no suspense of the power of alienation of land by the creation of successive life estates therein unless they are contingent. Any number of successive vested life estates may be created without violating the statute of perpetuities. The prohibition against creating more than two successive life estates in the same property applies to such estates, whether vested or contingent." It is to be observed that Chief Judge Andrews remarks that this statutory provision has no connection with the rule against perpetuities. But it is very apparent that in this statement he confines the rule of perpetuities to the law restricting the suspension of the power of alienation. I have used the term in the broader sense as comprehending any limitation on the power of creating future estates. This, however, is a mere matter of nomenclature, of no importance. The point is that the Revised Statutes make at least one additional limitation on such power. The question is whether there are not also other limitations, call them what you may.

Section 24, already quoted, concludes "and a fee may be limited on a fee, upon a contingency, which, if it should occur, must happen within the period prescribed in this Article" i.e., within two lives in being. This statutory authority for limiting a fee upon a fee is necessarily exclusive; otherwise, why should the statute declare that the contingency *must* occur within the specified period? It has no necessary connection with the provision restricting the suspension of the power of alienation. It is under this provision that the present case would fall if it were real estate.

I have said that the remainder in the present case would on the death of Mrs. Wilcox vest in her issue absolutely, subject to the gift over, but if I err in this view (See Greenland v. Waddell, 116 N.Y. 234) the only result would be that the remainder vested in the next of kin subject also to that gift. Under either view we have the case of a remainder in fee limited upon a remainder in fee upon a contingency which might not happen within the period of two lives in being.

Though this case is governed by the statutory provisions relative to estates in personal property, I have discussed the provisions relating to real estate, 1st, because by sections 1 and 2 of the Revised Statutes (1 R.S. 773) relative to expectant estates in such property, it is provided that "The absolute ownership of personal property shall not be suspended by any limitation or condition whatever, for a longer period than during the continuance and until the termination of not more than two lives in being at the date of the instrument containing such limitation or condition; or, if such instrument be a will, for not more than two lives in being at the death of the testator. *In all other respects, limitations of future or contingent interests in personal property" shall be subject to the rules governing future estates in land.* And, 2nd, if it were established that the sole statutory restriction on the power to create estates in realty was that the creation of such estates should not suspend the absolute power of alienation beyond the prescribed period, there would be force in the position that the absolute ownership of personal property was not suspended when there were persons in being, no matter in what manner or what the nature of their interests, who acting conjointly could transfer an indefeasible title. But if the proposition is established, as I think it is, that the inhibition on the suspension of the power of alienation is not the sole rule against perpetuities as to reality, it is evident that the term "absolute ownership" as applied to personalty must be interpreted in its ordinary and natural sense, and that the same is suspended where the title of one is defeasible in favor of another, and that neither one can be said to possess absolute ownership, even though both are in being at the time. . . .

I am, therefore, of opinion that for a contingent limitation of a remainder in personal property to be valid, the contingency must be such as necessarily to occur within two lives in being at the death of the testator. The limitation contained in this will on the death of all issue of the testator's daughter before arriving at the age of twenty-one years is, therefore, void.

The condition in which this case is presented to us creates some embarrassment. Any estate or interest in property as to which the testator dies intestate passes to his next of kin or heirs at law, depending on the character of the property, who are to be ascertained at the time of the testator's death. (Clark v. Cammann, 160 N.Y. 315.) The appellant here, Charles B. McCoy, claims as one of the heirs at law of William McCoy, a son of the testator who survived the latter. Any interest in the fund, therefore, passed to William McCoy's personal representatives (who are not parties to this proceeding) and not to his heirs at law. It is possible that the fund may have proceeded from the sale of real estate and, therefore, should be treated as such, but nothing of that kind appears in the record before us. But if the fund should be treated as real estate it would not affect the question before us, for, as already said, the gift over is not of the share of any of the issue of Frances upon its death before reaching majority, but on Frances not leaving any issue that might attain full age. The gift, therefore, would not fall within Section 16, p. 723, of the Revised Statutes, that of a single minority.

The decree of the surrogate and order of the Appellate Division should be reversed, and judgment rendered that the testator died intestate as to the remainder in the fund in controversy after the death of Frances, and that the same passed to his next of kin, with costs to all parties appearing in this court, payable out of the fund.[91]

EDWARD T. BARTLETT, J. (dissenting). [Dissenting opinion omitted.]

NOTE ON THE NEW YORK STATUTORY RULE AGAINST PERPETUITIES

The two-lives rule as it existed for many years in New York placed anyone who submitted himself to it at a distinct disadvantage from an estate planning standpoint. The disadvantage resulted from the fact that in a state governed by the common law rule against perpetuities, estates could be removed from subjection to estate taxes for a much longer period of time than was possible under the two-lives rule.

This disadvantage was lessened by the switch from a two-lives

---

[91] The separability of valid and invalid conditions is considered in 6 American Law of Property §24.54 (Casner ed. 1952).

Under the two-lives rule, if A creates a life interest in property and, then, by a separate conveyance disposes of his reversion, will the life estate originally created use up one of the allowable two lives in determining the validity of interests created by the transfer of the reversion? See New York Trust Co. v. Weaver, 298 N.Y. 1, 80 N.E.2d 56 (1948). Consider also Morgan v. Keyes, 302 N.Y. 439, 99 N.E.2d 230 (1951). — ED.

rule to a multiple-lives rule in 1958.[92]   The change was effective
from and after September 1, 1958, as to all inter vivos transfers
effective on or after that date and to estates or wills of persons dying on or after that date.   In 1959, New York further provided by
statute that when a trust was created by the exercise of a power of
appointment, the governing law, so far as the permissible number
of measuring lives was concerned, shall be the law in effect when
the power is exercised rather than when it was created.[93]   What
is the situation in New York with respect to interests created by a
revocable inter vivos trust where the instrument was executed before September 1, 1958, and the settlor dies after that date?

In 1960, New York undertook to gain equality with the states
following the common law rule against perpetuities, by adding the
twenty-one-year period to the multiple-lives rule.[94]   The effective
date of this change was April 12, 1960.   In addition, New York
undertook to give some advantages not available under the common law rule.   These advantages are as follows:

1. If a gift violates the rule against perpetuities because of an
   age contingency and it can be saved by cutting down the
   age contingency to age twenty-one, that will be done.[95]
2. A presumption is established to the effect that
   a. The creator of property interests intends all of them to
      be valid;
   b. A gift to a spouse means a spouse who is a person in be-
      ing at the effective date of the instrument, thereby do-
      ing away with the unborn widow case; and
   c. Where a gift is dependent upon the occurrence of a
      contingency relating to the probate of a will or the ad-
      ministration of an estate, the gift is to take effect only if
      the contingency occurs within twenty-one years of the
      effective date of the instrument.[96]

The present wording of Section 11 of the New York Personal
Property Law will be found infra page 1468, and that of Section 42
of the New York Real Property Law (Supp. 1960), infra page 1469.

[92] See N.Y. Laws 1958, c. 152, which amended New York Personal Property
Law §11, and Laws 1958, c. 153, which amended New York Real Property
Law §42.

[93] See N.Y. Laws 1959, c. 456, which amended Real Property Law §§178,
179.

[94] See N.Y. Laws 1960, c. 448, which amended both Personal Property Law
§11 and Real Property Law §42.

[95] See Personal Property Law §11-a and Real Property Law §42-b, both
added by N.Y. Laws 1960, c. 448.   The origin of this type of legislation in the
United States is found in the Massachusetts wait-and-see legislation discussed
in Note on Wait-and-See Statutes at page 655 infra.

[96] See Personal Property Law §11-b and Real Property Law §42-c, both
added by N.Y. Laws 1960, c. 448.

It should be kept in mind that the New York rule in its modern-ized form still retains the suspension of the power of alienation in-gredient, which is not present under the common law rule.[97]

PROBLEMS

11.37. A, a resident of New York, desires to establish a short-term trust so that the income from the trust property will be tax-able to the designated beneficiary during the period of the trust and, on the termination of the trust, the trust corpus will revert to A. How could such a trust have been established under the for-mer New York two-lives rule?

11.38. A conveys Blackacre, located in a jurisdiction which ap-plies the common rule against perpetuities, "to B for life, then to B's widow for life, then to B's children who are living on the death of the survivor of B and B's widow." At the time of the convey-ance B is married to W. If W predeceases B, is the gift to B's chil-dren valid? If W survives B, is the gift to B's children valid? [98]

[97] The two-lives rule which was in force in New York is thoroughly ex-amined in 6 American Law of Property §§25.7-25.35 (Casner ed. 1952). The influence of the New York statutory rule in other states and other statu-tory modifications of the common law rule are explored as follows: Arizona (§25.58); California (§§25.59-25.66); District of Columbia (§§25.83-25.86); Idaho (§25.67); Indiana (§§25.68-25.72); Kentucky (§25.87); Louisiana (§25.88); Mich-igan (§§25.36-25.47); Minnesota (§§25.48-25.53); Mississippi (§25.89); Mon-tana (§25.73); North Dakota (§§25.75-25.76); Oklahoma (§§25.77-25.81); South Dakota (§25.82); Wisconsin (§§25.54-25.57); Wyoming (§25.91). With respect to the states listed above, there is a trend toward eliminating statutory modifications of the common law rule. In 1945, Indiana restored the com-mon law rule; in 1949, Michigan repealed the statutory rule against the suspension of the power of alienation of real property and restored the com-mon law rule, so that now the common law rule is applicable to both real and personal property; and in 1951, California moved back to the common law rule, but the doctrine of the suspension of the power of alienation con-tinued to be significant until 1959 when its significance was eliminated by Cal. Laws 1959, c. 470, §1. In these three states, however, the statutory rules will continue for many years to be important because the changes are appli-cable only to documents executed after the restoration of the common law rule. See also Wyo. Laws 1949, c. 92, §1, in regard to the elimination of the suspension rules in that state. Kentucky restored the common law rule in 1960 and combined it with a wait-and-see approach. Ky. Laws 1960, S.B. 180. Montana has extended the period from lives in being to lives in being and twenty-one years and, though a provision requiring vesting has been added, the test as to suspension of the power of alienation remains. Mont. Rev. Codes Ann. §67-406(a), (b) (1947, Supp. 1959).

[98] If the conveyance is construed so that "B's widow" means W, B's present wife, then the gift to B's children living on her death is clearly valid. In Stryker v. Kennard, 339 Mass. 373, 159 N.E.2d 71 (1959), the court recognized that a gift to the widow of another is presumptively one only to that other's wife who was known to the transferor. The court, however, found evidence in the particular case to overcome the presumption and refused to pass on the validity of the remainders following the widow's life interest, because it

NEW ENGLAND TRUST CO. v. SANGER
337 Mass. 342, 149 N.E.2d 598 (1958)

SPALDING, J.

These are appeals from a decree of the Probate Court entered on a petition for instructions. The petition was brought by New England Trust Company, as trustee under an indenture of trust of Sabin P. Sanger, dated February 18, 1913 (hereinafter called the 1913 indenture), and as trustee under a declaration of trust of Sabin P. Sanger, dated April 29, 1930 (hereinafter called the 1930 declaration). The trustee sought instructions as to the distribution of the income and principal of these two trusts.

In the 1913 indenture Sabin P. Sanger, the settlor, declared that he held certain securities in trust.[99] Under article First, the income was to be accumulated during the life of Dr. Eugene B. Sanger (a brother of the settlor and hereinafter called Dr. Sanger) with a power in the trustee to pay to Dr. Sanger such portions of the income as the trustee in its uncontrolled discretion might deem proper. No question is here presented concerning Dr. Sanger's interest. The questions for decision arise out of the second and third articles, which are as follows: "Second: At the death of said Eugene B. Sanger said trustee shall pay said net income to the then surviving children of said Eugene B. Sanger in equal shares to each, the issue of any deceased child taking its parent's share of said income by right of representation. Third: At the death of the last surviving child of said Eugene B. Sanger the principal of said trust fund, with any accumulations thereto, free of all trust, shall be equally divided amongst the issue of the children of said Eugene B. Sanger, per stirpes and not per capita." The trust was irrevocable and there was no power to amend contained in the indenture.

In the course of time it became apparent to the settlor that certain provisions of the 1913 indenture might be repugnant to the rule against perpetuities. To remedy this defect the settlor executed the 1930 declaration. In this instrument the settlor, after

---

was not appropriate to give instructions then as to possible future duties of the trustee. Is there not always the possibility that the life interest in the widow might also fail on the ground of infectious invalidity (see the Sanger case printed in full above), so that the validity of the remainder interests must be determined in order to determine the validity of the prior interests? See New York Real Property Law §42-c and New York Personal Property Law §11-b, referred to supra note 96.

[99] (*Court footnote*) The settlor died on July 8, 1938, and the New England Trust Company was appointed trustee on October 7, 1938, by the Probate Court for Norfolk County.

reciting that doubts had arisen concerning the validity of certain gifts in the 1913 indenture, because of remoteness, provided as follows: "Now, therefore, in case any provision . . . [of the 1913 indenture] should be declared to be invalid and because of such invalidity any income or principal of the trust should revert in part or in whole to me or to my estate, I . . . declare that I hold in trust and shall be deemed to have held in trust from the date of this instrument, the properties thereby reverting, to pay over the net income accruing therefrom to the now living children of said Eugene B. Sanger and to their issue by right of representation until the death of the last survivor of the said children now living and thereupon to pay over the principal of the trust fund free of trust to the then living issue of such children by right of representation." The petition alleges that Dr. Sanger and two of his children were notified of the execution of this declaration prior to the settlor's death, but this allegation is denied by several of the respondents and the judge made no finding touching the matter, being of opinion that notice to the beneficiaries was not essential to its validity.

The family situation relevant to the two trusts is as follows: The settlor died in 1938. Dr. Sanger, the beneficiary under article First, died in 1945 and was survived by his three children. Two of them, Eugene B. Sanger, Junior, and Charlotte S. Averill, were alive when the 1913 indenture was executed; a third child (Sabin P. Sanger, Second) was born in 1919. These are the primary beneficiaries under article Second and will be sometimes referred to hereinafter as the children. The two eldest children, Charlotte and Eugene, Junior, died in 1947 and 1954, respectively. Charlotte was survived by two children, Richard and Constance. Sabin P. Sanger, Second, is still living and has three minor children. These two groups of children, the class intended to be benefited under article Third, will be referred to sometimes hereinafter as the issue. Eugene B. Sanger, Junior, Dr. Sanger's second child, had no children but he adopted two sons, Eugene B. Sanger, Third, and James M. D. Sanger.

After the death of Dr. Sanger, the income of the trust fund was paid in equal shares to his three children. After Charlotte's death, her share of the income was paid to her issue. The death of Dr. Sanger's second child, Eugene B., Junior, led to the present controversy. The two adopted sons of Eugene are not issue within the terms of either the 1913 indenture or the 1930 declaration and can take nothing under either instrument. (G.L. Ter. Ed.) c. 210, §8.[100] Gallagher v. Sullivan, 251 Mass. 552.

[100] (*Court footnote*) See now St. 1958. c. 121.

Eugene, Junior's share of the income has been accumulated since his death, and shortly thereafter the share of income paid to the issue of Charlotte was also accumulated, awaiting the settlement of this controversy.

The controversy centers upon who should receive the share of the income formerly paid to the deceased children, and upon the proper disposition of the principal on the death of the last surviving child, Sabin P. Sanger, Second. Certain members of the Sanger family and legal representatives of others are named as respondents in the petition. A guardian ad litem was appointed to represent the minor children of Sabin, Second, and any unborn or unascertained persons. Basically the respondents take two positions. Sabin, Second, the guardian ad litem, and Constance (Charlotte's daughter) contend that all gifts, following the gift of income to Dr. Sanger, fail and revert to the settlor's estate and pass under the terms of the 1930 declaration. Opposing this contention are the executors of the will of Eugene B. Sanger, Junior, and the guardian of his two adopted sons. The guardian argues that the 1930 declaration is an invalid trust, and that after the termination of the valid gifts in the 1913 indenture, the property reverts to the settlor's estate, and passes under the residuary clause in his will. The executors of Eugene, Junior, construe article Second as giving the principal to the children of Dr. Sanger, and contend that one third of the principal should now be given to the estate of Eugene B. Sanger, Junior. The wills of the settlor, Dr. Sanger, and Eugene Junior, are such that the two adopted sons of Eugene, Junior, would benefit if either of these contentions should prevail.

The judge entered a decree stating that the settlor's intent, as expressed in the 1913 indenture, was to create a class gift of income to the children of Dr. Sanger and their issue per stirpes until the death of the last survivor of such children, at which time the principal was to be paid to the issue per stirpes; that the settlor's intent was to benefit Dr. Sanger and his direct descendants only, each line of descent taking an equal share as long as it remained in existence; and that in 1930 the settlor reiterated this desire and provided a means of carrying it out in the event it could not be effectuated under the 1913 indenture. The decree declared that the gifts of principal in the 1913 indenture were invalid and are disposed of under the 1930 declaration. As to the gifts of income under article Second, the decree declared that all gifts following that to Dr. Sanger are to be treated as invalid, and passing under the 1930 declaration, for otherwise there would be either an unequal distribution among the different branches of the family, or gifts to those outside the family, both contrary to the settlor's intent. The decree further declared that the interests which did not pass under the 1913 indenture reverted to the settlor in 1913 and that these reversionary interests passed under the 1930 declaration, which, being a formal trust, was valid without notice to the beneficiaries. Accordingly, the trustee was instructed during the life of Sabin, Second, to pay Charlotte's share to her issue, to pay one half of Eugene, Junior's share to the issue of Charlotte, and to pay one half to Sabin, Second; the principal of the trust is to be held until the death of Sabin, Second, at which time it is to be distributed according to the provisions of the 1930 declaration.

We are of opinion that the decree was correct. As we shall point out later, some of the gifts in article Second and the gift of principal in article Third of the 1913 indenture violated the rule against perpetuities. Despite the contention of some respondents to the contrary, we think that the 1930 declaration set up a valid trust, capable of disposing, according to its terms, of all the property in which the settlor held a reversionary interest by reason of the partial invalidity of the 1913 indenture. The declaration was not an amendment of the indenture, but affected only property so reverting to the settlor.

Any failure, if such there was, of the settlor to notify the beneficiaries of the terms of the 1930 declaration was of no consequence. While, contrary to the prevailing rule, we have held that notice to the beneficiary is essential in certain types of informal trusts (O'Hara v. O'Hara, 291 Mass. 75, 78; Aronian v. Asadoorian, 315 Mass. 274, 276-277, and cases cited) the trend of our decisions has been to confine, rather than to extend, this rule. Even our rule has no application to a formal declaration of the sort here involved. Cohen v. Newton Savings Bank, 320 Mass. 90; Stern v. Stern, 330 Mass. 312, 317-318. See Scott on Trusts, 2d ed., §36; Restatement: Trusts, §36.

The guardian of the adopted children of Eugene argues that the 1930 declaration is obnoxious to the rule against perpetuities because it can have no effect until there has been a declaration of the invalidity of the 1913 indenture, and that may happen at a time beyond the period fixed by the rule. The language of the 1930 declaration on which this contention is grounded reads: "[I]n case any provision thereof should be declared to be invalid and because of such invalidity any income or principal of the trust should revert in part or in whole to me or to my estate."

This argument is untenable. While the expression, "in case," in the quoted clause often carries the flavor of a condition, we do not think it should be so interpreted here. It is plain that the settlor intended to create an effective trust of the reversionary inter-

ests. It is equally plain that there can be no trust unless there is
an existing trust res (Restatement: Trusts, §74), and that an interest which has not come into existence cannot be held in trust. Bennett v. Littlefield, 177 Mass. 294, 300. Restatement: Trusts: §75.
No matter what doubts the settlor may have entertained concerning the validity of portions of the 1913 trust, he actually held from
the moment of its creation the reversionary interests which were
disposed of by the 1930 declaration. Any inference of a trust
created on a condition to arise in the future is rebutted by the
words "I . . . declare that I hold in trust and shall be deemed to
have held in trust from the date of this instrument, the properties
thereby reverting." That event, the reverting of the properties,
had already occurred. An adjudication was not necessary to bring
it about; it took place by operation of law. The purpose of the
"in case" clause read as a whole, was to identify the property that
was to go into the trust and to explain how the settlor acquired it.
It was not a true condition and may be treated as surplusage. See
In re Shuckburgh's Settlement, [1901] 2 Ch. 794.

We turn now to a determination of what interests were invalid
under articles Second and Third of the 1913 indenture. There is
no doubt that the remainder to the issue under article Third is
void for remoteness. Indeed, this is conceded by all parties. The
determination of the issue who will take cannot be made until the
death of Dr. Sanger's children and such children may include children born after the creation of the 1913 indenture who may not
die within twenty-one years after the death of the surviving child
living in 1913. (In fact one child of Dr. Sanger, Sabin, Second,
was born after the creation of the 1913 trust.) Hence the gift of
the remainder to the settlor's issue was utterly void. Leake v. Robinson, 2 Meriv. 363; Sears v. Putnam, 102 Mass. 5; Hall v. Hall,
123 Mass. 120; Am. Law of Property, §24.26.

Article Second presents questions of more difficulty. The position of the executors of Eugene B. Sanger, Junior, is as follows.
A grammatical reading of article Second shows that the income is
to be paid only to those children or their issue who are alive at the
death of Dr. Sanger. It will be then, and only then, that the income beneficiaries can be determined. Issue of children dying
after the death of Dr. Sanger will not take under article Second.
The phrase "in equal shares" indicated a tenancy in common in
the income interest, and there is nothing in the 1913 indenture to
rebut this construction. A construction of article Second which
would give the issue an interest in the income when the parent
dies after Dr. Sanger, would offend against the rule against perpetuities. Under the familiar rule if it is possible to interpret a

provision either as valid or as invalid under the rule against perpetuities an interpretation which favors validity is to be adopted. Thus, on the death of an income beneficiary his share of the income, not being limited to life, will pass to his estate. The only limitation of these income interests is the remainder over in article Third, and because this is void, the indenture must be read without it. Under established principles (so runs the argument), where there is a gift of income of unlimited duration the gift carries with it the principal, and the beneficiary takes the fee.

The chief difficulty with this argument is that its major premise is untenable. We cannot agree that the settlor intended to give the children more than a life interest in the income. True, the executors' reading of article Second is literally correct from a grammatical standpoint, but the difficulty with such a reading is that it cuts too far. If the article is to be read literally, then as Sabin, Second, and Constance argue, the only point of time referred to for determining when income is to be paid is Dr. Sanger's death. Moreover the only income referred to is "said net income." These words refer back to article First in which the only income mentioned is the income accumulated and added to the principal prior to Dr. Sanger's death. Thus, under such a construction there then would be one payment of income at the death of Dr. Sanger to the children then living and the issue of deceased children; there would be no disposition of income thereafter accruing until the termination of the trust. Apart from this literal reading of article Second there is nothing in the indenture that justifies such a construction. Indeed, the instrument read as a whole compels a contrary construction. The trust here is the familiar family trust with provision for successive generations of the family as beneficiaries. We are of opinion that it was the settlor's intent that the children should have the income as long as they lived. A provision whereby there would be one distribution of income at Dr. Sanger's death and never again until the death of the surviving child would be most unusual, and to interpret article Second as calling for such a disposition would place too much emphasis on a preposition. Although the settlor said "at," we think that, sensibly construed, he meant "at and after." As we said in the recent case of Second Bank-State Street Trust Co. v. Wasserman, Mass., 148 N.E.2d 666, at page 669, " 'Grammatical construction may be altered, sentences and words transposed, and words supplied if necessary to give effect to the manifest intent' " of the settlor.

We are mindful, as Eugene, Junior's executors point out, that under the construction just mentioned article Second collides with the rule against perpetuities. The gift of income to the issue or to the surviving children will not vest ex necessitate within the period of the rule. Sears v. Putnam, 102 Mass. 5. That this consequence follows such a construction is not disputed. As stated above, Eugene, Junior's executors argue that we should avoid a construction which would violate the rule when a contrary construction, which would not, is possible. We are mindful of the rule of construction on which this contention rests. Second Bank-State Street Trust Co. v. Second Bank-State Street Trust Co., 335 Mass. 407, 412. But it ought not to be carried to the point of defeating the intent of the settlor. To avoid an interpretation that would violate the rule against perpetuities we shall not place a strained construction upon article Second which would have consequences never intended by the settlor. His intent was to benefit Dr. Sanger's direct descendants. The construction for which Eugene, Junior's executors contend would defeat that intent for reasons already pointed out and for the additional reason that the settlor's property would go to others than Dr. Sanger's descendants.

As the case now stands, all interests after the gift of income to the children for their lives are invalid, and after the death of each child his or her one-third share of the trust will be governed by the 1930 declaration. True, it will go to the persons whom the settlor intended to benefit, but there will be inequalities among the lines of descendants. Between the death of the first child and the death of the last, income will be paid under both trusts, and the surviving children will be receiving income from both. Thus, until his death, Sabin, Second, will be entitled to one third of the income of the trust under the 1913 indenture. Since the other two children have died their two-thirds shares of the income fall into, and are governed by, the 1930 declaration. Since Eugene, Junior's line has been eliminated (he having died without issue) Sabin, Second, will receive, in addition to his income under the 1913 indenture, one half the income under the 1930 declaration, or two thirds the entire income under both trusts. This, we think, does not accord with the settlor's intent, which was to benefit each line of descendants equally.

This inequality can be eliminated and full effect can be given to the settlor's original plan if all the interests in the 1913 indenture following the gift of income to Dr. Sanger are declared invalid under the principle sometimes called "infectious invalidity." [101] This

---

[101] (*Court footnote*) See Leach, Perpetuities in a Nutshell, 51 Harv. L. Rev. 638, 656; Am. Law of Property, §§24.47-24.52. We understand it to mean that the invalidity of certain gifts in a will or trust occurs in such circumstances that other gifts, valid in themselves, are infected by the invalidity of the bad gifts, and are also held invalid. In effect it is a rule of construction to carry out the presumed intent of the settlor or testator.

would eliminate the transition period during which the two trusts would concurrently operate under overlapping plans, and place the fund forthwith into the 1930 trust, where the entire fund would be administered in accordance with the real intent of the settlor. This is what the decree did, and we think it was right.

The doctrine of infectious invalidity has had little application in Massachusetts. In Bundy v. United States Trust Co., 257 Mass. 72, the donee of a testamentary power of appointment appointed the property to a trust, the primary beneficiaries of which were her two adopted daughters who were born after the creation of the power. Income of the trust was to be paid to these two daughters in the amounts which they required. Any unused income was to be paid to the secondary beneficiaries, the donee's cousins, one of whom was born before the creation of the power. On the death of the two adopted daughters, the principal was to go to their issue, and in default of such issue to the cousins in equal shares. The income interests to the adopted daughters, and the gift of principal to their issue were void for remoteness, and the court said, at page 80, that even if the interests given to the cousins could be separated from the invalid provisions "the effect of holding them valid would be to make the scheme of the testatrix almost hopelessly fragmentary; a construction we are not inclined to adopt." It was held that the property went to the donee's executor.

Our attention has not been directed to any other applications of the principle of infectious invalidity in Massachusetts, nor have we found any. On the contrary, it would appear at first blush that our decisions could not be reconciled with the doctrine. "The general rule is, that, if a limitation over is void for remoteness, it places all prior gifts in the same situation as if the devise over had been wholly omitted." Lovering v. Worthington, 106 Mass. 86, 88. Similar statements may be found in Fosdick v. Fosdick, 6 Allen, 41, 43; Greenough v. Osgood, 235 Mass. 235, 242; Amerige v. Attorney General, 324 Mass. 648, 656; and Second Bank-State Street Trust Co. v. Second Bank-State Street Trust Co., 335 Mass. 407. This doctrine was applied in Proprietors of the Church in Brattle Square v. Grant, 3 Gray, 142, 156, to hold that where there is a gift in fee simple, subject to be divested by a void condition subsequent, the gift takes effect absolutely and the condition is disregarded. See Am. Law of Property, §24.47. Professor Gray, in The Rule Against Perpetuities, 4th Ed., page 263, says, "And if anything is now well settled in the law it is that a life estate, good in itself, is not destroyed by the remainder over being bad for remoteness or any other reason." He cites Lovering v. Worthington, supra, as authority.

Whether the rule is well settled as an inexorable rule of law, as distinct from a rule of construction, is open to doubt. In none of the cases just mentioned did it appear that the testator's scheme would be more nearly carried out by striking down valid provisions. We do not think that the court intended to lay down a positive rule of law, applicable in any and all situations. The Lovering case only sets out the "general rule." The Brattle Church case speaks of the "general principle applicable to such cases" (3 Gray, at page 156).

The American Law of Property takes the position in §24.48 that there may be circumstances where the failure of a gift may so disrupt the dispositive scheme of the settlor or testator that he would prefer that valid prior gifts should also be struck down. The authors caution, however, that making such a determination is a delicate matter, and that valid interests should be struck down only on a clear showing that the alternative disposition, such as intestacy, residuary clause, or otherwise, would better carry out the settlor's scheme. This is in effect the position taken by the American Law Institute. Restatement: Property, §402.

We are in accord with these principles. Applying them here, we are of opinion that all gifts in article Second should be declared invalid. The settlor's plan for the income gifts under article Second is quite apparent. Each line of his brother's family is to get an equal share of the trust income until its termination. On the death of a child of the brother, that child's issue is to receive the parent's share. The distortion from this plan after the invalid parts are struck out and the valid parts given full effect is readily apparent and can be measured. On the other hand, if all the property passes under the 1930 declaration, there will be no distortion. All the gifts will take effect exactly as the settlor intended in 1913. We think that in these circumstances it would be inappropriate and unfair to apply the rule against perpetuities mechanically to the specific gifts which violate the rule, and then disregard the consequences of the application. We think that when it is clear that the settlor wanted the good and bad gifts to be made together, and an alternative scheme of disposition is available under which they can be made together in substantially the same form as the settlor intended, the good and the bad parts should not be regarded as severable, but should fall together. Restatement: Property, §402, illustration 3, comment g. Am. Law of Property, §24.52. Simes and Smith, Law of Future Interest, 2d Ed., §1262. In re Estate of Whitney, 176 Cal. 12, 19.

Doubtless, in most situations where there is a partial invalidity of a trust or a will, the relationship between the valid and the invalid gifts will not be readily apparent. There may be little in the instrument to indicate that the valid and the invalid are to be treated as a unit and generally the wiser course will be to give full effect to the valid provisions rather than to decide that another scheme will be closer to the settlor's intent.

The decree of the Probate Court is affirmed. Costs and expenses of the appeals are to be in the discretion of the Probate Court.

So ordered.[102]

MERCHANTS NATIONAL BANK v. CURTIS
98 N.H. 225, 97 A.2d 207 (1953)

[Margaret A. Harrington died survived by a son, Edward Harrington, a daughter, Delana B. Curtis, and a granddaughter, Margaret May Curtis. In her will she gave realty to her children for their lives and the remainder to her granddaughter in fee. The will further provided with respect to this realty:

"Fifth: In the event of either of my children having other heirs of their body, surviving them such heir or heirs shall share equally with Margaret May Curtis, and in that event I give, bequeath and devise my estate to them, and their heirs, on the death of my children.

"Sixth: If my Grand Daughter Margaret May Curtis or other grand children shall survive both of my children and shall have and leave no heirs of her or their body, then and in that event, I give, bequeath and devise all my estate unto my brothers and sisters then living and to the representatives of those not living, and to my late husband's niece, Almeda S. Goyscan formerly Almeda S. Harrington, in equal shares . . ."

Margaret May Curtis survived the two children of the testatrix and no other grandchildren of the testatrix were born. Margaret May Curtis died without issue. Query: Is the gift over to the other relatives of the testatrix valid under the rule against perpetuities?]

KENISON, Chief Justice. . . .

The Rule against Perpetuities, hereinafter called the rule, prevails in this state, Gale v. Gale, 85 N.H. 358, 159 A. 122, but it has never been "remorselessly applied" as advocated [sic] by Gray in "The Rule against Perpetuities" (4th ed.) §629. The genesis of the modified rule in New Hampshire began in 1891 with Edgerly v. Barker, 66 N.H. 434, 31 A. 900, 28 L.R.A. 328, when a gift of a

---

[102] In regard to the extent to which an invalid part of a disposition infects the whole because of the rule against perpetuities, see 6 American Law of Property §§24.47-24.53 (Casner ed. 1952). — ED.

remainder interest to grandchildren reaching forty years of age, which offended the rule, was cut down to a gift to grandchildren reaching twenty-one years of age so as to not offend the rule. This decision was bitterly assailed by Gray in his treatise (appendix G) since he thought it was a dangerous thing to tamper with this ancient English rule "which is concatenated with almost mathematical precision." Gray, supra, §871. Nevertheless, Edgerly v. Barker, supra, has been followed in subsequent decisions in this state and continues to remain in good standing here. Wentworth v. Wentworth, 77 N.H. 400, 92 A. 733; Flanders v. Parker, 80 N.H. 566, 120 A. 558; Gale v. Gale, supra; Amoskeag Trust Company v. Haskell, 96 N.H. 89, 91, 70 A.2d 210, 71 A.2d 408. See Quarles, The Cy Pres Doctrine; Its Application to Cases Involving the Rule against Perpetuities and Trusts for Accumulations, 21 N.Y.U.L.Q. Rev. 384 (1946). In England the same result has been achieved by legislation. Laws of Property Act, 1925, 39 & 40 Geo. V., c. 98, Sec. 163.

The rationale of the Barker case was that, wherever possible, a will should be construed to carry out the primary intent to accomplish a legal testamentary disposition even though the will may have inadvertently exposed a secondary intent to accomplish the testamentary disposition in an ineffective manner. That rationale has been applied in many recent will cases that have not involved the rule itself. "Traditionally, the courts of this jurisdiction have shown a signal regard for the intent of the testator . . . at times at the expense of other recognized principles deemed less cogent in their application. Cf. Edgerly v. Barker, 66 N.H. 434, 31 A. 900, 28 L.R.A. 328." Petition of Oliver Wolcott, 95 N.H. 23, 26, 56 A.2d 641, 643, 1 A.L.R.2d 1323. The same thought received expression in different language in Burtman v. Burtman, 97 N.H. 254, 258, 85 A.2d 892, 895: "Probably no jurisdiction has stood more steadfastly for giving effect to the intention of the testator rather than to arbitrary rules of law than New Hampshire." The refusal of this court to apply in unmodified form common law principles which defeat normal and reasonable estate plans has not been limited to wills but applies to conveyances as well. Therrien v. Therrien, 94 N.H. 66, 46 A.2d 538, 166 A.L.R. 1023.

The rule is a technical one, difficult of application and is often enforced to frustrate testamentary intent although the policy of the rule may not require such enforcement in a particular case. It is not surprising, therefore, that there has been an increasing tendency to avoid the application of the rule by various judicial techniques. There is a constructional preference for considering interests vested rather than contingent. Upton v. White, 92

N.H. 221, 29 A.2d 126. "The public interest in keeping *the destructive force of the rule against perpetuities within reasonable limits* is a considerable present factor supporting the public interest in that construction which accomplishes the earlier vesting." 3 Restatement, Property, §243 comment i. (Emphasis supplied.) If a gift is made upon alternative contingencies, one of which might be remote, while the other is not, the gift is valid where the second contingency actually happens. This doctrine is used to prevent the application of the rule in many cases. Annotation 64 A.L.R. 1077. "Essentially this represents a revulsion against the rule requiring absolute certainty of vesting as viewed from the creation of the interest. . . . Courts have a strong tendency to 'wait and see' wherever possible." 6 American Law of Property (1952) §24.54. These techniques have the salutary effect of avoiding the punitive and technical aspects of the rule but at the same time confirming the policy and purpose of the rule within reasonable limits. Wentworth & Co. v. Wentworth, 77 N.H. 400, 92 A. 733.

Clause sixth of the will is capable of at least two possible constructions. The first construction is that clause sixth created two contingencies upon which it would take effect: one to occur, if at all, on the death of Margaret May Curtis; the other to occur, if at all, on the death of unborn grandchildren. Since the first contingency actually occurred and is within the period of perpetuities, the gift may be considered valid. A closely parallel case is Springfield Safe Deposit & Trust Co. v. Ireland, 268 Mass. 62, 167 N.E. 261, 64 A.L.R. 1071. Under this construction the event occurs at the death of Margaret May Curtis, a life in being, and clause sixth would not be considered violative of the rule.

The second possible construction of this sixth clause is the one urged by the Bean-Quirin interests. They argue that the will gives the brothers and sisters an executory interest upon a single contingency which may occur at the death of as yet unborn grandchildren. While this is not the only construction that the clause is susceptible of, it is not a labored one. There is no doubt that, if there had been another grandchild who died after Margaret May Curtis without leaving heirs of his body, this event would have occurred beyond the period allowed by the rule against perpetuities.

Assuming this second construction to be permissible, we come to the crucial question whether we are justified in deciding the perpetuities issue on the facts which actually occurred rather than on facts that might have happened viewed as of the death of the testator. There is little case authority for deciding upon facts occurring after the testator's death in a case such as the one before us. However, recognized modern commentators present convincing arguments for doing so. Leach, Perpetuities in Perspective: Ending the Rule's Reign of Terror, 65 Harv. L. Rev. 721 (1952); 6 American Law of Property (1952) §24.10; and a full study by a Pennsylvania law revision commission resulted in a statute that permits such events to be considered. Pa. Estates Act of 1947, §4, Pa. Stat. Ann. (Purdon, 1947) tit. 20 §301.4. There is no precedent in this state that compels us to close our eyes to facts occurring after the death of the testator.

In the present case we are called on to determine the validity of a clause of a will that did not in fact tie up property beyond the permissible limit of lives in being plus twenty-one years. There is no logical justification for deciding the problem as of the date of the death of the testator on facts that might have happened rather than the facts which actually happened. It is difficult to see how the public welfare is threatened by a vesting that might have been postponed beyond the period of perpetuities but actually was not. The recent decision in Sears v. Coolidge, 329 Mass. 340, 108 N.E.2d 563, allows the court to take a "second look" under powers of appointment. While this is not direct authority for doing the same thing with a devise or bequest, it is bottomed on the same proposition that the glacial force of the rule will be avoided where the interests actually vest within the period of perpetuities. 6 American Law of Property, §24.35: When a decision is made at a time when the events have happened, the court should not be compelled to consider only what might have been and completely ignore what was. Analogy may be found in cases where the validity of a remainder interest is not considered until the facts existing on the death of the life tenant can be established. See Orr v. Moses, 94 N.H. 309, 52 A.2d 128; B. M. C. Durfee Trust Co. v. Taylor, 325 Mass. 201, 89 N.E.2d 777.

At the death of the survivor of the life tenants, Edward Harrington and Delana B. Curtis, both of whom were lives in being at testatrix' death, it became certain that no grandchildren of the testatrix would be born after her death. This in turn made it certain that the gift in clause sixth of the will would in fact vest at the death of Margaret May Curtis Reynolds Vreeland, also a life in being at testatrix' death. Consistent with the principles above stated, the facts existing at the death of the two life tenants are taken into consideration in applying the rule.

We therefore conclude that clause sixth does not violate the rule against perpetuities. The individuals who are entitled to participate in the distribution of the trust moneys and the extent of their interests are to be determined under this clause. . . .

Case discharged.

All concurred.[103]

NOTE ON WAIT-AND-SEE STATUTES

The aspect of the rule against perpetuities, whether the common law rule or one modeled on the New York statutory rule, that is the most controversial is the requirement that the validity of an interest is to be judged not on the basis of what does happen but on the basis of what might happen. It is this requirement that produces invalidity in certain situations because of the possibility that another child may be born, even though the parents are past the child-producing age or because a person may marry someone not yet born (the unborn widow case). No matter how remote and unlikely the contingency may be, if by any process of imagination it might occur, validity is to be judged on the assumption that the remote and unlikely does occur.

New Hampshire is the only jurisdiction that has judicially abandoned the what-might-happen approach in favor of a what-does-happen test for validity.

Pennsylvania took the lead in shifting by statute to the so-called wait-and-see doctrine.[104] In so doing, it adopted this approach for all situations. A somewhat more limited wait-and-see doctrine is typified by the Massachusetts statute, but that is broad enough to cover most situations which are likely to be presented.[105] The Massachusetts statute applies only to inter vivos instruments taking effect after January 1, 1955, to wills where the testator dies after that date, and to appointments made after June 10, 1954, the effective date of the act, including appointments by inter vivos instruments or wills under powers created before the effective date. If a revocable inter vivos trust governed by Massachusetts law was created before January 1, 1955, but the settlor dies after that date, will the Massachusetts statute apply to dispositions under the trust?

Connecticut in 1955,[106] Maine in 1955,[107] and Maryland in

---

[103] For comments on Merchants National Bank v. Curtis, see 53 Colum. L. Rev. 1158 (1953); 67 Harv. L. Rev. 355 (1953); 52 Mich. L. Rev. 305 (1953). — ED.

[104] Pa. Stat. Ann., tit. 20, §301.4 (Purdon). See also 6 American Law of Property §25.90 (Casner ed. 1952).

[105] See Mass. Ann. Laws, c. 184A, §§1-6, quoted infra page 1445. See Leach, Perpetuities Legislation, Massachusetts Style, 67 Harv. L. Rev. 1349 (1954).

[106] Conn. Gen. Stat. Rev. §§45-95-45-99 (1958).

[107] Me. Rev. Stat. Ann., c. 160, §§27-33 (1954, Supp. 1959).

1960 [108] followed in the footsteps of Massachusetts. A different twist to the wait-and-see approach was given in Vermont by the adoption in 1957 of a wide-open wait-and-see statute with a cy pres feature that calls for the disposition to be reformed, within the limits of the rule, to approximate most closely the intention of the creator of the interest, if, as events actually occur, the interest as originally limited is invalid.[109] In 1960, Kentucky restored the common law rule against perpetuities and at the same time adopted the Vermont-type statute.[110] Washington has also enacted a combination wait-and-see and cy pres statute.[111] It is reasonable to expect that there will be more and more legislation of the wait-and-see variety.[112]

It should be noted in passing that the Massachusetts-type statute has a provision that saves a gift from violating the rule against perpetuities where the invalidity is the result of an age contingency, by reducing the age to twenty-one if validity will thereby be produced. This change in the age contingency is made, however, only if, as events actually occur, it is necessary to do so to prevent a violation of the rule.[113]

What is the significance of this wait-and-see legislation so far as estate planning is concerned? It is certainly a comforting crutch to have in the background. It is very difficult, however, to imagine the situation where a lawyer would intentionally draft a disposition under which validity would be determined by whether certain events actually occur. In other words, under a properly drafted estate plan you should not have to wait and see whether a disposition is valid.[114]

RYAN v. WARD

192 Md. 342, 64 A.2d 258 (1949)

MARBURY, C.J., delivered the opinion of the Court.

On April 16, 1928, John R. Ward of Baltimore City executed and delivered a deed of trust to the Baltimore Trust Company

---

[108] Md. Code Ann., art. 16, §197A (1957, Supp. 1960).

[109] Vt. Stat. Ann., tit. 27, §§501-503 (1959), quoted infra page 1475.

[110] Ky. Laws 1960, S.B. 180.

[111] Wash. Laws 1959, c. 146.

[112] The situation in England is discussed in Leach, Perpetuities Reform by Legislation: England, 70 Harv. L. Rev. 1141 (1957).

[113] See Mass. Ann. Laws, c. 184A, §2, quoted infra page 1445.

[114] If the cy pres feature is not combined with the wait-and-see statute, how does the infectious invalidity principal considered in New England Trust Co. v. Sanger, printed supra page 642, work if you wait and see, and it turns out that a certain interest is invalid?

conveying to the latter certain personal property consisting of stocks and bonds. The record does not show the value of this personal property at the date of the deed of trust, but it appears that the corpus of the estate, as of September 26, 1945, was approximately $32,500. John R. Ward died on October 27, 1928 and Frank R. Ward, who was given a life estate by the terms of the deed of trust, died on September 26, 1945, as of which date the estate was valued as above set out. In 1934 the Baltimore Trust Company was removed as trustee by an order of the Circuit Court No. 2 of Baltimore City, and the Baltimore National Bank was appointed substituted trustee. The latter filed its bill of complaint in the Circuit Court of Baltimore City in 1946, asking for a construction of the deed of trust, and naming as parties all the living parties who might possibly have an interest in the matter, as well as the administratrix d.b.n.c.t.a. of the estate of John R. Ward. By the will of John R. Ward, all of his estate and property was left to his son, Frank R. Ward, if the latter survived him, which was the case. Frank R. Ward, who was a resident of New Jersey, left a will by which all of his estate was left to his wife, Olive Maria Ward, provided she survived him, which was the case. He also left three children, Ruth E. Ward, David E. Ward, and John F. Ward. Olive M. Ward is the executrix of the estate of Frank R. Ward and also the administratrix d.b.n.c.t.a. of the estate of John R. Ward. James J. Ryan was appointed by the court as guardian ad litem for all persons not in being whose interests might be affected by the proceedings. Answers were filed by the guardian ad litem, and the parties in being, and testimony was taken, after which the chancellor filed his decree holding some of the future interests good and some void. From this decree the guardian ad litem appeals here, and cross appeals were filed by all other parties.

The deed of trust gives the trustee full and complete power to manage, sell, reinvest, and otherwise deal with the trust estate, and to collect the dividends and profits and to pay over the entire net income in monthly installments to the grantor, John R. Ward, during the term of his natural life. It is further provided that ". . . during the life of the Grantor he shall have the right by one or more instruments in writing, personally signed by him and delivered to the Trustee, to withdraw from the operation of this Deed of Trust such sum or sums as he may in his absolute discretion see fit, such withdrawals, however, shall not be in excess of the sum of Fifteen Hundred Dollars ($1500.00) per annum during his lifetime, and to the extent of any sum or sums so

withdrawn, the principal of the trust hereby created shall be reduced accordingly, or expended entirely." It is further provided
by the deed of trust:

"From and after the death of the Grantor, the Trustee shall
pay over the net income derived therefrom in monthly instalments unto Frank R. Ward, son of the Grantor, during his lifetime, and upon the death of the Grantor's said son, Frank R.
Ward, or from and after the Grantor's death in case his said son
should predecease him, the Trustee shall pay the net income
derived from the trust fund unto the lineal descendants, per
stirpes, from time to time living, of the Grantor's said son until
the death of the last surviving child of the Grantor's said son, who
shall be living at the time of the Grantor's death, and upon the
death of the last surviving child of the Grantor's said son, who
shall be living at the time of the death of the Grantor, the trust
hereby created shall terminate, and the corpus or principal
thereof shall be by the Trustee conveyed, delivered and paid over
absolutely free, clear and discharged of any further trust, in equal
and even shares unto the then living children of the Grantor's
said son, and unto the issue then living of each then deceased
child of the Grantor's said son, so that each then living child of
the Grantor's said son shall take and receive, absolutely, one equal
share thereof, and the issue then living of each then deceased
child of the Grantor's said son shall take and receive, per stirpes,
and not per capita, one equal share thereof absolutely."

There is a spendthrift provision for both principal and income,
applicable after the death of the grantor, and it is also provided
that the Trustee shall have authority to receive any other funds
granted, devised, or bequeathed by the grantor or any other person for the uses of the trust created, with a proviso that during
the life of the grantor, at his written request, the Trustee is
directed to pay over to him the principal of any funds or property, or any part thereof, which may be received by the Trustee
as an addition to the original principal of the trust. This right
of withdrawal is limited to the additions to the trust fund.

The question before the court is whether any of the estates
attempted to be created by this deed of trust are in violation
of the rule against perpetuities. This rule requires that an interest or an estate, to be good, must vest not later than twenty-one
years, plus the usual period of gestation, after some life in being
at the time of its creation. In determining its applicability, the
court looks forward from the time of the taking effect of the instrument in question to determine whether a possible interest is

certain to vest within the prescribed period. Perkins v. Iglehart, 183 Md. 520, 39 A.2d 672. The rule was established by the courts to preserve the freedom of alienation, and to prevent restrictions of the circulation of property. Safe Deposit & Trust Co. v. Sheehan, 169 Md. 93, 179 A. 536.

Where an interest or an estate is created by will, the question is determined by looking forward from the date of the taking effect of the will which is, of course, the death of the testator, and not the date of the will. Gray's The Rule Against Perpetuities, 3rd Ed., Paragraph 231, p. 205; 4th Ed., Paragraph 231, p. 235. Where the interest or estate is created by deed, its effectiveness vel non is determined as of the time "when the deed became operative." Bowerman v. Taylor, 126 Md. 203 at page 212, 94 A. 652, 654; Goldberg v. Erich, 142 Md. 544, at page 548, 121 A. 365; Hawkins v. Ghent, 154 Md. 261, at page 265, 140 A. 212; Miller on Construction of Wills, Paragraph 323, p. 914.

The appellant Ryan suggests (without any citation of authority) that since there is an element of revocability in the deed, the effective date from which we must consider the succeeding estates is not the date of the execution and delivery of the deed, but the date of the death of the grantor. The element of revocability is the right of withdrawal of the original trust fund, not, however, to be "in excess of the sum of $1500.00 per annum during his lifetime" and the unlimited right of withdrawal of any funds or property, or any part thereof which may have been added to the trust estate from time to time. The terms of the provision authorizing the withdrawal of the original principal do not clearly indicate whether this right is cumulative or not, that is, whether the right must be exercised each year, if at all, or whether the grantor could withdraw at any time, not only the $1500 allowed during that year, but also $1500 for each previous year in which he had not exercised the right. Since, however, the grantor attempted to put a limitation upon his own actions, and did not reserve to himself the right to withdraw any or all of the original principal at any time he saw fit, while reserving that right as to subsequent additions, we hold that the right should be construed as non-cumulative, and lost as to the amount authorized to be withdrawn in any year, if not exercised during that year. We are not advised what was his age at the time he created it. No matter what it was, we cannot assume, viewing it prospectively, that he would not live long enough to withdraw the entire principal. Until the grantor actually died, therefore, he had the possible right to destroy the trust estate by withdrawals, although this destruction could be only partial until the end of twenty-two years.

Professor Gray, in his work "The Rule against Perpetuities" (3rd Ed., Paragraph 203, p. 175; 4th Ed., Paragraph 203, p. 193), states that ". . . a future interest, if destructible at the mere pleasure of the present owner of the property, is not regarded as an interest at all and the Rule does not concern itself with it." This statement is applied to revocable trusts in Paragraph 524.1 of the 4th Edition beginning on page 510.[115] This paragraph is the work of Roland Gray, son of the original author, who died in 1915. The 4th Edition was prepared in 1942. In paragraph 524.1 a case is suggested where a conveyance is made to A for life, with a power of revocation, A being the settlor, and, in default of exercise, to A's children at 25. If the period of the rule against perpetuities runs from the date of the conveyance, the ultimate limitation is too remote, but the author states that it seems to be correct to take A's death as the critical date, because A is at liberty to destroy the future interest. He cites the prevailing doctrine that the remoteness of limitations

---

[115] In Cook v. Horn, 214 Ga. 289, 104 S.E.2d 461 (1958), the court held that where the settlor retained the power to revoke the trust until his death, the period of the rule against perpetuities did not begin to run until he died.

In Fitzpatrick v. Mercantile-Safe Deposit and Trust Co., 220 Md. 534, 155 A.2d 702 (1959), an inter vivos trust was involved which provided that on the death or resignation of the original trustee, "full power is hereby reserved and given to her [the settlor] as if she were a feme sole to appoint by deed to be duly executed and recorded another trustee in his place and stead with all powers of the original trustee hereunder or at her option by such deed to cancel revoke rescind and annul this deed and thereupon in the latter case she shall stand seized and possessed to her own use of the property hereby conveyed or then held hereunder and the title thereto shall be as fully vested in her to all intents and for all purposes as if these presents had not been made." The trust was established in 1876; in 1895 the trustee died. Thirteen days later the settlor appointed a new trustee rather than cancel the trust as she might have done. The settlor died in 1924 and in her will she exercised a power to appoint by will which she possessed under the trust. All appointments under the will were valid if the validity of the interests created by the exercise of the power was judged from 1895 when the power of the settlor to cancel the trust expired, but some were invalid if their invalidity was judged from 1876, the date the trust was created. The court held the critical date to be 1895, because for thirteen days in that year the settlor had full power to revoke the trust. The fact that the power to revoke was initially contingent did not prevent the court from interrupting the running of the period of the rule when the contingency occurred and the full power to revoke vested.

The principle that the period of the rule against perpetuities begins to run from the date of the termination of the power to revoke (by death or release) is set forth in statutory form in New York Real Property Law §179-a, which was added by N.Y. Laws 1960, c. 448. For similar statutes, see Mont. Laws 1959, c. 213, and Wash. Laws 1959, c. 146. — ED.

under a general power to appoint by deed is to be reckoned from
the exercise of the power, as a reason why the same construction
by analogy, should be used in a revocable deed. In that connection he approves the reasoning of the Supreme Court of
Hawaii in the case of Manufacturers' Life Insurance Company v.
von Hamm-Young Company, 34 Hawaii 288. The case, decided
in 1937, involves the application of the rule against perpetuities
to a life insurance trust agreement. The settlor reserved the
right to revoke the trust agreement or change the beneficiary.
If the trust became effective at the time of its execution, there
was a possibility that the future interest might not vest within
the required period after that date. On the other hand, if the
future interest did not come into being until the death of the
settlor, no transgression of the rule could occur. The court, on
the authority of Gray and of other cases, determined that the
effective date from which to view the future interest was the
death of the settlor, on the ground that such interest was destructible at his pleasure up until that time.[116]

In the case of Hillyard v. Miller, 10 Pa. 326, 334, the learned
Chief Justice Gibson cited Lewis on Perpetuities, Chapter 12,
as giving the nearest approach to a perfect definition of a perpetuity. See Graham v. Whitridge, 99 Md. 248, at page 274,
57 A. 609; 58 A. 36, 66 L.R.A. 408. This definition included a
provision that the future limitation which would not necessarily
vest within the prescribed period should not be destructible by

---

[116] In Holmes v. John Hancock Mutual Life Insurance Co., 288 N.Y. 106,
41 N.E.2d 909 (1942), the insured adopted one of the optional methods of
settlement provided for in the policy, and the validity of the settlement
adopted was challenged on the ground that it constituted an unlawful suspension of the power of alienation. In rejecting this challenge the court at page
110 said:
"We may assume that if the proceeds of the policies constituted a trust
fund, these directions would be void under the provisions of section 11 of the
Personal Property Law (Cons. Laws, ch. 41). The insurance company does
not, however, hold the proceeds of the policy as a trust fund. By the terms
of the policy it has contracted to pay stipulated amounts, at stipulated times
and in stipulated manner. 'The obligation of the insurance company constitutes a debt from the company to . . . the beneficiary, under the policy.'
The stipulated payments 'are not income on personal property. They constitute deferred payments which the company agreed to make to the beneficiary. . . .' (Crossman Co. v. Rauch, 263 N.Y. 264, 273.) The provisions of
section 11 of the Personal Property Law have no application to such an
obligation." It should not be inferred from the comments in the preceding
paragraph that the rule against perpetuities has no application to contractual
rights. Sections 24.55-24.59 of 6 American Law of Property (Casner ed. 1952)
examine the applicability of the rule to options to purchase land, options in
leases which give the tenant the right to renew the lease or to purchase the
leased land, and contracts for future payments to unborn or unascertained
beneficiaries. — ED.

the person for the time being entitled to the property, except with the concurrence of the person interested in the contingent event. The Chief Justice said: "It was the indestructibility . . . of future trusts which forced upon the judges the rule against perpetuities, in order to set the bounds to the remoteness of, not only legal, but equitable limitations; and it acts upon perpetuities wherever they appear, except in conveyances in mortmain, or to charitable uses." That decision was used as a basis for holding that a deed of trust with a power to sell in the life tenant and use the proceeds was destructible, and therefore not subject to the rule against perpetuities. Miffin's Appeal, 121 Pa. 25, 15 A. 525, 1 L.R.A. 453, 6 Am. St. Rep. 781. See also Cooper's Estate, 150 Pa. 576, 24 A. 1057, 30 Am. St. Rep. 829. The Supreme Court of the United States, in the case of Goesele v. Bimeler, 14 How. 589, 14 L. Ed., 554, decided that an agreement by members of a religious society called "Separatists," composed of Germans who had emigrated to the United States, by the terms of which the parties renounced all individual ownership of property, present and future, and transferred such property to three directors, was not a perpetuity because the majority of the members might require sale of the property at any time and therefore, even though the articles of association provided for its continuance for an indefinite period of time, nevertheless it was destructible at any time by the will of the majority. In the case of Pultizer v. Livingston, 89 Me. 359, 36 A. 635, the court held that the rule against perpetuities did not apply to future interests which were destructible at the will and pleasure of the present owner. The deeds in question in that case contained express powers of revocation, and the court held that they were thereby removed from the operation of the rule against perpetuities. In the case of Equitable Trust Co. of New York v. Pratt, 117 Misc. 708, 193 N.Y.S. 152, the Supreme Court of New York had before it a trust agreement which provided that it was revocable at will. The New York statute, which took the place of the common law rule against perpetuities, provided that the absolute ownership of property should not be suspended for a longer period than two lives in being at the date of the instrument. In the case before it, there was a suspension for three lives on the face of the deed of trust, but the court held that as a result of the revocation clause, absolute ownership was not suspended at all during the life of the settlor, and therefore the New York statute did not commence to operate until after his death. In Lewis on Law of Perpetuity, Law Library Ed., Ch. XX, p. 483, it is stated that "the great aim of the laws against remoteness is secured in the immediate and unrestrained alienability of the property by means of a power of appointment." In an article in 45 Harvard Law Review, beginning at p. 896, the effect of the rule against perpetuities on insurance trusts is discussed, and the conclusion is reached that in calculating the period of perpetuity the courts have wisely excluded that period during which the property was subject to the absolute control of a single person. In another article in 51 Harvard Law Review by W. Barton Leach, entitled "Perpetuities in a Nutshell," at p. 638, it is stated: "So long as one person has the power at any time to make himself the sole owner (of the trust estate) there is no tying-up of the property and no violation of the policy of the rule against perpetuities." In 86 Univ. of Pa. Law Review 221, the decision of the Hawaii court above quoted is discussed and is stated to be the first decision on the question. The writer says that "unhampered by precedent, the Hawaiian court has enunciated a salutary rule which should be followed in this country."

A contrary view is taken by a member of the Ohio Bar in an article on "The Rule against Perpetuities as Applied to Living Trusts and Living Life Insurance Trusts" found in 11 University of Cincinnati Law Review beginning at p. 327.

Restatement, Property, Sec. 373, states "The period of time during which an interest is destructible, pursuant to the uncontrolled volition, and for the exclusive personal benefit of the person having such a power of destruction is not included in determining whether the limitation is invalid under the rule against perpetuities." Comment d states that the required destructibility exists only when some person possesses a complete power of disposition over the subject matter of the future interests, and can exercise this power of disposition for his own exclusive benefit. The destructibility prerequisite for an application of the rule stated in Sec. 373 can exist when the power of disposition (or revocation) is not presently exercisable at the time of its creation, provided that the period, during which the exercise of such power is postponed, does not invalidate all interest created by the exercise of such power, and thus, in effect, invalidate the power itself.

These cases and statements from recognized authorities amply sustain the proposition that, where a settlor has power during his lifetime to revoke or destroy the trust estate, the question whether interests, or any of them, created by a deed of trust are void because in violation of the rule against perpetuities, is to be determined as of the date of the settlor's death, and not as of the date when the deed of trust takes effect. It will be observed, however, that the cases cited involve situations where the trust is revocable at will, or could be destroyed by a single act of the settlor such as a change of beneficiary in an insurance policy, or a sale of the trust property and the use of the proceeds. It is stated in the article in 51 Harvard Law Review, already referred to, at p. 663:

"The situation is analogous to future interests after an estate tail, where the period of perpetuities is computed from the date of expiration of the estate tail; the power to disentail makes the tenant in tail the substantial owner and causes interests after the estate tail to be in substance gifts by the last tenant in tail at the time of expiration of his estate. The situation is also analogous to gifts in default of the exercise of a general power by deed or will, the period of perpetuities being computed from the expiration of the power — i.e., the death of the donee."

There is no case, so far as we have been able to find, which deals with a strictly limited power of withdrawal which can be exercised only over a period of years, and which cannot be used to destroy the entire estate until a number of years has elapsed. In the case before us, as we have shown, the estate could not be entirely destroyed during the first twenty-two years of its existence. There is some difference of opinion among the text writers whether the power to encroach upon the corpus is the same as the power to revoke. Professor Scott thinks it is. Trusts, Paragraph 330.11. Bogert thinks not. Vol. 4, Bogert on Trust and Trustees, Part 2, Sec. 994. The cases we have cited indicate that it is not the method of destruction but the destructibility which is the controlling factor. That being so, we are unable to say that in a case such as the one before us, the trust estate is destructible, as that word is used in connection with the Rule against Perpetuities. There is a possibility of ultimate destruction, but the estate is not destructible at the time of its creation, or at any one time thereafter. Any destruction must be by a gradual diminishing of the corpus, until, at the last, there is left only a balance equal to the amount which can be withdrawn in any year. At that time, the grantor can destroy the trust, but his right to do so is contingent upon the previous withdrawals, and does not become absolute until he has completed all such withdrawals, over a period of years. What would be the situation if the settlor were given power to revoke after twenty-two years, or power to withdraw the entire trust estate at that time, need not be decided, because we have no such situation here. It is our conclusion, therefore, that the rule against perpetuities operates upon the estates created, as of the date of the execution and delivery of the deed of trust.

There is, of course, no question that the beneficial life estate of Frank R. Ward, son of the grantor, was valid. Thereafter, the net income is to be paid *unto the lineal descendants per stirpes from time to time living* of Frank R. Ward until the death of the last surviving child of said Frank R. Ward who shall be living at the time of the death of the grantor. At that time, the trust is to terminate, and the residuary estates are to commence. It is apparent that Frank R. Ward could have had a son born prior to the death of John R. Ward, who could have been living at the death of John R. Ward, and who could have lived more than twenty-one years after the death of Frank R. Ward. The death of such child, if he were the last survivor of the children of Frank R. Ward, would fix the date of the ending of the trust estate and the commencement of the estates in remainder created by the deed of trust. It was quite within the bounds of possibility, at the time of the creation of the trust, that this date might be beyond a life and lives then in being and twenty-one years thereafter, plus the usual period of gestation. Consequently, it is agreed by everyone, and the court so held, that the remainders, after the termination of the trust estate, were void.

The gift of the beneficial estates pur autre vie, after the death of Frank R. Ward which gift, as we have shown, is to the lineal descendants per stirpes, *from time to time living,* of the grantor's son, might vest in one of those lineal descendants who was born more than twenty-one years after the death of Frank R. Ward, but before the death of his last surviving child. This is a class gift. In such a case, it is well recognized that if it "is good as to some members of the class, but is within the rule against perpetuities as to other members, the entire gift must fail. The general rule is that if a gift is void as to any of a class, it is void as to all of the class." Miller, Construction of Wills, Paragraph 328. The reason for this rule is that the courts cannot split into portions the gift to the class, and make these gifts what they were never intended to be by the grantor. Goldsborough v. Martin, 41 Md. 488, at page 502; Albert v. Albert, 68 Md. 352, 12 A. 11; Bowerman v. Taylor, 126 Md. 203, 94 A. 652.

The contention was made in this case, and upheld by the chancellor, that the gifts pur autre vie were not gifts to one class, but were gifts to three classes, since there were two sons and a daughter of Frank R. Ward who survived him and who were living at the time of the execution of the deed of trust. The

Chancellor said that, therefore, as to each of the classes represented by each of these children, they vested in the living children
within the period. This result cannot be reached by considering
what actually happened. It must be arrived at, if at all by considering what the grantor intended should happen.

In the case of Albert v. Albert, 68 Md. 352, 12 A. 11, 17; a
distinction, followed by this court in its subsequent decisions, is
made clear. In that case, Judge McSherry said (p. 373): "It is
undoubtedly true that where bequests are made to a *class,* and
some of the class are in esse and capable of taking without violating the rule, and some are not, the whole bequest must fail. . . .
But where the bequests have been made to individuals, some of
whom are capable of taking and some of whom are not, a different
consequence follows." The case of Wilson v. Wilson, 4 Jur. N.S.
1076, is given as an example of the latter class of cases, and these
words quoted from it: "Here, however, the children of each child
of J.L. form a separate class, and the share of each class is separately
ascertainable."

In the case of Turner v. Safe Deposit & Trust Co., 148 Md.
371, 129 A. 294, 295, the remainder of the estate was to be
divided by the trustee, after the death of the testator's wife, "into
as many parts as my brother Barreda shall have children living at
the time of the death of my dear wife, the child or children of any
deceased child . . . if any then living to be treated as representing
his or her parent." After the death of "each of said children" his
or her share was to become the absolute property of "his or her
children" then living, with a *per stirpes* provision for children of
deceased children. In the absence of children or descendants then
living, the share was to go to brothers and sisters and their descendants *per stirpes* then living. The Court held "The final limitations in legal remainder were to distinct classes of persons who
were to take the respective parts of the estate into which it was
to be separated" and followed the rule quoted from Gray on Perpetuities, 3rd Ed., sec. 391, that "when, on a gift to a class, the
number of the shares is definitely fixed within the time required
by the rule against perpetuities, the question of remoteness is to be
considered with reference to each share separately."

In the case of Bowerman v. Taylor, supra, there was a deed of
trust for the benefit of the settlor's wife, during his and her joint
lives and the lifetime of the survivor, and then to the use of all
of the children of the settlor and his wife, those now in being and
those who might thereafter be born, and the lawful issue of those
children surviving their parents, such issue taking *per stirpes,*
and, upon the death of any such children, their interest should

go to their heirs or issue if any, or, if not, their interest should revert to the common fund. There were seven children living at the time of the execution of this deed and no others were thereafter born. All but one of these children survived the grantor and this one died without issue. The court said the life estates following the death of the settlor and his wife were to vest in beneficiaries in existence at the time of the death of a person in being when the deed of trust took effect. The question was in reference to the remainders to the descendants of the children and issue. The court said that these remainders to the descendants of children who were in being when the deed became operative must necessarily vest within the period of the rule, because they are given to those only who are in existence at the death of the person who was living at the date of the deed. The other remainders sought to be created in favor of the descendants of unborn children and issue were in violation of the rule. This decision was made upon the theory that the final disposition of the estate was not to a single class of persons, some of whom might be incapable of taking, but to distinct classes, because upon the death of each of the secondary life tenants, that is, the children, his or her interest is given to his or her descendants absolutely, regardless of the continuance of the life interest of the other children. The remainders limited upon each life estate were disposed of separately by the terms of the deed, and the question of the capacity to take on the part of the descendants of any particular life tenant did not depend upon the status of others claiming under a similar relationship to a different beneficiary.

In the case of Safe Deposit & Trust Co. v. Sheehan, 169 Md. 93, 98, 179 A. 536, 539, a testator left the residue of his estate in trust, to pay the net income therefrom "unto such of the children of my son John and the descendants of his deceased children, *per stirpes* who may be living from time to time, as such income is received by my trustee; and upon the death of the last surviving child of my said son John . . . to divide the corpus of my trust estate and to . . . transfer . . . the same . . . between and among the descendants of my said son, John, living at that time, said division and transfer among said descendants, however, to be made *per stirpes* and not *per capita*." The court said that this class closed only at the death of the last surviving child of John and that since the last surviving child of John might not die until more than twenty-one years and nine months after a life or lives in being at the death of the testator, these provisions violated the rule against perpetuities and were void.

In the case of Vickery v. Maryland Trust Co., 188 Md. 178, 52

A.2d 100, there was a declaration of trust under which, after the death of the settlor, the income was to be paid in equal parts to the then surviving brothers and sisters, and to nephews and nieces, the nephews and nieces to take as a unit *per capita,* and the issue of any deceased nephew or niece to take the part which his or her respective parent would have taken if then living. From the death of the last survivor of the brothers, sisters, nephews, and nieces living at the time of the settlor's death, the principal of the estate should be divided among the nephews and nieces born after the settlor's decease, and the issue of all her nephews and nieces *per stirpes* and not *per capita.* It was considered by all parties and held by us that the ultimate remainders were void, and it was likewise agreed and held that the life interests of the brothers and sisters were valid. The question was the status of the life interest of the nephews and nieces and their issue. We held in that case that, while the share of the nephews and nieces was described as a unit, that was only for the purpose of fixing the quantum of their total share, and, that while the life interests of each nephew and niece and their issue must be dealt with separately, the limitation as to issue could not be sustained because the class of the issue was not closed, but would remain open to let in after born descendants beyond the period prescribed by the rule. We distinguished that case from the Bowerman case, supra, because the class of issue was not closed.

In the case of Reese v. Reese [Chism v. Reese], 190 Md. 311, 58 A.2d 643, we held that the testator had in mind those whom he knew, that is, those living at the time of his death, and that upon this interpretation all of the remainders had to vest, if at all, not later than the death of a son then living and therefore there was no violation of the rule against perpetuities. In the case of Evans v. Safe Deposit & Trust Co., 190 Md. 332, 58 A.2d 649, decided on the same day as the Reese case, and which was concerned with a deed of trust made by Samuel Scribner and wife, we discussed at length the general subject of class gifts, but found it unnecessary to decide whether in that case the gift was to a class or to designated individuals who were at the date of the deed the only living children of the grantor.

We are unable to find in the case before us, as did the chancellor, that the deed of trust before us created three classes. Even though it is true that there were only three children of Frank R. Ward living at the time of the execution of the deed of trust, the provision in that deed does not divide the estate into shares as was the situation in the Bowerman case, supra. The words "lineal descendants *per stirpes* from time to time living" do not create three classes. On the contrary, they create one. There is no gift to named children of Frank or even to children of Frank. The gift is to lineal descendants which includes others than children. In the case of Perkins v. Iglehart, 183 Md. 520, 39 A.2d 672, we held that a bequest to the children of a son then living and the descendants then living of his deceased children *per stirpes* created only one class, although a stronger argument to the contrary existed in that case than in the one before us.

As a result of our conclusion, we hold that the gifts pur autre vie are void and the trust estate has now ended. As John R. Ward, by his will, left all his property to Frank R. Ward, who was his only child, the trust property belongs to the latter's estate. As we said in Perkins v. Iglehart, supra, there is no necessity for the property to be administered through the estate of John R. Ward, thereby multiplying the costs and expenses. Distribution can be made directly by the trustee to Olive M. Ward, Executrix of the estate of Frank R. Ward, and such distribution will relieve the trustee of further responsibility.

Decree reversed and case remanded for the passage of a decree in accordance with this opinion. Costs to be paid out of the trust estate.[117]

STORRS v. BENBOW
3 De Gex, M. & G. 390 (Ch. 1853)

William Townsend by his will, dated the 31st March 1827, after certain specific legacies, gave the residue of his personal estate to Matthew Shaw, John Benbow, John Townsend, and Job Townsend, whom he appointed his executors, upon trust (after payment of all his just debts, funeral and testamentary expenses, and the several legacies thereinbefore by him bequeathed, together with the whole of the legacy duty and duties payable in respect to the several legacies and annuities by him therein given) to make certain investments for the benefit of various legatees: the testator directed the ultimate residue of his estate to be paid and divided amongst all and every his next of kin who should be living at the time of his decease share and

---

[117] For comments on Ryan v. Ward, see 47 Mich. L. Rev. 1126 (1949); 34 Minn. L. Rev. 152 (1950). Compare with Ryan v. Ward the case of Second Bank-State Street Trust Co. v. Second Bank-State Street Trust Co., 335 Mass. 407, 140 N.E.2d 201 (1957).

The application of the common law rule against perpetuities to revocable trusts is considered in 6 American Law of Property §24.59 (Casner ed. 1952). On gifts to classes under the rule against perpetuities, see id. §§24.26-24.29. — ED.

share alike to and for their his and her own respective use and benefit.

By a codicil to his will, dated the 14th November 1827, the testator disposed of his freehold copyhold and leasehold estates; and by a second codicil, dated the 10th March 1832, after bequeathing legacies of £500 each to four persons by name who were children of Alice Early a daughter of Henry one of the testator's brothers, he gave and bequeathed in the words and figures following, namely, — "Item. I direct my executors to pay by and out of my personal estate exclusively the sum of £500 a-piece to each child that may be born to either of the children of either of my brothers lawfully begotten to be paid to each of them on his or her attaining the age of twenty-one years without benefit of survivorship."

The testator died on the day of the date of the second codicil; and it appearing doubtful who might be entitled to claim legacies under the general bequest in the codicil, a suit was instituted in the name of William Townsend Storrs, an infant child of a daughter of one of the testator's brothers and who was born after his death, the bill in which prayed that the executors might be decreed to set apart from the general personal estate of the testator the sum of £500, and to invest the same on proper security at interest for the benefit of the Plaintiff until he should become entitled to receive the same and that the same might then be paid to him.

The cause came on to be heard before the Master of the Rolls (Sir John Leach), who made a decree therein, dated the 8th July 1833, declaring that the children in esse only at the time of the death of the testator were entitled to the legacies of £500 each, and referring it to the Master to inquire and state whether the Plaintiff was in esse at the time of the death of the testator. (See Storrs v. Benbow, 2 Myl. & K. 46.)

The Master by his report, dated the 20th November 1833, found that the Plaintiff was born on the 29th October 1832, and that the testator died on the 10th March 1832, and it therefore appeared to him and he found that the Plaintiff was in esse at the time of the death of the testator. This report was absolutely confirmed by an order, dated the 23d January 1834; and the administration of the testator's estate was proceeded with upon the footing of the decree, the executors considering that they would be justified in paying the £500 to the Plaintiff when he came of age.

Two other questions subsequently arose upon the clause above mentioned, and were brought at different times before the Court for decision. The first of these was, whether the four children of Alice Early, to whom legacies of £500 were bequeathed by name in the codicil, were also entitled to take similar legacies under the clause; and as to this the Vice-Chancellor Knight Bruce decided that the parties just named were not entitled to double legacies. (See Early v. Benbow, 2 Coll. 342.) The other question was whether a fifth child of Alice Early born after the date of the will but before the date of the second codicil was entitled to a legacy of £500 under the clause; and on this the Master of the Rolls (Sir John Romilly) decided that the child was not so entitled. (See Early v. Middleton, 14 Beav. 453.)

In the course of the discussions which thus took place doubts were suggested whether the clause in question was not altogether void for remoteness; and as the Plaintiff together with two other children similarly circumstanced with him were about shortly to come of age, and would then be entitled under the decree of Sir John Leach to the payment of legacies of £500 each, the representatives of the residuary legatees were advised to bring the question of construction again before the Court, by way of appeal from that decree. They accordingly appealed to the Lord Chancellor by petition under the 6th Order of the 7th August 1852 as to the enrollment of decrees, &c. (Note. — The application was first made by motion, but the parties were then directed to present a short petition stating the special circumstances of the case); and on the 21st January 1853 an order was made by the full Court of Appeal that the time for appealing from the decree of the 8th July 1833 should be enlarged until the first day of Easter term then next.

The representatives of the residuary legatees then presented their petition of appeal, praying that the decree of the 8th July 1833 might be reversed or altered, and that it might be declared that the bequest of the legacies of £500 each, contained in the second codicil, was void for remoteness, or that in the event which happened of the testator's death on the day of the date of the said codicil no legacy became payable under the bequest. This petition of appeal now came on to be heard before the Lord Chancellor.

The Lord Chancellor at the conclusion of the argument, intimated an opinion, that quacunque via, whether as a child in esse at the death of the testator, or as not born until after the date of the codicil, the Plaintiff would be entitled, but at the same time expressed some doubt as to the correctness of the holding of

Sir J. Leach confining the gift to children born in the testator's lifetime. His Lordship referred also to the Appellant's argument on the question of remoteness, and observed that he was not aware that the rule applicable to the case of the gift of a gross fund distributable between persons forming a class some of whom might be within and some beyond the limits allowed by law, had been extended to the gift of distinct legacies to a number of persons. His Lordship said that he would look into the authorities and dispose of the matter at a future day.

June 8. THE LORD CHANCELLOR. I was perfectly prepared to dispose of this case three months ago, but was told that the point was very much the same as that raised in Gooch v. Gooch (3 De G. M. & G. 366), and that the parties therefore wished the matter to stand over until the case was disposed of, thinking it might have a material bearing upon the present question. I confess however that this appears to me to be a perfectly clear case, and to be independent of any decision in Gooch v. Gooch.

The question arises upon a clause in a codicil which is in these words, — "Item. I direct my executors to pay by and out of my personal estate exclusively the sum of £500 a-piece to each child that may be born to either of the children of either of my brothers lawfully begotten to be paid to each of them on his or her attaining the age of twenty-one years without benefit of survivorship." This is a money legacy to each child of any nephew the testator had or might have. The testator had brothers living, but there might be legacies too remote, because the gift included legacies to children of a child not yet born.

The bill was filed twenty or thirty years ago; and the cause was heard before Sir John Leach. The argument then was, that the gift was too remote, but Sir John Leach thought that, according to the true construction of the clause children born in the lifetime of the testator were meant, and therefore he said the gift could not be too remote, for it only let in children that might be born between the date of the will and the death. A decree was accordingly made declaring that the children in esse only at the time of the death of the testator were entitled to the legacies, and it was referred to the Master to inquire, &c. The Master found that the Plaintiff was in esse in this sense, namely that the testator died in October and the Plaintiff was born six months afterwards; and I think he was so. The question then is whether he is entitled; I am of opinion that he certainly is, for he was a child in esse within the meaning put upon the clause by Sir John Leach.

There are three ways in which this gift might be interpreted;

it might mean children that were in esse at the date of the will; it might mean children that might come into esse in the lifetime of the testator; and it might mean children born at any time. I own it seems to me that this gentleman is entitled quacunque via. If it was to the children then in being, he would I think be probably within the meaning of such description; but if it was to children to come in esse in his lifetime and afterwards to be born, it seems to me that a child in ventre sa mere at the death of the testator was a child "hereafter to be born" within the meaning of the provision.

The rule that makes a limitation of this kind mean children at the death of the testator is one of convenience: a line must be drawn somewhere, otherwise the distribution of the testator's estate would be stopped, and executors would not know how to act; but that rule of convenience cannot be applied to exclude a child certainly within the meaning of the limitation in the absence of any contrary expressed intention of the testator. I think therefore that Sir John Leach was right, supposing the interpretation of the will to be what I have stated, and that this child certainly comes within the description. I must add however that I do not say that the gift was at all remote if it meant a child to be born at any time, because this is not the case of a class: it is a gift of a pecuniary legacy of a particular amount to every child of every nephew which the testator then had, or of every nephew that might be born after his death, and is therefore good as to the children of the nephews he then had, and bad as to the children of nephews to be born after his death.

It would be a mistake to compare this with Leake v. Robinson (2 Mer. 363) and other cases where the parties take as a class, for the difficulty which there arises as to giving it to some and not giving it to others does not apply here. The question of whether or not the children of afterborn nephews shall or shall not take, has no bearing at all upon the question of whether the child of an existing nephew takes: the legacy given to him cannot be bad because there is a legacy given under a similar description to a person who would not be able to take because the gift would be too remote. I give therefore no positive opinion upon the point of remoteness generally in this case, because I think that quacunque via, on the construction of the will, there is nothing to justify the exclusion from taking of a child who was conceived at the death of the testator and born six or seven months afterwards. If the words in question meant children who though not then in existence should be in existence at the death, the Plaintiff was in existence at the death; and if they meant children born at any time, he was born and must have been born if at all within such a time as made his legacy not remote. I am therefore of opinion that in any way he is entitled.[118]

PROBLEMS

11.39. T in his will gives Blackacre "to A for life, then to A's children who attain twenty-five." On T's death, A has two children. One is twenty-eight years of age and the other twenty-six. No other child is born to A. A dies. On A's death, are his children entitled to Blackacre in a jurisdiction which applies the common law rule against perpetuities? See Leake v. Robinson, 2 Mer. 363 (Ch. 1817).

11.40. T in his will gives $1000 "to each child of A, whenever born, if such child lives to attain the age of twenty-five." At T's death, A is living and has three children. One child is five years of age; the second child is three; and the third child is one. Two years after T's death A has a fourth child. A dies when the fourth child is five years of age. In a jurisdiction which applies the common law rule against perpetuities, will each of the four children be entitled to $1000 if he attains the age of twenty-five?

11.41. T in his will gives the residue of his estate to a trustee and directs him "to pay the income to my son A for life; on the death of my said son, to pay the net income in equal shares to my said son's children, and as each child of my said son dies, to pay to the issue then living of such deceased child of my said son, such issue to take per stirpes, the proportionate amount of the corpus that corresponds to the proportionate amount of the income such deceased child of my said son was enjoying prior to his death." On T's death A has two children living. Two more children are born to A after T dies. All four children of A survive A. In a jurisdiction which applies the common law rule against perpetuities, what interests under the trust violate that rule? See Cattlin v. Brown, 11 Hare 372 (Ch. 1853).

11.42. T in his will devises Blackacre to "my son A for life, then to A's first son for life, then to the first son of A's first son in fee provided he is born within twenty-one years after the death of A." Assume that no son has been born to A at the time of T's death. Is any part of the limitation invalid? See Whitby v. Mitchell, 42 Ch. D. 494 (1889), 44 Ch. D. 85 (C.A. 1890).[119]

---

[118] In connection with the rule against perpetuities and class gifts, re-examine at this point Earle Estate, printed in full supra page 502. — ED.

[119] It is provided by Mass. Ann. Laws, c. 184, §3 as follows: "A contingent remainder . . . shall . . . be subject to the rule respecting remoteness known as the rule against perpetuities, exclusive of any other supposed rule respecting limitations to successive generations or double possibilities . . ."

NOTE ON THE RULE AGAINST PERPETUITIES IN IDAHO AND WISCONSIN

If T should transfer property in trust with directions to the trustee to pay the income to T's issue living on each income payment date, such issue to take per stirpes, and the trust is to continue until no issue of T is living, all interests under this trust — one which might continue indefinitely — would violate the common law rule against perpetuities. If such a disposition in trust were valid, the trust property could be held perpetually for the benefit of T's descendant line without the imposition of any federal estate tax under present law as the benefits were enjoyed by successive generations.[120]

In 1957, Idaho enacted legislation which prohibits the suspension of the power of alienation of real property for longer than lives in being and twenty-five years and then provides: "there shall be no rule against perpetuities applicable to real or personal property, nor any rule prohibiting the placing of restraints on the alienation of personal property." [121] It would appear that a perpetual trust of the type described above could be validly set up in Idaho as to personal property, with an effective restraint on the alienation of the interests of T's descendants.[122]

In Wisconsin, a state in which the rule against perpetuities is concerned with the suspension of the power of alienation, it has been held that a trust of real and personal property does not suspend the power of alienation if the trustee is empowered to change the trust property or to sell and reinvest, and, furthermore, that remoteness of vesting is not prohibited in Wisconsin so long as there is no suspension of the power of alienation.[123] Thus, it appears that a perpetual trust of the type described above can be validly established under Wisconsin law if the trustee is given the necessary power of sale and reinvestment.[124]

The Idaho and Wisconsin situations, if allowed to continue, are certain to be covered in due course by an amendment to the federal estate tax law. The amendment will simply add another complexity to the already complex structure of the estate tax law.

[120] Section 2041(a)(3) of the 1954 Code, quoted infra page 1400, and discussed infra page 710, which was enacted to prevent appointive assets from escaping taxation perpetually in Delaware, has no application to the disposition described in the text.

[121] See Idaho Code Ann. §55-111 (1957), quoted infra page 1438.

[122] The situation in Idaho prior to the enactment of the 1957 legislation is discussed in 6 American Law of Property §25.67 (Casner ed. 1952).

[123] See Will of Walker, 258 Wis. 65, 45 N.W.2d 94 (1950).

[124] In regard to Wisconsin, see 6 American Law of Property §§25.54-25.57 (Casner ed. 1952).

It would be far better if Idaho and Wisconsin got into line with other states on perpetuity matters.

10.   RULE AGAINST ACCUMULATIONS

A trust which gives the trustee discretion to pay out income or to accumulate it (a discretionary accumulation trust) has an income tax advantage not available to a trust under which all of the income is required to be distributed.[125]   Consequently, this type of trust is quite widely employed in jurisdictions which have adopted the common law rule against accumulations.   In jurisdictions which have even more restrictive statutory rules in regard to accumulations, this type of trust can be used only in the limited situations provided for in the statute.[126]   Another type of accumulation trust is one where the trustee is required to retain the income for some designated period (a mandatory accumulation trust).   The use of this form of trust, however, should be very limited because of its inflexible nature. As a matter of fact, most of the objectives a person may have in mind in regard to accumulations can be accomplished under the more flexible discretionary accumulation trust.   Under the common law rule against accumulations, income may be accumulated and added to principal for a time not exceeding the period of the rule against perpetuities.[127]   Thus, under this rule, if the duration of the trust is limited to the period of the rule against perpetuities, no provisions in regard to the accumulation of income can be invalid.

In some states, the statutory rule relating to accumulations is based on the Thellusson Act [128] adopted in England in 1800.   This act permitted accumulation for any one of four alternative periods: (1) the life of the grantor, (2) a term in gross of twenty-one years from the death of the grantor or testator, (3) the minority of a person conceived at or before the death of the grantor or testator, or (4) the minority of a person who would for the time

---

[125] The income tax advantages of a discretionary accumulation trust are considered infra page 733.

[126] The statutes on accumulations, as well as the common law rule against accumulations, refer to directions to accumulate income.   However, it should be apparent that if a direction to accumulate income is invalid, a power to do the same thing would be invalid.   Thus the controlling local law as to accumulations is significant in determining the type of discretionary accumulation trust which can be validly established.   A power to pay out income or to accumulate it is also a power of appointment and as such it may be void ab initio under the applicable rule against perpetuities.   As to when a power of appointment is void ab initio under the rule against perpetuities, see the discussion at page 766 infra.

[127] See 6 American Law of Property §24.65 (Casner ed. 1952).

[128] 39 & 40 Geo. III, c. 98.

being, if of full age, be entitled to the income directed to be accumulated. If the accumulation is for a period in excess of the time allowed, the provision for the excess only is invalid.[129]

The original New York statute on accumulations established a much narrower rule than either the common law rule or the Thellusson Act.[130] This New York statute became the model for many other states.[131] New York and states which followed it placed their residents at a distinct disadvantage from a federal income tax standpoint because of the limited opportunity available to them to obtain the income tax advantages of discre-

---

[129] Illinois, Indiana and Pennsylvania adopted statutes modeled on the Thellusson Act. Illinois (in 1953) and Pennsylvania (in 1956) changed to the common law rule against accumulations. For a discussion of the Thellusson Act and the statutes modeled on it, see 6 American Law of Property §§25.100-25.106 (Casner ed. 1952).

Murphy v. Northern Trust Co., 17 Ill. 2d 518, 162 N.E.2d 428 (1959), was concerned with the disposition of income for a period in excess of the time allowed under the Illinois law as it was before the adoption of the common law rule against accumulations. Under the law such income should "go to and be received by such persons as would have been entitled thereto if such accumulation had not been directed." Under the circumstances, the court could not find that such persons were described in the instrument and thus held that the income became intestate property.

[130] New York Personal Property Law §16 and Real Property Law §61, as they were before the 1959 change, permitted accumulations only for the minority of the person to be benefited and any direction for any accumulation for a longer term was treated as limited to the minority of the beneficiary. Exceptions were made for accumulations for charities and employee-benefit plans, and the statute specifically provided that income of a trust used to pay premiums on policies of life, health, accident or disability insurance was not to be deemed an accumulation where the policies are held by the trust.

[131] Arizona, Michigan, Minnesota, North Dakota, South Dakota and Wisconsin followed the New York lead. The New York statute and the statutes based on it are discussed in 6 American Law of Property §§25.107-25.115 (Casner ed. 1952).

Michigan in 1952 broke ranks by repealing its statute on accumulations, thereby establishing the common law rule against accumulations.

It is provided by Wis. Stats. Ann. §230.37 (1957) that income from real and personal property may be accumulated for the benefit of any person or persons for such periods as may be directed by will or other written instrument sufficient to pass such property. This statutory provision should be considered in the light of the absence of a rule against perpetuities in Wisconsin to the extent described supra page 675.

In 1959, North Dakota repealed the statutory provisions which described the extent to which accumulations were permitted (N.D. Laws 1959, c. 330) but left on the books a provision which states that all directions for the accumulation of income, except such as are allowed by a designated chapter (the provisions in this chapter are the ones repealed), are void. The situation in North Dakota is obscure.

For the statutes in California, Montana and Nevada, see 6 American Law of Property §§25.116-25.118 (Casner ed. 1952). In 1951, California adopted the period of the common law rule against perpetuities as the period for accumulations. Cal. Civ. Code §§715.1, 715.2 (Deering, 1960).

tionary trusts.[132]   In 1959, New York moved to eliminate this disadvantage by permitting accumulations which commence and terminate within the period of the rule against perpetuities.[133] The effective date of this change was September 1, 1959. In 1960, however, New York specifically provided that the validity of a direction to accumulate, under an instrument exercising a power, is to be determined by the law in force at the time of the exercise of the power and not the law in force when the power was created.[134]

MOELLER v. KAUTZ
112 Conn. 481, 152 Atl. 886 (1931)

MALTBIE, J. This reservation brings before us for construction certain provisions of the will of Constand A. Moeller who died June 1st, 1914. The will was executed February 18th, 1913. After making provision for the payment of debts and funeral expenses it gives, devises and bequeaths all the residue of the testator's property to trustees "to hold the same upon the following trust, with power to sell all my real and personal property (except my stock in The Narragansett Brewing Company of Providence, Rhode Island, which I direct shall neither be sold nor exchanged) and to invest and reinvest the avails thereof for the purposes of this trust; all surplus income and all avails of sales of personal property or real property shall be invested in mortgages on improved real estate in the New England States, the same to be double security for the amount loaned, and interest to be paid semi-annually in cash, and insurance and all taxes to be paid by the mortgagor." The trustees are then directed to pay an annuity to each of the testator's nine children, $2500 during the first year after his death and increasing thereafter at the rate of $100 a year until the sum of $4000 is reached, "beyond which amount their annual payments are not to be increased; said income is to be paid to each one of said children as long as any one

[132] The income tax advantages of discretionary trusts are considered infra page 733.
[133] See N.Y. Laws 1959, c. 453, which accomplished the change in New York by appropriate amendments to Personal Property Law §§16 and 17, and by repealing §16-a, and by appropriate amendments to Real Property Law §§61 and 62, and by repealing §61-a.
See Note on the New York Statutory Rule Against Perpetuities, supra page 639, for a discussion of the present status of the New York rule against perpetuities, to which the rule against accumulations is now keyed.
[134] See N.Y. Laws 1960, c. 458, which added a new §179-c to the Real Property Law, to accomplish the result described in the text. The new section became effective as of April 12, 1960.

of them survives; in other words, the incomes as above directed, not exceeding four thousand ($4000) dollars a year, are to be paid to each of my said children up to the death of the last survivor, but none of the survivors is to receive more than is above directed." If any child died before the death of the last survivor his or her child or children or their issue were to receive the annuities provided for their parents, share and share alike. Upon the death of the last survivor of his children the testator gives all the rest and residue of this estate to his grandchildren per capita, and if any grandchild shall have died before the time of distribution leaving children the share of the parent is to be divided among them.

All nine children were alive at the testator's death, six were married and each had one or more children, and one had been married and divorced and had a living child. Since his death one daughter has died unmarried, one child has married, and a number of grandchildren of the testator have been born to the various children. At the time the will was made the ages of the testator's children varied from about forty-two years to about twenty-five years. The inventory of his estate amounted to slightly over $1,000,000 and his property was at his death substantially the same as at the time of the execution of the will; and assets to about the same amount stated in the inventory were delivered to the trustees in July, 1916. During the first year of the trust the gross income was $154,170.61, the net income was $66,456.63 and the surplus net income, $42,426.33. For the next two years the gross income was somewhat larger, while the surplus net income was $37,295.77 and $22,817.06, respectively. In the fourth year of the trust there was a large increase in the amount of income, the gross income amounting to $271,684.14 and the surplus net income to $123,171.14. Thereafter there was a very considerable shrinkage of income and the amount varied from year to year, in one year the income not being sufficient to pay the expenses of administration and the annuities. The trustees have invested the surplus net income as it accrued from year to year, and the approximate total now amounts to more that $350,000. We are asked to answer eight questions, but they may be summarized into two, first, is the net income of the trust above that needed to pay the annuities intestate estate and to be distributed as such from time to time or is it to be accumulated until the termination of the trust and then distributed under the will as a part of the principal; and secondly, if the latter, is such an accumulation illegal and void.

In Colonial Trust Co. v. Brown, 105 Conn. 261. 275, 135 Atl.

555, speaking of a large excess of income over the amount which would be required to meet certain annuities provided in the will then before us, we said: "In determining the disposition of such an excess of income, should it materialize, we must first search the will to see if we can find there disclosed any intent of the testator as to it. . . . We ought not, however, lightly to adopt a construction which will very likely result in an accumulation of income over a period of many years, in the aggregate amounting to an immense sum, accompanied, as it must be, with a denial of all the enjoyment of it to those in whom the beneficial interest is vested, and with an ultimate disposition to strangers to the blood of the testator's father or to descendants yet unborn." Turning to the will before us, we are at once struck by the fact that it is not silent as to any income which may be left in the hands of the trustees after the payment of the annuities. Immediately after the gift to the trustees, the grant to them of the power to sell all the property of the estate except certain stock, and the direction to invest and reinvest the trust fund, comes the provision quoted that "all surplus income" shall be invested, with the avails of the sale of assets, in mortgages of a certain type. Several things are noteworthy about this provision. The reference to "surplus income" shows that its existence was in the mind of the testator as something to be anticipated; the position of that reference at the beginning of the clause concerning the method of investment, before the reference to the avails of the sale of the property, indicates that it was a matter of no small importance in his mind; its conjunction with the reference to such avails shows that he looked upon it as just as much an integral part of the trust fund as they would be; and the provision for the investment in real estate mortgages with semiannual interest payments points to the fact that he regarded it as an asset not to be held for a temporary purpose but such a one as would be invested in long term securities. We cannot assent to the contention of counsel that this reference to surplus income was purely incidental, a mere passing thought in a mind centered upon directions as to the character of the investments to be made by the trustees, for, if that were so, it would have been more natural for him to use some general terms as to investments rather than specifically and primarily to mention such income; nor do we agree with them that the significance of that reference is lessened by its position before rather than after the gifts of annuities; indeed, that rather indicates that the surplus income was a matter very much in his mind and not a mere incident to the creation of the annuities.

This view is confirmed by the further statements in the will in connection with the increase in the amount of the annuities which emphasize the direction that the children are not to receive more than $4000 a year, showing that the testator not merely anticipated an excess of income but wanted to make it clear that his children were not to share in it. Indeed, he must have known that there was every likelihood of a very substantial surplus income; when he made his will his estate amounted to a little over $1,000,000, and this was also true at his death, while the total of the annuities he created would for the first year amount at most to $22,500 and they were to increase until a total of not over $36,000 was reached, beyond which amount he emphatically stated that they were not to go. It is evident that the likelihood of a surplus income above that needed for the annuities was in the testator's mind, that he could hardly have failed to realize that it would amount to a very substantial sum, and that, by his direction for its investment along with the avails of the sale of the property in the trust fund in the long term securities, he intended to incorporate it in the principal of that fund.

It is very likely true that the testator did not expect that there would be such a large increase in the income of the estate as actually accrued, or that there would be such a decrease in the purchasing power of the dollar as decidedly to shrink the real value of the annuities he gave. These circumstances cannot, however, justify a disregard of the plain words of the will and the intent he has expressed in it. Bartlett v. Sears, 81 Conn. 34, 40, 70 Atl. 33. Nor is it sufficient to overcome that intent that it may seem to us to be for the best interests of the grandchildren and great-grandchildren, who are ultimately to receive the principal of the trust, that the testator's children should receive the surplus income from time to time. The court cannot pass upon the wisdom of the provisions the testator has made; "its duty is to see that the testator's intention is consummated." South Norwalk Trust Co. v. St. John, 92 Conn. 168, 178, 101 Atl. 961. The emphasis which he put upon the restriction of the annual amount each of his children was to receive suggests a motive and one does not have to look far to find one that is at least legitimate. If any of his daughters did not marry, the provision he made would not be wholly inadequate for her reasonable support; and he may have thought it undesirable that his sons, or the husbands of his daughters, should they marry, should be relieved of the necessity of exercising initiative and industry; or he may have desired to build up, and pass over to his grandchildren an estate of sufficient size, so that, divided among them, it might still be expected to give each a very substantial sum.   Nor do we find anything in Colonial Trust Co. v. Brown, 105 Conn. 261, 135 Atl. 555, Shepard v. Union & New Haven Trust Co., 106 Conn. 627, 138 Atl. 809, and Belcher v. Phelps, 109 Conn. 7, 144 Atl. 659, which militates against our conclusion.   In the first case the court found expressed in the will an intent that any income above that needed for the payment of annuities should be used to discharge certain incumbrances on real estate which the trustees were directed to retain and to improve, but we discovered no intent expressed as to the disposition of the excess income after these purposes had been accomplished; and in the other two cases we point out that there was no direction for an accumulation nor any expression of an intent that the excess income should be accumulated and become a part of the principal of the trust.   Confronted with a will in which such an intent is expressed, we must give it effect, unless it violates some rule or principle of law.

The trust is to terminate and the principal of the fund is to be distributed at the death of the last survivor of the testator's children, and that creates a like limitation upon the period of accumulation.   It cannot therefore be extended beyond the time allowed by the rule against perpetuities for the vesting of estate. Colonial Trust Co. v. Brown, supra, p. 272.   By analogy to that rule, where statutory provisions do not control, the same limitations fixed by it are generally applied in determining the period over which funds are permitted to accumulate.   Thus in Hoadley v. Beardsley, 89 Conn. 270, 279, 93 Atl. 535, we stated it to be a well-established common-law principle that "trusts for accumulation must be strictly confined within the rules against perpetuities, and that, if such a trust exceeds those limits, it is void"; and in Wilson v. D'atro, 109 Conn. 563, 567, 145 Atl. 161, we applied that rule to hold invalid a provision for an accumulation over a period not measured by any life which extended for more than twenty-one years.   Counsel who are seeking a decision that the accumulation before us is illegal do not question this principle, but they do claim that we may hold a trust for accumulation illegal as unreasonable and against public policy even though it does not extend beyond the period allowed by the rule against perpetuities, and that we ought to do it in this case.   Previous to the enactment of the "Thellusson Act" in England in 1800 all accumulations which had come before the English court and which did not run beyond that period had been upheld and it is generally stated that the common law permitted accumulations not exceeding it.   Thellusson v. Woodford, 11 Ves. Jr. 112, 146; Odell v. Odell, 92 Mass. (10 Allen) 1, 5; Pray v. Hegeman, 92 N.Y. 508,

514; 1 Perry on Trusts (7th Ed.) Sec. 393; Lewin on Trusts (13th Ed.) p. 126. This is the general rule applicable in any except the most unusual situations. There is, however, in the courts a power, rarely to be exercised and only in a clear case, to declare void testamentary provisions of the nature of the one we are considering, aside from any violation of settled rules of law, because under the peculiar facts of the case they contravene a sound public policy. Colonial Trust Co. v. Brown, supra, p. 285. Thus it is the general rule that the limitations upon the period during which income may accumulate do not apply to charities, yet in Woodruff v. Marsh, 63 Conn. 125, 138, 26 Atl. 846, we recognized the right of the courts to curb the extent of accumulations for such purposes. See Colonial Trust Co. v. Waldron, 112 Conn. 216, 222, 152 Atl. 69; Girard Trust Co. v. Russell, 179 Fed. 446, 452. In Belcher v. Phelps, 109 Conn. 7, 18, 144 Atl. 659, we said that if the will then before us had provided for an accumulation "we should be obliged to determine whether the limitation imposed upon the enjoyment of this property through such accumulations was not an unreasonable restraint on alienation and in conflict with settled principles of public policy." We did not mean by this to suggest that any different principles were applicable to such accumulations than those we have stated, but we were merely giving a summary statement of them in the light of the basic principle underlying both the general rule and the possible exception.

The facts of the case before us certainly do not bring it within any exception to the general rule. The accumulation of excess income is large, but almost two-thirds of it accrued in the first four years of the trust, and that which has of late accrued from year to year has been relatively small in amount; indeed, if the interest earned upon the surplus income which had accrued in the early years of the trust and was then added to the principal were to be disregarded, there would be undoubtedly a much smaller surplus during the later years. Nor is the probable duration of the joint lives of the testator's children as fixed by the mortality tables, stated by counsel to be thirty-nine years longer, a time so unreasonable as to justify a defeat of the testator's intent.

To questions 1, 2, 3, 4, 6 and 7, we answer that the will does provide for the accumulation of the surplus income during the period of the trust and at its termination that income is to be distributed to those then entitled as a part of the principal of the fund, and that it is not therefore intestate estate to be distributed as such; and to question 5, we answer that the provision for the accumulation of the surplus income is not illegal and void. Question 8 is too general to justify an answer.

No costs will be taxed in this court to either party.
In this opinion the other judges concurred.[135]

11.   DURATION OF TRUSTS

In the absence of a statute, there is no rule which places a limit
on the duration of private trusts.[136]   The common law rule against
perpetuities requires only that interests under a trust vest within
the period of the rule, but the date of the termination of the trust
and the date of final vesting of interests under the trust do not
have to be the same.[137]   A well-drafted estate plan normally will
result in the date of final vesting of all interests under the trust
being the same as the date of the termination of the trust so as to
avoid the creation of any descendible future interests.

Although there may be no rule limiting the duration of a private trust, there clearly is some limit to the time during which
such a trust may be indestructible.[138]   If an attempt has been made
to make a trust indestructible for too long a period of time, the
effect is to eliminate the feature of indestructibility.[139]

[135] The validity of a provision regarding the accumulation of income in a
gift to a charity is considered infra page 876, and the rule against accumulations as applied to administrative provisions is dealt with infra page 1121.
See also in regard to the validity of provisions as to accumulations in employee benefit plans the comments at page 343, note 6, supra.

For an annotation on accumulations, see 152 A.L.R. 657 (1944). — ED.

[136] See 6 American Law of Property §24.67 (Casner ed. 1952).   California
Laws 1959, c. 270, adds a new §771 to the Civil Code, which provides that a
trust is not invalid merely because its duration may exceed the time within
which interests thereunder are required to vest, as long as all interests must
vest in time.

[137] Where the trust suspends the power of alienation while it endures, as
in New York because of Personal Property Law §15 (Real Property Law §103
is similar), quoted infra page 1468, the trust cannot endure beyond the period
of the rule when suspension of the power of alienation is the test.   In this
respect New York, even with its broadened rule against perpetuities, as described in Note on the New York Statutory Rule Against Perpetuities, supra
page 639, is not as liberal as a state governed by the common law rule against
perpetuities, but this is no handicap from an estate planning standpoint.

[138] A trust is indestructible when the beneficiaries thereunder cannot compel a termination of the trust, even though all are ascertained and all have
vested interests and all have attained their majority.   The leading case in the
United States which recognizes that a trust may be indestructible is Claflin v.
Claflin, 149 Mass. 19, 20 N.E. 454 (1889).   In England the doctrine of indestructibility of trusts is not recognized.   The circumstances under which
the beneficiaries can and cannot terminate the trust are considered in 3 Scott,
Trusts §337 (2d ed. 1956).

[139] California Laws 1959, c. 270 adds a new §771 to the Civil Code, which
provides that if a trust may endure beyond the period of the rule against
perpetuities, a provision therein that it may not be terminated is ineffective
in so far as it purports to be applicable beyond such time.   When a trust has
existed longer than the time within which future interests must vest, it may

PROBLEM

11.43. A transfers property to T in trust. The trust instrument directs T to pay the income to B for life and then to pay the income to B's first-born son for life (B has no son at the date of the transfer) and then to pay the principal to C and his heirs. The trust instrument contains the following provision: "The interest of each beneficiary in the income or principal of the trust under this instrument shall be free from the control or interference of any creditor of a beneficiary or any spouse of a married beneficiary and shall not be subject to attachment or susceptible of anticipation or alienation." Assume that under the governing state law the common law rule against perpetuities controls the validity of interests under a trust, that restraints on the alienation of both an equitable life interest and an equitable remainder are permitted, and that the doctrine of Claflin v. Claflin applies to a trust. Is any interest under the trust invalid because it may vest too remotely? Is the provision restraining the alienation of the interest in B's first-born son valid? Is the provision restraining the alienation of C's remainder interest valid? [140] After B's son has been born and has attained the age of twenty-one, can B, his son, and C by joining together compel a termination of the trust? [141]

12. ILLEGAL CONDITIONS

The estate plan which a person adopts can have considerable influence on the kinds of human beings the beneficiaries will become. Thus every estate plan should be tested as to whether its influence will be for good or bad so far as the characters of the individual beneficiaries are concerned. This testing will not always produce unanimity as to result but at least it is likely to bring to the forefront the obviously undesirable influences of particular property arrangements.

---

be terminated on the request of a majority of the beneficiaries, or on petition of anyone who would be affected by a termination if the court decides that it would be in the best interest of a majority of the persons who would be affected thereby. See also Cal. Laws 1959, c. 470, which provides for internal attack and attack by the Attorney General when a trust is set up to endure beyond the period of the rule against perpetuities.

See generally Morray, The Rule Against Prolonged Indestructibility of Private Trusts, 44 Ill. L. Rev. 467 (1949).

[140] For a consideration of time restrictions upon restraints on alienation which are otherwise valid, see 6 American Law of Property §24.66 (Casner ed. 1952).

[141] As to the limitations on the indestructibility of trusts, see id. §24.67.

The desire of a transferor to influence directly the life of a beneficiary by the imposition of a specific condition which must be met if he is to enjoy the benefits of the transfer is a not uncommon situation. This attempt to influence directly the life of the beneficiary will fail if it is against public policy. The effect of the failure will normally be to allow the beneficiary to enjoy the benefits of the transfer without complying with the condition.[142]

The legality of a condition which undertakes to restrain the beneficiary from alienating his interest has been considered.[143] The validity of a provision which is designed to prevent a contest of a will has also been noted.[144]

The most frequently occurring conditions are those which are designed to influence the beneficiary in some way in regard to his marital status. To what extent should a condition attached to a property disposition be deemed invalid as against public policy because it is designed to prevent the beneficiary from marrying a certain person or to break up an existing marriage? [145]

---

[142] If it is established that property held in the decedent's name was not owned beneficially by the decedent, then of course the value thereof is not includible in the decedent's gross estate under 1954 I.R.C. §2033, quoted infra page 1396. In Chandler v. United States, 177 F. Supp. 565 (D.N.H. 1959), securities were held in the name of the decedent under an illegal trust (illegal under controlling Massachusetts law because it was set up to defraud present and future creditors), but nevertheless a resulting trust to the settlor was proper under the circumstances and thus the value of the securities was not includible in the decedent's gross estate.

[143] See the discussion of restraints on alienation at page 620 supra.

[144] As to a provision which forfeits a beneficiary's interest if he contests the will, see page 53 supra, note 11. In regard to restraints on will contests generally, see 6 American Law of Property §§27.3-27.11 (Casner ed. 1952).

[145] Kovler v. Vagenheim, 333 Mass. 252, 130 N.E.2d 557 (1955), involved a contract made by a wife's brother to indemnify her husband for any money he was required to pay for the support or maintenance of his wife or children. After the divorce, the husband sought to enforce the contract to recover the amount he was required to pay for the support of his wife and child. It was argued that the contract was invalid because it tended to encourage divorce by enabling the husband to meet the expenses of divorce more easily. The court held that the contract was valid.

In Lantz v. Pence, 127 Ind. App. 620, 142 N.E.2d 456 (1957), the testator gave half of his residuary estate to his son "during the period of time that he and his present wife, Fern Pence, shall sustain to each other the relationship of husband and wife . . . ," and if his son survived the relationship, he was to take the property absolutely, and if he did not survive the relationship, the property was to go over to the testator's daughter or her children. The son divorced Fern in November of one year and remarried her in March of the next year. The court held that he became the absolute owner of the property as a result of the divorce, and the remarriage did not affect the result. No question was raised as to the possible illegality of the condition on the ground that it tended to induce a divorce.

In Fineman v. Central National Bank of Cleveland, 161 N.E.2d 557 (Cuyahoga Co. Prob. Ct., Ohio, 1959), a trust was created which was to terminate when the testator's son "shall be divorced from his present wife" or when

PROBLEMS

11.44. A gift may be valid if the testator's intention is not to induce a divorce or separation, but rather is to provide for the beneficiary in case such an event occurs. See Born v. Horstmann, 80 Cal. 452, 22 Pac. 338 (1889). Suppose that a trust is established under which the designated beneficiary is to receive the income until the death of her husband or until she and her husband are divorced, whichever first occurs, and then she is to receive the principal of the trust. Is such a trust one that tends to induce separation or divorce, or is it one which is designed only to provide for a beneficiary in case such an event occurs? See Patte v. Riggs National Bank of Washington, 124 F. Supp. 552 (D.D.C. 1954), *aff'd,* 218 F.2d 867 (D.C. Cir. 1955).

11.45. In Zdanowich v. Sherwood, 19 Conn. Super. 89, 110 A.2d 290 (1954), the testator made a gift to his wife, subject to the condition that if she ever gave any of the income of the property to a named son, the property interest in her was to end. Under Connecticut law a mother is liable for the support of even an adult son if he becomes unable to support himself. It was contended that the condition attached by the testator to the gift to his wife was void because it tended to defeat the policy in Connecticut as to the obligation of a mother to support her son. Should this contention prevail? [146]

11.46. T's will contained the following provision: "If any of my said children shall marry a person not born in the Hebrew faith, then I hereby revoke the gift or gifts and the provision or provisions herein made to or for such child." T dies in 1943. Prior to T's death, his son became acquainted with a young woman who was the daughter of Roman Catholic parents and had been brought up in her parents' faith. Subsequent to T's death she received religious instructions from rabbis. She became a convert to Judaism and received a certificate recognizing her conversion. Thereafter she and T's son went through a rabbinical marriage ceremony. Should T's son be deprived of his beneficial rights under a trust es-

---

she dies, and then the trust property was to go to the testator's son. The court held that the provision for terminating the trust was void as against public policy and that the son's interest in the trust property was indefeasibly vested.

See generally 6 American Law of Property §§27.12-27.23 (Casner ed. 1952).

[146] In Cummings v. Brenci, 334 Mass. 144, 134 N.E.2d 133 (1956), the court held that public policy did not prevent a wife from making an employment contract for part of her time and services for the lifetime of a middle-aged employer, although the contract might have an effect upon her marital relationship.

tablished under the will of his father?   See Gordon v. Gordon, 332 Mass. 197, 124 N.E.2d 228 (1955), *cert. denied,* 349 U.S. 947 (1955).[147]

[147] In Gordon v. Lewitsky, 333 Mass. 379, 131 N.E.2d 174 (1955), four of five daughters were trying to defeat the gift to the fifth daughter under the provision in a will which stated that the gift to any beneficiary who contested the validity of the will was revoked.   In the case of Gordon v. Gordon the fifth daughter had argued for the invalidity of the provision for forfeiture in the event of marriage to a non-Hebrew.   The court, however, held that the four daughters in the petition in Gordon v. Gordon had asked for a division into five shares and could not now change their position.

CHAPTER XII

Powers of Appointment Including Discretionary Trusts

Powers of appointment may take many different forms. Whatever the form, the person who has the power is not the beneficial owner of the interest subject to the power, but is vested with authority, either qualified or unqualified, to select the beneficial owner.[1] Through the proper employment of such powers, flexibility can be introduced into an estate plan. Decisions that must be made relate not only to whether powers should be created but also to whether powers possessed by the person whose estate is being planned should be exercised. Such decisions should be made in the light of their respective estate, gift, and income tax consequences.

It may not always be obvious that a person has a power of appointment. For example, if under the terms of a trust instrument the trustee has a power to appoint the principal of the trust for the benefit of designated individuals, and another person has the unrestricted power to remove or discharge the trustee and appoint himself as trustee, the person who has the power of removal has a power of appointment.[2]

If a discretionary trust is to be used, one, for example, where the trustee has discretion to spray income and principal among designated beneficiaries, it is very important for the long-range protection of the beneficiaries that the selection of successor trustees be placed in proper hands. Although the power to remove the trustee cannot be given to a beneficiary, if, after the removal of the trustee, the beneficiary can appoint himself as trustee without the beneficiary being deemed to have the discretionary powers of the trustee, with the resultant adverse tax consequences that flow from possessing a general power of appointment, the beneficiary

[1] The law of powers of appointment is developed in 5 American Law of Property §§23.1-23.66 (Casner ed. 1952). See also Halbach, The Use of Powers of Appointment in Estate Planning, 45 Iowa L. Rev. 691 (1960); Berger, The General Power of Appointment as an Interest in Property, 40 Neb. L. Rev. 104 (Dec. 1960).

[2] See Reg. §20.2041-1(b)(1), quoted infra page 1516.

may be given some hand in the selection of a successor trustee without such adverse tax consequences. Thus it seems clear that if a vacancy in the office of trustee occurs, a beneficiary may be authorized to name the successor trustee, as long as he cannot name himself as the trustee. In such a case he never moves into a position where he can take over the powers of the trustee himself and never has a voice in the determination of whether the powers in the trustee will be exercised. He never has a power of appointment exercisable by himself alone or by himself in conjunction with another. He would be acting improperly under his authorization and contrary to the prohibition that he not appoint himself, if he offered the trusteeship to any person on condition that that person, after appointment as trustee, would exercise the trustee's powers in some specified manner.

1.   RELEVANT FACTORS IN DETERMINING WHETHER
TO EXERCISE A POWER OF APPOINTMENT

a. *Basis*

Under Section 113(a)(5) of the 1939 Code, even if the value of appointive assets was includible in the gross estate of the donee of the power for estate tax purposes, the appointive property acquired a new basis as property passing from the donee by bequest or devise *only* if it passed "without full and adequate consideration under a general power of appointment exercised by will."[3]   When the value of the appointive assets was includible in the gross estate only if the power was exercised, as in the case of general powers created on or before October 21, 1942,[4] the estate tax cost of exercising the power had to be compared with the income tax advantage to the recipients of a new basis. If, however, the value of the appointive assets was includible in the donee's gross estate without regard to whether the power was exercised, there was no tax reason for not exercising it unless the old basis was more advantageous.

Section 1014(b)(4) of the 1954 Code[5] follows the old law by recognizing that a new basis is acquired by the recipient with respect to "property passing without full and adequate consideration un-

---

[3] Suppose that T established a trust in his will and that the trustee was to pay to A the income for his life and so much of the principal as A might demand, and, on A's death, was to pay the remaining principal to B and his heirs. A would not have a general power exercisable by will. The only way B could receive a new basis under the pre-1954 law was if A withdrew all of the assets from the trust in his lifetime and passed them to B under his will.

[4] See 1939 I.R.C. §811(f)(1). The corresponding section of the 1954 Code is §2041(a)(1) and is quoted infra page 1400.

[5] Quoted infra page 1382.

der a general power of appointment exercised by the decedent [donee of the power] by will." Section 1014(b)(9),[6] however, provides that "in the case of decedents dying after December 31, 1953, property acquired from the decedent by reason of death, form of ownership, or other conditions (including property acquired through the exercise or non-exercise of a power of appointment), if by reason thereof the property is required to be included in determining the value of the decedent's gross estate," acquires a new basis. The quoted language has largely, though not entirely, eliminated basis as a factor in determining whether to exercise a general power.[7]

In a few cases basis considerations may still induce the exercise of the general power. Suppose that a general power of appointment was created on or before October 21, 1942, and the value of the donee's owned and appointive assets totals $120,000, with the basis of the appointive assets very low in comparison with their present value. The only way the appointive assets can acquire a new basis, even under the 1954 Code, is by the exercise of the power, because only in that way will the appointive assets be included in the donee's gross estate. In such a case, the basis factor alone may possibly induce an exercise of the general power of appointment.

Suppose that A, before his death, exercises a general power to appoint by deed or by will in favor of B, and the value of the appointed property is included in A's gross estate as a gift in contemplation of death. Under Section 1014(b)(9), B takes as his basis the property's fair market value at the decedent's death (or its value on the alternate valuation date if that is used for valuing the decedent's gross estate).[8] Section 1014(b)(9) also provides that, where the property has been acquired before the death of the decedent, the basis shall be "reduced by the amount allowed to the taxpayer as deductions in computing taxable income . . . for exhaustion, wear and tear, obsolescence, amortization and depletion on such property before the death of the decedent." Section 1014(b)(9) applies only where no other paragraph of Section 1014 applies.

[6] Quoted infra page 1382.

[7] A new basis would now be acquired in a case like the one described in note 3 supra, even if the donee did not withdraw the assets from the trust in his lifetime.

[8] In regard to the extent to which the value at which property is included in the decedent's gross estate will control for the purpose of determining the basis, see McEwan v. Commissioner, 241 F.2d 887 (2d Cir. 1957), and material referred to at page 125 supra, note 41.

PROBLEM

12.1. A in his will bequeaths and devises the residue of his estate to T in trust. Under the terms of the trust, T is required to pay the income to B for life and, in addition, to pay B, from time to time, such amount or amounts of principal as B may request by an instrument in writing delivered to T in the lifetime of B. On B's death, the then remaining principal is to be paid to designated beneficiaries. B requests T to deliver to him all of the trust principal and T complies. Explain how you ascertain the basis in B's hands of the trust principal delivered to him by T. See Revenue Ruling 55-293, 1955-1 C.B. 352.

b. *Deduction for Debts, Expenses of Administration, and the Like*

In the absence of a statute, the mere existence of a general power of appointment does not subject the appointive property to claims of the donee's creditors. If the power is exercised, however, the creditors may be able to reach the appointive assets.[9] The 1939 Code did not allow an estate tax deduction for debts, expenses of administration, and the like, to the extent such items exceeded, at the time of the decedent's death, the value of property subject to claims.[10] Thus, under the 1939 Code a factor in determining whether to exercise a general power might be the importance of increasing the property subject to claims so that a full deduction would be allowable. Section 2053(c)(2)[11] of the 1954 Code allows a deduction for such an excess if "such deductions represent amounts paid before the date prescribed for the filing of the estate tax return." Accordingly, there should no longer be any need to exercise a general power of appointment to improve the picture as to those deductions. Section 2053(b),[12] allowing the deduction of "amounts representing expenses incurred in administering property not subject to claims which is included in the gross estate," may be of significance in connection with property passing in default of the exercise of a general power of appointment, or by the

---

[9] See Clapp v. Ingraham, 126 Mass. 200 (1879). It is brought out in 5 American Law of Property §23.16 (Casner ed. 1952) that the appointive assets can be reached to pay the donee's creditors only after the donee's owned property has been exhausted, unless the donee provides otherwise. See also note 21 infra.

[10] See 1939 I.R.C. 812(b).

[11] Quoted in full infra page 1403.

[12] Quoted infra page 1403.

exercise of a general power where such an exercise does not subject the assets to claims.

c. *Value of Appointive Assets Includible in Donee's Gross Estate Only If Power Is Exercised*

If a person has a general power of appointment created on or before October 21, 1942,[13] the value of the appointive assets will not be includible in his gross estate for federal estate tax purposes if he does not *exercise* the power.[14] If he exercises the power by his

[13] With respect to a power of appointment created on or before October 21, 1942, the power is a general one for federal estate tax purposes if it is exercisable in favor of the donee of the power, his creditors, his estate or creditors of his estate except that a power to consume, invade or appropriate property for the benefit of the donee of the power which is limited by an ascertainable standard relating to health, education, support or maintenance of the donee is not a general power, and a power exercisable by the donee only in conjunction with another is not a general power. See 1954 I.R.C. §2041(b)(1)(A), (B), quoted infra page 1401. For federal gift tax purposes, a power of appointment created on or before October 21, 1942, is a general one under the same circumstances that it would be a general one for federal estate tax purposes. See 1954 I.R.C. §2514(c)(1) and (2), quoted infra page 1421.

[14] See 1954 I.R.C. §2041(a)(1), quoted infra page 1400. It should be noted that the failure to exercise a pre-1942 general power or the complete release of such a power is not deemed an exercise thereof in favor of the takers in default of an exercise. Furthermore, if a pre-1942 general power has been partially released, so that it is no longer a general power, and the release took place before November 1, 1951, or, if the donee of the power was under a legal disability on October 21, 1942, the release occurred or occurs after November 1, 1951, but not later than six months after the termination of such disability, then the exercise of the power will not be deemed the exercise of a general power. In determining whether a gift has been made by the donee of a pre-1942 general power for federal gift tax purposes, he must be found to have exercised the power and the same tests as to exercise are applicable as when the question is whether the donee has exercised such a power for federal estate tax purposes. See 1954 I.R.C. §2514(a), quoted infra page 1420. See also Reg. §20.2041-2(e), quoted infra page 1520.

If it is desired to release a general power of appointment partially, care should be taken to use language of release rather than language that appears to exercise the power. In Emery v. United States, 153 F. Supp. 248 (D. Mass. 1957), what was in substance a partial release of a general power of appointment was accomplished by language which appeared to exercise the power, but the court held that it would disregard the form and give effect to the substance.

For a case in which a nonresident decedent's interest in property situated within the United States was determined, in accordance with controlling foreign law, to be the equivalent of a life interest with a power to invade corpus, and the value of the property over which she had the power was excluded from her gross estate because it was a pre-1942 power, see Estate of Hedwig Zietz, 34 T.C. 351 (1960). In Willy Zietz, 34 T.C. 369 (1960), the taxpayer was the one who took the property referred to in the preceding case and he claimed an income tax deduction for legal fees incurred to prevent the assessment of the estate tax. The deduction was allowed under 1954

will, or by a disposition which is of such a nature that, if it were a transfer of property owned by him, the property would be includible in his gross estate, the value of the appointive assets will be included in his gross estate. The donee should have some very compelling reason to justify exercising such a power and adding the value of the appointive assets to his gross estate.

A partial exercise of a pre-1942 general power may, or may not, require the inclusion of the value of the entire appointive property in the donee's gross estate. If the appointment is of a life interest in the whole, the value of the entire property is includible in the donee's gross estate. However, when the exercise affects only a part of the property, as where the donee has a power of appointment over a trust fund and appoints one half of it to a designated person, the value of the portion unaffected by the appointment is not includible in the donee's gross estate.[15]

I.R.C. §212, quoted infra page 1336, as an expenditure to conserve income-producing property.

Soars v. Graham, 163 F. Supp. 239 (M.D. Pa. 1957), considered a unique problem in relation to a pre-1942 power. Under Pennsylvania law prior to the enactment of the Estates Act of 1947, a gift to a person for life with a right to consume the subject matter of the gift, and with a remainder over of what was not consumed, was deemed to create a creditor-debtor relationship between the life beneficiary and the remainderman. The amount of the debt was the value of the subject matter of the gift on the date of the gift. Thus, if the subject matter of the gift increased in value, the increase was includible in the gross estate of the life beneficiary (the holder of the power), even though the power was a pre-1942 one. The Estates Act of 1947 changed the Pennsylvania law by providing that a life tenant in the situation under consideration will be deemed a trustee, and not a debtor to the remainderman. See Pa. Stat. Ann., tit. 20, §301.13 (Purdon), quoted infra page 1472. The case was affirmed in 256 F.2d 762 (3d Cir. 1958).

In Norris v. United States, 59-1 U.S.T.C. ¶11852 (E.D. Okla. 1959), the donee was given two separable powers with respect to the same property. Both powers were created before October, 1942. Under one power, the donee could appoint to "her children and their heirs" and under the other, to "such other beneficiaries as she may deem best." The court held that the second power was restricted and did not permit appointment to the donee's estate or her creditors, but even if it did, the exercise of the separable special power was not an exercise of the general power. Consequently, the value of the appointive assets was not includible in the donee's gross estate.

[15] See Rev. Rul. 54-59, 1954-1 C.B. 183, and Reg. §20.2041-2(f), quoted infra page 1520.

In Estate of Leo M. Gartland, 34 T.C. —, No. 89 (1960), the decedent had a pre-1942 general power to amend a trust under which the income was payable to him in such amounts as the trustee might deem advisable. The decedent amended the trust so as to require that the income be paid to him. In 1945 he released his general power. The court agreed with the Commissioner in holding that the amendment of the trust to require the payment of the income to the donee was an exercise of the power and was an exercise of such a nature that if he had transferred owned property, retaining the income for life, the value of the transferred property would have been includible in his gross estate under 1954 I.R.C. §2036. Thus the value of the trust property was includible in the decedent's gross estate notwithstanding the 1945 release.

If the donee does not want to exercise a pre-1942 power, it may not be enough just to ignore the power in his will. To keep from exercising his general power, he may have to negate specifically any intention to exercise it, because in many jurisdictions a general residuary clause in a will exercises such a power of appointment unless a contrary intent is manifested.[16]

A general provision negating the exercise of any power of appointment may produce undesirable results unless the provisions dealing with the payment of taxes are drawn with this negation in mind. If, for example, the provisions dealing with the payment of taxes throw the entire tax burden on the residuary estate and the decedent dies possessed of a post-1942 general power of appointment, so that the value of the appointive assets will be includible in his gross estate for estate tax purposes, even though the power is not exercised, the tax burden may wipe out most of the residuary estate. Such a result will be undesirable if the decedent anticipated that certain dependents would be adequately cared for out of his residuary estate.[17]

[16] See generally 5 American Law of Property §23.40 (Casner ed. 1952).

Merchants National Bank of Mobile v. United States, 156 F. Supp. 827 (S.D. Ala. 1957), held that under Alabama law the general residuary clause of a will did not exercise a power of appointment. The power involved was one which did not become exercisable by the donee unless she survived her husband, and her residuary clause established a trust under which she gave her husband a beneficial interest. These facts were noted by the court in deciding that the power had not been exercised. The case was affirmed sub nom. United States v. Merchants National Bank of Mobile, 261 F.2d 570 (5th Cir. 1958). In Second Bank-State Street Trust Co. v. Yale University Alumni Fund, 338 Mass. 520, 156 N.E.2d 57 (1959), a residuary clause operated as an exercise of a general testamentary power reserved by the testator in a revocable inter vivos trust established by him.

In Bartol v. McGinnes, 185 F. Supp. 659 (E.D. Pa. 1960), the issue was whether a pre-1942 general power of appointment had been exercised, so that the value of the appointive assets would be includible in the donee's gross estate. The state court had decided that the power had not been exercised. The state court's decision was deemed to be conclusive even though it reached its conclusion on the basis of extrinsic evidence as to the donee's intention, which should not have been considered.

The care with which a residuary clause must be drafted is illustrated in another situation, in Salter v. Salter, 338 Mass. 391, 155 N.E.2d 430 (1959), where the clause gave all "funds remaining" to designated persons, and the court held real property acquired after the will was executed did not pass under the residuary clause.

[17] Furthermore, appointive assets may be treated as owned by the donee of the power for state inheritance tax purposes (in some states he is so treated even if he has only a special power), and consequently, the tax clause with respect to the payment of such taxes should be drawn with this possibility in mind.

If the tax burden as to appointive assets must be borne by these assets, and a credit for the tax attributable to them is available under 1954 I.R.C. §2013, will the credit be available to the persons who pay the tax on the appointive assets or to the persons who pay the tax on the other assets of the decedent? It would seem that the credit would be allocated to the persons responsible,

PROBLEMS

12.2. A is the donee of a general power of appointment created before October 21, 1942. A executes a will in which he appoints the appointive assets to the persons who are designated as the takers in default. A dies and the appointees elect to take under the gift in default of appointment rather than under the appointment by A. Are the appointive assets includible in A's gross estate? See Barclay, Jr. v. United States, 175 F.2d 48 (3d Cir. 1949), *cert. denied,* 338 U.S. 849 (1949); Wilson v. Kraemer, 190 F.2d 341 (2d Cir. 1951), *cert. denied,* 342 U.S. 859 (1951); Keating v. Mayer, 236 F.2d 478 (3d Cir. 1956); Thompson v. United States, 148 F. Supp. 910 (E.D. Pa. 1957). Compare Commissioner v. Estate of Cardeza, 173 F.2d 19 (3d Cir. 1949). Section 20.2041-1(d) of the Regulations, quoted infra page 1518, also considers the situation dealt with in this problem.

12.3. A, who died before October 21, 1942, bequeathed and devised property to B, with the right to use and dispose of as much of the income and principal thereof as he might desire during his life, with remainder, if any, on his death to C and D. In order to maintain the identity of the property bequeathed and devised, B, C and D acting together conveyed the property to T in trust and the terms of the trust were identical with the terms of A's will in so far as B's rights and powers were concerned. B dies in 1961. Is the value of the property in the trust includible in B's gross estate for federal estate tax purposes? See Revenue Ruling 54-271, 1954-2 C.B. 294.

12.4. Prior to November 1, 1951, the donee of a pre-1942 general power of appointment executes a will which appoints the appointive assets to persons other than his creditors, his estate, or creditors of his estate. Shortly after executing his will but prior to November 1, 1951, he becomes hopelessly insane, so that the terms of his will can never be changed. He dies in 1961. Will the value of the appointive assets be includible in his gross estate? See Simons v. United States, 227 F.2d 168 (2d Cir. 1955), *cert. denied,* 350 U.S. 949 (1956).

12.5. A created a trust in 1940 under which the trustee was directed to pay the income to B for life, remainder as B appoints by a deed delivered to the trustee in B's lifetime. B exercised the power in 1960, reserving the right to revoke the exercise. One year later B revoked the exercise. B dies. Is the value of the ap-

---

in the final analysis, for the payment of the tax on the assets which give rise to the credit.

pointive assets includible in B's gross estate?   See Section 20.2041-2(c), Example (3) of the Regulations.

The 1954 Code specifically provides that a power of appointment created by a will which was executed on or before October 21, 1942, shall be considered as a power created on or before such date if the testator dies before July 1, 1949, without having republished his will, by codicil or otherwise, after October 21, 1942.[18] Whether or not a power of appointment created by an inter vivos instrument executed on or before October 21, 1942, is considered a power created on or before that date depends on the facts or circumstances of the particular case.[19]   A power of appointment is

[18] See 1954 I.R.C. §2041(b)(3), quoted infra page 1401.   Section 2514(f) of the 1954 Code, quoted infra page 1422, is the corresponding provision in the federal gift tax law.

[19] See Reg. §20.2041-1(e), quoted infra page 1519.

Merchants National Bank of Mobile v. United States, 156 F. Supp. 827 (S.D. Ala. 1957), held that a power of appointment granted by the terms of a revocable inter vivos trust which was executed prior to October 22, 1942, was created prior to that date, even though the settlor of the trust died after that date and the exercise of the power was contingent on the donee surviving the donor.   The donor of the power died in 1946 and the court referred to §2041(b)(3), quoted infra page 1401, as establishing a Congressional intent that such a power of appointment is to be deemed one created prior to Octo ber 22, 1942.   The case was affirmed sub nom. United States v. Merchants National Bank of Mobile, 261 F.2d 570 (5th Cir. 1958).

In Hubner v. United States, 187 F. Supp. 659 (S.D. Cal. 1959), a husband acquired a single premium policy and, when it matured, he elected to leave the proceeds with the company under an arrangement whereby he was to receive the interest thereon for his life, with power to withdraw the proceeds.   He also set up a revocable trust with the same terms.   All of this occurred before October 22, 1942.   He died in 1946.   In 1947 his wife released her power to withdraw the proceeds left with the insurance company and released her power to make withdrawals under the trust.   The court held that the wife's powers were created before October 22, 1942, and therefore no amounts were includible in her gross estate on her death in 1955, by virtue of the release of her powers in 1947.   The case was affirmed sub nom. United States v. Hubner, 285 F.2d 29 (9th Cir. 1960).

In Turner v. United States, 178 F. Supp. 239 (W.D. Mo. 1959), the interest option with right of withdrawal was selected by the decedent's husband for his wife as beneficiary of his insurance policies.   The selection, though revocable by the insured until his death, was made in 1935, and he died in 1948.   The court, following United States v. Merchants National Bank of Mobile, held that the power in the wife-beneficiary was created prior to October 22, 1942.   Estate of Ernestina Rosenthal, 34 T.C. 144 (1960), held that a general power with respect to life insurance proceeds was created prior to October 22, 1942, when the insured made the beneficiary designation prior to that date, although he died after that date and retained until his death the unconditional right to revoke or change the method of payment or the beneficiaries.   Hyman v. United States, 60-2 U.S.T.C. ¶11971 (S.D.N.Y. 1960), stressed the difference between the date a power is created and the date it becomes exercisable, in holding that a power was created before October 22,

not considered as created after October 21, 1942, merely because the power is not exercisable or the identity of its holders is not ascertainable until after that date.[20]

PROBLEMS

12.6. On February 1, 1942, A transfers property to T in trust. The trust instrument directs T to pay the income to B for life, then to pay the corpus as B may appoint by his will. A reserves a power to revoke the trust but he dies on June 1, 1961, without having revoked it. When was B's general power to appoint by will created? See Section 20.2041-1(e) of the Regulations, quoted infra page 1519, and cases discussed supra note 19. See also Revenue Ruling 277, 1953-2 C.B. 265.

12.7. On February 1, 1942, A transfers property to T in trust. The trust instrument directs T to pay the income to B for life, then to pay the corpus as B may appoint by his will and, in default of appointment, to pay the corpus to C and his heirs. The trust is irrevocable. A dies on June 1, 1961. In his will he gives the residue of his estate to T to hold under the terms of the trust created on February 1, 1942. When was B's general power to appoint by will created as to the assets added to the trust by A's will?

12.8. On February 1, 1942, A takes out a policy of insurance on his life. The settlement provision in the policy directs the insurance company to pay interest to B for B's life, but B is to have the right to withdraw all or part of the proceeds at any time. A dies on June 1, 1961. When was B's general power to withdraw the proceeds created? What difference, if any, would it make, so far as the date of the creation of B's power is concerned, if A never had the right to change the designated beneficiary under the policy but did have the right to obtain the cash surrender value of the policy or borrow on the policy? See Revenue Ruling 278, 1953-2 C.B. 267. See also the cases discussed supra note 19.

12.9. A in his will provides for the establishment of a trust, with B and C as trustees. The terms of the trust call for the payment of income to D for his life and then for the payment of the corpus to a charity. The trustees, however, are given the power to alter or amend the trust in any manner. A dies on June 1, 1942. The trust is established and B and C qualify as the trustees.

1942, when the insured, prior to that date, had selected an option which gave the decedent a general power of appointment, although the insured retained the right to change the beneficiary designation and did not die until after October 21, 1942.

20 See Reg. §20.2041-1(e), quoted infra page 1519.

a. C dies on June 1, 1960. Is all or any part of the value of the trust property includible in his gross estate for estate tax purposes?

b. After C's death in 1960, X is appointed trustee to succeed him. X dies on June 1, 1961. Is all or any part of the value of the trust property includible in his gross estate for estate tax purposes?

c. After X's death in 1961, Y is appointed trustee to succeed him. B dies on August 1, 1961. Is all or any part of the value of the trust property includible in his gross estate for estate tax purposes?

See Section 20.2041-1(e) of the Regulations, quoted infra page 1519.

d. *Gift in Default of Appointment*

In determining whether to exercise a power of appointment, the donee should examine carefully the instrument which created the power, to ascertain what will happen to the appointive assets if he does not exercise the power; in other words, he should examine the gift in default of appointment. The answers given to the following questions will indicate whether the power should be exercised:

1. Does the gift in default of appointment describe in clear and unambiguous language what is to happen to the appointive assets? If the language which describes the gift in default of appointment will have to be construed by a court to give it preciseness of meaning, it may be wise to exercise the power, to avoid the costs which will otherwise be incurred in obtaining a construction of the language.

2. Does the gift in default of appointment, when considered in conjunction with the plan for the disposition of the donee's owned assets, make an intelligent arrangement for the persons he is interested in benefiting?

3. If the gift in default of appointment provides for the continuation of a trust with respect to the appointive assets, is the managerial arrangement applicable to the appointive assets a sound one under all the circumstances?

4. Are there any tax advantages to be gained by exercising the power? The donee may be able, by an exercise of the power, to reduce the impact of taxation on the beneficiaries. For example, suppose that the donee has a power to appoint among his issue, and in default of appointment the appointive assets go outright to his son. By appointing the property to his son for life with a remainder to the son's is-

sue, the imposition of an estate tax with respect to the appointive assets on the death of the donee's son is avoided. If the donee does not exercise the power and his son takes the appointive assets outright, when the son dies and passes the property on to his children the value of the property will be included in his gross estate for federal estate tax purposes.

e. Miscellaneous Factors Which Bear on the Desirability of Exercising a Power

As has been pointed out, the exercise of a general power of appointment may cause the appointive assets to be reachable by the creditors of the donee.[21] It has also been pointed out that when a trustee exercises a power to pay out income and thereby discharges a legal obligation of the settlor to support some person, the settlor will be taxable on the income so used.[22] It will be seen that a trustee who has a power to apply the income of a trust to the support or maintenance of a person whom he is obligated to support or maintain will be taxable on the income to the extent the income is so applied.[23] Furthermore, it must be kept in mind that the five-year throwback rule[24] may produce undesirable income tax consequences when a power to pay out accumulated income is exercised.

If the life beneficiary of a trust has a power to appoint the trust assets by will and exercises the power by appointing the property outright to designated appointees, should the trustee of the appointive assets deliver the trust property directly to the designated appointees or should he deliver it to the executor of the donee? In Olney v. Balch,[25] where a general power of appointment was involved, the court held that the duty of the trustees is discharged by paying over the appointive assets to the executor of the donee.

---

[21] See note 9 supra.

In New York the debts of the donee's estate may not be paid from appointive assets, even though the power is general and is exercised. If the power is created by a New York decedent, the appointive assets will remain under the jurisdiction of the New York court and thus the New York rule is applicable, even though the donee is resident in another state. In Estate of Sadie G. Shea, N.Y.L.J., Sept. 17, 1959, p. 14 (Westchester County Surr.), the New York court allowed the appointive fund to be reached to pay the expenses incurred in connection with the probate of the donee's will in Connecticut, where the donee resided. It also allowed a claim by a Connecticut attorney for counsel fees. These costs were incurred in proving the exercise of the power, and the New York court relaxed its rule to this extent in permitting appointive assets to be reached.

[22] See page 186 supra. See also 1954 I.R.C. §677(b), quoted infra page 1375.

[23] See the discussion in relation to 1954 I.R.C. §678 at page 729 infra.

[24] The five-year throwback rule is considered infra page 742.

[25] 154 Mass. 318, 28 N.E. 258 (1891).

Thus it should be kept in mind that the exercise of a power may augment the amount of the property that will be placed under the control of the executor and hence may increase his fee.[26]

2. POINTS TO KEEP IN MIND IF IT IS DECIDED TO EXERCISE A POWER OF APPOINTMENT

The exercise of any power of appointment must be in accordance with the authority given the donee of the power by the donor. Thus the terms of the instrument creating the power must be closely examined to ascertain the methods of exercise permitted, the objects of the power, whether the power is exclusive or nonexclusive,[27] and the types of interests that can be created in the appointees. Of course it must be remembered that powers may be created after the date of the execution of a will purporting to exercise powers, and if the donee intends to exercise such after-created powers, this intention should be clearly indicated.[28] Even if the donor's instructions are fully complied with, another pitfall that must be kept constantly in mind is the rule against perpetuities.[29]

If the power is one to appoint by deed and is unrestricted as to objects, the donee is regarded as the owner of the appointive asssets

[26] The Olney case points out that the reason why it is appropriate for the trustee to pay the appointive asscts to the executor of the donee when the power is exercised is that the executor may need these assets to pay debts. Thus the reason is applicable only to general powers of appointment. It would seem that if a special power of appointment is exercised, it would not be apropriate for the trustee of the appointive assets to pay them to the donee's executor, and possibly, even though a general power of appointment is involved, it would not be proper to so pay them where it is clear that the donee's estate is solvent and therefore the appointive assets will not be needed to pay debts. Restatement of Property §329, Comment *h* is in accord with these observations. Boston Safe Deposit and Trust Co. v. Alfred University, 339 Mass. 82, 88, 157 N.E.2d 662, 667 (1959), contains this statement: "Although under a special power of appointment direct transfer of the appointed trust assets to the appointees is to be made (see Prescott v. Wordell, 319 Mass. 118, 120, 65 N.E.2d 19; Restatement: Property, §326), under this general power of appointment the appointed assets appropriately should be paid to Massachusetts ancillary executors of Mrs. Ames' [the donee's] will, or administrators with her will annexed."

[27] A power is nonexclusive when the donee is required to give something to each object of the power; a power is exclusive when the donee may exclude one or more of the objects from benefiting by the exercise of the power. See 5 American Law of Property §§23.57, 23.58 (Casner ed. 1952).

[28] The exercise of a power of appointment by a will executed before the power was created is considered in 5 American Law of Property §23.41 (Casner ed. 1952).

[29] As to the validity of interests created by the exercise of a power of appointment under the common law rule against perpetuities, see 6 id. §§24.33-24.35.

for the purpose of applying the rule against perpetuities to the interests created by the exercise of the power.[30] If, however, the power is one to appoint by will only, or if the power is restricted as to objects, then the significant date for measuring the period of the rule against perpetuities, so far as appointed interests are concerned, is the date the power was created.[31]

In determining whether the appointed interests, if they ever vest, must vest within the period of the rule, measuring from the date of the creation of the power, the actual facts as of the date the power is exercised may be taken into consideration (the so-called "second look" doctrine).[32] For example, A in his will transfers property to T in trust, with directions to pay the income to B for life, then to hold the principal for, or pay it to, such person or persons, in such amounts and proportions and upon or subject to such trusts, terms, powers or restrictions as B may appoint by will and, in default of appointment, to B's children equally. B exercises the power by appointing the property to T in trust, with directions to pay the income to his children for life and, on the death of B's last surviving child, to pay the principal to B's grandchildren then living, in equal shares. It is obvious that in a jurisdiction which applies the common law rule against perpetuities, a gift by A in his

---

[30] See 6 American Law of Property §24.33 (Casner ed. 1952); 4 Restatement of Property §391. For a codification of this principle, see Pa. Stat. Ann., tit. 20, §301.4(c) (Purdon). This principle is also applicable under the New York statutory rule against perpetuities. See 4 Restatement of Property, App., c. A, par. 36. The principle that the period of the rule against perpetuities is measured from the date the general power to appoint by deed is exercised is set out in statutory form in New York Real Property Law §179-a, which was added by N.Y. Laws 1960, c. 448.

[31] See 6 American Law of Property §24.34 (Casner ed. 1952); 4 Restatement of Property §392. This principle is also applicable under the New York statutory rule against perpetuities. See 4 Restatement of Property, App., c. A, par. 36. On the other hand, Delaware measures the period of perpetuities from the date of exercise, regardless of the type of power involved. Del. Code Ann., tit. 25, §501 (1953).

In Cleveland Trust Co. v. McQuade, 133 N.E.2d 664 (Cuyahoga County Prob. Ct., Ohio, 1955), the court reversed the authorities regarding the date when the period of the rule against perpetuities begins to run with respect to the interests created by the exercise of a general power to appoint by will and concluded that the period would begin to run and should begin to run from the date the power is exercised rather than the date the power is created. The case was reversed in 142 N.E.2d 249 (Ohio Ct. App. 1957).

[32] See 6 American Law of Property §24.35 (Casner ed. 1952); 4 Restatement of Property §392, Comment *b*. This principle is also applicable under the New York statutory rule against perpetuities. See 4 Restatement of Property, App., c. A, par. 30. The "second look" doctrine is set out in statutory form in New York Real Property Law §179-b, which was added by N.Y. Laws 1960, c. 448.

The Note on Wait-and-See Statutes, supra page 655, should be re-examined at this point because these statutes are also applicable to interests created by the exercise of a power of appointment.

will to the grandchildren of B living at the death of B's last surviving child would be invalid (assuming B survived A) because the gift to the grandchildren might not vest within twenty-one years after lives in being at A's death. In determining the validity of the gift to B's grandchildren under the exercise by B of his power of appointment, such a gift is not read back into A's will blindly. It is read back into A's will, but its validity is judged in the light of facts known as of B's death. Thus, if all of B's children were alive when A died, then the gift to B's grandchildren living on the death of B's last surviving child, must vest, if it ever vests, not later than lives in being as of A's death, and the gift is valid If, however, B had more children after A's death, and such after-born children are alive at B's death, then it cannot be said, even in the light of facts known at B's death, that the gift to B's grandchildren living on the death of B's last surviving child, must vest, if ever, not later than twenty-one years after lives in being as of A's death, and the gift is invalid.

The above discussion should make it apparent that whenever the estate plan calls for the mingling of owned and appointive assets and for their disposition under the same terms, care must be taken to provide for the vesting of all interests within the period of the rule against perpetuities as measured from the date of the creation of the power unless, of course, a general power to appoint by deed is involved.[33] Thus the blanket exercise of powers of appointment which may include appointive assets, without proper consideration being given to the circumstances existing at the date the power was created, should be strongly condemned.

SEARS v. COOLIDGE
329 Mass. 340, 108 N.E.2d 563 (1952)

WILKINS, Justice.

These two petitions under G.L. (Ter. Ed.) c. 231A seek binding declarations as to the validity of the provisions relating to income and to gifts of principal by way of remainder in a deed of trust executed by Thomas Jefferson Coolidge, late of Manchester, under date of February 12, 1913. The settlor died on November

---

[33] Another possible disadvantage of mingling owned and appointed assets is illustrated by Rev. Rul. 54-90, 1954-1 C.B. 194. In this ruling it is brought out that where a decedent had a power of appointment over certain property, the value of which is not includible in her gross estate, but which, by her will, was expressly made available along with probate assets for the payment of legacies, then all bequests, charitable and noncharitable, are considered payable pro rata out of probate assets and appointed assets, thus limiting the amount of the charitable deductions which may be allowed to that portion of the charitable bequest payable out of the probate assets.

17, 1920. In each case a decree was entered declaring that the life interests are valid; but that the gifts over of principal are invalid and void, and upon the termination of the trust the personal representatives of the settlor's estate are to receive the principal and any unpaid accumulated income. The petitioners, the trustees, and numerous other persons interested in the trust or in the settlor's estate appealed.

The net income of the trust was payable one third semi-annually to "such of the issue of my deceased son as shall be living at the time of each such semi-annual payment," and two thirds, divided into three parts payable semi-annually, one part each to Marian A. Sargent and to Sarah L. Newbold and after their death to their respective issue, and one to the living issue of Eleonora R. Sears, who were the petitioners Eleonora R. Sears and Frederick R. Sears.

The appeals relating to the life interests have been "waived and withdrawn." We are now concerned only with the decrees in so far as they affect the remainder interests. Whenever we refer to the appellants, we shall mean all or some of those who are seeking to establish the validity of the remainder interests. The facts are undisputed and, for the most part, are embodied in a written stipulation in the Probate Court. The evidence is reported.

The fundamental issue is whether the remainder interests violate the rule against perpetuities. Paragraph 5 of the trust instrument provides that the capital of the trust is to be distributed "in equal shares to and among my issue living" at the time of distribution. Distribution is to take place upon "whichever shall first happen" of two events: (1) "the death of the last survivor of those of my children, grandchildren and great grandchildren who shall be living at my death"; or (2) "the attainment of fifty years by the youngest surviving grandchild of mine who shall be living at my death." [34] The second event first happened. William A. Coolidge, the youngest grandchild living at the settlor's death, attained the age of fifty years on October 21, 1951.

Where a trust instrument contains two alternative conditions, of which the first might be too remote and the second, which

---

[34] (*Court footnote*) The full language of paragraph 5 is: "Upon the death of the last survivor of those of my children, grandchildren and great grandchildren who shall be living at my death, or upon the attainment of fifty years by the youngest surviving grandchild of mine who shall be living at my death, whichever shall first happen, the capital of the trust fund, as then existing, shall be conveyed, transferred and paid over in equal shares to and among my issue living at that time, such issue taking per stirpes and not per capita, and thereupon the trusts established by this instrument shall cease and determine." The same deed of trust was the subject of the decision in Dexter v. Treasurer & Receiver General, 243 Mass. 523, 137 N.E. 877.

actually occurs, is not too remote, the rule is not violated. Jackson v. Phillips, 14 Allen 539, 572-573; Stone v. Bradlee, 183 Mass. 165, 171-172, 66 N.E. 708; Gray v. Whittemore, 192 Mass. 367, 372, 78 N.E. 422, 10 L.R.A., N.S., 1143; Springfield Safe Deposit & Trust Co. v. Ireland, 268 Mass. 62, 67-68, 167 N.E. 261, 64 A.L.R. 1071. Accordingly, the appellants contend that the attainment by the youngest grandchild of the age of fifty years was certain to occur within the period required by the rule, and that as matter of construction the reference in paragraph 5 to "the youngest surviving grandchild of mine who shall be living at my death" must be read as if "grandchild" were qualified by "now living" or similar words. In support are adduced various facts in the settlor's family situation obvious to him when he executed the deed of trust. He was then eighty-one years of age and had been a widower for twelve years. At that time he had two living children, Marian A. Sargent, who was aged fifty-nine and had been a widow for twenty years, and Sarah L. Newbold, who was then fifty-five years of age. During the preceding year there had died two of his children, T. Jefferson Coolidge and Eleonora R. Sears. The settlor then had ten living grandchildren. Four were the minor sons of his deceased son. Two were the children of his deceased daughter, one being the petitioner, Eleonora R. Sears, and the other Frederick R. Sears, the administrator of whose estate is the petitioner Fiduciary Trust Company. One was the child of Marian A. Sargent, and three were the children of Sarah L. Newbold. The oldest grandchild was thirty-five and the youngest was seven. No further grandchildren were born in the settlor's lifetime, but the youngest of the ten died before the settlor.

The appellees argue, on the other hand, that it is not permissible thus to qualify the clause in paragraph 5, and for present purposes we accept their position on this point, and assume that the phrase "the youngest surviving grandchild of mine who shall be living at my death" is not to be interpreted as excluding grandchildren who might be born after the trust instrument was created.

The appellants make the contention that the settlor in the trust deed reserved a power which was at least equivalent to a special power of appointment, and that the validity of the remainders must in any event be determined in the light of the facts existing at his death when it was known that his only grandchildren had been lives in being at the time the trust was created. This has been referred to in the arguments as "a second look."

Paragraph 9 reads: "I reserve to myself power at all times to make any additions to the trust property, to change and alter any or all of the trusts herein set forth and to declare new uses and trusts of the property in any way or manner except such as will vest in myself the trust property or any beneficial interest therein, to name and appoint any other persons than those above specified or hereafter appointed as beneficiaries, whether by way of addition or substitution, and to appoint other trustees instead of or in addition to any or all of those above named. Every such change, alteration, nomination and appointment shall be made by my deed and shall take effect immediately upon the delivery thereof to any person who shall at the time be acting as a trustee under the provisions of these presents."

The point, which, so far as appears, has not been pressed upon an appellate court before, is based upon the analogy of Minot v. Paine, 230 Mass. 514, 120 N.E. 167, 1 A.L.R. 365. The theory is that at the settlor's death the expiration of the power to divert the property from the takers in default was the same in effect as an appointment of the remainders by the settlor's will.

The reserved power is, at the very least, akin to a power of appointment. National Shawmut Bank v. Joy, 315 Mass. 457, 474, 53 N.E.2d 113; Restatement: Property, sec. 318, comment i. See Saltonstall v. Treasurer & Receiver General, 256 Mass. 519, 524, 153 N.E. 4; Boston Safe Deposit & Trust Co. v. Commissioner of Corporations and Taxation, 294 Mass. 551, 554, 3 N.E.2d 33, 109 A.L.R. 854; State Street Trust Co. v. Crocker, 306 Mass. 257, 262, 28 N.E.2d 5, 128 A.L.R. 1166. And, for present purposes, we treat it as having attributes of a special power to appoint by deed.

In Minot v. Paine, the power to appoint was, in fact, exercised, and there was presented a question as to the effect of the language used by the donee of the power, who had become, in law, the agent of the donor for the purpose. At page 522 of 230 Mass., at page 170 of 120 N.E., it was said: "The donee in exercising the power is in effect writing the will of the donor respecting the appointed property. . . . The words used by the donee in exercising the power are to be construed and interpreted as to their meaning in the light of the facts as they are at the time the power is exercised. The will of the donor is projected forward to the time of the exercise of the power so as to receive the benefit of the facts which have appeared since his decease. . . . As applied to the exercise of a power of appointment the words of the rule are satisfied if it appears that in the light of facts as to relationship and longevity existent when the appointment is exercised, the estates created in truth will vest and take effect within the period limited by the rule, although this may not have been certain at the death of the donor of the power."

In the present instance, no appointment having been made, there were no words expressed by the holder of the reserved power to be read back into the deed of trust. That fact, however, should not be decisive. In every case where there is a power, whether it be exercised or not, there is the common feature that until the opportunity for its exercise ceases to exist, there will persist uncertainty as to the ultimate disposition of the property. Until then nothing final can be known as to what are the provisions for the vesting of the future interests, and it is with such vesting the policy of the rule is concerned. Proprietors of the Church in Brattle Square v. Grant, 3 Gray, 142, 152-153; Jackson v. Phillips, 14 Allen, 539, 572; Sears v. Putnam, 102 Mass. 5, 6-7; Hall v. Hall, 123 Mass. 120, 124; Gray v. Whittemore, 192 Mass. 367, 373, 78 N.E. 422, 10 L.R.A., N.S., 1143; Minot v. Paine, 230 Mass. 514, 522, 120 N.E. 167, 1 A.L.R. 365; Springfield Safe Deposit & Trust Co. v. Ireland, 268 Mass. 62, 66, 167 N.E. 261, 64 A.L.R. 1071; Fiduciary Trust Co. v. Mishou, 321 Mass. 615, 622-623, 75 N.E.2d 3. See Minot v. Treasurer & Receiver General, 207 Mass. 588, 592-593, 93 N.E. 973, 33 L.R.A., N.S., 236; Burnham v. Treasurer & Receiver General, 212 Mass. 165, 167, 98 N.E. 603.

Since it is permissible to make use of the circumstances known when a power, which is special or testamentary, is exercised to determine validity under the rule, it seems reasonable to afford the same opportunity in cases where such a power is not exercised. In the case of the trust instrument under consideration until it became too late for the settlor to exercise the reserved power no one could tell what might be the ultimate disposition of the trust property. As long as there remained a right to change, alter, and make new appointments, no instructions to the trustees or declaratory decree would ordinarily have been given as to the validity of the settlor's limitations. See National Shawmut Bank v. Morey, 320 Mass. 492, 497-500, 70 N.E.2d 316, 174 A.L.R. 871; Young v. Jackson, 321 Mass. 1, 7, 71 N.E.2d 386; Burn v. McAllister, 321 Mass. 660, 662, 75 N.E.2d 114. Upon his death it could be learned for the first time what definitely were to be the terms of the trust. It then could be seen for the first time that there was to be no failure to vest within the period limited by the rule. No further grandchildren had been born.[35] In these precise circum-

---

[35] In 1920 when Thomas Jefferson Coolidge died, his youngest living grandchild, William A. Coolidge, was then nineteen years of age. Thirty-one years later, on October 21, 1951, he was fifty. The court would obviously be correct in its statement that on the death of Thomas Jefferson Coolidge it became clear that no interest under the gift in default of appointment could vest too remotely, if no great-grandchildren as well as no grandchildren were born

stances there is no compelling decision which prevents taking advantage of facts known at the moment when the power ceased to be exercisable. American Law of Property, sec. 24.36. We are unwilling to apply the rule so as to invalidate the trust instrument.

The appellees strongly urge that the doctrine of a "second look" has no place in reading the original limitations in default of appointment, which were capable of examination when created, and which should retain the same meaning throughout. They argue that its adoption would be a nullification of the rule "that executory limitations are void unless they take effect ex necessitate and in all possible contingencies" within the prescribed period. Hall v. Hall, 123 Mass. 120, 124. But this rule, while recognized, was assuaged as to the exercise of a power of appointment in Minot v. Paine, 230 Mass. 514, 522, 120 N.E. 167, 1 A.L.R. 365. It was there deemed wise not to apply unmodified a remorseless technical principle to a case which it did not fit. That principle seems equally inappropriate here.

The decrees are reversed and the causes are remanded to the Probate Court for the entry of decrees in accordance with this opinion. Costs and expenses of appeal are to be in the discretion of the Probate Court.

So ordered.[36]

---

after the 1913 trust was executed and before Thomas died, so that the first of the alternative contingencies would be certain to occur in time. If great-grandchildren had been born, so that reliance would have to be placed on the second of the alternative contingencies, it would not be certain that the stipulated event would occur in time if distribution under this event would be made on the date when William A. Coolidge would have attained fifty years of age if he had died under that age because that date might occur more than twenty-one years after the death of Thomas in 1920 and more than twenty-one years after the death of any other person living in 1913 when the trust creating the power was established. The second alternative would be certain to occur in time if it is construed to mean that distribution would take place on the death of the surviving grandchild if no one of the grandchildren lived to attain fifty years of age. — ED.

[36] Comments on Sears v. Coolidge are found in 33 B.U.L. Rev. 119 (1953), 66 Harv. L. Rev. 937 (1953), 22 U. of Cin. L. Rev. 266 (1953). As a result of the claim that the provisions of the trust regarding income and principal were invalid in Sears v. Coolidge, the trustees withheld all income payments pending a determination of the validity of such provisions. The trustees paid under protest the income tax on the income withheld, and later claimed a refund on the ground that the income was payable in each year to the beneficiaries designated in the trust, and was therefore taxable to the beneficiaries and not to the trust. Should this claim for refund be allowed? See Higginson v. United States, 137 F. Supp. 240 (D. Mass. 1956), *aff'd sub nom.* United States v. Higginson, 238 F.2d 439 (1st Cir. 1956). See also Polt v. Commissioner, 233 F.2d 893 (2d Cir. 1956).

Fidelity Trust Co. v. United States, 57-2 U.S.T.C. ¶9850 (W.D. Pa. 1957), involved a trust under a will which provided for the payment of income to charities. The validity of the trust was questioned and a state court ordered

PROBLEMS

12.10. A in his will transfers property to T in trust. Under the terms of the trust, T is directed to pay the income to B for life, then to hold the principal for, or pay it to, such person or persons, in such amounts and proportions, and upon or subject to such trusts, terms, powers or restrictions as B may appoint by will. In default of appointment by B, T is to pay the principal to B's children who attain the age of twenty-five years. On A's death, B has two children living, C and D. C is ten years of age and D is five. Five years subsequent to A's death, another child, E, is born to B, and E is two years old when B dies. B's will does not exercise the power of appointment. Assuming that Massachusetts law controls and that B died in 1953, is the gift in default of appointment to B's children valid? Assuming that Massachusetts law controls and that A died in 1961, is the result the same? See Note on Wait-and-See Statutes, supra page 655.

12.11. Can you give an illustration of a case where an interest created by the exercise of a power of appointment will be invalid under the "second look" doctrine, but will be valid under the

the trustees to accumulate the income pending the outcome of the litigation. The District Court did not allow the trustees to take a charitable deduction on the basis of income permanently set aside for charitable purposes. The court pointed out that during the year in question the trustee was without power to apply income in any manner for the benefit of anyone. The case was affirmed in 253 F.2d 407 (3d Cir. 1958).

In Trust of John Walker, 30 T.C. 278 (1958), the donee of a power of appointment over a one-fourth share of a trust exercised the power by directing that the one-fourth share be held in another trust with another trustee and that a designated portion of the income of the new trust be paid to charity. In 1953, the trustee of the original trust withheld the payment of the one-fourth share to the new trust because of a dispute in a Pennsylvania court as to whether the power had been validly exercised. The one-fourth share was distributed to the new trust along with the income from the share on July 20, 1954, pursuant to the order of the Pennsylvania court. The Tax Court held that the original trust was not entitled to a charitable deduction for the income from the one-fourth share which was eventually to go to charity, because the original trust did not provide for income being permanently set aside for charitable purposes and also because there was no right in the trust set up by the donee of the power to have the income until the dispute over the exercise of the power had been settled by the Pennsylvania court and an order of distribution received by the original trustee.

In Martin Raymond Bowen, 34 T.C. —, No. 25 (1960), a will that passed property in 1939 was held invalid in 1948 and thus the recipients of the property in 1939 had to account for the property and the income therefrom for the period beginning in 1939. The court held that the 1939 recipients who had paid an income tax on the income from the property acquired in 1939 were entitled to a deduction in the year the income was given up. The one receiving the income so given up had to include the entire amount in his gross income in the year of receipt. In this connection, see 1954 I.R.C. §1341. — ED.

limited wait-and-see Massachusetts-type statute discussed in Note on Wait-and-See Statutes, supra page 655?

The 1954 Code contains a provision that makes estate tax consequences turn on whether the donee of a power exercises the power by creating another power of appointment which, under the applicable local law, can be validly exercised so as to postpone the vesting of an interest or to suspend the absolute power of alienation for a period ascertainable without regard to the date of the creation of the first power. If the donee of a power so exercises the power, the value of the appointive assets will be includible in the donee's gross estate regardless of the nature of the power if it is one created after October 21, 1942.[37] Presumably, if a nongeneral power of appointment created on or before October 21, 1942, is involved, its exempt character is not destroyed even though it is exercised by creating another power of appointment that can be exercised so as to create interests that will be measured as to their validity from the date the second power is exercised. The Code provision under consideration is sometimes referred to as the Delaware provision because in Delaware the period of perpetuities with respect to interests created by the exercise of any power, special or general, commences to run from the date the power is exercised.[38] If it were not for the special Code provision, property could be kept out of estate taxation perpetually in that state.[39]

The Delaware provision may have blocked the repeal of the federal estate and gift tax in Delaware but in so doing it has created a trap for residents in other states. The following two paragraphs illustrate this trap.

Suppose that T in his will gives the residue of his estate to a trustee. He directs the trustee to pay the net income to his son and, on his son's death, to hold or dispose of the property to or for the benefit of any one or more of the limited class composed of the son's issue as the son may appoint by his will. Suppose that the son then exercises his power by directing the trustee to hold the appointed property in trust and to pay the net income to his child for life. He also gives his child a power to appoint the

---

[37] See 1954 I.R.C. §2041(a)(3), quoted infra page 1400. The comparable provision operative with respect to the federal gift tax is §2514(d), quoted infra page 1421.

[38] See Del. Code Ann., tit. 25, §501 (1953).

[39] See Note on the Rule Against Perpetuities in Idaho and Wisconsin, supra page 675. Notice that the Code provisions referred to supra note 37 will not apply to the situation in Idaho or Wisconsin.

property by deed or by will to anyone.[40]   Here the original testator's son has exercised his power by creating another power in his
child, and since his child's power is a general power to appoint
either by deed or by will, the child can exercise it so as to postpone
the vesting of interests "for a period ascertainable without regard
to the date of the creation of the first power."

Suppose that A establishes a revocable inter vivos trust and that
under the terms of the trust, the income is to be paid to A's son
for life, and on the son's death, the trustee is to hold or dispose of
the trust property to or for the benefit of any one or more of the
limited class composed of the son's issue as the son may appoint
by his will.   Will the validity of interests created by the son by the
exercise of his power be determined on the basis of facts existing
on the date the revocable trust is executed or on the basis of facts
existing on the date of the settlor's death (or on the date he releases his power to revoke the trust if a release of such power is
made by him before his death)?   If the answer to this question is
that the validity of interests created by the son by the exercise of
his power will be determined on the basis of facts existing when
the settlor's power to revoke the trust ends, and the son exercises
his power after the death of his father by creating another power
of appointment, can the power of appointment created by the son
be exercised "so as to postpone the vesting of any estate or interest
in such property . . . for a period ascertainable without regard
to the date of the creation of the first power"?   The answer to this
last question may turn on whether the power in A's son is deemed
to be created when the revocable trust was executed or when the
power of revocation in the settlor of the revocable trust comes to
an end.

3.   RELEVANT FACTORS IN DETERMINING WHETHER
TO CREATE A POWER OF APPOINTMENT

It is through the creation of powers of appointment that flexibility to meet changing conditions is introduced into an estate
plan which involves future interests.   Normally such flexibility
is highly desirable because what may appear to be an appropriate
arrangement for one's family today may be inappropriate many
years from today, and an estate plan which involves future interests may continue in operation for many years.

---

[40] In some jurisdictions the donee of a special power of appointment may
not effectively exercise the power by creating a general power of appointment
in an object of the power.   See 5 American Law of Property §23.49 (Casner
ed. 1952).

The most important consideration in determining whether to create powers of appointment is the tax consequences of so doing. If the over-all tax picture can be improved through the creation of powers of appointment, a strong inducement exists for their creation. Furthermore, if the over-all tax picture is not impaired, even though it is not improved, through the creation of powers of appointment, a considerable inducement exists for their creation so as to introduce the desired flexibility in the estate plan.

In previous chapters,[41] consideration is given to the circumstances under which the creation of powers in an inter vivos trust causes the income from the trust property to be included in the gross income of the settlor for federal income tax purposes and causes the value of the trust property to be included in the settlor's gross estate for federal estate tax purposes. These tax consequences which may result from the creation of powers must be kept constantly in mind. In this chapter, however, it is assumed that such tax consequences are not involved. Such an assumption is a realistic one when powers of appointment are created (1) in a will, (2) in an inter vivos transfer which successfully eliminates the transferred property from the transferor's estate for both federal income and estate tax purposes, and (3) in an inter vivos transfer, as it is to operate from and after the transferor's death, though it is not effective to eliminate the transferred property from the transferor's estate for both federal income and estate tax purposes.

a. *Powers of Appointment Which Do Not Impair the Over-all Tax Picture*

(1) Estate and Gift Tax Consequences

The desired flexibility in an estate plan may call for a power of appointment with respect to the corpus, or a power of appointment with respect to the income, or both. The creation of a power of appointment does not impair the over-all tax picture if the tax picture of the donee of the power is not changed as a result of the creation of the power.

The donee's tax picture is changed as a result of the creation of the power if the donee is regarded as the owner of the appointive assets for federal estate and gift tax purposes. Only if the donee is given a general power of appointment is he so regarded.[42]

---

41 See page 153 supra and page 188 supra.
42 See 1954 I.R.C. §2041(a)(2), quoted infra page 1400. Notice that as to a general power of appointment created after October 21, 1942, the value of

Subject to some exceptions, a general power of appointment is one exercisable in favor of any one or more of the donee, the donee's estate, the donee's creditors or the creditors of the donee's estate.[43]

A power of appointment which can be exercised to meet charges enforceable against the donee's estate, such as death taxes, or which can be exercised for the purpose of discharging a legal obligation of the donee, such as a legal obligation to support certain persons, is a general power.[44]

Certain powers of appointment which enable the donee of the power to benefit himself are excepted from the category of general powers of appointment. Each one of these exceptions must be studied to determine its possible usefulness in an estate plan. The exceptions are as follows:

1. A power to consume, invade, or appropriate property for the benefit of the donee of the power which is limited by an ascertainable standard relating to health, education, support, or maintenance of the donee is not a general power of appointment for federal estate or gift tax purposes.[45] If this exception is to be utilized in an estate plan, care must be taken to provide the required standard.

---

the appointive assets are includible in the donee's gross estate for federal estate tax purposes, whether he exercises the power or not. If the power is exercised inter vivos or released, in determining whether the value of the appointive property has been removed from the donee's gross estate, he is treated as though he had made a transfer of owned property inter vivos. See Reg. §20.2041-3(d)(2), quoted infra page 1522. *A disclaimer or renunciation of a power is not deemed a release of the power.* There may even be a disclaimer or renunciation as to only a portion of the property subject to the power. See Reg. §20.2041-3(d)(6), quoted infra page 1523. Section 2514(b) of the 1954 Code, quoted infra page 1420, contains corresponding provisions which point out that the exercise inter vivos of a general power of appointment will be deemed a gift by the donee of the power for federal gift tax purposes.

[43] See 1954 I.R.C. §2041(b)(1), quoted infra page 1401. The corresponding definitional section in the federal gift tax law is 1954 I.R.C. §2514(c), quoted infra page 1421.

In Estate of Laura Brown Chisholm, 26 T.C. 253 (1956), the life beneficiary of a trust was given a power to appoint corpus to his issue or spouse, and in default of appointment, the trust corpus was to be paid to his estate and disposed of in accordance with his last will, or in the absence of a last will, the property was to vest in his heirs. The life beneficiary exercised his power and gave the property to his issue. The court held that the life beneficiary had only a limited power of appointment and that the property subject to the power was not includible in his gross estate. The fact that the gifts in default of the exercise of the power were to his estate or to his heirs did not change the character of the power. This result seems highly questionable in view of the fact that the life beneficiary could in effect give the property to anyone by letting it fall into his estate and go out under his will.

[44] See Reg. §20.2041-1(c)(1), quoted infra page 1517.

[45] See 1954 I.R.C. §2041(b)(1)(A), quoted infra page 1401, as to the federal estate tax and §2514(c)(1), quoted infra page 1421, as to the federal gift tax.

A power to use property for "the comfort, welfare or
happiness" of the holder of the power is not limited by the
requisite standard; whereas a power to use property for
"the maintenance in health and reasonable comfort" of
the holder of the power is recognized as limited by the
requisite standard.[46]

2. A power of appointment which is exercisable by the
donee only in conjunction with the creator of the power
is not a general power of appointment, even though the
power may be exercised in favor of the donee, his creditors,
his estate or creditors of his estate.[47] This exception has
little or no utility so far as estate planning is concerned
because, if used, the value of the appointive assets will be
includible in the gross estate of the creator of the power

---

[46] See Reg. §20.2041-1(c)(2), quoted infra page 1518.

In Barritt v. Tomlinson, 129 F. Supp. 642 (S.D. Fla. 1955), a husband devised all of his property to his wife for life, stating in his will: "I hereby give
. . . my said wife all the income from said estate absolutely and the right to
use all or any part of the principal that she might see fit." The will provided
for the disposition, on the wife's death, of the estate to named persons. The
husband died in 1944 and the wife in 1949. Is the value of the property received by the wife from her husband includible in her gross estate? The
court held that a proper interpretation of the husband's will indicated that
the power in the wife was only to invade principal for her support and maintenance and, as so limited, it was not a general power of appointment under
the law applicable between 1942 and 1951. The court thought it was also
excluded as a general power of appointment under the Powers of Appointment Act of 1951 because it was a power of withdrawal which was controlled
by an ascertainable standard. The court went on to say, however, that if such
a power is a general power of appointment under the 1951 act because no
ascertainable standard is involved, the 1951 act could not apply to the wife's
power, since she died in 1949.

The court in Kay v. Phinney, 59-1 U.S.T.C. ¶11869 (W.D. Tex. 1959), concluded that a power in the life beneficiary to consume, invade or appropriate
the property to the extent necessary for her health, support and maintenance
in accordance with her accustomed standard of living was not a general power
of appointment. The actual language which was construed by the District
Court as subject to such a standard was "to be used, occupied, enjoyed, conveyed and expended by" the life beneficiary as the life beneficiary desired.
The court was reversed sub nom. Phinney v. Kay, 275 F.2d 776 (5th Cir. 1960),
on the ground that such language gave the life beneficiary a general power of
appointment.

In Pittsfield National Bank v. United States, 181 F. Supp. 851 (D. Mass.
1960), the decedent was the life beneficiary under a testamentary trust established by his wife in 1947 and was entitled to receive income "together with
all or such part of the principal of same as he may from time to time request,
he to be the sole judge of his needs." The remainder was to go to their children. The court concluded that the decedent's power under applicable Massachusetts law was limited by an ascertainable standard because he could take
the principal only for his "*needs*." Thus it was not a general power under
§2041.

[47] See 1954 I.R.C. §2041(b)(1)(C)(i), quoted infra page 1401. The corresponding federal gift tax provision is §2514(c)(3)(A), quoted infra page 1421.

and it is unlikely that this will be a wanted tax result.[48]

3. A power of appointment which is exercisable by the donee only in conjunction with a person having a substantial interest in the property subject to the power, which is adverse to an exercise of the power in favor of the donee, is not a general power of appointment.[49] A co-holder of the power is not regarded as having an adverse interest merely because of his joint possession of the power nor merely because he is a permissible appointee under the power.[50] This exception is of little or no use in estate planning because it is highly unlikely that the desired flexibility will be introduced into the estate plan where the decision as to whether a power will be exercised will rest with one who will be adversely affected by the exercise. It should also be noted that if the co-holder of the power has an owned interest that will be adversely affected by an exercise of the power, the value of such an owned interest will be includible in his gross estate should he die.[51]

If the power of appointment is one exercisable by the donee only in conjunction with another person who is neither the creator of the power nor one who will be adversely affected by its exercise, and is exercisable in favor of such other person as well as the donee, the power is a general one only with respect to a fractional part of the property subject to the power. Such a fractional part is determined by dividing the value of the appointive property by the number of holders of the power in favor of whom it is exercisable.[52] If the objective is to introduce flexibility into the estate plan without impairing the tax picture, this partial exemption of the power from the category of a general one is not likely to be attractive.

[48] See 1954 I.R.C. §2038, quoted infra page 1397.

[49] See 1954 I.R.C. §2041(b)(1)(C)(ii), quoted infra page 1401. The corresponding federal gift tax provision is §2514(c)(3)(B), quoted infra page 1421.

[50] See Reg. §20.2041-3(c)(2), quoted infra page 1521.

[51] See Reg. §20.2041-1(b)(2), quoted infra page 1517; Reg. §20.2041-3(f), Ex. (4), quoted infra page 1524.

[52] See 1954 I.R.C. §2041(b)(1)(C)(iii), quoted infra page 1401. The corresponding provision in the federal gift tax law is §2514(c)(3)(C), quoted infra page 1421. See also Reg. §20.2041-3(c)(3), quoted infra page 1521.

New York Real Property Law §141, which applies equally to personal property, provides in substance that a power vested in a person as trustee to distribute corpus to himself cannot be exercised. If the power is vested in two or more trustees, it may be exercised by the trustee or trustees who cannot benefit from the exercise. Suppose that a New York resident creates a trust in his will, with his wife and another as trustees, and that under the trust the wife is to receive the income and the trustees are given a power to pay her principal. Does the wife in conjunction with another have a general power of appointment? See Rev. Rul. 54-153, 1954-1 C.B. 185.

As has been observed, a release of a general power of appointment created after October 21, 1942, is deemed an exercise of the power. Thus a release of such a power will be treated as though the donee owned the appointive assets and created all the interests in the property that will exist immediately after the release. The federal estate and gift tax consequences will be determined accordingly. A partial release of the power, that is, one which narrows the objects to which an appointment may be made, will leave the value of the appointive assets includible in the donee's gross estate and normally will not result in a completed gift for gift tax purposes.[53] It may be desirable to make a partial release of a general power of appointment so that if the power is exercised by the donee in his will, there will be a basis of claiming that creditors of the donee cannot reach the appointive assets, which they could do if he retained a general power of appointment until his death and exercised it.[54]

If it is unwise from a tax standpoint for the donee of a general power of appointment to accept the power, he should disclaim it promptly.[55] Once he is deemed to accept it, he cannot release it without the federal estate and gift tax consequences outlined above.

The 1954 Code provides that the lapse of a power of appointment created after October 21, 1942, during the life of the donee of the power is the same as a release of the power.[56] An exception to this general rule is made, however, in that a release of a power is deemed to have been made by virtue of a lapse of powers during any calendar year only to the extent that the property which could have been appointed by the exercise of such lapsed powers exceeded in value, at the time of such lapse, the greater of the following amounts: $5000 or 5 percent of the aggregate value of the assets out of which, or the proceeds out of which, the exercise of the lapsed powers could have been satisfied.[57] Stated another way, if a beneficiary under a trust is given the power to withdraw $5000 of principal annually, and if the beneficiary declines to make a withdrawal in any calendar year, so that the power for that year lapses, no adverse estate or gift tax consequences will

---

[53] See Reg. §20.2041-3(d)(1), quoted infra page 1522; Reg. §25.2514-3(c)(1), quoted infra page 1550.

[54] See page 692 supra, note 9.

For an example of a statute which provides that the donee of a power may release the power in the absence of any contrary manifestation of intent on the part of the donor of the power, see Mass. Ann. Laws, c. 204, §§27-32.

[55] As is pointed out supra note 42, a disclaimer is not deemed a release.

[56] See 1954 I.R.C. §2041(b)(2), quoted infra page 1401. The corresponding federal gift tax provision is §2514(e), quoted infra page 1421.

[57] See Reg. §20.2041-3(d)(3), (4) and (5), quoted infra page 1522.

result from such a lapse. In the year the donee dies, the $5000, or so much of it as has not been withdrawn in that year, will be includible in the donee's gross estate for federal estate tax purposes, but this is a small cost to pay for the added flexibility given the estate plan during the years the beneficiary lived. This exception to the lapse-release rule is very important in the field of estate planning.

Even though the donee's power is restricted so as to exclude himself, his creditors, his estate and creditors of his estate from benefiting by any exercise, he can be given a wide range of authority to confer benefits that will enable him to act with respect to the appointive assets in a manner not very different from the manner in which he can act with respect to owned assets. If the donee's power permits him to appoint by deed among various members of his family, he can carry out a program of inter vivos giving without the gift tax cost that attaches to such a program if owned assets are involved. Under a power to appoint by will to members of his family, he can make the same decisions as to the division of the property or as to whether the beneficiaries should receive the property outright or in trust, that he can make in connection with disposing of owned assets by his will.

Suppose that T, the testator, sets up a trust under his will, and that the terms of the trust require the net income to be paid to T's son, S, for life. The terms of the trust give S the power to appoint by deed the trust property to any one or more of his issue. If S exercises this power to appoint by deed, the effect will be to transfer to the appointee S's life interest in the trust property. Will S be deemed to have made a gift for federal gift tax purposes of the value of his life interest? The Regulations answer this question in the affirmative,[58] but one case has answered it in the negative.[59] Whether a gift for federal gift tax purposes of S's life interest occurs in the case under consideration or not, it may be highly desirable for S to possess the power to appoint by deed so as to give him the right to determine when his children will receive property.

---

[58] See Reg. §25.2514-3(e), quoted infra page 1551.

[59] In Self, Jr. v. United States, 142 F. Supp. 939 (Ct. Cl. 1956), the life income beneficiary under a trust was given the power to appoint by deed all or part of the trust property to or among his descendants. The life income beneficiary exercised this power and filed a gift tax return on the value of the right to receive the income for life. He then filed a refund claim. The court held that he was entitled to a refund of the gift tax paid, because he had only a limited power of appointment and, even though the exercise of this power resulted also in the termination of his income interest in the property transferred by the exercise of the power, such action on his part did not constitute a gift.

The existence of the power clearly produces no adverse estate tax effects on S's death.

In the situation examined in the preceding paragraph, is the possibility that S may make a gift for federal gift tax purposes lessened if the trust is one which gives the trustee the discretion to spray the income and principal among a group including S or to leave the income and principal in the trust? It would seem that the possibility would be lessened because S has only an expectancy as an object of the power in the trustee, and when he exercises his power to appoint by deed in favor of his children, he is eliminating only this expectancy, something that has no ascertainable value.

Although a particular power of appointment may be usable so far as the federal estate and gift tax consequences are concerned, a final decision whether it should be used should not be made until the federal income tax consequences of its use have been examined. The federal income tax and powers of appointment will be considered shortly.[60]

PROBLEMS

12.12. T in his will gives the residue of his estate to a trustee and directs the trustee "to pay the net income to my son for his life and on my son's death to pay the corpus as my son may appoint by his will." T dies in 1961.

    a. Within what period of time must T's son act to give up his power of appointment in order for his actions to be a disclaimer or renunciation of the power rather than a release of the power? [60a]

    b. If the son releases the power, has he made a gift for federal gift tax purposes? If so, has he made a gift of a present interest or a future interest?

    c. If the son releases the power, will the value of the trust property be includible in his gross estate for federal estate tax purposes?

---

[60] See the discussion beginning infra page 729.

[60a] Robert E. Cleary, 34 T.C. —, No. 76 (1960), held that a life beneficiary's purported renunciation of a trust under a will, which was made five years after the testator died, was not made within a reasonable period of time for an effective rejection of a bequest under New Jersey law. It was also noted that the beneficiary's request, as originally made, that her bequest should go to her children was oral and was not confirmed, in accordance with state law, until some seven years later. Under these circumstances the income of the trust was taxable to her, even though, in form, it was paid to her for her children. All the income tax years involved preceded the confirmation of her earlier oral request.

    d. If the son makes a partial release of the power so that he can appoint only to his issue, has he made a gift for federal gift tax purposes? Will the value of the trust property be includible in his gross estate for federal estate tax purposes?

    e. If T had died in 1941, would the answers to the above questions be the same?

12.13. T in his will gives the residue of his estate to a trustee and directs the trustee "to pay the net income to my son for his life and, in addition, to pay my said son from the corpus of the trust, from time to time, such amount or amounts as my said son may establish to be essential for his education, support and maintenance; on the death of my said son, to pay the then remaining corpus to my son's issue then living, such issue to take per stirpes; and if no issue of my said son is then living, to pay the then remaining corpus to the X charity." T dies in 1960. T's son dies in 1961. Will the value of the trust property be includible in the gross estate of T's son for federal estate tax purposes?

12.14. A makes an inter vivos transfer of property in 1961 to a trustee, and in the trust instrument the trustee is directed "to pay the net income to the settlor's son for life and, in addition, to pay to the settlor's said son from the corpus of the trust, from time to time, such amount or amounts as the settlor and the settlor's said son may direct by an instrument in writing signed by the settlor and the settlor's said son and delivered to the trustee during the joint lives of the settlor and the settlor's said son; if the settlor predeceases the settlor's said son, the aforementioned power to direct the payment of corpus to the settlor's said son shall be vested in the settlor's said son and in B during their joint lives; if B also predeceases the settlor's said son, the aforementioned power to direct the payment of the corpus to the settlor's said son shall be vested in the settlor's said son and C during their joint lives; the aforementioned power shall cease to exist on the death of the survivor of the settlor, B and C, even though the settlor's said son is alive at that time; on the death of the settlor's said son, to pay the net income to B for life; and on the death of the survivor of the settlor's said son and B, to pay the then remaining corpus to the issue then living of the settlor's said son, such issue to take per stirpes; and if no issue of the settlor's said son is then living, to pay the then remaining corpus to the X charity."

    a. The settlor's son predeceases the settlor. Will the value of the trust property be includible in the son's gross estate for federal estate tax purposes?

b. The settlor predeceases his son. Will the value of the trust property be includible in the settlor's gross estate for federal estate tax purposes?

c. The settlor dies, then the settlor's son dies. Will the value of the trust property be includible in the son's gross estate for federal estate tax purposes?

d. The settlor dies, then B dies. Will the value of the trust property, or any portion thereof, be includible in B's gross estate for federal estate tax purposes?

e. The settlor dies, then B dies, then the settlor's son dies. Will the value of the trust property, or any portion thereof, be includible in the son's gross estate for federal estate tax purposes?

f. The settlor dies, then B dies, then C dies. Has the settlor's son made a gift for federal gift tax purposes? If the settlor's son then dies, will the value of the trust property, or any portion thereof, be includible in his gross estate for federal estate tax purposes? Are the answers to the two preceding questions the same if the order of the deaths of B and C is reversed?

12.15. T in his will gives the residue of his estate to a trustee and directs the trustee "to pay the net income to my son for his life and, in addition, to pay my son from the corpus of the trust, from time to time, such amount or amounts as my son may request, provided, however, that the amount or amounts paid to my son in any calendar year pursuant to his request shall not exceed $5000." T's wife in her will gives the residue of her estate to a trustee and directs the trustee "to pay the net income to my son for his life and, in addition, to pay to my son from the corpus of the trust, from time to time, such amount or amounts as my son may request, provided, however, that the amount or amounts paid to my son in any calendar year pursuant to his request shall not exceed 5 percent of the value of the corpus." T dies and T's wife dies. Assume that the trust established by T has a corpus worth $80,000 and that the trust established by T's wife has a corpus worth $120,000. If S allows both powers of withdrawal to lapse within a year, what are the federal estate and gift tax consequences under the above assumptions as to value?

12.16. A establishes a trust which provides that if X predeceases B, the life beneficiary, and if no brother or sister of B survives B, the principal is to be distributed on B's death to such persons as X appoints by deed or by will. X predeceases B and later B dies, not survived by any brother or sister. X's will makes no specific reference to the power of appointment given him under the trust created by A but contains a general residuary clause.   Should any amount be included in X's gross estate because of the power of appointment given him in the trust established by A?   Will the answer to the previous question be changed in any respect if A established the trust on or before October 21, 1942?   If it is determined that any amount is includible in X's gross estate, how is that amount determined?   See Revenue Ruling 55-486, 1955-2 C.B. 605.

12.17.   A in his will established a trust of the residue of his estate.   Under the terms of the trust, all the income is to be paid to his wife for her life and she is given an unrestricted power to use, consume and dispose of the trust principal during her life.   From the date of A's death until her death, the wife is hopelessly insane. Will the value of the appointive assets be includible in the wife's gross estate on her death?   Does the trust established by A in his will qualify for the marital deduction? [61]   See Revenue Ruling 55-518, 1955-2 C.B. 384.

STATE STREET TRUST CO.
v. KISSEL
302 Mass. 328, 19 N.E.2d 25 (1939)

DOLAN, J.

This is an appeal from a decree entered in the Probate Court, instructing the petitioner as to its duties with relation to a certain trust estate, held by it as trustee under the fourth and residuary clause of the will of Julia Emma Bradford, late of Boston, deceased (hereinafter described as the testatrix), for the benefit of Samuel Dexter Bradford, who is now deceased.

The testatrix died on August 15, 1886, leaving as her heirs at law a son, John Henry Bradford, now deceased, and three grandchildren, Julia E. Bradford, Samuel Dexter Bradford, and Mary J. Kissel, who were the children of her deceased son, Samuel Dexter Bradford.   Her will was duly proved and allowed in 1886. Under its fourth and residuary clause she gave and devised one half of her residuary estate to her son, John H. Bradford, and the remaining one half to trustees in trust for the following purposes: "they shall hold the same as they receive it or in their discretion sell and invest the same in real estate or personal prop-

[61] The marital deduction is considered infra page 783.

In a letter ruling dated March 16, 1950, CCH Fed. Est. & Gift Tax Rep. ¶2070.30, it is recognized that property may be bequeathed or devised directly to the guardian of a surviving spouse who has been legally adjudicated incompetent, and in such case, the property will be deemed to pass from the decedent to his spouse for marital deduction purposes.

erty at their discretion, in a safe and prudent manner and after paying all expenses incident to the execution of the trust, together with a reasonable compensation for their own services, they shall pay or in their discretion apply and appropriate the net income thereof to the maintenance support and comfort, of such of my grandchildren, children of my deceased son Samuel Dexter Bradford, as shall survive me, share and share alike, for and during the period of their natural lives; the issue of any such deceased grandchild to take the parent's share; it being my purpose and intent that the said trust fund and the income thereof, shall not be liable for or chargeable with any debts contracted by them or either of them, and that they shall have no power to sell, assign, transfer or anticipate the same or any part thereof, but all payments of income shall be entirely within the absolute control and discretion of the trustees hereunder; and upon the death of each of such grandchildren, they shall pay over and distribute such portion of the principal of said trust fund as such grandchild dying was entitled to the income of during its life, to such person or persons as such grandchild by its last will and testament directs and appoints to receive the same, but in no event shall any part of said trust funds be liable for, or be paid or appropriated to or for any debts or liabilities of such grandchildren; and in case any such grandchild shall die and fail to make any such testamentary appointment; then and in such case said trustees shall pay over and distribute the share of such grandchild so dying to and among the issue of such grandchild; and in case such grandchild shall die, leaving no will and no issue, then and in such case the portion of the principal of said trust fund shall remain in and constitute a part of said trust fund; the income to be applied and the principal to be disposed of in like manner as though the then surviving grandchildren or grandchild if any, were the only ones or one for whose benefit this trust was created, so that such survivors or survivor shall receive or have applied for them or it an increased portion of income, and have the right to dispose of by will of an increased portion of capital; and in case of any of such grandchildren dying without a will and without issue and no one of such grandchildren surviving; then and in such case the portion of such trust fund, the income of which such grandchild so dying was at its death entitled to, the income thereof, shall go to my heirs at law in the same manner as they would take the same from me dying intestate."

The grandchild Julia E. Bradford, later Julia B. Armit, died September 10, 1923, and her share of the trust estate was distributed in accordance with the provisions of the will. Her children or their personal representatives are parties respondent. Mary J. Kissel, the appellant, is the sole surviving grandchild of the testatrix, the grandchild Samuel D. Bradford having deceased May 18, 1935, testate, leaving no widow or issue. His will dated October 22, 1934, was allowed in the Surrogate's Court of the County of Kings in the State of New York on December 31, 1935, and an authenticated copy thereof was filed and recorded in our county of Suffolk and letters testamentary were issued thereon to the Old Colony Trust Company and Jacob Rosenberg.

The pertinent provisions of the will of Samuel are as follows: "Third: As to the fund set apart and held in trust for my use during my life under the Will of my father, Samuel Dexter Bradford; and as to the fund set apart and held in trust for my use during my life under the Will of my grandmother, Julia Emma Bradford, and pursuant to the provisions of the said Wills, over and in respect to the respective principals of which funds I was given a power of testamentary appointment, I hereby exercise said power of appointment given to me in each of said Wills, and hereby give, devise and bequeath to Thelma Cooper, now residing at Hotel Empire, Broadway and 63rd Street, Borough of Manhattan, City and State of New York the sum of Thirty Thousand and 00/100 ($30,000.) dollars. In the event that the said Thelma Cooper should predecease me, then and in that event I give, devise and bequeath the said sum of $30,000. to the said Thelma Cooper's sister, Bessie Cooper, of 40 South Pine Street, Hazelton, Pennsylvania, and in the event of said sister's death, the said sum of $30,000. is to go to the estate of the said Thelma Cooper. Fourth: As to the fund set apart and held in trust for my use during my life under the Will of my father, Samuel Dexter Bradford, and as to the fund set apart and held in trust for my use during my life under the Will of my grandmother, Julia Emma Bradford, and pursuant to the provisions of the said Wills, over and in respect to the respective principals of which funds I was given a power of testamentary appointment, I hereby exercise said power of appointment given to me in each of said Wills, and hereby give, devise and bequeath to Jacob Rosenberg, of 70 Pine Street, Borough of Manhattan, City and State of New York, the sum of Five Thousand and 00/100 ($5,000.) dollars. Fifth: I give, devise and bequeath all the rest, residue and remainder of the said respective principals of the said trust funds to Percy D. Atherton of 541 Boylston Street, Boston, Massachusetts. Sixth: I am making no provision for any of my blood relatives for the reason that I do not feel that they have treated me with the kindness and consideration to which I was entitled."

The petition was heard on the facts therein alleged, statements and stipulations of counsel, and certain exhibits, all of which appear in the record. The judge filed a report of facts in substance as follows: At the time of the execution of the will of Samuel D. Bradford, hereinafter described as the donee, he was indebted to the appointee Rosenberg in the sum of $5,000; to the appointee Cooper in the sum of about $30,000; and to the residuary appointee Atherton in the sum of $23,490.50 and interest. The provisions for them were made by the donee in consequence of agreements made by him so to satisfy their claims. The Judge specifically found that the relation of debtor and creditors existed between the donee and them at the times of the execution of the will of the donee and of his death.

After hearing, the judge entered a decree to the effect that the power of appointment conferred upon the donee by the will of the testatrix was a general one; that it was validly exercised by the donee; that the provision in the fourth clause of the will of the testatrix "that after the exercise of the above mentioned power of appointment, no part of the trust property shall be appropriated for the payment of the debts of the donee of the power, is invalid as an improper limitation upon the general power of appointment"; and that the appointed property be paid to the executors in Massachusetts of the will of the donee of the power.

The respondent Mary J. Kissel appealed from this decree and now contends "that the provision in the clause of the will of Julia Emma Bradford granting a power of appointment to her grandchildren — '*but in no event shall any part of the said trust funds be liable for, or be paid or appropriated to or for any debts or liabilities of such grandchildren*' — was a limitation upon the power prohibiting an appointment by Bradford to creditors for the purpose of paying his debts to them, that the persons to whom Bradford appointed the trust property were creditors and that the appointment was made for the purpose of satisfying his debts to them, that accordingly no appointment within the scope of the power was made, and that in accordance with the terms of the will the trust fund was to be continued in trust for the benefit of this respondent."

It has long been settled in this Commonwealth that "when there was a general power of appointment, which it was absolutely in the donee's pleasure to execute or not, he might do it for any purpose whatever, and might appoint the money to be paid to his executors if he pleased, and, if he executed it voluntarily and without consideration, for the benefit of third persons, the money should be considered part of his assets, and his creditors should have the benefit of it." Clapp v. Ingraham, 126 Mass. 200, 202. While reference is made in the case just cited to an execution of the power "voluntarily and without consideration," it is also established in Vinton v. Pratt, 228 Mass. 468, a case which in the facts closely resembles the case at bar, that, where the donee of a testamentary power exercised it for the purpose of discharging his obligations upon a guaranty in writing, by the exercise of the power the property, if necessary, could be applied in satisfaction of the donee's debts. In that case, at page 470, it is said that this "has become a rule of property, and having been unchallenged for nearly forty years we cannot agree with the defendant, that it should be overset." We think that the rule is the same whether the appointment be made voluntarily as a benefaction, or upon a consideration.

The intention of the testatrix is to be gathered from a reading of her will as a whole considered in the light of the material circumstances known to her at the time of its execution. When thus ascertained, her intent must be given effect unless some positive rule of law forbids. Ware v. Minot, 202 Mass. 512. Thus considered, it appears that the will was executed and allowed over fifty years ago. Its provisions for the children of her son Samuel are identical. The will contains a specific spendthrift provision applicable to the shares of all the grandchildren during their respective lives, which embraces both the trust fund and the income therefrom. It is established in this Commonwealth that such a provision is valid. Broadway National Bank v. Adams, 133 Mass. 170. Boston Safe Deposit & Trust Co. v. Collier, 222 Mass. 390. We see no reason for departing from the principles set forth in those cases, and followed in Bucknam v. Bucknam, 294 Mass. 214. See also Burrage v. Bucknam, 301 Mass. 235. Immediately following this spendthrift provision effective during the lives of the grandchildren, the testatrix provided that "upon the death of each of such grandchildren . . . (the trustees) shall pay over and distribute such portion of the principal of said trust fund as such grandchild dying was entitled to the income of, during its life, to such person or persons as such grandchild by its last will and testament directs and appoints to receive the same, but in no event shall any part of said trust funds be liable for, or be paid or appropriated to or for any debts or liabilities of such grandchildren. . . ." Then follow the provisions in case, not of an exercise of the power by the donees in favor of creditors, but of default of appointment without qualification.

We are of opinion that it is manifest that the dominant inten-

tion of the testatrix was that, as during the lives of the respective
donees neither the trust fund nor the income therefrom should
be liable for any debts contracted by them, so also the testatrix
intended that upon their respective deaths, notwithstanding the
general power conferred upon them to appoint their shares by will,
the appointed property should not be paid to their creditors nor
appropriated to the satisfaction of their creditors' claims. We
think that her intent was the same whether the appointment was
exercised indirectly or expressly to creditors of the donees, or was
exercised to volunteers as pure benefactions, and that her clear
purpose was to extend the rules established by our decisions relating to spendthrift trusts during the lives of the beneficiaries,
beyond, notwithstanding the general power to appoint by will
conferred upon them. She was concerned not with who the appointees should be, but rather that in no event should the creditors of the donees reach the trust estate in satisfaction of their
claims. The power was a general one; the subsequent provision,
that the property appointed should not be appropriated to or for
any debts or liabilities of the donees, we think was a direction
to the trustees, who would be the only persons who could "pay,"
and a restriction upon them rather than a limitation upon the
power to appoint. Such an intent cannot be given effect. The
testatrix could not effectually thus give with one hand and take
away with the other.

In the case of Hill v. Treasurer & Receiver General, 229 Mass.
474, in the course of a careful analysis of the nature of general
powers of appointment, at page 476, the court said: "The doctrine that appointed property shall be regarded as assets of the
estate of the donee who has exercised a general power of appointment is purely equitable. It rests on the fundamental idea that a
man ought to pay his debts when he has the power to do so, rather
than to give property to those who are not his creditors. It is
not founded on the actual intent of the one who has exercised
the power. This principle of equity disregards the desires of the
donor in creating the power, deprives the donee of the untrammelled authority conferred upon him in terms, and to the extent
of its scope does violence to the manifest design of the donee in
exercising the appointment. It would operate even in the face
of his testamentary declaration to the contrary. Equity seizes the
property on its way from the donor to the appointee and applies
it to the satisfaction of the obligations of the appointor." We
think that these principles are decisive of the question before us;
that the desire of the donor in the case at bar to place a subsequent limitation on the general power once given must be dis-

regarded. In like manner, the actual intent of the donee who has exercised the power to satisfy in that manner certain of his creditors must be set aside, and they must take their places with the other creditors of his estate, which is insolvent, and must take their pro rata shares, not as appointees, but just as creditors.

The appointees in the case at bar have not appealed from the decree under consideration, and thus have evidenced their acceptance of what we have just said, although it sets at naught the intent of the donee. See Am. Law Inst. Restatement: Property, Sec. 452 and comment c, where, after stating the general equitable doctrine (which is the law of this Commonwealth), it is said: "The rule . . . applies in spite of the manifestation of a contrary intent by the donor or the donee or both. Thus it is immaterial that the donor provides in the instrument creating the power that the property covered thereby shall in no circumstances be appointed to the donee's creditors or subjected to their claims. It is also immaterial that the donee provides in the instrument of appointment that the property shall not be subjected to the claims of his creditors." Thus both attempts are condemned in this statement. Without intimating that all that is there said is not a correct statement of the law and one that would follow from what has been said by this court in such cases as Hill v. Treasurer & Receiver General, 229 Mass. 474, it goes further, we think, than we are required to go in the instant case, where the provision is not a specific one that the property shall not be appointed to the donee's creditors, but is one which follows the grant of the general power, and which provides against the payment or appropriation of the appointed property to or for any debts or liabilities of the grandchildren, the donees. In its essence, however, the comment in the Restatement, before referred to, includes the facts in the case at bar, and is consistent with the rule, which we have often repeated and have here followed, that the general power once given by the testatrix may not be limited by her so as to defeat the equitable doctrine that the property appointed shall be dealt with as assets of the donee's estate for the satisfaction of his debts, in so far as his individual estate is insufficient therefor. See Tuell v. Hurley, 206 Mass. 65.

Nothing is said in the decisions of this court sustaining spendthrift trusts as effective during the life of the beneficiary to whose interests as to either principal or income they applied, from which it may be inferred that such provisions, following the grant of a general power to appoint, are valid. "The purpose of a spendthrift trust, however phrased, is to provide a secure living for the beneficiary." Bucknam v. Bucknam, 294 Mass. 214, 219. Such provisions were effectively made by the testatrix in the case at bar affecting the interests in the trust fund which the donees of the power were to enjoy during their respective lives. We are of opinion that the testatrix could not thereafter, having conferred upon them a general power of appointment, legally make another form of spendthrift trust, to the end that the power having been exercised, the appointed property should still remain beyond the reach of the creditors of the donees. The purpose of the testatrix in this respect must be disregarded.

We have carefully considered the case of Fleming's Estate, 219 Penn. St. 422, which has been relied on by the appellant. We cannot follow it, since, if read in one light, it is opposed to the equitable doctrine before referred to as having been established in Clapp v. Ingraham, 126 Mass. 200, and, if read in the only other light possible, it is contrary to what we have already said in Old Colony Trust Co. v. Clarke, 291 Mass. 17. The case of Bundy v. United States Trust Co. of New York, 257 Mass. 72, is not inconsistent with the conclusion reached here, that the exercise of the power by the donee is valid.

The decree entered in the Probate Court instructing the petitioner to pay the appointed property involved to the executors in Massachusetts of the donee is correct. Olney v. Balch, 154 Mass. 318. Lovejoy v. Bucknam, 299 Mass. 446, 454. It is affirmed, and costs and expenses of this appeal as between solicitor and client are to be in the discretion of the Probate Court.

Ordered accordingly.[62]

PROBLEM

12.18. T in his will gives the residue of his estate to a trustee and directs the trustee "to pay the income to my son for life and, on the death of my said son, to pay the corpus as my said son may appoint by his will, provided always, however, that my said son shall not appoint to his estate, his creditors or creditors of his estate." T's will provides that in default of appointment the trust property is to go to his son's issue per stirpes and, if no issue, to the X charity. T dies. T's son dies, and his will does not exercise the power of appointment. In a state following State Street Trust Co. v. Kissel, will the value of the trust property be includible in the son's gross estate for federal estate tax purposes?

[62] Comments on State Street Trust Co. v. Kissel are found in 19 B.U.L. Rev. 340 (1939), 27 Geo. L.J. 815 (1939), 52 Harv. L. Rev. 1018 (1939), 37 Mich. L. Rev. 1343 (1939). — Ed.

(2) Income Tax Consequences

The preceding discussion has brought out the circumstances under which the tax picture of the donee of a power of appointment is the same as it would be in the absence of the power so far as federal estate and gift taxes are concerned. Attention is now directed to the federal income tax situation of the donee of a power of appointment, to ascertain when the existence of the power of appointment increases the donee's income tax load and when it leaves it unaffected.

In an earlier chapter,[63] an examination is made of the various situations under which the settlor of an inter vivos trust is taxable on the income from the trust property, even though such income may be paid to others, on the ground of dominion and control. The mere existence of certain powers to control beneficial enjoyment of the trust property may have such tax consequence. The earlier discussion of the rules applicable when the income tax situation of the settlor was under examination should be compared with the discussion at this point, where a person other than the settlor is involved.

Prior to enactment of the 1954 Code, no specific statutory provision set forth the circumstances under which persons other than the settlor would be taxed on the income from trust property as the substantial owners. But Section 22(a) of the 1939 Code, which was used to tax the settlor as the substantial owner under the Clifford regulations, was also used to tax persons other than the settlor who were not receiving the income.[64] Regulations on this point provided that where a person other than the settlor had a power exercisable solely by himself to vest corpus or the income in himself, the income was taxable to him. Furthermore, if he released the power or modified it, and the resultant arrangement was one under which he would be treated as the substantial owner of the trust property if he were the settlor, he would still be taxable.[65]

---

[63] See page 153 supra.

[64] Mallinckrodt v. Commissioner, 146 F.2d 1 (8th Cir. 1945), *cert. denied*, 324 U.S. 871 (1945).

In Smith v. United States, 265 F.2d 834 (5th Cir. 1959), the court held that the beneficiary under a testamentary trust was taxable on the income under 1939 I.R.C. §22(a), even though the income was left in the trust because it was determined that the will did not prescribe any standard limiting her control over the income of trust property.

[65] See Reg. 118, §39.22(a)-22, sometimes referred to as the Mallinckrodt regulations.

For example, suppose that A in his will established a trust, with T as trus-

The 1954 Code in substance codified the Regulations referred to in the preceding paragraph.[66] If a trust is established and a person other than the settlor has the power, exercisable solely by himself, to vest the corpus or the income therefrom in himself, he may prevent the income of the trust from being attributable to him by renouncing or disclaiming the power within a reasonable time after he first becomes aware of its existence.[67] The holder of the power is not deemed the owner for federal income tax purposes of the property subject to the power, however, if the power is not freely exercisable by him.[68]

What is the federal income tax situation of the donee of a power if he can apply the income of a trust to the support or maintenance of a person whom he is obligated to support or maintain? The Code provides that he is not taxed on the trust income merely because such a power exists, if he holds the power in the capacity of trustee or co-trustee, but he will be taxed on the trust income to the extent it is applied for such support and maintenance.[69] The

---

tee, under the terms of which the income was to be paid to B for life with remainder to C, but throughout B's life X could require the corpus to be paid to himself or anyone else. Under Reg. 118, §39.22(a)-22 the income was taxable to X, though paid to B. If X gave up the power to have the corpus paid to himself, but reserved the power to direct that it be paid to others, he would still be taxable because if he had been the settlor he would have been taxable on the income under the Clifford regulations. Reg. 118, §39.22(a)-21(d)(2)(iv)(b)(2).

[66] See 1954 I.R.C. §678, quoted infra page 1375. This section is applicable to testamentary as well as inter vivos trusts. See Reg. §1.678(a)-1(a).

[67] See 1954 I.R.C. §678(d), quoted infra page 1375.
The disclaimer or renunciation should produce no adverse federal estate or gift tax consequence. See the discussion at page 716 supra.

[68] See Funk v. Commissioner, 185 F.2d 127 (3d Cir. 1950); Falk v. Commissioner, 189 F.2d 806 (3d Cir. 1951), cert. denied, 342 U.S. 861 (1951); United States v. Smither, 205 F.2d 518 (5th Cir. 1953); Agnes R. May, 8 T.C. 860 (1947); Ruth W. Oppenheimer, 16 T.C. 515 (1951).
C. E. and Margaret Brehm, Trustees, Trust No. 3, 33 T.C. 734 (1960), considered a trust where the beneficiary was a minor and the beneficiary or his guardian was given power to terminate the trust, in whole or in part, at any time. The court held that the income of the trust was not taxable to the beneficiary under §678 during the minority of the beneficiary, since no guardian had been appointed. Under such circumstances the beneficiary did not have unfettered command over the trust property as required if §678 is to apply. The case was reversed sub nom. Trust No. 3, C. E. and Margaret Brehm, Trustees v. Commissioner, 285 F.2d 102 (7th Cir. 1960), and in reversing the court held that it was not necessary for a minor beneficiary to have a guardian in order to be deemed the owner under §678.

[69] See 1954 I.R.C. §678(c), quoted infra page 1375; Winton, Taxation of Nongrantors Under Trusts for Support of Their Dependents, 33 Taxes 804 (1955).
It should be kept in mind, however, that a power of appointment exercisable for the purpose of discharging a legal obligation of the holder of the

mere existence of the power, however, will cause the income to be taxable to the holder of the power if he does not hold it in the capacity of trustee or co-trustee.[70]

The person who is legally obligated to support another may be taxable on trust income which is in fact used to discharge such legal obligation pursuant to a mandate in the trust instrument,[71] or as the result of the exercise of a discretionary power given to another.[72]

The slight federal estate tax cost of giving a beneficiary the power to withdraw $5000 or 5 percent of the trust property has been considered.[73] The federal income tax cost to the beneficiary of giving him such a power must be examined before a decision is made to use the power in an estate plan.

If the power to withdraw $5000 or 5 percent is in a trust which directs the trustee to pay all the net income to the holder of the

---

power is a general power of appointment for federal estate and gift tax purposes. See Reg. §20.2041-1(c)(1), quoted infra page 1517.

[70] See Reg. §1.678(c)-1(b); Kamin et al., The Internal Revenue Code of 1954: Trusts, Estates, and Beneficiaries, 54 Colum. L. Rev. 1237, 1263 (1954).

It may be contended that the language of §678(c) which refers to a power enabling a person "in the capacity of trustee or co-trustee" to apply the income of the trust to the support or maintenance of a person he is obligated to support or maintain means that the power to so apply the income must be in such person alone, even though he is one of two trustees. Such an interpretation would eliminate the applicability of §678(c) if, for example, the father as trustee could only exercise the power in conjunction with another trustee. See Kamin et al., supra.

[71] Suppose that a grandfather establishes a trust and directs the trustee to apply the income to the support and maintenance of his grandson. Will the income be taxable to the father if he is trustee? If someone else is trustee? It may be contended that if the father is taxable when as trustee he exercises a power to apply the income to the support and maintenance of his son, he is likewise taxable when he, or someone else, as trustee, must do so. Cf. Commissioner v. Estate of Dwight, 205 F.2d 298 (2d Cir. 1953), *cert. denied,* 346 U.S. 871 (1953).

[72] Section 1.662(a)-4 of the Regulations recognizes that any amount which, pursuant to the terms of a will or a trust, may be used in full or partial discharge or satisfaction of a legal obligation of any person shall, to the extent so used, be included in the gross income of such person under §662(a)(1) or §662(a)(2), whichever is applicable, as though directly distributed to him as beneficiary, except when §71 (alimony payments) or §682 (income of an estate or trust in case of divorce) applies.

Section 1.662(a)-4 of the Regulations points out that normally the extent of the parent's legal obligation of support, including education, will be determined by the family's station in life and by the means of the parent, without consideration of the trust income in question.

In Lehman v. Commissioner, 234 F.2d 958 (2d Cir. 1956), *cert. denied,* 352 U.S. 926 (1956), the court held that annual payments which were made by the taxpayer's husband to her mother for and on behalf of the taxpayer, to discharge her obligation to support her mother, and which were made pursuant to a divorce settlement, were taxable to the taxpayer.

[73] See the discussion at page 716 supra.

power, the only additional income tax load the existence of the power could impose on the power holder would be with respect to income allocated to corpus, such as capital gains, which otherwise would be taxable to the trust. The existence of the power will cause the donee to be deemed the owner of a portion of the corpus and to be taxable on the portion of any income allocated to corpus that is attributable to such portion.[74] The Regulations state that when the portion of the trust corpus which the donee of the power is deemed to own is represented by a dollar amount ($5000 or 5 percent of the value of the trust property), a fraction of each item of capital gain is attributed to that portion. The numerator of the fraction is the dollar amount which can be withdrawn by the donee of the power, and the denominator is the fair market value of the trust corpus at the beginning of the taxable year in question.[75] This slight income tax cost should not be a deterrent to the use of the limited right of withdrawal in a trust under which the donee of the power is entitled to all the income.[76]

The use of the limited power of withdrawal is more questionable in a trust which gives the trustee discretion in regard to the distribution of income to the one who would have the limited power of withdrawal. The Regulations make it clear that if the donee's power is to withdraw from the income of the trust $5000 or 5 percent of the value of the trust property, the donee will be taxed on the amount of trust income he could withdraw, whether he withdraws it or not.[77] In a case where the trustee is given discretion to pay out or accumulate income, obviously the limited power of withdrawal would relate to corpus. In this case, probably the donee of the power should not be taxed on the ordinary trust income not distributed to him except to the extent it is attributable to the portion of the corpus he could withdraw. Thus the use of the limited power to withdraw corpus in a trust where the trustee is given discretion as to the distribution of income will cause the holder of the power to be taxed not only on a portion of the income allocated to corpus, such as capital gains, but also on at least a

[74] Section 678 of the 1954 Code applies when the power relates only to a portion of the trust property as well as when it relates to all the trust property.

[75] See Reg. §1.671-3(a)(3).

[76] If the power to withdraw $5000 is allowed to lapse in a particular year, will the donee of the power for future years be treated as the settlor of the trust to the extent of the portion of the corpus that is represented by the $5000 the donee has left in the trust? If he is, the income tax consequences with respect to such a portion will no longer be governed by §678 but may be governed by §§674, 676 and 677.

[77] See Reg. §1.671-3(b)(1) and (c).

portion of the ordinary income even though it is paid to someone else.[78]

H.R. 9662, which failed of passage in the Eighty-sixth Congress would make some significant changes in Section 678 of the 1954 Code if it is enacted.[79]

PROBLEMS

12.19. A establishes a trust which gives the trustee discretion to pay the income to W, his wife, or to accumulate it, and also gives W a power to withdraw $5000 of corpus in each calendar year. In the first year of the trust the value of the trust property at the beginning of the year is $100,000, the distributable net income of the trust is $4000 and the realized gains total $6000. The trustee makes no distribution to W. What amount of trust income should W include in her gross income for federal income tax purposes?

12.20. A establishes a trust which provides that one day after the end of the taxable year W, his wife, may withdraw an amount of corpus equal to the net income of the trust for the previous year. Describe the federal income tax consequences so far as W is concerned.

b. *Powers of Appointment Which Improve the Over-all Tax Picture — Discretionary Trusts*

If a husband creates a trust for the benefit of his wife, either inter vivos or in his will, and gives his wife a general power of appointment with respect to the corpus of the trust, the over-all tax picture may be improved because such a trust may qualify for the federal gift tax marital deduction or the federal estate tax marital deduction. In other words, though the wife will be regarded as the owner of the trust property for federal estate and gift tax purposes, the over-all tax picture may be improved by virtue of

---

[78] See Casner, Estate Planning — Beneficiary Controls of Trustee's Discretion as to Income or Corpus Distributions, 36 Trust Bull. No. 7, p. 51 (1957).

[79] H.R. 9662 would eliminate entirely §678 and insert in the Code a new §664. The effect of this new section would be to subject to the general operation of provisions governing taxation of trust income the situations where someone other than the settlor has a power to draw down income or corpus. Where the described power exists, the donee of the power would be deemed to have withdrawn the income or corpus in determining the income tax consequences. This new §664, however, would apply not only when the power of withdrawal is in the donee alone but also when it is in the donee "and one or more related or subordinate parties." The term "related or subordinate party" would have the same meaning it now has under 1954 I.R.C. §672(c), quoted infra page 1370, except that the term "person" would be substituted for the term "grantor" in each place it appears in that section.

the deduction available in determining the taxable gift made by the husband or in determining his taxable estate which will be subject to an estate tax. The next chapter is concerned with marital deduction gifts in an estate plan.

The over-all tax picture may be substantially improved by the establishment of a discretionary trust. Such a trust is limited in this discussion to one in which a power exists to pay out corpus or to determine who receives income, and in which the existence of the power does not cause the settlor or the power holder to be taxed on the income of the trust,[80] or cause the settlor or the power holder to be deemed the owner of the trust assets for federal estate or gift tax purposes.[81] Discretionary trusts have been used extensively to lessen the tax impact on income from family wealth. Under the 1939 Code, for example, if A provided in his will that the trustee was to pay the income to B, or to accumulate it and pay out accumulated income and corpus in his discretion, the income was taxable to B if the trustee elected to pay it to him; otherwise it was taxable to the trust.[82] If B did not need the income, the tax on it would probably be less if it were retained by the trust than if it were distributed to B and taxed as part of his net income. The income accumulated in one year and taxed to the trust could be paid out to B in the next year without any further tax.[83]

The 1954 Code, in general, does not eliminate or reduce that tax advantage. It recognizes the trust as a separate tax entity[84]

[80] The circumstances under which the existence of discretionary powers will cause trust income to be taxable to the settlor of an inter vivos trust are examined supra page 176. The extent to which the existence of discretionary powers will cause trust income to be taxable to the power holder (when he is someone other than the settlor) is considered supra page 729.

[81] The federal estate and gift tax consequences, so far as the settlor is concerned, resulting from the existence of discretionary powers are discussed supra page 188, and such consequences, so far as the power holder is concerned (when he is someone other than the settlor), are explained supra page 712.

[82] See 1939 I.R.C. §162(c).

[83] See 1939 I.R.C. §162(d), describing the so-called sixty-five-day rule in regard to distributions of income from previous years.

[84] See 1954 I.R.C. §641, quoted infra page 1361.

During the period between the occurrence of an event which causes a trust to terminate and the time the trust is considered as terminated, the income and the excess of capital gains over capital losses of the trust are in general considered as amounts required to be distributed for the year in which they are received. See Reg. §1.641(b)-3(c).

Revenue Ruling 58-267, 1958-1 C.B. 327, points out that an incompetent's estate which is managed by a guardian is not a tax entity separate and distinct from the incompetent for federal income tax purposes.

Where property is placed in trust with a proviso that on the termination of the trust, if an interest vests in a minor, the trustee shall retain such interest and invest and reinvest the principal, collect the income and apply such income, or as much as the trustee determines is needed, for the minor's

and sets up special rules for allowing certain credits against its tax and certain deductions in computing its taxable income.[85] It

---

support, the legal title to the property may be deemed to be in the minor, with what is called a power in trust in the trustee. In such a situation, should the trustee file a fiduciary return? Revenue Ruling 59-154, 1959-1 C.B. 160, answers this question in the affirmative.

[85] See 1954 I.R.C. §642, quoted infra page 1362.

The fact that a trust which is required to distribute all its income currently is allowed a deduction of $300, whereas one that gives the trustee discretion whether to distribute income or accumulate it is allowed a deduction of only $100, should have little influence on whether to select one type of trust or the other.

Under §642(c), a trust is allowed a deduction for charitable contributions without regard to the percentage limitation applicable to individuals. This deduction is one from gross income in computing the taxable income of the trust. H.R. 9662 would eliminate the charitable deduction under §642(c) and substitute a distribution deduction similar to the deduction allowed a trust for distributions to other beneficiaries.

Revenue Ruling 56-105, 1956-1 C.B. 209, holds in regard to §611(b)(3) "that where the manner in which the deduction for depletion may be apportioned and allocated between the income beneficiaries and the trust is, under the terms of the trust instrument, within the sole discretion of the trustees, they may properly allocate all of the depletion deduction to the beneficiaries and retain none for the trust although a substantial portion of the income from the depletable assets is retained by the trust." Revenue Ruling 56-105 is revoked by Rev. Rul. 60-47, I.R.B. 1960-6, 66, as the former is not in accord with §1.611-1(c)(4) of the Regulations, which provides in part: "No effect shall be given to any allocation of the depletion deduction which gives any beneficiary or the trustee a share of such deduction greater than his pro rata share of the trust income, irrespective of any provisions in the trust instrument, except as otherwise provided in this paragraph when the trust instrument or local law requires or permits the trustee to maintain a reserve for depletion." In Estate of Mary Jane Little, 30 T.C. 936 (1958), a will established a trust but its provisions did not mention the division of depletion and depreciation deductions between the income beneficiaries and the trust. One income beneficiary threatened to contest the will because the trustee had discretion as to what was income and what was corpus, and a compromise agreement was made under which the trustee was to allocate receipts between income and corpus according to the state law. The Texas Trust Act, which was controlling, provided that permissible depletion deductions should be treated as principal. Thus, under §§23(l) and 23(m) of the 1939 Code (1954 I.R.C. §§167(g) and 611(b)(3)) all deductions for depletion were to be taken by trust and none by income beneficiaries. The case was reversed sub nom. Estate of Mary Jane Little v. Commissioner, 274 F.2d 718 (9th Cir. 1960). The court decided that the original trust under the will controlled, and because it contained no provision relating directly to the depletion or depreciation deduction, the beneficiaries were entitled to their allocable shares of the deduction. In John R. Upton, 32 T.C. 301 (1959), the entire depletion deduction was granted to the trust where a court had construed the trust instrument as requiring a portion of the royalties to be allocated to corpus to protect the trust estate. The case was affirmed sub nom. Upton v. Commissioner, 60-2 U.S.T.C. ¶9711 (9th Cir. 1960). Brad Love Sneed, 34 T.C. —, No. 47 (1960), applied 1939 I.R.C. §23(m) (1954 I.R.C. §611(b)(3)) in a case where the income from a depletable asset was to remain in the trust and be invested and only income from the investment was to be distributed, and concluded that the trust estate was entitled to the depletion deduction.

In Rosalie M. Schubert, 33 T.C. 1048 (1960), a life income beneficiary

establishes a new concept called "distributable net income," which must be mastered to understand the income taxation of trusts.[86] To the extent that income is paid out or is required to be paid out, the trust is simply a conduit, and income in the hands of the beneficiary retains the same characteristics as it had in the hands of the trust. In ascertaining the amount of income taxable to the trust and the amount taxable to the beneficiary, trusts are divided into two categories — simple and complex. Sections 651 and 652[87] govern the taxability of simple trusts. A trust is simple if its terms require all income to be distributed currently and do not provide "that any amounts are to be paid, permanently set aside, or used for the purpose specified in section 642(c) (relating to deduction for charitable, etc., purposes)." [88] When a simple

---

under a trust claimed a deduction for depreciation where the trust property included land leased to a tenant under a long-term lease, on which the tenant had constructed a building, the estimated useful life of which extended beyond the lease. As an alternative the life income beneficiary sought to amortize the premium value of the lease because of the high rentals being paid. The court denied both claims. The case was affirmed in 61-1 U.S.T.C. ¶9217 (4th Cir. 1961).

H.R. 9662 would amend §642(h) to extend the deduction available to beneficiaries for unused loss carryovers and excess deductions on termination, to the termination of a single beneficiary's entire interest in a trust having different beneficiaries where such interest represents a separate share as determined under §663(c). The trust would lose the portion of the net operating loss carryover, capital loss carryover, and other excess deductions allocated to such a beneficiary. Further consideration of §642(h) appears infra page 1363.

[86] See 1954 I.R.C. §643, quoted infra page 1363.

H.R. 9662 would make it clear that in computing distributable net income the deduction under §691(c) for estate tax attributable to income in respect of a decedent is not allowed. Such a deduction is allowed to the persons taxable upon the income in respect of a decedent to which it is allocable.

Gains from the sale or exchange of capital assets are ordinarily excluded from distributable net income. Section 1.643(a)-3 of the Regulations spells out when such gains will be considered as paid, credited or required to be distributed to a beneficiary and hence includible in distributable net income. H.R. 9662 would specify in some detail in the Code when capital gains would be so includible.

All items of deductions other than capital losses and the personal exemption, whether paid from income or from corpus, are allowed primarily as deductions in computing distributable net income. Since distributable net income measures the amounts taxable to beneficiaries, so-called corpus deductions inure to the benefit of income beneficiaries rather than corpus beneficiaries. H.R. 9662 would change this and require corpus deductions to be applied first against income which is excluded from distributable net income, such as capital gains and, in certain cases, extraordinary income and taxable stock dividends. The excess of corpus deductions over excluded income would be allowed as a deduction in computing distributable net income.

[87] Quoted infra page 1364.

H.R. 9662 would modify §651(a) to reflect the different treatment of charitable beneficiaries.

[88] See the comments in note 87, supra, in regard to the change which would be made under H.R. 9662.

Section 1.651(a)-2 of the Regulations points out that if a trust instrument

trust is involved, in computing the taxable income of the trust, there is allowed as a deduction the amount of income for the taxable year which it is required to distribute currently, but such a deduction cannot exceed the amount of the distributable net income of the trust for that taxable year.[89]   The amount of income required to be distributed currently by a simple trust is includible in the gross income of the beneficiaries to whom it is required to be distributed, whether distributed or not, but the amount so includible cannot exceed the distributable net income of the trust.[90] The following are examples of simple trusts; notice that some of them are discretionary trusts.

> *Example 1.*   A trustee is directed to pay all income to A currently as long as A lives and then to pay the corpus to B or his estate.   The trustee has no discretion in regard to payments of income or corpus.[91]

---

provides that in determining the distributable income the trustee shall first retain a reserve for depreciation or otherwise make due allowance for keeping the trust corpus intact by retaining a reasonable amount of the current income for that purpose, such retention will not disqualify the trust from being a simple trust.

Revenue Ruling 59-346, 1959-2 C.B. 165, holds that where all the income of a trust is required to be distributed currently to a beneficiary who reports his income under the accrual method of accounting, such income earned by the trust to the date of the beneficiary's death is includible in his final return under §652(a).   Section 451(b) is not in conflict because amounts are not accrued by reason of the taxpayer's death but because of the operation of §652(a).

[89] Under §651(b), the distribution deduction allowed to the trust is the lesser of the income required to be distributed currently or the distributable net income, and the distributable net income is reduced for this purpose by exempt items.   If the distributable net income exceeds the income distribution, a distortion may result.   Suppose, for example, that the distributable net income was $10,000, but was reduced to $9000 after excluding exempt income.   In such a case, the trust could receive a deduction of $9000 for a $9000 distribution, although properly the deduction should be reduced to the extent the $9000 actually distributed would be deemed to consist of exempt income, as is provided in §661(c) for complex trusts.   This means the deduction to the trust should be $8100.   H.R. 9662 would bring about this result.

[90] If there are multiple beneficiaries and the amount distributable exceeds the distributable net income, each beneficiary includes in his gross income only a proportionate part of the amount.   The income distributed to the beneficiaries retains the same character in the hands of the beneficiaries that it had in the trust.

[91] The trust instrument as a whole must be carefully examined to determine whether the income beneficiary is entitled to all the income.   In Mueller v. Commissioner, 236 F.2d 537 (5th Cir. 1956), the trustees applied trust income in the reduction of a deficit incurred when carrying charges of trust leasehold properties exceeded income during a depression.   The trust instrument gave the trustees the power to pay the cost of preserving trust properties out of income.   Thus the court held that the income beneficiary was not entitled to the income in the years in which the trust income was used to reduce the above-mentioned deficit.

Example 2. A trustee is directed to pay all income to A currently as long as A lives and to pay A so much of the corpus from time to time as the trustee in his discretion may determine. On A's death, the trustee is to pay the remaining corpus to B or his estate. The trustee has no discretion as to income but has discretion as to the corpus. Such a trust is a simple trust, subject to the rules of Sections 651 and 652, in any year in which the trust does not distribute anything but current income. But in any year in which it distributes corpus it falls into the category of complex trusts.[92]

Example 3. A trustee is directed to pay out all the income currently but has discretion to pay the income to one or more members of a group consisting of A, A's wife, and A's issue, in such amounts as he shall determine. On A's death, he is to pay the corpus to B or his estate. This is a discretionary trust, which lessens the income tax impact on family wealth because by payment of income to several members of the family, rather than to one, a lower tax rate may be obtained. The trust is a simple trust; under Section 652 each beneficiary is taxed on what he receives, as under the 1939 Code. It may be designated a *mandatory spray trust.*[93]

Example 4. A trust contains a mandatory spray provision as to income and, in addition, gives the trustee discretion to spray corpus among the income beneficiaries. This trust, like the one in Example 2 above, is a simple trust in any year in which the trustee does not exercise his discretion to pay out corpus. It has the same income tax advantages as Example 3.

If a trust does not meet the test of a simple trust for income tax purposes, it is a complex trust. An understanding of the income taxation of complex trusts requires familiarity with the so-called tier system,[94] the throwback rule,[95] the types of distributions

[92] Section 1.651(a)-3 of the Regulations points out that a trust which is required to distribute all of its income currently does not qualify as a simple trust under §651 in the year of its termination, since in that year actual distributions of corpus will be made.

[93] Section 1.651(a)-2(b) of the Regulations specifically covers the situation referred to in Example 3 and recognizes that such a mandatory spray trust is a simple trust.

[94] Under the present law there are two tiers. Income of the trust is deemed to go out to beneficiaries in the first tier first, and then to those in the second tier. The first tier includes all beneficiaries to whom income is required to be distributed. The second includes all beneficiaries to whom other amounts are properly paid, credited or required to be distributed.

H.R. 9662 would set up three tiers. The first would include beneficiaries to whom income is required to be distributed or to whom only income can be distributed in the discretion of the trustee. The second would include beneficiaries to whom both income and corpus can be distributed in the dis-

which do not carry out distributable net income,[96] and the separate share rule.[97]   Generally speaking, the beneficiary is taxable on what he receives up to an amount that is not in excess of the distributable net income of the trust; while the trust gets a distribution deduction for what it distributes, and this cannot exceed the distributable net income of the trust.[98]   The following are examples of complex trusts; notice that some of them are not discretionary trusts.

> *Example 5.*   A trustee is directed to pay all the income to A currently as long as A lives and then to pay the corpus to the X charity.   In any year in which it realizes a gain, the trust, though not discretionary, is outside the category of a simple trust, since such a gain will be permanently set aside for charity.[99]

---

cretion of the trustee.   The third would include beneficiaries to whom only corpus can be paid.   A beneficiary to whom income is required to be distributed and to whom the trustee can in his discretion distribute corpus would be in the first tier so far as the income distribution was concerned and in the third so far as the corpus distribution was concerned.   Charitable distributees, however, would never rise above the third tier and would even drop to a fourth tier to the extent an amount is permanently set aside for charity and is not distributed.

[95] The throwback rule is discussed infra page 742.

[96] See 1954 I.R.C. §663, quoted infra page 1367.   This section is considered infra page 759.

[97] The separate share rule is examined infra page 751.

[98] See 1954 I.R.C. §§661, 662, quoted infra page 1365.

If there are multiple distributees, the distributable net income is allocated first to amounts that are in the first tier; if these distributions do not exhaust the distributable net income, it is allocated to amounts that are in the second tier.   If the amount distributed to any tier exceeds the distributable net income allocated to that tier, each distributee in that tier takes into his gross income only a proportionate part of the distributable net income.   The character rule applies in determining the nature of the income received by a distributee.

Attention is directed to the fact that where, under §§661 and 662, the trustee is directed to pay the beneficiary a specified amount annually, so that in effect the beneficiary has an annuity, the beneficiary will be taxable under §662(a)(1), if the annuity may be paid out of income or corpus, to the extent it is paid out of income for the taxable year.   Thus, as far as federal income taxes are concerned the result is the same whether the trust payment is set up in the form of an annuity payable out of income or corpus or in the form of a requirement that income be paid to the beneficiary plus an amount of corpus which will bring the payment up to a stated amount.   In Estate of Max Steinberger, N.Y.L.J., July 11, 1958, p. 3 (N.Y. County Surr.), it was pointed out that there is a difference in state income tax consequences because an annuity is a gift or bequest and is not taxable as income to the recipient, whereas a trust which pays all income to a person is not an annuity, though the income payment is to be supplemented by the payment of corpus to bring the total up to a certain amount.   The latter type of arrangement subjects the recipient to New York State income taxes.

[99] Section 1.651(a)-4 of the Regulations brings out that a trust with a charitable remainder is not disqualified for treatment as a simple trust if either

Example 6. A trustee is directed to accumulate the income for a specified period of time and then to pay the corpus and accumulated income to designated beneficiaries. This is a *mandatory accumulation trust.* The income will be taxed to the trust as a separate tax entity except during the year of final distribution (under the 1954 Code as under the 1939 Code), and except to the extent the trust may be caught by the five-year throwback rule in that year as well.

Example 7. A trustee is given uncontrolled discretion to pay the income to A or to accumulate it. On A's death, the trustee must pay the corpus and accumulated income to designated persons. This is a *discretionary accumulation trust.* It cannot be a simple trust, even in a year in which the income is all paid out, because the terms of the trust do not require that income be distributed currently. The income will be taxed to the trust if accumulated, and otherwise to the beneficiary (under the 1954 Code as under the 1939 Code), except to the extent the trust may be caught by the five-year throwback rule in the year of final distribution.[100]

Example 8. A discretionary accumulation trust is set up with a provision giving the trustee the power to pay the accumulated income and corpus to the income beneficiary. This is a *discretionary accumulation trust with discretionary distribution of accumulated income.* This trust is taxed as in Example 7 above, except that it may be caught by the five-year throwback rule also in years in which it pays out more than the distributable net income.

Example 9. A trustee is given discretion to pay the income to one or more members of a group consisting of A, A's wife, and A's living issue, at such times and in such amounts as the trustee in his uncontrolled discretion may determine, any income not so paid out to be accumulated. On A's death, the trustee is to pay the corpus and accumulated income to des-

---

the remainder is subject to a contingency, so that no deduction would be allowed for capital gains or other amounts added to corpus as amounts permanently set aside for charity, or the trust receives no capital gains or other income added to corpus for the taxable year for which such a deduction would be allowed.

[100] Flato v. Commissioner, 245 F.2d 413 (5th Cir. 1957), held that the trustee of a discretionary trust may exercise his discretion by determining to pay income to the beneficiary on request, and if his discretion is so exercised, the beneficiary will be taxed on the income, whether it is distributed to him or not. Even though the trustee has so exercised his discretion for prior years, he may change his mind for subsequent years so that income will not be distributed on the request of the beneficiary and hence will not be taxed to him unless it is in fact distributed to him.

ignated persons. This is a *discretionary spray and accumulation trust*. The income will be taxed to the trust if accumulated, and otherwise to the beneficiaries in the amounts received by each (under the 1954 Code as well as under the 1939 Code), except to the extent the trust may be caught by the five-year throwback rule in the year of final distribution.[101]

Example 10. A discretionary spray and accumulation trust is set up with a provision giving the trustee the power to spray the accumulated income and corpus among the income beneficiaries. This is a *discretionary spray and accumulation trust with discretionary distribution of accumulated income*. This trust is like Example 9 above except that the trust may get caught by the five-year throwback rule also in years in which it pays out more than the distributable net income.[102]

Example 11. A trustee is directed to pay all the income to A but is given discretion as to when to make payments. On A's death, the trustee is to pay the corpus to B or his estate. This is a *quasi-accumulation trust*.[103] The income will be taxed to the trust if not paid out in the taxable year, and

---

[101] Although the discretionary spray and accumulation trust has certain tax advantages, it may produce some undesirable tax consequences. If the spouse of the donor is one of the persons to whom income may be paid, the benefits of 1954 I.R.C. §2513, as to gift tax splitting, may be unavailable as to any interest in the trust from which the spouse may possibly benefit. Furthermore, if one of the persons to whom the income may be paid dies within ten years after the testator, no credit under 1954 I.R.C. §2013 will be available to the income beneficiary's estate because his interest under the trust is not capable of valuation (see Reg. §20.2013-4(a)). Also, the annual gift tax exclusion is not available as to any of the income interests because no one of them is a present interest. Revenue Ruling 59-9, 1959-1 C.B. 232, brings out that when a beneficiary receives a life interest that is capable of valuation, the value qualifies for credit for the tax on prior transfers under §2013, notwithstanding the fact that it is not included in the gross estate of the transferee-decedent.

[102] See note 101 supra.

If the group of income beneficiaries among whom the trustee is authorized to spray income and principal consists of A and his issue, and if it is desired to place some restriction on the trustee's discretion so that he cannot prefer the issue of A if A wants to receive the contemplated payment, it can be provided that the trustee shall not make distributions to the issue without the consent of A and that if his consent is not forthcoming, then the trustee must distribute to A or make no distribution as the trustee may determine. Such an arrangement will not cause the income to be taxable to A if it is not distributed to him, because A does not have the power alone to compel the payment of the income or corpus to himself. Will such a restriction, however, give A, in conjunction with the trustee, a general power of appointment for gift and estate tax purposes?

[103] The christening of this type of trust, as well as a discussion of its validity under a restricted rule against accumulation, is found in Mannheimer and

otherwise to the beneficiary (under the 1954 Code as well as under the 1939 Code), except that the trust may be caught by the five-year throwback rule in years in which it pays out more than the distributable net income, and in the year of final distribution.

These examples show that discretionary simple trusts retain their former tax advantages under the 1954 Code. The same is true of discretionary complex trusts, unless they fall within the five-year throwback rule. Thus, whether there is any income tax advantage in using a discretionary complex trust will depend on the extent to which trust drafting or trustee management may eliminate the applicability of the throwback rule, which applies only to complex trusts. Of course, there may be reasons justifying the use of a discretionary complex trust in an estate plan, even though no income tax advantage is likely.

(1) The Five-Year Throwback Rule

The operation of the five-year throwback rule[104] can best be explained by an illustration. Suppose that a trustee has discretionary power to pay out income and corpus to A. In 1955 the distributable net income of the trust is $10,000. In that year the trustee pays $5000 to A. Assume that the trust is subject to a tax of $1100[105] in 1955 on the undistributed portion of the distributable net income. The undistributed net income for the year 1955 is $10,000 (the distributable net income) minus $6100 (the amount distributed to A plus the tax paid by the trust), or $3900.[106]

Friedman, Income Tax Aspects of Various Will and Trust Arrangements, 30 Taxes 362, 371-375 (1952).

[104] See 1954 I.R.C. §§665-668, quoted infra page 1367. The significant changes in these sections which would be made by H.R. 9662 will be noted in connection with the discussion in the text.

[105] This figure is not strictly accurate but is rounded for ease of mathematical calculation.

Section 665(c) sets forth the rule for determining as of any time the taxes imposed on the trust for any particular taxable year. It should be noted that the only taxes imposed on the trust which are significant in connection with the five-year throwback rule are those properly allocable to the undistributed portion of the distributable net income. The Senate Finance Committee report gives this illustration: "For example, if a trust has capital gains which are allocable to corpus, the portion of the tax imposed on the trust which is properly allocable to such gains will not be included for the purposes of determining the amount of the taxes imposed on the trust . . ." S. Rep. No. 1622, 83d Cong., 2d Sess. 358 (1954).

[106] H.R. 9662, which would change charitable distributions from a deduction from the gross income of the trust in computing the taxable income of the trust to a distribution deduction, would not permit amounts permanently set aside for charitable purposes for which a distribution deduction is allowed to be taken into account to reduce undistributed net income.

In 1956 the distributable net income of the trust is again $10,000. In that year the trustee pays A $12,500, pursuant to his power to pay both income and capital. The trustee has made an accumulation distribution of $2500. This $2500 is taxable income to A, deemed to be paid out of the undistributed net income pot of the preceding year, since it is large enough to cover the payment.

In addition to the accumulation distribution, A is also deemed to have received an amount "equal to the taxes imposed on the trust for such taxable year multiplied by the ratio of the portion of the accumulation distribution to the undistributed net income of the trust for such year." [107] Thus A is deemed to receive additional income of $1100 (the amount of the taxes imposed on the trust for the preceding year) multiplied by 25/39 (ratio of the accumulation distribution to the undistributed net income) or $705.13. However, the tax on A as to the $2500 plus $705.13 "shall not be greater than the aggregate of the taxes attributable to those amounts had they been included in the gross income of" [108] A in 1955.[109]

A is allowed a credit against his 1956 taxes of a pro rata portion of the taxes imposed on the trust in 1955 in the amount "which would not have been payable by the trust for such preceding taxable year had the trust in fact made distributions" [110] to A in 1955 of the $2500 and the $705.13. If the trust had made those distributions in 1955, it would have paid A $8205.13, instead of $5000, and would have retained $1794.87 of the $10,000 distributable net income. The tax to the trust on the retained amount would have been $338.97. The difference between that amount

---

[107] 1954 I.R.C. §666(c).

[108] 1954 I.R.C. §668(a).

[109] The Senate Finance Committee report points out that "a beneficiary receiving a distribution in a taxable year which is subject to the provisions of this subpart will be subject to the application of this subpart as if such amount had been distributed in any preceding taxable years in accordance with section 666 even though during any of such preceding taxable years such beneficiary could not have been a beneficiary if such distribution had actually been made in such preceding taxable years." S. Rep. No. 1622, 83d Cong., 2d Sess. 360 (1954).

Section 1.668(a)-1(b) of the Regulations provides that the amounts treated under §666 as having been distributed by the trust on the last day of the preceding taxable year of the trust are included in the gross income of the beneficiary, even though as of that day the beneficiary would not have been entitled to receive them had they actually been distributed on that day.

H.R. 9662, in view of the fact that it adopts a three-tier system, would treat all recipients of an accumulation distribution as being in the third tier.

[110] 1954 I.R.C. §668(b).

H.R. 9662 would change the credit for taxes paid by the trust so that the credit would be the same as the amount of taxes deemed distributed.

and the $1100 the trust paid in taxes in 1955, or $761.03, is the credit available to A.[111]

What is the amount of the undistributed net income pot for 1955 after the 1956 distribution? Section 665 must be reapplied in the light of what occurred in 1956. The total amount paid out to the beneficiary and deemed taxable to him in relation to 1955 income is now $8205.13 ($5000 paid in 1955 and $3205.13 paid in 1956). This amount subtracted from the distributable net income for 1955 ($10,000) leaves $1794.87. However, the amount of the taxes imposed on the trust must also be taken out before the amount of 1955 undistributed net income is finally determined. Section 665(c) requires that the original amount of the taxes imposed on the trust with respect to 1955 income ($1100) be reduced by the credit allowed to the beneficiary in regard to any accumulation distribution, and credit here is $761.03.[112] Thus the taxes still imposed on the trust equal $338.97. When the amount is subtracted from $1794.87, the remainder is $1455.90, which is the undistributed net income pot now outstanding as to 1955.[113]

If no further accumulation distribution that can be attributed to 1955 is made until 1961, the undistributed net income of 1955 is no longer of significance,[114] because 1955 will not be one of the five preceding taxable years.

The above illustration should make it apparent that the income tax advantage of having the income from a discretionary trust in whole or in part taxed to the trust may be lost if the trustee exercises a power to pay out the accumulated income, when the exercise causes the distribution to be taxed as income to the distributee under the five-year throwback rule. It should be noted that, while the tax attributable to the accumulation distribution cannot be more than it would have been if the accumulation had not

---

[111] As a result of the accumulation distribution, the taxes imposed on the trust might conceivably be greater than the taxes imposed on the distributee in a particular year. In such a case the full amount of the available credit would not be used. Can a refund of the unused part be obtained? Section 667 denies a refund to the trust, but §668(b), which gives the beneficiary the credit, does not state whether the beneficiary is entitled to a refund if the credit exceeds the tax.

[112] Under H.R. 9662 this amount would be $705.13, the amount of the taxes paid by the trust which were deemed distributed.

[113] Under H.R. 9662 the undistributed net income pot would be slightly smaller.

[114] An accumulation distribution is initially allocated to the first preceding taxable year; if it exceeds the amount of the undistributed net income pot for that year, the excess is allocated to the second preceding taxable year, and so on until the entire accumulation distribution is allocated to the preceding taxable years. Of course, the allocation process ends after going back five preceding taxable years, and no part of the accumulation distribution not thus allocated is income to the distributee. See 1954 I.R.C. §666(a).

been made, it may be less if in the year of distribution the distributee's other income is less, even with the distributable net income of that year and the accumulation distribution, than it was in the year of original accumulation.[115]

Other provisions of the 1954 Code, which will now be discussed, restrict the area of operation of the five-year throwback rule. As a result of these restrictive provisions it is submitted that for all practical purposes the old income tax advantages of discretionary trusts are equally available under the 1954 Code. If this fact is established by the following discussion, the use of discretionary trusts in estate plans need not be curtailed to any extent by the throwback rule.

(a) *Final Distribution*

If the discretionary complex trust does not permit any distribution of corpus and accumulated income until the final distribution of the trust property,[116] then only the final distribution may invoke the five-year throwback rule. The same is true of the mandatory accumulation trust, and of the discretionary complex trust which permits distributions of corpus and accumulated income, if the trustee in fact makes no accumulation distributions during the existence of the trust.[117] In many case of discretionary trusts set up as part of an estate plan, only a final distribution of accumulated income is likely to be necessary or desirable. Thus the effect of the five-year throwback rule will be a limited one.

Section 665(b)(4) of the 1954 Code[118] provides that "amounts properly paid or credited to a beneficiary as a final distribution of the trust if such final distribution is made more than 9 years after the date of the last transfer to such trust" will not be subject to the five-year throwback rule.[119] Since it is unusual for a discretionary

[115] A change in the tax rates also might produce a lower income tax on the accumulation distribution than if the accumulation had not been made. Furthermore, the trust has the use of the difference between the total taxes paid by the beneficiary and the trust and what would have been payable by the beneficiary if no accumulation had been made.

[116] See Examples 7 and 9 at page 740 supra.

[117] See Examples 6 and 8 at page 740 supra.

[118] Quoted infra page 1368.

[119] The Senate Finance Committee report says: "This will prevent the setting up of trusts for the purpose of accumulating income and making final distributions within reasonably short periods so as to avoid" the five-year throwback rule. S. Rep. No. 1622, 83d Cong., 2d Sess. 358 (1954).

Suppose that A establishes twenty separate trusts, each for the benefit of his son S. The first trust is to terminate nine years and one day after its creation, and the accumulated income and principal are then to be paid to S. The second is to terminate ten years after its creation, and the accumulated income and principal are then to be paid to S. The termination date

complex trust to terminate within nine years of its establishment, the five-year throwback rule will probably be seldom applicable in regard to a final distribution. However, the possible applicability of Section 665(b)(4) should be considered in determining whether to make a testamentary "pour-over" into an existing discretionary trust whose remaining life may be brief.

Suppose that A establishes a revocable inter vivos trust with income to be paid to him for life. On A's death the trustee has discretion to pay out income and corpus from time to time among a defined group, with a final distribution of the corpus and accumulated income at some specified time and to designated beneficiaries. When does this nine-year period begin to run if no addition is made to the trust property — on A's death when the discretionary trust first begins to operate, or from the date the revocable inter vivos trust is established? Will the answer be the same if the inter vivos trust is irrevocable? Or suppose T in his will establishes a trust, with income to be paid to his wife for life, and a discretionary trust of the trust property to begin at her death. When does the nine-year period begin to run if no addition is made to the trust property — on T's death or on the death of his wife? Will the answer be the same if the discretionary trust is set up by the wife under a general power of appointment given her? While these questions are not definitively answered by Section 665(b)(4), the nine-year period probably begins to run from the date the discretionary trust goes into operation.

PROBLEMS

12.21 A desires to establish a short-term trust which will provide that the trustee may pay out the income to a designated beneficiary or accumulate it during the period the trust exists. On the termination of the trust, all accumulated income is to be paid to the designated person and the corpus is to revert to A. Explain why you should recommend to A that the short-term period for such a trust should be ten years and one day rather than ten years.

12.22. Suppose that A in his will establishes four discretionary trusts, one for each of his children, and provides that if a child dies

---

of each of the other eighteen trusts is fixed so that each year only one trust comes to an end and a final distribution of accumulated income and principal of such trust is made to S. Has A effectively nullified the five-year throwback rule for the twenty-year period?

H.R. 9662 would make the five-year throwback rule applicable only to the extent the final distribution is attributable to property transferred to the trust not more than nine years prior to such distribution and the income attributable to such transferred property.

without issue, the property in his trust shall go over to the other trusts. If one of A's children dies without issue and, within nine years thereafter, a final distribution of the trust for the benefit of another child is made, will the five-year throwback rule be applicable to the final distribution? See Section 1.665(b)-2(b)(4)(ii) of the Regulations.

(b) *Emergency Payments*

One of the principal reasons for giving the trustee of a discretionary trust employed in an estate plan the power to pay out corpus and accumulated income is to enable him to meet the emergency needs of the beneficiary. In fact it is usually contemplated, even if the trustee's discretion is not limited, that the distributions of corpus and accumulated income will normally be made only when the beneficiary's other resources are inadequate to meet necessary expenditures. If the trust is so operated, the five-year throwback rule will not apply. Section 665(b)(2) of the 1954 Code[120] excludes from the term "accumulation distribution" "amounts properly paid or credited to a beneficiary to meet the emergency needs of such beneficiary." [121]

Suppose that a trust gives the trustee discretion to pay out income and corpus, in such amounts as he may determine, among a group of defined beneficiaries. In the first year of the trust, the distributable net income is $10,000 and the trustee decides not to pay out any income. The tax on the trust properly allocable to the undistributed distributable net income is $2606; thus the undistributed net income for the first year is $7394. In the second year the distributable net income is again $10,000 and the trustee pays the beneficiary $14,000. It is established that the payment of $4000 in excess of distributable net income for the second year is

---

[120] Quoted infra page 1368.

[121] In discussing the meaning of emergency payments, the Senate Finance Committee report, says: "Whether or not a distribution falls within this paragraph depends upon the facts and circumstances causing such a distribution. A distribution based upon an unforeseen or unforeseeable combination of circumstances requiring immediate help to the beneficiary would qualify. However, the beneficiary must be in actual need of the distribution. The fact that a beneficiary has other sufficient resources would tend to negate the conclusion that a distribution was to meet his emergency needs." S. Rep. No. 1622, 83d Cong., 2d Sess. 357 (1954).

Section 1.665(b)-2(b)(2) of the Regulations provides that in order for a distribution to be an emergency distribution, the beneficiary must be in actual need of the distribution, and the fact that he had other sufficient resources will tend to negate the conclusion that a distribution was to meet his emergency needs. Ordinary distributions for the support, maintenance, or education of the beneficiary will not qualify as emergency distributions.

an emergency payment. Does such an emergency payment reduce the undistributed net income pot of the preceding taxable year? It is submitted that the amount in the pot is still $7394. By definition, the emergency payment is not an accumulation distribution; it should not diminish the amount in *any* undistributed net income pot for *any* preceding taxable year.[122]

(c) *Income Accumulated Before Birth of a Beneficiary or Before He Attains Twenty-one*

It is frequently desirable to terminate the trustee's discretion to accumulate income when the beneficiary of a discretionary trust for a minor attains twenty-one, and to require a distribution of the accumulated income. The desirability of this type of trust is apparently not diminished under the 1954 Code. Section 665(b)(1)[123] provides that "amounts paid, credited, or required to be distributed to a beneficiary as income accumulated before the birth of such beneficiary or before such beneficiary attains the age of 21" shall not be included as part of an accumulation distribution.[124]

The section provides that there is no accumulation distribution of income accumulated before the birth of the beneficiary, regardless of when accumulated income is paid out. Thus, if a trustee has discretion to distribute income and corpus among a designated group, some of whom are living and some of whom are unborn, distribution to a later-born beneficiary of income accumulated prior to his birth will not be subject to the five-year throwback rule. Of course, the problem may arise whether the distribution to the later-born beneficiary is traceable to an accumulation made prior to his birth. Suppose that there is a distribution to the later-born beneficiary when he is thirty years of age, and undistributed net income for the five preceding taxable years is outstanding. Can the distribution be traced to income accumulated prior to the beneficiary's birth? The same problem can arise where a discretionary trust is established for a minor beneficiary and the distribution is made when he reaches thirty. The Regulations take the position that the distribution will be deemed

---

[122] Section 1.665(b)-2(a) of the Regulations provides that amounts excluded from accumulation distributions do not reduce the amount of undistributed net income for the five years preceding the year of distribution.

[123] Quoted infra page 1368.

[124] See the discussion relating to §2503(c) trusts for minors at page 243 supra. Such a trust for a minor takes full advantage of this exception to the throwback rule.

to have been made from the most recently accumulated income.[125] If the terms of a discretionary trust for a minor require a distribution of all the accumulated income at twenty-one, of course no tracing problem is presented.

Suppose a distribution of all accumulated income occurs when the beneficiary is twenty-one and the trust continues, now with discretion in the trustee to distribute corpus to the beneficiary. When the beneficiary is twenty-two, the trustee pays the beneficiary more than the distributable net income for that year. The excess distribution cannot be from income accumulated before the beneficiary attained twenty-one because all such income is already distributed. Did the distribution at twenty-one, however, use up the undistributed net income pots for prior years? It would seem that it could not, because by definition it is not an accumulation distribution, and only such distributions would seem to diminish the undistributed net income pot of a preceding taxable year. The Regulations, however, do not tax such corpus distribution even though there is an undistributed net income pot.[126]

---

[125] The Senate Finance Committee report says: "It is anticipated that the Secretary or his delegate will by regulations prescribe rules for the determination of the source from which amounts are distributed by a trust to a beneficiary for the purposes of ascertaining whether such amounts are distributed as income accumulated before the birth of such beneficiary or before such beneficiary attained the age of 21." S. Rep. No. 1622, 83d Cong., 2d Sess. 357 (1954).
Section 1.665(b)-2(b)(1)(i) of the Regulations provides that a distribution is to be considered as paid, credited or required to be distributed to a beneficiary who is under twenty-one years of age or unborn when the income was accumulated, to the extent, and only to the extent, that there is no undistributed net income for taxable years preceding the year of distribution other than undistributed net income accumulated while the beneficiary was under twenty-one. If a distribution can be made from income accumulated either before or after a beneficiary reaches twenty-one, it will be considered as made from the most recently accumulated income, and it will be so considered, even though the governing instrument directs that distributions be charged first against the earliest accumulations.

[126] Section 1.665(b)-2(b)(1)(ii) of the Regulations provides that a distribution to a beneficiary of income accumulated before he reaches twenty-one will not reduce the undistributed net income includible in a future accumulation distribution to another beneficiary. However, all future distributions to the same beneficiary, or to another beneficiary to whom a distribution would be excepted because it relates to an accumulation before he reaches twenty-one, to the extent they could not be paid, credited or required to be distributed from other accumulated income, would be excepted from the definition of an accumulation distribution.

(d) *Amounts Paid When a Beneficiary Attains a Specified Age or Ages*

Section 665(b)(3)[127] rules out as accumulation distributions "amounts properly paid or credited to a beneficiary upon the beneficiary's attaining a specified age or ages if" *and only if* three conditions are met: (1) "the total number of such distributions cannot exceed 4 with respect to such beneficiary"; (2) "the period between each such distribution to such beneficiary is 4 years or more"; (3) "as of January 1, 1954, such distributions are required by the specific terms of the governing instrument." This exception, inapplicable to future estate plans, may be of importance to existing ones.[128]

(e) *The $2000 Annual Exclusion*

No distribution in excess of distributable net income is in an accumulation distribution unless the excess is more than $2000.[129] If it is $5000, including a $3000 emergency payment, no accumulation distribution will be involved either. But if the excess is $2001, and is not eliminated under any of the foregoing exceptions, then the whole amount is an accumulation distribution. Thus, in any year in which the distribution in excess of distributable net income is $2000 or less, the five-year throwback rule will not come into the picture.

Suppose that in the first year of a trust the undistributed net income pot contains $4000. In each of the next two years $2000 in excess of the distributable net income is distributed. These $2000 distributions are not accumulation distributions; hence the undistributed net income pot for the first year of the trust remains at $4000. Thus a distribution of more than $2000 in the fourth year may invoke the five-year throwback rule.[130]

---

[127] Quoted infra page 1368.

[128] H.R. 9662 would expand §665(b)(3) so as to make it applicable to amounts paid or credited to a beneficiary upon a specified date or dates as well as upon the beneficiary attaining a specified age or ages.

[129] See 1954 I.R.C. §665(b), quoted infra page 1368.

[130] H.R. 9662 would add a new exception to take care of required distributions from one trust to another trust upon the occurrence of an event unrelated to the termination of the distributing trust. The receiving trust, however, would pick up a proportionate amount of the undistributed net income pot of the distributing trust, and the undistributed net income pot of the distributing trust would be correspondingly reduced. This exception would take care of so-called "peel-off" trusts, where, on the birth of a child, a new trust is to "peel off" for him from the trusts for the other children.

(2) Separate Share Rule

Section 663(c)[131] provides that for the sole purpose of determining the amount of distributable net income in the application of Sections 661 and 662 to a trust having more than one beneficiary, "substantially separate and independent shares of different beneficiaries in the trust shall be treated as separate trusts." [132]   The Senate Finance Committee report gives the following example: Assume that a trust instrument provides that the trust income when not distributed to beneficiary A will be accumulated for his benefit and will ultimately be payable to his estate or appointees (including persons named as alternate takers in default of appointment).   The trust instrument also provides that the fiduciary may invade corpus from time to time to make payments to B, according to B's needs.   In a year in which the trustee accumulated the trust income for A but made a discretionary distribution of corpus to B, B would, but for the operation of this provision, be deemed taxable on the distribution to the extent of the trust's distributable net income.   Under this provision, if A is deemed to have a substantially separate and independent share in the trust, the trust income would be taxable to the fiduciary and B would receive the corpus distribution free of tax.[133]   Note that treating separate shares as separate trusts may affect the application of the five-year throwback rule to the case.

Since Section 663(c) permits a single trust to be treated as consisting of separate trusts only for the limited purpose outlined above, it cannot be applied to obtain more than one deduction for personal exemption or to permit the splitting of the trust's undis-

---

H.R. 9662 would also bring within the orbit of the throwback rule more situations where the trust is a foreign trust — for example, one set up by a United States citizen in a foreign country with a nonresident alien trustee — than where it is a domestic trust.   This would be accomplished by eliminating the $2000 annual exclusion and all other exceptions to the throwback rule where foreign trusts are involved and where the distribution to a United States citizen or resident from such trust consists of income from foreign sources or net capital gains which have not been subject to tax under 1954 I.R.C. §871.   See consideration of foreign trusts at page 1108 infra.

[131] Quoted infra page 1367.

[132] The Senate Finance Committee report provides: "The effect of this provision is to prevent a beneficiary from being subjected to tax on a distribution which represents a corpus distribution as to him but which would, except for this provision, be treated as a taxable distribution, since the trust income is being accumulated for another beneficiary to whom it will ultimately be made available."   S. Rep. No. 1622, 83d Cong., 2d Sess. 355 (1954).

[133] Ibid.

tributed net income into several shares to have it taxed at lower bracket rates.[134]

(3) Multiple Trusts

Under the 1939 Code, if the income of a discretionary trust could be sprayed among five named beneficiaries or accumulated, all the accumulated income was taxed to the trust. If, however, five separate trusts were established, each with a single income beneficiary, and the trustee had discretion to distribute income or to accumulate it, the accumulated income would be taxed to the five separate trusts.

The income tax advantage of multiple separate trusts is present to an even greater extent under the 1954 Code. If five separate trusts are set up, a distribution of $2000 in excess of distributable net income from each trust, or a total of $10,000, can be made without invoking the five-year throwback rule. But one trust with five beneficiaries would fall under the rule as soon as the excess surpassed $2000.[135]

The use of multiple trusts in situations where one trust is all that is required, in the hope that multiple-tax entities may be available with respect to the trust income that is not distributed is not recommended. Consider the following examples:

1. A owns a tract of land and his basis for income tax purposes is low compared to the market value of the land. A establishes sixty trusts, all identical in terms, and transfers to the trustee of each trust an undivided one-sixtieth interest in the land. Each trust directs the trustee to pay the income to A's son for life and on the death of A's son, to pay the corpus to A's issue then living, such issue to take per stirpes. The trustee sells the land. Will the capital gain realized on the sale be divided into sixty parts and each part taxed to one of the trusts as a separate tax entity?

2. A establishes Trust No. 1 to last for nine years and one day. During the period of the trust the income is to be

---

[134] Section 663(c) provides that the existence of substantially separate and independent shares and the manner of treatment as separate trusts, *including the application of subpart D,* shall be determined in accordance with regulations prescribed by the Secretary or his delegate. If a single trust with multiple beneficiaries qualifies for separate share treatment under §663(c), the operation of the $2000 annual exclusion under the throwback rule and the application of the exception to the throwback rule relating to final distributions will be affected.

[135] See note 134 supra.

paid to S or accumulated in the discretion of the trustee. On the termination of the trust, the principal and accumulated income are to be paid to S or his estate. On the following day A establishes Trust No. 2, which is identical with Trust No. 1 except that the termination date is ten years and one day after its creation. Will the accumulated income of Trust No. 1 be taxed to that trust as a separate tax entity and the accumulated income of Trust No. 2 be taxed to Trust No. 2 as a separate tax entity?

The answers to the questions raised above may not be clear under present law but it seems obvious that sooner or later legislation will be enacted to prevent such tax avoidance by the use of multiple trusts.[136]

McHARG v. FITZPATRICK
210 F.2d 792 (2d Cir. 1954)

L. HAND, Circuit Judge.

The plaintiffs, "Successor Trustees" under the will of Henry K. McHarg, deceased, sue the defendant, a former Collector of Internal Revenue for the District of Connecticut, to recover income taxes alleged to have been unlawfully collected. The only question is whether the income should have been computed on the basis of three separate trusts, or of a single trust; and that in turn depends upon Paragraph Thirteenth (a) of McHarg's will, which was admitted to probate in the courts of Connecticut, of which he had been a resident. In March, 1949, the plaintiffs filed an income tax return for the year 1948, in which they treated the total income arising under that paragraph as that of a single trust, and they paid the tax accordingly. On September 7, 1950, they filed a claim for refund of a part of this payment, then asserting that they had paid under a mistake, because the income of the property should have been treated as coming from three separate trusts. If this was right, it would concededly have resulted in an overpayment of about $10,000. The Commissioner of Internal Revenue disallowed the claim, and this action followed. The trustees never physically divided into separate parts the trust property described

---

[136] H.R. 9662 would require that under certain circumstances multiple trusts be taxed as a single trust. This would be accomplished by the addition of a new §641(c). The general rule would be that if the primary beneficiary or beneficiaries of the currently accumulated income or taxable income allocated to corpus of the separate trusts are substantially the same, the trust, subject to some other rules, would be taxed as one trust.

See Gordon, Multiple Trusts: The Consolidation Approach, 4 Wayne L. Rev. No. 1, p. 25 (1957).

in the paragraph; and until the year 1949 they had always reported the income, as though it came from a single trust; moreover, although on March 14, 1951, the Court of Probate of the District of Ridgefield, Connecticut, in passing their accounts for the year 1949, found that it was the intent of the testator to establish separate and independent trusts under the paragraph, it nonetheless declared that, for purposes of investment and accounting, the trustees might continue to administer the trusts as one. All four of the beneficiaries named in the paragraph were alive when the testator died, but his son died in 1943, and the principal of his share had been distributed to his issue per stirpes. The only relevant section of the Act[137] merely declares that "the taxes imposed by this chapter upon individuals shall apply to the income of estates or of any kind of property held in trust"; and that gives no guidance as to when "property held in trust" for more than one person is to be taxed as one trust, or as several.

The Supreme Court in United States Trust Co. of New York v. Commissioner of Internal Revenue, 296 U.S. 481, 487, 56 S. Ct. 329, 332, 80 L. Ed. 340 held that "it was not necessary to have such a physical division in order to carry out the clear intention of the parties. An undivided interest in property may constitute the corpus of a trust." And again: "Where there is an intention to create separate trusts, the fact that 'the trusts' are 'kept in one fund' does not necessarily defeat the intention and require the conclusion that there is but a single trust." This settled a point that until then had been in dispute: i.e., there may be separate trusts within §161(b) although the trustee is the same and the res in each is a separate undivided interest in the same mass of real and personal property. It decided nothing more save that in that particular instance there were three separate trusts; and that, given the initial ruling, could hardly be doubted. All of the many decisions on the subject do, indeed, hold that the settlor's intent is decisive; but their use of the word is left somewhat uncertain. They may only mean the intent to create those limitations that the settlor in fact does create, or they may include his added belief, or his purpose, that those limitations shall be treated as one trust, or as several; and it is indubitably the case that very often they appear to regard the second factor as relevant. It can be only for that reason that they have, for instance, so often laid stress upon whether the settlor used the singular, or the plural, in speaking of the limitations he sets up.[138] In spite of these expressions

---

[137] (*Court footnote*) Sec. 161(a), Title 26, U.S.C.

[138] (*Court footnote*) State Sav. Loan & Trust Co. v. Commissioner, 7 Cir., 63 F.2d 482; Huntington Nat. Bank v. Commissioner, 6 Cir., 90 F.2d 876;

(none of them, however, having been determinative), we cannot avoid believing that the second factor should have no place in deciding the issue. Obviously that issue is the tax actually imposed; and, whatever may be the proper differentia to determine whether there are one, or several, trusts, it would be anomalous to make any part of it the settlor's understanding of the legal effect of what he was doing — or of his purpose in doing it. It would of course be quite untrue — especially in the field of torts — to say that a man's purpose can never be a determinant of his civil liabilities; but, so far as we can recall, it is never a measure of his public duties. Income taxes are imposed upon persons because of what they receive from property held by them, or for their benefit; and it cannot be permissible to make them turn, either upon what rights the settlor supposed he had created, or what rights he may have wished to create, but did not. We do not believe that it would make the least difference in the case at bar, for example, how often, or how consistently, the testator used the singular or the plural, or that he used the word "shares" instead of "trusts" to describe the limitations set up in Paragraph Thirteenth (a). Incidentally, it is usually the pursuit of our *ignis fatuus* to try to find out whether he has meant to make one trust or more; and so it would be the case at bar. However, we refuse to enter upon that speculation, because we hold that, even if we were to succeed, the result would be irrelevant.

Coming then to the limitations in Paragraph Thirteenth (a), although we will not try to lay down any general principle by which the question can always be answered, it appears to us that the limitations plainly fall on the side of a plurality of trusts. The testator started with an unconditional devise and bequest to his trustee of a one-third undivided interest in the residue of his estate — less $20,000. That of course vested in the trustee the legal title to such an undivided "one-third part," quite as though the third had been distributed in kind. He then went on to describe the trustee's duties as follows. He was to subdivide "the same" — the undivided third — "into four equal shares," to collect the income "thereof": i.e., of the "shares," and "to pay the income of one of said shares" to his son, "during his life and upon his decease to divide and distribute the principal of said share, and I give, devise, and bequeath the same, to and among his lawful issue, per stirpes." Then there followed three successive directions, each couched in precisely the same words: one in favor of

MacManus v. Commissioner, 6 Cir., 131 F.2d 670; Hale v. Dominion National Bank, 6 Cir., 186 F.2d 374; Johnson v. United States, 65 Ct. Cl. 285; Fiduciary Trust Co. v. United States, D.C., 36 F. Supp. 653.

a granddaughter, a second in favor of a grandson, and the third in favor of another granddaughter; and the paragraph ended with a proviso that, if any grandchild should die "without lawful issue him or her surviving, then . . . to divide and distribute and I give, devise and bequeath all shares" thus "defeated to and among the lawful issue of my said son, per stirpes." Thus, although each "share" began with the testator's death, as was inevitable, and although there was but one trustee for all the "shares," no "share" had any other feature in common with any other "share." Each had only one beneficiary, and he or she had no possible interest in any other "share" while the res of that "share" was held in trust at all. The death of any beneficiary put an unconditional end to any equitable ownership of that "share." Indeed, the testator had been at unnecessary pains to make it clear that the succeeding estate or interest should be legal, not in any degree equitable; for he was not content with a mere direction to the trustee "to divide or distribute" the principal among a beneficiary's "lawful issue"; but — to make assurance doubly sure — he followed that direction with words of formal legal transfer: "I give, devise and bequeath." Furthermore, during the existence of the "share," qua "share," it was not to receive any addition from any of the other "shares"; nor was it to be drawn upon in favor of another "share." Each "share," during the whole period of its existence in trust, was as completely isolated from all the other "shares" in composition, in beneficiary, and in duration, as though they had all been set up by separate deeds in the testator's lifetime. Perhaps it would go too far to say that equitable limitations are to be deemed a separate trust within §161(b), if they retain their content for a period not determined by that of any similar concomitant limitations, without additions to them from others, or withdrawals from them to others, and without the interpolation of new beneficiaries, or the loss of any of their own beneficiaries. But it seems to us that, if these factors do all combine, as they did here; and if there are no other factors that make the limitations depend upon the course of any other set of limitations, the income of each set is to be treated as that of an individual. But, particularly, whatever may be the indicia that should settle the question, we repeat what we said at the outset: among those indicia is not the belief or desire of the settlor about what he has created. That is not for him to say; he may create what he likes, but he may not say how it shall be taxed.

Judgment affirmed.[139]

[139] In M. T. Straight Trust, 24 T.C. 69 (1955), *aff'd sub nom.* M. T. Straight's Trust, McCrea, Trustee v. Commissioner, 245 F.2d 327 (8th Cir. 1957), it was

PROBLEM

12.23. A in his will establishes a trust under which the income is to be paid to his wife, for her life, and on her death, the trust property is to be divided into four separate trusts, one for each of A's children. On the death of A's wife, will a transfer tax be payable with respect to the securities in the trust which are placed in the four separate trusts?

(4) Trusts Involving Multiple Income Beneficiaries

The nature of the income received by each beneficiary of a trust with multiple beneficiaries must be determined. Suppose a trust has $10,000 taxable income and $10,000 tax-exempt income. The trust has deductions of $500, one half of which are attributable to taxable and one half to tax-exempt income. The distributable net income is $19,500. This income is equally divided between A and B. A and B are each deemed to have received an amount consisting of the same proportions of taxable and tax-exempt income as are found in the distributable net income.[140] Thus A and B have each received $4875 tax-exempt income.

---

held that a state court determination reforming a trust instrument so as to establish thereunder separate trusts, when prior to the reformation a single trust was created, would have no retroactive effect for tax purposes. It was stated that Louise Savage Knapp Trust A, 46 B.T.A. 846 (1942), would not be followed. That case held that the reformation did have retroactive effect. See also Schall v. United States, 57-2 U.S.T.C. ¶9894 (D. Minn. 1957), where the court found that the settlor of a trust did not intend to create separate trusts for his minor children, who were the beneficiaries.

See Fort Worth National Bank v. United States, 137 F. Supp. 71 (N.D. Tex. 1956), where the court found that the intention of the testator was to create a single trust rather than multiple trusts, and in the course of its opinion distinguished McHarg v. Fitzpatrick.

In Frank C. Rand Trust, CCH T.C. Mem. 1960-216, the court upheld the taxpayer's contention that separate trusts were created under a will and indenture of trust. The language and provisions in the instruments indicated that this was the settlor's intention. The trusts were handled as separate trusts by the trustees. Orders for distribution of the assets by the Probate Court were on a basis of multiple trusts.

Multiple tax entities may be created by the use of multiple corporations. Section 482 provides, in substance, that in any case of two or more businesses owned or controlled directly or indirectly by the same interests, the Secretary may distribute, apportion, or allocate gross income, deductions, credits or allowances between or among such businesses, if he determines such action is necessary in order to prevent evasion of taxes or to reflect the income of any of such businesses clearly. Aldon Homes, Inc., 33 T.C. 582 (1959), is a case where several corporations were taxed as one. See also 1954 I.R.C. §§269 and 1551, which relate to this matter. — ED.

140 See 1954 I.R.C. §§652(b), 661(b) and 662(b), quoted beginning infra page 1365.

But suppose that one of the income beneficiaries is in a high income tax bracket and the other in a low one. It would be highly desirable, financially, for the beneficiary in the high income tax bracket to receive all the tax-exempt income; it would make much less difference to the other to receive only taxable income. Or suppose that one income beneficiary is a charity. If part of the tax-exempt income is allocated to the charity, the entire benefit of its tax-exempt character is lost because the charity will not be taxed in any case.

Thus, from an estate planning standpoint it is important to know to what extent the allocation of different classes of income among multiple income beneficiaries can be controlled. The sections of the Code which formulate the general rule of allocation all recognize that the general rule will not apply when "the terms of the trust specifically allocate different classes of income to different beneficiaries." [141]

The Regulations point out that an allocation pursuant to a provision in the trust instrument granting the trustee discretion to allocate different classes of income to different beneficiaries is not a specific allocation by the terms of the trust. Likewise an allocation pursuant to a provision directing the trustee to pay half the income to A, or $10,000 out of the income to A, and the balance of the income to B, but specifying that the trustee first allocate a specific class of income to A's share to the extent available, is not a specific allocation by the terms of the trust. On the other hand, an allocation pursuant to a provision directing the trustee to pay all of one class of income to A, and the balance of the income to B, is a specific allocation by the terms of the trust.[142]

(5) Restricting Certain Beneficiaries to Distributions of Corpus

Suppose that a trust gives the trustee discretion whether to pay out income to A or to accumulate it, and whether to pay out corpus to B. In the first year of the trust the distributable net income is $10,000. The trustee decides to pay nothing to A but to pay B $5000. For income tax purposes, B clearly receives income, not

---

[141] See 1954 I.R.C. §652(b), quoted infra page 1365; and §662(b), quoted infra page 1366.

H.R. 9662 would also recognize as equally effective an allocation of different classes of income to different beneficiaries pursuant to local law. This is referred to as a clarifying amendment which is not intended to change existing law.

[142] See Reg. §1.652(b)-2(b).

corpus.[143]   Suppose, instead, that the trustee decides to pay A $10,000 and B $5000. Two thirds of what each receives is taxable income.[144] In other words, where the trustee's discretion extends to both income and corpus payments, the identity of what a recipient receives cannot be controlled by any labels the trust instrument puts on such payments.

Distributable net income must first be used to meet required payments where the trust requires the current distribution of income.[145] Assume that a trust gives the trustee discretion to make payments of corpus to B, but provides that all income must be paid to A. In the first year of the trust the distributable net income is $10,000, which is paid to A, and $5000 is also paid to B. No part of the payment to B will be taxable income to him.[146]

Suppose that a trust requires that income be currently distributed to A and that $5000 of the corpus be currently distributed to B. Will any part of the $5000 payment be taxable income? Section 662(a) provides that "for the purposes of this section, the phrase 'the amount of income for the taxable year required to be distributed currently' includes any amount required to be paid out of income or corpus to the extent such amount is paid out of income for such taxable year." No part of the required payment to B could be taxable income if all income must be paid to A.

(6) Gift of Specific Sum or of Specific Property

Section 663(a)(1) [147] of the 1954 Code disallows as a deduction to a trust and eliminates as income to the recipient "any amount

---

[143] See 1954 I.R.C. §662(a)(2), quoted infra page 1366.

[144] See 1954 I.R.C. §662(a)(2), quoted infra page 1366.
Under the tier system in H.R. 9662, however, A would be in the first tier and would be taxable on the entire $10,000 he receives; B would be in the third tier and would not be taxable on any part of what he receives unless the throwback rule was applicable. See page 738 supra, note 94, which discusses the tier system under H.R. 9662.

[145] See 1954 I.R.C. §662(a)(1), quoted infra page 1366.

[146] Suppose that the trust requires the current distribution of income to a charity and gives the trustee discretion to make payments of corpus to an individual. In such a case the distributions to the individual would be tax-free. See Kamin et al., The Internal Revenue Code of 1954: Trusts, Estates and Beneficiaries, 54 Colum. L. Rev. 1237, 1259 (1954). Under H.R. 9662, which drops the charity into the third tier, even though income is required to be distributed to it, the distributable net income would be allocated proportionately between the charity and the corpus distributee. See page 738 supra, note 94, which discusses the tier system under H.R. 9662.

[147] Quoted infra page 1367.
H.R. 9662 would modify §663(a)(1) so as to permit gifts of a specific sum of money or of specific property without such gifts carrying out to the distributee any of the distributable net income of the year of distribution if they are distributed within one taxable year of the trust, provided the terms

which, under the terms of the governing instrument, is properly paid or credited as a gift or bequest of a specific sum of money or specific property and which is paid or credited all at once or in not more than three installments. For this purpose an amount which can be paid or credited only from the income of the . . . trust shall not be considered as a gift . . . of a specific sum of money." [148] Suppose that $100,000 is placed in trust and the terms of the trust require the trustee to pay $30,000 to a designated beneficiary — $10,000 on his attaining the age of twenty-five, $10,000 on his attaining thirty, and $10,000 on his attaining thirty-five. Subject to those directions, the trustee has discretion to pay the income to the designated beneficiary or to accumulate and add it to principal; he also has discretion to pay principal to the designated beneficiary from time to time. Since the $30,000 is not payable solely out of income, no part of it constitutes taxable income to the designated beneficiary.[149] Note that a payment which under Section 663(a)(1) is not taxable income will not invoke the five-year throwback rule.[150]

---

of the governing instrument do not require them to be paid in more than one taxable year. The three-installment exclusion of existing law would be changed so that the exclusion applies to all installments, however many there may be, paid before the close of the thirty-sixth calendar month which begins after the date of the death of the testator, provided that under the terms of the governing instrument no installment is required to be distributed after the close of such thirty-six-month period. The benefit of §663(a)(1) as changed would be available only to future testamentary trusts.

[148] The Senate Finance Committee report contains the following comments regarding Section 663(a)(1): "A distribution of $25,000 to beneficiary A, upon his attaining the age of 25 as provided in the trust instrument, would fall within the gift exclusion of this subsection; whereas, a distribution to A, upon his attaining the age of 25, of the accumulated income for the prior year or years of the trust under the terms of the trust instrument, would not be subject to the gift exclusion whether such amounts were payable only out of accumulated income or were payable either out of income or corpus." S. Rep. No. 1622, 83d Cong., 2d Sess. 354 (1954).

[149] Has there been a specific gift of a sum of money if the designated beneficiary must survive to the stipulated ages in order to be entitled to the various payments? In the case above, if the designated beneficiary must attain the stipulated ages in order for the amounts to vest in him, then he may receive nothing, or $10,000, or $20,000, or $30,000. Can it be said that a gift has been made to him "of a specific sum of money"? If the total gift vests in the designated beneficiary at once, and only distribution is postponed until the designated ages, then it would seem to be clear that a gift has been made "of a specific sum of money." See Kamin et al., The Internal Revenue Code of 1954: Trusts, Estates and Beneficiaries, 54 Colum. L. Rev. 1237, 1256 (1954). Section 1.663(a)-1(b)(4) of the Regulations makes it clear that a gift or bequest of a sum of money or of specific property is not disqualified solely because its payment is subject to a condition.

[150] If a trust requires a lump sum payment at some time during the existence of the trust (for example, $5000 to the beneficiary when he attains age twenty-five), and the trust has income on hand on the date of payment sufficient to meet the required payment, will the amount paid to the beneficiary

(7) Unused Loss Carryovers and Excess Deductions on Termination of Trust

Section 642(h) [151] of the 1954 Code has no counterpart in the 1939 Code. While the provision is of no special significance in the creation of discretionary trusts, it establishes a better tax atmosphere for any kind of trust by allowing the beneficiary who succeeds to the property of the trust on its termination to deduct the following items:

1. A net operating loss carryover
2. A capital loss carryover
3. Deductions for the last taxable year of the trust in excess of gross income for that year (not including, however, the $300 or $100 personal deduction and charitable deductions) [152]

---

be deemed income or corpus in his hands? Miriam C. Lindau, 21 T.C. 911 (1954), held such a payment to be corpus.

See also Adie v. Clausan, 128 F. Supp. 284 (D. Me. 1955). In this case a bequest payable in a lump sum out of income or corpus was deemed corpus in the hands of the designated beneficiary, the court purporting to follow the Lindau case.

Compare with the Lindau case, Harte v. United States, 152 F. Supp. 793 (S.D.N.Y. 1957), in which the taxpayer contested her grandfather's will and entered into a settlement under which dividends from specified shares of stock were to be used to make monthly payments to her. The court held that the monthly payments to her were income, and not excludable as an inheritance, because the payments under the settlement agreement were to be paid out of income. The case was affirmed in 252 F.2d 259 (2d Cir. 1958).

Revenue Ruling 57-214, 1957-1 C.B. 203, recognizes that a bequest of a dollar amount out of the residue to a trustee is a bequest of a specific sum of money within the meaning of §663(a)(1).

[151] Quoted infra page 1363. The changes which would be made by H.R. 9662 are considered supra page 735, note 85.

[152] In Swoboda v. United States, 156 F. Supp. 17 (E.D. Pa. 1957), the court held that a trust beneficiary could not deduct a net operating loss incurred by a business which was an asset of the trust, or a capital loss resulting from the sale of the business during the winding-up period of the trust but before the distribution of the corpus, because the trust was still in existence at the time the losses occurred. The case was affirmed in 258 F.2d 848 (3d Cir. 1958).

Revenue Ruling 59-100, 1959-1 C.B. 165, does not allow a beneficiary of a trust to avail himself of the dividend received credit and the dividend exclusion provided in §§34 and 116, respectively, where the trust in its last taxable year has excess deductions within the meaning of §642(h)(2). If a trust has no income to pass on to a beneficiary, as must be true if it has such excess deductions, there will be no dividend income attributable to such taxable year, which would be includible in the beneficiary's return and to which the dividend exclusion or credit may be applied.

Revenue Ruling 59-392 1959-2 C.B. 163, recognizes that a capital gains deduction allowable to a trust under §1202 also qualifies as an excess deduction which is allowable, upon the termination of a trust, to the beneficiaries under §642(h).

Revenue Ruling 57-31, 1957-1 C.B. 201, holds that where a residuary testa-

PROBLEMS

12.24. T in his will gives the residue of his estate to trustees and directs them to pay the income to his son for life and, on the son's death, to pay the corpus in a designated manner to the son's issue. The trust contains the following provision:

"I authorize and empower my disinterested trustees at any time or from time to time in their discretion to insure the life of my said son, the face amount of such insurance not to exceed $100,-000, the policy or policies of said insurance to be payable to the trustees of this trust at the time of my said son's death, to apply any and all dividends on said policy or policies to the payment of the premiums thereon and to pay the balance of said premiums from the income or the principal of this trust as the disinterested trustees shall deem best. The proceeds of said insurance shall be added to and disposed of as part of the principal of this trust. Any insurance taken out in the exercise of the foregoing power may be either term insurance or straight life insurance as my disinterested trustees may deem best. If at any time my disinterested trustees shall deem it unwise to continue any such insurance, they may surrender the policy or policies therefor, and the amount received upon such surrender shall be added to and disposed of as part of the principal of this trust."

---

mentary trust is a beneficiary succeeding to the property of an estate and has deductions in excess of its gross income after the allowance of the excess deductions from the estate as authorized by §642(h)(2), the amount in excess of the gross income of the trust is not deductible by the income beneficiaries of the trust; but, if the trust terminates in the same year, then such excess deductions will be available to the remaindermen under the trust. Revenue Ruling 60-134, I.R.B. 1960-15, 16, considers the allocation of the deduction allowed by §642(h) among the intestate takers of Louisiana property. Under Louisiana law the property passes to the descendants subject to the usufruct of the widow. Perfect usufruct is where the property is used by the wife until her death or remarriage and is then turned over to the children. Imperfect usufruct is where the property is such that it cannot be used and later turned over but its use involves its disappearance and in such case the widow must turn over on death or remarriage the same quantity, quality and value as she took over. The ruling recognizes that the phrase in §642(h) "beneficiaries succeeding to the estate or trust" has reference only to those persons who have a right to receive property as distinguished from a mere right to income from such property. The widow in effect gets only income from perfect usufruct but receives the property subject to imperfect usufruct and §642(h) operates accordingly.

Section 642(h) does not deal with net operating loss carrybacks (see §172). Mellott v. United States, 257 F.2d 798 (3d Cir. 1958), *cert. denied,* 358 U.S. 864 (1959), brings out that the heirs of an estate to whom estate income was currently distributable could not assert the benefits of a carryback of a net operating loss available to the estate under the 1939 Code.

If the disinterested trustees exercise their discretion and acquire insurance on the life of T's son,

    a. Will the income of the trust which is used to pay the premiums on the insurance be includible in the son's gross income for federal income tax purposes? [153]

    b. On the son's death, will the value of the proceeds of insurance on his life be includible in the son's gross estate for federal estate tax purposes?

    c. If the son has a special power of appointment over the trust property (including the proceeds of insurance on his life, which will be added to the trust property on his death), will the value of the proceeds of insurance be includible in the son's gross estate for federal estate tax purposes? See Karagheusian v. Commissioner, 233 F.2d 197 (2d Cir. 1956).

    d. Suppose that the son is one of the disinterested trustees and thus, as a trustee, has the incidents of ownership of the policy on his life. Will the value of the proceeds of the insurance be includible in his gross estate for federal estate tax purpose?

12.25. Suppose that a trustee is given discretion to invade the principal "as in his sole discretion he may deem wise whether because of insufficiency of income, personal need, or otherwise" of the designated beneficiary. Does such language impose any restriction on the trustee's discretion in regard to the payment of principal? See Matter of Bisconti, 306 N.Y. 442, 119 N.E.2d 34 (1954).[154]

---

[153] In answering this question bear in mind that the son may have to consent to the trustee's application for insurance on his life and that the son will have to give his consent to any required physical examination in connection with the procurement of the insurance. In other words, the son may be in a position to control the trustee in his determination to use part of the income to pay premiums on insurance on the life of the son. Also bear in mind that many states have statutes prohibiting the accumulation of income. Is such a power in the trustee valid in these states? See N.Y. Personal Property Law §16; Matter of Hartman, 126 Misc. 862, 215 N.Y. Supp. 802 (1926); In re Meyer's Estate, 119 N.Y.S.2d 737 (1953).

[154] When the trustee is given "uncontrolled discretion," are there any limits as to what he can do? In this connection see Kemp v. Paterson, 4 A.D.2d 153, 163 N.Y.S.2d 245 (1957), involving a trust, in which the trustees were authorized to distribute principal as they deemed for the "best interest" of the beneficiary. They decided that it would be in the best interest of the beneficiary to pay her all of the principal and terminate the trust so that she could utilize the funds for the better support and education of her children and obtain certain income tax and estate tax advantages. The court held that the trustees had exceeded their authorization. The following is a quotation from the court's opinion: "In our opinion the language used contemplated an occasional invasion prompted by unusual or unanticipated needs.

c. *Powers of Appointment and State Death Taxes*[155]

If the creation of a power of appointment results in the imposition of a state death tax which otherwise would not be imposed, then the power of appointment impairs the over-all tax picture. In a substantial number of states the tax statutes make no reference to powers of appointment or to the property covered by such powers. Under these statutes, as they have been construed, the donee of the power is not regarded as the owner of the appointive assets for state death tax purposes.[156] In a few states, the tax statutes specifically provide that property subject to a power of appointment shall be taxable in the estate of the donor of the power and not in the estate of the donee.[157] In these states, the use of the power of appointment trust for the estate tax marital deduction

---

There is no basis to construe this additional power to invade the principal as a power to summarily terminate the trust. To permit it would transgress the bounds of the power and in effect would constitute a rewriting of the trust by the trustees. The court is without power to sanction such action on the part of the trustees. Any invasion of principal must be related to the expressed and implied purpose of the trust. Here the proposed termination of the trust fails to meet that test." This case was affirmed (with three judges dissenting) in 6 N.Y.2d 40, 159 N.E.2d 661 (1959). See also Huntington National Bank v. Aladdin Crippled Children's Hospital Assn., 108 Ohio App. 234, 157 N.E.2d 138 (1959), where the court sustained, over the objections of the remainderman, the exercise of a power in the trustee, in his absolute and sole discretion, to invade principal for the benefit of the life tenant in the event of illness or incapacity.

In Finkbeiner v. Finkbeiner, — Ohio App. — , 165 N.E.2d 825 (1959), a testamentary trust gave the trustee "absolute and unqualified discretion" as to distribution of income and principal, and the court said: "While the trustee was given almost unlimited power to manage, control, and dispose of both the income and principal, as she saw fit, without the order of any court, including the power to discriminate among beneficiaries, so long as the trust endures, notwithstanding the plenitude of the power conferred on the trustee, it created a trust relationship."

Under what circumstances will a court require a trustee under a discretionary trust to make payments? See In re Lackmann's Estate, 156 Cal. App. 2d 674, 320 P.2d 186 (1958) (trustee required to pay state hospital for cost of maintaining beneficiary there as a patient).

Does the trustee have to take into account other property of a beneficiary in determining whether to make payments of income or principal to him? I should think not, when he is given "uncontrolled discretion." If the trustee is authorized to make payments for the support of a beneficiary, then the trust instrument should specify whether he can disregard the other resources of the beneficiary in making such payments. For a case which held the trustee properly took into account other funds of the beneficiary when the trust authorized payments for support, see Smith v. Gillikin, 201 Va. 149, 109 S.E.2d 121 (1959).

[155] Powers under state inheritance and estate taxes are considered in 5 American Law of Property §23.24 (Casner ed. 1952).

[156] See Emmons v. Shaw, 171 Mass. 410, 50 N.E. 1033 (1898).

[157] See, for example, Pa. Stat. Ann., tit. 72, §2301(d) (Purdon).

gift, rather than an outright gift, results in avoiding one state death tax.[158]

In a significant number of states, the tax statutes specifically provide that the exercise of a power of appointment, or the failure to exercise it, shall be deemed a transfer from the donee of the power and therefore taxable just as though the donee had owned the property. Many of these statutes make no distinction between general and special powers of appointment.[159]

The extent to which the creation of powers of appointment impairs the over-all tax picture in these jurisdictions depends on the state death tax that is imposed on the transfer from the donor of the power. If there is a tax on the full value of the property passing from the donor and another such tax when the donee dies, then the creation of the power impairs the over-all tax picture. But in view of the fact that state death taxes are not substantial in amount, the use of powers of appointment in otherwise appropriate cases is not likely to be curtailed by state death tax consequences.

PROBLEM

12.26. H dies domiciled in a jurisdiction which has a state inheritance tax statute but this statute contains no specific provision in regard to powers of appointment. H's will transfers the residue of his estate to T in trust. Under the terms of the trust, T is required to pay the net income to H's wife, W, for her life and then to pay the corpus as she may appoint by her will. In default of appointment, T is to pay the corpus to designated charitable institutions. W dies a few months after H, without exercising her

---

[158] The power of appointment trust as an estate tax marital deduction gift is considered infra page 839.

In Curtis v. Commissioner of Corporations and Taxation, 340 Mass. 169, 163 N.E.2d 151 (1959), the donee of a general power to appoint by will exercised the power by appointing the appointive assets to her executors to be disposed of as part of her assets. Her will set up a residuary trust under which the income was payable to a designated person for life. The Commissioner claimed a tax on the basis of the property passing outright from the donor of the power to the donee's estate and another tax on the succession to the property by the donee's beneficiary from the donee's estate. The court held that what the donee did did not differ from an exercise of the power in the donee's residuary clause and that for this reason the only tax was on the succession by the appointee from the donor of the power.

[159] See, for example, Ill. Rev. Stat., c. 120, §375 (1959); Estate of Mary W. Tompkins, CCH Inh., Est. & Gift Tax Rep. ¶19181 (Mo. 1960). See also Mass. Ann. Laws, c. 65, §2, which treats the donee of the power as the owner of the appointive assets for state inheritance tax purposes if the power of appointment is derived from a disposition of property made prior to September 1, 1907.

power to appoint by will. The state taxing authority claims an inheritance tax on the entire value of the trust principal in H's estate as property passing from him to W. The executor and the charitable remainderman urge that since the power of appointment in W was not exercised, only a life interest passed from H to W and that the tax should be assessed only on the value of the life interest, inasmuch as the remainder interest passed to tax-exempt institutions. Which position should prevail? See Boston Safe Deposit & Trust Co. v. Johnson, 151 Me. 152, 116 A.2d 656 (1955).

4. DRAFTING POWERS OF APPOINTMENT

If it is decided that a particular estate plan calls for the creation of powers of appointment, the powers must be drafted so that they are valid and so that their terms express clearly what the donee is authorized to do. The decision to create powers of appointment is frustrated if the drafting job is inadequately done.

a. *Validity (Rule Against Perpetuities)*

A power of appointment is invalid if no effective exercise of the power is possible. The most significant legal obstacle to effective exercise is the rule against perpetuities. In order to avoid this rule in creating a power of appointment, so that it is at least possible to make an effective exercise of the power, the draftsman must carefully distinguish between a power to appoint by deed which is unlimited as to objects (general power to appoint by deed) and a power which is either exercisable only by will or is limited as to objects (general testamentary power or any type of special power). A general power to appoint by deed will be invalid under the rule against perpetuities if the exercise of such a power is subject to a condition precedent which may not be performed, if it is ever to be performed, within the period of the rule. The fact that such a power may in fact be exercised beyond the period of the rule is not significant. The significant fact is when it becomes exercisable.[160]

Where a general testamentary power or any type of special

---

[160] See 6 American Law of Property §24.31 (Casner ed. 1952); 4 Restatement of Property §390(1). The following is an example of a general power to appoint by deed which is void ab initio in a jurisdiction in which the common law rule against perpetuities is in force: A transfers property to T in trust, with directions to pay the income to B for life, then to pay the income to B's first son for life, with a power in B's first son to appoint the principal by deed to anyone from and after the date he attains the age of twenty-five. B has no son at the date the trust is established.

power is involved, however, no effective exercise is possible if the power may in fact be exercised beyond the period of the rule.[161] In other words, the power must be so created that it will be exercised, if it ever is to be exercised, not later than a date which must occur before the expiration of the period of the rule against perpetuities.[162]

The draftsman should begin to worry about the rule against perpetuities in relation to the creation of a power whenever the donee of the power is not a life in being at the time of the creation of the power; or if the donee of the power is a life in being, whenever the exercise of the power may be made by a successor donee who may not be a life in being at the time of the creation of the power; or if the donee is a corporation and the power may be exercised for the benefit of persons not in being.

Another possible obstacle to the effective exercise of a power of appointment is the rule against accumulations. This rule must be kept in mind particularly when creating a power in a trustee to pay out or accumulate income.[163]

b. *Donor's Intentions with Respect to Exercise of Power*

The draftsman should spell out with considerable care the donor's intentions with respect to any exercise of the power of appointment. The more important things to be expressed clearly in this regard are the following:

1. *Method of exercise.* Is the power exercisable by deed or by will, or by both deed and will? If the power is exercisable by will, it should be clear whether this means a will valid under the law of the donor's domicile or the donee's domicile. Of course, if the appointive asset is land, the instrument has to meet the requirements of a will in the state where the land is located.[164] Further-

---

[161] See 6 American Law of Property §24.32 (Casner ed. 1952); 4 Restatement of Property §390(2). The following is an example of a general power to appoint by will which is void ab initio in a jurisdiction in which the common law rule against perpetuities is in force: A transfers property to T in trust, with directions to pay the income to B for life, then to pay the income to B's first son for life, then to distribute the principal to such persons as B's first son may appoint by his will. B has no son at the date the trust is established.

[162] Re-examine the wait-and-see statutes considered supra page 655 and determine to what extent they are relevant at this point.

[163] The common law rule against accumulations and statutory rules against accumulations are discussed supra page 676.

[164] See 3 Restatement of Property §356. For a case in which the will exercising the power was not valid in the donee's domicile but was valid in the donor's domicile, and it was held that the power was effectively exercised, see Pitman v. Pitman, 314 Mass. 465, 50 N.E.2d 69 (1943).

more, whether the power can be exercised by a will executed before the date of the creation of the power should be clearly stated.[165]

2. *Interests creatable in appointees.* May the donee of the power appoint the property in trust or on condition or must all appointments be outright? [166]

3. *Delegation of discretion.* May the donee delegate his discretion to others or is it personal to him? It is particularly important that the donor manifest his intention in this regard when powers are given to multiple trustees.[167]

4. *Creation of new powers.* May the donee create new powers of appointment when he exercises the power? Such an exercise of a power is in effect a delegation of discretion but, if it is not allowed, any appointment in trust will have to be rigid and inflexible.[168]

5. *Successor trustees.* May successor trustees exercise powers and discretions given to a trustee? [169]

6. *Objects of the power.* To whom may the donee appoint? In view of the fact that the objects of a power are normally described by a group designation, the draftsman faces most of the problems that are involved in making a gift directly to a class.[170] An appointment that indirectly benefits a non-object may be deemed a "fraud on the power." [171]

7. *Exclusive or nonexclusive.* Must the donee give something to each object of the power (nonexclusive power) or may he exclude one or more objects from any benefits (exclusive power)? [172]

8. *Effect of exercise on future rights of an object.* Does a benefit conferred on an object affect the object's future rights in the income or principal of the trust? It is particularly important to state clearly the donor's intention if a power is given to a trustee to augment payments of income out of principal. Otherwise the question may arise whether a payment of principal to one income

[165] See 5 American Law of Property §23.41 (Casner ed. 1952); 3 Restatement of Property §356.

Whenever a power is created by a will, it should be made clear whether the power can be exercised by a will of the donee executed either before the date on which the donor's will is executed or thereafter, but before the date of the donor's death.

[166] See 5 American Law of Property §23.48 (Casner ed. 1952); 3 Restatement of Property §§356, 358.

[167] See 3 Restatement of Property §357, Comment *b;* §359, Comment *d.*

[168] See 5 American Law of Property §23.49 (Casner ed. 1952); 3 Restatement of Property §§357, 359.

[169] See 1 Restatement of Trusts Second §196.

[170] Class gifts are discussed supra page 439.

[171] See 5 American Law of Property §§23.52-23.56 (Casner ed. 1952).

[172] See id. §§23.57, 23.58; 3 Restatement of Property §§360, 361.

beneficiary, which necessarily reduces the amount of future income, is to affect that income beneficiary's share of future income payments. Also, if the income beneficiary or his issue may share in the ultimate distribution of the principal, it should be stated clearly whether such payments are to affect the ultimate distribution of principal. Furthermore, if the trustee is given power to pay out or accumulate income, a question may arise, in the absence of a manifestation of intention, whether a payment of income to one of the possible beneficiaries, when he or his issue are to share in the ultimate distribution of principal and accumulated income, will affect the ultimate distribution.

9. *Release of the power.* May the donee release the power completely or partially? A clear manifestation of the donor's intention in this regard is very important in view of the fact that future changes in the tax laws may make an alteration of the power desirable.[173]

c. *Gift in Default of Appointment*

Some legal consequences depend upon whether the donee of a power exercises the power.[174] In view of this fact, it is highly desirable to provide a clear and unambiguous plan for the devolution of the appointive assets if the donee does not exercise the power. If such a plan is provided, the donee may in many cases find it unnecessary to exercise the power and he may thereby avoid any undesirable consequences which flow from an exercise of the power.

d. *Conflict of Laws* [175]

The draftsman of an estate plan must not lose sight of the fact that powers of appointment may present conflict of laws problems. The donor and the donee may not be domiciled in the same jurisdiction and this fact may necessitate a determination as to what law governs various questions presented in connection with a power of appointment. Also, the appointive assets may be located in a jurisdiction where neither the donor nor the donee is domiciled, and the significance of this fact may also have to be ascer-

[173] See 3 Restatement of Property §§334-336, as amended by 1948 Supplement 504-510. See particularly the collection of statutes relating to the release of powers of appointment at 508. See also 5 American Law of Property §§23.25-23.32 (Casner ed. 1952).

[174] See discussion at page 690 supra.

[175] Conflict of laws problems in regard to estate planning are dealt with generally in Chapter XVIII. See also Durand and Herterich, Conflict of Laws and the Exercise of Powers of Appointment, 42 Cornell L.Q. 185 (1957).

tained. Even though the donor, the donee and the appointive assets are all in the same jurisdiction at the time the power is created, this situation may not continue, and the possible effect of a change should not be overlooked.

The draftsman has some opportunity in the preparation of the estate plan to anticipate possible conflict of laws problems and to resolve them in advance by inserting appropriate provisions. In general, whenever the answer to a particular question depends on the intention of the donor or the donee, the terms of the estate plan should resolve the matter in unequivocal terms so that resort to state law will be unnecessary.

Are certain persons included in the description of objects of the power? If the objects of the power are described as the "children" of some designated person, this term may present doubts, for example, as to inclusion of adopted children or illegitimate children. The decisions and statutes in the various states are not uniform in defining the word "children." All states, however, recognize that the intention of the donor as to the persons included in the description of the objects of the power, if clearly manifested, will control. Thus the draftsman has the opportunity to avoid resort to the law of any state to give meaning to such a term.[176]

When the problem for consideration is whether the rule against

---

[176] In In re Flagler's Will, 4 Misc. 2d 705, 158 N.Y.S.2d 941 (1957), the donor of the power was domiciled in New York, the donee was domiciled in Pennsylvania at the time the donee's will was executed, and the donee died domiciled in Nevada. The court applied Pennsylvania law in determining that a gift to "issue" should be construed to be per stirpes rather than per capita. The court also held that the law of New York, the domicile of the donor, controlled as to the validity of the exercise of the power, including the validity of the exercise by a will purporting to dispose of all the donee's property. In Fidelity Union Trust Co. v. Caldwell, 137 N.J. Eq. 362, 44 A.2d 842 (1945), the court held that the donee's will must be executed in accordance with the law of the donor's domicile. In Matter of Deane, 4 N.Y.2d 326, 151 N.E.2d 184 (1958), a foreign will was construed in accordance with the law of New York, to determine whether a power of appointment was exercised when the donor was domiciled in New York and the appointive assets were located there. In Estate of Julia E. Eginton, N.Y.L.J., Oct. 19, 1959, p. 15 (N.Y. County Surr.), the donee of a general testamentary power died in California. The donor of the power was a New York resident. The donee exercised the power by appointing the appointive assets in trust and naming a California corporation as trustee. The California corporate executor-trustee requested the New York Surrogate to transmit the appointive property to it to become part of the general assets of the estate subject to the claims of all the creditors. The Surrogate refused to do so, holding that the trustee named by the donee must qualify and administer the trust in the donor's estate, and the California trustee could not do that. The Surrogate appointed another successor trustee. He said that the appointive assets could not be used to pay the donee's creditors unless the donee specifically directed that they be so used.

perpetuities or the rule against accumulations is violated in the creation or exercise of a power, a determination has to be made as to what state law is applicable. It is clear that if the appointive asset is land, the law of the jurisdiction where the land is located determines such questions of validity, and the draftsman must make certain that he has complied with the law of that jurisdiction. If, as is usually the case, the appointive asset is not land, the donor's domicile at the time of the creation of the power is likely to be controlling. If the power is created by an inter vivos trust, a manifestation of intention by the donor as to the state law which is to govern the validity of the creation and exercise of powers of appointment, so far as the rule against perpetuities and the rule against accumulations are concerned, may be given effect when the appointive property is to be managed in the jurisdiction whose law is thus chosen. Even if the power is created by a will, it has been recognized that the donor's intent as to governing law will likewise be carried out. In any event, the draftsman should give thought to this matter and consider the desirability of inserting a specific provision to the effect that all questions relating to the validity of the power shall be controlled by the law of a certain state, and that the donee of the power may choose the state that is to govern the validity of interests created by the exercise of the power.

If a trust is established by the donee when he exercises a power, some question may arise as to what state law is to govern the administration of the trust. If the donor has made it clear that the donee is authorized to establish administrative provisions in connection with the exercise of the power and the donee does establish such provisions, no conflicts problem need arise.

AMERIGE v. ATTORNEY GENERAL
324 Mass. 648, 88 N.E.2d 126 (1949)

SPALDING, J.

This is a petition for instructions by the trustees under the will of Mary Elizabeth Williams, late of Hopkinton. The case was heard in the Probate Court on a statement of agreed facts and was reserved and reported to this court without decision. G.L. (Ter. Ed.) c. 215, sec. 13.

The assets in the hands of the trustees, though treated as one fund, are derived from the following sources: property owned by Mary Elizabeth Williams, property which came to her from her father, James Leeds, and personal property and Massachusetts real estate from the estate of her uncle Timothy C. Leeds over which James Leeds had exercised a general testamentary power of appointment. It is with respect to the appointed property from Timothy Leeds's estate that the principal questions for decision have arisen.

Timothy Leeds died a resident of New York May 27, 1864. His will and codicil [177] were duly allowed in a Surrogate's Court in New York and ancillary Probate was granted here by the Probate Court for Suffolk County. By his will Timothy left one half of his property in trust for the benefit of his brother James for life ". . . and upon the decease of the said James, then to hold the said half part to the use of such person or persons and upon such trusts and conditions and for such purposes as he shall by his last will direct and appoint." The will contained an alternative disposition in the event James should die intestate.[178] James Leeds and his children Herbert C. Leeds, Mary Elizabeth Williams and Annie F. Boardman were living at Timothy's death but no child of Mary Elizabeth Williams had then been born.

By Timothy's will James Leeds and Samuel E. Guild, both of Boston, were named trustees. James was also the executor. The will provided that in case of the death or resignation of either of the trustees the persons holding the majority interest of the trust could appoint a successor trustee "subject however to the approval of the person who shall then hold the office of Judge of Probate for the County of Suffolk" in the Commonwealth of Massachusetts. The executor's inventory filed in the Surrogate's Court in New York showed personal property in the amount of $384,700.52. The executor's inventory filed in connection with the ancillary proceedings in Suffolk County disclosed Boston real estate valued at $50,000. The final account of James Leeds as executor and trustee of Timothy's estate was settled by a decree of the Surrogate's Court in New York on January 23, 1869. An accounting for the period October, 1868, to April, 1874, was filed in the Probate Court for Suffolk County.[179] Thereafter accountings of the Timothy Leeds trust were filed in the Probate Court for Suffolk County until the property was "transferred to the trustees . . . (under the will of) James Leeds during the accounting period ending March 2, 1911, and mingled with the general trust" created in James's will.

[177] (*Court footnote*) The codicil is not material to any of the questions presented for decision.

[178] The alternative disposition gave the property to the children of James, the share of a son to be paid to him at age twenty-one and the share of a daughter to be held for her benefit for her life and then to pass as she might appoint by will and, in default of appointment, to her heirs. — Ed.

[179] (*Court footnote*) The record states, "incidental account (was) filed in King's County, New York, as final accounting in that State."

James Leeds died March 22, 1875, a resident of Massachusetts, and his will and three codicils were allowed by the Probate Court for Suffolk County. The first codicil provided in part as follows: "I direct and appoint that the property which my brother Timothy C. Leeds empowered me by his last will and testament, shall be considered and held, in all respects, as part of my own property, and that, when I have bequeathed or devised a proportion or the residue of my estate, the estate of my brother, over which I have the power of appointment, shall be considered and devised and bequeathed as if they were a part of my estates." By the eighth article of his will James left one third of his estate to his trustees for the benefit of his daughter Mary Elizabeth Williams for life and upon her death "to hold the said estates real and personal to the uses of such person or persons as she shall by her last will or any instrument in the nature of one direct and appoint . . . and if she shall die intestate then to hold the said fund to the use of her children and the issue of any deceased children taking by representation." There were gifts over "upon default of such will, children and issue."

At his death James was survived by the following persons: his widow, who died in 1916, his son Herbert, two daughters, Annie Fearing Boardman and Mary Elizabeth Williams, and two grandchildren, Edward Shirley Goddard and Mary Elizabeth Goddard, who were the children of Mary Elizabeth Williams and were born subsequent to the death of Timothy.

Mary Elizabeth Williams died a resident of Massachusetts February 10, 1925, leaving no spouse and survived by her children Edward Shirley and Mary Elizabeth Goddard. She left a will, the seventh article of which provides in part as follows: "My said daughter Mary E. Goddard, and my said son Edward Shirley Goddard, were both born prior to the decease of my father, James Leeds late of Boston, Massachusetts, under whose will I have a power of appointment. All the rest, residue and remainder of my property, of every name and nature, real and personal, and any property over which I have the power of appointment by will, or otherwise, I give, devise and bequeath to the trustee . . . (named herein and their successors) but in trust nevertheless, for the following purposes, namely": to divide the residue into two equal shares and to hold one for each child during his or her life, and then to his or her issue, but in default of such issue, to hold the whole for the life of the survivor, and upon the death of the survivor to his or her issue, but if on the death of the survivor no issue of either be surviving, then to pay over the property discharged of all trusts in equal shares to the following charities:

Rotch's Travelling Scholarship, the Massachusetts Society for the Prevention of Cruelty to Animals, and the Animal Rescue League.

Under the terms of the seventh article as modified by a codicil, the trustees were empowered to pay to each child out of principal a sum not in excess of $10,000.

During the lifetime of Mary Elizabeth Goddard the income of her share of the trust created by the seventh article of her mother's will was paid to her and she also received payments out of principal amounting to $7,000. She died a resident of Boston, May 16, 1940, without issue, leaving a will and codicil.[180]

The trustees under the will of Mary Elizabeth Williams paid one half of the income of the trust to Edward Shirley Goddard until the death of Mary Elizabeth Goddard, and thereafter, until September 30, 1947, he received the entire income thereof. Since that date he has received one half of the income and the remaining income has been held by the trustees pending the outcome of the present proceeding. The trustees have paid to Edward, who is still living, sums out of principal amounting to $10,000.

The principal contentions of the parties interested in the disposition of the fund in question may be summarized as follows: The respondent Waters, who would take through a partial intestacy of Timothy, argues that the law of New York governs with respect to that percentage of the fund which is derived from Timothy's personalty, and accordingly the interests therein appointed after Mary Elizabeth Williams's life estate (namely, the Goddard life estates, the life estate to the survivor, the provision for payment of principal, the remainder to the Goddard issue, and the remainder to the charities) are invalid as violating the New York perpetuities statute; that the Massachusetts law applies to the realty, and by that law the interests after the Goddard life estates are invalid; that the doctrine of capture set forth in Fiduciary

[180] (Court footnote) Article Second of her will contained a recital to the effect that she understood that her mother, Mary Elizabeth Williams, had "a power and/or powers to dispose of certain property under the will of Timothy C. Leeds . . . and under the will of James Leeds . . . and (had) exercised the same under the Seventh Article of her will"; that it had been stated to her that there was some doubt as to the validity of the gifts over to the charitable corporations named in that article; and that she desired to carry out the provisions of that article as far as she was able after the decease of her brother Edward Shirley Goddard. She then went on to provide that "any and all property comprising the Timothy C. Leeds or James Leeds Funds, so called" which she had the right to appoint or dispose of whether it came to her or she had such right "under the will of Timothy C. Leeds and/or the will of James Leeds and/or the will of . . . (her) mother . . . Mary Elizabeth Williams" was to be held in trust to pay the income to Edward Shirley Goddard during his life and at his death to distribute the fund in equal shares to Rotch's Travelling Scholarship, the Massachusetts Society for the Prevention of Cruelty to Animals, and the Animal Rescue League.

Trust Co. v. Mishou, 321 Mass. 615, 624-625, does not apply to any of the interests; that the default clause in the will of James Leeds is not effective; and that the invalidly appointed property must be considered intestate property of Timothy. The Boardman group, who claim in part through Annie F. Boardman (a daughter of James Leeds), contend that the property should be distributed as intestate property of James by treating James as the donor of the power with respect to the personalty, to which the New York law applies, and by treating him as the donee as to the realty, to which Massachusetts law, including the doctrine of capture, applies. Edward Shirley Goddard argues that the law of New York applies to the personalty; that Mary Elizabeth Williams captured this property for her estate; and that there is a resulting trust to her estate. The executors of Mary Elizabeth Williams and of Mary Elizabeth Goddard urge that Massachusetts law determines the validity of the interests sought to be created with respect to both the rule against perpetuities and the consequences of a partially invalid appointment; and that this property was captured by Mary Elizabeth Williams and will go as a resulting trust to her estate. The executor of Mary Elizabeth Goddard contends in the alternative that the property is to go to the issue of Mary Elizabeth Williams by the default clause in James's will. The position of the charitable remaindermen and the guardian ad litem is that under the doctrine of allocation no percentage of the fund now in the hands of the trustees under the will of Mary Elizabeth Williams can be considered as coming from Timothy Leeds and that the appointment of Mary Elizabeth Williams is completely valid.[181]

1. As stated above, Timothy's property over which James and Mary Elizabeth Williams had powers of appointment comprised real estate situated in Massachusetts, and personal property. Questions relating to the validity and effect of the power contained in his will and questions arising out of the exercise of the power, in so far as they concern real estate, must be determined by the law where the real estate is situated. Restatement: Conflict of Laws, Sections 234, 235, 236. Beale, Conflict of Laws, Sections 234.1, 235.1. Sewall v. Wilmer, 132 Mass. 131, 138. Russell v. Joys, 227 Mass. 263, 267. Ligget v. Fidelity & Columbia Trust Co. 274 Ky. 387. Lawrence's Estate, 136 Pa. 354. No contention is made to the contrary. Thus the question whether the exercise of the power created interests in the real estate which are remote under

---

[181] (*Court footnote*) No contention is made by any of the respondents that any of the limitations in the will of Mary Elizabeth Williams are invalid with respect to property owned outright by James or herself.

the rule against perpetuities is to be governed by the law of this Commonwealth rather than by the law of Timothy's domicil, New York. Bundy v. United States Trust Co. 257 Mass. 72, 79. By section 42 of the real property law of New York (N.Y. Consol. Laws, c. 52) limitations extending beyond two lives in being are remote, whereas in Massachusetts the common law rule prevails.

Under the common law rule the interests which Mary Elizabeth Williams attempted to create after the life estates to her children Edward Shirley and Mary Elizabeth Goddard are remote. It is settled in this Commonwealth that "the remoteness of an appointment, made in the exercise of a power to appoint by will alone, so far as affected by the rule against perpetuities must be measured from the time of the creation and not the exercise of the power." Minot v. Paine, 230 Mass. 514, 523. Fiduciary Trust Co. v. Mishou, 321 Mass. 615, 622. The equitable life estate given to James Leeds and that which he gave by the appointment to his daughter Mary Elizabeth Williams were, of course, valid inasmuch as both were lives in being at Timothy's death. The life estates in the appointed property given by Mary Elizabeth Williams to her children Edward Shirley and Mary Elizabeth Goddard were valid since these vested at their mother's death. But the limitations beyond that, namely, those to the issue of the life tenants, the cross remainders, the gifts to the charities and the provisions with respect to payments of principal, were remote. None of these limitations was certain to take effect within twenty-one years from the death of Mary Elizabeth Williams. It is settled that a limitation over which violates the rule against perpetuities "will be considered as stricken out, leaving the prior disposition to operate as if a limitation over had never been made." Greenough v. Osgood, 235 Mass. 235, 242. Lovering v. Worthington, 106 Mass. 86, 88.

We pass now to the question of what disposition is to be made of that percentage of the fund derived from Timothy's real estate which Mary Elizabeth Williams did not properly appoint. The situation is one, we think, where the principle of capture becomes applicable. That principle is that "where the donee of a general power attempts to make an appointment that fails, but where, nevertheless, the donee has manifested an intent wholly to withdraw the appointive property from the operation of the instrument creating the power for all purposes and not merely for the purposes of the invalid appointment, the attempted appointment will commonly be effective to the extent of causing the appointive property to be taken out of the original instrument and to become in effect part of the estate of the donee of the power." Fiduciary

Trust Co. v. Mishou, 321 Mass. 615, 624.   Other cases applying this principle are Dunbar v. Hammond, 234 Mass. 554, Talbot v. Riggs, 287 Mass. 144, and Old Colony Trust Co. v. Allen, 307 Mass. 40.   See Gray, Rule against Perpetuities (4th Ed.) Sec. 540.1. And where, as here, the invalid appointments are in trust there will be a resulting trust to the estate of the donee of the power. Fiduciary Trust Co. v. Mishou, 321 Mass. 615, 624. Restatement: Property, Sec. 365, and Trusts, Sec. 426.   Scott on Trusts, Sec. 426. The complete blending by Mary Elizabeth Williams in her will of the appointive property with that which she owned outright shows her intent to capture the property for her own estate.   Since the remote limitations were in the residuary clause, the property cannot pass under that clause for the reasons which are set forth in Fiduciary Trust Co. v. Mishou, 321 Mass. 615, at pages 626 and 627.

2. With respect to that portion of the fund derived from Timothy's estate which was personal property, questions of considerable difficulty are presented.   At the outset it is necessary to decide what law is to govern.   Ordinarily in the case of personal property questions as to both form and substance relating to the validity and effect of an instrument exercising a power of appointment created by will are determined by the law of the domicil of the donor of the power.   Sewall v. Wilmer, 132 Mass. 131, 136-137. Walker v. Treasurer & Receiver General, 221 Mass. 600, 603. Bundy v. United States Trust Co. 257 Mass. 72, 79.   Hogarth-Swann v. Weed, 274 Mass. 125.   Boston Safe Deposit & Trust Co. v. Prindle, 290 Mass. 577, 581.   Pitman v. Pitman, 314 Mass 465, 470.   See Gray, Rule against Perpetuities (4th Ed.) Sec. 540.2. We are concerned here not with the validity of the instrument exercising the power or whether the power was exercised but rather with the nature and extent of the interests resulting from its exercise.   Whether the principle just stated is applicable here is of importance not only as to whether the New York [182] or Massachusetts rule against perpetuities is to govern but also as to whether the doctrine of capture, discussed above, is applicable.[183]

[182] (*Court footnote*)   See Personal Property Law, N.Y. Consol. Laws, c. 41, Sec. 11.   In New York, as in Massachusetts, for the purpose of applying the rule against perpetuities an appointment is measured from the time when the power is created.   Fargo v. Squiers, 154 N.Y. 250, 259.   Low v. Bankers Trust Co., 270 N.Y. 143, 148.

[183] (*Court footnote*)   Whether the doctrine of capture, as applied in this Commonwealth, obtains in New York is not clear.   We have found no case decided by the Court of Appeals in which the doctrine has been expressly adopted or repudiated.   In one case (Matter of Beaumont, 147 Misc. (N.Y.) 118) the court cites with apparent approval decisions in other jurisdictions which recognize the principle but it does not appear to have applied it. There are decisions, however, where the facts would seem to be such as would

While we do not doubt that the principle stated above is the one
ordinarily to be applied, we are of opinion that it ought not to
govern here. It has been said that the basis for the principle is
that the property subject to the power is considered as belonging
to the donor. See Pitman v. Pitman, 314 Mass. 465, 471. But this
is not always decisive. The intention, express or presumed, of the
donor has also been considered as a factor of importance. Sewall
v. Wilmer, 132 Mass. 131, 137. In Russell v. Joys, 227 Mass. 263,
the question for decision was whether a power of appointment
created by an instrument (an antenuptial agreement) made by a
Massachusetts resident, who was also the donee of the power, was
validly executed by a will admitted to probate in Wisconsin where
the donor-donee was domiciled at her death. In holding that the
question was to be determined by the law of Massachusetts the
court said, "On all the facts we are of opinion that the settlor
manifested an intention to have the trust administered, and the
validity of the appointment determined by the law of Massachusetts" (page 267). As bearing on the question of the donor's intent
the court took into consideration the facts that the donor was
domiciled here when the power was created, that the trustee
resided here, and that the property (originally real estate) was situated here. See also Greenough v. Osgood, 235 Mass. 235; Hutch-
ins v. Browne, 253 Mass. 55, 58. We are aware that the powers
of appointment in Russell v. Joys and Greenough v. Osgood were
contained in trusts created inter vivos and that in such trusts the
intent of the settlor has been accorded particular importance in
determining the choice of law. Wilmington Trust Co. v. Wilmington Trust Co. 26 Del. Ch. 397. Hutchinson v. Ross, 262
N.Y. 381. Land, Trusts in the Conflict of Laws, Section 21.1 and
24. But we think intent also of significance where a testator creates powers of appointment by testamentary trust.

In the case at bar there are several factors which shed light on
the intent of Timothy, the testator-donor. The trustees both were
residents of Massachusetts. One of them, James, was the donee of
the power. A substantial portion of the property consisted of real
estate situated here. Timothy's will provided that the appointment of successor trustees was to be "subject . . . to the approval
of the . . . Judge of Probate for the County of Suffolk" in the
Commonwealth of Massachusetts. We think it plain that he intended the trust to be administered here, as in fact it was. See Restatement: Conflict of Laws, Sec. 298. The trust, therefore, would

---

afford an opportunity for applying the doctrine but the court did not do so.
See Matter of Hayman, 134 Misc. (N.Y.) 803; In re Hellinger's Estate, 83 N.Y.
Sup. (2d) 10; In re Lather's Will, 64 N.Y. Sup. (2d) 757; Guaranty Trust Co.
v. New York Trust Co. 297 N.Y. 45. In none of these cases, however, was the
doctrine discussed.

be administered according to the law of this Commonwealth. Restatement: Conflict of Laws, Sec. 299. See Sewall v. Wilmer, 132 Mass. 131, 137; Codman v. Krell, 152 Mass. 214; Greenough v. Osgood, 235 Mass. 235. It is reasonable to infer that Timothy contemplated that the power given to James would be exercised here. Timothy manifested an intention not only that the trust be administered here and according to our law but also that that law should determine the extent and nature of the interests created by the exercise of the power created by his will.

An analogy furnishing support for the conclusion here reached may be found in cases dealing with testamentary trusts. Ordinarily the validity of a testamentary trust of personal property is determined by the law of the testator's domicil at the time of his death. Fellows v. Miner, 119 Mass. 541. McCurdy v. McCallum, 186 Mass. 464, 468. Restatement: Conflict of Laws, Sec. 295. Beale, Conflict of Laws, Sec. 295.1. But this principle has not been applied invariably. Thus where testamentary trusts of personal property were to be held and administered in a foreign State and were valid in such State but invalid in the State of the testator's domicil they have been upheld. Land, Trusts in the Conflict of Laws, Sections 18 and 19. Chamberlain v. Chamberlain, 43 N.Y. 424. Hope v. Brewer, 136 N.Y. 126. Matter of Sturgis, 164 N.Y. 485. Lanius v. Fletcher, 100 Tex. 550. Matter of Chappell's Estate, 124 Wash. 128. Parkhurst v. Roy, 7 Ont. App. 614. Fordyce v. Bridges, 2 Phil. Ch. 497. See Wilmington Trust Co. v. Wilmington Trust Co. 21 Del. Ch. 188. It is true that in most of these cases charitable trusts were involved but in two of them (Lanius v. Fletcher and Matter of Chappell's Estate) the trusts were not charitable. In some of the decisions the court gave considerable weight to the presumed intent of the testator. In Wilmington Trust Co. v. Wilmington Trust Co., 21 Del. Ch. 188, the rationale of the rule was said to rest "on the principle that since such questions of public policy as are embodied in the rule against perpetuities and in the mortmain statutes can be of legitimate interest only as to property intended to be held in the particular State where the public policy prevails, it becomes a matter of no concern to that State if public policy in another jurisdiction permits property to be received and held under more liberal regulations than in the former" (page 196). We see no reason why on principle the reasoning underlying these cases should not apply to a case like the present involving the exercise of a power of appointment. We hold, therefore, that the interests created by the limitations contained in the will of Mary Elizabeth Williams are to be determined by the law of Massachusetts. It follows that the personalty derived from Timothy's estate is to go as a resulting trust to the executor of the will of Mary Elizabeth Williams, to be distributed as intestate property. By applying the principle of capture this result would be reached under either the Massachusetts or the New York rule against perpetuities.

3. The charities, as noted above, advance the argument that none of the property appointed by Mary Elizabeth Williams is derived from property of Timothy. They invoke the principle that where the donee of a general power of appointment disposes of owned and appointive property as a single fund the appointive property is allocated to the various dispositions of such fund in such manner as to give the maximum effect to such dispositions. That principle is recognized by our decisions (Stone v. Forbes, 189 Mass. 163, 170-171; Minot v. Paine, 230 Mass. 514, 525) and by the American Law Institute in Sec. 363 of the Restatement: Property. Thus, it is argued, James Leeds dealt with his own and the appointive property as a single fund and to give the maximum effect to his dispositions the debts, expenses, legacies and residuary gifts must be charged against the appointive property and if this is done that property is exhausted and there is no property of Timothy remaining which Mary Elizabeth Williams could appoint. But that principle is not applicable here. In the case at bar there were successive donees of the power created by Timothy, James Leeds and Mary Elizabeth Williams. The appointments which violate the rule against perpetuities were made by Mary Elizabeth Williams, the second donee. None of the appointments made by James is invalid and no contention is made to the contrary. In all of the cases we have seen where the principle of allocation has been applied the valid and invalid dispositions have been made by the same person in the same will. To give the maximum effect to such dispositions under the principle of allocation the law is attempting to carry out the presumed intent of the testator. The doctrine ought not to be applied in the case of successive donees where the dispositions of the first donee are valid and those of the second invalid. It cannot reasonably be said that James contemplated that Mary Elizabeth Williams would exercise the power improperly with the result that he must be presumed to have intended that his dispositions be charged against the appointive property.

4. It becomes necessary to determine what proportion of the fund in question can be considered as having come from Timothy's estate. The respondents are not in agreement on this question. The following is stated in the stipulation of agreed facts: "The correct mathematical computation of the proportion of the funds in the hands of the trustee . . . (under the will of) Mary E. Williams derived from the various sources, tracing the specific assets specified in the foregoing paragraphs and striking proportions

in a general fund at each point indicated above at which funds were mingled, is as follows:

> Property of —
> Mary E. Williams 16%
> James Leeds 31%
> Timothy C. Leeds
>   Real Estate 6%
>   Personal Property 47%
>   100%"

The stipulation then states that "With regard to the foregoing computation the parties hereto admit only . . . (its) mathematical correctness . . . and do not admit that the method followed in making . . . (it) is correct as a matter of law." Some of the respondents urge that the appointive property ought to be determined on the basis of the foregoing percentages. Others, especially the charities, contend that these percentages are improper and suggest different ones.[184] The percentages arrived at by the charities are obtained by computing what percentage of the fund in question at the time of Mary Elizabeth Williams's death was owned by her outright. As to the balance they have figured the proportion of James's property and that which came from Timothy's estate on the basis of ratios which one bore to the other as of the death of James. In support of this position they rely on Fiduciary Trust Co. v. Mishou, 321 Mass. 615, 632-633. In the Mishou case the property owned by Mrs. Parker and the appointive property coming from the trust established in 1851 were mingled and became one fund shortly after Mrs. Parker's death in 1878. It was held that the proportions of owned and appointive funds should be established in so far as they could be traced, as of the time that they were mingled. Here the fund owned by James and that coming from Timothy's estate were held separately until the accounting period ending in 1911, when they were merged. Applying the principle of the Mishou case to the facts here, we are of opinion that the proportion of the fund attributable to Timothy's estate now held by the trustees of Mary Elizabeth Williams ought to be determined, if possible, on the basis of percentages fixed as of that time. No better method appears to be available. The percentages contained in the stipulation apparently were not established in that manner and on this record we

[184] *(Court footnote)* The suggested percentages are:

> Property of —
> Mary Elizabeth Williams 22.911%
> James Leeds . . . . , ...   40.812%
> Timothy C. Leeds 36.277%

are in no position to make the computation. The case, therefore, should be remanded to the Probate Court in order that the proportions be established by the method just outlined. In determining these proportions the debts, expenses and legacies ought to be chargeable against each fund on a pro rata basis. Fiduciary Trust Co. v. Mishou, 321 Mass. 615, 633. For the reasons set forth in the Mishou case there is no occasion here to apply the principle of exoneration illustrated by Tuell v. Hurley, 206 Mass. 65. The debts, expenses and legacies of Mary Elizabeth Williams ought also to be charged against each fund on a pro rata basis in computing the amount of appointive property in her estate.

5. Finally it has been argued that the payments of principal to Mary Elizabeth and Edward Shirley Goddard amounting in all to $17,000 should be treated as having been paid out of property other than that derived from Timothy's estate under the doctrine of allocation. But we are of opinion that that doctrine is not applicable. It is true, of course, that as to Timothy's property the limitations as to these payments were remote because measured from the creation of Timothy's power they might take effect more than twenty-one years after the death of Mary Elizabeth Williams, the last life in being. But in the view that we take of the case allocation is not necessary to save the payments. Edward Shirley and Mary Elizabeth Goddard became entitled to the appointive property as heirs and next of kin of Mary Elizabeth Williams at her death. Consequently, since they own the entire interest in that property, the payments of principal to them were not improper. Had they not become entitled to the property by reason of the resulting trusts a different question would be presented.

The case is remanded to the Probate Court for further proceedings in conformity with this opinion and the trustees are to be instructed in accordance therewith. Costs and expenses of appeal are to be in the discretion of the Probate Court.

So ordered.[185]

[185] See comments on Amerige v. Attorney General in 50 Colum. L. Rev. 239 (1950) and 63 Harv. L. Rev. 699 (1950).

For an annotation which considers the conflict of laws as to the exercise of powers of appointment, see 150 A.L.R. 519 (1944). For a statute which appears to recognize that when the testator intends the trust to be administered in and subject to the laws of the jurisdiction in which the selected trustee resides, such intent will be given effect, see Fla. Stat. §737.02 (1959).

The following statutes recognize that where a nonresident decedent provides in his will that testamentary dispositions of tangible or intangible property having a situs within the state should be construed and regulated by the laws of such state, the provision shall be given effect: Ill. Rev. Stat., c. 3, §241(b) (1959); N.Y. Decedent Estate Law §47.

Boston Safe Deposit and Trust Co. v. Alfred University, 339 Mass. 82, 157 N.E.2d 662 (1959), holds that Massachusetts has jurisdiction in regard to a trust where the trust was established by the will of a Florida decedent who named as the trustee a Massachusetts corporate fiduciary. — Ed.

CHAPTER XIII

The Marital Deduction

The consideration of the marital deduction in an estate plan is introduced at this point (immediately following the development of powers of appointment) because the most frequently employed marital deduction gift involves a general power of appointment. Marital deduction gifts, however, do not always involve a general power of appointment.

1. SOME HISTORICAL OBSERVATIONS

Prior to the Revenue Act of 1948, it was unwise from a tax standpoint (although it may have been wise from other standpoints) for a husband to make a gift to his wife in his will in such a form that the value of the gift would be includible in his wife's gross estate for federal estate tax purposes on her death (throughout this chapter the discussion will relate to a gift from a husband to his wife although what is said will be equally applicable in regard to a gift from a wife to her husband). The reason, of course, was that the subject matter of such a gift would be taxed in the husband's estate on his death and taxed again in his wife's estate on her subsequent death if she outlived him by five years. The natural tendency, therefore, in the pre-1948 era was for the husband to make a gift to his wife in his will in such a form that, on her death subsequent to his death, the subject matter of the gift could pass to his descendants without the imposition of an additional estate tax.

There were tax reasons in the pre-1948 era, however, which induced a husband to make an inter vivos gift to his wife in such a form that the value of the subject matter of the gift was removed from his gross estate for federal estate tax purposes, even though it thereby became includible in his wife's gross estate. Such an inter vivos gift would split the family wealth between him and his wife and during their joint lives the total income tax payable would be less than if he kept all the income-producing wealth. Such splitting also reduced the total estate tax payable as a result of their deaths. Normally the gift tax costs were worth sustaining to accomplish the income and estate tax savings.

The Revenue Act of 1948, which brought into existence the marital deduction with respect to both the federal estate tax and the federal gift tax and also introduced the split-income provisions of the federal income tax (when husband and wife file a joint return), required the tax thinking in the field of estate planning, so far as gifts from a husband to his wife are concerned, to be completely revised. In the post-1948 era it is frequently desirable from a tax standpoint for a husband to make a gift to his wife in his will in such a form that the value of the gift will be includible in his wife's gross estate for federal estate tax purposes on her death. It may be undesirable taxwise now for a husband to make inter vivos gifts to his wife, because no income tax savings result therefrom during their joint lives, and if his wife survives him, a gift to her in his will produces the desired estate tax savings.

Prior to 1942, the donee of a general power of appointment was treated as the owner of the appointive assets for federal estate tax purposes only if he exercised the power. In the pre-1942 era, therefore, general powers were frequently created, but exercised only if there was a good reason to do so. The donee of a general power of appointment created after October 21, 1942, however, is treated as the owner of the appointive assets for federal estate tax purposes whether he exercises the power or not. In fact, from 1942 to the Powers of Appointment Act of 1951, the donee of all powers, general or special, was so treated unless the power was narrowly restricted so as to come within the definition in the Internal Revenue Code of an exempt power. Thus from 1942 to the Revenue Act of 1948, only the narrowly restricted exempt powers were created unless special circumstances overcame the tax considerations. In 1948, however, with the introduction of the marital deduction, the general power of appointment came back into popularity when a husband made a gift in trust to his wife (since the enactment of the 1954 Code the gift may be of a legal life interest), even though thereby the appointive assets became a part of her gross estate for federal estate tax purposes. The narrowly restricted exempt power continued until 1951 as the type of power created in connection with nonmarital deduction gifts. The 1951 act did not affect the tax desirability of using the general power of appointment in connection with a marital deduction gift from a husband to his wife but allowed a person to create a broader power of appointment in a donee (one entitling the donee to appoint to anyone but himself, his estate, his creditors and creditors of his estate) without causing the appointive assets to be includible in the donee's gross estate for federal estate tax purposes.[1]

[1] Powers of appointment are considered in detail in Chapter XII.

2.   ESTATE TAX MARITAL DEDUCTION CONTRASTED WITH GIFT TAX MARITAL DEDUCTION

a. *Amount of Deduction*

A marital deduction is allowed in connection with both the federal estate tax and the federal gift tax. If an inter vivos gift is made by a husband to his wife in a form which satisfies the requirements for the gift tax marital deduction, one half of the value of the gift is allowed as a deduction in computing the net gifts made to the wife for that year.[2] In other words, one half of the value of the gift is regarded for gift tax purposes as having been owned by the wife before the husband made the gift to her. Thus, if a husband makes an outright inter vivos gift to his wife of $6000, he is only making a gift to her for federal gift tax purposes of $3000.[3]

The estate tax marital deduction is available with respect to all gifts by a husband to his wife, inter vivos or testamentary, which are in a form that satisfies the requirements for the estate tax marital deduction, if the value of such gifts is includible in the husband's gross estate for federal estate tax purposes.[4] The maximum allowable deduction, however, is 50 percent of the adjusted gross estate of the husband.[5]

The husband's adjusted gross estate is computed by subtracting from his gross estate the aggregate amount of deductions allowed by Sections 2053 and 2054 of the 1954 Code.[6] Some items deductible under Sections 2053 and 2054 may also meet the test of items deductible from the gross income of the estate for federal income tax purposes.[7] A double deduction is avoided by not permitting

---

[2] The gift tax marital deduction is not available if the husband is a nonresident noncitizen. See 1954 I.R.C. §2523(a), quoted infra page 1425.

[3] Special rules are established with respect to the operation of the gift tax marital deduction in connection with community property. See the discussion of community property at page 426 supra.

[4] See 1954 I.R.C. §2056(a), quoted infra page 1407.

[5] See 1954 I.R.C. §2056(c)(1), quoted infra page 1409.

[6] Quoted infra page 1403.
See 1954 I.R.C. §2056(c)(2)(A), quoted infra page 1409. Special rules are established for determining the adjusted gross estate when community property is involved. See the discussion of community property at page 426 supra.
Revenue Ruling 60-247, I.R.B. 1960-29, 17, points out that an estate tax deduction will not be allowed under 1954 I.R.C. §2053 for claims against a decedent's estate which have not been paid or will not be paid because the creditor waives payment, fails to file his claim as required by law, or otherwise fails to enforce payment. This ruling is relevant in determining a decedent's adjusted gross estate.

[7] Some of the expenses of administration (expenses of administration are

amounts allowable under Sections 2053 and 2054 as a deduction in computing the decedent's taxable estate for estate tax purposes to be taken as a deduction in computing the taxable income of the decedent's estate unless the right to take them as estate tax deductions is waived.[8] The husband's adjusted gross estate obviously will be affected as to its amount by whether his executor elects to take certain deductions as income or estate tax deductions.[9] Any action which raises or lowers the adjusted gross estate likewise raises or lowers the maximum allowable estate tax marital deduction because it will always be one half of whatever turns out to be the amount of the adjusted gross estate.[10]

Even though the maximum allowable estate tax marital deduction is affected by action of the executor which affects the amount of the adjusted gross estate, the total amount of the gifts to the wife which qualify for the deduction will not be affected by such action unless a formula is used which keys the total amount of such gifts to such maximum. For example, if a bequest is made to the wife in the amount of $100,000, the amount of this bequest as an estate tax marital deduction gift will remain the same whether the executor elects to treat certain deductions as income tax deductions or estate tax deductions. Likewise, where the wife is given one half of the residue, the valuation of that one half for estate tax marital deduction purposes is unaffected by how certain deductions are taken.[11] Where a formula is used to describe what passes to the wife and the formula is designed to produce the maximum allowable estate tax marital deduction, then the executor's deci-

---

deductible for estate tax purposes under §2053) may be expenses incurred for the production or collection of income or for the management, conservation or maintenance of property held for the production of income. Such expenses are deductible for income tax purposes under 1954 I.R.C. §212, quoted infra page 1336. See also 1954 I.R.C. §162, dealing with the deduction of expenses incurred in connection with carrying on a trade or business, which is allowed for income tax purposes.

[8] See 1954 I.R.C. §642(g), quoted infra page 1363.

[9] Assume that the husband's gross estate is $200,000 and §2053 deductions total $20,000, and of this amount $10,000 can be taken as an income tax deduction. If $5000 of the available $10,000 is used as an income tax deduction, the adjusted gross estate will be $185,000; whereas, if the entire $20,000 is taken as an estate tax deduction, the adjusted gross estate will be $180,000.

[10] See Rev. Rul. 55-643, 1955-2 C.B. 386 (dealing with the 1954 Code), and Rev. Rul. 55-225, 1955-1 C.B. 460 (dealing with the 1939 Code), both of which hold that the adjusted gross estate is determined by subtracting from the gross estate only the deductions actually taken under §§2053 and 2054. In accord is Estate of Walker P. Inman, N.Y.L.J., Dec. 15, 1959, p. 14 (N.Y. County Surr.). See also Bernstein, An Executor May Increase the Marital Deduction, 42 A.B.A.J. 577 (1956).

[11] In Estate of Newton B. T. Roney, 33 T.C. 801 (1960), the decedent's

sion actually affects what the wife is entitled to receive as an original matter under the disposition.

The executor is faced with a difficult decision when a formula estate tax marital deduction gift is involved and he must choose whether to take certain deductions as income or estate tax deductions. Where the residue is placed in trust, the decision may have its difficulties, even if no formula marital deduction gift is involved, because the effect of taking administration expenses as an income tax deduction may be to increase the estate taxes payable out of the principal of the estate and thereby to reduce what will eventually pass to the remainderman under the residuary trust. The question presented is whether an adjustment of some kind must be made between estate beneficiaries when the effect of the executor's election is to benefit one beneficiary at the expense of another. Some courts have so held.[12]

---

widow was residuary legatee, and as executrix of his estate she took certain administration expenses as an income tax deduction. In the estate tax return she claimed a marital deduction based on the value of the residuary estate, without any reduction for the administration expenses taken as an income tax deduction. The court held that administration expenses chargeable under state law to the residue had to be deducted in computing the value of the residue for marital deduction purposes, even though such expenses were properly taken as an income tax deduction.

In Estate of Edward H. Luehrmann, 33 T.C. 277 (1959), the decedent bequeathed the residue of his estate in trust, and under the trust the net income was to be paid to a named person for life and then the principal was to go to a charity. The executors claimed deductions for administration expenses on the estate's income tax return (see §642(g)) and accordingly waived their right to deduct them in computing the decedent's estate taxes. Under these circumstances, what is the value of the charitable remainder which is deductible for estate tax purposes? The court held that the administration expenses must be deducted from residue to determine the property in which the charity had a remainder interest. In other words, the value of the charitable remainder is not affected by the taking of administration expenses as an income tax deduction. The case was affirmed in 61-1 U.S.T.C. ¶11994 (8th Cir. 1961).

See also Rev. Rul. 55-225, 1955-1 C.B. 460, which points out that the executor's election to treat certain administration expenses as an income tax deduction is disregarded in determining the net value of the marital deduction gift to the surviving spouse.

[12] See Estate of Edwin H. Warms, 140 N.Y.S.2d 169 (N.Y. County Surr. Ct. 1955); Estate of Fred H. Bixby, 140 Cal. App. 2d 326, 295 P.2d 68 (1956).

In In re Samuel Levy's Estate, 9 Misc. 2d 561, 167 N.Y.S.2d 16 (1957), the executor elected to claim as deductions from estate income certain administration expenses which normally would have been available as estate tax deductions. The election increased the estate tax by over $7000 but produced an over-all tax saving of $25,000. The court, following the Warms case, directed the executor to credit the principal account with the estate tax saving which the principal would have enjoyed had the administration expenses been deducted from the estate corpus rather than from the estate income. In this case the testator made a pecuniary formula gift to his wife. The amount re-

Consideration should be given to the desirability of inserting in the will instructions to the executor in regard to the manner in which deductions should be taken when they may be taken either as income or estate tax deductions, and in regard to any adjustments which should be made between beneficiaries.[13]   In general, it would seem undesirable to dictate too rigidly the course of action which the executor should follow.[14]

---

ceived by his wife was increased because of the fact that the administration expenses were taken as an income tax deduction rather than as an estate tax deduction.   The court held that the estate tax deductions should not be credited to the widow's bequest, since it was freed of tax, and that the benefit of all deductions which would have been available to the estate principal should be credited to the residuary estate.

[13] In Fleming, From Peter to Paul, 96 Trusts & Estates 1089 (1957), there is a discussion of the adjustments which may be required if administration expenses are taken as income tax deductions.   The author suggests that consideration be given to the inclusion in the will of the following provision:

"I direct my executor to claim any expenses of administration of my estate as income tax deductions upon an income tax return or returns whenever in his sole judgment such action will achieve an over-all reduction in the income and death taxes for the benefit of my estate and of the income beneficiary or beneficiaries thereof.   I further direct that no compensating adjustments between income and principal or in the amount of the bequest under Article . . . [the formula bequest] shall be required or made as a result of such action."

As has been pointed out, when a formula marital deduction gift is used, the amount which passes to the wife is increased by any decision of the executor that increases the value of the decedent's adjusted gross estate.   If an executor was instructed to give the decedent's wife either $100,000 or $200,000 but he was given discretion to decide which amount the wife would receive, a marital deduction would be allowed for only $100,000, even though the executor decided to give the wife $200,000.   Otherwise a deduction would be permitted with respect to an amount that was within the power of a person other than the wife to divert from her, and as to the amount which could be so diverted the wife would have a terminable interest.   The power in the executor to affect the amount passing to the wife under a formula gift by taking certain estate tax deductions as income tax deductions and thereby increasing the adjusted gross estate might at first be thought to be a power to divert from the wife part of what finally passes to her: that is, the part which would not have passed to her if the deductions had been taken as estate tax deductions with the resultant decrease in the adjusted gross estate. This power in the executor is given by the terms of the Revenue Code itself and, like other powers created by operation of law, should not disqualify for the marital deduction any part of the gift to the wife.   Revenue Ruling 55-643, 1955-2 C.B. 386, agrees with this statement, saying, "The value of the interest which actually passes to the surviving spouse [under a formula gift] should not be reduced by the amounts of those items which are not allowed as deductions under section 2053."

[14] For a discussion of the relevant factors in determining whether an executor should take certain administration expenses as estate or income tax deductions, see Bronston, Income Tax Returns by an Executor, 43 Ill. B.J. 134 (1954).

In Rev. Rul. 240, 1953-2 C.B. 79, it is stated that a fiduciary managing a decedent's estate may hold off determining whether to deduct administration expenses on the estate tax return or on the income tax return for the full

PROBLEM

13.1. H makes the following outright inter vivos gifts:
   a. $10,000 to his wife
   b. $10,000 to his son
   c. $10,000 to his daughter
   d. $10,000 to the X charity

The inter vivos gifts are made by H just prior to his death and are obviously gifts in contemplation of death. On the date of his death the property owned by H consists solely of securities and is valued at $200,000. The value one year after H's death is the same. The deductions allowed by Sections 2053 and 2054 (funeral expenses, expenses of administration, debts, etc.) total $20,000. H's will gives all his property outright to his wife. What is the maximum allowable estate tax marital deduction in determining H's taxable estate for federal estate tax purposes?

b. *Relevant Factors in Choosing Between Estate Tax Marital Deduction Gifts and Gift Tax Marital Deduction Gifts*

The estate tax marital deduction is available only if the wife survives the husband. By making gift tax marital deduction gifts to his wife the husband can make certain that his taxable estate for estate tax purposes is reduced whether his wife survives him or not. Of course, he may have to pay some gift taxes to place approximately one half of his estate in his wife's estate by making gift tax marital deduction gifts, whereas if his wife survives him, he can place approximately one half of his estate in his wife's estate, without any estate tax thereon, by making estate tax marital deduction gifts.

It must be kept in mind that if gift tax marital deduction gifts are made to a wife, she does not get a new basis for the purpose of determining a capital gain in the event of a sale of the subject matter of the gift,[15] whereas she does get a new basis for such a purpose

---

limitation period. In other words, the fiduciary can wait until the estate tax has been computed and then determine whether the administration expenses should be taken as a deduction in the estate tax return or as a deduction under the income tax returns previously filed. If he decides to take the administration expenses as an income tax deduction, he will file the necessary waiver and a refund claim.

[15] Any gift tax that is paid may increase the basis. See 1954 I.R.C. §1015, quoted infra page 1383.

when the husband makes the gift to her by way of an estate tax marital deduction gift.[16]

3.   DESIRABILITY OF EQUALING OR EXCEEDING THE MAXIMUM ALLOWABLE ESTATE TAX MARITAL DEDUCTION

An analysis must be made of the present gross estates of the husband and his wife in order to determine the extent to which marital deduction gifts may be advantageous from a tax standpoint. If the wife's present gross estate equals or exceeds that of the husband, it must be kept in mind that while a marital deduction gift by him to her will reduce the estate taxes on his death, the value of such a gift will be added to the wife's gross estate and the total estate tax as a result of both of their deaths may be higher than if the husband had not made the marital deduction gift.

Even though the wife's gross estate equals or exceeds that of the husband, it may be proper to make marital deduction gifts to her because the resulting reduction in estate taxes payable on the husband's death will make available to his wife, during the period that she survives him, a larger portion of his estate than would otherwise be the case. If the wife's age and health are such that she is likely to survive the husband by a substantial period of time, her welfare may require that the maximum amount of his estate be available to her, even though she has an estate of her own equal to or in excess of his.

Furthermore, if the wife's age and health are such that she is likely to survive him by a substantial period of time, it may be desirable to make marital deduction gifts to her, even though her gross estate equals or exceeds his, on the theory that she will be able over the years to reduce her gross estate, at least to the extent the husband increases it, by inter vivos gifts within the allowable gift tax annual exclusion and within her over-all $30,000 gift tax exemption.

In determining whether to make marital deduction gifts to the wife, some thought must also be given to possible increases in her gross estate from other sources. It may be that she is likely to inherit substantial amounts from her parents and, if so, it may under all the circumstances be unwise from a tax standpoint to increase her gross estate by gifts from the husband. It should not be concluded that merely because the wife's parents are wealthy and she is likely to survive her parents, her gross estate will be in-

---

[16] See 1954 I.R.C. §1014, quoted infra page 1381.

creased. The wills of her parents may confer benefits on her in a manner that will not increase her gross estate. In other words, if an intelligent decision is to be reached in regard to the appropriateness of making marital deduction gifts to the wife, it may be highly desirable to find out what the wills of her parents provide.

If the husband makes estate tax marital deduction gifts to his wife in excess of the marital deduction allowance, he is increasing her gross estate by the amount of the excess without getting a deduction of that amount in determining his own taxable estate. Under the 1939 Code, double taxation in rapid succession might result as to such excess because the five-year moratorium with respect to property previously taxed did not apply to gifts from a husband to his wife (or vice versa).[17] The credit for taxes on prior transfers established by the 1954 Code,[18] however, does apply to gifts from a husband to his wife (or vice versa), and therefore, the likelihood of double taxation in rapid succession as to such excess is diminished.[19]

PROBLEM

13.2. If the wife has an estate of her own, when would it be appropriate to determine the amount of the marital deduction gift to her by a provision somewhat as follows?

"I direct that an appraisal be made to determine the value of my wife's adjusted gross estate as of the time of my death, and the amount (of the marital deduction gift) shall equal one half the excess of my adjusted gross estate over her adjusted gross estate as thus appraised."

4. DESCRIBING THE AMOUNT OF THE ESTATE TAX MARITAL DEDUCTION GIFT

The amount of the estate tax marital deduction gift, when the gift is other than of specific property, can be expressed in terms of

---

[17] See 1939 I.R.C. §812(c). Partial relief was granted in 1956 by the addition of §814 to the 1939 Code.

If the husband owned property previously taxed and used it to make up the whole or part of a marital deduction gift, what affect would this have on the deduction for property previously taxed under the 1939 Code? This matter is considered in Roth v. Welch, 183 F. Supp. 559 (S.D. Ohio, 1960).

[18] See §2013, quoted infra page 1391.

[19] It must be kept in mind, however, that the excess referred to in the text may be taxed in the husband's estate at a lower rate than when it is added to the wife's estate and, in such a case, the credit does not offset the tax in the wife's estate, so that in a real sense there is double taxation in rapid succession.

either a pecuniary gift or a fractional share of some designated fund. If the objective is to make a gift which, when added to other qualified gifts, will equal the maximum allowable deduction, the amount, whether expressed in terms of a pecuniary gift or in terms of a fractional share of some designated fund, must be determined with reference to a formula based upon the language of the Internal Revenue Code.[20] Otherwise, the value of the gift can only approximate what is needed to exhaust the deduction. So many variables affect the size of the adjusted gross estate that it will be entirely accidental if any estimated amount is precisely the sum needed.

The following are examples of various methods of expressing, in a will, the amount of a marital deduction gift:

1. Non-formula pecuniary gift

If my wife survives me, I give the sum of one hundred thousand dollars ($100,000) to . . .

COMMENTS

The non-formula pecuniary gift may be made outright to the wife or to a trust which qualifies for the estate tax marital deduction. In the absence of a contrary manifestation of intent, an outright pecuniary legacy does not earn interest for the beneficiary for some period of time, usually one year, after the testator's death.[21] A gift of $100,000 to be paid one year from date of death, without interest in the meantime, may not be deemed to be worth $100,000 for estate tax marital deduction purposes.[22] Thus consideration should be given to the inclusion of a provision to the effect that interest on the pecuniary legacy shall be payable from the date of the husband's death when the pecuniary legacy is an outright estate tax marital deduction gift. If the pecuniary legacy is payable to an estate tax marital deduction trust, however, the legacy is deemed to include income from the date of the testator's death in the absence of a contrary manifestation of intent, and thus

---

[20] If the gift made to the surviving spouse by will is 50 percent of the adjusted gross estate, the total amount passing to her will exceed the maximum allowable marital deduction if the gross estate of the deceased husband includes non-probate items which pass to his wife in a form that qualifies for the marital deduction. In King v. Citizens and Southern National Bank of Atlanta, 103 So.2d 689 (Fla. 1958), the court refused to construe such a bequest as one subject to being reduced by the non-probate items which passed to the wife and also held it was a general pecuniary legacy.

[21] See the discussion of pecuniary legacies at page 271 supra.

[22] See Reg. §20.2056(b)-4(a), quoted infra page 1534.

the valuation problem suggested with respect to the outright pecuniary legacy is not present.[23]

A non-formula pecuniary gift may originate in a revocable inter vivos trust as of the death of the settlor-husband and may be made payable outright to the settlor's wife or may be placed in a trust which, as of the husband's death, qualifies as an estate tax marital deduction trust.

If the property available to satisfy the pecuniary gifts is not sufficient to satisfy all of them, each one will abate proportionately unless the testator indicates otherwise. Will the fact that one of the pecuniary legacies is intended to be an estate tax marital deduction gift be enough to justify finding an intent on the part of the testator that it not abate along with the other pecuniary gifts?[24]

2. *Formula pecuniary gift*

If my wife survives me, I give to . . . the following:

An amount equal to the maximum estate tax marital deduction (allowable in determining the federal estate tax payable by reason of my death) minus the value for federal estate tax purposes of all items in my gross estate for federal estate tax purposes which qualify for said deduction and which pass or have passed from me to my said wife (the words "pass or have passed" shall have the same meaning as such words shall have under the provisions of the Internal Revenue Code in effect at the time of my death) under other provisions of this will, by right of survivorship with respect to jointly owned property, under settlement arrangements relating to life insurance proceeds, or otherwise than under this bequest. In making the computations necessary to determine the amount of this pecuniary estate tax marital deduction gift, values as finally determined for federal estate tax purposes shall control.

COMMENTS

The comments under the non-formula pecuniary gift are also applicable to the formula pecuniary gift.

The formula pecuniary gift starts off initially with a dollar amount equal to the maximum estate tax marital deduction, that

---

[23] See the discussion of pecuniary legacies at page 271 supra.

[24] In Estate of Joseph Goldman, 4 Misc. 2d 31, 153 N.Y.S.2d 140 (1956), the court held that all legacies abated pro rata, even though one was a marital deduction gift. Compare, however, In re Lewis' Will, 115 N.Y.S.2d 791 (1952).

is, a dollar amount equal to one half of the husband's adjusted gross estate. This amount must be reduced by other gifts to the wife which qualify for the estate tax marital deduction if the aggregate of deductible gifts is not to exceed the maximum deduction allowable.[25]

The husband's estate may be of such size that the maximum allowable marital deduction, when added to other deductions and the $60,000 estate tax exemption, will be more than is needed to eliminate the husband's taxable estate. If the wife has an estate of her own, it may be unwise to augment her gross estate by a greater amount than is necessary to eliminate the husband's taxable estate. In such a situation the following clause might be added to the formula pecuniary gift: "If the above-described amount is more than is necessary (along with credits, the exemption and other deductions) to eliminate any federal estate tax with respect to my gross estate, then the above-described amount shall be reduced so that it is equal in amount to the estate tax marital deduction that is necessary to eliminate such federal estate tax."

3. *Non-formula fractional share gift of the residue*

If my said wife survives me, I give to . . . one half ($\frac{1}{2}$) of my residuary estate.

COMMENTS

The described fractional share of the testator's residuary estate may be given outright to the wife or to a trust that qualifies for the estate tax marital deduction. In either case, since a gift of a share of the residue is involved, the beneficiary is entitled to the portion of estate income earned from the date of the testator's death that corresponds to the beneficiary's share of the residue, unless some other intent is manifested.[26]

---

[25] If the deceased spouse has made inter vivos gifts to the surviving spouse and they are held to be in contemplation of death, they will reduce the amount of the formula pecuniary gift if they are in a form which qualifies them for the marital deduction. See Matter of Clifford S. Walsh, N.Y.L.J., Aug. 6, 1958, p. 5 (Westchester County Surr. Ct.).

In Estate of John P. Hoelzel, 28 T.C. 384 (1957), the formula used required the reduction of one half of the adjusted gross estate by the portions of the decedent's gross estate which passed to his wife but did not constitute a part of his estate at his death. This language required the reduction of one half of the adjusted gross estate by the value of a life interest given to the wife under annuity and insurance contracts, even though such a life interest in the wife did not qualify for the marital deduction. In valuing the life interest, however, the court permitted the wife's actual life expectancy to be taken into consideration because of the fact that she had cancer.

[26] See the discussion of residuary gifts at page 80 supra.

A fractional share gift may be carved out of the trust fund in a revocable inter vivos trust as of the date of the settlor's death. The designated fractional share of the trust fund may be payable outright to the wife or may be placed in a trust which, as of the date of the settlor's death, qualifies for the estate tax marital deduction.

The residue against which the described fraction is to be applied may be defined in various ways. The significance of one definition as compared with another is considered later.[27]

4. *Formula fractional share gift of the residue*

If my said wife survives me, I give to . . . the following described fractional share of my residuary estate:

The numerator of the fraction shall be the maximum estate tax marital deduction (allowable in determining the federal estate tax payable by reason of my death) minus the value for federal estate tax purposes of all items in my gross estate which qualify for said deduction and which pass or have passed from me to my said wife (the words "pass or have passed" shall have the same meaning as such words shall have under the provisions of the Internal Revenue Code in effect at the time of my death) under other provisions of this will, by right of survivorship with respect to jointly owned property, under settlement arrangements relating to life insurance proceeds, or otherwise than under this fractional share gift of my residuary estate (in computing the numerator, the values as finally determined for federal estate tax purposes shall control); and the denominator of the fraction shall be the value of my residuary estate, and to the extent that the items initially in my residuary estate are included in my gross estate, the value at which they are included in my gross estate shall control, and to the extent they are not so included, their value at the time they would have been valued if they had been so included shall control in determining the denominator. When distribution is made, there shall be distributed the above-described fractional share of my residuary estate without regard to whether the total value of what is distributed is more or less than the numerator of the above-described fraction.

[27] With regard to defining the fund against which the fraction is to be applied, see the discussion at page 797 infra.

COMMENTS

The comments under the non-formula fractional share gift are also applicable to the formula fractional share gift.

It should be noted that a formula fractional share, as well as a formula pecuniary amount, might not be definitively determined within the period of the applicable rule against perpetuities because the federal estate tax proceedings might not have been concluded within that period. Will this fact result in a trust being invalid where the amount placed in trust is described as a fractional share of the residue? This fact relates only to the quantum of the estate which is subject to the trust and has nothing to do with the vesting of interests under the trust. If every interest under the trust must vest within the required time, the mere fact that the quantum of the interest might conceivably be ascertained beyond the period of the rule should not cause any violation of the rule. It is conceivable that the quantum of the interest of any taker under a residuary gift in a will might not be definitively ascertained within the period of the rule against perpetuities because the quantum going to such a taker normally depends upon the taxes and debts which are payable. Thus, if the quantum of an interest that vests in time also must be certain to be ascertained within the period of the rule, all residuary gifts under a will would be invalid.[28]

The residuary estate against which the fraction is to be applied may include property not in the husband's gross estate. Foreign realty and certain appointive assets included in the residue would be of this character. In the determination of the denominator, the language of the formula fractional share gift set out above calls for the valuation of such property as it would have been valued if it had been in the husband's gross estate.[29]

The words "items initially in my residuary estate" which are to be valued at gross estate values to determine the denominator may need some explanation. Such items are the ones which go to make up the residuary estate as it is initially constituted. A sale by the executor of an item in the original residue and a reinvestment of the proceeds of the sale will not change the items in the

---

[28] See 6 American Law of Property §24.23 (Casner ed 1952, Supp. 1960). In Connecticut a statute was enacted in 1953 which states that fractional share gifts do not violate the rule against perpetuities. See Conn. Gen. Stat. Rev. §45-174 (1958).

[29] Property in the residue which is not includible in the husband's gross estate should be excluded in allocating residuary property to make up the marital share. See the discussion at page 824 infra.

residue for the purpose of determining the denominator. If the sale is made during the first year following the husband's death, and the alternate valuation date is selected, the value of the item on the date it is sold will be the value at which the item is included "in my gross estate" and will control in ascertaining the denominator. In calculating the denominator, it should be kept in mind that whenever there has been a change in the original residuary items, it is always necessary to trace back to determine the value at which they were included in the gross estate.

Once the formula-obtained fraction is determined, it is applied at the date of distribution without regard to the value, on that date, of what will pass to the wife. The last sentence in the language used to describe the formula fractional share gift of the residue simply states what would be true if it were not there.[30]

5. DEFINING THE FUND AGAINST WHICH THE FRACTION IS TO BE APPLIED

A fractional share gift is not produced when the fund against which the fraction is to be applied is itself a fixed dollar amount. A gift of one half of $50,000 is not a fractional share gift but obviously is a gift of $25,000. Likewise a gift of an amount equal to one half of the husband's adjusted gross estate is a gift of a dollar amount because the ascertainment of the husband's adjusted gross estate is the ascertainment of a fixed dollar amount.[31]

---

[30] Many states exclude real estate from the estate distributable by the executor, unless personal property is insufficient to pay all valid claims and cash bequests. Suppose that the residuary estate includes real estate and that a formula fractional share gift of the residue is made. How much of the real estate in the residue will go into the marital deduction share? If real estate may be in the residue, should not the executor be given the specific power to allocate real estate to one or the other residuary shares as he in his uncontrolled discretion may determine?

[31] In Estate of Florence E. Bing, N.Y.L.J., March 16, 1960, p. 13 (N.Y. City Surr.), a will was involved which was executed after the federal estate tax marital deduction became available but before the New York State marital deduction was established. The decedent died, however, after New York had provided for marital deduction gifts. The will provided that the surviving spouse was to receive "that part of my residuary estate which shall be the amount by which: (1) the value of one-half of my adjusted gross estate (as finally determined whether as the result of acquiescence, compromise or litigation) as defined in Section 812(e)(2) of the Internal Revenue Code, or the equivalent section in force at my death . . . it being my intention that my estate shall have the benefit of the maximum marital deduction allowance for Federal Estate Tax purposes." In the New York estate tax proceedings, the estate was valued at a figure substantially higher than in the federal proceedings. The question was whether this gift to the wife was of a dollar amount, so that the amount of the marital deduction for New York tax purposes would be the same as for federal tax purposes. The court held that this gift was of a

If the fractional share marital deduction gift appears in a will, the residuary estate normally will be the fund against which the described fraction is to be applied. This means that there should be allocated to the marital deduction gift the described fractional share of each item in the residue. This allocation cannot be made until it is known what items initially will fall into the residue.

The maximum possible residue would be one which consists of all items disposed of by the decedent's will. If the will contains any specific bequests or devises, it is obvious that the items so bequeathed and devised will come out and the residue as initially constituted will at least exclude them. The decedent could intend that the fraction be applied against the property disposed of by the will, with no other exclusions, and, if so, the marital gift should be allocated the described fractional share of each item in a residue so constituted.

If the will contains some pecuniary legacies, the intention normally manifested is that they are to be satisfied before the residue is constituted.[32] Thus, until it is known what items disposed of by the will are to be used to satisfy the pecuniary legacies, it will not be known precisely what items initially will be found in the residue. In this situation, the executor, because of his power to select the items which will be used to satisfy the legacies, has some control over the items which will come to rest in the residue.[33] If the residue is defined as the items disposed of by the will minus specific bequests and devises and minus the items used to pay pecuniary legacies, then when it is so constituted, the fractional share marital gift should be allocated the described portion of each item initially in such residue.

The residue against which the described fraction is to be applied may be further restricted by excluding the items disposed of by the will which are used up in the payment of funeral expenses, debts and expenses of administration. If this is done, then the items which will initially come to rest in the residue will depend on what

"part" of the residuary estate and was "clearly a gift of a fractional interest to be determined in accordance with a formula." Thus the increases or decreases in value affect the fractional interest accordingly.

[32] An example of a case where the testator would intend that the residue be constituted before the pecuniary legacies are satisfied is one where the will gives the testator's wife one half of the residue and directs that out of the other half $10,000 be paid to A and $15,000 be paid to B.

[33] The testator could specify the order in which property in his estate is to be liquidated to pay pecuniary legacies (and other estate obligations) and thereby affect the executor's power to determine what items will come to rest initially in the residue, but such specification is not recommended because conditions existing at the time legacies are to be paid should determine what estate assets should be used to pay the legacies rather than some plan made years before by the testator.

is left after the executor has exercised his power to select the items to be liquidated to meet these estate obligations.

A further narrowing of what is meant by the residue is produced when the fraction is to be applied against a residue to be made up of what is left after taking out not only specific bequests and devises, the items used to satisfy pecuniary legacies and the items liquidated to pay funeral expenses, debts and expenses of administration but also after taking out the items liquidated to pay death taxes. It is obvious that each narrowing of the definition of the residue results in an increase in the power of the executor to determine what items will initially fall into the residue, to be allocated in accordance with the described fraction to the marital deduction gift.

The executor, if given appropriate investment powers, may make sales of estate items and may reinvest the proceeds so that the specific items in the residue at the time the fractional share thereof is in fact distributed to the surviving spouse may change from what they were when the residue as defined was initially constituted. If such is the case, the items in the residue at the time of distribution should be traced back to the items in the residue when it was initially constituted, to determine the proper proportion of each distributable item that should be distributed to the marital deduction gift.

Suppose that the surviving spouse is given one half of the residue and that the residue against which the fraction is to be applied is defined as what is left after taking out specific bequests and devises and pecuniary legacies but before paying funeral expenses, debts, expenses of administration and death taxes. Assume further that these latter payments are to be made out of the nonmarital one half of the residue. The residue as initially constituted consists of 1000 shares of the X Corporation, 1000 shares of the Y Corporation and 1000 shares of the Z Corporation. The executor elects to liquidate 400 shares of the X Corporation to pay death costs and receives a net amount after taxes of $40,000. The death costs which he pays total $36,000. He decides for investment reasons to sell 600 shares of the Y Corporation and buys 100 shares of the A Corporation with the net proceeds (the will authorizes such reinvestment). On the date of distribution, the executor has 600 shares of the X Corporation, 400 of the Y Corporation, 1000 shares of the Z Corporation, 100 shares of the A Corporation and $4000 in cash. He should allocate to the fractional share marital deduction gift 500 shares of the X Corporation, 200 shares of the Y Corporation, 500 shares of the Z Corporation and 50 shares of the A Corporation. An analysis of the property available for distribution discloses that

400 shares of the X Corporation were taken from the nonmarital share to pay death costs payable only out of the nonmarital share. Thus the original allocation to the marital portion of 500 shares of the X Corporation is not disturbed and the $4000 left from the liquidation of the shares in the X Corporation remain in the nonmarital share. The 600 shares of the Y Corporation sold for investment purposes, however, came equally from the marital and nonmarital shares, leaving their respective interests in the remaining 400 shares undisturbed, and the interest of the two shares in the A Corporation stock is the same as the interest each gives up in the Y Corporation stock that is sold; that means, one half of the A Corporation stock is distributable to each share.

If the illustration in the preceding paragraph is changed only in that the residue against which the described fraction is to be applied is what is left after also paying funeral expenses, debts, expenses of administration and death taxes, then the items in the residue as initially constituted would consist of 600 shares of the X Corporation, 1000 shares of the Y Corporation, 1000 shares of the Z Corporation and $4000 in cash. The fractional share marital deduction gift should receive one half of each item on distribution.[34]

If a non-formula fractional share marital deduction gift is to be employed (one half of the residue; one third of the residue, etc.), the amount of the available marital deduction will vary, depending on how the residue is defined. *We are assuming that the marital share of the defined residue will not have to contribute to the payment of estate costs which are not taken care of before the residue is constituted.* Thus one half of the residue, where the residue is defined as the property disposed of by the will minus only specific bequests and devises and the items used to pay pecuniary legacies, is obviously worth more than one half of the residue where the residue is defined as not only minus those items but also minus the items liquidated to pay funeral expenses, debts and expenses of administration. One half of the residue will be worth the least when the residue is to consist of what is left after eliminating all items mentioned above plus the items used to pay death taxes. In this last instance, the amount of the available marital deduction will

---

[34] If the items in the residue when it is initially constituted can only be changed as a result of sales or purchases for investment reasons, the fractional share marital deduction gift should receive one half of each item that is in fact distributable, and no tracing problem should be presented because, in the absence of some contrary manifestation of intent, it should be assumed that the executor would sell or purchase for investment purposes for all shares in the residue and thus the proportionate interest of each share of the residue in the items in the residue will not change as a result of sales or purchases.

not be known until the death taxes are determined and the death taxes cannot be determined until the amount of the marital deduction is known. If this circle is to be avoided, the residue must be defined in a manner that permits it to be constituted before the death taxes are paid.[35]

Unlike the result where the non-formula fractional share is used, where a formula fractional share marital deduction gift is made, the available marital deduction will not vary in amount no matter how the residue against which the fraction is to be applied is defined. This is true because the denominator of the formula-obtained fraction should always be the *value of the defined fund* against which the fraction is to be applied and the numerator should remain unchanged no matter how the fund is defined, so that the available marital deduction will always equal the numerator. For example, suppose that the numerator of the formula-obtained fraction is $70,000 and that the fund against which the fraction is to be applied is the residue determined before the payment of funeral expenses, debts, expenses of administration and death taxes. The value of the residue, based on estate tax values, is $180,000. The formula-obtained fraction is $70,000/$180,000 and the allowable marital deduction is $70,000/$180,000 × $180,000, or $70,000.

If the preceding illustration is changed only in that the residue is determined after the payment of all death costs except death taxes and the value of the residue, based on estate tax values, is $160,000, the formula-obtained fraction is $70,000/$160,000 and the allowable marital deduction is $70,000/$160,000 × $160,000, or $70,000.

When the formula-obtained fraction is employed, no circle should exist even if the residue against which the fraction is to be applied is defined as what is left after paying all death costs, including taxes. Since the described fraction is a self-adjusting one designed to produce the maximum available marital deduction, the death taxes should be determined initially on the assumption that the maximum deduction will be available.[36]

The fractional share marital deduction gift may be carved out of the funds in a revocable inter vivos trust established by the hus-

[35] Of course, if the residue is defined in a manner that permits it to be constituted before the death taxes are paid, and the marital share must then contribute to the payment of the tax bill, the available marital deduction will not be known until the death taxes are determined and the death taxes cannot be determined until the amount of the marital deduction is known.

[36] If, however, the formula-obtained fraction is to be applied against a residue determined before death taxes are taken out and the marital share thus ascertained is required to contribute to the payment of the taxes, the circle is present.

band. Such a trust, during the husband's life, may be funded or unfunded. If funded during his life and if not augmented on his death, the corpus of the trust as it exists at his death is the fund that corresponds to the residuary estate. If payments arising as a result of the husband's death are to be made out of this corpus, such as fixed dollar amounts comparable to a legacy or debts of the husband or taxes, then it must be specified whether the described fraction that produces the marital deduction gift is to be applied against the corpus before or after such payments are taken out, and the problems presented are identical with the problems considered in defining the residue.

A funded trust may be augmented on the death of the husband. Thus life insurance proceeds may be added to the trust, and the husband's will may pour property into it. The fractional share marital deduction gift may be carved out of the trust property as it existed before any such augmentations, with the property falling into the trust as a result of the husband's death being added to the nonmarital share under the trust. If this is intended, the terms of the trust should clearly so define the fund against which the fraction is to be applied and should direct the trustee to include in the nonmarital share all additions to the trust which come as a result of the husband's death. During the life of the husband, care must be taken to keep the trust funded to an amount that will produce the desired result when the described fraction is applied against it to produce the marital deduction gift. For example, if a formula-obtained fraction is employed, the corpus of the trust against which the fraction is to be applied must be kept up to an amount which exceeds the maximum allowable marital deduction, less other gifts which qualify for the deduction, or the numerator of the formula-obtained fraction will be larger than the denominator.

If the revocable inter vivos trust for all practical purposes remains unfunded during the life of the husband, as is the case when only a nominal amount is put in the trust during his life or when only insurance policies are made payable to it during his life, the defined fund against which the described fraction is to be applied will necessarily have to include some or all of the augmentations of the trust arising as a result of the death of the husband. Even though the trust is funded during the life of the husband, the defined fund may include such augmentations. It should be kept in mind that when the defined fund includes any augmentation of the trust resulting from a pour-over by the husband's will of his residuary estate, the residue poured over will normally be depleted by the payment of funeral expenses, debts, expenses of administration and death taxes so that the defined fund in the trust will be comparable to a gift of a fractional share of the residue when the residue is defined as what is left after the payment of all death costs.

Whether the revocable inter vivos trust is funded or not, it is possible to set up under the trust on the death of the husband a marital deduction gift, such as a power of appointment marital deduction trust,[37] and place therein a nominal amount such as one dollar. This empty shell can be filled by a pour-over from the husband's will of a fractional share of the residue of his estate. This arrangement presents all the problems of defining the residue which have been previously considered.

6.   EXCLUSION OF USE OF CERTAIN ITEMS IN DE-FINED FUND IN MAKING UP THE FRACTIONAL SHARE

It is desirable from a tax standpoint to exclude from the marital deduction share certain items of property. If the marital deduction gift is a fractional share of the residue and foreign realty is one of the items in the residue as it is defined, no portion of such realty should pass to the marital share because the value of any portion which so passes would not be available for the marital deduction. The marital deduction is not available with respect to property passing from the husband to the wife when the value of such property is not includible in the husband's gross estate and the value of foreign realty is not includible in his gross estate.[38] The foreign death tax credit may be lost with respect to the part of such a tax attributable to property subject to foreign death taxes which is distributable to a marital deduction gift, and hence it may be desirable to exclude such property from the marital share.[39] Some so-called terminable interests must be kept from marital deduction gifts or the amount of the available marital deduction will be reduced.[40]

The defined fund against which the fraction is to be applied may include these undesirable items initially, with a mandate that the fractional share of each undesirable item which otherwise

[37] Power of appointment marital deduction trusts are considered infra page 839.

[38] For a discussion of the requirement that the property used to satisfy a marital deduction gift must be includible in the husband's gross estate, see page 824 infra. Section 2031(a) of the 1954 Code, quoted infra page 1395, brings out that foreign realty is not includible in a decedent's gross estate. Appointive assets may be includible in a person's residuary estate, but not in his gross estate. See 1954 I.R.C. §2041, quoted infra page 1409.

[39] See 1954 I.R.C. §2014, quoted infra page 1393.

[40] Terminable interests are considered infra page 832.

would pass to the marital share shall be distributed to a share other than the marital share and property of equivalent value transferred from such other share to the marital share in place thereof. This mandate in effect sets up on the date of distribution a dollar claim in favor of the marital share equal in amount to the value, at that time, of the diverted property. Will the satisfaction of such dollar claim be treated the same for tax purposes as the satisfaction of any other dollar claim so that a taxable gain may be produced by its satisfaction? It is conceivable that the answer to this question is yes.[41]

Revenue Ruling 55-117 [42] is relevant in considering the question presented in the preceding paragraph. This ruling holds that no taxable gain is realized on the distribution of stock of a trust, and the basis of the stock in the hands of the distributee is the same as the basis of the stock in the trust under the following circumstances: A residuary trust under a will calls for the payment of the net income to the beneficiary until the beneficiary reaches a specified age, at which time she is to receive one fourth of the corpus of the trust as it is valued at that time; the balance of the corpus is to be retained and the net income is to be paid to the beneficiary until five more years elapse, at which time the trust is to terminate and the beneficiary is to receive the entire corpus; *the trustee on distribution is authorized to allot specific securities to any share or part;* the beneficiary has attained the specified age and the trustees, instead of giving her one fourth of each item in the corpus, propose to give her specific property equal in value to one fourth of the corpus. The ruling states: "The proposed distribution in the instant case, however, is not in satisfaction of an obligation of the trust for a definite amount of cash or equivalent value in securities, but is rather in the nature of a partial distribution of a share of the trust principal. Accordingly there is no sale or exchange."

Revenue Ruling 55-117 is concerned with a case where a single beneficiary is entitled to the entire corpus, part of it now and the balance later. Under these circumstances, no claim in favor of one of several beneficiaries is being satisfied by the distribution and consequently no tax consequences should turn on the selection of the property that is to be turned over to the single beneficiary to

---

[41] It should be noted that if the yes answer stands, the wife who receives property in satisfaction of such a dollar claim will pick up a new basis for the property so received, whereas the other share which is required to take the items excluded from the marital share probably will take the basis of the estate as to such items.

For a general discussion of the payment of formula and non-formula gifts by distributions in kind, see page 814 infra.

[42] 1955-1 C.B. 233.

meet the requirement of the particular partial distribution. The ruling may be interpreted to cover fractional share gifts with multiple beneficiaries but it is not clear at this stage that it will be so interpreted.[43]

The discussion so far in regard to the exclusion of the use of the undesirable items in making up the marital share has been on the basis that such items would have some influence on the ultimate benefit which the surviving spouse will receive, because the amount which the marital share will receive in place of its portion of the undesirable items is to be determined in the light of the value of such portion at the time of distribution. If the undesirable item that is present is a terminable interest that automatically decreases in value with the passage of time, it may be contended that the measurement of the amount which will be distributable to the marital share by the value of such an asset will affect the amount of the allowable marital deduction.

It must also be kept in mind that the available marital deduction will be cut down when the proceeds received on the sale of undesirable items may be used to satisfy a marital deduction gift. It may be contended that the mandate which requires the distribution to the nonmarital share of the undesirable items and the distribution to the marital share of other property of equivalent value is in effect directing the use of the proceeds of the sale of the undesirable items to satisfy the marital gift. The transfer of the undesirable items to the nonmarital share pursuant to the mandate is in no sense a sale and therefore the contention in the preceding sentence should not prevail.

The marital gift will be unaffected by the fluctuation in value of the undesirable items prior to the date of distribution if the mandate in regard to such items requires that they be initially allocated at estate tax values to the nonmarital share and that other property of equivalent value be initially allocated at estate tax values to the marital share. This arrangement, however, does not eliminate the possible contention that the proceeds of the sale of the undesirable items are being used to satisfy the marital gift. It should eliminate, however, the realization of any gain by the estate in satisfying the dollar amount which is owing to the marital share in place of its portion of the undesirable items.[44]

---

[43] It should be noted in passing that the ruling deals with a case where the fiduciary had discretion to allot specific property to a particular share, whereas the exclusion of the use of undesirable items in making up the marital share is mandatory. This difference, however, should not be significant. In connection with the problem considered in the text, examine references in note 47 infra.

[44] In this connection, see the discussion at page 814 infra in regard to the

The fund against which the described fraction is to be applied can be defined so as to exclude initially from the fund the undesirable items. For example, if one half of the residue is to pass to the testator's wife, the residue could be defined as what is left after taking out specific bequests and devises, pecuniary legacies, funeral expenses, debts, expenses of administration and the described undesirable items. The undesirable items could be given directly to the nonmarital share. This arrangement should eliminate any possibility of a gain being realized on the distribution of the marital share.

7. DISCRETION IN FIDUCIARY TO TRANSFER OUT OF MARITAL SHARE CERTAIN ITEMS AND SUBSTITUTE FROM THE NONMARITAL SHARE OTHER ITEMS OF EQUIVALENT VALUE

One objection sometimes made to fractional share marital deduction gifts is that property may be put under the control of the surviving spouse, which in the over-all family situation should not be put under her control. This may be true where stock in a closely held family business is or may be a significant item in the estate. A specific bequest of such property to persons other than the surviving spouse could be made with the marital deduction gift carved out of the remaining assets. In view of the fact that the valuation of such property is uncertain, the remaining assets may not turn out to be sufficient to cover the maximum allowable marital deduction. This decision to place or not to place such property in the marital deduction share can be postponed by leaving such property in the defined fund against which the fraction is to be applied and by giving the executor discretion on distribution to allocate such property to the nonmarital share and to transfer to the marital share from the nonmarital share property of equivalent value in place thereof.[45]

A discretionary power in the executor to exchange property as between the marital and nonmarital shares should not be a taxable exchange but it may be regarded as giving the executor the power to establish a dollar claim in favor of the marital share when property is taken from the marital share and given to the nonmarital

---

possible effect on a marital deduction gift where the fiduciary can satisfy a dollar amount by either a distribution in kind at estate tax values or a distribution of cash.

[45] Discretion in the fiduciary to allocate to the nonmarital share undesirable items such as terminable interests and property subject to foreign death taxes will not be enough to eliminate the undesirable consequences produced by the presence of such items. A mandate with respect to them is essential.

share. If so, the satisfaction of the dollar claim may conceivably produce a taxable gain.[46]

8.   EXCHANGE OF PROPERTY IN MARITAL AND NON-MARITAL SHARES WITH CONSENT OF OWNERS OF SUCH SHARES

When the time for distribution arrives, the distributees may request the executor to allocate the property as between them in a way other than that which would be required if each was to receive his proportionate share of each item originally in the defined fund (or if any distributable item was not originally in the defined fund, then as to it, in a way other than that which would be required if each was to receive his proportionate share of it based on tracing back to the item or items originally in the defined fund from which the distributable item in question stems). If this is done, the parties involved may have made a taxable exchange.[47] If so, each will be treated as though he sold the property to which he would have been entitled for the property he received in exchange. A gain or loss may be realized on such exchange but a new basis is acquired with respect to the property received on such exchange.

9.   COMPARISON OF FORMULA AND NON-FORMULA GIFTS

The preceding discussion has brought out that the non-formula fractional share gift of the husband's residuary estate may be one determined on the basis of a residue initially constituted before the payment of death taxes but after the payment of all other items, including debts and expenses of administration. If this is the situation, the executor needs to know the amount of the debts and expenses within fifteen months after the husband's death because at that time he must make a determination as to the amount of the marital deduction gift so that he can file the federal estate tax return and pay the tax. If the executor overestimates them, the marital deduction claimed will be lower than it should be and

---

[46] See discussion of Revenue Ruling 55-117 at page 804 supra. See also the references in note 47.

[47] The word "may" is used in the text instead of the word "will" designedly because under existing authority there is no taxable exchange.

A 1920 ruling, O.D. 667, 3 C.B. 52, and a 1935 case, M. L. Long, 35 B.T.A. 95, hold that a division of the residue, otherwise than proportionately by items, with the mutual consent of the beneficiaries does *not* constitute a taxable exchange. The question is whether these authorities are still healthy in the light of their age.

the deductions under Sections 2053 and 2054 claimed will be too high. In such a situation the total deductions taken will be greater than is allowed and the estate will be subject to a deficiency assessment with interest. For example, assume that the residue before the payment of taxes, debts and expenses of administration is $200,000 and that the latter two items are estimated at $20,000. If the marital deduction gift is one half of the residue after the deduction of the latter items, its value is $90,000. The total deductions taken would therefore be $110,000 — that is, $90,000 for the marital deduction and $20,000 under Sections 2053 and 2054. If the debts and expenses of administration finally amount to but $10,000, the marital deduction is $95,000 instead of $90,000, and deductions under Sections 2053 and 2054 are $10,000 instead of $20,000. Thus the total deductions allowed equal $105,000 instead of the $110,000 claimed on the return.

If the executor, however, underestimates the debts and expenses of administration, the marital deduction claimed will be higher than it should be and the deductions under Sections 2053 and 2054 will be too low. In such a situation the total deductions taken will also be too low and the estate will be entitled to a refund with interest. It would therefore seem advisable, if the executor must estimate the debts and expenses of administration in order to obtain a value for the marital deduction gift, that he should tend to underestimate, rather than overestimate, thereby avoiding a deficiency assessment and the accompanying interest charge.

The calculations of the marital deduction under the formula pecuniary gift and the formula fractional share gift present similar difficulties — that is, the formula cannot be applied without taking a position as to the amount of the deductions under Sections 2053 and 2054. The formula method may also confront the executor with other difficulties in calculating the amount of the marital deduction to be claimed in the final estate tax return. Thus the determination of the amount of the marital deduction gift under the formula requires the executor to make a decision as to the items to be included in the gross estate. If the decedent has made inter vivos gifts which may be deemed in contemplation of death, or has established inter vivos trusts which may be included in his gross estate under Sections 2035-2038, the executor must take a position as to their inclusion in or exclusion from the gross estate in order to calculate the amount of the marital deduction to be claimed. If the total estate tax will be increased by including such uncertain items in the gross estate, the executor should probably exclude them and proceed to calculate accordingly the amount of the marital deduction. Such a decision, however, should it prove incorrect, will cause the estate to be subjected to a deficiency determination with interest.[48]

If the executor excludes uncertain items from the gross estate, and these uncertain items are gifts to the wife which, if brought back into the gross estate, will qualify for the marital deduction, it may be that the wife's marital deduction trust will be zero under a formula gift. In this case the trustee will apparently be unable to make any payments of income to the wife out of any funds delivered to him to hold under the marital deduction trust, until it is definitely decided that the uncertain items excluded from the gross estate were properly excluded.

If a formula is used to describe the amount of the marital deduction gift, and additional nontestamentary assets which are includible in the gross estate are discovered after distribution has been made, the amount distributed in satisfaction of the marital deduction gift will be inaccurate either in favor of the wife if the newly discovered nontestamentary assets qualify for the marital deduction, or in favor of the other beneficiaries if the newly discovered nontestamentary assets do not qualify for the marital deduction.

It is possible, of course, that the total estate tax will not be increased by the inclusion of uncertain items in the gross estate. Thus, if an uncertain item is a gift to a charity, its inclusion in the gross estate will not increase the total tax bill. Indeed, its inclusion, with the resultant increase in the marital deduction under the formula, will decrease the total estate tax.[49] In such circumstances the natural tendency will be to attempt to increase the

---

[48] Suppose that the gross estate of the decedent is $200,000 if inter vivos gifts are excluded, and $300,000 if such gifts are included. If in either case deductions under §§2053 and 2054 amount to $20,000, the maximum estate tax marital deduction is $90,000 if the uncertain items are excluded, and $140,000 if the uncertain items are included. Thus, if the uncertain items are excluded in computing the estate tax due, the taxable estate is $30,000 ($200,000 less $90,000 less $20,000 less the $60,000 exemption); but, if it is later determined that these items should be included, the taxable estate is $80,000 ($300,000 less $140,000 less $20,000 less the $60,000 exemption), and the estate is subject to a deficiency determination with interest on the difference between a tax on $30,000 and a tax on $80,000. In determining the amount of any such deficiency, §2012 (gift tax paid may be credit against estate tax imposed) must be kept in mind.

[49] Suppose that the gross estate of the decedent is $200,000 if an inter vivos gift to a charity is excluded, and $300,000 if the gift is included. If in either case the deductions under §§2053 and 2054 amount to $20,000, the maximum estate tax marital deduction is $90,000 if the charitable gift is excluded, and $140,000 if it is included. However, since the charitable gift is also deductible under §2055 if it is included, it is to the advantage of the estate taxwise to include the charitable gift in the gross estate.

amount of the marital deduction gift by expanding the gross estate of the decedent.[50]

In the situations just discussed, the formula gift places the executor in the difficult position of making decisions that initially affect the amounts of the gifts to various beneficiaries. If his decisions as to items to be included in and excluded from the gross estate are questioned by the government, and the government's position is upheld, the various gifts are adjusted accordingly. Thus the executor in the final analysis does not have discretion to fix the amounts of the gifts to the various beneficiaries. In a situation where a formula gift is involved, however, the executor has some discretion in determining the amounts that the various beneficiaries will receive. Within certain limits, the executor may elect whether the controlling date in valuing property in the gross estate will be the date of the decedent's death or the date one year after the decedent's death.[51] If any item in the gross estate is dis-

---

[50] The government may find itself in what will be, for it, the unusual position of arguing that an inter vivos gift has removed the subject matter of a gift from the decedent's gross estate.

[51] See 1954 I.R.C. §2032, quoted infra page 1395.

In Rev. Rul. 54-445, 1954-2 C.B. 301, it is determined that a federal estate tax return filed in accordance with the values at date of death may be superseded by an amended return electing the optional valuation date if such an amended return is filed within fifteen months after the date of death or within an extension period duly granted, provided the personal representative is not estopped from changing his previously indicated election. The examples of estoppel which are given are where the representative has been discharged from personal liability pursuant to his request for a prompt determination of the tax (1954 I.R.C. §2204) and where the representative has entered into a closing agreement (1954 I.R.C. §7121). Section 20.2032-1(b)(2) of the Regulations, quoted infra page 1509, is in accord. Rosenfield v. United States, 156 F. Supp. 780 (E.D. Pa. 1957), deals with a case where the first administrator of an estate made an election, in a timely manner and in the form prescribed on the estate tax return, to have the assets valued on the optional valuation date. This election was made on the basis of advice of counsel who had mistakenly advised that the optional valuation applied only to the portion of the assets which had declined in value. The new administrator sought to revoke the election because the tax was higher as a result of using the optional valuation date, but the court held that the election was irrevocable, even though based on error and even though it resulted in the payment of a higher tax. The case was affirmed in 254 F.2d 940 (3d Cir. 1958), cert. denied, 358 U.S. 833 (1958).

In Rev. Rul. 55-333, 1955-1 C.B. 449, it is determined that §811(j) of the 1939 Code (§2032 of the 1954 Code is substantially the same) does not limit the executor's right to select the optional valuation date to the situation where the estate of the decedent has decreased in value during the one-year period following his death. The later date may be selected by the executor even when the estate has increased in value. Revenue Ruling 56-60, 1956-1 C.B. 443, points out that the optional valuation is not available if the decedent's estate is less than $60,000, because §2032 provides that the executor must select the optional valuation on the estate tax return (Form 706) and no estate tax return is called for by §6018(a)(1) unless the decedent's estate exceeds $60,000. If a return is filed when none is required, any material contributed, sold, exchanged, or otherwise disposed of during the year following the decedent's death, it must be valued on the date of such distribution, sale, exchange or other disposition if the alternate valuation date is selected.[52]   If he elects the lower valuation,

---

tained therein will have no force or effect.   In accord with the two rulings discussed in this paragraph is Reg. §20.2032-1(b)(1), quoted infra page 1509.

[52] If items in the gross estate are in the control of a person other than the executor and he transfers them during the first year, the executor will be bound by the value of the transferred property on the date of transfer if he elects the alternate valuation date.   Revenue Ruling 59-213, 1959-1 C.B. 244, holds that where jointly owned property included in a decedent's gross estate is transferred to a revocable trust by the surviving joint tenant, the transfer does not constitute a disposition of the property within the meaning of §2032, so that if the executor elects the alternate valuation date, the value of the trust property one year from the date of death will control.   The power to revoke the trust prevents the property from being "otherwise disposed of" during the year.   If the trustee sells the property and reinvests the proceeds, then a disposition would be made on the date of the sale for the purpose of §2032.

In Rev. Rul. 54-444, 1954-2 C.B. 300, it is determined that a distribution of the assets of the decedent's solely owned corporation to the executor in liquidation of the stock of the corporation, within a year after the decedent's death, constitutes a disposition of the stock of the company, and thus the date of such a distribution is the optional valuation date for federal estate tax purposes just as though the stock had been sold on that date.

Under Ohio law, a surviving spouse has the right to purchase from the estate of the deceased spouse property not specifically bequeathed.   In Estate of Walter O. Critchfield, 32 T.C. 844 (1959), the surviving spouse exercised her power to purchase some non-bequeathed stock and the probate court decreed the sale of the stock to her at $58 a share, the value at which it was appraised by a court-appointed appraiser.   The executor selected the alternate valuation date under §2032, and the court held that the fair market value of the stock on the date of sale controlled for estate tax purposes rather than what she paid for the stock.   The value on that date was $65 a share.

Some difficult problems may be presented as to valuation of gross estate items one year from date of death, when certain changes have occurred during the course of the year.   Revenue Ruling 58-576, 1958-2 C.B. 625, sets forth the applicable rules when the alternate valuation date is elected under §2032 and the following are involved: stock rights issued subsequent to death and sold before the year expires (proceeds of sale included); stock rights exercised before the year expires (value of rights on date exercised included); stock dividend received after death but before the year expires (value of stock dividend at end of year included); insurance policies where the beneficiary exercises his right to receive monthly payments rather than a lump sum (the amount included is the amount that would be paid in a lump sum); and mortgages where the principal payments are received after death and before the year expires (the value of the mortgage one year after death is included and payments on principal also included).   Revenue Ruling 58-576 was followed in Estate of John Schlosser, 32 T.C. 262 (1959), *aff'd sub nom.* Estate of John Schlosser v. Commissioner, 277 F.2d 268 (3d Cir. 1960); where it was held that a stock dividend received after death but before the year expired should be included.

Revenue Ruling 60-124, I.R.B. 1960-14, 12, holds that in determining the value of a decedent's gross estate, dividends declared before death on stock includible in the gross estate and payable to stockholders of record after the date of decedent's death must be considered in making an adjustment in the ex-dividend quotation of the stock at such date.   Such dividends are not

the total estate taxes normally will be lower, the marital deduction gift to the surviving spouse under the formula will be lower, and there will be a larger amount available for the nonmarital deduction gifts. If he elects the higher valuation, the total taxes normally will be higher, the marital deduction gift to the surviving spouse under the formula will be higher, and there will be less available for the nonmarital deduction gifts.[53] The executor may find himself under pressure from the surviving spouse to elect the higher valuation and under pressure from other beneficiaries to elect the lower valuation.[54] The executor is a fiduciary and he is liable to the persons damaged if he acts unreasonably in making his election, but his actions conceivably may be reasonable where he selects the higher valuation in order to increase the formula gift to the surviving spouse, even though thereby the total taxes on the estate are increased.

If the executor has sold estate assets during the first year and, on the basis of values at the date of the death of the decedent, has realized a gain, the selection of the optional valuation date may eliminate the gain and the tax which would otherwise be assessed on the estate on the gain. It may be that in a particular case a consideration of both the income and estate tax consequences will result in the estate being better off taxwise if the higher values on the optional valuation date are selected, so that no income tax will be payable in connection with the sale of the estate assets.

The problems which may thus be faced by the executor in calculating the amount of the marital deduction gift under the formula should be considered by the draftsman and, whenever it is possible, appropriate instructions should be given to the executor. With respect to the inclusion or exclusion of items from the

---

includible in the gross estate under the alternate method of valuing the gross estate either as a separate asset or as an adjustment of the ex-dividend quoted value of the stock. However, under the alternate method of valuing the gross estate, stock includible in the gross estate and selling ex-dividend is to be valued at its ex-dividend price one year from date of death (or any intermediate date) increased by the amount of dividends declared on stock during the alternate valuation period and payable subsequent to such period.

[53] See Reg. §20.2032-1(g), quoted infra page 1509.

[54] If the surviving spouse is the executor and she elects the lower valuation, she may be deemed to have released a nonexempt power of appointment, so that she will have made a gift for gift tax purposes under 1954 I.R.C. §2514, quoted infra page 1420. Thus it is unwise to name the surviving spouse, or any other person who may benefit himself by the election, as executor when the formula is used.

For another situation where the election made by the executor determines the amount of the marital deduction under the formula, see the discussion relating to the election by the executor whether to take certain deductions as estate or income tax deductions, at page 785 supra.

gross estate, the appropriateness of the following provision should be considered:

> If my executor in good faith decides that there is uncertainty as to the inclusion of particular property in my gross estate for federal estate tax purposes, he shall exclude such property from my gross estate in the estate tax return. My executor shall not be personally liable for any loss to my estate or to any beneficiary resulting from his decision made in good faith that there is uncertainty as to the inclusion of particular property in my gross estate.

With respect to the choice of dates for valuing the property in the gross estate when a formula gift is involved, consideration should be given to the desirability of inserting the following provision:

> Whenever my executor is given a choice of dates in valuing property in my gross estate, he shall elect the date which causes the lower federal estate tax on my estate.[55]

The non-formula pecuniary gift avoids the difficulties of calculating the amount of the marital deduction gift which are inherent in the non-formula fractional share gift and both types of formula gifts. Such a gift, however, is rigid and fixed in amount, whereas the formula gifts adjust to the size of the decedent's estate and the non-formula fractional share gift adjusts to the size of the designated fund out of which the fractional share is to come. This self-adjusting quality may often be very desirable.[56]

When a formula is used and the amount determined by the formula is placed in trust, the amount that will pass to the trust may turn out to be very small. It may be desirable to provide, in connection with formula gifts in trust, that unless the amount as finally determined exceeds some minimum, the gift will go outright rather than in trust.

---

[55] The lower valuation does not necessarily cause the lower estate tax. Suppose the value of the gross estate at the date of the decedent's death is $500,000, and, one year after his death, is $600,000, but the $100,000 increase is attributable entirely to securities specifically given to charities. In such circumstances the election of the higher valuation increases the marital deduction under the formula, and the charitable deduction absorbs all the increase in value of the gross estate, so that the total deductions make the taxes lower on the $600,000 valuation than would be the case on the $500,000 gross estate.

Bear in mind that a higher federal estate tax may be desirable if the result is to wipe out what would otherwise be a taxable gain realized as a result of a sale during the year following the husband's death.

[56] For a valuable factual analysis of experience with marital deduction gifts, see Lovell, The Marital Deduction — A Summary of Five Years' Administration, 33 Trust Bull. No. 2, p. 25 (1953).

10. PAYMENT OF FORMULA AND NON-FORMULA GIFTS IN KIND

In the absence of controlling provisions in the will, it is generally recognized that the executor is under a duty to convert into cash, as rapidly as is feasible, all personal property not specifically bequeathed.[57] It is usual, however, to authorize the executor to retain assets in the estate and to satisfy pecuniary legacies by a distribution in kind, and if a division into shares of the residue is directed, to make the division and distribution in kind. Such authorizations give the executor the discretion to proceed in the manner that is most intelligent under all the circumstances.[58] In this connection, it should be remembered that property sold by the executor within one year after the decedent's death must be included in the gross estate at its value at the time of sale if the executor chooses the optional date for valuing the gross estate.[59]

When the executor is authorized to satisfy a pecuniary legacy by a distribution in kind, the property so distributed is valued for this purpose, in the absence of any contrary provision in the will, at its value at the date of distribution.[60] The will, however, may authorize the executor to fix the value of the property distributed in kind.[61] But such a power in the executor may be deemed a power of appointment, and care must therefore be taken to make certain that it is an exempt power for gift and estate tax purposes,

---

[57] See In re Lazar's Estate, 139 Misc. 261, 247 N.Y. Supp. 230 (1930).

[58] On the termination of a trust of personal property, it is generally recognized that it is the duty of the trustee to convert the trust property into cash and distribute the cash rather than to distribute the trust property in kind. 3 Scott, Trusts §347 (2d ed. 1956). However, if at some designated time the trustee is directed to divide the trust property into shares and to hold each share in a separate trust, it has been recognized that he may divide in kind and allocate property in kind to the separate shares, and he may even be permitted to do this when certain shares are to contain a specified amount. Id. §347.6. It is usual to provide in the trust instrument that the trustee may distribute in kind on the termination of the trust and that he may divide and allocate in kind to each share when a division into shares is to be made.

[59] See note 52 supra.

[60] See Matter of Clark, 251 N.Y. 439, 167 N.E. 586 (1929). Also, when a trustee allocates in kind to a separate trust of a designated pecuniary amount, the value of the securities is to be established as of the date of the allocation. 3 Scott, Trusts §347.6 (2d ed. 1956). In In re Estate of Kantner, 50 N.J. Super. 582, 143 A.2d 243 (1958), the court construed a formula gift to be a formula pecuniary gift and required that a distribution in kind to satisfy the gift be on the basis of values at the date of the executor's application for distribution. See also 52 N.J. Super. 24, 144 A.2d 553 (1958), where the court refused to allow the executor's motion to have the valuation date set as the day when actual distribution would take place.

[61] Authority to fix values cannot be given to a fiduciary in New York. Decedent Estate Law §125.

lest unwanted tax consequences result. Furthermore, when the pecuniary gift is to qualify for the marital deduction, such a power in the executor may disqualify the gift for that purpose, for the executor may be deemed to have power to divert the property from the control of the surviving spouse, with the result that the spouse's interest would be a terminable one. Consequently, it is recommended that the executor not be given power to fix values in connection with a distribution in kind to satisfy a pecuniary gift designed to qualify for the estate tax marital deduction.[62]

The decedent may provide in his will that, if the executor satisfies a pecuniary gift by a distribution in kind, the value of the distributed property shall be the same as its basis rather than its value at the date of distribution. Thus the following sentence might be added to the language describing the amount of a formula or a non-formula pecuniary gift:

> The payment of this amount may be made wholly or partly in kind by transferring to . . . specific securities or other personal property at values which are the same as the basis of such property in the decedent's estate.[63]

But the question remains: Is such a provision desirable when a formula or non-formula pecuniary gift is made?

A provision like the one suggested permits the executor to examine the situation at the date of distribution and to decide how much shall be paid. If the value of certain property available for distribution is less than its basis in the decedent's estate, he can satisfy the designated pecuniary amount by a distribution in kind that is not then equal in value to the specified amount, or by a distribution in cash that is equal to it. If the value of certain property available for distribution is greater than its basis in the decedent's estate, he can pay off the pecuniary gift by distributing in kind property which exceeds in value the amount of the gift, or by distributing in cash the exact amount. Does the executor have in effect the power to fix values, so that there exist the same dangers that are present when he is given directly a power to fix values? There is no definitive answer to this question, but the

---

[62] Likewise the trustee of an inter vivos trust who is to establish a marital deduction trust of a designated pecuniary amount on the death of the settlor should not be given discretion to fix values.

[63] A similar provision in an inter vivos trust which calls for the establishment, upon the death of a settlor, of a marital deduction trust in a specified pecuniary amount might be as follows:

"The trustee may satisfy this amount wholly or partly by allocating in kind trust property at values which are the same as the basis of such property in the trust."

mere fact that it can be raised suggests the desirability of avoiding the problem by not requiring that property distributions be made at values which correspond to the basis of the distributed property in the decedent's estate.[64]   Agreement with such a conclusion results in the adoption of the following type of provision:

> The payment of this amount may be made wholly or partly in kind by transferring to . . . specific securities or other personal property at values current at the date of distribution.[65]

Of course the satisfaction of a pecuniary gift by a distribution in kind at values current at the date of distribution results in a capital gain to the estate of the decedent if the distributed assets have increased in value as compared with their basis in the decedent's estate, and a capital loss if they have decreased in value. But the basis to the distributee is the value of the distributed assets at the date of distribution.[66]   If the distribution in kind is made at values which correspond to the basis of the distributed property, the estate of the decedent should not have a capital gain or loss, regardless of the change in value of such assets, and the distributee should take over the basis that the assets had in the decedent's estate.

---

[64] The executor would not have a power to decide how much is to be paid if the provision under consideration is construed to require him to select the property distributed in kind so that its value when distributed will in fact be worth the designated dollar amount.   In In re Bush's Will, 2 A.D.2d 526, 156 N.Y.S.2d 897 (1956), the will gave the executor authority to satisfy gifts under the will by a distribution in kind on the basis of estate tax values.   A formula pecuniary marital deduction gift was made by the will.   The court held that the distribution and allocation of securities by the executor to satisfy the marital deduction gift should be made in such a manner that the marital deduction gift and the residuary trust would share proportionally in appreciation and depreciation of the several securities.   The court said that the authorization to the executor to use his discretion in making distribution in kind is in conflict with N.Y. Decedent Estate Law §125-2.   The case was affirmed in 3 N.Y.2d 908, 145 N.E.2d 872 (1957).   See also Estate of George S. Jephson, N.Y.L.J., Nov. 13, 1956 (N.Y. City Surr. Ct.).

[65] The provision set forth supra note 63 should be changed in a similar manner.

[66] See Commissioner v. Brinckerhoff, 168 F.2d 436 (2d Cir. 1948).

In Lindsay C. Howard, 23 T.C. 962 (1955), the taxpayer became entitled to receive one fifth of the net income accumulated between the time of the creation of the trust and the date he reached the age of twenty-one.   When he reached that age, the trustee distributed to him in kind certain shares of stock in satisfaction of his claim of one fifth of the accumulated net income.   It was held that the use of the stock by the trustee to satisfy the claim to the accumulated income was a "sale or other disposition" of the stock, and thus the distributee of the stock received a new basis equal to the amount of one fifth of the accumulated income which the transfer was made to satisfy.

When the marital deduction gift is a fractional share of the residue of the decedent's estate, and when the executor is authorized to retain assets and to divide and distribute in kind, a determination to distribute in kind results in the marital deduction gift receiving the designated fractional share of whatever assets are available at the time of distribution.[67] Of course the value of this fractional share for the purpose of the marital deduction is determined on the basis of gross estate values, and since the marital deduction gift receives what is in fact the designated fractional share of the residue at the date of distribution, the gift may receive assets worth more or less than the amount taken as a marital deduction.[68]

In the situation just discussed, any variation in value between the amount of the marital deduction and the value of what is distributed to the marital deduction gift is attributable solely to economic conditions. Clearly such variation cannot be the basis of claiming a larger marital deduction if the fractional share has increased in value. Nor can it be used by the Government as a basis for claiming a deficiency if the fractional share has decreased in value. Furthermore, a distribution in kind of the fractional share should not present any capital gain or loss problems to the estate, and the assets distributed should have the same basis that they had in the estate of the decedent.

When it has been determined that the estate tax marital deduction gift should be measured by a formula, it is normally better to use a formula fractional share gift rather than a formula pecuniary gift so as to avoid any possible realization of gain by the estate when distribution is made.[69] In choosing between these two types of formula gifts, it should also be kept in mind that a formula pecuniary gift is not a gift of a specific sum of money for

[67] The same is true when a fractional share of the corpus of an inter vivos trust is to be set up in a marital deduction trust on the death of the settlor.

[68] For example, suppose that a formula fractional share gift of the residue is made to the trustees, and by applying the formula the fractional share amounts to two fifths of the residue, and the value of this share, based on gross estate values, is $200,000. The marital deduction is $200,000. However, when the date for distribution of the residue arrives, the property in the residue may have decreased in value as compared with its valuation in the gross estate so that two fifths of the residue is less than $200,000, or it may have increased in value so that two fifths of the residue is more than $200,000. In either case the trust receives two fifths of the residue at the date of distribution.

[69] Revenue Ruling 56-270, 1956-1 C.B. 325, which is reaffirmed and clarified in Rev. Rul. 60-87, I.R.B. 1960-10, 18, and which is incorporated in Reg. §1.1014-4(a)(3), quoted infra page 1499, recognizes that an estate realizes a taxable gain when it distributes property which has a value in excess of its basis in satisfaction of a formula pecuniary gift.

the purpose of determining whether estate distributions carry out to the distributee any of the estate income for the year of distribution.[70]

It should be noted that when a distribution in kind is made in satisfaction of a pecuniary marital deduction gift, in the determination of the distributee's holding period, the period the estate held the distributed property is not included. The holding period of the distributee of a fractional share marital deduction gift, however, will include the period the property has been held by the decedent's estate.

11. VALUE TO THE WIFE OF AN ESTATE TAX MARITAL DEDUCTION GIFT

If the amount designated for the benefit of the wife is to be reduced by the payment of taxes (estate or inheritance), both the net worth of the gift to her and the allowable deduction are reduced accordingly.[71] That is to say, if the designated amount is to be fully deductible, the tax burdens must be placed on the nonmarital deduction gifts. This result can be accomplished in an instrument disposing of nonmarital deduction property by a provision which places all tax burdens upon such property.[72] If the

---

[70] See the discussion of income taxation of estates at page 77 supra.

Revenue Ruling 60-87, I.R.B. 1960-10, 18, referred to supra note 69, finds nothing inconsistent in the position that a formula pecuniary gift is a gift of a specific sum of money for the purpose of determining whether satisfaction of it by a distribution in kind subjects the estate to a tax on a gain, but is not a gift of a specific sum of money for the purpose of determining whether a distribution in satisfaction of it carries out to the distributee estate income for the year of distribution.

[71] See 1954 I.R.C. §2056(b)(4)(A), quoted infra page 1408.

In Estate of Raymond Parks Wheeler, 26 T.C. 466 (1956), the husband's will gave his wife his residuary estate, but it was determined that after the payment of administration expenses, debts and estate taxes, there would remain no assets to pass under the residuary gift, and consequently, no marital deduction could be allowed on the devise and bequest of the residuary estate to the decedent's wife.

[72] For a statute which undertakes to take into account marital deduction gifts in apportioning the tax load, see Mass. Ann. Laws, c. 65A, §5, as amended by Acts of 1948, c. 605, §1, quoted infra page 1444.

Under the New York Apportionment Act, no part of the estate tax will be apportioned to the wife's share if it qualifies for the marital deduction, unless the will directs otherwise. In Estate of Charles Juster, 25 T.C. 669 (1955), the court found that the will did direct otherwise when the language of the will provided that all legacies, bequests and devises should be free from any estate tax and all such taxes should be paid out of the principal of the testator's estate. The wife was given a share of the residue in a form that qualified for the marital deduction but the court held that her share of the residue would be determined after the residue had been diminished by the payment of all of the estate taxes. Compare In re Mattes' Will, 309 N.Y. 942,

dispositions made by the husband of his residuary estate do not set up any marital deduction gifts, all marital deduction gifts can be relieved from contributing to the payment of estate and inheritance taxes by a provision in the husband's will which directs that all such taxes shall be paid out of his residuary estate. The following is an example of such a provision:

> All estate taxes, federal or state, imposed by reason of my death, with respect to any property (whether disposed of by this will or not) required to be included in my gross estate for estate tax purposes, and interest or penalties thereon, shall be borne by my residuary estate.
>
> All legacy, succession, inheritance and like taxes (as distinguished from estate taxes), imposed by reason of my death, on property (whether disposed of by this will or not), and interest or penalties thereon, shall be borne by my residuary

---

132 N.E.2d 314 (1955); 12 Misc. 2d 502, 172 N.Y.S.2d 303 (N.Y. City Surr. 1958).

In Estate of Rosalie Cahn Morrison, 24 T.C. 965 (1955), it was determined that so far as the marital deduction was concerned, no reduction in value should be made as to property specifically bequeathed to the decedent's surviving spouse, because under the controlling law of Mississippi, estate taxes are not apportioned but are payable out of the residuary estate in the absence of any other provision in the will.

In Estate of Edward V. Babcock, 23 T.C. 888 (1955), it was determined that the Pennsylvania inheritance tax of 2 percent imposed on the share of the estate going to the decedent's widow and constituting a charge on the property received by her, and not on the estate of the decedent, had the effect of reducing the net value of the interest of the surviving spouse and must be subtracted in determining the marital deduction. No part of this tax is shifted to the estate or other beneficiaries by the Pennsylvania statute on apportionment of estate taxes. The Babcock case was reversed sub nom. Babcock v. Commissioner, 234 F.2d 837 (3d Cir. 1956), on the ground that the widow's share was subject to state inheritance taxes only if such taxes attributable to her share were not absorbed by the credit against the gross federal estate tax. The state inheritance tax in this case was less than the available credit.

In King v. Wiseman, 147 F. Supp. 156 (W.D. Okla. 1956), the court held that under Oklahoma law the taxes, debts and administration expenses were all payable out of the nonmarital deduction property, and thus the amount payable to the surviving spouse was not reduced on account of such items.

In Smith v. United States, 59-2 U.S.T.C. ¶11907 (W.D.S.C. 1959), the court followed the state court's determination that under South Carolina law the widow's fractional share of the husband's estate given to her under his will passed to her free of estate taxes.

If the property passing to the surviving spouse is subject to tax burdens which are eliminated by a volunteer paying the taxes, will the property passing to the surviving spouse be available for the marital deduction, undiminished in amount? Estate of Herman Hohensee, 25 T.C. 1258 (1956), holds that to the extent the amount received by the surviving spouse is increased because of the payment of the taxes by the volunteer, the property passes to the surviving spouse from the volunteer and not from the deceased spouse and thus is not available for the marital deduction.

estate. So far as practicable and reasonable, my executor shall pay as soon as convenient after my death any of the taxes referred to in the preceding sentence on future or contingent interests.

Of course such a provision is only effective to free marital deduction gifts from contributing to the tax bill if there are sufficient funds in the residuary estate to pay all taxes.

If a marital deduction gift of a fractional share of the residue is established by the husband's will, the will should make it clear that the designated fractional share is of the residue before the residue is diminished by the payment of taxes,[73] and then the fractional share so established should be exonerated from contributing to the payment of any taxes. If the form given above, which places the tax burdens on the residuary estate, is modified so as to require the taxes to be borne

by that portion of my residuary estate which is not disposed of by me in a manner that qualifies for the marital deduction allowed by the federal estate tax law applicable to my estate,

the marital deduction gift of a fractional share of the residue is exonerated from contributing to the payment of taxes if the balance of the residue is sufficient to pay all such taxes.[74]

---

[73] The discussion under the heading Defining the Fund Against Which the Fraction Is to Be Applied, supra page 797, illustrates the various ways in which the residue may be defined and the consequences of defining it in one way or another.

If the residue against which the designated fraction is to be applied is not carefully defined, the court will have to determine what it thinks the testator intended. In Thompson v. Wiseman, 233 F.2d 734 (10th Cir. 1956), the wife was given one third of the residue. The court held that her one third would be determined after the payment of debts, expenses of administration, and taxes out of the residue, because there was no provision in the will which indicated that the testator intended her one third of the residue to be determined before the payment of such obligations. See also page 62 supra, note 30, which deals with the determination of a widow's share on renunciation of her husband's will, and page 26 supra, note 58, which deals with the determination of the widow's share on intestacy. Both notes discuss whether her share is determined before or after the payment of death obligations.

[74] In Case v. Roebling, 42 N.J. Super. 545, 127 A.2d 409 (Ch. Div. 1956), the court construed a somewhat ambiguous provision as to payment of taxes to free the marital deduction gift from the burden of contributing to the tax bill, and thereby increased substantially the amount of the available marital deduction.

In Estate of Bernard M. Weiss, 19 CCH T.C. Mem. 1960-219, the decedent gave one half of the residue of his estate outright to his wife and placed the other one half in trust. His will stated that both federal and state death taxes were to be paid from the principal of the residue of his estate. Under these circumstances, the court held that the wife's share of the residue had to bear its share of the death taxes and that the marital deduction would be reduced accordingly.

The valuation of the interest passing to the surviving spouse as a marital deduction gift may be diminished by virtue of the fact that it is subject to some encumbrance.[75]   In such a situation the important determination in ascertaining the real value of what passes to the surviving spouse will be whether she can force the decedent spouse's estate to remove the encumbrance.[76]   If the

---

Whenever a marital deduction gift of a portion of the corpus of an inter vivos trust is established, the trust should contain a provision directing payment of any estate or inheritance taxes which may be payable upon the death of the settlor out of that portion of the corpus that is not placed in the marital deduction trust.

[75] See 1954 I.R.C. §2056(b)(4)(B), quoted infra page 1408.

[76] See Reg. §20.2056(b)-4(b), quoted infra page 1534.

In Estate of D. Byrd Gwinn, 25 T.C. 31 (1955), the decedent owned a life insurance policy in the face amount of $10,000 and his wife was designated as primary beneficiary.   At the time of the decedent's death this policy, along with other life insurance policies, was pledged with a bank as collateral for an indebtedness of the decedent amounting to $20,000.   The administrator paid the indebtedness, so that the widow received the proceeds of the policy in full.   The Commissioner contended that the full value of the policy did not qualify for the marital deduction because of the encumbrance outstanding against it on the date of the husband's death.   The court, however, held that the wife was entitled to require the payment of the indebtedness out of other assets of the estate, that if the administrator did not do this she would be subrogated to the rights of the bank against the estate, and that since the estate was solvent, the value of her rights under the policy should not be diminished by virtue of the existence of the encumbrance.   See Walzer v. Walzer, 1 A.D.2d 482, 151 N.Y.S.2d 550 (1956), in which the court recognized that where insurance policies are pledged to a bank as collateral for a loan, the presumption is that if the loan is satisfied out of the proceeds of the policy, the designated beneficiary will be subrogated to the bank's right against the insured's estate.   Such a presumption can be overcome only by facts affirmatively indicating the insured's intention to make the policies the exclusive source of payment.   The case was affirmed in 3 N.Y.2d 8, 143 N.E.2d 361 (1957).

In Estate of Fielder J. Coffin, 13 CCH T.C. Mem. 1149 (1954), the decedent took out a $50,000 insurance policy on his life and made his wife the beneficiary.   One third of the face amount of the policy was settled in such a manner as to qualify for the marital deduction.   The policy was assigned by the husband to his wife as security for a loan which she made to him.   In determining the amount of the marital deduction, it was decided that the one third of the face amount of the policy should be reduced proportionately by the indebtedness due on the policy.

If an insured borrows money from a life insurance company, it is generally held that the beneficiary named in the insurance policy is not entitled to reimbursement from the insured's estate for the amount of the loan because the loan by the insurance company is regarded as an advance on the insurance, and there is no underlying enforceable indebtedness.   See Fidelity Union Trust Co. v. Phillips, 5 N.J. Super. 529, 68 A.2d 574 (1949), aff'd, 4 N.J. 28, 71 A.2d 352 (1950); In re Schwartz' Estate, 369 Pa. 574, 87 A.2d 270 (1952). This result is codified in New York by statute.   See N.Y. Insurance Law §155-1(g).

In Wachovia Bank & Trust Co. v. United States, 163 F. Supp. 832 (Ct. Cl. 1958), the decedent and her husband acquired title to property as tenants by the entirety, each furnishing one half of the purchase price.   The purchase

surviving spouse can force the decedent spouse's estate to remove an encumbrance on property which passes to her, and the cost of the removal is deductible under Section 2053 of the 1954 Code, then, to the extent it is so deductible, it is a nondeductible interest for the purposes of the marital deduction. Otherwise a double deduction would be available in such cases.[77]

It is also advisable to make certain that other provisions applicable to the marital deduction gift do not diminish the net worth of the designated amount to the surviving spouse. For example, when property is put in trust by will, the beneficiary is normally entitled to income from the date of the decedent's death, even though the property is not distributed to the trustee until some period of time after that date.[78] The Regulations, however, provide that "An interest is not to be regarded as failing to satisfy the conditions set forth in paragraph (a)(1) and (2) of this section (that the spouse be entitled to all the income and that it be payable annually or more frequently) merely because the spouse is not entitled to the income from estate assets for the period before distribution of those assets by the executor, unless the executor is, by the decedent's will, authorized or directed to delay distribution beyond the period reasonably required for administration of the decedent's estate." [79] If, however, the surviving spouse is not entitled to the income from estate assets before the period of the distribution of those assets by the executor, the net worth of the gift to her is reduced and the marital deduction which can be taken for such gift is likewise reduced.[80] Of course, if no maxi-

---

money was obtained in part from a loan upon their joint note, secured by a deed of trust on the property. On the decedent's death, her executors paid one half of the remaining indebtedness out of the decedent's general estate and deducted the amount under 1939 I.R.C. §812(b)(4) (1954 I.R.C. §2053(a)(4)). The full value of one half of the tenancy by the entirety was included in the decedent's gross estate and the entire value of this one half was claimed as a marital deduction. The court allowed the marital deduction as claimed, because under the controlling state law the decedent's estate was obligated to discharge the encumbrance on the property in question. Estate of D. Byrd Gwinn, supra, was cited with approval.

[77] See Reg. §20.2056(a)-2(b)(2), quoted infra page 1530.

If, during the settlement of the estate, a loss deductible under 1954 I.R.C. §2054, quoted infra page 1405, occurs with respect to property in a marital deduction gift, then, to the extent of the deductible loss, that interest is a nondeductible interest for purposes of the marital deduction. See Reg. §20.2056(a)-2(b)(3), quoted infra page 1530.

[78] 3 Scott, Trusts §234 (2d ed. 1956).

[79] See §20.2056(b)-5(f)(9), quoted as a part of the text infra page 845.

[80] See Reg. §20.2056(b)-4(a), quoted infra page 1534.

In a Special Ruling dated Sept. 20, 1957, CCH Fed. Est. & Gift Tax Rep. ¶8127, §20.2056(b)-5(f)(9) of the Regulations is construed to mean that a will provision directing the payment of administration expenses, taxes, and so forth, with the income received during the period of administration from

mum limit has been placed on the time the income may be diverted pending the distribution of assets to the trustee, it is conceivable that the entire marital deduction may be lost so far as the trust is concerned, because it may be impossible to establish the amount of diminution in value due to the permissible diversion of income.[81] Consequently it is advisable, if a diversion of income pending the distribution of the assets to the trustee is allowed, to provide that under no circumstances shall the diversion take place over more than a stipulated period of time. With such a provision, at least a basis is given for obtaining a minimum value for the marital deduction gift.

If the estate tax marital deduction gift to the wife must contribute to the payment of expenses of administration, the net value of such a gift will be the amount left after making the contribution. In view of the fact that the expenses of administration are deductible for estate tax purposes, however, no increase in the amount of estate taxes will result from the marital deduction gift contributing to the payment of expenses of administration unless the amount of the marital deduction gift is reduced by the contribution below the maximum allowable marital deduction.

PROBLEMS

13.3. H in his will devises Blackacre to his wife, W. Blackacre is subject to a mortgage of $5000. The value of Blackacre at the time of H's death and also one year after his death is $20,000. What is the value of the estate tax marital deduction gift to W so far as Blackacre is concerned? See Mass. Ann. Laws, c. 191, §23, quoted infra page 1456.

13.4. If an estate tax marital deduction gift will be diminished in value by the amount of the federal estate taxes, the amount of such taxes cannot be determined until the exact amount of the estate tax marital deduction is ascertained, and the exact amount of the estate tax marital deduction cannot be ascertained until the amount of the federal estate taxes is known. How do you get out of this circle? See Section §20.2056(b)-4(c)(4) of the Regulations, quoted infra page 1535.

13.5. H in his will devises Blackacre to his son, S, for life with remainder to H's wife, W, and her heirs. The remainder to W is indefeasibly vested. How do you ascertain the value of the

---

property passing to the surviving spouse, will not operate to entirely defeat the marital deduction otherwise allowable with respect to such property but will only have the effect of reducing the amount of the marital deduction.

[81] See McLucas, Marital Deduction, 27 Taxes 1114, 1115 (1949).

estate tax marital deduction gift to W so far as Blackacre is concerned? See Revenue Ruling 54-470, 1954-2 C.B. 320; Section
20.2056(b)-4(d) of the Regulations, quoted infra page 1535.

12. GIFTS TO A WIFE WHICH QUALIFY FOR THE ESTATE TAX MARITAL DEDUCTION

a. *Value of Gift Includible in Husband's Gross Estate*

A gift by a husband to his wife can qualify for the estate tax
marital deduction only to the extent that the value of the gift is
includible in the husband's gross estate for federal estate tax purposes.[82]

PROBLEMS

13.6. H and W, his wife, purchase a family residence and the
title is taken in both their names as tenants by the entirety. The
purchase price of the house is $20,000. H furnishes one half of
the purchase price and W furnishes the other. H dies. The value
of the residence on the date of H's death and one year after his
death is $30,000. What is the amount of the available estate tax
marital deduction with respect to the family residence? See the
discussion of estate taxes with respect to concurrent interests at
page 409 supra.

13.7. H makes an inter vivos gift to his wife of 100 shares of
the common stock of the X Corporation. The value of the stock
at the date of the gift is $10,000. H dies. The inter vivos gift is
deemed a gift in contemplation of death. A hundred shares of
the common stock of the X Corporation are worth $8000 on the
date of H's death, and the value is the same one year after his
death. What is the amount of the available estate tax marital
deduction with respect to the common stock?

13.8. Under a qualified noncontributory employee benefit plan,
H elects to have the entire amount payable as a death benefit paid
to his wife, W, in a lump sum. At H's death, W is paid $20,000
as the payment due her under the plan. Will this payment to her
qualify for the estate tax marital deduction? See the discussion
of estate tax consequences with respect to employee death benefits
at page 355 supra.

[82] See 1954 I.R.C. §2056(a), quoted infra page 1407.

b. *Husband Must Be Resident or Citizen of United States*

If the husband is neither a citizen nor a resident of the United States, a gift by him to his wife cannot qualify for the estate tax marital deduction.[83] But if the husband is a resident though not a citizen, or is a citizen though not a resident, a gift by him to his wife can qualify for the estate tax marital deduction regardless of the status of his wife as to place of residence or citizenship.

c. *Wife Must Survive Husband*

A gift by a husband to his wife cannot qualify for the estate tax marital deduction, even though the value of the gift is includible in the husband's gross estate, if the wife does not survive her husband.[84] When the order of deaths of the husband and his wife cannot be established by proof, the Regulations provide that a presumption — whether supplied by local law or the husband's will or otherwise — that the husband was survived by his wife will satisfy this requirement to whatever extent the presumption causes the property in the marital deduction gift to be included in the gross estate of the wife.[85]

---

[83] There are no provisions allowing an estate tax marital deduction in 1954 I.R.C. §2106, quoted infra page 1412, which deals with the ascertainment, for federal estate tax purposes, of the taxable estate of a nonresident who is not a citizen of the United States. Section 2523(a) of the 1954 Code, quoted infra page 1425, specifically limits the gift tax marital deduction to a citizen or a resident.

[84] See 1954 I.R.C. §2056(a), quoted infra page 1407.

The person to whom an alleged marital deduction gift is made must in fact be the wife of the decedent. Revenue Ruling 58-66, 1958-1 C.B. 60, holds that a common law marriage is recognized for federal income tax purposes if it is recognized by the state in which it is entered into, and presumably, the common law wife would be similarly recognized for purposes of the estate tax marital deduction. Albert Gersten, 28 T.C. 756 (1957), and Revenue Ruling 29, 1953-1 C.B. 67, consider whether a husband and his second wife may file a joint federal income tax return when the husband's divorce from his first wife may not be recognized by all states. In Gersten v. Commissioner, 267 F.2d 195 (9th Cir. 1959), the Gersten case was affirmed on the point that a joint return could not be filed with the second wife where the marriage occurred during the pendency of an interlocutory decree, but was remanded on another point. In Irving A. Sheppard, 32 T.C. 942 (1959), the taxpayer's marriage was invalid under applicable state laws, and the court refused to allow him dependency exemptions for his alleged wife and alleged stepchildren.

[85] Section 20.2056(e)-2(e) of the Regulations, quoted infra page 1541, provides that if an estate tax return is required to be filed for the wife, the marital deduction will not be allowed in the husband's estate at the time of the final audit with respect to any property interest which has not been finally

It may be desirable, therefore, to anticipate the possibility that the order of the deaths of the husband and his wife will not be susceptible of proof and to attempt to establish a presumption that the wife is the survivor. A provision such as the following might be used in the husband's will:

> With respect to all items included in my gross estate for federal estate tax purposes which pass or have passed from me to my said wife under the provisions of this will or otherwise and which qualify for the estate tax marital deduction if my said wife survives me, I hereby declare that if the order of our deaths cannot be established by proof, my wife shall be deemed to have survived me.[86]

Such a provision is not appropriate unless under all the circumstances it is advisable taxwise for the marital deduction to be available in the husband's estate, and for the wife's gross estate to be correspondingly increased in size, even though she is not to have any period of beneficial enjoyment of the property. If the wife has no estate of her own, this result would normally be advisable taxwise, but if she does have a fairly sizable estate, it would normally not be desirable.

If the wife has little or no property, the estate tax bill will be much larger if she predeceases the husband, so that the marital deduction (as well as the wife's $60,000 estate tax exemption) will be lost to the family. One way to protect against the loss due to the wife predeceasing the husband is to insure the wife's life in an amount that will offset the increased tax bill resulting from her earlier death. Another way is for the husband to give his wife some of his property in his lifetime. Whatever will become subject to the wife's power of disposition should be dealt with in a manner that will not cause it to be included in the husband's gross estate on his subsequent death.

---

determined to be includible in the wife's gross estate. Thus, when the claim for the deduction is based on a presumption that the wife survived the husband, appropriate action should be taken in time to obtain a final determination that the marital deduction property is includible in the wife's gross estate.

[86] This provision undertakes to create a presumption that the wife survived as to items which have passed to her from her husband under the terms of an instrument other than the husband's will, such as an inter vivos trust. But if the local law allows the presumption to be effective as to property passing to the wife under the husband's will, the presumption might be deemed to have no effect on interests which have passed to her under an inter vivos trust. Thus inter vivos arrangements should contain a similar provision if the presumption is appropriate under the circumstances.

PROBLEM

13.9. H makes an inter vivos gift to W, his wife, of $10,000 in cash. W dies. H dies. The gift by H to W is deemed a gift in contemplation of death and, therefore, the value of the gift is includible in H's gross estate. What is the amount of the available estate tax marital deduction with respect to the gift by H to W? Will any credit be available to the estate of W for the estate tax paid on the $10,000 included in H's gross estate? See Section 2013 of the 1954 Code, quoted infra page 1391. Will any credit be available to H's estate for the gift tax paid on the gift to W? See Section 2012, quoted infra page 1390.

d. *Interest in Property Which Passes or Has Passed from the Husband to His Surviving Wife*

The language of the Internal Revenue Code is in substance that only interests in property which pass or have passed from the husband to his surviving wife can qualify for the estate tax marital deduction.[87] Interests in property are deemed to pass or to have passed from the husband to his surviving wife in a variety of situations. The following are typical:

1. When the wife, by surviving her husband, becomes the owner in severalty of property owned by the husband and wife as joint tenants or tenants by the entirety.
2. When H is the donee of a power of appointment and he exercises the power in favor of his wife or lets the appointive property go to his wife as the taker in default of appointment.
3. When H dies and his wife inherits property from him.[88]
4. When H dies and in his will bequeaths and devises property to his wife or in trust for the benefit of his wife.
5. When H makes an inter vivos transfer to his wife or in trust for his wife.
6. When H dies and the proceeds of his life insurance pass to

---

[87] See 1954 I.R.C. §2056(a), quoted infra page 1407.

[88] Suppose that a state statute provides that all personal property which is in the hands of the husband as head of the family shall be exempt from execution and shall be given to his surviving wife as her property and be exempt in her hands from execution. Does the personal property which the wife receives under such a statute pass to her by inheritance? Revenue Ruling 55-419, 1955-1 C.B. 458, answers this question in the affirmative and therefore concludes that the value of the property passing to the wife qualifies for the marital deduction.

his wife, or are paid to her under one of the options in the policy, or are paid to a trust for her benefit.[89]

It must be kept in mind that even though an interest in property is deemed to pass or to have passed from the husband to his surviving wife, the interest received by the wife may not qualify for the estate tax marital deduction because its value is not includible in the husband's gross estate, or because the wife may have been given no beneficial interest as, for example, when she received the interest in property as a trustee or subject to a binding agreement to dispose of it in favor of a third person, or because the interest in property given to the surviving wife may not pass the terminable interest test hereafter considered.[90]

If a wife disclaims the interest in property given to her by her husband, then the interest is deemed to pass from the husband to the persons entitled to receive it as a result of the disclaimer, but the converse is not true. That is, if another person disclaims an interest in property given to him by the husband and thereby the interest passes to the wife, the interest is not deemed to pass from the husband to the wife.[91] Since only interests in property which pass or have passed from the husband to the wife can qualify for the estate tax marital deduction, a disclaimer by the wife can lower the amount of the available estate marital deduction, but a disclaimer by a person other than the wife can never increase the amount.[92]

In the light of the circumstances which exist at the decedent's death, it may be undesirable from a tax standpoint to add the full amount of the estate tax marital deduction gift to the surviving spouse's gross estate. A disclaimer of all or part of such a gift eliminates the marital deduction accordingly and keeps the disclaimed property out of the surviving spouse's gross estate.[93]

---

[89] The definition of what interests in property will be deemed to pass from the decedent spouse to someone else is given in 1954 I.R.C. §2056(e), quoted infra page 1410.

[90] In Estate of Walter O. Critchfield, 32 T.C. 844 (1959), a wife exercised the power given her under Ohio law to purchase nonbequeathed property in her husband's estate. The Probate Court decreed that she could buy the particular property at $58 a share. When the transfer was made to her, however, the stock was worth $65, and it was at that value that the stock was included in the husband's gross estate. The executor claimed a marital deduction for the $7 per share difference, but the court disallowed the claim on the ground this benefit did not pass to the surviving spouse from the deceased spouse, and that, even if it did, the wife's right under Ohio law was a terminable one, as her death before the Probate Court fixed the terms of payment nullified her election.

[91] See 1954 I.R.C. §2056(d), quoted infra page 1410.

[92] See Reg. §20.2056(d)-1, quoted infra page 1538.

[93] If the amount of the marital deduction gift is based on an estimate, the disclaimer may be very significant if, as events turn out, the maximum marital

While it is probably true that the spouse can disclaim the benefits of such a gift, even though there is no mention of a disclaimer, a specific provision is desirable to eliminate any doubt as to whether she can disclaim only part of the gift, and to make it clear what disposition is to be made of the property disclaimed.

Some have suggested that such a disclaimer may amount to a gift by the surviving spouse for gift tax purposes.[94] But it certainly is not clear that this result will be reached. In any event, the mere insertion of a disclaimer provision does no harm and it provides the mechanism for the reduction or elimination of the gift if such a course of action turns out to be desirable.[95]

It must be kept in mind that the disclaimer as a method of adjusting the amount of the gift in the light of the circumstances existing at the decedent's death is available only if the spouse survives long enough to execute the necessary papers.[96]

---

deduction has been exceeded, for unless the excess is disclaimed it will be taxed in the estates of each spouse. Even if the formula is used and the exact maximum allowable deduction is attained, or even if the estimate method is employed and the total marital deduction gifts are less than the maximum allowable, the surviving spouse may have acquired an estate of her own, so that it may have become undesirable taxwise for her to take the full amount of the marital deduction gifts.

[94] See Note, Disclaimers in Federal Taxation, 63 Harv. L. Rev. 1047 (1950).

Suppose that the income beneficiary of a spendthrift trust purports to make a disclaimer of her right to part of the income from the trust. Is such a disclaimer effective in view of the spendthrift provision? In Gallagher v. Smith, 223 F.2d 218 (3d Cir. 1955), the decision of the District Court that the spendthrift provision in a will prevented the disclaimer from being binding, even though the Orphans' Court of Pennsylvania had held otherwise, was reversed on the ground that the state court's determination of the property rights of the parties under the will was conclusive, whether the proceeding before the state court was of an adversary or nonadversary character. It should be noted that the alleged disclaimer in this case was made several years after the will went into effect. See Wilmington Trust Co. v. Carpenter, printed in full supra page 556, and the notes appended to that case.

In Missouri, a new probate code which became operative on January 1, 1956, provides that an heir or devisee may renounce his succession to the real or personal property of a decedent but the renunciation shall be subject to the rights of creditors of the heir or devisee. In the case of an effective renunciation by the heir, the property descends as if he had died before the decedent. Mo. Ann. Stat. §474.490 (1952). See the discussion of disclaimers at page 29 supra.

[95] Section 2041(a)(2) of the 1954 Code, quoted infra page 1400, recognizes that a disclaimer of a power of appointment is not the same as a release of a power for estate tax purposes. A corresponding provision with regard to the federal gift tax appears in 1954 I.R.C. §2514(b), quoted infra page 1420. Examine Reg. §20.2041-3(d)(6), quoted infra page 1523. See Bowe, How to Provide for a Widow's Disclaimer Without Risking Gift Tax, 8 J. Taxation 68 (1958).

[96] In Rev. Rul. 59-123, 1959-1 C.B. 248, consideration was given to whether the estate of the husband might waive the benefits of the marital deduction and thereby keep the wife's gross estate smaller and at the same time give her

A wife may in some jurisdictions renounce her husband's will and claim her statutory share. Whether the statutory share qualifies for the estates tax marital deduction depends on its nature. The wife may receive as her statutory share a terminable interest which will not qualify. If the statutory share otherwise qualifies, it is deemed to pass from the husband to his wife, even though she becomes entitled to it only by renouncing his will.[97] Under some circumstances, the amount of the available estate tax marital deduction may be increased by a wife renouncing her husband's will and claiming her statutory share.

A contest may develop with respect to a dispositive instrument of the husband which transfers property included in the husband's gross estate. If the controversy is settled by giving the wife something that she would not otherwise have received, or by taking something from her that she would otherwise have received, what will be the effect so far as the marital deduction is concerned? It would seem clear that, for marital deduction purposes, what the wife gives up to settle the controversy should be treated as though she had disclaimed it.[98] If, on the other hand, the wife receives as a result of the settlement something she would not otherwise have received, the Regulations take the position that the interest will be deemed to pass from the deceased husband to the wife only if the transfer to her was a bona fide recognition of enforceable rights of the surviving spouse in her husband's estate.[99] Even if it is a bona fide recognition of her rights, it must pass to her in a form that meets the other requirements of a marital deduction gift.[100] Thus the road of compromise as a means of doing some

---

estate the credit under §2013, when she survived her husband for only a short period of time. It was held that the marital deduction could not be waived to obtain any other tax benefit or for any other purpose.

[97] See Reg. §20.2056(e)-2(c), quoted infra page 1541.

A Special Ruling dated November 21, 1956, CCH Fed. Est. & Gift Tax Rep. ¶8102, recognizes that when a wife in a community property state is required to make an election between the interest given her under her husband's will and her interest in the community property, and she elects to relinquish her interest in the community property, the property which passes to her under the will is deemed to pass from her husband to her. If the interest which passes to her under the will qualifies for the marital deduction, a deduction will be allowed to the extent that the value of such an interest exceeds the value of the community property interest which she has relinquished.

[98] See Reg. §20.2056(e)-2(d)(1), quoted infra page 1541.

See Estate of Thomas W. Tebb, 27 T.C. 671 (1957), for a case which holds that the interest under the husband's will which the widow gives up in connection with a compromise of a contemplated will contest is not an interest which passes from her husband to her. In this case nothing qualified for the marital deduction because what the widow received in place of what she gave up was a terminable interest.

[99] See Reg. §20.2056(e)-2(d)(2), quoted infra page 1541.

[100] In Estate of Gertrude P. Barrett, 22 T.C. 606 (1954), a settlement pay-

post-death estate planning is a rocky one so far as the marital deduction is concerned.[101]

PROBLEMS

13.10.　Under what circumstances will a wife in Massachusetts increase the amount of the available estate tax marital deduction gifts by renouncing her husband's will?　See Mass. Ann. Laws, c. 191, §15, quoted infra page 1455.

13.11.　H has a power to appoint certain property by his will to any one or more of a group consisting solely of his wife and his

---

ment was made by the executor of the wife's estate to the surviving husband to compromise his claim to a share in the estate so that the wife's will could be probated without a contest.　The settlement payment to the surviving husband qualified for the marital deduction, even though it had not been pursued in legal proceedings, because the Tax Court found as a fact that the husband's claim was a valid one, made in good faith and settled as a result of arm's-length negotiations.

In National Bank of Commerce of Norfolk v. United States 58-1 U.S.T.C. ¶11763 (E.D. Va. 1958), the defendant, shortly before his death in 1953, executed a will which, if it had been correctly typed from the dummy prepared by the lawyer, would have provided a power of appointment in his surviving wife under the trust created for her benefit, and the trust would have qualified for the marital deduction.　The decedent died before arrangements could be made to execute a corrected will.　In a state court proceeding brought by the surviving spouse against her daughter and her daughter's descendants, the court construed the will to give to the widow the power of appointment which would qualify the trust for the marital deduction.　The District Court held that the state court decree was conclusive in determining whether the trust provided for the necessary power of appointment.　Even though the daughter did not appeal from the state court decree, the District Court held that the state court proceeding was adversary in nature.

Estate of Leo J. Dutcher, 34 T.C. —, No. 95 (1960), held that a cash payment to the decedent's second wife under a settlement agreement with his children of a will controversy over her interest under the decedent's will qualified for the marital deduction.　The controversy had resulted in litigation in this case.

101 See the discussion of compromise agreements, which deals generally with the tax problems they raise, at page 74 supra.

A compromise agreement growing out of a will contest raises state inheritance tax questions.　One view is that the compromise agreement will be regarded, for purposes of determining state inheritance taxes, as allowing the will to take effect as written.　As representative of this view, see Jorgensen's Estate, 267 Wis. 1, 64 N.W.2d 430 (1954).　In other cases, however, the courts consider that the legatees under the will have renounced the interest that passes to the takers under the compromise agreement and on this basis determine the amount of the state inheritance taxes.　As representative of this view, see In re Kierstead's Estate, 122 Neb. 694, 241 N.W. 274 (1932).

In Maud H. Farrell, 13 CCH T.C. Mem. 239 (1954), the Tax Court held that transfers of property pursuant to agreements among beneficiaries named in the decedent's will and a relative not provided for in the will did not constitute the making of taxable gifts by the parties to such agreements, because the agreements, in the opinion of the Tax Court, were entered into at arm's length after extended negotiations.

issue. H exercises the power by appointing the property to his wife. Will the value of the appointed property be available for the estate tax marital deduction?

e. Terminable Interests

A non-trust gift by a husband to his wife of certain so-called terminable interests in property will not qualify for the estate tax marital deduction. The wife is given a terminable interest in property if upon the lapse of time, upon the occurrence of an event or contingency, or upon the failure of an event or contingency, the interest passing to the wife will terminate or fail.[102] It must be kept in mind, however, that not every non-trust gift of a terminable interest by a husband to his wife will fail to qualify for the estate tax marital deduction. Only gifts of certain terminable interests will fail to qualify.

The twofold test which, if met, produces the objectionable type of terminable interest is as follows:

[102] See 1954 I.R.C. §2056(b)(1), and (2), quoted infra page 1407. The comparable gift tax marital deduction section is §2523(b), (c) and is quoted infra page 1425.

In Estate of Hyman Kleinman, 25 T.C. 1245 (1956), aff'd sub nom. Estate of Kleinman v. Commissioner, 245 F.2d 235 (6th Cir. 1957), and Estate of Herman Hohensee, 25 T.C. 1258 (1956), the court held that a life interest in the surviving spouse was a terminable interest that did not qualify for the marital deduction.

Re-examine the discussion of joint and mutual wills at page 71 supra. See Estate of G. M. Peterson, 23 T.C. 1020 (1955), where there was involved a joint and mutual will executed by the decedent and his wife, whereby the estate of the first to die passed to the other, and the survivor's estate passed to their children. Under applicable Nebraska law, the effect of the will was to limit the widow's interest in property owned by her, or acquired by her from her husband, to that of a life tenant with power of use and disposition for her support, comfort and enjoyment only. The court held that no marital deduction was allowable. The case was reversed in 229 F.2d 741 (8th Cir. 1955) on the authority of the Awtry case referred to supra page 73, note 54.

If the gift to the wife is subject to a provision that if she sells the property given to her, she must offer it first to a designated person, will such a gift qualify for the marital deduction? Newton v. Wiseman, 58-2 U.S.T.C. ¶11816 (W.D. Okla. 1958), held that such a restriction did not disqualify the gift.

In Chritton v. United States, 59-2 U.S.T.C. ¶11883 (N.D. Ill. 1959), the decedent's wife was entitled under an antenuptial agreement to a life interest in certain residential property on the decedent's death. Subsequent to the decedent's death the wife agreed to accept in full satisfaction of her rights under the antenuptial agreement $10,000 of the sale price of the property, and the court refused to allow a marital deduction in the decedent's estate for the $10,000 payment because it was nothing more than a cash settlement for a terminable interest. Compare Crosby v. United States, discussed supra page 23, note 48. The court distinguished Estate of Gertrude P. Barrett, discussed supra page 830, note 100.

1. An interest in the property given to the wife passes or has passed (for less than an adequate or full consideration in money or money's worth) from the husband to a person other than his wife (or her estate),[103] and

2. By reason of such passing the other person (or his heirs or assigns) may possess or enjoy any part of such property after the termination or failure of the interest passing to the wife.

From the above it should be apparent that the following terminable interests which may be given by a husband to his wife are not of the objectionable type because they fail to meet the twofold test:

1. H sells Blackacre for an adequate money consideration to A and his heirs from and after the death of the survivor of H and W. H in his will devises his interest in Blackacre to W, his wife. H dies. A terminable interest passes from H to W but the interest in Blackacre which passed from H to A and which A will possess on the death of W is one for which A paid an adequate money consideration.

2. H's father devised Blackacre to him until the death of the survivor H and W (H's wife) with remainder to A and his heirs. H in his will devises his interest in Blackacre to W. H dies. A terminable interest passes from H to W but no interest in Blackacre passes or has passed from H to A, who will possess Blackacre on the death of W.

3. H buys a joint and survivor annuity under which he will receive certain payments for his life, and then W, his wife, will receive certain payments for her life. On the death of the survivor of H and W, all payments will cease. H dies and the value of the annuity for W is includible in H's gross estate. A terminable interest passes from H to W,

---

[103] The widow's allowance and the marital deduction are considered supra page 13. In Rev. Rul. 56-26, 1956-1 C.B. 447, it is held that a widow's allowance for support during the period of the settlement of her deceased husband's estate qualifies for the marital deduction when the husband's entire estate is given to the widow, even though the allowance will be terminated in the event of the widow's death, because on the termination of the allowance nothing passes to anyone other than the widow or her estate. The ruling reaffirms Rev. Rul. 83, 1953-1 C.B. 395, referred to supra page 13, which established the general principle that an allowance for the support of the widow qualifies for the marital deduction only if it is a vested right such as will, in the event of the widow's death at any moment of time following the husband's death, survive as an asset of her estate. When the widow is the only beneficiary of the estate, this test is met with respect to any support allowance that is granted.

but on the termination of W's interest no one else is entitled to enjoy or possess any part of the interest W was
enjoying.[104]

It must be kept in mind, however, that if H directs his executor
or the trustee of a trust to acquire for W, his wife, any type of
terminable interest, even one of the so-called nonobjectionable
types mentioned above, the amount spent by the executor or the
trustee of a trust for such an acquisition cannot qualify for the estate tax marital deduction.[105]

H may have among his assets one of the objectionable types of
terminable interests. For example, H may have given Blackacre
to A and his heirs subject only to the payment to H or his heirs or
assigns of a reasonable rental for twenty years. H now has among
his assets a terminable interest, and on the termination of the interest another person will enjoy what H has and that other person
received his interest in Blackacre from H for less than an adequate consideration (assuming rental payments are not really installment payments on a purchase price). If H in his will gives
his right to the rentals to W, his wife, the gift will not qualify for
the estate tax marital deduction.[106] Suppose, however, that H in

---

[104] See Reg. §20.2056(b)-1(g), Ex. (3), quoted infra page 1531.

The gift to the wife by the acquisition of the joint and survivor annuity is
one which the husband may enjoy after the termination of the wife's interest
and thus is not a gift that qualifies for the gift tax marital deduction. See
Reg. §25.2523(b)-1(c)(2), quoted infra page 1554.

[105] See 1954 I.R.C. §2056(b)(1)(C), quoted infra page 1407.

Suppose that in his will T does not direct his executor to acquire an annuity for his wife but rather gives an annuity of $10,000 a year to her. In
carrying out this disposition in T's will, his executor will be required to set
aside a fund which in the opinion of the court is sufficient in amount to provide the designated annuity. Suppose that W desires to take the amount set
aside for the annuity in a lump sum rather than to take it as an annuity.
Will the court allow her to do so? In In re Lanigan's Will, 174 Misc. 570,
21 N.Y.S.2d 550 (1940), the court held that under New York Decedent Estate
Law §47-b a lump sum election is allowed if the will makes the annuity assignable. In Matter of Jean Ferris, 3 N.Y.2d 70, 143 N.E.2d 505 (1957), *cert.
denied,* 355 U.S. 891 (1958), the court determined that when the commutation
of an annuity given by a will is proper, the appropriate date for arriving at
the capital value is the date of the testator's death. If the amount originally
set aside to provide the annuity turns out to be more than is needed as time
goes on, can the amount be revised from time to time in the future? See In
re Proctor's Will, 235 App. Div. 6, 255 N.Y. Supp. 722 (1932). Does the gift
of such an annuity qualify for the marital deduction?

In Morgenthaler v. First Atlantic National Bank, 80 So.2d 446 (Fla. 1955),
where a will specified that the annuity be purchased by the executor, the
court refused to allow a person to take the cost of an annuity in cash. The
court ordered the executor to purchase an annuity contract containing a
spendthrift clause so that the annuitant could not sell the annuity and acquire
a lump sum.

[106] See Reg. §20.2056(b)-1(g), Ex. (5), quoted infra page 1531.

his will bequeaths $20,000 to W. In this situation the value of the marital deduction gift will be reduced by the value of the objectionable terminable interest in H's general assets because whenever a gift to a wife is to be satisfied out of general assets, the objectionable terminable interests in such assets are deemed to be used first.[107]

In view of the comments made in the preceding paragraph, it may be desirable to include in an instrument which makes estate tax marital deduction gifts a provision somewhat as follows:

> Only assets which qualify for the estate tax marital deduction shall be used to pay estate tax marital deduction gifts hereunder or shall be sold to raise cash to make such payment.[108]

Normally, when a marital deduction trust is established, the same instrument also creates a nonmarital deduction trust with the same trustees. And it may be desirable to authorize the trustees to mingle the property of the two trusts for investment purposes, assigning to each trust an undivided interest in the mingled funds. Such an authorization clearly does not of itself disqualify the estate tax marital deduction gift. Suppose, however, that part of the assets of the nonmarital deduction trust are terminable interests which, if they could have been assigned initially to the marital deduction trust, would have caused the allowable deduction to be reduced to the extent of their value. Will an authorization to mingle the assets of the two trusts under such circumstances cause the allowable deduction to be reduced to the same extent that it would have been had it been possible to assign the terminable interests originally to the marital deduction trust? It would appear that the authorization to mingle the assets of the two trusts will not have such an effect; for the terminable interests provision does not prevent the trustee of a marital deduction trust from investing trust funds in terminable interests after the trust

---

[107] See 1954 I.R.C. §2056(b)(2), quoted infra page 1407.

[108] See Reg. §20.2056(b)-2(d), quoted infra page 1532, which recognizes that a provision such as the one suggested in the text will prevent the reduction for marital deduction purposes of a bequest which is to be satisfied out of general assets when such assets contain a terminable interest.

In Braun v. Central Trust Co., 158 Ohio St. 374, 109 N.E.2d 476 (1952), it was contended that a provision which required that the executor select only assets which qualify for the marital deduction was one which postponed the vesting of interests beyond the period allowed by the rule against perpetuities. The court rejected this contention. See also Conn. Gen. Stat. Rev. §45-174 (1958).

has been established, and when the trustee takes advantage of an authorization to mingle the funds of several trusts, he is simply selecting a method of investment.[109]

PROBLEMS

13.12. H in his will devises Blackacre to W, his wife, and her heirs "as long as Blackacre is used for residential purposes." H dies. Does the gift from H to W qualify for the estate tax marital deduction? See Brown v. Independent Baptist Church of Woburn, printed supra page 567.

13.13. H in his will devises Blackacre "to my wife W for her life, then to my said wife's heirs." H dies. Does the gift from H to W qualify for the estate tax marital deduction?

13.14. H in his will devises Blackacre "to my wife W for life, remainder to my son S and his heirs." H dies. S immediately gives his remainder to W. Does the gift from H to W qualify for the estate tax marital deduction?

13.15. H in his will devises Blackacre "to my wife W for life, remainder to my said wife's estate." H dies. Does the gift from H to W qualify for the estate tax marital deduction?

f. *Common Disaster Clauses*

Prior to the Revenue Act of 1948, which gave birth to the estate tax marital deduction, it was desirable to insert in a will a so-called common disaster clause in connection with a gift from a husband to a wife. The clause could take various forms but the form most frequently employed was that the gift to the wife would not take effect unless she survived her husband by thirty days. In the absence of such a clause, even though the wife survived the husband only a short period of time and received no benefit from the gift, the subject matter of the gift would pass through his estate to her estate and then through her estate to the persons to be benefited. Successive administrations with respect to the same property are expensive and also normally subject the property to state inheritance taxes in both estates. Of course, prior to the Revenue Act of 1948, the five-year moratorium as to property pre-

---

[109] See Reg. §20.2056(b)-1(f), quoted infra page 1531, which points out that a direction to the trustee to convert certain property into a terminable interest will disqualify for marital deduction purposes the property that is to be so converted, but that a general investment power authorizing investments in both terminable interests and other interests in property is not a direction to invest in a terminable interest.

viously taxed applied to gifts from a husband to his wife as well as to other gifts, so that such successive administrations did not subject the same property to federal estate taxes in both estates.

It may now be desirable taxwise, however, to allow the estate tax marital deduction gift to the wife to take effect if she survives her husband only by a few minutes. In fact, it may be desirable to go even further and provide that, if the husband and wife die under circumstances that make it impossible to determine which one survived, the wife will be presumed to have survived.[110] In other words, it may be desirable to add the value of the estate tax marital deduction gift to the wife's gross estate even though she does not live long enough to enjoy it, in order to take advantage of the deduction from the husband's gross estate in determining his taxable estate.

It should be kept in mind that if the husband makes the estate tax marital deduction gift to his wife in the form of a power of appointment arrangement, the subject matter of such a gift need not be administered in her estate so that the costs of successive administrations are not involved when she dies shortly after her husband.[111] In some states (Massachusetts is one), the appointive assets are not treated as owned by the donee of the power for state inheritance tax purposes, so that there will not be double state taxation in rapid succession if the wife dies shortly after her husband.[112]

Under some circumstances it may be desirable to make an estate tax marital deduction gift to the wife of some amount, no matter how short a period of time she survives her husband, and increase the amount if she survives for some stated period of time or does not die as a result of a common disaster which takes her husband's life. In that situation the common disaster clause is useful to govern the augmentation of the minimum amount. It can be provided that the increase will not apply if the wife does not survive the husband by six months; or that it will not apply if the wife dies in a common disaster that also takes the husband's life.[113] If the wife does survive by six months or does not die in

[110] For a discussion in regard to the requirement that the wife must survive her husband, see page 825 supra.

[111] As to whether the holder of appointive assets should deliver them to the estate of the donee of the power or directly to the persons entitled to receive them on the donee's death, see the discussion at page 700 supra.

[112] State inheritance taxes and appointive assets are considered supra page 764. Some states have provided for a marital deduction or exemption under their estate tax laws and inheritance tax laws. See the appropriate statutes in California, New York, South Carolina and South Dakota.

[113] See 1954 I.R.C. §2056(b)(3), quoted infra page 1408.

a common disaster, the gift to the wife will be available for the marital deduction. This is an exception to the terminable interest rule.

Suppose that the gift to the wife is subject to a requirement of survival to the occurrence of some event, and that the event actually occurs within six months after the husband's death. Will the terminable interest given to her come within the exception, so that the gift to her can qualify for the marital deduction if she meets the requirement of survival? The answer given in the Regulations is no, unless the stipulated event is one which can occur, if it ever occurs, only within six months after the husband's death.[114]

---

[114] See Reg. §20.2056(b)-3, quoted infra page 1532.

In Kellar v. Kasper, 53-2 U.S.T.C. ¶10919 (D.S.D. 1953), the court upheld as a marital deduction gift, a gift to the wife which was conditioned on her survivorship until the distribution, and distribution took place within six months after the husband's death. The District Court decision was reversed on appeal. Kasper v. Kellar, 217 F.2d 744 (8th Cir. 1954). The Court of Appeals, however, remanded the case for a determination as to whether, under the law of South Dakota, the language used in the husband's will had the legal effect of giving the widow an indefeasible interest as of the time of his death. The opinion of the Court of Appeals in Kellar v. Kasper was followed in California Trust Co. v. Riddell, 136 F. Supp. 7 (S.D. Cal. 1955), and Estate of Allen Clyde Street, 25 T.C. 673 (1955). In Kellar v. Kasper, 138 F. Supp. 738 (D.S.D. 1956), the court determined that under South Dakota law the gift to the decedent's wife "if living at the time of the distribution of my estate" required only that she survive her husband, and thus if she did, her death thereafter and before distribution would not defeat the gift. Thus the gift qualified for the marital deduction. Compare Reg. §20.2056(b)-3(d), Ex. (4), quoted infra page 1534.

In Steele v. United States, 146 F. Supp. 316 (D. Mont. 1956), the decedent's will provided that in the event his wife should not be living at the time of the decree of distribution of his estate, the property given to her should pass to other designated beneficiaries. The state court had held that the gift to the wife was not conditional on her surviving the decree of distribution, but vested in her by virtue of her surviving her husband. The court's determination was considered conclusive as to the question, and hence the gift to the wife qualified for the marital deduction. The state court's determination was also deemed controlling in Martinson v. Wright, 181 F. Supp. 534 (D. Idaho 1959).

Smith v. United States, 158 F. Supp. 344 (D. Colo. 1957), considered a devise to the testator's wife where the property given to her was to pass to others "in the event that my said wife should predecease me or, surviving me, die before distribution to her . . ." The court relied on Kellar v. Kaspar, supra, in holding that the gift to the wife qualified for the marital deduction because it vested in her indefeasibly as of the time of her husband's death.

In Roberts v. United States, 182 F. Supp. 957 (S.D. Cal. 1960), the decedent made a gift to his wife in one clause of his will which was unqualified if she survived him and was cohabitating with him as his wife at the time of his death. In the next and separate clause he made a gift to a stepson "in the event my wife, . . . should predecease me or die prior to the distribution of my estate, or our deaths should occur simultaneously." The Commissioner took the position that the second clause read in conjunction with the first showed an intent that the gift to the wife was subject to the condition that

g. *Separate Trust for the Benefit of the Wife*

The requirements which must be met if a separate trust established by the husband for the benefit of his wife is to qualify for the estate tax marital deduction are now to be examined.[115] The separate trust considered here is to be contrasted with a trust for the benefit of the wife of a portion of the trust assets. The portion trust arrangement is dealt with later.[116]

If the husband's assets include an objectionable terminable interest and this terminable interest is placed in the trust for the benefit of his wife, or is in the general assets which are available to satisfy the gift in trust — even though the terms of the trust otherwise qualify for the estate tax marital deduction — the value of the trust property will be diminished by the value of the terminable interest in determining the amount available for the estate tax marital deduction as a result of the establishment of the trust.[117] Thus he should exclude from the gift in trust any objec-

---

she be living at the time of distribution and thus was a disqualified terminable interest. The court held, however, that the first clause was a separate gift and was not subject to such a condition and thus qualified for the marital deduction.

The court in Estate of Frank Sbicca, 35 T.C. —, No. 14 (1960), held that a bequest to the decedent's wife "if she is living at the time of the entry of the Order of final distribution of my estate," with a gift over to others if she should not be living, was a terminable interest that did not qualify for the marital deduction.

Section 812(e)(1)(D) of the 1939 Code, which corresponds to §2056(b)(3) of the 1954 Code, was amended in 1958 to provide that an interest in a surviving spouse will not fail to qualify for the marital deduction, even though it was subject to termination upon the happening of an event or contingency, if within six months after the date of the decedent's death the event or contingency becomes impossible of occurrence and the decedent was judged incompetent before April 2, 1948, and was not restored to competency before his death.

Howells v. Fox, 251 F.2d 94 (10th Cir. 1957), *cert. denied,* 356 U.S. 974 (1958), considers a will in which property was given to the testator's wife "if she shall survive distribution of my estate." The court in applying California law seems to recognize that the death of the wife before distribution to her defeats the gift but that partial distributions made to her, though made without first securing an order of approval from the court, are valid when she dies before a final distribution has been made. The wife's estate contended that the partial distributions were void, so that a claim against her estate existed for the amount of such partial distributions and was deductible in determining her taxable estate for estate tax purposes. This contention did not prevail.

[115] The requirements which must be met if a gift in trust is to qualify for the gift tax marital deduction are basically the same.

[116] See the discussion of portion gifts with a power of appointment at page 861 infra.

[117] See 1954 I.R.C. §2056(b)(2), quoted infra page 1407.

tionable terminable interests which are subject to disposition by him.

If the gift in trust otherwise qualifies for the estate tax marital deduction, the trust will not be disqualified because the wife's rights under the trust are subject to termination or failure if she dies within a period not exceeding six months after her husband's death, or dies as a result of a common disaster which also causes the death of her husband. Of course, if the requirements as to survivorship are not met, so that the wife's rights under the trust fail or terminate, no estate tax marital deduction is available so far as the trust is concerned.[118]

A trust established by a husband for the benefit of his wife may or may not create a terminable interest in the wife. If the wife and her estate are the sole beneficiaries under the trust, she is not regarded as having a terminable interest and no problem is presented of qualifying the trust for the estate tax marital deduction regardless of its terms.[119] A trust under which all beneficial interests are in the wife and her estate is referred to in this discussion as an "estate trust." [120]

Even though all the interests under a trust established by a husband are not vested in his wife and her estate, the wife's interest under the trust may not be a terminable interest and, if it is not, her interest under the trust qualifies for the estate tax marital deduction. Thus if H in his will gives the residue of his estate to a trustee and directs the trustee "to pay the income to my sister A for her life, and on the death of my sister, to pay the corpus to my wife W absolutely," W's remainder interest under the trust is not a terminable interest.

If, however, the wife's interest under the trust established by her husband is terminable, the trust may nevertheless qualify for the estate tax marital deduction if certain specific requirements are met.[121] When such a trust does qualify, it is here referred to as a "power of appointment trust," to distinguish it from the "estate trust" mentioned above. When a power of appointment trust is created, the entire value of the trust property is available for the estate tax marital deduction, not just the value of the terminable interest of the wife under the trust. It also should be kept in mind that if an inter vivos trust is established by a husband and

---

[118] See 1954 I.R.C. §2056(b)(3), quoted infra page 1408.

[119] See 1954 I.R.C. §2056(b)(1), quoted infra page 1407.

[120] See Reg. §20.2056(e)-2(b), quoted infra page 1540.
The "estate trust" is recognized in Commissioner v. Ellis, 252 F.2d 109 (3d Cir. 1958).

[121] See 1954 I.R.C. §2056(b)(5), quoted infra page 1408. The corresponding gift tax marital deduction section is 1954 I.R.C. §2523(e), quoted infra page 1426.

the value of the trust property is includible in the husband's gross estate, the time when the requirements for a power of appointment trust must be satisfied is not when the trust is established but is at the death of the husband.

The following five conditions must be satisfied to establish a separate power of appointment trust:

1. The surviving spouse must be entitled for life to all the income from the corpus of the trust.

2. Such income must be payable annually or at more frequent intervals.

3. The surviving spouse must have the power, exercisable in favor of herself or of her estate, to appoint the entire corpus free of the trust.

4. Such a power in the surviving spouse must be exercisable by the spouse alone and (whether exercisable by will or during her life) must be exercisable in all events.

5. The corpus of the trust must not be subject to a power in any other person to appoint any part thereof to any person other than the surviving spouse.

The Regulations set out in detail what satisfies the five conditions which must be met to create a separate power of appointment marital deduction trust. They must be thoroughly examined if a power of appointment trust is to be employed, and therefore the pertinent parts are printed in full below.

SECTION 20.2056(b)-5. MARITAL DEDUCTION; LIFE ESTATE WITH POWER OF APPOINTMENT IN SURVIVING SPOUSE

Section 20.2056(b)-5. . . .

(e) *Application of local law.* In determining whether or not the conditions set forth in paragraph (a)(1) through (5) of this section are satisfied by the instrument of transfer, regard is to be had to the applicable provisions of the law of the jurisdiction under which the interest passes and, if the transfer is in trust, the applicable provisions of the law governing the administration of the trust. For example, silence of a trust instrument as to the frequency of payment will not be regarded as a failure to satisfy the condition set forth in paragraph (a)(2) of this section that income must be payable to the surviving spouse annually or more frequently unless the applicable law permits payment to be made less frequently than annually. The principles outlined in this paragraph and paragraphs (f) and (g) of this section which are applied in determining whether transfers in trust meet such conditions are equally applicable in ascertaining whether, in the case of interests not in trust, the surviving spouse has the equivalant in rights over income and over the property.

(f) *Right to income.* (1) If an interest is transferred in trust, the surviving spouse is "entitled for life to all of the income from the entire interest or a specific portion of the entire interest," for the purpose of the condition set forth in paragraph (a)(1) of this section, if the effect of the trust is to give her substantially that degree of beneficial enjoyment of the trust property during her life which the principles of the law of trusts accord to a person who is unqualifiedly designated as the life beneficiary of a trust.[122] Such degree of enjoyment is given only if it was the decedent's intention, as manifested by the terms of the trust instrument and the surrounding circumstances, that the trust should produce for the surviving spouse during her life such an income, or that the spouse should have such use of the trust property as is consistent with the value of the trust corpus and with its preservation. The designation of the spouse as sole income beneficiary for life of the entire interest or a specific portion of the entire interest will be sufficient to qualify the trust unless the terms of the trust and the surrounding circumstances considered as a whole evidence an intention to deprive the spouse of the requisite degree of enjoyment. In determining whether a trust evidences that intention, the treatment required or permitted with respect to individual items must be considered in relation to the entire system provided for the administration of the trust.

(2) If the over-all effect of a trust is to give to the surviving spouse such enforceable rights as will preserve to her the requisite degree of enjoyment, it is immaterial whether that result is effected by rules specifically stated in the trust instrument, or, in their absence, by the rules for the management of the trust property and the allocation of receipts and expenditures supplied by the State law. For example, a provision in the trust instrument for amortization of bond premium by appropriate periodic charges to interest will not disqualify the interest passing in trust even though there is no State law specifically authorizing amortization, or there is a State law denying amortization which is applicable only in the absence of such a provision in the trust instrument.

[122] In Estate of Allen L. Weisberger, 29 T.C. 217, (1957), a husband's will created a trust under which his widow had an unlimited testamentary power of appointment. She was also entitled to all the income, subject to the right of the trustee to divert to the husband's sons so much thereof as should, together with other income available to them, prove necessary for their maintenance and education. It was held that the trust did not qualify for the marital deduction, even though the diversion of income to the sons was unlikely because of other sources of income available to them. — Ed.

(3) In the case of a trust, the rules to be applied by the trustee in allocation of receipts and expenses between income and corpus must be considered in relation to the nature and expected productivity of the assets passing in trust, the nature and frequency of occurrence of the expected receipts, and any provisions as to change in the form of investments. If it is evident from the nature of the trust assets and the rules provided for management of the trust that the allocation to income of such receipts as rents, ordinary cash dividends, and interest will give to the spouse the substantial enjoyment during life required by the statute, provisions that such receipts as stock dividends and proceeds from the conversion of trust assets shall be treated as corpus will not disqualify the interest passing in trust. Similarly, provision for a depletion charge against income in the case of trust assets which are subject to depletion will not disqualify the interest passing in trust, unless the effect is to deprive the spouse of the requisite beneficial enjoyment. The same principle is applicable in the case of depreciation, trustees' commissions, and other charges.

(4) Provisions granting administrative powers to the trustees will not have the effect of disqualifying an interest passing in trust unless the grant of powers evidences the intention to deprive the surviving spouse of the beneficial enjoyment required by the statute. Such an intention will not be considered to exist if the entire terms of the instrument are such that the local courts will impose reasonable limitations upon the exercise of the powers. Among the powers which if subject to reasonable limitations will not disqualify the interest passing in trust are the power to determine the allocation or apportionment of receipts and disbursements between income and corpus, the power to apply the income or corpus for the benefit of the spouse, and the power to retain the assets passing to the trust. For example, a power to retain trust assets which consist substantially of unproductive property will not disqualify the interest if the applicable rules for the administration of the trust require, or permit the spouse to require, that the trustee either make the property productive or convert it within a reasonable time. Nor will such a power disqualify the interest if the applicable rules for administration of the trust require the trustee to use the degree of judgment and care in the exercise of the power which a prudent man would use if he were owner of the trust assets. Further, a power to retain a residence or other property for the personal use of the spouse will not disqualify the interest passing in trust.

(5) An interest passing in trust will not satisfy the condition set forth in paragraph (a)(1) of this section that the surviving spouse

be entitled to all the income if the primary purpose of the trust is to safeguard property without providing the spouse with the required beneficial enjoyment. Such trusts include not only trusts which expressly provide for the accumulation of the income but also trusts which indirectly accomplish a similar purpose. For example, assume that the corpus of a trust consists substantially of property which is not likely to be income producing during the life of the surviving spouse and that the spouse cannot compel the trustee to convert or otherwise deal with the property as described in subparagraph (4) of this paragraph. An interest passing to such a trust will not qualify unless the applicable rules for the administration require, or permit the spouse to require, that the trustee provide the required beneficial enjoyment, such as by payments to the spouse out of other assets of the trust.[123]

(6) If a trust is created during the decedent's life, it is immaterial whether or not the interest passing in trust satisfied the conditions set forth in paragraph (a)(1) through (5) of this section prior to the decedent's death. If a trust may be terminated during the life of the surviving spouse, under her exercise of a power of appointment or by distribution of the corpus to her, the interest passing in trust satisfies the condition set forth in paragraph (a)(1) of this section (that the spouse be entitled to all the income) if she (i) is entitled to the income until the trust terminates, or (ii) has the right, exercisable in all events, to have the corpus distributed to her at any time during her life.

(7) An interest passing in trust fails to satisfy the condition set forth in paragraph (a)(1) of this section, that the spouse be entitled to all the income, to the extent that the income is required to be accumulated in whole or in part or may be accumulated in the discretion of any person other than the surviving spouse;[124] to the extent that the consent of any person other than the surviving spouse is required as a condition precedent to distribution of the income; or to the extent that any person other than the surviving spouse

---

[123] When stock in a closely held corporation is placed in an intended marital deduction trust, and it is contemplated that the stock will be retained by the trustee without any power in the surviving spouse to direct otherwise, the past and probable future dividend payments will be a significant factor in determining whether the trust qualifies for the marital deduction. If the stock placed in the trust constitutes a minority interest, the power of the majority stockholder to control the flow of dividends to the trust may raise the question whether the wife has "substantially that degree of personal enjoyment of the trust property during her life which the principles of the law of trusts accord to a person who is unqualifiedly designated as the life beneficiary of the trust." In this connection examine In re Shupack's Will, cited supra page 65, note 33. — ED.

[124] If the estate trust is used, however, the income may be accumulated. — ED.

has the power to alter the terms of the trust so as to deprive her of her right to the income. An interest passing in trust will not fail to satisfy the condition that the spouse be entitled to all the income merely because its terms provide that the right of the surviving spouse to the income shall not be subject to assignment, alienation, pledge, attachment or claims of creditors.[125]

(8) In the case of an interest passing in trust, the terms "entitled for life" and "payable annually or at more frequent intervals," as used in the conditions set forth in paragraph (a)(1) and (2) of this section, require that under the terms of the trust the income referred to must be currently (at least annually; see paragraph (e) of this section) distributable to the spouse or that she must have such command over the income that it is virtually hers. Thus, the conditions in paragraph (a)(1) and (2) of this section are satisfied in this respect if, under the terms of the trust instrument, the spouse has the right exercisable annually (or more frequently) to require distribution to herself of the trust income, and otherwise the trust income is to be accumulated and added to corpus. Similarly, as respects the income for the period between the last distribution date and the date of the spouse's death, it is sufficient if that income is subject to the spouse's power to appoint. Thus, if the trust instrument provides that income accrued or undistributed on the date of the spouse's death is to be disposed of as if it had been received after her death, and if the spouse has a power of appointment over the trust corpus, the power necessarily extends to the undistributed income.[126]

(9) An interest is not to be regarded as failing to satisfy the conditions set forth in paragraph (a)(1) and (2) of this section (that the spouse be entitled to all the income and that it be payable annually or more frequently) merely because the spouse is not entitled to the income from estate assets for the period before distribution of those assets by the executor, unless the executor is, by the decedent's will, authorized or directed to delay distribution beyond the period reasonably required for administration of the decedent's estate.[127] As to the valuation of the property interest passing to

[125] The effectiveness of a spendthrift clause may turn on the nature of the power over the trust corpus which is given to the wife. See Griswold, Spendthrift Trusts 72 (2d ed. 1947). — ED.

[126] The income for the period between the last income distribution date and the date of the spouse's death can thus be kept out of the spouse's probate estate. On the pros and cons of avoiding probate, see the discussion at page 120 supra. — ED.

[127] One of the requirements to qualify a power of appointment marital deduction gift is that the income be "payable annually or at more frequent intervals." If a marital deduction trust is set up under a will, it is not likely that the trust will be established and in operation within a year after the

the spouse in trust where the right to income is expressly postponed, see §20.2056(b)-4.

(g) *Power of appointment in surviving spouse.* (1) The conditions set forth in paragraph (a) (3) and (4) of this section, that is, that the surviving spouse must have a power of appointment exercisable in favor of herself or her estate and exercisable alone and in all events, are not met unless the power of the surviving spouse to appoint the entire interest or a specific portion of it falls within one of the following categories:

(i) A power so to appoint fully exercisable in her own favor at any time following the decedent's death (as, for example, an unlimited power to invade); [128] or

---

husband's death, so that at least the initial income payments are not likely to be actually made until more than a year has gone by. Section 20.2056(b)-5(f)(9) of the Regulations makes it clear that the delay in payment of the income during administration of the estate will not disqualify the trust, and goes even farther by pointing out that the trust will not be disqualified if the wife is not *entitled* to the income for the period before distribution of the estate assets. In the absence of a provision to the contrary, when the trust is established, the wife will be entitled to an accounting for income back to the date of the husband's death. When an inter vivos trust calls for the establishment of a marital trust on the death of the husband-settlor, the marital trust can be promptly set up unless it is governed as to amount by a formula. In the latter case, the precise amount going into the trust cannot be determined normally within a year after the settlor's death and thus there may be a delay of more than a year before the income of the marital trust can be definitively paid to the wife. Such a delay, which is inherent in testamentary trusts and clearly recognized as permissible without disqualifying the marital trust, should likewise not disqualify the formula marital trust which comes in under an inter vivos trust on the settlor's death. On the establishment of the trust, however, the wife should be entitled to an accounting for income back to the husband-settlor's death. It would not be wise to rely on Reg. §20.2056(b)-5(f)(9) to justify excluding the wife from the right to the income for the period between the husband-settlor's death and the date the trust can be established. — Ed.

[128] In Estate of Harry A. Ellis, 26 T.C. 694 (1956), the decedent established a trust under his will. The decedent's wife was given the income for her life, but in any year in which the income was less than $5000, she was to receive $5000. In addition, should she require sums in excess of $5000 a year, such excess was to be paid to her monthly, and the document stated: "she and she alone shall be the judge as to how much shall be required." The court held that the trust qualified for the marital deduction, since the spouse was given an unlimited power to invade the principal. The case was reversed sub nom. Commissioner v. Ellis, 252 F.2d 109 (3d Cir. 1958), on the ground that under the applicable state law, the widow's power of invasion was limited to reasonable use and did not permit unlimited appointment to herself, but in view of the fact that the testator had provided that one half of the remainder should go to the widow's estate, the marital deduction was allowable with respect to one half of the trust property. Notice that the marital deduction is allowed under the 1939 Code with respect to a one-half interest under a single trust when, as here, the wife's interest in the one half is nonterminable because the remainder is payable to her estate. In Hoffman v. McGinnis, 277 F.2d 598 (3d Cir. 1960), the decedent in his will created a trust which provided that his surviving wife be given the income for her life and "the right to use and

spend any or all of the principal of my said estate, if she so desires," and that the trust was to terminate "as to that part of the principal so paid to her." In reversing the District Court, the Court of Appeals distinguished the Ellis case on the ground that in that case withdrawals from principal were authorized only as "required," while in the Hoffman case they were authorized as "desired." Furthermore, the court pointed out that in the Hoffman case the will provided that the trust would terminate as to that part of the principal paid to the widow, whereas in the Ellis case such a provision was absent.

In Matteson v. United States, 147 F. Supp. 535 (N.D.N.Y. 1956), the power given to the surviving wife under a trust, which gave her all the income, provided that if she ever found the income was not sufficient ("and of its sufficiency she shall be the sole judge"), the trustees should pay her principal in the amount she desired. The court held that this was not an unrestricted power but required a good faith determination by her of the insufficiency of income before she could call for payment of corpus. Thus the trust did not qualify for the marital deduction. The case was affirmed in 240 F.2d 517 (2d Cir. 1956), on the ground that the appeal was not taken in time.

The decedent's spouse in Estate of Theodore Geddings Tarver, 26 T.C. 490 (1956), was given the right to receive portions of the principal "as and when she may demand, for her use and/or the use or benefit of our children as she deems advisable." The court held that under the applicable South Carolina law, she was not given an unlimited right to invade corpus, and thus the trust did not qualify for the marital deduction. The case was affirmed sub nom. Estate of Tarver v. Commissioner, 255 F.2d 913 (4th Cir. 1958).

In Estate of Edward F. Pipe v. Commissioner, 241 F.2d 210 (2d Cir. 1957), *cert. denied,* 355 U.S. 814 (1957), the court considered a case where a legal life interest was given to the decedent's wife. In addition, she was given full power to use, enjoy, sell or dispose of the income and principal of the life estate or any part thereof for such purposes and in such a manner as she in her uncontrolled discretion might choose. The will provided that anything that remained unexpended at the time of her death was to pass to the designated remainderman. The court held that a power to consume was not an unlimited power to invade, because she had no power to deal with any unconsumed property. The court pointed out that the wife could not appoint the principal to herself or her estate because, as long as any of the principal of the estate remained, it was to pass to the named remainderman. In the light of this decision, a power to appoint by deed should specify that the donee may appoint the property to herself and free it from any claims of the remainderman. See, however, Lincoln Rochester Trust Co. v. United States, 188 F. Supp. 839 (W.D.N.Y. 1960), discussed infra note 138. There is a comment on the Pipe case in 57 Colum. L. Rev. 893 (1957).

The decedent in Cass v. Tomlinson, 57-1 U.S.T.C. ¶11692 (S.D. Fla. 1957), gave his wife the residue of his estate, "my said wife being empowered to sell, to convey, encumber and otherwise dispose of the same as to her may seem best . . ." The wife was also given a special power to appoint by will. The court held that the gift of the residue to the wife did not qualify for the marital deduction. The reason given was that she received only a life interest with administrative power to manage, to invest and reinvest the property. The court also concluded that the value of the property was not includible in the wife's gross estate on her death.

In Estate of Delia Crawford McGehee, 28 T.C. 412 (1957), a wife gave her entire estate in fee simple to her husband but provided that if at the time of his death, he should still own or possess any of the property, it was to pass to her brothers and sisters and to his brothers. The court held that she gave her husband only a life estate coupled with a power of disposition in fee during his lifetime and that such a gift did not qualify for the marital deduction. The court also pointed out that the property could not ripen into a fee interest in his hands so as to bring it within the scope of the estate tax, upon his subsequent death. The case was affirmed on this point (though reversed on another) sub nom. McGehee v. Commissioner 260 F.2d 818 (5th Cir. 1958). On rehearing, the case was reversed on this point, on the basis of the 1958 amendment referred to infra page 857, note 138, even though the Commissioner contended that the amendment did not change the result because of the provision for a gift over of the property if the spouse should still own any of the property at the time of his death. See 260 F.2d 823 (5th Cir. 1958).

The court in Dexter v. United States, 163 F. Supp. 442 (D. Mass. 1958), considered a trust under a will which authorized the trustees to make payments of principal to the deceased's wife "as she may request in writing," and in the instrument the decedent urged the trustees "in exercising the powers conferred upon them by this paragraph to bear in mind my earnest wish that it is my chief wish to protect my wife against privation rather than to maintain a maximum fund for final distribution." The court held that the wife did not have an unlimited power to invade corpus but that the trustees had a discretionary right to refuse to make a payment which the widow requested.

In Gordon v. United States, 163 F. Supp. 542 (W.D. Mo. 1958), the decedent's will left one half of the residue of his estate in trust with directions that the trustees pay the income to his widow for life, and stated, "In the event that the income from this trust shall be insufficient to meet living expenses or other requirements of said Minnie Gordon, she shall be entitled to withdraw such sums out of the corpus of this trust as may be required from time to time in her discretion." On the widow's death, the remaining principal and accumulated income were to pass to the decedent's children as his widow appointed by will and, in default of appointment, to the children equally. A marital deduction was claimed for the value of the trust property, the trust was established and the executor discharged. Thereafter, the Internal Revenue Service sent a ninety-day letter proposing to disallow the marital deduction. The trustees then filed a suit in the state court, and a decree issued ordering the trustees to convey the trust property to the widow, on the ground that at all times since her husband's death the trust property was subject to the complete control of the widow. The District Court held that the state court decree, in the absence of collusion, settled the property rights of the widow and, as settled, the interest given to her qualified for the marital deduction.

The testator in Keith v. Worcester County Trust Co., 338 Mass. 41, 153 N.E.2d 630 (1958), established a trust and said: "I authorize and empower my said trustees to make utilization of the principal for the foregoing purposes [support, etc.] at such times and to such extent as my said wife . . . desires." The court held that under this language the trustees were not required to comply with requests made by the wife.

In Estate of E. W. Noble, 31 T.C. 888 (1959), a trust was involved under which the widow received the income for life and was entitled to the corpus if she at any time deemed it "necessary or expedient in her discretion to use any of the corpus . . . for her maintenance, support and comfort." The widow's power to invade corpus was restricted, and hence the trust did not qualify for the marital deduction.

In Estate of Elwood Comer, 31 T.C. 1193 (1959), the wife was given a power to withdraw installments of principal in any amounts she deemed advisable for her maintenance, comfort and general welfare, and the court held that under the controlling Ohio law she did not have an unlimited power of invasion. Thus the interest given her under the trust did not qualify for the marital deduction.

Estate of Ralph G. May, 32 T.C. 386 (1959), considered a case involving a legal life interest in the wife with a right in her, exercisable in her sole discretion, "to invade and use principal not only for necessities but generally for her comfort, happiness and well-being," and the court held that the wife did not have an unlimited power to invade because the power was restricted to use and did not include the power to convey to herself or her estate. Hence, the

(ii) A power so to appoint exercisable in favor of her estate. Such a power, if exercisable during life, must be fully exercisable at any time during life, or, if exercisable by will,[129] must be fully exercisable irrespective of the time of her death (subject in either case to the provisions of §20.2053(b)-3, relating to interests conditioned on survival for a limited period); or

(iii) A combination of the powers described under subparagraphs (i) and (ii) of this subparagraph. For example, the surviving spouse may, until she attains the age of 50 years, have a power to appoint to herself and thereafter have a power to appoint to her estate. However, the condition that the spouse's power must be exercisable in all events is not satisfied unless irrespective of when the surviving spouse may die the entire interest or a specific portion of it will at the time of her death be subject to one power or the other (subject to the exception in §20.2053(b)-3, relating to interests contingent on survival for a limited period).

(2) The power of the surviving spouse must be a power to appoint the entire interest or a specific portion of it as unqualified owner (and free of the trust if a trust is involved, or free of the joint

---

interest did not qualify for the marital deduction. Although the decedent died before the 1954 Code went into effect, the legal life interest with a proper power could qualify for the marital deduction under the amendment of the 1939 Code referred to infra page 857, note 138. The case was affirmed sub nom. Estate of Ralph G. May v. Commissioner, 283 F.2d 853 (2d Cir. 1960).

In Estate of Thomas J. Semmes, 32 T.C. 1218 (1959), a marital deduction was denied where the widow was named as life income beneficiary and was given "sole power of management and control of the trust property" and was to "have the right to encroach upon the principal . . . for her own benefit, at any time she sees fit without accounting to my children." The remainder interest under the trust was given to the testator's children. The court concluded that the widow did not have the power to appoint the corpus in all events to herself as unqualified owner or appoint the corpus as a part of her estate. In Estate of Leo A. Bourke, CCH T.C. Mem. 1960-94, the testamentary trust gave the decedent's wife the income for life and required the trustees to pay her "such portion of the principal of the trust estate of this trust up to the whole thereof as [she] shall from time to time request in writing." The trust was to terminate on the death of the wife "unless sooner terminated by payment to my said wife of the whole of the principal of the trust estate . . ." The will contained a spendthrift clause. The Commissioner disallowed a marital deduction on the ground the wife had a terminable interest, but the court allowed the deduction. — ED.

129 If the wife is given a power to appoint the trust property by her will to such person or persons as she may select, the applicable state law may construe such a power as one which does not permit an appointment to be made to her estate. In Estate of William C. Allen, 29 T.C. 465 (1957), such a power, under applicable state law (Maryland), did not permit an appointment to be made to the wife's estate, or to herself, or in payment of her own debts, and the court held that the trust for the benefit of the wife did not qualify for the marital deduction. — ED.

tenancy if a joint tenancy is involved) or to appoint the entire interest or a specific portion of it as a part of her estate (and free of the trust if a trust is involved), that is, in effect, to dispose of it to whomsoever she pleases. Thus, if the decedent devised property to a son and the surviving spouse as joint tenants with right of survivorship and under local law the surviving spouse has a power of severance exercisable without consent of the other joint tenant, and by exercising this power could acquire a one-half interest in the property as a tenant in common, her power of severance will satisfy the condition set forth in paragraph (a)(3) of this section that she have a power of appointment in favor of herself or her estate. However, if the surviving spouse entered into a binding agreement with the decedent to exercise the power only in favor of their issue, that condition is not met. An interest passing in trust will not be regarded as failing to satisfy the conditon merely because takers in default of the surviving spouse's exercise of the power are designated by the decedent. The decedent may provide that, in default of exercise of the power, the trust shall continue for an additional period.

(3) A power is not considered to be a power exercisable by a surviving spouse alone and in all events as required by paragraph (a)(4) of this section if the exercise of the power in the surviving spouse to appoint the entire interest or a specific portion of it to herself or to her estate requires the joinder or consent of any other person. The power is not "exercisable in all events," if it can be terminated during the life of the surviving spouse by any event other than her complete exercise or release of it. Further, a power is not "exercisable in all events" if it may be exercised for a limited purpose only. For example, a power which is not exercisable in the event of the spouse's remarriage is not exercisable in all events. Likewise, if there are any restrictions, either by the terms of the instrument or under applicable local law, on the exercise of a power to consume property (whether or not held in trust) for the benefit of the spouse, the power is not exercisable in all events. Thus, if a power of invasion is exercisable only for the spouse's support, or only for her limited use, the power is not exercisable in all events. In order for a power of invasion to be exercisable in all events, the surviving spouse must have the unrestricted power exercisable at any time during her life to use all or any part of the property subject to the power, and to dispose of it in any manner. including the power to dispose of it by gift (whether or not she has power to dispose of it by will).[130]

(4) The power in the surviving spouse is exercisable in all events

---

[130] See note 128 supra. — Ed.

only if it exists immediately following the decedent's death.   For
example, if the power given to the surviving spouse is exercisable
during life, but cannot be effectively exercised before distribution
of the assets by the executor, the power is not exercisable in all
events.   Similarly, if the power is exercisable by will, but cannot
be effectively exercised in the event the surviving spouse dies before distribution of the assets by the executor, the power is not exercisable in all events.   However, an interest will not be disqualified by the mere fact that, in the event the power is exercised
during administration of the estate, distribution of the property to
the appointee will be delayed for the period of administration.   If
the power is in existence at all times following the decedent's
death, limitations of a formal nature will not disqualify an interest.
Examples of formal limitations on a power exercisable during life
are requirements that an exercise must be in a particular form,
that it must be filed with a trustee during the spouse's life, that
reasonable notice must be given, or that reasonable intervals must
elapse between successive partial exercises.[131]   Examples of formal
limitations on a power exercisable by will are that it must be exercised by a will executed by the surviving spouse after the decedent's death or that exercise must be by specific reference to the
power.[132]

[131] But see Estate of Thomas C. Werbe v. United States, 178 F. Supp. 704
(S.D. Ind. 1958), *aff'd;* 273 F.2d 201 (7th Cir. 1959), discussed infra page 872,
note 168. — ED.

[132] In Estate of Frank E. Tingley, 22 T.C. 402 (1954), it was held that no
marital deduction was allowable where the decedent left property in trust, and
the income was to be paid to his wife for life and she was to have the power
to request payment of any part or parts of the corpus for her own and absolute
use and consumption, but with the proviso that she was to lose this power and
that all of the income did not have to be distributed to her if she became
legally incapacitated or if a guardian, conservator or other custodian of her
estate or person should be appointed.   The court held that under these circumstances the power to invade corpus was not exercisable "in all events."   The
decision was affirmed sub nom. Starrett v. Commissioner 223 F.2d 163 (1st Cir.
1955).

Revenue Ruling 55-518, 1955-2 C.B. 384, held that, even though the surviving spouse was incompetent from the date of her husband's death until the
date of her death, a trust established by her husband in his will qualified for
the marital deduction when the surviving spouse was the lifetime income beneficiary and was given an unrestricted power to use, consume and dispose of
the trust principal during her lifetime.

In Miller v. Dowling, 56-2 U.S.T.C. ¶11646 (S.D.N.Y. 1956), the decedent
established a trust with his widow as one of the trustees, and under the terms
of the trust, the widow was entitled to the income and had the power to withdraw the corpus on demand.   The trustees had the power to terminate the
trust at any time, and on termination by the trustees, the property would be
distributed to the decedent's children.   As long as the widow was a trustee, she
could control the termination of the trust and the diversion of the trust property to the children, but if for any reason she was eliminated as a trustee
during her lifetime, there would be a power in others to divert the corpus to

(5) If the surviving spouse has the requisite power to appoint to herself or her estate, it is immaterial that she also has one or more lesser powers. Thus, if she has a testamentary power to appoint to her estate, she may also have a limited power of withdrawal or of appointment during her life. Similarly, if she has an unlimited power of withdrawal, she may have a limited testamentary power.

(h) *Requirement of survival for a limited period.* A power of appointment in the surviving spouse will not be treated as failing to meet the requirements of paragraph (a)(3) of this section even though the power may terminate, if the only conditions which would cause the termination are those described in paragraph (a) of §20.2056(b)-3, and if those conditions do not in fact occur. Thus, the entire interest or a specific portion of it will not be disqualified by reason of the fact that the exercise of the power in the spouse is subject to a condition of survivorship described in §20.2056(b)-3 if the terms of the condition, that is, the survivorship of the surviving spouse, or the failure to die in a common disaster, are fulfilled.

(j) *Existence of a power in another.* Paragraph (a)(5) of this section provides that a transfer described in paragraph (a) is nondeductible to the extent that the decedent created a power in the trustee or in any other person to appoint a part of the interest to any person other than the surviving spouse.[133] However, only

---

someone else. Nevertheless, the court held that the trust qualified for the marital deduction. — Ed.

[133] In Estate of Raymond Parks Wheeler, 26 T.C. 466 (1956), a marital deduction was not allowed where the decedent's wife was given the income for life and a power to requisition payments from the trust, and in addition, the trustee was given the power to invade corpus for the benefit of the decedent's children as well as for the benefit of his wife. The court pointed out that the power in the trustee to invade corpus for the benefit of the children made the trust subject to a power in someone else to appoint part of the property to a person other than the surviving spouse, and that such a power disqualified the trust for the marital deduction.

In Estate of Harry Gelb, CCH T.C. Mem. 1960-187, the income of a residuary trust was to go to the decedent's wife and the trustees were directed to invade principal, if necessary, to keep the annual return to the wife up to $10,000. The wife was given the power to appoint the principal. In addition the wife was to be paid for the support and education of her daughter amounts within the discretion of the trustees but they were not to exceed $5000 per year. Even though the wife was one of the trustees, the court held that the trust did not qualify for the marital deduction because the decedent clearly indicated that his daughter was to be provided for out of the trust and that the trustees would have to act in a fiduciary capacity in determining what to divert from the wife's control for the support of the daughter. Thus the power to invade corpus for the benefit of another defeated the marital deduction. In another case, Estate of Morton H. Spero, 34 T.C. —, No. 115 (1960), where the wife was a co-trustee, the court held that the trust did not qualify for the marital

powers in other persons which are in opposition to that of the surviving spouse will cause a portion of the interest to fail to satisfy the condition set forth in paragraph (a)(5) of this section. Thus, a power in a trustee to distribute corpus to or for the benefit of a surviving spouse will not disqualify the trust. Similarly, a power to distribute corpus to the spouse for the support of minor children will not disqualify the trust if she is legally obligated to support such children. The application of this paragraph may be illustrated by the following examples:

Example (1). Assume that a decedent created a trust, designating his surviving spouse as income beneficiary for life with an unrestricted power in the spouse to appoint the corpus during her life. The decedent further provided that in the event the surviving spouse should die without having exercised the power, the trust should continue for the life of his son with a power in the son to appoint the corpus. Since the power in the son could become exercisable only after the death of the surviving spouse, the interest is not regarded as failing to satisfy the condition set forth in paragraph (a)(5) of this section.[134]

Example (2). Assume that the decedent created a trust, designating his surviving spouse as income beneficiary for life and as donee of a power to appoint by will the entire corpus. The decedent further provided that the trustee could distribute 30 percent of the corpus to the decedent's son when he reached the age of 35 years. Since the trustee has a power to appoint 30 per-

---

deduction where the wife was entitled to all the income and had a general power to appoint by will the corpus, because the trustees had the power "to use so much of the principal of this trust as may be necessary at any time in their discretion, to provide reasonable needs and comfortable maintenance of my said wife, and any of my children, in the event that the income from this trust shall, in their discretion, be insufficient to provide properly for her or their comfortable care, maintenance and support." — ED.

[134] In Rev. Rul. 55-394, 1955-1 C.B. 458, it was held that a trust was not disqualified as a marital deduction trust merely because the trustee was directed to pay the corpus to the spouse if she were alive on a certain date. Although such a direction causes a termination of the power of appointment given the wife, it is not a termination that will disqualify the trust. Furthermore, it was held that the fact that the trust provided for a gift in default of appointment by the wife did not cause the trust to fail to satisfy the requirement that the surviving spouse must be able to appoint to herself or to her estate.

In Rev. Rul. 55-395, 1955-1 C.B. 458, a trust was considered in which the trustee was required to use the net income for the care, maintenance and support of the surviving spouse "in such fashion and state as she may desire," and in addition the trustee was given the power, in the event the income should be insufficient "to meet her desires and demands," to sell the trust assets and use the proceeds for such purposes. It was held that the trust did not qualify for the marital deduction because it did not confer upon the surviving spouse the power, exercisable by her alone and in all events, to appoint the corpus free of the trust. The trust provided that the property remaining in the trust on the death of the surviving spouse should go to designated beneficiaries. — ED.

cent of the entire interest for the benefit of a person other than the surviving spouse, only 70 percent of the interest placed in trust satisfied the condition set forth in paragraph (a)(5) of this section. If, in this case, the surviving spouse had a power, exercisable by her will, to appoint only one-half of the corpus as it was constituted at the time of her death, it should be noted that only 35 percent of the interest placed in the trust would satisfy the condition set forth in paragraph (a)(3) of this section.

PROBLEMS

13.16. H in his will purports to establish a separate estate tax marital deduction trust out of a fractional share of his residuary estate. His will contains a provision that income realized during administration from property used to pay debts, expenses of administration and taxes shall be added to corpus. Will such a provision prevent the trust from qualifying for the estate tax marital deduction? [135]

13.17. If a separate estate tax marital deduction trust is employed in an estate plan, what provision should you insert in the wife's will in regard to the payment of federal and state death taxes on her death?

13.18. H in his will establishes a separate estate tax marital de-

---

[135] See 3 Scott, Trusts §234.4 (2d ed. 1956) for a discussion of the various views as to the disposition of income from property used to pay debts, expenses of administration and taxes when the will contains no provision in this regard.

Suppose that the residue is divided into a marital deduction gift and a nonmarital deduction gift and that the will directs that all taxes shall be paid out of the nonmarital deduction share of the residue. Should any of the income earned by the property used to pay taxes go to the marital deduction gift? It is certainly arguable that the income was earned by funds which never were scheduled for the marital deduction gift and that thus all of the income should go to the nonmarital deduction share of the residue. Other possible solutions are that the income should be allocated on the basis of the original division of the residue before any part of the residue has been diverted to pay taxes. That is, if the marital deduction gift is two fifths of the original residue, then the marital deduction gift will receive two fifths of the income earned on the property used to pay taxes. It can also be contended that the income earned on the property used to pay taxes should be allocated on the basis of the division of the residue after taxes are paid. That is, if after the taxes have been paid, the amount of the net residue which passes to the marital deduction gift is three fifths of the net residue, then the marital deduction gift should receive three fifths of the income earned on property which has been used to pay taxes.

Waldrop v. United States, 137 F. Supp. 753 (Ct. Cl. 1956), recognizes that post-mortem income is not part of the decedent's gross estate and thus, even though it falls into the residue and passes to a charity, it cannot be the basis of any charitable deduction for the purpose of determining the amount of the estate tax. Likewise, adding income to the corpus of a marital deduction gift will not increase the amount of the deduction.

duction trust.   In addition to the general power to appoint by will given to his wife, W, under the trust, the trust contains the following provision: "During my wife's life, the trustees shall distribute to, or for the benefit of, any one or more of my issue who are living at the date of my death or are born thereafter, from the corpus of the trust, from time to time, such amount or amounts as my wife shall appoint by an instrument in writing delivered to the trustees in her lifetime.   Any appointment by my wife may be of such estates and interests and upon such terms, trusts, conditions, powers and limitations as my wife shall determine."   If W exercises her restricted power to appoint by deed, will such an exercise constitute a gift by her for federal gift tax purposes?   See E.T. 23, 1950-1 C.B. 133.   See also Section 25.2514-1(b)(2) quoted infra page 1549; Section 25.2514-3(e), Ex. (1), quoted infra page 1551, and Self, Jr. v. United States, 142 F. Supp. 939 (Ct. Cl. 1956).[136]

13.19.   H in his will establishes a trust under which the income is to be paid to his wife for life and "on the death of my wife, the then remaining principal and undistributed income shall be distributed to my wife's executors or administrators as a part of her estate and free of this trust."   The contention is made that the gift to the wife's executors or administrators violates the common law rule against perpetuities because they conceivably may not be appointed within the period of the rule.   Should such a contention prevail?   See 4 Restatement of Property §374, Comment *f*.   The contention is also made that the gift to the wife's executors or administrators is an attempted gift to her estate and that the estate of a person is not an entity capable of receiving a gift. Should such a contention prevail?   See In re Doyle's Estate, 107 Mont. 64, 80 P.2d 374 (1938).   Cf. In re Glass' Estate, 164 Cal. 765, 130 Pac. 868 (1913); Gardner v. Anderson, 114 Kan. 778, 227 Pac. 743 (1923).

13.20.   In determining whether to employ in an estate plan a separate power of appointment trust or an estate trust, point out the differences in the two types of trusts in regard to the following matters:

   a. The retention by the trustee of non-income-producing property
   b. The rights of the creditors of the wife to reach the trust property on her death

---

[136] When a surviving spouse is given both a general power to appoint by will and a special power to appoint by deed, as in Problem 13.18, it is possible for her to reduce her taxable estate by the exercise of the special power, but the gift tax cost to her may make this undesirable from her standpoint. If the trustee is directed to pay any gift taxes incurred by the exercise of the special power, it may be feasible for her to exercise the special power.

    c. The operation of the rule against perpetuities

    d. Probate expenses on the wife's death

    e. State death taxes on the wife's death

See the discussion of the points listed above in Casner, Estate Planning Under the Revenue Act of 1948 — The Regulations, 63 Harv. L. Rev. 99 (1949).

If a power of appointment marital deduction trust is established, additional problems may be presented on the death of the surviving spouse. The trustee of the original marital deduction trust may find himself in the position of having to work with someone who may not be compatible. Furthermore, the surviving spouse by exercising the power of appointment may create a number of separate trusts, so that the trustee may be confronted with the task of administering trusts of an entirely different nature from that of the original marital deduction trust, under which he accepted his responsibilities. In other words, the trustee who accepts the responsibilities under the original marital deduction trust should look forward to the situation with which he may be faced on the death of the surviving spouse if she exercises her power of appointment. He possibly should insist upon some protection regarding commissions under any trust created by the exercise of the power, and regarding his ability to resign as trustee if the arrangement resulting from the exercise of the power is not one under which he would like to continue to operate.

If the surviving spouse has no estate of her own, the exercise or nonexercise of the general power of appointment under a power of appointment marital deduction trust may place some duties on the trustee of the original marital deduction trust to see that taxes are paid, an estate tax return is filed, and other responsibilities in connection with the winding up of the surviving spouse's affairs are fulfilled. Legal questions may be presented and the problem will arise as to where the money is coming from to pay lawyer's fees and other expenses.

h. *Separate Legal Life Interest in the Wife Plus a General Power of Appointment*

Under the 1939 Code,[137] a transfer from husband to wife of a legal life interest in property coupled with a general power of appointment in the life tenant, with a remainder over to others in default of exercise, did not qualify for the marital deduction be-

---

[137] Section 812(e).

cause of the terminable interest rule.[138]   Such a transfer was unwise from a tax standpoint because the value of the transferred
property was includible in the wife's gross estate with no com-

[138] Section 210 of the Technical Changes Act of 1953 provides with regard
to decedents who die after December 31, 1947, and before April 3, 1948, that
whether property is held in trust or not, if the surviving spouse is entitled for
life to all the income from the property, payable annually or at more frequent
intervals, with power in the surviving spouse to use and consume such portion
of the property as the surviving spouse may need or desire for comfortable
support and maintenance, and with no power in any person other than the
surviving spouse to appoint any part of such property, the property so given
to the surviving spouse may qualify for the marital deduction. The purpose
of this amendment is to take care of the situation where a person died before
April 3, 1948, and thus did not have an opportunity to change his will in the
light of the enactment of the marital deduction provision which took effect
on April 3, 1948. In order to take advantage of this amendment, however,
the wife must elect to treat the property given her as subject to a general
power of appointment in her so that the property will be includible in her
gross estate when she dies. Her election must be made within one year after
the date of the enactment of this amendment. In Attix v. Robinson, 155 F.
Supp. 592 (D. Mont. 1957), the court applied §210 of the Technical Changes
Act of 1953 and held that a gift in trust qualified for the marital deduction
where the trust directed the appropriate court, upon proper application, to
order paid to the decedent's wife out of the principal whatever was necessary
to enable her to live comfortably. Furthermore, the court held that the widow
had properly made her election under §210 when she filed a refund claim
signed by her as executrix.

The court in Estate of Michael Melamid, 22 T.C. 966 (1954), considered a
will in which the decedent bequeathed his residuary estate to his wife for
life, with a remainder to his sons. The will authorized the wife to use so
much of the property as she might need for the way of life to which she had
become accustomed. The court held that the life interest in the wife plus
the power did not give her an absolute fee but only a terminable interest that
did not qualify for the marital deduction.

In Estate of Edward F. Pipe, 23 T.C. 99 (1954), the decedent gave his spouse
a legal life estate with an unlimited lifetime power over principal but expressly
prohibited the spouse from disposing of that part of the principal which was
unexpended at the time of her death. A gift over was made of anything
remaining at her death. In other words, the spouse had a general power to
appoint by deed but no power to appoint by will. It was decided that under
local law the spouse did not receive an absolute fee simple estate but had only
a terminable interest, and thus the value of the gift to her did not qualify
for the marital deduction under the 1939 Code. The case was affirmed sub
nom. Estate of Edward F. Pipe v. Commissioner, 241 F.2d 210 (2d Cir. 1957),
cert. denied, 355 U.S. 814 (1957).

In Estate of Julius Selling, 24 T.C. 191 (1955), the decedent made a bequest
to his wife of insurance renewal commissions payable over a period up to
nine years. The decedent's will provided that his wife had the right to dispose of the commission rights at any time and that any commissions unpaid
at her death (presumably if she had not disposed of such unpaid commissions)
should pass to the decedent's son. Applying the 1939 Code, the court held
that the wife was given a terminable interest and consequently the gift to her
of the renewal commissions did not qualify for the marital deduction.

The decedent in Estate of Harriet C. Evilsizor, 27 T.C. 710 (1957), devised
all of her real estate to her husband for life, with a remainder to her children,
and authorized her husband to sell, deed and transfer the real estate as he
should deem to be in his best interest. The court held that the husband

pensating marital deduction in the husband's estate. Likewise a
gift by a husband to his wife and son as joint tenants with the right
of survivorship did not qualify as to the wife's undivided one half

---

received only a life estate under Ohio law and that this life estate was not
enlarged into a fee simple by reason of the power of disposal. Hence the
gift to him did not qualify for the marital deduction under the 1939 Code.

The court in Davey v. Weber, 133 Colo. 365, 295 P.2d 688 (1956), held that
an unqualified power given to a life tenant to dispose of property devised by
will enlarged the life estate to a fee simple estate.

In Boyd v. Gray, 162 F. Supp. 307 (W.D. Ky. 1957), the testator's will gave
the residue of his estate to his wife to be used, enjoyed and disposed of by her
in any way she might choose, but if any of the property remained undisposed
of at her death, it was to pass to other designated beneficiaries. The court
held that under Kentucky law the wife received a life interest with a power
of disposal, and consequently, under the 1939 Code, which was controlling,
she had a terminable interest and the gift to her did not qualify for the marital
deduction. The case was remanded sub nom. Boyd v. Gray, 261 F.2d 914
(6th Cir. 1958), for consideration of the effect of the Technical Amendments
Act of 1958, §93 (referred to later in this note) upon the issues and the state
law involved. The District Court on reconsideration, as directed by the Court
of Appeals, held that the wife's power of disposition was in any manner she
might choose and thus the interest qualified for the marital deduction under
the provisions of the Technical Amendments Act of 1958. See Boyd v. Gray,
175 F. Supp. 57 (W.D. Ky. 1959).

In Estate of Wallace S. Howell, 28 T.C. 1193 (1957), where a decedent left
all of his property to his wife "to be used as she pleases, for her own support,
the residue after her life, to go to" a son or a grandson, no marital deduction
was allowed under 1939 I.R.C. §812(e)(1)(B). The fact that the state court
imposed an inheritance tax solely against the surviving spouse and not against
the remainderman was not deemed material.

The husband's will in Newton v. Wiseman, 58-2 U.S.T.C. ¶11816 (W.D.
Okla. 1958), gave certain stock to his wife but directed that if she decided to
sell the stock, his nephew as to have the first right to purchase it, and if she
"dies without disposing of such stock by sale within her lifetime," the stock
was to pass to the nephew. The court held that the wife's interest in the
stock was not a terminable one under 1939 I.R.C. §812(e)(1)(B), since she
could use the proceeds of the sale of the stock as she saw fit and "she can
dispose of it [the stock] by will as she sees fit."

In 1958, §812(e)(1)(F) of the 1939 Code was amended so as to make it identical with §2056(b)(5) of the 1954 Code. This amendment is to apply with
respect to decedents dying after April 1, 1948, and before August 17, 1954.
Despite statutes of limitation, one year after the date of enactment of this
amendment is allowed for filing claims, but no interest is allowed on any
refunds. See §93 of the Technical Amendments Act of 1958.

Lincoln Rochester Trust Co. v. United States, 188 F. Supp. 839 (W.D.N.Y.
1960), was concerned with a residuary gift to the testator's wife which gave
her "the life use of all the rest, residue and remainder of my estate, both
real and personal, wherever the same may be situated, with the right to use
any part of the principal thereof." The 1939 Code as amended by the Technical Amendments Act of 1958 was applicable. The court relied on H.R.
1027, 85th Cong., 1st Sess. (1957), relating to the Technical Amendments Act
of 1958, in holding that a power to consume was sufficient to qualify a gift
for the marital deduction. The Pipe case, discussed above in this note and
supra note 128, was deemed not controlling because it was decided before
the enactment of the Technical Amendments Act of 1958 and before the
date of H.R. 1027.

under the 1939 Code, even though she had the power to withdraw from the right of survivorship her undivided one half, because it was a terminable interest which might pass to the son on its termination. The 1954 Code has broadened allowable marital deduction gifts to include legal life interests coupled with a general power of appointment.[139] It seems clear that the general power of appointment, like in a power of appointment trust, may be a general power to appoint by will only, or by deed only, or by either deed or will.[140] The broadening provisions of the 1954 Code also have the effect of qualifying for the marital deduction the undivided one-half interest of the wife in the joint tenancy in the situation previously considered in this paragraph.[141]

There may be reasons why, in making a non-trust marital deduction gift, the spouse should be given a legal life interest with a general power of appointment rather than outright and complete ownership of the property:

1. The appointive property will not become a part of the probate estate of the spouse on her death and consequently need not be subject to the delays and expenses of probate administration.[142]

2. In many jurisdictions the appointive assets will not be subject to the claims of the wife's creditors upon her death unless the power is exercised.[143]

---

[139] See 1954 I.R.C. §2056(b)(5), quoted infra page 1408.

In Markoff v. United States, 60-2 U.S.T.C. ¶11960 (D.R.I. 1960), the testator devised the residue of his estate to his wife for life and thereafter "all of my said estate then remaining" to designated beneficiaries. Another clause in the will authorized the executrix, who was the testator's wife, to sell property if it became expedient to do so in the settlement of the estate. The court pointed out that under Rhode Island law, which was controlling, a life interest in personalty can be created except where the property is consumed by using it, and in that case, the bequest becomes absolute. Thus an automobile which was in the residue passed to the wife absolutely and qualified for the marital deduction. As to the balance of the residue, the court found that under Rhode Island law the wife had only a life interest and her only power of disposition was as executrix and thus she did not have the necessary power to qualify the balance of the residue for the marital deduction.

[140] Re-examine the cases cited supra page 846, note 128.

The requirement applicable to a separate power of appointment trust that the wife be entitled to all the income from the corpus of the trust is also applicable to a separate legal life interest with a power of appointment but should be deemed to be satisfied whenever the wife as the owner of the legal life interest is entitled to the use of the property involved if it is non-income-producing property. The requirement applicable to a separate power of appointment trust, namely, that the power be exercisable in all events, is also applicable here.

[141] See Reg. §20.2056(b)-5(g)(2), quoted supra page 849.

[142] The pros and cons of avoiding probate are considered supra page 120.

[143] See 5 American Law of Property §§23.14-23.19 (Casner ed. 1952).

3. In many jurisdictions the appointive assets will not be subject to state inheritance taxes on the death of the spouse.[144]
4. The appointive assets are not reachable by a surviving second husband of the spouse to satsify his marital rights.[145]

Such a gift of a legal life interest should be so drafted that the donee spouse will be able to make binding decisions in regard to the property. For example, the life tenant of a gift of land should be able to make leases that extend beyond the tenant's lifetime, to arrange for the development of the land, including the removal of oil, gas, solid minerals, and timber, to construct and tear down buildings, to settle boundary disputes, and so on. In other words, the life tenant should be given a complete charter of administration.[146]

When the spouse is given only a general power to appoint by will, it is vital that the charter include a power to sell a fee simple interest in the land by a deed executed by the life tenant alone. That provides a mechanism for the easy sale of the property if it becomes undesirable to continue to retain it. Instructions must also be given for the disposition of the net proceeds of the sale, since the general power is one only to appoint by will. The net proceeds probably should be poured into a trust that qualifies as a power of appointment trust for marital deductions purposes. Even if the general power is one to appoint by deed, a charter of administration is desirable so that these objectives may be accomplished without the donee spouse's first having to take over the complete ownership of the property.

If personal property is involved, the terms of the gift should specify that the spouse need not give security that the property will be forthcoming on her death. The charter of administration should provide adequate guidance for sales and reinvestments, the duty of the spouse to render accounts, and the allocations of receipts between income and principal.

It should be apparent from the foregoing that preparing an instrument conveying a legal life interest with a general power is not a simple drafting job. In fact, a trust arrangement is probably simpler, because the draftsman can draw on considerable experience in the types of powers and discretions that will provide a trustee with an adequate working charter.[147]

---

[144] Powers of appointment and state inheritance taxes are discussed supra page 764.

[145] See 5 American Law of Property §§23.20-23.22 (Casner ed. 1952).

[146] See the discussion of legal life interests at page 597 supra.

[147] Since successive legal interests are not frequently used, there is no similar body of experience. See Schuyler, Drafting Provisions for Legal Life Estates and the Marital Deduction, 44 Ill. B.J. 452 (1956).

For some marital deduction gifts a legal life interest with a general power is preferable to a trust. There is no need to set up a trust where the spouse can realize the benefits of the gift without the exercise of managerial judgment, as in the case of a gift of a family portrait or a life insurance agent's renewal commissions. A legal interest may be adequate where only the operation of the property requires managerial judgment, as in running a farm, or in collecting rent and repairing and maintaining premises used as rental property. The donee spouse may well be qualified to exercise the required judgment; but problems may arise if the spouse becomes incapacitated. A trust offers a better and more established framework where managerial judgment is required in regard to the sale and reinvestment of property. The spouse, of course, may be chosen as trustee.[148]

PROBLEMS

13.21. H's father devised Blackacre to him for life with a general power to appoint Blackacre by will and, in default of appointment, remainder to H's son, S. H in his will exercises the power by appointing Blackacre to his wife, W, for life with a general power to appoint Blackacre by her will. H dies. Does the gift from H to W qualify for the estate tax marital deduction?

13.22 H makes an inter vivos gift of Blackacre "to W [his wife] and S [his son] and their heirs as joint tenants." The son dies. H dies within three years. The gift by H is deemed one in contemplation of death. Does the gift from H to W qualify for the estate tax marital deduction? If S before his death had conveyed his interest in Blackacre to W, would the gift from H to W qualify for the estate tax marital deduction?

i. *Portion Gifts with a Power of Appointment*

Under the 1939 Code,[149] a power of appointment trust did not qualify for the marital deduction unless the donee-spouse was entitled to receive *all* the income from the corpus of the trust and to appoint the *entire* corpus free of the trust. Thus it was held that no part of a trust qualified for the estate tax marital deduction where the spouse was entitled to all the income from the

---

[148] A spendthrift provision with respect to the spouse's interest under a trust is valid in many jurisdictions, whereas a spendthrift provision with respect to a legal life interest is usually held invalid. See the consideration of restraints on the alienation of legal interests at page 620 supra.

[149] Section 812(e)(1)(F).

trust for her life but could appoint only so much of the trust corpus as equaled 50 percent of the value of the decedent husband's adjusted gross estate, less the value of property passing to her other than through the trust.[150]

The 1954 Code, however, provides that the gift qualifies if the donee-spouse "is entitled for life to all the income from the entire interest, or all the income from a specific portion thereof . . . with power in the surviving spouse to appoint the entire interest, or such specific portion . . ."[151] This raises an important estate planning consideration: When should a power of appointment marital deduction gift be made separate and distinct from other

---

[150] See Rev. Rul. 54-20, 1954-1 C.B. 195. See also Estate of Louis B. Hoffenberg, 22 T.C. 1185 (1954) (no part of trust qualified for marital deduction where wife was entitled to all income and had power to appoint two thirds of corpus), aff'd sub nom. Hoffenberg v. Commissioner, 223 F.2d 470 (2d Cir. 1955); Estate of Harrison P. Shedd, 23 T.C. 41 (1954) (no marital deduction allowed where wife was entitled to two thirds of income and had power to appoint one half of corpus), aff'd sub nom. Estate of Shedd v. Commissioner, 237 F.2d 345 (9th Cir. 1956), cert. denied, 352 U.S. 1024 (1957); Estate of Arthur Sweet, 24 T.C. 488 (1955) (no marital deduction allowed where wife entitled to all income but her power to appoint corpus was limited to one half of adjusted gross estate), aff'd sub nom. Sweet v. Commissioner, 234 F.2d 401 (10th Cir. 1956), cert. denied, 352 U.S. 878 (1956); Estate of Frank Clifford Bickers, 14 CCH T.C. Mem. 901 (1955) (no marital deduction allowed where wife was entitled to part of income and had power to appoint one half of corpus).

In Estate of Joseph A. Barry, Sr., 15 CCH T.C. Mem. 502 (1956), the court construed as separate trusts what looked like a single trust, and thereby saved the marital deduction gift under the 1939 Code. No marital deduction was allowed in Estate of William H. S. Warner, 15 CCH T.C. Mem. 1448 (1956), where the wife was entitled to all the income of a trust and had a power to appoint only a portion of the corpus. In Estate of Blanchard Houston Stallworth, Sr., 16 CCH T.C. Mem. 741 (1957), the wife was given one half of the income of a trust and the right to withdraw one half of the principal. The court held that the gift to her did not qualify for the marital deduction under the 1939 Code, even though a state court decree stated that the decedent intended to vest her with a fee simple title to a one-half interest in the trust property; the state court decree was not binding because it was obtained in a nonadversary proceeding and was collusive in that the parties joined together to procure a decree upon which to base a claim for a marital deduction. The case was affirmed sub nom. Estate of Blanchard Houston Stallworth, Sr. v. Commissioner, 260 F.2d 760 (5th Cir. 1958). On rehearing, the case was reversed on the basis of the 1958 amendment referred to below; see Estate of Blanchard Houston Stallworth, Sr. v. Commissioner, 58-2 U.S.T.C. ¶11832 (5th Cir. 1958). In Estate of John C. Zeman, 17 CCH T.C. Mem. 336 (1958), the deceased's wife was given the entire income of a residuary trust and the right to invade the trust corpus to the extent of $15,000; on her death, the trust was to terminate and the trust corpus was to pass to beneficiaries other than the wife or her estate. The court held that the trust did not qualify to any extent for the marital deduction under the 1939 Code.

See, however, Technical Amendments Act of 1958, §93, which is discussed supra page 858, note 138, and which gives some relief in the situations discussed above in this note.

[151] Section 2056(b)(5), quoted in full infra page 1408.

gifts (as had to be done under the 1939 law) and when should it
be a portion of a larger item?

If a legal life interest with a general power is to be employed
as a marital deduction gift, the portion gift naturally will be employed whenever the subject matter is not capable of being divided
into shares, as in the case of a farm, and the value of the whole
exceeds the projected gift. A gift to the wife of a life interest in
an undivided portion with a general power to appoint such portion may suffice. However, legal ownership in severalty is less
complex than legal concurrent ownership, since the spouse will
not have to deal with other concurrent owners in making decisions
regarding the property. Therefore the portion gift arrangement
should not be used where it is feasible to divide the property into
separate shares.

If the spouse gets a legal life interest in the entire property with
a general power of appointment over an undivided one half, she
may be given its exclusive management. The Regulations make
it clear that while the rights over the income and the power must
coexist in the same interest in property, it is not necessary that the
rights over the income or the power as to such an interest be in the
same proportion. If they are not in the same proportion, the marital deduction is limited to the smaller share.[152]

A single trust with a portion thereof qualifying as a power of
appointment trust has both advantages and disadvantages as
against separate trusts.[153] The principal advantage may be the
decreased cost of operating a single trust. Multiple separate trusts
may have tax advantages, however.[154]

Special problems must be dealt with if it is decided to employ a
portion gift.[155] One problem in making a marital deduction gift
is how to employ a formula to define the portion that exactly
equals the maximum allowable estate tax marital deduction. This
should present no greater difficulty than has been faced in the past
in establishing a separate trust of a fractional share of the residue
equal to the maximum deduction.[156] When the portion arrange-

---

[152] See Reg. §20.2056(b)-5(b), quoted infra page 1536.

[153] For an excellent statement of the considerations involved, see Lovell,
Marital Deduction Simplified, 93 Trusts & Estates 760 (1954).

[154] The possible tax advantages of multiple trusts are examined supra page
752.

[155] Lovell, supra note 153, deals with the drafting of portion gifts.

[156] Formula fractional share marital deduction gifts are considered supra
page 795.

The following example of a formula marital deduction clause which defines
the marital proportion of a marital trust was sent to me by Mr. Robert M.
Lovell of the Hanover Bank, New York City:

"If my wife survives me, I give, devise, and bequeath said residue to my
trustee hereinafter named under the following terms and conditions:

ment is used, the fractional share of the residue obtained by the formula method becomes not a separate trust, but a portion of a single trust.

Another problem is to avoid diminishing the value of the marital deduction portion when paying the deceased spouse's death obligations. When separate trusts are employed, such death obligations are specifically charged to the nonmarital deduction trust. The same procedure should be possible under the portion arrangement. For example, if the marital deduction fractional share of the residue, before the residue has been diminished by death obligations, is two fifths, and the death obligations use up one fifth of the residue, the final marital deduction portion will be one half.

How can the allocation to the marital deduction portion of disqualified terminable interests be avoided? [157] When separate trusts are employed, this is usually done by a provision stating, in substance, that only assets which qualify for the marital deduction shall be allotted in kind to the marital deduction trust or sold to provide cash to put in that trust. The portion concept may require that the marital deduction portion be considered a share of each individual asset subject to the single trust, and if so, it may not be possible to allocate away from the marital deduction portion disqualified terminable interests. Fortunately they are rarities in the estates of decedents.

---

(1) My trustee shall pay the net income to my wife or apply it for her benefit at least once annually and, in addition, shall pay to her or apply for her benefit so much of the principal as my trustee may deem necessary for her support and comfort. Principal paid or applied hereunder shall be charged against the portion established pursuant to subdivision (3) hereof until such portion is exhausted, and thereafter shall be charged against the remaining principal of this trust.

(2) I grant my said wife the right to withdraw during her lifetime and/or to appoint by her will to such persons or corporations as she chooses, including the executors or administrators of her estate, the portion of the principal defined hereinbelow.

(3) The portion of the principal referred to immediately above shall be determined by applying to the principal passing under this article a percentage determined as follows, using the values and deductions finally established for federal estate tax purposes: (a) subtract from the maximum marital deduction allowable in my estate an amount equal to the value of all property and interests in property which qualify for marital deduction and which pass or have passed to my wife otherwise than under this article and (b) divide the result thus obtained by the total value of my residuary estate passing hereunder. The percentage thus determined shall be redetermined immediately after each and every payment of principal to my wife or on her behalf pursuant to subdivisions (1) and (2) hereof.

(4) Upon the death of my wife any principal remaining which is not validly disposed of by her will as hereinabove provided shall be distributed as follows:"

[157] Disqualified terminable interests are described supra page 833.

Another problem is presented when the single trust permits an invasion of principal for the benefit of persons other than the spouse. Any such an invasion power must be qualified so that it cannot reduce the marital deduction portion. If a single trust starts out with a marital deduction portion of one half of the income and the power to appoint one half the corpus, an invasion of the principal of the other portion to the extent of one fourth of the total corpus would require an immediate prearranged change in the marital deduction portion so that in the future the spouse would receive two thirds of the income from the trust and the power to appoint two thirds of the remaining corpus. Such an arrangement can be spelled out, but it will probably be simpler to employ the separate trust arrangement.

Suppose that a residuary trust under a will provides that the testator's wife is to receive all the income and is to have a general power to appoint by will an undivided one half of the corpus. The trustee is given discretion to pay her all or any part of the corpus in such amounts as he may determine. In this case, the trust should provide whether payments of corpus made to the wife by the trustee are to be charged against the portion over which the wife has a power of appointment, against the nonappointive share, or against each share equally. Normally the appointive share should be charged first, because reducing its value reduces the value of the amount includible in the spouse's gross estate.

Can a portion be a specific amount? A by his will establishes a trust of the residue of his estate, the trustee to pay all the income to A's wife for her life, then to hold or dispose of a specified dollar amount (which could be determined by a formula, so as to be equal to the maximum allowable marital deduction) as A's wife appoints by will, and to pay the balance, plus the dollar amount if A's wife does not exercise her power, to designated beneficiaries. The advantage of this arrangement is that, whatever growth takes place in the trust property during the donee-spouse's lifetime, her gross estate will never include more than the dollar amount.[158] The Regulations take the position that if the annual income of the spouse is limited to a specific sum, or if she has a power to appoint only a specific sum out of a larger fund, the interest is not a deductible interest.[159]

---

[158] Conversely, there would be a disadvantage if there was a shrinkage in the worth of the trust property.

[159] See Reg. §20.2056(b)-5(c), quoted infra page 1536.

In Estate of Willard H. Cummings, 31 T.C. 986 (1959), the trust called for payment of the entire income to the decedent's spouse and she was given the right to withdraw $5000 annually. The court held that the Commissioner did not err in disallowing a claimed marital deduction.

A portion gift is not involved if the portion described is to be segregated from other portions and treated as a separate unit.[160] Thus a gift of $50,000 in trust is not a portion gift where the wife's right to income is limited to a specific sum. The described sum must be separately invested and the entire income from the investments must pass to the wife.

PROBLEMS

13.23. A in his will establishes a trust under which all of the income is to be paid to his wife, W, for her life. On her death, one third of the corpus is to be paid to her estate and two thirds is to be paid to other designated beneficiaries. To what extent, if at all, will the value of the trust property be available for the estate tax marital deduction if W survives H?

13.24. A in his will establishes a trust under which all the income is to be paid to his son, S, for his life. On the death of S the income is to be paid to W, A's wife, if she is then living. On the death of the survivor of S and W the trust property is to pass as W may appoint under a general power to appoint by will, and in default of appointment by her, the trust property is to pass to the issue of S then living, such issue to take per stirpes. To what extent, if at all, will the value of the trust property be available for the estate tax marital deduction if S and W survive H? If only W survives H?

13.25. A in his will establishes a trust under which all the income is to be paid to his wife, W, for her life. In addition W is given the power to withdraw in each calendar year the sum of $5000 or a sum equal to 5 percent of the value of the trust property, whichever sum is greater. To what extent, if at all, will the value of the trust property be available for the estate tax marital deduction if W survives H?

j. *Settlement of Life Insurance Proceeds*

The proceeds of insurance on the life of the husband may be settled in various ways so as to qualify for the estate tax marital deduction. If the wife is designated as the primary beneficiary and is to receive the proceeds in a lump sum, the settlement arrangement qualifies.[161] If the proceeds are to be paid to the trustee

[160] See Reg. §20.2056(b)-5(d), quoted infra page 1537.

[161] In Miller v. Dowling, 56-2 U.S.T.C. ¶11646 (S.D.N.Y. 1956), the decedent had transferred all incidents of ownership of a policy on his life to his wife before January 10, 1941, but had paid the premiums on the policy subsequent to that date, so that the portion of the proceeds on the policy which corresponded to the portion of the premiums paid by him subsequent to that date was in-

of an estate trust or the trustee of a power of appointment trust, the settlement arrangement qualifies. The problem of particular interest at this point is what settlement arrangements will qualify when the proceeds are left with the insurance company to be paid out under one of the options in the policy.

If the option which is adopted gives the wife a life annuity with no refund feature so that on her death nothing will pass to anyone else, her interest, though it is a terminable one, qualifies for the marital deduction because it is not a disqualified interest under the terminable interest rules.[162] If, however, the option adopted is one which calls for payments to the wife for a period certain and thereafter for her life, or for a period certain alone, with a contingent beneficiary designated to take the commuted value of any unpaid installments on the death of the wife, the arrangement will not qualify for the marital deduction because her interest will be a terminable one of the disqualified kind.[163]

---

cludible in his gross estate (see page 322 supra, note 69). Nevertheless, even though the entire proceeds of the policy were payable to the decedent's wife, no part of them was deemed available for the marital deduction.

[162] See the discussion of disqualified terminable interests at page 833 supra.

[163] See Rev. Rul. 55-733, 1955-2 C.B. 388.

In Reilly v. Commissioner, 239 F.2d 797 (3d Cir. 1957), however, the court held that the amount needed to guarantee the certain payments should be separated from the amount needed to provide the life annuity after the expiration of the period certain, because the option adopted was one requiring the payments to be made for a period certain and thereafter for the wife's life, and that the latter amount qualified for the marital deduction because no other person could succeed to the wife's interest in the life annuity. In accord are Meyer v. United States, 166 F. Supp. 629 (W.D.N.Y. 1958), and Sandperl v. United States, 59-2 U.S.T.C. ¶11893 (E.D. Mo. 1959); but the Meyer case was reversed in 275 F.2d 83 (2d Cir. 1959), the court, with one judge dissenting, refusing to follow the Third Circuit. The Court of Appeals decision in the Meyer case was affirmed in 81 Sup. Ct. 210 (1960), in a six-to-three decision. In Estate of John C. Zeman, 17 CCH T.C. Mem. 336 (1958), the court held that where the insurance proceeds were payable in monthly installments for the life of the insured's wife or for twenty years certain, with a provision that if the wife died within the 20-year period, the remaining installments were to be paid to the insured's daughter, and a provision that the commuted value of any unpaid installments should be paid to the estate of the survivor of the insured, his wife and his daughter, the wife's interest was a terminable one and the arrangement did not qualify for the marital deduction.

The court in Estate of Thomas J. White, 22 T.C. 641 (1954), considered a case in which the proceeds of life insurance on the life of the husband were settled under the installment option, with the wife as beneficiary, and on the death of the wife any unpaid amounts were to go as designated by the husband in the settlement arrangement. Evidently the husband had transferred all incidents of ownership of the policy to his wife but she had never changed the beneficiary arrangement. The court concluded that the arrangement did not qualify for the marital deduction, since the wife's interest was terminable and she did not have the power after her husband's death to qualify the arrangement under the power of appointment provisions.

A settlement arrangement which provides that on the death of the wife any unpaid installments will go to her estate is like the estate trust and qualifies for the marital deduction.[164]

A "power of appointment settlement arrangement" similar to the "power of appointment trust" can be adopted.[165] The power of appointment settlement arrangement may relate to a portion of the life insurance proceeds and thus the preceding comments applicable to portion gifts are also relevant here.[166] The Regulations must be thoroughly examined if a power of appointment settlement arrangement is to be employed, and therefore the pertinent parts are set out in full below.

[164] Revenue Ruling 57-423, 1957-2 C.B. 623, holds that the proceeds of life insurance policies issued under the World War Veterans' Act, 1924, or the National Service Life Insurance Act of 1940, qualify for the estate tax marital deduction, provided that at the death of the insured, such proceeds are payabe to the surviving spouse either in a lump sum or in monthly installments, with any balance at her death payable to her estate. Since neither of these modes of settlement is available under the provisions of the Servicemen's Indemnity Act of 1951, proceeds payable under that act will not qualify for the estate tax marital deduction.

In Second National Bank of Danville, Illinois v. Dallman, 209 F.2d 321 (7th Cir. 1954), a person who had procured insurance on his life designated his daughter as the beneficiary. The beneficiary designation provided that the principal amount should be retained by the insurance company during the life of the daughter and that during this period she should receive an annuity of 3 percent per annum upon the principal amount thus retained by the insurer. The beneficiary agreement also provided that the daughter was to have the right to designate a contingent beneficiary or beneficiaries during her lifetime, and that if she should not designate any contingent beneficiary, then on her death the principal should go to her executors, administrators, or assigns. The daughter did not designate any contingent beneficiary and thus the proceeds on her death were paid by the insurance company to her executors and administrators. The court held that the daughter had no interest in the principal retained by the insurance company which was includible in her gross estate under 1939 I.R.C. §811(a) (1954 I.R.C. §2033). The power of appointment that she had was a pre-1942 power, and since she did not exercise that power, the proceeds were not includible in her gross estate under §811(f) (1954 I.R.C. §2041). Revenue Ruling 55-277, 1955-1 C.B. 456, holds that the Second National Bank of Danville case will not be followed by the Internal Revenue Service, and the ruling recognizes that when the surviving spouse is entitled to the interest on life insurance proceeds left with the company and has the right to direct that the proceeds go to her executors or administrators, such an arrangement qualifies for the marital deduction.

[165] See 1954 I.R.C. §2056(b)(6), quoted infra page 1408.

For examples of power of appointment settlement arrangements, see examples of insurance settlement arrangements at page 292 supra.

[166] Portion gifts are considered beginning supra page 861.

SECTION 20.2056(b)-6. MARITAL DEDUCTION; LIFE INSURANCE OR ANNUITY PAYMENTS WITH POWER OF APPOINTMENT IN SURVIVING SPOUSE

(a) *In general.* Section 2056(b)(6) provides that an interest in property passing from a decedent to his surviving spouse, which consists of proceeds held by an insurer under the terms of a life insurance, endowment, or annuity contract, is a "deductible interest" to the extent that it satisfies all five of the following conditions (see paragraph (b) of this section if one or more of the conditions is satisfied as to only a portion of the proceeds):

(1) The proceeds, or a specific portion of the proceeds, must be held by the insurer subject to an agreement either to pay the entire proceeds or a specific portion thereof in installments, or to pay interest thereon, and all or a specific portion of the installments or interest payable during the life of the surviving spouse must be payable only to her.

(2) The installments or interest payable to the surviving spouse must be payable annually, or more frequently, commencing not later than 13 months after the decedent's death.

(3) The surviving spouse must have the power to appoint all or a specific portion of the amounts so held by the insurer to either herself or her estate.[167]

(4) The power in the surviving spouse must be exercisable by her alone and (whether exercisable by will or during life) must be exercisable in all events.

(5) The amounts or the specific portion of the amounts payable under such contract must not be subject to a power in any other person to appoint any part thereof to any person other than the surviving spouse.

(b) *Specific portion; deductible interest.* If the right to receive interest or installment payments or the power of appointment passing to the surviving spouse pertains only to a specific portion of the

---

[167] In Rev. Rul. 54-553, 1954-2 C.B. 303, it is stated that where the surviving spouse of a decedent is given the right to withdraw a specific portion of insurance proceeds retained by the insurer in a single fund, such an arrangement does not operate to create a separate fund of the portion of the proceeds subject to the power of appointment. Consequently, under the 1939 Code neither the entire proceeds nor any portion thereof qualifies for the estate tax marital deduction.

See also Estate of William Walker Wynekoop, 24 T.C. 167 (1955), which held that where life insurance proceeds were left with the company under the interest option (interest to be paid to the insured's wife), the arrangement qualified for the marital deduction because under Illinois law such an arrangement permits the surviving spouse to appoint the principal to herself. — ED.

proceeds held by the insurer, the marital deduction is allowed only to the extent that the rights of the surviving spouse in the specific portion meet the five conditions described in paragraph (a) of this section. While the rights to interest, or to receive payment in installments, and the power must coexist as to the proceeds of the same contract, it is not necessary that the rights to each be in the same proportion. If the rights to interest meeting the required conditions set forth in paragraph (a)(1) and (2) of this section extend over a smaller share of the proceeds than the share with respect to which the power of appointment requirements set forth in paragraph (a)(3) through (5) of this section are satisfied, the deductible interest is limited to the smaller share. Similarly, if the portion of the proceeds payable in installments is a smaller portion of the proceeds than the portion to which the power of appointment meeting such requirements relates, the deduction is limited to the smaller portion. In addition, if a power of appointment meeting all the requirements extends to a smaller portion of the proceeds than the portion over which the interest or installment rights pertain, the deductible interest cannot exceed the value of the portion to which such power of appointment applies. Thus, if the contract provides that the insurer is to retain the entire proceeds and pay all of the interest thereon annually to the surviving spouse and if the surviving spouse has a power of appointment meeting the specifications prescribed in paragraph (a)(3) through (5) of this section, as to only one-half of the proceeds held, then only one-half of the proceeds may be treated as a deductible interest. Correspondingly, if the rights of the spouse to receive installment payments or interest satisfying the requirements extend to only one-fourth of the proceeds and a testamentary power of appointment satisfying the requirements of paragraph (a)(3) through (5) of this section extends to all of the proceeds, then only one-fourth of the proceeds qualifies as a deductible interest. Further, if the surviving spouse has no right to installment payments (or interest) over any portion of the proceeds but a testamentary power of appointment which meets the necessary conditions over the entire remaining proceeds, then none of the proceeds qualifies for the deduction. In addition, if, from the time of the decedent's death, the surviving spouse has a power of appointment meeting all of the required conditions over three-fourths of the proceeds and the right to receive interest from the entire proceeds, but with a power in another person to appoint one-half of the entire proceeds, the value of the interest in the surviving spouse over only one-half of the proceeds will qualify as a deductible interest.

(c) *Applicable principles.* (1) The principles set forth in paragraph (c) of §20.2056 (b)-5 for determining what constitutes a "specific portion of the entire interest" for the purpose of section 2056-(b)(5) are applicable in determining what constitutes a "specific portion of all such amounts" for the purpose of section 2056(b)(6). However, the interest in the proceeds passing to the surviving spouse will not be disqualified by the fact that the installment payments or interest to which the spouse is entitled or the amount of the proceeds over which the power of appointment is exercisable may be expressed in terms of a specific sum rather than a fraction or a percentage of the proceeds provided it is shown that such sums are a definite or fixed percentage or fraction of the total proceeds.

(2) The provisions of paragraph (a) of this section are applicable with respect to a property interest which passed from the decedent in the form of proceeds of a policy of insurance upon the decedent's life, a policy of insurance upon the life of a person who predeceased the decedent, a matured endowment policy, or an annuity contract, but only in case the proceeds are to be held by the insurer. With respect to proceeds under any such contract which are to be held by a trustee, with power of appointment in the surviving spouse, see §20.2056(b)-5. As to the treatment of proceeds not meeting the requirements of §20.2056(b)-5 or of this section, see §20.2056(a)-2.

(3) In the case of a contract under which payments by the insurer commenced during the decedent's life, it is immaterial whether or not the conditions in subparagraphs (1) through (5) of paragraph (a) of this section were satisfied prior to the decedent's death.

(d) *Payments of installments or interest.* The conditions in subparagraphs (1) and (2) of paragraph (a) of this section relative to the payments of installments or interest to the surviving spouse are satisfied if, under the terms of the contract, the spouse has the right exercisable annually (or more frequently) to require distribution to herself of installments of the proceeds or a specific portion thereof, as the case may be, and otherwise such proceeds or interest are to be accumulated and held by the insurer pursuant to the terms of the contract. A contract which otherwise requires the insurer to make annual or more frequent payments to the surviving spouse following the decedent's death, will not be disqualified merely because the surviving spouse must comply with certain formalities in order to obtain the first payment. For example, the contract may satisfy the conditions in subparagraphs (1) and (2) of paragraph (a) of this section even though it requires the surviving spouse to furnish proof of death before the first payment is made. The condition in paragraph (a)(1) of this section is satisfied where interest on the proceeds or a specific portion thereof is payable, annually or more frequently, for a term, or until the occurrence of a specified event, following which the proceeds or a specific portion thereof are to be paid in annual or more frequent installments.

(e) *Powers of appointment.* (1) In determining whether the terms of the contract satisfy the conditions in subparagraphs (3), (4), or (5) of paragraph (a) of this section relating to a power of appointment in the surviving spouse or any other person, the principles stated in §20.2056(b)-5 are applicable. As stated in §20.2056-(b)-5, the surviving spouse's power to appoint is "exercisable in all events" only if it is in existence immediately following the decedent's death, subject, however, to the operation of §20.2056(b)-3 relating to interests conditioned on survival for a limited period.

(2) For examples of formal limitations on the power which will not disqualify the contract, see paragraph (g)(4) of §20.2056(b)-5.[168] If the power is exercisable from the moment of the decedent's death, the contract is not disqualified merely because the insurer may require proof of the decedent's death as a condition to making payment to the appointee. If the submission of proof of the decedent's death is a condition to the exercise of the power, the power will not be considered "exercisable in all events" unless in the event the surviving spouse had died immediately following the decedent, her power to appoint would have been considered to exist at the time of her death, within the meaning of section 2041-(a)(2). See paragraph (b) of §20.2041-3.[169]

[168] In Estate of Thomas C. Werbe v. United States, 178 F. Supp. 704 (S.D. Ind. 1958), insurance proceeds were settled so that the wife of the insured received interest for life and had a power to withdraw the amount left with the company, in whole or in part. In one set of policies the power of withdrawal could be exercised only on the payment date and on giving ninety days' notice; no more than four partial withdrawals could be made in one year; and no partial withdrawal of less than $50 could be made. In one policy, withdrawals could be made only on interest due dates; no withdrawal of less than $100 was permitted; and the compliance with the withdrawal request could be deferred for six months after receipt of the request. The court held that the settlement arrangement did not qualify for the marital deduction, as the wife had a terminable interest. The case was affirmed in 273 F.2d 201 (7th Cir. 1959). — Ed.

[169] In Rev. Rul. 54-121, 1954-1 C.B. 196, it is decided that if the payment of insurance proceeds to the surviving spouse is conditioned upon her being alive upon receipt by the insurer of due proof of the insured's death, the settlement arrangement with respect to the insurance proceeds will not qualify for the marital deduction. The exception relating to terminable interests which applies to gifts to a spouse conditioned upon her surviving for six months is not applicable because submission of due proof of the insured's death may occur either within the six-month period or thereafter, and in such a case the marital deduction is not available by reason of the so-called terminable interest rule. In accord is Eggleston v. Dudley, 154 F. Supp. 178 (W.D. Pa. 1957). The Eggleston case was reversed in 257 F.2d 398 (3d Cir. 1958), on the ground that the insurance settlement provisions were contradictory in

(3) It is sufficient for the purposes of the condition in paragraph (a)(3) of this section that the surviving spouse have the power to appoint amounts held by the insurer to herself or her estate if the surviving spouse has the unqualified power, exercisable in favor of herself or her estate, to appoint amounts held by the insurer which are payable after her death. Such power to appoint need not extend to installments or interest which will be paid to the spouse during her life. Further, the power to appoint need not be a power to require payment in a single sum. For example, if the proceeds of a policy are payable in installments, and if the surviving spouse has the power to direct that all installments payable after her death be paid to her estate, she has the requisite power.

(4) It is not necessary that the phrase "power to appoint" be used in the contract. For example, the condition in paragraph (a)(3) of this section that the surviving spouse have the power to appoint amounts held by the insurer to herself or her estate is satisfied by terms of a contract which give the surviving spouse a right which is, in substance and effect, a power to appoint to herself or her estate, such as a right to withdraw the amount remaining in the fund held by the insurer, or a right to direct that any amount held by the insurer under the contract at her death shall be paid to her estate.

PROBLEM

13.26. H makes an agreement with the insurer that the interest on the proceeds of insurance on his life is to be accumulated until the death of his wife, and then the proceeds and accumulated interest are to be paid to her estate. H dies. Will such a settlement arrangement qualify for the estate tax marital deduction? See Section 20.2056(e)-2(b) of the Regulations, quoted infra page 1540.

13. GIFTS TO A WIFE WHICH QUALIFY FOR THE
GIFT TAX MARITAL DEDUCTION

In general the requirements which must be satisfied to qualify a gift for the gift tax marital deduction are the same as those which must be satisfied to qualify a gift for the estate tax marital deduc-

---

regard to whether the surviving spouse was required to be alive when the company received due proof of her husband's death. The court construed the provisions as not requiring that she be alive at that time, so her interest under the insurance policies was not a terminable one. — ED.

tion.[170] Consequently, reference to the material on estate tax marital deduction gifts should be made at this point.[171]

PROBLEM

13.27. H acquires with his own funds United States Savings Bonds, Series E and G, and registers them in the name of W, his wife, payable on her death to H. Does the gift of the bonds to W qualify for the gift tax marital deduction? See Revenue Ruling 54-410, 1954-2 C.B. 321, and then consider whether the position taken in the ruling should be altered in view of Section 2523(e) of the 1954 Code.

[170] See 1954 I.R.C. §2523, quoted infra page 1425.

Notice particularly §2523(d), which specifically qualifies for the gift tax marital deduction property transferred by the donor to himself and his wife as joint tenants or tenants by the entirety. If the husband purchases a joint and survivor annuity, however, the gift to the wife does not qualify for the gift tax marital deduction. See Reg. §25.2523(b)-1(c)(2), quoted infra page 1554.

[171] See the discussion at page 824 supra.

A husband establishes a life insurance trust for the benefit of his wife, and the entire corpus of the trust consists of insurance policies on his life. He pays $5000 in premiums on the insurance held by the trustee. Can he claim that one half of the premium payment is a gift tax marital deduction gift? In Estate of Charles C. Smith, 23 T.C. 367 (1954), the court held that even though the insurance trust itself, by its terms, appeared to qualify for the gift tax marital deduction, it did not in fact so qualify because the husband never intended that the trust would provide any economic benefits to his wife prior to his death. There was no provision in the trust deed giving his wife the right to compel the trustee to convert the insurance policies into income-producing property. Thus it was held that the transfer of funds to pay premiums on the policies held in trust did not qualify for the gift tax marital deduction.

In Harbeck Halsted, 28 T.C. 1069 (1957), trusts were involved under which the beneficiary-wife was given the right to call for the corpus at any time, and it was held that payments made by the insured to the trustees to pay the premiums on the policies transferred to the trust were gifts of a present interest for the purposes of the annual exclusion. Such payments did not qualify for the gift tax marital deduction, however, because the terms of the trust provided that if the income from the property contributed to the trust — income which was primarily to be used to pay the premiums on the life insurance — exceeded the amount necessary to pay such premiums, the excess was to be paid to the settlor-husband. Thus the beneficiary-wife was not entitled to all of the income of the trust. Notice that this result was reached even though the beneficiary-wife had the power to call for the entire corpus of the trust.

In Berman v. Patterson, 171 F. Supp. 800 (N.D. Ala. 1959), the decedent claimed a marital deduction for gift tax purposes when he assigned policies of insurance on his life to his wife, with a proviso that if she predeceased him the policies would pass to his children. He claimed that the gift over to the children was void under Alabama law and thus the wife obtained an unqualified interest. The court held that the interest given to the children was valid and thus the wife's interest was terminable and did not qualify for the gift tax marital deduction.

CHAPTER XIV

Charitable Dispositions

In the formulation of an estate plan, consideration should always be given to the appropriateness, under all the circumstances, of making some charitable dispositions. The amount of wealth involved may be such that there can be no primary diversion of any amount to charitable purposes in the light of family responsibilities, but even in such cases, if future interests are created in the estate plan, an end limitation to a charity may be appropriate to provide for a final distribution on the remote contingency that all other beneficiaries may die before the period set for distribution.

Even though the amount of wealth is not substantial, the owner may not have any near relatives to whom he desires to give his property. In such a situation the estate plan may be concerned exclusively or largely with charitable dispositions.

If the amount of wealth involved is substantial, the dual planning of charitable dispositions and family dispositions may be a significant part of the estate planning job. In such cases the plan may involve inter vivos charitable transfers as well as testamentary charitable transfers.

This chapter obviously is not concerned with the selection of the charity, when charitable dispositions may be appropriate, because the selection depends on personal considerations. This chapter deals, rather, with the pitfalls which should be avoided if the charitable gift is to be effective, and with the tax considerations which should be kept in mind so that the amount available for charitable purposes will not be unnecessarily diminished by taxes. Incidentally, the net cost to the transferor of a charitable gift may be very little because of the deductions available to him for income, gift and estate tax purposes when the transferee is a charity, and this fact may be influential in determining whether a charitable gift should be made.[1]

[1] In regard to charitable dispositions generally, see Vestal, Critical Evaluation of the Charitable Trust as a Giving Device, 1957 Wash. U.L.Q. 196.

1.   STATE RESTRICTIONS ON CHARITABLE DISPOSITIONS

When charitable dispositions are made by will, the governing state law must be examined to ascertain whether any restriction exists as to the amount of property which can be given to a charity by will, or as to the length of time which must elapse before the death of the testator in order for charitable gifts in a will to be valid.[2]

2.   RULE AGAINST PERPETUITIES AND RULE AGAINST ACCUMULATIONS

The rule against perpetuities cannot be ignored in connection with charitable dispositions.   A contingent gift to a charity will violate the common law rule against perpetuities whenever a similar gift to an individual would violate that rule, except that a gift over from one charity to another on the happening of a remote contingency is not subject to the rule against perpetuities.[3]   The New York statutory rule against perpetuities similarly applies to contingent charitable gifts.[4]

There is no common law rule which limits the duration of a charitable trust.[5]   Thus, if the property becomes irrevocably devoted to charitable purposes under a valid trust, the fact that the trustee has the power to select the charitable purposes to be benefited from time to time is not an invalid power in the trustee, even though it may be exercised after the period of the rule against perpetuities.

In the absence of statutory provisions regarding accumulations for a charity, there is no restriction other than a general requirement that the directions as to accumulations be reasonable.[6]   If,

[2] See the discussion at page 142 supra.

[3] 6 American Law of Property §§24.37-24.41 (Casner ed. 1952); 4 Restatement of Property §§396, 397.   For a case which construes a gift to a charity as vested and not contingent, see Peakes v. Blakely, 333 Mass. 281, 130 N.E.2d 564 (1955).

[4] 4 Restatement of Property, App., c. A, ¶15.   The New York statutory rule against perpetuities is explained supra page 639.

[5] 4 Restatement of Property §398.   In New York, perpetual charitable trusts may be established.   Id., App., c. A, ¶15.

[6] 6 American Law of Property §24.42 (Casner ed. 1952).

In Franklin Foundation v. Attorney General, 340 Mass. 197, 163 N.E.2d 662 (1960), the court denied a request to terminate a charitable trust established by Benjamin Franklin in 1790.   The original amount in the trust was 1000 pounds and its present worth, with accumulations, was $1,578,098.

In Holdeen v. Ratterree, 60-2 U.S.T.C. ¶9671 (N.D.N.Y. 1960), a settlor of an inter vivos trust directed that the income of the trust should be accumulated for a long period of time and then the accumulated income and prin-

however, the gift is contingent on a fund accumulating to a certain amount and the period of accumulation is not restricted to the period of the rule against perpetuities, the gift to the charity is void under that rule. In some states there are statutory restrictions on accumulation for a charity.[7]

GRIMKE v. ATTORNEY GENERAL
206 Mass. 49, 91 N.E. 899 (1910)

KNOWLTON, C.J.

On June 18, 1895, Emmeline Cushing of Boston died, leaving a will containing a residuary clause which bequeaths and devises her property to trustees for the purposes expressed therein, as follows: "I have long entertained a desire of assisting colored people of my country who have been oppressed and down-trodden in the past, and are now unjustly treated, kept back and hindered in the race of life because of a cruel prejudice against them. Ever since my earliest recollection I have been interested in the welfare of colored people, and have felt that they had not had justice done them, and that in all benevolent operations the white man is the favored one, and receives by far the largest share of the bounty bestowed therefore I have not been governed or influenced in the least by any one, but have acted entirely as my conscience dictated in making this devise in trust. Several years ago I bequeathed my property to the Home Missionary Society in order that young colored men might be educated But there is so much spent for salaries and for elegant offices, comforts and luxuries for the officers in that institution, that I am disappointed. Therefore I make this change in order that the friends of colored persons may be my trustees believing that at my decease my plans may be more fully carried out to the end that the colored people by being assisted may become intelligent, industrious and thrifty citizens.

"My desire is that the residue of my estate shall be used in establishing what shall be known as the Cushing Industrial Home, where colored children may be taught by actual practice in every-

cipal should be paid to a charity. The court refused to allow an income tax deduction to the settlor for any part of the value of the property placed in the trust because of the remoteness of the possession and enjoyment of the gift by the charity. Here the delay in enjoyment by the charity was five hundred years. The court recognized that delay in enjoyment does not of itself destroy the charitable nature of the gift but when it is extended as in this case, no present charitable value is ascertainable. Because of the fact that the trust was void, the settlor was taxable on the capital gains and undistributed income, since he could recover them at any time. Holdeen v. Ratterree, 61-1 U.S.T.C. ¶ 9184 (N.D.N.Y. 1960).

[7] 6 American Law of Property §25.108 (Casner ed. 1952).

thing which in the opinion of my trustees, will tend to make home really comfortable, attractive and happy. My desire being that my property shall go to and for the use and benefit of colored people and none other, and in no event shall any portion of my property be applied to the use or benefit of Roman Catholics, or the support of any Roman Catholic institution." The value of the property that passed under this clause is $2,000. It appears that this is not at present sufficient to establish and maintain an industrial home for colored children as directed by the will, and that it is altogether problematical and uncertain how much money would be required, and how long it would take to accumulate the necessary funds for that purpose. The trustees bring this bill for instructions as to the disposition that should be made of the trust fund. [Footnote omitted.]

The case presents three questions: First, shall the property be held until, by reason of accumulations, it has become sufficient to carry out the provisions of the will in accordance with its terms? Second, shall the property be administered according to the doctrine of cy pres? Third, shall the fund be paid over to the heir at law on the ground that the gift has failed?

In reference to the first question, the facts are almost identical with those of Ely v. Attorney General, 202 Mass. 545. The amount in the hands of the trustees in that case was a little more than the trustees have in the present case, and the finding as to accumulation was in the exact words to which the parties have agreed as a statement of the facts in the present case. The court said in the opinion that "upon this finding, taken in connection with the other facts disclosed, . . . the trustees should not be instructed to hold the fund for accumulation, in the hope that some time, in the more or less distant future, they would be able to carry out literally the purpose of the testatrix, which evidently was intended to be executed in a short time after her death." This language is equally applicable to the present case.

The next question is whether the gift has failed altogether, or whether it should be administered in accordance with the doctrine of cy pres. This depends upon whether the language of the will indicates a general charitable intent, to be carried out for the benefit of young persons of the colored race, and particularly by giving them opportunities to obtain an industrial education, or whether the object of the testatrix was limited to a specific charity, which could only be administered by the establishment of a new institution, to be called the Cushing Industrial Home.[8] We think

---

[8] If the gift was contingent on the establishment of a new institution to be called the Cushing Industrial Home, this contingency might not be resolved

the will contains very plain indications of a general charitable intent in reference to colored people, and particularly in reference to the education and training of colored children. The first of the two paragraphs quoted above is of a very general character, showing that the testatrix had in mind the improvement of persons of African descent, "to the end that the colored people by being assisted may become intelligent, industrious and thrifty citizens." She changed her previous bequest to the Home Missionary Society for a particular reason applicable to that society alone. That bequest and the reason for changing it indicate that her real purpose was the education of young colored persons.

The last of the two quoted paragraphs, after stating her desire specifically, states in the broadest way her general purpose to have her property "go to and for the use and benefit of colored people and none other." The prohibition of the use of it for the "support of any Roman Catholic institution" is an indication that she thought of the possibility of a failure to establish and maintain the Cushing Industrial Home, and of its use for the support of some other institution. Her prohibition was only of the support of a Roman Catholic institution.

We are of opinion that a scheme should be framed for the use of this fund in accordance with the general intent of the testatrix, that shall accomplish her purpose as nearly as may be. For similar cases see Ely v. Attorney General, 202 Mass. 545; Weeks v. Hobson, 150 Mass. 377; Richardson v. Mullery, 200 Mass. 247; Attorney General v. Briggs, 164 Mass. 561; Sears v. Chapman, 158 Mass. 400.

So ordered.[9]

PROBLEM

14.1. A, who is domiciled in a jurisdiction which recognizes the common rule against perpetuities, provides as follows in his will: "I hereby devise Blackacre to the X Church provided the Church

---

until more than twenty-one years after lives in being at the time the testatrix died. — ED.

[9] Gray, the Rule Against Perpetuities §§604-609 (4th ed., Roland Gray, 1942), points out that in jurisdictions which do not recognize the power to administer a charitable trust cy pres, a gift to a charitable corporation to be created is void because of the rule against perpetuities unless the gift is to take effect if, and only if, the corporation is organized within the period of time allowed by the rule.

In Haggerty v. City of Oakland, 161 Cal. App. 2d 407, 326 P.2d 957 (1958), it was held that a lease for years which was to commence on the completion of a designated building (under construction when the lease was signed) violated the rule against perpetuities because the lease was subject to a condition precedent which might not occur within the period of the rule. — ED.

raises $100,000 for the purpose of building a church thereon, and if the X Church does not raise such sum, I give Blackacre to the Y Church." Within five years after A's death, the X Church raises $100,000. Would you advise the church to use this sum to erect a building on Blackacre? In connection with this problem consider the case of Edwards v. Hammond, quoted in full supra page 552.

3. FEDERAL TAX CONSIDERATIONS

a. *Income Taxes*

When a charitable disposition is made, the accomplishment of the following federal income tax objectives is normally desired:

1. Whether the charitable disposition is inter vivos or testamentary, the transferor wants the income derived from the gift property to be free of any income tax in the hands of the transferee. If the transferee meets the test of an exempt organization, the income will not be taxable as a general rule.[10] The exempt status of an organization may be

---

[10] See 1954 I.R.C. §501(c), quoted infra page 1356.

In Rev. Rul. 56-304, 1956-2 C.B. 306, it is held that a charitable foundation organized to carry on one or more of the purposes specified in §501(c)(3) is not precluded from making distributions of its funds to individuals, provided such distributions are made on a true charitable basis and in furtherance of the purposes for which it was organized. Adequate records and case histories should be maintained, however, "to show the name and address of each recipient of aid; the amount distributed to each; the purpose for which the aid was given; the manner in which the recipient was selected and the relationship, if any, between the recipient and (1) members, officers, or trustees of the organization, (2) a grantor or substantial contributor to the organization or a member of the family of either, and (3) a corporation controlled by a grantor or substantial contributor, in order that any or all distributions made to individuals can be substantiated upon request by the Internal Revenue Service."

William B. Chase, CCH T.C. Mem. 1960-49, is concerned with an incorporated foundation to which contributions were made by various companies owned or controlled by the taxpayer. The foundation adopted a scholarship program with employees of the participating companies, children of such employees and "deserving outsiders" being eligible to receive scholarships. In practice no awards were made to outsiders. The Commissioner argued that the foundation was not exempt because it was operated for the benefit of participating companies to increase employee morale and loyalty but the court found that under all the circumstances this was not so because there were reasons why no awards had been made to outsiders.

In Scripture Press Foundation v. United States, 285 F.2d 800 (Ct. Cl. 1961), a corporation organized as a nonprofit corporation, was denied tax-exempt status where it engaged in the publication and sale of religious literature and in free and voluntary instructional work at Sunday School meetings, because the volume of sales was so large in relation to the amounts expended in religious instructional activities.

Revenue Ruling 60-384, I.R.B. 1960-52, 19, recognizes that a wholly owned state or municipal instrumentality which is a separate entity and which is organized and operated exclusively for the purposes described in §501(c)(3)

lost if it engages in what are termed prohibited transactions.[11]   The exempt status may also be lost in any year in which amounts are accumulated out of income.[12]   Also, the so-called unrelated business income of an exempt organization will be taxable.[13]   If a trust or estate is involved which pays or permanently sets aside trust income or estate income for charitable purposes, a charitable deduction may be available to the trust or estate.[14]

---

may qualify for exemption from income tax under §501(a) as an organization described in §501(c)(3).

[11] See 1954 I.R.C. §503.   The prohibited transactions are described in §503(c), quoted infra page 1360.

[12] See 1954 I.R.C. §504(a), quoted infra page 1360.

Revenue Ruling 58-535, 1958-2 C.B. 270, holds that contributions to an organization exempt under §501(c)(3) are not income in applying §504.   Consequently, distributions made by the organization will first be charged against current income.   The extent to which a charitable corporation may pay off loans to it with the income from the borrowed funds without running afoul of §504 is illustrated in A. Shiffman, 32 T.C. 1073 (1959).   In this case a foundation purchased property for $1,150,000.   The purchase was made by borrowing $1,000,000 ($250,000 from an individual and $750,000 from an insurance company) at 5 percent interest and by receiving $154,000 in advance rentals.   The net income from the rental property was used to retire the debt.   The court held that such an accumulation of income by the foundation did not cause it to lose its exempt status.   The Bulletin of the A.B.A. Section on Taxation for April, 1960, states: "The Service has indicated that it will not approve articles of incorporation or indentures of trust organizations claiming exemption under §501(c)(3) of the Code if they contain an unlimited power to accumulate income.   The Service recognizes that such an organization must have some power to accumulate income but holds it must be limited by some standard such as reasonableness before exemption will be granted.   In effect, therefore, the Service is imposing the limitations of §504 in determining qualification under §501(c)(3)."

[13] See 1954 I.R.C. §§511-514.   In regard to unrelated business income, see Rev. Rul. 55-676, 1955-2 C.B. 266.   Revenue Ruling 58-547, 1958-2 C.B. 275, deals with income from a business lease (see §514) and points out that it may be unrelated business income even though the lessor and lessee are both charities.

See also Rev. Rul. 58-482, 1958-2 C.B. 273; Amon G. Carter Foundation v. United States, 58-1 U.S.T.C. ¶9342 (N.D. Tex. 1958), in which the court held that a corporation created and wholly owned by an exempt charitable organization had a separate existence, and that, consequently, the income of this separate corporation was not taxable to the exempt corporation as unrelated business income.

[14] See 1954 I.R.C. §642(c), quoted infra page 1362.   Income taxation of trusts is considered supra page 733.   Particular attention should be paid to the change in the treatment of charitable deductions in a trust if the tier system proposed by H.R. 9662, which failed of passage in the Eighty-sixth Congress, is later adopted.   The system is discussed supra page 738.   Section 681 of the 1954 Code places restrictions on the charitable deduction available to a trust where the trust has engaged in prohibited transactions, accumulated income, or received unrelated business income.   Section 642(c) requires that if the income is paid or permanently set aside for charitable purposes, it must be "pursuant to the terms of the governing instrument."   For a comment on the quoted language see Rev. Rul. 55-92, 1955-1 C.B. 390.   For a consideration of

2. When an inter vivos charitable disposition is made, the
   transferor does not want the income produced by the gift
   property after the transfer to be included in his gross income.[15]

---

the words "permanently set aside," which are used in §642(c), see Boston Safe
Deposit & Trust Co. v. United States, 129 F. Supp. 616 (D. Mass. 1955).

Section 642(c) also applies to estates. The operation of this section with respect to estate income is considered in Rev. Rul. 55-122, 1955-1 C.B. 390. The
changes in the handling of charitable deductions which would be made by
H.R. 9662, as explained supra page 738 so far as trusts are concerned, are also
relevant in connection with estates. Income taxation of estates is examined
generally in Chapter IV.

In Rockland Oil Co., 22 T.C. 1307 (1954), a will directed that the residue
of an estate was to go to a charity after the payment of two small bequests.
The testator left a large estate, which had many outstanding claims against it.
The question presented was whether the income of the estate which was accumulated prior to the period of distribution to the charity was subject to income taxes. The Commissioner's contention was that the claims against the
estate were so large that the ultimate charitable destination of the income was
uncertain. The court held that there was nothing in 1939 I.R.C. §162(a)
(1954 I.R.C. §642(c)) suggesting that its provisions were inapplicable if the estate was threatened by creditor's claims which might defeat the donor's intention.

See also Emanuelson, Jr. v. United States, 159 F. Supp. 34 (D. Conn. 1958),
dealing with income of an estate payable to a charity as the result of a compromise agreement settling a will dispute. In view of the Emanuelson case,
Rev. Rul. 55-122, 1955-1 C.B. 390, which had held that income passing to a
charity as the result of a compromise agreement was not deductible, was revoked by Rev. Rul. 59-15, 1959-1 C.B. 164, and it is now held that payments
to a charity made by an executor out of estate income which are attributable
to the part of the estate transferred to the charity under a compromise agreement are deductible under §642(c). The state court denied a charitable deduction for state inheritance tax purposes for the property passing to charities as a result of the compromise. See Emanuelson, Jr. v. Sullivan, Conn.
L.J., June 21, 1960, p. 4 (Conn. Sup. Ct. of Errors). Marquis v. United States,
173 F. Supp. 616 (Ct. Cl. 1959), holds that where a wife dies and gives property outright to her husband and then the husband dies and gives all his
property to charity, the income in the estate of the wife is not permanently
set aside for charitable purposes, even though when it is paid to the husband's
estate it will go to charity.

If a will contains a charitable gift, and a certain portion of income earned
by the estate during administration will pass to the charity, an income tax deduction is available to the estate. Under these circumstances, will the portion
of the income which is thus deductible be required to bear any part of the income tax payable by the estate? This question was considered in Rhode Island Hospital Trust Co. v. Sanders, 84 R.I. 347, 125 A.2d 100 (1956), and the
court held that no part of the estate income tax should be borne by the income allocable to the charitable gift.

In regard to whether income can be permanently set aside for charity in a
year in which there is a dispute as to whether the trust is entitled to income,
see Leon A. Beeghly Fund, 35 T.C. —, No. 56 (1960), which held that the
income would be regarded as permanently set aside in such a year when all of
the income was supposed to go to charity. Compare, however, Fidelity Trust
Co. v. United States, discussed supra page 708, note 36.

[15] It is necessary to re-examine at this point the material at pages 153-188

3. When an inter vivos charitable disposition is made, the transferor wants the value of the gift to be deductible, to the maximum extent allowable, from his gross income in the year in which the gift is made. The total deductions in any taxable year for charitable gifts by individuals is 20 percent of the donor's adjusted gross income, with an additional 10 percent allowed for charitable contributions to a church, an educational organization, a hospital, or a medical research organization.[16] The limitations described in

supra, describing the circumstances under which the income of an inter vivos trust is includible in the gross income of the settlor, and particularly the discussion at page 173 dealing with two-year trusts for a charity.

Emerson R. Miller, CCH T.C. Mem. 1960-267, held that the income of an irrevocable charitable trust was not includible in the settlor's gross income even though he was the trustee and had wide powers of management.

[16] See 1954 I.R.C. §170(a) and §170(b)(1), quoted infra page 1333.

Section 1.170-2(b)(1) of the Regulations points out that the additional 10 percent is not available for contributions "for the use of" a church, an educational organization or a hospital. Revenue Ruling 58-263, 1958-1 C.B. 146, holds that a nonprofit corporation whose primary purpose and activity is soliciting and distributing donations to improve the welfare of animals held for research does not qualify under any of the classes of organizations set forth in §170(b)(1)(A) and, further, that contributions made to the organization for the use of university medical schools will not qualify as contributions paid to the universities. Revenue Ruling 59-129, 1959-1 C.B. 58, holds that the Salvation Army is a church for the purposes of §170(b)(1)(A)(i). Revenue Rulings 60-110, I.R.B. 1960-13, 9, and 60-111, I.R.B. 1960-13, 10, examine the availability of the extra 10 percent deduction. In the former, the extra 10 percent was denied where contributions were made to a university endowment association organized and operated for the purpose of receiving and holding in trust, property given to the organization for the benefit of the university. In the latter ruling, however, where contributions were made to an association of educational institutions and the association invested the total contributions received in the calendar year in short-term notes, pending complete distribution to the member institutions early in the following year, the extra 10 percent deduction was allowed on the ground that the contributions were deemed to be made directly to the member institutions and not to some intermediate organization in trust for the use of the institutions.

A charitable deduction will be disallowed in the case of contributions to charitable organizations engaged in prohibited transactions (1954 I.R.C. §170 (e)) and of contributions to or for the use of Communist-controlled organizations (1954 I.R.C. §170 (e)).

In Mattie Fair, 27 T.C. 866 (1957), the court held that a gift to a charitable foundation of the perpetual right to build, own, and maintain five additional stories on an existing two-story building owned by the donor, plus the rights of access and support for such additional stories, involved the transfer of rights and interests which, if capable of valuation, would give rise to a deduction under 1939 I.R.C. §23(o) (1954 I.R.C. §170).

If stock is transferred to a charity, the fees paid to accomplish the transfer are deductible within the allowed limits as amounts paid for the benefit of the charity. They are not available, however, for the additional 10 percent because they are not paid directly to the charity. To get them within the additional 10 percent, the stock should be endorsed to the charity and then a separate gift should be made to the charity to cover the costs the charity is

the preceding sentence give way to an unlimited charitable deduction if the individual donor in the taxable year and in eight of the ten preceding years meets certain specified conditions.[17] If the donor makes a transfer to a trust and retains a reversionary interest in the corpus or income of the trust and this interest meets the 5 percent test as to value, no charitable deduction is allowed for such a transfer in trust.[18] The total deductions allowed a corporation, as distinguished from an individual, for charitable gifts are 5 percent of the corporation's taxable income.[19] In all

---

subjected to in completing the transfer. See CCH Fed. Tax Rep. 60-5, ¶8731.

Estate of O. J. Wardwell, 35 T.C. —, No. 53 (1960), denied a charitable deduction for income tax purposes where the payment was made primarily because of an anticipated benefit of an economic nature to the payor. In its holding the court referred to the Duberstein case, considered supra page 366, note 72. The taxpayer had endowed a room in the home for aged to which she had been admitted and the home had a policy of charging a lower room rental to one who had given a room. Under these circumstances, a deduction was not allowed.

[17] See 1954 I.R.C. §170(b)(1)(C), quoted infra page 1334.

[18] See 1954 I.R.C. §170(b)(1)(D), quoted infra page 1334.

Revenue Ruling 194, 1953-2 C.B. 128, provides that where a taxpayer irrevocably transfers property to a trust to be held for a period of ten years and ten days for the benefit of a charitable foundation, the taxpayer is entitled to a deduction of the present value of the property interest which was contributed to the trust. So far as situations where the grantor has a reversionary interest in trust property which meets the 5 percent test are concerned, this ruling is rendered obsolete by §170(b)(1)(D), but this section does not apply where the grantor has a reversionary interest in connection with the grant of a legal interest.

Section 1.170-2(d) of the Regulations provides in part as follows: "An interest of the grantor which, in any event, will terminate before the ripening of the assured charitable gift for which a deduction is claimed is not considered a reversionary interest for purposes of this section. For example, assume that a taxpayer conveyed property to a trust under the terms of which the income is payable to the taxpayer's wife for her life, and, if she predeceases him, to him for his life, and after the death of both the property is to be transferred to a charitable organization. The present value of the remainder interest in the property, taking into account the value of the life estates reserved to the taxpayer and his wife, may be allowed as a charitable deduction."

[19] See 1954 I.R.C. §170(b)(2) and (3), quoted infra page 1335.

If the corporation reports its taxable income on an accrual basis, a charitable contribution made by it after the close of its taxable year and on or before the fifteenth day of the third month following the close of its taxable year may be deducted in the taxable year. Wood-Mosaic Co. v. United States, 160 F. Supp. 636 (D. Ky. 1958), brings out that the deduction will not be allowed, even though made within two and a half months of the close of the taxable year, if the charity is not in existence in the taxable year. The deduction will be allowed in the taxable year in which it is made. The court also pointed out that there was no tangible evidence of any corporate action on the part of the directors of the company evidencing a fixed intention to make the contribution during the taxable year for which the deduction was claimed.

cases, whether the donor is an individual or a corporation, the deduction is available only if the gift meets the test of a charitable contribution as that term is defined in the Code.[20]

When a charitable gift is made, it may be to the advantage of the donor to place the highest value on the subject matter of the gift that is reasonably sustainable. In this way the maximum deduction for income tax purposes may be available to the donor.[21]

The case was affirmed in 272 F.2d 944 (6th Cir. 1959), *cert. denied,* 363 U.S. 803 (1960).

[20] See 1954 I.R.C. §170(c), quoted infra page 1336.

On the question of what are charitable contributions, see the following: Rev. Rul. 54-580, 1954-2 C.B. 97 (tuition paid for children attending parochial school not a charitable contribution); Rev. Rul. 55-269, 1955-1 C.B. 29 (payments made to subsidize dissemination of literature to charitable organizations not charitable contributions); Rev. Rul. 55-514, 1955-2 C.B. 55 (vendor of goods gave with sale of each item a certificate which he agreed to redeem for a certain amount when presented to him by a charitable organization to which purchaser of goods might deliver certificate; payments made by vendor in redemption of certificates not considered charitable contributions). On the question of whether an organization is attempting to influence legislation, see Seasongood v. Commissioner, 227 F.2d 907 (6th Cir. 1955).

In Rev. Rul. 56-138, 1956-1 C.B. 202, it is held that a trust organized primarily for the purpose of paying pensions to retired employees is not organized exclusively for charitable purposes, and hence contributions to it are not deductible under §170.

Revenue Ruling 56-329, 1956-2 C.B. 125, deals with §170(c)(4) and brings out that a contribution to a fraternal organization for purposes of acquiring, erecting and maintaining a building for the organization is not deductible because the contribution is not to be used exclusively for the charitable purposes referred to in §170(c)(4). Revenue Ruling 60-367, I.R.B. 1960-49, 11, however, points out that gifts made directly to a college for the purpose of acquiring or constructing a housing facility for a designated fraternity, title to which will be in the college, may be deductible.

Revenue Ruling 58-190, 1958-1 C.B. 15, considers §170(c)(5) and points out that contributions for the perpetual care of a particular lot or mausoleum crypt are not deductible under that section. Such contributions must be for the perpetual care of the cemetery as a whole in order to be deductible. Furthermore, the income of a trust which is used or permanently set aside for the care of a particular family burial lot is not deductible under §642(c).

John Joseph Cranley, Jr., CCH T.C. Mem. 1961-4, held that a doctor's contributions to a medical foundation were not deductible where the foundation had a dual operation, part being devoted to research and part to patients, so that it was not operated exclusively for scientific purposes. The court pointed out that the taxpayer had not proved that he did not benefit commercially from the foundation's work for patients.

[21] In Robert B. Dresser, 15 CCH T.C. Mem. 242 (1956), the donor valued property restricted to residential purposes at the value it might bring if it could be sold for commercial purposes. The court held that it had to be valued on the basis of residential property.

In Cooley v. Commissioner, 61-1 U.S.T.C. ¶9106 (2d Cir. 1960), the court held that automobiles given to charity had to be valued at the price paid for them, rather than at their higher retail value, when they were purchased subject to the specific condition that they be donated to charity.

Where a charitable corporation is organized or a charitable trust is established, it is customary to seek a ruling from the Internal Revenue Service determining that the corporation or the trust is exempt from federal income taxation. Normally the Service will not make a decision with respect to a newly formed organization until it has actually operated for such a period and to such an extent as to clearly demonstrate a bona fide operation for the purposes specified in the exemption statute. The Service has stated that an application for exemption should not be filed by an organization until it has had at least twelve months of active operation (not merely existence) for the purposes for which it was created.[22] Consequently, some risks are involved when contributions are made to an alleged charitable organization before a ruling in regard to its exempt status has been obtained.[23] If it should be determined that the organization is not exempt, gifts to the organization will not be deductible by the donor for income tax purposes, the income produced by the donated property will be taxable in

[22] Rev. Rul. 54-164, 1954-1 C.B. 88.

Section 6104(a) of the 1954 Code, which was added by §75 of the Technical Amendments Act of 1958, provides that an application for exemption of an organization under §501(a), together with any papers submitted in support of the application, shall be open to public inspection. Revenue Ruling 59-267, 1959-2 C.B. 382, holds that the term "application for exemption" does not include a request for a ruling as to whether a proposed transaction is a prohibited one under §503. Accordingly, documents submitted in connection with a request for a ruling with respect to the taxability of certain income under §511 (unrelated business income) are not subject to public inspection under §6104(a).

[23] In Lesavoy Foundation v. Commissioner, 238 F.2d 589 (3d Cir. 1956), the court held that the Commissioner went beyond the bounds of permissible discretion when he changed his mind as to the exemption to be granted to a foundation and made it liable for a tax bill so large as to wipe it out of existence. The court discussed 1954 I.R.C. §7805(b), which sets forth the general principle that the Commissioner, with the approval of the Secretary, may prescribe the extent, if any, to which a ruling relating to the Internal Revenue laws shall be applied without retroactive effect. See also Lorain Avenue Clinic, 31 T.C. 141 (1958), in regard to a review of the Commissioner's exercise of discretion in making the revocation of a charitable exemption retroactive.

Revenue Ruling 58-617, 1958-2 C.B. 260, points out that any material changes in the character of an exempt organization must be brought immediately to the attention of the District Director of Internal Revenue so that a determination may be made as to the effect of such changes on the exempt status of the organization. A ruling that the changes cause the exemption of the organization to be revoked may be retroactive to the date of the changes.

John Danz Charitable Trust, 32 T.C. 469 (1959), brings out that the doctrine of res judicata is not applicable so as to prevent a charitable organization, previously held to be nonexempt because of its operation of businesses, from claiming exemption in subsequent years under different factual situations. The case was affirmed sub nom. Commissioner v. John Danz Charitable Trust, 284 F.2d 726 (9th Cir. 1960).

the hands of the organization, and the donor may be liable for a gift tax.[24] A booklet is published which gives a list of the organizations which have been ruled to be exempt.[25]

[24] In Eddie Cigelman Corp., 14 CCH T.C. Mem. 1259 (1955), it was held that a corporation which, pending a ruling as to its exempt status, was to turn over to charitable purposes only that part of its net income which the controlling stockholder saw fit to have it pay, was not exempt because it was not organized for the purpose of turning over to charitable purposes the entire amount of its income less expenses. If the corporation never received its ex empt ruling, the income was to be held for noncharitable purposes.

In Perry v. United States, 160 F. Supp. 270 (Ct. Cl. 1958), the taxpayer made gifts in trust to a charity, on the condition that the subject matter of the gifts would be returned if the charity did not go forward with the building for which the gifts were intended. Later the subject matter of the gifts was returned to the donor pursuant to the condition, and the court held that in the year of the return the donor should add to his tax the amount by which his taxes in prior years had been decreased on account of deductions for contributions to the trust and that the basis of the returned property was its original cost to the donor. In T.I.R. 128, dated February 2, 1959, 59 CCH Fed. Tax Rep. ¶6307, the Internal Revenue Service says that the Perry decision conflicts with a long line of judicial authority holding that recoveries of previously deducted items constitute taxable income in the year of recovery to the extent a tax benefit was realized from the deduction, and that, consequently, the Perry case will not be followed as a precedent in the disposition of similar cases. The release is incorporated in Rev. Rul. 59-141, 1959-1 C.B. 17.

Maysteel Products, Inc., 33 T.C. 1021 (1960), is a case where the taxpayer purchased bonds at a premium, with the earliest call date upon thirty days' notice. After holding the bonds thirty days, the taxpayer made a gift of the bonds to charity. The taxpayer took a deduction for the amortization of the bond premium and a charitable deduction for the value of the bonds. The court denied the amortization of the bond premium because the only motive in the purchase and disposition of the bonds was to make a gift, and gift transactions do not give rise to deductions for bond premiums. The Maysteel Products case is followed in Fabreeka Products Co., 34 T.C. —, No. 30 (1960), Jack L. Sherman, 34 T.C. 303 (1960), Edwin A. Gallun, CCH T.C. Mem. 1960-104, Sadie S. Freedman, 34 T.C. —, No. 45 (1960), and Forrester A. Clark, CCH T.C. Mem. 1960-277. But compare Evans v. Dudley, 60-2 U.S.T.C. ¶9701 (W.D. Pa. 1960), which allowed the deduction for amortization and distinguished the preceding cases on the ground that the purchase of the bonds here was a real and legitimate purchase in the open market resulting in an appreciable change in the taxpayer's financial position.

Revenue Ruling 58-495, 1958-2 C.B. 27, holds that amounts earned by employees for services donated for charitable purposes are includible in their gross income, even though such amounts are paid directly to the charities by the employer pursuant to an agreement made before the services are rendered. But the value of services performed gratuitously for a charitable organization are not so includible. Compare, however, Rev. Rul. 58-515, 1958-2 C.B. 28 (compensation received by police officer from employment in private industry in the performance of his duties as an employee of the police department and remitted by him to the Police Pension Fund is not includible in his gross income).

[25] Cumulative List of Organizations Described in 170(c) of Internal Revenue Code of 1954, I.R.S. Pub. No. 78 (rev. ed. Oct. 31, 1954), printed by U.S. Government Printing Office.

PROBLEMS

14.2. It is possible for a person in at least one situation to have more money to spend if he makes a charitable gift than if he does not make one. Can you describe a situation which would produce this result?

14.3. A desires to establish during his lifetime a charitable trust. He plans to transfer to the trust approximately $100,000 worth of property. A owns 1000 shares of the X Corporation, which have a present value of $100,000. The basis of these shares to A is $20 a share. A also owns 1000 shares of the Y Corporation, which have a present value of $100,000. The basis of these shares to A is $120 a share. A also owns 1000 shares of the Z Corporation, which have a present value of $100,000. The basis of these shares to A is $80 a share. The drafting of the charitable trust is completed on December 1, but no decision has been made as to the property to be placed in the trust. Advise A regarding the establishment of the charitable trust from this point on. In connection with this problem consider Johnson v. Wiseman, 55-2 U.S.T.C. ¶9621 (W.D. Okla. 1955).

14.4. A pledges $1000 to the X Church, the pledge to be paid during 1960. In December, 1960, A discharges the pledge by delivering to the church ten shares of stock in the Y Company, which are worth $1000 on the date of delivery. If the basis of the stock in A's hands is $500, does A realize any taxable gain on this transaction? If the basis of the stock in A's hands is $1500, has A sustained a deductible loss on this transaction? See Revenue Ruling 55-410, 1955-1 C.B. 297. Assume that A dies before paying the pledge and A's executor pays it. Will the amount paid be deductible in determining A's taxable estate for estate tax purposes?

14.5. In which of the following instances does the gift qualify for the additional deduction of 10 percent of the adjusted gross income under Section 170(b)(1)(A), quoted infra page 1334?

    a. Contributions are made to federal, state and local governments for the expansion, development or creation of educational organizations or hospitals which are instrumentalities of such governments? See Revenue Ruling 55-453, 1955-2 C.B. 54.

    b. A charity fund-raising organization provides for payment of pledges by checks drawn in favor of a certain hospital or educational institution, and the checks are delivered to the fund-raising organization, which delivers the checks directly to the payee. See Revenue Ruling 55-1 1955-1 C.B. 26; Revenue Ruling 59-27, 1959-1 C.B. 57.

c. Contributions to a museum which maintains a regular faculty and has a curriculum and regularly enrolled students. See Revenue Ruling 55-219, 1955-1 C.B. 28; Revenue Ruling 56-262, 1956-1 C.B. 131; Revenue Ruling 58-433, 1958-2 C.B. 102.

d. Contributions to a rehabilitation center to acquire a building for use in treating handicapped individuals. See Revenue Ruling 55-268, 1955-1 C.B. 28.

14.6. Suppose that agricultural or manufactured products and property held for sale in the ordinary course of business are contributed to a charity. Describe the tax consequences of such a transaction so far as the donor is concerned. See Revenue Ruling 55-138, 1955-1 C.B. 223; Campbell v. Prothro, 209 F.2d 331 (5th Cir. 1954). See also Section 1.170-1(c) of the Regulations; Revenue Ruling 59-196, 1959-1 C.B. 56; Branscomb, Gifts and Other Dispositions of Crops, 46 A.B.A.J. 95 (1960).

14.7. A owns Blackacre in fee simple. His basis for federal income tax purposes with respect to Blackacre is $20,000. Blackacre is now worth $50,000. A borrows $30,000 from the X bank and executes a mortgage on Blackacre to secure the sum so borrowed. A then transfers Blackacre to a charity. He takes a charitable deduction for income tax purposes in the amount of $20,000, which does not exceed 20 percent of his adjusted gross income for the taxable year in which the gift is made. Does A realize a gain of $10,000, the amount by which the mortgage exceeds his basis?

b. *Gift Taxes*

When an inter vivos charitable disposition is made, the donor expects to be able to deduct the entire value of the gift in determining his taxable gifts for the year in which the gift is made.[26] It is important to know the date when the gift to the charity has

---

[26] See 1954 I.R.C. §2522(a) quoted infra page 1423.

In M. H. Davis, 22 T.C. 1091 (1954), the Tax Court allowed as exempt under the gift tax a transfer in trust for the benefit of a charitable foundation organized for social welfare work, even though the ultimate effect of some of the charitable work was realized in legislation for the improvement of social conditions. The Tax Court held that this fact did not characterize the work as an attempt to influence legislation.

Revenue Ruling 59-57, 1959-1 C.B. 626, holds that a contribution to a political party or to any candidate for public office does not constitute a gift to, or for the use of, the United States or any state, territory or political subdivision thereof, for exclusively public purposes within the meaning of §2522 (a)(1).

been completed, because the value of the subject matter of the gift on that date will be the amount to be taken into account in determining the income tax deduction.[27] Furthermore, the year in which the gift is completed is the year in which it should be reported for gift tax purposes.

PROBLEMS

14.8. On December 30, 1960, A delivers $50,000 to a solicitor who comes to his house to collect contributions for the Community Chest Fund. The solicitor does not turn over the contribution to the Community Chest Fund until January 2, 1961. In which year did A make a gift to the fund? See Revenue Ruling 55-192, 1955-1 C.B. 294.

14.9. If a charitable trust is established under which the charities to benefit are to be selected from time to time by the trustees, and the amount or amounts of income and principal to be paid to the selected charities are to be determined from time to time by the trustees, has the settlor of such a trust, if he is one of the trustees, made a completed gift to the charities at the time the trust is established? See Camp v. Commissioner, 195 F.2d 999 (1st Cir. 1952); Latta v. Commissioner, 212 F.2d 164 (3d Cir. 1954), cert. denied, 348 U.S. 825 (1954). See also Barber v. Edwards, 130 F. Supp. 83 (M.D. Ga. 1955), and note 38 infra.

c. Estate Taxes

If a testamentary charitable disposition is made, the testator will want the value of the gift to be deductible in determining his taxable estate for estate tax purposes.[28] If property passes to a charity

---

[27] See the discussion in regard to what constitutes a completed gift at page 218 supra. See also note 21 supra.

[28] See 1954 I.R.C. §2055, quoted infra page 1405.

On the question of what constitutes a bequest for charitable purposes, see Rev. Rul. 55-519, 1955-2 C.B. 386 (bequest for neglected and homeless animals deemed bequest for charitable purposes); Estate of Philip R. Thayer, 24 T.C. 384 (1955) (bequest to college alumni association deemed one for charitable purposes). The Thayer case is referred to with approval in Rev. Rul. 60-143, I.R.B. 1960-16, 20, where it is recognized that social and recreational activities carried on by an alumni association of a university which are incidental to its basic purpose of advancing the interests of the university do not of themselves preclude such an organization from tax exemption under §501(c)(3) as an association organized and operated exclusively for educational and charitable purposes.

In Estate of Harley J. Davis, 26 T.C. 549 (1956), a bequest in trust for the benefit of the student nurses then enrolled in or thereafter attending the Lutheran Hospital School of Nursing was deemed to be an educational bequest and thus deductible. Greiss v. United States, 146 F. Supp. 505 (N.D.

as a result of an estate beneficiary disclaiming a gift in his favor, the interest thus picked up by the charity may be deductible in determining the testator's taxable estate for federal estate tax pur-

---

Ill. 1956), held that a bequest was not to an organization operated exclusively for charitable, educational or scientific purposes, because part of the activities of the organization was to promote outdoor activities. Thus the deduction was not allowed.

In Williams v. United States, 158 F. Supp. 227 (N.D. Cal. 1957), a husband and wife made reciprocal wills under which the survivor was to receive the property of the first to die, and on the death of the survivor, their combined assets were to pass to charities. The husband died first, and before the administration of his estate was completed, his wife died. A charitable deduction was claimed in the husband's estate for the estate income received after the death of the wife, on the ground that the income was certain to pass to a charity. The court denied the deduction in the husband's estate on the ground that his will did not pass the income to charity. The case was affirmed in 251 F.2d 847 (9th Cir. 1958).

The court in Dulles v. Johnson, 155 F. Supp. 275 (S.D.N.Y. 1957), denied a charitable deduction for bequests to the New York County Lawyers Association, the Association of the Bar of the City of New York, and the New York State Bar Association on the ground that these organizations exist primarily to benefit members of the legal profession and to provide a method whereby their views and recommendations, as a body, on legislation of various kinds is made known to the legislatures. Such activities go well beyond education and the mere expression of opinions. Also, a bequest to the Association of the Bar of the City of New York "for its library and for research and exposition in law, and for other legal purposes" was held not deductible. The case was reversed on these points in 273 F.2d 362 (2d Cir. 1959). In addition, examine Rhode Island Hospital Trust Co. v. United States, 159 F. Supp. 204 (D.R.I. 1958), where a bequest to the Rhode Island Bar Association for advancing and upholding the standards of the profession of law, and for the prosecution and punishment of those members of the Bar who violated their obligations to the public and to the court, qualified for the charitable deduction, even though the Bar Association through a committee commented on proposed legislation. The court concluded that the gift to the Bar Association was in trust for the stated purposes and thus met the test of a charitable gift for estate tax purposes. The fact that a gift to the Bar Association for its general purposes might not have qualified was not material, but the court indicated that such a gift would have qualified because no substantial part of the activities of the Association was carrying on propaganda or otherwise attempting to influence legislation. Revenue Ruling 58-293, 1958-1 C.B. 146, deals with a bar association exempt from federal income taxation as a business league under §501(c)(6), and holds that gifts to a legal library maintained as a part of the activity of such an association are not deductible inasmuch as the association is not one of the organizations to which charitable contributions are deductible under §170(c). Revenue Ruling 59-152, 1959-1 C.B. 54, describes a state bar association created as an arm of the court to perform governmental functions, and holds that contributions to it are deductible for income, estate and gift tax purposes. In Massachusetts Medical Society v. Assessors of Boston, 340 Mass. 327, 164 N.E.2d 325 (1960), the court held that the Massachusetts Medical Society was not a charity and thus its real estate was not exempt from taxation.

Revenue Ruling 57-449, 1957-2 C.B. 622, holds that a bequest of a stated number of dollars to all individuals who are enrolled as students in a particular school is not deductible as a bequest for educational purposes unless the will as a whole may be construed as creating a trust for such purposes for the benefit of the students as distinguished from mere benevolence.

In League of Women Voters of the United States v. United States, 180

poses.[29] Unless the charitable gift is freed from contributing to the death cost burdens, it will be diminished in amount by such

---

F. Supp. 379 (Ct. Cl. 1960), *cert. denied,* 81 Sup. Ct. 57 (1960), the court held that a residuary gift to the League was not deductible as a charitable gift because the League's main purpose is influencing legislation.

Industrial National Bank of Providence v. United States, 60-2 U.S.T.C. ¶11972 (D.R.I. 1960), held that a bequest to the Providence Art Club, which maintained an art gallery, library, lounge, classrooms, rented studios and dining room, was made exclusively for educational purposes and thus was fully deductible. The operation of the dining room was incidental to the sponsorship of art exhibitions and the encouragement of skills and talents of artists.

It should be noted that an income tax deduction is not available to an individual under §170 when the gift is to a corporation, trust, or community chest, fund or foundation created or organized under the laws of a foreign country. However, a corporation organized under the laws of the United States evidently does not lose its exemption under §501 by virtue of the fact that it may make and does make gifts to foreign charities. Furthermore, a gift to a foreign charity may be deductible for federal gift tax purposes under §2522 and for federal estate tax purposes under §2055.

[29] See 1954 I.R.C. §2055(a), which brings out that the disclaimer must be made before the date prescribed for the filing of the estate tax return. Also, the complete termination before the date prescribed for the filing of the estate tax return of a power to consume, invade, or appropriate property for the benefit of an individual, before such power has been exercised, by reason of the death of such individual or for any other reason, is treated as a disclaimer in determining the availability of a charitable deduction.

Section 2055(b) as amended in 1956, quoted infra page 1405, enables a donee of a power to make available a charitable deduction in the estate of the donor of the power under limited circumstances by manifesting in a designated manner the intent to exercise the power in favor of a charity.

In Hight v. United States, 151 F. Supp. 202 (D. Conn. 1957), the decedent's will directed the transfer of the residue of her estate "to such charitable, benevolent, religious or educational institutions as my executors hereinafter named may determine." In view of the fact that the executors were authorized to expend the residue for "benevolent" institutions, a term the Connecticut court held was broader than the word "charitable," the transfer did not qualify as a deductible transfer for charitable purposes. The executors' attempt to disclaim the power to expend funds for benevolent institutions was not effective, since the executors could not change the legal interest established by the decedent's will. The case was reversed in 256 F.2d 795 (2d Cir. 1958). In reversing, the court held that the word "benevolent" in the decedent's will was coupled with the word "charitable" and was synonymous with that word, and that, moreover, factors indicated that the decedent intended the residuary estate to be used for tax-exempt institutions and that a state court decision with respect to the use of the word "benevolent" in a will could not be construed as preventing the residuary bequest from being a charitable one. The decision of the Court of Appeals was followed in Rosamond Gifford Charitable Corp. v. United States, 170 F. Supp. 239 (N.D.N.Y. 1958).

In Seubert v. Shaughnessy, 233 F.2d 134 (2d Cir. 1956), the court held that where a life beneficiary who had a power to withdraw principal filed an affidavit saying that she had "no intention of invading the principal of the decedent's estate for any purpose whatsoever," the affidavit did not constitute a disclaimer of the power of withdrawal.

Suppose that a bequest is made to the testator's wife which is designed to qualify for the marital deduction but the bequest is subject to the condition that if the wife does not survive by six months, the bequest to her shall pass

contributions and only the diminished amount will be deductible.[30]

A testamentary disposition in favor of a charity may be a bequest or devise of only a remainder interest or of only an income interest for a limited period, as well as of the complete interest in the property involved.[31]   An inter vivos transfer to charity also may be of an interest less than the complete interest in the property.

If a person wishes to have certain property pass to a charity on his death, it may be desirable for him to establish an irrevocable inter vivos trust in which he reserves to himself the income for life with the remainder to the charity.   Such an arrangement will not involve any gift tax because the only gift is of the remainder interest and that interest is given to a charity.[32]   If the property placed in the trust has a low basis, it can be sold by the trustees and no

---

to a charity.   The marital deduction will be available only if the wife survives her husband by six months (see discussion at page 836 supra).   No charitable deduction will be allowed when the wife survives her husband and then dies within six months, because the gift to the charity is subject to a condition as of the time of the testator's death, which makes it impossible to value it at that time.   The disclaimer provisions of §2055(a) do not help in this situation.

[30] Estate of Herman Hohensee, 25 T.C. 1258 (1956), brings out that no charitable deduction is available when the funds given to a charity are liable for death taxes and such taxes exceed the amount given to the charity, even though a volunteer pays the tax bill, because the charity receives the money from the volunteer and not from the decedent.

In Estate of Charles A. Brooks, 27 T.C. 295 (1956), there was uncertainty as to the amount of state inheritance taxes because of the fact that the amount could not be determined until it was known whether the life beneficiary exercised a power of appointment.   All death taxes were payable out of property passing to charities, and the court held that the charitable deduction would be reduced by the amount of state inheritance taxes which might ultimately be due.   The case was affirmed in 250 F.2d 937 (3d Cir. 1958).   See also Dulles v. Johnson, 273 F.2d 362 (2d Cir. 1959).

Estate of Edward H. Luehrmann, 33 T.C. 277 (1959), discussed supra page 787, considers the effect on the valuation of the remainder interest in a charity when the executor elects to take administration expenses as income tax deductions (§642(g)) rather than as estate tax deductions.   The case was affirmed in 60-1 U.S.T.C. ¶11994 (8th Cir. 1961).

[31] See Drye, Testamentary Gifts of Income to Charity, 13 Tax L. Rev. 49 (1957).   In this article, illustrations are given of the tax savings which in certain situations may result from making a testamentary gift of income to a charity for a limited period of time, with a remainder to individuals.   See also Reg. §1.170-1(d).

In Estate of George M. Moffett v. Commissioner, 269 F.2d 738 (4th Cir. 1959), the testator created a trust under which the income was to be paid to charity during the life of his wife and $50,000 per year was to be paid to his wife out of the principal.   A charitable deduction was allowed for the value of the income interest given to charity, the value being the present worth of the right to receive income from a diminishing fund for a period of thirty years (it would take thirty years to exhaust the principal in annual payments of $50,000 and the chance the wife would live thirty years was 290 in 1000).

[32] See Rev. Rul. 57-506, 1957-2 C.B. 65.

capital gains tax will be payable because the capital gain is permanently set aside for charitable purposes.[33] The value of the remainder that is given to charity will be deductible from the settlor's gross income to the extent allowable under Section 170 in the year in which the gift is made.[34] If the trust property is in-

[33] See 1954 I.R.C. §642(c), quoted infra page 1362.

Revenue Ruling 60-370, I.R.B. 1960-49, 15, holds that where the trustee is under an obligation, either express or implied, to sell or exchange the transferred property and to purchase tax-exempt securities, the transferor has given the trustee not appreciated property but, rather, the proceeds of the sale or exchange which he has required the trustee to consummate. Therefore, the gain from such a sale or exchange is includible in the gross income of the transferor in the taxable year in which the sale or exchange is consummated.

In Magnolia Development Corp., CCH T.C. Mem. 1960-177, the donor was held to be taxable on the gain, though the sale was made by a charity, where stock had been pledged by the donor to secure a loan at the time of the gift. The charity sold the stock and paid off the loan, and the court held that the substance of the transaction was a disposition by the taxpayer rather than by the charity.

When low-basis stock is given to a charity, the charitable deduction available for income tax purposes is determined on the basis of the full value of the stock, and the gain later realized by the sale of the stock is not taxable to the donor. But the same result is not obtained when a contribution is made by an employer to a qualified pension plan. In such a case, the employer can deduct the full value of the contributed stock but he is deemed to realize a gain in the amount of the difference between his basis and the value of the contributed stock. See United States v. General Shoe Corp., 60-2 U.S.T.C. ¶9678 (6th Cir. 1960).

[34] Revenue Ruling 57-506, 1957-2 C.B. 65, recognizes that the transfer of a remainder interest under a trust to a charitable organization constitutes a charitable contribution under §170. The amount of the charitable contribution cannot exceed the fair market value of the stock on the date of the transfer to the trust, less the value of the right of the life beneficiary to receive the designated amount of income from the trust. See also Rev. Rul. 57-507, 1957-2 C.B. 511; Rev. Rul. 57-562, 1957-2 C.B. 159; Reg. §1.170-1(d). Revenue Rulings 57-506 and 57-507 are distinguished in Rev. Rul. 59-47, 1959-1 C.B. 198, on a point other than the gift of the remainder to charity. Special Ruling, dated February 11, 1959, 59 CCH Fed. Tax Rep. ¶6356, holds that the additional deduction of 10 percent under §170(b)(1)(A) is available, although only a remainder interest is given to an educational organization.

In a Special Ruling dated March 12, 1958, 58 CCH Fed. Tax Rep. ¶6807, an irrevocable trust was examined under which income was to be paid to the grantor and then to a secondary beneficiary, and on the death of the survivor of the two, the principal and undistributed income was to go to a college, and the college was to be trustee. The following conclusions were set forth: (1) The present value of the remainder interest is deductible within the limits of §170(b)(1)(B) (whether the additional 10 percent under §170(b)(1)(A) will be available was reserved for a subsequent communication); (2) no gain or loss is realized by the grantor on the transfer (citing Rev. Rul. 55-275, 1955-1 C.B. 295); (3) capital gain realized on the sale of the contributed property will not be taxable to the grantor and, though includible in the gross income of the trust, will be deductible by the trust under §642(c); and (4) the trustee will be required to make an income tax return if the trust has any taxable income, or gross income is $600 or more, or any beneficiary is a resident alien.

If a trustee is given broad power to determine what is income and what is principal, the valuation of the remainder gift to the charity may be complicated.

vested in tax-exempt bonds, the income reserved to the settlor will be tax-free and he may have spendable income available to him that is greater in amount than what he had before making the gift of the remainder interest to charity.[35] The value of the trust property has not been removed from the settlor's gross estate because he has reserved the income for life, but this may be an advantage because the inclusion of the property in his gross estate will not increase his tax bill on his death. His estate tax may in fact be decreased, since the interest passing to the charity will be deductible, and at the same time the maximum marital deduction will be increased.[36]

Revenue Ruling 60-385, I.R.B. 1960-52, 15, brings out that the value of the charitable remainder cannot be determined, and hence no deduction will be available for income, estate or gift tax purposes if dividends representing capital gains are to be or may be distributed to the life beneficiary. Revenue Ruling 55-620, 1955-2 C.B. 56, which is contra, is revoked but the new ruling will not be applied to gifts made before January 1, 1961.

[35] But see Rev. Rul. 60-370 referred to supra note 33.

In Rev. Rul. 57-293, 1957-2 C.B. 153, it is held that where an owner of an art object transferred title thereto to charity by delivery of a formally executed and acknowledged deed of gift but reserves to himself the right to use the object during his life, a deduction of the present value of the remainder interest is available for federal income tax purposes. Likewise, it is held that where an undivided present interest in an art object is transferred to a charity by delivery of a formally executed and acknowledged deed of gift, a deduction of the fair market value of the undivided present interest will be available only if the deed contains unequivocal language of a present gift and transfers to the charity rights to possession, dominion, and control of the art object consistent with the creation of a tenancy in common as between the donor and the charity; the allowable deduction will be equal to that value which bears the same ratio to the value of the entire interest that the donated undivided present interest bears to the entire interest in the property. Revenue Ruling 58-455, 1958-2 C.B. 100, recognizes that the gift of an art object may consist of an undivided interest in remainder and that the value of the undivided interest may be deducted within the limits allowed by §170(b). Thus the owner of the art object may retain the use of the object for life and annually give an undivided remainder interest to charity so that the maximum benefit is obtained annually for income tax purposes.

Revenue Ruling 58-261, 1958-1 C.B. 143, is concerned with a situation where an undivided two-fifths interest in land was given to charity, and the donor planned to give the remaining three-fifths interest in succeeding taxable years, although he was in no way obligated to do so. The remaining three-fifths interest was under lease to the charity, with the understanding that if future gifts were made, the rent payable under the lease would be proportionately reduced. The fair market value of the two-fifths interest constitutes an allowable deduction from income to the extent provided by §170. The fair market value of the remaining three fifths will be deductible if and when it is donated to the charity. Revenue Ruling 58-260, 1958-1 C.B. 126, recognizes that a gift of an undivided one-fourth interest in a patent to a charity constitutes an allowable deduction as a charitable contribution to a charity to the extent provided in §170 in the taxable year in which the property is contributed.

[36] See Rev. Rul. 55-275, 1955-1 C.B. 295; Rev. Rul. 55-620, 1955-2 C.B. 56. See reference to Rev. Rul. 55-620 in note 34 supra.

Even if one desires to make a charitable gift during his lifetime without reserving any income benefits to himself, it may be advantageous for him to do so by means of a trust in which he retains the power to terminate the trust by paying out the corpus to charities during his lifetime.[37] In this way, he keeps the trust property in his gross estate for estate tax purposes and makes possible a larger marital deduction gift on his death and, consequently, a lower estate tax.[38]

PROBLEMS

14.10. Point out the difference in the tax consequences (1) if A establishes an irrevocable inter vivos trust reserving to himself the income for life and providing that on his death the income will be paid to his wife for her life, and that on the death of the survivor of A and his wife the principal will be paid to a designated charity; and (2) if A transfers property to a designated charity in return for the charity's promise to pay A an annuity of a stated amount for the balance of his life, and on his death to pay an annuity of a stated amount to his wife for the balance of her life. See Revenue Ruling 55-388, 1955-1 C.B. 233, and re-examine the material on family annuities at pages 261-266 supra.

14.11. T in his will gives the residue of his estate to a charitable corporation. The will provides that all federal estate taxes are to be paid out of the residue of his estate. T dies. The amount of the charitable deduction cannot be determined until the total amount of the taxes payable out of the residue of T's estate is ascertained, and the total amount of the taxes payable out of the residue of T's estate cannot be ascertained until the amount of the

---

[37] See Lober v. United States, quoted in full supra page 210.

[38] An informal letter from the Internal Revenue Service, not designed to be a ruling, which has come to my attention, expresses the conclusion that where the settlor of a trust can designate the charities to receive income and can terminate the trust at any time by a distribution of the corpus to charities, the value of the trust property will be includible in the settlor's gross estate under 1954 I.R.C. §2036 and also under §2038.

In Winthrop v. Meisels, 180 F. Supp. 29 (S.D.N.Y. 1959), the settlor of an inter vivos trust released his right to designate which charity would receive income under a trust that provided income was distributable to a charity for the first twenty years, with remainder to the members of his family. The settlor claimed that the relinquishment of his power constituted a charitable gift in the year of release but the court held that the relinquishment was of such slight value as not to amount to a payment to charity. Reference was made to §674(b)(4) as showing that the settlor is not the owner of anything when he has the power to determine the beneficial enjoyment of income irrevocably payable to charities. The case was affirmed in 281 F.2d 694 (2d Cir. 1960). In affirming, the court said that the charitable deduction was available when the trust was created.

charitable deduction is determined. How do you get out of this circle? See Section 20.2055-3 of the Regulations.

d. *Conditional Gift to a Charity*

The Regulations point out that if, as of the date of a gift, a transfer for charitable purposes is dependent upon the performance of some act or the happening of an event in order for the gift to become effective, no deduction is allowable unless the possibility that the charitable transfer will not become effective is so remote as to be negligible.[39] Furthermore, the deduction is not allowed in the case of a transfer in trust conveying to a charity a present interest in income if by reason of all the conditions and circumstances surrounding the transfer it appears that the charity may not receive the beneficial enjoyment of the interest.[40] The Sternberger case, which follows, deals with the conditional gift to a charity.

COMMISSIONER v. ESTATE OF LOUIS STERNBERGER
348 U.S. 187, 75 Sup. Ct. 229, 99 L. Ed. 246 (1955)

MR. JUSTICE BURTON delivered the opinion of the Court.

The issue here is whether, in determining a net estate for federal estate tax purposes, a deduction may be made on account of a charitable bequest that is to take effect only if decedent's childless 27-year-old daughter dies without descendants surviving her and her mother. For the reasons hereafter stated, we hold that it may not.

Louis Sternberger died testate June 25, 1947. His federal estate tax return discloses a gross estate of $2,406,541.71 and, for the additional estate tax, a net estate of $2,064,346.55. It includes assets owned by him at his death and others held by the Chase National Bank, respondent herein, under a revocable trust created by him. As the revocable trust makes provisions for charity that are for our

[39] See Reg. §§1.170-1(e), 20.2055-2(b) and 25.2522(a)-2(b).

[40] See Reg. §§1.170-1(e), 20.2055-2(b) and 25.2522(a)-2(b). Section 25.2522(a)-2(b) provides in part as follows: "For example, assume that assets placed in trust by the donor consist of stock in a corporation the fiscal policies of which are controlled by the donor and his family, that the trustees and remaindermen are likewise members of the donor's family, and that the governing instrument contains no adequate guarantee of the requisite income to the charitable organization. Under such circumstances, no deduction will be allowed. Similarly, if the trustees were not members of the donor's family but had no power to sell or otherwise dispose of closely held stock, or otherwise insure the requisite enjoyment of income to the charitable organization, no deduction will be allowed."

purposes identical with those in the will, this opinion applies to both dispositions.

The will places the residuary estate in trust during the joint lives of decedent's wife and daughter and for the life of the survivor of them. Upon the death of such survivor, the principal of the trust fund is payable to the then living descendants of the daughter. However, if there are no such descendants, one-half of the residue goes to certain collateral relatives of decedent and the other half to certain charitable corporations. If none of the designated relatives are living, the entire residue goes to the charitable corporations. [Footnote omitted.]

At decedent's death, his wife and daughter survived him. His wife was then 62 and his daughter 27. The latter married in 1942, was divorced in 1944, had not remarried and had not had a child.

In the estate tax return, decedent's executor, respondent herein, deducted $179,154.19 from the gross estate as the present value of the conditional bequest to charity of one-half of the residue. Respondent claimed no deduction for the more remote charitable bequest of the other half of the residue. The Commissioner of Internal Revenue disallowed the deduction and determined a tax deficiency on that ground. The Tax Court reversed the Commissioner. 18 T.C. 836. The Court of Appeals for the Second Circuit affirmed the Tax Court, 207 F.2d 600, on the authority of Meierhof v. Higgins, 2 Cir., 129 F.2d 1002. To resolve the resulting conflict with the Court of Appeals for the First Circuit in Newton Trust Co. v. Commissioner, 160 F.2d 175, we granted certiorari, 347 U.S. 932.

The controlling provisions of the Revenue Code are in substantially the same terms as when they were first enacted in 1919 [footnote omitted] and are as follows:

"SEC. 812. NET ESTATE

"For the purpose of the tax value of the net estate shall be determined, ... by deducting from the value of the gross estate — . . .

"(d) *Transfers for Public, Charitable, and Religious Uses.* The amount of all bequests, legacies, devises, or transfers . . . to or for the use of any corporation organized and operated exclusively for religious, charitable, scientific, literary, or educational purposes. . . ." I.R.C., 26 U.S.C.A. §812(d).

The Commissioner concedes that the corporations named in the will qualify as charitable corporations under the statute. There is no doubt, therefore, that if the bequest to them had been immediate and unconditional, its value would be deductible. The question before us is what, if any, charitable deduction may be

made despite (1) the deferment of the effective date of the charitable bequest until the deaths of both decedent's wife and daughter and (2) the conditioning of the bequest upon a lack of descendants of decedent's daughter surviving at that time. We find the
answer in the Treasury Regulations, which are of long standing
and strengthened by reenactments of I.R.C., §812(d), since their
promulgation. [Footnote omitted.]

1. *Section 81.44 of Treasury Regulations 105 would permit the
deduction of the present value of the bequest if it were an outright
bequest, merely deferred until the deaths of decedent's wife and
daughter.*

In their earliest form, the predecessors of these regulations, in
1919, recognized, in plain language, the propriety of the deduction
of the present value of a deferred, but assured, bequest to charity.
[Footnote omitted.] Section 81.44(d) of Treasury Regulations 105
does so with inescapable specificity:

"§81.44. *Transfers for public, charitable, religious, etc.,
uses. . . .*

"(d) If a trust is created for both a charitable and a private purpose, deduction may be taken of the value of the beneficial interest
in favor of the former only insofar as such interest is presently ascertainable, and hence severable from the interest in favor of the
private use. §811.10 indicates the principles to be applied in the
computation of the present worth of deferred uses, but such computation will not be made by the Commissioner on behalf of the
executor. *Thus, if money or property is placed in trust to pay the
income to an individual during his life, or for a term of years, and
then to pay or deliver the principal to the charitable corporation,
or to apply it to a charitable purpose, the present value of the remainder is deductible.* To determine the present value of such
remainder, use the appropriate factor in column 3 of Table A or B
of §81.10. *If the present worth of a remainder bequeathed for a
charitable use is dependent upon the termination of more than
one life, or in any other manner rendering inapplicable Table A
or B of §81.10, the claim for the deduction must be supported by a
full statement, in duplicate, of the computation of the present
worth made, in accordance with the principle set forth in §81.10,
by one skilled in actuarial computations.*" Emphasis supplied.)
26 C.F.R.

The very explicitness of the above provisions emphasizes their
restriction to "the computation of the present worth" of *assured*
bequests such as are the subject of each of the illustrations and
cross references in the section. The statute restricts charitable deductions to bequests to corporations "organized and *operated ex-*

clusively for . . . charitable . . . purposes." [Footnote omitted.] (Emphasis supplied.) Likewise, the above section of the regulations requires that the deductible value of "the beneficial interest in favor of" the designated charitable purpose be "severable from the interest in favor of the private use." There is no suggestion in the statute or in §81.44 of a deduction of funds other than those later to be used exclusively for charitable purposes.

2. *Section 81.46 of Treasury Regulations 105 permits no deduction for a conditional bequest to charity "unless the possibility that charity will not take is so remote as to be negligible."*

Here, also, the regulations in their earliest form, in 1919, were unequivocally restrictive. [Footnote omitted.] It was only after court decisions had demonstrated the need for doing so [footnote omitted] that the restrictions were restated so as expressly to permit deductions of bequests assured in fact but conditional in form.

Section 81.46 now provides expressly that no deduction is allowable for a conditional bequest to charity "unless the possibility that charity will not take is so remote as to be negligible." The whole section is significant:

"§81.46. *Conditional bequests.* (a) *If as of the date of decedent's death the transfer to charity is dependent upon the performance of some act or the happening of a precedent event in order that it might become effective, no deduction is allowable unless the possibility that charity will not take is so remote as to be negligible.* If an estate or interest has passed to or is vested in charity at the time of decedent's death and such right or interest would be defeated by the performance of some act or the happening of some event which appeared to have been highly improbable at the time of decedent's death, the deduction is allowable.

"(b) If the legatee, devisee, donee, or trustee is empowered to divert the property or fund, in whole or in part, to a use or purpose which would have rendered it, to the extent that it is subject to such power, not deductible had it been directly so bequeathed, devised, or given by the decedent, deduction will be limited to that portion, if any, of the property or fund which is exempt from an exercise of such power." (Emphasis supplied.) 26 C.F.R.

Sections 81.44 and 81.46 fully implement §812(d) of the code. In their early forms they were obviously mutually exclusive and easily reconcilable. The predecessor of §81.46 confined charitable deductions to outright, unconditional bequests to charity. It expressly excluded deductions for charitable bequests that were subject to conditions, either precedent or subsequent. While it encouraged assured bequests to charity, it offered no deductions for bequests that might never reach charity. Subsequent amendments have clarified and not changed that principle. Section 81.46(a) today yields to no condition unless the possibility that charity will not take is "negligible" or "highly improbable." Section 81.46(b) is equally strict. It relates to provisions whereby funds may be diverted in whole or in part to non-charitable uses, and it limits the tax deduction to that portion of each fund that cannot be so diverted. Where the principal of a bequest to charity thus may be invaded for private purposes, it is only the ascertainable and assured balance of the bequest to charity that is recognized for a tax deduction.

Respondent concedes that the chance that charity will not take is much more than negligible. Therefore, if §81.46(a) applies to the instant case, no charitable deduction is permissible.

Respondent claims, however, that §81.44 covers this case. In doing so, it reads §§81.44 and 81.46 together and, instead of confining them to their mutually exclusive subjects, makes them overlap. It applies §81.44 to some deferred *conditional* bequests. It does so in any case where it can compute, on approved actuarial standards, the degree of possibility that charity will receive the conditional bequest. Respondent then computes the present value of a corresponding percentage of the entire deferred bequest. In short, respondent claims an immediate tax deduction equal to the present value of whatever fraction of the bequest corresponds, actuarially, to the chance that charity may benefit from it.

This Court considered a somewhat comparable proposal in 1928. In Humes v. United States, 276 U.S. 487, a taxpayer sought a charitable deduction based on a bequest to charity that was conditional upon the death of decedent's 15-year-old niece, without issue, before reaching the age of 40. To sustain the proposal, the taxpayer sought to establish actuarially a measure of the chance that charity would receive the bequest and to find authority in the Revenue Code for the deduction of the present value of a corresponding percentage of the bequest. Speaking through Mr. Justice Brandeis, this Court found the actuarial computation inadequate. It, however, did not drop the matter there. It made the following statement:

"One may guess, or gamble on, or even insure against, any future event. The Solicitor General tells us that Lloyds of London will insure against having twins. But the fundamental question in the case at bar, is not whether this contingent interest can be insured against or its value guessed at, but what construction shall be given to a statute. Did Congress, in providing for the determination of the net estate taxable, intend that a deduction should be made for a contingency the *actual* value of which cannot be determined from any known data? Neither taxpayer, nor revenue officer — *even if equipped with all the aid which the actuarial art can supply* — could do more than guess at the value of this contingency. *It is clear that Congress did not intend that a deduction should be made for a contingent gift of that character."* (Emphasis supplied.)   Id., 276 U.S. at page 494.

Since the above was written, there have been advances in the actuarial art.   Today, actuarial estimates are employed more widely than they were then.   The computations now before us illustrate that advance.   They do not, however, lessen the necessity for statutory authorization for such a tax deduction.   The scope of the authority required by respondent can best be appreciated if examined in the revealing light of the specific circumstances of the present case.

The Tax Court and the Court of Appeals have approved respondent's actuarial computations as fairly reflecting the present value of one-half of a two-million-dollar residue, reduced in proportion to the chance that charity will receive it.   In making this estimate, respondent has computed the present value of the deferred bequest on the basis of 4% interest compounded annually and has used the following actuarial tables:

1. To determine the joint life expectancy of decedent's wife and daughter, the Combined Experience Mortality Table prescribed in §81.10 of the estate tax regulations.

2. To estimate the probability of remarriage of the daughter, the American Remarriage Table, published by the Casualty Actuarial Society.

3. To estimate the chance of a first child being born to decedent's daughter, a specially devised table which has been found by the Tax Court to have been prepared in accordance with accepted actuarial principles upon data derived from statistics published by the Bureau of the Census.[41]

On the basis of these tables, the Tax Court finds that the present value of the charitable remainder at the death of decedent is .18384 on the dollar if computed solely on the chances of his

---

[41] *(Court footnote)* Despite the conclusions of the Tax Court and the Court of Appeals to the contrary, the Government contends here that the proposed actuarial value of the conditional remainder to charity does not support the deduction.   We do not reach that issue, but the facts material to it are as follows: The Remarriage Table is based on a study of American experience conducted by a Committee of the Casualty Actuarial Society, 19 Proceedings of the Casualty Actuarial Society (1933), 279-349.   The table is based solely upon the remarriage experience of widows who, through the deaths of their husbands, become beneficiaries under workmen's compensation laws in states where they lose compensation benefits upon remarriage.   The reports relied upon cover experience for policy years 1921 to 1929, inclusive.   See id., at 286-288, 298.   See also, Myers, Further Remarriage Experience, 36 Proceedings of the Casualty Actuarial Society (1949), 73 et seq.   The specially devised table as to the probability of issue is based upon statistics, for white women in 47 states and the District of Columbia, indicating the degree of probability that such women, after they are 27 years old, will marry and have first-born

daughter's remarriage; .24094 on the dollar if computed on the chance that a legitimate descendant of his daughter will survive her; and .24058 on the dollar if computed on the chance that any legitimate or illegitimate descendant of his daughter will survive her.   It is this last estimate that respondent seeks to apply here.

If respondent is successful, it means the allowance of an immediate and irrevocable deduction of over $175,000 from the gross estate of decedent, although respondent admits there is a real possibility that charity will receive nothing.   The bequest, in fact, offers to the daughter an inducement of about $2,000,000 to remarry and leave a descendant.   To the extent that this inducement reduces the actuarially computed average probability that charity will receive this bequest, it further demonstrates the inappropriateness of authorizing charitable tax deductions based upon highly conditional bequests to charity.

An even clearer illustration of the effect of respondent's interpretation of the code readily suggests itself.   If decedent had here conditioned his bequest to charity solely on the death of his daughter before remarriage, the Remarriage Table would then fix the present value of the charitable remainder at .18384 on the dollar. The taxpayer would at once receive a substantial charitable deduction on that basis.   The daughter, however, would have a $2,000,000 inducement to remarry.   If she did so, her action would cancel the possibility that charity would receive anything from the bequest, but it would not cancel the tax deduction already allowed to the estate.   To whatever extent any person can defeat the fulfillment of any condition upon which a benefit to charity depends, to that extent the actuarial estimate that such benefit will reach charity is less dependable.   The allowance of such a tax reduction as is here sought would open a door to easy abuse.   The result might well be not so much to encourage gifts inuring to the benefit of charity as to encourage the writing of conditions into bequests which would assure charitable tax deductions without assuring benefits to charity.

We find no suggestion of authority for such a deduction in §812(d).   That section remains substantially the same as it was when Humes v. United States, supra, 276 U.S. 487, was decided. We also find no authorization for the deduction either in §81.46 or §81.44 of the regulations, as thus far discussed.   This relegates respondent to the following words now in §81.44(d):

"If the present worth of a remainder bequeathed for a charita-

children.   See the following Bureau of the Census publications for 1940; Vital Statistics of the United States, Pt. II, 89; Nativity and Parentage of the White Population — General Characteristics 110; Types of Families 9.   The instant computation assumes that such a child will survive its mother.   18 T.C. 836, 837-838.

ble use is dependent upon the termination of more than one life, or *in any other manner rendering inapplicable Table A or B of §81.10,* the claim for the deduction must be supported by a full statement, in duplicate, of the computation of the present worth made, in accordance with the principle set forth in §81.10, by one skilled in actuarial computations." (Emphasis supplied.)

In view of the statutory emphasis upon outright bequests and the long-standing exclusion of conditional bequest by §81.46 of the regulations (and its predecessors), we do not regard the above sentence as now invading the domain of §81.46 by extending the deduction to conditional bequests in a manner readily open to abuse. We regard the sentence as restricted to computations of deferred, but assured, bequests. Section 81.10(i) now deals at length with the valuation of remainders and reversionary interests and gives many examples of such computations. Every example, however, is one of the valuation of an assured bequest. The additional language in §81.44(d), quoted above, does not authorize the deduction, and §81.46 prohibits it. Such specific and established administrative interpretation of the statute is valid and "should not be overruled except for weighty reasons." Commissioner of Internal Revenue v. South Texas Co., 333 U.S. 496, 501.

This Court has not specifically faced the issue now before us since Humes v. United States, supra, but we see no reason to retreat from the views there stated. This Court finds no statutory authority for the deduction from a gross estate of any percentage of a conditional bequest to charity where there is no assurance that charity will receive the bequest or some determinable part of it. Where the amount of a bequest to charity has not been determinable, the deduction properly has been denied. Henslee v. Union Planters Nat. Bank, 335 U.S. 595, 598-600; Merchants Nat. Bank of Boston v. Commissioner, 320 U.S. 256, 259-263; and see Robinette v. Helvering, 318 U.S. 184, 189. Where the amount has been determinable, the deduction has, with equal propriety, been allowed where the designated charity has been sure to benefit from it. United States v. Provident Trust Co., 291 U.S. 272; Ithaca Trust Co. v. United States, 279 U.S. 151.

Some of the lower courts have squarely met the instant problem and denied the deduction. For example, the deduction was denied in the First Circuit where the court found that "it is not certain that the charity will take 50% of the corpus; only that it has a 50-50 chance of getting all or nothing." Newton Trust Co. v. Commissioner, 160 F.2d 175, 181. See also, Graff v. Smith, D.C., 100 F. Supp. 42; Hoagland v. Kavanagh, D.C., 36 F. Supp. 875; Wood v. United States, D.C., 20 F. Supp. 197. The administrative practice, as evidenced here by the action of the Commissioner, has been to deny the deduction.   See further, Paul, Federal Estate and Gift Taxation (1946 Supp.), 426-427.

The judgment of the Court of Appeals, accordingly, is reversed and the cause remanded for action in conformity with this opinion.

Reversed.

MR. JUSTICE REED, with whom MR. JUSTICE DOUGLAS joins, dissenting.   [Dissenting opinion omitted.] [42]

e. *Charitable Remainder with Power to Divert Corpus to the Life Beneficiary*

If a testator establishes a trust under which the income is to be paid to his wife and, in addition, the trustee is to pay her from time to time such amounts of the principal as may be necessary to

[42] For comments on Commissioner v. Estate of Louis Sternberger, see 55 Colum. L. Rev. 924 (1955) and 69 Harv. L. Rev. 197 (1955).

In Dean v. United States, 53-2 U.S.T.C. ¶10923 (D. Mass. 1953), the court allowed a charitable deduction when the gift to charity was subject to the condition that one or the other of persons aged sixty-seven and sixty-eight survive another person aged eighty-two.   The court referred to Reg. 105, §81.46, on conditional bequests to charities, which provides that no deduction of the value of such bequests is allowable unless the possibility that the charity will not take is so remote as to be negligible.   The court decided that the possibility of a person aged eighty-two surviving persons aged sixty-seven and sixty-eight was so remote as to be negligible.   In United States v. Dean, 224 F.2d 26 (1st Cir. 1955), the District Court was reversed on the ground that a person aged eighty-two has one chance in eleven of surviving persons aged sixty-seven and sixty-eight and that such a chance is not so remote as to be negligible.

It was determined in Rev. Rul. 55-483, 1955-2 C.B. 391, that where a remainder interest given to a charity under an irrevocable inter vivos trust was contingent on the life tenants (aged forty and fifty years on the date of the gift) both dying without being survived by issue, the gift to the charity was so uncertain that no gift tax deduction was allowable under 1954 I.R.C. §2522.   The ruling relied on the Sternberger case, pointing out that although that case involved the estate tax, its rationale is equally applicable to the gift tax.

For a case which found that the interest in the charity was indefeasibly vested, see Malcolm Lloyd, Jr., 24 T.C. 624 (1955).

In Estate of George M. Moffett, 31 T.C. 541 (1958), it was determined that where the life beneficiary was to be paid $50,000 per year out of a trust containing $1,500,000, and the life beneficiary was fifty years of age, the possibility that the charitable remainder would not take in possession was not so remote as to be negligible.   Thus the deduction for the charitable remainder was denied.   The case was affirmed sub nom. Estate of George M. Moffett v. Commissioner, 269 F.2d 738 (4th Cir. 1959).

In Estate of John C. Polster, 31 T.C. 874 (1959), a charitable gift was made which was to be used to provide funds for church properties, but not more than 25 percent of the cost could be provided from the gift.   The court held that the contingency that 75 percent of the cost had to come from other sources created a possibility that the charities would not take, which "was not so remote as to be negligible."   Therefore, no charitable deduction was allowed.   The case was reversed and remanded sub nom. Estate of John C. Polster v. Commissioner, 274 F.2d 358 (4th Cir. 1960) (court concluded that charitable gift was not contingent under applicable Maryland law because

provide her with adequate means to support and maintain herself, the value of the remainder interest in the trust is uncertain because there is no way to ascertain how much of the principal may be diverted to the testator's wife. Consequently, no charitable deduction may be available where such a remainder interest is given to charity.[43] The cases printed below are concerned with gifts of the type just described.

MERCHANTS NATIONAL BANK OF BOSTON v. COMMISSIONER OF INTERNAL REVENUE
320 U.S. 256, 64 Sup. Ct. 108, 88 L. Ed. 35 (1943)

Mr. Justice Rutledge delivered the opinion of the Court.

Ozro M. Field died in Massachusetts in 1936, leaving a gross estate of some $366,000. In his will he provided, after certain minor bequests, that the residue of his estate be held in trust, the income

---

there was no gift over and there was no language declaring gift void if beneficiary did not raise the other 75 percent).

Revenue Ruling 59-143, 1959-1 C.B. 247, considered a bequest to charity, which was contingent on the failure of issue by decedent's childless daughters who were fifty-nine and fifty-five at the decedent's death, and held that the statistical probability of children being born to a woman of fifty-five or older is so remote as to be negligible and thus a charitable deduction was available.

In Utley v. United States, 60-2 U.S.T.C. ¶11953 (S.D. Cal. 1960), a gift to a charity in an amount not to exceed a designated sum was held not to have sufficient certainty to permit a deduction for charitable purposes under §2055.

Benjamin Klopp, CCH T.C. Mem. 1960-185, involved a gift to the United States of a portion of a parcel of land owned by the taxpayer, and the title transferred was a determinable fee for so long as the land was used by the United States for the purpose of maintaining and operating facilities for the launching of anti-aircraft missiles. Certain easements over adjacent land were also given. A charitable deduction was allowed for the value of the determinable fee and the easements and also for what were termed severance damages to adjacent property. The full fee simple value of the land given was reduced slightly because of the determinable nature of the title.

In Lincoln National Bank and Trust Company of Fort Wayne v. United States, 60-2 U.S.T.C. ¶11963 (N.D. Ind. 1960), the testatrix's will bequeathed a portion of her estate to such charities "as may be selected and designated by my said nieces . . . such selection to be made . . . within six months of my death." There was no provision for the disposition of this portion if nieces did not make the selection. The nieces did make the selection but the Commissioner denied the claimed charitable deduction on the ground that the bequest was contingent and uncertain. The court held that the Commissioner was wrong. This result can be justified only if the court decided that the gift to charities would take place whether the nieces made the selection or not.

Bankers Trust Co. v. United States, 61-1 U.S.T.C. ¶11986 (S.D.N.Y. 1960), disallowed a charitable deduction for a remainder gift to charity where the remainder was contingent on the life beneficiary dying without issue when the life tenant, a woman, was forty-seven years of age, had been married for seventeen years and was childless. — Ed.

[43] See page 892 supra, note 29, which considers the use of a disclaimer as a means of making available a charitable deduction in a decedent's estate.

to go to his wife for life, and on her death all but $100,000 of the principal[44] to go "free and discharged of this trust" to certain named charities. Under the trust set up by the will, the trustee, petitioner here, was authorized to invade the corpus "at such time or times as my said Trustee shall in its sole discretion deem wise and proper for the comfort, support, maintenance, and/or happiness of my said wife, and it is my wish and will that in the exercise of its discretion with reference to such payments from the principal of the trust fund to my said wife, May L. Field, my said Trustee shall exercise its discretion with liberality to my said wife, and consider her welfare, comfort and happiness prior to claims of residuary beneficiaries under this trust."

In 1937 the trust realized gains of $100,900.31 from the sale of securities in its portfolio.

In filing estate and income tax returns petitioner, which was also Mr. Field's executor, sought to deduct $128,276.94 from the gross estate and the $100,900.31 from the 1937 income of the trust, on the theory that those sums constituted portions of a donation to charity and were therefore deductible respectively under sec. 303(a)(3) of the Revenue Act of 1926 (44 Stat. 72) [footnote omitted] and sec. 162(a) of the Revenue Act of 1936 (49 Stat. 1706). [Footnote omitted.]

The commissioner disallowed the deductions and determined deficiencies of $26,290.93 in estate tax and $42,825.69 in income tax for 1937, but on the taxpayer's petition for review the Board of Tax Appeals (now the Tax Court) upheld the latter's contentions. The Court of Appeals reversed the Board of Tax Appeals, 132 F.2d 483, and we granted certiorari because of an asserted conflict with decisions of other circuit courts[45] and this court.[46] 319 U.S. 734.

There is no question that the remaindermen here were charities. The case, at least under sec. 303(a)(3), turns on whether the bequest to the charities have, as of the testator's death, a "presently ascertainable" value or, put another way, on whether, as of that time, the extent to which the widow would divert the corpus from the charities could be measured accurately.

[44] *(Court footnote)* The $100,000 was to remain in trust, the income to go in equal shares to his three adopted children and a niece of his wife, and on the death of the last of these beneficiaries the corpus was also to go to the named charities.

[45] *(Court footnote)* Compare the decision below with Hartford-Connecticut Trust Co. v. Eaton, 36 F.2d 710 (C.C.A.2d); First National Bank v. Snead, 24 F.2d 186 (C.C.A.5th); Lucas v. Mercantile Trust Co., 43 F.2d 39 (C.C.A.8th); Commissioner v. Bank of America Assn., 133 F.2d 753 (C.C.A.9th); Commissioner v. F. G. Bonfils Trust, 115 F.2d 788 (C.C.A.10th).

[46] *(Court footnote)* See Ithaca Trust Co. v. United States, 279 U.S. 151.

Although Congress, in permitting estate tax deductions for charitable bequests, used the language of outright transfer, it apparently envisaged deductions in some circumstances where contingencies, not resolved at the testator's death, create the possibility that only a calculable portion of the bequest may reach ultimately its charitable destination.[47]   The Treasury has long accommodated the administration of the section to the narrow leeway thus allowed to charitable donors who wish to combine some private benefaction with their charitable gifts.   The limit of permissible contingencies has been blocked out in a more convenient administrative form in Treasury Regulations which provide that, where a trust is created for both charitable and private purposes the charitable bequest, to be deductible, must have, at the testator's death, a value "presently ascertainable, and hence severable from the interest in favor of the private use," [48] and, further to the extent that there is a power in a private donee or trustee to divert the property from the charity, "deduction will be limited to that portion, if any, of the property or fund which is exempt from an exercise of such power." [49]   These Regulations are appropriate implementations of sec. 303(a)(3), and, having been in effect under successive reenactments of that provision, define the framework of the inquiry in cases of this sort.   Cf. Helvering v. Winmill, 305 U.S. 79; Taft v. Commissioner, 304 U.S. 351.

Whatever may be said with respect to computing the present value of the bequest of the testator who dilutes his charity only to the extent of first affording specific private legatees the usufruct of his property for a fixed period, a different problem is presented by the testator who, preferring to *insure* the comfort and happiness of his private legatees, hedges his philanthropy, and permits invasion of the corpus for their benefit.   At the very least a possibility that part of the principal will be used is then created, and the present value of the remainder which the charity will receive becomes less readily ascertainable.   Not infrequently the standards by which the extent of permissible diversion of corpus is to be measured embrace factors which cannot be accounted for accurately by reliable statistical data and techniques.   Since, therefore, neither the amount which the private beneficiary will use nor the present

---

[47] *(Court footnote)*   E.g., the not unusual case of a bequest of income for life intervening between the testator and the charity, requiring computation, with the aid of reliable actuarial techniques and data, of present value from future worth.   Compare the provisions for charitable deductions in the Revenue Acts of 1918 — Sec. 403(a)(3) (40 Stat. 1098); 1921 — Sec. 403(a)(3) (42 Stat. 279); 1924 — Sec. 303(a)(3) (43 Stat. 306); 1926 — Sec. 303(a)(3) (44 Stat. 72).

[48] *(Court footnote)*   Treasury Regulations 80 (1934 ed.) Art. 44.

[49] *(Court footnote)*   Treasury Regulations 80 (1934 ed.) Art. 47.

value of the gift can be computed, deduction is not permitted. Cf. Humes v. United States, 276 U.S. 487.

For a deduction under sec. 303(a)(3) to be allowed, Congress and the Treasury require that a highly reliable appraisal of the amount the charity will receive be available, and made, at the death of the testator. Rough guesses, approximations, or even the relatively accurate valuations on which the market place might be willing to act are not sufficient. Cf. Humes v. United States, 276 U.S. 487, 494. Only where the conditions on which the extent of invasion of the corpus depends are fixed by reference to some readily ascertainable and reliably predictable facts do the amount which will be diverted from the charity and the present value of the bequest become adequately measurable. And, in these cases, the taxpayer has the burden of establishing that the amounts which will either be spent by the private beneficiary or reach the charity are thus accurately calculable. Cf. Bank of America Assn. v. Commissioner, 126 F.2d 48 (C.C.A.).

In this case the taxpayer could not sustain that burden. Decedent's will permitted invasion of the corpus of the trust for "the comfort, support, maintenance and/or happiness of my wife." It enjoined the trustee to be liberal in the matter, and to consider her "welfare, comfort and happiness prior to the claims of residuary beneficiaries," i.e., the charities.

Under this will the extent to which the principal might be used was not restricted by a fixed standard based on the widow's prior way of life. Compare Ithaca Trust Co. v. United States, 279 U.S. 151. Here, for example, her "happiness" was among the factors to be considered by the trustee. The sums which her happiness might require to be expended are of course affected by the fact that the trust income was not insubstantial and that she was sixty-seven years old with substantial independent means and no dependent children.[50] And the laws of Massachusetts may restrict the exer-

---

[50] *(Court footnote)* The Board of Tax Appeals found that decedent had adopted three children — two girls and a boy — before his marriage to the present Mrs. Field. She never adopted the children. The two girls were married to husbands fully able to support them, and the boy was nearly twenty-one at the testator's death.

Immediately after decedent's death the widow owned income-producing property worth about $104,000. Her total income from her own property and the trust, and the amounts she has actually expended have been as follows:

Period	Income	Expenditures
1936 (7 months)	$10,735.35	$ 1,853.99
1937	24,738.57	10,357.91
1938	17,480.85	11,055.91
1939	17,448.23	12,024.92
1940	16,959.66	13,389.31
	$87,362.66	$48,682.04

cise of the trustee's discretion somewhat more narrowly than a liberal reading of the will would suggest, although that is doubtful. Cf. Dana v. Dana, 185 Mass. 156, 70 N.E. 49, and compare Sparhawk v. Goldthwaite, 225 Mass. 414, 114 N.E. 718. Indeed one might well "guess, or gamble . . . , or even insure against" the principal being expended here. Cf. Humes v. United States, supra. But Congress has required a more reliable measure of possible expenditures and present value than is now available for computing what the charity will receive. The salient fact is that the purposes for which the widow could, and might wish to have the funds spent do not lend themselves to reliable prediction.[51] This is not a "standard fixed in fact and capable of being stated in definite terms of money." Cf. Ithaca Trust Co. v. United States, supra. Introducing the element of the widow's happiness and instructing the trustee to exercise its discretion with liberality to make her wishes prior to the claims of residuary beneficiaries brought into the calculation elements of speculation too large to be overcome, notwithstanding the widow's previous mode of life was modest and her own resources substantial. We conclude that the commissioner properly disallowed the deduction for estate tax purposes.

The deduction for income tax purposes stands on no better footing. Congress permitted a deduction of that part of gross income "which pursuant to the terms of the will . . . is during the taxable year . . . permanently set aside" for charitable purposes. In view of the explicit requirement that the income be permanently set aside, there is certainly no more occasion here than in the case of the estate tax to permit deduction of sums whose ultimate charitable destination is so uncertain.

Accordingly, the decision of the Court of Appeals is

Affirmed.

MR. JUSTICE DOUGLAS, with whom MR. JUSTICE JACKSON concurs, dissenting:

The Tax Court applied the correct rule of law in determining whether the gifts to charity were so uncertain as to disallow their deduction. That rule is that the deduction may be made if on the facts presented the amount of the charitable gifts are affected by "no uncertainty appreciably greater than the general uncertainty that attends human affairs." Ithaca Trust Co. v. United States 279 U.S. 151, 154. In that event the standard fixed by the will is "capable of being stated in definite terms of money." Id., p. 154. The

[51] *(Court footnote)* E.g., the Board found that since her husband's death, Mrs. Field purchased two automobiles and a fur coat, took two pleasure trips, gave financial assistance to a niece, helped send a grand nephew through medical school, and purchased a fur coat for one of her husband's daughters.

mere possibility of invasion of the corpus is not enough to defeat the deduction. The Tax Court applied that test to these facts. 45 B.T.A. 270, 273-274. Where its findings are supported by substantial evidence they are conclusive. We may modify or reverse such a decision only if it is "not in accordance with law." 44 Stat. 110, 26 U.S.C. sec. 1141(c)(i). See Wilmington Trust Co. v. Helvering, 316 U.S. 164, 168. The discretion to pay to the wife such principal amounts as the trustee deemed proper for her "happiness" introduces of course an element of uncertainty beyond that which existed in the Ithaca Trust Co. case. There the trustee only had authority to withdraw from the principal and pay to the wife a sum "necessary to suitably maintain her in as much comfort as she now enjoys." But the frugality and conservatism of this New England corporate trustee, the habits and temperament of this sixty-seven year old lady, her scale of living, the nature of the investments — these facts might well make certain what on the face of the will might appear quite uncertain. We should let that factual determination of the Tax Court stand, even though we would decide differently were we the triers of fact.[52]

BLODGET v. DELANEY

201 F.2d 589 (1st Cir. 1953)

WOODBURY, Circuit Judge.

This is an appeal from a judgment entered on motion dismissing an action brought for a refund of estate taxes. The question presented is whether on the facts alleged in the complaint it must be ruled as a matter of law that the value of certain charitable gifts in remainder could not be definitely ascertained as of the date of a testator's death, so that in consequence his estate cannot be allowed a deduction therefor under Section 812(d) of the Internal Revenue Code, 53 Stat. 1, 124, Title 26 U.S.C. Sec. 812(d).

The plaintiffs are the duly appointed executors and trustees under the will of a citizen and resident of the Commonwealth of Massachusetts who died on April 24, 1946. In Article Seventh of his will the testator left the residue of his estate to his trustees in trust "to pay over the net income therefrom to my said sister, Sarah L. Guild, if she survives me, quarterly or oftener in the discretion of said Trustees for and during the period of her natural life, and also to pay from the principal any amount in their discretion for

---

[52] For comments on Merchants National Bank of Boston v. Commissioner, see 29 Cornell L.Q. 406 (1944); 42 Mich. L. Rev. 1143 (1944); 92 U. of Pa. L. Rev. 325 (1944). In accord with the Merchants National Bank case is Henslee v. Union Planters National Bank & Trust Co., 335 U.S. 595, 69 Sup. Ct. 290, 93 L. Ed. 259 (1949), *rehearing denied,* 336 U.S. 915 (1949). — ED.

her comfort and welfare," with remainder upon her death one quarter to an individual, or if not living to his descendants, and three quarters — about $400,000 — in specified proportions to six admittedly charitable organizations. It is alleged in the complaint that the life tenant was born in 1862 and at the time the decedent's will was made, and also at the time of his death, was almost totally blind; that her activities had for many years "followed a definite and rigid routine and her future needs and expenses were capable of reasonably accurate and reliable calculation"; that her anticipated income from the trust under her brother's will and from approximately $500,000 owned by her outright was also capable of reasonably accurate calculation; that her anticipated annual income from all sources as of the date of the decedent's death "exceeded the maximum anticipated amount of any future expenses or requirements for her comfort and welfare"; and, furthermore, that her income from the above sources "exceeded all anticipated expenses which with any reasonable accuracy could be foreseen as needed to support and maintain her on any standard fairly comparable or equal to what she had been accustomed to over a long period of years."

The court below took the view that the standard set by the testator to guide the trustees in the exercise of their discretionary power to invade corpus rendered it impossible to make at the testator's death the "highly reliable appraisal" of the amounts the charities would eventually receive required by the rule of Merchants National Bank v. Commissioner, 320 U.S. 256, 261 (1943) for the allowance of a deduction under sec. 812(d). It therefore dismissed the plaintiff's action without passing upon or considering the question of the remoteness or imminence of actual invasion of the corpus by the trustees during the lifetime of the life tenant. See Newton Trust Co. v. Commissioner, 160 Fed. (2d) 175, 178, 180 (C.A. 1, 1947).

The plaintiffs herein contended below, and they contend here, that the language used by the testator, read with the limitations which Massachusetts law would put upon it, establish for the trustees a "standard . . . fixed in fact and capable of being stated in definite terms of money," so that this case is ruled by Ithaca Trust Co. v. United States, 279 U.S. 151, 154 (1929). Wherefore they contend that the judgment dismissing their action should be set aside, and the case remanded for determination of the question of the likelihood of invasion, and if likely, its probable extent.

In the will under consideration in the Ithaca Trust Co. case the testator gave the residue of his estate to his wife for life with authority to use any part of the principal "that may be necessary to suitably maintain her in as much comfort as she now enjoys," with remainder at her death in trust for admitted charities. The above quoted language, the court said, presented the question "whether the provision for the maintenance of the wife made the gifts to charity so uncertain that the deduction of the amount of those gifts from the gross estate . . . cannot be allowed." The court answered this question in the negative, saying:

"The principal that could be used was only so much as might be necessary to continue the comfort then enjoyed. The standard was fixed in fact and capable of being stated in definite terms of money. It was not left to the widow's discretion. The income of the estate at the death of the testator and even after debts and specific legacies had been paid was more than sufficient to maintain the widow as required. There was no uncertainty appreciably greater than the general uncertainty that attends human affairs."

In the subsequent Merchants National Bank case, supra, the court was confronted with quite different testamentary language. For in the will under consideration in that case the testator not only did not expressly restrict the exercise of the trustee's discretion to maintenance of the life beneficiary in the comfort she had previously enjoyed, but the testator also provided for invasion of the corpus by the trustee for her "comfort, support, maintenance, and/or happiness." And in addition the testator said that it was his "wish and will" that the trustee exercise his discretion "with liberality" toward the life beneficiary and "consider her welfare, comfort and happiness prior to claims to residuary beneficiaries under the trust." This language, the court held, made it impossible to fix a sufficiently definite valuation as of the testator's death of the amounts the charities would eventually receive to permit a deduction from the estate tax. It said, with citation of cases which we omit, that for a deduction to be allowed:

"Congress and the Treasury require that a highly reliable appraisal of the amount the charity will receive be available, and made, at the death of the testator. Rough guesses, approximations, or even the relatively accurate valuations on which the market place might be willing to act are not sufficient. . . . Only where the conditions on which the extent of invasion of the corpus depends are fixed by reference to some readily ascertainable and reliably predictable facts do the amount which will be diverted from the charity and the present value of the bequest become adequately measurable. And, in these cases, the taxpayer has the burden of establishing that the amounts which will either be spent by the private beneficiary or reach the charity are thus accurately calculable."

Then, pointing out that under the will the extent to which the trustee might invade the principal was not expressly restricted by a fixed standard based on the life beneficiary's way of life, as in the Ithaca Trust case, and emphasizing that the life beneficiary's "happiness" was among the factors to be considered by the trustee, the court summarized its conclusion on page 263 as follows:

"Introducing the element of the widow's happiness and instructing the trustee to exercise its discretion with liberality to make her wishes prior to the claims of residuary beneficiaries brought into the calculation elements of speculation too large to be overcome, notwithstanding the widow's previous mode of life was modest and her own resources substantial."

In the more recent case of Henslee v. Union Planters Bank, 335 U.S. 595 (1949) the court, considering substantially similar testamentary language, reached the same conclusion of nondeductibility, for in the will under consideration therein the testator authorized encroachment upon principal by the trustee "for the pleasure, comfort and welfare" of his mother, the life annuitant, and furthermore provided:

"The first object to be accomplished in the administration and management of my estate and this trust is to take care of and provide for my mother in such manner as she may desire and my executors and trustees are fully authorized and likewise directed to manage my estate primarily for this purpose."

The case at bar falls somewhere between the bounds set by the cases cited above. The testator here did not expressly limit his trustees' power to encroach upon principal only to the extent necessary to assure continuance of the life beneficiary's previous way of life as in the Ithaca Trust Co. case. But on the other hand our testator did not admonish his trustees to administer their trust with liberality toward the life beneficiary, or primarily in her interest, nor did he give them power of encroachment for her "happiness" or "pleasure." He simply gave them authority to invade corpus for his sister's "comfort and welfare" without further admonitions or directions. Thus the case is not free from doubt. On the whole, however, we are of the view that it falls within the rule of the Ithaca Trust Co. case rather than within the rule of the Merchants National Bank and Henslee cases. We therefore consider the plaintiff-appellants' position well taken.

Clearly we must interpret the testator's language as well as we can in conformity with the law of Massachusetts. Gammons v. Hassett, 121 Fed. (2d) 229, 231 (C.A. 1), cert. denied, 314 U.S. 673 (1941); Channing v. Hassett [200 F.2d 514 (1st Cir. 1952)]. Turning, therefore, to the law of that Commonwealth, it appears from the authorities cited in Gammons v. Hassett, supra, that the extent of a beneficiary's interest is determined by the intention of the testator ascertained by reading his language with reference to the circumstances surrounding its use. And it appears from Dana v. Dana, 185 Mass. 156 (1904) and Lumbert v. Fisher, 245 Mass. 190 (1923) that Massachusetts adheres to the general rule prevailing elsewhere that, absent indications to the contrary, one of the circumstances surrounding the use of a testamentary language to be considered in situations like the present is the beneficiary's station in life and accustomed pattern of living. We recognized Massachusetts' adherence to this rule of construction in Gammons v. Hassett, supra. But there we took the view that by coupling the word "desire" with the word "need," the testator indicated his intention to give the trustee broader power to use the principal than merely to perpetuate the life beneficiary's existing standard of living. We thought he attained that objective by the use of the word "need." So to avoid treating the word "desire" as mere surplusage, we held that the testator must have meant by the word "desire" to give the trustee a power of invasion of the principal "not restricted to a mere use of the corpus for the purpose of satisfying" the life beneficiary's needs as reflected by her prior standard of living. In subsequent cases in this circuit comparable words led us to the same result of nondeductibility, for in Commissioner v. Merchants National Bank, 132 Fed. (2d) 483 (C.A. 1, 1942) the testator had used the word "happiness"; in Industrial Trust Co. v. Commissioner, 151 Fed. (2d) 592 (C.A. 1, 1945), cert. denied, 327 U.S. 788 (C.A. 1, 1946), he had used the word "pleasure"; and in Newton Trust Co. v. Commissioner, 160 Fed. (2d) 175 (C.A. 1, 1947) the testamentary words were "for the use and benefit."

The words "comfort and welfare," with which we are now concerned, however, do not have such sweeping subjective connotations.

The Supreme Judicial Court of Massachusetts said in Stocker v. Foster, 178 Mass. 591 (1901) that although the word "comfort" may include a limited "mental element" in that it covers the "peace of mind which comes from a knowledge" that "physical comfort or support" is available, it nevertheless means primarily the "physical comfort" derived from the application of available funds to "physical comfort or support." See also Homans v. Foster, 232 Mass. 4 (1919). We therefore conclude that the word "comfort" has at the most only minor subjective connotations.

The word "welfare" presents a more difficult problem. It is not only a word whose general content of meaning cannot be defined with precision, but it is also one which so far as we know has not been construed, even in a different context and with reference to other circumstances, by the highest court of the Commonwealth of Massachusetts. No doubt in some contexts and used under some circumstances it covers more elements of the subjective than the word "comfort." Perhaps it does so here. But nevertheless it certainly is not as broad in its subjective sweep as "happiness," "desire," or "use and benefit." Surely it cannot possibly be construed to cover whim or caprice, or even to cover an invasion of principal by the trustee to satisfy the life beneficiary's wish to make a gift. Its precise meaning here eludes capture in a definition. We think there is strong indication in the Massachusetts cases cited above, however, particularly Dana v. Dana, that in view of the life beneficiary's advanced age, physical disability, and settled way of life, the highest court of that Commonwealth would hold that the testator did not intend by using it to authorize his trustees to invade capital to satisfy his sister's subjective yearnings, but intended to authorize them to go no further into capital than necessary to assure perpetuation of his sister's established way of life.

Moreover, a trustee, in addition to acting in good faith, is bound in the absence of instructions to the contrary to administer his trust with an eye to the remainder interest as well as to the interest of the life tenant. He cannot slight one interest for the benefit of the other; he must have scrupulous regard for the interests of both. Here the testator did not instruct his trustees to administer primarily for the life tenant, and if he had meant them to do so in spite of his failure to so instruct them, we think he certainly would have used some word, such as "happiness" or "desire," having far stronger subjective connotations than "welfare."

These considerations lead us to believe that the Supreme Judicial Court of Massachusetts would equate the meaning of "welfare" as used by the testator herein not so much to the meaning of "happiness," "desire" or "use and benefit," as to "maintenance" or "support." That is to say, we think that court on the basis of its prior decisions would hold that "comfort and welfare" as used in the will we are considering meant the physical comfort and state of physical well-being to which the life beneficiary had become accustomed; thus interpolating the "standard . . . fixed in fact and capable of being stated in definite terms of money" set out in words in the will under consideration in the Ithaca Trust Co. case.

Many other Courts of Appeals on like reasoning, and also taking into consideration the clear Congressional policy not to benefit the national revenue at the expense of charitable institutions, have in comparable factual situations reached the conclusion of deductibility.　First National Bank v. Snead, 24 Fed. (2d) 186 (C.A. 5, 1928); Hartford-Connecticut Trust Co. v. Eaton, 36 Fed. (2d) 710 (C.A. 2, 1929); Lucas v. Mercantile Trust Co., 43 Fed. (2d) 39 (C.A. 8, 1930); Commissioner v. Bank of America, 133 Fed. (2d) 753 (C.A. 9, 1943); Commissioner v. Robertson's Estate, 141 Fed. (2d) 855 (C.A. 4, 1944); Berry v. Kuhl, 174 Fed. (2d) 565 (C.A. 7, 1949); Lincoln Rochester Trust Co. v. Commissioner, 181 Fed. (2d) 424 (C.A. 2, 1950).　We find these cases persuasive.

We conclude, therefore, that the deduction claimed cannot be disallowed as a matter of law.

The judgment of the District Court is vacated and set aside and the case is remanded to that Court for further consistent proceedings; the appellants recover costs on appeal.

MAGRUDER, Chief Judge (concurring).

This is certainly a close case.　I do not dissent from the opinion and judgment of the court, though I am still somewhat troubled by the considerations expressed in my concurring opinion in Gammons v. Hassett, 121 Fed. (2d) 229, 234 (C.A. 1, 1941), cert. denied, 314 U.S. 673 (1941).

In Ithaca Trust Co. v. United States, 279 U.S. 151 (1929), the Court looked not at the trust instrument alone, but also at the extrinsic facts, and reached the conclusion that as of the moment of the testator's death there was no substantial likelihood that the corpus would be invaded for the benefit of the life tenant under the limited power of invasion conferred in the will; that the amounts which would ultimately be received by the charities in remainder were affected with "no uncertainty appreciably greater than the general uncertainty that attends human affairs." (P. 154.) On that factual conclusion, the charitable deduction was allowed. If there is a "clear Congressional policy not to benefit the national revenue at the expense of charitable institutions," it seems that the decided cases have drawn an unfortunate line in denying a charitable deduction wherever the power to invade corpus is conferred in terms embracing "factors which cannot be accounted for accurately by reliable statistical data and techniques" (320 U.S. at 261), even though on the existing facts and circumstances one might conclude to a moral certainty that the power would never be exercised and that the unimpaired remainder would go to the charity upon the death of the life tenant.　In Gammons v. Hassett, supra, at 234, I pointed out:

"Theoretically the contingency is broader and the chance of its occurrence less capable of estimation than in the Ithaca Trust case, because it depends upon the life tenant's desires as well as her needs.　But practically speaking, upon the facts in the present record as compared with the facts in the Ithaca Trust case, the charitable remaindermen are at least as well assured — perhaps somewhat better assured — of receiving the corpus intact upon the death of the life tenant."

Upon the facts appearing in Gammons v. Hassett it was indeed fantastic to suppose that the corpus would ever be invaded. Yet the charitable deduction was denied. Likewise, the charitable deduction was denied in Merchants National Bank v. Commissioner, 320 U.S. 256 (1943), the Court disregarding as irrelevant the conclusion of the Board of Tax Appeals that there was reason to believe that the life tenant would never want more than the income from the trust and that "the possibility of corpus being invaded is sufficiently remote to justify the deductions claimed." (45 B.T.A. 270, 174.) Instead of having to split hairs between "comfort and welfare" on the one hand and "comfort, support, maintenance, and/or happiness" on the other, it might seem more logical to adopt either of two alternatives: (1) To deny the charitable deduction unless the testator has given an indefeasible remainder to charity upon the death of the life tenant, or (2) to allow the deduction in full wherever it is properly found as a fact upon consideration of all the circumstances that the chance of invasion of the corpus is negligible, however broadly or narrowly the power to invade corpus may be expressed in the will.[53]

[53] It was determined in Rev. Rul. 54-285, 1954-2 C.B. 302, that the value of a remainder interest in favor of a charity was deductible from the gross estate of the decedent, even though the trustee was authorized to pay principal to the income beneficiary in such amounts as "the trustee in its sole discretion may from time to time deem necessary for her comfort, support, hospital or medical expenses." The income beneficiary was seventy-nine years of age and had substantial means of her own. The ruling uses this language: ". . . the trust instrument in the instant case impliedly fixes a definite standard, as the trustee is not authorized to use principal except for the proper comfort and support of the widow. As of the date of decedent's death the likelihood of any invasion of the principal for the proper comfort and support of the widow was so remote as to be negligible." The ruling further states: ". . . where the power of invasion is limited by such words as 'comfort and support' with no express standard or limitation in the will or instrument, such words should be interpreted as meaning comfort and support according to the standard of living enjoyed by the beneficiary prior to the decedent's death, if such interpretation is consistent with applicable local law, and other terminology in the will or instrument does not require some different interpretation."

Revenue Ruling 60-162, I.R.B. 1960-17, 14, considers the valuation of a remainder given to charity in depletable subsurface rights, including deposits of oil, gas, or minerals, or royalties, oil payments, leases, etc. It is recognized that a valuation of the remainder interest would have to be based on the maximum feasible rate at which the subsurface reserves could be withdrawn, since it is only the portion of the property which the charity is certain, or almost certain, to receive that qualifies for the charitable deduction.

In Mercantile-Safe Deposit and Trust Co. v. United States, 172 F. Supp. 72 (D. Md. 1959), the decedent established a trust in his will of the residue of his

PROBLEM

14.12. Section 2041(b)(1)(A) of the 1954 Code, quoted infra page 1401, provides in substance that a power in a person to consume, invade, or appropriate property for his own benefit which is

---

estate for the benefit of his sister, with power in the trustee to pay her only so much of the income as the trustee deemed necessary and proper for her reasonable living expenses, comfort, maintenance and general welfare in the light of all assets owned by her and all other income. On the sister's death, the trust property passed to charity. In view of the sister's other assets, it was highly remote that the income of this trust would ever be needed for the sister, and hence the court allowed the entire residuary estate to be deducted as a charitable bequest without taking out anything for the sister's life interest in the income.

In Hartford National Bank & Trust Co. v. United States, 58-1 U.S.T.C. ¶11736 (D. Conn. 1957), a state court in a nonadversary proceeding had construed the will in question to limit the invasion of principal to the support and maintenance of the life beneficiary. While the District Court held that it was not bound by the state court proceedings in this suit for a refund, the Commissioner was not entitled to a motion for a summary judgment. In Hartford National Bank & Trust Co. v. United States, 58-2 U.S.T.C. ¶11811 (D. Conn. 1958), the court found that the intention of the testatrix, as gleaned from the evidence of the family situation and habits of life and thought (all members of the family had lived frugal lives to preserve the property for their father's memory), was to limit the power to invade to provide reasonable support, even though the language of the will literally gave the trustees uncontrolled discretion as to invasions of corpus, and thus the charitable deduction was allowed.

The court in Estate of Elva W. Wilcox, 16 CCH T.C. Mem. 381 (1957), refused to allow a deduction for the remainder interest given to charity when the trustees had uncontrolled discretion to invade the trust corpus for funds with which to pay medical expenses incurred by the life beneficiaries. In Commerce Trust Co. v. United States, 167 F. Supp. 643 (W.D. Mo. 1958), the trustee was directed to pay the life beneficiary's expenses resulting from injury or illness, and the executor of the decedent's estate claimed a deduction for the value of the remainder, which was given to charity, computed on the hypothesis that the life beneficiary was totally disabled on the testator's death; but the court determined that the value of the remainder to charity was not ascertainable and refused to permit its valuation on the suggested hypothesis.

In the following cases the charitable deduction was denied because of the power to divert the corpus to the life beneficiary: Third National Bank and Trust Co. v. United States, 228 F.2d 772 (1st Cir. 1956); Gilfillan v. Kelm, 128 F. Supp. 291 (D. Minn. 1955). Bartlett v. Smith, 153 F. Supp. 674 (E.D. Pa. 1957); Merrill Trust Co. v. United States, 167 F. Supp. 474 (D. Me. 1958); Estate of Charles Herman Koinm, 16 CCH T.C. Mem. 728 (1957); Estate of Helen Thompson, 17 CCH T.C. Mem. 510 (1958).

In the following cases the charitable remainder was deemed capable of being valued, even though a power to divert corpus did exist: Lincoln Rochester Trust Co. v. McGowan, 217 F.2d 287 (2d Cir. 1954); Bowers v. South Carolina National Bank of Greenville, 228 F.2d 4 (4th Cir. 1955); Gilfillan v. Kelm, 128 F. Supp. 291 (D. Minn. 1955); Estate of L. O. Carlson, 21 T.C. 291 (1953); Estate of Joseph A. Schmitt, 14 CCH T.C. Mem. 579 (1955). See also Mercantile-Safe Deposit and Trust Co. v. United States, 141 F. Supp. 546 (D. Md. 1956); Jean S. Alexander, 25 T.C. 600 (1955); Estate of Oliver Lee, 28 T.C. 1259 (1957). — ED.

limited by an ascertainable standard relating to health, education, support or maintenance shall not be deemed a general power of appointment for purposes of the federal estate tax. Are the Merchants National Bank of Boston case and the Blodget case of any significance in determining whether a power is or is not a general power under this section?

f. *Indirect Gift to Charity*

DELANEY v. GARDNER
204 F.2d 855 (1st Cir. 1953)

HARTIGAN, Circuit Judge.

This is an appeal from a judgment entered in the United States District Court for the District of Massachusetts on June 19, 1952, for the taxpayers in an action brought for a refund of estate taxes.

The taxpayers are the two executors under the will of Olga E. Monks, a Massachusetts resident who died on April 22, 1944. The will was dated March 18, 1939 and was allowed by the Probate Court for Suffolk County, Massachusetts, on May 18, 1944. An estate tax return was duly filed and the tax paid about July 20, 1945.

On audit of the return, the Collector asserted a deficiency of $64,216.71, based on the disallowance of a deduction claimed, and the inclusion in Mrs. Monks' estate of an inter vivos transfer. The deficiencies were paid by the taxpayers on September 24 and December 30, 1946, and a claim for refund was filed on September 13, 1949. After the claim was disallowed on February 16, 1950, the plaintiffs commenced this action.

The two questions which we need to consider on this appeal concern (1) the deductibility of a claimed testamentary disposition to charity, and (2) the includibility in the gross estate of the value of securities transferred by the testator in her lifetime to a family corporation. [Only that portion of the opinion which deals with the first question is printed below.]

Article Second of the Will of Olga E. Monks provides:

"I give to my executors or administrators with the will annexed One Hundred Thousand ($100,000) Dollars, not subject to any trust, but in the hope that they will dispose of it at their absolute discretion and according to their own judgment, but giving due weight to any memoranda I may leave or any oral expressions by me to them made during my life."

A memorandum and accompanying identifying letter addressed to the executors, dated the same date as the will, were allowed by the Probate Court as a part of the will. The memorandum consisted of a list of individuals and institutions with amounts opposite their names and the letter read in part: "I have purposely not bound you to carry out any wishes I may express for I cannot foresee the future and have confidence that you will act wisely and will do as seems best, and possible when the time comes. I am, however, enclosing a list, of persons and institutions, who I should like to remember and the amounts I have assigned would at this time, seem to me suitable but as I have already said you are free to disregard my suggestions."

One of the executors, George Peabody Gardner, a nephew of the decedent Mrs. Monks, testified that this method of disposition was undertaken upon his advice, with his assurance to her that he and her sons, who were named as the other executors, would endeavor to carry out her desires. There was evidence that the executors distributed the gifts listed in the memorandum, with a few exceptions due to changed circumstances of particular individuals. Thirty-five thousand dollars of the amount so distributed was paid, prior to the filing of the Federal Estate Tax Return, to charitable or religious institutions within the meaning of §812(d) of the Internal Revenue Code.

The Commissioner ruled that these payments to religious or charitable institutions could not be deducted on the ground that they were not disclosed in the will and there was no legal obligation on the executors to pay them. The lower court overruled the Commissioner and allowed a refund on these items. It found that under the applicable law, the executors held the money for charities as constructive trustees and because the charities could compel compliance with Mrs. Monks' desires, then she had made charitable gifts deductible under §812(d) . . .

The first point urged on this appeal presents a nice issue of statutory interpretation. Internal Revenue Code §812(d), 26 U.S.C. §812(d), provides that there shall be deducted from the value of the gross estate the "amount of all bequests, legacies, devises, or transfers . . . to or for the use of . . ." charities. In this case the decedent has specifically detailed her wishes concerning the charities to be benefited upon her death by a memorandum and letter written on the same day as the execution of her will. Her executors accorded with her wishes exactly, and the charities have received precisely the amounts indicated by decedent. It is insisted, as the lower court has said, that if any one of the named charities had not received the exact amount intended, then it could compel the executors to pay over such amount, on the theory of a constructive trust. The Commissioner disputes this and says furthermore that even if the executors did have a legal obligation to pay over the money to the charities, it is still not deductible because any such payments would not be made under the terms of the will.

The argument for allowing this charitable deduction was well expressed in the following language in the opinion below: "While it did not pass by a bequest in express terms under the will of Mrs. Monks, it did pass to them from her estate by a transaction which in substance was the same. It was the expressed desire of Mrs. Monks that they should receive it. As a result of her will and of the promise which she had obtained from her executors, the charities had a legally enforceable right to receive the money. Regardless of the legal formulas employed, what Mrs. Monks wanted to do, and what she actually succeeded in doing, was to make a gift at her death of $35,000 from her estate to recognized charities. Her executors should be allowed to deduct that $35,000 as a charitable gift for tax purposes."

The language of §812(d) is not of very great assistance on this question. A word like "bequest" indicates that deductions should be limited to gifts which pass under the terms of the will, which is the strict construction urged upon us by the Commissioner. However, the section also says ". . . or transfers . . ." and this indicates a very broad applicability.

Turning to the legislative intent, it seems that the general purpose of §812(d) adds nothing to the indefinite content of its language. A Congressional intention to encourage gifts to charity, see 1 Paul, Federal Estate and Gift Tax, §12.04 (1942 ed.), does not offer much assistance. The theory of a constructive trust in this type of case rests on the testator's omission of a charitable gift in his will, relying on the promise of the constructive trustee. The asserted Congressional intention is not effectuated by putting unjust enrichment cases within the language Congress has employed to benefit charities. Therefore, we must look beyond the statutory language and its purpose to the decisions.

Many of the cases concerning the deductibility of a gift to a recognized charity have turned upon whether or not the gift was of an amount ascertainable at the time of the decedent's death. In Humes v. United States, 1928, 276 U.S. 487, it was held that where a gift to charity was contingent on a fifteen year old unmarried girl living until 40, or leaving issue, the gift was not deductible because it was too speculative, that is, due to the contingency the value of the bequest could not be determined from any known data. This precedent cast doubt upon the deductibility of gifts in remainder to charities where trust instruments provided for the invasion of the corpus of the trust and this doubt produced a string of cases recently reviewed in Blodget v. Delaney, 1 Cir., 1953, 201 F.2d 589. Also, the Humes decision governed the disallowance of a deduction in cases like First Trust Co. of St. Paul State Bank v. Reynolds, 8 Cir., 1943, 137 F.2d 518, where the court held that a charitable bequest conditioned on the consent of the decedent's wife was not deductible, although the consent was highly probable.

In Mississippi Valley Trust Co. v. Commissioner of Int. Rev. 8 Cir., 72 F.2d 197, certiorari denied 293 U.S. 604, rehearing denied 1934, 293 U.S. 631, a will contained a provision stating that decedent had expressed to his two sons his wishes concerning charitable gifts and therefore made none under the will but left the matter to the sons' sole discretion. Decedent had expressed a desire that his sons endow St. Louis University and the sons were willing to do so. Despite an order of the local probate court allowing the gift under the will, it was held that it was not deductible. Although the fatal uncertainty attached to that gift is evident in the particular circumstances, the opinion of the court intimates that the legal enforceability of a decedent's desire is the criterion for determining whether or not there has been a "bequest . . . or transfer."

The United States Court of Appeals for the Seventh Circuit, in Levey v. Smith, 103 F.2d 643, certiorari denied, 1939, 308 U.S. 578, held that a gift to a lodge, provided for in a will, was not deductible, but the language of the court indicates that a constructive trust may be deductible because the decision turns upon the failure to establish that the lodge held the gift on a constructive trust for charitable use. A similar case decided by the Second Circuit in the same year, Housman v. Commissioner of Internal Revenue, 2 Cir., 1939, 105 F.2d 973, likewise depended upon the existence of a constructive trust, but the question was whether a payment by a widow to her son was a taxable gift or the performance of a legal obligation.

A more recent decision in the Second Circuit offers a closer analogy than the Levey and Housman cases. In Commissioner of Internal Rev. v. Macaulay's Estate, 2 Cir., 1945, 150 F.2d 847, a case arising under §812(d) prior to the 1942 enactment of the parenthetical clause in the first sentence, a deduction was allowed for a renounced legacy which passed through a residuary clause providing for charities. The opinion at least indicates that as long as the charitable intention has been expressed in the will and is subsequently effectuated by the will, then §812(d) applies. That the applicability of §812(d) is limited to gifts passing by will is suggested by cases holding that local law which incorporates into probate compromised agreements over disputed wills cannot render deductible charitable dispositions agreed upon by disputants rather than made by decedent. Robbins v. Commissioner of Internal Revenue, 1 Cir., 1940, 111 F.2d 828. Cf. In re Sage's Estate, 3 Cir., 1941, 122 F.2d 480, 137 A.L.R. 658, certiorari denied 1942, 314 U.S. 699; Thompson's Estate v. Commissioner of Internal Revenue, 2 Cir., 1941, 123 F.2d 816; Dumont's Estate v. Commissioner of Internal Revenue, 3 Cir., 1945, 150 F.2d 691.

If local law cannot operate to transform compromised items into deductible bequests then it would seem that the correct reading of §812(d) would exclude charitable gifts which owe their existence to the court's willingness to probe the circumstances of a noncharitable bequest. The determinative point in construing "bequests, legacies, devises, or transfers" seems to be that since §812(d) offers to testators the privilege of deducting certain dispositions beneficial to society, then the policy underlying such a privilege would be best effectuated by requiring a clear and definite exercise of the privilege in the testamentary instrument.

In cases where the state statutes limit charitable bequests or legacies, gifts in excess of the allowable amount have been held to be deductible notwithstanding the fact that their effectiveness requires a waiver of statutory rights by the heirs. In Dimock v. Corwin, 2 Cir., 1938, 99 F.2d 799, a deduction for a fund to establish the Folger Shakespeare Memorial Library at Washington was upheld although waiver of statutory rights by the heirs was a condition of the effectiveness of the gift. The same decision has been rendered by the Fifth Circuit, rejecting the argument that the consenting heirs were the ones who made the gift. Commissioner of Internal Revenue v. First Nat. Bank of Atlanta, 5 Cir., 1939, 102 F.2d 129.

Thus, the pertinent determinations of the scope of §812(d) indicate that a charitable deduction should not be disallowed because cf a condition attached by operation of law, whereas it may be disallowed, as in Humes v. United States and First Trust Co. of St. Paul State Bank v. Reynolds, supra, when the testator himself makes the charitable gift conditional. No cases bearing more closely on the instant problem have been found. We must select a standard for deductibility somewhere between the certain extremes that the testator must intend a benefit to charity. Commissioner of Internal Rev. v. Macaulay's Estate, supra; and that a charity must receive the amount deducted. Heim v. Nee, D.C. Mo. 1937, 40 F. Supp. 594.

The government's brief states that a deduction is proper only if the terms of the will required the executors to make payments in specific amounts to institutions which fall within the class speci-

fied in the statute.   However, the only authority cited relates to
the government's contentions that the discretion lodged in these
executors make these gifts speculative and that it is doubtful
whether there really was a constructive trust.   Assuming the correctness of the district court's determination that Mrs. Monks' executors were constructive trustees, the gifts did not contain a speculative element.   And since we agree with the government's literal
reading of §812(d), we are free to make this assumption.   The taxpayers rely principally on the intimations of Levey v. Smith, supra,
and Housman v. Collector of Internal Revenue, supra, for the
proposition that the deduction should be based on the existence of
legal rights accruing to charitable institutions pursuant to the testator's intention.

We think that this proposition is broader than the language of
§812(d) and that it introduces an undesirable uncertainty into
charitable deductions.   Although the gifts in this case were testamentary in character, we think that the words "bequests, legacies,
devises, or transfers," considering the Congressional policy in attaching the deduction privilege to these gifts, make §812 (d) applicable only to those gifts which pass by the terms of a testamentary instrument.   Although the four corners of the will may be
abandoned to prevent the unjust enrichment of fraudulent executors, there is no justification for a similar abandonment of the will
in effectuating the language and purpose of §812(d).

By limiting deductions to transfers which pass under express
terms of the will, as Congress seems to have done, a clear line is
drawn which would be greatly obscured if we placed upon it the
frequently vague circumstances and apparently discretionary character of a constructive trust.

Furthermore, any constructive trust which might be imposed by
decree of a state court would be delimited by the terms of the oral
undertaking of the executors as expressed to their testator.   As we
read the record in this case, it seems pretty clear that the circumstances existing at the date of the death would not necessarily be
controlling.   If after the death and before the executors had got
around to making distribution, a radical change had occurred in
the circumstances of one of the charities, of such a nature that the
executors felt the testator, if living, would no longer want the
charity to take, it seems that the executors in perfect good faith
and consistently with their oral undertaking could withhold such
distribution and let the amount fall into the residuary estate.
This consideration raises an additional objection to saying that
the testator has made a bequest or transfer to or for the use of a
charity.

It was error for the district court to hold that the $35,000 was deductible under §812(d). . . .

The judgment of the District Court is vacated and the case is remanded to that Court for entry of judgment in conformity with this opinion.

WOODBURY, Circuit Judge (dissenting).

The question is close, but nevertheless I feel constrained to disagree with my associates as to the interpretation of §812(d) of the Internal Revenue Code.

I am persuaded that under Massachusetts law on the particular facts of this case enforceable constructive trusts for the benefit of each charity named in the memorandum in the amount set opposite the name of each arose at the death of the testatrix, as the court below held and as my associates are willing to concede. In this situation, I would allow a deduction under §812(d) from the gross estate in the total amount which the charities received.

The section under consideration provides that for the purpose of the tax the value of the net estate shall be determined by deducting from the value of the gross estate the "amount of all bequests, legacies, devises, or transfers . . . to or for the use of" charities such as those listed in the memorandum. If the statute provided only for the deduction of "bequests, legacies, devises . . . to" charities, I would agree with my associates' interpretation, for those words alone imply only the normal situation of a strictly testamentary gift directly to a charity. But the statute also includes "transfers . . . for the use of" charities, and to give these words additional meaning I think they should be construed to cover the transfer of money from an estate to a charity accomplished by the device of a constructive trust imposed by local law on a testamentary disposition because of a testator's reliance upon his legatee's agreement to hold the devise for the benefit of the charity. That is to say, it seems to me that what was in fact accomplished here falls squarely within the definition of transfers to the use of charities, and hence I think that deduction of the amounts which actually passed to the charities is authorized by §812(d) of the Internal Revenue Code.[54]

[54] For comments on Delaney v. Gardner, see 53 Colum. L. Rev. 1017 (1953) and 38 Minn. L. Rev. 287 (1954). See also Marine Midland Trust Company of Southern New York v. McGowan, 223 F.2d 408 (2d Cir. 1955), where the court commented on Delaney v. Gardner as follows: "While that case is distinguishable on the facts, we are not in accord with so much of the majority opinion as seems to hold testamentary transfers non-deductible when based upon a constructive trust for charitable purposes established by evidence dehors the will."

In Howell v. Dudley, 154 F. Supp. 571 (W.D. Pa. 1957), the decedent gave all of her property to her executrix, with instructions to carry out her wishes

PROBLEMS

14.13. A in his will leaves his residuary estate to "such charitable benevolent, religious or educational institutions as my executors hereinafter named may select." In determining the taxable estate, is any deduction permissible for such a gift of the residuary estate? See Cochran v. United States, 123 F. Supp. 362 (D. Conn. 1954).

14.14. A in his will requests designated beneficiaries to make suitable charitable gifts out of the property given to them in the will. In compliance with A's request, the beneficiaries make the charitable gifts. Will the amount of these gifts be deductible in determining A's taxable estate? See Revenue Ruling 55-335, 1955-1 C.B. 455.

14.15. A in his will makes a bequest to a person who has joined a religious organization and has taken his final vows of poverty, so that any property coming to him will pass to the religious organization. A dies. Will the amount of the bequest be deductible in determining A's taxable estate? See Revenue Ruling 55-759, 1955-2 C.B. 607; Revenue Ruling 55-760, 1955-2 C.B. 607; Estate of Margaret E. Callaghan, 33 T.C. 870 (1960); Estate of Charles J. Barry, 34 T.C. —, No. 20 (1960); Estate of May Bingham Cox, 19 CCH T.C. Mem. 1960-260.

14.16. A in his will gives the residue of his estate to certain charities in the amount that may be allocated to each by a named person within one year after A's death. To the extent that no allocation is made, his residuary estate is to pass to certain relatives. Is any charitable deduction available in determining A's taxable estate? See Danbury National Bank v. Fitzpatrick, 55-1 U.S.T.C. ¶11526 (D. Conn. 1955).

14.17. A's executor makes a payment of $1000 to a charity in satisfaction of A's unpaid pledge to the charity. Is this payment deductible in determining A's taxable estate? See Stanley T. Sochalski, 14 CCH T.C. Mem. 72 (1955).

---

as expressed in previous wills. The Orphans' Court of Pennsylvania held that, under the doctrine of incorporation by reference, the provisions of the former wills were valid and binding. Accordingly, the executrix paid a designated sum to Yale University. The District Court held that the state judgment was conclusive in determining federal tax liability, and thus the payment to Yale University was deductible as a charitable bequest. — ED.

4. STATE INCOME AND INHERITANCE TAX CONSIDERATIONS

If the charitable corporation to which a gift is made is one not organized under the laws of the state where the testator is domiciled, or if the charitable trust to which property is transferred may benefit charities located in another state, the charitable gift may be subject to state inheritance taxes in the state in which the testator is domiciled.[55]   In some states there are reciprocity statutes which in effect provide that a gift by a testator to an out-of-state charity will not be subject to a state inheritance tax by the testator's state if a gift by a resident of the state where the charity is located to a charity in the testator's state would not be taxed.[56]

If the settlor or someone else desires to pour over property from a will to an inter vivos charitable trust, the state inheritance tax laws must be examined to determine whether a gift by will to such a trust will be subject to the state inheritance tax.   If the trust gives the trustees discretion to select the charities to receive benefits and they are authorized to select either intrastate or out-of-state charities, a gift by will to such a trust may not be free of the state inheritance tax.[57]

An examination should be made of state income tax consequences with respect to the income from a trust devoted exclusively to charitable purposes.   In Massachusetts, prior to 1954, if the trustees of a charitable trust were given discretion to pay out or accumulate income and they decided not to pay out all the income in any particular year, the income thus accumulated was subject to the Massachusetts state income tax.   Strangely enough, the income of a Massachusetts charitable corporation has not been

---

[55] If a state inheritance tax is payable with respect to a charitable gift, a deduction may be available therefor in determining the taxable estate for federal estate tax purposes. See 1954 I.R.C. §2053(d), quoted infra page 1404.

[56] See, for example, Mass. Ann. Laws, c. 65, §1 (Supp. 1958), quoted infra page 1441.

If a testamentary gift is made to a charitable trust under which the trustee is to make payments of income and principal to such charities as may be selected by the trustee from time to time, the trustee may select charities in states which do not exempt from death taxation legacies and devises by its citizens for charitable purposes to be carried out within the testator's domicile. Is the entire gift in trust subject to state inheritance tax because of this possibility in a state which has a reciprocity statute?   Or will only so much of the gift as is in fact paid to charities in a nonreciprocity state be subject to a state inheritance tax?   The latter construction should control whenever it is not inconsistent with the express statutory language, because it is more in keeping with the general policy of encouraging charitable gifts by providing the statutory exemption from death taxation.

[57] See note 56 supra.

subject to the Massachusetts state income tax, even though all of it is not paid out in any particular year. Since 1954, the law as to charitable trusts has been the same as the rule applicable to charitable corporations.[58]

---

[58] See Mass. Ann. Laws, c. 62, §8(k).

In Hinkle v. State Tax Commission, CCH Mass. Tax Rep. ¶200-116 (App. Tax Bd. 1960), the income from a trust fund which was required to be paid to such charities as the trustee should select was exempt from taxation under §8(k), even though the charities to be benefited were not identified by name.

C H A P T E R   X V

Disposal of a Business Interest
or a Farm

When a person operates a business as sole proprietor, or is a partner in a business, or owns stock in a closely held corporation, the formulation of his estate plan normally presents special problems. The following questions should be considered in determining what disposition is to be made of his interest in a business:

1. Will the business have any going-concern value after his death?
2. Should he change the form of ownership of the business during his lifetime?
3. Is a member of his family qualified to succeed to his responsibilities with respect to the business?
4. Is it feasible for a trustee to succeed to his responsibilities with respect to the business and to carry it on for the benefit of his family?
5. Should his interest in the business be liquidated?
6. If the business should be liquidated, should an inter vivos agreement of sale be executed? If so, what method should be adopted to fix the price on the death of the owner and what provision should be made to give assurance that the buyer will be able to finance the purchase?
7. What value is likely to be placed on the business for death tax purposes?
8. Where will the estate of the owner of the business obtain funds to pay death taxes? [1]

Question 2 presents all the problems of business planning. In the discussion which follows, it will be assumed that the client's business is to remain in its present form, whether a sole proprietorship, a partnership or a corporation. The special problems, from

---

[1] These eight questions are examined in relation to sole proprietorships, partnerships and closely held corporations in Anderson, Disposition of Business Interests, 9 U. of Fla. L. Rev. 459 (1956).

See also Logan, Estate Planning for the Small Businessman, 8 Kan. L. Rev. 590 (1960).

an estate planning standpoint, presented by the business interest will be considered on the basis of such an assumption.

1. SOLE PROPRIETORSHIP

An examination of the nature of the business operated by a person as sole proprietor may reveal that on the owner's death nothing will be left but the physical assets used in the business and the accounts receivable. If the business involves only the rendition of personal service by the owner, such as a sales agency, it may have no going-concern value after his death. In such a case, however, it may be possible to make inter vivos agreements with others whereby, in return for action taken by the owner during his life, his family will receive after his death financial benefits through the others carrying on the business. For example, a food broker who holds the exclusive agency for the sale of certain foods in an area could make an agreement with an employee whereby the broker would undertake to arrange for his exclusive agencies to be granted to the employee on the broker's death, and the employee in turn would agree to pay the broker's wife, after her husband's death, a certain percentage of the gross income from operating the food brokerage business under the exclusive agencies thus granted to him.

Professional men, such as doctors and lawyers, who practice alone have nothing of value to pass on to others in relation to their practice but the worth of the physical assets and the accounts receivable, and consequently are presented with a problem similar to the one faced by the sole proprietor of a personal service business.[2]

---

[2] The legal profession and the medical profession are governed by very strict codes of conduct that make it difficult for anything to be sold by a member of the profession other than the bare physical assets.

Drinker, in Legal Ethics 161 (1953) states: "A lawyer's practice and good will may not be offered for sale." This statement is supported by formal Opinion 266 of the Standing Committee on Professional Ethics of the American Bar Association. This opinion is based on Canon 37 of the Canons of Professional Ethics adopted by the American Bar Association, which provides that it is the duty of a lawyer to preserve his clients' confidences and that this duty outlasts the lawyer's employment. The confidential information in a lawyer's files cannot be disclosed by the lawyer or by his estate without the client's express permission. Furthermore, Canon 27, which prohibits a lawyer from soliciting business, would be violated by the purchaser of a lawyer's practice because the purchaser would be seeking to have the clients of the selling lawyer continue their business with him.

The following further quotation from Mr. Drinker's book at page 189, is appropriate: "A lawyer's clients are not merchandise nor is a law practice the subject of barter. The purchase of a lawyer's practice and good will and

If, however, the sole proprietorship is of such a nature that the owner's death does not end the business, the disposal of a going business becomes an integral part of the owner's estate plan. Depending on what is appropriate under the circumstances, the disposal of the business involves (1) feasible arrangements for its sale, or (2) the transfer of the business to a member of the family for continued operation, or (3) the transfer of the business to a trustee for continued operation for the benefit of the owner's family.

If the decision is to sell the business as a going concern on the owner's death, consideration must be given to its marketability, to the desirability of making an inter vivos sales agreement with respect to the business, and to the powers which should be given

---

the payment therefor to him or to his estate by a percentage of the receipts from his business is improper, since this would constitute a division of his fees with laymen, forbidden by Canon 34. It would seem, however, that a reasonable agreement to pay the estate a proportion of the receipts for a reasonable period is a proper practical settlement for the lawyer's services on his retirement or death."

In Estate of Charles A. Riegelman, 27 T.C. 833 (1957), an agreement made by law partners provided that in the event of a partner's death, the partnership should continue and the deceased partner's estate should be entitled to share in the income of the continuing partnership for a specified time. The court held that the value of the estate's right to the post-death partnership earnings attributable to work done after the decedent's death was includible in his gross estate for federal estate tax purposes. The case was affirmed in 253 F.2d 315 (2d Cir. 1958). In affirming, the court referred to the estate's right to post-death partnership earnings as income in respect of a decedent. Mary Tighe, 33 T.C. 557 (1959), held that the amount received by the beneficiary of the decedent from the decedent's law partners pursuant to an agreement that the beneficiary was to receive $200 a month out of the profits of the firm for a period of five years was taxable income to the beneficiary and was not a payment that qualified as an employee's death benefit, because the decedent was a partner and not an employee.

The decedent in Winkle v. United States, 160 F. Supp. 348 (W.D. Pa. 1958), was a member of a partnership which had been established to last for ten years, and at the time of her death, three years and ten months of the original ten-year period remained. Under the terms of the partnership agreement, the death of a partner was not to disturb the partnership assets, but the deceased partner's estate was to share in the partnership income, though not in its management. The court held that the commuted value of the decedent's interest in the partnership income for the remaining period of three years and ten months was includible in the decedent's gross estate.

A partnership between a professional and a layman may be recognized for tax purposes even though the formation and conduct of such a partnership is contrary to law. See Beulah H. Nichols, 32 T.C. 1322 (1959).

See Boman v. Commissioner, 240 F.2d 767 (8th Cir. 1957), where a partnership of doctors established a charitable foundation, and the foundation leased its property to the partnership. Nevertheless, the exempt status of the foundation was upheld and contributions made by one of the doctors to the foundation were deductible as charitable contributions. Under this decision it may be possible for doctors to deduct currently the cost of a clinic and all its equipment through the medium of charitable contributions instead of capitalizing such costs and recovering them through depreciation. Reasonable rental payments would also be deductible.

to the executor so that he can appropriately operate the business pending its sale.[3]   If an inter vivos sales agreement is appropriate, thought must be given to how the purchaser is to finance his acquisition of the business.   If the executor is to undertake the sale of the business, he should not be put in the position of having to make a forced sale to raise funds to pay death taxes.   Therefore provision for the payment of such taxes out of other assets may be highly desirable.

If the decision is to transfer the business to a member of the family on the death of the owner, the executor should be given adequate powers to enable him to operate the business during the period of administration, and the availability of other funds to pay death taxes must be explored.

If the decision is to transfer the business on the death of the owner to a trustee to operate for the benefit of the family, the executor will have to carry on the business pending the transfer to the trustee; the trustee will have to have adequate powers and funds to operate the business; and the availability of other funds to pay death taxes must be considered.[4]

Whenever it is decided that the best plan is to transfer the sole proprietorship to a trust to be operated by the trustees, care should be taken to make certain that the resultant business arrangement will not be taxed as a corporation rather than as a trust.   Section 7701(a)(3) of the 1954 Code defines a corporation as including "associations, joint stock companies, and insurance companies." When the trust is used as the vehicle to operate a business it may be deemed an association and hence a corporation for tax purposes.

An arrangement will be treated as a trust for tax purposes if its purpose is to vest in the trustees the responsibility for the protection and conservation of property for beneficiaries who cannot share in the discharge of this responsibility and, therefore, are not associates in a joint enterprise for the conduct of business for profit.[5]   The principal characteristics of so-called business trusts which are taxable as corporations are the following:

1. They are created by beneficiaries simply as a device to carry on a profit-making business which normally would

---

[3] For examples of the types of powers which might appropriately be given to an executor or trustee who must deal with a going business, see Stephenson, Drafting Wills and Trust Agreements: Administrative Provisions, c. 7 (1952).

[4] For a discussion of various aspects of handling a business in a trust, see 33 Trust Bull. No. 7, p. 5 (1954).   See also Pfleiderer, Value of Estate Planning When Handling Businesses in Trust, 34 id. No. 4, p. 7 (1954); Tremayne, Jr., Estate Planning for the Man with a Business, 1955 Wash. U.L.Q. 40; McKenney, Some Estate Planning Considerations Involving Business Interests, 35 Trust Bull., No. 7, p. 55 (1956).

[5] See Reg. §301.7701-4(a), quoted infra page 1555.

have been carried on through business organizations which are classified as corporations or partnerships for tax purposes.[6]

2. The trust beneficiaries have transferable shares.

3. The liability of the beneficiaries is limited to the trust property.

4. The beneficiaries may remove the trustees.

5. The beneficiaries may terminate the trust.[7]

The desire to avoid the impact of corporate taxation has led to many attempts to use the trust device primarily for business purposes rather than for its primary purpose.[8]

[6] See Reg. §301.7701-4(b), quoted infra page 1556.

The mere fact that the trust corpus is not supplied by the beneficiaries is not sufficient reason in itself for classifying the arrangement as an ordinary trust rather than as an association or partnership.

[7] See Reg. §301.7701-2. The rules of §§301.7701-2 to 301.7701-4 are applicable only to taxable years beginning after December 31, 1960.

[8] If the trust is deemed to be an association of the beneficiaries in a joint enterprise for the transaction of business, the trust will be taxable as a corporation and thus will not be entitled to the benefit of 1954 I.R.C. §1202, which allows a deduction of 50 percent of capital gains. This point is discussed in connection with a trust of real property in Curt Teich Trust No. One, 25 T.C. 884 (1956). It would seem that a trust created by a will would usually not be deemed taxable as an association. See Estate of Herman Becker, 2 CCH T.C. Mem. 341 (1943).

Revenue Ruling 57-534, 1957-2 C.B. 924, comments on Reg. 118, §39.3797-3, applicable under the 1939 Code, and points out that a trust utilized by the beneficiaries as a medium to carry on a joint enterprise for their joint profit may constitute an association taxable as a corporation, even though the beneficiaries had no part in establishing the trust and are without power to modify the trust agreement or to terminate the trust. By this ruling, prior acquiescence in Living Funded Trust of Harry E. Lyman, 36 B.T.A. 161 (1937), is withdrawn. See Sams, Associations Taxable as Corporations — Real Estate Investors, 43 A.B.A.J. 651 (1957).

Elmer Irvin Trust, 29 T.C. 846 (1958), involved a trust created under a printed and copyrighted instrument prepared and distributed by the National Pure Trust Service. The court held that the trust created under this instrument was an association taxable as a corporation, where the trust instrument contained provisions specifying the number of trustees, their term of office, the manner in which they were to be removed, appointed or elected, and negotiable certificates of interest were issued on which the liability of the trustees was limited strictly to the assets of the trust. John I. Cooper, 17 CCH T.C. Mem. 127 (1958), aff'd sub nom. Cooper v. Commissioner, 262 F.2d 530 (10th Cir. 1958), cert. denied, 359 U.S. 944 (1959), held that a trust was an association taxable as a corporation, and emphasized that the trust was created to carry on a business enterprise, that its operation was not affected by the death of the trustees or beneficiaries, and that the beneficiaries had the right to transfer their interests. In Mullendore Trust Co. v. United States, 59-1 U.S.T.C. ¶9256 (N.D. Okla. 1959), a trust agreement was involved under which the beneficial interests were represented by negotiable certificates. During its liquidation period the trust continued to carry on its business because the trust assets — ranch land, livestock and corporate stocks — could not be readily distributed in kind. The court held that the trust was taxable as an association during its liquidation period. The case was affirmed in 271 F.2d 748 (10th Cir. 1959). Estate of Levi T. Scofield v. Commissioner, 266 F.2d

The best interests of the family may be served in some instances by the sole proprietor selling the business during his lifetime. In order for a sale to be consummated by him in his lifetime, it may be necessary, in connection with the sale, for him to give, a covenant not to compete with the purchaser.[9]

---

154 (6th Cir. 1959), concerned a trust that was taxed as an association, and the court stressed the presence of transferable shares, wide powers in the trustee, elimination of ordinary rules governing fiduciaries, limitation of liability of beneficiaries, power to remove trustee, etc. The trust had been set up by beneficiaries of a testamentary trust to manage land distributed to them on the termination of the testamentary trust. Rohman v. United States, 275 F.2d 120 (9th Cir. 1960), held that a trust was not taxable as an association where it lacked a business purpose and centralized management, though it had limited liability and transferability of interests.

In Stierwalt v. United States, 181 F. Supp. 770 (D. Wyo. 1960), the court quoted with approval from Fidelity-Bankers Trust Co. v. Helvering, 113 F.2d 14, 17 (D.C. Cir. 1940), as follows: "A Trust does not engage in business, for purposes of the tax, if its sole or principal object and activities are: (1) preservation of specified property; (2) liquidation of a trust estate; (3) distribution of income derived from another source. Clearly the same rule should apply if its function is exclusively to service the security for a loan. The ultimate question is whether the trust performs some nonbusiness function of this sort or operates a business enterprise as a going concern." In Caswal Corporation, A Corporation, CCH T.C. Mem. 1960-143, the court found that a trust existed and refused to tax it as an association because the trustee merely collected and transmitted rents, had some negotiations with tenants, and kept the property in repair.

[9] A, the owner of stock in a closely held corporation, sells the stock to B. At the time of the sale it is provided in the sales agreement that a certain portion of the sale price is to be allocated to an agreement by A not to enter into a competing business for a period of ten years. The tax effects of such an agreement are as follows: B, the buyer, is entitled to treat the covenant not to compete, and its cost, as a depreciable asset; on the other hand, the seller is required to report as ordinary income the portion of the price allocated to the covenant not to compete. See Clarence Clark Hamlin Trust v. Commissioner, 209 F.2d 761 (10th Cir. 1954); Commissioner v. Gazette Telegraph Co., 209 F.2d 926 (10th Cir. 1954). For additional cases dealing with covenants not to compete, see Wilson Athletic Goods Mfg. Co., Inc. v. Commissioner, 222 F.2d 355 (7th Cir. 1955); Dauksch v. Busey, 125 F. Supp. 130 (S.D. Ohio, 1954); Radio Medford, Inc. v. United States, 150 F. Supp. 641 (D. Ore. 1957); Rogers v. United States, 59-2 U.S.T.C. ¶9761 (D. Nev. 1959); Lee Ruwitch, 22 T.C. 1053 (1954); Frances Silberman, 22 T.C. 1240 (1954); D. & H. Bagel Bakery, Inc., 14 CCH T.C. Mem. 334 (1955); Estate of F. G. Masquelette, 14 CCH T.C. Mem. 879 (1955), *rev'd sub nom.* Masquelette v. Commissioner, 239 F.2d 322 (5th Cir. 1956); Sidney Alper, 15 CCH T.C. Mem. 1415 (1956); Richard Ullman, 29 T.C. 129 (1957), *aff'd sub nom.* Ullman v. Commissioner, 264 F.2d 305 (2d Cir. 1959); Andrew Newman, Inc., 16 CCH T.C. Mem. 1018 (1957); Standard Lumber and Hardware Co., 17 CCH T.C. Mem. 796 (1958).

Joseph Faulkner, 15 CCH T.C. Mem. 175 (1956), held that a stated amount received by the seller for a covenant not to compete was to be taxed as receipts from the sale of the business, and not as ordinary income, when the covenant was essential to protect the purchaser's investment and was not severable from the assets transferred.

Revenue Ruling 57-480, 1957-2 C.B. 47, points out that good will is a capital asset, and thus any gain resulting from its sale constitutes a capital gain. If the assignment of the exclusive right to use the firm name is accompanied by

Set forth below as Example 1 is a business purchase agreement funded with life insurance between a sole proprietor and one of his employees.[10]

EXAMPLE 1. *Business Purchase Agreement Between Sole Proprietor and Employee (with a Trustee)*

AGREEMENT made this .... day of ...., 19......, between John Jones of New York, N.Y. (hereafter referred to as Proprietor), Frank Richards of New York, N.Y. (hereafter referred to as Employee) and .... Trust Company of New York, N.Y. (hereafter referred to as Trustee).

---

a covenant by the assignor not to compete under another name, no part of the sales price attributable to such a covenant may be regarded as derived from the sale of good will. Revenue Ruling 60-301, I.R.B. 1960-38, 7, clarifies Rev. Rul. 57-480 by pointing out that where a business which is dependent solely upon the professional or other characteristics of the owner is sold, no portion of the sales price may be treated as the proceeds from the sale of good will, even though such a sale involves a valid assignment of the right to the exclusive use of the firm name. In United Finance and Thrift Corporation of Tulsa, 31 T.C. 278 (1958), the court made an allocation of the purchase price between good will and a covenant not to compete. The case was affirmed sub nom. United Finance and Thrift Corp. v. Commissioner, 282 F.2d 919 (4th Cir. 1960).

In Ray H. Schulz, 34 T.C. 235 (1960), the court found that the covenant not to compete was worthless under the circumstances because it would have been impossible for the seller to compete. Consequently, the amount allocated to the covenant was treated as a payment for the seller's share of the good will of the business and was a capital gain.

Harry Shwartz, CCH T.C. Mem. 1960-228, found that under all the circumstances there was no good-faith bargaining for the covenant not to compete, since the sellers had no intention of competing. Because covenant not to compete was nonseverable from the entire consideration, the sellers did not have to treat any part of the sale price as ordinary income.

Rees v. United States, 187 F. Supp. 924 (D. Ore. 1960), held that a dentist could sell his professional good will and the amount received would be a capital gain. The court relied on Masquelette v. Commissioner and Revenue Ruling 60-301, I.R.B. 1960-38, 7. It was recognized that good will may be transferred even though the right to the exclusive use of the firm name is not given and all of the good will is not sold. In Malcolm J. Watson, 35 T.C. — , No. 26 (1960), the court recognized the existence of saleable good will where a sale of an accounting practice was involved. George J. Aitken, 35 T.C. — , No. 29 (1960), concerned the sale of an insurance agent's expirations" (information records about previously sold policies) and the court held that these were capital assets.

[10] The sample business purchase agreements printed in this chapter as Examples 1-6 are all taken from a booklet published by the New York Life Insurance Company entitled "Business Purchase Agreements Funded With Life Insurance." The foreword to this booklet states that one of its primary purposes is to give "to lawyers some assistance in drawing business purchase agreements which involve the use of life insurance policies." The foreword also states, "the agreement must be drafted by the client's lawyer and he, alone, may give legal counsel and advice." The July, 1956, edition is referred to.

The Proprietor is the sole owner of a grocery business known as "The Village Market" located at 157 West 8th Street, New York, New York.

The Employee has been associated in said business with the Proprietor as an employee for a period of over five years.

The purpose of this Agreement is twofold: (a) to provide for the purchase by the Employee of the Proprietor's business at the time of his death; and (b) to provide funds necessary to carry out such purchase.

It is, therefore, mutually agreed by the Proprietor and Employee as follows:

1. The Proprietor agrees that he will not assign, encumber or dispose of "The Village Market" by sale or otherwise during his lifetime, without the written consent of the Employee.

[*Alternative 1:* If the Proprietor should desire to dispose of "The Village Market" during his lifetime, he shall first offer in writing to sell it to the Employee. The offer shall be based on a price determined in accordance with the provisions of Paragraph 5 hereof. If the offer is not accepted by the Employee within sixty days of receipt thereof, the Proprietor shall have the right to dispose of it to any other person but shall not sell it to any other person without giving the Employee the right to purchase it at a price and on the terms offered by such other person.]

2. The Employee shall deposit with the Trustee Policy No. .... issued by New York Life Insurance Company on the life of the Proprietor in the sum of $........................., with the Employee as applicant and owner and the Trustee as beneficiary. During the lifetime of the Proprietor and the continuance in force of this Agreement, the Employee agrees to pay premiums on the policy owned by him as they become due and to give proof of payment to the Trustee and the Proprietor within twenty days after the due date of each premium. If any premium is not paid within twenty days after its due date, the Proprietor shall have the right to pay such premium and be reimbursed therefor by the Employee. All dividends shall be applied on account of premiums. The New York Life Insurance Company is hereby authorized and directed to give the insured, upon his written request, any information with respect to the status of the policies on his life.

3. This Agreement shall extend to and shall include all additional policies issued pursuant hereto, such additional policies to be listed in Schedule A, attached hereto.

4. Upon the death of the Proprietor, his estate shall sell to the Employee and the Employee shall purchase all of the Proprietor's right, title and interest in "The Village Market." Said business

so sold shall include all real estate, furniture and fixtures, inventories and all other tangible and intangible property, including accounts receivable and cash in bank, owned in connection with the said business by the Proprietor. Said sale shall take effect as of the date of death of the Proprietor, and the purchase price shall be computed in accordance with the provisions of Paragraph 5 of this Agreement. It is agreed that upon the death of the Proprietor, the Employee shall be entitled to operate the said business but that title shall pass as of the close of business of the date of death of the Proprietor. The Employee shall be entitled to all of the profits of the business and suffer all the losses arising between the close of business on the date of death of the Proprietor and the consummation of this Agreement.

5. Unless and until changed as hereinafter provided, the total value of "The Village Market" for the purpose of determining the purchase price to be paid for the business, shall be $45,000. Said purchase price has been agreed upon by the parties as representing a fair value of all the assets of the business, tangible and intangible, including good will. Within thirty days following the end of each fiscal year, the parties shall redetermine the value of the business. Said value shall be endorsed on Schedule B, attached hereto. If the parties fail to redetermine said value for a particular year, the last previously stipulated value shall control, except that if no valuation has been agreed upon for a period of over one year before the death of the Proprietor, the value of the business shall be determined by the executor or administrator of the estate of the deceased Proprietor and the Employee. If, however, the Executor or Administrator of the estate of the deceased Proprietor and the Employee fail to reach an agreement as to such valuation, the value of the business shall be determined by arbitration: the Executor or Administrator of the estate of the deceased Proprietor and the Employee shall each appoint one arbitrator. If the two arbitrators cannot agree upon the valuation of the business, they shall appoint a third arbitrator and the decision of the majority shall be binding on both parties. The arbitrators shall consider as a basis for determining the value of the business, the valuation last agreed upon by the parties, and shall make adjustment to such basis by adding or subtracting from said value, a fair estimate of the increase or decrease of the valuation of the business between the date as of which the last valuation was made and the date of the death of the Proprietor. In no event, however, shall the value of "The Village Market" be less than the proceeds of life insurance purchased on the Proprietor's life by the Employee under this Agreement. The term "proceeds" is understood to include any

amount paid by reason of death by accidental means under any agreement for additional indemnity, as well as the face amount, plus any dividends and any additional amounts payable to the beneficiary.

6. The Employee agrees that the proceeds of the policies subject to this Agreement shall be applied toward the purchase price set forth above. The Trustee shall apply the proceeds in accordance with the terms of this Agreement. If the purchase price so set forth exceeds the proceeds of the life insurance, the balance of the purchase price shall be paid in twenty-four consecutive monthly payments beginning three months after the date of the Proprietor's death. The unpaid balance of the purchase price shall be evidenced by a series of negotiable promissory notes made by the Employee to the order of the estate of the Proprietor with interest at 5% per annum. Said notes shall provide for the acceleration of the due date of all unpaid notes in the series on default in the payment of any note or interest thereon and shall give the Employee the option of prepayment in whole or in part at any time.

7. The duties of the Trustee are as follows:

(a) To receive and safely hold the life insurance policy described herein and any that may be added, as described in Schedule A, attached hereto, and proof of payment of all premiums paid by the Employee, as required herein.

(b) Upon the death of the Proprietor to

(i) make claim for and collect the proceeds of the life insurance polices issued on the life of the Proprietor. The Trustee shall be under no obligation to institute any action to recover the proceeds of any of the polices, unless indemnified by the Employee for all expenses and attorney's fees connected therewith.

(ii) demand and receive from the Employee any notes required to be executed by him, as required herein.

(iii) deliver to the estate of the Proprietor the proceeds of the life insurance policies collected by it; any notes required herein to be executed or delivered by the Employee and an agreement executed by the Employee, indemnifying the estate of the Proprietor against all liabilities of the business, provided it receives simultaneously from the estate of the Proprietor such legal instruments as will convey to the Employee all the interest of the estate of the Proprietor in the business described herein.

(c) Upon termination of this Agreement other than by the death of the Proprietor, the Trustee shall deliver the policies described herein and in Schedule A, to the Employee. However, the Trustee shall be under no obligation to deliver such policies until it has received the compensation and reimbursement for expenses and counsel fees, if any, specified in paragraph 8 hereof.

8. The Trustee shall be paid as compensation a commission of .... percentage (......%) of all moneys which it collects as proceeds of life insurance on the death of the Proprietor. If this Agreement is terminated other than by the death of the Proprietor, the Trustee shall receive a fee of $........................., for its services in terminating the trust. The Trustee shall be reimbursed for all its reasonable expenses and counsel fees. The Trustee shall have the right to resign at any time upon ten days' notice to the Proprietor and the Employee, and the Proprietor and the Employee shall have the right to substitute another Trustee at any time by paying to the Trustee a fee of $......................... The Trustee's compensation, fees and expenses shall be divided and paid equally by the Proprietor and Employee.[11]

9. Upon the death of the Employee, the Proprietor shall have the right to purchase from the estate of the decedent any or all of the policies insuring his life, for a price equal to the interpolated terminal reserve thereof as of the date of death of the Employee, less any existing indebtedness charged against the policy, plus the proportionate part of the gross premium last paid before the date of death which covers the period extending beyond that date. This right may be exercised at any time within sixty days after the qualification of the legal representative of the deceased Employee by the payment of such price and, if the right is not so exercised within the time allowed, it shall lapse.

10. The Employee shall execute and deliver to the Trustee any promissory notes required herein to be executed by him as a part of the purchase price, together with a written agreement indemnifying the estate of the deceased Proprietor against all liabilities of the business. Upon the payment of the purchase price to the estate of the deceased Proprietor, in cash or in cash and notes, the estate shall execute and deliver to the Trustee all documents reasonably required to evidence such purchase; and all rights of the estate in the business and assets shall thereafter belong to the Employee.

11. This Agreement may be altered, amended or terminated by a writing signed by the Proprietor and the Employee, but no

[11] For an example of a corporate trustee's charges, see page 139 supra, note 83. — ED.

amendment shall be made affecting the duties of the Trustee without its consent thereto.   In the event of a termination of this Agreement before the death of the Proprietor, the Proprietor shall be entitled to an assignment to him of any policy on his life upon payment by him to the Employee within sixty days of such termination of a sum equal to the interpolated terminal reserve as of the date of transfer, less any existing indebtedness charged against the policy, plus the proportionate part of the gross premium last paid before the date of transfer which covers the period extending beyond that date.

12. This Agreement shall terminate on the occurrence of any of the following events:

   (a) Mutual agreement in writing of the Proprietor and Employee, and deposited with the Trustee.

   (b) Termination of the employment of the Employee whether voluntary or involuntary, upon deposit by the Proprietor with the Trustee of a notice in writing of such termination of employment.

   (c) Bankruptcy or insolvency of the Proprietor.

   (d) The death of the Employee prior to the death of the Proprietor.

   (e) Death of the Proprietor and Employee simultaneously or withing a period of thirty days.

   (f) At the option of the Proprietor if the Employee fails to pay the premiums within the grace period of the policy or policies of life insurance owned by him, for the purposes of this Agreement, or assigns, surrenders or borrows against said policy or policies, changes the beneficiary or makes the proceeds payable other than in a lump sum without the written consent of the Proprietor.

13. This Agreement shall be binding upon the Proprietor and the Employee, their heirs, legal representatives, successors and assigns.

14. Notwithstanding the provisions of this Agreement, New York Life Insurance Company is hereby authorized to act in accordance with the terms of any policies issued by it as if this Agreement did not exist, and payment or other performance of its contract obligations by said Company in accordance with the terms of any such policy shall completely discharge said Company from all claims, suits and demands of all persons whatsoever.

15. This Agreement shall be subject to and governed by the law of the State of ...., irrespective of the fact that one or more of the parties now is or may become a resident of a different state.

IN WITNESS WHEREOF, the parties hereto have executed this Agreement this .... day of ...., 19.......

....

....

....

Note. This Specimen Agreement can be readily extended to cover the situation where a business is to be sold to more than one employee. The lawyer drafting the agreement should provide for the possibility of one of the employees dying before the Proprietor.

SCHEDULE A

Schedule of Additional Life Insurance Policies

Name of Company   *Policy No.*   *Amount*   *Signature of Owners*

SCHEDULE B

Endorsements

Date of execution ....

Pursuant to Paragraph 5 of this Agreement, the Proprietor and the Employee do hereby determine that the total value of "The Village Market" as of this date is $..........................

....

....

NOTE ON THE EFECT OF AN AGREEMENT OF SALE ON THE VALUATION OF STOCK FOR ESTATE TAX PURPOSES

(1) *Introduction*

This note is inserted at this point, though it relates to the valuation for estate tax purposes of stock in a corporation rather than to the valuation for estate tax purposes of a sole proprietorship, because the governing principles applicable to the valuation of stock subject to an agreement of sale should be equally applicable when other types of business interests are subject to an agreement of sale.   As might be expected, most of the litigation has developed in connection with agreements of sale relating to closely held corporate stock and thus an analysis of this situation is likely to shed the most light on other situations.

(2)   *Tests Applied in Valuing Closely Held Stock*

Section 20.2031-2 of the Regulations [12] deals with the valuation of stocks and bonds for estate tax purposes.   The general rule, of course, is that the value of the stocks and bonds is the fair market value per share or per bond on the applicable valuation date.

When selling prices or bid-and-asked prices are unavailable, the fair market value is to be determined by taking the following factors into consideration:

(1) In the case of corporate or other bonds, the soundness of the security, the interest yield, the date of maturity, and other relevant factors; and

(2) In the case of shares of stock, the company's net worth, prospective earning power and dividend-paying capacity, and other relevant factors.

The other relevant factors are:

. . . the good will of the business; the economic outlook in the particular industry; the company's position in the industry and its management; the degree of control of the business represented by the block of stock to be valued; and the values of securities of corporations engaged in the same or similar lines of business which are listed on a stock exchange.   However, the weight to be accorded such comparisons or any other evidentiary factors considered in the determination of a value depends upon the facts of each case.   Complete financial and other data upon which the valuation is based should be submitted with the return, including copies of reports of any examinations of the company made by accountants, engineers, or any technical experts as of or near the applicable valuation date.

The tests outlined in the Regulations are far from precise yardsticks and the consequence is that in many cases the range of possible valuation of securities in a closely held company is quite broad.   The effect of this is that it is difficult to determine ahead

---

[12] Quoted in full infra page 1505.   See also Reg. §20.2031-3, quoted infra page 1507, which is concerned particularly with the valuation of a sole proprietorship and a partnership.

of time what the death costs may be and to plan for their payment.

Revenue Ruling 59-60, 1959-1 C.B. 237, sets forth in more detail than the Regulations an analysis of the factors which are significant in valuing closely held stock for estate tax purposes. In commenting on the dividend-paying history of the corporation and its significance in the valuation process, the ruling states:

> Primary consideration should be given to the dividend-paying capacity of the Company rather than to dividends actually paid in the past. Recognition must be given to the necessity of retaining a reasonable portion of profits in a company to meet competition. Dividend-paying capacity is a factor that must be considered in an appraisal, but dividends actually paid in the past may not have any relation to dividend-paying capacity. Specifically, the dividends paid by a closely held family company may be measured by the income needs of the stockholders or by their desire to avoid taxes on dividend receipts, instead of by the ability of the company to pay dividends. When an actual or effective controlling interest in a corporation is to be valued, the dividend factor is not a material element, since the payment of such dividends is discretionary with the controlling stockholders. The individual or group in control can substitute salaries and bonuses for dividends, thus reducing net income and understating the dividend-paying capacity of the company. It follows, therefore, that dividends are less reliable criteria of fair market value than other applicable factors.

As might very well be expected, the disputes over valuation of stock in closely held corporations have led in many instances to litigation.[13]

---

[13] See the following cases: Penn v. Commissioner, 219 F.2d 18 (9th Cir. 1955); Estate of Cora R. Fitts v. Commissioner, 237 F.2d 729 (8th Cir. 1956); Tucker v. Commissioner, 54-2 U.S.T.C. ¶10965 (E.D. Ark. 1954); Whittemore v. Fitzpatrick, 127 F. Supp. 710 (D. Conn. 1954); Kieckhefer, Sr. v. United States, 142 F. Supp. 615 (E.D. Wis. 1956); First Trust Co. v. United States, 59-1 U.S.T.C. ¶11843 (W.D. Mo. 1958); Gould v. Granquist, 59-1 U.S.T.C. ¶11857 (D. Ore. 1958); Bader v. United States, 172 F. Supp. 833 (S.D. Ill. 1959); Tuck v. United States, 172 F. Supp. 890 (N.D. Cal. 1959) aff'd, 282 F.2d 405 (9th Cir. 1960); Riley v. Meyers, 59-1 U.S.T.C. ¶11874 (N.D.N.Y. 1959); Roth v. Welch, 183 F. Supp. 559 (S.D. Ohio, 1960); Estate of George L. Cury, 23 T.C. 305 (1954); Estate of Thomas W. Tebb, 27 T.C. 671 (1957); Estate of Samuel Want, 29 T.C. 1223 (1958), modified, reversed and remanded on other points sub nom. Want v. Commissioner, 60-2 U.S.T.C. ¶11956 (2d Cir. 1960).

Bartram v. Graham, 157 F. Supp. 757 (D. Conn. 1957), dealt with the valuation of a minority interest of closely held stock for gift tax purposes and recognized that the minority position in a closely held corporation not traded on any market would undoubtedly cause most investors to seek a discount

Section 2031 of the 1954 Code contains a provision on valuation of unlisted stocks and securities but it is of little help. It simply says that "the value thereof shall be determined by taking into consideration, in addition to all other factors, the value of stock or securities of corporations engaged in the same or a similar line of business which are listed on an exchange."

The comments above on the valuation of closely held stock for estate tax purposes are also relevant when the valuation is for gift tax purposes. Section 25.2512-2 of the gift tax regulations corresponds to Section 20.2031-2 of the estate tax regulations mentioned above.

(3) *Effect of Options or Agreements to Buy on Valuation*

Section 20.2031-2(h) of the Regulations is the starting point for any discussion of the effect on valuation when the securities are subject to an option or contract to purchase. The language of the Regulations is as follows:

> Another person may hold an option or a contract to purchase securities owned by a decedent at the time of his death. The effect, *if any*, that is given to the option or contract price in determining the value of the securities for estate tax pur-

---

from liquidating values and, furthermore, that the time, effort and expense of disposing of a substantial number of shares should be taken into account. Therefore, the court allowed a 20 percent discount in determining the value of the stock.

In Hamilton v. Patterson, 58-1 U.S.T.C. ¶9256 (N.D. Ala. 1957), the value of stock in a closely held corporation which had been sold to the taxpayer became relevant in determining whether the taxpayer had realized any gain for income tax purposes. The taxpayer had received the stock at the value of $52,425, the Commissioner claimed its fair market value was $119,000, and the jury determined that its value was $57,420.

Estate of J. Luther Snyder v. United States, 182 F. Supp. 71 (W.D.N.C. 1960), involved the ascertainment of the value of closely held stock for gift tax purposes, and the value was determined by taking the average earnings per share for the five-year period preceding the gift and multiplying this figure by a rate of capitalization factor of nine (the normal rate of capitalization factor of ten was reduced by a 10 percent penalty factor, which was used to reflect the high price per share of the stock, the high rate per capital consumption rate, and the entire lack of an established market.) The case was reversed and remanded in 61-1 U.S.T.C. ¶11987 (4th Cir. 1961) and the Court of Appeals stated that stock cannot be reasonably valued by the application of any inflexible formula.

Bartol v. McGinnes, 185 F. Supp. 659 (E.D. Pa. 1960), shows how the valuation of listed securities may cause some difficulty, as where a block of stock held by the estate is such that if it were offered for sale all at once it would depress the market. In such a case the value for estate tax purposes will be the value determined in the light of the blockage factor.

poses depends upon the circumstances of the particular case. Little weight will be accorded a price contained in an option or contract under which the decedent is free to dispose of the underlying securities at any price he chooses during his lifetime. Such is the effect, for example, of an agreement on the part of a shareholder to purchase whatever shares of stock the decedent may own at the time of his death. Even if the decedent is not free to dispose of the underlying securities at other than the option or contract price, *such price will be disregarded* in determining the value of the securities unless it is determined under the circumstances of the particular case that *the agreement represents a bona fide business arrangement* and not a device to pass the decedent's shares to the natural objects of his bounty for less than an adequate and full consideration in money or money's worth. [Italics supplied.]

Revenue Ruling 59-60, 1959-1 C.B. 237, comments on the requirement that the agreement must represent a bona fide business arrangement as follows: "It is always necessary to consider the relationship of the parties, the relative number of shares held by the decedent, and other material facts, to determine whether the agreement represents a bona fide business arrangement or is a device to pass the decedent's shares to the natural objects of his bounty for less than an adequate and full consideration in money or money's worth."

Revenue Ruling 157, 1953-2 C.B. 255, involved a situation where the by-laws of a corporation provided that upon the death of a stockholder all of his stock should, at the option of the board of directors if exercised within thirty days, become the property of the corporation. Payment was to be made at a price agreed upon by and between the corporation and the legal representative of the deceased as the fair value of such stock, or if an agreement could not be reached, then the corporation might purchase the stock at a price to be determined as a fair value by a board of three appraisers. The by-laws further provided that in the determination of value *no allowance* would be made for any good will. These provisions were applicable only to the disposition of stock *after the death* of a stockholder. It was held that the agreement, though binding on the deceased shareholder's legal representative, did not preclude the Commissioner from evaluating the shareholder's interest in the business to include good will for estate tax purposes.

Revenue Ruling 54-76, 1954-1 C.B. 194, was concerned with a case where the corporation under its articles of organization reserved an option to repurchase its stock at a specific price before any transfer could be made to others. The ruling held: "Although valid and enforceable restrictions affecting the transfer of stock do not necessarily control value for federal estate tax purposes (see Rev. Rul. 157, I.R.B. 1953-17, 16), where a stockholder *acquires stock from the corporation subject to an option reserved to the corporation in the articles of organization* to repurchase the stock at a specific price before any sale or transfer, including any transfer at the death of the stockholder, can be validly made to others, the option price, *in the absence of other material circumstances* will be accepted as the fair market value at the date of death, especially where the option is exercised by the corporation." [Italics supplied.]   Revenue Ruling 54-76 is referrred to with approval in Revenue Ruling 59-60.

It should be noted that the gift tax regulations do not contain any language comparable to that found in Section 20.2031-2(h) of the Regulations applicable to the estate tax, which is quoted above. Revenue Ruling 189, 1953-2 C.B. 294, states: "Restrictions attaching to shares of corporate stock, providing that the owner may not sell, transfer, or otherwise dispose of the shares without first offering them for sale to certain interested persons at a fixed price, or at a price determined by the application of a particular formula, while a factor to be considered with all other pertinent factors of valuation, are not binding upon the Commissioner in determining fair market values for Federal gift tax purposes." The ruling cites in support of its conclusion James V. Commissioner,[14] Kline v. Commissioner,[15] Kraus v. United States,[16] Commissioner v. McCann,[17] Spitzer v. Commissioner.[18] The ruling is referred to with approval in Revenue Ruling 59-60. It should be noted, however, that in Kathleen I. Gibbs,[19] where gifts of stock in a closely held corporation were made by the donors to their son, who held enforceable options to purchase the stock at $1100 a share, it was held that, on the basis of expert testimony and the entire record, the value of the stock for gift tax purposes was $1100 per share rather than the $2500 per share figure which the Commissioner advanced.

An examination will now be made of various cases which have dealt with the effect on the valuation for estate tax purposes of an option or contract to purchase stock in a closely held corporation.

---

[14] 148 F.2d 236 (2d Cir. 1945).
[15] 130 F.2d 742 (3d Cir. 1942), *cert. denied,* 317 U.S. 697 (1943).
[16] 140 F.2d 510 (5th Cir. 1944).
[17] 146 F.2d 385 (2d Cir. 1944).
[18] 153 F.2d 967 (8th Cir. 1946).
[19] 18 CCH T.C. Mem. 178 (1959).

Some of the cases which will be considered involve an option or contract to purchase a partnership interest.

Broderick v. Gore.[20] The partnership agreement provided that if a partner should desire to withdraw, the remaining partners should have the exclusive right to purchase the interest of the retiring partner for a sum equal to the book value of the interest of the withdrawing partner in all the assets of the partnership as of the date of the withdrawal. The agreement further provided that if a partner should die, his interest in the partnership should be sold to the surviving partners and that they were to purchase it for a sum equal to the book value as of the date of death of the deceased partner. The Probate Court held that the agreement was binding on the estate and the surviving partners and determined that the book value was $345,897.53. The executors used this amount in the estate tax return. A deficiency was assessed on the ground that the fair market value of the decedent's interest in the partnership was $516,457.84. The Court of Appeals held that the agreement fixed the value and that that value controlled for estate tax purposes rather than the fair market value. The court stressed the fact that the deceased partner was bound by the agreement during his lifetime, as was his estate on his death. *Here the partners were a father and his sons.*

May v. McGowan.[21] The decedent and his son each owned 500 shares of stock in the corporation. They entered into an agreement which provided that during their joint lives neither would dispose of any of the stock without offering it to the other at a price of $100 per share. The agreement also gave the survivor the option to purchase the stock of the first to die on the same terms. In the case of the son, however, because he had agreed personally to guarantee to a bank its loan to the corporation, the option price of $100 per share was reduced by 1/500 of the indebtedness due the bank at the date of the exercise of the option. When the father died, the son was entitled to the father's shares for nothing and thus the father's executors put in his shares at zero for estate tax purposes. The agreement controlled in determining estate tax values, and in commenting on whether this determination and that of other cases leave a loophole, the court said: "If they leave a loophole for tax evasion in some cases, here the district court found there was no purpose to evade taxes. Such a loophole, if important, should be closed by legislative action rather than by disregarding the cases we have cited."

Armstrong's Estate v. Commissioner.[22] The owner of stock gave

20 224 F.2d 892 (10th Cir. 1955).
21 194 F.2d 396 (2d Cir. 1952).
22 146 F.2d 457 (7th Cir. 1945).

another the option to buy his stock for $25,000. During the life of the owner of the stock the agreement could terminate without mutual consent only if the holder of the option died or became insane or left the employ of the corporation. The option had to be exercised within five years after the death of the owner of the stock. If the option was exercised, the purchaser could not sell the stock without first offering it to the corporation at a price equal to one half of its book value. The option was exercised shortly after the death of the owner. In the owner's estate, the $25,000 price was *not* deemed controlling for estate tax purposes. The difference between the $25,000 figure and the real value was determined to be a gift to the purchaser and thus not effective to control the estate tax value.

Worcester County Trust Co. v. Commissioner.[23] The decedent owned stock which was subject to certain restrictions created by an amendment of the articles of incorporation prior to his death. The restrictions required that, before any transfer of the stock by anyone, the shares must first be offered to the corporation at book value "as appears from the books and records of the corporation as of the date of the close of the last prior month of the corporation plus interest from the date at the rate of six (6%) percent per annum, less any dividends thereon . . ." The restrictions did not apply to any transfer by an executor to legatees or next-of-kin of the deceased stockholder in the distribution of his estate. The corporation was not bound to buy. If it did not, the stock could be sold at any price. The executor included the stock in the decedent's estate for estate tax purposes at the value at which the stock would have to be offered to the corporation under the restrictive provisions. The Commissioner claimed a much higher valuation. The court held that the agreement did not set the value for estate tax purposes because "The amendment did not prohibit the sales of stock except at book values, nor did it fix book value as a call price at which at the behest of the corporation the stock must be sold. It fixed a limitation on the price obtainable by a shareholder for his shares only if he wished to sell and if the corporation at that time wished to buy." The court pointed out, however, that the restriction necessarily had a depressing effect on the value of the stock on the market.

Michigan Trust Co. v. United States.[24] The court instructed the jury that the price at which the decedent's stock could be purchased under an option which had to be exercised within four months after death, where evidently the decedent was not curtailed as to dispositions during his life, was not conclusive for estate tax

23 134 F.2d 578 (1st Cir. 1943).
24 58-2 U.S.T.C. ¶11819 (W.D. Mich. 1958).

purposes but could be taken into account along with all other evidence in determining the value of the stock.

Angela Fiorito.[25] A husband and wife and their two sons were partners and under the partnership agreement the husband gave his two sons an irrevocable option to buy his interest on his death (he could not transfer it during his life) for "the amount standing on the partnership books at the end of the month in which N. Fiorito dies after deducting all amounts due the partnership from N. Fiorito, but not including any allowance for good will, business on hand or any other item not shown in the capital account of N. Fiorito, according to recognized accounting practices." The court held the option price controlling for estate tax purposes. "But even though the price set in the agreement relates only to the price to be paid for an interest after the death of a partner, if the agreement effectively restricted a partner's right to sell his interest prior to death, the value of the partnership interest for estate tax purposes is limited by the option price for purchase of the interest after his death."

Estate of Orville B. Littick.[26] Three brothers, at a time when one was facing death from cancer, agreed that upon the death of any one of them, the corporation could buy his interest for $200,-000. None could sell his shares during his life. The $200,000 figure controlled for estate tax purposes. The court said: "Where for the purpose of keeping control of a business in its present management, the owners set up in *an arm's-length agreement,* which we consider this to be, the price at which the interest of a part owner is to be disposed of by his estate to the other owners, that price controls for estate tax purposes, regardless of the market value of the interest to be disposed of." (Italics supplied.)

Estate of Lionel Weil.[27] Under the terms of an agreement among partners, the decedent was prohibited from disposing of his partnership interest during his life, and the surviving partners were authorized and obligated to purchase the decedent's interest at a determinable price based on book value at his death. The court held that the amount fixed in the agreement controlled for estate tax purposes, saying, "It now seems well established that the value of property may be limited for estate tax purposes by an enforceable agreement which fixes the price to be paid therefor, and where the seller if he desires to sell during his lifetime can receive only the price theretofore agreed on." [28]

---

[25] 33 T.C. 440 (1959).
[26] 31 T.C. 181 (1958).
[27] 22 T.C. 1267 (1954).
[28] Additional cases dealing with the effect on estate tax values of an option or contract to purchase a business interest are Davis v. United States, 60-1

This survey of the Regulations, Revenue Rulings and litigated cases makes it apparent that the option or contract to purchase will *not* be controlling when:

1. The seller is free during his life to make any kind of sale he may choose to make, even though his estate is required to live up to the agreement with respect to what he owns at his death; or
2. The seller and his estate may choose whether or not to sell, even though, if either one sells, the property must be offered first to the corporation at some fixed price.

The requirement in the Regulations that the agreement must represent a bona fide business arrangement indicates that intra-family deals will be closely scrutinized to make certain that, in the guise of a sale, a gift is not in fact being made. Even though in the cases examined, agreements between close family members have, on the whole, stood up, one cannot be certain of the result when such an agreement sets a price that is unrealistic for a business arrangement.

The safest course of action is to provide in the agreement that the seller cannot dispose of the property during his life except to the one having the option or the one entitled to purchase under the contract of purchase; that any such lifetime disposition will be at the agreed price; that the seller's estate is required to sell at the behest of the buyer, or, better still, that the estate is required to sell and the buyer is required to buy; and, finally, that the price fixed is one that is realistic if the whole arrangement is looked at as a business deal.

If the seller has given an option at a price that is on the low side and if the buyer does *not* exercise his option (he is not bound to purchase), the buyer may be in some gift tax difficulties and his failure to act may undermine the whole agreement. In other words, an option clearly should not control the estate tax valuation when the option price was purposely set at a low figure, so as to get a low estate tax valuation, if there is any tacit understanding that the option will not be exercised by the buyer.

U.S.T.C. ¶11943 (D. Utah, 1960) (agreement controlling); Estate of George M. Trammel, 18 T.C. 662 (1952) (agreement not controlling).

In Land v. United States, 60-2 U.S.T.C. ¶11970 (S.D. Ala. 1960), the decedent was a partner in a business. The partnership agreement gave the other partners an option to buy a retiring partner's interest at two thirds of its value, prohibited any partner from selling his interest, and gave the surviving partners an option to buy the interest of a deceased partner at its *full* value. Under these circumstances the court held that the decedent's interest in the partnership would be included in his gross estate at a value equal to what he could have received for it during his life, that is, two thirds of its value, and not what his executors after his death could get for it.

(4) Risks of Setting Low Value in Option or Agreement

The major risk of setting a sale price in the option or contract to purchase at a low figure compared to the true market value is that the fixed price will be binding on the executor and he will have to sell at that price, but it will not be controlling for estate tax purposes. If such a result follows, the taxes on the estate may be more than the cash received for the sale of the stock.

Furthermore, in the described circumstances, the purchaser may be deemed a beneficiary of the estate to the extent of the difference between what he pays for the stock and what it is valued at in the decedent's estate. Under the so-called Apportionment Acts, he may have to pay the portion of the estate tax that is attributable to the difference. In Estate of Jacob Galewitz,[29] it was held that the decedent's son received a benefit in the amount of the difference between the price he paid for stock under an option and its real value. Consequently, he had to contribute to the payment of the estate tax bill under the New York Apportionment Act.

If the low value in the option or contract of purchase does not control for estate tax purposes, the buyer may nevertheless take as his basis the price he pays for the stock. The loss thus occasioned to the family unit is not only the diminution which results when the estate taxes are assessed on the higher value; a further diminution follows if, when the buyer sells, his realized gain is greater.

Even though the fixed low value controls for estate tax purposes, unless the purchase is being made by the decedent's own family, he is benefitting others by entering into such an agreement at the expense of his own family.

(5) Desirability of Option or Agreement That Sets Proper Value

An option or contract to purchase which establishes a realistic value for the stock of a decedent should be employed only if it is

---

[29] 3 A.D.2d 280, 160 N.Y.S.2d 564 (1957). In this case the testator and his son entered into a contract giving the survivor the option to purchase shares of stock in a family corporation at the price stated in the option. Neither party to the contract was in any way curtailed in his dealings with the stock during their joint lives. On the death of the testator, the son notified the personal representative that he desired to exercise the option. The testator's widow claimed that the contract was testamentary and void because of the fact that neither party was bound during his life to hold any of the stock until his death. The widow wanted the contract to be held unenforceable, presumably because the price in the option agreement was not, in her opinion, adequate in amount, and because her share in the estate would be larger if the agreement was unenforceable. The court held that the agreement was enforceable and was not a testamentary disposition.

desirable that the stock of a decedent pass to the designated purchasers. If the owner desires to have his stock held for the benefit of his family, he does not want to sign any agreement that may force his executor to sell it to others.

The mere fact that the agreement will fix estate tax values is of no major significance if the value fixed is to be realistic.   In fact, the existence of the agreement is a handicap because it prevents the possibility of obtaining a lower valuation through negotiation.[30]

The agreement of sale may be highly desirable when a sale will be required on the owner's death in order to obtain liquid funds. The agreement can assure both a purchaser and, if properly funded, the money to make the purchase.

PROBLEMS

15.1. If the employee referred to in the business purchase agreement in Example 1 dies before the proprietor, and the proprietor, pursuant to the provisions of paragraph 9 of the agreement, purchases from the employee's estate the policies of insurance on his life, what will be the income tax consequences when the proceeds of the policies are collected on the proprietor's death?   See Section 101(a)(2)(B) of the 1954 Code, quoted infra page 1329.

15.2. Under what circumstances, if any, would it be desirable to provide in a business purchase agreement like the one in Example 1 that, on the proprietor's death, the proceeds of the insurance should be paid out for the benefit of his wife under one of the options in the policy rather than for them to be turned over to his executors in a lump sum in payment for the business?

15.3. The business purchase agreement in Example 1 includes a trustee. A trustee, of course, is not essential to a business purchase agreement between an employer and an employee.   What are the advantages of having a trustee?

[30] In Belser and Leppard v. Edwards, 54-1 U.S.T.C. ¶10942 (M.D. Ga. 1954), the decedent entered into an agreement with an employee of the corporation in which the decedent owned all the stock, granting the employee an option to purchase a majority of the stock at a price to be determined in accordance with the formula set forth in the option. Pursuant to this purchase option, a majority of the stock was sold to the employee by the decedent's executors. The court sustained the Commissioner's finding that the value of the minority shares in the corporation which were retained by the decedent's estate was determinable in accordance with the formula set forth in the option. This case illustrates that an option given to buy stock in a closely held corporation at a certain price, where the option relates to only part of the stock, may be a dangerous thing because it will be used as the basis of fixing the value of the stock not subject to the option. If, as in this case, the inherent value of the stock is less than the price fixed in the option, the giving of the option produces a higher valuation for the gross estate than if the option had not been granted.

15.4. Should the wife of the employer be a party to a business purchase agreement like the one in Example 1?

15.5. Will the amount paid by the employee for the business, pursuant to the provisions of paragraph 5 of the business purchase agreement in Example 1, be conclusive as to the value of the business for federal estate tax purposes?

15.6. Paragraph 4 of the business purchase agreement in Example 1 provides that, among other things, the purchaser will be entitled to the accounts receivable of the business. To what extent, if at all, will the accounts receivable, when collected by the purchaser, be deemed ordinary income for federal income tax purposes? See Section 1221(4) of the 1954 Code. What portion, if any, of the purchase price received by the estate of the deceased proprietor will be ordinary income to the estate because it represents a sum paid for the accounts receivable? If any portion of the purchase price is deemed ordinary income to the estate because it represents a sum paid for accounts receivable, will it be income in respect of a decedent? See Section 691 of the 1954 Code, quoted infra page 1375.

2.   PARTNERSHIP[31]

If a person is a partner in a business, the partnership will be dissolved by the death of a partner unless the partners have agreed otherwise, and the deceased partner's estate will receive his share. In other words, on his death the partner may have nothing to pass

[31] The comments at pages 931-936 supra, which relate to the sole proprietorship are generally applicable to the partnership situation. In regard to professional partnerships, see page 931 supra, note 2. In addition to the Note on the Effect of an Agreement of Sale on the Valuation of Stock for Estate Tax Purposes, supra page 942, which includes references to several partnership cases on the valuation of a partnership interest, see Reg. §20.2031-3, quoted infra page 1507, and the cases cited below in this note. For comments on a covenant not to compete, see page 945 supra, note 9.

In Mandel v. Sturr, 57-1 U.S.T.C. ¶11688 (S.D.N.Y. 1957), an agreement was involved which was entered into by the decedent and another partner in a business. The agreement specified that upon the death of either partner, the surviving partner should purchase the interest of the deceased partner but that good will should not be considered an asset of the partnership for any purpose. The court held that in valuing the decedent's interest in the partnership for estate tax purposes, nothing should be included on account of good will. The case was reversed in part and remanded on another point in 266 F.2d 321 (2d Cir. 1959).

In Knipp v. Commissioner, 244 F.2d 436 (4th Cir. 1957), cert. denied, 355 U.S. 827 (1957), a partnership agreement was involved under which the distributive share of a deceased partner was limited to the amount of the salary due him at the time of his death. It was held that at the time of his death the decedent had no property interest in the partnership earnings because of the partnership agreement, and thus only the excess of his salary over his withdrawals was includible in his gross estate.

as a going concern to someone else but will be able to pass only the value of his share on dissolution. Of course, if the partnership agreement permits a deceased partner to select, within defined limits, his successor — though technically a new partnership results when a deceased partner selects his successor — in effect the deceased partner is transferring his interest in the going business to the person he selects.

The partnership agreement may provide that the surviving partners will carry on the business and pay to the estate of the deceased partner, over a period of years, a designated portion of the partnership earnings.[32]   In this connection it is relevant to examine the 1954 Code provisions which deal with payments made in installments by the partnership to a deceased partner's successor in complete liquidation of the deceased partner's interest.[33]

The use of the so-called family partnership, where the husband makes his wife a partner in his business in order that the income from the partnership may be split between them, was widespread prior to the Revenue Act of 1948, which introduced the split-income provisions of the federal income tax when husband and wife file a joint return. There was considerable uncertainty as to the accomplishment of the income tax objective by the establishment of such a partnership. The Supreme Court of the United States

[32] See, for example, Charles F. Coates, 7 T.C. 125 (1946); Sidney Hess, 12 T.C. 773 (1949). See also Rita A. Laube, 16 CCH T.C. Mem. 65 (1957), where, on the death of the taxpayer's husband, the partnership ended and a limited partnership came into operation, with the taxpayer as a limited partner. The court held that she had to report as her income the income to which she was entitled from the date of her husband's death. The case was affirmed in 253 F.2d 424 (3d Cir. 1958).

[33] See 1954 I.R.C. §736, quoted infra page 1380; §753, quoted infra page 1381.

Is the value of the right in the estate of the deceased partner to a share in the profits of the partnership carried on by the surviving partners includible in the gross estate of the deceased partner for federal estate tax purposes? If the value of such a right is so includible, is the estate entitled to an income tax deduction on account of the exhaustion of the right?   In Eleanor S. Howell, 24 T.C. 342 (1955), the decedent was a member of a theater partnership which required capital and exhaustible tangible property in the conduct of its business. The partnership agreement in effect at the time of the decedent's death gave the surviving partners the right to continue the business, using all partnership assets, until the end of the stated term of the partnership. The decedent's estate was to share equally in profits and losses with the surviving partners. For estate tax purposes, the value of this right was determined to be $45,000. It was held that exhaustion allowances were deductible. The court distinguished Estate of Boyd C. Taylor, 17 T.C. 627 (1951), *aff'd*, 200 F.2d 561 (6th Cir. 1952), on the ground that in that case capital and tangible assets were of no importance to the creation and retention of the partnership business and, consequently, the right in the estate to receive the deceased partner's share of income was not capital in nature and afforded no basis for depreciation, even though the value of such a right was includible in the gross estate of the deceased partner.

dealt with the matter in three cases.[34] In 1951, Congress undertook to deal with the taxation of family partnerships [35] and the 1951 provisions were incorporated in the 1954 Code.[36] Although generally there is today no income tax advantage in making the wife a partner in the family business, there may be an estate tax advantage in that the principal asset in the husband's estate will be split between his wife and himself, so that the order of their deaths no longer is significant in producing the lowest possible estate tax.[37] The continued use of the family partnership after 1948 to gain an income tax advantage has been in situations where children have been made partners or a trust that has been established for the benefit of some members of the family has become a partner in the family business.[38]

It may be highly desirable for the partners to make an inter vivos agreement whereby the surviving partners agree to purchase the interest of a deceased partner so as to avoid complete liquidation, which may be very damaging to the surviving partners. If an agreement of sale is made, thought must be given to financing the purchase of a deceased partner's interest by the surviving partners.

Set out below as Examples 2, 3 and 4 are business purchase agreements relating to partnerships which are funded with life insurance.

EXAMPLE 2. *Business Purchase Agreement*
Between Three Partners
(with a Trustee)

AGREEMENT made this .... day of ...., 19......, between Wilbur Thompson who resides at 123 First Avenue, New York, N.Y., John Anderson who resides at 456 Main Street, New York, N.Y., Thomas Grady who resides at 789 Broadway, New York, N.Y. (hereafter referred to as the Partners), and the

[34] Commissioner v. Tower, 327 U.S. 280, 66 Sup. Ct. 532, 90 L. Ed. 670 (1946); Lusthaus v. Commissioner, 327 U.S. 293, 66 Sup. Ct. 539, 90 L. Ed. 679 (1946); Commissioner v. Culbertson, 337 U.S. 733, 69 Sup. Ct. 1210, 93 L. Ed. 1659 (1949).

[35] See 1939 I.R.C. §191.

[36] See 1954 I.R.C. §704(e), quoted infra page 1378.

[37] See United States v. Neel, 235 F.2d 395 (10th Cir. 1956), which held that where a husband and wife had established a partnership, only one half of the value of the partnership assets were includible in the husband's gross estate when he died.

[38] Revenue Ruling 58-243, 1958-1 C.B. 255, holds that the fact that a husband and wife cannot legally be partners under state law does not necessarily prevent recognition of such a partnership for federal income tax purposes, and the fact that such a partnership would be valid under state law does not necessarily require its recognition for federal income tax purposes.

ABC Trust Company, a New York Corporation with its principal place of business in New York, N.Y. (hereafter referred to as the Trustee).

The Partners are general Partners in the partnership known as the "Reliable Grocery Stores" with stores in the City of New York. The interest of the Partners in said partnership is set forth as follows:

$$
\begin{array}{ll}
\text{Thompson} \dots\dots\dots\dots\dots & 33\tfrac{1}{3}\% \\
\text{Anderson} \dots\dots\dots\dots\dots & 33\tfrac{1}{3}\% \\
\text{Grady} \dots\dots\dots\dots\dots & 33\tfrac{1}{3}\%
\end{array}
$$

The purpose of this Agreement is twofold: (a) to provide for the purchase by the survivors of the decedent's interest in said partnership and (b) to provide the funds necessary to carry out such purchase.

It is, therefore, mutually agreed by the Partners as follows:

1. Each partner agrees that he will not assign, encumber or dispose of any portion of his partnership interest in the "Reliable Grocery Stores," by sale or otherwise, without the written consent of the other partners.

[*Alternative 1:* If any partner should desire to withdraw from the partnership during his lifetime, he shall first offer in writing to sell his entire interest to the other partners. The offer shall be based on a price determined in accordance with the provisions of Paragraph 5 hereof. Each partner shall have the right to purchase a portion of such interest in proportion that his partnership interest bears to the aggregate interests owned by all Partners excluding the selling partner or in any manner mutually agreeable to the remaining partners, except that the selling partner may not be compelled to sell less than his full interest. If the offer is not accepted by the other partners within sixty days of receipt thereof, the partner desiring to withdraw shall have the right to sell his interest to any other person but shall not sell such interest without giving the remaining partners the right to purchase such interest at a price and on the terms offered by such other person.]

2. The Partners shall deposit with the Trustee life insurance policies issued by the New York Life Insurance Company as follows:

    (a) Policy No. .... on the life of Thompson for $........................., with Anderson as applicant and owner, and the Trustee as beneficiary.

    (b) Policy No. .... on the life of Thompson for $........................., with Grady as applicant and owner, and the Trustee as beneficiary.

(c) Policy No. .... on the life of Anderson for $.........................., with Thompson as applicant and owner, and the Trustee as beneficiary.

(d) Policy No. .... on the life of Anderson for $.........................., with Grady as applicant and owner, and the Trustee as beneficiary.

(e) Policy No. .... on the life of Grady for $.........................., with Thompson as applicant and owner, and the Trustee as beneficiary.

(f) Policy No. .... on the life of Grady for $.........................., with Anderson as applicant and owner, and the Trustee as beneficiary.

During the lifetime of the Partners and the continuance in force of this Agreement, each partner agrees to pay premiums on the policies owned by him as they become due and to give proof of payment to the Trustee and to the insured within twenty days after the due date of each premium. If any premium is not paid within twenty days after its due date, the insured shall have the right to pay such premium and be reimbursed therefor by the owner. All dividends shall be applied on account of premiums. The New York Life Insurance Company is hereby authorized and directed to give the insured, upon his written request, any information with respect to the status of the policies on his life.

[*Alternative provision in lieu of the immediately preceding paragraph:* During the lifetime of the Partners and the continuance in force of this Agreement, each partner shall pay the premiums on the policies owned by him, as they become due, but no partner shall exercise any of the rights, privileges and benefits accruing under the policies owned by him, except as otherwise provided herein, or assign, encumber, borrow against or otherwise dispose of the policies without the written consent of the other partners. All dividends shall be applied on account of premiums or loan interest, if any. The New York Life Insurance Company is hereby authorized and directed to give the insured, upon his written request, any information with respect to the status of the policy on his life. Each partner shall give proof of payment to the Trustee and to the insured within twenty days after the due date of each premium. If any premium is not paid within twenty days after its due date, the insured partner shall have the right to pay such premium and be reimbursed therefor by the other partner.]

3. This Agreement shall extend to and shall include all additional policies issued pursuant hereto; such additional policies to be listed in Schedule A, attached hereto.

4. Upon the death of any partner, his estate shall sell the part-

nership interest then owned by the deceased partner to the surviving partners and each surviving partner shall purchase a portion
of such interest in the proportion that his interest bears to the
aggregate interests of all surviving partners. The purchase price
of such interest shall be computed in accordance with the provisions of Paragraph 5 of this Agreement.

5. Unless and until changed as hereinafter provided, the total
value of the "Reliable Grocery Stores" for the purpose of determining the purchase price to be paid for the interest of a deceased
partner shall be $99,000 and the value of each partner's respective
interest in said partnership shall be as follows:

Thompson	$33,000
Anderson	$33,000
Grady	$33,000

It has been mutually agreed that $10,000 of said purchase price
represents the good will of the Partnership as a going concern.
Within thirty days following the end of each fiscal year the
Partners shall redetermine the value of said partnership and their
respective interests therein. Such values shall be endorsed on
Schedule B, attached hereto. If the Partners fail to redetermine
said values for a particular year, the last previously stipulated
values shall control, except that if no valuation is agreed upon
for two consecutive years, the value of a partner's interests shall
be determined by the independent certified public accountant
regularly retained by the partnership for the auditing of its
books. If there is no such public accountant available or if he
fails to make a determination of such value, then the value shall be
determined by any other accountant who may be selected by mutual agreement of the surviving partners and the representative of
the deceased partner. In no event, however, shall the value of the
interest of a deceased partner be less than the proceeds of life insurance purchased on his life by the surviving partners under this
Agreement. The term "proceeds" is understood to include any
amount paid by reason of death by accidental means under any
agreement for additional indemnity, as well as the face amount,
plus any dividends and any additional amounts payable to the
beneficiary. The surviving partners shall be entitled to all the
profits of the business and suffer all the losses arising between
the date of death of the deceased partner and the consummation
of the sale of the interest of the deceased partner.

[*Alternative for a portion of 5:* Strike out all matter in Paragraph 5 following the fourth sentence and substitute the follow-

ing: If the Partners fail to redetermine said values for a particular
year, the last previously stipulated values shall control, except that
if no valuation is agreed upon for two consecutive years, the value
of a partner's interest shall be agreed upon by the representative of
the deceased partner and the surviving partners. If they do not
come to an agreement within thirty days after the death of a partner, the value of the deceased partner's interest shall be determined by arbitration as follows: The surviving partners and the
representative of the estate of the deceased shall each name one
arbitrator. If the two arbitrators cannot agree upon the value of
the interest of the deceased partner, they shall appoint a third arbitrator and the decision of the majority shall be binding on all parties. In no event, however, shall the value of the interest of a deceased partner be less than the proceeds of life insurance purchased
on his life by the surviving partners under this Agreement. The
term "proceeds" is understood to include any amount paid by reason of death by accidental means under any agreement for additional indemnity, as well as the face amount, plus any dividends
and any additional amounts payable to the beneficiary. The surviving partners shall be entitled to all the profits of the business
and suffer all the losses arising between the date of death of the deceased partner and the consummation of the sale of the interest of
the deceased partner.]

[Complete Alternative 5: The value of a deceased partner's interest for the purpose of this Agreement shall be an amount equal
to the sum of the following items:

    (a) The capital amount of the deceased partner's interest as
         shown by the books of the partnership at the end of the
         last fiscal year before his death;

    (b) Plus the decedent's share of the profits, or less the dece-
         dent's share of the losses of the partnership computed
         from the beginning of the fiscal year in which his death
         occurred to the last day of the month in which his death
         occurred, and less all withdrawals during such period.

The account books of the partnership kept in the usual course of
business and adjusted to take into account any errors and omissions shall be accepted by the surviving partners and the representative of the deceased partner as determining the true book
value and earnings of the partnership. The findings of any accountant they may select to determine such value and earnings as
shown by the account books shall be accepted. In no event, however, shall the value of the interest of a deceased partner be less
than the proceeds of life insurance purchased on his life by the
surviving partners under this Agreement. The term "proceeds" is

understood to include any amount paid by reason of death by accidental means under any agreement for additional indemnity, as well as the face amount, plus any dividends and any additional amounts payable to the beneficiary. The surviving partners shall be entitled to all the profits of the business and suffer all the losses arising between the last day of the month in which the death occurred and the consummation of the sale of the interest of the deceased partner.]

6. Each partner agrees that the proceeds of the policies owned by him for the purposes of this Agreement shall be applied toward the purchase price set forth above. The Trustee shall apply the proceeds in accordance with the terms of this Agreement. If the purchase price so set forth exceeds the proceeds of the life insurance, the balance of the purchase price shall be paid in twenty-four consecutive monthly payments beginning three months after the date of the decedent's death. The unpaid balance of the purchase price shall be evidenced by a series of negotiable promissory notes made by each of the surviving partners to the order of the estate of the deceased with interest at 5% per annum. Said notes shall provide for the acceleration of the due date of all unpaid notes in the series on default in the payment of any note or interest thereon and shall give the makers thereof the option of prepayment in whole or in part at any time.

7. The duties of the Trustee are as follows:

    (1) To receive and safely hold the life insurance policies described herein and any that may be added, as described in Schedule A attached hereto, and proof of payment of all premiums paid by the Partners as required herein.

    (2) Upon the death of a partner, to

        (a) make a claim for and collect the proceeds of the life insurance policies issued on the life of the deceased partner. The Trustee shall be under no obligation to institute any action to recover the proceeds of any of the policies unless indemnified by the surviving partners for all expenses and attorney's fees connected therewith.

        (b) demand and receive from the surviving partners any notes required to be executed by them as required herein.

        (c) deliver to the estate of the deceased partner (i) the proceeds of the life insurance policies collected by it; (ii) any notes required herein to be executed or delivered by the surviving partners; (iii) an agreement executed by the surviving partners, indemnifying the estate of the deceased partner against any liabilities of the partnership, provided it receives simultaneously from the estate of the deceased partner such legal instruments as will convey to the surviving partners all the interest of the estate of the decedent in the partnership described herein; and (iv) the policies owned by the decedent on the surviving partners.

(3) Upon termination of the Agreement other than by the death of one of the Partners, the Trustee shall deliver the policies described herein and in Schedule A, to their respective owners. However, the Trustee shall be under no obligation to deliver such policies until it has received the compensation and reimbursement for expenses and counsel fees, if any, as specified in paragraph 8.

8. The Trustee shall be paid as compensation a commission of .... percentage (........ %) of all moneys which it collects as proceeds of life insurance on the death of any partner. If this Agreement is terminated other than by the death of one of the Partners, the Trustee shall receive a fee of $........................, for its services in terminating the trust. The Trustee shall be reimbursed for all its reasonable expenses and counsel fees. The Trustee shall have the right to resign at any time upon ten days notice to the Partners, and the Partners shall have the right to substitute another Trustee at any time by paying to the Trustee a fee of $........................ The Trustee's compensation, fees and expenses shall be divided and paid equally by the Partners. For this purpose, the word partner shall include the legal representative of the deceased partner.

9. Upon the death of any partner, each surviving partner shall have the right to purchase from the estate of the decedent any or all of the policies insuring his life, for a price equal to the interpolated terminal reserve thereof as of the date of death of the partner, less any existing indebtedness charged against the policy, plus the proportionate part of the gross premium last paid before the date of death which covers the period extending beyond that date. This right may be exercised at any time within sixty days after the qualification of the legal representative of the deceased partner, by the payment of such price and if the right is not so exercised within the time allowed, it shall lapse.

10. The surviving partners and the executor or administrator of the deceased partner shall make, execute and deliver any documents necessary to transfer the ownership of the partnership assets and carry out this Agreement.

[*Alternative 10:* Each of the surviving partners shall execute and deliver to the Trustee any promissory notes required herein to be executed by him as a part of the purchase price, together with a written agreement indemnifying the estate against all liabilities of the partnership.   Upon the payment of the purchase price to the estate of the deceased partner, in cash, or in cash and notes, the estate shall execute and deliver to the Trustee all documents reasonably required to evidence such purchase; and all rights of the estate in the partnership, and in its business and assets, shall thereafter belong to the surviving partners.]

11. This Agreement may be altered, amended or terminated by a writing signed by all Partners, but no amendment shall be made affecting the duties of the Trustee without its consent thereto.   In the event of a termination of this Agreement before the death of any partner, each shall be entitled to an assignment to him of any policy on his life upon payment by him to the owner within sixty days of such termination of a sum equal to the interpolated terminal reserve as of the date of transfer less any existing indebtedness charged against the policy, plus the proportionate part of the gross premium last paid before the date of transfer which covers the period extending beyond that date.

12. This Agreement shall terminate on the occurrence of any of the following events:

    (a) Upon the death of any partner, except that the death of a partner shall not relieve his estate from the obligation to sell, or the surviving partners from their obligation to purchase, the interest of the deceased partner in accordance with the terms of this Agreement.

    (b) Cessation of the partnership business.

    (c) Bankruptcy, receivership or dissolution of the partnership.

    (d) Bankruptcy or insolvency of any partner.

    (e) Death of two partners simultaneously or within a period of thirty days.

    (f) At the option of any partner, if any other partner fails to pay the premiums within the grace period of the policy or policies of life insurance owned by him for the purposes of this Agreement, or assigns, surrenders or borrows against said policy or policies, changes the beneficiary or makes the proceeds payable other than in a lump sum without the written consent of all the Partners.

13. This Agreement shall be binding upon the Partners, their heirs, legal representatives, successors and assigns.

14. Notwithstanding the provisions of this Agreement, New York Life Insurance Company is hereby authorized to act in ac-

cordance with the terms of its policies as if this Agreement did not exist, and payment or other performance of its contract obligations by said Company in accordance with the terms of its policies shall completely discharge said Company from all claims, suits and demands of all persons whatsoever.

15. This Agreement shall be subject to and governed by the law of the State of ...., irrespective of the fact that one or more of the parties now is or may become a resident of a different state.

IN WITNESS WHEREOF, the parties hereto have executed this Agreement this .... day of ...., 19.........

....

....

....

....

SCHEDULE A

Schedule of Additional Life Insurance Policies

Name of Company   *Policy No.*   *Amount*   *Signature of Owners*

SCHEDULE B

Endorsements

Date of execution ....

Pursuant to Paragraph 5 of this Agreement, the parties do hereby determine that the total value of the partnership business as of this date is $........................., and the value of each partner's respective interest is:

Thompson .... $
Anderson .... $
Grady .... $

....

....

....

PROBLEMS

15.7. If one of the partners referred to in the business purchase agreement in Example 2 dies, and the surviving partners desire to continue the business and to use existing life insurance on their lives to fund a new agreement, what will be the income tax consequences, in view of the transferee for value rule, if each of the surviving partners purchases the existing policies on the life of the other? See Section 101(a)(2)(B) of the 1954 Code, quoted infra page 1329.

15.8. Will the amount paid by the surviving partners for the interest of the deceased partner, pursuant to the provisions of Paragraph 5 of the business purchase agreement in Example 2, be conclusive as to the value of the deceased partner's interest for federal estate tax purposes? See Problem 15.5, supra page 954.

15.9. What portion of the purchase price received by the estate of the deceased partner will be ordinary income to the estate? See Sections 731, 736, and 751 of the 1954 Code, quoted infra pages 1379, 1380, and 1381 respectively. If any portion of the purchase price is ordinary income to the estate of the deceased partner, will this income be income in respect of a decedent? See Section 753, quoted infra page 1381.

EXAMPLE 3.   *Business Purchase Agreement*
Where Insurance Policies Are
Owned by the Partnership

AGREEMENT made this .... day of ...., 19.........
between John Reynolds, Robert Olsen, William Rogers and Thomas Regan (hereinafter called the Partners) and "Reynolds and Olsen" (hereinafter called the Partnership).

The Partners are engaged in the wholesale and retail drug business in the City of New York, N.Y., under the Partnership name of "Reynolds and Olsen." The interest of each partner in said Partnership is set forth as follows:

> John Reynolds 30%
> Robert Olsen 30%
> William Rogers 20%
> Thomas Regan 20%

The purpose of this Agreement is twofold: (a) to provide for the purchase by the Partnership of the decedent's interest in said

Partnership and (b) to provide the funds necessary to carry out such purchase.

It is, therefore, mutually agreed as follows:

1. The Partnership is the applicant, owner and beneficiary of the following life insurance policies issued by New York Life Insurance Company:

Policy No. .... insuring the life of John Reynolds
in the amount of $....................

Policy No. .... insuring the life of Robert Olsen
in the amount of $....................

Policy No. .... insuring the life of William Rogers
in the amount of $....................

Policy No. .... insuring the life of Thomas Regan
in the amount of $....................

The Partnership shall pay all premiums on the insurance policies taken out pursuant to this Agreement. The Partnership shall give proof of payment of premiums to the Partners within twenty days after the due date of such premiums. If a premium is not paid within twenty days after its due date, the insured shall have the right to pay such premium and be reimbursed therefor by the Partnership. It is agreed that the Partnership shall hold such policies for the purpose of this Agreement and shall not borrow against such policies or pledge or otherwise encumber them without the consent of all of the Partners. The Partnership shall have the right to purchase additional insurance on the lives of any or all of the Partners; such additional policies to be listed in Schedule A, attached hereto.

2. Upon the death of any partner, the Partnership shall be continued by the surviving partners and the Partnership shall purchase for the account of the surviving partners, and the estate of the decedent shall sell, the interest of the decedent in the Partnership. Upon the completion of said purchase and sale, the estate of the deceased partner shall have no further interest in the Partnership or any of its assets.

3. No partner shall, during his lifetime, assign, encumber or dispose of his interest or any portion thereof in the Partnership, by sale or otherwise, without the written consent of the other partners.

4. This Agreement shall extend to and shall include all additional policies issued pursuant hereto; such additional policies to be listed in Schedule A, attached hereto.

5. Unless and until changed as hereinafter provided, it is agreed that for the purpose of determining the purchase price to be paid for the interest of a deceased partner the total value of all of the interests of the Partners in the Partnership is $120,000, and the value of each partner's respective interest in the Partnership is as follows:

> John Reynolds $36,000
> Robert Olsen $36,000
> William Rogers $24,000
> Thomas Regan $24,000

It has been mutually agreed that $10,000 of said purchase price represents the good will of the Partnership as a going concern. Within thirty days following the end of each fiscal year, the Partners shall redetermine the value of said Partnership and their respective interests therein.   Such values shall be endorsed on Schedule B, attached hereto.   If the Partners fail to redetermine said values for a particular year, the last previously stipulated values shall control, except that if the Partners have not so stipulated such values within the twelve months following the end of a fiscal year, the value of a deceased partner's interest shall be determined by the independent public accountant regularly retained by the Partnership for the auditing of its books. The accountant shall consider as a basis for determining the value of the interest of the decedent, the valuation last agreed upon by the Partners, and shall make adjustment to such basis by adding or subtracting from said value a fair estimate of the increase or decrease of the valuation of the business after the date as of which the last valuation was made and up to and including the date of the death of the partner.   If there is no such public accountant available or if he fails to make a determination of such valuation, then the value shall be determined by any other accountant who may be selected by mutual agreement of the Partnership and the representative of the deceased partner. In no event, however, shall the value of the interest of a deceased partner be less than the proceeds of the life insurance purchased on his life by the Partnership.   The term "proceeds" is understood to include any amount paid by reason of death by accidental means under any agreement for additional indemnity, as well as the face amount, plus any dividends and any additional amounts payable to the beneficiary.   The surviving partners shall be entitled to all of the profits of the business and suffer all of the losses arising between the close of business on the day of death of the deceased partner and the consummation of this Agreement. (See Note at end of Agreement.)

[*Alternative for a portion of 5:* Strike out all matter in paragraph 5 following the fourth sentence and substitute the following: If the Partners fail to redetermine said values for a particular year, the last previously stipulated value shall control except that if no valuation is agreed upon for two consecutive years, the value of a partner's interest shall be agreed upon by the representative of the deceased partner and the Partnership on behalf of the surviving partners. If they do not agree to a valuation within thirty days after the death of a partner, the value of the deceased partner's interest shall be determined by arbitration as follows: The Partnership on behalf of the surviving partners and the representative of the estate of the deceased partner shall each name one arbitrator. If the two arbitrators cannot agree upon a value, they shall appoint a third arbitrator and the decision of the majority shall be binding on all parties. In no event, however, shall the value of the interest of a deceased partner be less than the proceeds of the life insurance purchased on his life by the Partnership. The term "proceeds" is understood to include any amount paid by reason of death by accidental means under any agreement for additional indemnity, as well as the face amount, plus any dividends and any additional amounts payable to the beneficiary.]

[*Complete Alternative 5:* The value of a deceased partner's interest for the purpose of this Agreement shall be an amount equal to the sum of the following items:

  (a) The capital amount of the deceased partner's interest as shown by the books of the partnership at the end of the last fiscal year before his death;

  (b) plus the decedent's share of the profits, or less the decedent's share of the losses of the partnership computed from the beginning of the fiscal year in which his death occurred to the last day of the month in which his death occurred, and less all withdrawals during such period.

The account books of the partnership kept in the usual course of business and adjusted to take into account any errors and omissions shall be accepted by the surviving partner and the representative of the deceased partner as determining the true book value and earnings of the partnership. The findings of any accountant they may select to determine such value and earnings as shown by the account books shall be accepted. In no event, however, shall the value of the interest of a deceased partner be less than the proceeds of life insurance purchased on his life by the partnership under this Agreement. The term "proceeds" is understood to include any amount paid by reason of death by accidental means under any agreement for additional indemnity, as well as the face amount, plus any dividends and any additional amounts payable to the beneficiary. The surviving partners shall be entitled to all the profits of the business and suffer all the losses arising between the last day of the month in which the death occurred and the consummation of the sale of the interest of the deceased partner.]

6. Upon the death of a partner, the Partnership shall collect the proceeds of the policy or policies insuring the life of the deceased partner and shall pay such proceeds to the executor or administrator of the estate of the deceased partner upon receiving a Bill of Sale of the deceased partner's interest in the Partnership and a waiver of any right of accounting on the part of the surviving partners. At the same time, the surviving partners shall execute and deliver to the estate of the deceased partner an indemnifying agreement, indemnifying the estate of the deceased partner against any liability of the Partnership. Said sale shall take effect as of the close of business on the day of death of the deceased partner.

If the purchase price exceeds the proceeds of the life insurance, the balance of the purchase price shall be paid in twelve consecutive monthly payments beginning one month after the receipt of the Bill of Sale from the estate of the deceased partner. The unpaid balance of the purchase price shall be evidenced by a series of negotiable promissory notes made by the surviving partners to the order of the estate of the deceased with interest at 5% per annum. Said notes shall provide for the acceleration of the due date of all unpaid notes in the series on default in the payment of any note or interest thereon and shall give the maker thereof the option of prepayment in whole or in part at any time.

7. Any partner who is permitted to withdraw from the Partnership shall have the right to purchase the policy or policies on his life owned by the Partnership by paying an amount equal to the interpolated terminal reserve value of the policies as of the date of transfer, less any existing indebtedness charged against the policy, plus the proportionate part of the gross premium last paid before the date of transfer which covers the period extending beyond that date. This right shall lapse if not exercised within 30 days of such withdrawal.

8. The surviving partners and the executor or administrator of the deceased partner shall make, execute and deliver any documents necessary to carry out this Agreement. This Agreement

shall be binding upon the Partnership, the Partners, their legal representatives and assigns.

9. This Agreement may be altered, amended or terminated by a writing signed by a majority of the Partners. In the event of a termination of this Agreement before the death of a partner, each partner shall be entitled to purchase from the Partnership the policy or policies on his life upon payment of a sum equal to the interpolated terminal reserve of the policies as of the date of transfer, less any existing indebtedness charged against the policy, plus the proportionate part of the gross premium last paid before the date of transfer which covers the period extending beyond that date.

10. This Agreement shall terminate on the occurrence of any of the following events:

    (a) Cessation of the Partnership business.

    (b) Bankruptcy, receivership or dissolution of the Partnership.

    (c) Bankruptcy of any partner.

11. Notwithstanding the provisions of this Agreement, New York Life Insurance Company is hereby authorized to act in accordance with the terms of any policies issued by it as if this Agreement did not exist and payment or other performance of its contract obligations by said Company in accordance with the terms of any such policy shall completely discharge said Company from all claims, suits and demands of all persons whatsoever.

12. This Agreement shall be subject to and governed by the law of the State of..............., irrespective of the fact that one or more of the parties now is or may become a resident of a different state.

IN WITNESS WHEREOF, the parties hereto have executed this Agreement this .... day of ...., 19.........

Note: The parties should consider the advisability of including in the total value determined under paragraph 5, the cash values of all of the policies specified in this Agreement, and a further provision requiring the Partnership to pay in addition and in proportion to the deceased partner's interest in the Partnership, a portion of the excess of the proceeds of life insurance on the life of the deceased partner over the cash value of such policy at the date of his death.

SCHEDULE A

Schedule of Additional Life Insurance Policies

Name of Company   *Policy No.*   *Amount*   *Signature of Owners*

SCHEDULE B

Endorsements

Date of execution ....

Pursuant to Paragraph 5 of this Agreement, the parties do hereby determine that the total value of the Partnership business as of this date is $........................, and the value of each partner's respective interest is:

John Reynolds ....$
Robert Olsen ....$
William Rogers ....$
Thomas Regan ....$

....

....

....

....

PROBLEMS

15.10. When the partnership owns the insurance policies of a business purchase agreement, as in Example 3, and a partner dies, will the income tax basis of each surviving partner with respect to his partnership interest be increased as a result of the purchase of the deceased partner's interest with such insurance? See Section 705(a)(1)(B) of the 1954 Code, quoted infra page 1379, and compare therewith Paul Legallet, 41 B.T.A. 294 (1940).

15.11. When the insurance policies of a business purchase agreement are owned by the partnership, as in Example 3, the deceased partner will have paid part of the premiums on the insurance on his own life which is used by the partnership to buy out his interest and thus he is indirectly paying part of the purchase price. What provisions should be inserted in the business purchase agreement if it is desired to avoid this result?

15.12. When the partnership owns the insurance policies of a business purchase agreement, as in Example 3, will the deceased partner be deemed to have the incidents of ownership of the policies on his own life, exercisable in conjunction with the other partners, so that the value of these policies will be includible in his gross estate for estate tax purposes under Section 2042, quoted infra page 1402? See Estate of George H. Atkins, 2 T.C. 332 (1943); Estate of Frank H. Knipp, 25 T.C. 153 (1955).[39]

EXAMPLE 4. *Agreement Relating to Professional Partnership*

AGREEMENT made this .... day of ...., 19........, between James Kelleher, M.D., Robert Woodward, M.D., Sterling Given, M.D. and Richard Arnold, M.D., all residents of New York City, hereinafter referred to as the Partners.

The Partners are engaged in the practice of medicine, operating a medical clinic at 51 Madison Avenue, New York, New York.

This agreement is divided into two parts. Part I provides that, on the death of a partner, the Partnership is to continue

---

[39] Revenue Ruling 56-397, 1956-2 C.B. 599, holds that where a policy of insurance is acquired by a business associate on the life of the decedent for the purpose of purchasing the decedent's share in a business enterprise, the proceeds of the insurance are not includible in the decedent's gross estate, even though, at the same time and for the same purpose, the decedent acquired a similar policy of insurance on the life of the business associate. The ruling rejects the applicability of the reciprocal trust doctrine established by the Lehman case to this situation (see the discussion of the reciprocal trust doctrine at page 199 supra). The exact arrangement considered by the ruling involved two stockholders in a closely held corporation. The value of the policy which the decedent acquired on the life of his surviving business associate was includible in the decedent's gross estate.

Estate of George W. Dichtel, 30 T.C. 1258 (1958), illustrates what may be the most costly method of providing for the purchase of a deceased partner's interest by a surviving partner. In this case the partners agreed that the interest of the first to die would be purchased by the survivor. To provide the survivor with the necessary funds, each took out a policy of insurance on his own life and named the other as beneficiary. Each retained incidents of ownership in the policy on his own life. The face amount of the policy was includible in the gross estate of the insured. Nothing was said about the inclusion in his gross estate of the value of his interest in the partnership but evidently it was also includible. See also Hall v. Wheeler, 174 F. Supp. 418 (D. Me. 1959), referred to supra page 325.

among the surviving partners with provision for the continuation of income to the estate of the deceased partner, as provided therein.[40]　Part II provides that, on the death of a partner, the Partnership shall purchase his interest in the assets of the Partnership.

The following policies of life insurance, issued by the New York Life Insurance Company, have been purchased for a dual purpose: (1) to partially compensate the surviving partners for any loss resulting to them as a consequence of the loss, through death, of the services of an active partner; and (2) to carry out the purchase provided for in Part II hereof:

Policy No. .... insures the life of James Kelleher, M.D., in the amount of $..........................

Policy No. .... insures the life of Robert Woodward, M.D., in the amount of $..........................

Policy No. .... insures the life of Sterling Given, M.D., in the amount of $..........................

Policy No. .... insures the life of Richard Arnold, M.D., in the amount of $..........................

The Partnership is the applicant, owner and beneficiary of each of said policies of life insurance.　This Agreement shall extend to and shall include all additional policies issued pursuant hereto; such additional policies to be listed in Schedule A, attached hereto.

PART I

Continuation of Income to Estate of a Deceased Partner

1. Upon the death of a partner, the surviving partners shall continue the Partnership business without interruption.　The estate of the deceased partner shall participate in the net profits starting with the first day of the month following the month of death of the partner and continuing for a period of four years. The share of the estate of a deceased partner shall be equal to two-thirds of the net profits which the deceased partner would have received had he remained alive and continued as a partner. The share of net profits payable to the estate of the deceased partner shall be payable in monthly installments on the last day of

---

[40] As to whether it is ethical for a law firm to pay a deceased partner's estate a share of profits, see page 931 supra, note 2. — ED.

each month and shall be based upon the assumption that the Partnership profits for a current year will equal 85% of the Partnership profits for the last preceding year. Any necessary adjustment shall be made at the close of the calendar year (but not later than thirty days thereafter) with a final adjustment at the end of the four year period (such final adjustment shall be made not later than thirty days thereafter). The estate of the deceased partner shall not be required to repay any overpayment.

2. The executor or other legal representative of the deceased partner may instruct the Partnership to pay the income payable under this Part to the person legally entitled thereto under the Will of the deceased partner or under the applicable laws of descent and distribution.

PART II

Purchase and Sale of a Deceased Partner's Interest in the Assets of the Partnership

3. Upon the death of any partner, the Partnership shall purchase and the estate of the deceased partner shall sell the interest of the deceased partner in the Partnership. The value of the deceased partner's interest for the purpose of this Agreement shall be an amount equal to the sum of the following items:

    (a) The capital amount of the deceased partner's interest as shown by the books of the Partnership at the end of the last fiscal year before his death;

    (b) plus the decedent's share of the profits, or less the decedent's share of the losses of the Partnership computed from the beginning of the fiscal year in which his death occurred to the last day of the month in which his death occurred and less all withdrawals during such period.

The account books of the Partnership kept in the usual course of business and adjusted to take into account any errors and omissions shall be accepted by the surviving partners and the representative of the deceased partner as determining the true book value and earnings of the Partnership. Book value shall include the cash surrender values of all life insurance policies taken out by the Partnership pursuant to this Agreement and the proceeds of the policies insuring the life of a deceased partner in excess of their cash surrender values. The findings of any accountant they may select to determine such value and earnings as shown by the account books shall be accepted. If the parties cannot agree upon an acceptable account for such purpose, the surviving partners and the representative of the estate shall each name one arbitrator. If the two arbitrators cannot agree upon the value of the interest of the deceased partner, they shall appoint a third arbitrator, and the decision of the majority shall be binding on all parties.

Miscellaneous Provisions

4. The Partners agree that during their lives they will not assign, encumber or dispose of any portion of their respective Partnership interests by sale or otherwise without the written consent of the other partners.

5. When the estate of a deceased partner shall have received the purchase price provided for in Part II hereof, such estate shall have no further interest in the Partnership or in the Partnership assets other than the right to receive a share of the profits as provided in Part I hereof.

6. This Agreement may be altered, amended or terminated by a writing signed by a majority of the Partners. In the event of a termination of this Agreement before the death of any partner, each partner shall be entitled to purchase from the Partnership the policy or policies on his life upon payment of a sum equal to the interpolated terminal reserve of the policy or policies as of the date of transfer, less any existing indebtedness charged against the policies, plus the proportionate part of the gross premium last paid before the date of transfer which covers the period extending beyond that date.

7. This Agreement shall terminate on the occurrence of any of the following events:

    (a) Cessation of the Partnership business.

    (b) Bankruptcy, receivership or dissolution of the Partnership.

    (c) Bankruptcy of any partner.

8. This Agreement shall be binding upon the Partnership, the Partners, their legal representatives and assigns.

9. Notwithstanding the provisions of this Agreement, New York Life Insurance Company is hereby authorized to act in accordance with the terms of any policies issued by it as if this Agreement did not exist and payment or other performance of its contract obligations by said Company in accordance with the terms of any such policy shall completely discharge said Company from all claims, suits and demands of all persons whatsoever.

10. This Agreement shall be subject to and governed by the law of the State of ...., irrespective of the fact that one or

more of the parties now is or may become a resident of a different state.

IN WITNESS WHEREOF, the parties hereto have executed this Agreement this .... day of ...., 19.........

SCHEDULE A

Schedule of Additional Life Insurance Policies

Name of Company   *Policy No.*   *Amount*   *Signature of Owners*

3.   CLOSELY HELD CORPORATION

The closely held corporation is becoming more and more prevalent on the American business scene.   The estate planning problems presented when a significant portion of a client's estate consists of stock in such a corporation can be quite complex and very difficult of solution.

Stock in a closely held corporation presents an inherently difficult problem of valuation.   Inter vivos transfers and testamentary dispositions can be intelligently planned only if some fairly reliable estimate can be made as to the value of the property with which the dispositive instrument is to be concerned.   The valuation tests applied to closely held stock and the effectiveness of a buy-and-sell agreement to fix values for tax purposes have already been examined.[41]

[41] See Note on the Effect of an Agreement of Sale on the Valuation of Stock for Estate Tax Purposes, supra page 942.

See also Ness, Federal Estate Tax Consequences of Agreements and Options to Purchase on Death, 49 Colum. L. Rev. 796 (1949); O'Neal, Restrictions on Transfer of Stock in Closely Held Corporations; Planning and Drafting, 65 Harv. L. Rev. 773 (1952).

In Estate of Harry W. Hammond, 14 CCH T.C. Mem. 83 (1955), the settlor of a revocable trust authorized his trustees to sell fifty shares of the common stock of a closely held corporation to his son-in-law at a price of $200 a share. Prior to the consummation of the sale the settlor died.   It was held that the son-in-law did not acquire any indefeasible right to purchase the stock at such a price, and that the authorization to the trustees to sell to him at $200 a share consequently had no effect on the valuation of the stock for estate tax purposes.

a. *Sale of Stock on Death of Owner*

If it is assumed that some of the stock is to be held by the owner until his death and that a portion of it will have to be sold at that time to meet death costs, who will be the purchaser? The possible purchasers are some member of the decedent's family, the trustees of a family trust established inter vivos, the corporation itself, the surviving shareholders, a complete outsider. The one who is the most likely or the most desirable purchaser in the light of all the circumstances must be financially able to pay the estate a proper price.

Member of family as purchaser. A member of the decedent's family is not likely to have the necessary liquid funds to purchase the closely held stock from the decedent's estate unless insurance on the life of the decedent is owned by the family member and collected in a lump sum by him on the decedent's death. If a family member is selected as the desirable purchaser and appropriate insurance arrangements have been made to enable him to finance the purchase, unless he obligates himself to buy by entering into a contract, he may not go through with the purchase when the decedent dies. Also, it must be kept in mind that the selected family member may predecease the owner of the stock and the insurance he owns on the life of the owner of the stock will then become involved in his estate. If the stock is sold by the decedent's estate to a member of the family at a loss, the loss will be allowed to the estate if a bona fide sale is involved.[42]

Family trust as purchaser. An inter vivos trust can be estab-

---

[42] Section 1.1001-1(e) of the Regulations provides that where a transfer of property is in part a sale and in part a gift, a transferor has a gain to the extent that the amount realized by him exceeds his adjusted basis. However, no loss is sustained if the amount realized is less than the adjusted basis.

Section 267 of the 1954 Code, dealing with disallowance of deduction for loss with respect to transactions between related taxpayers, is not applicable where the sale is by the decedent's estate to someone. See also Rev. Rul. 56-222, 1956-1 C.B. 155.

In John B. Shethar, 28 T.C. 1222 (1957), a husband and wife separately owned securities which had declined in value, and they wished to have the benefit of deductible tax losses by selling these securities. At the same time, however, they did not desire to relinquish family control over the securities. Consequently, each purchased on the market an identical number of shares of the stock owned by the other and, the following day, each sold on the market the shares originally owned. The court held that the purchases and sales were part of a prearranged plan that amounted to an indirect sale between members of a family and the losses on the sales were disallowed.

Revenue Ruling 59-171, 1959-1 C.B. 65, holds that §267(b)(5) does not apply where the trustee of a separate trust sells, at a loss, to the trustee of another trust created by the same settlor securities owned personally by the first trustee and the purchase by the second trustee is for his own account.

lished to own insurance on the life of the owner of the stock, and the trustees can be authorized to purchase the decedent's stock from his estate. This arrangement does not assure that the purchase will be made, however, because the trustees may decide that it will not be in the best interest of the trust beneficiaries to buy the stock. It might not be wise to put the trustees under a mandate. Where the trust owns the insurance, deaths in the family prior to the death of the owner of the stock will not cause the life insurance to become involved in someone's estate.

Corporation as purchaser. The corporation may be obligated to buy the decedent's stock under a contract, or it may purchase the stock though not so obligated. In either case, the corporation must have the needed funds.[43] These can be acquired by accumulation of earnings, by acquiring life insurance on the owner of the stock or by borrowing.

Whenever a corporation accumulates earnings, it must be careful not to subject itself to the accumulated earnings tax.[44] If the corporation acquires insurance on the life of the owner of the stock, the premiums paid for the insurance will be accumulated income. While it is possible that arrangements made by a corporation to finance the purchase of its stock will be subject to the accumulated earnings tax,[45] in most cases such arrangements should escape that tax on the ground that the accumulation is for a proper business purpose, and not for the purpose of avoiding income tax with respect to its shareholders.[46]

[43] Topken, Loren & Schwartz, Inc. v. Schwartz, 249 N.Y. 206, 163 N.E. 735 (1928), held that a contract between a corporation and its employee, under which the corporation agreed to buy shares of its stock that the employee held on the termination of his employment, could not be specifically enforced by the corporation because the contract was not mutually binding and therefore lacked consideration. The court pointed out that the corporation could purchase the stock only if it had a surplus from which to make payment. Payment out of capital for the purchase of its stock would be illegal. Thus the promise, though binding on the employee, might or might not be binding on the employer.

[44] See 1954 I.R.C. §§531, 532, quoted infra page 1361.

[45] In Pelton Steel Casting Co., 28 T.C. 153 (1957), the court held that the purchase and retirement by a corporation of 80 percent of its outstanding stock was not a reasonable business need of its own but rather suited the personal or business needs of its shareholders, and that the purpose of the redemption scheme was to avoid imposition of a surtax on the shareholders. Consequently, the corporation was subject to a tax for its unlawful accumulation. The case was affirmed in 251 F.2d 278 (7th Cir. 1958), *cert. denied,* 356 U.S. 958 (1958). See also Penn Needle Art Co., 17 CCH T.C. Mem. 504 (1958); Mountain State Steel Foundries Inc., 18 CCH T.C. Mem. 306 (1959), *rev'd sub nom.* Mountain State Steel Foundries, Inc. v. Commissioner, 284 F.2d 737 (4th Cir. 1960), where it was held that the use of corporate funds to purchase stock from conflicting interests served a corporate purpose and did not indicate that disbursements in payment of stock amounted to an unreasonable accumulation of surplus by the corporation.

[46] See Emeloid Co., Inc. v. Commissioner, 189 F.2d 230 (3d Cir. 1951);

The premiums which a corporation pays to carry insurance on the life of one of its shareholders will be quite costly in the over-all picture if they are deemed dividends to the insured. Revenue Ruling 59-184[47] states that whenever a corporation purchases life insurance on the lives of its stockholders and the proceeds are to be used in payment for the stock of any stockholder, the premiums do not constitute income to any stockholder, even though the stockholder has the right to designate a beneficiary, if the right of the beneficiary to receive the proceeds is conditioned upon the transfer of the corporate stock to the corporation.[48]

Tremayne, Jr., Estate Planning for the Man with a Business, 1955 Wash. U.L.Q. 40, 57.

Bradford-Robinson Printing Co. v. United States, 58-1 U.S.T.C. ¶9262 (D. Colo. 1957), considered a case where a corporation established a self-insurance fund on its key members. The court held that the evidence showed that the fund was not established for the purpose of preventing the imposition of the surtax upon its stockholders.

[47] 1959-1 C.B. 65.

[48] See Paramount-Richards Theatres, Inc. v. Commissioner, 153 F.2d 602 (5th Cir. 1946); C. F. Smith Co., 13 CCH T.C. Mem. 607 (1954); Tremayne, Jr., Estate Planning for the Man with a Business, 1955 Wash. U.L.Q. 40, 56.

In Oreste Casale, 26 T.C. 1020 (1956), it was held that where a corporation entered into a deferred compensation agreement with its president and majority stockholder, the annual premium paid by the corporation for insurance on the life of the president to fund the deferred compensation agreement was a distribution to the president equivalent to a taxable dividend. The case was reversed *sub nom.* Casale v. Commissioner, 247 F.2d 440 (2d Cir. 1957), and in reversing, the Court of Appeals stressed the facts that the taxpayer got no immediate benefit from the policy and that the policy was a corporate asset subject to prior claims of corporate creditors in case of insolvency.

Henry E. Prunier, 28 T.C. 19 (1957), involved a corporation which paid premiums on policies of insurance on the lives of two of its principal stockholders. Each insured was named beneficiary in the policy on the other's life. In some of the policies, the named beneficiary had the exclusive right to change the beneficiary. Under an agreement entered into by the two stockholders, the proceeds of the policies on the life of each insured were to be used by the corporation to purchase the other's stock. The court held that the insurance premiums paid by the corporation on the policies issued on the life of each insured were includible in his taxable income. The case was reversed by the Court of Appeals, 248 F.2d 818 (1st Cir. 1957), and in reversing, the court held that the true beneficial owner of the policies under applicable Massachusetts law was the corporation and therefore the payment of the premiums by the corporation did not result in income to the stockholders.

In Sanders v. Fox, 149 F. Supp. 942 (D. Utah, 1957), the stockholders of the corporation entered into an agreement with the corporation by which the corporation paid premiums on insurance on the lives of the stockholders. The premiums were to be paid out of current earnings or surplus, and if there were none, the agreement would end and the policy would become ordinary assets of the corporation. The proceeds of the insurance were to be paid to the beneficiaries of the stockholders, as designated by them, if these beneficiaries would sell to the corporation the stock held by the insured at a price determined in accordance with an agreement. The minimum price for the stock, however, was set at the amount of the insurance proceeds. The court held that the premium payments made by the corporation were dividends to the stockholders. The total premiums allocated to the stockholders were prorated according to their holdings. Findings of fact and conclusions of law

The cost of redemption of stock by a corporation would be prohibitive in most cases if the redemption is deemed the equivalent of a dividend.[49] A redemption will not be deemed the equivalent of a dividend if it includes all the stock of the corporation owned by the shareholder.[50] But in determining whether all of the stock owned by the shareholder is redeemed, it must be kept in mind that the so-called attribution rules will attribute to certain shareholders stock actually owned by someone else.[51]

Insulation against dividend treatment is afforded if the redemption is under Section 303 of the 1954 Code.[52] This section is available to cover the redemption only if the following tests are met:

---

appear in 57-1 U.S.T.C. ¶9661 (D. Utah, 1957). The case was reversed in 253 F.2d 885 (10th Cir. 1958).

In William T. Pettit, Sr., CCH T.C. Mem. 1960-130, the taxpayer owned most of the stock in a corporation and the court held that he received compensation from the corporation in the amount of the payment on insurance premiums made by the corporation where the policy was on the life of the taxpayer and the proceeds were payable to his wife or his estate. No reference was made to who owned the policy.

[49] See 1954 I.R.C. §302.

In Erickson v. United States, 185 F. Supp. 938 (S.D. Ill. 1960), the redemption of stock by a corporation was deemed essentially equivalent to a dividend to the taxpayer. The taxpayer had bought all the stock of a deceased stockholder by borrowing the money, because the corporation was not then in a position to redeem the stock. Then, when the corporation was able to redeem, he transferred the stock to the creditor in payment of the loan and the stock was redeemed from the creditor. The court treated the transaction as though the stock had been sold by the taxpayer to the corporation and the proceeds used to pay off his debt. See, however, 189 F. Supp. 521, where the court entered judgment for the taxpayer.

[50] See 1954 I.R.C. §302(b)(3).

[51] See 1954 I.R.C. §318. In regard to the use of the revocable inter vivos trust to avoid attribution to the decedent's estate of stock owned by a beneficiary of the estate, see the discussion at page 133 supra.

See also the following rulings which deal with the income tax consequences of the redemption of stock by a corporation: Rev. Rul. 54-230, 1954-1 C.B. 114; Rev. Rul. 54-458, 1954-2 C.B. 167; Rev. Rul. 55-462, 1955-2 C.B. 221; Rev. Rul. 55-515, 1955-2 C.B. 222; Rev. Rul. 55-547, 1955-2 C.B. 571; Rev. Rul. 55-745, 1955-2 C.B. 223. On the question of stock being attributed to someone other than the owner under §318, see Rev. Rul. 56-103, 1956-1 C.B. 159.

Section 318(a)(3) provides that where a person has an option to acquire stock, such stock shall be considered as owned by that person. Consequently, if a person from whom stock is redeemed is, at the time of the redemption, given an option to purchase the "redeemed" stock, in whole or in part, the stock subject to the option will be considered to be owned by the person from whom the stock is redeemed, in determining, for the purpose of the substantially disproportionate test of §302(b)(2)(C), the shareholder's stock ownership after the redemption.

Revenue Ruling 59-233, 1959-2 C.B. 106, holds that the redemption of stock owned by a trust cannot qualify as a redemption to be treated as a termination of an interest under §302(b)(3), regardless of whether the trust has timely filed the agreement specified in §303(c)(2)(A)(iii).

[52] Quoted infra page 1338.

1. The stock redeemed is included in a decedent owner's gross estate.[53]
2. The distribution of corporate property must be made to a shareholder.
3. The distribution must be made after the decedent owner's death.
4. The distribution must be made within a stated period of time which will not end sooner than three years after the estate tax return is filed.
5. The value of all of the stock of the redeeming corporation which is included in determining the value of the decedent's gross estate must be either more than 35 percent of the value of the gross estate or more than 50 percent of the value of the taxable estate.[54]

From the nature of these tests, it should be apparent that the executor, by the way in which he administers a decedent's estate, may determine whether or not a redemption will be under Section 303. For example, the 35 percent or the 50 percent test might be met if the alternate valuation date is selected[55] but not if the gross estate is valued as of the date of the decedent's death. The size of the taxable estate will be smaller and hence the 50 percent test will be easier to meet if expenses of administration which can be taken either as income tax deductions or estate tax deductions are taken as the latter.[56]

The maximum amount distributable by the corporation which

---

[53] Section 303(c) of the 1954 Code, quoted infra page 1339, however, permits the redemption to be under §303 if "new stock" is involved and the basis of the "new stock" is determined by reference to the basis of the "old stock" and the "old stock" was included in the decedent's gross estate.

Section 115(g)(3) of the 1939 Code (1954 I.R.C. §303) required that the value of the stock be included in determining the value of the gross estate of the decedent. In Rev. Rul. 55-91, 1955-1 C.B. 364, it was determined that when stock of the A Corporation was included in the gross estate of the decedent and, after the decedent's death, stock of the B Corporation was received in a nontaxable reorganization which changed only the name of the A Corporation, the state of incorporation, and the number of shares of the corporate entity, the stock of the B Corporation was in substance the same as the stock in the A Corporation, and thus the test that the value of the stock must be included in determining the value of the gross estate of the decedent was met as to the B Corporation's stock which was redeemed to pay estate and inheritance taxes.

[54] If the decedent is survived by a wife, so that the marital deduction is available, it will be much easier to meet the test of 50 percent of the taxable estate.

A special rule is spelled out in 1954 I.R.C. §303(b)(2)(B), quoted infra page 1339, which makes it possible in very limited situations to treat the stock of two or more corporations as the stock of a single corporation in meeting the 35 percent and 50 percent tests.

[55] See 1954 I.R.C. §2032, quoted infra page 1395.

[56] See 1954 I.R.C. §642(g), quoted infra page 1363.

will be insulated from dividend treatment under Section 303 is the aggregate of the death taxes (including interest on such taxes) imposed because of the decedent owner's death and of the funeral and administration expenses allowable as deductions to his estate under Section 2053. It is what finally turns out to be the aggregate that controls.[57]

The stock does not have to be redeemed from the estate of the deceased owner in order for the redemption to be under Section 303. It can be redeemed from anyone as long as he received the stock from the decedent. He may have received it as an heir, legatee, donee, surviving joint tenant, appointee, taker in default of appointment or as trustee of a trust created by the decedent.[58]

There is no requirement that the money obtained by the person from whom the stock is redeemed be used to pay the death costs of the decedent. Several different redemptions may take place during the allowable period. Where different classes of stock are involved, the redemption may apply only to one class.

The extent to which Section 303 is useful in particular cases will depend, of course, on various factors. The number of shares redeemable without getting outside the protection of Section 303 may be difficult to determine without knowing exactly the value which will be placed on the stock.[59] Until a definite value has been placed on the stock, there may be uncertainty as to whether the 35 percent or the 50 percent test has been met. If the value of the

[57] In Rev. Rul. 55-592, 1955-2 C.B. 573, it was held that the amount received by the executors of an estate with respect to stock of a corporation which was sold to its wholly owned subsidiary did not constitute a dividend under 1939 I.R.C. §115(g)(3), to the extent that the amount received did not exceed the amount of estate and inheritance taxes, including interest, where the value of the stock in the corporation for estate tax purposes comprised more than 35 percent of the value of the gross estate.

Revenue Ruling 56-449, 1956-2 C.B. 180, holds that the language of §303(a)(2) with reference to funeral and administration expenses includes such expenses incurred and paid by an estate prior to August 16, 1954 (the effective date of 1954 I.R.C. §2053) provided that such expenses would otherwise be allowable as deductions to the estate under §2053. It is not material for this purpose whether allowable administrative expenses have been deducted by the estate on its income tax returns under the provisions of 1939 I.R.C. §162(e) or 1954 I.R.C. §642(g), or whether funeral and administration expenses are allowable on its estate tax return under the provisions of 1939 I.R.C. §812(b) or 1954 I.R.C. §2053.

[58] See Reg. §1.303-2(f), which brings out that §303 is not applicable where the stock is redeemed from a stockholder who has acquired it by gift or purchase from any person to whom the stock has passed from the decedent. Nor is the section applicable where stock is redeemed from a stockholder who has acquired it from the executor in satisfaction of a pecuniary bequest.

[59] The executor might protect himself by initially borrowing the money from the corporation so that he can repay any amount which exceeds the allowable amount under §303.

stock appreciates after the date it is valued for estate tax purposes and prior to the date it is redeemed, the person from whom it is redeemed will have realized a taxable gain. If a redemption deprives the estate and its beneficiaries of control of the corporation, it may be unwise to proceed under Section 303.[60] The future credit of the corporation might be impaired by the redemption to such an extent that the corporation should not redeem the stock.

The next hurdle to clear in the redemption of its stock by a corporation is to make certain that the redemption will not be a dividend to the other shareholders.[61]

---

[60] It might be possible to reorganize the corporation after the decedent's death so that the redemption could be made of nonvoting common. Such a redemption would not affect control.

[61] In Thomas F. Doran, 15 CCH T.C. Mem. 629 (1956), a corporation purchased insurance on the lives of its stockholders who were active in its management and operation. The proceeds received on the death of an insured stockholder were to be used to purchase his stock for the benefit of the surviving insured stockholders. A trust was established and the proceeds of the policies were made payable to the trustees, who were required to buy the stock of a deceased insured stockholder and to distribute it to the surviving insured stockholders. The court ruled that the trustees were agents of the corporation in receiving the proceeds of the policy and that the stockholders who received the purchased stock received income when the stock was purchased for their benefit. See also Golden v. Commissioner, 113 F.2d 590 (3d Cir. 1940). The Tax Court decision in the Doran case was reversed in 246 F.2d 934 (9th Cir. 1957). In reversing the Tax Court, the Court of Appeals held that there was no distribution of dividends by the corporation and that the stockholders were entitled to treat the proceeds of the insurance policy as exempt income. The Golden case was distinguished on the ground that in that case the corporation initially owned the policies and assigned them, whereas in the Doran case the corporation never owned or assigned any interest in the policies to the trustees and, therefore, could not have retained any incidents of ownership.

Joseph R. Holsey, 28 T.C. 962 (1957), dealt with a case where a person who owned 50 percent of the outstanding stock of a corporation was given an option to purchase the remaining stock held by another, and he assigned his option to the corporation. The corporation exercised the option, the consequence of which was to make the person who originally obtained the option the sole stockholder. The earned surplus of the corporation on the date the option was exercised was in excess of the option price. The corporation was an automobile sales agency. It was allegedly against the policy of the manufacturer of the cars sold to have divided ownership in a sales agency, and for this reason the option was exercised. The court held that the net effect of the transaction was the distribution of a dividend to the sole remaining stockholder. The case was reversed *sub nom.* Holsey v. Commissioner, 258 F.2d 865 (3d Cir. 1958), the court holding that the enhancement in value of the stockholder's stock was not equivalent to a dividend, as he had received no distribution and he would realize no income until a distribution was made to him by the corporation or he sold his stock. In T.I.R. 109, dated October 30, 1958, 58 CCH Fed. Tax Rep. ¶6780, the Internal Revenue Service announced that it will follow the Third Circuit's view in the Holsey case. Revenue Ruling 58-614, 1958-2 C.B. 920, incorporates T.I.R. 109. Revenue Ruling 59-286, 1959-2 C.B. 103, holds that a redemption of one shareholder's share at the

If the corporation takes out insurance on the life of the owner of the stock in order to have sufficient funds to redeem the stock on the owner's death, the augmentation of corporate assets by the collection of insurance proceeds will have an effect on the value of the stock.[62] If the corporation has contracted to buy the stock at a price fixed in the contract, consideration should be given to whether the contract price should reflect the increase in corporate worth as a result of the payment to the corporation of life insurance proceeds.

---

fair market value does not constitute a dividend to a remaining shareholder, even though the remaining shareholder was obligated to buy such stock or vote his stock for dissolution and liquidation of the corporation and he was relieved of that obligation by the redemption; if the stock is purchased by the remaining shareholder and paid for by the corporation, the payment will be considered a constructive dividend to the remaining shareholder. The Holsey case is referred to with approval in Niederkrome v. Commissioner, 266 F.2d 238 (9th Cir. 1958), *cert. denied,* 359 U.S. 945 (1959). For further proceedings with respect to Niederkrome, see Fred C. Niederkrome, CCH T.C. Mem. 1960-89. See also Wall v. United States, 164 F.2d 462 (4th Cir. 1947); Zipp v. Commissioner, 259 F.2d 119 (6th Cir. 1958), *cert. denied,* 359 U.S. 934 (1959). In John A. Decker, 32 T.C. 326 (1959), the surviving stockholders were obligated to purchase the stock of a deceased stockholder and the stock so purchased was immediately resold to the corporation for the purchase price (in one instance the money used to make the purchase from the estate of the deceased stockholder was borrowed from the corporation), and the court held the stockholders did not receive a taxable dividend. The case was affirmed sub nom. Commissioner v. Decker, 61-1 U.S.T.C. ¶9172 (6th Cir. 1960). It should be considered against the background of the statement in Rev. Rul. 58-614 that if stock is in reality purchased by a remaining stockholder and paid for by the corporation, then the payment will be considered a dividend to the stockholder who made the purchase, regardless of the form of the transaction. Compare with the Decker case, Schalk Chemical Co., 32 T.C. 879 (1959).

In Ducros v. Commissioner, 272 F.2d 49 (6th Cir. 1959), the court held that a stockholder could exclude insurance proceeds she received directly from an insurance company on the death of the president of a corporation, even though the corporation owned the policy and paid the premiums thereon. The insurance proceeds were not a dividend, since they were not paid to the stockholder by the corporation.

[62] In L. B. Foster Co. v. United States, 57-1 U.S.T.C. ¶9301 (W.D. Pa. 1956), a corporation acquired life insurance on its stockholders, and under an agreement with the stockholders, the life insurance proceeds were to be used to acquire the stock of a deceased stockholder. Under a settlement agreement, it was determined that the life insurance proceeds would be added to the assets of the corporation in valuing the stock of a deceased stockholder for estate tax purposes. The corporation paid its pro rata share of estate taxes imposed on the estate of the deceased stockholder, and the court held that such payment could not be considered as an ordinary business expense by the corporation. The case was affirmed in 248 F.2d 389 (3d Cir. 1957).

Land and Simmons Co. v. Arconti, — Md. —, 162 A.2d 478 (1960), interprets a buy-and-sell agreement between a corporation and its shareholders, where insurance was taken out by the corporation to fund the agreement, as requiring the inclusion in the corporate assets of the insurance proceeds in determining the total book value of the corporation on which the purchase price was based.

The purchase of its own stock by a corporation may offer an opportunity to pass on appreciated property without the corporation realizing a taxable gain. In such a situation, the distributee will acquire a new basis, so that the appreciation in value will go untaxed.[63]

The redemption of stock by a corporation may result in an increase in the value of the stock owned by other shareholders. These shareholders, however, obtain no improvement in the basis of their stock as a result of the purchase by the corporation.

Consideration should be given to the extent to which qualified profit-sharing trusts can be used as the medium for purchasing shares of deceased stockholders. Assume a profit-sharing trust which otherwise qualifies under Section 401(a). What is the effect on such qualification if the trust is authorized to enter into agreements with a shareholder to purchase his stock on his death, and the agreement is to be funded by insurance taken out by the trust on the life of the shareholders? Where the shareholder is also an employee, will the plan be discriminatory or not exclusively for the benefit of employees if the agreement is made by the trust? If either is so, will the objection be removed if the shareholder must waive his rights under the plan in order for the trust to make the agreement with him? Will the objection still be removed by such a required waiver if the purchase price of the stock in the agreement is based on a formula that takes into account a percentage of corporate earnings?

Surviving shareholders as purchasers. If the surviving shareholders are to be the purchasers of the stock of a deceased owner, they will probably have to depend on insurance proceeds to provide the funds to make the purchase. When the surviving shareholders are fairly numerous, the number of insurance policies which will be required, in working out a complete crisscross arrangement will be considerable.[64] The stock acquired from the decedent's estate by the surviving shareholders will have a new basis in their hands.

Complete outsider as purchaser. A sale of the stock of a deceased owner to a complete outsider may be damaging to the other shareholders. Whether such a sale is at all feasible, without being made at a substantial sacrifice, will depend on the nature of the

[63] See 1954 I.R.C. §311, quoted infra page 1339.

[64] If there are five shareholders, namely A, B, C, D and E, and the survivors are to purchase the stock of the first to die and the purchase agreement is to be funded with life insurance, A will take out policies on the lives of B, C, D and E; B will take out policies on the lives of A, C, D and E; and so on. When the crisscross arrangement is completed, twenty life insurance policies will be involved.

business and whether the stock to be offered for sale represents a controlling interest in the corporation.

Agreements of sale. Set out below are two examples of an agreement for the sale of stock in a closely held corporation.

EXAMPLE 5. *Business Purchase Agreement Between Two Stockholders*

AGREEMENT made this .... day of ...., 19........, between John Grant who resides at 123 First Avenue, New York, N.Y., (hereafter referred to as Grant) and William Ray who resides at 456 Main Street, New York, N.Y. (hereafter referred to as Ray).

Grant and Ray are the sole stockholders of the "Reliable Grocery Stores Company," a New York corporation (hereafter referred to as the Company), each owning 50% of the stock of the Company.

The purpose of this Agreement is twofold: (a) to provide for the purchase by the survivor of the decedent's stock interest in the Company; and (b) to provide the funds necessary to carry out such purchase.

It is, therefore, mutually agreed by Grant and Ray as follows:

1. Neither Grant nor Ray shall, during their joint lives, assign, encumber or dispose of any portion of their respective stock interests in the "Reliable Grocery Stores Company," by sale or otherwise, without the written consent of the other stockholder.

[*Alternative 1:* If either stockholder should desire to dispose of any of his stock in the Company during his lifetime, he shall first offer in writing to sell his stock to the other stockholder. The offer shall be based on a price determined in accordance with the provisions of paragraph 5 hereof. If the offer is not accepted by the other stockholder within sixty days of receipt thereof, the stockholder desiring to sell shall have the right to sell his stock to any other person, but shall not sell such stock without giving the remaining stockholder the right to purchase such stock at a price and on the terms offered by such other person.]

2. Grant is insured under Policy No. ...., issued by New York Life Insurance Company, for $..........................., and Ray is the applicant, owner and beneficiary thereof.

Ray is insured under Policy No. ...., issued by New York Life Insurance Company, for $..........................., and Grant is the applicant, owner and beneficiary thereof.

During the lifetime of both stockholders and the continuance in force of this Agreement, each stockholder agrees to pay premiums on the policy owned by him as they become due, and to give proof of payment to the insured within twenty days after the due date of each premium. If any premium is not paid within twenty days after its due date, the insured shall have the right to pay such premium and be reimbursed therefor by the owner. All dividends shall be applied on account of premiums or loan interest, if any. The New York Life Insurance Company is hereby authorized and directed to give the insured, upon his written request, any information with respect to the status of the policy on his life. The owner of each policy agrees to notify the insured in writing of any exercise of any of the rights, privileges or benefits of the policy on the life of the insured.

[*Alternative provision in lieu of the immediately preceding paragraph:* During the lifetime of both stockholders and the continuance in force of this Agreement, each stockholder shall pay the premiums on the policy owned by him, as they become due, but neither stockholder shall exercise any of the rights, privileges and benefits accruing under the policies owned by him, except as otherwise provided herein, or assign, encumber, borrow against or otherwise dispose of the policies without the consent of the other stockholder. All dividends shall be applied on account of premiums or loan interest, if any. The New York Life Insurance Company is hereby authorized and directed to give the insured, upon his written request, any information with respect to the status of the policy on his life. Each owner shall give proof of payment to the insured within twenty days after the due date of each premium. If any premium is not paid within twenty days after its due date, the insured shall have the right to pay such premium and be reimbursed therefor by the other stockholder.]

3. This Agreement shall extend to and shall include all additional policies issued pursuant hereto; such additional policies to be listed in Schedule A, attached hereto.

4. Upon the death of either stockholder, the survivor shall purchase and the estate of the decedent shall sell the stock interest now owned or hereafter acquired by the stockholder who is the first to die. The purchase price of such interest shall be computed in accordance with the provisions of paragraph 5 of this Agreement.

5. The outstanding capital stock of the Company consists of 1,000 shares which are owned and held by the stockholders as follows:

Grant .... 500 shares
Ray .... 500 shares

Unless and until changed as hereinafter provided, the value of each share of stock of the Company held by each stockholder shall be $100. Said value includes an amount mutually agreed upon as representing the good will of the Company as a going concern. Within thirty days following the end of each fiscal year, Grant and Ray shall redetermine the value of each share of stock. Such value shall be endorsed on Schedule B, attached hereto. If Grant and Ray fail to redetermine said value for a particular year, the last previously stipulated value shall control, except that if no valuation is agreed upon for two consecutive years, the value of a decedent's stock shall be agreed upon by the representative of the deceased stockholder and the surviving stockholder. If they do not come to an agreement within thirty days after the death of a stockholder, the value of the decedent's stock shall be determined by arbitration as follows: The surviving stockholder and the representative of the estate shall each name one arbitrator. If the two arbitrators cannot agree upon the value of the stock of the deceased stockholder, they shall appoint a third arbitrator and the decision of the majority shall be binding on both parties. In no event, however, shall the value of a decedent's stock be less than the proceeds of life insurance purchased on his life by the surviving stockholder under this Agreement. The term "proceeds" is understood to include any amount paid by reason of death by accidental means under any agreement for additional indemnity, as well as the face amount, plus any dividends and any additional amounts payable to the beneficiary.

[*Alternative 5:* The value of the outstanding capital stock of the Company for the purpose of this Agreement shall be its book value as of the end of the month in which the death of the stockholder occurs. The determination of the book value shall be made by the accountant then servicing the Company and such determination shall be conclusive on all parties. If there is no such accountant available or if he fails to make a determination of such valuation, then the value shall be determined by any other accountant who may be selected by mutual agreement of the surviving stockholder and the legal representative of the deceased stockholder. In no event, however, shall the value of a decedent's stock be less than the proceeds of life insurance purchased on his life by the surviving stockholder under this Agreement. The term "proceeds" is understood to include any amount paid by reason of death by accidental means under any agreement for additional indemnity, as well as the face amount, plus any dividends and any additional amounts payable to the beneficiary.]

6. Each stockholder agrees that the proceeds of the policies sub-

ject to this Agreement shall be applied toward the purchase price set forth above. If the purchase price so set forth exceeds the proceeds of the life insurance, the balance of the purchase price shall be paid in twenty-four consecutive monthly payments beginning three months after the date of the decedent's death. The unpaid balance of the purchase price shall be evidenced by a series of negotiable promissory notes made by the surviving stockholder to the order of the estate of the deceased with interest at 5% per annum. Said notes shall provide for the acceleration of the due date of all unpaid notes in the series on default in the payment of any note or interest thereon and shall give the maker thereof the option of prepayment in whole or in part at any time. All of the stock of the decedent covered by this Agreement shall be pledged with the decedent's estate as security for the payment of said notes, provided, however, that the surviving stockholder shall be entitled to exercise all rights of ownership in such stock prior to default in the payment of any note or interest thereon.

7. Upon the death of either stockholder, the surviving stockholder shall have the right to purchase from the estate of the decedent any or all of the policies insuring the life of the surviving stockholder for a price equal to the interpolated terminal reserve as of the date of death of the stockholder, less any existing indebtedness charged against the policy, plus the proportionate part of the gross premium last paid before the date of death which covers the period extending beyond that date. This right may be exercised at any time within sixty days after the qualification of the legal representative of the deceased stockholder by the payment of such price, and if the right is not so exercised within the time allowed, it shall lapse.

8. The surviving stockholder and the executor or administrator of the deceased stockholder shall make, execute and deliver any documents necessary to carry out this Agreement.

[*Alternative 8:* Upon the payment of the purchase price to the estate of the deceased stockholder, in cash or in cash and notes, the estate shall execute and deliver to the surviving stockholder all documents reasonably required to evidence such purchase; and all rights of the estate in the Company and in its business and assets, shall thereafter belong to the surviving stockholder.]

9. This Agreement may be altered, amended or terminated by a writing signed by both stockholders. In the event of a termination of this Agreement before the death of either stockholder, each shall be entitled to an assignment to him of any policy on his life upon payment by him to the owner within sixty days of such termination of a sum equal to the interpolated terminal reserve as

of the date of transfer, less any existing indebtedness charged against the policy, plus the proportionate part of the gross premium last paid before the date of transfer which covers the period extending beyond that date.

10. This Agreement shall terminate on the occurrence of any of the following events:

    (a) Bankruptcy, receivership or dissolution of the Company.

    (b) Death of both stockholders simultaneously or within a period of thirty days.

    (c) At the option of either stockholder, if the other stockholder fails to pay the premiums within the grace period of the policy or policies of life insurance owned by him for the purposes of this Agreement, or assigns, surrenders or borrows against said policy or policies, changes the beneficiary or makes the proceeds payable other than in a lump sum without the written consent of the insured stockholder.

11. This Agreement shall be binding upon the stockholders, their heirs, legal representatives, successors and assigns.

12. Notwithstanding the provisions of this Agreement, New York Life Insurance Company is hereby authorized to act in accordance with the terms of any policies issued by it as if this Agreement did not exist and payment, or other performance of its contract obligations, by said Company in accordance with the terms of any such policy shall completely discharge said Company from all claims, suits and demands of all persons whatsoever.

13. This Agreement shall be subject to and governed by the law of the State of ...., irrespective of the fact that one or more of the parties now is or may become a resident of a different state.

IN WITNESS WHEREOF, the parties hereto have executed this Agreement this .... day of ...., 19........

SCHEDULE A

Schedule of Additional Life Insurance Policies

Name of Company	*Policy No.*	*Amount*	*Signature of Owners*

SCHEDULE B

Endorsements

Date of execution ....

Pursuant to Paragraph 5 of this Agreement, the parties do hereby determine that the value of each share of stock as of this date is $...................., and the value of each stockholder's interest is:

Grant . . . . $
Ray . . . . $

PROBLEMS

15.13. Suppose that a business purchase agreement is executed by three stockholders instead of two, and that after the death of one, the surviving stockholders, in funding a new business purchase agreement between them, desire to use the existing insurance on their lives owned by the estate of the deceased stockholder. In view of the transferee for value rule, what will be the income tax consequences if each surviving stockholder purchases the existing policies on the life of the other? See Section 101(a)(2)(B) of the 1954 Code, quoted infra page 1329.

15.14. Will the amount paid by the surviving stockholder for the stock of the deceased stockholder, pursuant to the provisions of Paragraph 5 of the business purchase agreement in Example 5, be conclusive as to the value of the stock owned by the deceased stockholder for federal estate tax purposes?

EXAMPLE 6. *Stock Retirement Agreement*

AGREEMENT made this .... day of ...., 19........, between John Baird, William McCarthy and Thomas Ruhl (hereafter referred to as the Stockholders), and the "Reliable Grocery Stores Company, Inc.," a New York Corporation (hereafter referred to as the Company).

Baird, McCarthy and Ruhl are the sole Stockholders of the Company each owning one-third of the stock thereof.

The parties to this Agreement believe that it is to their mutual best interests to provide for continuity in the management and policies of the Company. Accordingly, the purpose of this Agreement is twofold: (a) to provide for the purchase by the Company of the decedent's stock interest therein; and (b) to provide the funds necessary to carry out such purchase.

It is, therefore, mutually agreed as follows:

1. No stockholder shall, during his lifetime, assign, encumber or dispose of any portion of his respective stock interest in the Company, by sale or otherwise, without the written consent of a duly authorized officer of the Company.

[*Alternative 1:* In the event that any stockholder should desire to dispose of any of his stock in the Company during his lifetime, he shall first offer to sell all of his stock for sale to the Company. The offer shall be based on a price determined in accordance with the provisions of Paragraph 5 hereof. Any share not purchased by the Company within sixty days after receipt of such offer shall be offered to the other stockholders, each of whom shall have the right to purchase such portion of the stock offered for sale as the number of shares owned by him at such date shall bear to the total number of shares owned by all the other stockholders, excluding the selling stockholder, provided, however, that if any stockholder does not purchase his full proportionate share of the stock, the unaccepted stock may be purchased by the other stockholders. If the offer is not accepted by the Company or other stockholders within sixty days of receipt thereof, the stockholder desiring to sell his stock shall have the right to sell it to any other person but shall not sell it without giving the Company and the remaining stockholders the right to purchase such stock at a price and on the terms offered by such other person.]

2. Baird is insured under Policy No. ...., issued by New York Life Insurance Company, for $........................, and the Company is the applicant, owner and beneficiary thereof.

McCarthy is insured under Policy No. ...., issued by New York Life Insurance Company, for $........................, and the Company is the applicant, owner and beneficiary thereof.

Ruhl is insured under Policy No. ...., issued by New York Life Insurance Company, for $........................, and the Company is the applicant, owner and beneficiary thereof.

The Company shall be the sole owner of the policies issued to it.

3. This Agreement shall extend to and shall include all additional policies issued pursuant hereto; such additional policies to be listed in Schedule A, attached hereto.

4. Upon the death of any stockholder, the Company shall purchase, and the estate of the decedent shall sell, all of the dece-

dent's stock in the Company now owned or hereafter acquired. The purchase price of such stock shall be computed in accordance with the provisions of Paragraph 5 of this Agreement.

5. The outstanding capital stock of the Company consists of 1500 shares which are owned and held by the stockholders as follows:

Baird	500 shares
McCarthy	500 shares
Ruhl	500 shares

Unless and until changed as hereinafter provided, the value of each share of stock of the Company held by each stockholder shall be $100. Said value includes an amount mutually agreed upon as representing the good will of the Company as a going concern. Within thirty days following the end of each fiscal year, the Company and the stockholders shall agree upon the value of each share of stock and such value shall be endorsed on Schedule B, attached hereto. If the parties fail to redetermine a value for a particular year, the last previously stipulated value shall control except that if the parties have not so stipulated a value within the twelve months following the end of a fiscal year, the value of each share of stock owned by a deceased stockholder shall be agreed upon by his representative and the Company. If they are unable to come to an agreement within thirty days after such death, the value of each share of stock of the deceased stockholder shall be determined by arbitration as follows: The Company and the representative of the estate shall each name one arbitrator. If the two arbitrators cannot agree upon the value of each share of stock of the deceased stockholder, they shall appoint a third arbitrator and the decision of the majority shall be binding on all parties.

[*Alternative 5:*   The value of the outstanding capital stock of the Company for the purpose of this Agreement shall be its book value as of the end of the month in which the death of a stockholder occurs. Book values shall include the cash surrender values of all life insurance policies taken out by the Company pursuant to this Agreement and the proceeds of the policies insuring the life of a deceased stockholder in excess of their cash surrender values. The determination of the book value shall be made by the accountant then servicing the Company and such determination shall be conclusive on all parties. If there is no such accountant available or if he fails to make a determination of such valuation, then the value shall be determined by any other accountant who may be selected by mutual agreement of the Company and the representative of the deceased stockholder. The term "proceeds" is understood to include any amount paid by reason of death by accidental means under any agreement for additional indemnity, as well as the face amount, plus any dividends and any additional amounts payable to the beneficiary.]

6. The Company agrees that the proceeds of the policies subject to this Agreement shall be applied towards the purchase price set forth above. If the purchase price so set forth exceeds the proceeds of the life insurance, the balance of the purchase price shall be paid in twenty-four consecutive monthly payments beginning three months after the date of the decedent's death. The unpaid balance of the purchase price shall be evidenced by a series of negotiable promissory notes made by the Company to the order of the estate of the deceased with interest at 5% per annum. Said notes shall provide for the acceleration of the due date of all unpaid notes in the series on default in the payment of any note or interest thereon and shall provide that upon default of any payment of interest or principal, all notes shall become due and payable immediately and shall give the maker thereof the option of prepayment in whole or in part at any time.

7. The Stockholders agree to endorse the certificate or certificates of stock held by them as follows:

"The sale or transfer of this certificate is subject to an agreement between the Reliable Grocery Stores Company, Inc., and Baird, McCarthy and Ruhl, dated .... day of ...., 19......... A copy of this agreement is on file in the office of the Secretary of said Company."

8. A duly authorized Officer of the Company and the executor or administrator of the deceased stockholder shall make, execute and deliver any documents necessary to carry out this Agreement. This Agreement shall be binding upon the Company and the Stockholders, their heirs, legal representatives, successors and assigns.

9. This Agreement may be altered, amended or terminated by a writing signed by the Company and all Stockholders.

10. This Agreement shall terminate on the occurrence of any of the following events:

    (a) Bankruptcy, receivership or dissolution of the Company.
    (b) Death of two or more stockholders simultaneously or within a period of thirty days.

11. Notwithstanding the provisions of this Agreement, New York Life Insurance Company is hereby authorized to act in accordance with the terms of any policies issued by it as if this Agreement did not exist, and payment or other performance of its contract obligations by said Company in accordance with the terms

of any such policy shall completely discharge said Company from all claims, suits and demands of all persons whatsoever.

12. This Agreement shall be subject to and governed by the law of the State of ...., irrespective of the fact that one or more of the parties now is or may become a resident of a different state.

IN WITNESS WHEREOF, the parties hereto have executed this Agreement this .... day of ...., 19..........

SCHEDULE A

Schedule of Additional Life Insurance Policies

Name of Company   *Policy No.*   *Amount*   *Signature of Owners*

SCHEDULE B

Endorsements

Date of execution ....

Pursuant to Paragraph 5 of this Agreement, the parties do hereby determine that the value of each share of stock as of this date is $........................, and the value of each stockholder's interest is:

Baird .... $

McCarthy .... $

Ruhl .... $

PROBLEMS

15.15. Suppose that after the death of one of three stockholders who have a stock retirement agreement like the one in Example 6, the two surviving stockholders desire to enter into a business purchase agreement like the one in Example 5, supra page

986. In funding the new agreement, they plan to use the existing life insurance on their lives which is owned by the corporation. In view of the transferee for value rule, what will be the income tax consequences, if each surviving stockholder purchases the existing policies on the life of the other? See Section 101(a)(2)(B) of the 1954 Code, quoted infra page 1329.

15.16. Suppose that a stock retirement agreement like the one in Example 6 is entered into but one of the stockholders is not insurable. If this stockholder sells to the corporation existing policies of insurance on his life, what will be the income tax consequences when the corporation collects the proceeds on his death? See Section 101(a)(2)(B), quoted infra page 1329.

15.17. Is the corporation entitled to an income tax deduction for the premiums it pays for the life insurance procured under a stock retirement agreement like the one in Example 6? See Section 264 of the 1954 Code, quoted infra page 1337.

15.18. Is there any possibility that stock retirement agreements like the one in Example 6 may be invalid because the corporation lacks power under the laws of the state of its incorporation to purchase its own stock? See Note, 59 Yale L.J. 1177 (1950).

b. *Postponement of Payment of Estate Taxes*

A sale of the decedent's stock in order to meet death costs may be unnecessary if the payment of the major item in such death costs, the federal estate tax, can be postponed. Such postponement may make it possible to raise the necessary funds in other ways and thereby keep the stock in the decedent's family.

A general section of the 1954 Code applicable to all estates permits the Secretary or his delegate to extend the time for payment of the estate tax for a period not in excess of ten years from the date prescribed for the payment of the tax, if he finds that payment on the prescribed date would result in undue hardship to the estate.[65] Interest at the rate of 4 percent is charged on the unpaid tax bill.[66] Estate plans should not, of course, be formulated in reliance on this general section of the Code because there can be no certainty that the extension will be granted.

Another section of the 1954 Code gives an extension of the time for the payment of the estate tax as a matter of right if certain prescribed tests are met.[67] This section may be available not

---

[65] See 1954 I.R.C. §6161(a)(2).

[66] See 1954 I.R.C. §6601(b). The general rule is that interest at the rate of 6 percent is charged on unpaid taxes. See §6601(a).

[67] See 1954 I.R.C. §6166, quoted infra page 1428. See also Reg. §§20.6166-1 to 20.6166-4.

only when the estate consists of stock in a closely held corporation but also when the estate has a sole proprietorship business or a partnership interest.[68]   Where a closely held business is in the decedent's gross estate, its value must exceed 35 percent of the value of the gross estate or 50 percent of the value of the taxable estate if the section is to apply.[69]   The decedent must be a citizen or resident of the United States.   When all requirements for the operation of the section are met, the executor must make his election to postpone the payment of the estate tax in accordance with its terms not later than the time for the filing of the estate tax return, including extensions thereof.   If an election is appropriately made, the maximum amount of the tax that can be postponed is an amount which bears the same ratio to the estate tax (reduced by the credits against the tax) as the value of the interest in the closely held business in the estate bears to the value of the gross estate.   The payment of the postponed amount can be made in two or more (but not exceeding ten) installments, the first of which must be made on or before the date for the payment of the estate tax and annually thereafter.   Interest at the rate of 4 percent is charged on the unpaid balance.

It will be the unusual case where estate planning should proceed on the basis that the best course of action is to rely on the section of the Code which gives the executor the right to elect to postpone the payment of the estate tax.   The tests which must be met if the section is to be available may be met now, but not at the time the decedent dies.   There may be uncertainty as to whether the 35 percent or the 50 percent test will be met, because of uncertainty as to the valuation of the closely held business. Even if it is clear that the section will be available, the long delay in closing the decedent's estate which will be involved if the maximum postponement is elected may be undesirable.[70]

It is possible to have stock of a corporation redeemed under

---

[68] Section 6166(c) of the 1954 Code, quoted infra page 1429, defines a closely held business (this type of business must be involved in order for the section to apply) as any sole proprietorship, a partnership where 20 percent or more of the total capital interest is included in the decedent's gross estate or where the partnership has ten or less partners, and any corporation where 20 percent or more in value of the voting stock is included in determining the decedent's gross estate or where the corporation has ten or less shareholders.

[69] Two or more closely held businesses may be regarded as a single business in applying the 35 percent or the 50 percent test under certain conditions. See 1954 I.R.C. §6166(d), quoted infra page 1429.

[70] If the estate is not closed, it continues to be available as a separate tax entity for federal income tax purposes.   It should be noted, however, that after the fourth taxable year an amount equal to the undistributed income of the estate for any taxable year must be paid on the unpaid tax bill.   See 1954 I.R.C. §6166(h)(2), quoted infra page 1431.

Section 303 of the 1954 Code and not to use the money to pay the estate tax but to postpone payment under Section 6166. If this is to be done, however, care must be taken to avoid the rules in the latter section which deal with the acceleration of the payment of the postponed tax which may result from the withdrawal of funds from the closely held business.[71]

c. *Disposition of Stock Not Sold*

To the extent that the closely held stock is not earmarked for sale on the owner's death, it is an asset to be integrated in the overall estate plan. It is, however, an asset that must be given special consideration in the process of integration because it may present problems not typical of other assets.

The corporation involved may be one that has elected under Subchapter S to have the taxable income of the corporation taxed directly to the shareholders.[72] Inter vivos transfers of such stock to a trust will destroy the election. Likewise, the bequest of the stock to a testamentary trust will eliminate the election from and after the time the executor in fact transfers the stock to the testamentary trustee.[73]

---

[71] See 1954 I.R.C. §6166(h)(1)(B), quoted infra page 1430. This provision rules out the significance of the withdrawal of business funds to make a distribution in redemption of stock under §303 only if an amount equal to the amount withdrawn from the corporation does not equal or exceed 50 percent of the value of the business. In other words, the withdrawal of funds from the business will not accelerate the payment of the unpaid tax if the aggregate withdrawals do not equal or exceed the 50 percent.

[72] See 1954 I.R.C. §§1371-1377, which were added by §64 of the Technical Amendments Act of 1958.

[73] If the corporation involved meets the test of a small business corporation as defined in §1371 and stock in the corporation is placed in trust, no election can be made, or can stand (as long as some of the stock is held by a trustee), to have the taxable income of the corporation taxed directly to the shareholders as provided in §§1372-1377. Section 1.1371-1(d)(2)(e) of the Regulations provides in part as follows: "The word 'trust' as used in this paragraph includes all trusts subject to the provisions of subchapter D, F, H or J (including subpart E thereof) of chapter 1 of the Code and voting trusts. Thus, even though the grantor is treated as the owner of all or any part of a trust, the corporation in which such trust is a shareholder does not meet the qualifications of a small business corporation." Revenue Ruling 59-235, 1959-2 C.B. 192, holds that a corporation having a partnership as a shareholder cannot qualify as a small business corporation within the meaning of §1371.

Technical Information Release, dated November 26, 1958, 58 CCH Fed. Tax Rep. ¶6818, considers various questions in regard to the election by a corporation under §1372 to have the corporate income taxed directly to the shareholders. For example, stock which is the community property of husband and wife is deemed owned by two shareholders for the purpose of determining whether there are more than ten shareholders, and both must consent to the election; stock held by two persons as tenants in common or as joint tenants or as tenants by the entirety is owned by two shareholders, and both

The nature of the asset involved requires careful thought as to where control of the stock should be placed. If it is dispersed among several members of the family, friction may develop in the operation of the business.[74] Control over the stock can be kept centralized by placing the stock in a trust. The corporation can be recapitalized with voting and nonvoting stock, and the voting stock can be placed where it would be in the best interest of the business enterprise.[75]

---

must consent to the election; stock which is to go into a testamentary trust is not held by a trust prior to the transfer to the trust by the executor, and thus an election could be made by the executor and the election would terminate when he transfers the stock to the trust; and stock transferred to a minor under the Uniform Gifts to Minors Act or the Gifts of Securities to Minors Act (see page 244 supra) is considered owned by an individual and not by a trust. In 1959, however, §1371(c) was added by §2(a) of Pub. L. 86-376, 73 Stat. 699, which provides that stock that is community property of a husband and wife and stock held by them as joint tenants, as tenants by the entirety, or as tenants in common, will be treated as though owned by one shareholder for purposes of determining whether a corporation meets the ten-or-less shareholders requirement. The addition is not retroactive. Revenue Ruling 59-187, 1959-1 C.B. 224, points out that §554 of the 1954 Code (relating to the constructive ownership of stock) has no applicability in determining the number of shareholders of a corporation under §1371.

An election by a corporation under §1372 to have the corporate income taxed directly to the shareholders will not cause the income to be so taxed for state income tax purposes. See Mass. Income Tax Ruling No. 22, Nov. 6, 1958, CCH Mass. State Tax Rep. ¶15-054 A, 10.

Where an unincorporated business enterprise elects to be taxed as a corporation under 1954 I.R.C. §1361, §1361(d) provides that a partner in such a business or the proprietor thereof shall not be considered an employee for the purposes of 1954 I.R.C. §401(a) (relating to employees' pension trusts, etc.). However, if an election is made under §1372 by a small business corporation to have the taxable income of the corporation taxed directly to the shareholders, no change is made in the status of the employees for the purposes of §401(a). Revenue Ruling 59-221, 1959-1 C.B. 225, holds that when an election is made under §1372, the shareholders do not receive self-employment income on which a self-employment tax is payable.

[74] Under some circumstances it may be desirable for the stockholder in his will to give some member of the family an option to buy his stock. In D. Winne Cadby, 24 T.C. 899 (1955), the taxpayer was bequeathed an option to purchase the testator's stock for a stipulated amount. This amount was less than the worth of the stock. The taxpayer sold the option and the question presented concerned the basis of the option for purposes of determining a gain or loss. The court held that the option obtained a new basis in the estate of the testator and that was its value. The value was determined to be the difference between the worth of the stock and the price at which the taxpayer was entitled to buy it.

[75] Before adopting the course of action outlined, a careful study should be made of 1954 I.R.C. §§305, 306. In connection with §306 stock, examine Rev. Rul. 55-746, 1955-2 C.B. 224.

In Rev. Rul. 56-223, 1956-1 C.B. 162, it was determined that even though the preferred stock qualified as §306 stock under §306(c), its disposition was not in pursuance of a plan having as one of its principal purposes the avoidance of federal income tax and thus was not subject to taxation at ordinary income rates. In accordance with a plan of recapitalization, new preferred

If inter vivos gifts of the stock are appropriate, it must be kept in mind that the gift tax cost may not be precisely determinable because of uncertainty as to the valuation of the stock.[76]

---

and common stock was issued in exchange for outstanding common stock. Prior to the reorganization an employee's trust created by the corporation had entered into an agreement with certain retiring employees to purchase their stock in the corporation over a six-year period. The sale of the new preferred stock by these employees pursuant to the agreement resulted in a capital gain or loss as the case might be. Since they sold to the trust both their preferred and common stock it was in no sense a preferred stock bailout.

Revenue Ruling 56-116, 1956-1 C.B. 164, holds that the provisions of §306(a)(1) are not applicable to the proceeds of the disposition of preferred stock issued in connection with a merger unless such a disposition is in anticipation after the issuance of the stock. Revenue Ruling 56-116 reached its result on the basis of the exception in §306(b)(4). Revenue Ruling 57-212, 1957-1 C.B. 114, considered whether the exception provided by §306(b)(4), which otherwise would be applicable on the basis of Rev. Rul. 56-116, was rendered inapplicable by operation of certain sinking fund provisions. It was held that the described sinking fund provisions did not have that effect.

Revenue Ruling 57-328, 1957-2 C.B. 229, holds that where an owner of common stock of a corporation receives a stock dividend payable in preferred stock and transfers the preferred stock to a charity, such a transfer or the subsequent sale of the stock by the charity involves no realization of income to the donor within the meaning of §306(a).

Revenue Ruling 60-1, I.R.B. 1960-1, 14, deals with a case where two corporations merged and shares of new preferred stock of the surviving corporation were issued to holders of preferred stock of one of the merging corporations. In holding that the shares of the new preferred stock did not constitute "306 stock," the ruling stresses the following factors: The old and new preferred stock related to a publicly held corporation; the new preferred was not largely owned by management; there was no single dominant group in the survivor corporation; only persons who owned 17.6 percent of the common after the merger also owned preferred, and all of them together owned only 24 percent of the preferred; and the net preferred was issued solely to owners of the old preferred and to meet the needs of the corporation, not the convenience of the shareholders.

See also Note, Control of Closely Held Family Corporations Through Charitable Foundations, 42 A.B.A.J. 278 (1956). A charitable foundation can be established and the nonvoting stock transferred to it and the voting stock kept in the family. In this way the death taxes may be reduced to the point where they can be paid without a sale of the closely held stock.

[76] On the valuation of stock for gift tax purposes, see Note on Effect of an Agreement of Sale on the Valuation of Stock for Estate Tax Purposes, supra page 942.

In Marjorie M. Merritt, 29 T.C. 149 (1957), the various members of a family who owned all the stock in a corporation entered into an agreement reserving to each a life interest in the stock which he owned, with provision for the disposition of the property on the death of each to his descendants, and if he had no descendants, to his brothers and sisters. Each reserved the right to receive all dividends in money, whether paid out of earnings or capital. The court held that such an agreement did not result in a completed gift by each member of the family because each had a power to divest the remaindermen of their interests by virtue of the reservation of their right to receive distributions of capital.

Under what circumstances will a transfer of property by a corporation to an

Furthermore, if, after the gift is made, the donor will have control of the corporation and, through this control, be able to influence the flow of dividends to the donee, will this produce any undesirable income or estate tax results? [77]

A closely held corporation will frequently have a very bad dividend-paying history because of the desirability from a tax standpoint of taking out the profit in salaries and using what is not so taken out to expand the business. If the stock in such a corporation is placed in a power of appointment marital deduction trust which is intended to qualify either for the gift tax marital deduction or the estate tax marital deduction, care must be taken to make certain that the non-income-producing nature of the asset placed in the trust will not prevent the trust from qualifying for the marital deduction.[78]

Whenever the stock in a closely held corporation is placed in the hands of a fiduciary, a detailed administrative plan should be worked out so that the fiduciary will not be handicapped in making the decisions that are required of the owner of such stock.

4. A FARM [79]

The disposal of a farm is considered at this point because it may present many of the problems discussed with respect to the closely

---

individual be deemed a gift to the individual from the stockholders of the corporation? Under what circumstances will a transfer by an individual to a corporation be deemed a gift to the stockholders of the corporation? Section 25.2511-1(h)(1) of the Regulations provides as follows: "A transfer of property by a corporation to B is a gift to B from the stockholders of the corporation. If B himself is a stockholder, the transfer is a gift to him from the other stockholders but only to the extent it exceeds B's own interest in such amount as a shareholder. A transfer of property by B to a corporation generally represents gifts by B to the other individual shareholders of the corporation to the extent of their proportionate interests in the corporation. However, there may be an exception to this rule, such as a transfer made by an individual to a charitable, public, political or similar organization which may constitute a gift to the organization as a single entity, depending upon the facts and circumstances in the particular case."

In White v. United States, 59-1 U.S.T.C. ¶11862 (E.D. Ark. 1959), a father who was president of a corporation in which his son was sole stockholder withdrew corporate funds in excess of his salary and gave an interest-bearing note to the corporation for the excess. A judgment on the note was obtained by the corporation but had not been paid. The arrangement was found to be a loan by the corporation and not a gift from the son to his father, and thus the son was allowed a refund on the gift taxes he had paid.

[77] In connection with this question, consider Reg. §20.2055-2(b), quoted infra page 1529.

[78] See Reg. §20.2056(b)-5(f)(4) and (5), quoted in text supra page 842.

[79] See generally, Logan, Estate Planning: The Special Problems of the Farmer in Dispositions by Will, 32 Rocky Mt. L. Rev. 329 (1960); Fleming

held business. The farm may be solely owned (like the sole proprietorship business), or it may be operated by a partnership, or it may be the principal asset of a corporation and the stock of the corporation will be the asset in the client's estate (closely held corporation).[80] In addition, the farm must be considered separately from other assets because it has its own peculiar problems.

If the farm is the major asset in a person's estate, careful thought must be given as to where liquid funds will come from to pay death costs. Farms located in certain areas are readily saleable assets and the sale of the farm by the executor to the highest bidder may in some cases be the best course of action to adopt. If a sale is desirable, it may be appropriate to provide for it in advance through a properly financed buy-and-sell agreement.[81] If the farm

---

et al., Estate Planning and Tax Planning for the Farmer and the Businessman, 45 Ill. B.J. 449 (1957).

[80] In Illinois there has developed what is known as the Illinois land trust. Under this arrangement the trustee holds the full title to the real estate, but the complete management of the property and the power to direct the trustee with respect to the title are in the beneficiaries. The reasons for using such a land trust, and a description of how it is established, are found in Garrett, Illinois Land Trusts, 36 Trust Bull. No. 4, p. 6 (1956).

[81] See the discussion in regard to sale of a closely held business at page 977 supra. If a buy-and-sell agreement is to be entered into, the price to be paid should reflect the worth of growing crops, harvested crops, farm equipment, livestock, etc., if these items are to pass with a sale of the farm.

Revenue Ruling 58-162, 1958-1 C.B. 234, holds that where a farmer using the cash receipts and disbursement method of accounting sells wheat under a bona fide arm's-length contract calling for payment in the taxable year following the year in which the wheat was delivered to the purchaser, in applying 1954 I.R.C. §451, the proceeds are includible in his gross income for the taxable year in which the payment is received. But compare Frank Cowden, Sr., 32 T.C. 853 (1959), where the court held that a cash-basis lessor was taxable, in the year a mineral lease was executed, on that portion of the consideration which represented a fixed bonus or advance royalty and which the lessee was then willing and able to pay, even though in deference to the lessor's wishes the parties agreed that payments were to be made in subsequent years.

Revenue Ruling 59-8, 1959-1 C.B. 202, considers the operation of 1954 I.R.C. §1033 when hail destroys a standing crop of wheat and the farmer uses the insurance money to purchase another standing crop of wheat. In such a case, a gain is recognized only to the extent that the amount realized from the insurance exceeds the cost of replacing the standing crop.

Section 1231(b)(4) of the 1954 Code points out that an unharvested crop on land used in trade or business and held for more than six months is considered as property used in a trade or business if the crop and land are sold at the same time to the same person. Prior to the enactment of the 1954 Code the law was different. See Wilson & Toomer Fertilizer Co. v. Fahs, 59-2 U.S.T.C. ¶9663 (S.D. Fla. 1959). Bidart Bros. v. United States, 262 F.2d 607 (9th Cir. 1959), cert. denied, 359 U.S. 1003 (1959), held that the sale of unharvested crops sold in one transaction to the same party who bought the taxpayer's lease is not a case where the crops and land are sold together, because a leasehold is not land for this purpose, so that the profit on such sale is ordinary income.

Section 1231(b)(3) points out that livestock held for twelve months or more

will present a difficult job of valuation, the buy-and-sell agreement may serve to fix the value for estate tax purposes.[82]

A sale of the farm may be avoided by borrowing the necessary funds to meet death costs and securing the loan by a mortgage on the farm. If this is contemplated, the executor should be specifically authorized to proceed in this manner.

The requirements of Section 6166 of the 1954 Code[83] may be met and the payment of the federal estate tax can be postponed.[84] If the farm is operated by a corporation, Section 303 of the 1954 Code[85] may be available.[86]

In most instances, the desire of the owner of the farm will be to arrange for its disposition in such a manner that it will continue to be an income-producing factor in the family picture. The order of beneficial enjoyment of the farm income will normally

---

for draft, breeding or dairy purposes is property used in a trade or business. United States v. Cook, 270 F.2d 725 (8th Cir. 1959), held that the livestock did not have to be sold alive when, as here, the mink involved could not commercially be sold alive.

See also Sales of Crop After Death of Farmer, 1956 CCH Fed. Tax Rep. ¶10929.

[82] In Frances M. Cullers, 14 CCH T.C. Mem. 925 (1955), the court considered the following factors in determining the valuation of farm land for gift tax purposes: the description of the farm and its condition, the appraisers' and witnesses' opinions as to value, the possibility of a tax assessment against the farm for construction of a bridge, and the price bid for an adjoining farm. The case was reversed in 237 F.2d 611 (8th Cir. 1956). In reversing, the court held that the taxpayer's valuation, which was based on an independent appraisal by a farm loan secretary, an agricultural college graduate, a farm owner and operator, and a person who was a farm owner, businessman and land trader, should be upheld because the qualifications of these appraisers had not been seriously challenged. For a discussion of the factors which are relevant in valuing a farm for estate tax purposes, see Estate of Hiram S. Brown, 15 CCH T.C. Mem. 1238 (1956).

See also Note on the Effect of an Agreement of Sale on the Valuation of Stock for Estate Tax Purposes at page 942 supra.

Section 2032 of the 1954 Code, dealing with the alternate valuation date for estate tax purposes, is applied in Revenue Ruling 58-436, 1958-2 C.B. 366, which is concerned with property fed to cattle during the alternate valuation period. Property on hand at the date of the decedent's death and the cattle were sold during such a period for a price in excess of their worth on the date of the decedent's death. The ruling holds that the property fed to the cattle must be valued on the date or dates it was fed to them and that the appreciation in value of the cattle during the alternate valuation period should be included in determining the value of the cattle. Furthermore, the value, as of the alternate valuation date, of feed on hand at the date of the decedent's death and the cost of labor, feed and supplies purchased after that date and prior to the alternate valuation date, and used in caring for the cattle prior to their sale are deductible under §2053(a)(2).

[83] Quoted infra page 1429.

[84] See the discussion of the postponement at the payment of the federal estate tax under §6166 at page 996 supra.

[85] Quoted infra page 1338.

[86] See the discussion of §303 at page 980 supra.

be the owner's wife first and then his children and their families.

The factors which will be influential in determining whether to give the wife a restricted or unrestricted interest in the farm and whether to make the gift to her in trust or in the form of a non-trust gift will be basically the same as when any other asset is involved. The same can be said with respect to the interests which should be passed on to the children and their families. The corporate trustees in farming communities are becoming more and more equipped to operate farms as a trust asset.[87] At the same time, it should be kept in mind that the farm is a type of asset that lends itself readily to the use of legal successive interests.[88]

If the farm is placed in trust or if legal successive interests are created therein, probably the most important consideration is the charter of administration that is given to the trustee or the holder of the legal present interest. The foresight and imagination that goes into preparation of this charter may determine the extent to which the asset is a benefit or a burden to the family. In this connection, it should be kept in mind that in the years to come the most effective uses which can be made of the land may be quite different from the present uses and that the subsurface rights may develop to be more important from an income-producing standpoint than the surface rights.[89]

[87] See Davis, Trust Service for Farmers, 32 Trust Bull. No. 3, p. 13 (1952); Robinson, Farm Management as a Trust Service, 32 id. No. 3, p. 42 (1952); Robinson, Handling Farms in Trust in the Mid-West, 35 id. No. 9, p. 3 (1956); Bury, Ranch Management as a Trust Service in the Southwest, 36 id. No. 4, p. 13 (1956); Savage, Farm and Ranch Operations in Trust, 37 id. No. 3, p. 27 (1957); Trowbridge, Farm Property Problems in the Pacific Northwest, 37 id. No. 2, p. 32 (1957).

Revenue Ruling 58-191, 1958-1 C.B. 149, points out that income received by a beneficiary of a trust which is derived from farming operations carried on by the trust cannot be used by the beneficiary for the purpose of computing the amount of his deductions for soil or water conservation expenditures in regard to his own farm within the purview of 1954 I.R.C. §175. However, on the termination of the trust, if the trust has deductions, including expenditures for soil or water conservation, in excess of gross income for the year of termination, then the excess (to the extent deductible by the trust) is allowable under §642(h)(2).

[88] Legal future interests are discussed supra page 597.

[89] In McLean and Draper, Handling Farms in Trust in the Southeast, 35 Trust Bull. No. 10, pp. 20, 23 (1956), the following trust provision is suggested when a farm is placed in trust:

"To continue and carry on any farming operation in which I may be financially interested at the time of my death and operate any other farm which may be acquired by the trust and, in so doing, by way of illustration and not limitation of its powers, to operate the farm with hired labor, tenants or share croppers; to lease or rent the farm for cash or for a share of the crops; to purchase or otherwise acquire farm machinery and equipment and livestock; to construct, repair, and improve farm buildings of all sorts needed, in its judgment, for the operation of the farm; to make or obtain loans or advances at the prevailing rate or rates of interest for farm purposes such as for

If the farm is placed in trust and the trust is intended to qualify for the marital deduction as a power of appointment trust, the requirement that the wife must be entitled to all the income and that it must be paid to her at least as often as annually should be kept in mind.[90] Will this requirement be met if the trustee can hold up the liquidation of harvested crops or can pick the time to sell various animals raised on the farm for sale? If the estate is large enough to have both a marital trust and a nonmarital trust, it may be advisable to place the farm in the nonmarital trust in order to give more flexibility to the fiduciary in the disbursement of income.

The dispositive provision which passes the farm to anyone should comprehensively describe what will go along with it. Specific reference in this regard should be made to tangible personal property regularly used in the operation of the farm, to unharvested crops, to harvested crops stored on the farm, to any assignable contracts which relate to the farm, to the livestock, etc.

If the farm is to go to one member of the family, with other members of the family receiving other property in the estate in place of an interest in the farm, or if the farm is divided up and each member of the family is allocated a specific portion, consideration should be given to withholding from such a plan the disposition of the subsurface rights. Such rights could become so valuable in the future as to make the plan of disposition a very unfair one for the family. The withheld subsurface rights (minerals, oil, gas, etc.) could be separately disposed of in a manner that would assure their equal division among all members of the family.

Inter vivos gifts may play an important part in the over-all estate plan where a farm and its fruits are the major assets in the estate. Undivided interests in the farm may be given annually

---

production, harvesting, or marketing, or for the construction, repair, or improvement of farm buildings, or for the purchase of farm machinery or equipment or livestock; to employ approved soil conservation practices in order to conserve, improve and maintain the fertility and productivity of the soil; to protect, manage and improve the timber and forest on the farm and sell the timber and forest products when it is to the best interest of my estate; to ditch and drain damp or wet fields and areas of the farm when and where needed; to engage in livestock production, if it is deemed advisable, and to construct such fences and buildings and plant such pastures and crops as may be necessary to carry on such a livestock program; and, in general, to employ the methods of carrying on the farming operations that are in common use by other landowners in the community in which the farm is located."

It may be highly desirable to allow the owner of a legal present interest to do practically everything that it would be appropriate for a trustee to do.

[90] Power of appointment marital deduction trusts are considered *supra* page 839.

to keep within the annual gift tax exclusion for present interests.[91] If inter vivos gifts of crops are made, will any amount be includible in the gross income of the donor for federal income tax purposes? [92] Where a gift of crops is made to a charity, will the entire value of the gift be deductible for income tax purposes if that value plus the value of other charitable gifts for the year does not exceed 20 percent of the donor's adjusted gross income? [93]

[91] The annual gift tax exclusion is discussed supra page 236.

[92] The answer to this question is found in Rev. Rul. 55-531, 1955-2 C.B. 520. See also Branscomb, Gifts and Other Dispositions of Crops, 46 A.B.A.J. 95 (1960).

[93] For the answer to this question, see Reg. §1.170-1(c), quoted infra page 1485.

CHAPTER XVI

Multiple State Death Taxation

If state death taxes can be and are imposed by several different states on the same items of property in a decedent's estate, the estate shrinkage due to taxes may be substantially increased. Whether additional shrinkage occurs will depend on whether the state death taxes imposed exceed the credit allowed against the federal estate taxes for state death taxes.[1] It is a part of the job of estate planning to prevent, in so far as feasible under the circumstances, the possibility of multiple state death taxation.

1. REAL ESTATE AND TANGIBLE PERSONAL PROPERTY

FRICK v. PENNSYLVANIA
268 U.S. 473, 45 Sup. Ct. 603, 69 L. Ed. 1058 (1925)

MR. JUSTICE VAN DEVANTER delivered the opinion of the Court.

These four cases involve the constitutional validity of particular features of a statute of Pennsylvania imposing a tax on the transfer of property by will or intestate laws. Act No. 258, Pa. Laws 1919, 521.

Henry C. Frick, domiciled in Pennsylvania, died testate December 2, 1919, leaving a large estate. By his will he disposed of the entire estate — giving about 53 per cent. for charitable and public purposes and passing the rest to or for the use of individual

---

[1] See 1954 I.R.C. §2011, quoted infra page 1388.

In order for the credit under §2011 to be available, evidence must be submitted to the District Director that the state death taxes have been paid. See Reg. §20.2011-1(c)(2).

Section 2011(c) provides in part as follows: "Refund based on the credit may (despite the provisions of sections 6511 and 6512) be made if claim therefor is filed within the period above described. Any such refund shall be made without interest." In Morgan Guaranty Trust Company of New York v. United States, 277 F.2d 466 (Ct. Cl. 1960), it was held that the estate was entitled to interest on the entire refund, since no part of the refund could be based upon the allowance of the credit for state taxes where the state taxes were paid prior to the filing of the estate tax return and no additional estate taxes were later paid.

See generally on the problems of this chapter Marsh, Multiple Death Taxation in the United States, 8 U.C.L.A.L. Rev. 69 (1961).

beneficiaries. Besides real and personal property in Pennsylvania, the estate included tangible personalty having an actual situs in New York, tangible personalty having a like situs in Massachusetts, and various stocks in corporations of States other than Pennsylvania. The greater part of the tangible personalty in New York,[2] having a value of $13,132,391.00, was given to a corporation of that State for the purposes of a public art gallery, and the other part,[3] having a value of $77,818.75, to decedent's widow. The tangible personalty in Massachusetts,[4] having a value of $325,534.25, was also given to the widow. The will was probated in Pennsylvania, and letters testamentary were granted there. It was also proved in New York and Massachusetts, and ancillary letters were granted in those States. Under the laws of the United States the executors were required to pay to it, and did pay, an estate tax of $6,338,898.68; and under the laws of Kansas, West Virginia and other States they were required to pay to such States, and did pay, large sums in taxes imposed as a prerequisite to effect transfer from a non-resident deceased of stocks in corporations of those States.[5]

The Pennsylvania statute provides that where a person domiciled in that State dies seized or possessed of property, real or personal, a tax shall be laid on the transfer of the property from him by will or intestate laws, whether the property be in that State or elsewhere; that the tax shall be 2 per cent. of the clear value of so much of the property as is transferred to or for the use of designated relatives of the decedent and 5 per cent. of the clear value of so much of it as is transferred to or for the use of others; and that the clear value shall be ascertained by taking the gross value of the estate and deducting therefrom the decedent's debts and the expenses of administration, but without making any deduction for taxes paid to the United States or to any other State.

In applying this statute to the Frick estate the taxing officers included the value of the tangible personalty in New York and Massachusetts in the clear value on which they computed the tax; and

---

[2] (*Court footnote*) This consisted of rare paintings, rugs, furniture, bronzes, porcelains and other art treasures known as "The Frick Collection" and housed in a building in New York City specially constructed for the purpose.

[3] (*Court footnote*) This consisted of furniture, household furnishings, automobiles, tools, etc., in Mr. Frick's New York house and garage.

[4] (*Court footnote*) This consisted of paintings, other objects of art, furniture, household furnishings, farming implements, etc., on Mr. Frick's estate at Prides Crossing.

[5] In regard to the jurisdiction of a state to tax the transfer of stock owned by a nonresident decedent in a corporation of the state, see Intangible Personal Property, infra page 1016. — ED.

in fixing that value refused to make any deduction on account of the estate tax paid to the United States or the stock-transfer taxes paid to other States. In proceedings which reached the Supreme Court of the State the action of the taxing officers and the resulting tax were upheld by that court, 277 Pa. 242. The matter was then brought here on writs of error under sec. 237 of the Judicial Code.

The plaintiffs in error are the executors and an interested legatee. They contended in the state court, and contend here, that in so far as the Pennsylvania statute attempts to tax the transfer of tangible personal property having an actual situs in States other than Pennsylvania it transcends the power of that State, and thereby contravenes the due process of law clause of the Fourteenth Amendment to the Constitution of the United States.

This precise question has not been presented to this Court before, but there are many decisions dealing with cognate questions which point the way to its solution. These decisions show, first, that the exaction by a State of a tax which it is without power to impose is a taking of property without due process of law in violation of the Fourteenth Amendment; secondly, that while a State may so shape its tax laws as to reach every object which is under its jurisdiction it cannot give them any extraterritorial operation; and, thirdly, that as respects tangible personal property having an actual situs in a particular State, the power to subject it to state taxation rests exclusively in that State, regardless of the domicil of the owner. [Citations omitted.]

In Union Refrigerator Transit Co. v. Kentucky [199 U.S. 194] the question presented was whether, consistently with the restriction imposed by the due process of law clause of the Fourteenth Amendment, the State of Kentucky could tax a corporation of that State upon its tangible personal property having an actual situs in other States. The question was much considered, prior cases were reviewed, and a negative answer was given. The grounds for the decision are reflected in the following excerpts from the opinion:

"It is also essential to the validity of a tax that the property shall be within the territorial jurisdiction of the taxing power. Not only is the operation of state laws limited to persons and property within the boundaries of the State, but property which is wholly and exclusively within the jurisdiction of another State, receives none of the protection for which the tax is supposed to be the compensation. This rule receives its most familiar illustration in the cases of land which, to be taxable, must be within the limits of the State. Indeed, we know of no case where a legislature has assumed to impose a tax upon land within the jurisdiction of another State, much less where such action has been defended by any court. It is said by this Court in the Foreign-held Bond case, 15 Wall. 300, 319, that no adjudication should be necessary to establish so obvious a proposition as that property lying beyond the jurisdiction of a State is not a subject upon which her taxing power can be legitimately exercised. The argument against the taxability of land within the jurisdiction of another State applies with equal cogency to tangible personal property beyond the jurisdiction. It is not only beyond the sovereignty of the taxing State, but does not and cannot receive protection under its laws. . . .

"The arguments in favor of the taxation of intangible property at the domicil of the owner have no application to tangible property. The fact that such property is visible, easily found and difficult to conceal, and the tax readily collectible, is so cogent an argument for its taxation at its situs, that of late there is a general consensus of opinion that it is taxable in the State where it is permanently located and employed and where it receives its entire protection, irrespective of the domicil of the owner. . . .

"The adoption of a general rule that tangible personal property in other States may be taxed at the domicil of the owner involves possibilities of an extremely serious character. Not only would it authorize the taxation of furniture and other property kept at country houses in other States or even in foreign countries, (and) of stocks of goods and merchandise kept at branch establishments when already taxed at the State of their situs, but of that enormous mass of personal property belonging to railways and other corporations which might be taxed in the State where they are incorporated, though their charters contemplated the construction and operation of roads wholly outside the State, and sometimes across the continent, and when in no other particular they are subject to its laws and entitled to its protection."

In United States v. Bennet, 232 U.S. 299, 306, where this Court had occasion to explain the restrictive operation of the due process of law clause of the Fourteenth Amendment, as applied to the taxation by one State of property in another, and to distinguish the operation of the like clause of the Fifth Amendment, as applied to the taxation by the United States of a vessel belonging to one of its citizens and located in foreign waters, it was said:

"The application to the States of the rule of due process relied upon comes from the fact that their spheres of activity are enforced and protected by the Constitution and therefore it is impossible for one State to reach out and tax property in another

without violating the Constitution, for where the power of the
one ends the authority of the other begins.   But this has no application to the Government of the United States so far as its admitted taxing power is concerned.   It is coextensive with the
limits of the United States; it knows no restriction except where
one is expressed in or arises from the Constitution and therefore
embraces all the attributes which appertain to sovereignty in the
fullest sense.   Indeed the existence of such a wide power is the essential resultant of the limitation restricting the States within
their allotted spheres . . ."

Other decisions show that the power to regulate the transmission, administration, and distribution of tangible personal property on the death of the owner rests with the State of its situs, and
that the laws of other States have no bearing save as that State
expressly or tacitly adopts them — their bearing then being attributable to such adoption and not to any force of their own.
[Citations omitted.]

The Pennsylvania statute is a tax law, not an escheat law.   This
is made plain by its terms and by the opinion of the state court.
The tax which it imposes is not a property tax but one laid on the
transfer of property on the death of the owner.   This distinction
is stressed by counsel for the State.   But to impose either tax the
State must have jurisdiction over the thing that is taxed, and to
impose either without such jurisdiction is mere extortion and in
contravention of due process of law.   Here the tax was imposed
on the transfer of tangible personalty having an actual situs in
other States — New York and Massachusetts.   This property, by
reason of its character and situs, was wholly under the jurisdiction
of those States and in no way under the jurisdiction of Pennsylvania.   True, its owner was domiciled in Pennsylvania, but this
neither brought it under the jurisdiction of that State nor subtracted anything from the jurisdiction of New York and Massachusetts.   In these respects the situation was the same as if the
property had been immovable realty.   The jurisdiction possessed
by the States of the situs was not partial but plenary, and included
power to regulate the transfer both inter vivos and on the death of
the owner, and power to tax both the property and the transfer.

Mr. Justice Story said in his work on Conflict of Laws, Sec. 550:
"A nation within whose territory any personal property is actually
situate has an entire dominion over it while therein, in point of
sovereignty and jurisdiction, as it has over immovable property
situate there.   It may regulate its transfer, and subject it to process and execution, and provide for and control the uses and disposition of it, to the same extent that it may exert its authority over

immovable property." And in Pullman's Car Company v. Pennsylvania, 141 U.S. 18, 22, where this Court held the actual situs of tangible personalty rather than the domicil of its owner to be the true test of jurisdiction and of power to tax, it was said: "No general principles of law are better settled, or more fundamental, than that the legislative power of every State extends to all property within its borders, and that only so far as the comity of that State allows can such property be affected by the law of any other State. The old rule expressed in the maxium mobilia sequuntur personam, by which personal property was regarded as subject to the law of the owner's domicil, grew up in the Middle Ages, when movable property consisted chiefly of gold and jewels, which could be easily carried by the owner from place to place, or secreted in spots known only to himself. In modern times, since the great increase in amount and variety of personal property, not immediately connected with the person of the owner, that rule has yielded more and more to the lex situs, the law of the place where the property is kept and used."

In support of the tax counsel for the State refer to statutes of New York and Massachusetts evidencing an election by those States to accept and give effect to the domiciliary law regulating the transfer of personal property of owners dying while domiciled in other States; and from this they contend that the transfer we are considering was brought under the jurisdiction of Pennsylvania and made taxable there. We think the contention is not sound. The statutes do not evidence a surrender or abandonment of jurisdiction, if that were admissible. On the contrary, they in themselves are an assertion of jurisdiction and an exercise of it. They declare what law shall apply and require the local courts to give effect to it. And it should be observed that here the property was administered in those courts and none of it was taken to the domiciliary State. Obviously the accepted domiciliary law could not in itself have any force or application outside that State. Only in virtue of its express or tacit adoption by the States of the situs could it have any force or application in them. Through its adoption by them it came to represent their will and this was the sole basis of its operation there. Burdick on American Constitution, Sec. 257. In keeping with this view New York and Massachusetts both provide for the taxation of transfer under the adopted domiciliary law; and they have imposed and collected such a tax on the transfer we are now considering.

Counsel for the State cite and rely on Blackstone v. Miller, 188 U.S. 189, and Bullen v. Wisconsin, 240 U.S. 625. Both cases related to intangible personalty, which has been regarded as on a different footing from tangible personalty. When they are read with this distinction in mind, and also in connection with other cases before cited, it is apparent that they do not support the tax in question.

We think it follows from what we have said that the transfer of the tangible personalty in New York and Massachusetts occurred under and in virtue of the jurisdiction and laws of those States and not under the jurisdiction and laws of Pennsylvania, and therefore that Pennsylvania was without power to tax it.

One ground on which the state court put its decision was that, in taxing the transfer of the property which the decedent owned in Pennsylvania, it was admissable to take as a basis for computing the tax the combined value of that property and the property in New York and Massachusetts. Of course, this was but the equivalent of saying that it was admissable to measure the tax by a standard which took no account of the distinction between what the State had power to tax and what it had no power to tax, and which necessarily operated to make the amount of the tax just what it would have been had the State's power included what was excluded by the Constitution. This ground, in our opinion, is not tenable. It would open the way for easily doing indirectly what is forbidden to be done directly, and would render important constitutional limitations of no avail. If Pennsylvania could tax according to such a standard other States could. It would mean, as applied to the Frick estate, that Pennsylvania, New York and Massachusetts could each impose a tax based on the value of the entire estate, although severally having jurisdiction of only parts of it. Without question each State had power to tax the transfer of so much of the estate as was under its jurisdiction, and also had some discretion in respect of the rate; but none could use that power and discretion in accomplishing an unconstitutional end, such as indirectly taxing the transfer of the part of the estate which was under the exclusive jurisdiction of others. [Citations omitted.]

The state court cited in support of its view Maxwell v. Bugbee, 250 U.S. 525, 539. The case is on the border line, as is evidenced by the dissent of four members of the Court. But it does not go so far as its citation by the state court suggests. The tax there in question was one imposed by New Jersey on the transfer of stock in a corporation of that State. The stock was part of the estate of a decedent who had resided elsewhere. The state statute, described according to its essence, provided for a tax graduated in rate according to the value of the entire estate, and required that where the estate was partly within and partly without the State the transfer of the part within should bear a proportionate part of what according to the graduated rate would be the tax on the whole. The only bearing which the property without the State had on the tax imposed in respect of the property within was that it affected the rate of the tax. Thus, if the entire estate had a value which put it within the class for which the rate was three per cent, that rate was to be applied to the value of the property within the State in computing the tax on its transfer, although its value separately taken would put it within the class for which the rate was two per cent. There was no attempt, as here, to compute the tax in respect of the part within the State on the value of the whole. The Court sustained the tax, but distinctly recognized that the State's power was subject to constitutional limitations, including the due process of law clause of the Fourteenth Amendment, and also that it would be a violation of that clause for a State to impose a tax on a thing within its jurisdiction "in such a way as to really amount to taxing that which is beyond its authority."

Another case cited by the state court is Plummer v. Coler, 178 U.S. 115, where it was held that a State, in taxing the transfer by will or descent of property within its jurisdiction, might lawfully measure the tax according to the value of the property, even though it included tax-exempt bonds of the United States; and this because the tax was not on the property but on the transfer. We think the case is not in point here. The objection to the present tax is that both the property and the transfer were within the jurisdiction of other States and without the jurisdiction of the taxing State.

For the reasons which have been stated it must be held that the Pennsylvania statute, in so far as it attempts to tax the transfer of tangible personalty having an actual situs in other States, contravenes the due process of law clause of the Fourteenth Amendment and is invalid. . . .[6]

In conclusion we hold, first, that the value of the tangible personalty in New York and Massachusetts should not have been included in determining the clear value on which the Pennsylvania tax was computed; . . .

Petitions for certiorari were presented in these cases, but as the cases are properly here on writs of error, the petitions will be denied.

Judgments reversed on writs of error.

Petitions for certiorari denied.[7]

[6] The portion of the opinion that deals with the other issues decided by the Court in this case is printed in the next section. — Ed.

[7] Comments on Frick v. Pennsylvania are found in 14 Geo. L.J. 396 (1926), 30 Ill. L. Rev. 492 (1926), 36 Yale L.J. 357 (1926). See also Bittker, The Taxation of Out-of-State Tangible Property, 56 Yale L.J. 640 (1947).

PROBLEMS

16.1. If a person dies domiciled in South Carolina, and in his will he directs his executor to sell his Pennsylvania real estate and he disposes of the proceeds of such a sale in his will, does South Carolina have jurisdiction to impose a death tax on the value of the real estate? Does Pennsylvania also have jurisdiction to impose a death tax on the value of the real estate? The answer to the first question was given in Land Title & Trust Co. v. South Carolina Tax Commission, 131 S.C. 192, 126 S.E. 189 (1925), where the South Carolina court held that South Carolina had jurisdiction to impose a death tax on the value of the Pennsylvania real estate. The court reached this result by applying the doctrine of equitable conversion as a result of the direction to sell the Pennsylvania real estate so that only cash and not real estate was disposed of by the will. The answer to the second question was given in Commonwealth v. Presbyterian Hospital, 287 Pa. 49, 134 Atl. 427 (1926), where the Pennsylvania court held that the real estate in Pennsylvania was also subject to the Pennsylvania death tax. See also In re Briebach's Estate, 132 Mont. 437, 318 P.2d 223 (1957).

Will the multiple state death taxation which was imposed on the Pennsylvania real estate stand up in the face of Frick v. Pennsylvania?

16.2. T is domiciled in Pennsylvania. He dies on a train traveling from Chicago, Illinois, to his home in Pennsylvania. At the time of his death, the train is in Indiana. When he dies, T, has valuable jewelry on his person. Does Pennsylvania have jurisdiction to impose a death tax on the jewelry? See Delaney v. Murchie, 177 F.2d 444 (1st Cir. 1949).

In Treichler v. Wisconsin, 338 U.S. 251, 70 Sup. Ct. 1, 94 L. Ed. 37 (1949), the Wisconsin emergency tax on inheritance was held to violate the due process clause of the Fourteenth Amendment so far as the tax was measured by tangible property outside of Wisconsin. In Rev. Rul. 56-230, 1956-1 C.B. 660, it was held, on the basis of Treichler v. Wisconsin, that where a state attempts to measure its additional estate tax by imposing a tax that will consume the entire 80 percent credit, and in so doing makes no distinction between different types of property includible in the decedent's gross estate, the total tax allowable as a credit may not exceed that portion of the available credit which is equal to the portion of the decedent's property with a taxable situs within the state.

In Dameron v. Brodhead, 345 U.S. 322 73 Sup. Ct. 721, 97 L. Ed. 322 (1953), a federal statute was held constitutional which stated, in substance, that personal property owned by a person who is absent from his domicile because of military orders shall not be deemed located in the place he resides, pursuant to such orders, for taxation purposes. — Ed.

16.3. T is domiciled in Pennsylvania. He is advised by his doctor that he will live only a few months. T owns tangible personal property of considerable value, and is informed by his attorney that the death tax imposed by Pennsylvania on his tangible personal property will exceed the credit allowed by Section 2011 of the 1954 Code. T moves all his tangible personal property to a warehouse in Nevada, which imposes no death taxes. T dies. Does Pennsylvania have jurisdiction to impose a death tax on the tangible personal property located in the warehouse in Nevada? See City Bank Farmers Trust Co. v. Schnader, 293 U.S. 112, 55 Sup. Ct. 29, 79 L. Ed. 228 (1934).

2. INTANGIBLE PERSONAL PROPERTY

When a person owns intangible personal property (for example, common stocks), it is conceivable that any one of the following states may claim that it has jurisdiction to impose a death tax on the value of such property:

1. The state in which such person is domiciled
2. The state of incorporation where common stock of a corporation is involved
3. The state in which the certificates of stock are located at the time of such person's death

The following cases deal with the jurisdiction of a state to impose a death tax on the value of intangible personal property.

FRICK v. PENNSYLVANIA
268 U.S. 473, 45 Sup. Ct. 603, 69 L. Ed. 1058 (1925)

MR. JUSTICE VAN DEVANTER delivered the opinion of the Court. . . . [For the portion of the opinion that is concerned with the jurisdiction to tax tangible personal property see page 1007 supra.]

The next question relates to the provision which requires that, in computing the value of the estate for the purpose of fixing the amount of the tax, stocks in corporations of other States shall be included at their full value without any deduction for transfer taxes paid to those States in respect of the same stocks.

The decedent owned many stocks in corporations of States, other than Pennsylvania, which subjected their transfer on death to a tax and prescribed means of enforcement which practically gave those States the status of lienors in possession.[8] As those

[8] *(Court footnote)* The nature of the tax and the provisions adopted for enforcing it are illustrated by c. 357, secs. 1, 2, 13, Laws Kansas 1915, p. 452; c. 33, secs. 1, 6, 7, Barnes' West Virginia Code, p. 586.

States had created the corporations issuing the stocks, they had power to impose the tax and to enforce it by such means, irrespective of the decedent's domicile and the actual situs of the stock certificates. Pennsylvania's jurisdiction over the stocks necessarily was subordinate to that power. Therefore to bring them into the adminstration in that State it was essential that the tax be paid. The executors paid it out of moneys forming part of the estate in Pennsylvania and the stocks were thereby brought into the administration there. We think it plain that such value as the stocks had in excess of the tax is all that could be regarded as within the range of Pennsylvania's taxing Power. Estate of Henry Miller, 184 Cal. 674, 683. So much of the value as was required to release the superior claim of the other States was quite beyond Pennsylvania's control. Thus the inclusion of the full value in the computation on which that State based its tax, without any deduction for the tax paid to the other States, was nothing short of applying that State's taxing power to what was not within its range. That the stocks, with their full value, were ultimately brought into the administration in that States does not help. They were brought in through the payment of the tax in the other States out of moneys of the estate in Pennsylvania. The moneys paid out just balanced the excess in stock value brought in. Yet in computating the tax in that State both were included.

We are of opinion that in so far as the statute requires that stocks in corporations of other States be included at their full value, without deducting the tax paid to those States, it exceeds the power of the State and thereby infringes the constitutional guaranty of due process of law.

The remaining question relates to the provision declaring that, in determining the value of the estate for the purpose of computing the tax, there shall be no deduction of the estate tax paid to the United States. The plaintiffs in error contend that this provision is invalid, first, as being inconsistent with the constitutional supremacy of the United States, and, secondly, as making the state tax in part a tax on the federal tax.

In support of the contention we are referred to several cases in which state courts have held the federal tax should be deducted in determining the value on which such a state tax is computed. But the cases plainly are not in point. In them the state courts were merely construing an earlier type of statute requiring that the state tax be computed on the clear or net value of the estate and containing no direction respecting the deduction of the federal tax. An earlier Pennsylvania statute of that type was so construed. Later statutes in the same States expressly forbidding any deduction of the federal tax have been construed according to their letter. This is true of the present Pennsylvania statute. The question here is not how the statute shall be construed but whether, as construed by the state court, it is open to the constitutional objections urged against it.

While the federal tax is called an estate tax and the state tax is called a transfer tax, both are imposed as excises on the transfer of property from a decedent and both take effect at the instant of transfer. Thus both are laid on the same subject, and neither has priority in time over the other. Subject to exceptions not material here, the power of taxation granted to the United States does not curtail or interfere with the taxing power of the several States. This power in the two governments is generally so far concurrent as to render it admissible for both, each under its own laws and for its own purposes, to tax the same subject at the same time. A few citations will make this plain. In Gibbons v. Ogden, 9 Wheat. 1, 199, Chief Justice Marshall, speaking for this Court, said: "Congress is authorized to lay and collect taxes etc., to pay the debts, and provide for the common defense and general welfare of the United States. This does not interfere with the power of the States to tax for the support of their own governments; nor is the exercise of this power by the States an exercise of any portion of the power that is granted to the United States. In imposing taxes for State purposes, they are not doing what Congress is empowered to do. Congress is not empowered to tax for those purposes which are within the exclusive province of the States. When, then, each government exercises the power of taxation, neither is exercising the power of the other." Mr Justice Story, in his Commentaries on the Constitution, sec. 1068, said: "The power of Congress, in laying taxes, is not necessarily or naturally inconsistent with that of the States. Each may lay a tax on the same property, without interfering with the action of the other." And in Knowlton v. Moore, 178 U.S. 41, 58-60, Mr. Justice White, speaking for this Court, said that "under our constitutional system both the national and state governments, moving in their respective orbits, have a common authority to tax many and diverse objects;" and he further pointed out that the transfer of property on death "is a usual subject of taxation" and one which falls within that common authority.

With this understanding of the power in virtue of which the two taxes are imposed, we are of opinion that neither the United States nor the State is under any constitutional obligation in determining the amount of its tax to make any deduction on account of the tax of the other. With both the matter of making such a deduction rests in legislative discretion. In their present statutes both direct that such a deduction be not made. It is not as if the tax of one, unless and until paid, presented an obstacle to the exertion of the power of the other. Here both had power to tax and both exercised it as of the same moment. Neither encroached on the sphere or power of the other. The estate out of which each required that its tax be paid is much more than ample for the payment of both taxes. No question of supremacy can arise in such a situation. Whether, if the estate were not sufficient to pay both taxes, that of the United States should be preferred (see Lane County v. Oregon, 7 Wall. 71, 77) need not be considered. That question is not involved here.

The objection that when no deduction is made on account of the federal tax the state tax becomes to that extent a tax on the federal tax and not a tax on the transfer is answered by what already has been said. But by way of repetition it may be observed that what the State is taxing is the transfer of particular property, not such property depleted by the federal tax. The two taxes were concurrently imposed and stand on the same plane, save as the United States possibly might have a preferred right of enforcement if the estate were insufficient to pay both.

In conclusion we hold . . . ; secondly, that in determining such clear value the stocks in corporations of other States should not have been included at their full value without deducting the transfer tax paid to such States in respect of those stocks; and thirdly, that there was no error in refusing to make any deduction from the clear value on account of the estate tax imposed by the United States.

Petitions for certiorari were presented in these cases, but as the cases are properly here on writs of error, the petitions will be denied.

Judgments reversed on writs of error.

Petitions for certiorari denied.

BLODGETT v. SILBERMAN

277 U.S. 1, 48 Sup. Ct. 410, 72 L. Ed. 749 (1928)

Review of a judgement of the Superior Court of Connecticut, levying a succession tax pursuant to the opinion and advice of the Supreme Court of Errors, 105 Conn. 192, on the transfer of property under the will of a resident of the State. The executors sued out a writ of error from this Court upon the ground that the taxing statute, as applied, violated the Fourteenth Amendment and the full faith and credit provision of the Constitution. The

Connecticut Tax Commission applied for a certiorari to so much of the judgment as denied to the State, because of the Fourteenth Amendment, the right to tax the transfer of certain securities of the United States and bank notes and coin.

MR. CHIEF JUSTICE TAFT delivered the opinion of the Court.

These two cases, which are really one, grow out of the operation of a transfer tax by the State of Connecticut. They are brought to this Court, one by certiorari, and one by writ of error. The questions presented are whether the tax on the transfer of certain parts of the large estate of Robert B. Hirsch was in violation of the due process clause of the Fourteenth Amendment to the Federal Constitution in that they were tangible property in New York and not in Connecticut. Hirsch died September 23, 1924, domiciled at Stamford, Connecticut, leaving a will with two codicils executed in accordance with the laws of both New York and Connecticut. The plaintiffs are the surviving executors of the will. Hirsch left real estate, chattels, cattle, horses and poultry in Connecticut, and also a debt due from a resident of Connecticut and a certificate of stock in a Connecticut corporation, as to all of which there is no dispute about the tax that was imposed. The great bulk of his estate, however, consisted of (1) a large interest, as general partner, appraised at $1,687,245.34, in the partnership of William Openhym & Sons, doing business in New York, and organize under the Limited Partnership Act of that State; (2) certificates of stock in New York, New Jersey and Canada corporations, appraised at $277,864.25; (3) bonds and Treasury certificates of indebtedness of the United States, appraised at $615,121.17; (4) a small savings bank account in New York; (5) a life insurance policy in the Mutual Life Insurance Company of New York payable to the estate; and (6) a small amount of bank bills and coin in a deposite box in New York. All the bonds and certificates of stock at the time of the decedent's death, and for a long time prior thereto, had been physically placed and kept in safe deposit boxes in New York City and were never in Connecticut. The partnership assets consisted of real estate in New York and also in Connecticut, merchandise, chattels, credits, and other personal property. The testator bequeathed the larger part of his estate to charitable and educational corporations organized under the laws of New York and existing in that State. The executors offered the will and codicils for probate in New York. They were admitted to probate in the Surrogate's Court in the County of New York, and thereafter the executors proceeded in the settlement of the estate in New York. They have paid from the funds of the estate legacies provided in the will and codicils amounting to $299,297.45. They have also paid the debts, the federal estate tax and the New York transfer or inheritance tax, which amounted to $19,166.04. The transfer report in that court exempted the legacies bequeathed to charitable and educational institutions in accord with New York law. The executors have paid to the trustees named in the will and codicils the amount therein mentioned for the benefit of certain persons named. The executors sold the stock standing in the name of the decedent and made transfer of the same to the purchaser, and the Mutual Life Insurance Company paid to the executors the proceeds of the policy. The National City Bank of New York paid to the executors the amount of a small deposit account therein to the credit of the decedent at the time of his death.

On January 8, 1925, the executors presented to the Court of Probate, for the Stamford district of Connecticut, an exemplified copy of the will and codicils from the record of the proceedings in the Surrogate's Court in New York, and on January 15, 1925, that Court received the will and codicils and accepted a bond for the executors and issued to them letters testamentary, made an order limiting the time for the presentation of claims, directed the filing of an inventory of all the property, including choses in action of the estate of the decedent, and appointed appraisers who made and filed the inventory of all the foregoing items of property belonging to the decedent at the time of his death.

On September 1, 1925, the executors filed in the Probate Court for the Stamford district, and with the tax commissoner for Connecticut, a statement under oath covering the property of the estate and the claimed deductions therefrom, all this for the purpose of determining the succession tax, if any, due the State of Connecticut. The tax commissioner thereafter filed a copy of his computation of the tax with the Probate Court, to which the executors made objection, but that court on December 4, 1925, made its order and decree approving the computation of $188,780.58, and directed the executors to pay this amount to the State Treasurer.

From this order the plaintiff executors took an appeal to the Superior Court of Fairfield County, and then by stipulation of the parties the case was reserved for the advice and direction of the Supreme Court of Errors as to what judgment, decree or decision should be made or rendered thereon by the Superior Court.

The chief questions considered by the Supreme Court of Errors were, first, whether the interest of the decedent in the partnership of Openhym & Sons was subject to a transfer tax in Connecticut, and second, whether the bonds of the United States and certificates of its indebtedness were to be deemed tangible property in New York and beyond the taxing jurisdiction of the State of Connecticut. There were other questions of taxable jurisdiction over other items of the estate, but we shall consider these two first.

The Supreme Court of Errors held, first, that the interest of the decedent in the partnership was a chose in action and intangible and the transfer thereof was subject to the tax imposed by the law of the decedent's domicil; second, that the bonds and certificates of the United States were tangible property having a situs in New York and were not within the taxable jurisdiction of Connecticut, but were to be regarded as in the same class of tangibles as the paintings, works of art and furniture considered in the case of Frick v. Pennsylvania, 268 U.S. 473. In that case, Pennsylvania, the State of Mr. Frick's domicil, sought to impose a transfer or succession tax on the paintings and other tangible personalty, which had always been in New York City, and it was held that they had an actual situs in New York and that, under the Fourteenth Amendment, Pennsylvania could impose no transfer or succession tax in respect of them. Applying what it conceived to be the principle of that case to the bonds of the United States and certificates of its indebtedness in this, the Supreme Court of Errors held that their transfer could not be taxed in Connecticut.

The Superior Court, following the advice of the Supreme Court of Errors, entered a judgment giving full effect to it. That is the final judgment in the case and it is the judgment now to be reviewed.

In No. 191 a writ of error was allowed by the Chief Justice of the Supreme Court of Errors and the Presiding Judge of the Superior Court of the State of Connecticut under Section 237 (a) of the Judicial Code, Act of February 13, 1925 (ch. 229, 43 Stat. 936, 937) to the final and consolidated judgment of the Superior Court of Connecticut as the highest court of the State in which a decision in the suit could be had, because there was drawn in question therein the validity of chapter 190, of the Public Acts of 1923 of Connecticut, on the ground of its being repugnant to the Constitution of the United States, and especially to the Fourteenth Amendment thereof, in that the statute as construed and applied by the Superior Court levied a succession tax on the transfer and succession of property and choses in action of the decedent which were within the jurisdiction of New York and not within the jurisdiction of Connecticut, the decedent's domicil.

In No. 190, the State Tax Commissioner applied for a writ of certiorari to the same consolidated judgment, and sought a reversal of that judgment in so far as it denied to the State of Connecticut, because of the Fourteenth Amendment to the Federal Constitution, the power and right created by its statute, chapter 190 of the Public Acts of 1923, to tax the transfer of the United States bonds and certificates of indebtedness and of $287.50 in bank notes and coin, all in a safe deposit box in the City and State of New York, as not within the taxing jurisdiction of Connecticut.

Had the Supreme Court of Errors put its ruling against the validity of part of the tax on the construction of the State Constitution or statute, we could not review that ruling, because it would have involved only a question of state law, but so far as the ruling was put on the ground that the State could not impose the tax consistently with the due process of law clause of the Fourteenth Amendment, a federal question is presented which we may consider, and when we have determined the federal questions, the cause will go back to the state court for further proceedings not inconsistent with our views on such federal questions.

The Connecticut Succession and Transfer Act, Ch. 190 of the Public Acts of 1923, says in its section 1:

"All property and any interest therein owned by a resident of this state at the time of his decease, and all real estate within this state owned by a nonresident of this state at the time of his decease, which shall pass by will or inheritance under the laws of this state; and all gifts of such property by deed, grant or other conveyance, made in contemplation of the death of the grantor or donor, or intended to take effect in possession or enjoyment at or after the death of such grantor or donor, shall be subject to the tax herein prescribed."

This is a tax not upon property but upon the right or privilege of succession to the property of a deceased person as is made clear in the opinion of the Supreme Court of Errors in this and prior cases. Silberman v. Blodgett, 105 Conn. 192; Corbin v. Townshend, 92 Conn. 501; Hopkins' Appeal, 77 Conn. 644; Warner v. Corbin, 91 Conn. 532; Gallup's Appeal, 76 Conn. 617; Nettleton's Appeal, 76 Conn. 235. These cases are all in accord with Knowlton v. Moore, 178 U.S. 41, 47, in which it was said by this Court that:

"Taxes of this general character are universally deemed to relate, not to property eo nomine, but to its passage by will or by descent in case of its intestacy, as distinguished from taxes imposed on property, real or personal as such, because of its ownership and possession. In other words, the public contribution which death duties exact is predicated on the passing of property as the result of death, as distinct from a tax on property dissociated from its transmission or receipt by will, or as the result of intestacy."

The power of the State of a man's domicil to impose a tax upon the succession to, or the transfer of, his intangible property, even when the evidences of such property are outside of the State at the time of his death, has been constantly asserted by the legislatures of the various States. The Supreme Court of Errors in its opinion in this case says that at the present time the inheritance tax laws of over four-fifths of the States impose a tax similar to that imposed by Connecticut. Frothingham v. Shaw, 175 Mass. 59; In re Estate of Zook, 317 Mo. 986; In re Sherwood's Estate, 122 Wash. 648; Mann v. Carter, 74 N.H. 345; People v. The Union Trust Company, 255 Ill. 168; In re Lines' Estate, 155 Pa. 378; In re Estate of Hodges, 170 Cal. 492; Commonwealth v. Williams' Executor, 102 Va. 778. The same principle was recognized by this Court in Carpenter v. Pennsylvania, 17 How. 456, before the adoption of the Fourteenth Amendment, and the principle was reaffirmed thereafter in Orr v. Gilman, 183 U.S. 278; Keeney v. New York, 222 U.S. 525; and Bullen v. Wisconsin, 240 U.S. 625. In the latter case the question arose as to the power of Wisconsin to impose a tax upon the succession to certain intangible property of one of its citizens, the evidences of which were held by a trust company in Illinois upon a revocable trust at the time of his death, and the power was sustained. Reference to the record in the case shows that the proprety included shares of stock in Missouri, New Jersey and Illinois corporations; stock in a national bank organized under the National Banking Act; mortage bonds and debentures issued by New Jersey, Illinois, Missouri, Utah and Kansas corporations; promissory notes of residents of Illinois and Minnesota; insurance policies issued by New York, Canadian and Wisconsin insurance companies; and money on deposit in two Illinois banks. The same principle was affirmed in the Frick case.

At common law the maxim "mobilia sequuntur personam" applied. There has been discussion and criticism of the application and enforcement of that maxim, but it is so fixed in the common law of this country and of England, in so far as it relates to intangible property, including choses in action, without regard to whether they are evidenced in writing or otherwise and whether the papers evidencing the same are found in the State of the domicil or elsewhere, and is so fully sustained by cases in this and other courts, that it must be treated as settled in this jurisdiction whether it approve itself to legal philosophic test or not.

Further this principle is not to be shaken by the inquiry into the question whether the transfer of such intangibles, like specialties, bonds or promissory notes, is subject to taxation in another jurisdiction. As to that we need not inquire. It is not the issue in this case. For present purposes it suffices that intangible personalty has such a situs at the domicil of its owner that its transfer on his death may be taxed there.

This brings us to the question whether the partnership interest of the decedent in William Openhym & Sons was a chose in action and intangible personalty. The partnership was a limited partnership organized in New York, the last agreement therefor having been executed in December, 1921. The New York partnership law then in force was Chapter 408, Laws of 1919.

Under Section 51, of this law, a partner is a co-owner with his partner of specific partnership property, holding this property as a tenant in partnership. Such tenancy confers certain rights with limitations. A partner has a right equal to that of his partners to possess specific partnership property for partnership purposes, but not otherwise. His right in specific partnership property is not assignable nor is it subject to attachment or execution upon a personal claim against him; upon his death the right to the specific property vests not in the partner's personal representative but in the surviving partner; his right in specific property is not subject to dower, curtesy, or allowance to widows, heirs or next of kin.

Section 52 specifically provides: "A partner's interest in the partnership is his share of the profits and surplus and the same is personal property."

Under Section 73, when any partner dies and the partnership continues, his personal representative may have the value of his interest at the date of dissolution ascertained and receive as an ordinary creditor an amount equal to the value of his interest in the partnership with interest.

Under Section 98, Chapter 640, Laws of 1922, the rights of a general partner in a limited partnership, which was the interest of the decedent here when he died, are identical with those of a general partner in a general partnership. And in regard to a limited partner's interest, Section 107 of the law specifically provides: "A limited partner's interest in the partnership is personal property."

It is very plain, therefore, that the interest of the decedent in the partnership of William Openhym & Sons was simply a right to share in what would remain of the partnership assets after its liabilities were satisfied. It was merely an interest in the surplus, a chose in action. It is an intangible and carries with it a right to an accounting.

There were among the holdings and property of the partnership, buildings and land. Although these statutes were passed after the decision in Darrow v. Calkins, 154 N.Y. 503, we have no reason for thinking that the partnership law of New York is now any different from what its Court of Appeals said it was in that case, pp. 515, 516, as follows:

"It is, however, generally conceded that the question whether partnership real estate shall be deemed absolutely converted into personalty for all purposes, or only converted pro tanto for the purpose of partnership equities, may be controlled by the express or implied agreement of the partners themselves, and that where by such agreement it appears that it was the intention of the partners that the lands should be treated and administered as personalty for all purposes, effect will be given thereto. In respect to real estate purchased for partnership purposes with partnership funds and used in the prosecution of the partnership business, the English rule of "out and out" conversion may be regarded as property applied on the ground of intention, even in jurisdictions which have not adopted that rule as applied to partnership real estate acquired under different circumstances and where no specific intention appeared. The investment of partnership funds in lands and chattels for the purpose of a partnership business, the fact that the two species of property are in most cases of this kind, so commingled that they can not be separated without impairing the value of each, has been deemed to justify the inference that under such circumstances the lands as well as the chattels were intended by the partners to constitute a part of the partnership stock and that both together should take the character of personalty for all purposes, and Judge Denio in Collumb v. Read expressed the opinion that to this extent the English rule of conversion prevailed here. That paramount consideration should be given to the intention of the partners when ascertained, is conceded by most of the cases."

It thus clearly appears that both under the partnership agreement and under the laws of the State of New York the interest of the partner was the right to receive a sum of money equal to his share of the net value of the partnership after a settlement, and this right to his share is a debt owing to him, a chose in action, and an intangible. We concur with the Supreme Court of Errors that as such it was subject to the transfer tax of Connecticut.

We come then to the second question, whether bonds of the United States and certificates of indebtedness of the United States deposited in a safe deposit box in New York City, and never removed from there, owned by the decedent at the time of his death, were intangibles which came within the rule already stated.

The argument is that such bonds, payable to bearer and transferable from hand to hand, have lost their character as choses in action and have taken on the qualities of physical property, and cases are cited to indicate that they can be made the subject of execution and constitute a basis for the jurisdiction of the courts and of taxing officers of the State in which the paper upon which the evidence of the debt or obligation is written, is found, although their owner lives and dies in another State.

The Supreme Court of Errors takes this view, citing Frick v. Pennsylvania, and holds that the transfer of the United States bonds and certificates is taxable in New York where they are, and only there. The Court cites, as sustaining its conclusion that the transfer of the bonds is only taxable in New York, the case of State Tax on Foreign-Held Bonds, 15 Wall. 300. This case is often cited to the point that Mr. Justice Field takes as indisputable (on page 319) that a State may not tax property that is not within its jurisdiction — a matter recognized in Frick v. Pennsylvania, 268 U.S. 473, 489; Union Refrigerator Transit Company v. Kentucky, 199 U.S. 194, 202, and Gloucester Ferry Co. v. Pennsylvania, 114 U.S. 196, 206. The effect of some of Mr. Justice Field's language in that case, and the exact point on which the decision there turned, have since been fully discussed by this Court and qualified in Savings & Loan Society v. Multnomah County, 169 U.S. 421, 428; New Orleans v. Stempel, 175 U.S. 309, 319, 320; and Blackstone v. Miller, 188 U.S. 189, 206. The tax there held invalid was a tax imposed by a statute of Pennsylvania upon the interest due a nonresident bond holder on bonds issued by a corporation of that State. It is now settled in these later cases that the point decided in the State Tax on Foreign-Held Bonds case was that the law of Pennsylvania in requiring the railroad company, which issued the bonds, to pay the state tax on them and deduct it from the interest due the nonresident owners, was as to them a law impairing the obligation of contracts under Murray v. Charleston, 96 U.S. 432. The case, therefore, is not authority for the proposition for which the Supreme Court of Errors cites it, to-wit: That such bonds are to be completely assimilated to tangible personal property. The other cases cited by the Supreme Court of Errors are New Orleans v.

Stempel, 175 U.S. 309, 321, and like cases which follow it in which a State, not that of the domicil of the owner, has been held to have the right to tax bonds, promissory notes, and other written evidences of choses in action with which business is there carried on for the owner, giving them what is sometimes called "a business situs"; but such cases have little or no bearing on the power of the State of a decedent's domicil to tax the transfer of his bonds which we are now considering.

The question here is whether bonds, unlike other choses in action, may have a situs different from the owner's domicil such as will render their transfer taxable in the State of that situs and in only that State. We think bonds are not thus distinguishable from other choses in action. It is not enough to show that the written or printed evidence of ownership may, by the law of the State in which they are physically present, be permitted to be taken in execution or dealt with as reaching that of which they are evidence, even without the presence of the owner. While bonds often are so treated, they are nevertheless in their essence only evidences of debt. The Supreme Court of Errors expressly admits that they are choses in action. Whatever incidental qualities may be added by usage of business or by statutory provision, this characteristic remains and shows itself by the fact that their destruction physically will not destroy the debt which they represent. They are representative and not the thing itself.

The case of Kirtland v. Hotchkiss, 100 U.S. 491, is in point. The case came to this Court from the Supreme Court of Errors of Connecticut and it involved the taxable status in that State of bonds held by one of its citizens and evidenced a debt owing to him by a citizen of Illinois. The court said, p. 498:

"The question does not seem to us to be very difficult of solution. The creditor, it is conceded, is a permanent resident within the jurisdiction of the State imposing the tax. The debt is property in his hands constituting a portion of his wealth, from which he is under the highest obligation, in common with his fellow-citizens of the same State, to contribute for the support of the government whose protection he enjoys.

"That debt, although a species of intangible property, may, for purposes of taxation, if not for all others, be regarded as situated at the domicile of the creditor. It is none the less property because its amount and maturity are set forth in a bond. That bond, wherever actually held or deposited, is only the evidence of the debt, and if destroyed, the debt — the right to demand payment of the money loaned, with the stipulated interest — remains. Nor is the debt, for the purposes of taxation, affected by the fact that it is secured by mortgage upon real estate situated in Illinois. The mortgage is but a security for the debt, and, as held in State Tax on Foreign-Held Bonds (supra), the right of the creditor "to proceed against the property mortgaged, upon a given contingency, to enforce by its sale the payment of his demand, . . . has no locality independent of the party in whom it resides. It may undoubtedly be taxed by the State when held by a resident therein," &c. Cooley on Taxation, 15, 63, 134, 270. The debt, then, having its situs at the creditor's residence, both he and it are, for the purposes of taxation, within the jurisdiction of the State."

The line which was drawn in the case of Frick v. Pennsylvania, supra, was one which was adopted from the decision of this Court in Union Refrigerator Transit Company v. Kentucky, 199 U.S. 194, and other cases cited in the same connection, where it was held that power of taxation could not extend to tangible chattels having an actual situs outside the jurisdiction, although the owner was within it. It was pointed out that this is not true of debts and choses in action, which usually have a taxable situs at the owner's domicil. In the Union Refrigerator case, this Court said, p. 205:

"In this class of cases the tendency of modern authorities is to apply the maxim mobilia sequuntur personam, and to hold that the property may be taxed at the domicil of the owner as the real situs of the debt, and also, more particularly in the case of mortgages, in the State where the property is retained."

The Court again said, p. 206:

"The arguments in favor of the taxation of intangible property at the domicil of the owner have no application to tangible property. The fact that such property is visible, easily found and difficult to conceal, and the tax readily collectible, is so cogent an argument for its taxation at its situs, that of late there is a general consensus of opinion that it is taxable in the State where it is permanently located and employed and where it receives its entire protection, irrespective of the domicil of the owner. We have, ourselves, held in a number of cases that such property permanently located in a State other than that of its owner is taxable there. Brown v. Houston, 114 U.S. 622; Coe v. Errol, 116 U.S. 517; Pullman's Car Co. v. Pennsylvania, 141 U.S. 18; Western Union Telegraph Company v. Massachusetts, 125 U.S. 530; Railroad Company v. Peniston, 18 Wall. 5; American Refrigerator Transit Company v. Hall, 174 U.S. 70; Pittsburgh Coal Company v. Bates, 156 U.S. 577; Old Dominion Steamship Company v. Virginia, 198 U.S. 299."

The Court continued, p. 206:

"There are doubtless cases in the state reports announcing the principle that the ancient maxim of mobilia sequuntur personam still applies to personal property, and that it may be taxed at the domicil of the owner, but upon examination they all or nearly all relate to intangible property, such as stocks, bonds, notes and other choses in action. We are cited to none applying this rule to tangible property, and after a careful examination have not been able to find any wherein the question is squarely presented. . . ."

The discussion in the Union Refrigerator case shows what this Court meant in the Frick case in holding that personal property in the form of paintings and furniture having an actual situs in one State could not be subjected to a transfer tax in another State, and emphasizes the inference that it did not apply to anything having as its essence an indebtedness or a chose in action and could not apply to property in the form of specialties or bonds or other written evidences of indebtedness whether governmental or otherwise, even though they passed from hand to hand. The analogy between furniture and bonds cannot be complete because bonds are representative only and are not the thing represented. They are at most choses in action and intangibles.

We think therefore that the Supreme Court of Errors in extending the rule of the Frick case from tangible personal property, like paintings, furniture or cattle, to bonds, is not warranted, and to that extent we must reverse its conclusion in denying to Connecticut the right to tax the transfer of the bonds and Treasury certificates. Of course this reasoning necessarily sustains the different view of that court that the transfer of certificates of stock in corporations of other States than Connecticut was taxable in the latter as the transfer of choses in action.

Among the other items is a savings bank account in New York which is certainly a chose in action and was properly treated as subject to the same rule. So, too, a life insurance policy payable to the estate was also of that character.

There was a small amount of cash, $287.48, in bank notes and coin in a safe deposit box in New York which the Supreme Court of Errors held not taxable in Connecticut. As to this, the contention on behalf of Connecticut is that it should be treated as attached to the person of the owner and subject to a transfer tax at the domicil. It is argued that it was not like coin or treasure in bulk, but like loose change, so to speak. To money of this amount usually and easily carried on the person, it is said that the doctrine of mobilia sequuntur personam has peculiar application in the historical derivation of the maxim. But we think that money, so definitely fixed and separated in its actual situs from the person of the owner as this was, is tangible property and can not be distinguished from the paintings and furniture held in the

Frick case to be taxable only in the jurisdiction where they were.

The results thus stated lead to our reversing the judgment of the Superior Court of Connecticut, in respect to the tax on the transfer of the bonds and certificates of indebtedness of the United States, and to our affirming the judgment in other respects.

It is further contended by the executors that the proceedings in the Connecticut court and the judgment therein fail to give full faith and credit to the public acts, records and proceedings of the State of New York, and that this is in violation of the Constitution of the United States. We do not think there is anything in this point. There is nothing in the proceedings in the Connecticut court that is inconsistent with those in the New York court. There is nothing to indicate that the New York court decided, assuming it had jurisdiction to decide, that there was no power in the State of Connecticut to impose a tax on the transfer that was taxed in Connecticut. More than that the proceedings and judgment in New York were not such as would conclude Connecticut even with the aid of the full faith and credit clause of the Constitution. Connecticut was not a party to those proceedings or to that judgment, nor was it in privity with any one who was a party.

Affirmed in part and reversed in part.[9]

PROBLEM

16.4. A is domiciled in State X. He owns and operates a sole proprietorship business in the adjoining State of Y. The assets of the sole proprietorship consist of the real property on which the business is conducted, tangible personal property used in the business, and accounts receivable. When A dies, to what extent, if any, can State X constitutionally impose a death tax on the sole proprietorship business which he owns and operates in State Y?

CURRY v. McCANLESS
307 U.S. 357, 59 Sup. Ct. 900, 83 L. Ed. 1339 (1939)

MR. JUSTICE STONE delivered the opinion of the Court.

The questions for decision are whether the States of Alabama

[9] Comments on Blodgett v. Silberman are found in 29 Colum. L. Rev. 782 (1929), 17 Geo. L.J. 149 (1929), 41 Harv. L. Rev. 1066 (1928), 27 Mich. L. Rev. 447 (1929), 2 So. Calif. L. Rev. 76 (1928).

In Thomas v. Virginia, 81 Sup. Ct. 229 (1960), the Supreme Court of the United States reversed a judgment of the Supreme Court of Appeals of Virginia which held that United States currency, owned by a domiciliary of Virginia and located at the time of his death in a safe-deposit box in his name in the District of Columbia, was intangible personal property and subject to the Virginia inheritance tax. Blodgett v. Silberman is referred to. — ED.

and Tennessee may each constitutionally impose death taxes upon the transfer of an interest in intangibles held in trust by an Alabama trustee but passing under the will of a beneficiary decedent domiciled in Tennessee; and which of the two states may tax in the event that it is determined that only one state may constitutionally impose the tax.

Decedent, a domiciled resident of Tennessee, by trust indenture transferred certain stocks and bonds upon specified trusts to Title Guarantee Loan & Trust Company, an Alabama corporation doing business in that state. So far as now material, the indenture provided that the net income of the trust property should be paid over to decedent during her lifetime. She reserved the power to remove the trustee and substitute another, which was never done; the power to direct the sale of the trust property and the investment of the proceeds; and the power to dispose of the trust estate by her last will and testament, in which event it was to be "handled and disposed of as directed" in her will. The indenture provided further that in default of disposition by will the property was to he held in trust for the benefit of her husband, son, and daughter. Until decedent's death the trust was administered by the trust company in Alabama and the paper evidences of the intangibles held by the trustee were at all times located in Alabama.

By her last will and testament decedent bequeathed the trust property to the trust company in trust for the benefit of her husband, son, and daughter, in different amounts and by different estates from those provided for by the trust indenture, with remainder interests over to the children of the son and the daughter respectively, and to his wife and her husband. By her will testatrix appointed a Tennessee trust company executor "as to all property which I may own in the State of Tennessee at the time of my death," and an Alabama trust company executor "as to all property which I may own in the State of Alabama and also as to all property which I may have the right to dispose of by last will and testament in said state." The will has been probated in Tennessee and in Alabama, and letters testamentary have issued to the two trust companies named as executors in the will.

The present suit was brought by the two executors in a chancery court of Tennessee against appellants, comprising the State Tax Commission of Alabama, and appellee, Commissioner of Finance and Taxation of the State of Tennessee, who are charged with the duty of collecting inheritance or succession taxes in their respective states. The bill of complaint prayed a declaratory judgment pursuant to the Tennessee Declaratory Judgments Act, Tennessee Code, 1932, secs. 8835-8847, determining what portions of the estate of decedent are taxable by the State of Tennessee and what portions by the State of Alabama.   Appellants and appellee appeared and by their answers and by stipulation recited in detail the facts already stated and admitted that the taxing officials of each state had imposed or asserted the right to impose an inheritance or death transfer tax on the trust property passing under decedent's will.

The chancery court of Tennessee decreed that the State of Alabama could lawfully impose the tax and that the inheritance tax law of Tennessee violated the Fourteenth Amendment in so far as it purported to impose a tax measured by the trust property disposed of by decedent's will.   The Supreme Court of Tennessee reversed, and entered its decree declaring the trust property disposed of by decedent's will to be "taxable in Tennessee and not taxable in Alabama for purposes of death succession or transfer taxes."   174 Tenn.; 118 S.W.2d 228.   The case comes here on an appeal from this decree taken by the taxing officials of Alabama under sec. 237(a) of the Judicial Code, 28 U.S.C. sec. 344(a).

Alabama has assessed a state inheritance tax on the trust property pursuant to Article XII, c. 2, of its General Revenue Act. Alabama Acts, 1935, pp. 434 et seq.   No transfer tax has been assessed upon the property by the Tennessee taxing officials, but they assert the right under the Tennessee statute to tax the transfer under decedent's will of the trust property.   Sections 1259 and 1260 of the Tennessee Code of 1932 impose a tax upon the transfer at death by a resident of the state of his intangible property wherever located, including transfers under powers of appointment.

Both the court of chancery of Tennessee and the Supreme Court of Tennessee, conceiving that the Fourteenth Amendment requires the transmission at death of intangibles to be taxed at their "situs" and there only, considered that the primary question for determination was the situs or location to be attributed to the intangibles of the trust estate at the time of decedent's death. After considering all of the relevant factors, the one court concluded that the situs of the intangibles was in Alabama, the other that is was in Tennessee.   Despite the impossibility in the circumstances of this case of attributing a single location to that which has no physical characteristics and which is associated in numerous intimate ways with both states, both courts have agreed that the Fourteenth Amendment compels the attribution to be made and that, once it is established by judicial pronouncement that the intangibles are in one state rather than the other, the due process clause forbids their taxation in any other.

The doctrine, of recent origin, that the Fourteenth Amendment precludes the taxation of any interest in the same intangible in more than one state has received support to the limited extent that it was applied in Farmers Loan & Trust Co. v. Minnesota, 280 U.S. 204; Baldwin v. Missouri, 281 U.S. 586; First National Bank v. Maine, 284 U.S. 312. Still more recently this Court has declined to give it completely logical application. [Footnote omitted.] It has never been pressed to the extreme now urged upon us, and we think that neither reason nor authority requires its acceptance in the circumstances of the present case.

That rights in tangibles — land and chattels — are to be regarded in many respects as localized at the place where the tangible itself is located for purposes of the jurisdiction of a court to make disposition of putative rights in them, for purposes of conflict of laws, and for purposes of taxation, is a doctrine generally accepted both in the common law and other legal systems before the adoption of the Fourteenth Amendment and since.[10] Originating, it has been thought, in the tendency of the mind to identify rights with their physical subjects, see Salmond, Jurisprudence (2nd ed.) 398, its survival and the consequent cleavage between the rules of law applicable to tangibles and those relating to intangibles are attributable to the exclusive dominion exerted over the tangibles themselves by the government within whose territorial limits they are found. Green v. Van Buskirk, 7 Wall. 139, 150; Pennoyer v. Neff, 95 U.S. 714; Arndt v. Griggs, 134 U.S. 316, 320-321. See McDonald v. Mabee, 243 U.S. 90, 91; cf. Harris v. Balk, 198 U.S. 215, 222; Frick v. Pennsylvania, supra, 497. The power of government and its agencies to possess and to exclude others from possessing tangibles, and thus to exclude them from enjoying rights in tangibles located within its territory, affords adequate basis for an exclusive taxing jurisdiction. When we speak of the jurisdiction to tax land or chattels as being exclusively in the state where they are physically located, we mean no more than that the benefit and protection of laws enabling the owner to enjoy the fruits of his ownership and the power to reach effectively the interest protected, for the purpose of subjecting them to payment of a tax, are so narrowly restricted to the state in whose territory the physical property is located as

[10] (*Court footnote*)   Green v. Van Buskirk, 5 Wall. 307; 7 Wall. 139; Pennoyer v. Neff, 95 U.S. 714; Arndt v. Griggs, 134 U.S. 316; Fall v. Eastin, 215 U.S. 1; Olmsted v. Olmsted, 216 U.S. 386; United States v. Guaranty Trust Co., 293 U.S. 340, 345-346; Paddell v. City of New York, 211 U.S. 446; St. Louis v. Ferry Co., 11 Wall. 423, 430; Frick v. Pennsylvania, 268 U.S. 473; see Story, Conflict of Laws (8th ed.), secs. 550, 551; Dicey, Conflict of Laws (5th ed.), pp. 418, et seq.; 583 et seq., 606 et seq.; 1 Beale, Conflict of Laws, sec. 48.1 et seq.; American Law Institute, Restatement of Conflict of Laws, secs. 48, 49; 2 Cooley, Taxation (4th ed.), secs. 447, 451.

to set practical limits to taxation by others.   Other states have been said to be without jurisdiction and so without constitutional power to tax intangibles if, because of their location elsewhere, those states can afford no substantial protection to the rights taxed and cannot effectively lay hold of any interest in the property in order to compel payment of the tax.   See Union Transit Co. v. Kentucky, 199 U.S. 194, 202; Frick v. Pennsylvania, 268 U.S. 473, 489 et seq. [Footnote omitted.]

Very different considerations, both theoretical and practical, apply to the taxation of intangibles, that is, rights which are not related to physical things.   Such rights are but relationships between persons, natural or corporate, which the law recognizes by attaching to them certain sanctions enforceable in courts.   The power of government over them and the protection which it gives them cannot be exerted through control of a physical thing.   They can be made effective only through control over and protection afforded to those persons whose relationships are the origin of the rights.   See Chicago, R.I. & P. Ry. Co. v. Sturm, 174 U.S. 710, 716; Harris v. Balk, 198 U.S. 215, 222.   Obviously, as sources of actual or potential wealth — which is an apprporite measure of any tax imposed on ownership or its exercise — they cannot be dissociated from the persons from whose relationships they are derived. These are not in any sense fictions.   They are indisputable realities.

The power to tax "is an incident of sovereignty, and is coextensive with that to which it is an incident.   All subjects over which the sovereign power of a state extends, are objects of taxation; but those over which it does not extend, are, upon the soundest principles, exempt from taxation."   McCulloch v. Maryland, 4 Wheat. 316, 429.   But this does not mean that the sovereign power of the states does not extend over intangibles of a domiciled resident because they have no physical location within its territory, or that its power to tax is lost because we may choose to say they are located elsewhere.   A jurisdiction which does not depend on physical presence within the state is not lost by declaring that it is absent.   From the beginning of our constitutional system control over the person at the place of his domicile and his duty there, common to all citizens, to contribute to the support of government have been deemed to afford an adequate constitutional basis for imposing on him a tax on the use and enjoyment of rights in intangibles measured by their value.   Until this moment that jurisdiction has not been thought to depend on any factor other than the domicile of the owner within the taxing state, or to compel the attribution to intangibles of a physical presence within its territory, as though they were chattels, in order to support the tax. Carpenter v. Pennsylvania, 17 How. 456; Kirtland v. Hotchkiss, 100 U.S. 491; Hawley v. Malden, 232 U.S. 1: Bullen v. Wisconsin, 240 U.S. 625; Cream of Wheat Co. v. Grand Forks, 253 U.S. 325; Blodgett v. Silberman, 277 U.S. 1; Farmers Loan & Trust Co. v. Minnesota, supra; Baldwin v. Missouri, supra; Beidler v. South Carolina, 282 U.S. 1; First National Bank v. Maine, supra; Virginia v. Imperial Coal Sales Co., 293 U.S. 15; Schuylkill Trust Co. v. Pennsylvania, 302 U.S. 506.

In cases where the owner of intangibles confines his activity to the place of his domicile it has been found convenient to substitute a rule for a reason, cf. New York ex rel. Cohn v. Graves, 300 U.S. 308, 313; First Bank Stock Corp. v. Minnesota, 301 U.S. 234, 241, by saying that his intangibles are taxed at their situs and not elsewhere, or, perhaps less artificially, by invoking the maxim mobilia sequuntur personam, Blodgett v. Silberman, supra; Baldwin v. Missouri, supra, which means only that it is the identity or association of intangibles with the person of their owner at his domicile which gives jurisdiction to tax. But when the taxpayer extends his activities with respect to his intangibles, so as to avail himself of the protection and benefit of the laws of another state, in such a way as to bring his person or property within the reach of the tax gatherer there, the reason for a single place of taxation no longer obtains, and the rule is not even a workable substitute for the reasons which may exist in any particular case to support the constitutional power of each state concerned to tax. Whether we regard the right of a state to tax as founded on power over the object taxed, as declared by Chief Justice Marshall in McCulloch v. Maryland, supra through dominion over tangibles or over persons whose relationships are the source of intangible rights; or on the benefit and protection conferred by the taxing sovereignty, or both, it is undeniable that the state of domicile is not deprived, by the taxpayer's activities elsewhere, of its constitutional jurisdiction to tax and consequently that there are many circumstance in which more than one state may have jurisdiction to impose a tax and measure it by some or all of the taxpayer's intangibles. Shares of corporate stock may be taxed at the domicile of the shareholder and also at that of the corporation which the taxing state has created and controls; and income may be taxed both by the state where it is earned and by the state of the recipient's domicile. [Footnote omitted.] Protection, benefit, and power over the subject matter are not confined to either state. The taxpayer who is domiciled in one state but carries on business in another is subject to a tax there measured by the value of the intangibles used in his business.   New Orleans v. Stempel, 175 U.S. 309; Bristol v. Washington County, 177 U.S. 133; State Board of Assessors v. Comptoir National, 191 U.S. 388; Metropolitan Life Ins Co. v. New Orleans, 205 U.S. 395; Liverpool & L. & G. Ins. Co. v. Board , 221 U.S. 346; Wheeling Steel Corp. v. Fox, 298 U.S. 193; cf. Blodgett v. Silberman, supra; Baldwin v. Missouri, supra.   But taxation of a corporation by a state where it does business, measured by the value of the intangibles used in its business there, does not preclude the state of incorporation from imposing a tax measured by all its intangibles.   Cream of Wheat Co. v. Grand Forks, supra, 329; [footnote omitted] see Fidelity & Columbia Trust Co. v. Louisville, 245 U.S. 54.

The practical obstacles and unwarranted curtailments of state power which may be involved in attempting to prevent the taxation of diverse legal interests in intangibles in more than a single place, through first ascribing to them a fictitious situs and then invoking the prohibition of the Fourteenth Amendment against their taxation elsewhere, are exemplified by the circumstances of the present case.   Here, for reasons of her own, the testatrix, although domiciled in Tennessee and enjoying the benefits of its laws, found it advantageous to create a trust of intangibles in Alabama by vesting legal title to the intangibles and limited powers of control over them in an Alabama trustee.   But she also provided that by resort to her power to dispose of property by will, conferred upon her by the law of the domicile, the trust could be terminated and the property pass under the will.   She thus created two sets of legal relationships resulting in distinct intangible rights, the one embodied in the legal ownership by the Alabama trustee of the intangibles, the other embodied in the equitable right of the decedent to control the action of the trustee with respect to the trust property and to compel it to pay over to her the income during her life, and in her power to dispose of the property at death.

Even if we could rightly regard these various and distinct legal interests, springing from distinct relationships, as a composite unitary interest and ascribe to it a single location in space, it is difficult to see how it could be said to be more in one state than in the other and upon what articulate principle the Fourteenth Amendment could be thought to have withdrawn from either state the taxing jurisdiction which it undoubtedly possessed before the adoption of the Amendment by conferring on one state, at the expense of the other, exclusive jurisdiction to tax.   See Paddell v. City of New York, 211 U.S. 446, 448.   If the "due process" of the Fifth Amendment does not require us to fix a single exclusive place of taxation of intangibles for the benefit of their foreign owner, who is entitled to its protection, Burnet v. Brooks, 288 U.S. 378; cf. Russian Volunteer Fleet v. United States, 282 U.S. 481, 489, the Fourteenth can hardly be thought to make us do so here, for the due process clause of each amendment is directed at the protection of the individual and he is entitled to its immunity as much against the state as against the national government.

If taxation is but a means of distributing the cost of government among those who are subject to its control and who enjoy the protection of its laws, see New York ex rel. Cohn v. Graves, supra, 313; First Bank Stock Corp. v. Minnesota, supra, 241, legal ownership of the intangibles in Alabama by the Alabama trustee would seem to afford adequate basis for imposing on it a tax measured by their value. We can find no more ground for saying that the Fourteenth Amendment relieves it, or the property which it holds and administers in Alabama, from bearing that burden, than for saying that they are constitutionally immune from paying any other expense which normally attaches to the administration of a trust in that state. This Court has never denied the constitutional power of the trustee's domicile to subject them to property taxation. Safe Deposit & Trust Co. v. Virginia, 280 U.S. 83; see cases collected in 30 Columbia Law Rev. 530; 2 Cooley, Taxation (8th ed.), sec. 602. And since Alabama may lawfully tax the property in the trustee's hands, we perceive no ground for saying that the Fourteenth Amendment forbids the state to tax the transfer of it or an interest in it to another merely because the transfer was effected by decedent's testamentary act in another state.

No more plausible ground is assigned for depriving Tennessee of the power to tax in the circumstances of this case. The decedent's power to dispose of the intangibles was a potential source of wealth which was property in her hands from which she was under the highest obligation, in common with her fellow citizens of Tennessee, to contribute to the support of the government whose protection she enjoyed. Exercise of that power, which was in her complete and exclusive control in Tennessee, was made a taxable event by the statutes of the state. Taxation of it must be taken to be as much within the jurisdiction of the state as taxation of the transfer of a mortgage on land located in another state and there subject to taxation at its full value. See Kirtland v. Hotchkiss, supra; cf. Paddell v. City of New York, supra.

For purposes of taxation, a general power of appointment, of which the testatrix here was both donor and donee, has hitherto been regarded by this Court as equivalent to ownership of the property subject to the power.   Chanler v. Kelsey, 205 U.S. 466; Bullen v. Wisconsin, supra, 630; Chase National Bank v. United States, 278 U.S. 327, 338; see Gray, Rule Against Perpetuities (3d ed. 1916), sec. 524.   [Footnote omitted.]   Whether the appointee derives title from the donor, under the common law theory, or from the donee by virtue of the exercise of the power, is here immaterial.   In either event the trustee's title under the will was derived from decedent, domiciled in Tennessee.   Cf. Wachovia Trust Co. v. Doughton, 272 U.S. 567.   There is no conflict here between the laws of the two states affecting the transmission of the trust property.   The title of the trustee under the original Alabama trust came to an end upon the exercise of the testatrix's power of appointment; and although the trustee after her death still had title to the securities, it was in by a new title as legatee under her will, and a new beneficial interest was created, both derived through the exercise of her power of disposition.   The resulting situation was no different from what it would have been if she had bequeathed the intangibles upon a new trust to a new and different trustee, either within or without the state of Alabama.   So far as the power of Tennessee to tax the exercise of the power of appointment is concerned, there is no substantial difference between the present case and any other case in which at the moment of death the evidences of intangibles passing under the will of a decedent domiciled in one state are physically present in another.   See Blodgett v. Silberman, supra; Baldwin v. Missouri, supra.

It has hitherto been the accepted law of this Court that the State of domicile may constitutionally tax the exercise or non-exercise at death of a general power of appointment, by one who is both donor and donee of the power, relating to securities held in trust in another state.   Bullen v. Wisconsin, supra.   If it be thought that it is identity of the intangibles with the person of the owner at the place of his domicile which gives power over them and hence "jurisdiction to tax," and this is the reason underlying the maxim mobilia sequuntur personam, it is certain here that the intangibles for some purposes are identified with the trustee, in their legal owner, at the place of its domicile and that in another and different relationship and for a different purpose — the exercise of the power of disposition at death, which is the equivalent of ownership — they are identified with the place of domicile of the testatrix, Tennessee.   In effecting her purposes, the testatrix brought some of the legal interests which she created within the control of one state by selecting a trustee there and others within the control of the other state by making her domicile there.   She necessarily invoked the aid of the law of both states, and her legatees, before they can secure and enjoy the benefits of succession, must invoke the law of both.

We can find nothing in the history of the Fourteenth Amendment and no support in reason, principle, or authority for saying that it prohibits either state, in the circumstances of this case, from laying the tax. On the contrary this Court, in sustaining the tax at the place of domicile in a case like the present, has declared that both the decedent's domicile and that of the trustee are free to tax. Bullen v. Wisconsin, supra, 631; cf. Keeney v. New York, 222 U.S. 525, 537; Guaranty Trust Co. v. Blodgett, 287 U.S. 509. That has remained the law of this Court until the present moment, and we see no reason for discarding it now. We find it impossible to say that taxation of intangibles can be reduced in every case to the mere mechanical operation of locating at a single place, and there taxing, every legal interest growing out of all the complex legal relationships which may be entered into between persons. This is the case because in point of actuality those interests may be too diverse in their relationships to various taxing jurisdictions to admit of unitary treatment without discarding modes of taxation long accepted and applied before the Fourteenth Amendment was adopted, and still recognized by this Court as valid. See Paddell v. New York, supra, 448. The Fourteenth Amendment cannot be carried out with such mechanical nicety without infringing powers which we think have not yet been withdrawn from the states. We have recently declined to press to a logical extreme the doctrine that the Fourteenth Amendment may be invoked to compel the taxation of intangibles by only a single state by attributing to them a situs within that state. [Footnote omitted.] We think it cannot be pressed so far here.

If we enjoyed the freedom of the farmers it is possible that we might, in the light of experience, devise a more equitable system of taxation than that which they gave us. But we are convinced that that end cannot be attained by the device of ascribing to intangibles in every case a locus for taxation in a single state despite the multiple legal interests to which they may give rise and despite the control over them or their transmission by any other state and its legitimate interest in taxing the one or the other. While fictions are sometimes invented in order to realize the judicial conceptions of justice, we cannot define the constitutional guaranty in terms of a fiction so unrelated to reality without creating as many tax injustices as we would avoid and without exercising a power to remake constitutional provisions which the Constitution has not given to the courts. See Bristol v. Washington County supra, 145; Kidd v. Alabama, 188 U.S. 730, 732, quoted with approval in Hawley v. Malden, supra, 13; Bullen v. Wisconsin, supra, 630; Fidelity & Columbia Trust Co. v. Louisville, supra, 58; Cream of Wheat Co. v. Grand Forks, supra, 330.

So far as the decree of the Supreme Court of Tennessee denies the power of Alabama to tax it is

Reversed.[11]

MR. JUSTICE REED wrote a concurring opinion.

MR. JUSTICE BUTLER wrote a dissenting opinion and MR. CHIEF JUSTICE HUGHES, MR. JUSTICE MCREYNOLDS and MR. JUSTICE ROBERTS joined in this dissenting opinion.

PROBLEMS

16.5. Assume that the decedent in Curry v. McCanless had reserved the right to income for life under the trust established in Alabama, but had not reserved any power to revoke the trust or to appoint the trust property by her will or to control the investment of the trust property. In other words, assume that the Alabama trust was irrevocable and completely beyond the control of the decedent except for the reservation of the life income. On the decedent's death, could Tennessee constitutionally impose a tax on the trust property?

16.6. Assume that the decedent in Curry v. McCanless had reserved only a special power to appoint by will and that in all other respects the facts were unchanged. On the decedent's death, could Tennessee constitutionally impose a tax on the Alabama trust property?

16.7. Assume that the Alabama trust had been established for the benefit of the decedent by someone other than the decedent, but that in all other respects the facts of the case were unchanged. On the decedent's death, could Tennessee constitutionally impose a tax on the Alabama trust property? See Graves v. Schmidlapp, 315 U.S. 657, 62 Sup. Ct. 870, 86 L. Ed 1097 (1942).

[11] Comments on Curry v. McCanless are found in 34 Ill. L. Rev. 359 (1939), 38 Mich. L. Rev. 81 (1939), 88 U. of Pa. L. Rev. 120 (1939).

Article 16, §3 of the New York State Constitution provides in part as follows: "Moneys, credits, securities and other intangible personal property within the state not employed in carrying on any business therein by the owner shall be deemed to be located at the domicile of the owner for purposes of taxation, and, if held in trust, shall not be deemed to be located in this state for purposes of taxation because of the trustee being domiciled in this state, provided that if no other state has jurisdiction to subject such property held in trust to death taxation, it may be deemed property having a taxable situs within this state for purposes of death taxation." — ED.

STATE TAX COMMISSION OF UTAH
v. ALDRICH
316 U.S. 174, 62 Sup. Ct. 1008, 86 L. Ed. 1358 (1942)

MR. JUSTICE DOUGLAS delivered the opinion of the Court.

The sole question presented by this case is whether the State of Utah is precluded by the Fourteenth Amendment from imposing a tax upon a transfer by death of shares of stock in a Utah corporation, forming part of the estate of a decedent who, at the time of his death, was domiciled in the State of New York and held there the certificates representing those shares.

In 1940, Edward S. Harkness died testate, being at that time domiciled in New York. His estate was probated in New York, where respondents were appointed executors. Respondents were also appointed administrators with the will annexed, in Utah. At the time of his death, Harkness was the owner of 10,000 shares of common stock and 400 shares of preferred stock of the Union Pacific Railroad Co., a Utah corporation. The certificates representing those shares were never within Utah. They were in the possession of Harkness in New York at the time of his death, and are now held by respondents. For many years, the Union Pacific Railroad Co. has kept its stock books and records and transfer agents in New York, and has not maintained any in Utah. These shares are the only property owned by decedent which is claimed to be within the jurisdiction of Utah. At the date of decedent's death, a New York statute allowed as a credit against the estate tax imposed by New York the amount of any constitutionally valid estate or inheritance tax paid to any other state within three years after the decedent's death. [Footnote omitted.]

Respondents sought a declaratory judgment in the Utah court holding that the transfer of the shares was not subject to tax by Utah under the provisions of its inheritance tax law. [Footnote omitted.] The trial court entered judgment for respondents. The Supreme Court of Utah, under the compulsion of First National Bank v. Maine, 284 U.S. 312, affirmed. 116 P.2d 923. We granted the petition for certiorari so that the constitutional basis of First National Bank v. Maine could be reexamined in the light of such recent decisions as Curry v. McCanless, 307 U.S. 357, and Graves v. Elliott, 307 U.S. 383. And see Commonwealth v. Stewart, 338 Pa. 12 A.2d 444, *aff'd* 312 U.S. 649.

There can be no doubt but that the judgment below should be affirmed if First National Bank v. Maine is to survive, as the judgment in that case prohibited the State of Maine from doing what the State of Utah is here attempting. But we do not think it should survive. And certainly it cannot if the principles which govern the Curry and Graves cases rest on firm constitutonal grounds.

First National Bank v. Maine, like its forerunners Farmers Loan & Trust Co. v. Minnesota, 280 U.S. 204, and Baldwin v. Missouri, 281 U.S. 586, read into the Fourteenth Amendment a "rule of immunity from taxation by more than one state." 284 U.S. p. 326. As we said in the Curry case, that doctrine is of recent origin. Prior to 1930, when Blackstone v. Miller, 188 U.S. 189, was overruled by Farmers Loan & Trust Co. v. Minnesota, the adjudications of this Court clearly demanded a result opposite from that which obtained in First National Bank v. Maine. That was recognized by the majority in the latter case (284 U.S. p. 321) — and properly so, because Blackstone v. Miller rejected the notion that there were constitutional objections to double taxation of intangibles by States which had command over them or their owner. And see Kidd v. Alabama, 188 U.S. 730, 732. Blackstone v. Miller permitted New York to tax the transfer of debts owed by New York citizens to a decedent who died domiciled in Illinois, although Illinois had taxed the entire succession. Mr. Justice Holmes, speaking for the Court, upheld the power of New York to collect the tax because the transfer of the debts "necessarily depends upon and involves the law of New York for its exercise." 188 U.S. p. 205. It was that view which the minority in First National Bank v. Maine championed. They maintained that there was no constitutional barrier to taxation by Maine of the transfer of the shares of stock of the Maine corporation, since the nature and extent of the decedent's interest in the shares were "defined by the laws of Maine, and his power to secure the complete transfer" was "dependent upon them." 284 U.S. p. 332. That view had been repeatedly expressed in other earlier cases touching on the rights of a State to tax intangibles over which it had command though the owner was a non-resident. Tappan v. Merchants' Nat. Bank, 19 Wall. 490, 503-504; Hawley v. Malden, 232 U.S. 1, 12; Baker v. Baker, Eccles & Co., 242 U.S. 394, 401; Frick v. Pennsylvania, 268 U.S. 473, 497; Rhode Island Hospital Trust Co. v. Doughton, 270 U.S. 69, 81. As stated by Chief Justice Marshall in McCulloch v. Maryland, 4 Wheat. 316, 429, the power to tax "is an incident of sovereignty, and is coextensive with that to which it is incident. All subjects over which the sovereign power of a state extends, are objects of taxation. . . ."

It was that view which we followed in the Curry case. We held that the Fourteenth Amendment did not prevent both Alabama and Tennessee from imposing death taxes upon the transfer of an interest in intangibles held in trust by an Alabama trustee but passing under the will of a beneficiary decedent domiciled in Tennessee. We stated that rights to intangibles "are but relationships between persons, natural or corporate, which the law recognizes by attaching to them certain sanctions enforceable in courts. The power of government over them and the protection which it gives them cannot be exerted through control of a physical thing. They can be made effective only through control over and protection afforded to those persons whose relationships are the origin of the rights. . . . Obviously, as sources of actual or potential wealth — which is an appropriate measure of any tax imposed on ownership or its exercise — they cannot be dissociated from the persons from whose relationships they are derived. These are not in any sense fictions. They are indisputable realities." 307 U.S. p. 366. We held that the power to tax intangibles was not restricted to one State, whether "we regard the right of a state to tax as founded on power over the object taxed, as declared by Chief Justice Marshall in McCulloch v. Maryland, supra, through dominion over tangibles or over persons whose relationships are the source of intangible rights; or on the benefit and protection conferred by the taxing sovereignty, or both." Id. pp. 367-368. And we added: "Shares of corporate stock may be taxed at the domicile of the shareholder and also at that of the corporation which the taxing state has created and controls; and income may be taxed both by the state where it is earned and by the state of the recipient's domicile. Protection, benefit, and power over the subject matter are not confined to either state." Id., pa. 368. In the recent case of Wisconsin v. J. C. Penney Co., 311 U.S. 435, 444, we gave renewed expression to the same view: "A state is free to pursue its own fiscal policies, unembarrassed by the Constitution, if by the practical operation of a tax the state has exerted its power in relation to opportunities which it has given, to protection which it has afforded, to benefits which it has conferred by the fact of being an orderly, civilized society." And see Graves v. Schmidlapp, 315 U.S. 657.

Furthermore, the rule of immunity against double taxation espoused by First National Bank v. Maine, had long been rejected in other cases. Kidd v. Alabama, supra; Fort Smith Lumber Co. v. Arkansas, 251 U.S. 532; Cream of Wheat Co. v. Grand Forks, 253 U.S. 325. We rejected it again only recently. Illinois Central R. Co. v. Minnesota, 309 U.S. 157. And as we pointed out in the Curry case, the reasons why the Fifth Amendment "does not require us to fix a single exclusive place of taxation of intangibles for the benefit of their foreign owner" (Burnet v. Brooks, 288 U.S. 378) are no less cogent in case of the Fourteenth.   307 U.S. pp. 369, 370.

The recent cases to which we have alluded are all distinguishable on their facts.   But their guiding principles are irreconcilable with the views expressed in First National Bank v. Maine. If we raised a constitutional barrier in this case after having let it down in the Curry case, we would indeed be drawing neat legal distinctions and refinements which certainly cannot be divined from the language of the Constitution.   Certainly any differences between the shares of stock in this case and the intangibles in the Curry case do not warrant differences in constitutional treatment so as to forbid taxation by two States in the one case and to permit it in the other.   If we perpetuated any such differences, we would be doing violence to the words "due process" by drawing lines where the Fourteenth Amendment fails to draw them.   Furthermore, the legal interests in the intangibles here involved are as diverse as they were in the intangibles in the Curry case.   And to say that these shares of stock were localized or had an exclusive situs in New York would be to indulge in the fiction which we rejected in the Curry case.   Any such attempt to fix their whereabouts in New York would disregard the intimate relationship which Utah has to this corporation and its shares.

More specifically, if the question is "whether the state has given anything for which it can ask return" (Wisconsin v. J. C. Penney Co., supra, p. 444), or whether the transfer depends upon and involves the law of Utah for its exercise (Blackstone v. Miller), there can be no doubt that Utah is not restrained by the Fourteenth Amendment from taxing this transfer.   The corporation owes its existence to Utah.   Utah law defines the nature and extent of the interest of the shareholders in the corporation.   Utah law affords protection for those rights.   Utah has power over the transfer by the corporation of its shares of stock.   Certainly that protection, benefit, and power over the shares would have satisfied the test of Blackstone v. Miller and Curry v. McCanless.   But it is said that we are here interested only in the factum of the transfer, and that the stockholder in the case at bar had no need to invoke the law of Utah to effect a complete transfer of his interest.   The argument is based on the fact that the transfer office is located outside Utah, and that, under the Uniform Stock Transfer Act which Utah has adopted (Rev. Stat. 1933 secs. 18-3-1 et seq.), the trend is to treat the shares as merged into the certificates in situations involving the ownership and transfer of the shares.   We do not stop to analyze the many cases which have been cited, nor to speculate as to how Utah would interpret its law in this regard. Suffice it to say that if that freedom of transfer exists as respondents claim, it stems from Utah law. It finds its ultimate source in the authority which Utah has granted. It is indeed a benefit which Utah has bestowed. For it alone Utah may constitutionally ask a return. In view of these realities, we cannot say with the majority in First National Bank v. Maine p. 327, that a "transfer from the dead to the living of any specific property is an event single in character and is effected under the laws, and occurs within the limits, of a particular state," so as to preclude Utah from imposing a tax on this transfer.

We are of course not unmindful of the notions expressed in Farmers Loan & Trust Co. v. Minnesota, and repeated in First National Bank v. Maine, that the view championed by Blackstone v. Miller disturbed the "good relations among the States" and had a "bad" practical effect which led many States "to avoid the evil by resort to reciprocal exemption laws." 280 U.S. p. 209. But, as stated by the minority in First National Bank v. Maine, "We can have no assurance that resort to the Fourteenth Amendment, as the ill-adapted instrument of such a reform, will not create more difficulties and injustices than it will remove." 284 U.S. p. 334. More basically, even though we believed that a different system should be designed to protect against multiple taxation, it is not our province to provide it. See Curry v. McCanless, supra, pp. 373-374. To do so would be to indulge in the dangerous assumption that the Fourteenth Amendment "was intended to give us carte blanche to embody our economic or moral beliefs in its prohibitions." Mrs. Justice Holmes, dissenting, Baldwin v. Missouri, supra, p. 595. It would violate the first principles of constitutional adjudication to strike down state legislation on the basis of our individual views or preferences as to policy, whether the state laws deal with taxes or other subjects of social or economic legislation.

For the reasons stated, we do not think that First National Bank v. Maine should survive. We overrule it. In line with our recent decisions in Curry v. McCanless, Graves v. Elliott and Graves v. Schmidlapp, we repeat that there is no constitutional rule of immunity from taxation of intangibles by more than one State. In case of shares of stock, "jurisdiction to tax" is not restricted to the domiciliary State. Another State which has extended benefits or protection, or which can demonstrate "the practical fact of its power" or sovereignty as respects the shares (Blackstone v. Miller, p. 205), may likewise constitutionally make its exaction. In other words, we restore these intangibles to the constitutional status

which they occupied up to a few years ago.   See Greves v. Shaw,
173 Mass. 205, 53 N.E. 372; Larson v. MacMiller, 56 Utah 84, 189
P. 579, and cases collected in 42 A.L.R. pp. 365 et seq.

We reverse the judgment below and remand the cause to the
Supreme Court of Utah for proceedings not inconsistent with this
opinion.

Reversed.[12]

Mr. Justice Frankfurter wrote a concurring opinion.

Mr. Justice Jackson wrote a dissenting opinion and Mr. Justice Roberts joined in this dissenting opinion.

3.   DOUBLE DOMICILE

If the jurisdiction of a state to impose death taxes in a particular case depends on whether the decedent is domiciled in that

---

[12] Comments on State Tax Commission of Utah v. Aldrich are to be found
in 28 Cornell L.Q. 74 (1942), 37 Ill. L. Rev. 280 (1942), 41 Mich. L. Rev. 351
(1942), 51 Yale L.J. 398 (1942).   See also Brown, Present Status of Multiple
Taxation of Intangible Property, 40 Mich. L. Rev. 806 (1942); Guterman,
Revitalization of Multiple State Death Taxation, 42 Colum. L. Rev. 1249
(1942); Howard, State Jurisdiction to Tax Intangibles; A Twelve-Year Cycle,
8 Mo. L. Rev. 155 (1943).

Shortly after the Aldrich case was decided, Utah, by Laws 1943, S.B. 132,
amended its inheritance tax law.   The revised provisions Utah Code Ann.
§59-12-9 (1953) are as follows:

"Where any property belonging to a foreign estate is subject to the payment of the tax herein provided for, such tax shall be assessed upon the
market value of such property remaining after the payment of such debts and
expenses as are chargeable to the property under the laws of this state, and,
in the event that the executor of such foreign estate files with the clerk of the
court in this state having ancillary jurisdiction statements in writing exhibit-
ing the true market value of the entire estate of the decedent, and the amount
of indebtedness for which the decedent has been adjudged liable at the time
of his death in other jurisdictions, which statements shall be in affidavit form
and sworn to by such executor, there shall also be deducted such proportion
of the said indebtedness of the decedent from the value of the property
within this state as the value of the property within this state bears to the
value of the entire estate; *provided,* that in all such cases where the property
within this state consists of personal property only, the statements hereinbefore provided for shall also be filed with the state tax commission.

"The tax imposed by this chapter in respect of personal property (except
tangible personal property having an actual situs in this state) shall not be
payable (a) if the decedent at the time of his death was a resident of a state
or territory of the United States, which at the time of his death did not impose a transfer tax or death tax of any character in respect of personal property of residents of this state (except tangible personal property having an
actual situs in such state or territory), or, (b) if the laws of the state or territory
of residence of the decedent at the time of his death contained a reciprocal
exemption provision under which non-residents were exempted from transfer
taxes or death taxes of every character in respect of personal property (except
tangible personal property having an actual situs therein), *provided* the state
or territory of residence of such non-residents allowed a similar exemption to
residents of the state or territory of residence of such decedent.   For the pur-

state, multiple state death taxation may result because two or more states may each decide independently that it is the state of domicile. Consider the following case in this connection.

WORCESTER COUNTY TRUST CO. v. RILEY
302 U.S. 292, 58 Sup. Ct. 185, 82 L. Ed. 268 (1937)

Mr. Justice Stone delivered the opinion of the Court.

The question for decision is whether the Federal Interpleader Act. sec. 24(26) of the Judicial Code as amended January 20, 1936, c. 13, sec. 1, 49 Stat. 1096, may be availed of for the litigation and final disposition of the rival claims of two states, each asserting through its officers the right to recover death taxes on the ground that decedent was last domiciled within its boundaries.

Petitioner is the duly qualified executor named in the last will of decedent, which has been probated in Massachusetts. Ancillary administration of the estate has been granted in California. Petitioner brought the present suit in the District Court for Massachusetts, joining as defendants Commissioner of Corporations and Taxation of the Commonwealth of Massachusetts, and respondents, officers of the State of California, all charged with the duty of adminstering death tax statutes of their respective states. The bill of complaint is founded upon the Interpleader Act and seeks the remedy which it affords.

Section 24(26) confers jurisdiction on the district courts in suits of interpleader or in the nature of interpleader, by plaintiffs who are under an obligation to the amount of $500 or more, the benefits of which are demanded by two or more adverse claimants who are citizens of different states. By subsection 26(a) "Such a suit in equity may be entertained although the titles or claims of the conflicting claimants do not have a common origin, or are not identical, but are adverse to and independent of one another." And by subsection 26 (a)(ii) and (d) complainant, upon satisfying jurisdictional requirements of the Act, and depositing the money or property in the registry of the court, or upon giving a prescribed bond, is entitled to a decree discharging him from further liability and enjoining the claimants from further proceedings in other courts to recover the sum claimed.

The bill of complaint alleges that decedent left bank deposits and other intangibles in California and Massachusetts, a substantial part of which has come into the possession or custody of petitioner; that respondents, the California taxing officials, have de-

---

pose of this section the District of Columbia and possessions of the United States shall be considered territories of the United States." — Ed.

termined and assert that decedent at death was domiciled in California, and that under the law of that state his estate is subject to death taxes upon all his intangibles; that respondents threaten to assess and collect there a tax in excess of any which would be due if decedent were domiciled in Massachusetts; that the Massachusetts Commissioner, in behalf of the state, asserts a similar claim that decedent at death was domiciled in Massachusetts, and that his estate is subject to taxes there upon all his intangibles; that it is impossible in law and in fact for decedent to have been domiciled in both states at the time of his death, or for his estate to be subject to death taxes in both states as asserted; and that the attempted collection of the tax is a threatened deprivation of property without due process of law and a denial of equal protection of the laws.   Petitioner prays that the Court order respondent officials of the two states to interplead their respective claims for the tax; that the Court determine the domicile of decedent, the amount of the tax, and the person or persons to whom it is payable; and that respondents be enjoined from any other proceedings to collect it.

Respondents, the California officers, appeared specially and moved to dismiss the complaint upon the ground, among others, that the suit was brought against respondents in their official capacity, and was in substance a suit against the state forbidden by the Eleventh Amendment.   The district court overruled this contention and granted a temporary injunction restraining defendants until further order of the court, from taking any action to assess the tax.   The Court of Appeals for the First Circuit reversed, 89 F.(2d) 59, holding that the maintenance of the suit is an infringement of the Eleventh Amendment, which provides that "The judicial power . . . shall not be construed to extend to any suit in law or equity, commenced or prosecuted against one of the United States by citizens of another state. . . ."   We granted certiorari, 299 U.S. 567, the decision below being of an important question of federal law which has not been but should be settled by this Court.   Supreme Court Rules, 38(5)(b).

Petitioner does not deny that a suit nominally against individuals, but restraining or otherwise affecting their action as state officers, may be in substance a suit against the state, which the Constitution forbids, Louisiana v. Jumel, 107 U.S. 711; Hagood v. Southern, 117 U.S.; In re Ayers, 123 U.S. 443; North Carolina v. Temple, 134 U.S. 22, 30; Smith v. Reeves, 178 U.S. 436; Lankford v. Platte Iron Works, 235 U.S. 461; Ex parte New York, No. 1, 256 U.S. 490, 500; Missouri v. Fiske, 290 U.S. 18, 28; see Cunningham v. Macon & Brunswick R. Co., 109 U.S. 446; cf. Wells v. Roper, 246 U.S. 335, or that generally suits to restrain action of state officials can, consistently with the constitutional prohibition, be prosecuted only when the action sought to be restrained is without the authority of state law or contravenes the statutes or Constitution of the United States. Cf. Ex parte Young, 209 U.S. 123; Scully v. Bird, 209 U.S. 481; Old Colony Trust Co. v. Seattle, 271 U.S. 426, with Louisiana v. Jumel, supra; Hagood v. Southern, supra; In re Ayers, supra; Lankford v. Platte Iron Works, supra. The Eleventh Amendment, which denies to the citizen the right to resort to a federal court to compel or restrain state action, does not preclude suit against a wrongdoer merely because he asserts that his acts are within an official authority which the state does not confer.

Petitioner's contention is that here the prospective official action of respondents involves a threatened violation of the Constitution for which state law can afford no sanction. It is said that as the officers of each state assert the right to collect the tax out of decedent's property within the state, they may succeed in establishing that right by a judicial determination in each that decedent was last domiciled there, cf. Dorrance's Estate, 309 Pa. 151; 163 Atl. 303; In re Estate of Dorrance, 115 N.J. Eq. 268; 170 Atl. 601; 116 N.J. Eq. 204; 172 Atl. 503, with New Jersey v. Pennsylvania, 287 U.S. 580; Dorrance v. Pennsylvania, 287 U.S. 660; Hill v. Martin, 296 U.S. 393, although he could not be domiciled in both; that neither state could constitutionally authorize its officials to impose the tax if decedent was last domiciled elsewhere, and petitioner is thus exposed to the danger of double taxation, which the Constitution forbids. See First National Bank v. Maine, 284 U.S. 312; Farmers Loan & Trust Co. v. Minnesota, 280 U.S. 204. As those officials threaten acts whose consequence may be taxation which is unauthorized by any valid state enactment, petitioner insists that the suit brought to restrain such action does not run against the state.

But this argument confuses the possibility of conflict of decisions of the courts of the two states, which the Constitution does not forestall, with other types of action by state officers which, because it passes beyond the limits of a lawful authority, is within the reach of the federal judicial power notwithstanding the Eleventh Amendment. This Court has held that state statutes, construed to impose death taxes upon the intangibles of decedents domiciled elsewhere, infringe the Fourteenth Amendment, and it has accordingly reversed judgments of state courts enforcing such liability. First National Bank v. Maine, supra; Farmers Loan & Trust Co. v. Minnesota, supra. But petitioner does not assert that there are such statutes in California or Massachuettts, or that the courts in those states have ever held or threaten to hold that their laws taxing inheritances apply to intangibles of those domiciled in other states.

Although the bill of complaint states that respondents, California officials, "have determined" that decedent was domiciled in California, it is not contended that they have or are assuming authority to assess the tax, independently of the judgment of the court. Under California statutes, inheritance taxes are assessed by judicial proceedings resulting, after full opportunity for presentation of evidence and a hearing, in a judgment which is reviewable on appeal by the state courts, and by this Court if it involves any denial of federal right. Secs. 14, 15, 16, 17 and 18, Cal. Inheritance Tax Act of June 3, 1921, Stats. 1921, p. 1500, as amended; see Stebbins v. Riley, 268 U.S. 137; Estate of Haskins, 170 Cal. 267; 149 Pac. 576; Estate of Brown, 196 Cal. 114; 236 Pac. 144.

Petitioner does not contend that respondents, the California officers, propose to do more than invoke the action of its courts to assess a lawful tax and to seek there a judicial determination that decedent was domiciled in California as the basis of its power to impose the tax. Nor is it denied that in so doing they are acting in the performance of official duty imposed upon them by state statutes, which conform to all constitutional requirements. Petitioner's real concern is that the judgment of the California court, if it should decide that decedent was domiciled there, may be erroneous or may conflict with that of the Massachusetts courts. But conflicting decisions upon the same issue of fact do not necessarily connote erroneous judicial action. Differences in proof and the latitude necessarily allowed to the trier of fact in each case to weigh and draw inferences from evidence and to pass upon the credibility of witnesses, might lead an appellate court to conclude that in none is the judgment erroneous. In any case the Constitution of the United States does not guarantee that the decisions of state courts shall be free from error, Central Land Co. v. Laidley, 159 U.S. 103; Tracy v. Ginzberg, 205 U.S. 170, or require that pronouncements shall be consistent. Milwaukee Electric Ry. & L. Co. v. Wisconsin ex rel. Milwaukee, 252 U.S. 100, 106. Neither the Fourteenth Amendment nor the full faith and credit clause requires uniformity in the decisions of the courts of different states as to the place of domicil, where the exertion of state power is dependent upon domicil within its boundaries. Thormann v. Frame, 176 U.S. 350; Overby v. Gordon, 177 U.S. 214; Burbank v. Ernst, 232 U.S. 162; Baker v. Baker, Eccles & Co., 242 U.S. 394;

Iowa v. Slimmer, 248 U.S. 115, 120, 121; cf. Tilt v. Kelsey, 207 U.S. 43. Hence it cannot be said that the threatened action of respondents involves any breach of state law or of the laws or Constitution of the United States. Since the proposed action is the performance of a duty imposed by the statute of the state upon state officials through whom alone the state can act, restraint of their action, which the bill of complaint prays, is restraint of state action, and the suit is in substance one against the state which the Eleventh Amendment forbids. We do not pass on the construction of the Interpleader Act or its applicability in other respects.

Unlike that in Ex parte Young, supra, and in the many cases which have followed it, the present suit is not founded on the asserted unconstitutionality of any state statute and the consequent want of lawful authority for official action taken under it. In City Bank Farmers Trust Co. v. Schnader, 291 U.S. 24, on which petitioner relies, it was held that the bill of complaint stated a cause of action in equity to enjoin a state official from proceeding to assess and collect an inheritance tax upon chattels alleged to have no tax situs within the state. The objection that the suit was one against the state within the meaning of the Eleventh Amendment was not urged or considered on the appeal to this Court.

Affirmed.[13]

---

[13] Comments on Worcester County Trust Co. v. Riley are to be found in 11 So. Calif. L. Rev. 329 (1938) and 86 U. of Pa. L. Rev. 306 (1938). See also Simons, Dangers of Double Domicile and Double Taxation, 20 Taxes 345 (1942).

For an example of a situation in which the Supreme Court of the United States resolved a conflict between states as to a person's domicile, see Texas v. Florida, 306 U.S. 398, 59 Sup. Ct. 563, 83 L. Ed. 817 (1939). In Massachusetts v. Missouri, 308 U.S. 1, 60 Sup. Ct. 39, 84 L. Ed. 3 (1939), a bill was instituted by Massachusetts against Missouri and certain citizens of Missouri, which alleged that Massachusetts had assessed a tax on a transfer by the decedent, who was one of its own citizens, and that to satisfy this tax it was necessary to resort to intangible assets of the decedent consisting of securities held by the individual defendants, as trustees, in Missouri. It was alleged that Missouri also levied a like tax on this property. The bill requested that the respective rights of the two states be adjudicated. It appeared that the property involved was sufficient to answer the claims of both states and that each state might constitutionally present its claim. Consequently, the court held that the bill did not present a justiciable controversy between the two states. Texas v. Florida was distinguished on the ground that in that case only a single tax could constitutionally be levied and there was danger that, through successful processing of the claims by several states in independent suits, enough of the estate would be absorbed to deprive some state of its lawful tax.

Revenue Ruling 60-88, I.R.B. 1960-10, 20, allows a credit for the amount paid to each of several states, where each is claiming the decedent was a domiciliary of that state, up to the maximum total credit permitted under 1954 I.R.C. §2011. The fact that, under a compromise agreement effected among the interested parties as to the amount of tax liability to each state, one of the

PROBLEM

16.8. In situations where mulitiple claims may be made with respect to the domicile of a person, what steps can be taken to increase the likelihood that he will be deemed domiciled in only one state? [14]

---

states is designated as the decedent's domicile will not alter the result. Revenue Ruling 56-230, 1956-1 C.B. 660, referred to supra page 1015, note 7, is distinguished on the ground that there a state not the domicile of the decedent was attempting to tax indirectly intangibles of the decedent located outside of the state in contravention of rules laid down by the Supreme Court. Mimeograph 3971, XI-2, C.B. 427 (1932), which states that no credit will be allowed to a decedent's estate for state taxes paid on intangible property after January 4, 1932, to a state other than that of the decedent's domicile, is amplified by Rev. Rul. 60-88.

[14] Some states have statutes designed to provide a mechanism which may be used to resolve conflicting state claims as to domicile. See Mass. Ann. Laws, c. 65B, §§1-7; Mich. Stat. Ann. §§7.592(1) to 7.592(7) (1960). For a comment on a Delaware statute, see 56 Harv. L. Rev. 482 (1942). See also Faught, Reciprocity in State Taxation as the Next Step in Empirical Legislation, 92 U. of Pa. L. Rev. 258 (1944).

CHAPTER XVII

Multiple State Income Taxation

When a person establishes a trust in his estate plan and the trustees and trust property are located in one state and the beneficiary who receives the income resides in another, can the income from the trust be taxed by each of the states involved? Consider the following cases in answering this question.

MAGUIRE v. TREFRY
253 U.S. 12, 40 Sup. Ct. 417, 64 L. Ed. 739 (1920)

MR. JUSTICE DAY delivered the opinion of the Court.

Massachusetts has a statute providing for a tax upon incomes (Gen. Acts Mass. 1916, c. 269). In the act imposing the tax it is provided: "If an inhabitant of this commonwealth receives income from one or more executors, administrators or trustees, none of whom is an inhabitant of this commonwealth or has derived his appointment from a court of this commonwealth, such income shall be subject to the taxes assessed by this act, according to the nature of the income received by the executors, administrators or trustees."

The plaintiff in error is a resident of the State of Massachusetts, and was taxed upon income from a trust created by the will of one Matilda P. MacArthur formerly of Philadelphia. The plaintiff in error under the will of the decedent was the beneficiary of a trust thereby created. The securities were held in trust by the Girard Trust Company of Philadelphia. Those which were directly taxable to the trustee were held exempt from taxation in Massachusetts under the terms of the statute of that State. The securities the income from which was held taxable in Massachusetts consisted of the bonds of three corporations and certain certificates of the Southern Railway Equipment Trust. These securities were held in the possession of the trustee in Philadelphia. The trust was being administered under the laws of Pennsylvania. The Supreme Judicial Court of Massachusetts held the tax to be valid. 230 Massachusetts, 503.

Of the nature of the tax the Chief Justice of Massachusetts, speaking for the Supreme Judicial Court, said: "The income tax is measured by reference to the riches of the person taxed actually made available to him for valuable use during a given period.   It establishes a basis of taxation directly proportionate to ability to bear the burden.   It is founded upon the protection afforded to the recipient of the income by the Government of the Commonwealth of his residence in his person, in his right to receive the income and in his enjoyment of the income when in his possession.   That government provides for him all the advantages of living in safety and in freedom and of being protected by law.   It gives security to life, liberty and the other privileges of dwelling in a civilized community.   It exacts in return a contribution to the support of that government measured by and based upon the income, in the fruition of which it defends him from unjust interference.   It is true of the present tax, as was said by Chief Justice Shaw in Bates v. Boston, 5 Cush. 93, at page 99, 'The assessment does not touch the fund, or control it; nor does it interfere with the trustee in the exercise of his proper duties; nor call him, nor hold him, to any accountability.   It affects only the income, after it has been paid by the trustee' to the beneficiary.''

We see no reason to doubt the correctness of this view of the nature and effect of the Massachusetts statute, and shall accept it for the purpose of considering the federal question before us, which arises from the contention of the plaintiff in error that the imposition of the tax was a denial of due process of law within the protection of the Fourteenth Amendment to the Federal Constitution, because it is alleged, the effect of the statute is to subject property to taxation which is beyond the limits and outside the jurisdiction of the State.   To support this contention the plaintiff in error relies primarily upon the decision of this court in Union Refrigerator Transit Co. v. Kentucky, 199 U.S. 194.   In that case we held that tangible, personal property, permanently located in another State than that of the owner, where it had acquired a situs, and was taxed irrespective of the domicile of the owner, — was beyond the taxing power of the State, and that an attempt to tax such property at the owner's domicile was a denial of due process of law under the Fourteenth Amendment. This ruling was made with reference to cars of the Transit Company permanently employed outside the State of the owner's residence.   In that case this court in the opinion of Mr. Justice Brown, speaking for it, expressly said that the taxation of intangible personal property was not involved.   (199 U.S. 211.)

It is true that in some instances we have held that bonds and bills and notes although evidences of debt have come to be regarded as property which may acquire a taxable situs at the place where they are kept, which may be elsewhere than at the domicile of the owner. These cases rest upon the principle that such instruments are more than mere evidences of debt, and may be taxed in the jurisdiction where located, and where they receive the protection of local law and authority. Blackstone v. Miller, 188 U.S. 189, 206. People ex rel. Jefferson v. Smith, 88 N.Y. 576, 585. At the last term we held in DeGanay v. Lederer, 250 U.S. 376, that stocks and bonds issued by domestic corporations, and mortgages on domestic real estate, although owned by an alien nonresident, but in the hands of an agent in this country with authority to deal with them, were subject to the Income Tax Law of October 3, 1913, 38 Stat. 166.

In the present case we are not dealing with the right to tax securities which have acquired local situs, but are concerned with the right of the State to tax the beneficiary of a trust at her residence, although the trust itself may be created and administered under the laws of another State.

In Fidelity & Columbia Trust Company v. Louisville, 245 U.S. 54, we held that a bank deposit of a resident of Kentucky in the bank of another State, where it was taxed, might be taxed as a credit belonging to the resident of Kentucky. In that case Union Refrigerator Transit Co. v. Kentucky, supra, was distinguished, and the principle was affirmed that the State of the owner's domicile might tax the credits of a resident although evidenced by debts due from residents of another State. This is the general rule recognized in the maxim "mobilia sequuntur personam," and justifying, except under exceptional circumstances, the taxation of credits and beneficial interests in property at the domicile of the owner. We have pointed out in other decisions that the principle of that maxim is not of universal application and may yield to the exigencies of particular situations. But we think it is applicable here.

It is true that the legal title of the property is held by the trustee in Pennsylvania. But it is so held for the benefit of the beneficiary of the trust, and such beneficiary has an equitable right, title and interest distinct from its legal ownership. "The legal owner holds the direct and absolute dominion over the property in the view of the law; but the income, profits, or benefits thereof in his hands, belong wholly, or in part, to others." 2 Story's Equity, 11th ed., sec. 964. It is this property right belonging to the beneficiary, realized in the shape of income, which is the subject matter of the tax under the statute of Massachusetts.

The beneficiary is domiciled in Massachusetts, has the protection of her laws, and there receives and holds the income from the trust property. We find nothing in the Fourteenth Amendment which prevents the taxation in Massachusetts of an interest of this character, thus owned and enjoyed by a resident of the State. The case presents no difference in principle from the taxation of credits evidenced by the obligations of persons who are outside of the State which are held taxable at the domicile of the owner. Kirtland v. Hotchkiss, 100 U.S. 491.

We find no error in the judgment and the same is
Affirmed.[1]

Dissenting, MR. JUSTICE McREYNOLDS.

GREENOUGH v. TAX ASSESSORS OF NEWPORT

331 U.S. 486, 67 Sup. Ct. 1400, 91 L. Ed. 1621 (1947)

MR. JUSTICE REED delivered the opinion of the Court.

Appellants are testamentary trustees of George H. Warren,

---

[1] The present Massachusetts statutory provisions concerned with the taxation of income from trusts provide in substance as follows:

  a. The trustees are required to pay a Massachusetts income tax on the trust income if it is payable to, or accumulated for the benefit of, inhabitants of Massachusetts where the trustees are
  (1) Trustees under a will of a person who died an inhabitant of Massachusetts; or
  (2) Trustees under a trust created by a person or persons, any one of whom was an inhabitant of Massachusetts at the time of the creation of the trust or at any time during the year for which the income is computed or who died an inhabitant of Massachusetts, if one or more of the trustees is an inhabitant of Massachusetts.
  b. The trustees are required to pay a Massachusetts income tax on income received from professions, employment, trade or business carried on within Massachusetts by the trustees, regardless of whether the persons to whom the income from the trust is payable, or for whose benefit it is accumulated, are residents or nonresidents of Massachusetts.
  c. Income received by trustees which is accumulated for the benefit of unborn or unascertained persons or persons with uncertain interests is taxed as if accumulated for the benefit of a known inhabitant of Massachusetts.

See Mass. Ann. Laws, c. 62, §10 (Supp. 1958).

An inhabitant of Massachusetts who receives or is entitled to receive trust income or to whom it is available must pay the tax on the income himself, if the tax is not payable by the trustees. See Mass. Ann. Laws, c. 62, §11. For an interpretation of this section as it was worded prior to an amendment in 1955, see State Tax Commission v. Fitts, — Mass. —, 165 N.E.2d 586 (1960).

The way in which the beneficiary's exemption under the Massachusetts income tax laws is handled when the trustee is required to pay the tax on trust income is covered by Mass. Ann. Laws, c. 62, §§12, 12A (Supp. 1959). In this regard, see State Tax Commission v. Blinder, 336 Mass. 698, 147 N.E.2d 796 (1958). — ED.

who died a resident of New York. His will was duly probated in that state and letters testamentary issued to appellants as executors. A duly authenticated copy of said will was filed and recorded in Rhode Island and there letters testamentary were also issued. Letters of trusteeship were granted to appellants by a surrogate's court in New York. None were needed or asked for or granted by Rhode Island. At all times pertinent to this appeal, appellants, as trustees under the will, held intangible personalty for the benefit of Constance W. Warren for her life and then to certain as yet undetermined future beneficiaries.

The evidences of the intangible property in the estate of George H. Warren and in the trust in question were at all times in New York. The life beneficiary and one of the trustees are residents of New York. The other trustee resides in Rhode Island. During the period in question, he did not, however, exercise his powers, as trustee, in Rhode Island.

A personal property tax of $50 was assessed by the City of Newport, Rhode Island, against the resident trustee upon one-half of the value of the corpus of the trust. The applicable assessment statute for ad valorem taxes appears in the margin.[2] At the time of this assessment, the property consisted of 500 shares of the capital stock of Standard Oil Company of New Jersey. The tax was paid by the trustees and this suit instituted, under appropriate state procedure, in the Superior Court of the County of Newport to recover the tax from the city. The Superior Court by decision denied the petition. A bill of exceptions was prosecuted by these petitioners to the Supreme Court of Rhode Island which overruled the exceptions and remitted the case to the superior court. [Footnote omitted.] Thereupon judgment was entered for the appellees and an appeal allowed to this Court. All questions of state procedures and of the applicability of the state stat-

---

[2] (*Court footnote*) General Laws of Rhode Island (1938), c. 30, Section 9:
"*Fifth.* Intangible personal property held in trust by any executor, administrator, or trustee, whether under an express or implied trust, the income of which is to be paid to any other person, shall be taxed to such executor, administrator, or trustee in the town where such other person resides; but if such other person resides out of the state, then in the town where the executor, administrator, or trustee resides; and if there be more than one such executor, administrator, or trustee, then in equal proportions to each of such executors, administrators, and trustees in the towns where they respectively reside." [The following language has been added to the Rhode Island statute: "provided, however, that in case of intangible personal property held by a resident trustee under a trust created by deed or will of a nonresident of this state, which property or the income therefrom is liable to taxation in the state of domicile of the creator of the trust and which property is not employed in carrying on any business within this state or has not acquired a business situs within this state, no city or town shall assess a tax to such trustee upon such property." See R.I. Gen. Laws Ann. §44-4-13 (1956).] — ED.

ute to the resident trustee in the circumstances of this case were foreclosed for us by the rulings of the Supreme Court of Rhode Island. [Footnote omitted.]

The appellants' contention throughout has been that the Rhode Island statute, under which the assessment was made, if applicable to the resident trustee, was unconstitutional under the due process clause of the Fourteenth Amendment to the Constitution of the United States. Their objection in the state courts and here is that Rhode Island cannot tax the resident trustee's proportionate part of these trust intangibles merely because that trustee resides in Rhode Island. Such a tax, they urge, is unconstitutional under the due process clause because it exacts payment measured by the value of property wholly beyond the reach of Rhode Island's power and to which that state does not give protection or benefit. Appellants specifically disclaim reliance upon the argument that the Rhode Island tax exposes them to the danger of other ad valorem taxes in another state. [Footnote omitted.] The same concession was made in the Supreme Court of Rhode Island. [Footnote omitted.] We therefore restrict our discussion and determination to the issue presented by appellants' insistence that Rhode Island cannot constitutionally collect this tax because the state rendered no equivalent for its exaction in protection of or benefit to the trust fund.

For the purpose of the taxation of those resident within her borders, Rhode Island has sovereign power unembarrassed by any restriction except those that emerge from the Constitution. Whether that power is exercised wisely or unwisely is the problem of each state. It may well be that sound fiscal policy would be promoted by a tax upon trust intangibles levied only by the state that is the seat of a testamentary trust. [Footnote omitted.] Or, it may be that the actual domicile of the trustee should be preferred for a single tax. Utilization by the states of modern reciprocal statutory tax provisions may more fairly distribute tax benefits and burdens, although the danger of competitive inducements for obtaining a settlor's favor are obvious. [Footnote omitted.] But our question here is whether or not a provision of the Constitution forbids this tax. Neither the expediency of the levy nor its economic effect on the economy of the taxing state is for our consideration. [Footnote omitted.] We are dealing with the totality of a state's authority in the exercise of its revenue raising powers.

The Fourteenth Amendment has been held to place a limit on a state's power to lay an ad valorem tax on its residents. [Footnote omitted.] Previous decisions of this Court have held that mere power over a resident does not permit a state to exact from him a property tax on his tangible property permanently located outside the jurisdiction of the taxing state. [Footnote omitted.] Such an exaction, the cases teach, would violate the due process clause of the Fourteenth Amendment, because no benefit or protection, adequate to support a tax exaction, is furnished by the state of residence. [Footnote omitted.] The domiciliary state of the owner of tangibles permanently located in another state, however, may require its resident to contribute to the government under which he lives by an income tax in which the income from the out-of-state property is an item of the taxpayer's gross income. It is immaterial, in such a case, that the property producing the income is located in another state. New York ex rel. Cohn v. Graves, 300 U.S. 308. And, where the tangible property of a corporation has no taxable situs outside the domicilary state, that state may tax the tangibles because the corporation exists under the law of its domicile. Southern Pacific Co. v. Kentucky, 222 U.S. 63. [Footnote omitted.]

The precedents, holding it unconstitutional for a state to tax tangibles of a resident that are permanently beyond its boundaries, have not been applied to intangibles where the documents of owner interest are beyond the confines of the taxing jurisdiction or where the choses in action are mere promises of a nonresident without documents. [Footnote omitted.] One reason that state taxation of a resident on his intangibles is justified is that when the taxpayer's wealth is represented by intangibles, the tax gatherer has difficulty in locating them and there is uncertainty as to which taxing district affords benefits or protection to the actual property that the intangibles represent. There may be no "papers." If the assessment is not made at the residence of the owner, intangibles may be overlooked easily by other assessors of taxes. A state is dependent upon its citizens for revenue. Wealth has long been accepted as a fair measure of a tax assessment. As a practical mode of collecting revenue, the states unrestricted by the federal Constitution have been accustomed to assess property taxes upon intangibles "wherever actually held or deposited," belonging to their citizens and regardless of the location of the debtor. [Footnote omitted.] So long as a state chooses to tax the value of intangibles as a part of a taxpayer's wealth, the location of the evidences of ownership is immaterial. If the location of the documents was controlling, their transfer to another jurisdiction would defeat the tax of the domiciliary state. As a matter of fact, there is more reason for the domiciliary state of the owner of the intangibles than for any other taxing jurisdiction to collect a property tax on the intangibles. Since the intangibles themselves have no real situs, the domicile of the owner is the nearest approximation, although other taxing jurisdictions may also have power to tax the same intangibles. [Footnote omitted.] Normally the intangibles are subject to the immediate control of the owner. This close relationship between the intangibles and the owner furnishes an adequate basis for the tax on the owner by the state of his residence as against any attack for violation of the Fourteenth Amendment. The state of the owner's residence supplies the owner with the benefits and protection inherent in the existence of an organized government. He may choose to expand his activities beyond its borders but the state of his residence is his base of operations. It is the place where he exercises certain privileges of citizenship and enjoys the protection of his domiciliary government. Does a similar relationship exist between a trustee and the intangibles of a trust?

The trustee of today moves freely from state to state. The settlor's residence may be one state, the seat of a trust another state and the trustee or trustees may live in still another jurisdiction or may constantly change their residence. [Footnote omitted.] The official life of a trustee is, of course, different from his personal. A trust, this Court has said, is "an abstraction." For federal income tax purposes it is sometimes dealt with as though it had a separate existence. Anderson v. Wilson, 289 U.S. 20, 27. This is because Congress has seen fit so to deal with the trust. This entity, the trust, from another point of view consists of separate interests, the equitable interest in the res of the beneficiary [footnote omitted] and the legal interest of the trustee. The legal interest of the trustee in the res is a distinct right. It enables a settlor to protect his beneficiaries from the burdens of ownership, while the beneficiary retains the right, through equity, to compel the legal owner to act in accordance with his trust obligations. The trustee as the owner of this legal interest in the res may incur obligations in the administration of the trust enforceable against him, personally. [Footnote omitted.] Nothing else appearing, the trustee is personally liable at law for contracts for the trust. [Footnote omitted.] This is the rule in Rhode Island. [Footnote omitted.] Specific performance may be decreed against him. [Footnote omitted.] Of course, the trustee when acting within his powers for the trust is entitled to exoneration or reimbursement [footnote omitted] and the trust res may be pursued in equity by the creditor for payment. [Footnote omitted.]

The Supreme Court of Rhode Island considered the argument that the laws of the state afforded no benefit or protection to the resident trustee.   Although nothing appeared as to any specific benefit or protection which the trustee had actually received, it concluded that the state was "ready, willing and capable" of furnishing either "if requested."   A resident trustee of a foreign trust would be entitled to the same advantages from Rhode Island laws as would any natural person there resident.   Greenough v. Tax Assessors, supra, 488, 47 A.2d at 631.   There may be matters of trust administration which can be litigated only in the courts of the state that is the seat of the trust.   For example, in the case of a testamentary trust, the appointment of trustees, settlement, termination and distribution under the provisions of the trust are to be carried out, normally, in the courts of decedent's domicile.   See Harrison v. Commissioner of Corporations, 272 Mass. 422, 427, 172 N.E. 605, 608.   But when testamentary trustees reside outside of the jurisdiction of the courts of the state of the seat of the trust, third parties dealing with the trustee on trust matters or beneficiaries may need to proceed directly against the trustee as an individual for matters arising out of his relation to the trust.   Or the resident trustee may need the benefit of the Rhode Island law to enforce trust claims against a Rhode Island resident.   As the trustee is a citizen of Rhode Island, the federal courts would not be open to the trustee for such causes of action where the federal jurisdiction depended upon diversity.   The citizenship of the trustee and not the seat of the trust or the residence of the beneficiary is the controlling factor.   [Footnote omitted.]   The trustee is suable like any other obligor.   There is no provision of the federal Constitution which forbids suits in state courts against a resident trustee of a trust created under the laws of a sister state.   Consequently, we must conclude that Rhode Island does offer benefit and protection through its law to the resident trustee as the owner of intangibles.   And, while it may logically be urged that these benefits and protection are no more than is offered a resident owner of land or chattels, permanently out of the state, the same reasons, hereinbefore stated on pages 492 and 493, apply that permit state property taxation of a resident owner of intangibles while denying a state power to tax similarly the resident's out-of-state realty.

No precedent from this Court called to our attention indicates that the federal Constitution contains provisions that forbid taxation by a state of intangibles in the hands of a resident testamentary trustee.   In Brooke v. Norfolk, 277 U.S. 27, the state property tax there invalidated, evidently as violative of the Fourteenth Amendment, was assessed to a life beneficiary, on a res, composed of intangibles, when both the testator and the trustee were residents of another state where the trust was administered.   Safe Deposit and Trust Company v. Virginia, 280 U.S. 83, held invalid a state's tax on a trust's intangibles, actually in the hands of the nonresident trustee and not subject to the control of the equitable owner, because it was an attempt to tax the trust res, intangibles actually in the hands of a nonresident trustee.   This was said to conflict with the Fourteenth Amendment as a tax on a thing beyond the jurisdiction of the taxing state.[3]   See also Graves v. Schmidlapp, 315 U.S. 657, 663, where the sovereign power of taxation was held to extend to a state resident who by will disposed of intangibles held by him as trustee with power of testamentary disposition under a nonresident trust.   Nothing in these cases leads to the conclusion that a state may not tax intangibles in the hands of a resident trustee of an out-of-state trust.[4]

State courts construe their statutes according to their understanding of state policy and apply them to such situations as their interpretation of the statutory language requires.   In so adjudging, they are the final judicial authority upon the meaning of their state law.   It is only in circumstances where their judgments collide with rights secured by the federal Constitution that we have power to protect or enforce the federal rights.   In adjudging the taxability under state law of a resident trustee's ownership of intangibles, without reliance upon the residence of settlor or beneficiary or the location of the intangibles, various conclusions have been reached under state law and without regard to the Constitution of the United States.   They are pertinent to our problem only as illustrations of the different viewpoints of state law.[5]

Nor do we think it constitutionally significant that the Rhode

[3] *(Court footnote)*   The power of a state to tax the equitable interest of a beneficiary in such circumstances was not presented. Id., pp. 92 and 95.

[4] *(Court footnote)*   Goodsite v. Lane, 139 F. 593 (C.C.A. 6th), holds that a state property tax on a trustee's intangibles for the sole reason that he resides in the taxing state is invalid.   It would seem this was so decided because of the Fourteenth Amendment.   We do not think this case gives proper recognition to the state's power to tax the owner of the legal title to the res.

[5] *(Court footnote)*   The state statute taxing property to the trustee validly applies to the resident trustee: Welch v. City of Boston, 221 Mass. 155, 109 N.E. 174; Harvard Trust Co. v. Commissioner of Taxation, 284 Mass. 225, 230, 187 N.E. 596, 598; Mackay v. San Francisco, 128 Cal. 678, 61 P. 382; Millsaps v. Jackson, 78 Miss. 537, 30 So. 756; McLellan v. Concord, 78 N.H. 89, 97 A. 552; Florida v. Beardsley, 77 Fla. 803, 82 So. 794.

The state tax statute is inapplicable to the resident trustee: Dorrance's Estate, 333 Pa. 162, 3 A.2d 682; Commonwealth v. Peebles, 134 Ky. 121, 135, 119 S.W. 774, 778; Darrow v. Coleman, 119 N.Y. 137, 23 N.E. 488; Rand v. Pittsfield, 70 N.H. 530, 49 A. 88.   Newcomb v. Paige, 224 Mass. 516, 113 N.E. 458, and Harrison v. Commissioner, 272 Mass. 422, 172 N.E. 605, declined taxation on the ground of comity and thus distinguished Welch v. City of Boston, supra, 272 Mass. 428-29, 172 N.E. 609.

Island trustee is not the sole trustee of the New York trust. The assessment, as the statute in question required, was only upon his proportionate interest, as a trustee, in the res. Whatever may have been the character of his title to the intangibles [footnote omitted] or the limitations on his sole administrative power over the trust, [footnote omitted] the resident trustee was the possessor of an interest in the intangibles, sufficient, as we have explained, to support a proportional tax for the benefit and protection afforded to that interest by Rhode Island.[6]

Affirmed.

MR. JUSTICE FRANKFURTER, concurring.

In view of the dissents elicited by the Court's opinion, I should like to state why I join it.

Rhode Island taxes its permanent residents in proportion to the value of their property. The State imposes the tax whether its residents own property outright or own it, legally speaking, in a fiduciary capacity. It is not questioned that the intangible assets in controversy could be included in the measure of the tax against the person of this trustee if he owned them outright. The doctrine that the power of taxation does not extend to chattels permanently situated outside a State though the owner was within it, Union Refrigerator Transit Co. v. Kentucky, 199 U.S. 194; Frick v. Pennsylvania, 268 U.S. 473, is inapplicable. The tax is challenged, as wanting in "due process," because the Rhode Island resident is merely trustee of these intangibles and the pieces of paper that evidence them are kept outside the State.

Rhode Island's system of taxing its residents — subjecting them to the same measure for ascertaining their ability to pay whether they hold property for themselves or for others — long antedated the Fourteenth Amendment. Rhode Island has imposed this tax, "it may be presumed, for the general advantages of living within the jurisdiction." Fidelity & Columbia Trust Co. v. Louisville, 245 U.S. 54, 58. It can hardly be deemed irrational to say, as Rhode Island apparently has said for a hundred years, that those advantages may be roughly measured, for fiscal purposes, by the wealth which a person controls, whatever his ultimate beneficial interest in the property. "The Fourteenth Amendment, itself a historical product did not destroy history for the State and substitute mechanical compartments of law all exactly alike." Jackman v. Rosenbaum Co. 260 U.S. 22, 31.

---

[6] (*Court footnote*) The state courts have reached varying conclusions under their statutes: See People ex rel. Beaman v. Feitner, 168 N.Y. 360, 61 N.E. 280; Mackay v. San Francisco, 128 Cal. 678, 61 P. 382; McLellan v. Concord, 78 N.H. 89, 97 A. 552; Dorrance's Estate, 333 Pa. 162, 3 A.2d 682; Newcomb v. Paige, 224 Mass. 516, 113 N.E. 458; Harrison v. Commissioner, 272 Mass. 422, 430-31. 172 N.E. 605, 609-10.

In any event, Rhode Island could in terms tax its residents for acting as trustees, and determine the amount of the tax as though a trustee owned his trust estate outright. Rhode Island has, in effect, done so by treating all Rhode Island resident alike in relation to their property holdings, regardless of their beneficial interests. That is the practical operation of the statute. It is that which controls constitutionality, and not the form in which a State has cast a tax. Lawrence v. State Tax Commission, 286 U.S. 276, 280; Wisconsin v. J. C. Penney Co., 311 U.S. 435, 443 et seq. Whether a Rhode Island trustee can go against his trust estate for the amount of the tax which Rhode Island exacts from him is of no concern to Rhode Island. Rhode Island's power to tax its residents is not contingent upon it. A trusteeship is a free undertaking.

Mr. JUSTICE JACKSON, dissenting.

If Rhode Island had laid a tax on one of its citizens individually, I should think it unassailable even if the basis for taxing him was that he held this trusteeship, and perhaps the tax on him could be measured by the value of the trust estate. In that case the state would tax only its own citizen. One is pretty much at the mercy of his own state as to the events or relationship for which it will tax him. If it wants to make the holding of a trusteeship taxable, I know of no federal grounds of objection. But that is not what is being done, nor what this decision authorizes.

If Rhode Island has taxed the individual, he might have sought reimbursement from the estate. Whether the estate was chargeable would be left to determination by the courts of the state supervising the trust. They might consider the nature of the tax to be a personal charge, as an income tax would doubtless be. Or they might find it to be an expense of administration, such as a transfer tax, and properly to be borne by the fund. But here no such decision is left to the courts which control the fund — the tax is laid on the trustee as such — the estate is the taxpayer.

Rhode Island claims the power to tax the estate solely because one of its trustees resides in that state. No property is in Rhode Island and its courts are not supervising administration of the trust. The estate is wholly located in New York and the trustees derive their authority, powers and title from its courts and to them must account.

I had not supposed that a trust fund became taxable in every state in which one of its trustees may reside. Of course, in this instance it is proposed to tax only one-half of the estate as only one of the two trustees is resident in Rhode Island. But this seems to be an act of grace if there is a right to tax at all. The trustee has no power over, or title to, any fraction of the trust property that he does not have over all of it.   If mere residence of a trustee is such a conductor of state authority that through him it reaches the estate, I see no reason why it should stop at a part, nor indeed why a trustee subject to the taxing power of several states, cf. Texas v. Florida, 306 U.S. 398, may not also subject the trust fund to several state taxes by merely moving about.

The decision is a hard blow to the practice of naming individual trustees.   It seems to me that there is no power in the state to lay the tax on the trust funds, despite unquestionable authority to tax its own citizen-trustee individually.

MR. JUSTICE MURPHY joins in this opinion.

MR. JUSTICE RUTLEDGE, with whom THE CHIEF JUSTICE concurs, dissenting.

I am in agreement with the views expressed by MR. JUSTICE JACKSON, except that I intimate no opinion concerning whether Rhode Island could lay a tax upon one of its residents for the privilege of acting as one of two or more trustees, when the state's only connection with the trust arises from the fact of his residence. This is not such a case.

Whether or not due process under the Fourteenth Amendment forbids state taxation of acts, transactions, events or property is essentially a practical matter and one of degree, depending upon the existence of sufficient factual connections, having economic and legal effects, between the taxing state and the subject of the tax.   I do not think the mere fact that one of a number of trustees resides in a state, without more, is a sufficiently substantial connection to justify a levy by that state upon the trust corpus, by an ad volorem tax either fractional or on the entirety of the res.

It may become necessary for claimants, beneficiaries or others to sue the trustee in Rhode Island or perhaps for him to join with other trustees in suing third persons there about trust matters. To that extent benefit and protection may be conferred upon the trust.   But those needs may arise in connection with any sort of business or activity, trust or other, located and conducted outside the state as largely as this trust's affairs.   I had not supposed that merely keeping open the state's courts to such claims would furnish a sufficient basis for bringing within its taxing grasp all property affected by the claims' assertion.   That the trust res here consists of intangibles does not seem to me a sufficiently substantial factor, in the circumstances presented, to justify so wide a reach of the state's taxing arm.

Mobilia sequuntur personam has its appropriate uses for sustaining the states' taxing powers affecting residents and their extrastate interests.   But when it is applied to the split ownership of a trust, not only as between trustee and beneficiary but also as among several trustees, to bring the trust res within the several states' powers of taxation, merely by virtue of the residence in each of one trustee and nothing more, the fiction I think is carried too far. Something more than affording a domiciliary basis for service of process, coupled with the split and qualified representative ownership of such a trustee, should be required to sustain the state's power to tax the trust res, whether for all or only a fraction of its value.

Finally, whatever might be true of a single trustee or of several residing in a single state, I should doubt the thesis that the interest of one of two or more trustees in a trust is more substantial than that of a beneficiary or receives greater protection or benefit from the state of his residence. And if the beneficiary's residence alone is insufficient to sustain a state's power to tax the corpus of the trust, cf. Brooke v. Norfolk, 277 U.S. 27, [footnote omitted] it would seem that the mere residence of one of a number of trustees hardly would supply a firmer foundation.[7]

---

[7] Comments on Greenough v. Tax Assessors of Newport are found in 47 Colum. L. Rev. 865 (1947), 33 Cornell L.Q. 305 (1947), 60 Harv. L. Rev. 1169 (1947).

For a consideration of federal legislation designed to free servicemen from both income and property taxes imposed by any state by virtue of their presence there as a result of military orders, see Dameron v. Brodhead, 345 U.S. 322, 73 Sup. Ct. 721, 97 L. Ed. 1041 (1953).

New York Laws 1960, c. 290 (Tax Law §363 (Supp. 1960)), which gives some relief against multiple state income taxation, provides as follows:

"Section 1. Subdivision two of section three hundred sixty-three of the tax law, as added by chapter one hundred twenty three of the laws of nineteen hundred fifty-seven, is hereby amended to read as follows:

"2. If any taxpayer who is a resident of the state has become liable to income tax to another state upon income for the calendar year nineteen hundred fifty-six, nineteen hundred fifty-seven, nineteen hundred fifty-eight, and nineteen hundred fifty-nine or for any fiscal year or period of less than one year ending during the calendar year nineteen hundred fifty-seven, nineteen hundred fifty-eight, nineteen hundred fifty-nine, and nineteen hundred sixty, derived from sources within such state and subject to taxation under this article, the tax commission shall credit the amount of income taxes payable by him under this article with such proportion thereof, not in excess of the amount of tax payable to such other state on such income, as his income subject to taxation in such state bears to his entire income subject to taxation under this article; provided (1) that such credit shall not be allowed if such other state allows residents of this state a credit against the taxes imposed by such state for taxes payable under this article substantially similar to the credit provided for by subdivision one of this section and (2) that the allowance of such credit shall not operate to reduce the taxes payable under this article to an amount less than would have been payable if the income from such other state had been excluded in computing net income and net capital gain.

"3. As used in this section, the word 'state' means any state, territory, or possession of the United States, and the District of Columbia." — ED.

CHAPTER XVIII

Estate Plans Which Cross State
or National Borders

1. STATE BORDERS

A person's estate plan may cross state borders in various ways.[1] Typical factors which bring several different states into the picture are as follows:

1. The transferor resides in one state and owns real property in another.
2. The donee of a power of appointment and the donor of the power reside in different states.[2]
3. The settlor of an inter vivos trust resides in one state and the trustee is located in another.
4. A person executes his will while a resident of one state and then dies a resident of another.[3]
5. The testator and the beneficiaries or the trustees under his will reside in different states.

It is conceivable that from time to time various questions may be raised about an estate plan, and when the plan crosses state borders, the laws in the several states involved may give conflicting answers. Such questions fall into one or another of the following categories:

1. Questions of interpretation of the language used in the estate plan
2. Questions relating to rules of law which give to certain

---

[1] See generally on the problems of this chapter, McAndrews v. Krause, 245 Minn. 85, 71 N.W.2d 153 (1955). See also Scoles, Conflict of Laws in Estate Planning, 9 U. of Fla. L. Rev. 388 (1956).

Multiple state death taxation and multiple state income taxation may result when an estate plan crosses state borders, and thus pages 1007-1053 and 1054-1067 should be re-examined in connection with the material in this chapter.

[2] For a discussion of powers of appointment and conflict of laws, see page 769 supra. That discussion should be read in conjunction with the material in this chapter, which also deals with powers of appointment.

[3] In some states, statutes have been enacted which make a will valid for all purposes if it is valid under the law of the place of its execution. See, for example, Mass. Ann. Laws, c. 191, §5, quoted infra page 1454.

words used in the estate plan a particular meaning regardless of intent
3. Questions relating to the administrative powers of the fiduciary in the estate plan
4. Questions relating to the validity of the provisions of the estate plan
5. Questions relating to the jurisdiction of a court to resolve disputes regarding the estate plan

a. *Questions of Interpretation*

When a question of interpretation is presented by an estate plan, the draftsman has employed language that lacks preciseness of meaning. It follows, therefore, that no question of interpretation will be presented, no matter how many state borders are crossed by an estate plan, if the transferor's intention is manifested in clear and unambiguous language. In other words, no problem as to governing state law in regard to questions of interpretation is raised by a properly drafted estate plan because no questions of interpretation will be presented by such a plan.[4]

PROBLEMS

18.1. A dies domiciled in State X. In his will he gives the residue of his estate to T in trust and directs T "to pay the net income to B for his life and, on B's death, to distribute the principal to B's children." B is a resident of State Y and T is also a resident of State Y. B moves to State Z and dies domiciled there.

Under the rules of construction recognized in State X, an adopted child is included in a gift "to children," no matter when the child is adopted; under the rules of construction recognized in State Y, an adopted child is included in a gift "to children" only if the child was adopted before the date the testator made his will; under the rules of construction recognized in State Z, an adopted child is not included in a gift "to children."

B is survived by two natural-born children and a child he adopted after A's death. To whom should T distribute the principal?

18.2. A dies domiciled in State X. In his will he gives the residue of his estate to T in trust and directs T "to pay the net income to B for his life, and, on B's death, to distribute one half

---

[4] The material at page 474, supra, should be re-examined at this point because it illustrates various situations where resort to litigation was necessary to determine what the transferor meant by the language he employed.

of the principal to B's issue and one half of the principal to C if he is then living, otherwise to C's heirs." B is a resident of State Y. C is a resident of State Z. T is a resident of State X. C dies and then B dies.

Under the rules of construction recognized in State X, issue take per capita; under the rules of construction recognized in State Y, issue take per stirpes. B is survived by two children and two grandchildren who are children of a deceased child of B. In what proportions should T distribute the half of the principal given to B's issue?

Under the rules of construction recognized in State X, heirs are ascertained on the death of the designated ancestor; under the rules of construction recognized in State Z, heirs are ascertained at the period of distribution. At C's death his heirs are two children. At B's death C's heirs are one child and the children of a deceased child. To whom should T distribute the half of the principal given to C's heirs?

18.3. A, a resident of State X, transfers property to T in trust. The terms of the trust direct T to pay the net income to A for his life and, on A's death, to distribute the trust property to "A's heirs." T is a resident of State Y. A moves to State Z and dies domiciled there.

State X recognizes the doctrine of worthier title as applied to inter vivos transfers.[5] States Y and Z have repudiated this doctrine and have established in its place as a rule of construction a presumption that an inter vivos transfer to the heirs of the transferor creates in such heirs an interest as purchasers.

A's heir on his death is his son S. A's will gives one half of the residue of his etate to S and the other one half to A's brother, B. Is S entitled to all of the trust property?

18.4. A dies domiciled in State X. In his will he devises Blackacre, located in State Y, "to B and his children." B is a resident of State Z and has no child on the date of A's death.

State X recognizes the rule in Wild's Case as a rule of construction.[6] State Y has established as a rule of construction that a gift to a parent and his children creates a life estate in the parent and a remainder in the children. State Z has adopted as a rule of construction that a gift to a parent and his children creates a vested interest in fee simple in the parent subject to partial divestiture as each child is born.

Does B have a fee tail estate, a life estate, or a fee simple estate subject to partial divestiture?

---

[5] The doctrine of worthier title as applied to inter vivos transfers is developed supra page 447.

[6] The rule in Wild's Case is considered supra page 467.

18.5. A dies domiciled in State X. In his will he devises Black-acre, located in State Y, "to B for life, then to C and his heirs, but if C dies without issue, to D and his heirs."   C and D are both residents of State Z.

State X has adopted the common law presumption that a gift over on failure of issue means a gift over on indefinite failure of issue.[7] State Y has repudiated the presumption in favor of indefinite failure of issue but has established a presumption that a gift over on failure of issue is substitutional rather than successive and where, as here, the gift over on failure of issue is attached to a remainder interest, the substitution of D for C will take effect if and only if C dies without issue before B. State Z has repudiated the presumption in favor of indefinite failure of issue but has established a presumption that a gift over on failure of issue is successive and not substitutional.[8]

Under what circumstances will D be entitled to the possession of Blackacre?

18.6. Under what circumstances should a dispositive instrument in an estate plan contain a provision in substance as follows: "The interpretation of the language of this instrument shall be controlled in all respects by the law of State X"?

    b. *Questions Relating to Rules of Law Which Give to Certain Words a Particular Meaning Regardless of Intent*

The draftsman of an estate plan should avoid the use of language that may bring into operation a rule of law which defeats intent. The outstanding example of such a rule of law is the rule in Shelley's Case.[9]

PROBLEM

18.7. A dies domiciled in State X. In his will he devises Black-acre, which is located in State Y, "to B for life, then to B's heirs."

    a. Assume that the rule in Shelley's Case is in force in State X but is not in force in State Y. What estate does B have in Blackacre?

---

[7] The common law presumption in favor of indefinite failure of issue is developed supra page 578.

[8] The difference between substitutional and successive gifts is examined supra page 578.

[9] The rule in Shelley's Case is considered supra page 441. Another example of a rule of law which gives to certain words a particular effect, regardless of intent, is the doctrine of worthier title as applied to testamentary dispositions, which is explained supra page 462.

b. Assume that the rule in Shelley's Case is in force in State Y but is not in force in State X. What estate does B have in Blackacre?

c. *Questions Relating to Administrative Powers*

The draftsman should spell out in detail the various administrative powers which the selected fiduciary (executor or trustee) is to have. To the extent that there is a failure to define the administrative powers of the selected fiduciary, the scope of his powers will be determined by state law, and if the estate plan crosses state borders, a determination has to be made as to what is the governing state law.[10]

PROBLEM

18.8. A dies domiciled in State X. In his will he gives the residue of his estate to T in trust and directs T "to pay the net income to B for life, and on B's death, to distribute the principal to C." T resides in State Y. B and C reside in State Z.

In the absence of a provision to the contrary in the will, State X restricts trustee's investments to a legal list, but State Y and Z have the prudent man rule.

In the absence of a provision to the contrary in a will, State Y requires stock dividends to be treated as principal, but States X and Z require stock dividends to be treated as income if paid out of surplus earned since the establishment of the trust.

What state law should T follow?

b. *Questions Relating to Validity*

(1) Formalities

Certain formalities must be complied with in the execution of a will.[11] What is the governing state law in regard to the formalities for the execution of a will when the will in some way or other crosses state borders?

PROBLEMS

18.9. A dies domiciled in State X. He leaves a will which disposes of personal property only and which he executed while he

[10] See Chapter XIX in regard to various administrative powers.
[11] The formalities which should be observed in the execution of a will to assure that it will be valid in all states are presented supra page 50.

was domiciled in State Y. The will satisfies the formalities for the execution of a will under the law of State Y, but not the formalities for the execution of a will under the law of State X. Is the will valid in State X? In connection with this problem see Massachusetts Annotated Laws, c. 191, §5, quoted infra page 1454.

18.10. A dies domiciled in State X. He leaves a will in which he disposes of real estate located in State Y. The will satisfies the formalities for the execution of a will under the law of State X but not the formalities for the execution of a will under the law of State Y. Is the will valid to dispose of the real estate located in State Y? In connection with this problem see Massachusetts Annotated Laws, c. 191, §5, quoted infra page 1454.

(2) Restrictions on Freedom of Disposition

State laws are not uniform as to the various restrictions which are placed on the freedom of disposition of property.[12] Thus, if an estate plan crosses state borders, what is the governing state law in determining the validity of the dispositions contained in it?

SHANNON v. IRVING TRUST CO.
275 N.Y. 95, 9 N.E.2d 792 (1937)

RIPPEY, J.

On December 13, 1929, a trust indenture was duly executed in the city of New York between Joseph G. Shannon, who was then a resident of Jersey City and domiciled within the State of New Jersey, and the Irving Trust Company, a corporation organized and existing under the laws of the State of New York with its principal office at 233 Broadway, New York city, as trustee, whereby an irrevocable trust was created for the benefit, among others, of Goewey F. Shannon, wife of the settlor, and plaintiff herein, John Shannon, the son of the settlor, both of which beneficiaries were then residents of and domiciled within the State of New Jersey. At the same time, the settlor delivered to the trustee various stocks, funds, securities and properties set forth in a schedule annexed to the instrument. Thereupon the trustee entered upon the administration of the trust at its office in the city of New

---

[12] Restrictions are placed on the freedom of disposition of property by the rule against perpetuities (see page 627 supra), by the rule against accumulations (see page 676 supra), by the rule against restraints on alienation (see page 620 supra), by a rule which prevents charitable gifts under certain circumstances (see page 142 supra), by a rule that invalidates conditions in restraint of marriage, etc. (see page 686 supra), and by a rule which relates to the period of time a trust may be indestructible (see page 684 supra).

York and has continued to administer it to the time of the commencement of this action. The trust created for the wife consisted of fixed items of income with the provision that all income in excess of the amount named should accumulate and become part of the principal of the trust. Up to December 26, 1933, when Goewey F. Shannon died, she continued to be a resident of and domiciled within the State of New Jersey and her sole heirs at law and next to kin, both under the laws of New Jersey and of New York, were her husband and son aforesaid. The trust instrument provided that upon her death the trustee should thereafter pay to the son, John Shannon, monthly, an aggregate annual income of $3,000 until the son should arrive at twenty-five years of age; that thereafter the income to the son, payable in monthly installments, should aggregate $5,000 per year until the son arrived at the age of thirty years; that thereafter the income to the son should be increased to $10,000 per year until he should arrive at the age of thirty-five years, after which time he should receive the full income from the trust estate for the balance of his life. All income in excess of the amounts thus payable to the son was directed to become a part of the trust estate. The trust instrument provided that, at the death of the son, the principal and accumulated income should pass to the issue of the son or, if the son should die without issue surviving, to the Hill School of Pottstown, Pa. At the time the trust was created, the plaintiff was a resident of and domiciled within the State of New Jersey and his domicile has continued in that State to the time of the commencement of the action. There accumulated in the hands of the trustee income in excess of the amount paid to the wife according to the terms of the trust in the sum of $6,370.16, and the sum of $10,608.72 in excess of the income paid to the son since the death of the wife. Other provisions of the trust instrument are not material, except the last clause, which reads as follows: "The Trustee shall receive for its services, its necessary expenses and the commissions allowed testamentary trustees by the laws of the State of New York instead of the laws of the State of New Jersey, but otherwise the laws of the State of New Jersey shall govern this trust indenture and any construction to be placed thereupon or interpretation thereof."

Upon submission to the Appellate Division in the first department pursuant to sections 546-548 of the Civil Practice Act, the plaintiff contended that the validity of the trust is to be determined by the laws of the State of New York and, inasmuch as the provisions for accumulations of income are void under section 16 of the Personal Property Law (Cons. Laws, ch. 41) of the State of

New York (Laws of 1909, ch. 45),[13] the accumulations should be paid over to him as the person presumptively entitled to the next eventual estate (St. John v. Andrews Institute for Girls, 191 N.Y. 254), while the defendants assert that the validity of the trust provisions is to be determined by the laws of the State of New Jersey, where the accumulations are valid. (Townsend v. Allen, 59 Hun, 622; *aff'd.*, 126 N.Y. 646). The Appellate Division found that the trust was valid and certified to this court that a question of law was involved which ought to be here reviewed.

Much confusion has existed concerning the law that controls the validity and administration of inter vivos trusts of intangible personal property where the domicile of the settlor is in one State and the situs and place of administration is in another. No invariable rule can be formulated for all cases involving varying facts. The domicile of the settlor is no longer the absolute and controlling consideration (Hutchison v. Ross, 262 N.Y. 381; Matter of Brown, 274 N.Y. 10). Where the domicile of the owner of the res and the actual and business situs of the trust do not coincide, the law applicable to the interpretation, construction and validity of the trust and the legal obligations arising out of it and to taxation depend upon facts involved in and circumstances surrounding the particular case. In such a situation, the express or clearly implied intent of the settlor may control. Thus, where the actual and business situs of the trust, intent of the settlor that his domiciliary law shall not be applied to test its validity and administration, and domicile of the trustee coincide, the law of the place of location and administration of the trust controls, regardless of the place of execution of the trust instrument. (Hutchison v. Ross, supra.)

In the case at bar the execution of the trust instrument, the location of the res, the domicile of the trustee and the place of administration of the trust are in the city of New York. The intent of the settlor that in all matters affecting the trust except remuneration of the trustee his domiciliary law shall govern is expressly stated in the body of the trust instrument. The intent is manifest; no uncertainty exists. The instrument should be construed and a determination of its validity made according to the law chosen by the settlor unless so to do is contrary to the public policy of this State.

It is unnecessary to enter into any extensive consideration of what is meant by the term "public policy" of the State. Its limi-

---

[13] The provisions for accumulations would not be invalid under the present law in regard to accumulations in New York. See the discussion at page 677 supra. — ED.

tations and extent under varying conditions in connection with enforcement here of foreign law have been fully considered by this court. (Cross v. United States Trust Co., 131 N.Y. 330; Loucks v. Standard Oil Co., 224 N.Y. 99; Mertz v. Mertz, 271 N.Y. 466; Hutchison v. Ross, supra, and antecedent decisions therein cited.) It has been held that a State can have no public policy except when it is to be found in its Constitution, statutes or judicial records. If our public policy is clearly defined in our Constitution or statutes, it must invariably control judicial decision. If not found in the Constitution or statutes of the State, it may be established by judicial decision. If guidance is still lacking, to enforce the laws of a sister State is not contrary to our public policy unless to do so would be manifestly injurious to the public interest or shocking to our morals or contrary to fundamental principles of justice or "deep rooted traditions of the common weal." (Hollis v. Drew Theological Seminary, 95 N.Y. 166.)

It is stipulated in this case that accumulation of income and addition thereof to the corpus of a trust are valid under the laws of the State of New Jersey. In McGill v. Trust Co. of New Jersey (94 N.J. Eq. 657) it is said: "The rule against perpetuities is in force in this state as a part of the common law (citing cases.) That rule requires that all future interests, legal or equitable, in realty (except dower and curtesy and rights of entry for conditions broken) or personalty, which are contingent and indestructible, must be such as necessarily to vest, if at all, within the term measured by the life or lives of a person or persons in being at the time of the creation of the interest and twenty-one years thereafter; otherwise they are invalid and void" (p. 664). Under that rule, the trust as to the corpus of the estate is valid. All accumulations of income in excess of the amounts specifically directed to be paid to plaintiff and his mother become a part of and pass with the corpus and are in aid of the ultimate gift. Inasmuch as the ultimate gift of the corpus is valid as vesting within the period of a life or lives in being at the date of the creation of the trust and twenty-one years, the provision for the accumulations of excess income is not void. (Van Riper v. Hilton, 78 N.J. Eq. 371.)

Consideration of the New Jersey law and our own relating to perpetuities and accumulations of income will indicate that our policy in that connection is substantially the same as that of New Jersey. This fact has been made clear when our law and that of other sister States have been involved. In Cross v. United States Trust Co. (supra), one Phoebe Jane Cross, whose residence and domicile were in the State of Rhode Island, died in New York city leaving a will executed in the State of New York and dated May 29, 1877, in which she created a trust of personal property for the benefit of her husband and each of her four children, with the United States Trust Company, a New York corporation, as trustee. The trust was invalid under the laws of New York at the domicile of the beneficiaries and trustees where it was to be administered, as "within the statutory prohibition against the suspension of the absolute ownership and power of disposition of personal property" (p. 337), but valid under the laws of the settlor's domicile when the will was made. Rhode Island had a statute in respect to perpetuities. In that case the court said: "The only material difference in the law of the two states on this subject is that in each a different rule is adopted for measuring the period within which absolute ownership may lawfully be suspended" (p. 342). "It does not follow that a trust created by the laws of another state is contrary to our public policy with respect to accumulations and the suspension of the absolute ownership, simply because the law of that state differs in some respects from ours. It may be assumed that all our sister states have enacted laws on this subject having the same general purpose in view as our own. Some of them permit a longer and others provide for a shorter period of suspension, but the policy of all is the same" (pp. 341, 342). To like effect are the decisions in Chamberlain v. Chamberlain (43 N.Y. 424) and Dammert v. Osborn (140 N.Y. 30), and see Hollis v. Drew Theological Seminary (supra). There can be no valid distinction raised between testamentary trusts and trusts inter vivos so far as questions of public policy are concerned. The general policy of New Jersey and New York to put some limitation on the absolute suspension of the power of alienation of property and the accumulation of income from trusts is the same. Difference arises only as to the ending of the period during which such power to suspend alienation and to provide for accumulation of income may be permitted.

Under the facts existing in the case at bar, after applying the tests above indicated, we find nothing in our public policy which forbids extending comity and applying the New Jersey law so as to carry out the wish of the settlor and sustain the trust. The positive direction contained in the trust instrument that the validity of the trust should be determined by the law of the settlor's domicile must prevail. Our decision here does not extend, however, beyond instances where conflict arises between the domiciliary law of the settlor and the law of the situs of the trust where the construction and validity of trusts inter vivos are involved.

The judgment should be affirmed, with costs.

CRANE, Ch. J., LEHMAN, O'BRIEN, HUBBS, LOUGHRAN and FINCH, JJ., concur.

Judgment affirmed.[14]

WILMINGTON TRUST CO. v. WILMINGTON TRUST CO.

26 Del. Ch. 397, 24 A.2d 309 (1942)

LAYTON, Chief Justice, delivering the opinion of the court:

The vexed question is one of conflict of law. Upon its determination depends the validity and effect of a deed of appointment under a power conferred by a trust agreement. The facts of the case and pertinent provisions of the writings involved have been fully stated in three opinions heretofore filed in the court below. They will be re-stated in the briefest possible way.

[14] See comment on Shannon v. Irving Trust Co. in 6 Duke B.A.J. 35 (1938). With Shannon v. Irving Trust Co. compare Matter of Clarkson, 201 Misc. 943, 107 N.Y.S.2d 289 (1951), in which the court held that New York law applied where the will of a California resident established a trust with a New York trustee, and the trust provisions violated the New York rule against accumulations but did not violate the California rule. The court pointed out that it originally took jurisdiction pursuant to N.Y. Surrogate's Court Act §45, subd. 3, which provides as follows:

"The surrogate's court of each county has jurisdiction, exclusive of every other surrogate's court, to take the proof of a will, and to grant letters testamentary thereupon, or to grant letters of administration, as the case requires, in either of the following cases: . . .

"3. Where the decedent, not being a resident of the state, died without the state, leaving personal property within that county, and no other; or leaving personal property which has since his death, come into that county, and no other, and remains unadministered; or leaving a cause of action against a resident of that county for damages for a wrongful act or negligence causing the death of the decedent and leaving no property in any other county."

The court used the following language at page 945: "Since the petitioning trustees have been appointed by this court and are administering the trust within this jurisdiction, by virtue of a decree of the California court ordering a transfer to such trustees, this court believes the law of this State to be controlling."

In connection with the action of the California court in ordering the transfer of the assets of a testamentary trust to a New York trustee, consider §1120 of Cal. Prob. Code (Deering, 1959), which provides that the Superior Court shall not lose jurisdiction of the estate when a trust created by a will continues after distribution. On the question of the transfer of the assets of a testamentary trust to a jurisdiction other than the domicile of the testator, examine also Mass. Ann. Laws, c. 206, §§29, 30, which provide a procedure for accomplishing such a transfer if all living parties interested as beneficiaries in a testamentary trust reside outside the Commonwealth.

In Rubin v. Irving Trust Co., 305 N.Y. 288, 113 N.E.2d 424 (1953), an oral contract not to revoke a will made in Florida by a New York resident was held to be unenforceable in New York, though the oral contract was valid in Florida. — ED.

On November 20, 1920, William H Donner, hereinafter referred to as the donor, then domiciled in Buffalo, New York, executed a deed of trust, conveying to his wife, Dora Browing Donner, certain shares of stock in trust for the benefit of his wife and his five children for their respective lives. Subject to certain conditions, the trust to the extent of each child's interest therein was to cease at death; but it was provided that the property and securities held under the trust to produce the incomer for such deceased child should be transferred and delivered to such lawful child or children or other lawful lineal descendants of the donor then surviving, and in such proportions, as such deceased child should appoint and designate by last will and testament, or other instrument, duly executed, sufficient for such purpose, or in default of appointment, to the lawful child or children or other lawful lineal descendants of the deceased child. Under certain restrictions, each child was empowered to devise not more than one-fourth of his or her share to such person or persons other than the said surviving children and lineal descendants, as he or she should appoint. The donor or any beneficiary was authorized to convey to the trustee additional money or property to be added to the principal of the trust, or to be added to any separate trust fund created or accumulating thereunder. The donor reserved to himself, or in the event of his death, to a majority of the adult beneficiaries, the right from time to time, to subdivide the trust into equal shares for the purpose of segregating into a separate trust or trusts the interests of any one or more of the beneficiaries. By the tenth paragraph of the trust agreement, a majority of the adult beneficiaries, subject to the approval of the donor during his lifetime, were authorized to change from time to time the trustee under the trust agreement, or under any of the separate trusts, to any trust company of any state, possessing certain qualifications, and in such event, it was directed that such successor trustee "shall hold the said trust estate subject to all the conditions herein to the same effect as though now named herein."

During the years 1921 to 1923, inclusive, the donor made substantial additions to the trust estate, and on January 16, 1924, the value of the securities held by the trustee exceeded $2,000,000.00.

By an instrument dated January 16, 1924, Dora Browing Donner, the wife of the donor and the trustee under the trust agreement, Robert Newsom Donner and Joseph W. Donner, sons of the donor, they being all of the adult beneficiaries under the trust agreement, constituted and appointed Wilmington Trust Company as the trustee to succeed Dora Browing Donner; and she, as trustee, was authorized and directed to transfer and deliver to the successor trustee all of the money, securities and property held by her under the trust agreement. On February 16, 1924, the principal of the trust was delivered to Wilmington Trust Company as successor trustee at the City of Wilmington; and since that time it has administered the trust.

Subsequent to the appointment of the successor trustee, large additions were made to the trust fund, and, inter alia, to a separate trust fund for the benefit of Joseph W. Donner, by the donor, by Dora Browing Donner, and by Joseph W. Donner himself.

On February 4, 1927, Joseph W. Donner, residing at Buffalo, New York, executed a last will and testament making no reference whatever to the power of appointment conferred on him by the trust agreement, nor to the property to which the power applied. He possessed property in his own right, however, upon which the will could operate. After making certain dispositions, he devised all of the residue of his estate to Marine Trust Company of Buffalo in trust for the benefit of his wife, Carroll E. Donner, for her life; and on her death, he devised and bequeathed the property constituting the trust fund to his children then living and to the issue then living of any deceased children, share and share alike, the issue of any deceased child to take the share of the parent.

On October 9, 1929, Joseph W. Donner executed an instrument in which express reference was made to the power of appointment conferred on him by the trust agreement. He appointed and designated his two children, Joseph W. Donner, Jr. and Carroll E. Donner, Jr., to receive all of his interest and share in the trust fund, that is, the share of the principal of the trust fund from which his income thereunder had been derived, including the separate trust fund thereunder, subject to certain conditions. He directed that all of the property and securities thereunder or thereafter subject to his power to devise or appoint should be held by the trustee as a separate trust fund under the article of trust for the benefit of his two children, the income to be paid to them in equal shares. It was provided that at the death of each of the children the trust was to cease to the extent of the deceased child's interest or share, and that all of the property and securities so held under the trust to produce income for such child should be transferred and delivered as such child should have devised or designated, or in default thereof, to his or her lawful lineal descendants, if any; otherwise to remain in trust for the benefit of the survivor of the children; and if there should be no survivor, the share should remain as part of the principal of the trust for the benefit of all of the cestui que trustents thereunder.

On November 9, 1929, Joseph W. Donner died, leaving to survive him his widow, and the two children. The will was probated in Erie County, New York; and the executors named, Marine Trust Company of Buffalo and the widow, Carroll E. Donner, duly qualified as such.

On January 23, 1931, William H. Donner, Jr., one of the sons of the donor, died while still a minor, unmarried, and without having executed the power of appointment conferred on him by the trust agreement.

In these circumstances, Wilmington Trust Company, as guardian for the two children of Joseph W. Donner, deceased, sued in the court below to compel Wilmington Trust Company, as successor trustee under the trust agreement of the donor, to account for and to pay over to the complainant the property which it held in trust for the benefit of the deceased. Marine Trust Company of Buffalo, and Carroll E. Donner, now Lady Carroll Tennyson, executors of the will of Joseph W. Donner, deceased, and Marine Trust Company of Buffalo, as trustee under the will, intervened as complainants. The successor trustee filed an answer. It also filed a cross-bill to which answers were filed by the original complainant and the intervenors.

At the first hearing before the late Chancellor no question of conflict of law was raised. It was agreed, apparently, that the validity and effect of the trust agreement were determinable under the law of this State. For reasons which are given in his opinion, reported in 21 Del. Ch. 102, 180 A. 597, Chancellor Wolcott concluded that the deed of appointment executed by Joseph W. Donner was a legitimate mode of executing the power conferred upon him by the trust agreement; that the limitation of equitable life interests to the two children of the appointor was valid; but that the limitation of the remainders to the childrens' appointees, and in default of appointment, to their lawful lineal descendants, was in violation of the rule against perpetuities, and invalid.

A re-hearing was granted. Pertinent provisions of the statutes of the State of New York and decisions construing them were made a part of the record. It was contended that the trust was governed by the law of New York, and, therefore, the validity and effect of the deed of appointment were to be adjudged by that law. In this state of the record, Chancellor Wolcott, in an opinion reported in 21 Del. Ch. 188, 186 A. 903, held that the trust was governed by the law of New York: that, under that law, the deed of appointment executed by Joseph W. Donner could not be sustained; that with respect to a one-fourth share of the trust estate of which Joseph W. Donner enjoyed the benefit for life, he had the unrestricted power of disposal, and that share passed under the residuary clause of his will; that as to the other three-fourths, the testator's attempt by the deed of appointment to appoint it in trust for his children for life remainder to their appointees or their lawful lineal descendants was void under the New York law against perpetuities; [15] and, therefore, the children of the testator were entitled absolutely to the three-fourths portion under the terms of the original trust agreement, their father, Joseph W. Donner, having failed to make a valid appointment.

No decree had been signed by the late Chancellor at the time of his death. An informal request for a rehearing was at that time before him, and a rehearing was granted by his successor, the present Chancellor. Some of the pleadings were reframed; and additional testimony, inter alia, a deposition of the donor, was introduced. The Chancellor held, in an opinion reported in 25 Del. Ch. 121, 15 A.2d 153, that on October 9, 1929, the date of the execution of the deed of appointment by Joseph W. Donner, the trust created by the donor was located in the State of Delaware; that the deed of appointment was a valid exercise of the power of appointment conferred on Joseph W. Donner by the terms of the trust deed of November 20, 1920; that the appointment in trust for life for the benefit of the two children of Joseph W. Donner was a valid exercise of that power; and, finally, that no share or interest of William H. Donner, Jr., who died on January 23, 1931, passed under the deed of appointment, or otherwise, to the two children of Joseph W. Donner, deceased.

From the decree entered, two appeals were taken, one by the guardian, the executors and the widow, individually, the other by the guardian, the executors, Marine Trust Company of Buffalo, trustee under the will of Joseph W. Donner, and the widow, individually.

The power of appointment exercised by Joseph W. Donner for the benefit of his two children had its origin in the donor's deed of trust; the provisions of the deed of appointment are viewed in law as though they had been embodied in that instrument; and the rights and interest appointed to the children are regarded as creations of the trust deed. Equitable Trust Co. v. Snader, 17 Del. Ch. 203, 151 A. 712. The validity of the deed of appointment and of the rights and interests assigned thereunder depend upon the law of the jurisdiction in which the trust had its seat when the power of appointment was exercised.

The diversity of judical opinion with respect to the discovery

----

[15] The more liberal rule against perpetuities now operative in New York is discussed supra page 639. — Ed.

of the jurisdiction under whose law the validity of a trust inter vivos of intangible personal property is to be determined is such that no useful purpose will be served by an attempted analysis of the decisions. Courts have variously looked to the domicile of the donor, the place of execution of the trust instrument, the situs of the trust property, the place of administration of the trust, the domicile of the trustee, the domicile of the beneficiaries, and to the intent or desire of the donor, or to a combination of some of these denominators, in deciding the troublesome question of conflict of law. In the case of a testamentary trust of personalty it is very generally held that the law of the testator's domicile is the governing law. In some jurisdictions the same rule is applied in the case of a living trust of personal property. Modern methods of transportation with a resulting change of business economy have tended, however, to obliterate state lines and to depreciate the importance of particular localities. The place of one's residence no longer is a sure indication of one's place of business; nor is ownership of property closely tied to residence. The domicile of the donor is, of course, a circumstance to be considered in the ascertainment of the seat of the trust; but courts, today, are not so much inclined to the uncompromising pursuit of abstract doctrine. They are disposed to take a more realistic and practical view of the problem; and the donor's domicile is no longer regarded as the decisive factor. The place of execution of the trust instrument and the domicile of the beneficiaries are not important indicia. The domicile of the trustee and the place of administration of the trust — quite generally the same place — are important factors; and the intent of the donor, if that can be ascertained, has been increasingly emphasized. Collection of the applicable decisions will be found in 89 A.L.R. 1033, and in a valuable article appearing in 89 University of Pennsylvania Law Review, 360.

Contracting parties, within definite limits, have some right of choice in the selection of the jurisdiction under whose law their contract is to be governed. And where the donor in a trust agreement has expressed his desire, or if it pleases, his intent to have his trust controlled by the law of a certain state, there seems to be no good reason why his intent should not be respected by the courts, if the selected jurisdiction has a material connection with the transaction. More frequently, perhaps, the trust instrument contains no expression of choice of jurisdiction; but, again, there is no sufficient reason why the donor's choice should be disregarded if his intention in this respect can be ascertained from an examination of attendant facts and circumstances, provided that the same substancial connection between the transaction and the intended jurisdiction shall be found to exist. These are the considered views of a writer of recognized authority who has done much to disentangle the mat of judicial decision. Cavers, Trusts Inter Vivos, and the Conflict of Laws, 44 Harvard Law Rev. 161, 195. See Hutchison v. Ross, 262 N.Y. 381, 187 N.E. 65, 89 A.L.R. 1007.

The late Chancellor [21 Del. Ch. 188, 186 A. 907] could "see no reason why the intent of a donor should not be allowed full play in the matter of selecting the jurisdiction under which the validity of a trust inter vivos is in all respects to be determined, provided of course the property composing the corpus be delivered to a trustee in the selected jurisdiction and there administered." This is but saying that the donor's intention shall prevail if there is a real connection between the selected jurisdiction and the transaction. The present Chancellor was in full accord with this view; and we, in turn, agree that if the intended jurisdiction is substantially linked to the trust, the intention or desire of the donor should be honored. Whether choice of jurisdiction has been affirmatively stated in the trust instrument, and is, therefore, directly provable, or whether the donor's intention is deducible from surrounding facts and circumstances, is a question of evidence and consequent proof; and in what manner the donor's intention is made to appear ought not to affect the result.

Originally the trust under consideration was a trust under the laws of the State of New York for the reason that every operative factor pointed solely to that State. But a change of trustee, not only as to character but as to location, was clearly contemplated and provided for in the trust instrument. At this point the divergence of view in the court below is first manifested. The late Chancellor took his stand squarely on the ground that a mere change of domicile of the trustee accompanied by a change of the location of the trust property does not change the status of the trust. He found nothing in the language of the trust instrument, nor in the surrounding facts and circumstances, which, as he said, pointed to a fundamental modification of the terms and conditions of the trust. He emphasized the fact that a change of jurisdiction would affect the rights and privileges of the beneficiaries. Expressly, with reference to the phrase contained in the tenth paragraph, *"to the same effect as though now named herein,"* he refused to accord it any other or further significance than as referring to the conditions as stated and existing at the time the trust was created.

The present Chancellor took a more liberal view. He was of opinion that, at the least, the italicized phrase was susceptible to more than one interpretation. In his view the phrase pointed to something more than mere administrative action; and with the aid, perhaps, of the donors testimony which is detailed in his opinion, he reached the conclusion that the donor had made provision for a shift of the situs of his trust, and for a re-creation of it under the laws of a jurisdiction to be selected by the adult beneficiaries with his approval.

There was no disagreement in the court below with respect to the general rules to be applied in ascertaining the situs of an inter vivos trust of personalty. The clash of opinion was with respect to a question of interpretation of language. We, after careful consideration, are of opinion that the narrow interpratation put upon the italicized phrase by the late Chancellor was unjustified.

It is a general rule of construction that no word or phrase shall be rejected, or treated as superfluous, redundant or meaningless, if to it a meaning can be given which is reasonable and consistent with the object and purpose of the writing considered as a whole. The donor was careful to provide for a change of trustee subject to his approval in his lifetime. In the event of such change he declared that the successor trustee should "hold the said trust estate subject to all the conditions herein *to the same effect as though now named herein."* The italicized language either has a significance of its own or it is to be considered as no more than a superfluous or redundant phrase. The late Chancellor, in holding that the phrase referred merely to conditions as stated and existing at the time of the execution of the trust agreement, treated it, virtually, as a redundancy, for if the donor had had in mind no more than that any successor trustee should be bound by the same conditions as was the original appointee, his purpose was clearly expressed by the phrase "subject to all the conditions herein." This phrase speaks of the present, of things that are. But existing and stated conditions were only one object of the donor's care. The effect of a change in the trustee, and, perhaps, the appointment of one in another jurisdiction, was also a matter of solicitude and prevision. Effect is the outcome, the fruit of an act. It points to the future, to things to come, to results and consequences. Conditions existing and the effect of a change of trustee are different fields of thought; and it is not to be supposed that language to which a precise, reasonable and consistent meaning can be assigned, was intended as merely tautological. As we view the donor's language, he very plainly declared that if the trustee should be changed, the successor trustee should not only be bound by the same conditions as were expressed in the trust deed, but also that the successor trustee should have the same status, and should be considered in all respects, as an original appointee. The phrase, reasonably considered, can have no other significance unless it is to be dismissed as a mere redundancy. If the donor, domiciled in New York, had, in the first instance, named Wilmington Trust Company as the guardian of his trust, and had delivered to it in this State the original corpus, making substancial additions thereto from time to time, the late Chancellor, as we read his opinion, would readily have accepted these facts and circumstances as sufficient evidence of the donor's intention to submit his trust to the law of this jurisdiction. The illustrative case put by him is almost precisely the same. "Suppose," said he, "a person domiciled in New York should travel by train to Delaware carrying with him a sum in cash, and in Delaware deposit his money with a Deleware resident under a specified trust to be there held and administered, and should then return to the state of his domicile, it would seem out of all reason to say that the law of New York rather than that of Delaware should govern the validity of the trust. If it were not so, domicile would become a straitjacket." We are of opinion that the phrase "to the same effect as though now named herein," as applied to the power to appoint a successor trustee in another state, must be accepted as authorizing a removal of the seat of the trust from its original location, and its re-establishment under the law of another jurisdiction. The paragraph is susceptible to interpretation from its terms. It is not necessary to invoke the aid of extraneous facts and circumstances in the discovery of the donor's intent.

There is no substancial reason why a donor, in dealing with that which is his own, may not provide for a change in the location of his trust with a consequent shifting of the controlling law. In an era of economic uncertainty, with vanishing returns from investments and with tax laws approaching confiscation, such a provision would seem to amount to no more than common foresight and prudence. The rights of beneficiaries may, it is true, be disturbed by a shift of jurisdiction, but if such change has been provided for, they have no more cause to complain than other persons who are the recipients of bounty under some condition or limitation.

The adult beneficiaries, with the donor's approval, transferred the seat of the trust from New York to Delaware. On October 9, 1920, when Joseph W. Donner availed himself of the power of appointment conferred on him by the trust agreement, the home of the trust was in this State, and, being subject then to local law, the validity and effect of his deed of appointment and of the rights and interests of the appointees thereunder are to be adjudged and determined by the law of Delaware.

Other conclusions reached by the Chancellor and the reasons for them are given at length in his opinion. They are approved; and the decree entered in the court below is in all respects affirmed.[16]

AMERIGE v. ATTORNEY GENERAL
324 Mass. 648, 88 N.E.2d 126 (1949)

[For opinion, see page 771 supra.]

PROBLEMS

18.11. A dies domiciled in State X. He leaves a will in which he bequeaths a stated sum of money to a charity located in State Y. His will was executed one month before his death.
  a. Assume that under the law in State X, charitable gifts are invalid if made in a will executed less than one year before the death of the testator, but that the law of State Y places no such restriction on charitable gifts. Is the gift to the charity invalid?
  b. Assume that under the law in State Y charitable gifts are invalid if made in a will executed less than one year before the death of the testator, but that the law of State X places no such restriction on charitable gifts. Is the gift to the charity invalid? [17]

18.12. A dies domiciled in State X. In his will he establishes a trust in which B is the life income beneficiary and in which there is a spendthrift provision. The trustee resides in State Y, and B resides in State Z. Under the law of State X, a spendthrift provision with respect to the interest of a life income beneficiary under a trust is valid. Under the laws of States Y and Z, such a spendthrift provision is invalid. Is the spendthrift provision valid? [18]

---

[16] For comments on the Wilmington Trust Co. case, see 30 Geo. L.J. 788 (1942), and 89 U. of Pa. L. Rev. 405 (1941). See also the annotation dealing with conflict of laws as to inter vivos trusts in 139 A.L.R. 1129 (1942). — ED.

[17] For comments on statutes which restrict testamentary dispositions to charities, see page 142 supra.

In In re Pratt's Trust 5 A.D.2d 501, 172 N.Y.S.2d 965(1958), gifts to charities were made by the exercise, in a Florida will, of a power under a New York inter vivos trust established by the testator, and the court held that the New York law controlled in determining the validity of the charitable gifts.

[18] For a state-by-state analysis as to the validity of spendthrift trusts, see 34 A.L.R.2d 1335 (1954). See also pages 620-627 supra.

18.13. A dies domiciled in State X. He leaves a will devising Blackacre, located in State Y, to a trustee who resides in State X. Under the terms of the trust he directs the trustee to sell Blackacre and to hold the proceeds in trust. Some of the interests under the trust are invalid under the statutory rule against perpetuities in force in State Y, but no interest under the trust is invalid under the common law rule against perpetuities which is in force in State X. Are any interests under the trust invalid?

e. *Jurisdictional Questions*

HANSON v. DENCKLA
357 U.S. 235, 78 Sup. Ct. 1228, 2 L. Ed. 2d 1283 (1958)

Mr. Chief Justice Warren delivered the opinion of the Court.[19]

This controversy concerns the right to $400,000, part of the corpus of a trust established in Delaware by a settlor who later became domiciled in Florida. One group of claimants, "legatees," urge that this property passed under the residuary clause of the settlor's will, which was admitted to probate in Florida. The Florida courts have sustained this position. Fla., 100 So.2d 378. Other claimants, "appointees" and "beneficiaries," contend that the property passed pursuant to the settlor's exercise of the inter vivos power of appointment created in the deed of trust. The Delaware courts adopted this position and refused to accord full faith and credit to the Florida determination because the Florida court had not acquired jurisdiction over an indispensable party, the Delaware trustee, Del., 128 A.2d 819. We noted probable jurisdiction in the Florida appeal, No. 107, 354 U.S. 919, and granted certiorari to the Delaware Supreme Court, No. 117, 354 U.S. 920.

The trust whose validity is contested here was created in 1935. Dora Browning Donner, then a domiciliary of Pennsylvania, executed a trust instrument in Delaware naming the Wilmington Trust Co., of Wilmington, Delaware, as trustee. The corpus was composed of securities. Mrs. Donner reserved the income for life, and stated that the remainder should be paid to such persons or upon such trusts as she should appoint by inter vivos or testamentary instrument. The trust agreement provided that Mrs. Donner could change the trustee, and that she could amend, alter or revoke the agreement at any time. A measure of control over trust ad-

---

[19] The Court's footnotes are omitted. — Ed.

ministration was assured by the provision that only with the consent of a trust "advisor" appointed by the settlor could the trustee (1) sell trust assets, (2) make investments, and (3) participate in any plan, proceeding, reorganization or merger involving securities held in the trust. A few days after the trust was established Mrs. Donner exercised her power of appointment. That appointment was replaced by another in 1939. Thereafter she left Pennsylvania and in 1944 became domiciled in Florida, where she remained until her death in 1952. Mrs. Donner's will was executed Dec. 3, 1949. On that same day she executed the inter vivos power of appointment whose terms are at issue here. After making modest appointments in favor of a hospital and certain family retainers (the "appointees"), she appointed the sum of $200,000 to each of two trusts previously established with another Delaware trustee, the Delaware Trust Co. The balance of the trust corpus, over $1,000,000 at the date of her death, was appointed to her executrix. That amount passed under the residuary clause of her will and is not at issue here.

The two trusts with the Delaware Trust Co. were created in 1948 by Mrs. Donner's daughter, Elizabeth Donner Hanson, for the benefit of Elizabeth's children, Donner Hanson and Joseph Donner Winsor. In identical terms they provide that the income not required for the beneficiary's support should be accumulated to age 25, when the beneficiary should be paid $\frac{1}{4}$ of the corpus and receive the income from the balance for life. Upon the death of the beneficiary the remainder was to go to such of the beneficiary's issue or Elizabeth Donner Hanson's issue as the beneficiary should appoint by inter vivos or testamentary instrument; in default of appointment to the beneficiary's issue alive at the time of his death, and if none to the issue of Elizabeth Donner Hanson.

Mrs. Donner died Nov. 20, 1952. Her will was admitted to probate in Florida, named Elizabeth Donner Hanson as executrix. She was instructed to pay all debts and taxes, including any which might be payable by reason of the property appointed under the power of appointment in the trust agreement with the Wilmington Trust Co. After disposing of personal and household effects, Mrs. Donner's will directed that the balance of her property (the $1,000,000 appointed from the Delaware trust) be paid in equal parts to two trusts for the benefit of her daughters Katherine N. R. Denckla and Dorothy B. R. Stewart.

This controversy grows out of the residuary clause that created the last-mentioned trusts. It begins:

"All the rest, residue and remainder of my estate, real, personal and mixed, whatsoever and wheresoever the same may be at the time of my death, including any and all property, rights and interest over which I may have power of appointment which prior to my death has not been effectively exercised by me or has been exercised by me in favor of my Executrix, I direct my Executrix to deal with as follows . . ."

Residuary legatees Denckla and Stewart, already the recipients of over $500,000 each, urge that the power of appointment over the $400,000 appointed to sister Elizabeth's children was not "effectively exercised" and that the property should accordingly pass to them. Fourteen months after Mrs. Donner's death these parties petitioned a Florida chancery court for a declaratory judgment "concerning what property passes under the residuary clause" of the will. Personal service was had upon the following defendants: (1) executrix Elizabeth Donner Hanson, (2) beneficiaries Donner Hanson and Joseph Donner Winsor and (3) potential beneficiary William Donner Roosevelt, also one of Elizabeth's children. Curtin Winsor, Jr., another of Elizabeth's children and also a potential beneficiary of the Delaware trusts, was not named as a party and was not served. About a dozen other defendants were nonresidents and could not be personally served. These included the Wilmington Trust Co. ("trustee"), the Delaware Trust Co. (to whom the $400,000 had been paid shortly after Mrs. Donner's death), certain individuals who were potential successors in interest to complainants Denckla and Stewart, and most of the named appointees in Mrs. Donner's 1949 appointment. A copy of the pleadings and a "Notice to Appear and Defend" were sent to each of these defendants by ordinary mail, and notice was published locally as required by the Florida statutes dealing with constructive service. With the exception of two individuals whose interests coincided with complainants Denckla and Stewart, none of the nonresident defendants made any appearance.

The appearing defendants (Elizabeth Donner Hanson and her children) moved to dismiss the suit because the exercise of jurisdiction over indispensable parties, the Delaware trustees, would offend Section 1 of the Fourteenth Amendment. The Chancellor ruled that he lacked jurisdiction over these nonresident defendants because no personal service was had and because the trust corpus was outside the territorial jurisdiction of the court. The cause was dismissed as to them. As far as parties before the court were concerned, however, he ruled that the power of appointment was testamentary and void under the applicable Florida law. In a decree dated Jan. 14, 1955, he ruled that the $400,000 passed under the residuary clause of the will.

After the Florida litigation began, but before entry of the decree, the executrix instituted a declaratory judgment action in Delaware to determine who was entitled to participate in the trust assets held in that State. Except for the addition of beneficiary Winsor and several appointees, the parties were substantially the same as in the Florida litigation. Nonresident defendants were notified by registered mail. All of the trust companies, beneficiaries, and legatees except Katherine N. R. Denckla, appeared and participated in the litigation. After the Florida court enjoined executrix Hanson from further participation, her children pursued their own interests. When the Florida decree was entered the legatees unsuccessfully urged it as res judicata of the Delaware dispute. In a decree dated Jan. 13, 1956, the Delaware Chancellor ruled that the trust and power of the appointment were valid under the applicable Delaware law, and that the trust corpus had properly been paid to the Delaware Trust Co. and the other appointees. — Del. —, 119 A.2d 901.

Alleging that she would be bound by the Delaware decree, the executrix moved the Florida Supreme Court to remand with instructions to dismiss the Florida suit then pending on appeal. No full faith and credit question was raised. The motion was denied. The Florida Supreme Court affirmed its Chancellor's conclusion that Florida law applied to determine the validity of the trust and power of appointment. Under that law the trust was invalid because the settlor had reserved too much power over the trustee and trust corpus, and the power of appointment was not independently effective to pass the property because it was a testamentary act not accompanied by the requisite formalities.[20] The Chancellor's conclusion that there was no jurisdiction over the trust companies, and other absent defendants was reversed. The court ruled that jurisdiction to construe the will carried with it "substantive" jurisdiction "over the persons of the absent defendents" even though the trust assets were not "physically in this state." Whether this meant jurisdiction over the person of the defendants or jurisdiction over the trust assets is open to doubt. In a motion for rehearing the beneficiaries and appointees urged for the first time that Florida should have given full faith and credit to the decision of the Delaware Chancellor. The motion was denied without opinion, Nov. 28, 1956.

The full faith and credit question was first raised in the Delaware litigation by an unsuccessful motion for new trial filed with

---

[20] The view of the Florida court as to what is a testamentary disposition does not present too encouraging a picture for the use of revocable inter vivos trusts in that state. See material relating to revocable inter vivos trusts as testamentary dispositions at page 95 supra. — ED.

the Chancellor, Jan. 20, 1956. After the Florida Supreme Court decision the matter was renewed by a motion to remand filed with the Delaware Supreme Court. In a decision of Jan. 14, 1957, that court denied the motion and affirmed its Chancellor in all respects. The Florida decree was held not binding for purposes of full faith and credit because the Florida court had no personal jurisdiction over the trust companies and no jurisdiction over the trust res.

The issues for our decision are, first, whether Florida erred in holding that it had jurisdiction over the nonresident defendants, and second, whether Delaware erred in refusing full faith and credit to the Florida decree. We need not determine whether Florida was bound to give full faith and credit to the decree of the Delaware Chancellor since the question was not seasonably presented to the Florida court. Radio Station WOW v. Johnson, 326 U.S. 120, 128.

No. 107, The Florida Appeal. The question of our jurisdiction was postponed until the hearing on the merits. The appeal is predicated upon the contention that as appealed to the facts of this case the Florida statute provided for constructive service is contrary to the Federal Constitution. 28 U.S.C. 28 §1257 (2). But in the state court appellants (the "beneficiaries") did not object that the statute was invalid as applied, but rather that the effect of the state court's exercise of jurisdiction in the circumstances of this case deprived them of a right under the Federal Constitution. Accordingly, we are without jurisdiction of the appeal and it must be dismissed. Wilson v. Cook, 327 U.S. 474, 482; Charleston Fed. Sav. & Loan Ass'n v. Alderson, 324 U.S. 182. Treating the papers whereon appeal was taken as a petition for certiorari, 28 U.S.C. §2103, certiorari is granted.

Relying upon the principle that a person cannot invoke the jurisdiction of this Court to vindicate the right of a third party, appellees urge that appellants lack standing to complain of defect of jurisdiction over the nonresident trust companies, who have made no appearance in this action. Florida adheres to the general rule that a trustee is an indispensable party to litigation involving the validity of the trust. In the absence of such a party a Florida court may not proceed to adjudicate the controversy. Since state law required the acquisition of jurisdiction over the nonresident trust company before the court was empowered to proceed with the action, any defendant affected by the court's judgment has that "direct and substantial personal interest in the outcome" that is necessary to challenge whether that jurisdiction was in fact acquired. Chicago v. Atchison, T. & S.F.R. Co., 357 U.S. 77.

Appellants charge that his judgment is offensive to the Due

Process Clause of the Fourteenth Amendment because the Florida court was without jurisdiction.   There is no suggestion that the court failed to employ a means of notice reasonably calculated to inform nonresident defendants of the pending proceedings, or denied them an opportunity to be heard in defense of their interests.   The alleged defect is the absence of those "affiliating circumstances" without which the courts of a State may not enter a judgment imposing obligations on persons (jurisdiction in personam) or affecting interests in property (jurisdiction in rem or quasi in rem).   While the in rem and in personam classifications do not exhaust all the situations that give rise to jurisdiction, they are adequate to describe the affiliating circumstances suggested here, and accordingly serve as a useful means of approach to this case.

In rem jurisdiction.   Founded on physical power, McDonald v. Mabee, 243 U.S. 90, 91, the in rem jurisdiction of a state court is limited by the extent of its power and by the coordinate authority of sister States.   The basis of the jurisdiction is the presence of the subject property within the territorial jurisdiction of the forum State.   Rose v. Himely, 4 Cranch 241, 277; Overby v. Gordon, 177 U.S. 214, 221-222.   Tangible property poses no problem for the application of this rule, but the situs of intangibles is often a matter of controversy.   In considering restrictions on the power to tax, this Court has concluded that "jurisdiction" over intangible property is not limited to a single State.   State Tax Commission of Utah v. Aldrich, 316 U.S. 174; Curry v. McCanless, 307 U.S. 357. Whether this type of "jurisdiction" with which this opinion deals may be exercised by more than one State we need not decide.   The parties seem to assume that the trust assets that form the subject matter of this action were located in Delaware and not in Florida. We can see nothing in the record contrary to that assumption, or sufficient to establish a situs in Florida.

The Florida court held that the presence of the subject property was not essential to its jurisdiction.   Authority over the probate and construction of its domiciliary's will, under which the assets might pass, was thought sufficient to confer the requisite jurisdiction.   But jurisdiction cannot be predicated upon the contingent role of this Florida will.   Whatever the efficacy of a so-called "in rem" jurisdiction over assets admittedly passing under a local will, a State acquires no in rem jurisdiction to adjudicate the validity of inter vivos disposition simply because its decision might augment an estate passing under a will probated in its courts.   If such a basis of jurisdiction were sustained, probate courts would enjoy nationwide service of process to adjudicate interests in property with which neither the State nor the decedent could claim any affiliation. The settlor-decedent's Florida domicile is equally unavailing as a basis for jurisdiction over the trust assets. For the purpose of jurisdiction in rem the maxim that personalty has its situs at the domicile of its owner is a fiction of limited utility. Green v. Van Buskirk, 7 Wall. 139, 150. The maxim is no less suspect when the domicile is that of a decedent. In analogous cases, this Court has rejected the suggestion that the probate decree of the State where decedent was domiciled has an in rem effect on personalty outside the forum State that could render it conclusive on the interests of nonresidents over whom there was no personal jurisdiction. Riley v. New York Trust Co., 315 U.S. 343, 353; Baker v. Baker, Eccles & Co., 242 U.S. 394, 401; Overby v. Gordon, 177 U.S. 24. The fact that the owner is or was domiciled within the forum State is not a sufficient affiliation with the property upon which to base jurisdiction in rem. Having concluded that Florida had no in rem jurisdiction, we proceed to consider whether a judgment purporting to rest on that basis is invalid in Florida and must therefore be reversed.

Prior to the Fourteenth Amendment an exercise of jurisdiction over persons or property outside the forum State was thought to be an absolute nullity, but the matter remained a question of state law over which this Court exercised no authority. With the adoption of that Amendment, any judgment purporting to bind the person of a defendant over whom the court had not acquired in personam jurisdiction was void within the State as well as without. Pennoyer v. Neff, 95 U.S. 714. Nearly a century has passed without this Court being called upon to apply that principle to an in rem judgment dealing with property outside the forum State. The invalidity of such a judgment within the forum State seems to have been assumed — and with good reason. Since a State is forbidden to enter a judgment attempting to bind a person over whom it has no jurisdiction, it has even less right to enter a judgment purporting to extinguish the interest of such a person in property over which the court has no jurisdiction. Therefore, so far as it purports to rest upon jurisdiction over the trust assets, the judgment of the Florida court cannot be sustained. Sadler v. Industrial Trust Co., 327 Mass. 10, 97 N.E.2d 169.

In personam jurisdiction. Appellees' stronger argument is for in personam jurisdiction over the Delaware trustee. They urge that the circumstances of this case amount to sufficient affiliation with the State of Florida to empower its court to exercise personal jurisdiction over this nonresident defendant. Principal reliance is placed upon McGee v. International Life Ins. Co., 355 U.S. 220. In McGee the Court noted the trend of expanding personal jurisdiction over nonresidents. As technological progress has increased the flow of commerce between States, the need for jurisdiction over nonresidents has undergone a similar increase. At the same time, progress in communications and transportation has made the defense of a suit in a foreign tribunal less burdensome. In response to these changes, the requirements for personal jurisdiction over nonresidents have evolved from the rigid rule of Pennoyer v. Neff, 95 U.S. 714, to the flexible standard of International Shoe Co. v. State of Washington, 326 U.S. 310. But it is a mistake to assume that this trend heralds the eventual demise of restriction on the personal jurisdiction of state courts. See Vanderbilt v. Vanderbilt, 354 U.S. 416, 418. Those restrictions are more than a guarantee of immunity from inconvenient or distant litigation. They are a consequence of territorial limitations on the power of the respective States. However minimal the burden of defending in a foreign tribunal, a defendant may not be called upon to do so unless he has had the "minimal contacts" with that State that are a prerequisite to its exercise of power over him. See International Shoe Co. v. State of Washington, 326 U.S. 310, 319.

We fail to find such contacts in the circumstances of this case. The defendant trust company has no office in Florida, and transacts no business there. None of the trust assets has ever been held or administered in Florida, and the record discloses no solicitation of business in that State either in person or by mail. Cf. International Shoe Co. v. State of Washington, 326 U.S. 310; McGee v. International Life Ins. Co., 355 U.S. 220; Travelers Health Ass'n v. Com. of Virginia ex rel. State Corporation Comm., 339 U.S. 643.

The cause of action in this case is not one that arises out of an act done or transaction consummated in the forum State. In that respect, it differs from McGee v. International Life Ins. Co. 355 U.S. 220, and the cases there cited. In McGee, the nonresident defendant solicited a reinsurance agreement with a resident of California. The offer was accepted in that State, and the insurance premiums were mailed from there until the insured's death. Noting the interest California has in providing effective redress for its residents when nonresidents insurers refuse to pay claims on insurance they have solicited in that State, the Court upheld jurisdiction because the suit "was based on a contract which had substantial connection with that State." In contrast, this action involves the validity of an agreement that was entered without any connection with the forum State. The agreement was executed in Delaware by a trust company incorporated in that State and a settlor domiciled in Pennsylvania. The first relationship Florida had to the agreement was years later when the settlor became domiciled there, and the trustee remitted the trust income to her in that State. From Florida Mrs. Donner carried on several bits of trust administration that may be compared to the mailing of premiums in McGee. But the record discloses no instance in which the *trustee* performed any acts in Florida that bear the same relationship to the agreement as the solicitation in McGee. Consequently, this suit cannot be said to be one to enforce an obligation that arose from a privilege the defendant exercised in Florida. Cf. International Shoe Co. v. State of Washington, 326 U.S. 310, 319. This case is also different from McGee in that there the State had enacted special legislation (Unauthorized Insurers Process Act, West's Ann. Cal. Insurance Code, §§1610 et seq.) to exercise what McGee called its "manifest interest" in providing effective redress for citizens who had been injured by nonresidents engaged in an activity that the State treats as exceptional and subjects to special regulation. Cf. Travelers Health Ass'n v. Com. of Virginia ex rel. State Corporation Comm., 339 U.S. 643, 647-649; Doherty & Co. v. Goodman, 249 U.S. 623, 627; Henry L. Hess v. Pawloski, 274 U.S. 352.

The execution in Florida of the powers of appointment under which the beneficiaries and appointees claim does not give Florida a substantial connection with the contract on which this suit is based. It is the validity of the trust agreement, not the appointment, that is at issue here. For the purpose of applying its rule that the validity of a trust is determined by the law of the State of its creation, Florida ruled that the appointment amounted to a "republication" of the original trust instrument in Florida. For choice-of-law purposes such a ruling may be justified, but we think it an insubstantial connection with the trust agreement for purposes of determining the question of personal jurisdiction over a nonresident defendant. The unilateral activity of those who claim some relationship with a nonresident defendant cannot satisfy the requirement of contact with the forum State. The application of that rule will vary with the quality and nature of the defendant's activity, but it is essential in each case that there be some act by which the defendant purposefully avails itself of the privilege of conducting activities within the forum State, thus invoking the benefits and protections of its laws. International Shoe Co. v. State of Washington, 326 U.S. 310, 319. The settlor's execution in Florida of her power of appointment cannot remedy the absence of such an act in this case.

It is urged that because the settlor and most of the appointees and beneficiaries were domiciled in Florida the courts of that State should be able to exercise personal jurisdiction over the nonresident trustees. This is a nonsequitur. With personal jurisdiction over the executor, legatees, and appointees, there is nothing in federal law to prevent Florida from adjudicating concerning the respective rights and liabilities of those parties. But Florida has not chosen to do so. As we understand its law, the trustee is an indispensable party over whom the court must acquire jurisdiction before it is empowered to enter judgment in a proceeding affecting the validity of a trust. It does not acquire that jurisdiction by being the "center of gravity" of the controversy, or the most convenient location for litigation. The issue is personal jurisdiction, not choice of law. It is resolved in this case by considering the acts of the trustee. As we have indicated, they are insufficient to sustain the jurisdiction.

Because it sustained jurisdiction over the nonresident trustees, the Florida Supreme Court found it unnecessary to determine whether Florida law made those defendants indispensable parties in the circumstances of this case. Our conclusion that Florida was without jurisdiction over the Delaware trustee, or over the trust corpus held in that State, requires that we make that determination in the first instance. As we have noted earlier, the Florida Supreme Court has repeatedly held that a trustee is an indispensable party without whom a Florida court has no power to adjudicate controversies affecting the validity of a trust. For that reason the Florida judgment must be reversed not only as to the nonresident trustees but also as to appellants, over whom the Florida court admittedly had jurisdiction.

No. 117, The Delaware Certiorari. The same reasons that compel reversal of the Florida judgment require affirmance of the Delaware one. Delaware is under no obligation to give full faith and credit to a Florida judgment because offensive to the Due Process Clause of the Fourteenth Amendment. 28 U.S.C. §1738. Even before passage of the Fourteenth Amendment this Court sustained state courts in refusing full faith and credit to judgments entered by courts that were without jurisdiction over nonresident defendants. D'Arcy v. Ketchum, 11 How. 165; Hall v. Lanning, 91 U.S. 160. See Baker v. Baker, Eccles & Co., 242 U.S. 394; Riley v. New York Trust Co., 315, U.S. 343. Since Delaware was entitled to conclude that Florida law made the trust company an indispensable party, it was under no obligation to give the Florida judgment any faith and credit — even against parties over whom Florida's jurisdiction was unquestioned.

It is suggested that this disposition is improper — that the Delaware case should be held while the Florida cause is remanded to give that court an opportunity to determine whether the trustee is an indispensable party in the circumstances of this case. But this is not a case like Herb v. Pitcairn, 324 U.S. 117, where it as appropriate to remand for the state court to clarify an ambiguity in its opinion that may reveal an adequate state ground that would deprive us of power to affect the result of the controversy. Nor is this a circumstance where the state court has never ruled on the question of state law that we are deciding. Although the question was left open in this case, there is ample Florida authority from which we may determine the appropriate answer.

The rule of primacy to the first final judgment is a necessary incident to the requirement of full faith and credit. Our only function is to determine whether judgments are consistent with the Federal Constitution. In determining the correctness of Delaware's judgment we look to what Delaware was entitled to conclude from the Florida authorities at the time the Delaware court's judgment was entered. To withhold affirmance of a correct Delaware judgment until Florida has had time to rule on another question would be participating in the litigation instead of adjudicating its outcome.

The judgment of the Delaware Supreme Court is affirmed, and the judgment of the Florida Supreme Court is reversed and the cause is remanded for proceeding not inconsistent with this opinion.

It is so ordered.[21]

Judgment of Delaware Supreme Court affirmed; judgment of Florida Supreme Court reversed and cause remanded with directions.

Mr. Justice Black, whom Mr. Justice Burton and Mr. Justice Brennan join, dissenting. [Dissenting opinion omitted.]

Mr. Justice Douglas dissenting. [Dissenting opinion omitted.]

2. NATIONAL BORDERS

Estate plans may cross national borders in any one of the following circumstances:

1. The transferor may be a citizen of the United States but a resident of a foreign country.
2. The transferor may be a citizen of a foreign country but a resident of the United States.
3. The transferor may be neither a resident nor a citizen of the United States, but the property subject to disposition may have a situs in the United States.

[21] For a comment on Hanson v. Denckla, see 72 Harv. L. Rev. 695 (1959). — Ed.

4. The transferor may be a citizen or resident of the United States, but the subject matter of the disposition may have a situs in a foreign country.
5. A beneficiary may be a citizen or a resident of a foreign country.
6. A citizen or a resident of the United States may establish a trust in a foreign country with a nonresident alien as trustee.

a. *Tax Matters*

When an estate plan crosses national borders in some manner special attention must be paid to the tax consequences. These may be such as to make it advantageous to push the plan across national borders. The discussion which follows will be concerned with estate taxes, gift taxes and income taxes in that order.

The federal estate tax provisions are divided into those applicable to estates of citizens or residents[22] and those applicable to nonresidents who are not citizens.[23] So far as citizens or residents are concerned, special consideration must be given to the matter of estate taxes when the estate plan will cross national borders, because of the fact that it will deal with property which has a foreign situs. To protect the citizen or the resident in this situation, the Code allows a credit against the federal estate tax in the amount of the death taxes paid to the foreign country with respect to property included in the decedent's gross estate and situated in the for-

[22] See 1954 I.R.C. §§2001-2056. See also §2208, quoted infra page 1416, which was added in 1958 and which brings out that a citizen of the United States who is a resident of a possession of the United States at the time of his death shall be deemed a citizen for purposes of the federal estate tax unless he acquired his citizenship solely by reason of his being a citizen of the possession or by reason of his birth or residence there.

See Commissioner v. Rivera's Estate, 214 F.2d 60 (2d Cir. 1954); Estate of Albert DeCaen Smallwood, 11 T.C. 740 (1948); Estate of Arthur S. Fairchild, 24 T.C. 408 (1955), which consider the exemption of a United States citizen from the federal estate tax when he became a citizen of the Virgin Islands (or Puerto Rico). This exemption is now curtailed by §2208.

In 1960 several additions were made to the Code which are relevant at this point: §2209, quoted infra page 1416, which is applicable to estates of decedents dying after September 14, 1960, and which is a companion to §2208 in that it defines as a nonresident noncitizen for estate tax purposes a person who acquires his United States citizenship solely by reason of his being a citizen of the possession of the United States in which he resides, or by reason of his birth or residence within that possession; §2501(c), quoted infra page 1416, which is the corresponding provision in the gift tax law; and §2106(a)(3)(B), quoted infra page 1414, which gives such a nonresident noncitizen a portion of the $60,000 exemption which corresponds to the portion of his gross estate within the United States, whereas a nonresident noncitizen normally is allowed only a $2000 exemption.

[23] See 1954 I.R.C. §§2101-2106, quoted infra page 1410.

eign country.²⁴ This foreign death tax may be lost in part when estate tax marital deduction gifts or charitable gifts are involved in the estate plan, unless there is excluded from such gifts property eligible for the credit.²⁵ A credit for a foreign death tax may be available under a death tax convention with the foreign country to which the payment is made.²⁶ In such a case, a credit is allowed either as provided by the convention or by the Code, whichever is the more beneficial to the estate.²⁷ For purposes of the foreign death tax credit, a possession of the United States is deemed a foreign country.²⁸

Foreign real estate is excluded from the gross estate of a citizen or a resident for federal estate tax purposes.²⁹ If real estate is acquired in a foreign country that does not impose a significant death tax, it can be passed on to beneficiaries designated in a will and they can sell the property and bring the net proceeds to the United States free of the federal estate tax.³⁰ Investment in for-

---

²⁴ See 1954 I.R.C. §2014, quoted infra page 1393. As to the foreign death taxes which may be payable, see Stewart, Canadian Taxation — A Review for Nonresidents, 104 J. Accountancy No. 5, p. 37 (1957).

²⁵ See Foreign Aspects of Taxation, 3 J. Taxation 376 (1955). In this connection notice that in 1959, §2053(d) of the 1954 Code, quoted infra page 1404, was amended to permit, under described circumstances, a deduction for death taxes paid to a foreign country with respect to certain charitable transfers and that a new §2014(f), quoted infra page 1393, was added at the same time, modifying the credit allowed under §2014 in any case where a deduction is allowed under §2053(d).

²⁶ A booklet entitled Outline of Death Duty and Gift Tax Treaties Between the United States and Other Countries has been published by the Internal Revenue Service and is reprinted in CCH Fed. Est. & Gift Tax Rep. ¶¶6100 et seq. See also Kanter, The United States Estate Tax Treaty Program, 9 Tax L. Rev. 401 (1954).

Revenue Ruling 56-251, 1956-1 C.B. 846, held that where a decedent was a citizen of the United States and died domiciled in France and had in his estate shares of stock in corporations organized in Canada, the Union of South Africa and the United Kingdom, and both the United States and France imposed a tax on these securities, the death tax convention between the United States and France did not prevent double taxation.

²⁷ See Reg. §20.2014-4(a)(1), quoted infra page 1503. Section 20.2014-1(a)(3), quoted infra page 1503, points out that no credit is allowable under §2014 in connection with property situated outside of the foreign country imposing the tax for which a credit is claimed, but that such a credit may be allowable under a death tax convention.

²⁸ See 1954 I.R.C. §2014(g), quoted infra page 1394. Thus the estate of one who is deemed a citizen of the United States for federal estate tax purposes, though he is a resident of a possession of the United States (see 1954 I.R.C. §2208, quoted infra page 1416), will be entitled to a foreign death tax credit with respect to the death taxes paid to the possession.

²⁹ See 1954 I.R.C. §2031(a), quoted infra page 1395. As to what constitutes real property, see Fair v. Commissioner, 91 F.2d 218 (3d Cir. 1937); Laird v. United States, 115 F. Supp. 931 (W.D. Wis. 1953); Estate of Margaret T. C. DePerigny, 9 T.C. 782 (1947). See also Rev. Rul. 65, 1953-1 C.B. 391.

³⁰ Will a new basis for the foreign real property be acquired by the bene-

eign real estate as a means of avoiding the federal estate tax is increasing, but it is unlikely that this method of tax avoidance will continue to be available very long. Because foreign real estate is not included in a decedent's gross estate, it should not be included in any gift designed to qualify for the estate tax marital deduction.[31]

A nonresident who is not a citizen of the United States is subject to a federal estate tax on that part of his gross estate which at the time of his death is situated in the United States.[32] He is not entitled to the foreign death tax credit which is available to a citizen or resident,[33] but he may be entitled to some credit for the tax paid to the United States in determining the death tax payable to his own country. The estate tax marital deduction is not available when the deceased spouse is a nonresident who is not a citizen, nor is the $60,000 exemption.

When does a noncitizen become a resident of the United States and therefore subject to the federal estate tax rules applicable to a citizen or a resident? He is a resident of the United States when he is domiciled in one of the states or the District of Columbia.[34]

What property owned by a nonresident who is not a citizen will be deemed to be situated in the United States? Stock owned by him and issued by a domestic corporation is in this category.[35] Funds deposited in a bank account in the United States by a nonresident who is not a citizen will be deemed situated here only if

---

ficiary under 1954 I.R.C. §1014, quoted infra page 1381, for federal income tax purposes so that any increase in value between the date the foreign realty is acquired and the date of the decedent's death will also escape income taxation?

[31] One of the requirements for an estate tax marital deduction gift is that the value of the property included in, or available to satisfy such a gift, be includible in the gross estate of the deceased spouse. See the discussion at page 824 supra.

[32] See 1954 I.R.C. §2103, quoted infra page 1411. See generally Reg. §§20.2101-1 et seq.

[33] See Reg. §20.2014-1(a)(1), quoted infra page 1502.

[34] See Reg. §20.0-1(b)(1) and (2), quoted infra page 1501, 1954 I.R.C. §7701(a)(9).

Revenue Ruling 58-70, 1958-1 C.B. 341, held that a citizen of a foreign country who had entered the United States as a temporary visitor was not domiciled in the United States for the purpose of the federal estate tax, where he had not taken any affirmative course of action to establish a domicile in the United States, although he may have formed an intent to do so.

[35] See 1954 I.R.C. §2104(a). In Curt E. Pulvermann, 30 T.C. 231 (1958), a nonresident alien owned bonds in a domestic corporation which were destroyed in an air raid on London in 1941. The Alien Property Custodian secured from the domestic corporation a reissue of the bonds in 1943 and sold them in 1944 after the death of the nonresident alien. The court held that no estate tax was due, since the bonds were not situated in the United States at the time of the decedent's death.

he is engaged in business in the United States.[36] Other items of property are specifically included or excluded by various Code provisions.[37]

The death tax conventions which exist between the United States and various foreign countries must be studied to ascertain whether the estate tax results described above have been modified.[38]

To the extent that it is possible, it may be desirable for a citizen or a resident to keep his property out of channels which will make it available for the payment of foreign death taxes. A beneficiary of an estate plan may be a nonresident of the United States and it may be highly desirable that the beneficial arrangement for him be such that the transferred property cannot be reached for the payment of foreign taxes to which the beneficiary may be subjected.[39]

---

[36] See 1954 I.R.C. §2105(b). Revenue Ruling 56-52, 1956-1 C.B. 448, holds that for estate tax purposes an ambassador or other diplomatic officer of a foreign country is not engaged in business in the United States at the time of his death solely by reason of his activities in this country as ambassador or other diplomatic officer.

Revenue Ruling 56-421, 1956-2 C.B. 602, holds that funds on deposit with the Treasurer of the United States which are held for the account of the Attorney General, the successor to the Alien Property Custodian, are includible in the gross estate of a nonresident decedent who is not a citizen of the United States and who is not engaged in business in the United States, because the Treasurer of the United States is not carrying on the banking business within the meaning of §2105(b). But in Estate of Ruth Waldstein, 35 T.C. — , No. 20 (1960), funds of a nonresident noncitizen taken by the Alien Property Custodian were withdrawn from a private bank and deposited in a Federal Reserve Bank, where they were when such person died, and the court held that for tax purposes the funds would be considered as still on deposit in the private bank and not includible in the decedent's gross estate. Bank of New York v. United States, 174 F. Supp. 911 (S.D.N.Y. 1957), held that trust income which had accumulated before the death of a nonresident alien beneficiary, and to which she had an absolute right, was money on deposit for a nonresident not doing business in the United States and, as such, was not subject to the estate tax. City Bank Farmers Trust Co. v. United States, 174 F. Supp. 583 (S.D.N.Y. 1959), considered a case where a New York trust company withheld income from a nonresident trust beneficiary because of the Trading with the Enemy Act and kept the withheld funds with other trust funds in its banking business. The court held that the undistributed income was "moneys deposited with any person carrying on the banking business" and thus was not includible in the nonresident decedent's gross estate.

[37] Property in a revocable transfer or a transfer in contemplation of death is situated in the United States if so situated either at the time of the transfer or at the time of the decedent's death. See 1954 I.R.C. §2104(b). Proceeds of life insurance on the life of a nonresident noncitizen are not deemed property within the United States. See 1954 I.R.C. §2105(a). Works of art on loan for exhibition are dealt with in §2105(c). United States bonds are covered by §2106(c). See generally Reg. §§20.2104, 20.2105.

[38] See page 1100 supra, note 26.

[39] In Estate of Nellie Hoyt McNeel, 170 N.Y.S.2d 893 (1957), the court held that United States assets of a decedent who was a citizen of the United States

The federal gift tax provisions also make a distinction, in determining whether a gift tax is payable, between gifts by citizens or residents and gifts by nonresidents who are not citizens.[40]   A donor who is a citizen of the United States and a resident of a possession thereof is regarded as a citizen in applying the federal gift tax provisions unless he acquired his citizenship solely by reason of his being a citizen of the possession or by reason of his birth or residence there.[41]

A citizen or a resident is subject to the federal gift tax provisions on transfers by gift, without regard to where the subject matter of the gift is located.[42]   Thus the transfer of foreign realty by gift is subject to such provisions, even though the realty could be transferred on death free of any estate tax.[43]

A nonresident who is not a citizen can be subjected to a gift tax on a transfer by gift only if the subject matter of the gift is situated within the United States,[44] and even though the subject matter of the gift is situated within the United States, if it is intangible property, he cannot be subjected to a gift tax unless he is engaged

---

but died domiciled in England need not be transmitted to England to pay the amount of the British death tax in excess of British assets when the decedent had made provision for the retention of these assets in the United States.

The New York courts have held that a New York fiduciary (executor or trustee) is not required to pay British death duties out of funds under control of the New York fiduciary.   See In re Guaranty Trust Company of New York, N.Y.L.J., Oct. 1, 1959, p. 12, and Estate of Diana M. Cubitt, N.Y.L.J., Oct. 22, 1959, p. 11.

[40] The word "resident" is defined in Reg. §25.2501-1(b) as an individual who has his domicile in one of the states or the District of Columbia at the time of the gift.

[41] See 1954 I.R.C. §2501(b), added in 1958.   See also §2501(c), referred to supra page 1099, note 22.

[42] See 1954 I.R.C. §2501(a); Reg. §25.2501-1(a).

[43] MacDonald v. United States, 139 F. Supp. 598 (D. Mass. 1956), held that real property situated outside the United States which was owned by a citizen of the United States was subject to gift tax on transfer.   The court stressed the fact that when the exclusion of such property from the estate tax was made in 1934, the gift tax regulations stated that foreign real property of a citizen was subject to the gift tax and no exclusion was inserted in the gift tax law.   The court also held that it was constitutional to impose a gift tax on foreign real property of a citizen.   Section 25.2501-1 of the Regulations is in accord.

[44] Section 2511(b) of the 1954 Code provides that shares of stock owned by a nonresident who is not a citizen shall be deemed property situated within the United States only if issued by a domestic corporation.

Jorgensen v. United States, 152 F. Supp. 73 (Ct. Cls. 1957), *cert. denied,* 355 U.S. 840 (1957), involved a gift of a New York bank account by a nonresident who was not a citizen.   A court had held that a bank account was property within the United States under 1939 I.R.C. §1000, even though it would not have been included in the donor's estate for estate tax purposes had he held it until the time of his death.   Changes made by §2501(a) of the 1954 Code to exempt such transfers were held to be substantive rather than declaratory of existing law.

in business in the United States during the calendar year in which the gift is made.[45]   When a nonresident who is not a citizen makes a gift to his wife that is subject to the federal gift tax provisions, the gift tax marital deduction is never available to him.[46]   The annual gift tax exclusion is available to a nonresident who is not a citizen,[47] but the $30,000 specific exemption is not.[48]

Gift tax treaties have been negotiated between the United States and various foreign countries.   These treaties must be examined to determine the extent to which the gift tax results described above have been modified or changed.[49]

In applying the provisions of the federal income tax law, a distinction must also be made between citizens or residents and nonresident aliens.   Citizens or residents, in certain situations, are allowed a credit for taxes paid to a foreign country.[50]   In

---

[45] See 1954 I.R.C. §2501(a), which lays down the general rule that where a nonresident who is not a citizen makes a transfer of intangible property by gift, he is not taxable if he was not engaged in business in the United States during the calendar year.   See also Reg. §25.2501-1(a).

Revenue Ruling 56-438, 1956-2 C.B. 604, holds that when §§2501 and 2511 are read together, it becomes apparent that a nonresident who is not a citizen of the United States is not subject to the federal gift tax on making a gift of shares of stock of a domestic corporation unless he was engaged in business in the United States during the calendar year in which the gift was made, even though §2511(b) provides that shares of stock owned by a nonresident who is not a citizen of the United States shall be deemed property within the United States when issued by a domestic corporation.

[46] See 1954 I.R.C. §2523, quoted infra page 1425.

[47] See 1954 I.R.C. §2503(b), quoted infra page 1418.

[48] See 1954 I.R.C. §2521, quoted infra page 1423.

[49] A booklet entitled Outline of Death Duty and Gift Tax Treaties Between the United States and Other Countries has been published by the Internal Revenue Service and is reprinted in CCH Fed. Est. & Gift Tax Rep. ¶¶6100 et seq.

[50] See 1954 I.R.C. §§901-905.

Revenue Ruling 57-153, 1957-1 C.B. 243, points out what is required of an alien resident of the United States or Puerto Rico in order that he may be entitled under §901(b)(3) to credit against his United States income tax for taxes paid or accrued during the taxable year to the foreign country of which he is a citizen.

Revenue Ruling 58-3, 1958-1 C.B. 263, holds that taxes imposed by the Federal Government of Mexico under the Mercantil Revenue Law of 1947 do not constitute income taxes within the meaning of §901 or taxes in lieu of income taxes within the meaning of §903 and hence are not allowable as a credit under §901.

Revenue Ruling 58-55, 1958-1 C.B. 266, holds that a foreign tax for the purpose of the credit under §901 is accruable for the taxable year to which it relates, even though the taxpayer contests the liability therefor and the tax is not paid until a later year.   Such an accrual, however, cannot be made until the contested liability is finally determined.   This ruling does not apply to the accrual of the deduction for foreign taxes under §164, a deduction that may be claimed only for the taxable year in which the liability for the foreign taxes is finally adjudicated.

Section 905(c) relates to refunds of foreign taxes to taxpayers and the result-

general, nonresident aliens who are not engaged in business within the United States are taxable only on income from **sources** within the United States.[51] Withholding requirements have been

---

ing redetermination of their United States tax liability. Revenue Ruling 58-244, 1958-1 C.B. 265, holds that, with respect to any additional tax due, the interest imposed by §6601 for the period prior to the refund of the foreign tax may be assessed and collected only to the extent that interest was paid by the foreign country on the refund for such period, and that the interest imposed by §6601 for the period from the date of the refund to the date of payment is collectible at the rate of 6 percent. Revenue Ruling 58-237, 1958-1 C.B. 534, holds that for the purposes of a redetermination of a tax resulting from a refund of foreign income taxes for which a credit has been allowed, the conversion of the refund to American dollars is made at the rate of exchange prevailing at the date of the refund.

Revenue Ruling 59-85, 1959-1 C.B. 188, is concerned with a case where a Belgian citizen residing in the United States paid income taxes to France on income arising in that country, and he was denied a credit under §901(b)(3) because the convention between Belgium and the United States allows a citizen of the United States residing in Belgium a credit against Belgian tax only with respect to income from sources within and taxed by the United States.

Revenue Ruling 59-101, 1959-1 C.B. 189, discusses various questions pertaining to the allowance of a credit under §901 for taxes paid or accrued to Puerto Rico under the "pay as you go" provisions of the Puerto Rican income tax of 1954.

In order for a tax paid to a foreign country to be allowable as a credit against the United States income tax under §901, it must be shown that the tax imposed under foreign law is a tax on income within the United States concept thereof, or is a tax paid in lieu of income tax under §903. See Rev. Rul. 56-658, 1956-2 C.B. 501. Revenue Ruling 59-192, 1959-1 C.B. 191, holds that certain described Cuban taxes constitute income taxes for which a credit is allowable.

Revenue Ruling 59-208, 1959-1 C.B. 192, holds that a foreign tax credit under §901 is allowable for German trade taxes paid, insofar as such taxes constitute a tax on business earnings. However, a credit is not allowable insofar as such taxes constitute a tax on business capital or wages paid.

Revenue Ruling 59-70, 1959-1 C.B. 186, and Rev. Rul. 60-56, I.R.B. 1960-6, 71, discuss certain Brazilian taxes and determine which ones are income taxes within the meaning of §901, so that a credit for their payment is allowable.

[51] See 1954 I.R.C. §§871-877, which deal with the taxation of nonresident alien individuals. Sections 861-864 determine what is and what is not income from sources within the United States.

Revenue Ruling 58-232, 1958-1 C.B. 261, holds that gains from the sale or exchange of capital assets of an estate of a deceased nonresident alien who was not engaged in trade or business in the United States are not subject to the tax imposed by §871(a)(2), irrespective of the presence in the United States of an ancillary and/or domiciliary representative of the estate during the year in which the gains were realized.

Revenue Ruling 59-167, 1959-1 C.B. 623, involves a nonresident foreign corporate trustee of a foreign trust which has as its sole beneficiary a nonresident alien individual and holds that the trustee is not required to file a fiduciary return where, for any year in which the trust is not engaged in business or trade in the United States, the gross income from sources within the United States is not more than $15,000 and the tax liability thereon is fully satisfied through withholding at the source. Also, the trustee is not required to file any return for the nonresident alien beneficiary for any year when he is not engaged in business or trade in the United States, none of the trust income is taxable to

established in regard to the tax on nonresident aliens.[52] The
income tax treaties which the United States has negotiated with
various countries may alter what would otherwise be the tax

---

him, and no gross income of his is derived from sources within the United
States.

No joint return by a husband and wife is proper if either is a nonresident
alien (see §6013(a)(1)) at any time during the taxable year. If both husband
and wife are nonresident aliens residing in a country where the income from
sources within the United States (the only income taxable to them under §872)
is regarded as community property, may they file separate federal income tax
returns? Revenue Ruling 59-199, 1959-1 C.B. 182, holds that the husband and
wife may file separate returns, each reporting one half of the income.

[52] See 1954 I.R.C. §§1441-1443.

Revenue Ruling 57-245, 1957-1 C.B. 286, holds that ancillary administration
in the United States of the estate of a nonresident alien decedent which is subject to domiciliary administration in a foreign country does not change the
status of the estate for federal income tax purposes from that of a nonresident
alien entity, so that dividends derived from such an estate are subject to withholding of United States income tax under §1441.

Revenue Ruling 57-299, 1957-2 C.B. 606, holds that where a nonresident
alien and his wife (a citizen of the United States residing in a foreign country) own stock of a domestic corporation either as joint tenants or tenants by
the entirety, any dividends paid on such stock will be considered as owned by
them in equal proportions, so that the corporation is required to withhold
the tax under §1441 only on that one half of the total dividend paid which is
considered as paid to the nonresident alien.

In a Special Ruling dated May 13, 1958, 58 CCH Fed. Tax Rep. ¶6522,
and in another Special Ruling dated May 13, 1958, 58 CCH Fed. Tax Rep.
¶6523, it is pointed out, with respect to a Cuban telephone company and a
Puerto Rican telephone company, that where less than 20 percent of the gross
income of each company was derived from sources within the United States,
payments of dividends and interest by such companies to such nonresident
alien individuals will not be subject to the withholding of federal income tax
under §1441 or §1442.

Revenue Ruling 59-177, 1959-1 C.B. 229, deals with a trust established in the
United States with a resident fiduciary, all the income of which is from
sources in the United States, and holds that the fiduciary is not required under §1441 to withhold income tax at the source on the amount of the distribution to a nonresident alien beneficiary which exceeds the beneficiary's proportionate share of the distributable net income of the trust.

Section 861(a)(1)(A) excludes interest on deposits with persons carrying on
the banking business from income from sources within the United States when
paid to persons not engaged in business within the United States. Revenue
Ruling 59-245, 1959-2 C.B. 172, considers a trust created in part by a nonresident alien and holds that interest on bank deposits paid to him, to the extent that they are attributed to him as owner pursuant to §677, are exempt
from tax under §871 and from withholding under §1441. However, to the extent that the person is deemed a donee-beneficiary of the trust, the interest is
deemed paid to the trustee and is taxable under §871 and subject to withholding under §1441.

Revenue Ruling 60-181, I.R.B. 1960-19, 16, holds that where the property of
a trust established under the laws of a foreign jurisdiction consists principally
of securities of United States corporations, and the securities are held, controlled, and traded in the United States on a domestic exchange by a trustee
who is a citizen and resident of this country, the trust is deemed to be a resident alien entity of the United States for federal income tax purposes.

situation with respect to citizens and residents and nonresidents who are not citizens.[53] A special section of the Code is applicable

[53] For a collection of the income tax conventions which are in force or in the process of negotiation, see 58 CCH Fed. Tax Rep. §6280.

Revenue Ruling 56-24, 1956-1 C.B. 851, interprets the word "day" as used in these treaties in relation to the tax consequences if a foreigner is present in the United States for a period not exceeding a designated number of days, to mean any portion of a day in which the foreigner is physically present within the country.

In Rev. Rul. 56-30, 1956-1 C.B. 646, consideration is given to the income tax consequences with respect to income received by a citizen and resident of the United States who is a beneficiary of a trust created in Australia, and the trust consists of Australian and American investments.

Revenue Ruling 59-56, 1959-1, C.B. 737, holds that, even though the tax conventions contain a provision that income from real property shall be subjected to tax only in the country where the property is situated, a citizen of the United States or a resident alien is, by reason of a saving clause in the convention, liable for the United States income tax on the income from such property. A credit against the United States income tax is allowable as provided in §901, subject to the limitation of §904.

In Marie G. Crerar, 26 T.C. 702 (1956), the taxpayer was a citizen of the United States but a resident of Canada, and most of her income was derived from two Illinois trusts of which the trustee was an Illinois corporation. In each case the trust principal consisted of stocks, bonds and real estate. All income from the trusts was earned in and derived from sources within the United States. The court held that the taxpayer's income was taxable at rates set forth in the Internal Revenue Code, rather than in the 1942 tax convention and the credit allowed her by the Commissioner for the income tax paid to Canada constituted all the allowable relief from double taxation.

The tax treaty between the United States and the United Kingdom exempts residents of the United Kingdom from the United States capital gains tax. In American Trust Co. v. Smyth, 141 F. Supp. 414 (N.D. Cal. 1956), it was held that this exemption does not apply to a United States trustee of a United States trust having life beneficiaries and remaindermen who are residents of the United Kingdom, where the capital gains of the trust are not currently distributable but are retained by the trustee. The case was reversed in 247 F.2d 149 (9th Cir. 1957).

Revenue Ruling 56-164, 1956-1 C.B. 848, construes the convention with the Netherlands and holds that after a visiting teacher from the Netherlands has been absent from the United States for one year he may return and enter upon another exemption period of two years.

Revenue Ruling 56-165, 1956-1 C.B. 849, construes the provision in the income tax convention with Switzerland which subjects to United States tax a Swiss enterprise which is engaged in trade or business in the United States. See also Elizabeth Herbert, 30 T.C. 26 (1958), which construes similar language in the income tax convention with the United Kingdom.

Section 894 recognizes that the taxation of nonresident alien individuals under §§871 et seq. may be modified by treaties. Revenue Ruling 58-63, 1958-1 C.B. 624, illustrates such a modification under the provisions of the income tax convention between the United States and France.

Revenue Ruling 55-211, 1955-1 C.B. 676, Rev. Rul. 55-508, 1955-2 C.B. 775, and Rev. Rul. 60-23, I.R.B. 1960-5, 75, consider the extent to which remuneration paid to visiting professors for research and teaching is exempt from federal income tax under the treaties with the United Kingdom, France and Japan.

In Inez De Amodio, 34 T.C. — , No. 92 (1960), the income tax convention with Switzerland was considered. The convention does not apply to a nonresident alien unless he is a resident of Switzerland and does not have a "per-to citizens of possessions of the United States,[54] and another covers income from sources within Puerto Rico.[55]

The taxable income of a trust is computed in the same manner as that of an individual. If the trust is a foreign trust, that is, the trust is administered in a foreign country by a nonresident alien trustee, the income of the trust which is retained by the trustee is taxable in the United States only to the extent that income received by a nonresident alien would be taxable.[56] This offers an opportunity to a citizen or a resident who is willing to establish a trust in a foreign country, with a nonresident alien trustee, and who is willing to forgo distributions from the trust, to avoid United States income taxes during the period the trust income is accumulated.[57] When distribution is made to the citizen or resident he will be taxed on the distribution just as any other trust distributee, with the benefit of a credit for his share of the foreign income taxes paid by the trust.[58] Because of the various exceptions to the throwback rule[59] and because capital gains are not normally includible in distributable net income,[60] the income retained by the foreign trust may escape United States taxation to a considerable extent when finally distributed. A proposal is now before Congress which is designed to remove some of the attractiveness of these foreign trusts.[61] It should be noted that if

---

manent establishment" in the United States. The court concluded that he was a resident of Switzerland and did not have a "permanent establishment" in the United States when he was carrying on business dealings through a broker or independent agent acting in the ordinary course of his business.

[54] See 1954 I.R.C. §932.

Revenue Ruling 60-291, I.R.B. 1960-36, 21, points out that United States citizens who are domiciled in the Virgin Islands and who qualify as inhabitants thereof are required to satisfy their income tax obligations under the applicable taxing statutes of the United States by filing their returns in the Virgin Islands and paying their tax there on income derived from all sources. H.R. 10960, passed by the Congress in 1960, contains a provision (1954 I.R.C. §934) which prevents the Virgin Islands from rebating taxes on income from sources within the United States.

[55] See 1954 I.R.C. §933.

[56] See 1954 I.R.C. §§871 et seq.

[57] If the foreign jurisdiction selected does not tax capital gains, no income tax may be payable by the trust if it invests only in growth stocks that are not paying current dividends.

[58] See 1954 I.R.C. §901(b)(4).

[59] The throwback rule and its exceptions are examined supra page 742.

[60] See 1954 I.R.C. §643(a)(3).

[61] H.R. 9662, which was reported favorably to the Senate by the Senate Finance Committee on June 18, 1960, but which failed of passage in the Eighty-sixth Congress, proposed appropriate amendments to the 1954 Code designed to eliminate the various exceptions to the throwback rule in connection with trust distributions of income from foreign sources and to cause the inclusion of net capital gains which have not been subject to tax under 1954 I.R.C. §871 in the distributable net income of a foreign trust, for the

stock or securities are transferred by a citizen or a resident to a foreign trust an excise tax is imposed on the transfer equal to $27\frac{1}{2}$ percent of the excess of the value of the stock or securities so transferred, over the adjusted basis of the stock or securities in the hands of the transferor.[62]

b. *Non-tax Matters*

If a United States citizen owns securities in a foreign corporation consideration, tax questions aside, should be given to the desirability of retaining the securities until his death, because of the delays and expenses that may be inherent in transferring them from his name to the name of his executor and from the name of his executor to the name of the distributee under the will.[63]

If a beneficiary under an estate plan is an alien, the controlling local state law must be examined to determine whether there are any restrictions on the ownership of property by aliens. In recent years, considerable concern has developed with respect to the transfer of property to a person who is a resident in one of the "iron curtain" countries, because it is not likely that any significant part of the transferred assets will be enjoyed by the intended beneficiary. Two types of statutes designed to deal with this situation have developed. One is represented by the California statute, under which the attempted gift is nullified completely unless the statutory conditions are met.[64] The other is represented by the New York statute, which is designed to prevent the money from being paid to the alien but does not result in depriving him of his substantive rights in the subject matter of the gift.[65] Massachusetts has a statute somewhat like New York's.[66]

---

purpose of computing undistributed net income which may be subject to the throwback rule. See §110 of H.R. 9662.

[62] See 1954 I.R.C. §1491.

[63] See Greene, Administration of British Assets in American Estates. 36 Trust Bull. No. 7, p. 39 (1957).

[64] See Cal. Prob. Code §§259-259.2 (Deering, 1959), quoted infra page 1437. The California legislation is reviewed in a comment in 25 So. Calif. L. Rev. 329 (1952).

Statutory provisions similar to those in California have been enacted in Iowa (Iowa Code §567.8 (1958)); Montana (Mont. Rev. Codes Ann. §§91-520, 91-521 (1947, Supp. 1959)); Nevada (Nev. Rev. Stat. §134.230 (1957)); and Oregon (Ore. Rev. Stat. §111.070 (1959)).

[65] See N.Y. Surrogate's Court Act §269-a, quoted infra page 1470. In Matter of Arnold Crymer, N.Y.L.J., Mar. 10, 1958, p. 11, the Surrogate's Court of Kings County interpreted Surrogate's Court Act §269 as permitting the court to authorize the executors of an estate to use reasonable amounts of a bequest to a resident of Hungary, not exceeding $100 a month, for shipment of food and

The Massachusetts statute was involved in In re Mazurowski, which is printed in full below.

In Matter of Grant-Suttie, printed in full infra page 1116, consideration is given to the controlling law, for purposes of the rule against perpetuities, when a citizen of a foreign country sets up a trust of assets located in the United States with a United States trustee.

In re FALICJA MAZUROWSKI
331 Mass. 33, 116 N.E.2d 854 (1954)

QUA, C.J.   One Leon Mazurowski of Springfield died intestate August 16, 1942, leaving personal property to be administered. A public administrator was appointed.   Mazurowski had a wife, a son, and two daughters in Poland.   In 1944 the administrator, upon his petition for distribution, was required to deposit the distributive shares of the wife and children in a savings bank for their benefit.   Allen v. Mazurowski, 317 Mass. 218.   These four petitions are now brought by the wife and children to require payment to them of the balances of these bank deposits.[67]

The petitioners are nationals of Poland.   The petitions, although apparently signed by them, were presented and are still pressed by the consul general of Poland in New York, who has "jurisdiction" over Massachusetts, and who claims the right to act for the petitioners and to receive the deposits in their behalf both by virtue of his consular office and under powers of attorney from them executed and authenticated in Poland.   In each case the trial judge made an order under G.L. (Ter. Ed.) c. 206, §27A, inserted by St. 1950, c. 265, requiring the appearance in person of each petitioner before the court "in order to assist in establishing such claimant's identity, right, and opportunity to

---

medicine packages to the legatee, provided proof of delivery was always obtained.

For a comparison of the California and New York legislation, see Chaitkin, The Rights of Residents of Russia and Its Satellites to Share in Estates of American Decedents, 25 So. Calif. L. Rev. 297 (1952).

The New York type of statute has been enacted in Connecticut (Conn. Gen. Stat. Rev. §45.278 (1958)); Maryland (Md. Code Ann., art. 93, §161 (1957)); Michigan (Mich. Stat. Ann. §27.3178(306a) (1943, Supp. 1959)); New Jersey (N.J. Rev. Stat. §3A:25-10 (1951)); Pennsylvania (Pa. State. Ann., tit. 20, §1156 (Purdon, Supp. 1959)); Rhode Island (R.I. Gen. Laws Ann. §33-13-13 (1956)).

[66] See Mass. Ann. Laws, c. 206, §§27A, 27B and 28, quoted infra page 1463.

[67] (Court footnote) Small amounts from these deposits have previously been paid under decree of the court to the alien property custodian, presumably for expenses in establishing the rights of the present petitioners in the previous litigation.

receive such fund." Each case was ordered continued until the appearance of the petitioner in court. The judge of probate found that it was practically impossible for any of the petitioners to come from Poland to the court at the present time, and that his orders in effect bar them from recovering the funds until some undeterminable future time, dependent upon the course of world events.

The petitioners, through the consul general, contend that the orders of the judge are in contravention of certain articles contained in the treaty between this country and Poland, proclaimed by the President July 10, 1933, 48 U.S. Sts. at Large, Part 2, page 1507, and that in so far as the statute under which the judge purported to act may appear to authorize such orders it is unconstitutional because of the provision of the second paragraph of art. 6 of the Constitution of the United States that "all treaties made, or which shall be made, under the authority of the United States, shall be the supreme law of the land; and the judges in every state shall be bound thereby, any thing in the constitution or laws of any state to the contrary notwithstanding."

The statute under which the judge acted reads as follows: "Section 27A. Whenever payment of a legacy or distributive share cannot be made to the person entitled thereto, or such person may not receive or have the opportunity to obtain said legacy or distributive share, the court, on petition of an interested party or in its discretion, may order that the money be deposited in a savings bank or other like institution, or invested in the manner provided in section twenty-five, and disposed of in the manner provided in section twenty-eight. When a claimant to such funds resides outside of the United States or its territories, the court in its discretion, in order to assist in establishing such claimant's identity, right and opportunity to receive such fund, may require the appearance in person before the court of such claimant." [68]

The orders appealed from were directly based upon the last sentence of the statute, but that sentence can hardly be considered without the first, and it seems necessary to deal with the statute as a whole.

The portions of the treaty with which the orders are said to conflict are found in the second paragraph of article 4, in the

---

[68] In 1956 a new §27B was added which authorizes the court to pay the legacy or distributive share to the executor, administrator or petitioning interested party for use by him in the purchase of goods in the form of necessaries of life, food, clothing and medicines, to be sent to the legatee or distributee through a recognized public or private agency, upon his written request, order, or assignment. See Mass. Ann. Laws, c. 206, §27B (Supp. 1959), quoted infra page 1463. — ED.

third paragraph of article 23, and in article 24. The passages in articles 23 and 24 relate to the right of consular officers as such to appear for their nationals in matters concerning the administration and distribution of estates and in their behalf to collect and receipt for their distributive shares. We are informed by the Department of State that the treaty was terminated January 5, 1952, pursuant to a notice given to the Polish government on July 5, 1951. All special powers and privileges of consular officers as such, not being property rights, came to an end with the termination of the treaty, and we need not further consider articles 23 and 24.

Article 4, however, in its second paragraph, purports to confer property rights which might survive the termination of the treaty. See Santovincenzo v. Egan, 284 U.S. 30. The paragraph reads, "Nationals of either High Contracting Party may have full power to dispose of their personal property of every kind within the territories of the other, by testament, donation, or otherwise, and their heirs, legatees and donees, of whatsoever nationality, whether resident or non-resident, shall succeed to such personal property, and may take possession thereof, either by themselves or by others acting for them, and retain and dispose of the same at their pleasure subject to the payment of such duties or charges only as the nationals of the High Contracting Party within whose territories such property may be or belong shall be liable to pay in like cases."

Provisions in treaties phrased in this manner apply only where the decedent was a national of the foreign country. Clark v. Allen, 331 U.S. 503, 514-516. The record fails to disclose whether in this instance the decedent was a Polish national. If he was not, the treaty gave no rights to his widow and next of kin. But even if the decedent was a Polish national, we do not understand that article 4 of the treaty gave to his widow and next of kin paramount rights to seize their shares in his estate regardless of the laws of this Commonwealth providing for the orderly settlement and distribution of the estates of deceased persons domiciled here. The foreign heir or distributee acquires his rights by the law of this Commonwealth and is bound by the provisions of that law as to the time and manner of distribution. Lyeth v. Hoey, 305 U.S. 188, 193. Irving Trust Co. v. Day, 314 U.S. 556, 562. United States v. Burnison, 339 U.S. 87, 91-92. The treaty did not purport to create special rights of succession in favor of aliens. Clark v. Allen, 331 U.S. 503, 517. No doubt the primary object and possibly the only effect in practice of the paragraph quoted from article 4 were to secure the nationals of the foreign State against discrimination.

The question then at once arises whether §27A is any more than a reasonable local regulation governing the distribution of the estates of deceased residents. In answering that question it becomes necessary to take into account conditions existing today in certain foreign countries, including Poland, which the Legislature no doubt had in mind in enacting the statute. See article entitled "Estates and 'The Iron Curtain' " in Mass. Law Q., Vol. 35 (1950), No. 2, page 34. The judge of probate ruled, we think rightly, that "Inasmuch as there was no adverse party" the responsibility rested upon the judge "to see that the property parties are entitled to receive the funds at their full value." Accordingly, acting sua sponte, he made inquiries from the Department of State and was advised that according to the information of that Department under Polish foreign exchange regulations dollar funds, whether remitted through banking channels or through a Polish consular officer, are retained by the Polish government and the persons to whom the remittances are directed receive Polish currency at the rate of approximately four zlotys to the dollar; and that the same regulations were understood to provide that permanent residents of that country must report to the government of Poland "against reimbursement in local currency" at the same rate. A recent communication to us from the Department of Justice confirms this information and further advises us that the prevailing free rate of exchange is approximately twenty zlotys to the dollar, and that United States government personnel in Poland are paid at the rate of twenty-five zlotys to the dollar. Moreover, by U.S.C. (1946 ed.) Title 31, §123, it is provided that no check or warrant drawn against funds of the United States shall be sent for delivery in a foreign country in any case in which the Secretary of the Treasury determines that postal, transportation or banking facilities in general, or local conditions in the country to which such check or warrant is to be delivered are such that there is not a reasonable assurance that the payee will actually receive such check or warrant and be able to negotiate the same for full value. The Secretary of the Treasury by Department Circular No. 655, as amended April 17, 1951, 16 Fed. Reg. 3479, determined that conditions in about a dozen named countries behind the "Iron Curtain," including Poland, were such "that there is not a reasonable assurance" that payees in those areas will actually receive such checks or warrants and be able to negotiate them for full value. There is no reason to suppose that a transfer of funds such as is sought by these petitions would meet with any better fate. We think that it was proper for the judge of probate to avail himself, and that it is proper for us to avail ourselves, of superior sources of information on such matters relating to foreign law and administrative regulations possessed by the high executive officers of the government, but not directly available to the courts or to litigants. Universal Adjustment Corp. v. Midland Bank, Ltd., 281 Mass. 303, 327. Matter of Braier, 305 N.Y. 148, at pages 157-158. G.L. (Ter. Ed.) c. 233, §70.

The result of the best information we have been able to obtain is that there is no reasonable assurance that money sent to many of the countries behind the "Iron Curtain" will be received by the payees at full value, and that as to Poland, the payees would receive no more than about twenty percent of full value, the remaining eighty percent being in effect confiscated by the Polish State.

When projected against this background §27A seems to us a reasonable and valid regulation of the final distribution of estates of deceased residents of this Commonwealth designed to preserve the property interests of the distributees. Such a regulation is binding upon distributees, even though enacted after the death of the decedent. "There is no vested right in a mode of procedure. Each succeeding legislature may establish a different one, providing only that in each are preserved the essential elements of protection." Backus v. Fort Street Union Depot Co., 169 U.S. 557, 570. Gibbes v. Zimmerman, 290 U.S. 326, 332. See Wilbur v. Gilmore, 21 Pick. 250, 252-253; Simmons v. Hanover, 23 Pick. 188, 193-194; Sohier v. Massachusetts General Hospital, 3 Cush. 483, 496; Jewett v. Phillips, 5 Allen 150; Magee v. Commissioner of Corporations & Taxation, 256 Mass. 512, 516-517; 36 L.R.A. (N.S.) 1029, note; Cooley, Constitutional Limitations (8th ed.) 754-756. The statute is in no sense discriminatory against nationals of Poland or of any other country. It would apply equally, under similar conditions, to a national of the United States residing in Poland or other foreign country.

For a number of years the surrogates of New York have upheld and applied in respect to distributees in various countries a statute of that State generally similar to the first sentence of §27A. Matter of Weidberg, 172 Misc. (N.Y.) 524 (Germany). Matter of Geffen, 199 Misc. (N.Y.) 756 (Lithuania). Matter of Yee Yoke Ban, 200 Misc. (N.Y.) 499 (China). Matter of Best, 200 Misc. (N.Y.) 332 (Soviet Union). In re Rysiakiewicz' Will, 114 N.Y. Supp. (2d) 504 (Poland). These and other similar decisions appear to have been confirmed by the Court of Appeals in Matter of Braier, 305 N.Y. 148 [69] (Hungary). See Estate of Blak, 65 Cal. App. (2d) 232.

There may be more doubt about the second sentence of the statute, under which the present orders were made, than about the first sentence. If these orders were in their nature final and if they irrevocably established that the petitioners could have the deposits only by coming here for them, a very different case would be presented. But the orders are merely temporary. They could be made in the first place only "in order to assist in establishing such claimant's identity, right and opportunity to receive such fund" and they can be continued in effect only as long as the judge still feels that the identity, right and opportunity of the petitioners to receive the funds are not otherwise sufficiently established. The world is still in a state of flux and uncertainty. It is still possible that more nearly normal relations will be resumed between nations. It is possible that a more realistic rate of exchange will be officially adopted in Poland. Many unforeseen events may profoundly alter present conditions. We do not think that we can as yet say that the deposit of the money and the orders of the court amount to a deprivation of the petitioners' property rather than a protection of it, especially as the present alternative seems to be that in order to receive twenty percent of their money they would be obliged to sacrifice the other eighty percent.

The result is that the consul general is not now entitled to receive the deposits either in his official capacity or as attorney in fact for the petitioners, and that the orders of the judge of probate must be affirmed.

Orders affirmed.[70]

[69] (*Court footnote*) The case sited deals in part with so-called "blocked" funds. No question of "blocking" arises in the case before us, since General License No. 97 of the Secretary of the Treasury, 13 Fed. Reg. 891, unblocked all funds in any account where the amount on February 1, 1948, did not exceed $5,000.

[70] The frozen funds of Leon Mazurowski's estate were released, without comment, under an order of the Probate Court of Hampden County, dated December 30, 1958, which directed that all sums due should be turned over to the Polish Consul General for payment to the Polish beneficiaries. See comments on In re Mazurowski in 48 Am. J. Int. Law 504 (1954), 53 Mich. L. Rev. 142 (1954), 102 U. of Pa. L. Rev. 945 (1954).

See generally Boyd, Treaties Governing the Succession to Real Property by Aliens, 51 Mich. L. Rev. 1001 (1953). — ED.

Matter of GRANT–SUTTIE
205 Misc. 640, 129 N.Y.S.2d 572 (1954)

Collins, S. Decedent was domiciled in the Province of Ontario, Canada. His will was proved in Canada and was admitted to probate in this country. The instrument treats his Canadian assets and his American assets separately and designates a distinct executor and trustee of each body of property. The ninth article of the will bequeaths testator's real and personal property comprising his American estate to the American executor in trust. In one contingency the trust will exist for the lives of four named persons and thereafter for a fixed period of years. In another contingency the trust will continue for the lives of five named persons and the issue of one of them. The trust provisions, whether regarded as creating a single trust or a primary trust and separable subordinate trusts, suspend the power of alienation for at least three lives in being at testator's death and a fixed period of slightly over fifteen years beyond testator's death. Concededly, if the New York rule against perpetuities is applicable to this will, the trust provisions, from whatever angle viewed, are replete with invalidity.[71] Fortunately for testator's testamentary scheme, the validity of the testamentary provisions is to be determined upon the basis of the law of his domicile (Decedent Estate Law, §47;[72] Cross v. United States Trust Co., 131 N.Y. 330; Bishop v. Bishop, 257 N.Y. 40).

The Canadian rule against perpetuities requires that every estate or interest must vest not later than twenty-one years after the determination of some life in being at the time of the crea-

[71] Under the present New York law in regard to the rule against perpetuities, the trust provisions would be valid. See the discussion of the present rule in New York at page 639 supra. — Ed.

[72] New York Decedent Estate Law §47 provides as follows: "The validity and effect of a testamentary disposition of real property, situated within the state, or of an interest in real property so situated, which would descend to the heir of an intestate, and the manner in which such property or such an interest descends, where it is not disposed of by will, are regulated by the laws of the state, without regard to the residence of the decedent. Except where special provision is otherwise made by law, the validity and effect of a testamentary disposition of any other property situated within the state, and the ownership and disposition of such property, where it is not disposed of by will, are regulated by the laws of the state or country, of which the decedent was a resident, at the time of his death. Whenever a decedent, being a citizen of the United States or a citizen or a subject of a foreign country, wherever resident, shall have declared in his will and testament that he elects that such testamentary dispositions shall be construed and regulated by the laws of this state, the validity and effect of such dispositions shall be determined by such laws." — Ed.

tion of the estate or interest. The additional term of twenty-one years may or may not be independent of a minority or may itself fix the term of suspension (8 Can. Ency. Digest [Ont. ed.], p. 454, Perpetuities; Ferguson v. Ferguson, 39 U.C.Q.B., 232, rev'd 1 Ont. App. 452, rev'd 2 Can. Sup. Ct. 497; Matter of Smith, 1942 Ont. Wkly. Notes 455; Matter of Miller, 1938 Ont. Wkly. Notes 118). The trust provisions of this will are in conformity with the law of testator's domicile and, insofar as they concern personal property in this jurisdiction, the provisions may be effectuated validly by the fiduciary appointed here.

While the validity of the trust provisions is to be determined by the law of testator's domicile, he has here expressed an intention, by the particular treatment of his American assets and the appointment of a New York trust company as trustee, that his assets in this jurisdiction are to be administered according to the law of this State (Matter of Berger, 183 Misc. 366; Matter of Shipman, 179 Misc. 303; Matter of McAuliffe, 167 Misc. 783; Matter of Vanneck, 158 Misc. 704; Matter of Keeler, 49 N.Y.S.2d 592; Restatement, Conflict of Laws, §298). Certain general powers are granted to the executor-trustee by the seventeenth article of the will. The authority there conferred is plainly expressed and there appears to be no exigency that requires a more precise definition of such powers at this time.

Inherent in testator's purpose to place the administration of the trust under the supervision of the courts of this State is the intention that the executor-trustee be compensated for its services in accordance with the law of the place of administration. This right of the executor-trustee to compensation is not challenged but an income beneficiary asserts that the fiduciary's compensation, both as executor and as trustee, should be borne by the capital fund alone. The court does not find this intention in the will. The provisions of section 285-a of the Surrogate's Court Act placing the burden of trustee's commissions are controlling in the absence of a testamentary direction to the contrary. Testator's will provides that the "whole of the income" be paid to a single individual until the death of such beneficiary when "one-half of the income" is to be paid to each of two other persons until the death of one of such persons when "the whole of the income" is to be paid to the survivor. The suggestion is made that, by use of the word "whole," testator meant that the gross income be paid out to trust beneficiaries and that trust corpus be charged with the expenses and burdens that, but for testator's use of the word "whole," would be borne by income. It seems quite clear that testator used the word "whole" in each instance as a direction for payment of trust income to a single individual as contrasted with the direction to divide the income between two persons. The locutions "whole income" and "one-half of the income" plainly express testator's distinction between the number of beneficiaries entitled to income under different contingencies and these expressions convey no thought as to the allocation of administrative expenses or other charges between income and corpus. There is no ambiguity in testator's use of the word "whole" and to try to read hidden meanings into the language would seem to be to completely distort testator's purpose. Questions arising in trust administrations as to the allocation of charges against either principal or income have been the subject of much judicial consideration and, in the absence of a testamentary direction, the equitable principle of adjusting charges in accordance with benefits received has always been held applicable. The application of equitable principles requires that, in the absence of an explicit mandate of a testator, the trust income beneficiary receive, not gross income, but instead, the net income that remains after deduction of all charges that equitably should be borne by income interests [citations omitted]. The court holds that commissions for the receipt of income, whether payable to the executor or to the trustee, are not chargeable to the principal of the estate. The objections to the failure to charge such commissions to principal are dismissed.

Submit decree on notice construing the will and settling the account.[73]

[73] See Molloy and Woodford, Estate Planning Techniques and the Ownership of Canadian Securities, 62 Yale L.J. 147 (1953). — Ed.

CHAPTER XIX

Administrative Provisions

The fiduciaries selected to administer an estate plan should be given a sensible and thorough working charter so that their administrative responsibilities can be performed in the manner that is most advantageous to the beneficiaries and, at the same time, is least costly to the estate involved. Whether the working charter should be one that gives the fiduciaries wide discretions in matters of administration, or one that minutely defines their permitted course of action, or one that is somewhere in between the two extremes depends on the circumstances. In general, it is believed that fiduciaries should be selected who are trustworthy and that considerable discretion should be given to them to meet the various problems of administration in the way which they believe will be for the best interest of all concerned.[1]

The administrative provisions which are adequate in certain situations may be inadequate in others. If a trust is established which has the function of operating a going business or of running a farm, the administrative provisions essential to the proper performance of such a function may be different than those essential to the performance of some other function.[2] In other words, the administrative provisions should be tailor-made to meet the particular situation.

The administrative provisions which are appropriate in a particular situation will be influenced somewhat by whether they relate to administration by an executor or by a trustee. An executor is basically a short-term fiduciary and a trustee is normally a long-term fiduciary. Obviously, administration of property over a long period of time is likely to result in many more administrative complexities than administration over a short period.

[1] See generally Stephenson, Drafting Wills and Trust Agreements: Administrative Provisions (1952).
[2] The special problems presented when a closely held business or a farm is to be dealt with in an estate plan are examined in Chapter XV.

1. Administrative Provisions and the Rule Against Perpetuities

If an administrative power given to a trustee may be exercised beyond the period of the governing rule against perpetuities, is such a power valid?[3] Suppose, for example, that T in his will devises the residue of his estate to a trustee and directs him "to pay the net income to A for his life; then to pay the net income to A's first son for his life; then to pay the corpus to the X charity." In a jurisdiction which applies the common law rule against perpetuities, no interest under the residuary trust in T's will may vest too remotely. Assuming, however, that A has no son at the death of T, the residuary trust may continue for more than twenty-one years after lives in being at the death of T. Consequently, the administrative powers given to the trustee of the residuary trust may be exercised beyond the period of the rule.

Even though a trust is limited in duration to the period of the governing rule against perpetuities, the normal process of winding up the trust will require its administration to go on for some limited time after the trust ends. If the administrative powers given to the trustee may be exercised during the winding-up period, the administrative powers may be exercised beyond the period of the rule.

Unless an alleged administrative power is really a power of appointment in disguise, it is submitted that the rule against perpetuities should not be applicable to it. Many administrative powers give the trustee power to determine to some extent the economic benefit a beneficiary receives. A liberal power as to investments gives the trustee the power to determine, by the risks that are taken in the investment of the principal, the amount of income which an income beneficiary receives and the amount which will eventually be distributed to the remaindermen. The power to determine, within limits, what is income and what is principal affects the income beneficiary and the remaindermen. The power to determine what charges shall be paid out of income and what charges out of principal also affects the income beneficiary and the remaindermen. Although these powers, and others, have an incidental effect on the economic benefits received by the beneficiaries, it is submitted that they are fundamentally

---

[3] See 6 American Law of Property §24.63 (Casner ed. 1952); Leach, Powers of Sale in Trustees and the Rule Against Perpetuities, 47 Harv. L. Rev. 948 (1934).

administrative powers and should not be classified as powers of appointment for the purposes of the rule against perpetuities.[4]

2. ADMINISTRATIVE PROVISIONS AND THE RULE AGAINST ACCUMULATIONS

Some administrative powers may give the fiduciary a power to accumulate income.[5] The power to use income to pay off a mortgage on part of the trust property, the power to use income to offset the loss to the principal when bonds are purchased at a premium,[6] and the power to determine what is income and what is principal may result in an accumulation of income. Whenever it is desired to give such administrative powers to a fiduciary, the governing state law must be examined to ascertain whether the rule against accumulations will be violated.[7]

3. ADMINISTRATIVE PROVISIONS AND TAX CONSIDERATIONS

a. *Income Taxes*

If the settlor of an inter vivos trust creates certain powers that are described as "administrative powers," the income of the trust will be taxable to him.[8] These powers relate to the power to deal with trust property for less than an adequate and full consideration; the power to borrow trust property; the power to vote or direct the voting of stock when the holdings of the settlor and the trust are significant from the viewpoint of voting control; the power to control investment of the trust funds to the extent that they consist of stock where the holdings of the settlor and the trust are significant from the viewpoint of voting control; and the power to reacquire the trust property by substituting other property of equivalent value. The presence of these powers will

[4] The circumstances under which a power of appointment is void ad initio because it may be exercised beyond the period of the rule against perpetuities is considered supra page 766.

[5] See 6 American Law of Property §25.109 (Casner ed. 1952).

[6] On the duty of a trustee to amortize the amount paid as a premium on bonds, see New England Trust Co. v. Eaton, 140 Mass. 532 (1886); Old Colony Trust Co. v. Comstock, 290 Mass. 377, 195 N.E. 389 (1935).

[7] For a consideration of the rule against accumulations, see pages 676-684 supra.

[8] See 1954 I.R.C. §675, quoted infra page 1373, and the discussion in regard thereto at page 183 supra.

not cause the income of the trust to be included in the settlor's gross income, however, if proper safeguards are used.[9]

An administrative power which gives the trustee considerable discretion as to whether the income beneficiary or the remainderman will receive a benefit may be deemed a power to control beneficial enjoyment. If it is so regarded, the income of the trust will be taxable to the settlor unless the power can be brought within one of the exceptions which allows such a power without such an income tax result.[10] One power expressly excepted in this regard is a power to allocate receipts and disbursements as between corpus and income, even though described in broad language.[11] If the exercise of a discretion under an administrative power may result in income or corpus vesting in the settlor, then the field of exceptions in which such powers can operate without the income being taxable to the settlor is extremely narrow.[12]

b. *Estate Taxes*

Administrative powers and their significance in relation to estate taxes is a problem that has two distinct aspects. The first deals with the relevance of administrative powers where the estate taxes on the estate of the creator of the powers are concerned. If the administrative powers are set up in an inter vivos transfer, will the transferor be deemed to have a Section 2036 or Section 2038 power,[13] so that the value of the transferred property will be includible in his gross estate for federal estate tax purposes? Recently many people were shocked by the answer given to this question by a court in a case where the settlor was a trustee and the trust contained fairly broad but rather typical administrative powers. The court said:

> Perhaps no single power conferred by the decedent on the trustees would be enough to warrant the inclusion of the corpora of the trusts in his estate. But we believe that the powers conferred on the trustees, considered as a whole, are so broad and all inclusive that within any limits a Massachusetts court of equity could impose, the trustees, within the scope of their discretionary powers, could very substan-

[9] The safeguards are spelled out in 1954 I.R.C. §675.

[10] See 1954 I.R.C. §674, quoted infra page 1371, and the comments thereon at page 176 supra.

[11] See 1954 I.R.C. §674(b)(8), quoted infra page 1373.

[12] See 1954 I.R.C. §§676, 677, quoted infra page 1374, and the consideration of these sections at page 184 supra.

[13] Section 2036 is quoted infra page 1396, and §2038, infra page 1397; §2036 powers and §2038 powers are examined supra page 188.

tially shift the economic benefits of the trusts between the life tenants and the remainderman.[14]

Clearly the administrative powers given a trustee must be closely scrutinized if the settlor is one of the trustees, where the objective is to remove the value of the transferred property from the settlor's gross estate for federal estate tax purposes.

The estate taxes payable by the estate of the creator of administrative powers will also be affected as to amount if the presence of the administrative powers eliminates a deduction which would otherwise be available in determining the taxable estate. The Regulations are fairly specific as to the types of administrative powers which can be used without disqualifying a power of appointment trust for the marital deduction.[15] It should also be kept in mind that a gift to a charity may not be fully deductible for estate tax purposes if the administrative powers permit a diversion of the benefits of the gift from the charity to some individual.[16]

The second aspect deals with the relevance of administrative powers where the estate taxes on the estate of the holder of the powers are concerned.[17] The holder of such powers may be deemed to have a power of appointment for estate tax purposes.[18] Even if he is deemed to have a power of appointment, its presence will not be significant to him, so far as estate taxes on his own estate are concerned, unless it is a general power of appointment, that is, one that permits him to benefit himself, his estate, his creditors or creditors of his estate by his exercise of it.[19]

c. *Gift Taxes*

Administrative powers may be significant in determining whether the transfer is a completed gift for gift tax purposes;[20]

[14] See State Street Trust Co. v. United States, 263 F.2d 635 (1st Cir. 1959).

[15] See particularly §20.2056(b)-5(f), quoted in text supra page 842.

[16] The deduction for income taxes purposes as well as for gift taxes purposes will also be similarly affected.

[17] If the creator of the powers and the holder of the powers are one and the same person, as when the settlor of a trust designates himself as trustee, then the discussion which relates to the relevance of administrative powers insofar as estate taxes on the estate of the creator of the powers are concerned is applicable.

[18] See Reg. §20.2041-1(b)(1), quoted infra page 1516, where it is recognized that the mere power of management, investment, custody of assets, or the power to allocate receipts and disbursements as between income and principal, exercisable in a fiduciary capacity, whereby the holder has no power to enlarge or shift any of the beneficial interests therein except as an incidental consequence of the discharge of fiduciary duties is not a power of appointment.

[19] General powers of appointment are considered supra page 689.

[20] As to when a gift is a completed one for gift tax purposes, see the mate-

whether a gift in trust qualifies for the gift tax marital deduction;[21] whether a gift is a present interest, so that the annual exclusion will be available with respect to it;[22] and whether the gift is deductible as a charitable gift.[23]

The case printed in full below is designed to illustrate the extent of the discretion a fiduciary may have under an administrative power.

DUMAINE v. DUMAINE
301 Mass. 214, 16 N.E.2d 625 (1938)

Cox, J. This is a bill in equity for instructions filed in the Supreme Judicial Court by the plaintiff, in his capacity as sole trustee under an indenture of trust dated April 11, 1932. The defendants are the plaintiff as an individual, Frederic C. Dumaine, Sr., and the trustees of a voluntary association, designated in the articles of association as "Dumaines," created and existing under the laws of New Hampshire. There is no dispute between the parties as to the material facts. The answers admit the allegations of the bill. The case was heard by a single justice who, at the request of the parties, reserved it for the full court upon the bill as amended and the answers. The sole question for determination is the power of the trustee under the following clause of the trust indenture: "The trustee under this instrument shall have full power and discretion to determine whether any money or other property received by him is principal or income without being answerable to any person for the manner in which he shall exercise that discretion." [24]

Frederic C. Dumaine, Jr., the plaintiff trustee, and Frederic C. Dumaine, Sr., a defendant, are the life tenants under the trust indenture and the trustees of "Dumaines," defendants, are the remaindermen. By the terms of the trust instrument certain

---

rial at page 216 supra. An administrative power in the settlor of a trust which enables the settlor to shift the economic benefits under the trust would be one that might cause the gift to be incomplete for gift tax purposes.

[21] See Reg. §25.2523(e)-1(f), which considers the types of administrative powers which can be inserted in a power of appointment marital deduction trust without disqualifying it for the gift tax marital deduction.

[22] The gift tax annual exclusion is examined supra page 236. An administrative power which in effect permits the trustee to accumulate income may make what would otherwise be a present interest under the trust a future interest.

[23] An administrative power that in effect allows the trustee to divert property from a gift to a charity may affect the valuation of the charitable gift.

[24] This power is usually given to a trustee but not always in such broad and unqualified language as is quoted in the text. — Ed.

property was conveyed to the plaintiff in trust "To hold, manage, invest and reinvest the same with all the powers hereinafter set forth, and, after paying the expenses of administering the trust in this instrument set forth," to pay the net income as therein directed. The trustee is not required to give any bond, and "No trustee under this instrument shall ever be held responsible for any act or omission of any other person nor for any loss or depreciation of any of the trust property unless such loss or depreciation shall have been directly caused by his own dishonesty or gross negligence. . . . He shall not be responsible for any loss which may occur if he shall have in his absolute and uncontrolled discretion mortgaged, pledged or otherwise encumbered any of the property of this trust fund for the benefit of 'Dumaines.' " Absolute and uncontrolled discretion is given the trustee as to the purchase and retention of securities. No trustee is ever to be liable to any person for any loss occasioned by depreciation of any security or property, and no person interested in the trust is entitled to proceed against the trustee on account of any such loss.

The bill was amended by adding an additional paragraph thereto: "7. The petitioner has sold certain shares of stock during the year 1938 at a profit over and above cost and is in doubt whether, as alleged by the Commissioner of Internal Revenue, he now under the trust instrument may in his discretion distribute the said profit to himself, as life tenant, as income." The defendants admit the allegations contained in this amendment. The prayers of the bill are (1) whether, under the provision of the trust indenture concerning which instruction is asked, the plaintiff has "the right to determine, contrary to the usual rules of law in this Commonwealth, what money or other property received by him, as trustee under said indenture, is principal or income, or whether said provision is to be construed as a limitation of the liability of the trustee without changing, for the purposes of the trust under said indenture, the usual rules of law of this Commonwealth as to what money or property, received by the trustee, is principal or income," and (2) "Whether or not the petitioner may in his discretion distribute to the life tenant gains from sales of securities." The defendant trustees in their brief state that "The precise question to be determined may be stated as follows: — Has the Petitioner, in his capacity as Trustee, the right and the power to distribute now to himself (in his personal capacity), 'as life tenant,' a profit derived during the year 1938 as the result of selling certain shares of stock, a part of the trust property, at a price 'over and above cost'?"

The purposes of the trust are clearly stated to be [1] "to pay so much of the net income as the trustee in his absolute and uncontrolled discretion shall determine, to said Frederic C. Dumaine, Jr. during his life, [2] and upon his death to pay such part of said net income as the trustee in his like absolute and uncontrolled discretion shall determine, to Frederic C. Dumaine . . . [3] and the balance of said income, if there be any at the end of any year, to carry to capital, [4] and upon the death of the survivor to pay over, transfer and convey the trust estate as then existing to the persons who at that time shall be the trustees of 'Dumaines' . . . to be held by said trustees upon the trusts set forth in said ['Dumaines'] instrument." These purposes, however, are subject to the power of the trustee "to apply any money or other property received by him, whether principal or income, for the protection of any of the rest of the trust fund and also for the protection of any or all of the trust fund of 'Dumaines' in such manner as he shall in his absolute and uncontrolled discretion deem best," and also subject to the power "to pledge, to borrow and to mortgage any of the property of which this trust fund may at any time consist for the benefit of 'Dumaines' . . . and to turn over to said 'Dumaines' the money raised thereby, all as he shall in his absolute and uncontrolled discretion deem best, not only for this trust but for the trust fund known as 'Dumaines.' " And there is also the provision, which is specifically under inquiry, that the trustee "shall have full power and discretion to determine whether any money or other property received by him is principal or income without being answerable to any person for the manner in which he shall exercise that discretion."

It has often been held that one of the principal requisites for the maintenance of a bill for instructions is the fiduciary possession of a fund of which some disposition is required to be made presently . [Citations omitted.] Our inquiry will be limited to the question raised by the amendment to the bill, that is, whether the trustee may, in his discretion, distribute to himself, as life tenant, as income, the profit derived by the sale of certain shares of stock in 1938, over and above their cost. The general rule is that, in case of a trust, gains resulting from the purchase and sale of securities are accretions belonging to the principal of the trust fund, rather than income.[25] [Citations omitted.] Such gains

---

[25] Such capital gains are included in the gross income of the trust for income tax purposes but, since they represent income normally allocated to corpus, they will not be deemed distributed, except under certain conditions, even though the trustee's distributions are in excess of the ordinary income of the trust. See the discussion relating to the income taxation of trusts at page 736 supra. — ED.

ordinarily do not belong to a beneficiary who is entitled to the "net income" under the trust. [Citation omitted.] It has been determined that gains from the sale of capital assets may be taxed as "income" within the meaning of a constitutional provision giving the Legislature authority to levy "a tax on income." [Citations omitted.] Reference is made to the discussion of the word "income," in Tax Commissioner v. Putnam, 227 Mass. 522. It is to be assumed that the settlor was familiar with these provisions of law at the time he executed the trust instrument, Tax Commissioner v. Putnam, 227 Mass. 522, 528, as well as the rule laid down in Minot v. Paine, 99 Mass. 101, as to stock dividends payable in cash or in stock being classified as income or principal. It is for us to determine, in so far as we are able, and sufficiently to answer the question raised, what the intention of the settlor was when he made use of the words contained in the clause under inquiry, for it is his intention which is the "controlling consideration" in determining the rights as between the life tenants and remaindermen. [Citations omitted.] And in making this determination, we must be guided by the well known principle of law that the whole instrument is to be considered, aided by the surrounding circumstances, due weight being given to all its language, with some meaning being given, if possible, to all parts, expressions and words used, discarding and disregarding no parts as meaningless, if any meaning can be given them consistently with the rest of the instrument. [Citations omitted.] Effect is to be given to the intent so ascertained unless some positive rule of law prevents. [Citation omitted.]

Trustees frequently are given power by the trust instrument to pay over a part of the principal to beneficiaries as to whom provision already has been made for payments of the income of the entire trust fund. This power may be conditional or unconditional. [Citation omitted.] A mere discretion to pay over such portion of principal as the trustee may "deem advisable," does not amount to an absolute power without limitation. It involves serious and responsible consideration. [Citation omitted.] In the case of Mayberry v. Carey, 268 Mass. 255, 257, a codicil of the will under inquiry provided: "For the purposes of the administration, settlement or distribution of my estate, I give my executor . . . and my administrator . . . and the trustee or trustees of each and every trust created by my will, the right to decide what is capital, what is income and what is net income . . . and their decision shall be final." It was held that the executor's determination as to net income was a proper exercise of his "discretionary power" and binding upon all parties, and that until the property

of the trust was turned over to the trustee, by the administrators
with the will annexed, the administrators were to exercise as to
that property the discretionary power given them by the codicil,
and also that the trustee was bound by the decision of the administrators as to what was net income. . . .

In the case of Minot v. Paine, 99 Mass. 101, 112, it was said,
in discussing the right of a beneficiary, who was entitled to income for life, to additional shares of stock distributed to the
trustee as dividends on stock already held, that "As to him [the
owner of stock], a stock dividend is an accretion to his capital;
and there is nothing to show that the testator intended that it
should be otherwise as between the successive takers of his
bounty." . . .

The defendant trustees do not appear to argue that a settlor
has no power to confer a discretion upon his trustees to determine
what is income and what is principal, but do contend that, under
the trust instrument in question, the trustee has no power to determine, contrary to established rules of law in this Commonwealth, what money or other property received by him as trustee
is principal or income.   This court has uniformly held that trustees in whom a discretion is vested are under an obligation to
exercise a "sound judgment and a reasonable and prudent discretion," Davis, appellant, 183 Mass. 499, 502; that kind of
"power and discretion which inheres in a fiduciary relation and
not that illimitable potentiality which an unrestrained individual possesses respecting his own property," Corkery v. Dorsey,
223 Mass. 97, 101; a "soundness of judgment which follows from
a due appreciation of trust responsibility," Boyden v. Stevens,
285 Mass. 176, 179, unless the settlor has expressed an intention
that the power of discretion conferred is such that "the court will
not interfere except upon clear proof that the trustees are abusing
their authority and acting in perversion of the trust."   Leverett
v. Barnwell, 214 Mass. 105, 108.   See National Exchange Bank v.
Sutton, 147 Mass. 131, 135.

In the case at bar it is pointed out that, in six instances in the
trust instrument, the trustee is given an "absolute and uncontrolled discretion" and that these comprehensive and conclusive
words do not appear in the clause under inquiry where the words
used are "full power and discretion."   Reverting to the terms of
the trust instrument, hereinbefore quoted, it is to be noted that if
at the end of any year there is a balance of income, it is to be
carried to capital, and that, during the lives of the life tenants
(compare North Adams National Bank v. Curtiss, 284 Mass.
330, 336), the trust property may be mortgaged or encumbered

for the benefit of "Dumaines," all of which manifests on the part of the settlor an interest in the remaindermen, possibly to the disadvantage of the life tenants. Compare Cammann v. Abbe, 258 Mass. 427, 429. Moreover, the life tenant's right to any part of the income depends upon how much the trustee shall determine in "his absolute and uncontrolled discretion" to pay. Then, too, the present trustee is the present life tenant and was the life tenant when the trust was created. Great powers, which powers will enure to his successor, are conferred upon him in the management of the trust. His liability for errors or omissions is posited only upon "his own dishonesty or gross negligence," and he is not required to furnish any bond.

On the other hand "full power and discretion" to determine whether any money or other property received by the trustee is principal or income, in the light of attendant circumstances and the language of the trust instrument as a whole, would have little significance if construed to mean a discretion so to determine only in cases where there is no settled law to guide. By the terms of the trust instrument he is to have that power and discretion "without being answerable to any person for the manner in which he shall exercise that discretion."

The court may properly have in mind that, when a settlor reposes a discretion in a trustee, he does so because he desires the honest judgment of the trustee, perhaps even to the exclusion of that of the court. In reposing a discretion he must be held to have known that human judgment is not infallible. It is not for the court to read into a trust instrument provisions which do not expressly appear or which do not arise by implication from the plain meaning of the words used, [citations omitted], and the court will not substitute its discretion for that of the trustee except when necessary to prevent an abuse of discretion. [Citations omitted.] It has been said that doubtless a trust might be created which by its terms would make his judgment, however unwise it might be, the final test. [Citations omitted.]

The power, if uncontrollable, to determine whether any money or other property received by the trustee is principal or income, coupled with the power to pay over to the present life tenant so much of the net income as in his absolute and uncontrolled discretion he shall determine, would give the trustee power to destroy the trust. The settlor had no such intention. In deciding the question which is before us, we think that the scope of our inquiry properly embraces the needs of the life tenants, the continuance of the trust until its manifest purposes are accomplished, and the protection and well-being of the "Dumaines," of which

latter trust the plaintiff is not only a trustee but also a beneficiary. We do not think the clause in issue confers an absolute
and uncontrolled discretion. Nor do we think that it limits the
trustee to the determination of the matter involved in cases where
there is a question of doubt or no rule of law to guide him. We
have nothing before us to show the amount of the trust fund.
The trust known as "Dumaines" was created on July 31, 1920,
twelve years prior to the trust involved. It made immediate provisions for the children of Frederic C. Dumaine, with ultimate
provisions for a substantial educational charity. The power is reserved, in the trust before us, in Frederic C. Dumaine, to make
additions to the trust property, and to appoint other trustees instead of or in addition to the one named in the instrument. The
trust known as "Dumaines" stands out as an important consideration in the mind of the settlor of the trust before us. Clearly he
contemplated no destruction of his trust by any discretionary act
of the trustee. But he did intend to give the trustee a power to
determine what was principal and income, although he refrained
from conferring that power as an absolute and uncontrolled discretion, and we regard this as significant, in the light shed upon
the inquiry by a consideration of all factors. The discretion conferred is not an empty one. It confers an important responsibility to make a determination which, if honestly exercised, calls for
no revision by the court. Am. Law Inst. Restatement: Trusts,
§§187, 233.

In the case of Tax Commissioner v. Putnam, 227 Mass. 522,
where it was held that gains received from sales of stock come
within the definitions of "income," as that word is used in the
Forty-fourth Amendment to the Constitution of the Commonwealth, which confers full power on the General Court to levy a
tax on income as therein provided, it was said that, in the case of
trust estates, profits and gains arising from the increase in value
of investments and realized by sale are treated as a part of the
principal and not as income. See Harrison v. Commissioner of
Corporations & Taxation, 272 Mass. 422, 425. The possibility of
conflicting interests between life tenants and remaindermen as to
what is principal and income is not of primary importance in
determining whether a certain gain to a trust estate is taxable as
income. It is important, however, to observe that in one connection a gain is classed as income and in another as principal and that
this court sees no inconsistency in such classifications. A settlor
of a trust must know that, unless he says something to the contrary in his trust instrument, the court's classification will be followed in the administration of his trust. We see no good reason

why he cannot be permitted to do that which the court itself can do by way of classification and also to delegate the power of classification to his trustee. If the delegation of power is comprehensive and sufficient, the court must respect it and make effectual the expressed intent of the settlor.

Upon consideration of the entire matter, we are of the opinion that the trustee under the clause in question has full power and discretion, after serious and responsible consideration, short of arbitrary or dishonest conduct or bad faith or fraud, when he has to determine whether any money or other property received by him is principal or income; and that upon this record there is nothing disclosed to prevent him from distributing to himself, in his personal capacity, the profit derived during the year 1938 as the result of selling certain shares of stock, a part of the trust property, at a price "over and above cost."

Decree is to be entered instructing the trustee accordingly, the details of which are to be fixed by a single justice. Costs as between solicitor and client are to be in the discretion of the single justice, to be paid out of the trust funds.

Ordered accordingly.[26]

PROBLEM

19.1. Will any undesirable tax consequences be produced if the executor under a will has any one or more of the following discretionary powers?

1. Discretion to determine whether items shall be included in the decedent's gross estate when the executor decides there is uncertainty as to their inclusion
2. Discretion as to whether the items in the decedent's gross

[26] For a comment on Dumaine v. Dumaine, See 25 Va. L. Rev. 242 (1938).

In 1956, Rhode Island enacted the following provision: "Every trustee under any trust instrument, whether heretofore or hereafter made, shall be entitled to reasonable expenses and costs incurred in the execution of the trust, and also reasonable compensation for services rendered as trustee, which expenses, costs and compensation may be charged annually or from time to time and may be equitably apportioned between principal and income in such manner as the trustee shall determine." R.I. Gen. Laws Ann. §18-6-1 (1956).

In Third National Bank & Trust Co. of Springfield v. Campbell, 336 Mass. 352, 145 N.E.2d 703 (1957), the trustee received cash dividends on real estate trust shares and these dividends were deemed exempt from federal income taxation because they were considered a return of capital. The distributions, however, did reduce the basis of the real estate shares, so that when they were later sold, a larger capital gains tax was payable. The court held that the cash dividends were distributable to the life income beneficiary, and that the entire capital gains tax resulting from the later sale of the shares was payable out of corpus. — Ed.

estate shall be valued on the date of his death or one year
after the date of his death

3. Discretion as to how estate expenditures which are allowable either as an income tax deduction or an estate tax
deduction shall be taken

4. ADMINISTRATIVE PROVISIONS IN REGARD TO
PAYMENT OF DEATH TAXES

The decedent may specify where the burden of various death
taxes will fall. Regardless of the plan which the decedent works
out, his executor is primarily responsible to see that such taxes are
paid to the extent that estate property comes to him.[27] If he has
paid more out of estate property in his hands than should be paid
out of such property, he may then take appropriate steps to place
the burden where, in the final analysis, it belongs.[28] Anyone
who receives property that is subject to death taxes may be held
liable to the extent of such property if the death taxes are not
paid by someone else.[29] If such a person pays more than he

[27] See 1954 I.R.C. §2002, quoted infra page 1388, which states explicitly that
the federal estate tax shall be paid by the executor. Section 20.2002-1 of the
Regulations, quoted infra page 1501, points out that this obligation of the
executor applies to the entire tax, regardless of the fact that the gross estate
consists in part of property which does not come within the possession of the
executor. Section 20.2203-1 of the Regulations, quoted infra page 1542, defines
the word "executor" as used in the Code.

Section 2204 of the 1954 Code, quoted infra page 1415, points out that the
executor may be discharged of his obligation with respect to the payment of
the federal estate tax by following the procedure outlined therein. Revenue
Ruling 57-424, 1957-2 C.B. 623, holds that where the assets of an inter vivos
trust created by a decedent are included in his gross estate for estate tax purposes, the trustees of the inter vivos trust are not entitled to discharge from
personal liability under the provisions of §2204. The provisions of this section are available only to an executor. Estate of Theodore Geddings Tarver
v. Commissioner, 255 F.2d 913 (4th Cir. 1958), held that §825(a) of the 1939
Code (which corresponds to §2204) operated only to discharge the executor
from personal liability and that, consequently, he continued liable in his
representative capacity despite the delay in notification of more than a year
as to any tax that might be due.

State inheritance taxes are normally payable out of the share given to a
beneficiary in the absence of a contrary manifestation of intent, but to the
extent that the beneficiary's share is to be paid to him by the executor, it
will be the executor's duty to withhold and pay to the state the tax on the
share.

[28] See, for example, 1954 I.R.C. §2206, quoted infra page 1415, which gives
to the executor the right to collect a portion of the tax bill from life insurance
beneficiaries, and §2207, quoted infra page 1415, which entitles him to collect
a portion of the tax bill from takers of appointive assets. These provisions
are inoperative, of course, if the decedent has freed these assets from sharing
in the burden of death taxes.

[29] In regard to the liability of persons who take gross estate items not includible in the probate estate, see 1954 I.R.C. §6324(a)(2), quoted infra page

should, he may have reimbursement from those who should have borne all or part of the burden.[30]

The thinking required with respect to the formulation of an estate plan is incomplete if the problem of paying death taxes has not been worked out and the burden placed where, in the best interest of all concerned, it should be placed. The placing of the burden where it belongs may be accomplished by the language of the estate plan or by a determination to allow the law to take its course in this regard.[31]

1432. See also §6901(a)(1), quoted infra page 1433, which concerns the liabilities of transferees and fiduciaries.

Sims v. Patterson, 183 F. Supp. 202 (N.D. Ala. 1959), considered the date from which interest is computed as against a transferee, and held that it is computed from the date when the statutory notice of deficiency is mailed, and not from the date when the property is acquired by the transferee. This case was decided under the 1939 Code but should be relevant in applying 1954 I.R.C. §6901. The case was affirmed in 281 F.2d 577 (5th Cir. 1960).

The liability of transferees for a tax is described in §6901. In this connection it should be noted that the period of limitations for assessment of transferee liability is, as against the initial transferee, within one year after the expiration of the period of limitations for assessment against the transferor. See §6901(c). In Melba Schuster, 32 T.C. 998 (1959), the widow, as a surviving joint tenant, received jointly owned property which was included in the decedent's gross estate and she was therefore subject to the transferee liability which was asserted within one year after the three-year statute (§6501(a)) had run against the executor. The transferee liability could be asserted even though the Commissioner had not asserted liability against the executor. (See also Estate of Louise A. Schneller, 18 CCH T.C. Mem. 654 (1959), where it was held that the Commissioner is not required to exhaust his remedies against the estate before proceeding with his claim against the transferee.) The reason the liability had not been asserted against the executor in the Schuster case was that Commissioner Andrews had determined that certain property in a revocable trust was not includible in the decedent's gross estate and then later, but after the three-year statute had run, Commissioner Harrington, who had succeeded Andrews, held that the property in such a trust was includible in the decedent's gross estate. The court held that the succeeding Commissioner was not bound by the determination of the prior Commissioner as to the law. In Patricia B. Englert, 32 T.C. 1008 (1959), the issue was whether the beneficiary to whom the assets of a trust (the one referred to above in the Schuster case) included in the decedent's gross estate were distributed could be subjected to transferee liability, and the court held the beneficiary could not be under the 1939 I.R.C. §827(b) (this court should reach the same result under §6324(a)(2), the corresponding provision under the 1954 Code). The final case in this cycle is First Western Bank and Trust Co., 32 T.C. 1017 (1959), which held that the trustee of the trust (the one referred to in the Schuster case) was subject to transferee liability, even though it had distributed the trust property after being informed by someone that the estate taxes were all paid.

[30] See 1954 I.R.C. §2205, quoted infra page 1415, which deals with reimbursement out of the estate when death taxes are paid by someone other than the executor.

[31] A decision to allow the law to take its course may have different effects in different jurisdictions. The controlling local law may have established a presumption that the death costs will all be payable out of the decedent's residuary estate unless he manifests a different intent. Many states have now

In determining where the burden of paying death taxes should be placed, the following considerations are relevant:

1. The availability of liquid funds[32]
2. The fact that certain property may have to be sold at a sacrifice if it is rapidly converted into liquid funds[33]
3. The fact that the marital deduction will be diminished in amount to the extent that marital deduction gifts are required to contribute to the payment of death taxes[34]
4. The fact that the deduction allowed for charitable gifts will be diminished in amount to the extent that charitable gifts are required to contribute to the payment of death taxes[35]
5. The value of the items in the gross estate which will not pass under the will[36]
6. The effect on the amounts received by various beneficiaries

---

enacted what are called apportionment acts, which apportion the tax among the various items which contribute to the tax. For an example of such an act see Mass. Ann. Laws, c. 65A, §5, quoted infra page 1444.

Suppose that the decedent's gross estate includes property located in a jurisdiction other than his domicile. Will the apportionment act in the domiciliary state enable the executor to collect a portion of the estate tax out of the assets in the other jurisdiction? In Isaacson v. Boston Safe Deposit & Trust Co., 325 Mass. 469, 91 N.E.2d 334 (1950), a Maine resident established a revocable inter vivos trust in Massachusetts, and the court held that the Maine Apportionment Act could not impose a liability for part of the federal estate tax on the trustee of the Massachusetts trust. Compare, however, the New York cases cited in the Massachusetts case. The Isaacson case is followed in Warfield v. Merchants National Bank of Boston, 337 Mass. 14, 147 N.E.2d 809 (1958), where an attempt was made to reach Massachusetts assets to pay the share of the tax allocated thereto under the New York Apportionment Act.

[32] If the available liquid funds are not adequate, it may be desirable to make provision for additional liquidity by acquiring more life insurance, through a systematic program of saving, or by entering into a buy-and-sell agreement. Buy-and-sell agreements are examined supra page 936.

[33] The closely held business is the typical asset which may have to be sacrificed if a quick sale is required. The plans which should be made in advance if such a business is to be sold on the death of the owner are explored supra page 976.

[34] See the discussion relating to marital deduction gifts at page 818 supra.

[35] See the discussion relating to charitable gifts at page 892 supra.

[36] If the entire death tax burden is placed on the residuary estate, and the gross estate items not included in the probate estate bulk large in comparison with the probate items, the residuary estate may be wiped out in the payment of the death taxes. If the testator's plan of disposition were based on the existence of a residuary estate for distribution to certain beneficiaries, his plan would be frustrated by the exhaustion of the estate in the payment of death taxes. In this regard it should be kept in mind that it may be difficult to predict in advance what items may be in the gross estate but not in the probate estate, and thus any probate fund that is charged with full responsibility for death costs may be in danger of substantial diminution or even elimination.

if the burden of paying death taxes is placed in one place rather than another[37]

The final decision as to the payment of the death taxes may be

1. To place the burden entirely on the residuary estate;[38] or
2. To place the burden on the residuary estate only as to property passing under the will;[39] or
3. To place the burden entirely on the property in a revocable inter vivos trust;[40] or
4. To give the trustee of a revocable inter vivos trust discretion to pay death taxes;[41] or
5. To apportion the death taxes on some basis.[42]

The decision as to where the burden of death costs shall finally come to rest should be expressed in clear and unambiguous lan-

---

[37] See note 36 supra.

[38] See note 36 supra. Suppose that the entire tax load is placed on the residuary estate and that it is insufficient in amount to pay the tax bill. What will be the result? In re Nesbitt's Estate, 158 Cal. App. 2d 630, 323 P.2d 474 (1958), faced this question where the will made a general bequest to charity and bequeathed personal property to an individual, and determined that the general bequest to charity took priority over the provision for payment of the inheritance tax due on the bequest to the individual. Thus the latter was required to bear the burden of the tax just as though the provision for the payment of the taxes out of the residue had never existed.

[39] This result will normally be reached as to federal estate taxes if nothing is said and the controlling local jurisdiction has an apportionment act.

[40] If the revocable inter vivos trust includes life insurance proceeds not subject to state inheritance taxes, it will be more costly to impose a mandate on the trustee to pay all death taxes, because such a mandate will increase the size of the residuary estate subject to such taxes over what it would be if the beneficiaries were entitled only to the residue left after the payment of the death taxes out of it. Such a mandate would also be highly undesirable if it required the payment of federal estate taxes out of the proceeds of an employee death benefit payable to the trustee when such proceeds would be subject to the federal estate tax under 1954 I.R.C. §2039, quoted infra page 1398, only if made payable to the employee's executor, because such a mandate might be deemed the equivalent of payment to the employee's executor.

[41] If a trustee has discretion as to the payment of death taxes he is the donee of a power of appointment. If the trustee can benefit himself by the way in which he exercises the discretion, he will have a general power of appointment and will be deemed the owner of the appointive assets for gift and estate tax purposes. The gift and estate tax consequences of general powers of appointment are considered supra page 712. Furthermore, a mere discretion in the trustee to pay death taxes should not prevent a diminution in marital deduction gifts and charitable gifts which are not freed of contributing to the payment of death taxes, even though the trustee exercises his discretion and in fact frees such gifts of their burden.

[42] If apportionment of death taxes is desired, the controlling local jurisdiction may, as to federal estate taxes, accomplish the job appropriately under its apportionment act. This act may free marital deduction gifts and charitable gifts which are not subject to the federal estate tax from any burden to contribute to the payment of such tax, but they may have to bear the state inheritance tax imposed on them and thus their amounts may be diminished for marital deduction and charitable deduction purposes unless some appropriate provision frees them of this burden.

guage in the appropriate dispositive instrument. Printed below are two cases where this goal was not attained.

MALDEN TRUST CO. v. BICKFORD
329 Mass. 567, 109 N.E.2d 453 (1952)

SPALDING, Justice.

Alice B. Simpson, a resident of Malden, died testate on September 14, 1949, leaving an estate appraised at just under $242,-000. At her death she held shares in a cooperative bank as trustee for one Mabel Fiske. She also was a joint owner of five savings accounts. The aggregate value of these shares and accounts was approximately $34,000. The beneficiary of the cooperative bank shares and each of the five joint owners of the savings accounts survived the testatrix, and, for convenience, will hereinafter be referred to as the respondents. Their interests in these accounts and shares were established by a prior decree which is not here challenged. The present controversy, which is between the respondents on the one hand, and Stanley Robbins, the residuary legatee and the appellant here, on the other, centers about the liability for Massachusetts and Federal inheritance and estate taxes imposed by the inclusion of the joint accounts and bank shares in the gross estate of the testatrix. G.L. (Ter. Ed.) c. 65, sec. 1; c. 65A, sec. 1; U.S.C. (1946 ed.) Title 26, sec. 811(c, e). The appellant's contention is that each of the respondents must pay the share of the inheritance and estate taxes attributable to the amount she is to receive, while the respondents' position is that these taxes must be paid out of the residue. To resolve the controversy, the executors brought this petition for instructions. The facts not being in dispute, the case was presented below on statements of counsel which constitute the basis for a voluntary report of material facts by the judge. A decree was entered ordering the taxes to be paid out of the residue, and the residuary legatee appealed.

The thirty-fourth article of the will of the testatrix contains the following provision: "I direct that all taxes of every kind upon the whole or any part of my estate, including inheritance, estate and transfer taxes, both state and federal, shall be paid from the residue of my estate, it being my desire that the legatees and devisee herein shall receive the full amount of their legacies and devise without the deduction of any tax." The respondents and the appellant were friends of the testatrix. All of the respondents were given legacies under the will and one was given also a devise. These gifts were in addition to their interests in the joint accounts and the cooperative bank shares. The appellant received a legacy of $5,000 apart from his gift of the residue. There were, in all, thirty-three legacies and devises.

The joint accounts and the cooperative bank shares, of course, were properly included in the gross estate of the testatrix for the purpose of computing the Federal and Massachusetts taxes, and no contention to the contrary is made. It is also clear that the testatrix had the right to shift the burden of those taxes as she saw fit. Beals v. Magenis, 307 Mass. 547, 550, 31 N.E.2d 20; Buffington v. Mason, 327 Mass. 195, 199, 97 N.E.2d 538. But unless the will provides otherwise the taxes, or at least those here involved, are to be apportioned in accordance with the statutes of this Commonwealth. Isaacson v. Boston Safe Deposit & Trust Co., 325 Mass. 469, 473, 91 N.E.2d 334, 16 A.L.R.2d 1277; Riggs v. Del Drago, 317 U.S. 95, 63 S. Ct. 109, 87 L. Ed. 106. It is plain that if the case is to be governed by these statutes, the pertinent provisions of which are set forth in the margin, [footnote omitted] the decree below cannot stand, for the burden of both the Massachusetts and Federal taxes would rest on the respondents.

The question, then, for decision is whether the will of the testatrix has shifted the burden of taxation on the joint accounts and the cooperative bank shares elsewhere. Stated differently, the question is whether the words "my estate" in the thirty-fourth article mean the probate estate of the testatrix or her taxable estate. We are of opinion that they mean the former. Since the case was submitted on agreed facts and documentary evidence we are in as good a position to decide the question as was the trial judge.

The direction in the thirty-fourth article to pay from the residue "all taxes of every kind upon the whole or any part of my estate, including inheritance, estate and transfer taxes, both state and federal" is very broad and if it stood alone a plausible argument could be made that the testatrix was referring to her taxable estate and not merely to her probate estate. See Martin v. New England Deaconess Hospital, 328 Mass. 259, 103 N.E.2d 240. But this language is qualified by the phrase "it being my desire that the legatees and devisee herein shall receive the full amount of their legacies and devise without the deduction of any tax." In the opinion of a majority of the court this limits the effect of the broad language which preceded it, and evinces an intent to exonerate from taxes only the gifts passing by will. See Whitlow v. Thomas, Ohio App., 86 N.E.2d 622; Commercial Trust Co. v. Thurber, 136 N.J. Eq. 471, 42 A.2d 571. There are instances, it is true, where general language employed in a will has been held not to be cut down by more specific language. The tenor of the instrument as a whole may be such as to indicate that the general language represents the true intent. See Taylor v. Albree, 309 Mass. 248, 34 N.E.2d 601; Old Colony Trust Co. v. Attorney General, 316 Mass. 530, 55 N.E.2d 948. But that, we think, is not the case here. Reading the will as a whole we are unable to discover anything which leads to the conclusion that the words "my estate" meant anything other than the probate estate.

The present case is distinguishable from Martin v. New England Deaconess Hospital, supra, on which the respondents rely. There the testator indicated that he was aware of the difference between property passing under the will and property which did not so pass but which, nevertheless, might be treated as part of his estate for tax purposes by saying, "I direct that any legacy and succession taxes, either state or federal, upon any devise or legacy in this will, *or upon the estate itself,* be paid . . . out of the residue of my estate" (emphasis supplied). Nor are the respondents aided by the decision in Buffington v. Mason, 327 Mass. 195, 97 N.E.2d 538, 541, on which reliance is also placed. In that case the will provided that "All inheritance taxes are to be paid from the residuum of my estate so that all legacies will be paid in full." One of the residuary legatees predeceased the testatrix, and her share passed by intestacy. It was contended that this share should bear the burden of all State and Federal taxes, so that the shares of the remaining residuary legatees would be paid in full. This contention was rejected not because the words "All inheritance taxes" were to be given the meaning which the respondents urge here, but rather because the entire scheme of the will manifested an intent to place the tax burden on the entire residue as distinguished from that portion of it which passed by intestacy. That case, we think, is distinguishable.

The respondents further argue that support for their contention may be found in circumstances attending the probate of the estate of Bradford P. Simpson, the husband of the testatrix. It appears that he died in 1941, leaving an estate of $236,000. His will contained a provision for the payment of taxes from the residue substantially similar to the clause here involved. He named his widow as executrix and residuary legatee, and, save for two small legacies, gave his entire estate to her. At the time of his death the testator and his wife were the joint owners of twenty-one savings accounts, and it appears that the inheritance and estate taxes imposed by reason of the inclusion of these joint accounts in his gross estate were paid out of the residue. The respondents urge that in making her will in 1948 with knowledge of these facts the testatrix must have intended a similar result. We cannot agree. Her payment of these taxes out of the residue was a matter of little or no significance. She was both the residuary legatee and the surviving owner of the joint accounts. Whether she paid the taxes out of one fund or the other could not have been contested by anyone, and to her it was a matter of no consequence.

It follows that the decree is to be reversed and a new decree is to be entered ordering each of the respondents to pay in accordance with G.L. (Ter. Ed.) c. 65A, secs. 5 and 5A, as appearing in St. 1948, c. 605, secs. 1 and 2, his or her proportionate share of the Federal estate tax imposed on the estate of the testatrix the proportionate share of the Massachusetts estate tax, if any, imposed by c. 65A, and the Massachusetts succession tax imposed on his or her interest in the joint account or cooperative bank shares as the case may be. Costs and expenses of appeal are to be in the discretion of the Probate Court.

So ordered.[43]

UNION AND NEW HAVEN TRUST CO. v. SULLIVAN

142 Conn. 685, 116 A.2d 908 (1955)

BALDWIN, Associate Justice.

This case has been reserved for advice to determine from which of two estates a federal estate tax shall be paid. The tax has been assessed with respect to property disposed of under a power of appointment.

The stipulated facts, taken from the pleadings and exhibits, follow: John Moran died a resident of New Haven on June 17, 1951. He left his wife, Agnes Moran, surviving, but no close blood relatives. He was seventy-eight years old. His wife was eighty-eight. They had been married fifty-four years. His will was dated December 28, 1950. After bequeathing his automobile, jewelry and apparel to his wife, and modest sums to four

---

[43] See also Carpenter v. Carpenter, 364 Mo. 782, 267 S.W.2d 632 (1954), and compare Morristown Trust Co. v. McCann, 19 N.J. 568, 118 A.2d 16 (1955). In Kershaw v. Kershaw, 84 R.I. 429, 125 A.2d 126 (1956), the testator provided that all death taxes "due from my estate" shall be paid out of the rest and residue of the estate. The court held that such language imposed on the residuary estate the burden of all taxes on all items in the decedent's gross estate. In Williams v. Stander, — Colo. —, 354 P.2d 492 (1960), the decedent's will directed that inheritance and other taxes payable "in respect of my said estate, or to any devise, legacy or distribution under this will or otherwise" be paid out of the estate, and the court held that this provision clearly indicated that taxes on property passing outside of the will should be paid by the estate. — ED.

persons who had worked for him or for two corporations in which he was interested, he provided, in article five, for the division of his residuary estate, amounting approximately to $2,000,000, into two trust funds. One, designated trust A, was to provide for his wife. The other, trust B, was a charitable trust in favor of certain religious and charitable organizations. [Footnote omitted.] Trust A was set up to provide a comfortable living for Mrs. Moran; all the income from it was payable to her. To make certain that she should not want, John Moran gave his trustees the power to apply the principal of trust A and so much of the income of trust B as they might deem necessary, without securing the consent of the beneficiaries of trust B, to her maintenance during her lifetime. He also gave her a general power of appointment over the principal of trust A. If she failed to exercise this power, the two trust funds were to be combined into one after her death, and the income was to be paid to the beneficiaries of trust B. None of the income from trust B was to be paid to the beneficiaries thereof until Mrs. Moran died. Thereafter, they were to receive the income until certain stock in The Guilford-Chester Water Company and The Clinton Electric Light and Power Company, two local utilities which John Moran controlled, was sold, or until twenty years after Mrs. Moran's death, whichever occurred first. The principal was then to be apportioned among them pursuant to percentages stated in the will.

John Moran's estate was valued for tax purposes at nearly $2,000,000. A federal estate tax of $71,316 has been assessed and paid. It is estimated that the state succession tax will be about $93,000. After all deductions, including federal and state taxes assessed against his estate and payable out of trust B, approximately $971,000 will be allocable to trust A and $798,000 to trust B.

In article eight, at the end of his will, John Moran provided for the payment of inheritance, transfer and estate taxes out of the funds allocable to trust B.[44] The interpretation of this article presents the issue in the case.

Agnes Moran died on March 30, 1952, before her husband's es-

---

[44] *(Court footnote)* "Article Eight. I hereby direct that all legacy, succession, inheritance, transfer and estate taxes, levied or assessed upon or with respect to any property which is included as a part of my gross estate for the purpose of any such tax, including, but limited to, the proceeds of any policy of insurance on my life, or any jointly owned property, shall be paid by my Executors solely out of the property comprising that portion of my estate described herein as Trust B, and shall not be pro-rated or apportioned among or charged against the respective devisees, legatees, beneficiaries, transferees or other recipients, nor charged against any other property passing or which may have passed to any of them and that my Executors shall not be required to seek reimbursement for any portion of any such tax from any such person."

tate was settled. Neither trust A nor trust B had been set up. She had made a will on July 13, 1951, twenty-six days after her husband's death, in which, in article six, she exercised the power of appointment given to her in her husband's will in favor of a brother and eight nieces and nephews. The power having been exercised in this manner, the estate of Mrs. Moran became subject to a federal estate tax estimated to be approximately $271,000. The allocation of the ultimate burden of so much of this tax as is attributable to the exercise of the power of appointment affords the basis for the present controversy. The questions presented in the reservation appear in full in the footnote.[45]

The answers to these questions require that we find and effectuate John Moran's intent with respect to the payment of this tax. We look to the will as an entirety and examine the particular words and language used in the light of the circumstances under which they were written. Chase National Bank v. Guthrie, 139 Conn. 178, 182, 90 A.2d 643. Do they express an intention that the funds in trust B shall be used to pay the federal estate tax assessed against the estate of Agnes Moran because she exercised the power of appointment? The will appears to have been prepared by an expert draftsman. At this point, it is well to state that John Moran disposed of his estate in the manner allowed by law to obviate the payment of large estate and inheritance taxes. The corpus of trust B is exempt as a bequest for charitable purposes. Int. Rev. Code of 1939, §812(d), as amended, 64 Stat. 959 (1950), 26 U.S.C.A. §812(d). By giving his widow a power of appointment over the corpus of trust A, from which she was to receive support during her lifetime, he qualified this corpus for the federal estate tax marital deduction provisions. Int. Rev. Code of 1939, §812 (e) (1)(A,F), added by 62 Stat. 118 (1948, 26 U.S.C.A. §812(e)(1)(A,F). In default of the exercise of the power, the corpus of trust A would pass to charitable purposes and would likewise be exempt from the federal estate tax.

Succession taxes are payable by the recipients of the property with respect to which the tax is assessed. Hackett v. Bankers Trust Co., 122 Conn. 107, 126, 187 A. 653; General Statutes, §§2052, 2060. Prior to 1945, estate taxes were payable out of

[45] *(Court footnote)* "(a) Should the portion of the Federal estate tax on the estate of Agnes Moran assessed with respect to the property disposed of by virtue of her exercise of her power of appointment under Article Five of the will of John Moran be paid out of assets comprising Trust B of the estate of John Moran or passing to the beneficiaries under Trust B?

"(b) Should the portion of the Federal estate tax on the estate of Agnes Moran assessed with respect to the property disposed of by virtue of her exercise of her power of appointment under Article Five of the will of John Moran be paid out of assets comprising Trust A of the estate of John Moran or passing to the beneficiaries under Trust A?"

the general estate. McLaughlin v. Green, 136 Conn. 138, 140, 69 A.2d 289; Ericson v. Childs, 124 Conn. 66, 81, 198 A. 176, 115 A.L.R. 907. Chapter 102 of the General Statutes, enacted in 1945, provides that estate taxes are payable pro-rata by the recipients of the taxable property in essentially the same manner as are succession taxes. The operation of these rules can be altered or avoided by testamentary direction. Starr v. Watrous, 116 Conn. 488, 451, 165 A. 459; Sherman v. Moore, 89 Conn. 190, 194, 93 A. 241. The testamentary direction, however, must be expressed in specific and unambiguous language because, in most cases, it can have a very material effect upon those who share in that part of the estate from which it is directed that the taxes are to be paid. McLaughlin v. Green, supra, 136 Conn. 142, 69 A.2d 291.

In article eight, John Moran directed that "all" taxes "levied or assessed upon or with respect to any property which is included as a part of [his] gross estate for the purpose of any such tax" should be paid solely out of the portion of his estate comprising trust B and that they should not "be prorated or apportioned among or charged against the respective devises, legatees, beneficiaries, transferees or other recipients, nor charged against any other property passing or which may have passed to any of them." It is true that the recipients of the corpus of trust A under the power of appointment exercised by Agnes Moran derive their title from John's, and not from Agnes', estate. McMurtry v. State, 111 Conn. 594, 601, 151 A. 252. This, however, is not determinative of our question. The value of the corpus of trust A is included in Agnes Moran's gross taxable estate, not because her estate had title to it but because she exercised a power of appointment over it. Int. Rev. Code of 1939, §811(f), as amended, 65 Stat. 91 (1951) 26 U.S.C.A. §811(f). Article eight by its very terms is concerned with taxes assessed with respect to property included in the gross estate of John Moran "for the purpose of any such tax," i.e. for the purpose of legacy, succession, inheritance, transfer and estate taxes on his estate. It anticipates the circumstances he believed would exist at the time of his death. It directs that the taxes so referred to shall be paid by his executors solely out of the property comprising the portion of his estate known as trust B and shall not be "charged against any other property passing or which may have passed to [his beneficiaries]." The will thus deliberately deals only with transfers already made or those to be made by its direction. It concerns only the taxes normally payable in the course of the settlement of John Moran's estate, and not the taxes to be assessed in the future with respect to some other person's gross taxable estate.

Although Agnes Moran was an aged woman, John could not foresee how long she might outlive him. He took every precaution to care for her. However, he could not know when or whether the power of appointment would be exercised. His widow might exercise it in favor of someone unknown to him. The amount of any tax on the exercise of the power of appointment or, indeed, whether there would be any tax was also problematical. A testator who caused a will to be drafted with such meticulous attention to the incidence of taxes could not conceivably have intended by article eight to leave so much to chance.

The language and the intent of article eight are not usual. This article is taken almost verbatim from the form recommended by the committee on bank and bar relations of the Connecticut Bar Association and the Connecticut Bankers Association in a pamphlet dated August 1, 1946. See 3 Locke & Kohn, Conn. Probate Practice, p. 160; McLaughlin v. Green, 136 Conn. 138, 145, 69 A.2d 289. This tax clause was obviously designed to nullify the effect of the statute on proration of federal and state estate taxes, now chapter 102 of the General Statutes, enacted the previous year. Sup. 1945, §§314h-319h, 322h. Since the proration statute by its terms covered only taxes on the decedent's own estate, it may fairly be inferred that the testator, by using the clause drafted by the joint committee, referred only to taxes on his own estate.

This is a case of first impression in Connecticut. The courts of Illinois, New York and Pennsylvania, however, have held, for reasons which appear persuasive to us, that clauses similar to the one in the case at bar do not apply to taxes assessed against the estate of a person to whom a testator had given a power of appointment. Page v. Wright, 342 Ill. App. 352, 356, 96 N.E.2d 634; Matter of Duryea's Estate, 277 N.Y. 310, 317, 14 N.E.2d 369, 124 A.L.R. 647; Matter of Vanderbilt's Estate, 180 Misc. 431, 436, 39 N.Y.S.2d 941, affirmed 295 N.Y. 964, 68 N.E.2d 50; In re Marvin's Estate, 26 Pa. Dist. & Co. 527, 533.

Accordingly, we answer question (a) "No." In the view we take of the case, question (b) cannot be answered categorically, at least without construing the tax clause in the will of Agnes Moran and considering the nature and devolution of her other taxable estate. Since the interpretation of her will has not been argued before us, we decline to answer the question.

No costs will be taxed in this court in favor of any party.

In this opinion the other judges concurred.[46]

---

[46] In Goodson v. United States, 151 F. Supp. 416 (D. Minn. 1957), the decedent's will stated: "it is my desire that any or all estate taxes . . . which

PROBLEM

19.2. If a will specifically negates the exercise of any power of appointment and provides that all death taxes, federal and state, shall be paid out of the residuary estate, what undesirable consequences may be produced?

5. ADMINISTRATIVE PROVISIONS IN REGARD TO FILING A JOINT INCOME TAX RETURN

When a husband or wife dies, the final income tax return for the decedent will include the decedent's income up to the date of his death. The decedent's estate will be the taxable entity with respect to income after the decedent's death. A joint income tax return for a husband and wife is permitted for the year in which the first one dies or for the year in which both of them die if they both die in the same year.[47] This joint return will include the

---

may be due at the time of my death or which may accrue by reason of my death on account of any [inter vivos] transfers, whether heretofore or hereafter made, shall be paid out of the property so transferred and shall not be paid out of the property passing under my will." It was determined that the word "desire" was sufficient to shift the burden of the tax payments on inter vivos transfers from the residuary estate under the will to the inter vivos transferees. The government had contended that the testator had no power to impose a share of the estate tax on the inter vivos transfers. The government made this contention because the residue went to charity, and if the entire tax load fell on the residue, the charitable deduction would be reduced and the total tax payable would be increased. The court concluded that under Minnesota law the testator could burden his donees with a share of the tax. The case was affirmed sub nom. United States v. Goodson, 253 F.2d 900 (8th Cir. 1958).

Estate of Theodore Geddings Tarver v. Commissioner, 255 F.2d 913 (4th Cir. 1958), held that the responsibility for the payment of the federal estate tax rests upon the executor in his representative capacity and that the government looks to him for the performance of this duty. Consequently, the executor cannot require the government to allocate a deficiency among the various items included in the gross estate of a decedent, and whether in the final analysis the tax burden should fall on one asset or another is a matter to be settled in appropriate proceedings in the state court between the interested parties in accordance with the applicable state law.

In Whitbeck v. Aldrich, — Mass. — , 169 N.E.2d 882 (1960), the testatrix's general estate was so depleted by paying death taxes that the remaining funds were insufficient to pay two pecuniary legacies in full and no funds were left to go into a trust created for the benefit of her sister, but the plain language of her will that all taxes on property payable by reason of her death, whether or not such property passed under will, was controlling. — Ed.

[47] See 1954 I.R.C. §6013(a)(3), quoted infra page 1428.

Revenue Ruling 57-368, 1957-2 C.B. 896, holds that a husband and wife who are separated under an interlocutory decree of divorce retain the relationship of husband and wife and are entitled to a joint return of income until the

income of the deceased spouse up to the date of his death and the income of the surviving spouse for the entire year or up to the date of her death if she dies within the year. The executor of the deceased spouse must decide whether to consent to the filing of a joint return with the surviving spouse.[48] A factor in making this decision will be the fact that the estate of the deceased spouse becomes liable for the entire tax payable under the joint return.[49]

If the estate of the deceased spouse pays the entire tax bill when a joint return is filed, will the total payment be deductible for estate tax purposes under Section 2053?[50] A deduction is allowed for only that portion of the tax bill that is properly attributed to the decedent's income.[51] If the decedent's estate and his surviving spouse are entitled to a refund on account of an overpayment of a joint income tax liability, the overpayment is an asset includible in the decedent's gross estate in the amount to which the estate

---

decree becomes final. Revenue Ruling 59-266, 1959-2 C.B. 377, considers the Wisconsin statute which provides that neither party to a divorce can marry until one year after the judgment of divorce but that the death of either party within one year will cause the marriage relation to be deemed severed immediately before such death. The ruling holds that under this statute the divorce decree is interlocutory until the year is up and so the husband and wife can file a joint return for a taxable year ending within such one-year period, but if one dies, the surviving spouse is precluded from filing a joint return with the deceased spouse for the year in which the death occurs.

[48] In Matter of the Estate of Frank J. Floyd, 51-2 U.S.T.C. ¶9415 (Pa. Orphans' Ct. 1951), a co-executrix was directed to join in the execution of a joint return on behalf of the decedent when the estate would benefit financially as a result of the income-splitting made possible by the joint return.

[49] Section 6013(d)(3) of the 1954 Code brings out that the liability under a joint return is joint and several.

The wife is primarily liable for the tax due on a joint return. The statute of limitations in the case of suits against one primarily liable for a tax is shorter than in the case of suits against a transferee of the one primarily liable. If the wife joins in a return and the husband dies and she succeeds to his property, can she be sued as a transferee of the husband's property, after the statute of limitations has run in her favor as one primarily liable? Floersch v. United States, 171 F. Supp. 260 (D.N.M. 1959), answers this question in the negative. The case was reversed and remanded sub nom. United States v. Floersch, 276 F.2d 714 (10th Cir. 1960), cert. denied, 81 Sup. Ct. 46 (1960).

E.T. 21, 1948-2 C.B. 156, establishes that no taxable gift occurs where one spouse pays all the income taxes due on a joint return. Section 25.2511-1(d) of the Regulations is in accord.

[50] Quoted infra page 1403.

[51] Section 20.2053-6(f) of the Regulations, quoted infra page 1527, describes how the portion of the tax bill properly attributable to the decedent's income is ascertained. See also Rev. Rul. 54-382, 1954-2 C.B. 279, which is modified by Rev. Rul. 56-290, 1956-1 C.B. 445. Revenue Ruling 56-290 is clarified in Rev. Rul. 57-78, 1957-1 C.B. 300, where it is pointed out that in making the computation, there is taken into account a tax computed on the income of the decedent for the balance of the year immediately prior to the date of his death (a fractional share) and a tax computed on the income of the surviving spouse for the entire year.

would be entitled under local law, as between the estate and the surviving spouse.[52]

Can gifts made by one spouse be treated as coming one half from each spouse by virtue of a consent given by the executor of a deceased spouse?[53] The Regulations answer this question in the affirmative as to gifts made by the surviving spouse prior to the date of the death of the deceased spouse.[54] Thus the executor may have to determine whether the requisite consent should be given with respect to gift tax matters as well as income tax matters.[55]

If reference is made in the deceased spouse's will to a joint income tax return or to the matter of consenting to have gifts made by the surviving spouse treated as though made in part by the deceased spouse, usually the executor should be given broad discretion as to the course of action to follow. In Illinois the executor will find guidance on these matters in statutory form.[56]

[52] See Reg. §20.2053-6(f), quoted infra page 1527.

Revenue Ruling 56-92, 1956-1 C.B. 564, holds that the amount of an overpayment of the tax on a joint return filed by a husband and wife may be credited against the tax liability of either spouse for a prior year. In Estate of Laura Brown Chisholm, 26 T.C. 253 (1956), it was held that when the decedent's widow and his executor filed a joint return, and the overpayment showing on the return was credited to the wife's tax liability for the next year, the amount of the overpayment was nevertheless includible in the decedent's gross estate because of the fact that it came from him.

In a Special Ruling dated August 9, 1957, CCH Fed. Est. & Gift Tax Rep. ¶8122, it was held that no part of a refund on an estimated tax on a joint return, a tax which was paid by the husband, passed from the husband to his surviving spouse solely because a joint return had been filed, and that, consequently, no marital deduction was allowable by reason of the refund.

In Matter of Eldridge Paul Illingworth, 56-2 U.S.T.C. ¶10004 (D.C. Ore. 1956), a wife claimed a share of a refund on a joint return which had been filed with her bankrupt husband. All of the income reported in the return belonged to the husband. The court held that under the circumstances the trustee in bankruptcy of the husband was entitled to the entire amount of the refund.

[53] See 1954 I.R.C. §2513, quoted infra page 1419, which deals with the gift-splitting allowed when a gift is made by a husband or wife to a third party.

[54] See Reg. §25.2513-1(b)(1), quoted infra page 1549.

[55] Section 2513(b) of the 1954 Code, quoted infra page 1420, is concerned with the manner in which, and the time at which, the consent must be signified. Section 2513(d), quoted infra page 1420, brings out that the liability for the gift taxes assessed when consent is given is joint and several.

[56] Chapter 3, §495a of Illinois Rev. Stat. (1959) provides as follows: "Except as otherwise authorized by the decedent in his will, an executor, administrator, guardian, or conservator, on his verified petition, by leave of the probate court, may join with the spouse of the decedent or ward or with the executor, administrator, guardian, or conservator of the spouse of the decedent or ward, in the making of a joint federal or state income or other tax return for the decedent or ward and his spouse and to consent for federal or state gift tax purposes to gifts made by the spouse of the decedent or ward as having been made one-half by the decedent or ward and one-half by his spouse. The court may order such notice of the time and place of the hearing on the petition to be given to any interested person as it deems expedient or the

PROBLEM

19.3. Under what circumstances, if any, is it appropriate to insert in the husband's will the following provision:

"I authorize and empower my executor to join with my wife, Mary, or her executor or administrator, in filing a joint federal or state income tax return of her income and my income for any period or periods for which such a return may be permitted. I further authorize and empower my executor to agree with my said wife, or her executor or administrator, (1) as to how the burden of the liability for the federal or state income tax, or interest thereon, arising out of the filing of a joint return by my executor and my said wife, or her executor or administrator, shall be borne as between my estate and my said wife or her estate, and (2) as to who, as between my said wife, or her estate and my estate shall be entitled (a) to any refund or credit of any federal or state income tax, or interest thereon, based on the filing of a joint return by my said wife and myself or by my executor and my said wife, or her executor or administrator, (b) to any refund or credit of any amount paid on account of any joint declaration of estimated federal or state income tax filed by my said wife and myself and of the interest on any such refund, and (c) to the benefit of any payment made by my said wife or myself on account of any joint or separate declaration of estimated federal or state income tax."

6.   ADMINISTRATIVE PROVISIONS IN REGARD TO ALLOWANCE OF TRUSTEE'S ACCOUNTS

If a trustee submits his accounts to a court for approval, all interested parties must be properly notified, and minors and unborn persons must be represented by guardians ad litem in order for the court decision as to the accounts to be legally binding on all concerned.[57] Such court approval of a trustee's accounts is expen-

---

court may hear the petition without notice. The court in its discretion may require the spouse of the decedent or ward or the executor, administrator, guardian or conservator of the spouse of the decedent or ward to give indemnity to the executor, administrator, guardian, or conservator of the decedent or ward in such amount, with such surety, and upon such conditions as the court deems proper. Unless there is fraud, accident, or mistake any liability incurred by the executor, administrator, guardian, or conservator by reason of such joinder or consent executed pursuant to the order of the court shall be incurred on behalf of the estate of the decedent or ward and not individually."

[57] For example, see Mass. Ann. Laws, c. 206, §24, quoted in part infra page 1462.

sive. Fees of attorneys and guardians ad litem, court costs, etc.,
may add up to a substantial amount. Is it possible to provide in
the trust instrument a method of approving the trustee's accounts
which will avoid such costs?

It is not uncommon to provide in an inter vivos trust (a non-
court trust) that the approval of the trustee's accounts by the income beneficiary shall be a complete discharge of the trustee as to
the matters covered by each account and shall bind all other persons, born or unborn, who may have any interest under the trust.
In a testamentary trust (a court trust), however, such a provision
as to the approval of the trustee's accounts is unusual, possibly because of the belief that no variations from the statutory provisions
as to the approval of a trustee's accounts is permissible with respect
to a trust under court supervision.[58]

PROBLEMS

19.4. A transfers property to T to hold in trust. The trust instrument provides that the net income is to be paid to A during
his life; on his death the net income is to be paid to his son for
his life; and on the son's death the corpus is to be distributed to
the son's issue then living, per stirpes. The trust is revocable by
A alone during his life. The trust instrument contains the following provisions:

"During the settlor's lifetime, the trustee shall render to the

---

[58] See generally Westfall, Nonjudicial Settlement of Trustees' Accounts, 71
Harv. L. Rev. 40 (1957).

In In re Claflin, 336 Mass. 578, 146 N.E.2d 914 (1958), the court considered
Mass. Ann. Laws, c. 206, §24, quoted infra page 1462, as it applies to the
allowance of the executors' accounts, and held that, in the absence of a conflict of interest between a testamentary trustee and the beneficiaries of the
testamentary trust, notice to the testamentary trustee of a petition for allowance of the executors' accounts is sufficient without giving additional notice
to the trust beneficiaries.

Second Bank-State Street Trust Co. v. Linsley, — Mass. — , 167 N.E.2d 624
(1960), considers the extent to which the beneficiary of a trust (a guardian ad
litem was actually involved) can require the records of the executors to be
produced at the time the trustee's accounts are offered for allowance on the
ground that it is necessary to examine the executors' accounts to determine
whether the trustee obtained everything he was entitled to from the executors. The court pointed out that the allowance of the executors' accounts
is not a complete bar to the investigation of the executors' records by the
trust beneficiary when the trustee alone was a party to the proceedings allowing the accounts. Once it appears, however, that the trustee did make a
reasonable investigation of the executors' records, a heavy burden will descend
on the guardian ad litem to justify further expenditure of time. Where the
will contains an exculpatory clause making the executors and trustee liable
only for willful conduct, then the guardian ad litem cannot require production of executors' records if he intends to show only negligence.

settlor annually an account of income and principal. The settlor's approval of said account shall, as to all matters and transactions covered by said account, be binding upon all who are then or may thereafter become entitled to the income or principal.

"After the death of the settlor, the trustee shall render to the settlor's said son annually an account of income and principal. The said son's approval of said account shall, as to all matters and transactions covered by such account, be binding upon all who are then or may thereafter become entitled to income or principal." [59]

A dies. A's son requests the trustee to pay him $10,000 out of the principal of the trust. The trustee points out to A's son that the terms of the trust do not permit payments of principal to him. A's son refers to the provision above quoted and tells the trustee that he will approve the trustee's account even though it shows a payment of principal to him. The trustee pays A's son the $10,000 out of principal and the son approves the trustee's account for the year in which the payment is made.

    a. A's son dies, survived by one minor child. The guardian of the minor sues the trustee to recover the $10,000 paid to A's son. Is the trustee liable?

    b. A's son dies, survived by one minor child. The guardian of the minor sues the estate of A's son to recover the $10,000 paid to A's son. Is the estate of A's son liable?

    c. Is the value of the trust property includible in the gross estate of A's son for federal estate tax purposes on the ground that A's son, in conjunction with another, had a general power of appointment?[60]

19.5. Draft a provision covering the approval of a trustee's accounts which will obviate the necessity of his obtaining court

---

[59] In Hillman v. Second Bank-State Street Trust Co., 338 Mass. 15, 21; 153 N.E.2d 651, 654 (1958), the court comments as follows in regard to a provision similar to the one to which this note is appended: ". . . The provision of article 6 that the approval of a trustee's accounts by some designated beneficiary shall be binding is not unusual in trust instruments, although it is perhaps unusual to place such a power of binding assent in the hands of a third person, not a beneficiary. . . . Nevertheless, even if we assume (without deciding) that under such a provision the power to assent, or to withhold consent, to trust accounts must be exercised, by the beneficiary or other person holding it, not arbitrarily but with good faith . . . and in a quasi fiduciary manner reasonably consistent with the trust purposes, the possession of the power does not make the person who possesses it a trustee, a party to the trust instrument, or even an adviser whose advice must be sought in advance, with respect to all matters affecting the trust."

[60] See Reg. §20.2041-1(b)(1), quoted infra page 1516, which provides that the right in a beneficiary to assent to a periodic accounting and thereby relieve the trustee from further accountability is not a power of appointment if the right of assent does not consist of any power or right to enlarge or shift the beneficial interest of any beneficiary therein.

approval but which, at the same time, will clearly avoid any reasonable basis of a claim that anyone has a general power of appointment in conjunction with the trustee.

7. ADMINISTRATIVE PROVISIONS IN REGARD TO PAYMENT OF DEBTS AND EXPENSES OF ADMINISTRATION

In the absence of any provisions in a will regarding the order in
which the property in the estate shall be used to pay debts and expenses of administration, the executor must resort to statutes or
judicial determinations to establish the order.[61]   Normally the
property that is not specifically devised or bequeathed should be
used to pay the debts and expenses of administration, and where
there is no provision in the will to the contrary, that result will
prevail.   If there is any likelihood that the property not specifically devised or bequeathed will be insufficient to pay debts and
expenses of administration, the testator should express in the will
the order in which specifically devised and bequeathed property
should be taken for such purposes.[62]

[61] In Dexter v. Jackson, 245 Mass. 333, 140 N.E. 267 (1923), the court states
that "the general rule is that all expenses of administration are to be paid
from the residue, even though they are incurred largely with reference to
certain legacies and not the will as a whole."
  The order in which property disposed of in a will is used to pay debts is
generally (1) personal property not specifically bequeathed, (2) real property
not specifically devised, and (3) real property and personal property specifically devised and bequeathed contributing ratably.
[62] If a will contains a provision directing the executor to pay the testator's
debts, a question may arise as to whether such a direction will require the
payment by the executor of claims that are unenforceable on some ground or
other, such as the statute of limitations.   Normally such a direction in the
will should not constitute a waiver of any defenses which may be available
in regard to claims against an estate, and it may be particularly significant in
the will of a wife because it may operate to relieve her husband and his estate of his legal duty to pay her debts and funeral expenses.   If the wife's
will contains a clause which directs that all debts be paid out of the residue,
will the expenses of the last illness of the wife, which normally would be
payable by the husband, be payable by the wife's executor?   See Foster v.
Reiss, 31 N.J. Super. 496, 107 A.2d 24 (1954), *rev'd on another point,* 18 N.J.
41, 112 A.2d 553 (1955).   Blackburn v. United States, 60-2 U.S.T.C. ¶11964
(S.D. Ind. 1960), holds that where a wife's will did not direct the payment of
her funeral expenses, such expenses were not deductible for estate tax purposes, even though her estate in fact did pay them, because they were not
payable out of her estate under Indiana law.
  A question may arise as to the expenditures which may be made by a decedent's personal representative to preserve the property under his care.   Such
expenditures properly made are expenses of administration deductible for
death tax purposes.   If, however, the expenditures for the preservation of
property benefit only a specific devisee as opposed to the estate as a whole,
they may not be deductible as administration expenses.

The property that is used to pay debts and expenses of administration may produce income between the date of the testator's death and the date the payments are made. If the testator in his will has divided the residue of his estate into shares and has given some outright and placed others in trust, how is the income from property used to pay debts and expenses of administration — income which becomes a part of the residue — to be divided between the shares given outright and those placed in trust? Is the portion of the income which goes to the shares placed in trust to be regarded as income in the trust or as principal? In the absence of a provision in the will which answers these questions, the answers must be found in a statute or in judicial determinations.[63]

PROBLEMS

19.6. T in his will devises Blackacre "to my son John in fee simple." He gives the residue of his estate (consisting of real property) to a trustee and directs him "to pay the income to my son John for his life, and on his death, to pay the corpus to the X charity." John is T's sole heir at his death. In the state in which Blackacre is located a statute is in force which provides: "Real estate not devised shall be first chargeable with the payment of debts, legacies or charges of administration in exoneration of real estate devised, unless a different intention appears by the will." [64] The X charity contends that Blackacre should be sold and the proceeds from the sale used to pay T's debts and the expenses of

---

[63] 3 Scott, Trusts §§234.4, 234.5 (2d ed. 1956). New York Personal Property Law §17b provides as follows: "Unless otherwise expressly provided by the will of a person dying after this act takes effect, all income from real and personal property earned during the period of administration of the estate of such testator and not payable to others or otherwise disposed of by the will shall be distributed pro rata as income among the beneficiaries of any trusts created out of the residuary estate of such testator and the other persons entitled to such residuary estate. None of such income shall, after such distribution, be added to the capital of the residuary estate the whole or any part of which is devised or bequeathed in trust or for life or for a term of years, but shall be paid ratably to the life beneficiary of a trust, or to the life tenant, or to the absolute residuary legatee, as the case may be. Unless otherwise directed in the will, income shall be payable to the life beneficiaries of trusts, or to life tenants from the date of testator's death. Nothing contained in this act shall affect the right of any person to income on any portion of the estate not part of the residuary estate of such testator." Maine enacted a statute substantially the same as the New York statute. See Me. Rev. Stat. Ann., c. 160, §34 (1954, Supp. 1959), quoted infra page 1440. See also comments at page 845, supra, in regard to the effect of a provision in a power of appointment marital deduction trust, which requires income realized during administration from property used to pay debts, expenses of administration and taxes to be added to corpus.

[64] Mass. Ann. Laws, c. 202, §4.

administering his estate instead of selling the real property in the trust, because John takes Blackacre by descent rather than by purchase under the will. Do you agree with the X charity? [65]

19.7. T makes various taxable gifts during his life but at no time files a federal gift tax return. After T's death, the amount of the federal gift taxes which should have been paid on such gifts (plus interest) is determined. In the absence of any provision in T's will regarding the payment of federal gift taxes which may be payable, what funds should be used to pay these taxes? See Section 25.2502-2 of the Regulations.

19.8. After T's death, a deficiency assessment is made in regard to federal income taxes for years prior to his death. In the absence of a provision in T's will regarding the payment of any deficiency, what funds should be used to pay the one assessed. See Revenue Ruling 56-6, 1956-1 C.B. 660.

8. ADMINISTRATIVE PROVISIONS IN REGARD TO INVESTMENTS

If the trust instrument does not give the trustee a charter of investment powers, the governing local law — statutes and cases — will determine his investment powers. The following opinion illustrates how the choice of language in a trust instrument regarding the trustee's investment powers may create an ambiguity that will require the trustee to ask the court for instructions.

MANUFACTURER'S TRUST CO. v. EARLE
32 N.J. Super. 262, 108 A.2d 115 (1954)

SULLIVAN, J.S.C.

Plaintiff-trustee has filed a suit asking this court to construe decedent's will. . . .

Do the provisions of decedent's will, particularly "Article Twenty-sixth: Section 1," limit the powers of investment granted to a trustee under the Prudent Man Investment Statute, N.J.S. 3A:15-18 et seq., N.J.S.A.? . . .

As to this first question, the problem arises because of the Prudent Man Investment Statute of the State, N.J.S. 3A:15-18 et seq., N.J.S.A., which permits a fiduciary to invest up to 40% of the principal of a trust in any type of investment subject only to the prudent man standard as set forth in N.J.S. 3A:15-19, N.J.S.A. The statute, however, further says in section 3A:15-25 that "If a

---

[65] See Ellis v. Page, printed in full supra page 462; 3 Restatement of Property §314(2), Comment j.

trust instrument prescribes, defines, limits or otherwise regulates" a trustee's powers and duties of investment, "the trust instrument shall control notwithstanding this article." To put it another way, the statute does not nor was it ever intended to countermand a trustor's instructions to his trustee as expressed in the trust instrument. Fidelity Union Trust Co. v. Price, 11 N.J. 90, 93 A.2d 321, 35 A.L.R.2d 980 (1952). In the case at hand the trustee is doubtful as to whether Article Twenty-sixth, Section 1, of decedent's will prescribes, defines, limits or otherwise regulates the trustee's powers and duties of investment within the meaning of N.J.S. 3A:15-25, N.J.S.A. supra. If it does, then the trustee may not avail itself of the liberal power of investment under the Prudent Man Investment Statute.

Article Twenty-sixth, Section 1, reads as follows:

"SECTION 1. It is my desire that all of the trusts herein provided for shall be set up within two years after this will shall have been admitted to probate and that the principal of each trust shall be and remain invested to the extent of at least two-thirds thereof in such securities as shall be legal investments for trust funds under the laws of the State of New Jersey and/or the State of New York, and to the extent of not to exceed one-third thereof in first and/or senior preferred stocks listed on the New York Stock Exchange upon which there shall have been no default in the payment of any regular dividend when due within five years immediately preceding their acquisition."

This article definitely contains specific provisions instructing and limiting the trustee in its investment policy and particularly with regard to any deviation from "legal investments for trust funds." If there were no provision indicating the extent to which a trustee might invest in securities other than "legal investments for trust funds," it might well be that the Prudent Man Investment Statute would apply. Where, however, the decedent has in effect drafted a Prudent Man Investment Statute of his own and included it in his will, specifying in what manner and to what extent his trustee may deviate from "legal investments for trust funds" as he knew and understood that provision to mean, the provisions of the will must prevail over the statute. In the first place, decedent wanted at least two-thirds of the corpus of each of the trusts invested "in such securities as shall be legal investments for trust funds under the laws of the State of New Jersey and/or the State of New York." He further provided that not more than one-third of corpus could be invested in certain preferred stocks. The fact that decedent made a distinction between "legal investments for trust funds" and other investments, and then specified the percentage of each that the trustee was to invest in, shows that he considered one class to be "legals" and the other "non-legals." It further shows that he was fully aware of the technical meaning of the phrase "legal investments for trust funds" and used it in exactly that sense. Likewise, in authorizing some liberalization of investment holdings by his trustee, he specified in what manner and to what extent. The provisions of N.J.S. 3A:15-26, N.J.S.A., therefore, do not apply to this situation because there are express provisions to the contrary contained in the trust instrument. No one can dispute the fact that today, generally speaking, it is legal for a trustee to invest in any kind of securities, and to that extent the term "legal investments" includes non-legals. Decedent, however, never understood that term to have such a broad meaning, and to try and read this latter construction into decedent's will would result in a conclusion that is almost the opposite of what decedent wrote and obviously intended. The will does anticipate that from time to time the laws relating to legal investments for trust funds may be changed, hence the use by decedent of the word "shall," which clearly indicates that the legality of investments is to be measured by the law at the time of the investment. Fidelity Union Trust Co. v. Price, supra. Likewise, it is apparent that in referring to "the laws of the State of New Jersey and/or the State of New York," the word "and" should be disregarded to give the clause the meaning intended.

To summarize, the results are:

The trustee may not avail itself of the investment provisions of the Prudent Man Investment Statute, N.J.S. 3A:15-18 et seq., N.J.S.A., and therefore may not invest in common stocks nor invest in any other non-legals except those specified in decedent's will and then only in the manner and to the extent indicated.

Preferred stock holdings, whether legals or non-legals, should not exceed one-third of corpus.

The provisions in decedent's will as to "legal investments" mean under the laws of the State of New Jersey or the State of New York . . .[66]

9. ADMINISTRATIVE PROVISIONS IN REGARD TO COMPROMISE OF DISPUTES

If the controlling local law imposes an inheritance tax on contingent future interests, it may be desirable to authorize some per-

---

[66] In the following cases it was held that the trustee could invest all or part of the trust assets in the trustee's common trust fund if the trust instrument did not prohibit such investment: Mechanicks National Bank of Concord v

son to compromise disputes with the taxing authorities in regard to the valuation of such interests.[67]   Other disputes may arise after a person dies which may have to be settled in some way by his personal representative.   Consideration should be given to the inclusion in a will of a provision which authorizes the executors "to compromise and settle any claims in favor of or against my estate upon such evidence as they may determine to be sufficient." [68]

10.   EFFECT OF CHANGE IN LAW AS TO FIDUCIARY ADMINISTRATION ON ADMINISTRATIVE PROVISIONS

If the governing instrument does not give the fiduciary a charter as to the administration of the trust or estate, then the controlling local law must be consulted.   For example, suppose that when the trust is established, the controlling local law requires the allocation of stock dividends between income and principal (the so-called Pennsylvania rule).   Subsequently the local law is changed by the adoption of the Uniform Principal and Income Act, which awards stock dividends to principal (the so-called Massachusetts rule).   If the trust instrument contains no directions as to the disposition of stock dividends, will the local law in force when the trust was established continue to control the disposition of such dividends after the local law has been changed by the adoption of the Uniform Principal and Income Act?   If the creator of the trust is deemed to adopt the law in force at the time the trust is established just as effectively as if he had spelled it out in the trust instrument, then a change in the local law should have no effect on the operation of the trust.   In the absence of a provision in the trust instrument, it is just as likely that the average person creating the trust would intend that the local law as it may exist from time to time will control.[69]   The issue of intent can be avoided only by giving the fiduciary a complete and comprehensive administrative charter.

D'Amours, 100 N.H. 461, 129 A.2d 859 (1957); Mechanicks National Bank of Concord v. Brady, 100 N.H. 469, 129 A.2d 857 (1957). — Ed.

[67] See the discussion regarding the payment of death taxes on future interests at page 435 supra.

[68] A provision authorizing an executor to compromise claims against an estate is considered in Edelstein v. Old Colony Trust Co., 336 Mass. 659, 147 N.E.2d 193 (1958).

[69] In re Allis' Will, 6 Wis. 2d 1, 94 N.W.2d 226 (1959), commented on in 73 Harv. L. Rev. 605 (1960), the court found that it was not unconstitutional to apply the recently adopted Uniform Income and Principal Act to existing trusts because the testatrix intended allocation of stock dividends in accordance with current laws of the state.

CHAPTER XX

The Selection of the Fiduciary

Every complete estate plan will involve a will, and the will should designate who is to serve as executor. Likewise a trustee must be selected whenever a trust is involved in an estate plan. If a minor child is a beneficiary, it may be necessary that he have a legal guardian, and the local law may permit the testator to select the guardian in his will.[1] The selection of these fiduciaries is one of the most important aspects of estate planning.

The fiduciary can be an individual or a corporation, or an individual and a corporation may be chosen as co-fiduciaries. If an individual is selected he may be a member of the immediate family involved, a more distant relative, a friend, someone who is not intimately associated with the family; or there may be a combination of such individuals. The range of choice is wide; the decision may be vital to the success of the estate plan.[2]

No intelligent selection of a fiduciary can be made without careful consideration of the duties the fiduciary is to perform.

[1] The statute in Massachusetts which permits the designation of a testamentary guardian restricts the privilege to a father or mother of a minor child and, even then, the designation is subject to the approval of a probate court. If neither parent is living, the testamentary guardian performs the required duties both with respect to the person and the property of the ward, but if one parent is living, then the guardian's duties relate only to the ward's property. See Mass. Ann. Laws, c. 201, §3, quoted infra page 1461. The Pennsylvania statute which is concerned with the appointment of a testamentary guardian is much more comprehensive than the one in Massachusetts. See Pa. Stat. Ann., tit. 20, §180.18b (Purdon, Supp. 1959).

[2] In Barnes v. Lee Savings Bank, 340 Mass. 87, 162 N.E.2d 666 (1959), the court reiterates the well-recognized rule that "when a debtor of an estate is appointed administrator or executor of his creditor, the debt is extinguished and treated as paid. The debt becomes part of the assets of the estate and the administrator or executor must account for the amount of such indebtedness." This rule generally is not applied in such a way as to eliminate a lien on the property of the debtor to the benefit of the other creditors of the debtor. In the Barnes case, however, the court eliminated a mortgage given by the debtor to the decedent when the debtor was appointed executor, and allowed a mortgagee junior to the decedent to benefit when the debtor was the sole beneficiary and there were no other creditors of the estate.

Obviously the selected fiduciary must be qualified to carry out the responsibilities of his office or the beneficiaries will suffer. In determining whether a person is qualified, however, it should be kept in mind that it is not necessarily essential that the fiduciary be qualified to perform the responsibilities of his office without assistance from others. Help and guidance from investment counsel may be obtained to assist the fiduciary in making decisions as to investments; attorneys are available to perform the necessary legal work;[3] and various qualified persons may be employed to keep the records.

1.   TAX CONSIDERATIONS

If a person establishes an inter vivos trust and desires thereby to remove the trust property from his estate for federal income and estate tax purposes, the accomplishment of this result may depend on the trustee he selects.[4] If the executor or the trustee is given discretionary powers and he can benefit himself by the exercise of such powers, he may be treated, for federal estate and

---

[3] In re Estate of Marks, 83 So.2d 853 (Fla. 1955), the could held that a provision in a will directing the executor to employ a certain attorney was not binding on the executor. The court observed that, of the several states which have passed on this question, only Louisiana has held that such a provision is binding on the executor.

In the California case of Estate of Thompson, 157 Cal. App. 2d 266, 320 P.2d 604 (1958), the District Court of Appeals held that an attorney who was serving as an executor could not collect both executor's fees and attorney's fees. The will directed that if the executor acted as his own attorney "he shall be allowed his fees as Executor, together with the fees which may be allowable to the attorney for the Executor." The court said that such a dual collection was against the public policy which forbids a person in whom fiduciary duties are vested to make a profit of them by employing himself. The court also pointed out that the executor was not bound by the testator's nomination of an attorney. The case was reversed in 50 Cal. 2d 613, 328 P.2d 1 (1958).

Haines v. George, 11 Ill. App. 359, 137 N.E.2d 555 (1956), held that where a will designated that a person should be the attorney for the executor, and the attorney was a witness to the will, he was precluded from receiving compensation for services rendered to the executor, because the local law did not permit a witness to a will to receive any financial remuneration by reason of the will.

[4] If the objective is to remove the income of the trust property from the settlor's gross income, the selection of the trustee is very important. See the discussion at page 176 supra. An examination of the material at page 188, supra, will make it apparent that in many cases this selection is also vital in order to eliminate the value of the trust property from the settlor's gross estate.

When the wrong trustee is chosen and, as a consequence, the value of the trust property remains in the settlor's gross estate or the income of the trust property is includible in his gross income, a gift for federal gift tax purposes may or may not be made. See the comments at page 218 supra.

gift tax purposes, as the owner of the property with respect to which such powers exist.[5]

PROBLEMS

20.1. If the settlor of an inter vivos trust desires to remove the trust property from his estate for federal income and estate tax purposes, determine under what circumstances such a result can be obtained with the following as trustee or trustees:

    a. The settlor as sole trustee

    b. The settlor's wife as sole trustee

    c. The settlor's son as sole trustee

    d. The settlor's lawyer as sole trustee

    e. A corporation as sole trustee

    f. Any combination of the above as trustees

20.2. If the testator desires to establish a trust in his will and to eliminate any possibility that the trustee will be treated as the owner of the trust property for federal estate and gift tax purposes, determine under what circumstances such a result can be obtained with the following as trustee or trustees:

    a. The testator's wife as sole trustee

    b. The testator's son as sole trustee

    c. The testator's lawyer as sole trustee

    d. A corporation as sole trustee

    e. Any combination of the above as trustees

20.3. If the testator desires to eliminate any possibility that his executor will be treated as the owner of any part of the estate property for federal estate and gift tax purposes, determine under what circumstances such a result can be obtained with the following as executor or executors:

    a. The testator's wife as sole executor

    b. The testator's son as sole executor

---

[5] In the situation described in the text the fiduciary may have a general power of appointment. General powers of appointment are considered supra page 689.

A power in the trustee to benefit himself may also cause the income of the trust property to be taxable to him, although it is distributed to someone else. See page 729 supra.

If a person who can be benefited by the exercise of the discretionary powers given to the fiduciary has a legally enforceable right to control the fiduciary's decisions, the powers of the fiduciary will be attributed to the beneficiary. It is not beyond the realm of possibility that the fiduciary's powers will also be attributed to the beneficiary, as a result of judicial or legislative developments, where the fiduciary, without exercising any independent judgment, simply follows instructions from the beneficiary, though he is not legally obligated to do so. See Casner, Responsibilities of the Corporate Trustees as to Discretionary Trusts, 32 Trust Bull. No. 7, p. 21 (1953).

   c. The testator's lawyer as sole executor
   d. A corporation as sole executor
   e. Any combination of the above as executors

2.   LEGAL RESTRICTIONS ON CHOICE

A person who lacks legal capacity, such as a minor or a mentally incompetent person, of course cannot serve as a fiduciary. Normally a nonresident is not disqualified to serve as executor but he may be required to designate a resident agent for service of process.[6] In some states, however, a nonresident individual is not qualified to serve as executor,[7] and in at least one state the statutory provision is broad enough to exclude a nonresident individual from serving as testamentary trustee.[8] In Virginia a resident executor and a resident testamentary trustee must be appointed to serve with a nonresident executor and a nonresident testamentary trustee.[9] The governing local law must be examined to determine what restrictions, if any, exist as to the appointment of a

---

[6] If a resident executor has been appointed and then moves to another state before completing his duties, he may be required to appoint a resident agent for service of process. For an example of a state statute which requires a nonresident executor to designate a resident agent for service of process, see Mass. Ann. Laws, c. 195, §§8-10, quoted infra page 1458.

[7] Illinois, after ruling out as executors the mentally incompetent, minors and criminals, also ruled out a nonresident of the state. See Ill. Rev. Stat., c. 3, §229 (1959), quoted infra page 1438. This type of statute, which is designed to preserve executors' fees for the local people, can be avoided to a considerable extent by eliminating as much as possible from a person's probate estate. See the discussion at page 120 supra.

[8] Michigan has declared that it is the public policy of the state to require all persons acting as fiduciary under appointment of a probate court to be amenable at all times to process issued out of the courts of the state and that, consequently, a person who is not a resident of the state and a citizen of the United States cannot serve as fiduciary. See Mich. Stat. Ann. §27.3178(278) (1943), quoted infra page 1465. It should be possible in Michigan, however, to select a nonresident as trustee of an inter vivos trust.

In Roby v. Smith, 131 Ind. 342, 30 N.E. 1093 (1891), it was held that an Indiana statute which prohibited the appointment of a nonresident trustee who was a citizen of the United States violated Article 4, Section 2, and the Fourteenth Amendment of the Constitution of the United States.

[9] See Va. Code Ann. §26-59 (1950, Supp. 1960), quoted infra page 1475. One should be completely free in selecting the trustee of an inter vivos trust in Virginia.

By Pa. Stat. Ann., tit. 20, §320.903 (Purdon), it is provided that when none of the trustees are residents of Pennsylvania, the court, after such notice as it shall direct, may appoint one or more additional trustees residing within the Commonwealth to serve with the nonresident trustees. Section 320.902, quoted infra page 1473, provides that the Secretary of the Commonwealth is automatically designated as one upon whom service of process and notice may be made as to all causes of action relating to the trust estate when the trustee is or becomes a nonresident.

foreign corporation as executor or testamentary trustee.[10] A person who owns property may become incompetent, so that a guardian will have to be appointed to manage his property. The state in which the incompetent resides may require that the guardian be a resident of the state.[11] Finally, it should be noted that aliens may not be allowed to serve as executor[12] or as testamentary trustee.[13]

If ancillary administration will be required in connection with a particular estate, thought should be given to the possibility of controlling the selection of the ancillary administrator.[14]

PROBLEMS

20.4. T, a resident of a state which does not permit a foreign trust company to serve as testamentary trustee, desires to establish a trust in his will and to have the trust administered under the supervision of the X Trust Company, a Massachusetts corporate trustee. His attorney advises him to designate as trustee that person who from time to time is the president of the X Trust Company. What is your reaction to such advice? In answering this

[10] New Hampshire is an example of a state which does not permit a foreign corporation to be appointed as trustee. See Bank of New York and Trust Company v. Tilton, 82 N.H. 81, 129 Atl. 492 (1925). See also Kan. Gen. Stat. Ann. §59-1701 (1949), quoted infra page 1440; La. Rev. Stat. Ann. §9:1871 (1950). Massachusetts is an example of a state that does allow such an appointment. See Mass. Ann. Laws, c. 167, §45A; c. 172, §52. But in Massachusetts, as well as in many other states which allow a foreign corporation to be appointed a fiduciary, the appointment can be made only if the jurisdiction in which the foreign corporation is located permits a Massachusetts corporation to serve as a fiduciary in that jurisdiction.

[11] Illinois permits a nonresident of the state to be appointed the conservator of the person of an incompetent but not the conservator of the incompetent's estate. See Ill. Rev. Stat., c. 3, §§271, 272 (1959), quoted infra page 1439. If a revocable inter vivos trust is established prior to the time the property owner becomes incompetent, a nonresident could be selected as trustee and could continue to manage the property after the incompetency. In this way the Illinois statute could be avoided.

The Virginia statute referred to in note 9, supra, permits a nonresident guardian to be designated for an incompetent person but requires the appointment of a resident guardian to serve with the nonresident.

[12] See Md. Ann. Code, art. 93, §59 (1957), quoted infra page 1441. See also the Michigan statute referred to supra note 8.

[13] See the Michigan statute referred to supra note 8. See also In re Fermer's Will, 177 Misc. 228, 30 N.Y.S.2d 248 (1941).

[14] The domiciliary executor will usually be appointed to take charge of the ancillary administration unless the local law prohibits such an appointment. A Kansas statute allows only banks or other corporations organized under the laws of Kansas which have their principal place of business in the state, to act as a fiduciary, but the statute expressly excepts ancillary proceedings from its operation. See Kan. Gen. Stat. Ann. §59-1701 (1949), quoted infra page 1440.

problem consider Kansas General Statutes Annotated §59-1701 (1949), quoted infra page 1440.

20.5. Point out the extent to which the restrictions on the choice of a fiduciary may be avoided by the establishment of a revocable inter vivos trust.

3.   CONTINUITY OF SUPERVISION

If it becomes essential to change from one fiduciary to another before the fiduciary's work is completed, an interruption in the continuity of the supervision of the property results and this may be undesirable.   Assurance of continuity of supervision is obtained by the selection of a corporate fiduciary.   A similar assurance of continuity may be obtained if the fiduciary is a partner in a law firm which may be expected to continue when a partner dies, by providing for the appointment of one of the other partners as successor fiduciary.

4.   PERSONAL ACQUAINTANCE WITH THE BENEFICIARIES

A fiduciary who is personally acquainted with the beneficiaries and their background may be able to perform the responsibilities of his office more understandingly than a stranger.   Sometimes, however, the beneficiaries may take advantage of a family friend in ways that in the long run may be detrimental to their own best interests.   Any fiduciary who is worthy of the name should become acquainted, if he is not already acquainted, with the beneficiaries and their background to the extent that is necessary to a proper performance of his duties.

5.   FIDUCIARY'S FEES

A factor to consider in the selection of a fiduciary is the fiduciary's fees.[15]   In determining the real significance of this factor, however, it must be kept in mind that the executor's fees are deductible for federal estate tax purposes[16] and that the trustee's fees are deductible for federal income tax purposes.[17]   In any event, if

[15] See the schedule of charges of a corporate executor and corporate trustee printed supra page 39, note 84; page 139, not 83; and page 283, note 8.

[16] See page 40 supra.   For the circumstances under which the executor's fees may be taken as a deduction in determining the net income of the estate for federal income tax purposes rather than as a deduction in determining the net estate for federal estate tax purposes, see page 785 supra.

[17] See page 121 supra.   If some of the trust income is not subject to federal

the fiduciary's work is not done satisfactorily, the financial loss to the estate involved may be far greater than the fees of an experienced and competent fiduciary.

6. PROVISIONS RELATING TO THE FIDUCIARY

In addition to the provisions in the estate plan which designate the fiduciaries, other provisions relating to them may be appropriate. In determining what these other provisions may be, consider the following questions:

1. Should the fiduciaries be excused from furnishing sureties on any bond? [18]

2. Should a simplified method be provided for the resignation of a fiduciary? [19]

3. Should the fiduciary be subject to removal by any of the beneficiaries? [20]

4. Should a simplified method be provided for the appointment of a successor fiduciary? [21]

5. If there are multiple fiduciaries, should a fiduciary be permitted to delegate his powers and discretions to a cofiduciary? [22]

---

income taxation (municipal bonds for example), only that part of the trustee's fees is deductible for federal income tax purposes which corresponds to the part of the total income that is taxable. See 1954 I.R.C. §265.

[18] The cost of sureties on any bond will come out of the estate being administered. This expense can be saved by selecting a fiduciary in which everyone has complete confidence and by excusing the fiduciary from furnishing sureties on any bond that is required.

[19] Every time a trustee steps out and a new trustee comes in, some expense is involved. Furthermore, the proper and orderly administration of the trust is impaired by frequent changes in the managerial staff. These factors indicate that it should not be easy for a fiduciary to give up his job. On the other hand, a responsible fiduciary does not drop his responsibilities without good reason, and if there is a good reason for changing control, the more easily the change can be accomplished, the better it is for all concerned.

[20] If a person has the power to remove a fiduciary and the fiduciary has discretionary powers, the person may, for federal tax purposes, be deemed to possess the discretionary powers nominally in the fiduciary. For comment on the tax consequences when a beneficiary has the power to remove a trustee, see page 689 supra.

[21] If the power to appoint a successor fiduciary is vested in a beneficiary and he is not excluded from appointing himself, some adverse tax consequences may be produced. See the discussion at page 690 supra.

[22] If certain powers and discretions are vested exclusively in the disinterested executors or in the disinterested trustees, a delegation by such fiduciaries should be permitted only to another disinterested executor or disinterested trustee.

A P P E N D I X I[1]

The Black Family Estate Plan (Third Revision)[2]

On ...., 19.............,[3] Richard Harry Black III and his wife visited the law firm of Andrew, James and Casner, located in ...., ...,[4] and conferred with Mr. Andrew, one of the senior partners, about their estate plans. After the conference, Mr. Andrew drew up the memoranda which are set out below.[5]

A. *Estate of Richard Harry Black III*

1. *Mr. Black's gross estate*
   a. *Tangible personal property*
      Note: The tangible personal property consists of the usual furnishings in a family residence and in a summer residence; two automobiles; a sailboat; personal effects such as clothing and jewelry; and other

---

[1] The estate plan in Appendix I is *not* presented as a model incapable of improvement. Rather it is simply a hypothetical attorney's work with respect to the factual situation presented. No mistakes, however, have been intentionally planted in the plan. The attorney's work should be the subject of critical examination from the following standpoints:
   1. The completeness of the factual background of the client's situation elicited by the attorney
   2. The soundness of the attorney's judgment in regard to his choice of methods to accomplish the client's objectives
   3. The correctness of the attorney's conception of the law applicable to the client's situation
   4. The adequacy of the draftsmanship of the attorney with respect to the instruments designed to accomplish the client's objectives

[2] The 1954 and 1955 Supplements to the First Edition of the text each contained a plan called the Black Family Estate Plan. Appendix I in the Second Edition of the text presented the Black Family Estate Plan (Second Revision). The plan as here presented is a third revision.

[3] Insert the date of the visit by Mr. and Mrs. Black.

[4] Insert the location of the law firm.

[5] The extent to which the comments made in memoranda may be evidence against a client at some later date should be appreciated. In this regard see 8 Wigmore, Evidence §2323 (McNaughton rev. 1961), which recognizes that the attorney-client privilege continues after the death of the client; as to the right in the personal representative to waive it, see id. §2329. See also Falsone v. United States, 205 F.2d 734 (5th Cir. 1953), *cert. denied,* 346 U.S. 864 (1953).

miscellaneous items.   The figure set opposite is only an estimate, for planning purposes, of the value of the tangible personal property owned by Mr. Black. $10,000

b. *Real Estate*

(1) *Family residence*

Note: The family residence is located at ....

...., ...

............................., ...[6]

The residence was purchased in 1944.   The purchase price was $20,000, and title to the property was taken in the following form: "Richard Harry Black III and Mildred Marie Black and their heirs as tenants by the entirety." [7]   Mr. Black paid $10,000 of the purchase price out of his own funds on the date the house was purchased, and he and his wife signed a note for the balance.   The note called for 4% interest payable annually and was secured by a mortgage on the house.   The mortgage was executed by Mr. Black and his wife. The note was due and payable in full in five years, with the privilege, however, in Mr. Black and his wife to pay off the note in whole or in part at any time.   During the first three years of the note, only interest was paid and this was paid out of funds belonging to Mr. Black.   At the end of the third year Mrs. Black paid $5000 on the note out of funds which had been given to her by her husband in the previous year.   The interest on the unpaid balance was paid by Mr. Black for the next two years out of his own funds.   At the end of the fifth year, when the balance of the note became due and payable, Mr. Black paid it out of his own funds.   In the summer of 1960, when the property was worth $30,000, an addition costing $15,000 was made to the house.   The entire cost of this addition was paid by Mrs. Black out of funds which she had inherited from her father. The assessed value of the house is now $30,000, but Mr. Black believes that the property could be sold for $49,000.   On the basis of this information, four sevenths of the present value of the house is included in Mr. Black's gross estate for planning purposes.[8]   28,000

[6] Insert the street address, city and state where the residence is located.

[7] If the jurisdiction where the residence is located does not recognize a tenancy by the entirety, change to a joint tenancy.

[8] The attorney has applied 1954 I.R.C. §2040.   He has concluded that the $5000 paid on the purchase price by Mrs. Black should be attributed to Mr. Black because

(2) *Summer residence*

> *Note:* Mr. Black bought a small summer place
> on ....,
> ...., ...
> ....,[9] in 1949. He paid $5000 for the prop-
> erty and took title in his own name. On the pres-
> ent market, this property is probably worth about
> $10,000.   10,000

(3) *Illinois farm*[10]

> *Note:* Mr. Black's mother originally came from
> Illinois, and her father, on his death in 1924, spe-
> cifically devised to her his 200-acre farm in Mc-
> Lean County in Illinois. In her will this farm
> was specifically devised to Mr. Black; James, his
> brother, received other property equal in value.
> A letter from a real-estate broker in Illinois in-
> dicates that this farm land today is worth $400
> an acre.[11]   80,000

c. *Bank accounts*

(1) *Checking account*

> *Note:* Mr. Black has only one checking account,
> which is at the ....
> ...., ...
> ...., ...[12]
> This account is in his name alone and the aver-
> age balance is $6000.   6,000

---

she acquired the $5000 from him for less than an adequate and full consideration in money or money's worth. Thus Mr. Black has contributed $20,000 (four sevenths of the total capital invested in the property) and Mrs. Black has contributed $15,000 (three sevenths of the total capital invested in the property). It should be noted that, at the time Mrs. Black made her $15,000 contribution, the value of the property was $30,000. This entire $30,000 value was attributable to Mr. Black's $20,000 contribution On this basis, it might be contended that the proportionate contributions by Mr. and Mrs. Black are two thirds and one third rather than four sevenths and three sevenths. See the discussion on this matter supra page 412. — Ed.

[9] Insert the street, city or town, and state where the summer residence is located. It is suggested that the summer residence be located in a state other than the one in which Mr. Black resides.

[10] If the jurisdiction selected for Mr. Black's domicile is Illinois, it is suggested that the farm be located in Iowa and that the subsequent material be modified to reflect this change.

[11] The valuation of real property for estate tax purposes is considered in O'Brien v. United States, 57-2 U.S.T.C. ¶11704 (N.D. Tex. 1957); Estate of M. Selnes v. United States, 58-1 U.S.T.C. ¶11749 (D. Minn. 1957); Byer v. Broderick, 59-2 U.S T.C. ¶11880 (D. Kan. 1959); Estate of Isaac W. Baldwin, 18 CCH T.C. Mem. 902 (1959) (court recognized that real property owned subject to clause which requires the owner to offer it to another at a stated price before selling it is a factor affecting value. In regard to the valuation of such property for gift tax purposes, see Buck v. United States, 154 F. Supp. 90 (D. Del. 1957). — Ed.

[12] Insert the name and location of the bank.

(2) *Savings accounts*

   Note: Mr. Black has two savings accounts: one with the ....
   ...., ...,[13] and the other with the ....
   ...., ...
   ....[14] Both of these accounts are joint accounts of Mr. Black and his wife, payable on the death of one to the survivor. All the money in these accounts has come from Mr. Black. The average balance in each account is $5000.   10,000

d. *Securities*

   (1) *Government bonds*

   Note: Mr. Black has acquired over the years with his own funds Series E Bonds having a face value of $4000. Bonds having a face value of $2000 are in the name of Mr. Black and his wife, payable on the death of one to the survivor; bonds having a face value of $2000 are in the name of Mr. Black, payable on his death to Mrs. Black. Although the present value of the bonds does not correspond with their face value, the face value is used for planning purposes.   4,000

   (2) *Stocks and bonds* (other than stock listed under item (3) immediately below)

   Note: Mr. Black has an account with the Jones and Jones investment house located in ....
   ...., ...[15]
   The securities are all owned outright by Mr. Black but title to the securities is in the name of High and Company, a nominee of the investment house. The present value of the securities in this account plus the uninvested cash is $250,000.   250,000

   (3) *Stock in Black Manufacturing Company*

   Note: The Black Manufacturing Company is a small incorporated business with offices in ....
   ...., ...
   ....[16] The state of incorporation of the company is ....[17]
   There are 2500 shares ($10 par value) of common stock of the Black Manufacturing Company outstanding. Mr. Black owns 1300 shares and his younger brother James owns the other 1200 shares.

---

[13] Insert the name and location of the bank.
[14] Insert the name and location of the bank.
[15] Insert the location of the investment house.
[16] Insert the location of the principal offices of the company.
[17] Insert the state of incorporation.

The Black brothers started the business in 1934. The company manufactures machine tools. It has had a slow but steady growth over the years. The stock has never been sold or valued for tax purposes. The financial statements of the company for the last ten years have been examined for the purpose of trying to arrive at a reasonable value of the common stock. Taking into account the net worth of the company and its earning and dividend-paying capacity as revealed by the financial statements, with some adjustments due to the fact that some of the earnings are the result of nonrecurring types of business, it is believed that the figure of $100 a share is a reasonable one.   130,000

e. *Life insurance*
   (1) *New York Life Insurance Policy No. 1,021,052*
      Note: This policy was acquired in 1933. It is an ordinary life policy. The guaranteed rate of interest is 3%. The face amount of the policy is $10,000. The proceeds are now payable to Mr. Black's wife as primary beneficiary and to his issue as secondary beneficiaries. The proceeds are now payable to the primary beneficiary under the first option of the policy, which provides that the proceeds shall be paid in equal monthly installments over a period of 10 years. If the primary beneficiary does not survive the insured, or survives the insured but dies before the end of the 10-year period, the proceeds, or the commuted value of the unpaid installments, are payable to the secondary beneficiaries on a per stirpes basis.   10,000

   (2) *Metropolitan Life Insurance Policy No. 2,032,051*
      Note: This policy was acquired in 1939. It is an ordinary life policy. The guaranteed rate of interest is 3%. The face amount of the policy is $10,000. The proceeds are now payable to Mr. Black's wife as primary beneficiary and to his issue as secondary beneficiaries. The proceeds are now payable under the second option of the policy, which provides for monthly payments for 10 years certain and thereafter during the life of Mrs. Black. If Mrs. Black dies before her husband, or survives him and dies before the 10-year certain period has expired, the proceeds, or the commuted value of the balance of the proceeds, will be paid in a lump sum to the secondary beneficiaries on a per stirpes basis.   10,000

(3) *Equitable Life Assurance Society of the United States Policy No. 3,014,652*

Note: This policy was acquired in 1943. It is an ordinary life policy. The guaranteed rate of interest is 3%. The face amount of the policy is $10,000. The proceeds are now payable to Mr. Black's wife as primary beneficiary and to his issue as secondary beneficiaries. The proceeds are now payable under the fifth option of the policy, which provides that the proceeds shall be paid to the primary beneficiary in monthly installments of $100 until the proceeds are exhausted. If Mrs. Black dies before her husband, or survives him and dies before the proceeds are exhausted, the proceeds, or the balance of the proceeds, will be paid in one sum to the secondary beneficiaries on a per stirpes basis.   10,000

(4) *John Hancock Mutual Life Insurance Company Policy No. 3,505,612*

Note: This policy was acquired in 1949. It is an endowment policy (20 payments) with a guaranteed rate of interest of $2\frac{1}{2}\%$. The face amount of the policy is $20,000. The proceeds are now payable to Mr. Black's wife as primary beneficiary and to his issue as secondary beneficiaries. The proceeds are now payable under the fourth option of the policy, which provides that monthly interest payments shall be made to Mrs. Black with the right in her to withdraw up to $5000 of the proceeds in any calendar year, and that on her death or on Mr. Black's death if she does not survive him, the balance of the proceeds held by the company shall be paid in a lump sum to the secondary beneficiaries on a per stirpes basis. Mr. Black has made no election as to the disposition of the proceeds of the policy if the policy matures before his death.   20,000

(5) *New England Mutual Life Insurance Company Policy No. 3,852,781*

Note: This policy was acquired in 1957. It is a 15-year term policy with the right in the insured to convert it to ordinary life at any time before the expiration of the 15-year period. The guaranteed rate of interest is $2\frac{1}{2}\%$. The face amount of the policy is $40,000. The proceeds are payable to Mr. Black's executors and administrators.   40,000

(6) *Group insurance*
      Note: The Black Manufacturing Company pro-
vides group insurance for all of its employees.
The amount payable on Mr. Black's death is $10,-
000. The proceeds are payable to Mr. Black's
executors and administrators.   10,000

Special comment: The first three policies listed above
pay double if Mr. Black dies an accidental death before
the age of 65. All dividends on the policies have been
used to reduce premiums. Thus the total face value of
the insurance policies is $100,000 if Mr. Black dies a nat-
ural death.

f. *Black Manufacturing Company Pension Plan*
      Note: The company has a qualified pension plan.
It is a pension trust funded with individual retirement income policies having an insurance feature.
No employee contributions are made to the plan.
      The death benefit in the event that Mr. Black dies
before retirement is $50,000 or the cash value at date
of death, whichever is larger. As of December 31 last
the cash value of the policies on Mr. Black's life was
$37,000. The rights of an employee under the plan
are 100% vested. At present, Mr. Black has named
his estate to receive in one sum any death benefit.
Under the plan, Mr. Black is free to name anyone as
the beneficiary in the event of his death before retirement and may stipulate that payment be made in one
lump sum or in installments. The trustee has made
no election as to the method of payment to Mr. Black
if he lives to retirement. The trustee may elect to
make a lump sum payment to an employee, or may
choose installment payments for a period certain and
thereafter for the balance of the employee's life, or a
joint and survivor annuity arrangement, or installments for a certain period only, or a life annuity with
or without refund. Mr. Black has control over the
selection of the beneficiary of any death benefit payable after his retirement. No figure is set opposite
because it is assumed that a change will be made in
the beneficiary designation with respect to the death
benefit so that the exemption for federal estate tax
purposes provided by 1954 I.R.C. §2039(c) will apply
to the death benefit.[18]

g. *Appointive assets*
      (1) *Under the will of the father of Mr. Black III*

[18] See the discussion at page 356 supra. — ED.

Note: Mr. Black's father (Richard Harry Black II) died in 1939, a resident of Boston, Massachusetts.[19] Under the father's will a trust was established of the residue of his estate. The trustee is the Old Line Trust Company, of Boston, Massachusetts. The terms of the trust direct that the income be paid to the mother of Mr. Black III for her life, and on her death the principal is to be divided into two equal shares. One share is to be held in trust for Mr. Black III for his life, and then it is to pass "to such person or persons as my said son shall appoint by will and in default of appointment to my said son's children." The trust of the other share is identical except that it relates to James, the brother of Mr. Black III. Their mother died in 1953. The property in the share held in trust for Mr. Black III is now valued at $100,000. In view of the fact that the appointive property is not includible in his gross estate unless he exercises the power, the $100,000 figure is not carried in the outer column.[20]

(2) *Under the will of the mother of Mr. Black III*

Note: As mentioned above, Mr. Black's mother died in 1953. She was a resident of Boston, Massachusetts, at the time of her death. Her will made certain specific devises, including the devise to Mr. Black III of the farm in Illinois,[21] which has been previously noted (an examination of her estate tax return reveals that the farm was included in her gross estate at a valuation of $200 an acre), and established trusts of the residue of her estate for the benefit of Mr. Black III and his brother James. The trustee is the Old Line Trust Company, of Boston, Massachusetts. The terms of the trust for the benefit of Mr. Black III direct the trustee to pay the income to him for life and then "to distribute the principal to, or for the benefit of, any one or more of the limited class consisting of my said son's wife, my said son's issue then living or born thereafter, spouses of my said son's issue and charities in such amounts and proportions and for such estates and interests and

[19] It is suggested that the location of the residence of Mr. Black's father not be changed regardless of the place of residence of Mr. Black.

[20] General powers of appointment created on or before October 21, 1942, are considered supra page 693. — Ed.

[21] If the location of the farm is changed to Iowa, the reference at this point should be to Iowa rather than to Illinois.

upon such terms, trust, conditions and limitations
and generally in such manner as my said son shall
by will appoint; and in default of appointment to
my said son's heirs." The terms of the trust for
the benefit of James are identical. The present
value of the property in the trust for Mr. Black
III is $100,000. This figure is not carried in the
outer column because of the restricted nature of
the power of Mr. Black.

h. *Probable inheritance*

   Note: Since both the mother and father of Mr.
   Black are dead, and his brother James is married and
   has three living children and six living grandchildren,
   Mr. Black has no expectations that his estate will be
   further augmented by inheritance.

i. *Annual income*

   Note: Mr. Black is president of the Black Manufacturing Company. His annual salary is $25,000, and
   the annual dividend declared on the stock of the company for the last five years has been $5 a share ($6500
   for Mr. Black). The net income from the trusts under
   the wills of his father and mother amounts annually
   to about $8000. The net income from his securities
   amounts annually to about $10,000. The net income
   from the Illinois[22] farm amounts annually to about
   $7500. Thus his total annual income now is ap-
   proximately $57,000.

j. *Inter vivos gifts*

   Note: Mr. Black has made no inter vivos gifts outside of the interests given his wife in their jointly
   owned property and the $5000 he gave her in 1946.
   He has never filed any gift tax return.

k. *Social security benefits*

   Note: Mr. Black will be entitled to the maximum
   social security benefits.

   Total gross estate $628,000

Special comment: The $628,000 figure is based on the assumption
that Mr. Black dies a natural death, so that the double indemnity
provisions of the life insurance will not apply, and on the assumption that the general power of appointment under the will of his
father is not exercised. Also, it should be noted that if Mr. Black
survives his wife, the entire value of the family residence ($49,000)
will be includible in his gross estate. Furthermore, his gross estate
may increase in value because the stock in the Black Manufacturing

---

22 If the location of the farm is changed to Iowa, the reference at this point
should be to Iowa rather than to Illinois.

Company may be valued for estate tax purposes at a figure higher than the one included in this memorandum, and the gross estate may also be increased in value because the value of the Illinois farm may be greater than the amount stipulated in this memorandum. On the other hand, the 15-year term policy in the amount of $40,000 drops out after 1972 and the $10,000 group policy continues in force only as long as Mr. Black is an employee of the corporation. Thus the gross estate may conceivably be $151,000 greater ($30,000 of additional insurance in the event of accidental death; $21,000 additional value with respect to the family residence if Mr. Black survives his wife; and $100,000 if Mr. Black exercises the power of appointment given him under the will of his father). Or the gross estate may conceivably be $50,000 less if neither the 15-year term policy nor the group policy is in force on his death.

2. *Mr. Black's adjusted gross estate*
   Note: The adjusted gross estate is the gross estate minus the deductions allowed by the Internal Revenue Code for expenses of administration, debts, funeral expenses, etc. We can only estimate the amount of the deductions. For planning purposes the sum of $28,000 seems a reasonable estimate of the deductions, so that the adjusted gross estate is $600,000. .... $600,000

3. *Maximum allowable marital deduction*
   Note: The maximum allowable marital deduction is one half of the adjusted gross estate. Thus the maximum allowable marital deduction is $300,000. .... $300,000

4. *Gifts to wife which qualify for the marital deduction*
   a. *Tangible personal property*
      Note: Mr. Black has decided to give all his tangible personal property to his wife in his will. Thus, even though the will has not been executed as yet, we can include for planning purposes the tangible personal property in the gifts which qualify for the marital deduction. $10,000

   b. *Real estate*
      Note: Mrs. Black will become the outright owner of the family residence if she survives her husband, because the residence is owned by them as tenants by the entirety.[23] Since only $28,000 of the value of the residence is included in the gross estate of Mr. Black, the marital deduction as to this item is limited to that amount. However, Mr. Black has decided to give his wife full control over the summer place in his will, so we can include for planning purposes the

---

[23] The reference at this point should be to a joint tenancy if the jurisdiction where the family residence is located does not recognize a tenancy by the entirety.

summer place in the gifts which qualify for the marital deduction.   38,000

c. *Savings accounts*

    Note: Mrs. Black will become the outright owner of the savings accounts if she survives her husband, because these accounts are payable to the survivor. Since the full amount in these accounts is included in the gross estate of Mr. Black because he furnished all the money in the accounts, the amount of the marital deduction gift is the entire amount in the accounts.   10,000

d. *Government bonds*

    Note: Mrs. Black will become the outright owner of the government bonds if she survives her husband, because these bonds are payable to the survivor. Since the full value of the bonds is included in the gross estate of Mr. Black, the amount of the marital deduction gift is the full value of such bonds.   4,000

    Total present marital deduction gifts $62,000

    Special comment: If the maximum allowable marital deduction is $300,000, additional marital deduction gifts in the amount of $238,000 will be needed in order to use up the maximum allowable marital deduction.

5. *Mr. Black's taxable estate*

  a. *If gross estate is $628,000 and wife survives*

    (1) *Allowable deductions and exemption*

      (a) Deductions for debts, expenses of administration, etc. (estimated) $28,000

      (b) Marital deduction (assuming additional marital deduction gifts are made so that maximum allowable marital deduction is available)   300,000

      (c) Exemption   60,000

        Total deductions and exemption $388,000

    (2) *Taxable estate* (gross estate minus allowable deductions and exemption — $628,000 minus $388,000 .... $240,000

  b. *If gross estate is $649,000 and wife does not survive*

    Note: It is assumed that Mrs. Black's estate plan will be such that there will be no significant augmentation of Mr. Black's gross estate if she predeceases him (she plans to give him her tangible personal property, but this item is disregarded in the subsequent calculations). The full value of the family residence, however, will be included in his gross estate, so that $21,000 is added to the $628,000 figure to make the above figure of $649,000.

(1) *Allowable deductions and exemption*
   (a) Deductions for debts, expenses of administration, etc. (estimated) $28,000

   (b) Exemption 60,000
         Total deductions and exemption $88,000

(2) *Taxable estate* (gross estate minus allowable deductions and exemption — $649,000 minus $88,000 $561,000

6. *Estimated taxes (federal and state)*

   Note: In addition to federal estate taxes, there will be state death taxes. The amount of the state death taxes will increase the total tax bill only to the extent that they exceed the credit for state death taxes allowed by 1954 I.R.C. §2011, quoted infra page 1388.[24]   We must keep in mind, however, that the property in the marital deduction gifts which escapes federal taxation if Mrs. Black survives Mr. Black may not escape state taxation. On the other hand, property such as life insurance proceeds which is subject to federal taxation may escape state taxation. The figures set out below are only preliminary general estimates for planning purposes but they include both federal and state taxes on the assumption that the state death taxes will not exceed by any substantial amount the credit for state death taxes.

   a. If taxable estate is $240,000 (credit for state death taxes, $3600) $62,700

   b. If taxable estate is $561,000 (credit for state death taxes, $14,840) $167,050

Special comment: If Mr. Black makes inter vivos gifts, his gross estate will be reduced by the value of such gifts plus the amount of the gift tax he will be required to pay. It must be kept in mind that the reduction in amount of Mr. Black's gross estate will likewise reduce the maximum allowable estate tax marital deduction.

---

  [24] State inheritance taxes may be assessed by the jurisdiction in which Mr. Black resides, by Illinois (or Iowa), where the farm is located, by the jurisdiction in which the summer place is located, and by the state of incorporation of the Black Manufacturing company. See consideration of this matter in Chapter XVI. — Ed.

B. *Estate of Mildred Marie Black, Wife of Richard Harry Black III*

1. *Mrs. Black's gross estate*
   a. *Tangible personal property*
      Note: Mrs. Black's tangible personal property consists principally of her personal effects such as clothing and jewelry. The figure set opposite is only an estimate, for planning purposes, of the value of the tangible personal property owned by Mrs. Black. .. $5,000

   b. *Real estate*
      Note: The payment by Mrs. Black of $5000 on the purchase price of the family residence (in 1947), which was made from funds given her in the previous year by her husband, does not cause any portion of the value of the family residence to be included in her gross estate. The payment by her of $15,000 in 1960, out of funds received from her father, for the cost of the addition to the house, does cause three sevenths of the value of the house to be includible in her gross estate if she predeceases her husband.[25]   21,000

   c. *Bank accounts*
      Note: No part of the bank accounts mentioned in the memorandum relating to Mr. Black's gross estate will be included in Mrs. Black's gross estate if she predeceases her husband, because she did not put into these accounts any of her own money. She has a savings account of her own, however, in which she now has $4000.   4,000

   d. *Securities*
      Note: No part of the value of the government bonds mentioned in the memorandum relating to Mr. Black's gross estate will be included in Mrs. Black's gross estate if she predeceases her husband, because she did not contribute to the purchase price of these bonds. She does have in her own name, however, securities which have a present value of $30,000.   30,000

   e. *Life insurance*
      John Hancock Mutual Life Insurance Policy No. 3,561,802
      Note: This policy was taken out by Mrs. Black in 1949 on the life of her husband. The guaranteed rate of interest is $2\frac{1}{2}\%$. The face amount of the policy is

---

[25] See page 1164 supra, note 8. Also compare with the attorney's position in regard to the $5000, Estate of Nathalie Koussevitsky, 5 T.C. 650, 659 (1945). — Ed.

$10,000. The proceeds are now payable to Mrs. Black outright as primary beneficiary and to her executors and administrators as secondary beneficiaries. Mrs. Black has paid all the premiums out of her own funds. The dividends on the policy have been used to reduce premiums. The present estate tax value of this policy is estimated for planning purposes at the figure set opposite.   3,000

f. *Probable inheritance*

Note: Mrs. Black's father died in 1948, a resident of New York City,[26] and in his will he made cash bequests to each of his children in the amount of $50,000 and established a trust of the residue of his estate. The trustee is the American Trust Company, of New York City. The trust provides that the net income is to be paid to Mrs. Black's mother for her life and that, on her death the principal is to be paid to "my surviving issue, such issue to take *per stirpes.*" Mrs. Black's mother is now living in New York City and is 79 years years of age. Mrs. Black is the only child of her father now living. A brother of hers died intestate in 1954, a resident of Massachusetts. This brother never married. Another brother died in 1959, a resident of New Jersey. This brother was survived by a wife and two children, all of whom are still living and are residents of New Jersey. The present value of the property in the trust established by the will of Mrs. Black's father is $300,000.

Mrs. Black's mother has some property of her own and Mrs. Black understands that her mother's will provides that all of her property will go outright and in equal shares "to my great-grandchildren."

From the above, it is apparent that Mrs. Black's gross estate may be augmented on the death of her mother, not from property owned outright by her mother but rather from the property which is now being held in trust under her father's will. The amount Mrs. Black will receive from the trust established by her father depends on the construction given to the words in his will providing for the distribution of principal on the death of Mrs. Black's mother. Her father's will provides that on the mother's death the principal is to be paid to "my surviving issue, such issue to take *per stirpes.*" Does the word "surviving" relate to the date of her father's death or to the date of her mother's death? If it relates to the date of her

---

[26] It is suggested that the location of the residence of Mrs. Black's father not be changed, regardless of the place of residence of Mrs. Black.

father's death, then the brother who died intestate in 1954, without ever having married, had a vested interest which passed to his heir, who was his mother, and Mrs. Black is entitled only to one third of the trust property. If, however, "surviving" relates to the date of her mother's death, the trust property will be divided into two shares, one for Mrs. Black and one for the children of the brother who died in 1959. Of course, if no issue of the brother who died in 1959 survives Mrs. Black's mother, Mrs. Black will be entitled to all of the trust property if she survives her mother. For planning purposes we shall assume that the word "surviving" relates to the date of her mother's death and that issue of her brother who died in 1959 will survive her mother, so that Mrs. Black will receive one half of the trust property on the death of her mother if she survives her mother. 150,000

g. *Inter vivos gifts*

> *Note:* Mrs. Black has made no inter vivos gifts outside of the interest given to her husband in their family residence. She has never filed any gift tax return.
>
> Total gross estate if Mrs. Black survives her mother $213,000
>
> Total gross estate if Mrs. Black predeceases her mother $63,000

Special comment: If Mrs. Black survives her husband, her gross estate will be augmented by the amount she receives from him in a form that will cause the value of such property to be added to her gross estate. If her husband gives her property in such a form that it is equal in value to the estimated maximum marital deduction as developed in the memorandum relating to his estate, Mrs. Black's gross estate will be augmented by $300,000 if she survives her husband. Also her gross estate will be augmented by the amount she will take under the gift in default of appointment in the will of Mr. Black's mother if Mr. Black does not exercise his power to appoint (since Mr. Black will undoubtedly exercise this power, any augmentation of Mrs. Black's gross estate from this source is hereinafter ignored). Furthermore, it must be kept in mind that if Mrs. Black survives her husband, she will collect the face amount of the policy on his life which she owns, and thus her gross estate will be increased by $7000 from this source.

If Mr. Black reduces his gross estate by inter vivos gifts, presumably to persons other than his wife, the maximum allowable marital deduction with respect to his estate will decrease, and consequently the augmentation of his wife's gross estate, if she survives him, will decrease, provided he limits the gifts to his wife that augment her gross estate to the maximum marital deduction.

2. *Mrs. Black's adjusted gross estate*

    Note: This calculation is relevant only if Mrs. Black predeceases her husband but survives her mother, and thus it will be made with relation to her possible gross estate on this assumption.

    a. *If Mrs. Black survives her mother, so that her gross estate is $213,000*

        Note: The adjusted gross estate is the gross estate minus the deductions allowed by the Internal Revenue Code for expenses of administration, debts, funeral expenses, etc. We can only estimate the amount of the deductions. For planning purposes the sum of $13,000 seems a reasonable estimate of the deductions, so that the adjusted gross estate is $200,000. .... $200,000

3. *Maximum allowable marital deduction*
    a. *If adjusted gross estate is $200,000* $100,000

4. *Gifts to husband which qualify for the marital deduction*
    Note: Mrs. Black does not plan to augment her husband's gross estate by her will except to the extent of the value of her tangible personal property. The gift of the tangible personal property qualifies for the marital deduction ($5000).

    a. *Real estate* (value of family residence to extent that it is included in Mrs. Black's gross estate). $21,000

5. *Mrs. Black's taxable estate*
    a. *If gross estate is $63,000*
        Note: Obviously her taxable estate will be zero because the $60,000 exemption and the expenses of administration, etc., total more than the gross estate. Even in this situation, however, there may be some state death taxes.

    b. *If gross estate is $213,000*
      (1) *Allowable deductions and exemption*
        (a) Deductions for debts, expenses of administration, etc. (estimated) $13,000

        (b) Marital deduction 26,000

        (c) Exemption 60,000
              Total deductions and exemption $99,000

      (2) *Taxable estate* (gross estate minus deductions and exemption — $213,000 minus $99,000) $114,000

    c. *If gross estate is $370,000* (Mrs. Black survives her husband, but not her mother, and he makes gifts to her equaling the maximum marital deduction. The above figure takes into account the $7000 augmentation of her gross estate resulting from the collection of the face amount of the life insurance policy which she owns on the life of her husband.)

(1) *Allowable deductions and exemption*

    (a) Deductions for debts, expenses of administration, etc. (estimated) $25,000

    (b) Exemption 60,000

              Total deductions and exemption $85,000

(2) *Taxable estate* (gross estate minus deductions and exemption — $370,000 minus $85,000) $285,000

d. *If gross estate is $520,000* (Mrs. Black survives her husband and her mother.)

(1) *Allowable deductions and exemption*

    (a) Deductions for debts, expenses of administration, etc. (estimated) $30,000

    (b) Exemption 60,000

              Total deductions and exemption $90,000

(2) *Taxable estate* (gross estate minus deductions and exemption — $520,000 minus $90,000) $430,000

6. *Estimated taxes*

Note: In addition to federal estate taxes, there will be state death taxes. The amount of the state death taxes will increase the total tax bill only to the extent that they exceed the credit for state death taxes. We must keep in mind that the marital deduction gifts to Mrs. Black may be in a form that will not be subject to state death taxes on her death. The figures set out below are only preliminary general estimates for planning purposes, but they include both federal and state taxes on the assumption that the state death taxes will not exceed by any substantial amount the credit for state death taxes.

a. If taxable estate is $114,000 (credit for state death taxes, $784) $24,900

b. If taxable estate is $285,000 (credit for state death taxes, $5040) $76,900

c. If taxable estate is $430,000 (credit for state death taxes, $9680) $123,300

Special comment: The above analysis indicates that the range of death taxes with respect to Mrs. Black's estate is from zero (death taxes will actually never be zero because there will be some state death taxes, even though there are no federal death taxes) to approximately $124,-000. The top figure will decrease if Mr. Black makes inter vivos gifts that decrease his gross estate and do not augment his wife's gross estate, provided we assume that the estate tax marital deduction gifts to Mrs. Black do not exceed the maximum allowable marital deduction.

C. *Family Picture*

1. *Richard Harry Black III* is 55 years of age. He is in good health. His father died of a heart attack at the age of 65. His mother died of pneumonia at the age of 73.

2. *Mildred Marie Black* (wife of Richard Harry Black III) is 53 years of age. She is in good health. Her father died at the age of 72 as the result of an accident. As has already been mentioned, her mother is still living and is 79 years old.

3. *Richard Harry Black IV* (son of Richard Harry Black III and Mildred Marie Black) is 30 years of age. His home is in ...., ...,[27] and he is a junior executive in the Black Manufacturing Company. His annual salary at present is $10,000. He carries about $50,000 worth of life insurance. His owned property is nominal. Richard Harry Black III does not think that his son has made any will, and he does not know how the life insurance proceeds are payable.

4. *Dorothy Ann Black* (wife of Richard Harry Black IV) is 28 years of age. Dorothy and Richard were married ten years ago, just before Richard went into the Army, and the marriage has turned out very well. Dorothy's parents are both living and are fairly wealthy, so that she should inherit some property in the future. She owns a small amount of income-producing property now. She and Richard have two children, and though no child has been born to them during the last three years, certainly more children are a possibility. Richard Harry Black III does not know whether Dorothy has made any will but he does not think it likely that she has.

5. *James Harry Black* (son of Dorothy and Richard IV) is 5 years of age.

6. *Dorothy Marie Black* (daughter of Dorothy and Richard IV) is 3 years of age.

7. *Margaret Black Logan* (daughter of Richard Harry Black III and Mildred Marie Black) is 28 years of age. She lives with her husband (Robert Gerald Logan) in Philadelphia, Pennsylvania. Margaret's present husband is her second husband. Ten years ago she married a man named Adam Rudolph. This marriage was the result of a quick romance and her parents were opposed to it because, for some reason or other, they never liked Rudolph. Margaret obtained a Reno divorce five years ago and immediately married Logan. Rudolph had no money, so there was no property settlement of any kind at the time of the divorce. Rudolph agreed, however, to give Margaret the custody of their one child. Mar-

[27] Insert the location of the residence of Mr. Black's son. He should reside in the same locality as his father.

garet's second marriage seems to be a very happy one, and her parents are very fond of Logan.

8. *Robert Gerald Logan* (Margaret's husband) is 35 years of age. He is a doctor and has a reasonably good practice. Richard Harry Black III does not know what Logan's income is but he does know that Logan has no expectation of any significant inheritance from his parents. He assumes Logan has some life insurance but does not know whether he has made a will.

9. *Adam Rudolph, Jr.* (son of Margaret and Adam Rudolph) is 9 years of age.

10. *Millicent Logan* (daughter of Margaret and Robert Gerald Logan) is 2 years of age.

11. *Richard Harry Logan* (son of Margaret and Robert Gerald Logan) is 6 months old.

12. *Other relatives.* Richard Harry Black III has one brother, James Robert Black, who is 53 years of age. James is married and has three children and six grandchildren. Mildred Marie Black's mother is still living. Her two brothers are deceased but the two children of one brother are now living. There are no other relatives that are close to the family.

13. *Servants.* No employees have been with the family for any substantial period except a gardener named Joseph Ricardo, who has been working for them on a part-time basis for seventeen years.

14. *Charitable interests.* Richard Harry Black III and his wife are interested in many charities.

D.   Matters Discussed with Mr. and Mrs. Black

1. *Liquid funds needed on death of Mr. Black*

Liquid funds should be readily available on Mr. Black's death to meet federal and state death taxes, expenses of administration of his estate, debts and funeral expenses. On the basis of the memorandum relating to Mr. Black's estate, it is estimated that the maximum amount of liquid funds which may be required is $195,050 ($167,050 plus $28,000). The actual amount required may be even greater than this maximum because the items in his gross estate may be valued at higher figures than the ones used in the memorandum, and because the expenses of administration may be greater than estimated. On the other hand, the actual amount required may be much less than the maximum if Mr. Black's gross estate is decreased by inter vivos gifts and if his taxable estate is decreased because his wife survives him and the marital deduction becomes available. Even if inter vivos gifts are made, the maximum may not be significantly reduced if Mr. Black should die within three years, because such inter vivos gifts may be deemed gifts in contemplation of death. Thus arrangements now made with respect to Mr. Black's estate should be such that liquid funds, at least in the amount of the estimated maximum, remain available to meet obligations arising on his death.

The following assets in his estate should not be regarded as liquid funds available to meet death obligations because they are assets which Mr. Black does not want sold:

   a. The tangible personal property (worth $10,000)
   b. The common stock of the Black Manufacturing Company (worth $130,000)
   c. The Illinois farm (worth $80,000)

The following assets in his estate should be regarded as liquid funds available to meet death obligations only if he survives Mrs. Black, because otherwise they go outright to Mrs. Black and should pass to her free and clear of his death obligations:

   a. The family residence (worth $49,000)
   b. The joint bank accounts (worth $10,000)
   c. The government bonds (worth $4000)
   d. The summer residence (worth $10,000)

The following assets in his estate should be regarded as liquid funds available to meet death obligations whether or not he survives Mrs. Black:

   a. Life insurance proceeds ($100,000)
   b. Securities now held by the Jones and Jones investment house (worth $250,000)
   c. The death benefit under the Black Manufacturing Company Pension Plan ($50,000)
   d. The amount in Mr. Black's checking account ($6000)

The presently available liquid assets are adequate to meet the foreseeable death obligations of Mr. Black's estate. If he makes inter vivos arrangements that decrease his gross estate, or if Mrs. Black survives him, so that the marital deduction is available, such liquid assets are substantially in excess of what may be needed.

With regard to Mrs. Black, she has ample liquid assets to meet obligations arising as a result of her death so far as any property she may own outright at her death is concerned. If she survives her husband, however, and if her gross estate is substantially augmented by marital deduction gifts from him in the form of power of appointment arrangements, it may be necessary to throw back on such gifts some part of her death obligations. If that is necessary, care must be taken not to produce a situation that will force a sale outside of the family of any of the common stock of the Black Manufacturing Company or of the Illinois farm.

2. *The common stock of the Black Manufacturing Company*

Mr. Black stated that he and his brother James are both interested in so arranging their affairs that the control of the Black Manufacturing Company will not get into the hands of strangers to the family. It is contemplated that the arrangement worked out with respect to Mr. Black's holdings in the Black Manufacturing Company will also be adopted by his brother James. We discussed the feasibility of an agreement whereby the corporation, or the surviving brother, would buy the common stock of the Black Manufacturing Company owned by the first of the two brothers to die, but Mr. Black did not think that such an agreement was appropriate in this case.[28] We also discussed the possibility of the corporation redeeming some of the common stock of the Black Manufacturing Company to pay death taxes assessed against his or his brother's estate, but Mr. Black thinks that it is unlikely that it will be desirable from the family standpoint for any such redemption to take place.[29]

We considered the possibility of a recapitalization of the corporation involving a reduction of the par value of the presently existing common from $10 par value to, say, $.50 par value, an increase of the authorized common from 2500 shares to 50,000 shares — such increase to be accomplished by creating 47,500 shares of nonvoting common of $.50 par value — and a distribution of a stock dividend of the nonvoting common to holders of the voting common on a pro rata basis. Such recapitalization would give more flexibility in the disposition of the common stock of the corporation because the voting control could be arranged along definite lines without tying up such a large segment of the wealth of Mr.

---

[28] Buy-and-sell agreements are considered supra page 936. — ED.

[29] See the discussion of 1954 I.R.C. §303 at page 980 supra. See also the comments on §6166 at page 996 supra. In limited situations §6166 permits an extension of the time for the payment of the estate tax attributable to investments in closely held business enterprises. — ED.

Black along the same lines.[30] Mr. Black, however, rejected this approach to the problem after careful consideration.

It was finally agreed to work out the disposition of the common stock of the Black Manufacturing Company through a trust with a corporate trustee and some member or members of the Black family as co-trustee or co-trustees and with very specific provisions regarding the sale of the common stock in the trust, in the event a sale becomes necessary, these provisions going as far as possible in the direction of assuring that purchasers of the stock will be members of the Black family. It was pointed out to Mr. Black that as a result of placing the stock in a trust, no election could be made under 1954 I.R.C. §§1371-1377 to change the taxable status of the corporation.

3. The Illinois farm[31]

Mr. Black wants his family to enjoy the financial benefits from the farm as long as possible, because he thinks that farm land is a secure investment. He does not think that any member of his family other than his wife is sufficiently familiar with or interested in farming problems to manage the farm. Thus he wants the farm placed in a trust, after the death of his wife, to be managed by a local corporate trustee for the benefit of his family.

4. Other income-producing property

Mr. Black's other income-producing property consists, in the main, of his $250,000 in securities now being managed by the Jones and Jones investment house. He is convinced that some part of his property should be given away during his lifetime and the necessary gift tax paid, provided that adequate liquid funds will remain to take care of obligations which may arise at the time of his death, so that it will be unnecessary to sell any of the common stock of the Black Manufacturing Company.

---

30 See Commissioner v. Sunnen, 333 U.S. 591 (1948). See also Overton v. Commissioner, 162 F.2d 155 (2d Cir. 1947); Anderson v. Commissioner, 164 F.2d 870 (7th Cir. 1947). Compare Bishop v. Shaughnessy, 95 F. Supp. 759 (N.D.N.Y. 1951). Notice also §544(a)(2) of the 1954 Code, which points out that, for purposes of determining whether a corporation is a personal holding company, in so far as such a determination is based on stock ownership, "An individual shall be considered as owning the stock owned, directly or indirectly, by or for his family or by or for his partner. For purposes of this paragraph, the family of an individual includes only his brothers and sisters (whether by the whole or half blood), spouse, ancestors, and lineal descendants."

Revenue Ruling 57-132, 1957-1 C.B. 115, considered a plan of reorganization which resulted in the issuance of voting common stock and nonvoting common stock, where the nonvoting common was redeemable at the discretion of the corporation at a price equal to 110 percent of its book value. The ruling held that the nonvoting common constituted §306 stock within the meaning of §306(c)(1)(B), since such stock was redeemable and, therefore, was not common stock for the purposes of that subsection. — ED.

31 If the location of the farm is changed to Iowa, the reference at this point should be to Iowa rather than to Illinois.

5. *Appointive assets*

I explained to Mr. Black that if he exercises the general power to appoint by will given him under the will of his father, the value of the appointive assets will be included in his gross estate; whereas if he does not exercise such power, the value of the appointive assets will not be included in his gross estate. I also pointed out to him that the gift in default of appointment outright to his "children" means that one half of the appointive assets will go to each of his children and that if one of them predeceases him that child's one half will pass in accordance with his or her will, because each child now has a vested interest in one half of the appointive assets, subject only to divestiture by an exercise of Mr. Black's power to appoint by will. Mr. Black decided that he will not exercise his general power.

I explained to Mr. Black that he can exercise the special power to appoint by will given him under the will of his mother without thereby increasing his gross estate for federal estate tax purposes. I pointed out that if he fails to exercise the power, the appointive assets will go outright to his wife, son and daughter, each taking one third if all three survive him, because they will be his heirs and the gift in default of appointment is to his heirs. I advised him to exercise the power.

6. *Life insurance*

I suggested that the proceeds of the New York Life policy ($10,000), of the Metropolitan Life Insurance policy ($10,000), of the Equitable Life policy ($10,000) and of the John Hancock policy ($20,000) be settled with Mrs. Black as the primary beneficiary under the option which provides for monthly payments for 10 years certain and thereafter during the life of Mrs. Black. Under the settlement arrangement Mrs. Black should be given a power to dispose of the commuted value of the unpaid installments in any manner so that the settlement arrangement with respect to these policies will qualify for the marital deduction. In the absence of any other direction by Mrs. Black, the commuted value of the unpaid installments should be made payable in a lump sum to the insurance trust hereinafter referred to. I pointed out that under this arrangement we take advantage of the $1000 annual interest exclusion applicable to installment payments when the beneficiary is the spouse of the insured. Furthermore, the amount that will be included in the wife's gross estate on her death is annually diminished by the installment payments, assuming that she spends or otherwise disposes of the full amount of each installment that she receives. I recommended that the proceeds of the New England Mutual term policy ($40,000) and the group insurance ($10,000) be made payable to an insurance trust and that the terms of the insurance trust permit the trustee to pay death obligations of Mr. Black, or to buy assets in his estate, or to make loans to his executor. In this way, the $50,000 of insurance may be made available to meet death obligations but at the same time it will not go through Mr. Black's probate estate and thus will not be subject to state inheritance taxes and probate expenses.

I also discussed with Mr. Black the tax consequences under present law if he takes in a lump sum the proceeds of the John Hancock endowment policy, if the policy matures before his death, as compared with the result if he adopts one of the installment options. No decision was made at this time as to this matter.

7. *Death benefit under the Black Manufacturing Company Pension Plan*

The death benefit under the pension plan is now payable to Mr. Black's estate. If it continues to be payable to his estate, the entire amount will be subject to federal estate taxes; whereas if it is payable otherwise than to his estate, §2039(c) of the 1954 Code will eliminate the entire amount from his estate for estate tax purposes. Consequently, the death benefit should be made payable in a lump sum to the insurance trust mentioned above. In this way, the death benefit will be available to satisfy the needs of the estate for liquid funds but at the same time full advantage will be taken of §2039. I pointed out that since the death benefit will not be includible in gross estate, no part of it should be available to satisfy any gift to his wife which is to qualify for the marital deduction. We also discussed the methods of payment available to Mr. Black under the pension plan on his retirement. No decision was made at this time as to which method of payment should be requested.

8. *Trust of present interest for minor grandchildren*

I explained to Mr. Black the $3000 annual gift tax exclusion as to gifts of present interests. I described to him the type of trust which can be established under §2503(c) for the benefit of a minor and which is deemed to contain only a present interest so far as the gift tax is concerned.

9. *Revocable inter vivos trust*

I explained to Mr. Black the advantages of establishing a revocable inter vivos trust. I pointed out that the insurance trust mentioned above can be combined with the revocable inter vivos trust.

10. *Temporary allocation of income*

Short-term trusts and their use in making a temporary allocation of income to other member of the family were discussed. In view of the fact that Mr. Black plans to retire at 65 or 66, I pointed out that he could augment the present income of his two children now while his earning capacity is at its height and, at about the time his earned income would cease, get back the property that would be used to increase the income of his children.

E. Conclusions

1. *Inter vivos gifts*

   a. All the common stock of the Black Manufacturing Company is to to be placed in an irrevocable inter vivos trust with Mr. Black, his son and a corporation as co-trustees. The powers given to the trustees are to be restricted to the corporate trustee to whatever extent is necessary to prevent the income of the trust property from being taxable to Mr. Black,[32] and to prevent the value of the trust property from being includible in his gross estate for federal estate tax purposes,[33] and to prevent Mr. Black's son from being treated as the owner of the trust property for income or gift or estate tax purposes.[34] This decision was made with full knowledge of the fact that the securities placed in the trust would not get a new basis, except to the extent the basis is improved as a result of a gift tax which is paid in connection with the transfer, and that §303 (redemption of stock to pay death obligations) would not be available after the establishment of the trust. Mr. and Mrs. Black are to have no present or future beneficial interest under the trust. The gift tax payable on this gift (taking into account prior gifts made by Mr. and Mrs. Black to each other) is approximately $7000 if the valuation of the common stock at $100 a share stands up and if Mrs. Black consents to have one half of the gift charged to her for gift tax purposes under §2513.

   b. A charitable trust is to be established with Mr. and Mrs. Black and their son as trustees, and securities worth approximately $50,000 are to be placed in this trust. The securities chosen are to be ones with a low basis.

   c. A present interest trust is to be established for each grandchild of Mr. Black in order that he and his children may make gifts to the respective trusts for the purpose of taking advantage of the $3000 annual gift tax exclusion.

   d. A 10-year trust is to be established with Mr. Black as trustee, and securities worth $50,000 are to be placed in this trust. The net income is to be paid in equal shares to Mr. Black's two children. In view of the fact that the major interest of each child under the trust will be a present interest, so that the annual exclusion is available as to the value of the 10-year interest in each child, and in view of the fact that Mrs. Black will consent

---

[32] See the discussion at page 176 supra. — ED.

[33] In regard to the estate tax danger if the settlor is included as a trustee of an irrevocable inter vivos trust, see comments at page 193 supra and particularly those concerning State Street Trust Co. v. United States at page 195 supra, note 96. — ED.

[34] For a discussion of the circumstances under which the donee of a power will be treated as the owner of the appointive assets for tax purposes, see pages 689-764 supra. — ED.

to have one half of the gift to each child charged to her under §2513, the gift tax payable with respect to the short-term trust will be nominal in amount.

2. *Revocable inter vivos trust*

After the dispositions described above have been made, the securities and cash remaining are to be placed in a revocable inter vivos trust with Mr. Black, his son and me as co-trustees. The life insurance proceeds (except to the extent that the proceeds of certain policies are to be paid to Mrs. Black under the option calling for payments to her for 10 years certain and thereafter for her life) and the death benefit under the pension plan are to be made payable to this trust. The terms of the trust will qualify in part at least for the marital deduction at the time of Mr. Black's death. The trust will also contain appropriate provisions regarding the use of trust funds to pay death taxes and other death obligations when he dies.

3. *Will of Mr. Black*

a. It will dispose of the Illinois farm[35] in such a way as to qualify for the marital deduction.

b. It will exercise his power under the will of his mother.

c. It will pour the residue over to the revocable inter vivos trust.

4. *Will of Mrs. Black*

a. It will provide for the payment of premiums on the insurance policy on the life of her husband in the event that she predeceases him and will make certain that the incidents of ownership of the policy do not pass to her husband.

b. It will provide for payment of taxes on property disposed of by her will and on any real property included in her gross estate, which is not disposed of by her will.

c. It will create a trust of the residue.

5. *Executors and trustees under wills*

a. Mr. Black's son and I are to be co-executors of his will.

b. The Illinois Trust Company of Bloomington, Illinois, is to be trustee of the Illinois farm.

c. The trustee designated in the will of Mr. Black's mother is to continue as trustee to the extent that any trust is created by Mr. Black's exercise of his special power of appointment.

d. Mrs. Black's son and I are to be co-executors under her will and co-trustees of any trust under her will.

6. *Summary of effect of conclusions*

a. Assuming that Mr. Black lives more than three years, so that the inter vivos gifts cannot be attacked as gifts in contemplation of death, his gross estate will be permanently reduced by $187,000

---

[35] If the location of the farm is changed to Iowa, the reference at this point should be to Iowa rather than to Illinois.

($130,000 — the value of the stock in the Black Manufacturing Company; $50,000 — the amount placed in the charitable foundation [Is the attorney correct in excluding the $50,000 from the gross estate? If he is not, the marital deduction will be larger than he has estimated.[36] — ED.]; and $7000 in gift taxes). During the 10-year period the short-term trust is in force, his gross estate will be temporarily reduced in amount by the value of the outstanding short-term interest. His annual income will be reduced by about $11,000 but about $2000 of this reduction will come back to him at the end of ten years. His maximum estimated tax bill of $167,050 will be reduced to $105,380. If Mrs. Black survives Mr. Black, so that the maximum marital deduction is available, the estimated tax will be reduced from $62,700 to $34,650 (if the $50,000 placed in the charitable foundation is included in Mr. Black's gross estate, thereby increasing the maximum marital deduction, the estimated tax is reduced to $27,150).

b. Mrs. Black's maximum gross estate (if she survives both her husband and her mother) will be reduced from $520,000 to $426,500, assuming that the gifts from Mr. Black to Mrs. Black on his death do not exceed the maximum allowable marital deduction (if the $50,000 placed in the charitable foundation is included in Mr. Black's gross estate, thereby increasing the maximum marital reduction, the reduction will be from $520,000 to $451,500). Consequently, the maximum estimated tax on her estate will be reduced from $123,300 to $94,500.

[36] See the discussion at page 896 supra. — ED.

F.   *Black Family Trusts*

I, RICHARD HARRY BLACK III, of ....,
....[37] (hereinafter called the "settlor"), hereby
transfer in ...., ...[38]
thirteen hundred (1300) shares of the common stock of the Black
Manufacturing Company (represented by Certificates No. 1 through
No. 13) to RICHARD HARRY BLACK III,[39] RICHARD HARRY
BLACK IV,[40] and ....,
of ...., ...[41] (hereinafter
called the "trustees"); the trusts under this instrument cannot be al-
tered, amended, revoked or terminated by the settlor and he retains no
beneficial interest, vested or contingent, hereunder; this instrument
creates what may be called "THE BLACK FAMILY TRUSTS"; and
at the request of the settlor, the trustees agree to hold the said common stock and all additions thereto, in trust, as follows:

FIRST: The settlor requests the trustees, although no duty is imposed on them in this regard, to retain as an investment of the trusts
created by this instrument the common stock or other securities of the
Black Manufacturing Company, and the common stock or other securities of any concern which shall succeed to the whole or a substantial
part of the assets or business of the Black Manufacturing Company,
placed in the trusts hereunder, even though such an amount of securities of one company may not be considered suitable as an investment
for trustees.   Furthermore, if at any time there are trust funds to be
invested, the settlor requests the trustees, although no duty is imposed
on them in this regard, to purchase, if available, and retain as an investment of the trusts created hereunder the common stock or other
securities of the Black Manufacturing Company and the common stock
or other securities of any concern which shall succeed to the whole or
a substantial part of the assets or business of the Black Manufacturing
Company.

In the event the trustees decide to make purchases as mentioned in
the preceding paragraph, such purchases may be made from any source,
including the settlor, the settlor's wife, the settlor's son, the settlor's
daughter, any issue of the settlor's son, any issue of the settlor's daughter, the settlor's brother, the wife of the settlor's brother, any issue of
the settlor's brother, or the trustees of any trust established by the
settlor or by the settlor's wife or by any issue of the settlor or by the

(1)

---

[37] Insert the city and state where Mr. Black resides.

[38] Insert the city and state where the transfer is made.

[39] In regard to the inclusion of the settlor as one of the trustees, see notes 32 and
33 supra. — ED.

[40] Richard Harry Black IV is also a beneficiary under the trust, and with respect
to the tax problems when a beneficiary is also a trustee, see note 34 supra. — ED.

[41] Insert the name and location of the corporate fiduciary.

settlor's brother or by the wife of the settlor's brother or by any issue of the settlor's brother. In each case, however, the decision of the corporate trustee as to the price which should be paid for such acquisitions shall be conclusive.

In the event that the trustees decide to sell any of the common stock or other securities of the Black Manufacturing Company, or the common stock or other securities of any concern which shall succeed to the whole or a substantial part of the assets or business of the Black Manufacturing Company, such sale shall be made at a price deemed adequate by the corporate trustee and such sale shall be made to one or more of the following if one or more of the following is ready and willing to purchase at such price, and otherwise to the general public at such price: the settlor, the settlor's wife, the settlor's son, the settlor's daughter, any issue of the settlor's son, any issue of the settlor's daughter, the settlor's brother, the wife of the settlor's brother, any issue of the settlor's brother, or the trustees of any trust established by the settlor or by the settlor's wife or by any issue of the settlor or by the settlor's brother or by the wife of the settlor's brother or by any issue of the settlor's brother.[42]

In the event that the corporate trustee exercises its power to distribute corpus to the beneficiary of any trust hereunder, the settlor requests the corporate trustee, although no duty is imposed on it in this regard, to avoid a distribution in kind of the common stock or other securities of the Black Manufacturing Company, or the common stock or other securities of any concern which shall succeed to the whole or a substantial part of the assets or business of the Black Manufacturing Company, whenever in the opinion of the corporate trustee such distribution in kind will result in an undesirable dispersion of the control of the corporation.

On the termination of any trust hereunder, the settlor requests the trustees, although no duty is imposed on them in this regard, to avoid a distribution in kind of the common stock or other securities of the Black Manufacturing Company, or the common stock or other securities of any concern which shall succeed to the whole or a substantial part of the assets or business of the Black Manufacturing Company, whenever in the opinion of the trustees such distribution in kind will result in an undesirable dispersion of the control of the corporation.

Any individual trustee hereunder or any officer of the corporate trustee hereunder (as well as any beneficiary hereunder) may serve as an officer of the Black Manufacturing Company or of any concern which shall succeed to the whole or a substantial part of the assets or business of the Black Manufacturing Company.

Any power or discretion given to the trustees under this Article FIRST or under any other Article in this instrument shall be exer-

(2)

---

[42] If the sale results in a loss, deduction for the loss will be disallowed if §267 of the 1954 Code is applicable. The operation of this section must be kept in mind whenever stock in a closely held corporation is sold or bought by a trust. — ED.

cisable only by the trustee or trustees other than the settlor whenever such restriction is necessary in order to prevent the income of the trust, in whole or in part, from being attributable to the settlor for federal income tax purposes, or to prevent the value of the trust property, in whole or in part, from being includible in the settlor's gross estate for federal estate tax purposes, or to prevent the settlor from being deemed to have made a gift, in whole or in part, for federal gift tax purposes when such power is exercised.

SECOND: The property originally placed in trust hereunder shall be divided into two equal shares. One equal share shall be known as "Richard IV's share" and the other equal share shall be known as "Margaret's share." Property subsequently transferred to the trustees to be held in trust hereunder shall be allocated among the various trusts in accordance with the directions given in the instrument of transfer.

THIRD: Richard IV's share shall be divided into as many equal shares as there are children of the settlor's son, Richard Harry Black IV, living on the date this instrument is executed. One of such equal shares shall be allocated to each living child of the settlor's said son and each share so allocated shall be held in a separate trust in accordance with the provisions hereinafter set forth in this Article THIRD. If a new child is born to the settlor's said son or if a new child is finally adopted by the settlor's said son, a new separate trust shall be established for him or her on the date of the birth or final adoption of such child. The trustees shall transfer to the new separate trust a portion of the trust property of each of the then existing separate trusts under this Article THIRD, such portion to be ascertained as though the following steps were taken:

> The trust property in all the then existing separate trusts, including undistributed income, is mingled in one trust fund; and

> Each contributing separate trust is allocated an undivided interest in the mingled fund that is equal to such trust's proportionate contribution to the mingled fund (the corporate trustee's determination as to each trust's undivided interest is to be conclusive on all concerned); and

> The mingled fund is divided into as many equal shares as there are trusts under this Article THIRD, including the new separate trust; and

> One such equal share is transferred from the mingled fund to the new separate trust; and

> The balance of the mingled fund is distributed to the contributing trusts, each receiving the portion of such balance that corresponds to its undivided interest in the original mingled fund.[43]

The corporate trustee's determination that the new separate trust has

(3)

---

[43] When separate trusts are established for the primary benefit of each member of a described group while it is still possible for more members to be born, usually some mechanism should be provided which will produce a new trust for each after-

received what it is entitled to receive and that the directions given above have been complied with shall be conclusive on all concerned. Each separate trust for a child of the settlor's said son shall be designated and known by the name of the child to whom the equal share is allocated, followed by the word "Trust," e.g., "THE JAMES HARRY BLACK TRUST." Each separate trust for a child of the settlor's said son is as follows:

1. During the lifetime of the settlor's said son, the net income in whole or in part may be paid to, or applied for the benefit of, any one or more of the group consisting of the settlor's said son, the wife of the settlor's said son, the child of the settlor's said son to whom the share held in this separate trust is allocated, the spouse of such child and the issue living from time to time of such child, in such amount or amounts as the corporate trustee in its uncontrolled discretion may determine; any net income in any year which is not paid to, or applied for the benefit of, any one or more of such group shall be added to the principal at the end of each year; and, in addition, the principal in whole or in part may be paid to, or applied for the benefit of, any one or more of such group, from time to time, in such amount or amounts and for such estates and interests and outright or upon such terms, trusts, conditions and limitations, provided that no beneficial interest is created in anyone outside of such group by any such payment, as the corporate trustee in its uncontrolled discretion may determine;[44] and furthermore, in addition to such payments as may be made under the preceding provisions, from and after the death of the settlor, the principal (other than life insurance on the life of the settlor's said son) in whole or in part shall be paid to, or applied for the benefit of, any one or more of such group other than the settlor's said son, from time to time, in such amount or amounts and for such estates and interests and outright or upon such terms, trusts, conditions and limitations,

(4)

---

born member. The procedure described in the trust under consideration will produce a trust for the new member but it will not necessarily result in complete equality of treatment for all members of the group. If, for example, the principal of one of the original trusts has been depleted at the time the new trust is to be established, the share which will go into the new trust will not be as large as it would have been if it had been determined prior to any diversion of principal.

The income tax consequences in the year a new trust peels off must be explored. Under the peel-off arrangement spelled out in the instrument under consideration, it is submitted that the distribution out of the mingled fund to the new separate trust should carry to the new trust only its proportionate share of the distributable net income of the year of distribution. The new trust should also, on some basis or other, take over a proportionate share of the undistributed net income of the old trusts for purposes of the throwback rule and the old trusts should have their undistributed net income correspondingly reduced in amount. H.R. 9662, which failed of passage in the Eighty-sixth Congress, would describe in the Internal Revenue Code the income tax result outlined above so far as peel-off trusts are concerned. See comments at page 750 supra, note 130. — ED.

44 See page 763 supra, note 154. — ED.

provided that no beneficial interest is created in anyone outside of such group (excluding from such group the settlor's said son), as the settlor's said son shall specify in an instrument or instruments in writing delivered to the trustees in his lifetime (nothing contained herein shall be construed as authorizing the settlor's said son to discharge his legal obligations by any directions he may give as to the payment of the principal); payments of income and principal to the issue of such child of the settlor's said son pursuant to the above provisions shall not be taken into account in any later division of the principal and undistributed income into shares for the benefit of such issue unless the settlor's said son or such child of the settlor's said son directs otherwise in the exercise of any power of appointment hereinafter given to the settlor's said son or to such child of the settlor's said son.[45]

2. On the death of the settlor's said son, the then remaining principal and undistributed income shall be paid to, or held for the benefit of, such one or more of the group consisting of the widow of the settlor's said son, the issue of the settlor living at the death of the settlor's said son or born thereafter, and spouses of the settlor's issue, including spouses of issue who predecease the settlor's said son as well as spouses of issue who are born after the death of the settlor's said son, as the settlor's said son shall appoint by a will, executed after the date of this instrument, which refers specifically to this power. The exercise of this power by the settlor's said son, however, shall not apply to the proceeds of any life insurance on the life of the settlor's said son payable to this trust. Subject to the above restrictions, in the exercise of this power of appointment the settlor's said son may appoint outright or in trust; he may select the trustee or trustees if he appoints in trust; he may create new powers of appointment in a trustee or trustees or in any other appointee; he may, if he appoints in trust, establish such administrative powers for the trustee as he deems appropriate; he may create life interests or other limited interests in an appointee with future interests in favor of other appointees; he may impose lawful conditions on an appointment; he may appoint by his will different types of interests to selected appointees; he may impose lawful spendthrift provisions; and generally he may appoint by his will in any manner, provided always, however, that no appointment shall benefit directly or indirectly persons other than members of the restricted group who are the objects of this power, and that nothing herein shall

(5)

---

[45] If the corporate trustee is given discretion to pay income and principal to the spouses of the issue of such child, then the provision to which this note is appended should make it clear whether a distribution to the spouse of an issue is to be taken into account when the principal and undistributed income are divided into shares for the benefit of the issue. — ED.

be construed as authorizing the settlor's said son to appoint to himself, his creditors, his estate or creditors of his estate.

3. On the death of the settlor's said son, to whatever extent the then remaining principal and undistributed income are not effectively appointed by the settlor's said son pursuant to his power to appoint by will, if the child of the settlor's said son to whom the share held in this separate trust is allocated is then living, such remaining principal and undistributed income shall be held in a separate trust as follows:

(a) During the lifetime of such child of the settlor's said son, the net income in whole or in part may be paid to, or applied for the benefit of, any one or more of the group consisting of the widow of the settlor's said son, such child of the settlor's said son, the spouse of such child and the issue living from time to time of such child, in such amount or amounts as the corporate trustee in its uncontrolled discretion may determine; in any year, any net income which is not paid to, or applied for the benefit of, any one or more of such group shall be added to the principal at the end of the year; and, in addition, the principal in whole or in part may be paid to, or applied for the benefit of, any one or more of such group, from time to time, in such amount or amounts and for such estates and interests and outright or upon such terms, trusts, conditions and limitations, provided that no beneficial interest is created in anyone outside of such group by any such payment, as the corporate trustee in its uncontrolled discretion may determine; payments of income and principal to the issue of such child of the settlor's said son pursuant to the above provisions shall not be taken into account in any later division of the principal and undistributed income into shares for the benefit of such issue unless such child of the settlor's said son directs otherwise in the exercise of any power of appointment hereinafter given to such child of the settlor's said son.

(b) On the death of such child of the settlor's said son, the then remaining principal and undistributed income shall be paid to, or held for the benefit of, such one or more of the group consisting of the widow of the settlor's said son, the spouse of such child of the settlor's said son, the issue of the settlor living at the death of such child of the settlor's said son or born thereafter, and spouses of the settlor's issue, including spouses of issue who predecease such child of the settlor's said son as well as spouses of issue who are born after the death of such child of the settlor's said son, as such child of the settlor's said son shall appoint by a will, executed after the death of the settlor's said son, which refers specifically to this power. The exercise of this power by such child, however, shall not

(6)

apply to the proceeds of any life insurance on the life of such child which are payable to this trust. Subject to the above restrictions, in the exercise of this power of appointment such child may appoint outright or in trust; such child may select the trustee or trustees if an appointment in trust is made; such child may create new powers of appointment in a trustee or trustees or in any other appointee; such child may, if an appointment in trust is made, establish such administrative powers for the trustee as such child deems appropriate; such child may create life interests or other limited interests in an appointee with future interests in favor of other appointees; such child may impose lawful conditions on an appointment; such child may appoint by will different types of interests to selected appointees; such child may impose lawful spend-thrift provisions; and generally such child may appoint by will in any manner, provided always, however, that no appointment shall benefit directly or indirectly persons other than members of the restricted group who are the objects of this power, and that nothing herein shall be construed as authorizing such child to appoint to himself or herself, his or her creditors, his or her estate or creditors of his or her estate.

(c) On the death of such child of the settlor's said son, to whatever extent the then remaining principal and undistributed income are not effectively appointed by such child pursuant to such child's power to appoint by will, if issue of such child of the settlor's said son are then living, such remaining principal and undistributed income shall be held or disposed of for the benefit of such issue in accordance with the provisions of Article FIFTH of this instrument; and if no issue of such child of the settlor's said son is then living, such remaining principal and undistributed income shall be paid to the issue then living of the settlor's said son, such issue to take *per stirpes,* provided always, however, that any payment of principal and undistributed income directed to be made to an issue of the settlor's said son to whom income may be distributed under a trust established by this instrument, or established by the exercise of any power of appointment under this instrument, shall not be made outright to such issue but instead shall be added to the principal of such trust (if there are several such trusts, such payment shall be divided among them in equal shares) and administered as a part thereof; and if no issue of such child of the settlor's said son is then living and no issue of the settlor's said son is then living, such remaining principal and undistributed income shall be paid to the issue then living of the settlor's daughter, Margaret Black Logan, such issue to take *per stirpes,* provided always, however, that any payment of principal and undistributed income directed to be made to an issue of the settlor's said daughter to whom income may be distributed under a trust established by this instrument, or established by the exercise of any power of appointment under this instrument, shall not be made outright to such issue but instead shall be added to the principal of such trust (if there are several such trusts, such payment shall be divided among them in equal shares) and administered as a part thereof; and if no issue of such child of the settlor's said son is then living and no issue of the settlor's said son is then living and no issue of the settlor's said daughter is then living, such remaining principal and undistributed income shall be paid to the settlor's issue then living, such issue to take *per stirpes;* and if no issue of the settlor is then living, such remaining principal and undistributed income shall be paid to the issue then living of the settlor's brother James, such issue to take *per stirpes;* and if no issue of the settlor is then living and no issue of the settlor's said brother is then living, one half of such remaining principal and undistributed income shall be paid to the settlor's heirs as purchasers hereunder and the other one half shall be paid to the heirs of the settlor's wife, Mildred Marie Black, as purchasers hereunder.

4. On the death of the settlor's said son, to whatever extent the then remaining principal and undistributed income are not effectively appointed by the settlor's said son pursuant to his power to appoint by will, if the child of the settlor's said son to whom the share held in this separate trust is allocated is not then living but issue of such child of the settlor's said son are then living, such remaining principal and undistributed income shall be held or disposed of for the benefit of such issue in accordance with the provisions of Article FIFTH of this instrument; and if no issue of such child of the settlor's said son is then living, such remaining principal and undistributed income shall be paid to the issue then living of the settlor's said son, such issue to take *per stirpes,* provided always, however, that any payment of principal and undistributed income directed to be made to an issue of the settlor's said son to whom income may be distributed under a trust established by this instrument, or established by the exercise of any power of appointment under this instrument, shall not be made outright to such issue but instead shall be added to the principal of such trust (if there are several such trusts, such payment shall be divided among them in equal shares) and administered as a part thereof; and if no issue of such child of the settlor's said son is then living and no issue of the settlor's said son is then living, such remaining principal and undistributed income shall be paid to the issue then living of the settlor's said daughter, such issue to take *per stirpes,* provided always, however, that any payment

(8)

of principal and undistributed income directed to be made to an issue of the settlor's said daughter to whom income may be distributed under a trust established by this instrument, or established by the exercise of any power of appointment under this instrument, shall not be made outright to such issue but instead shall be added to the principal of such trust (if there are several such trusts, such payment shall be divided among them in equal shares) and administered as a part thereof; and if no issue of such child of the settlor's said son is then living and no issue of the settlor's said son is then living and no issue of the settlor's said daughter is then living, such remaining principal and undistributed income shall be paid to the settlor's issue then living, such issue to take *per stirpes;* and if no issue of the settlor is then living, such remaining principal and undistributed income shall be paid to the issue then living of the settlor's said brother, such issue to take *per stirpes;* and if no issue of the settlor is then living and no issue of the settlor's said brother is then living, one half of such remaining principal and undistributed income shall be paid to the settlor's heirs as purchasers hereunder and the other one half shall be paid to the heirs of the settlor's said wife as purchasers hereunder.

FOURTH: Margaret's share shall be divided into as many equal shares as there are children of the settlor's daughter, Margaret Black Logan, living on the date this instrument is executed. One of such equal shares shall be allocated to each living child of the settlor's said daughter and each share so allocated shall be held in a separate trust in accordance with the provisions hereinafter set forth in this Article FOURTH. If a new child is born to the settlor's said daughter or if a new child is finally adopted by the settlor's said daughter, a new separate trust shall be established for him or her on the date of the birth or final adoption of such child. The trustees shall transfer to the new separate trust a portion of the trust property of each of the then existing separate trusts under this Article FOURTH, such portion to be ascertained as though the following steps were taken:

The trust property in all the then existing separate trusts, including undistributed income, is mingled in one trust fund; and

Each contributing separate trust is allocated an undivided interest in the mingled fund that is equal to such trust's proportionate contribution to the mingled fund (the corporate trustee's determination as to each trust's undivided interest is to be conclusive on all concerned); and

The mingled fund is divided into as many equal shares as there are trusts under this Article FOURTH, including the new separate trust; and

One such equal share is transferred from the mingled fund to the new separate trust; and

The balance of the mingled fund is distributed to the contributing trusts, each receiving the portion of such balance that corresponds to its undivided interest in the original mingled fund.[46]

Each separate trust for a child of the settlor's said daughter shall be designated and known by the name of the child to whom the equal share is allocated, followed by the word "Trust," e.g., "THE ADAM RUDOLPH, JR., TRUST." Each separate trust for a child of the settlor's said daughter is as follows:

1. During the lifetime of the settlor's said daughter, the net income in whole or in part may be paid to, or applied for the benefit of, any one or more of the group consisting of the settlor's said daughter, the spouse of the settlor's said daughter, the child of the settlor's said daughter to whom the share held in this separate trust is allocated, the spouse of such child and the issue living from time to time of such child, in such amount or amounts as the corporate trustee in its uncontrolled discretion may determine; any net income in any year which is not paid to, or applied for the benefit of, any one or more of such group shall be added to the principal at the end of each year; and, in addition, the principal in whole or in part may be paid to, or applied for the benefit of, any one or more of such group, from time to time, in such amount or amounts and for such estates and interests and outright or upon such terms, trusts, conditions and limitations, provided that no beneficial interest is created in anyone outside of such group by any such payment, as the corporate trustee in its uncontrolled discretion may determine;[47] and furthermore, in addition to such payments as may be made under the preceding provisions, from and after the death of the settlor, the principal (other than life insurance on the life of the settlor's said daughter) in whole or in part shall be paid to, or applied for the benefit of, any one or more of such group other than the settlor's said daughter, from time to time, in such amount or amounts and for such estates and interests and outright or upon such terms, trusts, conditions and limitations, provided that no beneficial interest is created in anyone outside such group (excluding from such group the settlor's said daughter), as the settlor's said daughter shall specify in an instrument or instruments in writing delivered to the trustees in her lifetime (nothing contained herein shall be construed as authorizing the settlor's said daughter to discharge her legal obligations by any directions she may give as to the payment of principal); payments of income and principal to the issue of such child of the settlor's said daughter pursuant to the above provisions shall not be taken into account in any later division of the principal and undistributed income into shares for the benefit of such issue unless the settlor's said daughter or such child of the settlor's said daughter directs otherwise in the exercise of any

(10)

---

[46] See note 43 supra. — ED.
[47] See page 763 supra, note 154. — ED.

power of appointment hereinafter given to the settlor's said daughter or to such child of the settlor's said daughter.[48]

2. On the death of the settlor's said daughter, the then remaining principal and undistributed income shall be paid to, or held for the benefit of, such one or more of the group consisting of the spouse of the settlor's said daughter, the issue of settlor living at the death of the settlor's said daughter or born thereafter, and spouses of the settlor's issue, including spouses of issue who predecease the settlor's said daughter as well as spouses of issue who are born after the death of the settlor's said daughter, as the settlor's said daughter shall appoint by a will, executed after the date of this instrument, which refers specifically to this power. The exercise of this power by the settlor's said daughter, however, shall not apply to the proceeds of any life insurance on the life of the settlor's said daughter payable to this trust. Subject to the above restrictions, in the exercise of this power of appointment the settlor's said daughter may appoint outright or in trust; she may select the trustee or trustees if she appoints in trust; she may create new powers of appointment in a trustee or trustees or in any other appointee; she may, if she appoints in trust, establish such administrative powers for the trustee as she deems appropriate; she may create life interests or other limited interests in an appointee with future interests in favor of other appointees; she may impose lawful conditions on an appointment; she may appoint by her will different types of interests to selected appointees; she may impose lawful spendthrift provisions; and generally she may appoint by her will in any manner, provided always, however, that no appointment shall benefit directly or indirectly persons other than members of the restricted group who are the objects of this power, and that nothing herein shall be construed as authorizing the settlor's said daughter to appoint to herself, her creditors, her estate or creditors of her estate.

3. On the death of the settlor's said daughter, to whatever extent the then remaining principal and undistributed income are not effectively appointed by the settlor's said daughter pursuant to her power to appoint by will, if the child of the settlor's said daughter to whom the share held in this separate trust is allocated is then living, such remaining principal and undistributed income shall be held in a separate trust as follows:

(a) During the lifetime of such child of the settlor's said daughter, the net income in whole or in part may be paid to, or applied for the benefit of, any one or more of the group consisting of such child of the settlor's said daughter, the spouse of such child and the issue living from time to time of such child, in such amount or amounts as the corporate trustee in its un-

(11)

---

[48] See note 45 supra. — Ed.

controlled discretion may determine; in any year, any net income which is not paid to, or applied for the benefit of, any one or more of such group shall be added to the principal at the end of the year; and, in addition, the principal in whole or in part may be paid to, or applied for the benefit of, any one or more of such group, from time to time, in such amount or amounts and for such estates and interests and outright or upon such terms, trusts, conditions and limitations, provided that no beneficial interest is created in anyone outside of such group by any such payment, as the corporate trustee in its uncontrolled discretion may determine; payments of income and principal to the issue of such child of the settlor's said daughter pursuant to the above provisions shall not be taken into account in any later division of the principal and undistributed income into shares for the benefit of such issue unless such child of the settlor's said daughter directs otherwise in the exercise of any power of appointment hereinafter given to such child of the settlor's said daughter.

(b) On the death of such child of the settlor's said daughter, the then remaining principal and undistributed income shall be paid to, or held for the benefit of, such one or more of the group consisting of the spouse of the settlor's said daughter, the spouse of such child of the settlor's said daughter, the issue of the settlor living at the death of such child of the settlor's said daughter or born thereafter, and spouses of the settlor's issue, including spouses of issue who predecease such child of the settlor's said daughter as well as spouses of issue who are born after the death of such child of the settlor's said daughter, as such child of the settlor's said daughter shall appoint by a will, executed after the death of the settlor's said daughter which refers specifically to this power. The exercise of this power by such child, however, shall not apply to the proceeds of any life insurance on the life of such child which are payable to this trust. Subject to the above restrictions, in the exercise of this power of appointment such child may appoint outright or in trust; such child may select the trustee or trustees if an appointment in trust is made; such child may create new powers of appointment in a trustee or trustees or in any other appointee; such child may, if an appointment in trust is made, establish such administrative powers for the trustee as such child deems appropriate; such child may create life interests or other limited interests in an appointee with future interests in favor of other appointees; such child may impose lawful conditions on an appointment; such child may appoint by will different types of interests to selected appointees; such child may impose lawful spendthrift

(12)

provisions; and generally such child may appoint by will in any manner, provided always, however, that no appointment shall benefit directly or indirectly persons other than members of the restricted group who are the objects of this power, and that nothing herein shall be construed as authorizing such child to appoint to himself or herself, his or her creditors, his or her estate or creditors of his or her estate.

(c) On the death of such child of the settlor's said daughter, to whatever extent the then remaining principal and undistributed income are not effectively appointed by such child pursuant to such child's power to appoint by will, if issue of such child of the settlor's said daughter are then living, such remaining principal and undistributed income shall be held or disposed of for the benefit of such issue in accordance with the provisions of Article FIFTH of this instrument; and if no issue of such child of the settlor's said daughter is then living, such remaining principal and undistributed income shall be paid to the issue then living of the settlor's said daughter, such issue to take *per stirpes,* provided always, however, that any payment of principal and undistributed income directed to be made to an issue of the settlor's said daughter to whom income may be distributed under a trust established by this instrument, or established by the exercise of any power of appointment under this instrument, shall not be made outright to such issue but instead shall be added to the principal of such trust (if there are several such trusts, such payment shall be divided among them in equal shares) and administered as a part thereof; and if no issue of such child of the settlor's said daughter is then living and no issue of the settlor's said daughter is then living, such remaining principal and undistributed income shall be paid to the issue then living of the settlor's said son, such issue to take *per stirpes,* provided always, however, that any payment of principal and undistributed income directed to be made to an issue of the settlor's said son to whom income may be distributed under a trust established by this instrument, or established by the exercise of any power of appointment under this instrument, shall not be made outright to such issue but instead shall be added to the principal of such trust (if there are several such trusts, such payment shall be divided among them in equal shares) and administered as a part thereof; and if no issue of such child of the settlor's said daughter is then living and no issue of the settlor's said daughter is then living and no issue of the settlor's said son is then living, such remaining principal and undistributed income shall be paid to the settlor's issue then living, such issue to take *per stirpes;* and if no issue of the settlor is then living, such remaining principal and

(13)

undistributed income shall be paid to the issue then living of the settlor's said brother, such issue to take *per stirpes;* and if no issue of the settlor is then living and no issue of the settlor's said brother is then living, one half of such remaining principal and undistributed income shall be paid to the settlor's heirs as purchasers hereunder and the other one half shall be paid to the heirs of the settlor's said wife as purchasers hereunder.

4. On the death of the settlor's said daughter, to whatever extent the then remaining principal and undistributed income are not effectively appointed by the settlor's said daughter pursuant to her power to appoint by will, if the child of the settlor's said daughter to whom the share held in this separate trust is allocated is not then living but issue of such child of the settlor's said daughter are then living, such remaining principal and undistributed income shall be held or disposed of for the benefit of such issue in accordance with the provisions of Article FIFTH of this instrument; and if no issue of such child of the settlor's said daughter is then living, such remaining principal and undistributed income shall be paid to the issue then living of the settlor's said daughter, such issue to take *per stirpes,* provided always, however, that any payment of principal and undistributed income directed to be made to an issue of the settlor's said daughter to whom income may be distributed under a trust established by this instrument, or established by the exercise of any power of appointment under this instrument, shall not be made outright to such issue but instead shall be added to the principal of such trust (if there are several such trusts, such payment shall be divided among them in equal shares) and administered as a part thereof; and if no issue of such child of the settlor's said daughter is then living and no issue of the settlor's said daughter is then living, such remaining principal and undistributed income shall be paid to the issue then living of the settlor's said son, such issue to take *per stirpes,* provided always, however, that any payment of principal and undistributed income directed to be made to an issue of the settlor's said son to whom income may be distributed under a trust established by this instrument, or established by the exercise of any power of appointment under this instrument, shall not be made outright to such issue but instead shall be added to the principal of such trust (if there are several such trusts, such payment shall be divided among them in equal shares) and administered as a part thereof; and if no issue of such child of the settlor's said daughter is then living and no issue of the settlor's said daughter is then living and no issue of the settlor's said son is then living, such remaining principal and undistributed income shall be paid to the settlor's issue then living, such issue to take *per stirpes;* and if no issue of the settlor is then living, such

remaining principal and undistributed income shall be paid to the issue then living of the settlor's said brother, such issue to take *per stirpes;* and if no issue of the settlor is then living and no issue of the settlor's said brother is then living, one-half of such remaining principal and undistributed income shall be paid to the settlor's heirs as purchasers hereunder and the other one half shall be paid to the heirs of the settlor's said wife as purchasers hereunder.

FIFTH: Whenever the remaining principal and undistributed income of any trust hereunder are to be held or disposed of for the benefit of the issue of a deceased child of the settlor's said son, or for the benefit of the issue of a deceased child of the settlor's said daughter, in accordance with the provisions of this Article FIFTH, the trustees are directed as follows in regard thereto:

1. If no child of such deceased child is living who is under the age of twenty-one (21) years, the trust property shall be paid to the issue then living of such deceased child, such issue to take *per stirpes.*

2. If a child of such deceased child is living who is under the age of twenty-one (21) years, the trust property shall be held in a separate trust for the benefit of the issue of such deceased child as follows:

   (a) Until no child of such deceased child is living who is under the age of twenty-one (21) years, the net income in whole or in part may be paid to or applied for the benefit of, any one or more of the group consisting of the spouse of such deceased child and the issue of such deceased child who are living from time to time, in such amount or amounts as the corporate trustee in its uncontrolled discretion may determine; any net income in any year which is not paid to, or applied for the benefit of, any one or more of such group shall be added to the principal at the end of the year; and, in addition, the principal in whole or in part may be paid to, or applied for the benefit of, any one or more of such group, from time to time, in such amount or amounts and for such estates and interests and outright or upon such terms, trusts, conditions and limitations, provided that no beneficial interest is created in anyone outside of such group by any such payment, as the corporate trustee in its uncontrolled discretion may determine; payments of income and principal to the issue of such deceased child pursuant to the above provisions shall not be taken into account in any later division of the principal and undistributed income into shares for the benefit of such issue.

   (b) When no child of such deceased child is living who is under the age of twenty-one (21) years, the then remaining principal and undistributed income shall be paid to the issue then living of such deceased child, such issue to take *per stirpes;* and if no issue of such deceased child is then living, the then re-

(15)

maining principal and undistributed income shall be paid to the issue then living of the settlor's said son, if such deceased child is a child of the settlor's said son, or to the issue then living of the settlor's said daughter, if such deceased child is a child of the settlor's said daughter, such issue to take *per stirpes*, provided always, however, that any payment of principal and undistributed income directed to be made to one of such issue to whom income may be distributed under a trust established by this instrument, or established by the exercise of any power of appointment under this instrument, shall not be made outright to such issue but instead shall be added to the principal of such trust (if there are several such trusts, such payment shall be divided among them in equal shares) and administered as a part thereof; and if no issue of such deceased child is then living and no issue of the settlor's said son is then living, if such deceased child is a child of the settlor's said son, or no issue of the settlor's said daughter is then living, if such deceased child is a child of the settlor's said daughter, the then remaining principal and undistributed income shall be paid to the issue then living of the settlor's said son, if such deceased child is not a child of the settlor's said son, or to the issue then living of the settlor's said daughter, if such deceased child is not a child of the settlor's said daughter, such issue to take *per stirpes*, provided always, however, that any payment of principal and undistributed income directed to be made to one of such issue to whom income may be distributed under a trust established by this instrument, or established by the exercise of any power of appointment under this instrument, shall not be made outright to such issue but instead shall be added to the principal of such trust (if there are several such trusts, such payment shall be divided among them in equal shares) and administered as a part thereof; and if no issue of such deceased child is then living and no issue of the settlor's said son is then living and no issue of the settlor's said daughter is then living, the then remaining principal and undistributed income shall be paid to the settlor's issue then living, such issue to the then remaining principal and undistributed income shall take *per stirpes;* and if no issue of the settlor is then living, be paid to the issue then living of the settlor's said brother, such issue to take *per stirpes;* and if no issue of the settlor is then living and no issue of the settlor's said brother is then living, one half of the then remaining principal and undistributed income shall be paid to the settlor's heirs as purchasers hereunder and the other one half shall be paid to the heirs of the settlor's said wife as purchasers hereunder.

SIXTH: Notwithstanding the directions given as to the distribution of income and principal in Articles THIRD, FOURTH and FIFTH

(16)

of this instrument, any trust established by said Articles shall terminate, if it has not previously terminated, twenty-one (21) years after the death of the survivor of the following persons living on the date this instrument is executed:

1. Richard Harry Black III, the settlor;
2. Mildred Marie Black, wife of the settlor;
3. Richard Harry Black IV, son of the settlor;
4. Dorothy Ann Black, daughter-in-law of the settlor;
5. Margaret Black Logan, daughter of the settlor;
6. Robert Gerald Logan, son-in-law of the settlor;
7. James Harry Black, grandchild of the settlor;
8. Dorothy Marie Black, grandchild of the settlor;
9. Adam Rudolph, Jr., grandchild of the settlor;
10. Millicent Logan, grandchild of the settlor;
11. Richard Harry Logan, grandchild of the settlor;

and the then remaining principal and undistributed income of such trust shall be paid to the settlor's issue then living to whom income payments could be made under such trust immediately prior to its termination under this Article SIXTH, such issue to take *per stirpes.*

Furthermore, each power to appoint given under the provisions of Articles THIRD, FOURTH and FIFTH of this instrument shall be exercisable by the designated donee if, and only if, the power is exercised prior to twenty-one (21) years after the death of the survivor of the persons named in the preceding paragraph.

SEVENTH: If income payments are ever required to be made under any trust established by this instrument, they shall be made at times fixed by the corporate trustee but at least as often as quarterly.

The interest of each beneficiary in the income or principal of a trust under this instrument shall be free from the control or interference of any creditor of a beneficiary or of any spouse of a married beneficiary and shall not be subject to attachment or susceptible of anticipation or alienation. Nothing contained in this paragraph shall be construed as restricting in any way the exercise of any power of appointment granted hereunder.

EIGHTH: The whole or any part of the income or principal paid hereunder to any minor or to any other person who in the opinion of the corporate trustee is incapacitated through illness, age or other cause may be applied by the corporate trustee in its discretion for such beneficiary's comfort, maintenance, support or education. Any such application may be made at such time and in such manner as it deems advisable, whether by direct payment of such beneficiary's expenses or by payment to a person selected by the corporate trustee to receive payment for such beneficiary; in each case the receipt of such person to whom payment is made or entrusted shall be a complete discharge of the trustees in respect thereof. Whenever any payment hereunder is required to be made to a minor, the interest so required to be paid shall be indefeasibly vested in the minor but the trustees may retain the amount payable until the minor attains his majority or dies, whichever first occurs, and the trustees may pay the income and principal to the minor in such amount or amounts and from time to time as the trustees may determine, and if the minor lives to attain his majority, then when he attains his majority the trustees shall pay the then remaining principal and undistributed income to him, and if the minor dies before attaining his majority, then on the minor's death the trustees shall pay the then remaining principal and undistributed income to the minor's estate.

NINTH: The trustees are authorized to mingle the trust property of the separate trusts established by this instrument, allotting to each separate trust an undivided interest in the mingled funds that shall always be equal to that trust's proportionate contribution (as adjusted from time to time as a result of accumulations of income, payments of principal and additions to principal) to the mingled funds.

TENTH: References in this instrument to "child" or "children" mean lawful blood descendants in the first degree of the parent designated, and references to "issue" mean lawful blood descendants in the first, second or any other degree of the ancestor designated, provided always, however, that

1. An adopted child and such adopted child's lawful blood descendants shall be considered in this instrument as lawful blood descendants of the adopting parent or parents and of anyone who is by blood or adoption an ancestor of the adopting parent or of either of the adopting parents and shall not be considered descendants of the adopted child's natural parents, except that where a child is adopted by a spouse of one of his or her natural parents such child shall be considered a descendant of such natural parent as well as a descendant of the adopting parent; and
2. A child born to persons who are openly living together as husband and wife after the performance of a marriage ceremony between them and such child's lawful blood descendants shall be considered in this instrument as lawful blood descendants of such child's parents and of any ancestor of such child's parents, regardless of the fact that a purported divorce of one or both of such persons with reference to a prior marriage is invalid.

A child in gestation, who is later born alive, shall be regarded in this instrument as a child in being during the period of gestation, in determining whether any person has died without leaving issue surviving him or her, and in determining, on the termination of any trust hereunder, whether such child is entitled to share in the disposition of the then remaining principal and undistributed income of such trust, but for other purposes such child's rights shall accrue from date of birth.

References in this instrument to "wife," "widow" and "spouse" mean the person who answers to such description on the assumption that all decrees of divorce rendered by a court of record wherever located are valid. References in this instrument to "widow" mean the surviving spouse of a deceased male. Furthermore, a decision of the corpo-

(18)

rate trustee made in good faith as to whether a person is the described "wife" or "widow" or "spouse" shall be conclusive for all purposes.

Whenever distribution is to be made to designated "issue" on a *per stirpes* basis, the property shall be distributed to the persons and in the proportions that personal property of the named ancestor would be distributed under the laws of the .... of ....[49] in force at the time stipulated for distribution if the named ancestor had died intestate at such time, domiciled in such State, not married and survived only by such issue.

Whenever the corporate trustee has discretion to pay income or principal to designated "issue," payment may be made to or for the benefit of an issue of the second or more remote degree even though payment is also made, or could be made, to the parent of such issue.

Whenever any person is given hereunder a power to appoint to designated "issue," an appointment may be made to issue of the second or more remote degree even though an appointment is also made, or could be made, to the parent of such issue.

References in this instrument to "settlor's heirs" mean those persons, other than creditors, who would take the personal property of the settlor under the laws of the .... of ....[50] if the settlor had died intestate at the time stipulated for distribution, not married and domiciled in such State. In determining who such persons are, it shall be assumed that all decrees of divorce rendered by a court of record, wherever located, are valid. Distribution to such persons shall be made in the manner and in the proportion that personal property of the settlor would be distributed under the laws of the .... of ....[51] if the settlor had died intestate at the time stipulated for distribution, not married, owning the property available for distribution and no other property and domiciled in such State.

References in this instrument to the "heirs of the settlor's wife, Mildred Marie Black" or to the "heirs of the settlor's said wife" mean those persons, other than creditors, who would take the personal property of the settlor's said wife under the laws of the .... of ....[52] if the settlor's said wife had died intestate at the time stipulated for distribution, not married and domiciled in such State. In determining who such persons are, it shall be assumed that all decrees of divorce rendered by a court of record, wherever located, are valid. Distribution to such persons shall be made in the manner and in the proportion that personal property of the settlor's said wife would be distributed under the laws of the .... of ....[53] if the settlor's said wife had died intestate at the time stipulated for distribu-

(19)

---

[49] Insert the state which is to govern.
[50] Insert the state which is to govern.
[51] Insert the state which is to govern.
[52] Insert the state which is to govern.
[53] Insert the state which is to govern.

tion, not married, owning the property available for distribution and no other property and domiciled in such State.

ELEVENTH: The corporate trustee of any trust established by this instrument and the donee of any power of appointment hereunder may disclaim or release in whole or in part any power given exclusively to it, him or her. If a disclaimer or release relates to the corporate trustee's discretion to pay out or accumulate income, then after such disclaimer or release, the net income of the trust shall be paid to the settlor's said son when the corporate trustee in the exercise of its discretion, prior to its disclaimer or release, could have paid the income to the settlor's said son, and to the settlor's said daughter when the corporate trustee in the exercise of its discretion, prior to its disclaimer or release, could have paid the income to the settlor's said daughter, and to that child of the settlor's said son or to that child of the settlor's said daughter to whom the corporate trustee in the exercise of its discretion, prior to its disclaimer or release, could have paid the income when the income could not have been paid either to the settlor's said son or to the settlor's said daughter, and to the issue of that deceased child of the settlor's said son or to the issue of that deceased child of the settlor's said daughter to whom the corporate trustee in the exercise of its discretion, prior to its disclaimer or release, could have paid the income when the income could not have been paid either to the settlor's said son or to the settlor's said daughter or to a child of either the settlor's said son or his said daughter, such issue who are living at each income payment date to take *per stirpes.*

In addition to any other method of disclaimer or release recognized by law, the holder of the power may disclaim or release the power in whole or in part by delivering to the trustees an instrument in writing declaring the power holder's intention in this regard.

TWELFTH: Each trust hereunder is a .... [54] trust, made in that State, and is to be governed and construed and administered according to its laws and shall continue to be so governed and construed and administered even though administered elsewhere within the United States or abroad.

THIRTEENTH: The trustees shall each year render an account of their administration of each trust hereunder to the oldest living issue of the settlor to whom income of such trust may be distributed (or such issue's guardian). Such person's (or the guardian's) written approval of such account shall, as to all matters and transactions stated therein or shown thereby, be final and binding upon all persons (whether in being or not) who are then or may thereafter become interested in, or entitled to share in, either the income or the principal of such trust, provided always, however, that nothing contained in this Article THIRTEENTH shall be deemed to give such person (or the guardian) acting in conjunction with the trustees the power to alter, amend, revoke or terminate such trust.[55]

(20)

[54] Insert the state which is to govern.
[55] The validity in New York of a provision relating to the approval of accounts

FOURTEENTH: No trustee hereunder who has contributed to the trust property shall be entitled to compensation for his services as trustee. All other trustees shall be entitled to a reasonable compensation for their services.

FIFTEENTH: Notwithstanding the directions heretofore given to the trustees acting together and to the corporate trustee acting alone as to the distribution of income and principal of any trust under Articles THIRD, FOURTH and FIFTH, but subject to the directions given to the trustees as to the distribution of income and principal in Article SIXTH, the corporate trustee of each separate trust under this instrument is authorized at any time or from time to time in its uncontrolled discretion to insure the life of any income beneficiary of such trust (that is, any person to whom the corporate trustee in its discretion may pay income or any person to whom the trustees are required to pay the income) for such amount or amounts as the corporate trustee may determine. The proceeds of the policy or policies of said insurance shall be made payable to the trustees of the trust of which the insured is an income beneficiary. The corporate trustee may apply any or all dividends on said policy or policies of insurance to the payment of premiums thereon and shall pay the balance of the premiums out of the income or principal of the trust of which the insured is an income beneficiary. The corporate trustee may at any time or from time to time surrender such policy or policies of insurance and obtain the cash surrender value. The proceeds of such policy or policies of insurance, whether collected before or after the death of the insured, shall be added to the principal of the trust of which the insured is an income beneficiary. The corporate trustee may take out term insurance or straight life insurance or endowment insurance or any other kind of life insurance under the authorization to it contained in this Article FIFTEENTH. In making any distribution of trust property, distribution shall not be made to any insured of a policy on his or her life or of any proceeds of such policy.

SIXTEENTH: With respect to any liability which must be satisfied out of the property held in trust hereunder, the amount necessary to satisfy such liability may be obtained by borrowing, and pledging or mortgaging trust property to secure the sum borrowed, or by selling trust property, or by both methods, bearing in mind the provisions of Article FIRST of this instrument in the event that a sale of any of the common stock or other securities of the Black Manufacturing Company, or the common stock or other securities of any concern which shall succeed to the whole or a substantial part of the assets or business of the Black Manufacturing Company, is necessary in order to obtain the cash necessary to meet such liability; provided always, however,

(21)

---

such as the provision to which this footnote is appended is considered in Matter of Crane, 34 N.Y.S.2d 9 (1942), *aff'd sub nom.* Application of Central Hanover Bank & Trust Co., 266 App. Div. 726, 41 N.Y.S.2d 940 (1943), *leave to appeal denied,* 266 App. Div. 846, 43 N.Y.S.2d 851 (1943). On the approval of accounts, see page 1148 supra, note 58. — ED.

that the same amount of property shall be taken from each separate trust hereunder to provide the necessary security for the sum borrowed, and that the same amount of income and principal shall be diverted from each separate trust hereunder to pay the debt and the interest thereon, and that if trust property is sold to raise the cash necessary to meet such liability, the same amount of property shall be taken from each separate trust hereunder to be sold. The decision of the corporate trustee shall be conclusive as to the method adopted to provide the funds necessary to meet such liability.

SEVENTEENTH: In extension and not in limitation of the powers given them by law or other provisions of this instrument, but subject to the provisions of Articles FIRST and SIXTEENTH, the trustees of each trust established hereunder shall have the following powers with respect to such trust and its property, in each case to be exercised from time to time in their discretion and without order or license of court:

1. To retain indefinitely any investments and to invest and reinvest in stocks, shares and obligations of corporations, of unincorporated associations or trusts and of investment companies,[56] or in a common trust fund without giving notice to any beneficiary,[57] or in any other kind of personal or real property, notwithstanding the fact that any or all of the investments made or retained are of a character or size which but for this express authority would not be considered proper for trustees;

2. To make loans with adequate interest and with adequate security, unless the loan is made to one to whom the corporate trustee has

(22)

[56] In order for regulated investment companies to enjoy certain tax benefits, they must distribute annually at least 90 percent of earnings from income and capital gains. The distribution should be accompanied by a statement which advises the shareholder of the proportion of the dividend that is attributable to investment income and to capital gains. Should the trustee who receives the distribution pay the entire dividend to the life income beneficiary or only the proportion that is attributable to investment income? Unless the trustee has discretion as to the distribution of income and principal, the trust instrument should instruct the trustee in this regard, as there is conflict in the authorities concerning situations where there are no instructions. See Rosenburg v. Lombardi, 222 Md. 346, 160 A.2d 601 (1960), which held that the income beneficiary was entitled to a portion of the dividend that was attributable to the capital gain. — Ed.

[57] If trust assets are invested in a common trust fund, §584 of the 1954 Code should be kept in mind, and particularly §584(e), which provides that the withdrawal of any participating interest in a common trust fund by a participant is treated as a sale or exchange of such interest by the participant. Revenue Ruling 57-335, 1957-2 C.B. 322, considers the consequences of §584(e) in several different situations. In Wiggin v. United States, 59-1 U.S.T.C. ¶9309 (D. Mass. 1959), it was held that an intertrust transfer of participating units in a common trust fund from a testamentary trust, on its termination, to an inter vivos trust created by the beneficiary at that time was not a withdrawal of a participating interest within the meaning of §584(e), where no funds changed hands, there was no surrender of indicia of ownership, and nothing was received by the beneficiary. The court refused to follow Rev. Rul. 57-335, on which the government relied. Technical Information Release 169, dated August 3, 1959, states that Rev. Rul. 57-335 will be modified to the extent that it is inconsistent with Wiggin v. United States. The release

discretion to distribute the income or principal of such trust, in which case the loan may be made without adequate interest or adequate security, provided always, however, that the powers given in this Section 2 shall be exercisable only by the corporate trustee;

3. To sell, to exchange, to lease and to make contracts concerning real or personal property for such considerations and upon such terms as to credit or otherwise as the corporate trustee may determine, which leases and contracts may extend beyond the term of the trust; to give options therefor; to execute deeds, transfers, leases and other instruments of any kind;

4. To hold bonds, shares or other securities in bearer form, or in the name of the trustees or in the name of one or more but less than all of the trustees or in the name of a nominee, without indication of any fiduciary capacity; to deposit cash in a checking or savings account in a bank, without indication of any fiduciary capacity;

5. To give general or special proxies or powers of attorney for voting or acting in respect of shares or securities, which may be discretionary and with power of substitution; to deposit shares or securities with, or transfer them to, protective committees or similar bodies; to join in any reorganization and to pay assessments or subscriptions called for in connection with shares or securities held by them;

6. To improve or develop real estate; to construct, alter or repair buildings or structures on real estate; to settle boundary lines and easements and other rights with respect to real estate; to partition and to join with co-owners and others in dealing with real estate in any way;

7. To employ investment counsel, custodians of trust property, brokers, agents and attorneys;

8. Subject to the provisions of Article SECOND, to receive additions to the trusts under this instrument by gift or will or otherwise, and to hold and administer the same under the provisions hereof;

9. To pay as income the whole of the interest, dividends, rent or similar receipts from property, whether wasting or not and although bought or taken at a value above par, but if they see fit,

(23)

---

is incorporated in Rev. Rul. 59-414, 1959-2 C.B. 156. Revenue Ruling 60-256, I.R.B. 1960-31, 10, produces the promised modification by holding that a transfer of units of participation in a common trust fund from one trust, of which the taxpayer is sole beneficiary, to another trust, of which the taxpayer is also the sole beneficiary, does not constitute a "withdrawal" of a participating interest within the meaning of §584(e), provided no funds change hands, there is no surrender of indicia of ownership, nothing is received by the taxpayer, and the trustee of the two trusts is the same.

Revenue Ruling 60-240, I.R.B. 1960-28, 11, brings out that though a merger of two common trust funds will not in and of itself cause either the funds or the participants to realize any gain or loss, distributions of cash or securities to participants in order to eliminate fractional units will be treated as proceeds from the sale or exchange of the fractional units. — ED.

when property is bought or taken at a value above par, they may retain a portion of the income to offset such loss to the principal; to treat as income or principal or to apportion between them stock dividends, extra dividends, rights to take stock or securities, and proceeds from the sale of real estate, although such real estate may have been wholly or partly unproductive; to charge to income or principal or to apportion between them any expense of making and changing investments, investment counsel's compensation, custodians' compensation, brokers' commissions, agents' compensation, attorneys' fees, insurance premiums, repairs or improvements, taxes, depreciation charges and trustees' compensation; and generally to determine all questions as between income and principal and to credit or charge to income or principal or to apportion between them any receipt or gain and any charge, disbursement or loss as is deemed advisable in the circumstances of each case as it arises, nothwithstanding any statute or rule of law for distinguishing income from principal or any determination of the courts; provided always, however, that the powers and discretion given in this Section 9 shall be exercisable only by the corporate trustee;

10. When paying trust principal or dividing or distributing any trust fund, to make such payment, division or distribution wholly or partly in kind by allotting and transferring specific securities or other personal or real property or undivided interests therein as a part or the whole of any one or more shares or payments, at current values;

11. To keep any or all of the trust property at any place or places in ....[58] or elsewhere within the United States or abroad or with a depositary or custodian at such place or places.

All powers given to the trustees by this instrument are exercisable by the trustees only in a fiduciary capacity. No power given to the trustees hereunder shall be construed to enable the settlor or any person to purchase, exchange, or otherwise deal with or dispose of the principal or the income therefrom for less than an adequate consideration in money or money's worth. The trustees shall not use the income or principal of any trust hereunder to pay premiums on insurance on the life of the settlor.

Powers and discretions vested in the trustees under this Article or under any other Article in this instrument shall be vested in the trustees, exclusive of the settlor, whenever this is necessary to prevent the value of the trust property from being includible in whole or in part in the settlor's gross estate for federal estate tax purposes.

EIGHTEENTH: No bond shall be required of the original trustees hereunder or of any successor trustee, or if a bond is required by law, no surety on such bond shall be required.

(24)

---

[58] Insert the state where the corporate fiduciary is located.

If a vacancy in the office of individual trustee occurs, the remaining trustees or trustee (other than the settlor) shall appoint by an instrument in writing to fill such vacancy one of the following:

1. Issue of Richard Harry Black IV;
2. Margaret Black Logan;
3. Mildred Marie Black;
4. Issue of Margaret Black Logan;
5. James Robert Black (brother of the settlor); and
6. Issue of James Robert Black.

If no one of the above-listed persons is eligible or available to serve as trustee at the time a vacancy in the office of individual trustee occurs, the vacancy shall not then be filled but shall be filled at such time in the future as one of the above-listed persons becomes eligible or available to fill such vacancy. In other words, there shall always be two individual trustees whenever there are eligible and available from the above list of persons individuals to serve as trustees hereunder.

If a vacancy in the office of corporate trustee occurs, the remaining trustees or trustee (other than the settlor) shall appoint by an instrument in writing a corporation to fill such vacancy. If there is no such remaining trustee, a corporation shall be appointed to fill such vacancy by an instrument in writing signed by the oldest living issue of the settlor, or such issue's guardian.

A trustee may resign at any time by an instrument in writing delivered to the remaining trustees or trustee, and if there is no remaining trustee, by an instrument in writing delivered to the oldest living issue of the settlor, or such issue's guardian.

The approval of all the trustees in office shall be required in order to act in any matter affecting the trust except such matters as are herein vested exclusively in the corporate trustee. If a vacancy in the office of trustee exists, the trustee or trustees in office may act pending the filling of the vacancy, provided always, however, that only a corporate trustee can act with respect to matters vested exclusively in it.

References in this instrument to "trustees" shall be deemed to include not only the original trustees but also any successor trustee, and all powers and discretions vested in the trustees shall be vested in and exercisable by any such successor trustee except that the powers and discretions vested herein in the corporate trustee shall be vested in, and exercisable by, only a successor corporate trustee.

No one dealing with the trustees need inquire concerning the validity of anything they purport to do, or need see to the application of any money paid or any property transferred to or upon the order of the trustees.[59]

(25)

[59] Illinois has simplified the transfer of securities by and to a fiduciary, and the consequence of this simplification is to make unnecessary a provision such as the one to which this footnote is appended in situations covered by the new legislation. See Ill. Rev. Stat., c. 32, §§439.50-439.57 (1959), added in 1957. The Model Fiduciaries' Securities Transfer Act adopted in Illinois has also been adopted in Connecticut (Conn. Gen. Stat. Rev. §§33-67 to 33-71 (1958)) and Delaware (Del. Code Ann., tit. 12, §§4301-4307 (1953, Supp. 1958)). A similar law entitled Uniform Act for the Simpli-

No trustee shall be responsible for the acts or omissions of another of the trustees or for allowing another of the trustees to have custody or control of the funds, securities or property.   Each of them shall be responsible only for his, her, or its acts or omissions in bad faith.   Furthermore, a successor trustee shall not be liable for any action taken by the trustees prior to the time such successor becomes a trustee.

A trustee may, by an instrument in writing, delegate all or any powers and discretions to a co-trustee or to co-trustees for a period of one year or less at a time and may renew such delegation from time to time; provided always, however, that the powers and discretions vested exclusively in the corporate trustee shall not be delegated.

NINETEENTH: To the same effect as if it were the original, anyone may rely upon a copy certified by a notary public to be a counterpart of this instrument (and of the writings, if any, endorsed thereon or attached thereto).   Anyone may rely upon any statement of fact certified by anyone who appears from the original document or a certified copy to be a trustee hereunder.

IN WITNESS WHEREOF, RICHARD HARRY BLACK III as settlor has hereunto set his hand and seal, and RICHARD HARRY BLACK III and RICHARD HARRY BLACK IV, in token of their acceptance of the trusts hereby created, have caused their hands and seals to be hereto affixed, and ....

........................[60], in token of its acceptance of the trusts hereby created, has caused these presents to be executed and its corporate seal to be affixed hereto by James Johnston, its Vice President, thereunto duly authorized, all as of this .... day of ....

................................, 19..............[61]

/s/ *Richard Harry Black III* [Scal]

SETTLOR AND TRUSTEE

/s/ *Richard Harry Black IV* [Seal]

TRUSTEE

-------------------------------------[62]

[Corporate Seal]   By /s/ *James Johnston*

                                    VICE PRESIDENT

(26)

---

fication of Fiduciary Transfer has been enacted in California, Colorado, Georgia, Idaho, Maine, Maryland, Michigan, Missouri, Nevada, New Mexico, New York, North Carolina, Rhode Island, South Carolina, Tennessee, Texas, Virginia, Wisconsin, and Wyoming.   See Christy, The Model Fiduciaries' Securities Transfer Act, 37 Trust Bull. No. 8, p. 10 (1958).   See also the Uniform Act for Simplification of Fiduciary Security Transfers, enacted in 1959 in New York (General Business Law, art. 23-C). — ED.

[60] Insert the name of the corporate fiduciary.
[61] Insert the date on which the trust is executed.
[62] Insert the name of the corporate fiduciary.

Attest:
/s/ *Marie Almond*
....

.... of.. [63]
....................................,[64] ss.   ....
                                              ...., 19............ [65]

Then personally appeared the above-named **RICHARD HARRY
BLACK III** and acknowledged the foregoing instrument to be his free
act and deed, before me,

                              /s/ *Robert Lewis*

                                        NOTARY PUBLIC
[Notarial Seal]

        ROBERT LEWIS Notary Public
        My commission expires ...., 19............ [66]

.... of .... [67]
....................................,[68] ss.   ....
                                              ...., 19............ [69]

Then personally appeared the above-named **RICHARD HARRY
BLACK IV** and acknowledged the foregoing instrument to be his free
act and deed, before me,

                              /s/ *Robert Lewis*

                                        NOTARY PUBLIC
[Notarial Seal]

        ROBERT LEWIS Notary Public
        My commission expires ...., 19............ [70]

.... of .... [71]
....................................,[72] ss.   ....
                                              ...., 19............ [73]

(27)

[63] Insert the state in which the acknowledgment is taken.
[64] Insert the county in which the acknowledgment is taken.
[65] Insert the city in which and the date on which the acknowledgment is taken.
[66] Insert the date on which the notary's commission expires.
[67] Insert the state in which the acknowledgment is taken.
[68] Insert the county in which the acknowledgment is taken.
[69] Insert the city in which and the date on which the acknowledgment is taken.
[70] Insert the date on which the notary's commission expires.
[71] Insert the state in which the acknowledgment is taken.
[72] Insert the county in which the acknowledgment is taken.
[73] Insert the city in which and the date on which the acknowledgment is taken.

Then personally appeared ....[74]
by James Johnston, its Vice President, thereunto duly authorized, who
acknowledged the foregoing instrument to be the free act and deed
of said ....,[75]
before me,

/s/ *Robert Lewis*

NOTARY PUBLIC

[Notarial Seal]

ROBERT LEWIS Notary Public
My commission expires ...., 19........[76]

(28)

[74] Insert the name of the corporate fiduciary.
[75] Insert the name of the corporate fiduciary.
[76] Insert the date on which the notary's commission expires.

G.   *The Black Family Foundation*

I, RICHARD HARRY BLACK III, of ....,
....,[77] hereby transfer the property listed in
Schedule A attached hereto to **RICHARD HARRY BLACK III,**
MILDRED MARIE BLACK and **RICHARD HARRY BLACK IV,**
of ...., ...[78] (hereinafter
called the "trustees"); and the trustees hereby agree to hold such prop-
erty and all additions thereto, in trust, as follows:

FIRST: This trust is an irrevocable charitable trust and may be
known as "THE BLACK FAMILY FOUNDATION."

SECOND: There shall always be at least three trustees hereunder.
The trustees in office may from time to time determine the number of
trustees, if any, in excess of three. Whenever the number of trustees
in office is less than three, the remaining trustees or trustee shall
promptly appoint a successor trustee or successor trustees to fill the
vacancy or vacancies. Whenever the trustees in office determine that
the number of trustees shall exceed three, the trustees in office shall
promptly appoint an additional trustee or additional trustees to give
effect to such determination. A corporation may be appointed a successor trustee or an additional trustee. Appointments of successor trustees or additional trustees shall be by an instrument in writing signed
by the trustees or trustee in office, and such instrument shall be kept attached to the executed original of this trust held by the trustees.

Every successor trustee and every additional trustee shall forthwith
upon his appointment, without the necessity of any act of transfer or
action by any court, become vested with title to the trust assets jointly
with the other trustees or trustee and become vested with and have all
the same powers and obligations as if he were one of the original
trustees. He shall not, however, be liable for the acts of the trustees
prior to the time he takes office.

No bond shall be required of the original trustees, of any successor
trustee or of any additional trustee, or if a bond is required by law,
no surety on such bond shall be required.

The trustees or trustee for the time being in office shall have full
authority to act even though a vacancy or vacancies exist.

If the number of trustees in office is less than three, the action of all
the trustees shall be required in order to act in any matter affecting the
trust. If the number of trustees is three or more, the action of a majority shall be sufficient in order to act with respect to any matter affecting the trust, provided always, however, that any trustee in office
may from time to time, by an instrument in writing signed by him or
her, delegate to any one or more of the other trustees his or her authority to act either generally or specifically with respect to any matter or

(1)

---

[77] Insert the city and state where Mr. Black resides.
[78] Insert the city and state where Richard Harry Black IV resides.

matters affecting the trust and may, by an instrument in writing signed by him or her, recall and revoke any such delegation. The instruments referred to in the previous sentence shall be kept attached to the executed original of this trust held by the trustees.

Any trustee may resign at any time by an instrument in writing delivered to the remaining trustees or trustee, and such writing shall be kept attached to the executed original of this trust held by the trustees.

THIRD: The net income and principal shall be disposed of as follows:

1. The trustees shall from time to time pay such portions or the whole of the net income and/or principal to such one or more charitable organizations (as hereinafter defined) as the trustees in their uncontrolled discretion shall determine. At the end of each year any net income not paid out shall be paid out within six months after the end of such year.[79]

2. This trust shall terminate whenever all its income and principal have been paid out.

3. The "charitable organizations" to which payments of income and/or principal may be made under this trust are confined to corporations, trusts, or community chests, funds, or foundations which are created or organized in the United States or in any possession thereof, or under the laws of the United States, any state or territory, the District of Columbia, or any possession of the United States; which are organized and operated exclusively for religious, charitable, scientific, literary or educational purposes, or for the prevention of cruelty to children or animals; with respect to which no part of the net earnings inures to the benefit of any private shareholder or individual; and with respect to which no substantial part of the activities is carrying on propaganda or otherwise attempting to influence legislation.[80]

(2)

[79] See page 881 supra, note 12, where it is pointed out that an unlimited power to accumulate income may prevent the trust from being granted an exempt status. — Ed.

[80] The Articles of Incorporation of the Ford Foundation (as amended to April 1, 1954) describe the purposes of the Foundation as follows:

"To receive and administer funds for *scientific, educational, and charitable purposes, all for the public welfare,* and for no other purposes, and to that end to take and hold, by bequest, devise, gift, purchase, or lease, either absolutely or in trust for such objects and purposes or any of them, any property, real, personal, or mixed, without limitation as to amount or value, except such limitations, if any, as may be imposed by law; to sell, convey, and dispose of any such property and to invest and re-invest the principal thereof, and to deal with and expend the income therefrom for any of the before mentioned purposes, without limitation, except such limitations, if any, as may be contained in the instrument under which such property is received; to receive any property, real, personal, or mixed, in trust, under the terms of any will, deed of trust, or other trust instrument for the foregoing purposes or any of them (but for no other purposes), and in administering the same to carry out the directions and exercise the powers contained in the trust instrument under which the property is received, including the expenditure of the principal, as well as the income, for one or more of such purposes, if authorized or directed in the

4. The "charitable organizations" (as defined above) to which payments of income and/or principal may be made under this trust may be further restricted from time to time by an instrument in writing signed by the trustees, which shall be kept attached to the executed original of this trust held by the trustees. When such further restriction has been imposed in the manner described in the preceding sentence, such further restriction shall be irrevocable.

5. The trustees may amend this trust in any way that from time to time may be necessary to cause the income to be exempt from federal and state income taxation. Such amendment shall be by an instrument in writing signed by the trustees, which shall be kept attached to the executed original of this trust held by the trustees. Such an amendment, if made, shall be irrevocable.

FOURTH: The trustees serving hereunder shall be entitled to reasonable compensation, but in no event shall Richard Harry Black III ever receive any compensation, and no trustee serving hereunder shall be entitled to any compensation from and after the date he or she makes a contribution to the trust.

FIFTH: In extension and not in limitation of the powers given them by law or other provisions of this instrument, the trustees hereunder shall have the following powers with respect to this trust and its property, in each case to be exercised from time to time in their discretion and without order or license of court:

1. To retain indefinitely any investments and to invest and reinvest in stocks, shares and obligations of corporations, of unincorporated associations or trusts and of investment companies, or in a common trust fund, or in any other kind of personal or real property, notwithstanding the fact that any or all of the investments made or retained are of a character or size which but for this express authority would not be considered proper for trustees;

2. To sell, to exchange, to lease and to make contracts concerning real or personal property, which leases and contracts may extend beyond the term of the trust; to give options therefor; to execute deeds, transfers, leases and other instruments of any kind;

3. To hold the trust property in the names of the trustees or in the

(3)

trust instrument under which it is received; to receive, take title to, hold, and use the proceeds and income of stocks, bonds, obligations, or other securities of any corporation or corporations, domestic or foreign, but only for the foregoing purposes, or some of them; and, in general, to exercise any, all and every power for which a non-profit corporation known as a Foundation, organized under the provisions of the Michigan General Corporation Act for scientific, educational, and charitable purposes, all for the public welfare, can be authorized to exercise, but not any other power. No part of the activities of this corporation shall be the carrying on of propaganda or otherwise attempting to influence legislation." — Ed.

name of one of the trustees but only with indication of fiduciary capacity unless the trustee in whose name the trust property is held is a bank or trust company, in which case the trust property may be held without indication of fiduciary capacity; to hold the trust property in the name of a nominee of a bank or trust company which is a trustee or custodian of the trust property; to deposit cash in a checking or savings account in a bank but only with indication of fiduciary capacity; provided always, however, that the trust property shall at all times be physically held in such a manner as to make it clearly identifiable as the property of this trust;[81]

4. To give general or special proxies or powers of attorney for voting or acting in respect of shares or securities, which may be discretionary and with power of substitution; to deposit shares or securities with, or transfer them to, protective committees or similar bodies; to join in any reorganization and to pay assessments or subscriptions called for in connection with shares or securities held by them;

5. To construct, alter or repair buildings or structures on real estate; to settle boundary lines and easements and other rights with respect to real estate; to partition and to join with co-owners and others in dealing with real estate;

6. To employ investment counsel, custodians of trust property, brokers, agents and attorneys;

7. To receive additions to the trust under this instrument by gift or will or otherwise, and to hold and administer to same under the provisions hereof;

8. To pay as income the whole of the interest, dividends, rent or similar receipts from property, whether wasting or not and although bought or taken at a value above par, but if they see fit, when property is bought or taken at a value above par, they may retain a portion of the income to offset such loss to the principal; to treat as income or principal or to apportion between them stock dividends, extra dividends, rights to take stock or securities and proceeds from the sale of real estate, although such real estate may have been wholly or partly unproductive; to charge to income or principal or to apportion between them any expense of making or changing investments, investment counsel's com-

(4)

[81] Although no formal ruling has been issued to date, the Internal Revenue Service has refused to recognize as an exempt charitable trust one in which the trustees are given the power to hold securities in their individual names without indication of their fiduciary capacity. It has come to my attention that, in a recent ruling granting exempt status to a charitable trust, the following paragraph was included: "This ruling is made with the understanding that any funds, securities or other property now owned or acquired in the future will be held and maintained strictly in the name of the trustees with full disclosure of the fiduciary relationship, or in the name of such nominee as may be appointed exclusively by a bank or trust company acting as custodian for the Trust." — Ed.

pensation, custodians' compensation, brokers' commissions, agents' compensation, attorneys' fees, insurance premiums, repairs or improvements, taxes, depreciation charges and trustees' compensation; and generally to determine all questions as between income and principal and to credit or charge to income or principal or to apportion between them any receipt or gain and any charge, disbursement or loss as is reasonable in the circumstances of each case as it arises;

9. To make distributions in cash or in kind or partly in cash and partly in kind;

10. To keep any or all of the trust property at any place or places in ....[82] or elsewhere within the United States or abroad or with a depositary or custodian in such place or places.

No power given to the trustees under this instrument shall be construed to enable the settlor or any person to purchase, exchange, or otherwise deal with or dispose of the principal or the income therefrom for less than an adequate consideration in money or money's worth; to permit the settlor or any other contributor to the trust to borrow income or principal; or to authorize loans to a person other than the settlor or any other contributor to the trust except on the basis of an adequate interest charge and with adequate security. It is the settlor's intention that contributions to this charitable trust be deductible for federal income, gift and estate tax purposes, and that the income of this charitable trust be exempt from federal income taxation, and that the provisions of this instrument be construed so that these intentions will be effectuated.

SIXTH: The powers and discretions herein given to the trustees are exercisable by them only in a fiduciary capacity in furtherance of the charitable purposes of this trust and not otherwise.

SEVENTH: No one dealing with the trustees need inquire concerning the validity of anything they purport to do, or need see to the application of any money paid or any property transferred to or upon the order of the trustees.

EIGHTH: A trustee hereunder shall not be liable for an act, misfeasance or default of any co-trustee or of any prior trustee or of any agent or of any other person but shall be liable only for his or her own personal and willful act, misfeasance or default.

NINTH: This is a ....[83] trust, made in that State, and is to be governed and construed and administered according to its laws and shall continue to be so governed and construed and administered even though it is administered elsewhere within the United States or abroad.

TENTH: To the same effect as if it were the original, anyone may rely upon a copy certified by a notary public to be a counterpart of this

(5)

---

[82] Insert the state where the settlor resides.
[83] Insert the state which is to govern.

instrument (and of the writings, if any, endorsed thereon or attached thereto). Anyone may rely upon any statement of fact certified by anyone who appears from the original document or a certified copy to be a trustee hereunder.

IN WITNESS WHEREOF, RICHARD HARRY BLACK III as settlor has hereunto set his hand and seal, and **RICHARD HARRY BLACK III, MILDRED MARIE BLACK** and **RICHARD HARRY BLACK IV**, in token of their acceptance of the trust hereby created, have caused their hands and seals to be hereto affixed all as of this .... day of ...., 19............[84]

/s/ *Richard Harry Black III* [Seal]

SETTLOR AND TRUSTEE

/s/ *Mildred Marie Black* [Seal]

TRUSTEE

/s/ *Richard Harry Black IV* [Seal]

TRUSTEE

.... of ....[85]
......................,[86] ss.   ....
.............................., 19............[87]

Then personally appeared the above-named RICHARD HARRY BLACK III and acknowledged the foregoing instrument to be his free act and deed, before me,

/s/ *Robert Lewis*

NOTARY PUBLIC

[Notarial Seal]

ROBERT LEWIS Notary Public
My commission expires ...., 19............[88]

.... of ....[89]
......................,[90] ss   ....
.............................., 19............[91]

(6)

[84] Insert the date on which the trust is executed.
[85] Insert the state in which the acknowledgment is taken.
[86] Insert the county in which the acknowledgment is taken.
[87] Insert the city in which and the date on which the acknowledgment is taken.
[88] Insert the date on which the notary's commission expires.
[89] Insert the state in which the acknowledgment is taken.
[90] Insert the county in which the acknowledgment is taken.
[91] Insert the city in which and the date on which the acknowledgment is taken.

Then personally appeared the above-named MILDRED MARIE BLACK and acknowledged the foregoing instrument to be her free act and deed, before me,

/s/ *Robert Lewis*

NOTARY PUBLIC

[Notarial Seal]

    ROBERT LEWIS Notary Public
    My commission expires _____, 19_____[92]

_____ of _____[93]

_____,[94] ss.

              _____

              _____, 19_____[95]

Then personally appeared the above-named RICHARD HARRY BLACK IV and acknowledged the foregoing instrument to be his free act and deed, before me,

/s/ *Robert Lewis*

NOTARY PUBLIC

[Notarial Seal]

    ROBERT LEWIS Notary Public
    My commission expires _____, 19_____[96]

(7)

[92] Insert the date on which the notary's commission expires.
[93] Insert the state in which the acknowledgment is taken.
[94] Insert the county in which the acknowledgment is taken.
[95] Insert the city in which and the date on which the acknowledgment is taken.
[96] Insert the date on which the notary's commission expires.

SCHEDULE A

[*Note:* Assume that on this page the various securities placed in this trust are listed.   Mr. Black selected securities in his account with the Jones and Jones investment house which are worth approximately $50,000 and placed these securities in this trust.   The securities he selected are, in the main, those which had a low basis.]

H. *Present Interest Trust for a Minor*[97]

I, RICHARD HARRY BLACK III, of ....,
....[98] (hereinafter called the "settlor"), hereby transfer Five Dollars ($5) to JAMES ROBERT BLACK (hereinaftei called the "trustee"); and at the request of the settlor, the trustee agrees to hold the said sum of money and all additions thereto, in trust, as follows:

FIRST: This trust cannot be altered, amended, revoked, or termi- nated by the settlor, and may be known as "THE JAMES HARRY BLACK PRESENT INTEREST TRUST."

SECOND: The trust property and the income therefrom may be expended in whole or in part by, or for the benefit of, James Harry Black, grandchild of the settlor, from time to time, in such amount or amounts, as the trustee in his uncontrolled discretion may determine, until the said grandchild attains the age of twenty-one (21) years or dies, whichever first occurs. If the said grandchild lives to attain the age of twenty-one (21) years, then when he attains that age, the trustee shall pay the then remaining principal and undistributed income to the said grandchild free and clear of any trust unless the said grandchild directs otherwise. If the said grandchild dies before attaining the age of twenty-one (21) years, then on the death of the said grandchild, the trustee shall pay the then remaining principal and undistributed in- come to, or hold the same for the benefit of, such person or persons or the estate of the said grandchild, in such amounts and proportions and for such estates and interests and outright or upon such terms, trusts, conditions and limitations as the said grandchild shall appoint by his will; and if, or to the extent that, the said grandchild does not effec- tively exercise his power to appoint by will, the trustee shall pay the then remaining principal and undistributed income in equal shares to the settlor's grandchildren then living, and if no grandchild of the set- tlor is then living, to the estate of the said grandchild. A child adopted by a child of the settlor shall be deemed a grandchild of the settlor for the purposes of this instrument. Also a divorce granted by a court of record shall be valid for all purposes in applying the provisions of this instrument.

THIRD: In extension and not in limitation of the powers given him by law or other provisions of this instrument, the trustee hereunder shall have the following powers with respect to the trust established hereunder and the trust property, in each case to be exercised from time to time in his discretion and without order or license of court:

(1)

---

[97] Only the present interest trust for grandchild James Harry Black is set out here. Identical trusts were executed for each grandchild. It is understood that no contributions are to be made to any of these trusts by the person named as trus- tee. — ED.

[98] Insert the city and state where Mr. Black resides.

1. To retain indefinitely any investments and to invest and reinvest in stocks, shares and obligations of corporations, of unincorporated associations or trusts and of investment companies (all dividends which represent capital gains shall be added to principal), or in any other kind of personal or real property;
2. To sell, to exchange, to lease and to make contracts concerning real or personal property, which leases and contracts may extend beyond the term of the trust; to give options therefor; to execute deeds, transfers, leases and other instruments of any kind;
3. To hold bonds, shares or other securities in bearer form, or in the name of the trustee or in the name of a nominee, without indication of any fiduciary capacity;
4. To deposit cash in a bank or banks in the name of the trustee without any indication of his fiduciary capacity;
5. To give general or special proxies or powers of attorney for voting or acting in respect of shares or securities, which may be discretionary and with power of substitution; to deposit shares or securities with, or transfer them to, protective committees or similar bodies; to join in any reorganization and to pay assessments or subscriptions called for in connection with shares or securities held by the trustee;
6. To employ investment counsel, custodians of trust property, brokers, agents and attorneys;
7. To receive additions to the trust under this instrument by gift or will or otherwise, and to hold and administer the same under the provisions hereof;
8. To make distributions in cash or in kind or partly in cash and partly in kind.

All powers given to the trustee by this instrument are exercisable by the trustee only in a fiduciary capacity. No power given to the trustee hereunder shall be construed to enable the settlor or any person to purchase, exchange, or otherwise deal with or dispose of the principal or income therefrom for less than an adequate consideration in money or money's worth; to permit the settlor or any other contributor to the trust to borrow income or principal; or to authorize loans to a person other than the settlor or any other contributor to the trust except on the basis of an adequate interest charge and with adequate security. The trustee shall not use the income or principal of the trust to pay premiums on insurance on the life of the settlor.

FOURTH: No bond shall be required of the original trustee hereunder or of any successor trustee, or if a bond is required by law, no surety shall be required on such bond.

If a vacancy in the office of trustee occurs, an individual shall be appointed to fill such vacancy by an instrument in writing signed by the legal guardian of said grandchild. No one who has contributed property to this trust and no one who is legally obligated to support said grandchild shall be appointed a trustee hereunder.

(2)

The trustee may resign at any time by an instrument in writing delivered to the legal guardian of the said grandchild.

References in this instrument to "trustee" shall be deemed to include not only the original trustee but also any successor trustee, and all powers and discretions vested in the trustee shall be vested in and exercisable by any such successor trustee. A successor trustee shall not be liable for the acts of a prior trustee.

No one dealing with the trustee need inquire concerning the validity of anything he purports to do, or need see to the application of any money paid or any property transferred to or upon the order of the trustee.

FIFTH: This is a ....[99] trust, made in that State, and is to be governed and construed and administered according to its laws and shall continue to be so governed and construed and administered even though administered elsewhere within the United States or abroad.

SIXTH: To the same effect as if it were the original, anyone may rely upon a copy certified by a notary public to be a counterpart of this instrument (and of the writings, if any, endorsed thereon or attached thereto). Anyone may rely upon any statement of fact certified by anyone who appears from the original document or a certified copy to be a trustee hereunder.

IN WITNESS WHEREOF, RICHARD HARRY BLACK III as settlor has hereunto set his hand and seal, and JAMES ROBERT BLACK, in token of his acceptance of the trust hereby created, has caused his hand and seal to be hereto affixed, all as of this .... day of ...., 19...........[100]

/s/ *Richard Harry Black III* [Seal]

SETTLOR

/s/ *James Robert Black* [Seal]

TRUSTEE

.... of ....[101]
....,[102] ss.   ....
...., 19...........[103]

Then personally appeared the above-named RICHARD HARRY

(3)

---

[99] Insert the state which is to govern.
[100] Insert the date on which the trust is executed.
[101] Insert the state in which the acknowledgment is taken.
[102] Insert the county in which the acknowledgment is taken.
[103] Insert the city in which and the date on which the acknowledgment is taken.

BLACK III, who acknowledged the foregoing instrument to be his free act and deed, before me,

/s/ *Robert Lewis*
....
NOTARY PUBLIC

[Notarial Seal]

ROBERT LEWIS Notary Public
My commission expires ...., 19.............[104]

.... of ....[105]
.................................,[106] ss.   ....
...., 19.............[107]

Then personally appeared the above-named JAMES ROBERT BLACK, who acknowledged the foregoing instrument to be his free act and deed, before me,

/s/ *Robert Lewis*
....
NOTARY PUBLIC

[Notarial Seal]

ROBERT LEWIS Notary Public
My commission expires ...., 19.............[108]

(4)

---

[104] Insert the date on which the notary's commission expires.
[105] Insert the state in which the acknowledgment is taken.
[106] Insert the county in which the acknowledgment is taken.
[107] Insert the city in which and the date on which the acknowledgment is taken.
[108] Insert the date on which the notary's commission expires.

I. *Short-Term Trust*

DECLARATION OF TRUST made this ....
day of ...., 19............,[109] by **RICHARD HARRY
BLACK III**, of ...., ...,[110]
who hereby declares that on the aforesaid date he delivered to himself
as trustee the property listed in Schedule A attached hereto, which
property is to be held in trust hereunder; and furthermore, he hereby
declares that said property and all property hereafter added to the
same from any source, or hereafter acquired by him as trustee hereunder, and all proceeds and investments thereof, shall be held by him
or his successor or successors, in trust, as follows:

FIRST: This trust shall terminate ten (10) years and one (1) day
after the aforesaid date unless Richard Harry Black IV and Margaret
Black Logan, children of the said Richard Harry Black III, both die
prior to that time, in which case this trust shall terminate on the death
of the survivor of the said children. The said Richard Harry Black
III shall have no power to alter, amend, revoke or terminate this trust
prior to the date of termination as set forth in the preceding sentence
but he may postpone the date of termination specified in the preceding
sentence.

SECOND: During the continuance of this trust, the net income shall
be paid in equal shares to the said children while both of them are
living and shall be paid to the survivor while only one of them is living. Income payments shall be made at least as often as quarterly.

THIRD: On the termination of this trust, the principal shall be
paid to the said Richard Harry Black III; or if he has assigned his
interest, to the person or persons then entitled under such assignment; or if he is not then living and has not assigned his interest
during his lifetime, to his executors or administrators.

FOURTH: The interest of the said children in the income from
this trust shall be free from the control or interference of any creditor
or of any spouse and shall not be subject to attachment or susceptible
of anticipation or alienation.

FIFTH: The trustee shall each year render an account of his administration of this trust to the said Richard Harry Black III if he is
living and is not serving as a trustee, and if the said Richard Harry
Black III is not living or if living is serving as a trustee, to the said
children if both of them are living, otherwise to the one that is living.
The written approval of the person or persons to whom the account
must be rendered shall, as to all matters and transactions stated therein
or shown thereby, be final and binding upon all persons (whether in
being or not) who are then or may thereafter become interested in, or

(1)

---

109 Insert the date when the trust is executed.
110 Insert the city and state where Mr. Black resides.

entitled to share in, the income or principal of the trust, provided always, however, that nothing contained in this Article FIFTH shall be deemed to give anyone acting in conjunction with the trustee the power to alter or amend the terms of this trust.

SIXTH: In extension and not in limitation of the powers he will have by law or other provisions of this DECLARATION OF TRUST, the trustee shall have the following powers and discretions with respect to this trust and its property, in each case to be exercised from time to time in his discretion and without order or license of court:

1. To retain indefinitely any investments and to invest and reinvest in stocks, shares and obligations of corporations, of unincorporated associations or trusts and of investment companies, or in any other kind of personal or real property, notwithstanding the fact that any or all of the investments made or retained are of a character or size which but for this express authority would not be considered proper for trustees;

2. To sell, to exchange, to lease and to make contracts concerning the trust property, which leases and contracts may extend beyond the term of the trust; to give options therefor; to execute deeds, transfers, leases and other instruments of any kind;

3. To hold bonds, shares or other securities in bearer form, or in the name of the trustee or in the name of a nominee, without indication of any fiduciary capacity; to deposit cash in a checking or savings account in a bank, without indication of any fiduciary capacity;

4. To give general or special proxies or powers of attorney for voting or acting in respect of shares or securities, which may be discretionary and with power of substitution; to deposit shares or securities with, or transfer them to, protective committees or similar bodies; to join in any reorganization and to pay assessments or subscriptions called for in connection with shares or securities held by him;

5. To employ investment counsel, custodians of trust property, brokers, agents and attorneys;

6. To receive additions to the trust hereunder and to hold and administer the same under the provisions hereof;

7. To make distributions in cash or in kind or partly in cash and partly in kind.

All powers given to the trustee by this instrument are exercisable by the trustee only in a fiduciary capacity. No power given to the trustee hereunder shall be construed to enable the said Richard Harry Black III or any person to purchase, exchange, or otherwise deal with or dispose of the principal or income therefrom for less than an adequate consideration in money or money's worth; to permit the said Richard Harry Black III to borrow income or principal; or to authorize loans to a person other than the said Richard Harry Black III except on the

(2)

basis of an adequate interest charge and with adequate security. The trustee shall not use the income or principal of the trust to pay premiums on insurance on the life of the settlor.

SEVENTH: No bond shall be required of the original trustee or of any successor trustee, or if a bond is required by law, no surety on such bond shall be required.

If the said Richard Harry Black III dies, or for any reason is unable to serve or ceases to serve as trustee, the said Richard Harry Black IV is hereby designated trustee. If the said Richard Harry Black IV dies, declines to serve or for any reason is unable to serve or ceases to serve as trustee, the said Margaret Black Logan is hereby designated trustee.

A trustee may resign at any time by an instrument in writing indicating his intention in this regard, which instrument in writing shall be delivered to the said Richard Harry Black III if he is living and competent, and if he is not living or if living is not competent, by such an instrument in writing which shall be delivered to the said Richard Harry Black IV if he is living and competent, and if he is not living or if living is not competent, by such an instrument in writing which shall be delivered to the said Margaret Black Logan if she is living and competent.

References in this instrument to "trustee" shall be deemed to include not only the original trustee but also any successor trustee, and all powers and discretions vested in the trustee shall be vested in and be exercisable by any such successor trustee. A successor trustee shall not be liable for the acts of a prior trustee.

No one dealing with the trustee need inquire concerning the validity of anything he purports to do, or need see to the application of any money paid or any property transferred to or upon the order of the trustee.

EIGHTH: This trust is a .... trust,[111] made in that State, and is to be governed and construed and administered according to its laws and shall continue to be so governed and construed and administered though administered elsewhere in the United States or abroad.

NINTH: To the same effect as if it were the original, anyone may rely upon a copy certified by a notary public to be a counterpart of this instrument (and of the writings, if any, endorsed thereon or attached thereto). Anyone may rely upon any statement of fact certified by anyone who appears from the original document or a certified copy to be a trustee hereunder.

SIGNED AND SEALED by the above-named RICHARD HARRY BLACK III on the date first above written.

/s/ *Richard Harry Black III* [Seal]

(3)

111 Insert the state which is to govern.

-- of --[112]

--,[113] ss.   --
                                        --------------------------------------, 19----------[114]

Then personally appeared the above-named **RICHARD HARRY BLACK III** and acknowledged the foregoing instrument to be his free act and deed, before me,

/s/ *Robert Lewis*

NOTARY PUBLIC

[Notarial Seal]

ROBERT LEWIS Notary Public
My commission expires --, 19----------[115]

The undersigned hereby acknowledge receipt of a copy of this instrument.

/s/ *Richard Harry Black IV* [Seal]

/s/ *Margaret Black Logan* [Seal]

(4)

112 Insert the state in which the acknowledgment is taken.
113 Insert the county in which the acknowledgment is taken.
114 Insert the city in which and the date on which the acknowledgment is taken.
115 Insert the date on which the notary's commission expires.

SCHEDULE A

[*Note:* Assume that on this page the various securities placed in this trust are listed.   Mr. Black selected securities in his account with the Jones and Jones investment house which are worth approximately $50,000 and placed these securities in this trust.   He avoided, as far as possible, placing in the trust any securities which had a basis in excess of the present market.]

J.   *The Richard Harry Black III Revocable Trust*

I, RICHARD HARRY BLACK III, of ....
....[116] (hereinafter called the "settlor"), hereby
transfer in ....[117] the
property listed in Schedule A attached hereto to RICHARD HARRY
BLACK III, RICHARD HARRY BLACK IV and ROBERT J.
ANDREW of ...., ...[118]
(hereinafter called the "trustees"); and the settlor also desires or may
desire to have the proceeds of one or more policies of insurance on
his life payable to the trustees hereunder; and at the request of the
settlor, the trustees agree to hold such property and such life insurance
proceeds and all additions thereto from whatever source in trust as
follows:

FIRST: This trust may be known as "THE RICHARD HARRY
BLACK III TRUST," and can be amended, altered, revoked or terminated by the settlor in the manner hereinafter described.

SECOND: The trustees shall dispose of the net income and principal
as the settlor may direct the trustees from time to time by an instrument in writing signed by the settlor and delivered to the trustees in
the lifetime of the settlor, provided always, however, that if, in the
opinion of the disinterested trustee, the settlor is incapacitated through
illness, age or other cause, the disinterested trustee may in his uncontrolled discretion, from time to time, while he believes such incapacity
continues, apply all or any part of the net income or principal toward
the support, care and benefit of the settlor and the settlor's wife, Mildred Marie Black, in such amount or amounts and in such manner as
he may determine without regard to the settlor's other means or the
other means of the settlor's said wife. Any net income in any year
which is not disposed of by the terms of the preceding sentence shall
be added to the principal of the trust at the end of each year.

THIRD: The settlor reserves the right at any time or times to
amend, alter, revoke or terminate this trust, in whole or in part, or
any provision thereof, by an instrument in writing signed by the settlor
and delivered to the trustees in the lifetime of the settlor. If this trust
is revoked in its entirety, the revocation shall take effect upon the
delivery of the required writing to the trustees. On the revocation of
this trust in its entirety, the trustees shall pay or transfer to the settlor,
or as the settlor may direct in the instrument of revocation, all of the
trust fund.

The settlor's will may provide for additions to a trust hereunder and
consequently the settlor's will should be examined in connection with

(1)

---

[116] Insert the city and state where Mr. Black resides.
[117] Insert the city and state in which the transfer is made.
[118] Insert the place of residence of Mr. Andrew.

the making of any alteration, amendment or revocation of this instrument to determine what changes, if any, should be made in the settlor's will in the light of such alteration, amendment or revocation of this instrument.

FOURTH: The settlor reserves the right by his own act alone, without the consent or approval of the trustees, to sell, assign or hypothecate any policies of insurance upon his life made payable to the trustees, to exercise any option or privilege granted by such policies, including, but without limitation of the generality of the foregoing, the right to change the beneficiary of such policies, to borrow any sum in accordance with the provisions of such policies and to receive all payments, dividends, surrender values, benefits or privileges of any kind which may accrue on account of such policies during his lifetime. Furthermore, the trustees agree to deliver to the settlor on his written request any of such policies deposited with the trustees hereunder.

If, in the opinion of the disinterested trustee, the settlor is incapacitated through illness, age or other cause, the disinterested trustee may in his uncontrolled discretion pay any premiums on insurance on the life of the settlor.[119]

FIFTH: The trustees shall use their best efforts to collect the proceeds of any policies of insurance upon the settlor's life made payable to the trustees hereunder when any of such policies shall, to the knowledge of the trustees, have matured, but they shall not be required to take any legal proceedings until indemnified. The trustees shall have no responsibility, except as above specified, as to any of such policies, or the premiums thereon.[120]

SIXTH: The trustees shall render to the settlor annually an account of income and principal. The settlor's written approval of said account shall as to all matters and transactions covered by said account be binding upon all who are then or who may thereafter become entitled to the income or principal.

SEVENTH: On the death of the settlor, if the settlor's said wife survives him, the following described fractional share of the trust fund (for the purposes of this Article SEVENTH the words "trust fund" shall include only the trust property as it exists immediately prior to the settlor's death, including undistributed income, plus the proceeds

(2)

---

[119] It might be desirable for all concerned if the disinterested trustee could have the incidents of ownership of the policies on the life of the settlor during any period the settlor is incapacitated. If the incidents of ownership are transferred to the trustees at the time the trust is established (rather than just having the trustees named as beneficiaries in the policies), the control over the incidents of ownership could be vested in the disinterested trustee during any period the settlor is incapacitated. — ED.

[120] If the trustees are designated as the beneficiaries of the policies on the life of the settlor, the beneficiary designations should specify contingent beneficiaries to take the proceeds in the event that the trust is revoked by the settlor and hence is not in existence on his death. — ED.

of insurance on the life of the settlor which are payable to the trustees hereunder) shall be placed in a separate trust to be known as "THE MILDRED MARIE BLACK MARITAL DEDUCTION TRUST":

The numerator of the fraction shall be the maximum estate tax marital deduction (allowable in determining the federal estate tax payable by reason of the settlor's death) minus the value for federal estate tax purposes of all items in the settlor's gross estate which qualify for said deduction and which pass or have passed to the settlor's said wife from the settlor (the words "pass or have passed" shall have the same meaning as such words shall have under the provisions of the Internal Revenue Code in effect at the time of the settlor's death) under other provisions of this instrument, under the provisions of the settlor's will, by right of survivorship with respect to jointly owned property, under settlement arrangements relating to life insurance proceeds not payable to the trustees hereunder, or otherwise than under this Article SEVENTH (in computing the numerator, the values as finally determined for federal estate tax purposes shall control);[121] and the denominator of the fraction shall be the value of the trust fund, and to the extent that the items in the trust fund as originally constituted are included in the settlor's gross estate their value for federal estate tax purposes shall control in determining the denominator, and to the extent that such items are not so included, their value at the time they would have been valued if they had been so included shall control in determining the denominator.[122]

If the numerator of the above-described fraction equals or exceeds the denominator, the entire trust fund shall be placed in THE MILDRED MARIE BLACK MARITAL DEDUCTION TRUST. This separate trust is not one of a specified dollar amount and its provisions shall be construed accordingly.[123] The trustees are directed as follows with

(3)

[121] The value of the adjusted gross estate must be determined before the numerator can be ascertained. The value of the adjusted gross estate will differ if the executor elects to take certain expenses of administration as income tax deductions rather than estate tax deductions. The executor's selection of the alternate valuation date rather than the date of the settlor's death will affect the value of the adjusted gross estate. The parenthetical statement in the trust instrument is designed to make it clear that the computation of the numerator will be controlled by whatever finally turns out to be the values for federal estate tax purposes of such items as must be valued in order to determine the maximum allowable marital deduction. — ED.

[122] The definition of the words "trust fund" for the purposes of Article Seventh make it extremely unlikely that there will be any items in that fund as originally constituted that will not be included in the settlor's gross estate. The only possible item would seem to be foreign real estate. — ED.

[123] When a formula fractional share marital deduction gift is made, one of the objectives is to make possible a distribution in kind without subjecting the trust to a capital gain if the value of the distributed property at the date of distribution to the separate trust is greater than its basis. — ED.

respect to THE MILDRED MARIE BLACK MARITAL DEDUC-
TION TRUST:[124]

1. The trustees shall pay the net income from the time of the settlor's death to the settlor's said wife for her life; and, in addition,
the trustees shall pay to the settlor's said wife, or as she directs,
from the principal of the trust, from time to time, such amount
or amounts or all of the principal as the settlor's said wife may
specify in an instrument or instruments in writing delivered to
the trustees in her lifetime. If, in the opinion of the disinterested
trustee, the settlor's said wife is incapacitated through illness, age
or other cause, the disinterested trustee may in his uncontrolled
discretion, from time to time, while he believes such incapacity
continues, apply all or any part of the principal toward the support, care and benefit of the settlor's said wife, in such amount or
amounts and in such manner as he may determine without regard
to the other means of the settlor's said wife.

2. On the death of the settlor's said wife, the trustees shall pay the
then remaining principal and the income for the period between
the last income distribution date and the date of the death of the
settlor's said wife to, or hold the same for the benefit of, such person or persons or the estate of the settlor's said wife, in such
amounts and proportions and for such estates and interests and
outright or upon such terms, trust, conditions and limitations, as
the settlor's said wife shall appoint by a will, executed after the
settlor's death, referring specifically to the power herein given to
the settlor's said wife.[125]

(4)

[124] If the estate tax marital deduction is modified or eliminated by future legislation prior to the settlor's death, the settlor will have to amend the trust. It does not
appear to be feasible to provide an alternative disposition to cover such a future
contingency.

The trustee will not be able to determine precisely the portion of the trust fund
that is to go into the marital trust until the amount of the settlor's adjusted gross
estate is ascertained. This very likely will not be known until after at least one
tax year has passed. To whom will the income of the marital trust be taxable for
the tax years that pass prior to the time a definitive determination is made as to
the portion of the trust fund that will be placed in the marital trust? It is believed
that such income will be taxable to the settlor's wife, and if the estimate of the
income for such years that is taxable to her is too high, she would claim a refund
on the tax paid on the estimate; if it is too low, she would amend her return when
the right amount became known and would pay the additional tax. The trust
would take corresponding action as to any income on which it paid a tax or failed
to pay a tax.

If the marital trust established on the settlor's death is limited to a nominal
amount and the trust so established is increased to the desired size by a pour-over
from the settlor's will, the income attributable to the pour-over share would be
taxable to the estate until distribution, and such a tax result might be more beneficial during the period of administration than the one described in the preceding
paragraph. Income taxation of estates is considered in Chapter IV, and income
taxation of trusts is examined in Chapter XII. — ED.

[125] New York Real Property Law §170 provides as follows: "Where the grantor

3. On the death of the settlor's said wife, if, or to the extent that, the settlor's said wife does not exercise her power to appoint by will, the trustees shall dispose of the then remaining principal and the income for the period between the last income distribution date and the date of the death of the settlor's said wife as follows:

   (a) If issue of the settlor are then living or a widow of a deceased son of the settlor is then living who has not remarried, the trustees shall add the same to the fund disposed of by Section 2 of Article EIGHTH.

   (b) If no issue of the settlor is then living and no widow of a deceased son of the settlor is then living who has not remarried, the trustee shall pay the same to THE BLACK FAMILY FOUNDATION, created by an indenture of trust, dated ...., 19............,[126] if it is then in existence, otherwise to ....[127]

4. There shall not be allocated to this separate trust any property, or the proceeds of any property, which do not qualify for the estate tax marital deduction or which are subject to foreign death taxes. Furthermore, income in respect of a decedent (or the right to income in respect of a decedent) shall not be allocated to this separate trust. In place of that which would be allocated to this separate trust but for the exclusion directed by the two preceding sentences, there shall be allocated other property of equivalent value.

5. The settlor intends that the value for federal estate tax purposes of the property of this trust shall be available for the marital deduction allowed by the federal estate tax law applicable to his estate and all questions applicable to this trust shall be resolved accordingly.[128] To this end, the powers and discretions of the trustees with respect to the property in this trust shall not be exercised or exercisable, during the period that the settlor's said wife

(5)

---

of a power has directed any formality to be observed in its execution, in addition to those which would be sufficient by law to pass the estate, the observance of such additional formality is not necessary to the valid execution of the power, except that if the grantor has explicitly directed that no instrument shall be effective to exercise the power unless it contains a reference to the specific power, an instrument which lacks such reference will not validly exercise the power."

[126] Insert the date when the indenture of trust was executed.

[127] Insert the name of a charity.

[128] In re Lieberman's Will, 2 Misc. 2d 833, 840, 147 N.Y.S.2d 815, 822 (1955), contains the following language: "The expressly declared intention of testator to obtain the maximum marital deduction allowable ordinarily imports an intention that estate taxes shall not be deducted in the computation of the net estate. To the extent that a spouse does not receive at least one half of the taxable estate free of tax the estate would be burdened with a greater tax than would otherwise be imposed, and the estate would not obtain the maximum benefit of the marital deduction to the extent of such additional tax." — ED.

survives him, except in a manner consistent with the settlor's intentions as expressed in the preceding sentence.

6. For the purposes of this Article SEVENTH, in determining whether the settlor's said wife survives him, if the order of their deaths cannot be established by proof, the settlor's said wife shall be deemed to have survived him. If the settlor's said wife does not survive him by six (6) months, the numerator of the above-described fraction shall be reduced by a sum equal to one half of the amount by which the value of the adjusted gross estate of the settlor's said wife exceeds the value of the items in the settlor's gross estate (which are also in his said wife's gross estate) which qualify for the estate tax marital deduction in determining the settlor's taxable estate for federal estate tax purposes.

7. If the settlor's said wife disclaims, in whole or in part, her interest in and power over any property placed in this estate tax marital deduction trust, the trustees shall add the property or the portion thereof to which such disclaimer of interest and power pertains to the trust property disposed of by Article EIGHTH of this instrument, such property so added to be disposed of as though it were a part of the trust property disposed of by Article EIGHTH from the date of the settlor's death. In addition to any method of disclaimer recognized by law, the settlor's said wife may disclaim by an instrument in writing signed by her and delivered to the trustees.

EIGHTH: On the death of the settlor, the trust property (the words "trust property" shall include all property held in trust under this instrument except that which is required to be placed in the separate trust under Article SEVENTH either by the preceding provisions of this instrument or by the terms of any instrument which directs that property be held in trust under this instrument) shall be held in trust or disposed of as follows:

1. During the lifetime of the settlor's said wife, the disinterested trustee may pay to, or apply for the benefit of, any one or more of the group consisting of the settlor's said wife and the settlor's issue who are living from time to time, such amount or amounts of the net income or all of the net income as the disinterested trustee in his uncontrolled discretion may determine; any net income in any year which is not paid to, or applied for the benefit of, any one or more of said group shall be added to the principal of the trust at the end of the year; in addition, the disinterested trustee may pay to, or apply for the benefit of, any one or more of said group, from the principal of the trust, from time to time, such amount or amounts or all of the principal as he in his uncontrolled discretion may determine; payments of income and principal to the issue of the settlor pursuant to the above provisions shall be taken into account, in the manner hereinafter

(6)

provided, in any division of the principal and undistributed income into shares for the benefit of such issue on the death of the settlor's said wife.[129]

2. On the death of the settlor's said wife, or on the settlor's death if the settlor's said wife does not survive him, if issue of the settlor are then living or a widow of a deceased son of the settlor is then living who has not remarried, the trustees shall assume they have trust property comprised of the then remaining principal and undistributed income plus the amount added by paragraph (a) of Section 3 of Article SEVENTH and the payments made to the settlor's issue under Section 1 above minus the payments made to a deceased child of the settlor and to such deceased child's issue under Section 1 above if such deceased child has no issue then living and no widow then living who has not remarried, and the trustees shall divide such assumed trust property into as many equal shares as there are children of the settlor then living and children of the settlor then deceased with issue then living and sons of the settlor then deceased who have no issue then living but have a widow then living who has not remarried. The trustees shall allocate to each living son of the settlor out of the then remaining principal and undistributed income (as augmented by the addition thereto pursuant to the terms of paragraph (a) of Section 3 of Article SEVENTH) one of such equal shares minus the payments made to such son and to such son's issue under Section 1 above, and the trustees shall hold such share in a separate trust in accordance with the provisions of paragraph (a) of this Section 2. The trustees shall allocate to each living daughter of the settlor out of the then remaining principal and undistributed income (as augmented by the addition thereto pursuant to the terms of paragraph (a) of Section 3 of Article SEVENTH) one of such equal shares minus the payments made to such daughter and to such daughter's issue under Section 1 above, and the trustees shall hold such share in a separate trust in accordance with the provisions of paragraph (b) of this Section 2. The trustees shall allocate to the issue of each deceased child of the settlor out of the then remaining principal and undistributed income (as augmented by the addition thereto pursuant to the terms of paragraph (a) of Section 3 of Article SEVENTH) one of such equal shares minus the payments made

(7)

---

[129] The payments to the issue of the settlor which must be taken into account may have been accumulation distributions (see 1954 I.R.C., §665), so that all or a pro rata portion of the taxes paid by the trust will be deemed distributed (§666) and so that the distributee will be entitled to a credit for taxes paid by the trust (§668(b)). Is the payment to be taken into account limited to the dollars actually paid to the distributee by the trustee or is it the amount includible in the distributee's gross income for income tax purposes under the five-year throwback rule? Only the amount paid should be taken into account. — ED.

to such deceased child and to such deceased child's issue under Section 1 above, and the trustees shall hold or dispose of such share for the benefit of the issue of such deceased child of the settlor in accordance with the provisions of paragraph (c) of this Section 2. The trustees shall allocate to the widow of each deceased son of the settlor, if such widow has not remarried and such deceased son has no issue then living, out of the then remaining principal and undistributed income (as augmented by the addition thereto pursuant to the terms of paragraph (a) of Section 3 of Article SEVENTH) one of such equal shares minus the payments made to such deceased son and to such deceased son's issue under Section 1 above, and the trustees shall hold such share in a separate trust in accordance with the provisions of paragraph (d) of this Section 2. If the then remaining principal and undistributed income (as augmented by the addition thereto pursuant to the terms of paragraph (a) of Section 3 of Article SEVENTH) are not sufficient to provide the separate shares designated above, such separate shares shall abate proportionately.

(a) The separate trust for each living son of the settlor is as follows:

    (i) During the lifetime of such son, the disinterested trustee may pay the net income in whole or in part to, or apply it for the benefit of, any one or more of the group consisting of such son, such son's wife and such son's issue who are living from time to time, in such amount or amounts as the disinterested trustee in his uncontrolled discretion may determine; any net income in any year which is not paid to, or applied for the benefit of, any one or more of said group shall be added to the principal at the end of the year; in addition, the disinterested trustee may pay principal in whole or in part to, or apply the same for the benefit of, any one or more of said group, from time to time, in such amount or amounts and for such estates and interests and outright or upon such terms, trusts, conditions and limitations, provided that no beneficial interest is created in anyone outside of such group by such payment, as he in his uncontrolled discretion may determine; payments of income and principal to such son's issue pursuant to the above provisions shall be taken into account, in the manner hereinafter provided, in the division of the principal and undistributed income into shares for the benefit of such issue on the death of such son unless such son directs otherwise in the exercise of the power of appointment given him by subparagraph (ii) of this paragraph (a).

    (ii) On the death of such son, the trustees shall pay the then remaining principal and undistributed income to, or hold the same for the benefit of, such person or persons (and charitable organizations), other than the estate of such son and creditors of such son or of such son's estate, as such son shall appoint by a will, executed after the death of the survivor of the settlor and the settlor's said wife, which refers specifically to this power. The exercise of this power by such son, however, shall not apply to the proceeds of any life insurance on the life of such son payable to this trust. Subject to the above restrictions in the exercise of this power of appointment, such son may appoint outright or in trust; he may select the trustee or trustees if he appoints in trust; he may create new powers of appointment in the trustee or trustees or in any other appointee; he may, if he appoints in trust, establish such administrative powers for the trustee or trustees as he deems appropriate; he may create a life interest or other limited interests in an appointee with future interests in favor of other appointees; he may impose lawful conditions on an appointment; he may appoint different types of interests to selected appointees; he may impose lawful spendthrift provisions on an appointee; and generally he may appoint by will in any manner, provided always, however, that no appointment shall benefit directly or indirectly such son or the estate of such son or such son's creditors or creditors of such son's estate.

(iii) On the death of such son, to whatever extent the then remaining principal and undistributed income are not effectively appointed by such son pursuant to his power to appoint by will, the trustees shall hold or dispose of such remaining principal and undistributed income for the benefit of such son's issue in accordance with the provisions of paragraph (c) of this Section 2; and if no issue of such son is then living, the trustees shall hold such remaining principal and undistributed income in a separate trust for the benefit of the widow of such son in accordance with the provisions of paragraph (d) of this Section 2; and if no issue of such son is then living and no widow of such son is then living, the trustees shall pay such remaining principal and undistributed income to the settlor's issue then living, such issue to take *per stirpes*, provided always, however, that any payment of principal and undistributed income directed to be made to an issue to whom income may be distributed under a trust established by this instrument, or established by the exercise of any power of appointment under this instrument, shall not be

(9)

made outright to such issue but instead shall be added to the principal of such trust (if there are several such trusts, such payment shall be divided among them in equal shares) and administered as a part thereof; and if no issue of such son is then living and no widow of such son is then living and no issue of the settlor is then living, the trustees shall pay such remaining principal and undistributed income to THE BLACK FAMILY FOUNDATION, created by an indenture of trust, dated ...., 19............,[130] if it is then in existence, otherwise to ....[131]

(b) The separate trust for each living daughter of the settlor is as follows:

(i) During the lifetime of such daughter, the disinterested trustee may pay the net income in whole or in part to, or apply it for the benefit of, any one or more of the group consisting of such daughter and such daughter's issue who are living from time to time, in such amount or amounts as the disinterested trustee in his uncontrolled discretion may determine; any net income in any year which is not paid to, or applied for the benefit of, any one or more of said group shall be added to the principal at the end of the year; in addition, the disinterested trustee may pay the principal in whole or in part to, or apply it for the benefit of, any one or more of said group, from time to time, in such amount or amounts and for such estates and interests and outright or upon such terms, trusts, conditions and limitations, provided that no beneficial interest is created in anyone outside of such group by such payment, as he in his uncontrolled discretion may determine; payments of income and principal to such daughter's issue pursuant to the above provisions shall be taken into account, in the manner hereinafter provided, in the division of the principal and undistributed income into shares for the benefit of such issue on the death of such daughter unless such daughter directs otherwise in the exercise of the power of appointment given her by subparagraph (ii) of this paragraph (b).

(ii) On the death of such daughter, the trustees shall pay the then remaining principal and undistributed income to, or hold the same for the benefit of, such one or more of such daughter's issue living at her death or born thereafter and charitable organizations as such daughter shall appoint by a will, executed after the death of the survivor of the set-

(10)

---

[130] Insert the date when the indenture of trust was executed.
[131] Insert the name of a charity.

tlor and the settlor's said wife, which refers specifically to this power. The exercise of this power by such daughter, however, shall not apply to the proceeds of any life insurance on the life of such daughter payable to this trust. Subject to the above restrictions in the exercise of this power of appointment, the settlor's said daughter may appoint outright or in trust; she may select the trustee or trustees if she appoints in trust; she may create new powers of appointment in a trustee or trustees or in any other appointee; she may, if she appoints in trust, establish such administrative powers for the trustee or trustees as she deems appropriate; she may create life interests or other limited interests in some of the appointees with future interests in favor of other appointees; she may impose lawful conditions on an appointment; she may appoint to one or more of the objects of this power to the exclusion of other objects and she may appoint different types of interests to different objects; she may impose lawful spendthrift provisions; and generally she may appoint by will in any manner, provided always, however, that no appointment shall benefit directly or indirectly one not an object of this power and that nothing herein shall be construed as authorizing her to appoint to herself, her creditors, her estate, or creditors of her estate.

(iii) On the death of such daughter, to whatever extent the then remaining principal and undistributed income are not effectively appointed by such daughter pursuant to her power to appoint by will, the trustees shall hold or dispose of such remaining principal and undistributed income for the benefit of such daughter's issue in accordance with the provisions of paragraph (c) of this Section 2; and if no issue of such daughter is then living, the trustees shall pay such remaining principal and undistributed income to the settlor's issue then living, such issue to take *per stirpes,* provided always, however, that any payment of principal and undistributed income directed to be made to an issue to whom income may be distributed under a trust established by this instrument, or established by the exercise of any power of appointment under this instrument, shall not be made outright to such issue but instead shall be added to the principal of such trust (if there are several such trusts, such payment shall be divided among them in equal shares) and administered as a part thereof; and if no issue of such daughter is then living and no issue of the settlor is then living, the trustees shall pay such remaining principal and undistributed income to THE BLACK

(11)

FAMILY FOUNDATION, created by an indenture of trust, dated ...., 19............,[132] if it is then in existence, otherwise to ....[133]

(c) When the preceding provisions direct the trustees to hold or dispose of a described fund for the benefit of the issue of a deceased child of the settlor, the trustees are directed as follows with respect to such described fund:

(i) The trustees shall assume that they have trust property comprised of such described fund plus the payments made to the issue of such deceased child of the settlor under Section 1 above and under paragraphs (a) or (b) of this Section 2 minus the payments made to a deceased child of such deceased child of the settlor and to the issue of such deceased child of such deceased child of the settlor under Section 1 above and under paragraphs (a) or (b) of this Section 2 if such deceased child of such deceased child of the settlor has no issue then living, and the trustees shall divide such assumed trust property into as many equal shares as there are children of such deceased child of the settlor then living and children deceased of such deceased child of the settlor who have issue then living. The trustees shall pay to each living child of such deceased child of the settlor who has attained the age of thirty (30) years out of such described fund one of such equal shares minus the payments made to such living child of such deceased child of the settlor and to the issue of such living child of such deceased child of the settlor under Section 1 above and under paragraphs (a) or (b) of this Section 2. The trustees shall allocate to each living child of such deceased child of the settlor who has not attained the age of thirty (30) years out of such described fund one of such equal shares minus the payments made to such living child of such deceased child of the settlor and to the issue of such living child of such deceased child of the settlor under Section 1 above and under paragraphs (a) or (b) of this Section 2, and the trustees shall hold such share in a separate trust in accordance with the provisions of subparagraph (ii) of this paragraph (c). The trustees shall allocate to the issue of each deceased child of such deceased child of the settlor out of such described fund one of such equal shares minus the payments made to such deceased child of such deceased child of the settlor and to the issue of such deceased child of such deceased child of the settlor under Section 1 above and under paragraphs (a) or (b) of this Section 2, and the

(12)

---

[132] Insert the date when the indenture of trust was executed.
[133] Insert the name of a charity.

trustees shall hold such share in a separate trust in accordance with the provisions of subparagraph (iii) of this paragraph (c). If such described fund is not sufficient in amount to provide the separate shares designated above, such separate shares shall abate proportionately.

(ii) The separate trust for each child of a deceased child of the settlor who has not attained the age of thirty (30) years is as follows:

(aa) Until such child attains the age of thirty (30) years or dies, whichever first occurs, the trustees shall pay the net income to such child; and, in addition, after such child has attained the age of twenty-one (21) years, the trustees shall pay to such child, from the principal of the trust, from time to time, such amount or amounts as such child may request by an instrument in writing delivered to the trustees in the lifetime of such child, provided always, however, that the aggregate amount of principal paid to such child pursuant to such child's request shall not exceed the sum of $5000 in any calendar year; furthermore, the disinterested trustee may pay to such child, from the principal of the trust, from time to time, before and after such child attains the age of twenty-one (21) years, such amount or amounts or all of the principal as he in his uncontrolled discretion may determine without any restriction on the aggregate amount which may be paid to such child in any calendar year.

(bb) If such child lives to attain the age of thirty (30) years, then when such child attains that age, the trustees shall pay the then remaining principal and undistributed income to such child.

(cc) If such child dies before attaining the age of (30) years, then on the death of such child, the trustees shall hold the then remaining principal and undistributed income in a separate trust for the issue of such child in accordance with the provisions of subparagraph (iii) of this paragraph (c); and if no issue of such child is then living, the trustees shall pay the then remaining principal and undistributed income to the issue then living of that deceased child of the settlor who is the parent of such child, such issue to take *per stirpes,* provided always, however, that any payment of principal and undistributed income directed to be made to an issue of such deceased child of the settlor to whom income may be distributed under a trust established by this instrument, or established by the ex-

(13)

ercise of any power of appointment under this instrument, shall not be made outright to such issue but instead shall be added to the principal of such trust (if there are several such trusts, such payment shall be divided among them in equal shares) and administered as a part thereof; and if no issue of such child is then living and no issue of such deceased child of the settlor is then living, the trustees shall hold the then remaining principal and undistributed income in a separate trust for the widow of such deceased child of the settlor, if such widow has not remarried, in accordance with the provisions of paragraph (d) of this Section 2; and if no issue of such child is then living and no issue of such deceased child of the settlor is then living and no widow of such deceased child of the settlor is then living who has not remarried, the trustees shall pay the then remaining principal and undistributed income to the settlor's issue then living, such issue to take *per stirpes,* provided always, however, that any payment of principal and undistributed income directed to be made to an issue to whom income may be distributed under a trust established by this instrument, or established by the exercise of any power of appointment under this instrument, shall not be made outright to such issue but instead shall be added to the principal of such trust (if there are several such trusts, such payment shall be divided among them in equal shares) and administered as a part thereof; and if no issue of such child is then living and no issue of such deceased child of the settlor is then living and no widow of such deceased child of the settlor is then living who has not remarried and no issue of the settlor is then living, the trustees shall pay the then remaining principal and undistributed income to THE BLACK FAMILY FOUNDATION, created by an indenture of trust, dated ...., 19............,[134] if it is then in existence, otherwise to ....
....[135]

(iii) When the preceding provisions direct that a designated share or the then remaining principal and undistributed income be held in a separate trust for the issue of a deceased child of a certain deceased child of the settlor, the trustees shall pay such share or such remaining principal

(14)

---

[134] Insert the date when the indenture of trust was executed.
[135] Insert the name of a charity.

and undistributed income to such issue then living, such issue to take *per stirpes,* if no child of the deceased child of such deceased child of the settlor is living who is under the age of twenty-one (21) years, but if a child of the deceased child of such deceased child of the settlor is living who is under the age of twenty-one (21) years, then the trustees are directed as follows with respect to such share or such remaining principal and undistributed income:

(aa) Until no child of the deceased child is living who is under the age of twenty-one (21) years, the disinterested trustee may pay the net income in whole or in part to, or apply it for the benefit of, the issue of the deceased child who are living from time to time, in such amount or amounts as the disinterested trustee in his uncontrolled discretion may determine but whatever amount or amounts of income are paid to such issue shall be paid to such issue living at the time of each payment on a *per stirpes* basis; any net income in any year which is not paid to, or applied for the benefit of, such issue shall be added to the principal at the end of the year; and, in addition, the disinterested trustee may pay the principal in whole or in part to, or apply it for the benefit of, such issue, from time to time, in such amount or amounts as he in his uncontrolled discretion may determine but whatever amount or amounts of principal are paid to such issue shall be paid to such issue living at the time of each payment on a *per stirpes* basis.

(bb) When no child of the deceased child is living who is under the age of twenty-one (21) years, the trustees shall pay the then remaining principal and undistributed income to the issue then living of the deceased child, such issue to take *per stirpes;* and if no issue of the deceased child is then living, the trustees shall pay the then remaining principal and undistributed income to the issue then living of such deceased child of the settlor, such issue to take *per stirpes,* provided always, however, that any payment of principal and undistributed income directed to be made to an issue of such deceased child of the settlor to whom income may be distributed under a trust established by this instrument, or established by the exercise of any power of appointment under this instrument, shall not be made outright to such issue but instead shall be added to the principal of such trust (if there are several such trusts, such payment shall be divided

(15)

among them in equal shares) and administered as a part thereof; and if no issue of the deceased child is then living and no issue of such deceased child of the settlor is then living, the trustees shall hold the then remaining principal and undistributed income in a separate trust for the widow of such deceased child of the settlor, if such widow has not remarried, in accordance with the provisions of paragraph (d) of this Section 2; and if no issue of the deceased child is then living and no issue of such deceased child of the settlor is then living and no widow of such deceased child of the settlor is then living who has not remarried, the trustees shall pay the then remaining principal and undistributed income to the settlor's issue then living, such issue to take *per stirpes,* provided always, however, that any payment of principal and undistributed income directed to be made to an issue to whom income may be distributed under a trust established by this instrument, or established by the exercise of any power of appointment under this instrument, shall not be made outright to such issue but instead shall be added to the principal of such trust (if there are several such trusts, such payment shall be divided among them in equal shares) and administered as a part thereof; and if no issue of the deceased child is then living and no issue of such deceased child of the settlor is then living and no widow of such deceased child of the settlor is then living who has not remarried and no issue of the settlor is then living, the trustees shall pay the then remaining principal and undistributed income to THE BLACK FAMILY FOUNDATION, created by an indenture of trust, dated ...., 19............,[136] if it is then in existence, otherwise to ....
....[137]

(d) The separate trust for the widow of each deceased son of the settlor, when, pursuant to the above provisions in this Section 2, such a separate trust is to be established, is as follows:

(i) Until the death or remarriage of such widow, whichever first occurs, the trustees shall pay the net income to such widow; and, in addition, the disinterested trustee may pay the principal in whole or in part to, or apply it for the benefit of, such widow, from time to time, in such amount

(16)

---

[136] Insert the date when the indenture of trust was executed.
[137] Insert the name of a charity.

or amounts as he may determine are necessary for such widow's support and maintenance.

(ii) On the death or remarriage of such widow, whichever first occurs, the trustees shall pay the then remaining principal and undistributed income to the settlor's issue then living, such issue to take *per stirpes,* provided always, however, that any payment of principal directed to be made to an issue to whom income may be distributed under a trust established by this instrument, or established by the exercise of any power of appointment under this instrument, shall not be made outright to such issue but instead shall be added to the principal of such trust (if there are several such trusts, such payment shall be divided among them in equal shares) and administered as a part thereof; and if no issue of the settlor is then living, the trustees shall pay the then remaining principal and undistributed income to THE BLACK FAMILY FOUNDATION, created by an indenture of trust, dated ....,

19............,[138] if it is then in existence, otherwise to ....
....[139]

3. On the death of the settlor's said wife, or on the settlor's death if the settlor's said wife does not survive him, if no issue of the settlor is then living and no widow of a deceased son of the settlor is then living who has not remarried, the trustees shall pay the then remaining principal and undistributed income to THE BLACK FAMILY FOUNDATION, created by an indenture of trust, dated ...., 19............,[140] if it is then in existence, otherwise to ....
..............................[141]

NINTH: Notwithstanding the directions heretofore given to the trustees acting together and to the disinterested trustee acting alone as to the distribution of income and principal under the terms of this instrument, any trust established by this instrument shall terminate, if it has not previously terminated, twenty-one (21) years after the death of the survivor of the following named persons living on the date this instrument is executed:[142]

1. Richard Harry Black III, the settlor;

(17)

[138] Insert the date when the indenture of trust was executed.
[139] Insert the name of a charity.
[140] Insert the date when the indenture of trust was executed.
[141] Insert the name of a charity.
[142] When a revocable trust is involved, it should be permissible to measure the period of the rule against perpetuities from the date the power of revocation ceases to exist. Unless the controlling local law, either by statute or judicial decision, is clear on this point, the safer course of action is to terminate all trusts twenty-one years after the death of the survivor of persons living on the date the revocable trust was executed. — ED.

2. Mildred Marie Black, wife of the settlor;
3. Richard Harry Black IV, son of the settlor;
4. Dorothy Ann Black, daughter-in-law of the settlor;
5. Margaret Black Logan, daughter of the settlor;
6. Robert Gerald Logan, son-in-law of the settlor;
7. James Harry Black, grandchild of the settlor;
8. Dorothy Marie Black, grandchild of the settlor;
9. Adam Rudolph, Jr., grandchild of the settlor;
10. Millicent Logan, grandchild of the settlor;
11. Richard Harry Logan, grandchild of the settlor;

and the trustees of such trust shall pay the then remaining principal and undistributed income of such trust to that child of the settlor to whom income payments under such trust could be made in the discretion of the disinterested trustee immediately prior to its termination under this Article NINTH; and if income payments could not be made to a child of the settlor under such trust immediately prior to its termination under this Article NINTH, the trustees of such trust shall pay the then remaining principal and undistributed income of such trust to the child of the deceased child of the settlor to whom the income was payable under such trust immediately prior to its termination under this Article NINTH; and if income payments could not be made to a child of the settlor and were not payable to a child of a deceased child of the settlor under such trust immediately prior to its termination under this Article NINTH, the trustees of such trust shall pay the then remaining principal and undistributed income of such trust to the issue of that deceased child of a deceased child of the settlor to whom income payments could be made in the discretion of the disinterested trustee under such trust immediately prior to its termination under this Article NINTH, such issue to take *per stirpes;* and if income payments could not be made to a child of the settlor and were not payable to a child of a deceased child of the settlor and could not be made to the issue of a deceased child of a deceased child of the settlor under such trust immediately prior to its termination under this Article NINTH, the trustees of such trust shall pay the then remaining principal and undistributed income of such trust to THE BLACK FAMILY FOUNDATION, created by an indenture of trust, dated ...., 19............,[143] if it is then in existence, otherwise to ....[144]

Furthermore, each power to appoint given under the provisions of this instrument shall be exercisable by the designated donee if, and only if, the power is exercised prior to the termination of the trust under this Article NINTH.

TENTH: Income payments which the trustees are required to make

(18)

---

[143] Insert the date when the indenture of trust was executed.
[144] Insert the name of a charity.

to a beneficiary under the provisions of this instrument shall be made at times fixed by the disinterested trustee but at least as often as quarterly.

ELEVENTH: The interest of each beneficiary in the income or principal of a trust under this instrument shall be free from the control or interference of any creditor of a beneficiary or of any spouse of a married beneficiary and shall not be subject to attachment or susceptible of anticipation or alienation.[145]   Nothing contained in this paragraph shall be construed as restricting in any way the exercise of any power of appointment granted hereunder.

TWELFTH: The whole or any part of the income or principal payable hereunder to any minor or to any other person who in the opinion of the disinterested trustee is incapacitated through illness, age or other cause may be applied by the disinterested trustee in his discretion for such beneficiary's comfort, maintenance, support or education. Any such application may be made at such time and in such manner as he deems advisable, whether by direct payment of such beneficiary's expenses or by payment to a person selected by the disinterested trustee to receive payment for such beneficiary; in each case the receipt of such beneficiary or other person to whom payment is made or entrusted shall be a complete discharge of the trustees in respect thereof.   If the disinterested trustee exercises his power under this Article to apply the income of the marital deduction trust under Article SEVENTH, he must apply all of the income for the benefit of the settlor's said wife. Whenever any payment hereunder is required to be made to a minor, the interest so required to be paid shall be indefeasibly vested in the minor but the trustees may retain the amount payable until the minor attains his majority or dies, whichever first occurs, and the trustees may pay the income and principal to the minor in such amount or amounts and from time to time as the trustees may determine, and if the minor lives to attain his majority, then when he attains his majority the trustees shall pay the then remaining principal and undistributed income to him, and if the minor dies before attaining his majority, then on the minor's death the trustees shall pay the then remaining principal and undistributed income to the minor's estate.

THIRTEENTH: The trustees are authorized to mingle the trust property of the separate trusts established by this instrument, allotting to each separate trust an undivided interest in the mingled funds, that

(19)

---

[145] It should be noted that in Section 1 of Article Seventh the settlor's wife is given an unlimited power of withdrawal, and that in subdivision (aa) of subparagraph (ii) of paragraph c of Section 2 of Article Eighth a child of the deceased child of the settlor is given the power to withdraw $5000 of principal annually. What effect will these powers have on the spendthrift provision to which this note is appended, when this provision purports to be applicable to the trusts under which the designated beneficiaries have these powers?   See Griswold, Spendthrift Trusts §83.1, p. 72 (2d ed. 1947). — ED.

shall always be equal to that trust's proportionate contribution (as adjusted from time to time as a result of accumulations of income, payments of principal and additions to principal) to the mingled funds.

FOURTEENTH: References in this instrument to "child," "children," "son," and "daughter" mean lawful blood descendants in the first degree of the parent designated, and references to "issue" mean lawful blood descendants in the first, second or any other degree of the ancestor designated, provided always, however, that

1. An adopted child and such adopted child's lawful blood descendants shall be considered in this instrument as lawful blood descendants of the adopting parent or parents and of anyone who is by blood or adoption an ancestor of the adopting parent or of either of the adopting parents and shall not be considered descendants of the adopted child's natural parents, except that where a child is adopted by a spouse of one of his or her natural parents such child shall be considered a descendant of such natural parent as well as a descendant of the adopting parent; and

2. A child born to persons who are openly living together as husband and wife after the performance of a marriage ceremony between them and such child's lawful blood descendants shall be considered in this instrument as lawful blood descendants of such child's parents and of any ancestor of such child's parents, regardless of the fact that a purported divorce of one or both of such persons with reference to a prior marriage is invalid.

FIFTEENTH: References in this instrument to "widow" mean the surviving spouse of a deceased male and references to "wife" and "widow" mean the person who answers to such description on the assumption that all decrees of divorce rendered by a court of record wherever located are valid. Furthermore, a decision of the disinterested trustee made in good faith as to whether a person is a widow of a deceased male and as to whether such widow has remarried shall be conclusive for all purposes. The disinterested trustee may assume that a widow of a deceased male has not remarried if he has no actual notice of her remarriage.

A child in gestation, who is later born alive, shall be regarded in this instrument as a child in being during the period of gestation, in determining whether any person has died without leaving issue surviving him or her, and in determining, on the termination of any trust hereunder, whether such child is entitled to share in the disposition of the then remaining principal and undistributed income of such trust, but for other purposes such child's rights shall accrue from date of birth.

References in this instrument to a "minor" mean a person under the age of twenty-one (21) years.

SIXTEENTH: Whenever distribution is to be made to designated "issue" on a *per stirpes* basis, the property shall be distributed to the persons and in the proportions that personal property of the named

(20)

ancestor would be distributed under the laws of the ....
.... of .... [146] in force at the time stipulated for distribution if the named ancestor had died intestate at such
time, domiciled in such State, not married and survived only by such
issue.

Whenever the disinterested trustee has discretion to pay income or
principal to designated "issue" (except when the discretion can be exercised only in favor of designated "issue" on a *per stirpes* basis, in
which case payment, if made, must be made to such issue in accordance
with the terms of the preceding paragraph), payments may be made to
or for the benefit of issue of the second or more remote degree even
though payment is also made or could be made to the parent of such
issue.

Whenever any person is given hereunder a power to appoint by will
to designated "issue," an appointment may be made to issue of the second or more remote degree even though an appointment is also made,
or could be made, to the parent of such issue.

SEVENTEENTH: The disinterested trustee of any trust established
by this instrument and the donee of any power of appointment hereunder may disclaim or release in whole or in part any power given exclusively to him or her. If the disclaimer or release relates to the disinterested trustee's discretion to pay out or accumulate income, then
after such disclaimer or release, the net income of the trust shall be
paid to the settlor's said wife if she is a person to whom the disinterested trustee in his discretion could have paid the income prior to his
disclaimer or release, and to a certain child of the settlor if the settlor's
said wife is not then living and such child of the settlor is a person to
whom the disinterested trustee in his discretion could have paid the
income prior to his disclaimer or release, and to the issue of a certain
deceased child of a deceased child of the settlor who are living at the
time of each income payment, on a *per stirpes* basis, when the disinterested trustee in his discretion could have paid the income to such
issue prior to his disclaimer or release and the settlor's said wife is not
then living and the child of the settlor who is the ancestor of such issue
is not then living.

In addition to any other method of disclaimer or release recognized
by law, the holder of the power may disclaim or release the power in
whole or in part by delivering to the trustees or trustee an instrument
in writing declaring the power holder's intention in this regard.

EIGHTEENTH: Notwithstanding the directions heretofore given
to the trustees and to the disinterested trustee in Article EIGHTH
with respect to the distribution of income and principal of any trust
under Article EIGHTH, and with respect to any distributable share
under Article EIGHTH, but subject to the directions given to the trustees as to the distribution of income and principal in Article NINTH,

(21)

---

[146] Insert the state which is to govern.

the disinterested trustee is authorized in his uncontrolled discretion to use the income and principal of each separate trust and of each distributable share under Article EIGHTH, provided the same proportionate amount is taken from each separate trust and from each distributable share, from time to time, as follows:

1. To pay the funeral expenses of the settlor and to pay the debts and expenses of administration of the settlor's estate and to pay all federal and state taxes in the nature of income, estate, inheritance, succession, transfer, gift or like taxes arising or owing on the settlor's death (including the right to compromise and to pay as soon as convenient after the settlor's death any of such taxes on future or contingent interests), except estate taxes attributable to the value of appointive assets included in the settlor's gross estate when the settlor was granted the power of appointment by someone other than himself, without requiring any reimbursement from the settlor's executors or administrators or other persons receiving property as a result of the settlor's death. Such payments may be made to the person entitled or authorized to receive and receipt for such payments upon a certificate from the settlor's executors or administrators stating the amount due and payable, and the disinterested trustee shall in no way be bound to inquire into the legality or amount of any payments so certified by the settlor's executors or administrators. Payments made in the bona fide belief that they are pursuant to this Article EIGHTEENTH shall not be open to question by anyone.[147]

2. To purchase and to retain as investments any securities or other property, real or personal, belonging to the estate of the settlor.

3. To make loans to the settlor's executors or administrators on such terms as the disinterested trustee deems advisable.

NINETEENTH: With respect to any liability which arises as a result of the death of the settlor that relates to items included in the settlor's gross estate but not in his probate estate, the trustees shall pay such liability to the extent that the property disposed of by Article EIGHTH is sufficient to discharge such liability, and the amount

(22)

---

[147] Note that the death benefit under the Black Manufacturing Company Pension Plan may be a part of the property subject to the terms of Article Eighteenth. Will this fact cause the death benefit to be deemed payable to the employee's executor or administrator under §2039? It is believed that this would not be the case because the payment of such funds to the executor or administrator of the employee is in the *uncontrolled discretion* of the disinterested trustee. In this connection, see §20.2042-1(b)(1) of the Regulations, quoted infra page 1525.

If the disinterested trustee exercises the discretion given him to pay certain death costs, a distribution for such purposes will carry out distributable net income of the trust for the year of distribution, as it is in effect a distribution directly for the benefit of the estate and indirectly for the benefit of the estate beneficiaries who will receive more as a consequence of estate assets being relieved of the obligations paid by the disinterested trustee.

See page 339 supra, note 106, in regard to life insurance proceeds which may be used to pay death costs. — Ed.

necessary to satisfy such liability shall be obtained by borrowing, and pledging or mortgaging property in each separate trust under Article EIGHTH and in each distributable share under Article EIGHTH to secure the sum borrowed, or by selling property in each separate trust under Article EIGHTH and in each distributable share under Article EIGHTH, or by both methods; provided always, however, that the same proportionate amount of property shall be taken from each separate trust under Article EIGHTH and from each distributable share under Article EIGHTH to provide the necessary security for the sum borrowed, and that the same proportionate amount of income and principal shall be diverted from each separate trust under Article EIGHTH and from each distributable share under Article EIGHTH to pay the debt and the interest thereon, and that if property is sold to raise the cash necessary to meet the liability, the same proportionate amount of property shall be taken from each separate trust under Article EIGHTH and from each distributable share under Article EIGHTH to be sold. The decision of the disinterested trustee shall be conclusive as to the method adopted to provide the funds necessary to meet the liability.[148]

TWENTIETH: Notwithstanding the directions heretofore given to the trustees and to the disinterested trustee in Article EIGHTH with respect to the distribution of income and principal of a trust under Article EIGHTH, but subject to the directions given to the trustees as to the distribution of income and principal in Article NINTH, the disinterested trustee is authorized in his uncontrolled discretion to use the income and principal of a separate trust under Article EIGHTH, from time to time, as follows:

1. To pay the funeral expenses of a deceased income beneficiary of such separate trust and to pay the debts and expenses of administration of such deceased income beneficiary, and to pay all federal and state taxes in the nature of income, estate, inheritance, succession, transfer, gift or like taxes arising or owing on the death of such deceased income beneficiary (including the right to compromise and to pay as soon as convenient after such deceased in-

(23)

---

[148] Article Nineteenth imposes a liability on the described trust assets to meet death costs imposed on all non-probate items. Thus, if the settlor and his wife own real property as tenants by the entirety and the settlor furnished the consideration for the acquisition of such property, so that its full value will be includible in his gross estate, any death costs that might be imposed on such property under the controlling local law will be picked up and paid by the trustees pursuant to the directions contained in Article Nineteenth. Part of the assets which may be used to pay liabilities which would fall on trust property and other non-probate property may be derived from employee death benefits which are not includible in the settlor's gross estate under §2039 unless they are paid to the settlor's executors. Will the direction to use such property to discharge the described liabilities constitute payment of such property to the settlor's executors? In view of the fact that Article Nineteenth does not direct the payment of what are primarily the obligations of the settlor's probate property, the answer to the question should be no. — ED.

come beneficiary's death any of such taxes on future or contingent interests), except estate taxes attributable to the value of appointive assets included in the deceased income beneficiary's gross estate when the deceased income beneficiary was granted the power of appointment by someone other than himself, without requiring any reimbursement from such deceased income beneficiary's executors or administrators or other persons receiving property as a result of such deceased income beneficiary's death, provided always, however, that such payments shall be made only from the separate trust of which the decedent was an income beneficiary. Such payments may be made to the person entitled or authorized to receive and receipt for such payments upon a certificate from the deceased income beneficiary's executors or administrators stating the amount due and payable, and the disinterested trustee shall in no way be bound to inquire into the legality or the amount of any payments so certified by the deceased income beneficiary's administrators or executors. Payments made in the bona fide belief that they are pursuant to this Article TWENTIETH shall not be open to question by anyone.[149]

2. To purchase and to retain as investments of the separate trust of which the decedent was an income beneficiary any security or other property, real or personal, belonging to the estate of the deceased income beneficiary.

3. To make loans out of the separate trust of which the decedent was an income beneficiary to the deceased income beneficiary's executors or administrators on such terms as the disinterested trustee deems advisable.

The words "deceased income beneficiary" as used in this Article TWENTIETH mean any deceased person who, during his or her lifetime, was entitled to receive income of the separate trust in question or to whom income of the separate trust in question could be paid in the discretion of the disinterested trustee.

TWENTY-FIRST: Notwithstanding the directions heretofore given to the trustees and to the disinterested trustee with respect to the distribution of income and principal of any trust under Article EIGHTH, but subject to the directions given to the trustees as to the distribution of income and principal in Article NINTH, the disinterested trustee of each separate trust under Article EIGHTH is authorized at any time or from time to time in his uncontrolled discretion to insure the life of any income beneficiary of such trust for such amount or amounts as he

(24)

---

[149] Note that proceeds of insurance on the life of the income beneficiary may be a part of the property subject to the terms of Article Twentieth. Will this fact cause such life insurance proceeds to be deemed payable to the executor or administrator of the insured? It is believed that this would not be the case because the payment of such funds to the executor or administrator of the insured is in the uncontrolled discretion of the distinterested trustee. In this connection, see §20-2042-1(b)(1) of the Regulations, quoted infra page 1525. — ED.

may determine. The proceeds of the policy or policies of said insurance shall be made payable to the trustees of the trust of which the insured is an income beneficiary. The disinterested trustee may apply any or all dividends on said policy or policies of insurance to the payment of premiums thereon and shall pay the balance of the premiums out of the income or principal of the trust of which the insured is an income beneficiary. The disinterested trustee may at any time or from time to time surrender such policy or policies of insurance and obtain the cash surrender value. The proceeds of such policy or policies of insurance, whether collected before or after the death of the insured, shall be added to the principal of the trust of which the insured is an income beneficiary. The disinterested trustee may take out term insurance or straight life insurance or endowment insurance or any other kind of life insurance under the authorization to him contained in this Article TWENTY-FIRST. In making any distribution of trust property, distribution shall not be made to any insured of a policy on his or her life or of any proceeds of such policy.

The words "income beneficiary" as used in this Article TWENTY-FIRST mean any person who is entitled to receive income of a separate trust in Article EIGHTH or to whom income of a separate trust in Article EIGHTH could be paid in the discretion of the disinterested trustee.

TWENTY-SECOND: After the death of the settlor, the trustees shall each year render an account of their administration of each trust under this instrument to the settlor's said wife, and if she is not living, to the oldest living issue of the settlor to whom income of such trust may be distributed (or such issue's guardian). Such person's (or the guardian's) written approval of such account shall, as to all matters and transactions stated therein or shown thereby, be final and binding upon all persons (whether in being or not) who are then or may thereafter become interested in, or entitled to share in, either the income or the principal of such trust, provided always, however, that nothing contained in this Article TWENTY-SECOND shall be deemed to give such person acting in conjunction with the trustees the power to alter, amend, revoke or terminate such trust.

TWENTY-THIRD: The settlor requests the trustees, although no duty is imposed on them in this regard, to purchase and retain as an investment of the trust or trusts created hereunder the common stock or other securities of the Black Manufacturing Company and the common stock or other securities of any concern which succeeds to the whole or a substantial part of the assets or business of the Black Manufacturing Company. In the event that the trustees decide to make purchases as mentioned in the preceding sentence, such purchases may be made from any source, including the settlor, the settlor's wife, any issue of the settlor, the settlor's brother, the wife of the settlor's brother, any issue of the settlor's brother or the trustees of any trust established

(25)

by the settlor or by the settlor's wife or by any issue of the settlor or by the settlor's brother or by the wife of the settlor's brother or by any issue of the settlor's brother. In each case, however, the decision of the disinterested trustee as to the price which should be paid for such acquisitions shall be conclusive.

In the event that the trustees decide to sell any of the common stock or other securities of the Black Manufacturing Company, or the common stock or other securities of any concern which shall succeed to the whole or a substantial part of the assets or business of the Black Manufacturing Company, such sale shall be made at a price deemed adequate by the disinterested trustee, and such sale shall be made to one or more of the following if one or more of the following is ready and willing to purchase at the price deemed adequate by the disinterested trustee, and otherwise to the general public at such price: the settlor, the settlor's wife, any issue of the settlor, the settlor's brother, the wife of the settlor's brother, any issue of the settlor's brother, or the trustees of any trust established by the settlor or by the settlor's wife or by any issue of the settlor or by the settlor's brother or by the wife of the settlor's brother or by any issue of the settlor's brother.[150]

In the event that the disinterested trustee exercises his power to distribute corpus to the beneficiary of any trust hereunder, the settlor requests the disinterested trustee, although no duty is imposed on him in this regard, to avoid a distribution in kind of the common stock or other securities of the Black Manufacturing Company, or the common stock or other securities of any concern which shall succeed to the whole or a substantial part of the assets or business of the Black Manufacturing Company, whenever in the opinion of the disinterested trustee such distribution in kind will result in an undesirable dispersion of the control of the corporation.

On the termination of any trust hereunder, the settlor requests the trustees, although no duty is imposed on them in this regard, to avoid a distribution in kind of the common stock or other securities of the Black Manufacturing Company, or the common stock or other securities of any concern which shall succeed to the whole or a substantial part of the assets or business of the Black Manufacturing Company, whenever in the opinion of the trustees such distribution in kind will result in an undesirable dispersion of the control of the corporation.

Any individual trustee hereunder (as well as any issue of the settlor or the settlor's brother or any issue of the settlor's brother) may serve as an officer of the Black Manufacturing Company or of any concern which shall succeed to the whole or a substantial part of the assets or business of the Black Manufacturing Company.

TWENTY-FOURTH: In extension and not in limitation of the powers given them by law or other provisions of this instrument (but subject to the restrictions of Article SEVENTH, during the period that

(26)

[150] See page 1191 supra, note 42. — Ed.

the settlor's said wife survives him, in regard to the trust established by Article SEVENTH and subject to the provisions of Article TWENTY-THIRD), the trustees of each trust established hereunder shall have the following powers with respect to such trust and its property, in each case to be exercised from time to time in the discretion of the trustees and without order or license of court:

1. To retain indefinitely any investments and to invest and reinvest in stocks, shares and obligations of corporations, of unincorporated associations or trusts and of investment companies,[151] or in a common trust fund without giving notice to any beneficiary,[152] or any other kind of personal or real property, notwithstanding the fact that any or all of the investments made or retained are of a character or size which but for this express authority would not be considered proper for trustees;

2. To make loans with adequate interest and with adequate security, unless the loan is made to one to whom the disinterested trustee has discretion to distribute the income or principal of such trust, in which case the loan may be made without adequate interest or adequate security, provided always, however, that the powers given in this Section 2 shall be exercisable only by the disinterested trustee;

3. To sell, to exchange, to lease and to make contracts concerning real or personal property for such considerations and upon such terms as to credit or otherwise as the disinterested trustee may determine, which leases and contracts may extend beyond the term of any trust; to give options therefor; to execute deeds, transfers, leases and other instruments of any kind;

4. To hold bonds, shares or other securities in bearer form, or in the name of the trustees or in the name of one of the trustees or in the name of a nominee, without indication of any fiduciary capacity; to deposit cash in a checking or savings account in a bank, without indication of any fiduciary capacity;

5. To give general or special proxies or powers of attorney for voting or acting in respect of shares or securities, which may be discretionary and with power of substitution; to deposit shares or securities with, or transfer them to, protective committees or similar bodies; to join in any reorganization and to pay assessments or subscriptions called for in connection with shares or securities held by them;

6. To improve or develop real estate; to construct, alter or repair buildings or structures on real estate; to settle boundary lines and easements and other rights with respect to real estate; to partition and to join with co-owners and others in dealing with real estate in any way;

(27)

---

[151] See page 1211 supra, note 56. — ED.
[152] See page 1211 supra, note 57. — ED.

7. To employ investment counsel, custodians of trust property, brokers, agents and attorneys;

8. To receive additions to any trusts under this instrument by gift or will or otherwise, and to hold and administer the same under the provisions hereof;

9. To pay as income the whole of the interest, dividends, rent or similar receipts from property, whether wasting or not and although bought or taken at a value above par, but if they see fit when property is bought or taken at a value above par, they may retain a portion of the income to offset such loss to the principal; to treat as income or principal or to apportion between them stock dividends, extra dividends, rights to take stock or securities, and proceeds from the sale of real estate, although such real estate may have been wholly or partly unproductive; to charge to income or principal or to apportion between them investment counsel's compensation, custodians' compensation, brokers' commissions, agents' compensation, attorneys' fees, insurance premiums, repairs or improvements, taxes (income, estate, inheritance or any other taxes), depreciation charges and trustees' compensations; and generally to determine all questions as between income and principal and to credit or charge to income or principal or to apportion between them any receipt or gain and any charge, disbursement or loss as is deemed advisable in the circumstances of each case as it arises, notwithstanding any statute or rule of law for distinguishing income from principal or any determination of the courts; provided always, however, that the powers and discretions given in this Section 9 shall be exercisable only by the disinterested trustee;

10. When dividing or distributing any trust fund, to make such division or distribution wholly or partly in kind by allotting and transferring specific securities or other personal or real property or undivided interests therein as a part or the whole of any one or more shares or payments at current values;

11. To keep any or all of the trust property at any place or places in ....[153] or elsewhere within the United States or abroad or with a depositary or custodian at such place or places.

TWENTY-FIFTH: No bond shall be required of the original trustees hereunder or of any successor trustee, or if a bond is required by law, no surety on such bond shall be required.

There shall always be a disinterested trustee of each trust under this instrument. If a vacancy in the office of disinterested trustee occurs, a successor disinterested trustee shall be appointed by the partners in the law firm of Andrew, James and Casner, or by the partners in whatever law firm is the successor to the firm of Andrew, James and Casner. Ap-

(28)

---

[153] Insert the state where the disinterested trustee is located.

pointments of successor trustees shall be by an instrument in writing.

If a vacancy in the office of interested trustee occurs, the remaining trustees or trustee shall appoint by an instrument in writing to fill such vacancy one of the following:

1. Issue of Richard Harry Black IV;
2. Margaret Black Logan;
3. Mildred Marie Black; and
4. Issue of Margaret Black Logan.

If no one of the above-listed persons is eligible or available to serve as trustee at the time a vacancy in the office of interested trustee occurs, the vacancy shall not then be filled but shall be filled at such time in the future as one of the above-listed persons becomes eligible or available to fill such vacancy. In other words, there shall always be two interested trustees whenever there are eligible and available from the above list of persons individuals to serve as trustees hereunder.

A trustee may resign at any time by an instrument in writing delivered to the remaining trustees or trustee, and if there is no remaining trustee, by an instrument in writing delivered to persons who are authorized to appoint his successor.

The approval of all the trustees in office (if a vacancy in the office of trustee exists, the trustee or trustees in office may act pending the filling of the vacancy) shall be required in order to act in any matter affecting the trust except such matters as are herein vested exclusively in the disinterested trustee.

References in this instrument to "trustees" shall be deemed to include not only the original trustees but also any successor trustee, and all powers and discretions vested in the trustees shall be vested in and exercisable by any such successor trustee except that the powers and discretions vested herein in the disinterested trustee shall be vested in, and exercisable by, only a successor disinterested trustee.

References in this instrument to "disinterested trustee" mean the trustee hereunder who has no interest vested or contingent in the trust property and who cannot be benefited by the exercise of the powers vested exclusively in the disinterested trustee. In addition, the disinterested trustee must be one who can possess the powers vested exclusively in the disinterested trustee without causing trust income or principal to be attributable to a trust beneficiary for federal income, gift or estate tax purposes prior to the distribution of the trust income or principal to the beneficiary.

No one dealing with the trustees need inquire concerning the validity of anything they purport to do, or need see to the application of any money paid or any property transferred to or upon the order of the trustees.

No trustee shall be responsible for the acts or omissions of the co-trustees or for allowing the co-trustees to have custody or control of the funds, securities or property. Each trustee shall be responsible only for his or her acts or omissions in bad faith. Furthermore, a successor trustee shall not be liable for any action taken by the trustees prior to the time such successor trustee becomes a trustee.

A trustee may, by an instrument in writing, delegate all or any powers and discretions to a co-trustee or to co-trustees for a period of one year or less at a time and may renew such delegation from time to time; provided always, however, that the powers and discretions vested exclusively in the disinterested trustee shall not be delegated.

TWENTY-SIXTH: Each trust hereunder is a ....[154] trust made in that State, and is to be governed and construed and administered according to its laws and shall continue to be so governed and construed and administered even though administered elsewhere within the United States or abroad.

TWENTY-SEVENTH: To the same effect as if it were the original, anyone may rely upon a copy certified by a notary public to be a true copy of this instrument (and of the writings, if any, endorsed thereon or attached thereto). Anyone may rely upon any statement of fact certified by anyone who appears from the original document or a certified copy thereof to be a trustee hereunder.

IN WITNESS WHEREOF, RICHARD HARRY BLACK III as settlor has hereunto set his hand and seal, and RICHARD HARRY BLACK III, RICHARD HARRY BLACK IV and ROBERT J. ANDREW, in token of their acceptance of the trusts hereby created, have hereunto set their hands and seals, all as of this .... day of ...., 19...........[155]

/s/ *Richard Harry Black III* [Seal]

SETTLOR AND TRUSTEE

/s/ *Richard Harry Black IV* [Seal]

TRUSTEE

/s/ *Robert J. Andrew* [Seal]

TRUSTEE

.... of ....[156]
.........................,[157] SS.   ....
...., 19...........[158]

(30)

[154] Insert the state where the disinterested trustee is located.
[155] Insert the date on which the trust is executed.
[156] Insert the state in which the acknowledgment is taken.
[157] Insert the county in which the acknowledgment is taken.
[158] Insert the city in which and the date on which the acknowledgment is taken.

Then personally appeared the above-named RICHARD HARRY BLACK III and acknowledged the foregoing instrument to be his free act and deed, before me,

/s/ *Robert Lewis*

NOTARY PUBLIC

[Notarial Seal]

ROBERT LEWIS Notary Public
My commission expires ...., 19............[159]

.... of ....[160]
.............................,[161] ss.   ....
...................................., 19............[162]

Then personally appeared the above-named RICHARD HARRY BLACK IV and acknowledged the foregoing instrument to be his free act and deed, before me,

/s/ *Robert Lewis*

NOTARY PUBLIC

[Notarial Seal]

ROBERT LEWIS Notary Public
My commission expires ...., 19............[163]

.... of ....[164]
.............................,[165] ss.   ....
...................................., 19............[166]

Then personally appeared the above-named ROBERT J. ANDREW and acknowledged the foregoing instrument to be his free act and deed, before me,

/s/ *Robert Lewis*

NOTARY PUBLIC

[Notarial Seal]

ROBERT LEWIS Notary Public
My commission expires ...., 19............[167]

(31)

[159] Insert the date on which the notary's commission expires.
[160] Insert the state in which the acknowledgment is taken.
[161] Insert the county in which the acknowledgment is taken.
[162] Insert the city in which and the date on which the acknowledgment is taken.
[163] Insert the date on which the notary's commission expires.
[164] Insert the state in which the acknowledgment is taken.
[165] Insert the county in which the acknowledgment is taken.
[166] Insert the city in which and the date on which the acknowledgment is taken.
[167] Insert the date on which the notary's commission expires.

SCHEDULE A

[*Note:* Assume that on this page the various securities and cash placed in this trust are listed. Mr. Black closed out his account with the Jones and Jones investment house, and after placing securities worth approximately $50,000 in the Black Family Foundation and securities worth approximately $50,000 in the short-term trust, and after paying a gift tax of approximately $7000, he has left securities worth approximately $143,000 from the Jones and Jones investment account, which he placed in this trust. He also designated the trustees of this trust as the beneficiaries of his life insurance ($50,000 made payable to this trust as primary beneficiary and $50,000 made payable to this trust as secondary beneficiary). He also made the death benefit under the Black Manufacturing Company Pension Plan payable to the trustees of this trust. He plans to add to this trust from time to time any surplus annual income.]

K. *Will of Richard Harry Black III*

I, RICHARD HARRY BLACK III, of ....,
....,[168] make this my last will, hereby revoking
all wills and codicils heretofore made by me.

FIRST: My tangible personal property owned by me at the time of
my death, including furniture, clothing, jewelry, silver, books, pictures, china, automobiles and their equipment, boats and their equipment, and articles of personal or household use or ornament (and all
policies of insurance on such tangible personal property), excepting
therefrom, however, any tangible personal property of mine regularly
used in connection with my real property disposed of by Article
THIRD of this will, and not including money, securities or the like,
I give absolutely to my wife, Mildred Marie Black, if she survives me
by thirty (30) days, and if she does not so survive me, I give the same
absolutely to my issue who so survive me, such issue to take *per stirpes.*

I express the hope that my said wife or my said issue will dispose of
said tangible personal property according to my wishes, however my
wishes may be made known to her or to them, but I expressly declare
that I do not intend to create any trust in law or in equity with respect
to said tangible personal property.

In the event that my said wife does not survive me by thirty (30) days
and more than one issue of mine do so survive me, so that a division
of my said tangible personal property into shares is required by the
provisions of this Article FIRST, the following steps shall be taken to
accomplish such division:

1. My disinterested executor shall place a value on each item of my
   tangible personal property disposed of by this Article FIRST.

2. Each issue of mine entitled to a share (or such person as may be
   designated by my disinterested executor to represent such issue)
   shall alternately select the items of tangible personal property he
   or she desires, the first item to be selected by my oldest issue (or
   such issue's representative) entitled to a share.

3. When an issue of mine entitled to a share (or such issue's representative) has selected items of tangible personal property which
   total in value his or her share, he or she shall have no further
   right of selection.

4. Items of tangible personal property not selected by the above
   method shall be sold by my executors (issue of mine to have
   the first right of purchase at such sale) and the net proceeds of

Richard Harry Black III   *R.J.A.*
                                 D.R.J.
                                 A.J.C.

(1)

[168] Insert the city and state where Mr. Black resides.

the sale shall be divided among my issue so that the cash plus the items of tangible personal property selected by an issue of mine will total in value such issue's share.

The decision of my disinterested executor made in good faith as to the items of my tangible personal property which are excepted from this Article FIRST and which therefore pass under said Article THIRD of this will shall be conclusive on all concerned.

Property and cash distributable to a minor under this Article FIRST may be distributed by my executors to such minor personally, or to such minor's legal guardian, or to some other person selected by my executors to receive such property for such minor, and the receipt of such minor, or such minor's legal guardian, or such other person, shall be a complete discharge of my executors in regard to such distribution.[169]

The person to whom property is distributed under this Article FIRST for the benefit of a minor shall decide from time to time whether such property shall be retained for eventual distribution to the minor or whether some or all of it shall be sold and the proceeds of the sale held for the minor. Such person's decision in this regard shall be conclusive on all concerned.

The cost of moving any tangible personal property disposed of under this Article FIRST to the destination desired by the beneficiary shall be borne by the beneficiary.

SECOND: If my said wife survives me by thirty (30) days, I give to her absolutely all real property owned by me at the time of my death in the _____ of _____,[170] and if my said wife does not so survive me, said real property shall be added to my residuary estate and shall be disposed of as hereinafter provided.

THIRD: My real property located in the State of Illinois[171] and all my tangible personal property regularly used in connection therewith (including all policies of insurance on such tangible personal property), which real and personal property are owned by me at my death, I give as follows:

1. If my said wife survives me, I give said real property and said

Richard Harry Black III   **R.J.A.**
D.R.J.
A.J.C.

(2)

---

[169] Suppose that the testator desires to have his executor select the persons to receive his tangible personal property. He may do so by giving the property outright to the executor, with an expression as to his wishes; or by giving the executor a special power of appointment over such property; or by giving the executor a general power of appointment over such property; or by establishing a trust of said property with the executor as trustee. See Wills — Devise to Executor for Further Distribution — Application of Trust and Power Doctrines, 56 Mich. L. Rev. 1167 (1958). — Ed.

[170] Insert the state where the summer residence is located.

[171] The reference to Illinois should be changed to Iowa if the farm is located in Iowa.

tangible personal property to my said wife to have and to hold during her lifetime; and, in addition, I give to my said wife, acting alone, the power to convey said real property in fee simple by deed to anyone, including herself, and the power to convey said tangible personal property absolutely by deed to anyone, including herself; such conveyance of said real property or said tangible personal property by my said wife may be of the beneficial legal ownership or may be in trust; a conveyance of the beneficial legal ownership may be for such estates and interests and upon such terms, conditions and limitations as my said wife may determine; such conveyance in trust may result in the creation of such beneficial interests under the trust as my said wife may determine. If my said wife as a result of the exercise of her power to convey said real property by deed, or the exercise of her power to convey said tangible personal property by deed, receives any funds in return for such conveyance, she shall be free to use and dispose of such funds in any manner she determines.[172] It is my intention that the value for federal estate tax purposes of said real property and said personal property shall be available for the marital deduction allowed by the federal estate tax law applicable to my estate. For the purposes of this Article THIRD, if my said wife and I die under circumstances where the order of our deaths cannot be established by proof, my said wife shall be deemed to have survived me.

2. During the period of time that my said wife survives me, in addition to the powers given my said wife in Section 1 above, she is authorized as follows with respect to said real property:

(a) To make such arrangements as she deems appropriate for the operation of said real property, including, without limiting the generality of the foregoing, the employment of a corporation or individual as a farm manager, and the leasing of said real property on such terms as she deems appropriate. A lease of said real property made by my said wife may include or exclude, as she deems appropriate, the right to use said tangible personal property, and such lease shall be valid and effective for the entire period of the lease, even though my said wife dies before the expiration of the lease; the benefits of said lease shall inure to the remainderman on the death of

                               R.J.A.

Richard Harry Black III   *D.R.J.*

                               A.J.C.

(3)

---

[172] In view of the fact that the wife is given unlimited power of disposition with respect to the tangible personal property, there should be no need to insert a specific provision excusing her from giving bond for the protection of the remaindermen. In regard to the requirement of a bond by the owner of a legal present interest in personal property, see pages 597 to 618 supra. — ED.

my said wife unless my said wife by the exercise of her power under Section 1 above has vested the ownership of said real property and said tangible personal property in herself or in someone else.

(b) To make such arrangements as she deems appropriate with respect to the development of said real property, including, without limiting the generality of the foregoing, the removal of oil or gas, the removal of any solid minerals, the cutting of timber, the removal of any building, the construction of any building, and the settlement of boundary disputes. Such arrangements made by my said wife shall be binding on the remainderman and the benefits of any such arrangements shall inure to the remainderman on the death of my said wife unless my said wife by the exercise of her power under Section 1 above has vested the ownership of said real property and said tangible personal property in herself or in someone else.

(c) To mortgage said real property to secure any sums which she may borrow.

3. On the death of my said wife, if my said wife survives me, to the extent that she has not exercised the powers given her under Sections 1 and 2, or on my death if my said wife does not survive me, if issue of mine are then living, I give said real property and said tangible personal property to the ILLINOIS TRUST COMPANY, of Bloomington, Illinois,[173] to hold in trust as follows:

(a) Unless the trust sooner terminates by the distribution of all the trust property pursuant to the power in the trustee to distribute the trust property, the trust shall terminate twenty-one (21) years after the death of the survivor of my said wife and my issue living at my death, or when my said wife is deceased and no issue of mine is living, whichever event first occurs.

(b) During the continuance of the trust, the trustee shall pay the net income to my issue living from time to time, such issue to take *per stirpes;* and, in addition, the trustee may pay to my issue living from time to time, such issue to take *per stirpes* any such payment made by the trustee, from the principal of the trust, from time to time, such amount or amounts or all of the principal as the trustee in its uncontrolled discretion may determine.

(c) On the termination of the trust, the trustee shall distribute the then remaining principal to my issue then living, such

Richard Harry Black III   R.J.A.
D.R.J.
A.J.C.

(4)

----

[173] An Iowa trust company should be named if the farm is located in Iowa.

issue to take *per stirpes;* and if no issue of mine is then living, the trustee shall distribute the then remaining principal to THE BLACK FAMILY FOUNDATION created by indenture of trust dated ...., 19............,[174] if said Foundation is then in existence, otherwise to my heirs.

(d) It is my desire that, throughout the duration of the trust, the trustee retain the real property which comes to it as trustee hereunder. The real property which will most likely pass to the trustee hereunder is farm land. While the trustee is authorized to sell such real property if it believes such sale is in the best interest of the beneficiaries, it is my earnest hope that such sale will not be deemed necessary and that eventually the real property will be available to pass in kind to the ultimate distributees of the principal. In the event that the trustee decides that a sale of such real property should be made, the trustee shall attempt to sell such real property to one or more of my issue before offering such real property for sale to the public generally. If any one or more of my issue desires to buy such real property, the trustee is authorized to provide liberal terms for the financing of such purchase by such issue of mine. In view of the fact that the trust principal will most likely consist of real property which is farm land, I give the trustee the following powers in regard thereto:

(i) The trustee is authorized to retain throughout the duration of the trust any real property which comes to it as trustee hereunder though the retention of such real property by the trustee may not be regarded as a proper trust investment in the absence of this express authorization.

(ii) The trustee is authorized to lease said real property on such terms as it deems appropriate and any such lease shall be binding and effective for the full term of such lease though such term extends beyond the duration of this trust.

(iii) The trustee is authorized to employ a farm manager to supervise the operation of farm land in the trust but in such case the trustee's compensation shall be reduced by the amount paid to the farm manager for his services.

(iv) The trustee is authorized to carry on both a crop and livestock program in the operation of the farm and generally to carry on any program of farming that is recognized in the locality where the farm land is situated as good farm-

Richard Harry Black III
R.J.A.
D.R.J.
A.J.C.

(5)

---

[174] Insert the date when the indenture of trust was executed.

ing practice; in this connection the trustee's determination as to the amount of income and cash principal which should be used to pay the expenses of the farming program adopted shall be conclusive on all concerned. Furthermore, the trustee is authorized to borrow money to pay such expenses and to place a mortgage on the farm land and the farm buildings to secure funds borrowed and to pay such indebtedness out of the income and cash principal.

(v) The trustee is authorized to keep farm buildings in repair, to build new farm buildings, to keep the soil fertile and generally to do such other things as are normally regarded as good farming practice in the locality where the farm land is situated; in this connection the trustee's determination as to the amount of income and cash principal which should be used to pay the expenses of the upkeep of farm buildings and of the land and to pay for the construction of new farm buildings shall be conclusive on all concerned. Furthermore, the trustee is authorized to borrow money to pay such expenses and such construction costs and to place a mortgage on the farm land and the farm buildings to secure funds borrowed and to pay such indebtedness out of income and cash principal.

(vi) The trustee is authorized to make such arrangements as it deems appropriate with respect to the development of said real property, including, without limiting the generality of the foregoing, the removal of oil or gas, the removal of any solid minerals, the cutting of timber, the removal of any building and the settlement of boundary disputes. Furthermore, the trustee is authorized to borrow money to pay for such arrangements and to place a mortgage on the farm land and the farm buildings to secure funds borrowed and to pay such indebtedness out of the income and cash principal.

(vii) The trustee's determination as to whether cash received in the operation of farm land is income or principal shall be conclusive on all concerned.

(viii) The trustee's compensation with respect to real property held in the trust shall equal ten percent (10%) of the gross cash received by it from the operation and management of such real property, including cash received from the sale of crops and livestock, such compensation to be paid out of income or cash principal as the trustee may determine. The trustee's compensation with respect to the manage-

	R.J.A.
Richard Harry Black III	D.R.J.
	A.J.C.

(6)

ment of other than real property held in the trust shall be in accordance with local Illinois[175] practice.

(ix) Other powers hereinafter given in this will to a trustee of a trust under this will shall also be applicable to the trust under this Article THIRD to the extent that such powers are not inconsistent with the powers above set forth.

4. On the death of my said wife, if my said wife survives me, to the extent that she has not exercised the powers given her under Sections 1 and 2, or on my death if my said wife does not survive me, if no issue of mine is then living, I give said real property and said tangible personal property to THE BLACK FAMILY FOUNDATION created by indenture of trust dated ...., 19.............,[176] if said Foundation is then in existence, otherwise to my heirs.

FOURTH: Under the will of my late mother, who died in 1953, a trust was established for my benefit with the Old Line Trust Company, of Boston, Massachusetts, as trustee. On my death the trustee is directed to distribute the principal to, or for the benefit of, any one or more of the limited class consisting of my wife, my issue then living or born thereafter, spouses of my issue and charities in such amounts and proportions and for such estates and interests and upon such terms, trusts, conditions and limitations and generally in such manner as I shall appoint by will. I hereby exercise said power of appointment by directing the said trustee to hold or dispose of the principal of said trust as follows:

1. If my children, Richard Harry Black IV and Margaret Black Logan, both survive me, to pay the principal in equal shares to my said children.

2. If only one of my said children survives me and the one who predeceases me leaves no issue who survive me, to pay the principal to the child of mine who survives me.

3. If only one of my said children survives me and the one who predeceases me leaves issue who survive me, to pay one half of the principal to the child who survives me and to hold one half of the principal in trust for the issue of my deceased child in accordance with the provisions of Section 7 of this Article FOURTH.

4. If neither of my said children survives me and only one of my said children leaves issue who survive me, to hold the principal in trust for the issue of my deceased child in accordance with the provisions of Section 7 of this Article FOURTH.

5. If neither of my said children survives me but each of my said

R.J.A.

Richard Harry Black III   *D.R.J.*

A.J.C.

(7)

---

[175] The reference to Illinois should be changed to Iowa if the farm is located in Iowa.

[176] Insert the date when the indenture of trust was executed.

children leaves issue who survive me, to hold one half of the principal in trust for the issue of one deceased child of mine and to hold the other half of the principal in trust for the issue of my other deceased child in accordance with the provisions of Section 7 of this Article FOURTH.

6. If no issue of mine survives me, to pay the net income to my said wife for her life and on the death of my said wife, or on my death if my said wife does not survive me, to pay the principal to THE BLACK FAMILY FOUNDATION created by indenture of trust dated _____, 19_____,[177] if it is then in existence, and appointment to it is permissible, otherwise to _____ ---[178]

7. The trustee is directed as follows with respect to the trust for the issue of a deceased child of mine:

(a) The trustee shall divide the trust property into as many equal shares as there are children of such deceased child of mine who survive me and deceased children of such deceased child of mine who leave issue who survive me. The trustee shall pay one of such equal shares to the issue of a deceased child of such deceased child of mine, such issue to take *per stirpes;* and the trustee shall hold in a separate trust one of such equal shares for each living child of such deceased child of mine as follows:

(i) If such child has attained the age of thirty (30) years, the trustee shall pay the trust fund to such child.

(ii) If such child has not attained the age of thirty (30) years then the trustee shall accumulate the income until such child attains the age of thirty (30) years, or until twenty-one (21) years after the death of the survivor of myself and my children, or until such child dies, whichever event first occurs, provided that if the event first to occur occurs within nine (9) years and one day after my death, then the income shall be accumulated until nine (9) years and one day after my death.[179] When the period of accumulation designated in the preceding sentence has come to an end, the trustee shall pay to such child the principal and accumulated income; if such child is not then living, the trustee

Richard Harry Black III   *R.J.A.*
                               D.R.J.
                               A.J.C.

(8)

---

[177] Insert the date when the indenture of trust was executed.

[178] Insert the name of a charity.

[179] The nine-year period is inserted to take advantage of 1954 I.R.C. §665(b)(4), quoted infra page 1368. Is this nine-year period essential in view of the fact that the trust created by the exercise of the power is a continuation of the trust created under the will of the testator's mother, who died in 1953? — ED.

shall pay the principal and accumulated income to such child's issue then living, such issue to take *per stirpes;* if such child is not then living and no issue of such child is then living, the trustee shall pay the principal and accumulated income to the issue then living of such deceased child of mine, such issue to take *per stirpes,* provided always, however, that if an issue of such deceased child of mine who would be entitled to a share is one for whom another share is then being held in trust under this Section 7, the share of such issue shall be added to the share being held in trust for such issue and henceforth administered accordingly; if such child is not then living and no issue of such child is then living and no issue of such deceased child of mine is then living, the trustee shall pay the principal and accumulated income to my issue then living, such issue to take *per stirpes,* provided always, however, that if an issue of mine who would be entitled to a share is one for whom another share is then being held in trust under this Section 7, the share of such issue shall be added to the share being held in trust for such issue and henceforth administered accordingly; if such child is not then living and no issue of such child is then living and no issue of such deceased child of mine is then living and no issue of mine is then living and my said wife is not then living, the trustee shall pay the principal and accumulated income to THE BLACK FAMILY FOUNDATION created by indenture of trust dated ...., 19............,[180] if it is then in existence, and appointment to it is permissible, otherwise to ....
..................;[181] if such child is not then living and no issue of such child is then living and no issue of such deceased child of mine is then living and no issue of mine is then living but my said wife is then living, the trustee shall hold the principal and accumulated income in trust as follows:

(aa) To pay the net income therefrom to my said wife for her life.

(bb) On the death of my said wife, to pay the entire trust fund to THE BLACK FAMILY FOUNDATION, created by indenture of trust dated ....

Richard Harry Black III
                R.J.A.
                D.R.J.
                A.J.C.

(9)

---

[180] Insert the date when the indenture of trust was executed.
[181] Insert the name of a charity.

..............., 19.............,[182] if it is then in existence, and appointment to it is permissible, otherwise to ....
....[183]

FIFTH: The following provisions are applicable to each of the preceding Articles in this will to the extent that they are not inconsistent with any of the provisions of such preceding Articles; and, in addition, so far as Article FOURTH is concerned, they are applicable only to the extent that they are permissible provisions under the terms of the power of appointment given me by the will of my late mother.

1. Income payments which the trustee is required to make to a beneficiary shall be made at times fixed by the trustee but at least as often as quarterly.

2. The interest of each beneficiary in the income or principal of a trust shall be free from the control or interference of any creditor of a beneficiary or of any spouse of a married beneficiary and shall not be subject to attachment or susceptible of anticipation or alienation. Nothing contained in this Section 2 shall be construed as restricting in any way the exercise of any power of appointment granted hereunder.

3. The whole or any part of the income or principal paid to any minor or to any other person who in the opinion of the trustee is incapacitated through illness, age or other cause may be applied by the trustee in its discretion for such beneficiary's comfort, maintenance, support or education. Any such application may be made at such time and in such manner as the trustee deems advisable, whether by direct payment of such beneficiary's expenses or by payment to a person selected by the trustee to receive payment for such beneficiary; in each case the receipt of such person to whom payment is made or entrusted shall be a complete discharge of the trustee in respect thereof. Whenever any payment hereunder is required to be made to a minor, the interest so required to be paid shall be indefeasibly vested in the minor but the trustees may retain the amount payable until the minor attains his majority or dies, whichever first occurs, and the trustees may pay the income and principal to the minor in such amount or amounts and from time to time as the trustees may determine, and if the minor lives to attain his majority, then when he attains his majority the trustees shall pay the then remaining principal and undistributed income to him, and if the minor dies before attaining his majority, then on the minor's death the trustees shall pay

Richard Harry Black III   **R.J.A.**
                              D.R.J.
                              A.J.C.

(10)

[182] Insert the date when the indenture of trust was executed.
[183] Insert the name of a charity.

the then remaining principal and undistributed income to the minor's estate.

4. The trustee is authorized to mingle the trust property of the separate trusts established by Article FOURTH of this will, allotting to each separate trust an undivided interest in the mingled funds, that shall always be equal to that trust's proportionate contribution (as adjusted from time to time as a result of accumulations of income, payments of principal and accumulated income and additions to principal) to the mingled funds.

5. References to "child" or "children" mean lawful blood descendants in the first degree of the parent designated, and references to "issue" mean lawful blood descendants in the first, second or any other degree of the ancestor designated, provided always, however, that

  (a) An adopted child and such adopted child's lawful blood descendants shall be considered as lawful blood descendants of the adopting parent or parents and of anyone who is by blood or adoption an ancestor of the adopting parent or of either of the adopting parents and shall not be considered descendants of the adopted child's natural parents, except that where a child is adopted by a spouse of one of his or her natural parents such child shall be considered a descendant of such natural parent as well as a descendant of the adopting parent; and

  (b) A child born to persons who are openly living together as husband and wife after the performance of a marriage ceremony between them and such child's lawful blood descendants shall be considered as lawful blood descendants of such child's parents and of any ancestor of such child's parents, regardless of the fact that a purported divorce of one or both of such persons with reference to a prior marriage is invalid.

6. Whenever distribution is to be made to designated "issue" on a *per stirpes* basis, the property shall be distributed to the persons and in the proportions that personal property of the named ancestor would be distributed under the laws of the .... of ....[184] in force at the time stipulated for distribution if the named ancestor had died intestate at such time, domiciled in such State, not married and survived only by such issue.

7. References under the provisions of Article THIRD of this will to "my heirs" mean those persons, other than creditors, who

	R.J.A.
Richard Harry Black III	D.R.J.
	A.J.C.

(11)

---

[184] Insert the state which is to govern.

would take my personal property under the laws of the ....
.... of ....[185] if I had died intestate at
the time stipulated for distribution and domiciled in such State.
In determining who such persons are, it shall be assumed that all
decrees of divorce rendered by a court of record, wherever located, are valid. Distribution to such persons shall be made in
the manner and in the proportion that personal property of mine
would be distributed under the laws of the ....
of ....[186] if I had died intestate at the time
stipulated for distribution, owning the property available for distribution and no other property and domiciled in such State.

8. A child in gestation, who is later born alive, shall be regarded in
this will as a child in being during the period of gestation, in
determining whether any person has died without leaving issue
surviving him or her, and in determining, on the termination of
any trust hereunder, whether such child is entitled to share in
required distributions of principal, but for other purposes such
child's right shall accrue from date of birth.

SIXTH: Reference is made to **THE RICHARD HARRY BLACK
III TRUST**, which was created by indenture of trust dated ....
.............................., 19............,[187] and to Article SEVENTH thereof, which
establishes an estate tax marital deduction trust if my said wife survives
me. It is my intention that the value of the said estate tax marital
deduction trust when combined with the value of other gross estate
items which qualify for the marital deduction and which pass or have
passed from me to my said wife will equal the maximum estate tax
marital deduction allowable to my estate for federal estate tax purposes on the basis of values as finally determined for federal estate
tax purposes. If for any reason my intention as expressed in the preceding sentence will not be accomplished unless an additional amount
passes from me to my said wife, I hereby give such additional amount
to THE RICHARD HARRY BLACK III TRUST, to be added to
the principal of the trust created by said Article SEVENTH, as, when
added to such principal, will effectuate my intention. To whatever
extent it is necessary, in order to give validity to this pour-over from
my will to said trust, that changes made in said trust not be applicable
to the poured-over property, such changes shall be inapplicable.

There shall not be used to satisfy the above-described amount any
property, or the proceeds of any property, which do not qualify for the
estate tax marital deduction or which are subject to foreign death

	R.J.A.
Richard Harry Black III	*D.R.J.*
	A.J.C.

(12)

---

[185] Insert the state which is to govern.
[186] Insert the state which is to govern.
[187] Insert the date when the indenture of trust was executed.

taxes. Furthermore, income in respect of a decedent (or the right to income in respect of a decedent) shall not be so used.

I intend that the value for federal estate tax purposes of the amount described above in this Article SIXTH shall be available for the marital deduction allowed by the federal estate tax law applicable to my estate and that all questions applicable to this amount shall be resolved accordingly.[188]

Nothing shall pass under this Article SIXTH if the order of the deaths of my said wife and me cannot be established by proof.

My said wife may disclaim in whole or in part the amount described above and in the event of such disclaimer, said amount, or the portion thereof to which the disclaimer applies, shall be added to my residuary estate and disposed of as hereinafter provided.

SEVENTH: All the rest and residue of my property of whatever kind and wherever located that I own at my death, including any of the foregoing gifts in this will which for any reason fail to take effect, but not including property over which I shall then have any power of appointment (it being my intention not to exercise any power of appointment I may have except as it may be exercised specifically by other provisions of this will), all of which is herein referred to as my residuary estate, I give, devise and bequeath as follows:

1. Ten percent (10%) of my residuary estate, or Two Thousand Dollars ($2000), whichever is smaller in amount, such determination to be made on the basis of the value of my residuary estate as of the date of my death and before it has been diminished by the payment of any death costs, to Joseph Ricardo, if he is in my employ at the time of my death. No interest shall be paid on this legacy regardless of the time the payment thereof is delayed.

2. The balance of my residuary estate, or all of my residuary estate if the said Joseph Ricardo is not in my employ at the time of my death, to THE RICHARD HARRY BLACK III TRUST, to be held or disposed of in accordance with the provisions of Article EIGHTH thereof; to whatever extent it is necessary, in order to give validity to this pour-over from my will to said trust, that changes made in said trust not be applicable to the poured-over property, such changes shall be inapplicable.

EIGHTH: Article EIGHTEENTH of THE RICHARD HARRY BLACK III TRUST authorizes the disinterested trustee in his uncontrolled discretion to use the income and principal of each separate trust and of each distributable share under Article EIGHTH of said trust, provided the same proportionate amount is taken from each separate

R.J.A.

Richard Harry Black III   D.R.J.

A.J.C.

(13)

[188] See page 1239 supra, note 128. — ED.

trust and from each distributable share, to pay my funeral expenses, my debts, expenses of administration of my estate, all federal and state taxes in the nature of income, estate, inheritance, succession, transfer, gift or like taxes arising or owing on my death (including the right to compromise and to pay as soon as convenient after my death any of such taxes on future or contingent interests), except estate taxes attributable to the value of appointive assets included in my gross estate when I was granted the power of appointment by someone other than myself.

All estate taxes, federal and state, imposed by reason of my death with respect to any property disposed of by this will, which are not paid by the disinterested trustee referred to above, and any interest thereon, shall be borne by that portion of my residuary estate disposed of by Article SEVENTH, Section 2 of this will.

All legacy, succession, inheritance and like taxes (as distinguished from estate taxes) imposed by reason of my death on property disposed of by this will, which are not paid by the disinterested trustee referred to above, and any interest thereon, shall be borne by that portion of my residuary estate disposed of by said Article SEVENTH, Section 2. So far as practicable and reasonable, my disinterested executor shall settle and compromise and shall pay as soon as convenient after my death any of the taxes referred to in the preceding sentence on future or contingent interests.[189]

My funeral expenses, my debts and the expenses of administration of my estate, to the extent that they are not paid by the disinterested trustee referred to above, shall be borne by that portion of my residuary estate disposed of by said Article SEVENTH, Section 2.

If the obligations referred to in this Article EIGHTH are required to be met to any extent out of the property disposed of by Article THIRD of this will, I hope that the necessary funds will be raised by a loan and a mortgage placed on the property disposed of by said Article THIRD to secure the loan rather than by a sale of such property.[190]

If my said wife survives me, and obligations similar to the ones de-

Richard Harry Black III   **R.J.A.**
D.R.J.
A.J.C.

(14)

---

[189] It should be noted that the paragraph in the will to which this note is appended, and the preceding paragraph, provide for the payment of various death taxes out of the described portion of the residuary estate only with respect to the taxes which are imposed on property disposed of by the will. In anticipation of this, Article Nineteenth of "The Richard Harry Black III Trust" (see page 1256 supra) assumes the tax burden with respect to all taxes imposed on property not disposed of by the will. — ED.

[190] In the light of what is stated supra note 189, no death cost burdens should fall on the property disposed of by Article Third so long as the portion of the residuary estate charged with such burdens is sufficient in amount to cover them. — ED.

scribed in this Article EIGHTH arise on my said wife's death and are required to be met to any extent out of the property then held in trust under Article THIRD of this will, I hope that the necessary funds will be raised by the trustee by a loan and a mortgage placed on the trust property to secure the loan rather than by a sale of such property.[191]

NINTH: I give to my disinterested executor the following powers and discretions:

1. If my disinterested executor in good faith decides that there is uncertainty as to the inclusion of particular property in my gross estate for federal estate tax purposes, he shall exclude such property from my gross estate in the estate tax return. My disinterested executor shall not be liable for any loss to my estate or to any beneficiary, if such loss results from his decision made in good faith that there is uncertainty as to the inclusion of particular property in my gross estate.[192]

2. The decision of my disinterested executor as to the date which should be selected for the valuation of property in my gross estate for federal estate tax purposes shall be conclusive on all concerned.

3. When a choice is available as to whether certain deductions shall be taken as income tax deductions or estate tax deductions, the decision of my disinterested executor in this regard shall be conclusive on all concerned and no adjustment of income and principal accounts in the estate shall be made as a result of such decision.[193]

Richard Harry Black III	*R.J.A.*
	D.R.J.
	A.J.C.

(15)

---

[191] See Article Second of Mrs. Black's will at page 1290 infra, which undertakes to relieve the property held in trust under Article Third of Mr. Black's will from any tax burdens on Mrs. Black's death. — ED.

[192] If this provision is not included, the executor runs some risk of being personally liable for interest due on any deficiency assessment made as a result of excluding an item from the gross estate. See Hooker v. Hoskyns, 328 P.2d 404 (Okla. 1958). — ED.

[193] It should be noted that the power of decision in each of the three sections in Article Ninth is vested in the disinterested executor. To this extent the inclusion of the sections is probably desirable. However, the wisdom of including the direction in Section 1 which is given to the disinterested executor as to the exclusion of property from the gross estate is highly questionable, and the appropriateness of the direction in regard to the adjustment of income and principal accounts in Section 3 should be determined only after considering some alternatives. One alternative might be to direct the disinterested executor to make a proper adjustment, and to provide that his determination as to what constitutes a proper adjustment would be conclusive on all concerned. Another might be to give the disinterested executor discretion to determine whether any adjustment should be made.

In Fleming, From Peter to Paul, 96 Trusts & Estates 1089 (1957), the following form is suggested with respect to the problem dealt with in Section 3: "I direct my

My executors are authorized to make partial or complete distributions to estate beneficiaries from time to time during administration; to distribute unequal amounts to similar beneficiaries from time to time during administration; and to make such other distributions during administration as they may determine. Nothing contained in this paragraph shall be construed as authorizing my executors to vary the dispositive provisions in this will.

TENTH: I request my executors, although no duty is imposed on them in this regard, to retain as an investment the common stock or other securities of the Black Manufacturing Company which come to them as a part of my estate, and the common stock or other securities of any concern that shall succeed to the whole or a substantial part of the assets or business of the Black Manufacturing Company, which common stock or other securities come to them as a part of my estate, even though such an amount of securities of one company may not be considered suitable as an investment by executors. Furthermore, if at any time there are estate funds to be invested, I request my executors, although no duty is imposed on them in this regard, to purchase and retain as an investment of the estate the common stock or other securities of the Black Manufacturing Company and the common stock or other securities of any concern which shall succeed to the whole or a substantial part of the assets or business of the Black Manufacturing Company.

In the event my executors decide to make purchases as mentioned in the preceding paragraph, such purchases may be made from any source, including my said wife, my said son, my said daughter, any issue of my said son, any issue of my said daughter, my brother, the wife of my brother, any issue of my brother, or the trustees of any trust established by me or by my said wife or by any issue of mine or by my brother or by the wife of my brother or by any issue of my brother. In each case, however, the decision of my disinterested executor as to the price which should be paid for such acquisitions shall be conclusive.

In the event that my executors decide to sell any of the common stock or other securities of the Black Manufacturing Company, or the common stock or other securities of any concern which shall succeed to the whole or a substantial part of the assets or business of the Black

	R.J.A.
Richard Harry Black III	*D.R.J.*
	A.J.C.

(16)

---

executor to claim any expenses of administration of my estate as income tax deductions upon an income tax return or returns whenever in his sole judgment such action will achieve an overall reduction in the income and death taxes for the benefit of my estate and of the income beneficiary or beneficiaries thereof. I further direct that no compensating adjustments between income and principal or in the amount of the bequest under ARTICLE ----------------(formula bequest) shall be required or made as a result of such action." — ED.

Manufacturing Company, such sale shall be made at a price deemed adequate by my disinterested executor and such sale shall be made to one or more of the following if one or more of the following is ready and willing to purchase at the price deemed adequate by my disinterested executor, and otherwise to the general public at such price: my said wife, my said son, my said daughter, any issue of my said son, any issue of my said daughter, my brother, the wife of my brother, any issue of my brother, or the trustees of any trust established by me or by my said wife or by any issue of mine or by my brother or by the wife of my brother or by any issue of my brother.[194]

Any executor hereunder (as well as any issue of mine, or my brother or any issue of my brother) may serve as an officer of the Black Manufacturing Company or of any concern which shall succeed to the whole or a substantial part of the assets or business of the Black Manufacturing Company.

ELEVENTH: In extension and not in limitation of the powers given by law or other provisions of this will (but subject to the restrictions of Articles SIXTH, NINTH and TENTH of this will), my executors shall have the following powers with respect to the settlement of my estate, and the trustee of each trust under Articles THIRD and FOURTH hereof shall have the following powers with respect to such trust and its property, in each case to be exercised from time to time in the discretion of my executors and the trustee and without order or license of court:

1. To retain indefinitely any investments and to invest and reinvest in stocks, shares and obligations of corporations, of unincorporated associations or trusts and of investment companies,[195] or in a common trust fund without giving notice to any beneficiary,[196] or in any other kind of personal or real property, notwithstanding the fact that any or all of the investments made or retained are of a character or size which but for this express authority would not be considered proper for executors or trustees;

2. To sell, to exchange, to lease and to make contracts concerning real or personal property for such considerations and upon such terms as to credit or otherwise as my disinterested executor or the trustee may determine, which leases and contracts may extend beyond the term of the settlement of my estate or the term of any trust; to give options therefor; to execute deeds, transfers, leases and other instruments of any kind;

3. To hold bonds, shares or other securities in bearer form, or in

R.J.A.

Richard Harry Black III   **D.R.J.**

A.J.C.

(17)

---

[194] See page 1191 supra, note 42. — ED.
[195] See page 1211 supra, note 56. — ED.
[196] See page 1211 supra, note 57. — ED.

the name of the executors or in the name of one of the executors or in the name of the trustee or in the name of a nominee, without indication of any fiduciary capacity; to deposit cash in a checking or savings account in a bank, without indication of any fiduciary capacity;

4. To give general or special proxies or powers of attorney for voting or acting in respect of shares or securities, which may be discretionary and with power of substitution; to deposit shares or securities with, or transfer them to, protective committees or similar bodies; to join in any reorganization and to pay assessments or subscriptions called for in connection with shares or securities held by my executors or the trustee;

5. To improve or develop real estate; to construct, alter or repair buildings or structures on real estate; to settle boundary lines and easements and other rights with respect to real estate; to partition and to join with co-owners and others in dealing with real estate in any way;

6. To employ investment counsel, custodians of estate property and trust property, brokers, agents and attorneys;

7. To receive additions to any trusts under this will by gift or will or otherwise, and to hold and administer the same under the provisions hereof;

8. To pay as income the whole of the interest, dividends, rent or similar receipts from property, whether wasting or not and although bought or taken at a value above par, but if it is deemed advisable when property is bought or taken at a value above par, a portion of the income may be retained to offset such loss to the principal; to treat as income or principal or to apportion between them stock dividends, extra dividends, rights to take stock or securities, and proceeds from the sale of real estate, although such real estate may have been wholly or partly unproductive; to charge to income or principal or to apportion between them investment counsel's compensation, custodians' compensation, brokers' commissions, agents' compensations, attorneys' fees, insurance premiums, repairs or improvements, taxes (income, estate, inheritance or any other taxes), depreciation charges, executors' and trustee's compensation; and generally to determine all questions as between income and principal and to credit or charge to income or principal or to apportion between them any receipt or gain and any charge, disbursement or loss as is deemed advisable in the circumstances of each case as it arises, notwithstanding any statute or rule of law for distinguishing income from principal or any determination of the courts; provided always, however, that the powers and discretions given in this

Richard Harry Black III   *R.J.A.*
D.R.J.
A.J.C.

(18)

Section 8 shall be exercisable only by my disinterested executor and the trustee;

9. When paying legacies or dividing or distributing my estate or any trust fund, to make such payments, division or distribution wholly or partly in kind by allotting and transferring specific securities or other personal or real property or undivided interests therein as a part or the whole of any one or more payments or shares at current values;

10. To keep any or all of the estate property or the trust property at any place or places in ....[197] or elsewhere within the United States or abroad or with a depositary or custodian at such place or places.

The above provisions are applicable to the trusts established by Article FOURTH of this will only to the extent that they are permissible provisions under the terms of the power of appointment given me in the will of my late mother. Furthermore, the above provisions are applicable to the trust established by Article THIRD of this will only to the extent that they are not inconsistent with the terms of such Article.

TWELFTH: I authorize and empower my disinterested executor to join with my said wife or her executor or administrator, in filing a joint federal or state income tax return of the income of my said wife and myself for any period or periods for which such a return may be permitted. I further authorize and empower my disinterested executor to agree with my said wife or her executor or administrator,

1. As to how the burden of the liability for federal or state income tax, or interest thereon, arising out of the filing of a joint return by my disinterested executor and my said wife or her executor or administrator, shall be borne as between my estate and my said wife or her estate, and

2. As to who, as between my said wife or her estate and my estate, shall be entitled

   (a) To any refund or credit of any federal or state income tax, or interest thereon, based on the filing of a joint return by my said wife and myself or by my executor and my said wife or her executor or administrator,

   (b) To any refund or credit of any amount paid on account of any joint declaration of estimated federal or state income tax filed by my said wife and myself, and of the interest on any such refund, and

   (c) To the benefit of any payment made by my said wife or myself on account of any joint or separate declaration of estimated federal or state income tax.

	R.J.A.
Richard Harry Black III	D.R.J.
	A.J.C.

(19)

---

[197] Insert the state where Mr. Black resides.

My disinterested executor may exercise the foregoing powers in such manner as he shall in his absolute and uncontrolled discretion deem best, whether in the interest of my said wife or her estate or in the interest of my estate.

I authorize and empower my disinterested executor to consent for federal gift tax purposes to gifts made by my said wife as having been made one half by me and one half by her.[198]

THIRTEENTH: I name my son, RICHARD HARRY BLACK IV, and ROBERT J. ANDREW of ...., ...
........................,[199] to be executors of my will. No bond shall be required of my said son or said ROBERT J. ANDREW as executors, or if a bond is required by law, no surety on such bond shall be required.

To the extent that it is necessary to appoint a representative of my estate in Illinois, I name ILLINOIS TRUST COMPANY, of Bloomington, Illinois,[200] to be such representative and no bond shall be required of the said ILLINOIS TRUST COMPANY in this capacity, or if a bond is required by law, no surety on such bond shall be required.

References in this will to "executors" mean the executor or executors for the time being in office or the administrator or administrators with the will annexed for the time being in office.

References in this will to "disinterested executor" mean the executor hereunder who has no interest vested or contingent in the property disposed of by this will and who cannot be benefited by the exercise or nonexercise of the powers vested exclusively in the disinterested executor.

	R.J.A.
Richard Harry Black III	*D.R.J.*
	A.J.C.

(20)

[198] Section 25.2513-2(c) of the Regulations provides as follows in regard to the consent referred to: "The executor or administrator of a deceased spouse, or the guardian or committee of a legally incompetent spouse, as the case may be, may signify the consent."

Sections 25.2513-1(b)(1) of the Regulations provides in part as follows: "Where the consent is signified by an executor or administrator of a deceased spouse, the consent is not effective with respect to gifts made by the surviving spouse during the portion of the calendar year that his spouse was deceased."

Section 25.2513-4 of the Regulations provides as follows: "If consent to the application of the provisions of section 2513 is signified as provided in §25.2513-2, and not revoked as provided in §25.2513-3, the liability with respect to the entire gift tax of each spouse for such calendar year is joint and several. See paragraph (d) of §25.2511-1."

Section 25.2511-1(d) of the Regulations points out that no gift is made if one spouse pays the entire gift tax assessed when the gifts are considered as made half by each spouse in accordance with the provisions of §2513, quoted infra page 1419. — ED.

[199] Insert the place of residence of Robert J. Andrew.

[200] References here to Illinois and Illinois Trust Company should be changed to Iowa and to an Iowa trust company if the farm is located in Iowa.

References in this will to "trustee" include not only the original trustee but also any successor trustee who may from time to time be named by competent authority, and all powers and discretions vested in the trustee shall be vested in and exercised by any such successor trustee. No bond shall be required of the trustee or any successor trustee, or if a bond is required by law, no surety on such bond shall be required.

No one dealing with my executors or the trustee need inquire concerning the validity of anything that they purport to do or need see to the application of any money paid or any property transferred to or upon the order of my executors or the trustee.

An executor and a trustee shall be responsible only for such executor's of such trustee's own acts and omissions in bad faith. Furthermore, a successor executor or successor trustee shall not be liable for any action taken by the executors or a trustee prior to the time such successor executor becomes an executor or such successor trustee becomes a trustee.

An executor may delegate any powers and discretions which he has as executor to the co-executors by an instrument in writing, provided always, however, that the powers and discretions vested exclusively in the disinterested executor shall not be delegated.

FOURTEENTH: The trustee designated in Article THIRD of this will and the trustee designated in Article FOURTH of this will may resign by an instrument in writing which expresses such intention and which is delivered to my oldest living issue, or such issue's legal guardian.

If a vacancy in the office of trustee occurs with respect to the trust under said Article THIRD or a trust under said Article FOURTH, a trustee, individual or corporate, shall be appointed to fill such vacancy by an instrument in writing which designates such appointee and which is signed by my oldest living issue, or such issue's legal guardian.

No person who has any interest vested or contingent in the trust property or who may benefit by the exercise of any of the powers given the trustee shall be appointed a trustee.

IN WITNESS WHEREOF, I hereunto set my hand and seal this .... day of ...., 19............[201] For identification I have signed each of the foregoing 20 pages of this will, which consists of 22 pages.

/s/ *Richard Harry Black III* [Seal]

Signed, sealed, published and declared by the above-named RICH-ARD HARRY BLACK III as and for his last will, in the presence of us three who, at his request, in his presence and in the presence of

(21)

----

[201] Insert the date on which the will is executed.

one another, hereto subscribe our names as witnesses thereof, all on the date last above written, and each of us hereby declares that in his opinion the said RICHARD HARRY BLACK III is of sound and disposing mind and memory.

Name	Address[202]
/s/ Roger J. Avis	........................., ...
/s/ Donald R. James	........................., ...
/s/ Albert J. Casner	........................., ...

(22)

---

[202] Insert the address of each witness.

L. *Will of Mildred Marie Black*

I, MILDRED MARIE BLACK, of ....,
....,[203] wife of Richard Harry Black III, make
this my last will, hereby revoking all wills and codicils heretofore made
by me.

FIRST: My tangible personal property owned by me at the time of
my death, including furniture, books, automobiles and their equipment, boats and their equipment, jewelry, and articles of personal or
household use or ornament (and all policies of insurance on such tangible personal property), but not including money, securities or the
like, I give absolutely to my said husband, if he survives me by thirty
(30) days; and if my said husband does not so survive me, I give the
same absolutely to my issue who so survive me, such issue to take *per
stirpes.*

I express the hope that my said husband or my said issue will dispose of said tangible personal property according to my wishes, however my wishes may be made known to him or to them, but I expressly
declare that I do not intend to create any trust in law or in equity with
respect to said tangible personal property.

In the event that my said husband does not survive me by thirty (30)
days and more than one issue of mine do so survive me, so that a
division of my said tangible personal property into shares is required
by the provisions of this Article FIRST, the following steps shall be
taken to accomplish such division:

1. My disinterested executor shall place a value on each item of my
   tangible personal property.
2. Each issue of mine entitled to a share (or such person as may be
   designated by my disinterested executor to represent such issue)
   shall alternately select the items of tangible personal property he
   or she desires, the first item to be selected by my oldest issue (or
   such issue's representative) entitled to a share.
3. When an issue of mine entitled to a share (or such issue's representative) has selected items of tangible personal property which
   total in value his or her share, he or she shall have no further
   right of selection.
4. Items of tangible personal property not selected by the above
   method shall be sold by my executors (issue of mine to have
   the first right of purchase at such sale) and the net proceeds of the
   sale shall be divided among my issue so that the cash plus the

Mildred Marie Black	*R.J.A.*
	D.R.J.
	A.J.C.

(1)

[203] Insert the city and state where Mrs. Black resides.

items of tangible personal property selected by an issue of mine will total in value such issue's share.

Property and cash distributable to a minor under this Article FIRST may be distributed by my executors to such minor personally, or to such minor's legal guardian, or to some other person selected by my executors to receive such property for such minor, and the receipt of such minor, or such minor's legal guardian, or such other person, shall be a complete discharge of my executors in regard to such distribution.[204]

The person to whom property is distributed under this Article FIRST for the benefit of a minor shall decide from time to time whether such property shall be retained for eventual distribution to the minor or whether some or all of it shall be sold and the proceeds of the sale held for the minor. Such person's decision in this regard shall be conclusive on all concerned.

The cost of moving any tangible personal property disposed of under this Article FIRST to the destination desired by the beneficiary shall be borne by the beneficiary.

SECOND: All the rest and residue of my property of whatever kind and wherever located that I own at my death, but not including property over which I shall then have any power of appointment (it being my intention not to exercise any power of appointment I may have), all of which is hereinafter referred to as my residuary estate, I give, devise and bequeath as follows:

1. All estate taxes, federal and state, imposed by reason of my death with respect to any property disposed of by this will and imposed, by reason of my death, with respect to any real property or tangible personal property, though not disposed of by this will, whether held in trust or not, which is required to be included in my gross estate for estate tax purposes, and any interest thereon, shall be paid out of my residuary estate.

2. All legacy, succession, inheritance and like taxes (as distinguished from estate taxes) imposed by reason of my death on property disposed of by this will and on any real property or tangible personal property not disposed of by this will, whether held in trust or not, and any interest thereon, shall be paid out of my residuary estate. So far as is practicable and reasonable, my disinterested executor shall settle and compromise and shall pay as soon as convenient after my death any of the taxes referred to in the preceding sentence on future or contingent interests.

3. My funeral expenses, my debts and the expenses of administration of my estate shall be paid out of my residuary estate.

	R.J.A.
Mildred Marie Black	D.R.J.
	A.J.C.

(2)

---

[204] See page 1268 supra, note 169. — ED.

4. The balance of my residuary estate (said balance means my residuary estate minus the payments called for by Sections 1, 2 and 3 of this Article SECOND), if issue of mine survive me, I give to my trustees hereinafter named and their successor or successors, and my trustees shall divide the trust property into as many equal shares as there are children of mine who survive me and children of mine who predecease me leaving issue who survive me, and my trustees shall allocate one of such equal shares to each living child of mine and each share so allocated shall be held in a separate trust in accordance with the provisions of paragraph (a) of this Section 4; and my trustees shall allocate one of such equal shares to the issue of each deceased child of mine and shall pay such share to such issue then living if no child of such deceased child of mine is living who is under the age of twenty-one (21) years, such issue to take *per stirpes,* and if a child of such deceased child of mine is living who is under the age of twenty-one (21) years, then such share shall be held in a separate trust for the benefit of the issue of such deceased child of mine in accordance with the provisions of paragraph (b) of this Section 4.

(a) With respect to the separate trust for each living child of mine, my trustees are directed as follows:

(i) My trustees shall pay the net income to such child for such child's life; and, in addition, my trustees shall pay to such child, from the principal of the trust, from time to time, such amount or amounts as such child may request by an instrument or instruments in writing delivered to my trustees in the lifetime of such child, provided always, however, that the aggregate amount of principal paid to such child pursuant to such child's request shall not exceed the sum of Five Thousand Dollars ($5000) in any calendar year; furthermore, my disinterested trustee may pay to such child, from the principal of the trust, from time to time, such amount or amounts or all of the principal as he in his uncontrolled discretion may determine, without any restriction on the aggregate amount which may be paid to such child in any calendar year.

(ii) On the death of such child, my trustees shall pay the then remaining principal and undistributed income to the issue of such child then living if no child of such child is living who is under the age of twenty-one (21) years, such issue to take *per stirpes;* and if a child of such child is living who is under the age of twenty-one (21) years, my trustees shall hold the then remaining principal and undistributed income in a separate trust for the issue of such child in

Mildred Marie Black *R.J.A.*
D.R.J.
A.J.C.

(3)

accordance with the provisions of paragraph (b) of this Section 4; and if no issue of such child is then living, my trustees shall pay the then remaining principal and undistributed income to my issue then living, such issue to take *per stirpes,* provided always, however, that an issue of mine who is then entitled to income under any other trust established by this Section 4 or who is then a member of a group to whom income is distributable under any other trust established by this Section 4 shall not receive his or her share outright, but such share shall be added to the principal of such other trust and be governed accordingly; and if no issue of such child is then living and no issue of mine is then living, my trustees shall pay the then remaining principal and undistributed income to my heirs.

(b) With respect to the separate trust for the issue of each deceased child of mine, my trustees are directed as follows:

(i) Until no child of such deceased child is living who is under the age of twenty-one (21) years, my disinterested trustee shall pay out all the net income in each calendar year to, or apply the same for the benefit of, any one or more of the issue of such deceased child who are living from time to time, in such amount or amounts as my disinterested trustee in his uncontrolled discretion may determine; in addition, my disinterested trustee may pay to, or apply for the benefit of, any one or more of the issue of such deceased child who are living from time to time, from the principal of the trust, from time to time, such amount or amounts or all of the principal as he in his uncontrolled discretion may determine; payments of income and principal to the issue of such deceased child pursuant to the above provisions shall not be taken into account in any later division of the principal and undistributed income into shares for the benefit of such issue.

(ii) When no child of such deceased child is living who is under the age of twenty-one (21) years, the trustees shall pay the then remaining principal and undistributed income to the issue then living of such deceased child, such issue to take *per stirpes;* and if no issue of such deceased child is then living, the trustees shall pay the then remaining principal and undistributed income to my issue then living, such issue to take *per stirpes,* provided always, however, that an issue of mine who is then entitled to the income under any other trust established by this Section 4

Mildred Marie Black   *R.J.A.*
                          D.R.J.
                          A.J.C.

(4)

or who is then a member of a group to whom income is distributable under any other trust established by this Section 4 shall not receive his or her share outright, but such share shall be added to the principal of such other trust and be governed accordingly; and if no issue of such deceased child is then living and no issue of mine is then living, the trustees shall pay the then remaining principal and undistributed income to my heirs.

5. The balance of my residuary estate (said balance means my residuary estate minus the payments called for by Sections 1, 2 and 3 of this Article SECOND), if no issue of mine survives me, shall be paid to my heirs.

6. Income payments which my trustees are required to make to a beneficiary under the provisions of this Article SECOND shall be made at times fixed by my disinterested trustee but at least as often as quarterly.

7. The interest of each beneficiary in the income or principal of a trust under this Article SECOND shall be free from the control or interference of any creditor of a beneficiary or of any spouse of a married beneficiary and shall not be subject to attachment or susceptible of anticipation or alienation.

8. The whole or any part of the income or principal paid to any minor or to any other person who in the opinion of my disinterested trustee is incapacitated through illness, age or other cause may be applied by my disinterested trustee in his discretion for such beneficiary's comfort, maintenance, support or education. Any such application may be made at such time and in such manner as my disinterested trustee deems advisable, whether by direct payment of such beneficiary's expenses or by payment to a person selected by my disinterested trustee to receive payment for such beneficiary; in each case the receipt of such person to whom payment is made or entrusted shall be a complete discharge of my disinterested trustee in respect thereof. Whenever any payment hereunder is required to be made to a minor, the interest so required to be paid shall be indefeasibly vested in the minor but the trustees may retain the amount payable until the minor attains his majority or dies, whichever first occurs, and the trustees may pay the income and principal to the minor in such amount or amounts and from time to time as the trustees may determine, and if the minor lives to attain his majority, then when he attains his majority the trustees shall pay the then remaining principal and undistributed income to him, and if the minor dies before attaining his majority, then on the minor's death the trustees shall

Mildred Marie Black　　　*R.J.A.*
　　　　　　　　　　　　D.R.J.
　　　　　　　　　　　　A.J.C.

(5)

pay the then remaining principal and undistributed income to the minor's estate.

9. My trustees are authorized to mingle the trust property of the separate trusts established by this Article SECOND, allotting to each separate trust an undivided interest in the mingled fund, which undivided interest shall always be equal to that trust's proportionate contribution (as adjusted from time to time as a result of payments of principal) to the mingled funds.

10. References under the provisions of this Article SECOND to "my heirs" mean those persons, other than creditors, who would take my personal property under the laws of the .... of .... [205] if I had died intestate at the time stipulated for distribution, not survived by my said husband and domiciled in such State. In determining who such persons are, it shall be assumed that all decrees of divorce rendered by a court of record, wherever located, are valid. Distribution to such persons shall be made in the manner and in the proportion that personal property of mine would be distributed under the laws of the .... of .... [206] if I had died intestate at the time stipulated for distribution, owning the property available for distribution and no other property, not survived by my said husband and domiciled in such State.

THIRD: References in this will to "child" and "children" mean lawful blood descendants in the first degree of the parent designated, and references to "issue" mean lawful blood descendants in the first, second or any other degree of the ancestor designated, provided always, however, that

1. An adopted child and such adopted child's lawful blood descendants shall be considered in this will as lawful blood descendants of the adopting parent or parents and of anyone who is by blood or adoption an ancestor of the adopting parent or of either of the adopting parents and shall not be considered descendants of the adopted child's natural parents, except that where a child is adopted by a spouse of one of his or her natural parents such child shall be considered a descendant of such natural parent as well as a descendant of the adopting parent; and

2. A child born to persons who are openly living together as husband and wife after the performance of a marriage ceremony between them and such child's lawful blood descendants shall be considered in this will as lawful blood descendants of such child's

<table>
<tr><td></td><td>R.J.A.</td></tr>
<tr><td>Mildred Marie Black</td><td>D.R.J.</td></tr>
<tr><td></td><td>A.J.C.</td></tr>
</table>

(6)

[205] Insert the state which is to govern.
[206] Insert the state which is to govern.

parents and of any ancestor of such child's parents, regardless of the fact that a purported divorce of one or both of such persons with reference to a prior marriage is invalid.

A child in gestation, who is later born alive, shall be regarded in this will as a child in being during the period of gestation, in determining whether any person has died without leaving issue surviving him or her, and in determining, on the termination of any trust hereunder, whether such child is entitled to share in required distributions of principal, but for other purposes such child's right shall accrue from date of birth.

References in this will to a "minor" mean a person under the age of twenty-one (21) years.

Whenever distribution is to be made to designated issue on a *per stirpes* basis, the property shall be distributed to the persons and in the proportions that personal property of the named ancestor would be distributed under the laws of the .... of .... [207] in force at the time stipulated for distribution if the named ancestor had died intestate at such time, domiciled in such State, not married and survived only by such issue.

Whenever my disinterested trustee is required to distribute all the net income among designated issue but has discretion to select one or more of the designated issue to receive the income, payments may be made to or for the benefit of any issue of the second or more remote degree even though payment is also made or could be made to the parent of such issue.

FOURTH: I now own a policy of insurance on the life of my said husband. I have paid and expect to continue to pay out of my own funds all premiums on said policy, and I now possess and expect to retain all incidents of ownership with respect to said policy. If I predecease my said husband, said policy will become a part of the residue of my estate. With respect to said policy, I authorize my disinterested executor, while said policy is a part of my estate, and my disinterested trustee, while said policy is a part of the trust funds of any trust established by Article SECOND of this will, to do any of the following things with respect to said policy, the authorizations here given to prevail, notwithstanding anything to the contrary in other provisions of my will:

1. To continue said policy in force and to pay the premiums on said policy out of income or principal;
2. To obtain the cash surrender value of said policy and add it to principal;

Mildred Marie Black   **R.J.A.**
                          D.R.J.
                          A.J.C.

(7)

---

[207] Insert the state which is to govern.

3. To convert said policy to paid-up insurance; and
4. To deal with said policy in any other way that my disinterested executor or my disinterested trustee in his uncontrolled discretion may determine is in the best interest of all concerned.

FIFTH: I request my executors and my trustees, although no duty is imposed on them in this regard, to retain as an investment of my estate, or as an investment of any trust created by this will, the common stock or other securities of the Black Manufacturing Company which are in my estate at the time of my death and are placed by my executors in any trust established by this will, and the common stock or other securities of any concern that shall succeed to the whole or a substantial part of the assets or business of the Black Manufacturing Company, which common stock or other securities are in my estate at the time of my death and are placed by my executors in any trust established by this will, even though such an amount of securities of one company may not be considered suitable as an investment by executors or trustees. Furthermore, if at times there are estate funds or trust funds to be invested, I request my executors and my trustees, although no duty is imposed on them in this regard, to purchase and retain as an investment of my estate or of any trust established by this will the common stock or other securities of the Black Manufacturing Company and the common stock or other securities of any concern which shall succeed to the whole or a substantial part of the assets or business of the Black Manufacturing Company.

In the event that my executors or my trustees decide to make purchases as mentioned in the preceding paragraph, such purchases may be made from any source, including my said husband, my issue, my said husband's brother, the wife of my said husband's brother, any issue of my said husband's brother, or the trustees of any trust established by my said husband or by my issue or by my said husband's brother or by the wife of my said husband's brother or by any issue of my said husband's brother. In each case, however, the decision of my disinterested executor or my disinterested trustee as to the price which should be paid for such acquisitions shall be conclusive.

In the event that my executors or my trustees decide to sell any of the common stock or other securities of the Black Manufacturing Company, or the common stock or other securities of any concern which shall succeed to the whole or a substantial part of the assets or business of the Black Manufacturing Company, such sale shall be made at a price deemed adequate by my disinterested executor or my disinterested trustee and such sale shall be made to one or more of the following if one or more of the following is ready and willing to purchase at the price deemed adequate by my disinterested executor or my disin-

Mildred Marie Black   **R.J.A.**
D.R.J.
A.J.C.

(8)

terested trustee, and otherwise to the general public at such price: my said husband, my issue, my said husband's brother, the wife of my said husband's brother, any issue of my said husband's brother, or the trustees of any trust established by my said husband or by my issue or by my said husband's brother or by the wife of my said husband's brother or by any issue of my said husband's brother.[208]

In the event that my disinterested trustee exercises his power to distribute corpus to the beneficiary of any trust under my will, I request my disinterested trustee, although no duty is imposed on him in this regard, to avoid a distribution in kind of the common stock or other securities of the Black Manufacturing Company, or the common stock or other securities of any concern which shall succeed to the whole or a substantial part of the assets or business of the Black Manufacturing Company, whenever in the opinion of my disinterested trustee such distribution in kind will result in an undesirable dispersion of the control of the corporation. When any part of my estate is distributed, or on the termination of any trust under this will, I request my executors and my trustees, although no duty is imposed on them in this regard, to avoid a distribution in kind of the common stock or other securities of the Black Manufacturing Company, or the common stock or other securities of any concern which shall succeed to the whole or a substantial part of the assets or business of the Black Manufacturing Company, whenever in the opinion of my executors or my trustees such distribution in kind will result in an undesirable dispersion of the control of the corporation.

Any executor or any trustee under this will (as well as my said husband or any issue of mine or my said husband's brother, or any issue of my said husband's brother) may serve as an officer of the Black Manufacturing Company or of any concern which shall succeed to the whole or a substantial part of the assets or business of the Black Manufacturing Company.

SIXTH: I give to my disinterested executor the following powers and discretions:

1. If my disinterested executor in good faith decides that there is uncertainty as to the inclusion of particular property in my gross estate for federal estate tax purposes, he shall exclude such property from my gross estate in the estate tax return. My disinterested executor shall not be liable for any loss to my estate or to any beneficiary, if such loss results from his decision made in good faith that there is uncertainty as to the inclusion of particular property in my gross estate.[209]

	R.J.A.
Mildred Marie Black	*D.R.J.*
	A.J.C.

(9)

208 See page 1191 supra, note 42. — ED.
209 See page 1281 supra, note 192. — ED.

2. The decision of my disinterested executor as to the date which should be selected for the valuation of property in my gross estate for federal estate tax purposes shall be conclusive on all concerned.

3. When a choice is available as to whether certain deductions shall be taken as income tax deductions or estate tax deductions, the decision of my disinterested executor in this regard shall be conclusive on all concerned and no adjustment of income and principal accounts in the estate shall be made as a result of such decision.[210]

My executors are authorized to make partial or complete distributions to estate beneficiaries from time to time during administration; to distribute unequal amounts to similar beneficiaries from time to time during administration; and to make such other distributions during administration as they may determine. Nothing contained in this paragraph shall be construed as authorizing my executors to vary the dispositive provisions in this will.

SEVENTH: In extension and not in limitation of the powers given by law or other provisions of this will (but subject to the restrictions of Articles FIFTH and SIXTH), my executors shall have the following powers with respect to the settlement of my estate, and the trustees of each trust under this will shall have the following powers with respect to such trust and its property, in each case to be exercised from time to time in the discretion of my executors and my trustees and without order or license of court:

1. To retain indefinitely any investments and to invest and reinvest in stocks, shares and obligations of corporations, of unincorporated associations or trusts and of investment companies,[211] or in a common trust fund without giving notice to any beneficiary,[212] or in any other kind of personal or real property, notwithstanding the fact that any or all of the investments made or retained are of a character or size which but for this express authority would not be considered proper for executors or trustees;

2. To sell, to exchange, to lease and to make contracts concerning real or personal property for such considerations and upon such terms as to credit or otherwise as my disinterested executor or my disinterested trustee may determine, which leases and contracts may extend beyond the term of the settlement of my estate or the term of any trust; to give options therefor; to execute deeds, transfers, leases and other instruments of any kind;

Mildred Marie Black   **R.J.A.**
                             D.R.J.
                             A.J.C.

(10)

---

[210] See page 1281 supra, note 193. — Ed.
[211] See page 1211 supra, note 56. — Ed.
[212] See page 1211 supra, note 57. — Ed.

3. To hold bonds, shares or other securities in bearer form, or in the name of the executors or in the name of one of the executors or in the name of the trustees or in the name of one of the trustees or in the name of a nominee, without indication of any fiduciary capacity; to deposit cash in a checking or savings account in a bank, without indication of any fiduciary capacity;

4. To give general or special proxies or powers of attorney for voting or acting in respect of shares or securities, which may be discretionary and with power of substitution; to deposit shares or securities with, or transfer them to, protective committees or similar bodies; to join in any reorganization and to pay assessments or subscriptions called for in connection with shares or securities held by my executors or my trustees;

5. To improve or develop real estate; to construct, alter or repair buildings or structures on real estate; to settle boundary lines and easements and other rights with respect to real estate; to partition and to join with co-owners and others in dealing with real estate in any way;

6. To employ investment counsel, custodians of estate property and trust property, brokers, agents and attorneys;

7. To receive additions to any trusts under this will by gift or will or otherwise, and to hold and administer the same under the provisions hereof;

8. To pay as income the whole of the interest, dividends, rent or similar receipts from property, whether wasting or not and although bought or taken at a value above par, but if it is deemed advisable when property is bought or taken at a value above par, a portion of the income may be retained to offset such loss to the principal; to treat as income or principal or to apportion between them stock dividends, extra dividends, rights to take stock or securities, and proceeds from the sale of real estate, although such real estate may have been wholly or partly unproductive; to charge to income or principal or to apportion between them investment counsel's compensation, custodians' compensation, brokers' commissions, agents' compensation, attorneys' fees, insurance premiums, repairs or improvements, taxes (income, estate, inheritance or any other taxes), depreciation charges, executors' and trustees' compensation; and generally to determine all questions as between income and principal and to credit or charge to income or principal or to apportion between them any receipt or gain and any charge, disbursement or loss as is deemed advisable in the circumstances of each case as it arises, notwithstanding any statute or rule of law for distinguishing income

Mildred Marie Black   *R.J.A.*
                           D.R.J.
                           A.J.C.

(11)

from principal or any determination of the courts; provided always, however, that the powers and discretions given in this Section 8 shall be exercisable only by my disinterested executor and my disinterested trustee;

9. When paying legacies or dividing or distributing my estate or any trust fund, to make such payments, division or distribution wholly or partly in kind by allotting and transferring specific securities or other personal or real property or undivided interests therein as a part or the whole of any one or more payments or shares at current values;

10. To keep any or all of the estate property or the trust property at any place or places in _____ [213] or elsewhere within the United States or abroad or with a depositary or custodian at such place or places.

EIGHTH: I authorize and empower my disinterested executor to join with my said husband or his executor or administrator, in filing a joint federal or state income tax return of the income of my said husband and myself for any period or periods for which such a return may be permitted. I further authorize and empower my disinterested executor to agree with my said husband or his executor or administrator,

1. As to how the burden of the liability for federal or state income tax, or interest thereon, arising out of the filing of a joint return by my disinterested executor and my said husband or his executor or administrator, shall be borne as between my estate and my said husband or his estate, and

2. As to who, as between my said husband or his estate and my estate, shall be entitled

 (a) To any refund or credit of any federal or state income tax, or interest thereon, based on the filing of a joint return by my said husband and myself or by my executor and my said husband or his executor or administrator,

 (b) To any refund or credit of any amount paid on account of any joint declaration of estimated federal or state income tax filed by my said husband and myself, and of the interest on any such refund, and

 (c) To the benefit of any payment made by my said husband and myself on account of any joint or separate declaration of estimated federal or state income tax.

My disinterested executor may exercise the foregoing powers in such manner as he shall in his absolute and uncontrolled discretion deem best, whether in the interest of my said husband or his estate or in the interest of my estate.

	R.J.A.
Mildred Marie Black	*D.R.J.*
	A.J.C.

(12)

---

[213] Insert the state where Mrs. Black resides.

I authorize and empower my disinterested executor to consent for federal gift tax purposes to gifts made by my said husband as having been made one half by me and one half by him.[214]

NINTH: I name my son, RICHARD HARRY BLACK IV, and ROBERT J. ANDREW,[215] of ...., ...

.................,[216] to be executors of my will and trustees of each trust under my will. No bond shall be required of my said son or said ROBERT J. ANDREW as executors and trustees, or if a bond is required by law, no surety on such bond shall be required.

There shall always be a disinterested trustee of each trust under this will. If a vacancy in the office of disinterested trustee occurs, a successor disinterested trustee shall be appointed by the partners in the law firm of Andrew, James and Casner, or by the partners in whatever law firm is the successor to the firm of Andrew, James and Casner. Appointments of successor trustees shall be by an instrument in writing.

If a vacancy in the office of interested trustee occurs, the remaining trustee shall appoint by an instrument in writing to fill such vacancy one of the following:

1. Issue of Richard Harry Black IV;
2. Margaret Black Logan;
3. Issue of Margaret Black Logan;
4. James Robert Black (brother of my said husband); and
5. Issue of James Robert Black.

If no one of the above-listed persons is eligible or available to serve as

Mildred Marie Black	*R.J.A.*
	D.R.J.
	A.J.C.

(13)

214 See page 1286 supra, note 198. — ED.

215 It should be noted that Robert J. Andrew, the attorney for Richard Harry Black III and the draftsman of the revocable inter vivos trust, the will of Mr. Black III and the will of Mildred Marie Black, is named as a fiduciary in each of these documents. Is it ever improper for the lawyer-draftsman to name himself as a fiduciary in the documents he drafts? The following quotation is from Drinker, Legal Ethics 94 (1953):

"A question is sometimes raised as to the propriety of a lawyer's inserting in the will a legacy to himself, or a provision appointing him executor or trustee, or one directing his executors to employ him as counsel for the estate. This, of course, depends on the surrounding circumstances. If they are such that the lawyer might reasonably be accused of using undue influence, he will be wise to have the provision inserted in a codicil drawn by another lawyer. Where, however, a testator is entirely competent and the relation has been a longstanding one, and where the suggestion originates with testator, there is no necessity of having another lawyer in the case of a reasonable legacy, or of a provision appointing the draftsman executor, or of a direction that he be retained by the executors. In the case of the latter provision it should be clearly explained to the testator that it will not be binding on the executor, who will be free to choose his own counsel, since the lawyer has no vested interest in representing the estate of one whose will he has drawn. The lawyer may not properly get the executors named, who are also witnesses to the will, to sign a retainer agreement with him." (The footnotes appended to this passage have been omitted.) — ED.

216 Insert the place of residence of Robert J. Andrew.

trustee at the time a vacancy in the office of interested trustee occurs, the vacancy shall not then be filled but shall be filled at such time in the future as one of the above-listed persons becomes eligible or available to fill such vacancy. In other words, there shall always be one interested trustee whenever there is eligible and available, from the above-listed persons, an individual to serve as trustee hereunder.

No bond shall be required of any successor appointed as above provided, or if a bond is required by law, no surety on such bond shall be required.

A trustee may resign at any time by an instrument in writing which expresses such intention and which is delivered to the remaining trustee, and if there is no remaining trustee, by such an instrument in writing delivered to my oldest living issue, or such issue's legal guardian.

The action of all the trustees in office shall be required in order to act in any matter affecting any trust hereunder except such matters as are herein vested exclusively in the disinterested trustee.

References in this will to "executors" mean the executor or executors for the time being in office or the administrator or administrators with the will annexed for the time being in office.

References in this will to "trustees" shall be deemed to include not only the original trustees but also any successor trustee, and all powers and discretions vested in the trustees shall be vested in and exercisable by any such successor trustee except that the powers and discretions vested exclusively in the disinterested trustee shall be vested in, and exercisable by, only a successor disinterested trustee.

References in this will to "disinterested executor" or "disinterested trustee" mean the executor or the trustee who has no interest vested or contingent in the property disposed of by this will and who cannot be benefited by the exercise or nonexercise of the powers vested exclusively in the disinterested executor or the disinterested trustee.

No one dealing with my executors or my trustees need inquire concerning the validity of anything that they purport to do or need see to the application of any money paid or any property transferred to or upon the order of my executors or my trustees.

No executor or trustee shall be responsible for the acts or omissions of the co-executor or co-trustee or for allowing the co-executor or co-trustee to have custody or control of the funds, securities or property. Each of them shall be responsible only for his acts or omissions in bad faith. Furthermore, a successor executor or successor trustee shall not be liable for any action taken by the executors or trustees prior to the time such successor executor becomes an executor or such successor trustee becomes a trustee.

	R.J.A.
Mildred Marie Black	D.R.J.
	A.J.C.

(14)

An executor or a trustee may delegate any powers and discretions which he has as executor or trustee to a co-executor or to a co-trustee by an instrument in writing; provided always, however, that the powers and discretions vested exclusively in the disinterested executor or disinterested trustee shall not be delegated.

IN WITNESS WHEREOF, I hereunto set my hand and seal this
.... day of ...., 19............[217]
For identification I have signed each of the foregoing 14 pages of this will, which consists of 15 pages.

/s/ *Mildred Marie Black* [Seal]
....

Signed, sealed, published and declared by the above-named MILDRED MARIE BLACK as and for her last will, in the presence of us three who, at her request, in her presence and in the presence of one another, hereto subscribe our names as witnesses thereof, all on the date last above written, and each of us hereby declares that in his opinion the said MILDRED MARIE BLACK is of sound and disposing mind and memory.

Name	*Address* [218]
/s/ *Roger J. Avis*	............................, ...
/s/ *Donald R. James*	............................, ...
/s/ *Albert J. Casner*	............................, ...

(15)

[217] Insert the date on which the will is executed.
[218] Insert the address of each witness.

APPENDIX II

The Stevens Family Estate[1]

A. *Estate of William Stevens*

1. *Mr. Stevens' separate and community property*
  a. *Tangible personal property*

   Note: The tangible personal property includes the
   furnishings of a residence and a summer home, an
   automobile and a station wagon, and other miscellaneous personal items. Mr. Stevens, who is a biblio-
   phile, has a collection of first editions worth approximately $5000. All of the tangible personal property
   was paid for by Mr. Stevens out of earnings since his
   marriage and is presumed to be community property. The figure given is an estimate of the value of
   the personal property, which includes the collection
   of first editions. .... $ 15,000

   Special comment: Tangible personal property may
   be owned outright by one spouse as his or her separate
   property or by both spouses as community property.
   The problem is one of keeping accurate records so that
   it can be determined which property is community and
   which is separate. Since all property is presumed to be
   community, the task of proving the separate nature of
   property may be almost impossible unless such records
   are kept. Here all personal property was paid for with
   earnings since the marriage, and the correct assumption is that all the property is community.

  b. *Real estate*

   Note: The Stevens real estate consists of two pieces
   of property, a family residence and a summer home.
   (1) *Family residence*

---

[1] The analysis of the Stevens family estate is set forth for the purpose of illustrating the considerations which are relevant in planning an estate in a community
property state. This analysis is based on a similar analysis found in a manuscript
entitled "Estate Planning in Louisiana," prepared by Professor Leonord Oppenheim
of the Tulane University Law School in New Orleans, Louisiana, which was submitted by him to the Committee on Graduate Studies of the Harvard Law School,
in partial fulfillment of the requirements for the degree of Doctor of Juridical Science. See the discussion of community property at page 426 supra.

Note: The family residence is located at No. 6 Audubon Avenue in New Orleans, Louisiana. The residence was purchased by Mr. Stevens in 1935 for $35,000. He paid $10,000 as a down payment and took a 10-year mortgage on the balance due. The down payment was made with community funds and the mortgage was also paid off with community earnings. Although the title is in William Stevens' name, the family residence is community property. The assessed value of the property is $40,000, but Mr. Stevens believes that it could be sold for $70,000 and he has been offered that amount. . . . . $ 70,000

(2) *Summer home*
Note: In 1937, Mr. Stevens purchased a summer home at Bay St. Louis, Mississippi, for $5000. He used money which he had inherited from his father, Walter Stevens, to buy the property and took title in his own name. At the present time the property is worth about $10,000. The summer home is part of the separate property of Mr. Stevens. . . . . $ 10,000

c. *Bank accounts*
(1) *Checking account*
Note: Mr. Stevens has a checking account in his own name in the Second National Bank of New Orleans, in which he deposits community funds. The average balance in this account is about $3000. . . . . $ 3,000

(2) *Savings account*
Note: Mr. Stevens also has a savings account in his own name in the First National Bank of New Orleans. The balance in that account is $15,000 and consists entirely of money which he inherited from his father. This money is his separate property. . . . . $ 15,000

Special comment: In Louisiana it is not possible to set up a joint bank account which will achieve the same result as at common law. While the joint bank account at common law serves to take the property out of the probate estate, this is not true in Louisiana. The only effect of the joint bank account is to permit either party to withdraw funds upon his or her signature alone. However, if the funds in a bank account are separate property, the account remains separate property. Great care should be taken to avoid any mingling of separate and community funds in a bank account.

d. *Securities*
   (1) *Government bonds*
      Note: Mr. Stevens owns $10,000 worth of government bonds which are in the name of himself and wife, payable on the death of either party to the survivor. Of these bonds, $5000 worth was purchased by Mr. Stevens with money which he inherited from his father, and the other $5000 worth was purchased over a period of time with community earnings. .... $ 10,000

   Special comment: Five thousand dollars' worth of the government bonds is the separate property of Mr. Stevens and the other $5000 worth must be treated as community property for all intents and purposes. While the Louisiana courts have not interfered with the contract between the United States Government and the purchasers of government bonds, they have protected the wife's community interest in such bonds and have thus treated them as though they were community property.

   (2) *Stocks and bonds*
      Note: Mr. Stevens has two accounts with Harper & Green Investment Co., Accounts A and B.
      (a) *Account A*
         Note: Account A contains securities which Mr. Stevens inherited from his father and mother, as well as cash obtained from the sale of securities received from the same source, and new securities which were purchased from time to time. At present the value of these securities and the uninvested cash amounts to $200,000. .... $200,000

      (b) *Account B*
         Note: Account B consists of securities which Mr. Stevens has purchased with community earnings. At the present time, the value of the securities and the uninvested cash amounts to $250,000. .... $250,000

   Special comment: Mr. Stevens has exercised great care in keeping the two accounts separate. At no time have securities been transferred from one account to the other, nor have funds from the accounts been mingled. Therefore he has preserved the separate nature of Account A. Although under Louisiana law the dividends received from the securities in Account A are community property, the securities and cash obtained from the sale of the securities in this account are the separate property of Mr. Stevens. As to Account B, both dividends and securities, as well as cash received from the sale of securities, are community property. In accordance with Mr. Stevens' instructions, the securities in both accounts are nonspeculative and can be readily sold on the market. Mr. Stevens has considered the accounts as sound investments in a highly liquid state.

e. *Life insurance*

　Note: Mr. Stevens has four life insurance policies with a total face value of $140,000. For purposes of discussion these policies will be designated A, B, C and D.

(1) *Policy A*

　Note: This policy was taken out in 1915, before Mr. Stevens' marriage, with the New England Mutual Life Insurance Company and is Policy No. 400,469. It is an ordinary life policy with a guaranteed rate of interest of 3% and a face value of $10,000. The proceeds are payable to Mr. Stevens' executors and administrators. .. $ 10,000

(2) *Policy B*

　Note: This policy was taken out in 1919 with the New York Life Insurance Company and is Policy No. 929,805. It is an ordinary life policy with a guaranteed rate of interest of 3% and a face value of $35,000. The proceeds are payable to Mary Ann Stevens, his wife, with Mr. Stevens' children as secondary beneficiaries. The proceeds are payable under Option D of the policy, which provides for equal monthly payments over a period of 15 years. .... $ 35,000

(3) *Policy C*

　Note: This policy was taken out in 1929 with the Prudential Life Insurance Company of America and is Policy No. 1,532,682. It is an ordinary life policy with a guaranteed rate of interest of 3% and a face value of $50,000. The proceeds are payable under Option 3 of the policy, which provides that the interest is to be paid to Mary Ann Stevens during her lifetime in monthly installments, and that upon her death the principal is to be paid to Mr. Stevens' children. ..... $ 50,000

(4) *Policy* D

    Note: This policy was taken out in 1936 with the Metropolitan Life Insurance Company and is Policy No. 2,836,392. It is an ordinary life policy with a guaranteed rate of interest of 3% and a face value of $45,000. The proceeds are payable under an agreement with the insurance company whereby Mary Ann Stevens will have an annuity for life with guaranteed semiannual payments for a period of 10 years. The agreement also provides that if Mary Ann Stevens dies within the 10-year period, the remaining payments will be made to Mr. Stevens' children. $ 45,000

Special comment: We will assume that as to Policy A, Mr. Stevens has paid all premiums after marriage out of his separate funds and that the premiums on the other three policies were paid out of community funds. We shall also assume that all four policies have double indemnity clauses in case of accidental death of the insured, and waiver of premium clauses in case of disability, and that Mr. Stevens still has full rights in regard to all policies.

f. *Probable inheritance*

    Note: Mr. Stevens' father and mother are both dead and he has no prospects of inheritance from other relatives. Unless his wife or some of his children predecease him and he receives property from them, his estate will not be augmented by way of inheritance.

g. *Business connections and income*

    Note: Mr. Stevens is vice president of the Acme Manufacturing Company, at an annual salary of $24,000. The company has no retirement plan. In addition to his salary Mr. Stevens receives an income of $18,000 per year from his accounts with Harper & Green Investment Co. Thus he has at present an annual income of $42,000.

h. *Inter vivos gifts*

    Note: Mr. Stevens has made no inter vivos gifts of any consequence to his wife or children.

i. *Social security benefits*

    Note: Mr. Stevens will be entitled to maximum social security benefits under the applicable federal law.

2. *Summary of separate and community property*

    Tangible personal property (community) .... $ 15,000

Real estate
 Family residence (community) 70,000
 Summer home (separate) 10,000
Bank accounts
 Checking account (community) 3,000
 Savings account (separate) 15,000
Securities
 Government bonds (community) 5,000
 Government bonds (separate) 5,000
 Stocks and bonds (separate) 200,000
 Stocks and bonds (community) 250,000
Insurance
 Policy A (separate) 10,000
 Policies B, C and D (community) 130,000

  Total separate and community property $713,000

3. *Mr. Stevens' gross estate*
 Tangible personal property (one-half interest) .... $ 7,500
 Community real estate (one-half interest) 35,000
 Separate real estate 10,000
 Community checking account (one-half interest) ... 1,500
 Separate savings account 15,000
 Separate government bonds 5,000
 Community government bonds (one-half interest) .. 2,500
 Separate securities 200,000
 Community securities (one-half interest) 125,000
 Separate insurance — Policy A 10,000
 Community insurance — Policies B, C and D (one-
  half interest) 65,000

  Total gross estate $476,500

Special comment: The gross estate of Mr. Stevens has been calculated without regard to the double indemnity provisions in the life insurance policies.

4. *Mr. Stevens' adjusted gross estate*[2]
 Separate real estate .... $ 10,000
 Separate savings account 15,000
 Separate govenment bonds 5,000
 Separate securities 200,000
 Separate insurance — Policy A 10,000

  Total $240,000
 Less §§2053, 2054 deductions[3] 17,125

  Adjusted gross estate $222,875

[2] 1954 I.R.C. §§2056(c)(2)(B),(C), quoted infra page 1409. These sections set forth the rules for computing the adjusted gross estate of estates composed partly of community property.

[3] The figure of $17,125 was arrived at by estimating §§2053, 2054 deductions as $34,000 and then following the formula as set out in §2056(c)(2)(B)(iv), quoted infra page 1409.

5. *Maximum allowable marital deduction*

> *Note:* The maximum allowable marital deduction is one half of the adjusted gross estate. Thus the maximum allowable marital deduction is $111,-437.50. .... **$111,437.50**

6. *Gifts to wife which will qualify for the marital deduction*

> *Note:* An important fact concerning the marital deduction in a community property state is that the decedent may use community or separate property when providing for the marital deduction. The classification of separate or community is significant only in determining the adjusted gross estate, but so long as the légitime is protected, there is no restriction which would preclude a bequest of community property as a part of a marital deduction. In Mr. Stevens' estate the only problem is to select carefully the property which would be most suitable for marital deduction purposes. For example, it may be advisable for Mr. Stevens to bequeath his interest in the family home to Mrs. Stevens so that she can dispose of it if necessary, instead of her owning an undivided one-half interest and being the usufructuary of the other half.

> The problem of the marital deduction is somewhat different in Louisiana than in the average common law state. Where the estate plan seeks to achieve maximum tax savings in a common law state, the marital deduction may be one important way to accomplish that end. In Louisiana, however, as well as in other community property states, the decedent must have separate property before the marital deduction will apply. In many instances the only property owned by the spouses is community property and the marital deduction is not available. Of course, where the separate property is of appreciable value, the marital deduction clearly becomes significant. This again highlights the necessity for keeping careful records of the nature of property owned by the spouses and for avoiding acts such as mingling separate property with community property, which will destroy the separate status of such property.

7. *Mr. Stevens' taxable estate where gross estate is $476,500*

   a. *Allowable deductions and exemption*

     (1) §§2053, 2054 deductions .... $ 34,000.00

     (2) Maximum marital deduction 111,437.50

     (3) Exemption 60,000.00

           Total deductions and exemption $205,437.50

   b. *Taxable estate* (gross estate less allowable deductions and exemption — $476,500 less $205,437.50) $271,062.50

B.   *Estate of Mary Ann Stevens, Wife of William Stevens*

1. *General comments*

Mary Ann Stevens owns a small amount of separate property. This consists of jewelry and clothing worth approximately $2500. Of course she has a one-half interest in all of the community property, which must be carefully considered in the planning of her estate.

Mrs. Stevens' father died in 1940, leaving no property of any consequence. Her mother is still living but will leave very little property at her death. Mrs. Stevens has two brothers, who are both successful businessmen. They are both married and have families of their own. Therefore, it is unlikely that Mrs. Stevens' estate will be augmented by inheritance other than from her husband or children. In planning her estate we must consider two possibilities: first, and more likely, that she will survive her husband, and second, that she will predecease her husband.

2. *Mrs. Stevens' gross estate if she survives her husband*
   a. *Tangible personal property*
   Note: The value of the tangible personal property owned by Mrs. Stevens is $2500. In addition to her interest in the personal property owned by the community, which is $7500, she will become the owner of her husband's share under his will. ...... $ 17,500

   b. *Real estate*
   Note: Mrs. Stevens' interest in the community realty amounts to $35,000 and she will become the owner of the remaining $35,000 interest under the will of her husband. 70,000

   c. *Checking account and government bonds*
   Note: Mrs. Stevens has a community interest of $1500 in the checking account. She will become the outright owner of the government bonds by surviving her husband. 11,500

   d. *Securities other than government bonds*
   Note: Mrs. Stevens has a one-half interest in the community securities, which amounts to $125,000. 125,000

   e. *Life insurance*
   Note: Since policies B, C and D are community property, Mrs. Stevens will have a one-half community interest in the proceeds. 65,000

   f. *Marital deduction gifts*
   Note: If Mr. Stevens makes additional gifts to his wife, so that the total gifts to her equal the maxi-

mum marital deduction, her gross estate will be augmented by the amount of the difference between $111,437.50 (the maximum allowable marital deduction) and the items listed above which will pass to her in a form which qualifies for the marital deduction ($35,000, the value of the interest in the family residence, which passes to her, plus $7500 worth of tangible personal property and $7500 worth of government bonds). The difference equals $61,437.50. ....   61,437.50

Total gross estate $350,437.50

Special comment: Although some of the insurance policies (Policies B, C and D) provide for the payment of proceeds directly to Mrs. Stevens, a new arrangement will be made as to the proceeds.

3. *Mrs. Stevens' taxable estate if she survives her husband and has a gross estate of $350,437.50*
   a. *Allowable deductions and exemption*
   (1) §§2053, 2054 deductions (estimated) .... $ 30,000.00

   (2) Exemption 60,000.00

   Total deductions and exemption .... $ 90,000.00

   b. *Taxable estate* (gross estate less allowable deductions and exemption — $350,437.50 less $90,000) .. $260,437.50

4. *Mrs. Stevens' gross estate if she predeceases her husband*
   Note: Again it should be pointed out that in a community property state the wife's estate will be taxed so far as her community interest is concerned. If the wife owns separate property other than gifts of community property from her husband, it may be desirable to make provision for the marital deduction. In the case of Mrs. Stevens, the marital deduction is not available, since she owns no separate property other than $2500 worth of personal effects which were gifts from her husband out of community funds.
   a. *Tangible personal property*
   Note: The value of the tangible personal property owned by Mrs. Stevens is $2500. In addition her interest in the personal property owned by the community amounts to $7500. .... $ 10,000

   b. *Real estate*
   Note: Mrs. Stevens' interest in the community realty amounts to $35,000.   35,000

   c. *Checking account and government bonds*
   Note: Mrs. Stevens has a community interest of $1500 in the checking account plus a community in-

terest in the bonds purchased with community
funds, amounting to $2500.   4,000

d. *Securities other than government bonds*
    Note: Mrs. Stevens has a one-half interest in the
community securities, which amounts to $125,000.   125,000

e. *Life insurance*
    Note: Since Policies B, C and D are community
property, Mrs. Stevens will have a community interest in these policies. In the situation where the wife
predeceases her husband, the interest is half the
value of the policies at the time of the wife's death.
For purposes of planning, the round figure of $20,-
000 will be taken as such value.   20,000

     Total gross estate **$194,000**

5. *Mrs. Stevens' taxable estate if she predeceases her hus-*
band and has a gross estate of $194,000
  a. *Allowable deductions and exemption*
    (1) §§2053, 2054 deductions (estimated) .... $ 20,000

    (2) Exemption   60,000

      Total deductions and exemption .... **$ 80,000**

  b. *Taxable estate* (gross estate less allowable deductions and exemption — $194,000 less $80,000) **$114,000**

A P P E N D I X   I I I

A Small Estate

An estate that is between $60,000 and $120,000 in value and is owned by a husband whose wife has no estate of her own is one to which special attention should be given. The husband usually desires that the entire estate be available to his wife during the period she survives him, or available to himself if he survives his wife, and that what is left when both have died go to their children. Such an estate usually can be so arranged that no federal estate tax will be payable on the death of either the husband or the wife, no matter in which order they die, and at the same time, for all practical purposes, the entire estate will be available to the survivor of the husband and the wife.

Suppose the husband's estate is as follows:

1. Tangible personalty .... $ 2,000
2. Real estate (family residence, with title in name of husband and wife as tenants by the entirety — purchase money came from husband) 20,000
3. Life insurance 40,000
4. Securities and bank accounts 40,000

　　　Total $102,000

On the advice of the husband's attorney the following steps are taken:

1. The husband gives to his wife the $40,000 in securities and cash, and a gift tax return is filed. No gift tax, of course, is payable.
2. The husband establishes a life insurance trust, to which the proceeds of the life insurance policies are payable if his wife survives him. The trust is one where the value of the property in the trust is not includible in the wife's gross estate on her death. She is trustee of the trust. If the wife does not survive the husband, the proceeds of the policies are made payable to the issue.
3. The husband's will pours the residue of his estate into the insurance trust if his wife survives him.
4. The wife's will establishes a trust with her husband as trustee (if he survives her) and the terms of the trust are such that the value of the trust property is not includible in the husband's gross estate on his death.

Under this arrangement, if it is assumed that the husband lives three years after the gift to his wife, so that the gift cannot be attacked as in contemplation of death, the gross estate of the wife will be approximately $60,000 in value, if she survives her husband (less if she predeceases him), and the gross estate of the husband will be approximately the same in value whether he survives his wife or predeceases her. The documents are set out below.

A.   *The Insurance Trust*

I, [insert name and address of husband], hereinafter referred to as the "donor," desire to have the proceeds of one or more policies of insurance on my life payable to [insert name of wife], if she survives me, to hold as trustee hereunder; and at the request of the donor, the trustee agrees to hold such life insurance proceeds and all additions thereto in trust as follows:

FIRST: The donor reserves the right at any time or times to amend, alter or revoke this trust, in whole or in part, or any provision thereof, by an instrument in writing signed by the donor and delivered to the trustee in the lifetime of the donor.

The donor's will may provide for additions to this trust and, consequently, the donor's will should be examined in connection with the making of any alteration, amendment or revocation of this instrument, to determine what changes, if any, should be made in the donor's will in the light of such alteration, amendment or revocation of this instrument.

SECOND: The donor reserves the right by his own act alone, without the consent or approval of the trustee, to sell, assign or hypothecate any policies of insurance upon his life made payable to the trustee, to exercise any option or privilege granted by such policies, including, but without limitation of the generality of the foregoing, the right to change the beneficiaries of such policies, to borrow any sum in accordance with the provisions of such policies, and to receive all payments, dividends, surrender values, benefits or privileges of any kind which may accrue on account of such policies during his lifetime.   Furthermore, the trustee agrees to deliver to the donor on his written request any of such policies deposited with the trustee hereunder.

THIRD: On the death of the donor, the trustee shall collect the proceeds of any policies upon the donor's life made payable to the trustee hereunder and shall hold in trust the amount so collected plus any additions thereto pursuant to the terms of the donor's will as follows:

1. The trustee shall pay the net income to, or apply it for the benefit of, the donor's wife [insert name] for her life; and, in addition, the trustee shall pay to, or apply for the benefit of, the donor's said wife, from the principal of the trust, from time to time, such amount or amounts as are necessary for the support and maintenance of the donor's said wife in the manner to which she has been accustomed, and such amount or amounts as are necessary to maintain the donor's said wife in good health.

2. On the death of the donor's said wife, the then remaining principal and undistributed income shall be paid to the donor's issue then living, such issue to take *per stirpes;* and if no issue of the donor is then living, the then remaining principle and undistributed income shall be paid to the donor's heirs. [If appro-

priate, the trust may be continued for the benefit of the donor's issue.]

FOURTH: Income payments to the donor's said wife shall be made quarterly from the date of the donor's death.

The interest of each beneficiary in the income or principal shall be free from the control or interference of any creditor of a beneficiary or any spouse of a married beneficiary and shall not be subject to attachment or susceptible of anticipation or alienation.

FIFTH: References in this instrument to "issue" mean lawful blood descendants in the first, second or any other degree of the ancestor designated, provided always, however, that

1. An adopted child and such adopted child's lawful blood descendants shall be considered in this instrument as lawful blood descendants of the adopting parent or parents and of anyone who is by blood or adoption an ancestor of the adopting parent or of either of the adopting parents and shall not be considered descendants of such adopted child's natural parents; and

2. A child born to persons who are openly living together as husband and wife after the performance of a marriage ceremony between them and such child's lawful blood descendants shall be considered in this instrument as lawful blood descendants of such child's parents and of any ancestor of such child's parents, regardless of the fact that a purported divorce of one or both of such persons with reference to a prior marriage is invalid.

References in this instrument to "donor's heirs" mean those persons, other than creditors, who would take the personal property of the donor under the laws of the [insert name of controlling state] if the settlor had died intestate at the time stipulated for distribution, not married and domiciled in such State. In determining who such persons are, it shall be assumed that all decrees of divorce rendered by a court of record, wherever located, are valid. Distribution to such persons shall be made in the manner and in the proportion that personal property of the donor would be distributed under the laws of the [insert name of controlling state] if the donor had died intestate at the time stipulated for distribution, owning the property available for distribution and no other property, not married and domiciled in such State.

SIXTH: [This article contains the administrative powers given to the trustee. For a similar article see Article Twenty-fourth of The Richard Harry Black III Trust (page 1260 supra). In view of the fact that the income beneficiary is the trustee, care must be taken to make certain that no administrative power will give the trustee uncontrolled discretion to benefit herself by its exercise, or such power may be a general power for tax purposes.]

SEVENTH: No bond shall be required of the original trustee hereunder or of any successor trustee, or if a bond is required by law, no surety on such bond shall be required.

If a vacancy in the office of trustee occurs, the donor's said wife, or her guardian, shall select as trustee a corporation or a person who has no beneficial interest hereunder, and if the donor's said wife is not living when the vacancy occurs, such selection shall be made by the oldest living issue of the donor, or such issue's guardian.

References in this instrument to "trustee" shall be deemed to include not only the original trustee hereunder but also any successor trustee, and all powers and discretions vested in the trustee shall be vested in and exercisable by any such successor trustee.

No one dealing with the trustee need inquire concerning the validity of anything she purports to do, or need see to the application of any money paid or property transferred to or upon the order of the trustee.

The trustee shall be responsible only for her own acts or omissions in bad faith.

IN WITNESS WHEREOF, [insert name of donor] as donor has hereunto set his hand and seal, and [insert name of donor's wife], in token of her acceptance of the trust hereby created, has hereunto set her hand and seal, all on this [insert date when trust is executed].

[The signature of the donor and his wife and their acknowledgments should follow at this point. See, for example, The Richard Harry Black III Trust (page 1235 supra).]

B.   *The Husband's Will*

I, [insert name and address of husband], make this my last will, hereby revoking all wills and codicils heretofore made by me.

FIRST: My tangible personal property, including furniture, clothing, automobiles and their equipment, and articles of personal or household use or ornament, but not including money, securities or the like, I give absolutely to my wife [insert name of wife], if she survives me by thirty (30) days, and if she does not so survive me, I give the same absolutely to my issue who so survive me, such issue to take *per stirpes.*

I express the hope that my said wife or my said issue will dispose of said tangible personal property according to my wishes, however my wishes may be made known to her or to them, but I expressly declare that I do not intend to create any trust in law or in equity with respect to said tangible personal property.

SECOND: All the rest and residue of my property of whatever kind or wherever located that I own at my death, but not including property over which I shall then have any power of appointment, all of which is hereinafter referred to as my residuary estate, I give, devise and bequeath as follows:

1. All estate taxes, federal and state, imposed by reason of my death with respect to any property required to be included in my gross estate for estate tax purposes (other than property so included because I have a power of appointment over the same given me by someone other than myself), and any interest thereon, shall be paid out of my residuary estate.

2. All legacy, succession, inheritance and like taxes (as distinguished from estate taxes) imposed by reason of my death on property, whether disposed of by this will or not (other than property over which I have a power of appointment given me by someone other than myself), and any interest thereon, shall be paid out of my residuary estate. So far as is practicable and reasonable, my executor shall settle and compromise and pay as soon as convenient after my death any of the taxes referred to in the preceding sentence on future or contingent interests.

3. My funeral expenses, my debts and the expenses of administration of my estate shall be paid out of my residuary estate.

4. The balance of my residuary estate (said balance means my residuary estate minus the payments called for by Sections 1, 2 and 3 of this Article SECOND), I give as follows:

   (a) If my said wife survives me, I give said balance to the trustee of the trust of which I am donor and which trust was created by indenture of trust dated [insert date of insurance trust], to be added to the principal thereof and disposed of accordingly.

   (b) If my said wife does not survive me, I give said balance to my issue who survive me, such issue to take *per stirpes.* [If the insurance trust continues for the benefit of the issue, the balance should be poured over, even though wife does not survive.]

   (c) If my said wife does not survive me and no issue of mine survives me, I give said balance to my heirs.

THIRD: [This article defines the word "issue" and the words "my heirs" in the same manner as these words are defined in Article Fifth of the insurance trust (page 1317 supra).]

FOURTH: Property and cash distributable to a minor under this will may be distributed by my executor to such minor personally or to such minor's legal guardian or to some other person for such minor, and the receipt of such minor or such minor's legal guardian or such other person shall be a complete discharge of my executor in regard to such distribution.

FIFTH: In extension and not in limitation of the powers given by law or other provisions of this will, my executor shall have the following powers with respect to the settlement of my estate, in each case to be exercised from time to time in the discretion of my executor and without order or license of court: [insert the powers of the executor, which should be basically the same as the powers given the trustee in the insurance trust (page 1316 supra)].

SIXTH: I name my said wife to be guardian of the person and property of each minor child of mine, and if my said wife dies, declines to serve or ceases to serve as such guardian, I name [insert name of friend or relative who is to serve as guardian under these circumstances] to be guardian of the person and property of each minor child of mine. I request that no bond be required of the persons above named as guardian, or if a bond is required by law, I request that no surety on such bond be required.

SEVENTH: I name my said wife to be executor of my will. If my said wife dies, declines to serve or ceases to serve as my executor, I name my oldest living issue, or such issue's legal guardian, to be executor of my will. No bond shall be required of the persons named as executor, or if a bond is required by law, no surety shall be required on such bond.

References in this will to "executor" mean the executor for the time being in office or the administrator with the will annexed for the time being in office.

No one dealing with my executor need inquire concerning the validity of anything that is done or need see to the application of any money paid or property transferred to or upon the order of my executor.

My executor shall be responsible only for her own acts or omissions in bad faith.

IN WITNESS WHEREOF, I hereunto set my hand and seal this [insert the date when the will is executed]. For identification I have signed each of the foregoing .... pages of this will, which consists of .... pages.

                /s/ *[Name of testator]* [Seal]

Signed, sealed, published and declared by the above-named [insert name of testator] as and for his last will, in the presence of us three who, at his request, in his presence and in the presence of one another, hereto subscribe our names as witnesses thereof, all on the date last above written.

[Insert names and addresses of witnesses.]

Name	*Address*
....	...., ...
....	...., ...
....	...., ...

[In executing his will the testator should sign each page and the witnesses should place their initials beside the testator's signature. See, for example, the will of Richard Harry Black III (pages 1267-1288 supra).]

C. *The Wife's Will*

I, [insert name and address of wife], make this my last will, hereby revoking all wills and codicils heretofore made by me.

FIRST: [The wife's Article First will be like Article First in the husband's will.]

SECOND: All the rest and residue of my property of whatever kind and wherever located that I own at my death, but not including property over which I shall then have any power of appointment, all of which is hereinafter referred to as my residuary estate, I give, devise, and bequeath as follows:

1. All estate taxes, federal or state, imposed by reason of my death with respect to any property required to be included in my gross estate for estate tax purposes (other than property so included because I have a power of appointment over it given me by someone other than myself), and any interest thereon, shall be paid out of my residuary estate.

2. All legacy, succession, inheritance and like taxes (as distinguished from estate taxes) imposed by reason of my death on property, whether disposed of by this will or not (other than property over which I have a power of appointment given me by someone other than myself), and any interest thereon, shall be paid out of my residuary estate. So far as is practicable and reasonable, my executor shall settle and compromise and pay as soon as convenient after my death any of the taxes referred to in the preceding sentence on future or contingent interests.

3. My funeral expenses, my debts and the expenses of administration of my estate shall be paid out of my residuary estate.

4. The balance of my residuary estate (said balance means my residuary estate minus the payments called for by Sections 1, 2 and 3 of this Article SECOND), I give as follows:

   (a) If my said husband survives me, I give said balance to my trustee hereinafter named and his successor or successors, in trust, as follows:

   (i) The trustee shall pay the net income to, or apply it for the benefit of, my said husband for his life; and, in addition, the trustee shall pay to, or apply for the benefit of, my said husband, from the principal of the trust, from time to time, such amount or amounts as are necessary for the support and maintenance of my said husband in the manner to which he has been accustomed and such amount or amounts as are necessary to maintain my said husband in good health.

   (ii) On the death of my said husband the then remaining principal and undistributed income shall be paid to my issue then living, such issue to take *per stirpes,* and if no issue of mine is then living, the same shall be paid to my heirs. [If the trust under the insurance trust is continued for the issue, this trust should continue for the issue.]

(b) If my said husband does not survive me, I give said balance to my issue who survive me, such issue to take *per stirpes*. [See comment in brackets at end of subparagraph (ii) above.]

(c) If my said husband does not survive me and no issue of mine survives me, I give said balance to my heirs.

THIRD: [The wife's Article Third will be like Article Third of the husband's will.]

FOURTH: [The wife's Article Fourth will be like Article Fourth of the husband's will.]

FIFTH: In extension and not in limitation of the powers given by law or other provisions of this will, my executor shall have the following powers with respect to the settlement of my estate, and the trustee of each trust under this will shall have the following powers with respect to such trust and its property, in each case to be exercised from time to time in the discretion of my executor and my trustee and without order or license of court: [insert administrative powers similar to the administrative powers in the insurance trust (page 1316 supra), making the powers applicable to both trustee and executor].

SIXTH: [The wife's Article Sixth will be like Article Sixth of the husband's will.]

SEVENTH: I name my said husband to be executor of my will and trustee of the trust under my will. If my said husband dies, declines to serve or ceases to serve as my executor, I name my oldest living issue, or such issue's legal guardian, to be executor. If a vacancy in the office of trustee occurs, my said husband, or his guardian, shall select as trustee a corporation or a person who has no beneficial interest under the trust, and if my said husband is not living when the vacancy occurs, such selection shall be made by my oldest living issue, or such issue's guardian. No bond shall be required of my executor and trustee, whether original or successor, or if a bond is required by law, no surety on such bond shall be required.

References in this will to "executor" mean the executor for the time being in office or the administrator with the will annexed for the time being in office.

References in this will to "trustee" shall be deemed to include not only the original trustee but also any successor trustee, and all powers and discretions vested in the trustee shall be vested in and exercisable by any such successor trustee.

No one dealing with my executor or my trustee need inquire concerning the validity of anything that is done or need see to the application of any money paid or property transferred to or upon the order of my executor or my trustee.

My executor and trustee shall be responsible only for his acts and omissions in bad faith.

IN WITNESS WHEREOF, I hereunto set my hand and seal this [insert the date when the will is executed]. For identification I have signed each of the foregoing .... pages of this will, which consists of .... pages.

/s/ [*Name of testatrix*] [Seal]

Signed, sealed, published and declared by the above-named (insert name of testatrix) as and for her last will, in the presence of us three who, at her request, in her presence and in the presence of one another, hereto subscribe our names as witnesses thereof, all on the date last above written.

[Insert names and addresses of witnesses.]

Name	*Address*
--	------------------------------, ------------------------
--	------------------------------, ------------------------
--	------------------------------, ------------------------

[In executing her will the testatrix should sign each page and the witnesses should place their initials beside the testatrix's signature. See, for example, the will of Richard Harry Black III (pages 1267-1288 supra).]

Selected Provisions from the Internal Revenue Code of 1954[1]

Sec. 61. Gross Income Defined.

(a) *General Definition.* — Except as otherwise provided in this subtitle, gross income means all income from whatever source derived, including (but not limited to) the following items:

(1) Compensation for services, including fees, commissions, and similar items;

(2) Gross income derived from business;

(3) Gains derived from dealings in property;

(4) Interest;

(5) Rents;

(6) Royalties;

(7) Dividends;

(8) Alimony and separate maintenance payments;

(9) Annuities;

(10) Income from life insurance and endowment contracts;

(11) Pensions;

(12) Income from discharge of indebtedness;

(13) Distributive share of partnership gross income;

(14) Income in respect of a decedent; and

(15) Income from an interest in an estate or trust.

(b) *Cross References.* —

For items specifically included in gross income, see part II (sec. 71 and following). For items specifically excluded from gross income, see part III (sec. 101 and following).

Sec. 72. Annuities; Certain Proceeds of Endowment and Life Insurance Contracts.

(a) *General Rule for Annuities.* — Except as otherwise provided in this chapter, gross income includes any amount received as an annuity (whether for a period certain or during one or more lives) under an annuity, endowment, or life insurance contract.

(b) *Exclusion Ratio.* — Gross income does not include that part of any amount received as an annuity under an annuity, endowment, or life insurance contract which bears the same ratio to such amount as the investment in the contract (as of the annuity starting date) bears to the expected return under the contract (as of such date). This subsection shall not apply to any amount to which subsection (d)(1) (relating to certain employee annuities) applies.

[1] As of September 14, 1960. The amendments made by the Eighty-sixth Congress are included.

(c) *Definitions.* —

(1) *Investment in the contract.* — For purposes of subsection (b), the investment in the contract as of the annuity starting date is —

(A) the aggregate amount of premiums or other consideration paid for the contract, minus

(B) the aggregate amount received under the contract before such date, to the extent that such amount was excludable from gross income under this subtitle or prior income tax laws.

(2) *Adjustment in investment where there is refund feature.* — If —

(A) the expected return under the contract depends in whole or in part on the life expectancy of one or more individuals;

(B) the contract provides for payments to be made to a beneficiary (or to the estate of an annuitant) on or after the death of the annuitant or annuitants; and

(C) such payments are in the nature of a refund of the consideration paid,

then the value (computed without discount for interest) of such payments on the annuity starting date shall be subtracted from the amount determined under paragraph (1). Such value shall be computed in accordance with actuarial tables prescribed by the Secretary or his delegate. For purposes of this paragraph and of subsection (e)(2)(A), the term "refund of the consideration paid" includes amounts payable after the death of an annuitant by reason of a provision in the contract for a life annuity with minimum period of payments certain, but (if part of the consideration was contributed by an employer) does not include that part of any payment to a beneficiary (or to the estate of the annuitant) which is not attributable to the consideration paid by the employee for the contract as determined under paragraph (1)(A).

(3) *Expected return.* — For purposes of subsection (b), the expected return under the contract shall be determined as follows:

(A) *Life expectancy.* — If the expected return under the contract, for the period on and after the annuity starting date, depends in whole or in part on the life expectancy of one or more individuals, the expected return shall be computed with reference to actuarial tables prescribed by the Secretary or his delegate.

(B) *Installment payments.* — If subparagraph (A) does not apply, the expected return is the aggregate of the amounts receivable under the contract as an annuity.

(4) *Annuity starting date.* — For purposes of this section, the annuity starting date in the case of any contract is the first day of the first period for which an amount is received as an annuity under the contract; except that if such date was before January 1, 1954, then the annuity starting date is January 1, 1954.

(d) *Employees' Annuities.* —

(1) *Employee's contributions recoverable in 3 years.* — Where —

(A) part of the consideration for an annuity, endowment, or life insurance contract is contributed by the employer, and

(B) during the 3-year period beginning on the date (whether or not before January 1, 1954) on which an amount is first received under the contract as an annuity, the aggregate amount receivable by the employee under the terms of the contract is equal to or greater than the consideration for the contract contributed by the employee, then all amounts received as an annuity under the contract shall be excluded from gross income until there has been so excluded (under this paragraph and prior income tax laws) an amount equal to the consideration for the contract contributed by the employee. Thereafter all amounts so received under the contract shall be included in gross income.

(2) *Special rules for application of paragraph (1).* — For purposes of paragraph (1), if the employee died before any amount was received as an annuity under the contract, the words "receivable by the employee" shall be read as "receivable by a beneficiary of the employee".

(3) *Cross reference.* —

For certain rules for determining whether amounts contributed by employer are includible in the gross income of the employee, see part I of subchapter D (sec. 401 and following, relating to pension, profit-sharing, and stock bonus plans, etc.).

(e) *Amounts Not Received as Annuities.* —

(1) *General rule.* — If any amount is received under an annuity, endowment, or life insurance contract, if such amount is not received as an annuity, and if no other provision of this subtitle applies, then such amount —

(A) if received on or after the annuity starting date, shall be included in gross income; or

(B) if subparagraph (A) does not apply, shall be included in gross income, but only to the extent that it (when added to amounts previously received under the contract which were excludable from gross income under this subtitle or prior income tax laws) exceeds the aggregate premiums or other consideration paid.

For purposes of this section, any amount received which is in the nature of a dividend or similar distribution shall be treated as an amount not received as an annuity.

(2) *Special rules for application of paragraph (1).* — For purposes of paragraph (1), the following shall be treated as amounts not received as an annuity:

(A) any amount received, whether in a single sum or otherwise, under a contract in full discharge of the obligation under the contract which is in the nature of a refund of the consideration paid for the contract; and

(B) any amount received under a contract on its surrender, redemption, or maturity.

In the case of any amount to which the preceding sentence applies, the rule of paragraph (1)(B) shall apply (and the rule of paragraph (1)(A) shall not apply).

(3) *Limit on tax attributable to receipt of lump sum.* — If a lump sum is received under an annuity, endowment, or life insurance contract, and the part which is includible in gross income is determined under paragraph (1), then the tax attributable to the inclusion of such part in gross income for the taxable year shall not be greater than the aggregate of the taxes attributable to such part had it been included in the gross income of the taxpayer ratably over the taxable year in which received and the preceding 2 taxable years.

(f) *Special Rules for Computing Employees' Contributions.* — In computing, for purposes of subsection (c)(1)(A), the aggregate amount of premiums or other consideration paid for the contract, for purposes of subsection (d)(1), the consideration for the contract contributed by the employee, and for purposes of subsection (e)(1)(B), the aggregate premiums or other consideration paid, amounts contributed by the employer shall be included, but only to the extent that —

(1) such amounts were includible in the gross income of the employee under this subtitle or prior income tax laws; or

(2) if such amounts had been paid directly to the employee at the time they were contributed, they would not have been includible in the gross income of the employee under the law applicable at the time of such contribution.

(g) *Rules for Transferee Where Transfer Was for Value.* — Where any contract (or any interest therein) is transferred (by assignment or otherwise) for a valuable consideration, to the extent that the contract (or interest therein) does not, in the hands of the transferee, have a basis which is determined by reference to the basis in the hands of the transferor, then —

(1) for purposes of this section, only the actual value of such consideration, plus the amount of the premiums and other consideration paid by the transferee after the transfer, shall be taken into account in computing the aggregate amount of the premiums or other consideration paid for the contract;

(2) for purposes of subsection (c)(1)(B), there shall be taken into account only the aggregate amount received under the contract by the transferee before the annuity starting date, to the extent that such amount was excludable from gross income under this subtitle or prior income tax laws; and

(3) the annuity starting date is January 1, 1954, or the first day of the first period for which the transferee received an amount under the contract as an annuity, whichever is the later.

For purposes of this subsection, the term "transferee" includes a beneficiary of, or the estate of, the transferee.

(h) *Option to Receive Annuity in Lieu of Lump Sum.* — If —

(1) a contract provides for payment of a lump sum in full discharge of an obligation under the contract, subject to an option to receive an annuity in lieu of such lump sum;

(2) the option is exercised within 60 days after the day on which such lump sum first became payable; and

(3) part or all of such lump sum would (but for this subsection) be includible in gross income by reason of subsection (e)(1),

then, for purposes of this subtitle, no part of such lump sum shall be considered as includible in gross income at the time such lump sum first became payable.

(i) *Joint and Survivor Annuities Where First Annuitant Died in 1951, 1952, or 1953.* — Where an annuitant died after December 31, 1950, and before January 1, 1954, and the basis of a surviving annuitant's interest in the joint and survivor annuity contract was determinable under section 113(a)(5) of the Internal Revenue Code of 1939, then —

(1) subsection (d) shall not apply with respect to such contract;

(2) for purposes of this section, the aggregate amount of premiums or other consideration paid for the contract is the basis of the contract determined under such section 113(a)(5);

(3) for purposes of subsection (c)(1)(B), there shall be taken into account only the aggregate amount received by the surviving annuitant under the contract before the annuity starting date, to the extent that such amount was excludable from gross income under this subtitle or prior income tax laws; and

(4) the annuity starting date is January 1, 1954, or the first day of the first period for which the surviving annuitant received an amount under the contract as an annuity, whichever is the later.

(j) *Interest.* — Notwithstanding any other provision of this section, if any amount is held under an agreement to pay interest thereon, the interest payments shall be included in gross income.

(k) *Payments in Discharge of Alimony.* —

(1) *In general.* — This section shall not apply to so much of any payment under an annuity, endowment, or life insurance contract (or any interest therein) as is includible in the gross income of the wife under section 71 or section 682 (relating to income of an estate or trust in case of divorce, etc.).

(2) *Cross reference.* —

For definition of "wife", see section 7701(a)(17).

(1) *Face-Amount Certificates.* — For purposes of this section, the term "endowment contract" includes a face-amount certificate, as defined in section 2(a)(15) of the Investment Company Act of 1940 (15 U.S.C., sec. 80a-2), issued after December 31, 1954.

(m) *Cross Reference.* —

For limitation on adjustments to basis of annuity contracts sold, see section 1021.

Sec. 101. Certain Death Benefits.

(a) *Proceeds of Life Insurance Contracts Payable by Reason of Death.* —

(1) *General rule.* — Except as otherwise provided in paragraph (2) and in subsection (d), gross income does not include amounts received (whether in a single sum or otherwise) under a life insurance contract, if such amounts are paid by reason of the death of the insured.

(2) *Transfer for valuable consideration.* — In the case of a transfer for a valuable consideration, by assignment or otherwise, of a life insurance contract or any interest therein, the amount excluded from gross income by paragraph (1) shall not exceed an amount equal to the sum of the actual value of such consideration and the premiums and other amounts subsequently paid by the transferee. The preceding sentence shall not apply in the case of such a transfer —

(A) if such contract or interest therein has a basis for determining gain or loss in the hands of a transferee determined in whole or in part by reference to such basis of such contract or interest therein in the hands of the transferor, or

(B) if such transfer is to the insured, to a partner of the insured, to a partnership in which the insured is a partner, or to a corporation in which the insured is a shareholder or officer.

(b) *Employees' Death Benefits.* —

(1) *General rule.* — Gross income does not include amounts received (whether in a single sum or otherwise) by the beneficiaries or the estate of an employee, if such amounts are paid by or on behalf of an employer and are paid by reason of the death of the employee.

(2) *Special rules for paragraph (1).* —

(A) *$5,000 limitation.* — The aggregate amounts excludable under paragraph (1) with respect to the death of any employee shall not exceed $5,000.

(B) *Nonforfeitable rights.* — Paragraph (1) shall not apply to amounts with respect to which the employee possessed, immediately before his death, a nonforfeitable right to receive the amounts while living. This subparagraph shall not apply to total distributions payable (as defined in section 402(a)(3)) which are paid to a distributee within one taxable year of the distributee by reason of the employee's death —

(i) by a stock bonus, pension, or profit-sharing trust described in section 401(a) which is exempt from tax under section 501(a),

(ii) under an annuity contract under a plan which meets the requirements of paragraphs (3), (4), (5), and (6) of section 401(a), or

(iii) under an annuity contract purchased by an employer which is an organization referred to in section 503(b)(1), (2), or (3) and which is exempt from tax under section 501(a), but only with respect to that portion of such total distributions payable which bears the same ratio to the amount of such total distributions payable which is (without regard to this subsection) includible in gross income, as the amounts contributed by the employer for such annuity contract which are excludable from gross income under section 403(b) bear to the total amounts contributed by the employer for such annuity contract.

(C) *Joint and survivor annuities.* — Paragraph (1) shall not apply to amounts received by a surviving annuitant under a joint and survivor's annuity contract after the first day of the first period for which an amount was received as an annuity by the employee (or would have been received if the employee had lived).

(D) *Other annuities.* — In the case of any amount to which section 72 (relating to annuities, etc.) applies, the amount which is excludable under paragraph (1) (as modified by the preceding subparagraphs of this paragraph) shall be determined by reference to the value of such amount as of the day on which the employee died. Any amount so excludable under paragraph (1) shall, for purposes of section 72, be treated as additional consideration paid by the employee.

(c) *Interest.* — If any amount excluded from gross income by subsection (a) or (b) is held under an agreement to pay interest thereon, the interest payments shall be included in gross income.

(d) *Payment of Life Insurance Proceeds at a Date Later Than Death.* —

(1) *General rule.* — The amounts held by an insurer with respect to any beneficiary shall be prorated (in accordance with such regulations as may be prescribed by the Secretary or his delegate) over the period or periods with respect to which such payments are to be made. There shall be excluded from the gross income of such beneficiary in the taxable year received —

(A) any amount determined by such proration, and

(B) in the case of the surviving spouse of the insured, that portion of the excess of the amounts received under one or more agreements specified in paragraph (2)(A) (whether or not payment of any part of such amounts is guaranteed by the insurer) over the amount determined in subparagraph (A) of this paragraph which is not greater than $1,000 with respect to any insured.

Gross income includes, to the extent not excluded by the preceding sentence, amounts received under agreements to which this subsection applies.

(2) *Amount held by an insurer.* — An amount held by an insurer with respect to any beneficiary shall mean an amount to which subsection (a) applies which is —

(A) held by any insurer under an agreement provided for in the life insurance contract, whether as an option or otherwise, to pay such amount on a date or dates later than the death of the insured, and

(B) is equal to the value of such agreement to such beneficiary

(i) as of the date of death of the insured (as if any option exercised under the life insurance contract were exercised at such time), and

(ii) as discounted on the basis of the interest rate and mortality tables used by the insurer in calculating payments under the agreement.

(3) *Surviving spouse.* — For purposes of this subsection, the term "surviving spouse" means the spouse of the insured as of the date of death, including a spouse legally separated but not under a decree of absolute divorce.

(4) *Application of subsection.* — This subsection shall not apply to any amount to which subsection (c) is applicable.

(e) *Alimony, Etc., Payments.* —

(1) *In general.* — This section shall not apply to so much of any payment as is includible in the gross income of the wife under section 71 (relating to alimony) or section 682 (relating to income of an estate or trust in case of divorce, etc.).

(2) *Cross reference.* —

For definition of "wife" see section 7701(a)(17).

(f) *Effective Date of Section.* — This section shall apply only to amounts received by reason of the death of an insured or an employee occurring after the date of enactment of this title. Section 22(b)(1) of the Internal Revenue Code of 1939 shall apply to amounts received by reason of the death of an insured or an employee occurring on or before such date.

Sec. 102. Gifts and Inheritances.

(a) *General Rule.* — Gross income does not include the value of property acquired by gift, bequest, devise, or inheritance.

(b) *Income.* — Subsection (a) shall not exclude from gross income —

(1) the income from any property referred to in subsection (a); or

(2) where the gift, bequest, devise, or inheritance is of income from property, the amount of such income.

Where, under the terms of the gift, bequest, devise, or inheritance, the payment, crediting, or distribution thereof is to be made at intervals, then, to the extent that it is paid or credited or to be distributed out of income from property, it shall be treated for purposes of paragraph (2) as a gift, bequest, devise, or inheritance of income from property. Any amount included in the gross income of a beneficiary under subchapter J shall be treated for purposes of paragraph (2) as a gift, bequest, devise, or inheritance of income from property.

Sec. 104. Compensation for Injuries or Sickness.

(a) *In General.* — Except in the case of amounts attributable to (and not in excess of) deductions allowed under section 213 (relating to medical, etc., expenses) for any prior taxable year, gross income does not include —

(1) amounts received under workmen's compensation acts as compensation for personal injuries or sickness;

(2) the amount of any damages received (whether by suit or agreement) on account of personal injuries or sickness;

(3) amounts received through accident or health insurance for personal injuries or sickness (other than amounts received by an employee, to the extent such amounts (A) are attributable to contributions by the employer which were not includible in the gross income of the employee, or (B) are paid by the employer); and

(4) amounts received as a pension, annuity, or similar allowance for per-

sonal injuries or sickness resulting from active service in the armed forces of any country or in the Coast and Geodetic Survey or the Public Health Service.

(b) *Cross References.* —

(1) For exclusion from employee's gross income of employer contributions to accident and health plans, see section 106.

(2) For exclusion of part of disability retirement pay from the application of subsection (a)(4) of this section, see section 402(h) of the Career Compensation Act of 1949 (37 U.S.C. 272(h)).

Sec. 105. Amounts Received Under Accident and Health Plans.

(a) *Amounts Attributable to Employer Contributions.* — Except as otherwise provided in this section, amounts received by an employee through accident or health insurance for personal injuries or sickness shall be included in gross income to the extent such amounts (1) are attributable to contributions by the employer which were not includible in the gross income of the employee, or (2) are paid by the employer.

(b) *Amounts Expended for Medical Care.* — Except in the case of amounts attributable to (and not in excess of) deductions allowed under section 213 (relating to medical, etc., expenses) for any prior taxable year, gross income does not include amounts referred to in subsection (a) if such amounts are paid, directly or indirectly, to the taxpayer to reimburse the taxpayer for expenses incurred by him for the medical care (as defined in section 213(e)) of the taxpayer, his spouse, and his dependents (as defined in section 152).

(c) *Payments Unrelated to Absence From Work.* — Gross income does not include amounts referred to in subsection (a) to the extent such amounts —

(1) constitute payment for the permanent loss or loss of use of a member or function of the body, or the permanent disfigurement, of the taxpayer, his spouse, or a dependent (as defined in section 152), and

(2) are computed with reference to the nature of the injury without regard to the period the employee is absent from work.

(d) *Wage Continuation Plans.* — Gross income does not include amounts referred to in subsection (a) if such amounts constitute wages or payments in lieu of wages for a period during which the employee is absent from work on account of personal injuries or sickness; but this subsection shall not apply to the extent that such amounts exceed a weekly rate of $100. In the case of a period during which the employee is absent from work on account of sickness, the preceding sentence shall not apply to amounts attributable to the first 7 calendar days in such period unless the employee is hospitalized on account of sickness for at least one day during such period. If such amounts are not paid on the basis of a weekly pay period, the Secretary or his delegate shall by regulations prescribe the method of determining the weekly rate at which such amounts are paid.

(e) *Accident and Health Plans.* — For purposes of this section and section 104 —

(1) amounts received under an accident or health plan for employees, and

(2) amounts received from a sickness and disability fund for employees maintained under the law of a State, a Territory, or the District of Columbia,

shall be treated as amounts received through accident or health insurance.

(f) *Rules for Application of Section 213.* — For purposes of section 213(a) (relating to medical, dental, etc., expenses) amounts excluded from gross income under subsection (c) or (d) shall not be considered as compensation (by insurance or otherwise) for expenses paid for medical care.

Sec. 106. Contributions by Employer to Accident and Health Plans.

Gross income does not include contributions by the employer to accident or health plans for compensation (through insurance or otherwise) to his employees for personal injuries or sickness.

Sec. 116. Partial Exclusion of Dividends Received by Individuals.

(a) *Exclusion From Gross Income.* — Effective with respect to any taxable year ending after July 31, 1954, gross income does not include amounts received by an individual as dividends from domestic corporations, to the extent that the dividends do not exceed $50. If the dividends received in a taxable year exceed $50, the exclusion provided by the preceding sentence shall apply to the dividends first received in such year.

(b) *Certain Dividends Excluded.* — Subsection (a) shall not apply to any dividend from —

(1) a corporation organized under the China Trade Act, 1922 (see sec. 941); or

(2) a corporation which, for the taxable year of the corporation in which the distribution is made, or for the next preceding taxable year of the corporation, is —

(A) a corporation exempt from tax under section 501 (relating to certain charitable, etc., organizations) or section 521 (relating to farmers' cooperative associations); or

(B) a corporation to which section 931 (relating to income from sources within possessions of the United States) applies.

(c) *Special Rules for Certain Distributions.* — For purposes of subsection (a) —

(1) Any amount allowed as a deduction under section 591 (relating to deduction for dividends paid by mutual savings banks, etc.) shall not be treated as a dividend.

(2) A dividend received from a regulated investment company shall be subject to the limitations prescribed in section 854.

(d) *Certain Nonresident Aliens Ineligible for Exclusion.* — Subsection (a) does not apply to a nonresident alien individual with respect to whom a tax is imposed for the taxable year under section 871(a).

Sec. 170. Charitable, Etc., Contributions and Gifts.

(a) *Allowance of Deduction.* —

(1) *General rule.* — There shall be allowed as a deduction any charitable contribution (as defined in subsection (c)) payment of which is made within the taxable year. A charitable contribution shall be allowable as a deduction only if verified under regulations prescribed by the Secretary or his delegate.

(2) *Corporations on accrual basis.* — In the case of a corporation reporting its taxable income on the accrual basis, if —

(A) the board of directors authorizes a charitable contribution during any taxable year, and

(B) payment of such contribution is made after the close of such taxable year and on or before the 15th day of the third month following the close of such taxable year,

then the taxpayer may elect to treat such contribution as paid during such taxable year. The election may be made only at the time of the filing of the return for such taxable year, and shall be signified in such manner as the Secretary or his delegate shall by regulations prescribe.

(b) *Limitations.* —

(1) *Individuals.* — In the case of an individual the deduction provided in subsection (a) shall be limited as provided in subparagraphs (A), (B), (C), and (D).

(A.) *Special rule.* — Any charitable contribution to —

(i) a church or a convention or association of churches,

(ii) an educational organization referred to in section 503 (b) (2), or

(iii) a hospital referred to in section 503(b)(5) or to a medical research organization (referred to in section 503(b)(5)) directly engaged in the continuous active conduct of medical research in conjunction with a hospital, if during the calendar year in which the contribution is made such organization is committed to spend such contributions for such research before January 1 of the fifth calendar year which begins after the date such contribution is made,

shall be allowed to the extent that the aggregate of such contributions does not exceed 10 percent of the taxpayer's adjusted gross income computed without regard to any net operating loss carryback to the taxable year under section 172.

(B) *General limitation.* — The total deductions under subsection (a) for any taxable year shall not exceed 20 percent of the taxpayer's adjusted gross income computed without regard to any net operating loss carryback to the taxable year under section 172. For purposes of this subparagraph, the deduction under subsection (a) shall be computed without regard to any deduction allowed under subparagraph (A) but shall take into account any charitable contributions to the organizations described in clauses (i), (ii), and (iii) which are in excess of the amount allowable as a deduction under subparagraph (A).

(C) *Unlimited deduction for certain individuals.* — The limitation in subparagraph (B) shall not apply in the case of an individual if, in the taxable year and in 8 of the 10 preceding taxable years, the amount of the charitable contributions, plus the amount of income tax (determined without regard to chapter 2, relating to tax on self-employment income) paid during such year in respect of such year or preceding taxable years, exceeds 90 percent of the taxpayer's taxable income for such year, computed without regard to —

(i) this section,

(ii) section 151 (allowance of deductions for personal exemptions), and

(iii) any net operating loss carryback to the taxable year under section 172.

In lieu of the amount of income tax paid during any such year, there may be substituted for that year the amount of income tax paid in respect of such year, provided that any amount so included in the year in respect of which payment was made shall not be included in any other year.

(D) *Denial of deduction in case of certain transfers in trust.* — No deduction shall be allowed under this section for the value of any interest in property transferred after March 9, 1954, to a trust if —

(i) the grantor has a reversionary interest in the corpus or income of that portion of the trust with respect to which a deduction would (but for this subparagraph) be allowable under this section; and

(ii) at the time of the transfer the value of such reversionary interest exceeds 5 percent of the value of the property constituting such portion of the trust.

For purposes of this subparagraph, a power exercisable by the grantor or a nonadverse party (within the meaning of section 672(b)), or both, to revest in the grantor property or income therefrom shall be treated as a reversionary interest.

(2) *Corporations.* — In the case of a corporation, the total deductions under subsection (a) for any taxable year shall not exceed 5 percent of the taxpayer's taxable income computed without regard to —

(A) this section,

(B) part VIII (except section 248),

(C) any net operating loss carryback to the taxable year under section 172, and

(D) section 922 (special deduction for Western Hemisphere trade corporations).

Any contribution made by a corporation in a taxable year to which this section applies in excess of the amount deductible in such year under the foregoing limitation shall be deductible in each of the two succeeding taxable years in order of time, but only to the extent of the lesser of the two following amounts: (i) the excess of the maximum amount deductible for such succeeding taxable year under the foregoing limitation over the contributions made in such year; and (ii) in the case of the first succeeding taxable year the amount of such excess contribution, and in the case of the second succeeding taxable year the portion of such excess contribution not deductible in the first succeeding taxable year.

(3) *Special rule for corporations having net operating loss carryovers.* — In applying the second sentence of paragraph (2) of this subsection, the excess of —

(A) the contributions made by a corporation in a taxable year to which this section applies, over

(B) the amount deductible in such year under the limitation in the first sentence of such paragraph (2),

shall be reduced to the extent that such excess reduces taxable income (as computed for purposes of the second sentence of section 172(b)(2)) and increases a net operating loss carryover under section 172 to a succeeding taxable year.

(4) *Reduction for certain interest.* — If, in connection with any charitable contribution, a liability is assumed by the recipient or by and other person, or if a charitable contribution is of property which is subject to a liability, then, to the extent necessary to avoid the duplication of amounts, the amount taken into account for purposes of this section as the amount of the charitable contribution —

(A) shall be reduced for interest (i) which has been paid (or is to be paid) by the taxpayer, (ii) which is attributable to the liability, and (iii) which is attributable to any period after the making of the contribution, and

(B) in the case of a bond, shall be further reduced for interest (i) which has been paid (or is to be paid) by the taxpayer on indebtedness incurred or continued to purchase or carry such bond, and (ii) which is attributable to any period before the making of the contribution.

The reduction pursuant to subparagraph (B) shall not exceed the interest (including interest equivalent) on the bond which is attributable to any period before the making of the contribution and which is not (under the taxpayer's method of accounting) includible in the gross income of the taxpayer for any taxable year. For purposes of this paragraph, the term "bond" means any bond, debenture, note, or certificate or other evidence of indebtedness.

(c) *Charitable Contribution Defined.* — For purposes of this section, the term "charitable contribution" means a contribution or gift to or for the use of —

(1) A State, a Territory, a possession of the United States, or any political subdivision of any of the foregoing, or the United States or the District of Columbia, but only if the contribution or gift is made for exclusively public purposes.

(2) A corporation, trust, or community chest, fund, or foundation —

(A) created or organized in the United States or in any possession thereof, or under the law of the United States, any State or Territory, the District of Columbia, or any possession of the United States;

(B) organized and operated exclusively for religious, charitable, scientific, literary, or educational purposes or for the prevention of cruelty to children or animals;

(C) no part of the net earnings of which inures to the benefit of any private shareholder or individual; and

(D) no substantial part of the activities of which is carrying on propaganda, or otherwise attempting, to influence legislation.

A contribution or gift by a corporation to a trust, chest, fund, or foundation shall be deductible by reason of this paragraph only if it is to be used within the United States or any of its possessions exclusively for purposes specified in subparagraph (B).

(3) A post or organization of war veterans, or an auxiliary unit or society of, or trust or foundation for, any such post or organization —

(A) organized in the United States or any of its possessions, and

(B) no part of the net earnings of which inures to the benefit of any private shareholder or individual.

(4) In the case of a contribution or gift by an individual, a domestic fraternal society, order, or association, operating under the lodge system, but only if such contribution or gift is to be used exclusively for religious, charitable, scientific, literary, or educational purposes, or for the prevention of cruelty to children or animals.

(5) A cemetery company owned and operated exclusively for the benefit of its members, or any corporation chartered solely for burial purposes as a cemetery corporation and not permitted by its charter to engage in any business not necessarily incident to that purpose, if such company or corporation is not operated for profit and no part of the net earnings of such company or corporation inures to the benefit of any private shareholder or individual.

Sec. 212. Expenses for Production of Income.

In the case of an individual, there shall be allowed as a deduction all the ordinary and necessary expenses paid or incurred during the taxable year —

(1) for the production or collection of income;

(2) for the management, conservation, or maintenance of property held for the production of income; or

(3) in connection with the determination, collection, or refund of any tax.

Sec. 264. Certain Amounts Paid in Connection With Insurance Contracts.

(a) *General Rule.* — No deduction shall be allowed for —

(1) Premiums paid on any life insurance policy covering the life of any officer or employee, or of any person financially interested in any trade or business carried on by the taxpayer, when the taxpayer is directly or indirectly a beneficiary under such policy.

(2) Any amount paid or accrued on indebtedness incurred or continued to purchase or carry a single premium life insurance, endowment, or annuity contract.

Paragraph (2) shall apply in respect of annuity contracts only as to contracts purchased after March 1, 1954.

(b) *Contracts Treated as Single Premium Contracts.* — For purposes of subsection (a) (2), a contract shall be treated as a single premium contract —

(1) if substantially all the premiums on the contract are paid within a period of 4 years from the date on which the contract is purchased, or

(2) if an amount is deposited after March 1, 1954, with the insurer for payment of a substantial number of future premiums on the contract.

Sec. 267. Losses, Expenses, and Interest With Respect to Transactions Between Related Taxpayers.

(a) *Deductions Disallowed.* — No deduction shall be allowed —

(1) *Losses.* — In respect of losses from sales or exchanges of property (other than losses in cases of distributions in corporate liquidations), directly or indirectly, between persons specified within any one of the paragraphs of subsection (b).

(2) *Unpaid expenses and interest.* — In respect of expenses, otherwise deductible under section 162 or 212, or of interest, otherwise deductible under section 163, —

(A) If within the period consisting of the taxable year of the taxpayer and $2\frac{1}{2}$ months after the close thereof (i) such expenses or interest are not paid, and (ii) the amount thereof is not includible in the gross income of the person to whom the payment is to be made; and

(B) If, by reason of the method of accounting of the person to whom the payment is to be made, the amount thereof is not, unless paid, includible in the gross income of such person for the taxable year in which or with which the taxable year of the taxpayer ends; and

(C) If, at the close of the taxable year of the taxpayer or at any time within $2\frac{1}{2}$ months thereafter, both the taxpayer and the person to whom the payment is to be made are persons specified within any one of the paragraphs of subsection (b).

(b) *Relationships.* — The persons referred to in subsection (a) are:

(1) Members of a family, as defined in subsection (c) (4);

(2) An individual and a corporation more than 50 percent in value of the outstanding stock of which is owned, directly or indirectly, by or for such individual;

(3) Two corporations more than 50 percent in value of the outstanding stock of each of which is owned, directly or indirectly, by or for the same individual, if either one of such corporations, with respect to the taxable year of the corporation preceding the date of the sale or exchange was, under the law applicable to such taxable year, a personal holding company or a foreign personal holding company;

(4) A grantor and a fiduciary of any trust;

(5) A fiduciary of a trust and a fiduciary of another trust, if the same person is a grantor of both trusts;

(6) A fiduciary of a trust and a beneficiary of such trust;

(7) A fiduciary of a trust and a beneficiary of another trust, if the same person is a grantor of both trusts;

(8) A fiduciary of a trust and a corporation more than 50 percent in value of the outstanding stock of which is owned, directly or indirectly, by or for the trust or by or for a person who is a grantor of the trust; or

(9) A person and an organization to which section 501 (relating to certain educational and charitable organizations which are exempt from tax) applies and which is controlled directly or indirectly by such person or (if such person is an individual) by members of the family of such individual.

(c) *Constructive Ownership of Stock.* — For purposes of determining, in applying subsection (b), the ownership of stock —

(1) Stock owned, directly or indirectly, by or for a corporation, partnership, estate, or trust shall be considered as being owned proportionately by or for its shareholders, partners, or beneficiaries;

(2) An individual shall be considered as owning the stock owned, directly or indirectly, by or for his family;

(3) An individual owning (otherwise than by the application of paragraph (2) any stock in a corporation shall be considered as owning the stock owned, directly or indirectly, by or for his partner;

(4) The family of an individual shall include only his brothers and sisters (whether by the whole or half blood), spouse, ancestors, and lineal descendants; and

(5) Stock constructively owned by a person by reason of the application of paragraph (1) shall, for the purpose of applying paragraph (1), (2), or (3), be treated as actually owned by such person, but stock constructively owned by an individual by reason of the application of paragraph (2) or (3) shall not be treated as owned by him for the purpose of again applying either of such paragraphs in order to make another the constructive owner of such stock.

(d) *Amount of Gain Where Loss Previously Disallowed.* — If —

(1) in the case of a sale or exchange of property to the taxpayer a loss sustained by the transferor is not allowable to the transferor as a deduction by reason of subsection (a) (1) (or by reason of section 24 (b) of the Internal Revenue Code of 1939); and

(2) after December 31, 1953, the taxpayer sells or otherwise disposes of such property (or of other property the basis of which in his hands is determined directly or indirectly by reference to such property) at a gain, then such gain shall be recognized only to the extent that it exceeds so much of such loss as is properly allocable to the property sold or otherwise disposed of by the taxpayer. This subsection applies with respect to taxable years ending after December 31, 1953. This subsection shall not apply if the loss sustained by the transferor is not allowable to the transferor as a deduction by reason of section 1091 (relating to wash sales) or by reason of section 118 of the Internal Revenue Code of 1939.

Sec. 303. Distributions in Redemption of Stock to Pay Death Taxes.

(a) *In General.* — A distribution of property to a shareholder by a corporation in redemption of part or all of the stock of such corporation which (for Federal estate tax purposes) is included in determining the gross estate of a decedent, to the extent that the amount of such distribution does not exceed the sum of —

(1) the estate, inheritance, legacy, and succession taxes (including any interest collected as a part of such taxes) imposed because of such decedent's death, and

(2) the amount of funeral and administration expenses allowable as deductions to the estate under section 2053 (or under section 2106 in the case of the estate of a decedent nonresident, not a citizen of the United States),

shall be treated as a distribution in full payment in exchange for the stock so redeemed.

(b) *Limitations on Application of Subsection (a).* —

(1) *Period for distribution.* — Subsection (a) shall apply only to amounts distributed after the death of the decedent and —

(A) within the period of limitations provided in section 6501 (a) for the assessment of the Federal estate tax (determined without the application of any provision other than section 6501 (a)), or within 90 days after the expiration of such period, or

(B) if a petition for redetermination of a deficiency in such estate tax has been filed with the Tax Court within the time prescribed in section 6213, at any time before the expiration of 60 days after the decision of the Tax Court becomes final.

(2) *Relationship of stock to decedent's estate.* —

(A) *In general.* — Subsection (a) shall apply to a distribution by a corporation only if the value (for Federal estate tax purposes) of all of the stock of such corporation which is included in determining the value of the decedent's gross estate is either —

(i) more than 35 percent of the value of the gross estate of such decedent, or

(ii) more than 50 percent of the taxable estate of such decedent.

(B) *Special rule for stock of two or more corporations.* — For purposes of the 35 percent and 50 percent requirements of subparagraph (A) stock of two or more corporations, with respect to each of which there is included in determining the value of the decedent's gross estate more than 75 percent in value of the outstanding stock, shall be treated as the stock of a single corporation. For the purpose of the 75 percent requirement of the preceding sentence, stock which, at the decedent's death, represents the surviving spouse's interest in property held by the decedent and the surviving spouse as community property shall be treated as having been included in determining the value of the decedent's gross estate.

(c) *Stock With Substituted Basis.* — If —

(1) a shareholder owns stock of a corporation (referred to in this subsection as "new stock") the basis of which is determined by reference to the basis of stock of a corporation (referred to in this subsection as "old stock"),

(2) the old stock was included (for Federal estate tax purposes) in determining the gross estate of a decedent, and

(3) subsection (a) would apply to a distribution of property to such shareholder in redemption of the old stock,

then, subject to the limitation specified in subsection (b) (1), subsection (a) shall apply in respect of a distribution in redemption of the new stock.

Sec. 311.   Taxability of Corporation on Distribution.

(a) *General Rule.* — Except as provided in subsections (b) and (c) of this section and section 453 (d), no gain or loss shall be recognized to a corporation on the distribution, with respect to its stock, of —

(1) its stock (or rights to acquire its stock), or

(2) property.

(b) *LIFO Inventory.* —

(1) *Recognition of gain.* — If a corporation inventorying goods under the method provided in section 472 (relating to last-in, first-out inventories) distributes inventory assets (as defined in paragraph (2) (A)), then the amount (if any) by which —

(A) the inventory amount (as defined in paragraph (2) (B)) of such assets under a method authorized by section 471 (relating to general rule for inventories), exceeds

(B) the inventory amount of such assets under the method provided in section 472,

shall be treated as gain to the corporation recognized from the sale of such inventory assets.

(2) *Definitions.* — For purposes of paragraph (1) —

(A) *Inventory assets.* — The term "inventory assets" means stock in trade of the corporation, or other property of a kind which would properly be included in the inventory of the corporation if on hand at the close of the taxable year.

(B) *Inventory amount.* — The term "inventory amount" means, in the case of inventory assets distributed during a taxable year, the amount of such inventory assets determined as if the taxable year closed at the time of such distribution.

(3) *Method of determining inventory amount.* — For purposes of this subsection, the inventory amount of assets under a method authorized by section 471 shall be determined —

(A) if the corporation uses the retail method of valuing inventories under section 472, by using such method, or

(B) if subparagraph (A) does not apply, by using cost or market, whichever is lower.

(c) *Liability in Excess of Basis.* — If —

(1) a corporation distributes property to a shareholder with respect to its stock,

(2) such property is subject to a liability, or the shareholder assumes a liability of the corporation in connection with the distribution, and

(3) the amount of such liability exceeds the adjusted basis (in the hands of the distributing corporation) of such property,

then gain shall be recognized to the distributing corporation in an amount equal to such excess as if the property distributed had been sold at the time of the distribution. In the case of a distribution of property subject to a liability which is not assumed by the shareholder, the amount of gain to be recognized under the preceding sentence shall not exceed the excess, if any, of the fair market value of such property over its adjusted basis.

Sec. 401. Qualified Pension, Profit-sharing, and Stock Bonus Plans.

(a) *Requirements for Qualification.* — A trust created or organized in the United States and forming part of a stock bonus, pension, or profit-sharing plan of an employer for the exclusive benefit of his employees or their beneficiaries shall constitute a qualified trust under this section —

(1) if contributions are made to the trust by such employer, or employees, or both, or by another employer who is entitled to deduct his contributions under section 404(a)(3)(B) (relating to deduction for contributions to profit-sharing and stock bonus plans), for the purpose of distributing

to such employees or their beneficiaries the corpus and income of the fund accumulated by the trust in accordance with such plan;

(2) if under the trust instrument it is impossible, at any time prior to the satisfaction of all liabilities with respect to employees and their beneficiaries under the trust, for any part of the corpus or income to be (within the taxable year or thereafter) used for, or diverted to, purposes other than for the exclusive benefit of his employees or their beneficiaries;

(3) if the trust, or two or more trusts, or the trust or trusts and annuity plan or plans are designated by the employer as constituting parts of a plan intended to qualify under this subsection which benefits either —

(A) 70 percent or more of all the employees, or 80 percent or more of all the employees who are eligible to benefit under the plan if 70 percent or more of all the employees are eligible to benefit under the plan, excluding in each case employees who have been employed not more than a minimum period prescribed by the plan, not exceeding 5 years, employees whose customary employment is for not more than 20 hours in any one week, and employees whose customary employment is for not more than 5 months in any calendar year, or

(B) such employees as qualify under a classification set up by the employer and found by the Secretary or his delegate not to be discriminatory in favor of employees who are officers, shareholders, persons whose principal duties consist in supervising the work of other employees, or highly compensated employees;
and

(4) if the contributions or benefits provided under the plan do not discriminate in favor of employees who are officers, shareholders, persons whose principal duties consist in supervising the work of other employees, or highly compensated employees.

(5) A classification shall not be considered discriminatory within the meaning of paragraph (3)(B) or (4) merely because it excludes employees the whole of whose remuneration constitutes "wages" under section 3121 (a) (1) (relating to the Federal Insurance Contributions Act) or merely because it is limited to salaried or clerical employees. Neither shall a plan be considered discriminatory within the meaning of such provisions merely because the contributions or benefits of or on behalf of the employees under the plan bear a uniform relationship to the total compensation, or the basic or regular rate of compensation, of such employees, or merely because the contributions or benefits based on that part of an employee's remuneration which is excluded from "wages" by section 3121(a)(1) differ from the contributions or benefits based on employee's remuneration not so excluded, or differ because of any retirement benefits created under State or Federal law.

(6) A plan shall be considered as meeting the requirements of paragraph (3) during the whole of any taxable year of the plan if on one day in each quarter it satisfied such requirements.

(b) *Certain Retroactive Changes in Plan.* — A stock bonus, pension, profit-sharing, or annuity plan shall be considered as satisfying the requirements of paragraphs (3), (4), (5), and (6) of subsection (a) for the period beginning with the date on which it was put into effect and ending with the 15th day of the third month following the close of the taxable year of the employer in which the plan was put in effect, if all provisions of the plan which are necessary to satisfy such requirements are in effect by the end of such period and have been made effective for all purposes with respect to the whole of such period.

(c) *Cross Reference.* —
     For exemption from tax of a trust qualified under this section, see section 501(a).

Sec. 402. Taxability of Beneficiary of Employees' Trust.

(a) *Taxability of Beneficiary of Exempt Trust.* —

(1) *General rule.* — Except as provided in paragraphs (2) and (4), the amount actually distributed or made available to any distributee by any employees' trust described in section 401(a) which is exempt from tax under section 501(a) shall be taxable to him, in the year in which so distributed or made available, under section 72 (relating to annuities) except that section 72(e)(3) shall not apply. The amount actually distributed or made available to any distributee shall not include net unrealized appreciation in securities of the employer corporation attributable to the amount contributed by the employee. Such net unrealized appreciation and the resulting adjustments to basis of such securities shall be determined in accordance with regulations prescribed by the Secretary or his delegate.

(2) *Capital gains treatment for certain distributions.* — In the case of an employees' trust described in section 401(a), which is exempt from tax under section 501(a), if the total distributions payable with respect to any employee are paid to the distributee within 1 taxable year of the distributee on account of the employee's death or other separation from the service, or on account of the death of the employee after his separation from the service, the amount of such distribution, to the extent exceeding the amounts contributed by the employee (determined by applying section 72(f)), which employee contributions shall be reduced by any amounts theretofore distributed to him which were not includible in gross income, shall be considered a gain from the sale or exchange of a capital asset held for more than 6 months. Where such total distributions include securities of the employer corporation, there shall be excluded from such excess the net unrealized appreciation attributable to that part of the total distributions which consists of the securities of the employer corporation so distributed. The amount of such net unrealized appreciation and the resulting adjustments to basis of the securities of the employer corporation so distributed shall be determined in accordance with regulations prescribed by the Secretary or his delegate.

(3) *Definitions.* — For purposes of this subsection —

     (A) The term "securities" means only shares of stock and bonds or debentures issued by a corporation with interest coupons or in registered form.

     (B) The term "securities of the employer corporation" includes securities of a parent or subsidiary corporation (as defined in section 421(d)(2) and (3)) of the employer corporation.

     (C) The term "total distributions payable" means the balance to the credit of an employee which becomes payable to a distributee on account of the employee's death or other separation from the service, or on account of his death after separation from the service.

(4) *Distributions by United States to nonresident aliens.* — The amount includible under paragraph (1) or (2) of this subsection in the gross income of a nonresident alien individual with respect to a distribution made by the United States in respect of services performed by an employee of the United States shall not exceed an amount which bears the same ratio to the amount includible in gross income without regard to this paragraph as —

(A) the aggregate basic salary paid by the United States to such employee for such services, reduced by the amount of such basic salary which was not includible in gross income by reason of being from sources without the United States, bears to

(B) the aggregate basic salary paid by the United States to such employee for such services.

In the case of distributions under the Civil Service Retirement Act (5 U.S.C. 2251), the term "basic salary" shall have the meaning provided in section 1(d) of such Act.

(b) *Taxability of Beneficiary of Non-Exempt Trust.* — Contributions to an employees' trust made by an employer during a taxable year of the employer which ends within or with a taxable year of the trust for which the trust is not exempt from tax under section 501(a) shall be included in the gross income of an employee for the taxable year in which the contribution is made to the trust in the case of an employee whose beneficial interest in such contribution is nonforfeitable at the time the contribution is made. The amount actually distributed or made available to any distributee by any such trust shall be taxable to him, in the year in which so distributed or made available, under section 72 (relating to annuities) except that section 72(e)(3) shall not apply.

(c) *Taxability of Beneficiary of Certain Foreign Situs Trusts.* — For purposes of subsections (a) and (b), a stock bonus, pension, or profit-sharing trust which would qualify for exemption from tax under section 501(a) except for the fact that it is a trust created or organized outside the United States shall be treated as if it were a trust exempt from tax under section 501(a).

(d) *Certain Employees' Annuities.* — Notwithstanding subsection (b) or any other provision of this subtitle, a contribution to a trust by an employer shall not be included in the gross income of the employee in the year in which the contribution is made if —

(1) such contribution is to be applied by the trustee for the purchase of annuity contracts for the benefit of such employee;

(2) such contribution is made to the trustee pursuant to a written agreement entered into prior to October 21, 1942, between the employer and the trustee, or between the employer and the employee; and

(3) under the terms of the trust agreement the employee is not entitled during his lifetime, except with the consent of the trustee, to any payments under annuity contracts purchased by the trustee other than annuity payments.

The employee shall include in his gross income the amounts received under such contracts for the year received as provided in section 72 (relating to annuities) except that section 72(e)(3) shall not apply. This subsection shall have no application with respect to amounts contributed to a trust after June 1, 1949, if the trust on such date was exempt under section 165(a) of the Internal Revenue Code of 1939. For purposes of this subsection, amounts paid by an employer for the purchase of annuity contracts which are transferred to the trustee shall be deemed to be contributions made to a trust or trustee and contributions applied by the trustee for the purchase of annuity contracts; the term "annuity contracts purchased by the trustee" shall include annuity contracts so purchased by the employer and transferred to the trustee; and the term "employee" shall include only a person who was in the employ of the employer, and was covered by the agreement referred to in paragraph (2), prior to October 21, 1942.

(e) *Certain Plan Terminations.* — For purposes of subsection (a)(2), distributions made after December 31, 1953, and before January 1, 1955, as a result of the complete termination of a stock bonus, pension, or profit-sharing plan of an employer which is a corporation, if the termination of the plan is incident to the complete liquidation, occurring before the date of enactment of this title, of the corporation, whether or not such liquidation is incident to a reorganization as defined in section 368(a), shall be considered to be distributions on account of separation from service.

Sec. 403. Taxation of Employee Annuities.

(a) *Taxability of Beneficiary Under a Qualified Annuity Plan.* —

(1) *General rule.* — Except as provided in paragraph (2), if an annuity contract is purchased by an employer for an employee under a plan which meets the requirements of section 404(a)(2) (whether or not the employer deducts the amounts paid for the contract under such section), the employee shall include in his gross income the amounts received under such contract for the year received as provided in section 72 (relating to annuities) except that section 72(e)(3) shall not apply.

(2) *Capital gains treatment for certain distributions.* —

(A) *General rule.* — If —

(i) an annuity contract is purchased by an employer for an employee under a plan which meets the requirements of section 401(a)(3), (4), (5), and (6);

(ii) such plan requires that refunds of contributions with respect to annuity contracts purchased under such plan be used to reduce subsequent premiums on the contracts under the plan; and

(iii) the total amounts payable by reason of an employee's death or other separation from the service, or by reason of the death of an employee after the employee's separation from the service, are paid to the payee within one taxable year of the payee,

then the amount of such payments, to the extent exceeding the amount contributed by the employee (determined by applying section 72(f)), which employee contributions shall be reduced by any amounts theretofore paid to him which were not includible in gross income, shall be considered a gain from the sale or exchange of a capital asset held for more than 6 months.

(B) *Definition.* — For purposes of subparagraph (A), the term "total amounts" means the balance to the credit of an employee which becomes payable to the payee by reason of the employee's death or other separation from the service, or by reason of his death after separation from the service.

(b) *Taxability of Beneficiary Under Annuity Purchased by Section 501(c)(3) Organization.* —

(1) *General rule.* — If —

(A) an annuity contract is purchased for an employee by an employer described in section 501(c)(3) which is exempt from tax under section 501(a),

(B) such annuity contract is not subject to subsection (a), and

(C) the employee's rights under the contract are nonforfeitable, except for failure to pay future premiums,

then amounts contributed by such employer for such annuity contract on or after such rights become nonforfeitable shall be excluded from the gross income of the employee for the taxable year to the extent that the aggregate of such amounts does not exceed the exclusion allowance for such taxable year. The employee shall include in his gross income the amounts received under such contract for the year received as provided in section 72 (relating to annuities) except that section 72(e)(3) shall not apply.

(2) *Exclusion allowance.* — For purposes of this subsection, the exclusion allowance for any employee for the taxable year is an amount equal to the excess, if any, of —

(A) the amount determined by multiplying (i) 20 percent of his includible compensation, by (ii) the number of years of service, over

(B) the aggregate of the amounts contributed by the employer for annuity contracts and excludable from the gross income of the employee for any prior taxable year.

(3) *Includible compensation.* — For purposes of this subsection, the term "includible compensation" means, in the case of any employee, the amount of compensation which is received from the employer described in section 501(c)(3) and exempt from tax under section 501(a), and which is includible in gross income (computed without regard to sections 105(d) and 911) for the most recent period (ending not later than the close of the taxable year) which under paragraph (4) may be counted as one year of service. Such term does not include any amount contributed by the employer for any annuity contract to which this subsection applies.

(4) *Years of service.* — In determining the number of years of service for purposes of this subsection, there shall be included —

(A) one year for each full year during which the individual was a full-time employee of the organization purchasing the annuity for him, and

(B) a fraction of a year (determined in accordance with regulations prescribed by the Secretary or his delegate) for each full year during which such individual was a part-time employee of such organization and for each part of a year during which such individual was a full-time or part-time employee of such organization.

In no case shall the number of years of service be less than one.

(5) *Application to more than one annuity contract.* — If for any taxable year of the employee this subsection applies to 2 or more annuity contracts purchased by the employer, such contracts shall be treated as one contract.

(6) *Forfeitable rights which become nonforfeitable.* — For purposes of this subsection and section 72(f) (relating to special rules for computing employees' contributions to annuity contracts), if rights of the employee under an annuity contract described in subparagraphs (A) and (B) of paragraph (1) change from forfeitable to nonforfeitable rights, then the amount (determined without regard to this subsection) includible in gross income by reason of such change shall be treated as an amount contributed by the employer for such annuity contract as of the time such rights become nonforfeitable.

(c) *Taxability of Beneficiary Under a Nonqualified Annuity.* — If an annuity contract purchased by an employer for an employee is not subject to subsection (a) and the employee's rights under the contract are nonforfeitable, except for failure to pay future premiums, the amount contributed by the employer for such annuity contract on or after such rights become nonforfeitable shall be included in the gross income of the employee in the year in which the amount is contributed. The employee shall include in his gross income the amounts received under such contract for the year received as provided in section 72 (relating to annuities) except that section 72(e)(3) shall not apply.

(d) *Taxability of Beneficiary Under Certain Forfeitable Contracts Purchased by Exempt Organizations.* — Notwithstanding the first sentence of subsection (c), if rights of an employee under an annuity contract purchased by an employer which is exempt from tax under section 501(a) or 521(a) change from forfeitable to nonforfeitable rights, the value of such contract on the date of such change (to the extent attributable to amounts contributed by the employer after December 31, 1957) shall, except as provided in subsection (b), be included in the gross income of the employee in the year of such change.

Sec. 404. Deduction for Contributions of an Employer to an Employees' Trust or Annuity Plan and Compensation Under a Deferred-Payment Plan.

(a) *General Rule.* — If contributions are paid by an employer to or under a stock bonus, pension, profit-sharing, or annuity plan, or if compensation is paid or accrued on account of any employee under a plan deferring the receipt of such compensation, such contributions or compensation shall not be deductible under section 162 (relating to trade or business expenses) or section 212 (relating to expenses for the production of income); but, if they satisfy the conditions of either of such sections, they shall be deductible under this section, subject, however, to the following limitations as to the amounts deductible in any year:

(1) *Pension trusts.* — In the taxable year when paid, if the contributions are paid into a pension trust, and if such taxable year ends within or with a taxable year of the trust for which the trust is exempt under section 501(a), in an amount determined as follows:

(A) an amount not in excess of 5 percent of the compensation otherwise paid or accrued during the taxable year to all the employees under the trust, but such amount may be reduced for future years if found by the Secretary or his delegate upon periodical examinations at not less that 5-year intervals to be more than the amount reasonably necessary to provide the remaining unfunded cost of past and current service credits of all employees under the plan, plus

(B) any excess over the amount allowable under subparagraph (A) necessary to provide with respect to all of the employees under the trust the remaining unfunded cost of their past and current service credits distributed as a level amount, or a level percentage of compensation, over the remaining future service of each such employee, as determined under regulations prescribed by the Secretary or his delegate, but if such remaining unfunded cost with respect to any 3 individuals is more than 50 percent of such remaining unfunded cost, the amount of such unfunded cost attributable to such individuals shall be distributed over a period of at least 5 taxable years, or

(C) in lieu of the amounts allowable under subparagraphs (A) and (B) above, an amount equal to the normal cost of the plan, as determined under regulations prescribed by the Secretary or his delegate, plus, if past service or other supplementary pension or annuity credits are provided by the plan, an amount not in excess of 10 percent of the cost which would be required to completely fund or purchase such pension or annuity credits as of the date when they are included in the plan, as determined under regulations prescribed by the Secretary or his delegate, except that in no case shall a deduction be allowed for any amount (other than the normal cost) paid in after such pension or annuity credits are completely funded or purchased.

(D) Any amount paid in a taxable year in excess of the amount deductible in such year under the foregoing limitations shall be deductible in the succeeding taxable years in order of time to the extent of the

difference between the amount paid and deductible in each such succeeding year and the maximum amount deductible for such year in accordance with the foregoing limitations.

(2) *Employees' annuities.* — In the taxable year when paid, in an amount
determined in accordance with paragraph (1), if the contributions are paid
toward the purchase of retirement annuities and such purchase is a part of
a plan which meets the requirements of section 401(a)(3), (4), (5), and (6),
and if refunds of premiums, if any, are applied within the current taxable
year or next succeeding taxable year towards the purchase of such retirement annuities.

(3) *Stock bonds and profit-sharing trusts.* —

(A) *Limits on deductible contributions.* — In the taxable year when
paid, if the contributions are paid into a stock bonus or profit-sharing
trust, and if such taxable year ends within or with a taxable year of the
trust with respect to which the trust is exempt under section 501(a), in
an amount not in excess of 15 percent of the compensation otherwise paid
or accrued during the taxable year to all employees under the stock
bonus or profit-sharing plan. If in any taxable year there is paid into
the trust, or a similar trust then in effect, amounts less than the amounts
deductible under the preceding sentence, the excess, or if no amount is
paid, the amounts deductible, shall be carried forward and be deductible
when paid in the succeeding taxable years in order of time, but the
amount so deductible under this sentence in any such succeeding taxable
year shall not exceed 15 percent of the compensation otherwise paid or
accrued during such succeeding taxable year to the beneficiaries under
the plan. In addition, any amount paid into the trust in any taxable
year in excess of the amount allowable with respect to such year under
the preceding provisions of this subparagraph shall be deductible in the
succeeding taxable years in order of time, but the amount so deductible
under this sentence in any one such succeeding taxable year together
with the amount allowable under the first sentence of this subparagraph
shall not exceed 15 percent of the compensation otherwise paid or
accrued during such taxable year to the beneficiaries under the plan.
The term "stock bonus or profit-sharing trust", as used in this subparagraph, shall not include any trust designed to provide benefits upon
retirement and covering a period of years, if under the plan the amounts
to be contributed by the employer can be determined actuarially as provided in paragraph (1). If the contributions are made to 2 or more
stock bonus or profit-sharing trusts, such trusts shall be considered a
single trust for purposes of applying the limitations in this subparagraph.

(B) *Profit-sharing plan of affiliated group.* — In the case of a profit-
sharing plan, or a stock bonus plan in which contributions are determined
with reference to profits, of a group of corporations which is an affiliated
group within the meaning of section 1504, if any member of such affiliated
group is prevented from making a contribution which it would otherwise
have made under the plan, by reason of having no current or accumulated
earnings or profits or because such earnings or profits are less than
the contributions which it would otherwise have made, then so much of
the contribution which such member was so prevented from making may
be made, for the benefit of the employees of such member, by the other
members of the group, to the extent of current or accumulated earnings
or profits, except that such contribution by each such other member
shall be limited, where the group does not file a consolidated return,

to that proportion of its total current and accumulated earnings or profits remaining after adjustment for its contribution deductible without regard to this subparagraph which the total prevented contribution bears to the total current and accumulated earnings or profits of all the members of the group remaining after adjustment for all contributions deductible without regard to this subparagraph. Contributions made under the preceding sentence shall be deductible under subparagraph (A) of this paragraph by the employer making such contribution, and, for the purpose of determining amounts which may be carried forward and deducted under the second sentence of subparagraph (A) of this paragraph in succeeding taxable years, shall be deemed to have been made by the employer on behalf of whose employees such contributions were made.

(4) *Trusts created or organized outside the United States.* — If a stock bonus, pension, or profit-sharing trust would qualify for exemption under section 501(a) except for the fact that it is a trust created or organized outside the United States, contributions to such a trust by an employer which is a resident, or corporation, or other entity of the United States, shall be deductible under the preceding paragraphs.

(5) *Other plans.* — In the taxable year when paid, if the plan is not one included in paragraph (1), (2), or (3), if the employees' rights to or derived from such employer's contribution or such compensation are nonforfeitable at the time the contribution or compensation is paid.

(6) *Taxpayers on accrual basis.* — For purposes of paragraphs (1), (2), and (3), a taxpayer on the accrual basis shall be deemed to have made a payment on the last day of the year of accrual if the payment is on account of such taxable year and is made not later than the time prescribed by law for filing the return for such taxable year (including extensions thereof).

(7) *Limit of deduction.* — If amounts are deductible under paragraphs (1) and (3), or (2) and (3), or (1), (2), and (3), in connection with 2 or more trusts, or one or more trusts and an annuity plan, the total amount deductible in a taxable year under such trusts and plans shall not exceed 25 percent of the compensation otherwise paid or accrued during the taxable year to the persons who are the beneficiaries of the trusts or plans. In addition, any amount paid into such trust or under such annuity plans in any taxable year in excess of the amount allowable with respect to such year under the preceding provisions of this paragraph shall be deductible in the succeeding taxable years in order of time, but the amount so deductible under this sentence in any one such succeeding taxable year together with the amount allowable under the first sentence of this paragraph shall not exceed 30 percent of the compensation otherwise paid or accrued during such taxable years to the beneficiaries under the trusts or plans. This paragraph shall not have the effect of reducing the amount otherwise deductible under paragraphs (1), (2), and (3), if no employee is a beneficiary under more than one trust, or a trust and an annuity plan.

(b) *Method of Contributions, Etc., Having the Effect of a Plan.* — If there is no plan but a method of employer contributions or compensation has the effect of a stock bonus, pension, profit-sharing, or annuity plan, or similar plan deferring the receipt of compensation, subsection (a) shall apply as if there were such a plan.

(c) *Certain Negotiated Plans.* — If contributions are paid by an employer —

(1) under a plan under which such contributions are held in trust for the purpose of paying (either from principal or income or both) for the benefit of employees and their families and dependents at least medical or hospital care, and pensions on retirement or death of employees; and

(2) such plan was established prior to January 1, 1954, as a result of an agreement between employee representatives and the Government of the United States during a period of Government operation, under seizure powers, of a major part of the productive facilities of the industry in which such employer is engaged,

such contributions shall not be deductible under this section nor be made nondeductible by this section, but the deductibility thereof shall be governed solely by section 162 (relating to trade or business expenses). This subsection shall have no application with respect to amounts contributed to a trust on or after any date on which such trust is qualified for exemption from tax under section 501(a).

(d) *Carryover of Unused Deductions.* — The amount of any unused deductions or contributions in excess of the deductible amounts for taxable years to which this part does not apply which under section 23(p) of the Internal Revenue Code of 1939 would be allowable as deductions in later years had such section 23(p) remained in effect, shall be allowable as deductions in taxable years to which this part applies as if such section 23(p) were continued in effect for such years. However, the deduction under the preceding sentence shall not exceed an amount which, when added to the deduction allowable under subsection (a) for contributions made in taxable years to which this part applies, is not greater than the amount which would be deductible under subsection (a) if the contributions which give rise to the deduction under the preceding sentence were made in a taxable year to which this part applies.

Sec. 421. Employee Stock Options.

(a) *Treatment of Restricted Stock Options.* — If a share of stock is transferred to an individual pursuant to his exercise after 1949 of a restricted stock option, and no disposition of such share is made by him within 2 years from the date of the granting of the option nor within 6 months after the transfer of such share to him —

(1) no income shall result at the time of the transfer of such share to the individual upon his exercise of the option with respect to such share;

(2) no deduction under section 162 (relating to trade or business expenses) shall be allowable at any time to the employer corporation, a parent or subsidiary corporation of such corporation, or a corporation issuing or assuming a stock option in a transaction to which subsection (g) is applicable, with respect to the share so transferred; and

(3) no amount other than the price paid under the option shall be considered as received by any of such corporations for the share so transferred.

This subsection and subsection (b) shall not apply unless (A) the individual, at the time he exercises the restricted stock option, is an employee of either the corporation granting such option, a parent or subsidiary corporation of such corporation, or a corporation or a parent or subsidiary of such corporation issuing or assuming a stock option in a transaction to which subsection (g) is applicable, or (B) the option is exercised by him within 3 months after the date he ceases to be an employee of such corporations. In applying paragraphs (2) and (3) of subsection (d) for purposes of the preceding sentence, there shall be substituted for the term "employer corporation" wherever it appears in such paragraphs the term "grantor corporation," or the term "corporation issuing or assuming a stock option in a transaction to which subsection (g) is applicable," as the case may be.

(b) *Special Rule Where Option Price Is Between 85 Percent and 95 Percent of Value of Stock.* — If no disposition of a share of stock acquired by an individual on his exercise after 1949 of a restricted stock option is made by him within 2 years from the date of the granting of the option nor within 6 months after the transfer of such share to him, but, at the time the restricted stock option was granted, the option price (computed under subparagraph (d)(1)(A)) was less than 95 percent of the fair market value at such time of such share, then, in the event of any disposition of such share by him, or in the event of his death (whenever occurring) while owning such share, there shall be included as compensation (and not as gain upon the sale or exchange of a capital asset) in his gross income, for the taxable year in which falls the date of such disposition or for the taxable year closing with his death, whichever applies —

(1) in the case of a share of stock acquired under an option qualifying under clause (i) of subparagraph (d)(1)(A), an amount equal to the amount (if any) by which the option price is exceeded by the lesser of —

(A) the fair market value of the share at the time of such disposition or death, or

(B) the fair market value of the share at the time the option was granted; or

(2) in the case of stock acquired under an option qualifying under clause (ii) of subparagraph (d)(1)(A), an amount equal to the lesser of —

(A) the excess of the fair market value of the share at the time of such disposition or death over the price paid under the option, or

(B) the excess of the fair market value of the share at the time the option was granted over the option price (computed as if the option had been exercised at such time).

In the case of the disposition of such share by the individual, the basis of the share in his hands at the time of such disposition shall be increased by an amount equal to the amount so includible in his gross income.

(c) *Acquisition of New Stock.* — If stock is received by an individual in a distribution to which section 305, 354, 355, 356, or 1036, or so much of section 1031 as relates to section 1036, applies and such distribution was made with respect to stock transferred to him upon his exercise of the option, such stock shall be considered as having been transferred to him on his exercise of such option. A similar rule shall be applied in the case of a series of such distributions.

(d) *Definitions.* — For purposes of this section —

(1) *Restricted stock option.* — The term "restricted stock option" means an option granted after February 26, 1945, to an individual, for any reason connected with his employment by a corporation, if granted by the employer corporation or its parent or subsidiary corporation, to purchase stock of any of such corporations, but only if —

(A) at the time such option is granted —

(i) the option price is at least 85 percent of the fair market value at such time of the stock subject to the option, or

(ii) in the case of a variable price option, the option price (computed as if the option had been exercised when granted) is at least 85 percent of the fair market value of the stock at the time such option is granted; and

(B) such option by its terms is not transferable by such individual otherwise than by will or the laws of descent and distribution, and is exercisable, during his lifetime, only by him; and

(C) such individual, at the time the option is granted, does not own stock possessing more than 10 percent of the total combined voting power of all classes of stock of the employer corporation or of its parent or subsidiary corporation. This subparagraph shall not apply if at the time such option is granted the option price is at least 110 percent of the fair market value of the stock subject to the option and such option either by its terms is not exercisable after the expiration of 5 years from the date such option is granted or is exercised within one year after the date of enactment of this title. For purposes of this subparagraph —

(i) such individual shall be considered as owning the stock owned, directly or indirectly, by or for his brothers and sisters (whether by the whole or half blood), spouse, ancestors, and lineal descendants; and

(ii) stock owned, directly or indirectly, by or for a corporation, partnership, estate, or trust, shall be considered as being owned proportionately by or for its shareholders, partners, or beneficiaries; and

(D) such option by its terms is not exercisable after the expiration of 10 years from the date such option is granted, if such option has been granted on or after June 22, 1954.

(2) *Parent corporation.* — The term "parent corporation" means any corporation (other than the employer corporation) in an unbroken chain of corporations ending with the employer corporation if, at the time of the granting of the option, each of the corporations other than the employer corporation owns stock possessing 50 percent or more of the total combined voting power of all classes of stock in one of the other corporations in such chain.

(3) *Subsidiary corporation.* — The term "subsidiary corporation" means any corporation (other than the employer corporation) in an unbroken chain of corporations beginning with the employer corporation if, at the time of the granting of the option, each of the corporations other than the last corporation in the unbroken chain owns stock possessing 50 percent or more of the total combined voting power of all classes of stock in one of the other corporations in such chain.

(4) *Disposition.* —

(A) *General rule.* — Except as provided in subparagraph (B), the term "disposition" includes a sale, exchange, gift, or a transfer of legal title, but does not include —

(i) a transfer from a decedent to an estate or a transfer by bequest or inheritance;

(ii) an exchange to which section 354, 355, 356, or 1036 (or so much of section 1031 as relates to section 1036) applies; or

(iii) a mere pledge or hypothecation.

(B) *Joint tenancy.* — The acquisition of a share of stock in the name of the employee and another jointly with the right of survivorship or a subsequent transfer of a share of stock into such joint ownership shall not be deemed a disposition, but a termination of such joint tenancy (except to the extent such employee acquires ownership of such stock) shall be treated as a disposition by him occurring at the time such joint tenancy is terminated.

(5) *Stockholder approval.* — If the grant of an option is subject to approval by stockholders, the date of grant of the option shall be determined as if the option had not been subject to such approval.

(6) *Exercise by estate.* —

(A) *In general.* — If a restricted stock option is exercised subsequent to the death of the employee by the estate of the decedent, or by a person who acquired the right to exercise such option by bequest or inheritance or by reason of the death of the decedent, the provisions of this section shall apply to the same extent as if the option had been exercised by the decedent, except that —

(i) the holding period and employment requirements of subsection (a) shall not apply, and

(ii) any transfer by the estate of stock acquired shall be considered a disposition of such stock for purposes of subsection (b).

(B) *Deduction for estate tax.* — If an amount is required to be included under subsection (b) in gross income of the estate of the deceased employee or of a person described in subparagraph (A), there shall be allowed to the estate or such person a deduction with respect to the estate tax attributable to the inclusion in the taxable estate of the deceased employee of the net value for estate tax purposes of the restricted stock option. For this purpose, the deduction shall be determined under section 691(c) as if the option acquired from the deceased employee were an item of gross income in respect of the decedent under section 691 and as if the amount includible in gross income under subsection (b) of this section were an amount included in gross income under section 691 in respect of such item of gross income.

(C) *Basis of shares acquired.* — In the case of a share of stock acquired by the exercise of an option to which subparagraph (A) applies —

(i) the basis of such share shall include so much of the basis of the option as is attributable to such share; except that the basis of such share shall be reduced by the excess (if any) of the amount, which would have been includible in gross income under subsection (b) if the employee had exercised the option and held such share at the time of his death, over the amount which is includible in gross income under subsection (b); and

(ii) the last sentence of subsection (b) shall apply only to the extent that the amount includible in gross income under such subsection exceeds so much of the basis of the option as is attributable to such share.

(7) *Variable price option.* — The term "variable price option" means an option under which the purchase price of the stock is fixed or determinable under a formula in which the only variable is the fair market value of the stock at any time during a period of 6 months, which includes the time the option is exercised; except that in the case of options granted after September 30, 1958, such term does not include any such option in which such formula provides for determining such price by reference to the fair market value of the stock at any time before the option is exercised if such value may be greater than the average fair market value of the stock during the calendar month in which the option is exercised.

(e) *Modification, Extension, or Renewal of Option.* —

(1) *Rules of application.* — For purposes of subsection (d), if the terms of any option to purchase stock are modified, extended, or renewed, the following rules shall be applied with respect to transfers of stock made on the exercise of the option after the making of such modification, extension, or renewal —

(A) such modification, extension, or renewal shall be considered as the granting of a new option,

(B) the fair market value of such stock at the time of the granting of such option shall be considered as —

(i) the fair market value of such stock on the date of the original granting of the option,

(ii) the fair market value of such stock on the date of the making of such modification, extension, or renewal, or

(iii) the fair market value of such stock at the time of the making of any intervening modification, extension, or renewal,

whichever is the highest.

Subparagraph (B) shall not apply if the aggregate of the monthly average fair market values of the stock subject to the option for the 12 consecutive calendar months before the date of the modification, extension, or renewal, divided by 12, is an amount less than 80 percent of the fair market value of such stock on the date of the original granting of the option or the date of the making of any intervening modification, extension, or renewal, whichever is the highest.

(2) *Definition of modification.* — The term "modification" means any change in the terms of the option which gives the employee additional benefits under the option, but such term shall not include a change in the terms of the option —

(A) attributable to the issuance or assumption of an option under subsection (g); or

(B) to permit the option to qualify under subsection (d)(1)(B).

If an option is exercisable after the expiration of 10 years from the date such option is granted, subparagraph (B) shall not apply unless the terms of the option are also changed to make it not exercisable after the expiration of such period.

(f) *Effect of Disqualifying Disposition.* — If a share of stock, acquired by an individual pursuant to his exercise of a restricted stock option, is disposed of by him within 2 years from the date of the granting of the option or within 6 months after the transfer of such share to him, then any increase in the income of such individual or deduction from the income of his employer corporation for the taxable year in which such exercise occurred attributable to such disposition, shall be treated as an increase in income or a deduction from income in the taxable year of such individual or of such employer corporation in which such disposition occurred.

Sec. 453. Installment Method.

(a) *Dealers in Personal Property.* — Under regulations prescribed by the Secretary or his delegate, a person who regularly sells or otherwise disposes of personal property on the installment plan may return as income therefrom in any taxable year that proportion of the installment payments actually received in that year which the gross profit, realized or to be realized when payment is completed, bears to the total contract price.

(b) *Sales of Realty and Casual Sales of Personalty.* —

(1) *General rule.* — Income from —

(A) a sale or other disposition of real property, or

(B) a casual sale or other casual disposition of personal property (other than property of a kind which would properly be included in the inventory of the taxpayer if on hand at the close of the taxable year) for a price exceeding $1,000,

may (under regulations prescribed by the Secretary or his delegate) be returned on the basis and in the manner prescribed in subsection (a).

(2) *Limitation.* — Paragraph (1) shall apply —

(A) In the case of a sale or other disposition during a taxable year beginning after December 31, 1953 (whether or not such taxable year ends after the date of enactment of this title), only if in the taxable year of the sale or other disposition —

(i) there are no payments, or

(ii) the payments (exclusive of evidences of indebtedness of the purchaser) do not exceed 30 per cent of the selling price.

(B) In the case of a sale or other disposition during a taxable year beginning before January 1, 1954, only if the income was (by reason of section 44(b) of the Internal Revenue Code of 1939) returnable on the basis and in the manner prescribed in section 44(a) of such code.

(c) *Change From Accrual to Installment Basis.* —

(1) *General rule.* — If a taxpayer entitled to the benefits of subsection (a) elects for any taxable year to report his taxable income on the installment basis, then in computing his taxable income for such year (referred to in this subsection as "year of change") or for any subsequent year —

(A) installment payments actually received during any such year on account of sales or other dispositions of property made in any taxable year before the year of change shall not be excluded; but

(B) the tax imposed by this chapter for any taxable year (referred to in this subsection as "adjustment year") beginning after December 31, 1953, shall be reduced by the adjustment computed under paragraph (2).

(2) *Adjustment in tax for amounts previously taxed.* — In determining the adjustment referred to in paragraph (1) (B), first determine, for each taxable year before the year of change, the amount which equals the lesser of —

(A) the portion of the tax for such prior taxable year which is attributable to the gross profit which was included in gross income for such prior taxable year, and which by reason of paragraph (1) (A) is includible in gross income for the taxable year, or

(B) the portion of the tax for the adjustment year which is attributable to the gross profit described in subparagraph (A).

The adjustment referred to in paragraph (1) (B) for the adjustment year is the sum of the amounts determined under the preceding sentence.

(3) *Rule for applying paragraph (2).* — For purposes of paragraph (2), the portion of the tax for a prior taxable year, or for the adjustment year, which is attributable to the gross profit described in such paragraph is that amount which bears the same ratio to the tax imposed by this chapter (or by the corresponding provisions of prior revenue laws) for such taxable year (computed without regard to paragraph (2)) as the gross profit described in such paragraph bears to the gross income for such taxable year. For purposes of the preceding sentence, the provisions of chapter 1 (other than of subchapter D, relating to excess profits tax, and of subchapter E, relating to self-employment income) of the Internal Revenue Code of 1939 shall be treated as the corresponding provisions of the Internal Revenue Code of 1939.

(d) *Gain or Loss on Disposition of Installment Obligations.* —

(1) *General rule.* — If an installment obligation is satisfied at other than its face value or distributed, transmitted, sold, or otherwise disposed of, gain or loss shall result to the extent of the difference between the basis of the obligation and —

(A) the amount realized, in the case of satisfaction at other than face value or a sale or exchange, or

(B) the fair market value of the obligation at the time of distribution, transmission, or disposition, in the case of the distribution, transmission, or disposition otherwise than by sale or exchange.

Any gain or loss so resulting shall be considered as resulting from the sale or exchange of the property in respect of which the installment obligation was received.

(2) *Basis of obligation.* — The basis of an installment obligation shall be the excess of the face value of the obligation over an amount equal to the income which would be returnable were the obligation satisfied in full.

(3) *Special rule for transmission at death.* — Except as provided in section 691 (relating to recipients of income in respect of decedents), this subsection shall not apply to the transmission of installment obligations at death.

(4) *Effect of distribution in certain liquidations.* —

(A) *Liquidations to which section 332 applies.* — If —

(i) an installment obligation is distributed by one corporation to another corporation in the course of a liquidation, and

(ii) under section 332 (relating to complete liquidations of subsidiaries) no gain or loss with respect to the receipt of such obligation is recognized in the case of the recipient corporation,

then no gain or loss with respect to the distribution of such obligation shall be recognized in the case of the distributing corporation.

(B) *Liquidations to which section 337 applies.* — If —

(i) an installment obligation is distributed by a corporation in the course of a liquidation, and

(ii) under section 337 (relating to gain or loss on sales or exchanges in connection with certain liquidations) no gain or loss would have been recognized to the corporation if the corporation had sold or exchanged such installment obligation on the day of such distribution,

then no gain or loss shall be recognized to such corporation by reason of such distribution.

(5) *Life insurance companies.* — In the case of a disposition of an installment obligation by any person other than a life insurance company (as defined in section 801(a)) to such an insurance company or to a partnership of which such an insurance company is a partner, no provision of this subtitle providing for the nonrecognition of gain shall apply with respect to any gain resulting under paragraph (1). If a corporation which is a life insurance company for the taxable year was (for the preceding taxable year) a corporation which was not a life insurance company, such corporation shall, for purposes of this paragraph and paragraph (1), be treated as having transferred to a life insurance company, on the last day of the preceding taxable year, all installment obligations which it held on such last day. A partnership of which a life insurance company becomes a partner shall, for purposes of this paragraph and paragraph (1), be treated as having transferred to a life insurance company, on the last day of the preceding taxable year of such partnership, all installment obligations which it holds at the time such insurance company becomes a partner.

Sec. 501. Exemption From Tax on Corporations, Certain Trusts, Etc.

(a) *Exemption From Taxation.* — An organization described in subsection (c) or (d) or section 401 (a) shall be exempt from taxation under this subtitle unless such exemption is denied under section 502, 503, or 504.

(b) *Tax on Unrelated Business Income.* —An organization exempt from taxation under subsection (a) shall be subject to tax to the extent provided in part II of this subchapter (relating to tax on unrelated income), but, notwithstanding part II, shall be considered an organization exempt from income taxes for the purpose of any law which refers to organizations exempt from income taxes.

(c) *List of Exempt Organizations.* — The following organizations are referred to in subsection (a):

(1) Corporations organized under Act of Congress, if such corporations are instrumentalities of the United States and if, under such Act, as amended and supplemented, such corporations are exempt from Federal income taxes.

(2) Corporations organized for the exclusive purpose of holding title to property, collecting income therefrom, and turning over the entire amount thereof, less expenses, to an organization which itself is exempt under this section.

(3) Corporations, and any community chest, fund, or foundation, organized and operated exclusively for religious, charitable, scientific, testing for public safety, literary, or educational purposes, or for the prevention of cruelty to children or animals, no part of the net earnings of which inures to the benefit of any private shareholder or individual, no substantial part of the activities of which is carrying on propaganda, or otherwise attempting, to influence legislation, and which does not participate in, or intervene in (including the publishing or distributing of statements), any political campaign on behalf of any candidate for public office.

(4) Civic leagues or organizations not organized for profit but operated exclusively for the promotion of social welfare, or local associations of employees, the membership of which is limited to the employees of a designated person or persons in a particular municipality, and the net earnings of which are devoted exclusively to charitable, educational, or recreational purposes.

(5) Labor, agricultural, or horticultural organizations.

(6) Business leagues, chambers of commerce, real-estate boards, or boards of trade, not organized for profit and no part of the net earnings of which inures to the benefit of any private shareholder or individual.

(7) Clubs organized and operated exclusively for pleasure, recreation, and other nonprofitable purposes, no part of the net earnings of which inures to the benefit of any private shareholder.

(8) Fraternal beneficiary societies, orders, or associations —

(A) operating under the lodge system or for the exclusive benefit of the members of a fraternity itself operating under the lodge system, and

(B) providing for the payment of life, sick, accident, or other benefits to the members of such society, order, or association or their dependents.

(9) Voluntary employees' beneficiary associations providing for the payment of life, sick, accident, or other benefits to the members of such association or their dependents, if —

(A) no part of their net earnings inures (other than through such payments) to the benefit of any private shareholder or individual, and

(B) 85 percent or more of the income consists of amounts collected from members and amounts contributed to the association by the employer of the members for the sole purpose of making such payments and meeting expenses.

(10) Voluntary employees' beneficiary associations providing for the pay-

ment of life, sick, accident, or other benefits to the members of such association or their dependents or their designated beneficiaries, if —

(A) admission to membership in such association is limited to individuals who are officers or employees of the United States Government, and

(B) no part of the net earnings of such association inures (other than through such payments) to the benefit of any private shareholder or individual.

(11) Teachers' retirement fund associations of a purely local character, if —

(A) no part of their net earnings inures (other than through payment of retirement benefits) to the benefit of any private shareholder or individual, and

(B) the income consists solely of amounts received from public taxation, amounts received from assessments on the teaching salaries of members, and income in respect of investments.

(12) Benevolent life insurance associations of a purely local character, mutual ditch or irrigation companies, mutual or cooperative telephone companies, or life organizations; but only if 85 percent or more of the income consists of amounts collected from members for the sole purpose of meeting losses and expenses.

(13) Cemetery companies owned and operated exclusively for the benefit of their members or which are not operated for profit; and any corporation chartered solely for burial purposes as a cemetery corporation and not permitted by its charter to engage in any business not necessarily incident to that purpose, no part of the net earnings of which inures to the benefit of any private shareholder or individual.

(14) Credit unions without capital stock organized and operated for mutual purposes and without profit; and corporations or associations without capital stock organized before September 1, 1957, and operated for mutual purposes and without profit for the purpose of providing reserve funds for, and insurance of, shares of deposits in —

(A) domestic building and loan associations,

(B) cooperative banks without capital stock organized and operated for mutual purposes and without profit, or

(C) mutual savings banks not having capital stock represented by shares.

(15) Mutual insurance companies or associations other than life or marine (including interinsurers and reciprocal underwriters) if the gross amount received during the taxable year from the items described in section 822(b) (other than paragraph (1)(D) thereof) and premiums (including deposits and assessments) does not exceed $75,000.

(16) Corporations organized by an association subject to part III of this subchapter or members thereof, for the purpose of financing the ordinary crop operations of such members or other producers, and operated in conjunction with such association. Exemption shall not be denied any such corporation because it has capital stock, if the dividend rate of such stock is fixed at not to exceed the legal rate of interest in the State of incorporation or 8 percent per annum, whichever is greater, on the value of the consideration for which the stock was issued, and if substantially all such stock (other than nonvoting preferred stock, the owners of which are not entitled or permitted to participate, directly or indirectly, in the profits of the corporation, on dissolution or otherwise, beyond the fixed dividends) is owned

by such association, or members thereof; nor shall exemption be denied any such corporation because there is accumulated and maintained by it a reserve required by State law or a reasonable reserve for any necessary purpose.

(17)(A) A trust or trusts forming part of a plan providing for the payment of supplemental unemployment compensation benefits, if —

(i) under the plan, it is impossible, at any time prior to the satisfaction of all liabilities with respect to employees under the plan, for any part of the corpus or income to be (within the taxable year or thereafter) used for, or diverted to, any purpose other than the providing of supplemental unemployment compensation benefits,

(ii) such benefits are payable to employees under a classification which is set forth in the plan and which is found by the Secretary or his delegate not to be discriminatory in favor of employees who are officers, shareholders, persons whose principal duties consist of supervising the work of other employees, or highly compensated employees, and

(iii) such benefits do not discriminate in favor of employees who are officers, shareholders, persons whose principal duties consist of supervising the work of other employees, or highly compensated employees. A plan shall not be considered discriminatory within the meaning of this clause merely because the benefits received under the plan bear a uniform relationship to the total compensation, or the basic or regular rate of compensation, of the employees covered by the plan.

(B) In determining whether a plan meets the requirements of subparagraph (A), any benefits provided under any other plan shall not be taken into consideration, except that a plan shall not be considered discriminatory —

(i) merely because the benefits under the plan which are first determined in a nondiscriminatory manner within the meaning of subparagraph (A) are then reduced by any sick, accident, or unemployment compensation benefits received under State or Federal law (or reduced by a portion of such benefits if determined in a nondiscriminatory manner), or

(ii) merely because the plan provides only for employees who are not eligible to receive sick, accident, or unemployment compensation benefits under State or Federal law the same benefits (or a portion of such benefits if determined in a nondiscriminatory manner) which such employees would receive under such laws if such employees were eligible for such benefits, or

(iii) merely because the plan provides only for employees who are not eligible under another plan (which meets the requirements of subparagraph (A)) of supplemental unemployment compensation benefits provided wholly by the employer the same benefits (or a portion of such benefits if determined in a nondiscriminatory manner) which such employees would receive under such other plan if such employees were eligible under such other plan, but only if the employees eligible under both plans would make a classification which would be nondiscriminatory within the meaning of subparagraph (A).

(C) A plan shall be considered to meet the requirements of subparagraph (A) during the whole of any year of the plan if on one day in each quarter it satisfies such requirements.

(D) The term "supplemental unemployment compensation benefits" means only —

(i) benefits which are paid to an employee because of his involuntary separation from the employment of the employer (whether or not such separation is temporary) resulting directly from a reduction in force, the discontinuance of a plant or operation, or other similar conditions, and

(ii) sick and accident benefits subordinate to the benefits described in clause (i).

(E) Exemption shall not be denied under subsection (a) to any organization entitled to such exemption as an association described in paragraph (9) of this subsection merely because such organization provides for the payment of supplemental unemployment benefits (as defined in subparagraph (D)(i).

(d) *Religious and Apostolic Organizations.* — The following organizations are referred to in subsection (a): Religious or apostolic associations or corporations, if such associations or corporations have a common treasury or community treasury, even if such associations or corporations engage in business for the common benefit of the members, but only if the members thereof include (at the time of filing their returns) in their gross income their entire prorata shares, whether distributed or not, of the taxable income of the association or corporation for such year. Any amount so included in the gross income of a member shall be treated as a dividend received.

(e) *Cross Reference.* —

For nonexemption of Communist-controlled organizations, see section 11(b) of the Internal Security Act of 1950 (64 Stat. 997; 50 U.S.C. 790 (b)).

Sec. 503. Requirements for Exemption.

(a) *Denial of Exemption to Organizations Engaged in Prohibited Transactions.* —

(1) *General rule.* —

(A) An organization described in section 501(c)(3) which is subject to the provisions of this section shall not be exempt from taxation under section 501(a) if it has engaged in a prohibited transaction after July 1, 1950.

(B) An organization described in section 501(c)(17) which is subject to the provisions of this section shall not be exempt from taxation under section 501(a) if it has engaged in a prohibited transaction after December 31, 1959.

(C) An organization described in section 401(a) which is subject to the provisions of this section shall not be exempt from taxation under section 501(a) if it has engaged in a prohibited transaction after March 1, 1954.

(2) *Taxable years affected.* — An organization described in section 501(c)(3) or (17) or section 401(a) shall be denied exemption from taxation under section 501(a) by reason of paragraph (1) only for taxable years after the taxable year during which it is notified by the Secretary or his delegate that it has engaged in a prohibited transaction, unless such organization entered into such prohibited transaction with the purpose of diverting corpus or income of the organization from its exempt purposes, and such transaction involved a substantial part of the corpus or income of such organization.

(b) *Organizations to Which Section Applies.* — This section shall apply to any organization described in section 501(c)(3) or (17) or section 401(a) except —

(1) a religious organization (other than a trust);

(2) an educational organization which normally maintains a regular faculty and curriculum and normally has a regularly enrolled body of pupils or students in attendance at the place where its educational activities are regularly carried on;

(3) an organization which normally receives a substantial part of its support (exclusive of income received in the exercise or performance by such organization of its charitable, educational, or other purpose or function constituting the basis for its exemption under section 501(a)) from the United States or any State or political subdivision thereof or from direct or indirect contributions from the general public;

(4) an organization which is operated, supervised, controlled, or principally supported by a religious organization (other than a trust) which is itself not subject to the provisions of this section; and

(5) an organization the principal purposes or functions of which are the providing of medical or hospital care or medical education or medical research or agricultural research.

(c) *Prohibited Transactions.* — For purposes of this section, the term "prohibited transaction" means any transaction in which an organization subject to the provisions of this section —

(1) lends any part of its income or corpus, without the receipt of adequate security and a reasonable rate of interest, to;

(2) pays any compensation, in excess of a reasonable allowance for salaries or other compensation for personal services actually rendered, to;

(3) makes any part of its services available on a preferential basis to;

(4) makes any substantial purchase of securities or any other property, for more than adequate consideration in money or money's worth, from;

(5) sells any substantial part of its securities or other property, for less than an adequate consideration in money or money's worth, to; or

(6) engages in any other transaction which results in a substantial diversion of its income or corpus to;

the creator of such organization (if a trust); a person who has made a substantial contribution to such organization; a member of the family (as defined in section 267(c)(4)) of an individual who is the creator of such trust or who has made a substantial contribution to such organization; or a corporation controlled by such creator or person through the ownership, directly or indirectly, of 50 percent or more of the total combined voting power of all classes of stock entitled to vote or 50 percent or more of the total value of shares of all classes of stock of the corporation.

Sec. 504. Denial of Exemption.

(a) *General Rule.* — In the case of any organization described in section 501(c)(3) to which section 503 is applicable, exemption under section 501 shall be denied for the taxable year if the amounts accumulated out of income during the taxable year or any prior taxable year and not actually paid out by the end of the taxable year —

(1) are unreasonable in amount or duration in order to carryout the charitable, educational, or other purpose or function constituting the basis for exemption under section 501(a) of an organization described in section 501(c)(3); or

(2) are used to a substantial degree for purposes or functions other than those constituting the basis for exemption under section 501(a) of an organization described in section 501(c)(3); or

(3) are invested in such a manner as to jeopardize the carrying out of the

charitable, educational, or other purpose or function constituting the basis for exemption under section 501(a) of an organization described in section 501(c)(3).

Paragraph (1) shall not apply to income attributable to property of a decedent dying before January 1, 1951, which is transferred under his will to a trust created by such will. In the case of a trust created by the will of a decedent dying on or after January 1, 1951, if income is required to be accumulated pursuant to the mandatory terms of the will creating the trust, paragraph (1) shall apply only to income accumulated during a taxable year of the trust beginning more than 21 years after the date of death of the last life in being designated in the trust instrument.

(b) *Cross References.* —

For limitation on charitable contributions in case of unreasonable accumulations by certain trusts, see section 681(c)(2).

Sec. 531. Imposition of Accumulated Earnings Tax.

In addition to other taxes imposed by this chapter, there is hereby imposed for each taxable year on the accumulated taxable income (as defined in section 535) of every corporation described in section 532, an accumulated earnings tax equal to the sum of —

(1) $27\frac{1}{2}$ percent of the accumulated taxable income not in excess of $100,000, plus

(2) $38\frac{1}{2}$ percent of the accumulated taxable income in excess of $100,000.

Sec. 532. Corporations Subject to Accumulated Earnings Tax.

(a) *General Rule.* — The accumulated earnings tax imposed by section 531 shall apply to every corporation (other than those described in subsection (b)) formed or availed of for the purpose of avoiding the income tax with respect to its shareholders or the shareholders of any other corporation, by permitting earnings and profits to accumulate instead of being divided or distributed.

(b) *Exceptions.* — The accumulated earnings tax imposed by section 531 shall not apply to —

(1) a personal holding company (as defined in section 542),

(2) a foreign personal holding company (as defined in section 552), or

(3) a corporation exempt from tax under subchapter F (section 501 and following).

Sec. 641. Imposition of Tax.

(a) *Application of Tax.* — The taxes imposed by this chapter on individuals shall apply to the taxable income of estates or of any kind of property held in trust, including —

(1) income accumulated in trust for the benefit of unborn or unascertained persons or persons with contingent interests, and income accumulated or held for future distribution under the terms of the will or trust;

(2) income which is to be distributed currently by the fiduciary to the beneficiaries, and income collected by a guardian of an infant which is to be held or distributed as the court may direct;

(3) income received by estates of deceased persons during the period of administration or settlement of the estate; and

(4) income which, in the discretion of the fiduciary, may be either distributed to the beneficiaries or accumulated.

(b) *Computation and Payment.* — The taxable income of an estate or trust shall be computed in the same manner as in the case of an individual, except as otherwise provided in this part. The tax shall be computed on such taxable income and shall be paid by the fiduciary.

Sec. 642. Special Rules for Credits and Deductions.

(a) *Credits Against Tax.* —

(1) *Partially Tax-exempt Interest.* — An estate or trust shall be allowed the credit against tax for partially tax-exempt interest provided by section 35 only in respect of so much of such interest as is not properly allocable to any beneficiary under section 652 or 662. If the estate or trust elects under section 171 to treat as amortizable the premium on bonds with respect to the interest on which the credit is allowable under section 35, such credit (whether allowable to the estate or trust or to the beneficiary) shall be reduced under section 171(a)(3).

(2) *Foreign taxes.* — An estate or trust shall be allowed the credit against tax for taxes imposed by foreign countries and possessions of the United States, to the extent allowed by section 901, only in respect of so much of the taxes described in such section as is not properly allocable under such section to the beneficiaries.

(3) *Dividends received by individuals.* — An estate or trust shall be allowed the credit against tax for dividends received provided by section 34 only in respect of so much of such dividends as is not properly allocable to any beneficiary under section 652 or 662. For purposes of determining the time of receipt of dividends under section 34 and section 116, the amount of dividends properly allocable to a beneficiary under section 652 or 662 shall be deemed to have been received by the beneficiary ratably on the same dates that the dividends were received by the estate or trust.

(b) *Deduction for Personal Exemption.* — An estate shall be allowed a deduction of $$600. A trust which, under its governing instrument, is required to distribute all of its income currently shall be allowed a deduction of $300. All other trusts shall be allowed a deduction of $100. The deductions allowed by this subsection shall be in lieu of the deductions allowed under section 151 (relating to deduction for personal exemption).

(c) *Deduction for Amounts Paid or Permanently Set Aside for a Charitable Purpose.* — In the case of an estate or trust (other than a trust meeting the specifications of subpart B) there shall be allowed as a deduction in computing its taxable income (in lieu of the deductions allowed by section 170(a), relating to deduction for charitable, etc., contributions and gifts) any amount of the gross income, without limitation, which pursuant to the terms of the governing instrument is, during the taxable year, paid or permanently set aside for a purpose specified in section 170(c), or is to be used exclusively for religious, charitable, scientific, literary, or educational purposes, or for the prevention of cruelty to children or animals, or for the establishment, acquisition, maintenance or operation of a public cemetery not operated for profit. For this purpose, to the extent that such amount consists of gain from the sale or exchange of capital assets held for more than 6 months, proper adjustment of the deduction otherwise allowable under this subsection shall be made for any deduction allowable to the estate or trust under section 1202 (relating to deduction for excess of capital gains over capital losses). In the case of a trust, the deduction allowed by this subsection shall be subject to section 681 (relating to unrelated business income and prohibited transactions).

(d) *Net Operating Loss Deduction.* — The benefit of the deduction for net operating losses provided by section 172 shall be allowed to estates and trusts under regulations prescribed by the Secretary or his delegate.

(e) *Deduction for Depreciation and Depletion.* — An estate or trust shall be allowed the deduction for depreciation and depletion only to the extent not allowable to beneficiaries under sections 167(g) and 611(b).

(f) *Amortization of Emergency or Grain Storage Facilities.* — The benefit of the deductions for amortization of emergency and grain storage facilities provided by sections 168 and 169 shall be allowed to estates and trusts in the same manner as in the case of an individual. The allowable deduction shall be apportioned between the income beneficiaries and the fiduciary under regulations prescribed by the Secretary or his delegate.

(g) *Disallowance of Double Deductions.* — Amounts allowable under section 2053 or 2054 as a deduction in computing the taxable estate of a decedent shall not be allowed as a deduction in computing the taxable income of the estate, unless there is filed, within the time and in the manner and form prescribed by the Secretary or his delegate, a statement that the amounts have not been allowed as deductions under section 2053 or 2054 and a waiver of the right to have such amounts allowed at any time as deductions under section 2053 or 2054. This subsection shall not apply with respect to deductions allowed under part II (relating to income in respect of decedents).

(h) *Unused Loss Carryovers and Excess Deductions on Termination Available to Beneficiaries.* — If on the termination of an estate or trust, the estate or trust has —

(1) a net operating loss carryover under section 172 or a capital loss carryover under section 1212, or

(2) for the last taxable year of the estate or trust deductions (other than the deductions allowed under subsections (b) or (c)) in excess of gross income for such year,

then such carryover or such excess shall be allowed as a deduction, in accordance with regulations prescribed by the Secretary or his delegate, to the beneficiaries succeeding to the property of the estate or trust.

(i) *Cross Reference.* —

For disallowance of standard deduction in case of estates and trusts see section 142(b)(4).

Sec. 643. Definitions Applicable to Subparts A, B, C, and D.

(a) *Distributable Net Income.* — For purposes of this part, the term "distributable net income" means, with respect to any taxable year, the taxable income of the estate or trust computed with the following modifications —

(1) *Deduction for distributions.* — No deduction shall be taken under sections 651 and 661 (relating to additional deductions).

(2) *Deduction for personal exemption.* — No deduction shall be taken under section 642(b) (relating to deduction for personal exemptions).

(3) *Capital gains and losses.* — Gains from the sale or exchange of capital assets shall be excluded to the extent that such gains are allocated to corpus and are not (A) paid, credited, or required to be distributed to any beneficiary during the taxable year, or (B) paid, permanently set aside, or to be used for the purposes specified in section 642(c). Losses from the sale or exchange of capital assets shall be excluded, except to the extent such losses are taken into account in determining the amount of gains from the sale or exchange of capital assets which are paid, credited, or required to be distributed to any beneficiary during the taxable year. The deduction under section 1202 (relating to deduction for excess of capital gains over capital losses) shall not be taken into account.

(4) *Extraordinary dividends and taxable stock dividends.* — For purposes only of subpart B (relating to trusts which distribute current income only),

there shall be excluded those items of gross income constituting extraordinary dividends or taxable stock dividends which the fiduciary, acting in good faith, does not pay or credit to any beneficiary by reason of his determination that such dividends are allocable to corpus under the terms of the governing instrument and applicable local law.

(5) *Tax-exempt interest.* — There shall be included any tax-exempt interest to which section 103 applies, reduced by any amounts which would be deductible in respect of disbursements allocable to such interest but for the provisions of section 265 (relating to disallowance of certain deductions).

(6) *Foreign income.* — In the case of a foreign trust, there shall be included the amounts of gross income from sources without the United States, reduced by any amounts which would be deductible in respect of disbursements allocable to such income but for the provisions of section 265(1) (relating to disallowance of certain deductions).

(7) *Dividends.* — There shall be included the amount of any dividends excluded from gross income pursuant to section 116 (relating to partial exclusion of dividends received).

If the estate or trust is allowed a deduction under section 642(c), the amount of the modifications specified in paragraphs (5) and (6) shall be reduced to the extent that the amount of income which is paid, permanently set aside, or to be used for the purposes specified in section 642(c) is deemed to consist of items specified in those paragraphs. For this purpose, such amount shall (in the absence of specific provisions in the governing instrument) be deemed to consist of the same proportion of each class of items of income of the estate or trust as the total of each class bears to the total of all classes.

(b) *Income.* — For purposes of this subpart and subparts B, C, and D, the term "income", when not preceded by the words "taxable", "distributable net", "undistributed net", or "gross", means the amount of income of the estate or trust for the taxable year determined under the terms of the governing instrument and applicable local law. Items of gross income constituting extraordinary dividends or taxable stock dividends which the fiduciary, acting in good faith, determines to be allocable to corpus under the terms of the governing instrument and applicable local law shall not be considered income.

(c) *Beneficiary.* — For purposes of this part, the term "beneficiary" includes heir, legatee, devisee.

Sec. 651. Deduction for Trusts Distributing Current Income Only.

(a) *Deduction.* — In the case of any trust the terms of which —

(1) provide that all of its income is required to be distributed currently, and

(2) do not provide that any amounts are to be paid, permanently set aside, or used for the purposes specified in sections 642(c) (relating to deduction for charitable, etc., purposes),

there shall be allowed as a deduction in computing the taxable income of the trust the amount of the income for the taxable year which is required to be distributed currently. This section shall not apply in any taxable year in which the trust distributes amounts other than amounts of income described in paragraph (1).

(b) *Limitation on Deduction.* — If the amount of income required to be distributed currently exceeds the distributable net income of the trust for the taxable year, the deduction shall be limited to the amount of the distributable net income. For this purpose, the computation of distributable net income shall not include items of income which are not included in the gross income of the trust and the deductions allocable thereto.

Sec. 652. **Inclusion of Amounts in Gross Income of Beneficiaries of Trusts Distributing Current Income Only.**

(a) *Inclusion.* — Subject to subsection (b), the amount of income for the taxable year required to be distributed currently by a trust described in section 651 shall be included in the gross income of the beneficiaries to whom the income is required to be distributed, whether distributed or not. If such amount exceeds the distributable net income, there shall be included in the gross income of each beneficiary an amount which bears the same ratio to distributable net income as the amount of income required to be distributed to such beneficiary bears to the amount of income required to be distributed to all beneficiaries.

(b) *Character of Amounts.* — The amounts specified in subsection (a) shall have the same character in the hands of the beneficiary as in the hands of the trust. For this purpose, the amounts shall be treated as consisting of the same proportion of each class of items entering into the computation of distributable net income of the trust as the total of each class bears to the total distributable net income of the trust, unless the terms of the trust specifically allocate different classes of income to different beneficiaries. In the application of the preceding sentence, the items of deduction entering into the computation of distributable net income shall be allocated among the items of distributable net income in accordance with regulations prescribed by the Secretary or his delegate.

(c) *Different Taxable Years.* — If the taxable year of a beneficiary is different from that of the trust, the amount which the beneficiary is required to include in gross income in accordance with the provisions of this section shall be based upon the amount of income of the trust for any taxable year, or years of the trust ending within or with his taxable year.

Sec. 661. **Deduction for Estates and Trusts Accumulating Income or Distributing Corpus.**

(a) *Deduction.* — In any taxable year there shall be allowed as a deduction in computing the taxable income of an estate or trust (other than a trust to which subpart B applies), the sum of —

(1) any amount of income for such taxable year required to be distributed currently (including any amount required to be distributed which may be paid out of income or corpus to the extent such amount is paid out of income for such taxable year); and

(2) any other amounts properly paid or credited or required to be distributed for such taxable year;

but such deduction shall not exceed the distributable net income of the estate or trust.

(b) *Character of Amounts Distributed.* — The amount determined under subsection (a) shall be treated as consisting of the same proportion of each class of items entering into the computation of distributable net income of the estate or trust as the total of each class bears to the total distributable net income of the estate or trust in the absence of the allocation of different classes of income under the specific terms of the governing instrument. In the application of the preceding sentence, the items of deduction entering into the computation of distributable net income (including the deduction allowed under section 642(c)) shall be allocated among the items of distributable net income in accordance with regulations prescribed by the Secretary or his delegate.

(c) *Limitation on Deduction.* — No deduction shall be allowed under subsection (a) in respect of any portion of the amount allowed as a deduction under that subsection (without regard to this subsection) which is treated under subsection (b) as consisting of any item of distributable net income which is not included in the gross income of the estate or trust.

Sec. 662. Inclusion of Amounts in Gross Income of Beneficiaries of Estates and Trusts Accumulating Income or Distributing Corpus.

(a) *Inclusion.* — Subject to subsection (b), there shall be included in the gross income of a beneficiary to whom an amount specified in section 661(a) is paid, credited, or required to be distributed (by an estate or trust described in section 661), the sum of the following amounts:

(1) *Amounts required to be distributed currently.* — The amount of income for the taxable year required to be distributed currently to such beneficiary, whether distributed or not. If the amount of income required to be distributed currently to all beneficiaries exceeds the distributable net income (computed without the deduction allowed by section 642(c), relating to deduction for charitable, etc. purposes) of the estate or trust, then, in lieu of the amount provided in the preceding sentence, there shall be included in the gross income of the beneficiary an amount which bears the same ratio to distributable net income (as so computed) as the amount of income required to be distributed currently to such beneficiary bears to the amount required to be distributed currently to all beneficiaries. For purposes of this section, the phrase "the amount of income for the taxable year required to be distributed currently" includes any amount required to be paid out of income or corpus to the extent such amount is paid out of income for such taxable year.

(2) *Other amounts distributed.* — All other amounts properly paid, credited, or required to be distributed to such beneficiary for the taxable year. If the sum of —

(A) the amount of income for the taxable year required to be distributed currently to all beneficiaries, and

(B) all other amounts properly paid, credited, or required to be distributed to all beneficiaries

exceeds the distributable net income of the estate or trust, then, in lieu of the amount provided in the preceding sentence, there shall be included in the gross income of the beneficiary an amount which bears the same ratio to distributable net income (reduced by the amounts specified in (A)) as the other amounts properly paid, credited or required to be distributed to the beneficiary bear to the other amounts properly paid, credited, or required to be distributed to all beneficiaries.

(b) *Character of Amounts.* — The amounts determined under subsection (a) shall have the same character in the hands of the beneficiary as in the hands of the estate or trust. For this purpose, the amounts shall be treated as consisting of the same proportion of each class of items entering into the computation of distributable net income as the total of each class bears to the total distributable net income of the estate or trust unless the terms of the governing instrument specifically allocate different classes of income to different beneficiaries. In the application of the preceding sentence, the items of deduction entering into the computation of distributable net income (including the deduction allowed under section 642(c)) shall be allocated among the items of distributable net income in accordance with regulations prescribed by the Secretary or his delegate. In the application of this subsection to the amount determined under paragraph (1) of subsection (a), distributable net income shall be computed without regard to any portion of the deduction under section 642(c) which is not attributable to income of the taxable year.

(c) *Different Taxable Years.* — If the taxable year of a beneficiary is different from that of the estate or trust, the amount to be included in the gross income of the beneficiary shall be based on the distributable net income of the estate or trust and the amounts properly paid, credited, or required to be distributed to the beneficiary during any taxable year or years of the estate or trust ending within or with his taxable year.

Sec. 663. Special Rules Applicable to Sections 661 and 662.
(a) *Exclusions.* — There shall not be included as amounts falling within section 661(a) or 662(a) —

(1) *Gifts, bequests, etc.* — Any amount which, under the terms of the governing instrument, is properly paid or credited as a gift or bequest of a specific sum of money or of specific property and which is paid or credited all at once or in not more than 3 installments. For this purpose an amount which can be paid or credited only from the income of the estate or trust shall not be considered as a gift or bequest of a specific sum of money.

(2) *Charitable, etc., distributions.* — Any amount paid or permanently set aside or otherwise qualifying for the deduction provided in section 642(c) (computed without regard to section 681).

(3) *Denial of double deduction.* — Any amount paid, credited, or distributed in the taxable year, if section 651 or section 661 applied to such amount for a preceding taxable year of an estate or trust because credited or required to be distributed in such preceding taxable year.

(b) *Distributions in First Sixty-five Days of Taxable Year.* —
(1) *General rule.* — If within the first 65 days of any taxable year of a trust, an amount is properly paid or credited, such amount shall be considered paid or credited on the last day of the preceding taxable year.

(2) *Limitation.* — This subsection shall apply only to a trust —
(A) which was in existence prior to January 1, 1954,
(B) which, under the terms of its governing instrument, may not distribute in any taxable year amounts in excess of the income of the preceding taxable year, and
(C) on behalf of which the fiduciary elects to have this subsection apply.

The election authorized by subparagraph (C) shall be made for the first taxable year to which this part is applicable in accordance with such regulations as the Secretary or his delegate shall prescribe and shall be made not later than the time prescribed by law for filing the return for such year (including extensions thereof). If such election is made with respect to a taxable year, this subsection shall apply to all amounts properly paid or credited within the first 65 days of all subsequent taxable years of such trust.

(c) *Separate Shares Treated as Separate Trusts.* — For the sole purpose of determining the amount of distributable net income in the application of sections 661 and 662, in the case of a single trust having more than one beneficiary, substantially separate and independent shares of different beneficiaries in the trust shall be treated as separate trusts. The existence of such substantially separate and independent shares and the manner of treatment as separate trusts, including the application of subpart D, shall be determined in accordance with regulations prescribed by the Secretary or his delegate.

Sec. 665. Definitions Applicable to Subpart D.
(a) *Undistributed Net Income.* — For purposes of this subpart, the term "undistributed net income" for any taxable year means the amount by which

distributable net income of the trust for such taxable year exceeds the sum of —

(1) the amounts for such taxable year specified in paragraphs (1) and (2) of section 661(a); and

(2) the amount of taxes imposed on the trust.

(b) *Accumulation Distribution.* — For purposes of this subpart, the term "accumulation distribution" for any taxable year of the trust means the amount (if in excess of $2,000) by which the amounts specified in paragraph (2) of section 661(a) for such taxable year exceed distributable net income reduced by the amounts specified in paragraph (1) of section 661(a). For purposes of this subsection, the amount specified in paragraph (2) of section 661(a) shall be determined without regard to section 666 and shall not include —

(1) amounts paid, credited, or required to be distributed to a beneficiary as income accumulated before the birth of such beneficiary or before such beneficiary attains the age of 21;

(2) amounts properly paid or credited to a beneficiary to meet the emergency needs of such beneficiary;

(3) amounts properly paid or credited to a beneficiary upon such beneficiary's attaining a specified age or ages if —

(A) the total number of such distributions cannot exceed 4 with respect to such beneficiary,

(B) the period between each such distribution to such beneficiary is 4 years or more, and

(C) as of January 1, 1954, such distributions are required by the specific terms of the governing instrument; and

(4) amounts properly paid or credited to a beneficiary as a final distribution of the trust if such final distribution is made more than 9 years after the date of the last transfer to such trust.

(c) *Taxes Imposed on the Trust.* — For purposes of this subpart, the term "taxes imposed on the trust" means the amount of the taxes which are imposed for any taxable year on the trust under this chapter (without regard to this subpart) and which, under regulations prescribed by the Secretary or his delegate, are properly allocable to the undistributed portion of the distributable net income. The amount determined in the preceding sentence shall be reduced by any amount of such taxes allowed, under sections 667 and 668, as a credit to any beneficiary on account of any accumulation distribution determined for any taxable year.

(d) *Preceding Taxable Year.* — For purposes of this subpart, the term "preceding taxable year" does not include any taxable year of the trust to which this part does not apply. In the case of a preceding taxable year with respect to which a trust qualifies (without regard to this subpart) under the provisions of subpart B, for purposes of the application of this subpart to such trust for such taxable year, such trust shall, in accordance with regulations prescribed by the Secretary or his delegate, be treated as a trust to which subpart C applies.

Sec. 666. Accumulation Distribution Allocated to 5 Preceding Years.

(a) *Amount Allocated.* — In the case of a trust which for a taxable year beginning after December 31, 1953, is subject to subpart C, the amount of the accumulation distribution of such trust for such taxable year shall be deemed to be an amount within the meaning of paragraph (2) of section 661(a) distributed on the last day of each of the 5 preceding taxable years to the extent that such amount exceeds the total of any undistributed net incomes for any taxable years intervening between the taxable year with respect to which the accumulation distribution is determined and such preceding taxable year. The amount deemed to be distributed in any such preceding taxable year under the preceding sentence shall not exceed the undistributed net income of such preceding taxable year. For purposes of this subsection, undistributed net income for each of such 5 preceding taxable years shall be computed without regard to such accumulation distribution and without regard to any accumulation distribution determined for any succeeding taxable year.

(b) *Total Taxes Deemed Distributed.* — If any portion of an accumulation distribution for any taxable year is deemed under subsection (a) to be an amount within the meaning of paragraph (2) of section 661(a) distributed on the last day of any preceding taxable year, and such portion of such accumulation distribution is not less than the undistributed net income for such preceding taxable year, the trust shall be deemed to have distributed on the last day of such preceding taxable year an additional amount within the meaning of paragraph (2) of section 661(a). Such additional amount shall be equal to the taxes imposed on the trust for such preceding taxable year. For purposes of this subsection, the undistributed net income and the taxes imposed on the trust for such preceding taxable year shall be computed without regard to such accumulation distribution and without regard to any accumulation distribution determined for any succeeding taxable year.

(c) *Pro Rata Portion of Taxes Deemed Distributed.* — If any portion of an accumulation distribution for any taxable year is deemed under subsection (a) to be an amount within the meaning of paragraph (2) of section 661(a) distributed on the last day of any preceding taxable year and such portion of the accumulation distribution is less than the undistributed net income for such preceding taxable year, the trust shall be deemed to have distributed on the last day of such preceding taxable year an additional amount within the meaning of paragraph (2) of section 661(a). Such additional amount shall be equal to the taxes imposed on the trust for such taxable year multiplied by the ratio of the portion of the accumulation distribution to the undistributed net income of the trust for such year. For purposes of this subsection, the undistributed net income and the taxes imposed on the trust for such preceding taxable year shall be computed without regard to the accumulation distribution and without regard to any accumulation distribution determined for any succeeding taxable year.

Sec. 667. Denial of Refund to Trusts.

The amount of taxes imposed on the trust under this chapter, which would not have been payable by the trust for any preceding taxable year had the trust in fact made distributions at the times and in the amounts deemed under section 666, shall not be refunded or credited to the trust, but shall be allowed as a credit under section 668(b) against the tax of the beneficiaries who are treated as having received the distributions. For purposes of the preceding sentence, the amount of taxes which may not be refunded or credited to the trust shall be an amount equal to the excess of (1) the taxes imposed on the trust for any preceding taxable year (computed without regard to the accumulation distribution for the taxable year) over (2) the amount of taxes for such preceding taxable year imposed on the undistributed portion of distributable net income of the trust for such preceding taxable year after the application of this subpart on account of the accumulation distribution determined for such taxable year.

Sec. 668. Treatment of Amounts Deemed Distributed in Preceding Years.

(a) *Amounts Treated as Received in Prior Taxable Years.* — The total of the amounts which are treated under section 666 as having been distributed by the trust in a preceding taxable year shall be included in the income of a beneficiary or beneficiaries of the trust when paid, credited, or required to be distributed to the extent that such total would have been included in the income of such beneficiary or beneficiaries under section 662(a)(2) and (b) if such total had been paid to such beneficiary or beneficiaries on the last day of such preceding taxable year. The portion of such total included under the preceding sentence in the income of any beneficiary shall be based upon the same ratio as determined under the second sentence of section 662(a)(2) for the taxable year in respect of which the accumulation distribution is determined, except that proper adjustment of such ratio shall be made, in accordance with regulations prescribed by the Secretary or his delegate, for amounts which fall within paragraphs (1) through (4) of section 665(b). The tax of the beneficiaries attributable to the amounts treated as having been received on the last day of such preceding taxable year of the trust shall not be greater than the aggregate of the taxes attributable to those amounts had they been included in the gross income of the beneficiaries on such day in accordance with section 662(a)(2) and (b).

(b) *Credit for Taxes Paid by Trust.* — The tax imposed on beneficiaries under this chapter shall be credited with a pro rata portion of the taxes imposed on the trust under this chapter for such preceding taxable year which would not have been payable by the trust for such preceding taxable year had the trust in fact made distributions to such beneficiaries at the times and in the amounts specified in section 666.

Sec. 671. Trust Income, Deductions, and Credits Attributable to Grantors and Others as Substantial Owners.

Where it is specified in this subpart that the grantor or another person shall be treated as the owner of any portion of a trust, there shall then be included in computing the taxable income and credits of the grantor or the other person those items of income, deductions, and credits against tax of the trust which are attributable to that portion of the trust to the extent that such items would be taken into account under this chapter in computing taxable income or credits against the tax of an individual. Any remaining portion of the trust shall be subject to subparts A through D. No items of a trust shall be included in computing the taxable income and credits of the grantor or of any other person solely on the grounds of his dominion and control over the trust under section 61 (relating to definition of gross income) or any other provision of this title, except as specified in this subpart.

Sec. 672. Definitions and Rules.

(a) *Adverse Party.* — For purposes of this subpart, the term "adverse party" means any person having a substantial beneficial interest in the trust which would be adversely affected by the exercise or nonexercise of the power which he possesses respecting the trust. A person having a general power of appointment over the trust property shall be deemed to have a beneficial interest in the trust.

(b) *Nonadverse Party.* — For purposes of this subpart, the term "nonadverse party" means any person who is not an adverse party.

(c) *Related or Subordinate Party.* — For purposes of this subpart, the term "related or subordinate party" means any nonadverse party who is —

(1) the grantor's spouse if living with the grantor;

(2) any one of the following: The grantor's father, mother, issue, brother or sister; an employee of the grantor; a corporation or any employee of a corporation in which the stock holdings of the grantor and the trust are significant from the viewpoint of voting control; a subordinate employee of a corporation in which the grantor is an executive.

For purposes of sections 674 and 675, a related or subordinate party shall be presumed to be subservient to the grantor in respect of the exercise or non-exercise of the powers conferred on him unless such party is shown not to be subservient by a preponderance of the evidence.

(d) *Rule Where Power Is Subject to Condition Precedent.* — A person shall be considered to have a power described in this subpart even though the exercise of the power is subject to a precedent giving of notice or takes effect only on the expiration of a certain period after the exercise of the power.

Sec. 673. Reversionary Interests.

(a) *General Rule.* — The grantor shall be treated as the owner of any portion of a trust in which he has a reversionary interest in either the corpus or the income therefrom if, as of the inception of that portion of the trust, the interest will or may reasonably be expected to take effect in possession or enjoyment within 10 years commencing with the date of the transfer of that portion of the trust.

(b) *Exception Where Income Is Payable to Charitable Beneficiaries.* — Subsection (a) shall not apply to the extent that the income of a portion of a trust in which the grantor has a reversionary interest is, under the terms of the trust, irrevocably payable for a period of at least 2 years (commencing with the date of the transfer) to a designated beneficiary, which beneficiary is of a type described in section 170(b)(1)(A)(i), (ii), or (iii).

(c) *Reversionary Interest Taking Effect at Death of Income Beneficiary.* — The grantor shall not be treated under subsection (a) as the owner of any portion of a trust where his reversionary interest in such portion is not to take effect in possession or enjoyment until the death of the person or persons to whom the income therefrom is payable.

(d) *Postponement of Date Specified for Reacquisition.* — Any postponement of the date specified for the reacquisition of possession or enjoyment of the reversionary interest shall be treated as a new transfer in trust commencing with the date on which the postponement is effected and terminating with the date prescribed by the postponement. However, income for any period shall not be included in the income of the grantor by reason of the preceding sentence if such income would not be so includible in the absence of such postponement.

Sec. 674. Power to Control Beneficial Enjoyment.

(a) *General Rule.* — The grantor shall be treated as the owner of any portion of a trust in respect of which the beneficial enjoyment of the corpus or the income therefrom is subject to a power of disposition, exercisable by the grantor or a nonadverse party, or both, without the approval or consent of any adverse party.

(b) *Exceptions for Certain Powers.* — Subsection (a) shall not apply to the following powers regardless of by whom held:

(1) *Power to apply income to support of a dependent.* — A power described in section 677(b) to the extent that the grantor would not be subject to tax under that section.

(2) *Power affecting beneficial enjoyment only after expiration of 10-year period.* — A power, the exercise of which can only affect the beneficial enjoyment of the income for a period commencing after the expiration of a period such that a grantor would not be treated as the owner under section 673 if the power were a reversionary interest; but the grantor may be treated as the owner after the expiration of the period unless the power is relinquished.

(3) *Power exercisable only by will.* — A power exercisable only by will, other than a power in the grantor to appoint by will the income of the trust where the income is accumulated for such disposition by the grantor or may be so accumulated in the discretion of the grantor or a nonadverse party, or both, without the approval or consent of any adverse party.

(4) *Power to allocate among charitable beneficiaries.* — A power to determine the beneficial enjoyment of the corpus or the income therefrom if the corpus or income is irrevocably payable for a purpose specified in section 170(c) (relating to definition of charitable contributions).

(5) *Power to distribute corpus.* — A power to distribute corpus either —

(A) to or for a beneficiary or beneficiaries or to or for a class of beneficiaries (whether or not income beneficiaries) provided that the power is limited by a reasonably definite standard which is set forth in the trust instrument; or

(B) to or for any current income beneficiary, provided that the distribution of corpus must be chargeable against the proportionate share of corpus held in trust for the payment of income to the beneficiary as if the corpus constituted a separate trust.

A power does not fall within the powers described in this paragraph if any person has a power to add to the beneficiary or beneficiaries or to a class of beneficiaries designated to receive the income or corpus, except where such action is to provide for after-born or after-adopted children.

(6) *Power to withhold income temporarily.* — A power to distribute or apply income to or for any current income beneficiary or to accumulate the income for him, provided that any accumulated income must ultimately be payable —

(A) to the beneficiary from whom distribution or application is withheld, to his estate, or to his appointees (or persons named as alternate takers in default of appointment) provided that such beneficiary possesses a power of appointment which does not exclude from the class of possible appointees any person other than the beneficiary, his estate, his creditors, or the creditors of his estate, or

(B) on termination of the trust, or in conjunction with a distribution of corpus which is augmented by such accumulated income, to the current income beneficiaries in shares which have been irrevocably specified in the trust instrument.

Accumulated income shall be considered so payable although it is provided that if any beneficiary does not survive a date of distribution which could reasonably have been expected to occur within the beneficiary's lifetime, the share of the deceased beneficiary is to be paid to his appointees or to one or more designated alternate takers (other than the grantor or the grantor's estate) whose shares have been irrevocably specified. A power does not fall within the powers described in this paragraph if any person has a power to add to the beneficiary or beneficiaries or to a class of beneficiaries designated to receive the income or corpus except where such action is to provide for after-born or after-adopted children.

(7) *Power to withhold income during disability of a beneficiary.* — A power exercisable only during —

(A) the existence of a legal disability of any current income beneficiary, or

(B) the period during which any income beneficiary shall be under the age of 21 years,

to distribute or apply income to or for such beneficiary or to accumulate and add the income to corpus. A power does not fall within the powers described in this paragraph if any person has a power to add to the beneficiary or beneficiaries or to a class of beneficiaries designated to receive the income or corpus, except where such action is to provide for after-born or after-adopted children.

(8) *Power to allocate between corpus and income.* — A power to allocate receipts and disbursements as between corpus and income, even though expressed in broad language.

(c) *Exception for Certain Powers of Independent Trustees.* — Subsection (a) shall not apply to a power solely exercisable (without the approval or consent of any other person) by a trustee or trustees, none of whom is the grantor, and no more than half of whom are related or subordinate parties who are subservient to the wishes of the grantor —

(1) to distribute, apportion, or accumulate income to or for a beneficiary or beneficiaries, or to, for, or within a class of beneficiaries; or

(2) to pay out corpus to or for a beneficiary or beneficiaries or to or for a class of beneficiaries (whether or not income beneficiaries).

A power does not fall within the powers described in this subsection if any person has a power to add to the beneficiary or beneficiaries or to a class of beneficiaries designated to receive the income or corpus, except where such action is to provide for after-born or after-adopted children.

(d) *Power to Allocate Income if Limited by a Standard.* — Subsection (a) shall not apply to a power solely exercisable (without the approval or consent of any other person) by a trustee or trustees, none of whom is the grantor or spouse living with the grantor, to distribute, apportion, or accumulate income to or for a beneficiary or beneficiaries, or to, for, or within a class of beneficiaries, whether or not the conditions of paragraph (6) or (7) of subsection (b) are satisfied, if such power is limited by a reasonably definite external standard which is set forth in the trust instrument. A power does not fall within the powers described in this subsection if any person has a power to add to the beneficiary or beneficiaries or to a class of beneficiaries designated to receive the income or corpus except where such action is to provide for after-born or after-adopted children.

Sec. 675. Administrative Powers.

The grantor shall be treated as the owner of any portion of a trust in respect of which —

(1) *Power to deal for less than adequate and full consideration.* — A power exercisable by the grantor or a nonadverse party, or both, without the approval or consent of any adverse party enables the grantor or any person to purchase, exchange, or otherwise deal with or dispose of the corpus or the income therefrom for less than an adequate consideration in money or money's worth.

(2) *Power to borrow without adequate interest or security.* — A power exercisable by the grantor or a nonadverse party, or both, enables the grantor to borrow the corpus or income, directly or indirectly, without adequate in-

terest or without adequate security except where a trustee (other than the grantor) is authorized under a general lending power to make loans to any person without regard to interest or security.

(3) *Borrowing of the trust funds.* — The grantor has directly or indirectly borrowed the corpus or income and has not completely repaid the loan, including any interest, before the beginning of the taxable year. The preceding sentence shall not apply to a loan which provides for adequate interest and adequate security, if such loan is made by a trustee other than the grantor and other than a related or subordinate trustee subservient to the grantor.

(4) *General powers of administration.* — A power of administration is exercisable in a nonfiduciary capacity by any person without the approval or consent of any person in a fiduciary capacity. For purposes of this paragraph, the term "power of administration" means any one or more of the following powers: (A) a power to vote or direct the voting of stock or other securities of a corporation in which the holdings of the grantor and the trust are significant from the viewpoint of voting control; (B) a power to control the investment of the trust funds either by directing investments or reinvestments, or by vetoing proposed investments or reinvestments, to the extent that the trust funds consist of stocks or securities of corporations in which the holdings of the grantor and the trust are significant from the viewpoint of voting control; or (C) a power to reacquire the trust corpus by substituting other property of an equivalent value.

Sec. 676. Power to Revoke.

(a) *General Rule.* — The grantor shall be treated as the owner of any portion of a trust, whether or not he is treated as such owner under any other provision of this part, where at any time the power to revest in the grantor title to such portion is exercisable by the grantor or a nonadverse party, or both.

(b) *Power Affecting Beneficial Enjoyment Only After Expiration of 10-Year Period.* — Subsection (a) shall not apply to a power the exercise of which can only affect the beneficial enjoyment of the income for a period commencing after the expiration of a period such that a grantor would not be treated as the owner under section 673 if the power were a reversionary interest. But the grantor may be treated as the owner after the expiration of such period unless the power is relinquished.

Sec. 677. Income for Benefit of Grantor.

(a) *General Rule.* — The grantor shall be treated as the owner of any portion of a trust, whether or not he is treated as such owner under section 674, whose income without the approval or consent of any adverse party is, or, in the discretion of the grantor or a nonadverse party, or both, may be —

(1) distributed to the grantor;

(2) held or accumulated for future distribution to the grantor; or

(3) applied to the payment of premiums on policies of insurance on the life of the grantor (except policies of insurance irrevocably payable for a purpose specified in section 170(c) (relating to definition of charitable contributions)).

This subsection shall not apply to a power the exercise of which can only affect the beneficial enjoyment of the income for a period commencing after the expiration of a period such that the grantor would not be treated as the owner under section 673 if the power were a reversionary interest; but the grantor may be treated as the owner after the expiration of the period unless the power is relinquished.

(b) *Obligations of Support.* — Income of a trust shall not be considered taxable to the grantor under subsection (a) or any other provision of this chapter merely because such income in the discretion of another person, the trustee, or the grantor acting as trustee or co-trustee, may be applied or distributed for the support or maintenance of a beneficiary whom the grantor is legally obligated to support or maintain, except to the extent that such income is so applied or distributed. In cases where the amounts so applied or distributed are paid out of corpus or out of other than income for the taxable year, such amounts shall be considered to be an amount paid or credited within the meaning of paragraph (2) of section 661(a) and shall be taxed to the grantor under section 662.

Sec. 678. Person Other Than Grantor Treated as Substantial Owner.

(a) *General Rule.* — A person other than the grantor shall be treated as the owner of any portion of a trust with respect to which:

(1) such person has a power exercisable solely by himself to vest the corpus or the income therefrom in himself, or

(2) such person has previously partially released or otherwise modified such a power and after the release or modification retains such control as would, within the principles of sections 671 to 677, inclusive, subject a grantor of a trust to treatment as the owner thereof.

(b) *Exception Where Grantor Is Taxable.* — Subsection (a) shall not apply with respect to a power over income, as originally granted or thereafter modified, if the grantor of the trust is otherwise treated as the owner under sections 671 to 677, inclusive.

(c) *Obligations of Support.* — Subsection (a) shall not apply to a power which enables such person, in the capacity of trustee or co-trustee, merely to apply the income of the trust to the support or maintenance of a person whom the holder of the power is obligated to support or maintain except to the extent that such income is so applied. In cases where the amounts so applied or distributed are paid out of corpus or out of other than income of the taxable year, such amounts shall be considered to be an amount paid or credited within the meaning of paragraph (2) of section 661(a) and shall be taxed to the holder of the power under section 662.

(d) *Effect of Renunciation or Disclaimer.* — Subsection (a) shall not apply with respect to a power which has been renounced or disclaimed within a reasonable time after the holder of the power first became aware of its existence.

Sec. 691. Recipients of Income in Respect of Decedents.

(a) *Inclusion in Gross Income.* —

(1) *General rule.* — The amount of all items of gross income in respect of a decedent which are not properly includible in respect of the taxable period in which falls the date of his death or a prior period (including the amount of all items of gross income in respect of a prior decedent, if the right to receive such amount was acquired by reason of the death of the prior decedent or by bequest, devise, or inheritance from the prior decedent) shall be included in the gross income, for the taxable year when received, of:

(A) the estate of the decedent, if the right to receive the amount is acquired by the decedent's estate from the decedent;

(B) the person who, by reason of the death of the decedent, acquires the right to receive the amount, if the right to receive the amount is not acquired by the decedent's estate from the decedent; or

(C) the person who acquires from the decedent the right to receive the amount by bequest, devise, or inheritance, if the amount is received after a distribution by the decedent's estate of such right.

(2) *Income in case of sale, etc.* — If a right, described in paragraph (1), to receive an amount is transferred by the estate of the decedent or a person who received such right by reason of the death of the decedent or by bequest, devise, or inheritance from the decedent, there shall be included in the gross income of the estate or such person, as the case may be, for the taxable period in which the transfer occurs, the fair market value of such right at the time of such transfer plus the amount by which any consideration for the transfer exceeds such fair market value. For purposes of this paragraph, the term "transfer" includes sale, exchange, or other disposition, or the satisfaction of an installment obligation at other than face value, but does not include transmission at death to the estate of the decedent or a transfer to a person pursuant to the right of such person to receive such amount by reason of the death of the decedent or by bequest, devise, or inheritance from the decedent.

(3) *Character of income determined by reference to decedent.* — The right, described in paragraph (1), to receive an amount shall be treated, in the hands of the estate of the decedent or any person who acquired such right by reason of the death of the decedent, or by bequest, devise, or inheritance from the decedent, as if it had been acquired by the estate or such person in the transaction in which the right to receive the income was originally derived and the amount includible in gross income under paragraph (1) or (2) shall be considered in the hands of the estate or such person to have the character which it would have had in the hands of the decedent if the decedent had lived and received such amount.

(4) *Installment obligations acquired from decedent.* — In the case of an installment obligation received by a decedent on the sale or other disposition of property, the income from which was properly reportable by the decedent on the installment basis under section 453, if such obligation is acquired by the decedent's estate from the decedent or by any person by reason of the death of the decedent or by bequest, devise, or inheritance from the decedent —

(A) an amount equal to the excess of the face amount of such obligation over the basis of the obligation in the hands of the decedent (determined under section 453(d)) shall, for the purpose of paragraph (1), be considered as an item of gross income in respect of the decedent; and

(B) such obligation shall, for purposes of paragraphs (2) and (3), be considered a right to receive an item of gross income in respect of the decedent, but the amount includible in gross income under paragraph (2) shall be reduced by an amount equal to the basis of the obligation in the hands of the decedent (determined under section 453(d)).

(b) *Allowance of Deductions and Credit.* — The amount of any deduction specified in section 162, 163, 164, 212, or 611 (relating to deductions for expenses, interest, taxes, and depletion) or credit specified in section 33 (relating to foreign tax credit), in respect of a decedent which is not properly allowable to the decedent in respect of the taxable period in which falls the date of his death, or a prior period, shall be allowed:

(1) *Expenses, interest, and taxes.* — In the case of a deduction specified in section 162, 163, 164, or 212 and a credit specified in section 33, in the taxable year when paid —

(A) to the estate of the decedent; except that

(B) if the estate of the decedent is not liable to discharge the obligation to which the deduction or credit relates, to the person who, by reason of the death of the decedent or by bequest, devise, or inheritance acquires, subject to such obligation, from the decedent an interest in property of the decedent.

(2) *Depletion.* — In the case of the deduction specified in section 611, to the person described in subsection (a)(1)(A), (B), or (C) who, in the manner described therein, receives the income to which the deduction relates, in the taxable year when such income is received.

(c) *Deduction for Estate Tax.* —

(1) *Allowance of deduction.* —

(A) *General rule.* — A person who includes an amount in gross income under subsection (a) shall be allowed, for the same taxable year, as a deduction an amount which bears the same ratio to the estate tax attributable to the net value for estate tax purposes of all the items described in subsection (a)(1) as the value for estate tax purposes of the items of gross income or portions thereof in respect of which such person included the amount in gross income (or the amount included in gross income, whichever is lower) bears to the value for estate tax purposes of all the items described in subsection (a)(1).

(B) *Estates and trusts.* — In the case of an estate or trust, the amount allowed as a deduction under subparagraph (A) shall be computed by excluding from the gross income of the estate or trust the portion (if any) of the items described in subsection (a)(1) which is properly paid, credited, or to be distributed to the beneficiaries during the taxable year. This subparagraph shall apply to the same taxable years, and to the same extent, as is provided in section 683.

(2) *Method of computing deduction.* — For purposes of paragraph (1) —

(A) The term "estate tax" means the tax imposed on the estate of the decedent or any prior decedent under section 2001 or 2101, reduced by the credits against such tax.

(B) The net value for estate tax purposes of all the items described in subsection (a)(1) shall be the excess of the value for estate tax purposes of all the items described in subsection (a)(1) over the deductions from the gross estate in respect of claims which represent the deductions and credit described in subsection (b). Such net value shall be determined with regard to the provisions of section 421(d)(6)(B), relating to the deduction for estate tax with respect to restricted stock options.

(C) The estate tax attributable to such net value shall be an amount equal to the excess of the estate tax over the estate tax computed without including in the gross estate such net value.

(d) *Amounts Received by Surviving Annuitant Under Joint and Survivor Annuity Contract.* —

(1) *Deduction for estate tax.* — For purposes of computing the deduction under subsection (c)(1)(A), amounts received by a surviving annuitant —

(A) as an annuity under a joint and survivor annuity contract where the decedent annuitant died after December 31, 1953, and after the annuity starting date (as defined in section 72(c)(4)), and

(B) during the surviving annuitant's life expectancy period,
shall, to the extent included in gross income under section 72, be considered
as amounts included in gross income under subsection (a).

(2) *Net value for estate tax purposes.* — In determining the net value for
estate tax purposes under subsection (c)(2)(B) for purposes of this subsection, the value for estate tax purposes of the items described in paragraph
(1) of this subsection shall be computed —

(A) by determining the excess of the value of the annuity at the date
of the death of the deceased annuitant over the total amount excludible
from the gross income of the surviving annuitant under section 72 during the surviving annuitant's life expectancy period, and

(B) by multiplying the figure so obtained by the ratio which the value
of the annuity for estate tax purposes bears to the value of the annuity at
the date of the death of the deceased.

(3) *Definitions.* — For purposes of this subsection —

(A) The term "life expectancy period" means the period beginning
with the first day of the first period for which an amount is received by
the surviving annuitant under the contract and ending with the close of
the taxable year with or in which falls the termination of the life expectancy of the surviving annuitant. For purposes of this subparagraph,
the life expectancy of the surviving annuitant shall be determined, as of
the date of the death of the deceased annuitant, with reference to actuarial tables prescribed by the Secretary or his delegate.

(B) The surviving annuitant's expected return under the contract
shall be computed, as of the death of the deceased annuitant, with reference to actuarial tables prescribed by the Secretary or his delegate.

(e) *Cross Reference.* —

For application of this section to income in respect of a deceased partner, see section 753.

Sec. 704. Partner's Distributive Share.

(e) *Family Partnerships.* —

(1) *Recognition of interest created by purchase or gift.* — A person shall
be recognized as a partner for purposes of this subtitle if he owns a capital
interest in a partnership in which capital is a material income-producing
factor, whether or not such interest was derived by purchase or gift from
any other person.

(2) *Distributive share of donee includible in gross income.* — In the case
of any partnership interest created by gift, the distributive share of the
donee under the partnership agreement shall be includible in his gross income, except to the extent that such share is determined without allowance
of reasonable compensation for services rendered to the partnership by the
donor, and except to the extent that the portion of such share attributable
to donated capital is proportionately greater than the share of the donor
attributable to the donor's capital. The distributive share of a partner in
the earnings of the partnership shall not be diminished because of absence
due to military service.

(3) *Purchase of interest by member of family.* — For purposes of this section, an interest purchased by one member of a family from another shall
be considered to be created by gift from the seller, and the fair market
value of the purchased interest shall be considered to be donated capital.
The "family" of any individual shall include only his spouse, ancestors, and
lineal descendants, and any trusts for the primary benefit of such persons.

Sec. 705. Determination of Basis of Partner's Interest.

(a) *General Rule.* — The adjusted basis of a partner's interest in a partnership shall, except as provided in subsection (b), be the basis of such interest determined under section 722 (relating to contributions to a partnership) or section 742 (relating to transfers of partnership interests) —

(1) increased by the sum of his distributive share for the taxable year and prior taxable years of —

(A) taxable income of the partnership as determined under section 703(a),

(B) income of the partnership exempt from tax under this title, and

(C) the excess of the deductions for depletion over the basis of the property subject to depletion; and

(2) decreased (but not below zero) by distributions by the partnership as provided in section 733 and by the sum of his distributive share for the taxable year and prior taxable years of —

(A) losses of the partnership, and

(B) expenditures of the partnership not deductible in computing its taxable income and not properly chargeable to capital account.

(b) *Alternative Rule.* — The Secretary or his delegate shall prescribe by regulations the circumstances under which the adjusted basis of a partner's interest in a partnership may be determined by reference to his proportionate share of the adjusted basis of partnership property upon a termination of the partnership.

Sec. 731. Extent of Recognition of Gain or Loss on Distribution.

(a) *Partners.* — In the case of a distribution by a partnership to a partner —

(1) gain shall not be recognized to such partner, except to the extent that any money distributed exceeds the adjusted basis of such partner's interest in the partnership immediately before the distribution, and

(2) loss shall not be recognized to such partner, except that upon a distribution in liquidation of a partner's interest in a partnership where no property other than that described in subparagraph (A) or (B) is distributed to such partner, loss shall be recognized to the extent of the excess of the adjusted basis of such partner's interest in the partnership over the sum of —

(A) any money distributed, and

(B) the basis to the distributee, as determined under section 732, of any unrealized receivables (as defined in section 751(c)) and inventory (as defined in section 751(d)(2)).

Any gain or loss recognized under this subsection shall be considered as gain or loss from the sale or exchange of the partnership interest of the distributee partner.

(b) *Partnerships.* — No gain or loss shall be recognized to a partnership on a distribution to a partner of property, including money.

(c) *Exceptions.* — This section shall not apply to the extent otherwise provided by section 736 (relating to payments to a retiring partner or a deceased partner's successor in interest) and section 751 (relating to unrealized receivables and inventory items).

Sec. 736. Payments to a Retiring Partner or a Deceased Partner's Successor in Interest.

(a) *Payments Considered as Distributive Share or Guaranteed Payment.* — Payments made in liquidation of the interest of a retiring partner or a deceased partner shall, except as provided in subsection (b), be considered —

(1) as a distributive share to the recipient of partnership income if the amount thereof is determined with regard to the income of the partnership, or

(2) as a guaranteed payment described in section 707(c) if the amount thereof is determined without regard to the income of the partnership.

(b) *Payments for Interest in Partnership.* —

(1) *General rule.* — Payments made in liquidation of the interest of a retiring partner or a deceased partner shall, to the extent such payments (other than payments described in paragraph (2)) are determined, under regulations prescribed by the Secretary or his delegate, to be made in exchange for the interest of such partner in partnership property, be considered as a distribution by the partnership and not as a distributive share or guaranteed payment under subsection (a).

(2) *Special rules.* — For purposes of this subsection, payments in exchange for an interest in partnership property shall not include amounts paid for —

(A) unrealized receivables of the partnership (as defined in section 751(c)), or

(B) good will of the partnership, except to the extent that the partnership agreement provides for a payment with respect to good will.

Sec. 751. Unrealized Receivables and Inventory Items.

(a) *Sale or Exchange of Interest in Partnership.* — The amount of any money, or the fair market value of any property, received by a transferor partner in exchange for all or a part of his interest in the partnership attributable to —

(1) unrealized receivables of the partnership, or

(2) inventory items of the partnership which have appreciated substantially in value,

shall be considered as an amount realized from the sale or exchange of property other than a capital asset.

(b) *Certain Distributions Treated as Sales or Exchanges.* —

(1) *General rule.* — To the extent a partner receives in a distribution —

(A) partnership property described in subsection (a)(1) or (2) in exchange for all or a part of his interest in other partnership property (including money), or

(B) partnership property (including money) other than property described in subsection (a)(1) or (2) in exchange for all or a part of his interest in partnership property described in subsection (a)(1) or (2),

such transactions shall, under regulations prescribed by the Secretary or his delegate, be considered as a sale or exchange of such property between the distributee and the partnership (as constituted after the distribution).

(2) *Exceptions.* — Paragraph (1) shall not apply to —

(A) a distribution of property which the distributee contributed to the partnership, or

(B) payments, described in section 736(a), to a retiring partner or successor in interest of a deceased partner.

(c) *Unrealized Receivables.* — For purposes of this subchapter, the term "unrealized receivables" includes, to the extent not previously includible in income under the method of accounting used by the partnership, any rights (contractual or otherwise) to payment for —

(1) goods delivered, or to be delivered, to the extent the proceeds there-

from would be treated as amounts received from the sale or exchange of property other than a capital asset, or

(2) services rendered, or to be rendered.

(d) *Inventory Items Which Have Appreciated Substantially in Value.* —

(1) *Substantial appreciation.* — Inventory items of the partnership shall be considered to have appreciated substantially in value if their fair market value exceeds —

(A) 120 percent of the adjusted basis to the partnership of such property, and

(B) 10 percent of the fair market value of all partnership property, other than money.

(2) *Inventory items.* — For purposes of this subchapter the term "inventory items" means —

(A) property of the partnership of the kind described in section 1221(1),

(B) any other property of the partnership which, on sale or exchange by the partnership, would be considered property other than a capital asset and other than property described in section 1231, and

(C) any other property held by the partnership which, if held by the selling or distributee partner, would be considered property of the type described in subparagraph (A) or (B).

Sec. 753.   Partner Receiving Income in Respect of Decedent.

The amount includible in the gross income of a successor in interest of a deceased partner under section 736(a) shall be considered income in respect of a decedent under section 691.

Sec. 1012.   Basis of Property — Cost.

The basis of property shall be the cost of such property, except as otherwise provided in this subchapter and subchapters C (relating to corporate distributions and adjustments), K (relating to partners and partnerships), and P (relating to capital gains and losses).   The cost of real property shall not include any amount in respect of real property taxes which are treated under section 164(d) as imposed on the taxpayer.

Sec. 1014.   Basis of Property Acquired From a Decedent.

(a) *In General.* — Except as otherwise provided in this section, the basis of property in the hands of a person acquiring the property from a decedent or to whom the property passed from a decedent shall, if not sold, exchanged, or otherwise disposed of before the decedent's death by such person, be the fair market value of the property at the date of the decedent's death, or, in the case of an election under either section 2032 or section 811(j) of the Internal Revenue Code of 1939 where the decedent died after October 21, 1942, its value at the applicable valuation date prescribed by those sections.

(b) *Property Acquired From the Decedent.* — For purposes of subsection (a), the following property shall be considered to have been acquired from or to have passed from the decedent:

(1) Property acquired by bequest, devise, or inheritance, or by the decedent's estate from the decedent;

(2) Property transferred by the decedent during his lifetime in trust to pay the income for life to or on the order or direction of the decedent, with the right reserved to the decedent at all times before his death to revoke the trust;

(3) In the case of decedents dying after December 31, 1951, property

transferred by the decedent during his lifetime in trust to pay the income for life to or on the order or direction of the decedent with the right reserved to the decedent at all times before his death to make any change in the enjoyment thereof through the exercise of a power to alter, amend, or terminate the trust;

(4) Property passing without full and adequate consideration under a general power of appointment exercised by the decedent by will;

(5) In the case of decedents dying after August 26, 1937, property acquired by bequest, devise, or inheritance or by the decedent's estate from the decedent, if the property consists of stock or securities of a foreign corporation, which with respect to its taxable year next preceding the date of the decedent's death was, under the law applicable to such year, a foreign personal holding company. In such case, the basis shall be the fair market value of such property at the date of the decedent's death or the basis in the hands of the decedent, whichever is lower;

(6) In the case of decedents dying after December 31, 1947, property which represents the surviving spouse's one-half share of community property held by the decedent and the surviving spouse under the community property laws of any State, Territory, or possession of the United States or any foreign country, if at least one-half of the whole of the community interest in such property was includible in determining the value of the decedent's gross estate under chapter 11 of subtitle B (section 2001 and following, relating to estate tax) or section 811 of the Internal Revenue Code of 1939;

(7) In the case of decedents dying after October 21, 1942, and on or before December 31, 1947, such part of any property, representing the surviving spouse's one-half share of property held by a decedent and the surviving spouse under the community property laws of any State, Territory, or possession of the United States or any foreign country, as was included in determining the value of the gross estate of the decedent, if a tax under chapter 3 of the Internal Revenue Code of 1939 was payable on the transfer of the net estate of the decedent. In such case, nothing in this paragraph shall reduce the basis below that which would exist if the Revenue Act of 1948 had not been enacted;

(8) In the case of decedents dying after December 31, 1950, and before January 1, 1954, property which represents the survivor's interest in a joint and survivor's annuity if the value of any part of such interest was required to be included in determining the value of decedent's gross estate under section 811 of the Internal Revenue Code of 1939;

(9) In the case of decedents dying after December 31, 1953, property acquired from the decedent by reason of death, form of ownership, or other conditions (including property acquired through the exercise or non-exercise of a power of appointment), if by reason thereof the property is required to be included in determining the value of the decedent's gross estate under chapter 11 of subtitle B or under the Internal Revenue Code of 1939. In such case, if the property is acquired before the death of the decedent, the basis shall be the amount determined under subsection (a) reduced by the amount allowed to the taxpayer as deductions in computing taxable income under this subtitle or prior income tax laws for exhaustion, wear and tear, obsolescence, amortization, and depletion on such property before the death of the decedent. Such basis shall be applicable to the property commencing on the death of the decedent. This paragraph shall not apply to —

(A) annuities described in section 72;

(B) property to which paragraph (5) would apply if the property had been acquired by bequest; and

(C) property described in any other paragraph of this subsection.

(c) *Property Representing Income in Respect of a Decedent.* — This section shall not apply to property which constitutes a right to receive an item of income in respect of a decedent under section 691.

Sec. 1015. Basis of Property Acquired by Gifts and Transfers in Trust.

(a) *Gifts After December 31, 1920.* — If the property was acquired by gift after December 31, 1920, the basis shall be the same as it would be in the hands of the donor or the last preceding owner by whom it was not acquired by gift, except that if such basis (adjusted for the period before the date of the gift as provided in section 1016) is greater than the fair market value of the property at the time of the gift, then for the purpose of determining loss the basis shall be such fair market value. If the facts necessary to determine the basis in the hands of the donor or the last preceding owner are unknown to the donee, the Secretary or his delegate shall, if possible, obtain such facts from such donor or last preceding owner, or any other person cognizant thereof. If the Secretary or his delegate finds it impossible to obtain such facts, the basis in the hands of such donor or last preceding owner shall be the fair market value of such property as found by the Secretary or his delegate as of the date or approximate date at which, according to the best information that the Secretary or his delegate is able to obtain, such property was acquired by such donor or last preceding owner.

(b) *Transfer in Trust After December 31, 1920.* — If the property was acquired after December 31, 1920, by a transfer in trust (other than by a transfer in trust by a gift, bequest, or devise), the basis shall be the same as it would be in the hands of the grantor increased in the amount of gain or decreased in the amount of loss recognized to the grantor on such transfer under the law applicable to the year in which the transfer was made.

(c) *Gift or Transfer in Trust Before January 1, 1921.* — If the property was acquired by gift or transfer in trust on or before December 31, 1920, the basis shall be the fair market value of such property at the time of such acquisition.

(d) *Increased Basis for Gift Tax Paid.* —

(1) *In general.* — If —

(A) the property is acquired by gift on or after the date of the enactment of the Technical Amendments Act of 1958, the basis shall be the basis determined under subsection (a), increased (but not above the fair market value of the property at the time of the gift) by the amount of gift tax paid with respect to such gift, or

(B) the property was acquired by gift before the date of the enactment of the Technical Amendments Act of 1958 and has not been sold, exchanged, or otherwise disposed of before such date, the basis of the property shall be increased on such date by the amount of gift tax paid with respect to such gift, but such increase shall not exceed an amount equal to the amount by which the fair market value of the property at the time of the gift exceeded the basis of the property in the hands of the donor at the time of the gift.

(2) *Amount of tax paid with respect to gift.* — For purposes of paragraph (1), the amount of gift tax paid with respect to any gift is an amount which bears the same ratio to the amount of gift tax paid under chapter 12 with respect to all gifts made by the donor for the calendar year in which

such gift is made as the amount of such gift bears to the taxable gifts (as defined in section 2503(a) but computed without the deduction allowed by section 2521) made by the donor during such calendar year. For purposes of the preceding sentence, the amount of any gift shall be the amount included with respect to such gift in determining (for the purposes of section 2503(a)) the total amount of gifts made during the calendar year, reduced by the amount of any deduction allowed with respect to such gift under section 2522 (relating to charitable deduction) or under section 2523 (relating to marital deduction).

(3) *Gifts treated as made one-half by each spouse.* — For purposes of paragraph (1), where the donor and his spouse elected, under section 2513 to have the gift considered as made one-half by each, the amount of gift tax paid with respect to such gift under chapter 12 shall be the sum of the amounts of tax paid with respect to each half of such gift (computed in the manner provided in paragraph (2)).

(4) *Treatment as adjustment to basis.* — For purposes of section 1016 (b), an increase in basis under paragraph (1) shall be treated as an adjustment under section 1016(a).

(5) *Application to gifts before 1955.* — With respect to any property acquired by gift before 1955, references in this subsection to any provision of this title shall be deemed to refer to the corresponding provision of the Internal Revenue Code of 1939 or prior revenue laws which was effective for the year in which such gift was made.

Sec. 1033. Involuntary Conversions.

(a) *General Rule.* — If property (as a result of its destruction in whole or in part, theft, seizure, or requisition or condemnation or threat or imminence thereof) is compulsorily or involuntarily converted —

(1) *Conversion into similar property.* — Into property similar or related in service or use to the property so converted, no gain shall be recognized.

(2) *Conversion into money where disposition occurred prior to 1951.* — Into money, and the disposition of the converted property occurred before January 1, 1951, no gain shall be recognized if such money is forthwith in good faith, under regulations prescribed by the Secretary or his delegate, expended in the acquisition of other property similar or related in service or use to the property so converted, or in the acquisition of control of a corporation owning such other property, or in the establishment of a replacement fund. If any part of the money is not so expended, the gain shall be recognized to the extent of the money which is not so expended (regardless of whether such money is received in one or more taxable years and regardless of whether or not the money which is not so expended constitutes gain). For purposes of this paragraph and paragaph (3), the term "disposition of the converted property" means the destruction, theft, seizure, requisition, or condemnation of the converted property, or the sale or exchange of such property under threat or imminence of requisition or condemnation. For purposes of this paragraph and paragraph (3), the term "control" means the ownership of stock possessing at least 80 percent of the total combined voting power of all classes of stock entitled to vote and at least 80 percent of the total number of shares of all other classes of stock of the corporation.

(3) *Conversion into money where disposition occurred after 1950.* — Into money or into property not similar or related in service or use to the converted property, and the disposition of the converted property (as defined in paragraph (2)) occurred after December 31, 1950, the gain (if any) shall

be recognized except to the extent hereinafter provided in this paragraph:

(A) *Nonrecognition of gain.* — If the taxpayer during the period specified in subparagraph (B), for the purpose of replacing the property so converted, purchases other property similar or related in service or use to the property so converted, or purchases stock in the acquisition of control of a corporation owning such other property, at the election of the taxpayer the gain shall be recognized only to the extent that the amount realized upon such conversion (regardless of whether such amount is received in one or more taxable years) exceeds the cost of such other property or such stock. Such election shall be made at such time and in such manner as the Secretary or his delegate may by regulations prescribe. For purposes of this paragraph —

(i) no property or stock acquired before the disposition of the converted property shall be considered to have been acquired for the purpose of replacing such converted property unless held by the taxpayer on the date of such disposition; and

(ii) the taxpayer shall be considered to have purchased property or stock only if, but for the provisions of subsection (c) of this section, the unadjusted basis of such property or stock would be its cost within the meaning of section 1012.

(B) *Period within which property must be replaced.* — The period referred to in subparagraph (A) shall be the period beginning with the date of the disposition of the converted property, or the earliest date of the threat or imminence or requisition or condemnation of the converted property, which ever is the earlier, and ending —

(i) one year after the close of the first taxable year in which any part of the gain upon the conversion is realized, or

(ii) subject to such terms and conditions as may be specified by the Secretary or his delegate, at the close of such later date as the Secretary or his delegate may designate on application by the taxpayer. Such application shall be made at such time and in such manner as the Secretary or his delegate may by regulations prescribe.

(C) *Time for assessment of deficiency attributable to gain upon conversion.* — If a taxpayer has made the election provided in subparagraph (A), then —

(i) the statutory period for the assessment of any deficiency, for any taxable year in which any part of the gain on such conversion is realized, attributable to such gain shall not expire prior to the expiration of 3 years from the date the Secretary or his delegate is notified by the taxpayer (in such manner as the Secretary or his delegate may by regulations prescribe) of the replacement of the converted property or of an intention not to replace, and

(ii) such deficiency may be assessed before the expiration of such 3-year period notwithstanding the provisions of section 6212(c) or the provisions of any other law or rule of law which would otherwise prevent such assessment.

(D) *Time for assessment of other deficiencies attributable to election.* — If the election provided in subparagraph (A) is made by the taxpayer and such other property or such stock was purchased before the beginning of the last taxable year in which any part of the gain upon such conversion is realized, any deficiency, to the extent resulting from such election, for any taxable year ending before such last taxable year may be assessed (notwithstanding the provisions of section 6212(c) or 6501 or the provisions of any other law or rule of law which would otherwise prevent such assessment) at any time before the expiration of the period within which a deficiency for such last taxable year may be assessed.

(b) *Residence of Taxpayer.* — Subsection (a) shall not apply, in the case of property used by the taxpayer as his principal residence, if the destruction, theft, seizure, requisition, or condemnation of the residence, or the sale or exchange of such residence under threat or imminence thereof, occurred after December 31, 1950, and before January 1, 1954.

(c) *Basis of Property Acquired Through Involuntary Conversion.* — If the property was acquired, after February 28, 1913, as the result of a compulsory or involuntary conversion described in subsection (a)(1) or (2), the basis shall be the same as in the case of the property so converted, decreased in the amount of any money received by the taxpayer which was not expended in accordance with the provisions of law (applicable to the year in which such conversion was made) determining the taxable status of the gain or loss upon such conversion, and increased in the amount of gain or decreased in the amount of loss to the taxpayer recognized upon such conversion under the law applicable to the year in which such conversion was made. This subsection shall not apply in respect of property acquired as a result of a compulsory or involuntary conversion of property used by the taxpayer as his principal residence if the destruction, theft, seizure, requisition, or condemnation of such residence, or the sale or exchange of such residence under threat or imminence thereof, occurred after December 31, 1950, and before January 1, 1954. In the case of property purchased by the taxpayer in a transaction described in subsection (a)(3) which resulted in the nonrecognition of any part of the gain realized as the result of a compulsory or involuntary conversion, the basis shall be the cost of such property decreased in the amount of the gain not so recognized; and if the property purchased consists of more than one piece of property, the basis determined under this sentence shall be allocated to the purchased properties in proportion to their respective costs.

(d) *Property Sold Pursuant to Reclamation Laws.* — For purposes of this subtitle, if property lying within an irrigation project is sold or otherwise disposed of in order to conform to the acreage limitation provisions of Federal reclamation laws, such sale or disposition shall be treated as an involuntary conversion to which this section applies.

(e) *Livestock Destroyed by Disease.* — For purposes of this subtitle, if livestock are destroyed by or on account of disease, or are sold or exchanged because of disease, such destruction or such sale or exchange shall be treated as an involuntary conversion to which this section applies.

(f) *Livestock Sold on Account of Drought.* — For purposes of this subtitle, the sale or exchange of livestock (other than poultry) held by a taxpayer for draft, breeding, or dairy purposes in excess of the number the taxpayer would sell if he followed his usual business practices shall be treated as an involuntary conversion to which this section applies if such livestock are sold or exchanged by the taxpayer solely on account of drought.

(g) *Condemnation of Real Property Held for Productive Use in Trade or Business or for Investment.* —

(1) *Special rule.* — For purposes of subsection (a), if real property (not including stock in trade or other property held primarily for sale) held for productive use in trade or business or for investment is (as the result of its seizure, requisition, or condemnation, or threat or imminence thereof) compulsorily or involuntarily converted, property of a like kind to be held either for productive use in trade or business or for investment shall be

treated as property similar or related in service or use to the property so converted.

(2) *Limitations.* —

(A) *Purchase of stock.* — Paragraph (1) shall not apply to the purchase of stock in the acquisition of control of a corporation described in subsection (a)(3)(A).

(B) *Conversions before January 1, 1958.* — Paragraph (1) shall apply with respect to the compulsory or involuntary conversion of any real property only if the disposition of the converted property (within the meaning of subsection (a)(2)) occurs after December 31, 1957.

(h) *Cross References.* —

(1) For determination of the period for which the taxpayer has held property involuntarily converted, see section 1223.

(2) For treatment of gains from involuntary conversions as capital gains in certain cases, see section 1231(a).

Sec. 1035.   Certain Exchanges of Insurance Policies.

(a) *General Rules.* — No gain or loss shall be recognized on the exchange of —

(1) a contract of life insurance for another contract of life insurance or for an endowment or annuity contract; or

(2) a contract of endowment insurance (A) for another contract of endowment insurance which provides for regular payments beginning at a date not later than the date payments would have begun under the contract exchanged, or (B) for an annuity contract; or

(3) an annuity contract for an annuity contract.

(b) *Definitions.* — For the purpose of this section —

(1) *Endowment contract.* — A contract of endowment insurance is a contract with a life insurance company as defined in section 801 which depends in part on the life expectancy of the insured, but which may be payable in full in a single payment during his life.

(2) *Annuity contract.* — An annuity contract is a contract to which paragraph (1) applies but which may be payable during the life of the annuitant only in installments.

(3) *Life insurance contract.* — A contract of life insurance is a contract to which paragraph (1) applies but which is not ordinarily payable in full during the life of the insured.

(c) *Cross References.* —

(1) For rules relating to recognition of gain or loss where an exchange is not solely in kind, see subsections (b) and (c) of section 1031.

(2) For rules relating to the basis of property acquired in an exchange described in subsection (a), see subsection (d) of section 1031.

Sec. 2001.   Rate of Tax.

A tax computed in accordance with the following table is hereby imposed on the transfer of the taxable estate, determined as provided in section 2051, of every decedent, citizen or resident of the United States dying after the date of enactment of this title:

If the taxable estate is:	The tax shall be:
Not over $5,000	3% of the taxable estate.
Over $5,000 but not over $10,000	$150, plus 7% of excess over $5,000.

If the taxable estate is:	The tax shall be:
Over $10,000 but not over $20,000.......	$500, plus 11% of excess over $10,000.
Over $20,000 but not over $30,000........	$1,600, plus 14% of excess over $20,000.
Over $30,000 but not over $40,000........	$3,000, plus 18% of excess over $30,000.
Over $40,000 but not over $50,000........	$4,800, plus 22% of excess over $40,000.
Over $50,000 but not over $60,000........	$7,000, plus 25% of excess over $50,000.
Over $60,000 but not over $100,000.......	$9,500, plus 28% of excess over $60,000.
Over $100,000 but not over $250,000......	$20,700, plus 30% of excess over $100,000.
Over $250,000 but not over $500,000......	$65,700, plus 32% of excess over $250,000.
Over $500,000 but not over $750,000......	$145,700, plus 35% of excess over $500,000.
Over $750,000 but not over $1,000,000.....	$233,200, plus 37% of excess over $750,000.
Over $1,000,000 but not over $1,250,000...	$325,700, plus 39% of excess over $1,000,000.
Over $1,250,000 but not over $1,500,000...	$423,200, plus 42% of excess over $1,250,000.
Over $1,500,000 but not over $2,000,000...	$528,200, plus 45% of excess over $1,500,000.
Over $2,000,000 but not over $2,500,000...	$753,200, plus 49% of excess over $2,000,000.
Over $2,500,000 but not over $3,000,000...	$998,200, plus 53% of excess over $2,500,000.
Over $3,000,000 but not over $3,500,000...	$1,263,200, plus 56% of excess over $3,000,000.
Over $3,500,000 but not over $4,000,000...	$1,543,200, plus 59% of excess over $3,500,000.
Over $4,000,000 but not over $5,000,000...	$1,838,200, plus 63% of excess over $4,000,000.
Over $5,000,000 but not over $6,000,000...	$2,468,200, plus 67% of excess over $5,000,000.
Over $6,000,000 but not over $7,000,000...	$3,138,200, plus 70% of excess over $6,000,000.
Over $7,000,000 but not over $8,000,000...	$3,838,200, plus 73% of excess over $7,000,000.
Over $8,000,000 but not over $10,000,000..	$4,568,200, plus 76% of excess over $8,000,000.
Over $10,000,000......................	$6,088,200, plus 77% of excess over $10,000,000.

Sec. 2002. Liability for Payment.
The tax imposed by this chapter shall be paid by the executor.

Sec. 2011. Credit for State Death Taxes.
(a) *In General.* — The tax imposed by section 2001 shall be credited with

the amount of any estate, inheritance, legacy, or succession taxes actually paid to any State or Territory or the District of Columbia, in respect of any property included in the gross estate (not including any such taxes paid with respect to the estate of a person other than the decedent).

(b) *Amount of Credit.* — The credit allowed by this section shall not exceed the appropriate amount stated in the following table:

If the taxable estate is:	The maximum tax credit shall be:
Not over $90,000	8/10ths of 1% of the amount by which the taxable estate exceeds $40,000.
Over $90,000 but not over $140,000	$400 plus 1.6% of the excess over $90,000.
Over $140,000 but not over $240,000	$1,200 plus 2.4% of the excess over $140,000.
Over $240,000 but not over $440,000	$3,600 plus 3.2% of the excess over $240,000.
Over $440,000 but not over $640,000	$10,000 plus 4% of the excess over $440,000.
Over $640,000 but not over $840,000	$18,000 plus 4.8% of the excess over $640,000.
Over $840,000 but not over $1,040,000	$27,600 plus 5.6% of the excess over $840,000.
Over $1,040,000 but not over $1,540,000	$38,800 plus 6.4% of the excess over $1,040,000.
Over $1,540,000 but not over $2,040,000	$70,800 plus 7.2% of the excess over $1,540,000.
Over $2,040,000 but not over $2,540,000	$106,800 plus 8% of the excess over $2,040,000.
Over $2,540,000 but not over $3,040,000	$146,800 plus 8.8% of the excess over $2,540,000.
Over $3,040,000 but not over $3,540,000	$190,800 plus 9.6% of the excess over $3,040,000.
Over $3,540,000 but not over $4,040,000	$238,800 plus 10.4% of the excess over $3,540,000.
Over $4,040,000 but not over $5,040,000	$290,800 plus 11.2% of the excess over $4,040,000.
Over $5,040,000 but not over $6,040,000	$402,800 plus 12% of the excess over $5,040,000.
Over $6,040,000 but not over $7,040,000	$522,800 plus 12.8% of the excess over $6,040,000.
Over $7,040,000 but not over $8,040,000	$650,800 plus 13.6% of the excess over $7,040,000.
Over $8,040,000 but not over $9,040,000	$786,800 plus 14.4% of the excess over $8,040,000.
Over $9,040,000 but not over $10,040,000	$930,800 plus 15.2% of the excess over $9,040,000.
Over $10,040,000	$1,082,800 plus 16% of the excess over $10,040,000.

(c) *Period of Limitations on Credit.* — The credit allowed by this section shall include only such taxes as were actually paid and credit therefor claimed within 4 years after the filing of the return required by section 6018, except that —

(1) If a petition for redetermination of a deficiency has been filed with the Tax Court within the time prescribed in section 6213(a), then within such 4-year period or before the expiration of 60 days after the decision of the Tax Court becomes final.

(2) If, under section 6161, an extension of time has been granted for payment of the tax shown on the return, or of a deficiency, then within such 4-year period or before the date of the expiration of the period of the extension.

(3) If a claim for refund or credit of an overpayment of tax imposed by this chapter has been filed within the time prescribed in section 6511, then within such 4-year period or before the expiration of 60 days from the date of mailing by certified mail or registered mail by the Secretary or his delegate to the taxpayer of a notice of the disallowance of any part of such claim, or before the expiration of 60 days after a decision by any court of competent jurisdiction becomes final with respect to a timely suit instituted upon such claim, whichever is later.

Refund based on the credit may (despite the provisions of sections 6511 and 6512) be made if claim therefor is filed within the period above provided. Any such refund shall be made without interest.

(d) *Basic Estate Tax.* — The basic estate tax and the estate tax imposed by the Revenue Act of 1926 shall be 125 percent of the amount determined to be the maximum credit provided by subsection (b). The additional estate tax shall be the difference between the tax imposed by section 2001 or 2101 and the basic estate tax.

(e) *Limitation in Cases Involving Deduction Under Section 2053(d).* — In any case where a deduction is allowed under section 2053(d) for an estate, succession, legacy, or inheritance tax imposed by a State or Territory or the District of Columbia upon a transfer for public, charitable, or religious uses described in section 2055 or 2106(a)(2), the allowance of the credit under this section shall be subject to the following conditions and limitations:

(1) The taxes described in subsection (a) shall not include any estate, succession, legacy, or inheritance tax for which such deduction is allowed under section 2053(d).

(2) The credit shall not exceed the lesser of —

(A) the amount stated in subsection (b) on a taxable estate determined by allowing such deduction authorized by section 2053(d), or

(B) that proportion of the amount stated in subsection (b) on a taxable estate determined without regard to such deduction authorized by section 2053(d) as (i) the amount of the taxes described in subsection (a), as limited by the provisions of paragraph (1) of this subsection, bears to (ii) the amount of the taxes described in subsection (a) before applying the limitation contained in paragraph (1) of this subsection.

(3) If the amount determined under subparagraph (B) of paragraph (2) is less than the amount determined under subparagraph (A) of that paragraph, then for purposes of subsection (d) such lesser amount shall be the maximum credit provided by subsection (b).

Sec. 2012. Credit for Gift Tax.

(a) *In General.* — If a tax on a gift has been paid under chapter 12 (sec. 2501 and following), or under corresponding provisions of prior laws, and thereafter on the death of the donor any amount in respect of such gift is required to be included in the value of the gross estate of the decedent for purposes of this chapter, then there shall be credited against the tax imposed by section 2001 the amount of the tax paid on a gift under chapter 12, or under corresponding provisions of prior laws, with respect to so much of the property which constituted the gift as is included in the gross estate, except that the amount of such credit shall not exceed an amount which bears the same ratio to the tax imposed by section 2001 (after deducting from such tax the credit for State death taxes provided by section 2011) as the value (at the time of the gift or at the time of the death, whichever is lower) of so much of the property which constituted the gift as is included in the gross estate bears to the value of the entire gross estate reduced by the aggregate amount of the charitable and marital deductions allowed under sections 2055, 2056, and 2106(a)(2).

(b) In applying, with respect to any gift, the ratio stated in subsection (a), the value at the time of the gift or at the time of the death, referred to in such ratio, shall be reduced —

(1) by such amount as will properly reflect the amount of such gift which was excluded in determining (for purposes of section 2503(a)), or of corresponding provisions of prior laws, the total amount of gifts made during the year in which the gift was made;

(2) if a deduction with respect to such gift is allowed under section 2056(a) (relating to marital deduction) — then by an amount which bears the same ratio to such value (reduced as provided in paragraph (1) of this subsection) as the aggregate amount of the marital deductions allowed under section 2056(a) bears to the aggregate amount of such marital deductions computed without regard to subsection (c) thereof; and

(3) if a deduction with respect to such gift is allowed under sections 2055 or 2106(a)(2) (relating to charitable deduction) — then by the amount of such value, reduced as provided in paragraph (1) of this subsection.

(c) Where the decedent was the donor of the gift but, under the provisions of section 2513, or corresponding provisions of prior laws, the gift was considered as made one-half by his spouse —

(1) the term "the amount of the tax paid on a gift under chapter 12", as used in subsection (a), includes the amounts paid with respect to each half of such gift, the amount paid with respect to each being computed in the manner provided in subsection (d); and

(2) in applying, with respect to such gift, the ratio stated in subsection (a), the value at the time of the gift or at the time of the death, referred to in such ratio, includes such value with respect to each half of such gift, each such value being reduced as provided in paragraph (1) of subsection (b).

(d) (1) For purposes of subsection (a), the amount of tax paid on a gift under chapter 12, or under corresponding provisions of prior laws, with respect to any gift shall be an amount which bears the same ratio to the total tax paid for the year in which the gift was made as the amount of such gift bears to the total amount of taxable gifts (computed without deduction of the specific exemption) for such year.

(2) For purposes of paragraph (1), the "amount of such gift" shall be the amount included with respect to such gift in determining (for the purposes of section 2503(a), or of corresponding provisions of prior laws) the total amount of gifts made during such year, reduced by the amount of any deduction allowed with respect to such gift under section 2522, or under corresponding provisions of prior laws (relating to charitable deduction), or under section 2523 (relating to marital deduction).

Sec. 2013. Credit for Tax on Prior Transfers.

(a) *General Rule.* — The tax imposed by section 2001 shall be credited with all or a part of the amount of the Federal estate tax paid with respect to the transfer of property (including property passing as a result of the exercise or non-exercise of a power of appointment) to the decedent by or from a person (herein designated as a "transferor") who died within 10 years before, or within 2 years after, the decedent's death. If the transferor died within 2 years of the death of the decedent, the credit shall be the amount determined under subsections (b) and (c). If the transferor predeceased the decedent by more than 2 years, the credit shall be the following percentage of the amount so determined —

(1) 80 percent, if within the third or fourth years preceding the decedent's death;

(2) 60 percent, if within the fifth or sixth years preceding the decedent's death;

(3) 40 percent, if within the seventh or eighth years preceding the decedent's death; and

(4) 20 percent, if within the ninth or tenth years preceding the decedent's death.

(b) *Computation of Credit.* — Subject to the limitation prescribed in subsection (c), the credit provided by this section shall be an amount which bears the same ratio to the estate tax paid (adjusted as indicated hereinafter) with respect to the estate of the transferor as the value of the property transferred bears to the taxable estate of the transferor (determined for purposes of the estate tax) decreased by any death taxes paid with respect to such estate and increased by the exemption provided for by section 2052 or section 2106(a)(3), or the corresponding provisions of prior laws, in determining the taxable estate of the transferor for purposes of the estate tax. For purposes of the preceding sentence, the estate tax paid shall be the Federal estate tax paid increased by any credits allowed against such estate tax under section 2012, or corresponding provisions of prior laws, on account of gift tax, and for any credits allowed against such estate tax under this section on account of prior transfers where the transferor acquired property from a person who died within 10 years before the death of the decedent.

(c) *Limitation on Credit.* —

(1) *In general.* — The credit provided in this section shall not exceed the amount by which —

(A) the estate tax imposed by section 2001 or section 2101 (after deducting the credits for State death taxes, gift tax, and foreign death taxes provided for in sections 2011, 2012, and 2014) computed without regard to this section, exceeds

(B) such tax computed by excluding from the decedent's gross estate the value of such property transferred and, if applicable, by making the adjustment hereinafter indicated.

If any deduction is otherwise allowable under section 2055 or section 2106(a)(2) (relating to charitable deduction) then, for the purpose of the computation indicated in subparagraph (B), the amount of such deduction shall be reduced by that part of such deduction which the value of such property transferred bears to the decedent's entire gross estate reduced by the deductions allowed under sections 2053 and 2054, or section 2106(a)(1) (relating to deduction for expenses, losses, etc.). For purposes of this section, the value of such property transferred shall be the value as provided for in subsection (d) of this section.

(2) *Two or more transferors.* — If the credit provided in this section relates to property received from 2 or more transferors, the limitation provided in paragraph (1) of this subsection shall be computed by aggregating

the value of the property so transferred to the decedent. The aggregate limitation so determined shall be apportioned in accordance with the value of the property transferred to the decedent by each transferor.

(d) *Valuation of Property Transferred.* — The value of property transferred to the decedent shall be the value used for the purpose of determining the Federal estate tax liability of the estate of the transferor but —

(1) there shall be taken into account the effect of the tax imposed by section 2001 or 2101, or any estate, succession, legacy, or inheritance tax, on the net value to the decedent of such property;

(2) where such property is encumbered in any manner, or where the decedent incurs any obligation imposed by the transferor with respect to such property, such encumbrance or obligation shall be taken into account in the same manner as if the amount of a gift to the decedent of such property was being determined; and

(3) if the decedent was the spouse of the transferor at the time of the transferor's death, the net value of the property transferred to the decedent shall be reduced by the amount allowed under section 2056 (relating to marital deductions), or the corresponding provision of prior law, as a deduction from the gross estate of the transferor.

(e) *Property Defined.* — For purposes of this section, the term "property" includes any beneficial interest in property, including a general power of appointment (as defined in section 2041).

Sec. 2014. Credit for Foreign Death Taxes.

(a) *In General.* — The tax imposed by section 2001 shall be credited with the amount of any estate, inheritance, legacy, or succession taxes actually paid to any foreign country in respect of any property situated within such foreign country and included in the gross estate (not including any such taxes paid with respect to the estate of a person other than the decedent). If the decedent at the time of his death was not a citizen of the United States, credit shall not be allowed under this section unless the foreign country of which such decedent was a citizen or subject, in imposing such taxes, allows a similar credit in the case of a citizen of the United States resident in such country.   The determination of the country within which property is situated shall be made in accordance with the rules applicable under subchapter B (sec. 2101 and following) in determining whether property is situated within or without the United States.

(b) *Limitations on Credit.* — The credit provided in this section with respect to such taxes paid to any foreign country —

(1) shall not, with respect to any such tax, exceed an amount which bears the same ratio to the amount of such tax actually paid to such foreign country as the value of property which is —

(A) situated within such foreign country,

(B) subjected to such tax, and

(C) included in the gross estate

bears to the value of all property subjected to such tax; and

(2) shall not, with respect to all such taxes, exceed an amount which bears the same ratio to the tax imposed by section 2001 (after deducting from such tax the credits provided by sections 2011 and 2012) as the value of property which is —

(A) situated within such foreign country,

(B) subjected to the taxes of such foreign country, and

(C) included in the gross estate

bears to the value of the entire gross estate reduced by the aggregate amount of the deductions allowed under sections 2055 and 2056.

(c) *Valuation of Property.* —

(1) The values referred to in the ratio stated in subsection (b)(1) are the values determined for purposes of the tax imposed by such foreign country.

(2) The values referred to in the ratio stated in subsection (b)(2) are the values determined under this chapter; but, in applying such ratio, the value of any property described in subparagraphs (A), (B), and (C) thereof shall be reduced by such amount as will properly reflect, in accordance with regulations prescribed by the Secretary or his delegate, the deductions allowed in respect of such property under sections 2055 and 2056 (relating to charitable and marital deductions).

(d) *Proof of Credit.* — The credit provided in this section shall be allowed only if the taxpayer establishes to the satisfaction of the Secretary or his delegate —

(1) the amount of taxes actually paid to the foreign country,

(2) the amount and date of each payment thereof,

(3) the description and value of the property in respect of which such taxes are imposed, and

(4) all other information necessary for the verification and computation of the credit.

(e) *Period of Limitation.* — The credit provided in this section shall be allowed only for such taxes as were actually paid and credit therefor claimed within 4 years after the filing of the return required by section 6018, except that —

(1) If a petition for redetermination of a deficiency has been filed with the Tax Court within the time prescribed in section 6213(a), then within such 4-year period or before the expiration of 60 days after the decision of the Tax Court becomes final.

(2) If, under section 6161, an extension of time has been granted for payment of the tax shown on the return, or of a deficiency, then within such 4-year period or before the date of the expiration of the period of the extension.

Refund based on such credit may (despite the provisions of sections 6511 and 6512) be made if claim therefor is filed within the period above provided. Any such refund shall be made without interest.

(f) *Additional Limitation in Cases Involving a Deduction Under Section 2053(d).* — In any case where a deduction is allowed under section 2053(d) for an estate, succession, legacy, or inheritance tax imposed by and actually paid to any foreign country upon a transfer by the decedent for public, charitable, or religious uses described in section 2055, the property described in subparagraphs (A), (B), and (C) of paragraphs (1) and (2) of subsection (b) of this section shall not include any property in respect of which such deduction is allowed under section 2053(d).

(g) *Possession of United States Deemed a Foreign Country.* — For purposes of the credits authorized by this section, each possession of the United States shall be deemed to be a foreign country.

Sec. 2015.   Credit for Death Taxes on Remainders.

Where an election is made under section 6163(a) to postpone payment of the tax imposed by section 2001 or 2101, such part of any estate, inheritance, legacy, or succession taxes allowable as a credit under section 2011 or 2014, as is attributable to a reversionary or remainder interest may be allowed as a credit against the tax attributable to such interest, subject to the limitations on the amount of the credit contained in such sections, if such part is paid, and credit therefor claimed, at any time before the expiration of the time for payment of the tax imposed by section 2001 or 2101 as postponed and extended under section 6163.

Sec. 2016. Recovery of Taxes Claimed as Credit.

If any tax claimed as a credit under section 2011 or 2014 is recovered from any foreign country, any State, any Territory or possession of the United States, or the District of Columbia, the executor, or any other person or persons recovering such amount, shall give notice of such recovery to the Secretary or his delegate at such time and in such manner as may be required by regulations prescribed by him, and the Secretary or his delegate shall (despite the provisions of section 6501) redetermine the amount of the tax under this chapter and the amount, if any, of the tax due on such redetermination, shall be paid by the executor or such person or persons, as the case may be, on notice and demand. No interest shall be assessed or collected on any amount of tax due on any redetermination by the Secretary or his delegate, resulting from a refund to the executor of tax claimed as a credit under section 2014, for any period before the receipt of such refund, except to the extent interest was paid by the foreign country on such refund.

Sec. 2031. Definition of Gross Estate.

(a) *General.* — The value of the gross estate of the decedent shall be determined by including to the extent provided for in this part, the value at the time of his death of all property, real or personal, tangible or intangible, wherever situated, except real property situated outside of the United States.

(b) *Valuation of Unlisted Stock and Securities.* — In the case of stock and securities of a corporation the value of which, by reason of their not being listed on an exchange and by reason of the absence of sales thereof, cannot be determined with reference to bid and asked prices or with reference to sales prices, the value thereof shall be determined by taking into consideration, in addition to all other factors, the value of stock or securities of corporations engaged in the same or a similar line of business which are listed on an exchange.

Sec. 2032. Alternate Valuation.

(a) *General.* — The value of the gross estate may be determined, if the executor so elects, by valuing all the property included in the gross estate as follows:

(1) In the case of property distributed, sold, exchanged, or otherwise disposed of, within 1 year after the decedent's death such property shall be valued as of the date of distribution, sale, exchange, or other disposition.

(2) In the case of property not distributed, sold, exchanged, or otherwise disposed of, within 1 year after the decedent's death such property shall be valued as of the date 1 year after the decedent's death.

(3) Any interest or estate which is affected by mere lapse of time shall be included at its value as of the time of death (instead of the later date) with adjustment for any difference in its value as of the later date not due to mere lapse of time.

(b) *Special Rules.* — No deduction under this chapter of any item shall be allowed if allowance for such item is in effect given by the alternate valuation provided by this section. Wherever in any other subsection or section of this chapter reference is made to the value of property at the time of the decedent's death, such reference shall be deemed to refer to the value of such property used in determining the value of the gross estate. In case of an election made by the executor under this section, then —

(1) for purposes of the charitable deduction under section 2055 or 2106(a)(2), any bequest, legacy, devise, or transfer enumerated therein, and

(2) for the purpose of the marital deduction under section 2056, any interest in property passing to the surviving spouse,

shall be valued as of the date of the decedent's death with adjustment for any difference in value (not due to mere lapse of time or the occurrence or non-occurrence of a contingency) of the property as of the date 1 year after the decedent's death (substituting, in the case of property distributed by the executor or trustee, or sold, exchanged, or otherwise disposed of, during such 1-year period, the date thereof).

(c) *Time of Election.* — The election provided for in this section shall be exercised by the executor on his return if filed within the time prescribed by law or before the expiration of any extension of time granted pursuant to law for the filing of the return.

Sec. 2033. Property in Which the Decedent Had an Interest.

The value of the gross estate shall include the value of all property (except real property situated outside of the United States) to the extent of the interest therein of the decedent at the time of his death.

Sec. 2034. Dower or Curtesy Interests.

The value of the gross estate shall include the value of all property (except real property situated outside of the United States) to the extent of any interest therein of the surviving spouse, existing at the time of the decedent's death as dower or curtesy, or by virtue of a statute creating an estate in lieu of dower or curtesy.

Sec. 2035. Transactions in Contemplation of Death.

(a) *General Rule.* — The value of the gross estate shall include the value of all property (except real property situated outside of the United States) to the extent of any interest therein of which the decedent has at any time made a transfer (except in case of a bona fide sale for an adequate and full consideration in money or money's worth), by trust or otherwise, in contemplation of his death.

(b) *Application of General Rule.* — If the decedent within a period of 3 years ending with the date of his death (except in case of a bona fide sale for an adequate and full consideration in money or money's worth) transferred an interest in property, relinquished a power, or exercised or released a general power of appointment, such transfer, relinquishment, exercise, or release shall, unless shown to the contrary, be deemed to have been made in contemplation of death within the meaning of this section and sections 2038 and 2041 (relating to revocable transfers and powers of appointment); but no such transfer, relinquishment, exercise, or release made before such 3-year period shall be treated as having been made in contemplation of death.

Sec. 2036. Transfers With Retained Life Estate.

(a) *General Rule.* — The value of the gross estate shall include the value of all property (except real property situated outside of the United States) to the extent of any interest therein of which the decedent has at any time made a transfer (except in case of a bona fide sale for an adequate and full consideration in money or money's worth), by trust or otherwise, under which he has retained for his life or for any period not ascertainable without reference to his death or for any period which does not in fact end before his death —

(1) the possession or enjoyment of, or the right to the income from, the property, or

(2) the right, either alone or in conjunction with any person, to designate the persons who shall possess or enjoy the property or the income therefrom.

(b) *Limitation on Application of General Rule.* — This section shall not apply to a transfer made before March 4, 1931; nor to a transfer made after March 3, 1931, and before June 7, 1932, unless the property transferred would have been includible in the decedent's gross estate by reason of the amendatory language of the joint resolution of March 3, 1931 (46 Stat. 1516).

Sec. 2037. Transfers Taking Effect at Death.

(a) *General Rule.* — The value of the gross estate shall include the value of all property (except real property situated outside of the United States) to the extent of any interest therein of which the decedent has at any time after September 7, 1916, made a transfer (except in case of a bona fide sale for an adequate and full consideration in money or money's worth), by trust or otherwise, if —

(1) possession or enjoyment of the property can, through ownership of such interest, be obtained only by surviving the decedent, and

(2) the decedent has retained a reversionary interest in the property (but in the case of a transfer made before October 8, 1949, only if such reversionary interest arose by the express terms of the instrument of transfer), and the value of such reversionary interest immediately before the death of the decedent exceeds 5 percent of the value of such property.

(b) *Special Rules.* — For purposes of this section, the term "reversionary interest" includes a possibility that property transferred by the decedent —

(1) may return to him or his estate, or

(2) may be subject to a power of disposition by him,

but such term does not include a possibility that the income alone from such property may return to him or become subject to a power of disposition by him. The value of a reversionary interest immediately before the death of the decedent shall be determined (without regard to the fact of the decedent's death) by usual methods of valuation, including the use of tables of mortality and actuarial principles, under regulations prescribed by the Secretary or his delegate. In determining the value of a possibility that property may be subject to a power of disposition by the decedent, such possibility shall be valued as if it were a possibility that such property may return to the decedent or his estate. Notwithstanding the foregoing, an interest so transferred shall not be included in the decedent's gross estate under this section if possession or enjoyment of the property could have been obtained by any beneficiary during the decedent's life through the exercise of a general power of appointment (as defined in section 2041) which in fact was exercisable immediately before the decedent's death.

Sec. 2038. Revocable Transfers.

(a) *In General.* — The value of the gross estate shall include the value of all property (except real property situated outside of the United States) —

(1) *Transfers after June 22, 1936.* — To the extent of any interest therein

of which the decedent has at any time made a transfer (except in case of a bona fide sale for an adequate and full consideration in money or money's worth), by trust or otherwise, where the enjoyment thereof was subject at the date of his death to any change through the exercise of a power (in whatever capacity exercisable) by the decedent alone or by the decedent in conjunction with any other person (without regard to when or from what source the decedent acquired such power), to alter, amend, revoke, or terminate, or where any such power is relinquished in contemplation of decedent's death.

(2) *Transfers on or before June 22, 1936.* — To the extent of any interest therein of which the decedent has at any time made a transfer (except in case of a bona fide sale for an adequate and full consideration in money or money's worth), by trust or otherwise, where the enjoyment thereof was subject at the date of his death to any change through the exercise of a power, either by the decedent alone or in conjunction with any person, to alter, amend, or revoke, or where the decedent relinquished any such power in contemplation of his death. Except in the case of transfers made after June 22, 1936, no interest of the decedent of which he has made a transfer shall be included in the gross estate under paragraph (1) unless it is includible under this paragraph.

(b) *Date of Existence of Power.* — For purposes of this section, the power to alter, amend, revoke, or terminate shall be considered to exist on the date of the decedent's death even though the exercise of the power is subject to a precedent giving of notice or even though the alteration, amendment, revocation, or termination takes effect only on the expiration of a stated period after the exercise of the power, whether or not on or before the date of the decedent's death notice has been given or the power has been exercised. In such cases proper adjustment shall be made representing the interests which would have been excluded from the power if the decedent had lived, and for such purpose, if the notice has not been given or the power has not been exercised on or before the date of his death, such notice shall be considered to have been given, or the power exercised, on the date of his death.

(c) *Effect of Disability in Certain Cases.* — For purposes of this section, in the case of a decedent who was (for a continuous period beginning not less than 3 months before December 31, 1947, and ending with his death) under a mental disability to relinquish a power, the term "power" shall not include a power the relinquishment of which on or after January 1, 1940, and on or before December 31, 1947, would, by reason of section 1000(e) of the Internal Revenue Code of 1939, be deemed not to be a transfer of property for purposes of chapter 4 of the Internal Revenue Code of 1939.

Sec. 2039. Annuities.

(a) *General.* — The gross estate shall include the value of an annuity or other payment receivable by any beneficiary by reason of surviving the decedent under any form of contract or agreement entered into after March 3, 1931 (other than as insurance under policies on the life of the decedent), if, under such contract or agreement, an annuity or other payment was payable to the decedent, or the decedent possessed the right to receive such annuity or payment, either alone or in conjunction with another for his life or for any period not ascertainable without reference to his death or for any period which does not in fact end before his death.

(b) *Amount Includible.* — Subsection (a) shall apply to only such part of the value of the annuity or other payment receivable under such contract or agreement as is proportionate to that part of the purchase price therefor contributed by the decedent. For purposes of this section, any contribution by the decedent's employer or former employer to the purchase price of such contract or agreement (whether or not to an employee's trust or fund forming part of a pension, annuity, retirement, bonus or profit-sharing plan) shall be considered to be contributed by the decedent if made by reason of his employment.

(c) *Exemption of Annuities Under Certain Trusts and Plans.* — Notwithstanding the provisions of this section or of any provision of law, there shall be excluded from the gross estate the value of an annuity or other payment receivable by any beneficiary (other than the executor) under —

(1) an employees' trust (or under a contract purchased by an employees' trust) forming part of a pension, stock bonus, or profit-sharing plan which, at the time of the decedent's separation from employment (whether by death or otherwise), or at the time of termination of the plan if earlier, met the requirements of section 401(a);

(2) a retirement annuity contract purchased by an employer (and not by an employees' trust) pursuant to a plan which, at the time of decedent's separation from employment (by death or otherwise), or at the time of termination of the plan if earlier, met the requirements of section 401(a)(3), (4), (5), and (6); or

(3) a retirement annuity contract purchased for an employee by an employer which is an organization referred to in section 503(b)(1), (2), or (3), and which is exempt from tax under section 501(a).

If such amounts payable after the death of the decedent under a plan described in paragraph (1) or (2) or under a contract described in paragraph (3) are attributable to any extent to payments or contributions made by the decedent, no exclusion shall be allowed for that part of the value of such amounts in the proportion that the total payments or contributions made by the decedent bears to the total payments or contributions made. For purposes of this subsection, contributions or payments made by the decedent's employer or former employer under a trust or plan described in paragraph (1) or (2) shall not be considered to be contributed by the decedent, and contributions or payments made by the decedent's employer or former employer toward the purchase of an annuity contract described in paragraph (3) shall, to the extent excludable from gross income under section 403(b), not be considered to be contributed by the decedent.

Sec. 2040. Joint Interests.

The value of the gross estate shall include the value of all property (except real property situated outside of the United States) to the extent of the interest therein held as joint tenants by the decedent and any other person, or as tenants by the entirety by the decedent and spouse, or deposited, with any person carrying on the banking business, in their joint names and payable to either or the survivor, except such part thereof as may be shown to have originally belonged to such other person and never to have been received or acquired by the latter from the decedent for less than an adequate and full consideration in money or money's worth: *Provided,* That where such property or any part thereof, or part of the consideration with which such property was acquired, is shown to have been at any time acquired by such other person from the decedent for less than an adequate and full consideration in money or money's worth, there shall be excepted only such part of the value of such property as is proportionate to the consideration furnished by such other person: *Provided further,* That where any property has been acquired by gift, bequest, devise, or inheritance, as a tenancy by the entirety by the decedent and spouse, then to the extent of one-half of the value thereof, or, where so acquired by the decedent and any other person as joint tenants and their interests are not otherwise specified or fixed by law, then to the extent of the value of a fractional part to be determined by dividing the value of the property by the number of joint tenants.

Sec. 2041. Powers of Appointment.

(a) *In General.* — The value of the gross estate shall include the value of all property (except real property situated outside of the United States) —

(1) *Powers of appointment created on or before October 21, 1942.* — To the extent of any property with respect to which a general power of appointment created on or before October 21, 1942, is exercised by the decedent —

(A) by will, or

(B) by a disposition which is of such nature that if it were a transfer of property owned by the decedent, such property would be includible in the decedent's gross estate under sections 2035 to 2038, inclusive;

but the failure to exercise such a power or the complete release of such a power shall not be deemed an exercise thereof. If a general power of appointment created on or before October 21, 1942, has been partially released so that it is no longer a general power of appointment, the exercise of such power shall not be deemed to be the exercise of a general power of appointment if —

(i) such partial release occurred before November 1, 1951, or

(ii) the donee of such power was under a legal disability to release such power on October 21, 1942, and such partial release occurred not later than 6 months after the termination of such legal disability.

(2) *Powers created after October 21, 1942.* — To the extent of any property with respect to which the decedent has at the time of his death a general power of appointment created after October 21, 1942, or with respect to which the decedent has at any time exercised or released such a power of appointment by a disposition which is of such nature that if it were a transfer of property owned by the decedent, such property would be includible in the decedent's gross estate under sections 2035 to 2038, inclusive. A disclaimer or renunciation of such a power of appointment shall not be deemed a release of such power. For purposes of this paragraph (2), the power of appointment shall be considered to exist on the date of the decedent's death even though the exercise of the power is subject to a precedent giving of notice or even though the exercise of the power takes effect only on the expiration of a stated period after its exercise, whether or not on or before the date of the decedent's death notice has been given or the power has been exercised.

(3) *Creation of another power in certain cases.* — To the extent of any property with respect to which the decedent —

(A) by will, or

(B) by a disposition which is of such nature that if it were a transfer of property owned by the decedent such property would be includible in the decedent's gross estate under section 2035, 2036, or 2037,

exercises a power of appointment created after October 21, 1942, by creating another power of appointment which under the applicable local law can be validly exercised so as to postpone the vesting of any estate or interest in such property, or suspend the absolute ownership or power of alienation of such property, for a period ascertainable without regard to the date of the creation of the first power.

(b) *Definitions.* — For purposes of subsection (a) —

(1) *General power of appointment.* — The term "general power of appointment" means a power which is exercisable in favor of the decedent, his estate, his creditors, or the creditors of his estate; except that —

(A) A power to consume, invade, or appropriate property for the benefit of the decedent which is limited by an ascertainable standard relating to the health, education, support, or maintenance of the decedent shall not be deemed a general power of appointment.

(B) A power of appointment created on or before October 21, 1942, which is exercisable by the decedent only in conjunction with another person shall not be deemed a general power of appointment.

(C) In the case of a power of appointment created after October 21, 1942, which is exercisable by the decedent only in conjunction with another person —

(i) If the power is not exercisable by the decedent except in conjunction with the creator of the power — such power shall not be deemed a general power of appointment.

(ii) If the power is not exercisable by the decedent except in conjunction with a person having a substantial interest in the property, subject to the power, which is adverse to exercise of the power in favor of the decedent — such power shall not be deemed a general power of appointment. For the purposes of this clause a person who, after the death of the decedent, may be possessed of a power of appointment (with respect to the property subject to the decedent's power) which he may exercise in his own favor shall be deemed as having an interest in the property and such interest shall be deemed adverse to such exercise of the decedent's power.

(iii) If (after the application of clauses (i) and (ii)) the power is a general power of appointment and is exercisable in favor of such other person — such power shall be deemed a general power of appointment only in respect of a fractional part of the property subject to such power, such part to be determined by dividing the value of such property by the number of such persons (including the decedent) in favor of whom such power is exercisable.

For purposes of clauses (ii) and (iii), a power shall be deemed to be exercisable in favor of a person if it is exercisable in favor of such person, his estate, his creditors, or the creditors of his estate.

(2) *Lapse of power.* — The lapse of a power of appointment created after October 21, 1942, during the life of the individual possessing the power shall be considered a release of such power. The preceding sentence shall apply with respect to the lapse of powers during any calendar year only to the extent that the property, which could have been appointed by exercise of such lapsed powers, exceeded in value, at the time of such lapse, the greater of the following amounts:

(A) $5,000, or

(B) 5 percent of the aggregate value, at the time of such lapse, of the assets out of which, or the proceeds of which, the exercise of the lapsed powers could have been satisfied.

(3) *Date of creation of power.* — For purposes of this section, a power of appointment created by a will executed on or before October 21, 1942,

shall be considered a power created on or before such date if the person executing such will dies before July 1, 1949, without having republished such will, by codicil or otherwise, after October 21, 1942.

Sec. 2042. Proceeds of Life Insurance.

The value of the gross estate shall include the value of all property —

(1) *Receivable by the executor.* — To the extent of the amount receivable by the executor as insurance under policies on the life of the decedent.

(2) *Receivable by other beneficiaries.* — To the extent of the amount receivable by all other beneficiaries as insurance under policies on the life of the decedent with respect to which the decedent possessed at his death any of the incidents of ownership, exercisable either alone or in conjunction with any other person. For purposes of the preceding sentence, the term "incident of ownership" includes a reversionary interest (whether arising by the express terms of the policy or other instrument or by operation of law) only if the value of such reversionary interest exceeded 5 percent of the value of the policy immediately before the death of the decedent. As used in this paragraph, the term "reversionary interest" includes a possibility that the policy, or the proceeds of the policy, may return to the decedent or his estate, or may be subject to a power of disposition by him. The value of a reversionary interest at any time shall be determined (without regard to the fact of the decedent's death) by usual methods of valuation, including the use of tables of mortality and actuarial principles, pursuant to regulations prescribed by the Secretary or his delegate. In determining the value of a possibility that the policy or proceeds thereof may be subject to a power of disposition by the decedent, such possibility shall be valued as if it were a possibility that such policy or proceeds may return to the decedent or his estate.

Sec. 2043. Transfers for Insufficient Consideration.

(a) *In General.* — If any one of the transfers, trusts, interests, rights, or powers enumerated and described in sections 2035 to 2038, inclusive, and section 2041 is made, created, exercised, or relinquished for a consideration in money or money's worth, but is not a bona fide sale for an adequate and full consideration in money or money's worth, there shall be included in the gross estate only the excess of the fair market value at the time of death of the property otherwise to be included on account of such transaction, over the value of the consideration received therefor by the decedent.

(b) *Marital Rights Not Treated as Consideration.* — For purposes of this chapter, a relinquishment or promised relinquishment of dower or curtesy, or of a statutory estate created in lieu of dower or curtesy, or of other marital rights in the decedent's property or estate, shall not be considered to any extent a consideration "in money or money's worth."

Sec. 2044. Prior Interests.

Except as otherwise specifically provided therein, sections 2034 to 2042, inclusive, shall apply to the transfers, trusts, estates, interests, rights, powers, and relinquishment of powers, as severally enumerated and described therein, whenever made, created, arising, existing, exercised, or relinquished.

Sec. 2051. Definition of Taxable Estate.

For purposes of the tax imposed by section 2001, the value of the taxable estate shall be determined by deducting from the value of the gross estate the exemption and deductions provided for in this part.

Sec. 2052. Exemption.

For purposes of the tax imposed by section 2001, the value of the taxable estate shall be determined by deducting from the value of the gross estate an exemption of $60,000.

Sec. 2053. Expenses, Indebtedness, and Taxes.

(a) *General Rule.* — For purposes of the tax imposed by section 2001, the value of the taxable estate shall be determined by deducting from the value of the gross estate such amounts —

(1) for funeral expenses,

(2) for administration expenses,

(3) for claims against the estate, and

(4) for unpaid mortgages on, or any indebtedness in respect of, property where the value of the decedent's interest therein, undiminished by such mortgage or indebtedness, is included in the value of the gross estate, as are allowable by the laws of the jurisdiction, whether within or without the United States, under which the estate is being administered.

(b) *Other Administration Expenses.* — Subject to the limitations in paragraph (1) of subsection (c), there shall be deducted in determining the taxable estate amounts representing expenses incurred in administering property not subject to claims which is included in the gross estate to the same extent such amounts would be allowable as a deduction under subsection (a) if such property were subject to claims, and such amounts are paid before the expiration of the period of limitation for assessment provided in section 6501.

(c) *Limitations.* —

(1) *Limitations applicable to subsections (a) and (b).* —

(A) *Consideration for claims.* — The deduction allowed by this section in the case of claims against the estate, unpaid mortgages, or any indebtedness shall, when founded on a promise or agreement, be limited to the extent that they were contracted bona fide and for an adequate and full consideration in money or money's worth; except that in any case in which any such claim is founded on a promise or agreement of the decedent to make a contribution or gift to or for the use of any donee described in section 2055 for the purposes specified therein, the deduction for such claims shall not be so limited, but shall be limited to the extent that it would be allowable as a deduction under section 2055 if such promise or agreement constituted a bequest.

(B) *Certain taxes.* — Any income taxes on income received after the death of the decedent, or property taxes not accrued before his death, or any estate, succession, legacy, or inheritance taxes, shall not be deductible under this section.

(2) *Limitations applicable only to subsection (a).* — In the case of the amounts described in subsection (a), there shall be disallowed the amount by which the deductions specified therein exceed the value, at the time of the decedent's death, of property subject to claims, except to the extent that such deductions represent amounts paid before the date prescribed for the filing of the estate tax return. For purposes of this section, the term "property subject to claims" means property includible in the gross estate of the decedent which. or the avails of which, would under the applicable

law, bear the burden of the payment of such deductions in the final adjustment and settlement of the estate, except that the value of the property shall be reduced by the amount of the deduction under section 2054 attributable to such property.

(d) *Certain State and Foreign Death Taxes.* —

(1) *General rule.* — Notwithstanding the provisions of subsection (c)(1) (B) of this section, for purposes of the tax imposed by section 2001 the value of the taxable estate may be determined, if the executor so elects before the expiration of the period of limitation for assessment provided in section 6501, by deducting from the value of the gross estate the amount (as determined in accordance with regulations prescribed by the Secretary or his delegate) of —

(A) any estate, succession, legacy, or inheritance tax imposed by a State or Territory or the District of Columbia upon a transfer by the decedent for public, charitable, or religious uses described in section 2055 or 2106(a)(2), and

(B) any estate, succession, legacy, or inheritance tax imposed by and actually paid to any foreign country, in respect of any property situated within such foreign country and included in the gross estate of a citizen or resident of the United States, upon a transfer by the decedent for public, charitable, or religious uses described in section 2055.

The determination under subparagraph (B) of the country within which property is situated shall be made in accordance with the rules applicable under subchapter B (sec. 2101 and following) in determining whether property is situated within or without the United States. Any election under this paragraph shall be exercised in accordance with regulations prescribed by the Secretary or his delegate.

(2) *Condition for allowance of deduction.* — No deduction shall be allowed under paragraph (1) for a State death tax or a foreign death tax specified therein unless the decrease in the tax imposed by section 2001 which results from the deduction provided in paragraph (1) will inure solely for the benefit of the public, charitable, or religious transferees described in section 2055 or section 2106(a)(2). In any case where the tax imposed by section 2001 is equitably apportioned among all the transferees of property included in the gross estate, including those described in sections 2055 and 2106(a)(2) (taking into account any exemptions, credits, or deductions allowed by this chapter), in determining such decrease, there shall be disregarded any decrease in the Federal estate tax which any transferees other than those described in sections 2055 and 2106(a)(2) are required to pay.

(3) *Effect on credits for state and foreign death taxes of deduction under this subsection.* —

(A) *Election.* — An election under this subsection shall be deemed a waiver of the right to claim a credit, against the Federal estate tax, under a death tax convention with any foreign country for any tax or portion thereof in respect of which a deduction is taken under this subsection.

(B) *Cross references.* —

See section 2011(e) for the effect of a deduction taken under this subsection on the credit for State death taxes, and see section 2014(f) for the effect of a deduction taken under this subsection on the credit for foreign death taxes.

(e) *Marital Rights.* —

For provisions that <u>relinquishment of marital rights shall not be</u>

~~deemed a consideration~~ "in money or money's worth," see section 2043(b).

Sec. 2054. Losses.

For purposes of the tax imposed by section 2001, the value of the taxable estate shall be determined by deducting from the value of the gross estate losses incurred during the settlement of estates arising from fires, storms, ship-wrecks, or other casualties, or from theft, when such losses are not compensated for by insurance or otherwise.

Sec. 2055. Transfers for Public, Charitable, and Religious Uses.

(a) *In General.* — For purposes of the tax imposed by section 2001, the value of the taxable estate shall be determined by deducting from the value of the gross estate the amount of all bequests, legacies, devises, or transfers (including the interest which falls into any such bequest, legacy, devise, or transfer as a result of an irrevocable disclaimer of a bequest, legacy, devise, transfer, or power, if the disclaimer is made before the date prescribed for the filing of the estate tax return) —

(1) to or for the use of the United States, any State, Territory, any political subdivision thereof, or the District of Columbia, for exclusively public purposes;

(2) to or for the use of any corporation organized and operated exclusively for religious, charitable, scientific, literary, or educational purposes, including the encouragement of art and the prevention of cruelty to children or animals, no part of the net earnings of which inures to the benefit of any private stockholder or individual, and no substantial part of the activities of which is carrying on propaganda, or otherwise attempting, to influence legislation;

(3) to a trustee or trustees, or a fraternal society, order, or association operating under the lodge system, but only if such contributions or gifts are to be used by such trustee or trustees, or by such fraternal society, order, or association, exclusively for religious, charitable, scientific, literary, or educational purposes, or for the prevention of cruelty to children or animals, and no substantial part of the activities of such trustee or trustees, or of such fraternal society, order, or association, is carrying on propaganda, or otherwise attempting, to influence legislation; or

(4) to or for the use of any veterans' organization incorporated by Act of Congress, or of its departments or local chapters or posts, no part of the net earnings of which inures to the benefit of any private shareholder or individual.

For purposes of this subsection, the complete termination before the date prescribed for the filing of the estate tax return of a power to consume, invade or appropriate property for the benefit of an individual before such power has been exercised by reason of the death of such individual or for any other reason shall be considered and deemed to be an irrevocable disclaimer with the same full force and effect as though he had filed such irrevocable disclaimer.

(b) *Powers of Appointment.* —

(1) *General rule.* — Property includible in the decedent's gross estate under section 2041 (relating to powers of appointment) received by a donee described in this section shall, for purposes of this section, be considered a bequest of such decedent.

(2) *Special rule for certain bequests subject to power of appointment.* — For purposes of this section, in the case of a bequest in trust, if the surviv-

ing spouse of the decedent is entitled for life to all of the net income from the trust and such surviving spouse has a power of appointment over the corpus of such trust exercisable by will in favor of, among others, organizations described in subsection (a)(2), such bequests in trust, reduced by the value of the life estate, shall, to the extent such power is exercised in favor of such organizations, be deemed a transfer to such organizations by the decedent if —

(A) no part of the corpus of such trust is distributed to a beneficiary during the life of the surviving spouse;

(B) such surviving spouse was over 80 years of age at the date of the decedent's death;

(C) such surviving spouse by affidavit executed within one year after the death of the decedent specifies the organizations described in subsection (a)(2) in favor of which he intends to exercise the power of appointment and indicates the amount or proportion each such organization is to receive; and

(D) the power of appointment is exercised in favor of such organization and in the amounts or proportions specified in the affidavit required under subparagraph (C).

The affidavit referred to in subparagraph (C) shall be attached to the estate tax return of the decedent and shall constitute a sufficient basis for the allowance of the deduction under this paragraph in the first instance subject to a later disallowance of the deduction if the conditions herein specified are not complied with.

(c) *Death Taxes Payable Out of Bequests.* — If the tax imposed by section 2001, or any estate, succession, legacy, or inheritance taxes, are, either by the terms of the will, by the law of the jurisdiction under which the estate is administered, or by the law of the jurisdiction imposing the particular tax, payable in whole or in part out of the bequests, legacies, or devises otherwise deductible under this section, then the amount deductible under this section shall be the amount of such bequests, legacies, or devises reduced by the amount of such taxes.

(d) *Limitation on Deduction.* — The amount of the deduction under this section for any transfer shall not exceed the value of the transferred property required to be included in the gross estate.

(e) *Disallowance of Deductions in Certain Cases.* —

For disallowance of certain charitable, etc., deductions otherwise allowable under this section, see sections 503 and 681.

(f) *Other Cross References.* —

(1) For option as to time for valuation for purpose of deduction under this section, see section 2032.

(2) For exemption of bequests to or for benefit of Library of Congress, see section 5 of the Act of March 3, 1925, as amended (56 Stat. 765; 2 U.S.C. 161).

(3) For construction of bequests for benefit of the library of the Post Office Department as bequests to or for the use of the United States, see section 2 or the Act of August 8, 1946 (60 Stat. 924; 5 U.S.C. 393).

(4) For exemption of bequests for benefit of Office of Naval Records and Library, Navy Department, see section 2 of the Act of March 4, 1937 (50 Stat. 25; 5 U.S.C. 419b).

(5) For exemption of bequests to or for benefit of National Park Service, see section 5 of the Act of July 10, 1935 (49 Stat. 478; 16 U.S.C. 19c).

(6) For construction of devises or bequests accepted by the Secretary of State under the Foreign Service Act of 1946 as devises or bequests to or for the use of the United States, see section 1021(e) of that Act (60 Stat. 1032; 22 U.S.C. 809).

(7) For construction of gifts or bequests of money accepted by the Attorney General for credit to "Commissary Funds, Federal Prisons" as gifts or bequests to or for the use of the United States, see section 2 of the Act of May 15, 1952, 66 Stat. 73, as amended by the Act of July 9, 1952, 66 Stat. 479 (31 U.S.C. 725s-4).

(8) For payment of tax on bequests of United States obligations to the United States, see section 24 of the Second Liberty Bond Act, as amended (59 Stat. 48, §4; 31 U.S.C. 757e).

(9) For construction of bequests for benefit of or use in connection with the Naval Academy as bequests to or for the use of the United States, see section 3 of the Act of March 31, 1944 (58 Stat. 135; 34 U.S.C. 1115b).

(10) For exemption of bequests for benefit of Naval Academy Museum, see section 4 of the Act of March 26, 1938 (52 Stat. 119; 34 U.S.C. 1119).

(11) For exemption of bequests received by National Archives Trust Fund Board, see section 7 of the National Archives Trust Fund Board Act (55 Stat. 582; 44 U.S.C. 300gg).

Sec. 2056. Bequests, Etc., to Surviving Spouse.

(a) *Allowance of Marital Deduction.* — For purposes of the tax imposed by section 2001, the value of the taxable estate shall, except as limited by subsections (b), (c), and (d), be determined by deducting from the value of the gross estate an amount equal to the value of any interest in property which passes or has passed from the decedent to his surviving spouse, but only to the extent that such interest is included in determining the value of the gross estate.

(b) *Limitation in the Case of Life Estate or Other Terminable Interest.* —

(1) *General rule.* — Where, on the lapse of time, on the occurrence of an event or contingency, or on the failure of an event or contingency to occur, an interest passing to the surviving spouse will terminate or fail, no deduction shall be allowed under this section with respect to such interest —

(A) if an interest in such property passes or has passed (for less than an adequate and full consideration in money or money's worth) from the decedent to any person other than such surviving spouse (or the estate of such spouse); and

(B) if by reason of such passing such person (or his heirs or assigns) may possess or enjoy any part of such property after such termination or failure of the interest so passing to the surviving spouse;
and no deduction shall be allowed with respect to such interest (even if such deduction is not disallowed under subparagraphs (A) and (B)) —

(C) if such interest is to be acquired for the surviving spouse, pursuant to directions of the decedent, by his executor or by the trustee of a trust. For purposes of this paragraph, an interest shall not be considered as an interest which will terminate or fail merely because it is the ownership of a bond, note, or similar contractual obligation, the discharge of which would not have the effect of an annuity for life or for a term.

(2) *Interest in unidentified assets.* — Where the assets (included in the decedent's gross estate) out of which, or the proceeds of which, an interest

passing to the surviving spouse may be satisfied include a particular asset or assets with respect to which no deduction would be allowed if such asset or assets passed from the decedent to such spouse, then the value of such interest passing to such spouse shall, for purposes of subsection (a), be reduced by the aggregate value of such particular assets.

(3) *Interest of spouse conditional on survival for limited period.* — For purposes of this subsection, an interest passing to the surviving spouse shall not be considered as an interest which will terminate or fail on the death of such spouse if —

(A) such death will cause a termination or failure of such interest only if it occurs within a period not exceeding 6 months after the decedent's death, or only if it occurs as a result of a common disaster resulting in the death of the decedent and the surviving spouse, or only if it occurs in the case of either such event; and

(B) such termination or failure does not in fact occur.

(4) *Valuation of interest passing to surviving spouse.* — In determining for purposes of subsection (a) the value of any interest in property passing to the surviving spouse for which a deduction is allowed by this section —

(A) there shall be taken into account the effect which the tax imposed by section 2001, or any estate, succession, legacy, or inheritance tax, has on the net value to the surviving spouse of such interest; and

(B) where such interest or property is encumbered in any manner, or where the surviving spouse incurs any obligation imposed by the decedent with respect to the passing of such interest, such encumbrance or obligation shall be taken into account in the same manner as if the amount of a gift to such spouse of such interest were being determined.

(5) *Life estate with power of appointment in surviving spouse.* — In the case of an interest in property passing from the decedent, if his surviving spouse is entitled for life to all the income from the entire interest, or all the income from a specific portion thereof, payable annually or at more frequent intervals, with power in the surviving spouse to appoint the entire interest, or such specific portion (exercisable in favor of such surviving spouse, or of the estate of such surviving spouse, or in favor of either, whether or not in each case the power is exercisable in favor of others), and with no power in any other person to appoint any part of the interest, or such specific portion, to any person other than the surviving spouse —

(A) the interest or such portion thereof so passing shall, for purposes of subsection (a), be considered as passing to the surviving spouse, and

(B) no part of the interest so passing shall, for purposes of paragraph (1)(A), be considered as passing to any person other than the surviving spouse.

This paragraph shall apply only if such power in the surviving spouse to appoint the entire interest, or such specific portion thereof, whether exercisable by will or during life, is exercisable by such spouse alone and in all events.

(6) *Life insurance or annuity payments with power of appointment in surviving spouse.* — In the case of an interest in property passing from the decedent consisting of proceeds under a life insurance, endowment, or annuity contract, if under the terms of the contract such proceeds are payable in installments or are held by the insurer subject to an agreement to pay interest thereon (whether the proceeds, on the termination of any interest payments, are payable in a lump sum or in annual or more frequent installments), and such installment or interest payments are payable

annually or at more frequent intervals, commencing not later than 13 months after the decedent's death, and all amounts, or a specific portion of all such amounts, payable during the life of the surviving spouse are payable only to such spouse, and such spouse has the power to appoint all amounts, or such specific portion, payable under such contract (exercisable in favor of such surviving spouse, or of the estate of such surviving spouse, or in favor of either, whether or not in each case the power is exercisable in favor of others), with no power in any other person to appoint such amounts to any person other than the surviving spouse —

(A) such amounts shall, for purposes of subsection (a), be considered as passing to the surviving spouse, and

(B) no part of such amounts shall, for purposes of paragraph (1)(A), be considered as passing to any person other than the surviving spouse. This paragraph shall apply only if, under the terms of the contract, such power in the surviving spouse to appoint such amounts, whether exercisable by will or during life, is exercisable by such spouse alone and in all events.

(c) *Limitation on Aggregate of Deductions.* —

(1) *General rule.* — The aggregate amount of the deductions allowed under this section (computed without regard to this subsection) shall not exceed 50 percent of the value of the adjusted gross estate, as defined in paragraph (2).

(2) *Computation of adjusted gross estate.* —

(A) *General rule.* — Except as provided in subparagraph (B) of this paragraph, the adjusted gross estate shall, for purposes of subsection (c)(1), be computed by subtracting from the entire value of the gross estate the aggregate amount of the deductions allowed by sections 2053 and 2054.

(B) *Special rule in cases involving community property.* — If the decedent and his surviving spouse at any time, held property as community property under the law of any State, Territory, or possession of the United States, or of any foreign country, then the adjusted gross estate shall, for purposes of subsection (c)(1), be determined by subtracting from the entire value of the gross estate the sum of —

(i) the value of property which is at the time of the death of the decedent held as such community property; and

(ii) the value of property transferred by the decedent during his life, if at the time of such transfer the property was held as such community property; and

(iii) the amount receivable as insurance under policies on the life of the decedent, to the extent purchased with premiums or other consideration paid out of property held as such community property; and

(iv) an amount which bears the same ratio to the aggregate of the deductions allowed under sections 2053 and 2054 which the value of the property included in the gross estate, diminished by the amount subtracted under clauses (i), (ii), and (iii) of this subparagraph, bears to the entire value of the gross estate.

For purposes of clauses (i), (ii), and (iii), community property (except property which is considered as community property solely by reason of the provisions of subparagraph (C) of this paragraph) shall be considered as not "held as such community property" as of any moment of time, if, in case of the death of the decedent at such moment, such property (and not merely one-half thereof) would be or would have been includible in determining the value of his gross estate without regard to the provisions of section 402(b) of the Revenue Act of 1942. The amount to be subtracted under clauses (i), (ii), or (iii) shall not exceed the value of the interest in the property described therein which is included in determining the value of the gross estate.

(C) *Community property — conversion into separate property.* —

(i) *After December 31, 1941.* — If after December 31, 1941, property held as such community property (unless considered by reason of subparagraph (B) of this paragraph as not so held) was by the decedent and the surviving spouse converted, by one transaction or a series of transactions, into separate property of the decedent and his spouse (including any form of co-ownership by them), the separate property so acquired by the decedent and any property acquired at any time by the decedent in exchange therefor (by one exchange or a series of exchanges) shall, for the purposes of clauses (i), (ii), and (iii) of subparagraph (B), be considered as "held as such community property."

(ii) *Limitation.* — Where the value (at the time of such conversion) of the separate property so acquired by the decedent exceeded the value (at such time) of the separate property so acquired by the decedent's spouse, the rule in clause (i) shall be applied only with respect to the same portion of such separate property of the decedent as the portion which the value (as of such time) of such separate property so acquired by the decedent's spouse is of the value (as of such time) of the separate property so acquired by the decedent.

(d) *Disclaimers.* —

(1) *By surviving spouse.* — If under this section an interest would, in the absence of a disclaimer by the surviving spouse, be considered as passing from the decedent to such spouse, and if a disclaimer of such interest is made by such spouse, then such interest shall, for the purposes of this section, be considered as passing to the person or persons entitled to receive such interest as a result of the disclaimer.

(2) *By any other person.* — If under this section an interest would, in the absence of a disclaimer by any person other than the surviving spouse, be considered as passing from the decedent to such person, and if a disclaimer of such interest is made by such person and as a result of such disclaimer the surviving spouse is entitled to receive such interest, then such interest shall, for purposes of this section, be considered as passing, not to the surviving spouse, but to the person who made the disclaimer, in the same manner as if the disclaimer had not been made.

(e) *Definition.* — For purposes of this section, an interest in property shall be considered as passing from the decedent to any person if and only if —

(1) such interest is bequeathed or devised to such person by the decedent;

(2) such interest is inherited by such person from the decedent;

(3) such interest is the dower or curtesy interest (or statutory interest in lieu thereof) of such person as surviving spouse of the decedent;

(4) such interest has been transferred to such person by the decedent at any time;

(5) such interest was, at the time of the decedent's death, held by such person and the decedent (or by them and any other person) in joint ownership with right of survivorship;

(6) the decedent had a power (either alone or in conjunction with any person) to appoint such interest and if he appoints or has appointed such interest to such person, or if such person takes such interest in default on the release or nonexercise of such power; or

(7) such interest consists of proceeds of insurance on the life of the decedent receivable by such person.

Except as provided in paragraph (5) or (6) of subsection (b), where at the time of the decedent's death it is not possible to ascertain the particular person or persons to whom an interest in property may pass from the decedent, such interest shall, for purposes of subparagraphs (A) and (B) of subsection (b)(1), be considered as passing from the decedent to a person other than the surviving spouse.

Sec. 2101.   Tax Imposed.

(a) *In General.* — A tax computed in accordance with the table contained in section 2001 is hereby imposed on the transfer of the taxable estate, determined as provided in section 2106, of every decedent nonresident not a citizen of the United States dying after the date of enactment of this title.

(b) *Property Held by Alien Property Custodian.* —

> For taxes in connection with property or interests transferred to or vested in the Alien Property Custodian, see section 36 of the Trading with the Enemy Act, as added by the Act of August 8, 1946 (60 Stat. 929; 50 U.S.C. App. 36).

Sec. 2102.   Credits Against Tax.

The tax imposed by section 2101 shall be credited with the amounts determined in accordance with sections 2011 to 2013, inclusive (relating to State death taxes, gift tax, and tax on prior transfers).

Sec. 2103.   Definition of Gross Estate.

For the purpose of the tax imposed by section 2101, the value of the gross estate of every decedent nonresident not a citizen of the United States shall be that part of his gross estate (determined as provided in section 2031) which at the time of his death is situated in the United States.

Sec. 2104.   Property Within the United States.

(a) *Stock in Corporation.* — For purposes of this subchapter shares of stock owned and held by a nonresident not a citizen of the United States shall be deemed property within the United States only if issued by a domestic corporation.

(b) *Revocable Transfers and Transfers in Contemplation of Death.* — For purposes of this subchapter, any property of which the decedent has made a transfer, by trust or otherwise, within the meaning of sections 2035 to 2038, inclusive, shall be deemed to be situated in the United States, if so situated either at the time of the transfer or at the time of the decedent's death.

Sec. 2105.   Property Without the United States.

(a) *Proceeds of Life Insurance.* — For purposes of this subchapter, the amount receivable as insurance on the life of a nonresident not a citizen of the United States shall not be deemed property within the United States.

(b) *Bank Deposits.* — For purposes of this subchapter, any moneys deposited with any person carrying on the banking business, by or for a nonresident not a citizen of the United States who was not engaged in business in the United States at the time of his death shall not be deemed property within the United States.

(c) *Works of Art on Loan for Exhibition.* — For purposes of this subchapter, works of art owned by a nonresident not a citizen of the United States shall not be deemed property within the United States if such works of art are —

(1) imported into the United States solely for exhibition purposes,

(2) loaned for such purposes, to a public gallery or museum, no part of the net earnings of which inures to the benefit of any private stockholder or individual, and

(3) at the time of the death of the owner, on exhibition, or en route to or from exhibition, in such a public gallery or museum.

Sec. 2106. Taxable Estate.

(a) *Definition of Taxable Estate.* — For purposes of the tax imposed by section 2101, the value of the taxable estate of every decedent nonresident not a citizen of the United States shall be determined by deducting from the value of that part of his gross estate which at the time of his death is situated in the United States —

(1) *Expenses, losses, indebtedness, and taxes.* — That proportion of the deductions specified in sections 2053 and 2054 (other than the deductions described in the following sentence) which the value of such part bears to the value of his entire gross estate, wherever situated. Any deduction allowable under section 2053 in the case of a claim against the estate which was founded on a promise or agreement but was not contracted for an adequate and full consideration in money or money's worth shall be allowable under this paragraph to the extent that it would be allowable as a deduction under paragraph (2) if such promise or agreement constituted a bequest.

(2) *Transfers for public, charitable, and religious uses.* —

(A) *In general.* — The amount of all bequests, legacies, devises, or transfers (including the interest which falls into any such bequest, legacy, devise, or transfer as a result of an irrevocable disclaimer of a bequest, legacy, devise, transfer, or power, if the disclaimer is made before the date prescribed for the filing of the estate tax return) —

(i) to or for the use of the United States, any State, Territory, any political subdivision thereof, or the District of Columbia, for exclusively public purposes;

(ii) to or for the use of any domestic corporation organized and operated exclusively for religious, charitable, scientific, literary, or educational purposes, including the encouragement of art and the prevention of cruelty to children or animals, no part of the net earnings of which inures to the benefit of any private stockholder or individual, and no substantial part of the activities of which is carrying on propaganda, or otherwise attempting, to influence legislation; or

(iii) to a trustee or trustees, or a fraternal society, order, or association operating under the lodge system, but only if such contributions or gifts are to be used within the United States by such trustee or trustees, or by such fraternal society, order, or association, exclusively for religious, charitable, scientific, literary, or educational purposes, or for the prevention of cruelty to children or animals, and no substantial part of the activities of such trustee or trustees, or of such fraternal society, order, or association, is carrying on propaganda, or otherwise attempting, to influence legislation.

(B) *Powers of appointment* — Property includible in the decedent's gross estate under section 2041 (relating to powers of appointment) received by a donee described in this paragraph shall, for purposes of this paragraph, be considered a bequest of such decedent.

(C) *Death taxes payable out of bequest.* — If the tax imposed by section 2101, or any estate, succession, legacy, or inheritance taxes, are, either by the terms of the will, by the law of the jurisdiction under which the estate is administered, or by the law of the jurisdiction imposing the particular tax, payable in whole or in part out of the bequests, legacies, or devises otherwise deductible under this paragraph, then the amount deductible under this paragraph shall be the amount of such bequests, legacies, or devises reduced by the amount of such taxes.

(D) *Limitation on deduction.* — The amount of the deduction under this paragraph for any transfer shall not exceed the value of the transferred property required to be included in the gross estate.

(E) *Disallowance of deductions in certain cases.* —

For disallowance of certain charitable, etc., deductions otherwise allowable under this paragraph [section], see sections 503 and 681.

(F) *Other cross references.* —

(1) For option as to time for valuation for purpose of deduction under this paragraph [section], see section 2032.

(2) For exemption of bequests to or for benefit of Library of Congress, see section 5 of the Act of March 3, 1925, as amended (56 Stat. 765; 2 U.S.C. 161).

(3) For construction of bequests for benefit of the library of the Post Office Department as bequests to or for the use of the United States, see section 2 of the Act of August 8, 1946 (60 Stat. 924; 5 U.S.C. 393).

(4) For exemption of bequests for benefit of Office of Naval Records and Library, Navy Department, see section 2 of the Act of March 4, 1937 (50 Stat. 25; 5 U.S.C. 419b).

(5) For exemption of bequests to or for benefit of National Park Service, see section 5 of the Act of July 10, 1935 (49 Stat. 478; 16 U.S.C. 19c).

(6) For construction of devises or bequests accepted by the Secretary of State under the Foreign Service Act of 1946 as devises or bequests to or for the use of the United States, see section 1021 (e) of that Act (60 Stat. 1032; 22 U.S.C. 809).

(7) For construction of gifts or bequests of money accepted by the Attorney General for credit to "Commissary Funds, Federal Prisons" as gifts or bequests to or for the use of the United States, see section 2 of the Act of May 15, 1952, 66 Stat. 73, as amended by the Act of July 9, 1952, 66 Stat. 479 (31 U.S.C. 725s-4).

(8) For payment of tax on bequests of United States obligations to the United States, see section 24 of the Second Liberty Bond Act, as amended (59 Stat. 48, §4; 31 U.S.C. 757e).

(9) For construction of bequests for benefit of or use in connection with the Naval Academy as bequests to or for the use of the United States, see section 3 of the Act of March 31, 1944 (58 Stat. 135; 34 U.S.C. 1115b).

(10) For exemption of bequests for benefit of Naval Academy Museum, see section 4 of the Act of March 26, 1938 (52 Stat. 119; 34 U.S.C. 1119).

(11) For exemption of bequests received by National Archives

Trust Fund Board, see section 7 of the National Archives Trust Fund Board Act (55 Stat. 582; 44 U.S.C. 300gg).

(3) *Exemption.* —

(A) *General rule.* — An exemption of $2,000.

(B) *Residents of possessions of the United States.* — In the case of a decedent who is considered to be a "nonresident not a citizen of the United States" under the provisions of section 2209, the exemption shall be the greater of (i) $2,000, or (ii) that proportion of the exemption authorized by section 2052 which the value of that part of the decedent's gross estate which at the time of his death is situated in the United States bears to the value of his entire gross estate wherever situated.

(b) *Condition of Allowance of Deductions.* — No deduction shall be allowed under paragraphs (1) and (2) of subsection (a) in the case of a nonresident not a citizen of the United States unless the executor includes in the return required to be filed under section 6018 the value at the time of his death of that part of the gross estate of such nonresident not situated in the United States.

(c) *United States Bonds.* — For purposes of section 2103, the value of the gross estate (determined as provided in section 2031) of a decedent who was not engaged in business in the United States at the time of his death —

(1) shall not include obligations issued by the United States before March 1, 1941; and

(2) shall include obligations issued by the United States on or after March 1, 1941.

Sec. 2201. Members of the Armed Forces Dying During an Induction Period.

The additional estate tax as defined in section 2011(d) shall not apply to the transfer of the taxable estate of a citizen or resident of the United States dying during an induction period (as defined in sec. 112(c)(5)), while in active service as a member of the Armed Forces of the United States, if such decedent —

(1) was killed in action while serving in a combat zone, as determined under section 112(c); or

(2) died as a result of wounds, disease, or injury suffered, while serving in a combat zone (as determined under section 112(c)), and while in line of duty, by reason of a hazard to which he was subjected as an incident of such service.

Sec. 2202. Missionaries in Foreign Service.

Missionaries duly commissioned and serving under boards of foreign missions of the various religious denominations in the United States, dying while in the foreign missionary service of such boards, shall not, by reason merely of their intention to permanently remain in such foreign service, be deemed nonresidents of the United States, but shall be presumed to be residents of the State or the District of Columbia wherein they respectively resided at the time of their commission and their departure for such foreign service.

Sec. 2203. Definition of Executor.

The term "executor" wherever it is used in this title in connection with the estate tax imposed by this chapter means the executor or administrator of the decedent, or, if there is no executor or administrator appointed, qualified, and acting within the United States, then any person in actual or constructive possession of any property of the decedent.

Sec. 2204. Discharge of Executor From Personal Liability.

If the executor makes written application to the Secretary or his delegate for determination of the amount of the tax and discharge from personal liability therefor, the Secretary or his delegate (as soon as possible, and in any event within 1 year after the making of such application, or, if the application is made before the return is filed, then within 1 year after the return is filed, but not after the expiration of the period prescribed for the assessment of the tax in section 6501) shall notify the executor of the amount of the tax. The executor, on payment of the amount of which he is notified, shall be discharged from personal liability for any deficiency in tax thereafter found to be due and shall be entitled to a receipt or writing showing such discharge.

Sec. 2205. Reimbursement Out of Estate.

If the tax or any part thereof is paid by, or collected out of, that part of the estate passing to or in the possession of any person other than the executor in his capacity as such, such person shall be entitled to reimbursement out of any part of the estate still undistributed or by a just and equitable contribution by the persons whose interest in the estate of the decedent would have been reduced if the tax had been paid before the distribution of the estate or whose interest is subject to equal or prior liability for the payment of taxes, debts, or other charges against the estate, it being the purpose and intent of this chapter that so far as is practicable and unless otherwise directed by the will of the decedent the tax shall be paid out of the estate before its distribution.

Sec. 2206. Liability of Life Insurance Beneficiaries.

Unless the decedent directs otherwise in his will, if any part of the gross estate on which tax has been paid consists of proceeds of policies of insurance on the life of the decedent receivable by a beneficiary other than the executor, the executor shall be entitled to recover from such beneficiary such portion of the total tax paid as the proceeds of such policies bear to the sum of the taxable estate and the amount of the exemption allowed in computing the taxable estate, determined under section 2051. If there is more than one such beneficiary, the executor shall be entitled to recover from such beneficiaries in the same ratio. In the case of such proceeds receivable by the surviving spouse of the decedent for which a deduction is allowed under section 2056 (relating to marital deduction), this section shall not apply to such proceeds except as to the amount thereof in excess of the aggregate amount of the marital deductions allowed under such section.

Sec. 2207. Liability of Recipient of Property Over Which Decedent Had Power of Appointment.

Unless the decedent directs otherwise in his will, if any part of the gross estate on which the tax has been paid consists of the value of property included in the gross estate under section 2041, the executor shall be entitled to recover from the person receiving such property by reason of the exercise, nonexercise, or release of a power of appointment such portion of the total tax paid as the value of such property bears to the sum of the taxable estate and the amount of the exemption allowed in computing the taxable estate, determined under section 2052, or section 2106 (a), as the case may be. If there is more than one such person, the executor shall be entitled to recover from such persons in the same ratio. In the case of such property received by the surviving spouse of the decedent for which a deduction is allowed under section 2056 (relating to marital deduction), this section shall not apply to such property except as to the value thereof reduced by an amount equal to the excess of the aggregate amount of the marital deductions allowed under section 2056 over the amount of proceeds of insurance upon the life of the decedent receivable by the surviving spouse for which proceeds a marital deduction is allowed under such section.

Sec. 2208. Certain Residents of Possessions Considered Citizens of the United States.

A decedent who was a citizen of the United States and a resident of a possession thereof at the time of his death shall, for purposes of the tax imposed by this chapter, be considered a "citizen" of the United States within the meaning of that term wherever used in this title unless he acquired his United States citizenship solely by reason of (1) his being a citizen of such possession of the United States, or (2) his birth or residence within such possession of the United States.

Sec. 2209. Certain Residents of Possessions Considered Nonresidents Not Citizens of the United States.

A decedent who was a citizen of the United States and a resident of a possession thereof at the time of his death shall, for purposes of the tax imposed by this chapter, be considered a "nonresident not a citizen of the United States" within the meaning of that term wherever used in this title, but only if such person acquired his United States citizenship solely by reason of (1) his being a citizen of such possession of the United States, or (2) his birth or residence within such possession of the United States.

Sec. 2501. Imposition of Tax.

(a) *General Rule.* — For the calendar year 1955 and each calendar year thereafter a tax, computed as provided in section 2502, is hereby imposed on the transfer of property by gift during such calendar year by any individual, resident or nonresident, except transfers of intangible property by a nonresident not a citizen of the United States and who was not engaged in business in the United States during such calendar year.

(b) *Certain Residents of Possessions Considered Citizens of the United States.* — A donor who is a citizen of the United States and a resident of a possession thereof shall, for purposes of the tax imposed by this chapter, be considered a "citizen" of the United States withing the meaning of that term wherever used in this title unless he acquired his United States citizenship solely by reason of (1) his being a citizen of such possession of the United States, or (2) his birth or residence within such possession of the United States.

(c) *Certain Residents of Possessions Considered Nonresidents Not Citizens of the United States.* — A donor who is a citizen of the United States and a resident of a possession thereof shall, for purposes of the tax imposed by this chapter, be considered a "nonresident not a citizen of the United States" within the meaning of that term wherever used in this title, but only if such donor acquired his United States citizenship solely by reason of (1) his being a citizen of such possession of the United States, or (2) his birth or residence within such possession of the United States.

(d) *Cross Reference.* —

(1) for increase in basis of property acquired by gift for gift tax paid, see section 1015(d).

(2) For exclusion of transfers of property outside the United States by a nonresident who is not a citizen of the United States, see section 2511(a).

Sec. 2502. Rate of Tax.

(a) *Computation of Tax.* — The tax imposed by section 2501 for each calendar year shall be an amount equal to the excess of —

(1) a tax, computed in accordance with the rate schedule set forth in this subsection, on the aggregate sum of the taxable gifts for such calendar year and for each of the preceding calendar years, over

(2) a tax, computed in accordance with such rate schedule, on the aggregate sum of the taxable gifts for each of the preceding calendar years.

RATE SCHEDULE

If the taxable gifts are:	The tax shall be:
Not over $5,000	$2\frac{1}{4}\%$ of the taxable gifts.
Over $5,000 but not over $10,000........	$112.50, plus $5\frac{1}{4}\%$ of excess over $5,000.
Over $10,000 but not over $20,000........	$375, plus $8\frac{1}{4}\%$ of excess over $10,000.
Over $20,000 but not over $30,000........	$1,200, plus $10\frac{1}{2}\%$ of excess over $20,000.
Over $30,000 but not over $40,000........	$2,250, plus $13\frac{1}{2}\%$ of excess over $30,000.
Over $40,000 but not over $50,000........	$3,600, plus $16\frac{1}{2}\%$ of excess over $40,000.
Over $50,000 but not over $60,000........	$5,250, plus $18\frac{3}{4}\%$ of excess over $50,000.
Over $60,000 but not over $100,000.......	$7,125, plus 21% of excess over $60,000.
Over $100,000 but not over $250,000......	$15,525, plus $22\frac{1}{2}\%$ of excess over $100,000.
Over $250,000 but not over $500,000......	$49,275, plus 24% of excess over $250,000.
Over $500,000 but not over $750,000......	$109,275, plus $26\frac{1}{4}\%$ of excess over $500,000.
Over $750,000 but not over $1,000,000....	$174,900, plus $27\frac{3}{4}\%$ of excess over $750,000.
Over $1,000,000 but not over $1,250,000...	$244,275, plus $29\frac{1}{4}\%$ of excess over $1,000,000.
Over $1,250,000 but not over $1,500,000...	$317,400, plus $31\frac{1}{2}\%$ of excess over $1,250,000.
Over $1,500,000 but not over $2,000,000...	$396,150, plus $33\frac{3}{4}\%$ of excess over $1,500,000.
Over $2,000,000 but not over $2,500,000...	$564,900, plus $36\frac{3}{4}\%$ of excess over $2,000,000.
Over $2,500,000 but not over $3,000,000...	$748,650, plus $39\frac{3}{4}\%$ of excess over $2,500,000.
Over $3,000,000 but not over $3,500,000...	$947,400, plus 42% of excess over $3,000,000.

If the taxable gifts are:	The tax shall be:
Over $3,500,000 but not over $4,000,000...	$1,157,400, plus 44¼% of excess over $3,500,000.
Over $4,000,000 but not over $5,000,000...	$1,378,650, plus 47¼% of excess over $4,000,000.
Over $5,000,000 but not over $6,000,000...	$1,851,150, plus 50¼% of excess over $5,000,000.
Over $6,000,000 but not over $7,000,000...	$2,353,650, plus 52½% of excess over $6,000,000.
Over $7,000,000 but not over $8,000,000...	$2,878,650, plus 54¾% of excess over $7,000,000.
Over $8,000,000 but not over $10,000,000..	$3,426,150, plus 57% of excess over $8,000,000.
Over $10,000,000	$4,566,150, plus 57¾% of excess over $10,000,000.

(b) *Calendar Year.* — The term "calendar year" includes only the calendar year 1932 and succeeding calendar years, and, in the case of the calendar year 1932, includes only the portion of such year after June 6, 1932.

(c) *Preceding Calendar Years.* — The term "preceding calendar years" means the calendar year 1932 and all calendar years intervening between the calendar year 1932 and the calendar year for which the tax is being computed.

(d) *Tax To Be Paid by Donor.* — The tax imposed by section 2501 shall be paid by the donor.

Sec. 2503.   Taxable Gifts.

(a) *General Definition.* — The term "taxable gifts" means the total amount of gifts made during the calendar year, less the deductions provided in sub-chapter C (sec. 2521 and following).

(b) *Exclusions From Gifts.* — In the case of gifts (other than gifts of future interests in property) made to any person by the donor during the calendar year 1955 and subsequent calendar years, the first $3,000 of such gifts to such person shall not, for purposes of subsection (a), be included in the total amount of gifts made during such year. Where there has been a transfer to any person of a present interest in property, the possibility that such interest may be diminished by the exercise of a power shall be disregarded in apply-ing this subsection, if no part of such interest will at any time pass to any other person.

(c) *Transfer for the Benefit of Minor.* — No part of a gift to an individual who has not attained the age of 21 years on the date of such transfer shall be considered a gift of a future interest in property for purposes of subsection (b) if the property and the income therefrom —

(1) may be expended by, or for the benefit of, the donee before his attaining the age of 21 years, and

(2) will to the extent not so expended —

(A) pass to the donee on his attaining the age of 21 years, and

(B) in the event the donee dies before attaining the age of 21 years, be payable to the estate of the donee or as he may appoint under a general power of appointment as defined in section 2514(c).

Sec. 2504.   Taxable Gifts for Preceding Years.

(a) *In General.* — In computing taxable gifts for the calendar year 1954 and preceding calendar years for the purpose of computing the tax for the calen-dar year 1955 or any calendar year thereafter, there shall be treated as gifts such transfers as were considered to be gifts under the gift tax laws applicable to the years in which the transfers were made and there shall be allowed such deductions as were provided for under such laws, except that specific exemption in the amount, if any, allowable under section 2521 shall be applied in all computations in respect of the calendar year 1954 and previous calendar years for the purpose of computing the tax for the calendar year 1955 or any calendar year thereafter.

(b) *Exclusions From Gifts for Preceding Years.* — In the case of gifts made to any person by the donor during the calendar year 1954 and preceding calendar years, the amount excluded, if any, by the provisions of gift tax laws applicable to the years in which the gifts were made shall not, for purposes of subsection (a), be included in the total amount of the gifts made during such year.

(c) *Valuation of Certain Gifts for Preceding Calendar Years.* — If the time has expired within which a tax may be assessed under this chapter or under corresponding provisions of prior laws, on the transfer of property by gift made during a preceding calendar year, as defined in section 2502(c), and if a tax under this chapter or under corresponding provisions of prior laws has been assessed or paid for such preceding calendar year, the value of such gift made in such preceding calendar year shall, for purposes of computing the tax under this chapter for the calendar year 1955 and subsequent calendar years, be the value of such gift which was used in computing the tax for the last preceding calendar year, for which a tax under this chapter or under corresponding provisions of prior laws was assessed or paid.

(d) *Net Gifts.* — For years before the calendar year 1955, the term "net gifts" as used in corresponding provisions of prior laws shall be read as "taxable gifts" for purposes of this chapter.

Sec. 2511. Transfers in General.

(a) *Scope.* — Subject to the limitations contained in this chapter, the tax imposed by section 2501 shall apply whether the transfer is in trust or otherwise, whether the gift is direct or indirect, and whether the property is real or personal, tangible or intangible; but in the case of a nonresident not a citizen of the United States, shall apply to a transfer only if the property is situated within the United States.

(b) *Stock in Corporation.* — Shares of stock owned and held by a nonresident not a citizen of the United States shall be deemed property within the United States only if issued by a domestic corporation.

Sec. 2512. Valuation of Gifts.

(a) If the gift is made in property, the value thereof at the date of the gift shall be considered the amount of the gift.

(b) Where property is transferred for less than an adequate and full consideration in money or money's worth, then the amount by which the value of the property exceeded the value of the consideration shall be deemed a gift, and shall be included in computing the amount of gifts made during the calendar year.

Sec. 2513. Gifts by Husband or Wife to Third Party.

(a) *Considered as Made One-Half by Each.* —

(1) *In general.* — A gift made by one spouse to any person other than his spouse shall, for the purposes of this chapter, be considered as made one-half by him and one-half by his spouse, but only if at the time of the gift

each spouse is a citizen or resident of the United States. This paragraph shall not apply with respect to a gift by a spouse of an interest in property if he creates in his spouse a general power of appointment, as defined in section 2514(c), over such interest. For purposes of this section, an individual shall be considered as the spouse of another individual only if he is married to such individual at the time of the gift and does not remarry during the remainder of the calendar year.

(2) *Consent of both spouses.* — Paragraph (1) shall apply only if both spouses have signified (under the regulations provided for in subsection (b)) their consent to the application of paragraph (1) in the case of all such gifts made during the calendar year by either while married to the other.

(b) *Manner and Time of Signifying Consent.* —

(1) *Manner.* — A consent under this section shall be signified in such manner as is provided under regulations prescribed by the Secretary or his delegate.

(2) *Time.* — Such consent may be so signified at any time after the close of the calendar year in which the gift was made, subject to the following limitations —

(A) the consent may not be signified after the 15th day of April following the close of such year, unless before such 15th day no return has been filed for such year by either spouse, in which case the consent may not be signified after a return for such year is filed by either spouse;

(B) the consent may not be signified after a notice of deficiency with respect to the tax for such year has been sent to either spouse in accordance with section 6212(a).

(c) *Revocation of Consent.* — Revocation of a consent previously signified shall be made in such manner as is provided under regulations prescribed by the Secretary or his delegate, but the right to revoke a consent previously signified with respect to a calendar year —

(1) shall not exist after the 15th day of April following the close of such year if the consent was signified on or before such 15th day; and

(2) shall not exist if the consent was not signified until after such 15th day.

(d) *Joint and Several Liability for Tax.* — If the consent required by subsection (a)(2) is signified with respect to a gift made in any calendar year, the liability with respect to the entire tax imposed by this chapter of each spouse for such year shall be joint and several.

Sec. 2514. Powers of Appointment.

(a) *Powers Created on or Before October 21, 1942.* — An exercise of a general power of appointment created on or before October 21, 1942, shall be deemed a transfer of property by the individual possessing such power; but the failure to exercise such a power or the complete release of such a power shall not be deemed an exercise thereof. If a general power of appointment created on or before October 21, 1942, has been partially released so that it is no longer a general power of appointment, the subsequent exercise of such power shall not be deemed to be the exercise of a general power of appointment if —

(1) such partial release occurred before November 1, 1951, or

(2) the donee of such power was under a legal disability to release such power on October 21, 1942, and such partial release occurred not later than six months after the termination of such legal disability.

(b) *Powers Created After October 21, 1942.* — The exercise or release of a general power of appointment created after October 21, 1942, shall be deemed a transfer of property by the individual possessing such power. A disclaimer or renunciation of such a power of appointment shall not be deemed a release of such power.

(c) *Definition of General Power of Appointment.* — For purposes of this section, the term "general power of appointment" means a power which is exercisable in favor of the individual possessing the power (hereafter in this subsection referred to as the "possessor"), his estate, his creditors, or the creditors of his estate; except that —

(1) A power to consume, invade, or appropriate property for the benefit of the possessor which is limited by an ascertainable standard relating to the health, education, support, or maintenance of the possessor shall not be deemed a general power of appointment.

(2) A power of appointment created on or before October 21, 1942, which is exercisable by the possessor only in conjunction with another person shall not be deemed a general power of appointment.

(3) In the case of a power of appointment created after October 21, 1942, which is exercisable by the possessor only in conjunction with another person —

(A) if the power is not exercisable by the possessor except in conjunction with the creator of the power — such power shall not be deemed a general power of appointment;

(B) if the power is not exercisable by the possessor except in conjunction with a person having a substantial interest, in the property subject to the power, which is adverse to exercise of the power in favor of the possessor — such power shall not be deemed a general power of appointment. For the purposes of this subparagraph a person who, after the death of the possessor, may be possessed of a power of appointment (with respect to the property subject to the possessor's power) which he may exercise in his own favor shall be deemed as having an interest in the property and such interest shall be deemed adverse to such exercise of the possessor's power;

(C) if (after the application of subparagraphs (A) and (B)) the power is a general power of appointment and is exercisable in favor of such other person — such power shall be deemed a general power of appointment only in respect of a fractional part of the property subject to such power, such part to be determined by dividing the value of such property by the number of such persons (including the possessor in favor of whom such power is exercisable.

For purposes of subparagraphs (B) and (C), a power shall be deemed to be exercisable in favor of a person if it is exercisable in favor of such person, his estate, his creditors, or the creditors of his estate.

(d) *Creation of Another Power in Certain Cases.* — If a power of appointment created after October 21, 1942, is exercised by creating another power of appointment which, under the applicable local law, can be validly exercised so as to postpone the vesting of any estate or interest in the property which was subject to the first power, or suspend the absolute ownership or power of alienation of such property, for a period ascertainable without regard to the date of the creation of the first power, such exercise of the first power shall, to the extent of the property subject to the second power, be deemed a transfer of property by the individual possessing such power.

(e) *Lapse of Power.* — The lapse of a power of appointment created after October 21, 1942, during the life of the individual possessing the power shall be considered a release of such power. The rule of the preceding sentence shall apply with respect to the lapse of powers during any calendar year only to the extent that the property which could have been appointed by exercise of such lapsed powers exceeds in value the greater of the following amounts:

(1) $5,000, or

(2) 5 percent of the aggregate value of the assets out of which, or the proceeds of which, the exercise of the lapsed powers could be satisfied.

(f) *Date of Creation of Power.* — For purposes of this section a power of appointment created by a will executed on or before October 21, 1942, shall be considered a power created on or before such date if the person executing such will dies before July 1, 1949, without having republished such will, by codicil or otherwise, after October 21, 1942.

Sec. 2515. Tenancies by the Entirety.

(a) *Creation.* — The creation of a tenancy by the entirety in real property, either by one spouse alone or by both spouses, and additions to the value thereof in the form of improvements, reductions in the indebtedness thereon, or otherwise, shall not be deemed transfers of property for purposes of this chapter, regardless of the proportion of the consideration furnished by each spouse, unless the donor elects to have such creation of a tenancy by the entirety treated as a transfer, as provided in subsection (c).

(b) *Termination.* — In the case of the termination of a tenancy by the entirety, other than by reason of the death of a spouse, the creation of which, or additions to which, were not deemed to be transfers by reason of subsection (a), a spouse shall be deemed to have made a gift to the extent that the proportion of the total consideration furnished by such spouse multiplied by the proceeds of such termination (whether in form of cash, property, or interests in property) exceeds the value of such proceeds of termination received by such spouse.

(c) *Exercise of Election.* — The election provided by subsection (a) shall be exercised by including such creation of a tenancy by the entirety or additions made to the value thereof as a transfer by gift, to the extent such transfer constitutes a gift, determined without regard to this section, in the gift tax return of the donor for the calendar year in which such tenancy by the entirety was created or additions made to the value thereof, filed within the time prescribed by law, irrespective of whether or not the gift exceeds the exclusion provided by section 2503(b).

(d) *Certain Joint Tenancies Included.* — For purposes of this section, the term "tenancy by the entirety" includes a joint tenancy between husband and wife with right of survivorship.

Sec. 2516. Certain Property Settlements.

Where husband and wife enter into a written agreement relative to their marital and property rights and divorce occurs within 2 years thereafter (whether or not such agreement is approved by the divorce decree), any transfers of property or interests in property made pursuant to such agreement —

(1) to either spouse in settlement of his or her marital or property rights, or

(2) to provide a reasonable allowance for the support of issue of the marriage during minority,

shall be deemed to be transfers made for a full and adequate consideration in money or money's worth.

Sec. 2517. Certain Annuities Under Qualified Plans.

(a) *General Rule.* — The exercise or nonexercise by an employee of an election or option whereby an annuity or other payment will become payable to any beneficiary at or after the employee's death shall not be considered a transfer for purposes of this chapter if the option or election and annuity or other payment is provided for under —

(1) an employees' trust (or under a contract purchased by an employees' trust) forming part of a pension, stock bonus, or profit-sharing plan which, at the time of such exercise or nonexercise, or at the time of termination of the plan if earlier, met the requirements of section 401(a);

(2) a retirement annuity contract purchased by an employer (and not by an employees' trust) pursuant to a plan which, at the time of such exercise or nonexercise, or at the time of termination of the plan if earlier, met the requirements of section 401(a)(3), (4), (5), and (6); or

(3) a retirement annuity contract purchased for an employee by an employer which is an organization referred to in section 503(b)(1), (2), or (3), and which is exempt from tax under section 501(a).

(b) *Transfers Attributable to Employee Contributions.* — If the annuity or other payment referred to in subsection (a) is attributable to any extent to payments or contributions made by the employee, then subsection (a) shall not apply to that part of the value of such annuity or other payment which bears the same proportion to the total value of the annuity or other payment as the total payments or contributions made by the employee bear to the total payments or contributions made. For purposes of the preceding sentence, payments or contributions made by the employee's employer or former employer toward the purchase of an annuity contract described in subsection (a)(3) shall, to the extent not excludable from gross income under section 403(b), be considered to have been made by the employee.

(c) *Employee Defined.* — For purposes of this section, the term "employee" includes a former employee.

Sec. 2521. Specific Exemption.

In computing taxable gifts for the calendar year, there shall be allowed [as] a deduction in the case of a citizen or resident an exemption of $30,000, less the aggregate of the amounts claimed and allowed as specific exemption in the computation of gift taxes for the calendar year 1932 and all calendar years intervening between that calendar year and the calendar year for which the tax is being computed under the laws applicable to such years.

Sec. 2522. Charitable and Similar Gifts.

(a) *Citizens or Residents.* — In computing taxable gifts for the calendar year, there shall be allowed as a deduction in the case of a citizen or resident the amount of all gifts made during such year to or for the use of —

(1) the United States, any State, Territory, or any political subdivision thereof, or the District of Columbia, for exclusively public purposes;

(2) a corporation, or trust, or community chest, fund, or foundation, organized and operated exclusively for religious, charitable, scientific, literary, or educational purposes, including the encouragement of art and the prevention of cruelty to children or animals, no part of the net earnings of which inures to the benefit of any private shareholder or individual, and no substantial part of the activities of which is carrying on propaganda, or otherwise attempting, to influence legislation;

(3) a fraternal society, order, or association, operating under the lodge

system, but only if such gifts are to be used exclusively for religious, charitable, scientific, literary, or educational purposes, including the encouragement of art and the prevention of cruelty to children or animals;

(4) posts or organizations of war veterans, or auxiliary units or societies of any such posts or organizations, if such posts, organizations, units, or societies are organized in the United States or any of its possessions, and if no part of their net earnings inures to the benefit of any private shareholder or individual.

(b) *Nonresidents.* — In the case of a nonresident not a citizen of the United States, there shall be allowed as a deduction the amount of all gifts made during such year to or for the use of —

(1) the United States, any State, Territory, or any political subdivision thereof, or the District of Columbia, for exclusively public purposes;

(2) a domestic corporation organized and operated exclusively for religious, charitable, scientific, literary, or educational purposes, including the encouragement of art and the prevention of cruelty to children or animals, no part of the net earnings of which inures to the benefit of any private shareholder or individual, and no substantial part of the activities of which is carrying on propaganda, or otherwise attempting, to influence legislation;

(3) a trust, or community chest, fund, or foundation, organized and operated exclusively for religious, charitable, scientific, literary, or educational purposes, including the encouragement of art and the prevention of cruelty to children or animals, no substantial part of the activities of which is carrying on propaganda, or otherwise attempting, to influence legislation; but only if such gifts are to be used within the United States exclusively for such purposes;

(4) a fraternal society, order, or association, operating under the lodge system, but only if such gifts are to be used within the United States exclusively for religious, charitable, scientific, literary, or educational purposes, including the encouragement of art and the prevention of cruelty to children or animals;

(5) posts or organizations of war veterans, or auxiliary units or societies of any such posts or organizations, if such posts, organizations, units, or societies are organized in the United States or any of its possessions, and if no part of their net earnings inures to the benefit of any private shareholder or individual.

(c) *Disallowance of Deductions in Certain Cases.* —

For disallowance of certain charitable, etc., deductions otherwise allowable under this section, see sections 503 and 681.

(d) *Other Cross References.* —

(1) For exemption of gifts to or for benefit of Library of Congress, see section 5 of the Act of March 3, 1925, as amended (56 Stat. 765; 2 U.S.C. 161).

(2) For construction of gifts for benefit of library of Post Office Department as gifts to or for the use of the United States, see section 2 of the Act of August 8, 1946 (60 Stat. 924; 5 U.S.C. 393).

(3) For exemption of gifts for benefit of Office of Naval Records and Library, Navy Department, see section 2 of the Act of March 4, 1937 (50 Stat. 25; 5 U.S.C. 419b).

(4) For exemption of gifts to or for benefit of National Park Service, see section 5 of the Act of July 10, 1935 (49 Stat. 478; 16 U.S.C. 19c).

(5) For construction of gifts accepted by the Secretary of State under the Foreign Service Act of 1946 as gifts to or for the use of the United

States, see section 1021(e) of that Act (60 Stat. 1032; 22 U.S.C. 809).

(6) For construction of gifts or bequests of money accepted by the Attorney General for credit to "Commissary Funds, Federal Prisons" as gifts or bequests to or for the use of the United States, see section 2 of the Act of May 15, 1952, 66 Stat. 73, as amended by the Act of July 9, 1952, 66 Stat. 479 (31 U.S.C. 725s-4).

(7) For payment of tax on gifts of United States obligations to the United States, see section 24 of the Second Liberty Bond Act, as amended (59 Stat. 48, §4; 31 U.S.C. 757e).

(8) For construction of gifts for benefit of or use in connection with Naval Academy as gifts to or for the use of the United States, see section 3 of the Act of March 31, 1944 (58 Stat. 135; 34 U.S.C. 1115b).

(9) For exemption of gifts for benefit of Naval Academy Museum, see section 4 of the Act of March 26, 1938 (52 Stat. 119; 34 U.S.C. 1119).

(10) For exemption of gifts received by National Archives Trust Fund Board, see section 7 of the National Archives Trust Fund Board Act (55 Stat. 582; 44 U.S.C. 300gg).

Sec. 2523. Gift to Spouse.

(a) *In General.* — Where a donor who is a citizen or resident transfers during the calendar year by gift an interest in property to a donee who at the time of the gift is the donor's spouse, there shall be allowed as a deduction in computing taxable gifts for the calendar year an amount with respect to such interest equal to one-half of its value.

(b) *Life Estate or Other Terminable Interest.* — Where, on the lapse of time, on the occurrence of an event or contingency, or on the failure of an event or contingency to occur, such interest transferred to the spouse will terminate or fail, no deduction shall be allowed with respect to such interest —

(1) if the donor retains in himself, or transfers or has transferred (for less than an adequate and full consideration in money or money's worth) to any person other than such donee spouse (or the estate of such spouse), an interest in such property, and if by reason of such retention or transfer the donor (or his heirs or assigns) or such person (or his heirs or assigns) may possess or enjoy any part of such property after such termination or failure of the interest transferred to the donee spouse; or

(2) if the donor immediately after the transfer to the donee spouse has a power to appoint an interest in such property which he can exercise (either alone or in conjunction with any person) in such manner that the appointee may possess or enjoy any part of such property after such termination or failure of the interest transferred to the donee spouse. For purposes of this paragraph, the donor shall be considered as having immediately after the transfer to the donee spouse such power to appoint even though such power cannot be exercised until after the lapse of time, upon the occurrence of an event or contingency, or on the failure of an event or contingency to occur.

An exercise or release at any time by the donor, either alone or in conjunction with any person, of a power to appoint an interest in property, even though not otherwise a transfer, shall, for purposes of paragraph (1), be considered as a transfer by him. Except as provided in subsection (e), where at the time of the transfer it is impossible to ascertain the particular person or persons who may receive from the donor an interest in property so transferred by him, such interest shall, for purposes of paragraph (1), be considered as transferred to a person other than the donee spouse.

(c) *Interest in Unidentified Assets.* — Where the assets out of which, or the proceeds of which, the interest transferred to the donee spouse may be satisfied include a particular asset or assets with respect to which no deduction would be allowed if such asset or assets were transferred from the donor to such spouse, then the value of the interest transferred to such spouse shall, for purposes of subsection (a), be reduced by the aggregate value of such particular assets.

(d) *Joint Interests.* — If the interest is transferred to the donee spouse as sole joint tenant with the donor or as tenant by the entirety, the interest of the donor in the property which exists solely by reason of the possibility that the donor may survive the donee spouse, or that there may occur a severance of the tenancy, shall not be considered for purposes of subsection (b) as an interest retained by the donor in himself.

(e) *Life Estate With Power of Appointment in Donee Spouse.* — Where the donor transfers an interest in property, if by such transfer his spouse is entitled for life to all of the income from the entire interest, or all the income from a specific portion thereof, payable annually or at more frequent intervals, with power in the donee spouse to appoint the entire interest, or such specific portion (exercisable in favor of such donee spouse, or of the estate of such donee spouse, or in favor of either, whether or not in each case the power is exercisable in favor of others), and with no power in any other person to appoint any part of such interest, or such portion, to any person other than the donee spouse —

   (1) the interest, or such portion, so transferred shall, for purposes of subsection (a) be considered as transferred to the donee spouse, and

   (2) no part of the interest, or such portion, so transferred shall, for purposes of subsection (b)(1), be considered as retained in the donor or transferred to any person other than the donee spouse.

This subsection shall apply only if, by such transfer, such power in the donee spouse to appoint the interest, or such portion, whether exercisable by will or during life, is exercisable by such spouse alone and in all events.

(f) *Community Property.* —

   (1) A deduction otherwise allowable under this section shall be allowed only to the extent that the transfer can be shown to represent a gift of property which is not, at the time of the gift, held as community property under the law of any State, Territory, or possession of the United States, or of any foreign country.

   (2) For purposes of paragraph (1), community property (except property which is considered as community property solely by reason of paragraph (3)) shall not be considered as "held as community property" if the entire value of such property (and not merely one-half thereof) is treated as the amount of the gift.

   (3) If during the calendar year 1942 or in succeeding calendar years, property held as such community property (unless considered by reason of paragraph (2) as not so held) was by the donor and the donee spouse converted, by one transaction or a series of transactions, into separate property of the donor and such spouse (including any form of co-ownership by them), the separate property so acquired by the donor and any property acquired at any time by the donor in exchange therefor (by one exchange or a series of exchanges) shall, for purposes of paragraph (1), be considered as "held as community property."

   (4) Where the value (at the time of such conversion) of the separate property so acquired by the donor exceeded the value (at such time) of the sepa-

rate property so acquired by such spouse, paragraph (3) shall apply only with respect to the same portion of such separate property of the donor as the portion which the value (as of such time) of such separate property so acquired by such spouse is of the value (as of such time) of the separate property so acquired by the donor.

Sec. 2524.   Extent of Deductions.

The deductions provided in sections 2522 and 2523 shall be allowed only to the extent that the gifts therein specified are included in the amount of gifts against which such deductions are applied.

Sec. 4321.   Imposition of Tax.

There is hereby imposed on each sale or transfer of share or certificates of stock, or of rights to subscribe for or to receive shares or certificates, issued by a corporation, a tax at the rate of 4 cents on each $100 (or major fraction thereof) of the actual value of the certificates, of the shares where no certificates are sold or transferred, or of the rights, as the case may be.   In no case shall the tax so imposed on any sale or transfer be —

(1) more than 8 cents on each share, or

(2) less than 4 cents on the sale or transfer.

Sec. 4343.   Transfers by Operation of Law.

(a) *Exempt Transfers.* — The taxes imposed by sections 4321 and 4331 shall not apply to any delivery or transfer of any of the instruments referred to in such sections —

(1) *Decedents.* — From a decedent to his executor or administrator.

Sec. 4344.   Certain Other Transfers.

(b) *Worthless Stock and Obligations.* — The taxes imposed by sections 4321 and 4331 shall not apply to any delivery or transfer of any of the instruments referred to in such sections by an executor or administrator to a legatee, heir, or distributee, if it is shown to the satisfaction of the Secretary or his delegate that the value of such instrument is not greater than the amount of the tax which would otherwise be imposed on such delivery or transfer.

(c) *Transfers Between Certain Revocable Trusts.* — The taxes imposed by sections 4321 and 4331 shall not apply to any delivery or transfer of any of the instruments referred to in such sections by one revocable trust to another revocable trust if —

(1) the grantor of both trusts is the same person, and

(2) at the time of such delivery or transfer, such grantor is treated under section 676 as the owner of both trusts.

For purposes of the preceding sentence, if 2 or more grantors are treated under section 676 as owners in the same relative proportions or both trusts, such grantors shall be treated as the same person.

Sec. 6013.   Joint Returns of Income Tax by Husband and Wife.

(a) *Joint Returns.* — A husband and wife may make a single return jointly of income taxes under subtitle A, even though one of the spouses has neither gross income nor deductions, except as provided below:

(1) no joint return shall be made if either the husband or wife at any time during the taxable year is a nonresident alien;

(2) no joint return shall be made if the husband and wife have different taxable years; except that if such taxable years begin on the same day and

end on different days because of the death of either or both, then the joint return may be made with respect to the taxable year of each. The above exception shall not apply if the surviving spouse remarries before the close of his taxable year, nor if the taxable year of either spouse is a fractional part of a year under section 443(a)(1);

(3) in the case of death of one spouse or both spouses the joint return with respect to the decedent may be made only by his executor or administrator; except that in the case of the death of one spouse the joint return may be made by the surviving spouse with respect to both himself and the decedent if no return for the taxable year has been made by the decedent, no executor or administrator has been appointed, and no executor or administrator is appointed before the last day prescribed by law for filing the return of the surviving spouse. If an executor or administrator of the decedent is appointed after the making of the joint return by the surviving spouse, the executor or administrator may disaffirm such joint return by making, within - year after the last day prescribed by law for filing the return of the surviving spouse, a separate return for the taxable year of the decedent with respect to which the joint return was made, in which case the return made by the survivor shall constitute his separate return.

Sec. 6163. Extension of Time for Payment of Estate Tax on Value of Reversionary or Remainder Interest in Property.

(a) *Extension Permitted.* — If the value of a reversionary or remainder interest in property is included under chapter 11 in the value of the gross estate, the payment of the part of the tax under chapter 11 attributable to such interest may, at the election of the executor, be postponed until 6 months after the termination of the precedent interest or interests in the property, under such regulations as the Secretary or his delegate may prescribe.

(b) *Extension To Prevent Undue Hardship.* — If the Secretary or his delegate finds that the payment of the tax at the expiration of the period of postponement provided for in subsection (a) would result in undue hardship to the estate, he may extend the time for payment for a reasonable period not in excess of 2 years from the expiration of such period of postponement.

(c) *Cross References.* —

(1) *Interest.* —

For provisions requiring the payment of interest for the period of such extension, see section 6601(b).

(2) *Security.* —

For authority of the Secretary or his delegate to require security in the case of such extension, see section 6165.

Sec. 6165. Bonds Where Time To Pay Tax or Deficiency Has Been Extended.

In the event the Secretary or his delegate grants any extension of time within which to pay any tax or any deficiency therein, the Secretary or his delegate may require the taxpayer to furnish a bond in such amount (not exceeding double the amount with respect to which the extension is granted) conditioned upon the payment of the amount extended in accordance with the terms of such extension.

Sec. 6166. Extension of Time for Payment of Estate Tax Where Estate Consists Largely of Interest in Closely Held Business.

(a) *Extension Permitted.* — If the value of an interest in a closely held business which is included in determining the gross estate of a decedent who was (at the date of his death) a citizen or resident of the United States exceeds either —

(1) 35 percent of the value of the gross estate of such decedent, or

(2) 50 percent of the taxable estate of such decedent,

the executor may elect to pay part or all of the tax imposed by section 2001 in two or more (but not exceeding 10) equal installments. Any such election shall be made not later than the time prescribed by section 6075(a) for filing the return of such tax (including extensions thereof), and shall be made in such manner as the Secretary or his delegate shall by regulations prescribe. If an election under this section is made, the provisions of this subtitle shall apply as though the Secretary or his delegate were extending the time for pay·ment of the tax. For purposes of this section, value shall be value determined for Federal estate tax purposes.

(b) *Limitation.* — The maximum amount of tax which may be paid in in·stallments as provided in this section shall be an amount which bears the same ratio to the tax imposed by section 2001 (reduced by the credits against such tax) as the value of the interest in a closely held business which qualifies under subsection (a) bears to the value of the gross estate.

(c) *Closely Held Business.* — For purposes of this section, the term "interest in a closely held business" means —

(1) an interest as a proprietor in a trade or business carried on as a proprietorship.

(2) an interest as a partner in a partnership carrying on a trade or business, if —

(A) 20 percent or more of the total capital interest in such partnership is included in determining the gross estate of the decedent, or

(B) such partnership had 10 or less partners,

(3) stock in a corporation carrying on a trade or business, if —

(A) 20 percent or more in value of the voting stock of such corporation is included in determining the gross estate of the decedent, or

(B) such corporation had 10 or less shareholders.

For purposes of this subsection, determinations shall be made as of the time immediately before the decedent's death.

(d) *Special Rule for Interests in Two or More Closely Held Businesses.* — For purposes of subsections (a), (b), and (h)(1), interests in two or more closely held businesses, with respect to each of which there is included in determining the value of the decedent's gross estate more than 50 percent of the total value of each such business, shall be treated as an interest in a single closely held business. For purposes of the 50 percent requirement of the preceding sentence, an interest in a closely held business which represents the surviving spouse's interest in property held by the decedent and the surviving spouse as community property shall be treated as having been included in determining the value of the decedent's gross estate.

(e) *Date for Payment of Installments.* — If an election is made under subsection (a), the first installment shall be paid on or before the date prescribed by section 6151(a) for payment of the tax, and each succeeding installment shall be paid on or before the date which is one year after the date prescribed by this subsection for payment of the preceding installment.

(f) *Proration of Deficiency to Installments.* — If an election is made under subsection (a) to pay any part of the tax imposed by section 2001 in install·ments and a deficiency has been assessed, the deficiency shall (subject to the limitation provided by subsection (b)) be prorated to such installments. The part of the deficiency so prorated to any installment the date for payment of which has not arrived shall be collected at the same time as, and as a part of, such installment. The part of the deficiency so prorated to any installment the date for payment of which has arrived shall be paid upon notice and demand from the Secretary or his delegate. This subsection shall not apply if the deficiency is due to negligence, to intentional disregard of rules and regulations, or to fraud with intent to evade tax.

(g) *Time for Payment of Interest.* — If the time for payment of any amount of tax has been extended under this section, interest payable under section 6601 on any unpaid portion of such amount shall be paid annually at the same time as, and as a part of, each installment payment of the tax. Interest, on that part of a deficiency prorated under this section to any installment the date for payment of which has not arrived, for the period before the date fixed for the last installment preceding the assessment of the deficiency, shall be paid upon notice and demand from the Secretary or his delegate. In applying section 6601(b) (relating to the application of the 4-percent rate of interest in the case of certain extensions of time to pay estate tax) in the case of a deficiency, the entire amount which is prorated to installments under this section shall be treated as an amount of tax the payment of which is extended under this section.

(h) *Acceleration of Payment.* —

(1) *Withdrawal of funds from business; disposition of interest.* —

(A) If —

(i) aggregate withdrawals of money and other property from the trade or business, an interest in which qualifies under subsection (a), made with respect to such interest, equal or exceed 50 percent of the value of such trade or business, or

(ii) 50 percent or more in value of an interest in a closely held business which qualifies under subsection (a) is distributed, sold, exchanged, or otherwise disposed of,

then the extension of time for payment of tax provided in this section shall cease to apply, and any unpaid portion of the tax payable in installments shall be paid upon notice and demand from the Secretary or his delegate.

(B) In the case of a distribution in redemption of stock to which section 303 (or so much of section 304 as relates to section 303) applies —

(i) subparagraph (A)(i) does not apply with respect to withdrawals of money and other property distributed; and for purposes of such subparagraph the value of the trade or business shall be considered to be such value reduced by the amount of money and other property distributed, and

(ii) subparagraph (A)(ii) does not apply with respect to the stock redeemed; and for purposes of such subparagraph the interest in the closely held business shall be considered to be such interest reduced by the value of the stock redeemed.

This subparagraph shall apply only if, on or before the date prescribed by subsection (e) for payment of the first installment which becomes due after the date of the distribution, there is paid an amount of the tax imposed by section 2001 not less than the amount of money and other property distributed.

(C) Subparagraph (A)(ii) does not apply to an exchange of stock pursuant to a plan of reorganization described in subparagraph (D), (E), or (F) of section 368(a)(1) nor to an exchange to which section 355 (or so much of section 356 as relates to section 355) applies; but any stock received in such an exchange shall be treated for purposes of such subparagraph as an interest qualifying under subsection (a).

(D) Subparagraph (A)(ii) does not apply to a transfer of property of the decedent by the executor to a person entitled to receive such property under the decedent's will or under the applicable law of descent and distribution.

(2) *Undistributed income of estate.* —

(A) If an election is made under this section and the estate has undistributed net income for any taxable year after its fourth taxable year, the executor shall, on or before the date prescribed by law for filing the income tax return for such taxable year (including extensions thereof), pay an amount equal to such undistributed net income in liquidation of the unpaid portion of the tax payable in installments.

(B) For purposes of subparagraph (A), the undistributed net income of the estate for any taxable year is the amount by which the distributable net income of the estate for such taxable year (as defined in section 643) exceeds the sum of —

(i) the amounts for such taxable year specified in paragraphs (1) and (2) of section 661(a) (relating to deduction for distributions, etc.);

(ii) the amount of tax imposed for the taxable year on the estate under chapter 1; and

(iii) the amount of the Federal estate tax (including interest) paid by the executor during the taxable year (other than any amount paid pursuant to this paragraph).

(3) *Failure to pay installment.* — If any installment under this section is not paid on or before the date fixed for its payment by this section (including any extension of time for the payment of such installment), the unpaid portion of the tax payable in installments shall be paid upon notice and demand from the Secretary or his delegate.

(i) *Transitional Rules.* —

(1) *In general.* — If —

(A) a deficiency in the tax imposed by section 2001 is assessed after the date of the enactment of this section, and

(B) the estate qualifies under paragraph (1) or (2) of subsection (a), the executor may elect to pay the deficiency in installments. This subsection shall not apply if the deficiency is due to negligence, to intentional disregard of rules and regulations, or to fraud with intent to evade tax.

(2) *Time of election.* — An election under this subsection shall be made not later than 60 days after issuance of notice and demand by the Secretary or his delegate for the payment of the deficiency, and shall be made in such manner as the Secretary or his delegate shall by regulations prescribe.

(3) *Effect of election on payment.* — If an election is made under this subsection, the deficiency shall (subject to the limitation provided by subsection (b) be prorated to the installments which would have been due if an election had been timely made under this section at the time the estate tax return was filed. The part of the deficiency so prorated to any installment the date for payment of which would have arrived shall be paid at the time of the making of the election under this subsection. The portion of the deficiency so prorated to installments the date for payment of which would not have so arrived shall be paid at the time such installments would have been due if such an election had been made.

(4) *Application of subsection (h)(2).* — In the case of an election under this subsection, subsection (h)(2) shall not apply with respect to undistributed net income for any taxable year ending before January 1, 1960.

(j) *Regulations.* — The Secretary or his delegate shall prescribe such regulations as may be necessary to the application of this section.

(k) *Cross References.* —

(1) *Interest.* —

For provisions requiring the payment of interest at the rate of 4 percent per annum for the period of an extension, see section 6601(b).

(2) *Security.* —

For authority of the Secretary or his delegate to require security in the case of an extension under this section, see section 6165.

(3) *Period of limitation.* —

For extension of the period of limitation in the case of an extension under this section, see section 6503(d).

Sec. 6324. Special Liens for Estate and Gift Taxes.

(a) *Liens for Estate Tax.* — Except as otherwise provided in subsection (c) (relating to transfers of securities) —

(1) *Upon gross estate.* — Unless the estate tax imposed by chapter 11 is sooner paid in full, it shall be a lien for 10 years upon the gross estate of the decedent, except that such part of the gross estate as is used for the payment of charges against the estate and expenses of its administration, allowed by any court having jurisdiction thereof, shall be divested of such lien.

(2) *Liability of transferees and others.* — If the estate tax imposed by chapter 11 is not paid when due, then the spouse, transferee, trustee (except the trustee of an employee's [*sic*] trust which meets the requirements of section 401(a)), surviving tenant, person in possession of the property by reason of the exercise, nonexercise, or release of a power of appointment, or beneficiary, who receives, or has on the date of the decedent's death, property included in the gross estate under sections 2034 to 2042, inclusive, to the extent of the value, at the time of the decedent's death, of such property, shall be personally liable for such tax. Any part of such property transferred by (or transferred by a transferee of) such spouse, transferee, trustee, surviving tenant, person in possession of property by reason of the exercise, nonexercise, or release of a power of appointment, or beneficiary, to a bona fide purchaser, mortgagee, or pledgee, for an adequate and full consideration in money or money's worth shall be divested of the lien provided in paragraph (1) and a like lien shall then attach to all the property of such spouse, transferee, trustee, surviving tenant, person in possession, beneficiary, or transferee of any such person, except any part transferred to a bona fide purchaser, mortgagee, or pledgee for an adequate and full consideration in money or money's worth.

(3) *Continuance after discharge of executor.* — The provisions of section 2204 (relating to discharge of executor from personal liability) shall not operate as a release of any part of the gross estate from the lien for any deficiency that may thereafter be determined to be due, unless such part of the gross estate (or any interest therein) has been transferred to a bona fide purchaser, mortgagee, or pledgee for an adequate and full consideration in money, or money's worth, in which case such part (or such interest) shall not be subject to a lien or to any claim or demand for any such

deficiency, but the lien shall attach to the consideration received from such purchaser, mortgagee, or pledgee by the heirs, legatees, devisees, or distributees.

(b) *Lien for Gift Tax.* — Except as otherwise provided in subsection (c) (relating to transfers of securities), the gift tax imposed by chapter 12 shall be a lien upon all gifts made during the calendar year, for 10 years from the time the gifts are made. If the tax is not paid when due, the donee of any gift shall be personally liable for such tax to the extent of the value of such gift. Any part of the property comprised in the gift transferred by the donee (or by a transferee of the donee) to a bona fide purchaser, mortgagee, or pledgee for an adequate and full consideration in money or money's worth shall be divested of the lien herein imposed and the lien, to the extent of the value of such gift, shall attach to all the property (including after-acquired property) of the donee (or the transferee) except any part transferred to a bona fide purchaser, mortgagee, or pledgee for an adequate and full consideration in money or money's worth.

(c) *Exception in Case of Securities.* — The lien imposed by subsection (a) or (b) shall not be valid with respect to a security, as defined in section 6323(c)(2), as against any mortgagee, pledgee, or purchaser of any such security, for an adequate and full consideration in money or money's worth, if at the time of such mortgage, pledge, or purchase such mortgagee, pledgee, or purchaser is without notice or knowledge of the existence of such lien.

Sec. 6601. Interest on Underpayment, Nonpayment, or Extensions of Time for Payment, of Tax.

(a) *General Rule.* — If any amount of tax imposed by this title (whether required to be shown on a return, or to be paid by stamp or by some other method) is not paid on or before the last date prescribed for payment, interest on such amount at the rate of 6 percent per annum shall be paid for the period from such last date to the date paid.

(b) *Extensions of Time for Payment of Estate Tax.* — If the time for payment of an amount of tax imposed by chapter 11 is extended as provided in section 6161(a)(2) or 6166, or if the time for payment of an amount of such tax is postponed or extended as provided by section 6163, interest shall be paid at the rate of 4 percent, in lieu of 6 percent as provided in subsection (a).

Sec. 6901. Transferred Assets.

(a) *Method of Collection.* — The amounts of the following liabilities shall, except as hereinafter in this section provided, be assessed, paid and collected in the same manner and subject to the same provisions and limitations as in the case of the taxes with respect to which the liabilities were incurred:

(1) *Income, estate, and gift taxes.* —

(A) *Transferees.* — The liability, at law or in equity, of a transferee of property —

(i) of a taxpayer in the case of a tax imposed by subtitle A (relating to income taxes),

(ii) of a decedent in the case of a tax imposed by chapter 11 (relating to estate taxes), or

(iii) of a donor in the case of a tax imposed by chapter 12 (relating to gift taxes),

in respect of the tax imposed by subtitle A or B.

(B) *Fiduciaries.* — The liability of a fiduciary under section 3467 of the Revised Statutes (31 U.S.C. 192) in respect of the payment of any tax described in subparagraph (A) from the estate of the taxpayer, the decedent, or the donor, as the case may be.

(2) *Other taxes.* — The liability, at law or in equity of a transferee of property of any person liable in respect of any tax imposed by this title (other than a tax imposed by subtitle A or B), but only if such liability arises on the liquidation of a partnership or corporation, or on a reorganization within the meaning of section 368(a).

(b) *Liability.* — Any liability referred to in subsection (a) may be either as to the amount of tax shown on a return or as to any deficiency or underpayment of any tax.

(c) *Period of Limitations.* — The period of limitations for assessment of any such liability of a transferee or a fiduciary shall be as follows:

(1) *Initial transferee.* — In the case of the liability of an initial transferee, within 1 year after the expiration of the period of limitation for assessment against the transferor;

(2) *Transferee of transferee.* — In the case of the liability of a transferee of a transferee, within 1 year after the expiration of the period of limitation for assessment against the preceding transferee, but not more than 3 years after the expiration of the period of limitation for assessment against the initial transferor;

except that if, before the expiration of the period of limitation for the assessment of the liability of the transferee, a court proceeding for the collection of the tax or liability in respect thereof has been begun against the initial transferor or the last preceding transferee, respectively, then the period of limitation for assessment of the liability of the transferee shall expire 1 year after the return of execution in the court proceeding.

(3) *Fiduciary.* — In the case of the liability of a fiduciary, not later than 1 year after the liability arises or not later than the expiration of the period for collection of the tax in respect of which such liability arises, whichever is the later.

(d) *Extension by Agreement.* —

(1) *Extension of time for assessment.* — If before the expiration of the time prescribed in subsection (c) for the assessment of the liability, the Secretary or his delegate and the transferee or fiduciary have both consented in writing to its assessment after such time, the liability may be assessed at any time prior to the expiration of the period agreed upon. The period so agreed upon may be extended by subsequent agreements in writing made before the expiration of the period previously agreed upon. For the purpose of determining the period of limitation on credit or refund to the transferee or fiduciary of overpayments of tax made by such transferee or fiduciary or overpayments of tax made by the transferor of which the transferee or fiduciary is legally entitled to credit or refund, such agreement and any extension thereof shall be deemed an agreement and extension thereof referred to in section 6511(c).

(2)(3) *Extension of time for credit or refund.* — If the agreement is executed after the expiration of the period of limitation for assessment against the taxpayer with reference to whom the liability of such transferee or fiduciary arises, then in applying the limitations under section 6511(c) on the amount of the credit or refund, the periods specified in section 6511(b)(2) shall be increased by the period from the date of such expiration to the date of the agreement.

(e) *Period for Assessment Against Transferor.* — For purposes of this section, if any person is deceased, or is a corporation which has terminated its existence, the period of limitation for assessment against such person shall be the period that would be in effect had death or termination of existence not occurred.

(f) *Suspension of Running of Period of Limitations.* — The running of the period of limitations upon the assessment of the liability of a transferee or fiduciary shall, after the mailing to the transferee or fiduciary of the notice provided for in section 6212 (relating to income, estate, and gift taxes), be suspended for the period during which the Secretary or his delegate is prohibited from making the assessment in respect of the liability of the transferee or fiduciary (and in any event, if a proceeding in respect of the liability is placed on the docket of the Tax Court, until the decision of the Tax Court becomes final), and for 60 days thereafter.

(g) *Address for Notice of Liability.* — In the absence of notice to the Secretary or his delegate under section 6903 of the existence of a fiduciary relationship, any notice of liability enforceable under this section required to be mailed to such person, shall, if mailed to the person subject to the liability at his last known address, be sufficient for purposes of this title, even if such person is deceased, or is under a legal disability, or, in the case of a corporation, has terminated its existence.

(h) *Definition of Transferee.* — As used in this section, the term "transferee" includes donee, heir, legatee, devisee, and distributee, and with respect to estate taxes, also includes any person who, under section 6324(a)(2), is personally liable for any part of such tax.

(i) *Extension of Time.* —

For extensions of time by reason of armed service in a combat zone, see section 7508.

Sec. 7101.   Form of Bonds.

Whenever, pursuant to the provisions of this title (other than sections 7485 and 6803(a)(1)), or rules or regulations prescribed under authority of this title, a person is required to furnish a bond or security —

(1) *General rule.* — Such bond or security shall be in such form and with such surety or sureties as may be prescribed by regulations issued by the Secretary or his delegate.

(2) *United States bonds and notes in lieu of surety bonds.* — The person required to furnish such bond or security may, in lieu thereof, deposit bonds or notes of the United States as provided in 6 U.S.C. 15.

APPENDIX V

Selected Provisions from State Statutes

ALABAMA

Code 1958

Title 47, §64. Removal of personalty. The tenant for life in personalty, cannot remove it beyond the jurisdiction of this state without the consent of the remainderman. If he attempts to do so, the remainderman or reversioner is entitled to the writ of ne exeat to restrain him.

Title 61, §10. When child born or adopted after will takes as in case of intestacy. Whenever a testator has a child born after the making of his will, either in his lifetime or after his death, or adopted after the making of his will, and no provision is made in the will in any way for such contingency, such birth or adoption operates as a revocation of the will, so far as to allow such child to take the same share of the estate of the testator as if he had died intestate.

CALIFORNIA

Probate Code (Deering) 1959

§53. Holographic will: Form: Execution: Printed matter as part of will. A holographic will is one that is entirely written, dated and signed by the hand of the testator himself. It is subject to no other form, and need not be witnessed. No address, date or other matter written, printed or stamped upon the document, which is not incorporated in the provisions which are in the handwriting of the decedent, shall be considered as any part of the will.

§122. References to death or survivorship: Time to which words refer. Words in a will referring to death or survivorship, simply, relate to the time of the testator's death, unless possession is actually postponed, when they must be referred to the time of possession.

§201.5. Personal property: Real property situated in state. Upon the death of any married person domiciled in this State one-half of the following property in his estate shall belong to the surviving spouse and the other one-half of such property is subject to the testamentary disposition of the decedent, and in the absence thereof goes to the surviving spouse: all personal property wherever situated and all real property situated in this State heretofore or hereafter (a) acquired by the decedent while domiciled elsewhere which would have been the community property of the decedent and the surviving spouse had the decedent been domiciled in this State at the time of its acquisition or (b) acquired in exchange for real or personal property wherever situated and so acquired. All such property is subject to the debts of the decedent and to administration and disposal under the provisions of Division 3 of this code.

As used in this section personal property does not include and real property does include leasehold interests in real property.

§259. Right of nonresident aliens to take realty: Dependence on reciprocal rights. The right of aliens not residing within the United States or its territories to take real property in this State by succession or testamentary disposition, upon the same terms and conditions as residents and citizens of the United States is dependent in each case upon the existence of a reciprocal right upon the part of citizens of the United States to take real property upon the same terms and conditions as residents and citizens of the respective countries of which such aliens are residents and the right of aliens not residing in the United States or its territories to take personal property in this State by succession or testamentary disposition, upon the same terms and conditions as residents and citizens of the United States is dependent in each case upon the existence of a reciprocal right upon the part of citizens of the United States to take personal property upon the same terms and conditions as residents and citizens of the respective countries of which such aliens are residents

§259.1. Burden of proof as to reciprocal rights. The burden shall be upon such nonresident aliens to establish the existence of the reciprocal rights set forth in Section 259.

§259.2. When property escheats. If such reciprocal rights are not found to exist and if no heirs other than such aliens are found eligible to take such property, the property shall be disposed of as escheated property.

CONNECTICUT

General Statutes 1958

§45-173 [Supp. 1959]. Reference to document creating trusts. No devise or bequest given in any will or codicil or republication thereof in any codicil shall be deemed invalid by reason of any reference therein to any document creating a trust, which document was in existence at the time of the execution of such will or codicil and is identified in such will or codicil by reference to the names of the parties who executed such document and the date of such execution, and such a devise or bequest may be made to the trustee or trustees of such trust; provided, if such trust by its terms may be revoked or amended, such devise or bequest shall be deemed invalid if, subsequent to the execution of such will or codicil, the trust is revoked or amended, provided mere addition to or withdrawal of any or all assets from such trust or a change of the trustee or trustees of such trust, if such amendment is in accordance with the terms thereof, shall not be deemed a revocation or amendment within the meaning of the provisions hereof. Such reference in a will or codicil to such trust document by which a devise or bequest is made to such trust shall not thereby cause such trust or such part of the assets thereof distributed to it by such devise or bequest to be subject to the jurisdiction of the probate court in which such will or codicil is admitted to probate.

GEORGIA

Code Annotated 1955

§85-708. Vesting of remainders favored. The law favors the vesting of remainders in all cases of doubt. In construing wills, words of survivorship shall refer to the death of the testator in order to vest remainders, unless a manifest intention to the contrary shall appear.

IDAHO

Code Annotated 1957

§55-111. Suspension of power of alienation. The absolute power of alienation of real property cannot be suspended by any limitation or condition
whatever, for a longer period than during the continuance of the lives of the
persons in being at the creation of the limitation or condition, and 25 years
thereafter; there shall be no rule against perpetuities applicable to real or
personal property, nor any rule prohibiting the placing of restraints on the
alienation of personal property; no trust heretofore or hereafter created,
either testamentary or inter vivos, shall be declared void, but shall be so
construed as to eliminate parts violating the above provisions, and in such a
way that the testator's or trustor's wishes are carried out to the greatest extent permitted by this act; that there shall be no presumption that a person
is capable of having children at any stage of adult life.

ILLINOIS

Revised Statutes 1959

Chapter 3, §194a. Testamentary additions to trusts. By a will signed and
attested as provided in this Act a testator may devise and bequeath real
and personal estate to a trustee of a trust which is evidenced by a written
instrument in existence when the will is made and which is identified in the
will, even though the trust is subject to amendment, modification, revocation
or termination. Unless the will provides otherwise the estate so devised and
bequeathed shall be governed by the terms and provisions of the instrument
creating the trust including any amendments or modifications in writing
made at any time before or after the making of the will and before the death
of the testator.

§200. Devise or legacy to deceased devisee or legatee. When a devise or
legacy is to a descendant of the testator who dies before the testator and
there is no provision in the will for that contingency, the descendants of the
devisee or legatee take per stirpes the estate so devised or bequeathed. When
a devise or legacy is to a class, and any member of the class dies before the
testator and there is no provision in the will for that contingency, the members of the class who survive the testator take the share or shares which the
deceased member would have taken had he survived the testator, except that
if the deceased member of the class is a descendant of the testator, the descendants of the deceased member take per stirpes the share or shares which
the deceased member would have taken had he survived the testator. Except
as above provided, when a devise or legacy lapses, by reason of the death of
the devisee or legatee before the testator, and there is no provision in the
will for that contingency, the estate so devised or bequeathed shall be included in and pass as part of the residue under the will, and if the devise or
legacy is or becomes part of the residue, the estate so devised or bequeathed
shall pass to and be taken by the legatees or devisees, or those remaining, if
any, of the residue in proportions and upon estates corresponding to their
respective interests in the residue.

§229. Who may act as executor. A person is not qualified to act as
executor of any will who is of unsound mind or an adjudged incompetent
under this Act or has been convicted of a crime rendering him infamous or

is a non-resident of this State or, if a male, is less than twenty-one years of age or, if a female, is less than eighteen years of age. Any corporation qualified to accept and execute trusts in this State is qualified to act as executor of a will.

§271. Control of estate — Custody of person — Different conservators. The conservatorship of the incompetent's estate may be appointed to one person and the conservatorship of the incompetent's person to another. Any corporation qualified to accept and execute trusts in this State is qualified to act as conservator of the incompetent's estate.

§272. Residence of conservator. A non-resident of this State may be appointed as conservator of the person of an incompetent person but not as conservator of his estate.

Chapter 30, §188. Abolition of worthier title and of rule that grantor cannot create limitation in favor of own heirs. Where a deed, will or other instrument purports to create any present or future interest in real or personal property in the heirs of the maker of the instrument, the heirs shall take, by purchase and not by descent, the interest that the instrument purports to create. The doctrine of worthier title and the rule of the common law that a grantor cannot create a limitation in favor of his own heirs are abolished.

§189. Application of act. This Act shall apply only to instruments which become effective after the effective date of this Act.

INDIANA

Statutes Annotated (Burns) 1953

§6-601(c). Rules for interpretation of wills. A devise of real or personal estate, whether directly or in trust, to the testator's or another designated person's "heirs" or "next of kin" or "relatives," or "family," or to "the persons thereunto entitled under the intestate laws" or to persons described by words of similar import, shall mean those persons, including the spouse, who would take under the intestate laws if the testator or other designated person were to die intestate at the time when such class is to be ascertained, domiciled in this state, and owning the estate so devised. With respect to a devise which does not take effect at the testator's death, the time when such class is to be ascertained shall be the time when the devise is to take effect in enjoyment.

§6-601(d). Rules for interpretation of wills. In construing a will making a devise to a person or persons described by relationship to the testator or to another, any person adopted during minority before the death of the testator shall be considered the child of his adopting parent or parents and not the child of his natural or previous adopting parents: Provided, that if a natural parent or previous adopting parent shall have married the adopting parent before the testator's death, the adopted person shall also be considered the child of such natural or previous adopting parent. Any person adopted when an adult by the testator shall be considered the child of the testator, but no other person shall be entitled to establish relationship to the testator through such child.

§6-601(e). Rules for interpretation of wills. In construing a will making a devise to a person described by relationship to the testator or to another, an illegitimate person shall be considered the child of his mother, and also of his father, if, but only if, his right to inherit from his father is, or has been, established in the manner provided in section 205 [§6-205] of this code. [The reference should be to section 207 [§6-207]. ED.]

§6-604. Renunciation by heir or devisee. At any time within three (3) months after the appointment of the personal representative an heir or devisee may renounce his succession to all or any portion of the real or personal property of a decedent by filing a renunciation in court, except that no such renunciation shall be effective if it is objected to within thirty (30) days by a creditor of the heir or devisee and if the court finds that the creditor is prejudiced thereby. In case of an effective renunciation by the heir, or devisee, the property affected thereby shall descend as if he had died before the decedent, but the succession so renounced shall be subject to the same Indiana inheritance tax that would have been assessed if there were no renunciation.

KANSAS

General Statutes Annotated 1949

§58-505. Common law rules inapplicable (rule in Wild's case). In the case of instruments disposing of property of which the following is a type: "A to B and his children," the doctrine of the common law known as the rule in Wild's case shall not hereafter apply, and the instrument shall create a life interest in B and a remainder in his children. The rule here prescribed applies when the expression is "children," or "issue," or words of similar import.

§59-1701. Corporate fiduciaries. No bank or other corporation, unless it is organized under the laws of and has its principal place of business in this state, or is a national bank located in this state, shall be appointed or authorized directly or indirectly to act as a fiduciary in this state, except in ancillary proceedings; and no officer, employee or agent of such bank or corporation shall be permitted to act as a fiduciary in this state, whether such officer, employee or agent is a resident or a nonresident of this state, when in fact such officer, employee or agent is acting as such fiduciary on behalf of such bank or corporation; nor shall any bank or other corporation be appointed guardian of the person of a ward.

MAINE

Revised Statutes Annotated 1954

Chapter 160, §34 [Supp. 1959]. Income earned during period of administration. Unless otherwise expressly provided by the will of a testator dying after the effective date of this act, all net income from real and personal property earned during the period of administration of the estate of such testator and not payable to others or otherwise disposed of by the will shall be distributed pro rata to or for the benefit of the immediate income beneficiaries of any trusts created out of the residuary estate of such testator and to other persons entitled to such residuary estate. None of such income shall, after such distribution, be added to the principal of the residuary estate the whole or any part of which is devised or bequeathed in trust or for life or for a term of years, but shall be paid ratably to the income beneficiary of a trust, or to the tenant for life or for a term of years, or to the absolute residuary distributee, as the case may be. Unless otherwise directed in the will, income shall be payable to the life beneficiaries of trusts, or to life tenants from the date of testator's death. Nothing contained in this section shall affect the right of any person to income on any portion of the estate not part of the residuary estate of such testator.

MARYLAND

Code Annotated 1957

Article 93, §59.   Executors disqualified. If any person named as executor in a will shall be, at the time when administration ought to be granted, under the age of eighteen years or of unsound mind, incapable according to law of making a contract, or convicted of any crime rendering him infamous according to law, or if any person named as executor shall not be a citizen of the United States, letters testamentary or of administration (as the case may require) may be granted in the same manner as if such person had not been named in the will.

§354.   Death of devisee or legatee in lifetime of testator — Does not cause lapse. No devise, legacy or bequest shall lapse or fail of taking effect by reason of the death of any devisee or legatee (actually and specially named as devisee or legatee, or who is or shall be mentioned, described, or in any manner referred to, or designated or identified as devisee or legatee in any will, testament or codicil) in the lifetime of the testator, but every such devise, legacy or bequest shall have the same effect and operation in law to transfer the right, estate and interest in the property mentioned in such devise or bequest as if such devisee or legatee had survived the testator.

§355.   Same — Applicable to two or more persons as a class. In all wills executed after July 1, 1929, unless a contrary intention is expressly stated in the will, the provisions of §354 in regard to lapse shall apply to all devises and bequests to two or more persons as a class in the same manner as though such devises or bequests had been made to such persons by their individual names.

MASSACHUSETTS

Annotated Laws

Chapter 65, §1 [Supp. 1959].   Taxation of legacies and successions; rates of tax; exemptions. All property within the jurisdiction of the commonwealth, corporeal or incorporeal, and any interest therein, belonging to inhabitants of the commonwealth, and all real estate or any interest therein and all tangible personal property within the commonwealth belonging to persons who are not inhabitants of the commonwealth, except such an interest in such real estate as is represented by a mortgage or by a transferable certificate of participation or share of an association, partnership or trust, which shall pass by will, or by laws regulating intestate succession, or by deed, grant or gift, except in cases of a bona fide purchase for full consideration in money or money's worth, made in contemplation of the death of the grantor or donor or made or intended to take effect in possession or enjoyment after his death, and any beneficial interest therein which shall arise or accrue by survivorship in any form of joint ownership, or in any tenancy by the entirety in which the decedent contributed during his life any part of the property held in such joint ownership or tenancy by the entirety or of the purchase price thereof, to any person, absolutely or in trust, except (1) to or for the use of charitable, educational or religious societies or institutions which are organized under the laws of, or charitable, educational or religious societies or institutions, incorporated or unincorporated, whose principal charitable, educational or religious objects are solely carried out within, or whose charitable, educational or religious objects are principally and usually carried out within, or whose charitable, educational or religious activities are principally and usually carried out within the commonwealth; or which are organized under the laws of, or whose principal charitable, educational or religious objects are carried out within any other state or states of the United States which exempt from similar taxation legacies and devises by its citizens to or for the use of such societies or institutions which are organized under the laws of, or whose principal charitable, educational or religious objects are carried out within the commonwealth; or (2) for the saying, singing, performance or celebration of religious rites, rituals, services or ceremonies whether to be conducted within or without the commonwealth; or (3) for or upon trust for any charitable purposes to be carried out within the commonwealth and/or within any other state or states of the United States which exempt from similar taxation legacies and devises by its citizens for charitable purposes to be carried out within this commonwealth; or (4) to or for the use of the commonwealth or any town therein for public purposes, shall be subject to a tax at the percentage rates fixed by the following table:

Relationship of Beneficiary to Deceased.	RATE PER CENTUM OF TAX ON VALUE OF PROPERTY OF INTEREST.								
	On Value not over $10,000.	On Excess above $10,000, not over $25,000.	On Excess above $25,000, not over $50,000.	On Excess above $50,000, not over $100,000.	On Excess above $100,000, not over $250,000.	On Excess above $250,000, not over $500,000.	On Excess above $500,000, not over $750,000.	On Excess above $750,000, not over $1,000,000.	On Excess above $1,000,000.
CLASS A. Husband, wife, father, mother; child, adopted child, adoptive parent, grandchild	1%	2%	3%	4%	5%	6%	7%	8%	9%
CLASS B. Lineal ancestor, except father or mother; lineal descendant, except child or grandchild; lineal descendant of adopted child; lineal ancestor of adoptive parent; wife or widow of a son; husband of a daughter	2%	3%	5%	6%	7%	8%	9%	10%	11%
CLASS C. Brother, sister, half brother, half sister, nephew, niece, stepchild or step-parent	4%	6%	8%	10%	11%	12%	13%	14%	15%
CLASS D. All others	6%	8%	9%	10%	11%	12%	13%	14%	15%

Provided, however, that in the case of any beneficial interest arising or accruing by survivorship of a husband or wife in a tenancy by the entirety in single family residential property occupied by such husband and wife as a domicile, there shall be allowed an exemption of such property to the extent of its value, and in multiple family residential property so occupied there shall be allowed an exemption of such property to the extent of twenty-five thousand dollars of its value.

Provided, however, that no property or interest therein, which shall pass or accrue to or for the use of a person in Class A, except a grandchild of the deceased, unless its value exceeds ten thousand dollars, and no other property or interest therein, unless its value exceeds one thousand dollars, shall be subject to the tax imposed by this chapter, and no tax shall be exacted upon any property or interest so passing or accruing which shall reduce the value of such property or interest below said amounts.

All property and interests therein which shall pass from a decedent to the same beneficiary by any one or more of the methods hereinbefore specified and all beneficial interests which shall accrue in the manner hereinbefore provided to such beneficiary on account of the death of such decedent shall be united and treated as a single interest for the purpose of determining the tax hereunder.

§13. **Tax to be assessed upon value, etc.** Except as otherwise provided in this and the following section, the tax imposed by this chapter shall be assessed upon the value of the property at the time of the death of the decedent. In case of a devise, descent, bequest or grant to take effect in possession or enjoyment after the expiration of one or more life estates or of a term of years, the tax shall be assessed on the value of the property or interest therein coming to the beneficiary at the time when he becomes entitled to the same in possession or enjoyment. The value of an annuity or a life interest in any such property, or any interest therein less than an absolute interest, shall be determined by the "American Experience Tables" at four per cent compound interest; but when an annuity or a life interest is terminated by the death of the annuitant or life tenant, and the tax upon such interest is not due and has not been paid in advance, the value of said interest for the purposes of taxation under this chapter shall be the amount of the annuity or income actually paid or payable to the annuitant or life tenant during the period for which he was entitled to the annuity or was in possession of the life estate.

§14 [Supp. 1959]. **Persons entitled to future interests may pay tax in advance, etc.** Any person entitled to a future interest in any property may pay the tax on account of the same at any time before such tax would be due under this chapter, and in such cases the tax shall be assessed upon the value of the interest at the time of payment, and such value shall be determined by the commissioner as provided in this chapter. Whenever it is impossible to compute the present value of any interest, the commissioner may, with the approval of the state tax commission, effect such settlement of the tax as he shall deem to be for the best interests of the commonwealth, and payment of the sum so agreed upon shall be a full satisfaction of such tax.

§15. **Deposit, etc., in lieu of tax.** In case of a devise, bequest or grant of real or personal property made or intended to take effect in possession or enjoyment after the death of the grantor, to take effect in possession or come into actual enjoyment after the expiration of one or more life estates or a term of years, whether conditioned upon the happening of a contingency, dependent upon the exercise of a discretion, subject to a power of appointment, or otherwise, the taxes upon which have not yet become due, the executor, administrator, trustee or grantee may (a) deposit with the state treasurer bonds or other negotiable obligations of the commonwealth or of the United States of America of such aggregate face amount as the commissioner may from time to time deem necessary to adequately secure payment of such taxes, or (b) any executor, administrator, trustee or grantee, or any person interested in such devise, bequest or grant may give bond to a judge of the probate court having jurisdiction of the estate of the decedent, in such amount and with such sureties as said court may approve, conditioned that the obligor shall notify the commissioner when said taxes become due and shall then pay the same to the commonwealth. In case of a deposit of bonds or other negotiable obligations with the state treasurer hereunder, he shall pay to such executor, administrator, trustee or grantee as aforesaid or persons entitled thereto the interest accruing thereon and, if such taxes shall be paid in full when due, shall return such bonds or obligations to the persons entitled thereto, but if such taxes shall not be paid when due, the state treasurer may sell all or any part of such bonds or obligations to satisfy such taxes and shall return to the persons entitled thereto all the proceeds of such sale, and all such bonds or obligations, remaining in his hands after satisfying such taxes.

Chapter 65A, §5 [Supp. 1959]. Equitable apportionment of tax among persons interested in estate. Whenever it appears upon any accounting, or in any appropriate action or proceeding, that an executor, administrator, trustee or other person acting in a fiduciary capacity, has paid or may be required to pay an estate tax levied or assessed under the provisions of this chapter, or under the provisions of any estate tax law of the United States heretofore or hereafter enacted, upon the transfer of the estate of any person who at the time of his death was an inhabitant of this commonwealth, the net amount of said tax shall be apportioned among and borne by recipients and beneficiaries of the property and interests included in the gross estate in the following manner: —

1. If any portion of the estate passed under the will of the decedent, such proportion of the net amount of the tax so levied or assessed shall, except as otherwise provided or directed by the will, be charged to and paid from the general funds of the estate as the net amount of the property passing under the will and included in the measure of such tax, exclusive of property over which the decedent had any power of appointment as defined from time to time by the estate tax laws of the United States, bears to the amount of the net estate as hereafter defined in this section.

2. If any portion of the property with respect to which such tax is levied or assessed is held under the terms of any trust created inter-vivos or is subject to such a power of appointment, such proportion of the net amount of the tax so levied or assessed shall, except as otherwise provided or directed by the trust instrument with respect to the fund established thereby, or by the decedent's will, be charged to and paid from the corpus of the trust property or the property subject to such power of appointment, as the case may be, as the net amount of the property of such trust or property subject to such power of appointment and included in the measure of such tax bears to the amount of the net estate as hereafter defined in this section. The amount so charged shall not be apportioned between temporary and remainder estates.

3. The balance of the net amount of the tax so levied or assessed, or if paragraphs one and two are inapplicable the whole of the net amount of such tax shall, except as otherwise provided or directed by the decedent's will be equitably apportioned among and charged to and paid by the recipients and beneficiaries of property or interests included in the measure of such tax and passing or arising otherwise than under the will of the decedent or by virtue of any such trust or by the exercise or non-exercise of any such power of

appointment in the proportion that the net amount of such property or interests bears to the amount of the net estate as hereafter defined in this section; provided, that where any provision is made whereby any person is given an interest in income or an estate for years or for life or other temporary interest in any property or fund the amount so charged to such recipients or beneficiaries shall not be apportioned between temporary and remainder estates but shall be charged to and paid out of the corpus of such property or fund; and provided, further, that any apportionment made under this section shall accord with applicable estate tax laws of the United States where such laws specify with respect to an apportionment.

4. The term "net estate" as used in this section shall mean the gross estate as defined by the applicable estate tax laws of the United States less the deductions, other than specific exemptions, allowed by the provisions of such laws.

Chapter 183, §3 [Supp. 1959]. Estate created without writing to have effect of estate at will. An estate or interest in land created without an instrument in writing signed by the grantor or by his attorney shall have the force and effect of an estate at will only, and no estate or interest in land shall be assigned, granted or surrendered unless by such writing or by operation of law.

Chapter 184, §6. Effect of words "die without issue," etc. In a limitation of real or personal property by deed, will or other instrument in writing, executed after April thirtieth, eighteen hundred and eighty-eight, the words "die without issue," or "die without leaving issue," or "have no issue," or "die without heirs of the body," or other words importing either a want or failure of issue of any person in his lifetime or at the time of his death, or an indefinite failure of his issue, shall, unless a contrary intention clearly appears by the instrument creating such limitation, mean a want or failure of issue in the lifetime or at the time of the death of such person, and not an indefinite failure of his issue.

Chapter 184A, §1. Basis of determining validity of interest; "life estate." In applying the rule against perpetuities to an interest in real or personal property limited to take effect at or after the termination of one or more life estates in, or lives of, persons in being when the period of said rule commences to run, the validity of the interest shall be determined on the basis of facts existing at the termination of such one or more life estates or lives. In this section an interest which must terminate not later than the death of one or more persons is a "life estate" even though it may terminate at an earlier time.

§2. Age contingency reduced, when. If an interest in real or personal property would violate the rule against perpetuities as modified by section 1 because such interest is contingent upon any person attaining or failing to attain an age in excess of twenty-one, the age contingency shall be reduced to twenty-one as to all persons subject to the same age contingency.

§3. Fee simple determinable in land, etc., when to become fee simple absolute; Exceptions. A fee simple determinable in land or a fee simple in land subject to a right of entry for condition broken shall become a fee simple absolute if the specified contingency does not occur within thirty years from the date when such fee simple determinable or such fee simple subject to a right of entry becomes possessory. If such contingency occurs within said thirty years the succeeding interest, which may be an interest in a person other than the person creating the interest or his heirs, shall become possessory or the right of entry exercisable notwithstanding the rule against perpetuities. But if a fee simple determinable in land or a fee simple in land subject to a right of entry for condition broken is so limited that the specified contingency must occur, if at all, within the period of the rule against perpetuities, said interests shall take effect as limited. This section shall not apply where both such fee simple determinable and such succeeding interest, or both such fee simple and such right of entry are for public, charitable or religious purposes; nor shall it apply to a deed, gift or grant of the commonwealth or any political subdivision thereof.

§4. **Chapter applicable to legal and equitable interests.** This chapter shall apply to both legal and equitable interests.

§5. **Chapter not to invalidate, etc., terms of certain limitations.** Except as provided in the first sentence of section three, this chapter shall not be construed to invalidate or modify the terms of any limitation which would have been valid prior to January first, nineteen hundred and fifty-five.

§6. **Effect of partial invalidity, unconstitutionality, etc.** If any of the provisions of this chapter shall be held invalid or unconstitutional in relation to any of the applications thereof, such invalidity or unconstitutionality shall not affect other applications thereof or other provisions thereof; and to this end the provisions of this chapter are declared to be severable.

This act applies only to inter vivos instruments taking effect after January 1, 1955, to wills where the testator dies after that date, and to appointments made after June 10, 1954, the effective date of the act, including appointments by inter vivos instrument or wills under powers created before said effective date.

Chapter 188, §1. Nature of homestead estate. A householder who has a family shall be entitled to acquire an estate of homestead to the extent of four thousand dollars in value in the land and buildings thereon owned or rightly possessed by lease or otherwise and occupied by him as a residence; and such estate shall be exempt from the laws of conveyance, descent and devise and from attachment, levy on execution and sale for the payment of his debts or legacies, except —

(1) Sale for taxes.

(2) Attachment, levy and sale in the following cases:

(a) For a debt contracted previous to the acquisition of said estate of homestead.

(b) For a debt contracted for the purchase thereof.

(c) Upon an execution issued from the probate court to enforce its decree that a husband pay a certain amount weekly or otherwise to support his wife or minor children.

(d) Where buildings on land not owned by the householder are attached, levied upon or sold for the ground rent of the lot of land whereon they stand.

§2. **Mode of acquisition.** To acquire such estate of homestead, the fact that it is designed to be held as such shall be set forth in the deed of conveyance by which the property is acquired; or, after the title has been acquired, such design may be declared by a writing duly signed, sealed and acknowledged and recorded in the registry of deeds for the county or district in which the property is situated. The acquisition of a new estate of homestead shall defeat and discharge any such previous estate.

§3. **Wife or minor child may occupy in certain cases.** In a case in which the probate court has entered a decree that the wife is living apart from her husband for justifiable cause, or the custody of his minor children or minor child has been decreed to some person other than him, and the husband owns or holds a homestead estate, the probate court may by its decree grant to his wife or minor children, or to both, the right to use, occupy and enjoy such homestead estate until the further order of the court. The recording of the order of the probate court granting to the wife or minor children, or to both, the right to use, occupy and enjoy said homestead estate, together with the description thereof, in the registry of deeds for the county or district where the land lies, shall operate to prevent the husband from disposing of said estate until such time as the probate court may revoke said decree.

§4. **Continuence after death of householder.** The estate of homestead existing at the death of a householder shall continue for the benefit of his widow and minor children, and shall be held and enjoyed by them, if one of them or a purchaser under section eight occupies the premises, until the youngest child is twenty-one and until the marriage or death of the widow; and if a widow or minor children are entitled to an estate of homestead as provided herein, it may be set off to them in the same manner as dower. But all the right, title and interest of the deceased in the premises in which such estate exists, except the estate of homestead thus continued, shall be subject to the laws relating to devise, descent, dower and sale for the payment of debts and legacies.

§5. **Previous mortgage, etc., unaffected.** No estate of homestead shall affect a mortgage, lien or other encumbrance previously existing.

§6. **Estate subject to prior mortgage.** Property which is subject to a mortgage executed before an estate of homestead was acquired therein, or executed afterward and containing a release thereof, shall be subject to an estate of homestead, except as against the mortgagee and those claiming under him, in the same manner as if there were no such mortgage. If the owner of the equity in such property redeems the mortgage, he shall not be allowed to claim under it against the owner of the estate of homestead, his widow, heirs or assigns; but if said owner of the estate of homestead, his widow, heirs or assigns offers to redeem the residue above the homestead estate and the mortgage from a sale or set-off on execution and the judgment creditor has redeemed the mortgage, the amount paid for such redemption of the mortgage, with interest and expenses, shall be included in the amount to be paid for the redemption of said residue.

§7. **Release of rights.** Except as provided in section seven A, no conveyance of property in which an estate of homestead exists, and no release or waiver of such estate, shall convey the part so held and exempted, or defeat the right of the owner or of his wife and children to a homestead therein, unless such conveyance is by a deed in which the wife of the owner joins for the purpose of releasing such right in the manner in which she may release her dower, unless such right is released as provided in chapter two hundred and nine;[1] but a deed duly executed without such release shall be valid to pass, according to its terms, any title or interest in the property beyond the estate of homestead.

§7A. **Same subject.** The provisions of section one A of chapter one hundred and eighty-nine[2] relative to the release of rights of or to dower or curtesy shall, so far as applicable, apply to the release of rights under this chapter.

§8. **Sale of rights of widow, etc.** The widow and the guardian of the minor children, if he has obained a license therefor from the probate court

---

[1] Chapter 209, §§18 and 19 provide a method whereby a guardian of an insane wife may be authorized to release an estate of homestead, and give the Probate Court power to order a certain portion of the proceeds, not exceeding $4000, set aside and paid over to the guardian to be invested in a homestead. — ED.

[2] See page 1449 infra. — ED.

as in the sale of land of minors, may join in a sale of an estate of homestead; or if there is no widow entitled to rights therein, the guardian may, upon obtaining such license, make sale of such estate; and the widow may make such sale if there are no minor children. The purchaser shall enjoy and possess the premises for the full time that the widow and children or either of them might have continued to hold and enjoy them if no sale had been made. The probate court may apportion the proceeds of the sale among the parties entitled thereto.

§9. **Set-off if holder insolvent.** If the property of a debtor is assigned under the laws relative to insolvent debtors, and such debtor claims, and it appears to the court wherein the proceedings in insolvency are pending, that he is entitled to hold a part therefore as a homestead and that the property in which such estate of homestead exists is of greater value than four thousand dollars, the court shall cause the property to be appraised by three disinterested appraisers, one of whom shall be appointed by the insolvent, one by the assignee and the third by the court; or if either the assignee or insolvent neglects to appoint, the court shall appoint for him. The appraisers shall be sworn faithfully and impartially to appraise the property, and shall appraise and set off an estate of homestead therein to the insolvent debtor in the manner prescribed in section eighteen of chapter two hundred and thirty-six in case of a judgment debtor;[3] and the residue shall vest in and be disposed of by the assignee in the same manner as property which is not exempt by law from levy on execution. The appraisers shall be entitled to the same fees, to be paid out of the estate in insolvency, as are allowed to an appraiser of land seized upon execution.

§10. **Existing rights saved.** All existing estates of homestead which have been acquired under any law heretofore in force shall continue to be held and enjoyed notwithstanding the repeal of such law.

Chapter 189, §1. **Nature of Estate; How claimed.** A husband shall upon the death of his wife hold for his life one third of all land owned by her at any time during coverture. Such estate shall be known as his tenancy by curtesy, and the law relative to dower shall be applicable to curtesy, and no conveyance by a married woman of real property shall, except as provided in section thirty-five of chapter two hundred and nine,[4] extinguish or impair

---

[3] Chapter 236, §18 provides as follows: "If a judgment creditor requires an execution to be levied on property which is claimed by the debtor to be as a homestead exempt from such levy, and if the officer holding such execution is of opinion that the premises are of greater value than four thousand dollars, appraisers shall be appointed to appraise the property in the manner provided by section six. If, in the judgment of the appraisers, the premises are of greater value than four thousand dollars, they shall set off to the judgment debtor so much of the premises, including the dwelling house, in whole or in part, as shall appear to them to be of the value of four thousand dollars; and the residue of the property shall be levied upon and disposed of in like manner as land not exempt from levy on execution; and if the property levied on is subject to a mortgage, it may be set off or sold subject to the mortgage and to the estate of homestead, in like manner as land subject to a mortgage only." — ED.

[4] Chapter 209, §35 provides: "If a court having jurisdiction has entered a decree that a married woman has been deserted by her husband or is living apart from him for justifiable cause, she may convey her real estate in the same manner and with the same effect as if she were sole; and the surviving husband shall not be entitled under section fifteen of chapter one hundred and ninety-one to waive the provisions of a will made by her or to claim such portion of her estate as he would take if she had died intestate, nor shall he be entitled upon her death, if she leaves a will, to his

his tenancy by curtesy in such property unless he joins in the conveyance or otherwise releases his right. A wife shall, upon the death of her husband, hold her dower at common law in her deceased husband's land. Such estate shall be known as her tenancy by dower. To be entitled to such curtesy or dower the surviving husband or wife shall file his or her election and claim therefor in the registry of probate within six months after the date of the approval of the bond of the executor or administrator of the deceased, and shall thereupon hold instead of the interest in real property given in section one of chapter one hundred and ninety, curtesy or dower, respectively, otherwise such estate shall be held to be waived. Such curtesy and dower may be assigned by the probate court in the same manner as dower is now assigned, and the tenant by curtesy or dower shall be entitled to the possession and profits of one undivided third of the real estate of the deceased from her or his death until the assignment of curtesy or dower, and to all remedies therefor which the heirs of the deceased have in the residue of the estate. Rights of curtesy which existed on December thirty-first, nineteen hundred and one, may be claimed and held in the manner above provided, but in such case the husband shall take no other interest in the real or personal property of his wife; and, except as preserved herein, curtesy as it existed prior to January first, nineteen hundred and two, is abolished.

§1A. **Release by joining in deed.** A deed conveying land which is signed by the spouse of a grantor, said spouse being competent so to act, shall be held to release the right of such spouse of or to dower or curtesy in such land, unless such right is expressly reserved in said deed.

§2. **No curtesy as against purchase money mortgages.** If a deed of land is made to a married woman, who at the time of its execution, mortgages such land to the grantor to secure the payment of the whole or a part of the purchase money, or to a third person to obtain the whole or a part of such purchase money, her seisin shall not give her husband an estate by the curtesy as against such mortgagee.

§3. **Wife not dowable, nor widower entitled to curtesy, in wild land.** A widow shall not be entitled to dower, nor a widower to curtesy, in wild land of which her or his spouse dies seized, except wood lots or other land used with the farm or dwelling house of the deceased spouse, nor in such land which is conveyed by him or her although it is afterward cleared.

§4. **Dower in husband's right of redemption.** If, upon a mortgage made by a husband, his wife has released her right of dower, or if a husband is seized of land subject to a mortgage which is valid and effectual as against his wife, she shall nevertheless be entitled to dower in the land mortgaged as against every person except the mortgagee and those claiming under him. If the heir or other person who claims under the husband redeems the mortgage, the widow shall either repay such part of the money which was paid by the person so redeeming as shall be equal to the proportion which her interest in the land mortgaged bears to the whole value thereof or, at her election, she shall be entitled to dower according to the value of the estate after deducting the money paid for redemption.

§5. **Release of dower.** A married woman may bar her right of dower in land conveyed by her husband or by operation of law by joining in the deed conveying the land or by releasing the land by a subsequent deed executed

---

tenancy by curtesy in her estate, as provided in section one of chapter one hundred and eighty-nine." — Ed.

either separately or jointly with her husband. Her dower may also be released in the manner provided in chapter two hundred and nine.

§6. Signing of instruments by married women under twenty-one. The signature of a married woman under twenty-one affixed by her to any instrument relating to the conveyance of land of her husband shall have the same effect as if she were over that age.

§7. Dower barred by jointure before marriage. A woman may be barred of her dower in all the land of her husband by a jointure settled on her with her assent before her marriage, if such jointure consists of a freehold estate in land for her life at least and is to take effect in possession or profits immediately upon the death of her husband. Her assent to such jointure shall be expressed, if she is of full age, by her becoming a party to the conveyance by which it is settled, or, if a minor, by her joining with her father or guardian in such conveyance.

§8. Dower barred by pecuniary provision. A pecuniary provision, made for the benefit of an intended wife and in lieu of dower, shall, if assented to as provided in the preceding section, bar her dower in all the land of her husband.

§9. Jointure made without wife's assent or after marriage effective unless waived. Such jointure or pecuniary provision, if made after marriage, or made before marriage and without the assent of the intended wife, shall bar her dower, unless within six months after the death of her husband she makes her election to waive such jointure or provision. If the husband dies while absent from his wife, she shall have six months after notice of his death within which to make such election; and she shall in all cases have six months after notice of the existence of such jointure or provision within which to make such election.

§10. Assignment of dower or other undivided interest. If a widow is entitled by law, by deed of jointure, or under the will of her husband, to an undivided interest in his land either for life or during widowhood, such interest may be assigned to her, in whatever counties the land lies, by the probate court for the county in which the estate of her husband is settled. Such assignment may be made upon her petition or, if she does not petition therefor within one year after the decease of her husband, upon petition by an heir or devisee of her husband, by any person having an estate in the land subject to such interest, or by the guardian or conservator of any such heir, devisee or person, or by an executor or administrator if the probate court finds that the personal property will probably be insufficient to pay the debts and legacies of the decedent or charges of administration.

§11. Manner of assignment. Upon such petition, the court shall issue a warrant to three disinterested persons as commissioners, who shall be sworn to perform their duty faithfully and impartially and who shall set off the widow's interest by metes and bounds if it can be so done without damage to the whole estate. But if the estate out of which a widow's interest is to be assigned consists of a mill or other tenement which cannot be divided without damage to the whole, such interest may be assigned out of the rents or profits thereof, to be had and received by the widow as a tenant in common with the other owners of the estate.

§12. Where husband is tenant in common. If a widow is entitled to an undivided interest in land which is owned by her husband as tenant in common, the probate court, upon petition by her or by any person entitled to petition for assignment of her interest in her husband's land, after notice as in case of other partitions, may empower the commissioners to make partition of the land so owned in common, and then to assign the widow her interest in the portion set off to the estate of her husband.

§13. Widow may claim her interest after occupying in common with heirs. If a widow is entitled to an interest in land of which her husband died seized, she may, without having her interest assigned, continue to occupy such land with the heirs or devisees of the deceased, or to receive her share of the rents or profits thereof, so long as such heirs or devisees do not object thereto; and when the heirs or devisees or any of them desire to hold or occupy their share in severalty, the widow may claim her interest and shall have it assigned to her.

§14. Limitation for claim of interest in realty. No surviving husband or widow of a deceased person shall make claim for an interest in the real estate of such deceased, or begin any proceeding for the recovery thereof, unless such claim or action is made or begun within twenty years after the decease of the wife or husband, or after he or she has ceased to occupy or receive the profits of his or her share of such real estate, except that if at the time of such decease the surviving husband or widow is absent from the commonwealth, under twenty-one, insane or imprisoned, he or she may make such claim or begin such proceeding at any time within twenty years after such disability ceases.

§15. Re-endowment of woman if evicted. If a woman is lawfully evicted of land which has been assigned to her as dower or settled upon her as jointure, or is deprived of the provision made for her by will or otherwise in lieu of dower, she may be endowed anew in like manner as if such assignment, jointure or other provision had not been made.

§16 [Supp. 1959]. Dower or curtesy barred after ten years from recording of conveyance unless notice of claim thereof recorded. After the expiration of a period of ten years from the recording of any conveyance no spouse of any party making the conveyance shall make any claim to dower or curtesy in the land conveyed unless within such period the spouse has recorded in the registry of deeds for the county or district where the land lies a notice identifying the conveyance and the place in the public records of its recording and stating that dower or curtesy may be claimed in the land thereby conveyed. A reference to such notice shall be noted on the margin of the record of the conveyance.

Chapter 190, §1 [Supp. 1959]. Share of surviving husband or wife. A surviving husband or wife shall, after the payment of the debts of the deceased and the charges of his last sickness and funeral and of the settlement of his estate, and subject to chapter one hundred and ninety-six, be entitled to the following share in his real and personal property not disposed of by will:

(1) If the deceased leaves kindred and no issue, and it appears on determination by the probate court, as hereinafter provided, that the whole estate does not exceed twenty-five thousand dollars in value, the surviving husband or wife shall take the whole thereof; otherwise such survivor shall take twenty-five thousand dollars and one half of the remaining personal and one half of the remaining real property. If the personal property is insufficient to pay said twenty-five thousand dollars, the deficiency shall, upon the petition of any party in interest, be paid from the sale or mortgage, in the manner provided for the payment of debts or legacies, of any interest of the deceased in real property which he could have conveyed at the time of his death; and the surviving husband or wife shall be permitted, subject to the approval of the court, to purchase at any such sale, notwithstanding the fact that he or she is the administrator of the estate of the deceased person. A further sale

or mortgage of any real estate of the deceased may later be made to provide for any deficiency still remaining. Whenever it shall appear, upon petition to the probate court of any party in interest, and after such notice as the court shall order, and after a hearing thereon, that the whole amount of the estate of the deceased, as found by the inventory and upon such other evidence as the court shall deem necessary, does not exceed the sum of twenty-five thousand dollars over and above the amount necessary to pay the debts and charges of administration, the court shall itself by decree determine the value of said estate, which decree shall be binding upon all parties. If additional property is later discovered, the right or title to the estate covered by such decree shall not be affected thereby, but the court may make such further orders and decrees as are necessary to effect the distribution herein provided for.

(2) If the deceased leaves issue, the survivor shall take one third of the personal and one third of the real property.

(3) If the deceased leaves no issue and no kindred, the survivor shall take the whole.[5]

§2. **Distribution of personal property.** The personal property of a deceased person not lawfully disposed of by will shall, after the payment of his debts and the charges of his last sickness and funeral and of the settlement of the estate, and subject to the preceding section and to chapter one hundred and ninety-six, be distributed among the persons and in the proportions hereinafter prescribed for the descent of real property.

§3. **Descent of real property.** When a person dies seized of land, tenements or hereditaments, or of any right thereto, or entitled to any interest therein, in fee simple or for the life of another, not having lawfully devised the same, they shall descend, subject to his debts and to the rights of the husband or wife and minor children of the deceased as provided in this and in the two preceding chapters and in chapter one hundred and ninety-six, as follows:

(1) In equal shares to his children and to the issue of any deceased child by right of representation; and if there is no surviving child of the intestate then to all his other lineal descendants. If all such descendants are in the same degree of kindred to the intestate, they shall share the estate equally; otherwise, they shall take according to the right of representation.

(2) If he leaves no issue, in equal shares to his father and mother.

(3) If he leaves no issue and no mother, to his father.

(4) If he leaves no issue and no father, to his mother.

(5) If he leaves no issue and no father or mother, to his brothers and sisters and to the issue of any deceased brother or sister by right of representation; and, if there is no surviving brother or sister of the intestate, to all the issue of his deceased brothers and sisters. If all such issue are in the same degree of kindred to the intestate, they shall share the estate equally, otherwise, according to the right of representation.

(6) If he leaves no issue, and no father, mother, brother or sister, and no issue of any deceased brother or sister, then to his next of kin in equal degree; but if there are two or more collateral kindred in equal degree claiming through different ancestors, those claiming through the nearest ancestor shall be preferred to those claiming through an ancestor more remote.

(7) [Supp. 1959] If an intestate leaves no kindred and no widow or husband, his estate shall escheat to the commonwealth, provided, however, if

[5] As to estates of persons who died prior to January 1, 1957, substitute for all references to "twenty-five thousand dollars" the words "ten thousand dollars." — ED.

such intestate is a veteran who died while a member of the Soldiers' Home in Massachusetts or the Soldiers' Home in Holyoke, his estate shall inure to the benefit of the legacy fund or legacy account of the soldiers' home of which he was a member.

§4. Degrees of kindred. Degrees of kindred shall be computed according to the rules of the civil law; and the kindred of the half blood shall inherit equally with those of the whole blood in the same degree.

§5. Illegitimate child to be heir of his mother. An illegitimate child shall be heir of his mother and of any maternal ancestor, and the lawful issue of an illegitimate person shall represent such person and take by descent any estate which such person would have taken if living.

§6. Mother to be heir of illegitimate child. If an illegitimate child dies intestate and without issue who may lawfully inherit his estate, such estate shall descend to his mother or, if she is not living, to the persons who would have been entitled thereto by inheritance through his mother if he had been a legitimate child.

§7. When illegitimate child to be deemed legitimate. An illegitimate child whose parents have intermarried and whose father has acknowledged him as his child or has been adjudged his father under chapter two hundred and seventy-three shall be deemed legitimate and shall be entitled to take the name of his parents to the same extent as if born in lawful wedlock.

§8. Taking by right of representation; posthumous children. Inheritance or succession by right of representation is the taking by the descendants of a deceased heir of the same share or right in the estate of another person as their parent would have taken if living. Posthumous children shall be considered as living at the death of their parent.

Chapter 190A, §1. Disposition of property in absence of evidence of survivorship. Where title to property or the devolution thereof depends upon priority of death and there is no sufficient evidence that the persons concerned have died otherwise than simultaneously the property of each person shall be disposed of as if he had survived, except as otherwise provided in this chapter.

§2. Beneficiaries of another person's disposition of property. Where two or more beneficiaries are designated to take successively or alternatively by reason of survivorship under another person's disposition of property and there is no sufficient evidence that these beneficiaries have died otherwise than simultaneously the property thus disposed of shall be divided into as many equal portions as there are successive or alternate beneficiaries, and the portion allocable to each beneficiary shall be distributed as if he had survived all the other beneficiaries.

§3. Joint tenants or tenants by the entirety. Where there is no sufficient evidence that two joint tenants or tenants by the entirety have died otherwise than simultaneously the property so held shall be distributed one half as if one had survived and one half as if the other survived. Where more than two joint tenants have died and there is no sufficient evidence that they died otherwise than simultaneously the property so held shall be divided into as many equal shares as there were joint tenants and the share allocable to each shall be distributed as if he had survived all the others.

§4. Insurance policies or contracts. Where the insured and the beneficiary in a policy or contract of life or endowment insurance or insurance against accident have died and there is no sufficient evidence that they have died otherwise than simultaneously the proceeds of the policy or contract shall be payable as if the insured had survived the beneficiary.

§5. Provision in will, etc., rendering chapter inapplicable. This chapter shall not apply to a will, living trust or deed wherein provision has been made for distribution different from the distribution under this chapter, or to a policy or contract of insurance wherein provision has been made for payment of its proceeds different from such payment under this chapter.

§6.   Interpretation.   This chapter shall be so construed and interpreted as to effectuate its general purpose to make uniform the law in those states which enact it.

§7.   Effect of partial invalidity.   If any of the provisions of this chapter or the application thereof to any persons or circumstances is held invalid such invalidity shall not affect other provisions or applications of the chapter which can be given effect without the invalid provisions or application, and to this end the provisions of this chapter are declared severable.

§8.   How chapter cited.   This chapter may be cited as the Uniform Simultaneous Death Law.

Chapter 191, §1.   By whom and how wills may be made.   Every person of full age and sound mind may by his last will in writing, signed by him or by a person in his presence and by his express direction, and attested and subscribed in his presence by three or more competent witnesses, dispose of his property, real and personal, except an estate tail, and except as is provided in this chapter and in chapters one hundred and eighty-eight and one hundred and eighty-nine and in section one of chapter two hundred and nine. A married woman, in the same manner and with the same effect, may make a will.

§2.   Competency of witness; Validity of devise or legacy to witness regulated.   Any person of sufficient understanding shall be deemed to be a competent witness to a will, notwithstanding any common law disqualification for interest or otherwise; but a beneficial devise or legacy to a subscribing witness or to the husband or wife of such witness shall be void unless there are three other subscribing witnesses to the will who are not similarly benefited thereunder.

§3.   Subsequent incompetency of witness.   If a witness to a will is competent at the time of his attestation, his subsequent incompetency shall not prevent the probate and allowance of such will.

§4.   Wills made in accordance with law at time of execution.   A will made and executed in conformity with law existing at the time of its execution shall have the same effect as if made pursuant to this chapter.

§5.   Wills made out of the commonwealth.   A last will and testament executed in the mode prescribed by law, either of the place where the will is executed or of the testator's domicile, shall be deemed to be legally executed, and shall be of the same force and effect as if executed in the mode prescribed by the laws of this commonwealth; provided, that such last will and testament is in writing and subscribed by the testator.

§6.   Nuncupative will.   A soldier in actual military service or a mariner at sea may dispose of his personal property by a nuncupative will.

§8.   Revocation.   No will shall be revoked except by burning, tearing, cancelling or obliterating it with the intention of revoking it, by the testator himself or by a person in his presence and by his direction; or by some other writing signed, attested and subscribed in the same manner as a will; or by subsequent changes in the condition or circumstances of the testator from which a revocation is implied by law.

§9.   Revocation by marriage; Exception.   The marriage of a person shall act as a revocation of a will made by him previous to such marriage, unless it appears from the will that it was made in contemplation thereof.   If the will is made in the exercise of a power of appointment and the real and personal property subject to the appointment would not, without the appointment, pass to the persons who would have been entitled to it if it had been the estate and property of the testator making the appointment and he had died intestate, so much of the will as makes the appointment shall not be revoked by the marriage.

§10. **Deposit of wills.** A will enclosed in a sealed wrapper, with an endorsement thereon of the name and residence of the testator and of the day when and the person by whom it was deposited, and with or without the name of a person to whom the will is to be delivered after the death of the testator, shall, on the payment of one dollar, be received by the register of probate in the county where the testator lives, who shall give a certificate of the receipt thereof, and shall keep such will; and the same shall not be opened until it is delivered to a person entitled to receive it or is otherwise disposed of as hereinafter provided.

§11. **Custody and delivery of such wills.** During the life of the testator such will shall be delivered only to him or in accordance with his order in writing duly verified by the oath of a subscribing witness; and after his death it shall be delivered to the person named in the endorsement, if such person demands it.

§12. **Will not called for, to be opened at first probate court.** If the will is not called for by the person, if any, named in the endorsement, it shall be publicly opened at the first probate court held after notice of the testator's death, and shall be retained in the registry until so opened. If the jurisdiction of the case belongs to another court, it shall be delivered to the executors or other persons entitled to the custody thereof, to be by them presented for probate in such other court.

§15 [Supp. 1959]. **Right to waive will; Effect of waiver.** The surviving husband or wife of a deceased person, except as provided in section thirty-five or thirty-six of chapter two hundred and nine, within six months after the probate of the will of such deceased, may file in the registry of probate a writing signed by him or by her, waiving any provisions that may have been made in it for him or for her, or claiming such portion of the estate of the deceased as he or she is given the right to claim under this section, and if the deceased left issue, he or she shall thereupon take one third of the personal and one third of the real property; and if the deceased left kindred but no issue, he or she shall take ten thousand dollars and one half of the remaining personal and one half of the remaining real property; except that in either case if he or she would thus take real and personal property to an amount exceeding ten thousand dollars in value, he or she shall receive, in addition to that amount, only the income during his or her life of the excess of his or her share of such estate above that amount, the personal property to be held in trust and the real property vested in him or her for life, from the death of the deceased. If the deceased left no issue or kindred, the surviving husband or wife shall take ten thousand dollars and one half of the remaining personal and one half of the remaining real property absolutely. If the real and personal property of the deceased which the surviving husband or wife takes under the foregoing provisions exceeds ten thousand dollars in value, and the surviving husband or wife is to take only ten thousand dollars absolutely, the ten thousand dollars above given absolutely shall be paid out of that part of the personal property in which the husband or wife is interested; and if such part is insufficient the deficiency shall, upon the petition of any person interested, be paid from the sale or mortgage in fee, in the manner provided for the payment of debts or legacies, of that part of the real property in which he or she is interested. Such sale or mortgage may be made either before or after such part is set off from the other real property of the deceased for the life of the husband or widow. If, after probate of such will, legal proceedings have been instituted wherein its validity or effect is drawn in question, the probate court may, within six months, on petition and after such notice as it orders, extend the time for filing the aforesaid claim and waiver until the expiration of six months from the termination of such proceedings.

§16. **Appointment of trustees to hold husband's or widow's share.** The probate court may upon application of a person interested appoint one or more trustees, who shall be subject to chapter two hundred and three so far as applicable, to hold during the life of a husband or widow any personal property to the income of which he or she may be entitled under the preceding section.

§17. **Husband not to have curtesy or widow dower in addition to provision of will, unless, etc.** A husband shall not be entitled to his curtesy in addition to the provisions of his wife's will, nor a widow to her dower in addition to the provisions of her husband's will, unless such plainly appears by the will to have been the intention of the testator.

§20. **Child not provided for in will.** If a testator omits to provide in his will for any of his children, whether born before or after the testator's death, or for the issue of a deceased child, whether born before or after the testator's death, they shall take the same share of his estate which they would have taken if he had died intestate, unless they have been provided for by the testator in his lifetime or unless it appears that the omission was intentional and not occasioned by accident or mistake.

§22. **Devisee or legatee dying before testator.** If a devise or legacy is made to a child or other relation of the testator, who dies before the testator, but leaves issue surviving the testator, such issue shall, unless a different disposition is made or required by the will, take the same estate which the person whose issue they are would have taken if he had survived the testator.

§23. **Devises of real estate subject to mortgage.** In all wills made subsequent to January first, nineteen hundred and ten, a specific devise of real estate subject to a mortgage given by the testator, unless the contrary shall plainly appear by his will, shall be deemed to be the devise of the interest only which the testator had at the time of his decease in such real estate over and above such mortgage, and if the note or obligation of the testator secured by such mortgage be paid out of his other property after his decease, the executor of his will or the administrator with the will annexed of his estate shall, at the request of any person interested and by leave of the probate court, sell such real estate specifically devised for the purpose of satisfying the estate of the testator for the amount so paid, together with the costs and expenses thereof.

§25. **Contribution to make up portion of posthumous or omitted child.** If a child, or the issue of a child, omitted in the will takes under section twenty a portion of the estate of a testator, such portion shall be taken from all the devisees and legatees in proportion to and not exceeding the value of what they respectively receive under such will, unless in consequence of a specific devise or legacy or of some other provision of the will a different apportionment is found necessary to give effect to the testator's intention relative to that part of his estate which passes by his will.

Chapter 193, §1. Administration, to whom granted. Administration of the estate of a person deceased intestate shall be granted to one or more of the persons hereinafter mentioned and in the order named, if competent and suitable for the discharge of the trust and willing to undertake it, unless the court deems it proper to appoint some other person:

First, The widow or surviving husband of the deceased.

Second, The next of kin or their guardians or conservators as the court shall determine.

Third, If none of the above are competent or if they all renounce the administration or without sufficient cause neglect for thirty days after the death of the intestate to take administration of his estate, one or more of the principal creditors, after public notice upon the petition.

Fourth, If there is no widow, husband or next of kin within the commonwealth, a public administrator.

§2. When granted to next of kin without notice. Administration of the estate of an intestate may be granted to one or more of the next of kin or any suitable person, if the husband or widow and all the next of kin resident in the commonwealth, who are of full age and legal capacity, consent in writing thereto. Notice of the petition may be dispensed with as if all parties entitled thereto had signified their assent or waived notice.

§6. Letters of administration to be revoked on probate of a will. If, after the granting of letters of administration as upon an intestate estate, a will of the person deceased is duly proved and allowed, such letters shall be revoked; and the executor or an administrator with the will annexed may demand, collect and sue for all the personal property of the deceased which remains unadministered.

§7. Administration with the will annexed. If no executor is named in a will, or if all the executors therein named are dead or incompetent or refuse to accept the trust, or if, after being duly cited therefor, the executor neglects to accept the trust, or if he neglects for thirty days after the probate of the will to give bond according to law, the court shall commit administration of the estate, with the will annexed, to any person interested in the will of said deceased, to any creditor of the deceased or to any suitable person; but after the expiration of said thirty days, and before letters of administration with the will annexed have been granted, the court may grant letters testamentary to any person named as executor who gives the bond required by law. If a person named as executor in a will petitions for the probate of the same and dies, declines or becomes unable to act before final decree is entered on said petition, any person interested in the will of said deceased, or any creditor of the deceased, or any suitable person, may, on petition, be allowed to enter and to prosecute the original petition for probate, to apply for letters of administration with the will annexed, and to act and proceed in any proposed compromises under sections fifteen and sixteen of chapter two hundred and four. If it appears that there are no known heirs or legatees or devisees under the will of the deceased, a public administrator of the county shall be appointed to the trust.

§8. Administration with the will annexed may be granted when executor is a minor. If a person named as executor is at the time of the probate of the will under the age of twenty-one, administration with the will annexed may be granted during his minority, unless there is another executor who accepts the trust.

§9. Administration de bonis non. If a sole or surviving executor or administrator dies, resigns or is removed before having fully administered an estate, and there is personal property of the deceased not administered to the amount of twenty dollars, or debts to that amount remaining due from the estate, or anything remaining to be performed in execution of the will, or if there is an order of distribution in accordance with section twenty-eight of chapter two hundred and six, the probate court shall grant letters of administration, with the will annexed, or otherwise as the case may require, to one or more suitable persons to administer the goods and estate of the deceased not already administered. If it appears that there are no known heirs of the deceased, a public administrator of the county shall be appointed to the trust.

§10. **Special administrators.** If the judge of probate deems it necessary or expedient, he may, at any time and place, with or without notice, appoint a special administrator, who, in case of an appeal from the decree appointing him, shall nevertheless proceed in the execution of his duties until it is otherwise ordered by the supreme judicial court, and may in like manner discharge him. Such appointment and discharge shall be entered forthwith on the records of the court and notice thereof given to the executor or administrator, if any.

Chapter 195, §8. Agent of non-resident executor or administrator. An executor or administrator who is appointed in, but resides out of, the commonwealth shall not enter upon the duties of his trust nor be entitled to receive his letter of appointment until he shall, by a writing filed in the registry of probate for the county where he is appointed, have appointed an agent residing in the commonwealth, and, by such writing, shall have agreed that the service of any legal process against him as such executor or administrator, or that the service of any such process against him in his individual capacity in any action founded upon or arising out of any of his acts or omissions as such executor or administrator, shall, if made on said agent, have like effect as if made on him personally within the commonwealth, and such service shall have such effect. Said writing shall state the name and address of the agent. An executor or administrator who, after his appointment, removes from, and resides without, the commonwealth shall so appoint a like agent.

§9. **New appointment of agent.** If an agent appointed under the preceding section dies or removes from the commonwealth before the final settlement of the accounts of his principal, another appointment shall be made and filed as above provided, and the powers of an agent appointed under this or the preceding section shall not be revoked prior to the final settlement of the estate unless another appointment shall be made as before provided.

§10. **Failure to appoint agent, effect.** Failure by an executor or administrator to comply with any provision of the two preceding sections shall be cause for removal.

§12. **Acts of executor or administrator before removal to be valid.** If an executor or administrator is removed or if letters of administration are revoked, all previous sales, whether of real or personal property, made lawfully by the executor or administrator and with good faith on the part of the purchaser, and all other lawful acts done by such executor or administrator, shall remain valid and effectual.

§16 [Supp. 1959]. **Estates consisting of no more than eight hundred dollars of personal property.** If an inhabitant of the commonwealth dies leaving an estate consisting entirely of personal property the total value of which does not exceed eight hundred dollars, his surviving spouse, child, parent, brother or sister if of full age and legal capacity and an inhabitant of the commonwealth, or, in the case of a person who at his decease was receiving relief or support under chapter one hundred and seventeen or assistance under chapter one hundred and eighteen, one hundred and eighteen A or one hundred and Eighteen D, any person designated to act as a voluntary administrator of the estate of such person by the board of public welfare of the town from which such person at his decease was receiving such relief, support or assistance, may, after the expiration of thirty days from the death of the decedent, provided no petition for letters testamentary or letters of administration has been filed with the probate court of the county in which the decedent resided, file with said probate court upon a form prescribed by the court a statement verified by oath or affirmation containing (a) the name and residential address of the affiant, (b) the name, residence and date of death of the deceased, (c) the relationship of the affiant to the deceased, (d) a schedule showing every asset of the estate known to the affiant and the estimated value of each such asset, (e) a statement that the affiant has undertaken to act as voluntary administrator of the estate of the deceased and will administer the same according to law and apply the proceeds thereof in conformity with this section and (f) the names and addresses of surviving joint owners of property with the deceased, known to the affiant. The oath required by this section shall not be governed by section one A of chapter two hundred and sixty-eight.

Upon presentation of such statement, accompanied by a certificate of the death of the deceased by a public officer and payment of a fee of three dollars or such amount as may be specified in section forty of chapter two hundred and sixty-two, the register of probate shall docket these documents as a part of the permanent records of the court. Upon payment of a fee of one dollar the register shall, and if no other probate proceeding for administration of such estate is pending in said court, issue an attested copy of a statement duly filed under this section.

Upon the presentation of a copy of such a statement duly attested by the register of probate, the tender of a proper receipt in writing and the surrender of any policy, passbook, note, certificate or other evidentiary instrument, a voluntary administrator may, as the legal representative of the deceased and his estate, receive payment of any debt or obligation in the nature of a debt, or delivery of any chattel or asset, scheduled in such statement. Payments and deliveries made under this section shall discharge the liability of the debtor, obligor or deliverer to all persons with respect to such debt, chattel, obligation or other asset unless, at the time of such payment or delivery, a written demand has been made upon said debtor, obligor or deliverer by a duly appointed executor or administrator.

A voluntary administrator may sell any chattel so received and negotiate or assign any chose in action to convert the same to cash in a reasonable amount.

A voluntary administrator shall, as far as possible out of the assets which come into his hands, first discharge the necessary expenses of the funeral and last sickness of the deceased and the necessary expenses of administration without fee for his services, and then pay the debts of the deceased in the order specified in section one of chapter one hundred and ninety-eight and any other debts of the estate, and then distribute the balance, if any, to the surviving spouse, or, if there is no surviving spouse, to the persons and in the proportions prescribed by clauses (1), (2), (3), (4) and (5) of section three of chapter one hundred and ninety.

A voluntary administrator shall be liable as an executor in his own wrong to all persons aggrieved by his administration of the estate, and, if letters testamentary or letters of administration are at any time granted, shall be liable as such an executor to the rightful executor or administrator.

For the purpose of paragraph (6) of section one hundred and thirteen A of chapter one hundred and seventy-five and section two of chapter ninety, a voluntary administrator shall be deemed to be the legal representative of the estate of the decedent until an executor or administrator is appointed.

Chapter 196, §1. Apparel of widow and children; Quarantine. Articles of apparel and ornaments of the widow and minor children of a deceased person shall belong to them respectively. The widow may remain in the house of her husband for not more than six months next succeeding his death without being chargeable for rent.

§2. Allowance of necessaries. Such parts of the personal property of a deceased person as the probate court, having regard to all the circumstances of the case, may allow as necessaries to his widow for herself and for his family under her care, or if there is no widow or if the deceased was a woman, to the minor children of the deceased, not exceeding one hundred dollars to any child, and also such provisions and other articles as are necessary for the reasonable sustenance of his family, if the deceased was a man, or of her minor children, if the deceased was a woman, and the use of the house of the deceased and of the furniture therein for six months next succeeding his or her death, shall not be taken as assets for the payment of debts, legacies or charges of administration. After exhausting the personal property, real property may be sold or mortgaged to provide the amount of allowance decreed in the same manner as it is sold or mortgaged for the payment of debts, if a decree authorizing such sale or mortgage is made, upon the petition of any party in interest, within one year after the approval of the bond of the executor or administrator.

§3. Advancements treated as estate of intestate, when. Property, real or personal, which is given by an intestate in his lifetime as an advancement to a child or other lineal descendant shall be considered as part of the intestate's estate in the division and distribution of such estate among his issue, and shall be taken by such child or other descendant toward his share of such estate; but he shall not be required to restore any part thereof, although it exceeds his share. The widow shall be entitled only to her share in the residue after deducting the value of the advancement.

§4. Same subject. If such advancement is made in real property, the value thereof shall be considered as part of the real property to be divided; if it is in personal property, it shall be considered as part of the personal property; and if in either case it exceeds the share of real or personal property, respectively, which would have come to the heir so advanced, he shall not restore any part of it, but shall receive so much less out of the other part of the estate as will make his whole share equal to the shares of the other heirs who are in the same degree with him.

§5. Proof of advancement. Gifts and grants shall be held to have been made as advancements, if they are expressed in the gift or grant to be so made, or if charged in writing as such by the intestate, or acknowledged in writing as such by the party receiving them.

§6. Value of advancement, how ascertained. If the value of an advancement is expressed in the conveyance, in the charge thereof made by the intestate or in the acknowledgment by the person receiving it, such value shall be adopted in the division and distribution of the estate; otherwise it shall be determined according to the value when the property was given.

§7. Death of person receiving advancement before intestate. If a child or other lineal descendant who has received an advancement dies before the intestate, leaving issue, the advancement shall be considered as part of the intestate's estate in the division and distribution of such estate, and the value thereof shall be taken by the representative of the heir to whom the advancement was made toward his share of the estate, as if the advancement had been made directly to him.

§8. **Determination of questions of advancement.** The probate court in which the estate of a deceased person is settled may hear and determine all questions of advancements arising relative to such estate, or such questions may be heard and determined upon a petition for partition; but if such question arises upon a petition for partition, the court may suspend proceedings until the question has been decided in the probate court in which the estate of the deceased is settled.

Chapter 201, §3. Testamentary guardian. A father or mother may by will appoint, subject to approval of the probate court, a guardian for a minor child whether born at the time of making the will or afterward, to continue during minority or for a less time. A testamentary guardian appointed by will of a parent shall have the same powers and perform the same duties relative to the property of the ward, and, if the other parent is not living, relative to the person of the ward, as a guardian appointed under section two. If application is made to the probate court for the appointment of a testamentary guardian after the appointment of a guardian, whether testamentary or otherwise, has been made by such court, notice of such application shall be given to such guardian previously appointed, and thereafter the court may remove said guardian so first appointed and appoint in his place the person applying for an appointment as testamentary guardian or any suitable person or it may appoint the person making such application to serve as guardian with the guardian already appointed by said court.

§45 [Supp. 1959]. **Election, waiver, or exercise of power by guardian, etc.** If property, rights or benefits given by will or by law depend upon the election, waiver or other act of a person incompetent by reason of mental illness or minority to perform the same, his guardian may make such election or waiver or perform such act; provided, that no waiver of the provisions of a will under this section shall be valid until approved by the probate court after notice to such persons, if any, as the court shall deem proper and a hearing thereon, and provided also that if a power is vested in a mentally ill person for his own benefit, or his consent is required for the exercise of any power where the power of consent is in the nature of a beneficial interest in himself, his guardian may, by order of the probate court, made after notice to such persons, if any, as the court shall deem proper, exercise the power or give the consent in such manner as shall be authorized or directed by the order. If, in any case where the guardian of a ward incompetent by reason of mental illness or minority has not waived the provisions of the will of the ward's spouse or brought a petition under this section for approval of a waiver of the provisions thereof and a guardian ad litem has been appointed under section one B of chapter one hundred and ninety-two, such guardian ad litem is of opinion that a waiver of the provisions thereof is for the benefit and for the best interests of the ward, and the guardian fails to take such action after written demand made upon him, such guardian ad litem as next friend may waive the provisions thereof, subject to the approval of the probate court as hereinbefore provided.

Chapter 203, §3A. Certain employer trusts exempted from operation of rule against perpetuities or suspension of power of alienation of title to property. A trust created by an employer as part of a stock bonus, pension, disability, death benefit or profit sharing plan for the benefit of some or all of his employees, to which contributions are made by the employer or employees, or both, for the purpose of distributing to the employees the earnings or the principal, or both earnings and principal, of the fund held in trust, may continue in perpetuity or for such time as may be necessary to accomplish the purpose for which it is created, and shall not be invalid as violating any rule of law against perpetuities or suspension of the power of alienation of the title to property.

Chapter 204, §15. Compromise of wills. The supreme judicial court or the probate court may authorize the persons named as executors in an instrument purporting to be the last will of a person deceased, or the petitioners for administration with such will annexed, to adjust by arbitration or compromise any controversy between the persons who claim as devisees or legatees under such will and the persons entitled to the estate of the deceased under the laws regulating the descent and distribution of intestate estates, to which arbitration or compromise the persons named as executors, or the petitioners for administration with the will annexed, as the case may be, those claiming as devisees or legatees whose interests will in the opinion of the court be affected by the proposed arbitration or compromise, and those claiming the estate as intestate, shall be parties.

§16. Protection of contingent interests. If the court finds that any future contingent interests which would arise under said will if admitted to probate would be affected by the arbitration or compromise, it shall appoint some person to represent such interests in such controversy, and the court shall have like power as to any bequests made in the will for charitable purposes, if no trustees have been appointed in such will; in both cases with such conditions as to costs as the court orders.

§17. Effect of compromise. An award or compromise made in writing in any such case, if found by the court to be just and reasonable in relation to the parties in being and in its effect upon any future contingent interests that might arise under such will and upon any bequests to charities made in the same, shall be valid and binding upon such interests and upon such bequests, as well as upon the interests of all persons in being, but it shall not impair the claims of creditors.

Chapter 205, §4. Exemption of executor, etc., from giving sureties. An executor shall be exempt from giving a surety on his bond if the testator has ordered or requested such exemption or that no bond be required, and an executor, administrator or an administrator with the will annexed shall be so exempt if all the persons interested in the estate of full age and legal capacity, other than creditors, certify to the probate court their consent thereto; but not until all creditors of the estate, and the guardian or conservator of any person under disability interested therein, have been notified and have had opportunity to show cause against the same. The probate court may, however, upon or after the granting of letters testamentary or letters of administration require bond, with sufficient sureties, and failure to furnish the same within such time as the court orders shall constitute a declination of or a resignation from the trust.

Chapter 206, §24. Notice of application for allowance of account; Representative of person unborn, unascertained, etc.; Final determination. Upon application for the allowance of an account filed in the probate court such notice as the court may order shall be given by publication, unless all persons interested receive actual notice, and by delivering or mailing by registered mail a copy of the citation to the attorney general if there are public charitable interests, to the department of mental health and to the Veterans Administration if interested, and . . .

(4) For accounts of trustees to all persons to or for whom income has been paid or accumulated or in the discretion of the trustee might have been paid or accumulated during the period covered by the account, and to those persons who during such period have received or were entitled to receive or in the discretion of the trustee might have received principal, and to all persons who at the mailing or delivery of such notice, in default of any appointment or otherwise, would be entitled to share in the income or principal if an existing tenancy for life or for years had then terminated or the trust estate were then distributable in whole or in part;

(5) For accounts of special administrators or in other kinds of fiduciary accounts or where the court deems special circumstances exist to such persons as the court may direct; and in all cases to the executor or administrator of any deceased person entitled to notice or to those in being who have succeeded to the interest of such deceased person, and to other persons who are or may become interested and who shall have filed with the accountant and the register of probate a request in writing for notice of proceedings on accounts. The written assent to an account or the waiver in writing of notice thereof by a person interested or by his guardian or legal representative shall be deemed equivalent to notice.

If there are other persons interested to whom such notice has not been given by delivery or registered mail, or if the interests of persons unborn, unascertained or legally incompetent to act in their own behalf are not represented except by the accountant, the court shall appoint as guardian ad litem a competent and disinterested person to represent such interests and persons, and such guardian ad litem shall without further notice or action by the court also represent with respect to such account all interested persons who may be born after the date of his appointment. It shall not be necessary, unless the court shall so order, to designate by name persons represented by the guardian ad litem other than those who are entitled to notice by delivery or registered mailing. The guardian ad litem so appointed shall make oath to perform his duties faithfully and impartially and shall be entitled to such reasonable compensation as the court shall allow.

After a final decree has been entered on any account hereunder it shall not be impeached except for fraud or manifest error.

In the case of a minor entitled to notice by delivery or mailing hereunder who is under the age of fourteen at the date of the citation, such notice may be delivered or mailed to the legal or natural guardian of said minor or if the court shall so direct to some other person in his behalf.

§27A. **Disposition of certain legacies or distributive shares of estates of deceased persons.** Whenever payment of a legacy or distributive share cannot be made to the person entitled thereto, or such person may not receive or have the opportunity to obtain said legacy or distributive share, the court, on petition of an interested party or in its discretion, may order that that money be deposited in a savings bank or other like institution, or invested in the manner provided in section twenty-five, and disposed of in the manner provided in section twenty-eight. When a claimant to such funds resides outside of the United States or its territories, the court in its discretion, in order to assist in establishing such claimant's identity, right and opportunity to receive such fund, may require the appearance in person before the court of such claimant.

§27B [Supp. 1959]. **Some subject; when legatees or distributees reside in countries under Communist control.** Whenever payment of a legacy or distributive share is to be made to a person who is domiciled in a country or state outside of the United States or its territories, in which the court, in its discretion, finds that there is not a reasonable assurance that such legatee or distributee will actually receive payment of his legacy or distributive share in substantially full value, the court, upon petition of the executor, administrator, or an interested party, or in its discretion, may order that such legacy or distributive share be paid, in whole or in part, to said executor, administrator, or interested party for use by him in the purchase of goods in the form of necessaries of life, food, clothing and medicines, to be sent to such legatee or distributee through a recognized public or private agency, upon his written request, order, or assignment.

§28. **Final disposition of deposits.** The probate court may, on petition of any person interested and after public notice, order all money or the proceeds thereof which have been deposited or invested by its authority and which shall have remained unclaimed for twenty years from the date of such deposit or investment to be paid to the residuary legatee, if any, of the testator to whose estate the money belonged, or, if such residuary legatee is dead, to his heirs living at the time of such distribution; and if no such residuary legatee or any of his heirs are then living, or if the deceased died intestate, said money and the proceeds thereof shall be disposed of and distributed among the persons entitled thereto and in the manner provided by chapter one hundred and ninety. The court shall first require from the persons to whom such money shall be ordered paid a sufficient bond of indemnity, with two sufficient sureties to be approved by it, conditioned to repay to the persons for whose benefit such deposit or investment was originally made, or to the personal representatives of such persons, all money paid over by the order of the court under this section.

Chapter 210, §7. Rights of adopted child as to succession to property. A person adopted in accordance with this chapter shall take the same share of the property which the adopting parent could dispose of by will as he would have taken if born to such parent in lawful wedlock, and he shall stand in regard to the legal descendants, but to no other of the kindred of such adopting parent, in the same position as if so born to him. If the person adopted dies intestate, his property acquired by himself or by gift or inheritance from his adopting parent or from the kindred of such parent shall be distributed according to chapters one hundred and ninety and one hundred and ninety-six among the persons who would have been his kindred if he had been born to his adopting parent in lawful wedlock; and property received by gift or inheritance from his natural parents or kindred shall be distributed in the same manner as if no act of adoption had taken place. The apportionment and distribution shall be ascertained by the court. A person shall not by adoption lose his right to inherit from his natural parents or kindred.

The court may decree that the rights of succession to property under this section shall vest in the person adopted as of the date of the filing of the petition for adoption.

§9. **Rights in this commonwealth of a child adopted in another state.** An inhabitant of another state, adopted as a child in accordance with the laws thereof, shall upon proof of such fact be entitled in this commonwealth to the same rights of succession to property as he would have had in the state where he was adopted, except so far as such rights are in conflict with this chapter.

§10. **Effect of second adoption.** If the child has been previously adopted, all the legal consequences of the former decree shall, upon a subsequent adoption, determine, except so far as any interest in property may have vested in the adopted child, and a decree to that effect shall be entered on the records of the court.

Chapter 260, §31A. Certain proceedings based upon the right of entry for condition broken or possibility of reverter, when prohibited. No proceeding based upon any right of entry for condition broken or possibility of reverter, to which a fee simple or fee simple determinable in land is subject, created before the second day of January, nineteen hundred and fifty-five, shall be maintained either at law or in equity in any court after the first day of January, nineteen hundred and sixty-six, unless on or before the first day of January nineteen hundred and sixty-six, (a) the condition has been broken or the reverter has occurred, and a person or persons having the right of entry or reverter shall have taken possession of the land, and in the case of entry made after January first, nineteen hundred and fifty-seven, shall have filed a certificate of entry pursuant to section nineteen of chapter one hundred and eighty-four, or (b) a person or persons having the right of entry, or who would have it if the condition were broken, or would be entitled if the reverter occurred, or one of them if there be more than one, shall by himself, or by his attorney, agent, guardian, conservator or parent, have filed in the registry of deeds, or in the case of registered land, in the registry of the land court, for the district in which the land is situated, a statement in writing, duly sworn to, describing the land and the nature of the right and the deed or other instrument creating it, and where it may be found if recorded or registered, and, in case of registered land, naming the holder or holders of the outstanding certificate of title and stating the number of said certificate, and, in case of land not registered, naming the person or persons appearing of record to own the fee subject to such right or possibility, or shown by the records of the tax assessors at the last prior assessment date to be the owner or owners thereof.

Such statement shall be received and recorded or registered upon payment of the fee required by law, and shall be indexed in the grantor index under the person or persons so named, and in case of registered land, noted on the certificate of title. The register and assistant recorder shall also keep a separate list of such statements.

This section shall apply to all such rights whether or not the owner thereof is a corporation or a charity or a government or governmental subdivision, or is under any disability or out of the commonwealth, and it shall apply notwithstanding any recitals in deeds or other instruments heretofore or hereafter recorded, unless a statement is filed as above provided. Nothing in this section shall be construed to extend the period of any other applicable statute of limitations or to authorize the bringing of any proceeding to enforce any right which has been or may be barred by lapse of time or for any other reason.

MICHIGAN

Statutes Annotated 1943

§27.3178 (278). Policy of state that fiduciaries be amenable to process; non-residents and persons not citizens of United States not to act as fiduciaries. It is hereby declared to be the public policy of this state to require that all persons acting in a representative capacity under appointment of a probate court, as fiduciary, shall at all times be amenable to process issued out of the courts of this state, and to that end no person shall hereafter be deemed suitable and competent to act as a fiduciary, who is not a resident of this state and a citizen of the United States: Provided, That nothing herein shall be construed to limit the power of the court to appoint any bank or trust company authorized to do business in this state.

MISSOURI

Annotated Statutes 1952

§474.150-1 [Supp. 1959].   Gifts in fraud of marital rights — Presumption on conveyances.   Any gift made by a person, whether dying testate or intestate, in fraud of the marital rights of his surviving spouse to share in his estate, shall, at the election of the surviving spouse, be treated as a testamentary disposition and may be recovered from the donee and persons taking from him without adequate consideration and applied to the payment of the spouse's share, as in case of his election to take against the will.

NEBRASKA

Revised Statutes 1943

§76-111.   Estates; definite failure of issue, defined.   Whenever property is limited upon the death of any person without "heirs" or "heirs of the body" or "issue" general or special, or "descendants" or "offspring" or "children" or any such relative described by other terms, such limitation, unless a different intent is effectively manifested, is a limitation to take effect only when such person dies not having such relative living at the time of his death or in gestation and born alive thereafter, and is not a limitation to take effect upon the indefinite failure of such relatives; nor, unless a different intent is effectively manifested, does it mean that death without such relative, in order to be material, must occur in the lifetime of the creator of the interest.

§76-114.   Estates; testamentary conveyance to the heirs or next of kin of the conveyor; doctrine of worthier title abolished.   When any property is limited, mediately or immediately, in an otherwise effective testamentary conveyance, in form or in effect, to the heirs or next of kin of the conveyor, or to a person or persons who on the death of the conveyor are some or all of his heirs or next of kin, such conveyees acquire the property by purchase and not by descent.

§76-115.   Estates; inter vivos conveyance to the heirs or next of kin of the conveyor; effect.   When any property is limited, in an otherwise effective conveyance inter vivos, in form or in effect, to the heirs or next of kin of the conveyor, which conveyance creates one or more prior interests in favor of a person or persons in existence, such conveyance operates in favor of such heirs or next of kin by purchase and not by descent.

NEW JERSEY

Revised Statutes 1951

§3A:3-10.   After-born children; When total intestacy results.   A will, made when a testator had no issue living wherein any issue he might have is not provided for or mentioned, shall be void and the testator be deemed to die intestate if, at his death, he leave a child or issue or leave his wife enceinte of a child which shall be born.

§3A:3-16. Words importing estate in fee not to prevent further devise or bequest. In any devise or bequest of real or personal property set forth in the will of a testator dying after January 1, 1952, the giving to one person of an indeterminate or other interest in the property or an estate in fee therein or absolute ownership thereof, together with a power, absolute or otherwise, to dispose of the property, shall not be construed to render void a limitation over of the property to another person which is to take effect in the event that the first named devisee or legatee shall not have disposed of the property during his lifetime. In all such cases, the testator's intent shall be given effect.

NEW YORK

Decedent Estate Law

§17. Devise or bequest to certain societies, associations, corporations or purposes. No person having a husband, wife, child, or descendant or parent, shall, by his or her last will and testament, devise or bequeath to any benevolent, charitable, literary, scientific, religious or missionary society, association, corporation or purpose, in trust or otherwise, more than one-half part of his or her estate, after the payment of his or her debts, and such devise or bequest shall be valid to the extent of one-half, and no more. The validity of a devise or bequest for more than such one-half may be contested only by a surviving husband, wife, child, descendant or parent. When payment of a devise or bequest to such society, association, corporation or purpose is postponed, in computing the one-half part of such society, association, corporation or purpose, no allowance may be made for such postponement for any interest or gains or losses which may accrue after the testator's death. The value of an annuity or life estate, legal or equitable, shall not be computed upon the actual duration of the life, but shall be computed upon the actuarial value according to the American Experience Table of Mortality at the rate of four per centum per annum. Such value shall be deducted from the fund or property, which is subject to the annuity or life estate, in order to ascertain the value of a future estate or remainder interest passing to such society, association, corporation or purpose.

§21. Manner of execution of will. Every last will and testament of real or personal property, or both, shall be executed and attested in the following manner:

1. It shall be subscribed by the testator at the end of the will.

2. Such subscription shall be made by the testator in the presence of each of the attesting witnesses, or shall be acknowledged by him, to have been so made, to each of the attesting witnesses.

3. The testator, at the time of making such subscription, or at the time of acknowledging the same, shall declare the instrument so subscribed, to be his last will and testament.

4. There shall be at least two attesting witnesses, each of whom shall sign his name as a witness, at the end of the will, at the request of the testator.

§22. Witnesses to will to write names and places of residence. The witnesses to any will, shall write opposite to their names their respective places of residence; and every person who shall sign the testator's name to any will by his direction, shall write his own name as a witness to the will. Whoever shall neglect to comply with either of these provisions, shall forfeit fifty dollars, to be recovered by any person interested in the property devised or bequeathed, who will sue for the same. Such omission shall not affect the validity of any will; nor shall any person liable to the penalty aforesaid, be excused or incapacitated on, that account, from testifying respecting the execution of such will.

§47-f [Supp. 1960]. **Designation of trustee to receive proceeds of life insurance policy and taxation thereof.** 1. Life insurance may be made payable to a trustee to be named as beneficiary in the policy and the proceeds of such insurance shall be paid to such trustee and be held and disposed of by the trustee as provided in a trust agreement made by the insured during his lifetime. It shall not be necessary to the validity of any such trust agreement or declaration of trust that it have a trust corpus other than the right of the trustee to receive such insurance proceeds as beneficiary.

2. A policy of life insurance may designate as beneficiary a trustee or trustees named by will, if the designation is made in accordance with the provisions of the policy and the requirements of the insurance company. Upon qualification and issuance of letters of trusteeship the proceeds of such insurance shall be payable to the trustee or trustees to be held and disposed of under the terms of the will as they exist as of the date of the death of the testator and in the same manner as other testamentary trusts are administered; but if no qualified trustee makes claim to the proceeds from the insurance company within eighteen months after the death of the insured, or if satisfactory evidence is furnished to the insurance company within such eighteen month period showing that there is or will be no trustee to receive the proceeds, payment shall be made by the insurance company to the executors, administrators or assigns of the insured, unless otherwise provided by agreement with the insurance company during the lifetime of the insured.

3. The proceeds of the insurance as received by the trustee or trustees shall not be subject to debts of the insured nor to transfer or estate tax to any greater extent than if such proceeds were payable to the beneficiary or beneficiaries named in the trust and not to the estate of the insured.

4. Such insurance proceeds so held in trust may be commingled with any other assets which may properly come into such trust.

5. Nothing in this act shall affect the validity of any life insurance policy beneficiary designation heretofore made naming trustees of trusts established by will.

Personal Property Law

§11 [Supp. 1960]. **Suspension of ownership.** The absolute ownership of personal property shall not be suspended by any limitation or condition, for a longer period than during the continuance and until the termination of lives in being at the date of the instrument containing such limitation or condition, or, if such instrument be a last will and testament, for lives in being at the death of the testator, and a term of not more than twenty-one years. Lives in being shall include a child begotten before the creation of the estate but born thereafter. In no case shall the lives measuring the permissible period be so designated or so numerous as to make proof of their end unreasonably difficult. In other respects limitations of future or contingent interests in personal property, are subject to the rules prescribed in relation to future estates in real property.

§15. **Personal property not alienable in certain cases.** 1. The right of the beneficiary to enforce the performance of a trust to receive the income of personal property, and to apply it to the use of any person, can not be transferred by assignment or otherwise. But the right and interest of the beneficiary of any other trust in personal property, including the beneficiary of a trust in personal property under a plan of reorganization pursuant to chapter seven hundred forty-five of the laws of nineteen hundred thirty-three, as enacted or amended, [see Unconsolidated Laws §§4871 et seq.] and/or pursuant to chapter nineteen of the laws of nineteen hundred thirty-five, as enacted or amended, [see Unconsolidated Laws §§4801 et seq.] and/or pursuant to sections one hundred nineteen to one hundred twenty-three, both inclusive, of the real property law or pursuant to section seventy-seven-b of the national bankruptcy act, [see 11 U.S.C.A. §207, note] may be transferred. Provided, however, that when the proceeds of a life insurance policy, becoming a claim by death of the insured, are left with the insurance company under a trust or other agreement, the benefits accruing thereunder after the death of the insured shall not be transferable, nor subject to communication or incumbrance, nor to legal process except in an action to recover for necessaries, if the parties to the trust or other agreement so agree.

2. The provisions of this section shall not impair or affect any right existing on March twenty-fifth, nineteen hundred and three, nor impair or affect the rights of creditors under section fifty-two of the domestic relations law.

§17b. **Distribution of income earned during period of administration.** Unless otherwise expressly provided by the will of a person dying after this act takes effect, all income from real and personal property earned during the period of administration of the estate of such testator and not payable to others or otherwise disposed of by the will shall be distributed pro rata as income among the beneficiaries of any trusts created out of the residuary estate of such testator and the other persons entitled to such residuary estate. None of such income shall, after such distribution, be added to the capital of the residuary estate the whole or any part of which is devised or bequeathed in trust or for life or for a term of years, but shall be paid ratably to the life beneficiary of a trust, or to the life tenant, or to the absolute residuary legatee, as the case may be. Unless otherwise directed in the will, income shall be payable to the life beneficiaries of trusts, or to life tenants from the date of testator's death. Nothing contained in this act shall affect the right of any person to income on any portion of the estate not part of the residuary estate of such testator.

Real Property Law

§42 [Supp. 1960]. **Suspension of power of alienation.** The absolute power of alienation is suspended, when there are no persons in being by whom an absolute fee in possession can be conveyed. Every future estate shall be void in its creation, which shall suspend the absolute power of alienation, by any limitation or condition whatever, for a longer period than during the continuance of lives in being at the creation of the estate and a term of not more than twenty-one years. Lives in being shall include a child begotten before the creation of the estate but born thereafter. In no case shall the lives measuring the permissible period be so designated or so numerous as to make proof of their end unreasonably difficult.

§56. **Posthumous children.** Where a future estate is limited to heirs, or issue, or children, posthumous children shall be entitled to take in the same manner as if living at the death of their parents; and a future estate, dependent on the contingency of the death of any person without heirs, or issue, or children, shall be defeated by the birth of a posthumous child of such person, capable of taking by descent.

§141. **Capacity to take and execute a power.** A power may be vested in any person capable in law of holding, but cannot be exercised by a person not capable of transferring real property. A power, vested in a person in his capacity as trustee of an express trust, to distribute principal to himself cannot be exercised by him; if the power is vested in two or more trustees, it may be executed by the trustee or trustees who are not so disqualified; if there is no trustee qualified to execute the power, its execution devolves on the supreme court, except that if the power is created by a testamentary instrument the surrogate's court having jurisdiction over the estate of the grantor of the power shall have coordinate jurisdiction with the supreme court in respect of the execution thereof.

Surrogate's Court Act

§269-a. **Deposit in Court for benefit of a legatee, distributee or beneficiary.** Where it shall appear that a legatee, distributee or beneficiary of a trust would not have the benefit or use or control of the money or other property due him, or where other special circumstances make it appear desirable that such payment should be withheld, the decree may direct that such money or other property be paid into the surrogate's court for the benefit of such legatee, distributee, beneficiary of a trust or such person or persons who may thereafter appear to be entitled thereto. Such money or other property so paid into court shall be paid out only by the special order of the surrogate or pursuant to the judgment of a court of competent jurisdiction.

NORTH CAROLINA

General Statutes 1950

§28-149, 13(b) [Supp. 1959]. **Order of distribution.** In case of renunciation or disclaimer by any heir at law or other person entitled to receive any benefits from said estate, the property of said estate shall be distributed among the other heirs at law or persons entitled to receive the same, and in the event there are no other children as heirs at law or persons entitled to receive said estate or any part thereof, the said estate shall descend and be distributed to the next of kin.

OHIO

Revised Code (Page), 1954

§2107.06. **Bequest to charitable purpose.** If a testator dies leaving issue, or an adopted child, or the lineal descendants of either, and the will of such testator gives, devises, or bequeaths such testator's estate, or any part thereof, to a benevolent, religious, educational, or charitable purpose, or to any other state or country, or to a county, municipal corporation, or other corporation, or to an association in any state or country, or to persons, municipal corporations, corporations, or associations in trust for such purposes, whether such trust appears on the face of the instrument making such gift, devise or bequest or not, such will as to such gift, devise, or bequest, shall be invalid unless it was executed at least one year prior to the death of the testator.

§2113.58. **Protection of remainderman's interest in personal property.** When by a last will and testament the use or income of personal property is given to a person for a term of years or for life and some other person has an interest in such property as remainderman, the probate court, unless such last will and testament otherwise provides, may deliver such personal property to the person having the limited estate, with or without bond, as the court may determine; or the court may order that such property be held by the executor or some other trustee, with or without bond, for the benefit of the person having the limited estate. If bond is required of the person having the limited estate, or of the trustee, it may be increased or decreased, and if bond is not required in the first instance it may be required by the court at any time prior to the termination of the limited estate.

OREGON

Revised Statutes 1957

§114.070. Devise or bequest to trustee of existing trust. A devise or bequest in a will duly executed pursuant to the provisions of this chapter may be made in form or substance to the trustee of a trust in existence at the date of the testator's death and established by written instrument executed prior to the execution of such will. Such devise or bequest shall not be invalid because the trust is amendable by the settlor or any other person or persons, provided that the will or the last codicil thereto was executed subsequent to the time of execution of the trust instrument and all amendments thereto.

PENNSYLVANIA

Statutes Annotated (Purdon)

Title 20, §192. Signature by mark. If the testator be unable to sign his name, for any reason other than the extremity of his last sickness, a will to which his name is subscribed in his presence, by his direction and authority, and to which he makes his mark or cross, unless unable so to do, — in which case the mark or cross shall not be required; — shall be as valid as though he had signed his name thereto: Provided, That such will shall be proved by the oaths or affirmations of two or more competent witnesses.

§301.7a [Supp. 1959]. Designation of insurance beneficiaries not testamentary. The designation of beneficiaries of life insurance shall not be considered testamentary, regardless of whether the insurance contract designates the ultimate beneficiaries or makes the proceeds payable, directly or indirectly, to a trustee of a trust under a will or under a separate trust instrument which designates the ultimate beneficiaries, and regardless of whether any such trust is amendable or revocable, or both, or is funded or unfunded, and notwithstanding a reservation to the settlor of all rights of ownership in the insurance contracts. Unless otherwise expressly provided in the conveyance, funds or other property so passing to a trust under a will shall become and be a part of the testamentary trust to be administered and disposed of in accordance with the provisions thereof, without forming any part of the testator's estate for administration by his personal representative.

§301.11 [Supp. 1959]. Conveyances to defeat marital rights.

(a) *In general.* A conveyance of assets by a person who retains a power of appointment by will, or a power of revocation or consumption over the principal thereof, shall at the election of his surviving spouse, be treated as a testamentary disposition so far as the surviving spouse is concerned to the extent to which the power has been reserved, but the right of the surviving spouse shall be subject to the rights of any income beneficiary whose interest in income becomes vested in enjoyment prior to the death of the conveyor.

The provisions of this subsection shall not apply to any contract of life insurance purchased by a decedent, whether payable in trust or otherwise.

(b) *Determination of share.* The spouse may elect to take against any such conveyance and shall be entitled to one-third thereof if the conveyor is survived by more than one child, or by one or more children and the issue of a deceased child or children, or by the issue of more than one deceased child, and in all other circumstances one-half thereof.

(c) *Election against other conveyances.* A spouse electing under this section also must elect to take against the will, if he is a beneficiary thereunder, and against all other conveyances within the scope of subsection (a) of which he is a beneficiary.

(d) *Procedure.* The election to treat a conveyance as testamentary shall be made in the same manner as an election to take against the will. If there is a will, such election shall be made within the same time limitations as an election to take against the will. If there is no will, such election shall be made within one year of the conveyor's death, and the orphans' court, on application of the surviving spouse made within such period, may extend the time for making the election. It can be made only if there has been no forfeiture of the right to make an election. The court having jurisdiction of the deceased conveyor's estate shall determine the rights of the surviving spouse in the property included in the conveyance.

§301.13. Limited estates in personalty and in the proceeds of the conversion of the real estate. A person having a present interest in personal property, or in the proceeds of the conversion of real estate, which is not in trust, and which is subject to a future interest, shall be deemed to be a trustee of such property, and not a debtor to the remainderman, with the ordinary powers and duties of a trustee, except that he shall not be required to change the form of the investment to an investment authorized for Pennsylvania fiduciaries, nor shall he be entitled to compensation as trustee. Such person, unless given a power of consumption or excused from entering security by the terms of the conveyance, shall be required to enter such security for the protection of persons entitled to the future interests as the court in its discretion shall direct. If a person having a present interest shall not enter security as directed, the court shall appoint a trustee who shall enter such security as the court shall direct, and who shall exercise all the ordinary powers and duties of a trustee, except that he shall not be required to change the form of the investment to an investment authorized for Pennsylvania fiduciaries.

§301.14. Rules of interpretation. In the absence of a contrary intent appearing therein, conveyances shall be construed, as to real and personal estate in accordance with the following rules:

(1) *Meaning of "heirs" and "next of kin," etc. — Time of ascertaining class.* A conveyance of real or personal property, whether directly or in trust, to the conveyor's or another designated person's "heirs", or "next of kin", or "relatives" or "family" or to "the persons thereunto entitled under the intestate laws", or to persons described by words of similar import, shall mean those persons, including the spouse, who would take under the intestate laws if such conveyor or other designated person were to die intestate at the time when such class is to be ascertained, a resident of the Commonwealth, and owning the property so conveyed: Provided, That the share of a spouse other than the spouse of the conveyor, shall not include the ten thousand dollar allowance under the intestate laws. The time when such class is to be ascertained shall be when the conveyance to the class is to take effect in enjoyment.

(2) *Meaning of "die without issue" and similar phrases.* In any conveyance

of real or personal estate, the words "die without issue", "die without leaving issue", "have no issue", or other words importing either a want or failure of issue of any person in his lifetime or at the time of his death, or an indefinite failure of his issue, shall be construed to mean a want or failure of issue in his lifetime or at his death, and not an indefinite failure of his issue.

(3) *Adopted children.* In construing a conveyance to a person or persons described by relationship to the conveyor or to another, any person adopted before the effective date of the conveyance shall be considered the child of his adopting parent or parents and not the child of his natural parents: Provided, That if a natural parent shall have married the adopting parent before the effective date of the conveyance, the adopted person shall also be considered the child of such natural parent.

(4) *Illegitimates.* In construing a conveyance to a person or persons described by relationship to the conveyor or to another, an illegitimate person shall be considered the child of his mother and not of his father: Provided, That when the parents of a person born illegitimate shall have married each other he shall thereafter be considered legitimate.

§320.902. **Nonresident trustee.** If a trustee is or becomes a nonresident of the Commonwealth, the acceptance of the trusteeship or the act of becoming a nonresident, as the case may be, shall constitute the Secretary of the Commonwealth his attorney-in-fact upon whom service of process and notices may be made as to all causes of action relating to the trust estate.

§320.903. **Resident co-trustee.** When no trustee shall be a resident of the Commonwealth, the court, after such notice as it shall direct, may appoint one or more additional trustees resident within the Commonwealth to serve with the nonresident trustee or trustees.

RHODE ISLAND

General Laws Annotated 1956

§33-6-33 [Supp. 1959]. **Gifts to trustee of existing trust.** A devise, bequest or appointment in a will validly executed under the provisions of this chapter may be made in form or substance to the trustee or trustees of a trust in writing executed by the testator or any other person or persons prior to and in existence at the time of the execution of such will and identified in such will, whatever the size or character of the corpus of the trust (including an unfunded life insurance trust, although the settlor has reserved any or all rights of ownership in the insurance policies). Such devise, bequest or appointment shall not be invalid because such trust is amendable or revocable, or both, by the settlor or any other person or persons; nor because the trust instrument or any amendment thereto was not executed in the manner required for wills; nor because the trust was amended after the execution of such will. Unless such will provides otherwise, the property so devised, bequeathed or appointed shall not be deemed held under a testamentary trust, but shall become and be a part of the principal of such trust to which it is given to be administered and disposed of in accordance with the terms and provisions of such trust to which it is given, including any amendments, as it appears in writing at the death of the testator. In the event of complete termination of such trust prior to the testator's death such devise or bequest shall lapse and such appointment fail unless such will directs otherwise.

§34-5-1. **Inheritance or devise of real estate.** An heir of a decedent, or his executors or administrators, may disclaim and renounce the inheritance of real estate and a devisee, or his executors or administrators, may disclaim and renounce a devise of real estate, at any time within six (6) months after the death of the decedent, provided, he has not theretofore conveyed such inheritance to another by an instrument duly recorded in the office of the person having charge of the recording of deeds in the city or town in which the real estate is situated, or another person has not obtained through him a right to, or interest in, or title to said real estate or to the possession thereof by an instrument duly recorded in the office of the person having charge of the recording of deeds in the city or town in which the real estate is situated, by filing his disclaimer and renunciation in the office of the person having charge of the recording of deeds in the city or town in which the real estate is situated and if probate proceedings are commenced in the estate of the decedent such disclaimer and renunciation shall also be filed in the office of the clerk of the probate court in which such probate proceedings are instituted within six (6) months after such probate proceedings are begun.

§34-5-2. **Inheritance or legacy of personal property.** One of the next of kin of a decedent, or his executors or administrators, may disclaim and renounce the inheritance of personal property at any time and a legatee, or his executors or administrators, may disclaim and renounce a legacy of personal property at any time within six (6) months after the death of the decedent, provided, he has not theretofore conveyed such inheritance to another or another person has not obtained through him a right to, or interest in, or title to said personal estate or to the possession thereof by filing his disclaimer and renunciation in the office of the clerk of a probate court that had jurisdiction of the estate of the decedent at the date of his death and if probate proceedings are commenced in the estate of the decedent such disclaimer and renunciation shall also be filed in the office of the clerk of the probate court in which such probate proceedings are instituted within six (6) months after such probate proceedings are begun.

§34-5-3. **Estate less than absolute ownership of personal property.** . . .

§34-5-4. **Less than fee interest in real estate.** . . .

§34-5-5. **Reversion or remainder in real estate.** . . .

§34-5-6. **Reversion or remainder in personal property.** . . .

§34-5-7. **Inheritance of real estate by virtue of previous disclaimer.** . . .

§34-5-8. **Inheritance of personal property by virtue of previous disclaimer.** . . .

§34-5-9. **Disclaimer by person under disability.** . . .

§34-5-10. **Effect of disclaimer on passage of title — recording of real estate disclaimers.** Upon such a disclaimer and renunciation no title or right of any kind shall pass to or from the person making the disclaimer and renunciation. Such disclaimer and renunciation insofar as it relates to real estate shall not be effective unless recorded in the office of the person having charge of the recording of deeds in the city or town in which the real estate is situated.

§34-5-11. **Title to property disclaimed.** Upon the filing of such disclaimer and renunciation of the inheritance of real or personal estate or of the reversion or remainder in fee or in absolute ownership in the same, the real estate or personal estate so disclaimed and renounced shall pass to the heirs or the next of kin of the decedent, testator, grantor or donor in the same proportions that it would have passed had the person making the renunciation died before the decedent, testator, grantor or donor and the decedent, testator, grantor, or donor had died seised and possessed of said real estate and personal property unless otherwise provided by the will or inter vivos instrument.

§34-5-12. **Addition to other rights of disclaimer.** The provisions of this chapter relative to disclaimer and renunciation are in addition to and not in derogation of existing rights of disclaimer and renunciation.

TENNESSEE

Code Annotated 1955

§32-306. Death of devisee or legatee prior to testator — Issue taking. Whenever the devisee or legatee to whom, or any member of a class to which, an immediate devise or bequest is made, dies before the testator, or is dead at the making of the will, leaving issue which survives the testator, said issue shall take the estate or interest devised or bequeathed which the devisee or legatee or the member of the class, as the case may be, would have taken, had he survived the testator, unless a different disposition thereof is made or required by the will.

VERMONT

Statutes Annotated 1959

Title 27, §501. Reformation of interests violating rule against perpetuities. Any interest in real or personal property which would violate the rule against perpetuities shall be reformed, within the limits of that rule, to approximate most closely the intention of the creator of the interest. In determining whether an interest would violate said rule and in reforming an interest the period of perpetuities shall be measured by actual rather than possible events.

§502. Application of subchapter. This subchapter shall apply only to inter vivos instruments and wills taking effect after the subchapter becomes operative and to appointments made after the subchapter becomes operative including appointments by inter vivos instrument or will under powers created before the subchapter becomes operative. This subchapter shall apply to both legal and equitable interests.

§503. Effect on prior interests. This subchapter shall not be construed to invalidate or modify the terms of any interest which would have been valid prior to its enactment.

VIRGINIA

Code Annotated 1950

§26-59 [Supp. 1960]. Non-resident fiduciaries must have resident co-fiduciaries. No person not a resident of this State nor any corporation not authorized to do business in this State shall be appointed or allowed to qualify or act as personal representative, or trustee under a will, of any decedent, or appointed as guardian of an infant or committee of any person non compos mentis, unless there be also appointed to serve with the non-resident personal representative, trustee, guardian or committee, a person resident in this State or corporation authorized to do business in this State; and in the event such resident personal representative, trustee, or guardian ceases, for any reason to act, then a new resident personal representative, trustee, or guardian shall be appointed in the same manner as provided in §26-48; provided that when the non-resident guardian or committee is the parent of the infant or person non compos mentis, the resident guardian appointed under this section shall have no control over the person of the ward. Nothing in this section shall be construed to impair the validity of any appointment or qualification made prior to June seventeenth, nineteen hundred and twenty-four, nor to affect in any way the other provisions of this chapter or of §64-123. The provisions of this section shall not authorize or allow any appointment or qualification prohibited by §6-9.

§55-7. **Power of disposal in life tenant not to defeat remainder unless exercised.** If any interest in or claim to real estate or personal property be disposed of by deed or will for life, with a limitation in remainder over, and in the same instrument there be conferred expressly or by implication a power upon the life tenant in his lifetime or by will to dispose absolutely of such property, the limitation in remainder over shall not fail, or be defeated, except to the extent that the life tenant shall have lawfully exercised such power of disposal. A deed of trust or mortgage executed by the life tenant shall not be construed to be an absolute disposition of the estate thereby conveyed unless there be a sale thereunder.

WASHINGTON

Revised Code 1959

§11.12.050. **Subsequent marriage of testator — divorce.** If, after making any will, the testator shall marry and the wife, or husband, shall be living at the time of the death of the testator, such will shall be deemed revoked, unless provision shall have been made for such survivor by marriage settlement, or unless such survivor be provided for in the will or in such way mentioned therein as to show an intention not to make such provision, and no other evidence to rebut the presumption of revocation shall be received. A divorce, subsequent to the making of a will, shall revoke the will as to the divorced spouse.

WEST VIRGINIA

Code 1955

§4095a [Supp. 1960]. **Disclaimer of gifts under wills or property passing by intestacy.** Any devisee or beneficiary who is sui juris, shall have the right, within two months from the date on which the will is admitted to probate, to disclaim such devise or bequest. If the will be contested, or the order admitting it to probate be appealed from, such disclaimer may be made within two months of the final decision on such contest or appeal. The devise or bequest so disclaimed shall pass as the will directs where there is a provision for disclaimer contained in the will making a specific alternative disposition of such property, and, in the absence of any such provision said devise or bequest shall pass as if the person so disclaiming had immediately predeceased the testator.

Any heir-at-law or distributee under the laws of descent and distribution who is sui juris, shall have the right, within two months of the date of death of the decedent, to disclaim such real or personal property. The property so disclaimed shall pass by the laws of descent and distribution of this state as if the person so disclaiming had immediately predeceased the decedent.

Any such disclaimer shall be made by a writing signed by the person so disclaiming and acknowledged in such manner as would authorize a deed to be admitted to record and shall be filed and recorded in the office of the clerk of the county court by which the will is admitted to probate or, in the event of intestacy, in the office of the clerk of the county court in which the decedent's estate is administered; and in either event, such disclaimer shall be recorded with fiduciary orders and/or probate documents. Said gift or property so disclaimed shall be considered as never having vested in any manner whatsoever in the person so disclaiming.

WISCONSIN

Statutes Annotated 1957

§206.52. **Trusts created by life insurance.**

(1) Life insurance may be made payable to a trustee to be named as beneficiary in the policy and the proceeds of such insurance shall be paid to such trustee and be held and disposed of by the trustee as provided in a trust agreement or declaration of trust made by the insured during his lifetime. It shall not be necessary to the validity of any such trust agreement or declaration of trust that it have a trust corpus other than the right of the trustee to receive such insurance proceeds as beneficiary.

(2) A policy of life insurance may designate as beneficiary a trustee or trustees named or to be named by will, if the designation is made in accordance with the provisions of the policy and the requirements of the insurance company. The trustee or trustees may be appointed immediately after the proving of the will, and upon appointment and qualification the proceeds of such insurance shall be paid to the trustee or trustees to be held and disposed of under the terms of the will as they exist at the death of the testator and in accordance with ch. 323; but if no qualified trustee makes claim to the proceeds from the insurance company within one year after the death of the insured, or if satisfactory evidence is furnished the insurance company within one such year period showing that no trustee can qualify to receive the proceeds, payment shall be made by the insurance company to the executors, administrators or assigns of the insured, unless otherwise provided by agreement with the insurance company during the lifetime of the insured. The proceeds of the insurance as collected by the trustee or trustees shall not be subject to debts of the insured and inheritance tax to any greater extent than if such proceeds were payable to any other named beneficiary other than the estate of the insured. For purposes of trust administration such proceeds shall be subject to the court jurisdiction over the trust in the same manner as though they had been payable to the estate of the insured, but shall not otherwise be considered as payable to the estate of the insured. Such proceeds shall be listed for tax purposes only, as required under §312.01, in the general inventory of the estate. Such insurance proceeds so held in trust may be commingled with any other assets which may properly come into such trust as provided in the will. Enactment of this section shall not invalidate previous life insurance policy beneficiary designations naming trustees of trusts established by will.

(3) The fact that the insured may reserve or have the right to borrow on the policy or to surrender the same shall not affect the validity of any such trust further than the amounts so borrowed or withdrawn are involved, and the remainder of the moneys due on such policy at the death of the insured shall go to the trustee to be handled and administered in accordance with the trust provisions.

§237.01(8) [**Supp. 1960**]. **How to descend.** If a person to whom property would otherwise descend under this chapter or be distributed under ch. 318 renounces all or any part of such property within 180 days after receiving notice of the death of the intestate by filing a declaration of such renunciation with the county court of the county in which the intestate resided at his death, then no interest in the property or part thereof so renounced shall be deemed to have vested in such person and such property or part thereof shall descend or be distributed as if such person had predeceased the intestate.

§238.06. **How wills to be executed.** No will made within this state since the first day of January, 1896, except such nuncupative wills as are mentioned in this chapter, shall be effectual to pass any estate, whether real or personal, or to charge or in any way affect the same unless it be in writing and signed by the testator or by some person in his presence and by his express direction, and attested and subscribed in the presence of the testator by two or more competent witnesses in the presence of each other; if the witnesses are competent at the time of such attesting their subsequent incompetency, from whatever cause it may arise, shall not prevent the probate and allowance of the will if it be otherwise satisfactorily proved.

Treasury Regulations Under the 1954 Code

Sec. 1.61-2(d)

(2) *Property transferred to employee; insurance premiums paid by employer.* Except as otherwise provided in section 421 and the regulations thereunder (relating to employee stock options), if property is transferred by an employer to an employee for an amount less than its fair market value, regardless of whether the transfer is in the form of a sale or exchange, the difference between the amount paid for the property and the amount of its fair market value at the time of the transfer is compensation and shall be included in the gross income of the employee. In computing the gain or loss from the subsequent sale of such property, its basis shall be the amount paid for the property increased by the amount of such difference included in gross income. Generally, life insurance premiums paid by an employer on the lives of his employees, where the proceeds of such insurance are payable to the beneficiaries of such employees, are part of the gross income of the employees. However, premiums paid by an employer on policies of group term life insurance covering the lives of his employees are not gross income to the employees, even if they designate the beneficiaries. For special rules relating to the exclusion of contributions by an employer to accident and health plans, see section 106 and the regulations thereunder.

Sec. 1.101-1

(b) *Transfers of life insurance policies.* (1) In the case of a transfer, by assignment or otherwise, of a life insurance policy or any interest therein for a valuable consideration, the amount of the proceeds attributable to such policy or interest which is excludable from the transferee's gross income is generally limited to the sum of (i) the actual value of the consideration for such transfer, and (ii) the premiums and other amounts subsequently paid by the transferee (see section 101(a)(2) and example (1) of subparagraph (5) of this paragraph). However, this limitation on the amount excludable from the transferee's gross income does not apply (except in certain special cases involving a series of transfers), where the basis of the policy or interest transferred, for the purpose of determining gain or loss with respect to the transferee, is determinable, in whole or in part, by reference to the basis of such policy or interest in the hands of the transferor (see section 101(a)(2)(A) and examples (2) and (4) of subparagraph (5) of this paragraph). Neither does the limitation apply where the policy or interest therein is transferred to the insured, to a partner of the insured, to a partnership in which the insured is a partner, or to a corporation in which the insured is a shareholder or officer (see section 101(a)(2)(B)). For rules relating to gratuitous transfers, see subparagraph (2) of this paragraph. For special rules with respect to certain cases where a series of transfers is involved, see subparagraph (3) of this paragraph.

(2) In the case of a gratuitous transfer, by assignment or otherwise, of a life insurance policy or any interest therein, as a general rule the amount of the proceeds attributable to such policy or interest which is excludable from the transferee's gross income under section 101(a) is limited to the sum of (i) the amount which would have been excludable by the transferor (in accordance with this section) if no such transfer had taken place, and (ii) any premiums and other amounts subsequently paid by the transferee. See example (6) of subparagraph (5) of this paragraph. However, where the gratuitous transfer in question is made by or to the insured, a partner of the insured, a partnership in which the insured is a partner, or a corporation in which the insured is a shareholder or officer, the entire amount of the proceeds attributable to the policy or interest transferred shall be excludable from the transferee's gross income (see section 101(a)(2)(B) and example (7) of subparagraph (5) of this paragraph).

(3) In the case of a series of transfers, if the last transfer of a life insurance policy or an interest therein is for a valuable consideration —

(i) The general rule is that the final transferee shall exclude from gross income, with respect to the proceeds of such policy or interest therein, only the sum of —

(a) The actual value of the consideration paid by him, and

(b) The premiums and other amounts subsequently paid by him;

(ii) If the final transfer is to the insured, to a partner of the insured, to a partnership in which the insured is a partner, or to a corporation in which the insured is a shareholder or officer, the final transferee shall exclude the entire amount of the proceeds from gross income;

(iii) Except where subdivision (ii) of this subparagraph applies, if the basis of the policy or interest transferred, for the purpose of determining gain or loss with respect to the final transferee, is determinable, in whole or in part, by reference to the basis of such policy or interest therein in the hands of the transferor, the amount of the proceeds which is excludable by the final transferee is limited to the sum of —

(a) The amount which would have been excludable by his transferor if no such transfer had taken place, and

(b) Any premiums and other amounts subsequently paid by the final transferee himself.

(4) For the purposes of section 101(a)(2) and subparagraphs (1) and (3) of this paragraph, a "transfer for a valuable consideration" is any absolute transfer for value of a right to receive all or a part of the proceeds of a life insurance policy. Thus, the creation, for value, of an enforceable contractual right to receive all or a part of the proceeds of a policy may constitute a transfer for a valuable consideration of the policy or an interest therein. On the other hand, the pledging or assignment of a policy as collateral security is not a transfer for a valuable consideration of such policy or an interest therein, and section 101 is inapplicable to any amounts received by the pledgee or assignee.

(5) The application of this paragraph may be illustrated by the following examples:

Example (1). A pays premiums of $500 for an insurance policy in the face amount of $1,000 upon the life of B, and subsequently transfers the policy to C for $600. C receives the proceeds of $1,000 upon the death of B. The amount which C can exclude from his gross income is limited to $600 plus any premiums paid by C subsequent to the transfer.

Example (2). The X Corporation purchases for a single premium of $500 an insurance policy in the face amount of $1,000 upon the life of A, one of its employees, naming the X Corporation as beneficiary. The X Corporation transfers the policy to the Y Corporation in a tax-free reorganization (the policy having a basis for determining gain or loss in the hands of the Y Corporation determined by reference to its basis in the hands of the X Corporation). The Y Corporation receives the proceeds of $1,000 upon the death of A. The entire $1,000 is to be excluded from the gross income of the Y Corporation.

Example (3). The facts are the same as in example (2) except that, prior to the death of A, the Y Corporation transfers the policy to the Z Corporation for $600. The Z Corporation receives the proceeds of $1,000 upon the death of A. The amount which the Z Corporation can exclude from its gross income is limited to $600 plus any premiums paid by the Z Corporation subsequent to the transfer of the policy to it.

Example (4). The facts are the same as in example (3) except that, prior to the death of A, the Z Corporation transfers the policy to the M Corporation in a tax-free reorganization (the policy having a basis for determining gain or loss in the hands of the M Corporation determined by reference to its basis in the hands of the Z Corporation). The M Corporation receives the proceeds of $1,000 upon the death of A. The amount which the M Corporation can exclude from its gross income is limited to $600 plus any premiums paid by the Z Corporation and the M Corporation subsequent to the transfer of the policy to the Z Corporation.

Example (5). The facts are the same as in example (3) except that, prior to the death of A, the Z Corporation transfers the policy to the N Corporation, in which A is a shareholder. The N Corporation receives the proceeds of $1,000 upon the death of A. The entire $1,000 is to be excluded from the gross income of the N Corporation.

Example (6). A pays premiums of $500 for an insurance policy in the face amount of $1,000 upon his own life and subsequently transfers the policy to his wife B for $600. B later transfers the policy without consideration to C, who is the son of A and B. C receives the proceeds of $1,000 upon the death of A. The amount which C can exclude from his gross income is limited to $600 plus any premiums paid by B and C subsequent to the transfer of the policy to B.

Example (7). The facts are the same as in example (6) except that, prior to the death of A, C transfers the policy without consideration to A, the insured. A's estate receives the proceeds of $1,000 upon the death of A. The entire $1,000 is to be excluded from the gross income of A's estate.

Sec. 1.101-2(d)(3)(ii)

Example (2). The trustee of the X Corporation noncontributory, "qualified," profit-sharing plan is required under the provisions of the plan to pay to the beneficiary of B, an employee of the X Corporation who died on July 1, 1955, the benefit due on account of the death of B. The provisions of the profit-sharing plan give each participating employee, in case of termination of employment, a 10 percent vested interest in the amount accumulated in his account for each year of participation in the plan, but, in case of death, the entire credit to the participant's account is to be paid to his beneficiary. At the time of B's death, he had been a participant for five years. The accumulation in his account was $8,000, and the amount which would have been distributable to him in the event of termination of employment was $4,000 (50 percent of $8,000). After his death, $8,000 is paid to his beneficiary in a lump sum. (It may be noted that these are the same facts as in example (5) of subparagraph (2) of this paragraph except that the employee has been a participant for five years instead of three and the plan is a "qualified" plan.) It is immaterial that the employee had a nonforfeitable right to $4,000, because the payment of the $8,000 to the beneficiary is the payment of the "total distributions payable" within one taxable year of the distributee to which subdivision (i) of this subparagraph applies. Assuming no other death benefits are involved, the beneficiary may exclude $5,000 of the $8,000 payment from gross income.

Sec. 1.101-3. Interest payments

(a) *Applicability of Section 101(c)*. Section 101(c) provides that if any amount excluded from gross income by section 101(a) (relating to life insurance proceeds) or section 101(b) (relating to employees' death benefits) is held under an agreement to pay interest thereon, the interest payments shall be included in gross income. This provision applies to payments made (either by an insurer or by or on behalf of an employer) of interest earned on any amount so excluded from gross income which is held without substantial diminution of the principal amount during the period when such interest payments are being made or credited to the beneficiaries or estate of the insured or the employee. For example, if a monthly payment is $100, of which $99 represents interest and $1 represents diminution of the principal amount, the principal amount shall be considered held under an agreement to pay interest thereon and the interest payment shall be included in the gross income of the recipient. Section 101(c) applies whether the election to have an amount held under an agreement to pay interest thereon is made by the insured or employee or by his beneficiaries or estate, and whether or not an interest rate is explicitly stated in the agreement. Section 101(d), relating to the payment of life insurance proceeds at a date later than death, shall not apply to any amount to which section 101(c) applies. See section 101(d)(4).

(b) *Determinations of "present value."* For the purpose of determining whether section 101(c) or section 101(d) applies, the present value (at the time of the insured's death) of any amount which is to be paid at a date later than death shall be determined by the use of the interest rate and mortality tables used by the insurer in determining the size of the payments to be made.

Sec. 1.101-4

(b) . . .

(3) Notwithstanding any other provision of this section, if the policy was transferred for a valuable consideration, the total "amount held by an insurer" cannot exceed the sum of the consideration paid plus any premiums or other consideration paid subsequent to the transfer if the provisions of section 101(a)(2) and paragraph (b) of §1.101-1 limit the excludability of the proceeds to such total.

(c) *Treatment of payments for life to a sole beneficiary.* If the contract provides for the payment of a specified lump sum, but, pursuant to an agreement between the beneficiary and the insurer, payments are to be made during the life of the beneficiary in lieu of such lump sum, the lump sum shall be divided by the life expectancy of the beneficiary determined in accordance with the mortality table used by the insurer in determining the benefits to be paid. However, if payments are to be made to the estate or beneficiary of the primary beneficiary in the event that the primary beneficiary dies before receiving a certain number of payments or a specified total amount, such lump sum shall be reduced by the present value (at the time of the insured's death) of amounts which may be paid by reason of the guarantee, in accordance with the provisions of paragraph (e) of this section, before making this calculation. To the extent that payments received in each taxable year do not exceed the amount found from the above calculation, they are "prorated amounts" of the "amount held by an insurer" and are excludable from the gross income of the beneficiary without regard to whether he lives beyond the life expectancy used in making the calculation. If the contract in question does not provide for the payment of a specific lump sum upon the death of the insured as one of the alternative methods of payment, the present value (at the time of the death of the insured) of the payments to be made the beneficiary, determined in accordance with the interest rate and mortality table used by the insurer in determining the benefits to be paid, shall be used in the above calculation in lieu of a lump sum.

(d) *Treatment of payments to two or more beneficiaries.* (1) *Unrelated payments.* If payments are to be made to two or more beneficiaries, but the payments to be made to each are to be made without regard to whether or not payments are made or continue to be made to the other beneficiaries, the present value (at the time of the insured's death) of such payments to each beneficiary shall be determined independently for each such beneficiary. The present value so determined shall then be divided by the term for which the payments are to be made. If the payments are to be made for the life of the beneficiary, the divisor shall be the life expectancy of the beneficiary. To the extent that payments received by a beneficiary do not exceed the amount found from the above calculation, they are "prorated amounts" of the "amount held by an insurer" with respect to such beneficiary and are excludable from the gross income of the beneficiary without regard to whether he lives beyond any life expectancy used in making the calculation. For the purpose of the calculation described above, both the "present value" of the payments to be made periodically and the "life expectancy" of the beneficiary shall be determined in accordance with the interest rate and mortality table used by the insurer in determining the benefits to be paid. If payments are to be made to the estate or beneficiary of a primary beneficiary in the event that such beneficiary dies before receiving a certain number of payments or a specified total amount, the "present value" of payments to such beneficiary shall not include the present value (at the time of the insured's death) of amounts which may be paid by reason of such a guarantee. See paragraph (e) of this section.

(2) *Related payments.* If payments to be made to two or more beneficiaries are in the nature of a joint and survivor annuity (as described in paragraph (b) of §1.72-5), the present value (at the time of the insured's death) of the payments to be made to all such beneficiaries shall be divided by the life expectancy of such beneficiaries as a group. To the extent that the payments received by a beneficiary do not exceed the amount found from the above calculation, they are "prorated amounts" of the "amount held by an insured" with respect to such beneficiary and are excludable from the gross income of the beneficiary without regard to whether all the beneficiaries involved live beyond the life expectancy used in making the calculation. For the purpose of the calculation described above, both the "present value" of the payments to be made periodically and the "life expectancy" of all the beneficiaries as a group shall be determined in accordance with the interest rate and mortality table used by the insurer in determining the benefits to be paid. If the contract provides that certain payments are to be made in the event that all the beneficiaries of the group die before a specified number of payments or a specified total amount is received by them, the present value of payments to be

made to the group shall not include the present value (at the time of the insured's death) of amounts which may be paid by reason of such a guarantee. See paragraph (e) of this section.

(3) *Payments to secondary beneficiaries.* Payments made by reason of the death of a beneficiary (or beneficiaries) under a contract providing that such payments shall be made in the event that the beneficiary (or beneficiaries) die before receiving a specified number of payments or a specified total amount shall be excluded from the gross income of the recipient to the extent that such payments are made solely by reason of such guarantee.

(e) *Treatment of present value of guaranteed payments.* In the case of payments which are to be made for a life or lives under a contract providing that further amount shall be paid upon the death of the primary beneficiary (or beneficiaries) in the event that such beneficiary (or beneficiaries) die before receiving a specified number of payments or a specified total amount, the present value (at the time of the insured's death) of all payments to be made under the contract shall not include, for purposes of prorating the amount held by the insurer, the present value of the payments which may be made to the estate or beneficiary of the primary beneficiary. In such a case, any lump sum amount used to measure the value of the amount held by an insurer with respect to the primary beneficiary must be reduced by the value at the time of the insured's death of any amounts which may be paid by reason of the guarantee provided for a secondary beneficiary or the estate of the primary beneficiary before prorating such lump sum over the life or lives of the primary beneficiaries. Such present value (of the guaranteed payment) shall be determined by the use of the interest rate and mortality tables used by the insurer in determining the benefits to be paid.

(f) *Treatment of payments not paid periodically.* Payments made to beneficiaries other than periodically shall be included in the gross income of the recipients, but only to the extent that they exceed amounts payable at the time of the death of the insured to each such beneficiary or, where no such amounts are specified, the present value of such payments at that time.

(g) . . .

Example (7). A life insurance policy provides for the payment of $75,000 in a lump sum to the beneficiary, A, at the death of the insured. A, upon the insured's death, however, selects an option for the payment of $4,000 per year for life, with a guarantee that any part of the $75,000 lump sum not paid to A before his death shall be paid to B (or his estate), A's beneficiary. Assuming that, under the criteria used by the insurer in determining the benefits to be paid, the present value of the guaranteed amount to B is $13,500 and that A's life expectancy is 25 years, the lump sum shall be reduced by the present value of the guarantee to B ($75,000 less $13,500, or $61,500) and divided by A's life expectancy ($61,500 divided by 25, or $2,460). Hence, $2,460 of each $4,000 payment is excludable from A's gross income. If A is the surviving spouse of the insured and no other contracts of insurance whose proceeds are to be paid to her at a date later than death are involved, A shall exclude $3,460 of each $4,000 payment from gross income in any taxable year in which but one such payment is received. Under these facts, if any amount is paid to B by reason of the fact that A dies before receiving a total of $75,000, the residue of the lump sum paid to B shall be excluded from B's gross income since it is wholly in lieu of the present value of such guarantee plus the present value of the payments to be made to the first beneficiary, and is therefore entirely an "amount held by an insurer" paid at a date later than death (see paragraph (d)(3) of this section).

Example (8). Assume, that an insurance policy does not provide for the payment of a lump sum, but provides for the payment of $1,200 per year for a beneficiary's life upon the death of the insured, and also provides that if ten payments are not made to the beneficiary before death a secondary beneficiary (whether named by the insured or by the first beneficiary) shall receive the remainder of the ten payments in similar installments. If, according to the criteria used by the insurance company in determining the benefits, the present value of the payments to the first beneficiary is $12,000 and the life expectancy of such beneficiary is 15 years, $800 of each payment received by the first beneficiary is excludable from gross income. Assuming that the same figures obtain even though the payments are to be made at the rate of $100 per month, the yearly exclusion remains the same unless more or less than twelve months' installments are received by the beneficiary in a particular taxable year. In such a case two-thirds of the total received in the particular taxable year with respect to such beneficiary shall be excluded from gross income. Under either of the above alternatives, any amount received by the second beneficiary by reason of the guarantee of ten payments is fully excludable from the beneficiary's gross income since it is wholly in lieu of the present value of such guarantee plus the present value of the payments to be made to the first beneficiary and is therefore entirely an "amount held by an insurer" paid at a date later than death (see paragraph (d)(3) of this section).

Sec. 1.170-1

(b) *Time of making contribution.* Ordinarily a contribution is made at the time delivery is effected. In the case of a check, the unconditional delivery (or mailing) of a check which subsequently clears in due course will constitute an effective contribution on the date of delivery (or mailing). If a taxpayer unconditionally delivers a properly endorsed stock certificate to a charitable donee or the donee's agent, the gift is completed on the date of delivery. If the donor delivers the certificate to his bank or broker as the donor's agent, or to the issuing corporation or its agent, for transfer into the name of the donee, the gift is completed on the date the stock is transferred on the books of the corporation.

(c) *Contribution in property.* If a contribution is made in property other than money, the amount of the deduction is determined by the fair market value of the property at the time of the contribution. The fair market value is the price at which the property would change hands between a willing buyer and a willing seller, neither being under any compulsion to buy or sell and both having reasonable knowledge of relevant facts. If the contribution is made in property of a type which the taxpayer sells in the course of his business, the fair market value is the price which the taxpayer would have received if he had sold the contributed property in the lowest usual market in which he customarily sells, at the time and place of the contribution (and in the case of a contribution of goods in quantity, in the quantity contributed). The usual market of a manufacturer or other producer consists of the wholesalers or other distributors to or through whom he customarily sells, unless he sells only at retail in which event it is his retail customers. If a donor makes a charitable contribution of, for example, stock in trade at a time when he could not reasonably have been expected to realize its usual selling price, the value of the gift is not the usual selling price but is the amount for which the quantity of merchandise contributed would have been sold by the donor at the time of the contribution. Costs and expenses incurred in the year of contribution in producing or acquiring the contributed property are not deductible and are not a part of the cost of goods sold. Similarly, to the extent that costs and expenses incurred in a prior taxable year in producing or acquiring the contributed property are reflected in the cost of goods sold in the year of contribution, cost of goods sold must be reduced by such costs and expenses. Transfers of property to an organization described in section 170(c) which bear a direct relationship to the taxpayer's business and are made with a reasonable expectation of financial return commensurate with the amount of the transfer may constitute allowable deductions as trade or business expenses rather than as charitable contributions. See section 162 and the regulations thereunder.

Sec. 1.212-1

(e) A deduction under section 212 is subject to the restrictions and limitations in sections 261 through 273, relating to items not deductible. Thus, no deduction is allowable under section 212 for any amount allocable to the production or collection of one or more classes of income which are not includible in gross income, or for any amount allocable to the management, conservation, or maintenance of property held for the production of income which is not included in gross income. See section 265. Nor does section 212 allow the deduction of any expenses which are disallowed by any of the provisions of subtitle A of the Internal Revenue Code of 1954, even though such expenses may be paid or incurred for one of the purposes specified in section 212.

Sec. 1.401-1. Qualified pension, profit-sharing and stock bonus plans

(a) *Introduction*. (1) Sections 401 through 404 relate to pension, profit-sharing, stock bonus, and annuity plans, and compensation paid under a deferred-payment plan. Section 401(a) prescribes the requirements which must be met for qualification of a trust forming part of a pension, profit-sharing, or stock bonus plan.

(2) A qualified pension, profit-sharing, or stock bonus plan is a definite written program and arrangement which is communicated to the employees and which is established and maintained by an employer —

(i) In the case of a pension plan, to provide for the livelihood of the employees or their beneficiaries after the retirement of such employees through the payment of benefits determined without regard to profits (see §1.401-1(b)(1)(i));

(ii) In the case of a profit-sharing plan, to enable employees or their beneficiaries to participate in the profits of the employer's trade or business, or in the profits of an affiliated employer who is entitled to deduct his contributions to the plan under section 404(a)(3)(B), pursuant to a definite formula for allocating the contributions and for distributing the funds accumulated under the plan (see §1.401(b)(1)(ii)); and

(iii) In the case of a stock bonus plan, to provide employees or their beneficiaries benefits similar to those of profit-sharing plans, except that such benefits are distributable in stock of the employer, and that the contributions by the employer are not necessarily dependent upon profits. If the employer's contributions are dependent upon profits, the plan may enable employees or their beneficiaries to participate not only in the profits of the employer, but also in the profits of an affiliated employer who is entitled to deduct his contributions to the plan under section 404(a)(3)(B) (see §1.401-1(b)(1)(iii)).

(3) In order for a trust forming part of a pension, profit-sharing, or stock bonus plan to constitute a qualified trust under section 401(a), the following tests must be met:

(i) It must be created or organized in the United States, as defined in section 7701(a)(9), and it must be maintained at all times as a domestic trust in the United States;

(ii) It must be part of a pension, profit-sharing, or stock bonus plan established by an employer for the exclusive benefit of his employees or their beneficiaries (see §1.401-1(b)(2) through (5));

(iii) It must be formed or availed of for the purpose of distributing to the employees or their beneficiaries the corpus and income of the fund accumulated by the trust in accordance with the plan;

(iv) It must be impossible under the trust instrument at any time before the satisfaction of all liabilities with respect to employees and their beneficiaries under the trust, for any part of the corpus or income to be used for, or diverted to, purposes other than for the exclusive benefit of the employees or their beneficiaries (see §1.401-2);

(v) It must be part of a plan which benefits prescribed percentages of the employees, or which benefits such employees as qualify under a classification set up by the employer and found by the Commissioner not to be discriminatory in favor of certain specified classes of employees (see §1.401-3); and

(vi) It must be part of a plan under which contributions or benefits do not discriminate in favor of certain specified classes of employees (see §1.401-4).

(b) *General rules.* (1)(i) A pension plan within the meaning of section 401(a) is a plan established and maintained by an employer primarily to provide systematically for the payment of definitely determinable benefits to his employees over a period of years, usually for life, after retirement. Retirement benefits generally are measured by, and based on, such factors as years of service and compensation received by the employees. The determination of the amount of retirement benefits and the contributions to provide such benefits are not dependent upon profits. Benefits are not definitely determinable if funds arising from forfeitures on termination of service, or other reason, may be used to provide increased benefits for the remaining participants instead of being used to reduce the amount of contributions by the employer. A plan designed to provide benefits for employees or their beneficiaries to be paid upon retirement or over a period of years after retirement will, for the purposes of section 401(a), be considered a pension plan if the employer contributions under the plan can be determined actuarially on the basis of definitely determinable benefits, or, as in the case of money purchase pension plans, such contributions are fixed without being geared to profits. A pension plan may provide for the payment of a pension due to disability and may also provide for the payment of incidental death benefits through insurance or otherwise. However, a plan is not a pension plan if it provides for the payment of benefits not customarily included in a pension plan such as layoff benefits or benefits for sickness, accident, hospitalization, or medical expenses.

(ii) A profit-sharing plan is a plan established and maintained by an employer to provide for the participation in his profits by his employees or their beneficiaries. The plan must provide a definite predetermined formula for allocating the contributions made to the plan among the participants and for distributing the funds accumulated under the plan after a fixed number of years, the attainment of a stated age, or upon the prior occurrence of some event such as layoff, illness, disability, retirement, death, or severance of employment. A formula for allocating the contributions among the participants is definite if, for example, it provides for an allocation in proportion to the basic compensation of each participant. A plan (whether or not it contains a definite predetermined formula for determining the profits to be shared with the employees) does not qualify under section 401(a) if the contributions to the plan are made at such times or in such amounts that the plan in operation discriminates in favor of officers, shareholders, persons whose principal duties consist in supervising the work of other employees, or highly compensated employees. For the rules with respect to discrimination, see §§1.401-3 and 1.401-4. A profit-sharing plan within the meaning of section 401 is primarily a plan of deferred compensation, but the amounts allocated to the account of a participant may be used to provide for him or his family incidental life or accident or health insurance.

(iii) A stock bonus plan is a plan established and maintained by an employer to provide benefits similar to those of a profit-sharing plan, except that the contributions by the employer are not necessarily dependent upon profits and the benefits are distributable in stock of the employer company. For the purpose of allocating and distributing the stock of the employer which is to be shared among his employees or their beneficiaries, such a plan is subject to the same requirements as a profit-sharing plan.

Sec. 1.402(a)-1(a)

(2) If a trust described in section 401(a) and exempt under section 501(a) purchases an annuity contract for an employee and distributes it to the employee in a year for which the trust is exempt, the contract containing a cash surrender value which may be available to an employee by surrendering the contract, such cash surrender value will not be considered income to the employee unless and until the contract is surrendered. If, however, the contract distributed by such an exempt trust is a retirement income, endowment, or other life insurance contract and is distributed after October 26, 1956, the entire cash value of such contract at the time of distribution must be included in the distributee's income in accordance with the provisions of section 402(a), except to the extent that, within 60 days after the distribution of such contract, all or any portion of such value is irrevocably converted into a contract under which no part of any proceeds payable on death at any time would be excludable under section 101(a) (relating to life insurance proceeds).

(3)(i) If a trust described in section 401(a) and exempt under section 501(a) purchases under the plan retirement income, endowment, or other contracts providing life insurance protection, payable upon the death of the employee participant, and either —

(a) The proceeds of such life insurance are payable to a beneficiary of the employee participant, other than the trust, or

(b) In case such proceeds are payable to the trust, by the terms of the plan the trustee is required to pay over all of such proceeds to a beneficiary of the employee participant,

then, the portion of the premiums paid for the life insurance protection provided under such contracts from either the contributions of the employer or earnings of the trust will constitute income to the employee for the year or years in which the contributions or earnings are applied toward the purchase of such life insurance. If the amount payable upon death at any time during the year exceeds the cash value of the insurance policy at the end of the year, the entire amount of such excess will be considered current life insurance protection. The cost of such insurance will be considered to be a reasonable net premium cost, as determined by the Commissioner, for such amount for the appropriate period. The amount thus to be included in the gross income of the employee under this subdivision shall be considered as premiums or other consideration paid or contributed by the employee only with respect to any benefits attributable to the contract providing the life insurance protection.

(ii) The determination of the cost of life insurance protection may be illustrated by the following example:

Example. A policy purchased under a qualified plan for an employee provides an annuity of $100 per month upon retirement at age 65, with a mini-

mum death benefit of $10,000. The insurance payable if death occurred in
the first year would be $10,000. The cash value at the end of the first year
is 0. The net insurance is therefore $10,000 minus 0, or $10,000. Assuming
that the Commissioner has determined that a reasonable net premium for the
employee's age is $5.85 per $1,000, the premium for $10,000 of life insurance
is therefore $58.50, and this is the amount to be reported as income by the
employee for the year. The balance of the premium is the amount contributed for the annuity, which is not taxable to the employee under a plan meeting the requirements of section 401(a), except as provided under section
402(a). Assuming that the cash value at the end of the second year is $500,
the net insurance would then be $9,500 for the second year. With a net
1-year term rate of $6.30 for the employee's age in the second year, the amount
to be reported as income to the employee would be $59.85.

Sec. 1.402(a)-1(a)(4)(ii)

(b) In the case of a retirement income, endowment, or other life insurance
contract under which there is a reserve accumulation which is intended to
fund pension or other deferred benefits under a pension or profit-sharing
plan, such reserve accumulation constitutes the source of the cash value of the
contract and approximates the amount of such cash value. The portion of
the proceeds paid upon the death of the insured employee which is equal to
the cash value immediately before death is not excludable from gross income
under section 101(a). The remaining portion, if any, of the proceeds paid to
the beneficiary by reason of the death of the insured employee — that is, the
amount in excess of the cash value — constitutes current insurance protection
and is excludable under section 101(a).

(c) The death benefit under an annuity contract, or the portion of the
death proceeds under a retirement income, endowment, or other life insurance contract which is equal to the cash value of the contract immediately before death, constitutes a distribution from the trust consisting in whole or in
part of deferred compensation and is taxable to the beneficiary in accordance
with section 402(a) and the provisions of this paragraph, except to the extent
that the limited exclusion from income provided in section 101(b) is applicable.

Sec. 1.402(a)-1(a)(6)

(iv) If the "total distributions payable" are paid or includible in the gross
income of several distributees within one taxable year on account of the employee's death or other separation from the service or on account of his death
after separation from the service, the capital gains treatment is applicable.
The total distributions payable are paid within one taxable year of the distributees when, for example, a portion of such total is distributed in cash to
one distributee and the balance is used to purchase an annuity contract which
is distributed to the other distributee. However, if the share of any distributee is not paid or includible in his gross income within the same taxable
year in which the shares of the other distributees are paid or includible in
their gross income, none of the distributees is entitled to the capital gains
treatment, since the total distributions payable are not paid or includible in
the distributees' gross income within one taxable year. For example, if the
total distributions payable are made available to each of two distributees and
one elects to receive his share in cash while the other makes a timely election
under section 72(h) to receive his share in installment payments from the
trust, the capital gains treatment does not apply to either distributee.

Sec. 1.402(b)-1. Treatment of beneficiary of a trust not exempt under
section 501(a)

(a) Taxation by reason of employer contributions. — (1) Except as provided in section 402(d), any contribution made by an employer on behalf of an employee to a trust during a taxable year of the employer which ends within or with a taxable year of the trust for which the trust is not exempt under section 501(a), shall be included in income of the employee for his taxable year during which the contribution is made if the employee's beneficial interest in the contribution is nonforfeitable at the time the contribution is made. If the employee's beneficial interest in the contribution is forfeitable at the time the contribution is made even though his interest becomes nonforfeitable later, the amount of such contribution is not required to be included in the income of the employee at the time his interest becomes nonforfeitable.

(2)(i) An employee's beneficial interest in the contribution is nonforfeitable within the meaning of sections 402(b), 403(b), and 404(a)(5) at the time the contribution is made if there is no contingency under the plan which may cause the employee to lose his rights in the contribution. For example, if under the terms of a pension plan, an employee upon termination of his services before the retirement date, whether voluntarily or involuntarily, is entitled to a deferred annuity contract to be purchased with the employer's contributions made on his behalf, or is entitled to annuity payments which the trustee is obligated to make under the terms of the trust instrument based on the contributions made by the employer on his behalf, the employee's beneficial interest in such contributions is nonforfeitable.

(ii) On the other hand, if, under the terms of a pension plan, an employee will lose the right to any annuity purchased from, or to be provided by, contributions made by the employer if his services should be terminated before retirement, his beneficial interest in such contributions is forfeitable.

(iii) The mere fact that an employee may not live to the retirement date, or may live only a short period after the retirement date, and may not be able to enjoy the receipt of annuity or pension payments, does not make his beneficial interest in the contributions made by the employer on his behalf forfeitable. If the employer's contributions have been irrevocably applied to purchase an annuity contract for the employee, or if the trustee is obligated to use the employer's contributions to provide an annuity for the employee provided only that the employee is alive on the dates the annuity payments are due, the employee's rights in the employer's contributions are nonforfeitable.

(b) *Taxation of distributions from trust not exempt under section 501(a).* — Any amount actually distributed or made available to any distributee by an employees' trust which is not exempt under section 501(a) for the taxable year of the trust in which the distribution is made shall be taxable in the year in which so distributed or made available, under section 72 (relating to annuities), except that section 72(e)(3) shall not apply. If, for example, the distribution from such a trust consists of an annuity contract, the amount of the distribution shall be considered to be the entire value of the contract at the time of distribution, and such value is includible in the gross income of the distributee at the time of the distribution to the extent that such value exceeds the investment in the contract determined by applying sections 72 and 101(b). The distributions by such an employees' trust shall be taxed as provided in section 72, whether or not the employee's rights to the contributions were nonforfeitable when the contributions were made or at any time thereafter. For rules relating to the treatment of employer contributions to a non-exempt trust as part of the consideration paid by the employee, see section 72(f). For rules relating to the treatment of the limited exclusion allowable under section 101(b)(2)(D) as additional consideration paid by the employee, see the regulations under that section.

Sec. 1.403(b)-1. Taxability of beneficiary under a nonqualified annuity

(a) Except as provided in section 402(d), if an employer purchases an annuity contract and if the amounts paid for the contract are not subject to §1.403(a)-1(a), the amount of such contribution shall be included in the income of the employee for the taxable year during which such contribution is made if, at the time the contribution is made, the employee's rights under the annuity contract are nonforfeitable, except for failure to pay future premiums. If the employee's rights under the annuity contract in such a case were forfeitable at the time the employer's contribution was made for the annuity contract, even though they become nonforfeitable later, the amount of such contribution is not required to be included in the income of the employee at the time his rights under the contract become nonforfeitable. As to what constitutes nonforfeitable rights of an employee, see §1.402(b)-1. The amounts received by or made available to the employee under the annuity contract shall be included in the gross income of the employee for the taxable year in which received or made available, as provided in section 72 (relating to annuities) except that section 72(e)(3) shall not apply. For rules relating to the treatment of employer contributions as part of the consideration paid by the employee, see section 72(f). See also section 101(b)(2)(D) for rules relating to the treatment of the limited exclusion provided thereunder as part of the consideration paid by the employee.

(b) If an employer has purchased annuity contracts and transferred the same to a trust or if an employer has made contributions to a trust for the purpose of providing annuity contracts for his employees as provided in section 402(d) (see §1.402(d)-1(a)), the amount so paid or contributed is not required to be included in the income of the employee, but any amount received by or made available to the employee under the annuity contract shall be includible in the gross income of the employee for the taxable year in which received or made available, as provided in section 72 (relating to annuities), except that section 72(e)(3) shall not apply. In such case the amount paid or contributed by the employer shall not constitute consideration paid by the employee for such annuity contract in determining the amount of annuity payments required to be included in his gross income under section 72 unless the employee has paid income tax for any taxable year beginning before January 1, 1949, with respect to such payment or contribution by the employer for such year and such tax is not credited or refunded to the employee. In the event such tax has been paid and not credited or refunded the amount paid or contributed by the employer for such year shall constitute consideration paid by the employee for the annuity contract in determining the amount of the annuity required to be included in the income of the employee under section 72.

Sec. 1.642(g)-1. Disallowance of double deductions; in general.

Amounts allowable under section 2053(a)(2) (relating to administration expenses) or under section 2054 (relating to losses during administration) as deductions in computing the taxable estate of a decedent are not allowed as deductions in computing the taxable income of the estate unless there is filed a statement, in duplicate, to the effect that the items have not been allowed as deductions from the gross estate of the decedent under section 2053 or 2054 and that all rights to have such items allowed at any time as deductions under section 2053 or 2054 are waived. The statement should be filed with the return for the year for which the items are claimed as deductions or with the district director of internal revenue for the internal revenue district in which the return was filed, for association with the return. The statement may be filed at any time before the expiration of the statutory period of limitation applicable to the taxable year for which the deduction is sought. Allowance of a deduction in computing an estate's taxable income is not precluded by claiming a deduction in the estate tax return, so long as the estate tax deduction is not finally allowed and the statement is filed. However, after a statement is filed under section 642(g) with respect to a particular item or portion of an item, the item cannot thereafter be allowed as a deduction for estate tax purposes since the waiver operates as a relinquishment of the right to have the deduction allowed at any time under section 2053 or 2054.

Sec. 1.661(a)-2. Deduction for distributions to beneficiaries

(a) In computing the taxable income of an estate or trust there is allowed under section 661(a) as a deduction for distributions to beneficiaries the sum of —

(1) The amount of income for the taxable year which is required to be distributed currently, and

(2) Any other amounts properly paid or credited or required to be distributed for such taxable year.

However, the total amount deductible under section 661(a) cannot exceed the distributable net income as computed under section 643(a) and as modified by section 661(c). See §1.661(c)-1.

(b) The term "income required to be distributed currently" includes any amount required to be distributed which may be paid out of income or corpus (such as an annuity), to the extent it is paid out of income for the taxable year. See §1.651(a)-2 which sets forth additional rules which are applicable in determining whether income of an estate or trust is required to be distributed currently.

(c) The term "any other amounts properly paid or credited or required to be distributed" includes all amounts properly paid, credited, or required to be distributed by an estate or trust during the taxable year other than income required to be distributed currently. Thus, the term includes the payment of an annuity to the extent it is not paid out of income for the taxable year, and a distribution of property in kind (see paragraph (f) of this section below). However, see section 663(a) and regulations thereunder for distributions which are not included. Where the income of an estate or trust may be accumulated or distributed in the discretion of the fiduciary, or where the fiduciary has a power to distribute corpus to a beneficiary, any such discretionary distribution would qualify under section 661(a)(2). The term also includes an amount applied or distributed for the support of a dependent of a grantor or of a trustee or cotrustee under the circumstances described in section 677(b) or section 678(c) out of corpus or out of other than income for the taxable year.

(d) The terms "income required to be distributed currently" and "any other amounts properly paid or credited or required to be distributed" also include any amount used to discharge or satisfy any person's legal obligation as that term is used in §1662(a)-4.

(e) The terms "income required to be distributed currently" and "any other amounts properly paid or credited or required to be distributed" do not include amounts required to be paid by a decedent's estate pursuant to a court order or decree as an allowance or award under local law for the support of the decedent's widow or other dependent for a limited period during the administration of the estate, except to the extent such amounts are payable out of and chargeable to income under the order or decree or local law. The term "any other amounts properly paid or credited or required to be distributed" does not include the value of any interest in real estate owned by a decedent, title to which under local law passes directly from the decedent to his heirs or devisees.

Sec. 1.662(a)-4.   Amounts used in discharge of a legal obligation.   Any amount which, pursuant to the terms of a will or trust instrument, is used in full or partial discharge or satisfaction of a legal obligation of any person is included in the gross income of such person under section 662(a)(1) or (2), whichever is applicable, as though directly distributed to him as a beneficiary, except in cases to which section 71 (relating to alimony payments) or section 682 (relating to income of a trust in case of divorce, etc.) applies.   The term "legal obligation" includes a legal obligation to support another person if, and only if, the obligation is not affected by the adequacy of the dependent's own resources.   For example, a parent has a "legal obligation" within the meaning of the preceding sentence to support his minor child if under local law property or income from property owned by the child cannot be used for his support so long as his parent is able to support him.   On the other hand, if under local law a mother may use the resources of a child for the child's support in lieu of supporting him herself, no obligation of support exists within the meaning of this paragraph, whether or not income is actually used for support.   Similarly, since under local law a child ordinarily is obligated to support his parent only if the parent's earnings and resources are insufficient for the purpose, no obligation exists whether or not the parent's earnings and resources are sufficient.   In any event, the amount of trust income which is included in the gross income of a person obligated to support a dependent is limited by the extent of his legal obligation under local law.   In the case of a parent's obligation to support his child, to the extent that the parent's legal obligation of support, including education, is determined under local law by the family's station in life and by the means of the parent, it is to be determined without consideration of the trust income in question.

Sec. 1.673(a)-1.   Reversionary interests; income payable to beneficiaries other than certain charitable organizations; general rule

(a) Under section 673(a), a grantor, in general, is treated as the owner of any portion of a trust in which he has a reversionary interest in either the corpus or income if, as of the inception of that portion of the trust, the grantor's interest will or may reasonably be expected to take effect in possession or enjoyment within 10 years commencing with the date of transfer of that portion of the trust.   However, the following types of reversionary interests are excepted from the general rule of the preceding sentence:

(1) A reversionary interest after the death of the income beneficiary of a trust (see paragraph (b) below); and

(2) A reversionary interest in a charitable trust meeting the requirements of section 673(b) (see §1.673(b)-1).

Even though the duration of the trust may be such that the grantor is not treated as its owner under section 673, and therefore is not taxed on the ordinary income, he may nevertheless be treated as an owner under section 677(a)(2) if he has a reversionary interest in the corpus.   In the latter case, items of income, deduction, and credit allocable to corpus, such as capital gains and losses, will be included in the portion he owns.   See §1.671-3 and the regulations under section 677.   See §1.673(d)-1 with respect to a postponement of the date specified for reacquisition of a reversionary interest.

(b) Section 673(c) provides that a grantor is not treated as the owner of any portion of a trust by reason of section 673 if his reversionary interest in the portion is not to take effect in possession or enjoyment until the death of the person or persons to whom the income of the portion is payable, regardless of the life expectancies of the income beneficiaries. If his reversionary interest is to take effect on or after the death of an income beneficiary or upon the expiration of a specific term of years, whichever is earlier, the grantor is treated as the owner if the specific term of years is less than 10 years (but not if the term is 10 years or longer).

(c) Where the grantor's reversionary interest in a portion of a trust is to take effect in possession or enjoyment by reason of some event other than the expiration of a specific term of years or the death of the income beneficiary, the grantor is treated as the owner of the portion if the event may reasonably be expected to occur within 10 years from the date of transfer of that portion, but he is not treated as the owner under section 673 if the event may not reasonably be expected to occur within 10 years from that date. For example, if the reversionary interest in any portion of a trust is to take effect on or after the death of the grantor (or any person other than the person to whom the income is payable) the grantor is treated under section 673 as the owner of the portion if the life expectancy of the grantor (or other person) is less than 10 years on the date of transfer of the portion, but not if the life expectancy is 10 years or longer. If the reversionary interest in any portion is to take effect on or after the death of the grantor (or any person other than the person to whom the income is payable) or upon the expiration of a specific term of years, whichever is earlier, the grantor is treated as the owner of the portion if on the date of transfer of the portion either the life expectancy of the grantor (or other person) or the specific term is less than 10 years; however, if both the life expectancy and the specific term are 10 years or longer the grantor is not treated as the owner of the portion under section 673. Similarly, if the grantor has a reversionary interest in any portion which will take effect at the death of the income beneficiary or the grantor, whichever is earlier, the grantor is not treated as an owner of the portion unless his life expectancy is less than 10 years.

(d) It is immaterial that a reversionary interest in corpus or income is subject to a contingency if the reversionary interest may, taking the contingency into consideration, reasonably be expected to take effect in possession or enjoyment within 10 years. For example, the grantor is taxable where the trust income is to be paid to the grantor's son for 3 years, and the corpus is then to be returned to the grantor if he survives that period, or to be paid to the grantor's son if he is already deceased.

(e) See section 671 and §§1.671-2 and 1.671-3 for rules for treatment of items of income, deduction, and credit when a person is treated as the owner of all or only a portion of a trust.

Sec. 1.673(b)-1.　Income payable to charitable beneficiaries

(a) Pursuant to section 673(b) a grantor is not treated as an owner of any portion of a trust under section 673, even though he has a reversionary interest which will take effect within 10 years, to the extent that, under the terms of the trust, the income of the portion is irrevocably payable for a period of at least 2 years (commencing with the date of the transfer) to a designated beneficiary of the type described in section 170(b)(1)(A) (i), (ii), or (iii); that is, to a church or a convention or association of churches, or to certain educational organizations or hospitals. For definitions of these terms see the regulations under section 170.

(b) Income must be irrevocably payable to a designated beneficiary for at least 2 years commencing with the date of the transfer before the benefit of section 673(b) will apply. Thus, section 673(b) will not apply if income of a trust is irrevocably payable to University A for 1 year and then to University B for the next year; or if income of a trust may be allocated among two or more charitable beneficiaries in the discretion of the trustee or any other person. On the other hand, section 673(b) will apply if half the income of a trust is irrevocably payable to University A and the other half is irrevocably payable to University B for two years.

Sec. 1.677(a)-1. Income for benefit of grantor; general rule

(a) Section 677 deals with situations in which a grantor of a trust is treated as the owner of a portion of the trust because he has retained an interest in the income from that portion. See section 671 and §§1.671-2 and 1.671-3 for rules for treatment of items of income, deduction, and credit when a person is treated as the owner of all or only a portion of a trust.

(b) Under section 677, the grantor is treated in any taxable year as the owner of a portion of a trust (whether or not he is treated as an owner under section 674) of which the income for the taxable year or for a period not coming within the exception described in paragraph (e) of this section is, or in the discretion of the grantor or a nonadverse party, or both, (without the approval or consent of any adverse party) may be —

(1) Distributed to the grantor;

(2) Held or accumulated for future distribution to the grantor; or

(3) Applied to the payment of premiums on policies of insurance on the life of the grantor, except policies of insurance irrevocably payable for a charitable purpose specified in section 170(c).

(c) Therefore, under the general rule of section 677 the grantor is treated as the owner of a portion of a trust if he has retained any interest which might, without the approval or consent of an adverse party, enable him to have the income from the portion, at some time, distributed to him either actually or constructively (subject to the exception described in paragraph (e) of this section). Constructive distribution to the grantor includes payment to another in obedience to his direction and payment of premiums upon policies of insurance on the grantor's life (other than policies of insurance irrevocably payable for charitable purposes). If the grantor strips himself permanently and definitively of every interest described in the first sentence of this paragraph, he is not treated as an owner under section 677 after that divesting. The word "interest" as used in the first sentence of this paragraph does not include the possibility that the grantor might receive back from a beneficiary an interest in a trust by inheritance, or as a surviving spouse under a statutory right of election or a similar right.

(d) Under section 677 a grantor is, in general, treated as owner of a portion of a trust whose income is, or in the discretion of the grantor or a nonadverse party, or both, may be, applied in discharge of a legal obligation of the grantor. However, see §1.677(b)-1 for special rules for trusts whose income may not be applied for the discharge of any legal obligation of the grantor other than the support or maintenance of a beneficiary whom the grantor is legally obligated to support.

(e) The last sentence of section 677(a) provides an exception to the general rule when a discretionary right can only affect the beneficial enjoyment of the income of a trust received after a period of time which is such that a grantor would not be treated as an owner under section 673 if the power were a reversionary interest. See §§1.673(a)-1 and 1.673(b)-1. For example, if the ordinary income of a trust is payable to B for 10 years and then in the grantor's discretion income or corpus may be paid to B or to the grantor, the grantor is not treated as an owner with respect to ordinary income under section 677 during the first 10 years. He will be treated as an owner under section 677 after the expiration of the 10-year period unless the power is relinquished. If the beginning of the period during which the grantor may substitute beneficiaries is postponed, the rules set forth in §1.673(d)-1 are applicable in order to determine whether the grantor should be treated as an owner during the period following the postponement.

(f) However, if income is accumulated in any taxable year for future distribution to the grantor, section 677(a)(2) treats the grantor as an owner for that taxable year. The exception set forth in the last sentence of section 677(a) does not apply merely because the grantor must await the expiration of a period of time before he can receive or exercise discretion over previously accumulated income of the trust, even though the period is such that the grantor would not be treated as an owner under section 673 if a reversionary interest were involved. Thus, if income (including capital gains) of a trust is to be accumulated for 10 years and then will be, or at the discretion of the grantor may be, distributed to the grantor, the grantor is treated as the owner of the trust from its inception.

(g) The application of section 677(a) may be illustrated by the following examples:

Example (1). G creates an irrevocable trust which provides that the ordinary income is to be payable to himself for life and that on his death the corpus shall be distributed to a designated charity. Except for the right to receive income, G retains no right or power which would cause him to be treated as an owner under sections 671-677. Under the applicable local law capital gains must be applied to corpus. During the taxable year 1955 the trust has the following items of gross income and deductions:

Dividends	$5,000
Capital gain	1,000
Expenses allocable to income	200
Expenses allocable to corpus	100

Since G has a right to receive income he is treated as an owner of a portion of the trust under section 677. Accordingly, he should include the $5,000 of dividends, $200 income expense, and $100 corpus expense in the computation of his taxable income for 1955. He should not include the $1,000 capital gain since that is not attributable to the portion of the trust that he owns. See §1.671-3. The tax consequences of the capital gain are governed by the provisions of sections 641-668 (subparts A, B, C, and D). Had the trust sustained a capital loss in any amount the loss would likewise not be included in the computation of G's taxable income, but would also be governed by the provisions of sections 641-668.

Example (2). G creates a trust whose ordinary income is payable to his adult son. Ten years from the date of transfer or on the death of his son, whichever is earlier, corpus is to revert to G. In addition, G retains a discretionary right to receive $5,000 of ordinary income each year. (Absent the exercise of this right all the ordinary income is to be distributed to his son.) G retains no other right or power which would cause him to be treated as an owner under subpart E. Under the terms of the trust instrument and applicable local law capital gains must be applied to corpus. During the taxable year 1955 the trust had the following items of income and deductions:

Dividends	$10,000
Capital gain	2,000
Expenses allocable to income	400
Expenses allocable to corpus	200

Since the capital gain is held or accumulated for future distributions to G, he is treated under section 677(a)(2) as an owner of a portion of the trust to which the gain is attributable. Therefore, he must include the capital gain in the computation of his taxable income. (Had the trust sustained a capital loss in any amount, G would likewise include that loss in the computation of his taxable income.) In addition, because of G's discretionary right (whether exercised or not) he is treated as the owner of a portion of the trust which will permit a distribution of income to him of $5,000. Accordingly, G includes dividends of $5,208.33 and income expenses of $208.33 in computing his taxable income, determined in the following manner:

Total dividends	$10,000
Less: Expenses allocable to income	400
Distributable income of the trust	9,600
Portion of dividends attributable to G (5,000/9,600 × $10,000)	5,208.33
Portion of income expenses attributable to G (5,000/9,600 × $400)	208.33
Amount of income subject to discretionary right	$ 5,000.00

Sec. 1.677(b)-1. Trusts for support

(a) Section 677(b) provides in effect that a grantor is not treated as the owner of a trust merely because its income may in the discretion of any person except the grantor not acting as trustee or cotrustee be applied or distributed for the support or maintenance of a beneficiary, such as the wife or child of the grantor, whom the grantor is legally obligated to support. If income of the current year of the trust is actually so applied or distributed the grantor may be treated as the owner of any portion of the trust under section 677 to that extent, even though it might have been applied or distributed for other purposes.

(d) The exception provided in section 677(b) relates solely to the satisfaction of the grantor's legal obligation to support or maintain a beneficiary. Consequently, the general rule of section 677(a) is applicable when in the discretion of the grantor or nonadverse parties income of a trust may be applied in discharge of a grantor's obligations other than his obligation of support or maintenance falling within section 677(b). Thus, if the grantor creates a trust the income of which may in the discretion of a nonadverse party be applied in the payment of the grantor's debts, such as the payment of his rent or other household expenses, he is treated as an owner of the trust regardless of whether the income is actually so applied.

(e) The general rule of section 677(a), and not section 677(b), is applicable if discretion to apply or distribute income of a trust rests solely in the grantor, or in the grantor in conjunction with other persons, unless in either case the grantor has such discretion as trustee or cotrustee.

Sec. 1.1014-3. Other basis rules

(a) *Fair market value.* For purposes of this section and §1.1014-1, the value of property as of the date of the decedent's death as appraised for the purpose of the Federal estate tax or the alternate value as appraised for such purpose, whichever is applicable, shall be deemed to be its fair market value. If no estate tax return is required to be filed under section 6018 (or under section 821 or 864 of the Internal Revenue Code of 1939) the value of the property appraised as of the date of the decedent's death for the purpose of State inheritance or transmission taxes shall be deemed to be its fair market value and no alternate valuation date shall be applicable.

(d) *Reinvestments of property transferred during life.* Where property is transferred by a decedent during life and the property is sold, exchanged, or otherwise disposed of before the decedent's death by the person who acquired the property from the decedent, the general rule stated in §1.1014-1(a) shall not apply to such property. However, in such a case, the basis of any property acquired by such donee in exchange for the original property, or of any property acquired by the donee through reinvesting the proceeds of the sale of the original property, shall be the fair market value of the property thus acquired at the date of the decedent's death (or applicable alternate valuation date) if the property thus acquired is properly included in the decedent's gross estate for Federal estate tax purposes. These rules also apply to property acquired by the donee in any further exchanges or in further reinvestments. For example, on January 1, 1956, the decedent made a gift of real property to a trust for the benefit of his children, reserving to himself the power to revoke the trust at will. Prior to the decedent's death the trustee sold the real property and invested the proceeds in stock of the Y company at $50 per share. At the time of the decedent's death the value of such stock was $75 per share. The corpus of the trust was required to be included in the decedent's gross estate owing to his reservation of the power of revocation. The basis of the Y company stock following the decedent's death is $75 per share. Moreover, if the trustee sold the Y company stock before the decedent's death for $65 a share and reinvested the proceeds in Z company stock which increased in value to $85 per share at the time of the decedent's death, the basis of the Z company stock following the decedent's death would be $85 per share.

Sec. 1.1014-4. **Uniformity of basis; adjustment to basis**

(a) *In general.* (1) The basis of property acquired from a decedent, as determined under section 1014(a), is uniform in the hands of every person having possession or enjoyment of the property at any time under the will or other instrument or under the laws of descent and distribution. The principle of uniform basis means that the basis of the property (to which proper adjustments must, of course, be made) will be the same, or uniform, whether the property is possessed or enjoyed by the executor or administrator, the heir, the legatee or devisee, or the trustee or beneficiary of a trust created by a will or an inter vivos trust. In determining the amount allowed or allowable to a taxpayer in computing taxable income as deductions for depreciation or depletion under section 1016(a)(2), the uniform basis of the property shall at all times be used and adjusted. The sale, exchange, or other disposition by a life tenant or remainderman of his interest in property will, for purposes of this section, have no effect upon the uniform basis of the property in the hands of those who acquired it from the decedent. Thus, gain or loss on sale of trust assets by the trustee will be determined without regard to the prior sale of any interest in the property. Moreover, any adjustment for depreciation shall be made to the uniform basis of the property without regard to such prior sale, exchange, or other disposition.

(2) Under the law governing wills and the distribution of the property of decedents, all titles to property acquired by bequest, devise, or inheritance relate back to the death of the decedent, even though the interest of the person taking the title was, at the date of death of the decedent, legal, equitable, vested, contingent, general, specific, residual, conditional, executory, or

otherwise. Accordingly, there is a common acquisition date for all titles to property acquired from a decedent within the meaning of section 1014, and, for this reason, a common or uniform basis for all such interests. For example, if distribution of personal property left by a decedent is not made until one year after his death, the basis of such property in the hands of the legatee is its fair market value at the time when the decedent died, and not when the legatee actually received the property. If the bequest is of the residue to trustees in trust, and the executors do not distribute the residue to such trustees until five years after the death of the decedent, the basis of each piece of property left by the decedent and thus received, in the hands of the trustees, is its fair market value at the time when the decedent dies. If the bequest is to trustees in trust to pay to A during his lifetime the income of the property bequeathed, and after his death to distribute such property to the survivors of a class, and upon A's death the property is distributed to the taxpayer as the sole survivor, the basis of such property, in the hands of the taxpayer, is its fair market value at the time when the decedent died. The purpose of the Internal Revenue Code in prescribing a general uniform basis rule for property acquired from a decedent is, on the one hand, to tax the gain, in respect of such property, to him who realizes it (without regard to the circumstance that at the death of the decedent it may have been quite uncertain whether the taxpayer would take or gain anything); and, on the other hand, not to recognize as gain any element of value resulting solely from the circumstance that the possession or enjoyment of the taxpayer was postponed. Such postponement may be, for example, until the administration of the decedent's estate is completed, until the period of the possession or enjoyment of another has terminated, or until an uncertain event has happened. It is the increase or decrease in the value of property reflected in a sale or other disposition which is recognized as the measure of gain or loss.

(3) The principles stated in subparagraphs (1) and (2) of this paragraph do not apply to property transferred by an executor, administrator or trustee, to an heir, legatee, devisee or beneficiary under circumstances such that the transfer constitutes a sale or exchange. In such a case, gain or loss must be recognized by the transferor to the extent required by the revenue laws, and the transferee acquires a basis equal to the fair market value of the property on the date of the transfer. Thus, for example, if the trustee of a trust created by will transfers to a beneficiary, in satisfaction of a specific bequest of $10,000, securities which had a fair market value of $9,000 on the date of the decedent's death (the applicable valuation date) and $10,000 on the date of the transfer, the trust realizes a taxable gain of $1,000 and the basis of the securities in the hands of the beneficiary would be $10,000. As a further example, if the executor of an estate transfers to a trust property worth $200,-000, which had a fair market value of $175,000 on the date of the decedent's death (the applicable valuation date), in satisfaction of the decedent's bequest in trust for the benefit of his wife of cash or securities to be selected by the executor in an amount sufficient to utilize the marital deduction to the maximum extent authorized by law (after taking into consideration any other property qualifying for the marital deduction), capital gain in the amount of $25,000 would be realized by the estate and the basis of the property in the hands of the trustees would be $200,000. If, on the other hand, the decedent bequeathed a fraction of his residuary estate to a trust for the benefit of his wife, which fraction will not change regardless of any fluctuations in value of property in the decedent's estate after his death, no gain or loss would be

realized by the estate upon transfer of property to the trust, and the basis of the property in the hands of the trustee would be its fair market value on the date of the decedent's death or on the alternate valuation date.

Sec. 1.1014-6. Special rule for adjustments to basis where property is acquired from a decedent prior to his death

(a) *In general.* (1) The basis of property described in section 1014(b)(9) which is acquired from a decedent prior to his death shall be adjusted for depreciation, obsolescence, amortization, and depletion allowed the taxpayer on such property for the period prior to the decedent's death. Thus, in general, the adjusted basis of such property will be its fair market value at the decedent's death, or the applicable alternate valuation date, less the amount allowed (determined with regard to section 1016(a)(2)(B)) to the taxpayer as deductions for exhaustion, wear and tear, obsolescence, amortization and depletion for the period held by the taxpayer prior to the decedent's death. The deduction allowed for a taxable year in which the decedent dies shall be an amount properly allocable to that part of the year prior to his death. For a discussion of the basis adjustment required by section 1014(b)(9) where property is held in trust, see paragraph (c) of this section.

(2) Where property coming within the purview of subparagraph (1) of this paragraph was held by the decedent and his surviving spouse as tenants by the entirety or as joint tenants with right of survivorship, and joint income tax returns were filed by the decedent and the surviving spouse in which the deductions referred to in subparagraph (1) were taken, there shall be allocated to the surviving spouse's interest in the property that proportion of the deductions allowed for each period for which the joint returns were filed which her income from the property bears to the total income from the property. Each spouse's income from the property shall be determined in accordance with local law.

(3) The application of this paragraph may be illustrated by the following examples:

Example (2). On July 1, 1952, H purchased for $30,000 income-producing property which he conveyed to himself and W, his wife, as tenants by the entirety. Under local law each spouse was entitled to one-half of the income therefrom. H died on January 1, 1955, at which time the fair market value of the property was $40,000. The entire value of the property was included in H's gross estate. H and W filed joint income tax returns for the years 1952, 1953, and 1954. The total depreciation allowance for the year 1952 was $500 and for each of the other years 1953 and 1954 was $1,000. One-half of the $2,500 depreciation will be allocated to W. The adjusted basis of the property in W's hands [as] of January 1, 1955, was $38,750 ($40,000, value on the date of H's death, less $1,250, depreciation allocated to W for periods before H's death). However, if, under local law, all of the income from the property was allocable to H, no adjustment under this paragraph would be required and W's basis for the property as of the date of H's death would be $40,000.

Sec. 1.1371-1. Definition of small business corporation

(a) *In general.* For purposes of subchapter S of chapter 1 of the Code and §§1.1371 through 1.1377-3, the term "small business corporation" means a domestic corporation which is not a member of an affiliated group of corporations (as defined in section 1504) and which does not have —

(1) More than 10 shareholders,

(2) As a shareholder a person (other than an estate) who is not an individual,

(3) A nonresident alien as a shareholder, and

(4) More than one class of stock.

(e) *Shareholders must be individuals or estates.* A corporation in which any shareholder is a corporation, trust, or partnership does not qualify as a small business corporation. The word "trust" as used in this paragraph includes all trusts subject to the provisions of subchapter D, F, H, or J (including subpart E thereof) of chapter 1 of the Code and voting trusts. Thus, even though the grantor is treated as the owner of all or any part of a trust, the corporation in which such trust is a shareholder does not meet the qualifications of a small business corporation.

Sec. 20.0-1

(b) *Scope of regulations* — (1) *Estates of citizens or residents.* Subchapter A of chapter 11 of the Code pertains to the taxation of the estate of a person who was a citizen or a resident of the United States at the time of his death. The term "resident" means a decedent who, at the time of his death, had his domicile in the United States. The term "United States," as used in the Estate Tax Regulations, includes only the States, and the District of Columbia. The term also includes the territories of Alaska and Hawaii prior to their admission as states. See section 7701(a)(9). A person acquires a domicile in a place by living there, for even a brief period of time, with no definite present intention of later removing therefrom. Residence without the requisite intention to remain indefinitely will not suffice to constitute domicile, nor will intention to change domicile effect such a change unless accompanied by actual removal. For meaning of the term "citizen of the United States" as applied in a case, where the decedent was a resident of a possession of the United States, see §20.2208-1. The regulations pursuant to subchapter A are set forth in §§20.2001-1 through 20.2056(e)-3.

(2) *Estates of nonresidents not citizens.* Subchapter B of chapter 11 of the Code pertains to the taxation of the estate of a person who was a nonresident not a citizen of the United States at the time of his death. A "nonresident" is a decedent who, at the time of his death, had his domicile outside the United States under the principles set forth in subparagraph (1) of this paragraph. (See, however, section 2202 with respect to missionaries in foreign service.) The regulations pursuant to subchapter B are set forth in §§20.2101-1 through 20.2106-2 of this part.

Sec. 20.0-2. General description of tax

(a) *Nature of tax.* The Federal estate tax is neither a property tax nor an inheritance tax. It is a tax imposed upon the transfer of the entire taxable estate and not upon any particular legacy, devise, or distributive share. Escheat of a decedent's property to the State for lack of heirs is a transfer which causes the property to be included in the decedent's gross estate.

Sec. 20.2002-1. Liability for payment of tax. The Federal estate tax imposed both with respect to the estates of citizens or residents and with respect to estates of nonresidents not citizens is payable by the executor or administrator of the decedent's estate. This duty applies to the entire tax, regardless of the fact that the gross estate consists in part of property which does not come within the possession of the executor or administrator. If there is no executor or administrator appointed, qualified and acting in the United States, any person in actual or constructive possession of any property of the decedent is required to pay the entire tax to the extent of the value of the property in his possession. See section 2203, defining the term "executor." The personal liability of the executor or such other person is described in section 3467 of the Revised Statutes (31 U.S.C. 192) as follows:

"Every executor, administrator, or assignee, or other person, who pays, in whole or in part, any debt due by the person or estate for whom or for which he acts before he satisfies and pays the debts due to the United States from such person or estate, shall become answerable in his own person and estate to the extent of such payments for the debts so due to the United States, or for so much thereof as may remain due and unpaid."

As used in said section, the word "debt" includes a beneficiary's distributive share of an estate. Thus, if the executor pays a debt due by the decedent's estate or distributes any portion of the estate before all the estate tax is paid, he is personally liable, to the extent of the payment or distribution, for so much of the estate tax as remains due and unpaid. In addition, section 6324(a)(2) provides that if the estate tax is not paid when due, then the spouse, transferee, trustee (except the trustee of an employee's trust which meets the requirements of section 401(a)), surviving tenant, person in possession of the property by reason of the exercise, nonexercise, or release of a power of appointment, or beneficiary, who receives, or has on the date of the decedent's death, property included in the gross estate under sections 2034 through 2042, is personally liable for the tax to the extent of the value, at the time of the decedent's death, of such property. See also the following related sections of the Internal Revenue Code: section 2204, discharge of executor from personal liability; section 2205, reimbursement out of estate; sections 2206 and 2207, liability of life insurance beneficiaries and recipients of property over which decedent had power of appointment; sections 6321 through 6325, concerning liens for taxes; and section 6901(a)(1), concerning the liabilities of transferees and fiduciaries.

Sec. 20.2014-1. Credit for foreign death taxes

(a) *In general.* (1) A credit is allowed under section 2014 against the Federal estate tax for any estate, inheritance, legacy, or succession taxes actually paid to any foreign country (hereinafter referred to as "foreign death taxes"). The credit is allowed only for foreign death taxes paid (i) with respect to property situated within the country to which the tax is paid, (ii) with respect to property included in the decedent's gross estate, and (iii) with respect to the decedent's estate. The credit is allowable to the estate of a decedent who was a citizen of the United States at the time of his death. The credit is also allowable to the estate of a decedent who was a resident but not a citizen of the United States at the time of his death if the country of which the decedent was a national, in imposing death taxes, allows a similar credit to the estates of citizens of the United States resident in that country. See paragraph (b)(1) of §20.0-1 for definition of the term "resident." The credit is not allowable to the estate of a decedent who was neither a citizen nor a resident of the United States at the time of his death. The credit is allowable not only for death taxes paid to foreign countries which are states in the international sense, but also for death taxes paid to possessions or political subdivisions of foreign states. With respect to the estate of a decedent dying after September 2, 1958, the term "foreign country," as used in this section and in §§20.2014-2 to 20.2014-6 includes a possession of the United States. See §§20.2011-1 and 20.2011-2 for the allowance of a credit for death taxes paid to a possession of the United States in the case of a decedent dying before September 3, 1958. No credit is allowable for interest or penalties paid in connection with foreign death taxes.

(2) In addition to the credit for foreign death taxes under section 2014, similar credits are allowed under death tax conventions with certain foreign

countries. If credits against the Federal estate tax are allowable under section 2014, or under section 2014 and one or more death tax conventions, for death taxes paid to more that one country, the credits are combined and the aggregate amount is credited against the Federal estate tax, subject to the limitation provided for in paragraph (c) of §20.2014-4. For application of the credit in cases involving a death tax convention, see §20.2014-4.

(3) No credit is allowable under section 2014 in connection with property situated outside of the foreign country imposing the tax for which credit is claimed. However, such a credit may be allowable under certain death tax conventions. In the case of a tax imposed by a political subdivision of a foreign country, credit for such tax shall be allowed with respect to property having a situs in that foreign country, even though, under the principles described in this subparagraph, such property has a situs in a political subdivision different from the one imposing the tax. Whether or not particular property of a decedent is situated in the foreign country imposing the tax is determined in accordance with the same principles that would be applied in determining whether or not similar property of a nonresident decedent not a citizen of the United States is situated within the United States for Federal estate tax purposes. See §§20.2104-1 and 20.2105-1. For example, under §20.2104-1, a bond for the payment of money is not within the United States unless it is physically located in the United States. Accordingly, a bond is deemed situated in the foreign country imposing the tax only if it is physically located in that country. Similarly, under §20.2104-1, shares of stock are deemed to be situated in the United States only if issued by a domestic (United States) corporation. Thus, a share of corporate stock is regarded as situated in the foreign country imposing the tax only if the issuing corporation is incorporated in that country. Further, under §20.2105-1, moneys deposited with any person carrying on the banking business by or for a nonresident not a citizen of the United States who was not engaged in business in the United States at the time of death are not deemed situated in the United States. Therefore, an account with a foreign bank in the country imposing the tax is not considered to be situated in that country under corresponding circumstances.

Sec. 20.2014-4. **Application of credit in cases involving a death tax convention**

(a) *In general.* (1) If credit for a particular foreign death tax is authorized by a death tax convention, there is allowed either the credit provided for by the convention or the credit provided for by section 2014, whichever is the more beneficial to the estate. The application of this paragraph may be illustrated by the following example:

Example. (i) Decedent, a citizen of the United States and a domiciliary of Country X at the time of his death, left a gross estate of $1,000,000 which includes: shares of stock issued by a Country X corporation, valued at $400,-000; bonds issued by a Country X corporation physically located in the United States, valued at $350,000; and real estate located in the United States, valued at $250,000. Expenses, indebtedness, etc., amounted to $50,000. Decedent left his entire estate to his son. There is in effect a death tax convention between the United States and Country X which provides for allowance of credit by the United States for succession duties imposed by the national government of Country X. The gross Federal estate tax is $307,200 and the credit for State death taxes is $33,760. Country X imposed a net succession duty on the stocks and bonds of $180,000. Under the situs rules described in paragraph (a)(3) of §20.2014-1, the shares of stock comprise the only property deemed to be situated in Country X. Under the convention, both the stocks and the bonds are deemed to be situated in Country X.

(ii) (a) The credit authorized by the convention for death taxes imposed by Country X is computed as follows:

(1) Country X tax attributable to property situated in Country X and subjected to tax by both countries

$$\frac{(\$750,000}{(\$750,000} \times \$180,000) \dots\dots\dots\dots\dots\dots\dots\dots\dots\dots \mathbf{\$180,000}$$

(2) Federal estate tax attributable to property situated in Country X and subjected to tax by both countries

$$\frac{(\ \$750,000}{(\$1,000,000} \times \$273,440) \dots\dots\dots\dots\dots\dots\dots\dots\dots \ 205,080$$

(3) Credit (subdivision (1) or (2), whichever is less) $\dots\dots\dots$ 180,000

(b) The credit authorized by section 2014 for death taxes imposed by Country X is computed as follows:

(1) "First limitation" computed under §20.2014-2

$$\frac{(\$400,000}{(\$750,000} \times \$180,000) \dots\dots\dots\dots\dots\dots\dots\dots\dots\dots \mathbf{\$96,000}$$

(2) "Second limitation" computed under §20.2014-3

$$\frac{(\ \$400,000}{(\$1,000,000} \times \$273,440) \dots\dots\dots\dots\dots\dots\dots\dots\dots \ 109,376$$

(3) Credit (subdivision (1) or (2), whichever is less) $\dots\dots\dots\dots$ 96,000

(iii) On the basis of the facts contained in this example, the credit of $180,000 authorized by the convention is the more beneficial to the estate.

Sec. 20.2031-1

(b) *Valuation of property in general.* The value of every item of property includible in a decedent's gross estate under sections 2031 through 2044 is its fair market value at the time of the decedent's death, except that if the executor elects the alternate valuation method under section 2032, it is the fair market value thereof at the date, and with the adjustments, prescribed in that section. The fair market value is the price at which the property would change hands between a willing buyer and a willing seller, neither being under any compulsion to buy or to sell and both having reasonable knowledge of relevant facts. The fair market value of a particular item of property includible in the decedent's gross estate is not to be determined by a forced sale price. The value is generally to be determined by ascertaining as a basis the fair market value as of the applicable valuation date of each unit of the property. For example, in the case of shares of stock or bonds, such unit of property is generally a share of stock or a bond. Livestock, farm machinery, harvested and growing crops must generally be itemized and the value of each item separately returned. Property shall not be returned at the value at which it is assessed for local tax purposes unless that value represents the fair market value as of the applicable valuation date. All relevant facts and elements of value as of the applicable valuation date shall be considered in every case. See §§20.2031-2 through 20.2031-8 for further information concerning the valuation of particular kinds of property.

Sec. 20.2031-2. Valuation of stocks and bonds

(a) *In general.* The value of stocks and bonds is the fair market value per share or bond on the applicable valuation date.

(b) *Based on selling prices.* If there is a market for stocks or bonds, on a stock exchange, in an over-the-counter market, or otherwise, the mean between the highest and lowest quoted selling prices on the valuation date is the fair market value per share or bond. If there were no sales on the valuation date, but there were sales on dates within a reasonable period both before and after the valuation date, the fair market value is determined by taking a weighted average of the means between the highest and lowest sales on the nearest date before and the nearest date after the valuation date. The average is to be weighted inversely by the respective numbers of trading days between the selling dates and the valuation date. For example, assume that sales of stock nearest the valuation date (Friday, June 15) occurred two trading days before (Wednesday, June 13) and three trading days after (Wednesday, June 20) and that on these days the mean sale prices per share were $10 and $15, respectively. The price of $12 is taken as representing the fair market value of a share of the stock as of the valuation date $\left(\dfrac{(3 \times 10) + (2 \times 15)}{5} \right)$. If, instead, the mean sale prices per share on June 13 and June 20 were $15 and $10, respectively, the price of $13 is taken as representing the fair market value $\left(\dfrac{(3 \times 15) + (2 \times 10)}{5} \right)$. As a further example, assume that the decedent died on Sunday, October 7, and that Saturday and Sunday were not trading days. If sales of stock occurred on Friday, October 5, at mean sale prices per share of $20 and on Monday, October 8, at mean sale prices per share of $23, then the fair market value per share of stock as of the valuation date is $21.50. If stocks or bonds are listed on more than one exchange, the records of the exchange where the stocks or bonds are principally dealt in should be employed. In valuing listed securities, the executor should be careful to consult accurate records to obtain values as of the applicable valuation date. If quotations of unlisted securities are obtained from brokers, or evidence as to their sale is obtained from officers of the issuing companies, copies of the letters furnishing such quotations or evidence of sale should be attached to the return.

(c) *Based on bid and asked prices.* If the provisions of paragraph (b) of this section are inapplicable because actual sales are not available during a reasonable period beginning before and ending after the valuation date, the fair market value may be determined by taking the mean between the bona fide bid and asked prices on the valuation date, or if none, by taking a weighted average of the means between the bona fide bid and asked prices on the nearest trading date before and the nearest trading date after the valuation date, if both such nearest dates are within a reasonable period. The average is to be determined in the manner described in paragraph (b) of this section.

(d) *Based on incomplete selling prices or bid and asked prices.* If the provisions of paragraphs (b) and (c) of this section are inapplicable because no actual sale prices or bona fide bid and asked prices are available on a date within a reasonable period before the valuation date, but such prices are available on a date within a reasonable period after the valuation date, or vice versa, then the mean between the highest and lowest available sale prices or bid and asked prices may be taken as the value.

(e) *Where selling prices or bid and asked prices do not reflect fair market value.* If it is established that the value of any bond or share of stock determined on the basis of selling or bid and asked prices as provided under paragraphs (b), (c), and (d) of this section does not reflect the fair market value thereof, then some reasonable modification of that basis or other relevant facts and elements of value are considered in determining the fair market value. Where sales at or near the date of death are few or of a sporadic nature, such sales alone may not indicate fair market value. In certain exceptional cases, the size of the block of stock to be valued in relation to the number of shares changing hands in sales may be relevant in determining whether selling prices reflect the fair market value of the block of stock to be valued. If the executor can show that the block of stock to be valued is so large in relation to the actual sales on the existing market that it could not be liquidated in a reasonable time without depressing the market, the price at which the block could be sold as such outside the usual market, as through an underwriter, may be a more accurate indication of value than market quotations. Complete data in support of any allowance claimed due to the size of the block of stock being valued shall be submitted with the return. On the other hand, if the block of stock to be valued represents a controlling interest, either actual or effective, in a going business, the price at which other lots change hands may have little relation to its true value.

(f) *Where selling prices or bid and asked prices are unavailable.* If the provisions of paragraphs (b), (c), and (d) of this section are inapplicable because actual sale prices and bona fide bid and asked prices are lacking, then the fair market value is to be determined by taking the following factors into consideration:

(1) In the case of corporate or other bonds, the soundness of the security, the interest yield, the date of maturity, and other relevant factors; and

(2) In the case of shares of stock, the company's net worth, prospective earning power and dividend-paying capacity, and other relevant factors. Some of the "other relevant factors" referred to in subparagraphs (1) and (2) of this paragraph are: the good will of the business; the economic outlook in the particular industry; the company's position in the industry and its management; the degree of control of the business represented by the block of stock to be valued; and the values of securities of corporations engaged in the same or similar lines of business which are listed on a stock exchange. However, the weight to be accorded such comparisons or any other evidentiary factors considered in the determination of a value depends upon the facts of each case. Complete financial and other data upon which the valuation is based should be submitted with the return, including copies of reports of any examinations of the company made by accountants, engineers, or any technical experts as of or near the applicable valuation date.

(g) *Pledged securities.* The full value of securities pledged to secure an indebtedness of the decedent is included in the gross estate. If the decedent had a trading account with a broker, all securities belonging to the decedent and held by the broker at the date of death must be included at their fair market value as of the applicable valuation date. Securities purchased on margin for the decedent's account and held by a broker must also be returned at their fair market value as of the applicable valuation date. The amount of the decedent's indebtedness to a broker or other person with whom securities were pledged is allowed as a deduction from the gross estate in accordance with the provisions of §20.2053-1 or §20.2106-1 (for estates of nonresidents not citizens).

(h) *Securities subject to an option or contract to purchase.* Another person may hold an option or a contract to purchase securities owned by a decedent at the time of his death. The effect, if any, that is given to the option or contract price in determining the value of the securities for estate tax purposes depends upon the circumstances of the particular case. Little weight will be accorded a price contained in an option or contract under which the decedent is free to dispose of the underlying securities at any price he chooses during his lifetime. Such is the effect, for example, of an agreement on the part of a shareholder to purchase whatever shares of stock the decedent may own at the time of his death. Even if the decedent is not free to dispose of the underlying securities at other than the option or contract price, such price will be disregarded in determining the value of the securities unless it is determined under the circumstances of the particular case that the agreement represents a bona fide business arrangement and not a device to pass the decedent's shares to the natural objects of his bounty for less than an adequate and full consideration in money or money's worth.

(j) *Stock sold "ex-dividend."* In any case where a dividend is declared on a share of stock before the decedent's death but payable to stockholders of record on a date after his death and the stock is selling "ex-dividend" on the date of the decedent's death, the amount of the dividend is added to the ex-dividend quotation in determining the fair market value of the stock as of the date of the decedent's death.

Sec. 20.2031-3. Valuation of interests in businesses. The fair market value of any interest of a decedent in a business, whether a partnership or a proprietorship, is the net amount which a willing purchaser, whether an individual or a corporation, would pay for the interest to a willing seller, neither being under any compulsion to buy or to sell and both having reasonable knowledge of relevant facts. The net value is determined on the basis of all relevant factors including —

(a) A fair appraisal as of the applicable valuation date of all the assets of the business, tangible and intangible, including good will;

(b) The demonstrated earning capacity of the business; and

(c) The other factors set forth in paragraphs (f) and (h) of §20.2031-2 relating to the valuation of corporate stock, to the extent applicable.

Special attention should be given to determining an adequate value of the good will of the business in all cases in which the decedent has not agreed, for an adequate and full consideration in money or money's worth, that his interest passes at his death to, for example, his surviving partner or partners. Complete financial and other data upon which the valuation is based should be submitted with the return, including copies of reports of examinations of the business made by accountants, engineers, or any technical experts as of or near the applicable valuation date.

Sec. 20.2031-6

(c) *Disposition of household effects prior to investigation.* If it is desired to effect distribution or sale of any portion of the household or personal effects of the decedent in advance of an investigation by an officer of the Internal Revenue Service, information to that effect shall be given to the district director. The statement to the district director shall be accompanied by an appraisal of such property, under oath, and by a written statement of the executor, containing a declaration that it is made under the penalties of perjury, regarding the completeness of the list of such property and the qualifications of the appraiser, as heretofore described. If a personal inspection by an officer of the Internal Revenue Service is not deemed necessary, the executor will be so advised. This procedure is designed to facilitate disposition of such property and to obviate future expense and inconvenience to the estate by affording the district director an opportunity to make an investigation should one be deemed necessary prior to sale or distribution.

Sec. 20.2031-8. Valuation of certain life insurance and annuity contracts

(a) The value of a contract for the payment of an annuity, or an insurance policy on the life of a person other than the decedent, issued by a company regularly engaged in the selling of contracts of that character is established through the sale by that company of comparable contracts. An annuity payable under a combination annuity contract and life insurance policy on the decedent's life (e.g., a "retirement income" policy with death benefit) under which there was no insurance element at the time of the decedent's death (see paragraph (d) of §20.2039-1) is treated like a contract for the payment of an annuity for purposes of this section.

(b) As valuation of an insurance policy through sale of comparable contracts is not readily ascertainable when, at the date of the decedent's death, the contract has been in force for some time and further premium payments are to be made, the value may be approximated by adding to the interpolated terminal reserve at the date of the decedent's death the proportionate part of the gross premium last paid before the date of the decedent's death which covers the period extending beyond that date. If, however, because of the unusual nature of the contract such an approximation is not reasonably close to the full value of the contract, this method may not be used.

(c) The application of this section may be illustrated by the following examples. In each case involving an insurance contract, it is assumed that there are no accrued dividends or outstanding indebtedness on the contract.

Example (3). Z died holding the incidents of ownership in a life insurance policy on the life of his wife. The policy was an ordinary life policy issued nine years and four months prior to Z's death and at a time when Z's wife was 35 years of age. The gross annual premium is $2,811 and the decedent died four months after the last premium due date. The value of the insurance policy at the date of Z's death is computed as follows:

Terminal reserve at end of tenth year	$14,601.00
Terminal reserve at end of ninth year	12,965.00
Increase	1,636.00
One-third of such increase	
(Z having died four months following the last preceding premium due date) is	545.33
Terminal reserve at end of ninth year	12,965.00
Interpolated terminal reserve at date of Z's death	13,510.33
Two-thirds of gross premium	
($\frac{2}{3} \times$ $2,811)	1,874.00
Value of the insurance policy	15,384.33

Sec. 20.2032-1

(b) *Method and effect of election.* (1) While it is the purpose of section 2032 to permit a reduction in the amount of tax that would otherwise be payable if the gross estate has suffered a shrinkage in its aggregate value in the year following the decedent's death, the alternate valuation method is not automatic but must be elected. Furthermore, the alternate valuation method may be elected whether or not there has been a shrinkage in the aggregate value of the estate. However, the election is not effective for any purpose unless the value of the gross estate at the time of the decedent's death exceeded $60,000, so that an estate tax return is required to be filed under section 6018.

(2) If the alternate valuation method under section 2032 is to be used, section 2032(c) requires that the executor must so elect on the estate tax return required under section 6018, filed within 15 months from the date of the decedent's death or within the period of any extension of time granted by the district director under section 6081. In no case may the election be exercised, or a previous election changed, after the expiration of such time. If the election is made, it applies to all the property included in the gross estate, and cannot be applied to only a portion of the property.

(g) *Effect of election on deductions.* If the executor elects the alternate valuation method under section 2032, any deduction for administration expenses under section 2053(b) (pertaining to property not subject to claims) or losses under section 2054 (or section 2106(a)(1), relating to estates of nonresidents not citizens) is allowed only to the extent that it is not otherwise in effect allowed in determining the value of the gross estate. Furthermore, the amount of any charitable deduction under section 2055 (or section 2106(a)(2), relating to the estates of nonresidents not citizens) or the amount of any marital deduction under section 2056 is determined by the value of the property with respect to which the deduction is allowed as of the date of the decedent's death, adjusted, however, for any difference in its value as of the date one year after death, or as of the date of its distribution, sale, exchange, or other disposition, whichever first occurs. However, no such adjustment may take into account any difference in value due to lapse of time or to the occurrence or nonoccurrence of a contingency.

Sec. 20.2033-1. Property in which the decedent had an interest

(a) *In general.* The gross estate of a decedent who was a citizen or resident of the United States at the time of his death includes under section 2033 the value of all property, whether real or personal, tangible or intangible, and wherever situated, beneficially owned by the decedent at the time of his death, except real property situated outside of the United States. Real property situated in the United States is included whether it came into the possession and control of the executor or administrator or passed directly to heirs or devisees. Various statutory provisions which exempt bonds, notes, bills, and certificates of indebtedness of the Federal Government or its agencies and the interest thereon from taxation are generally not applicable to the estate tax, since such tax is an excise tax on the transfer of property at death and is not a tax on the property transferred.

(b) *Miscellaneous examples.* A cemetery lot owned by the decedent is part of his gross estate, but its value is limited to the salable value of that part of the lot which is not designed for the interment of the decedent and the members of his family. Property subject to homestead or other exemptions under local law is included in the gross estate. Notes or other claims held by the decedent are likewise included even though they are cancelled by the decedent's will. Interest and rents accrued at the date of the decedent's death constitute a part of the gross estate. Similarly, dividends which are payable to the decedent or his estate by reason of the fact that on or before the date of the decedent's death he was a stockholder of record (but which have not been collected at death) constitute a part of the gross estate.

Sec. 20.2035-1

(e) *Valuation.* The value of an interest in transferred property includible in a decedent's gross estate under this section is the value of the interest as of the applicable valuation date. In this connection, see sections 2031, 2032, and the regulations thereunder. However, if the transferee has made improvements or additions to the property, any resulting enhancement in the value of the property is not considered in ascertaining the value of the gross estate. Similarly, neither income received subsequent to the transfer nor property purchased with such income is considered.

Sec. 20.2036-1.   Transfers with retained life estate

(a) *In general.* A decedent's gross estate includes under section 2036 the value of any interest in property transferred by the decedent after March 3, 1931, whether in trust or otherwise, except to the extent that the transfer was for an adequate and full consideration in money or money's worth (see §20.2043-1), if the decedent retained or reserved (1) for his life, or (2) for any period not ascertainable without reference to his death (if the transfer was made after June 6, 1932), or (3) for any period which does not in fact end before his death —

(i) The use, possession, right to the income, or other enjoyment of the transferred property, or

(ii) The right, either alone or in conjunction with any other person or persons, to designate the person or persons who shall possess or enjoy the transferred property or its income (except that, if the transfer was made before June 7, 1932, the right to designate must be retained by or reserved to the decedent alone).

If the decedent retained or reserved an interest or right with respect to all of the property transferred by him, the amount to be included in his gross estate under section 2036 is the value of the entire property, less only the value of any outstanding income interest which is not subject to the decedent's interest or right and which is actually being enjoyed by another person at the time of the decedent's death. If the decedent retained or reserved an interest or right with respect to a part only of the property transferred by him, the amount to be included in his gross estate under section 2036 is only a corresponding proportion of the amount described in the preceding sentence. An interest or right is treated as having been retained or reserved if at the time of the transfer there was an understanding, express or implied, that the interest or right would later be conferred.

Sec. 20.2036-1(b)

(2) The "use, possession, right to the income, or other enjoyment of the transferred property" is considered as having been retained by or reserved to the decedent to the extent that the use, possession, right to the income, or other enjoyment is to be applied toward the discharge of a legal obligation of the decedent, or otherwise for his pecuniary benefit. The term "legal obligation" includes a legal obligation to support a dependent during the decedent's lifetime.

(3) The phrase "right . . . to designate the person or persons who shall possess or enjoy the transferred property or the income therefrom" includes a reserved power to designate the person or persons to receive the income from the transferred property, or to possess or enjoy nonincome-producing property, during the decedent's life or during any other period described in paragraph (a) of this section. With respect to such a power, it is immaterial (i) whether the power was exercisable alone or only in conjunction with another person or persons, whether or not having an adverse interest; (ii) in what capacity the power was exercisable by the decedent or by another person or persons in conjunction with the decedent; and (iii) whether the exercise of the power was subject to a contingency beyond the decedent's control which did not occur before his death (e.g., the death of another person

during the decedent's lifetime). The phrase, however, does not include a power over the transferred property itself which deos not affect the enjoyment of the income received or earned during the decedent's life. (See, however, section 2038 for the inclusion of property in the gross estate on account of such a power.) Nor does the phrase apply to a power held solely by a person other than the decedent. But, for example, if the decedent reserved the unrestricted power to remove or discharge a trustee at any time and appoint himself as trustee, the decedent is considered as having the powers of the trustee.

Sec. 20.2037-1. Transfers taking effect at death

(a) *In general.* A decedent's gross estate includes under section 2037 the value of any interest in property transferred by the decedent after September 7, 1916, whether in trust or otherwise, except to the extent that the transfer was for an adequate and full consideration in money or money's worth (see §20.2043-1), if —

(1) Possession or enjoyment of the property could, through ownership of the interest, have been obtained only by surviving the decedent,

(2) The decedent had retained a possibility (hereinafter referred to as a "reversionary interest") that the property, other than the income alone, would return to the decedent or his estate or would be subject to a power of disposition by him, and

(3) The value of the reversionary interest immediately before the decedent's death exceeded 5 percent of the value of the entire property.

However, if the transfer was made before October 8, 1949, section 2037 is applicable only if the reversionary interest arose by the express terms of the instrument of transfer and not by operation of law (see paragraph (f) of this section). See also paragraph (g) of this section with respect to transfers made between November 11, 1935, and January 29, 1940. The provisions of section 2037 do not apply to transfers made before September 8, 1916.

(c) *Retention of reversionary interest.* (1) As indicated in paragraph (a) of this section, the value of an interest in transferred property is not included in a decedent's gross estate under section 2037 unless the decedent had retained a reversionary interest in the property, and the value of the reversionary interest immediately before the death of the decedent exceeded 5 percent of the value of the property.

(2) For purposes of section 2037, the term "reversionary interest" includes a possibility that property transferred by the decedent may return to him or his estate and a possibility that property transferred by the decedent may become subject to a power of disposition by him. The term is not used in a technical sense, but has reference to any reserved right under which the transferred property shall or may be returned to the grantor. Thus, it encompasses an interest arising either by the express terms of the instrument of transfer or by operation of law. (See, however, paragraph (f) of this section, with respect to transfers made before October 8, 1949.) The term "reversionary interest" does not include rights to income only, such as the right to receive the income from a trust after the death of another person. (However, see section 2036 for the inclusion of property in the gross estate on account of such rights.) Nor does the term "reversionary interest" include the possibility that the decedent during his lifetime might have received back an interest in transferred property by inheritance through the estate of another person. Similarly, a statutory right of a spouse to receive a portion of whatever estate a decedent may leave at the time of his death is not a "reversionary interest."

(3) For purposes of this section, the value of the decedent's reversionary

interest is computed as of the moment immediately before his death, without regard to whether or not the executor elects the alternate valuation method under section 2032 and without regard to the fact of the decedent's death. The value is ascertained in accordance with recognized valuation principles for determining the value for estate tax purposes of future or conditional interests in property. (See §§20.2031-1, 20.2031-7, and 20.2031-9.) For example, if the decedent's reversionary interest was subject to an outstanding life estate in his wife, his interest is valued according to the actuarial rules set forth in §20.2031-7. On the other hand, if the decedent's reversionary interest was contingent on the death of his wife without issue surviving and if it cannot be shown that his wife is incapable of having issue (so that his interest is not subject to valuation according to the actuarial rules in §20.2031-7), his interest is valued according to the general rules set forth in §20.2031-1. A possibility that the decedent may be able to dispose of property under certain conditions is considered to have the same value as a right of the decedent to the return of the property under those same conditions.

(4) In order to determine whether or not the decedent retained a reversionary interest in transferred property of a value in excess of 5 percent, the value of the reversionary interest is compared with the value of the transferred property, including interests therein which are not dependent upon survivorship of the decedent. For example, assume that the decedent, A, transferred property in trust with the income payable to B for life and with the remainder payable to C if A predeceases B, but with the property to revert to A if B predeceases A. Assume further that A does, in fact, predecease B. The value of A's reversionary interest immediately before his death is compared with the value of the trust corpus, without deduction of the value of B's outstanding life estate. If, in the above example, A had retained a reversionary interest in one-half only of the trust corpus, the value of his reversionary interest would be compared with the value of one-half of the trust corpus, again without deduction of any part of the value of B's outstanding life estate.

(f) . . .

(2) The decedent's reversionary interest will be considered to have arisen by the express terms of the instrument of transfer and not by operation of law if the instrument contains an express disposition which affirmatively creates the reversionary interest, even though the terms of the disposition do not refer to the decedent or his estate, as such. For example, where the disposition is, in its terms, to the next of kin of the decedent and such a disposition, under applicable local law, constitutes a reversionary interest in the decedent's estate, the decedent's reversionary interest will be considered to have arisen by the express terms of the instrument of transfer and not by operation of law.

Sec. 20.2038-1. Revocable transfers

(a) *In general.* A decedent's gross estate includes under section 2038 the value of any interest in property transferred by the decedent, whether in trust or otherwise, if the enjoyment of the interest was subject at the date of the decedent's death to any change through the exercise of a power by the decedent to alter, amend, revoke, or terminate, or if the decedent relinquished such a power in contemplation of death. However, section 2038 does not apply —

(1) To the extent that the transfer was for an adequate and full consideration in money or money's worth (see §20.2043-1);

(2) If the decedent's power could be exercised only with the consent of

all parties having an interest (vested or contingent) in the transferred property, and if the power adds nothing to the rights of the parties under local law; or

(3) To a power held solely by a person other than the decedent. But, for example, if the decedent had the unrestricted power to remove or discharge a trustee at any time and appoint himself trustee, the decedent is considered as having the powers of the trustee. However, this result would not follow if he only had the power to appoint himself trustee under limited conditions which did not exist at the time of his death. (See last two sentences of paragraph (b) of this section.)

Except as provided, it is immaterial in what capacity the power was exercisable by the decedent or by another person or persons in conjunction with the decedent; whether the power was exercisable alone or only in conjunction with another person or persons, whether or not having an adverse interest (unless the transfer was made before June 2, 1924; see paragraph (d) of this section); and at what time or from what source the decedent acquired his power (unless the transfer was made before June 23, 1936; see paragraph (c) of this section). Section 2038 is applicable to any power affecting the time or manner of enjoyment of property or its income, even though the identity of the beneficiary is not affected. For example, section 2038 is applicable to a power reserved by the grantor of a trust to accumulate income or distribute it to A, and to distribute corpus to A, even though the remainder is vested in A or his estate, and no other person has any beneficial interest in the trust. However, only the value of an interest in property subject to a power to which section 2038 applies is included in the decedent's gross estate under section 2038.

(b) *Date of existence of power.* A power to alter, amend, revoke, or terminate will be considered to have existed at the date of the decedent's death even though the exercise of the power was subject to a precedent giving of notice or even though the alteration, amendment, revocation, or termination would have taken effect only on the expiration of a stated period after the exercise of the power, whether or not on or before the date of the decedent's death notice had been given or the power had been exercised. In determining the value of the gross estate in such cases, the full value of the property transferred subject to the power is discounted for the period required to elapse between the date of the decedent's death and the date upon which the alteration, amendment, revocation, or termination could take effect. In this connection, see especially §20.2031-7. However, section 2038 is not applicable to a power the exercise of which was subject to a contingency beyond the decedent's control which did not occur before his death (e.g., the death of another person during the decedent's life). See, however, section 2036(a)(2) for the inclusion of property in the decedent's gross estate on account of such a power.

(c) *Transfers made before June 23, 1936.* Notwithstanding anything to the contrary in paragraphs (a) and (b) of this section, the value of an interest in property transferred by a decedent before June 23, 1936, is not included in his gross estate under section 2038 unless the power to alter, amend, revoke, or terminate was reserved at the time of the transfer. For purposes of this paragraph, the phrase "reserved at the time of the transfer" has reference to a power (arising either by the express terms of the instrument of transfer or by operation of law) to which the transfer was subject when made and which continued to the date of the decedent's death (see paragraph (b) of this section) to be exercisable by the decedent alone or by the decedent in conjunction with any other person or persons. The phrase also has reference to any understanding, express or implied, had in connection with the making of the transfer that the power would later be created or conferred.

Sec. 20.2039-1

(d) *Insurance under policies on the life of the decedent.* If an annuity or other payment receivable by a beneficiary under a contract or agreement is in substance the proceeds of insurance under a policy on the life of the decedent, section 2039(a) and (b) does not apply. For the extent to which such an annuity or other payment is includible in a decedent's gross estate, see section 2042 and §20.2042-1. A combination annuity contract and life insurance policy on the decedent's life (e.g., a "retirement income" policy with death benefits) which matured during the decedent's lifetime so that there was no longer an insurance element under the contract at the time of the decedent's death is subject to the provisions of section 2039(a) and (b). On the other hand, the treatment of a combination annuity contract and life insurance policy on the decedent's life which did not mature during the decedent's lifetime depends upon the nature of the contract at the time of the decedent's death. The nature of the contract is generally determined by the relation of the reserve value of the policy to the value of the death benefit at the time of the decedent's death. If the decedent dies before the reserve value equals the death benefit, there is still an insurance element under the contract. The contract is therefore considered, for estate tax purposes, to be an insurance policy subject to the provisions of section 2042. However, if the decedent dies after the reserve value equals the death benefit, there is no longer an insurance element under the contract. The contract is therefore considered to be a contract for an annuity or other payment subject to the provisions of section 2039(a) and (b) or some other section of part III of subchapter A of chapter 11. Notwithstanding the relation of the reserve value to the value of the death benefit, a contract under which the death benefit could never exceed the total premiums paid, plus interest, contains no insurance element.

Example. Pursuant to a retirement plan established January 1, 1945, the employer purchased a contract from an insurance company which was to provide the employee, upon his retirement at age 65, with an annuity of $100 per month for life, and which was to provide his designated beneficiary, upon the employee's death after retirement, with a similar annuity for life. The contract further provided that if the employee should die before reaching the retirement age, a lump sum payment of $20,000 would be paid to his designated beneficiary in lieu of the annuity described above. The plan at no time met the requirements of section 401(a) (relating to qualified plans). Assume that the reserve value of the contract at the retirement age would be $20,000. If the employee died after reaching the retirement age, the death benefit to the designated beneficiary would constitute an annuity, the value of which would be includible in the employee's gross estate under section 2039(a) and (b). If, on the other hand, the employee died before reaching his retirement age, the death benefit to the designated beneficiary would constitute insurance under a policy on the life of the decedent since the reserve value would be less than the death benefit. Accordingly, its includibility would depend upon section 2042 and §20.2042-1.

Sec. 20.2039-2

(b) *Plans to which section 2039(c) applies.* Section 2039(c) excludes from a decedent's gross estate, to the extent provided in paragraph (c) of this section, the value of an annuity or other payment receivable by any beneficiary (except the value of an annuity or other payment receivable by or for the benefit of the decedent's estate) under —

(1) An employees' trust (or under a contract purchased by an employees' trust) forming part of a pension, stock bonus, or profit-sharing plan which, at the time of the decedent's separation from employment (whether by death or otherwise), or at the time of the earlier termination of the plan, met the requirements of section 401(a), or

(2) A retirement annuity contract purchased by an employer (and not by an employees' trust) pursuant to a plan which, at the time of decedent's separation from employment (by death or otherwise), or at the time of the earlier termination of the plan, met the requirements of section 401(a)(3) through (6).

For the meaning of the term "annuity or other payment," see paragraph (b) of §20.2039-1. For the meaning of the phrase "receivable by or for the benefit of the decedent's estate," see paragraph (b) of §20.2042-1. The application of this paragraph may be illustrated by the following examples in each of which it is assumed that the amount stated to be excludable from the decedent's gross estate is determined in accordance with paragraph (c) of this section:

Example (3). Pursuant to a pension plan, the employer made contributions to a trust which were used by the trustee to purchase a contract from an insurance company for the benefit of an employee. The contract was to provide the employee, upon his retirement at age 65, with an annuity of $100 per month for life, and was to provide his designated beneficiary, upon the employee's death after retirement, with a similar annuity for life. The contract further provided that if the employee should die before reaching the retirement age, a lump sum payment equal to the greater of (a) $10,000 or (b) the reserve value of the policy would be paid to his designated beneficiary in lieu of the annuity described above. Assume that the employee died before reaching the retirement age and that at such time the plan met the requirements of section 401(a). Since the designated beneficiary's lump sum payment was receivable under a qualified pension plan, no part of such lump sum payment is includible in the decedent's gross estate by reason of the provisions of section 2039(c). It should be noted that for purposes of the exclusion under section 2039(c), it is immaterial whether or not such lump sum payment constitutes the proceeds of life insurance under the principles set forth in paragraph (d) of §20.2039-1.

Sec. 20.2040-1. Joint interests

(a) *In general.* A decedent's gross estate includes under section 2040 the value of property held jointly at the time of the decedent's death by the decedent and another person or persons with right of survivorship, as follows:

(1) To the extent that the property was acquired by the decedent and the other joint owner or owners by gift, devise, bequest, or inheritance, the decedent's fractional share of the property is included.

(2) In all other cases, the entire value of the property is included except such part of the entire value as is attributable to the amount of the consideration in money or money's worth furnished by the other joint owner or owners. See §20.2043-1 with respect to adequacy of consideration. Such part of the entire value is that portion of the entire value of the property at the decedent's death (or at the alternate valuation date described in section 2032) which the consideration in money or money's worth furnished by the other joint owner or owners bears to the total cost of acquisition and capital additions. In determining the consideration furnished by the other joint owner or owners, there is taken into account only that portion of such consideration which is shown not to be attributable to money or other property acquired by the other joint owner or owners from the decedent for less than a full and adequate consideration in money or money's worth.

The entire value of jointly held property is included in a decedent's gross estate unless the executor submits facts sufficient to show that property was not acquired entirely with consideration furnished by the decedent, or was acquired by the decedent and the other joint owner or owners by gift, bequest, devise, or inheritance.

(b) *Meaning of "property held jointly."* Section 2040 specifically covers property held jointly by the decedent and any other person (or persons), property held by the decedent and spouse as tenants by the entirety, and a deposit of money, or a bond or other instrument, in the name of the decedent and any other person and payable to either or the survivor. The section applies to all classes of property, whether real or personal, and regardless of when the joint interests were created. Furthermore, it makes no difference that the survivor takes the entire interest in the property by right of survivorship and that no interest therein forms a part of the decedent's estate for purposes of administration. The section has no application to property held by the decedent and any other person (or persons) as tenants in common.

(c) *Examples.* The application of this section may be explained in the following examples in each of which it is assumed that the other joint owner or owners survived the decedent:

(1) If the decedent furnished the entire purchase price of the jointly held property, the value of the entire property is included in his gross estate;

(2) If the decedent furnished a part only of the purchase price, only a corresponding portion of the value of the property is so included;

(3) If the decedent furnished no part of the purchase price, no part of the value of the property is so included;

(4) If the decedent, before the acquisition of the property by himself and the other joint owner, gave the latter a sum of money or other property which thereafter became the other joint owner's entire contribution to the purchase price, then the value of the entire property is so included, notwithstanding the fact that the other property may have appreciated in value due to market conditions between the time of the gift and the time of the acquisition of the jointly held property;

(5) If the decedent, before the acquisition of the property by himself and the other joint owner, transferred to the latter for less than an adequate and full consideration in money or money's worth other income-producing property, the income from which belonged to and became the other joint owner's entire contribution to the purchase price, then the value of the jointly held property less that portion attributable to the income which the other joint owner did furnish is included in the decedent's gross estate;

(6) If the property originally belonged to the other joint owner and the decedent purchased his interest from the other joint owner, only that portion of the value of the property attributable to the consideration paid by the decedent is included;

(7) If the decedent and his spouse acquired the property by will or gift as tenants by the entirety, one-half of the value of the property is included in the decedent's gross estate; and

(8) If the decedent and his two brothers acquired the property by will or gift as joint tenants, one-third of the value of the property is so included.

Sec. 20.2041-1

(b) *Definition of "power of appointment"* — (1) *In general.* The term "power of appointment" includes all powers which are in substance and effect powers of appointment regardless of the nomenclature used in creating the power and regardless of local property law connotations. For example, if a trust instrument provides that the beneficiary may appropriate or consume the principal of the trust, the power to consume or appropriate is a power of appointment. Similarly, a power given to a decedent to affect the beneficial enjoyment of trust property or its income by altering, amending, or revoking the trust instrument or terminating the trust is a power of appointment. If the community property laws of a State confer upon the wife a power of testamentary disposition over property in which she does not have a vested interest she is considered as having a power of appointment. A power in a donee to remove or discharge a trustee and appoint himself may be a power of appointment. For example, if under the terms of a trust instrument, the trustee or his successor has the power to appoint the principal of the trust for the benefit of individuals including himself, and the decedent has the unrestricted power to remove or discharge the trustee at any time and appoint any other person including himself, the decedent is considered as having a power of appointment. However, the decedent is not considered to have a power of appointment if he only had the power to appoint a successor, including himself, under limited conditions which did not exist at the time of his death, without an accompanying unrestricted power of removal. Similarly, a power to amend only the administrative provisions of a trust instrument, which cannot substantially affect the beneficial enjoyment of the trust property or income, is not a power of appointment. The mere power of management, investment, custody of assets, or the power to allocate receipts and disbursements as between income and principal, exercisable in a fiduciary capacity, whereby the holder has no power to enlarge or shift any of the beneficial interests therein except as an incidental consequence of the discharge of such fiduciary duties is not a power of appointment. Further, the right in a beneficiary of a trust to assent to a periodic accounting, thereby relieving the trustee from further accountability, is not a power of appointment if the right of assent does not consist of any power or right to enlarge or shift the beneficial interest of any beneficiary therein.

(2) *Relation to other sections.* For purposes of §§20.2041-1 to 20.2041-3, the term "power of appointment" does not include powers reserved by the decedent to himself within the concept of sections 2036 to 2038. (See §§20.2036-1 to 20.2038-1.) No provision of section 2041 or of §§20.2041-1 to 20.2041-3 is to be construed as in any way limiting the application of any other section of the Internal Revenue Code or of these regulations. The power of the owner of a property interest already possessed by him to dispose of his interest, and nothing more, is not a power of appointment, and the interest is includible in his gross estate to the extent it would be includible under section 2033 or some other provision of part III of subchapter A of chapter 11. For example, if a trust created by S provides for payment of the income to A for life with power in A to appoint the remainder by will and, in default of such appointment for payment of the income to A's widow, W, for her life and for payment of the remainder to A's estate, the value of A's interest in the remainder is includible in his gross estate under section 2033 regardless of its includibility under section 2041.

(c) *Definition of "general power of appointment"* — (1) *In general.* The term "general power of appointment" as defined in section 2041(b)(1) means any power of appointment exercisable in favor of the decedent, his estate, his creditors, or the creditors of his estate, except (i) joint powers, to the extent provided in §§20.2041-2 and 20.2041-3, and (ii) certain powers limited by an ascertainable standard, to the extent provided in subparagraph (2) of this paragraph. A power of appointment exercisable to meet the estate tax, or any other taxes, debts, or charges which are enforceable against the estate, is included within the meaning of a power of appointment exercisable in favor of the decedent's estate, his creditors, or the creditors of his estate. A power of appointment exercisable for the purpose of discharging a legal obligation of the decedent or for his pecuniary benefit is considered a power of appointment exercisable in favor of the decedent or his creditors. However, for purposes of §§20.2041-1 to 20.2041-3, a power of appointment not otherwise considered to be a general power of appointment is not treated as a general power of appointment merely by reason of the fact that an appointee may, in fact, be a creditor of the decedent or his estate. A power of appointment is not a general power if by its terms it is either —

    (a) Exercisable only in favor of one or more designated persons or classes other than the decedent or his creditors, or the decedent's estate or the creditors of his estate, or

    (b) Expressly not exercisable in favor of the decedent or his creditors, or the decedent's estate or the creditors of his estate.

A decedent may have two powers under the same instrument, one of which is a general power of appointment and the other of which is not. For example, a beneficiary may have a power to withdraw trust corpus during his life, and a testamentary power to appoint the corpus among his descendants. The testamentary power is not a general power of appointment.

    (2) *Powers limited by an ascertainable standard.* A power to consume, invade, or appropriate income or corpus, or both, for the benefit of the decedent which is limited by an ascertainable standard relating to the health, education, support, or maintenance of the decedent is, by reason of section 2041(b)(1)(A), not a general power of appointment. A power is limited by such a standard if the extent of the holder's duty to exercise and not to exercise the power is reasonably measurable in terms of his needs for health, education, or support (or any combination of them). As used in this subparagraph, the words "support" and "maintenance" are synonymous and their meaning is not limited to the bare necessities of life. A power to use property for the comfort, welfare, or happiness of the holder of the power is not limited by the requisite standard. Examples of powers which are limited by the requisite standard are powers exercisable for the holder's "support," "support in reasonable comfort," "maintenance in health and reasonable comfort," "support in his accustomed manner of living," "education, including college and professional education," "health," and "medical, dental, hospital and nursing expenses and expenses of invalidism." In determining whether a power is limited by an ascertainable standard, it is immaterial whether the beneficiary is required to exhaust his other income before the power can be exercised.

    (d) *Definition of "exercise."* Whether a power of appointment is in fact exercised may depend upon local law. For example, the residuary clause of a will may be considered under local law as an exercise of a testamentary power of appointment in the absence of evidence of a contrary intention drawn from the whole of the testator's will. However, regardless of local law, a power of appointment is considered as exercised for purposes of section 2041 even though the exercise is in favor of the taker in default of appointment, and irrespective of whether the appointed interest and the interest in default of appointment are identical or whether the appointee renounces any right to take under the appointment. A power of appointment is also considered as exercised even though the disposition cannot take effect until the occurrence of an event after the exercise takes place, if the exercise is irrevocable and, as of the time of the exercise, the condition was not impossible of occurrence. For example, if property is left in trust to A for life, with a power in B to appoint the remainder by will, and B dies before A, exercising his power by appointing the remainder to C if C survives A, B is considered to have exercised his power if C is living at B's death. On the other hand, a testamentary power of appointment is not considered as exercised if it is exercised subject to the occurrence during the decedent's life of an express or implied condition which did not in fact occur. Thus, if in the preceding example, C dies before B, B's power of appointment would not be considered to have been exercised. Similarly, if a trust provides for income to A for life, remainder as A appoints by will, and A appoints a life estate in the property to B and does not otherwise exercise his power, but B dies before A, A's power is not considered to have been exercised.

(e) *Time of creation of power.* A power of appointment created by will is, in general, considered as created on the date of the testator's death. However, section 2041(b)(3) provides that a power of appointment created by a will executed on or before October 21, 1942, is considered a power created on or before that date if the testator dies before July 1, 1949, without having republished the will, by codicil or otherwise, after October 21, 1942. Whether or not a power of appointment created by an intervivos instrument executed on or before October 21, 1942, is considered a power created on or before that date depends upon the facts and circumstances of the particular case. For example, assume that A created a revocable trust before October 21, 1942, providing for payment of income to B for life with remainder as B shall appoint by will. If A dies after October 21, 1942, without having exercised his power of revocation, B's power of appointment is considered a power created after October 21, 1942. On the other hand, assume that C created an irrevocable intervivos trust before October 21, 1942, naming T as trustee and providing for payment of income to D for life with remainder to E. Assume further that T was given the power to pay corpus to D and the power to appoint a successor trustee. If T resigns after October 21, 1942, and appoints D as successor trustee, D is considered to have a power of appointment created before October 21, 1942. As another example, assume that F created an irrevocable intervivos trust before October 21, 1942, providing for payment of income to G for life with remainder as G shall appoint by will, but in default of appointment income to H for life with remainder as H shall appoint by will. If G dies after October 21, 1942, without having exercised his power of appointment, H's power of appointment is considered a power created before October 21, 1942, even though it was only a contingent interest until G's death. If, in this last example, G had exercised his power of appointment by creating a similar power in I, I's power of appointment would be considered a power created after October 21, 1942. A power of appointment is not considered as created after October 21, 1942, merely because the power is not exercisable or the identity of its holders is not ascertainable until after that date.

Sec. 20.2041-2

(d) *Release or lapse.* A failure to exercise a general power of appointment created on or before October 21, 1942, or a complete release of such a power is not considered to be an exercise of a general power of appointment. The phrase "a complete release" means a release of all powers over all or a portion of the property subject to a power of appointment, as distinguished from the reduction of a power of appointment to a lesser power. Thus, if the decedent completely relinquished all powers over one-half of the property subject to a power of appointment, the power is completely released as to that one-half.

If at or before the time a power of appointment is relinquished, the holder of the power exercises the power in such a manner or to such an extent that the relinquishment results in the reduction, enlargement, or shift in a beneficial interest in property, the relinquishment will be considered to be an exercise and not a release of the power. For example, assume that A created a trust in 1940 providing for payment of the income to B for life and, upon B's death, remainder to C. Assume further that B was given the unlimited power to amend the trust instrument during his lifetime. If B amended the trust in 1948 by providing that upon his death the remainder was to be paid to D, and if he further amended the trust in 1950 by deleting his power to amend the trust, such relinquishment will be considered an exercise and not a release of a general power of appointment. On the other hand, if the 1948 amendment became ineffective before or at the time of the 1950 amendment, or if B in 1948 merely amended the trust by changing the purely ministerial powers of the trustee, his relinquishment of the power in 1950 will be considered as a release of a power of appointment.

(e) *Partial release.* If a general power of appointment created on or before October 21, 1942, is partially released so that it is not thereafter a general power of appointment, a subsequent exercise of the partially released power is not an exercise of a general power of appointment if the partial release occurs before whichever is the later of the following dates:

(1) November 1, 1951, or

(2) If the decedent was under a legal disability to release the power on October 21, 1942, the day after the expiration of 6 months following the termination of such legal disability.

However, if a general power created on or before October 21, 1942, is partially released on or after the later of these dates, a subsequent exercise of the power will cause the property subject to the power to be included in the holder's gross estate, if the exercise is such that if it were a disposition of property owned by the decedent it would cause the property to be included in his gross estate. The legal disability referred to in this paragraph is determined under local law and may include the disability of an insane person, a minor, or an unborn child. The fact that the type of general power of appointment possessed by the decedent actually was not generally releasable under the local law does not place the decedent under a legal disability within the meaning of this paragraph. In general, however, it is assumed that all general powers of appointment are releasable, unless the local law on the subject is to the contrary, and it is presumed that the method employed to release the power is effective, unless it is not in accordance with the local law relating specifically to releases or, in the absence of such local law, is not in accordance with the local law relating to similar transactions.

(f) *Partial exercise.* If a general power of appointment created on or before October 21, 1942, is exercised only as to a portion of the property subject to the power, section 2041 is applicable only to the value of that portion. For example, if a decedent had a general power of appointment exercisable by will created on or before October 21, 1942, over a trust fund valued at $200,000 at the date of his death, and if the decedent exercised his power either to the extent of directing the distribution of one-half of the trust property to B or of directing the payment of $100,000 to B, the trust property would be includible in the decedent's gross estate only to the extent of $100,000.

Sec. 20.2041-3

(c) *Joint powers created after October 21, 1942.* The treatment of a power of appointment created after October 21, 1942, which is exercisable only in conjunction with another person is governed by section 2041(b)(1)(C), which provides as follows:

(1) Such a power is not considered a general power of appointment if it is not exercisable by the decedent except with the consent or joinder of the creator of the power.

(2) Such power is not considered a general power of appointment if it is not exercisable by the decedent except with the consent or joinder of a person having a substantial interest in the property subject to the power which is adverse to the exercise of the power in favor of the decedent, his estate, his creditors, or the creditors of his estate. An interest adverse to the exercise of a power is considered as substantial if its value in relation to the total value of the property subject to the power is not insignificant. For this purpose, the interest is to be valued in accordance with the actuarial principles set forth in §20.2031-7 or, if it is not susceptible to valuation under those provisions, in accordance with the general principles set forth in §20.2031-1. A taker in default of appointment under a power has an interest which is adverse to an exercise of the power. A coholder of the power has no adverse interest merely because of his joint possession of the power nor merely because he is a permissible appointee under a power. However, a coholder of a power is considered as having an adverse interest where he may possess the power after the decedent's death and may exercise it at that time in favor of himself, his estate, his creditors, or the creditors of his estate. Thus, for example, if X, Y, and Z held a power jointly to appoint among a group of persons which includes themselves and if on the death of X the power will pass to Y and Z jointly, then Y and Z are considered to have interests adverse to the exercise of the power in favor of X. Similarly, if on Y's death the power will pass to Z, Z is considered to have an interest adverse to the exercise of the power in favor of Y. The application of this subparagraph may be further illustrated by the following additional examples in each of which it is assumed that the value of the interest in question is substantial:

Example (1). The decedent and R were trustees of a trust under the terms of which the income was to be paid to the decedent for life and then to M for life, and the remainder was to be paid to R. The trustees had power to distribute corpus to the decedent. Since R's interest was substantially adverse to an exercise of the power in favor of the decedent the latter did not have a general power of appointment. If M and the decedent were the trustees, M's interest would likewise have been adverse.

Example (2). The decedent and L were trustees of a trust under the terms of which the income was to be paid to L for life and then to M for life, and the remainder was to be paid to the decedent. The trustees had power to distribute corpus to the decedent during L's life. Since L's interest was adverse to an exercise of the power in favor of the decedent, the decedent did not have a general power of appointment. If the decedent and M were the trustees, M's interest would likewise have been adverse.

Example (3). The decedent and L were trustees of a trust under the terms of which the income was to be paid to L for life. The trustees could designate whether corpus was to be distributed to the decedent or to A after L's death. L's interest was not adverse to an exercise of the power in favor of the decedent, and the decedent therefore had a general power of appointment.

(3) A power which is exercisable only in conjunction with another person, and which after application of the rules set forth in subparagraphs (1) and (2) of this paragraph constitutes a general power of appointment, will be treated as though the holders of the power who are permissible appointees of the

property were joint owners of property subject to the power. The decedent, under this rule, will be treated as possessed of a general power of appointment over an aliquot share of the property to be determined with reference to the number of joint holders, including the decedent, who (or whose estates or creditors) are permissible appointees. Thus, for example, if X, Y, and Z hold an unlimited power jointly to appoint among a group of persons, including themselves, but on the death of X the power does not pass to Y and Z jointly, then Y and Z are not considered to have interests adverse to the exercise of the power in favor of X. In this case X is considered to possess a general power of appointment as to one-third of the property subject to the power.

(d) *Releases, lapses, and disclaimers of general powers of appointment.* (1) Property subject to a general power of appointment created after October 21, 1942, is includible in the gross estate of a decedent under section 2041(a)(2) even though he does not have the power at the date of his death, if during his life he exercised or released the power under circumstances such that, if the property subject to the power had been owned and transferred by the decedent, the property would be includible in the decedent's gross estate under section 2035, 2036, 2037, or 2038. Further, section 2041(b)(2) provides that the lapse of a power of appointment is considered to be a release of the power to the extent set forth in subparagraph (3) of this paragraph. A release of a power of appointment need not be formal or express in character. The principles set forth in §20.2041-2 for determining the application of the pertinent provisions of sections 2035 through 2038 to a particular exercise of a power of appointment are applicable for purposes of determining whether or not an exercise or release of a power of appointment created after October 21, 1942, causes the property to be included in a decedent's gross estate under section 2041(a)(2). If a general power of appointment created after October 21, 1942, is partially released, a subsequent exercise or release of the power under circumstances described in the first sentence of this subparagraph, or its possession at death, will nevertheless cause the property subject to the power to be included in the gross estate of the holder of the power.

(2) Section 2041(a)(2) is not applicable to the complete release of a general power of appointment created after October 21, 1942, whether exercisable during life or by will, if the release was not made in contemplation of death within the meaning of section 2035, and if after the release the holder of the power retained no interest in or control over the property subject to the power which would cause the property to be included in his gross estate under sections 2036 through 2038 if the property had been transferred by the holder.

(3) The failure to exercise a power of appointment created after October 21, 1942, within a specified time, so that the power lapses, constitutes a release of the power. However, section 2041(b)(2) provides that such a lapse of a power of appointment during any calendar year during the decedent's life is treated as a release for purposes of inclusion of property in the gross estate under section 2041(a)(2) only to the extent that the property which could have been appointed by exercise of the lapsed power exceeds the greater of (i) $5,000 or (ii) 5 percent of the aggregate value, at the time of the lapse, of the assets out of which, or the proceeds of which, the exercise of the lapsed power could have been satisfied. For example, assume that A transferred $200,000 worth of securities in trust providing for payment of income to B for life with remainder to B's issue. Assume further that B was given a non-cumulative right to withdraw $10,000 a year from the principal of the trust fund (which neither increased nor decreased in value prior to B's death). In

such case, the failure of B to exercise his right of withdrawal will not result in estate tax with respect to the power to withdraw $10,000 which lapses each year before the year of B's death. At B's death there will be included in his gross estate the $10,000 which he was entitled to withdraw for the year in which his death occurs less any amount which he may have taken during that year. However, if in the above example B had possessed the right to withdraw $15,000 of the principal annually, the failure to exercise such power in any year will be considered a release of the power to the extent of the excess of the amount subject to withdrawal over 5 percent of the trust fund (in this example, $5,000, assuming that the trust fund is worth $200,000 at the time of the lapse). Since each lapse is treated as though B had exercised dominion over the trust property by making a transfer of principal reserving the income therefrom for his life, the value of the trust property (but only to the extent of the excess of the amount subject to withdrawal over 5 percent of the trust fund) is includible in B's gross estate (unless before B's death he has disposed of his right to the income under circumstances to which sections 2035 through 2038 would not be applicable). The extent to which the value of the trust property is included in the decedent's gross estate is determined as provided in subparagraph (4) of this paragraph.

(4) The purpose of section 2041(b)(2) is to provide a determination, as of the date of the lapse of the power, of the proportion of the property over which the power lapsed which is an exempt disposition for estate tax purposes and the proportion which, if the other requirements of sections 2035 through 2038 are satisfied, will be considered as a taxable disposition. Once the taxable proportion of any disposition at the date of lapse has been determined, the valuation of that proportion as of the date of the decedent's death (or, if the executor has elected the alternate valuation method under section 2032, the value as of the date therein provided), is to be ascertained in accordance with the principles which are applicable to the valuation of transfers of property by the decedent under the corresponding provisions of sections 2035 through 2038. For example, if the life beneficiary of a trust had a right exercisable only during one calendar year to draw down $50,000 from the corpus of a trust, which he did not exercise, and if at the end of the year the corpus was worth $800,000, the taxable portion over which the power lapsed is $10,000 (the excess of $50,000 over 5 percent of the corpus), or $\frac{1}{80}$ of the total value. On the decedent's death, if the total value of the corpus of the trust (excluding income accumulated after the lapse of the power) on the applicable valuation date was $1,200,000, $15,000 ($\frac{1}{80}$ of $1,200,000) would be includible in the decedent's gross estate. However, if the total value was then $600,000, only $7,500 ($\frac{1}{80}$ of $600,000) would be includible.

(5) If the failure to exercise a power, such as a right of withdrawal, occurs in more than a single year, the proportion of the property over which the power lapsed which is treated as a taxable disposition will be determined separately for each such year. The aggregate of the taxable proportions for all such years, valued in accordance with the above principles, will be includible in the gross estate by reason of the lapse. The includible amount, however, shall not exceed the aggregate value of the assets out of which, or the proceeds of which, the exercise of the power could have been satisfied, valued as of the date of the decedent's death (or, if the executor has elected the alternate valuation method under section 2032, the value as of the date therein provided).

(6) A disclaimer or renunciation of a general power of appointment is not considered to be a release of the power. The disclaimer of renunciation must

be unequivocal and effective under local law. A disclaimer is a complete and unqualified refusal to accept the rights to which one is entitled. There can be no disclaimer or renunciation of a power after its acceptance. In any case where a power is purported to be disclaimed or renounced as to only a portion of the property subject to the power, the determination as to whether or not there has been a complete and unqualified refusal to accept the rights to which one is entitled will depend on all the facts and circumstances of the particular case, taking into account the recognition and effectiveness of such a disclaimer under local law. Such rights refer to the incidents of the power and not to other interests of the decedent in the property. If effective under local law, the power may be disclaimed or renounced without disclaiming or renouncing such other interests. In the absence of facts to the contrary, the failure to renounce or disclaim within a reasonable time after learning of its existence will be presumed to constitute an acceptance of the power.

(f) *Examples.* The application of this section may be further illustrated by the following examples, in each of which it is assumed, unless otherwise stated, that S has transferred property in trust after October 21, 1942, with the remainder payable to R at L's death, and that neither L nor R has any interest in or power over the enjoyment of the trust property except as is indicated separately in each example:

Example (4). Income was payable to L during his lifetime. R has an unrestricted power to cause corpus to be distributed to L. R dies before L. In such case, R has only a power to dispose of his remainder interest, the value of which is includible in his gross estate under section 2033, and nothing in addition would be includible under section 2041. If in this example R's remainder were contingent on his surviving L, nothing would be includible in his gross estate under either section 2033 or 2041. While R would have a power of appointment, it would not be a general power.

Sec. 20.2042-1. Proceeds of life insurance

(a) *In general.* (1) Section 2042 provides for the inclusion in a decedent's gross estate of the proceeds of insurance on the decedent's life (i) receivable by or for the benefit of the estate (see paragraph (b) of this section), and (ii) receivable by other beneficiaries (see paragraph (c) of this section). The term "insurance" refers to life insurance of every description, including death benefits paid by fraternal beneficial societies operating under the lodge system.

(2) Proceeds of life insurance which are not includible in the gross estate under section 2042 may, depending upon the facts of the particular case, be includible under some other section of part III of subchapter A of chapter 11. For example, if the decedent possessed incidents of ownership in an insurance policy on his life but gratuitously transferred all rights in the policy in contemplation of death, the proceeds would be includible under section 2035. Section 2042 has no application to the inclusion in the gross estate of the value of rights in an insurance policy on the life of a person other than the decedent, or the value of rights in a combination annuity contract and life insurance policy on the decedent's life (i.e., a "retirement income" policy with death benefit or an "endowment" policy) under which there was no insurance element at the time of the decedent's death (see paragraph (d) of §20.2039-1).

(3) The amount to be included in the gross estate under section 2042 is the full amount receivable under the policy. If the proceeds of the policy are made payable to a beneficiary in the form of an annuity for life or for a term of years, the amount to be included in the gross estate is the one sum payable at death under an option which could have been exercised either by the in-

sured or by the beneficiary, or if no option was granted, the sum used by the insurance company in determining the amount of the annuity.

(b) *Receivable by or for the benefit of the estate.* (1) Section 2042 requires the inclusion in the gross estate of the proceeds of insurance on the decedent's life receivable by the executor or administrator, or payable to the decedent's estate. It makes no difference whether or not the estate is specifically named as the beneficiary under the terms of the policy. Thus, if under the terms of an insurance policy the proceeds are receivable by another beneficiary but are subject to an obligation, legally binding upon the other beneficiary, to pay taxes, debts, or other charges enforceable against the estate, then the amount of such proceeds required for the payment in full (to the extent of the beneficiary's obligation) of such taxes, debts, or other charges is includible in the gross estate. Similarly, if the decedent purchased an insurance policy in favor of another person or a corporation as collateral security for a loan or other accommodation, its proceeds are considered to be receivable for the benefit of the estate. The amount of the loan outstanding at the date of the decedent's death, with interest accrued to that date, will be deductible in determining the taxable estate. See §20.2053-4.

(c) *Receivable by other beneficiaries.* (1) Section 2042 requires the inclusion in the gross estate of the proceeds of insurance on the decedent's life not receivable by or for the benefit of the estate if the decedent possessed at the date of his death any of the incidents of ownership in the policy, exercisable either alone or in conjunction with any other person. However, if the decedent did not possess any of such incidents of ownership at the time of his death nor transfer them in contemplation of death, no part of the proceeds would be includible in his gross estate under section 2042. Thus, if the decedent owned a policy of insurance on his life and, 4 years before his death, irrevocably assigned his entire interest in the policy to his wife retaining no reversionary interest therein (see subparagraph (3) of this paragraph), the proceeds of the policy would not be includible in his gross estate under section 2042.

(2) For purposes of this paragraph, the term "incidents of ownership" is not limited in its meaning to ownership of the policy in the technical legal sense. Generally speaking, the term has reference to the right of the insured or his estate to the economic benefits of the policy. Thus, it includes the power to change the beneficiary, to surrender or cancel the policy, to assign the policy, to revoke an assignment, to pledge the policy for a loan, or to obtain from the insurer a loan against the surrender value of the policy, etc. Similarly, the term includes a power to change the beneficiary reserved to a corporation of which the decedent is sole stockholder.

(3) The term "incidents of ownership" also includes a reversionary interest in the policy or its proceeds, whether arising by the express terms of the policy or other instrument or by operation of law, but only if the value of the reversionary interest immediately before the death of the decedent exceeded 5 percent of the value of the policy. As used in this subparagraph, the term "reversionary interest" includes a possibility that the policy or its proceeds may return to the decedent or his estate and a possibility that the policy or its proceeds may become subject to a power of disposition by him. In order to determine whether or not the value of a reversionary interest immediately before the death of the decedent exceeded 5 percent of the value of the policy the principles contained in paragraph (c) (3) and (4) of §20.2037-1 insofar as applicable, shall be followed under this subparagraph. In that connection there must be specifically taken into consideration any incidents of owner

ship held by others immediately before the decedent's death which would affect the value of the reversionary interest. For example, the decedent would not be considered to have a reversionary interest in the policy of a value in excess of 5 percent if the power to obtain the cash surrender value existed in some other person immediately before the decedent's death and was exercisable by such other person alone and in all events. The terms "reversionary interest" and "incidents of ownership" do not include the possibility that the decedent might receive a policy or its proceeds by inheritance through the estate of another person, or as a surviving spouse under a statutory right of election or a similar right.

(4) A decedent is considered to have an "incident of ownership" in an insurance policy on his life held in trust if, under the terms of the policy, the decedent (either alone or in conjunction with another person or persons) has the power (as trustee or otherwise) to change the beneficial ownership in the policy or its proceeds, or the time or manner of enjoyment thereof, even though the decedent has no beneficial interest in the trust. Moreover, assuming the decedent created the trust, such a power may result in the inclusion in the decedent's gross estate under section 2036 or 2038 of other property transferred by the decedent to the trust if, for example, the decedent has the power to surrender the insurance policy and if the income otherwise used to pay premiums on the policy would become currently payable to a beneficiary of the trust in the event that the policy were surrendered.

Sec. 20.2053-3

(b) *Executor's commissions.* (1) The executor or administrator, in filing the estate tax return, may deduct his commissions in such an amount as has actually been paid, or in an amount which at the time of filing the estate tax return may reasonably be expected to be paid, but no deduction may be taken if no commissions are to be collected. If the amount of the commissions has not been fixed by decree of the proper court, the deduction will be allowed on the final audit of the return, to the extent that all three of the following conditions are satisfied:

(i) The district director is reasonably satisfied that the commissions claimed will be paid;

(ii) The amount claimed as a deduction is within the amount allowable by the laws of the jurisdiction in which the estate is being administered; and

(iii) It is in accordance with the usually accepted practice in the jurisdiction to allow such an amount in estates of similar size and character.

If the deduction is disallowed in whole or in part on final audit, the disallowance will be subject to modification as the facts may later require. If the deduction is allowed in advance of payment and payment is thereafter waived, it shall be the duty of the executor to notify the district director and to pay the resulting tax, together with interest.

(2) A bequest or devise to the executor in lieu of commissions is not deductibile. If, however, the decedent fixed by his will the compensation payable to the executor for services to be rendered in the administration of the estate, deduction may be taken to the extent that the amount so fixed does not exceed the compensation allowable by the local law or practice.

Sec. 20.2053-6

(d) *Gift taxes.* Unpaid gift taxes on gifts made by a decedent before his death are deductible. If a gift is considered as made one-half by the decedent and one-half by his spouse under section 2513, the entire amount of the gift tax, unpaid at the decedent's death, attributable to a gift in fact made by the decedent is deductible. No portion of the tax attributable to a gift in fact made by the decedent's spouse is deductible except to the extent that the obligation is enforced against the decedent's estate and his estate has no effective right of contribution against his spouse. (See section 2012 and §20.2012-1 with respect to credit for gift taxes paid upon gifts of property included in a decedent's gross estate.)

(f) *Income taxes.* Unpaid income taxes are deductible if they are on income property includible in an income tax return of the decedent for a period before his death. Taxes on income received after the decedent's death are not deductible. If income received by a decedent during his lifetime is included in a joint income tax return filed by the decedent and his spouse, or by the decedent's estate and his surviving spouse, the portion of the joint liability for the period covered by the return for which a deduction would be allowed is the amount for which the decedent's estate would be liable under local law, as between the decedent and his spouse, after enforcement of any effective right of reimbursement or contribution. . . .

Sec. 20.2053-8. Deduction for expenses in administering property not subject to claims

(a) Expenses incurred in administering property included in a decedent's gross estate but not subject to claims fall within the second category of deductions set forth in §20.2053-1, and may be allowed as deductions if they —

(1) Would be allowed as deductions in the first category if the property being administered were subject to claims; and

(2) Were paid before the expiration of the period of limitation for assessment provided in section 6501.

Usually, these expenses are incurred in connection with the administration of a trust established by a decedent during his lifetime. They may also be incurred in connection with the collection of other assets or the transfer or clearance of title to other property included in a decedent's gross estate for estate tax purposes but not included in his probate estate.

(b) These expenses may be allowed as deductions only to the extent that they would be allowed as deductions under the first category if the property were subject to claims. See §20.2053-3. The only expenses in administering property not subject to claims which are allowed as deductions are those occasioned by the decedent's death and incurred in settling the decedent's interest in the property or vesting good title to the property in the beneficiaries. Expenses not coming within the description in the preceding sentence but incurred on behalf of the transferees are not deductible.

(c) The principles set forth in paragraphs (b), (c), and (d) of §20.2053-3 (relating to the allowance of executor's commissions, attorney's fees, and miscellaneous administration expenses of the first category) are applied in determining the extent to which trustee's commissions, attorney's and accountant's fees, and miscellaneous administration expenses are allowed in connection with the administration of property not subject to claims.

(d) The application of this section may be illustrated by the following examples:

Example (1). In 1940, the decedent made an irrevocable transfer of property to the X Trust Company, as trustee. The instrument of transfer provided that the trustee should pay the income from the property to the decedent for the duration of his life and, upon his death, distribute the corpus of the trust among designated beneficiaries. The property was included in the decedent's gross estate under the provisions of section 2036. Three months after the date of death, the trustee distributed the trust corpus among the beneficiaries, except for $6,000 which it withheld. The amount withheld represented $5,000 which it retained as trustee's commissions in connection with the termination of the trust and $1,000 which it had paid to an attorney for representing it in connection with the termination. Both the trustee's commissions and the attorney's fees were allowable under the law of the jurisdiction in which the trust was being administered, were reasonable in amount, and were in accord with local custom. Under these circumstances, the estate is allowed a deduction of $6,000.

Example (2). In 1945, the decedent made an irrevocable transfer of property to Y Trust Company, as trustee. The instrument of transfer provided that the trustee should pay the income from the property to the decedent during his life. If the decedent's wife survived him, the trust was to continue for the duration of her life, with Y Trust Company and the decedent's son as co-trustees, and with income payable to the decedent's wife for the duration of her life. Upon the death of both the decedent and his wife, the corpus is to be distributed among designated remaindermen. The decedent was survived by his wife. The property was included in the decedent's gross estate under the provisions of section 2036. In accordance with local custom, the trustee made an accounting to the court as of the date of the decedent's death. Following the death of the decedent, a controversy arose among the remaindermen as to their respective rights under the instrument of transfer, and a suit was brought in court to which the trustee was made a party. As a part of the accounting, the court approved the following expenses which the trustee had paid within 3 years following the date of death: $10,000, trustee's commissions; $5,000, accountant's fees; $25,000, attorney's fees; and $2,500, representing fees paid to the guardian of a remainderman who was a minor. The trustee's commissions and accountant's fees were for services in connection with the usual issues involved in a trust accounting as also were one-half of the attorney's and guardian's fees. The remainder of the attorney's and guardian's fees were for services performed in connection with the suit brought by the remaindermen. The amount allowed as a deduction is the $28,750 ($10,000, trustee's commissions; $5,000, accountant's fees; $12,500, attorney's fees; and $1,250, guardian's fees) incurred as expenses in connection with the usual issues involved in a trust accounting. The remaining expenses are not allowed as deductions since they were incurred on behalf of the transferees.

Example (3). Decedent in 1950 made an irrevocable transfer of property to the Z Trust Company, as trustee. The instrument of transfer provided that the trustee should pay the income from the property to the decedent's wife for the duration of her life. If the decedent survived his wife the trust corpus was to be returned to him but if he did not survive her, then upon the death of the wife, the trust corpus was to be distributed among their children. The decedent predeceased his wife and the transferred property, less the value of the wife's outstanding life estate, was included in his gross estate under the provisions of section 2037 since his reversionary interest therein immediately before his death was in excess of 5 percent of the value of the property. At the wife's request, the court ordered the trustee to render an accounting of the trust property as of the date of the decedent's death. No deduction will be allowed the decedent's estate for any of the expenses incurred in connection with the trust accounting, since the expenses were incurred on behalf of the wife.

Example (4). If, in the preceding example, the decedent died without other property and no executor or administrator of his estate was appointed, so that it was necessary for the trustee to prepare an estate tax return and participate in its audit, or if the trustee required accounting proceedings for its own protection in accordance with local custom, trustees', attorneys' and guardians' fees in connection with the estate tax or accounting proceedings would be deductible to the same extent that they would be deductible if the property were subject to claims. Deductions incurred under similar circumstances by a surviving joint tenant or the recipient of life insurance proceeds would also be deductible.

Sec. 20.2055-1. Deduction for transfers for public, charitable, and religious uses; in general

(a) *General rule.* A deduction is allowed under section 2055(a) from the gross estate of a decedent who was a citizen or resident of the United States at the time of his death for the value of property included in the decedent's gross estate and transferred by the decedent during his lifetime or by will —

(1) To or for the use of the United States, any State, Territory, any political subdivision thereof, or the District of Columbia, for exclusively public purposes;

(2) To or for the use of any corporation or association organized and operated exclusively for religious, charitable, scientific, literary, or educational purposes (including the encouragement of art and the prevention of cruelty to children or animals), if no part of the net earnings of the corporation or association inures to the benefit of any private stockholder or individual (other than as a legitimate object of such purposes), and no substantial part of its activities is carrying on propaganda, or otherwise attempting, to influence legislation;

(3) To a trustee or trustees, or a fraternal society, order, or association operating under the lodge system, if the transferred property is to be used exclusively for religious, charitable, scientific, literary, or educational purposes (or for the prevention of cruelty to children or animals), and if no substantial part of the activities of such transferee is carrying on propaganda, or otherwise attempting, to influence legislation; or

(4) To or for the use of any veterans' organization incorporated by Act of Congress, or of any of its departments, local chapters, or posts, no part of the net earnings of which inures to the benefit of any private shareholder or individual.

The deduction is not limited, in the case of estates of citizens or residents of the United States, to transfers to domestic corporations or associations, or to trustees for use within the United States. Nor is the deduction subject to percentage limitations such as are applicable to the charitable deduction under the income tax. However, sections 503(e) and 681(b)(5) provide that no deduction is allowed for transfers to organizations or trusts described in subparagraphs (2) and (3) of this paragraph which have engaged in certain "prohibited transactions" (see §20.2055-4).

Sec. 20.2055-2

(b) *Transfers subject to a condition or a power.* If, as of the date of a decedent's death, a transfer for charitable purposes is dependent upon the performance of some act or the happening of a precedent event in order that it might become effective, no deduction is allowable unless the possibility that the charitable transfer will not become effective is so remote as to be negligible. If an estate or interest has passed to or is vested in charity at the time of a decedent's death and the estate or interest would be defeated by the performance of some act or the happening of some event, the occurrence of which appeared to have been highly improbable at the time of the decedent's death, the deduction is allowable. If the legatee, devisee, donee, or trustee is empowered to divert the property or fund, in whole or in part, to a use or purpose which would have rendered it, to the extent that it is subject to such power, not deductible had it been directly so bequeathed, devised, or given by the decedent, the deduction will be limited to that portion, if any, of the property or fund which is exempt from an exercise of the power. The deduction is not allowed in the case of a transfer in trust conveying to charity a present interest in income if by reason of all the conditions and circumstances surrounding the transfer it appears that the charity may not receive the beneficial enjoyment of the interest. For example, assume that assets placed in trust by the decedent consist of stock in a corporation the fiscal policies of which are controlled by the decedent and his family, that the trustees and remaindermen are likewise members of the decedent's family, and that the governing instrument contains no adequate guarantee of the requisite income to the charitable organization. Under such circumstances, no deduction will be allowed. Similarly, if the trustees are not members of the decedent's family but have no power to sell or otherwise dispose of the closely held stock, or otherwise insure the requisite enjoyment of income to the charitable organization, no deduction will be allowed.

(d) *Payments in compromise.* If a charitable organization assigns or surrenders a part of a transfer to it pursuant to a compromise agreement in settlement of controversy, the amount so assigned or surrendered is not deductible as a transfer to that charitable organization.

Sec. 20.2056(a)-2

(b) An interest passing to a decedent's surviving spouse is a "deductible interest" if it does not fall within one of the following categories of "nondeductible interests":

(1) Any property interest which passed from the decedent to his surviving spouse is a "nondeductible interest" to the extent it is not included in the decedent's gross estate.

(2) If a deduction is allowed under section 2053 (relating to deductions for expenses and indebtedness) by reason of the passing of a property interest from the decedent to his surviving spouse, such interest is, to the extent of the deduction under section 2053, a "nondeductible interest." Thus, a property interest which passed from the decedent to his surviving spouse in satisfaction of a deductible claim of the spouse against the estate is, to the extent of the claim, a "nondeductible interest" (see §20.2056(b)-4). Similarly, amounts deducted under section 2053(a)(2) for commissions allowed to the surviving spouse as executor are "nondeductible interests." As to the valuation, for the purpose of the marital deduction, of any property interest which passed from the decedent to his surviving spouse subject to a mortgage or other encumbrance, see §20.2056(b)-4.

(3) If during settlement of the estate a loss deductible under section 2054 occurs with respect to a property interest, then that interest is, to the extent of the deductible loss, a "nondeductible interest" for the purpose of the marital deduction.

Sec. 20.2056(b)-1. **Marital deduction; limitation in case of life estate or other "terminable interest"**

(a) *In general.* Section 2056(b) provides that no marital deduction is allowed with respect to certain property interests, referred to generally as "terminable interests," passing from a decedent to his surviving spouse. The phrase "terminable interest" is defined in paragraph (b) of this section. However, the fact that an interest in property passing to a decedent's surviving spouse is a "terminable interest" makes it nondeductible only (1) under the circumstances described in paragraph (c) of this section, and (2) if it does not come within one of the exceptions referred to in paragraph (d) of this section.

(b) *"Terminable interests."* A "terminable interest" in property is an interest which will terminate or fail on the lapse of time or on the occurrence or the failure to occur of some contingency. Life estates, terms for years, annuities, patents, and copyrights are therefore terminable interests. However, a bond, note, or similar contractual obligation, the discharge of which would not have the effect of an annuity or a term for years, is not a terminable interest.

(f) *Direction to acquire a terminable interest.* No marital deduction is allowed with respect to a property interest which a decedent directs his executor or a trustee to convert after his death into a terminable interest for his surviving spouse. The marital deduction is not allowed even though no interest in the property subject to the terminable interest passes to another person and even though the interest would otherwise come within the exceptions described in §§20.2056(b)-5 and 20.2056(b)-6 (relating to life estates and life insurance and annuity payments with powers of appointment). However, a general investment power, authorizing investments in both terminable interests and other property, is not a direction to invest in a terminable interest.

(g) *Examples.* The application of this section may be illustrated by the following examples, in each of which it is assumed that the property interest which passed from the decedent to a person other than his surviving spouse did not pass for an adequate and full consideration in money or money's worth:

Example (3). H during his lifetime purchased an annuity contract providing for payments to himself for life and then to W for life if she should survive him. Upon the death of the survivor of H and W, the excess, if any, of the cost of the contract over the annuity payments theretofore made was to be refunded to A. The interest which passed from H to W is a nondeductible interest since A may possess or enjoy a part of the property following the termination of the interest of W. If, however, the contract provided for no refund upon the death of the survivor of H and W, or provided that any refund was to go to the estate of the survivor, then the interest which passed from H to W is (to the extent it is included in H's gross estate) a deductible interest.

Example (5). H transferred real property to A by gift, reserving the right to the rentals of the property for a term of 20 years. H died within the 20-year term, bequeathing the right to the remaining rentals to a trust for the benefit of W. The terms of the trust satisfy the five conditions stated in §20.2056(b)-5, so that the property interest which passed in trust is considered to have passed from H to W. However, the interest is a nondeductible interest since it will terminate upon the expiration of the term and A will thereafter possess or enjoy the property.

Example (8). Assume that pursuant to local law an allowance for support is payable to the decedent's surviving spouse during the period of the administration of the decedent's estate, but that upon her death or remarriage during such period her right to any further allowance will terminate. Assume further that the surviving spouse is sole beneficiary of the decedent's estate. Under such circumstances, the allowance constitutes a deductible interest since any part of the allowance not receivable by the surviving spouse during her lifetime will pass to her estate under the terms of the decedent's will. If, in this example, the decedent bequeathed only one-third of his residuary estate to his surviving spouse, then two-thirds of the allowance for support would constitute a nondeductible terminable interest.

Sec. 20.2056(b)-2. **Marital deduction; interest in unidentified assets**

(a) Section 2056(b)(2) provides that if an interest passing to a decedent's surviving spouse may be satisfied out of assets (or their proceeds) which include a particular asset that would be a nondeductible interest if it passed from the decedent to his spouse, the value of the interest passing to the spouse is reduced, for the purpose of the marital deduction, by the value of the particular asset.

(b) In order for section 2056(b)(2) to apply, two circumstances must coexist, as follows:

(1) The property interest which passed from the decedent to his surviving spouse must be payable out of a group of assets included in the gross estate. Examples of property interests payable out of a group of assets are a general legacy, a bequest of the residue of the decedent's estate or of a portion of the residue, and a right to a share of the corpus of a trust upon its termination.

(2) The group of assets out of which the property interest is payable must include one or more particular assets which, if passing specifically to the surviving spouse, would be nondeductible interests. Therefore, section 2056 (b)(2) is not applicable merely because the group of assets includes a terminable interest, but would only be applicable if the terminable interest were nondeductible under the provisions of §20.2056(b)-1.

(c) If both of the circumstances set forth in paragraph (b) of this section are present, the property interest payable out of the group of assets is (except as to any excess of its value over the aggregate value of the particular asset or assets which would not be deductible if passing specifically to the surviving spouse) a nondeductible interest.

(d) The application of this section may be illustrated by the following example:

Example. A decedent bequeathed one-third of the residue of his estate to his wife. The property passing under the decedent's will included a right to the rentals of an office building for a term of years, reserved by the decedent under a deed of the building by way of gift to his son. The decedent did not make a specific bequest of the right to such rentals. Such right, if passing specifically to the wife, would be a nondeductible interest (see example (5) of paragraph (g) of §20.2056(b)-1). It is assumed that the value of the bequest of one-third of the residue of the estate to the wife was $85,000, and that the right to the rentals was included in the gross estate at a value of $60,000. If the decedent's executor had the right under the decedent's will or local law to assign the entire lease in satisfaction of the bequest, the bequest is a nondeductible interest to the extent of $60,000. If the executor could only assign a one-third interest in the lease in satisfaction of the bequest, the bequest is a nondeductible interest to the extent of $20,000. If the decedent's will provided that his wife's bequest could not be satisfied with a nondeductible interest, the entire bequest is a deductible interest. If, in this example, the asset in question had been foreign real estate not included in the decedent's gross estate, the results would be the same.

Sec. 20.2056(b)-3. **Marital deduction; interest of spouse conditioned on survival for limited period**

(a) *In general.* Generally, no marital deduction is allowable if the interest passing to the surviving spouse is a terminable interest as defined in paragraph (b) of §20.2056(b)-1. However, section 2056(b)(3) provides an exception to this rule so as to allow a deduction if (1) the only condition under which it will terminate is the death of the surviving spouse within 6 months after the decedent's death, or her death as a result of a common disaster which also resulted in the decedent's death, and (2) the condition does not in fact occur.

(b) *Six months' survival.* If the only condition which will cause the interest taken by the surviving spouse to terminate is the death of the surviving spouse and the condition is of such nature that it can occur only within 6 months following the decedent's death, the exception provided by section 2056(b)(3) will apply, provided the condition does not in fact occur. However, if the condition (unless it relates to death as a result of a common disaster) is one which may occur either within the 6-month period or thereafter, the exception provided by section 2056(b)(3) will not apply.

(c) *Common disaster.* If a property interest passed from the decedent to his surviving spouse subject to the condition that she does not die as a result of a common disaster which also resulted in the decedent's death, the exception provided by section 2056(b)(3) will not be applied in the final audit of the return if there is still a possibility that the surviving spouse may be deprived of the property interest by operation of the common disaster provision as given effect by the local law.

(d) *Examples.* The application of this section may be illustrated by the following examples:

Example (1). A decedent bequeathed his entire estate to his spouse on condition that she survive him by 6 months. In the event his spouse failed to survive him by 6 months, his estate was to go to his niece and her heirs. The decedent was survived by his spouse. It will be observed that, as of the time of the decedent's death, it was possible that the niece would, by reason of the interest which passed to her from the decedent, possess or enjoy the estate after the termination of the interest which passed to the spouse. Hence, under the general rule set forth in §20.2056(b)-1, the interest which passed to the spouse would be regarded as a nondeductible interest. If the surviving spouse in fact died within 6 months after the decedent's death, that general rule is to be applied, and the interest which passed to the spouse is a nondeductible interest. However, if the spouse in fact survived the decedent by 6 months, thus extinguishing the interest of the niece, the case comes within the exception provided by section 2056(b)(3), and the interest which passed to the spouse is a deductible interest. (It is assumed for the purpose of this example that no other factor which would cause the interest to be nondeductible is present.)

Example (2). The facts are the same as in example (1) except that the will provided that the estate was to go to the niece either in case the decedent and his spouse should both die as a result of a common disaster, or in case the spouse should fail to survive the decedent by 3 months. It is assumed that the decedent was survived by his spouse. In this example, the interest which passed from the decedent to his surviving spouse is to be regarded as a nondeductible interest if the surviving spouse in fact died either within 3 months after the decedent's death or as a result of a common disaster which also resulted in the decedent's death. However, if the spouse in fact survived the decedent by 3 months, and did not thereafter die as a result of a common disaster which also resulted in the decedent's death, the exception provided under section 2056(b)(3) will apply and the interest will be deductible.

Example (3). The facts are the same as in example (1) except that the will provided that the estate was to go to the niece if the decedent and his spouse should both die as a result of a common disaster and if the spouse failed to survive the decedent by 3 months. If the spouse in fact survived the decedent by 3 months, the interest of the niece is extinguished, and the interest passing to the spouse is a deductible interest.

Example (4). A decedent devised and bequeathed his residuary estate to his wife if she was living on the date of distribution of his estate. The devise and bequest is a nondeductible interest even though distribution took place within 6 months after the decedent's death and the surviving spouse in fact survived the date of distribution.

Sec. 20.2056(b)-4. Marital deduction; valuation of interest passing to surviving spouse

(a) *In general.* The value, for the purpose of the marital deduction, of any deductible interest which passed from the decedent to his surviving spouse is to be determined as of the date of the decedent's death, except that if the executor elects the alternate valuation method under section 2032 the valuation is to be determined as of the date of the decedent's death but with the adjustment described in paragraph (a)(3) of §20.2032-1. The marital deduction may be taken only with respect to the net value of any deductible interest which passed from the decedent to his surviving spouse, the same principles being applicable as if the amount of a gift to the spouse were being determined. In determining the value of the interest in property passing to the spouse account must be taken of the effect of any material limitations upon her right to income from the property. An example of a case in which this rule may be applied is a bequest of property in trust for the benefit of the decedent's spouse but the income from the property from the date of the decedent's death until distribution of the property to the trustee is to be used to pay expenses incurred in the administration of the estate.

(b) *Property interest subject to an encumbrance or obligation.* If a property interest passed from the decedent to his surviving spouse subject to a mortgage or other encumbrance, or if an obligation is imposed upon the surviving spouse by the decedent in connection with the passing of a property interest, the value of the property interest is to be reduced by the amount of the mortgage, other encumbrance, or obligation. However, if under the terms of the decedent's will or under local law the executor is required to discharge, out of other assets of the decedent's estate, a mortgage or other encumbrance on property passing from the decedent to his surviving spouse, or is required to reimburse the surviving spouse for the amount of the mortgage or other encumbrance, the payment or reimbursement constitutes an additional interest passing to the surviving spouse. The passing of a property interest subject to the imposition of an obligation by the decedent does not include a bequest, devise, or transfer in lieu of dower, curtesy, or of a statutory estate created in lieu of dower or curtesy, or of other marital rights in the decedent's property or estate. The passing of a property interest subject to the imposition of an obligation by the decedent does, however, include a bequest, etc., in lieu of the interest of his surviving spouse under community property laws unless such interest was, immediately prior to the decedent's death, a mere expectancy. (As to the circumstances under which the interest of the surviving spouse is regarded as a mere expectancy, see §20.2056(c)-2.) The following examples are illustrative of property interests which passed from the decedent to his surviving spouse subject to the imposition of an obligation by the decedent:

Example (1). A decedent devised a residence valued at $25,000 to his wife, with a direction that she pay $5,000 to his sister. For the purpose of the marital deduction, the value of the property interest passing to the wife is only $20,000.

Example (2). A decedent devised real property to his wife in satisfaction of a debt owing to her. The debt is a deductible claim under section 2053. Since the wife is obligated to relinquish the claim as a condition to acceptance of the devise, the value of the devise is, for the purpose of the marital deduction, to be reduced by the amount of the claim.

Example (3). A decedent bequeathed certain securities to his wife in lieu of her interest in property held by them as community property under the law of the State of their residence. The wife elected to relinquish her community property interest and to take the bequest. For the purpose of the marital deduction, the value of the bequest is to be reduced by the value of the community property interest relinquished by the wife.

(c) *Effect of death taxes.* (1) In the determination of the value of any property interest which passed from the decedent to his surviving spouse, there must be taken into account the effect which the Federal estate tax, or any estate, succession, legacy, or inheritance tax, has upon the net value to the surviving spouse of the property interest.

(2) For example, assume that the only bequest to the surviving spouse is $100,000 and the spouse is required to pay a State inheritance tax in the amount of $1,500. If no other death taxes affect the net value of the bequest, the value, for the purpose of the marital deduction, is $98,500.

(3) As another example, assume that a decedent devised real property to his wife having a value for Federal estate tax purposes of $100,000 and also bequeathed to her a nondeductible interest for life under a trust. The State of residence valued the real property at $90,000 and the life interest at $30,000, and imposed an inheritance tax (at graduated rates) of $4,800 with respect to the two interests. If it is assumed that the inheritance tax on the devise is required to be paid by the wife, the amount of tax to be ascribed to the devise is

$$\frac{90,000}{120,000} \times \$4,800 = \$3,600.$$

Accordingly, if no other death taxes affect the net value of the bequest, the value, for the purpose of the marital deduction, is $100,000 less $3,600, or $96,400.

(4) If the decedent bequeaths his residuary estate, or a portion of it, to his surviving spouse, and his will contains a direction that all death taxes shall be payable out of the residuary estate, the value of the bequest, for the purpose of the marital deduction, is based upon the amount of the residue as reduced pursuant to such direction, if the residuary estate, or a portion of it, is bequeathed to the surviving spouse, and by the local law the Federal estate tax is payable out of the residuary estate, the value of the bequest, for the purpose of the marital deduction, may not exceed its value as reduced by the Federal estate tax. Methods of computing the deduction, under such circumstances, are set forth in supplemental instructions to the estate tax return.

(d) *Remainder interests.* If the income from property is made payable to another individual for life, or for a term of years, with remainder absolutely to the surviving spouse or to her estate, the marital deduction is based upon the present value of the remainder. The present value of the remainder is to be determined in accordance with the rules stated in §20.2031-7. For example, if the surviving spouse is to receive $50,000 upon the death of a person aged 31 years, the present value of the remainder is $14,466. If the remainder is such that its value is to be determined by a special computation (see paragraph (e) of §20.2031-7), a request for a specific factor may be submitted to the Commissioner. The request should be accompanied by a statement of the date of birth of each person, the duration of whose life may affect the value of the remainder, and copies of the relevant instruments. The Commissioner may, if conditions permit, supply the factor requested. If the Commissioner does not furnish the factor, the claim for deduction must be supported by a full statement of the computation of the present value made in accordance with the principles set forth in the applicable paragraphs of §20.2031-7.

Sec. 20.2056(b)-5

(b) *Specific portion; deductible amount.* If either the right to income or the power of appointment passing to the surviving spouse pertains only to a specific portion of a property interest passing from the decedent, the marital deduction is allowed only to the extent that the rights in the surviving spouse meet all of the five conditions described in paragraph (a) of this section. While the rights over the income and the power must coexist as to the same interest in property, it is not necessary that the rights over the income or the power as to such interest be in the same proportion. However, if the rights over income meeting the required conditions set forth in paragraph (a) (1) and (2) of this section extend over a smaller share of the property interest than the share with respect to which the power of appointment requirements set forth in paragraph (a) (3) through (5) of this section are satisfied, the deductible interest is limited to the smaller share. Correspondingly, if a power of appointment meeting all the requirements extends to a smaller portion of the property interest than the portion over which the income rights pertain, the deductible interest cannot exceed the value of the portion to which such power of appointment applies. Thus, if the decedent leaves to his surviving spouse the right to receive annually all of the income from a particular property interest and a power of appointment meeting the specifications prescribed in paragraph (a) (3) through (5) of this section as to only one-half of the property interest, then only one-half of the property interest is treated as a deductible interest. Correspondingly, if the income interest of the spouse satisfying the requirements extends to only one-fourth of the property interest and a testamentary power of appointment satisfying the requirements extends to all of the property interest, then only one-fourth of the interest in the spouse qualifies as a deductible interest. Further, if the surviving spouse has no right to income from a specific portion of a property interest but a testamentary power of appointment which meets the necessary conditions over the entire interest, then none of the interest qualifies for the deduction. In addition, if, from the time of the decedent's death, the surviving spouse has a power of appointment meeting all of the required conditions over three-fourths of the entire property interest and the prescribed income rights over the entire interest, but with a power in another person to appoint one-half of the entire interest, the value of the interest in the surviving spouse over only one-half of the property interest will qualify as a deductible interest.

(c) *Definition of "specific portion."* A partial interest in property is not treated as a specific portion of the entire interest unless the rights of the surviving spouse in income and as to the power constitute a fractional or percentile share of a property interest so that such interest or share in the surviving spouse reflects its proportionate share of the increment or decline in the whole of the property interest to which the income rights and the power relate. Thus, if the right of the spouse to income and the power extend to one-half or a specified percentage of the property, or the equivalent, the interest is considered as a specific portion. On the other hand, if the annual income of the spouse is limited to a specific sum, or if she has a power to appoint only a specific sum out of a larger fund, the interest is not a deductible interest. Even though the rights in the surviving spouse may not be expressed in terms of a definite fraction or percentage, a deduction may be allowable if it is shown that the effect of local law is to give the spouse rights which are identical to those she would have acquired if the size of the share had been expressed in terms of a definite fraction or percentage. The following examples illustrate the application of this and the preceding paragraphs of this section:

Example (1). The decedent transferred to a trustee 500 identical shares of X Company stock. He provided that during the lifetime of the surviving spouse the trustee should pay her annually one-half of the trust income or $6,000, whichever is the larger. The spouse was also given a general power of appointment, exercisable by her last will over the sum of $160,000 or over three-fourths of the trust corpus, whichever should be of larger value. Since there is no certainty that the trust income will not vary from year to year, for purposes of paragraphs (a) and (b) of this section, an annual payment of a specified sum, such as the $6,000 provided for in this case, is not considered as representing the income from a definite fraction or a specific portion of the entire interest if that were the extent of the spouse's interest. However, since the spouse is to receive annually at least one-half of the trust income, she will, for purposes of paragraphs (a) and (b) of this section, be considered as receiving all of the income from one-half of the entire interest in the stock. Inasmuch as there is no certainty that the value of the stock will be the same on the date of the surviving spouse's death as it was on the date of the decedent's death, for purposes of paragraphs (a) and (b) of this section, a specified sum, such as the $160,000 provided for in this case, is not considered to be a definite fraction of the entire interest. However, since the surviving spouse has a general power of appointment over at least three-fourths of the trust corpus, she is considered as having a general power of appointment over three-fourths of the entire interest in the stock.

Example (2). The decedent bequeathed to a trustee an office building and 250 identical shares of Y Company stock. He provided that during the lifetime of the surviving spouse the trustee should pay her annually three-fourths of the trust income. The spouse was given a general power of appointment, exercisable by will, over the office building and 100 shares of the stock. By the terms of the decedent's will the spouse is given all the income from a definite fraction of the entire interest in the office building and in the stock. She also has a general power of appointment over the entire interest in the office building. However, since the amount of property represented by a single share of stock would be altered if the corporation split its stock, issued stock dividends, made a distribution of capital, etc., a power to appoint 100 shares at the time of the surviving spouse's death is not the same necessarily as a power to appoint 100/250 of the entire interest which the 250 shares represented on the date of the decedent's death. If it is shown in this case that the effect of local law is to give the spouse a general power to appoint not only the 100 shares designated by the decedent but also 100/250 of any shares or amounts which are distributed by the corporation and included in the corpus, the requirements of this paragraph will be satisfied and the surviving spouse will be considered as having a general power to appoint 100/250 of the entire interest in the 250 shares.

(d) *Definition of "entire interest."* Since a marital deduction is allowed for each qualifying separate interest in property passing from the decedent to his surviving spouse (subject to the percentage limitation contained in

§§20.2056(c)-1 and 20.2056(c)-2 concerning the aggregate amount of the deductions), for purposes of paragraphs (a) and (b) of this section, each property interest with respect to which the surviving spouse received some rights is considered separately in determining whether her rights extend to the entire interest or to a specific portion of the entire interest. A property interest which consists of several identical units of property (such as a block of 250 shares of stock, whether the ownership is evidenced by one or several certificates) is considered one property interest, unless certain of the units are to be segregated and accorded different treatment, in which case each segregated group of items is considered a separate property interest. The bequest of a specified sum of money constitutes the bequest of a separate property interest if immediately following distribution by the executor and thenceforth it, and the investments made with it, must be so segregated or accounted for as to permit its identification as a separate item of property. The application of this paragraph may be illustrated by the following examples:

Example (1). The decedent transferred to a trustee three adjoining farms, Blackacre, Whiteacre, and Greenacre. His will provided that during the lifetime of the surviving spouse the trustee should pay her all of the income from the trust. Upon her death, all of Blackacre, a one-half interest in Whiteacre, and a one-third interest in Greenacre were to be distributed to the person or persons appointed by her in her will. The surviving spouse is considered as being entitled to all of the income from the entire interest in Blackacre, all of the income from the entire interest in Whiteacre, and all of the income from the entire interest in Greenacre. She also is considered as having a power of appointment over the entire interest in Blackacre, over one-half of the entire interest in Whiteacre, and over one-third of the entire interest in Greenacre.

Example (2). The decedent bequeathed $250,000 to C, as trustee. C is to invest the money and pay all of the income from the investments to W, the decedent's surviving spouse, annually. W was given a general power, exercisable by will, to appoint one-half of the corpus of the trust. Here, immediately following distribution by the executor, the $250,000 will be sufficiently segregated to permit its identification as a separate item, and the $250,000 will constitute an entire property interest. Therefore, W has a right to income and a power of appointment such that one-half of the entire interest is a deductible interest.

Example (3). The decedent bequeathed 100 shares of Z Corporation stock to D, as trustee. W, the decedent's surviving spouse, is to receive all of the income of the trust annually and is given a general power, exercisable by will, to appoint out of the trust corpus the sum of $25,000. In this case the $25,000 is not, immediately following distribution, sufficiently segregated to permit its identification as a separate item of property in which the surviving spouse has the entire interest. Therefore, the $25,000 does not constitute the entire interest in a property for the purpose of paragraphs (a) and (b) of this section.

Sec. 20.2056(d)-1. Marital deduction; effect of disclaimers

(a) *By a surviving spouse.* If a decedent's surviving spouse makes a disclaimer of any property interest which would otherwise be considered as having passed from the decedent to her, the disclaimed interest is to be considered as having passed from the decedent to the person or persons entitled to receive the interest as a result of the disclaimer. A disclaimer is a complete and unqualified refusal to accept the rights to which one is entitled. It is, therefore, necessary to distinguish between the surviving spouse's disclaimer of a property interest and her acceptance and subsequent disposal of a property interest. For example, if proceeds of insurance are payable to the surviving spouse and she refuses them so that they consequently pass to an alternate beneficiary designated by the decedent, the proceeds are considered as having passed from the decedent to the alternate beneficiary. On the other hand, if the surviving spouse directs the insurance company to hold the proceeds at interest during her life and, upon her death, to pay the principal sum to another person designated by her, thus effecting a transfer of a remainder interest, the proceeds are considered as having passed from the decedent to his spouse. See paragraph (c) of §20.2056(e)-2 with respect to a spouse's exercise or failure to exercise a right to take against a decedent's will.

(b) *By a person other than a surviving spouse.* It is unnecessary to distinguish, for the purpose of the marital deduction, between a disclaimer by a person other than the surviving spouse and a transfer by such person. If the surviving spouse becomes entitled to receive an interest in property from the decedent as a result of a disclaimer made by some other person, the interest is, nevertheless, considered as having passed from the decedent, not to the surviving spouse, but to the person who made the disclaimer, as though the disclaimer had not been made. If, as a result of a disclaimer made by a person other than the surviving spouse, a property interest passes to the surviving spouse under circumstances which meet the conditions set forth in §20.2056(b)-5 (relating to a life estate with a power of appointment), the rule stated in the preceding sentence applies, not only with respect to the portion of the interest which beneficially vests in the surviving spouse, but also with respect to the portion over which she acquires a power to appoint. The rule applies also in the case of proceeds under a life insurance, endowment, or annuity contract, which, as a result of a disclaimer made by a person other than the surviving spouse, are held by the insurer subject to the conditions set forth in §20.2056(b)-6.

Sec. 20.2056(e)-1.   **Marital deduction; definition of "passed from the decedent"**

(a) The following rules are applicable in determining the person to whom any property interest "passed from the decedent":

(1) Property interests devolving upon any person (or persons) as surviving co-owner with the decedent under any form of joint ownership under which the right of survivorship existed are considered as having passed from the decedent to such person (or persons).

(2) Property interests at any time subject to the decedent's power to appoint (whether alone or in conjunction with any person) are considered as having passed from the decedent to the appointee under his exercise of the power, or, in case of the lapse, release or nonexercise of the power, as having passed from the decedent to the taker in default of exercise.

(3) The dower or curtesy interest (or statutory interest in lieu thereof) of the decedent's surviving spouse is considered as having passed from the decedent to his spouse. *Dower*

(4) The proceeds of insurance upon the life of the decedent are considered as having passed from the decedent to the person who, at the time of the decedent's death, was entitled to receive the proceeds.

(5) Any property interest transferred during life, bequeathed or devised by the decedent, or inherited from the decedent, is considered as having passed to the person to whom he transferred, bequeathed, or devised the interest, or to the person who inherited the interest from him.

(6) The survivor's interest in an annuity or other payment described in

section 2039 (see §§20.2039-1 and 20.2039-2) is considered as having passed from the decedent to the survivor only to the extent that the value of such interest is included in the decedent's gross estate under that section. If only a portion of the entire annuity or other payment is included in the decedent's gross estate and the annuity or other payment is payable to more than one beneficiary, then the value of the interest considered to have passed to each beneficiary is that portion of the amount payable to each beneficiary that the amount of the annuity or other payment included in the decedent's gross estate bears to the total value of the annuity or other payment payable to all beneficiaries.

Sec. 20.2056(e)-2. Marital deduction; definition of "passed from the decedent to his surviving spouse"

(a) *In general.* In general, the definition stated in §20.2056(e)-1 is applicable in determining the property interests which "passed from the decedent to his surviving spouse." Special rules are provided, however, for the following:

(1) In the case of certain interests with income for life to the surviving spouse with power of appointment in her (see §20.2056(b)-5);

(2) In the case of proceeds held by the insurer under a life insurance, endowment, or annuity contract with power of appointment in the surviving spouse (see §20.2056(b)-6);

(3) In case of the disclaimer of an interest by the surviving spouse or by any other person (see §20.2056(d)-1);

(4) In case of an election by the surviving spouse (see paragraph (c) of this section); and

(5) In case of a controversy involving the decedent's will, see paragraph (d) of this section.

A property interest is considered as passing to the surviving spouse only if it passed to her as beneficial owner, except to the extent otherwise provided in §§20.2056(b)-5 and 20.2056(b)-6 in the case of certain life estates and insurance and annuity contracts with powers of appointment. For this purpose, where a property interest passed from the decedent in trust, such interest is considered to have passed from him to his surviving spouse to the extent of her beneficial interest therein. The deduction may not be taken with respect to a property interest which passed to such spouse merely as trustee, or subject to a binding agreement by the spouse to dispose of the interest in favor of a third person. An allowance or award paid to a surviving spouse pursuant to local law for her support during the administration of the decedent's estate constitutes a property interest passing from the decedent to his surviving spouse. In determining whether or not such an interest is deductible, however, see generally the terminable interest rules of §20.2056(b)-1 and especially example (8) of paragraph (g) of that section.

(b) *Examples.* The following illustrate the provisions of paragraph (a) of this section:

(1) A property interest bequeathed in trust by H (the decedent) is considered as having passed from him to W (his surviving spouse) —

(i) If the trust income is payable to W for life and upon her death the corpus is distributable to her executors or administrators;

(ii) If W is entitled to the trust income for a term of years following which the corpus is to be paid to W or her estate;

(iii) If the trust income is to be accumulated for a term of years or for W's life and the augmented fund paid to W or her estate; or

(iv) If the terms of the transfer satisfy the requirements of §20.2056(b)-5.

(2) If H devised property —

(i) To A for life with remainder absolutely to W or her estate, the remainder interest is considered to have passed from H to W;

(ii) To W for life with remainder to her estate, the entire property is considered as having passed from H to W; or

(iii) Under conditions which satisfy the provisions of §20.2056(b)-5, the entire property is considered as having passed from H to W.

(3) Proceeds of insurance upon the life of H are considered as having passed from H to W if the terms of the contract —

(i) Meet the requirements of §20.2056(b)-6;

(ii) Provide that the proceeds are payable to W in a lump sum;

(iii) Provide that the proceeds are payable in installments to W for life and after her death any remaining installments are payable to her estate;

(iv) Provide that interest on the proceeds is payable to W for life and upon her death the principal amount is payable to her estate; or

(v) Provide that the proceeds are payable to a trustee under an arrangement whereby the requirements of section 2056(b)(5) are satisfied.

(c) *Effect of election by surviving spouse.* This paragraph contains rules applicable if the surviving spouse may elect between a property interest offered to her under the decedent's will or other instrument and a property interest to which she is otherwise entitled (such as dower, a right in the decedent's estate, or her interest under community property laws) of which adverse disposition was attempted by the decedent under the will or other instrument. If the surviving spouse elects to take against the will or other instrument, then the property interests offered thereunder are not considered as having "passed from the decedent to his surviving spouse" and the dower or other property interest retained by her is considered as having so passed (if it otherwise so qualifies under this section). If the surviving spouse elects to take under the will or other instrument, then the dower or other property interest relinquished by her is not considered as having "passed from the decedent to his surviving spouse" (irrespective of whether it otherwise comes within the definition stated in paragraph (a) of this section) and the interest taken under the will or other instrument is considered as having so passed (if it otherwise so qualifies). As to the valuation of the property interest taken under the will or other instrument, see paragraph (b) of §20.2056(b)-4.

(d) *Will contests.* (1) If as a result of a controversy involving the decedent's will, or involving any bequest or devise thereunder, his surviving spouse assigns or surrenders a property interest in settlement of the controversy, the interest so assigned or surrendered is not considered as having "passed from the decedent to his surviving spouse."

(2) If as a result of the controversy involving the decedent's will, or involving any bequest or devise thereunder, a property interest is assigned or surrendered to the surviving spouse, the interest so acquired will be regarded as having "passed from the decedent to his surviving spouse" only if the assignment or surrender was a bona fide recognition of enforceable rights of the surviving spouse in the decedent's estate. Such a bona fide recognition will be presumed where the assignment or surrender was pursuant to a decision of a local court upon the merits in an adversary proceeding following a genuine and active contest. However, such a decree will be accepted only to the extent that the court passed upon the facts upon which deductibility of the property interests depends. If the assignment or surrender was pursuant to a decree rendered by consent, or pursuant to an agreement not to contest the will or not to probate the will, it will not necessarily be accepted as a bona fide evaluation of the rights of the spouse.

(e) *Survivorship.* If the order of deaths of the decedent and his spouse cannot be established by proof, a presumption (whether supplied by local law, the decedent's will, or otherwise) that the decedent was survived by his spouse will be recognized as satisfying paragraph (b)(1) of §20.2056(a)-1, but only to the extent that it has the effect of giving to the spouse an interest in property includible in her gross estate under part III of subchapter A of chapter 11. Under these circumstances, if an estate tax return is required to be filed for the estate of the decedent's spouse, the marital deduction will not be allowed in the final audit of the estate tax return of the decedent's estate with respect to any property interest which has not been finally determined to be includible in the gross estate of his spouse.

Sec. 20.2203-1. Definition of executor. The term "executor" means the executor or administrator of the decedent's estate. However, if there is no executor or administrator appointed, qualified and acting within the United States, the term means any person in actual or constructive possession of any property of the decedent. The term "person in actual or constructive possession of any property of the decedent" includes, among others, the decedent's agents and representatives; safe-deposit companies, warehouse companies, and other custodians of property in this country; brokers holding, as collateral, securities belonging to the decedent; and debtors of the decedent in this country.

Sec. 25.2503-3. Future interests in property

(a) No part of the value of a gift of a future interest may be excluded in determining the total amount of gifts made during the calendar year. "Future interests" is a legal term, and includes reversions, remainders, and other interests or estates, whether vested or contingent, and whether or not supported by a particular interest or estate, which are limited to commence in use, possession or enjoyment at some future date or time. The term has no reference to such contractual rights as exist in a bond, note (though bearing no interest until maturity), or in a policy of life insurance, the obligations of which are to be discharged by payments in the future. But a future interest or interests in such contractual obligations may be created by the limitations contained in a trust or other instrument of transfer used in effecting a gift.

(b) An unrestricted right to the immediate use, possession, or enjoyment of property or the income from property (such as a life estate or term certain) is a present interest in property. An exclusion is allowable with respect to a gift of such an interest (but not in excess of the value of the interest). If a donee has received a present interest in property, the possibility that such interest may be diminished by the transfer of a greater interest in the same property to the donee through the exercise of a power is disregarded in computing the value of the present interest, to the extent that no part of such interest will at any time pass to any other person (see example (4) of paragraph (c) of this section). For an exception to the rule disallowing an exclusion for gifts of future interests in the case of certain gifts to minors, see §25.2503-4.

(c) The operation of this section may be illustrated by the following examples:

Example (1). Under the terms of a trust created by A the trustee is directed to pay the net income to B, so long as B shall live. The trustee is authorized in his discretion to withhold payments of income during any period he deems advisable and add such income to the trust corpus. Since B's right to receive the income payments is subject to the trustee's discretion, it is not a present interest and no exclusion is allowable with respect to the transfer in trust.

Example (2). C transfers certain insurance policies on his own life to a trust created for the benefit of D. Upon C's death the proceeds of the policies are to be invested and the net income therefrom paid to D during his lifetime. Since the income payments to D will not begin until after C's death the transfer in trust represents a gift of a future interest in property against which no exclusion is allowable.

Example (3). Under the terms of a trust created by E the net income is to be distributed to E's three children in such shares as the trustee, in his uncontrolled discretion, deems advisable. While the terms of the trust provide that all of the net income is to be distributed, the amount of income any one of the three beneficiaries will receive rests entirely within the trustee's discretion and cannot be presently ascertained. Accordingly, no exclusions are allowable with respect to the transfers to the trust.

Example (4). Under the terms of a trust the net income is to be paid to F for life, with the remainder payable to G on F's death. The trustee has the uncontrolled power to pay over the corpus to F at any time. Although F's present right to receive the income may be terminated, no other person has the right to such income interest. Accordingly, the power in the trustee is disregarded in determining the value of F's present interest. The power would not be disregarded to the extent that the trustee during F's life could distribute corpus to persons other than F.

Example (5). The corpus of a trust created by J consists of certain real property, subject to a mortgage. The terms of the trust provide that the net income from the property is to be used to pay the mortgage. After the mortgage is paid in full the net income is to be paid to K during his lifetime. Since K's right to receive the income payments will not begin until after the mortgage is paid in full the transfer in trust represents a gift of a future interest in property against which no exclusion is allowable.

Example (6). L pays premiums on a policy of insurance on his life. All the incidents of ownership in the policy (including the right to surrender the policy) are vested in M. The payment of premiums by L constitutes a gift of a present interest in property.

Sec. 25.2503-4. Transfer for the benefit of a minor

(a) Section 2503(c) provides that no part of a transfer for the benefit of a donee who has not attained the age of 21 years on the date of the gift will be considered a gift of a future interest in property if the terms of the transfer satisfy all of the following conditions:

(1) Both the property itself and its income may be expended by or for the benefit of the donee before he attains the age of 21 years;

(2) Any portion of the property and its income not disposed of under (1) will pass to the donee when he attains the age of 21 years; and

(3) Any portion of the property and its income not disposed of under (1) will be payable either to the estate of the donee or as he may appoint under a general power of appointment as defined in section 2514(c) if he dies before attaining the age of 21 years.

(b) Either a power of appointment exercisable by the donee by will or a power of appointment exercisable by the donee during his lifetime will satisfy the conditions set forth in paragraph (a)(3) of this section. However, if the transfer is to qualify for the exclusion under this section, there must be no restrictions of substance (as distinguished from formal restrictions of the type described in paragraph (g)(4) of §25.2523(e)-1) by the terms of the instrument of transfer on the exercise of the power by the donee. However, if the minor is given a power of appointment exercisable during lifetime or is given a power of appointment exercisable by will, the fact that under the local law a minor is under a disability to exercise an intervivos power or to execute a will does not cause the transfer to fail to satisfy the conditions of section 2503(c). Further, a transfer does not fail to satisfy the conditions of section 2503(c) by reason of the mere fact that —

(1) There is left to the discretion of a trustee the determination of the amounts, if any, of the income or property to be expended for the benefit of the minor and the purpose for which the expenditure is to be made, provided there are no substantial restrictions under the terms of the trust instrument on the exercise of such discretion;

(2) The donee, upon reaching age 21, has the right to extend the term of the trust; or

(3) The governing instrument contains a disposition of the property or income not expended during the donee's minority to persons other than the donee's estate in the event of the default of appointment by the donee.

(c) A gift to a minor which does not satisfy the requirements of section 2503(c) may be either a present or a future interest under the general rules of §25.2503-3. Thus, for example, a transfer of property in trust with income required to be paid annually to a minor beneficiary and corpus to be distributed to him upon his attaining the age of 25 is a gift of a present interest with respect to the right to income but is a gift of a future interest with respect to the right to corpus.

Sec. 25.2504-1

(d) If interpretations of the gift tax law in prior calendar years resulted in the erroneous inclusion of property for gift tax purposes which should have been excluded, or the erroneous exclusion of property which should have been included, adjustments must be made in order to arrive at the correct aggregate of taxable gifts for preceding years. However, see section 1000(e) and (g) of the 1939 Code relating to certain discretionary trusts and reciprocal trusts.

Sec. 25.2511-1. Transfers in general

(a) The gift tax applies to a transfer by way of gift whether the transfer is in trust or otherwise, whether the gift is direct or indirect, and whether the property is real or personal, tangible or intangible. For example, a taxable transfer may be effected by the creation of a trust, the forgiving of a debt, the assignment of a judgment, the assignment of the benefits of an insurance policy, or the transfer of cash, certificates of deposit, or Federal, State or municipal bonds. Statutory provisions which exempt bonds, notes, bills and certificates of indebtedness of the Federal Government or its agencies and the interest thereon from taxation are not applicable to the gift tax, since the gift tax is an excise tax on the transfer, and is not a tax on the subject of the gift.

(b) In the case of a nonresident not a citizen who was not engaged in business in the United States (see §25.2501-1) during the calendar year, the tax is imposed only if the gift consisted of real estate or tangible personal property situated within the United States at the time of transfer. See §§25.2501-1 and 25.2511-3.

(c) The gift tax also applies to gifts indirectly made. Thus, all transactions whereby property or property rights or interests are gratuitously passed or conferred upon another, regardless of the means or device employed, constitute gifts subject to tax. See further §25.2512-8. Where the law governing the administration of the decedent's estate gives a beneficiary, heir, or next-of-kin a right to completely and unqualifiedly refuse to accept ownership of property transferred from a decedent (whether the transfer is effected by the decedent's will or by the law of descent and distribution of intestate property), a refusal to accept ownership does not constitute the making of a gift if the refusal is made within a reasonable time after knowledge of the existence of the transfer. The refusal must be unequivocable and effective under the local law. There can be no refusal of ownership of property after its acceptance. Where the local law does not permit such a refusal, any disposition by the beneficiary, heir, or next-of-kin whereby ownership is transferred gratuitously to another constitutes the making of a gift by the beneficiary, heir, or next-of-kin. In any case where a refusal is purported to relate to only a part of the property, the determination of whether or not there has been a complete and unqualified refusal to accept ownership will depend on all of the facts and circumstances in each particular case, taking into account the recognition and effectiveness of such a purported refusal under the local law. In the absence of facts to the contrary, if a person fails to refuse to accept a transfer to him of ownership of a decedent's property within a reasonable time after learning of the existence of the transfer, he will be presumed to have accepted the property. In illustration, if Blackacre was devised to A under the decedent's will (which also provided that all lapsed legacies and devices shall go to B, the residuary beneficiary), and under the local law A could refuse to accept ownership in which case title would be considered as never having passed to A, A's refusal to accept Blackacre within a reasonable time of learning of the devise will not constitute the making of a gift by A to B. However, if a decedent who owned Greenacre died intestate with C and D as his only heirs, and under local law the heir of an intestate cannot, by refusal to accept, prevent himself from becoming an owner of intestate property, any gratuitous disposition by C (by whatever term it is known) whereby he gives up his ownership of a portion of Greenacre and D acquires the whole thereof constitutes the making of a gift by C to D.

(e) If a donor transfers by gift less than his entire interest in property, the gift tax is applicable to the interest transferred. The tax is applicable, for example, to the transfer of an undivided half interest in property, or to the transfer of a life estate when the grantor retains the remainder interest, or vice versa. However, if the donor's retained interest is not susceptible of measurement on the basis of generally accepted valuation principles, the gift tax is applicable to the entire value of the property subject to the gift. Thus, if a donor, aged 65 years, transfers a life estate in property to A, aged 25 years, with remainder to A's issue, or in default of issue, with reversion to the donor, the gift tax will normally be applicable to the entire value of the property.

(h) The following are examples of transactions resulting in taxable gifts and in each case it is assumed that the transfers were not made for an adequate and full consideration in money or money's worth:

(2) The transfer of property to B if there is imposed upon B the obligation of paying a commensurate annuity to C is a gift to C.

(3) The payment of money or the transfer of property to B in consideration of B's promise to render a service to C is a gift to C, or to both B and C, depending on whether the service to be rendered to C is or is not an adequate and full consideration in money or money's worth for that which is received by B. See section 2512(b) and the regulations thereunder.

(5) If A with his own funds purchases property and has the title conveyed to himself and B as joint owners, with rights of survivorship (other than a joint ownership described in example (4)) but which rights may be defeated by either party severing his interest, there is a gift to B in the amount of half the value of the property. However, see §25.2515-1 relative to the crea-

tion of a joint tenancy (or tenancy by the entirety) between husband and wife in real property with rights of survivorship which, unless the donor elects otherwise, is not considered as a transfer includible for Federal gift tax purposes at the time of the creation of the joint tenancy. See §25.2515-2 with respect to determining the extent to which the creation of a tenancy by the entirety constitutes a taxable gift if the donor elects to have the creation of the tenancy so treated. See also §25.2523(d)-1 with respect to the marital deduction allowed in the case of the creation of a joint tenancy or a tenancy by the entirety.

(9) Where property held by a husband and wife as community property is used to purchase insurance upon the husband's life and a third person is revocably designated as beneficiary and under the State law the husband's death is considered to make absolute the transfer by the wife, there is a gift by the wife at the time of the husband's death of half the amount of the proceeds of such insurance.

(10) If under a pension plan (pursuant to which he has an unqualified right to an annuity) an employee has an option to take either a retirement annuity for himself alone or a smaller annuity for himself with a survivorship annuity payable to his wife, and irrevocable election by the employee to take the reduced annuity in order that an annuity may be paid, after the employee's death, to his wife results in the making of a gift. However, see section 2517 and the regulations thereunder for the exemption from gift tax of amounts attributable to employers' contributions under qualified plans and certain other contracts.

Sec. 25.2511-2. Cessation of donor's dominion and control

(a) The gift tax is not imposed upon the receipt of the property by the donee, nor is it necessarily determined by the measure of enrichment resulting to the donee from the transfer, nor is it conditioned upon ability to identify the donee at the time of the transfer. On the contrary, the tax is a primary and personal liability of the donor, is an excise upon his act of making the transfer, is measured by the value of the property passing from the donor, and attaches regardless of the fact that the identity of the donee may not then be known or ascertainable.

(b) As to any property, or part thereof or interest therein, of which the donor has so parted with dominion and control as to leave in him no power to change its disposition, whether for his own benefit or for the benefit of another, the gift is complete. But if upon a transfer of property (whether in trust or otherwise) the donor reserves any power over its disposition, the gift may be wholly incomplete, or may be partially complete and partially incomplete, depending upon all the facts in the particular case. Accordingly, in every case of a transfer of property subject to a reserved power, the terms of the power must be examined and its scope determined. For example, if a donor transfers property to another in trust to pay the income to the donor or accumulate it in the discretion of the trustee, and the donor retains a testamentary power to appoint the remainder among his descendants, no portion of the transfer is a completed gift. On the other hand, if the donor had not retained the testamentary power of appointment, but instead provided that the remainder should go to X or his heirs, the entire transfer would be a completed gift. However, if the exercise of the trustee's power in favor of the grantor is limited by a fixed or ascertainable standard (see paragraph (g)(2) of §25.2511-1), enforceable by or on behalf of the grantor, then the gift is incomplete to the extent of the ascertainable value of any rights thus retained by the grantor.

(c) A gift is incomplete in every instance in which a donor reserves the power to revest the beneficial title to the property in himself. A gift is also incomplete if and to the extent that a reserved power gives the donor the power to name new beneficiaries or to change the interests of the beneficiaries as between themselves unless the power is a fiduciary power limited by a fixed or ascertainable standard. Thus, if an estate for life is transferred but, by an exercise of a power, the estate may be terminated or cut down by the donor to one of less value, and without restriction upon the extent to which the estate may be so cut down, the transfer constitutes an incomplete gift. If in this example the power was confined to the right to cut down the estate for life to one for a term of five years, the certainty of an estate for not less than that term results in a gift to that extent complete.

(d) A gift is not considered incomplete, however, merely because the donor reserves the power to change the manner or time of enjoyment. Thus, the creation of a trust the income of which is to be paid annually to the donee for a period of years, the corpus being distributable to him at the end of the period, and the power reserved by the donor being limited to a right to require that, instead of the income being so payable, it should be accumulated and distributed with the corpus to the donee at the termination of the period, constitutes a completed gift.

(e) A donor is considered as himself having a power if it is exercisable by him in conjunction with any person not having a substantial adverse interest in the disposition of the transferred property or the income therefrom. A trustee, as such, is not a person having an adverse interest in the disposition of the trust property or its income.

(f) The relinquishment or termination of a power to change the beneficiaries of transferred property, occurring otherwise than by the death of the donor (the statute being confined to transfers by living donors), is regarded as the event which completes the gift and causes the tax to apply. For example, if A transfers property in trust for the benefit of B and C but reserves the power as trustee to change the proportionate interests of B and C, and if A thereafter has another person appointed trustee in place of himself, such later relinquishment of the power by A to the new trustee completes the gift of the transferred property, whether or not the new trustee has a substantial adverse interest. The receipt of income or of other enjoyment of the transferred property by the transferee or by the beneficiary (other than by the donor himself) during the interim between the making of the initial transfer and the relinquishment or termination of the power operates to free such income or other enjoyment from the power, and constitutes a gift of such income or of such other enjoyment taxable as of the calendar year of its receipt. If property is transferred in trust to pay the income to A for life with remainder to B, powers to distribute corpus to A, and to withhold income from A for future distribution to B, are powers to change the beneficiaries of the transferred property.

(g) If a donor transfers property to himself as trustee (or to himself and some other person, not possessing a substantial adverse interest, as trustees), and retains no beneficial interest in the trust property and no power over it except fiduciary powers, the exercise or nonexercise of which is limited by a fixed or ascertainable standard, to change the beneficiaries of the transferred property, the donor has made a completed gift and the entire value of the transferred property is subject to the gift tax.

(h) If a donor delivers a properly indorsed stock certificate to the donee or the donee's agent, the gift is completed for gift tax purposes on the date of delivery. If the donor delivers the certificate to his bank or broker as his agent, or to the issuing corporation or its transfer agent, for transfer into the name of the donee, the gift is completed on the date the stock is transferred on the books of the corporation.

(j) If the donor contends that a power is of such nature as to render the gift incomplete, and hence not subject to the tax as of the calendar year of the initial transfer, the transaction shall be disclosed in the return and evidence showing all relevant facts, including a copy of the instrument of transfer, should be submitted.

Sec. 25.2512-6. Valuation of certain life insurance and annuity contracts. The value of a life insurance contract or of a contract for the payment of an annuity issued by a company regularly engaged in the selling of contracts of that character is established through the sale of the particular contract by the company, or through the sale by the company of comparable contracts. As valuation of an insurance policy through sale of comparable contracts is not readily ascertainable when the gift is of a contract which has been in force for some time and on which further premium payments are to be made, the value may be approximated by adding to the interpolated terminal reserve at the date of the gift the proportionate part of the gross premium last paid before the date of the gift which covers the period extending beyond that date. If, however, because of the unusual nature of the contract such approximation is not reasonably close to the full value, this method may not be used.

The following examples, so far as relating to life insurance contracts, are of gifts of such contracts on which there are no accrued dividends or outstanding indebtedness.

Example (1). A donor purchases from a life insurance company for the benefit of another a life insurance contract or a contract for the payment of an annuity. The value of the gift is the cost of the contract.

Example (2). An annuitant purchased from a life insurance company a single payment annuity contract by the terms of which he was entitled to receive payments of $1,200 annually for the duration of his life. Five years subsequent to such purchase, and when of the age of 50 years, he gratuitously assigns the contract. The value of the gift is the amount which the company would charge for an annuity contract providing for the payment of $1,200 annually for the life of a person 50 years of age.

Example (3). A donor owning a life insurance policy on which no further payments are to be made to the company (e.g., a single premium policy or paid-up policy) makes a gift of the contract. The value of the gift is the amount which the company would charge for a single premium contract of the same specified amount on the life of a person of the age of the insured.

Example (4). A gift is made four months after the last premium due date of an ordinary life insurance policy issued nine years and four months prior to the gift thereof by the insured, who was 35 years of age at date of issue. The gross annual premium is $2,811. The computation follows:

Terminal reserve at end of tenth year	$14,601.00
Terminal reserve at end of ninth year	12,965.00
Increase	1,636.00
One-third of such increase (the gift having been made four months following the last preceding premium due date), is	545.33
Terminal reserve at end of ninth year	12,965.00
Interpolated terminal reserve at date of gift	13,510.33
Two-thirds of gross premium ($2,811)	1,874.00
Value of the gift	15,384.33

Sec. 25.2513-1

(b) The provisions of this section will apply to gifts made during a particular calendar year only if both spouses signify their consent to treat all gifts made to third parties during that calendar year by both spouses while married to each other as having been made one-half by each spouse. As to the manner and time for signifying consent see §25.2513-2. Such consent, if signified with respect to any calendar year, is effective with respect to all gifts made to third parties during such year except as follows:

(1) If the consenting spouses were not married to each other during a portion of the calendar year, the consent is not effective with respect to any gifts made during such portion of the calendar year. Where the consent is signified by an executor or administrator of a deceased spouse, the consent is not effective with respect to gifts made by the surviving spouse during the portion of the calendar year that his spouse was deceased.

(2) If either spouse was a nonresident not a citizen of the United States during any portion of the calendar year, the consent is not effective with respect to any gift made during that portion of the calendar year.

(3) The consent is not effective with respect to a gift by one spouse of a property interest over which he created in his spouse a general power of appointment (as defined in section 2514(c)).

(4) If one spouse transferred property in part to his spouse and in part to third parties, the consent is effective with respect to the interest transferred to third parties only insofar as such interest is ascertainable at the time of the gift and hence severable from the interest transferred to his spouse. See §25.2512-5 for the principles to be applied in the valuation of annuities, life estates, terms for years, remainders and reversions.

(5) The consent applies alike to gifts made by one spouse alone and to gifts made partly by each spouse, provided such gifts were to third parties and do not fall within any of the exceptions set forth in subparagraphs (1) through (4) of this paragraph. The consent may not be applied only to a portion of the property interest constituting such gifts. For example, a wife may not treat gifts made by her spouse from his separate property to third parties as having been made one-half by her if her spouse does not consent to treat gifts made by her to third parties during the same calendar year as having been made one-half by him. If the consent is effectively signified on either the husband's return or the wife's return, all gifts made by the spouses to third parties (except as described in subparagraphs (1) through (4) of this paragraph), during the calendar year will be treated as having been made one-half by each spouse.

Sec. 25.2513-2

(c) The executor or administrator of a deceased spouse, or the guardian or committee of a legally incompetent spouse, as the case may be, may signify the consent.

Sec. 25.2514-1

(b) . . .

(2) *Relation to other sections.* For purposes of §§25.2514-1 through 25.2514-3, the term "power of appointment" does not include powers reserved by a donor to himself. No provision of section 2514 or of §§25.2514-1 through 25.2514-3 is to be construed as in any way limiting the application of any other section of the Internal Revenue Code or of these regulations. The power of the owner of a property interest already possessed by him to dispose of his interest, and nothing more, is not a power of appointment, and the interest is includible in the amount of his gifts to the extent it would be includible under section 2511 or other provisions of the Internal Revenue Code. For

example, if a trust created by S provides for payment of the income to A for life with power in A to appoint the entire trust property by deed during her lifetime to a class consisting of her children, and a further power to dispose of the entire corpus by will to anyone, including her estate, and A exercises the inter vivos power in favor of her children, she has necessarily made a transfer of her income interest which constitutes a taxable gift under section 2511(a), without regard to section 2514. This transfer also results in a relinquishment of her general power to appoint by will, which constitutes a transfer under section 2514 if the power was created after October 21, 1942.

(c) *Definition of "general power of appointment"* — (1) *In general.* The term "general power of appointment" as defined in section 2514(c) means any power of appointment exercisable in favor of the person possessing the power (referred to as the "possessor"), his estate, his creditors, or the creditors of his estate, except (i) joint powers, to the extent provided in §§25.2514-2 and 25.2514-3 and (ii) certain powers limited by an ascertainable standard, to the extent provided in subparagraph (2) of this paragraph. A power of appointment exercisable to meet the estate tax, or any other taxes, debts, or charges which are enforceable against the possessor or his estate, is included within the meaning of a power of appointment exercisable in favor of the possessor, his estate, his creditors, or the creditors of his estate. A power of appointment exercisable for the purpose of discharging a legal obligation of the possessor or for his pecuniary benefit is considered a power of appointment exercisable in favor of the possessor or his creditors. However, for purposes of §§25.2514-1 through 25.2514-3, a power of appointment not otherwise considered to be a general power of appointment is not treated as a general power of appointment merely by reason of the fact that an appointee may, in fact, be a creditor of the possessor or his estate. A power of appointment is not a general power if by its terms it is either —

(a) Exercisable only in favor of one or more designated persons or classes other than the possessor or his creditors, or the possessor's estate or the creditors of his estate, or

(b) Expressly not exercisable in favor of the possessor or his creditors, the possessor's estate or the creditors of his estate. A beneficiary may have two powers under the same instrument, one of which is a general power of appointment and the other of which is not. For example, a beneficiary may have a general power to withdraw a limited portion of trust corpus during his life, and a further power exercisable during his lifetime to appoint the corpus among his children. The latter power is not a general power of appointment (but its exercise may cause a release of the former power; see example in paragraph (b)(2) of this section).

Sec. 25.2514-3

(c) *Partial releases, lapses, and disclaimers of general powers created after October 21, 1942.* (1) The general principles set forth in §25.2511-2 for determining whether a donor of property (or of a property right or interest) has divested himself of all or any portion of his interest therein to the extent necessary to effect a completed gift are applicable in determining whether a partial release of a power of appointment constitutes a taxable gift. Thus, if a general power of appointment is partially released so that thereafter the donor may still appoint among a limited class of persons not including himself the partial release does not effect a complete gift, since the possessor of the power has retained the right to designate the ultimate beneficiaries of the property over which he holds the power and since it is only the termination of such control which completes a gift.

(e) *Examples.* The application of this section may be further illustrated by the following examples in each of which it is assumed, unless otherwise stated, that S has transferred property in trust after October 21, 1942, with the remainder payable to R at L's death, and that neither L nor R has any interest in or power over the enjoyment of the trust property except as is indicated separately in each example:

Example (1). The income is payable to L for life. L has the power to cause the income to be paid to R. The exercise of the right constitutes the making of a transfer of property under section 2511. L's power does not constitute a power of appointment since it is only a power to dispose of his income interest, a right otherwise possessed by him.

Example (2). The income is to be accumulated during L's life. L has the power to have the income distributed to himself. If L's power is limited by an ascertainable standard (relating to health, etc.) as defined in paragraph (c)(2) of §25.2514-1, the lapse of such power will not constitute a transfer of property for gift tax purposes. If L's power is not so limited, its lapse or release during L's lifetime may constitute a transfer of property for gift tax purposes. See especially paragraph (c)(4) of §25.2514-3.

Example (3). The income is to be paid to L for life. L has a power, exercisable at any time, to cause corpus to be distributed to himself. L has a general power of appointment over the remainder interest, the release of which constitutes a transfer for gift tax purposes of the remainder interest. If in this example L had a power to cause the corpus to be distributed only to X, L would have a power of appointment which is not a general power of appointment, the exercise or release of which would not constitute a transfer of property for purposes of the gift tax.

Example (4). The income is payable to L for life. R has the right to cause the corpus to be distributed to L at any time. R's power is not a power of appointment, but merely a right to dispose of his remainder interest, a right already possessed by him. In such a case, the exercise of the right constitutes the making of a transfer of property under section 2511 of the value, if any, of his remainder interest. See paragraph (c) of §25.2511-1.

Example (5). The income is to be paid to L. R has the right to appoint the corpus to himself at any time. R's general power of appointment over the corpus includes a general power to dispose of L's income interest therein. The lapse or release of R's general power over the income interest during his life may constitute the making of a transfer of property. See especially paragraph (c)(4) of §25.2514-3.

Sec. 25.2515-1

(c) . . .

(2) *Proportion of consideration attributable to appreciation.* Any general appreciation (appreciation due to fluctuations in market value) in the value of the property occurring between two successive contribution dates which can readily be measured and which can be determined with reasonable certainty to be allocable to any particular contribution or contributions previously furnished is to be treated, for the purpose of the computations in §§25.2515-3 and 25.2515-4, as though it were additional consideration furnished by the person who furnished the prior consideration. Any general depreciation in value is treated in a comparable manner. For the purpose of the first sentence of this subparagraph, successive contribution dates are the two consecutive dates on which any contributions to the tenancy are made, not necessarily by the same party. Further, appreciation allocable to the prior consideration falls in the same class as the prior consideration to which

it relates. The application of this subparagraph may be illustrated by the following examples:

Example (2). In 1955 real property was purchased by H and W and conveyed to them as tenants by the entirety. The purchase price of the property was $15,000 of which H contributed $10,000 and W, $5,000. In 1960 when the fair market value of the property is $21,000, W makes improvements thereto of $5,000. The property then is sold for $26,000. The appreciation in value of $6,000 results in an additional contribution of $4,000 (10,000/15,000 × $6,000) by H, and an additional contribution by W of $2,000 (5,000/15,000 × $6,000). H's total contribution to the tenancy is $14,000 ($10,000 + $4,000) and W's total contribution is $12,000 ($5,000 + $2,000 + $5,000).

(d) *Gift upon termination of tenancy by the entirety* — (1) *In general.* Upon the termination of the tenancy, whether created before, during, or subsequent to the calendar year 1955, a gift may result, depending upon the disposition made of the proceeds of the termination (whether the proceeds be in the form of cash, property, or interests in property). A gift may result notwithstanding the fact that the contribution of either spouse to the tenancy was treated as a gift. See §25.2515-3 for the method of determining the amount of any gift which may result from the termination of the tenancy in those cases in which no portion of the consideration contributed was treated as a gift by the spouses in the year in which furnished. See §25.2515-4 for the method of determining the amount of any gift which may result from the termination of the tenancy in those cases in which all or a portion of the consideration contributed was treated as constituting a gift by the spouses in the year in which furnished. See §25.2515-2 for the procedure to be followed by a donor who elects under section 2515(c) to treat the creation of a tenancy by the entirety (or the making of additions to its value) as a transfer subject to the gift tax in the year in which the transfer is made, and for the method of determining the amount of the gift.

(2) *Termination* — (i) *In general.* Except as indicated in subdivision (ii) of this subparagraph, a termination of a tenancy is effected when all or a portion of the property so held by the spouses is sold, exchanged, or otherwise disposed of, by gift or in any other manner, or when the spouses through any form of conveyance or agreement become tenants in common of the property or otherwise alter the nature of their respective interests in the property formerly held by them as tenants by the entirety. In general, any increase in the indebtedness on a tenancy constitutes a termination of the tenancy to the extent of the increase in the indebtedness. However, such an increase will not constitute a termination of the tenancy to the extent that the increase is offset by additions to the tenancy within a reasonable time after such increase. Such additions (to the extent of the increase in the indebtedness) shall not be treated by the spouses as contributions within the meaning of paragraph (c) of this section.

(ii) *Exchange or reinvestment.* A termination is not considered as effected to the extent that the property subject to the tenancy is exchanged for other real property, the title to which is held by the spouses in an identical tenancy. For this purpose, a tenancy is considered identical if the proportionate values of the spouses' respective rights (other than any change in the proportionate values resulting solely from the passing of time) are identical to those held in the property which was sold. In addition the sale, exchange, (other than an exchange described above), or other disposition of property held as tenants by the entirety is not considered as a termination if all three of the following conditions are satisfied:

(a) There is no division of the proceeds of the sale, exchange or other disposition of the property held as tenants by the entirety;

(b) On or before the due date for the filing of a gift tax return for the calendar year in which the property held as tenants by the entirety was sold, exchanged, or otherwise disposed of, the spouses enter into a binding contract for the purchase of other real property; and

(c) After the sale, exchange, or other disposition of the former property and within a reasonable time after the date of the contract referred to in subdivision (b), such other real property actually is acquired by the spouses and held by them in an identical tenancy.

To the extent that all three of the conditions set forth in this subdivision are not met (whether by reason of the death of one of the spouses or for any other reason), the provisions of the preceding sentence shall not apply, and the sale, exchange or other disposition of the property will constitute a termination of the tenancy. As used in subdivision (c) the expression "a reasonable time" means the time which, under the particular facts in each case, is needed for those matters which are incident to the acquisition of the other property (i.e., perfecting of title, arranging for financing, construction, etc.). The fact that proceeds of a sale are deposited in the name of one tenant or of both tenants separately or jointly as a convenience does not constitute a division within the meaning of subdivision (a) if the other requirements of this subdivision are met. The proceeds of a sale, exchange, or other disposition of property held as tenants by the entirety will be deemed to have been used for the purchase of other real property if applied to the purchase or construction of improvements which themselves constitute real property and which are additions to other real property held by the spouses in a tenancy identical to that in which they held the property which was sold, exchanged, or otherwise disposed of.

Sec. 25.2515-2. Tenancies by the entirety; transfers treated as gifts; manner of election and valuation

(a) The election to treat the creation of a tenancy by the entirety in real property, or additions made to its value, as constituting a gift in the year in which effected, shall be exercised by including the value of such gifts in the gift tax return of the donor for the calendar year in which the tenancy was created, or the additions in value were made to the property. See section 6019 and the regulations thereunder. The election may be exercised only in a return filed within the time prescribed by law, or before the expiration of any extension of time granted pursuant to law for the filing of the return. See section 6075 for the time for filing the gift tax return, and section 6081 for extensions of time for filing the return, together with the regulations thereunder. In order to make the election, a gift tax return must be filed for the calendar year in which the tenancy was created, or additions in value thereto made, even though the value of the gift involved does not exceed the amount of the exclusion provided by section 2503(b).

(b) If the donor spouse exercises the election as provided in paragraph (a) of this section, the amount of the gift at the creation of the tenancy is the amount of his contribution to the tenancy less the value of his retained interest in it, determined as follows:

(1) If under the law of the jurisdiction governing the rights of the spouses, either spouse, acting alone, can bring about a severance of his or her interest in the property, the value of the donor's retained interest is one-half the value of the property.

(2) If, under the law of the jurisdiction governing the rights of the spouses

each is entitled to share in the income or other enjoyment of the property but neither, acting alone, may defeat the right of the survivor of them to the whole of the property, the amount of retained interest of the donor is determined by use of the appropriate actuarial factors for the spouses at their respective attained ages at the time the transaction is effected.

(c) Factors representing the respective interests of the spouses, under a tenancy by the entirety, at their attained ages at the time of the transaction may be found in, or readily computed with the use of the tables contained in, the actuarial pamphlet referred to in paragraph (e) of §25.2512-5. State law may provide that the husband only is entitled to all of the income or other enjoyment of the real property held as tenants by the entirety, and the wife's interest consists only of the right of survivorship with no right of severance. In such a case, a special factor may be needed to determine the value of the interests of the respective spouses. See paragraph (e) of §25.2512-5 for the procedure for obtaining special factors from the Commissioner in cases requiring their use.

(d) The application of this paragraph may be illustrated by the following example:

Example. A husband with his own funds acquires real property valued at $10,000 and has it conveyed to himself and his wife as tenants by the entirety. Under the law of the jurisdiction governing the rights of the parties, each spouse is entitled to share in the income from the property but neither spouse acting alone could bring about a severance of his or her interest. The husband elects to treat the transfer as a gift in the year in which effected. At the time of transfer, the ages of the husband and wife are 45 and 40, respectively, on their birthdays nearest to the date of transfer. The value of the gift to the wife is $5,502.90, computed as follows:

Value of property transferred	$10,000.00
Less $10,000 × .44971 (factor for value of donor's retained rights)	4,497.10
Value of gift	$ 5,502.90

Sec. 25.2521-1. Specific exemption

(a) In determining the amount of taxable gifts for the calendar year there may be deducted, if the donor was a resident or citizen of the United States at the time the gifts were made, a specific exemption of $30,000, less the sum of the amounts claimed and allowed as an exemption in prior calendar years. The exemption, at the option of the donor, may be taken in the full amount of $30,000 in a single calendar year, or be spread over a period of years in such amounts as the donor sees fit, but after the limit has been reached no further exemption is allowable. Except as otherwise provided in a tax convention between the United States and another country, a donor who was a nonresident not a citizen of the United States at the time the gift or gifts were made is not entitled to this exemption.

Sec. 25.2523(b)-1(c)

(2) In general, the principles illustrated by the examples under paragraph (b) of this section are applicable in determining whether the marital deduction may be taken with respect to a property interest transferred to the donee spouse subject to the retention by the donor of an interest in the same property. The application of this paragraph may be further illustrated by the following example:

Example. The donor purchased three annuity contracts for the benefit of his wife and himself. The first contract provided for payments to the wife for life, with refund to the donor in case the aggregate payments made to the wife were less than the cost of the contract. The second contract provided for payments to the donor for life, and then to the wife for life if she survived the donor. The third contract provided for payments to the donor and his wife for their joint lives and then to the survivor of them for life. No marital deduction may be taken with respect to the gifts resulting from the purchases of the contracts since, in the case of each contract, the donor may possess or enjoy a part of the property after the termination or failure of the interest transferred to the wife.

Sec. 25.2523(d)-1. **Joint interests.** Section 2523(d) provides that if a property interest is transferred to the donee spouse as sole joint tenant with the donor or as a tenant by the entirety, the interest of the donor in the property which exists solely by reason of the possibility that the donor may survive the donee spouse, or that there may occur a severance of the tenancy, is not for the purposes of section 2523(b), to be considered as an interest retained by the donor in himself. Under this provision, the fact that the donor may, as surviving tenant, possess or enjoy the property after the termination of the interest transferred to the donee spouse does not preclude the allowance of the marital deduction with respect to the latter interest. Thus, if the donor purchased real property in the name of himself and wife as tenants by the entirety, or as joint tenants with right of survivorship and, pursuant to the provisions of section 2515(c), elected to treat such transaction as a completed gift in the calendar year effected, a marital deduction equal to one-half the value of the interest of the donee spouse in such property may be taken. See paragraph (c) of §25.2523(b)-1, and section 2524.

Sec. 25.2523(e)-1(g)

(2) The power of the donee spouse must be a power to appoint the entire interest or a specific portion of it as unqualified owner (and free of the trust if a trust is involved, or free of the joint tenancy if a joint tenancy is involved) or to appoint the entire interest or a specific portion of it as a part of her estate (and free of the trust if a trust is involved), that is, in effect, to dispose of it to whomsoever she pleases. Thus, if the donor transferred property to a son and the donee spouse as joint tenants with right of survivorship and under local law the donee spouse has a power of severance exercisable without consent of the other joint tenant, and by exercising this power could acquire a one-half interest in the property as a tenant in common, her power of severance will satisfy the condition set forth in paragraph (a)(3) of this section that she have a power of appointment in favor of herself or her estate. However, if the donee spouse entered into a binding agreement with the donor to exercise the power only in favor of their issue, that condition is not met. An interest transferred in trust will not be regarded as failing to satisfy the condition merely because takers in default of the donee spouse's exercise of the power are designated by the donor. The donor may provide that, in default of exercise of the power, the trust shall continue for an additional period.

Sec. 301.7701-4. **Trusts**

(a) *Ordinary trusts.* In general, the term "trust" as used in the Internal Revenue Code refers to an arrangement created either by a will or by an inter vivos declaration whereby trustees take title to property for the purpose of protecting or conserving it for the beneficiaries under the ordinary rules applied in chancery or probate courts. Usually the beneficiaries of such a trust do no more than accept the benefits thereof and are not the voluntary planners or creators of the trust arrangement. However, the beneficiaries of such a trust may be the persons who create it and it will be recognized as a trust under the Internal Revenue Code if it was created for the purpose of protecting or conserving the trust property for beneficiaries who stand in the same relation to the trust as they would if the trust had been created by others for them. Generally speaking, an arrangement will be treated as a trust under the Internal Revenue Code if it can be shown that the purpose of the arangement is to vest in trustees responsibility for the protection and conservation of property for beneficiaries who cannot share in the discharge of this responsibility and, therefore, are not associates in a joint enterprise for the conduct of business for profit.

(b) *Business trusts.* There are other arrangements which are known as trusts because the legal title to property is conveyed to trustees for the benefit of beneficiaries, but which are not classified as trusts for purposes of the Internal Revenue Code because they are not simply arrangements to protect or conserve the property for the beneficiaries. These trusts, which are often known as business or commercial trusts, generally are created by the beneficiaries simply as a device to carry on a profit-making business which normally would have been carried on through business organizations that are classified as corporations or partnerships under the Internal Revenue Code. However, the fact that the corpus of the trust is not supplied by the beneficiaries is not sufficient reason in itself for classifying the arrangement as an ordinary trust rather than as an association or partnership. The fact that any organization is technically cast in the trust form, by conveying title to property to trustees for the benefit of persons designated as beneficiaries, will not change the real character of the organization if applying the principles set forth in §§301.7701-2 and 301.7701-3, the organization more nearly resembles an association or a partnership than a trust.

A P P E N D I X   V I I

Participation by Laymen in
Estate Planning

To the extent that estate planning involves the practice of law, only lawyers are authorized to do the work. In this connection, lawyers must keep in mind Canon 47 of the Canons of Professional Ethics of the American Bar Association, which provides as follows: "No lawyer shall permit his professional services, or his name, to be used in aid of, or to make possible, the unauthorized practice of law by any lay agency, personal or corporate."

Set forth below are various matters that relate to the participation by laymen in estate planning.

1. OPINION OF AMERICAN BAR ASSOCIATION COMMITTEE ON UNAUTHORIZED PRACTICE OF THE LAW IN REGARD TO ESTATE PLANNING

This Committee has received inquiries concerning the propriety of the conduct of corporations and individuals who are not lawyers but who, through advertisements, brochures, orally or otherwise, solicit legal work or hold themselves out to the public as being available to give legal assistance in the field of estate planning or to do the whole job of planning an estate.

The phrase "estate planning" has come into existence in recent years to refer to the orderly arrangement of an individual's assets so as to provide most effectively for the economic needs of himself while living and of those dependent upon him after his death. At the outset it should be recognized that there are certain lay activities which are legitimate aspects of estate planning and which do not involve legal work, but which are in the nature of an analysis of the facts and assets of an estate in relation to economic needs, and may extend to giving general information as to laws affecting the disposition of estates, though without any specific application thereof to a particular estate or individual situation. These activities may be properly performed by persons who are not lawyers, and are discussed later in this opinion. In general, however, pursued to its proper conclusion, estate planning necessarily involves the application of legal principles of the law of wills and decedents' estates, the law of trusts and future interests, the law of real and personal property, the law of taxation, practice in the probate and chancery courts, or other fields of law. When such is the case, the work involved in estate planning includes legal research, the giving of legal advice or the drafting of legal instruments.

There can thus be no question that estate planning, except where it is in the nature of an analysis of the facts and assets of an estate as above described, involves legal work and constitutes the practice of law. When engaged in by an individual who is not a lawyer, or by a corporation, it is the unauthorized practice of law. Nor does it become any the less the practice of law because the suggestion is made that the legal advice given or legal work done should be reviewed by an attorney. It is well settled that both corporations and laymen are prohibited from practicing law directly, and that they may not practice law indirectly by hiring lawyers to practice law for them. Accordingly, neither corporations nor laymen may engage in estate planning by soliciting the legal work involved and then hiring lawyers to perform it. This is also the unauthorized practice of law. In addition, under Canon 47 of the Canons of Professional Ethics of the American Bar Association no lawyer shall permit his professional services, or his name, to be used in aid of, or to make possible, the unauthorized practice of law by any lay agency, personal or corporate.

It is elementary that under Canon 27 lawyers are forbidden to solicit legal employment by circulars, advertisements, or otherwise. Thus, no lawyer may solicit legal work in the field of estate planning or be employed to do such work for a corporation or a layman which does. But the public could not be protected by prohibiting the lawyer from soliciting legal work in the field of estate planning, if at the same time laymen and lay agencies were permitted, in any guise, to advertise a claimed legal competence in this field. It should be clear, therefore, that the holding out by any lay agency to the public, directly or indirectly, overtly or subtly, of its willingness to perform legal services in the field of estate planning is itself the unauthorized practice of law. Also, no lay agency may hold itself out to the public as willing to do the whole job of "estate planning" without becoming engaged in the unauthorized practice of law.

In addition, the lawyer-client relationship requires a duty of absolute loyalty to the client, and undivided allegiance. Under Canons 6 and 35 of the Canons of Professional Ethics the lawyer cannot permit his professional services to be controlled or exploited by a lay agency intervening between him and his client.

Also, under Canon 34 lawyers may not divide fees with laymen, and this principle applies to fees for legal work in the field of estate planning. Moreover, the sharing by a layman of a lawyer's fees constitutes the unauthorized practice of law.

Illustrative of the treatment of the subject in the courts is the decision of the Superior Court of Cook County, Illinois, in Chicago Bar Association v. Financial Planning, Inc.,[1] decided March 21, 1958, in which the court held that certain estate planning services involved the giving of "legal advice on some of the most important problems which can arise during a man's lifetime and after his death," adding that "Even if this advice were confined to tax savings alone, it still would amount to the practice of law . . ." and "the contention that the advice is comprised merely of suggestions, and is always subject to be reviewed by a lawyer, is no excuse for the conduct of the defendants. The practice of law should be confined to lawyers without the interposition of unauthorized practitioners who solicit this business directly or indirectly."

The decree in this case permanently enjoined the defendants, their agents and employees from:

    (a) Giving legal counsel and advice,
    (b) Rendering legal opinions,
    (c) Preparing, drafting and construing legal documents,

---

[1] This case is reported in 26 Law Week 2662, and 24 Unauthorized Practice News, No. 2, page 29.

(d) Preparing estate plans which embody legal analysis, counsel and advice,

(e) Holding themselves out as persons who prepare estate plans embodying legal analysis, counsel and advice,

(f) Charging and collecting fees for legal counsel, advice, or services rendered by them, or their agents, or employees,

(g) From practicing law in any form, or holding themselves out as having a right to practice law, or soliciting employment to prepare estate plans embodying legal analysis, counsel and advice, or from charging, or collecting fees, or payments for legal services rendered by said defendants and each of them or their agents, or employees.

It is not intended by the opinion of this Committee to proscribe activities of those groups which serve various fields related to estate planning unless they involve the performance of legal services as outlined herein. Activities geared to motivating the individual concerned to do something about his affairs and to seek the advice of his own lawyer as early as possible, preferably from the outset, with regard to the development of an over-all estate plan, are in the public interest. Advice on matters of law with respect to a particular factual situation of the individual concerned, however, must not be given.

The activities of lay groups described above should conform to the standards of propriety set forth in the several Statements of Principles developed through the conference method between the American Bar Association and various business and professional groups. Moreover, because of the shadowy borderline between an analysis of facts and assets of an estate and the application of legal principles to them, it is clearly within the spirit of the several Statements of Principles that the activities of these groups should be performed in close cooperation with the client's own attorney. It is contemplated that any disputes which may arise with respect to the activities of such business and professional groups shall be governed by such Statements of Principles. The understandings reached in these Principles have served to encourage the public to seek proper legal guidance, the lay groups not to transgress upon the sphere of activity properly reserved for the legal profession, and to bring about better understanding and cooperation between these groups and the Bar.

F. Trowbridge vom Baur,
  Chairman, *Washington, D.C.*
Wayland B. Cedarquist,
  Chicago, Illinois
E. N. Eisenhower,
  Tacoma, Washington
Jonathan F. Ellis,
  Winsted, Connecticut

Terrell Marshall,
  Little Rock, Arkansas
H. H. Perry, Jr.,
  Albany, Georgia
Raymond Reisler,
  Brooklyn, New York

2. STATEMENT ON ESTATE PLANNING BY NATIONAL CONFERENCE OF LAWYERS AND REPRESENTATIVES OF AMERICAN BANKERS ASSOCIATION, TRUST DIVISION

The Statement of General Policies adopted by the National Conference Group formed by the American Bar Association and the Trust Division of the American Bankers Association on September 27, 1941 and thereafter approved by both Associations is hereby reaffirmed.

The proper planning of an individual's estate, so as to provide for the orderly arrangement of his property and affairs in such manner as to take care of his needs and those he may wish to benefit after his death, is definitely in the public interest. Trust institutions and lawyers working together can be of great public aid in this field. The consideration of an estate plan requires expert and considered knowledge as to the investments and as to the way in which investments are to be dealt with in an estate plan. Corporate fiduciaries, through their broad experience in relation to these matters, are of substantial assistance. The setting up of the estate plan sometimes requires conferences which have to do with the kind and character of the assets of the estate in question. In connection with these matters, there are bound to arise, sometimes at the outset and certainly in the course of the planning of the estate, numerous legal problems involving law of all kinds in which it is essentially necessary for the person seeking to plan his estate to have competent legal advice. The harmonious understanding of the proper functions of corporate fiduciaries and lawyers in matters of this kind has been developed and made great progress since the creation of our National Conference.

A trust institution is granted charter powers to act as fiduciary and to conduct a trust business. It may analyze the assets and estates of its customers and discuss with them the problems, other than those involving the giving of legal advice, of disposition of such assets and estates and the services and facilities of the trust institutions that may be used in aid of carrying out such dispositions. The experience acquired by trust institutions in handling trust estates of various kinds is of great value in assisting a person planning his estate. Hence trust institutions are often consulted by their customers in relation to these matters. However, any such discussions involving the disposition of the assets and estates of such customers should be general and preliminary only and subject to the consultation and advice of the customer's own lawyer.

The primary purpose of participation in estate planning by the trust institution should be to motivate its customer to initiate the arrangements for the orderly disposition of his assets and to confer with his own lawyer or a lawyer of his choosing regarding those arrangements. In reviewing the assets and estate of its customer, the trust institution should at the earliest practicable date include the customer's own lawyer in the development of the plan.

Because the formulation and execution of a plan for the disposition of a customer's assets necessarily involves the application of legal principles, of the law of wills and decedent's estates, the law of trusts and future interests, the law of real and personal property, and the law of taxation, as well as practice in the Probate and Chancery Courts, and other fields of law, advice in respect thereto is the responsibility of the customer's own lawyer.

Accordingly, there should be no implication in its advertising by a trust institution that legal services will be rendered by it or that the services of a lawyer are unnecessary or only ministerial. Trust company advertising should be dignified and should not overstate or overemphasize its qualifications in this field.

Since the adoption of the original Statement of General Policies on September 27, 1941 and the creation of this National Conference Group, it is gratifying to note the very great cooperation that has developed between corporate fiduciaries and lawyers in rendering this important mutual service to the American public.

Representing the American Bar Association

Thomas J. Boodell, Co-Chairman
A. James Casner
Andrew Hourigan, Jr.
Edwin M. Otterbourg
Joseph Trachtman

Representing the American Bankers Association, Trust Division

Don H. McLucas, Co-Chairman
Harry M. Bardt
Carlysle A. Bethel
William H. Gambrell
Joseph W. White

3. STATEMENT OF PRINCIPLES FORMULATED BY THE NATIONAL CONFERENCE OF LAWYERS AND REPRESENTATIVES OF AMERICAN BANKERS ASSOCIATION, TRUST DIVISION

Statement of General Policies [2]

Trust institutions are corporations engaged in the business of administering estates and trusts and in other trust activities, and acting as agents in all appropriate cases. Legal services are required in connection with many phases of trust business. Trust institutions are not authorized to engage in the practice of law. For the protection of the public and in aid of the administration of justice, the practice of law has, by the courts and legislatures, been delegated and restricted to attorneys at law, members of the bar. Attorneys at law constitute a professional group that performs essential legal functions in the conduct of trust business and have a community of interest with trust institutions in the common aim of service to the public.

It is in the interest of the public that proper principles, with respect to functions of trust institutions in relation to the practice of law and to functions of attorneys at law with relation to trust business, be set forth and agreed upon by trust institutions and members of the bar to guide trust institutions and attorneys at law alike in their important relationships in this public service and as a basis for agreements between trust institutions and groups or associations of attorneys at law. Therefore, to that end, the following declaration of policies is adopted by the National Conference

[2] Adopted on September 27, 1941, by the National Conference Group composed of five representatives of the American Bar Association and five representatives of the American Bankers Association, Trust Division. Approved by the Executive Committee of the Trust Division of the American Bankers Association on September 29, 1941, and approved by the American Bar Association on October 1, 1941. — ED.

Group, a joint Committee of the American Bar Association and the Trust Division of the American Bankers Association.

I. Trust institutions should neither perform services which constitute the practice of law nor otherwise engage in such practice; therefore, they should not draw wills or other legal documents or perform services in the administration of estates and trusts where such acts by law or local procedure are considered the practice of law.

II. The development of trust business by a trust institution should be on the basis of assistance to the customer in the use of the institution's trust services and facilities as related to his business or financial matters.

In all legal questions which may arise in the development of trust business, the trust institution should advise the customer to confer with his own lawyer or a lawyer of his own choosing.

III. The trust institution should respect and not interfere with the professional relationship existing between an attorney and his client, and an attorney should respect and not interfere with the business relationship existing between a trust institution and its customer. It is recognized, however, that in all cases the interest of the client is paramount. An attorney at law must reserve the right to advise his client with respect to the choice of a fiduciary. The attorney should not seek to displace the institution of the client's choice by inducing the appointment of some other institution or individual unless the attorney believes the client's affairs demand services peculiar to some particular institution or individual, or where the attorney believes that the true interest of the client will suffer if such substitution is not made.

If the trust institution is requested by its customer to recommend counsel, any counsel so recommended should be in a position to advise the customer disinterestedly, and it is preferable that the trust institution, when making such recommendations of counsel to its customer, submit, without recommending one above another, the names of several attorneys in whom it has confidence, leaving the choice of the selection to the customer.

IV. A trust institution, qualified and authorized by law as a legitimate business enterprise, has an inherent right to advertise its trust services in appropriate ways. It should not, directly or indirectly, offer to give legal advice or render legal services, and there should be no invitation to the public, either direct or by inference in such advertisement, to bring their legal problems to the trust institution. Its advertisement should be dignified and the qualifications of the institution should not be overstated or overemphasized, and it should not be implied in any advertisement that the services of a lawyer are only secondary or ministerial, or that by the employment of the services of the trust institution, the employment of counsel to advise the customer is unnecessary.

V. In the employment of counsel, the trust institution should endeavor, in the absence of compelling reasons to the contrary, to engage the attorney who drew the instrument, or who represented the testator or donor, to perform any legal work required in the course of trust or estate administration. . . .

The National Conference Group hereby recommends to state and local bar and trust organizations the creation of joint conference committees, composed equally of representatives of the trust institutions and the bar associations, for the purpose of implementing and making effective the carrying out of these principles and the amicable and cooperative solution of disputes or misunderstandings in relation thereto.

Statement on Advertising [3]

The National Conference Group formed by the American Bar Association and the American Bankers Association Trust Division believes it in the public interest that, in the services rendered by corporate fiduciaries and by lawyers, there should be cooperation and harmony in order that the public may be best served.

It deems it desirable at this time again to call to the attention of corporate fiduciaries and lawyers of the country the following points in the Statement of Principles of Trust Institutions heretofore adopted by the Trust Division and approved by the Executive Council of the American Bankers Association on April 11, 1933:

Advertising. A trust institution has the same right as any other business enterprise to advertise its trust services in appropriate ways. Its advertisements should be dignified and not overstate or overemphasize the qualifications of the trust institutions. There should be no implication that legal services will be rendered. There should be no reflection, expressed or implied, upon other trust institutions or individuals, and the advertisements of all trust institutions should be mutually helpful.

Relationship with Bar. Attorneys at law constitute a professional group that perform essential functions in relation to trust business, and have a community of interest with trust institutions in the common end of service to the public. The maintenance of harmonious relations between trust institutions and members of the bar is in the best interests of both and of the public as well. It is a fundamental principle of this relationship that trust institutions should not engage in the practice of law.

The National Conference Group recommends to corporate fiduciaries that in accordance with the foregoing, particular care should be taken that advertisements should contain no direct or implied statement that corporate fiduciaries offer to render legal services, or that the services of a lawyer are only secondary or ministerial. . . .

A study made by this Group of numerous statements of principle adopted by state and local associations of corporate fiduciaries and by bar associations throughout the country, indicates that the principles underlying the above recommendations are generally accepted, and this statement is published as a reminder of the importance of carrying these principles into practical effect.

4. STATEMENT OF PRINCIPLES FORMULATED BY THE NATIONAL CONFERENCE OF LAWYERS AND LIFE UNDERWRITERS

Statement [4]

In recent years, much of the actual negotiation of the sale of life insurance contracts involves estate planning. The acquisition of life insurance has

[3] This statement was drawn up and published by the National Conference Group in the fall of 1940. — ED.

[4] The National Conference of Lawyers and Life Underwriters was constituted on

become a complex problem by its ever increasing relation to plans of testamentary disposition, wills and living trusts, to partnerships and close corporation contracts, and to problems of taxation. The solution of such problems requires a man to make far-reaching decisions. These decisions often are, or, upon the happening of death, become, irrevocable. The American public should therefore receive not only expert insurance service and disinterested advice but also skilled and disinterested legal guidance and advice when necessary; both are often required in problems arising out of negotiation for and use of life insurance, and when this is the case, the simultaneous and harmonious attention of a representative of each profession in solving the problems of the same client will provide the safest and most efficient service.

Fair dealing with the public and an observance of laws which have been enacted throughout the United States require that all legal service and advice should at all times be given by an individual trained in the law and duly licensed to practice; anyone who gives legal advice should be solely devoted to the interest of his client and permit no personal consideration whatsoever to weaken his exclusive loyalty to his client.

In this connection, it might well be remembered that the courts consider communications between an attorney and his client as privileged; that is, they do not compel their disclosure, while communications between a life underwriter and his client are not so considered. This distinction should, for the protection of the public, be borne in mind by the members of both professions.

For the guidance of life underwriters and of lawyers, and to insure that the public shall be protected by receiving authorized and disinterested legal advice on life insurance problems, such as those hereinabove referred to, the National Conference states:

I

The National Conference considers it to be in the interest of cooperation between life underwriters and lawyers and of better service to the public, that all lawyers be guided by the opinion of the American Bar Association's Standing Committee on Professional Ethics and Grievances, dated February 10, 1940, issued in reply to an inquiry from that Association's Standing Committee on Unauthorized Practice of Law. That opinion in full is as follows:

In the opinion of the Committee, the Lawyer's conduct in each of the following situations is ethically improper and should be condemned:

1. A life underwriter recommends a certain transaction, for example, the purchase of business life insurance. The client presents the proposed transaction to his attorney for approval or disapproval. The attorney then demands of the life underwriter, as a condition for his approval, a share in the life underwriter's commission.

2. An attorney promises a life underwriter to recommend him to the attorney's clients, provided the life underwriter will pay to the attorney a share of his commissions resulting from any business obtained from the lawyer's clients.

It should be noted, in this connection, that in most of the states participation in commissions on life insurance contracts by any person other

---

July 17, 1946, by representatives of the American Bar Association and the National Association of Life Underwriters upon due authorization by the governing bodies of the two associations. — ED.

than a duly licensed life insurance agent, has been condemned by statute or by court decision and has been declared unethical for life underwriters by their professional organizations.

3. A life underwriter proposes a certain life insurance plan to a prospective client; the client submits the proposed plan to his attorney for his legal opinion. The attorney approves the plan, but for reasons of personal advantage to himself advises the client to divert the business and to purchase the necessary life insurance not through the underwriter who submitted the plan but through another underwriter whom the attorney recommends although the interests of the client do not require such substitution.

4. An attorney promises an underwriter that if he, the underwriter, will induce his clients to refer legal business to the attorney, the attorney will pay to the underwriter a share of the fees resulting from such business.

5. To advertise himself and to promote his sale of life insurance, a life underwriter desires to use a lawyer's legal opinion in relation to a specific plan by using the lawyer's name and opinion in a general circular or as a selling document. At the underwriter's request, a lawyer furnishes such an opinion knowing (a), that the attorney's name will be thus advertised and utilized by the underwriter, and (b), that the opinion may mislead the person to whom it is exhibited to his detriment unless it is adapted to the facts of his particular case. This form of business solicitation by life underwriters has been condemned by their profession and by this Association's Committee on Unauthorized Practice of the Law.

I I

The National Conference considers it to be in the interest of cooperation between life underwriters and lawyers and of better service to the public, that all life underwriters be guided by the following principles:

(1) A life underwriter has no right to practice law or to give legal advice or to hold himself out as having such rights. He should not attempt to do so directly or indirectly. Therefore, he must never prepare for execution by his client legal documents of any kind, such as wills or codicils thereto, trust agreements, corporation charters, minutes, by-laws or business insurance agreements. When submitting an involved mode of settlement, or one which may affect a client's prior disposition of property by his Last Will and Testament, the life underwriter should suggest that the same be submitted to the client's attorney for approval.

In estate planning, all transfers of property, except simple modes of settlement under life insurance policies or changes of beneficiary thereof, should be recommended subject to the approval of the client's attorney. Since these decisions should in the final analysis be subject to the approval of the client's attorney, it is important for the life underwriter to collaborate with his client's attorney as early as possible in the negotiations so as to afford his client the safest and most effective service.

It is improper for a life underwriter, in submitting to his client an estate planning report, to attach thereto or insert therein any forms of legal instruments or of specific legal clauses.

(2) A life underwriter should never dissuade a client from seeking the advice of legal counsel. It is improper for a life underwriter to attempt to divert legal business from one attorney to another.

(3) It is improper for a life underwriter to furnish attorneys who will give legal advice to the life underwriter's clients or prospective clients.

(4) A life underwriter must never share or participate in an attorney's fee; a life underwriter must not pay directly or indirectly any part of his commission to an attorney or any other person not a life underwriter, whether or not such sharing in commissions is known to be insured.

It should be noted, in this connection, that in most of the states participation in commissions on life insurance contracts, by any person other than a duly licensed life insurance agent, has been condemned by statute or by court decision and has been declared unethical for life underwriters by their professional organizations.

(5) A life underwriter may properly obtain legal advice or a written legal opinion from an attorney for his own guidance; it is improper conduct, however, to circularize any such legal opinion, or to use it as a selling document.

Nothing herein contained is intended to restrict or limit the life underwriter's legitimate activities in measuring the client's need for life insurance, determining the amount and type needed, developing a comprehensive life insurance program in relation to the client's other plans and affairs, and selling such insurance; the ethics of his profession require him not to recommend the purchase of additional insurance unless needed. Such activities are for the benefit of those insured and their dependents only insofar as they are consistent with the foregoing statement of principles.

III

The National Conference of Lawyers and Life Underwriters recommends to state, district and local bar associations and to state and local associations of life underwriters that cooperative action be taken by them to secure adherence to the principles contained in this Statement and to dispose of misunderstandings between the two groups. The National Conference is authorized to act in an advisory capacity as a clearing house for suggestions and complaints, to aid in establishing, as far as may be practical, a country-wide recognition of these principles, and to aid in the setting up of similar conference groups in the various states and localities. It gladly offers its services in this respect to state, district and local associations of the bar and life underwriters.

Approved by

> THE NATIONAL CONFERENCE OF
> LAWYERS AND LIFE UNDERWRITERS

February 8, 1948

Ratified by

> THE AMERICAN BAR ASSOCIATION

February 24, 1948

> THE NATIONAL ASSOCIATION OF
> LIFE UNDERWRITERS

March 16, 1948

5.   STATEMENT OF PRINCIPLES WITH RESPECT TO
DISSEMINATION OF LEGAL INFORMATION BY HOME
OFFICE COUNSEL OF LIFE INSURANCE COMPANY

Statement [5]

1.   Disseminating Legal Information and Specimen Legal Documents on the Initiative of Home Counsel

A. *Information Bulletins.* — Home office counsel occasionally prepare information bulletins for distribution among the agents of the insurance company. A bulletin may describe recent developments in federal income, estate or gift tax laws.

The proper protection of the public in connection with the sale of life insurance requires that life insurance agents be as well informed as possible about legal matters that have a particular bearing on life insurance. The agent should be cautioned not to give legal advice to clients on the basis of these bulletins, but to use them for his own edification. Any discussion with clients of underlying legal principles should always be made subject to confirmation by the client's counsel.

B. *Specimen Legal Document.* — Home office counsel may properly prepare legal documents to which the insurance company is a party — for example, settlement provisions under one of the options in the insurance policy. However, preparation of legal documents to which the insurance company is not a party and that are concerned with the purchase of life insurance in a particular case or the disposition of insurance proceeds of a particular policy after the proceeds have been paid out by the company are not, in the opinion of the Conference, within the proper sphere of a home office counsel's operations.

The Conference believes that the company may furnish the insurance agent with specimen legal documents that are related to the purchase of life insurance or the disposition of insurance proceeds. The agent should be informed that these specimen legal documents are prepared and disseminated for reference by the client's own counsel in drafting the particular document. Specimen documents furnished an agent should clearly indicate that they are sample forms and that the client's own counsel should be consulted. The legal document which is to be executed must be drawn by the client's own counsel.

2.   Furnishing an Agent, on the Request of the Agent, Legal Information in Regard to a Specific Situation

The inquiries which an agent may address to home office counsel which can only be answered by giving the agent legal information may relate to a wide variety of situations. The appropriateness of the home office counsel answering the inquiry and the form which an answer should take when an answer is appropriate depend on the particular inquiry.

A. *Inquiry relating to a provision in a policy.* — The home office counsel

[5] Approved by the House of Delegates of the American Bar Association and by the Executive Committee of the American Life Convention and the Board of Directors of the Life Insurance Association of America. — ED.

should readily give an interpretation of the meaning of any language in an existing or specimen insurance policy. Such interpretation can be incorporated in a letter sent to the agent and the agent should be free to show such a letter to a client or to give the client a copy of such a letter.

If the inquiry from the agent regarding a provision in the policy involves the legal consequences of a particular provision, such as whether the settlement provision qualifies for the marital deduction under the federal estate tax law, the Conference believes that it is appropriate for the home office counsel to express to the agent his opinion with the suggestion that this be confirmed by client's counsel.

B. *Inquiry relating to provisions of legal documents other than the policy of insurance.* — If an inquiry from an agent relates to the meaning of a legal document for the purpose of determining whether the purchase of insurance of a certain type is authorized, the Conference believes that the home office counsel may properly advise the agent whether the insurance company will consider an application for insurance under such legal document, whether it will accept a premium payment, and the reasons for its conclusion.

If the inquiry from the agent refers to the tax consequences of a particular legal document in so far as the life insurance is concerned, the Conference believes that it is appropriate for home office counsel to express his opinion to the agent provided home office counsel states that his opinion should be confirmed by client's counsel.

C. *Participation of home office counsel in sales interview with agent and counsel.* — The Conference believes that when home office counsel is asked to participate in a sales interview with an agent and a client, the home office counsel should strongly urge that the client's counsel be present, both for the benefit of the client and home office counsel. The presence of home office counsel, in such an interview, will inevitably lead to the discussion of legal questions which the client might reasonably be expected to rely on in the planning of his affairs.

D. *Inquiry seeking suggestions for a particular estate plan.* — If the inquiry from the agent seeks specific suggestions which might be made to a client so that he will have an intelligent estate plan, the Conference believes that the home office counsel should confine his opinion to the aspects of the plan as it relates to insurance, with the recommendation that the client see his attorney for the formulation of the over-all estate plan.

3. **Furnishing a Person Who Is Already Insured or a Person Who Is a Prospective Client for Insurance, on the Request of such Person, Legal Advice in Regard to a Specific Situation**

When a specific inquiry is made by an insured or a prospective insured on a legal problem relating to his existing or contemplated insurance, the Conference believes that it is within the province of home office counsel to answer the inquiry, but that it is clearly improper for it to render legal advice on noninsurance subjects.

4. **Inquiry from Client's Counsel**

The Conference believes that the home office counsel should encourage the agent, insured or prospective insured to have the client's counsel direct inquiries to home office counsel.

The membership of the Conference is as follows:

Representing the American Bar Association

Thomas J. Boodell, Co-Chairman, Chicago, Illinois
Warren H. Resh, Co-Secretary, Madison, Wisconsin
Cuthbert S. Baldwin, New Orleans, Louisiana
A. James Casner, Cambridge, Massachusetts
Abraham N. Davis, New York, New York
E. N. Eisenhower, Tacoma, Washington
John D. Randall, Cedar Rapids, Iowa

Representing the American Life Convention and the Life Insurance Association of America

John Barker, Jr., Co-Chairman, Vice President and General Counsel, New England Mutual Life Insurance Company, Boston, Massachusetts
H. S. Redeker, Co-Secretary, General Counsel, Fidelity Mutual Life Insurance Company, Philadelphia, Pennsylvania
Vincent B. Coffin, Senior Vice President, Connecticut Mutual Life Insurance Company, Hartford, Connecticut
Deane C. Davis, President, National Life Insurance Company, Montpelier, Vermont
Roger Hull, Executive Vice President, Mutual Life Insurance Company of New York, New York
Powell B. McHaney, President, General American Life Insurance Company, St. Louis, Missouri
H. Bruce Palmer, Executive Vice President, Mutual Benefit Life Insurance Company, Newark, New Jersey
Sylvester C. Smith, Jr., General Counsel, Prudential Insurance Company of America, Newark, New Jersey
Walter Weissinger, Agency Vice President, New York Life Insurance Company, New York 10, New York
William P. Worthington, Executive Vice President, Home Life Insurance Company, New York, New York

6. STATEMENT OF PRINCIPLES FORMULATED BY THE NATIONAL CONFERENCE OF LAWYERS AND CERTIFIED PUBLIC ACCOUNTANTS

Preamble [6]

In our present complex society, the average citizen conducting a business is confronted with a myriad of governmental laws and regulations which cover every phase of human endeavor and raise intricate and perplexing problems. These are further complicated by the tax incidents attendant upon all business transactions. As a result, citizens in increasing numbers have sought the professional services of lawyers and certified public account-

---

[6] Approved by the National Conference of Lawyers and Certified Public Accountants on February 8, 1951, and in the same year by the Board of Governors and the House of Delegates of the American Bar Association on February 24 and 27, respectively, and by the Council of the American Institute of Accountants on May 8. — ED.

ants. Each of these groups is well qualified to serve the public in its respective field. The primary function of the lawyer is to advise the public with respect to the legal implications involved in such problems, whereas the certified public accountant has to do with the accounting aspects thereof. Frequently the legal and accounting phases are so interrelated and interdependent and overlapping that they are difficult to distinguish. Particularly is this true in the field of income taxation where questions of law and accounting have sometimes been inextricably intermingled. As a result, there has been some doubt as to where the functions of one profession end and those of the other begin.

For the guidance of members of each profession the National Conference of Lawyers and Certified Public Accountants recommends the following statement of principles relating to practice in the field of federal income taxation:

1. Collaboration of Lawyers and Certified Public Accountants Desirable

It is in the best public interest that services and assistance in federal income tax matters be rendered by lawyers and certified public accountants, who are trained in their fields by education and experience, and for whose admission to professional standing there are requirements as to education, citizenship and high moral character. They are required to pass written examinations and are subject to rules of professional ethics, such as those of the American Bar Association and American Institute of Accountants, which set a high standard of professional practice and conduct, including prohibition of advertising and solicitation. Many problems connected with business require the skills of both lawyers and certified public accountants and there is every reason for a close and friendly cooperation between the two professions. Lawyers should encourage their clients to seek the advice of certified public accountants whenever accounting problems arise and certified public accountants should encourage clients to seek the advice of lawyers whenever legal questions are present.

2. Preparation of Federal Income Tax Returns

It is a proper function of a lawyer or a certified public accountant to prepare federal income tax returns.

When a lawyer prepares a return in which questions of accounting arise, he should advise the taxpayer to enlist the assistance of a certified public accountant.

When a certified public accountant prepares a return in which questions of law arise, he should advise the taxpayer to enlist the assistance of a lawyer.

3. Ascertainment of Probable Tax Effects of Transactions

In the course of the practice of law and in the course of the practice of accounting, lawyers and certified public accountants are often asked about the probable tax effects of transactions.

The ascertainment of probable tax effects of transactions frequently is within the function of either a certified public accountant or a lawyer. However, in many instances, problems arise which require the attention of a member of one or the other profession, or members of both. When such ascertainment raises uncertainties as to the interpretation of law (both tax law and general law), or uncertainties as to the application of law to the transaction involved, the certified public accountant should advise the taxpayer to enlist the services of a lawyer. When such ascertainment involves difficult questions of classifying and summarizing the transaction in a significant manner and in terms of money, or interpreting the financial results thereof, the lawyer should advise the taxpayer to enlist the services of a certified public accountant.

In many cases, therefore, the public will be best served by utilizing the joint skills of both professions.

4. Preparation of Legal and Accounting Documents

Only a lawyer may prepare legal documents such as agreements, conveyances, trust instruments, wills, or corporate minutes, or give advice as to the legal sufficiency or effect thereof, or take the necessary steps to create, amend or dissolve a partnership, corporation, trust, or other legal entity.

Only an accountant may properly advise as to the preparation of financial statements included in reports or submitted with tax returns, or as to accounting methods and procedures.

5. Prohibited Self-designations

An accountant should not describe himself as a "tax consultant" or "tax expert" or use any similar phrase. Lawyers, similarly, are prohibited by the canons of ethics of the American Bar Association and the opinions relating thereto, from advertising a special branch of law practice.

6. Representation of Taxpayers Before Treasury Department

Under Treasury Department regulations lawyers and certified public accountants are authorized, upon a showing of their professional status, and subject to certain limitations as defined in the Treasury rules, to represent taxpayers in proceedings before that Department. If, in the course of such proceedings, questions arise involving the application of legal principles, a lawyer should be retained, and if, in the course of such proceedings accounting questions arise, a certified public accountant should be retained.

7. Practice Before the Tax Court of the United States

Under the Tax Court rules non-lawyers may be admitted to practice.

However, since upon issuance of a formal notice of deficiency by the Commissioner of Internal Revenue a choice of legal remedies is afforded the taxpayer under existing law (either before the Tax Court of the United States, a United States District Court, or the Court of Claims), it is in the best interest of the taxpayer that the advice of a lawyer be sought if further proceedings are contemplated. It is not intended hereby to foreclose the right of non-lawyers to practice before the Tax Court of the United States pursuant to its rules.

Here also, as in proceedings before the Treasury Department, the taxpayer, in many cases, is best served by the combined skills of both lawyers and certified public accountants, and the taxpayers, in such cases, should be advised accordingly.

8. Claims for Refund

Claims for refund may be prepared by lawyers or certified public accountants, provided, however, that where a controversial legal issue is involved or where the claim is to be made the basis of litigation, the services of a lawyer should be obtained.

9. Criminal Tax Investigations

When a certified public accountant learns that his client is being specially investigated for possible criminal violation of the Income Tax Law, he should advise his client to seek the advice of a lawyer as to his legal and constitutional rights.

Conclusion

This statement of principles should be regarded as tentative and subject to revision and amplification in the light of future experience. The principal purpose is to indicate the importance of voluntary cooperation between our professions, whose members should use their knowledge and skills to the best advantage of the public. It is recommended that joint committees representing the local societies of both professions be established. Such committees might well take permanent form as local conferences of lawyers and certified public accountants patterned after this conference, or could take the form of special committees to handle a specific situation.

Index